J. W. McKENZIE

Specialists in antiquarian, secondhand cricket books, particularly John Wisden's Cricketers' Almanack

BOOKS AND COLLECTIONS BOUGHT

12 STONELEIGH PARK ROAD
EWELL, EPSOM, SURREY KT19 0QT
ENGLAND

CATALOGUES SENT ON REQUEST

TEL: 081-393 7700
FAX: 081-393 1694

PREFACE

If anyone doubted that the amount of cricket being played around the world has been increasing – and doing so in inverse proportion to those watching, it seems – he or she need only compare the pages of this *Wisden* with those of the 1990 edition. Nor is this increase limited to countries other than the United Kingdom. Although it is frequently said that there is too much cricket, the TCCB managed last year to squeeze a short tour by Sri Lanka into a fixture list already containing Test-match tours by New Zealand and India. Each year, it appears, the season begins earlier and finishes later. With the first game commencing on April 13, the season in 1991 has its earliest start since 1903 (also April 13), while the final game, a new fixture over four days between the new county champions and the Sheffield Shield winners, is scheduled to start on September 23. One ramification of the profusion, as far as *Wisden* is concerned, is an increase in the number of pages from 1296 in 1990 to 1360 in 1991.

Even so, the demands on space continue. More schools, with fixtures against schools currently in *Wisden*, ask to be included. Among them this year was Richard Huish, of Taunton, the first state school to win the Barclays Under-17 competition: one of their players appeared for Somerset in the final of the Bain Clarkson Trophy. Prompted perhaps by Rachael Heyhoe Flint's application for membership of MCC, Roedean School submitted their averages for the season, pointing out quite correctly that there was an absence of girls' schools in the section. Their letter arriving two months after the closing date, an editorial dilemma was postponed for a year.

For their co-operation my thanks are extended to the secretariats of MCC and the TCCB, to the county secretaries and their staffs, and in particular to the county scorers and statisticians, whose checking of scorecards is so valuable. I would also like to pay tribute to the work of Roy Smart, who developed the computer program which set up for *Wisden* a data base of the summer's cricket and, in addition to producing averages and other statistical highlights, provided the facility to send scorecards on disk to our typesetters, SB Datagraphics.

Once again I am indebted to the many journalists and statisticians who help in so many ways. To P. N. Sundaresan, who sent details of cricket in India to *Wisden* from the 1967 edition until last year's, I offer *Wisden's* thanks for his generous help to three editors. As always, Christine Forrest's contribution has been tireless, and Gordon Burling has again read the majority of the proofs with his customary diligence. Finally, a welcome to Harriet Monkhouse, who has joined John Wisden as an editor and whose assistance has already altered the work-pattern of more than a decade. For that I am especially grateful.

GRAEME WRIGHT

Eastcote
Middlesex

LIST OF CONTRIBUTORS

The editor acknowledges with gratitude the assistance in the preparation of the Almanack by the following:

Jack Arlidge (Sussex)
John Arlott (Books)
David Armstrong
Chris Aspin (Lancashire Leagues)
Philip Bailey
Jack Bannister (Warwickshire)
Simon Barnes
Colin Bateman
Brian Bearshaw (Lancashire)
Sir William Becher
Michael Berry
Edward Bevan (Glamorgan)
J. Watson Blair (Scotland)
Dick Brittenden
Robert Brooke (Births and Deaths)
Gordon Burling
C. R. Buttery (New Zealand)
John Callaghan (Yorkshire)
Terry Cooper (Middlesex)
Geoffrey Copinger
Tony Cozier (West Indies)
Brian Croudy
Jon Culley (Leicestershire)
Pat Culpan
Norman de Mesquita
Patrick Eagar
Paton Fenton (Oxford University)
David Field (Surrey)
Bill Frindall (Records)
Nigel Fuller (Essex)
Ghulam Mustafa Khan
David Hallett (Cambridge University)
David Hardy (The Netherlands)
Peter Hargreaves (Denmark)
Bob Harragan (Welsh Schools)
Chris Harte
Les Hatton
Frank Heydenrych (South Africa)
Eric Hill (Somerset)
Ted and Mary-Anne Hirst
Dr Grenville Holland (UAU)
Brian Hunt
Ken Ingman (ESCA)
Kate Jenkins
Abid Ali Kazi (Pakistan)
Michael Kennedy
John Kitchin (Obituaries)
Stephanie Lawrence
Alan Lee
David Leggat
Nick Lucy (Nottinghamshire)
John MacKinnon (Australia)
John Minshull-Fogg
R. Mohan (India)
Chris Moore (Worcestershire)
Dudley Moore (Kent)
Gerald Mortimer (Derbyshire)
Don Mosey
David Munden
Mike Neasom (Hampshire)
David Norrie
Graham Otway
Alwyn Pichanick (Zimbabwe)
Qamar Ahmed
Andrew Radd (Northamptonshire)
Rex Roberts
Carol Salmon (Women's Cricket)
Geoffrey Saulez
Derek Scott (Ireland)
Roy Smart
Bill Smith
Peter Smith
Richard Streeton
John Thicknesse
Sudhir Vaidya (India)
Gerry Vaidyasekera (Sri Lanka)
David Walsh (HMC Schools)
Geoffrey Wheeler (Gloucestershire)
John Woodcock
Peter Wynne-Thomas

Thanks are accorded also to the following for checking the scorecards of first-class matches: M. R. L. W. Ayers, L. Beaumont, G. R. Blackburn, Mrs C. Byatt, L. V. Chandler, B. H. Clarke, W. Davies, B. T. Denning, J. Foley, V. H. Isaacs, B. H. Jenkins, D. Kendix, D. A. Oldam, S. W. Tacey and R. D. Wilkinson.

CONTENTS

Preface	3
Index	7
Notes by the Editor	42
Don't Blame the Ball by Jack Bannister	48
Sir Leonard Hutton by John Woodcock	53
Sir Richard Hadlee by Don Mosey	57
Five Cricketers of the Year	65
Lancashire's Revival – Is it Enough? by Michael Kennedy	75
A Genuinely Great Cricketer by Simon Barnes	79
Test Cricketers 1877-1990	85
Cricket Records	129
Features of 1990	273
First-Class Averages, 1990	280
Individual Scores of 100 and Over, 1990	287
Ten Wickets in a Match, 1990	292
The Cricket Council, TCCB and NCA	293
The New Zealanders in England, 1990	294
The Indians in England, 1990	318
The Sri Lankans in England, 1990	344
The Unibind ICC Trophy, 1990	354
Marylebone Cricket Club, 1990	364
Other Matches at Lord's, 1990	369
Britannic Assurance County Championship, 1990	378
The First-Class Counties in 1990	386
Oxford and Cambridge Universities in 1990	667
Other Matches, 1990	696
NatWest Bank Trophy, 1990	704
Benson and Hedges Cup, 1990	729
Refuge Assurance League, 1990	761
Refuge Assurance Cup, 1990	846
Minor Counties Championship, 1990	849
Second Eleven Championship, 1990	868
Bain Clarkson Trophy, 1990	889
The UAU Championship, 1990	891
The Lancashire Leagues, 1990	894
Irish and Scottish Cricket in 1990	896
Pakistan Young Cricketers in England, 1990	902
Esso/NAYC Under-19 County Festivals, 1990	907
Schools Cricket in 1990	909
England in the West Indies, 1989-90	967
England A in Kenya and Zimbabwe, 1989-90	989
The Indians in Pakistan, 1989-90	1000
The New Zealanders in Australia, 1989-90	1012
The Sri Lankans in Australia, 1989-90	1017
The Pakistanis in Australia, 1989-90	1029
The Indians in New Zealand, 1989-90	1040
The Australians in New Zealand, 1989-90	1056
Sharjah Champions Trophy, 1989-90	1058
Nehru Cup, 1989-90	1063
Benson and Hedges World Series Cup, 1989-90	1077
Austral-Asia Cup, 1989-90	1088
Overseas Domestic Cricket in 1989-90	1095
Women's Cricket, 1990	1204
Births and Deaths of Cricketers	1207
Obituaries	1253
The Laws of Cricket	1287
International Cricket Conference	1317
Qualification and Registration	1321
Meetings in 1990	1325
Cricket Books, 1990 by John Arlott	1329
Fixtures, 1991	1348

INDEX

Note: For reasons of space, certain entries which appear in alphabetical order in sections of the Almanack are not included in this index. These include names that appear in Test Cricketers, Births and Deaths of Cricketers, individual batting and bowling performances in the 1990 first-class season, and Oxford and Cambridge Blues.

c. = catches; d. = dismissals; p'ship = partnership; r. = runs; w. = wickets.
** Signifies not out or an unbroken partnership.*

A

Aamer Malik (Pak.):– 2 hundreds on début, *136;* 2 Test hundreds, *255.*

Aamer Wasim (Sialkot):– LBW hat-trick, *159.*

Aaqib Javed (Pak.):– Test début at 16, *197.*

Abdul Azeem (H'bad):– 303* v Tamil Nadu, *134.*

Abdul Kadir (Pak.):– Test p'ship record, *239.*

Abdul Qadir (Pak.):– 230 w. in Tests, *189;* 131 w. in one-day ints, *266;* 103 w. in Pakistan season, *161;* 10 w. or more in Test (4), *225, 239;* 9 w. in Test innings, *185;* All-round in Tests, *191;* Test p'ship record, *259.*

Abel, R. (Eng.):– 33,124 r., *143;* 3,309 r. in season, *140;* Highest for Surrey, *135;* 74 hundreds, *139;* 357* v Somerset, *133, 135;* 2 Test hundreds, *201, 209;* Carrying bat in Test, *181;* 379 for 1st wkt, *150.*

Absolom, C. A. (Eng.):– Obstructing the field, *155.*

Adcock, N. A. T. (SA):– 104 w. in Tests, *188;* 26 w. in series, *212;* Test p'ship record, *241.*

Addresses of representative bodies, *1315-6.*

Adhikari, H. R. (Ind.):– Test captain, *244;* 1 Test hundred, *246;* Test p'ship records, *236, 256.*

Afaq Hussain (Pak.):– Test p'ship record, *239.*

Aftab Baloch (Pak.):– Test début at 16, *197;* 428 v Baluchistan, *133.*

Agha Zahid (HBL):– 2 hundreds in match (2), *137.*

Agnew, J. P. (Eng.): – Career figures, *1324.*

Ahad Khan (Pak. Rlwys):– 9 w. for 7 r., *157.*

Alabaster, J. C. (NZ):– 8 w. in Test, *242;* Test p'ship record, *244.*

Alderman, T. M. (Aust.):– 153 w. in Tests, *188;* 42 w. in series, *187, 207;* 41 w. in series, *187;* 10 w. or more in Test, *206;* Test p'ship record, *239.*

Alexander, F. C. M. (WI):– Test captain, *213, 244, 247;* 1 Test hundred, *231;* 23 d. in series, *193;* 5 c. in Test innings, *192.*

Ali Zia (UBL):– 2 hundreds in match (2), *137.*

Alim-ud-Din (Pak.):– 2 Test hundreds, *224, 255.*

Allan, P. J. (Aust.):– 10 w. in innings, *156.*

Allcott, C. F. W. (NZ):– 190* for 8th wkt, *153;* Test p'ship record, *242.*

Allen, D. A. (Eng.):– 122 w. in Tests, *187;* Test p'ship records, *225.*

Allen, Sir G. O. B. (Eng.):– Test captain, *200, 213, 220;* Test cricket at 45, *198;* 1 Test hundred, *218;* 10 w. in innings, *156;* 10 w. or more in Test (1), *223;* 246 for 8th wkt v New Zealand, *184, 219.*

Alletson, E. B. (Notts.):– Fast scoring, *145;* 34 r. in over, *147.*

Alley, W. E. (Som.):– 3,019 r. in season, *140.*

Alleyne, M. W. (Glos.):– 256 in 1990, *273.*

Allom, M. J. C. (Eng.):– Test hat-trick, *189, 220.*

Allott, P. J. W. (Eng.):– 116 for 10th wkt, *277;* Test p'ship records, *222, 226.*

Altaf Shah (HBFC):– 355 for 5th wkt, *152.*

Amarnath, L. (Ind.):– Test captain, *235, 244, 254;* Hundred on Test début, *174, 221;* 410 for 3rd wkt, *152.*

Amarnath, M. (Ind.):– 4,378 r. in Tests, *179;* 11 Test hundreds, *236, 246, 255, 257;* 2,234 r. in overseas season, *141;* 1,077 Test r. in year, *177;* Test p'ship records, *236, 246, 256, 257.*

Amarnath, S. (Ind.):– Hundred on Test début, *175, 250;* Test p'ship record, *250.*

Ambrose, C. E. L. (WI):– 12 w. in match, *277;* 10 w. in Test, *216;* 8 w. in Test innings, *185.*

Ames, L. E. G. (Eng.):– Obituary, *1254-6;* 37,248 r., *143;* 2,434 r. in Tests, *178;* 1,000 r. (17), *141;* 3,058 r. in season, *140;* 102 hundreds, *138;* 8 Test hundreds, *201, 209, 214, 218;* 2 hundreds in match (3), *137;* 1,121 d., *168;* 100 d. in season (3), *167;* 8 d. in Test, *192;* 2,482 r. and 104 d. in season, 1,919 r. and 122 d. in season, 1,795 r. and 128 d. in season, *165;* 246 for 8th wkt v New Zealand, *184, 219;* Test p'ship records, *184, 211, 219.*

Amin Lakhani (Pak. Univs):– Double hat-trick, *159.*

Amir Elahi (Ind. and Pak.):– Test p'ship record, *256.*

Amiss, D. L. (Eng.):– 43,423 r., *142;* 7,040 r. in Sunday League, *843;* 3,612 r. in Tests, *177;* 1,950 r. in GC/NWB, *725;* 1,379 Test r. in year, *176;* 1,000 r. (24), *140;* 102 hundreds, *138;* 11 Test hundreds, *214, 218, 221, 224;* 2 hundreds in match (2), *137;* 262* v West Indies, *174, 214.*

Anderson, J. H. (SA):– Test captain, *227*.
Anderson, R. W. (NZ):– Test p'ship record, *252*.
Andrew, K. V. (Eng.):– 7 d. in innings, *165*.
Andrews, C. W. (Qld):– 335 for 7th wkt, *153*.
Anil Dalpat (Pak.):– 10 d. in match, *167;* Test p'ship record, *253*.
Anwar Iqbal (H'bad):– Hit the ball twice, *155*.
Anwar Miandad (IDBP):– Hit the ball twice, *155*.
Appearances in Test cricket:– As captain, *128;* Most, *128, 198;* Most consecutive, *199*.
Appleyard, R. (Eng.):– 200 w. in season, *160;* 4 w. for 7 r. in Test innings, *186*.
Apte, M. L. (Ind.):– 1 Test hundred, *246*.
Archer, R. G. (Aust.):– 1 Test hundred, *230;* Test p'ship records, *232*.
Arkwright, H. A.:– 18 w. v Gentlemen of Kent, *158*.
Arif Butt (Pak.):– Test p'ship record, *253*.
Arif-ud-Din (UBL):– 10 d. in match, *167;* 7 d. in innings, *166*.
Armstrong, N. F. (Leics.):– Obituary, *1256-7;* 36 hundreds, *140*.
Armstrong, W. W. (Aust.):– Test captain, *200;* All-round, *165;* 2,863 r. in Tests, *178;* 2,172 r. v England, *208;* 45 hundreds, *139;* 6 Test hundreds, *203, 228;* Hundred and double-hundred, *136;* 303* v Somerset, *134;* Carrying bat in Test, *181;* 428 for 6th wkt, *152;* Test p'ship record, *229*.
Arnold, E. G. (Eng.):– All-round, *165;* Wkt with 1st ball on Test début, *189;* 393 for 5th wkt, *152*.
Arnold, G. G. (Eng.):– 115 w. in Tests, *187;* Most w. in GC/NWB Trophy, *726*.
Arnold, J. (Eng.):– 37 hundreds, *140*.
Arshad Ali (Sukkur):– Obstructing the field, *155*.
Arshad Pervez (HBL):– 37 hundreds, *140;* 426 for 2nd wkt, *151*.
Arun Lal (Ind.):– Test p'ship record, *257*.
Ashdown, W. H. (Kent):– Highest for Kent, *135;* 332 v Essex, *133;* 307* in day, *146;* 305* v Derbyshire, *135;* 39 hundreds, *139*.
Ashes, The:– *200-8;* History of, *263*.
Ashraf Ali (Pak.):– Test p'ship record, *259*.
Asif Iqbal (Pak.):– Test captain, *254;* 3,575 r. in Tests, *180;* 45 hundreds, *139;* 11 Test hundreds, *224, 238, 248, 252, 255;* 350 for 4th wkt v New Zealand, *152, 184, 252;* 190 for 9th wkt, *153, 184, 225;* Test p'ship records, *225, 248, 252-3*.
Asif Masood (Pak.):– Test p'ship record, *225*.
Aslam Ali (UBL):– 456 for 3rd wkt, *149, 152*.
Aslett, D. G. (Kent):– Hundred on début, *135*.
Astill, W. E. (Eng.):– All-round, *165;* 2,431 w., *162;* 100 w. (9), *161*.
Athar Khan (Allied Bank):– Handled the ball, *154*.
Atherton, M. A. (Eng.):– Cricketer of the Year, *69-70;* 2 Test hundreds, *218, 221;* 364 for 3rd wkt, *277;* Test p'ship record, *222*.
Athey, C. W. J. (Eng.):– 35 hundreds, *140;* 4 successive hundreds, *138;* 2 hundreds in match (2), *137, 275;* 1 Test hundred, *224*.
Atkins, P. D. (Surrey):– Hundred on début, *136*.
Atkinson, D. St E. (WI):– Test captain, *229, 242;* Test hundred, *231;* All-round in Test, *191;* 347 for 7th wkt v Australia, *153, 184, 232;* Test p'ship records, *232, 243*.
Atkinson, G. (Som.):– 1st wkt hundreds, *151*.
Atkinson, J. C. M. (CUCC and Som.):– Captain of Cambridge, *676*.
Attewell, W. (Eng.):– 1,950 w., *162;* 100 w. (10), *161*.
Australia:– Australia in Test cricket (*see p. 132*); Austral-Asia Cup, *1088-94;* B & H World Series Cup, *1077-87;* Definition of first-class matches, *1319;* Domestic season 1989-90, *1095-132;* Highest individual Test innings, *174;* Highest Test innings, *194;* Leading batsmen in Tests, *178;* Leading bowlers in Tests, *188;* Lowest Test innings, *196;* Most consecutive Test appearances, *198;* Most Test appearances, *128;* Most Test appearances as captain, *128;* Nehru Cup, *1063-74;* Oldest Test player, *198;* Representative body, *1315;* Summary of Tests, *199;* Summary of one-day ints, *264;* Test cricketers (1877-1990), *97-105;* Youngest and oldest on Test début, *197-8*.
Austral-Asia Cup, 1989-90, *1088-94*.
Ayaz Jilani (PACO):– Hat-trick, *159, 1189*.
Aymes, A. N. (Hants):– 10 d. in match, *167*.
Azad, K. (Ind.):– Handled the ball, *154*.
Azhar Abbas (B'pur):– 10 d. in match, *167*.
Azharuddin, M. (Ind.):– Cricketer of the Year, *65-7;* Test captain, *220, 249;* 2,953 r. (avge 51.80) in Tests, *180, 181;* 4 hundreds in succession, *138;* 10 Test hundreds, *175, 221, 250, 255, 257;* Hundred on Test début, *175, 221;* 5 c. in Test innings, *193;* Test p'ship records, *222, 256, 257*.
Aziz Malik (Lahore Div.):– Hit the ball twice, *155*.

B

Bacchus, S. F. A. F. (WI):– 250 v India, *174, 245*.
Bacher, A. (SA):– Test captain, *227*.
Badcock, C. L. (Aust.):– 325 v Victoria, *133;* 1 Test hundred, *203*.
Badcock, F. T. (NZ):– Test p'ship record, *242*.
Baichan, L. (WI):– Hundred on Test début, *175, 248;* Hundred and double-hundred, *136;* 2 hundreds in match (2), *137*.

Baig, A. A. (Ind.):– Hundred on Test début, *175, 221;* Test p'ship record, *236.*
Bailey, R. J. (Eng.):– 10,000 r., *279;* 204* in 1990, *273.*
Bailey, T. E. (Eng.):– All-round, *164, 165, 191;* 28,641 r., *143;* 2,290 r. in Tests, *178;* 1,000 r. (17), *141;* 1 Test hundred, *218;* Slow batting in Test, *183;* 2,082 w., *163;* 132 w. in Tests, *187;* 100 w. (9), *161;* 10 w. in innings, *156;* 10 w. or more in Test (1), *216;* Test p'ship record, *225.*
Bainbridge, P. (Glos.):– Career figures, *1324.*
Bain Clarkson Trophy, *889-90;* Fixtures, 1991, *1358-9.*
Bairstow, D. L. (Eng.):– Career figures, *1324;* 1,099 d., *168;* 255 d. in Sunday League, *845;* 11 c. in match, *166;* 7 c. in innings, *166.*
Bakewell, A. H. (Eng.):– 1 Test hundred, *214;* 8 c. in match, *168.*
Balaskas, X. C. (SA):– 1 Test hundred, *241.*
Banerjee, S. N. (Ind.):– 249 for 10th wkt, *154.*
Bangladesh:– Austral-Asia Cup, 1989-90, *1088-90;* ICC Trophy, *354-7, 359, 361-2;* Representative body, *1316.*
Banks, D. A. (Worcs. and Warwicks.):– Hundred on début, *135.*
Bannerman, C. (Aust.):– Hundred on Test début, *174, 203.*
Bannister, J. D. (Warwicks.):– 10 w. in innings, *156.*
Baptiste, E. A. E. (WI):– Test p'ship record, *216.*
Barber, R. W. (Eng.):– 1 Test hundred, *201;* Test p'ship record, *225.*
Bardsley, W. (Aust.):– Test captain, *200;* 2,469 r. in Tests, *178;* 53 hundreds, *139;* 6 Test hundreds, *203, 228;* 2 hundreds in same Test, *176, 203;* Carrying bat in Test, *181;* Test p'ship record, *229.*
Barker, G. (Essex):– 1,000 r. (15), *141;* Hundred on début, *135.*
Barlow, E. J. (SA):– 2,516 r. in Tests, *178;* 43 hundreds, *139;* 6 Test hundreds, *210, 228;* 341 for 3rd wkt v Australia, *152, 184, 229.*
Barlow, R. G. (Eng.):– Hit the ball twice, *155;* 4 hat-tricks, *159.*
Barnes, S. F. (Eng.):– 189 w. in Tests, *187;* 106 w. v Australia, *208;* 104 w. in overseas season, *161;* 49 w. and 34 w. in series, *187, 212;* 17 w. in Test, *157, 186;* 14 w. in Test, *186;* 10 w. or more in Test (7), *206, 212;* 9 w. in Test innings, *185;* 8 w. in Test innings (2), *185.*
Barnes, S. G. (Aust.):– 3 Test hundreds, *203, 235;* 405 for 5th wkt v England, *152, 184, 205;* Test p'ship records, *205, 236.*
Barnes, W. (Eng.):– 1 Test hundred, *201.*
Barnett, C. J. (Eng.):– 25,389 r., *144;* 48 hundreds, *139;* 2 Test hundreds, *201;* 11 sixes in innings, *148.*
Barnett, K. J. (Eng.):– Captain of Derbyshire, *386;* 3 hundreds in succession, *273;* Test p'ship record, *226.*
Barratt, E. (Surrey):– 10 w. in innings, *155.*
Barrett, J. E. (Aust.):– Carrying bat in Test, *181.*
Barrington, K. F. (Eng.):– 31,714 r., *142;* 6,806 r. (avge 58.67) in Tests, *177, 180;* 2,111 r. v Australia, *208;* 1,039 Test r. in year, *177;* 1,000 r. (15), *141;* 76 hundreds, *139;* 20 Test hundreds, *181, 201, 209, 214, 218, 221, 224;* 256 v Australia, *174, 201;* 64 c. in season, *168;* 369 for 2nd wkt v New Zealand, *184, 219;* Test p'ship records, *211, 219, 225.*
Barrow, I. (WI):– 1 Test hundred, *215.*
Bartlett, G. A. (NZ):– Test p'ship records, *242.*
Bartlett, R. J. (Som.):– Hundred on début, *136.*
Barton, P. T. (NZ):– 1 Test hundred, *241.*
Base, S. J. (Derbys.):– 107 for 10th wkt, *277.*
Basit Ali (Karachi Blues and PACO):– 2 hundreds in match (2), *137, 138, 1184, 1188.*
Bates, W. (Eng.):– Test hat-trick, *189;* 14 w. in Test, *186, 206.*
Beard, D. A. (N. Districts):– Hat-trick, *159, 1164.*
Beck, J. E. F. (NZ):– Test p'ship record, *242.*
Bedfordshire, *849, 850, 853-4.*
Bedi, B. S. (Ind.):– Test captain, *220, 235, 244, 249, 254;* 1,560 w., *163;* 266 w. in Tests, *189;* 10 w. or more in Test (1), *237;* Test p'ship records, *246, 250.*
Bedser, A. V. (Eng.):– 1,924 w., *162;* 236 w. in Tests, *187;* 104 w. v Australia, *208;* 100 w. (11), *161;* 39 w. in series, *187;* 14 w. in Test, *186, 206;* 10 w. or more in Test (5), *206, 212, 223.*
Bell, A. J. (SA):– Test p'ship record, *211.*
Benaud, J. (Aust.):– 1 Test hundred, *238.*
Benaud, R. (Aust.):– Test captain, *200, 227, 229, 235, 237;* Fast scoring, *182;* 11 sixes in innings, *148;* 2,201 r. in Tests, *178;* 3 Test hundreds, *228, 230;* 248 w. in Tests, *188;* 106 w. in overseas season, *161;* 10 w. or more in Test (1), *237;* 3 w. for 0 r. in Test innings, *186;* All-round in Tests, *190, 191;* Test p'ship records, *229, 232.*
Benefits in 1991, *292.*
Benjamin, S. (Rajasthan):– 7 d. in innings, *166.*
Benjamin, W. K. M. (WI):– Test p'ship record, *248.*
Benson and Hedges Cup:– *729-60;* Fixtures, 1991, *1348-51.*
Benson and Hedges Trophy (SA), *1145-8.*
Benson and Hedges World Series Cup (Aust.), *1077-87.*
Benson, M. R. (Kent):– Captain of Kent, *468;* 268 for 3rd wkt, *277.*
Bensted, E. C. (Qld):– 335 for 7th wkt, *153.*
Berkshire:– *711, 849, 851, 852, 853;* v Oxford Univ., *670.*
Berry, L. G. (Leics.):– 30,225 r., *142;* 1,000 r. (18), *141;* 45 hundreds, *139.*
Berry, R. (Eng.):– 10 w. in innings, *156.*

Best, C. A. (WI):– 1 Test hundred, *215*.
Bestwick, W. (Derbys.):– 10 w. in innings, *156*.
Betancourt, N. (WI):– Test captain, *213;* Oldest West Indian on début, *197*.
Bhandarkar, K. V. (M'tra):– 455 for 2nd wkt, *149, 151*.
Bicknell, D. J. (Surrey):– 321 and 256 for 1st wkt, *276;* 413 for 2nd wkt, *277*.
Bicknell, M. P. (Surrey):– 205 for 8th wkt, *277*.
Binks, J. G. (Eng.):– 1,071 d., *168;* 107 d. in season, *167;* 5 c. in Test innings, *193;* 412 consecutive Champ. appearances, *272*.
Binny, R. M. H. (Ind.):– 451 for 1st wkt, *149, 150, 151;* Test p'ship record, *256*.
Bird, M. C. (Eng.):– 2 hundreds in match v Eton, *370;* Test p'ship record, *211*.
Bisset, M. (SA):– Test captain, *208*.
Blackham, J. McC. (Aust.):– Test captain, *200;* Test p'ship record, *205*.
Blackie, D. D. (Aust.):– Test cricket at 46, *198;* Oldest Australian Test début, *197*.
Blakey, R. J. (Yorks.):– 9 c. in match, *278;* 6 d. in innings, *278*.
Bland, C. H. G. (Sussex):– 10 w. in innings, *156*.
Bland, K. C. (SA):– 3 Test hundreds, *210, 228;* Test p'ship record, *241*.
Bligh, Hon. Ivo (Lord Darnley) (Eng.):– Test captain, *200;* The Ashes, *263*.
Blues:– Both universities, *373;* List of (1946-90), Cambridge, *692;* Oxford, *688*.
Blunt, R. C. (NZ):– 338* v Canterbury, *133, 146, 154;* 184 for 10th wkt, *154*.
Blythe, C. (Eng.):– 2,506 w., *162, 163;* 215 w. in season, *160;* 100 w. (14), *161;* 100 w. in Tests, *187;* 17 w. in day, *158;* 17 w. in match, *157, 158;* 15 w. in Test, *186, 212;* 10 w. or more in Test (4), *206, 212;* 10 w. in innings, *156;* 8 w. in Test innings, *186*.
Board, J. H. (Eng.):– 1,207 d., *168*.
Bolus, J. B. (Eng.):– 25,598 r., *144;* 39 hundreds, *139*.
Bonnor, G. J. (Aust.):– 1 Test hundred, *203*.
Boock, S. L. (NZ):– Test p'ship record, *234*.
Boon, D. C. (Aust.):– 3,186 r. in Tests, *178;* 8 Test hundreds, *203, 230, 233, 235;* Carrying bat in Test, *181;* Test p'ship record, *236*.
Boon, T. J. (Leics.):– 1st wkt hundreds, *276*.
Booth, A. (Lancs. II):– 253 v Lincolnshire, *270*.
Booth, B. C. (Aust.):– Test captain, *200;* 5 Test hundreds, *203, 228 230*.
Booth, R. (Worcs.):– 1,126 d., *168;* 100 d. in season (2), *167*.
Borde, C. G. (Ind.):– Test captain, *235;* 3,061 r. in Tests, *179;* 1,604 r. in Indian season, *141;* 5 Test hundreds, *246, 250, 255*.
Border, A. R. (Aust.):– Test captain, *200, 230, 233, 235, 237, 239;* 115 Tests, *128, 198;* 112 consecutive Tests, *198;* 21,261 r. (avge 53.15), *145;* 8,701 r. (avge 53.38) in Tests, *178, 181;* 5,263 r. in one-day ints, *265;* 2,834 r. v England, *208;* 1,099, 1,073 and 1,000 Test r. in year, *177;* 61 hundreds, *139;* 23 Test hundreds, *181, 203, 230, 233, 235, 238;* 4 hundreds in succession, *138;* 2 hundreds in same Test (2), *175;* 2 hundreds in match (2), *137, 175;* 10 w. or more in Test, *232;* 125 c. in Tests, *194;* 96 c. in one-day ints, *267;* Test p'ship records, *234, 236, 239*.
Borland, A. F. (Natal):– 4 w. with consecutive balls, *158*.
Bosanquet, B. J. T. (Eng.):– All-round, *163;* 2 hundreds in match (2), *137;* 8 w. in Test innings, *186*.
Botham, I. T. (Eng.):– Test captain, *200, 213;* 65 consecutive Tests, *198;* 5,119 r. in Tests, *177;* 1,095 Test r. in year, *177;* 14 Test hundreds, *201, 218, 221, 224;* Fast scoring, *182, 183;* 32 r. and 30 r. in over, *147;* 80 sixes in season, *148;* 13 sixes in Sunday League innings, *844;* 12 sixes in innings, *148;* 376 w. in Tests, *187;* 148 w. v Australia, *208;* 118 w. in one-day ints, *266;* 10 w. or more in Test (4), *206, 219, 223;* 8 w. in Test innings (2), *185;* 112 c. in Tests, *194;* All-round in Tests, *191, 192;* All-round in one-day ints, *267;* Test p'ship record, *222*.
Bowden, M. P. (Eng.):– Test captain, *209*.
Bowes, W. E. (Eng.):– 1,639 w., *162;* 100 w. (9), *161*.
Bowl, The (SA), *1140-3*.
Bowler, P. D. (Leics. and Derbys.):– Hundred on début, *136;* 210 in 1990, *273*.
Bowley, E. H. (Eng.):– 28,378 r., *143;* 1,000 r. (15), *141;* 52 hundreds, *139;* 1 Test hundred, *218;* 490 for 1st wkt, *149, 150*.
Bowley, F. L. (Worcs.):– 38 hundreds, *139*.
Boyce, K. D. (WI):– 10 w. or more in Test (1), *216;* Best bowling in Sunday League, *845;* Test p'ship record, *246*.
Boycott, G. (Eng.):– Test captain, *217, 223;* 48,426 r. (avge 56.83), *142, 144;* 8,114 r. in Tests, *177;* 2,945 r. v Australia, *208;* 1,000 r. (26), *140-1;* 151 hundreds, *138;* 22 Test hundreds, *181, 201, 209, 214, 218, 221, 224;* 13 hundreds in season, *138;* 2 hundreds in match (3), *137;* Avge of 102.53 in English season, *142;* Carrying bat in Test, *181;* 1st wkt hundreds, *150;* Test p'ship record, *205*.
Boyd-Moss, R. J. (CUCC and Northants):– 2 hundreds in match (2), *137;* 3 hundreds v Oxford, *373*.
Bracewell, J. G. (NZ):– 1 Test hundred, *218;* 102 w. in Tests, *188;* 12 w. in match, *277;* 10 w. or more in Test, *234;* All-round in Tests, *191;* Test p'ship records, *219, 234*.
Bradburn, W. P. (NZ):– Test p'ship record, *242*.
Bradley, W. M. (Eng.):– Wkt with 1st ball on Test début, *189;* 3 hat-tricks, *159*.
Bradman, Sir D. G. (Aust.):– Test captain, *200, 235;* Fast scoring, *182, 183;* 28,067 r. (avge 95.14), *143, 144;* 6,996 r. (avge 99.94) in Tests, *178, 180;* 5,028 r. v

Bradman, Sir D. G. (Aust.):– *contd* England, *208;* 1,690 r. in Australian season, *141;* 1,025 Test r. in year, *177;* 1,005 r. in 5 consecutive Tests, *177;* 1,000 r. (April 30-May 31), *147;* 1,000 r. (16), *141;* 974 r. in series, *176, 206;* 452* v Queensland, *133;* 369 v Tasmania, *133, 146;* 357 v Victoria, *133;* 340* v Victoria, *133;* 334 v England, *133, 135, 173, 203;* 309* in day, *146;* 304 v England, *134, 174, 203;* 300 r. in 213 min., *146;* 309 and 271 r. in day v England, *183;* 299* v South Africa, *174, 228;* 278 at Lord's, *269;* 270 and 254 v England, *174, 203;* 117 hundreds, *138;* 29 Test hundreds, *181, 203, 228, 230, 235;* 13 hundreds in season, *138;* 6 hundreds in succession, *138;* 4 hundreds in succession, *138;* 2 hundreds in same Test, *176, 235;* 2 hundreds in match (4), *137;* Hundred and double-hundred, *136;* 10 successive fifties, *138;* Average of 115.66 in English season, *142;* 50 boundaries in innings, *149;* 30 r. in over, *148;* 451 for 2nd wkt, *149, 151, 184, 205;* 301 for 2nd wkt v England, *184;* 388 for 4th wkt v England, *184, 205;* 405 for 5th wkt, *152, 184, 205;* 346 for 6th wkt v England, *184, 205;* Test p'ship records, *205, 229, 236.*

Brain, W. H. (Glos.):– w-k hat-trick, *159, 166.*

Braund, L. C. (Eng.):– All-round, *165;* 3 Test hundreds, *201, 209;* 8 w. in Test innings, *185.*

Brayshaw, I. J. (W. Aust.):– 10 w. in innings, *156.*

Brearley, J. M. (Eng.):– Test captain, *200, 217, 220, 223;* 25,185 r., *144;* 312* v North Zone in day, *134, 146;* 45 hundreds, *139.*

Brearley, W. (Eng.):– 17 w. in match, *157;* 4 w. with consecutive balls, *158.*

Briasco, P. S. (C. Dist.):– 317 for 2nd wkt, *151.*

Briers, N. E. (Leics.):– Captain of Leicestershire, *499;* Carrying bat in 1990, *276;* 1st wkt hundreds, *276.*

Briggs, J. (Eng.):– 1 Test hundred, *201;* Test hat-trick, *189;* 2,221 w., *162;* 118 w. in Tests, *187;* 100 w. (12), *161;* 15 w. in Test, *186, 212;* 10 w. or more in Test (4), *206, 212;* 10 w. in innings, *156;* 8 w. for 11 r. in Test innings, *185, 186;* 7 w. for 17 r. in Test innings, *186.*

Bright, R. J. (Aust.):– 10 w. or more in Test (1), *239;* Test p'ship record, *236.*

Broad, B. C. (Eng.):– 37 hundreds, *140;* 6 Test hundreds, *201, 218, 224;* 227* in 1990, *273;* Hundred before lunch, *275;* 285 for 4th wkt, *277;* Test p'ship record, *226.*

Brockwell, W. (Eng.):– 379 for 1st wkt, *150.*

Bromfield, H. D. (SA):– Test p'ship record, *241.*

Bromley-Davenport, H. R. (Eng.):– Test p'ship record, *211.*

Brookes, D. (Eng.):– 30,874 r., *142;* 1,000 r. (17), *141;* 71 hundreds, *139.*

Brown, A. S. (Glos.):– 7 c. in innings, *168.*

Brown, F. R. (Eng.):– Test captain, *200, 209, 213, 217.*

Brown, G. (Eng.):– 25,649 r., *144;* 37 hundreds, *140.*

Brown, J. (Scotland):– 7 d. in innings, *165.*

Brown, J. T. (Eng.):– 1 Test hundred, *201;* 311 v Sussex, *134;* 300 v Derbyshire, *135;* 554 and 378 for 1st wkt, *149-50.*

Brown, K. R. (Middx):– 200* in 1990, *273.*

Brown, S. M. (Middx):– 1st wkt hundreds, *151.*

Brown, W. A. (Aust.):– Test captain, *233;* 13,838 r. (avge 51.44), *145;* 39 hundreds, *139;* 4 Test hundreds, *203, 228;* Carrying bat in Test, *181;* Test p'ship record, *229.*

Buckinghamshire, *705, 849, 851, 852-3, 854-5.*

Burge, P. J. (Aust.):– Handled the ball, *154;* 2,290 r. in Tests, *178;* 38 hundreds, *139;* 4 Test hundreds, *203.*

Burgess, M. G. (NZ):– Test captain, *217, 233, 251;* 2,684 r. in Tests, *179;* 5 Test hundreds, *218, 243, 252;* Test p'ship records, *234, 252.*

Burke, J. W. (Aust.):– 3 Test hundreds, *203, 228, 235;* Hundred on Test début, *175, 203;* Slow batting in Test, *183.*

Burke, S. F. (SA):– 10 w. or more in Test (1), *242.*

Burki, J. (Pak.):– Test captain, *223;* 3 Test hundreds, *224;* Test p'ship records, *225.*

Burns, W. B. (Worcs.):– 102* and hat-trick v Gloucestershire, *164;* 8 c. in match, *168;* 393 for 5th wkt, *152.*

Burton, G. (Eng.):– 10 w. in innings, *155.*

Butcher, A. R. (Eng.):– Cricketer of the Year, *67-8;* Captain of Glamorgan, *419;* 20,000 r., *279;* 42 hundreds, *139;* 1st wkt hundreds, *276;* 256 and 255* for 1st wkt, *276.*

Butcher, B. F. (WI):– 3,104 r. in Tests, *179;* 7 Test hundreds, *215, 231, 245;* 335 for 5th wkt, *152.*

Butler, H. J. (Eng.):– 3 hat-tricks, *159.*

Butler, S. E. (OUCC):– All 10 Cambridge w., *155, 373;* 15 Cambridge w., *373.*

Butt, H. R. (Eng.):– 1,228 d., *168.*

C

Cairns, B. L. (NZ):– 130 w. in Tests, *188;* 10 w. or more in Test (1), *219;* Test p'ship record, *219.*

Callers-Pegasus Festival, *698-9.*

Calthorpe, Hon. F. S. G. (Eng.):– Test captain, *213.*

Camacho, G. S. (WI):– Slow scoring in Test, *183.*

Cambridge University 1990:– *676-87;* Blues, *692-5* (*Also see Oxford v Cambridge*).

Cambridgeshire:– *849, 850, 855-6;* v Cambridge Univ., *683.*

Cameron, F. J. (NZ):– Test p'ship record, *242*.
Cameron, H. B. (SA):– Test captain, *209*; Fifty in 14 min., *145*; Test p'ship record, *241*.
Captains in Test cricket, *128* (*Also see individual series*).
Career records, *279*; of players not retained, *1324*.
Carew, G. M. (WI):– 1 Test hundred, *215*.
Carew, M. C. (WI):– 1 Test hundred, *243*.
Carr, A. W. (Eng.):– Test captain, *200, 209*; 45 hundreds, *139*.
Carr, D. B. (Eng.):– Test captain, *220*.
Carrying bat through innings:– in a Test match, *181*; in 1990, *276*.
Carson, W. N. (Auck.):– 445 for 3rd wkt, *152*.
Cartwright, T. W. (Eng.):– 1,536 w., *163*; 100 w. (8), *161*.
Catches in 1990, *278, 580*.
Catterall, R. H. (SA):– 3 Test hundreds, *210*.
Cave, H. B. (NZ):– Test captain, *242, 249, 251*; 239 for 9th wkt, *153*.
Central Lancashire League, 1990, *894-5*.
Chaman Lal (Mehandra College):– 502* v Government College, *270*.
Chandrasekhar, B. S. (Ind.):– 242 w. in Tests, *189*; 35 w. in series, *187*; 10 w. or more in Test (2), *237, 247*; 8 w. in Test innings, *185*; Test p'ship records, *222*.
Chapman, A. P. F. (Eng.):– Test captain, *200, 209, 213*; 1 Test hundred, *201*; Hundreds at Lord's, *373*.
Chapman, J. (Derbys.):– 283 for 9th wkt, *153*.
Chappell, G. S. (Aust.):– Test captain, *200, 230, 233, 235, 237, 239*; 24,535 r. (avge 52.20), *145*; 7,110 r. (avge 53.86) in Tests, *178, 180*; 2,619 r. v England, *208*; 74 hundreds, *139*; 24 Test hundreds, *181, 203, 230, 233, 235, 238*; 2 hundreds in same Test, *175, 230, 233*; 2 separate hundreds (4), *137*; Hundred and double-hundred, *136*; Hundred on Test début, *175, 203*; 122 c. in Tests, *194*; 14 c. in series, *194*; 7 c. in Test, *194*; Test p'ship records, *239*.
Chappell, I. M. (Aust.):– Test captain, *200, 230, 233, 237*; 5,345 r. in Tests, *178*; 2,138 r. v England, *208*; 71 consecutive Tests, *198*; 59 hundreds, *139*; 14 Test hundreds, *203, 230, 233, 235, 238*; 2 hundreds in same Test, *176, 233*; 2 hundreds in match (3), *137*; 105 c. in Tests, *194*; 6 c. in Test, *194*; Test p'ship records, *232, 234*.
Chapple, M. E. (NZ):– Test captain, *217*; Test p'ship record, *242*.
Chatfield, E. J. (NZ):– 140 w. in one-day ints, *266*; 123 w. in Tests, *188*; 10 w. or more in Test (1), *244*.
Chatterjee, P. (Bengal):– 10 w. in innings, *156*.
Chauhan, C. P. S. (Ind.):– 2,084 r. in Tests, *180*; 405 for 1st wkt, *150*; Test p'ship records, *222, 236, 246*.
Cheetham, J. E. (SA):– Test captain, *209, 227, 240*; Test p'ship records, *241*.
Chemplast-Kailis Cup, *1178*.
Cheshire, *849, 852, 856*.
Chidgey, G. J. (Free Foresters):– Hundred on début, *135*.
Chipperfield, A. G. (Aust.):– 1 Test hundred, *228*; Test p'ship record, *229*.
Christiani, R. J. (WI):– 1 Test hundred, *245*.
Christy, J. A. J. (SA):– 1 Test hundred, *241*; Test p'ship records, *241*.
Chubb, G. W. A. (SA):– Oldest South African Test début, *198*.
Clapp, R. J. (Som.):– Most w. in Sunday League season, *845*.
Clark, E. A. (Middx):– Hundred on début, *135*.
Clarke, A. R. (Sussex):– Career figures, *1324*.
Clarke, S. T. (WI):– 3 hat-tricks, *159*; Test p'ship record, *248*.
Claughton, J. A. (OUCC):– Hundred on début, *135*.
Clay, J. C. (Eng.):– 17 w. in match, *157*.
Clinton, G. S. (Surrey):– Career figures, *1324*; 321 for 1st wkt, *276*.
Close, D. B. (Eng.):– Test captain, *213, 220, 223*; Test cricket at 45, *198*; Youngest England Test player, *197*; 34,994 r., *143*; 1,000 r. (20), *141*; 52 hundreds, *139*; 813 c., *169*.
Club Cricket Championship, *375-6*.
Club Cricket Conference, *1316*.
Cockspur Cup, *375-6*.
Coe, S. (Leics.):– Highest for Leicestershire, *135*.
Coen, S. K. (SA):– 305 for 2nd wkt, *151*.
Collinge, R. O. (NZ):– 116 w. in Tests, *188*; 151 for 10th wkt v Pakistan, *184, 252*; Test p'ship records, *184, 250, 252*.
Collins, A. E. J. (Clifton Coll.):– 628* v North Town, *270*.
Collins, G. C. (Kent):– 10 w. in innings, *156*.
Collins, H. L. (Aust.):– Test captain, *200, 227*; 4 Test hundreds, *203, 228*; Hundred on Test début, *174*.
Combined Services:– Address, *1316*; v Cambridge Univ., *687*; v NCA Young Cricketers, *374*; v Oxford Univ., *675*; v Pakistan Young Cricketers, *903*.
Combined Univs:– In B & H Cup, *729, 741-8, 760*.
Commaille, J. M. M. (SA):– 305 for 2nd wkt, *151*.
Compton, D. C. S. (Eng.):– Fast scoring, *146, 182, 183*; 38,942 r. (avge 51.85), *142, 145*; 5,807 r. (avge 50.06) in Tests, *177, 181*; 3,816 r. in season, *140*; 1,159 Test r. in year, *177*; 1,000 r. (17), *141*; 753 r. in series, *212*; 123 hundreds, *138*; 18 hundreds in season, *138*; 17 Test hundreds, *201, 209, 214, 218, 224*; 4 successive hundreds, *138*; 2 hundreds in same Test, *176, 201*; 2 hundreds in match (3), *137*; 300 v NE Transvaal in 181 min.,

Compton, D. C. S. (Eng.):– *contd* *134, 146;* 278 v Pakistan, *174, 224;* 273 r. in day v Pakistan, *183;* Avge of 90.85 in English season, *142;* 424* for 3rd wkt, *152;* 370 for 3rd wkt v South Africa, *184, 211;* Test p'ship records, *205, 211, 225.*

Coney, J. V. (NZ):– Test captain, *217, 233, 242, 251;* 2,668 r. in Tests, *179;* 3 Test hundreds, *218, 234, 252;* Test p'ship records, *219, 234, 244, 254.*

Congdon, B. E. (NZ):– Test captain, *217, 233, 242, 251;* 3,448 r. in Tests, *179;* 7 Test hundreds, *218, 234, 243;* Test p'ship records, *219, 234, 244, 250.*

Coningham, A. (Aust.):– Wkt with 1st ball on Test début, *189.*

Connolly, A. N. (Aust.):– 102 w. in Tests, *188.*

Consecutive Test appearances, *199.*

Constantine, Lord Learie (WI):– 107 and hat-trick, *164.*

Contractor, N. J. (Ind.):– Test captain, *220, 244, 254;* 1 Test hundred, *236;* 4 successive hundreds, *138;* 152 and 102* on début, *136.*

Cook, C. (Eng.):– 100 w. (9), *161.*

Cook, G. (Eng.):– Career figures, *1324;* 37 hundreds, *140;* 94 c. in Sunday League, *845;* 24 c. in GC/NWB Trophy, *727.*

Cook, S. J. (Som. and Tvl):– 902 r. in Sunday League season, *844;* 43 hundreds, *139;* 313* v Glamorgan, *134, 273;* 4 hundreds in succession, *138;* 2 hundreds in match (2), *137;* First to 1,000 r. and 2,000 r. in 1990, *276;* 285* for 3rd wkt, *277.*

Copson, W. H. (Derbys.):– 5 w. in 6 balls, *159;* 4 w. with consecutive balls, *158;* 3 hat-tricks, *159.*

Cornford, W. L. (Eng.):– 1,017 d., *168.*

Cornwall, *849, 852, 856-7.*

Corrall, P. (Leics.):– 10 d. in match, *166.*

Cosier, G. J. (Aust.):– 2 Test hundreds, *230, 238;* Hundred on Test début, *175, 230;* Test p'ship records, *236.*

Cosstick, S. (Vic.):– 6 w. for 1 r., *157.*

County caps in 1990, *632.*

County Championship:– in 1990, *378-85;* Appearances, *272;* Champion counties, *382;* Constitution of, *272;* Fixtures, 1991, *1348-54;* Match results 1864-1990, *383;* Over-rate and run-rate, *401;* Positions 1890-1990, *384-5.*

Cowdrey, C. S. (Eng.):– Test captain, *213;* Captain of Kent, *468.*

Cowdrey, G. R. (Kent):– 268 for 3rd wkt, *277;* 258 for 4th wkt, *277.*

Cowdrey, M. C. (Eng.):– Test captain, *200, 209, 213, 220, 223;* 42,719 r., *142;* 7,624 r. in Tests, *177;* 2,433 r. v Australia, *208;* 1,000 r. (27), *140-1;* 114 Tests, *128, 198;* 107 hundreds, *138;* 22 Test hundreds, *181, 202, 209, 214, 218, 221, 224;* 2 hundreds in match (3), *137;* 307 v South Australia, *134;* 120 c. in Tests, *194;* 6 c. in Test, *194;* 411 for 4th wkt v West Indies, *184, 216;* Test p'ship records, *216, 219, 225.*

Cowie, J. (NZ):– 10 w. or more in Test (1), *219;* Test p'ship record, *219.*

Cowper, R. M. (Aust.):– 10,595 r. (avge 53.78), *145;* 2,061 r. in Tests, *178;* 5 Test hundreds, *203, 230, 235;* 307 v England, *134, 135, 174, 203;* Test p'ship record, *239.*

Cox, G. (Sussex):– 50 hundreds, *139.*

Cox, G. R. (Surrey):– 17 w. in match, *157;* 5 w. for 0 r., *157.*

Cox, J. (Tasmania):– 2 hundreds in match, *138, 1117-8.*

Craig, I. D. (Aust.):– Test captain, *227;* Youngest Australian Test player, *197.*

Cranston, K. (Eng.):– Test captain, *213.*

Crapp, J. F. (Eng.):– 38 hundreds, *139.*

Crawford, W. P. A. (Aust.):– Test p'ship record, *236.*

Cricket Council, *293.*

Cricketer Cup winners, *564.*

Cricketers of the Year, *65-74* (*See also* Births and Deaths of Cricketers).

Crisp, R. J. (SA):– 4 w. with consecutive balls (2), *158;* 3 hat-tricks, *159.*

Croft, C. E. H. (WI):– Slow scoring in Test, *183;* 125 w. in Tests, *188;* 8 w. in Test innings, *185;* Test p'ship records, *216, 232.*

Cromb, I. B. (NZ):– Test p'ship record, *242.*

Crowe, J. J. (NZ):– Test captain, *217, 233, 253;* 3 Test hundreds, *218, 243, 254;* Slow scoring in Test, *183;* Slow Test hundred, *183, 254;* 246* for 6th wkt, *153;* Test p'ship records, *244, 254.*

Crowe, M. D. (NZ):– 15,512 r. (avge 57.23), *144;* 3,384 r. in Tests, *179;* 1,676 r. in NZ season, *141;* 54 hundreds, *139;* 11 Test hundreds, *218, 234, 243, 250, 252;* Slow scoring in Test, *183;* Test p'ship records, *219, 234, 244.*

Cumberland, *849, 851, 857-8.*

Cunis, R. S. (NZ):– Test p'ship records, *244, 252.*

Curran, K. M. (Glos.):– All-round in 1990, *278;* 229 for 7th wkt, *277.*

Currie Cup (SA), *1133-5, 1137-40.*

Curtis, T. S. (Eng.):– 264 for 2nd wkt, *277.*

D

Dacre, C. C. (Auck.):– 2 hundreds in match (2), *137.*

Dalton, E. L. (SA):– 2 Test hundreds, *210;* Test p'ship record, *211.*

Daniel, W. W. (WI):– Best bowling in B & H Cup, *759.*

Darling, J. (Aust.):– Test captain, *200, 227;* 3 Test hundreds, *203.*

Dates of Formation of County Clubs, including Minor Counties, *271-2.*

Davidson, A. K. (Aust.):– 186 w. in Tests, *188;* 10 w. or more in Test (2), *232, 237;* All-round in Tests, *191;* Test p'ship record, *232.*

Davidson, G. (Derbys.):– Highest for Derbyshire, *135.*

Davies, D. E. (Glam.):– All-round, *164;* Highest for Glamorgan, *135;* 26,564 r., *143;* 1,000 r. (16), *141;* 139 and hat-trick v Leicestershire, *164;* 1st wkt hundreds, *151.*
Davies, T. (Glam.):– 6 d. in NWB Trophy innings, *727.*
Davis, C. A. (WI):– 4 Test hundreds, *215, 243, 245;* Test avge of 54.20, *180;* Test p'ship record, *243.*
Davis, I. C. (Aust.):– 1 Test hundred, *238;* Test p'ship record, *239.*
Davison, B. F. (Leics. and Tas.):– 27,453 r., *143;* 53 hundreds, *139.*
Dawkes, G. O. (Derbys.):– 1,043 d., *168;* w-k hat-trick, *159, 166.*
Dean, H. (Eng.):– 100 w. (8), *161;* 17 w. in match, *157.*
Deed, J. A. (Kent II):– 252 v Surrey II, *270.*
DeFreitas, P. A. J. (Eng.):– Man of Match in NWB Trophy final, *724.*
Deloitte Ratings, *988.*
de Mel, A. L. F. (SL):– 59 w. in Tests, *189;* Test p'ship records, *227, 258.*
Dempster, C. S. (NZ):– 35 hundreds, *140;* 2 Test hundreds, *218;* Test p'ship record, *219.*
Denmark:– Cricket in, *1201;* ICC Trophy, *354-6, 357-8, 359.*
Denness, M. H. (Eng.):– Test captain, *200, 213, 217, 220, 223;* 25,886 r., *144;* 1,000 r. (15), *141;* 4 Test hundreds, *202, 218, 221;* Test p'ship record, *219.*
Dennett, G. E. (Glos.):– 2,147 w., *162, 163;* 201 w. in season, *160;* 100 w. (12), *161;* 10 w. in innings, *156.*
Denton, D. (Eng.):– 36,479 r., *143, 144;* 1,000 r. (21), *141;* 69 hundreds, *139;* 1 Test hundred, *210;* 2 hundreds in match (3), *137.*
Depeiza, C. C. (WI):– 1 Test hundred, *231;* 347 for 7th wkt v Australia, *153, 184, 232.*
Derbyshire:– *378, 386-401;* Championship positions, *384-5;* Highest score, *169;* Highest individual score, *135;* Lowest score, *170;* Refuge Assurance League winners, *761.*
Derbyshire II, *868, 872-3, 889.*
Desai, R. B. (Ind.):– Test p'ship records, *250, 256.*
Desai, S. (Karn.):– 451* for 1st wkt, *149, 150, 151.*
de Silva, D. S. (SL):– Test captain, *253;* Oldest Sri Lankan Test début, *198;* Test p'ship records, *240, 258, 259.*
de Silva, E. A. R. (SL):– Test p'ship record, *258.*
de Silva, P. A. (SL):– 3 Test hundreds, *240, 259;* 221* in 1990, *273;* 263 for 4th wkt, *277;* Test p'ship records, *258, 259.*
Devon, *706-7, 849, 851, 858.*
Dexter, E. R. (Eng.):– Test captain, *200, 213, 217, 220, 223;* 4,502 r. in Tests, *177;* 1,038 Test r. in year, *177;* 51 hundreds, *139;* 8 Test hundreds, *202, 210, 214, 218, 221, 224;* Test p'ship records, *225.*
Dias, R. L. (SL):– 3 Test hundreds, *254, 257, 259;* Test p'ship records, *227, 254, 258, 259.*
Dick, A. E. (NZ):– 23 d. in series, *193;* Test p'ship record, *242.*
Dildar Malik (Multan):– 7 d. in innings, *166.*
Dilley, G. R. (Eng.):– 138 w. in Tests, *187.*
Dipper, A. E. (Glos.):– 1,000 r. (15), *141;* 53 hundreds, *139.*
Dodemaide, A. I. C. (Aust.):– All-round in 1990, *278;* Test p'ship record, *234.*
Doggart, G. H. G. (Eng.):– 215* on début, *135.*
D'Oliveira, B. L. (Eng.):– 2,484 r. in Tests, *178;* 43 hundreds, *139;* 5 Test hundreds, *202, 218, 221, 224.*
D'Oliveira, D. B. (Worcs.):– 264 for 3rd wkt, *277;* 226 for 6th wkt, *277.*
Dollery, H. E. (Eng.):– 1,000 r. (15), *141;* 50 hundreds, *139.*
Donnelly, M. P. (NZ):– 1 Test hundred, *218;* Hundreds at Lord's, *373.*
Dorreen, N. (Cant.):– 265 for 7th wkt, *153.*
Dorset, *707-8, 849, 851, 858-9.*
Doshi, D. R. (Ind.):– 114 w. in Tests, *189.*
Double, The, *165, 190-1, 278.*
Double-hundreds in 1990, *273.*
Douglas, J. (Middx):– 1st wkt hundreds, *151.*
Douglas, J. W. H. T. (Eng.):– Test captain, *200-1, 208;* All-round, *165;* 1 Test hundred, *210;* 3 hat-tricks, *159;* 1,893 w., *162;* Test p'ship record, *211.*
Dowling, G. T. (NZ):– Test captain, *217, 242, 249, 251;* 2,306 r. in Tests, *179;* 3 Test hundreds, *250;* Test p'ship records, *250.*
Downes, A. D. (Otago):– 4 w. with consecutive balls, *158.*
Downton, P. R. (Eng.):– 20 d. in series, *193;* Test p'ship record, *226.*
Drake, A. (Yorks.):– 10 w. in innings, *156;* 4 w. with consecutive balls, *158.*
Ducat, A. (Eng.):– 52 hundreds, *139;* 306* in day v Oxford Univ., *134, 146;* 50 boundaries in innings, *149.*
Duchess of Norfolk's XI:– v New Zealanders, *298.*
Duckworth, G. (Eng.):– 1,095 d., *168;* 107 d. in season, *167.*
Duff, R. A. (Aust.):– 2 Test hundreds, *203;* Hundred on Test début, *174, 203.*
Dujon, P. J. L. (WI):– 2,994 r. in Tests, *179;* 5 Test hundreds, *215, 231, 245, 248;* 223 d. in Tests, *193;* 188 d. in one-day ints, *266;* 20 d. in series (2), *193;* All-round in one-day ints, *267;* Test p'ship record, *248.*
Duleep Trophy (Ind.), *1178.*
Duleepsinhji, K. S. (Eng.):– Highest for Sussex, *135;* 50 hundreds, *139;* 4 successive hundreds, *138;* 3 Test hundreds, *202, 218;* 2 hundreds in match (3), *137;* Hundred and double-hundred, *136;* 333 v Northamptonshire, *133, 135.*

Dunell, O. R. (SA):– Test captain, *208*.
Durani, S. A. (Ind.):– 1 Test hundred, *246;* 10 w. or more in Test (1), *223*.
Durham:– *710, 849, 850, 859-60;* Election to f-c status, *1327*.
Durham Univ.:– UAU Championship winners, *893;* v MCC, *697;* v Scotland B, *900*.
Dymock, G. (Aust.):– 10 w. or more in Test (1), *237*.
Dyson, A. H. (Glam.):– 305 consecutive Championship appearances, *272;* 1st wkt hundreds, *151*.
Dyson, J. (Aust.):– 2 Test hundreds, *203, 230*.

E

Eady, C. J. (Tas.):– 566 v Wellington, *270*.
East, D. E. (Essex):– 8 d. in innings, *165*.
East, R. J. (OFS):– 7 d. in innings, *166*.
Edgar, B. A. (NZ):– 3 Test hundreds, *234, 243, 252;* Slow scoring in Test, *183;* Test p'ship record, *219*.
Edmonds, P. H. (Eng.):– 125 w. in Tests, *187;* 4 w. for 6 r. in Test innings, *186;* Test p'ship record, *222*.
Edrich, J. H. (Eng.):– Test captain, *200;* 39,790 r., *142;* 5,138 r. in Tests, *177;* 2,644 r. v Australia, *208;* 1,000 r. (21), *141;* 103 hundreds, *138;* 12 Test hundreds, *202, 214, 218, 221;* 2 hundreds in match (4), *137;* 310* v New Zealand, *134, 174, 218;* 57 boundaries in innings, *149;* 1st wkt hundreds, *150;* 369 for 2nd wkt v New Zealand, *184, 219*.
Edrich, W. J. (Eng.):– 36,965 r., *143;* 3,539 r. (avge 80.43) in season, *140, 142;* 2,440 r. in Tests, *178;* 1,010 r. (April 30-May 31), *147;* 1,000 r. (15), *141;* 86 hundreds, *139;* 6 Test hundreds, *202, 210, 218;* 424* for 3rd wkt, *152;* 370 for 3rd wkt v South Africa, *184, 211;* Test p'ship records, *211*.
Edwards, R. (Aust.):– 2 Test hundreds, *203*.
Elliott, G. (Vic.):– 9 w. for 2 r., *157*.
Elliott, H. (Eng.):– 1,206 d., *168;* 10 d. in match, *166*.
Ellison, R. M. (Eng.):– 10 w. or more in Test (1), *206;* Test p'ship record, *226*.
Emburey, J. E. (Eng.):– Test captain, *213;* 138 w. in Tests, *187;* 270 w. in Sunday League, *845;* All-round in Tests, *191*.
Emmett, G. M. (Eng.):– 25,602 r., *144;* 37 hundreds, *140;* 2 hundreds in match (2), *137*.
Emmett, T. (Eng.):– 1,571 w., *162;* 16 w. in day, *158*.
Endean, W. R. (SA):– Handled the ball, *154;* 3 Test hundreds, *210, 228, 241;* Test p'ship records, *229, 241*.
Engineer, F. M. (Ind.):– 2,611 r. in Tests, *180;* 2 Test hundreds, *221, 246;* Test p'ship records, *222, 250*.
England:– Definition of first-class matches, *368, 1319;* England in Test cricket (*see p. 132*); England v Rest of the World, *227;* Highest individual Test innings, *174;* Highest Test innings, *194;* Hon. MCC members, *368;* Leading batsmen in Tests, *177;* Leading bowlers in Tests, *187;* Lowest Test innings, *196;* Most consecutive Test appearances, *198;* Most Test appearances, *128;* Most Test appearances as captain, *128;* Nehru Cup, *1063-75;* Oldest Test player, *198;* Qualification and registration of players, *1321-3;* Representative body, *1315;* Summary of Tests, *199;* Summary of one-day ints, *264;* Test cricketers (1877-1990), *85-97;* Youngest and oldest on Test début, *197-8*.
England Under-17:– v Pakistan Young Cricketers, *902*.
England Young Cricketers:– in Australia, *999;* v Pakistan Young Cricketers, *902-6*.
English XI in South Africa, 1989-90, *1135, 1148-51*.
English Schools Cricket Association:– Address, *1316;* 1990 season, *909-10, 912;* v Pakistan Young Cricketers, *903, 904, 910*.
Errata in *Wisden*, *1327*.
Essex:– *378, 402-18;* Championship positions, *384-5;* Esso/NAYC Under-19 winners, *908;* Highest score, *169;* Highest individual score, *135;* Lowest score, *170;* Scarborough Festival Trophy, *701*.
Essex II, *868, 869, 873-4, 889*.
Esso/NAYC Under-19 County Festivals, *907-8*.
Eton v Harrow, *369-70*.
European Cup (Women), *1204-6*.
Evans, T. G. (Eng.):– 2,439 r. in Tests, *178;* 2 Test hundreds, *214, 221;* Slow scoring in Test, *183;* 1,066 d., *168;* 219 d. in Tests, *193;* 75 d. v Australia, *207;* 20 d. in series, *193*.
Exeter Univ.:– UAU Championship finalists, *893*.

F

Fagg, A. E. (Eng.):– 27,291 r., *143;* 58 hundreds, *139;* 2 double-hundreds, *136;* 2 hundreds in match (2), *137*.
FAI Cup (Aust.), *1131-2*.
Fairbairn, A. (Middx):– Hundred on début, *135, 136*.
Fairbrother, N. H. (Eng.):– 10,000 r., *279;* 366 v Surrey, *133, 273;* 311* in day, *146, 275;* 203* in 1990, *273;* Hundred before lunch, *275;* 52 boundaries in innings, *149, 276;* 364 for 3rd wkt, *277*.
Falkner, N. J. (Surrey):– Hundred on début, *135*.
Family connections, *261-3*.
Fane, F. L. (Eng.):– Test captain, *200, 209;* 1 Test hundred, *210*.
Farnes, K. (Eng.):– 10 w. or more in Test (1), *206*.
Farrimond, W. (Eng.):– 7 d. in innings, *165*.
Faulkner, G. A. (SA):– 4 Test hundreds, *210, 228;* All-round in Test, *190*.

Favell, L. E. (Aust.):– 1 Test hundred, *235;* 2 hundreds in match (2), *137.*
Fazal Mahmood (Pak.):– Test captain, *237, 247, 254;* 139 w. in Tests, *189;* 10 w. or more in Test (3), *225, 239, 249.*
Fender, P. G. H. (Eng.):– All-round, *165;* Hundred in 35 minutes, *145.*
Ferguson, W. (WI):– 10 w. or more in Test (1), *216.*
Fernandes, M. P. (WI):– Test captain, *213.*
Fernando, L. R. (SL):– 10 c. in match, *167.*
Ferris, J. J. (Aust. and Eng.):– 10 w. or more in Test (1), *212.*
Fielder, A. (Eng.):– 10 w. in innings, *156;* 235 for 10th wkt, *154.*
Fielding statistics, 1990, *278, 580.*
Findlay, T. M. (WI):– Test p'ship record, *243.*
Fingleton, J. H. (Aust.):– 5 Test hundreds, *203, 228;* 346 for 6th wkt v England, *184, 205;* Test p'ship records, *205, 229.*
First-class match defined, *368, 1319-20.*
First-wicket hundreds, *150-1.*
First-wicket partnerships, *150.*
Fisher, H. (Yorks.):– LBW hat-trick, *159.*
Fishlock, L. B. (Eng.):– 25,376 r., *144;* 56 hundreds, *139;* 2 hundreds in match (4), *137.*
Flavell, J. A. (Eng.):– 1,529 w., *163;* 100 w. (8), *161;* 3 hat-tricks, *159;* LBW hat-trick, *159.*
Fleetwood-Smith, L. O'B. (Aust.):– 10 w. or more in Test (1), *206.*
Fletcher, K. W. R. (Eng.):– Test captain, *220, 226;* 37,665 r., *142;* 3,272 r. in Tests, *178;* 1,090 Test r. in year, *177;* 1,000 r. (20), *141;* 63 hundreds, *139;* 7 Test hundreds, *202, 214, 218, 221, 224;* Slow Test hundred, *183;* Test p'ship records, *219, 222.*
Folley, I. (Lancs.):– Career figures, *1324.*
Fordham, A. (Northants):– 206* in 1990, *273;* 393 for 3rd wkt, *277.*
Formation of counties, *271-2.*
Foster, F. R. (Eng.):– Highest for Warwickshire, *135;* 305* for Warwickshire in day, *134, 135, 146.*
Foster, M. L. C. (WI):– 1 Test hundred, *231;* Test p'ship record, *232.*
Foster, N. A. (Eng.):– 10 w. or more in Test (1), *223;* 8 w. in Test innings, *186;* Most w. in 1990, *278;* Test p'ship records, *226.*
Foster, R. E. (Eng.):– Test captain, *208;* 2 hundreds in match (3), *137;* 300 r. on Test début, *175;* 287 v Australia on Test début, *134, 174, 202;* Test p'ship record, *205.*
Foster, W. L. (Worcs.):– 2 hundreds in match, *137.*
Four w. with consecutive balls, *158.*
Fourth innings, highest totals, *171.*
Fowler, G. (Eng.):– 3 Test hundreds, *214, 218, 221;* Test p'ship records, *219, 222.*
Frank, C. N. (SA):– 1 Test hundred, *228;* Test p'ship record, *229.*
Franklin, T. J. (NZ):– 1 Test hundred, *218;* Test p'ship record, *250.*
Fredericks, R. C. (WI):– 4,334 r. in Tests, *179;* 40 hundreds, *139;* 8 Test hundreds, *215, 231, 243, 245, 248;* 2 hundreds in match (3), *137;* Fast Test fifty, *182;* Fast Test hundred, *182;* Test p'ship records, *243, 248.*
Free Foresters:– v Cambridge Univ., *685;* v Oxford Univ., *673.*
Freeman, A. P. (Eng.):– 3,776 w., *161;* 2,090 w. in eight seasons, *161;* 1,122 w. in four seasons, *161;* 304 w. in season, *160;* 200 w. (8), *160;* 100 w. (17), *161;* 100 w. by June 13, *161;* 17 w. in match (2) *157;* 10 w. in innings (3), *156;* 10 w. or more in Test (3), *212, 216;* 3 hat-tricks, *159.*
Freeman, D. L. (NZ):– Youngest New Zealand Test player, *197.*
French, B. N. (Eng.):– 10 d. in match, *167.*
Fry, C. B. (Eng.):– Test captain, *200, 208;* 30,886 r. (avge 50.22), *143, 145;* Aggregate of 3,147 r., *140;* 94 hundreds, *139;* 13 hundreds in season, *138;* 6 and 4 successive hundreds, *138;* 2 Test hundreds, *202, 210;* 2 hundreds in match (5), *137;* Hundred and double-hundred, *136;* Avge of 81.30 in English season, *142;* 1st wkt hundreds, *151.*
Funston, K. J. (SA):– Test p'ship record, *241.*
Future tours, *363.*

G

Gaekwad, A. D. (Ind.):– 2 Test hundreds, *246, 255;* Test p'ship record, *246.*
Gaekwad, D. K. (Ind.):– Test captain, *220.*
Gallian, J. E. R. (Lancs.):– Wkt with 1st ball in f-c cricket, *278.*
Ganteaume, A. G. (WI):– Hundred on Test début, *174, 215.*
Gard, T. (Som.): Career figures, *1324.*
Garner, J. (WI):– 259 w. in Tests, *188;* 146 w. in one-day ints, *266;* Test p'ship records, *232, 243, 248.*
Garnett, E. (Berks.):– 282 v Wiltshire, *270.*
Gartrell, R. B. (Tas.):– Handled the ball, *154.*
Gatting, M. W. (Eng.):– Test captain, *200, 213, 217, 220, 223;* Captain of Middlesex, *516;* 3,870 r. in Tests, *177;* 58 hundreds, *139;* 9 Test hundreds, *202, 218, 221, 224;* Test p'ship record, *222.*
Gavaskar, S. M. (Ind.):– Test captain, *128, 220, 235, 244, 249, 254, 256;* 125 Tests, *128, 198;* 106 consecutive Tests, *198;* 25,834 r. (avge 51.46), *144, 145;* 10,122 r. (avge 51.12) in Tests, *179, 181;* 2,121 r. in overseas season, *141;* 1,555 and 1,310 Test r. in year, *176;* 774 r. in series, *176;* 81 hundreds, *139;* 34 Test hundreds, *181, 221, 236, 246, 250, 255, 257;* 2 hundreds in same Test (3), *137, 175, 246, 255;* Hundred and double-hundred, *136;* 236* v West Indies, *174, 246;* Slow scoring in Test, *183;* Carrying bat in Test, *181;* 340 v Bengal, *133;* 108 c. in Tests, *194;* 421

Gavaskar, S. M. (Ind.):– *contd*
for 1st wkt, *150;* 344* for 2nd wkt v West Indies, *184, 246;* Test p'ship records, *222, 236, 246, 250, 255, 257.*
Geary, G. (Eng.):– 2,063 w., *162;* 100 w. (11), *161;* 10 w. in innings, *156;* 10 w. or more in Test (1), *212.*
Geddes Grant Shield (WI), *1154, 1157.*
Ghavri, K. D. (Ind.):– 109 w. in Tests, *189;* Test p'ship records, *236.*
Ghosh, A. (Bihar):– 10 d. in match, *167.*
Ghulam Ahmed (Ind.):– Test captain, *244, 249;* 10 w. or more in Test (1), *237;* Test p'ship record, *256.*
Gibb, P. A. (Eng.):– 2 Test hundreds, *210;* Hundred on Test début, *174;* Test p'ship record, *211.*
Gibb, P. J. M. (Tvl):– 342 for 4th wkt, *152.*
Gibbons, H. H. I. (Worcs.):– 44 hundreds, *139.*
Gibbs, G. L. R. (WI):– 390 for 1st wkt, *150, 151.*
Gibbs, L. R. (WI):– 309 w. in Tests, *188;* 10 w. or more in Test (2), *216;* 8 w. in Test innings, *185;* Hat-trick v Australia, *190.*
Giffen, G. (Aust.):– Test captain, *200;* All-round, *163, 165;* All-round in Tests, *191;* 1 Test hundred, *203;* 113 and hat-trick v Lancashire, *164;* 103 w. in Tests, *188, 208;* 17 w. in match, *157;* 10 w. in innings, *155;* 10 w. or more in Test (1), *206;* 3 hat-tricks, *159.*
Gifford, N. (Eng.):– 2,068 w., *162;* 284 w. in Sunday League, *845;* Test p'ship records, *219, 222.*
Gilbert, D. R. (Aust.):– Test p'ship record, *236.*
Gill, J. R. (Ireland):– Hundred on début, *135.*
Gillette Cup winners, *728.*
Gilligan, A. E. R. (Eng.):– Test captain, *200, 209;* 10 w. or more in Test (1), *212;* 6 w. for 7 r. in Test innings, *186;* Test p'ship record, *211.*
Gilligan, A. H. H. (Eng.):– Test captain, *217.*
Gilmour, G. J. (Aust.):– 1 Test hundred, *233;* Test p'ship records, *234.*
Gimblett, H. (Eng.):– 310 v Sussex, *134;* 50 hundreds, *139;* 2 hundreds in match (2), *137.*
Gladwin, C. (Eng.):– 100 w. (12), *161.*
Glamorgan:– *387, 419-34;* Championship positions, *384-5;* Highest score, *169;* Highest individual score, *135;* Lowest score, *170.*
Glamorgan II, *868, 869, 874-5, 889.*
Gloucestershire:– *387, 435-50;* Championship positions, *384-5;* Highest score, *169;* Highest individual score, *135;* Lowest score, *170.*
Gloucestershire II, *868, 869, 875-6, 889.*
Goddard, J. D. C. (WI):– Test captain, *213, 229, 242, 244;* 502* for 4th wkt, *149;* Test p'ship record, *243.*
Goddard, T. L. (SA):– Test captain, *209, 227, 240;* 2,516 r. in Tests, *178;* 1 Test hundred, *210;* Carrying bat in Test, *181;* 123 w. in Tests, *188;* All-round in Tests, *191.*
Goddard, T. W. (Eng.):– 2,979 w., *161;* 200 w. (4), *160;* 100 w. (16), *161;* 17 w. in day, *158;* 17 w. in match, *157;* 10 w. in innings, *156;* 6 hat-tricks, *159;* Test hat-trick, *190.*
Goel, R. (Haryana):– 7 w. for 4 r., *157.*
Gomes, H. A. (WI):– 3,171 r. in Tests, *179;* 9 Test hundreds, *215, 231, 245;* Test p'ship records, *216, 232.*
Gomez, G. E. (WI):– Test captain, *213;* 1 Test hundred, *245;* 10 w. or more in Test (1), *232;* 434 for 3rd wkt, *152;* Test p'ship record, *246.*
Gooch, G. A. (Eng.):– "A Genuinely Great Cricketer" by Simon Barnes, *79;* Test captain, *213, 217, 220, 226;* Captain of Essex, *402;* 31,363 r, *143, 279;* 5,910 r. in Tests, *177;* 6,324 r. in Sunday League, *843;* 1,264 Test r. in year, *177;* 1,000 Test r. in English season, *176;* 752 r. in series, *176;* 1,000 r. (15), *141;* Average of 101.70 in English season, *142;* Highest aggregate since 1969, *140;* 456 r. in Test, *222;* 333 v India at Lord's, *133, 173, 269, 273;* 215 in 1990, *273;* 82 hundreds, *139;* 12 Test hundreds, *202, 214, 218, 221;* 8 one-day int. hundreds, *265;* 2 hundreds in same Test, *176;* Hundred and double-hundred, *137;* 2 hundreds in match (2), *137, 275;* 3 hundreds in succession, *273;* 30 r. in over, *148;* Record score in B & H Cup, *758,* in Sunday League, *843;* 1st wkt hundreds, *150, 276;* 403 for 2nd wkt, *277;* 351 for 2nd wkt v Australia, *184;* 308 for 3rd wkt v India, *184, 222, 277;* Test p'ship records, *222, 226.*
Goonatillake, H. M. (SL):– Test p'ship record, *259.*
Gould, I. J. (Middx, Auck. and Sussex):– Career figures, *1324.*
Govan, J. W. (Scotland and Northants):– Career figures, *1324.*
Gover, A. R. (Eng.):– 200 w. (2), *160;* 100 w. (8), *161;* 4 w. with consecutive balls, *158.*
Gower, D. I. (Eng.):– Test captain, *200, 213, 220, 223, 226;* 7,674 r. in Tests, *177;* 2,862 r. v Australia, *208;* 1,061 and 1,059 Test r. in year, *177;* 46 hundreds, *139;* 16 Test hundreds, *202, 214, 218, 221, 224;* 7 one-day int. hundreds, *265;* 351 for 2nd wkt v Australia, *184;* 331 for 2nd wkt v Australia, *184;* 256 for 3rd wkt, *277;* Test p'ship records, *224, 226.*
Grace, Dr E. M. (Eng.):– 192* and 10 w., *157, 163.*
Grace, Dr W. G. (Eng.):– Test captain, *200;* All-round, *164, 165;* Highest for Gloucestershire, *135;* Test cricket at 50, *198;* Throwing the cricket ball, *271;* 54,896 r., *142, 144, 165;* 2,739 r. in season, *140;* 1,000 r. (28), *140;* 1,000 r. in May, *146;* 126 hundreds, *138;* 2 Test hundreds, *202;* Hundred on Test début, *174;* 2

Grace, Dr W. G. (Eng.):– *contd* hundreds in match (3), *137;* 344 v Kent, *133;* 318* v Yorkshire, *133, 135;* 301 v Sussex, *134;* 130 and 102* at Canterbury, *137;* 123 and hat-trick v Kent, *164;* 104 and 10 w., *163;* 2,876 w., *163, 165;* 100 w. (10), *161;* 17 w. in match, *157;* 10 w. in innings, *155, 157;* 887 c., *169;* 1st wkt hundreds, *151*.
Graham, H. (Aust.):– 2 Test hundreds, *203;* Hundred on Test début, *174*.
Grant, G. C. (WI):– Test captain, *213, 229*.
Grant, R. S. (WI):– Test captain, *213*.
Graveney, D. A. (Glos.):– Career figures, *1324*.
Graveney, J. K. (Glos.):– 10 w. in innings, *156*.
Graveney, T. W. (Eng.):– Test captain, *200;* 47,793 r., *142;* 4,882 r. in Tests, *177;* 1,000 r. (22), *141;* 122 hundreds, *138;* 11 Test hundreds, *202, 214, 221, 224;* 2 hundreds in match (3), *137;* 258 v West Indies, *174, 214;* Test p'ship records, *215, 216, 225*.
Gray, J. R. (Hants):– 1st wkt hundreds, *151*.
Greatbatch, M. J. (NZ):– 2 Test hundreds, *218, 234;* Hundred on Test début, *175, 218;* 2 hundreds in match, *275;* Test avge of 53.94, *180;* Test p'ship records, *219, 234, 250*.
Green, A. M. (Sussex and OFS):– Career figures, *1324*.
Greenidge, C. G. (WI):– Test captain, *247;* Fast scoring, *183;* 36,434 r., *143;* 6,344 r. in Sunday League, *843;* 7,134 r. in Tests, *179;* 4,981 r. in one-day ints, *265;* 1,149 Test r. in year, *177;* 90 hundreds, *139;* 18 Test hundreds, *215, 231, 243, 245, 248;* 11 hundreds in Sunday League, *843;* 11 one-day int. hundreds, *265;* 4 successive hundreds, *138;* 2 hundreds in match (4), *137;* 2 hundreds in same Test, *176, 215;* Hundred on Test début, *175, 245;* 1,000 r. (17), *141;* Avge of 82.23 in English season, *142;* 13 sixes in innings (2), *148;* Test p'ship records, *216, 232, 243, 246, 248*.
Gregory, C. W. (Aust.):– 383 v Queensland, *133;* 318 r. in day, *146;* 55 boundaries in innings, *149*.
Gregory, D. W. (Aust.):– Test captain, *200*.
Gregory, J. M. (Aust.):– 2 Test hundreds, *203, 228;* Fastest Test hundred, *182;* All-round in Test, *190*.
Gregory, R. J. (Surrey):– 39 hundreds, *139*.
Gregory, S. E. (Aust.):– Test captain, *199, 227;* 2,282 r. in Tests, *178;* 2,193 r. v England, *208;* 4 Test hundreds, *203;* Test p'ship record, *205*.
Greig, A. W. (Eng.):– Test captain, *200, 213, 220;* 3,599 r. in Tests, *177;* 8 Test hundreds, *202, 214, 218, 221;* 141 w. in Tests, *187;* 10 w. or more in Test (2), *216, 219;* 8 w. in Test innings, *185;* All-round in Tests, *190, 191;* 6 c. in Test, *194;* Test p'ship records, *216, 222*.
Greig, I. A. (Eng.):– Captain of Surrey, *581;* Hundred before lunch, *275;* 291 in 1990, *273;* 205 for 8th wkt, *277*.
Grieves, K. J. (Lancs.):– 63 c. in season, *168;* 8 c. in match, *168*.
Griffin, G. M. (SA):– Hat-trick v England, *190*.
Griffith, H. C. (WI):– 138 for 10th wkt, *154*.
Griffith, S. C. (Eng.):– Hundred on Test début, *174, 214*.
Griffiths, The Rt Hon. The Lord:– President of MCC, *364*.
Grimmett, C. V. (Aust.):– 216 w. in Tests, *188;* 44 w. in series, *187;* 14 w. v South Africa, *186;* 10 w. in innings, *156;* 10 w. or more in Test (7), *206, 229, 232;* Test p'ship record, *229*.
Grounds, Test match, *260-1*.
Grout, A. T. W. (Aust.):– 187 d. in Tests, *193;* 76 d. v England, *207;* 23 d. in series, *193;* 8 d. in innings, *165;* 8 d. in Test, *192;* 6 d. in Test innings, *192*.
Guise, J. L. (Winchester):– 278 v Eton, *270*.
Gul Mahomed (Ind.):– 319 v Holkar, *133, 152;* 577 for 4th wkt, *149, 152*.
Gulfraz Khan (Pak. Rlwys):– 12 sixes in innings, *148;* 240 for 8th wkt, *153*.
Gunn, G. (Eng.):– Test cricket at 50, *198;* 35,208 r., *143;* 1,000 r. (20), *141;* 62 hundreds, *139;* 2 Test hundreds, *202;* 2 hundreds in match (3), *137;* Hundred on Test début, *174;* (and G. V. Gunn) Hundreds in same match, *137;* 1st wkt hundreds, *151*.
Gunn, J. (Eng.):– All-round, *165;* 40 hundreds, *139*.
Gunn, W. (Eng.):– 25,691 r., *144;* 48 hundreds, *139;* 1 Test hundred, *202*.
Gupte, M. S. (M'tra):– 405 for 1st wkt, *150*.
Gupte, S. P. (Ind.):– 149 w. in Tests, *189;* 10 w. in innings, *156;* 10 w. or more in Test (1), *247;* 9 w. in Test innings, *185, 247*.
Gurusinha, A. P. (SL):– 1 Test hundred, *259;* Test p'ship record, *259*.
Guy, J. W. (NZ):– 1 Test hundred, *250;* Test p'ship record, *250*.

H

Haaris Khan (Karachi Blues):– Hat-trick, *159, 1182*.
Hadlee, D. R. (NZ):– Test p'ship records, *234, 252*.
Hadlee, Sir R. J. (NZ):– "Sir Richard Hadlee" by Don Mosey, *57;* All-round, *165;* All-round in Tests, *191;* All-round in one-day ints, *267;* 86 Tests, *128, 198;* 3,124 r. in Tests, *179;* 2 Test hundreds, *243, 254;* 431 w. in Tests, *188;* 158 w. in one-day ints, *266;* 15 w. in Test, *186, 234;* 10 w. or more in Test (9), *186, 219, 234, 244, 251;* 9 w. in Test innings, *185;* 246* for 6th wkt, *153;* Test p'ship records, *234, 250, 252, 254*.

Hadlee, W. A. (NZ):– Test captain, *217, 233;* 1 Test hundred, *218.*
Hafeez, A. (Ind. and Pak.), *see* Kardar, A. H.
Haig, N. E. (Eng.):– All-round, *165.*
Haigh, S. (Eng.):– 2,012 w., *162;* 100 w. (11), *161;* 6 w. for 11 r. in Test innings, *184;* 5 hat-tricks, *159;* 4 w. with consecutive balls, *158.*
Halangoda, M. B. (SSC):– Hat-trick, *159, 1192, 1196.*
Hall, A. E. (SA):– 10 w. or more in Test (1), *212.*
Hall, W. W. (WI):– 192 w. in Tests, *188;* 10 w. or more in Test (1), *247;* Hat-trick v Pakistan, *190;* Test p'ship record, *246.*
Hallam, M. R. (Leics.):– 2 hundreds in match (3), *137;* Hundred and double-hundred (2), *136.*
Halliwell, E. A. (SA):– Test captain, *208, 227;* Test p'ship record, *229.*
Hallows, C. (Eng.):– 1,000 r. in May, *146;* 55 hundreds, *139;* 2 hundreds in match (2), *137;* 1st wkt hundreds, *150.*
Hamence, R. A. (Aust.):– 2 hundreds in match (2), *137.*
Hammond, W. R. (Eng.):– Test captain, *200, 209, 213, 217, 220;* 50,551 r. (avge 56.10), *142, 144;* 7,249 r. (avge 58.45) in Tests, *177, 180;* 3,323 r. in season, *140;* 2,852 r. v Australia, *208;* 1,042 r. in May, *146;* 1,000 r. (22), *141;* 905 r. in series, *176, 206;* 167 hundreds, *138;* 22 Test hundreds, *181, 202, 203, 210, 214, 218, 221;* 15 and 13 hundreds in season, *138;* 4 successive hundreds, *138;* 2 hundreds in match (7), *137;* 2 hundreds and 10 c. in match, *168;* 2 hundreds in same Test, *176, 202;* 336* v New Zealand, *133, 173, 218;* 317 v Nottinghamshire, *133;* 302* and 302 v Glamorgan, *134;* 295 r. in day in Test, *183;* 251 v Australia, *174;* Avge of 84.90 in English season, *142;* Fast scoring, *182, 183;* 819 c., *169;* 78 c. and 65 c. in season, *168;* 10 c. in match, *168;* Test p'ship records, *205, 211, 215, 219, 222.*
Hampshire:– *378, 451-67;* Championship positions, *384-5;* Highest score, *169;* Highest individual score, *135;* Lowest score, *170;* Scarborough Festival Trophy winners, *700-2.*
Hampshire II, *868, 869, 876-7, 889.*
Hampshire, J. H. (Eng.):– 28,059 r., *143;* 1,000 r. (15), *141;* 43 hundreds, *139;* Hundred on Test début, *175, 214.*
Hanif Mohammad (Pak.):– Test captain, *223, 237, 251;* Test début at 17, *197;* Longest first-class innings, *133, 134;* 17,059 r. (avge 52.32), *145;* 3,915 r. in Tests, *180;* 55 hundreds, *139;* 12 Test hundreds, *224, 238, 248, 252, 255;* 2 hundreds in match (3), *137;* 2 hundreds in same Test, *176, 224;* 499 v Bahawalpur, *133;* 337 v West Indies, *133, 173, 248;* 64 boundaries in innings, *149;* Slow batting in Test, *183;* Test p'ship records, *225, 248, 253, 256.*
Hanumant Singh (Ind.):– Hundred on Test début, *175, 221;* Hundred and double-hundred, *136;* Test p'ship record, *250.*
Harden, R. J. (Som.):– 256 for 4th wkt, *277.*
Hardie, B. R. (Scotland and Essex):– Career figures, *1324.*
Hardinge, H. T. W. (Eng.):– 33,519 r., *143;* 1,000 r. (18), *141;* 75 hundreds, *139;* 4 successive hundreds, *138;* 2 hundreds in match (4), *137;* Hundred and double-hundred, *136.*
Hardstaff, J. jun. (Eng.):– Obituary, *1263;* 31,847 r., *143;* 83 hundreds, *139;* 4 Test hundreds, *202, 218, 221;* Test p'ship records, *205, 219.*
Haroon Rashid (Pak.):– 3 Test hundreds, *224, 259;* Test p'ship records, *225, 259.*
Harper, R. A. (WI):– 12 sixes in innings, *148.*
Harris, 4th Lord (Eng.):– Test captain, *199.*
Harris, C. B. (Notts.):– 1st wkt hundreds, *151.*
Harris, M. J. (Middx and Notts.):– 41 hundreds, *139;* 2 hundreds in match (3), *137.*
Harris, P. G. Z. (NZ):– Test p'ship record, *242.*
Harrison, G. D. (Ireland):– 9 w. in innings, *277, 897.*
Harrogate Festival, *656-7, 696-7.*
Harrow v Eton, *369-70.*
Hart, R. T. (C. Dist.):– 317 for 2nd wkt, *151.*
Hartigan, R. J. (Aust.):– Hundred on Test début, *174, 203;* Test p'ship record, *205.*
Harvey, R. N. (Aust.):– Test captain, *200;* 21,699 r. (avge 50.93), *145;* 6,149 r. in Tests, *178;* 2,416 r. v England, *208;* 834 r. in series, *176;* 67 hundreds, *139;* 21 Test hundreds, *181, 203, 228, 230, 235;* 6 c. in Test, *194;* Test p'ship records, *229, 232.*
Harvey-Walker, A. J. (Derbys.):– Hundred on début, *135.*
Hassett, A. L. (Aust.):– Test captain, *200, 227, 229;* 16,890 r. (avge 58.24), *144;* 3,073 r. in Tests, *178;* 59 hundreds, *139;* 10 Test hundreds, *203, 228, 230, 235;* 2 hundreds in match (2), *137;* Test p'ship records, *205, 229.*
Hastings, B. F. (NZ):– 4 Test hundreds, *234, 243, 252;* 151 for 10th wkt v Pakistan, *184, 252;* Test p'ship records, *184, 234, 244, 252.*
Hathorn, C. M. H. (SA):– 1 Test hundred, *210.*
Hat-tricks:– *159;* Double, *159;* in one-day ints, *266;* in Test matches, *189;* All caught, *159;* All LBW, *159;* All stumped, *159;* Three and more, *159;* in 1990, *277.*
Havewalla, D. R. (BB and CI Rlwys):– 515 v St Xavier's, *270.*
Hawke, 7th Lord (Eng.):– Test captain, *208;* 292 for 8th wkt, *153.*
Hawke, N. J. N. (Aust.):– 10 w. or more in Test (1) *232.*

Hawkesworth, W. (Otago):– 184 for 10th wkt, *154*.

Hayes, E. G. (Eng.):– 27,318 r., *143;* 1,000 r. (16), *141;* 48 hundreds, *139*.

Hayes, F. C. (Eng.):– Hundred on Test début, *175, 214;* 34 r. in over, *147*.

Hayes, J. A. (NZ):– Obstructing the field, *151*.

Hayhurst, A. N. (Som.):– 258 for 2nd wkt, *277*.

Haynes, D. L. (WI):– Cricketer of the Year, *70-2;* Test captain, *213;* 72 consecutive Tests, *198;* 6,471 r. in one-day ints, *265;* 5,711 r. in Tests, *179;* 38 hundreds, *139;* 16 one-day int. hundreds, *265;* 13 Test hundreds, *215, 231, 243, 245;* 2 hundreds in match, *275;* Carrying bat in & batting through Test innings, *181;* Hundred before lunch, *275;* 220* & 255* in 1990, *273;* Handled the ball, *154;* 306 for 1st wkt, *276;* Test p'ship records, *216, 232, 243, 246*.

Hayward, T. W. (Eng.):– 43,551 r., *142;* 3,518 r. in season, *140;* 1,000 r. (20), *141;* 1,000 r. (April 16-May 31), *147;* 104 hundreds, *138;* 13 hundreds in season, *138;* 4 successive hundreds, *137, 138;* 3 Test hundreds, *202, 210;* 2 hundreds in match (3), *137;* 315* v Lancashire, *134;* 1st wkt hundreds, *150-1*.

Hazare, V. S. (Ind.):– Test captain, *220, 244;* 18,621 r. (avge 58.19), *144;* 2,192 r. in Tests, *180;* 60 hundreds, *139;* 7 Test hundreds, *221, 236, 246, 255;* 2 hundreds in same Test, *176, 236;* 2 hundreds in match (3), *137;* 316* v Baroda, *134, 153;* 309 v Hindus, *134;* 577 for 4th wkt, *149, 152;* 245 for 9th wkt, *153;* Test p'ship records, *222, 236*.

Headley, G. A. (WI):– Test captain, *213;* 2,190 r. (avge 60.83) in Tests, *179, 180;* 10 Test hundreds, *215, 231;* 2 hundreds in same Test, *175, 215;* 2 hundreds in match (2), *137;* 344* v Lord Tennyson's XI, *133, 152;* 270* v England, *174, 215;* Hundred on Test début, *174, 215;* 487* for 6th wkt, *149, 152*.

Headley, R. G. A. (WI):– 1st wkt hundreds, *150*.

Healy, I. A. (Aust.):– 51 d. in one-day ints, *266*.

Hearn, P. (Kent):– Hundred on début, *135*.

Hearne, J. T. (Eng.):– 3,061 w., *161;* 200 w. (3), *160;* 100 w. (15), *161;* 100 w. by June 12, *161;* 10 w. or more in Test (1), *206;* 4 hat-tricks, *159;* Hat-trick v Australia, *189;* Test p'ship record, *211*.

Hearne, J. W. (Eng.):– All-round, *164, 165;* 37,252 r., *143;* 1,000 r. (19), *141;* 96 hundreds, *139;* 1 Test hundred, *202*.

Hegg, W. K. (Lancs.):– 11 d. in match, *166;* 7 d. in innings, *166*.

Hemmings, E. E. (Eng.):– 10 w. in innings, *156;* 258 w. in Sunday League, *845*.

Henderson, M. (NZ):– Wkt with 1st ball on Test début, *189*.

Henderson, W. A. (NE Tvl):– 7 w. for 4 r., *157;* 5 w. in 6 balls, *159;* 4 w. with consecutive balls, *158*.

Hendren, E. H. (Eng.):– Test cricket at 46, *198;* 57,611 r. (avge 50.80), *142, 145;* 3,525 r. in Tests, *177;* 3,311 r. in season, *140;* 1,765 r. in West Indies, *141;* 1,000 r. (25), *140;* 170 hundreds, *138;* 13 hundreds in season, *138;* 7 Test hundreds, *202, 210, 214;* 2 hundreds in match (4), *137;* 301* v Worcestershire, *134;* 277* at Lord's, *269;* 754 c., *169;* Test p'ship record, *205*.

Hendriks, J. L. (WI):– Test p'ship record, *232*.

Hendry, H. L. (Aust.):– 1 Test hundred, *204;* 325* v New Zealanders, *133*.

Hertfordshire:– *709, 849, 850, 852, 860;* Esso/NAYC Under-19 finalists, *908*.

Hick, G. A. (Zimb., Worcs. and N. Dist.):– 15,080 r. (avge 64.17), *144;* 1,000 r. (April 17-May 29), *147;* Highest for Worcestershire, *135;* 405* v Somerset, *133;* 252* in 1990, *273;* 54 hundreds, *139;* Hundred and double-hundred, *137, 275;* 2 hundreds in match (2), *137, 275;* 500 r. without being dismissed, *275;* Average of 90.26 in English season, *142;* 11 sixes in innings, *148;* 264 for 2nd wkt, *277;* 264 for 3rd wkt, *277*.

Hickton, W. (Lancs.):– 10 w. in innings, *155*.

Hide, J. B. (Sussex):– 4 w. with consecutive balls, *158*.

Higgs, K. (Eng.):– 1,536 w., *162;* 4 w. for 5 r. in Test innings, *186;* 3 hat-tricks, *159;* Test p'ship record, *216*.

Highest aggregates:– Individual, *140, 141;* Team, *169, 194, 267-8*.

Highest individual scores:– *133-4, 269-70;* in Tests, *174;* in one-day ints, *265;* in 1990, *273*.

Highest innings totals:– in Tests, *194;* in one-day ints, *267;* in 1990, *278*.

Highest match aggregates in 1990, *279*.

Highest partnerships:– *149-54;* in one-day ints, *265;* in 1990, *276-7*.

Highest total for each county:– Individual, *135;* Team, *169*.

Hilditch, A. M. J. (Aust.):– 2 Test hundreds, *204, 230;* Handled the ball, *154*.

Hill, A. (Eng.):– 3 hat-tricks, *159*.

Hill, A. J. L. (Eng.):– 1 Test hundred, *210*.

Hill, C. (Aust.):– Test captain, *200, 227;* 3,412 r. in Tests, *178;* 2,660 r. v England, *208;* 1,061 Test r. in year, *177;* 45 hundreds, *139;* 7 Test hundreds, *204, 228;* 365* v NSW, *133, 153;* 232 for 9th wkt, *153;* Test p'ship records, *205*.

Hinds, F. (A. B. St Hill's XI):– 10 w. in innings, *156*.

Hinkly, E. (Kent):– 10 w. in innings, *155*.

Hinks, S. G. (Kent):– 234 in 1990, *273;* 366 for 2nd wkt, *277;* 258 for 4th wkt, *277*.

Hirst, G. H. (Eng.):– All-round, *164, 165;* Highest for Yorkshire, *135;* 36,323 r., *143, 144;* 1,000 r. (19), *141;* 60 hundreds, *139;* 341 v Leicestershire, *133, 135;* 2 hundreds

Hirst, G. H. (Eng.):– *contd*
and 5 w. twice v Somerset, *163;* 54 boundaries in innings, *149;* 2,739 w., *162, 163;* 208 w. in season, *160;* 100 w. (15), *161.*

Hirwani, N. D. (Ind.):– 16 w. in Test, *186, 247;* 8 w. in Test innings (2), *185.*

HMC Schools in 1990, *911, 913.*

Hoad, E. L. G. (WI):– Test captain, *213;* 138 for 10th wkt, *154.*

Hobbs, Sir J. B. (Eng.):– Test cricket at 47, *198;* 61,237 r. (avge 50.65), *142, 144, 145;* 5,410 r. (avge 56.94) in Tests, *177, 180;* 3,636 r. v Australia, *208;* 3,024 r. in season, *140;* 1,000 r. (26), *140;* 197 hundreds, *138;* 16 hundreds in season, *138;* 15 Test hundreds, *202, 210, 214;* 4 successive hundreds, *138;* 2 hundreds in match (6), *137;* 316* v Middlesex at Lord's, *134, 269;* Avge of 82 in English season, *142;* 428 for 1st wkt, *150;* 1st wkt hundreds, *150;* 323 for 1st wkt v Australia, *184, 205.*

Hobbs, R. N. S. (Eng.):– Hundred in 44 minutes, *145.*

Hogan, T. G. (Aust.):– Best bowling v Sri Lanka, *240;* Test p'ship record, *232.*

Hogg, R. M. (Aust.):– 123 w. in Tests, *188;* 41 w. in series, *187, 206;* 10 w. or more in Test (2), *206;* Test p'ship record, *232.*

Holder, V. A. (WI):– 109 w. in Tests, *188;* Test p'ship record, *248.*

Holding, M. A. (WI):– 249 w. in Tests, *188;* 142 w. in one-day ints, *266;* 14 w. in Test, *186, 216;* 11 w. in Test, *232;* 8 w. in Test innings, *185, 216;* Best bowling in GC/NWB Trophy, *726;* Test p'ship record, *216.*

Holford, D. A. J. (WI):– 1 Test hundred, *215;* Test p'ship records, *216, 232.*

Holland, R. G. (Aust.):– 10 w. or more in Test (2), *232, 234.*

Hollies, W. E. (Eng.):– 2,323 w., *162;* 100 w. (14), *161;* 10 w. in innings, *156.*

Holmes, P. (Eng.):– Test cricket at 45, *198;* 30,573 r., *143;* 1,000 r. (15), *141;* 67 hundreds, *139;* 315* v Middlesex at Lord's, *134, 269;* 302* v Hampshire, *134;* 555 for 1st wkt, *149, 150, 151;* 1st wkt hundreds, *151.*

Holt Cup final, *852-3.*

Holt, J. K. (WI):– 2 Test hundreds, *215, 245;* Test p'ship record, *216.*

Honours' List in 1990, *597.*

Hooker, J. E. H. (NSW):– 4 w. with consecutive balls, *158;* 307 for 10th wkt, *154.*

Hookes, D. W. (Aust.):– 1 Test hundred, *240;* 4 successive hundreds, *138;* 2 hundreds in match (3), *137;* 306* v Tasmania, *134, 152;* Hundred in 43 minutes off 34 balls, *145;* 462* for 4th wkt, *149, 152.*

Hooper, C. L. (WI):– 1 Test hundred, *245.*

Horan, T. (Aust.):– Test captain, *200;* 1 Test hundred, *204.*

Hornby, A. H. (Lancs.):– Hundred in 43 minutes, *145.*

Hornby, A. N. (Eng.):– Test captain, *199-200.*

Hordern, H. V. (Aust.):– 10 w. or more in Test (2), *206, 207.*

Horner, N. F. (Warwicks.):– 377* for 1st wkt, *150.*

Howard, N. D. (Eng.):– Test captain, *220.*

Howarth, G. P. (NZ):– Test captain, *217, 233, 242, 249, 251, 253;* 2,531 r. in Tests, *179;* 6 Test hundreds, *218, 243, 250, 252;* 2 hundreds in same Test, *176, 218;* Test p'ship records, *244, 252.*

Howarth, H. J. (NZ):– Test p'ship records, *234.*

Howell, H. (Eng.):– 10 w. in innings, *156.*

Howell, W. P. (Aust.):– 17 w. in match, *157;* 10 w. in innings, *156.*

Howorth, R. (Eng.):– All-round, *165;* 100 w. (9), *161;* Wkt with 1st ball on Test début, *189.*

Hubble, J. C. (Kent):– 10 d. in match, *166.*

Hughes, D. P. (Lancs.):– Captain of Lancashire, *484;* 94 c. in Sunday League, *845.*

Hughes, K. J. (Aust.):– Test captain, *200, 230, 235, 237;* 4,415 r. in Tests, *178;* 1,163 Test r. in year, *177;* 9 Test hundreds, *204, 231, 235, 238;* Test p'ship records, *236, 239.*

Hughes, M. G. (Aust.):– 8 w. in Test innings, *185;* Hat-trick v West Indies, *190;* 10 w. or more in Test (1) *232;* Test p'ship record, *232.*

Huish, F. H. (Kent):– 1,310 d., *167;* 100 d. in season (2), *167;* 10 d. in match, *166.*

Humpage, G. W. (Warwicks.):– Career figures, *1324;* 13 sixes in innings, *148;* 470 for 4th wkt, *149, 152.*

Hundreds:– In 1990, *287-92;* Before lunch in 1990, *275;* Fastest, *146;* Fastest in 1990, *275;* Fastest in Tests, *182;* Most individual (35 or more), *138-9;* Most in one-day ints, *265;* Most in season, *138;* Most in Tests, *181;* On début, *135-6, 175;* On début in 1990, *273;* Slowest in Tests, *183;* 4 or more in succession, *138;* 2 in match, *136-7, 275.*

Hundred and double-hundred:– in match, *136;* in a Test, *176.*

Hunte, C. C. (WI):– 3,245 r. in Tests, *179;* 8 Test hundreds, *215, 231, 245, 248;* Hundred on Test début, *175, 248;* 260 v Pakistan, *174, 248;* Carrying bat in Test, *181;* 446 for 2nd wkt, *151, 184, 248;* Test p'ship record, *248.*

Hunter, D. (Yorkshire):– 1,253 d., *167.*

Hutchings, K. L. (Eng.):– 1 Test hundred, *202.*

Hutton, Sir Leonard (Eng.):– "Sir Leonard Hutton" by John Woodcock, *53;* Obituary, *1269-71;* Test captain, *200, 213, 217, 220, 223;* 40,140 r. (avge 55.51), *142, 144;* 6,971 r. (avge 56.67) in Tests, *177, 180;* 3,429 r. in season, *140;* 2,428 r. v Australia, *208;* 1,294 r. and 1,050 r. in month, *147;* 1,000 r. (17), *141;* 129

Hutton, Sir Leonard (Eng.):– *contd* hundreds, *138;* 19 Test hundreds, *202, 210, 214, 218, 221;* 2 hundreds in match (3), *137;* 364 v Australia, *133, 135, 173, 202;* Carrying bat in Test (2), *181;* Obstructing the field, *155;* 1st wkt hundreds, *150;* 359 for 1st wkt v South Africa, *184, 211;* 382 for 2nd wkt v Australia, *184, 205;* Test p'ship records, *205, 211, 215.*

I

Ibadulla, Khalid (Pak.):– Hundred on Test début, *175, 238;* Obstructing the field, *155;* 377* for 1st wkt, *150;* Test p'ship record, *239.*
Ibrahim, K. C. (Ind.):– 274 for 7th wkt, *153.*
Iddon, J. (Eng.):– 46 hundreds, *139.*
Ijaz Ahmed (Lahore Greens):– Obstructing the field, *155.*
Ijaz Ahmed (Pak.):– 2 Test hundreds, *238;* Test p'ship record, *225.*
Ijaz Butt (Pak.):– Slow batting in Test, *183.*
Ijaz Faqih (Pak.):– 1 Test hundred, *255;* 107 w. in Pakistan season, *161;* Test p'ship record, *256.*
Ikin, B. J. (Griq. West):– LBW hat-trick, *159.*
Illingworth, R. (Eng.):– Test captain, *200, 213, 217, 220, 223;* All-round, *165;* All-round in Tests, *191;* 2 Test hundreds, *214, 221;* 2,072 w., *162;* 122 w. in Tests, *187;* 100 w. (10), *161;* Test p'ship record, *222.*
Imran Adil (Bahawalpur):– 10 w. in innings, *157, 1180-1, 1183.*
Imran Khan (Pak.):– Test captain, *223, 237, 247, 251, 254, 258;* 3,541 r. in Tests, *180;* 6 Test hundreds, *224, 238, 248, 255;* 358 w. in Tests, *189;* 165 w. in one-day ints, *266;* 40 w. in series, *187;* 14 w. in Test, *186, 260;* 10 w. or more in Test (6), *225, 239, 249, 256, 260;* 8 w. in Test innings (2), *185, 256, 260;* All-round in one-day ints, *267;* All-round in Tests, *190, 191;* Test p'ship records, *239, 256, 259.*
Imran Zia (Bahawalpur):– 10 d. in match, *167, 1181;* 7 d. in innings, *166, 1181.*
Imtiaz Ahmed (Pak.):– Test captain, *223, 237;* 2,079 r. in Tests, *180;* 300* v Commonwealth XI, *134;* 3 Test hundreds, *248, 252, 255;* 308 for 7th wkt v New Zealand, *153, 184, 253;* Test p'ship records, *253, 256.*
India:– Austral-Asia Cup, *1088-92;* Definition of first-class matches, *1320;* Domestic season 1989-90, *1167-78;* Highest individual Test innings, *174;* Highest Test innings, *194;* India in Test cricket (*see p. 132*); Leading batsmen in Tests, *179;* Leading bowlers in Tests, *189;* Lowest Test innings, *196;* Most consecutive Test appearances, *198;* Most Test appearances, *128;* Most Test appearances as captain, *128;* Nehru Cup, *1063-76;* Representative body, *1315;* Sharjah Champions Trophy, *1058-62;* Summary of Tests, *199;* Summary of one-day ints, *264;* Test cricketers (1932-90), *118-23;* Youngest and oldest on Test début, *197-8.*
India v Sri Lanka, 1990-91, *1011.*
Individual hundreds (35 or more), *138-9.*
Inman, C. C. (Leics.):– 50 in 8 min., *145;* 32 r. in over, *147.*
Insole, D. J. (Eng.):– 25,241 r., *144;* 54 hundreds, *139;* 1 Test hundred, *210.*
International Cricket Council:– Addresses of members, *1315-6;* Constitution and Membership, *1317;* Meetings, *1326.*
Intikhab Alam (Pak.):– Test captain, *223, 237, 247, 251;* Test début at 17, *197;* 1 Test hundred, *224;* 1,571 w., *163;* 125 w. in Tests, *189;* 10 w. or more in Test (2), *253;* Wkt with 1st ball on Test début, *189;* All-round in Tests, *191;* 190 for 9th wkt v England, *153, 184, 225;* Test p'ship records, *225, 239, 253.*
Iqbal Qasim (Pak.):– 171 w. in Tests, *189;* 10 w. or more in Test (2), *239, 256;* Test p'ship records, *239, 253, 256, 259.*
Iqtidar Ali (Allied Bank):– Hit the ball twice, *155.*
Irani Cup (Ind.), *1178.*
Iredale, F. A. (Aust.):– 2 Test hundreds, *204.*
Ireland:– v MCC, *697, 896-7;* v New Zealanders, *299-300, 896;* v Scotland, *699-700, 897;* v Wales, *897;* v Worcestershire, *896;* in NatWest Bank Trophy, *709, 897;* Representative body, *1316.*
Irish Cricket in 1990, *896-8.*
Ironmonger, H. (Aust.):– Oldest Australian Test player, *198;* Test début at 46, *197;* 10 w. or more in Test (2), *229, 232;* 5 w. for 6 r. in Test innings, *186.*
Irvine, B. L. (SA):– 1 Test hundred, *228.*
Israr Ali (B'pur):– 6 w. for 1 r., *157.*
I Zingari results, 1990, *615.*

J

Jackman, R. D. (Eng.):– 234 w. in Sunday League, *845;* 3 hat-tricks, *159.*
Jackson, A. A. (Aust.):– Hundred v England on Test début, *174, 204.*
Jackson, Hon. Sir F. S. (Eng.):– Test captain, *200;* 5 Test hundreds, *202.*
Jackson, H. L. (Eng.):– 1,733 w., *162;* 100 w. (10), *161.*
Jaisimha, M. L. (Ind.):– 2,056 r. in Tests, *180;* 3 Test hundreds, *221, 236;* Slow batting in Test, *183.*
Jalal-ud-Din (Pak.):– Hat-trick in one-day int., *266;* Handled the ball, *154.*
Jameson, J. A. (Eng.):– 465* for 2nd wkt, *149, 151.*
Jamshedji, R. J. D. (Ind.):– Oldest Indian Test début, *197.*
Jardine, D. R. (Eng.):– Test captain, *200, 213, 217, 220;* 35 hundreds, *140;* 1 Test hundred, *214;* Avge of 91.09 in English season, *142;* Test p'ship record, *205.*

Jarman, B. N. (Aust.):– Test captain, *200;* 10 d. in match, *166;* Test p'ship record, *236.*
Jarvis, K. B. S. (Kent and Glos.):– Career figures, *1324.*
Jarvis, T. W. (NZ):– 1 Test hundred, *243;* Slow batting in Test, *183;* 387 for 1st wkt v West Indies, *150, 151, 184, 244.*
Javed Miandad (Pak.):– Test captain, *223, 237, 247, 251, 258;* 104 Tests, *128, 198;* 27,010 r. (avge 54.67), *143, 145;* 7,891 r. (avge 56.36) in Tests, *180;* 5,610 r. in one-day ints, *265;* 53 consecutive Tests, *199;* 78 hundreds, *139;* 23 Test hundreds, *181, 224, 238, 248, 252, 255, 259;* 2 hundreds in match (4), *137;* 2 hundreds in same Test, *176, 252;* Hundred on Test début, *175, 252;* 311 v National Bank, *134;* 280* v India, *174, 255;* 271 v New Zealand, *174, 252;* 260 v England, *174, 224;* 58 c. in one-day ints, *267;* 8 c. in match, *168;* 451 for 3rd wkt v India, *149, 184, 256;* 388 for 4th wkt v Sri Lanka, *184, 259;* Test p'ship records, *225, 239, 252-3, 256, 259.*
Javed Mohammad (Multan):– Hit the ball twice, *155.*
Jefferies, S. T. (Hants and W. Prov.):– 10 w. in innings, *157;* Best bowling in B & H Cup final, *759.*
Jenkins, R. O. (Eng.):– Double hat-trick, *159;* 3 hat-tricks, *159.*
Jennings, R. V. (Tvl):– 10 d. in match (3), *167.*
Jessop, G. L. (Eng.):– All-round, *164;* Fastest English Test hundred, *182, 202;* Hundreds in 40 and 42 min., *145;* 26,698 r., *143;* 53 hundreds, *139;* 2 hundreds in match (4), *137;* 1 Test hundred, *182, 202;* 200 r. in 120 min. and 130 min., *146.*
Jesty, T. E. (Hants, Surrey and Lancs.):– 32 r. in over, *147;* 249 w. in Sunday League, *845.*
John Player League winners, *846.*
Johnson, H. H. H. (WI):– 10 w. or more in Test (1), *216.*
Johnson, I. W. (Aust.):– Test captain, *200, 229, 235, 237;* 109 w. in Tests, *188;* All-round in Tests, *191;* Test p'ship records, *232, 236.*
Johnson, J. S. (Shropshire):– Hundred on début, *135.*
Johnson, L. A. (Northants):– 10 d. in match (2), *166.*
Johnson, T. F. (WI):– Wkt with 1st ball on Test début, *189.*
Johnston, W. A. (Aust.):– Avge of 102 in English season, *142;* 160 w. in Tests, *188.*
Jones, A. (Glam.):– 36,049 r., *143;* 1,000 r. (23), *141;* 56 hundreds, *139;* 2 hundreds in match (3), *137.*
Jones, A. H. (NZ):– 2 Test hundreds, *234, 250;* Test p'ship record, *234.*
Jones, A. O. (Eng.):– Test captain, *200;* 391 for 1st wkt, *150.*
Jones, D. M. (Aust.):– 2,637 r. in Tests (avge 50.70), *178, 181;* 1,099 Test r. in year, *177;* 3,857 r. in one-day ints, *265;* 9 Test hundreds, *204, 231, 235, 238, 240;* 2 hundreds in same Test, *176, 1036;* 2 hundreds in match, *138, 1036;* Avge of 88.82 in English season, *142;* 12 sixes in innings, *148;* Test p'ship records, *232, 236, 240.*
Jones, E. (Aust.):– 10 w. or more in Test (1), *207.*
Jones, E. W. (Glam.):– 223 d. in Sunday League, *845;* 7 d. in innings, *166.*
Jones, S. A. (Boland):– 259 for 6th wkt, *153.*
Jordon, R. C. (Vic.):– 10 d. in match, *167.*
Joshi, P. G. (Ind.):– Test p'ship record, *256.*
Julien, B. D. (WI):– 2 Test hundreds, *215, 248;* Test p'ship records, *216, 248.*
Jupp, V. W. C. (Eng.):– All-round, *164, 165;* 1,658 w., *162;* 102 and hat-trick, *164;* 100 w. (10), *161;* 5 hat-tricks, *159.*

K

Kallicharran, A. I. (WI):– Career figures, *1324;* Test captain, *230, 244;* 32,650 r., *143;* 4,399 r. in Tests, *179;* 87 hundreds, *139;* 12 Test hundreds, *215, 231, 243, 245, 248;* 2 hundreds in match (2), *137;* Hundred and double-hundred, *137;* Hundred on Test début, *175, 243;* Record score in GC/NWB Trophy, *725;* 303 for 3rd wkt v England, *184;* 470 for 4th wkt, *149, 152;* Test p'ship records, *232, 243, 246.*
Kamal Najamuddin (Kar.):– 10 d. in match, *167;* 418 for 1st wkt, *150.*
Kambli, V. G. (Sharadashram Vidyamandir School):– 664* for 3rd wkt, *271.*
Kanhai, R. B. (WI):– Test captain, *213, 230;* 28,774 r., *143;* 6,227 r. in Tests, *179;* 83 hundreds, *139;* 15 Test hundreds, *215, 231, 245, 248;* 256 v India, *174, 245;* 2 hundreds in same Test, *176, 231;* Avge of 82.53 in English season, *142;* 465* for 2nd wkt, *149, 151;* Test p'ship records, *232, 246, 248.*
Kapil Dev (Ind.):– Test captain, *220, 235, 244, 254, 256;* 4,521 r. in Tests, *179;* 66 consecutive Tests, *198;* 8 Test hundreds, *221, 236, 246, 257;* Fast scoring, *182;* 4 successive sixes, *276;* 371 w. in Tests, *189;* 185 w. in one-day ints, *266;* 10 w. or more in Test (2), *247, 256;* 9 w. in Test innings, *185, 247;* 8 w. in Test innings (2), *185, 186;* All-round in one-day ints, *267;* All-round in Tests, *191;* 57 c. in one-day ints, *267;* Test p'ship records, *222, 236, 256, 257.*
Kardar, A. H. (Ind. and Pak.):– Test captain, *223, 237, 247, 251, 254;* Test p'ship record, *248.*
Keeton, W. W. (Eng.):– Highest for Notts., *135;* 54 hundreds, *139;* 312* v Middlesex, *134, 135;* 1st wkt hundreds, *151.*
Kelleway, C. (Aust.):– 3 Test hundreds, *204, 228;* All-round in Test, *190;* Test p'ship records, *229.*
Kelly, J. J. (Aust.):– 8 d. in Test, *192.*

Kennedy, A. S. (Eng.):– All-round, *164, 165;* 2,874 w., *162;* 205 w. in season, *160;* 100 w. (15), *161;* 10 w. in innings, *156;* 3 hat-tricks, *159.*
Kenny, R. B. (Ind.):– Test p'ship record, *236.*
Kent:– *378, 468-83;* Championship positions, *384-5;* Highest score, *169;* Highest individual score, *135;* Lowest score, *170;* Seeboard Trophy winners, *702-3.*
Kent II:– *868, 870, 877-8, 889.*
Kenya:– in ICC Trophy, *355-6, 357, 358-9, 361;* CA v England A, *992.*
Kenyon, D. (Eng.):– 37,002 r., *143;* 1,000 r. (19), *141;* 74 hundreds, *139.*
Kerr, R. B. (Qld):– 388 for 1st wkt, 150.
Khalid Alvi (Kar.):– 418 for 1st wkt, *150.*
Khalid Javed (Pak. Rlwys):– Obstructing the field, *155.*
Khalid Hassan (Pak.):– Test début at 16, *197.*
Khalid Irtiza (UBL):– 456 for 3rd wkt, *149, 152.*
Killick, E. H. (Sussex):– 344 consecutive Championship appearances, *272.*
Kilner, R. (Eng.):– All-round, *165.*
King, C. L. (WI):– 1 Test hundred, *243.*
King, J. H. (Eng.):– Hit the ball twice, *155;* 25,121 r., *144;* 2 hundreds in match (2), *137.*
Kinneir, S. P. (Eng.):– Test début at 40, *198.*
Kippax, A. F. (Aust.):– 12,762 r. (avge 57.22), *144;* 43 hundreds, *139;* 2 Test hundreds, *204, 231;* 2 hundreds in match (2), *137;* 315* v Queensland, *134;* 307 for 10th wkt, *154.*
Kirmani, S. M. H. (Ind.):– 2,759 r. in Tests, *180;* 2 Test hundreds, *221, 236;* 198 d. in Tests, *193;* 6 d. in Test innings, *192;* Test p'ship records, *222, 236, 246, 250, 256.*
Kirsten, N. (Border):– 7 d. in innings, *165.*
Kirsten, P. N. (Derbys. and W. Prov.):– 46 hundreds, *139;* 4 successive hundreds, *138;* 2 hundreds in match (3), *137.*
Kline, L. F. (Aust.):– Hat-trick v South Africa, *190.*
Knight, B. R. (Eng.):– All-round, *165;* 2 Test hundreds, *218, 221;* Test p'ship record, *219.*
Knott, A. P. E. (Eng.):– 4,389 r. in Tests, *177;* 65 consecutive Tests, *198;* 5 Test hundreds, *202, 214, 218, 224;* 1,344 d., *167;* 269 d. in Tests, *193;* 105 d. v Australia, *207;* 65 d. in GC/NWB Trophy, *727;* 24 d. in series, *193;* 5 d. in Test innings, *192;* Test p'ship records, *205, 216, 219.*
Kripal Singh, A. G. (Ind.):– Hundred on Test début, *175, 250;* Test p'ship record, *250.*
Kripal Singh, Arjan (Tamil Nadu):– 302* v Goa, *134.*
Kunderan, B. K. (Ind.):– 2 Test hundreds, *221.*
Kuruppu, D. S. B. P. (SL):– 201* v NZ on Test début, *174, 175, 184, 254;* Slowest double-hundred, *184;* Test p'ship record, *227.*

L

Labrooy, G. F. (SL):– Test p'ship records, *227.*
Lacey, Sir F. E. (Hants):– 323* v Norfolk, *270.*
Laird, B. M. (Aust.):– Test p'ship record, *234.*
Laker, J. C. (Eng.):– 1,944 w., *162;* 193 w. in Tests, *187;* 100 w. (11), *161;* 46 w. in series, *187, 207;* 19 w. in Test, *157, 186, 206;* 10 w. in innings (2), *156;* 10 w. in Test innings, *156, 185, 186;* 10 w. or more in Test (3), *206, 212;* 9 w. in Test innings, *185, 186;* 10 w. for 53 r. and 9 w. for 37 r. in Test innings, *185, 186;* 8 w. for 2 r., *157;* 4 hat-tricks, *159.*
Lakspray Trophy (SL):– *1192-3, 1194-8.*
Lamb, A. J. (Eng.):– Test captain, *213;* Captain of Northamptonshire, *532;* 3,981 r. in Tests, *177;* 3,306 r. in one-day ints, *265;* 66 hundreds, *139;* 14 Test hundreds, *202, 214, 218, 221, 224;* 6 c. in Test, *194;* 30 r. in over, *148;* 235 in 1990, *273;* 308 for 3rd wkt v India, *184, 222, 277;* 393 for 3rd wkt, *277;* 355 for 5th wkt, *152;* Test p'ship records, *222, 226.*
Lamba, R. (Ind.):– 320 v West Zone, *133.*
Lambert, W. (Sussex):– 107 and 157 v Epsom (1817), *137.*
Lancashire:– *378, 484-98;* B & H Cup winners, *757;* Championship positions, *384-5;* Highest score, *169;* Highest individual score, *135;* Lowest score, *170;* NatWest Bank Trophy winners, *724.*
Lancashire II:– *868, 870, 878, 889-90;* Bain Clarkson Trophy winners, *889-90.*
Lancashire League, 1990, *894-5.*
Lance, H. R. (SA):– 174 for 10th wkt, *154;* Test p'ship record, *229.*
Langford, B. A. (Som.):– Most economical analysis in Sunday League, *845.*
Langley, G. R. A. (Aust.):– 21 d. in series, *193;* 9 d. in Test, *192.*
Langridge, James (Eng.):– All-round, *164, 165;* 31,716 r., *143;* 1,000 r. (20), *141;* 42 hundreds, *139;* 1,530 w., *163.*
Langridge, J. G. (Sussex):– 34,380 r., *143;* 1,000 r. (17), *141;* 76 hundreds, *139;* 4 successive hundreds, *138;* 2 hundreds in match (2), *137;* 784 c., *169;* 69 c. in season, *168;* 490 for 1st wkt, *149, 150.*
Langton, A. B. C. (SA):– Test p'ship record, *211.*
Larkins, W. (Eng.):– 49 hundreds, *139;* 207 in 1990, *273.*
Larsen, G. R. (Wgtn):– 341 for 5th wkt, *152.*
Larwood, H. (Eng.):– 100 w. (8), *161;* 10 w. or more in Test (1), *206;* Test p'ship record, *205.*
Laver, F. (Aust.):– 8 w. in Test innings, *185.*

Lawrence, D. V. (Eng.):– Hat-trick in 1990, *277;* Test p'ship record, *226.*
Lawrence, G. B. (SA):– 8 w. in Test innings, *185.*
Lawrence Trophy, *275.*
Lawry, W. M. (Aust.):– Test captain, *200, 227, 230, 235;* 18,734 r. (avge 50.90), *145;* 5,234 r. in Tests, *178;* 2,233 r. v England, *208;* 1,056 Test r. in year, *177;* 50 hundreds, *139;* 13 Test hundreds, *204, 228, 231, 235;* Carrying bat in Test (2), *181;* 382 for 1st wkt v West Indies, *150, 184, 232;* 336 for 4th wkt v West Indies, *184, 232;* Test p'ship records, *232.*
Lawson, G. F. (Aust.):– 180 w. in Tests, *188;* 10 w. or more in Test (2), *207, 232;* 8 w. in Test innings, *186;* Test p'ship record, *239.*
League Cricket Conference:– v Indians, *321.*
Le Couteur, P. R. (OUCC):– 160 and 11 w. v Cambridge, *373.*
Lee, F. S. (Som.):– 1st wkt hundreds, *151.*
Lee, H. W. (Eng.):– Test début at 40, *198;* 37 hundreds, *140;* 2 hundreds in match (2), *137.*
Lee, J. W. (Som.):– 1st wkt hundreds, *151.*
Lees, W. K. (NZ):– 1 Test hundred, *252;* 8 d. in Test, *192;* Test p'ship record, *252.*
Leggat, I. B. (NZ):– 239 for 9th wkt, *153.*
Legge, G. B. (Eng.):– 1 Test hundred, *218.*
Leicestershire:– *378, 499-515;* Championship positions, *384-5;* Highest score, *169;* Highest individual score, *135;* Lowest score, *170.*
Leicestershire II, *868, 870, 879, 889.*
Lester, E. (Yorks.):– 2 hundreds in match (2), *137.*
Lever, J. K. (Eng.):– 1,722 w., *162;* 386 w. in Sunday League, *845*; 10 w. or more in Test (1), *223.*
Lever, P. (Eng.):– Test p'ship records, *219, 222.*
Leveson Gower, Sir H. D. G. (Eng.):– Test captain, *208.*
Lewis, A. R. (Eng.):– Test captain, *220, 223;* 1 Test hundred, *221;* 1st wkt hundreds, *151.*
Lewis, J. J. B. (Essex):– Hundred on début, *136, 273.*
Leyland, M. (Eng.):– 33,660 r., *143;* 2,764 r. in Tests, *178;* 1,000 r. (17), *141;* 80 hundreds, *139;* 9 Test hundreds, *202, 210;* 382 for 1st wkt v Australia, *184, 205.*
Lillee, D. K. (Aust.):– 355 w. in Tests, *188;* 167 w. v England, *207;* 103 w. in one-day ints, *266;* 39 w. in series, *187;* 10 w. or more in Test (7), *207, 232, 234, 239;* Test p'ship record, *239.*
Lilley, A. A. (Eng.):– Hit the ball twice, *155;* 84 d. v Australia, *207.*
Lilley, A. W. (Essex):– Hundred on début, *135.*
Lillywhite, James jun. (Eng.):– Test captain, *199;* 10 w. in innings, *155.*
Lincolnshire, *708, 849, 850, 852-3, 860-1.*
Lindenberg, H. C. (Border):– Hat-trick, *159, 1142.*
Lindsay, D. T. (SA):– 3 Test hundreds, *228;* 30 r. in over, *148;* 24 d. in series, *192;* 8 d. in Test, *192;* 6 d. in Test innings, *192;* All-round in Test, *191;* Test p'ship records, *229, 241.*
Lindsay, N. V. (SA):– 221 for 9th wkt, *153.*
Lindwall, R. R. (Aust.):– Test captain, *235;* 2 Test hundreds, *204, 231;* 228 w. in Tests, *188;* 114 w. v England, *208;* All-round in Tests, *191.*
Linton, G. N. (B'dos):– Handled the ball, *154.*
Llewellyn, C. B. (SA):– All-round, *165;* 10 w. or more in Test (1), *229;* 2 hundreds in match (2), *137;* Test p'ship record, *229.*
Lloyd, C. H. (WI):– Test captain, *128, 213, 230, 242, 244, 247;* 31,232 r., *143;* 7,515 r. in Tests, *179;* 79 hundreds, *139;* 19 Test hundreds, *215, 231, 245, 248;* Fast scoring, *146, 183;* 161 for 9th wkt, *153, 246;* 335 for 5th wkt, *152;* Test p'ship records, *246, 248.*
Lloyd, D. (Eng.):– 38 hundreds, *139;* Double-hundred v India, *221.*
Lloyd, T. A. (Eng.):– Captain of Warwickshire, *616.*
Loader, P. J. (Eng.):– Hat-trick v West Indies, *190.*
Lock, G. A. R. (Eng.):– 2,844 w., *162;* 200 w. in season (2), *160;* 174 w. in Tests, *187;* 100 w. (14), *161;* 10 w. in innings, *156;* 10 w. or more in Test (3), *216, 219;* 4 hat-tricks, *159;* 830 c., *169;* 64 c. in season, *168;* 8 c. in match, *168.*
Lockwood, W. H. (Eng.):– 10 w. or more in Test (1), *206;* 3 hat-tricks, *159.*
Logie, A. L. (WI):– 2 Test hundreds, *245.*
Lohmann, G. A. (Eng.):– Hat-trick v South Africa, *189;* 1,841 w., *162;* 200 w., (3), *160;* 112 w. in Tests, *187;* 100 w. (8), *161;* 35 w. in series, *187;* 15 w. in Test, *186;* 10 w. or more in Test (5), *206, 212;* 9 w. in Test innings, *185, 186;* 8 w. in Test innings (3), *185;* 9 w. for 28 r. in Test innings, *185, 186;* 8 w. for 7 r. in Test innings, *185, 186.*
Long, A. (Surrey and Sussex):– 1,046 d., *168;* 11 d. in match, *166;* 7 d. in innings, *166.*
Lord's Cricket Ground:– *269-70;* Matches in 1990, *366-77.*
Loughborough Univ.:– v Cambridge Univ., *679.*
Lowest innings totals:– in Tests, *196;* in one-day ints, *268;* in 1990, *279.*
Lowest match aggregates, *170, 197.*
Lowry, T. C. (NZ):– Test captain, *217.*
Loxton, S. J. E. (Aust.):– 1 Test hundred, *228.*
Luckhurst, B. W. (Eng.):– 48 hundreds, *139;* 4 Test hundreds, *202, 221, 224.*
Lyons, J. J. (Aust.):– 1 Test hundred, *204.*

M

Macartney, C. G. (Aust.):– 2,131 r. in Tests, *178;* 49 hundreds, *139;* 7 Test hundreds, *204, 228;* 4 successive hundreds, *138;* 2 hundreds in match (2), *137;* 345 v Nottinghamshire, *133, 135, 146;* 300 r. in 205 min., *146;* 51 boundaries in innings, *149;* 10 w. or more in Test (1), *207.*
Macaulay, G. G. (Eng.):– 1,837 w., *162;* 211 w. in season, *160;* 100 w. (10), *161;* 4 hat-tricks, *159;* Wkt with 1st ball on Test début, *189.*
McCabe, S. J. (Aust.):– 2,748 r. in Tests, *178;* 6 Test hundreds, *204, 228.*
McCool, C. L. (Aust.):– 1 Test hundred, *204.*
McCosker, R. B. (Aust.):– 4 Test hundreds, *204, 231, 238;* 2 hundreds in match (3), *137.*
McCubbin, G. R. (Tvl):– 221 for 9th wkt, *153.*
McDermott, C. J. (Aust.):– 8 w. in Test innings, *186;* Test p'ship record, *234.*
McDonald, C. C. (Aust.):– 3,107 r. in Tests, *178;* 5 Test hundreds, *204, 228, 231;* Test p'ship records, *229, 232.*
McDonald, E. A. (Aust.):– 205 w. in season, *160;* 3 hat-tricks, *159.*
McDonnell, P. S. (Aust.):– Test captain, *200;* 3 Test hundreds, *204.*
McEwan, K. S. (Essex and W. Prov.): 26,309 r., *144;* 73 hundreds, *139.*
McEwan, S. M. (Worcs.):– Hat-trick in 1990, *277.*
McGibbon, A. R. (NZ):– Test p'ship record, *250.*
McGirr, H. M. (NZ):– Oldest New Zealand Test début, *198.*
McGlew, D. J. (SA):– Test captain, *209, 227, 240;* 2,440 r. in Tests, *179;* 7 Test hundreds, *210, 228, 241;* Slow Test hundred, *183;* 255* v New Zealand, *174, 241;* Carrying bat in Test, *181;* Test p'ship records, *229, 241.*
McGregor, S. N. (NZ):– 1 Test hundred, *252;* Test p'ship record, *242.*
Mackay, K. D. (Aust.):– Slow batting in Test, *183;* Test p'ship record, *229.*
Mackay-Coghill, D. (Tvl):– 174 for 10th wkt, *154.*
McKenzie, G. D. (Aust.):– 246 w. in Tests, *188;* 10 w. or more in Tests (3), *232, 237;* 8 w. in Test innings, *185;* Test p'ship records, *229, 236.*
MacLaren, A. C. (Eng.):– Test captain, *200;* Highest for Lancashire, *135;* 47 hundreds, *139;* 5 Test hundreds, *202;* 424 v Somerset, *133, 135;* 65 boundaries in innings, *149.*
Maclean, J. A. (Aust.):– 7 d. in innings, *166.*
McLean, R. A. (SA):– 2,120 r. in Tests, *179;* 5 Test hundreds, *210, 241;* Test p'ship records, *241.*
McLeod, C. E. (Aust.):– 1 Test hundred, *204.*
McMorris, E. D. A. (WI):– 1 Test hundred, *245;* Test p'ship record, *246.*
McSweeney, E. B. (Wgtn):– 341 for 5th wkt, *152.*
McWatt, C. A. (WI):– Test p'ship record, *216.*
Madan Lal (Ind.):– Test p'ship records, *222, 256, 257.*
Madugalle, R. S. (SL):– Test captain, *226, 239;* 1 Test hundred, *257;* Test p'ship records, *258, 259.*
Mahmood Rashid (UBL):– Obstructing the field, *155.*
Mailey, A. A. (Aust.):– 36 w. in series, *187;* 10 w. in innings, *156;* 10 w. or more in Test (2), *207;* 9 w. in Test innings, *185;* Test p'ship record, *205.*
Majid Khan (Pak.):– Test captain, *223;* 27,444 r., *143;* 3,931 r. in Tests, *180;* 73 hundreds, *139;* 8 Test hundreds, *238, 248, 252;* Fast Test hundred, *182;* 30 r. in over, *148;* 13 sixes in innings, *148;* 389 for 1st wkt, *150;* Test p'ship records, *239, 248, 252, 253, 259.*
Makepeace, J. W. H. (Eng.):– 25,799 r., *144;* 43 hundreds, *139;* 1 Test hundred, *202.*
Malcolm, D. E. (Eng.):– 10 w. in Test, *216.*
Mallender, N. A. (Som.):– 183 for 9th wkt, *277.*
Mallett, A. A. (Aust.):– 132 w. in Tests, *188;* 10 w. or more in Test (1), *237;* 8 w. in Test innings, *185.*
Maninder Singh (Ind.):– Test cricket at 17, *197;* 10 w. or more in Test (2), *256, 258.*
Manjrekar, S. V. (Ind.):– 3 Test hundreds, *246, 255;* Test p'ship records, *256.*
Manjrekar, V. L. (Ind.):– 3,208 r. in Tests, *179;* 38 hundreds, *139;* 7 Test hundreds, *221, 246, 250;* Test p'ship records, *222, 250.*
Mankad, A. V. (Ind.):– 12,980 r. (avge 50.90), *145.*
Mankad, V. (Ind.):– Test captain, *244, 254;* 2,109 r. in Tests, *180;* 5 Test hundreds, *221, 236, 250;* 162 w. in Tests, *189;* 10 w. or more in Test (2), *223, 256;* 8 w. in Test innings (2), *185, 223, 256;* All-round in Tests, *190, 191;* 413 for 1st wkt v New Zealand, *150, 184, 250.*
Mann, A. L. (Aust.):– 1 Test hundred, *235.*
Mann, F. G. (Eng.):– Test captain, *209, 217;* 1 Test hundred, *210.*
Mann, F. T. (Eng.):– Test captain, *209*; Fifty in 14 min., *145.*
Mansoor Akhtar (Pak.):– 1 Test hundred, *238;* 561 for 1st wkt, *149, 150, 151;* 389 for 1st wkt, *150;* Test p'ship record, *239.*
Maqsood Kundi (MCB):– 196* for 10th wkt, *154.*
Marks, V. J. (Eng.):– Test p'ship record, *225.*
Marriott, C. S. (Eng.):– 10 w. or more in Test (1), *216.*
Marsh, G. R. (Aust.):– 2,129 r. in Tests, *178;* 4 Test hundreds, *204, 233, 235;* 7 one-day int. hundreds, *265;* 355* v South

Marsh, G. R. (Aust.):– *contd* Australia, *133;* 55 boundaries in innings, *149;* 431 for 1st wkt, *150;* 329 for 1st wkt v England, *184, 205;* Test p'ship records, *205, 234, 236.*

Marsh, R. W. (Aust.):– 3,633 r. in Tests, *178;* 3 Test hundreds, *204, 233, 238;* 355 d. in Tests, *193;* 148 d. v England, *207;* 1,220 r. and 124 d. in one-day ints, *266, 267;* 28 d., 26 d., 23 d. and 21 d. in series, *192-3;* 11 d. and 10 d. in match, *166, 167;* 9 d. and 8 d. (4) in Test, *192;* 6 d. in Test innings, *192.*

Marshall, M. D. (WI):– 329 w. in Tests, *188*; 137 w. in one-day ints, *266;* 10 w. or more in Test (4), *216, 232, 244, 247;* 35 w. in series, *187;* Most w. since 1969, *161;* All-round in Tests, *191;* Test p'ship records, *243, 246.*

Marshall, R. E. (WI):– 35,725 r., *143;* 1,000 r. (18), *141;* 68 hundreds, *139;* 1st wkt hundreds, *151.*

Martin, F. (Eng.):– 10 w. or more in Test (1), *206;* 4 w. with consecutive balls, *158.*

Martin, F. R. (WI):– 1 Test hundred, *231.*

Martindale, E. A. (WI):– 255 for 8th wkt, *153.*

Marx, W. F. E. (Tvl):– 240 on début, *136.*

Marylebone Cricket Club, The:– *364-8;* Honorary England cricketers, *368;* v Cambridge Univ., *685;* v Durham Univ., *697;* v Ireland, *697, 896-7;* v New Zealanders, *299;* v Oxford Univ., *673;* v Scotland, *368, 899;* v Wales, *700.*

MCC Schools:– v MCC, *367;* v National Association of Young Cricketers, *373-4.*

MCC Schools Festival, 1990, *911-3.*

MCC Young Cricketers:– v MCC, *367;* v Pakistan Young Cricketers, *903.*

Masood Anwar (R'pindi and United Bank):– Hat-trick, *159, 1180, 1186;* 8 c. in match, *168.*

Masood Iqbal (HBL):– 7 d. in innings, *166.*

Massie, H. H. (Aust.):– Test captain, *200.*

Massie, R. A. L. (Aust.):– 16 w. in Test, *186, 207;* 10 w. or more in Test (1), *207;* 8 w. in Test innings (2), *185, 207;* Test p'ship record, *239.*

Matthews, F. C. L. (Notts.):– 17 w. in match, *157.*

Matthews, G. R. J. (Aust.):– 3 Test hundreds, *233, 235;* 10 w. or more in Test (1), *237;* Test p'ship records, *234, 236, 239.*

Matthews, T. J. (Aust.):– Double hat-trick in Test, *159, 189;* 4 hat-tricks, *159.*

May, P. B. H. (Eng.):– Test captain, *128, 200, 209, 213, 217, 220;* 27,592 r. (avge 51.00), *143, 145;* 4,537 r. in Tests, *177;* 85 hundreds, *139;* 13 Test hundreds, *202, 210, 214, 218, 221;* 4 successive hundreds, *138;* 2 hundreds in match (3), *137;* Hundred on Test début, *175, 210;* 285* v West Indies, *174, 214;* 411 for 4th wkt v WI, *184, 216.*

Maynard, M. P. (Eng.):– Hundred on début, *135;* 50 in 14 min., *145;* 30 r. in over, *148.*

Mayne, E. R. (Aust.):– 456 for 1st wkt, *149, 150, 151.*

Mead, C. P. (Eng.):– 55,061 r., *142;* 3,179 r. in season, *140;* 1,000 r. (27), *140;* 665 Championship appearances, *272;* 153 hundreds, *138;* 13 hundreds in season, *138;* 4 Test hundreds, *202, 210;* 2 hundreds in match (3), *137;* Hundred and double-hundred, *136.*

Mead, W. (Eng.):– 1,916 w., *162;* 100 w. (10), *161;* 17 w. in match, *157, 158.*

Meckiff, I. (Aust.):– Test p'ship record, *229.*

Medlycott, K. T. (Surrey):– Hundred on début, *135.*

Meetings in 1990:– ICC, *1326;* MCC, *364-6;* TCCB, *1325, 1326-7.*

Mehra, M. (Ind. Rlwys):– Obstructing the field, *155.*

Mehra, V. L. (Ind.):– Test cricket at 17, *197.*

Melville, A. (SA):– Test captain, *209;* 4 Test hundreds, *210;* 2 hundreds in same Test, *176, 210;* 319 for 3rd wkt v England, *184, 211;* 299 for 7th wkt, *153.*

Mendis, G. D. (Sussex and Lancs.):– 36 hundreds, *140.*

Mendis, L. R. D. (SL):– Test captain, *128, 226, 239, 253, 256, 258;* 4 Test hundreds, *226, 257;* 2 hundreds in same Test, *176, 257;* Test p'ship records, *227, 258, 259.*

Mercer, J. (Sussex, Glam. and Northants):– 1,591 w., *162;* 100 w. (9), *161;* 10 w. in innings, *156.*

Merchant, U. M. (Bombay):– 360 for 5th wkt, *152.*

Merchant, V. M. (Ind.):– 13,248 r. (avge 71.22), *144;* 4 successive hundreds, *138;* 44 hundreds, *139;* 3 Test hundreds, *221;* 359* v Maharashtra, *133, 153;* 142 and hat-trick, *164;* 371 for 6th wkt, *152.*

Metcalfe, A. A. (Yorks.):– Hundred on début, *135;* 2 hundreds in match, *275;* Hundred before lunch, *275;* 293* for 3rd wkt, *277.*

Metson, C. P. (Glam.):– 6 d. in innings (2), *278.*

Middlesex:– *378, 516-31;* Championship positions, *384-5;* Highest score, *169;* Highest individual score, *135;* Lowest score, *170;* Refuge Assurance Cup winners, *848.*

Middlesex II, *868, 870, 879-80, 889.*

Middlesex Young Cricketers:– v Pakistan Young Cricketers, *902.*

Middleton, T. C. (Hants):– 292 for 1st wkt, *276.*

Milburn, C. (Eng.):– Obituary, *1273-5;* 2 Test hundreds, *214, 224;* Test p'ship record, *215.*

Miller, G. (Eng.):– Career figures, *1324;* Slow batting in Test, *183;* 107 for 10th wkt, *277.*

Miller, K. R. (Aust.):– 2,958 r. in Tests, *178;* 41 hundreds, *139;* 7 Test hundreds, *204, 231;* 170 w. in Tests, *188;* 10 w. or more in Test (1), *207;* All-round in Tests, *190, 191;* Test p'ship records, *229, 232.*
Mills, J. E. (NZ):– Hundred on Test début, *174, 219;* 190* for 8th wkt, *153;* Test p'ship record, *219.*
Mills, P. T. (Glos.):– 5 w. for 0 r., *157.*
Milton, C. A. (Eng.):– 32,150 r., *143;* 1,000 r. (16), *141;* 56 hundreds, *139;* 2 hundreds in match (2), *137;* Hundred on Test début, *175, 218;* 758 c., *169;* 63 c. in season, *168;* 8 c. in match, *168.*
Milton, W. H. (SA):– Test captain, *208.*
Minor Counties:– *849-67;* B & H Cup, *729, 736-40;* Championship winners, *867;* Fixtures, 1991, *1359-60;* Formation, *272;* Highest individual scores, *270;* NWB Trophy, *727;* Representative body, *1316;* Umpires, *418;* v Indians, *326-7.*
Miran Bux (Pak.):– Test début at 47, *197;* Oldest Pakistan Test player, *198.*
Mitchell, A. (Eng.):– 44 hundreds, *139;* 4 successive hundreds, *138.*
Mitchell, B. (SA):– 3,471 r. in Tests, *178;* 8 Test hundreds, *210, 241;* 2 hundreds in same Test, *176, 210;* 6 c. in Test, *194;* 299 for 7th wkt, *153;* Test p'ship records, *211, 241.*
Mitchell, F. (Eng. and SA):– Test captain, *208, 227.*
Mitchell, T. B. (Eng.):– 100 w. (10), *161;* 10 w. in innings, *156.*
Modi, R. S. (Ind.):– 1 Test hundred, *246;* 410 for 3rd wkt, *152;* 371 for 6th wkt, *152.*
Mohammad Farooq (Pak.):– Test p'ship record, *253.*
Mohammad Ilyas (Pak.):– 1 Test hundred, *252;* Test p'ship record, *252.*
Mohammad Iqbal (Muslim Model HS):– 475* v Islamia HS *270.*
Mohapatra, S. (Orissa):– Hat-trick, *159.*
Mohol, S. N. (M'tra):– 4 w. with consecutive balls, *158.*
Mohsin Khan (Pak.):– 2,709 r. in Tests, *180;* 1,029 Test r. in year, *177;* 7 Test hundreds, *224, 238, 255, 259;* Handled the ball, *154;* 426 for 2nd wkt, *151;* Test p'ship records, *225, 239, 259.*
Mold, A. W. (Eng.):– 1,673 w., *162;* 200 w. (2), *160;* 100 w. (9), *161;* 4 w. with consecutive balls, *158.*
Moles, A. J. (Warwicks.):– 224* in 1990, *273.*
Moloney, D. A. R. (NZ):– Test p'ship record, *219.*
Moody, T. M. (Aust.):– 1 Test hundred, *240;* 100 in 26 min., *145, 275;* 50 in 11 min., *145;* Average of 89.46 in English season, *142.*
Mooney, F. L. H. (NZ):– Test p'ship record, *219.*
Moore, R. H. (Hants):– Highest for Hampshire, *135;* 316 v Warwickshire in day, *134, 135, 146.*
More, K. S. (Ind.):– 56 d. in one-day ints, *266;* 5 st. in Test innings, *192;* 6 st. in Test, *192;* Test p'ship record, *270.*
Morgan, H. E. (Glam.):– 254 v Monmouthshire, *270.*
Morkel, D. P. B. (SA):– 222 for 8th wkt, *153.*
Moroney, J. R. (Aust.):– 2 hundreds in same Test, *176, 228.*
Morris, A. R. (Aust.):– Test captain, *200, 230;* 12,614 r. (avge 53.67), *145;* 3,533 r. in Tests, *178;* 2,080 r. v England, *208;* 46 hundreds, *139;* 12 Test hundreds, *204, 228, 231, 236;* 2 hundreds in same Test, *176, 204;* 2 hundreds in match (2), *137;* 148 and 111 on début, *136;* 301 for 2nd wkt v England, *184;* Test p'ship record, *236.*
Morris, H. (Glam.):– 2 hundreds in match (2), *137, 275;* 1st wkt hundreds, *276;* 256 and 255* for 1st wkt, *276.*
Morris, J. E. (Eng.):– 2 hundreds in match, *275.*
Morris, R. E. (OUCC):– Captain of Oxford, *667.*
Morrison, J. F. M. (NZ):– 1 Test hundred, *234.*
Mortimore, J. B. (Eng.):– All-round, *165;* 1,807 w., *162.*
Moss, A. E. (Cant.):– 10 w. in innings on début, *155.*
Moss, J. K. (Aust.):– 390* for 3rd wkt, *152.*
Motz, R. C. (NZ):– 100 w. in Tests, *188.*
Moxon, M. D. (Eng.):– Captain of Yorkshire, *649;* Hundred on début, *135;* 218* in 1990, *273.*
Mudassar Nazar (Pak.):– 4,114 r. in Tests, *180;* 42 hundreds, *139;* 10 Test hundreds, *224, 252, 255;* Slowest Test hundred, *183;* 761 r. in series, *176;* Carrying bat in Test, *181;* 111 w. in one-day ints, *266;* All-round in one-day ints, *267;* Average of 82.50 in English season, *142;* 451 for 3rd wkt, *149, 184, 256;* 389 for 1st wkt, *150;* Test p'ship records, *225, 252, 256, 259.*
Mukherjee, S. (Bengal):– Hat-trick, *159, 1177.*
Murdoch, W. L. (Aust. and Eng.):– Test captain, *199-200;* 2 Test hundreds, *204;* 321 v Victoria, *133.*
Murray, A. R. A. (SA):– 1 Test hundred, *241;* Test p'ship record, *241.*
Murray, D. A. (WI):– 10 d. in match, *167;* 9 d. in Test, *192.*
Murray, D. L. (WI):– Test captain, *230;* 189 d. in Tests, *193;* 24 d. in series, *192;* Test p'ship records, *232, 246, 248.*
Murray, J. T. (Eng.):– 1,025 r. and 104 d. in season, *165;* 1 Test hundred, *214;* Slow batting in Test, *183;* 1,527 d., *167;* 100 d. in season (2), *167;* 6 d. in Test innings, *192;* Test p'ship record, *216.*
Mushtaq Ali (Ind.):– 2 Test hundreds, *221, 246.*
Mushtaq Mohammad (Pak.):– Test captain, *237, 247, 251, 254;* Youngest Test player, *197;* 31,091 r., *143;* 3,643 r. in Tests, *180;*

Mushtaq Mohammad (Pak.):– *contd* 1,000 r. (15), *141;* 72 hundreds, *139;* 10 Test hundreds, *224, 238, 248, 252, 255;* 303* v Karachi Univ., *134;* All-round in Tests, *190;* 350 for 4th wkt v New Zealand, *152, 184, 252;* Test p'ship records, *225, 248, 252.*
Mycroft, W. (Derbys.):– 17 w. in match, *157.*

N

Nadeem Yousuf (MCB):– 196* for 10th wkt, *154.*
Nadkarni, R. G. (Ind.):– 1 Test hundred, *222;* 10 w. or more in Test (1), *237;* Test p'ship records, *222, 250.*
Nagarwalla, N. D. (M'tra):– 245 for 9th wkt, *153.*
Nanan, R. (WI):– Test p'ship record, *248.*
Nash, G. (Lancs.):– 4 w. with consecutive balls, *158.*
Nash, M. A. (Glam.):– Fastest hundred in B & H Cup, *758.*
Nasim-ul-Ghani (Pak.):– Test début at 16, *197;* 1 Test hundred, *224;* Test p'ship record, *225.*
National Association of Young Cricketers:– v MCC Schools, *373-4;* v Pakistan Young Cricketers, *905.*
National Club Championship, *375-6.*
National Cricket Association:– *293;* Address, *1316;* England Amateur XI v Pakistan Young Cricketers, *902;* Young Cricketers v Combined Services, *374.*
National Power Awards, *648.*
National Village Championship, *376-7.*
NatWest Bank Trophy:– *705-28;* Fixtures, 1991, *1350-3.*
Nayudu, C. K. (Ind.):– Test captain, *220;* 11 sixes in innings, *148.*
Nayyar, R. (H. Pradesh):– Handled the ball, *154.*
Nazar Mohammad (Pak.):– 1 Test hundred, *255;* Carrying bat in Test, *181.*
Neale, P. A. (Worcs.):– Captain of Worcestershire, *633.*
Nehru Cup, *1063-76.*
Netherlands, The:– Cricket in, *1202-3;* ICC Trophy finalists, *362-3;* Representative body, *1316.*
Newham, W. (Eng.):– 344 for 7th wkt, *153.*
Newman, J. A. (Hants):– All-round, *165;* 2,032 w., *162, 163;* 100 w. (9), *161.*
Newport, P. J. (Eng.):– Test p'ship record, *226.*
New Zealand:– Austral-Asia Cup, 1989-90, *1088-93;* Definition of first-class matches, *1320;* Domestic season 1989-90, *1158-66;* Highest individual Test innings, *174;* Highest Test innings, *195;* Leading batsmen in Tests, *179;* Leading bowlers in Tests, *188;* Lowest Test innings, *196;* Most consecutive Test appearances, *199;* Most Test appearances, *128;* Most Test appearances as captain, *128;* New Zealand in Test cricket (*see p. 132*); Representative body, *1315;* Summary of Tests, *199;* Summary of one-day ints, *264;* Test cricketers (1929-90), *114-8;* Youngest and Oldest on Test début, *197-8.*
Nicholas, M. C. J. (Hants):– Captain of Hampshire, *451.*
Nicholls, R. B. (Glos.):– 1,000 r. (15), *141;* 395 for 1st wkt, *150.*
Nichols, M. S. (Eng.):– All-round, *165;* 1,833 w., *162;* 100 w. (11), *161.*
Nicolson, J. F. W. (Natal):– 424 for 1st wkt, *150, 151.*
Nimbalkar, B. B. (M'tra):– 443* v Western Indian States, *133, 151;* 50 boundaries in innings, *149;* 455 for 2nd wkt, *149, 151.*
Nissan Shield (SA), *1144-5.*
Nixon, P. A. (Leics.):– 6 d. in innings, *278.*
Noble, M. A. (Aust.):– Test captain, *200;* 37 hundreds, *140;* 1 Test hundred, *204;* 121 w. in Tests, *188;* 10 w. or more in Test (2), *207;* 7 w. for 17 r. in Test innings, *186;* All-round in Tests, *191;* 428 for 6th wkt, *152.*
Noreiga, J. M. (WI):– 9 w. in Test innings, *185.*
Norfolk, *714, 849, 850, 861-2.*
Northamptonshire:– *378, 532-47;* Championship positions, *384-5;* Highest score, *169;* Highest individual score, *135;* Lowest score, *170.*
Northamptonshire II:– *868, 871, 880-1, 889;* v Pakistan Young Cricketers, *903.*
Northumberland, *849, 851, 862.*
Nottinghamshire:– *378, 548-64;* Championship positions, *384-5;* Highest score, *169;* Highest individual score, *135;* Lowest score, *170.*
Nottinghamshire II:– *868, 871, 881-2;* v Scotland B, *900.*
Nourse, A. D. (SA):– Test captain, *209, 227;* 12,472 r. (avge 51.53), *145;* 2,960 r. (avge 53.81) in Tests, *178, 181;* 621 r. in series, *212;* 41 hundreds, *139;* 9 Test hundreds, *210, 228;* 319 for 3rd wkt v England, *184, 211.*
Nourse, A. W. (SA):– Handled the ball, *154;* Oldest South African Test player, *198;* 45 consecutive Tests, *199;* 2,234 r. in Tests, *179;* 38 hundreds, *139;* 1 Test hundred, *228;* 304* v Transvaal, *134;* 53 boundaries in innings, *149;* Test p'ship records, *229.*
Nunes, R. K. (WI):– Test captain, *213.*
Nupen, E. P. (SA):– Test captain, *209;* 10 w. or more in Test (1), *212;* Test p'ship record, *211.*
Nurse, S. M. (WI):– 2,523 r. in Tests, *179;* 6 Test hundreds, *215, 231, 243;* 258 v New Zealand, *174, 243;* Test p'ship record, *216.*

O

Oates, T. W. (Notts.):– 10 d. in match, *166.*
O'Brien, Sir T. C. (Eng.):– Test captain, *209.*

Ochse, A. E. (SA):– Youngest South African Test player, *197*.
O'Connor, J. (Eng.):– 28,764 r., *143;* 1,000 r. (16), *141;* 72 hundreds, *139*.
O'Keeffe, K. J. (Aust.):– Test p'ship records, *234, 239*.
Old, C. M. (Eng.):– Fast scoring, *146;* 143 w. in Tests, *187;* 4 w. in 5 balls v Pakistan, *225*.
Oldest players on Test début, *198*.
Oldest Test players, *198*.
Oldfield, N. (Eng.):– 38 hundreds, *139*.
Oldfield, W. A. (Aust.):– 130 d. in Tests, *193;* 90 d. v England, *207*.
Oldroyd, E. (Yorks.):– 36 hundreds, *140*.
O'Neill, N. C. (Aust.):– 13,859 r. (avge 50.95), *145;* 2,779 r. in Tests, *178;* 45 hundreds, *139;* 6 Test hundreds, *204, 231, 236, 238*.
O'Reilly, W. J. (Aust.):– 144 w. in Tests, *188;* 102 w. v England, *208;* 10 w. or more in Test (3), *207;* Test p'ship record, *229*.
O'Shaughnessy, S. J. (Lancs. and Worcs.):– Hundred in 35 minutes, *146*.
Over-rates in County Championship, *401*.
Owen-Smith, H. G. (SA):– Obituary, *1275-6;* 1 Test hundred, *210;* Test p'ship record, *211*.
Oxford v Cambridge, *371-3*.
Oxford & Cambridge Universities:– v New Zealanders, *313-4;* in B & H Cup, *760*.
Oxford University 1990:– *667-76;* Blues, *688-91*.
Oxfordshire:– *712-3, 849, 851, 862-3;* v Oxford Univ., *671*.

P

Page, M. L. (NZ):– Test captain, *217, 240;* 1 Test hundred, *219*.
Pairaudeau, B. H. (WI):– Hundred on Test début, *175, 245;* Test p'ship record, *246*.
Pakistan:– Austral-Asia Cup winners, *1088-94;* B & H World Series Cup, *1077-87;* Definition of first-class matches, *1320;* Domestic season 1989-90, *1179-91;* Highest individual Test innings, *174;* Highest Test innings, *194;* Leading batsmen in Tests, *180;* Leading bowlers in Tests, *189;* Lowest Test innings, *196;* Most Test appearances, *128;* Most consecutive Test appearances, *199;* Most Test appearances as captain, *128;* Nehru Cup winners, *1063-76;* Oldest Test player, *198;* Pakistan in Test cricket (*see p. 132*); Representative body, *1315;* Sharjah Champions Trophy, *1058-62;* Summary of Tests, *199;* Summary of one-day ints, *264;* Test cricketers (1952-90), *123-6;* Youngest and oldest on Test début, *197-8*.
Pakistan v New Zealand, 1990-91, *1166*.
Pakistan v West Indies, 1990-91, *1039*.
Pakistan Young Cricketers in England, *902-6*.
Palmer, G. E. (Aust.):– 10 w. or more in Test (2), *207*.
Palmer, G. V. (Som.):– Career figures, *1324*.
Pandya, A. (S'tra):– Handled the ball, *154*.
Parfitt, P. H. (Eng.):– 26,924 r., *143;* 1,000 r. (15), *141;* 58 hundreds, *139;* 7 Test hundreds, *210, 218, 221, 224;* 2 hundreds in match (2), *137;* Test p'ship records, *219, 225*.
Parikh, R. B. (Baroda):– 2 hundreds in match, *138, 1176*.
Parkar, G. A. (Ind.):– 421 for 1st wkt, *150*.
Parkar, Z. (Bombay):– 10 d. in match, *167*.
Parker, C. W. L. (Glos.):– 3,278 w., *161;* 200 w. (5), *160;* 100 w. (16), *161;* 100 w. by June 12, *161;* 17 w. in match, *157;* 10 w. in innings, *156;* 6 hat-tricks, *159;* Double hat-trick, *159*.
Parker, J. M. (NZ):– Test captain, *251;* 3 Test hundreds, *219, 234, 250;* Test p'ship record, *234*.
Parker, P. W. G. (Eng.):– Captain of Sussex, *598;* 40 hundreds, *139;* 32 r. in over, *147*.
Parkhouse, W. G. A. (Eng.):– 1,000 r. (15), *141*.
Parkin, C. H. (Eng.):– 200 w. (2), *160*.
Parkinson's World XI, M.:– v Indians, *342-3;* v Yorkshire, *700*.
Parks, H. W. (Sussex):– 42 hundreds, *139*.
Parks, J. H. (Eng.):– All-round, *164;* 3,003 r. in season, *140;* 41 hundreds, *139*.
Parks, J. M. (Eng.):– 36,673 r., *143;* 1,000 r. (20), *141;* 51 hundreds, *139;* 2 Test hundreds, *210, 214;* 1,181 d., *168;* 114 d. in Tests, *193;* 8 d. in Test, *192;* Test p'ship records, *211, 216*.
Parks, R. J. (Hants):– 10 d. in match, *167*.
Parsons, Revd J. H. (Warwicks.):– 38 hundreds, *139*.
Partnerships:– First-wicket, *150;* Highest, *149;* Highest for each country, *151-4;* Highest in one-day ints, *265;* Highest in Tests, *184* (*see individual series for records v countries*); In 1990, *276-7*.
Passailaigue, C. C. (WI):– 487* for 6th wkt, *149, 152*.
Pataudi (sen.), Nawab of (Eng. and Ind.):– Test captain, *220;* 4 successive hundreds, *138;* Hundred on Test début, *174, 202*.
Pataudi (jun.), Nawab of (Ind.):– Test captain, *220, 235, 244, 249;* 2,793 r. in Tests, *180;* 6 Test hundreds, *222, 236, 250;* 2 hundreds in match (2), *137;* Slow batting in Test, *183*.
Patel, B. P. (Ind.):– 37 hundreds, *140;* 1 Test hundred, *246;* Test p'ship records, *246, 250*.
Patel, J. M. (Ind.):– 14 w. in Test, *186, 237;* 9 w. in Test innings, *185, 237*.
Patil, S. M. (Ind.):– 4 Test hundreds, *222, 236, 255;* Test p'ship record, *256, 257*.
Patron's Trophy (Pak.):– *1179, 1182-5;* One-day, *1191*.
Patterson, B. M. W. (Scotland):– Hundred on début, *136*.

Paynter, E. (Eng.):– 653 r. in series, *212;* 45 hundreds, *139;* 4 Test hundreds, *202, 210;* 2 hundreds in match (2), *137;* 2 hundreds in same Test, *176, 210;* 322 v Sussex, *133;* Test avge of 59.23, *180;* Test p'ship records, *205*.

Payton, W. R. D. (Notts.):– 39 hundreds, *139*.

Peach, H. A. (Surrey):– Fast scoring, *146;* 4 w. with consecutive balls, *158*.

Pearse, D. K. (Natal):– Handled the ball, *154*.

Pearson, A. J. G. (CUCC and Som.):– 10 w. in innings, *156*.

Peate, E. (Eng.):– 214 w. in season, *160;* 8 w. for 5 r., *157*.

Peel, R. (Eng.):– 1,753 w., *162, 163;* 102 w. in Tests, *187;* 100 w. (8), *161;* 10 w. or more in Test (2), *206;* 292 for 8th wkt, *153*.

Pegler, S. J. (SA):– Fifty in 14 min., *145;* Test p'ship record, *229*.

Pellew, C. E. (Aust.):– 2 Test hundreds, *204*.

Perks, R. T. D. (Worcs.):– 2,233 w., *162;* 100 w. (16), *161*.

Perrin, P. A. (Essex):– Highest for Essex, *135;* 29,709 r., *143;* 1,000 r. (18), *141;* 66 hundreds, *139;* 2 hundreds in match (4), *137;* 343* v Derbyshire, *133, 135;* 68 boundaries in innings, *149*.

Pervez Akhtar (Pak. Rlwys):– 337* v Dera Ismail Khan, *133*.

Pervez Sajjad (Pak.):– 4 w. for 5 r. in Test innings, *184*.

Petherick, P. J. (NZ):– Hat-trick v Pakistan, *190*.

Phadkar, D. G. (Ind.):– 2 Test hundreds, *222, 236*.

Philip, I. L. (Scotland):– Hundred on début, *136*.

Phillips, H. (Sussex):– 10 d. in match, *166*.

Phillips, R. B. (Qld):– 7 d. in innings, *166*.

Phillips, W. B. (Aust.):– Hundred on Test début, *175, 238;* 2 Test hundreds, *231, 238;* 462* for 4th wkt, *149, 152;* Test p'ship records, *234, 239*.

Pickett, H. (Essex):– 10 w. in innings, *156*.

Pinch, C. (S. Aust.):– 2 hundreds in match (2), *137*.

Piper, K. J. (Warwicks.):– 6 d. in innings, *278*.

Pithey, A. J. (SA):– 1 Test hundred, *210;* Test p'ship record, *211*.

Place, W. (Eng.):– 36 hundreds, *140;* 1 Test hundred, *214*.

Playle, W. R. (NZ):– Slow Test batting, *183*.

Pocock, P. I. (Eng.):– 1,607 w., *162;* 5 w. in 6 balls, *159;* 4 w. with consecutive balls, *158;* Test p'ship record, *216*.

Pollard, P. R. (Notts.):– 1st wkt hundreds, *150*.

Pollard, V. (NZ):– 2 Test hundreds, *219;* Test p'ship records, *219, 244*.

Pollock, P. M. (SA):– 116 w. in Tests, *188;* 10 w. or more in Test (1), *212;* 341 for 3rd wkt v Australia, *184, 229;* Test p'ship records, *229, 241*.

Pollock, R. G. (SA):– Handled the ball, *154;* 20,940 r. (avge 54.67), *145;* 2,256 r. (avge 60.97) in Tests, *179, 180;* 64 hundreds, *139;* 7 Test hundreds, *210, 228;* 2 hundreds in match (2), *137;* 274 v Australia, *174, 228;* 341 for 3rd wkt, *152;* Test p'ship records, *229*.

Ponsford, W. H. (Aust.):– 13,819 r. (avge 65.18), *144;* 2,122 r. in Tests, *178;* 47 hundreds, *139;* 7 Test hundreds, *204, 231;* Hundred on Test début, *174, 204;* 437 v Queensland, *133;* 429 v Tasmania, *133;* 352 v New South Wales, *133;* 336 v South Australia, *133;* 334 r. in day, *146;* 281* at Lord's, *269;* 266 v England, *174, 204;* 456 for 1st wkt, *149, 150;* 375 for 1st wkt, *150;* 451 for 2nd wkt v England, *149, 151, 184, 205;* 388 for 4th wkt v England, *184, 205*.

Pooley, E. (Surrey):– 12 d. and 10 d. in matches, *166*.

Poore, M. B. (NZ):– Test p'ship record, *242*.

Poore, R. M. (Hants):– 304 v Somerset, *134, 153;* Avge of 91.23 in English season, *142;* 411 for 6th wkt, *152*.

Popplewell, N. F. M. (Som.):– Hundred in 41 minutes, *146*.

Pougher, A. D. (Eng.):– 5 w. for 0 r., *157*.

Powell, J. L. (Cant.):– 265 for 7th wkt, *153*.

Prasanna, E. A. S. (Ind.):– 189 w. in Tests, *189;* 10 w. or more in Tests (2), *237, 251;* 8 w. in Test innings, *185, 251*.

Price, W. F. F. (Eng.):– 7 d. in innings, *165*.

Prichard, P. J. (Essex):– 245 in 1990, *273;* 403 for 2nd wkt, *277*.

Prideaux, R. M. (Eng.):– 25,136 r., *144;* 41 hundreds, *139;* 2 hundreds in match (2), *137;* 1st wkt hundreds, *151*.

Pritchard, T. L. (Warwicks.):– 3 hat-tricks, *159*.

Procter, M. J. (SA):– 48 hundreds, *139;* 6 successive hundreds, *138;* 30 r. in over, *147;* Hundred and hat-trick (2), *164;* 4 hat-tricks, *159;* LBW hat-trick (2), *159*.

Prodger, J. M. (Kent):– 8 c. in match, *168*.

Prout, J. A. (Wesley Coll.):– 459 v Geelong College, *270*.

Public Schools, highest score, *270*.

Pullar, G. (Eng.):– 41 hundreds, *139;* 4 Test hundreds, *210, 221, 224;* Test p'ship record, *225*.

Q

Qasim Omar (Pak.):– 3 Test hundreds, *238, 255, 259;* 2 hundreds in match (2), *137;* Hundred and double-hundred, *137;* 397 for 3rd wkt v Sri Lanka, *184, 259;* Test p'ship records, *239, 256, 259*.

Quaid-e-Azam Trophy (Pak.):– *1180, 1185-91;* One-day, *1191*.

Rushby, T. (Surrey):– 10 w. in innings, *156.*
Rushmere, M. W. (E. Prov.):– 2 hundreds in match, *138, 1150.*
Russell, A. C. (C.A.G.) (Eng.):– 27,358 r., *143;* 71 hundreds, *139;* 5 Test hundreds, *202, 210;* 2 hundreds in match (3), *137;* 2 hundreds in same Test, *176, 210;* Test p'ship record, *211.*
Russell, R. C. (Eng.):– 1 Test hundred, *202;* w-k hat-trick, *166;* 229 for 7th wkt, *277;* Test p'ship record, *226.*
Russell, W. E. (Eng.):– 25,525 r., *144;* 41 hundreds, *139.*
Rutherford, K. R. (NZ):– 317 in day v D. B. Close's XI, *134, 146;* 53 boundaries in innings, *149;* 1 Test hundred, *219;* Test p'ship records, *219, 234.*
Ryall, R. J. (W. Prov.):– 10 d. in match, *167.*
Ryder, J. (Aust.):– Test captain, *200;* 3 Test hundreds, *204, 228;* Test avge of 51.62, *181.*

S

Saadat Ali (Income Tax):– Hundred and double-hundred, *136;* 1,649 r. in Pakistan season, *141.*
Sadiq Mohammad (Pak.):– 2,579 r. in Tests, *180;* 50 hundreds, *139;* 5 Test hundreds, *224, 238, 252;* 4 successive hundreds, *138;* 2 hundreds in match (3), *137;* Test p'ship record, *252.*
Saeed Ahmed (Pak.):– Test captain, *223;* 2,991 r. in Tests, *180;* 5 Test hundreds, *238, 248, 252, 255;* 4 successive hundreds, *138;* Test p'ship records, *248, 252.*
Saggers, R. A. (Aust.):– 21 d. in series, *193;* 10 d. in match, *166;* 7 d. in innings, *165.*
Saini, S. S. (Delhi):– 4 w. with consecutive balls, *158.*
Sajjad Akbar (Sargodha and PNSC):– 104 w. in Pakistan season, *161, 1180, 1182.*
Salah-ud-Din (Pak.):– Hundred and double-hundred, *136;* 353 for 6th wkt, *153;* Test p'ship record, *253.*
Salim Malik (Pak.):– 2,718 r. in Tests, *180;* 7 Test hundreds, *224, 252, 255, 259;* Hundred on Test début, *175, 259;* Test p'ship records, *225, 239, 248, 256, 259.*
Salim Yousuf (Pak.):– 91 d. in one-day ints, *266;* Test p'ship records, *225, 248, 259.*
Sandham, A. (Eng.):– 41,284 r., *142;* 1,000 r. (20), *141;* 107 hundreds, *138;* 2 Test hundreds, *214;* 325 v West Indies, *133, 173, 214;* 219 v Australians, *135;* 428 for 1st wkt, *150;* 1st wkt hundreds, *150.*
Sandhu, B. S. (Ind.):– Test p'ship record, *246.*
Sardesai, D. N. (Ind.):– 2,001 r. in Tests, *180;* 5 Test hundreds, *246, 250;* Slow Test hundred, *183;* Test p'ship records, *246, 250.*
Sarfraz Nawaz (Pak.):– 177 w. in Tests, *189;* 10 w. or more in Test (1), *239;* 9 w. in Test innings, *185, 239;* All-round in Tests, *191;* Test p'ship records, *225, 248.*
Sarwate, C. T. (Ind.):– 236 for 8th wkt, *153;* 249 for 10th wkt, *154.*
Scarborough Festival:– *342-3, 664-5, 700-2;* Address of Secretary, *1316.*
Scarborough Festival Trophy, *700-2.*
Schofield, R. M. (C. Dist.):– Obituary, *1279;* 7 d. in innings, *166.*
Scotland:– v England Amateur XI, *899;* v Indians, *327-8, 899;* v Ireland, *699-700, 899;* v MCC, *368, 899;* in B & H Cup, *729, 749-52, 898-9;* in NatWest Bank Trophy, *707, 899;* Representative body, *1316.*
Scott, C. W. (Notts.):– 10 d. in match, *167.*
Scott, H. J. H. (Aust.):– Test captain, *200;* 1 Test hundred, *204.*
Scottish Cricket in 1990, *898-901.*
Scotton, W. H. (Eng.):– Handled the ball, *154;* Test p'ship record, *205.*
Sealy, J. E. D. (WI):– Youngest West Indian Test player, *197.*
Second XI Championship:– *868-87;* Championship winners, *887;* Fixtures, 1991, *1356-8.*
Seeboard Trophy:– *702-3;* Fixtures, 1991, *1353.*
Serjeant, C. S. (Aust.):– 1 Test hundred, *231.*
Seymour, James (Kent):– 27,237 r., *143;* 1,000 r. (16), *141;* 53 hundreds, *139;* 2 hundreds in match (2), *137.*
Shackleton, D. (Eng.):– 2,857 w., *161;* 100 w. (20), *162;* 8 w. for 4 r., *157.*
Shacklock, F. J. (Notts.):– 4 w. with consecutive balls, *158.*
Shafiq Ahmed (Pak.):– 52 hundreds, *139;* 2 hundreds in match (2), *137;* Hundred and double-hundred, *136;* 389 for 1st wkt, *150.*
Shahid Israr (Pak.):– 7 d. in innings, *166.*
Shahid Mahmood (Pak.):– 10 w. in innings, *156.*
Sharjah Champions Trophy, 1989-90, *1058-62.*
Sharma, Chetan (Ind.):– 10 w. or more in Test (1), *222;* Hat-trick in one-day int., *266;* Test p'ship records, *222, 257.*
Sharma, Gopal (Ind.):– Test p'ship record, *257.*
Sharp, J. (Eng.):– 38 hundreds, *140;* 1 Test hundred, *202.*
Sharp, J. C. (Melb. GS):– 506* v Geelong College, *270.*
Sharpe, P. J. (Eng.):– 1 Test hundred, *218;* 71 c. in season, *168;* 24 c. in GC/NWB Trophy, *727.*
Shastri, R. J. (Ind.):– Test captain, *244;* 3,372 r. in Tests, *179;* 10 Test hundreds, *222, 236, 246, 255;* 200 r. in 113 min., *146;* 36 r. in over, *147;* 13 sixes in innings, *148;* 143 w. in Tests, *189;* 114 w. in one-day ints, *266;* All-round in Tests, *191;* All-round in one-day ints, *267;* 251 for 1st wkt, *276;* Test p'ship records, *222, 236, 246, 256.*

Shaw, A. (Eng.):– Test captain, *199;* 2,027 w., *162;* 201 w. in season, *160;* 100 w. (9), *161;* 10 w. in innings, *155;* Double hat-trick, *159;* 3 hat-tricks, *159.*
Sheahan, A. P. (Aust.):– 2 Test hundreds, *236, 238.*
Sheffield Shield (Aust.), *1095-131.*
Shell Cup (NZ), *1159, 1165-6.*
Shell Shield (WI):– Winners, *1156.*
Shell Trophy (NZ), *1158-9, 1161-4.*
Shepherd, D. J. (Glam.):– 2,218 w., *162;* 100 w. (12), *161.*
Shepherd, D. R. (Glos.):– Hundred on début, *135.*
Shepherd, J. N. (WI):– 267 w. in Sunday League, *845.*
Shepherd, T. F. (Surrey):– 42 hundreds, *139.*
Sheppard, Rt Rev. D. S. (Eng.):– Test captain, *223;* 45 hundreds, *139;* 3 Test hundreds, *202, 221.*
Sherwell, P. W. (SA):– Test captain, *208, 227;* 1 Test hundred, *210.*
Shillingford, G. C. (WI):– Test p'ship record, *243.*
Shillingford, I. T. (WI):– 1 Test hundred, *248.*
Shoaib Mohammad (Pak.):– 4 Test hundreds, *252, 255;* Slow scoring in Test, *183;* Test p'ship records, *225, 252.*
Shodhan, D. H. (Ind.):– Hundred on Test début, *175, 255.*
Shrewsbury, A. (Eng.):– Test captain, *200;* 26,505 r., *143;* 59 hundreds, *139;* 3 Test hundreds, *202;* 6 c. in Test, *194;* 391 for 1st wkt, *150.*
Shropshire, *706, 849, 851, 863.*
Sidhu, N. S. (Ind.):– 2 Test hundreds, *246, 250;* 251 for 1st wkt, *276;* Test p'ship record, *256.*
Siedle, I. J. (SA):– 1 Test hundred, *211;* 424 for 1st wkt, *150, 151;* Test p'ship record, *211.*
Sikander Bakht (Pak.):– 10 w. or more in Test (1), *256;* 8 w. in Test innings, *185, 256.*
Silva, S. A. R. (SL):– 2 Test hundreds, *226, 257;* 34 d. in Tests, *193;* 22 d. in series, *193;* 9 d. in Test (2), *192;* 6 d. in Test innings, *192;* All-round in Test, *191;* Test p'ship records, *227, 258.*
Simmons, J. (Lancs.):– 307 w. in Sunday League, *845;* 79 w. in GC/NWB Trophy, *726;* Most econ. analysis in GC/NWB Trophy, *727;* 25 c. in GC/NWB Trophy, *727.*
Simpson, R. B. (Aust.):– Test captain, *200, 227, 230, 235, 237;* 21,029 r. (avge 56.22), *144;* 4,869 r. in Tests, *178;* 2,063 r. in overseas season, *141;* 1,381 Test r. in year, *176;* 60 hundreds, *139;* 10 Test hundreds, *204, 228, 231, 236, 238;* 2 hundreds in same Test, *176, 238;* 2 hundreds in match (2), *137;* 359 v Queensland, *133;* 311 v England, *134, 174, 204;* 110 c. in Tests, *194;* 13 c. in series (2), *194;* 382 for 1st wkt v West Indies, *150, 184, 232.*
Simpson, R. T. (Eng.):– 30,546 r., *143;* 64 hundreds, *139;* 4 Test hundreds, *202, 210, 218, 224;* Test p'ship records, *215, 219.*
Sims, Sir Arthur (Australian XI):– 433 for 8th wkt, *153.*
Sims, J. M. (Eng.):– 1,581 w., *162;* 100 w. (8), *161;* 10 w. in innings, *156.*
Sinclair, B. W. (NZ):– Test captain, *217, 249;* 3 Test hundreds, *219, 241, 252;* Test p'ship records, *242, 252.*
Sinclair, J. H. (SA):– 3 Test hundreds, *211, 228;* All-round in Test, *190.*
Singer Inter-Provincial Tournament (SL):– *1193, 1198.*
Singh, R. P. (Holkar):– 236 for 8th wkt, *153.*
Singla, A. (Haryana):– Hat-trick, *159, 1174.*
Sivaramakrishnan, L. (Ind.):– Youngest Indian Test player, *197;* 10 w. or more in Test (1), *223;* Test p'ship record, *257.*
Slack, J. K. E. (CUCC):– Hundred on début, *135.*
Smailes, T. F. (Eng.):– 10 w. in innings, *156.*
Smales, K. (Notts.):– 10 w. in innings, *156.*
Smart, C. C. (Glam.):– 32 r. in over, *147.*
Smith, A. C. (Eng.):– Test p'ship record, *219.*
Smith, Sir C. Aubrey (Eng.):– Test captain, *208.*
Smith, C. I. J. (Eng.):– Fifty in 11 min. and 14 min., *145.*
Smith, C. L. (Eng.):– 41 hundreds, *139;* 264 for 1st wkt, *276.*
Smith, E. J. (Eng.):– 7 d. in innings, *165.*
Smith, H. D. (NZ):– Wkt with 1st ball on Test début, *189.*
Smith, I. D. S. (NZ):– 2 Test hundreds, *219, 250;* 151 d. in Tests, *193;* All-round in Test, *191;* 65 d. in one-day ints, *266;* Test p'ship records, *244, 250.*
Smith, M. J. (Middx):– 40 hundreds, *139.*
Smith, M. J. K. (Eng.):– Test captain, *200, 209, 213, 217, 220;* 39,832 r., *142;* 3,245 r. in season, *140;* 2,278 r. in Tests, *178;* 1,000 r. (20), *141;* 69 hundreds, *139;* 3 Test hundreds, *210, 214, 221;* 3 hundreds v Cambridge, *373;* Test p'ship records, *216.*
Smith, M. S. (Natal):– 7 d. in innings, *165.*
Smith, O. G. (WI):– 4 Test hundreds, *215, 231, 245;* Hundred on Test début, *175, 231;* All-round in Test, *190;* Test p'ship records, *243, 248.*
Smith, P. A. (Warwicks.): Hat-trick in 1990, *277.*
Smith, R. (Essex):– All-round, *165.*
Smith, R. A. (Eng.):– 10,000 r., *279;* 4 Test hundreds, *202, 221;* Hundred before lunch, *275;* Test avge of 53.73, *180;* 256 for 3rd wkt, *277;* Test p'ship record, *226.*
Smith, S. G. (Northants):– All-round, *165;* 4 w. with consecutive balls, *158.*
Smith, T. P. B. (Eng.):– 1,697 w., *162.*
Smith, V. I. (SA):– 6 w. for 1 r., *157.*
Smith, W. C. (Surrey):– 247 w. in season, *160.*

Snedden, M. C. (NZ):– 114 w. in one-day ints, *266;* Test p'ship records, *234, 250.*
Snooke, S. J. (SA):– Test captain, *208;* 1 Test hundred, *228;* 10 w. or more in Test (1), *212;* 8 w. in Test innings, *185.*
Snow, J. A. (Eng.):– 202 w. in Tests, *187;* 10 w. or more in Test (1), *216;* Test p'ship record, *216.*
Sobers, Sir G. S. (WI):– Test captain, *213, 230, 242, 244;* Test début at 17, *197;* 85 consecutive Tests, *198;* 28,315 r. (avge 54.87), *143, 144;* 8,032 r. (avge 57.78) in Tests, *179, 180;* 1,193 Test r. in year, *177;* 1,000 r. (15), *141;* 824 r. in series, *176;* 86 hundreds, *139;* 26 Test hundreds, *181, 215, 231, 243, 245, 248;* 2 hundreds in same Test, *176, 248;* 2 hundreds in match (2), *137;* 365* v Pakistan, *133, 151, 173, 248;* 36 r. in over, *147;* 235 w. in Tests, *188;* All-round in Tests, *190, 191, 192;* 109 c. in Tests, *194;* 6 c. in Test, *194;* 446 for 2nd wkt, *151, 184, 248;* 399 for 4th wkt v England, *184, 216;* Test p'ship records, *216, 243, 248.*
Solkar, E. D. (Ind.):– 1 Test hundred, *246;* 6 c. in Test, *194;* Test p'ship record, *246.*
Solomon, J. S. (WI):– 1 Test hundred, *245;* Hundreds in first three first-class innings, *136.*
Somerset:– *378, 565-80;* Championship positions, *384-5;* Highest score, *169;* Highest individual score, *135;* Lowest score, *170.*
Somerset II:– *868, 871, 882-3, 889-90;* Bain Clarkson Trophy finalists, *889-90.*
Sookram Memorial Trophy (WI), *1157.*
South Africa:– Domestic season 1989-90, *1133-51;* Highest individual Test innings, *174;* Highest Test innings, *195;* Leading batsmen in Tests, *178;* Leading bowlers in Tests, *188;* Lowest Test innings, *196;* Most consecutive Test appearances, *199;* Most Test appearances, *128;* Most Test appearances as captain, *128;* Oldest Test player, *198;* Representative bodies, *1315;* South Africa in Test cricket (*see p. 132*); Summary of Tests, *199;* Test cricketers (1888-1970), *105-9;* Youngest and oldest on Test début, *197-8.*
Southerton, J. (Eng.):– Oldest Test début, *197;* Test cricket at 49, *198;* 1,681 w., *162;* 210 w. in season, *161;* 100 w. (10), *161;* 16 w. in day, *158.*
Spofforth, F. R. (Aust.):– 207 w. in season, *160;* 14 England w. in match, *186, 207;* 10 w. or more in Test (4), *207;* 7 w. for 3 r., *157;* Test hat-trick, *189;* 4 hat-tricks, *159.*
Spooner, R. H. (Eng.):– 1 Test hundred, *210.*
Squires, H. S. (Surrey):– 37 hundreds, *140.*
Srikkanth, K. (Ind.):– Test captain, *254;* 3,541 r. in one-day ints, *265;* 2 Test hundreds, *236, 255;* Test p'ship record, *256.*
Sri Lanka:– Austral-Asia Cup, *1088-93;* B & H World Series Cup, *1077-86;* Definition of first-class matches, *1320;* Domestic season 1989-90, *1192-8;* Highest individual Test innings, *174;* Highest Test innings, *195;* Leading batsman in Tests, *180;* Leading bowler in Tests, *189;* Lowest Test innings, *196;* Most consecutive Test appearances, *199;* Most Test appearances, *128;* Most Test appearances as captain, *128;* Nehru Cup, *1063-74;* Representative body, *1315;* Sri Lanka in Test cricket (*see p. 132*); Summary of Tests, *199;* Summary of one-day ints, *264;* Test cricketers (1982-90), *126-7;* Youngest and oldest on Test début, *197-8.*
Srinath, J. (Karnataka):– Hat-trick, *159, 1174.*
Stackpole, K. R. (Aust.):– 2,807 r. in Tests, *178;* 7 Test hundreds, *204, 228, 231, 233, 236.*
Staffordshire, *711-2, 849, 850, 864.*
Stanyforth, Lt-Col. R. T. (Eng.):– Test captain, *209.*
Statham, J. B. (Eng.):– 2,260 w., *162;* 252 w. in Tests, *187;* 100 w. (13), *161;* 10 w. or more in Test (1), *212;* 3 hat-tricks, *159.*
Status of matches in UK, *368.*
Steel, A. G. (Eng.):– Test captain, *200;* 2 Test hundreds, *202.*
Steele, D. S. (Eng.):– 1 Test hundred, *214.*
Steele, J. F. (Leics. and Glam.):– 101 c. in Sunday League, *845;* 390 for 1st wkt, *150.*
Stephenson, F. D. (Notts.):– All-round, *163, 165.*
Stephenson, H. W. (Som.):– 1,082 d., *168.*
Stephenson, J. P. (Eng.):– 202* in 1990, *273;* 1st wkt hundreds, *150, 276.*
Stevens, G. T. S. (Eng.):– Test captain, *209;* 466* v Lambda, *270;* 10 w. or more in Test (1), *216.*
Stewart, A. J. (Eng.):– 11 d. in match, *166.*
Stewart, M. J. (Eng.):– 26,492 r., *143;* 1,000 r. (15), *141;* 49 hundreds, *139;* 77 c. and 61 c. in season, *168;* 7 c. in innings, *168.*
Stewart, W. J. (Warwicks.):– 17 sixes in match, *148.*
Steyn, S. S. L. (W. Prov.):– 222 for 8th wkt, *153.*
Stimpson, P. J. (Worcs.):– 1st wkt hundreds, *150.*
Stocks, F. W. (Notts.):– Hundred on début, *135.*
Stoddart, A. E. (Eng.):– Test captain, *200;* 2 Test hundreds, *203;* 485 v Stoics, *270;* 1st wkt hundreds, *151.*
Stollmeyer, J. B. (WI):– Test captain, *213, 230, 244;* 2,159 r. in Tests, *179;* 4 Test hundreds, *231, 243, 245;* 324 v British Guiana, *133, 152;* 434 for 3rd wkt, *152.*
Storie, A. C. (Northants and Warwicks.):– Hundred on début, *135.*
Straw, T. (Worcs.):– Obstructing the field (2), *155.*
Stricker, L. A. (SA):– Test p'ship record, *229.*
Strudwick, H. (Eng.):– Test cricket at 46, *198;* 1,497 d., *167;* 21 d. in series, *193.*
Strydom, J. J. (E. Prov.):– 355 for 5th wkt, *152.*

Stumpings in 1990, *580*.
Subba Row, R. (Eng.):– Chairman of Cricket Council and TCCB, *293;* Highest for Northamptonshire, *135;* 3 Test hundreds, *203, 214;* 300 v Surrey, *134, 135*.
Suffolk, *713, 849, 851, 864-5*.
Sunderam, P. (Rajasthan):– 10 w. in innings, *157*.
Super Wills Cup (Pak.), *1191*.
Surrey:– *378, 581-97;* Championship positions, *384-5;* Highest score, *169;* Highest individual score, *135;* Lowest score, *170;* Seeboard Trophy, *702-3;* Tilcon Trophy, *696*.
Surrey II, *868, 871, 883-4, 889*.
Sussex:– *378, 598-615;* Championship positions, *384-5;* Highest score, *169;* Highest individual score, *135;* Lowest score, *170;* Seeboard Trophy, *702;* Tilcon Trophy, *696*.
Sussex II:– *868, 871-2, 884-5, 889;* Second Eleven champions, *868*.
Sutcliffe, B. (NZ):– Test captain, *240, 242;* 2,727 r. in Tests, *179;* 44 hundreds, *139;* 5 Test hundreds, *219, 250;* 2 hundreds in match (4), *137;* Hundred and double-hundred, *136;* 385 v Canterbury, *133;* 355 v Auckland, *133;* 1st wkt hundreds, *150;* Test p'ship records, *219, 242, 250*.
Sutcliffe, H. (Eng.):– 50,138 r. (avge 51.95), *142, 144, 145;* 4,555 r. (avge 60.73) in Tests, *177, 180;* 3,336 r. in season, *140;* 2,741 r. v Australia, *208;* 1,000 r. (24), *140;* 149 hundreds, *138;* 16 Test hundreds, *203, 210, 218;* 13 and 14 hundreds in season, *138;* 4 successive hundreds, *138;* 2 hundreds in same Test (2), *175, 203, 210;* 2 hundreds in match (4), *137;* 313 v Essex, *134, 151;* Avge of 96.96 in English season, *142;* 1st wkt hundreds, *150-1;* 555 for 1st wkt, *149, 150, 151*.
Suttle, K. G. (Sussex):– 30,225 r., *143;* 1,000 r. (17), *141;* 49 hundreds, *139;* 423 consecutive Championship appearances, *272*.
Sydenham, D. A. D. (Surrey):– 4 w. in 5 balls in GC/NWB Trophy, *726*.

T

Taber, H. B. (Aust.):– 20 d. in series, *193;* 12 d. in match, *166;* 8 d. in Test, *192;* 7 d. in innings, *166*.
Taberer, H. M. (SA):– Test captain, *227*.
Tahir Naqqash (Pak.):– Test p'ship record, *259*.
Talat Ali (Pak.):– Hundred and double-hundred, *136*.
Tallon, D. (Aust.):– 20 d. in series, *193;* 12 d. in match, *166;* 7 d. in innings, *165*.
Tamil Nadu:– v Western Australia, *1178*.
Tancred, A. B. (SA):– Carrying bat in Test, *181*.
Tancred, L. J. (SA):– Test captain, *209, 227;* Test p'ship record, *229*.
Tarilton, P. H. (B'dos):– 304* v Trinidad, *134*.
Tariq Baig (Lahore City):– 2 hundreds in match, *138, 1185*.
Tariq Bashir (HBFC):– 355 for 5th wkt, *152*.
Tarrant, F. A. (Vic. and Middx):– All-round, *164, 165;* 100 w. (8), *161;* 5 hat-tricks, *159;* 4 w. with consecutive balls, *158*.
Taslim Arif (Pak.):– 1 Test hundred, *238;* 10 d. in match, *167;* 7 d. in innings, *166;* Test p'ship record, *239*.
Tate, M. W. (Eng.):– All-round, *164, 165;* All-round in Tests, *191;* 1 Test hundred, *210;* 2,784 w., *162;* 200 w. (3), *160;* 155 w. in Tests, *187;* 116 w. in overseas season, *161;* 100 w. (14), *161;* 38 w. in series, *207;* 10 w. or more in Test (1), *206;* 3 hat-tricks, *159;* Wkt with 1st ball on Test début, *189*.
Tattersall, R. (Eng.):– 100 w. (8), *161;* 10 w. or more in Test (1), *212*.
Tauseef Ahmed (Pak.):– Test p'ship record, *259*.
Tavaré, C. J. (Eng.):– Captain of Somerset, *565;* 20,000 r., *279;* 39 hundreds, *139;* 2 Test hundreds, *218, 221;* Slow scoring in Test, *183;* 49 c. in season, *168;* 219 in 1990, *273;* 285* for 3rd wkt, *277;* 256 for 4th wkt, *277;* 183 for 9th wkt *277;* Test p'ship record, *219*.
Tayfield, H. J. (SA):– 170 w. in Tests, *188;* 37 w. in series, *187, 212;* 26 w. in series, *212;* 13 w. in Test (2), *186, 212, 229;* 9 w. in Test innings, *185;* 8 w. in Test innings, *185;* 6 w. for 13 r. in Test innings, *186;* Test p'ship record, *241*.
Taylor, B. (Essex):– 1,294 d., *167;* 301 consec. Championship appearances, *272*.
Taylor, B. R. (NZ):– 2 Test hundreds, *243, 250;* Hundred on Test début, *175, 250;* 111 w. in Tests, *188;* All-round in Test, *190;* Test p'ship record, *250*.
Taylor, D. D. (NZ):– 1st wkt hundreds, *150*.
Taylor, H. W. (SA):– Test captain, *128, 208, 227;* 2,936 r. in Tests, *178;* 582 r. in series, *212;* 7 Test hundreds, *211;* Test p'ship record, *211*.
Taylor, J. M. (Aust.):– 1 Test hundred, *204;* Test p'ship record, *205*.
Taylor, L. B. (Leics. and Natal):– Career figures, *1324*.
Taylor, M. A. (Aust.):– 1,219 Test r. in year, *177;* 839 r. in series, *176;* 6 Test hundreds, *204, 238, 240;* 2 hundreds in match (2), *137, 138, 1129-30;* Test avge of 64.72, *180;* 329 for 1st wkt v England, *184, 205*.
Taylor, N. R. (Kent):– Hundred on début, *135;* Hundred and double-hundred, *137, 275;* 204 in 1990, *273;* 366 for 2nd wkt, *277*.
Taylor, R. W. (Eng.):– 1,649 d., *167;* 236 d. in Sunday League, *845;* 174 d. in Tests, *193;* 66 d. in GC/NWB Trophy, *727;* 20 d. in series, *193;* 10 d. in Test, *192;* 10 d. in match (2), *166, 167;* 7 d. in Test innings, *192;* 7 d. in innings (3), *166;* 7 d.

Taylor, R. W. (Eng.):– *contd*
in Sunday League innings, *845;* 6 d. in GC/NWB Trophy innings, *727;* Test p'ship records, *222, 225, 226.*
Tendulkar, S. R. (Ind.):– Test cricket at 16, *197;* 1 Test hundred, *222;* 664* for 3rd wkt, *271;* Test p'ship record, *250.*
Tennyson, Hon. L. H. (Lord Tennyson) (Eng.):– Test captain, *200.*
Terry, V. P. (Eng.):– 10,000 r., *279;* 292 and 264 for 1st wkt, *276.*
Test and County Cricket Board:– Meetings, *1325, 1326-7;* Officers, *293;* Under-25 XI v Indians, *321.*
Test match grounds, *260-1.*
Test matches, duration of and qualification for, *1318.*
Texaco Trophy matches:– in 1990, *304-5, 329-31;* in 1991, *1349.*
Thompson, G. J. (Eng.):– 1,591 w., *162;* 100 w. (8), *161;* Hat-trick of c., *159.*
Thomson, J. R. (Aust.):– 200 w. in Tests, *188;* 100 w. v England, *208.*
Thomson, K. (NZ):– Test p'ship record, *250.*
Thomson, N. I. (Eng.):– 1,597 w., *162;* 100 w. (12), *161;* 10 w. in innings, *156.*
Thorne, D. A. (Warwicks. and OUCC):– Career figures, *1324.*
Thousand runs in May, *147.*
Throwing records, *271.*
Tied matches, *172-3, 268.*
Tilcon Trophy:– *696-7;* Fixtures, 1991, *1350.*
Tillekeratne, H. P. (SL):– 263 for 4th wkt, *277.*
Titmus, F. J. (Eng.):– All-round, *165;* All-round in Tests, *191;* 2,830 w., *162;* 153 w. in Tests, *187;* 100 w. (16), *161.*
Todd, L. J. (Kent):– 38 hundreds, *140.*
Tolchard, R. W. (Eng.):– 1,037 d., *168.*
Toogood, G. J. (OUCC):– 149 and 10 w. v Cambridge, *373.*
Toohey, P. M. (Aust.):– 1 Test hundred, *231.*
Toshack, E. R. H. (Aust.):– 10 w. or more in Test (1), *237;* 5 w. for 2 r. in Test innings, *186.*
Tours, Future, *363.*
Townsend, C. L. (Eng.):– All-round, *164.*
Townsend, L. F. (Eng.):– All-round, *164, 165.*
Trans-Tasman Trophy, *233.*
Tribe, G. E. (Aust.):– All-round, *165;* 100 w. (8), *161.*
Trott, A. E. (Aust. and Eng.):– All-round, *164;* Double hat-trick, *159;* Hit over Lord's Pavilion, *270;* 1,674 w., *162;* 200 w. (2), *160;* 10 w. in innings, *156;* 8 w. in Test innings, *185;* 4 w. with consecutive balls, *158.*
Trott, G. H. S. (Aust.):– Test captain, *200;* 1 Test hundred, *204.*
Troup, G. B. (NZ):– 10 w. or more in Test (1), *244.*
Trueman, F. S. (Eng.):– 2,304 w., *162;* 307 w. in Tests, *187;* 100 w. (12), *161;* 10 w. or more in Test (3), *206, 216;* 8 w. in Test innings, *185;* 4 hat-tricks, *159;* Test p'ship record, *225.*
Trumble, H. (Aust.):– Test captain, *200;* 141 w. in Tests, *188;* 10 w. or more in Test (3), *207;* 8 w. in Test innings, *185;* 2 Test hat-tricks, *189;* 3 hat-tricks, *159;* Test p'ship record, *205.*
Trumper, V. T. (Aust.):– 3,163 r. in Tests, *178;* 2,263 r. v England, *208;* 42 hundreds, *139;* 8 Test hundreds, *204, 228;* 300* v Sussex, *134;* 200 r. in 131 min., *146;* 433 for 8th wkt, *153;* Test p'ship record, *229.*
Tuckett, L. (SA):– Test p'ship record, *211.*
Tunnicliffe, J. (Yorks.):– 70 c., 66 c., 64 c. and 63 c. in season, *168;* 554 and 378 for 1st wkt, *149, 150.*
Turner, A. (Aust.):– 1 Test hundred, *231;* Test p'ship record, *239.*
Turner, C. T. B. (Aust.):– 283 w. in season, *160;* 106 w. in Australian season, *161;* 101 w. in Tests, *188, 208;* 17 w. in match, *157;* 10 w. or more in Test (2), *207;* 6 w. for 15 r. in Test innings, *186.*
Turner, D. R. (Hants):– Career figures, *1324;* 6,639 r. in Sunday League, *843.*
Turner, G. M. (NZ):– Test captain, *233, 249, 251;* 34,346 r., *143;* 6,144 r. in Sunday League, *843;* 2,991 r. in Tests, *179;* 1,000 r. (18), *141;* 1,000 r. (April 24-May 31), *147;* 103 hundreds, *138;* 7 Test hundreds, *234, 243, 250, 252;* 2 hundreds in same Test, *176, 234;* 2 hundreds in match (6), *137;* 311* v Warwickshire in day, *134, 146;* 259 v West Indies, *174, 243;* Avge of 90.07 in English season, *142;* Carrying bat in Test (2), *181;* 387 for 1st wkt v West Indies, *150, 151, 184, 244;* Test p'ship records, *234, 244, 252.*
Turner, J. B. (Minor Counties):– Hundred on début, *135.*
Turner, S. (Essex):– 303 w. in Sunday League, *845.*
Tyldesley, E. (Eng.):– 38,874 r., *142;* 3,024 r. in season, *140;* 1,000 r. (19), *141;* 102 hundreds, *138;* 3 Test hundreds, *210, 214;* 4 successive hundreds, *138;* 2 hundreds in match (2), *137;* 10 successive fifties, *138;* Test avge of 55.00, *180.*
Tyldesley, J. T. (Eng.):– 37,897 r., *142;* 3,041 r. in season, *140;* 1,000 r. (19), *141;* 86 hundreds, *139;* 4 Test hundreds, *203, 210;* 2 hundreds in match (3), *137.*
Tyldesley, R. K. (Eng.):– 1,509 w., *163;* 100 w. (10), *161;* 5 w. for 0 r., *157;* 4 w. with consecutive balls, *158.*
Tyler, E. J. (Som.):– 10 w. in innings, *156.*
Tyson, F. H. (Eng.):– 10 w. or more in Test (1), *206.*

U

UAU Championship, 1990, *891-3.*
Ulyett, G. (Eng.):– 1 Test hundred, *203;* 4 w. with consecutive balls, *158.*

Umpires for 1991, *418*.
Umpires, Association of Cricket, *1316*.
Umrigar, P. R. (Ind.):– Test captain, *235, 244, 249;* 16,154 r. (avge 52.28), *145;* 3,631 r. in Tests, *179;* 49 hundreds, *139;* 12 Test hundreds, *222, 246, 250, 255;* All-round in Test, *190;* Test p'ship records, *250*.
Underwood, D. L. (Eng.):– 2,465 w., *162;* 346 w. in Sunday League, *845;* 297 w. in Tests, *187;* 105 w. v Australia, *208;* 100 w. (10), *161;* 10 w. or more in Test (6), *206, 219, 225;* 8 w. in Test innings, *185;* 6 w. for 12 r. in Test innings, *186*.

V

Valentine, A. L. (WI):– 139 w. in Tests, *188;* 10 w. or more in Test (2), *216;* 8 w. in Test innings, *186, 216*.
Valentine, B. H. (Eng.):– 35 hundreds, *140;* 2 Test hundreds, *210, 221;* Hundred on Test début, *174, 221*.
Vance, R. H. (NZ):– 77 r. conceded in over, *148*.
van der Bijl, P. G. V. (SA):– 1 Test hundred, *211*.
van der Merwe, P. L. (SA):– Test captain, *209, 227;* Test p'ship record, *229*.
Van Ryneveld, C. B. (SA):– Test captain, *209, 227;* Test p'ship record, *211*.
Veivers, T. R. (Aust.):– Test p'ship records, *236, 239*.
Veletta, M. R. J. (Aust.):– 431 for 1st wkt, *150*.
Vengsarkar, D. B. (Ind.):– Test captain, *244, 249;* 16,095 r. (avge 51.58), *145;* 6,703 r. in Tests, *179;* 3,508 r. in one-day ints, *265;* 1,174 Test r. in year, *177;* 50 hundreds, *139;* 17 Test hundreds, *222, 236, 246, 255, 257;* Slow Test batting, *183;* 344* for 2nd wkt v West Indies, *184, 246;* Test p'ship records, *236, 246, 257*.
Venkataraghavan, S. (Ind.):– Test captain, *220, 244;* 156 w. in Tests, *189;* 10 w. or more in Test (1), *251;* 8 w. in Test innings, *185, 251*.
Verity, H. (Eng.):– 1,956 w., *162;* 200 w. (3), *160;* 144 w. in Tests, *187;* 100 w. (9), *161;* 17 w. in day, *158;* 17 w. in match, *157;* 15 Australian w. in match, *186, 206;* 10 w. in innings (2), *156;* 10 w. or more in Test (2), *186, 206, 223;* 8 w. in Test innings, *185, 206*.
Viljoen, K. G. (SA):– 2 Test hundreds, *211, 228*.
Village Championship, *376-7*.
Vine, J. (Eng.):– 25,171 r., *144;* 399 consecutive Championship appearances, *272;* 1st wkt hundreds, *151;* Test p'ship record, *205*.
Virgin, R. T. (Som. and Northants):– 37 hundreds, *140;* 1st wkt hundreds, *151*.
Viswanath, G. R. (Ind.):– Test captain, *220, 254;* 87 consecutive Tests, *198;* 6,080 r. in Tests, *179;* 1,388 Test runs in year, *176;* 44 hundreds, *139;* 14 Test hundreds, *222, 236, 246, 250, 255;* Hundred on début, *136;* Hundred on Test début, *136, 175, 236;* 415 for 3rd wicket, *184, 222;* 316 for 3rd wkt v England, *184, 222;* Test p'ship records, *222, 236, 246*.
Vivian, H. G. (NZ):– 1 Test hundred, *241;* Test p'ship record, *242*.
Vizianagram, Maharaj Kumar of, Sir Vijay A. (Ind.):– Test captain, *220*.
Voce, W. (Eng.):– 1,558 w., *163;* 10 w. or more in Test (2), *206, 216*.
Vogler, A. E. E. (SA):– 36 w. in series, *187;* 16 w. in day, *158;* 10 w. in innings, *156;* 10 w. or more in Test (1), *212;* 6 c. in Test, *194*.

W

Wade, H. F. (SA):– Test captain, *209, 227*.
Wade, W. W. (SA):– 1 Test hundred, *211*.
Wadekar, A. L. (Ind.):– Test captain, *220, 244;* 2,113 r. in Tests, *180;* 36 hundreds, *140;* 1 Test hundred, *250;* 323 v Mysore, *133;* Test p'ship record, *222*.
Wadsworth, K. J. (NZ):– Test p'ship record, *244*.
Waheed Mirza (Sind):– 324 v Quetta, *133, 151;* 561 for 1st wkt, *149, 150, 151*.
Waite, J. H. B. (SA):– 2,405 r. in Tests, *179;* 50 Tests, *128, 198;* 4 Test hundreds, *211, 228, 241;* 141 d. in Tests, *193;* 26 d. in series, *192;* Test p'ship records, *211, 229*.
Walcott, C. L. (WI):– 11,820 r. (avge 56.55), *144;* 3,798 r. (avge 56.68) in Tests, *179, 180;* 827 r. in series, *176;* 40 hundreds, *139;* 15 Test hundreds, *215, 231, 243, 245, 248;* 2 hundreds in same Test, *175, 231;* 2 hundreds in match (2), *137;* 314* v Trinidad, *134, 152;* 574* for 4th wkt, *149, 152;* Test p'ship records, *243, 246, 248*.
Wales:– in Minor Counties Championship, *849, 851, 865;* v Ireland, *897;* v MCC, *700*.
Walker, A. K. (Notts.):– 4 w. with consecutive balls, *158*.
Walker, M. H. N. (Aust.):– 138 w. in Tests, *188;* 8 w. in Test innings, *185;* 6 w. for 15 r. in Test innings, *186;* Test p'ship record, *239*.
Walker, P. M. (Eng.):– 73 c., 69 c. and 65 c. in season, *168;* 8 c. in match, *168*.
Walker, V. E. (Middx):– 108 and 10 w., *163;* 10 w. in innings (2), *155*.
Walkley, E. (S. Aust.):– 232 for 9th wkt, *153*.
Wall, T. W. (Aust.):– 10 w. in innings, *156*.
Wallace, W. M. (NZ):– Test captain, *240;* 324 for 4th wkt, *152*.
Walsh, C. A. (WI):– 134 w. in Tests, *188;* 101 w. in one-day ints, *266;* 10 w. or more in Test, *247;* 8 w. in innings, *277;* Hat-trick v Australia, *190*.
Walters, C. F. (Eng.):– Test captain, *200;* 1 Test hundred, *221*.

Walters, K. D. (Aust.):– 5,357 r. in Tests, *178;* 45 hundreds, *139;* 15 Test hundreds, *204, 231, 233, 236, 238;* 2 hundreds in same Test, *176, 231;* Hundred and double-hundred, *136;* Hundred on Test début, *175, 204;* 250 v New Zealand, *174, 233;* 336 for 4th wkt v West Indies, *184, 232;* Test p'ship records, *232, 234.*

Waqar Hassan (Pak.):– 1 Test hundred, *252;* 308 for 7th wkt v New Zealand, *153, 184, 253.*

Waqar Younis (Pak.):– Test cricket at 17, *197.*

Ward, Alan (Eng.):– 4 w. in 4 balls in Sunday League, *845.*

Ward, Albert (Eng.):– 1 Test hundred, *203.*

Ward, D. M. (Surrey):– 263 and 208 in 1990, *273;* 256 for 1st wkt, *276;* 413 for 3rd wkt, *277.*

Ward, J. T. (NZ):– Test p'ship record, *250.*

Ward, W. (MCC):– 278 at Lord's, *269.*

Wardle, J. H. (Eng.):– 1,846 w., *162;* 102 w. in Tests, *187;* 100 w. (10), *161;* 10 w. or more in Test (1), *212;* 4 w. for 7 r. in Test innings, *186.*

Warnapura, B. (SL):– Test captain, *226, 256, 258;* Test p'ship record, *227.*

Warner, Sir P. F. (Eng.):– Test captain, *200, 208;* 29,028 r., *143;* 60 hundreds, *139;* Hundred on Test début, *174, 210;* Carrying bat in Test, *181.*

Warren, A. (Eng.):– 283 for 9th wkt, *153.*

Warwickshire:– *378, 616-32;* Championship positions, *384-5;* Highest score, *169;* Highest individual score, *135;* Lowest score, *170;* Seeboard Trophy, *702-3;* Tilcon Trophy winners, *696-7.*

Warwickshire II, *868, 872, 885, 889.*

Washbrook, C. (Eng.):– 34,101 r., *143;* 2,569 r. in Tests, *178;* 1,000 r. (20), *141;* 76 hundreds, *139;* 6 Test hundreds, *203, 210, 214, 218;* 1st wkt hundreds, *150;* 359 for 1st wkt v South Africa, *184, 211;* Test p'ship records, *211, 215.*

Wasim Akram (Pak.):– 1 Test hundred, *238;* 111 w. in Tests, *189;* 130 w. in one-day ints, *266;* 10 w. or more in Test (2), *239, 253;* 2 hat-tricks in one-day ints, *266;* All-round in Tests, *190;* Test p'ship records, *239, 256.*

Wasim Bari (Pak.):– Test captain, *223;* 228 d. in Tests, *193;* 62 d. in one-day ints, *266;* 8 d. in Test, *192;* 7 d. in Test innings, *166, 192;* 7 d. in innings (2), *166;* Test p'ship records, *239, 248, 256.*

Wasim Raja (Pak.):– 2,821 r. in Tests, *180;* 4 Test hundreds, *224, 248, 255;* Test p'ship records, *248.*

Wass, T. G. (Notts.):– 1,666 w., *162;* 100 w. (10), *161;* 16 w. in day (2), *158.*

Wasu, H. (Vidarbha):– Obstructing the field, *155.*

Watkins, A. J. (Eng.):– 2 Test hundreds, *210, 221.*

Watkins, J. R. (Aust.):– Test p'ship record, *239.*

Watkinson, M. (Lancs.):– Man of match in B & H Cup final, *757.*

Watson, F. B. (Lancs):– 50 hundreds, *139;* 300* v Surrey, *134;* 1st wkt hundreds, *151.*

Watson, W. (Eng.):– 25,670 r., *144;* 55 hundreds, *139;* 2 Test hundreds, *203, 214.*

Watson-Smith, R. (Border):– 183* and 125* in first two first-class innings, *136.*

Watts, E. A. (Surrey):– 10 w. in innings, *156.*

Waugh, M. E. (NSW and Essex):– Cricketer of the Year, *72-4;* 204 and 207* in 1990, *273.*

Waugh, S. R. (Aust.):– 3 Test hundreds, *204, 240;* Test p'ship records, *234, 240.*

Wazir Mohammad (Pak.):– Test p'ship records, *248.*

Weekes, E. D. (WI):– 12,010 r. (avge 55.34), *144;* 4,455 r. (avge 58.61) in Tests, *179, 180;* 779 r. in series, *176;* 36 hundreds, *140;* 15 Test hundreds, *215, 231, 243, 245, 248;* 5 successive hundreds, *138;* 2 hundreds in same Test, *176, 245;* 304* v Cambridge Univ., *134;* Avge of 79.65 in English season, *142;* 338 for 3rd wkt v England, *184, 216;* Test p'ship records, *216, 243, 246, 248.*

Weekes, K. H. (WI):– 1 Test hundred, *215.*

Weerasinghe, C. D. U. S. (SL):– Youngest Sri Lankan Test player, *197.*

Wellard, A. W. (Eng.):– All-round, *165;* 1,614 w., *162;* 66 sixes in season, *148;* 30 r. and 31 r. in over, *147, 148;* 100 w. (8), *161.*

Wellham, D. M. (Aust.)–: Hundred on début, *136;* Hundred on Test début, *136, 175, 204.*

Wells, J. (Kent):– 4 w. with consecutive balls, *158.*

Wessels, K. C. (Aust.):– 16,633 r. (avge 50.40), *145;* 46 hundreds, *139;* 4 Test hundreds, *204, 231, 238, 240;* 2 hundreds in match (2), *137;* Hundred on Test début, *175, 204;* 388 for 1st wkt, *150.*

Western Australia:– v Tamil Nadu, *1178.*

West Indies:– Definition of first-class matches, *1320;* Domestic season 1989-90, *1152-7;* Highest individual Test innings, *174;* Highest Test innings, *194;* Leading batsmen in Tests, *179;* Leading bowlers in Tests, *188;* Lowest Test innings, *196;* Most consecutive Test appearances, *198;* Most Test appearances, *128;* Most Test appearances as captain, *128;* Nehru Cup, *1063-76;* Oldest Test player, *198;* Representative body, *1315;* Sharjah Champions Trophy, *1058-62;* Summary of Tests, *199;* Summary of one-day ints, *264;* Test cricketers (1928-90), *110-4;* West Indies in Test cricket (*see p. 132*); Youngest and oldest on Test début, *197-8.*

West Indies B in Zimbabwe, *1200-1.*

Wettimuny, S. (SL):– 2 Test hundreds, *226, 259;* 190 v England, *226, 269;* Carrying bat in Test, *181;* Longest innings in

Wettimuny, S. (SL):– *contd*
Lord's Test, *269;* Test p'ship records, *227, 254, 258, 259.*
Whatmore, D. F. (Aust.):– 6 c. in Test, *194.*
White, C. de L. (Border):– Hat-trick of c., *159.*
White, G. C. (SA):– 2 Test hundreds, *211.*
White, J. C. (Eng.):– Test captain, *200, 209;* 2,356 w., *162;* 100 w. (14), *161;* 16 w. in day, *158;* 10 w. in innings, *156;* 10 w. or more in Test (1), *206;* 8 w. in Test innings, *185;* 4 w. for 7 r. in Test innings, *186.*
Whitehead, H. (Leics.):– 380 for 1st wkt, *150.*
Whitehouse, J. (Warwicks.):– Hundred on début, *135.*
Whitelaw, P. E. (Auck.):– 445 for 3rd wkt, *152.*
Whiteside, J. P. (Leics.):– Obstructing the field, *155.*
Whittaker, G. J. (Surrey):– 253* v Gloucestershire II, *270.*
Whitty, W. J. (Aust.):– 37 w. in series, *187;* Test p'ship record, *229.*
Whysall, W. W. (Eng.):– 51 hundreds, *139;* 4 successive hundreds, *138;* 2 hundreds in match (2), *137;* 1st wkt hundreds, *151.*
Wicket-keeping records:– *165-9, 192-3, 266;* in 1990, *278, 580.*
Wicket records (1st to 10th), *151-4.*
Wiener, J. M. (Aust.):– 390* for 3rd wkt, *152.*
Wight, G. L. (British Guiana):– 390 for 1st wkt, *150, 151.*
Wijesuriya, R. G. C. E. (SL):– Test p'ship record, *259.*
Wild, D. J. (Northants):– Career figures, *1324.*
Wiles, C. A. (WI):– Test début at 40, *198.*
Willey, P. (Eng.):– 6,353 r. in Sunday League, *843;* 44 hundreds, *139;* 2 Test hundreds, *214.*
Williams, A. B. (WI):– 2 Test hundreds, *231, 245;* Hundred on Test début, *175, 231.*
Williams, E. A. V. (WI):– 255 for 8th wkt, *153.*
Willis, R. G. D. (Eng.):– Test captain, *200, 217, 220, 223;* 325 w. in Tests, *187;* 128 w. v Australia, *208;* 8 w. in Test innings, *185;* Test p'ship records, *222, 225.*
Wills Cup (Pak.), *1179, 1191.*
Wilson, A. E. (Glos.):– 10 d. in match, *166.*
Wilson, D. (Eng.):– 30 r. in over, *148;* 3 hat-tricks, *159.*
Wilson, E. R. (Eng.):– Test début at 41, *197.*
Wilson, G. A. (Worcs.):– 3 hat-tricks, *159.*
Wilson, J. V. (Yorks.):– 61 c. in season, *168.*
Wiltshire:– *713-4, 849, 851, 866;* v Oxford Univ., *676.*
Winslow, P. L. (SA):– 1 Test hundred, *211;* 30 r. in over, *148;* Test p'ship record, *211.*
Wisden, J. (Sussex):– 10 w. in innings, *155.*
Wisden Trophy, *213.*
Women's Cricket Association, Address of Secretary, *1316.*
Wood, C. J. B. (Leics.):– 37 hundreds, *140;* 2 separate hundreds, *137;* 380 for 1st wkt, *150.*
Wood, G. M. (Aust.):– 3,374 r. in Tests, *178;* 9 Test hundreds, *204, 231, 233, 236, 238;* Test p'ship record, *234.*
Wood, H. (Eng.):– 1 Test hundred, *210;* Test p'ship record, *211.*
Woodfull, W. M. (Aust.):– Test captain, *200, 227, 229;* 13,388 r. (avge 64.99), *144;* 2,300 r. in Tests, *178;* 49 hundreds, *139;* 7 Test hundreds, *204, 228;* Carrying bat in Test (2), *181;* 375 for 1st wkt, *150.*
Woods, S. M. J. (Eng. and Aust.):– 10 w. in innings, *155.*
Woolley, C. N. (Northants):– 326 consecutive Championship appearances, *272.*
Woolley, F. E. (Eng.):– All-round, *164, 165;* Test cricket at 47, *198;* 58,969 r., *142, 144;* 3,352 r. in season, *140;* 3,283 r. in Tests, *178;* 1,000 r. (28), *140;* 707 Championship appearances, *272;* 145 hundreds, *138;* 5 Test hundreds, *203, 210;* 4 successive hundreds, *138;* 305* v Tasmania, *134, 146;* 300 r. in 205 min., *146;* 2,068 w., *162, 163;* 100 w. (8), *161;* 10 w. or more in Test (1), *206;* 1,018 c., *169;* 6 c. in Test, *194;* 235 for 10th wkt, *154;* Test p'ship record, *205.*
Woolmer, R. A. (Eng.):– 3 Test hundreds, *203.*
Wootton, G. (Notts.):– 10 w. in innings, *155.*
Worcestershire:– *378, 633-48;* Championship positions, *384-5;* Highest score, *169;* Highest individual score, *135;* Lowest score, *170;* Scarborough Festival Trophy, *700.*
Worcestershire II, *868, 872, 886, 889.*
World Cup Finals, *268.*
Worrell, Sir F. M. M. (WI):– Test captain, *213, 229, 244;* 15,025 r. (avge 54.24), *145;* 3,860 r. in Tests, *179;* 39 hundreds, *139;* 9 Test hundreds, *215, 231, 243, 245;* 308* v Trinidad, *134;* 261 v England, *174, 215;* Carrying bat in Test, *181;* 338 for 3rd wkt v England, *184, 216;* 574* and 502* for 4th wkt, *149, 150, 152;* 399 for 4th wkt v England, *184, 216;* Test p'ship records, *216, 243, 246.*
Worrell, Frank, Trophy, *230.*
Worthington, T. S. (Eng.):– 1 Test hundred, *221;* Test p'ship record, *222.*
Wright, A. J. (Glos.):– Captain of Gloucestershire, *435.*
Wright, C. W. (Eng.):– Test p'ship record, *211.*
Wright, D. V. P. (Eng.):– 2,056 w., *162;* 108 w. in Tests, *187;* 100 w. (10), *161;* 10 w. or more in Test (1), *212;* 7 hat-tricks, *159.*
Wright, J. G. (NZ):– Test captain, *217, 233, 249, 251;* 4,377 r. in Tests, *179;* 3,416 r. in one-day ints, *265;* 55 hundreds, *139;* 10 Test hundreds, *219, 234, 243, 250, 252;* Test p'ship records, *234, 244, 250, 252.*

Wyatt, R. E. S. (Eng.):– Test captain, *200, 209, 213, 217;* 39,405 r., *142;* 1,000 r. (18), *141;* 85 hundreds, *139;* 2 Test hundreds, *210;* 124 and hat-trick v Ceylon, *164*.
Wynyard, E. G. (Eng.):– 411 for 6th wkt, *152*.

Y

Yadav, N. S. (Ind.):– 102 w. in Tests, *189;* Test p'ship records, *236, 250*.
Yajurvindra Singh (Ind.):– 7 c. in Test, *194;* 5 c. in Test innings, *193*.
Yallop, G. N. (Aust.):– Test captain, *200, 237;* 2,756 r. in Tests, *178;* 8 Test hundreds, *204, 236, 238;* 2 hundreds in match (2), *137;* 268 v Pakistan, *174, 238;* Test p'ship records, *239*.
Yardley, B. (Aust.):– 126 w. in Tests, *188;* 10 w. or more in Test (1), *232*.
Yardley, N. W. D. (Eng.):– Test captain, *200, 209, 213;* Test p'ship record, *211*.
Yarnold, H. (Worcs.):– 110 d. in season, *167;* 7 d. in innings, *165*.
Yashpal Sharma (Ind.):– 2 Test hundreds, *222, 236;* 316 for 3rd wkt v England, *184, 222;* Test p'ship records, *222, 246, 256*.
Yates, G. (Lancs.):– 116 for 10th wkt, *277*.
Yorkshire:– *378, 649-65;* Championship positions, *384-5;* Highest score, *169;* Highest individual score, *135;* Lowest score, *170;* v Michael Parkinson's World XI, *700;* Scarborough Festival Trophy, *701;* Tilcon Trophy, *696-7;* v Yorkshiremen, *703*.
Yorkshire II, *868, 872, 866-7, 889*.
Young Cricketer of the Year, *467*.
Young, B. A. (N. Dist.):– 7 d. in innings, *166*.
Young, D. M. (Worcs. and Glos.):– 40 hundreds, *139;* 395 for 1st wkt, *150*.
Young, J. A. (Eng.):– 100 w. (8), *161*.
Youngest Test players, *197*.
Younis Ahmed (Pak.):– 26,063 r., *144;* 46 hundreds, *139;* Slow scoring in Test, *183*.
Yuile, B. W. (NZ):– Test p'ship record, *252*.

Z

Zaheer Abbas (Pak.):– Test captain, *223, 237, 251, 254;* 34,843 r. (avge 51.54), *143, 145;* 5,062 r. in Tests, *180;* 1,000 r. (17), *141;* 108 hundreds, *138;* 12 Test hundreds, *224, 238, 252, 255, 259;* 7 one-day int. hundreds, *265;* 4 successive hundreds, *138;* 2 hundreds in match (8), *137;* Hundred and double-hundred (4), *136, 137;* 274 v England, *174, 224;* Avge of 88.69 in English season, *142;* 30 r. in over, *148;* Fast scoring, *183;* Hit the ball twice, *155;* 353 for 6th wkt, *153;* Test p'ship records, *225, 239, 248, 256, 259*.
Zahoor Elahi (ADBP):– 2 hundreds in match, *138, 1187*.
Zimbabwe:– 1989-90 season, *1199-201;* ICC Trophy winners, *362-3;* Representative body, *1316*.
Zimbabweans in England, 1990:– v Essex, *407;* v Gloucestershire, *440;* v Lancashire, *490;* v Sussex, *603;* v Yorkshire, *654*.
Zulch, J. W. (SA):– 2 Test hundreds, *228;* Carrying bat in Test, *181*.
Zulfiqar Ahmed (Pak.):– 10 w. or more in Test (1), *253;* Test p'ship record, *256*.

INDEX OF FILLERS

Addresses of Representative Bodies, *1315-6*.
Ashes, The, *263*.
Career Figures of Players Retiring or Not Being Retained, *1324*.
County Benefits Awarded in 1991, *292*.
County Caps Awarded in 1990, *632*.
Cricketer Cup Winners, 1967-90, *564*.
Deloitte Ratings, *988*.
England Young Cricketers in Australia, 1989-90, *999*.
Errata in *Wisden*, *1327*.
Fielding in 1990, *580*.
Future Tours, *363*.
Honours' List, 1990, *597*.
India v Sri Lanka, 1990-91, *1011*.
I Zingari Results, 1990, *615*.
National Power Awards, 1990, *648*.
Overs Bowled and Runs Scored in the Britannic Assurance Championship, 1990, *401*.
Pakistan v New Zealand, 1990-91, *1166*.
Pakistan v West Indies, 1990-91, *1039*.
Status of Matches in UK, *368*.
Umpires for 1991, *418*.
Young Cricketer of the Year, *467*.

NOTES BY THE EDITOR

If only the introduction to these Notes could have echoed those written for the 1929 *Wisden*. A record number of hundreds in the English season under review, success for England in the home Test matches, the Ashes series in Australia already won as the Almanack went to press. It was not to be. Injuries to key England players in Australia, particularly to the captain, Graham Gooch, were a factor in England's failure to regain the Ashes during the winter. But more worrying were avoidable technical deficiencies and the attitude of the team in Gooch's absence. When, early on, the wheels fell off, it seemed that no-one knew how to put them back on, leaving the mule-team to drag the waggon backwards and forwards across Australia on its axles. To those who watch county cricket regularly, and critically, this will have come as less of a surprise than it may have to the gentleman who wrote, in the autumn, "A fine season. A settled English captain, settled England openers, a successful team. Good County Championship season. Excellent over-limit season. Not such gloomy introductory Notes next year, please."

The profession of cricketer

At the press conference, in March 1987, at which the Test and County Cricket Board announced the appointment of Micky Stewart as England team manager for three years from April 1 that year, it was suggested to Mr Stewart that England's success on their recent tour of Australia owed something to their itinerary: until the final Test, the first-class matches were uninterrupted by one-day internationals, which were all played at the end of the tour. Able to concentrate on one form of the game at a time, England won the Test series 2-1 and both one-day tournaments. Might it not, Mr Stewart was asked, be more difficult for the players to maintain such form in a domestic programme which required them to alternate between the first-class and the one-day game throughout the season. If I remember correctly, his reply was to the effect that the players were professional cricketers: they knew how to adjust. If little else has emerged from the past winter's tour of Australia, two things have. The Australians made sure that England did not have such a sensible itinerary two tours running, and England's cricketers did not find it an easy matter to adjust. Nothing new there.

They are professional cricketers. What does this mean? I think that today it means they are cricketers who play the game of cricket as a livelihood, as opposed to playing it as a recreation. They are in a job, in the same way that a Civil Servant or a bank clerk is in a job. There is not the same security, of course, but that is a hazard of the occupation – and there is more than there was. The danger is that in regarding cricket as a job rather than a sport, players not only derive a nine to five mentality towards cricket but also become accustomed to defeat. In limited-overs cricket – and there is so much of it – someone has to lose. Given that fact, what is wrong with losing? It becomes part of the job. There is as little discredit attached to defeat as there is to any job done poorly these days. The public, too, becomes accustomed to a winner and a loser, and the value of a draw loses its significance. It is, after all, better than losing, and yet in the County Championship the draw brings no reward other than the negative one of denying victory to the opposing team. I feel it should. Those who can't be winners don't always have to be losers: many of us try to live honourably drawn lives and have to work hard to do so.

What "professional cricketers" no longer means is that they are professionals as opposed to amateurs. I wonder, though, what kind of professional cricketer Mr Stewart was thinking of. I suspect he had in mind the kind of professional cricketer he was himself: the county cricketer to whom the job was secondary to the enjoyment of playing cricket and to the opportunity to practise his skills against his peers at the highest level. It was his livelihood, it was his work, but it was not just a job.

In modern times the game provides a greater reward. Not riches by any means; but since the advent of sponsorship and income from off-field activities by the counties, the established player can expect better remuneration and greater security. A car is provided; away from home the teams stay in hotels. It is not an uncomfortable life. The player who maintains his average from season to season can remain an average player for a good number of summers. Indeed there is something of the chocolate cream soldier about him. Young players, adventurous and ambitious, come through, but not so many as to upset the order of things. As in the Civil Service, it takes a genuine talent to unsettle the time-servers: a few years of apprenticeship in the Second Eleven knocks off the confidence and cockiness of youth and produces in good time the county cricketer – the professional cricketer.

The consequence of this is a county game that rather meanders along from one season to the next with a carefully regulated change of personnel. And while there are some very good cricketers, there are a lot of fairly ordinary ones. It is not surprising that the overall standard of first-class cricket played and occasionally watched is not particularly high. It would be interesting to know how many English county cricketers would hold a place in a first-class side in Australia, the West Indies or in the Currie Cup in South Africa.

Under the auspices of the TCCB and the National Cricket Association, a programme has been launched to develop and maintain higher standards. Cricketers are monitored in their age-groups, the aim being to build a sound base for a pyramid, the apex of which is the England team. Inherent in this, however, is that to reach the apex, the young cricketer has to commit himself to the life of a professional county cricketer. And on the pyramid, county cricket is not so much the final step to the top as a broad plateau which many cricketers traverse summer after summer. It can be argued that the greater the number who are on the plateau, the better are those who go on to reach the apex. The evidence suggests otherwise.

Time to think anew

Perhaps the plateau should be smaller, making the competition for places on it greater. For this to happen, the structure of county cricket would have to change. And while at present it is inconceivable that the first-class counties would agree to any such change, it is possible that the coming years will show change to be inevitable. A lot will depend on how English cricket views its role on the small stage of international cricket: a star performer or a player of supporting parts.

It will be said that this reflects undue concern with Test cricket; that the County Championship serves a purpose other than being a nursery for Test cricketers. Perhaps, and then again perhaps not. Without the income that international cricket produces, and the interest it arouses, the subsidy to first-class cricket would be cut drastically and the diet of one-day cricket would be increased. That the economic health of English cricket in its fully professional form depends on the image the game projects, on and off the field, should not be in dispute. I am surprised sometimes that the players themselves are not more aware how important this is. International success is part of that image.

The intended elevation of Durham from minor county to first-class status in 1992 brings with it an opportunity to reshape the County Championship more radically than merely by an increase in the number of counties for the first time since 1921. One possible change is the introduction of a Championship consisting of seventeen four-day games per county; this, basically, is the recommendation of the TCCB's England, Cricket and Marketing committees, which was rejected by a majority of the counties last spring. Whether this is sufficient to bring about a more competitive Championship is another matter.

What about dividing the counties into two leagues of nine, with the teams in each league playing the others home and away? Worthwhile prizemoney, plus the prospect of promotion and relegation, might provide the keen competition which to me seems to be missing from much County Championship cricket. The nature of the cricket would demand a higher standard from the leading players: the potential England players. It is élitist, no doubt, but the alternative is mediocrity.

Another possible change is in the way cricketers are employed. No doubt Durham, the newcomers, will be hoping to attract experienced players from other counties. It would not be unexpected if some of those who retired at the end of 1990 were to reappear in Durham's colours in 1992, their absence from the game in 1991 having anticipated the obstacle of contested registrations.

What would be enterprising is an initiative which opens the way for young cricketers who want to try themselves in the first-class game but do not wish to commit themselves to a career as a professional cricketer. Durham have sought, and must continue to seek, sponsorship to pay their players. But what if companies were to provide that sponsorship in players rather than in money? A cricketer, in the employ of a local firm, could be available for the season, while at the same time having a career outside cricket which offers him long-term prospects. Indeed, his employment need not be dependent simply on his cricket but also on his other skills. The sponsoring company, in turn, would benefit from the presence on its staff of a county cricketer. The county cricket club would have a cricketer who could look to playing his natural game and not to maintaining a good enough average to keep his contract. It would, I believe, give more cricketers the opportunity to pursue every boy's ambition to play for his country.

Attitude as well as ability

Whatever their value, such thoughts are meaningless if the cricketers themselves are found wanting. It is worrying that young cricketers, who look to have had a good grounding in the basics of batting and bowling, pick up and retain technical faults between youth cricket and first-class cricket. What are the county coaches doing? Impressionable youngsters are being allowed to ape their seniors without the period of consolidation which has led to the senior player developing his particular style. Gooch, for example, did not start out with his raised-bat style: that was a development, not a beginning.

For a young batsman to emulate him because he is successful is rather like a writer setting out to write in the style of James Joyce's *Ulysses* without even having the mastery of the Joyce who wrote *Dubliners*.

But it is in their running between the wickets and their fielding that cricketers reveal much about their approach to the game and their coaching. In his tribute to Sir Leonard Hutton on pages 53 to 55, John Woodcock writes: "Studying under Sutcliffe in his early days for Yorkshire would have shown him the need for conviction in calling and let him into the secrets of the short single." Few batsmen today look to have learned how to take the pace off the ball; to make the fielder come in for the ball while the batsmen run their single quickly. Perhaps heavier bats have cost them that touch; they give the ball away to the fielder. If so it is poor cricket, for it has taken from the batsman the tactical advantage of upsetting field placings. Similarly in the field: too often one sees fieldsmen waiting for the ball to come to them rather than "attacking" it and putting the batsman under pressure when judging a run. Such things come naturally to a few; for most they require practice and awareness. Both appear to be at a premium.

That bowling skills are in short supply was demonstrated starkly last season. In time they will return. In an age when spelling is not considered important by some teachers, it is hardly surprising that the standard of spelling has deteriorated. So it is with the skills that bowlers need. The TCCB has acted positively to make the bowler, and not the ball or the pitch, the wicket-taker. They should be commended, not criticised, for acting decisively and for having the resolve to resist the cries for leniency. Their determination to maintain acceptable standards of behaviour is also correct. If some cricketers find the disciplinary measures repressive, it is probably not too late for them to become football hooligans.

It used to be said that when English batting is at a low ebb, look first at the strength of English bowling. And English batting, over the seventeen counties, is technically poor. Good bowlers show it up, as they did even in the batsmen's conditions of 1990. Sadly for England's selectors, none of those bowlers was eligible for England. And that is the problem to which the TCCB has addressed itself.

Getting to the pitch

In 1928, when there were 312 first-class games, there was an aggregate of 1,000 or more runs in 72 of those games. Last summer, 1,000 runs were posted in 108 of the 241 first-class games and there were 428 individual hundreds, which passed the previous record of 414 in 1928. However, the 32 double-hundreds in 1990 did not quite match the record 34 in 1933, another summer when good weather produced an improvement in conditions for batsmen. To what extent the balance swung from the bowlers to the batsmen last summer can be seen from a comparison of County Championship aggregates: 154,232 runs and 5,260 wickets in 1989; 179,360 runs and 4,632 wickets in 1990. Perhaps to encourage the endeavours of the bowlers in the coming years, the TCCB might limit the weight of bats. In addition to widening the range of strokeplay, this would reduce the instances of the bat making up with power what the batsman lacks in skill.

Although in 1928 the heavy run-getting struck the dominant note for the editor of *Wisden*, "the outstanding achievements were accomplished by a bowler and wicket-keeper, A. P. Freeman taking 304 wickets and so beating

Tom Richardson's record of 290 (made in 1895) and Leslie Ames disposing of 121 batsmen" – a total upgraded to 122 in recent years, I notice. Freeman, a leg-spinner, bowled more than 1,900 overs that season and averaged a wicket every six and a half overs. But of greater significance than the number of overs he bowled was the benefit he received from the hard wickets of that summer. I doubt that he would have had quite the same strike-rate on the pitches of 1990. Despite all the sunshine, they were in the main slow enough for batsmen playing from the crease to watch the turn and adjust accordingly. England's batsmen, although inexperienced against this kind of bowling, illustrated that against the Indian leg-spinners.

In an attempt to find a more uniform, ideal pitch, experimental pitches have been laid down at ten county grounds, using several different combinations of loam and grass seed. The TCCB hopes they will be ready for use towards the end of the 1991 season. What is needed, I suspect, is a break from cricket to give groundsmen time to relay not just a pitch here and there but the entire square. Since the end of the Second World War there have been 45 summers of cricket: 45 autumns of top-dressing and remaking, with the result that layers of soils have been pressed together, binding in some places and not binding in others. This irregular binding, it seems, is a major cause of uneven bounce. Another problem is that to keep the pitch together, groundsmen have to water more, with the result that matches start on pitches containing too much moisture to provide pace early on or help for the spinners in the later stages.

Last year there was a move by Derbyshire, Kent, Northamptonshire and Yorkshire for a return to uncovered pitches in Championship cricket. It was not supported by the other counties. Given a summer such as that of 1990, and the difficulties which some groundsmen have in getting topsoil to bind, it strikes me that if pitches were not covered overnight, the players could arrive on the final day to find that the surface was blowing away. If it did rain, in all probability the ball would go through the top so quickly that batsmen would be calling for their heaviest bats, not to hit the ball with but to bash the pitch into some kind of shape. It sounds like a groundsman's nightmare.

As to the argument that batsmen would improve their skills on such pitches, I agree in theory. In practice I am less than certain. From what I saw last summer when pitch and ball had a chance to conspire, a good number of batsmen are more likely to get out than grit it out. Mike Gatting's innings at Derby was an example of how to bat in such conditions, but it was also a rare exception.

Pity the poor umpire

It is not as if the players aren't capable of making life difficult for themselves. Groundsmen have noticed an increasing tendency among batsmen to run on the pitch and damage it with their spikes. And such was the umpires' concern at the practice of roughening one side of the ball that the TCCB last summer felt it necessary to bring in stiffer penalties for the offence, in line with those for picking the seam. In either instance the umpire can now replace the ball with one of inferior condition to that previously used. It makes one wonder whence the provenance of the malpractices alleged by the New Zealand and West Indian touring teams in Pakistan late last year. In England last summer there were one or two bowlers who swung the ball much more effectively in their second spell than in their opening one. It is yet another example of how the spirit of the game, as well as the Law, is violated. It is yet another item to tax the umpires' vigilance.

When I first wrote the editor's Notes for *Wisden*, in the 1987 edition, I advocated an international panel of umpires. It would, I wrote then, "cost money, but Test matches are cricket's money-spinner. They are also the world's window on the sport." Just how little money is spun by Test cricket, and how much an international panel of umpires would cost, has become apparent in recent months. A sum of around half a million pounds a year has been estimated (less than £75,000 per country), but without sponsorship that is beyond the budget of world cricket. Sponsorship not being forthcoming, nor for the present is the panel of umpires, even though the International Cricket Council voted six to one in favour of its mandatory use in Test cricket. Australia opposed the motion, partly because of the cost and in part because they did not believe such a move would raise the standard of international umpiring.

I was disappointed that ICC's proposal precluded members of the panel from standing in matches played by their own country. It had seemed to me that it was not neutrality that was so necessary as the umpires' independence from the national boards of control which have appointed and paid them, and will now continue to do so. It was my conjecture that placing the umpires under the auspices of ICC would give them the security to control the game without any kind of outside pressure. It was not my thinking that an Australian should never stand in Australia, or that a Sri Lankan umpire could not take part in a Test match involving Sri Lanka.

An incident at Melbourne in January 1990, in the tour match between Victoria and the Pakistanis, highlights the problems facing an umpire who stands by the grace of a local governing body. After a final warning for following through on the pitch, the Pakistani leg-spinner, Mushtaq Ahmed, was barred from bowling by the umpire following a further transgression. This resulted in the Pakistani team, with their manager, Intikhab Alam, at the head, walking off the field, and the match did not resume until a compromise was reached which allowed Mushtaq to continue bowling. On the face of it, the authority of the umpire was undermined. Let us assume that something similar had happened in a Test match there, and that the touring team had threatened to go home, not only with the Test series unfinished but with the crowd-drawing World Series one-day games still to be played. Would the umpire feel more confident of making a similar decision (and being appointed to stand again) if he had been chosen by the Australian Board or if he was a member of an ICC panel?

Although for the moment there will not be an independent panel of umpires, ICC will have a paid referee at all international matches from October 1991. He will have powers, including the imposition of fines and the suspension of players, to discipline anyone who contravenes the Code of Conduct being drawn up by ICC. The referee, it has been stressed, will be there to support the umpires and will not be able to overrule a decision or interfere with the course of a game. It would be interesting to know what action he could have taken in the aforementioned hypothesis, or what he will do in the event of pitches being prepared to enhance the prospects of the home country. The Code of Conduct will cover "sledging", dissent, over-rates and, one hopes, short-pitched bowling. But it is a sad commentary on the game's players, and on those who have administered the game nationally, that the Code of Conduct has been deemed necessary. Such are the times in which we live.

DON'T BLAME THE BALL

By JACK BANNISTER

Facts and figures may be irrefutable. But just as beauty is often in the eye of the beholder, so too are analysis and interpretation. This is particularly so when the dramatic swing in balance between bat and ball in the English domestic season of 1990 is examined.

Only four counties lacked an individual County Championship double-hundred, while no fewer than 25 batsmen shared 30 Championship scores of 200 or more, including two triple-hundreds. There were seven Championship totals over 600, including two of more than 700 and Lancashire's 863 at The Oval – the second-highest score in the Championship (the highest for 94 years) and the ninth-largest in first-class cricket anywhere in the world.

The occurrence of such a pronounced change in favour of batsmen did not come about simply by coincidence. The previous winter, concerned at the declining standards of play in English first-class cricket, the Test and County Cricket Board had brought in new conditions with regard to the seam of the ball and the preparation of pitches. It was the former, the "new" nine-strand ball, which received universal criticism from players and spectators alike. Bowlers claimed that the big reduction from the previous fifteen-strand ball had rendered ineffective techniques which, in recent years, had produced a rich harvest of wickets. And certainly the division of batting and bowling bonus points won by the seventeen counties in the Britannic Assurance County Championship seemed to reinforce the general complaint that the dominance by batsmen had resulted in too many contrived finishes following a surfeit of meaningless cricket in the preceding days.

Season	*Batting Points*	*Bowling Points*
1987	916	1,154
1988	819	1,118
1989	828	1,141
1990	1,048	909

The above table shows that, in the three seasons from 1987 to 1989, an average of 283 more bowling bonus points than batting bonus points were won. And yet in 1990 the difference in favour of the bat was only 139. Over the years, parity has always eluded the authorities, but the smallest differential in four years suggests that they are on the right lines. This is especially so, given that the effect of the despised "new" ball could not really be evaluated accurately because of the additional influence of better pitches and an exceptionally hot and dry summer.

Before the declining quality of modern bowling standards comes under the microscope, another clutch of statistics – bowling ones, this time – shows that the shock to the systems of most county bowlers was almost terminal. In 1989, of all those who bowled more than 200 overs and took ten wickets in Championship cricket, thirteen secured their wickets at an average of less than 20 runs apiece. In 1990 only Ian Bishop and Malcolm Marshall managed this. In 1989, using the same qualification, 38 bowlers secured their wickets at an average cost of less than 26, but in 1990 only five did so, with Curtly Ambrose, Waqar Younis and Ole Mortensen completing a nap-hand of bowlers ineligible for England. In 1989, ten bowlers took 70 wickets or more in the Championship – all of them seamers – whereas in 1990 only five bowlers accomplished this: Neil Foster, Courtney Walsh, Marshall, Tim Munton and Richard Illingworth. Another telling statistic is that in 1989 24 bowlers took 60 or more wickets, but only one spinner, whereas in 1990, of the ten bowlers who passed this mark, three were slow left-arm spinners: Illingworth, Philip Tufnell and Richard Davis.

Most of the bowlers whose results declined so spectacularly last year shouted "foul", but their *cri de coeur* was really a self-critical lament rather than a justifiable complaint that they had been treated unfairly. Even allowing for the fact that the most sharp-witted cricketers need more than one season to adjust to what was, arguably, the biggest change in equipment for two decades, the best bowlers still took wickets. And while the critics of the less helpful ball could claim that fewer matches produced outright results – 93 last year compared with 103 in 1989 – they cannot argue with what is probably the most revealing statistic of all – the extra amount of spin bowling in 1990.

The following list of spinners is a fair representation of most counties' slow-bowling strength (or lack thereof), and the sixteen, except for Barnett and Williams in the first year, all bowled a minimum of 200 overs in the County Championship in 1989 and 1990: Kim Barnett, John Childs, David Graveney, Raj Maru, Davis, John Emburey, Tufnell, Nick Cook, Richard Williams, Eddie Hemmings, Andy Afford, Ian Swallow, Keith Medlycott, Ian Salisbury, Illingworth and Phil Carrick.

Season	*Overs Bowled*	*Wickets Taken*
1989	7,216.2	607
1990	9,931.2	693

Surely these figures prove the worth of the decision of the cricket committee of the TCCB to put a stop to too many cheap wickets on too many sub-standard pitches. Admittedly the strike-rate declined from a wicket in every twelve overs to one in fourteen, but even this shows that captains were prepared to put their faith in spin once it became clear that ordinary medium-pace bowling, previously so effective from one new ball to another, produced nothing more than easy runs.

The real benefits to English cricket from a more equal contest between bat and ball will manifest themselves only slowly, because a whole new generation of bowlers is having to go right back to the beginning and learn many of the arts of bowling which were in danger of disappearing completely. Of course, the old days of bowlers taking big totals of wickets have gone, now that the Championship programme comprises only 72 days. And if the lobby which wants an entire programme of four-day Championship cricket has its way, even that total will be reduced by eight days. Consequently, valid comparisons with giants of yesteryear are impossible.

Since the proliferation of regular one-day cricket in the English domestic season from 1969, today's bowlers lack the opportunity to bowl the same number of overs as the leading wicket-takers either side of the Second World War. The current 72-day programme allows for a maximum of just under 8,000 overs in the 22 games played by each county; i.e., 4,000 overs per side. In the days of 32 three-day games, in which at least 120 overs a day were the norm, a seasonal maximum of more than 11,000 overs gave each set of bowlers well over 5,000 overs to share out. Hence the 59 instances of 28 bowlers taking 200 wickets or more in an English season. Eight of those instances were performed by the Kent leg-spinner, "Tich" Freeman, the only man this century to bowl more than 2,000 overs in a season, which he did in 1933 when he took 298 wickets, six fewer than his record of 304 in 1928. This means that he bowled approximately 80 per cent of his county's overs from one end. After the resumption of first-class cricket in 1946, however, only Tony Lock (twice), Tom Goddard and Bob Appleyard passed the 200 mark.

The decline in bowling standards started around twenty years ago, with at least four factors responsible: poor pitches, overseas players, one-day cricket and a more helpful ball, though not necessarily in that order. Thankfully, the TCCB, if not quite at a stroke, gave their policy on pitches some teeth; and whatever the criticism of introducing the nine-strand ball at the same time, the combination of the two has undoubtedly shown up the average modern bowler for what he is: an unimaginative purveyor of the kind of seam bowling which relies more on containment than penetration.

The Reader balls used until 1989 made life easy for such bowlers. They just had to point it and wait for the hand-grenade to explode. Subtleties, such as swinging the ball, varying the point of delivery and change of pace – arts learned, it seems, much more readily by overseas bowlers – were ignored, simply because they were unnecessary. Now they are required, and any bowler who cannot master what used to be ordinary basics will have to look for another job. However, Warwickshire's Munton has set an example for his fellow seam bowlers to copy. His own captain, Andy Lloyd, confessed that he thought Munton was the last sort of bowler to prosper with the 1990 ball. He was delighted by his bowler's determination to learn to swing the ball and to develop the ability to adjust his point of delivery, and so his line, when necessary.

For 1990, the two principal ball manufacturers, Reader and Duke, produced two different balls, despite the firm specifications given them. (These included nine strands only, and a reduction in the height of the seam from the circumference from 0.9 to 0.7 millimetres – a difference of 22 per cent.) The Reader ball contained a golf-ball-type core, which meant it retained its shape better than the softer Duke, which still had a cork-bound centre. However, Duke's used looser stitching which, when waxed, gave a more prominent seam and much more swing. In addition to the moans from the seam bowlers, there was also a general complaint that the flatter seam did not give slow bowlers the grip necessary to obtain more purchase. But that is a teething problem which should be solved by the manufacturers, as well as by some extra determination from a breed of bowlers who, in recent years, had been almost actively discouraged.

The cricketers, through their Association, and the captains begged the TCCB to relent and increase the strands for 1991 either to twelve or fifteen. However, the cricket committee stuck to its guns. That means a lot of hard work for many young bowlers, the benefit of which will be reaped at international level as soon as they develop a more repetitive technique. At the moment, Angus Fraser glitters like a lone jewel among much dross in English cricket. And if it irritates the modern cricketer to remind him that there were half a dozen Frasers in county cricket in the first 25 years after the Second World War, so be it.

Now that it is no longer sufficient for seam bowlers to point and release, they will have to learn the mechanics of a good hand action. With most bowlers, the position of the feet dictates the body position which, in turn, governs the hand action at the moment of release. Nevertheless, history is littered with exceptions to the rule – the unorthodox open-chested bowler who still possessed a hand action to bowl the out-swinger, and vice versa. I watched Tom Cartwright, originally a batsman for Warwickshire, turn seam bowling into an art, simply by taking the construction of a flawless hand action to the ultimate. With an "old" ball (i.e., before the seam was *increased*) he took 1,058 wickets for Warwickshire in the later part of the 1950s and in the 1960s.

The "new" ball is similar to that used 30 years ago. The major difference in the game, though, is that pitches were uncovered then. The arguments against reverting to this environment are many, yet if the run-ups were also uncovered, fears that fast bowlers would be lethal after rain would be unfounded. Uncovered pitches brought about more rounded techniques for both batsmen and bowlers. With the ball, accuracy and a repetitive method were essential. But while that debate continues, unquestionably the TCCB has got it right with regard to the ball. The Board must not now bow to pressure to abandon a brave experiment which, if responded to with similar courage by county bowlers, will bring the rich reward of better standards for bowlers and batsmen alike.

[*Patrick Eagar*

SIR LEONARD HUTTON

A CRICKETING LEGEND

By JOHN WOODCOCK

Between the end of the First World War in 1918 and the start of the Second in 1939, English cricket produced three great batsmen – Walter Hammond, Leonard Hutton and Denis Compton. Each one was endowed with a wonderful talent, Hammond's enabling him to play with rare splendour, Compton's with an irresistible *joie de vivre* and Hutton's with a style that was all-embracing. Although Herbert Sutcliffe had a comparable record, compiled between the wars, he was not in the same way a product of the 1920s or 1930s, having been on the point of breaking through in 1914.

Len Hutton died on September 6, 1990, at the age of 74. He had slipped into Lord's only five days earlier, to watch the final of the NatWest Bank Trophy from Paul Getty's box in the Mound Stand. He had been there, too, for the Test match against India in July, and seen Graham Gooch get to within 31 runs of his own most famous record, the 364 with which he tormented Australia at The Oval in 1938.

Hutton retained until the end the unassuming manner which marked his apprenticeship. Sir Jack Hobbs had been the same; as disarmingly unboastful after being knighted as before. There was also about Sir Len an apparent frailty at the crease, a characteristic which caused his son, Richard, who also played for Yorkshire and England, frequent anxiety until he was old and wise enough to recognise the artistry it disguised.

For the benefit of those who never saw Hutton bat, I have been trying to think of someone playing today who puts one in mind of him, and I am not sure that I can. This is surprising, for he was essentially orthodox and resolutely conventional. Except that he gives more of an impression of hitting the ball, and less of stroking it, than Hutton did, Stephen Waugh, the gifted Australian of similar build, probably comes as near to it as anyone. Mohammad Azharuddin is another who possesses that intuition which gives the great natural players such a start to life. There was something quite uncanny about the way, for example, in which Hutton coped with the mysteries of Sonny Ramadhin's spin while carrying his bat against West Indies at The Oval in 1950, just as there was in his handling of Jack Iverson's when doing the same against Australia at Adelaide only six months later. He was, hereabouts, at the meridian of his powers. So, besides Ramadhin and Iverson, were Keith Miller and Ray Lindwall. In fair weather and foul, at home and overseas, if Len failed the chances were that England would.

Whether his character was influenced by being born at Fulneck, the village near Pudsey where there was an isolated Moravian community ("protestants of rare missionary zeal") is a matter for conjecture. To some extent it probably was, their significance being quite considerable. But cricket, too, was a family religion. Those who didn't take to it would have been put back if that had been possible, and being chosen for Yorkshire when still a month short of his eighteenth birthday – his first match was against Cambridge University at Fenner's in May 1934 – made Hutton the youngest player to appear for the county since George Hirst in 1889. He came into a side that had won the Championship for the previous three years – Yorkshire had not been out of the first four since 1911 – and, although they finished a disappointing fifth in 1934, to play regularly for them in those days gave a young man a distinct advantage. If the same applied today, Richard Blakey and Ashley Metcalfe would, I am sure, be nearer to playing for England than they probably are.

In Hutton's case, the transition from callow youth, cap steeply tilted, to one of the world's most accomplished batsmen was achieved in an extraordinarily short time. Yorkshire colts getting a game for the county side in the middle 1930s were left in no doubt that they were there to be seen and not heard. It was an austere school, and Hutton was an astute observer. Within four years of joining it he had become a household name. Nothing was more remarkable about his *tour de force* at The Oval than that he was only just 22 at the time.

Then came the war, claiming several summers when Hutton's play would still have carried the bloom of youth, and leaving him, as the result of a training accident, with his left arm two inches shorter than the right. With the return of peace, the mantle that had been Hammond's passed to Hutton, whose batting, despite having been laid up for so long, had matured. Between 1934 and 1939 he had scored 11,658 runs at an average of 48.98. From 1945, when he played his next first-class innings, to his retirement in 1955 he made another 28,292 at 58.81. Although, hardly surprisingly, he himself felt handicapped by his disabled arm – its shortening was clearly visible – he made miraculously light of it. If Compton and Bill Edrich were the spirit of the immediate post-war years, Hutton was looked to to provide the stability. Between the three of them they did wonders for our rehabilitation.

That Compton rather than Hutton was made Freddie Brown's vice-captain in Australia in 1950-51 was for reasons of compatibility. When, in 1952, a more egalitarian age was dawning and a captain was being sought to succeed Brown, Len was the clear choice (although he had never led Yorkshire), and it fell to him to regain the Ashes in England in 1953 and then retain them in Australia two years later. In Australia he was quick to see the possibilities of a Statham-Tyson combination, despite Tyson's rather lumbering early efforts and although it meant leaving out Alec Bedser, which he did without the consideration due to so great a figure in the game.

Hutton was not, in fact, an easy communicator. It could be said that he distanced himself from his side when at times they needed a stronger lead. This was particularly so in the West Indies in 1953-54 on the first of his two tours as captain. On the other hand, they were in awe of him as a player, and that was a help. Just as Sir Henry Cotton dignified the status of the professional golfer, so Hutton did of the professional cricketer.

Still good enough to make 145 against Australia at Lord's in 1953 – an innings described by Neville Cardus as "one of the most regal and highly pedigreed ever seen in an England and Australia Test match" – and to average an astonishing 96.71 against West Indies that winter, by the summer of 1954 Len was suddenly finding it much more of an effort to summon the skill and nerve and concentration needed both to captain England and to make runs. There were also suggestions that, although his side had staged an epic recovery in the West Indies, they had not covered themselves with glory in other respects. There were, accordingly, calls for a change of captain. These, happily, were resisted, and off to Australia he went in September 1954 for his third and last tour there as a player. In the event it took so much out of him, once England had been horribly beaten in the First Test – not least because Hutton had put Australia in – that, within a few months of his getting home in the spring of 1955, he put his bats away. His back was playing him up, and after the heat and burden of the last two years a quiet retirement in Surrey, with a golf course nearby, had an obvious appeal. Famous Yorkshireman that he was, the south, with its less competitive responses, suited him better than the north.

For a decade Len Hutton was the model for English batsmen. As a first movement he slid his right foot back and across towards the middle stump, from where, basically, he did what came naturally. He had a lovely stance, as still as it was relaxed. He would play right back but seldom right forward, preferring to let the ball come to him and playing it very late. Between bat and pad there was sometimes, dare I say it, a gap – the forward "prop" had yet to come into fashion – and through it he was liable to be bowled by an off-break. Early in the season, undergraduates at Oxford and Cambridge were known to get him out this way.

There were occasions, too, when, because of his arm, he played his cover drive not leaning into the ball so much as reaching for it. But his timing and balance were such that it was still pleasing to the eye. He had all the strokes if he wanted them, though only when no risk was involved did he loft the ball. In his nineteen Test hundreds he hit only two sixes, and one of those was to what was then the shortest straight boundary in Test cricket – Jamaica's Sabina Park. It was a drive off Gary Sobers, bowling orthodox left-arm spin.

Hutton never greatly cared for leaving his crease to the spinners, of whom there were vastly more then than there are now. Had he done so, the chances are that the generation which followed him, led by Peter May, Colin Cowdrey and Tom Graveney, would themselves have ventured forth rather more. Like all instinctively good judges of a run, he never looked to be in a hurry between the wickets. Studying under Sutcliffe in his early days for Yorkshire would have shown him the need for conviction in calling and let him into the secrets of the short single.

A broken nose gave Len a misleadingly rugged appearance. But to go with it he had a winning smile and blue eyes which regularly twinkled with his own brand of sometimes cryptic humour. He was full of paradoxes: self-contained yet vulnerable, reserved yet quizzical, shrewd yet enigmatic, gentle yet tenacious. He wanted to be judged as a person as much as in his role as a cricketer, and it may truthfully be said that, like Hobbs before him, he attracted widespread and genuine affection.

I see him on board ship in 1950 and again in 1954, bound for Australia and wrapped in contemplation. I see him working the ball around, seldom plundering the bowling, rather picking up runs as he went – a late cut here, a placed single there, and then, sometimes after a long wait, the cover drive that was his special glory. The modern game would have given us, inevitably, a different player: he would have had no chance to surpass himself, as he sometimes so memorably did, on drying pitches, and it is as dreadful to think of him in a helmet as it is to think of Compton, Hammond or W.G. in one.

I see him near the end of his tether, as a lot of us were, before the Ashes were safely in England's keeping in Australia in 1954-55. And I shall remember him at the Lord's Test match against India last year, going quietly and a little wearily off into the twilight, content, I fancy, that his record score for England was still intact, though certain to have been just as affable had it not been. He was not one to shower compliments around, but by then he knew when they were due and duly paid them. A cricketing legend, he won as many hearts with his beguiling albeit watchful charm as with the mastery of his batting.

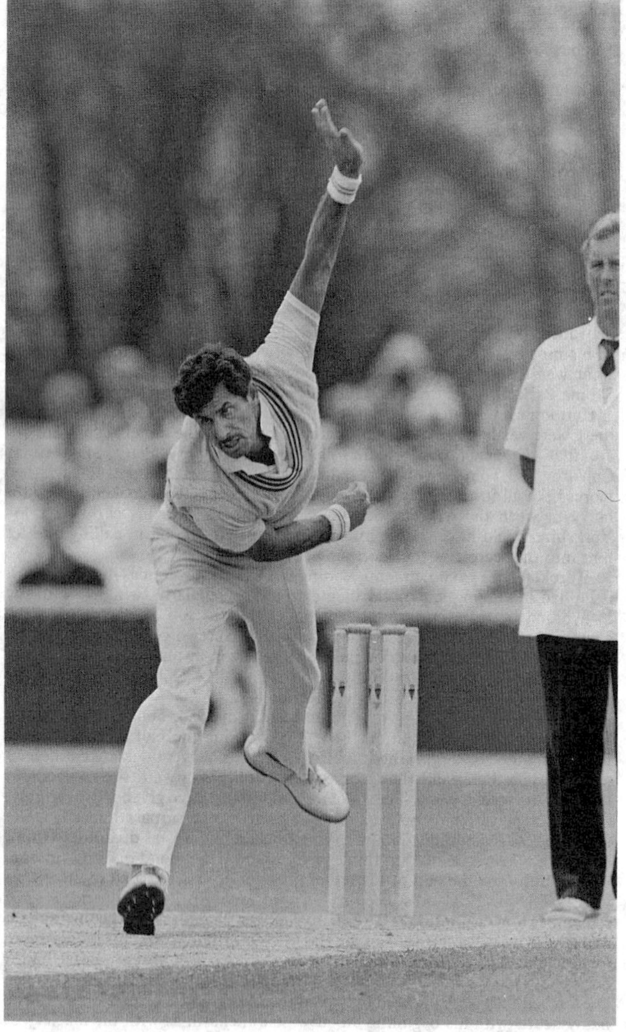

[Patrick Eagar

SIR RICHARD HADLEE

"VERY HAPPY, RELIEVED, PROUD"

By DON MOSEY

The international bowling career of Richard John Hadlee, KBE, by his own assessment may be divided into three distinct periods: the first five years when he was "erratic, inconsistent and without a great idea of how to get through three days, let alone four, or five"; the years 1977 to 1980 when, according to Glenn Turner, he "came of age"; and the final decade, when he positively raced to his record number of 431 Test wickets by summoning every resource of experience and guile.

It began on February 2, 1973, at the Basin Reserve, Wellington, where he took two wickets in the match against Pakistan for 112 runs, and it ended on July 10, 1990, at Edgbaston, Birmingham, when he was handed the ball with which he had taken five wickets in an innings for the 36th time. From that modest start he had averaged five wickets a match over the 86 Tests in which he had played in the subsequent seventeen and a half years, and he retired "very happy, relieved, proud".

That he was the most intelligent fast bowler the world has seen there can be little doubt or argument. He did not have the bumptious lovableness of Botham, the small boy's hero; he rarely, if ever, showed the fire and fury of Trueman in his pomp; he never besmirched his reputation with the gimmickry or histrionics of Lillee (the bowler he most admired). What Hadlee brought to fast bowling in the second half of his career was deep thought, intense academic study and immense concentration. Not only did he spend hours watching video-tapes of Lillee, considering the approach, the delivery, the grip, the release; he spent even more time searching for weaknesses in the defensive armoury of the greatest batsmen of his day, in the manner of a surgeon studying X-rays before probing for the source of the problem.

Hadlee's basic delivery (if, in fact, there was one) would be the ball which moved away from the bat after pitching on to an angled seam. He called it, in Southern hemisphere style, a leg-cutter – a delivery which in English terms requires a specific movement of the fingers at the moment of release – but such was his control and his ability to land the ball exactly as required that he might be said to have perfected a simplified version of the leg-cutter. He could nip one back the other way, usually from a little wider in the bowling crease to pose problems of line-judgement. Swing was not always the most potent weapon, but when atmospheric conditions were right his quicker ball moved late and away towards the slips; his slower ball, the one he called the "dangly", swung into the batsman. He used the quick bouncer sparingly, keeping it always in reserve to invest it with the additional element of surprise. There was subtlety in everything he did.

Hadlee's "placing" of these differing deliveries in the course of an over was as meticulously thoughtful as every other aspect of his campaign, for that is what a bowling spell was to him. In the manner of the great spin bowlers of earlier years, he plotted the downfall of his opponents on lines of long-term strategy, without necessarily feeling that each individual delivery deserved a wicket on its own merits. It was simply a factor in the Grand Design, a skirmish in the battle to put the batsman on the foot, back or front, where he was less assured or – the ultimate victory – to catch him in no-man's-land. There has been no greater fascination in modern cricket than watching an over from Richard Hadlee when there was some response from the pitch or some help in the atmosphere.

So great has been the impact of his bowling, for Nottinghamshire and for New Zealand, that it is possible to pay less regard to his batting than it merits. Yet on figures alone he stands among the greatest of post-war all-rounders. Only Botham, Kapil Dev and Imran Khan join him in the ranks of those who have scored more than 3,000 runs while taking more than 300 wickets in Test matches. His "double" in the County Championship of 1984 was the first to be performed in England since 1967 (by Fred Titmus), in an age when the feat seemed to be beyond modern cricketers. And consider his averages in accomplishing it: 1,179 runs at 51.26, 117 wickets costing 14.05 each. They are astonishing figures. In the 1987 NatWest Bank Trophy final, the game seemed irretrievably lost to Nottinghamshire when it spilled over into a second day because of rain; Hadlee's 70 not out from 61 balls on the Monday resulted in a victory which was something more than improbable.

At Test level, his eleven wickets for 102 and 51 runs in the first innings helped New Zealand to the victory which decided the 1979-80 series against West Indies; in the following match he completed a maiden Test century (as well as rounding off his Test "double") off 92 balls from Roberts, Holding, Garner and Croft. In February 1984, in Christchurch, he took eight wickets for 44 runs and scored 99 runs from 81 balls on a pitch where England mustered *totals* of only 82 and 93.

Even in a career as illustrious as his, however, there have been disappointments. "If the ultimate satisfaction for a bowler is to do the hat-trick, then the *ultimate* ultimate must be to take all ten wickets in an innings, and I never did that." The nearest Hadlee came to all ten was when he took nine for 52 in the innings victory over Australia in Brisbane in November 1985. But as he caught the tenth batsman, took six for 71 in the second innings, and in between hit 54 runs, that can scarcely amount to a deep disappointment. "No. That was, I suppose, as near-perfect a performance as one hopes to achieve, and one in which the whole team shared. Brilliant catches were held and the batting was consistent." It was a result which left Australia stunned.

For the real disappointment of his Test life, one has to turn to events in his own country, most particularly a widespread failure by press and public to understand and accept his adoption of the short run after 1980. There was a rather naïve insistence that New Zealand's principal strike bowler should *look* fast by continuing an approach from 25 yards. While sheer physical necessity demanded that he reduce this, Hadlee felt a sense of outrage that his professionalism was being questioned. The shaft which went deepest was a well-turned journalistic phrase of Don Cameron, the country's leading cricket-writer, who wrote of ". . . New Zealand's heaviest artillery operating off a pop-gun run-up". Ten years after the words were written, Richard Hadlee quotes them in a crescendo of indignant incredulity. It was that change which transformed him from a good Test bowler into a great one.

As his career developed, so did his public persona and the need for a highly developed sense of public relations. He acknowledges with gratitude the debt he owes to Grahame Felton, a management consultant in Christchurch, who changed the whole Hadlee character after a near-breakdown in 1983. His naturally strong personality became even more positive; he seemed able almost to anticipate all but the most asinine of questions, and in consequence an interview with Richard Hadlee has usually been a rewarding experience for the questioner. His replies are reasoned, succinct, humorous (where appropriate) and always to the point. If he has not suffered fools gladly, no-one but a fool would condemn him.

His is a character which his fellow New Zealanders have perhaps found easier to respect than to regard with warm affection, though his autobiography achieved a massive sale. His countrymen are less effusive about sporting heroes than in some other parts of the world. As a result of this, criticism at home, especially when ill-informed, has tended to irritate him more than might otherwise have been the case. (In this, he would find a ready ally in Glenn Turner.) One accusation of cupidity – the matter of a car awarded for an outstanding performance – was built up to a *cause célèbre* in New Zealand. Yet if one searches for the real heart of the man, one comes to his confession at the end of the 1980 season with Nottinghamshire: "I felt a cheat. I had had three awful seasons since first joining the club and commitments to New Zealand meant that I hadn't given Notts value for money. I was embarrassed to collect my pay-cheque." Hadlee has always been practical and pragmatic in financial matters, but he would shudder at the thought of anyone believing him capable of short-changing his employers or his colleagues.

He has been as industrious a worker outside cricket as he was on the field, involving himself in authorship, broadcasting (presenting his own programme), publicity and promotion, television commercials, journalism and public speaking. To these activities he now adds the commercial cultivation of exotic flowers, and it will be no surprise to anyone if that, in due course, becomes a highly successful enterprise. If Richard Hadlee appears to have the golden touch, it is largely because he works so hard for his success. Edison may well have been looking a century into the future when he defined genius as one per cent inspiration and 99 per cent perspiration.

The final distinction of a knighthood in the 1990 Birthday Honours' list came as near as anything has to overwhelming the man. He admits to "dreaming dreams" as a child without any real expectation of fulfilment. Personally, I have a few doubts about that. Richard John Hadlee seems always to have had a strong sense of his own destiny. At 39, feeling "very happy, relieved, proud", he could look forward to the second half of a life in which all things were possible. There will be no raised eyebrows – from New Zealand to Nottingham – at what he achieves.

While Hadlee's conversation is animated, bright and witty, it is perhaps a little difficult to think of him indulging his sense of humour in the middle of a Test match. When he bowled Devon Malcolm to end England's first innings at Edgbaston, however, he was laughing so much at the batsman's simulated aggression that he found it difficult to direct the ball at the target. The umpire, John Holder, confessed that *he* was laughing so heartily that it would have been difficult to answer an lbw appeal. Fortunately for the dignity of the game and of a distinguished career, the end of the second innings was a more serious matter, for that final five-wicket performance put New Zealand in with a chance of victory. It would have been unthinkable to look back on a bowling performance by Sir Richard Hadlee as any sort of laughing matter. The last spell of all put matters into perspective. Hadlee bade farewell to the game on a more characteristically thoughtful – and successful – note.

SIR RICHARD HADLEE

TEST CAREER – BATTING

		T	*I*	*NO*	*R*	*HI*	*100s*	*50s*	*Avge*	*Ct*
1972-73	v Pakistan†	1	1	0	46	46	0	0	46.00	2
1973	v England	1	2	1	4	4*	0	0	4.00	0
1973-74	v Australia	3	6	0	68	20	0	0	11.33	2
	v Australia†	2	3	0	37	23	0	0	12.33	1
1975-76	v India†	2	2	0	45	33	0	0	22.50	0
1976-77	v Pakistan	3	6	2	214	87	0	1	53.50	2
	v India	3	6	0	60	21	0	0	10.00	1
	v Australia†	2	4	0	143	81	0	1	35.75	2
1977-78	v England†	3	6	1	80	39	0	0	16.00	0
1978	v England	3	6	0	32	11	0	0	5.33	3
1978-79	v Pakistan†	3	5	1	115	53*	0	1	28.75	1
1979-80	v West Indies†	3	4	0	178	103	1	1	44.50	1
1980-81	v Australia	3	6	2	98	51*	0	1	24.50	1
	v India†	3	4	0	29	20	0	0	7.25	2
1981-82	v Australia†	3	5	1	92	40	0	0	23.00	2
1982-83	v Sri Lanka†	2	3	1	59	30	0	0	29.50	1
1983	v England	4	8	2	301	92*	0	3	50.16	1
1983-84	v England†	3	4	0	144	99	0	1	36.00	3
	v Sri Lanka	3	4	0	75	29	0	0	18.75	3
1984-85	v Pakistan†	3	4	0	131	89	0	1	32.75	0
	v West Indies	4	7	1	137	39*	0	0	22.83	1
1985-86	v Australia	3	4	0	111	54	0	1	27.75	2
	v Australia†	3	3	1	105	72*	0	1	52.50	2
1986	v England	3	3	0	93	68	0	1	31.00	0
1986-87	v West Indies†	3	4	2	74	35*	0	0	37.00	2
	v Sri Lanka	1	1	1	151	151*	1	0	—	1
1987-88	v Australia	3	6	1	111	36	0	0	22.20	0
	v England†	1	1	0	37	37	0	0	37.00	0
1988-89	v India	3	6	1	61	31	0	0	12.20	1
	v Pakistan†	2	3	1	53	32	0	0	26.50	0
1989-90	v India†	3	2	0	115	87	0	1	57.50	0
	v Australia†	1	1	0	18	18	0	0	18.00	0
1990	v England	3	4	0	107	86	0	1	26.75	2
		86	134	19	3,124	151*	2	15	27.16	39

* *Signifies not out.* † *Series played in New Zealand.*

Highest innings: 151* v Sri Lanka at Colombo (CCC), 1986-87.

TEST CAREER – BOWLING

		T	*O*	*M*	*R*	*W*	*BB*	*Avge*	*5W/i*
1972-73	v Pakistan†	1	*25	0	112	2	2-84	56.00	0
1973	v England	1	45	8	143	1	1-79	143.00	0
1973-74	v Australia	3	*66.7	9	255	7	4-33	36.42	0
	v Australia†	2	*50.4	7	225	10	4-71	22.50	0
1975-76	v India†	2	*48.3	4	197	12	7-23	16.41	1‡

		T	O	M	R	W	BB	Avge	5W/i
1976-77	v Pakistan	3	*75.2	2	447	10	5-121	44.70	1
	v India	3	127	18	437	13	4-95	33.61	0
	v Australia†	2	*72	7	354	6	3-155	59.00	0
1977-78	v England†	3	*121.3	26	371	15	6-26	24.73	1‡
1978	v England	3	121.1	31	270	13	5-84	20.76	1
1978-79	v Pakistan†	3	*117.6	13	414	18	5-62	23.00	2
1979-80	v West Indies†	3	161.3	50	361	19	6-68	19.00	2‡
1980-81	v Australia	3	147.3	35	364	19	6-57	19.15	2
	v India†	3	119.3	37	288	10	5-47	28.80	1
1981-82	v Australia†	3	91.5	25	226	14	6-100	16.14	2
1982-83	v Sri Lanka†	2	77.3	27	141	10	4-33	14.10	0
1983	v England	4	232	65	559	21	6-53	26.61	2
1983-84	v England†	3	109.5	33	232	12	5-28	19.33	1
	v Sri Lanka	3	117.5	47	230	23	5-29	10.00	2‡
1984-85	v Pakistan†	3	118.5	29	306	16	6-51	19.12	1
	v West Indies	4	143	31	409	15	4-53	27.26	0
1985-86	v Australia	3	169.3	42	401	33	9-52	12.15	5§
	v Australia†	3	157.5	36	387	16	7-116	24.18	1
1986	v England	3	153.5	42	390	19	6-80	20.52	2‡
1986-87	v West Indies†	3	113.1	20	354	17	6-50	20.82	2
	v Sri Lanka	1	38.5	10	102	4	4-102	25.50	0
1987-88	v Australia	3	156	44	353	18	5-67	19.61	3‡
	v England†	1	18	3	50	0	0-50	—	0
1988-89	v India	3	100.5	25	252	18	6-49	14.00	2‡
	v Pakistan†	2	82	21	169	5	4-101	33.80	0
1989-90	v India†	3	105.5	24	319	12	4-69	26.58	0
	v Australia†	1	41.2	8	109	7	5-39	15.57	1
1990	v England	3	133.5	24	384	16	5-53	24.00	1
		86	2,883.3 & *577.1	803	9,611	431	9-52	22.29	36

* *Eight-ball overs.* † *Series played in New Zealand.*

‡ *Signifies ten wickets in a match once; § twice. Sir Richard Hadlee took ten wickets in a Test match nine times.*

Best bowling: 9-52 v Australia at Brisbane, 1985-86.

SUMMARY v EACH COUNTRY

	T	O	M	R	W	BB	Avge	5W/i
v Australia	23	*189.3 & 764	213	2,674	130	9-52	20.56	14§
v England	21	*121.3 & 813.4	232	2,399	97	6-26	24.73	8‡
v India	14	*48.3 & 453.1	108	1,493	65	7-23	22.96	4‡
v Pakistan	12	*218 & 200.5	65	1,448	51	6-51	28.39	4
v West Indies	10	417.4	101	1,124	51	6-50	22.03	4†
v Sri Lanka	6	234.1	84	473	37	5-29	12.78	2†
	86	2,883.3 & *577.1	803	9,611	431	9-52	22.29	36

* *Eight-ball overs.* † *Signifies ten wickets in a match once; ‡ twice; § three times.*

FIVE WICKETS IN AN INNINGS/TEN WICKETS IN A MATCH

4-35 }
7-23 } v India, Wellington, 1975-76.
5-121 v Pakistan, Lahore, 1976-77.
4-74 }
6-26 } v England, Wellington, 1977-78.
5-84 v England, Lord's, 1978.
5-62 v Pakistan, Christchurch, 1978-79.
5-104 v Pakistan, Auckland, 1978-79.
5-34 }
6-68 } v West Indies, Dunedin, 1979-80.
5-87 v Australia, Perth, 1980-81.
6-57 v Australia, Melbourne, 1980-81.
5-47 v India, Christchurch, 1980-81.
5-63 v Australia, Auckland, 1981-82.
6-100 v Australia, Christchurch, 1981-82.
6-53 v England, The Oval, 1983.
5-93 v England, Lord's, 1983.
5-28 v England, Christchurch, 1983-84.
5-73 }
5-29 } v Sri Lanka, Colombo (CCC), 1983-84.
6-51 v Pakistan, Dunedin, 1984-85.
9-52 }
6-71 } v Australia, Brisbane, 1985-86.
5-65 v Australia, Sydney, 1985-86.
5-65 }
6-90 } v Australia, Perth, 1985-86.
7-116 v Australia, Christchurch, 1985-86.
6-80 v England, Lord's, 1986.
6-80 }
4-60 } v England, Nottingham, 1986.
6-105 v West Indies, Auckland, 1986-87.
6-50 v West Indies, Christchurch, 1986-87.
5-68 v Australia, Adelaide, 1987-88.
5-109 }
5-67 } v Australia, Melbourne, 1987-88.
5-65 v India, Bangalore, 1988-89.
6-49 }
4-39 } v India, Bombay, 1988-89.
5-39 v Australia, Wellington, 1989-90.
5-53 v England, Birmingham, 1990.

FIRST-CLASS CAREER – BATTING

		M	*I*	*NO*	*R*	*HI*	*100s*	*50s*	*Avge*	*Ct*
1971-72		3	3	1	16	11	0	0	8.00	2
1972-73		6	8	1	126	50	0	1	18.00	7
	(Australia)	1	1	0	9	9	0	0	9.00	0
1973		12	7	2	74	30	0	0	14.80	0
1973-74		3	5	1	71	23	0	0	17.75	1
	(Australia)	7	11	0	197	49	0	0	17.90	3
1974-75		1	2	1	47	33	0	0	47.00	1
1975-76		9	12	3	200	53*	0	1	22.22	3
1976-77		7	11	1	328	81	0	2	32.80	4
	(Pakistan)	5	8	2	224	87	0	1	37.33	2
	(India)	3	6	0	60	21	0	0	10.00	1
1977-78		10	20	4	346	77	0	2	21.62	2
1978		17	21	4	342	101*	1	0	20.11	10
1978-79		10	16	4	329	79*	0	3	27.41	3
1979		12	16	4	193	41	0	0	16.08	5
1979-80		3	4	0	178	103	1	1	44.50	1
	(Australia)	6	10	3	160	33*	0	0	22.85	4
1980		8	9	1	231	68	0	1	28.87	4
1980-81		3	4	0	29	20	0	0	7.25	2
	(Australia)	5	8	2	249	103	1	1	41.50	2
1981		21	26	3	745	142*	1	3	32.39	14
1981-82		10	18	3	500	83*	0	3	33.33	5
1982		18	28	2	807	131	2	4	31.03	16
1982-83		4	7	1	171	46	0	0	28.50	5
1983		13	15	2	596	103	1	5	45.84	6
1983-84		6	9	1	305	99	0	2	38.12	7
	(Sri Lanka)	4	4	0	75	29	0	0	18.75	3
1984		24	31	8	1,179	210*	2	7	51.26	23
1984-85		8	12	2	221	89	0	1	22.10	0
	(West Indies)	4	7	1	137	39*	0	0	22.83	1
1985		19	29	11	592	73*	0	5	32.88	17

		M	*I*	*NO*	*R*	*HI*	*100s*	*50s*	*Avge*	*Ct*
1985-86		3	3	1	105	72*	0	1	52.50	2
	(Australia)	5	6	0	151	54	0	1	25.16	3
1986		17	21	5	813	129*	2	4	50.81	6
1986-87		11	17	5	281	50*	0	1	23.41	9
	(Sri Lanka)	1	1	1	151	151*	1	0	—	1
1987		21	28	7	1,111	133*	2	6	52.90	16
1987-88		1	1	0	37	37	0	0	37.00	0
	(Australia)	5	8	3	151	36	0	0	30.20	1
1988-89		3	4	1	90	37	0	0	30.00	0
	(India)	4	7	2	88	31	0	0	17.60	2
1989-90		4	3	0	133	87	0	1	44.33	0
1990		5	6	0	204	90	0	2	34.00	4
		342	473	93	12,052	210*	14	59	31.71	198

** Signifies not out.*

Note: Sir Richard Hadlee appeared for Nottinghamshire from 1978 to 1987, and for Tasmania in 1979-80. In New Zealand he played for Canterbury.

Highest innings: 210*, Nottinghamshire v Middlesex at Lord's, 1984.

FIRST-CLASS CAREER – BOWLING

		O	*M*	*R*	*W*	*BB*	*Avge*	*5W/i*	*10W/m*
1971-72		*55	9	194	10	4-42	19.40	0	0
1972-73		*144	18	550	30	4-25	18.33	0	0
	(Australia)	*26	3	80	1	1-32	80.00	0	0
1973		355.1	72	1,058	38	5-56	27.84	1	0
1973-74		*79.5	11	340	16	4-64	21.25	0	0
	(Australia)	*175.7	18	728	16	4-33	45.50	0	0
1974-75		*27	6	82	3	2-32	27.33	0	0
1975-76		*222.7	31	751	40	7-23	18.77	2	1
1976-77		*181.5	20	721	18	3-21	40.05	0	0
	(Pakistan)	*109.5	3	610	18	5-47	33.88	2	0
	(India)	127	18	437	13	4-95	33.61	0	0
1977-78		*266.1	56	860	42	6-26	20.47	3	1
1978		497.1	120	1,269	78	7-77	16.26	6	2
1978-79		*299.1	56	909	50	6-28	18.18	4	0
1979		317	103	753	47	7-23	16.02	2	0
1979-80		161.3	50	361	19	6-68	19.00	2	1
	(Australia)	173.2	36	477	13	5-55	36.69	1	0
1980		222.1	82	410	29	5-32	14.13	1	0
1980-81		119.3	37	288	10	5-47	28.80	1	0
	(Australia)	229.3	52	567	27	6-57	21.00	3	0
1981		708.4	231	1,564	105	7-25	14.89	4	0
1981-82		424.2	131	867	59	6-26	14.69	7	0
1982		403.5	123	889	61	7-25	14.57	4	0
1982-83		152.5	52	277	23	6-43	12.04	1	1
1983		431.3	123	1,065	49	6-53	21.73	3	0
1983-84		181.5	62	329	24	5-28	13.70	1	0
	(Sri Lanka)	128.5	49	258	24	5-29	10.75	2	1
1984		772.2	248	1,645	117	7-35	14.05	6	1
1984-85		287.3	88	652	38	6-51	17.15	3	0
	(West Indies)	143	33	409	15	4-53	27.26	0	0
1985		473.5	136	1,026	59	8-41	17.38	2	0
1985-86		157.5	36	387	16	7-116	24.18	1	0
	(Australia)	241.3	65	537	37	9-52	14.51	5	2
1986		547.3	150	1,215	76	6-31	15.98	7	2
1986-87		407.2	106	935	62	7-49	15.08	8	1
	(Sri Lanka)	38.5	10	102	4	4-102	25.50	0	0
1987		591	189	1,227	97	6-20	12.64	9	2

		O	M	R	W	BB	Avge	5W/i	10W/m
1987-88		18	3	50	0	0-50	—	0	0
	(Australia)	237.4	63	564	29	5-30	19.44	5	2
1988-89		113	32	234	7	4-101	33.42	0	0
	(India)	124.5	30	307	27	9-55	11.37	3	1
1989-90		147.1	32	428	19	5-39	22.52	1	0
1990		201.5	39	586	24	5-27	24.41	2	0
		9,137.2 & *1,586.7	2,832	26,998	1,490	9-52	18.11	102	18

* *Eight-ball overs.*

Best bowling: 9-52, New Zealand v Australia at Brisbane, 1985-86.

LIMITED-OVERS CAREER – BATTING

	M	I	NO	R	HI	50s	Avge	Ct
One-day Internationals	115	98	17	1,749	79	4	21.59	27

Highest innings: 79 v England at Adelaide, 1982-83.

	M	I	NO	R	HI	50s	Avge	Ct
John Player/Refuge Assurance League	96	82	21	1,618	100*	3	26.52	32
Benson and Hedges Cup	44	37	9	920	70	5	32.85	15
Gillette Cup/NatWest Bank Trophy .	19	17	3	412	70*	3	29.42	11
Australian domestic competition	9	7	1	86	30	0	14.33	3
New Zealand domestic competition ..	29	25	3	396	63	1	18.00	11

* *Signifies not out.*

Highest innings: 100*, Nottinghamshire v Gloucestershire at Cheltenham, 1982. This was Sir Richard Hadlee's only hundred in limited-overs matches.

LIMITED-OVERS CAREER – BOWLING

	Balls	R	W	BB	Avge	4W/i
One-day Internationals	6,182	3,407	158	5-25	21.56	6

Best bowling: 5-25 v Sri Lanka at Bristol, 1983.

	Balls	R	W	BB	Avge	4W/i
John Player/Refuge Assurance League	4,100	2,532	125	6-12	20.25	4
Benson and Hedges Cup	2,476	1,144	74	4-13	15.45	3
Gillette Cup/NatWest Bank Trophy .	1,184	480	32	5-17	15.00	1
Australian domestic competition	457	222	13	3-13	17.07	0
New Zealand domestic competition ..	1,545	647	46	4-15	14.06	3

Best bowling: 6-12, Nottinghamshire v Lancashire at Nottingham, 1980.

Statistics compiled by Philip Bailey.

WHERE WAS THE PROTECTION?

[*Patrick Eagar*

England's Robin Smith avoids yet another West Indies bouncer in the Antigua Test. As the barrage against him continued, the umpire did not intervene, even though such bowling not only was *likely to inflict physical injury* (Law 42.8) but actually did so.

THE 1990 NEW ZEALAND TEAM IN ENGLAND

[*Patrick Eagar*

Back row: A. C. Parore, D. K. Morrison, K. R. Rutherford, M. W. Priest. *Middle row:* R. S. Cunis (*coach*), T. J. Franklin, S. A. Thomson, A. H. Jones, M. J. Greatbatch, J. P. Millmow, P. N. Culpan (*scorer*), M. R. Plummer (*physiotherapist*). *Front row:* J. J. Crowe, M. C. Snedden, J. G. Bracewell, I. N. Taylor (*manager*), J. G. Wright (*captain*), M. D. Crowe (*vice-captain*), Sir Richard Hadlee, I. D. S. Smith.

THE 1990 INDIAN TEAM IN ENGLAND

[*Graham Morris*

Back row: Dr Ali Irani (*physiotherapist*), S. K. Sharma, S. L. V. Raju, W. V. Raman, A. S. Wassan, B. S. Bedi (*cricket manager*), A. Kumble, N. D. Hirwani, S. R. Tendulkar, N. R. Mongia, M. K. Mantri (*manager*). *Front row:* M. Prabhakar, K. S. More, D. B. Vengsarkar, M. Azharuddin (*captain*), R. J. Shastri (*vice-captain*), Kapil Dev, N. S. Sidhu, S. V. Manjrekar.

THE DEVASTATING EFFECT OF THE FAST, IN-SWINGING YORKER

[*Adam Scott*

The fast, full-pitched swing bowling of Waqar Younis for Surrey in 1990 led to the coining of a new word on the county circuit – Wackered! Leicestershire's Tim Boon (*left*), Peter Willey and James Whitaker learned its meaning during an eighteen-ball blitz on a hot August Saturday at The Oval.

CRICKET'S YOUNGEST TEEMED STAR

[*Patrick Eagar*

At sixteen India's youngest Test cricketer, at seventeen the maker of a Test hundred against England at Old Trafford: Sachin Tendulkar has the cricket world waiting to acclaim his prowess.

BEHIND THE SCREENS AT LORD'S

[*Patrick Eagar*

Masked by extended sightscreens, the construction of the Compton and Edrich stands at Lord's continued throughout the summer of 1990.

AND THAT WAS ALL THE FAREWELL

[Patrick Eagar

[Patrick Eagar

Alvin Kallicharran and Yorkshire wicket-keeper David Bairstow left the first-class game after two decades at Edgbaston and Headingley respectively.

FIVE CRICKETERS OF THE YEAR

[*David Munden*

A. R. Butcher (Glamorgan)

FIVE CRICKETERS OF THE YEAR

[*David Munden*

M. E. Waugh (Essex)

FIVE CRICKETERS OF THE YEAR

[*David Munden*

M. A. Atherton (Lancashire and England)

FIVE CRICKETERS OF THE YEAR

[*Patrick Eagar*

D. L. Haynes (Middlesex)

FIVE CRICKETERS OF THE YEAR

[*Patrick Eagar*

M. Azharuddin (India)

FIVE CRICKETERS OF THE YEAR

MOHAMMAD AZHARUDDIN

Last summer, a new definition was given to oriental artistry as Mohammad Azharuddin, India's captain, time and again placed the ball through square leg and mid-wicket with a wristy turn of the bat at the instant of impact. Line seemed to mean little, length everything, as he feasted on England's bowling with hundreds at Lord's and Old Trafford to follow successively on one against New Zealand in Auckland. They set the crackers bursting in the cosmopolitan neighbourhood of Vithalwadi, in celebration not just of Azharuddin's success, but also of the return of the touch which five years earlier had launched his international career so spectacularly. Three hundreds against England in his first three Tests. That was early in 1985, and the 21-year-old was hailed as a prophet among the Indian pantheon of batting demi-gods. He was also beginning the struggle to cope with the expectations of a nation and his awe of his own reputation.

MOHAMMAD AZHARUDDIN was born on February 8, 1963 in Hyderabad, capital city of the Deccan plateau state of Andhra Pradesh. A doting grandfather was the first to spot the youngster's passion for cricket, and at the All Saints missionary school, Brother Joseph inculcated in him a love of the game. It was as a seam bowler, who could make the ball swing in a banana arc, that the young Azharuddin began playing for All Saints, but he progressed quickly to bat at No. 3, besides being the third seamer, for Hyderabad Schools in the South Zone inter-state schools tournament. In 1979-80 he turned out for South Zone Schools against the visiting English Schools side, and in 1981-82, at the age of eighteen, he made his first-class début in the Ranji Trophy. Such exposure was rather easily attained in a Hyderabad side which was going through a transition, but the experience shaped his batting even as it toughened him mentally.

National recognition came on the heels of a double-hundred for South Zone in January 1984, in the Duleep Trophy, with a place on the Under-25 tour of Zimbabwe. He did not make the short tour of Pakistan in October that year, but only because it was thought that Pakistan was no place for blooding youngsters. His breakthrough came later in the season after David Gower's England team, beaten in the First Test, had come back to square the series in Delhi. In contentious circumstances Kapil Dev was dropped from the side and Azharuddin was brought in to replace Sandeep Patil for the Calcutta Test. The rest is history.

The soft-spoken, almost shy young man was also an instant hit in the limited-overs game. Critics in Australia raved about his essentially back-foot play, which they thought had gone out of fashion along with good manners on the field. His fielding, too, made him invaluable to the side, a factor which came to his aid when his form could not match the impossibly high levels he had set in his first international season. Azharuddin is emphatic that he did not start out as a naturally gifted fielder and that he had to work hard to attain the standards he has today.

While there were centuries to be made on the plumb pitches at home, there were none abroad until his first visit to Pakistan in 1989-90. By then, following an unhappy tour of the West Indies, where fast and short-pitched bowling had provided a searching test of his technique, his place in the side was in doubt. Indeed, it was only because Raman Lamba was forced to withdraw from the First Test because of a broken toe that he played. He saved his place for the next Test with a record-equalling five catches in Pakistan's first innings – four of them brilliant ones in the slips, where he had not always stood – but batting on a hard wicket had meant a return to the horrors of his "blind" ducking against genuine fast bowling.

Advice from colleagues to stand up and hook if bowlers were trying to corner him with bouncers was not really what an uncertain and unwilling player of the hook needed to hear. Sounder advice came from the former Pakistan batsman, Zaheer Abbas, who advocated a readjustment of his grip. By wrapping his right hand further round the handle, Azharuddin found he could stroke the ball with greater control and assurance. In the second innings of the Faisalabad Test, having been dismissed for 0 in the first innings, he made his first century away from home. In the course of it, he found his confidence and his true touch returning. Changes in selection were soon to thrust him further into the limelight, and although he had little experience of leading sides, he was made captain for the tour of New Zealand in early 1990.

Such is Azharuddin's nature, however, that he takes everything in his stride, not making a drama out of a crisis, or even a crisis out of the drama that is so often Indian cricket. He set about tackling his new responsibilities with the modesty that is a refreshing trait: the devout Muslim probably believed in just praying extra hard and leaving his young team to play to the best of their resources. Such a style was disastrous to begin with, but soon enough Azharuddin learned to assert himself as captain.

The Auckland Test, the last of the New Zealand series, brought a sensational twist to his career as a batsman, for it saw the fruition of his counter-attacking style. Suddenly, everything he did came right and a truly majestic innings of 192 unfolded. Marked by straight- and on-driving of a very high order, the innings was supreme also in that it was the highest by an Indian captain abroad. His match- and series-winning half-century at Trent Bridge in the second of last summer's Texaco one-dayers was a further indication of how completely "Azhar" had rediscovered himself.

Having made his name as a stylist who used the power of his wrists to create the mesmeric effect of strokes played late, he had often been struggling in his attempt to put percentages ahead of style. It was an index of his re-emerging batting personality that he should score the centuries which fascinated Englishmen so. He explained away the seeming desperation which sparked India's strokeplay in the defeat at Lord's as the need for aggression which has always acted as a tonic for him. "It's not as if we were always hitting the ball as if we wanted to take the cover off it. But there was so much loose bowling, especially from Malcolm, that it was easy to send the ball speeding down the slope." But at Old Trafford, and again at The Oval, where a century seemed his for the taking, Azharuddin reached the very heights of artistic batting. The Old Trafford hundred pleased him particularly. "I always knew that the ball was going where I aimed to hit it." Watching some of the power developed, especially off the back foot, it was hard to believe he was playing with one of the lightest bats in modern cricket.

Since childhood, Azharuddin has believed in turning out neatly at a cricket match, be it a hit in the park or a Test. Notice how he always goes out to toss in a blazer. By his manner, he also promises to re-establish sporting standards in the game as well as sartorial ones. Certainly, if India's tour of England was a resounding success for the game, Azharuddin can take pride in being a leading contributor to it. This summer his contract with Derbyshire will see the oriental charmer return to England, with his one-year-old son, Asaduddin, in tow. The future beckons brightly. His only regret is that his grandfather, who used to stand under the trees on the boundary line watching him, did not live to see him play Test cricket. – R. Mohan.

ALAN BUTCHER

When Surrey decided not to renew Alan Butcher's contract in 1986, he thought seriously of retiring from first-class cricket. Instead, he accepted an offer to join Glamorgan, for whom his consistent batting and, latterly, his astute captaincy have been an inspiration. Moreover, and importantly, he began to enjoy his cricket again, something he had not experienced with Surrey for some seasons. Last season he thrived on his responsibilities as captain. While Glamorgan, who had propped up the County Championship for two years, rose to eighth, their best position for twenty years, the elegant left-hander, who many thought should have played for England more often than his solitary appearance in 1979, had his most successful season, finishing with an aggregate of 2,116 runs for an average of 58.77. He hit six Championship hundreds, but it was his unbeaten 104 against Middlesex in the NatWest Bank Trophy quarter-final at Lord's which best epitomised his many qualities. Glamorgan's early-order batsmen, including Viv Richards, were dismissed cheaply, but Butcher, on a slow, unresponsive pitch, countered the formidable Middlesex attack and batted throughout the innings. Despite the home side's emphatic nine-wicket win, this captain's innings earned him the Man of the Match award.

ALAN RAYMOND BUTCHER was born in Croydon on January 7, 1954, and after playing for Beckenham Under-11s he spent five and a half years in South Australia, where the family emigrated. He made a considerable impression with the Glenelg youth team, winning their Junior Cricketer award for outstanding performances, and was selected for the South Australia Under-15 side, and later for an all-Australia representative team. South Australia Under-15s included David Hookes, and had Alan's family decided to reside permanently in Australia he would almost certainly have played for his state team, and through qualification he would have been eligible for his adopted country.

After the family's return to England, he played for Surrey Young Cricketers before joining the county staff in 1972, having played two Sunday League games at the end of the previous season. In a Surrey side boasting a batting line-up which included John Edrich, Mike Edwards, Younis Ahmed, Graham Roope and Stewart Storey, he was selected primarily as a left-arm medium-fast bowler who batted at No. 8 or No. 9. In only his third first-class game he took six for 48 against Hampshire at Guildford, his wickets including Barry Richards, Gordon Greenidge and Roy Marshall, while two years later, in 1974, his three for 11 in Surrey's Benson and Hedges Cup semi-final against Lancashire was followed by an eleven-over spell in the final which yielded 23 runs as Leicestershire were beaten by 27 runs. However, the lively left-arm in-swingers are now only sparingly used, although some orthodox slow left-arm is occasionally revived in an attempt to break a partnership.

Butcher began opening the innings for Surrey midway through the 1975 season, partnering Edrich, a batsman whom he admired for his ability to concentrate fully, never to appear ruffled and never to play any differently. The following season he achieved his first Championship century, against Warwickshire at Edgbaston, and his consistent batting over the next three seasons earned him an England cap against India at The Oval in 1979. He made 14 and 20, succumbing to the spin of Venkataraghavan in the first innings and the swing of Ghavri in the second, but he was not given another chance at that level, although he was called up for a one-day international against Australia in 1980. Mike Brearley, who captained England in that 1979 series, rated Butcher as one of the best players of fast bowling in the county game, a view shared by many over the last fifteen years. His seasons' aggregates varied between 1,300 and 1,700, on good, bad and indifferent pitches, especially those at The Oval in the mid-1970s which lacked bounce and pace. Strangely, apart from a period when Geoff Howarth opened the Surrey innings with him, Butcher has always been involved in a left-handed opening combination. Grahame Clinton followed Edrich, and since he joined Glamorgan Butcher and Hugh Morris have developed a productive partnership which has yielded 4,845 runs at an average of 56.00, including eighteen century stands.

Readers of the coaching manual will not find many faults with Butcher's technique. He is well balanced, the weight evenly distributed on either foot enabling him to launch into a half-volley from the quicker bowlers or position himself for the hook and cut. Most batsmen of small stature, and most left-handers, favour the latter, and Butcher's trademark is the slash past gully. While it sometimes gets him out, it also brings him lots of runs, and he revelled in the stroke last summer on flat pitches from which the ball rarely deviated. An abiding memory was Mike Gatting's field-placing when Butcher was batting at Lord's with a short Tavern boundary on his off side. There were two gullies slightly backward of square, with a third fielder in front and another posted ten yards deeper. Butcher relished the challenge and followed his century in the NatWest game several days earlier with fifties in the Championship and Sunday League matches.

Although Butcher's strokeplay is characterised by an attacking approach, he is always prepared to graft when the occasion demands. In 1980 he scored 107 before lunch for Surrey at The Oval, ironically against Glamorgan; nine years later, on the same ground, he frustrated his former county with a superb defensive innings of 88 not out that occupied 84 overs. On a pitch which provided exaggerated bounce and turn on the last day, he showed unwavering patience and concentration, denying himself any liberties and saving the game for his adopted county. It is this tough competitiveness, allied to his professionalism and sportsmanship, which has always endeared him to his fellow-players. In addition to these qualities, he has shown that he possesses a shrewd cricket brain and the ability to be an inspiring leader. – Edward Bevan.

MIKE ATHERTON

It is quite possible that Mike Atherton would not yet have played Test cricket had Mike Gatting not taken a group of fellow-dissidents to South Africa in the winter of 1989-90. The announcement of a party which included eight players who had taken part in the 1989 series against Australia came during the Old Trafford Test. There were two Tests against Australia to go, and one of the new recruits, for the game at Trent Bridge, was Atherton, then 21 years old and having just completed his third and final year at Cambridge. His début was the sort of which nightmares are made – out second ball to the sixth ball of the match. Atherton's reaction was to respond with, "It bothered other people more than me. I hadn't suddenly become a bad player with one duck." He was top scorer in the second innings with 47, scored 12 and 14 in the final Test, and missed out on the tour of West Indies.

There was talk of protecting him, putting him in cotton wool, and he finished up instead with the gentler pleasures of Zimbabwean bowling. He was disappointed: he did not want to be protected, and hoped he had been omitted on the simple grounds of other players being better. But Zimbabwe helped his development, which continued in England in 1990 when he played in all six Tests and scored 735 runs in eleven innings, with hundreds at Trent Bridge, against New Zealand, and Old Trafford, against India, where he joined Geoff Pullar as the only Lancastrians to score centuries for England on their home ground. This was Atherton's first season as a full-time professional after three years split between Cambridge and Lancashire, and he responded with a total of 1,924 runs in first-class cricket for an average of 71.25.

MICHAEL ANDREW ATHERTON was born on March 23, 1968, a Mancunian like two of Lancashire's greatest players, Archie MacLaren and Brian Statham. He learned his cricket with Woodhouses, the Lancashire and Cheshire League club where his father also played. He was at Manchester Grammar School for seven years and his batting blossomed to take him into the Lancashire Schools', English Public Schools' and English Schools' teams. David Moss, his cricket mentor at Manchester Grammar School, recalled seeing Atherton play cricket at the age of nine and hoping he would pass his entrance examination so that the school would also benefit from his batting talent.

He captained the first team for three years, starting when he was fifteen, and for a time he, Mark Crawley and Gary Yates, all of whom played for Lancashire last year, were the first three in the batting order. Leadership qualities developed, and Mike went on to captain English Schools, Lancashire Federation and Young England – in Sri Lanka and Australia, where he had charge of such rising talent as Martin Bicknell, Mark Alleyne, Warren Hegg, Nasser Hussain, Chris Lewis, Mark Ramprakash, and Peter Martin.

Atherton went to Cambridge in 1987 and made his first-class début in a weak University side which sank to 20 for seven against a strong Essex team bristling with such bowling abilities as those of Neil Foster, John Lever, Hugh Page, Geoff Miller and John Childs. The team also included Graham Gooch and Keith Fletcher, who were later to play important parts in Atherton's progress. Batting at No. 3, he scored 73 not out in a total of 135 in the first innings and 33 out of 71 in the second. His first century was not far behind. In his fifth match, opening the innings, Atherton carried his bat for 109 not out in a total of 185 against Derbyshire, an innings he looks back on with pleasure. He also opened the batting in the University Match at Lord's and scored 7 and 0 in the drawn game. Mark Crawley, on the other hand, scored 140 for Oxford.

The second half of the season belonged to Lancashire, a pattern he was to follow in his three years at Cambridge. There was a two-week gap in Championship fixtures, so he went into the second team and scored 110 in the match against Somerset at Taunton. His first-team début came at Southport on July 22, 1987, and after Warwickshire had been bowled out for 116 on a soft, drying pitch, he scored 53 in 61 overs and shared in a stand of 108 with Fairbrother, helping Lancashire to a ten-wicket win in two days. He had come to stay, and he played important parts in Lancashire's run of six wins at the end of the season which almost swept them to the Championship. With 602 runs in eleven games for Lancashire to add to his 411 for Cambridge, he sneaked past 1,000 runs in his first season in first-class cricket.

For those of us witnessing him for the first time, it was not just his class which shone through; it was the temperament, his ability to adjust to any situation and play accordingly. Atherton captained Cambridge in his next two years and was also captain of Combined Universities, who beat Surrey and the mighty Worcestershire in the qualifying stage of the 1989 Benson and Hedges Cup before losing by 3 runs to Somerset in the quarter-finals. His best summer at Cambridge was in 1988, when he scored two hundreds in a total of 665 runs. Yet Lancashire, with a rare show of misjudgement, refused to play him immediately he returned to Old Trafford, ignoring him for three Championship matches. His reaction was to score two centuries in the eight matches left to him and to finish top of the county's averages.

However, 1990 was to be the true testing time: a full, demanding season with Lancashire, not just in Championship cricket but in limited-overs cricket, too. He started the Championship season with scores of 50, 191, 93 and 51, the one-day matches with 63, 44, 5, 69 not out and 76 not out, and by the end of May he had scored 856 runs in all competitions. Moreover, that did not include a century denied him in a washed-out Benson and Hedges Cup game with Hampshire. The recall to Test cricket was a near formality, although now it was as opener to leave the position of No. 3 available for Graeme Hick in 1991. Atherton showed his taste for the game at its highest level with innings of 151, 0, 54, 82 and 70 against New Zealand; 8, 72, 131, 74, 7 and 86 against India; a grand total of 735 runs and an average of 66.81. Not bad for starters. – Brian Bearshaw.

DESMOND HAYNES

The death of Wilf Slack in January 1989 left a void in the Middlesex team, both on and off the field. The acquisition of the West Indian opening batsman, Desmond Haynes, for the 1989 season undoubtedly filled the on-field vacancy, and it quickly became apparent that he was the ideal man to have in the dressing-room as well.

During 1989, Middlesex had a system of fines for such things as late arrival, or not wearing a blazer or tie, with John Emburey in charge of levying the fines. However, when he was away on Test-match duty –

Middlesex at the time were playing two Championship matches at Uxbridge – Haynes took it upon himself to bring to book his colleagues' misdemeanours. He did so with relish. He would be seen, lurking behind a pillar in the Uxbridge pavilion, waiting to leap out and surprise some unsuspecting young cricketer with the news that he owed a pound or two to the kitty.

This made it obvious that he was very much a part of the team, and he made no secret of the fact that his assimilation was made easier because of the West Indian members of the Middlesex side, most of whom he had met at some stage of his career. Emburey and Mike Gatting, of course, had been international opponents. He also found his introduction to county cricket made easier by virtue of the fact that the county was in the running for honours throughout the season. He thought that it would not have been quite so enjoyable playing for a county that was not in contention for at least one of the season's titles.

That first season was a good, rather than outstanding, one for Haynes. He scored 1,446 first-class runs at an average of just over 45, and his three centuries included the first double-century of his career – 206 not out against Kent at Uxbridge. In the limited-overs competitions, he made a fine start, winning the Gold Award in a Benson and Hedges group match against Surrey on his début for the county. In addition, he was Man of the Match on his first appearance in the NatWest Bank Trophy, scoring 83 against Durham at Darlington. He failed to score in the second round of the NatWest, against Nottinghamshire at Uxbridge, but this was only one of five ducks in seven innings which followed the award of his county cap. He returned to form with 88 in the quarter-finals, 80 in the semi-finals and 50 in the final. The Sunday game was not quite so much to his liking and he passed 50 only twice in ten games.

His avowed intention, at the end of 1989, was to score 2,000 first-class runs for Middlesex in 1990. He achieved that target with plenty to spare in what was an outstanding season. It culminated in Middlesex winning the County Championship and his being named both the Britannic Assurance and Nixdorf Middlesex Player of the Year.

DESMOND LEO HAYNES was born in the Holders Hill district of Barbados on February 15, 1956, the eldest of three brothers. There was no cricket-playing tradition in his family but, "Everyone in the area played cricket, and it's still very strong in high schools in the West Indies". He played in the Barbados Under-15 schools competition and made his first-class début for Barbados in January 1977. The following season, against Australia, came his first Test appearance for West Indies, and he has represented them nearly 100 times in Tests, as well as appearing in more than 170 limited-overs internationals. His opening partnership with Gordon Greenidge has left all others in its wake, and with Haynes showing no lessening of his skills or his enthusiasm in his mid-30s, there seems no reason why his international career should not continue for some years. Last winter, in the absence of Viv Richards, he captained West Indies in Pakistan and drew favourable comments for the way he led the side on a difficult tour.

He was one of many batsmen to take full advantage of last year's conditions, which were so much in favour of the bat, but he is realistic enough to accept that the ideal is somewhere between 1989 and 1990 in terms of which ball should be used in English cricket. He certainly started 1990 with a bang. Barely off the plane, he scored 107 not out on the first Sunday of the season at Old Trafford, won Gold Awards in the first two Benson and Hedges matches (80 against Minor Counties and 131 at Hove), and also hit 116 in the second innings of Middlesex's opening Championship match, against Essex at Lord's. Before the end of April, he had scored 358 runs in five innings in the three competitions. He was to score five more half-centuries in the Refuge Assurance League and one more in the Cup, 75 not out and 149 not out in the NatWest Trophy and, most important for Middlesex, 2,036 Championship runs at an average of 63.62. Besides two hundreds in the match against the New Zealanders at Lord's, he hit six Championship hundreds, two of them, against Essex and Sussex, unbeaten double-centuries. He passed 50 on a further seven occasions and was consistency itself.

But it was not just the runs he scored, it was the way in which he scored them. Never slowly and always most attractively, without a slog in sight. His cover driving, a combination of timing and barely evident power, remained in the mind's eye as a particular adornment of his batting. He was a most enthusiastic fielder and even took a couple of Championship wickets, as well as providing several useful spells of bowling in the limited-overs game.

He wished he had played county cricket some years ago. "I would have liked to have come to it a bit earlier, but most counties are looking for an overseas fast bowler rather than a batsman. Gordon [Greenidge] was a different case. He grew up over here and he was also playing at a time when counties could use more overseas players."

Desmond Haynes has a high regard for his Middlesex team-mates. "There is a very good attitude, particularly on the part of the younger players such as Mark Ramprakash and Mike Roseberry. Keith Brown doesn't get the credit he deserves, and I would single him out for special mention. He is reliable, difficult to get out and always seems to be able to play the right sort of innings for the situation." His Middlesex colleagues all spoke in glowing terms of their West Indian opening batsman, not only with regard to the runs he scored, but to his readiness to offer help and advice without having to be asked. Yet at the end of last season there was some doubt as to whether the Middlesex committee would offer him a new contract for 1992, after the West Indies tour in 1991. Ask any Middlesex supporter, however, and you would get an unhesitating vote of confidence in Desmond Haynes, as well as the fervent hope that he would be playing for the county once again. – Norman de Mesquita.

MARK WAUGH

Australian cricket has two nurseries for its finest young players. One is in the verdant grounds of Adelaide's glorious Oval, where the Australian Cricket Academy prepares a balanced squad of fourteen teenage prospects every year. The other is 12,000 miles away, in a country small enough to slip into Australia's back pocket, but where the opportunities for cricketers are big: England, of course, where the beer is warm, the climate cold and the Poms live.

Despite these drawbacks, Allan Border, Australia's captain, knows the value to a young cricketer's education of English cricket, with its diversity of players, pitches and pubs (for what would the game be without the bar-room analyst?). Border himself spent a few years enjoying all three with Essex, and his Australian team has benefited from the skills of such as Steve Waugh and Terry Alderman, both of them graduates of the County Championship.

But while Border may have a deep affection for Essex, there was also some self-interest in the telephone call he made to Lancashire late in the summer of 1988. An investment for the future, as it were. Border was soon to leave England for training camp Down Under, prior to Australia's tour to Pakistan, and he was wondering if Mark Waugh would like to fill in at Essex for him for the rest of the season. Waugh, playing in Bolton League cricket, could hardly believe the conversation. You had to be either an established Test cricketer or a South African to get one of the plum jobs as an overseas professional at a county club. At 23, he was neither.

Waugh took the chance and did well. Well enough to be back in 1989 to watch with a mixture of anticipation and excitement as brother Steve, "A.B." and his Australian mates conquered England in the Ashes series. It was becoming a formidable batting line-up to break into. Back home, however, he topped the Sheffield Shield averages with New South Wales and forced Steve out of the Australian one-day side. "One of us had to go, and brotherly love stops short when it comes to playing for your country." Last summer he returned to Chelmsford to complete his education in readiness for the call-up to Test cricket.

He scored 2,072 first-class runs at an average of 76.74 which, even in a summer of indulgence for batsmen, showed him to be a performer of the highest calibre. He is the type who can have 30 on the board without the bowlers realising he has his pads strapped on. Undemonstrative, compact and still at the crease, he works the ball rather than crashing it about. And being a high-quality cricketer, he could supplement his batting with some useful medium-pace bowling and safe, adaptable fielding. Twice he improved on his highest score, first with 204 against Gloucestershire at Ilford and then with an unbeaten 207 against Yorkshire at Middlesbrough two months later. He also turned in career-best bowling figures of five for 37 against Northamptonshire late in the season and was voted Player of the Year by Essex supporters accustomed to fine batsmen from overseas.

What gave Waugh the greatest pleasure were his innings against the best bowlers in the world. His double-hundred against Gloucestershire came off an attack including Courtney Walsh; he scored 126 against Derbyshire and Ian Bishop, 125 against Hampshire and Malcolm Marshall, a one-day century against Lancashire and Wasim Akram, and 79 not out against Surrey's Pakistan Test discovery, Waqar Younis. "I'm confident I can handle it now", he said, explaining the satisfaction those scores had given him. "You never know as you progress in cricket how you will cope with the next step up. I realise that facing one West Indian quick at Ilford or Colchester may be different from facing four in Kingston, but the whole season has helped my confidence. I've faced those guys and survived. I feel ready for the next step when – if – it comes."

MARK EDWARD WAUGH was born in the Sydney suburb of Canterbury on June 2, 1965 a few moments after Steve went out to bat first for Rodger and Beverley Waugh. Next in the order was Dean, now 22 and following in Mark's footsteps in the Bolton League. At No. 4 is Danny, a sixteen-year-old in Sydney grade cricket: his older brothers think he is the best yet. The four Waugh boys had little option but be good at sport in a country which thrives on the outdoor life, has the ideal climate, and supplies its youth with excellent and cheap facilities. They also descend from a lineage rich in ball skills. One grandfather played rugby league for New South Wales Country; father Rodger once beat Tony Roche to win the New South Wales under-14 tennis title, and a few years later he picked up a national doubles title; mother Bev was a highly regarded tennis player, winning state and national titles as a teenager and later becoming a leading squash player in the state.

The Waugh twins were naturally good at soccer, tennis and cricket. Mark was playing Sheffield Shield cricket by twenty, a season later than Steve, but even then the brothers' careers were no longer running parallel. Already Steve was forging ahead into the Australian Test side, and after he had shown the benefits of county cricket at Somerset, Mark followed him to England to learn. At Essex it did not take long for the dressing-room wit to devise a nickname for the newcomer: "Afghan". Afghanistan, the forgotten war – simple when you know how. Relaxed and open, whereas Steve can be wary and cool, Mark soon found the company of Pringle, Hardie and Lilley as stimulating as the real ale he was being introduced to by a seriously social Essex side.

In this funny game, all cricketers have their little quirks, and Mark Waugh, for all his boy-next-door traits, has a ritual which is among the odder ones in the game. Like a Battle of Britain fighter pilot who painted swastikas outside his cockpit for every enemy aircraft downed, Waugh draws little matchstick men on his thigh pad for every century scored, with the name of the opponents below. Last summer another nine joined the ranks, and at that rate he may soon have enough for an army. – Colin Bateman.

LANCASHIRE'S REVIVAL – IS IT ENOUGH?

By MICHAEL KENNEDY

If Lancashire cricket is a religion for some of its supporters, we experience the doubts as well as the certainties of belief. Thanks to Cardus's imaginative prose, the giants of the distant past still have vivid life. We can almost delude ourselves that we saw MacLaren, Brearley, Spooner, J. T. Tyldesley, Johnny Briggs and Cecil Parkin. I did see Paynter and Washbrook before the war and have the brightest memories of the unfulfilled genius of Norman Oldfield, on the verge of greatness when war robbed him of six years, after which he took umbrage over pay and left Old Trafford (a mistake, as he later admitted).

Memories of watching Lancashire in the 45 seasons since the war are a mixture of frustration and elation: the former because of the maladroit administration which, for twenty years, sabotaged the efforts of several not always very wisely selected captains; the latter because of the pleasures afforded by such players as Washbrook, Statham, Clive Lloyd, Pullar, Tattersall, Hayes (the biggest "if only" of them all), Jack Simmons, the untiring Dick Pollard, Bond and Abrahams. So much talent and yet, until the advent of the one-day competitions, so little to show for it.

Thus, for someone born within a mile of the county cricket ground, the revival of Lancashire's fortunes under the captaincy of David Hughes has lifted the heart, especially as it has occurred during the presidency of Cyril Washbrook, illustrious link between the Lancashire of pre-1939 and the post-war side. Since Hughes was appointed captain at the end of 1986, Lancashire have been second, ninth, fourth and sixth in the County Championship, won the NatWest Bank Trophy and the Benson and Hedges Cup in the same season, 1990, and have been Refuge Assurance League champions in 1989 and runners-up in 1990; they were the first winners of the Refuge Assurance Cup in 1988. It is an impressive record, and all the more impressive when one recalls Lancashire's dismal eleven years in the County Championship from 1976 to 1986 when the highest they finished was twelfth.

If ever proof was needed that an inspired captain can re-motivate a team that has lost its bearings and confidence, then it was provided by Hughes in 1987, just as it was by Mike Brearley for England in 1981. The two cases are remarkably similar, since many people would have argued that neither was worth his place in the side on playing ability alone. Yet look what happened! Hughes was a legend because of the 1971 Gillette Cup semi-final against Gloucestershire at Old Trafford, when he struck Mortimore for 24 in an over in the gathering darkness of a late-July evening, but during the 1980s his form slipped and he played most of his cricket in the Second Eleven. In 1986 he played for the first team in only three one-day matches and was ready to resign, but delayed sending in his letter until he had captained Lancashire's second team to victory in the Second Eleven Championship. Lancashire finished 53 points ahead of the runners-up, Warwickshire, and were undefeated. Hughes's part in the team's success was considerable: he had a batting average of 41.44, scoring 746 runs with a top score of 119 not out; he was second in the bowling averages, with 46 wickets at an average of 15.43. Lancashire's senior side had a wretched Championship season in 1986, but reached the NatWest Trophy final, only to be defeated by Sussex. A few days later, Jack Bond and Peter Lever, manager and coach respectively, were dismissed. Two months later Clive Lloyd was replaced as captain by the 39-year-old Hughes, to general Red Rose astonishment.

But the committee which made these changes was itself under fire, and in February 1987 its chairman since 1969, Cedric Rhoades, was compelled to resign. He was replaced by a former player, Bob Bennett; and Alan Ormrod, who had joined Lancashire in 1984 after more than twenty years with Worcestershire and was Hughes's *aide-de-camp* in the Second Eleven triumph of 1986, became coach/manager. The Bennett-Hughes-Ormrod triumvirate has converted Lancashire into a team for which a run of success in the 1990s has been predicted by many commentators, not all of them northern in origin.

Hughes's leadership has been compared with that of the best amateur captains from between the wars. There is no doubt who is the boss when he is on the field, and his 100 per cent commitment to the game and to Lancashire has communicated itself to the other players, who now take the field with a spring in their step. The metamorphosis in 1987 will remain a glorious page in Lancashire's annals: the dejected side which had been fifteenth in the table the previous season now ended in second place, failing only at the last moment to draw level with Nottinghamshire by not gaining the full eight bonus points against Essex at Chelmsford. The 1988 season was disappointing by comparison, but the sense of buoyancy was maintained, and a new international star joined the side in Wasim Akram of Pakistan. After the retirement in 1986 of the great Clive Lloyd, Lancashire had lacked a glamorous figure of this stature and high hopes were built on Wasim.

The 1988 side was of special appeal, for it contained a piquant mixture of the old guard with the new. Hughes and the irrepressible Jack Simmons were survivors from the Lancashire team of the 1970s which, under the captaincy first of Bond and then of David Lloyd, twice finished third in the Championship, won the Gillette Cup three years running and again in 1975, and were regarded as the "one-day kings". The names of Barry Wood, Harry Pilling, Farokh Engineer, Frank Hayes, Peter Lee, Peter Lever and Ken Shuttleworth were a litany for Lancashire schoolboys as those of the pre-1939 players were for my generation.

Experience was also brought to the 1988 side by the batsmen, Graeme Fowler, Gehan Mendis and Trevor Jesty, and the diligent seam bowler, Paul Allott. They represented the "middle generation", as it were. The players of the future were the Cambridge University captain, Michael Atherton, who headed the batting averages although he played only fourteen innings (he had scored 602 runs for the county in 1987); Neil Fairbrother, a member of the side since 1982 and capped for England in 1987; the all-rounder, Mike Watkinson, another 1982 débutant; and the wicket-keeper, Warren Hegg, a more than useful batsman. In 1989 Phillip DeFreitas transferred to Lancashire from Leicestershire and David Lloyd's son, Graham, scored three centuries in essentially his first first-class season, drawing, it is said, from David Hughes the characteristically dry comment: "Good innings, lad. I don't know who coached you, but it can't have been your father!"

The 1990 season, still fresh in memory, belonged above all to Fairbrother. His aggressive batting for Lancashire, heading the county first-class averages with 1,681 runs at 80.04, reminded older spectators of another little left-hander, Eddie Paynter, and made all the more inexplicable his failure in the

Test matches. The inevitable question was asked: does he lack the temperament for the big occasion? One is hesitant to be dogmatic, remembering the early Test careers of W. J. Edrich, Dennis Amiss and Mike Gatting. Yet one must doubt if he will receive many more chances, simply because there is a long queue of batsmen good enough to be picked for England, and the pressure to succeed means a low threshold of tolerance of failure. But about Atherton's temperament, there can be no doubt whatsoever; and if John Crawley remains with Lancashire (his elder brother, Mark, having already sadly refused the offer of a three-year contract), the batting strength should be formidable a season or two hence.

However high we Lancastrians throw our hats in the air over the team's successes last season, we are not really satisfied – nor, I am sure, is David Hughes – by one-day success. Lancashire have not won the County Championship outright since 1934, when Ernest Tyldesley scored 2,487 runs and Iddon more than 2,000, Len Hopwood did the double, and Frank Booth took 101 wickets. Their golden period was the five years from 1926 to 1930, when they won the Championship four times (three in succession) and were runners-up in 1929. Lancashire's batting side was strong in those years, with Harry Makepeace, Ernest Tyldesley, Charlie Hallows and Frank Watson, but they won because of their bowling, spearheaded by the wonderful Australian fast bowler, E. A. McDonald, who (in all matches) took 182 wickets in 1925, 175 in 1926, 150 in 1927 (a wet summer, so he turned to spin), 190 in 1928, 142 in 1929 and 108 in 1930. In those years, the Championship comprised up to 30 matches. McDonald was complemented by Dick Tyldesley, with Iddon, Hopwood and Sibbles in support – a combination of fast bowling, flight and spin. Yet the side was considered to play unattractive cricket, and in 1930 no less a partisan than Neville Cardus wrote that he hoped Gloucestershire would win the title!

In Lancashire's Championship hat-trick year, 1928, a total of 139 players scored 414 centuries. Such a batsmen's bonanza did not recur until last year, when 156 players scored 428 hundreds. But in 1928 Kent's "Tich" Freeman, a spin bowler, took 300 wickets and many bowlers passed the 100 wickets mark. In 1990 not one bowler in the land took 100 wickets; and whereas Atherton, Fairbrother and Mendis all averaged more than 50 with the bat, the most wickets taken for Lancashire were 47 by Watkinson at a cost of 33.57. DeFreitas's 34 wickets cost him 37.20 apiece and Wasim's 16 were even more expensive.

If Lancashire are to win the Championship, they must find bowlers who can be as consistent as McDonald and Tyldesley – and, of course, as Brian Statham was throughout his career from 1950 to 1968. Three attempts, in the persons of Croft, Holding and Patterson, to find a contemporary equivalent to McDonald have misfired on the benign Old Trafford post-war wicket. No successor to Statham for accuracy or silken grace has arisen. Wasim Akram and DeFreitas have only fitfully produced the form expected of them. Allott is in the second half of his career. Watkinson and Atherton offer the kind of variety that is needed, but a venomous strike bowler – preferably home-grown, like Statham – is an urgent requirement. Until he is found, no Lancashire supporter can be confident that the recent achievements of the Hughes-Ormrod partnership will be rewarded with the only accolade that matters – to be county champions.

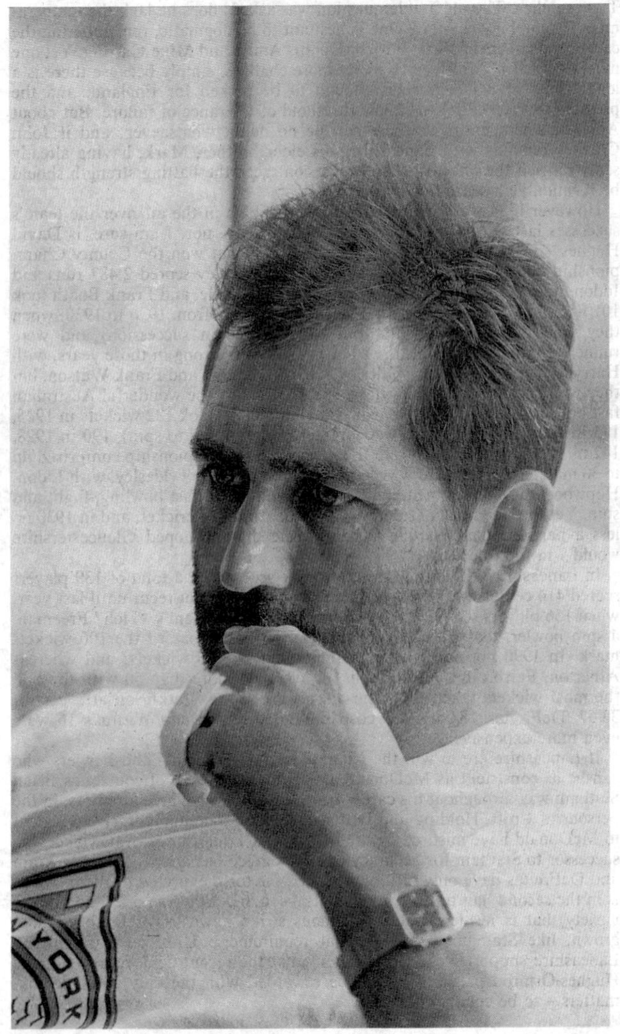

[Patrick Eagar

A GENUINELY GREAT CRICKETER

AN ASSESSMENT OF GRAHAM GOOCH

By SIMON BARNES

Ian Botham has, in his time, managed to make a fair amount of trouble for himself. But not even Botham managed to get himself banned from Test cricket for three years, or made himself the hate-focus of an international political campaign, or caused an entire tour to be cancelled. Graham Gooch has done all those things. How extraordinary then, how absolutely extraordinary, to consider that this is the man we must begin to think of as the most important cricketer of his generation, and the most effective captain of England since Mike Brearley.

Yes, Gooch said famously, we've got the makings of a goodish side. The point is that this was not an understatement: it was an exact assessment of the facts. Gooch's achievement has been to maximise the resources of that goodish side. It has been a triumph of nothing less than leadership, and this from a man who resigned as captain of Essex because captaincy was affecting his form.

It is clear that captaincy affected his form as captain of England in the summer of 1990. To be accurate, captaincy inspired him. It took him to the enormous achievement of his innings of 333 against India at Lord's, and his breaking of Sir Donald Bradman's record for Test runs scored in an English summer.

Gooch had always been a man in search of greatness; he achieved that immodest aim last summer. He achieved greatness as a player – at the age of 37. Such preposterous scores are normally for younger men. The fitness, the reflexes, the ability to concentrate for session after session: these are things that the years take away from you. But they have not taken them from Gooch. Gooch is a fanatic for mere fitness, a passionate lover of work for its own sake, a true glutton for austerity. Furthermore, he has achieved something quite close to greatness as a leader. Before he was given the captaincy, England's cricket had become the material of cheap jokes: material the more discriminating joke-crackers avoided. A quip about England's defeats was simply too obvious, too hoary a joke.

The joke reached its apex in 1988, "the summer of the five captains". This was perhaps the most inept display of man-management in the history of sport; a summer in which Gatting, Emburey, Cowdrey, Gooch himself and Pringle all led England in the field, four of them as official appointees. When Gooch was asked to lead England in India, the tour was promptly cancelled because of Gooch's South African connections. Disaster followed disaster. After the West Indian hammering and the Indian débâcle, there came another traumatic summer. The opponents were Australia. England, captained now by Gower, were not only beaten but trampled on. For Gooch, as for Gower, the summer was a personal disaster. There was scarcely a scoreboard, it seemed, that did not carry details of Gooch lbw b Alderman, for not a lot. Gooch volunteered to stand down, to make room for fresh blood, and his offer was accepted. Perhaps that one incident summed up his summer: a personal nadir, a personal black hole. For some cricketers it would have been a disaster of career-ending proportions. Instead, Gooch used it as a springboard into greatness.

There is a case for saying that Headingley 1981 is one of the greatest disasters to have hit England's cricket. Certainly, it lunged into a pattern of self-destructiveness as the echoes of that extraordinary year died away. The England team became based around an Inner Ring, with Botham at its heart: Botham, self-justified by his prodigious feats during that unforgettable summer. To be accepted, you had to hate the press, hate practice, enjoy a few beers and what have you, and generally be one hell of a good ol' boy. Like all cliques, the England clique was defined by exclusion. Nothing could be more destructive to team spirit than a team within a team, but that was the situation in the England camp for years. It was the same at Somerset. It was the presence of an Inner Ring which created the furore in which Vivian Richards and Joel Garner were not offered new contracts, and Botham himself resigned. It needed the right man at the right time to destroy this unpleasant and destructive atmosphere in the England team. The old members of the Inner Ring were being lost to time, one by one. It needed someone to indicate that it was gone forever; that this was a new start, a new way forward. This was Gooch's moment, and he accepted it avidly.

It happened in India in the autumn of 1989. India had rejected an England team under Gooch's captaincy a year before. Now they accepted one. The Test-playing countries had at last come to an agreement about players with South African histories. Gooch was officially forgiven. The way was clear for the remaking of the England cricket team. The tour itself, a four-week trip for the Nehru Cup, a six-nation one-day tournament, was thought by all wise critics to be a complete waste of time. The widely used *mot juste* for the competition was "spurious". It was not spurious at all for Gooch.

It was on a practice ground in Delhi that one became aware of strong forces at work. The weather was hot, but the pace of the practice was still hotter. It was all sweat and Gatorade: everyone was competing as to who sweated the most. Micky Stewart, the manager, was like a man come into his own, taking fielding practice with all the camp affectations of a sergeant-major. It looked as if Stewart was having his way at last, but he was not. Gooch was. The two of them plainly saw eye to eye; not something that had always been the case with Stewart and his captains. They were dubbed "the Cockney Mafia" almost within hours.

The prevailing ethic of the old Inner Ring was that if you are as massively talented as us, you don't have to work as hard as ordinary players. Gooch has always believed that the difference between ordinariness and excellence lies in hard work. And if work will make that difference, then it is folly to be idle. He does not seek mindless conformity from his players. More than most team sports, cricket requires a motley bunch of assorted shapes, sizes, temperaments, talents and social backgrounds. What Gooch has managed is to inspire his own motley bunch with the same desire to work to a common goal: what is more, to work in the belief that the goal is attainable.

That has been his miracle. The results in the West Indies in the early months of 1990 did not surprise him. It was only everybody else who was surprised by the win and the near-win under his captaincy. Gooch would, I think, have escaped from the series on level terms at worst, had it not been for the injuries to himself and to Angus Fraser. Instead, England lost 2-1. The two 1-0 wins in the following summer's three-Test series against New

Zealand and India were consolidation. Suddenly, England had acquired the habit of winning Test matches. That was miracle enough to be going on with.

The central experience of Gooch's professional life was his trip to South Africa in 1982. He went to play on that "rebel" tour in the hopelessly naïve belief that he would not receive any form of punishment. He was made captain of the rebel team, though not as a recognition of any leading part in the plotting and deception involved in the setting-up of this tour: it was more an expression of the dressing-room's feelings about having Geoffrey Boycott as captain. But the responsibilities of the captaincy were not restricted to cricketing decisions. Gooch did not expect that. The captaincy made Gooch the spokesman of the tour. "Gooch's men" and "Gooch's rebel tour" were phrases that tripped nicely off page and microphone. Gooch himself had to face cameras and interviews: this was, as far as the Republic was concerned, a major public relations exercise. These were muddy waters, and Gooch hid behind his role of professional sportsman. "We're just here to play cricket, we're just professional cricketers." Would that life were as simple.

Gooch and his fellow-rebels were banned from Test cricket for three years. I am sure he still feels that this was desperately unjust; I suspect that even now, he finds this "wrong" an inspiration. For whereas many of his colleagues on that South African venture were well-known players slightly over the hill, Gooch was in his prime. His adventures robbed him of three years in which he might have established himself as the greatest batsman of his generation. Instead, he played for Essex and Western Province. Still, his career has been characterised as much by its troughs as by its peaks. He began his Test career with a pair in 1975; he chose not to tour Australia in 1986-87 because his wife, Brenda, was pregnant with twins; and Terry Alderman has turned up to blight his life more than once or twice. He even began his *annus mirabilis* of 1990 with a "king duck" against New Zealand.

Perhaps Gooch's greatest asset of all has been his ability to give equal treatment to Kipling's twin imposters, Triumph and Disaster. He remains consistent in everything in his life except shaving. His capricious changes from a clean shave, Zapata moustache, designer stubble or full beard have been the nearest he has come to a change of facial expression in fifteen years. But he is not an easy person. He does not forget those who, he believes, have done wrong by him. He has no appreciation of the necessary symbiosis of professional sport and mass media. His achievement in cutting down the number of compulsory captain's press conferences during a home Test from three to one was regarded as a major coup.

The chairman of the England selectors, Ted Dexter, when in his journalistic avatar, famously described Gooch as having the charisma of a wet fish. This has been thrown back at Dexter times without number, but it is, in fact, a fair remark – from a media person. All the same, Gooch cannot have achieved his success without great gifts of communication. It just so happens that these gifts are not apparent to those outside the charmed circle of his team. Nor does his team find Gooch's gifts readily communicable to the outside world. The nearest anyone ever gets to an explanation is to say that he leads "by example". But this means little. Plenty of leaders have worked themselves silly while inspiring only contempt. Gooch simply has, at a point that must be alarmingly close to the end of his cricketing life, come into his own. He has reconstructed and re-inspired the England cricket team: and it seems that he has done a similar job on himself. Yet he remains as hostile to outsiders as ever, and the team is probably even less approachable now than it was in Botham's time. There is still an Inner Ring: the difference is that Gooch appears to have made everyone in the team a member of it.

Right from the first moment that he took charge in Delhi, Gooch made it clear that he wanted to be judged only by results. In those terms, he has established himself as a genuinely great cricketer. His achievement in remaking the England team might yet be even more significant, and in this much larger area he again bears the stamp of incipient greatness.

G. A. GOOCH – TEST CAREER

		T	*I*	*NO*	*R*	*HI*	*100s*	*50s*	*Avge*	*Ct*
1975	v Australia	2	4	0	37	31	0	0	9.25	2
1978	v Pakistan	2	2	0	74	54	0	1	37.00	2
1978	v New Zealand	3	5	2	190	91*	0	2	63.33	1
1978-79	v Australia	6	11	0	246	74	0	1	22.36	9
1979	v India	4	5	0	207	83	0	2	41.40	6
1979-80	v Australia	2	4	0	172	99	0	2	43.00	1
	v India	1	2	1	57	49*	0	0	57.00	1
1980	v West Indies	5	10	0	394	123	1	2	39.40	5
	v Australia	1	2	0	24	16	0	0	12.00	0
1980-81	v West Indies	4	8	0	460	153	2	1	57.50	3
1981	v Australia	5	10	0	139	44	0	0	13.90	1
1981-82	v India	6	10	1	487	127	1	4	54.11	4
	v Sri Lanka	1	2	0	53	31	0	0	26.50	1
1985	v Australia	6	9	0	487	196	1	2	54.11	4
1985-86	v West Indies	5	10	0	276	53	0	4	27.60	6
1986	v India	3	6	0	175	114	1	0	29.16	5
	v New Zealand	3	5	0	268	183	1	0	53.60	6
1987-88	v Pakistan	3	6	0	225	93	0	2	37.50	3
1988	v West Indies	5	10	0	459	146	1	3	45.90	6
	v Sri Lanka	1	2	0	111	75	0	1	55.50	3
1989	v Australia	5	9	0	183	68	0	2	20.33	4
1989-90	v West Indies	2	4	1	128	84	0	1	42.66	2
1990	v New Zealand	3	5	0	306	154	1	1	61.20	3
	v India	3	6	0	752	333	3	2	125.33	4
		81	147	5	5,910	333	12	33	41.61	82

* *Signifies not out.*

Highest innings: 333 v India at Lord's, 1990.

Bowling: G. A. Gooch has taken 15 wickets for 717 runs (1,803 balls) at an average of 47.80. His best bowling figures are 2-12 v India at Delhi, 1981-82.

Note: In the 1990 calendar year, G. A. Gooch scored 1,264 runs (average 79.00) from seventeen innings in nine Test matches.

SUMMARY v EACH COUNTRY

	T	*I*	*NO*	*R*	*HI*	*100s*	*50s*	*Avge*	*Ct*
v Australia	27	49	0	1,288	196	1	7	26.28	21
v West Indies	21	42	1	1,717	153	4	11	41.87	22
v India	17	29	2	1,678	333	5	8	62.14	20
v New Zealand	9	15	2	764	183	2	3	58.76	10
v Pakistan	5	8	0	299	93	0	3	37.37	5
v Sri Lanka	2	4	0	164	75	0	1	41.00	4
	81	147	5	5,910	333	12	33	41.61	82

G. A. GOOCH – FIRST-CLASS CAREER

	M	I	NO	R	HI	100s	50s	Avge	Ct
1973	1	1	0	18	18	0	0	18.00	1
1974	15	25	3	637	114*	1	2	28.95	4
1975	24	42	0	1,147	100	1	7	27.30	16
1976	21	34	4	1,273	136	3	6	42.43	17
1977	23	37	6	837	105*	1	5	27.00	11
1978	21	33	3	1,254	129	2	9	41.80	22
1978-79 (Australia)	13	23	1	514	74	0	3	23.36	13
1979	17	25	2	838	109	1	6	36.43	28
1979-80 (Australia)	6	12	2	582	115	1	6	58.20	8
(India)	1	2	1	57	49*	0	0	57.00	1
1980	19	35	5	1,437	205	6	2	47.90	17
1980-81 (West Indies)	7	13	0	777	153	4	1	59.76	4
1981	16	31	0	1,345	164	5	5	43.38	11
1981-82 (India)	11	18	3	867	127	2	6	57.80	9
(Sri Lanka)	2	3	0	100	47	0	0	33.33	1
(South Africa)	4	7	0	396	109	1	3	56.57	6
1982	23	38	1	1,632	149	3	12	44.10	25
1982-83 (South Africa)	9	18	3	597	126	2	1	39.80	11
1983	26	38	1	1,481	174	4	7	40.02	35
1983-84 (South Africa)	7	13	1	615	171	2	1	51.25	5
1984	26	45	7	2,559	227	8	13	67.34	27
1985	21	33	2	2,208	202	7	9	71.22	25
1985-86 (West Indies)	9	18	0	443	53	0	5	24.61	10
1986	19	32	0	1,221	183	3	5	38.15	22
1987	24	41	6	1,361	171	3	7	38.88	20
1987-88 (Pakistan)	3	6	0	225	93	0	2	37.50	3
1988	21	37	1	2,324	275	6	15	64.55	28
1989	18	31	1	1,256	158	3	9	41.86	25
1989-90 (West Indies)	6	11	1	616	239	1	4	61.60	6
1990	18	30	3	2,746	333	12	8	101.70	16
	431	732	57	31,363	333	82	159	46.46	427

* *Signifies not out.*

Highest innings: 333, England v India at Lord's, 1990.

Bowling: G. A. Gooch has taken 213 wickets for 7,339 runs (16,329 balls) at an average of 34.45. His best bowling figures are 7-14, Essex v Worcestershire at Ilford, 1982.

G. A. GOOCH – LIMITED-OVERS CAREER

	M	I	NO	R	HI	100s	50s	Avge
One-day Internationals	85	83	5	3,305	142	8	19	42.37

Highest innings: 142 v Pakistan at Karachi, 1987-88.

	M	I	NO	R	HI	100s	50s	Avge
John Player/Refuge Assurance League	209	206	19	6,324	176	10	40	33.81
Benson and Hedges Cup	87	86	10	3,954	198*	9	28	52.02
Gillette Cup/NatWest Bank Trophy .	39	38	2	1,820	144	5	10	50.55
Nissan Shield (SA)	9	9	0	297	60	0	3	33.00
Benson and Hedges Trophy (SA)	11	11	0	546	106	1	3	49.63

* *Signifies not out.*

Highest innings: 198*, Essex v Sussex at Hove, 1982.

G. A. GOOCH in 1990

	M	*I*	*NO*	*R*	*HI*	*100s*	*50s*	*Avge*
First-class matches								
v New Zealand	3	5	0	306	154	1	1	61.20
v India	3	6	0	752	333	3	2	125.33
Britannic Assurance Championship	11	18	2	1,586	215	7	5	99.12
Other	1	1	1	102	102*	1	0	—
Limited-overs matches								
v New Zealand	2	2	1	167	112*	1	1	167.00
v India	2	2	0	52	45	0	0	26.00
Refuge Assurance League	10	10	0	386	136	1	3	38.60
Benson and Hedges Cup	4	4	1	285	102	1	2	95.00
NatWest Bank Trophy	2	2	1	247	144	2	0	247.00
Others	2	2	0	167	105	1	1	83.50
	40	52	6	4,050	333	18	15	88.04

* *Signifies not out.* *Statistics compiled by Philip Bailey.*

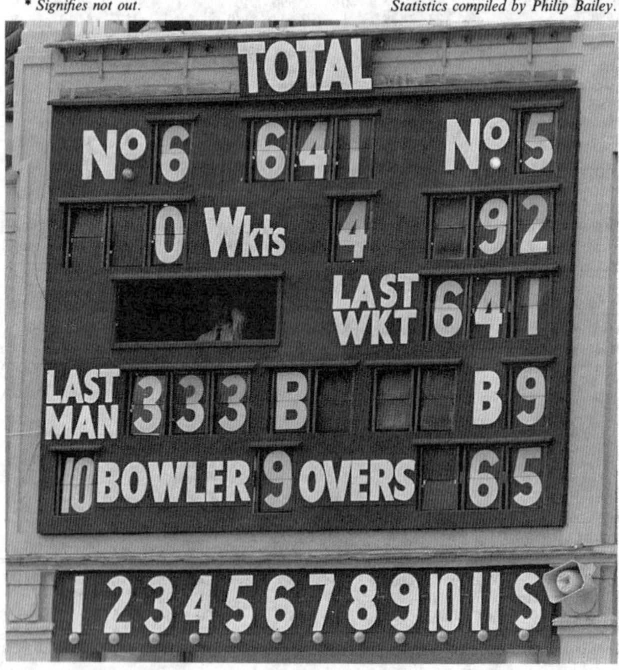

[*Patrick Eagar*

The scoreboard at Lord's following Gooch's dismissal for 333 against India in July 1990.

TEST CRICKETERS

FULL LIST FROM 1877 TO AUGUST 28, 1990

These lists have been compiled on a home and abroad basis, appearances abroad being printed in *italics*.

Abbreviations. E: England. A: Australia. SA: South Africa. WI: West Indies. NZ: New Zealand. In: India. P: Pakistan. SL: Sri Lanka.

All appearances are placed in this order of seniority. Hence, any England cricketer playing against Australia in England has that achievement recorded first and the remainder of his appearances at home (if any) set down before passing to matches abroad. Although the distinction between amateur and professional was abolished in 1963, initials of English professionals before that date are still given in brackets. The figures immediately following each name represent the total number of appearances in *all* Tests.

Where the season embraces two different years, the first year is given; i.e. 1876 indicates 1876-77.

ENGLAND

Number of Test cricketers: 546

Abel (R.) 13: v A 1888 (3) 1896 (3) 1902 (2); *v A 1891 (3); v SA 1888 (2)*
Absolom, C. A. 1: *v A 1878*
Agnew, J. P. 3: v A 1985 (1); v WI 1984 (1); v SL 1984 (1)
Allen (D. A.) 39: v A 1961 (4) 1964 (1); v SA 1960 (2); v WI 1963 (2) 1966 (1); v P 1962 (4); *v A 1962 (1) 1965 (4); v SA 1964 (4); v WI 1959 (5); v NZ 1965 (3); v In 1961 (5); v P 1961 (3)*
Allen, G. O. B. 25: v A 1930 (1) 1934 (2); v WI 1933 (1); v NZ 1931 (3); v In 1936 (3); *v A 1932 (5) 1936 (5); v WI 1947 (3); v NZ 1932 (2)*
Allom, M. J. C. 5: *v SA 1930 (1); v NZ 1929 (4)*
Allott, P. J. W. 13: v A 1981 (1) 1985 (4); v WI 1984 (3); v In 1982 (2); v SL 1984 (1); *v In 1981 (1); v SL 1981 (1)*
Ames (L. E. G.) 47: v A 1934 (5) 1938 (2); v SA 1929 (1) 1935 (4); v WI 1933 (3); v NZ 1931 (3) 1937 (3); v In 1932 (1); *v A 1932 (5) 1936 (5); v SA 1938 (5); v WI 1929 (4) 1934 (4); v NZ 1932 (2)*
Amiss, D. L. 50: v A 1968 (1) 1975 (2) 1977 (2); v WI 1966 (1) 1973 (3) 1976 (1); v NZ 1973 (3); v In 1967 (2) 1971 (1) 1974 (3); v P 1967 (1) 1971 (3) 1974 (3); *v A 1974 (5) 1976 (1); v WI 1973 (5) v NZ 1974 (2); v In 1972 (3) 1976 (5); v P 1972 (3)*
Andrew (K. V.) 2: v WI 1963 (1); *v A 1954 (1)*
Appleyard (R.) 9: v A 1956 (1); v SA 1955 (1); v P 1954 (1); *v A 1954 (4); v NZ 1954 (2)*
Archer, A. G. 1: *v SA 1898*
Armitage (T.) 2: *v A 1876 (2)*
Arnold (E. G.) 10: v A 1905 (4); v SA 1907 (2); *v A 1903 (4)*
Arnold, G. G. 34: v A 1972 (3) 1975 (1); v WI 1973 (3); v NZ 1969 (1) 1973 (3); v In 1974 (2); v P 1967 (2) 1974 (3); *v A 1974 (4); v WI 1973 (3); v NZ 1974 (2); v In 1972 (4); v P 1972 (3)*
Arnold (J.) 1: v NZ 1931
Astill (W. E.) 9: *v SA 1927 (5); v WI 1929 (4)*
Atherton, M. A. 8: v A 1989 (2); v NZ 1990 (3); v In 1990 (3)
Athey, C. W. J. 23: v A 1980 (1); v WI 1988 (1); v NZ 1986 (3); v In 1986 (2); v P 1987 (4); *v A 1986 (5) 1987 (1); v WI 1980 (2); v NZ 1987 (1); v P 1987 (3)*
Attewell (W.) 10: v A 1890 (1); *v A 1884 (5) 1887 (1) 1891 (3)*

Bailey, R. J. 4: v WI 1988 (1); *v WI 1989 (3)*
Bailey, T. E. 61: v A 1953 (5) 1956 (4); v SA 1951 (2) 1955 (5); v WI 1950 (2) 1957 (4); v NZ 1949 (4) 1958 (4); v P 1954 (3); *v A 1950 (4) 1954 (5) 1958 (5); v SA 1956 (5); v WI 1953 (5); v NZ 1950 (2) 1954 (2)*
Bairstow, D. L. 4: v A 1980 (1); v WI 1980 (1); v In 1979 (1); *v WI 1980 (1)*
Bakewell (A. H.) 6: v SA 1935 (2); v WI 1933 (1); v NZ 1931 (2); *v In 1933 (1)*

Balderstone J. C. 2: v WI 1976 (2)
Barber, R. W. 28: v A 1964 (1) 1968 (1); v SA 1960 (1) 1965 (3); v WI 1966 (2); v NZ 1965 (3); *v A 1965 (5); v SA 1964 (4); v In 1961 (5); v P 1961 (3)*
Barber (W.) 2: v SA 1935 (2)
Barlow, G. D. 3: v A 1977 (1); *v In 1976 (2)*
Barlow (R. G.) 17: v A 1882 (1) 1884 (3) 1886 (3); *v A 1881 (4) 1882 (4) 1886 (2)*
Barnes (S. F.) 27: v A 1902 (1) 1909 (3) 1912 (3); v SA 1912 (3); *v A 1901 (3) 1907 (5) 1911 (5); v SA 1913 (4)*
Barnes (W.) 21: v A 1880 (1) 1882 (1) 1884 (2) 1886 (2) 1888 (3) 1890 (2); *v A 1882 (4) 1884 (5) 1886 (1)*
Barnett (C. J.) 20: v A 1938 (3) 1948 (1); v SA 1947 (3); v WI 1933 (1); v NZ 1937 (3); v In 1936 (1); *v A 1936 (5); v In 1933 (3)*
Barnett, K. J. 4: v A 1989 (3); v SL 1988 (1)
Barratt (F.) 5: v SA 1929 (1); *v NZ 1929 (4)*
Barrington (K. F.) 82: v A 1961 (5) 1964 (5) 1968 (3); v SA 1955 (2) 1960 (4) 1965 (3); v WI 1963 (5) 1966 (2); v NZ 1965 (2); v In 1959 (5) 1967 (3); v P 1962 (4) 1967 (3); *v A 1962 (5) 1965 (5); v SA 1964 (5); v WI 1959 (5) 1967 (5); v NZ 1962 (3); v In 1961 (5) 1963 (1); v P 1961 (2)*
Barton (V. A.) 1: *v SA 1891*
Bates (W.) 15: *v A 1881 (4) 1882 (4) 1884 (5) 1886 (2)*
Bean (G.) 3: *v A 1891 (3)*
Bedser (A. V.) 51: v A 1948 (5) 1953 (5); v SA 1947 (2) 1951 (5) 1955 (1); v WI 1950 (3); v NZ 1949 (2); v In 1946 (3) 1952 (4); v P 1954 (2); *v A 1946 (5) 1950 (5) 1954 (1); v SA 1948 (5); v NZ 1946 (1) 1950 (2)*
Benson, M. R. 1: v In 1986
Berry (R.) 2: v WI 1950 (2)
Binks, J. G. 2: *v In 1963 (2)*
Bird M. C. 10: *v SA 1909 (5) 1913 (5)*
Birkenshaw J. 5: *v WI 1973 (2); v In 1972 (2); v P 1972 (1)*
Bligh, Hon. I. F. W. 4: *v A 1882 (4)*
Blythe (C.) 19: v A 1905 (1) 1909 (2); v SA 1907 (3); *v A 1901 (5) 1907 (1); v SA 1905 (5) 1909 (2)*
Board (J. H.) 6: *v SA 1898 (2) 1905 (4)*
Bolus, J. B. 7: v WI 1963 (2); *v In 1963 (5)*
Booth (M. W.) 2: *v SA 1913 (2)*
Bosanquet, B. J. T. 7: v A 1905 (3); *v A 1903 (4)*
Botham, I. T. 97: v A 1977 (2) 1980 (1) 1981 (6) 1985 (6) 1989 (3); v WI 1980 (5) 1984 (5); v NZ 1978 (3) 1983 (4) 1986 (1); v In 1979 (4) 1982 (3); v P 1978 (3) 1982 (3) 1987 (5); v SL 1984 (1); *v A 1978 (6) 1979 (3) 1982 (5) 1986 (4); v WI 1980 (4) 1985 (5); v NZ 1977 (3) 1983 (3); v In 1979 (1) 1981 (6); v P 1983 (1); v SL 1981 (1)*
Bowden, M. P. 2: *v SA 1888 (2)*
Bowes (W. E.) 15: v A 1934 (3) 1938 (2); v SA 1935 (4); v WI 1939 (2); v In 1932 (1) 1946 (1); *v A 1932 (1); v NZ 1932 (1)*
Bowley (E. H.) 5: v SA 1929 (2); *v NZ 1929 (3)*
Boycott, G. 108: v A 1964 (4) 1968 (3) 1972 (2) 1977 (3) 1980 (1) 1981 (6); v SA 1965 (2); v WI 1966 (4) 1969 (3) 1973 (3) 1980 (5); v NZ 1965 (2) 1969 (3) 1973 (3) 1978 (2); v In 1967 (2) 1971 (1) 1974 (1) 1979 (4); v P 1967 (1) 1971 (2); *v A 1965 (5) 1970 (5) 1978 (6) 1979 (3); v SA 1964 (5); v WI 1967 (5) 1973 (5) 1980 (4); v NZ 1965 (2) 1977 (3); v In 1979 (1) 1981 (4); v P 1977 (3)*
Bradley, W. M. 2: v A 1899 (2)
Braund (L. C.) 23: v A 1902 (5); v SA 1907 (3); *v A 1901 (5) 1903 (5) 1907 (5)*
Brearley, J. M. 39: v A 1977 (5) 1981 (4); v WI 1976 (2); v NZ 1978 (3); v In 1979 (4); v P 1978 (3); *v A 1976 (1) 1978 (6) 1979 (3); v In 1976 (5) 1979 (1); v P 1977 (2)*
Brearley, W. 4: v A 1905 (2) 1909 (1); v SA 1912 (1)
Brennan, D. V. 2: v SA 1951 (2)
Briggs (John) 33: v A 1886 (3) 1888 (3) 1893 (2) 1896 (1) 1899 (1); *v A 1884 (5) 1886 (2) 1887 (1) 1891 (3) 1894 (5) 1897 (5); v SA 1888 (2)*
Broad, B. C. 25: v A 1989 (2); v WI 1984 (4) 1988 (2); v P 1987 (4); v SL 1984 (1); *v A 1986 (5) 1987 (1); v NZ 1987 (3); v P 1987 (3)*
Brockwell (W.) 7: v A 1893 (1) 1899 (1); *v A 1894 (5)*
Bromley-Davenport, H. R. 4: *v SA 1895 (3) 1898 (1)*
Brookes (D.) 1: *v WI 1947*
Brown (A.) 2: *v In 1961 (1); v P 1961 (1)*
Brown, D. J. 26: v A 1968 (4); v SA 1965 (2); v WI 1966 (1) 1969 (3); v NZ 1969 (1); v In 1967 (2): *v A 1965 (4); v WI 1967 (4); v NZ 1965 (2); v P 1968 (3)*

Brown, F. R. 22: v A 1953 (1); v SA 1951 (5); v WI 1950 (1); v NZ 1931 (2) 1937 (1) 1949 (2); v In 1932 (1); *v A 1950 (5); v NZ 1932 (2) 1950 (2)*
Brown (G.) 7: v A 1921 (3); *v SA 1922 (4)*
Brown (J. T.) 8: v A 1896 (2) 1899 (1); *v A 1894 (5)*
Buckenham (C. P.) 4: *v SA 1909 (4)*
Butcher, A. R. 1: v In 1979
Butcher, R. O. 3: *v WI 1980 (3)*
Butler (H. J.) 2: v SA 1947 (1); *v WI 1947 (1)*
Butt (H. R.) 3: *v SA 1895 (3)*

Calthorpe, Hon. F. S. G. 4: *v WI 1929 (4)*
Capel, D. J. 15: v A 1989 (1); v WI 1988 (2); v P 1987 (1); *v A 1987 (1); v WI 1989 (4); v NZ 1987 (3); v P 1987 (3)*
Carr, A. W. 11: v A 1926 (4); v SA 1929 (2); *v SA 1922 (5)*
Carr, D. B. 2: *v In 1951 (2)*
Carr, D. W. 1: v A 1909
Cartwright, T. W. 5: v A 1964 (2); v SA 1965 (1); v NZ 1965 (1); *v SA 1964 (1)*
Chapman, A. P. F. 26: v A 1926 (4) 1930 (4); v SA 1924 (2); v WI 1928 (3); *v A 1924 (4) 1928 (4); v SA 1930 (5)*
Charlwood (H. R. J.) 2: *v A 1876 (2)*
Chatterton (W.) 1: *v SA 1891*
Childs, J. H. 2: v WI 1988 (2)
Christopherson, S. 1: v A 1884
Clark (E. W.) 8: v A 1934 (2); v SA 1929 (1); v WI 1933 (2); *v In 1933 (3)*
Clay, J. C. 1: v SA 1935
Close (D. B.) 22: v A 1961 (1); v SA 1955 (1); v WI 1957 (2) 1963 (5) 1966 (1) 1976 (3); v NZ 1949 (1); v In 1959 (1) 1967 (3); v P 1967 (3); *v A 1950 (1)*
Coldwell (L. J.) 7: v A 1964 (2); v P 1962 (2); *v A 1962 (2); v NZ 1962 (1)*
Compton (D. C. S.) 78: v A 1938 (4) 1948 (5) 1953 (5) 1956 (1); v SA 1947 (5) 1951 (4) 1955 (5); v WI 1939 (3) 1950 (1); v NZ 1937 (1) 1949 (4); v In 1946 (3) 1952 (2); v P 1954 (4); *v A 1946 (5) 1950 (4) 1954 (4); v SA 1948 (5) 1956 (5); v WI 1953 (5); v NZ 1946 (1) 1950 (2)*
Cook (C.) 1: v SA 1947
Cook, G. 7: v In 1982 (3); *v A 1982 (3); v SL 1981 (1)*
Cook, N. G. B. 15: v A 1989 (3); v WI 1984 (3); v NZ 1983 (2); *v NZ 1983 (1); v P 1983 (3) 1987 (3)*
Cope, G. A. 3: *v P 1977 (3)*
Copson (W. H.) 3: v SA 1947 (1); v WI 1939 (2)
Cornford (W. L.) 4: *v NZ 1929 (4)*
Cottam, R. M. H. 4: *v In 1972 (2); v P 1968 (2)*
Coventry, Hon. C. J. 2: *v SA 1888 (2)*
Cowans, N. G. 19: v A 1985 (1); v WI 1984 (1); v NZ 1983 (4); *v A 1982 (4); v NZ 1983 (2); v In 1984 (5); v P 1983 (2)*
Cowdrey, C. S. 6: v WI 1988 (1); *v In 1984 (5)*
Cowdrey, M. C. 114: v A 1956 (5) 1961 (4) 1964 (3) 1968 (4); v SA 1955 (1) 1960 (5) 1965 (3); v WI 1957 (5) 1963 (2) 1966 (4); v NZ 1958 (4) 1965 (3); v In 1959 (5); v P 1962 (4) 1967 (2) 1971 (1); *v A 1954 (5) 1958 (5) 1962 (5) 1965 (4) 1970 (3) 1974 (5); v SA 1956 (5); v WI 1959 (5) 1967 (5); v NZ 1954 (2) 1958 (2) 1962 (3) 1965 (3) 1970 (1); v In 1963 (3); v P 1968 (3)*
Coxon (A.) 1: v A 1948
Cranston, J. 1: v A 1890
Cranston, K. 8: v A 1948 (1); v SA 1947 (3); *v WI 1947 (4)*
Crapp (J. F.) 7: v A 1948 (3); *v SA 1948 (4)*
Crawford, J. N. 12: v SA 1907 (2); *v A 1907 (5); v SA 1905 (5)*
Curtis, T. S. 5: v A 1989 (3); v WI 1988 (2)
Cuttell (W. R.) 2: *v SA 1898 (2)*

Dawson, E. W. 5: *v SA 1927 (1); v NZ 1929 (4)*
Dean (H.) 3: v A 1912 (2); v SA 1912 (1)
DeFreitas, P. A. J. 17: v A 1989 (1); v WI 1988 (3); v NZ 1990 (2); v P 1987 (1); *v A 1986 (4); v WI 1989 (2); v NZ 1987 (2); v P 1987 (2)*
Denness, M. H. 28: v A 1975 (1); v NZ 1969 (1); v In 1974 (3); v P 1974 (3); *v A 1974 (5); v WI 1973 (5); v NZ 1974 (2); v In 1972 (5); v P 1972 (3)*
Denton (D.) 11: v A 1905 (1); *v SA 1905 (5) 1909 (5)*

Dewes, J. G. 5: v A 1948 (1); v WI 1950 (2); *v A 1950 (2)*
Dexter, E. R. 62: v A 1961 (5) 1964 (5) 1968 (2); v SA 1960 (5); v WI 1963 (5); v NZ 1958 (1) 1965 (2); v In 1959 (2); v P 1962 (5); *v A 1958 (2) 1962 (5); v SA 1964 (5); v WI 1959 (5); v NZ 1958 (2) 1962 (3); v In 1961 (5); v P 1961 (3)*
Dilley, G. R. 41: v A 1981 (3) 1989 (2); v WI 1980 (3) 1988 (4); v NZ 1983 (1) 1986 (2); v In 1986 (2); v P 1987 (4); *v A 1979 (2) 1986 (4) 1987 (1); v WI 1980 (4); v NZ 1987 (3); v In 1981 (4); v P 1983 (1) 1987 (1)*
Dipper (A. E.) 1: v A 1921
Doggart, G. H. G. 2: v WI 1950 (2)
D'Oliveira, B. L. 44: v A 1968 (2) 1972 (5); v WI 1966 (4) 1969 (3); v NZ 1969 (3); v In 1967 (2) 1971 (3); v P 1967 (3) 1971 (3); *v A 1970 (6); v WI 1967 (5); v NZ 1970 (2); v P 1968 (3)*
Dollery (H. E.) 4: v A 1948 (2); v SA 1947 (1); v WI 1950 (1)
Dolphin (A.) 1: *v A 1920*
Douglas, J. W. H. T. 23: v A 1912 (1) 1921 (5); v SA 1924 (1); *v A 1911 (5) 1920 (5) 1924 (1); v SA 1913 (5)*
Downton, P. R. 30: v A 1981 (1) 1985 (6); v WI 1984 (5) 1988 (3); v In 1986 (1); v SL 1984 (1); *v WI 1980 (3) 1985 (5); v In 1984 (5)*
Druce, N. F. 5: *v A 1897 (5)*
Ducat (A.) 1: v A 1921
Duckworth (G.) 24: v A 1930 (5); v SA 1924 (1) 1929 (4) 1935 (1); v WI 1928 (1); v In 1936 (3); *v A 1928 (5); v SA 1930 (3); v NZ 1932 (1)*
Duleepsinhji, K. S. 12: v A 1930 (4); v SA 1929 (1); v NZ 1931 (3); *v NZ 1929 (4)*
Durston (F. J.) 1: v A 1921

Edmonds, P. H. 51: v A 1975 (2) 1985 (5); v NZ 1978 (3) 1983 (2) 1986 (3); v In 1979 (4) 1982 (3) 1986 (2); v P 1978 (3) 1987 (5); *v A 1978 (1) 1986 (5); v WI 1985 (3); v NZ 1977 (3); v In 1984 (5); v P 1977 (2)*
Edrich, J. H. 77: v A 1964 (3) 1968 (5) 1972 (5) 1975 (4); v SA 1965 (1); v WI 1963 (3) 1966 (1) 1969 (3) 1976 (2); v NZ 1965 (1) 1969 (3); v In 1967 (2) 1971 (3) 1974 (3); v P 1971 (3) 1974 (3); *v A 1965 (5) 1970 (6) 1974 (4); v WI 1967 (5); v NZ 1965 (3) 1970 (2) 1974 (2); v In 1963 (2); v P 1968 (3)*
Edrich, W. J. 39: v A 1938 (4) 1948 (5) 1953 (3); v SA 1947 (4); v WI 1950 (2); v NZ 1949 (4); v In 1946 (1); v P 1954 (1); *v A 1946 (5) 1954 (4); v SA 1938 (5); v NZ 1946 (1)*
Elliott (H.) 4: v WI 1928 (1); *v SA 1927 (1); v In 1933 (2)*
Ellison, R. M. 11: v A 1985 (2); v WI 1984 (1); v In 1986 (1); v SL 1984 (1); *v WI 1985 (3); v In 1984 (3)*
Emburey, J. E. 60: v A 1980 (1) 1981 (4) 1985 (6) 1989 (3); v WI 1980 (3) 1988 (3); v NZ 1978 (1) 1986 (2); v In 1986 (3); v P 1987 (4); v SL 1988 (1); *v A 1978 (4) 1986 (5) 1987 (1); v WI 1980 (4) 1985 (4); v NZ 1987 (3); v In 1979 (1) 1981 (3); v P 1987 (3); v SL 1981 (1)*
Emmett (G. M.) 1: v A 1948
Emmett (T.) 7: *v A 1876 (2) 1878 (1) 1881 (4)*
Evans, A. J. 1: v A 1921
Evans (T. G.) 91: v A 1948 (5) 1953 (5) 1956 (5); v SA 1947 (5) 1951 (3) 1955 (3); v WI 1950 (3) 1957 (5); v NZ 1949 (4) 1958 (5); v In 1946 (1) 1952 (4) 1959 (2); v P 1954 (4); *v A 1946 (4) 1950 (5) 1954 (4) 1958 (3); v SA 1948 (3) 1956 (5); v WI 1947 (4) 1953 (4); v NZ 1946 (1) 1950 (2) 1954 (2)*

Fagg (A. E.) 5: v WI 1939 (1); v In 1936 (2); *v A 1936 (2)*
Fairbrother, N. H. 7: v NZ 1990 (3); v P 1987 (1); *v NZ 1987 (2); v P 1987 (1)*
Fane, F. L. 14: *v A 1907 (4); v SA 1905 (5) 1909 (5)*
Farnes, K. 15: v A 1934 (2) 1938 (4); *v A 1936 (2); v SA 1938 (5); v WI 1934 (2)*
Farrimond (W.) 4: v SA 1935 (1); *v SA 1930 (2); v WI 1934 (1)*
Fender, P. G. H. 13: v A 1921 (2); v SA 1924 (2) 1929 (1); *v A 1920 (3); v SA 1922 (5)*
Ferris, J. J. 1: *v SA 1891*
Fielder (A.) 6: *v A 1903 (2) 1907 (4)*
Fishlock (L. B.) 4: v In 1936 (2) 1946 (1); *v A 1946 (1)*
Flavell (J. A.) 4: v A 1961 (2) 1964 (2)
Fletcher, K. W. R. 59: v A 1968 (1) 1972 (1) 1975 (2); v WI 1973 (3); v NZ 1969 (2) 1973 (3); v In 1971 (2) 1974 (3); v P 1974 (3); *v A 1970 (5) 1974 (5) 1976 (1); v WI 1973 (4); v NZ 1970 (1) 1974 (2); v In 1972 (5) 1976 (3) 1981 (6); v P 1968 (3) 1972 (3); v SL 1981 (1)*
Flowers (W.) 8: v A 1893 (1); *v A 1884 (5) 1886 (2)*
Ford, F. G. J. 5: *v A 1894 (5)*

Foster, F. R. 11: v A 1912 (3); v SA 1912 (3); *v A 1911 (5)*
Foster, N. A. 28: v A 1985 (1) 1989 (3); v WI 1984 (1) 1988 (2); v NZ 1983 (1) 1986 (1); v In 1986 (1); v P 1987 (5); v SL 1988 (1); *v A 1987 (1); v WI 1985 (3); v NZ 1983 (2); v In 1984 (2); v P 1983 (2) 1987 (2)*
Foster, R. E. 8: v SA 1907 (3); *v A 1903 (5)*
Fothergill (A. J.) 2: *v SA 1888 (2)*
Fowler, G. 21: v WI 1984 (5); v NZ 1983 (2); v P 1982 (1); v SL 1984 (1); *v A 1982 (3); v NZ 1983 (2); v In 1984 (5); v P 1983 (2)*
Fraser, A. R. C. 8: v A 1989 (3); v In 1990 (3); *v WI 1989 (2)*
Freeman (A. P.) 12: v SA 1929 (3); v WI 1928 (3); *v A 1924 (2); v SA 1927 (4)*
French, B. N. 16: v NZ 1986 (3); v In 1986 (2); v P 1987 (4); *v A 1987 (1); v NZ 1987 (3); v P 1987 (3)*
Fry, C. B. 26: v A 1899 (5) 1902 (3) 1905 (4) 1909 (3) 1912 (3); v SA 1907 (3) 1912 (3); *v SA 1895 (2)*

Gatting, M. W. 68: v A 1980 (1) 1981 (6) 1985 (6) 1989 (1); v WI 1980 (4) 1984 (1) 1988 (2); v NZ 1983 (2) 1986 (3); v In 1986 (3); v P 1982 (3) 1987 (5); *v A 1986 (5) 1987 (1); v WI 1980 (1) 1985 (1); v NZ 1977 (1) 1983 (2) 1987 (3); v In 1981 (5) 1984 (5); v P 1977 (1) 1983 (3) 1987 (3)*
Gay, L. H. 1: *v A 1894*
Geary (G.) 14: v A 1926 (2) 1930 (1) 1934 (2); v SA 1924 (1) 1929 (2); *v A 1928 (4); v SA 1927 (2)*
Gibb, P. A. 8: v In 1946 (2); *v A 1946 (1); v SA 1938 (5)*
Gifford, N. 15: v A 1964 (2) 1972 (3); v NZ 1973 (2); v In 1971 (2); v P 1971 (2); *v In 1972 (2); v P 1972 (2)*
Gilligan, A. E. R. 11: v SA 1924 (4); *v A 1924 (5); v SA 1922 (2)*
Gilligan, A. H. H. 4: *v NZ 1929 (4)*
Gimblett (H.) 3: v WI 1939 (1); v In 1936 (2)
Gladwin (C.) 8: v SA 1947 (2); v NZ 1949 (1); *v SA 1948 (5)*
Goddard (T. W.) 8: v A 1930 (1); v WI 1939 (2); v NZ 1937 (2); *v SA 1938 (3)*
Gooch, G. A. 81: v A 1975 (2) 1980 (1) 1981 (5) 1985 (6) 1989 (5); v WI 1980 (5) 1988 (5); v NZ 1978 (3) 1986 (3) 1990 (3); v In 1979 (4) 1986 (3) 1990 (3); v P 1978 (2); v SL 1988 (1); *v A 1978 (6) 1979 (2); v WI 1980 (4) 1985 (5) 1989 (2); v In 1979 (1) 1981 (6); v P 1987 (3); v SL 1981 (1)*
Gover (A. R.) 4: v NZ 1937 (2); v In 1936 (1) 1946 (1)
Gower, D. I. 109: v A 1980 (1) 1981 (5) 1985 (6) 1989 (6); v WI 1980 (1) 1984 (5) 1988 (4); v NZ 1978 (3) 1983 (4) 1986 (3); v In 1979 (4) 1982 (3) 1986 (2) 1990 (3); v P 1978 (3) 1982 (3) 1987 (5); v SL 1984 (1); *v A 1978 (6) 1979 (3) 1982 (5) 1986 (5); v WI 1980 (4) 1985 (5); v NZ 1983 (3); v In 1979 (1) 1981 (6) 1984 (5); v P 1983 (3); v SL 1981 (1)*
Grace, E. M. 1: v A 1880
Grace, G. F. 1: v A 1880
Grace, W. G. 22: v A 1880 (1) 1882 (1) 1884 (3) 1886 (3) 1888 (3) 1890 (2) 1893 (2) 1896 (3) 1899 (1); *v A 1891 (3)*
Graveney (T. W.) 79: v A 1953 (5) 1956 (2) 1968 (5); v SA 1951 (1) 1955 (5); v WI 1957 (4) 1966 (4) 1969 (1); v NZ 1958 (4); v In 1952 (4) 1967 (3); v P 1954 (3) 1962 (4) 1967 (3); *v A 1954 (2) 1958 (5) 1962 (3); v WI 1953 (5) 1967 (5); v NZ 1954 (2) 1958 (2); v In 1951 (4); v P 1968 (3)*
Greenhough (T.) 4: v SA 1960 (1); v In 1959 (3)
Greenwood (A.) 2: *v A 1876 (2)*
Greig, A. W. 58: v A 1972 (5) 1975 (4) 1977 (5); v WI 1973 (3) 1976 (5); v NZ 1973 (3); v In 1974 (3); v P 1974 (3); *v A 1974 (6) 1976 (1); v WI 1973 (5); v NZ 1974 (2); v In 1972 (5) 1976 (5); v P 1972 (3)*
Greig, I. A. 2: v P 1982 (2)
Grieve, B. A. F. 2: *v SA 1888 (2)*
Griffith, S. C. 3: *v SA 1948 (2); v WI 1947 (1)*
Gunn (G.) 15: v A 1909 (1); *v A 1907 (5) 1911 (5); v WI 1929 (4)*
Gunn (J.) 6: v A 1905 (1); *v A 1901 (5)*
Gunn (W.) 11: v A 1888 (2) 1890 (2) 1893 (3) 1896 (1) 1899 (1); *v A 1886 (2)*

Haig, N. E. 5: v A 1921 (1); *v WI 1929 (4)*
Haigh (S.) 11: v A 1905 (2) 1909 (1) 1912 (1); *v SA 1898 (2) 1905 (5)*
Hallows (C.) 2: v A 1921 (1); v WI 1928 (1)
Hammond, W. R. 85: v A 1930 (5) 1934 (5) 1938 (4); v SA 1929 (4) 1935 (5); v WI 1928 (3) 1933 (3) 1939 (3); v NZ 1931 (3) 1937 (3); v In 1932 (1) 1936 (2) 1946 (3); *v A 1928 (5) 1932 (5) 1936 (5) 1946 (4); v SA 1927 (5) 1930 (5) 1938 (5); v WI 1934 (4); v NZ 1932 (2) 1946 (1)*
Hampshire, J. H. 8: v A 1972 (1) 1975 (1); v WI 1969 (2); *v A 1970 (2); v NZ 1970 (2)*

Hardinge (H. T. W.) 1: v A 1921
Hardstaff (J.) 5: *v A 1907 (5)*
Hardstaff (J. jun.) 23: v A 1938 (2) 1948 (1); v SA 1935 (1); v WI 1939 (3); v NZ 1937 (3); v In 1936 (2) 1946 (2); *v A 1936 (5) 1946 (1); v WI 1947 (3)*
Harris, Lord 4: v A 1880 (1) 1884 (2); *v A 1878 (1)*
Hartley, J. C. 2: *v SA 1905 (2)*
Hawke, Lord 5: *v SA 1895 (3) 1898 (2)*
Hayes (E. G.) 5: v A 1909 (1); v SA 1912 (1); *v SA 1905 (3)*
Hayes, F. C. 9: v WI 1973 (3) 1976 (2); *v WI 1973 (4)*
Hayward (T. W.) 35: v A 1896 (2) 1899 (5) 1902 (1) 1905 (5) 1909 (1); v SA 1907 (3); *v A 1897 (5) 1901 (5) 1903 (5); v SA 1895 (3)*
Hearne (A.) 1: *v SA 1891*
Hearne (F.) 2: *v SA 1888 (2)*
Hearne (G. G.) 1: *v SA 1891*
Hearne (J. T.) 12: v A 1896 (3) 1899 (3); *v A 1897 (5); v SA 1891 (1)*
Hearne (J. W.) 24: v A 1912 (3) 1921 (1) 1926 (1); v SA 1912 (2) 1924 (3); *v A 1911 (5) 1920 (2) 1924 (4); v SA 1913 (3)*
Hemmings, E. E. 15: v A 1989 (1); v NZ 1990 (3); v In 1990 (3); v P 1982 (2); *v A 1982 (3) 1987 (1); v NZ 1987 (1); v P 1987 (1)*
Hendren (E. H.) 51: v A 1921 (2) 1926 (5) 1930 (2) 1934 (4); v SA 1924 (5) 1929 (4); v WI 1928 (1); *v A 1920 (5) 1924 (5) 1928 (5); v SA 1930 (5); v WI 1929 (4) 1934 (4)*
Hendrick, M. 30: v A 1977 (3) 1980 (1) 1981 (2); v WI 1976 (2) 1980 (2); v NZ 1978 (2); v In 1974 (3) 1979 (4); v P 1974 (2); *v A 1974 (2) 1978 (5); v NZ 1974 (1) 1977 (1)*
Heseltine, C. 2: v SA 1895 (2)
Higgs, K. 15: v A 1968 (1); v WI 1966 (5); v SA 1965 (1); v In 1967 (1); v P 1967 (3); *v A 1965 (1); v NZ 1965 (3)*
Hill (A.) 2: *v A 1876 (2)*
Hill, A. J. L. 3: *v SA 1895 (3)*
Hilton (M. J.) 4: v SA 1951 (1); v WI 1950 (1); *v In 1951 (2)*
Hirst (G. H.) 24: v A 1899 (1) 1902 (4) 1905 (3) 1909 (4); v SA 1907 (3); *v A 1897 (4) 1903 (5)*
Hitch (J. W.) 7: v A 1912 (1) 1921 (1); v SA 1912 (1); *v A 1911 (3) 1920 (1)*
Hobbs (J. B.) 61: v A 1909 (3) 1912 (3) 1921 (1) 1926 (5) 1930 (5); v SA 1912 (3) 1924 (4) 1929 (1); v WI 1928 (2); *v A 1907 (4) 1911 (5) 1920 (5) 1924 (5) 1928 (5); v SA 1909 (5) 1913 (5)*
Hobbs, R. N. S. 7: v In 1967 (3); v P 1967 (1) 1971 (1); *v WI 1967 (1); v P 1968 (1)*
Hollies (W. E.) 13: v A 1948 (1); v SA 1947 (3); v WI 1950 (2); v NZ 1949 (4); *v WI 1934 (3)*
Holmes, E. R. T. 5: v SA 1935 (1); *v WI 1934 (4)*
Holmes (P.) 7: v A 1921 (1); v In 1932 (1); *v SA 1927 (5)*
Hone, L. 1: *v A 1878*
Hopwood (J. L.) 2: v A 1934 (2)
Hornby, A. N. 3: v A 1882 (1) 1884 (1); *v A 1878 (1)*
Horton (M. J.) 2: v In 1959 (2)
Howard, N. D. 4: *v In 1951 (4)*
Howell (H.) 5: v A 1921 (1); v SA 1924 (1); *v A 1920 (3)*
Howorth (R.) 5: v SA 1947 (1); *v WI 1947 (4)*
Humphries (J.) 3: *v A 1907 (3)*
Hunter (J.) 5: *v A 1884 (5)*
Hussain, N. 3: *v WI 1989 (3)*
Hutchings, K. L. 7: v A 1909 (2); *v A 1907 (5)*
Hutton (L.) 79: v A 1938 (3) 1948 (4) 1953 (5); v SA 1947 (5) 1951 (5); v WI 1939 (3) 1950 (3); v NZ 1937 (3) 1949 (4); v In 1946 (3) 1952 (4); v P 1954 (2); *v A 1946 (5) 1950 (5) 1954 (5); v SA 1938 (4) 1948 (5); v WI 1947 (2) 1953 (5); v NZ 1950 (2) 1954 (2)*
Hutton, R. A. 5: v In 1971 (3); v P 1971 (2)

Iddon (J.) 5: v SA 1935 (1); *v WI 1934 (4)*
Igglesden, A. P. 1: v A 1989
Ikin (J. T.) 18: v SA 1951 (3) 1955 (1); v In 1946 (2) 1952 (2); *v A 1946 (5); v NZ 1946 (1); v WI 1947 (4)*
Illingworth (R.) 61: v A 1961 (2) 1968 (3) 1972 (5); v SA 1960 (4); v WI 1966 (2) 1969 (3) 1973 (3); v NZ 1958 (1) 1965 (1) 1969 (3) 1973 (3); v In 1959 (2) 1967 (3) 1971 (3); v P 1962 (1) 1967 (1) 1971 (3); *v A 1962 (2) 1970 (6); v WI 1959 (5); v NZ 1962 (3) 1970 (2)*
Insole, D. J. 9: v A 1956 (1); v SA 1955 (1); v WI 1950 (1) 1957 (1); *v SA 1956 (5)*

Jackman, R. D. 4: v P 1982 (2); *v WI 1980 (2)*
Jackson, F. S. 20: v A 1893 (2) 1896 (3) 1899 (5) 1902 (5) 1905 (5)
Jackson (H. L.) 2: v A 1961 (1); v NZ 1949 (1)
Jameson, J. A. 4: v In 1971 (2); *v WI 1973 (2)*
Jardine, D. R. 22: v WI 1928 (2) 1933 (2); v NZ 1931 (3); v In 1932 (1); *v A 1928 (5) 1932 (5); v NZ 1932 (1); v In 1933 (3)*
Jarvis, P. W. 6: v A 1989 (2); v WI 1988 (2); *v NZ 1987 (2)*
Jenkins (R. O.) 9: v WI 1950 (2); v In 1952 (2); *v SA 1948 (5)*
Jessop, G. L. 18: v A 1899 (1) 1902 (4) 1905 (1) 1909 (2); v SA 1907 (3) 1912 (2); *v A 1901 (5)*
Jones, A. O. 12: v A 1899 (1) 1905 (2) 1909 (2); *v A 1901 (5) 1907 (2)*
Jones, I. J. 15: v WI 1966 (2); *v A 1965 (4); v WI 1967 (5); v NZ 1965 (3); v In 1963 (1)*
Jupp (H.) 2: *v A 1876 (2)*
Jupp, V. W. C. 8: v A 1921 (2); v WI 1928 (2); *v SA 1922 (4)*

Keeton (W. W.) 2: v A 1934 (1); v WI 1939 (1)
Kennedy (A. S.) 5: *v SA 1922 (5)*
Kenyon (D.) 8: v A 1953 (2); v SA 1955 (3); *v In 1951 (3)*
Killick, E. T. 2: v SA 1929 (2)
Kilner (R.) 9: v A 1926 (4); v SA 1924 (2); *v A 1924 (3)*
King (J. H.) 1: v A 1909
Kinneir (S. P.) 1: *v A 1911*
Knight (A. E.) 3: *v A 1903 (3)*
Knight (B. R.) 29: v A 1968 (2); v WI 1966 (1) 1969 (3); v NZ 1969 (2); v P 1962 (2); *v A 1962 (1) 1965 (2); v NZ 1962 (3) 1965 (2); v In 1961 (4) 1963 (5); v P 1961 (2)*
Knight, D. J. 2: v A 1921 (2)
Knott, A. P. E. 95: v A 1968 (5) 1972 (5) 1975 (4) 1977 (5) 1981 (2); v WI 1969 (3) 1973 (3) 1976 (5) 1980 (4); v NZ 1969 (3) 1973 (3); v In 1971 (3) 1974 (3); v P 1967 (2) 1971 (3) 1974 (3); *v A 1970 (6) 1974 (6) 1976 (1); v WI 1967 (2) 1973 (5); v NZ 1970 (1) 1974 (2); v In 1972 (5) 1976 (5); v P 1968 (3) 1972 (3)*
Knox, N. A. 2: v SA 1907 (2)

Laker (J. C.) 46: v A 1948 (3) 1953 (3) 1956 (5); v SA 1951 (2) 1955 (1); v WI 1950 (1) 1957 (4); v NZ 1949 (1) 1958 (4); v In 1952 (4); v P 1954 (1); *v A 1958 (4); v SA 1956 (5); v WI 1947 (4) 1953 (4)*
Lamb, A. J. 67: v A 1985 (6) 1989 (1); v WI 1984 (5) 1988 (4); v NZ 1983 (4) 1986 (1) 1990 (3); v In 1982 (3) 1986 (2) 1990 (3); v P 1982 (3); v SL 1984 (1) 1988 (1); *v A 1982 (5) 1986 (5); v WI 1985 (5) 1989 (4); v NZ 1983 (3); v In 1984 (5); v P 1983 (3)*
Langridge (James) 8: v SA 1935 (1); v WI 1933 (2); v In 1936 (1) 1946 (1); *v In 1933 (3)*
Larkins, W. 10: v A 1981 (1); v WI 1980 (3); *v A 1979 (1); v WI 1989 (4); v In 1979 (1)*
Larter (J. D. F.) 10: v SA 1965 (2); v NZ 1965 (1); v P 1962 (1); *v NZ 1962 (3); v In 1963 (3)*
Larwood (H.) 21: v A 1926 (2) 1930 (3); v SA 1929 (3); v WI 1928 (2); v NZ 1931 (1); *v A 1928 (5) 1932 (5)*
Lawrence, D. V. 1: v SL 1988
Leadbeater (E.) 2: *v In 1951 (2)*
Lee (H. W.) 1: *v SA 1930*
Lees (W. S.) 5: *v SA 1905 (5)*
Legge G. B. 5: *v SA 1927 (1); v NZ 1929 (4)*
Leslie, C. F. H. 4: *v A 1882 (4)*
Lever, J. K. 21: v A 1977 (3); v WI 1980 (1); v In 1979 (1) 1986 (1); *v A 1976 (1) 1978 (1) 1979 (1); v NZ 1977 (1); v In 1976 (5) 1979 (1) 1981 (2); v P 1977 (3)*
Lever, P. 17: v A 1972 (1) 1975 (1); v In 1971 (1); v P 1971 (3); *v A 1970 (5) 1974 (2); v NZ 1970 (2) 1974 (2)*
Leveson Gower, H. D. G. 3: *v SA 1909 (3)*
Levett, W. H. V. 1: *v In 1933*
Lewis, A. R. 9: v NZ 1973 (1); *v In 1972 (5); v P 1972 (3)*
Lewis, C. C. 3: v NZ 1990 (1); v In 1990 (2)
Leyland (M.) 41: v A 1930 (3) 1934 (5) 1938 (1); v SA 1929 (5) 1935 (4); v WI 1928 (1) 1933 (1); v In 1936 (2); *v A 1928 (1) 1932 (5) 1936 (5); v SA 1930 (5); v WI 1934 (3)*
Lilley (A. A.) 35: v A 1896 (3) 1899 (4) 1902 (5) 1905 (5) 1909 (5); v SA 1907 (3); *v A 1901 (5) 1903 (5)*
Lillywhite (James jun.) 2: *v A 1876 (2)*
Lloyd, D. 9: v In 1974 (2); v P 1974 (3); *v A 1974 (4)*

Lloyd, T. A. 1: v WI 1984
Loader (P. J.) 13: v SA 1955 (1); v WI 1957 (2); v NZ 1958 (3); v P 1954 (1); *v A 1958 (2); v SA 1956 (4)*
Lock (G. A. R.) 49: v A 1953 (2) 1956 (4) 1961 (3); v SA 1955 (3); v WI 1957 (3) 1963 (3); v NZ 1958 (5); v In 1952 (2); v P 1962 (3); *v A 1958 (4); v SA 1956 (1); v WI 1953 (5) 1967 (2); v NZ 1958 (2); v In 1961 (5); v P 1961 (2)*
Lockwood (W. H.) 12: v A 1893 (2) 1899 (1) 1902 (4); *v A 1894 (5)*
Lohmann (G. A.) 18: v A 1886 (3) 1888 (3) 1890 (2) 1896 (1); *v A 1886 (2) 1887 (1) 1891 (3); v SA 1895 (3)*
Lowson (F. A.) 7: v SA 1951 (2) 1955 (1); *v In 1951 (4)*
Lucas, A. P. 5: v A 1880 (1) 1882 (1) 1884 (2); *v A 1878 (1)*
Luckhurst, B. W. 21: v A 1972 (4); v WI 1973 (2); v In 1971 (3); v P 1971 (3); *v A 1970 (5) 1974 (2); v NZ 1970 (2)*
Lyttelton, Hon. A. 4: v A 1880 (1) 1882 (1) 1884 (2)

Macaulay (G. G.) 8: v A 1926 (1); v SA 1924 (1); v WI 1933 (2); *v SA 1922 (4)*
MacBryan, J. C. W. 1: v SA 1924
McConnon (J. E.) 2: v P 1954 (2)
McGahey, C. P. 2: *v A 1901 (2)*
MacGregor, G. 8: v A 1890 (2) 1893 (3); *v A 1891 (3)*
McIntyre (A. J. W.) 3: v SA 1955 (1); v WI 1950 (1); *v A 1950 (1)*
MacKinnon, F. A. 1: *v A 1878*
MacLaren, A. C. 35: v A 1896 (2) 1899 (4) 1902 (5) 1905 (4) 1909 (5); *v A 1894 (5) 1897 (5) 1901 (5)*
McMaster, J. E. P. 1: *v SA 1888*
Makepeace (J. W. H.) 4: *v A 1920 (4)*
Malcolm, D. E. 11: v A 1989 (1); v NZ 1990 (3); v In 1990 (3); *v WI 1989 (4)*
Mann, F. G. 7: v NZ 1949 (2); *v SA 1948 (5)*
Mann, F. T. 5: *v SA 1922 (5)*
Marks, V. J. 6: v NZ 1983 (1); v P 1982 (1); *v NZ 1983 (1); v P 1983 (3)*
Marriott, C. S. 1: v WI 1933
Martin (F.) 2: v A 1890 (1); *v SA 1891 (1)*
Martin, J. W. 1: v SA 1947
Mason, J. R. 5: *v A 1897 (5)*
Matthews (A. D. G.) 1: v NZ 1937
May, P. B. H. 66: v A 1953 (2) 1956 (5) 1961 (4); v SA 1951 (2) 1955 (5); v WI 1957 (5); v NZ 1958 (5); v In 1952 (4) 1959 (3); v P 1954 (4); *v A 1954 (5) 1958 (5); v SA 1956 (5); v WI 1953 (5) 1959 (3); v NZ 1954 (2) 1958 (2)*
Maynard, M. P. 1: v WI 1988
Mead (C. P.) 17: v A 1921 (2); *v A 1911 (4) 1928 (1); v SA 1913 (5) 1922 (5)*
Mead (W.) 1: v A 1899
Midwinter (W. E.) 4: *v A 1881 (4)*
Milburn, C. 9: v A 1968 (2); v WI 1966 (4); v In 1967 (1); v P 1967 (1); *v P 1968 (1)*
Miller, A. M. 1: *v SA 1895*
Miller, G. 34: v A 1977 (2); v WI 1976 (1) 1984 (2); v NZ 1978 (2); v In 1979 (3) 1982 (1); v P 1978 (3) 1982 (1); *v A 1978 (6) 1979 (1) 1982 (5); v WI 1980 (1); v NZ 1977 (3); v P 1977 (3)*
Milligan, F. W. 2: *v SA 1898 (2)*
Millman (G.) 6: v P 1962 (2); *v In 1961 (2); v P 1961 (2)*
Milton (C. A.) 6: v NZ 1958 (2); v In 1959 (2); *v A 1958 (2)*
Mitchell (A.) 6: v SA 1935 (2); v In 1936 (1); *v In 1933 (3)*
Mitchell, F. 2: *v SA 1898 (2)*
Mitchell (T. B.) 5: v A 1934 (2); v SA 1935 (1); *v A 1932 (1); v NZ 1932 (1)*
Mitchell-Innes, N. S. 1: v SA 1935
Mold (A. W.) 3: v A 1893 (3)
Moon, L. J. 4: *v SA 1905 (4)*
Morley (F.) 4: v A 1880 (1); *v A 1882 (3)*
Morris, J. E. 3: v In 1990 (3)
Mortimore (J. B.) 9: v A 1964 (1); v In 1959 (2); *v A 1958 (1); v NZ 1958 (2); v In 1963 (3)*
Moss (A. E.) 9: v A 1956 (1); v SA 1960 (2); v In 1959 (3); *v WI 1953 (1) 1959 (2)*
Moxon, M. D. 10: v A 1989 (1); v WI 1988 (2); v NZ 1986 (2); v P 1987 (1); *v A 1987 (1); v NZ 1987 (3)*
Murdoch, W. L. 1: *v SA 1891*

Murray, J. T. 21: v A 1961 (5); v WI 1966 (1); v In 1967 (3); v P 1962 (3) 1967 (1); *v A 1962 (1); v SA 1964 (1); v NZ 1962 (1) 1965 (1); v In 1961 (3); v P 1961 (1)*

Newham (W.) 1: *v A 1887*
Newport, P. J. 2: v A 1989 (1); v SL 1988 (1)
Nichols (M. S.) 14: v A 1930 (1); v SA 1935 (4); v WI 1933 (1) 1939 (1); *v NZ 1929 (4); v In 1933 (3)*

Oakman (A. S. M.) 2: v A 1956 (2)
O'Brien, Sir T. C. 5: v A 1884 (1) 1888 (1); *v SA 1895 (3)*
O'Connor (J.) 4: v SA 1929 (1); *v WI 1929 (3)*
Old, C. M. 46: v A 1975 (3) 1977 (2) 1980 (1) 1981 (2); v WI 1973 (1) 1976 (2) 1980 (1); v NZ 1973 (2) 1978 (1); v In 1974 (3); v P 1974 (3) 1978 (3); *v A 1974 (2) 1976 (1) 1978 (1); v WI 1973 (4) 1980 (1); v NZ 1974 (1) 1977 (2); v In 1972 (4) 1976 (4); v P 1972 (1) 1977 (1)*
Oldfield (N.) 1: v WI 1939

Padgett (D. E. V.) 2: v SA 1960 (2)
Paine (G. A. E.) 4: *v WI 1934 (4)*
Palairet, L. C. H. 2: v A 1902 (2)
Palmer, C. H. 1: *v WI 1953*
Palmer, K. E. 1: *v SA 1964*
Parfitt (P. H.) 37: v A 1964 (4) 1972 (3); v SA 1965 (2); v WI 1969 (1); v NZ 1965 (2); v P 1962 (5); *v A 1962 (2); v SA 1964 (5); v NZ 1962 (3) 1965 (3); v In 1961 (2) 1963 (3); v P 1961 (2)*
Parker (C. W. L.) 1: v A 1921
Parker, P. W. G. 1: v A 1981
Parkhouse (W. G. A.) 7: v WI 1950 (2); v In 1959 (2); *v A 1950 (2); v NZ 1950 (1)*
Parkin (C. H.) 10: v A 1921 (4); v SA 1924 (1); *v A 1920 (5)*
Parks (J. H.) 1: v NZ 1937
Parks (J. M.) 46: v A 1964 (5); v SA 1960 (5) 1965 (3); v WI 1963 (4) 1966 (4); v NZ 1965 (3); v P 1954 (1); *v A 1965 (5); v SA 1964 (5); v WI 1959 (1) 1967 (3); v NZ 1965 (2); v In 1963 (5)*
Pataudi sen., Nawab of, 3: v A 1934 (1); *v A 1932 (2)*
Paynter (E.) 20: v A 1938 (4); v WI 1939 (2); v NZ 1931 (1) 1937 (2); v In 1932 (1); *v A 1932 (3); v SA 1938 (5); v NZ 1932 (2)*
Peate (E.) 9: v A 1882 (1) 1884 (3) 1886 (1); *v A 1881 (4)*
Peebles, I. A. R. 13: v A 1930 (2); v NZ 1931 (3); *v SA 1927 (4) 1930 (4)*
Peel (R.) 20: v A 1888 (3) 1890 (1) 1893 (1) 1896 (1); *v A 1884 (5) 1887 (1) 1891 (3) 1894 (5)*
Penn, F. 1: v A 1880
Perks (R. T. D.) 2: v WI 1939 (1); *v SA 1938 (1)*
Philipson, (H.) 5: *v A 1891 (1) 1894 (4)*
Pigott, A. C. S. 1: *v NZ 1983*
Pilling (R.) 8: v A 1884 (1) 1886 (1) 1888 (1); *v A 1881 (4) 1887 (1)*
Place (W.) 3: *v WI 1947 (3)*
Pocock, P. I. 25: v A 1968 (1); v WI 1976 (2) 1984 (2); v SL 1984 (1); *v WI 1967 (2) 1973 (4); v In 1972 (4) 1984 (5); v P 1968 (1) 1972 (3)*
Pollard (R.) 4: v A 1948 (2); v In 1946 (1); *v NZ 1946 (1)*
Poole (C. J.) 3: *v In 1951 (3)*
Pope (G. H.) 1: v SA 1947
Pougher (A. D.) 1: *v SA 1891*
Price, J. S. E. 15: v A 1964 (2) 1972 (1); v In 1971 (3); v P 1971 (1); *v SA 1964 (4); v In 1963 (4)*
Price (W. F. F.) 1: v A 1938
Prideaux, R. M. 3: v A 1968 (1); *v P 1968 (2)*
Pringle, D. R. 21: v A 1989 (2); v WI 1984 (3) 1988 (4); v NZ 1986 (1); v In 1982 (3) 1986 (3); v P 1982 (1); v SL 1988 (1); *v A 1982 (3)*
Pullar (G.) 28: v A 1961 (5); v SA 1960 (3); v In 1959 (3); v P 1962 (2); *v A 1962 (4); v WI 1959 (5); v In 1961 (3); v P 1961 (3)*

Quaife (W. G.) 7: v A 1899 (2); *v A 1901 (5)*

Radford, N. V. 3: v NZ 1986 (1); v In 1986 (1); *v NZ 1987 (1)*
Radley, C. T. 8: v NZ 1978 (3); v P 1978 (3); *v NZ 1977 (2)*

Randall, D. W. 47: v A 1977 (5); v WI 1984 (1); v NZ 1983 (3); v In 1979 (3) 1982 (3); v P 1982 (3); *v A 1976 (1) 1978 (6) 1979 (2) 1982 (4); v NZ 1977 (3) 1983 (3); v In 1976 (4); v P 1977 (3) 1983 (3)*
Ranjitsinhji, K. S. 15: v A 1896 (2) 1899 (5) 1902 (3); *v A 1897 (5)*
Read, H. D. 1: v SA 1935
Read (J. M.) 17: v A 1882 (1) 1890 (2) 1893 (1); *v A 1884 (5) 1886 (2) 1887 (1) 1891 (3); v SA 1888 (2)*
Read, W. W. 18: v A 1884 (2) 1886 (3) 1888 (3) 1890 (2) 1893 (2); *v A 1882 (4) 1887 (1); v SA 1891 (1)*
Relf (A. E.) 13: v A 1909 (1); *v A 1903 (2); v SA 1905 (5) 1913 (5)*
Rhodes (H. J.) 2: v In 1959 (2)
Rhodes (W.) 58: v A 1899 (3) 1902 (5) 1905 (4) 1909 (4) 1912 (3) 1921 (1) 1926 (1); v SA 1912 (3); *v A 1903 (5) 1907 (5) 1911 (5) 1920 (5); v SA 1909 (5) 1913 (5); v WI 1929 (4)*
Richards, C. J. 8: v WI 1988 (2); v P 1987 (1); *v A 1986 (5)*
Richardson (D. W.) 1: v WI 1957
Richardson (P. E.) 34: v A 1956 (5); v WI 1957 (5) 1963 (1); v NZ 1958 (4); *v A 1958 (4); v SA 1956 (5); v NZ 1958 (2); v In 1961 (5); v P 1961 (3)*
Richardson (T.) 14: v A 1893 (1) 1896 (3); *v A 1894 (5) 1897 (5)*
Richmond (T. L.) 1: v A 1921
Ridgway (F.) 5: *v In 1951 (5)*
Robertson (J. D.) 11: v SA 1947 (1); v NZ 1949 (1); *v WI 1947 (4); v In 1951 (5)*
Robins, R. W. V. 19: v A 1930 (2); v SA 1929 (1) 1935 (3); v WI 1933 (2); v NZ 1931 (1) 1937 (3); v In 1932 (1) 1936 (2); *v A 1936 (4)*
Robinson, R. T. 29: v A 1985 (6) 1989 (1); v In 1986 (1); v P 1987 (5); v SL 1988 (1); *v A 1987 (1); v WI 1985 (4); v NZ 1987 (3); v In 1984 (5); v P 1987 (2)*
Roope, G. R. J. 21: v A 1975 (1) 1977 (2); v WI 1973 (1); v NZ 1973 (3) 1978 (1); v P 1978 (3); *v NZ 1977 (3); v In 1972 (2); v P 1972 (2) 1977 (3)*
Root (C. F.) 3: v A 1926 (3)
Rose, B. C. 9: v WI 1980 (3); *v WI 1980 (1); v NZ 1977 (2); v P 1977 (3)*
Royle, V. P. F. A. 1: *v A 1878*
Rumsey, F. E. 5: v A 1964 (1); v SA 1965 (1); v NZ 1965 (3)
Russell (A. C.) 10: v A 1921 (2); *v A 1920 (4); v SA 1922 (4)*
Russell, R. C. 17: v A 1989 (6); v NZ 1990 (3); v In 1990 (3); v SL 1988 (1); *v WI 1989 (4)*
Russell, W. E. 10: v SA 1965 (1); v WI 1966 (2); v P 1967 (1); *v A 1965 (1); v NZ 1965 (3); v In 1961 (1); v P 1961 (1)*

Sandham (A.) 14: v A 1921 (1); v SA 1924 (2); *v A 1924 (2); v SA 1922 (5); v WI 1929 (4)*
Schultz, S. S. 1: *v A 1878*
Scotton (W. H.) 15: v A 1884 (1) 1886 (3); *v A 1881 (4) 1884 (5) 1886 (2)*
Selby (J.) 6: *v A 1876 (2) 1881 (4)*
Selvey, M. W. W. 3: v WI 1976 (2); *v In 1976 (1)*
Shackleton (D.) 7: v SA 1951 (1); v WI 1950 (1) 1963 (4); *v In 1951 (1)*
Sharp (J.) 3: v A 1909 (3)
Sharpe (J. W.) 3: v A 1890 (1); *v A 1891 (2)*
Sharpe, P. J. 12: v A 1964 (2); v WI 1963 (3) 1969 (3); v NZ 1969 (3); *v In 1963 (1)*
Shaw (A.) 7: v A 1880 (1); *v A 1876 (2) 1881 (4)*
Sheppard, Rev. D. S. 22: v A 1956 (2); v WI 1950 (1) 1957 (2); v In 1952 (2); v P 1954 (2) 1962 (2); *v A 1950 (2) 1962 (5); v NZ 1950 (1) 1963 (3)*
Sherwin (M.) 3: v A 1888 (1); *v A 1886 (2)*
Shrewsbury (A.) 23: v A 1884 (3) 1886 (3) 1890 (2) 1893 (3); *v A 1881 (4) 1884 (5) 1886 (2) 1887 (1)*
Shuter, J. 1: v A 1888
Shuttleworth, K. 5: v P 1971 (1); *v A 1970 (2); v NZ 1970 (2)*
Sidebottom, A. 1: v A 1985
Simpson, R. T. 27: v A 1953 (3); v SA 1951 (3); v WI 1950 (3); v NZ 1949 (2); v In 1952 (2); v P 1954 (3); *v A 1950 (5) 1954 (1); v SA 1948 (1); v NZ 1950 (2) 1954 (2)*
Simpson-Hayward, G. H. 5: *v SA 1909 (5)*
Sims (J. M.) 4: v SA 1935 (1); v In 1936 (1); *v A 1936 (2)*
Sinfield (R. A.) 1: v A 1938
Slack, W. N. 3: v In 1986 (1); *v WI 1985 (2)*
Smailes (T. F.) 1: v In 1946
Small, G. C. 13: v A 1989 (1); v WI 1988 (1); v NZ 1986 (2) 1990 (3); *v A 1986 (2); v WI 1989 (4)*
Smith, A. C. 6: *v A 1962 (4); v NZ 1962 (2)*

Smith, C. A. 1: *v SA 1888*
Smith (C. I. J.) 5: v NZ 1937 (1); *v WI 1934 (4)*
Smith, C. L. 8: v NZ 1983 (2); v In 1986 (1); *v NZ 1983 (2); v P 1983 (3)*
Smith (D.) 2: v SA 1935 (2)
Smith D. M. 2: *v WI 1985 (2)*
Smith (D. R.) 5: *v In 1961 (5)*
Smith (D. V.) 3: v WI 1957 (3)
Smith (E. J.) 11: v A 1912 (3); v SA 1912 (3); *v A 1911 (4); v SA 1913 (1)*
Smith (H.) 1: v WI 1928
Smith, M. J. K. 50: v A 1961 (1) 1972 (3); v SA 1960 (4) 1965 (3); v WI 1966 (1); v NZ 1958 (3) 1965 (3); v In 1959 (2); *v A 1965 (5); v SA 1964 (5); v WI 1959 (5); v NZ 1965 (3); v In 1961 (4) 1963 (5); v P 1961 (3)*
Smith, R. A. 18: v A 1989 (5); v WI 1988 (2); v NZ 1990 (3); v In 1990 (3); v SL 1988 (1); *v WI 1989 (4)*
Smith (T. P. B.) 4: v In 1946 (1); *v A 1946 (2); v NZ 1946 (1)*
Smithson (G. A.) 2: *v WI 1947 (2)*
Snow, J. A. 49: v A 1968 (5) 1972 (5) 1975 (4); v SA 1965 (1); v WI 1966 (3) 1969 (3) 1973 (1) 1976 (3); v NZ 1965 (1) 1969 (2) 1973 (3); v In 1967 (3) 1971 (2); v P 1967 (1); *v A 1970 (6); v WI 1967 (4); v P 1968 (2)*
Southerton (J.) 2: *v A 1876 (2)*
Spooner, R. H. 10: v A 1905 (2) 1909 (2) 1912 (3); v SA 1912 (3)
Spooner (R. T.) 7: v SA 1955 (1); *v In 1951 (5); v WI 1953 (1)*
Stanyforth, R. T. 4: *v SA 1927 (4)*
Staples (S. J.) 3: *v SA 1927 (3)*
Statham (J. B.) 70: v A 1953 (1) 1956 (3) 1961 (4); v SA 1951 (2) 1955 (4) 1960 (5) 1965 (1); v WI 1957 (3) 1963 (2); v NZ 1958 (2); v In 1959 (3); v P 1954 (4) 1962 (3); *v A 1954 (5) 1958 (4) 1962 (5); v SA 1956 (4); v WI 1953 (4) 1959 (3); v NZ 1950 (1) 1954 (2); v In 1951 (5)*
Steel, A. G. 13: v A 1880 (1) 1882 (1) 1884 (3) 1886 (3) 1888 (1); *v A 1882 (4)*
Steele, D. S. 8: v A 1975 (3); v WI 1976 (5)
Stephenson, J. P. 1: v A 1989
Stevens, G. T. S. 10: v A 1926 (2); *v SA 1922 (1) 1927 (5); v WI 1929 (2)*
Stevenson, G. B. 2: *v WI 1980 (1); v In 1979 (1)*
Stewart, A. J. 7: v NZ 1990 (3); *v WI 1989 (4)*
Stewart (M. J.) 8: v WI 1963 (4); v P 1962 (2); *v In 1963 (2)*
Stoddart, A. E. 16: v A 1893 (3) 1896 (2); *v A 1887 (1) 1891 (3) 1894 (5) 1897 (2)*
Storer (W.) 6: v A 1899 (1); *v A 1897 (5)*
Street (G. B.) 1: *v SA 1922*
Strudwick (H.) 28: v A 1921 (2) 1926 (5); v SA 1924 (1); *v A 1911 (1) 1920 (4) 1924 (5); v SA 1909 (5) 1913 (5)*
Studd, C. T. 5: v A 1882 (1); *v A 1882 (4)*
Studd, G. B. 4: *v A 1882 (4)*
Subba Row, R. 13: v A 1961 (5); v SA 1960 (4); v NZ 1958 (1); v In 1959 (1); *v WI 1959 (2)*
Sugg (F. H.) 2: v A 1888 (2)
Sutcliffe (H.) 54: v A 1926 (5) 1930 (4) 1934 (4); v SA 1924 (5) 1929 (5) 1935 (2); v WI 1928 (3) 1933 (2); v NZ 1931 (2); v In 1932 (1); *v A 1924 (5) 1928 (4) 1932 (5); v SA 1927 (5); v NZ 1932 (2)*
Swetman (R.) 11: v In 1959 (3); *v A 1958 (2); v WI 1959 (4); v NZ 1958 (2)*

Tate (F. W.) 1: v A 1902
Tate (M. W.) 39: v A 1926 (5) 1930 (5); v SA 1924 (5) 1929 (3) 1935 (1); v WI 1928 (3); v NZ 1931 (1); *v A 1924 (5) 1928 (5); v SA 1930 (5); v NZ 1932 (1)*
Tattersall (R.) 16: v A 1953 (1); v SA 1951 (5); v P 1954 (1); *v A 1950 (2); v NZ 1950 (2); v In 1951 (5)*
Tavaré, C. J. 31: v A 1981 (2) 1989 (1); v WI 1980 (2) 1984 (1); v NZ 1983 (4); v In 1982 (3); v P 1982 (3); v SL 1984 (1); *v A 1982 (5); v NZ 1983 (2); v In 1981 (6); v SL 1981 (1)*
Taylor (K.) 3: v A 1964 (1); v In 1959 (2)
Taylor, L. B. 2: v A 1985 (2)
Taylor, R. W. 57: v A 1981 (3); v NZ 1978 (3) 1983 (4); v In 1979 (3) 1982 (3); v P 1978 (3) 1982 (3); *v A 1978 (6) 1979 (3) 1982 (5); v NZ 1970 (1) 1977 (3) 1983 (3); v In 1979 (1) 1981 (6); v P 1977 (3) 1983 (3); v SL 1981 (1)*
Tennyson, Hon. L. H. 9: v A 1921 (4); *v SA 1913 (5)*
Terry, V. P. 2: v WI 1984 (2)

Thomas, J. G. 5: v NZ 1986 (1); *v WI 1985 (4)*
Thompson (G. J.) 6: v A 1909 (1); *v SA 1909 (5)*
Thomson, N. I. 5: *v SA 1964 (5)*
Titmus (F. J.) 53: v A 1964 (5); v SA 1955 (2) 1965 (3); v WI 1963 (4) 1966 (3); v NZ 1965 (3); v P 1962 (2) 1967 (2); *v A 1962 (5) 1965 (5) 1974 (4); v SA 1964 (5); v WI 1967 (2); v NZ 1962 (3); v In 1963 (5)*
Tolchard, R. W. 4: *v In 1976 (4)*
Townsend, C. L. 2: v A 1899 (2)
Townsend, D. C. H. 3: *v WI 1934 (3)*
Townsend (L. F.) 4: *v WI 1929 (1); v In 1933 (3)*
Tremlett (M. F.) 3: *v WI 1947 (3)*
Trott (A. E.) 2: *v SA 1898 (2)*
Trueman (F. S.) 67: v A 1953 (1) 1956 (2) 1961 (4) 1964 (4); v SA 1955 (1) 1960 (5); v WI 1957 (5) 1963 (5); v NZ 1958 (5) 1965 (2); v In 1952 (4) 1959 (5); v P 1962 (4); *v A 1958 (3) 1962 (5); v WI 1953 (3) 1959 (5); v NZ 1958 (2) 1962 (2)*
Tufnell, N. C. 1: *v SA 1909*
Turnbull, M. J. 9: v WI 1933 (2); v In 1936 (1); *v SA 1930 (5); v NZ 1929 (1)*
Tyldesley (E.) 14: v A 1921 (3) 1926 (1); v SA 1924 (1); v WI 1928 (3); *v A 1928 (1): v SA 1927 (5)*
Tyldesley (J. T.) 31: v A 1899 (2) 1902 (5) 1905 (5) 1909 (4); v SA 1907 (3); *v A 1901 (5) 1903 (5); v SA 1898 (2)*
Tyldesley (R. K.) 7: v A 1930 (2); v SA 1924 (4); *v A 1924 (1)*
Tylecote, E. F. S. 6: v A 1886 (2); *v A 1882 (4)*
Tyler (E. J.) 1: *v SA 1895*
Tyson (F. H.) 17: v A 1956 (1); v SA 1955 (2); v P 1954 (1); *v A 1954 (5) 1958 (2); v SA 1956 (2); v NZ 1954 (2) 1958 (2)*

Ulyett (G.) 25: v A 1882 (1) 1884 (3) 1886 (3) 1888 (2) 1890 (1); *v A 1876 (2) 1878 (1) 1881 (4) 1884 (5) 1887 (1); v SA 1888 (2)*
Underwood, D. L. 86: v A 1968 (4) 1972 (2) 1975 (4) 1977 (5); v WI 1966 (2) 1969 (2) 1973 (3) 1976 (5) 1980 (1); v NZ 1969 (3) 1973 (1); v In 1971 (1) 1974 (3); v P 1967 (2) 1971 (1) 1974 (3); *v A 1970 (5) 1974 (5) 1976 (1) 1979 (3); v WI 1973 (4); v NZ 1970 (2) 1974 (2); v In 1972 (4) 1976 (5) 1979 (1) 1981 (6); v P 1968 (3) 1972 (2); v SL 1981 (1)*

Valentine, B. H. 7: *v SA 1938 (5); v In 1933 (2)*
Verity (H.) 40: v A 1934 (5) 1938 (4); v SA 1935 (4); v WI 1933 (2) 1939 (1); v NZ 1931 (2) 1937 (1); v In 1936 (3); *v A 1932 (4) 1936 (5); v SA 1938 (5); v NZ 1932 (1); v In 1933 (3)*
Vernon, G. F. 1: *v A 1882*
Vine (J.) 2: *v A 1911 (2)*
Voce (W.) 27: v NZ 1931 (1) 1937 (1); v In 1932 (1) 1936 (1) 1946 (1); *v A 1932 (4) 1936 (5) 1946 (2); v SA 1930 (5); v WI 1929 (4); v NZ 1932 (2)*

Waddington (A.) 2: *v A 1920 (2)*
Wainwright (E.) 5: v A 1893 (1); *v A 1897 (4)*
Walker (P. M.) 3: v SA 1960 (3)
Walters, C. F. 11: v A 1934 (5); v WI 1933 (3); *v In 1933 (3)*
Ward, A. 5: v WI 1976 (1); v NZ 1969 (3); v P 1971 (1)
Ward (A.) 7: v A 1893 (2); *v A 1894 (5)*
Wardle (J. H.) 28: v A 1953 (3) 1956 (1); v SA 1951 (2) 1955 (3); v WI 1950 (1) 1957 (1); v P 1954 (4); *v A 1954 (4); v SA 1956 (4); v WI 1947 (1) 1953 (2); v NZ 1954 (2)*
Warner, P. F. 15: v A 1909 (1) 1912 (1); v SA 1912 (1); *v A 1903 (5); v SA 1898 (2) 1905 (5)*
Warr, J. J. 2: *v A 1950 (2)*
Warren (A. R.) 1: v A 1905
Washbrook (C.) 37: v A 1948 (4) 1956 (3); v SA 1947 (5); v WI 1950 (2); v NZ 1937 (1) 1949 (2); v In 1946 (3); *v A 1946 (5) 1950 (5); v SA 1948 (5); v NZ 1946 (1) 1950 (1)*
Watkins (A. J.) 15: v A 1948 (1); v NZ 1949 (1); v In 1952 (3); *v SA 1948 (5); v In 1951 (5)*
Watson (W.) 23: v A 1953 (3) 1956 (2); v SA 1951 (5) 1955 (1); v NZ 1958 (2); v In 1952 (1); *v A 1958 (2); v WI 1953 (5); v NZ 1958 (2)*
Webbe, A. J. 1: *v A 1878*
Wellard (A. W.) 2: v A 1938 (1); v NZ 1937 (1)
Wharton (A.) 1: v NZ 1949
Whitaker, J. J. 1: *v A 1986*
White (D. W.) 2: v *P 1961 (2)*

White, J. C. 15: v A 1921 (1) 1930 (1); v SA 1929 (3); v WI 1928 (1); *v A 1928 (5); v SA 1930 (4)*
Whysall (W. W.) 4: v A 1930 (1); *v A 1924 (3)*
Wilkinson (L. L.) 3: *v SA 1938 (3)*
Willey, P. 26: v A 1980 (1) 1981 (4) 1985 (1); v WI 1976 (2) 1980 (5); v NZ 1986 (1); v In 1979 (1); *v A 1979 (3); v WI 1980 (4) 1985 (4)*
Williams, N. F. 1: v In 1990
Willis, R. G. D. 90: v A 1977 (5) 1981 (6); v WI 1973 (1) 1976 (2) 1980 (4) 1984 (3); v NZ 1978 (3) 1983 (4); v In 1974 (1) 1979 (3) 1982 (3); v P 1974 (1) 1978 (3) 1982 (2); *v A 1970 (4) 1974 (5) 1976 (1) 1978 (6) 1979 (3) 1982 (5); v WI 1973 (3); v NZ 1970 (1) 1977 (3) 1983 (3); v In 1976 (5) 1981 (5); v P 1977 (3) 1983 (1); v SL 1981 (1)*
Wilson, C. E. M. 2: *v SA 1898 (2)*
Wilson, D. 6: *v NZ 1970 (1); v In 1963 (5)*
Wilson, E. R. 1: *v A 1920*
Wood (A.) 4: v A 1938 (1); v WI 1939 (3)
Wood, B. 12: v A 1972 (1) 1975 (3); v WI 1976 (1); v P 1978 (1); *v NZ 1974 (2); v In 1972 (3); v P 1972 (1)*
Wood, G. E. C. 3: v SA 1924 (3)
Wood (H.) 4: v A 1888 (1); *v SA 1888 (2) 1891 (1)*
Wood (R.) 1: *v A 1886*
Woods S. M. J. 3: *v SA 1895 (3)*
Woolley (F. E.) 64: v A 1909 (1) 1912 (3) 1921 (5) 1926 (5) 1930 (2) 1934 (1); v SA 1912 (3) 1924 (5) 1929 (3); v NZ 1931 (1); v In 1932 (1); *v A 1911 (5) 1920 (5) 1924 (5); v SA 1909 (5) 1913 (5) 1922 (5); v NZ 1929 (4)*
Woolmer, R. A. 19: v A 1975 (2) 1977 (5) 1981 (2); v WI 1976 (5) 1980 (2); *v A 1976 (1); v In 1976 (2)*
Worthington (T. S.) 9: v In 1936 (2); *v A 1936 (3); v NZ 1929 (4)*
Wright, C. W. 3: *v SA 1895 (3)*
Wright (D. V. P.) 34: v A 1938 (3) 1948 (1); v SA 1947 (4); v WI 1939 (3) 1950 (1); v NZ 1949 (1); v In 1946 (2); *v A 1946 (5) 1950 (5); v SA 1938 (3) 1948 (3); v NZ 1946 (1) 1950 (2)*
Wyatt, R. E. S. 40: v A 1930 (1) 1934 (4); v SA 1929 (2) 1935 (5); v WI 1933 (2); v In 1936 (1); *v A 1932 (5) 1936 (2); v SA 1927 (5) 1930 (5); v WI 1929 (2) 1934 (4); v NZ 1932 (2)*
Wynyard, E. G. 3: v A 1896 (1); *v SA 1905 (2)*

Yardley, N. W. D. 20: v A 1948 (5); v SA 1947 (5); v WI 1950 (3); *v A 1946 (5); v SA 1938 (1); v NZ 1946 (1)*
Young (H. I.) 2: v A 1899 (2)
Young (J. A.) 8: v A 1948 (3); v SA 1947 (1); v NZ 1949 (2); *v SA 1948 (2)*
Young, R. A. 2: *v A 1907 (2)*

AUSTRALIA

Number of Test cricketers: 348

a'Beckett, E. L. 4: v E 1928 (2); v SA 1931 (1); *v E 1930 (1)*
Alderman, T. M. 36: v E 1982 (1); v WI 1981 (2) 1984 (3) 1988 (2); v NZ 1989 (1); v P 1981 (3) 1989 (2); v SL 1989 (2); *v E 1981 (6) 1989 (6); v WI 1983 (3); v NZ 1981 (3) 1989 (1); v P 1982 (1)*
Alexander, G. 2: v E 1884 (1); *v E 1880 (1)*
Alexander, H. H. 1: v E 1932
Allan, F. E. 1: v E 1878
Allan, P. J. 1: v E 1965
Allen, R. C. 1: v E 1886
Andrews, T. J. E. 16: v E 1924 (3); *v E 1921 (5) 1926 (5); v SA 1921 (3)*
Archer, K. A. 5: v E 1950 (3); v WI 1951 (2)
Archer, R. G. 19: v E 1954 (4); v SA 1952 (1); *v E 1953 (3) 1956 (5); v WI 1954 (5); v P 1956 (1)*
Armstrong, W. W. 50: v E 1901 (4) 1903 (3) 1907 (5) 1911 (5) 1920 (5); v SA 1910 (5); *v E 1902 (5) 1905 (5) 1909 (5) 1921 (5); v SA 1902 (3)*

Badcock, C. L. 7: v E 1936 (3); *v E 1938 (4)*
Bannerman, A. C. 28: v E 1878 (1) 1881 (3) 1882 (4) 1884 (4) 1886 (1) 1887 (1) 1891 (3); *v E 1880 (1) 1882 (1) 1884 (3) 1888 (3) 1893 (3)*
Bannerman, C. 3: v E 1876 (2) 1878 (1)

Bardsley, W. 41: v E 1911 (4) 1920 (5) 1924 (3); v SA 1910 (5); *v E 1909 (5) 1912 (3) 1921 (5) 1926 (5); v SA 1912 (3) 1921 (3)*
Barnes, S. G. 13: v E 1946 (4); v In 1947 (3); *v E 1938 (1) 1948 (4); v NZ 1945 (1)*
Barnett, B. A. 4: *v E 1938 (4)*
Barrett, J. E. 2: *v E 1890 (2)*
Beard, G. R. 3: *v P 1979 (3)*
Benaud, J. 3: v P 1972 (2); *v WI 1972 (1)*
Benaud, R. 63: v E 1954 (5) 1958 (5) 1962 (5); v SA 1952 (4) 1963 (4); v WI 1951 (1) 1960 (5); *v E 1953 (3) 1956 (5) 1961 (4); v SA 1957 (5); v WI 1954 (5); v In 1956 (3) 1959 (5); v P 1956 (1) 1959 (3)*
Bennett, M. J. 3: v WI 1984 (2); *v E 1985 (1)*
Blackham, J. McC. 35: v E 1876 (2) 1878 (1) 1881 (4) 1882 (4) 1884 (2) 1886 (1) 1887 (1) 1891 (3) 1894 (1); *v E 1880 (1) 1882 (1) 1884 (3) 1886 (3) 1888 (3) 1890 (2) 1893 (3)*
Blackie, D. D. 3: v E 1928 (3)
Bonnor, G. J. 17: v E 1882 (4) 1884 (3); *v E 1880 (1) 1882 (1) 1884 (3) 1886 (2) 1888 (3)*
Boon, D. C. 48: v E 1986 (4) 1987 (1); v WI 1984 (3) 1988 (5); v NZ 1985 (3) 1987 (3) 1989 (1); v In 1985 (3); v P 1989 (2); v SL 1987 (1) 1989 (2); *v E 1985 (4) 1989 (6); v NZ 1985 (3) 1989 (1); v In 1986 (3); v P 1988 (3)*
Booth, B. C. 29: v E 1962 (5) 1965 (3); v SA 1963 (4); v P 1964 (1); *v E 1961 (2) 1964 (5); v WI 1964 (5); v In 1964 (3); v P 1964 (1)*
Border, A. R. 115: v E 1978 (3) 1979 (3) 1982 (5) 1986 (5) 1987 (1); v WI 1979 (3) 1981 (3) 1984 (5) 1988 (5); v NZ 1980 (3) 1985 (3) 1987 (3) 1989 (1); v In 1980 (3) 1985 (3); v P 1978 (2) 1981 (3) 1983 (5) 1989 (3); v SL 1987 (1) 1989 (2); *v E 1980 (1) 1981 (6) 1985 (6) 1989 (6); v WI 1983 (5); v NZ 1981 (3) 1985 (3) 1989 (1); v In 1979 (6) 1986 (3); v P 1979 (3) 1982 (3) 1988 (3); v SL 1982 (1)*
Boyle, H. F. 12: v E 1878 (1) 1881 (4) 1882 (1) 1884 (1); *v E 1880 (1) 1882 (1) 1884 (3)*
Bradman, D. G. 52: v E 1928 (4) 1932 (4) 1936 (5) 1946 (5); v SA 1931 (5); v WI 1930 (5); v In 1947 (5); *v E 1930 (5) 1934 (5) 1938 (4) 1948 (5)*
Bright, R. J. 25: v E 1979 (1); v WI 1979 (1); v NZ 1985 (1); v In 1985 (3); *v E 1977 (3) 1980 (1) 1981 (5); v NZ 1985 (2); v In 1986 (3); v P 1979 (3) 1982 (2)*
Bromley, E. H. 2: v E 1932 (1); *v E 1934 (1)*
Brown, W. A. 22: v E 1936 (2); v In 1947 (3); *v E 1934 (5) 1938 (4) 1948 (2); v SA 1935 (5); v NZ 1945 (1)*
Bruce, W. 14: v E 1884 (2) 1891 (3) 1894 (4); *v E 1886 (2) 1893 (3)*
Burge, P. J. 42: v E 1954 (1) 1958 (1) 1962 (3) 1965 (4); v SA 1963 (5); v WI 1960 (2); *v E 1956 (3) 1961 (5) 1964 (5); v SA 1957 (1); v WI 1954 (1); v In 1956 (3) 1959 (2) 1964 (3); v P 1959 (2) 1964 (1)*
Burke, J. W. 24: v E 1950 (2) 1954 (2) 1958 (5); v WI 1951 (1); *v E 1956 (5); v SA 1957 (5); v In 1956 (3); v P 1956 (1)*
Burn, K. E. 2: *v E 1890 (2)*
Burton, F. J. 2: v E 1886 (1) 1887 (1)

Callaway, S. T. 3: v E 1891 (2) 1894 (1)
Callen, I. W. 1: v In 1977
Campbell, G. D. 4: v P 1989 (1); v SL 1989 (1); *v E 1989 (1); v NZ 1989 (1)*
Carkeek, W. 6: *v E 1912 (3); v SA 1912 (3)*
Carlson, P. H. 2: v E 1978 (2)
Carter, H. 28: v E 1907 (5) 1911 (5) 1920 (2); v SA 1910 (5); *v E 1909 (5) 1921 (4); v SA 1921 (2)*
Chappell, G. S. 87: v E 1970 (5) 1974 (6) 1976 (1) 1979 (3) 1982 (5); v WI 1975 (6) 1979 (3) 1981 (3); v NZ 1973 (3) 1980 (3); v In 1980 (3); v P 1972 (3) 1976 (3) 1981 (3) 1983 (5); *v E 1972 (5) 1975 (4) 1977 (5) 1980 (1); v WI 1972 (5); v NZ 1973 (3) 1976 (2) 1981 (3); v P 1979 (3); v SL 1982 (1)*
Chappell, I. M. 75: v E 1965 (2) 1970 (6) 1974 (6) 1979 (2); v WI 1968 (5) 1975 (6) 1979 (1); v NZ 1973 (3); v In 1967 (4); v P 1964 (1) 1972 (3); *v E 1968 (5) 1972 (5) 1975 (4); v SA 1966 (5) 1969 (4); v WI 1972 (5); v NZ 1973 (3); v In 1969 (5)*
Chappell, T. M. 3: *v E 1981 (3)*
Charlton, P. C. 2: *v E 1890 (2)*
Chipperfield, A. G. 14: v E 1936 (3); *v E 1934 (5) 1938 (1); v SA 1935 (5)*
Clark, W. M. 10: v In 1977 (5); v P 1978 (1); *v WI 1977 (4)*
Colley, D. J. 3: *v E 1972 (3)*
Collins, H. L. 19: v E 1920 (5) 1924 (5); *v E 1921 (3) 1926 (3); v SA 1921 (3)*
Coningham, A. 1: v E 1894

Connolly, A. N. 29: v E 1965 (1) 1970 (1); v SA 1963 (3); v WI 1968 (5); v In 1967 (3); *v E 1968 (5); v SA 1969 (4); v In 1964 (2); 1969 (5)*
Cooper, B. B. 1: v E 1876
Cooper, W. H. 2: v E 1881 (1) 1884 (1)
Corling, G. E. 5: *v E 1964 (5)*
Cosier, G. J. 18: v E 1976 (1) 1978 (2); v WI 1975 (3); v In 1977 (4); v P 1976 (3); *v WI 1977 (3); v NZ 1976 (2)*
Cottam, W. J. 1: v E 1886
Cotter, A. 21: v E 1903 (2) 1907 (2) 1911 (4); v SA 1910 (5); *v E 1905 (3) 1909 (5)*
Coulthard, G. 1: v E 1881
Cowper, R. M. 27: v E 1965 (4); v In 1967 (4); v P 1964 (1); *v E 1964 (1) 1968 (4); v SA 1966 (5); v WI 1964 (5); v In 1964 (2); v P 1964 (1)*
Craig, I. D. 11: v SA 1952 (1); *v E 1956 (2); v SA 1957 (5); v In 1956 (2); v P 1956 (1)*
Crawford, W. P. A. 4: *v E 1956 (1); v In 1956 (3)*

Darling, J. 34: v E 1894 (5) 1897 (5) 1901 (3); *v E 1896 (3) 1899 (5) 1902 (5) 1905 (5); v SA 1902 (3)*
Darling, L. S. 12: v E 1932 (2) 1936 (1); *v E 1934 (4); v SA 1935 (5)*
Darling, W. M. 14: v E 1978 (4); v In 1977 (1); v P 1978 (1); *v WI 1977 (3); v In 1979 (5)*
Davidson, A. K. 44: v E 1954 (3) 1958 (5) 1962 (5); v WI 1960 (4); *v E 1953 (5) 1956 (2) 1961 (5); v SA 1957 (5); v In 1956 (1) 1959 (5); v P 1956 (1) 1959 (3)*
Davis, I. C. 15: v E 1976 (1); v NZ 1973 (3); v P 1976 (3); *v E 1977 (3); v NZ 1973 (3) 1976 (2)*
Davis, S. P. 1: *v NZ 1985*
De Courcy, J. H. 3: *v E 1953 (3)*
Dell, A. R. 2: v E 1970 (1); v NZ 1973 (1)
Dodemaide, A. I. C. 8: v E 1987 (1); v WI 1988 (2); v NZ 1987 (1); v SL 1987 (1); *v P 1988 (3)*
Donnan, H. 5: v E 1891 (2); *v E 1896 (3)*
Dooland, B. 3: v E 1946 (2); v In 1947 (1)
Duff, R. A. 22: v E 1901 (4) 1903 (5); *v E 1902 (5) 1905 (5); v SA 1902 (3)*
Duncan, J. R. F. 1: v E 1970
Dyer, G. C. 6: v E 1986 (1) 1987 (1); v NZ 1987 (3); v SL 1987 (1)
Dymock, G. 21: v E 1974 (1) 1978 (3) 1979 (3); v WI 1979 (2); v NZ 1973 (1); v P 1978 (1); *v NZ 1973 (2); v In 1979 (5); v P 1979 (3)*
Dyson, J. 30: v E 1982 (5); v WI 1981 (2) 1984 (3); v NZ 1980 (3); v In 1977 (3) 1980 (3); *v E 1981 (5); v NZ 1981 (3); v P 1982 (3)*

Eady, C. J. 2: v E 1901 (1); *v E 1896 (1)*
Eastwood, K. H. 1: v E 1970
Ebeling, H. I. 1: *v E 1934*
Edwards, J. D. 3: *v E 1888 (3)*
Edwards, R. 20: v E 1974 (5); v P 1972 (2); *v E 1972 (4) 1975 (4); v WI 1972 (5)*
Edwards, W. J. 3: v E 1974 (3)
Emery, S. H. 4: *v E 1912 (2); v SA 1912 (2)*
Evans, E. 6: v E 1881 (2) 1882 (1) 1884 (1); *v E 1886 (2)*

Fairfax, A. G. 10: v E 1928 (1); v WI 1930 (5); *v E 1930 (4)*
Favell, L. E. 19: v E 1954 (4) 1958 (2); v WI 1960 (4); *v WI 1954 (2); v In 1959 (4); v P 1959 (3)*
Ferris, J. J. 8: v E 1886 (2) 1887 (1); *v E 1888 (3) 1890 (2)*
Fingleton, J. H. 18: v E 1932 (3) 1936 (5); v SA 1931 (1); *v E 1938 (4); v SA 1935 (5)*
Fleetwood-Smith, L. O'B. 10: v E 1936 (3); *v E 1938 (4); v SA 1935 (3)*
Francis, B. C. 3: *v E 1972 (3)*
Freeman, E. W. 11: v WI 1968 (4); v In 1967 (2); *v E 1968 (2); v SA 1969 (2); v In 1969 (1)*
Freer, F. W. 1: v E 1946

Gannon, J. B. 3: v In 1977 (3)
Garrett, T. W. 19: v E 1876 (2) 1878 (1) 1881 (3) 1882 (3) 1884 (3) 1886 (2) 1887 (1); *v E 1882 (1) 1886 (3)*
Gaunt, R. A. 3: v SA 1963 (1); *v E 1961 (1); v SA 1957 (1)*
Gehrs, D. R. A. 6: v E 1903 (1); v SA 1910 (4); *v E 1905 (1)*
Giffen, G. 31: v E 1881 (3) 1882 (4) 1884 (3) 1891 (3) 1894 (5); *v E 1882 (1) 1884 (3) 1886 (3) 1893 (3) 1896 (3)*
Giffen, W. F. 3: v E 1886 (1) 1891 (2)

Gilbert, D. R. 9: v NZ 1985 (3); v In 1985 (2); *v E 1985 (1); v NZ 1985 (1); v In 1986 (2)*
Gilmour, G. J. 15: v E 1976 (1); v WI 1975 (5); v NZ 1973 (2); v P 1976 (3); *v E 1975 (1); v NZ 1973 (1) 1976 (2)*
Gleeson, J. W. 29: v E 1970 (5); v WI 1968 (5); v In 1967 (4); *v E 1968 (5) 1972 (3); v SA 1969 (4); v In 1969 (3)*
Graham, H. 6: v E 1894 (2); *v E 1893 (3) 1896 (1)*
Gregory, D. W. 3: v E 1876 (2) 1878 (1)
Gregory, E. J. 1: v E 1876
Gregory, J. M. 24: v E 1920 (5) 1924 (5) 1928 (1); *v E 1921 (5) 1926 (5); v SA 1921 (3)*
Gregory, R. G. 2: v E 1936 (2)
Gregory, S. E. 58: v E 1891 (1) 1894 (5) 1897 (5) 1901 (5) 1903 (4) 1907 (2) 1911 (1); *v E 1890 (2) 1893 (3) 1896 (3) 1899 (5) 1902 (5) 1905 (3) 1909 (5) 1912 (3); v SA 1902 (3) 1912 (3)*
Grimmett, C. V. 37: v E 1924 (1) 1928 (5) 1932 (3); v SA 1931 (5); v WI 1930 (5); *v E 1926 (3) 1930 (5) 1934 (5); v SA 1935 (5)*
Groube, T. U. 1: *v E 1880*
Grout, A. T. W. 51: v E 1958 (5) 1962 (2) 1965 (5); v SA 1963 (5); v WI 1960 (5); *v E 1961 (5) 1964 (5); v SA 1957 (5); v WI 1964 (5); v In 1959 (4) 1964 (1); v P 1959 (3) 1964 (1)*
Guest, C. E. J. 1: v E 1962

Hamence, R. A. 3: v E 1946 (1); v In 1947 (2)
Hammond, J. R. 5: *v WI 1972 (5)*
Harry, J. 1: v E 1894
Hartigan, R. J. 2: v E 1907 (2)
Hartkopf, A. E. V. 1: v E 1924
Harvey, M. R. 1: v E 1946
Harvey, R. N. 79: v E 1950 (5) 1954 (5) 1958 (5) 1962 (5); v SA 1952 (5); v WI 1951 (5) 1960 (4); v In 1947 (2); *v E 1948 (2) 1953 (5) 1956 (5) 1961 (5); v SA 1949 (5) 1957 (4); v WI 1954 (5); v In 1956 (3) 1959 (5); v P 1956 (1) 1959 (3)*
Hassett, A. L. 43: v E 1946 (5) 1950 (5); v SA 1952 (5); v WI 1951 (4); v In 1947 (4); *v E 1938 (4) 1948 (5) 1953 (5); v SA 1949 (5); v NZ 1945 (1)*
Hawke, N. J. N. 27: v E 1962 (1) 1965 (4); v SA 1963 (4); v In 1967 (1); v P 1964 (1); *v E 1964 (5) 1968 (2); v SA 1966 (2); v WI 1964 (5); v In 1964 (1); v P 1964 (1)*
Hazlitt, G. R. 9: v E 1907 (2) 1911 (1); *v E 1912 (3); v SA 1912 (3)*
Healy, I. A. 21: v WI 1988 (5); v NZ 1989 (1); v P 1989 (3); v SL 1989 (2); *v E 1989 (6); v NZ 1989 (1); v P 1988 (3)*
Hendry, H. S. T. L. 11: v E 1924 (1) 1928 (4); *v E 1921 (4); v SA 1921 (2)*
Hibbert, P. A. 1: v In 1977
Higgs, J. D. 22: v E 1978 (5) 1979 (1); v WI 1979 (1); v NZ 1980 (3); v In 1980 (2); *v WI 1977 (4); v In 1979 (6)*
Hilditch, A. M. J. 18: v E 1978 (1); v WI 1984 (2); v NZ 1985 (1); v P 1978 (2); *v E 1985 (6); v In 1979 (6)*
Hill, C. 49: v E 1897 (5) 1901 (5) 1903 (5) 1907 (5) 1911 (5); v SA 1910 (5); *v E 1896 (3) 1899 (3) 1902 (5) 1905 (5); v SA 1902 (3)*
Hill, J. C. 3: *v E 1953 (2); v WI 1954 (1)*
Hoare, D. E. 1: v WI 1960
Hodges, J. H. 2: v E 1876 (2)
Hogan, T. G. 7: v P 1983 (1); *v WI 1983 (5); v SL 1982 (1)*
Hogg, R. M. 38: v E 1978 (6) 1982 (3); v WI 1979 (2) 1984 (4); v NZ 1980 (2); v In 1980 (2); v P 1978 (2) 1983 (4); *v E 1981 (2); v WI 1983 (4); v In 1979 (6); v SL 1982 (1)*
Hohns, T. V. 7: v WI 1988 (2); *v E 1989 (5)*
Hole, G. B. 18: v E 1950 (1) 1954 (3); v SA 1952 (4); v WI 1951 (5); *v E 1953 (5)*
Holland, R. G. 11: v WI 1984 (3); v NZ 1985 (3); v In 1985 (1); *v E 1985 (4)*
Hookes, D. W. 23: v E 1976 (1) 1982 (5); v WI 1979 (1); v NZ 1985 (2); v In 1985 (2); *v E 1977 (5); v WI 1983 (5); v P 1979 (1); v SL 1982 (1)*
Hopkins, A. J. Y. 20: v E 1901 (2) 1903 (5); *v E 1902 (5) 1905 (3) 1909 (2); v SA 1902 (3)*
Horan, T. P. 15: v E 1876 (1) 1878 (1) 1881 (4) 1882 (4) 1884 (4); *v E 1882 (1)*
Hordern, H. V. 7: v E 1911 (5); v SA 1910 (2)
Hornibrook, P. M. 6: v E 1928 (1); *v E 1930 (5)*
Howell, W. P. 18: v E 1897 (3) 1901 (4) 1903 (3); *v E 1899 (5) 1902 (1); v SA 1902 (2)*
Hughes, K. J. 70: v E 1978 (6) 1979 (3) 1982 (5); v WI 1979 (3) 1981 (3) 1984 (4); v NZ 1980 (3); v In 1977 (2) 1980 (3); v P 1978 (2) 1981 (3) 1983 (5); *v E 1977 (1) 1980 (1) 1981 (6); v WI 1983 (5); v NZ 1981 (3); v In 1979 (6); v P 1979 (3) 1982 (3)*

Hughes, M. G. 23: v E 1986 (4); v WI 1988 (4); v NZ 1987 (1) 1989 (1); v In 1985 (1); v P 1989 (3); v SL 1987 (1) 1989 (2); *v E 1989 (6)*
Hunt, W. A. 1: v SA 1931
Hurst, A. G. 12: v E 1978 (6); v NZ 1973 (1); v In 1977 (1); v P 1978 (2); *v In 1979 (2)*
Hurwood, A. 2: v WI 1930 (2)

Inverarity, R. J. 6: v WI 1968 (1); *v E 1968 (2) 1972 (3)*
Iredale, F. A. 14: v E 1894 (5) 1897 (4); *v E 1896 (2) 1899 (3)*
Ironmonger, H. 14: v E 1928 (2) 1932 (4); v SA 1931 (4); v WI 1930 (4)
Iverson, J. B. 5: v E 1950 (5)

Jackson, A. 8: v E 1928 (2); v WI 1930 (4); *v E 1930 (2)*
Jarman, B. N. 19: v E 1962 (3); v WI 1968 (4); v In 1967 (4); v P 1964 (1); *v E 1968 (4); v In 1959 (1); 1964 (2)*
Jarvis, A. H. 11: v E 1884 (3) 1894 (4); *v E 1886 (2) 1888 (2)*
Jenner, T. J. 9: v E 1970 (2) 1974 (2); v WI 1975 (1); *v WI 1972 (4)*
Jennings, C. B. 6: *v E 1912 (3); v SA 1912 (3)*
Johnson I. W. 45: v E 1946 (4) 1950 (5) 1954 (4); v SA 1952 (1); v WI 1951 (4); v In 1947 (4); *v E 1948 (4) 1956 (5); v SA 1949 (5); v WI 1954 (5); v NZ 1945 (1); v In 1956 (2); v P 1956 (1)*
Johnson, L. J. 1: v In 1947
Johnston W. A. 40: v E 1950 (5) 1954 (4); v SA 1952 (5); v WI 1951 (5); v In 1947 (4); *v E 1948 (5) 1953 (3); v SA 1949 (5); v WI 1954 (4)*
Jones, D. M. 34: v E 1986 (5) 1987 (1); v WI 1988 (3); v NZ 1987 (3) 1989 (1); v P 1989 (3); v SL 1987 (1) 1989 (2); *v E 1989 (6); v WI 1983 (2); v NZ 1989 (1); v In 1986 (3); v P 1988 (3)*
Jones, E. 19: v E 1894 (1) 1897 (5) 1901 (2); *v E 1896 (3) 1899 (5) 1902 (2); v SA 1902 (1)*
Jones, S. P. 12: v E 1881 (2) 1884 (4) 1886 (1) 1887 (1); *v E 1882 (1) 1886 (3)*
Joslin, L. R. 1: v In 1967

Kelleway, C. 26: v E 1911 (4) 1920 (5) 1924 (5) 1928 (1); v SA 1910 (5); *v E 1912 (3); v SA 1912 (3)*
Kelly, J. J. 36: v E 1897 (5) 1901 (5) 1903 (5); *v E 1896 (3) 1899 (5) 1902 (5) 1905 (5); v SA 1902 (3)*
Kelly, T. J. D. 2: v E 1876 (1) 1878 (1)
Kendall, T. 2: v E 1876 (2)
Kent, M. F. 3: *v E 1981 (3)*
Kerr, R. B. 2: v NZ 1985 (2)
Kippax, A. F. 22: v E 1924 (1) 1928 (5) 1932 (1); v SA 1931 (4); v WI 1930 (5); *v E 1930 (5) 1934 (1)*
Kline L. F. 13: v E 1958 (2); v WI 1960 (2); *v SA 1957 (5); v In 1959 (3); v P 1959 (1)*

Laird, B. M. 21: v E 1979 (2); v WI 1979 (3) 1981 (3); v P 1981 (3); *v E 1980 (1); v NZ 1981 (3); v P 1979 (3) 1982 (3)*
Langley, G. R. A. 26: v E 1954 (2); v SA 1952 (5); v WI 1951 (5); *v E 1953 (4) 1956 (3); v WI 1954 (4); v In 1956 (2); v P 1956 (1)*
Laughlin, T. J. 3: v E 1978 (1); *v WI 1977 (2)*
Laver, F. 15: v E 1901 (1) 1903 (1); *v E 1899 (4) 1905 (5) 1909 (4)*
Lawry, W. M. 67: v E 1962 (5) 1965 (5) 1970 (5); v SA 1963 (5); v WI 1968 (5); v In 1967 (4); v P 1964 (1); *v E 1961 (5) 1964 (5) 1968 (4); v SA 1966 (5) 1969 (4); v WI 1964 (5); v In 1964 (3) 1969 (5); v P 1964 (1)*
Lawson, G. F. 46: v E 1982 (5) 1986 (1); v WI 1981 (1) 1984 (5) 1988 (1); v NZ 1980 (1) 1985 (2) 1989 (1); v P 1983 (5); v SL 1989 (1); *v E 1981 (3) 1985 (6) 1989 (6); v WI 1983 (5); v P 1982 (3)*
Lee, P. K. 2: v E 1932 (1); v SA 1931 (1)
Lillee, D. K. 70: v E 1970 (2) 1974 (6) 1976 (1) 1979 (3) 1982 (1); v WI 1975 (5) 1979 (3) 1981 (3); v NZ 1980 (3); v In 1980 (3); v P 1972 (3) 1976 (3) 1981 (3) 1983 (5); *v E 1972 (5) 1975 (4) 1980 (1) 1981 (6); v WI 1972 (1); v NZ 1976 (2) 1981 (3); v P 1979 (3); v SL 1982 (1)*
Lindwall, R. R. 61: v E 1946 (4) 1950 (5) 1954 (4) 1958 (2); v SA 1952 (4); v WI 1951 (5); v In 1947 (5); *v E 1948 (5) 1953 (5) 1956 (4); v SA 1949 (4); v WI 1954 (5); v NZ 1945 (1); v In 1956 (3) 1959 (2); v P 1956 (1) 1959 (2)*
Love, H. S. B. 1: v E 1932
Loxton, S. J. E. 12: v E 1950 (3); v In 1947 (1); *v E 1948 (3); v SA 1949 (5)*
Lyons, J. J. 14: v E 1886 (1) 1891 (3) 1894 (3) 1897 (1); *v E 1888 (1) 1890 (2) 1893 (3)*

McAlister, P. A. 8: v E 1903 (2) 1907 (4); *v E 1909 (2)*
Macartney, C. G. 35: v E 1907 (5) 1911 (1) 1920 (2); v SA 1910 (4); *v E 1909 (5) 1912 (3) 1921 (5) 1926 (5); v SA 1912 (3) 1921 (2)*

McCabe, S. J. 39: v E 1932 (5) 1936 (5); v SA 1931 (5); v WI 1930 (5); *v E 1930 (5) 1934 (5) 1938 (4); v SA 1935 (5)*
McCool, C. L. 14: v E 1946 (5); v In 1947 (3); *v SA 1949 (5) v NZ 1945 (1)*
McCormick, E. L. 12: v E 1936 (4); *v E 1938 (3); v SA 1935 (5)*
McCosker, R. B. 25: v E 1974 (3) 1976 (1) 1979 (2); v WI 1975 (4) 1979 (1); v P 1976 (3); *v E 1975 (4) 1977 (5); v NZ 1976 (2)*
McDermott, C. J. 24: v E 1986 (1) 1987 (1); v WI 1984 (2) 1988 (2); v NZ 1985 (2) 1987 (3); v In 1985 (2); v SL 1987 (1); *v E 1985 (6); v NZ 1985 (2); v In 1986 (2)*
McDonald, C. C. 47: v E 1954 (2) 1958 (5); v SA 1952 (5); v WI 1951 (1) 1960 (5); *v E 1956 (5) 1961 (3); v SA 1957 (5); v WI 1954 (5); v In 1956 (2) 1959 (5); v P 1956 (1) 1959 (3)*
McDonald, E. A. 11: v E 1920 (3); *v E 1921 (5); v SA 1921 (3)*
McDonnell, P. S. 19: v E 1881 (4) 1882 (3) 1884 (2) 1886 (2) 1887 (1); *v E 1880 (1) 1884 (3) 1888 (3)*
McIlwraith, J. 1: *v E 1886*
Mackay K. D. 37: v E 1958 (5) 1962 (3); v WI 1960 (5); *v E 1956 (3) 1961 (5); v SA 1957 (5); v In 1956 (3) 1959 (5); v P 1959 (3)*
McKenzie, G. D. 60: v E 1962 (5) 1965 (4) 1970 (3); v SA 1963 (5); v WI 1968 (5); v In 1967 (2); v P 1964 (1); *v E 1961 (3) 1964 (5) 1968 (5); v SA 1966 (5) 1969 (3); v WI 1964 (5); v In 1964 (3) 1969 (5); v P 1964 (1)*
McKibbin, T. R. 5: v E 1894 (1) 1897 (2); *v E 1896 (2)*
McLaren, J. W. 1: v E 1911
Maclean, J. A. 4: v E 1978 (4)
McLeod, C. E. 17: v E 1894 (1) 1897 (5) 1901 (2) 1903 (3); *v E 1899 (1) 1905 (5)*
McLeod, R. W. 6: v E 1891 (3); *v E 1893 (3)*
McShane, P. G. 3: v E 1884 (1) 1886 (1) 1887 (1)
Maddocks, L. V. 7: v E 1954 (3); *v E 1956 (2); v WI 1954 (1); v In 1956 (1)*
Maguire, J. N. 3: v P 1983 (1); *v WI 1983 (2)*
Mailey, A. A. 21: v E 1920 (5) 1924 (5); *v E 1921 (3) 1926 (5); v SA 1921 (3)*
Mallett, A. A. 38: v E 1970 (2) 1974 (5) 1979 (1); v WI 1968 (1) 1975 (6) 1979 (1); v NZ 1973 (3); v P 1972 (2); *v E 1968 (1) 1972 (2) 1975 (4) 1980 (1); v SA 1969 (1); v NZ 1973 (3); v In 1969 (5)*
Malone, M. F. 1: *v E 1977*
Mann, A. L. 4: v In 1977 (4)
Marr, A. P. 1: v E 1884
Marsh, G. R. 36: v E 1986 (5) 1987 (1); v WI 1988 (5); v NZ 1987 (3); v In 1985 (3); v P 1989 (2); v SL 1987 (1); *v E 1989 (6); v NZ 1985 (3) 1989 (1); v In 1986 (3); v P 1988 (3)*
Marsh, R. W. 96: v E 1970 (6) 1974 (6) 1976 (1) 1979 (3) 1982 (5); v WI 1975 (6) 1979 (3) 1981 (3); v NZ 1973 (3) 1980 (3); v In 1980 (3); v P 1972 (3) 1976 (3) 1981 (3) 1983 (5); *v E 1972 (5) 1975 (4) 1977 (5) 1980 (1) 1981 (6); v WI 1972 (5); v NZ 1973 (3) 1976 (2) 1981 (3); v P 1979 (3) 1982 (3)*
Martin, J. W. 8: v SA 1963 (1); v WI 1960 (3); *v SA 1966 (1); v In 1964 (2); v P 1964 (1)*
Massie, H. H. 9: v E 1881 (4) 1882 (3) 1884 (1); *v E 1882 (1)*
Massie, R. A. L. 6: v P 1972 (2); *v E 1972 (4)*
Matthews, C. D. 3: v E 1986 (2); v WI 1988 (1)
Matthews, G. R. J. 21: v E 1986 (4); v WI 1984 (1); v NZ 1985 (3); v In 1985 (3); v P 1983 (2); *v E 1985 (1); v WI 1983 (1); v NZ 1985 (3); v In 1986 (3)*
Matthews, T. J. 8: v E 1911 (2); *v E 1912 (3); v SA 1912 (3)*
May, T. B. A. 7: v WI 1988 (3); v NZ 1987 (1); *v P 1988 (3)*
Mayne, E. R. 4: *v E 1912 (1); v SA 1912 (1) 1921 (2)*
Mayne, L. C. 6: *v SA 1969 (2); v WI 1964 (3); v In 1969 (1)*
Meckiff, I. 18: v E 1958 (4); v SA 1963 (1); v WI 1960 (2); *v SA 1957 (4); v In 1959 (5); v P 1959 (2)*
Meuleman, K. D. 1: *v NZ 1945*
Midwinter, W. E. 8: v E 1876 (2) 1882 (1) 1886 (2); *v E 1884 (3)*
Miller, K. R. 55: v E 1946 (5) 1950 (5) 1954 (4); v SA 1952 (4); v WI 1951 (5); v In 1947 (5); *v E 1948 (5) 1953 (5) 1956 (5); v SA 1949 (5); v WI 1954 (5); v NZ 1945 (1); v P 1956 (1)*
Minnett, R. B. 9: v E 1911 (5); *v E 1912 (1); v SA 1912 (3)*
Misson, F. M. 5: v WI 1960 (3); *v E 1961 (2)*
Moody, T. M. 4: v NZ 1989 (1); v P 1989 (1); v SL 1989 (2)
Moroney, J. R. 7: v E 1950 (1); v WI 1951 (1); *v SA 1949 (5)*
Morris, A. R. 46: v E 1946 (5) 1950 (5) 1954 (4); v SA 1952 (5); v WI 1951 (4); v In 1947 (4); *v E 1948 (5) 1953 (5); v SA 1949 (5); v WI 1954 (4)*
Morris, S. 1: v E 1884

Moses, H. 6: v E 1886 (2) 1887 (1) 1891 (2) 1894 (1)
Moss, J. K. 1: v P 1978
Moule, W. H. 1: *v E 1880*
Murdoch, W. L. 18: v E 1876 (1) 1878 (1) 1881 (4) 1882 (4) 1884 (1); *v E 1880 (1) 1882 (1) 1884 (3) 1890 (2)*
Musgrove, H. 1: v E 1884

Nagel, L. E. 1: v E 1932
Nash, L. J. 2: v E 1936 (1); v SA 1931 (1)
Nitschke, H. C. 2: v SA 1931 (2)
Noble, M. A. 42: v E 1897 (4) 1901 (5) 1903 (5) 1907 (5); *v E 1899 (5) 1902 (5) 1905 (5) 1909 (5); v SA 1902 (3)*
Noblet, G. 3: v SA 1952 (1); v WI 1951 (1); *v SA 1949 (1)*
Nothling, O. E. 1: v E 1928

O'Brien, L. P. J. 5: v E 1932 (2) 1936 (1); *v SA 1935 (2)*
O'Connor, J. D. A. 4: v E 1907 (3); *v E 1909 (1)*
O'Donnell, S. P. 6: v NZ 1985 (1); *v E 1985 (5)*
Ogilvie, A. D. 5: v In 1977 (3); *v WI 1977 (2)*
O'Keeffe, K. J. 24: v E 1970 (2) 1976 (1); v NZ 1973 (3); v P 1972 (2) 1976 (3); *v E 1977 (3); v WI 1972 (5); v NZ 1973 (3) 1976 (2)*
Oldfield, W. A. 54: v E 1920 (3) 1924 (5) 1928 (5) 1932 (4) 1936 (5); v SA 1931 (5); v WI 1930 (5); *v E 1921 (1) 1926 (5) 1930 (5) 1934 (5); v SA 1921 (1) 1935 (5)*
O'Neill, N. C. 42: v E 1958 (5) 1962 (5); v SA 1963 (4); v WI 1960 (5); *v E 1961 (5) 1964 (4); v WI 1964 (4); v In 1959 (5) 1964 (2); v P 1959 (3)*
O'Reilly, W. J. 27: v E 1932 (5) 1936 (5); v SA 1931 (2); *v E 1934 (5) 1938 (4); v SA 1935 (5); v NZ 1945 (1)*
Oxenham, R. K. 7: v E 1928 (3); v SA 1931 (1); v WI 1930 (3)

Palmer, G. E. 17: v E 1881 (4) 1882 (4) 1884 (2); *v E 1880 (1) 1884 (3) 1886 (3)*
Park, R. L. 1: v E 1920
Pascoe, L. S. 14: v E 1979 (2); v WI 1979 (1) 1981 (1); v NZ 1980 (3); v In 1980 (3); *v E 1977 (3) 1980 (1)*
Pellew, C. E. 10: v E 1920 (4); *v E 1921 (5); v SA 1921 (1)*
Phillips, W. B. 27: v WI 1984 (2); v NZ 1985 (3); v In 1985 (3); v P 1983 (5); *v E 1985 (6); v WI 1983 (5); v NZ 1985 (3)*
Philpott, P. I. 8: v E 1965 (3); *v WI 1964 (5)*
Ponsford, W. H. 29: v E 1924 (5) 1928 (2) 1932 (3); v SA 1931 (4); v WI 1930 (5); *v E 1926 (2) 1930 (4) 1934 (4)*
Pope, R. J. 1: v E 1884

Rackemann, C. G. 11: v E 1982 (1); v WI 1984 (1); v NZ 1989 (1); v P 1983 (2) 1989 (3); v SL 1989 (1); *v WI 1983 (1); v NZ 1989 (1)*
Ransford, V. S. 20: v E 1907 (5) 1911 (5); v SA 1910 (5); *v E 1909 (5)*
Redpath, I. R. 66: v E 1965 (1) 1970 (6) 1974 (6); v SA 1963 (1); v WI 1968 (5) 1975 (6); v In 1967 (3); v P 1972 (3); *v E 1964 (5) 1968 (5); v SA 1966 (5) 1969 (4); v WI 1972 (5); v NZ 1973 (3); v In 1964 (2) 1969 (5); v P 1964 (1)*
Reedman, J. C. 1: v E 1894
Reid, B. A. 18: v E 1986 (5); v NZ 1987 (2); v In 1985 (3); *v NZ 1985 (3); v In 1986 (2); v P 1988 (3)*
Renneberg, D. A. 8: v In 1967 (3); *v SA 1966 (5)*
Richardson, A. J. 9: v E 1924 (4); *v E 1926 (5)*
Richardson, V. Y. 19: v E 1924 (3) 1928 (2) 1932 (5); *v E 1930 (4); v SA 1935 (5)*
Rigg, K. E. 8: v E 1936 (3); v SA 1931 (4); v WI 1930 (1)
Ring, D. T. 13: v SA 1952 (5); v WI 1951 (5); v In 1947 (1); *v E 1948 (1) 1953 (1)*
Ritchie, G. M. 30: v E 1986 (4); v WI 1984 (1); v NZ 1985 (3); v In 1985 (2); *v E 1985 (6); v WI 1983 (5); v NZ 1985 (3); v In 1986 (3); v P 1982 (3)*
Rixon, S. J. 13: v WI 1984 (3); v In 1977 (5); *v WI 1977 (5)*
Robertson, W. R. 1: v E 1884
Robinson, R. D. 3: *v E 1977 (3)*
Robinson, R. H. 1: v E 1936
Rorke, G. F. 4: v E 1958 (2); *v In 1959 (2)*

Rutherford, J. W. 1: *v In 1956*
Ryder, J. 20: v E 1920 (5) 1924 (3) 1928 (5); *v E 1926 (4); v SA 1921 (3)*

Saggers, R. A. 6: *v E 1948 (1); v SA 1949 (5)*
Saunders, J. V. 14: v E 1901 (1) 1903 (2) 1907 (5); *v E 1902 (4); v SA 1902 (2)*
Scott, H. J. H. 8: v E 1884 (2); *v E 1884 (3) 1886 (3)*
Sellers, R. H. D. 1: *v In 1964*
Serjeant, C. S. 12: v In 1977 (4); *v E 1977 (3); v WI 1977 (5)*
Sheahan, A. P. 31: v E 1970 (2); v WI 1968 (5); v NZ 1973 (2); v In 1967 (4); v P 1972 (2); *v E 1968 (5) 1972 (2); v SA 1969 (4); v In 1969 (5)*
Shepherd, B. K. 9: v E 1962 (2); v SA 1963 (4); v P 1964 (1); *v WI 1964 (2)*
Sievers, M. W. 3: v E 1936 (3)
Simpson, R. B. 62: v E 1958 (1) 1962 (5) 1965 (3); v SA 1963 (5); v WI 1960 (5); v In 1967 (3) 1977 (5); v P 1964 (1); *v E 1961 (5) 1964 (5); v SA 1957 (5) 1966 (5); v WI 1964 (5) 1977 (5); v In 1964 (3); v P 1964 (1)*
Sincock, D. J. 3: v E 1965 (1); v P 1964 (1); *v WI 1964 (1)*
Slater, K. N. 1: v E 1958
Sleep, P. R. 14: v E 1986 (3) 1987 (1); v NZ 1987 (3); v P 1978 (1) 1989 (1); v SL 1989 (1); *v In 1979 (2); v P 1982 (1) 1988 (1)*
Slight, J. 1: *v E 1880*
Smith, D. B. M. 2: *v E 1912 (2)*
Smith, S. B. 3: *v WI 1983 (3)*
Spofforth, F. R. 18: v E 1876 (1) 1878 (1) 1881 (1) 1882 (4) 1884 (3) 1886 (1); *v E 1882 (1) 1884 (3) 1886 (3)*
Stackpole, K. R. 43: v E 1965 (2) 1970 (6); v WI 1968 (5); v NZ 1973 (3); v P 1972 (1); *v E 1972 (5); v SA 1966 (5) 1969 (4); v WI 1972 (4); v NZ 1973 (3); v In 1969 (5)*
Stevens, G. B. 4: *v In 1959 (2); v P 1959 (2)*

Taber, H. B. 16: v WI 1968 (1); *v E 1968 (1); v SA 1966 (5); 1969 (4); v In 1969 (5)*
Tallon, D. 21: v E 1946 (5) 1950 (5); v In 1947 (5); *v E 1948 (4) 1953 (1); v NZ 1945 (1)*
Taylor, J. M. 20: v E 1920 (5) 1924 (5); *v E 1921 (5) 1926 (3); v SA 1921 (2)*
Taylor, M. A. 15: v WI 1988 (2); v NZ 1989 (1); v P 1989 (3); v SL 1989 (2); *v E 1989 (6); v NZ 1989 (1)*
Taylor, P. L. 10: v E 1986 (1) 1987 (1); v WI 1988 (2); v P 1989 (2); v SL 1987 (1); *v NZ 1989 (1); v P 1988 (2)*
Thomas, G. 8: v E 1965 (3); *v WI 1964 (5)*
Thompson, N. 2: v E 1876 (2)
Thoms, G. R. 1: v WI 1951
Thomson, A. L. 4: v E 1970 (4)
Thomson, J. R. 51: v E 1974 (5) 1979 (1) 1982 (4); v WI 1975 (6) 1979 (1) 1981 (2); v In 1977 (5); v P 1972 (1) 1976 (1) 1981 (3); *v E 1975 (4) 1977 (5) 1985 (2); v WI 1977 (5); v NZ 1981 (3); v P 1982 (3)*
Thurlow, H. M. 1: v SA 1931
Toohey, P. M. 15: v E 1978 (5) 1979 (1); v WI 1979 (1); v In 1977 (5); *v WI 1977 (3)*
Toshack, E. R. H. 12: v E 1946 (5); v In 1947 (2); *v E 1948 (4); v NZ 1945 (1)*
Travers, J. P. F. 1: v E 1901
Tribe, G. E. 3: v E 1946 (3)
Trott, A. E. 3: v E 1894 (3)
Trott, G. H. S. 24: v E 1891 (3) 1894 (5) 1897 (5); *v E 1888 (3) 1890 (2) 1893 (3) 1896 (3)*
Trumble, H. 32: v E 1894 (1) 1897 (5) 1901 (5) 1903 (4); *v E 1890 (2) 1893 (3) 1896 (3) 1899 (5) 1902 (3); v SA 1902 (1)*
Trumble, J. W. 7: v E 1884 (4); *v E 1886 (3)*
Trumper, V. T. 48: v E 1901 (5) 1903 (5) 1907 (5) 1911 (5); v SA 1910 (5); *v E 1899 (5) 1902 (5) 1905 (5) 1909 (5); v SA 1902 (3)*
Turner, A. 14: v WI 1975 (6); v P 1976 (3); *v E 1975 (3); v NZ 1976 (2)*
Turner, C. T. B. 17: v E 1886 (2) 1887 (1) 1891 (3) 1894 (3); *v E 1888 (3) 1890 (2) 1893 (3)*

Veivers, T. R. 21: v E 1965 (4); v SA 1963 (3); v P 1964 (1); *v E 1964 (5); v SA 1966 (4); v In 1964 (3); v P 1964 (1)*
Veletta, M. R. J. 8: v E 1987 (1); v WI 1988 (2); v NZ 1987 (3); v P 1989 (1); v SL 1987 (1)

Waite, M. G. 2: *v E 1938 (2)*
Walker, M. H. N. 34: v E 1974 (6); 1976 (1); v WI 1975 (3); v NZ 1973 (1); v P 1972 (2) 1976 (2); *v E 1975 (4); 1977 (5); v WI 1972 (5); v NZ 1973 (3) 1976 (2)*

Wall, T. W. 18: v E 1928 (1) 1932 (4); v SA 1931 (3); v WI 1930 (1); *v E 1930 (5) 1934 (4)*
Walters, F. H. 1: v E 1884
Walters, K. D. 74: v E 1965 (5) 1970 (6) 1974 (6) 1976 (1); v WI 1968 (4); v NZ 1973 (3) 1980 (3); v In 1967 (2) 1980 (3); v P 1972 (1) 1976 (3); *v E 1968 (5) 1972 (4) 1975 (4) 1977 (5); v SA 1969 (4); v WI 1972 (5); v NZ 1973 (3) 1976 (2); v In 1969 (5)*
Ward, F. A. 4: v E 1936 (3); *v E 1938 (1)*
Watkins, J. R. 1: v P 1972
Watson, G. D. 5: *v E 1972 (2); v SA 1966 (3)*
Watson, W. 4: v E 1954 (1); *v WI 1954 (3)*
Waugh, S. R. 39: v E 1986 (5) 1987 (1); v WI 1988 (5); v NZ 1987 (3) 1989 (1); v In 1985 (2); v P 1989 (3); v SL 1987 (1) 1989 (2); *v E 1989 (6); v NZ 1985 (3) 1989 (1); v In 1986 (3); v P 1988 (3)*
Wellham, D. M. 6: v E 1986 (1); v WI 1981 (1); v P 1981 (2); *v E 1981 (1) 1985 (1)*
Wessels, K. C. 24: v E 1982 (4); v WI 1984 (5); v NZ 1985 (1); v P 1983 (5); *v E 1985 (6); v WI 1983 (2); v SL 1982 (1)*
Whatmore, D. F. 7: v P 1978 (2); *v In 1979 (5)*
Whitney, M. R. 4: v WI 1988 (1); v NZ 1987 (1); *v E 1981 (2)*
Whitty, W. J. 14: v E 1911 (2); v SA 1910 (5); *v E 1909 (1) 1912 (3); v SA 1912 (3)*
Wiener, J. M. 6: v E 1979 (2); v WI 1979 (2); *v P 1979 (2)*
Wilson, J. W. 1: *v In 1956*
Wood, G. M. 59: v E 1978 (6) 1982 (1); v WI 1981 (3) 1984 (5) 1988 (3); v NZ 1980 (3); v In 1977 (1) 1980 (3); v P 1978 (1) 1981 (3); *v E 1980 (1) 1981 (6) 1985 (5); v WI 1977 (5) 1983 (1); v NZ 1981 (3); v In 1979 (2); v P 1982 (3) 1988 (3); v SL 1982 (1)*
Woodcock, A. J. 1: v NZ 1973
Woodfull, W. M. 35: v E 1928 (5) 1932 (5); v SA 1931 (5); v WI 1930 (5); *v E 1926 (5) 1930 (5) 1934 (5)*
Woods, S. M. J. 3: *v E 1888 (3)*
Woolley, R. D. 2: *v WI 1983 (1); v SL 1982 (1)*
Worrall, J. 11: v E 1884 (1) 1887 (1) 1894 (1) 1897 (1); *v E 1888 (3) 1899 (4)*
Wright, K. J. 10: v E 1978 (2); v P 1978 (2); *v In 1979 (6)*

Yallop, G. N. 39: v E 1978 (6); v WI 1975 (3) 1984 (1); v In 1977 (1); v P 1978 (1) 1981 (1) 1983 (5); *v E 1980 (1) 1981 (6); v WI 1977 (4); v In 1979 (6); v P 1979 (3); v SL 1982 (1)*
Yardley, B. 33: v E 1978 (4) 1982 (5); v WI 1981 (3); v In 1977 (1) 1980 (2); v P 1978 (1) 1981 (3); *v WI 1977 (5); v NZ 1981 (3); v In 1979 (3); v P 1982 (2); v SL 1982 (1)*

Zoehrer, T. J. 10: v E 1986 (4); *v NZ 1985 (3); v In 1986 (3)*

SOUTH AFRICA

Number of Test cricketers: 235

Adcock, N. A. T. 26: v E 1956 (5); v A 1957 (5); v NZ 1953 (5) 1961 (2); *v E 1955 (4) 1960 (5)*
Anderson, J. H. 1: v A 1902
Ashley, W. H. 1: v E 1888

Bacher, A. 12: v A 1966 (5) 1969 (4); *v E 1965 (3)*
Balaskas, X. C. 9: v E 1930 (2) 1938 (1); v A 1935 (3); *v E 1935 (1); v NZ 1931 (2)*
Barlow, E. J. 30: v E 1964 (5); v A 1966 (5) 1969 (4); v NZ 1961 (5); *v E 1965 (3); v A 1963 (5); v NZ 1963 (3)*
Baumgartner, H. V. 1: v E 1913
Beaumont, R. 5: v E 1913 (2); *v E 1912 (1); v A 1912 (2)*
Begbie, D. W. 5: v E 1948 (3); v A 1949 (2)
Bell, A. J. 16: v E 1930 (3); *v E 1929 (3) 1935 (3); v A 1931 (5); v NZ 1931 (2)*
Bisset, M. 3: v E 1898 (2) 1909 (1)
Bissett, G. F. 4: v E 1927 (4)
Blanckenberg, J. M. 18: v E 1913 (5) 1922 (5); v A 1921 (3); *v E 1924 (5)*
Bland, K. C. 21: v E 1964 (5); v A 1966 (1); v NZ 1961 (5); *v E 1965 (3); v A 1963 (4); v NZ 1963 (3)*
Bock, E. G. 1: v A 1935
Bond, G. E. 1: v E 1938

Botten, J. T. 3: *v E 1965 (3)*
Brann, W. H. 3: v E 1922 (3)
Briscoe, A. W. 2: v E 1938 (1); v A 1935 (1)
Bromfield, H. D. 9: v E 1964 (3); v NZ 1961 (5); *v E 1965 (1)*
Brown, L. S. 2: *v A 1931 (1); v NZ 1931 (1)*
Burger, C. G. de V. 2: v A 1957 (2)
Burke, S. F. 2: v E 1964 (1); v NZ 1961 (1)
Buys, I. D. 1: v E 1922

Cameron, H. B. 26: v E 1927 (5) 1930 (5); *v E 1929 (4) 1935 (5); v A 1931 (5); v NZ 1931 (2)*
Campbell, T. 5: v E 1909 (4); *v E 1912 (1)*
Carlstein, P. R. 8: v A 1957 (1); *v E 1960 (5); v A 1963 (2)*
Carter, C. P. 10: v E 1913 (2); v A 1921 (3); *v E 1912 (2) 1924 (3)*
Catterall, R. H. 24: v E 1922 (5) 1927 (5) 1930 (4); *v E 1924 (5) 1929 (5)*
Chapman, H. W. 2: v E 1913 (1); v A 1921 (1)
Cheetham, J. E. 24: v E 1948 (1); v A 1949 (3); v NZ 1953 (5); *v E 1951 (5) 1955 (3); v A 1952 (5); v NZ 1952 (2)*
Chevalier, G. A. 1: v A 1969
Christy, J. A. J. 10: v E 1930 (1); *v E 1929 (2); v A 1931 (5); v NZ 1931 (2)*
Chubb, G. W. A. 5: *v E 1951 (5)*
Cochran, J. A. K. 1: v E 1930
Coen, S. K. 2: v E 1927 (2)
Commaille, J. M. M. 12: v E 1909 (5) 1927 (2); *v E 1924 (5)*
Conyngham, D. P. 1: v E 1922
Cook, F. J. 1: v E 1895
Cooper, A. H. C. 1: v E 1913
Cox, J. L. 3: v E 1913 (3)
Cripps, G. 1: v E 1891
Crisp, R. J. 9: v A 1935 (4); *v E 1935 (5)*
Curnow, S. H. 7: v E 1930 (3); *v A 1931 (4)*

Dalton, E. L. 15: v E 1930 (1) 1938 (4); v A 1935 (1); *v E 1929 (1) 1935 (4); v A 1931 (2); v NZ 1931 (2)*
Davies, E. Q. 5: v E 1938 (3); v A 1935 (2)
Dawson, O. C. 9: v E 1948 (4); *v E 1947 (5)*
Deane, H. G. 17: v E 1927 (5) 1930 (2); *v E 1924 (5) 1929 (5)*
Dixon, C. D. 1: v E 1913
Dower, R. R. 1: v E 1898
Draper, R. G. 2: v A 1949 (2)
Duckworth, C. A. R. 2: v E 1956 (2)
Dumbrill, R. 5: v A 1966 (2); *v E 1965 (3)*
Duminy, J. P. 3: v E 1927 (2); *v E 1929 (1)*
Dunell, O. R. 2: v E 1888 (2)
Du Preez, J. H. 2: v A 1966 (2)
Du Toit, J. F. 1: v E 1891
Dyer, D. V. 3: *v E 1947 (3)*

Elgie, M. K. 3: v NZ 1961 (3)
Endean, W. R. 28: v E 1956 (5); v A 1957 (5); v NZ 1953 (5); *v E 1951 (1) 1955 (5); v A 1952 (5); v NZ 1952 (2)*

Farrer, W. S. 6: v NZ 1961 (3); *v NZ 1963 (3)*
Faulkner, G. A. 25: v E 1905 (5) 1909 (5); *v E 1907 (3) 1912 (3) 1924 (1); v A 1910 (5) 1912 (3)*
Fellows-Smith, J. P. 4: *v E 1960 (4)*
Fichardt, C. G. 2: v E 1891 (1) 1895 (1)
Finlason, C. E. 1: v E 1888
Floquet, C. E. 1: v E 1909
Francis, H. H. 2: v E 1898 (2)
Francois, C. M. 5: v E 1922 (5)
Frank, C. N. 3: v A 1921 (3)
Frank, W. H. B. 1: v E 1895
Fuller, E. R. H. 7: v A 1957 (1); *v E 1955 (2); v A 1952 (2); v NZ 1952 (2)*

Fullerton, G. M. 7: v A 1949 (2); *v E 1947 (2) 1951 (3)*
Funston, K. J. 18: v E 1956 (3); v A 1957 (5); v NZ 1953 (3); *v A 1952 (5); v NZ 1952 (2)*

Gamsy, D. 2: v A 1969 (2)
Gleeson, R. A. 1: v E 1895
Glover, G. K. 1: v E 1895
Goddard, T. L. 41: v E 1956 (5) 1964 (5); v A 1957 (5) 1966 (5) 1969 (3); *v E 1955 (5) 1960 (5); v A 1963 (5); v NZ 1963 (3)*
Gordon, N. 5: v E 1938 (5)
Graham, R. 2: v E 1898 (2)
Grieveson, R. E. 2: v E 1938 (2)
Griffin, G. M. 2: *v E 1960 (2)*

Hall, A. E. 7: v E 1922 (4) 1927 (2) 1930 (1)
Hall, G. G. 1: v E 1964
Halliwell, E. A. 8: v E 1891 (1) 1895 (3) 1898 (1); v A 1902 (3)
Halse, C. G. 3: *v A 1963 (3)*
Hands, P. A. M. 7: v E 1913 (5); v A 1921 (1); *v E 1924 (1)*
Hands, R. H. M. 1: v E 1913
Hanley, M. A. 1: v E 1948
Harris, T. A. 3: v E 1948 (1); *v E 1947 (2)*
Hartigan, G. P. D. 5: v E 1913 (3); *v E 1912 (1); v A 1912 (1)*
Harvey, R. L. 2: v A 1935 (2)
Hathorn, C. M. H. 12: v E 1905 (5); v A 1902 (3); *v E 1907 (3); v A 1910 (1)*
Hearne, F. 4: v E 1891 (1) 1895 (3)
Hearne, G. A. L. 3: v E 1922 (2); *v E 1924 (1)*
Heine, P. S. 14: v E 1956 (5); v A 1957 (4); v NZ 1961 (1); *v E 1955 (4)*
Hime, C. F. W. 1: v E 1895
Hutchinson, P. 2: v E 1888 (2)

Ironside, D. E. J. 3: v NZ 1953 (3)
Irvine, B. L. 4: v A 1969 (4)

Johnson, C. L. 1: v E 1895

Keith, H. J. 8: v E 1956 (3); *v E 1955 (4); v A 1952 (1)*
Kempis, G. A. 1: v E 1888
Kotze, J. J. 3: v A 1902 (2); *v E 1907 (1)*
Kuys, F. 1: v E 1898

Lance, H. R. 13: v A 1966 (5) 1969 (3); v NZ 1961 (2); *v E 1965 (3)*
Langton, A. B. C. 15: v E 1938 (5); v A 1935 (5); *v E 1935 (5)*
Lawrence, G. B. 5: v NZ 1961 (5)
Le Roux, F. le S. 1: v E 1913
Lewis, P. T. 1: v E 1913
Lindsay, D. T. 19: v E 1964 (3); v A 1966 (5) 1969 (2); *v E 1965 (3); v A 1963 (3); v NZ 1963 (3)*
Lindsay, J. D. 3: *v E 1947 (3)*
Lindsay, N. V. 1: v A 1921
Ling, W. V. S. 6: v E 1922 (3); v A 1921 (3)
Llewellyn, C. B. 15: v E 1895 (1) 1898 (1); v A 1902 (3); *v E 1912 (3); v A 1910 (5) 1912 (2)*
Lundie, E. B. 1: v E 1913

Macaulay, M. J. 1: v E 1964
McCarthy, C. N. 15: v E 1948 (5); v A 1949 (5); *v E 1951 (5)*
McGlew, D. J. 34: v E 1956 (1); v A 1957 (5); v NZ 1953 (5) 1961 (5); *v E 1951 (2) 1955 (5) 1960 (5); v A 1952 (4); v NZ 1952 (2)*
McKinnon, A. H. 8: v E 1964 (2); v A 1966 (2); v NZ 1961 (1); *v E 1960 (1) 1965 (2)*
McLean, R. A. 40: v E 1956 (5) 1964 (2); v A 1957 (4); v NZ 1953 (4) 1961 (5); *v E 1951 (3) 1955 (5) 1960 (5); v A 1952 (5); v NZ 1952 (2)*
McMillan, Q. 13: v E 1930 (5); *v E 1929 (2); v A 1931 (4); v NZ 1931 (2)*
Mann, N. B. F. 19: v E 1948 (5); v A 1949 (5); *v E 1947 (5) 1951 (4)*
Mansell, P. N. F. 13: *v E 1951 (2) 1955 (4); v A 1952 (5); v NZ 1952 (2)*
Markham, L. A. 1: v E 1948

Marx, W. F. E. 3: v A 1921 (3)
Meintjes, D. J. 2: v E 1922 (2)
Melle, M. G. 7: v A 1949 (2); *v E 1951 (1); v A 1952 (4)*
Melville, A. 11: v E 1938 (5) 1948 (1); *v E 1947 (5)*
Middleton, J. 6: v E 1895 (2) 1898 (2); v A 1902 (2)
Mills, C. 1: v E 1891
Milton, W. H. 3: v E 1888 (2) 1891 (1)
Mitchell, B. 42: v E 1930 (5) 1938 (5) 1948 (5); v A 1935 (5); *v E 1929 (5) 1935 (5) 1947 (5); v A 1931 (5); v NZ 1931 (2)*
Mitchell, F. 3: *v E 1912 (1); v A 1912 (2)*
Morkel, D. P. B. 16: v E 1927 (5); *v E 1929 (5); v A 1931 (5); v NZ 1931 (1)*
Murray, A. R. A. 10: v NZ 1953 (4); *v A 1952 (4); v NZ 1952 (2)*

Nel, J. D. 6: v A 1949 (5) 1957 (1)
Newberry, C. 4: v E 1913 (4)
Newson, E. S. 3: v E 1930 (1) 1938 (2)
Nicholson, F. 4: v A 1935 (4)
Nicolson, J. F. W. 3: v E 1927 (3)
Norton, N. O. 1: v E 1909
Nourse, A. D. 34: v E 1938 (5) 1948 (5); v A 1935 (5) 1949 (5); *v E 1935 (4) 1947 (5) 1951 (5)*
Nourse, A. W. 45: v E 1905 (5) 1909 (5) 1913 (5) 1922 (5); v A 1902 (3) 1921 (3); *v E 1907 (3) 1912 (3) 1924 (5); v A 1910 (5) 1912 (3)*
Nupen, E. P. 17: v E 1922 (4) 1927 (5) 1930 (3); v A 1921 (2) 1935 (1); *v E 1924 (2)*

Ochse, A. E. 2: v E 1888 (2)
Ochse, A. L. 3: v E 1927 (1); *v E 1929 (2)*
O'Linn, S. 7: v NZ 1961 (2); *v E 1960 (5)*
Owen-Smith, H. G. 5: *v E 1929 (5)*

Palm, A. W. 1: v E 1927
Parker, G. M. 2: *v E 1924 (2)*
Parkin, D. C. 1: v E 1891
Partridge, J. T. 11: v E 1964 (3); *v A 1963 (5); v NZ 1963 (3)*
Pearse, O. C. 3: *v A 1910 (3)*
Pegler, S. J. 16: v E 1909 (1); *v E 1912 (3) 1924 (5); v A 1910 (4) 1912 (3)*
Pithey, A. J. 17: v E 1956 (3) 1964 (5); *v E 1960 (2); v A 1963 (4); v NZ 1963 (3)*
Pithey, D. B. 8: v A 1966 (2); *v A 1963 (3); v NZ 1963 (3)*
Plimsoll, J. B. 1: *v E 1947*
Pollock, P. M. 28: v E 1964 (5); v A 1966 (5) 1969 (4); v NZ 1961 (3); *v E 1965 (3); v A 1963 (5); v NZ 1963 (3)*
Pollock, R. G. 23: v E 1964 (5); v A 1966 (5) 1969 (4); *v E 1965 (3); v A 1963 (5); v NZ 1963 (1)*
Poore, R. M. 3: v E 1895 (3)
Pothecary, J. E. 3: *v E 1960 (3)*
Powell, A. W. 1: v E 1898
Prince, C. F. H. 1: v E 1898
Procter, M. J. 7: v A 1966 (3) 1969 (4)
Promnitz, H. L. E. 2: v E 1927 (2)

Quinn, N. A. 12: v E 1930 (1); *v E 1929 (4); v A 1931 (5); v NZ 1931 (2)*

Reid, N. 1: v A 1921
Richards, A. R. 1: v E 1895
Richards, B. A. 4: v A 1969 (4)
Richards, W. H. 1: v E 1888
Robertson, J. B. 3: v A 1935 (3)
Rose-Innes, A. 2: v E 1888 (2)
Routledge, T. W. 4: v E 1891 (1) 1895 (3)
Rowan, A. M. B. 15: v E 1948 (5); *v E 1947 (5) 1951 (5)*
Rowan, E. A. B. 26: v E 1938 (4) 1948 (4); v A 1935 (3); 1949 (5); *v E 1935 (5) 1951 (5)*
Rowe, G. A. 5: v E 1895 (2) 1898 (2); v A 1902 (1)

Samuelson, S. V. 1: v E 1909
Schwarz, R. O. 20: v E 1905 (5) 1909 (4); *v E 1907 (3) 1912 (1); v A 1910 (5) 1912 (2)*
Seccull, A. W. 1: v E 1895

Seymour, M. A. 7: v E 1964 (2); v A 1969 (1); *v A 1963 (4)*
Shalders, W. A. 12: v E 1898 (1) 1905 (5); v A 1902 (3); *v E 1907 (3)*
Shepstone, G. H. 2: v E 1895 (1) 1898 (1)
Sherwell, P. W. 13: v E 1905 (5); *v E 1907 (3); v A 1910 (5)*
Siedle, I. J. 18: v E 1927 (1) 1930 (5); v A 1935 (5); *v E 1929 (3) 1935 (4)*
Sinclair, J. H. 25: v E 1895 (3) 1898 (2) 1905 (5) 1909 (4); v A 1902 (3); *v E 1907 (3); v A 1910 (5)*
Smith, C. J. E. 3: v A 1902 (3)
Smith, F. W. 3: v E 1888 (2) 1895 (1)
Smith, V. I. 9: v A 1949 (3) 1957 (1); *v E 1947 (4) 1955 (1)*
Snooke, S. D. 1: *v E 1907*
Snooke, S. J. 26: v E 1905 (5) 1909 (5) 1922 (3); *v E 1907 (3) 1912 (3); v A 1910 (5) 1912 (2)*
Solomon, W. R. 1: v E 1898
Stewart, R. B. 1: v E 1888
Stricker, L. A. 13: v E 1909 (4); *v E 1912 (2); v A 1910 (5) 1912 (2)*
Susskind, M. J. 5: *v E 1924 (5)*

Taberer, H. M. 1: v A 1902
Tancred, A. B. 2: v E 1888 (2)
Tancred, L. J. 14: v E 1905 (5) 1913 (1); v A 1902 (3); *v E 1907 (1) 1912 (2); v A 1912 (2)*
Tancred, V. M. 1: v E 1898
Tapscott, G. L. 1: v E 1913
Tapscott, L. E. 2: v E 1922 (2)
Tayfield, H. J. 37: v E 1956 (5); v A 1949 (5) 1957 (5); v NZ 1953 (5); *v E 1955 (5) 1960 (5); v A 1952 (5); v NZ 1952 (2)*
Taylor, A. I. 1: v E 1956
Taylor, D. 2: v E 1913 (2)
Taylor, H. W. 42: v E 1913 (5) 1922 (5) 1927 (5) 1930 (4); v A 1921 (3); *v E 1912 (3) 1924 (5) 1929 (3); v A 1912 (3) 1931 (5); v NZ 1931 (1)*
Theunissen, N. H. G. de J. 1: v E 1888
Thornton, P. G. 1: v A 1902
Tomlinson, D. S. 1: *v E 1935*
Traicos, A. J. 3: v A 1969 (3)
Trimborn, P. H. J. 4: v A 1966 (3) 1969 (1)
Tuckett, L. 9: v E 1948 (4); *v E 1947 (5)*
Tuckett, L. R. 1: v E 1913
Twentyman-Jones, P. S. 1: v A 1902

van der Bijl, P. G. V. 5: v E 1938 (5)
Van der Merwe, E. A. 2: v A 1935 (1); *v E 1929 (1)*
Van der Merwe, P. L. 15: v E 1964 (2); v A 1966 (5); *v E 1965 (3); v A 1963 (3); v NZ 1963 (2)*
Van Ryneveld, C. B. 19: v E 1956 (5); v A 1957 (4); v NZ 1953 (5); *v E 1951 (5)*
Varnals, G. D. 3: v E 1964 (3)
Viljoen, K. G. 27: v E 1930 (3) 1938 (4) 1948 (2); v A 1935 (4); *v E 1935 (4) 1947 (5); v A 1931 (4); v NZ 1931 (1)*
Vincent, C. L. 25: v E 1927 (5) 1930 (5); *v E 1929 (4) 1935 (4); v A 1931 (5); v NZ 1931 (2)*
Vintcent, C. H. 3: v E 1888 (2) 1891 (1)
Vogler, A. E. E. 15: v E 1905 (5) 1909 (5); *v E 1907 (3); v A 1910 (2)*

Wade, H. F. 10: v A 1935 (5); *v E 1935 (5)*
Wade, W. W. 11: v E 1938 (3) 1948 (5); v A 1949 (3)
Waite, J. H. B. 50: v E 1956 (5); 1964 (2); v A 1957 (5); v NZ 1953 (5) 1961 (5); *v E 1951 (4) 1955 (5) 1960 (5); v A 1952 (5) 1963 (4); v NZ 1952 (2) 1963 (3)*
Walter, K. A. 2: v NZ 1961 (2)
Ward, T. A. 23: v E 1913 (5) 1922 (5); v A 1921 (3); *v E 1912 (2) 1924 (5); v A 1912 (3)*
Watkins, J. C. 15: v E 1956 (2); v A 1949 (3); v NZ 1953 (3); *v A 1952 (5); v NZ 1952 (2)*
Wesley, C. 3: *v E 1960 (3)*
Westcott, R. J. 5: v A 1957 (2); v NZ 1953 (3)
White, G. C. 17: v E 1905 (5) 1909 (4); *v E 1907 (3) 1912 (2); v A 1912 (3)*
Willoughby, J. T. I. 2: v E 1895 (2)
Wimble, C. S. 1: v E 1891
Winslow, P. L. 5: v A 1949 (2); *v E 1955 (3)*
Wynne, O. E. 6: v E 1948 (3); v A 1949 (3)

Zulch, J. W. 16: v E 1909 (5) 1913 (3); v A 1921 (3); *v A 1910 (5)*

WEST INDIES

Number of Test cricketers: 195

Achong, E. 6: v E 1929 (1) 1934 (2); *v E 1933 (3)*
Alexander, F. C. M. 25: v E 1959 (5); v P 1957 (5); *v E 1957 (2); v A 1960 (5); v In 1958 (5); v P 1958 (3)*
Ali, Imtiaz 1: v In 1975
Ali, Inshan 12: v E 1973 (2); v A 1972 (3); v In 1970 (1); v P 1976 (1); v NZ 1971 (3); *v E 1973 (1); v A 1975 (1)*
Allan, D. W. 5: v A 1964 (1); v In 1961 (2); *v E 1966 (2)*
Ambrose, C. E. L. 20: v E 1989 (3); v In 1988 (4); v P 1987 (3); *v E 1988 (5); v A 1988 (5)*
Arthurton, K. L. T. 5: v In 1988 (4); *v E 1988 (1)*
Asgarali, N. 2: *v E 1957 (2)*
Atkinson, D. St E. 22: v E 1953 (4); v A 1954 (4); v P 1957 (1); *v E 1957 (2); v A 1951 (2); v NZ 1951 (1) 1955 (4); v In 1948 (4)*
Atkinson, E. St E. 8: v P 1957 (3); *v In 1958 (3); v P 1958 (2)*
Austin, R. A. 2: v A 1977 (2)

Bacchus, S. F. A. F. 19: v A 1977 (2); *v E 1980 (5); v A 1981 (2); v In 1978 (6); v P 1980 (4)*
Baichan, L. 3: *v A 1975 (1); v P 1974 (2)*
Baptiste, E. A. E. 10: v E 1989 (1); v A 1983 (3); *v E 1984 (5); v In 1983 (1)*
Barrett, A. G. 6: v E 1973 (2); v In 1970 (2); *v In 1974 (2)*
Barrow, I. 11: v E 1929 (1) 1934 (1); *v E 1933 (3) 1939 (1); v A 1930 (5)*
Bartlett, E. L. 5: *v E 1928 (1); v A 1930 (4)*
Benjamin, W. K. M. 8: v In 1988 (1); v P 1987 (3); *v E 1988 (3); v In 1987 (1)*
Best, C. A. 6: v E 1985 (3) 1989 (3)
Betancourt, N. 1: v E 1929
Binns, A. P. 5: v A 1954 (1); v In 1952 (1); *v NZ 1955 (3)*
Birkett, L. S. 4: *v A 1930 (4)*
Bishop, I. R. 8: v E 1989 (4); v In 1988 (4)
Boyce, K. D. 21: v E 1973 (4); v A 1972 (4); v In 1970 (1); *v E 1973 (3); v A 1975 (4); v In 1974 (3); v P 1974 (2)*
Browne, C. R. 4: v E 1929 (2); *v E 1928 (2)*
Butcher, B. F. 44: v E 1959 (2) 1967 (5); v A 1964 (5); *v E 1963 (5) 1966 (5) 1969 (3); v A 1968 (5); v NZ 1968 (3); v In 1958 (5) 1966 (3); v P 1958 (3)*
Butler, L. 1: v A 1954
Butts, C. G. 7: v NZ 1984 (1); *v NZ 1986 (1); v In 1987 (3); v P 1986 (2)*
Bynoe, M. R. 4: *v In 1966 (3); v P 1958 (1)*

Camacho, G. S. 11: v E 1967 (5); v In 1970 (2); *v E 1969 (2); v A 1968 (2)*
Cameron, F. J. 5: *v In 1948 (5)*
Cameron, J. H. 2: *v E 1939 (2)*
Carew, G. M. 4: v E 1934 (1) 1947 (2); *v In 1948 (1)*
Carew, M. C. 19: v E 1967 (1); v NZ 1971 (3); v In 1970 (3); *v E 1963 (2) 1966 (1) 1969 (1); v A 1968 (5); v NZ 1968 (3)*
Challenor, G. 3: *v E 1928 (3)*
Chang, H. S. 1: *v In 1978*
Christiani, C. M. 4: v E 1934 (4)
Christiani, R. J. 22: v E 1947 (4) 1953 (1); v In 1952 (2); *v E 1950 (4); v A 1951 (5); v NZ 1951 (1); v In 1948 (5)*
Clarke, C. B. 3: *v E 1939 (3)*
Clarke, S. T. 11: v A 1977 (1); *v A 1981 (1); v In 1978 (5); v P 1980 (4)*
Constantine, L. N. 18: v E 1929 (3) 1934 (3); *v E 1928 (3) 1933 (1) 1939 (3); v A 1930 (5)*
Croft, C. E. H. 27: v E 1980 (4); v A 1977 (2); v P 1976 (5); *v E 1980 (3); v A 1979 (3) 1981 (3); v NZ 1979 (3); v P 1980 (4)*

Da Costa, O. C. 5: v E 1929 (1) 1934 (1); *v E 1933 (3)*
Daniel, W. W. 10: v A 1983 (2); v In 1975 (1); *v E 1976 (4); v In 1983 (3)*
Davis, B. A. 4: v A 1964 (4)
Davis, C. A. 15: v A 1972 (2); v NZ 1971 (5); v In 1970 (4); *v E 1969 (3); v A 1968 (1)*

Davis, W. W. 15: v A 1983 (1); v NZ 1984 (2); v In 1982 (1); *v E 1984 (1); v In 1983 (6) 1987 (4)*
De Caires, F. I. 3: v E 1929 (3)
Depeiza, C. C. 5: v A 1954 (3); *v NZ 1955 (2)*
Dewdney, T. 9: v A 1954 (2); v P 1957 (3); *v E 1957 (1); v NZ 1955 (3)*
Dowe, U. G. 4: v A 1972 (1); v NZ 1971 (1); v In 1970 (2)
Dujon, P. J. L. 68: v E 1985 (4) 1989 (4); v A 1983 (5); v NZ 1984 (4); v In 1982 (5) 1988 (4); v P 1987 (3); *v E 1984 (5) 1988 (5); v A 1981 (3) 1984 (5) 1988 (5); v NZ 1986 (3); v In 1983 (6) 1987 (4); v P 1986 (3)*

Edwards, R. M. 5: *v A 1968 (2); v NZ 1968 (3)*

Ferguson, W. 8: v E 1947 (4) 1953 (1); *v In 1948 (3)*
Fernandes, M. P. 2: v E 1929 (1); *v E 1928 (1)*
Findlay, T. M. 10: v A 1972 (1); v NZ 1971 (5); v In 1970 (2); *v E 1969 (2)*
Foster, M. L. C. 14: v E 1973 (1); v A 1972 (4) 1977 (1); v NZ 1971 (3); v In 1970 (2); v P 1976 (1); *v E 1969 (1) 1973 (1)*
Francis, G. N. 10: v E 1929 (1); *v E 1928 (3) 1933 (1); v A 1930 (5)*
Frederick, M. C. 1: v E 1953
Fredericks, R. C. 59: v E 1973 (5); v A 1972 (5); v NZ 1971 (5); v In 1970 (4) 1975 (4); v P 1976 (5); *v E 1969 (3) 1973 (3) 1976 (5); v A 1968 (4) 1975 (6); v NZ 1968 (3); v In 1974 (5); v P 1974 (2)*
Fuller, R. L. 1: v E 1934
Furlonge, H. A. 3: v A 1954 (1); *v NZ 1955 (2)*

Ganteaume, A. G. 1: v E 1947
Garner, J. 58: v E 1980 (4) 1985 (5); v A 1977 (2) 1983 (5); v NZ 1984 (4); v In 1982 (4); v P 1976 (5); *v E 1980 (5) 1984 (5); v A 1979 (3) 1981 (3) 1984 (5); v NZ 1979 (3) 1986 (2); v P 1980 (3)*
Gaskin, B. B. M. 2: v E 1947 (2)
Gibbs, G. L. R. 1: v A 1954
Gibbs, L. R. 79: v E 1967 (5) 1973 (5); v A 1964 (5) 1972 (5); v NZ 1971 (2); v In 1961 (5) 1970 (1); v P 1957 (4); *v E 1963 (5) 1966 (5) 1969 (3) 1973 (3); v A 1960 (3) 1968 (5) 1975 (6); v NZ 1968 (3); v In 1958 (1) 1966 (3) 1974 (5); v P 1958 (3) 1974 (2)*
Gilchrist, R. 13: v P 1957 (5); *v E 1957 (4); v In 1958 (4)*
Gladstone, G. 1: v E 1929
Goddard, J. D. C. 27: v E 1947 (4); *v E 1950 (4) 1957 (5); v A 1951 (4); v NZ 1951 (2) 1955 (3); v In 1948 (5)*
Gomes, H. A. 60: v E 1980 (4) 1985 (5); v A 1977 (3) 1983 (2); v NZ 1984 (4); v In 1982 (5); *v E 1976 (2) 1984 (5); v A 1981 (3) 1984 (5); v NZ 1986 (3); v In 1978 (6) 1983 (6); v P 1980 (4) 1986 (3)*
Gomez, G. E. 29: v E 1947 (4) 1953 (4); v In 1952 (4); *v E 1939 (2) 1950 (4); v A 1951 (5); v NZ 1951 (1); v In 1948 (5)*
Grant, G. C. 12: v E 1934 (4); *v E 1933 (3); v A 1930 (5)*
Grant, R. S. 7: v E 1934 (4); *v E 1939 (3)*
Gray, A. H. 5: *v NZ 1986 (2); v P 1986 (3)*
Greenidge, A. E. 6: v A 1977 (2); *v In 1978 (4)*
Greenidge, C. G. 100: v E 1980 (4) 1985 (5) 1989 (4); v A 1977 (2) 1983 (5); v NZ 1984 (4); v In 1982 (5) 1988 (4); v P 1976 (5) 1987 (3); *v E 1976 (5) 1980 (5) 1984 (5) 1988 (4); v A 1975 (2) 1979 (3) 1981 (2) 1984 (5) 1988 (5); v NZ 1979 (3) 1986 (3); v In 1974 (5) 1983 (6) 1987 (3); v P 1986 (3)*
Greenidge, G. A. 5: v A 1972 (3); v NZ 1971 (2)
Grell, M. G. 1: v E 1929
Griffith, C. C. 28: v E 1959 (1) 1967 (4); v A 1964 (5); *v E 1963 (5) 1966 (5); v A 1968 (3); v NZ 1968 (2); v In 1966 (3)*
Griffith, H. C. 13: v E 1929 (3); *v E 1928 (3) 1933 (2); v A 1930 (5)*
Guillen, S. C. 5: *v A 1951 (3); v NZ 1951 (2)*

Hall, W. W. 48: v E 1959 (5) 1967 (4); v A 1964 (5); v In 1961 (5); *v E 1963 (5) 1966 (5); v A 1960 (5) 1968 (2); v NZ 1968 (1); v In 1958 (5) 1966 (3); v P 1958 (3)*
Harper, R. A. 24: v E 1985 (2); v A 1983 (4); v NZ 1984 (1); *v E 1984 (5) 1988 (3); v A 1984 (2) 1988 (1); v In 1983 (2) 1987 (1); v P 1986 (3)*
Haynes, D. L. 89: v E 1980 (4) 1985 (5) 1989 (4); v A 1977 (2) 1983 (5); v NZ 1984 (4); v In 1982 (5) 1988 (4); v P 1987 (3); *v E 1980 (5) 1984 (5) 1988 (4); v A 1979 (3) 1981 (3) 1984 (5) 1988 (5); v NZ 1979 (3) 1986 (3); v In 1983 (6) 1987 (4); v P 1980 (4) 1986 (3)*

Headley, G. A. 22: v E 1929 (4) 1934 (4) 1947 (1) 1953 (1); *v E 1933 (3) 1939 (3); v A 1930 (5); v In 1948 (1)*
Headley, R. G. A. 2: *v E 1973 (2)*
Hendriks, J. L. 20: v A 1964 (4); v In 1961 (1); *v E 1966 (3) 1969 (1); v A 1968 (5); v NZ 1968 (3); v In 1966 (3)*
Hoad, E. L. G. 4: v E 1929 (1); *v E 1928 (1) 1933 (2)*
Holder, V. A. 40: v E 1973 (1); v A 1972 (3) 1977 (3); v NZ 1971 (4); v In 1970 (3) 1975 (1); v P 1976 (1); *v E 1969 (3) 1973 (2) 1976 (4); v A 1975 (3); v In 1974 (4) 1978 (6); v P 1974 (2)*
Holding, M. A. 60: v E 1980 (4) 1985 (4); v A 1983 (3); v NZ 1984 (3); v In 1975 (4) 1982 (5); *v E 1976 (4) 1980 (5) 1984 (4); v A 1975 (5) 1979 (3) 1981 (3) 1984 (3); v NZ 1979 (3) 1986 (1); v In 1983 (6)*
Holford, D. A. J. 24: v E 1967 (4); v NZ 1971 (5); v In 1970 (1) 1975 (2); v P 1976 (1); *v E 1966 (5); v A 1968 (2); v NZ 1968 (3); v In 1966 (1)*
Holt, J. K. 17: v E 1953 (5); v A 1954 (5); *v In 1958 (5); v P 1958 (2)*
Hooper, C. L. 19: v E 1989 (3); v P 1987 (3); *v E 1988 (5); v A 1988 (5); v In 1987 (3)*
Howard, A. B. 1: v NZ 1971
Hunte, C. C. 44: v E 1959 (5); v A 1964 (5); v In 1961 (5); v P 1957 (5); *v E 1963 (5) 1966 (5); v A 1960 (5); v In 1958 (5) 1966 (3); v P 1958 (1)*
Hunte, E. A. C. 3: v E 1929 (3)
Hylton, L. G. 6: v E 1934 (4); *v E 1939 (2)*

Johnson, H. H. H. 3: v E 1947 (1); *v E 1950 (2)*
Johnson, T. F. 1: *v E 1939*
Jones, C. M. 4: v E 1929 (1) 1934 (3)
Jones, P. E. 9: v E 1947 (1); *v E 1950 (2); v A 1951 (1); v In 1948 (5)*
Julien, B. D. 24: v E 1973 (5); v In 1975 (4); v P 1976 (1); *v E 1973 (3) 1976 (2); v A 1975 (3); v In 1974 (4); v P 1974 (2)*
Jumadeen, R. R. 12: v A 1972 (1) 1977 (2); v NZ 1971 (1); v In 1975 (4); v P 1976 (1); *v E 1976 (1); v In 1978 (2)*

Kallicharran, A. I. 66: v E 1973 (5); v A 1972 (5) 1977 (5); v NZ 1971 (2); v In 1975 (4); v P 1976 (5); *v E 1973 (3) 1976 (3) 1980 (5); v A 1975 (6) 1979 (3); v NZ 1979 (3); v In 1974 (5) 1978 (6); v P 1974 (2) 1980 (4)*
Kanhai, R. B. 79: v E 1959 (5) 1967 (5) 1973 (5); v A 1964 (5) 1972 (5); v In 1961 (5) 1970 (5); v P 1957 (5); *v E 1957 (5) 1963 (5) 1966 (5) 1973 (3); v A 1960 (5) 1968 (5); v In 1958 (5) 1966 (3); v P 1958 (3)*
Kentish, E. S. M. 2: v E 1947 (1) 1953 (1)
King, C. L. 9: v P 1976 (1); *v E 1976 (3) 1980 (1); v A 1979 (1); v NZ 1979 (3)*
King, F. M. 14: v E 1953 (3); v A 1954 (4); v In 1952 (5); *v NZ 1955 (2)*
King, L. A. 2: v E 1967 (1); v In 1961 (1)

Lashley, P. D. 4: *v E 1966 (2); v A 1960 (2)*
Legall, R. 4: v In 1952 (4)
Lewis, D. M. 3: v In 1970 (3)
Lloyd, C. H. 110: v E 1967 (5) 1973 (5) 1980 (4); v A 1972 (3) 1977 (2) 1983 (4); v NZ 1971 (2); v In 1970 (5) 1975 (4) 1982 (5); v P 1976 (5); *v E 1969 (3) 1973 (3) 1976 (5) 1980 (4) 1984 (5); v A 1968 (4) 1975 (6) 1979 (2) 1981 (3) 1984 (5); v NZ 1968 (3) 1979 (3); v In 1966 (3) 1974 (5) 1983 (6); v P 1974 (2) 1980 (4)*
Logie, A. L. 40: v E 1989 (3); v A 1983 (1); v NZ 1984 (4); v In 1982 (5) 1988 (4); v P 1987 (3); *v E 1988 (5); v A 1988 (5); v NZ 1986 (3); v In 1983 (3) 1987 (4)*

McMorris, E. D. A. 13: v E 1959 (4); v In 1961 (4); v P 1957 (1); *v E 1963 (2) 1966 (2)*
McWatt, C. A. 6: v E 1953 (5); v A 1954 (1)
Madray, I. S. 2: v P 1957 (2)
Marshall, M. D. 68: v E 1980 (1) 1985 (5) 1989 (2); v A 1983 (4); v NZ 1984 (4); v In 1982 (5) 1988 (3); v P 1987 (2); *v E 1980 (4) 1984 (4) 1988 (5); v A 1984 (5) 1988 (5); v NZ 1986 (3); v In 1978 (3) 1983 (6); v P 1980 (4) 1986 (3)*
Marshall, N. E. 1: v A 1954
Marshall, R. E. 4: *v A 1951 (2); v NZ 1951 (2)*
Martin, F. R. 9: v E 1929 (1); *v E 1928 (3); v A 1930 (5)*
Martindale, E. A. 10: v E 1934 (4); *v E 1933 (3) 1939 (3)*
Mattis, E. H. 4: v E 1980 (4)

Mendonca, I. L. 2: v In 1961 (2)
Merry, C. A. 2: *v E 1933 (2)*
Miller, R. 1: v In 1952
Moodie, G. H. 1: v E 1934
Moseley, E. A. 2: v E 1989 (2)
Murray, D. A. 19: v E 1980 (4); v A 1977 (3); *v A 1981 (2); v In 1978 (6); v P 1980 (4)*
Murray, D. L. 62: v E 1967 (5) 1973 (5); v A 1972 (4) 1977 (2); v In 1975 (4); v P 1976 (5); *v E 1963 (5) 1973 (3) 1976 (5) 1980 (5); v A 1975 (6) 1979 (3); v NZ 1979 (3); v In 1974 (5); v P 1974 (2)*

Nanan, R. 1: *v P 1980*
Neblett, J. M. 1: v E 1934
Noreiga, J. M. 4: v In 1970 (4)
Nunes, R. K. 4: v E 1929 (1); *v E 1928 (3)*
Nurse, S. M. 29: v E 1959 (1) 1967 (5); v A 1964 (4); v In 1961 (1); *v E 1966 (5); v A 1960 (3) 1968 (5); v NZ 1968 (3); v In 1966 (2)*

Padmore, A. L. 2: v In 1975 (1); *v E 1976 (1)*
Pairaudeau, B. H. 13: v E 1953 (2); v In 1952 (5): *v E 1957 (2); v NZ 1955 (4)*
Parry, D. R. 12: v A 1977 (5); *v NZ 1979 (1); v In 1978 (6)*
Passailaigue, C. C. 1: v E 1929
Patterson, B. P. 18: v E 1985 (5) 1989 (1); v P 1987 (1); *v E 1988 (2); v A 1988 (4); v In 1987 (4); v P 1986 (1)*
Payne, T. R. O. 1: v E 1985
Phillip, N. 9: v A 1977 (3); *v In 1978 (6)*
Pierre, L. R. 1: v E 1947

Rae, A. F. 15: v In 1952 (2); *v E 1950 (4); v A 1951 (3); v NZ 1951 (1); v In 1948 (5)*
Ramadhin, S. 43: v E 1953 (5) 1959 (4); v A 1954 (4); v In 1952 (4); *v E 1950 (4) 1957 (5); v A 1951 (5) 1960 (2); v NZ 1951 (2) 1955 (4); v In 1958 (2); v P 1958 (2)*
Richards, I. V. A. 111: v E 1980 (4) 1985 (5) 1989 (3); v A 1977 (2) 1983 (5); v NZ 1984 (4); v In 1975 (4) 1982 (5) 1988 (4); v P 1976 (5) 1987 (2); *v E 1976 (4) 1980 (5) 1984 (5) 1988 (5); v A 1975 (6) 1979 (3) 1981 (3) 1984 (5) 1988 (5); v NZ 1986 (3); v In 1974 (5) 1983 (6) 1987 (4); v P 1974 (2) 1980 (4) 1986 (3)*
Richardson, R. B. 49: v E 1985 (5) 1989 (4); v A 1983 (5); v NZ 1984 (4); v In 1988 (4); v P 1987 (3); *v E 1988 (3); v A 1984 (5) 1988 (5); v NZ 1986 (3); v In 1983 (1) 1987 (4); v P 1986 (3)*
Rickards, K. R. 2: v E 1947 (1); *v A 1951 (1)*
Roach, C. A. 16: v E 1929 (4) 1934 (1); *v E 1928 (3) 1933 (3); v A 1930 (5)*
Roberts, A. M. E. 47: v E 1973 (1) 1980 (3); v A 1977 (2); v In 1975 (2) 1982 (5); v P 1976 (5); *v E 1976 (5) 1980 (3); v A 1975 (5) 1979 (3) 1981 (2); v NZ 1979 (2); v In 1974 (5) 1983 (2); v P 1974 (2)*
Roberts, A. T. 1: *v NZ 1955*
Rodriguez, W. V. 5: v E 1967 (1); v A 1964 (1); v In 1961 (2); *v E 1963 (1)*
Rowe, L. G. 30: v E 1973 (5); v A 1972 (3); v NZ 1971 (4); v In 1975 (4); *v E 1976 (2); v A 1975 (6) 1979 (3); v NZ 1979 (3)*

St Hill, E. L. 2: v E 1929 (2)
St Hill, W. H. 3: v E 1929 (1); *v E 1928 (2)*
Scarlett, R. O. 3: v E 1959 (3)
Scott, A. P. H. 1: v In 1952
Scott, O. C. 8: v E 1929 (1); *v E 1928 (2); v A 1930 (5)*
Sealey, B. J. 1: *v E 1933*
Sealy, J. E. D. 11: v E 1929 (2) 1934 (4); *v E 1939 (3); v A 1930 (2)*
Shepherd, J. N. 5: v In 1970 (2); *v E 1969 (3)*
Shillingford, G. C. 7: v NZ 1971 (2); v In 1970 (3); *v E 1969 (2)*
Shillingford, I. T. 4: v A 1977 (1); v P 1976 (3)
Shivnarine, S. 8: v A 1977 (3); *v In 1978 (5)*
Simmons, P. V. 2: v P 1987 (1); *v In 1987 (1)*
Singh, C. K. 2: v E 1959 (2)
Small, J. A. 3: v E 1929 (1); *v E 1928 (2)*
Small, M. A. 2: v A 1983 (1); *v E 1984 (1)*
Smith, C. W. 5: v In 1961 (1); *v A 1960 (4)*
Smith, O. G. 26: v A 1954 (4); v P 1957 (5); *v E 1957 (5); v NZ 1955 (4); v In 1958 (5); v P 1958 (3)*

Sobers, G. S. 93: v E 1953 (1) 1959 (5) 1967 (5) 1973 (4); v A 1954 (4) 1964 (5); v NZ 1971 (5); v In 1961 (5); 1970 (5); v P 1957 (5); *v E 1957 (5) 1963 (5) 1966 (5) 1969 (3) 1973 (3); v A 1960 (5) 1968 (5); v NZ 1955 (4) 1968 (3); v In 1958 (5) 1966 (3); v P 1958 (3)*
Solomon, J. S. 27: v E 1959 (2); v A 1964 (4); v In 1961 (4); *v E 1963 (5); v A 1960 (5); v In 1958 (4); v P 1958 (3)*
Stayers, S. C. 4: v In 1961 (4)
Stollmeyer, J. B. 32: v E 1947 (2) 1953 (5); v A 1954 (2); v In 1952 (5); *v E 1939 (3) 1950 (4); v A 1951 (5); v NZ 1951 (2); v In 1948 (4)*
Stollmeyer, V. H. 1: *v E 1939*

Taylor, J. 3: v P 1957 (1); *v In 1958 (1); v P 1958 (1)*
Trim, J. 4: v E 1947 (1); *v A 1951 (1); v In 1948 (2)*

Valentine, A. L. 36: v E 1953 (3); v A 1954 (3); v In 1952 (5) 1961 (2); v P 1957 (1); *v E 1950 (4) 1957 (2); v A 1951 (5) 1960 (5); v NZ 1951 (2) 1955 (4)*
Valentine, V. A. 2: *v E 1933 (2)*

Walcott, C. L. 44: v E 1947 (4) 1953 (5) 1959 (2); v A 1954 (5); v In 1952 (5); v P 1957 (4); *v E 1950 (4) 1957 (5); v A 1951 (3); v NZ 1951 (2); v In 1948 (5)*
Walcott, L. A. 1: v E 1929
Walsh, C. A. 37: v E 1985 (1) 1989 (3); v NZ 1984 (1); v In 1988 (4); v P 1987 (3); *v E 1988 (5); v A 1984 (5) 1988 (5); v NZ 1986 (3); v In 1987 (4); v P 1986 (3)*
Watson, C. 7: v E 1959 (5); v In 1961 (1); *v A 1960 (1)*
Weekes, E. D. 48: v E 1947 (4) 1953 (4); v A 1954 (5) v In 1952 (5); v P 1957 (5); *v E 1950 (4) 1957 (5); v A 1951 (5); v NZ 1951 (2) 1955 (4); v In 1948 (5)*
Weekes, K. H. 2: *v E 1939 (2)*
White, W. A. 2: v A 1964 (2)
Wight, C. V. 2: v E 1929 (1); *v E 1928 (1)*
Wight, G. L. 1: v In 1952
Wiles, C. A. 1: *v E 1933*
Willett, E. T. 5: v A 1972 (3); *v In 1974 (2)*
Williams, A. B. 7: v A 1977 (3); *v In 1978 (4)*
Williams, E. A. V. 4: v E 1947 (3); *v E 1939 (1)*
Wishart, K. L. 1: v E 1934
Worrell, F. M. M. 51: v E 1947 (3) 1953 (4) 1959 (4); v A 1954 (4); v In 1952 (5) 1961 (5); *v E 1950 (4) 1957 (5) 1963 (5); v A 1951 (5) 1960 (5); v NZ 1951 (2)*

NEW ZEALAND

Number of Test cricketers: 171

Alabaster, J. C. 21: v E 1962 (2); v WI 1955 (1); v In 1967 (4); *v E 1958 (2); v SA 1961 (5); v WI 1971 (2); v In 1955 (4); v P 1955 (1)*
Allcott, C. F. W. 6: v E 1929 (2); v SA 1931 (1); *v E 1931 (3)*
Anderson, R. W. 9: v E 1977 (3); *v E 1978 (3); v P 1976 (3)*
Anderson, W. M. 1: v A 1945
Andrews, B. 2: *v A 1973 (2)*

Badcock, F. T. 7: v E 1929 (3) 1932 (2); v SA 1931 (2)
Barber, R. T. 1: v WI 1955
Bartlett, G. A. 10: v E 1965 (2); v In 1967 (2); v P 1964 (1); *v SA 1961 (5)*
Barton, P. T. 7: v E 1962 (3); *v SA 1961 (4)*
Beard, D. D. 4: v WI 1951 (2) 1955 (2)
Beck, J. E. F. 8: v WI 1955 (4); *v SA 1953 (4)*
Bell, W. 2: *v SA 1953 (2)*
Bilby, G. P. 2: v E 1965 (2)
Blain, T. E. 3: *v E 1986 (1); v In 1988 (2)*
Blair, R. W. 19: v E 1954 (1) 1958 (2) 1962 (2); v SA 1952 (2) 1963 (3); v WI 1955 (2); *v E 1958 (3); v SA 1953 (4)*
Blunt, R. C. 9: v E 1929 (4); v SA 1931 (2); *v E 1931 (3)*
Bolton, B. A. 2: v E 1958 (2)
Boock, S. L. 30: v E 1977 (3) 1983 (2) 1987 (1); v WI 1979 (3) 1986 (2); v P 1978 (3) 1984 (2) 1988 (1); *v E 1978 (3); v A 1985 (1); v WI 1984 (3); v P 1984 (3); v SL 1983 (3)*

Bracewell, B. P. 6: v P 1978 (1) 1984 (1); *v E 1978 (3); v A 1980 (1)*
Bracewell, J. G. 41: v E 1987 (3); v A 1985 (2) 1989 (1); v WI 1986 (3); v In 1980 (1) 1989 (2); v P 1988 (2); *v E 1983 (4) 1986 (3) 1990 (3); v A 1980 (3) 1985 (2) 1987 (3); v WI 1984 (1); v In 1988 (3); v P 1984 (2); v SL 1983 (2) 1986 (1)*
Bradburn, W. P. 2: v SA 1963 (2)
Brown, V. R. 2: *v A 1985 (2)*
Burgess, M. G. 50: v E 1970 (1) 1977 (3); v A 1973 (1) 1976 (2); v WI 1968 (2); v In 1967 (4) 1975 (3); v P 1972 (3) 1978 (3); *v E 1969 (2) 1973 (3) 1978 (3); v A 1980 (3); v WI 1971 (5); v In 1969 (3) 1976 (3); v P 1969 (3) 1976 (3)*
Burke, C. 1: v A 1945
Burtt, T. B. 10: v E 1946 (1) 1950 (2); v SA 1952 (1); v WI 1951 (2); *v E 1949 (4)*
Butterfield, L. A. 1: v A 1945

Cairns, B. L. 43: v E 1974 (1) 1977 (1) 1983 (3); v A 1976 (1) 1981 (3); v WI 1979 (3); v In 1975 (1) 1980 (3); v P 1978 (3) 1984 (3); v SL 1982 (2); *v E 1978 (2) 1983 (4); v A 1973 (1) 1980 (3) 1985 (1); v WI 1984 (2); v In 1976 (2); v P 1976 (2); v SL 1983 (2)*
Cairns, C. L. 1: *v A 1989*
Cameron, F. J. 19: v E 1962 (3); v SA 1963 (3); v P 1964 (3); *v E 1965 (2); v SA 1961 (5); v In 1964 (1); v P 1964 (2)*
Cave, H. B. 19: v E 1954 (2); v WI 1955 (3); *v E 1949 (4) 1958 (2); v In 1955 (5); v P 1955 (3)*
Chapple, M. E. 14: v E 1954 (1) 1965 (1); v SA 1952 (1) 1963 (3); v WI 1955 (1); *v SA 1953 (5) 1961 (2)*
Chatfield, E. J. 43: v E 1974 (1) 1977 (1) 1983 (3) 1987 (3); v A 1976 (2) 1981 (1) 1985 (3); v WI 1986 (3); v P 1984 (3) 1988 (2); v SL 1982 (2); *v E 1983 (3) 1986 (1); v A 1985 (2) 1987 (2); v WI 1984 (4); v In 1988 (3); v P 1984 (1); v SL 1983 (2) 1986 (1)*
Cleverley, D. C. 2: v SA 1931 (1); v A 1945 (1)
Collinge, R. O. 35: v E 1970 (2) 1974 (2) 1977 (3); v A 1973 (3); v In 1967 (2) 1975 (3); v P 1964 (3) 1972 (2); *v E 1965 (3) 1969 (1) 1973 (3) 1978 (1); v In 1964 (2) 1976 (1); v P 1964 (2) 1976 (2)*
Colquhoun, I. A. 2: v E 1954 (2)
Coney, J. V. 52: v E 1983 (3); v A 1973 (2) 1981 (3) 1985 (3); v WI 1979 (3) 1986 (3); v In 1980 (3); v P 1978 (3) 1984 (3); v SL 1982 (2); *v E 1983 (4) 1986 (3); v A 1973 (2) 1980 (2) 1985 (3); v WI 1984 (4); v P 1984 (3); v SL 1983 (3)*
Congdon, B. E. 61: v E 1965 (3) 1970 (2) 1974 (2) 1977 (3); v A 1973 (3) 1976 (2); v WI 1968 (3); v In 1967 (4) 1975 (3); v P 1964 (3) 1972 (3); *v E 1965 (3) 1969 (3) 1973 (3) 1978 (3); v A 1973 (3); v WI 1971 (5); v In 1964 (3) 1969 (3); v P 1964 (1) 1969 (3)*
Cowie, J. 9: v E 1946 (1); v A 1945 (1); *v E 1937 (3) 1949 (4)*
Cresswell G. F. 3: v E 1950 (2); *v E 1949 (1)*
Cromb, I. B. 5: v SA 1931 (2); *v E 1931 (3)*
Crowe, J. J. 39: v E 1983 (3) 1987 (2); v A 1989 (1); v WI 1986 (3); v P 1984 (3) 1988 (2); v SL 1982 (2); *v E 1983 (2) 1986 (3); v A 1985 (3) 1987 (3) 1989 (1); v WI 1984 (4); v P 1984 (3); v SL 1983 (3) 1986 (1)*
Crowe, M. D. 51: v E 1983 (3) 1987 (3); v A 1981 (3) 1985 (3); v WI 1986 (3); v In 1989 (3); v P 1984 (3) 1988 (2); *v E 1983 (4) 1986 (3) 1990 (3); v A 1985 (3) 1987 (3) 1989 (1); v WI 1984 (4); v P 1984 (3); v SL 1983 (3) 1986 (1)*
Cunis, R. S. 20: v E 1965 (3) 1970 (2); v SA 1963 (1); v WI 1968 (3); *v E 1969 (1); v WI 1971 (5); v In 1969 (3); v P 1969 (2)*

D'Arcy, J. W. 5: *v E 1958 (5)*
Dempster, C. S. 10: v E 1929 (4) 1932 (2); v SA 1931 (2); *v E 1931 (2)*
Dempster, E. W. 5: v SA 1952 (1); *v SA 1953 (4)*
Dick, A. E. 17: v E 1962 (3); v SA 1963 (2); v P 1964 (2); *v E 1965 (2); v SA 1961 (5); v P 1964 (3)*
Dickinson, G. R. 3: v E 1929 (2); v SA 1931 (1)
Donnelly, M. P. 7: *v E 1937 (3) 1949 (4)*
Dowling, G. T. 39: v E 1962 (3) 1970 (2); v In 1967 (4); v SA 1963 (1); v WI 1968 (3); v P 1964 (2); *v E 1965 (3) 1969 (3); v SA 1961 (4); v WI 1971 (2); v In 1964 (4) 1969 (3); v P 1964 (2) 1969 (3)*
Dunning, J. A. 4: v E 1932 (1); *v E 1937 (3)*

Edgar, B. A. 39: v E 1983 (3); v A 1981 (3) 1985 (3); v WI 1979 (3); v In 1980 (3); v P 1978 (3); v SL 1982 (2); *v E 1978 (3) 1983 (4) 1986 (3); v A 1980 (3) 1985 (3); v P 1984 (3)*
Edwards, G. N. 8: v E 1977 (1); v A 1976 (2); v In 1980 (3); *v E 1978 (2)*
Emery, R. W. G. 2: v WI 1951 (2)

Fisher, F. E. 1: v SA 1952
Foley, H. 1: v E 1929
Franklin, T. J. 15: v E 1987 (3); v A 1985 (1) 1989 (1); v In 1989 (3); *v E 1983 (1) 1990 (3); v In 1988 (3)*
Freeman, D. L. 2: v E 1932 (2)

Gallichan, N. 1: *v E 1937*
Gedye, S. G. 4: v SA 1963 (3); v P 1964 (1)
Gillespie, S. R. 1: v A 1985
Gray, E. J. 10: *v E 1983 (2) 1986 (3); v A 1987 (1); v In 1988 (1); v P 1984 (2); v SL 1986 (1)*
Greatbatch, M. J. 14: v E 1987 (2); v A 1989 (1); v In 1989 (3); v P 1988 (1); *v E 1990 (3); v A 1989 (1); v In 1988 (3)*
Guillen, S. C. 3: v WI 1955 (3)
Guy, J. W. 12: v E 1958 (2); v WI 1955 (2); *v SA 1961 (2); v In 1955 (5); v P 1955 (1)*

Hadlee, D. R. 26: v E 1974 (2) 1977 (1); v A 1973 (3) 1976 (1); v In 1975 (3); v P 1972 (2); *v E 1969 (2) 1973 (3); v A 1973 (3); v In 1969 (3); v P 1969 (3)*
Hadlee, Sir R. J. 86: v E 1977 (3) 1983 (3) 1987 (1); v A 1973 (2) 1976 (2) 1981 (3) 1985 (3) 1989 (1); v WI 1979 (3) 1986 (3); v In 1975 (2) 1980 (3) 1989 (3); v P 1972 (1) 1978 (3) 1984 (3) 1988 (2); v SL 1982 (2); *v E 1973 (1) 1978 (3) 1983 (4) 1986 (3) 1990 (3); v A 1973 (3) 1980 (3) 1985 (3) 1987 (3); v WI 1984 (4); v In 1976 (3) 1988 (3); v P 1976 (3); v SL 1983 (3) 1986 (1)*
Hadlee, W. A. 11: v E 1946 (1) 1950 (2); v A 1945 (1); *v E 1937 (3) 1949 (4)*
Harford, N. S. 8: *v E 1958 (4); v In 1955 (2); v P 1955 (2)*
Harford, R. I. 3: v In 1967 (3)
Harris, P. G. Z. 9: v P 1964 (1); *v SA 1961 (5); v In 1955 (1); v P 1955 (2)*
Harris, R. M. 2: v E 1958 (2)
Hastings, B. F. 31: v E 1974 (2); v A 1973 (3); v WI 1968 (3); v In 1975 (1); v P 1972 (3); *v E 1969 (3) 1973 (3); v A 1973 (3); v WI 1971 (5); v In 1969 (2); v P 1969 (3)*
Hayes, J. A. 15: v E 1950 (2) 1954 (1); v WI 1951 (2); *v E 1958 (4); v In 1955 (5); v P 1955 (1)*
Henderson, M. 1: v E 1929
Horne, P. A. 3: v WI 1986 (1); *v A 1987 (1); v SL 1986 (1)*
Hough, K. W. 2: v E 1958 (2)
Howarth, G. P. 47: v E 1974 (2) 1977 (3) 1983 (3); v A 1976 (2) 1981 (3); v WI 1979 (3); v In 1980 (3); v P 1978 (3) 1984 (3); v SL 1982 (2); *v E 1978 (3) 1983 (4); v A 1980 (2); v WI 1984 (4); v In 1976 (2); v P 1976 (2); v SL 1983 (3)*
Howarth, H. J. 30: v E 1970 (2) 1974 (2); v A 1973 (3) 1976 (2); v In 1975 (2); v P 1972 (3); *v E 1969 (3) 1973 (2); v WI 1971 (5); v In 1969 (3); v P 1969 (3)*

James, K. C. 11: v E 1929 (4) 1932 (2); v SA 1931 (2); *v E 1931 (3)*
Jarvis, T. W. 13: v E 1965 (1); v P 1972 (3); *v WI 1971 (4); v In 1964 (2); v P 1964 (3)*
Jones, A. H. 17: v E 1987 (1); v A 1989 (1); v In 1989 (3); v P 1988 (2); *v E 1990 (3); v A 1987 (3); v In 1988 (3); v SL 1986 (1)*

Kerr, J. L. 7: v E 1932 (2); v SA 1931 (1); *v E 1931 (2) 1937 (2)*
Kuggeleijn, C. M. 2: *v In 1988 (2)*

Lees, W. K. 21: v E 1977 (2); v A 1976 (1); v WI 1979 (3); v P 1978 (3); v SL 1982 (2); *v E 1983 (2); v A 1980 (2); v In 1976 (3); v P 1976 (3)*
Leggat, I. B. 1: *v SA 1953*
Leggat, J. G. 9: v E 1954 (1); v SA 1952 (1); v WI 1951 (1) 1955 (1); *v In 1955 (3); v P 1955 (2)*
Lissette, A. F. 2: v WI 1955 (2)
Lowry, T. C. 7: v E 1929 (4); *v E 1931 (3)*

MacGibbon, A. R. 26: v E 1950 (2) 1954 (2); v SA 1952 (1); v WI 1955 (3); *v E 1958 (5); v SA 1953 (5); v In 1955 (5); v P 1955 (3)*
McEwan, P. E. 4: v WI 1979 (1); *v A 1980 (2); v P 1984 (1)*
McGirr, H. M. 2: v E 1929 (2)
McGregor, S. N. 25: v E 1954 (2) 1958 (2); v SA 1963 (3); v WI 1955 (4); v P 1964 (2); *v SA 1961 (5); v In 1955 (4); v P 1955 (3)*
McLeod E. G. 1: v E 1929
McMahon T. G. 5: v WI 1955 (1); *v In 1955 (3); v P 1955 (1)*
McRae, D. A. N. 1: v A 1945

Matheson, A. M. 2: v E 1929 (1); *v E 1931 (1)*
Meale, T. 2: *v E 1958 (2)*
Merritt, W. E. 6: v E 1929 (4); *v E 1931 (2)*
Meuli, E. M. 1: v SA 1952
Milburn, B. D. 3: v WI 1968 (3)
Miller, L. S. M. 13: v SA 1952 (2); v WI 1955 (3); *v E 1958 (4); v SA 1953 (4)*
Mills, J. E. 7: v E 1929 (3) 1932 (1); *v E 1931 (3)*
Moir, A. M. 17: v E 1950 (2) 1954 (2) 1958 (2); v SA 1952 (1); v WI 1951 (2) 1955 (1); *v E 1958 (2); v In 1955 (2); v P 1955 (3)*
Moloney D. A. R. 3: *v E 1937 (3)*
Mooney, F. L. H. 14: v E 1950 (2); v SA 1952 (2); v WI 1951 (2); *v E 1949 (3); v SA 1953 (5)*
Morgan, R. W. 20: v E 1965 (2) 1970 (2); v WI 1968 (1); v P 1964 (2); *v E 1965 (3); v WI 1971 (3); v In 1964 (4); v P 1964 (3)*
Morrison, B. D. 1: v E 1962
Morrison, D. K. 16: v E 1987 (3); v A 1989 (1); v In 1989 (3); v P 1988 (1); *v E 1990 (3); v A 1987 (3) 1989 (1); v In 1988 (1)*
Morrison, J. F. M. 17: v E 1974 (2); v A 1973 (3) 1981 (3); v In 1975 (3); *v A 1973 (3); v In 1976 (1); v P 1976 (2)*
Motz, R. C. 32: v E 1962 (2) 1965 (3); v SA 1963 (2); v WI 1968 (3); v In 1967 (4); v P 1964 (3); *v E 1965 (3) 1969 (3); v SA 1961 (5); v In 1964 (3); v P 1964 (1)*
Murray, B. A. G. 13: v E 1970 (1); v In 1967 (4); *v E 1969 (2); v In 1969 (3); v P 1969 (3)*

Newman J. 3: v E 1932 (2); v SA 1931 (1)

O'Sullivan, D. R. 11: v In 1975 (1); v P 1972 (1); *v A 1973 (3); v In 1976 (3); v P 1976 (3)*
Overton, G. W. F. 3: *v SA 1953 (3)*

Page, M. L. 14: v E 1929 (4) 1932 (2); v SA 1931 (2); *v E 1931 (3) 1937 (3)*
Parker, J. M. 36: v E 1974 (2) 1977 (3); v A 1973 (3) 1976 (2); v WI 1979 (3); v In 1975 (3); v P 1972 (1) 1978 (2); *v E 1973 (3) 1978 (2); v A 1973 (3) 1980 (3); v In 1976 (3); v P 1976 (3)*
Parker, N. M. 3: *v In 1976 (2); v P 1976 (1)*
Parore, A. C. 1: *v E 1990*
Patel, D. N. 8: v WI 1986 (3); v P 1988 (1); *v A 1987 (3) 1989 (1)*
Petherick, P. J. 6: v A 1976 (1); *v In 1976 (3); v P 1976 (2)*
Petrie, E. C. 14: v E 1958 (2) 1965 (3); *v E 1958 (5); v In 1955 (2); v P 1955 (2)*
Playle, W. R. 8: v E 1962 (3); *v E 1958 (5)*
Pollard, V. 32: v E 1965 (3) 1970 (1); v WI 1968 (3); v In 1967 (4); v P 1972 (1); *v E 1965 (3) 1969 (3) 1973 (3); v In 1964 (4) 1969 (1); v P 1964 (3) 1969 (3)*
Poore, M. B. 14: v E 1954 (1); v SA 1952 (1); *v SA 1953 (5); v In 1955 (4); v P 1955 (3)*
Priest, M. W. 1: *v E 1990*
Puna, N. 3: v E 1965 (3)

Rabone, G. O. 12: v E 1954 (2); v SA 1952 (1); v WI 1951 (2); *v E 1949 (4); v SA 1953 (3)*
Redmond, R. E. 1: v P 1972
Reid, J. F. 19: v A 1985 (3); v In 1980 (3); v P 1978 (1) 1984 (3); *v A 1985 (3); v P 1984 (3); v SL 1983 (3)*
Reid, J. R. 58: v E 1950 (2) 1954 (2) 1958 (2) 1962 (3); v SA 1952 (2) 1963 (3); v WI 1951 (2) 1955 (4); v P 1964 (3); *v E 1949 (2) 1958 (5) 1965 (3); v SA 1953 (5) 1961 (5); v In 1955 (5) 1964 (4); v P 1955 (3) 1964 (3)*
Roberts, A. D. G. 7: v In 1975 (2); *v In 1976 (3); v P 1976 (2)*
Roberts, A. W. 5: v E 1929 (1); v SA 1931 (2); *v E 1937 (2)*
Robertson, G. K. 1: v A 1985
Rowe, C. G. 1: v A 1945
Rutherford, K. R. 22: v E 1987 (2); v A 1985 (3) 1989 (1); v WI 1986 (2); v In 1989 (3); *v E 1986 (1) 1990 (2); v A 1987 (1); v WI 1984 (4); v In 1988 (2); v SL 1986 (1)*

Scott, R. H. 1: v E 1946
Scott, V. J. 10: v E 1946 (1) 1950 (2); v A 1945 (1); v WI 1951 (2); *v E 1949 (4)*
Shrimpton, M. J. F. 10: v E 1962 (2) 1965 (3) 1970 (2); v SA 1963 (1); *v A 1973 (2)*
Sinclair, B. W. 21: v E 1962 (3) 1965 (3); v SA 1963 (3); v In 1967 (2); v P 1964 (2); *v E 1965 (3); v In 1964 (2); v P 1964 (3)*
Sinclair, I. M. 2: v WI 1955 (2)

Smith, F. B. 4: v E 1946 (1); v WI 1951 (1); *v E 1949 (2)*
Smith, H. D. 1: v E 1932
Smith, I. D. S. 55: v E 1983 (3) 1987 (3); v A 1981 (3) 1985 (3) 1989 (1); v WI 1986 (3); v In 1980 (3) 1989 (3); v P 1984 (3) 1988 (2); *v E 1983 (2) 1986 (2) 1990 (2); v A 1980 (1) 1985 (3) 1987 (3) 1989 (1); v WI 1984 (4); v In 1988 (3); v P 1984 (3); v SL 1983 (3) 1986 (1)*
Snedden, C. A. 1: v E 1946
Snedden, M. C. 25: v E 1983 (1) 1987 (2); v A 1981 (3) 1989 (1); v WI 1986 (1); v In 1980 (3) 1989 (3); v SL 1982 (2); *v E 1983 (1) 1990 (3); v A 1985 (1) 1987 (1) 1989 (1); v In 1988 (1); v SL 1986 (1)*
Sparling, J. T. 11: v E 1958 (2) 1962 (1); v SA 1963 (2); *v E 1958 (3); v SA 1961 (3)*
Stirling, D. A. 6: *v E 1986 (2); v WI 1984 (1); v P 1984 (3)*
Sutcliffe, B. 42: v E 1946 (1) 1950 (2) 1954 (2) 1958 (2); v SA 1952 (2); v WI 1951 (2) 1955 (2); *v E 1949 (4) 1958 (4) 1965 (1); v SA 1953 (5); v In 1955 (5) 1964 (4); v P 1955 (3) 1964 (3)*

Taylor, B. R. 30: v E 1965 (1); v WI 1968 (3); v In 1967 (3); v P 1972 (3); *v E 1965 (2) 1969 (2) 1973 (3); v WI 1971 (4); v In 1964 (3) 1969 (2); v P 1964 (3) 1969 (1)*
Taylor, D. D. 3: v E 1946 (1); v WI 1955 (2)
Thomson, K. 2: v In 1967 (2)
Thomson, S. A. 1: v In 1989
Tindill, E. W. T. 5: v E 1946 (1); v A 1945 (1); *v E 1937 (3)*
Troup, G. B. 15: v A 1981 (2) 1985 (2); v WI 1979 (3); v In 1980 (2); v P 1978 (2); *v A 1980 (2); v WI 1984 (1); v In 1976 (1)*
Truscott, P. B. 1: v P 1964
Turner, G. M. 41: v E 1970 (2) 1974 (2); v A 1973 (3) 1976 (2); v WI 1968 (3); v In 1975 (3); v P 1972 (3); v SL 1982 (2); *v E 1969 (2) 1973 (3); v A 1973 (2); v WI 1971 (5); v In 1969 (3) 1976 (3); v P 1969 (1) 1976 (2)*

Vance, R. H. 4: v E 1987 (1); v P 1988 (2); *v A 1989 (1)*
Vivian, G. E. 5: *v WI 1971 (4); v In 1964 (1)*
Vivian, H. G. 7: v E 1932 (1); v SA 1931 (1); *v E 1931 (2) 1937 (3)*

Wadsworth, K. J. 33: v E 1970 (2) 1974 (2); v A 1973 (3); v In 1975 (3); v P 1972 (3); *v E 1969 (3) 1973 (3); v A 1973 (3); v WI 1971 (5); v In 1969 (3); v P 1969 (3)*
Wallace, W. M. 13: v E 1946 (1) 1950 (2); v A 1945 (1); v SA 1952 (2); *v E 1937 (3) 1949 (4)*
Ward, J. T. 8: v SA 1963 (1); v In 1967 (1); v P 1964 (1); *v E 1965 (1); v In 1964 (4)*
Watson, W. 3: *v E 1986 (2); v A 1989 (1)*
Watt, L. 1: v E 1954
Webb, M. G. 3: v E 1970 (1); v A 1973 (1); *v WI 1971 (1)*
Webb, P. N. 2: v WI 1979 (2)
Weir, G. L. 11: v E 1929 (3) 1932 (2); v SA 1931 (2); *v E 1931 (3) 1937 (1)*
Whitelaw, P. E. 2: v E 1932 (2)
Wright, J. G. 71: v E 1977 (3) 1983 (3) 1987 (3); v A 1981 (3) 1985 (2) 1989 (1); v WI 1979 (3) 1986 (3); v In 1980 (3) 1989 (3); v P 1978 (3) 1984 (3) 1988 (2); v SL 1982 (2); *v E 1978 (2) 1983 (3) 1986 (3) 1990 (3); v A 1980 (3) 1985 (3) 1987 (3) 1989 (1); v WI 1984 (4); v In 1988 (3); v P 1984 (3); v SL 1983 (3)*

Yuile, B. W. 17: v E 1962 (2); v WI 1968 (3); v In 1967 (1); v P 1964 (3); *v E 1965 (1); v In 1964 (3) 1969 (1); v P 1964 (1) 1969 (2)*

INDIA

Number of Test cricketers: 192

Abid Ali, S. 29: v E 1972 (4); v A 1969 (1); v WI 1974 (2); v NZ 1969 (3); *v E 1971 (3) 1974 (3); v A 1967 (4); v WI 1970 (5); v NZ 1967 (4)*
Adhikari, H. R. 21: v E 1951 (3); v A 1956 (2); v WI 1948 (5) 1958 (1); v P 1952 (2); *v E 1952 (3); v A 1947 (5)*
Amarnath, L. 24: v E 1933 (3) 1951 (3); v WI 1948 (5); v P 1952 (5); *v E 1946 (3); v A 1947 (5)*
Amarnath, M. 69: v E 1976 (2) 1984 (5); v A 1969 (1) 1979 (1) 1986 (3); v WI 1978 (2) 1983 (3) 1987 (3); v NZ 1976 (3); v P 1983 (2) 1986 (5); v SL 1986 (2); *v E 1979 (2) 1986 (2); v A 1977 (5) 1985 (3); v WI 1975 (4) 1982 (5); v NZ 1975 (3); v P 1978 (3) 1982 (6) 1984 (2); v SL 1985 (2)*

Amarnath, S. 10: v E 1976 (2): *v WI 1975 (2); v NZ 1975 (3); v P 1978 (3)*
Amar Singh 7: v E 1933 (3); *v E 1932 (1) 1936 (3)*
Amir Elahi 1: *v A 1947*
Ankola, S. A. 1: *v P 1989*
Apte, A. L. 1: *v E 1959*
Apte, M. L. 7: v P 1952 (2); *v WI 1952 (5)*
Arshad Ayub 13: v WI 1987 (4); v NZ 1988 (3); *v WI 1988 (4); v P 1989 (2)*
Arun, B. 2: v SL 1986 (2)
Arun Lal 16: v WI 1987 (4); v NZ 1988 (3); v P 1986 (1); v SL 1982 (1); *v WI 1988 (4); v P 1982 (3)*
Azad, K. 7: v E 1981 (3); v WI 1983 (2); v P 1983 (1); *v NZ 1980 (1)*
Azharuddin, M. 40: v E 1984 (3); v A 1986 (3); v WI 1987 (3); v NZ 1988 (3); v P 1986 (5); v SL 1986 (1); *v E 1986 (3) 1990 (3); v A 1985 (3); v WI 1988 (3); v NZ 1989 (3); v P 1989 (4); v SL 1985 (3)*

Baig, A. A. 10: v A 1959 (3); v WI 1966 (2); v P 1960 (3); *v E 1959 (2)*
Banerjee, S. A. 1: v WI 1948
Banerjee, S. N. 1: v WI 1948
Baqa Jilani, M. 1: *v E 1936*
Bedi, B. S. 67: v E 1972 (5) 1976 (5); v A 1969 (5); v WI 1966 (2) 1974 (4) 1978 (3); v NZ 1969 (3) 1976 (3); *v E 1967 (3) 1971 (3) 1974 (3) 1979 (3); v A 1967 (2) 1977 (5); v WI 1970 (5) 1975 (4); v NZ 1967 (4) 1975 (2); v P 1978 (3)*
Bhandari, P. 3: v A 1956 (1); v NZ 1955 (1); *v P 1954 (1)*
Bhat, A. R. 2: v WI 1983 (1); v P 1983 (1)
Binny, R. M. H. 27: v E 1979 (1); v WI 1983 (6); v P 1979 (6) 1983 (2) 1986 (3); *v E 1986 (3); v A 1980 (1) 1985 (2); v NZ 1980 (1); v P 1984 (1); v SL 1985 (1)*
Borde, C. G. 55: v E 1961 (5) 1963 (5); v A 1959 (5) 1964 (3) 1969 (1); v WI 1958 (4) 1966 (3); v NZ 1964 (4); v P 1960 (5); *v E 1959 (4) 1967 (3); v A 1967 (4); v WI 1961 (5); v NZ 1967 (4)*

Chandrasekhar, B. S. 58: v E 1963 (4) 1972 (5) 1976 (5); v A 1964 (2); v WI 1966 (3) 1974 (4) 1978 (4); v NZ 1964 (2) 1976 (3); *v E 1967 (3) 1971 (3) 1974 (2) 1979 (1); v A 1967 (2) 1977 (5); v WI 1975 (4); v NZ 1975 (3); v P 1978 (3)*
Chauhan, C. P. S. 40: v E 1972 (2); v A 1969 (1) 1979 (6); v WI 1978 (6); v NZ 1969 (2); v P 1979 (6); *v E 1979 (4); v A 1977 (4) 1980 (3); v NZ 1980 (3); v P 1978 (3)*
Chowdhury, N. R. 2: v E 1951 (1); v WI 1948 (1)
Colah, S. H. M. 2: v E 1933 (1); *v E 1932 (1)*
Contractor, N. J. 31: v E 1961 (5); v A 1956 (1) 1959 (5); v WI 1958 (5); v NZ 1955 (4); v P 1960 (5); *v E 1959 (4); v WI 1961 (2)*

Dani, H. T. 1: v P 1952
Desai, R. B. 28: v E 1961 (4) 1963 (2); v A 1959 (3); v WI 1958 (1); v NZ 1964 (3); v P 1960 (5); *v E 1959 (5); v A 1967 (1); v WI 1961 (3); v NZ 1967 (1)*
Dilawar Hussain 3: v E 1933 (2); *v E 1936 (1)*
Divecha, R. V. 5: v E 1951 (2); v P 1952 (1); *v E 1952 (2)*
Doshi, D. R. 33: v E 1979 (1) 1981 (6); v A 1979 (6); v P 1979 (6) 1983 (1); v SL 1982 (1); *v E 1982 (3); v A 1980 (3); v NZ 1980 (2); v P 1982 (4)*
Durani, S. A. 29: v E 1961 (5) 1963 (5) 1972 (3); v A 1959 (1) 1964 (3); v WI 1966 (1); v NZ 1964 (3); *v WI 1961 (5) 1970 (3)*

Engineer, F. M. 46: v E 1961 (4) 1972 (5); v A 1969 (5); v WI 1966 (1) 1974 (5); v NZ 1964 (4) 1969 (2); *v E 1967 (3) 1971 (3) 1974 (3); v A 1967 (4); v WI 1961 (3); v NZ 1967 (4)*

Gadkari, C. V. 6: *v WI 1952 (3); v P 1954 (3)*
Gaekwad, A. D. 40: v E 1976 (4) 1984 (3); v WI 1974 (3) 1978 (5) 1983 (6); v NZ 1976 (3); v P 1983 (3); *v E 1979 (2); v A 1977 (1); v WI 1975 (3) 1982 (5); v P 1984 (2)*
Gaekwad, D. K. 11: v WI 1958 (1); v P 1952 (2) 1960 (1); *v E 1952 (1) 1959 (4); v WI 1952 (2)*
Gaekwad, H. G. 1: v P 1952
Gandotra, A. 2: v A 1969 (1); v NZ 1969 (1)
Gavaskar, S. M. 125: v E 1972 (5) 1976 (5) 1979 (1) 1981 (6) 1984 (5); v A 1979 (6) 1986 (3); v WI 1974 (2) 1978 (6) 1983 (6); v NZ 1976 (3); v P 1979 (6) 1983 (3) 1986 (4); v SL 1982 (1) 1986 (3); *v E 1971 (3) 1974 (3) 1979 (4) 1982 (3) 1986 (3); v A 1977 (5) 1980 (3) 1985 (3); v WI 1970 (4) 1975 (4) 1982 (5); v NZ 1975 (3) 1980 (3); v P 1978 (3) 1982 (6) 1984 (2); v SL 1985 (3)*

Ghavri, K. D. 39: v E 1976 (3) 1979 (1); v A 1979 (6); v WI 1974 (3) 1978 (6); v NZ 1976 (2); v P 1979 (6); *v E 1979 (4); v A 1977 (3) 1980 (3); v NZ 1980 (1); v P 1978 (1)*
Ghorpade, J. M. 8: v A 1956 (1); v WI 1958 (1); v NZ 1955 (1); *v E 1959 (3); v WI 1952 (2)*
Ghulam Ahmed 22: v E 1951 (2); v A 1956 (2); v WI 1948 (3) 1958 (2); v NZ 1955 (1); v P 1952 (4); *v E 1952 (4); v P 1954 (4)*
Gopalan, M. J. 1: v E 1933
Gopinath, C. D. 8: v E 1951 (3); v A 1959 (1); v P 1952 (1); *v E 1952 (1); v P 1954 (2)*
Guard, G. M. 2: v A 1959 (1); v WI 1958 (1)
Guha, S. 4: v A 1969 (3); *v E 1967 (1)*
Gul Mahomed 8: v P 1952 (2); *v E 1946 (1); v A 1947 (5)*
Gupte, B. P. 3: v E 1963 (1); v NZ 1964 (1); v P 1960 (1)
Gupte, S. P. 36: v E 1951 (1) 1961 (2); v A 1956 (3); v WI 1958 (5); v NZ 1955 (5); v P 1952 (2) 1960 (3); *v E 1959 (5); v WI 1952 (5); v P 1954 (5)*
Gursharan Singh 1: *v NZ 1989*

Hafeez, A. 3: *v E 1946 (3)*
Hanumant Singh 14: v E 1963 (2); v A 1964 (3); v WI 1966 (2); v NZ 1964 (4) 1969 (1); *v E 1967 (2)*
Hardikar, M. S. 2: v WI 1958 (2)
Hazare, V. S. 30: v E 1951 (5); v WI 1948 (5); v P 1952 (3); *v E 1946 (3) 1952 (4); v A 1947 (5); v WI 1952 (5)*
Hindlekar, D. D. 4: *v E 1936 (1) 1946 (3)*
Hirwani, N. D. 13: v WI 1987 (1); v NZ 1988 (3); *v E 1990 (3); v WI 1988 (3); v NZ 1989 (3)*

Ibrahim, K. C. 4: v WI 1948 (4)
Indrajitsinhji, K. S. 4: v A 1964 (3); v NZ 1969 (1)
Irani, J. K. 2: *v A 1947 (2)*

Jahangir Khan, M. 4: *v E 1932 (1) 1936 (3)*
Jai, L. P. 1: v E 1933
Jaisimha, M. L. 39: v E 1961 (5) 1963 (5); v A 1959 (1) 1964 (3); v WI 1966 (2); v NZ 1964 (4) 1969 (1); v P 1960 (4); *v E 1959 (1); v A 1967 (2); v WI 1961 (4) 1970 (3); v NZ 1967 (4)*
Jamshedji, R. J. 1: v E 1933
Jayantilal, K. 1: *v WI 1970*
Joshi, P. G. 12: v E 1951 (2); v A 1959 (1); v WI 1958 (1); v P 1952 (1) 1960 (1); *v E 1959 (3); v WI 1952 (3)*

Kanitkar, H. S. 2: v WI 1974 (2)
Kapil Dev 109: v E 1979 (1) 1981 (6) 1984 (4); v A 1979 (6) 1986 (3); v WI 1978 (6) 1983 (6) 1987 (4); v NZ 1988 (3); v P 1979 (6) 1983 (3) 1986 (5); v SL 1982 (1) 1986 (3); *v E 1979 (4) 1982 (3) 1986 (3) 1990 (3); v A 1980 (3) 1985 (3); v WI 1982 (5) 1988 (4); v NZ 1980 (3) 1989 (3); v P 1978 (3) 1982 (6) 1984 (2) 1989 (4); v SL 1985 (3)*
Kardar, A. H. (*see* Hafeez)
Kenny, R. B. 5: v A 1959 (4); v WI 1958 (1)
Kirmani, S. M. H. 88: v E 1976 (5) 1979 (1) 1981 (6) 1984 (5); v A 1979 (6); v WI 1978 (6) 1983 (6); v NZ 1976 (3); v P 1979 (6) 1983 (3); v SL 1982 (1); *v E 1982 (3); v A 1977 (5) 1980 (3) 1985 (3); v WI 1975 (4) 1982 (5); v NZ 1975 (3) 1980 (3); v P 1978 (3) 1982 (6) 1984 (2)*
Kischenchand, G. 5: v P 1952 (1); *v A 1947 (4)*
Kripal Singh, A. G. 14: v E 1961 (3) 1963 (2); v A 1956 (2) 1964 (1); v WI 1958 (1); v NZ 1955 (4); *v E 1959 (1)*
Krishnamurthy, P. 5: *v WI 1970 (5)*
Kulkarni, R. R. 3: v A 1986 (1); v P 1986 (2)
Kulkarni, U. N. 4: *v A 1967 (3); v NZ 1967 (1)*
Kumar, V. V. 2: v E 1961 (1); v P 1960 (1)
Kumble, A. 1: *v E 1990*
Kunderan, B. K. 18: v E 1961 (1) 1963 (5); v A 1959 (3); v WI 1966 (2); v NZ 1964 (1); v P 1960 (2); *v E 1967 (2); v WI 1961 (2)*

Lall Singh 1: *v E 1932*
Lamba, R. 4: v WI 1987 (1); v SL 1986 (3)

Madan Lal 39: v E 1976 (2) 1981 (6); v WI 1974 (2) 1983 (3); v NZ 1976 (1); v P 1983 (3); v SL 1982 (1); *v E 1974 (2) 1982 (3) 1986 (1); v A 1977 (2); v WI 1975 (4) 1982 (2); v NZ 1975 (3); v P 1982 (3) 1984 (1)*

Maka, E. S. 2: v P 1952 (1); *v WI 1952 (1)*
Malhotra, A. 7: v E 1981 (2) 1984 (1); v WI 1983 (3); *v E 1982 (1)*
Maninder Singh 34: v A 1986 (3); v WI 1983 (4) 1987 (3); v P 1986 (4); v SL 1986 (3); *v E 1986 (3); v WI 1982 (3); v P 1982 (5) 1984 (1) 1989 (3); v SL 1985 (2)*
Manjrekar, S. V. 15: v WI 1987 (1); *v E 1990 (3); v WI 1988 (4); v NZ 1989 (3); v P 1989 (4)*
Manjrekar, V. L. 55: v E 1951 (2) 1961 (5) 1963 (4); v A 1956 (3) 1964 (3); v WI 1958 (4); v NZ 1955 (5) 1964 (1); v P 1952 (3) 1960 (5); *v E 1952 (4) 1959 (2); v WI 1952 (4) 1961 (5); v P 1954 (5)*
Mankad, A. V. 22: v E 1976 (1); v A 1969 (5); v WI 1974 (1); v NZ 1969 (2) 1976 (3); *v E 1971 (3) 1974 (1); v A 1977 (3); v WI 1970 (3)*
Mankad, V. 44: v E 1951 (5); v A 1956 (3); v WI 1948 (5) 1958 (2); v NZ 1955 (4); v P 1952 (4); *v E 1946 (3) 1952 (3); v A 1947 (5); v WI 1952 (5); v P 1954 (5)*
Mansur Ali Khan (*see* Pataudi)
Mantri, M. K. 4: v E 1951 (1); *v E 1952 (2); v P 1954 (1)*
Meherhomji, K. R. 1: *v E 1936*
Mehra, V. L. 8: v E 1961 (1) 1963 (2); v NZ 1955 (2); *v WI 1961 (3)*
Merchant, V. M. 10: v E 1933 (3) 1951 (1); *v E 1936 (3) 1946 (3)*
Milkha Singh, A. G. 4: v E 1961 (1); v A 1959 (1); v P 1960 (2)
Modi, R. S. 10: v E 1951 (1); v WI 1948 (5); v P 1952 (1); *v E 1946 (3)*
More, K. S. 34: v A 1986 (2); v WI 1987 (4); v NZ 1988 (3); v P 1986 (5); v SL 1986 (3); *v E 1986 (3) 1990 (3); v WI 1988 (4); v NZ 1989 (3); v P 1989 (4)*
Muddiah, V. M. 2: v A 1959 (1); v P 1960 (1)
Mushtaq Ali, S. 11: v E 1933 (2) 1951 (1); v WI 1948 (3); *v E 1936 (3) 1946 (2)*

Nadkarni, R. G. 41: v E 1961 (1) 1963 (5); v A 1959 (5) 1964 (3); v WI 1958 (1) 1966 (1); v NZ 1955 (1) 1964 (4); v P 1960 (4); *v E 1959 (4); v A 1967 (3); v WI 1961 (5); v NZ 1967 (4)*
Naik, S. S. 3: v WI 1974 (2); *v E 1974 (1)*
Naoomal Jeoomal 3: v E 1933 (2); *v E 1932 (1)*
Narasimha Rao, M. V. 4: v A 1979 (2); v WI 1978 (2)
Navle, J. G. 2: v E 1933 (1); *v E 1932 (1)*
Nayak, S. V. 2: *v E 1982 (2)*
Nayudu, C. K. 7: v E 1933 (3); *v E 1932 (1) 1936 (3)*
Nayudu, C. S. 11: v E 1933 (2) 1951 (1); *v E 1936 (2) 1946 (2); v A 1947 (4)*
Nazir Ali, S. 2: v E 1933 (1); *v E 1932 (1)*
Nissar, Mahomed 6: v E 1933 (2); *v E 1932 (1) 1936 (3)*
Nyalchand, S. 1: v P 1952

Pai, A. M. 1: v NZ 1969
Palia, P. E. 2: *v E 1932 (1) 1936 (1)*
Pandit, C. S. 3: v A 1986 (2); *v E 1986 (1)*
Parkar, G. A. 1: *v E 1982*
Parkar, R. D. 2: v E 1972 (2)
Parsana, D. D. 2: v WI 1978 (2)
Patankar, C. T. 1: v NZ 1955
Pataudi sen., Nawab of, 3: *v E 1946 (3)*
Pataudi jun., Nawab of (now Mansur Ali Khan) 46: v E 1961 (3) 1963 (5) 1972 (3); v A 1964 (3) 1969 (5); v WI 1966 (3) 1974 (4); v NZ 1964 (4) 1969 (3); *v E 1967 (3); v A 1967 (3); v WI 1961 (3); v NZ 1967 (4)*
Patel, B. P. 21: v E 1976 (5); v WI 1974 (3); v NZ 1976 (3); *v E 1974 (2); v A 1977 (2); v WI 1975 (3); v NZ 1975 (3)*
Patel, J. M. 7: v A 1956 (2) 1959 (3); v NZ 1955 (1); *v P 1954 (1)*
Patel, R. 1: v NZ 1988
Patiala, Yuvraj of, 1: v E 1933
Patil, S. M. 29: v E 1979 (1) 1981 (4) 1984 (2); v WI 1983 (2); v P 1979 (2) 1983 (3); v SL 1982 (1); *v E 1982 (2); v A 1980 (3); v NZ 1980 (3); v P 1982 (4) 1984 (2)*
Patil, S. R. 1: v NZ 1955
Phadkar, D. G. 31: v E 1951 (4); v A 1956 (1); v WI 1948 (4) 1958 (1); v NZ 1955 (4); v P 1952 (2); *v E 1952 (4); v A 1947 (4); v WI 1952 (4); v P 1954 (3)*
Prabhakar, M. 12: v E 1984 (2); *v E 1990 (3); v NZ 1989 (3); v P 1989 (4)*
Prasanna, E. A. S. 49: v E 1961 (1) 1972 (3) 1976 (4); v A 1969 (5); v WI 1966 (1) 1974 (5); v NZ 1969 (3); *v E 1967 (3) 1974 (2); v A 1967 (4) 1977 (4); v WI 1961 (1) 1970 (3) 1975 (1); v NZ 1967 (4) 1975 (3); v P 1978 (2)*
Punjabi, P. H. 5: *v P 1954 (5)*

Rai Singh, K. 1: *v A 1947*
Rajinder Pal 1: v E 1963
Rajindernath, V. 1: v P 1952
Rajput, L. S. 2: *v SL 1985 (2)*
Raju, S. L. V. 2: *v NZ 1989 (2)*
Raman, W. V. 6: v WI 1987 (1); v NZ 1988 (1); *v WI 1988 (1); v NZ 1989 (3)*
Ramaswami, C. 2: *v E 1936 (2)*
Ramchand, G. S. 33: v A 1956 (3) 1959 (5); v WI 1958 (3); v NZ 1955 (5); v P 1952 (3); *v E 1952 (4); v WI 1952 (5); v P 1954 (5)*
Ramji, L. 1: v E 1933
Rangachary, C. R. 4: v WI 1948 (2); *v A 1947 (2)*
Rangnekar, K. M. 3: *v A 1947 (3)*
Ranjane, V. B. 7: v E 1961 (3) 1963 (1); v A 1964 (1); v WI 1958 (1); *v WI 1961 (1)*
Razdan, V. 2: *v P 1989 (2)*
Reddy, B. 4: *v E 1979 (4)*
Rege, M. R. 1: v WI 1948
Roy, A. 4: v A 1969 (2); v NZ 1969 (2)
Roy, Pankaj 43: v E 1951 (5); v A 1956 (3) 1959 (5); v WI 1958 (5); v NZ 1955 (3); v P 1952 (3) 1960 (1); *v E 1952 (4) 1959 (5); v WI 1952 (4); v P 1954 (5)*
Roy, Pranab 2: v E 1981 (2)

Sandhu, B. S. 8: v WI 1983 (1); *v WI 1982 (4); v P 1982 (3)*
Sardesai, D. N. 30: v E 1961 (1) 1963 (5) 1972 (1); v A 1964 (3) 1969 (1); v WI 1966 (2); v NZ 1964 (3); *v E 1967 (1) 1971 (3); v A 1967 (2); v WI 1961 (3) 1970 (5)*
Sarwate, C. T. 9: v E 1951 (1); v WI 1948 (2); *v E 1946 (1); v A 1947 (5)*
Saxena, R. C. 1: *v E 1967*
Sekar, T. A. P. 2: *v P 1982 (2)*
Sen, P. 14: v E 1951 (2); v WI 1948 (5); v P 1952 (2); *v E 1952 (2); v A 1947 (3)*
Sengupta, A. K. 1: v WI 1958
Sharma, Ajay 1: v WI 1987
Sharma, Chetan 23: v E 1984 (3); v A 1986 (2); v WI 1987 (3); v SL 1986 (2); *v E 1986 (2); v A 1985 (2); v WI 1988 (4); v P 1984 (2); v SL 1985 (3)*
Sharma, Gopal 4: v E 1984 (1); v P 1986 (2); *v SL 1985 (1)*
Sharma, P. 5: v E 1976 (2); v WI 1974 (2); *v WI 1975 (1)*
Sharma, Sanjeev 2: v NZ 1988 (1); *v E 1990 (1)*
Shastri, R. J. 72: v E 1981 (6) 1984 (5); v A 1986 (3); v WI 1983 (6) 1987 (4); v NZ 1988 (3); v P 1983 (2) 1986 (5); v SL 1986 (3); *v E 1982 (3) 1986 (3) 1990 (3); v A 1985 (3); v WI 1982 (5) 1988 (4); v NZ 1980 (3); v P 1982 (2) 1984 (2) 1989 (4); v SL 1985 (3)*
Shinde, S. G. 7: v E 1951 (3); v WI 1948 (1); *v E 1946 (1) 1952 (2)*
Shodhan, R. H. 3: v P 1952 (1); *v WI 1952 (2)*
Shukla, R. C. 1: v SL 1982
Sidhu, N. S. 17: v WI 1983 (2); v NZ 1988 (3); *v E 1990 (3); v WI 1988 (4); v NZ 1989 (1); v P 1989 (4)*
Sivaramakrishnan, L. 9: v E 1984 (5); *v A 1985 (2); v WI 1982 (1); v SL 1985 (1)*
Sohoni, S. W. 4: v E 1951 (1); *v E 1946 (2); v A 1947 (1)*
Solkar, E. D. 27: v E 1972 (5) 1976 (1); v A 1969 (4); v WI 1974 (4); v NZ 1969 (1); *v E 1971 (3) 1974 (3); v WI 1970 (5) 1975 (1)*
Sood, M. M. 1: v A 1959
Srikkanth, K. 39: v E 1981 (4) 1984 (2); v A 1986 (3); v WI 1987 (4); v NZ 1988 (3); v P 1986 (5); v SL 1986 (3); *v E 1986 (3); v A 1985 (3); v P 1982 (2) 1989 (4); v SL 1985 (3)*
Srinivasan, T. E. 1: *v NZ 1980*
Subramanya, V. 9: v WI 1966 (2); v NZ 1964 (1); *v E 1967 (2); v A 1967 (2); v NZ 1967 (2)*
Sunderram, G. 2: v NZ 1955 (2)
Surendranath, R. 11: v A 1959 (2); v WI 1958 (2); v P 1960 (2); *v E 1959 (5)*
Surti, R. F. 26: v E 1963 (1); v A 1964 (2) 1969 (1); v WI 1966 (2); v NZ 1964 (1) 1969 (2); v P 1960 (2); *v E 1967 (2); v A 1967 (4); v WI 1961 (5); v NZ 1967 (4)*
Swamy, V. N. 1: v NZ 1955

Tamhane, N. S. 21: v A 1956 (3) 1959 (1); v WI 1958 (4); v NZ 1955 (4); v P 1960 (2); *v E 1959 (2); v P 1954 (5)*
Tarapore, K. K. 1: v WI 1948
Tendulkar, S. R. 10: *v E 1990 (3); v NZ 1989 (3); v P 1989 (4)*

Umrigar, P. R. 59: v E 1951 (5) 1961 (4); v A 1956 (3) 1959 (3); v WI 1948 (1) 1958 (5); v NZ 1955 (5); v P 1952 (5) 1960 (5); *v E 1952 (4) 1959 (4); v WI 1952 (5) 1961 (5); v P 1954 (5)*

Vengsarkar, D. B. 110: v E 1976 (1) 1979 (1) 1981 (6) 1984 (5); v A 1979 (6) 1986 (2); v WI 1978 (6) 1983 (5) 1987 (3); v NZ 1988 (3); v P 1979 (5) 1983 (1) 1986 (5); v SL 1982 (1) 1986 (3); *v E 1979 (4) 1982 (3) 1986 (3) 1990 (3); v A 1977 (5) 1980 (3) 1985 (3); v WI 1975 (2) 1982 (5) 1988 (4); v NZ 1975 (3) 1980 (3) 1989 (2); v P 1978 (3) 1982 (6) 1984 (2); v SL 1985 (3)*

Venkataraghavan, S. 57: v E 1972 (2) 1976 (1); v A 1969 (5) 1979 (3); v WI 1966 (2) 1974 (2) 1978 (6); v NZ 1964 (4) 1969 (2) 1976 (3); v P 1983 (2); *v E 1967 (1) 1971 (3) 1974 (2) 1979 (4); v A 1977 (1); v WI 1970 (5) 1975 (3) 1982 (5); v NZ 1975 (1)*

Venkataramana, M. 1: *v WI 1988*

Viswanath, G. R. 91: v E 1972 (5) 1976 (5) 1979 (1) 1981 (6); v A 1969 (4) 1979 (6); v WI 1974 (5) 1978 (6); v NZ 1976 (3); v P 1979 (6); v SL 1982 (1); *v E 1971 (3) 1974 (3) 1979 (4) 1982 (3); v A 1977 (5) 1980 (3); v WI 1970 (3) 1975 (4); v NZ 1975 (3) 1980 (3); v P 1978 (3) 1982 (6)*

Viswanath, S. 3: *v SL 1985 (3)*

Vizianagram, Maharaj Sir Vijaya 3: *v E 1936 (3)*

Wadekar, A. L. 37: v E 1972 (5); v A 1969 (5); v WI 1966 (2); v NZ 1969 (3); *v E 1967 (3) 1971 (3) 1974 (3); v A 1967 (4); v WI 1970 (5); v NZ 1967 (4)*

Wassan, A. S. 4: *v E 1990 (1); v NZ 1989 (3)*

Wazir Ali, S. 7: v E 1933 (3); *v E 1932 (1) 1936 (3)*

Yadav, N. S. 35: v E 1979 (1) 1981 (1) 1984 (4); v A 1979 (5) 1986 (3); v WI 1983 (3); v P 1979 (5) 1986 (4); v SL 1986 (2); *v A 1980 (2) 1985 (3); v NZ 1980 (1); v P 1984 (1)*

Yajurvindra Singh 4: v E 1976 (2); v A 1979 (1); *v E 1979 (1)*

Yashpal Sharma 37: v E 1979 (1) 1981 (2); v A 1979 (6); v WI 1983 (1); v P 1979 (6) 1983 (3); v SL 1982 (1); *v E 1979 (3) 1982 (3); v A 1980 (3); v WI 1982 (5); v NZ 1980 (1); v P 1982 (2)*

Yograj Singh 1: *v NZ 1980*

Note: Hafeez, on going later to Oxford University, took his correct name, Kardar.

PAKISTAN

Number of Test cricketers: 117

Aamer Malik 12: v E 1987 (2); v A 1988 (1); v In 1989 (4); *v A 1989 (2); v WI 1987 (1); v NZ 1988 (2)*

Aaqib Javed 2: *v A 1989 (1); v NZ 1988 (1)*

Abdul Kadir 4: v A 1964 (1); *v A 1964 (1); v NZ 1964 (2)*

Abdul Qadir 63: v E 1977 (3) 1983 (3) 1987 (3); v A 1982 (3) 1988 (3); v WI 1980 (2) 1986 (3); v NZ 1984 (3); v In 1982 (5) 1984 (1) 1989 (4); v SL 1985 (3); *v E 1982 (3) 1987 (4); v A 1983 (5); v WI 1987 (3); v NZ 1984 (2) 1988 (2); v In 1979 (3) 1986 (3); v SL 1985 (2)*

Afaq Hussain 2: v E 1961 (1); *v A 1964 (1)*

Aftab Baloch 2: v WI 1974 (1); v NZ 1969 (1)

Aftab Gul 6: v E 1968 (2); v NZ 1969 (1); *v E 1971 (3)*

Agha Saadat Ali 1: v NZ 1955

Agha Zahid 1: v WI 1974

Akram Raza 1: v In 1989

Alim-ud-Din 25: v E 1961 (2); v A 1956 (1) 1959 (1); v WI 1958 (1); v NZ 1955 (3); v In 1954 (5); *v E 1954 (3) 1962 (3); v WI 1957 (5); v In 1960 (1)*

Amir Elahi 5: *v In 1952 (5)*

Anil Dalpat 9: v E 1983 (3); v NZ 1984 (3); *v NZ 1984 (3)*

Anwar Hussain 4: *v In 1952 (4)*

Anwar Khan 1: *v NZ 1978*

Arif Butt 3: *v A 1964 (1); v NZ 1964 (2)*

Ashraf Ali 8: v E 1987 (3); v In 1984 (2); v SL 1981 (2) 1985 (1)

Asif Iqbal 58: v E 1968 (3) 1972 (3); v A 1964 (1); v WI 1974 (2); v NZ 1964 (3) 1969 (3) 1976 (3); v In 1978 (3); *v E 1967 (3) 1971 (3) 1974 (3); v A 1964 (1) 1972 (3) 1976 (3) 1978 (2); v WI 1976 (5); v NZ 1964 (3) 1972 (3) 1978 (2); v In 1979 (6)*

Asif Masood 16: v E 1968 (2) 1972 (1); v WI 1974 (2); v NZ 1969 (1); *v E 1971 (3) 1974 (3); v A 1972 (3) 1976 (1)*

Asif Mujtaba 3: v E 1987 (1); v WI 1986 (2)
Azeem Hafeez 18: v E 1983 (2); v NZ 1984 (3); v In 1984 (2); *v A 1983 (5); v NZ 1984 (3); v In 1983 (3)*
Azhar Khan 1: v A 1979
Azmat Rana 1: v A 1979

Burki, J. 25: v E 1961 (3); v A 1964 (1); v NZ 1964 (3) 1969 (1); *v E 1962 (5) 1967 (3); v A 1964 (1); v NZ 1964 (3); v In 1960 (5)*

D'Souza, A. 6: v E 1961 (2); v WI 1958 (1); *v E 1962 (3)*

Ehtesham-ud-Din 5: v A 1979 (1); *v E 1982 (1); v In 1979 (3)*

Farooq Hamid 1: *v A 1964*
Farrukh Zaman 1: v NZ 1976
Fazal Mahmood 34: v E 1961 (1); v A 1956 (1) 1959 (2); v WI 1958 (3); v NZ 1955 (2); v In 1954 (4); *v E 1954 (4) 1962 (2); v WI 1957 (5); v In 1952 (5) 1960 (5)*

Ghazali, M. E. Z. 2: *v E 1954 (2)*
Ghulam Abbas 1: *v E 1967*
Gul Mahomed 1: v A 1956

Hanif Mohammad 55: v E 1961 (3) 1968 (3); v A 1956 (1) 1959 (3) 1964 (1); v WI 1958 (1); v NZ 1955 (3) 1964 (3) 1969 (1); v In 1954 (5); *v E 1954 (4) 1962 (5) 1967 (3); v A 1964 (1); v WI 1957 (5); v NZ 1964 (3); v In 1952 (5) 1960 (5)*
Haroon Rashid 23: v E 1977 (3); v A 1979 (2) 1982 (3); v In 1982 (1); v SL 1981 (2); *v E 1978 (3) 1982 (1); v A 1976 (1) 1978 (1); v WI 1976 (5); v NZ 1978 (1)*
Haseeb Ahsan 12: v E 1961 (2); v A 1959 (1); v WI 1958 (1); *v WI 1957 (3); v In 1960 (5)*

Ibadulla, K. 4: v A 1964 (1); *v E 1967 (2); v NZ 1964 (1)*
Ijaz Ahmed 16: v E 1987 (3); v A 1988 (3); *v E 1987 (4); v A 1989 (3); v WI 1987 (2); v In 1986 (1)*
Ijaz Butt 8: v A 1959 (2); v WI 1958 (3); *v E 1962 (3)*
Ijaz Faqih 5: v WI 1980 (1); *v A 1981 (1); v WI 1987 (2); v In 1986 (1)*
Imran Khan 82: v A 1979 (2) 1982 (3); v WI 1980 (4) 1986 (3); v NZ 1976 (3); v In 1978 (3) 1982 (6) 1989 (4); v SL 1981 (1) 1985 (3); *v E 1971 (1) 1974 (3) 1982 (3) 1987 (5); v A 1976 (3) 1978 (2) 1981 (3) 1983 (2) 1989 (3); v WI 1976 (5) 1987 (3); v NZ 1978 (2) 1988 (2); v In 1979 (5) 1986 (5); v SL 1985 (3)*
Imtiaz Ahmed 41: v E 1961 (3); v A 1956 (1) 1959 (3); v WI 1958 (3); v NZ 1955 (3); v In 1954 (5); *v E 1954 (4) 1962 (4); v WI 1957 (5); v In 1952 (5) 1960 (5)*
Intikhab Alam 47: v E 1961 (2) 1968 (3) 1972 (3); v A 1959 (1) 1964 (1); v WI 1974 (2); v NZ 1964 (3) 1969 (3) 1976 (3); *v E 1962 (3) 1967 (3) 1971 (3) 1974 (3); v A 1964 (1) 1972 (3); v WI 1976 (1); v NZ 1964 (3) 1972 (3); v In 1960 (3)*
Iqbal Qasim 50: v E 1977 (3) 1987 (3); v A 1979 (3) 1982 (2) 1988 (3); v WI 1980 (4); v NZ 1984 (3); v In 1978 (3) 1982 (2); v SL 1981 (3); *v E 1978 (3); v A 1976 (3) 1981 (2); v WI 1976 (2); v NZ 1984 (1); v In 1979 (6) 1983 (1) 1986 (3)*
Israr Ali 4: v A 1959 (2); *v In 1952 (2)*

Jalal-ud-Din 6: v A 1982 (1); v In 1982 (2) 1984 (2); v SL 1985 (1)
Javed Akhtar 1: *v E 1962*
Javed Miandad 104: v E 1977 (3) 1987 (3); v A 1979 (3) 1982 (3) 1988 (3); v WI 1980 (4) 1986 (3); v NZ 1976 (3) 1984 (3); v In 1978 (3) 1982 (6) 1984 (2) 1989 (4); v SL 1981 (3) 1985 (3); *v E 1978 (3) 1982 (3) 1987 (5); v A 1976 (3) 1978 (2) 1981 (3) 1983 (5) 1989 (3); v WI 1976 (1) 1987 (3); v NZ 1978 (3) 1984 (3) 1988 (2); v In 1979 (6) 1983 (3) 1986 (4); v SL 1985 (3)*

Kardar, A. H. 23: v A 1956 (1); v NZ 1955 (3); v In 1954 (5); *v E 1954 (4); v WI 1957 (5); v In 1952 (5)*
Khalid Hassan 1: *v E 1954*
Khalid Wazir 2: *v E 1954 (2)*
Khan Mohammad 13: v A 1956 (1); v NZ 1955 (3); v In 1954 (4); *v E 1954 (2); v WI 1957 (2); v In 1952 (1)*

Liaqat Ali 5: v E 1977 (2); v WI 1974 (1); *v E 1978 (2)*

Mahmood Hussain 27: v E 1961 (1); v WI 1958 (3); v NZ 1955 (1); v In 1954 (5); *v E 1954* (*2*) *1962* (*3*)*; v WI 1957* (*3*)*; v In 1952* (*4*) *1960* (*5*)
Majid Khan 63: v E 1968 (3) 1972 (3); v A 1964 (1) 1979 (3); v WI 1974 (2) 1980 (4); v NZ 1964 (3) 1976 (3); v In 1978 (3) 1982 (1); v SL 1981 (1); *v E 1967* (*3*) *1971* (*2*) *1974* (*3*) *1982* (*1*)*; v A 1972* (*3*) *1976* (*3*) *1978* (*2*) *1981* (*3*)*; v WI 1976* (*5*)*; v NZ 1972* (*3*) *1978* (*2*)*; v In 1979* (*6*)
Mansoor Akhtar 19: v A 1982 (3); v WI 1980 (2); v In 1982 (3); v SL 1981 (1); *v E 1982* (*3*) *1987* (*5*)*; v A 1981* (*1*) *1989* (*1*)
Manzoor Elahi 4: v NZ 1984 (1); v In 1984 (1); *v In 1986* (*2*)
Maqsood Ahmed 16: v NZ 1955 (2); v In 1954 (5); *v E 1954* (*4*)*; v In 1952* (*5*)
Mathias, Wallis 21: v E 1961 (1); v A 1956 (1) 1959 (2); v WI 1958 (3); v NZ 1955 (1); *v E 1962* (*3*)*; v WI 1957* (*5*)*; v In 1960* (*5*)
Miran Bux 2: v In 1954 (2)
Mohammad Aslam 1: *v E 1954*
Mohammad Farooq 7: v NZ 1964 (3); *v E 1962* (*2*)*; v In 1960* (*2*)
Mohammad Ilyas 10: v E 1968 (2); v NZ 1964 (3); *v E 1967* (*1*)*; v A 1964* (*1*)*; v NZ 1964* (*3*)
Mohammad Munaf 4: v E 1961 (2); v A 1959 (2)
Mohammad Nazir 14: v E 1972 (1); v WI 1980 (4); v NZ 1969 (3)*; v A 1983* (*3*)*; v In 1983* (*3*)
Mohsin Kamal 7: v E 1983 (1); v SL 1985 (1); *v E 1987* (*4*)*; v SL 1985* (*1*)
Mohsin Khan 48: v E 1977 (1) 1983 (3); v A 1982 (3); v WI 1986 (3); v NZ 1984 (2); v In 1982 (6) 1984 (2); v SL 1981 (2) 1985 (2); *v E 1978* (*3*) *1982* (*3*)*; v A 1978* (*1*) *1981* (*2*) *1983* (*5*)*; v NZ 1978* (*1*) *1984* (*3*)*; v In 1983* (*3*)*; v SL 1985* (*3*)
Mudassar Nazar 76: v E 1977 (3) 1983 (1) 1987 (3); v A 1979 (3) 1982 (3) 1988 (3); v WI 1986 (2); v NZ 1984 (3); v In 1978 (2) 1982 (6) 1984 (2); v SL 1981 (1) 1985 (3) ; *v E 1978* (*3*) *1982* (*3*) *1987* (*5*)*; v A 1976* (*1*) *1978* (*1*) *1981* (*3*) *1983* (*5*)*; v WI 1987* (*3*)*; v NZ 1978* (*1*) *1984* (*3*) *1988* (*2*)*; v In 1979* (*5*) *1983* (*3*)*; v SL 1985* (*3*)
Mufasir-ul-Haq 1: *v NZ 1964*
Munir Malik 3: v A 1959 (1); *v E 1962* (*2*)
Mushtaq Ahmed 1: *v A 1989*
Mushtaq Mohammad 57: v E 1961 (3) 1968 (3) 1972 (3); v WI 1958 (1) 1974 (2); v NZ 1969 (2) 1976 (3); v In 1978 (3); *v E 1962* (*5*) *1967* (*3*) *1971* (*3*) *1974* (*3*)*; v A 1972* (*3*) *1976* (*3*) *1978* (*2*)*; v WI 1976* (*5*)*; v NZ 1972* (*2*) *1978* (*3*)*; v In 1960* (*5*)

Nadeem Abbasi 3: v In 1989 (3)
Nadeem Ghauri 1: *v A 1989*
Nasim-ul-Ghani 29: v E 1961 (2); v A 1959 (2) 1964 (1); v WI 1958 (3); *v E 1962* (*5*) *1967* (*2*)*; v A 1964* (*1*) *1972* (*1*)*; v WI 1957* (*5*)*; v NZ 1964* (*3*)*; v In 1960* (*4*)
Naushad Ali 6: v NZ 1964 (3); *v NZ 1964* (*3*)
Naved Anjum 1: v In 1989
Nazar Mohammad 5: *v In 1952* (*5*)
Nazir Junior (*see* Mohammad Nazir)
Niaz Ahmed 2: v E 1968 (1); *v E 1967* (*1*)

Pervez Sajjad 19: v E 1968 (1) 1972 (2); v A 1964 (1); v NZ 1964 (3) 1969 (3); *v E 1971* (*3*)*; v NZ 1964* (*3*) *1972* (*3*)

Qasim Omar 26: v E 1983 (3); v WI 1986 (3); v NZ 1984 (3); v In 1984 (2); v SL 1985 (3); *v A 1983* (*5*)*; v NZ 1984* (*3*)*; v In 1983* (*1*)*; v SL 1985* (*3*)

Ramiz Raja 31: v E 1983 (2) 1987 (3); v A 1988 (3); v WI 1986 (3); v In 1989 (4); v SL 1985 (1); *v E 1987* (*2*)*; v A 1989* (*2*)*; v WI 1987* (*3*)*; v In 1986* (*5*)*; v SL 1985* (*3*)
Rashid Khan 4: v SL 1981 (2); *v A 1983* (*1*)*; v NZ 1984* (*1*)
Rehman, S. F. 1: *v WI 1957*
Rizwan-uz-Zaman 11: v WI 1986 (1); v SL 1981 (2); *v A 1981* (*1*)*; v NZ 1988* (*2*)*; v In 1986* (*5*)

Sadiq Mohammad 41: v E 1972 (3) 1977 (2); v WI 1974 (1) 1980 (3); v NZ 1969 (3) 1976 (3); v In 1978 (1); *v E 1971* (*3*) *1974* (*3*) *1978* (*3*)*; v A 1972* (*3*) *1976* (*2*)*; v WI 1976* (*5*)*; v NZ 1972* (*3*)*; v In 1979* (*3*)
Saeed Ahmed 41: v E 1961 (3) 1968 (3); v A 1959 (3) 1964 (1); v WI 1958 (3); v NZ 1964 (3); *v E 1962* (*5*) *1967* (*3*) *1971* (*1*)*; v A 1964* (*1*) *1972* (*2*)*; v WI 1957* (*5*)*; v NZ 1964* (*3*)*; v In 1960* (*5*)
Salah-ud-Din 5: v E 1968 (1); v NZ 1964 (3) 1969 (1)
Saleem Jaffer 10: v E 1987 (1); v A 1988 (2); v WI 1986 (1); v In 1989 (1); *v WI 1987* (*1*)*; v NZ 1988* (*2*)*; v In 1986* (*2*)
Salim Altaf 21: v E 1972 (3); v NZ 1969 (2); v In 1978 (1); *v E 1967* (*2*) *1971* (*2*)*; v A 1972* (*3*) *1976* (*2*)*; v WI 1976* (*3*)*; v NZ 1972* (*3*)

Salim Malik 57: v E 1983 (3) 1987 (3); v A 1988 (3); v WI 1986 (1); v NZ 1984 (3); v In 1982 (6) 1984 (2) 1989 (4); v SL 1981 (2) 1985 (3); *v E 1987 (5); v A 1983 (3) 1989 (1); v WI 1987 (3); v NZ 1984 (3) 1988 (2); v In 1983 (2) 1986 (5); v SL 1985 (3)*
Salim Yousuf 28: v A 1988 (3); v WI 1986 (3); v In 1989 (1); v SL 1981 (1) 1985 (2); *v E 1987 (5); v A 1989 (3); v WI 1987 (3); v NZ 1988 (2); v In 1986 (5)*
Sarfraz Nawaz 55: v E 1968 (1) 1972 (2) 1977 (2) 1983 (3); v A 1979 (3); v WI 1974 (2) 1980 (2); v NZ 1976 (3); v In 1978 (3) 1982 (6); *v E 1974 (3) 1978 (2) 1982 (1); v A 1972 (2) 1976 (2) 1978 (2) 1981 (3) 1983 (3); v WI 1976 (4); v NZ 1972 (3) 1978 (3)*
Shafiq Ahmad 6: v E 1977 (3); v WI 1980 (2); *v E 1974 (1)*
Shafqat Rana 5: v E 1968 (2); v A 1964 (1); v NZ 1969 (2)
Shahid Israr 1: v NZ 1976
Shahid Mahboob 1: v In 1989
Shahid Mahmood 1: *v E 1962*
Shahid Saeed 1: v In 1989
Sharpe, D. 3: v A 1959 (3)
Shoaib Mohammad 29: v E 1983 (1) 1987 (1); v A 1988 (3); v NZ 1984 (1); v In 1989 (4); v SL 1985 (1); *v E 1987 (4); v A 1989 (3); v WI 1987 (3); v NZ 1984 (1) 1988 (2); v In 1983 (2) 1986 (3)*
Shuja-ud-Din 19: v E 1961 (2); v A 1959 (3); v WI 1958 (3); v NZ 1955 (3); v In 1954 (5); *v E 1954 (3)*
Sikander Bakht 26: v E 1977 (2); v WI 1980 (1); v NZ 1976 (1); v In 1978 (2) 1982 (1); *v E 1978 (3) 1982 (2); v A 1978 (2) 1981 (3); v WI 1976 (1); v NZ 1978 (3); v In 1979 (5)*

Tahir Naqqash 15: v A 1982 (3); v In 1982 (2); v SL 1981 (3); *v E 1982 (2); v A 1983 (1); v NZ 1984 (1); v In 1983 (3)*
Talat Ali 10: v E 1972 (3); *v E 1978 (2); v A 1972 (1); v NZ 1972 (1) 1978 (3)*
Taslim Arif 6: v A 1979 (3); v WI 1980 (2); *v In 1979 (1)*
Tauseef Ahmed 31: v E 1983 (2) 1987 (2); v A 1979 (3) 1988 (3); v WI 1986 (3); v NZ 1984 (1); v In 1984 (1); v SL 1981 (3) 1985 (1); *v E 1987 (2); v A 1989 (3); v NZ 1988 (1); v In 1986 (4); v SL 1985 (2)*

Waqar Hassan 21: v A 1956 (1) 1959 (1); v WI 1958 (1); v NZ 1955 (3); v In 1954 (5); *v E 1954 (4); v WI 1957 (1); v In 1952 (5)*
Waqar Younis 5: v In 1989 (2); *v A 1989 (3)*
Wasim Akram 32: v E 1987 (2); v WI 1986 (2); v In 1989 (4); v SL 1985 (3); *v E 1987 (5); v A 1989 (3); v WI 1987 (3); v NZ 1984 (2); v In 1986 (5); v SL 1985 (3)*
Wasim Bari 81: v E 1968 (3) 1972 (3) 1977 (3); v A 1982 (3); v WI 1974 (2) 1980 (2); v NZ 1969 (3) 1976 (2); v In 1978 (3) 1982 (6); *v E 1967 (3) 1971 (3) 1974 (3) 1978 (3) 1982 (3); v A 1972 (3) 1976 (3) 1978 (2) 1981 (3) 1983 (5); v WI 1976 (5); v NZ 1972 (3) 1978 (3); v In 1979 (6) 1983 (3)*
Wasim Raja 57: v E 1972 (1) 1977 (3) 1983 (3); v A 1979 (3); v WI 1974 (2) 1980 (4); v NZ 1976 (1) 1984 (1); v In 1982 (1) 1984 (1); v SL 1981 (3); *v E 1974 (2) 1978 (3) 1982 (1); v A 1978 (1) 1981 (3) 1983 (2); v WI 1976 (5); v NZ 1972 (3) 1978 (3) 1984 (2); v In 1979 (6) 1983 (3)*
Wazir Mohammad 20: v A 1956 (1) 1959 (1); v WI 1958 (3); v NZ 1955 (2); v In 1954 (5); *v E 1954 (2); v WI 1957 (5); v In 1952 (1)*

Younis Ahmed 4: v NZ 1969 (2); *v In 1986 (2)*

Zaheer Abbas 78: v E 1972 (2) 1983 (3); v A 1979 (2) 1982 (3); v WI 1974 (2) 1980 (3); v NZ 1969 (1) 1976 (3) 1984 (3); v In 1978 (3) 1982 (6) 1984 (2); v SL 1981 (1) 1985 (2); *v E 1971 (3) 1974 (3) 1982 (3); v A 1972 (3) 1976 (3) 1978 (2) 1981 (2) 1983 (5); v WI 1976 (3); v NZ 1972 (3) 1978 (2) 1984 (2); v In 1979 (5) 1983 (3)*
Zakir Khan 2: v In 1989 (1); *v SL 1985 (1)*
Zulfiqar Ahmed 9: v A 1956 (1); v NZ 1955 (3); *v E 1954 (2); v In 1952 (3)*
Zulqarnain 3: *v SL 1985 (3)*

SRI LANKA

Number of Test cricketers: 45

Ahangama, F. S. 3: v In 1985 (3)
Amalean, K. N. 2: v P 1985 (1); *v A 1987 (1)*
Amerasinghe, A. M. J. G. 2: v NZ 1983 (2)
Anurasiri, S. D. 4: v NZ 1986 (1); v P 1985 (2); *v In 1986 (1)*

de Alwis, R. G. 11: v A 1982 (1); v NZ 1983 (3); v P 1985 (2); *v A 1987 (1); v NZ 1982 (1); v In 1986 (3)*
de Mel, A. L. F. 17: v E 1981 (1); v A 1982 (1); v In 1985 (3); v P 1985 (3); *v E 1984 (1); v In 1982 (1) 1986 (1); v P 1981 (3) 1985 (3)*
de Silva, D. S. 12: v E 1981 (1); v A 1982 (1); v NZ 1983 (3); *v E 1984 (1); v NZ 1982 (2); v In 1982 (1); v P 1981 (3)*
de Silva, E. A. R. 7: v In 1985 (1); v P 1985 (1); *v A 1989 (2); v In 1986 (3)*
de Silva, G. R. A. 4: v E 1981 (1); *v In 1982 (1); v P 1981 (2)*
de Silva, P. A. 17: v In 1985 (3); v P 1985 (3); *v E 1984 (1) 1988 (1); v A 1987 (1) 1989 (2); v In 1986 (3); v P 1985 (3)*
Dias, R. L. 20: v E 1981 (1); v A 1982 (1); v NZ 1983 (2) 1986 (1); v In 1985 (3); v P 1985 (1); *v E 1984 (1); v In 1982 (1) 1986 (3); v P 1981 (3) 1985 (3)*

Fernando, E. R. N. S. 5: v A 1982 (1); v NZ 1983 (2); *v NZ 1982 (2)*

Goonatillake, H. M. 5: v E 1981 (1); *v In 1982 (1); v P 1981 (3)*
Gunasekera, Y. 2: *v NZ 1982 (2)*
Guneratne, R. P. W. 1: v A 1982
Gurusinha, A. P. 9: v NZ 1986 (1); v P 1985 (2); *v A 1989 (2); v In 1986 (3); v P 1985 (1)*

Jayasekera, R. S. A. 1: *v P 1981*
Jeganathan, S. 2: *v NZ 1982 (2)*
John, V. B. 6: v NZ 1983 (3); *v E 1984 (1); v NZ 1982 (2)*
Jurangpathy, B. R. 2: v In 1985 (1); *v In 1986 (1)*

Kaluperuma, L. W. 2: v E 1981 (1); *v P 1981 (1)*
Kaluperuma, S. M. S. 4: v NZ 1983 (3); *v A 1987 (1)*
Kuruppu, D. S. B. P. 3: v NZ 1986 (1); *v E 1988 (1); v A 1987 (1)*
Kuruppuarachchi, A. K. 2: v NZ 1986 (1); v P 1985 (1)

Labrooy, G. F. 5: *v E 1988 (1); v A 1987 (1) 1989 (2); v In 1986 (1)*

Madugalle, R. S. 21: v E 1981 (1); v A 1982 (1); v NZ 1983 (3) 1986 (1); v In 1985 (3); *v E 1984 (1) 1988 (1); v A 1987 (1); v NZ 1982 (2); v In 1982 (1); v P 1981 (3) 1985 (3)*
Madurasinghe, A. W. R. 1: *v E 1988*
Mahanama, R. S. 6: v NZ 1986 (1); v P 1985 (2); *v A 1987 (1) 1989 (2)*
Mendis, L. R. D. 24: v E 1981 (1); v A 1982 (1); v NZ 1983 (3) 1986 (1); v In 1985 (3); v P 1985 (3); *v E 1984 (1) 1988 (1); v In 1982 (1) 1986 (3); v P 1981 (3) 1985 (3)*

Ramanayake, C. P. H. 4: *v E 1988 (1); v A 1987 (1) 1989 (2)*
Ranasinghe, A. N. 2: *v In 1982 (1); v P 1981 (1)*
Ranatunga, A. 26: v E 1981 (1); v A 1982 (1); v NZ 1983 (3) 1986 (1); v In 1985 (3); v P 1985 (3); *v E 1984 (1) 1988 (1); v A 1987 (1) 1989 (2); v In 1982 (1) 1986 (3); v P 1981 (2) 1985 (3)*
Ranatunga, D. 2: *v A 1989 (2)*
Ratnayake, R. J. 15: v A 1982 (1); v NZ 1983 (1) 1986 (1); v In 1985 (3); v P 1985 (1); *v A 1989 (1); v NZ 1982 (2); v In 1986 (2); v P 1985 (3)*
Ratnayeke, J. R. 22: v NZ 1983 (2) 1986 (1); v P 1985 (3); *v E 1984 (1) 1988 (1); v A 1987 (1) 1989 (2); v NZ 1982 (2); v In 1982 (1) 1986 (3); v P 1981 (2) 1985 (3)*

Samarasekera, M. A. R. 2: *v E 1988 (1); v A 1989 (1)*
Silva, S. A. R. 9: v In 1985 (3); v P 1985 (1); *v E 1984 (1) 1988 (1); v NZ 1982 (1); v P 1985 (2)*

Tillekeratne, H. P. 1: *v A 1989*

Warnapura, B. 4: v E 1981 (1); *v In 1982 (1); v P 1981 (2)*
Warnaweera, K. P. J. 1: v P 1985
Weerasinghe, C. D. U. S. 1: v In 1985
Wettimuny, M. D. 2: *v NZ 1982 (2)*
Wettimuny, S. 23: v E 1981 (1); v A 1982 (1); v NZ 1983 (3); v In 1985 (3); v P 1985 (3); *v E 1984 (1); v NZ 1982 (2); v In 1986 (3); v P 1981 (3) 1985 (3)*
Wickremasinghe, A. G. D. 1: *v A 1989*
Wijesuriya, R. G. C. E. 4: *v P 1981 (1) 1985 (3)*

TWO COUNTRIES

Twelve cricketers have appeared for two countries in Test matches, namely:

Amir Elahi, *India and Pakistan.*
J. J. Ferris, *Australia and England.*
S. C. Guillen, *West Indies and NZ.*
Gul Mahomed, *India and Pakistan.*
F. Hearne, *England and South Africa.*
A. H. Kardar, *India and Pakistan.*
W. E. Midwinter, *England and Australia.*
F. Mitchell, *England and South Africa.*
W. L. Murdoch, *Australia and England.*
Nawab of Pataudi, sen., *England and India.*
A. E. Trott, *Australia and England.*
S. M. J. Woods, *Australia and England.*

MOST TEST APPEARANCES FOR EACH COUNTRY

England: M. C. Cowdrey 114.
Australia: A. R. Border 115.
South Africa: J. H. B. Waite 50.
West Indies: I. V. A. Richards 111.
New Zealand: Sir R. J. Hadlee 86.
India: S. M. Gavaskar 125.
Pakistan: Javed Miandad 104.
Sri Lanka: A. Ranatunga 26.

MOST TEST APPEARANCES AS CAPTAIN FOR EACH COUNTRY

England: P. B. H. May 41.
Australia: A. R. Border 52.
South Africa: H. W. Taylor 18.
West Indies: C. H. Lloyd 74.
New Zealand: J. R. Reid 34.
India: S. M. Gavaskar 47.
Pakistan: Imran Khan 42.
Sri Lanka: L. R. D. Mendis 19.

ENGLAND v REST OF THE WORLD

The following were awarded England caps for playing against the Rest of the World in England in 1970, although the five matches played are now generally considered not to have rated as full Tests: D. L. Amiss (1), G. Boycott (2), D. J. Brown (2), M. C. Cowdrey (4), M. H. Denness (1), B. L. D'Oliveira (4), J. H. Edrich (2), K. W. R. Fletcher (4), A. W. Greig (3), R. Illingworth (5), A. Jones (1), A. P. E. Knott (5), P. Lever (1), B. W. Luckhurst (5), C. M. Old (2), P. J. Sharpe (1), K. Shuttleworth (1), J. A. Snow (5), D. L. Underwood (3), A. Ward (1), D. Wilson (2).

CRICKET RECORDS

Amended by BILL FRINDALL to end of the 1990 season in England

Unless stated to be of a minor character, all records apply only to first-class cricket including some performances in the distant past which have always been recognised as of exceptional merit.

* Denotes not out or an unbroken partnership.

(A), (SA), (WI), (NZ), (I), (P) or (SL) indicates either the nationality of the player, or the country in which the record was made.

FIRST-CLASS RECORDS

BATTING RECORDS

Highest Individual Scores ... 133
Highest Scores in England and Australia ... 134
Highest for Each First-class County ... 135
Hundred on Début in British Isles ... 135
Two Double-Hundreds in a Match ... 136
Hundred and Double-Hundred in a Match ... 136
Two Separate Hundreds in a Match ... 137
Four Hundreds or More in Succession ... 138
Most Hundreds in a Season ... 138
Most Hundreds in a Career ... 138
3,000 Runs in a Season ... 140
1,000 Runs in a Season Most Times ... 140
Highest Aggregates Outside England ... 141
Highest Averages in an English Season ... 142
25,000 Runs in a Career ... 142
Career Average over 50 ... 144
Fast Scoring ... 145
300 Runs in One Day ... 146
1,000 Runs in May ... 146
1,000 Runs in Two Separate Months ... 147
Most Runs Scored off One Over ... 147
Most Sixes in an Innings ... 148
Most Sixes in a Season ... 148
Most Boundaries in an Innings ... 149
Highest Partnerships ... 149
Partnerships for First Wicket ... 150
First-Wicket Hundreds in Both Innings ... 150
Partnership Records for All Countries ... 151
Out Handled the Ball ... 154
Out Obstructing the Field ... 155
Out Hit the Ball Twice ... 155

BOWLING RECORDS

Ten Wickets in One Innings ... 155
Outstanding Analyses ... 157
Most Wickets in a Match ... 157
Sixteen or More Wickets in a Day ... 158
Four Wickets with Consecutive Balls ... 158
Hat-tricks ... 159
200 Wickets in a Season ... 160
100 Wickets in a Season Most Times ... 161
100 Wickets in a Season Outside England ... 161
1,500 Wickets in a Career ... 161

ALL-ROUND RECORDS

Hundred and Ten Wickets in One Innings 163
Two Hundred Runs and Sixteen Wickets 163
Hundred in Each Innings and Five Wickets Twice 163
Hundred in Each Innings and Ten Wickets 163
Hundred and Hat-trick 164
Season Doubles 164
20,000 Runs and 2,000 Wickets in a Career 165

WICKET-KEEPING RECORDS

Most Dismissals in an Innings 165
Wicket-keepers' Hat-tricks 166
Most Dismissals in a Match 166
Most Dismissals in a Season 167
Most Dismissals in a Career 167

FIELDING RECORDS

Most Catches in an Innings 168
Most Catches in a Match 168
Most Catches in a Season 168
Most Catches in a Career 169

TEAM RECORDS

Highest Totals 169
Highest for Each First-class County 169
Lowest Totals 170
Lowest for Each First-class County 170
Highest Match Aggregates 171
Lowest Aggregate in a Completed Match 171
Highest Fourth-Innings Totals 171
Largest Victories 172
Tied Matches 172
Matches Begun and Finished on First Day 173

TEST MATCH RECORDS

BATTING RECORDS

Highest Individual Test Innings 173
Hundred on Test Début 174
300 Runs in First Test 175
Two Separate Hundreds in a Test 175
Hundred and Double-Hundred in Same Test 176
Most Runs in a Series 176
1,000 Test Runs in a Calendar Year 176
Most Runs in a Career 177
Highest Averages 180
Most Hundreds 181
Carrying Bat Through Test Innings 181

Fastest Fifties 182
Fastest Hundreds 182
Fastest Double-Hundreds 182
Fastest Triple-Hundreds 183
Most Runs in a Day by a Batsman 183
Slowest Individual Batting 183
Slowest Hundreds 183
Highest Partnerships for each Wicket 184
Partnerships of 300 and Over 184

BOWLING RECORDS

Most Wickets in an Innings 185
Outstanding Innings Analyses 186
Most Wickets in a Match and in a Series 186
Most Wickets in a Career 187
Wicket with First Ball in Test Cricket 189
Hat-tricks 189
Most Balls Bowled in a Test 190

ALL-ROUND RECORDS

100 Runs and Five Wickets in an Innings 190
100 Runs and Five Dismissals in an Innings 191
100 Runs and Ten Wickets in a Test 191
1,000 Runs and 100 Wickets in a Career 191
1,000 Runs, 100 Wickets and 100 Catches 192

WICKET-KEEPING RECORDS

Most Dismissals in an Innings, in a Match, in a Series and in a Career 192

FIELDING RECORDS

Most Catches in an Innings, in a Match, in a Series and in a Career 193

TEAM RECORDS

Highest Innings Totals 194
Highest Fourth-Innings Totals 195
Most Runs in a Day (Both Sides and One Side) 195
Most Wickets in a Day 196
Highest Match Aggregates 196
Lowest Innings Totals 196
Fewest Runs in a Full Day's Play 196
Lowest Match Aggregates 197
Youngest Test Players 197
Oldest Players on Test Début 197
Oldest Test Players 198
Most Test Match Appearances 198
Most Consecutive Test Appearances 198

TEST SERIES

Summary of All Test Matches 199
England v Australia 199
England v South Africa 208
England v West Indies 213
England v New Zealand 217
England v India 220
England v Pakistan 223
England v Sri Lanka 226
England v Rest of the World 227
Australia v South Africa 227
Australia v West Indies 229
Australia v New Zealand 233
Australia v India 235
Australia v Pakistan 237
Australia v Sri Lanka 239
South Africa v New Zealand 240
West Indies v New Zealand 242
West Indies v India 244
West Indies v Pakistan 247
New Zealand v India 249
New Zealand v Pakistan 251
New Zealand v Sri Lanka 253
India v Pakistan 254
India v Sri Lanka 256
Pakistan v Sri Lanka 258
Test Match Grounds 260
Families in Test Cricket 261

LIMITED-OVERS INTERNATIONAL RECORDS

Summary of all Limited-Overs Internationals 264
3,500 or More Runs 265
Highest Individual Score for Each Country 265
Seven or More Hundreds 265
Highest Partnership for Each Wicket 265
100 or More Wickets 266
Best Bowling for Each Country 266
Hat-tricks 266
Wicket-keeping and Fielding Records 266
All-round 267
Highest Innings Totals 267
Highest Totals Batting Second 267
Highest Match Aggregates 268
Lowest Innings Totals 268
Largest Victories 268
Tied Matches 268
World Cup Finals 268

MISCELLANEOUS

Large Attendances 269
Lord's Cricket Ground 269
Highest Scores in Minor Counties and Other Matches 270
Highest Partnership in Minor Cricket 271
Record Hit 271
Throwing the Cricket Ball 271
Formation Dates of County and Minor County Clubs 271
Constitution of County Championship 272
Most County Championship Appearances 272
Most Consecutive County Championship Appearances 272

FIRST-CLASS RECORDS

BATTING RECORDS

HIGHEST INDIVIDUAL SCORES

499	Hanif Mohammad	Karachi v Bahawalpur at Karachi	1958-59
452*	D. G. Bradman	NSW v Queensland at Sydney	1929-30
443*	B. B. Nimbalkar	Maharashtra v Kathiawar at Poona	1948-49
437	W. H. Ponsford	Victoria v Queensland at Melbourne	1927-28
429	W. H. Ponsford	Victoria v Tasmania at Melbourne	1922-23
428	Aftab Baloch	Sind v Baluchistan at Karachi	1973-74
424	A. C. MacLaren	Lancashire v Somerset at Taunton	1895
405*	G. A. Hick	Worcestershire v Somerset at Taunton	1988
385	B. Sutcliffe	Otago v Canterbury at Christchurch	1952-53
383	C. W. Gregory	NSW v Queensland at Brisbane	1906-07
369	D. G. Bradman	South Australia v Tasmania at Adelaide	1935-36
366	N. H. Fairbrother	Lancashire v Surrey at The Oval	1990
365*	C. Hill	South Australia v NSW at Adelaide	1900-01
365*	G. S. Sobers	West Indies v Pakistan at Kingston	1957-58
364	L. Hutton	England v Australia at The Oval	1938
359*	V. M. Merchant	Bombay v Maharashtra at Bombay	1943-44
359	R. B. Simpson	NSW v Queensland at Brisbane	1963-64
357*	R. Abel	Surrey v Somerset at The Oval	1899
357	D. G. Bradman	South Australia v Victoria at Melbourne	1935-36
356	B. A. Richards	South Australia v Western Australia at Perth	1970-71
355*	G. R. Marsh	Western Australia v South Australia at Perth	1989-90
355	B. Sutcliffe	Otago v Auckland at Dunedin	1949-50
352	W. H. Ponsford	Victoria v NSW at Melbourne	1926-27
350	Rashid Israr	Habib Bank v National Bank at Lahore	1976-77
345	C. G. Macartney	Australians v Nottinghamshire at Nottingham	1921
344*	G. A. Headley	Jamaica v Lord Tennyson's XI at Kingston	1931-32
344	W. G. Grace	MCC v Kent at Canterbury	1876
343*	P. A. Perrin	Essex v Derbyshire at Chesterfield	1904
341	G. H. Hirst	Yorkshire v Leicestershire at Leicester	1905
340*	D. G. Bradman	NSW v Victoria at Sydney	1928-29
340	S. M. Gavaskar	Bombay v Bengal at Bombay	1981-82
338*	R. C. Blunt	Otago v Canterbury at Christchurch	1931-32
338	W. W. Read	Surrey v Oxford University at The Oval	1888
337*	Pervez Akhtar	Railways v Dera Ismail Khan at Lahore	1964-65
337†	Hanif Mohammad	Pakistan v West Indies at Bridgetown	1957-58
336*	W. R. Hammond	England v New Zealand at Auckland	1932-33
336	W. H. Ponsford	Victoria v South Australia at Melbourne	1927-28
334	D. G. Bradman	Australia v England at Leeds	1930
333	K. S. Duleepsinhji	Sussex v Northamptonshire at Hove	1930
333	G. A. Gooch	England v India at Lord's	1990
332	W. H. Ashdown	Kent v Essex at Brentwood	1934
331*	J. D. Robertson	Middlesex v Worcestershire at Worcester	1949
325*	H. L. Hendry	Victoria v New Zealanders at Melbourne	1925-26
325	A. Sandham	England v West Indies at Kingston	1929-30
325	C. L. Badcock	South Australia v Victoria at Adelaide	1935-36
324	J. B. Stollmeyer	Trinidad v British Guiana at Port-of-Spain	1946-47
324	Waheed Mirza	Karachi Whites v Quetta at Karachi	1976-77
323	A. L. Wadekar	Bombay v Mysore at Bombay	1966-67
322	E. Paynter	Lancashire v Sussex at Hove	1937
322	I. V. A. Richards	Somerset v Warwickshire at Taunton	1985
321	W. L. Murdoch	NSW v Victoria at Sydney	1881-82
320	R. Lamba	North Zone v West Zone at Bhilai	1987-88
319	Gul Mahomed	Baroda v Holkar at Baroda	1946-47
318*	W. G. Grace	Gloucestershire v Yorkshire at Cheltenham	1876
317	W. R. Hammond	Gloucestershire v Nottinghamshire at Gloucester	1936

317	K. R. Rutherford	New Zealanders v D. B. Close's XI at Scarborough	1986
316*	J. B. Hobbs	Surrey v Middlesex at Lord's	1926
316*	V. S. Hazare	Maharashtra v Baroda at Poona	1939-40
316	R. H. Moore	Hampshire v Warwickshire at Bournemouth	1937
315*	T. W. Hayward	Surrey v Lancashire at The Oval	1898
315*	P. Holmes	Yorkshire v Middlesex at Lord's	1925
315*	A. F. Kippax	NSW v Queensland at Sydney	1927-28
314*	C. L. Walcott	Barbados v Trinidad at Port-of-Spain	1945-46
313*	S. J. Cook	Somerset v Glamorgan at Cardiff	1990
313	H. Sutcliffe	Yorkshire v Essex at Leyton	1932
313	W. V. Raman	Tamil Nadu v Goa at Panaji	1988-89
312*	W. W. Keeton	Nottinghamshire v Middlesex at The Oval‡	1939
312*	J. M. Brearley	MCC Under 25 v North Zone at Peshawar	1966-67
311*	G. M. Turner	Worcestershire v Warwickshire at Worcester	1982
311	J. T. Brown	Yorkshire v Sussex at Sheffield	1897
311	R. B. Simpson	Australia v England at Manchester	1964
311	Javed Miandad	Karachi Whites v National Bank at Karachi	1974-75
310*	J. H. Edrich	England v New Zealand at Leeds	1965
310	H. Gimblett	Somerset v Sussex at Eastbourne	1948
309	V. S. Hazare	The Rest v Hindus at Bombay	1943-44
308*	F. M. M. Worrell	Barbados v Trinidad at Bridgetown	1943-44
307	M. C. Cowdrey	MCC v South Australia at Adelaide	1962-63
307	R. M. Cowper	Australia v England at Melbourne	1965-66
306*	A. Ducat	Surrey v Oxford University at The Oval	1919
306*	E. A. B. Rowan	Transvaal v Natal at Johannesburg	1939-40
306*	D. W. Hookes	South Australia v Tasmania at Adelaide	1986-87
305*	F. E. Woolley	MCC v Tasmania at Hobart	1911-12
305*	F. R. Foster	Warwickshire v Worcestershire at Dudley	1914
305*	W. H. Ashdown	Kent v Derbyshire at Dover	1935
304*	A. W. Nourse	Natal v Transvaal at Johannesburg	1919-20
304*	P. H. Tarilton	Barbados v Trinidad at Bridgetown	1919-20
304*	E. D. Weekes	West Indians v Cambridge University at Cambridge	1950
304	R. M. Poore	Hampshire v Somerset at Taunton	1899
304	D. G. Bradman	Australia v England at Leeds	1934
303*	W. W. Armstrong	Australians v Somerset at Bath	1905
303*	Mushtaq Mohammad	Karachi Blues v Karachi University at Karachi	1967-68
303*	Abdul Azeem	Hyderabad v Tamil Nadu at Hyderabad	1986-87
302*	P. Holmes	Yorkshire v Hampshire at Portsmouth	1920
302*	W. R. Hammond	Gloucestershire v Glamorgan at Bristol	1934
302*	Arjan Kripal Singh	Tamil Nadu v Goa at Panaji	1988-89
302	W. R. Hammond	Gloucestershire v Glamorgan at Newport	1939
302	L. G. Rowe	West Indies v England at Bridgetown	1973-74
301*	E. H. Hendren	Middlesex v Worcestershire at Dudley	1933
301	W. G. Grace	Gloucestershire v Sussex at Bristol	1896
300*	V. T. Trumper	Australians v Sussex at Hove	1899
300*	F. B. Watson	Lancashire v Surrey at Manchester	1928
300*	Imtiaz Ahmed	PM's XI v Commonwealth XI at Bombay	1950-51
300	J. T. Brown	Yorkshire v Derbyshire at Chesterfield	1898
300	D. C. S. Compton	MCC v N. E. Transvaal at Benoni	1948-49
300	R. Subba Row	Northamptonshire v Surrey at The Oval	1958

† *Hanif Mohammad batted for 16 hours 10 minutes – the longest innings in first-class cricket.*
‡ *Played at The Oval because Lord's was required for Eton v Harrow.*

Note: W. V. Raman (313) and Arjan Kripal Singh (302*) provide the only instance of two triple-hundreds in the same innings.

HIGHEST FOR TEAMS

For English Teams in Australia

307	M. C. Cowdrey	MCC v South Australia at Adelaide	1962-63
287	R. E. Foster	England v Australia at Sydney	1903-04

Against Australians in England

364	L. Hutton	England v Australia at The Oval	1938
219	A. Sandham	Surrey at The Oval (record for any county)	1934

For Australian Teams in England

345	C. G. Macartney	v Nottinghamshire at Nottingham	1921
334	D. G. Bradman	Australia v England at Leeds	1930

Against English Teams in Australia

307	R. M. Cowper	Australia v England at Melbourne	1965-66
280	A. J. Richardson	South Australia v MCC at Adelaide	1922-23

For Each First-Class County

Derbyshire	274	G. Davidson v Lancashire at Manchester	1896
Essex	343*	P. A. Perrin v Derbyshire at Chesterfield	1904
Glamorgan	287*	D. E. Davies v Gloucestershire at Newport	1939
Gloucestershire	318*	W. G. Grace v Yorkshire at Cheltenham	1876
Hampshire	316	R. H. Moore v Warwickshire at Bournemouth	1937
Kent	332	W. H. Ashdown v Essex at Brentwood	1934
Lancashire	424	A. C. MacLaren v Somerset at Taunton	1895
Leicestershire	252*	S. Coe v Northamptonshire at Leicester	1914
Middlesex	331*	J. D. Robertson v Worcestershire at Worcester	1949
Northamptonshire	300	R. Subba Row v Surrey at The Oval	1958
Nottinghamshire	312*	W. W. Keeton v Middlesex at The Oval†	1939
Somerset	322	I. V. A. Richards v Warwickshire at Taunton	1985
Surrey	357*	R. Abel v Somerset at The Oval	1899
Sussex	333	K. S. Duleepsinhji v Northamptonshire at Hove	1930
Warwickshire	305*	F. R. Foster v Worcestershire at Dudley	1914
Worcestershire	405*	G. A. Hick v Somerset at Taunton	1988
Yorkshire	341	G. H. Hirst v Leicestershire at Leicester	1905

† *Played at The Oval because Lord's was required for Eton v Harrow.*

HUNDRED ON DEBUT IN BRITISH ISLES

(The following list does not include instances of players who have previously appeared in first-class cricket outside the British Isles or who performed the feat before 1946. Particulars of the latter are in *Wisdens* prior to 1984.)

114	F. W. Stocks	Nottinghamshire v Kent at Nottingham	1946
108	A. Fairbairn	Middlesex v Somerset at Taunton	†‡1947
124	P. Hearn	Kent v Warwickshire at Gillingham	1947
215*	G. H. G. Doggart	Cambridge University v Lancashire at Cambridge	1948
106	J. R. Gill	Ireland v MCC at Dublin	1948
107*	G. Barker	Essex v Canadians at Clacton	†1954
135	J. K. E. Slack	Cambridge University v Middlesex at Cambridge	1954
100*	E. A. Clark	Middlesex v Cambridge University at Cambridge	1959
113	G. J. Chidgey	Free Foresters v Cambridge U. at Cambridge	1962
108	D. R. Shepherd	Gloucestershire v Oxford University at Oxford	1965
110*	A. J. Harvey-Walker	Derbyshire v Oxford University at Burton upon Trent	†1971
173	J. Whitehouse	Warwickshire v Oxford University at Oxford	1971
106	J. B. Turner	Minor Counties v Pakistanis at Jesmond	1974
112	J. A. Claughton	Oxford University v Gloucestershire at Oxford	†1976
100*	A. W. Lilley	Essex v Nottinghamshire at Nottingham	†1978
146*	J. S. Johnson	Minor Counties v Indians at Wellington	1979
110	N. R. Taylor	Kent v Sri Lankans at Canterbury	1979
146*	D. G. Aslett	Kent v Hampshire at Bournemouth	1981
116	M. D. Moxon	Yorkshire v Essex at Leeds	†1981
100	D. A. Banks	Worcestershire v Oxford University at Oxford	1983
122	A. A. Metcalfe	Yorkshire v Nottinghamshire at Bradford	1983
117*	K. T. Medlycott	Surrey v Cambridge University at Banstead	§1984
101*	N. J. Falkner	Surrey v Cambridge University at Banstead	§1984
106	A. C. Storie	Northamptonshire v Hampshire at Northampton	†1985
102	M. P. Maynard	Glamorgan v Yorkshire at Swansea	1985

117*	R. J. Bartlett	Somerset v Oxford University at Oxford	1986
100*	P. D. Bowler	Leicestershire v Hampshire at Leicester	1986
145	I. L. Philip	Scotland v Ireland at Glasgow	1986
114*	P. D. Atkins	Surrey v Cambridge University at The Oval	1988
100	B. M. W. Patterson	Scotland v Ireland at Dumfries	1988
116*	J. J. B. Lewis	Essex v Surrey at The Oval	1990

† *In his second innings.*

‡ *A. Fairbairn (Middlesex) in 1947 scored hundreds in the second innings of his first two matches in first-class cricket: 108 as above, 110* Middlesex v Nottinghamshire at Nottingham.*

§ *The only instance in England of two players performing the feat in the same match.*

Notes: A number of players abroad have also made a hundred on a first appearance.

The highest innings on début was hit by W. F. E. Marx when he made 240 for Transvaal against Griqualand West at Johannesburg in 1920-21.

There are three instances of a cricketer making two separate hundreds on début: A. R. Morris, New South Wales, 148 and 111 against Queensland in 1940-41, N. J. Contractor, Gujarat, 152 and 102* against Baroda in 1952-53, and Aamer Malik, Lahore "A", 132* and 110* against Railways in 1979-80.

J. S. Solomon, British Guiana, scored a hundred in each of his first three innings in first-class cricket: 114* v Jamaica; 108 v Barbados in 1956-57; 121 v Pakistanis in 1957-58.

R. Watson-Smith, Border, scored 310 runs before he was dismissed in first-class cricket, including not-out centuries in his first two innings: 183* v Orange Free State and 125* v Griqualand West in 1969-70.

G. R. Viswanath and D. M. Wellham alone have scored a hundred on both their début in first-class cricket and in Test cricket. Viswanath scored 230 for Mysore v Andhra in 1967-68 and 137 for India v Australia in 1969-70. Wellham scored 100 for New South Wales v Victoria in 1980-81 and 103 for Australia v England in 1981.

TWO DOUBLE-HUNDREDS IN A MATCH

A. E. Fagg	244	202*	Kent v Essex at Colchester	1938

HUNDRED AND DOUBLE-HUNDRED IN A MATCH

C. B. Fry	125	229	Sussex v Surrey at Hove	1900
W. W. Armstrong	157*	245	Victoria v South Australia at Melbourne.	1920-21
H. T. W. Hardinge	207	102*	Kent v Surrey at Blackheath	1921
C. P. Mead	113	224	Hampshire v Sussex at Horsham	1921
K. S. Duleepsinhji	115	246	Sussex v Kent at Hastings	1929
D. G. Bradman	124	225	Woodfull's XI v Ryder's XI at Sydney	1929-30
B. Sutcliffe	243	100*	New Zealanders v Essex at Southend	1949
M. R. Hallam	210*	157	Leicestershire v Glamorgan at Leicester	1959
M. R. Hallam	203*	143*	Leicestershire v Sussex at Worthing	1961
Hanumant Singh	109	213*	Rajasthan v Bombay at Bombay	1966-67
Salah-ud-Din	256	102*	Karachi v East Pakistan at Karachi	1968-69
K. D. Walters	242	103	Australia v West Indies at Sydney	1968-69
S. M. Gavaskar	124	220	India v West Indies at Port-of-Spain	1970-71
L. G. Rowe	214	100*	West Indies v New Zealand at Kingston	1971-72
G. S. Chappell	247*	133	Australia v New Zealand at Wellington	1973-74
L. Baichan	216*	102	Berbice v Demerara at Georgetown	1973-74
Zaheer Abbas	216*	156*	Gloucestershire v Surrey at The Oval	1976
Zaheer Abbas	230*	104*	Gloucestershire v Kent at Canterbury	1976
Zaheer Abbas	205*	108*	Gloucestershire v Sussex at Cheltenham	1977
Saadat Ali	141	222	Income Tax v Multan at Multan	1977-78
Talat Ali	214*	104	PIA v Punjab at Lahore	1978-79
Shafiq Ahmed	129	217*	National Bank v MCB at Karachi	1978-79
D. W. Randall	209	146	Nottinghamshire v Middlesex at Nottingham	1979
Zaheer Abbas	215*	150*	Gloucestershire v Somerset at Bath	1981

Qasim Omar	210*	110	MCB v Lahore at Lahore	1982-83
A. I. Kallicharran	200*	117*	Warwickshire v Northamptonshire at Birmingham	1984
Rizwan-uz-Zaman	139	217*	PIA v PACO at Lahore	1989-90
G. A. Gooch	333	123	England v India at Lord's	1990
G. A. Hick	252*	100*	Worcestershire v Glamorgan at Abergavenny	1990
N. R. Taylor	204	142	Kent v Surrey at Canterbury	1990

TWO SEPARATE HUNDREDS IN A MATCH

Eight times: Zaheer Abbas.

Seven times: W. R. Hammond.

Six times: J. B. Hobbs, G. M. Turner.

Five times: C. B. Fry.

Four times: D. G. Bradman, G. S. Chappell, J. H. Edrich, L. B. Fishlock, T. W. Graveney, C. G. Greenidge, H. T. W. Hardinge, E. H. Hendren, Javed Miandad, G. L. Jessop, P. A. Perrin, B. Sutcliffe, H. Sutcliffe.

Three times: L. E. G. Ames, G. Boycott, I. M. Chappell, D. C. S. Compton, M. C. Cowdrey, D. Denton, K. S. Duleepsinhji, R. E. Foster, R. C. Fredericks, S. M. Gavaskar, W. G. Grace, G. Gunn, M. R. Hallam, Hanif Mohammad, M. J. Harris, T. W. Hayward, V. S. Hazare, D. W. Hookes, L. Hutton, A. Jones, P. N. Kirsten, R. B. McCosker, P. B. H. May, C. P. Mead, Rizwan-uz-Zaman A. C. Russell, Sadiq Mohammad, J. T. Tyldesley.

Twice: Agha Zahid, Ali Zia, D. L. Amiss, C. W. J. Athey, L. Baichan, Basit Ali, A. R. Border, B. J. T. Bosanquet, R. J. Boyd-Moss, S. J. Cook, C. C. Dacre, G. M. Emmett, A. E. Fagg, L. E. Favell, H. Gimblett, G. A. Gooch, C. Hallows, R. A. Hamence, A. L. Hassett, G. A. Headley, G. A. Hick, A. I. Kallicharran, J. H. King, A. F. Kippax, J. G. Langridge, H. W. Lee, E. Lester, C. B. Llewellyn, C. G. Macartney, C. A. Milton, A. R. Morris, H. Morris, P. H. Parfitt, Nawab of Pataudi jun., E. Paynter, C. Pinch, R. G. Pollock, R. M. Prideaux, Qasim Omar, W. Rhodes, B. A. Richards, I. V. A. Richards, R. T. Robinson, Pankaj Roy, James Seymour, Shafiq Ahmed, R. B. Simpson, G. S. Sobers, M. A. Taylor, E. Tyldesley, C. L. Walcott, K. C. Wessels, W. W. Whysall, G. N. Yallop.

Notes: W. Lambert scored 107 and 157 for Sussex v Epsom at Lord's in 1817 and it was not until W. G. Grace made 130 and 102* for South of the Thames v North of the Thames at Canterbury in 1868 that the feat was repeated.

T. W. Hayward (Surrey) set up a unique record in 1906 when in one week – six days – he hit four successive hundreds, 144 and 100 v Nottinghamshire at Nottingham and 143 and 125 v Leicestershire at Leicester.

L. G. Rowe is alone in scoring hundreds in each innings on his first appearance in Test cricket: 214 and 100* for West Indies v New Zealand at Kingston in 1971-72.

Zaheer Abbas (Gloucestershire) set a unique record in 1976 by twice scoring a double hundred and a hundred in the same match without being dismissed: 216* and 156* v Surrey at The Oval and 230* and 104* v Kent at Canterbury. In 1977 he achieved this feat for a third time, scoring 205* and 108* v Sussex at Cheltenham, and in 1981 for a fourth time, scoring 215* and 150* v Somerset at Bath.

M. R. Hallam (Leicestershire), opening the batting each time, achieved the following treble: 210* and 157 v Glamorgan at Leicester, 1959; 203* and 143* v Sussex at Worthing, 1961; 107* and 149* v Worcestershire at Leicester, 1965. In the last two matches he was on the field the whole time.

C. J. B. Wood, 107* and 117* for Leicestershire v Yorkshire at Bradford in 1911, and S. J. Cook, 120* and 131* for Somerset v Nottinghamshire at Nottingham in 1989, are alone in carrying their bats and scoring hundreds in each innings.

W. L. Foster, 140 and 172*, and R. E. Foster, 134 and 101*, for Worcestershire v Hampshire at Worcester in July 1899, were the first brothers each to score two separate hundreds in the same first-class match.

The brothers I. M. Chappell, 145 and 121, and G. S. Chappell, 247* and 133, for Australia v New Zealand at Wellington in 1973-74, became the first players on the same side each to score a hundred in each innings of a Test match.

G. Gunn, 183, and G. V. Gunn, 100*, for Nottinghamshire v Warwickshire at Birmingham in 1931, provide the only instance of father and son each hitting a century in the same innings of a first-class match.

Most recent instances

In 1989-90

Basit Ali (2)	106	127	Karachi Blues v Multan at Karachi.
	128*	157	PACO v ADBP at Lahore.
J. Cox	175	102	Tasmania v New South Wales at Hobart.
D. M. Jones	116	121*	Australia v Pakistan at Adelaide.
R. B. Parikh	198	115*	Baroda v Gujarat at Baroda.
Rizwan-uz-Zaman	139	217*	PIA v PACO at Lahore.
M. W. Rushmere	150*	151*	SA Invitation XI v English XI at Pietermaritzburg.
Tariq Baig	103	103	Lahore City v Bahawalpur at Lahore.
M. A. Taylor	127	100	New South Wales v Queensland at Sydney.
Zahoor Elahi	122	133	ADBP v PNSC at Rawalpindi.

In 1990: See Features of 1990.

FOUR HUNDREDS OR MORE IN SUCCESSION

Six in succession: C. B. Fry 1901; D. G. Bradman 1938-39; M. J. Procter 1970-71.

Five in succession: E. D. Weekes 1955-56.

Four in succession: C. W. J. Athey 1987; M. Azharuddin 1984-85; A. R. Border 1985; D. G. Bradman 1931-32, 1948-49; D. C. S. Compton 1946-47; N. J. Contractor 1957-58; S. J. Cook 1989; K. S. Duleepsinhji 1931; C. B. Fry 1911; C. G. Greenidge 1986; W. R. Hammond 1936-37, 1945-46; H. T. W. Hardinge 1913; T. W. Hayward 1906; J. B. Hobbs 1920, 1925; D. W. Hookes 1976-77; P. N. Kirsten 1976-77; J. G. Langridge 1949; C. G. Macartney 1921; K. S. McEwan 1977; P. B. H. May 1956-57; V. M. Merchant 1941-42; A. Mitchell 1933; Nawab of Pataudi sen. 1931; L. G. Rowe 1971-72; Pankaj Roy 1962-63; Rizwan-uz-Zaman 1989-90; Sadiq Mohammad 1976; Saeed Ahmed 1961-62; H. Sutcliffe 1931, 1939; E. Tyldesley 1926; W. W. Whysall 1930; F. E. Woolley 1929; Zaheer Abbas 1970-71, 1982-83.

Note: The most fifties in consecutive innings is ten – by E. Tyldesley in 1926 and by D. G. Bradman in the 1947-48 and 1948 seasons.

MOST HUNDREDS IN A SEASON

Eighteen: D. C. S. Compton in 1947. These included six hundreds against the South Africans in which matches his average was 84.78. His aggregate for the season was 3,816, also a record.

Sixteen: J. B. Hobbs in 1925, when aged 42, played 16 three-figure innings in first-class matches. It was during this season that he exceeded the number of hundreds obtained in first-class cricket by W. G. Grace.

Fifteen: W. R. Hammond in 1938.

Fourteen: H. Sutcliffe in 1932.

Thirteen: G. Boycott in 1971, D. G. Bradman in 1938, C. B. Fry in 1901, W. R. Hammond in 1933 and 1937, T. W. Hayward in 1906, E. H. Hendren in 1923, 1927 and 1928, C. P. Mead in 1928, and H. Sutcliffe in 1928 and 1931.

MOST HUNDREDS IN A CAREER

(35 or more)

	Hundreds Total	Abroad	100th 100		Hundreds Total	Abroad	100th 100
J. B. Hobbs	197	22	1923	D. G. Bradman ...	117	41†	1947-48
E. H. Hendren ...	170	19	1928-29	I. V. A. Richards .	109	90†	1988-89
W. R. Hammond .	167	33	1935	Zaheer Abbas	108	70†	1982-83
C. P. Mead	153	8	1927	M. C. Cowdrey ...	107	27	1973
G. Boycott	151	27	1977	A. Sandham	107	20	1935
H. Sutcliffe	149	14	1932	T. W. Hayward	104	4	1913
F. E. Woolley	145	10	1929	J. H. Edrich	103	13	1977
L. Hutton	129	24	1951	G. M. Turner	103	85†	1982
W. G. Grace	126	1	1895	L. E. G. Ames	102	13	1950
D. C. S. Compton .	123	31	1952	D. L. Amiss	102	15	1986
T. W. Graveney ..	122	31	1964	E. Tyldesley	102	8	1934

† *"Abroad" for D. G. Bradman is outside Australia; for Zaheer Abbas, outside Pakistan; for G. M. Turner, outside New Zealand; for I. V. A. Richards, outside the West Indies.*

E. H. Hendren, D. G. Bradman and I. V. A. Richards scored their 100th hundreds in Australia, Zaheer Abbas scored his in Pakistan. Zaheer Abbas and G. Boycott did so in Test matches.

Name	100s
J. W. Hearne	96
C. B. Fry	94
C. G. Greenidge	90
A. I. Kallicharran	87
W. J. Edrich	86
G. S. Sobers	86
J. T. Tyldesley	86
P. B. H. May	85
R. E. S. Wyatt	85
J. Hardstaff, jun.	83
R. B. Kanhai	83
G. A. Gooch	82
S. M. Gavaskar	81
M. Leyland	80
B. A. Richards	80
C. H. Lloyd	79
Javed Miandad	78
K. F. Barrington	76
J. G. Langridge	76
C. Washbrook	76
H. T. W. Hardinge	75
R. Abel	74
G. S. Chappell	74
D. Kenyon	74
K. S. McEwan	73
Majid Khan	73
Mushtaq Mohammad	72
J. O'Connor	72
W. G. Quaife	72
K. S. Ranjitsinhji	72
D. Brookes	71
A. C. Russell	71
D. Denton	69
M. J. K. Smith	69
R. E. Marshall	68
R. N. Harvey	67
P. Holmes	67
J. D. Robertson	67
A. J. Lamb	66
P. A. Perrin	66
R. G. Pollock	64
R. T. Simpson	64
K. W. R. Fletcher	63
G. Gunn	62
A. R. Border	61
V. S. Hazare	60
G. H. Hirst	60
R. B. Simpson	60
P. F. Warner	60
I. M. Chappell	59
A. L. Hassett	59
A. Shrewsbury	59
A. E. Fagg	58
M. W. Gatting	58
P. H. Parfitt	58
W. Rhodes	58
L. B. Fishlock	56
A. Jones	56
C. A. Milton	56
C. Hallows	55
Hanif Mohammad	55
W. Watson	55
J. G. Wright	55
M. D. Crowe	54
G. A. Hick	54
D. J. Insole	54
W. W. Keeton	54
W. Bardsley	53
B. F. Davison	53
A. E. Dipper	53
G. L. Jessop	53
James Seymour	53
E. H. Bowley	52
D. B. Close	52
A. Ducat	52
Shafiq Ahmed	52
E. R. Dexter	51
J. M. Parks	51
W. W. Whysall	51
G. Cox jun.	50
H. E. Dollery	50
K. S. Duleepsinhji	50
H. Gimblett	50
W. M. Lawry	50
Sadiq Mohammad	50
D. B. Vengsarkar	50
F. B. Watson	50
W. Larkins	49
C. G. Macartney	49
M. J. Stewart	49
K. G. Suttle	49
P. R. Umrigar	49
W. M. Woodfull	49
C. J. Barnett	48
W. Gunn	48
E. G. Hayes	48
B. W. Luckhurst	48
M. J. Procter	48
C. E. B. Rice	48
A. C. MacLaren	47
W. H. Ponsford	47
D. I. Gower	46
J. Iddon	46
P. N. Kirsten	46
A. R. Morris	46
C. T. Radley	46
D. W. Randall	46
K. C. Wessels	46
Younis Ahmed	46
W. W. Armstrong	45
Asif Iqbal	45
L. G. Berry	45
J. M. Brearley	45
A. W. Carr	45
C. Hill	45
N. C. O'Neill	45
E. Paynter	45
Rev. D. S. Sheppard	45
K. D. Walters	45
H. H. I. Gibbons	44
V. M. Merchant	44
A. Mitchell	44
P. E. Richardson	44
B. Sutcliffe	44
G. R. Viswanath	44
P. Willey	44
E. J. Barlow	43
S. J. Cook	43
B. L. D'Oliveira	43
J. H. Hampshire	43
A. F. Kippax	43
J. W. H. Makepeace	43
A. R. Butcher	42
James Langridge	42
Mudassar Nazar	42
H. W. Parks	42
T. F. Shepherd	42
V. T. Trumper	42
M. J. Harris	41
K. R. Miller	41
A. D. Nourse	41
J. H. Parks	41
R. M. Prideaux	41
G. Pullar	41
W. E. Russell	41
C. L. Smith	41
R. C. Fredericks	40
J. Gunn	40
P. W. G. Parker	40
M. J. Smith	40
C. L. Walcott	40
D. M. Young	40
W. H. Ashdown	39
J. B. Bolus	39
W. A. Brown	39
R. J. Gregory	39
W. R. D. Payton	39
J. R. Reid	39
R. T. Robinson	39
C. J. Tavaré	39
F. M. M. Worrell	39
F. L. Bowley	38
P. J. Burge	38
J. F. Crapp	38
D. L. Haynes	38
D. Lloyd	38
V.L. Manjrekar	38
A. W. Nourse	38
N. Oldfield	38
Rev. J. H. Parsons	38
W. W. Read	38

J. Sharp	38	H. W. Lee	37	E. Oldroyd	36
L. J. Todd	38	M. A. Noble	37	W. Place	36
J. Arnold	37	B. P. Patel	37	A. L. Wadekar	36
Arshad Pervez	37	H. S. Squires	37	E. D. Weekes	36
B. C. Broad	37	R. T. Virgin	37	C. W. J. Athey	35
G. Brown	37	C. J. B. Wood	37	C. S. Dempster	35
G. Cook	37	N. F. Armstrong	36	D. R. Jardine	35
G. M. Emmett	37	G. D. Mendis	36	B. H. Valentine	35

3,000 RUNS IN A SEASON

	Season	*I*	*NO*	*R*	*HI*	*100s*	*Avge*
D. C. S. Compton	1947	50	8	3,816	246	18	90.85
W. J. Edrich	1947	52	8	3,539	267*	12	80.43
T. W. Hayward	1906	61	8	3,518	219	13	66.37
L. Hutton	1949	56	6	3,429	269*	12	68.58
F. E. Woolley	1928	59	4	3,352	198	12	60.94
H. Sutcliffe	1932	52	7	3,336	313	14	74.13
W. R. Hammond	1933	54	5	3,323	264	13	67.81
E. H. Hendren	1928	54	7	3,311	209*	13	70.44
R. Abel	1901	68	8	3,309	247	7	55.15
W. R. Hammond	1937	55	5	3,252	217	13	65.04
M. J. K. Smith	1959	67	11	3,245	200*	8	57.94
E. H. Hendren	1933	65	9	3,186	301*	11	56.89
C. P. Mead	1921	52	6	3,179	280*	10	69.10
T. W. Hayward	1904	63	5	3,170	203	11	54.65
K. S. Ranjitsinhji	1899	58	8	3,159	197	8	63.18
C. B. Fry	1901	43	3	3,147	244	13	78.67
K. S. Ranjitsinhji	1900	40	5	3,065	275	11	87.57
L. E. G. Ames	1933	57	5	3,058	295	9	58.80
J. T. Tyldesley	1901	60	5	3,041	221	9	55.29
C. P. Mead	1928	50	10	3,027	180	13	75.67
J. B. Hobbs	1925	48	5	3,024	266*	16	70.32
E. Tyldesley	1928	48	10	3,024	242	10	79.57
W. E. Alley	1961	64	11	3,019	221*	11	56.96
W. R. Hammond	1938	42	2	3,011	271	15	75.27
E. H. Hendren	1923	51	12	3,010	200*	13	77.17
H. Sutcliffe	1931	42	11	3,006	230	13	96.96
J. H. Parks	1937	63	4	3,003	168	11	50.89
H. Sutcliffe	1928	44	5	3,002	228	13	76.97

Notes: W. G. Grace scored 2,739 runs in 1871 – the first batsman to reach 2,000 runs in a season. He made ten hundreds and twice exceeded 200, with an average of 78.25 in all first-class matches. At the time, the over consisted of four balls.

The highest aggregate in a season since the reduction of County Championship matches in 1969 is 2,746 by G. A. Gooch (30 innings) in 1990.

1,000 RUNS IN A SEASON MOST TIMES

(Includes Overseas Tours and Seasons)

28 times: W. G. Grace 2,000 (6); F. E. Woolley 3,000 (1), 2,000 (12).
27 times: M. C. Cowdrey 2,000 (2); C. P. Mead 3,000 (2), 2,000 (9).
26 times: G. Boycott 2,000 (3); J. B. Hobbs 3,000 (1), 2,000 (16).
25 times: E. H. Hendren 3,000 (3), 2,000 (12).
24 times: D. L. Amiss 2,000 (3); W. G. Quaife 2,000 (1); H. Sutcliffe 3,000 (3), 2,000 (12).

23 times: A. Jones.

22 times: T. W. Graveney 2,000 (7); W. R. Hammond 3,000 (3), 2,000 (9).

21 times: D. Denton 2,000 (5); J. H. Edrich 2,000 (6); W. Rhodes 2,000 (2).

20 times: D. B. Close; K. W. R. Fletcher; G. Gunn; T. W. Hayward 3,000 (2), 2,000 (8); James Langridge 2,000 (1); J. M. Parks 2,000 (3); A. Sandham 2,000 (8); M. J. K. Smith 3,000 (1), 2,000 (5); C. Washbrook 2,000 (2).

19 times: J. W. Hearne 2,000 (4); G. H. Hirst 2,000 (3); D. Kenyon 2,000 (7); E. Tyldesley 3,000 (1), 2,000 (5); J. T. Tyldesley 3,000 (1), 2,000 (4).

18 times: L. G. Berry 2,000 (1); H. T. W. Hardinge 2,000 (5); R. E. Marshall 2,000 (6); P. A. Perrin; G. M. Turner 2,000 (3); R. E. S. Wyatt 2,000 (5).

17 times: L. E. G. Ames 3,000 (1), 2,000 (5); T. E. Bailey 2,000 (1); D. Brookes 2,000 (6); D. C. S. Compton 3,000 (1), 2,000 (5); C. G. Greenidge 2,000 (1); L. Hutton 3,000 (1), 2,000 (8); J. G. Langridge 2,000 (11); M. Leyland 2,000 (3); K. G. Suttle 2,000 (1), Zaheer Abbas 2,000 (2).

16 times: D. G. Bradman 2,000 (4); D. E. Davies 2,000 (1); E. G. Hayes 2,000 (2); C. A. Milton 2,000 (1); J. O'Connor 2,000 (4); C. T. Radley; I. V. A. Richards 2,000 (1); James Seymour 2,000 (1).

15 times: G. Barker; K. F. Barrington 2,000 (3); E. H. Bowley 2,000 (4); M. H. Denness; A. E. Dipper 2,000 (5); H. E. Dollery 2,000 (2); W. J. Edrich 3,000 (1), 2,000 (8); G. A. Gooch 2,000 (4); J. H. Hampshire; P. Holmes 2,000 (7); Mushtaq Mohammad; R. B. Nicholls 2,000 (1); P. H. Parfitt 2,000 (3); W. G. A. Parkhouse 2,000 (1); B. A. Richards 2,000 (1); J. D. Robertson 2,000 (9); G. S. Sobers; M. J. Stewart 2,000 (1).

Notes: F. E. Woolley reached 1,000 runs in 28 consecutive seasons (1907-1938). C. P. Mead did so 27 seasons in succession (1906-1936).

Outside England, 1,000 runs in a season has been reached most times by D. G. Bradman (in 12 seasons in Australia).

Three batsmen have scored 1,000 runs in a season in each of four different countries: G. S. Sobers in West Indies, England, India and Australia; M. C. Cowdrey and G. Boycott in England, South Africa, West Indies and Australia.

HIGHEST AGGREGATES OUTSIDE ENGLAND

In Australia	*Season*	*I*	*NO*	*R*	*HI*	*100s*	*Avge*
D. G. Bradman	1928-29	24	6	1,690	340*	7	93.88
In South Africa							
J. R. Reid	1961-62	30	2	1,915	203	7	68.39
In West Indies							
E. H. Hendren	1929-30	18	5	1,765	254*	6	135.76
In New Zealand							
M. D. Crowe	1986-87	21	3	1,676	175*	8	93.11
In India							
C. G. Borde	1964-65	28	3	1,604	168	6	64.16
In Pakistan							
Saadat Ali	1983-84	27	1	1,649	208	4	63.42
In Sri Lanka							
A. Ranatunga	1985-86	16	2	739	135*	3	52.78

Note: In more than one country, the following aggregates of over 2,000 runs have been recorded.

M. Amarnath (P/I/WI)	1982-83	34	6	2,234	207	9	79.78
J. R. Reid (SA/A/NZ).	1961-62	40	2	2,188	203	7	57.57
S. M. Gavaskar (I/P) .	1978-79	30	6	2,121	205	10	88.37
R. B. Simpson (I/P/A/WI)	1964-65	34	4	2,063	201	8	68.76

HIGHEST AVERAGES IN AN ENGLISH SEASON

(Qualification: 12 innings)

	Season	*I*	*NO*	*R*	*HI*	*100s*	*Avge*
D. G. Bradman	1938	26	5	2,429	278	13	115.66
G. Boycott	1979	20	5	1,538	175*	6	102.53
W. A. Johnston	1953	17	16	102	28*	0	102.00
G. A. Gooch	1990	30	3	2,746	333	12	101.70
G. Boycott	1971	30	5	2,503	233	13	100.12
D. G. Bradman	1930	36	6	2,960	334	10	98.66
H. Sutcliffe	1931	42	11	3,006	230	13	96.96
R. M. Poore	1899	21	4	1,551	304	7	91.23
D. R. Jardine	1927	14	3	1,002	147	5	91.09
D. C. S. Compton	1947	50	8	3,816	246	18	90.85
G. A. Hick	1990	35	9	2,347	252*	8	90.26
G. M. Turner	1982	16	3	1,171	311*	5	90.07
D. G. Bradman	1948	31	4	2,428	187	11	89.92
T. M. Moody	1990	15	2	1,163	168	7	89.46
D. M. Jones	1989	20	3	1,510	248	5	88.82
Zaheer Abbas	1981	36	10	2,306	215*	10	88.69
K. S. Ranjitsinhji	1900	40	5	3,065	275	11	87.57
D. R. Jardine	1928	17	4	1,133	193	3	87.15
W. R. Hammond	1946	26	5	1,783	214	7	84.90
D. G. Bradman	1934	27	3	2,020	304	7	84.16
R. B. Kanhai	1975	22	9	1,073	178*	3	82.53
Mudassar Nazar	1982	16	6	825	211*	4	82.50
C. G. Greenidge	1984	16	3	1,069	223	4	82.23
J. B. Hobbs	1928	38	7	2,542	200*	12	82.00
C. B. Fry	1903	40	7	2,683	234	9	81.30
W. J. Edrich	1947	52	8	3,539	267*	12	80.43

25,000 RUNS IN A CAREER

Dates in italics denote the first half of an overseas season; i.e. *1945* denotes the 1945-46 season.

	Career	*R*	*I*	*NO*	*HI*	*100s*	*Avge*
J. B. Hobbs	1905-34	61,237	1,315	106	316*	197	50.65
F. E. Woolley	1906-38	58,969	1,532	85	305*	145	40.75
E. H. Hendren	1907-38	57,611	1,300	166	301*	170	50.80
C. P. Mead	1905-36	55,061	1,340	185	280*	153	47.67
W. G. Grace	1865-1908	54,896	1,493	105	344	126	39.55
W. R. Hammond	1920-51	50,551	1,005	104	336*	167	56.10
H. Sutcliffe	1919-45	50,138	1,088	123	313	149	51.95
G. Boycott	1962-86	48,426	1,014	162	261*	151	56.83
T. W. Graveney	1948-*71*	47,793	1,223	159	258	122	44.91
T. W. Hayward	1893-1914	43,551	1,138	96	315*	104	41.79
D. L. Amiss	1960-87	43,423	1,139	126	262*	102	42.86
M. C. Cowdrey	1950-76	42,719	1,130	134	307	107	42.89
A. Sandham	1911-*37*	41,284	1,000	79	325	107	44.82
L. Hutton	1934-60	40,140	814	91	364	129	55.51
M. J. K. Smith	1951-75	39,832	1,091	139	204	69	41.84
W. Rhodes	1898-1930	39,802	1,528	237	267*	58	30.83
J. H. Edrich	1956-78	39,790	979	104	310*	103	45.47
R. E. S. Wyatt	1923-57	39,405	1,141	157	232	85	40.04
D. C. S. Compton	1936-64	38,942	839	88	300	123	51.85
E. Tyldesley	1909-36	38,874	961	106	256*	102	45.46
J. T. Tyldesley	1895-1923	37,897	994	62	295*	86	40.66
K. W. R. Fletcher	1962-88	37,665	1,167	170	228*	63	37.77

	Career	*R*	*I*	*NO*	*HI*	*100s*	*Avge*
J. W. Hearne	1909-36	37,252	1,025	116	285*	96	40.98
L. E. G. Ames	1926-51	37,248	951	95	295	102	43.51
D. Kenyon	1946-67	37,002	1,159	59	259	74	33.63
W. J. Edrich	1934-58	36,965	964	92	267*	86	42.39
J. M. Parks	1949-76	36,673	1,227	172	205*	51	34.76
D. Denton	1894-1920	36,479	1,163	70	221	69	33.37
C. G. Greenidge	1970-90	36,434	860	72	273*	90	46.23
G. H. Hirst	1891-1929	36,323	1,215	151	341	60	34.13
A. Jones	1957-83	36,049	1,168	72	204*	56	32.89
W. G. Quaife	1894-1928	36,012	1,203	185	255*	72	35.37
R. E. Marshall	*1945*-72	35,725	1,053	59	228*	68	35.94
G. Gunn	1902-32	35,208	1,061	82	220	62	35.96
D. B. Close	1949-86	34,994	1,225	173	198	52	33.26
Zaheer Abbas	*1965-86*	34,843	768	92	274	108	51.54
J. G. Langridge	1928-55	34,380	984	66	250*	76	37.45
G. M. Turner	*1964-82*	34,346	792	101	311*	103	49.70
C. Washbrook	1933-64	34,101	906	107	251*	76	42.67
M. Leyland	1920-48	33,660	932	101	263	80	40.50
H. T. W. Hardinge	1902-33	33,519	1,021	103	263*	75	36.51
R. Abel	1881-1904	33,124	1,007	73	357*	74	35.46
I. V. A. Richards	*1971*-90	33,033	708	50	322	109	50.20
A. I. Kallicharran	*1966*-90	32,650	834	86	243*	87	43.64
C. A. Milton	1948-74	32,150	1,078	125	170	56	33.73
J. D. Robertson	1937-59	31,914	897	46	331*	67	37.50
J. Hardstaff, jun.	1930-55	31,847	812	94	266	83	44.35
James Langridge	1924-53	31,716	1,058	157	167	42	35.20
K. F. Barrington	1953-68	31,714	831	136	256	76	45.63
G. A. Gooch	1973-90	31,363	732	57	333	82	46.46
C. H. Lloyd	*1963*-86	31,232	730	96	242*	79	49.26
Mushtaq Mohammad	*1956*-85	31,091	843	104	303*	72	42.07
C. B. Fry	1892-*1921*	30,886	658	43	258*	94	50.22
D. Brookes	1934-59	30,874	925	70	257	71	36.10
P. Holmes	1913-35	30,573	810	84	315*	67	42.11
R. T. Simpson	*1944*-63	30,546	852	55	259	64	38.32
L. G. Berry	1924-51	30,225	1,056	57	232	45	30.25
K. G. Suttle	1949-71	30,225	1,064	92	204*	49	31.09
P. A. Perrin	1896-1928	29,709	918	91	343*	66	35.92
P. F. Warner	1894-1929	29,028	875	75	244	60	36.28
R. B. Kanhai	*1954-81*	28,774	669	82	256	83	49.01
J. O'Connor	1921-39	28,764	903	79	248	72	34.90
T. E. Bailey	1945-67	28,641	1,072	215	205	28	33.42
E. H. Bowley	1912-34	28,378	859	47	283	52	34.94
B. A. Richards	*1964-82*	28,358	576	58	356	80	54.74
G. S. Sobers	*1952*-74	28,315	609	93	365*	86	54.87
A. E. Dipper	1908-32	28,075	865	69	252*	53	35.27
D. G. Bradman	*1927-48*	28,067	338	43	452*	117	95.14
J. H. Hampshire	1961-84	28,059	924	112	183*	43	34.55
P. B. H. May	1948-63	27,592	618	77	285*	85	51.00
B. F. Davison	*1967-87*	27,453	766	79	189	53	39.96
Majid Khan	*1961-84*	27,444	700	62	241	73	43.01
A. C. Russell	1908-30	27,358	717	59	273	71	41.57
E. G. Hayes	1896-1926	27,318	896	48	276	48	32.21
A. E. Fagg	1932-57	27,291	803	46	269*	58	36.05
James Seymour	1900-26	27,237	911	62	218*	53	32.08
Javed Miandad	*1973-89*	27,010	584	90	311	78	54.67
P. H. Parfitt	1956-*73*	26,924	845	104	200*	58	36.33
G. L. Jessop	1894-1914	26,698	855	37	286	53	32.63
D. E. Davies	1924-54	26,564	1,032	80	287*	32	27.90
A. Shrewsbury	1875-1902	26,505	813	90	267	59	36.65
M. J. Stewart	1954-72	26,492	898	93	227*	49	32.90

	Career	*R*	*I*	*NO*	*HI*	*100s*	*Avge*
C. T. Radley	1964-87	26,441	880	134	200	46	35.44
K. S. McEwan	*1972-89*	26,309	698	66	218	73	41.62
Younis Ahmed	*1961-86*	26,063	762	118	221*	46	40.47
P. E. Richardson	1949-65	26,055	794	41	185	44	34.60
M. H. Denness	1959-80	25,886	838	65	195	33	33.48
S. M. Gavaskar	*1966*-87	25,834	563	61	340	81	51.46
J. W. H. Makepeace	1906-30	25,799	778	66	203	43	36.23
D. W. Randall	1972-90	25,727	754	69	237	46	37.55
W. Gunn	1880-1904	25,691	850	72	273	48	33.02
W. Watson	1939-64	25,670	753	109	257	55	39.86
G. Brown	1908-33	25,649	1,012	52	232*	37	26.71
G. M. Emmett	1936-59	25,602	865	50	188	37	31.41
J. B. Bolus	1956-75	25,598	833	81	202*	39	34.03
W. E. Russell	1956-72	25,525	796	64	193	41	34.87
C. E. B. Rice	*1969-89*	25,417	732	118	246	48	41.39
C. J. Barnett	1927-*53*	25,389	821	45	259	48	32.71
L. B. Fishlock	1931-52	25,376	699	54	253	56	39.34
D. J. Insole	1947-63	25,241	743	72	219*	54	37.61
J. M. Brearley	1961-83	25,185	768	102	312*	45	37.81
J. Vine	1896-1922	25,171	920	79	202	34	29.92
R. M. Prideaux	1958-*74*	25,136	808	75	202*	41	34.29
J. H. King	1895-1926	25,122	988	69	227*	34	27.33

Note: Some works of reference provide career figures which differ from those in this list, owing to the exclusion or inclusion of matches recognised or not recognised as first-class by *Wisden*. Those figures are:

	Career	*R*	*I*	*NO*	*HI*	*100s*	*Avge*
J. B. Hobbs	1905-34	61,760	1,325	107	316*	199	50.66
F. E. Woolley	1906-38	58,959	1,530	84	305*	145	40.77
W. G. Grace	1865-1908	54,211	1,478	104	344	124	39.45
H. Sutcliffe	1919-45	50,670	1,098	124	313	151	52.02
W. Rhodes	1898-1930	39,969	1,534	237	267*	58	30.58
D. Denton	1894-1920	36,440	1,161	70	221	69	33.40
G. H. Hirst	1891-1929	36,356	1,217	152	341	60	34.13

CAREER AVERAGE OVER 50

(Qualification: 10,000 runs)

Avge		*Career*	*I*	*NO*	*R*	*HI*	*100s*
95.14	D. G. Bradman	*1927-48*	338	43	28,067	452*	117
71.22	V. M. Merchant	*1929-51*	229	43	13,248	359*	44
65.18	W. H. Ponsford	*1920-34*	235	23	13,819	437	47
64.99	W. M. Woodfull	*1921-34*	245	39	13,388	284	49
64.17	G. A. Hick	*1983*-90	269	34	15,080	405*	54
58.24	A. L. Hassett	*1932-53*	322	32	16,890	232	59
58.19	V. S. Hazare	*1934-66*	365	45	18,621	316*	60
57.23	M. D. Crowe	*1979*-90	321	50	15,512	242*	54
57.22	A. F. Kippax	*1918-35*	256	33	12,762	315*	43
56.83	G. Boycott	1962-86	1,014	162	48,426	261*	151
56.55	C. L. Walcott	*1941-63*	238	29	11,820	314*	40
56.37	K. S. Ranjitsinhji	1893-1920	500	62	24,692	285*	72
56.22	R. B. Simpson	*1952-77*	436	62	21,029	359	60
56.10	W. R. Hammond	1920-51	1,005	104	50,551	336*	167
55.51	L. Hutton	1934-60	814	91	40,140	364	129
55.34	E. D. Weekes	*1944*-64	241	24	12,010	304*	36
54.87	G. S. Sobers	*1952*-74	609	93	28,315	365*	86

Avge		*Career*	*I*	*NO*	*R*	*HI*	*100s*
54.74	B. A. Richards	*1964-82*	576	58	28,358	356	80
54.67	Javed Miandad	*1973-89*	584	90	27,010	311	78
54.67	R. G. Pollock	*1960-86*	437	54	20,940	274	64
54.24	F. M. M. Worrell	*1941*-64	326	49	15,025	308*	39
53.78	R. M. Cowper	*1959-69*	228	31	10,595	307	26
53.67	A. R. Morris	*1940-63*	250	15	12,614	290	46
53.15	A. R. Border	*1976-89*	476	76	21,261	205	61
52.32	Hanif Mohammad	*1951-75*	371	45	17,059	499	55
52.27	P. R. Umrigar	*1944-67*	350	41	16,154	252*	49
52.20	G. S. Chappell	*1966-83*	542	72	24,535	247*	74
51.95	H. Sutcliffe	1919-45	1,088	123	50,138	313	149
51.85	D. C. S. Compton	1936-64	839	88	38,942	300	123
51.58	D. B. Vengsarkar	*1975*-90	360	48	16,095	210	50
51.54	Zaheer Abbas	*1965-86*	768	92	34,843	274	108
51.53	A. D. Nourse	*1931-52*	269	27	12,472	260*	41
51.46	S. M. Gavaskar	*1966*-87	563	61	25,834	340	81
51.44	W. A. Brown	*1932-49*	284	15	13,838	265*	39
51.00	P. B. H. May	1948-63	618	77	27,592	285*	85
50.95	N. C. O'Neill	*1955-67*	306	34	13,859	284	45
50.93	R. N. Harvey	*1946-62*	461	35	21,699	231*	67
50.90	W. M. Lawry	*1955-71*	417	49	18,734	266	50
50.90	A. V. Mankad	*1963-82*	326	71	12,980	265	31
50.80	E. H. Hendren	1907-38	1,300	166	57,611	301*	170
50.65	J. B. Hobbs	1905-34	1,315	106	61,237	316*	197
50.22	C. B. Fry	1892-*1921*	658	43	30,886	258*	94
50.20	I. V. A. Richards	*1971*-90	708	50	33,033	322	109

FAST FIFTIES

Minutes			
11	C. I. J. Smith (66)	Middlesex v Gloucestershire at Bristol	1938
14	S. J. Pegler (50)	South Africans v Tasmania at Launceston	1910-11
14	F. T. Mann (53)	Middlesex v Nottinghamshire at Lord's	1921
14	H. B. Cameron (56)	Transvaal v Orange Free State at Johannesburg	1934-35
14	C. I. J. Smith (52)	Middlesex v Kent at Maidstone	1935

Note: The following fast fifties were scored in contrived circumstances when runs were given from full tosses and long hops to expedite a declaration: C. C. Inman (8 minutes), Leicestershire v Nottinghamshire at Nottingham, 1965; T. M. Moody (11 minutes), Warwickshire v Glamorgan at Swansea, 1990; M. P. Maynard (14 minutes), Glamorgan v Yorkshire at Cardiff, 1987.

FASTEST HUNDREDS

Minutes			
35	P. G. H. Fender (113*)	Surrey v Northamptonshire at Northampton	1920
40	G. L. Jessop (101)	Gloucestershire v Yorkshire at Harrogate	1897
42	G. L. Jessop (191)	Gentlemen of South v Players of South at Hastings	1907
43	A. H. Hornby (106)	Lancashire v Somerset at Manchester	1905
43	D. W. Hookes (107)	South Australia v Victoria at Adelaide	1982-83
44	R. N. S. Hobbs (100)	Essex v Australians at Chelmsford	1975

Notes: The fastest recorded hundred in terms of balls received was scored off 34 balls by D. W. Hookes (above).

Research of the scorebook has shown that P. G. H. Fender scored his hundred from between 40 and 46 balls. He contributed 113 to an unfinished sixth-wicket partnership of 171 in 42 minutes with H. A. Peach.

E. B. Alletson (Nottinghamshire) scored 189 out of 227 runs in 90 minutes against Sussex at Hove in 1911. It has been estimated that his last 139 runs took 37 minutes.

The following fast hundreds were scored in contrived circumstances when runs were given from full tosses and long hops to expedite a declaration: T. M. Moody (26 minutes), Warwickshire v Glamorgan at Swansea, 1990; S. J. O'Shaughnessy (35 minutes), Lancashire v Leicestershire at Manchester, 1983; C. M. Old (37 minutes), Yorkshire v Warwickshire at Birmingham, 1977; N. F. M. Popplewell (41 minutes), Somerset v Gloucestershire at Bath, 1983.

FASTEST DOUBLE-HUNDREDS

Minutes			
113	R. J. Shastri (200*)	Bombay v Baroda at Bombay	1984-85
120	G. L. Jessop (286)	Gloucestershire v Sussex at Hove	1903
120	C. H. Lloyd (201*)	West Indians v Glamorgan at Swansea	1976
130	G. L. Jessop (234)	Gloucestershire v Somerset at Bristol	1905
131	V. T. Trumper (293)	Australians v Canterbury at Christchurch	1913-14

FASTEST TRIPLE-HUNDREDS

Minutes			
181	D. C. S. Compton (300)	MCC v N. E. Transvaal at Benoni	1948-49
205	F. E. Woolley (305*)	MCC v Tasmania at Hobart	1911-12
205	C. G. Macartney (345)	Australians v Nottinghamshire at Nottingham	1921
213	D. G. Bradman (369)	South Australia v Tasmania at Adelaide	1935-36

300 RUNS IN ONE DAY

345	C. G. Macartney	Australians v Nottinghamshire at Nottingham	1921
334	W. H. Ponsford	Victoria v New South Wales at Melbourne	1926-27
333	K. S. Duleepsinhji	Sussex v Northamptonshire at Hove	1930
331*	J. D. Robertson	Middlesex v Worcestershire at Worcester	1949
325*	B. A. Richards	S. Australia v W. Australia at Perth	1970-71
322†	E. Paynter	Lancashire v Sussex at Hove	1937
322	I. V. A. Richards	Somerset v Warwickshire at Taunton	1985
318	C. W. Gregory	New South Wales v Queensland at Brisbane	1906-07
317	K. R. Rutherford	New Zealanders v D. B. Close's XI at Scarborough	1986
316†	R. H. Moore	Hampshire v Warwickshire at Bournemouth	1937
315*	R. C. Blunt	Otago v Canterbury at Christchurch	1931-32
312*	J. M. Brearley	MCC Under 25 v North Zone at Peshawar	1966-67
311*	G. M. Turner	Worcestershire v Warwickshire at Worcester	1982
311*	N. H. Fairbrother	Lancashire v Surrey at The Oval	1990
309*	D. G. Bradman	Australia v England at Leeds	1930
307*	W. H. Ashdown	Kent v Essex at Brentwood	1934
306*	A. Ducat	Surrey v Oxford University at The Oval	1919
305*	F. R. Foster	Warwickshire v Worcestershire at Dudley	1914

† *E. Paynter's 322 and R. H. Moore's 316 were scored on the same day: July 28, 1937.*

1,000 RUNS IN MAY

	Runs	*Avge*
W. G. Grace, May 9 to May 30, 1895 (22 days):		
13, 103, 18, 25, 288, 52, 257, 73*, 18, 169	1,016	112.88
Grace was within two months of completing his 47th year.		
W. R. Hammond, May 7 to May 31, 1927 (25 days):		
27, 135, 108, 128, 17, 11, 99, 187, 4, 30, 83, 7, 192, 14	1,042	74.42
Hammond scored his 1,000th run on May 28, thus equalling Grace's record of 22 days.		
C. Hallows, May 5 to May 31, 1928 (27 days):		
100, 101, 51*, 123, 101*, 22, 74, 104, 58, 34*, 232	1,000	125.00

1,000 RUNS IN APRIL AND MAY

T. W. Hayward, April 16 to May 31, 1900: 120*, 55, 108, 131*, 55, 193, 120, 5, 6, 3, 40, 146, 92	1,074	97.63
D. G. Bradman, April 30 to May 31, 1930: 236, 185*, 78, 9, 48*, 66, 4, 44, 252*, 32, 47*	1,001	143.00
On April 30 Bradman scored 75 not out.		
D. G. Bradman, April 30 to May 31, 1938: 258, 58, 137, 278, 2, 143, 145*, 5, 30*	1,056	150.85
Bradman scored 258 on April 30, and his 1,000th run on May 27.		
W. J. Edrich, April 30 to May 31, 1938: 104, 37, 115, 63, 20*, 182, 71, 31, 53*, 45, 15, 245, 0, 9, 20*	1,010	84.16
Edrich scored 21 not out on April 30. All his runs were scored at Lord's.		
G. M. Turner, April 24 to May 31, 1973: 41, 151*, 143, 85, 7, 8, 17*, 81, 13, 53, 44, 153*, 3, 2, 66*, 30, 10*, 111	1,018	78.30
G. A. Hick, April 17 to May 29, 1988: 61, 37, 212, 86, 14, 405*, 8, 11, 6, 7, 172	1,019	101.90
Hick scored a record 410 runs in April, and his 1,000th run on May 28.		

1,000 RUNS IN TWO SEPARATE MONTHS

Only four batsmen, C. B. Fry, K. S. Ranjitsinhji, H. Sutcliffe and L. Hutton, have scored over 1,000 runs in each of two months in the same season. L. Hutton, by scoring 1,294 in June 1949, made more runs in a single month than anyone else. He also made 1,050 in August 1949.

MOST RUNS SCORED OFF ONE OVER

(All instances refer to six-ball overs)

36	G. S. Sobers	off M. A. Nash, Nottinghamshire v Glamorgan at Swansea (six sixes)	1968
36	R. J. Shastri	off Tilak Raj, Bombay v Baroda at Bombay (six sixes)	1984-85
34	E. B. Alletson	off E. H. Killick, Nottinghamshire v Sussex at Hove (46604446; including two no-balls)	1911
34	F. C. Hayes	off M. A. Nash, Lancashire v Glamorgan at Swansea (646666)	1977
32	I. T. Botham	off I. R. Snook, England XI v Central Districts at Palmerston North (466466)	1983-84
32	C. C. Inman	off N. W. Hill, Leicestershire v Nottinghamshire at Nottingham (466664; full tosses were provided for him to hit)	1965
32	T. E. Jesty	off R. J. Boyd-Moss, Hampshire v Northamptonshire at Southampton (666662)	1984
32	P. W. G. Parker	off A. I. Kallicharran, Sussex v Warwickshire at Birmingham (466664)	1982
32	I. R. Redpath	off N. Rosendorff, Australians v Orange Free State at Bloemfontein (666644)	1969-70
32	C. C. Smart	off G. Hill, Glamorgan v Hampshire at Cardiff (664664)	1935
31	M. H. Bowditch (1) and M. J. Procter (30)	off A. A. Mallett, Western Province v Australians at Cape Town (Procter hit five sixes)	1969-70
31	A. W. Wellard	off F. E. Woolley, Somerset v Kent at Wells (666661)	1938
30	I. T. Botham	off P. A. Smith, Somerset v Warwickshire at Taunton (4466460 including one no-ball)	1982

30	D. G. Bradman	off A. P. Freeman, Australians v England XI at Folkestone (466464)	1934
30	H. B. Cameron	off H. Verity, South Africans v Yorkshire at Sheffield (444666)	1935
30	G. A. Gooch	off S. R. Gorman, Essex v Cambridge U. at Cambridge (662664)	1985
30	A. J. Lamb	off A. I. Kallicharran, Northamptonshire v Warwickshire at Birmingham (644664)	1982
30	D. T. Lindsay	off W. T. Greensmith, South African Fezela XI v Essex at Chelmsford (066666 to win the match)	1961
30	Majid Khan	off R. C. Davis, Pakistanis v Glamorgan at Swansea (606666)	1967
30	M. P. Maynard	off K. Sharp, Glamorgan v Yorkshire at Cardiff (464466) (runs were offered to expedite a declaration)	1987
30	A. W. Wellard	off T. R. Armstrong, Somerset v Derbyshire at Wells (066666)	1936
30	D. Wilson	off R. N. S. Hobbs, Yorkshire v MCC at Scarborough (466266)	1966
30	P. L. Winslow	off J. T. Ikin, South Africans v Lancashire at Manchester (446646)	1955
30	Zaheer Abbas	off D. Breakwell, Gloucestershire v Somerset at Taunton (466626)	1979

Notes: The greatest number of runs scored off an eight-ball over is 34 (40446664) by R. M. Edwards off M. C. Carew, Governor-General's XI v West Indians at Auckland, 1968-69.

In a Shell Trophy match against Canterbury at Christchurch in 1989-90, R. H. Vance (Wellington), acting on the instructions of his captain, deliberately conceded 77 runs in an over of full tosses which contained seventeen no-balls and, owing to the umpire's miscalculation, only five legitimate deliveries.

MOST SIXES IN AN INNINGS

15	J. R. Reid (296)	Wellington v N. Districts at Wellington	1962-63
13	Majid Khan (147*)	Pakistanis v Glamorgan at Swansea	1967
13	C. G. Greenidge (273*)	D. H. Robins' XI v Pakistanis at Eastbourne	1974
13	C. G. Greenidge (259)	Hampshire v Sussex at Southampton	1975
13	G. W. Humpage (254)	Warwickshire v Lancashire at Southport	1982
13	R. J. Shastri (200*)	Bombay v Baroda at Bombay	1984-85
12	Gulfraz Khan (207)	Railways v Universities at Lahore	1976-77
12	I. T. Botham (138*)	Somerset v Warwickshire at Birmingham	1985
12	R. A. Harper (234)	Northamptonshire v Gloucestershire at Northampton	1986
12	D. M. Jones (248)	Australians v Warwickshire at Birmingham	1989
11	C. K. Nayudu (153)	Hindus v MCC at Bombay	1926-27
11	C. J. Barnett (194)	Gloucestershire v Somerset at Bath	1934
11	R. Benaud (135)	Australians v T. N. Pearce's XI at Scarborough	1953
11	G. A. Hick (405*)	Worcestershire v Somerset at Taunton	1988

Note: W. J. Stewart (Warwickshire) hit seventeen sixes in the match v Lancashire, at Blackpool, 1959; ten in his first innings of 155 and seven in his second innings of 125.

MOST SIXES IN A SEASON

80	I. T. Botham	1985
66	A. W. Wellard	1935

Note: A. W. Wellard hit 50 or more sixes in a season four times. His number of sixes in 1935 has in the past been given as 72, but later research has caused this to be adjusted.

MOST BOUNDARIES IN AN INNINGS

68	P. A. Perrin (343*)	Essex v Derbyshire at Chesterfield	1904
65	A. C. MacLaren (424)	Lancashire v Somerset at Taunton	1895
64	Hanif Mohammad (499)	Karachi v Bahawalpur at Karachi	1958-59
57	J. H. Edrich (310*)	England v New Zealand at Leeds	1965
55	C. W. Gregory (383)	NSW v Queensland at Brisbane	1906-07
55	G. R. Marsh (355*)	Western Australia v South Australia at Perth	1989-90
54	G. H. Hirst (341)	Yorkshire v Leicestershire at Leicester	1905
53	A. W. Nourse (304*)	Natal v Transvaal at Johannesburg	1919-20
53	K. R. Rutherford (317)	New Zealanders v D. B. Close's XI at Scarborough.	1986
52	N. H. Fairbrother (366)	Lancashire v Surrey at The Oval	1990
51	C. G. Macartney (345)	Australians v Nottinghamshire at Nottingham	1921
50	D. G. Bradman (369)	South Australia v Tasmania at Adelaide	1935-36
50	A. Ducat (306*)	Surrey v Oxford University at The Oval	1919
50	B. B. Nimbalkar (443*)	Maharashtra v Kathiawar at Poona	1948-49
50	J. R. Reid (296)	Wellington v N. Districts at Wellington	1962-63
50	I. V. A. Richards (322)	Somerset v Warwickshire at Taunton	1985

Note: Boundaries include sixes.

HIGHEST PARTNERSHIPS

577	V. S. Hazare (288) and Gul Mahomed (319), fourth wicket, Baroda v Holkar at Baroda	1946-47
574*	F. M. M. Worrell (255*) and C. L. Walcott (314*), fourth wicket, Barbados v Trinidad at Port-of-Spain	1945-46
561	Waheed Mirza (324) and Mansoor Akhtar (224*), first wicket, Karachi Whites v Quetta at Karachi	1976-77
555	P. Holmes (224*) and H. Sutcliffe (313), first wicket, Yorkshire v Essex at Leyton	1932
554	J. T. Brown (300) and J. Tunnicliffe (243), first wicket, Yorkshire v Derbyshire at Chesterfield	1898
502*	F. M. M. Worrell (308*) and J. D. C. Goddard (218*), fourth wicket, Barbados v Trinidad at Bridgetown	1943-44
490	E. H. Bowley (283) and J. G. Langridge (195), first wicket, Sussex v Middlesex at Hove	1933
487*	G. A. Headley (344*) and C. C. Passailaigue (261*), sixth wicket, Jamaica v Lord Tennyson's XI at Kingston	1931-32
470	A. I. Kallicharran (230*) and G. W. Humpage (254), fourth wicket, Warwickshire v Lancashire at Southport	1982
465*	J. A. Jameson (240*) and R. B. Kanhai (213*), second wicket, Warwickshire v Gloucestershire at Birmingham	1974
462*	D. W. Hookes (306*) and W. B. Phillips (213*), fourth wicket, South Australia v Tasmania at Adelaide	1986-87
456	W. H. Ponsford (248) and E. R. Mayne (209), first wicket, Victoria v Queensland at Melbourne	1923-24
456	Khalid Irtiza (290) and Aslam Ali (236), third wicket, United Bank v Multan at Karachi	1975-76
455	K. V. Bhandarkar (205) and B. B. Nimbalkar (443*), second wicket, Maharashtra v Kathiawar at Poona	1948-49
451	D. G. Bradman (244) and W. H. Ponsford (266), second wicket, Australia v England, Fifth Test, at The Oval	1934
451*	S. Desai (218*) and R. M. H. Binny (211*), first wicket, Karnataka v Kerala at Chikmagalur	1977-78
451	Mudassar Nazar (231) and Javed Miandad (280*), third wicket, Pakistan v India, Fourth Test, at Hyderabad	1982-83

PARTNERSHIPS FOR FIRST WICKET

561	Waheed Mirza and Mansoor Akhtar, Karachi Whites v Quetta at Karachi	1976-77
555	P. Holmes and H. Sutcliffe, Yorkshire v Essex at Leyton	1932
554	J. T. Brown and J. Tunnicliffe, Yorkshire v Derbyshire at Chesterfield	1898
490	E. H. Bowley and J. G. Langridge, Sussex v Middlesex at Hove	1933
456	E. R. Mayne and W. H. Ponsford, Victoria v Queensland at Melbourne	1923-24
451*	S. Desai and R. M. H. Binny, Karnataka v Kerala at Chikmagalur	1977-78
431	M. R. J. Veletta and G. R. Marsh, Western Australia v South Australia at Perth	1989-90
428	J. B Hobbs and A. Sandham, Surrey v Oxford University at The Oval	1926
424	J. F. W. Nicholson and I. J. Siedle, Natal v Orange Free State at Bloemfontein	1926-27
421	S. M. Gavaskar and G. A. Parkar, Bombay v Bengal at Bombay	1981-82
418	Kamal Najamuddin and Khalid Alvi, Karachi v Railways at Karachi	1980-81
413	V. Mankad and Pankaj Roy, India v New Zealand at Madras (world Test record)	1955-56
405	C. P. S. Chauhan and M. S. Gupte, Maharashtra v Vidarbha at Poona	1972-73
395	D. M. Young and R. B. Nicholls, Gloucestershire v Oxford University at Oxford	1962
391	A. O. Jones and A. Shrewsbury, Nottinghamshire v Gloucestershire at Bristol	1899
390	G. L. Wight and G. L. R. Gibbs, B. Guiana v Barbados at Georgetown	1951-52
390	B. Dudleston and J. F. Steele, Leicestershire v Derbyshire at Leicester	1979
389	Majid Khan and Shafiq Ahmed, Punjab A v Sind A at Karachi	1974-75
389	Mudassar Nazar and Mansoor Akhtar, United Bank v Rawalpindi at Lahore	1981-82
388	K. C. Wessels and R. B. Kerr, Queensland v Victoria at St Kilda, Melbourne	1982-83
387	G. M. Turner and T. W. Jarvis, New Zealand v West Indies at Georgetown	1971-72
382	R. B. Simpson and W. M. Lawry, Australia v West Indies at Bridgetown	1964-65
380	H. Whitehead and C. J. B. Wood, Leicestershire v Worcestershire at Worcester	1906
379	R. Abel and W. Brockwell, Surrey v Hampshire at The Oval	1897
378	J. T. Brown and J. Tunnicliffe, Yorkshire v Sussex at Sheffield	1897
377*	N. F. Horner and Khalid Ibadulla, Warwickshire v Surrey at The Oval	1960
375	W. H. Ponsford and W. M. Woodfull, Victoria v New South Wales at Melbourne	1926-27

FIRST-WICKET HUNDREDS IN BOTH INNINGS

There have been three instances of two double-century opening stands in the same match: B. Sutcliffe and D. D. Taylor, 220 and 286 for Auckland v Canterbury at Auckland in 1948-49; P. R. Pollard and R. T. Robinson, 222 and 282 for Nottinghamshire v Kent at Nottingham in 1989; and G. A. Gooch and J. P. Stephenson, 227 and 220 for Essex v Northamptonshire at Northampton in 1990.

T. W. Hayward and J. B. Hobbs in 1907 accomplished a performance without parallel by scoring over 100 together for Surrey's first wicket four times in one week: 106 and 125 v Cambridge University at The Oval, and 147 and 105 v Middlesex at Lord's.

L. Hutton and C. Washbrook, in three consecutive Test match innings which they opened together for England v Australia in 1946-47, made 138 in the second innings at Melbourne, and 137 and 100 at Adelaide. They also opened with 168 and 129 at Leeds in 1948.

J. B. Hobbs and H. Sutcliffe, in three consecutive Test match innings which they opened together for England v Australia in 1924-25, made 157 and 110 at Sydney and 283 at Melbourne. On 26 occasions – 15 times in Test matches – Hobbs and Sutcliffe took part in a three-figure first-wicket partnership. Seven of these stands exceeded 200.

G. Boycott and J. H. Edrich, in three consecutive Test match innings which they opened together for England v Australia in 1970-71, made 161* in the second innings at Melbourne, and 107 and 103 at Adelaide.

In 1971 R. G. A. Headley and P. J. Stimpson of Worcestershire shared in first-wicket hundred partnerships on each of the first four occasions they opened the innings together: 125 and 147 v Northamptonshire at Worcester, 102 and 128* v Warwickshire at Birmingham.

J. B. Hobbs during his career, which extended from 1905 to 1934, helped to make 100 or more for the first wicket in first-class cricket 166 times – 15 of them in 1926, when in consecutive innings he helped to make 428, 182, 106 and 123 before a wicket fell. As many as 117 of the 166 stands were made for Surrey. In all first-class matches Hobbs and A. Sandham shared 66 first-wicket partnerships of 100 or more runs.

P. Holmes and H. Sutcliffe made 100 or more runs for the first wicket of Yorkshire on 69 occasions; J. B. Hobbs and A. Sandham for Surrey on 63 occasions; W. W. Keeton and C. B. Harris of Nottinghamshire on 46; T. W. Hayward and J. B. Hobbs of Surrey on 40; G. Gunn and W. W. Whysall of Nottinghamshire on 40; J. D. Robertson and S. M. Brown of Middlesex on 34; C. B. Fry and J. Vine of Sussex on 33; R. E. Marshall and J. R. Gray of Hampshire on 33; and D. E. Davies and A. H. Dyson of Glamorgan on 32.

J. Douglas and A. E. Stoddart in 1896 scored over 150 runs for the Middlesex first wicket three times within a fortnight. In 1901, J. Iremonger and A. O. Jones obtained over 100 for the Nottinghamshire first wicket four times within eight days, scoring 134 and 144* v Surrey at The Oval, 238 v Essex at Leyton, and 119 v Derbyshire at Welbeck.

J. W. Lee and F. S. Lee, brothers, for Somerset in 1934, scored over 100 runs thrice in succession in the County Championship.

W. G. Grace and A. E. Stoddart, in three consecutive innings against the Australians in 1893, made over 100 runs for each opening partnership.

C. Hallows and F. B. Watson, in consecutive innings for Lancashire in 1928, opened with 200, 202, 107, 118; reached three figures twelve times, 200 four times.

H. Sutcliffe, in the period 1919-1939 inclusive, shared in 145 first-wicket partnerships of 100 runs or more.

There were four first-wicket hundred partnerships in the match between Somerset and Cambridge University at Taunton in 1960. G. Atkinson and R. T. Virgin scored 172 and 112 for Somerset and R. M. Prideaux and A. R. Lewis 198 and 137 for Cambridge University.

PARTNERSHIP RECORDS FOR ALL COUNTRIES

Best First-Wicket Stands

Pakistan	561	Waheed Mirza (324) and Mansoor Akhtar (224*), Karachi Whites v Quetta at Karachi	1976-77
English	555	P. Holmes (224*) and H. Sutcliffe (313), Yorkshire v Essex at Leyton	1932
Australian	456	W. H. Ponsford (248) and E. R. Mayne (209), Victoria v Queensland at Melbourne	1923-24
Indian	451*	S. Desai (218*) and R. M. H. Binny (211*), Karnataka v Kerala at Chikmagalur	1977-78
South African	424	J. F. W. Nicolson (252*) and I. J. Siedle (174), Natal v Orange Free State at Bloemfontein	1926-27
West Indian	390	G. L. Wight (262*) and G. L. R. Gibbs (216), British Guiana v Barbados at Georgetown	1951-52
New Zealand	387	G. M. Turner (259) and T. W. Jarvis (182), New Zealand v West Indies at Georgetown	1971-72

Best Second-Wicket Stands

English	465*	J. A. Jameson (240*) and R. B. Kanhai (213*), Warwickshire v Gloucestershire at Birmingham	1974
Indian	455	K. V. Bhandarkar (205) and B. B. Nimbalkar (443*), Maharashtra v Kathiawar at Poona	1948-49
Australian	451	W. H. Ponsford (266) and D. G. Bradman (244), Australia v England at The Oval	1934
West Indian	446	C. C. Hunte (260) and G. S. Sobers (365*), West Indies v Pakistan at Kingston	1957-58
Pakistan	426	Arshad Pervez (220) and Mohsin Khan (220), Habib Bank v Income Tax Dept at Lahore	1977-78
New Zealand	317	R. T. Hart (167*) and P. S. Briasco (157), Central Districts v Canterbury at New Plymouth	1983-84
South African	305	S. K. Coen (165) and J. M. M Commaille (186), Orange Free State v Natal at Bloemfontein	1926-27

Best Third-Wicket Stands

Pakistan ...... 456 Khalid Irtiza (290) and Aslam Ali (236), United Bank v Multan at Karachi 1975-76

New Zealand .. 445 P. E. Whitelaw (195) and W. N. Carson (290), Auckland v Otago at Dunedin (in 268 minutes) 1936-37

West Indian ... 434 J. B. Stollmeyer (324) and G. E. Gomez (190), Trinidad v British Guiana at Port-of-Spain 1946-47

English .... 424* W. J. Edrich (168*) and D. C. S. Compton (252*), Middlesex v Somerset at Lord's 1948

Indian .... 410 L. Amarnath (262) and R. S. Modi (156), India in England v The Rest at Calcutta 1946-47

Australian ..... 390* J. M. Wiener (221*) and J. K. Moss (200*), Victoria v Western Australia at St Kilda, Melbourne 1981-82

South African .. 341 E. J. Barlow (201) and R. G. Pollock (175), South Africa v Australia at Adelaide 1963-64

Best Fourth-Wicket Stands

Indian .... 577 V. S. Hazare (288) and Gul Mahomed (319), Baroda v Holkar at Baroda 1946-47

West Indian ... 574* C. L. Walcott (314*) and F. M. M. Worrell (255*), Barbados v Trinidad at Port-of-Spain 1945-46

English .... 470 A. I. Kallicharran (230*) and G. W. Humpage (254), Warwickshire v Lancashire at Southport 1982

Australian ..... 462* D. W. Hookes (306*) and W. B. Phillips (213*), South Australia v Tasmania at Adelaide 1986-87

Pakistan ...... 350 Mushtaq Mohammad (201) and Asif Iqbal (175), Pakistan v New Zealand at Dunedin 1972-73

South African .. 342 E. A. B. Rowan (196) and P. J. M. Gibb (203), Transvaal v N. E. Transvaal at Johannesburg 1952-53

New Zealand .. 324 J. R. Reid (188*) and W. M. Wallace (197), New Zealanders v Cambridge University at Cambridge 1949

Best Fifth-Wicket Stands

Australian ..... 405 S. G. Barnes (234) and D. G. Bradman (234), Australia v England at Sydney 1946-47

English .... 393 E. G. Arnold (200*) and W. B. Burns (196), Worcestershire v Warwickshire at Birmingham 1909

Indian .... 360 U. M. Merchant (217) and M. N. Raiji (170), Bombay v Hyderabad at Bombay 1947-48

Pakistan ...... 355 Altaf Shah (276) and Tariq Bashir (196), House Building Finance Corporation v Multan at Multan 1976-77

South African .. 355 A. J. Lamb (294) and J. J. Strydom (107), OFS v Eastern Province at Bloemfontein 1987-88

New Zealand .. 341 G. R. Larsen (161) and E. B. McSweeney (205*), Wellington v Central Districts at Levin 1987-88

West Indian ... 335 B. F. Butcher (151) and C. H. Lloyd (201*), West Indians v Glamorgan at Swansea 1969

Best Sixth-Wicket Stands

West Indian ... 487* G. A. Headley (344*) and C. C. Passailaigue (261*), Jamaica v Lord Tennyson's XI at Kingston 1931-32

Australian ..... 428 M. A. Noble (284) and W. W. Armstrong (172*), Australians v Sussex at Hove 1902

English .... 411 R. M. Poore (304) and E. G. Wynyard (225), Hampshire v Somerset at Taunton 1899

Indian .... 371 V. M. Merchant (359*) and R. S. Modi (168), Bombay v Maharashtra at Bombay 1943-44

Pakistan	353	Salah-ud-Din (256) and Zaheer Abbas (197), Karachi v East Pakistan at Karachi	1968-69
South African	259	S. A. Jones (209*) and O. Henry (125), Boland v Border at East London	1987-88
New Zealand	246*	J. J. Crowe (120*) and R. J. Hadlee (151*), New Zealand v Sri Lanka at Colombo (CCC)	1986-87

Best Seventh-Wicket Stands

West Indian	347	D. St E. Atkinson (219) and C. C. Depeiza (122), West Indies v Australia at Bridgetown	1954-55
English	344	K. S. Ranjitsinhji (230) and W. Newham (153), Sussex v Essex at Leyton	1902
Australian	335	C. W. Andrews (253) and E. C. Bensted (155), Queensland v New South Wales at Sydney	1934-35
Pakistan	308	Waqar Hassan (189) and Imtiaz Ahmed (209), Pakistan v New Zealand at Lahore	1955-56
South African	299	B. Mitchell (159) and A. Melville (153), Transvaal v Griqualand West at Kimberley	1946-47
Indian	274	K. C. Ibrahim (250) and K. M. Rangnekar (138), Bijapur XI v Bengal XI at Bombay	1942-43
New Zealand	265	J. L. Powell (164) and N. Dorreen (105*), Canterbury v Otago at Christchurch	1929-30

Best Eighth-Wicket Stands

Australian	433	A. Sims (184*) and V. T. Trumper (293), An Australian XI v Canterbury at Christchurch	1913-14
English	292	R. Peel (210*) and Lord Hawke (166), Yorkshire v Warwickshire at Birmingham	1896
West Indian	255	E. A. V. Williams (131*) and E. A. Martindale (134), Barbados v Trinidad at Bridgetown	1935-36
Pakistan	240	Gulfraz Khan (207) and Raja Sarfraz (102), Railways v Universities at Lahore	1976-77
Indian	236	C. T. Sarwate (235) and R. P. Singh (88), Holkar v Delhi and District at Delhi	1949-50
South African	222	D. P. B. Morkel (114) and S. S. L. Steyn (261*), Western Province v Border at Cape Town	1929-30
New Zealand	190*	J. E. Mills (104*) and C. F. W. Allcott (102*), New Zealanders v Civil Service at Chiswick	1927

Best Ninth-Wicket Stands

English	283	J. Chapman (165) and A. Warren (123), Derbyshire v Warwickshire at Blackwell	1910
Indian	245	V. S. Hazare (316*) and N. D. Nagarwalla (98), Maharashtra v Baroda at Poona	1939-40
New Zealand	239	H. B. Cave (118) and I. B. Leggat (142*), Central Districts v Otago at Dunedin	1952-53
Australian	232	C. Hill (365*) and E. Walkley (53), South Australia v New South Wales at Adelaide	1900-01
South African	221	N. V. Lindsay (160*) and G. R. McCubbin (97), Transvaal v Rhodesia at Bulawayo	1922-23
Pakistan	190	Asif Iqbal (146) and Intikhab Alam (51), Pakistan v England at The Oval	1967
West Indian	161	C. H. Lloyd (161*) and A. M. E. Roberts (68), West Indies v India at Calcutta	1983-84

Best Tenth-Wicket Stands

Australian	307	A. F. Kippax (260*), and J. E. H. Hooker (62), New South Wales v Victoria at Melbourne	1928-29
Indian	249	C. T. Sarwate (124*) and S. N. Banerjee (121), Indians v Surrey at The Oval	1946
English	235	F. E. Woolley (185) and A. Fielder (112*), Kent v Worcestershire at Stourbridge	1909
Pakistan	196*	Nadim Yousuf (202*) and Maqsood Kundi (109*) Muslim Commercial Bank v National Bank at Lahore	1981-82
New Zealand	184	R. C. Blunt (338*) and W. Hawkesworth (21), Otago v Canterbury at Christchurch	1931-32
South African	174	H. R. Lance (168) and D. Mackay-Coghill (57*), Transvaal v Natal at Johannesburg	1965-66
West Indian	138	E. L. G. Hoad (149*) and H. C. Griffith (84), West Indians v Sussex at Hove	1933

Note: All the English record wicket partnerships were made in the County Championship.

OUT HANDLED THE BALL

J. Grundy	MCC v Kent at Lord's	1857
G. Bennett	Kent v Sussex at Hove	1872
W. H. Scotton	Smokers v Non-Smokers at East Melbourne	1886-87
C. W. Wright	Nottinghamshire v Gloucestershire at Bristol	1893
E. Jones	South Australia v Victoria at Melbourne	1894-95
A. W. Nourse	South Africans v Sussex at Hove	1907
E. T. Benson	MCC v Auckland at Auckland	1929-30
A. W. Gilbertson	Otago v Auckland at Auckland	1952-53
W. R. Endean	South Africa v England at Cape Town	1956-57
P. J. Burge	Queensland v New South Wales at Sydney	1958-59
Dildar Awan	Services v Lahore at Lahore	1959-60
Mahmood-ul-Hasan	Karachi University v Railways-Quetta at Karachi	1960-61
Ali Raza	Karachi Greens v Hyderabad at Karachi	1961-62
Mohammad Yusuf	Rawalpindi v Peshawar at Peshawar	1962-63
A. Rees	Glamorgan v Middlesex at Lord's	1965
Pervez Akhtar	Multan v Karachi Greens at Sahiwal	1971-72
Javed Mirza	Railways v Punjab at Lahore	1972-73
R. G. Pollock	Eastern Province v Western Province at Cape Town	1973-74
C. I. Dey	Northern Transvaal v Orange Free State at Bloemfontein	1973-74
Nasir Valika	Karachi Whites v National Bank at Karachi	1974-75
Haji Yousuf	National Bank v Railways at Lahore	1974-75
Masood-ul-Hasan	PIA v National Bank B at Lyallpur	1975-76
D. K. Pearse	Natal v Western Province at Cape Town	1978-79
A. M. J. Hilditch	Australia v Pakistan at Perth	1978-79
Musleh-ud-Din	Railways v Lahore at Lahore	1979-80
Jalal-ud-Din	IDBP v Habib Bank at Bahawalpur	1981-82
Mohsin Khan	Pakistan v Australia at Karachi	1982-83
D. L. Haynes	West Indies v India at Bombay	1983-84
K. Azad	Delhi v Punjab at Amritsar	1983-84
Athar A. Khan	Allied Bank v HBFC at Sialkot	1983-84
A. Pandya	Saurashtra v Baroda at Baroda	1984-85
G. N. Linton	Barbados v Windward Islands at Bridgetown	1985-86
R. B. Gartrell	Tasmania v Victoria at Melbourne	1986-87
R. Nayyar	Himachal Pradesh v Punjab at Una	1988-89

OUT OBSTRUCTING THE FIELD

C. A. Absolom	Cambridge University v Surrey at The Oval	1868
T. Straw	Worcestershire v Warwickshire at Worcester	1899
T. Straw	Worcestershire v Warwickshire at Birmingham	1901
J. P. Whiteside	Leicestershire v Lancashire at Leicester	1901
L. Hutton	England v South Africa at The Oval	1951
J. A. Hayes	Canterbury v Central Districts at Christchurch	1954-55
D. D. Deshpande	Madhya Pradesh v Uttar Pradesh at Benares	1956-57
M. Mehra	Railways v Delhi at Delhi	1959-60
K. Ibadulla	Warwickshire v Hampshire at Coventry	1963
Qaiser Khan	Dera Ismail Khan v Railways at Lahore	1964-65
Ijaz Ahmed	Lahore Greens v Lahore Blues at Lahore	1973-74
Qasim Feroze	Bahawalpur v Universities at Lahore	1974-75
T. Quirk	Northern Transvaal v Border at East London	1978-79
Mahmood Rashid	United Bank v Muslim Commercial Bank at Bahawalpur	1981-82
Arshad Ali	Sukkur v Quetta at Quetta	1983-84
H. Wasu	Vidarbha v Rajasthan at Akola	1984-85
Khalid Javed	Railways v Lahore at Lahore	1985-86

OUT HIT THE BALL TWICE

H. E. Bull	MCC v Oxford University at Lord's	1864
H. R. J. Charlwood	Sussex v Surrey at Hove	1872
R. G. Barlow	North v South at Lord's	1878
P. S. Wimble	Transvaal v Griqualand West at Kimberley	1892-93
G. B. Nicholls	Somerset v Gloucestershire at Bristol	1896
A. A. Lilley	Warwickshire v Yorkshire at Birmingham	1897
J. H. King	Leicestershire v Surrey at The Oval	1906
A. P. Binns	Jamaica v British Guiana at Georgetown	1956-57
K. Bavanna	Andhra v Mysore at Guntur	1963-64
Zaheer Abbas	PIA A v Karachi Blues at Karachi	1969-70
Anwar Miandad	IDBP v United Bank at Lahore	1979-80
Anwar Iqbal	Hyderabad v Sukkur at Hyderabad	1983-84
Iqtidar Ali	Allied Bank v Muslim Commercial Bank at Lahore	1983-84
Aziz Malik	Lahore Division v Faisalabad at Sialkot	1984-85
Javed Mohammad	Multan v Karachi Whites at Sahiwal	1986-87

BOWLING RECORDS

TEN WICKETS IN ONE INNINGS

	O	*M*	*R*		
E. Hinkly (Kent)				v England at Lord's	1848
*J. Wisden (North)				v South at Lord's	1850
V. E. Walker (England)	43	17	74	v Surrey at The Oval	1859
V. E. Walker (Middlesex)	44.2	5	104	v Lancashire at Manchester	1865
G. Wootton (All England)	31.3	9	54	v Yorkshire at Sheffield	1865
W. Hickton (Lancashire)	36.2	19	46	v Hampshire at Manchester	1870
S. E. Butler (Oxford)	24.1	11	38	v Cambridge at Lord's	1871
James Lillywhite (South)	60.2	22	129	v North at Canterbury	1872
A. Shaw (MCC)	36.2	8	73	v North at Lord's	1874
E. Barratt (Players)	29	11	43	v Australians at The Oval	1878
G. Giffen (Australian XI)	26	10	66	v The Rest at Sydney	1883-84
W. G. Grace (MCC)	36.2	17	49	v Oxford University at Oxford	1886
G. Burton (Middlesex)	52.3	25	59	v Surrey at The Oval	1888
†A. E. Moss (Canterbury)	21.3	10	28	v Wellington at Christchurch	1889-90
S. M. J. Woods (Cambridge U.)	31	6	69	v Thornton's XI at Cambridge	1890
T. Richardson (Surrey)	15.3	3	45	v Essex at The Oval	1894

	O	*M*	*R*		
H. Pickett (Essex)	27	11	32	v Leicestershire at Leyton	1895
E. J. Tyler (Somerset)	34.3	15	49	v Surrey at Taunton	1895
W. P. Howell (Australians)	23.2	14	28	v Surrey at The Oval	1899
C. H. G. Bland (Sussex)	25.2	10	48	v Kent at Tonbridge	1899
J. Briggs (Lancashire)	28.5	7	55	v Worcestershire at Manchester	1900
A. E. Trott (Middlesex)	14.2	5	42	v Somerset at Taunton	1900
F. Hinds (A. B. St Hill's XI)	19.1	6	36	v Trinidad at Port-of-Spain	1900-01
A. Fielder (Players)	24.5	1	90	v Gentlemen at Lord's	1906
E. G. Dennett (Gloucestershire).	19.4	7	40	v Essex at Bristol	1906
A. E. E. Vogler (E. Province)	12	2	26	v Griqualand West at Johannesburg	1906-07
C. Blythe (Kent)	16	7	30	v Northamptonshire at Northampton	1907
A. Drake (Yorkshire)	8.5	0	35	v Somerset at Weston-super-Mare	1914
W. Bestwick (Derbyshire)	19	2	40	v Glamorgan at Cardiff	1921
A. A. Mailey (Australians)	28.4	5	66	v Gloucestershire at Cheltenham	1921
C. W. L. Parker (Glos.)	40.3	13	79	v Somerset at Bristol	1921
T. Rushby (Surrey)	17.5	4	43	v Somerset at Taunton	1921
J. C. White (Somerset)	42.2	11	76	v Worcestershire at Worcester	1921
G. C. Collins (Kent)	19.3	4	65	v Nottinghamshire at Dover	1922
H. Howell (Warwickshire)	25.1	5	51	v Yorkshire at Birmingham	1923
A. S. Kennedy (Players)	22.4	10	37	v Gentlemen at The Oval	1927
G. O. B. Allen (Middlesex)	25.3	10	40	v Lancashire at Lord's	1929
A. P. Freeman (Kent)	42	9	131	v Lancashire at Maidstone	1929
G. Geary (Leicestershire)	16.2	8	18	v Glamorgan at Pontypridd	1929
C. V. Grimmett (Australians)	22.3	8	37	v Yorkshire at Sheffield	1930
A. P. Freeman (Kent)	30.4	8	53	v Essex at Southend	1930
H. Verity (Yorkshire)	18.4	6	36	v Warwickshire at Leeds	1931
A. P. Freeman (Kent)	36.1	9	79	v Lancashire at Manchester	1931
V. W. C. Jupp (Northants)	39	6	127	v Kent at Tunbridge Wells	1932
H. Verity (Yorkshire)	19.4	16	10	v Nottinghamshire at Leeds	1932
T. W. Wall (South Australia)	12.4	2	36	v New South Wales at Sydney	1932-33
T. B. Mitchell (Derbyshire)	19.1	4	64	v Leicestershire at Leicester	1935
J. Mercer (Glamorgan)	26	10	51	v Worcestershire at Worcester	1936
T. W. Goddard (Glos.)	28.4	4	113	v Worcestershire at Cheltenham	1937
T. F. Smailes (Yorkshire)	17.1	5	47	v Derbyshire at Sheffield	1939
E. A. Watts (Surrey)	24.1	8	67	v Warwickshire at Birmingham	1939
*W. E. Hollies (Warwickshire)	20.4	4	49	v Nottinghamshire at Birmingham	1946
J. M. Sims (East)	18.4	2	90	v West at Kingston	1948
T. E. Bailey (Essex)	39.4	9	90	v Lancashire at Clacton	1949
J. K. Graveney (Glos.)	18.4	2	66	v Derbyshire at Chesterfield	1949
R. Berry (Lancashire)	36.2	9	102	v Worcestershire at Blackpool	1953
S. P. Gupte (President's XI)	24.2	7	78	v Combined XI at Bombay	1954-55
J. C. Laker (Surrey)	46	18	88	v Australians at The Oval	1956
J. C. Laker (England)	51.2	23	53	v Australia at Manchester	1956
G. A. R. Lock (Surrey)	29.1	18	54	v Kent at Blackheath	1956
K. Smales (Nottinghamshire)	41.3	20	66	v Gloucestershire at Stroud	1956
P. Chatterjee (Bengal)	19	11	20	v Assam at Jorhat	1956-57
J. D. Bannister (Warwickshire)	23.3	11	41	v Comb. Services at Birmingham	1959
A. J. G. Pearson (Cambridge University)	30.3	8	78	v Leicestershire at Loughborough	1961
N. I. Thomson (Sussex)	34.2	19	49	v Warwickshire at Worthing	1964
P. J. Allan (Queensland)	15.6	3	61	v Victoria at Melbourne	1965-66
I. J. Brayshaw (W. Australia)	17.6	4	44	v Victoria at Perth	1967-68
Shahid Mahmood (Karachi Whites)	25	5	58	v Khairpur at Karachi	1969-70
E. E. Hemmings (International XI)	49.3	14	175	v West Indies XI at Kingston	1982-83
P. Sunderam (Rajasthan)	22	5	78	v Vidarbha at Jodhpur	1985-86

	O	*M*	*R*		
S. T. Jefferies (W. Province)	22.5	7	59	v Orange Free State at Cape Town	1987-88
Imran Adil (Bahawalpur)	22.5	3	92	v Faisalabad at Faisalabad	1989-90

** J. Wisden and W. E. Hollies achieved the feat without the direct assistance of a fielder. Wisden's ten were all bowled; Hollies bowled seven and had three leg-before-wicket.*
† On debut in first-class cricket.

Note: The following instances were achieved in 12-a-side matches:

E. M. Grace (MCC)	32.2	7	69	v Gents of Kent at Canterbury	1862
W. G. Grace (MCC)	46.1	15	92	v Kent at Canterbury	1873

OUTSTANDING ANALYSES

	O	*M*	*R*	*W*		
H. Verity (Yorkshire)	19.4	16	10	10	v Nottinghamshire at Leeds	1932
G. Elliott (Victoria)	19	17	2	9	v Tasmania at Launceston	1857-58
Ahad Khan (Railways)	6.3	4	7	9	v Dera Ismail Khan at Lahore	1964-65
J. C. Laker (England)	14	12	2	8	v The Rest at Bradford	1950
D. Shackleton (Hampshire)	11.1	7	4	8	v Somerset at Weston-super-Mare	1955
E. Peate (Yorkshire)	16	11	5	8	v Surrey at Holbeck	1883
F. R. Spofforth (Australians)	8.3	6	3	7	v England XI at Birmingham	1884
W. A. Henderson (N.E. Transvaal)	9.3	7	4	7	v Orange Free State at Bloemfontein	1937-38
Rajinder Goel (Haryana)	7	4	4	7	v Jammu and Kashmir at Chandigarh	1977-78
V. I. Smith (South Africans)	4.5	3	1	6	v Derbyshire at Derby	1947
S. Cosstick (Victoria)	21.1	20	1	6	v Tasmania at Melbourne	1868-69
Israr Ali (Bahawalpur)	11	10	1	6	v Dacca U. at Bahawalpur	1957-58
A. D. Pougher (MCC)	3	3	0	5	v Australians at Lord's	1896
G. R. Cox (Sussex)	6	6	0	5	v Somerset at Weston-super-Mare	1921
R. K. Tyldesley (Lancashire)	5	5	0	5	v Leicestershire at Manchester	1924
P. T. Mills (Gloucestershire)	6.4	6	0	5	v Somerset at Bristol	1928

MOST WICKETS IN A MATCH

19-90	J. C. Laker	England v Australia at Manchester	1956
17-48	C. Blythe	Kent v Northamptonshire at Northampton	1907
17-50	C. T. B. Turner	Australians v England XI at Hastings	1888
17-54	W. P. Howell	Australians v Western Province at Cape Town	1902-03
17-56	C. W. L. Parker	Gloucestershire v Essex at Gloucester	1925
17-67	A. P. Freeman	Kent v Sussex at Hove	1922
17-89	W. G. Grace	Gloucestershire v Nottinghamshire at Cheltenham	1877
17-89	F. C. L. Matthews	Nottinghamshire v Northants at Nottingham	1923
17-91	H. Dean	Lancashire v Yorkshire at Liverpool	1913
17-91	H. Verity	Yorkshire v Essex at Leyton	1933
17-92	A. P. Freeman	Kent v Warwickshire at Folkestone	1932
17-103	W. Mycroft	Derbyshire v Hampshire at Southampton	1876
17-106	G. R. Cox	Sussex v Warwickshire at Horsham	1926
17-106	T. W. Goddard	Gloucestershire v Kent at Bristol	1939
17-119	W. Mead	Essex v Hampshire at Southampton	1895
17-137	W. Brearley	Lancashire v Somerset at Manchester	1905
17-159	S. F. Barnes	England v South Africa at Johannesburg	1913-14
17-201	G. Giffen	South Australia v Victoria at Adelaide	1885-86
17-212	J. C. Clay	Glamorgan v Worcestershire at Swansea	1937

Notes: H. A. Arkwright took eighteen wickets for 96 runs in a 12-a-side match for Gentlemen of

MCC v Gentlemen of Kent at Canterbury in 1861.

W. Mead took seventeen wickets for 205 runs for Essex v Australians at Leyton in 1893, the year before Essex were raised to first-class status.

F. P. Fenner took seventeen wickets for Cambridge Town Club v University of Cambridge at Cambridge in 1844.

SIXTEEN OR MORE WICKETS IN A DAY

17-48	C. Blythe	Kent v Northamptonshire at Northampton	1907
17-91	H. Verity	Yorkshire v Essex at Leyton	1933
17-106	T. W. Goddard	Gloucestershire v Kent at Bristol	1939
16-38	T. Emmett	Yorkshire v Cambridgeshire at Hunslet	1869
16-52	J. Southerton	South v North at Lord's	1875
16-69	T. G. Wass	Nottinghamshire v Lancashire at Liverpool	1906
16-38	A. E. E. Vogler	E. Province v Griqualand West at Johannesburg	1906-07
16-103	T. G. Wass	Nottinghamshire v Essex at Nottingham	1908
16-83	J. C. White	Somerset v Worcestershire at Bath	1919

FOUR WICKETS WITH CONSECUTIVE BALLS

J. Wells	Kent v Sussex at Brighton	1862
G. Ulyett	Lord Harris's XI v New South Wales at Sydney	1878-79
G. Nash	Lancashire v Somerset at Manchester	1882
J. B. Hide	Sussex v MCC and Ground at Lord's	1890
F. J. Shacklock	Nottinghamshire v Somerset at Nottingham	1893
A. D. Downes	Otago v Auckland at Dunedin	1893-94
F. Martin	MCC and Ground v Derbyshire at Lord's	1895
A. W. Mold	Lancashire v Nottinghamshire at Nottingham	1895
W. Brearley†	Lancashire v Somerset at Manchester	1905
S. Haigh	MCC v Army XI at Pretoria	1905-06
A. E. Trott‡	Middlesex v Somerset at Lord's	1907
F. A. Tarrant	Middlesex v Gloucestershire at Bristol	1907
A. Drake	Yorkshire v Derbyshire at Chesterfield	1914
S. G. Smith	Northamptonshire v Warwickshire at Birmingham	1914
H. A. Peach	Surrey v Sussex at The Oval	1924
A. F. Borland	Natal v Griqualand West at Kimberley	1926-27
J. E. H. Hooker†	New South Wales v Victoria at Sydney	1928-29
R. K. Tyldesley†	Lancashire v Derbyshire at Derby	1929
R. J. Crisp	Western Province v Griqualand West at Johannesburg	1931-32
R. J. Crisp	Western Province v Natal at Durban	1933-34
A. R. Gover	Surrey v Worcestershire at Worcester	1935
W. H. Copson	Derbyshire v Warwickshire at Derby	1937
W. A. Henderson	N.E. Transvaal v Orange Free State at Bloemfontein	1937-38
F. Ridgway	Kent v Derbyshire at Folkestone	1951
A. K. Walker§	Nottinghamshire v Leicestershire at Leicester	1956
S. N. Mohol	Board of Control President's XI v Minister for Small Savings' XI at Poona	1965-66
P. I. Pocock	Surrey v Sussex at Eastbourne	1972
S. S. Saini†	Delhi v Himachal Pradesh at Delhi	1988-89

† *Not all in the same innings.*

‡ *Trott achieved another hat-trick in the same innings of this, his benefit match.*

§ *Walker dismissed Firth with the last ball of the first innings and Lester, Tompkin and Smithson with the first three balls of the second innings, a feat without parallel.*

Notes: In their match with England at The Oval in 1863, Surrey lost four wickets in the course of a four-ball over from G. Bennett.

Sussex lost five wickets in the course of the final (six-ball) over of their match with Surrey at Eastbourne in 1972. P. I. Pocock, who had taken three wickets in his previous over, captured four more, taking in all seven wickets with eleven balls, a feat unique in first-class matches. (The eighth wicket fell to a run-out.)

HAT-TRICKS

Double Hat-Trick

Besides Trott's performance, which is given in the preceding section, the following instances are recorded of players having performed the hat-trick twice in the same match, Rao doing so in the same innings.

A. Shaw	Nottinghamshire v Gloucestershire at Nottingham	1884
T. J. Matthews	Australia v South Africa at Manchester	1912
C. W. L. Parker	Gloucestershire v Middlesex at Bristol	1924
R. O. Jenkins	Worcestershire v Surrey at Worcester	1949
J. S. Rao	Services v Northern Punjab at Amritsar	1963-64
Amin Lakhani	Combined XI v Indians at Multan	1978-79

Five Wickets with Six Consecutive Balls

W. H. Copson	Derbyshire v Warwickshire at Derby	1937
W. A. Henderson	NE Transvaal v Orange Free State at Bloemfontein	1937-38
P. I. Pocock	Surrey v Sussex at Eastbourne	1972

Most Hat-Tricks

Seven times: D. V. P. Wright.
Six times: T. W. Goddard, C. W. L. Parker.
Five times: S. Haigh, V. W. C. Jupp, A. E. G. Rhodes, F. A. Tarrant.
Four times: R. G. Barlow, J. T. Hearne, J. C. Laker, G. A. R. Lock, G. G. Macaulay, T. J. Matthews, M. J. Procter, T. Richardson, F. R. Spofforth, F. S. Trueman.
Three times: W. M. Bradley, H. J. Butler, S. T. Clarke, W. H. Copson, R. J. Crisp, J. W. H. T. Douglas, J. A. Flavell, A. P. Freeman, G. Giffen, K. Higgs, A. Hill, W. A. Humphries, R. D. Jackman, R. O. Jenkins, A. S. Kennedy, W. H. Lockwood, E. A. McDonald, T. L. Pritchard, J. S. Rao, A. Shaw, J. B. Statham, M. W. Tate, H. Trumble, D. Wilson, G. A. Wilson.

Unusual Hat-Tricks

All "Stumped":	by W. H. Brain off C. L. Townsend, Gloucestershire v Somerset at Cheltenham	1893
All "Caught":	by G. J. Thompson off S. G. Smith, Northamptonshire v Warwickshire at Birmingham	1914
	by C. de L. White off R. Beesly, Border v Griqualand West at Queenstown	1946-47
	by G. O. Dawkes (wicket-keeper) off H. L. Jackson, Derbyshire v Worcestershire at Kidderminster	1958
All "LBW":	H. Fisher, Yorkshire v Somerset at Sheffield	1932
	J. A. Flavell, Worcestershire v Lancashire at Manchester	1963
	M. J. Procter, Gloucestershire v Essex at Westcliff	1972
	B. J. Ikin, Griqualand West v OFS at Kimberley	1973-74
	M. J. Procter, Gloucestershire v Yorkshire at Cheltenham	1979
	Aamer Wasim, Zone C v Lahore at Lahore	1985-86

Most recent instances

In 1989-90

Ayaz Jilani	PACO v United Bank at Sialkot.
D. A. Beard	Northern Districts v Central Districts at Nelson.
Haaris Khan	Karachi Blues v Lahore City at Lahore.
M. B. Halangoda	Sinhalese SC v Sinha SC at Sinhalese SC, Colombo.
H. C. Lindenberg	Border v Natal B at East London.
Masood Anwar	United Bank v National Bank at Karachi.
S. Mukherjee	Bengal v Hyderabad at Secunderabad (*on début*).
R. J. Ratnayake	Western Province v Southern Province at Galle.
A. Singla	Haryana v Services at Gurgaon.
J. Srinath	Karnataka v Hyderabad at Secunderabad (*on début*).

In 1990: See Features of 1990.

200 WICKETS IN A SEASON

	Season	*O*	*M*	*R*	*W*	*Avge*
A. P. Freeman	1928	1,976.1	423	5,489	304	18.05
A. P. Freeman	1933	2,039	651	4,549	298	15.26
T. Richardson	1895‡	1,690.1	463	4,170	290	14.37
C. T. B. Turner**	1888†	2,427.2	1,127	3,307	283	11.68
A. P. Freeman	1931	1,618	360	4,307	276	15.60
A. P. Freeman	1930	1,914.3	472	4,632	275	16.84
T. Richardson	1897‡	1,603.4	495	3,945	273	14.45
A. P. Freeman	1929	1,670.5	381	4,879	267	18.27
W. Rhodes	1900	1,553	455	3,606	261	13.81
J. T. Hearne	1896	2,003.1	818	3,670	257	14.28
A. P. Freeman	1932	1,565.5	404	4,149	253	16.39
W. Rhodes	1901	1,565	505	3,797	251	15.12
T. W. Goddard	1937	1,478.1	359	4,158	248	16.76
W. C. Smith	1910	1,423.3	420	3,225	247	13.05
T. Richardson	1896‡	1,656.2	526	4,015	246	16.32
A. E. Trott	1899‡	1,772.4	587	4,086	239	17.09
T. W. Goddard	1947	1,451.2	344	4,119	238	17.30
M. W. Tate	1925	1,694.3	472	3,415	228	14.97
J. T. Hearne	1898‡	1,802.2	781	3,120	222	14.05
C. W. L. Parker	1925	1,512.3	478	3,311	222	14.91
G. A. Lohmann	1890‡	1,759.1	737	2,998	220	13.62
M. W. Tate	1923	1,608.5	331	3,061	219	13.97
C. F. Root	1925	1,493.2	416	3,770	219	17.21
C. W. L. Parker	1931	1,320.4	386	3,125	219	14.26
H. Verity	1936	1,289.3	463	2,847	216	13.18
G. A. R. Lock	1955	1,408.4	497	3,109	216	14.39
C. Blythe	1909	1,273.5	343	3,128	215	14.54
E. Peate	1882†	1,853.1	868	2,466	214	11.52
A. W. Mold	1895‡	1,629	598	3,400	213	15.96
W. Rhodes	1902	1,306.3	405	2,801	213	13.15
C. W. L. Parker	1926	1,739.5	556	3,920	213	18.40
J. T. Hearne	1893‡	1,741.4	667	3,492	212	16.47
A. P. Freeman	1935	1,503.2	320	4,562	212	21.51
G. A. R. Lock	1957	1,194.1	449	2,550	212	12.02
A. E. Trott	1900	1,547.1	363	4,923	211	23.33
G. G. Macaulay	1925	1,338.2	307	3,268	211	15.48
H. Verity	1935	1,279.2	453	3,032	211	14.36
J. Southerton	1870†	1,876.5	709	3,074	210	14.63
G. A. Lohmann	1888†	1,649.1	783	2,280	209	10.90
C. H. Parkin	1923	1,356.2	356	3,543	209	16.95
G. H. Hirst	1906	1,306.1	271	3,434	208	16.50
F. R. Spofforth	1884†	1,577	653	2,654	207	12.82
A. W. Mold	1894‡	1,288.3	456	2,548	207	12.30
C. W. L. Parker	1922	1,294.5	445	2,712	206	13.16
A. S. Kennedy	1922	1,346.4	366	3,444	205	16.80
M. W. Tate	1924	1,469.5	465	2,818	205	13.74
E. A. McDonald	1925	1,249.4	282	3,828	205	18.67
A. P. Freeman	1934	1,744.4	440	4,753	205	23.18
C. W. L. Parker	1924	1,303.5	411	2,913	204	14.27
G. A. Lohmann	1889‡	1,614.1	646	2,714	202	13.43
H. Verity	1937	1,386.2	487	3,168	202	15.68
A. Shaw	1878†	2,630	1,586	2,203	202	10.89
E. G. Dennett	1907	1,216.2	305	3,227	201	16.05
A. R. Gover	1937	1,219.4	191	3,816	201	18.98
C. H. Parkin	1924	1,162.5	357	2,735	200	13.67
T. W. Goddard	1935	1,553	384	4,073	200	20.36
A. R. Gover	1936	1,159.2	185	3,547	200	17.73
T. W. Goddard	1939§	819	139	2,973	200	14.86
R. Appleyard	1951	1,313.2	391	2,829	200	14.14

† *Indicates 4-ball overs;* ‡ *5-ball overs. All others were 6-ball overs except* § *8-ball overs.*
** *Exclusive of matches not reckoned as first-class.*

Notes: In four consecutive seasons (1928-31), A. P. Freeman took 1,122 wickets, and in eight consecutive seasons (1928-35), 2,090 wickets. In each of these eight seasons he took over 200 wickets.

T. Richardson took 1,005 wickets in four consecutive seasons (1894-97).

In 1896, J. T. Hearne took his 100th wicket as early as June 12. In 1931, C. W. L. Parker did the same and A. P. Freeman obtained his 100th wicket a day later.

The most wickets in a season since the reduction of Championship matches in 1969 is 134 by M. D. Marshall (822 overs) in 1982.

100 WICKETS IN A SEASON MOST TIMES

(Includes Overseas Tours and Seasons)

23 times: W. Rhodes 200 wkts (3).

20 times: D. Shackleton (In successive seasons – 1949 to 1968 inclusive).

17 times: A. P. Freeman 300 wkts (1), 200 wkts (7).

16 times: T. W. Goddard 200 wkts (4), C. W. L. Parker 200 wkts (5), R. T. D. Perks, F. J. Titmus.

15 times: J. T. Hearne 200 wkts (3), G. H. Hirst 200 wkts (1), A. S. Kennedy 200 wkts (1).

14 times: C. Blythe 200 wkts (1), W. E. Hollies, G. A. R. Lock 200 wkts (2), M. W. Tate 200 wkts (3), J. C White.

13 times: J. B. Statham.

12 times: J. Briggs, E. G. Dennett 200 wkts (1), C. Gladwin, D. J. Shepherd, N. I. Thomson, F. S. Trueman.

11 times: A. V. Bedser, G. Geary, S. Haigh, J. C. Laker, M. S. Nichols, A. E. Relf.

10 times: W. Attewell, W. G. Grace, R. Illingworth, H. L. Jackson, V. W. C. Jupp, G. G. Macaulay 200 wkts (1), W. Mead, T. B. Mitchell, T. Richardson 200 wkts (3), J. Southerton 200 wkts (1), R. K. Tyldesley, D. L. Underwood, J. H. Wardle, T. G. Wass, D. V. P. Wright.

9 times: W. E. Astill, T. E. Bailey, W. E. Bowes, C. Cook, R. Howorth, J. Mercer, A. W. Mold 200 wkts (2), J. A. Newman, C. F. Root 200 wkts (1), A. Shaw 200 wkts (1), H. Verity 200 wkts (3).

8 times: T. W. Cartwright, H. Dean, J. A. Flavell, A. R. Gover 200 wkts (2), H. Larwood, G. A. Lohmann 200 wkts (3), R. Peel, J. M. Sims, F. A. Tarrant, R. Tattersall, G. J. Thompson, G. E. Tribe, A. W. Wellard, F. E. Woolley, J. A. Young.

100 WICKETS IN A SEASON OUTSIDE ENGLAND

W		*Season*	*Country*	*R*	*Avge*
116	M. W. Tate	1926-27	India/Ceylon	1,599	13.78
107	Ijaz Faqih	1985-86	Pakistan	1,719	16.06
106	C. T. B. Turner	1887-88	Australia	1,441	13.59
106	R. Benaud	1957-58	South Africa	2,056	19.39
104	S. F. Barnes	1913-14	South Africa	1,117	10.74
104	Sajjad Akbar	1989-90	Pakistan	2,328	22.38
103	Abdul Qadir	1982-83	Pakistan	2,367	22.98

1,500 WICKETS IN A CAREER

Dates in italics denote the first half of an overseas season; i.e. *1970* denotes the 1970-71 season.

	Career	*W*	*R*	*Avge*
W. Rhodes	1898-1930	4,187	69,993	16.71
A. P. Freeman	1914-36	3,776	69,577	18.42
C. W. L. Parker	1903-35	3,278	63,817	19.46
J. T. Hearne	1888-1923	3,061	54,352	17.75
T. W. Goddard	1922-52	2,979	59,116	19.84
W. G. Grace	1865-1908	2,876	51,545	17.92

	Career	*W*	*R*	*Avge*
A. S. Kennedy	1907-36	2,874	61,034	21.23
D. Shackleton	1948-69	2,857	53,303	18.65
G. A. R. Lock	1946-*70*	2,844	54,709	19.23
F. J. Titmus	1949-82	2,830	63,313	22.37
M. W. Tate	1912-37	2,784	50,571	18.16
G. H. Hirst	1891-1929	2,739	51,282	18.72
C. Blythe	1899-1914	2,506	42,136	16.81
D. L. Underwood	1963-87	2,465	49,993	20.28
W. E. Astill	1906-39	2,431	57,783	23.76
J. C. White	1909-37	2,356	43,759	18.57
W. E. Hollies	1932-57	2,323	48,656	20.94
F. S. Trueman	1949-69	2,304	42,154	18.29
J. B. Statham	1950-68	2,260	36,995	16.36
R. T. D. Perks	1930-55	2,233	53,770	24.07
J. Briggs	1879-1900	2,221	35,430	15.95
D. J. Shepherd	1950-72	2,218	47,302	21.32
E. G. Dennett	1903-26	2,147	42,571	19.82
T. Richardson	1892-1905	2,104	38,794	18.43
T. E. Bailey	1945-67	2,082	48,170	23.13
R. Illingworth	1951-83	2,072	42,023	20.28
N. Gifford	1960-88	2,068	48,731	23.56
F. E. Woolley	1906-38	2,068	41,066	19.85
G. Geary	1912-38	2,063	41,339	20.03
D. V. P. Wright	1932-57	2,056	49,307	23.98
J. A. Newman	1906-30	2,032	51,111	25.15
†A. Shaw	1864-97	2,027	24,580	12.12
S. Haigh	1895-1913	2,012	32,091	15.94
H. Verity	1930-39	1,956	29,146	14.90
W. Attewell	1881-1900	1,950	29,896	15.33
J. C. Laker	1946-*64*	1,944	35,791	18.41
A. V. Bedser	1939-60	1,924	39,279	20.41
W. Mead	1892-1913	1,916	36,388	18.99
A. E. Relf	1900-21	1,897	39,724	20.94
P. G. H. Fender	1910-36	1,894	47,458	25.05
J. W. H. T. Douglas	1901-30	1,893	44,159	23.32
J. H. Wardle	1946-*67*	1,846	35,027	18.97
G. R. Cox	1895-1928	1,843	42,136	22.86
G. A. Lohmann	1884-97	1,841	25,295	13.73
J. W. Hearne	1909-36	1,839	44,926	24.42
G. G. Macaulay	1920-35	1,837	32,440	17.65
M. S. Nichols	1924-39	1,833	39,666	21.63
J. B. Mortimore	1950-75	1,807	41,904	23.18
C. Cook	1946-64	1,782	36,578	20.52
R. Peel	1882-99	1,753	28,442	16.22
H. L. Jackson	1947-63	1,733	30,101	17.36
J. K. Lever	1967-89	1,722	41,772	24.25
T. P. B. Smith	1929-52	1,697	45,059	26.55
J. Southerton	1854-79	1,681	24,290	14.44
A. E. Trott	*1892*-1911	1,674	35,317	21.09
A. W. Mold	1889-1901	1,673	26,010	15.54
T. G. Wass	1896-1920	1,666	34,092	20.46
V. W. C. Jupp	1909-38	1,658	38,166	23.01
C. Gladwin	1939-58	1,653	30,265	18.30
W. E. Bowes	1928-47	1,639	27,470	16.76
A. W. Wellard	1927-50	1,614	39,302	24.35
P. I. Pocock	1964-86	1,607	42,648	26.53
N. I. Thomson	1952-72	1,597	32,867	20.58
J. Mercer	1919-47	1,591	37,210	23.38
G. J. Thompson	1897-1922	1,591	30,058	18.89
J. M. Sims	1929-53	1,581	39,401	24.92
T. Emmett	1866-88	1,571	21,314	13.56

	Career	*W*	*R*	*Avge*
Intikhab Alam	*1957-82*	1,571	43,474	27.67
B. S. Bedi	*1961-81*	1,560	33,843	21.69
W. Voce	1927-52	1,558	35,961	23.08
A. R. Gover	1928-48	1,555	36,753	23.63
T. W. Cartwright	1952-77	1,536	29,357	19.11
K. Higgs	1958-86	1,536	36,267	23.61
James Langridge	1924-53	1,530	34,524	22.56
J. A. Flavell	1949-67	1,529	32,847	21.48
C. F. Root	1910-33	1,512	31,933	21.11
R. K. Tyldesley	1919-35	1,509	25,980	17.21

† *The figures for A. Shaw exclude one wicket for which no analysis is available.*

Note: Some works of reference provide career figures which differ from those in this list, owing to the exclusion or inclusion of matches recognised or not recognised as first-class by *Wisden*. Those figures are:

	Career	*W*	*R*	*Avge*
W. Rhodes	1898-1930	4,204	70,322	16.72
W. G. Grace	1865-1908	2,808	50,982	18.15
G. H. Hirst	1891-1929	2,742	51,372	18.73
C. Blythe	1899-1914	2,503	42,099	16.81
E. G. Dennett	1903-26	2,151	42,640	19.82
F. E. Woolley	1906-38	2,066	41,058	19.87
J. A. Newman	1906-30	2,054	51,397	25.03
R. Peel	1882-99	1,776	28,758	16.19

ALL-ROUND RECORDS

HUNDRED AND TEN WICKETS IN ONE INNINGS

V. E. Walker, England v Surrey at The Oval; 20*, 108, ten for 74, and four for 17. 1859
W. G. Grace, MCC v Oxford University at Oxford; 104, two for 60, and ten for 49. 1886

Note: E. M. Grace, for MCC v Gentlemen of Kent in a 12-a-side match at Canterbury in 1862, scored 192* and took five for 77 and ten for 69.

TWO HUNDRED RUNS AND SIXTEEN WICKETS

G. Giffen, South Australia v Victoria at Adelaide; 271, nine for 96, and seven for 70. 1891-92

HUNDRED IN EACH INNINGS AND FIVE WICKETS TWICE

G. H. Hirst, Yorkshire v Somerset at Bath; 111, 117*, six for 70, and five for 45. 1906

HUNDRED IN EACH INNINGS AND TEN WICKETS

B. J. T. Bosanquet, Middlesex v Sussex at Lord's; 103, 100*, three for 75, and eight for 53 1905
F. D. Stephenson, Nottinghamshire v Yorkshire at Nottingham; 111, 117, four for 105, and seven for 117 1988

HUNDRED AND HAT-TRICK

G. Giffen, Australians v Lancashire at Manchester; 13, 113, and six for 55 including hat-trick 1884
W. E. Roller, Surrey v Sussex at The Oval; 204, four for 28 including hat-trick, and two for 16. (Unique instance of 200 and hat-trick.) 1885
W. B. Burns, Worcestershire v Gloucestershire at Worcester; 102*, three for 56 including hat-trick, and two for 21 1913
V. W. C. Jupp, Sussex v Essex at Colchester; 102, six for 61 including hat-trick, and six for 78 1921
R. E. S. Wyatt, MCC v Ceylon at Colombo; 124 and five for 39 including hat-trick. 1926-27
L. N. Constantine, West Indians v Northamptonshire at Northampton; seven for 45 including hat-trick, 107 (five 6s), and six for 67 1928
D. E. Davies, Glamorgan v Leicestershire at Leicester; 139, four for 27, and three for 31 including hat-trick 1937
V. M. Merchant, Dr C. R. Pereira's XI v Sir Homi Mehta's XI at Bombay; 1, 142, three for 31 including hat-trick, and no wicket for 17 1946-47
M. J. Procter, Gloucestershire v Essex at Westcliff-on-Sea; 51, 102, three for 43, and five for 30 including hat-trick (all lbw) 1972
M. J. Procter, Gloucestershire v Leicestershire at Bristol; 122, no wkt for 32, and seven for 26 including hat-trick 1979

Note: W. G. Grace, for MCC v Kent in a 12-a-side match at Canterbury in 1874, scored 123 and took five for 82 and six for 47 including a hat-trick.

SEASON DOUBLES

2,000 RUNS AND 200 WICKETS

1906 G. H. Hirst 2,385 runs and 208 wickets

3,000 RUNS AND 100 WICKETS

1937 J. H. Parks 3,003 runs and 101 wickets

2,000 RUNS AND 100 WICKETS

	Season	*R*	*W*		*Season*	*R*	*W*
W. G. Grace	1873	2,139	106	F. E. Woolley	1914	2,272	125
W. G. Grace	1876	2,622	129	J. W. Hearne	1920	2,148	142
C. L. Townsend	1899	2,440	101	V. W. C. Jupp	1921	2,169	121
G. L. Jessop	1900	2,210	104	F. E. Woolley	1921	2,101	167
G. H. Hirst	1904	2,501	132	F. E. Woolley	1922	2,022	163
G. H. Hirst	1905	2,266	110	F. E. Woolley	1923	2,091	101
W. Rhodes	1909	2,094	141	L. F. Townsend	1933	2,268	100
W. Rhodes	1911	2,261	117	D. E. Davies	1937	2,012	103
F. A. Tarrant	1911	2,030	111	James Langridge	1937	2,082	101
J. W. Hearne	1913	2,036	124	T. E Bailey	1959	2,011	100
J. W. Hearne	1914	2,116	123				

1,000 RUNS AND 200 WICKETS

	Season	*R*	*W*		*Season*	*R*	*W*
A. E. Trott	1899	1,175	239	M. W. Tate	1923	1,168	219
A. E. Trott	1900	1,337	211	M. W. Tate	1924	1,419	205
A. S. Kennedy	1922	1,129	205	M. W. Tate	1925	1,290	228

1,000 RUNS AND 100 WICKETS

Sixteen times: W. Rhodes.
Fourteen times: G. H. Hirst.
Ten times: V. W. C. Jupp.
Nine times: W. E. Astill.
Eight times: T. E. Bailey, W. G. Grace, M. S. Nichols, A. E. Relf, F. A. Tarrant, M. W. Tate†, F. J. Titmus, F. E. Woolley.
Seven times: G. E. Tribe.
Six times: P. G. H. Fender, R. Illingworth, James Langridge.
Five times: J. W. H. T. Douglas, J. W. Hearne, A. S. Kennedy, J. A. Newman.
Four times: E. G. Arnold, J. Gunn, R. Kilner, B. R. Knight.
Three times: W. W. Armstrong (Australians), L. C. Braund, G. Giffen (Australians), N. E. Haig, R. Howorth, C. B. Llewellyn, J. B. Mortimore, Ray Smith, S. G. Smith, L. F. Townsend, A. W. Wellard.

† *M. W. Tate also scored 1,193 runs and took 116 wickets for MCC in first-class matches on the 1926-27 MCC tour of India and Ceylon.*

Note: R. J. Hadlee (1984) and F. D. Stephenson (1988) are the only players to perform the feat since the reduction of County Championship matches. A complete list of those performing the feat before then will be found on p. 202 of the 1982 *Wisden*.

WICKET-KEEPERS' DOUBLE

	Season	*R*	*D*
L. E. G. Ames	1928	1,919	122
L. E. G. Ames	1929	1,795	128
L. E. G. Ames	1932	2,482	104
J. T. Murray	1957	1,025	104

20,000 RUNS AND 2,000 WICKETS IN A CAREER

	Career	*R*	*Avge*	*W*	*Avge*	*'Doubles'*
W. E. Astill	1906-39	22,731	22.55	2,431	23.76	9
T. E. Bailey	1945-67	28,642	33.42	2,082	23.13	8
W. G. Grace	1865-1908	54,896	39.55	2,876	17.92	8
G. H. Hirst	1891-1929	36,323	34.13	2,739	18.72	14
R. Illingworth	1951-83	24,134	28.06	2,072	20.28	6
W. Rhodes	1898-1930	39,802	30.83	4,187	16.71	16
M. W. Tate	1912-37	21,717	25.01	2,784	18.16	8
F. J. Titmus	1949-82	21,588	23.11	2,830	22.37	8
F. E. Woolley	1906-38	58,969	40.75	2,068	19.85	8

WICKET-KEEPING RECORDS

MOST DISMISSALS IN AN INNINGS

8 (all ct)	A. T. W. Grout	Queensland v Western Australia at Brisbane	1959-60
8 (all ct)†	D. E. East	Essex v Somerset at Taunton	1985
7 (4ct, 3st)	E. J. Smith	Warwickshire v Derbyshire at Birmingham	1926
7 (6ct, 1st)	W. Farrimond	Lancashire v Kent at Manchester	1930
7 (all ct)	W. F. F. Price	Middlesex v Yorkshire at Lord's	1937
7 (3ct, 4st)	D. Tallon	Queensland v Victoria at Brisbane	1938-39
7 (all ct)	R. A. Saggers	New South Wales v Combined XI at Brisbane	1940-41
7 (1ct, 6st)	H. Yarnold	Worcestershire v Scotland at Dundee	1951
7 (4ct, 3st)	J. Brown	Scotland v Ireland at Dublin	1957
7 (6ct, 1st)	N. Kirsten	Border v Rhodesia at East London	1959-60
7 (all ct)	M. S. Smith	Natal v Border at East London	1959-60
7 (all ct)	K. V. Andrew	Northamptonshire v Lancashire at Manchester	1962

7 (all ct)	A. Long	Surrey v Sussex at Hove	1964
7 (all ct)	R. M. Schofield	Central Districts v Wellington at Wellington	1964-65
7 (all ct)	R. W. Taylor	Derbyshire v Glamorgan at Derby	1966
7 (6ct, 1st)	H. B. Taber	New South Wales v South Australia at Adelaide	1968-69
7 (6ct, 1st)	E. W. Jones	Glamorgan v Cambridge University at Cambridge.	1970
7 (6ct, 1st)	S. Benjamin	Central Zone v North Zone at Bombay	1973-74
7 (all ct)	R. W. Taylor	Derbyshire v Yorkshire at Chesterfield	1975
7 (6ct, 1st)	Shahid Israr	Karachi Whites v Quetta at Karachi	1976-77
7 (4ct, 3st)	Wasim Bari	PIA v Sind at Lahore	1977-78
7 (all ct)	J. A. Maclean	Queensland v Victoria at Melbourne	1977-78
7 (5ct, 2st)	Taslim Arif	National Bank v Punjab at Lahore	1978-79
7 (all ct)	Wasim Bari	Pakistan v New Zealand at Auckland	1978-79
7 (all ct)	R. W. Taylor	England v India at Bombay	1979-80
7 (all ct)	D. L. Bairstow	Yorkshire v Derbyshire at Scarborough	1982
7 (6ct, 1st)	R. B. Phillips	Queensland v New Zealanders at Bundaberg	1982-83
7 (3ct, 4st)	Masood Iqbal	Habib Bank v Lahore at Lahore	1982-83
7 (3ct, 4st)	Arif-ud-Din	United Bank v PACO at Sahiwal	1983-84
7 (6ct, 1st)	R. J. East	OFS v Western Province B at Cape Town	1984-85
7 (all ct)	B. A. Young	Northern Districts v Canterbury at Christchurch	1986-87
7 (all ct)	D. J. Richardson	Eastern Province v OFS at Bloemfontein	1988-89
7 (6ct, 1st)	Dildar Malik	Multan v Faisalabad at Sahiwal	1988-89
7 (all ct)	W. K. Hegg	Lancashire v Derbyshire at Chesterfield	1989
7 (all ct)	Imran Zia	Bahawalpur v Faisalabad at Faisalabad	1989-90

† *The first eight wickets to fall.*

WICKET-KEEPERS' HAT-TRICKS

W. H. Brain, Gloucestershire v Somerset at Cheltenham, 1893 – three stumpings off successive balls from C. L. Townsend.

G. O. Dawkes, Derbyshire v Worcestershire at Kidderminster, 1958 – three catches off successive balls from H. L. Jackson.

R. C. Russell, Gloucestershire v Surrey at The Oval, 1986 – three catches off successive balls from C. A. Walsh and D. V. Lawrence (2).

MOST DISMISSALS IN A MATCH

12 (8ct, 4st)	E. Pooley	Surrey v Sussex at The Oval	1868
12 (9ct, 3st)	D. Tallon	Queensland v New South Wales at Sydney	1938-39
12 (9ct, 3st)	H. B. Taber	New South Wales v South Australia at Adelaide.	1968-69
11 (all ct)	A. Long	Surrey v Sussex at Hove	1964
11 (all ct)	R. W. Marsh	Western Australia v Victoria at Perth	1975-76
11 (all ct)	D. L. Bairstow	Yorkshire v Derbyshire at Scarborough	1982
11 (all ct)	W. K. Hegg	Lancashire v Derbyshire at Chesterfield	1989
11 (all ct)	A. J. Stewart	Surrey v Leicestershire at Leicester	1989
10 (5ct, 5st)	H. Phillips	Sussex v Surrey at The Oval	1872
10 (2ct, 8st)	E. Pooley	Surrey v Kent at The Oval	1878
10 (9ct, 1st)	T. W. Oates	Nottinghamshire v Middlesex at Nottingham	1906
10 (1ct, 9st)	F. H. Huish	Kent v Surrey at The Oval	1911
10 (9ct, 1st)	J. C. Hubble	Kent v Gloucestershire at Cheltenham	1923
10 (8ct, 2st)	H. Elliott	Derbyshire v Lancashire at Manchester	1935
10 (7ct, 3st)	P. Corrall	Leicestershire v Sussex at Hove	1936
10 (9ct, 1st)	R. A. Saggers	New South Wales v Combined XI at Brisbane	1940-41
10 (all ct)	A. E. Wilson	Gloucestershire v Hampshire at Portsmouth	1953
10 (7ct, 3st)	B. N. Jarman	South Australia v New South Wales at Adelaide.	1961-62
10 (all ct)	L. A. Johnson	Northamptonshire v Sussex at Worthing	1963
10 (all ct)	R. W. Taylor	Derbyshire v Hampshire at Chesterfield	1963
10 (8ct, 2st)	L. A. Johnson	Northamptonshire v Warwickshire at Birmingham	1965

10 (9ct, 1st)	R. C. Jordon	Victoria v South Australia at Melbourne	1970-71
10 (all ct)	R. W. Marsh†	Western Australia v South Australia at Perth	1976-77
10 (6ct, 4st)	Taslim Arif	National Bank v Punjab at Lahore	1978-79
10 (9ct, 1st)	Arif-ud-Din	United Bank v Karachi B at Karachi	1978-79
10 (all ct)	R. W. Taylor	England v India at Bombay	1979-80
10 (all ct)	R. J. Parks	Hampshire v Derbyshire at Portsmouth	1981
10 (9ct, 1st)	A. Ghosh	Bihar v Assam at Bhagalpur	1981-82
10 (8ct, 2st)	Z. Parkar	Bombay v Maharashtra at Bombay	1981-82
10 (all ct)	R. V. Jennings	Transvaal v Arosa Sri Lankans at Johannesburg	1982-83
10 (9ct, 1st)	Kamal Najamuddin	Karachi v Lahore at Multan	1982-83
10 (all ct)	D. A. Murray	West Indies XI v South Africa at Port Elizabeth.	1983-84
10 (7ct, 3st)	Azhar Abbas	Bahawalpur v Lahore City Greens at Bahawalpur	1983-84
10 (7ct, 3st)	B. N. French	Nottinghamshire v Oxford University at Oxford.	1984
10 (8ct, 2st)	R. J. Ryall	Western Province v Transvaal at Cape Town	1984-85
10 (all ct)	S. J. Rixon	Australian XI v South Africa at Johannesburg	1985-86
10 (8ct, 2st)	Anil Dalpat	Karachi v United Bank at Lahore	1985-86
10 (all ct)	R. V. Jennings	Transvaal v Northern Transvaal at Verwoerdburg	1986-87
10 (all ct)	S. J. Rixon	Australian XI v South Africa at Johannesburg	1986-87
10 (all ct)	R. V. Jennings	Transvaal v Orange Free State at Johannesburg	1986-87
10 (9ct, 1st)	C. J. Richards	Surrey v Sussex at Guildford	1987
10 (all ct)	C. W. Scott	Nottinghamshire v Derbyshire at Derby	1988
10 (all ct)	D. J. Richardson	Eastern Province v OFS at Bloemfontein	1988-89
10 (all ct)	A. N. Aymes	Hampshire v Oxford University at Oxford	1989
10 (all ct)	L. R. Fernando	Moratuwa v Panadura at Moratuwa	1989-90
10 (all ct)	Imran Zia	Bahawalpur v Faisalabad at Faisalabad	1989-90
10 (9ct, 1st)	D. J. Richardson	Eastern Province v N. Transvaal at Verwoerdburg	1989-90

† *Marsh also scored a hundred (104), a unique "double".*

MOST DISMISSALS IN A SEASON

128 (79ct, 49st)	L. E. G. Ames	Kent	1929
122 (70ct, 52st)	L. E. G. Ames	Kent	1928
110 (63ct, 47st)	H. Yarnold	Worcestershire	1949
107 (77ct, 30st)	G. Duckworth	Lancashire	1928
107 (96ct, 11st)	J. G. Binks	Yorkshire	1960
104 (40ct, 64st)	L. E. G. Ames	Kent	1932
104 (82ct, 22st)	J. T. Murray	Middlesex	1957
102 (69ct, 33st)	F. H. Huish	Kent	1913
102 (95ct, 7st)	J. T. Murray	Middlesex	1960
101 (62ct, 39st)	F. H. Huish	Kent	1911
101 (85ct, 16st)	R. Booth	Worcestershire	1960
100 (91ct, 9st)	R. Booth	Worcestershire	1964

MOST DISMISSALS IN A CAREER

Dates in italics denote the first half of an overseas season; i.e. *1914* denotes the 1914-15 season.

	Career	*M*	*Ct*	*St*	*Total*
R. W. Taylor	1960-88	639	1,473	176	1,649
J. T. Murray	1952-75	635	1,270	257	1,527
H. Strudwick	1902-27	675	1,242	255	1,497
A. P. E. Knott	1964-85	511	1,211	133	1,344
F. H. Huish	1895-1914	497	933	377	1,310
B. Taylor	1949-73	572	1,083	211	1,294
D. Hunter	1889-1909	548	906	347	1,253

	Career	*M*	*Ct*	*St*	*Total*
H. R. Butt	1890-1912	550	953	275	1,228
J. H. Board	1891-*1914*	525	852	355	1,207
H. Elliott	1920-47	532	904	302	1,206
J. M. Parks	1949-76	739	1,088	93	1,181
R. Booth	1951-70	468	948	178	1,126
L. E. G. Ames	1926-51	593	703	418	1,121
D. L. Bairstow	1970-90	459	961	138	1,099
G. Duckworth	1923-47	504	753	343	1,096
H. W. Stephenson	1948-64	462	748	334	1,082
J. G. Binks	1955-75	502	895	176	1,071
T. G. Evans	1939-69	465	816	250	1,066
A. Long	1960-80	452	922	124	1,046
G. O. Dawkes	1937-61	482	895	148	1,043
R. W. Tolchard	1965-83	483	912	125	1,037
W. L. Cornford	1921-47	496	675	342	1,017

FIELDING RECORDS

(Excluding wicket-keepers)

Most Catches in an Innings

7	M. J. Stewart	Surrey v Northamptonshire at Northampton	1957
7	A. S. Brown	Gloucestershire v Nottinghamshire at Nottingham	1966

Most Catches in a Match

10	W. R. Hammond†	Gloucestershire v Surrey at Cheltenham	1928
8	W. B. Burns	Worcestershire v Yorkshire at Bradford	1907
8	A. H. Bakewell	Northamptonshire v Essex at Leyton	1928
8	W. R. Hammond	Gloucestershire v Worcestershire at Cheltenham	1932
8	K. J. Grieves	Lancashire v Sussex at Manchester	1951
8	C. A. Milton	Gloucestershire v Sussex at Hove	1952
8	G. A. R. Lock	Surrey v Warwickshire at The Oval	1957
8	J. M. Prodger	Kent v Gloucestershire at Cheltenham	1961
8	P. M. Walker	Glamorgan v Derbyshire at Swansea	1970
8	Javed Miandad	Habib Bank v Universities at Lahore	1977-78
8	Masood Anwar	Rawalpindi v Lahore Division at Rawalpindi	1983-84

† *Hammond also scored a hundred in each innings.*

Most Catches in a Season

78	W. R. Hammond	1928
77	M. J. Stewart	1957
73	P. M. Walker	1961
71	P. J. Sharpe	1962
70	J. Tunnicliffe	1901
69	J. G. Langridge	1955
69	P. M. Walker	1960
66	J. Tunnicliffe	1895
65	W. R. Hammond	1925
65	P. M. Walker	1959
65	D. W. Richardson	1961
64	K. F. Barrington	1957
64	G. A. R. Lock	1957
63	J. Tunnicliffe	1896
63	J. Tunnicliffe	1904
63	K. J. Grieves	1950
63	C. A. Milton	1956
61	J. V. Wilson	1955
61	M. J. Stewart	1958

Note: The most catches by a fielder since the reduction of County Championship matches in 1969 is 49 by C. J. Tavaré in 1979.

Most Catches in a Career

Dates in italics denote the first half of an overseas season; i.e. *1970* denotes the 1970-71 season.

1,018	F. E. Woolley (1906-38)	784	J. G. Langridge (1928-55)
887	W. G. Grace (1865-1908)	764	W. Rhodes (1898-1930)
830	G. A. R. Lock (1946-*70*)	758	C. A. Milton (1948-74)
819	W. R. Hammond (1920-51)	754	E. H. Hendren (1907-38)
813	D. B. Close (1949-86)		

TEAM RECORDS

HIGHEST TOTALS

1,107	Victoria v New South Wales at Melbourne	1926-27
1,059	Victoria v Tasmania at Melbourne	1922-23
951-7 dec.	Sind v Baluchistan at Karachi	1973-74
918	New South Wales v South Australia at Sydney	1900-01
912-8 dec.	Holkar v Mysore at Indore	1945-46
910-6 dec.	Railways v Dera Ismail Khan at Lahore	1964-65
903-7 dec.	England v Australia at The Oval	1938
887	Yorkshire v Warwickshire at Birmingham	1896
863	Lancashire v Surrey at The Oval	1990
860-6 dec.†	Tamil Nadu v Goa at Panaji	1988-89
849	England v West Indies at Kingston	1929-30
843	Australians v Oxford and Cambridge Universities Past and Present at Portsmouth	1893

† *Tamil Nadu's final total of 912-6 dec. included 52 penalty runs from their opponents' failure to meet the required bowling rate by 13 overs.*

Note: North Zone totalled 868 v West Zone at Bhilai in 1987-88. However, this included 68 penalty runs for West Zone's failure to meet the required bowling rate by 17 overs.

HIGHEST FOR EACH FIRST-CLASS COUNTY

Derbyshire	645	v Hampshire at Derby	1898
Essex	761-6	v Leicestershire at Chelmsford	1990
Glamorgan	587-8	v Derbyshire at Cardiff	1951
Gloucestershire	653-6	v Glamorgan at Bristol	1928
Hampshire	672-7	v Somerset at Taunton	1899
Kent	803-4	v Essex at Brentwood	1934
Lancashire	863	v Surrey at The Oval	1990
Leicestershire	701-4	v Worcestershire at Worcester	1906
Middlesex	642-3	v Hampshire at Southampton	1923
Northamptonshire	636-6	v Essex at Chelmsford	1990
Nottinghamshire	739-7	v Leicestershire at Nottingham	1903
Somerset	675-9	v Hampshire at Bath	1924
Surrey	811	v Somerset at The Oval	1899
Sussex	705-8	v Surrey at Hastings	1902
Warwickshire	657-6	v Hampshire at Birmingham	1899
Worcestershire	633	v Warwickshire at Worcester	1906
Yorkshire	887	v Warwickshire at Birmingham	1896

LOWEST TOTALS

12	Oxford University v MCC and Ground at Oxford	†1877
12	Northamptonshire v Gloucestershire at Gloucester	1907
13	Auckland v Canterbury at Auckland	1877-78
13	Nottinghamshire v Yorkshire at Nottingham	1901
14	Surrey v Essex at Chelmsford	1983
15	MCC v Surrey at Lord's	1839
15	Victoria v MCC at Melbourne	†1903-04
15	Northamptonshire v Yorkshire at Northampton	†1908
15	Hampshire v Warwickshire at Birmingham	1922
	(Following on, Hampshire scored 521 and won by 155 runs.)	
16	MCC and Ground v Surrey at Lord's	1872
16	Derbyshire v Nottinghamshire at Nottingham	1879
16	Surrey v Nottinghamshire at The Oval	1880
16	Warwickshire v Kent at Tonbridge	1913
16	Trinidad v Barbados at Bridgetown	1942-43
16	Border v Natal at East London (first innings)	1959-60
17	Gentlemen of Kent v Gentlemen of England at Lord's	1850
17	Gloucestershire v Australians at Cheltenham	1896
18	The Bs v England at Lord's	1831
18	Kent v Sussex at Gravesend	†1867
18	Tasmania v Victoria at Melbourne	1868-69
18	Australians v MCC and Ground at Lord's	†1896
18	Border v Natal at East London (second innings)	1959-60
19	Sussex v Surrey at Godalming	1830
19	Sussex v Nottinghamshire at Hove	†1873
19	MCC and Ground v Australians at Lord's	1878
19	Wellington v Nelson at Nelson	1885-86

† *Signifies that one man was absent.*

Note: At Lord's in 1810, The Bs, with one man absent, were dismissed by England for 6.

LOWEST TOTAL IN A MATCH

34	(16 and 18) Border v Natal at East London	1959-60
42	(27 and 15) Northamptonshire v Yorkshire at Northampton	1908

Note: Northamptonshire batted one man short in each innings.

LOWEST FOR EACH FIRST-CLASS COUNTY

Derbyshire	16	v Nottinghamshire at Nottingham	1879
Essex	30	v Yorkshire at Leyton	1901
Glamorgan	22	v Lancashire at Liverpool	1924
Gloucestershire	17	v Australians at Cheltenham	1896
Hampshire	15	v Warwickshire at Birmingham	1922
Kent	18	v Sussex at Gravesend	1867
Lancashire	25	v Derbyshire at Manchester	1871
Leicestershire	25	v Kent at Leicester	1912
Middlesex	20	v MCC at Lord's	1864
Northamptonshire	12	v Gloucestershire at Gloucester	1907
Nottinghamshire	13	v Yorkshire at Nottingham	1901
Somerset	25	v Gloucestershire at Bristol	1947
Surrey	14	v Essex at Chelmsford	1983
Sussex	19	v Nottinghamshire at Hove	1873
Warwickshire	16	v Kent at Tonbridge	1913
Worcestershire	24	v Yorkshire at Huddersfield	1903
Yorkshire	23	v Hampshire at Middlesbrough	1965

HIGHEST MATCH AGGREGATES

2,376 for 38 wickets	Maharashtra v Bombay at Poona	1948-49
2,078 for 40 wickets	Bombay v Holkar at Bombay	1944-45
1,981 for 35 wickets	England v South Africa at Durban	1938-39
1,929 for 39 wickets	New South Wales v South Australia at Sydney	1925-26
1,911 for 34 wickets	New South Wales v Victoria at Sydney	1908-09
1,905 for 40 wickets	Otago v Wellington at Dunedin	1923-24

In England

1,723 for 31 wickets	England v Australia at Leeds	1948
1,650 for 19 wickets	Surrey v Lancashire at The Oval	1990
1,641 for 16 wickets	Glamorgan v Worcestershire at Abergavenny	1990
1,614 for 30 wickets	England v India at Manchester	1990
1,603 for 28 wickets	England v India at Lord's	1990
1,601 for 29 wickets	England v Australia at Lord's	1930
1,570 for 29 wickets	Essex v Kent at Chelmsford	1988
1,530 for 19 wickets	Essex v Leicestershire at Chelmsford	1990
1,509 for 36 wickets	Somerset v Worcestershire at Taunton	1990
1,507 for 28 wickets	England v West Indies at The Oval	1976
1,502 for 28 wickets	MCC v New Zealanders at Lord's	1927

LOWEST AGGREGATE IN A COMPLETED MATCH

105 for 31 wickets	MCC v Australians at Lord's	1878

Note: The lowest aggregate since 1900 is 158 for 22 wickets, Surrey v Worcestershire at The Oval, 1954.

HIGHEST FOURTH-INNINGS TOTALS

(Unless otherwise stated, the side making the runs won the match.)

654-5	England v South Africa at Durban (After being set 696 to win. The match was left drawn on the tenth day.)	1938-39
604	Maharashtra v Bombay at Poona (After being set 959 to win.)	1948-49
576-8	Trinidad v Barbados at Port-of-Spain (After being set 672 to win. Match drawn on fifth day.)	1945-46
572	New South Wales v South Australia at Sydney (After being set 593 to win.)	1907-08
529-9	Combined XI v South Africans at Perth (After being set 579 to win. Match drawn on fourth day.)	1963-64
518	Victoria v Queensland at Brisbane (After being set 753 to win.)	1926-27
507-7	Cambridge University v MCC and Ground at Lord's	1896
502-6	Middlesex v Nottinghamshire at Nottingham (Game won by an unfinished stand of 271; a county record.)	1925
502-8	Players v Gentlemen at Lord's	1900
500-7	South African Universities v Western Province at Stellenbosch	1978-79

LARGEST VICTORIES

Largest Innings Victories

Inns and 851 runs:	Railways (910-6 dec.) v Dera Ismail Khan (Lahore)	1964-65
Inns and 666 runs:	Victoria (1,059) v Tasmania (Melbourne)	1922-23
Inns and 656 runs:	Victoria (1,107) v New South Wales (Melbourne)	1926-27
Inns and 605 runs:	New South Wales (918) v South Australia (Sydney)	1900-01
Inns and 579 runs:	England (903-7 dec.) v Australia (The Oval)	1938
Inns and 575 runs:	Sind (951-7 dec.) v Baluchistan (Karachi)	1973-74
Inns and 527 runs:	New South Wales (713) v South Australia (Adelaide)	1908-09
Inns and 517 runs:	Australians (675) v Nottinghamshire (Nottingham)	1921

Largest Victories by Runs Margin

685 runs:	New South Wales (235 and 761-8 dec.) v Queensland (Sydney)	1929-30
675 runs:	England (521 and 342-8 dec.) v Australia (Brisbane)	1928-29
638 runs:	New South Wales (304 and 770) v South Australia (Adelaide)	1920-21
625 runs:	Sargodha (376 and 416) v Lahore Municipal Corporation (Faisalabad)	1978-79
609 runs:	Muslim Commercial Bank (575 and 282-0 dec.) v WAPDA (Lahore).	1977-78
571 runs:	Victoria (304 and 649) v South Australia (Adelaide)	1926-27
562 runs:	Australia (701 and 327) v England (The Oval)	1934

Victory Without Losing a Wicket

Lancashire (166-0 dec. and 66-0) beat Leicestershire by ten wickets (Manchester)	1956
Karachi A (277-0 dec.) beat Sind A by an innings and 77 runs (Karachi)	1957-58
Railways (236-0 dec. and 16-0) beat Jammu and Kashmir by ten wickets (Srinagar)	1960-61
Karnataka (451-0 dec.) beat Kerala by an innings and 186 runs (Chikmagalur)	1977-78

TIED MATCHES IN FIRST-CLASS CRICKET

There have been 37 tied matches since the First World War.

Somerset v Sussex at Taunton 1919
(The last Sussex batsman was not allowed to bat under Law 45 [subsequently Law 17 and now Law 31].)
Orange Free State v Eastern Province at Bloemfontein 1925-26
(Eastern Province had two wickets to fall.)
Essex v Somerset at Chelmsford 1926
(Although Essex had one man to go in, MCC ruled that the game should rank as a tie. The ninth wicket fell half a minute before time.)
Gloucestershire v Australians at Bristol 1930
Victoria v MCC at Melbourne 1932-33
(Victoria's third wicket fell to the last ball of the match when one run was needed to win.)
Worcestershire v Somerset at Kidderminster 1939
Southern Punjab v Baroda at Patiala 1945-46
Essex v Northamptonshire at Ilford 1947
Hampshire v Lancashire at Bournemouth 1947
D. G. Bradman's XI v A. L. Hassett's XI at Melbourne 1948-49
Hampshire v Kent at Southampton 1950
Sussex v Warwickshire at Hove 1952
Essex v Lancashire at Brentwood 1952
Northamptonshire v Middlesex at Peterborough 1953
Yorkshire v Leicestershire at Huddersfield 1954
Sussex v Hampshire at Eastbourne 1955
Victoria v New South Wales at Melbourne 1956-57
T. N. Pearce's XI v New Zealanders at Scarborough 1958
Essex v Gloucestershire at Leyton 1959

Australia v West Indies (First Test) at Brisbane 1960-61
Bahawalpur v Lahore B at Bahawalpur 1961-62
Hampshire v Middlesex at Portsmouth 1967
England XI v England Under-25 XI at Scarborough 1968
Yorkshire v Middlesex at Bradford 1973
Sussex v Essex at Hove 1974
South Australia v Queensland at Adelaide 1976-77
Central Districts v England XI at New Plymouth 1977-78
Victoria v New Zealanders at Melbourne 1982-83
Muslim Commercial Bank v Railways at Sialkot 1983-84
Sussex v Kent at Hastings 1984
Northamptonshire v Kent at Northampton 1984
Eastern Province B v Boland at Albany SC, Port Elizabeth 1985-86
Natal B v Eastern Province B at Pietermaritzburg 1985-86
India v Australia (First Test) at Madras 1986-87
Gloucestershire v Derbyshire at Bristol 1987
Bahawalpur v Peshawar at Bahawalpur 1988-89
Wellington v Canterbury at Wellington 1988-89

Note: Since 1948 a tie has been recognised only when the scores are level with all the wickets down in the fourth innings. This ruling applies to all grades of cricket, and in the case of a one-day match to the second innings, provided that the match has not been brought to a further conclusion.

MATCHES BEGUN AND FINISHED ON FIRST DAY

Since 1900. A fuller list may be found in the Wisden *of 1981 and preceding editions.*

Yorkshire v Worcestershire at Bradford, May 7 1900
MCC and Ground v London County at Lord's, May 20 1903
Transvaal v Orange Free State at Johannesburg, December 30 1906
Middlesex v Gentlemen of Philadelphia at Lord's, July 20 1908
Gloucestershire v Middlesex at Bristol, August 26 1909
Eastern Province v Orange Free State at Port Elizabeth, December 26 1912
Kent v Sussex at Tonbridge, June 21 1919
Lancashire v Somerset at Manchester, May 21 1925
Madras v Mysore at Madras, November 4 1934
Ireland v New Zealanders at Dublin, September 11 1937
Derbyshire v Somerset at Chesterfield, June 11 1947
Lancashire v Sussex at Manchester, July 12 1950
Surrey v Warwickshire at The Oval, May 16 1953
Somerset v Lancashire at Bath, June 6 (H. T. F. Buse's benefit) 1953
Kent v Worcestershire at Tunbridge Wells, June 15 1960

TEST MATCH RECORDS

BATTING RECORDS

HIGHEST INDIVIDUAL INNINGS

365* G. S. Sobers, West Indies v Pakistan at Kingston 1957-58
364 L. Hutton, England v Australia at The Oval 1938
337 Hanif Mohammad, Pakistan v West Indies at Bridgetown 1957-58
336* W. R. Hammond, England v New Zealand at Auckland 1932-33
334 D. G. Bradman, Australia v England at Leeds 1930
333 G. A. Gooch, England v India at Lord's 1990
325 A. Sandham, England v West Indies at Kingston 1929-30

311	R. B. Simpson, Australia v England at Manchester	1964
310*	J. H. Edrich, England v New Zealand at Leeds	1965
307	R. M. Cowper, Australia v England at Melbourne	1965-66
304	D. G. Bradman, Australia v England at Leeds	1934
302	L. G. Rowe, West Indies v England at Bridgetown	1973-74
299*	D. G. Bradman, Australia v South Africa at Adelaide	1931-32
291	I. V. A. Richards, West Indies v England at The Oval	1976
287	R. E. Foster, England v Australia at Sydney	1903-04
285*	P. B. H. May, England v West Indies at Birmingham	1957
280*	Javed Miandad, Pakistan v India at Hyderabad	1982-83
278	D. C. S. Compton, England v Pakistan at Nottingham	1954
274	R. G. Pollock, South Africa v Australia at Durban	1969-70
274	Zaheer Abbas, Pakistan v England at Birmingham	1971
271	Javed Miandad, Pakistan v New Zealand at Auckland	1988-89
270*	G. A. Headley, West Indies v England at Kingston	1934-35
270	D. G. Bradman, Australia v England at Melbourne	1936-37
268	G. N. Yallop, Australia v Pakistan at Melbourne	1983-84
266	W. H. Ponsford, Australia v England at The Oval	1934
262*	D. L. Amiss, England v West Indies at Kingston	1973-74
261	F. M. M. Worrell, West Indies v England at Nottingham	1950
260	C. C. Hunte, West Indies v Pakistan at Kingston	1957-58
260	Javed Miandad, Pakistan v England at The Oval	1987
259	G. M. Turner, New Zealand v West Indies at Georgetown	1971-72
258	T. W. Graveney, England v West Indies at Nottingham	1957
258	S. M. Nurse, West Indies v New Zealand at Christchurch	1968-69
256	R. B. Kanhai, West Indies v India at Calcutta	1958-59
256	K. F. Barrington, England v Australia at Manchester	1964
255*	D. J. McGlew, South Africa v New Zealand at Wellington	1952-53
254	D. G. Bradman, Australia v England at Lord's	1930
251	W. R. Hammond, England v Australia at Sydney	1928-29
250	K. D. Walters, Australia v New Zealand at Christchurch	1976-77
250	S. F. A. F. Bacchus, West Indies v India at Kanpur	1978-79

The highest individual innings for other countries are:

236*	S. M. Gavaskar, India v West Indies at Madras	1983-84
201*	D. S. B. P. Kuruppu, Sri Lanka v New Zealand at Colombo (CCC)	1986-87

HUNDRED ON TEST DEBUT

C. Bannerman (165*)	Australia v England at Melbourne	1876-77
W. G. Grace (152)	England v Australia at The Oval	1880
H. Graham (107)	Australia v England at Lord's	1893
†K. S. Ranjitsinhji (154*)	England v Australia at Manchester	1896
†P. F. Warner (132*)	England v South Africa at Johannesburg	1898-99
†R. A. Duff (104)	Australia v England at Melbourne	1901-02
R. E. Foster (287)	England v Australia at Sydney	1903-04
G. Gunn (119)	England v Australia at Sydney	1907-08
†R. J. Hartigan (116)	Australia v England at Adelaide	1907-08
†H. L. Collins (104)	Australia v England at Sydney	1920-21
W. H. Ponsford (110)	Australia v England at Sydney	1924-25
A. A. Jackson (164)	Australia v England at Adelaide	1928-29
†G. A. Headley (176)	West Indies v England at Bridgetown	1929-30
J. E. Mills (117)	New Zealand v England at Wellington	1929-30
Nawab of Pataudi sen. (102)	England v Australia at Sydney	1932-33
B. H. Valentine (136)	England v India at Bombay	1933-34
†L. Amarnath (118)	India v England at Bombay	1933-34
†P. A. Gibb (106)	England v South Africa at Johannesburg	1938-39
S. C. Griffith (140)	England v West Indies at Port-of-Spain	1947-48
A. G. Ganteaume (112)	West Indies v England at Port-of-Spain	1947-48

†J. W. Burke (101*)	Australia v England at Adelaide	1950-51
P. B. H. May (138)	England v South Africa at Leeds	1951
R. H. Shodhan (110)	India v Pakistan at Calcutta	1952-53
B. H. Pairaudeau (115)	West Indies v India at Port-of-Spain	1952-53
†O. G. Smith (104)	West Indies v Australia at Kingston	1954-55
A. G. Kripal Singh (100*)	India v New Zealand at Hyderabad	1955-56
C. C. Hunte (142)	West Indies v Pakistan at Bridgetown	1957-58
C. A. Milton (104*)	England v New Zealand at Leeds	1958
†A. A. Baig (112)	India v England at Manchester	1959
Hanumant Singh (105)	India v England at Delhi	1963-64
Khalid Ibadulla (166)	Pakistan v Australia at Karachi	1964-65
B. R. Taylor (105)	New Zealand v India at Calcutta	1964-65
K. D. Walters (155)	Australia v England at Brisbane	1965-66
J. H. Hampshire (107)	England v West Indies at Lord's	1969
†G. R. Viswanath (137)	India v Australia at Kanpur	1969-70
G. S. Chappell (108)	Australia v England at Perth	1970-71
‡L. G. Rowe (214, 100*)	West Indies v New Zealand at Kingston	1971-72
A. I. Kallicharran (100*)	West Indies v New Zealand at Georgetown	1971-72
R. E. Redmond (107)	New Zealand v Pakistan at Auckland	1972-73
†F. C. Hayes (106*)	England v West Indies at The Oval	1973
†C. G. Greenidge (107)	West Indies v India at Bangalore	1974-75
†L. Baichan (105*)	West Indies v Pakistan at Lahore	1974-75
G. J. Cosier (109)	Australia v West Indies at Melbourne	1975-76
S. Amarnath (124)	India v New Zealand at Auckland	1975-76
Javed Miandad (163)	Pakistan v New Zealand at Lahore	1976-77
†A. B. Williams (100)	West Indies v Australia at Georgetown	1977-78
†D. M. Wellham (103)	Australia v England at The Oval	1981
†Salim Malik (100*)	Pakistan v Sri Lanka at Karachi	1981-82
K. C. Wessels (162)	Australia v England at Brisbane	1982-83
W. B. Phillips (159)	Australia v Pakistan at Perth	1983-84
§M. Azharuddin (110)	India v England at Calcutta	1984-85
D. S. B. P. Kuruppu (201*)	Sri Lanka v New Zealand at Colombo (CCC)	1986-87
†M. J. Greatbatch (107*)	New Zealand v England at Auckland	1987-88

† *In his second innings of the match.*
‡ *L. G. Rowe is the only batsman to score a hundred in each innings on début.*
§ *M. Azharuddin is the only batsman to score hundreds in each of his first three Tests.*

Note: L. Amarnath and S. Amarnath provide the only instance of a father and son scoring a hundred on début.

300 RUNS IN FIRST TEST

314	L. G. Rowe (214, 100*)	West Indies v New Zealand at Kingston	1971-72
306	R. E. Foster (287, 19)	England v Australia at Sydney	1903-04

TWO SEPARATE HUNDREDS IN A TEST

Three times: S. M. Gavaskar v West Indies (1970-71), v Pakistan (1978-79), v West Indies (1978-79).

Twice in one series: C. L. Walcott v Australia (1954-55).

Twice: H. Sutcliffe v Australia (1924-25), v South Africa (1929); G. A. Headley v England (1929-30 and 1939); G. S. Chappell v New Zealand (1973-74), v West Indies (1975-76); ‡A. R. Border v Pakistan (1979-80), v New Zealand (1985-86).

Once: W. Bardsley v England (1909); A. C. Russell v South Africa (1922-23); W. R. Hammond v Australia (1928-29); E. Paynter v South Africa (1938-39); D. C. S. Compton v Australia (1946-47); A. R. Morris v England (1946-47); A. Melville v England (1947); B. Mitchell v England (1947); D. G. Bradman v India (1947-48); V. S. Hazare v Australia (1947-48); E. D. Weekes v India (1948-49); J. Moroney v South Africa (1949-50); G. S. Sobers v Pakistan (1957-58); R. B. Kanhai v Australia (1960-61); Hanif Mohammad v England (1961-62); R. B. Simpson v Pakistan (1964-65); K. D. Walters v West Indies (1968-69); †L. G. Rowe v New Zealand (1971-72); I. M. Chappell v New Zealand (1973-74); G. M. Turner v Australia (1973-74); C. G. Greenidge v England (1976); G. P. Howarth v England (1977-78); L. R. D. Mendis v India (1982-83); Javed Miandad v New Zealand (1984-85); D. M. Jones v Pakistan (1989-90); G. A. Gooch v India (1990).

† *L. G. Rowe's two hundreds were on his Test début.*

‡ *A. R. Border scored 150* and 153 against Pakistan to become the first batsman to score 150 in each innings of a Test match.*

HUNDRED AND DOUBLE-HUNDRED IN SAME TEST

K. D. Walters (Australia)	242 and 103 v West Indies at Sydney	1968-69
S. M. Gavaskar (India)	124 and 220 v West Indies at Port-of-Spain	1970-71
†L. G. Rowe (West Indies)	214 and 100* v New Zealand at Kingston	1971-72
G. S. Chappell (Australia)	247* and 133 v New Zealand at Wellington	1973-74
‡G. A. Gooch (England)	333 and 123 v India at Lord's	1990

† *On Test début.*

‡ *G. A. Gooch became the first to score a hundred and a triple-hundred in the same first-class match.*

MOST RUNS IN A SERIES

	T	*I*	*NO*	*R*	*HI*	*100s*	*Avge*		
D. G. Bradman	5	7	0	974	334	4	139.14	A v E	1930
W. R. Hammond	5	9	1	905	251	4	113.12	E v A	1928-29
M. A. Taylor	6	11	1	839	219	2	83.90	A v E	1989
R. N. Harvey	5	9	0	834	205	4	92.66	A v SA	1952-53
I. V. A. Richards	4	7	0	829	291	3	118.42	WI v E	1976
C. L. Walcott	5	10	0	827	155	5	82.70	WI v A	1954-55
G. S. Sobers	5	8	2	824	365*	3	137.33	WI v P	1957-58
D. G. Bradman	5	9	0	810	270	3	90.00	A v E	1936-37
D. G. Bradman	5	5	1	806	299*	4	201.50	A v SA	1931-32
E. D. Weekes	5	7	0	779	194	4	111.28	WI v I	1948-49
†S. M. Gavaskar	4	8	3	774	220	4	154.80	I v WI	1970-71
Mudassar Nazar	6	8	2	761	231	4	126.83	P v I	1982-83
D. G. Bradman	5	8	0	758	304	2	94.75	A v E	1934
D. C. S. Compton	5	8	0	753	208	4	94.12	E v SA	1947
‡G. A. Gooch	3	6	0	752	333	3	125.33	E v I	1990

† *Gavaskar's aggregate was achieved in his first Test series.*

‡ *G. A. Gooch is alone in scoring 1,000 runs in Test cricket during an English season with 1,058 runs in eleven innings against New Zealand and India in 1990.*

1,000 TEST RUNS IN A CALENDAR YEAR

	T	*I*	*NO*	*R*	*HI*	*100s*	*Avge*	*Year*
I. V. A. Richards (WI)	11	19	0	1,710	291	7	90.00	1976
S. M. Gavaskar (I)	18	27	1	1,555	221	5	59.80	1979
G. R. Viswanath (I)	17	26	3	1,388	179	5	60.34	1979
R. B. Simpson (A)	14	26	3	1,381	311	3	60.04	1964
D. L. Amiss (E)	13	22	2	1,379	262*	5	68.95	1974

	T	*I*	*NO*	*R*	*HI*	*100s*	*Avge*	*Year*
S. M. Gavaskar (I)	18	32	4	1,310	236*	5	46.78	1983
G. A. Gooch (E)	9	17	1	1,264	333	4	79.00	1990‡
M. A. Taylor (A)	11	20	1	1,219	219	4	64.15	1989†
G. S. Sobers (WI)	7	12	3	1,193	365*	5	132.55	1958
D. B. Vengsarkar (I)	18	27	4	1,174	146*	5	51.04	1979
K. J. Hughes (A)	15	28	4	1,163	130*	2	48.45	1979
D. C. S. Compton (E)	9	15	1	1,159	208	6	82.78	1947
C. G. Greenidge (WI)	14	22	4	1,149	223	4	63.83	1984
A. R. Border (A)	11	20	3	1,099	196	4	64.64	1985
D. M. Jones (A)	11	18	3	1,099	216	4	73.26	1989
I. T. Botham (E)	14	22	0	1,095	208	3	49.77	1982
K. W. R. Fletcher (E)	13	22	4	1,090	178	2	60.55	1973
M. Amarnath (I)	14	24	1	1,077	120	4	46.82	1983
A. R. Border (A)	14	27	3	1,073	162	3	44.70	1979
C. Hill (A)	12	21	2	1,061	142	2	55.84	1902
D. I. Gower (E)	14	25	2	1,061	114	1	46.13	1982
D. I. Gower (E)	14	25	1	1,059	136	2	44.12	1986
W. M. Lawry (A)	14	27	2	1,056	157	2	42.24	1964
S. M. Gavaskar (I)	9	15	2	1,044	205	4	80.30	1978
K. F. Barrington (E)	12	22	2	1,039	132*	3	51.95	1963
E. R. Dexter (E)	11	15	1	1,038	205	2	74.14	1962
K. F. Barrington (E)	10	17	4	1,032	172	4	79.38	1961
Mohsin Khan (P)	10	17	3	1,029	200	4	73.50	1982
D. G. Bradman (A)	8	13	4	1,025	201	5	113.88	1948
S. M. Gavaskar (I)	11	20	1	1,024	156	4	53.89	1976
A. R. Border (A)	11	19	3	1,000	140	5	62.50	1986

† *The year of his début.* ‡ *Amended to December 1990.*

Notes: The earliest date for completing 1,000 runs is May 3 by M. Amarnath in 1983.

D. G. Bradman (A) scored 1,005 runs in five consecutive Tests, all against England, in 1936-37 and 1938: 13, 270, 26, 212, 169, 51, 144*, 18, 102*.

MOST RUNS IN A CAREER

(Qualification: 2,000 runs)

ENGLAND

	T	*I*	*NO*	*R*	*HI*	*100s*	*Avge*
G. Boycott	108	193	23	8,114	246*	22	47.72
D. I. Gower	109	189	15	7,674	215	16	44.10
M. C. Cowdrey	114	188	15	7,624	182	22	44.06
W. R. Hammond	85	140	16	7,249	336*	22	58.45
L. Hutton	79	138	15	6,971	364	19	56.67
K. F. Barrington	82	131	15	6,806	256	20	58.67
G. A. Gooch	81	147	5	5,910	333	12	41.61
D. C. S. Compton	78	131	15	5,807	278	17	50.06
J. B. Hobbs	61	102	7	5,410	211	15	56.94
J. H. Edrich	77	127	9	5,138	310*	12	43.54
I. T. Botham	97	154	5	5,119	208	14	34.35
T. W. Graveney	79	123	13	4,882	258	11	44.38
H. Sutcliffe	54	84	9	4,555	194	16	60.73
P. B. H. May	66	106	9	4,537	285*	13	46.77
E. R. Dexter	62	102	8	4,502	205	9	47.89
A. P. E. Knott	95	149	15	4,389	135	5	32.75
A. J. Lamb	67	118	10	3,981	139	13	36.86
M. W. Gatting	68	117	14	3,870	207	9	37.57
D. L. Amiss	50	88	10	3,612	262*	11	46.30
A. W. Greig	58	93	4	3,599	148	8	40.43
E. H. Hendren	51	83	9	3,525	205*	7	47.63

	T	I	NO	R	HI	100s	Avge
F. E. Woolley	64	98	7	3,283	154	5	36.07
K. W. R. Fletcher	59	96	14	3,272	216	7	39.90
M. Leyland	41	65	5	2,764	187	9	46.06
C. Washbrook	37	66	6	2,569	195	6	42.81
B. L. D'Oliveira	44	70	8	2,484	158	5	40.06
D. W. Randall	47	79	5	2,470	174	7	33.37
W. J. Edrich	39	63	2	2,440	219	6	40.00
T. G. Evans	91	133	14	2,439	104	2	20.49
L. E. G. Ames	47	72	12	2,434	149	8	40.56
W. Rhodes	58	98	21	2,325	179	2	30.19
T. E. Bailey	61	91	14	2,290	134*	1	29.74
M. J. K. Smith	50	78	6	2,278	121	3	31.63
P. E. Richardson	34	56	1	2,061	126	5	37.47

AUSTRALIA

	T	I	NO	R	HI	100s	Avge
A. R. Border	115	199	36	8,701	205	23	53.38
G. S. Chappell	87	151	19	7,110	247*	24	53.86
D. G. Bradman	52	80	10	6,996	334	29	99.94
R. N. Harvey	79	137	10	6,149	205	21	48.41
K. D. Walters	74	125	14	5,357	250	15	48.26
I. M. Chappell	75	136	10	5,345	196	14	42.42
W. M. Lawry	67	123	12	5,234	210	13	47.15
R. B. Simpson	62	111	7	4,869	311	10	46.81
I. R. Redpath	66	120	11	4,737	171	8	43.45
K. J. Hughes	70	124	6	4,415	213	9	37.41
R. W. Marsh	96	150	13	3,633	132	3	26.51
A. R. Morris	46	79	3	3,533	206	12	46.48
C. Hill	49	89	2	3,412	191	7	39.21
G. M. Wood	59	112	6	3,374	172	9	31.83
D. C. Boon	48	88	7	3,186	200	8	39.33
V. T. Trumper	48	89	8	3,163	214*	8	39.04
C. C. McDonald	47	83	4	3,107	170	5	39.32
A. L. Hassett	43	69	3	3,073	198*	10	46.56
K. R. Miller	55	87	7	2,958	147	7	36.97
W. W. Armstrong	50	84	10	2,863	159*	6	38.68
K. R. Stackpole	43	80	5	2,807	207	7	37.42
N. C. O'Neill	42	69	8	2,779	181	6	45.55
G. N. Yallop	39	70	3	2,756	268	8	41.13
S. J. McCabe	39	62	5	2,748	232	6	48.21
D. M. Jones	34	59	8	2,637	216	9	51.70
W. Bardsley	41	66	5	2,469	193*	6	40.47
W. M. Woodfull	35	54	4	2,300	161	7	46.00
P. J. Burge	42	68	8	2,290	181	4	38.16
S. E. Gregory	58	100	7	2,282	201	4	24.53
R. Benaud	63	97	7	2,201	122	3	24.45
C. G. Macartney	35	55	4	2,131	170	7	41.78
G. R. Marsh	36	66	3	2,129	138	4	33.79
W. H. Ponsford	29	48	4	2,122	266	7	48.22
R. M. Cowper	27	46	2	2,061	307	5	46.84

SOUTH AFRICA

	T	I	NO	R	HI	100s	Avge
B. Mitchell	42	80	9	3,471	189*	8	48.88
A. D. Nourse	34	62	7	2,960	231	9	53.81
H. W. Taylor	42	76	4	2,936	176	7	40.77
E. J. Barlow	30	57	2	2,516	201	6	45.74
T. L. Goddard	41	78	5	2,516	112	1	34.46

	T	I	NO	R	HI	100s	Avge
D. J. McGlew	34	64	6	2,440	255*	7	42.06
J. H. B. Waite	50	86	7	2,405	134	4	30.44
R. G. Pollock	23	41	4	2,256	274	7	60.97
A. W. Nourse	45	83	8	2,234	111	1	29.78
R. A. McLean	40	73	3	2,120	142	5	30.28

WEST INDIES

	T	I	NO	R	HI	100s	Avge
G. S. Sobers	93	160	21	8,032	365*	26	57.78
I. V. A. Richards	111	166	10	7,990	291	24	51.21
C. H. Lloyd	110	175	14	7,515	242*	19	46.67
C. G. Greenidge	100	170	15	7,134	223	18	46.02
R. B. Kanhai	79	137	6	6,227	256	15	47.53
D. L. Haynes	89	153	17	5,711	184	14	41.99
E. D. Weekes	48	81	5	4,455	207	15	58.61
A. I. Kallicharran	66	109	10	4,399	187	12	44.43
R. C. Fredericks	59	109	7	4,334	169	8	42.49
F. M. M. Worrell	51	87	9	3,860	261	9	49.48
C. L. Walcott	44	74	7	3,798	220	15	56.68
R. B. Richardson	49	83	7	3,515	194	10	46.25
C. C. Hunte	44	78	6	3,245	260	8	45.06
H. A. Gomes	60	91	11	3,171	143	9	39.63
B. F. Butcher	44	78	6	3,104	209*	7	43.11
P. J. L. Dujon	68	96	11	2,994	139	5	35.22
S. M. Nurse	29	54	1	2,523	258	6	47.60
G. A. Headley	22	40	4	2,190	270*	10	60.83
J. B. Stollmeyer	32	56	5	2,159	160	4	42.33
L. G. Rowe	30	49	2	2,047	302	7	43.55

NEW ZEALAND

	T	I	NO	R	HI	100s	Avge
J. G. Wright	71	126	6	4,377	185	10	36.47
B. E. Congdon	61	114	7	3,448	176	7	32.22
J. R. Reid	58	108	5	3,428	142	6	33.28
M. D. Crowe	51	83	7	3,384	188	11	44.52
Sir R. J. Hadlee	86	134	19	3,124	151*	2	27.16
G. M. Turner	41	73	6	2,991	259	7	44.64
B. Sutcliffe	42	76	8	2,727	230*	5	40.10
M. G. Burgess	50	92	6	2,684	119*	5	31.20
J. V. Coney	52	85	14	2,668	174*	3	37.57
G. P. Howarth	47	83	5	2,531	147	6	32.44
G. T. Dowling	39	77	3	2,306	239	3	31.16

INDIA

	T	I	NO	R	HI	100s	Avge
S. M. Gavaskar	125	214	16	10,122	236*	34	51.12
D. B. Vengsarkar	110	175	22	6,703	166	17	43.81
G. R. Viswanath	91	155	10	6,080	222	14	41.93
Kapil Dev	109	158	13	4,521	163	7	31.17
M. Amarnath	69	113	10	4,378	138	11	42.50
P. R. Umrigar	59	94	8	3,631	223	12	42.22
R. J. Shastri	72	109	14	3,372	187	10	35.49
V. L. Manjrekar	55	92	10	3,208	189*	7	39.12
C. G. Borde	55	97	11	3,061	177*	5	35.59

	T	*I*	*NO*	*R*	*HI*	*100s*	*Avge*
M. Azharuddin	40	60	3	2,953	199	10	51.80
Nawab of Pataudi jun.	46	83	3	2,793	203*	6	34.91
S. M. H. Kirmani	88	124	22	2,759	102	2	27.04
F. M. Engineer	46	87	3	2,611	121	2	31.08
Pankaj Roy	43	79	4	2,442	173	5	32.56
V. S. Hazare	30	52	6	2,192	164*	7	47.65
A. L. Wadekar	37	71	3	2,113	143	1	31.07
V. Mankad	44	72	5	2,109	231	5	31.47
C. P. S. Chauhan	40	68	2	2,084	97	0	31.57
M. L. Jaisimha	39	71	4	2,056	129	3	30.68
D. N. Sardesai	30	55	4	2,001	212	5	39.23

PAKISTAN

	T	*I*	*NO*	*R*	*HI*	*100s*	*Avge*
Javed Miandad	104	158	18	7,891	280*	22	56.36
Zaheer Abbas	78	124	11	5,062	274	12	44.79
Mudassar Nazar	76	116	8	4,114	231	10	38.09
Majid Khan	63	106	5	3,931	167	8	38.92
Hanif Mohammad ...	55	97	8	3,915	337	12	43.98
Mushtaq Mohammad .	57	100	7	3,643	201	10	39.17
Asif Iqbal	58	99	7	3,575	175	11	38.85
Imran Khan	82	118	22	3,541	136	6	36.88
Saeed Ahmed	41	78	4	2,991	172	5	40.41
Wasim Raja	57	92	14	2,821	125	4	36.16
Salim Malik	57	79	14	2,718	119*	7	41.81
Mohsin Khan	48	79	6	2,709	200	7	37.10
Sadiq Mohammad	41	74	2	2,579	166	5	35.81
Imtiaz Ahmed	41	72	1	2,079	209	3	29.28

SRI LANKA: The highest aggregate is 1,621, average 36.84, by A. Ranatunga in 26 Tests.

HIGHEST AVERAGES

(Qualification: 20 innings)

Avge		*T*	*I*	*NO*	*R*	*HI*	*100s*
99.94	D. G. Bradman (A)	52	80	10	6,996	334	29
64.72	M. A. Taylor (A)	15	27	2	1,618	219	6
60.97	R. G. Pollock (SA)	23	41	4	2,256	274	7
60.83	G. A. Headley (WI)	22	40	4	2,190	270*	10
60.73	H. Sutcliffe (E)	54	84	9	4,555	194	16
59.23	E. Paynter (E)	20	31	5	1,540	243	4
58.67	K. F. Barrington (E)	82	131	15	6,806	256	20
58.61	E. D. Weekes (WI)	48	81	5	4,455	207	15
58.45	W. R. Hammond (E)	85	140	16	7,249	336*	22
57.78	G. S. Sobers (WI)	93	160	21	8,032	365*	26
56.94	J. B. Hobbs (E)	61	102	7	5,410	211	15
56.68	C. L. Walcott (WI)	44	74	7	3,798	220	15
56.67	L. Hutton (E)	79	138	15	6,971	364	19
56.36	Javed Miandad (P)........	104	158	18	7,891	280*	22
55.00	E. Tyldesley (E)	14	20	2	990	122	3
54.20	C. A. Davis (WI)	15	29	5	1,301	183	4
53.94	M. J. Greatbatch (NZ)	14	21	4	917	146*	2
53.86	G. S. Chappell (A)	87	151	19	7,110	247*	24

Avge		*T*	*I*	*NO*	*R*	*HI*	*100s*
53.81	A. D. Nourse (SA)	34	62	7	2,960	231	9
53.73	R. A. Smith (E)	18	34	8	1,397	143	4
53.38	A. R. Border (A)	115	199	36	8,701	205	23
51.80	M. Azharuddin (I)	40	60	3	2,953	199	10
51.70	D. M. Jones (A)	34	59	8	2,637	216	9
51.62	J. Ryder (A)	20	32	5	1,394	201*	3
51.21	I. V. A. Richards (WI)	111	166	10	7,990	291	24
51.12	S. M. Gavaskar (I)	125	214	16	10,122	236*	34
50.06	D. C. S. Compton (E)	78	131	15	5,807	278	17

MOST HUNDREDS

Total		*E*	*A*	*SA*	*WI*	*NZ*	*I*	*P*	*SL*
34	S. M. Gavaskar (I)	4	8	—	13	2	—	5	2
29	D. G. Bradman (A)	19	—	4	2	—	4	—	—
26	G. S. Sobers (WI)	10	4	—	—	1	8	3	—
24	G. S. Chappell (A)	9	—	—	5	3	1	6	0
24	I. V. A. Richards (WI)	8	5	—	—	1	8	2	—
23	A. R. Border (A)	7	—	—	2	4	4	6	0
22	W. R. Hammond (E)	—	9	6	1	4	2	—	—
22	M. C. Cowdrey (E)	—	5	3	6	2	3	3	—
22	G. Boycott (E)	—	7	1	5	2	4	3	—
22	Javed Miandad (P)	1	6	—	2	7	5	—	1
21	R. N. Harvey (A)	6	—	8	3	—	4	0	—
20	K. F. Barrington (E)	—	5	2	3	3	3	4	—

CARRYING BAT THROUGH TEST INNINGS

(Figures in brackets show side's total)

A. B. Tancred	26*	(47)	South Africa v England at Cape Town	1888-89
J. E. Barrett	67*	(176)	Australia v England at Lord's	1890
R. Abel	132*	(307)	England v Australia at Sydney	1891-92
P. F. Warner	132*	(237)	England v South Africa at Johannesburg	1898-99
W. W. Armstrong	159*	(309)	Australia v South Africa at Johannesburg	1902-03
J. W. Zulch	43*	(103)	South Africa v England at Cape Town	1909-10
W. Bardsley	193*	(383)	Australia v England at Lord's	1926
W. M. Woodfull	30*	(66)‡	Australia v England at Brisbane	1928-29
W. M. Woodfull	73*	(193)†	Australia v England at Adelaide	1932-33
W. A. Brown	206*	(422)	Australia v England at Lord's	1938
L. Hutton	202*	(344)	England v West Indies at The Oval	1950
L. Hutton	156*	(272)	England v Australia at Adelaide	1950-51
Nazar Mohammad	124*	(331)	Pakistan v India at Lucknow	1952-53
F. M. M. Worrell	191*	(372)	West Indies v England at Nottingham	1957
T. L. Goddard	56*	(99)	South Africa v Australia at Cape Town	1957-58
D. J. McGlew	127*	(292)	South Africa v New Zealand at Durban	1961-62
C. C. Hunte	60*	(131)	West Indies v Australia at Port-of-Spain	1964-65
G. M. Turner	43*	(131)	New Zealand v England at Lord's	1969
W. M. Lawry	49*	(107)	Australia v India at Delhi	1969-70
W. M. Lawry	60*	(116)†	Australia v England at Sydney	1970-71
G. M. Turner	223*	(386)	New Zealand v West Indies at Kingston	1971-72
I. R. Redpath	159*	(346)	Australia v New Zealand at Auckland	1973-74
G. Boycott	99*	(215)	England v Australia at Perth	1979-80
S. M. Gavaskar	127*	(286)	India v Pakistan at Faisalabad	1982-83
Mudassar Nazar	152*	(323)	Pakistan v India at Lahore	1982-83
S. Wettimuny	63*	(144)	Sri Lanka v New Zealand at Christchurch	1982-83
D. C. Boon	58*	(103)	Australia v New Zealand at Auckland	1985-86
D. L. Haynes	88*	(211)	West Indies v Pakistan at Karachi	1986-87

† *One man absent.* ‡ *Two men absent.*

Notes: G. M. Turner (223*) holds the record for the highest score by a player carrying his bat through a Test innings. He is also the youngest player to do so, being 22 years 63 days old when he first achieved the feat (1969).

Nazar Mohammad and Mudassar Nazar provide the only instance of a father and son carrying their bat through a Test innings.

D. L. Haynes (55 and 105) opened the batting and was last man out in each innings for West Indies v New Zealand at Dunedin, 1979-80.

FASTEST FIFTIES

Minutes			
28	J. T. Brown	England v Australia at Melbourne	1894-95
29	S. A. Durani	India v England at Kanpur	1963-64
30	E. A. V. Williams	West Indies v England at Bridgetown	1947-48
30	B. R. Taylor	New Zealand v West Indies at Auckland	1968-69
33	C. A. Roach	West Indies v England at The Oval	1933
34	C. R. Browne	West Indies v England at Georgetown	1929-30

The fastest fifties in terms of balls received (where recorded) are:

Balls			
30	Kapil Dev	India v Pakistan at Karachi (2nd Test)	1982-83
32	I. T. Botham	England v New Zealand at The Oval	1986
32	I. V. A. Richards	West Indies v India at Kingston	1982-83
33	R. C. Fredericks	West Indies v Australia at Perth	1975-76
33	Kapil Dev	India v Pakistan at Karachi	1978-79
33	Kapil Dev	India v England at Manchester	1982
33	I. V. A. Richards	West Indies v England at St John's	1985-86

FASTEST HUNDREDS

Minutes			
70	J. M. Gregory	Australia v South Africa at Johannesburg	1921-22
75	G. L. Jessop	England v Australia at The Oval	1902
78	R. Benaud	Australia v West Indies at Kingston	1954-55
80	J. H. Sinclair	South Africa v Australia at Cape Town	1902-03
81	I. V. A. Richards	West Indies v England at St John's	1985-86
86	B. R. Taylor	New Zealand v West Indies at Auckland	1968-69

The fastest hundreds in terms of balls received (where recorded) are:

Balls			
56	I. V. A. Richards	West Indies v England at St John's	1985-86
67	J. M. Gregory	Australia v South Africa at Johannesburg	1921-22
71	R. C. Fredericks	West Indies v Australia at Perth	1975-76
74	Kapil Dev	India v Sri Lanka at Kanpur	1986-87
76	G. L. Jessop	England v Australia at The Oval	1902
77	Majid Khan	Pakistan v New Zealand at Karachi	1976-77

FASTEST DOUBLE-HUNDREDS

Minutes			
214	D. G. Bradman	Australia v England at Leeds	1930
223	S. J. McCabe	Australia v England at Nottingham	1938
226	V. T. Trumper	Australia v South Africa at Adelaide	1910-11
234	D. G. Bradman	Australia v England at Lord's	1930
240	W. R. Hammond	England v New Zealand at Auckland	1932-33
241	S. E. Gregory	Australia v England at Sydney	1894-95
245	D. C. S. Compton	England v Pakistan at Nottingham	1954

The fastest double-hundreds in terms of balls received (where recorded) are:

Balls			
220	I. T. Botham	England v India at The Oval	1982
232	C. G. Greenidge ...	West Indies v England at Lord's	1984
240	C. H. Lloyd	West Indies v India at Bombay	1974-75
241	Zaheer Abbas	Pakistan v India at Lahore	1982-83
242	D. G. Bradman ...	Australia v England at The Oval	1934
242	I. V. A. Richards ..	West Indies v Australia at Melbourne	1984-85

FASTEST TRIPLE-HUNDREDS

Minutes			
288	W. R. Hammond ..	England v New Zealand at Auckland	1932-33
336	D. G. Bradman ...	Australia v England at Leeds	1930

MOST RUNS IN A DAY BY A BATSMAN

309	D. G. Bradman	Australia v England at Leeds	1930
295	W. R. Hammond	England v New Zealand at Auckland	1932-33
273	D. C. S. Compton	England v Pakistan at Nottingham	1954
271	D. G. Bradman	Australia v England at Leeds	1934

SLOWEST INDIVIDUAL BATTING

2* in 80 minutes	C. E. H. Croft, West Indies v Australia at Brisbane	1979-80
3* in 100 minutes	J. T. Murray, England v Australia at Sydney	1962-63
5 in 102 minutes	Nawab of Pataudi jun, India v England at Bombay	1972-73
7 in 123 minutes	G. Miller, England v Australia at Melbourne	1978-79
9 in 125 minutes	T. W. Jarvis, New Zealand v India at Madras	1964-65
10* in 133 minutes	T. G. Evans, England v Australia at Adelaide	1946-47
16* in 147 minutes	D. B. Vengsarkar, India v Pakistan at Kanpur	1979-80
17* in 166 minutes	G. M. Ritchie, Australia v India at Sydney	1985-86
18 in 194 minutes	W. R. Playle, New Zealand v England at Leeds	1958
19 in 217 minutes	M. D. Crowe, New Zealand v Sri Lanka at Colombo (SSC)	1983-84
28* in 250 minutes	J. W. Burke, Australia v England at Brisbane	1958-59
31 in 264 minutes	K. D. Mackay, Australia v England at Lord's	1956
34* in 271 minutes	Younis Ahmed, Pakistan v India at Ahmedabad	1986-87
35 in 332 minutes	C. J. Tavaré, England v India at Madras	1981-82
55 in 336 minutes	B. A. Edgar, New Zealand v Australia at Wellington ...	1981-82
57 in 346 minutes	G. S. Camacho, West Indies v England at Bridgetown ...	1967-68
58 in 367 minutes	Ijaz Butt, Pakistan v Australia at Karachi	1959-60
60 in 390 minutes	D. N. Sardesai, India v West Indies at Bridgetown	1961-62
62 in 408 minutes	Ramiz Raja, Pakistan v West Indies at Karachi	1986-87
68 in 458 minutes	T. E. Bailey, England v Australia at Brisbane	1958-59
99 in 505 minutes	M. L. Jaisimha, India v Pakistan at Kanpur	1960-61
105 in 575 minutes	D. J. McGlew, South Africa v Australia at Durban	1957-58
114 in 591 minutes	Mudassar Nazar, Pakistan v England at Lahore	1977-78
120* in 609 minutes	J. J. Crowe, New Zealand v Sri Lanka, Colombo (CCC) .	1986-87
158 in 648 minutes	C. T. Radley, England v New Zealand at Auckland	1977-78
163 in 720 minutes	Shoaib Mohammad, Pakistan v New Zealand at Wellington	1988-89
337 in 970 minutes	Hanif Mohammad, Pakistan v West Indies at Bridgetown	1957-58

SLOWEST HUNDREDS

557 minutes	Mudassar Nazar, Pakistan v England at Lahore	1977-78
545 minutes	D. J. McGlew, South Africa v Australia at Durban	1957-58
515 minutes	J. J. Crowe, New Zealand v Sri Lanka, Colombo (CCC)	1986-87
488 minutes	P. E. Richardson, England v South Africa at Johannesburg	1956-57

Notes: The slowest hundred for any Test in England is 458 minutes (329 balls) by K. W. R.

Fletcher, England v Pakistan, The Oval, 1974.

The slowest double-hundred in a Test was scored in 777 minutes (548 balls) by D. S. B. P. Kuruppu for Sri Lanka v New Zealand at Colombo (CCC), 1986-87, on his début. It is also the slowest-ever first-class double-hundred.

HIGHEST PARTNERSHIPS FOR EACH WICKET

413 for 1st	V. Mankad (231)/Pankaj Roy (173)........	I v NZ	Madras	1955-56
451 for 2nd	W. H. Ponsford (266)/D. G. Bradman (244).	A v E	The Oval	1934
451 for 3rd	Mudassar Nazar (231)/Javed Miandad (280*)	P v I	Hyderabad	1982-83
411 for 4th	P. B. H. May (285*)/M. C. Cowdrey (154)..	E v WI	Birmingham	1957
405 for 5th	S. G. Barnes (234)/D. G. Bradman (234) ...	A v E	Sydney	1946-47
346 for 6th	J. H. W. Fingleton (136)/D. G. Bradman (270)	A v E	Melbourne	1936-37
347 for 7th	D. St E. Atkinson (219)/C. C. Depeiza (122)	WI v A	Bridgetown	1954-55
246 for 8th	L. E. G. Ames (137)/G. O. B. Allen (122) ..	E v NZ	Lord's	1931
190 for 9th	Asif Iqbal (146)/Intikhab Alam (51)	P v E	The Oval	1967
151 for 10th	B. F. Hastings (110)/R. O. Collinge (68*)...	NZ v P	Auckland	1972-73

PARTNERSHIPS OF 300 AND OVER

451	for 2nd	W. H. Ponsford (266)/D. G. Bradman (244) ...	A v E	The Oval	1934
451	for 3rd	Mudassar Nazar (231)/Javed Miandad (280*) ..	P v I	Hyderabad	1982-83
446	for 2nd	C. C. Hunte (260)/G. S. Sobers (365*)	WI v P	Kingston	1957-58
413	for 1st	V. Mankad (231)/Pankaj Roy (173)	I v NZ	Madras	1955-56
411	for 4th	P. B. H. May (285*)/M. C. Cowdrey (154)	E v WI	Birmingham	1957
405	for 5th	S. G. Barnes (234)/D. G. Bradman (234)	A v E	Sydney	1946-47
399	for 4th	G. S. Sobers (226)/F. M. M. Worrell (197*) ...	WI v E	Bridgetown	1959-60
397	for 3rd	Qasim Omar (206)/Javed Miandad (203*)	P v SL	Faisalabad	1985-86
388	for 4th	W. H. Ponsford (181)/D. G. Bradman (304) ...	A v E	Leeds	1934
387	for 1st	G. M. Turner (259)/T. W. Jarvis (182)	NZ v WI	Georgetown	1971-72
382	for 2nd	L. Hutton (364)/M. Leyland (187)	E v A	The Oval	1938
382	for 1st	W. M. Lawry (210)/R. B. Simpson (201)	A v WI	Bridgetown	1964-65
370	for 3rd	W. J. Edrich (189)/D. C. S. Compton (208) ...	E v SA	Lord's	1947
369	for 2nd	J. H. Edrich (310*)/K. F. Barrington (163)	E v NZ	Leeds	1965
359	for 1st	L. Hutton (158)/C. Washbrook (195)	E v SA	Johannesburg	1948-49
351	for 2nd	G. A. Gooch (196)/D. I. Gower (157)	E v A	The Oval	1985
350	for 4th	Mushtaq Mohammad (201)/Asif Iqbal (175) ...	P v NZ	Dunedin	1972-73
347	for 7th	D. St E. Atkinson (219)/C. C. Depeiza (122) ..	WI v A	Bridgetown	1954-55
346	for 6th	J. H. Fingleton (136)/D. G. Bradman (270) ...	A v E	Melbourne	1936-37
344*	for 2nd	S. M. Gavaskar (182*)/D. B. Vengsarkar (157*)	I v WI	Calcutta	1978-79
341	for 3rd	E. J. Barlow (201)/R. G. Pollock (175)	SA v A	Adelaide	1963-64
338	for 3rd	E. D. Weekes (206)/F. M. M. Worrell (167) ...	WI v E	Port-of-Spain	1953-54
336	for 4th	W. M. Lawry (151)/K. D. Walters (242)	A v WI	Sydney	1968-69
331	for 2nd	R. T. Robinson (148)/D. I. Gower (215)	E v A	Birmingham	1985
329	for 1st	G. R. Marsh (138)/M. A. Taylor (219)	A v E	Nottingham	1989
323	for 1st	J. B. Hobbs (178)/W. Rhodes (179)	E v A	Melbourne	1911-12
319	for 3rd	A. Melville (189)/A. D. Nourse (149).........	SA v E	Nottingham	1947
316†	for 3rd	G. R. Viswanath (222)/Yashpal Sharma (140) .	I v E	Madras	1981-82
308	for 7th	Waqar Hassan (189)/Imtiaz Ahmed (209)	P v NZ	Lahore	1955-56
308	for 3rd	R. B. Richardson (154)/I. V. A. Richards (178)	WI v A	St John's	1983-84
308	for 3rd	G. A. Gooch (333)/A. J. Lamb (139)	E v I	Lord's	1990
303	for 3rd	I. V. A. Richards (232)/A. I. Kallicharran (97) .	WI v E	Nottingham	1976
301	for 2nd	A. R. Morris (182)/D. G. Bradman (173*)	A v E	Leeds	1948

† 415 runs were scored for this wicket in two separate partnerships: D. B. Vengsarkar retired hurt when he and Viswanath had added 99 runs.

BOWLING RECORDS

MOST WICKETS IN AN INNINGS

10-53	J. C. Laker	England v Australia at Manchester	1956
9-28	G. A. Lohmann	England v South Africa at Johannesburg	1895-96
9-37	J. C. Laker	England v Australia at Manchester	1956
9-52	R. J. Hadlee	New Zealand v Australia at Brisbane	1985-86
9-56	Abdul Qadir	Pakistan v England at Lahore	1987-88
9-69	J. M. Patel	India v Australia at Kanpur	1959-60
9-83	Kapil Dev	India v West Indies at Ahmedabad	1983-84
9-86	Sarfraz Nawaz	Pakistan v Australia at Melbourne	1978-79
9-95	J. M. Noreiga	West Indies v India at Port-of-Spain	1970-71
9-102	S. P. Gupte	India v West Indies at Kanpur	1958-59
9-103	S. F. Barnes	England v South Africa at Johannesburg	1913-14
9-113	H. J. Tayfield	South Africa v England at Johannesburg	1956-57
9-121	A. A. Mailey	Australia v England at Melbourne	1920-21
8-7	G. A. Lohmann	England v South Africa at Port Elizabeth	1895-96
8-11	J. Briggs	England v South Africa at Cape Town	1888-89
8-29	S. F. Barnes	England v South Africa at The Oval	1912
8-29	C. E. H. Croft	West Indies v Pakistan at Port-of-Spain	1976-77
8-31	F. Laver	Australia v England at Manchester	1909
8-31	F. S. Trueman	England v India at Manchester	1952
8-34	I. T. Botham	England v Pakistan at Lord's	1978
8-35	G. A. Lohmann	England v Australia at Sydney	1886-87
8-38	L. R. Gibbs	West Indies v India at Bridgetown	1961-62
8-43†	A. E. Trott	Australia v England at Adelaide	1894-95
8-43	H. Verity	England v Australia at Lord's	1934
8-43	R. G. D. Willis	England v Australia at Leeds	1981
8-45	C. E. L. Ambrose	West Indies v England at Bridgetown	1989-90
8-51	D. L. Underwood	England v Pakistan at Lord's	1974
8-52	V. Mankad	India v Pakistan at Delhi	1952-53
8-53	G. B. Lawrence	South Africa v New Zealand at Johannesburg	1961-62
8-53†	R. A. L. Massie	Australia v England at Lord's	1972
8-55	V. Mankad	India v England at Madras	1951-52
8-56	S. F. Barnes	England v South Africa at Johannesburg	1913-14
8-58	G. A. Lohmann	England v Australia at Sydney	1891-92
8-58	Imran Khan	Pakistan v Sri Lanka at Lahore	1981-82
8-59	C. Blythe	England v South Africa at Leeds	1907
8-59	A. A. Mallett	Australia v Pakistan at Adelaide	1972-73
8-60	Imran Khan	Pakistan v India at Karachi	1982-83
8-61†	N. D. Hirwani	India v West Indies at Madras	1987-88
8-65	H. Trumble	Australia v England at The Oval	1902
8-68	W. Rhodes	England v Australia at Melbourne	1903-04
8-69	H. J. Tayfield	South Africa v England at Durban	1956-57
8-69	Sikander Bakht	Pakistan v India at Delhi	1979-80
8-70	S. J. Snooke	South Africa v England at Johannesburg	1905-06
8-71	G. D. McKenzie	Australia v West Indies at Melbourne	1968-69
8-72	S. Venkataraghavan	India v New Zealand at Delhi	1964-65
8-75†	N. D. Hirwani	India v West Indies at Madras	1987-88
8-76	E. A. S. Prasanna	India v New Zealand at Auckland	1975-76
8-79	B. S. Chandrasekhar	India v England at Delhi	1972-73
8-81	L. C. Braund	England v Australia at Melbourne	1903-04
8-83	J. R. Ratnayeke	Sri Lanka v Pakistan at Sialkot	1985-86
8-84†	R. A. L. Massie	Australia v England at Lord's	1972
8-85	Kapil Dev	India v Pakistan at Lahore	1982-83
8-86	A. W. Greig	England v West Indies at Port-of-Spain	1973-74
8-87	M. G. Hughes	Australia v West Indies at Perth	1988-89
8-92	M. A. Holding	West Indies v England at The Oval	1976
8-94	T. Richardson	England v Australia at Sydney	1897-98
8-103	I. T. Botham	England v West Indies at Lord's	1984

8-104†	A. L. Valentine ...	West Indies v England at Manchester	1950
8-106	Kapil Dev	India v Australia at Adelaide	1985-86
8-107	B. J. T. Bosanquet .	England v Australia at Nottingham	1905
8-107	N. A. Foster	England v Pakistan at Leeds	1987
8-112	G. F. Lawson	Australia v West Indies at Adelaide	1984-85
8-126	J. C. White	England v Australia at Adelaide	1928-29
8-141	C. J. McDermott ..	Australia v England at Manchester	1985
8-143	M. H. N. Walker ..	Australia v England at Melbourne	1974-75

† *On Test début.*

OUTSTANDING ANALYSES

	O	*M*	*R*	*W*		
J. C. Laker (E)	51.2	23	53	10	v Australia at Manchester	1956
G. A. Lohmann (E)	14.2	6	28	9	v South Africa at Johannesburg	1895-96
J. C. Laker (E)	16.4	4	37	9	v Australia at Manchester	1956
G. A. Lohmann (E)	9.4	5	7	8	v South Africa at Port Elizabeth	1895-96
J. Briggs (E)	14.2	5	11	8	v South Africa at Cape Town ..	1888-89
J. Briggs (E)	19.1	11	17	7	v South Africa at Cape Town ..	1888-89
M. A. Noble (A)	7.4	2	17	7	v England at Melbourne	1901-02
W. Rhodes (E)	11	3	17	7	v Australia at Birmingham	1902
A. E. R. Gilligan (E)	6.3	4	7	6	v South Africa at Birmingham .	1924
S. Haigh (E)	11.4	6	11	6	v South Africa at Cape Town ..	1898-99
D. L. Underwood (E)	11.6	7	12	6	v New Zealand at Christchurch	1970-71
H. J. Tayfield (SA)	14	7	13	6	v New Zealand at Johannesburg.	1953-54
C. T. B. Turner (A)	18	11	15	6	v England at Sydney	1886-87
M. H. N. Walker (A)	16	8	15	6	v Pakistan at Sydney	1972-73
E. R. H. Toshack (A)	2.3	1	2	5	v India at Brisbane	1947-48
H. Ironmonger (A)	7.2	5	6	5	v South Africa at Melbourne ...	1931-32
Pervez Sajjad (P)	12	8	5	4	v New Zealand at Rawalpindi .	1964-65
K. Higgs (E)	9	7	5	4	v New Zealand at Christchurch.	1965-66
P. H. Edmonds (E)	8	6	6	4	v Pakistan at Lord's	1978
J. C. White (E)	6.3	2	7	4	v Australia at Brisbane	1928-29
J. H. Wardle (E)	5	2	7	4	v Australia at Manchester	1953
R. Appleyard (E)	6	3	7	4	v New Zealand at Auckland ..	1954-55
R. Benaud (A)	3.4	3	0	3	v India at Delhi	1959-60

MOST WICKETS IN A MATCH

19-90	J. C. Laker	England v Australia at Manchester	1956
17-159	S. F. Barnes	England v South Africa at Johannesburg	1913-14
16-136†	N. D. Hirwani	India v West Indies at Madras	1987-88
16-137†	R. A. L. Massie ...	Australia v England at Lord's	1972
15-28	J. Briggs	England v South Africa at Cape Town	1888-89
15-45	G. A. Lohmann ..	England v South Africa at Port Elizabeth	1895-96
15-99	C. Blythe	England v South Africa at Leeds	1907
15-104	H. Verity	England v Australia at Lord's	1934
15-123	R. J. Hadlee	New Zealand v Australia at Brisbane	1985-86
15-124	W. Rhodes	England v Australia at Melbourne	1903-04
14-90	F. R. Spofforth	Australia v England at The Oval	1882
14-99	A. V. Bedser	England v Australia at Nottingham	1953
14-102	W. Bates	England v Australia at Melbourne	1882-83
14-116	Imran Khan	Pakistan v Sri Lanka at Lahore	1981-82
14-124	J. M. Patel	India v Australia at Kanpur	1959-60
14-144	S. F. Barnes	England v South Africa at Durban	1913-14
14-149	M. A. Holding	West Indies v England at The Oval	1976
14-199	C. V. Grimmett ...	Australia v South Africa at Adelaide	1931-32

† *On Test début.*

Notes: The best for South Africa is 13-165 by H. J. Tayfield against Australia at Melbourne, 1952-53.
The best for Sri Lanka is 9-125 by R. J. Ratnayake against India at Colombo (PSS), 1985-86.

MOST WICKETS IN A SERIES

	T	*R*	*W*	*Avge*		
S. F. Barnes	4	536	49	10.93	England v South Africa	1913-14
J. C. Laker	5	442	46	9.60	England v Australia	1956
C. V. Grimmett	5	642	44	14.59	Australia v South Africa	1935-36
T. M. Alderman	6	893	42	21.26	Australia v England	1981
R. M. Hogg	6	527	41	12.85	Australia v England	1978-79
T. M. Alderman	6	712	41	17.36	Australia v England	1989
Imran Khan	6	558	40	13.95	Pakistan v India	1982-83
A. V. Bedser	5	682	39	17.48	England v Australia	1953
D. K. Lillee	6	870	39	22.30	Australia v England	1981
M. W. Tate	5	881	38	23.18	England v Australia	1924-25
W. J. Whitty	5	632	37	17.08	Australia v South Africa	1910-11
H. J. Tayfield	5	636	37	17.18	South Africa v England	1956-57
A. E. E. Vogler	5	783	36	21.75	South Africa v England	1909-10
A. A. Mailey	5	946	36	26.27	Australia v England	1920-21
G. A. Lohmann	3	203	35	5.80	England v South Africa	1895-96
B. S. Chandrasekhar	5	662	35	18.91	India v England	1972-73
M. D. Marshall	5	443	35	12.65	West Indies v England	1988

MOST WICKETS IN A CAREER

(Qualification: 100 wickets)

ENGLAND

	T	*Balls*	*R*	*W*	*Avge*	*5 W/i*	*10 W/m*
I. T. Botham	97	21,281	10,633	376	28.27	27	4
R. G. D. Willis	90	17,357	8,190	325	25.20	16	—
F. S. Trueman	67	15,178	6,625	307	21.57	17	3
D. L. Underwood	86	21,862	7,674	297	25.83	17	6
J. B. Statham	70	16,056	6,261	252	24.84	9	1
A. V. Bedser	51	15,918	5,876	236	24.89	15	5
J. A. Snow	49	12,021	5,387	202	26.66	8	1
J. C. Laker	46	12,027	4,101	193	21.24	9	3
S. F. Barnes	27	7,873	3,106	189	16.43	24	7
G. A. R. Lock	49	13,147	4,451	174	25.58	9	3
M. W. Tate	39	12,523	4,055	155	26.16	7	1
F. J. Titmus	53	15,118	4,931	153	32.22	7	—
H. Verity	40	11,173	3,510	144	24.37	5	2
C. M. Old	46	8,858	4,020	143	28.11	4	—
A. W. Greig	58	9,802	4,541	141	32.20	6	2
G. R. Dilley	41	8,192	4,107	138	29.76	6	—
J. E. Emburey	60	14,227	5,105	138	36.99	6	—
T. E. Bailey	61	9,712	3,856	132	29.21	5	1
W. Rhodes	58	8,231	3,425	127	26.96	6	1
P. H. Edmonds	51	12,028	4,273	125	34.18	2	—
D. A. Allen	39	11,297	3,779	122	30.97	4	—
R. Illingworth	61	11,934	3,807	122	31.20	3	—
J. Briggs	33	5,332	2,094	118	17.74	9	4
G. G. Arnold	34	7,650	3,254	115	28.29	6	—
G. A. Lohmann	18	3,821	1,205	112	10.75	9	5
D. V. P. Wright	34	8,135	4,224	108	39.11	6	1
R. Peel	20	5,216	1,715	102	16.81	6	2
J. H. Wardle	28	6,597	2,080	102	20.39	5	1
C. Blythe	19	4,546	1,863	100	18.63	9	4

AUSTRALIA

	T	Balls	R	W	Avge	5 W/i	10 W/m
D. K. Lillee	70	18,467	8,493	355	23.92	23	7
R. Benaud	63	19,108	6,704	248	27.03	16	1
G. D. McKenzie	60	17,681	7,328	246	29.78	16	3
R. R. Lindwall	61	13,650	5,251	228	23.03	12	—
C. V. Grimmett	37	14,513	5,231	216	24.21	21	7
J. R. Thomson	51	10,535	5,601	200	28.00	8	—
A. K. Davidson	44	11,587	3,819	186	20.53	14	2
G. F. Lawson	46	11,118	5,501	180	30.56	11	2
K. R. Miller	55	10,461	3,906	170	22.97	7	1
W. A. Johnston	40	11,048	3,826	160	23.91	7	—
T. M. Alderman	35	9,152	4,083	153	26.68	13	1
W. J. O'Reilly	27	10,024	3,254	144	22.59	11	3
H. Trumble	32	8,099	3,072	141	21.78	9	3
M. H. N. Walker	34	10,094	3,792	138	27.47	6	—
A. A. Mallett	38	9,990	3,940	132	29.84	6	1
B. Yardley	33	8,909	3,986	126	31.63	6	1
R. M. Hogg	38	7,633	3,503	123	28.47	6	2
M. A. Noble	42	7,159	3,025	121	25.00	9	2
I. W. Johnson	45	8,780	3,182	109	29.19	3	—
G. Giffen	31	6,391	2,791	103	27.09	7	1
A. N. Connolly	29	7,818	2,981	102	29.22	4	—
C. T. B. Turner	17	5,179	1,670	101	16.53	11	2

SOUTH AFRICA

	T	Balls	R	W	Avge	5 W/i	10 W/m
H. J. Tayfield	37	13,568	4,405	170	25.91	14	2
T. L. Goddard	41	11,736	3,226	123	26.22	5	—
P. M. Pollock	28	6,522	2,806	116	24.18	9	1
N. A. T. Adcock	26	6,391	2,195	104	21.10	5	—

WEST INDIES

	T	Balls	R	W	Avge	5 W/i	10 W/m
M. D. Marshall	68	15,221	6,831	329	20.76	22	4
L. R. Gibbs	79	27,115	8,989	309	29.09	18	2
J. Garner	58	13,169	5,433	259	20.97	7	—
M. A. Holding	60	12,680	5,898	249	23.68	13	2
G. S. Sobers	93	21,599	7,999	235	34.03	6	—
A. M. E. Roberts	47	11,136	5,174	202	25.61	11	2
W. W. Hall	48	10,421	5,066	192	26.38	9	1
S. Ramadhin	43	13,939	4,579	158	28.98	10	1
A. L. Valentine	36	12,953	4,215	139	30.32	8	2
C. A. Walsh	37	7,177	3,201	134	23.88	5	1
C. E. H. Croft	27	6,165	2,913	125	23.30	3	—
V. A. Holder	40	9,095	3,627	109	33.27	3	—

NEW ZEALAND

	T	Balls	R	W	Avge	5 W/i	10 W/m
Sir R. J. Hadlee	86	21,918	9,611	431	22.29	36	9
B. L. Cairns	43	10,628	4,280	130	32.92	6	1
E. J. Chatfield	43	10,360	3,958	123	32.17	3	1
R. O. Collinge	35	7,689	3,392	116	29.24	3	—
B. R. Taylor	30	6,334	2,953	111	26.60	4	—
J. G. Bracewell	41	8,403	3,653	102	35.81	4	1
R. C. Motz	32	7,034	3,148	100	31.48	5	—

INDIA

	T	*Balls*	*R*	*W*	*Avge*	*5 W/i*	*10 W/m*
Kapil Dev	109	23,037	11,199	371	30.18	21	2
B. S. Bedi	67	21,364	7,637	266	28.71	14	1
B. S. Chandrasekhar	58	15,963	7,199	242	29.74	16	2
E. A. S. Prasanna	49	14,353	5,742	189	30.38	10	2
V. Mankad	44	14,686	5,236	162	32.32	8	2
S. Venkataraghavan	57	14,877	5,634	156	36.11	3	1
S. P. Gupte	36	11,284	4,403	149	29.55	12	1
R. J. Shastri	72	15,103	5,914	143	41.35	2	—
D. R. Doshi	33	9,322	3,502	114	30.71	6	—
K. D. Ghavri	39	7,042	3,656	109	33.54	4	—
N. S. Yadav	35	8,349	3,580	102	35.09	3	—

PAKISTAN

	T	*Balls*	*R*	*W*	*Avge*	*5 W/i*	*10 W/m*
Imran Khan	82	19,290	8,188	358	22.87	23	6
Abdul Qadir	63	16,592	7,458	230	32.42	15	5
Sarfraz Nawaz	55	13,927	5,798	177	32.75	4	1
Iqbal Qasim	50	13,019	4,807	171	28.11	8	2
Fazal Mahmood	34	9,834	3,434	139	24.70	13	4
Intikhab Alam	47	10,474	4,494	125	35.95	5	2
Wasim Akram	32	7,017	2,967	111	26.72	8	2

SRI LANKA: The highest aggregate is 59 wickets, average 36.94, by A. L. F. de Mel in 17 Tests.

WICKET WITH FIRST BALL IN TEST CRICKET

	Batsman dismissed			
A. Coningham	A. C. MacLaren	A v E	Melbourne	1894-95
W. M. Bradley	F. Laver	E v A	Manchester	1899
E. G. Arnold	V. T. Trumper	E v A	Sydney	1903-04
G. G. Macaulay	G. A. L. Hearne	E v SA	Cape Town	1922-23
M. W. Tate	M. J. Susskind	E v SA	Birmingham	1924
M. Henderson	E. W. Dawson	NZ v E	Christchurch	1929-30
H. D. Smith	E. Paynter	NZ v E	Christchurch	1932-33
T. F. Johnson	W. W. Keeton	WI v E	The Oval	1939
R. Howorth	D. V. Dyer	E v SA	The Oval	1947
Intikhab Alam	C. C. McDonald	P v A	Karachi	1959-60

HAT-TRICKS

F. R. Spofforth	Australia v England at Melbourne	1878-79
W. Bates	England v Australia at Melbourne	1882-83
J. Briggs	England v Australia at Sydney	1891-92
G. A. Lohmann	England v South Africa at Port Elizabeth	1895-96
J. T. Hearne	England v Australia at Leeds	1899
H. Trumble	Australia v England at Melbourne	1901-02
H. Trumble	Australia v England at Melbourne	1903-04
T. J. Matthews† / T. J. Matthews	Australia v South Africa at Manchester	1912
M. J. C. Allom‡	England v New Zealand at Christchurch	1929-30

T. W. Goddard	England v South Africa at Johannesburg	1938-39
P. J. Loader	England v West Indies at Leeds	1957
L. F. Kline	Australia v South Africa at Cape Town	1957-58
W. W. Hall	West Indies v Pakistan at Lahore	1958-59
G. M. Griffin	South Africa v England at Lord's	1960
L. R. Gibbs	West Indies v Australia at Adelaide	1960-61
P. J. Petherick‡	New Zealand v Pakistan at Lahore	1976-77
C. A. Walsh§	West Indies v Australia at Brisbane	1988-89
M. G. Hughes§	Australia v West Indies at Perth	1988-89

† *T. J. Matthews did the hat-trick in each innings of the same match.*
‡ *On Test début.*
§ *Not all in the same innings.*

MOST BALLS BOWLED IN A TEST

S. Ramadhin (West Indies) sent down 774 balls in 129 overs against England at Birmingham, 1957. It was the most delivered by any bowler in a Test, beating H. Verity's 766 for England against South Africa at Durban, 1938-39. In this match Ramadhin also bowled the most balls (588) in any single first-class innings, including Tests.

It should be noted that six balls were bowled to the over in the Australia v England Test series of 1928-29 and 1932-33, when the eight-ball over was otherwise in force in Australia.

ALL-ROUND RECORDS

100 RUNS AND FIVE WICKETS IN AN INNINGS

England					
A. W. Greig	148	6-164	v West Indies	Bridgetown	1973-74
I. T. Botham	103	5-73	v New Zealand	Christchurch	1977-78
I. T. Botham	108	8-34	v Pakistan	Lord's	1978
I. T. Botham	114	6-58 / 7-48	v India	Bombay	1979-80
I. T. Botham	149*	6-95	v Australia	Leeds	1981
I. T. Botham	138	5-59	v New Zealand	Wellington	1983-84
Australia					
C. Kelleway	114	5-33	v South Africa	Manchester	1912
J. M. Gregory	100	7-69	v England	Melbourne	1920-21
K. R. Miller	109	6-107	v West Indies	Kingston	1954-55
R. Benaud	100	5-84	v South Africa	Johannesburg	1957-58
South Africa					
J. H. Sinclair	106	6-26	v England	Cape Town	1898-99
G. A. Faulkner	123	5-120	v England	Johannesburg	1909-10
West Indies					
D. St E. Atkinson	219	5-56	v Australia	Bridgetown	1954-55
O. G. Smith	100	5-90	v India	Delhi	1958-59
G. S. Sobers	104	5-63	v India	Kingston	1961-62
G. S. Sobers	174	5-41	v England	Leeds	1966
New Zealand					
B. R. Taylor†	105	5-86	v India	Calcutta	1964-65
India					
V. Mankad	184	5-196	v England	Lord's	1952
P. R. Umrigar	172*	5-107	v West Indies	Port-of-Spain	1961-62
Pakistan					
Mushtaq Mohammad	201	5-49	v New Zealand	Dunedin	1972-73
Mushtaq Mohammad	121	5-28	v West Indies	Port-of-Spain	1976-77
Imran Khan	117	6-98 / 5-82	v India	Faisalabad	1982-83
Wasim Akram	123	5-100	v Australia	Adelaide	1989-90

† *On début.*

100 RUNS AND FIVE DISMISSALS IN AN INNINGS

D. T. Lindsay	182	6ct	SA v A	Johannesburg	1966-67
I. D. S. Smith	113*	4ct, 1st	NZ v E	Auckland	1983-84
S. A. R. Silva	111	5ct	SL v I	Colombo (PSS)	1985-86

100 RUNS AND TEN WICKETS IN A TEST

A. K. Davidson	44 80	5-135 6-87	A v WI	Brisbane	1960-61
I. T. Botham	114	6-58 7-48	E v I	Bombay	1979-80
Imran Khan	117	6-98 5-82	P v I	Faisalabad	1982-83

1,000 RUNS AND 100 WICKETS IN A CAREER

	Tests	*Runs*	*Wkts*	*Tests for Double*
England				
T. E. Bailey	61	2,290	132	47
I. T. Botham	97	5,119	376	21
J. E. Emburey	60	1,540	138	46
A. W. Greig	58	3,599	141	37
R. Illingworth	61	1,836	122	47
W. Rhodes	58	2,325	127	44
M. W. Tate	39	1,198	155	33
F. J. Titmus	53	1,449	153	40
Australia				
R. Benaud	63	2,201	248	32
A. K. Davidson	44	1,328	186	34
G. Giffen	31	1,238	103	30
I. W. Johnson	45	1,000	109	45
R. R. Lindwall	61	1,502	228	38
K. R. Miller	55	2,958	170	33
M. A. Noble	42	1,997	121	27
South Africa				
T. L. Goddard	41	2,516	123	36
West Indies				
M. D. Marshall	68	1,457	329	49
G. S. Sobers	93	8,032	235	48
New Zealand				
J. G. Bracewell	41	1,001	102	41
Sir R. J. Hadlee	86	3,124	431	28
India				
Kapil Dev	109	4,521	371	25
V. Mankad	44	2,109	162	23
R. J. Shastri	72	3,372	143	44
Pakistan				
Abdul Qadir	63	1,022	230	62
Imran Khan	82	3,541	358	30
Intikhab Alam	47	1,493	125	41
Sarfraz Nawaz	55	1,045	177	55

1,000 RUNS, 100 WICKETS AND 100 CATCHES

	Tests	Runs	Wkts	Ct
I. T. Botham	97	5,119	376	112
G. S. Sobers	93	8,032	235	109

WICKET-KEEPING RECORDS

Most Dismissals in an Innings

7 (all ct)	Wasim Bari	Pakistan v New Zealand at Auckland	1978-79
7 (all ct)	R. W. Taylor	England v India at Bombay	1979-80
6 (all ct)	A. T. W. Grout	Australia v South Africa at Johannesburg	1957-58
6 (all ct)	D. T. Lindsay	South Africa v Australia at Johannesburg	1966-67
6 (all ct)	J. T. Murray	England v India at Lord's	1967
6 (5ct, 1st)	S. M. H. Kirmani	India v New Zealand at Christchurch	1975-76
6 (all ct)	R. W. Marsh	Australia v England at Brisbane	1982-83
6 (all ct)	S. A. R. Silva	Sri Lanka v India at Colombo (SSC)	1985-86

Note: The most stumpings in an innings is 5 by K. S. More for India v West Indies at Madras in 1987-88.

Most Dismissals in One Test

10 (all ct)	R. W. Taylor	England v India at Bombay	1979-80
9 (8ct, 1st)	G. R. A. Langley	Australia v England at Lord's	1956
9 (all ct)	D. A. Murray	West Indies v Australia at Melbourne	1981-82
9 (all ct)	R. W. Marsh	Australia v England at Brisbane	1982-83
9 (all ct)	S. A. R. Silva	Sri Lanka v India at Colombo (SSC)	1985-86
9 (8ct, 1st)	S. A. R. Silva	Sri Lanka v India at Colombo (PSS)	1985-86
8 (all ct)	J. J. Kelly	Australia v England at Sydney	1901-02
8 (6ct, 2st)	L. E. G. Ames	England v West Indies at The Oval	1933
8 (all ct)	G. R. A. Langley	Australia v West Indies at Kingston	1954-55
8 (6ct, 2st)	A. T. W. Grout	Australia v Pakistan at Lahore	1959-60
8 (all ct)	A. T. W. Grout	Australia v England at Lord's	1961
8 (all ct)	J. M. Parks	England v New Zealand at Christchurch	1965-66
8 (all ct)	D. T. Lindsay	South Africa v Australia at Johannesburg	1966-67
8 (7ct, 1st)	H. B. Taber	Australia v South Africa at Johannesburg	1966-67
8 (all ct)	Wasim Bari	Pakistan v England at Leeds	1971
8 (all ct)	R. W. Marsh	Australia v West Indies at Melbourne	1975-76
8 (all ct)	R. W. Marsh	Australia v New Zealand at Christchurch	1976-77
8 (7ct, 1st)	R. W. Marsh	Australia v India at Sydney	1980-81
8 (all ct)	W. K. Lees	New Zealand v Sri Lanka at Wellington	1982-83
8 (all ct)	R. W. Marsh	Australia v England at Adelaide	1982-83

Notes: S. A. R. Silva made 18 dismissals in two successive Tests.

The most stumpings in a match is 6 by K. S. More for India v West Indies at Madras in 1987-88.

Most Dismissals in a Series

(*Played in 5 Tests unless otherwise stated*)

28 (all ct)	R. W. Marsh	Australia v England	1982-83
26 (23ct, 3st)	J. H. B. Waite	South Africa v New Zealand	1961-62
26 (all ct)	R. W. Marsh	Australia v West Indies (6 Tests)	1975-76
24 (22ct, 2st)	D. L. Murray	West Indies v England	1963
24 (all ct)	D. T. Lindsay	South Africa v Australia	1966-67

24 (21ct, 3st)	A. P. E. Knott	England v Australia (6 Tests)	1970-71
23 (16ct, 7st)	J. H. B. Waite	South Africa v New Zealand	1953-54
23 (22ct, 1st)	F. C. M. Alexander	West Indies v England	1959-60
23 (20ct, 3st)	A. T. W. Grout	Australia v West Indies	1960-61
23 (21ct, 2st)	A. E. Dick	New Zealand v South Africa	1961-62
23 (21ct, 2st)	R. W. Marsh	Australia v England	1972
23 (22ct, 1st)	A. P. E. Knott	England v Australia (6 Tests)	1974-75
23 (all ct)	R. W. Marsh	Australia v England (6 Tests)	1981
22 (all ct)	S. J. Rixon	Australia v India	1977-78
22 (21ct, 1st)	S. A. R. Silva	Sri Lanka v India (3 Tests)	1985-86
21 (15ct, 6st)	H. Strudwick	England v South Africa	1913-14
21 (13ct, 8st)	R. A. Saggers	Australia v South Africa	1949-50
21 (16ct, 5st)	G. R. A. Langley	Australia v West Indies	1951-52
21 (20ct, 1st)	A. T. W. Grout	Australia v England	1961
21 (all ct)	R. W. Marsh	Australia v Pakistan	1983-84
20 (16ct, 4st)	D. Tallon	Australia v England	1946-47
20 (16ct, 4st)	G. R. A. Langley	Australia v West Indies (4 Tests)	1954-55
20 (18ct, 2st)	T. G. Evans	England v South Africa	1956-57
20 (17ct, 3st)	A. T. W. Grout	Australia v England	1958-59
20 (19ct, 1st)	H. B. Taber	Australia v South Africa	1966-67
20 (18ct, 2st)	R. W. Taylor	England v Australia (6 Tests)	1978-79
20 (19ct, 1st)	P. J. L. Dujon	West Indies v Australia	1983-84
20 (19ct, 1st)	P. R. Downton	England v Australia (6 Tests)	1985
20 (all ct)	P. J. L. Dujon	West Indies v England	1988

Most Dismissals in a Career

	T	*Ct*	*St*	*Total*
R. W. Marsh (Australia)	96	343	12	355
A. P. E. Knott (England)	95	250	19	269
Wasim Bari (Pakistan)	81	201	27	228
P. J. L. Dujon (West Indies)	68	218	5	223
T. G. Evans (England)	91	173	46	219
S. M. H. Kirmani (India)	88	160	38	198
D. L. Murray (West Indies)	62	181	8	189
A. T. W. Grout (Australia)	51	163	24	187
R. W. Taylor (England)	57	167	7	174
I. D. S. Smith (New Zealand)	55	143	8	151
J. H. B. Waite (South Africa)	50	124	17	141
W. A. Oldfield (Australia)	54	78	52	130
J. M. Parks (England)	46	103	11	114

Notes: The records for P. J. L. Dujon and J. M. Parks each include two catches taken when not keeping wicket in two and three Tests respectively.

S. A. R. Silva (33ct, 1st) has made most dismissals for Sri Lanka.

FIELDING RECORDS

(Excluding wicket-keepers)

Most Catches in an Innings

5	V. Y. Richardson	Australia v South Africa at Durban	1935-36
5	Yajurvindra Singh	India v England at Bangalore	1976-77
5	M. Azharuddin	India v Pakistan at Karachi	1989-90

Most Catches in One Test

7	G. S. Chappell	Australia v England at Perth	1974-75
7	Yajurvindra Singh	India v England at Bangalore	1976-77
6	A. Shrewsbury	England v Australia at Sydney	1887-88
6	A. E. E. Vogler	South Africa v England at Durban	1909-10
6	F. E. Woolley	England v Australia at Sydney	1911-12
6	J. M. Gregory	Australia v England at Sydney	1920-21
6	B. Mitchell	South Africa v Australia at Melbourne	1931-32
6	V. Y. Richardson	Australia v South Africa at Durban	1935-36
6	R. N. Harvey	Australia v England at Sydney	1962-63
6	M. C. Cowdrey	England v West Indies at Lord's	1963
6	E. D. Solkar	India v West Indies at Port-of-Spain	1970-71
6	G. S. Sobers	West Indies v England at Lord's	1973
6	I. M. Chappell	Australia v New Zealand at Adelaide	1973-74
6	A. W. Greig	England v Pakistan at Leeds	1974
6	D. F. Whatmore	Australia v India at Kanpur	1979-80
6	A. J. Lamb	England v New Zealand at Lord's	1983

Most Catches in a Series

15	J. M. Gregory	Australia v England	1920-21
14	G. S. Chappell	Australia v England (6 Tests)	1974-75
13	R. B. Simpson	Australia v South Africa	1957-58
13	R. B. Simpson	Australia v West Indies	1960-61

Most Catches in a Career

A. R. Border (Australia)	125 in 115 matches
G. S. Chappell (Australia)	122 in 87 matches
M. C. Cowdrey (England)	120 in 114 matches
I. V. A. Richards (West Indies)	116 in 111 matches
I. T. Botham (England)	112 in 97 matches
R. B. Simpson (Australia)	110 in 62 matches
W. R. Hammond (England)	110 in 85 matches
G. S. Sobers (West Indies)	109 in 93 matches
S. M. Gavaskar (India)	108 in 125 matches
I. M. Chappell (Australia)	105 in 75 matches

TEAM RECORDS

HIGHEST INNINGS TOTALS

903-7 dec.	England v Australia at The Oval	1938
849	England v West Indies at Kingston	1929-30
790-3 dec.	West Indies v Pakistan at Kingston	1957-58
758-8 dec.	Australia v West Indies at Kingston	1954-55
729-6 dec.	Australia v England at Lord's	1930
708	Pakistan v England at The Oval	1987
701	Australia v England at The Oval	1934
699-5	Pakistan v India at Lahore	1989-90
695	Australia v England at The Oval	1930
687-8 dec.	West Indies v England at The Oval	1976
681-8 dec.	West Indies v England at Port-of-Spain	1953-54
676-7	India v Sri Lanka at Kanpur	1986-87
674-6	Pakistan v India at Faisalabad	1984-85
674	Australia v India at Adelaide	1947-48
668	Australia v West Indies at Bridgetown	1954-55
659-8 dec.	Australia v England at Sydney	1946-47
658-8 dec.	England v Australia at Nottingham	1938
657-8 dec.	Pakistan v West Indies at Bridgetown	1957-58
656-8 dec.	Australia v England at Manchester	1964

654-5	England v South Africa at Durban	1938-39
653-4 dec.	England v India at Lord's	1990
652-7 dec.	England v India at Madras	1984-85
652-8 dec.	West Indies v England at Lord's	1973
652	Pakistan v India at Faisalabad	1982-83
650-6 dec.	Australia v West Indies at Bridgetown	1964-65

The highest innings for the countries not mentioned above are:

622-9 dec.	South Africa v Australia at Durban	1969-70
553-7 dec.	New Zealand v Australia at Brisbane	1985-86
491-7 dec.	Sri Lanka v England at Lord's	1984

HIGHEST FOURTH-INNINGS TOTALS

To win

406-4	India (needing 403) v West Indies at Port-of-Spain	1975-76
404-3	Australia (needing 404) v England at Leeds	1948
362-7	Australia (needing 359) v West Indies at Georgetown	1977-78
348-5	West Indies (needing 345) v New Zealand at Auckland	1968-69
344-1	West Indies (needing 342) v England at Lord's	1984

To tie

347	India v Australia at Madras	1986-87

To draw

654-5	England (needing 696 to win) v South Africa at Durban	1938-39
429-8	India (needing 438 to win) v England at The Oval	1979
423-7	South Africa (needing 451 to win) v England at The Oval	1947
408-5	West Indies (needing 836 to win) v England at Kingston	1929-30

To lose

445	India (lost by 47 runs) v Australia at Adelaide	1977-78
440	New Zealand (lost by 38 runs) v England at Nottingham	1973
417	England (lost by 45 runs) v Australia at Melbourne	1976-77
411	England (lost by 193 runs) v Australia at Sydney	1924-25

MOST RUNS IN A DAY (BOTH SIDES)

588	England (398-6), India (190-0) at Manchester (2nd day)	1936
522	England (503-2), South Africa (19-0) at Lord's (2nd day)	1924
508	England (221-2), South Africa (287-6) at The Oval (3rd day)	1935

MOST RUNS IN A DAY (ONE SIDE)

503	England (503-2) v South Africa at Lord's (2nd day)	1924
494	Australia (494-6) v South Africa at Sydney (1st day)	1910-11
475	Australia (475-2) v England at The Oval (1st day)	1934
471	England (471-8) v India at The Oval (1st day)	1936
458	Australia (458-3) v England at Leeds (1st day)	1930
455	Australia (455-1) v England at Leeds (2nd day)	1934

MOST WICKETS IN A DAY

27	England (18-3 to 53 out and 62) v Australia (60) at Lord's (2nd day)	1888
25	Australia (112 and 48-5) v England (61) at Melbourne (1st day)	1901-02

HIGHEST MATCH AGGREGATES

Runs	*Wkts*			*Days played*
1,981	35	South Africa v England at Durban	1938-39	10†
1,815	34	West Indies v England at Kingston	1929-30	9‡
1,764	39	Australia v West Indies at Adelaide	1968-69	5
1,753	40	Australia v England at Adelaide	1920-21	6
1,723	31	England v Australia at Leeds	1948	5
1,661	36	West Indies v Australia at Bridgetown	1954-55	6

† *No play on one day.* ‡ *No play on two days.*

LOWEST INNINGS TOTALS

26	New Zealand v England at Auckland	1954-55
30	South Africa v England at Port Elizabeth	1895-96
30	South Africa v England at Birmingham	1924
35	South Africa v England at Cape Town	1898-99
36	Australia v England at Birmingham	1902
36	South Africa v Australia at Melbourne	1931-32
42	Australia v England at Sydney	1887-88
42	New Zealand v Australia at Wellington	1945-46
42†	India v England at Lord's	1974
43	South Africa v England at Cape Town	1888-89
44	Australia v England at The Oval	1896
45	England v Australia at Sydney	1886-87
45	South Africa v Australia at Melbourne	1931-32
47	South Africa v England at Cape Town	1888-89
47	New Zealand v England at Lord's	1958

The lowest innings for the countries not mentioned above are:

53	West Indies v Pakistan at Faisalabad	1986-87
62	Pakistan v Australia at Perth	1981-82
93	Sri Lanka v New Zealand at Wellington	1982-83

† *Batted one man short.*

FEWEST RUNS IN A FULL DAY'S PLAY

95 At Karachi, October 11, 1956. Australia 80 all out; Pakistan 15 for two (first day, 5½ hours).

104 At Karachi, December 8, 1959. Pakistan 0 for no wicket to 104 for five v Australia (fourth day, 5½ hours).

106 At Brisbane, December 9, 1958. England 92 for two to 198 all out v Australia (fourth day, 5 hours). *England were dismissed five minutes before the close of play, leaving no time for Australia to start their second innings.*

112 At Karachi, October 15, 1956. Australia 138 for six to 187 all out; Pakistan 63 for one (fourth day, 5½ hours).

115 At Karachi, September 19, 1988. Australia 116 for seven to 165 all out and 66 for five following on v Pakistan (fourth day, 5½ hours).

117 At Madras, October 19, 1956. India 117 for five v Australia (first day, 5½ hours).

117 At Colombo (SSC), March 21, 1984. New Zealand 6 for no wicket to 123 for four (fifth day, 5 hours, 47 minutes).

In England

151 At Lord's, August 26, 1978. England 175 for two to 289 all out; New Zealand 37 for seven (third day, 6 hours).

159 At Leeds, July 10, 1971. Pakistan 208 for four to 350 all out; England 17 for one (third day, 6 hours).

LOWEST MATCH AGGREGATES

(For a completed match)

Runs	*Wkts*			*Days played*
234	29	Australia v South Africa at Melbourne	1931-32	3†
291	40	England v Australia at Lord's	1888	2
295	28	New Zealand v Australia at Wellington	1945-46	2
309	29	West Indies v England at Bridgetown	1934-35	3
323	30	England v Australia at Manchester	1888	2

† *No play on one day.*

YOUNGEST TEST PLAYERS

Years	*Days*			
15	124	Mushtaq Mohammad	Pakistan v West Indies at Lahore	1958-59
16	189	Aaqib Javed	Pakistan v New Zealand at Wellington	1988-89
16	205	S. R. Tendulkar	India v Pakistan at Karachi	1989-90
16	221	Aftab Baloch	Pakistan v New Zealand at Dacca	1969-70
16	248	Nasim-ul-Ghani	Pakistan v West Indies at Bridgetown	1957-58
16	352	Khalid Hassan	Pakistan v England at Nottingham	1954
17	118	L. Sivaramakrishnan	India v West Indies at St John's	1982-83
17	122	J. E. D. Sealy	West Indies v England at Bridgetown	1929-30
17	189	C. D. U. S. Weerasinghe	Sri Lanka v India at Colombo (PSS)	1985-86
17	193	Maninder Singh	India v Pakistan at Karachi	1982-83
17	239	I. D. Craig	Australia v South Africa at Melbourne	1952-53
17	245	G. S. Sobers	West Indies v England at Kingston	1953-54
17	265	V. L. Mehra	India v New Zealand at Bombay	1955-56
17	300	Hanif Mohammad	Pakistan v India at Delhi	1952-53
17	341	Intikhab Alam	Pakistan v Australia at Karachi	1959-60
17	364	Waqar Younis	Pakistan v India at Karachi	1989-90

Note: The youngest Test players for countries not mentioned above are: England – D. B. Close, 18 years 149 days, v New Zealand at Manchester, 1949; New Zealand – D. L. Freeman, 18 years 197 days, v England at Christchurch, 1932-33; South Africa – A. E. Ochse, 19 years 1 day, v England at Port Elizabeth, 1888-89.

OLDEST PLAYERS ON TEST DEBUT

Years	*Days*			
49	119	J. Southerton	England v Australia at Melbourne	1876-77
47	284	Miran Bux	Pakistan v India at Lahore	1954-55
46	253	D. D. Blackie	Australia v England at Sydney	1928-29
46	237	H. Ironmonger	Australia v England at Brisbane	1928-29
42	242	N. Betancourt	West Indies v England at Port-of-Spain	1929-30
41	337	E. R. Wilson	England v Australia at Sydney	1920-21
41	27	R. J. D. Jamshedji	India v England at Bombay	1933-34

Years	*Days*			
40	345	C. A. Wiles	West Indies v England at Manchester . .	1933
40	216	S. P. Kinneir . . .	England v Australia at Sydney	1911-12
40	110	H. W. Lee	England v South Africa at Johannesburg	1930-31
40	56	G. W. A. Chubb	South Africa v England at Nottingham .	1951
40	37	C. Ramaswami . .	India v England at Manchester	1936

Note: The oldest Test player on début for New Zealand was H. M. McGirr, 38 years 101 days, v England at Auckland, 1929-30; for Sri Lanka, D. S. de Silva, 39 years 251 days, v England at Colombo (PSO), 1981-82.

OLDEST TEST PLAYERS

(Age on final day of their last Test match)

Years	*Days*			
52	165	W. Rhodes	England v West Indies at Kingston . . .	1929-30
50	327	H. Ironmonger	Australia v England at Sydney	1932-33
50	320	W. G. Grace	England v Australia at Nottingham . . .	1899
50	303	G. Gunn	England v West Indies at Kingston . . .	1929-30
49	139	J. Southerton	England v Australia at Melbourne	1876-77
47	302	Miran Bux	Pakistan v India at Peshawar	1954-55
47	249	J. B. Hobbs	England v Australia at The Oval	1930
47	87	F. E. Woolley	England v Australia at The Oval	1934
46	309	D. D. Blackie	Australia v England at Adelaide	1928-29
46	206	A. W. Nourse	South Africa v England at The Oval . . .	1924
46	202	H. Strudwick	England v Australia at The Oval	1926
46	41	E. H. Hendren	England v West Indies at Kingston . . .	1934-35
45	245	G. O. B. Allen	England v West Indies at Kingston . . .	1947-48
45	215	P. Holmes	England v India at Lord's	1932
45	140	D. B. Close	England v West Indies at Manchester .	1976

MOST TEST MATCH APPEARANCES

For	*Total*		*E*	*A*	*SA*	*WI*	*NZ*	*I*	*P*	*SL*
England	114	M. C. Cowdrey	—	43	14	21	18	8	10	—
Australia	115	A. R. Border	36	—	—	21	17	15	22	4
South Africa	50	J. H. B. Waite	21	14	—	—	15	—	—	—
West Indies	111	I. V. A. Richards	31	29	—	—	7	28	16	—
New Zealand	86	Sir R. J. Hadlee	21	23	—	10	—	14	12	6
India	125	S. M. Gavaskar	38	20	—	27	9	—	24	7
Pakistan	104	Javed Miandad	17	25	—	11	14	28	—	9
Sri Lanka	26	A. Ranatunga	3	4	—	—	4	7	8	—

MOST CONSECUTIVE TEST APPEARANCES

112	A. R. Border (Australia)	March 1979 to March 1990
106	S. M. Gavaskar (India)	January 1975 to February 1987
87	G. R. Viswanath (India)	March 1971 to February 1983
85	G. S. Sobers (West Indies)	April 1955 to April 1972
72	D. L. Haynes (West Indies)	December 1979 to June 1988
71	I. M. Chappell (Australia)	January 1966 to February 1976
66	Kapil Dev (India)	October 1978 to December 1984
65	I. T. Botham (England)	February 1978 to March 1984
65	A. P. E. Knott (England)	March 1971 to August 1977

The most consecutive Test appearances for the countries not mentioned above are:

58†	J. R. Reid (New Zealand)	July 1949 to July 1965
53	Javed Miandad (Pakistan)	December 1977 to January 1984
45†	A. W. Nourse (South Africa) ...	October 1902 to August 1924
22	A. Ranatunga (Sri Lanka)	April 1983 to December 1989

† *Indicates complete Test career.*

SUMMARY OF ALL TEST MATCHES

To end of 1990 season in England

		Tests	*Won by*								*Tied*	*Drawn*
			E	*A*	*SA*	*WI*	*NZ*	*I*	*P*	*SL*		
England	v Australia	269	88	101	–	–	–	–	–	–	–	80
	v South Africa	102	46	–	18	–	–	–	–	–	–	38
	v West Indies	99	22	–	–	41	–	–	–	–	–	36
	v New Zealand	69	31	–	–	–	4	–	–	–	–	34
	v India	78	31	–	–	–	–	11	–	–	–	36
	v Pakistan	47	13	–	–	–	–	–	5	–	–	29
	v Sri Lanka	3	2	–	–	–	–	–	–	0	–	1
Australia	v South Africa	53	–	29	11	–	–	–	–	–	–	13
	v West Indies	67	–	28	–	22	–	–	–	–	1	16
	v New Zealand	26	–	10	–	–	6	–	–	–	–	10
	v India	45	–	20	–	–	–	8	–	–	1	16
	v Pakistan	34	–	12	–	–	–	–	9	–	–	13
	v Sri Lanka	4	–	3	–	–	–	–	–	0	–	1
South Africa	v New Zealand	17	–	–	9	–	2	–	–	–	–	6
West Indies	v New Zealand	24	–	–	–	8	4	–	–	–	–	12
	v India	62	–	–	–	26	–	6	–	–	–	30
	v Pakistan	25	–	–	–	9	–	–	6	–	–	10
New Zealand	v India	31	–	–	–	–	6	12	–	–	–	13
	v Pakistan	29	–	–	–	–	3	–	10	–	–	16
	v Sri Lanka	6	–	–	–	–	4	–	–	0	–	2
India	v Pakistan	44	–	–	–	–	–	4	7	–	–	33
	v Sri Lanka	7	–	–	–	–	–	2	–	1	–	4
Pakistan	v Sri Lanka	9	–	–	–	–	–	–	5	1	–	3
		1,150	233	203	38	106	29	43	42	2	2	452

	Tests	*Won*	*Lost*	*Drawn*	*Tied*	*Toss Won*
England	667	233	180	254	–	330
Australia	498	203	144	149	2	250
South Africa	172	38	77	57	–	80
West Indies	277	106	66	104	1	145
New Zealand	202	29	80	93	–	100
India	267	43	91	132	1	132
Pakistan	188	42	42	104	–	98
Sri Lanka	29	2	16	11	–	15

ENGLAND v AUSTRALIA

	Captains					
Season	*England*	*Australia*	*T*	*E*	*A*	*D*
1876-77	James Lillywhite	D. W. Gregory	2	1	1	0
1878-79	Lord Harris	D. W. Gregory	1	0	1	0
1880	Lord Harris	W. L. Murdoch	1	1	0	0
1881-82	A. Shaw	W. L. Murdoch	4	0	2	2
1882	A. N. Hornby	W. L. Murdoch	1	0	1	0

THE ASHES

Season	*Captains* *England*	*Australia*	*T*	*E*	*A*	*D*	*Held by*
1882-83	Hon. Ivo Bligh	W. L. Murdoch	4*	2	2	0	E
1884	Lord Harris[1]	W. L. Murdoch	3	1	0	2	E
1884-85	A. Shrewsbury	T. Horan[2]	5	3	2	0	E
1886	A. G. Steel	H. J. H. Scott	3	3	0	0	E
1886-87	A. Shrewsbury	P. S. McDonnell	2	2	0	0	E
1887-88	W. W. Read	P. S. McDonnell	1	1	0	0	E
1888	W. G. Grace[3]	P. S. McDonnell	3	2	1	0	E
1890†	W. G. Grace	W. L. Murdoch	2	2	0	0	E
1891-92	W. G. Grace	J. McC. Blackham	3	1	2	0	A
1893	W. G. Grace[4]	J. McC. Blackham	3	1	0	2	E
1894-95	A. E. Stoddart	G. Giffen[5]	5	3	2	0	E
1896	W. G. Grace	G. H. S. Trott	3	2	1	0	E
1897-98	A. E. Stoddart[6]	G. H. S. Trott	5	1	4	0	A
1899	A. C. MacLaren[7]	J. Darling	5	0	1	4	A
1901-02	A. C. MacLaren	J. Darling[8]	5	1	4	0	A
1902	A. C. MacLaren	J. Darling	5	1	2	2	A
1903-04	P. F. Warner	M. A. Noble	5	3	2	0	E
1905	Hon. F. S. Jackson	J. Darling	5	2	0	3	E
1907-08	A. O. Jones[9]	M. A. Noble	5	1	4	0	A
1909	A. C. MacLaren	M. A. Noble	5	1	2	2	A
1911-12	J. W. H. T. Douglas	C. Hill	5	4	1	0	E
1912	C. B. Fry	S. E. Gregory	3	1	0	2	E
1920-21	J. W. H. T. Douglas	W. W. Armstrong	5	0	5	0	A
1921	Hon. L. H. Tennyson[10]	W. W. Armstrong	5	0	3	2	A
1924-25	A. E. R. Gilligan	H. L. Collins	5	1	4	0	A
1926	A. W. Carr[11]	H. L. Collins[12]	5	1	0	4	E
1928-29	A. P. F. Chapman[13]	J. Ryder	5	4	1	0	E
1930	A. P. F. Chapman[14]	W. M. Woodfull	5	1	2	2	A
1932-33	D. R. Jardine	W. M. Woodfull	5	4	1	0	E
1934	R. E. S. Wyatt[15]	W. M. Woodfull	5	1	2	2	A
1936-37	G. O. B. Allen	D. G. Bradman	5	2	3	0	A
1938†	W. R. Hammond	D. G. Bradman	4	1	1	2	A
1946-47	W. R. Hammond[16]	D. G. Bradman	5	0	3	2	A
1948	N. W. D. Yardley	D. G. Bradman	5	0	4	1	A
1950-51	F. R. Brown	A. L. Hassett	5	1	4	0	A
1953	L. Hutton	A. L. Hassett	5	1	0	4	E
1954-55	L. Hutton	I. W. Johnson[17]	5	3	1	1	E
1956	P. B. H. May	I. W. Johnson	5	2	1	2	E
1958-59	P. B. H. May	R. Benaud	5	0	4	1	A
1961	P. B. H. May[18]	R. Benaud[19]	5	1	2	2	A
1962-63	E. R. Dexter	R. Benaud	5	1	1	3	A
1964	E. R. Dexter	R. B. Simpson	5	0	1	4	A
1965-66	M. J. K. Smith	R. B. Simpson[20]	5	1	1	3	A
1968	M. C. Cowdrey[21]	W. M. Lawry[22]	5	1	1	3	A
1970-71†	R. Illingworth	W. M. Lawry[23]	6	2	0	4	E
1972	R. Illingworth	I. M. Chappell	5	2	2	1	E
1974-75	M. H. Denness[24]	I. M. Chappell	6	1	4	1	A
1975	A. W. Greig[25]	I. M. Chappell	4	0	1	3	A
1976-77‡	A. W. Greig	G. S. Chappell	1	0	1	0	—
1977	J. M. Brearley	G. S. Chappell	5	3	0	2	E
1978-79	J. M. Brearley	G. N. Yallop	6	5	1	0	E
1979-80‡	J. M. Brearley	G. S. Chappell	3	0	3	0	—
1980‡	I. T. Botham	G. S. Chappell	1	0	0	1	—
1981	J. M. Brearley[26]	K. J. Hughes	6	3	1	2	E
1982-83	R. G. D. Willis	G. S. Chappell	5	1	2	2	A
1985	D. I. Gower	A. R. Border	6	3	1	2	E
1986-87	M. W. Gatting	A. R. Border	5	2	1	2	E
1987-88‡	M. W. Gatting	A. R. Border	1	0	0	1	—
1989	D. I. Gower	A. R. Border	6	0	4	2	A
	In Australia		140	51	67	22	
	In England		129	37	34	58	
	Totals		269	88	101	80	

* *The Ashes were awarded in 1882-83 after a series of three matches which England won 2-1. A fourth unofficial match was played, each innings being played on a different pitch, and this was won by Australia.*

† *The matches at Manchester in 1890 and 1938 and at Melbourne (Third Test) in 1970-71 were abandoned without a ball being bowled and are excluded.*

‡ *The Ashes were not at stake in these series.*

Notes: The following deputised for the official touring captain or were appointed by the home authority for only a minor proportion of the series:

[1]A. N. Hornby (First). [2]W. L. Murdoch (First), H. H. Massie (Third), J. McC. Blackham (Fourth). [3]A. G. Steel (First). [4]A. E. Stoddart (First). [5]J. McC. Blackham (First). [6]A. C. MacLaren (First, Second and Fifth). [7]W. G. Grace (First). [8]H. Trumble (Fourth and Fifth). [9]F. L. Fane (First, Second and Third). [10]J. W. H. T. Douglas (First and Second). [11]A. P. F. Chapman (Fifth). [12]W. Bardsley (Third and Fourth). [13]J. C. White (Fifth). [14]R. E. S. Wyatt (Fifth). [15]C. F. Walters (First). [16]N. W. D. Yardley (Fifth). [17]A. R. Morris (Second). [18]M. C. Cowdrey (First and Second). [19]R. N. Harvey (Second). [20]B. C. Booth (First and Third). [21]T. W. Graveney (Fourth). [22]B. N. Jarman (Fourth). [23]I. M. Chappell (Seventh). [24]J. H. Edrich (Fourth). [25]M. H. Denness (First). [26]I. T. Botham (First and Second).

HIGHEST INNINGS TOTALS

For England in England: 903-7 dec. at The Oval 1938
in Australia: 636 at Sydney 1928-29

For Australia in England: 729-6 dec. at Lord's 1930
in Australia: 659-8 dec. at Sydney 1946-47

LOWEST INNINGS TOTALS

For England in England: 52 at The Oval 1948
in Australia: 45 at Sydney 1886-87

For Australia in England: 36 at Birmingham 1902
in Australia: 42 at Sydney 1887-88

INDIVIDUAL HUNDREDS

For England (192)

R. Abel (1)
132*‡ Sydney 1891-92
L. E. G. Ames (1)
120 Lord's 1934
R. W. Barber (1)
185 Sydney 1965-66
W. Barnes (1)
134 Adelaide 1884-85
C. J. Barnett (2)
129 Adelaide 1936-37
126 Nottingham . 1938
K. F. Barrington (5)
132* Adelaide 1962-63
101 Sydney 1962-63
256 Manchester . 1964
102 Adelaide 1965-66
115 Melbourne .. 1965-66

I. T. Botham (4)
119* Melbourne .. 1979-80
149* Leeds 1981
118 Manchester . 1981
138 Brisbane 1986-87
G. Boycott (7)
113 The Oval ... 1964
142* Sydney 1970-71
119* Adelaide 1970-71
107 Nottingham . 1977
191 Leeds 1977
128* Lord's 1980
137 The Oval ... 1981
L. C. Braund (2)
103* Adelaide 1901-02
102 Sydney 1903-04

J. Briggs (1)
121 Melbourne .. 1884-85
B. C. Broad (4)
162 Perth 1986-87
116 Adelaide 1986-87
112 Melbourne .. 1986-87
139 Sydney 1987-88
J. T. Brown (1)
140 Melbourne .. 1894-95
A. P. F. Chapman (1)
121 Lord's 1930
D. C. S. Compton (5)
102† Nottingham . 1938
147 }
103* } Adelaide 1946-47
184 Nottingham . 1948
145* Manchester . 1948

M. C. Cowdrey (5)
102 Melbourne .. 1954-55
100* Sydney 1958-59
113 Melbourne .. 1962-63
104 Melbourne .. 1965-66
104 Birmingham . 1968
M. H. Denness (1)
188 Melbourne .. 1974-75
E. R. Dexter (2)
180 Birmingham . 1961
174 Manchester . 1964
B. L. D'Oliveira (2)
158 The Oval 1968
117 Melbourne .. 1970-71
K. S. Duleepsinhji (1)
173† Lord's 1930
J. H. Edrich (7)
120† Lord's 1964
109 Melbourne .. 1965-66
103 Sydney 1965-66
164 The Oval ... 1968
115* Perth 1970-71
130 Adelaide 1970-71
175 Lord's 1975
W. J. Edrich (2)
119 Sydney 1946-47
111 Leeds 1948
K. W. R. Fletcher (1)
146 Melbourne .. 1974-75
R. E. Foster (1)
287† Sydney 1903-04
C. B. Fry (1)
144 The Oval ... 1905
M. W. Gatting (3)
160 Manchester . 1985
100* Birmingham . 1985
100 Adelaide 1986-87
G. A. Gooch (1)
196 The Oval ... 1985
D. I. Gower (7)
102 Perth 1978-79
114 Adelaide 1982-83
166 Nottingham . 1985
215 Birmingham . 1985
157 The Oval ... 1985
136 Perth 1986-87
106 Lord's 1989
W. G. Grace (2)
152† The Oval ... 1880
170 The Oval ... 1886
T. W. Graveney (1)
111 Sydney 1954-55
A. W. Greig (1)
110 Brisbane 1974-75
G. Gunn (2)
119† Sydney 1907-08
122* Sydney 1907-08
W. Gunn (1)
102* Manchester . 1893
W. R. Hammond (9)
251 Sydney 1928-29
200 Melbourne .. 1928-29
119* } Adelaide 1928-29
177 }
113 Leeds 1930
112 Sydney 1932-33
101 Sydney 1932-33
231* Sydney 1936-37
240 Lord's 1938
J. Hardstaff jun. (1)
169* The Oval ... 1938
T. W. Hayward (2)
130 Manchester . 1899
137 The Oval ... 1899
J. W. Hearne (1)
114 Melbourne .. 1911-12
E. H. Hendren (3)
127* Lord's 1926
169 Brisbane 1928-29
132 Manchester . 1934
J. B. Hobbs (12)
126* Melbourne .. 1911-12
187 Adelaide 1911-12
178 Melbourne .. 1911-12
107 Lord's 1912
122 Melbourne .. 1920-21
123 Adelaide 1920-21
115 Sydney 1924-25
154 Melbourne .. 1924-25
119 Adelaide 1924-25
119 Lord's 1926
100 The Oval ... 1926
142 Melbourne .. 1928-29
K. L. Hutchings (1)
126 Melbourne .. 1907-08
L. Hutton (5)
100† Nottingham . 1938
364 The Oval ... 1938
122* Sydney 1946-47
156*‡ Adelaide 1950-51
145 Lord's 1953
Hon. F. S. Jackson (5)
103 The Oval ... 1893
118 The Oval ... 1899
128 Manchester . 1902
144* Leeds 1905
113 Manchester . 1905
G. L. Jessop (1)
104 The Oval ... 1902
A. P. E. Knott (2)
106* Adelaide 1974-75
135 Nottingham . 1977
A. J. Lamb (1)
125 Leeds 1989
M. Leyland (7)
137† Melbourne .. 1928-29
109 Lord's 1934
153 Manchester . 1934
110 The Oval ... 1934
126 Brisbane 1936-37
111* Melbourne .. 1936-37
187 The Oval ... 1938
B. W. Luckhurst (2)
131 Perth 1970-71
109 Melbourne .. 1970-71
A. C. MacLaren (5)
120 Melbourne .. 1894-95
109 Sydney 1897-98
124 Adelaide 1897-98
116 Sydney 1901-02
140 Nottingham . 1905
J. W. H. Makepeace (1)
117 Melbourne .. 1920-21
P. B. H. May (3)
104 Sydney 1954-55
101 Leeds 1956
113 Melbourne .. 1958-59
C. P. Mead (1)
182* The Oval ... 1921
Nawab of Pataudi sen. (1)
102† Sydney 1932-33
E. Paynter (1)
216* Nottingham . 1938
D. W. Randall (3)
174† Melbourne .. 1976-77
150 Sydney 1978-79
115 Perth 1982-83
K. S. Ranjitsinhji (2)
154*† Manchester . 1896
175 Sydney 1897-98
W. W. Read (1)
117 The Oval ... 1884
W. Rhodes (1)
179 Melbourne .. 1911-12
C. J. Richards (1)
133 Perth 1986-87
P. E. Richardson (1)
104 Manchester . 1956
R. T. Robinson (2)
175† Leeds 1985
148 Birmingham . 1985
A. C. Russell (3)
135* Adelaide 1920-21
101 Manchester . 1921
102* The Oval ... 1921
R. C. Russell (1)
128* Manchester . 1989
J. Sharp (1)
105 The Oval ... 1909
Rev. D. S. Sheppard (2)
113 Manchester . 1956
113 Melbourne .. 1962-63
A. Shrewsbury (3)
105* Melbourne .. 1884-85
164 Lord's 1886
106 Lord's 1893
R. T. Simpson (1)
156* Melbourne .. 1950-51
R. A. Smith (2)
143 Manchester . 1989
101 Nottingham . 1989
A. G. Steel (2)
135* Sydney 1882-83
148 Lord's 1884

A. E. Stoddart (2)
134 Adelaide 1891-92
173 Melbourne .. 1894-95
R. Subba Row (2)
112† Birmingham . 1961
137 The Oval ... 1961
H. Sutcliffe (8)
115† Sydney 1924-25
176 } Melbourne .. 1924-25
127 }
143 Melbourne .. 1924-25
161 The Oval ... 1926
135 Melbourne .. 1928-29
161 The Oval ... 1930
194 Sydney 1932-33
J. T. Tyldesley (3)
138 Birmingham . 1902
100 Leeds 1905
112* The Oval ... 1905
G. Ulyett (1)
149 Melbourne .. 1881-82
A. Ward (1)
117 Sydney 1894-95
C. Washbrook (2)
112 Melbourne .. 1946-47
143 Leeds 1948
W. Watson (1)
109† Lord's 1953
F. E. Woolley (2)
133* Sydney 1911-12
123 Sydney 1924-25
R. A. Woolmer (3)
149 The Oval ... 1975
120 Lord's 1977
137 Manchester . 1977

† *Signifies hundred on first appearance in England–Australia Tests.*
‡ *Carried his bat.*
Note: In consecutive innings in 1928-29, W. R. Hammond scored 251 at Sydney, 200 and 32 at Melbourne, and 119* and 177 at Adelaide.

For Australia (211)

W. W. Armstrong (4)
133* Melbourne .. 1907-08
158 Sydney 1920-21
121 Adelaide 1920-21
123* Melbourne .. 1920-21
C. L. Badcock (1)
118 Melbourne .. 1936-37
C. Bannerman (1)
165*† Melbourne .. 1876-77
W. Bardsley (3)
136 } The Oval ... 1909
130 }
193*‡ Lord's 1926
S. G. Barnes (2)
234 Sydney 1946-47
141 Lord's 1948
G. J. Bonnor (1)
128 Sydney 1884-85
D. C. Boon (2)
103 Adelaide 1986-87
184* Sydney 1987-88
B. C. Booth (2)
112 Brisbane 1962-63
103 Melbourne .. 1962-63
A. R. Border (7)
115 Perth 1979-80
123* Manchester . 1981
106* The Oval ... 1981
196 Lord's 1985
146* Manchester . 1985
125 Perth 1986-87
100* Adelaide 1986-87
D. G. Bradman (19)
112 Melbourne .. 1928-29
123 Melbourne .. 1928-29
131 Nottingham . 1930
254 Lord's 1930
334 Leeds 1930
232 The Oval ... 1930
103* Melbourne .. 1932-33
304 Leeds 1934
244 The Oval ... 1934
270 Melbourne .. 1936-37
212 Adelaide 1936-37
169 Melbourne .. 1936-37
144* Nottingham . 1938
102* Lord's 1938
103 Leeds 1938
187 Brisbane 1946-47
234 Sydney 1946-47
138 Nottingham . 1948
173* Leeds 1948
W. A. Brown (3)
105 Lord's 1934
133 Nottingham . 1938
206*‡ Lord's 1938
P. J. Burge (4)
181 The Oval ... 1961
103 Sydney 1962-63
160 Leeds 1964
120 Melbourne .. 1965-66
J. W. Burke (1)
101*† Adelaide 1950-51
G. S. Chappell (9)
108† Perth 1970-71
131 Lord's 1972
113 The Oval ... 1972
144 Sydney 1974-75
102 Melbourne .. 1974-75
112 Manchester . 1977
114 Melbourne .. 1979-80
117 Perth 1982-83
115 Adelaide 1982-83
I. M. Chappell (4)
111 Melbourne .. 1970-71
104 Adelaide 1970-71
118 The Oval ... 1972
192 The Oval ... 1975
H. L. Collins (3)
104† Sydney 1920-21
162 Adelaide 1920-21
114 Sydney 1924-25
R. M. Cowper (1)
307 Melbourne .. 1965-66
J. Darling (3)
101 Sydney 1897-98
178 Adelaide 1897-98
160 Sydney 1897-98
R. A. Duff (2)
104† Melbourne .. 1901-02
146 The Oval ... 1905
J. Dyson (1)
102 Leeds 1981
R. Edwards (2)
170* Nottingham . 1972
115 Perth 1974-75
J. H. Fingleton (2)
100 Brisbane 1936-37
136 Melbourne .. 1936-37
G. Giffen (1)
161 Sydney 1894-95
H. Graham (2)
107† Lord's 1893
105 Sydney 1894-95
J. M. Gregory (1)
100 Melbourne .. 1920-21
S. E. Gregory (4)
201 Sydney 1894-95
103 Lord's 1896
117 The Oval ... 1899
112 Adelaide 1903-04
R. J. Hartigan (1)
116† Adelaide 1907-08
R. N. Harvey (6)
112† Leeds 1948
122 Manchester . 1953
162 Brisbane 1954-55
167 Melbourne .. 1958-59
114 Birmingham . 1961
154 Adelaide 1962-63
A. L. Hassett (4)
128 Brisbane 1946-47
137 Nottingham . 1948
115 Nottingham . 1953
104 Lord's 1953

H. S. T. L. Hendry (1)
112 Sydney 1928-29
A. M. J. Hilditch (1)
119 Leeds 1985
C. Hill (4)
188 Melbourne .. 1897-98
135 Lord's 1899
119 Sheffield 1902
160 Adelaide 1907-08
T. P. Horan (1)
124 Melbourne .. 1881-82
K. J. Hughes (3)
129 Brisbane 1978-79
117 Lord's 1980
137 Sydney 1982-83
F. A. Iredale (2)
140 Adelaide 1894-95
108 Manchester . 1896
A. A. Jackson (1)
164† Adelaide 1928-29
D. M. Jones (3)
184* Sydney 1986-87
157 Birmingham . 1989
122 The Oval ... 1989
C. Kelleway (1)
147 Adelaide 1920-21
A. F. Kippax (1)
100 Melbourne .. 1928-29
W. M. Lawry (7)
130 Lord's 1961
102 Manchester . 1961
106 Manchester . 1964
166 Brisbane 1965-66
119 Adelaide 1965-66
108 Melbourne .. 1965-66
135 The Oval ... 1968
R. R. Lindwall (1)
100 Melbourne .. 1946-47
J. J. Lyons (1)
134 Sydney 1891-92
C. G. Macartney (5)
170 Sydney 1920-21
115 Leeds 1921
133* Lord's 1926
151 Leeds 1926
109 Manchester . 1926
S. J. McCabe (4)
187* Sydney 1932-33
137 Manchester . 1934
112 Melbourne .. 1936-37
232 Nottingham . 1938
C. L. McCool (1)
104* Melbourne .. 1946-47
R. B. McCosker (2)
127 The Oval ... 1975
107 Nottingham . 1977

C. C. McDonald (2)
170 Adelaide 1958-59
133 Melbourne .. 1958-59
P. S. McDonnell (3)
147 Sydney 1881-82
103 The Oval ... 1884
124 Adelaide 1884-85
C. E. McLeod (1)
112 Melbourne .. 1897-98
G. R. Marsh (2)
110† Brisbane 1986-87
138 Nottingham . 1989
R. W. Marsh (1)
110* Melbourne .. 1976-77
K. R. Miller (3)
141* Adelaide 1946-47
145* Sydney 1950-51
109 Lord's 1953
A. R. Morris (8)
155 Melbourne .. 1946-47
122 }
124* } Adelaide 1946-47
105 Lord's 1948
182 Leeds 1948
196 The Oval ... 1948
206 Adelaide 1950-51
153 Brisbane 1954-55
W. L. Murdoch (2)
153* The Oval ... 1880
211 The Oval ... 1884
M. A. Noble (1)
133 Sydney 1903-04
N. C. O'Neill (2)
117 The Oval ... 1961
100 Adelaide 1962-63
C. E. Pellew (2)
116 Melbourne .. 1920-21
104 Adelaide 1920-21
W. H. Ponsford (5)
110† Sydney 1924-25
128 Melbourne .. 1924-25
110 The Oval ... 1930
181 Leeds 1934
266 The Oval ... 1934
V. S. Ransford (1)
143* Lord's 1909
I. R. Redpath (2)
171 Perth 1970-71
105 Sydney 1974-75
A. J. Richardson (1)
100 Leeds 1926
V. Y. Richardson (1)
138 Melbourne .. 1924-25
G. M. Ritchie (1)
146 Nottingham . 1985

J. Ryder (2)
201* Adelaide 1924-25
112 Melbourne .. 1928-29
H. J. H. Scott (1)
102 The Oval ... 1884
R. B. Simpson (2)
311 Manchester . 1964
225 Adelaide 1965-66
K. R. Stackpole (3)
207 Brisbane 1970-71
136 Adelaide 1970-71
114 Nottingham . 1972
J. M. Taylor (1)
108 Sydney 1924-25
M. A. Taylor (2)
136† Leeds 1989
219 Nottingham . 1989
G. H. S. Trott (1)
143 Lord's 1896
V. T. Trumper (6)
135* Lord's 1899
104 Manchester . 1902
185* Sydney 1903-04
113 Adelaide 1903-04
166 Sydney 1907-08
113 Sydney 1911-12
K. D. Walters (4)
155† Brisbane 1965-66
115 Melbourne .. 1965-66
112 Brisbane 1970-71
103 Perth 1974-75
S. R. Waugh (2)
177* Leeds 1989
152* Lord's 1989
D. M. Wellham (1)
103† The Oval ... 1981
K. C. Wessels (1)
162† Brisbane 1982-83
G. M. Wood (3)
100 Melbourne .. 1978-79
112 Lord's 1980
172 Nottingham . 1985
W. M. Woodfull (6)
141 Leeds 1926
117 Manchester . 1926
111 Sydney 1928-29
107 Melbourne .. 1928-29
102 Melbourne .. 1928-29
155 Lord's 1930
G. N. Yallop (3)
102† Brisbane 1978-79
121 Sydney 1978-79
114 Manchester . 1981

† *Signifies hundred on first appearance in England–Australia Tests.*

‡ *Carried his bat.*

Notes: D. G. Bradman's scores in 1930 were 8 and 131 at Nottingham, 254 and 1 at Lord's, 334 at Leeds, 14 at Manchester, and 232 at The Oval.

D. G. Bradman scored a hundred in eight successive Tests against England in which he batted – three in 1936-37, three in 1938 and two in 1946-47. He was injured and unable to bat at The Oval in 1938.

W. H. Ponsford and K. D. Walters each hit hundreds in their first two Tests.

C. Bannerman and H. Graham each scored their maiden hundred in first-class cricket in their first Test.

No right-handed batsman has obtained two hundreds for Australia in a Test match against England, and no left-handed batsman for England against Australia.

H. Sutcliffe, in his first two games for England, scored 59 and 115 at Sydney and 176 and 127 at Melbourne in 1924-25. In the latter match, which lasted into the seventh day, he was on the field throughout except for 86 minutes, namely 27 hours and 52 minutes.

C. Hill made 98 and 97 at Adelaide in 1901-02, and F. E. Woolley 95 and 93 at Lord's in 1921.

H. Sutcliffe in 1924-25, C. G. Macartney in 1926 and A. R. Morris in 1946-47 made three hundreds in consecutive innings.

J. B. Hobbs and H. Sutcliffe shared eleven first-wicket three-figure partnerships.

L. Hutton and C. Washbrook twice made three-figure stands in each innings, at Adelaide in 1946-47 and at Leeds in 1948.

H. Sutcliffe, during his highest score of 194, v Australia in 1932-33, took part in three stands each exceeding 100, viz. 112 with R. E. S. Wyatt for the first wicket, 188 with W. R. Hammond for the second wicket, and 123 with the Nawab of Pataudi sen. for the third wicket. In 1903-04 R. E. Foster, in his historic innings of 287, added 192 for the fifth wicket with L. C. Braund, 115 for the ninth with A. E. Relf, and 130 for the tenth with W. Rhodes.

When L. Hutton scored 364 at The Oval in 1938 he added 382 for the second wicket with M. Leyland, 135 for the third wicket with W. R. Hammond and 215 for the sixth wicket with J. Hardstaff jun.

D. C. S. Compton and A. R. Morris at Adelaide in 1946-47 provide the only instance of a player on each side hitting two separate hundreds in a Test match.

G. S. and I. M. Chappell at The Oval in 1972 provide the first instance in Test matches of brothers each scoring hundreds in the same innings.

RECORD PARTNERSHIPS FOR EACH WICKET

For England

323 for 1st	J. B. Hobbs and W. Rhodes at Melbourne	1911-12
382 for 2nd†	L. Hutton and M. Leyland at The Oval	1938
262 for 3rd	W. R. Hammond and D. R. Jardine at Adelaide	1928-29
222 for 4th	W. R. Hammond and E. Paynter at Lord's	1938
206 for 5th	E. Paynter and D. C. S. Compton at Nottingham	1938
215 for 6th	L. Hutton and J. Hardstaff jun. at The Oval	1938
	G. Boycott and A. P. E. Knott at Nottingham	1977
143 for 7th	F. E. Woolley and J. Vine at Sydney	1911-12
124 for 8th	E. H. Hendren and H. Larwood at Brisbane	1928-29
151 for 9th	W. H. Scotton and W. W. Read at The Oval	1884
130 for 10th†	R. E. Foster and W. Rhodes at Sydney	1903-04

For Australia

329 for 1st	G. R. Marsh and M. A. Taylor at Nottingham	1989
451 for 2nd†	W. H. Ponsford and D. G. Bradman at The Oval	1934
276 for 3rd	D. G. Bradman and A. L. Hassett at Brisbane	1946-47
388 for 4th†	W. H. Ponsford and D. G. Bradman at Leeds	1934
405 for 5th†‡	S. G. Barnes and D. G. Bradman at Sydney	1946-47
346 for 6th†	J. H. Fingleton and D. G. Bradman at Melbourne	1936-37
165 for 7th	C. Hill and H. Trumble at Melbourne	1897-98
243 for 8th†	R. J. Hartigan and C. Hill at Adelaide	1907-08
154 for 9th†	S. E. Gregory and J. McC. Blackham at Sydney	1894-95
127 for 10th†	J. M. Taylor and A. A. Mailey at Sydney	1924-25

† *Denotes record partnership against all countries.*

‡ *Record fifth-wicket partnership in first-class cricket.*

MOST RUNS IN A SERIES

England in England	732 (average 81.33)	D. I. Gower	1985
England in Australia	905 (average 113.12)	W. R. Hammond ..	1928-29
Australia in England	974 (average 139.14)	D. G. Bradman ...	1930
Australia in Australia	810 (average 90.00)	D. G. Bradman ...	1936-37

TEN WICKETS OR MORE IN A MATCH

For England (37)

13-163 (6-42, 7-121)	S. F. Barnes, Melbourne	1901-02
14-102 (7-28, 7-74)	W. Bates, Melbourne	1882-83
10-105 (5-46, 5-59)	A. V. Bedser, Melbourne	1950-51
14-99 (7-55, 7-44)	A. V. Bedser, Nottingham	1953
11-102 (6-44, 5-58)	C. Blythe, Birmingham	1909
11-176 (6-78, 5-98)	I. T. Botham, Perth	1979-80
10-253 (6-125, 4-128)	I. T. Botham, The Oval	1981
11-74 (5-29, 6-45)	J. Briggs, Lord's	1886
12-136 (6-49, 6-87)	J. Briggs, Adelaide	1891-92
10-148 (5-34, 5-114)	J. Briggs, The Oval	1893
10-104 (6-77, 4-27)†	R. M. Ellison, Birmingham	1985
10-179 (5-102, 5-77)†	K. Farnes, Nottingham	1934
10-60 (6-41, 4-19)	J. T. Hearne, The Oval	1896
11-113 (5-58, 6-55)	J. C. Laker, Leeds	1956
19-90 (9-37, 10-53)	J. C. Laker, Manchester	1956
10-124 (5-96, 5-28)	H. Larwood, Sydney	1932-33
11-76 (6-48, 5-28)	W. H. Lockwood, Manchester	1902
12-104 (7-36, 5-68)	G. A. Lohmann, The Oval	1886
10-87 (8-35, 2-52)	G. A. Lohmann, Sydney	1886-87
10-142 (8-58, 2-84)	G. A. Lohmann, Sydney	1891-92
12-102 (6-50, 6-52)†	F. Martin, The Oval	1890
10-58 (5-18, 5-40)	R. Peel, Sydney	1887-88
11-68 (7-31, 4-37)	R. Peel, Manchester	1888
15-124 (7-56, 8-68)	W. Rhodes, Melbourne	1903-04
10-156 (5-49, 5-107)†	T. Richardson, Manchester	1893
11-173 (6-39, 5-134)	T. Richardson, Lord's	1896
13-244 (7-168, 6-76)	T. Richardson, Manchester	1896
10-204 (8-94, 2-110)	T. Richardson, Sydney	1897-98
11-228 (6-130, 5-98)†	M. W. Tate, Sydney	1924-25
11-88 (5-58, 6-30)	F. S. Trueman, Leeds	1961
10-130 (4-45, 6-85)	F. H. Tyson, Sydney	1954-55
10-82 (4-37, 6-45)	D. L. Underwood, Leeds	1972
11-215 (7-113, 4-102)	D. L. Underwood, Adelaide	1974-75
15-104 (7-61, 8-43)	H. Verity, Lord's	1934
10-57 (6-41, 4-16)	W. Voce, Brisbane	1936-37
13-256 (5-130, 8-126)	J. C. White, Adelaide	1928-29
10-49 (5-29, 5-20)	F. E. Woolley, The Oval	1912

For Australia (36)

10-151 (5-107, 5-44)	T. M. Alderman, Leeds	1989
10-239 (4-129, 6-110)	L. O'B. Fleetwood-Smith, Adelaide	1936-37
10-160 (4-88, 6-72)	G. Giffen, Sydney	1891-92
11-82 (5-45, 6-37)†	C. V. Grimmett, Sydney	1924-25
10-201 (5-107, 5-94)	C. V. Grimmett, Nottingham	1930
10-122 (5-65, 5-57)	R. M. Hogg, Perth	1978-79
10-66 (5-30, 5-36)	R. M. Hogg, Melbourne	1978-79
12-175 (5-85, 7-90)†	H. V. Hordern, Sydney	1911-12

10-161 (5-95, 5-66)	H. V. Hordern, Sydney	1911-12
10-164 (7-88, 3-76)	E. Jones, Lord's	1899
11-134 (6-47, 5-87)	G. F. Lawson, Brisbane	1982-83
10-181 (5-58, 5-123)	D. K. Lillee, The Oval	1972
11-165 (6-26, 5-139)	D. K. Lillee, Melbourne	1976-77
11-138 (6-60, 5-78)	D. K. Lillee, Melbourne	1979-80
11-159 (7-89, 4-70)	D. K. Lillee, The Oval	1981
11-85 (7-58, 4-27)	C. G. Macartney, Leeds	1909
10-302 (5-160, 5-142)	A. A. Mailey, Adelaide	1920-21
13-236 (4-115, 9-121)	A. A. Mailey, Melbourne	1920-21
16-137 (8-84, 8-53)†	R. A. L. Massie, Lord's	1972
10-152 (5-72, 5-80)	K. R. Miller, Lord's	1956
13-77 (7-17, 6-60)	M. A. Noble, Melbourne	1901-02
11-103 (5-51, 6-52)	M. A. Noble, Sheffield	1902
10-129 (5-63, 5-66)	W. J. O'Reilly, Melbourne	1932-33
11-129 (4-75, 7-54)	W. J. O'Reilly, Nottingham	1934
10-122 (5-66, 5-56)	W. J. O'Reilly, Leeds	1938
11-165 (7-68, 4-97)	G. E. Palmer, Sydney	1881-82
10-126 (7-65, 3-61)	G. E. Palmer, Melbourne	1882-83
13-110 (6-48, 7-62)	F. R. Spofforth, Melbourne	1878-79
14-90 (7-46, 7-44)	F. R. Spofforth, The Oval	1882
11-117 (4-73, 7-44)	F. R. Spofforth, Sydney	1882-83
10-144 (4-54, 6-90)	F. R. Spofforth, Sydney	1884-85
12-89 (6-59, 6-30)	H. Trumble, The Oval	1896
10-128 (4-75, 6-53)	H. Trumble, Manchester	1902
12-173 (8-65, 4-108)	H. Trumble, The Oval	1902
12-87 (5-44, 7-43)	C. T. B. Turner, Sydney	1887-88
10-63 (5-27, 5-36)	C. T. B. Turner, Lord's	1888

† *Signifies ten wickets or more on first appearance in England–Australia Tests.*

Note: J. Briggs, J. C. Laker, T. Richardson in 1896, R. M. Hogg, A. A. Mailey, H. Trumble and C. T. B. Turner took ten wickets or more in successive Tests. J. Briggs was omitted, however, from the England team for the first Test match in 1893.

MOST WICKETS IN A SERIES

England in England	46 (average 9.60)	J. C. Laker	1956
England in Australia	38 (average 23.18)	M. W. Tate	1924-25
Australia in England	42 (average 21.26)	T. M. Alderman (6 Tests)	1981
Australia in Australia	41 (average 12.85)	R. M. Hogg (6 Tests)	1978-79

WICKET-KEEPING – MOST DISMISSALS

	M	*Ct*	*St*	*Total*
†R. W. Marsh (Australia)	42	141	7	148
A. P. E. Knott (England)	34	97	8	105
†W. A. Oldfield (Australia)	38	59	31	90
A. A. Lilley (England)	32	65	19	84
A. T. W. Grout (Australia)	22	69	7	76
T. G. Evans (England)	31	63	12	75

† *The number of catches by R. W. Marsh (141) and stumpings by W. A. Oldfield (31) are respective records in England–Australia Tests.*

SCORERS OF OVER 2,000 RUNS

	T	I	NO	R	HI	Avge
D. G. Bradman	37	63	7	5,028	334	89.78
J. B. Hobbs	41	71	4	3,636	187	54.26
G. Boycott	38	71	9	2,945	191	47.50
D. I. Gower	37	67	3	2,862	215	44.71
W. R. Hammond	33	58	3	2,852	251	51.85
A. R. Border	36	66	17	2,834	196	57.83
H. Sutcliffe	27	46	5	2,741	194	66.85
C. Hill	41	76	1	2,660	188	35.46
J. H. Edrich	32	57	3	2,644	175	48.96
G. S. Chappell	35	65	8	2,619	144	45.94
M. C. Cowdrey	43	75	4	2,433	113	34.26
L. Hutton	27	49	6	2,428	364	56.46
R. N. Harvey	37	68	5	2,416	167	38.34
V. T. Trumper	40	74	5	2,263	185*	32.79
W. M. Lawry	29	51	5	2,233	166	48.54
S. E. Gregory	52	92	7	2,193	201	25.80
W. W. Armstrong	42	71	9	2,172	158	35.03
I. M. Chappell	30	56	4	2,138	192	41.11
K. F. Barrington	23	39	6	2,111	256	63.96
A. R. Morris	24	43	2	2,080	206	50.73

BOWLERS WITH 100 WICKETS

	T	Balls	R	W	5 W/i	Avge
D. K. Lillee	29	8,516	3,507	167	11	21.00
I. T. Botham	36	8,479	4,093	148	9	27.65
H. Trumble	31	7,895	2,945	141	9	20.88
R. G. D. Willis	35	7,294	3,346	128	7	26.14
M. A. Noble	39	6,845	2,860	115	9	24.86
R. R. Lindwall	29	6,728	2,559	114	6	22.44
W. Rhodes	41	5,791	2,616	109	6	24.00
S. F. Barnes	20	5,749	2,288	106	12	21.58
C. V. Grimmett	22	9,224	3,439	106	11	32.44
D. L. Underwood	29	8,000	2,770	105	4	26.38
A. V. Bedser	21	7,065	2,859	104	7	27.49
G. Giffen	31	6,325	2,791	103	7	27.09
W. J. O'Reilly	19	7,864	2,587	102	8	25.36
R. Peel	20	5,216	1,715	102	6	16.81
C. T. B. Turner	17	5,195	1,670	101	11	16.53
J. R. Thomson	21	4,951	2,418	100	5	24.18

ENGLAND v SOUTH AFRICA

	Captains					
Season	England	South Africa	T	E	SA	D
1888-89	C. A. Smith[1]	O. R. Dunell[2]	2	2	0	0
1891-92	W. W. Read	W. H. Milton	1	1	0	0
1895-96	Lord Hawke[3]	E. A. Halliwell[4]	3	3	0	0
1898-99	Lord Hawke	M. Bisset	2	2	0	0
1905-06	P. F. Warner	P. W. Sherwell	5	1	4	0
1907	R. E. Foster	P. W. Sherwell	3	1	0	2
1909-10	H. D. G. Leveson Gower[5]	S. J. Snooke	5	2	3	0
1912	C. B. Fry	F. Mitchell[6]	3	3	0	0
1913-14	J. W. H. T. Douglas	H. W. Taylor	5	4	0	1

	Captains					
Season	*England*	*South Africa*	*T*	*E*	*SA*	*D*
1922-23	F. T. Mann	H. W. Taylor	5	2	1	2
1924	A. E. R. Gilligan[7]	H. W. Taylor	5	3	0	2
1927-28	R. T. Stanyforth[8]	H. G. Deane	5	2	2	1
1929	J. C. White[9]	H. G. Deane	5	2	0	3
1930-31	A. P. F. Chapman	H. G. Deane[10]	5	0	1	4
1935	R. E. S. Wyatt	H. F. Wade	5	0	1	4
1938-39	W. R. Hammond	A. Melville	5	1	0	4
1947	N. W. D. Yardley	A. Melville	5	3	0	2
1948-49	F. G. Mann	A. D. Nourse	5	2	0	3
1951	F. R. Brown	A. D. Nourse	5	3	1	1
1955	P. B. H. May	J. E. Cheetham[11]	5	3	2	0
1956-57	P. B. H. May	C. B. van Ryneveld[12]	5	2	2	1
1960	M. C. Cowdrey	D. J. McGlew	5	3	0	2
1964-65	M. J. K. Smith	T. L. Goddard	5	1	0	4
1965	M. J. K. Smith	P. L. van der Merwe	3	0	1	2
	In South Africa		58	25	13	20
	In England		44	21	5	18
	Totals		102	46	18	38

Notes: The following deputised for the official touring captain or were appointed by the home authority for only a minor proportion of the series:

[1]M. P. Bowden (Second). [2]W. H. Milton (Second). [3]Sir T. C. O'Brien (First). [4]A. R. Richards (Third). [5]F. L. Fane (Fourth and Fifth). [6]L. J. Tancred (Second and Third). [7]J. W. H. T. Douglas (Fourth). [8]G. T. S. Stevens (Fifth). [9]A. W. Carr (Fourth and Fifth). [10]E. P. Nupen (First), H. B. Cameron (Fourth and Fifth). [11]D. J. McGlew (Third and Fourth). [12]D. J. McGlew (Second).

HIGHEST INNINGS TOTALS

For England in England: 554-8 dec. at Lord's 1947
in South Africa: 654-5 at Durban 1938-39

For South Africa in England: 538 at Leeds 1951
in South Africa: 530 at Durban 1938-39

LOWEST INNINGS TOTALS

For England in England: 76 at Leeds 1907
in South Africa: 92 at Cape Town 1898-99

For South Africa in England: 30 at Birmingham 1924
in South Africa: 30 at Port Elizabeth 1895-96

INDIVIDUAL HUNDREDS

For England (87)

R. Abel (1)
120 Cape Town . 1888-89
L. E. G. Ames (2)
148* The Oval ... 1935
115 Cape Town . 1938-39
K. F. Barrington (2)
148* Durban 1964-65
121 Johannesburg 1964-65

G. Boycott (1)
117 Pt Elizabeth . 1964-65
L. C. Braund (1)
104† Lord's 1907
D. C. S. Compton (7)
163† Nottingham . 1947
208 Lord's 1947
115 Manchester . 1947
113 The Oval ... 1947
114 Johannesburg 1948-49
112 Nottingham . 1951
158 Manchester . 1955

M. C. Cowdrey (3)
101 Cape Town . 1956-57
155 The Oval ... 1960
105 Nottingham . 1965

D. Denton (1)
104 Johannesburg 1909-10
E. R. Dexter (1)
172 Johannesburg 1964-65
J. W. H. T. Douglas (1)
119† Durban 1913-14
W. J. Edrich (3)
219 Durban 1938-39
189 Lord's 1947
191 Manchester . 1947
F. L. Fane (1)
143 Johannesburg 1905-06
C. B. Fry (1)
129 The Oval . . . 1907
P. A. Gibb (2)
106† Johannesburg 1938-39
120 Durban 1938-39
W. R. Hammond (6)
138* Birmingham . 1929
101* The Oval . . . 1929
136* Durban 1930-31
181 Cape Town . 1938-39
120 Durban 1938-39
140 Durban 1938-39
T. W. Hayward (1)
122 Johannesburg 1895-96
E. H. Hendren (2)
132 Leeds 1924
142 The Oval . . . 1924
A. J. L. Hill (1)
124 Cape Town . 1895-96
J. B. Hobbs (2)
187 Cape Town . 1909-10
211 Lord's 1924
L. Hutton (4)
100 Leeds 1947
158 Johannesburg 1948-49
123 Johannesburg 1948-49
100 Leeds 1951
D. J. Insole (1)
110* Durban 1956-57
M. Leyland (2)
102 Lord's 1929
161 The Oval . . . 1935
F. G. Mann (1)
136* Pt Elizabeth . 1948-49
P. B. H. May (3)
138† Leeds 1951
112 Lord's 1955
117 Manchester . 1955
C. P. Mead (3)
102 Johannesburg 1913-14
117 Pt Elizabeth . 1913-14
181 Durban 1922-23
P. H. Parfitt (1)
122* Johannesburg 1964-65
J. M. Parks (1)
108* Durban 1964-65
E. Paynter (3)
117 } †Johannesburg 1938-39
100 }
243 Durban 1938-39
G. Pullar (1)
175 The Oval . . . 1960
W. Rhodes (1)
152 Johannesburg 1913-14
P. E. Richardson (1)
117† Johannesburg 1956-57
R. W. V. Robins (1)
108 Manchester . 1935
A. C. Russell (2)
140 } Durban 1922-23
111 }
R. T. Simpson (1)
137 Nottingham . 1951
M. J. K. Smith (1)
121 Cape Town . 1964-65
R. H. Spooner (1)
119† Lord's 1912
H. Sutcliffe (6)
122 Lord's 1924
102 Johannesburg 1927-28
114 Birmingham . 1929
100 Lord's 1929
104 } The Oval . . . 1929
109* }
M. W. Tate (1)
100* Lord's 1929
E. Tyldesley (2)
122 Johannesburg 1927-28
100 Durban 1927-28
J. T. Tyldesley (1)
112 Cape Town . 1898-99
B. H. Valentine (1)
112 Cape Town . 1938-39
P. F. Warner (1)
132*†‡Johannesburg 1898-99
C. Washbrook (1)
195 Johannesburg 1948-49
A. J. Watkins (1)
111 Johannesburg 1948-49
H. Wood (1)
134* Cape Town . 1891-92
F. E. Woolley (3)
115* Johannesburg 1922-23
134* Lord's 1924
154 Manchester . 1929
R. E. S. Wyatt (2)
113 Manchester . 1929
149 Nottingham . 1935

For South Africa (58)

E. J. Barlow (1)
138 Cape Town . 1964-65
K. C. Bland (2)
144* Johannesburg 1964-65
127 The Oval . . . 1965
R. H. Catterall (3)
120 Birmingham . 1924
120 Lord's 1924
119 Durban 1927-28
E. L. Dalton (2)
117 The Oval . . . 1935
102 Johannesburg 1938-39
W. R. Endean (1)
116* Leeds 1955
G. A. Faulkner (1)
123 Johannesburg 1909-10
T. L. Goddard (1)
112 Johannesburg 1964-65
C. M. H. Hathorn (1)
102 Johannesburg 1905-06
D. J. McGlew (2)
104* Manchester . 1955
133 Leeds 1955
R. A. McLean (3)
142 Lord's 1955
100 Durban 1956-57
109 Manchester . 1960
A. Melville (4)
103 Durban 1938-39
189 } Nottingham . 1947
104* }
117 Lord's 1947
B. Mitchell (7)
123 Cape Town . 1930-31
164* Lord's 1935
128 The Oval . . . 1935
109 Durban 1938-39
120 } The Oval . . . 1947
189* }
120 Cape Town . 1948-49
A. D. Nourse (7)
120 Cape Town . 1938-39
103 Durban 1938-39
149 Nottingham . 1947
115 Manchester . 1947
112 Cape Town . 1948-49
129* Johannesburg 1948-49
208 Nottingham . 1951
H. G. Owen-Smith (1)
129 Leeds 1929
A. J. Pithey (1)
154 Cape Town . 1964-65
R. G. Pollock (2)
137 Pt Elizabeth . 1964-65
125 Nottingham . 1965
E. A. B. Rowan (2)
156* Johannesburg 1948-49
236 Leeds 1951
P. W. Sherwell (1)
115 Lord's 1907

I. J. Siedle (1)		
141	Cape Town	1930-31
J. H. Sinclair (1)		
106	Cape Town	1898-99
H. W. Taylor (7)		
109	Durban	1913-14
176	Johannesburg	1922-23
101	Johannesburg	1922-23
102	Durban	1922-23
101	Johannesburg	1927-28
121	The Oval	1929
117	Cape Town	1930-31
P. G. V. van der Bijl (1)		
125	Durban	1938-39
K. G. Viljoen (1)		
124	Manchester	1935
W. W. Wade (1)		
125	Pt Elizabeth	1948-49
J. H. B. Waite (1)		
113	Manchester	1955
G. C. White (2)		
147	Johannesburg	1905-06
118	Durban	1909-10
P. L. Winslow (1)		
108	Manchester	1955

† *Signifies hundred on first appearance in England–South Africa Tests.*
‡ *P. F. Warner carried his bat through the second innings.*

Notes: The highest score by a South African batsman on début is 93* by A. W. Nourse at Johannesburg in 1905-06.

P. N. F. Mansell made 90 at Leeds in 1951, the best on début in England.

A. Melville's four hundreds were made in successive Test innings.

H. Wood scored the only hundred of his career in a Test match.

RECORD PARTNERSHIP FOR EACH WICKET

For England

359 for 1st†	L. Hutton and C. Washbrook at Johannesburg	1948-49
280 for 2nd	P. A. Gibb and W. J. Edrich at Durban	1938-39
370 for 3rd†	W. J. Edrich and D. C. S. Compton at Lord's	1947
197 for 4th	W. R. Hammond and L. E. G. Ames at Cape Town	1938-39
237 for 5th	D. C. S. Compton and N. W. D. Yardley at Nottingham	1947
206* for 6th	K. F. Barrington and J. M. Parks at Durban	1964-65
115 for 7th	M. C. Bird and J. W. H. T. Douglas at Durban	1913-14
154 for 8th	C. W. Wright and H. R. Bromley-Davenport at Johannesburg	1895-96
71 for 9th	H. Wood and J. T. Hearne at Cape Town	1891-92
92 for 10th	A. C. Russell and A. E. R. Gilligan at Durban	1922-23

For South Africa

260 for 1st†	I. J. Siedle and B. Mitchell at Cape Town	1930-31
198 for 2nd†	E. A. B. Rowan and C. B. van Ryneveld at Leeds	1951
319 for 3rd	A. Melville and A. D. Nourse at Nottingham	1947
214 for 4th†	H. W. Taylor and H. G. Deane at The Oval	1929
157 for 5th†	A. J. Pithey and J. H. B. Waite at Johannesburg	1964-65
171 for 6th	J. H. B. Waite and P. L. Winslow at Manchester	1955
123 for 7th	H. G. Deane and E. P. Nupen at Durban	1927-28
109* for 8th	B. Mitchell and L. Tuckett at The Oval	1947
137 for 9th†	E. L. Dalton and A. B. C. Langton at The Oval	1935
103 for 10th†	H. G. Owen-Smith and A. J. Bell at Leeds	1929

† *Denotes record partnership against all countries.*

MOST RUNS IN A SERIES

England in England	753 (average 94.12)	D. C. S. Compton	1947
England in South Africa	653 (average 81.62)	E. Paynter	1938-39
South Africa in England	621 (average 69.00)	A. D. Nourse	1947
South Africa in South Africa	582 (average 64.66)	H. W. Taylor	1922-23

TEN WICKETS OR MORE IN A MATCH

For England (23)

11-110 (5-25, 6-85)†	S. F. Barnes, Lord's	1912
10-115 (6-52, 4-63)	S. F. Barnes, Leeds	1912
13-57 (5-28, 8-29)	S. F. Barnes, The Oval	1912
10-105 (5-57, 5-48)	S. F. Barnes, Durban	1913-14
17-159 (8-56, 9-103)	S. F. Barnes, Johannesburg	1913-14
14-144 (7-56, 7-88)	S. F. Barnes, Durban	1913-14
12-112 (7-58, 5-54)	A. V. Bedser, Manchester	1951
11-118 (6-68, 5-50)	C. Blythe, Cape Town	1905-06
15-99 (8-59, 7-40)	C. Blythe, Leeds	1907
10-104 (7-46, 3-58)	C. Blythe, Cape Town	1909-10
15-28 (7-17, 8-11)	J. Briggs, Cape Town	1888-89
13-91 (6-54, 7-37)†	J. J. Ferris, Cape Town	1891-92
10-207 (7-115, 3-92)	A. P. Freeman, Leeds	1929
12-171 (7-71, 5-100)	A. P. Freeman, Manchester	1929
12-130 (7-70, 5-60)	G. Geary, Johannesburg	1927-28
11-90 (6-7, 5-83)	A. E. R. Gilligan, Birmingham	1924
10-119 (4-64, 6-55)	J. C. Laker, The Oval	1951
15-45 (7-38, 8-7)†	G. A. Lohmann, Port Elizabeth	1895-96
12-71 (9-28, 3-43)	G. A. Lohmann, Johannesburg	1895-96
11-97 (6-63, 5-34)	J. B. Statham, Lord's	1960
12-101 (7-52, 5-49)	R. Tattersall, Lord's	1951
12-89 (5-53, 7-36)	J. H. Wardle, Cape Town	1956-57
10-175 (5-95, 5-80)	D. V. P. Wright, Lord's	1947

For South Africa (6)

11-112 (4-49, 7-63)†	A. E. Hall, Cape Town	1922-23
11-150 (5-63, 6-87)	E. P. Nupen, Johannesburg	1930-31
10-87 (5-53, 5-34)	P. M. Pollock, Nottingham	1965
12-127 (4-57, 8-70)	S. J. Snooke, Johannesburg	1905-06
13-192 (4-79, 9-113)	H. J. Tayfield, Johannesburg	1956-57
12-181 (5-87, 7-94)	A. E. E. Vogler, Johannesburg	1909-10

† *Signifies ten wickets or more on first appearance in England–South Africa Tests.*

Note: S. F. Barnes took ten wickets or more in his first five Tests v South Africa and in six of his seven Tests v South Africa. A. P. Freeman and G. A. Lohmann took ten wickets or more in successive matches.

MOST WICKETS IN A SERIES

England in England	34 (average 8.29)	S. F. Barnes	1912
England in South Africa	49 (average 10.93)	S. F. Barnes	1913-14
South Africa in England	26 (average 21.84)	H. J. Tayfield	1955
South Africa in England	26 (average 22.57)	N. A. T. Adcock	1960
South Africa in South Africa	37 (average 17.18)	H. J. Tayfield	1956-57

ENGLAND v WEST INDIES

Season	Captains: England	West Indies	T	E	WI	D
1928	A. P. F. Chapman	R. K. Nunes	3	3	0	0
1929-30	Hon. F. S. G. Calthorpe	E. L. G. Hoad[1]	4	1	1	2
1933	D. R. Jardine[2]	G. C. Grant	3	2	0	1
1934-35	R. E. S. Wyatt	G. C. Grant	4	1	2	1
1939	W. R. Hammond	R. S. Grant	3	1	0	2
1947-48	G. O. B. Allen[3]	J. D. C. Goddard[4]	4	0	2	2
1950	N. W. D. Yardley[5]	J. D. C. Goddard	4	1	3	0
1953-54	L. Hutton	J. B. Stollmeyer	5	2	2	1
1957	P. B. H. May	J. D. C. Goddard	5	3	0	2
1959-60	P. B. H. May[6]	F. C. M. Alexander	5	1	0	4

THE WISDEN TROPHY

Season	Captains: England	West Indies	T	E	WI	D	Held by
1963	E. R. Dexter	F. M. M. Worrell	5	1	3	1	WI
1966	M. C. Cowdrey[7]	G. S. Sobers	5	1	3	1	WI
1967-68	M. C. Cowdrey	G. S. Sobers	5	1	0	4	E
1969	R. Illingworth	G. S. Sobers	3	2	0	1	E
1973	R. Illingworth	R. B. Kanhai	3	0	2	1	WI
1973-74	M. H. Denness	R. B. Kanhai	5	1	1	3	WI
1976	A. W. Greig	C. H. Lloyd	5	0	3	2	WI
1980	I. T. Botham	C. H. Lloyd[8]	5	0	1	4	WI
1980-81†	I. T. Botham	C. H. Lloyd	4	0	2	2	WI
1984	D. I. Gower	C. H. Lloyd	5	0	5	0	WI
1985-86	D. I. Gower	I. V. A. Richards	5	0	5	0	WI
1988	J. E. Emburey[9]	I. V. A. Richards	5	0	4	1	WI
1989-90‡	G. A. Gooch[10]	I. V. A. Richards[11]	4	1	2	1	WI
	In England		54	14	24	16	
	In West Indies		45	8	17	20	
	Totals		99	22	41	36	

† The Second Test, at Georgetown, was cancelled owing to political pressure.
‡ The Second Test, at Georgetown, was abandoned without a ball being bowled and is excluded.

Notes: The following deputised for the official touring captain or were appointed by the home authority for only a minor proportion of the series:

[1]N. Betancourt (Second), M. P. Fernandes (Third), R. K. Nunes (Fourth). [2]R. E. S. Wyatt (Third). [3]K. Cranston (First). [4]G. A. Headley (First), G. E. Gomez (Second). [5]F. R. Brown (Fourth). [6]M. C. Cowdrey (Fourth and Fifth). [7]M. J. K. Smith (First), D. B. Close (Fifth). [8]I. V. A. Richards (Fifth). [9]M. W. Gatting (First), C. S. Cowdrey (Fourth), G. A. Gooch (Fifth). [10]A. J. Lamb (Fourth and Fifth). [11]D. L. Haynes (Third).

HIGHEST INNINGS TOTALS

For England in England: 619-6 dec. at Nottingham 1957
in West Indies: 849 at Kingston 1929-30

For West Indies in England: 687-8 dec. at The Oval 1976
in West Indies: 681-8 dec. at Port-of-Spain 1953-54

LOWEST INNINGS TOTALS

For England in England: 71 at Manchester 1976
in West Indies: 103 at Kingston 1934-35

For West Indies in England: 86 at The Oval 1957
in West Indies: 102 at Bridgetown 1934-35

INDIVIDUAL HUNDREDS

For England (85)

L. E. G. Ames (3)
105 Port-of-Spain 1929-30
149 Kingston ... 1929-30
126 Kingston ... 1934-35
D. L. Amiss (4)
174 Port-of-Spain 1973-74
262* Kingston ... 1973-74
118 Georgetown . 1973-74
203 The Oval ... 1976
A. H. Bakewell (1)
107† The Oval ... 1933
K. F. Barrington (3)
128† Bridgetown . 1959-60
121 Port-of-Spain 1959-60
143 Port-of-Spain 1967-68
G. Boycott (5)
116 Georgetown . 1967-68
128 Manchester . 1969
106 Lord's 1969
112 Port-of-Spain 1973-74
104* St John's ... 1980-81
D. C. S. Compton (2)
120† Lord's 1939
133 Port-of-Spain 1953-54
M. C. Cowdrey (6)
154† Birmingham . 1957
152 Lord's 1957
114 Kingston ... 1959-60
119 Port-of-Spain 1959-60
101 Kingston ... 1967-68
148 Port-of-Spain 1967-68
E. R. Dexter (2)
136*† Bridgetown . 1959-60
110 Georgetown . 1959-60
J. H. Edrich (1)
146 Bridgetown . 1967-68
T. G. Evans (1)
104 Manchester . 1950
K. W. R. Fletcher (1)
129* Bridgetown . 1973-74
G. Fowler (1)
106 Lord's 1984

G. A. Gooch (4)
123 Lord's 1980
116 Bridgetown . 1980-81
153 Kingston ... 1980-81
146 Nottingham . 1988
D. I. Gower (1)
154* Kingston ... 1980-81
T. W. Graveney (5)
258 Nottingham . 1957
164 The Oval ... 1957
109 Nottingham . 1966
165 The Oval ... 1966
118 Port-of-Spain 1967-68
A. W. Greig (3)
148 Bridgetown . 1973-74
121 Georgetown . 1973-74
116 Leeds 1976
S. C. Griffith (1)
140† Port-of-Spain 1947-48
W. R. Hammond (1)
138 The Oval ... 1939
J. H. Hampshire (1)
107† Lord's 1969
F. C. Hayes (1)
106*† The Oval ... 1973
E. H. Hendren (2)
205* Port-of-Spain 1929-30
123 Georgetown . 1929-30
J. B. Hobbs (1)
159 The Oval ... 1928
L. Hutton (5)
196† Lord's 1939
165* The Oval ... 1939
202*‡ The Oval ... 1950
169 Georgetown . 1953-54
205 Kingston ... 1953-54
R. Illingworth (1)
113 Lord's 1969
D. R. Jardine (1)
127 Manchester . 1933
A. P. E. Knott (1)
116 Leeds 1976

A. J. Lamb (6)
110 Lord's 1984
100 Leeds 1984
100* Manchester . 1984
113 Lord's 1988
132 Kingston ... 1989-90
119 Bridgetown . 1989-90
P. B. H. May (3)
135 Port-of-Spain 1953-54
285* Birmingham . 1957
104 Nottingham . 1957
C. Milburn (1)
126* Lord's 1966
J. T. Murray (1)
112† The Oval ... 1966
J. M. Parks (1)
101*† Port-of-Spain 1959-60
W. Place (1)
107 Kingston ... 1947-48
P. E. Richardson (2)
126 Nottingham . 1957
107 The Oval ... 1957
J. D. Robertson (1)
133 Port-of-Spain 1947-48
A. Sandham (2)
152† Bridgetown . 1929-30
325 Kingston ... 1929-30
M. J. K. Smith (1)
108 Port-of-Spain 1959-60
D. S. Steele (1)
106† Nottingham . 1976
R. Subba Row (1)
100† Georgetown . 1959-60
E. Tyldesley (1)
122† Lord's 1928
C. Washbrook (2)
114† Lord's 1950
102 Nottingham . 1950
W. Watson (1)
116† Kingston ... 1953-54
P. Willey (2)
100* The Oval ... 1980
102* St John's 1980-81

For West Indies (96)

I. Barrow (1)
105 Manchester . 1933
C. A. Best (1)
164 Bridgetown . 1989-90
B. F. Butcher (2)
133 Lord's 1963
209* Nottingham . 1966
G. M. Carew (1)
107 Port-of-Spain 1947-48
C. A. Davis (1)
103 Lord's 1969
P. J. L. Dujon (1)
101 Manchester . 1984
R. C. Fredericks (3)
150 Birmingham . 1973
138 Lord's 1976
109 Leeds 1976
A. G. Ganteaume (1)
112† Port-of-Spain 1947-48
H. A. Gomes (2)
143 Birmingham . 1984
104* Leeds 1984
C. G. Greenidge (7)
134, 101 Manchester . 1976
115 Leeds 1976
214* Lord's 1984
223 Manchester . 1984
103 Lord's 1988
149 St John's . . . 1989-90
D. L. Haynes (5)
184 Lord's 1980
125 The Oval . . . 1984
131 St John's 1985-86
109 Bridgetown . 1989-90
167 St John's . . . 1989-90
G. A. Headley (8)
176† Bridgetown . 1929-30
114, 112 Georgetown . 1929-30
223 Kingston . . . 1929-30
169* Manchester . 1933
270* Kingston . . . 1934-35
106, 107 Lord's 1939
D. A. J. Holford (1)
105* Lord's 1966
J. K. Holt (1)
166 Bridgetown . 1953-54
C. C. Hunte (3)
182 Manchester . 1963
108* The Oval . . . 1963
135 Manchester . 1966
B. D. Julien (1)
121 Lord's 1973
A. I. Kallicharran (2)
158 Port-of-Spain 1973-74
119 Bridgetown . 1973-74
R. B. Kanhai (5)
110 Port-of-Spain 1959-60
104 The Oval . . . 1966
153 Port-of-Spain 1967-68
150 Georgetown . 1967-68
157 Lord's 1973
C. H. Lloyd (5)
118† Port-of-Spain 1967-68
113* Bridgetown . 1967-68
132 The Oval . . . 1973
101 Manchester . 1980
100 Bridgetown . 1980-81
S. M. Nurse (2)
137 Leeds 1966
136 Port-of-Spain 1967-68
A. F. Rae (2)
106 Lord's 1950
109 The Oval . . . 1950
I. V. A. Richards (8)
232† Nottingham . 1976
135 Manchester . 1976
291 The Oval . . . 1976
145 Lord's 1980
182* Bridgetown . 1980-81
114 St John's . . . 1980-81
117 Birmingham . 1984
110* St John's 1985-86
R. B. Richardson (2)
102 Port-of-Spain 1985-86
160 Bridgetown . 1985-86
C. A. Roach (2)
122 Bridgetown . 1929-30
209 Georgetown . 1929-30
L. G. Rowe (3)
120 Kingston . . . 1973-74
302 Bridgetown . 1973-74
123 Port-of-Spain 1973-74
O. G. Smith (2)
161† Birmingham . 1957
168 Nottingham . 1957
G. S. Sobers (10)
226 Bridgetown . 1959-60
147 Kingston . . . 1959-60
145 Georgetown . 1959-60
102 Leeds 1963
161 Manchester . 1966
163* Lord's 1966
174 Leeds 1966
113* Kingston . . . 1967-68
152 Georgetown . 1967-68
150* Lord's 1973
C. L. Walcott (4)
168* Lord's 1950
220 Bridgetown . 1953-54
124 Port-of-Spain 1953-54
116 Kingston . . . 1953-54
E. D. Weekes (3)
141 Kingston . . . 1947-48
129 Nottingham . 1950
206 Port-of-Spain 1953-54
K. H. Weekes (1)
137 The Oval . . . 1939
F. M. M. Worrell (6)
131* Georgetown . 1947-48
261 Nottingham . 1950
138 The Oval . . . 1950
167 Port-of-Spain 1953-54
191*‡ Nottingham . 1957
197* Bridgetown . 1959-60

† Signifies hundred on first appearance in England–West Indies Tests. S. C. Griffith provides the only instance for England of a player hitting his maiden century in first-class cricket in his first Test.
‡ Carried his bat.

RECORD PARTNERSHIPS FOR EACH WICKET

For England

212 for 1st	C. Washbrook and R. T. Simpson at Nottingham	1950
266 for 2nd	P. E. Richardson and T. W. Graveney at Nottingham	1957
264 for 3rd	L. Hutton and W. R. Hammond at The Oval	1939
411 for 4th†	P. B. H. May and M. C. Cowdrey at Birmingham	1957
130* for 5th	C. Milburn and T. W. Graveney at Lord's	1966

163 for 6th	A. W. Greig and A. P. E. Knott at Bridgetown	1973-74
197 for 7th†	M. J. K. Smith and J. M. Parks at Port-of-Spain	1959-60
217 for 8th	T. W. Graveney and J. T. Murray at The Oval	1966
109 for 9th	G. A. R. Lock and P. I. Pocock at Georgetown	1967-68
128 for 10th	K. Higgs and J. A. Snow at The Oval	1966

For West Indies

298 for 1st†	C. G. Greenidge and D. L. Haynes at St John's	1989-90
287* for 2nd	C. G. Greenidge and H. A. Gomes at Lord's	1984
338 for 3rd†	E. D. Weekes and F. M. M. Worrell at Port-of-Spain	1953-54
399 for 4th†	G. S. Sobers and F. M. M. Worrell at Bridgetown	1959-60
265 for 5th†	S. M. Nurse and G. S. Sobers at Leeds	1966
274* for 6th†	G. S. Sobers and D. A. J. Holford at Lord's	1966
155* for 7th‡	G. S. Sobers and B. D. Julien at Lord's	1973
99 for 8th	C. A. McWatt and J. K. Holt at Georgetown	1953-54
150 for 9th	E. A. E. Baptiste and M. A. Holding at Birmingham	1984
67* for 10th	M. A. Holding and C. E. H. Croft at St John's	1980-81

† *Denotes record partnership against all countries.*
‡ *231 runs were added for this wicket in two separate partnerships: G. S. Sobers retired ill and was replaced by K. D. Boyce when 155 had been added.*

TEN WICKETS OR MORE IN A MATCH

For England (11)

11-98 (7-44, 4-54)	T. E. Bailey, Lord's	1957
10-93 (5-54, 5-39)	A. P. Freeman, Manchester	1928
13-156 (8-86, 5-70)	A. W. Greig, Port-of-Spain	1973-74
11-48 (5-28, 6-20)	G. A. R. Lock, The Oval	1957
10-137 (4-60, 6-77)	D. E. Malcolm, Port-of-Spain	1989-90
11-96 (5-37, 6-59)†	C. S. Marriott, The Oval	1933
10-142 (4-82, 6-60)	J. A. Snow, Georgetown	1967-68
10-195 (5-105, 5-90)†	G. T. S. Stevens, Bridgetown	1929-30
11-152 (6-100, 5-52)	F. S. Trueman, Lord's	1963
12-119 (5-75, 7-44)	F. S. Trueman, Birmingham	1963
11-149 (4-79, 7-70)	W. Voce, Port-of-Spain	1929-30

For West Indies (12)

10-127 (2-82, 8-45)	C. E. L. Ambrose, Bridgetown	1989-90
11-147 (5-70, 6-77)†	K. D. Boyce, The Oval	1973
11-229 (5-137, 6-92)	W. Ferguson, Port-of-Spain	1947-48
11-157 (5-59, 6-98)†	L. R. Gibbs, Manchester	1963
10-106 (5-37, 5-69)	L. R. Gibbs, Manchester	1966
14-149 (8-92, 6-57)	M. A. Holding, The Oval	1976
10-96 (5-41, 5-55)†	H. H. H. Johnson, Kingston	1947-48
10-92 (6-32, 4-60)	M. D. Marshall, Lord's	1988
11-152 (5-66, 6-86)	S. Ramadhin, Lord's	1950
10-123 (5-60, 5-63)	A. M. E. Roberts, Lord's	1976
11-204 (8-104, 3-100)†	A. L. Valentine, Manchester	1950
10-160 (4-121, 6-39)	A. L. Valentine, The Oval	1950

† *Signifies ten wickets or more on first appearance in England–West Indies Tests.*

Note: F. S. Trueman took ten wickets or more in successive matches.

ENGLAND v NEW ZEALAND

	Captains					
Season	*England*	*New Zealand*	*T*	*E*	*NZ*	*D*
1929-30	A. H. H. Gilligan	T. C. Lowry	4	1	0	3
1931	D. R. Jardine	T. C. Lowry	3	1	0	2
1932-33	D. R. Jardine[1]	M. L. Page	2	0	0	2
1937	R. W. V. Robins	M. L. Page	3	1	0	2
1946-47	W. R. Hammond	W. A. Hadlee	1	0	0	1
1949	F. G. Mann[2]	W. A. Hadlee	4	0	0	4
1950-51	F. R. Brown	W. A. Hadlee	2	1	0	1
1954-55	L. Hutton	G. O. Rabone	2	2	0	0
1958	P. B. H. May	J. R. Reid	5	4	0	1
1958-59	P. B. H. May	J. R. Reid	2	1	0	1
1962-63	E. R. Dexter	J. R. Reid	3	3	0	0
1965	M. J. K. Smith	J. R. Reid	3	3	0	0
1965-66	M. J. K. Smith	B. W. Sinclair[3]	3	0	0	3
1969	R. Illingworth	G. T. Dowling	3	2	0	1
1970-71	R. Illingworth	G. T. Dowling	2	1	0	1
1973	R. Illingworth	B. E. Congdon	3	2	0	1
1974-75	M. H. Denness	B. E. Congdon	2	1	0	1
1977-78	G. Boycott	M. G. Burgess	3	1	1	1
1978	J. M. Brearley	M. G. Burgess	3	3	0	0
1983	R. G. D. Willis	G. P. Howarth	4	3	1	0
1983-84	R. G. D. Willis	G. P. Howarth	3	0	1	2
1986	M. W. Gatting	J. V. Coney	3	0	1	2
1987-88	M. W. Gatting	J. J. Crowe[4]	3	0	0	3
1990	G. A. Gooch	J. G. Wright	3	1	0	2
	In New Zealand		32	11	2	19
	In England		37	20	2	15
	Totals		69	31	4	34

Notes: The following deputised for the official touring captain or were appointed by the home authority for only a minor proportion of the series:

[1]R. E. S. Wyatt (Second). [2]F. R. Brown (Third and Fourth). [3]M. E. Chapple (First). [4]J. G. Wright (Third).

HIGHEST INNINGS TOTALS

For England in England: 546-4 dec. at Leeds 1965
in New Zealand: 593-6 dec. at Auckland 1974-75

For New Zealand in England: 551-9 dec. at Lord's 1973
in New Zealand: 537 at Wellington 1983-84

LOWEST INNINGS TOTALS

For England in England: 158 at Birmingham 1990
in New Zealand: 64 at Wellington 1977-78

For New Zealand in England: 47 at Lord's 1958
in New Zealand: 26 at Auckland 1954-55

INDIVIDUAL HUNDREDS

For England (71)

G. O. B. Allen (1)
122† Lord's 1931
L. E. G. Ames (2)
137† Lord's 1931
103 Christchurch. 1932-33
D. L. Amiss (2)
138*† Nottingham . 1973
164* Christchurch. 1974-75
M. A. Atherton (1)
151† Nottingham . 1990
T. E. Bailey (1)
134* Christchurch. 1950-51
K. F. Barrington (3)
126† Auckland ... 1962-63
137 Birmingham . 1965
163 Leeds 1965
I. T. Botham (3)
103 Christchurch. 1977-78
103 Nottingham . 1983
138 Wellington .. 1983-84
E. H. Bowley (1)
109 Auckland ... 1929-30
G. Boycott (2)
115 Leeds 1973
131 Nottingham . 1978
B. C. Broad (1)
114† Christchurch. 1987-88
D. C. S. Compton (2)
114 Leeds 1949
116 Lord's 1949
M. C. Cowdrey (2)
128* Wellington .. 1962-63
119 Lord's 1965
M. H. Denness (1)
181 Auckland ... 1974-75
E. R. Dexter (1)
141 Christchurch. 1958-59
B. L. D'Oliveira (1)
100 Christchurch. 1970-71

K. S. Duleepsinhji (2)
117 Auckland ... 1929-30
109 The Oval ... 1931
J. H. Edrich (3)
310*† Leeds 1965
115 Lord's 1969
155 Nottingham . 1969
W. J. Edrich (1)
100 The Oval ... 1949
K. W. R. Fletcher (2)
178 Lord's 1973
216 Auckland ... 1974-75
G. Fowler (1)
105† The Oval ... 1983
M. W. Gatting (1)
121 The Oval ... 1986
G. A. Gooch (2)
183 Lord's 1986
154 Birmingham . 1990
D. I. Gower (4)
111† The Oval ... 1978
112* Leeds 1983
108 Lord's 1983
131 The Oval 1986
A. W. Greig (1)
139† Nottingham . 1973
W. R. Hammond (4)
100* The Oval ... 1931
227 Christchurch. 1932-33
336* Auckland ... 1932-33
140 Lord's 1937
J. Hardstaff jun. (2)
114† Lord's 1937
103 The Oval ... 1937
L. Hutton (3)
100 Manchester . 1937
101 Leeds 1949
206 The Oval ... 1949

B. R. Knight (1)
125† Auckland ... 1962-63
A. P. E. Knott (1)
101 Auckland ... 1970-71
A. J. Lamb (2)
102*† The Oval ... 1983
137* Nottingham . 1983
G. B. Legge (1)
196 Auckland ... 1929-30
P. B. H. May (3)
113* Leeds 1958
101 Manchester . 1958
124* Auckland ... 1958-59
C. A. Milton (1)
104*† Leeds 1958
P. H. Parfitt (1)
131*† Auckland ... 1962-63
C. T. Radley (1)
158 Auckland ... 1977-78
D. W. Randall (2)
164 Wellington .. 1983-84
104 Auckland ... 1983-84
P. E. Richardson (1)
100† Birmingham . 1958
J. D. Robertson (1)
121† Lord's 1949
P. J. Sharpe (1)
111 Nottingham . 1969
R. T. Simpson (1)
103† Manchester . 1949
H. Sutcliffe (2)
117† The Oval ... 1931
109* Manchester . 1931
C. J. Tavaré (1)
109† The Oval ... 1983
C. Washbrook (1)
103* Leeds 1949

For New Zealand (34)

J. G. Bracewell (1)
110 Nottingham . 1986
M. G. Burgess (2)
104 Auckland ... 1970-71
105 Lord's 1973
J. V. Coney (1)
174* Wellington .. 1983-84
B. E. Congdon (3)
104 Christchurch. 1965-66
176 Nottingham . 1973
175 Lord's 1973

J. J. Crowe (1)
128 Auckland ... 1983-84
M. D. Crowe (3)
100 Wellington .. 1983-84
106 Lord's 1986
143 Wellington .. 1987-88
C. S. Dempster (2)
136 Wellington .. 1929-30
120 Lord's 1931
M. P. Donnelly (1)
206 Lord's 1949

T. J. Franklin (1)
101 Lord's 1990
M. J. Greatbatch (1)
107*† Auckland ... 1987-88
W. A. Hadlee (1)
116 Christchurch. 1946-47
G. P. Howarth (3)
122 } Auckland ... 1977-78
102 }
123 Lord's 1978

J. E. Mills (1)
117† Wellington .. 1929-30
M. L. Page (1)
104 Lord's 1931
J. M. Parker (1)
121 Auckland ... 1974-75
V. Pollard (2)
116 Nottingham . 1973
105* Lord's 1973

J. R. Reid (1)
100 Christchurch. 1962-63
K. R. Rutherford (1)
107* Wellington .. 1987-88
B. W. Sinclair (1)
114 Auckland ... 1965-66
I. D. S. Smith (1)
113* Auckland ... 1983-84

B. Sutcliffe (2)
101 Manchester . 1949
116 Christchurch. 1950-51
J. G. Wright (3)
130 Auckland ... 1983-84
119 The Oval ... 1986
103 Auckland ... 1987-88

† *Signifies hundred on first appearance in England–New Zealand Tests.*

RECORD PARTNERSHIPS FOR EACH WICKET

For England

223 for 1st	G. Fowler and C. J. Tavaré at The Oval	1983
369 for 2nd	J. H. Edrich and K. F. Barrington at Leeds	1965
245 for 3rd	W. R. Hammond and J. Hardstaff jun. at Lord's	1937
266 for 4th	M. H. Denness and K. W. R. Fletcher at Auckland	1974-75
242 for 5th	W. R. Hammond and L. E. G. Ames at Christchurch	1932-33
240 for 6th†	P. H. Parfitt and B. R. Knight at Auckland	1962-63
149 for 7th	A. P. E. Knott and P. Lever at Auckland	1970-71
246 for 8th†	L. E. G. Ames and G. O. B. Allen at Lord's	1931
163* for 9th†	M. C. Cowdrey and A. C. Smith at Wellington	1962-63
59 for 10th	A. P. E. Knott and N. Gifford at Nottingham	1973

For New Zealand

276 for 1st	C. S. Dempster and J. E. Mills at Wellington	1929-30
131 for 2nd	B. Sutcliffe and J. R. Reid at Christchurch	1950-51
210 for 3rd	B. A. Edgar and M. D. Crowe at Lord's	1986
155 for 4th	M. D. Crowe and M. J. Greatbatch at Wellington	1987-88
177 for 5th	B. E. Congdon and V. Pollard at Nottingham	1973
134 for 6th	K. R. Rutherford and J. G. Bracewell at Wellington	1987-88
104 for 7th	B. Sutcliffe and V. Pollard at Birmingham	1965
104 for 8th	D. A. R. Moloney and A. W. Roberts at Lord's	1937
118 for 9th	J. V. Coney and B. L. Cairns at Wellington	1983-84
57 for 10th	F. L. H. Mooney and J. Cowie at Leeds	1949

† *Denotes record partnership against all countries.*

TEN WICKETS OR MORE IN A MATCH

For England (7)

11-140 (6-101, 5-39)	I. T. Botham, Lord's	1978
10-149 (5-98, 5-51)	A. W. Greig, Auckland	1974-75
11-65 (4-14, 7-51)	G. A. R. Lock, Leeds	1958
11-84 (5-31, 6-53)	G. A. R. Lock, Christchurch	1958-59
11-70 (4-38, 7-32)†	D. L. Underwood, Lord's	1969
12-101 (6-41, 6-60)	D. L. Underwood, The Oval	1969
12-97 (6-12, 6-85)	D. L. Underwood, Christchurch	1970-71

For New Zealand (4)

10-144 (7-74, 3-70)	B. L. Cairns, Leeds	1983
10-140 (4-73, 6-67)	J. Cowie, Manchester	1937
10-100 (4-74, 6-26)	R. J. Hadlee, Wellington	1977-78
10-140 (6-80, 4-60)	R. J. Hadlee, Nottingham	1986

† *Signifies ten wickets or more on first appearance in England–New Zealand Tests.*

Note: D. L. Underwood took twelve wickets in successive matches against New Zealand in 1969 and 1970-71.

HAT-TRICK AND FOUR WICKETS IN FIVE BALLS

M. J. C. Allom, in his first Test match, v New Zealand at Christchurch in 1929-30, dismissed C. S. Dempster, T. C. Lowry, K. C. James, and F. T. Badcock to take four wickets in five balls (w-www).

ENGLAND v INDIA

Season	England (Captains)	India (Captains)	T	E	I	D
1932	D. R. Jardine	C. K. Nayudu	1	1	0	0
1933-34	D. R. Jardine	C. K. Nayudu	3	2	0	1
1936	G. O. B. Allen	Maharaj of Vizianagram	3	2	0	1
1946	W. R. Hammond	Nawab of Pataudi sen.	3	1	0	2
1951-52	N. D. Howard[1]	V. S. Hazare	5	1	1	3
1952	L. Hutton	V. S. Hazare	4	3	0	1
1959	P. B. H. May[2]	D. K. Gaekwad[3]	5	5	0	0
1961-62	E. R. Dexter	N. J. Contractor	5	0	2	3
1963-64	M. J. K. Smith	Nawab of Pataudi jun.	5	0	0	5
1967	D. B. Close	Nawab of Pataudi jun.	3	3	0	0
1971	R. Illingworth	A. L. Wadekar	3	0	1	2
1972-73	A. R. Lewis	A. L. Wadekar	5	1	2	2
1974	M. H. Denness	A. L. Wadekar	3	3	0	0
1976-77	A. W. Greig	B. S. Bedi	5	3	1	1
1979	J. M. Brearley	S. Venkataraghavan	4	1	0	3
1979-80	J. M. Brearley	G. R. Viswanath	1	1	0	0
1981-82	K. W. R. Fletcher	S. M. Gavaskar	6	0	1	5
1982	R. G. D. Willis	S. M. Gavaskar	3	1	0	2
1984-85	D. I. Gower	S. M. Gavaskar	5	2	1	2
1986	M. W. Gatting[4]	Kapil Dev	3	0	2	1
1990	G. A. Gooch	M. Azharuddin	3	1	0	2
	In England		38	21	3	14
	In India		40	10	8	22
	Totals		78	31	11	36

Notes: The 1932 Indian touring team was captained by the Maharaj of Porbandar but he did not play in the Test match.

The following deputised for the official touring captain or were appointed by the home authority for only a minor proportion of the series:

[1]D. B. Carr (Fifth). [2]M. C. Cowdrey (Fourth and Fifth). [3]Pankaj Roy (Second). [4]D. I. Gower (First).

HIGHEST INNINGS TOTALS

For England in England: 653-4 dec. at Lord's 1990
in India: 652-7 dec. at Madras 1984-85

For India in England: 606-9 dec. at The Oval 1990
in India: 553-8 dec. at Kanpur 1984-85

LOWEST INNINGS TOTALS

For England in England: 101 at The Oval 1971
in India: 102 at Bombay 1981-82

For India in England: 42 at Lord's 1974
in India: 83 at Madras 1976-77

INDIVIDUAL HUNDREDS

For England (70)

D. L. Amiss (2)
188 Lord's 1974
179 Delhi 1976-77
M. A. Atherton (1)
131 Manchester 1990
K. F. Barrington (3)
151* Bombay 1961-62
172 Kanpur 1961-62
113* Delhi 1961-62
I. T. Botham (5)
137 Leeds 1979
114 Bombay 1979-80
142 Kanpur 1981-82
128 Manchester 1982
208 The Oval 1982
G. Boycott (4)
246*† Leeds 1967
155 Birmingham 1979
125 The Oval 1979
105 Delhi 1981-82
M. C. Cowdrey (3)
160 Leeds 1959
107 Calcutta 1963-64
151 Delhi 1963-64
M. H. Denness (2)
118 Lord's 1974
100 Birmingham 1974
E. R. Dexter (1)
126* Kanpur 1961-62
B. L. D'Oliveira (1)
109† Leeds 1967
J. H. Edrich (1)
100* Manchester 1974
T. G. Evans (1)
104 Lord's 1952
K. W. R. Fletcher (2)
113 Bombay 1972-73
123* Manchester 1974
G. Fowler (1)
201 Madras 1984-85
M. W. Gatting (3)
136 Bombay 1984-85
207 Madras 1984-85
183* Birmingham 1986
G. A. Gooch (5)
127 Madras 1981-82
114 Lord's 1986
333 }
123 } Lord's 1990
116 Manchester 1990
D. I. Gower (2)
200*† Birmingham 1979
157* The Oval 1990
T. W. Graveney (2)
175† Bombay 1951-52
151 Lord's 1967
A. W. Greig (3)
148 Bombay 1972-73
106 Lord's 1974
103 Calcutta 1976-77
W. R. Hammond (2)
167 Manchester 1936
217 The Oval 1936
J. Hardstaff jun. (1)
205* Lord's 1946
L. Hutton (2)
150 Lord's 1952
104 Manchester 1952
R. Illingworth (1)
107 Manchester 1971
B. R. Knight (1)
127 Kanpur 1963-64
A. J. Lamb (3)
107 The Oval 1982
139 Lord's 1990
109 Manchester 1990
A. R. Lewis (1)
125 Kanpur 1972-73
D. Lloyd (1)
214* Birmingham 1974
B. W. Luckhurst (1)
101 Manchester 1971
P. B. H. May (1)
106 Nottingham 1959
P. H. Parfitt (1)
121 Kanpur 1963-64
G. Pullar (2)
131 Manchester 1959
119 Kanpur 1961-62
D. W. Randall (1)
126 Lord's 1982
R. T. Robinson (1)
160 Delhi 1984-85
D. S. Sheppard (1)
119 The Oval 1952
M. J. K. Smith (1)
100† Manchester 1959
R. A. Smith (2)
100*† Lord's 1990
121* Manchester 1990
C. J. Tavaré (1)
149 Delhi 1981-82
B. H. Valentine (1)
136† Bombay 1933-34
C. F. Walters (1)
102 Madras 1933-34
A. J. Watkins (1)
137*† Delhi 1951-52
T. S. Worthington (1)
128 The Oval 1936

For India (56)

L. Amarnath (1)
118† Bombay 1933-34
M. Azharuddin (5)
110† Calcutta 1984-85
105 Madras 1984-85
122 Kanpur 1984-85
121 Lord's 1990
179 Manchester 1990
A. A. Baig (1)
112† Manchester 1959
F. M. Engineer (1)
121 Bombay 1972-73
S. M. Gavaskar (4)
101 Manchester 1974
108 Bombay 1976-77
221 The Oval 1979
172 Bangalore 1981-82
Hanumant Singh (1)
105† Delhi 1963-64
V. S. Hazare (2)
164* Delhi 1951-52
155 Bombay 1951-52
M. L. Jaisimha (2)
127 Delhi 1961-62
129 Calcutta 1963-64
Kapil Dev (2)
116 Kanpur 1981-82
110 The Oval 1990
S. M. H. Kirmani (1)
102 Bombay 1984-85
B. K. Kunderan (2)
192 Madras 1963-64
100 Delhi 1963-64
V. L. Manjrekar (3)
133 Leeds 1952
189* Delhi 1961-62
108 Madras 1963-64
V. Mankad (1)
184 Lord's 1952
V. M. Merchant (3)
114 Manchester 1936
128 The Oval 1946
154 Delhi 1951-52
Mushtaq Ali (1)
112 Manchester 1936

R. G. Nadkarni (1)
122* Kanpur 1963-64
Nawab of Pataudi jun. (3)
103 Madras 1961-62
203* Delhi 1963-64
148 Leeds 1967
S. M. Patil (1)
129* Manchester . 1982
D. G. Phadkar (1)
115 Calcutta 1951-52
Pankaj Roy (2)
140 Bombay 1951-52
111 Madras 1951-52

R. J. Shastri (4)
142 Bombay 1984-85
111 Calcutta 1984-85
100 Lord's 1990
187 The Oval ... 1990
S. R. Tendulkar (1)
119* Manchester . 1990
P. R. Umrigar (3)
130* Madras 1951-52
118 Manchester . 1959
147* Kanpur 1961-62
D. B. Vengsarkar (5)
103 Lord's 1979
157 Lord's 1982
137 Kanpur 1984-85
126* Lord's 1986
102* Leeds 1986
G. R. Viswanath (4)
113 Bombay 1972-73
113 Lord's 1979
107 Delhi 1981-82
222 Madras 1981-82
Yashpal Sharma (1)
140 Madras 1981-82

† *Signifies hundred on first appearance in England–India Tests.*

Notes: G. A. Gooch's match aggregate of 456 (333 and 123) for England at Lord's in 1990 is the record in Test matches and provides the only instance of a batsman scoring a triple-hundred and a hundred in the same first-class match. His 333 is the highest innings in any match at Lord's.

M. Azharuddin scored hundreds in each of his first three Tests.

RECORD PARTNERSHIPS FOR EACH WICKET

For England

225 for 1st	G. A. Gooch and M. A. Atherton at Manchester	1990
241 for 2nd	G. Fowler and M. W. Gatting at Madras	1984-85
308 for 3rd	G. A. Gooch and A. J. Lamb at Lord's	1990
266 for 4th	W. R. Hammond and T. S. Worthington at The Oval	1936
254 for 5th†	K. W. R. Fletcher and A. W. Greig at Bombay	1972-73
171 for 6th	I. T. Botham and R. W. Taylor at Bombay	1979-80
125 for 7th	D. W. Randall and P. H. Edmonds at Lord's	1982
168 for 8th	R. Illingworth and P. Lever at Manchester	1971
83 for 9th	K. W. R. Fletcher and N. Gifford at Madras	1972-73
70 for 10th	P. J. W. Allott and R. G. D. Willis at Lord's	1982

For India

213 for 1st	S. M. Gavaskar and C. P. S. Chauhan at The Oval	1979
192 for 2nd	F. M. Engineer and A. L. Wadekar at Bombay	1972-73
316 for 3rd†‡	G. R. Viswanath and Yashpal Sharma at Madras	1981-82
222 for 4th†	V. S. Hazare and V. L. Manjrekar at Leeds	1952
214 for 5th†	M. Azharuddin and R. J. Shastri at Calcutta	1984-85
130 for 6th	S. M. H. Kirmani and Kapil Dev at The Oval	1982
235 for 7th†	R. J. Shastri and S. M. H. Kirmani at Bombay	1984-85
128 for 8th	R. J. Shastri and S. M. H. Kirmani at Delhi	1981-82
104 for 9th	R. J. Shastri and Madan Lal at Delhi	1981-82
51 for 10th	R. G. Nadkarni and B. S. Chandrasekhar at Calcutta	1963-64
	S. M. H. Kirmani and Chetan Sharma at Madras	1984-85

† *Denotes record partnership against all countries.*

‡ *415 runs were added between the fall of the 2nd and 3rd wickets: D. B. Vengsarkar retired hurt when he and Viswanath had added 99 runs.*

TEN WICKETS OR MORE IN A MATCH

For England (7)

10-78 (5-35, 5-43)†	G. O. B. Allen, Lord's	1936
11-145 (7-49, 4-96)†	A. V. Bedser, Lord's	1946
11-93 (4-41, 7-52)	A. V. Bedser, Manchester	1946
13-106 (6-58, 7-48)	I. T. Botham, Bombay	1979-80
11-163 (6-104, 5-59)†	N. A. Foster, Madras	1984-85
10-70 (7-46, 3-24)†	J. K. Lever, Delhi	1976-77
11-153 (7-49, 4-104)	H. Verity, Madras	1933-34

For India (4)

10-177 (6-105, 4-72)	S. A. Durani, Madras	1961-62
12-108 (8-55, 4-53)	V. Mankad, Madras	1951-52
10-188 (4-130, 6-58)	Chetan Sharma, Birmingham	1986
12-181 (6-64, 6-117)†	L. Sivaramakrishnan, Bombay	1984-85

† *Signifies ten wickets or more on first appearance in England–India Tests.*

Note: A. V. Bedser took eleven wickets in a match in the first two Tests of his career.

ENGLAND v PAKISTAN

Season	*England* (Captains)	*Pakistan* (Captains)	*T*	*E*	*P*	*D*
1954	L. Hutton[1]	A. H. Kardar	4	1	1	2
1961-62	E. R. Dexter	Imtiaz Ahmed	3	1	0	2
1962	E. R. Dexter[2]	Javed Burki	5	4	0	1
1967	D. B. Close	Hanif Mohammad	3	2	0	1
1968-69	M. C. Cowdrey	Saeed Ahmed	3	0	0	3
1971	R. Illingworth	Intikhab Alam	3	1	0	2
1972-73	A. R. Lewis	Majid Khan	3	0	0	3
1974	M. H. Denness	Intikhab Alam	3	0	0	3
1977-78	J. M. Brearley[3]	Wasim Bari	3	0	0	3
1978	J. M. Brearley	Wasim Bari	3	2	0	1
1982	R. G. D. Willis[4]	Imran Khan	3	2	1	0
1983-84	R. G. D. Willis[5]	Zaheer Abbas	3	0	1	2
1987	M. W. Gatting	Imran Khan	5	0	1	4
1987-88	M. W. Gatting	Javed Miandad	3	0	1	2
	In England		29	12	3	14
	In Pakistan		18	1	2	15
	Totals		47	13	5	29

Notes: The following deputised for the official touring captain or were appointed by the home authority for only a minor proportion of the series:

[1]D. S. Sheppard (Second and Third). [2]M. C. Cowdrey (Third). [3]G. Boycott (Third). [4]D. I. Gower (Second). [5]D. I. Gower (Second and Third).

HIGHEST INNINGS TOTALS

For England in England:	558-6 dec. at Nottingham	1954
in Pakistan:	546-8 dec. at Faisalabad	1983-84
For Pakistan in England:	708 at The Oval	1987
in Pakistan:	569-9 dec. at Hyderabad	1972-73

LOWEST INNINGS TOTALS

For England in England: 130 at The Oval 1954
in Pakistan: 130 at Lahore 1987-88

For Pakistan in England: 87 at Lord's 1954
in Pakistan: 191 at Faisalabad 1987-88

INDIVIDUAL HUNDREDS

For England (41)

D. L. Amiss (3)
112 Lahore 1972-73
158 Hyderabad .. 1972-73
183 The Oval ... 1974
C. W. J. Athey (1)
123 Lord's 1987
K. F. Barrington (4)
139† Lahore 1961-62
148 Lord's 1967
109* Nottingham . 1967
142 The Oval ... 1967
I. T. Botham (2)
100† Birmingham . 1978
108 Lord's 1978
G. Boycott (3)
121* Lord's 1971
112 Leeds 1971
100* Hyderabad .. 1977-78
B. C. Broad (1)
116 Faisalabad .. 1987-88
D. C. S. Compton (1)
278 Nottingham . 1954

M. C. Cowdrey (3)
159† Birmingham . 1962
182 The Oval ... 1962
100 Lahore 1968-69
E. R. Dexter (2)
205 Karachi 1961-62
172 The Oval ... 1962
B. L. D'Oliveira (1)
114* Dacca 1968-69
K. W. R. Fletcher (1)
122 The Oval ... 1974
M. W. Gatting (2)
124 Birmingham . 1987
150* The Oval ... 1987
D. I. Gower (2)
152 Faisalabad .. 1983-84
173* Lahore 1983-84
T. W. Graveney (3)
153 Lord's 1962
114 Nottingham . 1962
105 Karachi 1968-69

A. P. E. Knott (1)
116 Birmingham . 1971
B. W. Luckhurst (1)
108*† Birmingham . 1971
C. Milburn (1)
139 Karachi 1968-69
P. H. Parfitt (4)
111 Karachi 1961-62
101* Birmingham . 1962
119 Leeds 1962
101* Nottingham . 1962
G. Pullar (1)
165 Dacca 1961-62
C. T. Radley (1)
106† Birmingham . 1978
D. W. Randall (1)
105 Birmingham . 1982
R. T. Robinson (1)
166† Manchester . 1987
R. T. Simpson (1)
101 Nottingham . 1954

For Pakistan (30)

Alim-ud-Din (1)
109 Karachi 1961-62
Asif Iqbal (3)
146 The Oval ... 1967
104* Birmingham . 1971
102 Lahore 1972-73
Hanif Mohammad (3)
111 }
104 } Dacca 1961-62
187* Lord's 1967
Haroon Rashid (2)
122† Lahore 1977-78
108 Hyderabad .. 1977-78
Imran Khan (1)
118 The Oval ... 1987

Intikhab Alam (1)
138 Hyderabad .. 1972-73
Javed Burki (3)
138† Lahore 1961-62
140 Dacca 1961-62
101 Lord's 1962
Javed Miandad (1)
260 The Oval ... 1987
Mohsin Khan (2)
200 Lord's 1982
104 Lahore 1983-84
Mudassar Nazar (3)
114† Lahore 1977-88
124 Birmingham . 1987
120 Lahore 1987-88

Mushtaq Mohammad (3)
100* Nottingham . 1962
100 Birmingham . 1971
157 Hyderabad .. 1972-73
Nasim-ul Ghani (1)
101 Lord's 1962
Sadiq Mohammad (1)
119 Lahore 1972-73
Salim Malik (2)
116 Faisalabad .. 1983-84
102 The Oval ... 1987
Wasim Raja (1)
112 Faisalabad .. 1983-84
Zaheer Abbas (2)
274† Birmingham . 1971
240 The Oval ... 1974

† *Signifies hundred on first appearance in England–Pakistan Tests.*

Note: Three batsmen – Majid Khan, Mushtaq Mohammad and D. L. Amiss – were dismissed for 99 at Karachi, 1972-73: the only instance in Test matches.

RECORD PARTNERSHIPS FOR EACH WICKET

For England

198 for 1st	G. Pullar and R. W. Barber at Dacca	1961-62
248 for 2nd	M. C. Cowdrey and E. R. Dexter at The Oval	1962
201 for 3rd	K. F. Barrington and T. W. Graveney at Lord's	1967
188 for 4th	E. R. Dexter and P. H. Parfitt at Karachi	1961-62
192 for 5th	D. C. S. Compton and T. E. Bailey at Nottingham	1954
153* for 6th	P. H. Parfitt and D. A. Allen at Birmingham	1962
167 for 7th	D. I. Gower and V. J. Marks at Faisalabad	1983-84
99 for 8th	P. H. Parfitt and D. A. Allen at Leeds	1962
76 for 9th	T. W. Graveney and F. S. Trueman at Lord's	1962
79 for 10th	R. W. Taylor and R. G. D. Willis at Birmingham	1982

For Pakistan

173 for 1st	Mohsin Khan and Shoaib Mohammad at Lahore	1983-84
291 for 2nd†	Zaheer Abbas and Mushtaq Mohammad at Birmingham	1971
180 for 3rd	Mudassar Nazar and Haroon Rashid at Lahore	1977-78
234 for 4th	Javed Miandad and Salim Malik at The Oval	1987
197 for 5th	Javed Burki and Nasim-ul-Ghani at Lord's	1962
145 for 6th	Mushtaq Mohammad and Intikhab Alam at Hyderabad	1972-73
89 for 7th	Ijaz Ahmed and Salim Yousuf at The Oval	1987
130 for 8th†	Hanif Mohammad and Asif Iqbal at Lord's	1967
190 for 9th†	Asif Iqbal and Intikhab Alam at The Oval	1967
62 for 10th	Sarfraz Nawaz and Asif Masood at Leeds	1974

† *Denotes record partnership against all countries.*

TEN WICKETS OR MORE IN A MATCH

For England (2)

11-83 (6-65, 5-18)†	N. G. B. Cook, Karachi	1983-84
13-71 (5-20, 8-51)	D. L. Underwood, Lord's	1974

For Pakistan (6)

10-194 (5-84, 5-110)	Abdul Qadir, Lahore	1983-84
13-101 (9-56, 4-45)	Abdul Qadir, Lahore	1987-88
10-186 (5-88, 5-98)	Abdul Qadir, Karachi	1987-88
10-211 (7-96, 3-115)	Abdul Qadir, The Oval	1987
12-99 (6-53, 6-46)	Fazal Mahmood, The Oval	1954
10-77 (3-37, 7-40)	Imran Khan, Leeds	1987

† *Signifies ten wickets or more on first appearance in England–Pakistan Tests.*

FOUR WICKETS IN FIVE BALLS

C. M. Old, v Pakistan at Birmingham in 1978, dismissed Wasim Raja, Wasim Bari, Iqbal Qasim and Sikander Bakht to take four wickets in five balls (ww-ww).

ENGLAND v SRI LANKA

Captains

Season	*England*	*Sri Lanka*	*T*	*E*	*SL*	*D*
1981-82	K. W. R. Fletcher	B. Warnapura	1	1	0	0
1984	D. I. Gower	L. R. D. Mendis	1	0	0	1
1988	G. A. Gooch	R. S. Madugalle	1	1	0	0
	In England		2	1	0	1
	In Sri Lanka		1	1	0	0
	Totals		3	2	0	1

INNINGS TOTALS

Highest innings total for England: 429 at Lord's 1988
for Sri Lanka: 491-7 dec. at Lord's 1984

Lowest innings total for England: 223 at Colombo (PSS) 1981-82
for Sri Lanka: 175 at Colombo (PSS) 1981-82

INDIVIDUAL HUNDREDS

For England (1)

A. J. Lamb (1)
107† Lord's 1984

For Sri Lanka (3)

L. R. D. Mendis (1)
111 Lord's 1984

S. A. R. Silva (1)
102*† Lord's 1984

S. Wettimuny (1)
190 Lord's 1984

† *Signifies hundred on first appearance in England–Sri Lanka Tests.*

BEST BOWLING

Best bowling in an innings for England: 6-33 by J. E. Emburey at Colombo (PSS) 1981-82
for Sri Lanka: 4-70 by A. L. F. de Mel at Colombo (PSS) 1981-82

RECORD PARTNERSHIPS FOR EACH WICKET

For England

73 for 1st	G. A. Gooch and R. T. Robinson at Lord's	1988
131 for 2nd	G. A. Gooch and R. C. Russell at Lord's	1988
85 for 3rd	B. C. Broad and D. I. Gower at Lord's	1984
87 for 4th	K. J. Barnett and A. J. Lamb at Lord's	1988
38 for 5th	A. J. Lamb and R. A. Smith at Lord's	1988
87 for 6th	A. J. Lamb and R. M. Ellison at Lord's	1984
49 for 7th	A. J. Lamb and P. R. Downton at Lord's	1984
9 for 8th	R. W. Taylor and P. J. W. Allott at Colombo (PSS)	1981-82
37 for 9th	P. J. Newport and N. A. Foster at Lord's	1988
9 for 10th	N. A. Foster and D. V. Lawrence at Lord's	1988

For Sri Lanka

43 for 1st	D. S. B. P. Kuruppu and S. A. R. Silva at Lord's	1988
83 for 2nd	B. Warnapura and R. L. Dias at Colombo (PSS)	1981-82
101 for 3rd	S. Wettimuny and R. L. Dias at Lord's	1984
148 for 4th	S. Wettimuny and A. Ranatunga at Lord's	1984
150 for 5th†	S. Wettimuny and L. R. D. Mendis at Lord's	1984
138 for 6th	S. A. R. Silva and L. R. D. Mendis at Lord's	1984
59 for 7th	L. R. D. Mendis and J. R. Ratnayeke at Lord's	1988
27* for 8th	A. L. F. de Mel and J. R. Ratnayeke at Lord's	1984
12 for 9th	J. R. Ratnayeke and G. F. Labrooy at Lord's	1988
64 for 10th†	J. R. Ratnayeke and G. F. Labrooy at Lord's	1988

† *Denotes record partnership against all countries.*

ENGLAND v REST OF THE WORLD

In 1970, owing to the cancellation of the South African tour to England, a series of matches was arranged, with the trappings of a full Test series, between England and the Rest of the World. It was played for the Guinness Trophy.

The following players represented the Rest of the World: E. J. Barlow (5), F. M. Engineer (2), L. R. Gibbs (4), Intikhab Alam (5), R. B. Kanhai (5), C. H. Lloyd (5), G. D. McKenzie (3), D. L. Murray (3), Mushtaq Mohammad (2), P. M. Pollock (1), R. G. Pollock (5), M. J. Procter (5), B. A. Richards (5), G. S. Sobers (5).

A list of players who appeared for England in these matches may be found on page 128.

AUSTRALIA v SOUTH AFRICA

	Captains					
Season	*Australia*	*South Africa*	*T*	*A*	*SA*	*D*
1902-03*S*	J. Darling	H. M. Taberer[1]	3	2	0	1
1910-11*A*	C. Hill	P. W. Sherwell	5	4	1	0
1912*E*	S. E. Gregory	F. Mitchell[2]	3	2	0	1
1921-22*S*	H. L. Collins	H. W. Taylor	3	1	0	2
1931-32*A*	W. M. Woodfull	H. B. Cameron	5	5	0	0
1935-36*S*	V. Y. Richardson	H. F. Wade	5	4	0	1
1949-50*S*	A. L. Hassett	A. D. Nourse	5	4	0	1
1952-53*A*	A. L. Hassett	J. E. Cheetham	5	2	2	1
1957-58*S*	I. D. Craig	C. B. van Ryneveld[3]	5	3	0	2
1963-64*A*	R. B. Simpson[4]	T. L. Goddard	5	1	1	3
1966-67*S*	R. B. Simpson	P. L. van der Merwe	5	1	3	1
1969-70*S*	W. M. Lawry	A. Bacher	4	0	4	0
	In South Africa		30	15	7	8
	In Australia		20	12	4	4
	In England		3	2	0	1
	Totals		53	29	11	13

S Played in South Africa. A Played in Australia. E Played in England.

Notes: The following deputised for the official touring captain or were appointed by the home authority for only a minor proportion of the series:

[1]J. H. Anderson (Second), E. A. Halliwell (Third). [2]L. J. Tancred (Third). [3]D. J. McGlew (First). [4]R. Benaud (First).

HIGHEST INNINGS TOTALS

For Australia in Australia: 578 at Melbourne	1910-11
in South Africa: 549-7 dec. at Port Elizabeth	1949-50
For South Africa in Australia: 595 at Adelaide	1963-64
in South Africa: 622-9 dec. at Durban	1969-70

LOWEST INNINGS TOTALS

For Australia in Australia: 153 at Melbourne 1931-32
in South Africa: 75 at Durban 1949-50

For South Africa in Australia: 36† at Melbourne 1931-32
in South Africa: 85 at Johannesburg 1902-03

† *Scored 45 in the second innings giving the smallest aggregate of 81 (12 extras) in Test cricket.*

INDIVIDUAL HUNDREDS

For Australia (55)

W. W. Armstrong (2)
159*‡ Johannesburg 1902-03
132 Melbourne .. 1910-11
W. Bardsley (3)
132† Sydney 1910-11
121 Manchester . 1912
164 Lord's 1912
R. Benaud (2)
122 Johannesburg 1957-58
100 Johannesburg 1957-58
B. C. Booth (2)
169† Brisbane 1963-64
102* Sydney 1963-64
D. G. Bradman (4)
226† Brisbane 1931-32
112 Sydney 1931-32
167 Melbourne .. 1931-32
299* Adelaide 1931-32
W. A. Brown (1)
121 Cape Town . 1935-36
J. W. Burke (1)
189 Cape Town . 1957-58
A. G. Chipperfield (1)
109† Durban 1935-36
H. L. Collins (1)
203 Johannesburg 1921-22
J. H. Fingleton (3)
112 Cape Town . 1935-36
108 Johannesburg 1935-36
118 Durban 1935-36
J. M. Gregory (1)
119 Johannesburg 1921-22
R. N. Harvey (8)
178 Cape Town . 1949-50
151* Durban 1949-50
100 Johannesburg 1949-50
116 Pt Elizabeth . 1949-50
109 Brisbane 1952-53
190 Sydney 1952-53
116 Adelaide 1952-53
205 Melbourne .. 1952-53
A. L. Hassett (3)
112† Johannesburg 1949-50
167 Pt Elizabeth . 1949-50
163 Adelaide 1952-53
C. Hill (3)
142† Johannesburg 1902-03
191 Sydney 1910-11
100 Melbourne .. 1910-11
C. Kelleway (2)
114 Manchester . 1912
102 Lord's 1912
W. M. Lawry (1)
157 Melbourne .. 1963-64
S. J. E. Loxton (1)
101† Johannesburg 1949-50
C. G. Macartney (2)
137 Sydney 1910-11
116 Durban 1921-22
S. J. McCabe (2)
149 Durban 1935-36
189* Johannesburg 1935-36
C. C. McDonald (1)
154 Adelaide 1952-53
J. Moroney (2)
118 } Johannesburg 1949-50
101* }
A. R. Morris (2)
111 Johannesburg 1949-50
157 Pt Elizabeth . 1949-50
K. E. Rigg (1)
127† Sydney 1931-32
J. Ryder (1)
142 Cape Town . 1921-22
R. B. Simpson (1)
153 Cape Town . 1966-67
K. R. Stackpole (1)
134 Cape Town . 1966-67
V. T. Trumper (2)
159 Melbourne .. 1910-11
214* Adelaide 1910-11
W. M. Woodfull (1)
161 Melbourne .. 1931-32

For South Africa (36)

E. J. Barlow (5)
114† Brisbane 1963-64
109 Melbourne .. 1963-64
201 Adelaide 1963-64
127 Cape Town . 1969-70
110 Johannesburg 1969-70
K. C. Bland (1)
126 Sydney 1963-64
W. R. Endean (1)
162* Melbourne .. 1952-53
G. A. Faulkner (3)
204 Melbourne .. 1910-11
115 Adelaide 1910-11
122* Manchester . 1912
C. N. Frank (1)
152 Johannesburg 1921-22
B. L. Irvine (1)
102 Pt Elizabeth . 1969-70
D. T. Lindsay (3)
182 Johannesburg 1966-67
137 Durban 1966-67
131 Johannesburg 1966-67
D. J. McGlew (2)
108 Johannesburg 1957-58
105 Durban 1957-58
A. D. Nourse (2)
231 Johannesburg 1935-36
114 Cape Town . 1949-50
A. W. Nourse (1)
111 Johannesburg 1921-22
R. G. Pollock (5)
122 Sydney 1963-64
175 Adelaide 1963-64
209 Cape Town . 1966-67
105 Pt Elizabeth . 1966-67
274 Durban 1969-70
B. A. Richards (2)
140 Durban 1969-70
126 Pt Elizabeth . 1969-70
E. A. B. Rowan (1)
143 Durban 1949-50
J. H. Sinclair (2)
101 Johannesburg 1902-03
104 Cape Town . 1902-03
S. J. Snooke (1)
103 Adelaide 1910-11
K. G. Viljoen (1)
111 Melbourne .. 1931-32
J. H. B. Waite (2)
115 Johannesburg 1957-58
134 Durban 1957-58
J. W. Zulch (2)
105 Adelaide 1910-11
150 Sydney 1910-11

† *Signifies hundred on first appearance in Australia–South Africa Tests.*
‡ *Carried his bat.*

RECORD PARTNERSHIPS FOR EACH WICKET

For Australia

233 for 1st	J. H. Fingleton and W. A. Brown at Cape Town	1935-36
275 for 2nd	C. C. McDonald and A. L. Hassett at Adelaide	1952-53
242 for 3rd	C. Kelleway and W. Bardsley at Lord's	1912
168 for 4th	R. N. Harvey and K. R. Miller at Sydney	1952-53
143 for 5th	W. W. Armstrong and V. T. Trumper at Melbourne	1910-11
107 for 6th	C. Kelleway and V. S. Ransford at Melbourne	1910-11
160 for 7th	R. Benaud and G. D. McKenzie at Sydney	1963-64
83 for 8th	A. G. Chipperfield and C. V. Grimmett at Durban	1935-36
78 for 9th	D. G. Bradman and W. J. O'Reilly at Adelaide	1931-32
	K. D. Mackay and I. Meckiff at Johannesburg	1957-58
82 for 10th	V. S. Ransford and W. J. Whitty at Melbourne	1910-11

For South Africa

176 for 1st	D. J. McGlew and T. L. Goddard at Johannesburg	1957-58
173 for 2nd	L. J. Tancred and C. B. Llewellyn at Johannesburg	1902-03
341 for 3rd†	E. J. Barlow and R. G. Pollock at Adelaide	1963-64
206 for 4th	C. N. Frank and A. W. Nourse at Johannesburg	1921-22
129 for 5th	J. H. B. Waite and W. R. Endean at Johannesburg	1957-58
200 for 6th†	R. G. Pollock and H. R. Lance at Durban	1969-70
221 for 7th	D. T. Lindsay and P. L. van der Merwe at Johannesburg	1966-67
124 for 8th†	A. W. Nourse and E. A. Halliwell at Johannesburg	1902-03
85 for 9th	R. G. Pollock and P. M. Pollock at Cape Town	1966-67
53 for 10th	L. A. Stricker and S. J. Pegler at Adelaide	1910-11

† *Denotes record partnership against all countries.*

TEN WICKETS OR MORE IN A MATCH

For Australia (5)

14-199 (7-116, 7-83)	C. V. Grimmett, Adelaide	1931-32
10-88 (5-32, 5-56)	C. V. Grimmett, Cape Town	1935-36
10-110 (3-70, 7-40)	C. V. Grimmett, Johannesburg	1935-36
13-173 (7-100, 6-73)	C. V. Grimmett, Durban	1935-36
11-24 (5-6, 6-18)	H. Ironmonger, Melbourne	1931-32

For South Africa (2)

10-116 (5-43, 5-73)	C. B. Llewellyn, Johannesburg	1902-03
13-165 (6-84, 7-81)	H. J. Tayfield, Melbourne	1952-53

Note: C. V. Grimmett took ten wickets or more in three consecutive matches in 1935-36.

AUSTRALIA v WEST INDIES

	Captains						
Season	*Australia*	*West Indies*	*T*	*A*	*WI*	*T*	*D*
1930-31*A*	W. M. Woodfull	G. C. Grant	5	4	1	0	0
1951-52*A*	A. L. Hassett[1]	J. D. C. Goddard[2]	5	4	1	0	0
1954-55*W*	I. W. Johnson	D. St E. Atkinson[3]	5	3	0	0	2
1960-61*A*	R. Benaud	F. M. M. Worrell	5	2	1	1	1

THE FRANK WORRELL TROPHY

Season	Australia (Captains)	West Indies (Captains)	T	A	WI	T	D	Held by
1964-65*W*	R. B. Simpson	G. S. Sobers	5	1	2	0	2	WI
1968-69*A*	W. M. Lawry	G. S. Sobers	5	3	1	0	1	A
1972-73*W*	I. M. Chappell	R. B. Kanhai	5	2	0	0	3	A
1975-76*A*	G. S. Chappell	C. H. Lloyd	6	5	1	0	0	A
1977-78*W*	R. B. Simpson	A. I. Kallicharran[4]	5	1	3	0	1	WI
1979-80*A*	G. S. Chappell	C. H. Lloyd[5]	3	0	2	0	1	WI
1981-82*A*	G. S. Chappell	C. H. Lloyd	3	1	1	0	1	WI
1983-84*W*	K. J. Hughes	C. H. Lloyd[6]	5	0	3	0	2	WI
1984-85*A*	A. R. Border[7]	C. H. Lloyd	5	1	3	0	1	WI
1988-89*A*	A. R. Border	I. V. A. Richards	5	1	3	0	1	WI
	In Australia		42	21	14	1	6	
	In West Indies		25	7	8	0	10	
	Totals		67	28	22	1	16	

A Played in Australia. W Played in West Indies.

Notes: The following deputised for the official touring captain or were appointed by the home authority for only a minor proportion of the series:

[1]A. R. Morris (Third). [2]J. B. Stollmeyer (Fifth). [3]J. B. Stollmeyer (Second and Third). [4]C. H. Lloyd (First and Second). [5]D. L. Murray (First). [6]I. V. A. Richards (Second). [7]K. J. Hughes (First and Second).

HIGHEST INNINGS TOTALS

For Australia in Australia: 619 at Sydney 1968-69
in West Indies: 758-8 dec. at Kingston 1954-55

For West Indies in Australia: 616 at Adelaide 1968-69
in West Indies: 573 at Bridgetown 1964-65

LOWEST INNINGS TOTALS

For Australia in Australia: 76 at Perth 1984-85
in West Indies: 90 at Port-of-Spain 1977-78

For West Indies in Australia: 78 at Sydney 1951-52
in West Indies: 109 at Georgetown 1972-73

INDIVIDUAL HUNDREDS

For Australia (67)

R. G. Archer (1)
128 Kingston ... 1954-55
R. Benaud (1)
121 Kingston ... 1954-55
D. C. Boon (1)
149 Sydney 1988-89
B. C. Booth (1)
117 Port-of-Spain 1964-65
A. R. Border (2)
126 Adelaide 1981-82
100* Port-of-Spain 1983-84
D. G. Bradman (2)
223 Brisbane 1930-31
152 Melbourne .. 1930-31

G. S. Chappell (5)
106 Bridgetown . 1972-73
123 } ‡Brisbane ... 1975-76
109* }
182* Sydney 1975-76
124 Brisbane 1979-80
I. M. Chappell (5)
117† Brisbane 1968-69
165 Melbourne .. 1968-69
106* Bridgetown . 1972-73
109 Georgetown . 1972-73
156 Perth 1975-76
G. J. Cosier (1)
109† Melbourne .. 1975-76

R. M. Cowper (2)
143 Port-of-Spain 1964-65
102 Bridgetown . 1964-65
J. Dyson (1)
127*† Sydney 1981-82
R. N. Harvey (3)
133 Kingston ... 1954-55
133 Port-of-Spain 1954-55
204 Kingston ... 1954-55
A. L. Hassett (2)
132 Sydney 1951-52
102 Melbourne .. 1951-52
A. M. J. Hilditch (1)
113† Melbourne .. 1984-85

K. J. Hughes (2)
130*† Brisbane 1979-80
100* Melbourne .. 1981-82
D. M. Jones (1)
216 Adelaide 1988-89
A. F. Kippax (1)
146† Adelaide 1930-31
W. M. Lawry (4)
210 Bridgetown . 1964-65
105 Brisbane 1968-69
205 Melbourne .. 1968-69
151 Sydney 1968-69
R. R. Lindwall (1)
118 Bridgetown . 1954-55
R. B. McCosker (1)
109* Melbourne .. 1975-76
C. C. McDonald (2)
110 Port-of-Spain 1954-55
127 Kingston ... 1954-55
K. R. Miller (4)
129 Sydney 1951-52
147 Kingston ... 1954-55
137 Bridgetown . 1954-55
109 Kingston ... 1954-55
A. R. Morris (1)
111 Port-of-Spain 1954-55
N. C. O'Neill (1)
181† Brisbane 1960-61
W. B. Phillips (1)
120 Bridgetown . 1983-84
W. H. Ponsford (2)
183 Sydney 1930-31
109 Brisbane 1930-31
I. R. Redpath (4)
132 Sydney 1968-69
102 Melbourne .. 1975-76
103 Adelaide 1975-76
101 Melbourne .. 1975-76
C. S. Serjeant (1)
124 Georgetown . 1977-78
R. B. Simpson (1)
201 Bridgetown . 1964-65
K. R. Stackpole (1)
142 Kingston ... 1972-73
P. M. Toohey (1)
122 Kingston ... 1977-78
A. Turner (1)
136 Adelaide 1975-76
K. D. Walters (6)
118 Sydney 1968-69
110 Adelaide 1968-69
242 } Sydney 1968-69
103 }
102* Bridgetown . 1972-73
112 Port-of-Spain 1972-73
K. C. Wessels (1)
173 Sydney 1984-85
G. M. Wood (2)
126 Georgetown . 1977-78
111 Perth 1988-89

‡ *G. S. Chappell is the only player to score hundreds in both innings of his first Test as captain.*

For West Indies (69)

F. C. M. Alexander (1)
108 Sydney 1960-61
D. St E. Atkinson (1)
219 Bridgetown . 1954-55
B. F. Butcher (3)
117 Port-of-Spain 1964-65
101 Sydney 1968-69
118 Adelaide 1968-69
C. C. Depeiza (1)
122 Bridgetown . 1954-55
P. J. L. Dujon (2)
130 Port-of-Spain 1983-84
139 Perth 1984-85
M. L. C. Foster (1)
125† Kingston ... 1972-73
R. C. Fredericks (1)
169 Perth 1975-76
H. A. Gomes (6)
101† Georgetown . 1977-78
115 Kingston ... 1977-78
126 Sydney 1981-82
124* Adelaide 1981-82
127 Perth 1984-85
120* Adelaide 1984-85
C. G. Greenidge (3)
120* Georgetown . 1983-84
127 Kingston ... 1983-84
104 Adelaide 1988-89
D. L. Haynes (4)
103* Georgetown . 1983-84
145 Bridgetown . 1983-84
100 Perth 1988-89
143 Sydney 1988-89
G. A. Headley (2)
102* Brisbane 1930-31
105 Sydney 1930-31
C. C. Hunte (1)
110 Melbourne .. 1960-61
A. I. Kallicharran (4)
101 Brisbane 1975-76
127 Port-of-Spain 1977-78
126 Kingston ... 1977-78
106 Adelaide 1979-80
R. B. Kanhai (5)
117 } Adelaide 1960-61
115 }
129 Bridgetown . 1964-65
121 Port-of-Spain 1964-65
105 Bridgetown . 1972-73
C. H. Lloyd (6)
129† Brisbane 1968-69
178 Georgetown . 1972-73
149 Perth 1975-76
102 Melbourne .. 1975-76
121 Adelaide 1979-80
114 Brisbane 1984-85
F. R. Martin (1)
123* Sydney 1930-31
S. M. Nurse (2)
201 Bridgetown . 1964-65
137 Sydney 1968-69
I. V. A. Richards (5)
101 Adelaide 1975-76
140 Brisbane 1979-80
178 St John's 1983-84
208 Melbourne .. 1984-85
146 Perth 1988-89
R. B. Richardson (5)
131* Bridgetown . 1983-84
154 St John's 1983-84
138 Brisbane 1984-85
122 Melbourne .. 1988-89
106 Adelaide 1988-89
L. G. Rowe (1)
107 Brisbane 1975-76
O. G. Smith (1)
104† Kingston ... 1954-55
G. S. Sobers (4)
132 Brisbane 1960-61
168 Sydney 1960-61
110 Adelaide 1968-69
113 Sydney 1968-69
J. B. Stollmeyer (1)
104 Sydney 1951-52
C. L. Walcott (5)
108 Kingston ... 1954-55
126 } Port-of-Spain 1954-55
110 }
155 } Kingston ... 1954-55
110 }
E. D. Weekes (1)
139 Port-of-Spain 1954-55
A. B. Williams (1)
100† Georgetown . 1977-78
F. M. M. Worrell (1)
108 Melbourne .. 1951-52

† *Signifies hundred on first appearance in Australia–West Indies Tests.*

Note: F. C. M. Alexander and C. C. Depeiza scored the only hundreds of their careers in a Test match.

RECORD PARTNERSHIPS FOR EACH WICKET

For Australia

382 for 1st†	W. M. Lawry and R. B. Simpson at Bridgetown	1964-65
298 for 2nd	W. M. Lawry and I. M. Chappell at Melbourne	1968-69
295 for 3rd†	C. C. McDonald and R. N. Harvey at Kingston	1954-55
336 for 4th	W. M. Lawry and K. D. Walters at Sydney	1968-69
220 for 5th	K. R. Miller and R. G. Archer at Kingston	1954-55
206 for 6th	K. R. Miller and R. G. Archer at Bridgetown	1954-55
134 for 7th	A. K. Davidson and R. Benaud at Brisbane	1960-61
137 for 8th	R. Benaud and I. W. Johnson at Kingston	1954-55
114 for 9th	D. M. Jones and M. G. Hughes at Adelaide	1988-89
97 for 10th	T. G. Hogan and R. M. Hogg at Georgetown	1983-84

For West Indies

250* for 1st	C. G. Greenidge and D. L. Haynes at Georgetown	1983-84
167 for 2nd	D. L. Haynes and R. B. Richardson at Adelaide	1988-89
308 for 3rd	R. B. Richardson and I. V. A. Richards at St John's	1983-84
198 for 4th	L. G. Rowe and A. I. Kallicharran at Brisbane	1975-76
210 for 5th	R. B. Kanhai and M. L. C. Foster at Kingston	1972-73
165 for 6th	R. B. Kanhai and D. L. Murray at Bridgetown	1972-73
347 for 7th†‡	D. St E. Atkinson and C. C. Depeiza at Bridgetown	1954-55
82 for 8th	H. A. Gomes and A. M. E. Roberts at Adelaide	1981-82
122 for 9th	D. A. J. Holford and J. L. Hendriks at Adelaide	1968-69
56 for 10th	J. Garner and C. E. H. Croft at Brisbane	1979-80

† *Denotes record partnership against all countries.*
‡ *Record seventh-wicket partnership in first-class cricket.*

TEN WICKETS OR MORE IN A MATCH

For Australia (11)

11-96 (7-46, 4-50)	A. R. Border, Sydney	1988-89
11-222 (5-135, 6-87)†	A. K. Davidson, Brisbane	1960-61
11-183 (7-87, 4-96)†	C. V. Grimmett, Adelaide	1930-31
10-115 (6-72, 4-43)	N. J. N. Hawke, Georgetown	1964-65
10-144 (6-54, 4-90)	R. G. Holland, Sydney	1984-85
13-217 (5-130, 8-87)	M. G. Hughes, Perth	1988-89
11-79 (7-23, 4-56)	H. Ironmonger, Melbourne	1930-31
11-181 (8-112, 3-69)	G. F. Lawson, Adelaide	1984-85
10-127 (7-83, 3-44)	D. K. Lillee, Melbourne	1981-82
10-159 (8-71, 2-88)	G. D. McKenzie, Melbourne	1968-69
10-185 (3-87, 7-98)	B. Yardley, Sydney	1981-82

For West Indies (3)

10-113 (7-55, 3-58)	G. E. Gomez, Sydney	1951-52
11-107 (5-45, 6-62)	M. A. Holding, Melbourne	1981-82
10-107 (5-69, 5-38)	M. D. Marshall, Adelaide	1984-85

† *Signifies ten wickets or more on first appearance in Australia–West Indies Tests.*

AUSTRALIA v NEW ZEALAND

	Captains					
Season	*Australia*	*New Zealand*	*T*	*A*	*NZ*	*D*
1945-46*N*	W. A. Brown	W. A. Hadlee	1	1	0	0
1973-74*A*	I. M. Chappell	B. E. Congdon	3	2	0	1
1973-74*N*	I. M. Chappell	B. E. Congdon	3	1	1	1
1976-77*N*	G. S. Chappell	G. M. Turner	2	1	0	1
1980-81*A*	G. S. Chappell	G. P. Howarth[1]	3	2	0	1
1981-82*N*	G. S. Chappell	G. P. Howarth	3	1	1	1

TRANS-TASMAN TROPHY

	Captains						
Season	*Australia*	*New Zealand*	*T*	*A*	*NZ*	*D*	*Held by*
1985-86*A*	A. R. Border	J. V. Coney	3	1	2	0	NZ
1985-86*N*	A. R. Border	J. V. Coney	3	0	1	2	NZ
1987-88*A*	A. R. Border	J. J. Crowe	3	1	0	2	A
1989-90*A*†	A. R. Border	J. G. Wright	1	0	0	1	—
1989-90*N*†	A. R. Border	J. G. Wright	1	0	1	0	—
	In Australia		13	6	2	5	
	In New Zealand		13	4	4	5	
	Totals		26	10	6	10	

A Played in Australia. N Played in New Zealand.

† *The Trans-Tasman Trophy was not at stake in these series.*

Note: The following deputised for the official touring captain: [1]M. G. Burgess (Second).

HIGHEST INNINGS TOTALS

For Australia in Australia: 521-9 dec. at Perth 1989-90
in New Zealand: 552 at Christchurch 1976-77

For New Zealand in Australia: 553-7 dec. at Brisbane 1985-86
in New Zealand: 484 at Wellington 1973-74

LOWEST INNINGS TOTALS

For Australia in Australia: 162 at Sydney 1973-74
in New Zealand: 103 at Auckland 1985-86

For New Zealand in Australia: 121 at Perth 1980-81
in New Zealand: 42 at Wellington 1945-46

INDIVIDUAL HUNDREDS

For Australia (23)

D. C. Boon (2)
143 Brisbane 1987-88
200 Perth 1989-90
A. R. Border (4)
152* Brisbane 1985-86
140 } Christchurch. 1985-86
114* }
205 Adelaide 1987-88
G. S. Chappell (3)
247* } Wellington .. 1973-74
133 }
176 Christchurch. 1981-82
I. M. Chappell (2)
145 } Wellington .. 1973-74
121 }
G. J. Gilmour (1)
101 Christchurch. 1976-77
G. R. Marsh (1)
118 Auckland ... 1985-86
R. W. Marsh (1)
132 Adelaide 1973-74
G. R. J. Matthews (2)
115† Brisbane 1985-86
130 Wellington .. 1985-86
I. R. Redpath (1)
159*‡ Auckland ... 1973-74
K. R. Stackpole (1)
122† Melbourne .. 1973-74
K. D. Walters (3)
104* Auckland ... 1973-74
250 Christchurch. 1976-77
107 Melbourne .. 1980-81
G. M. Wood (2)
111† Brisbane 1980-81
100 Auckland ... 1981-82

For New Zealand (17)

J. V. Coney (1)
101* Wellington . . 1985-86

B. E. Congdon (2)
132 Wellington . . 1973-74
107* Christchurch. 1976-77

M. D. Crowe (3)
188 Brisbane 1985-86
137 Christchurch. 1985-86
137 Adelaide 1987-88

B. A. Edgar (1)
161 Auckland . . . 1981-82

M. J. Greatbatch (1)
146*† Perth 1989-90

B. F. Hastings (1)
101 Wellington . . 1973-74

A. H. Jones (1)
150 Adelaide 1987-88

J. F. M. Morrison (1)
117 Sydney 1973-74

J. M. Parker (1)
108 Sydney 1973-74

J. F. Reid (1)
108† Brisbane 1985-86

G. M. Turner (2)
101 } Christchurch. 1973-74
110* }

J. G. Wright (2)
141 Christchurch. 1981-82
117* Wellington . . 1989-90

† *Signifies hundred on first appearance in Australia–New Zealand Tests.*
‡ *Carried his bat.*

Notes: G. S. and I. M. Chappell at Wellington in 1973-74 provide the only instance in Test matches of brothers both scoring a hundred in each innings and in the same Test.

RECORD PARTNERSHIPS FOR EACH WICKET

For Australia

106 for 1st	B. M. Laird and G. M. Wood at Auckland	1981-82
168 for 2nd	G. R. Marsh and W. B. Phillips at Auckland	1985-86
264 for 3rd	I. M. Chappell and G. S. Chappell at Wellington	1973-74
116 for 4th	A. R. Border and S. R. Waugh at Adelaide	1987-88
213 for 5th	G. M. Ritchie and G. R. J. Matthews at Wellington	1985-86
197 for 6th	A. R. Border and G. R. J. Matthews at Brisbane	1985-86
217 for 7th†	K. D. Walters and G. J. Gilmour at Christchurch	1976-77
93 for 8th	G. J. Gilmour and K. J. O'Keeffe at Auckland	1976-77
61 for 9th	A. I. C. Dodemaide and C. J. McDermott at Melbourne	1987-88
60 for 10th	K. D. Walters and J. D. Higgs at Melbourne	1980-81

For New Zealand

107 for 1st	G. M. Turner and J. M. Parker at Auckland	1973-74
128* for 2nd	J. G. Wright and A. H. Jones at Wellington	1989-90
224 for 3rd	J. F. Reid and M. D. Crowe at Brisbane	1985-86
229 for 4th†	B. E. Congdon and B. F. Hastings at Wellington	1973-74
88 for 5th	J. V. Coney and M. G. Burgess at Perth	1980-81
109 for 6th	K. R. Rutherford and J. V. Coney at Wellington	1985-86
132* for 7th	J. V. Coney and R. J. Hadlee at Wellington	1985-86
88* for 8th	M. J. Greatbatch and M. C. Snedden at Perth	1989-90
73 for 9th	H. J. Howarth and D. R. Hadlee at Christchurch	1976-77
124 for 10th	J. G. Bracewell and S. L. Boock at Sydney	1985-86

† *Denotes record partnership against all countries.*

TEN WICKETS OR MORE IN A MATCH

For Australia (2)

10-174 (6-106, 4-68)	R. G. Holland, Sydney	1985-86
11-123 (5-51, 6-72)	D. K. Lillee, Auckland	1976-77

For New Zealand (4)

10-106 (4-74, 6-32)	J. G. Bracewell, Auckland	1985-86
15-123 (9-52, 6-71)	R. J. Hadlee, Brisbane	1985-86
11-155 (5-65, 6-90)	R. J. Hadlee, Perth	1985-86
10-176 (5-109, 5-67)	R. J. Hadlee, Melbourne	1987-88

AUSTRALIA v INDIA

	Captains						
Season	*Australia*	*India*	*T*	*A*	*I*	*T*	*D*
1947-48*A*	D. G. Bradman	L. Amarnath	5	4	0	0	1
1956-57*I*	I. W. Johnson[1]	P. R. Umrigar	3	2	0	0	1
1959-60*I*	R. Benaud	G. S. Ramchand	5	2	1	0	2
1964-65*I*	R. B. Simpson	Nawab of Pataudi jun.	3	1	1	0	1
1967-68*A*	R. B. Simpson[2]	Nawab of Pataudi jun.[3]	4	4	0	0	0
1969-70*I*	W. M. Lawry	Nawab of Pataudi jun.	5	3	1	0	1
1977-78*A*	R. B. Simpson	B. S. Bedi	5	3	2	0	0
1979-80*I*	K. J. Hughes	S. M. Gavaskar	6	0	2	0	4
1980-81*A*	G. S. Chappell	S. M. Gavaskar	3	1	1	0	1
1985-86*A*	A. R. Border	Kapil Dev	3	0	0	0	3
1986-87*I*	A. R. Border	Kapil Dev	3	0	0	1	2
	In Australia		20	12	3	0	5
	In India		25	8	5	1	11
	Totals		45	20	8	1	16

A Played in Australia. I Played in India.

Notes: The following deputised for the official touring captain or were appointed by the home authority for only a minor proportion of the series:

[1]R. R. Lindwall (Second). [2]W. M. Lawry (Third and Fourth). [3]C. G. Borde (First).

HIGHEST INNINGS TOTALS

For Australia in Australia: 674 at Adelaide 1947-48
in India: 574-7 dec. at Madras 1986-87

For India in Australia: 600-4 dec. at Sydney 1985-86
in India: 517-5 dec. at Bombay 1986-87

LOWEST INNINGS TOTALS

For Australia in Australia: 83 at Melbourne 1980-81
in India: 105 at Kanpur 1959-60

For India in Australia: 58 at Brisbane 1947-48
in India: 135 at Delhi 1959-60

INDIVIDUAL HUNDREDS

For Australia (45)

S. G. Barnes (1)
112 Adelaide 1947-48
D. C. Boon (3)
123† Adelaide 1985-86
131 Sydney 1985-86
122 Madras 1986-87
A. R. Border (4)
162† Madras 1979-80
124 Melbourne .. 1980-81
163 Melbourne .. 1985-86
106 Madras 1986-87
D. G. Bradman (4)
185† Brisbane 1947-48
132, 127* Melbourne .. 1947-48
201 Adelaide 1947-48
J. W. Burke (1)
161 Bombay 1956-57
G. S. Chappell (1)
204† Sydney 1980-81
I. M. Chappell (2)
151 Melbourne .. 1967-68
138 Delhi 1969-70
R. M. Cowper (2)
108 Adelaide 1967-68
165 Sydney 1967-68
L. E. Favell (1)
101 Madras 1959-60
R. N. Harvey (4)
153 Melbourne .. 1947-48
140 Bombay 1956-57
114 Delhi 1959-60
102 Bombay 1959-60
A. L. Hassett (1)
198* Adelaide 1947-48
K. J. Hughes (2)
100 Madras 1979-80
213 Adelaide 1980-81
D. M. Jones (1)
210† Madras 1986-87
W. M. Lawry (1)
100 Melbourne .. 1967-68
A. L. Mann (1)
105 Perth 1977-78
G. R. Marsh (1)
101 Bombay 1986-87
G. R. J. Matthews (1)
100* Melbourne .. 1985-86

A. R. Morris (1)
100* Melbourne .. 1947-48
N. C. O'Neill (2)
163 Bombay 1959-60
113 Calcutta 1959-60
G. M. Ritchie (1)
128† Adelaide 1985-86
A. P. Sheahan (1)
114 Kanpur 1969-70

R. B. Simpson (4)
103 Adelaide 1967-68
109 Melbourne .. 1967-68
176 Perth 1977-78
100 Adelaide 1977-78
K. R. Stackpole (1)
103† Bombay 1969-70
K. D. Walters (1)
102 Madras 1969-70

G. M. Wood (1)
125 Adelaide 1980-81
G. N. Yallop (2)
121† Adelaide 1977-78
167 Calcutta 1979-80

For India (31)

M. Amarnath (2)
100 Perth 1977-78
138 Sydney 1985-86
N. J. Contractor (1)
108 Bombay 1959-60
S. M. Gavaskar (8)
113† Brisbane 1977-78
127 Perth 1977-78
118 Melbourne .. 1977-78
115 Delhi 1979-80
123 Bombay 1979-80
166* Adelaide 1985-86
172 Sydney 1985-86
103 Bombay 1986-87
V. S. Hazare (2)
116 } Adelaide 1947-48
145 }

M. L. Jaisimha (1)
101 Brisbane 1967-68
Kapil Dev (1)
119 Madras 1986-87
S. M. H. Kirmani (1)
101* Bombay 1979-80
V. Mankad (2)
116 Melbourne .. 1947-48
111 Melbourne .. 1947-48
Nawab of Pataudi jun. (1)
128*† Madras 1964-65
S. M. Patil (1)
174 Adelaide 1980-81
D. G. Phadkar (1)
123 Adelaide 1947-48
G. S. Ramchand (1)
109 Bombay 1956-57

R. J. Shastri (1)
121* Bombay 1986-87
K. Srikkanth (1)
116 Sydney 1985-86
D. B. Vengsarkar (2)
112 Bangalore ... 1979-80
164* Bombay 1986-87
G. R. Viswanath (4)
137† Kanpur 1969-70
161* Bangalore ... 1979-80
131 Delhi 1979-80
114 Melbourne .. 1980-81
Yashpal Sharma (1)
100* Delhi 1979-80

† *Signifies hundred on first appearance in Australia–India Tests.*

RECORD PARTNERSHIPS FOR EACH WICKET

For Australia

217 for 1st	D. C. Boon and G. R. Marsh at Sydney	1985-86
236 for 2nd	S. G. Barnes and D. G. Bradman at Adelaide	1947-48
222 for 3rd	A. R. Border and K. J. Hughes at Madras	1979-80
178 for 4th	D. M. Jones and A. R. Border at Madras	1986-87
223* for 5th	A. R. Morris and D. G. Bradman at Melbourne	1947-48
151 for 6th	T. R. Veivers and B. N. Jarman at Bombay	1964-65
66 for 7th	G. R. J. Matthews and R. J. Bright at Melbourne	1985-86
73 for 8th	T. R. Veivers and G. D. McKenzie at Madras	1964-65
87 for 9th	I. W. Johnson and W. P. A. Crawford at Madras	1956-57
77 for 10th	A. R. Border and D. R. Gilbert at Melbourne	1985-86

For India

192 for 1st	S. M. Gavaskar and C. P. S. Chauhan at Bombay	1979-80
224 for 2nd	S. M. Gavaskar and M. Amarnath at Sydney	1985-86
159 for 3rd	S. M. Gavaskar and G. R. Viswanath at Delhi	1979-80
159 for 4th	D. B. Vengsarkar and G. R. Viswanath at Bangalore	1979-80
109 for 5th	A. A. Baig and R. B. Kenny at Bombay	1959-60
298* for 6th†	D. B. Vengsarkar and R. J. Shastri at Bombay	1986-87
132 for 7th	V. S. Hazare and H. R. Adhikari at Adelaide	1947-48
127 for 8th	S. M. H. Kirmani and K. D. Ghavri at Bombay	1979-80
57 for 9th	S. M. H. Kirmani and K. D. Ghavri at Sydney	1980-81
	Kapil Dev and N. S. Yadav at Madras	1986-87
94 for 10th	S. M. Gavaskar and N. S. Yadav at Adelaide	1985-86

† *Denotes record partnership against all countries.*

TEN WICKETS OR MORE IN A MATCH

For Australia (8)

11-105 (6-52, 5-53)	R. Benaud, Calcutta	1956-57
12-124 (5-31, 7-93)	A. K. Davidson, Kanpur	1959-60
12-166 (5-99, 7-67)	G. Dymock, Kanpur	1979-80
10-91 (6-58, 4-33)†	G. D. McKenzie, Madras	1964-65
10-151 (7-66, 3-85)	G. D. McKenzie, Melbourne	1967-68
10-144 (5-91, 5-53)	A. A. Mallett, Madras	1969-70
10-249 (5-103, 5-146)	G. R. J. Matthews, Madras	1986-87
11-31 (5-2, 6-29)†	E. R. H. Toshack, Brisbane	1947-48

For India (6)

10-194 (5-89, 5-105)	B. S. Bedi, Perth	1977-78
12-104 (6-52, 6-52)	B. S. Chandrasekhar, Melbourne	1977-78
10-130 (7-49, 3-81)	Ghulam Ahmed, Calcutta	1956-57
11-122 (5-31, 6-91)	R. G. Nadkarni, Madras	1964-65
14-124 (9-69, 5-55)	J. M. Patel, Kanpur	1959-60
10-174 (4-100, 6-74)	E. A. S. Prasanna, Madras	1969-70

† *Signifies ten wickets or more on first appearance in Australia–India Tests.*

AUSTRALIA v PAKISTAN

Captains

Season	*Australia*	*Pakistan*	*T*	*A*	*P*	*D*
1956-57*P*	I. W. Johnson	A. H. Kardar	1	0	1	0
1959-60*P*	R. Benaud	Fazal Mahmood[1]	3	2	0	1
1964-65*P*	R. B. Simpson	Hanif Mohammad	1	0	0	1
1964-65*A*	R. B. Simpson	Hanif Mohammad	1	0	0	1
1972-73*A*	I. M. Chappell	Intikhab Alam	3	3	0	0
1976-77*A*	G. S. Chappell	Mushtaq Mohammad	3	1	1	1
1978-79*A*	G. N. Yallop[2]	Mushtaq Mohammad	2	1	1	0
1979-80*P*	G. S. Chappell	Javed Miandad	3	0	1	2
1981-82*A*	G. S. Chappell	Javed Miandad	3	2	1	0
1982-83*P*	K. J. Hughes	Imran Khan	3	0	3	0
1983-84*A*	K. J. Hughes	Imran Khan[3]	5	2	0	3
1988-89*P*	A. R. Border	Javed Miandad	3	0	1	2
1989-90*A*	A. R. Border	Imran Khan	3	1	0	2
	In Pakistan		14	2	6	6
	In Australia		20	10	3	7
	Totals		34	12	9	13

A Played in Australia. *P Played in Pakistan.*

Notes: The following deputised for the official touring captain or were appointed by the home authority for only a minor proportion of the series:

[1]Imtiaz Ahmed (Second). [2]K. J. Hughes (Second). [3]Zaheer Abbas (First, Second and Third).

HIGHEST INNINGS TOTALS

For Australia in Australia:	585 at Adelaide	1972-73
in Pakistan:	617 at Faisalabad	1979-80
For Pakistan in Australia:	624 at Adelaide	1983-84
in Pakistan:	501-6 dec. at Faisalabad	1982-83

LOWEST INNINGS TOTALS

For Australia in Australia: 125 at Melbourne 1981-82
in Pakistan: 80 at Karachi 1956-57

For Pakistan in Australia: 62 at Perth 1981-82
in Pakistan: 134 at Dacca 1959-60

INDIVIDUAL HUNDREDS

For Australia (37)

J. Benaud (1)
142 Melbourne .. 1972-73
A. R. Border (6)
105† Melbourne .. 1978-79
150* }
153 } Lahore 1979-80
118 Brisbane 1983-84
117* Adelaide 1983-84
113* Faisalabad .. 1988-89
G. S. Chappell (6)
116* Melbourne .. 1972-73
121 Melbourne .. 1976-77
235 Faisalabad .. 1979-80
201 Brisbane 1981-82
150* Brisbane 1983-84
182 Sydney 1983-84
I. M. Chappell (1)
196 Adelaide 1972-73
G. J. Cosier (1)
168 Melbourne .. 1976-77

I. C. Davis (1)
105† Adelaide 1976-77
K. J. Hughes (2)
106 Perth 1981-82
106 Adelaide 1983-84
D. M. Jones (2)
116 }
121* } Adelaide 1989-90
R. B. McCosker (1)
105 Melbourne .. 1976-77
R. W. Marsh (1)
118† Adelaide 1972-73
N. C. O'Neill (1)
134 Lahore 1959-60
W. B. Phillips (1)
159† Perth 1983-84
I. R. Redpath (1)
135 Melbourne .. 1972-73

G. M. Ritchie (1)
106* Faisalabad .. 1982-83
A. P. Sheahan (1)
127 Melbourne .. 1972-73
R. B. Simpson (2)
153 }
115 } †Karachi 1964-65
M. A. Taylor (2)
101† Melbourne .. 1989-90
101* Sydney 1989-90
K. D. Walters (1)
107 Adelaide 1976-77
K. C. Wessels (1)
179 Adelaide 1983-84
G. M. Wood (1)
100 Melbourne .. 1981-82
G. N. Yallop (3)
172 Faisalabad .. 1979-80
141 Perth 1983-84
268 Melbourne .. 1983-84

For Pakistan (31)

Asif Iqbal (3)
152* Adelaide 1976-77
120 Sydney 1976-77
134* Perth 1978-79
Hanif Mohammad (2)
101* Karachi 1959-60
104 Melbourne .. 1964-65
Ijaz Ahmed (2)
122 Faisalabad .. 1988-89
121 Melbourne .. 1989-90
Imran Khan (1)
136 Adelaide 1989-90
Javed Miandad (6)
129* Perth 1978-79
106* Faisalabad .. 1979-80
138 Lahore 1982-83

131 Adelaide 1983-84
211 Karachi 1988-89
107 Faisalabad .. 1988-89
Khalid Ibadulla (1)
166† Karachi 1964-65
Majid Khan (3)
158 Melbourne .. 1972-73
108 Melbourne .. 1978-79
110* Lahore 1979-80
Mansoor Akhtar (1)
111 Faisalabad .. 1982-83
Mohsin Khan (3)
135 Lahore 1982-83
149 Adelaide 1983-84
152 Melbourne .. 1983-84

Mushtaq Mohammad (1)
121 Sydney 1972-73
Qasim Omar (1)
113 Adelaide 1983-84
Sadiq Mohammad (2)
137 Melbourne .. 1972-73
105 Melbourne .. 1976-77
Saeed Ahmed (1)
166 Lahore 1959-60
Taslim Arif (1)
210* Faisalabad .. 1979-80
Wasim Akram (1)
123 Adelaide 1989-90
Zaheer Abbas (2)
101 Adelaide 1976-77
126 Faisalabad .. 1982-83

† *Signifies hundred on first appearance in Australia–Pakistan Tests.*

RECORD PARTNERSHIPS FOR EACH WICKET

For Australia

134 for 1st	I. C. Davis and A. Turner at Melbourne	1976-77
259 for 2nd	W. B. Phillips and G. N. Yallop at Perth	1983-84
203 for 3rd	G. N. Yallop and K. J. Hughes at Melbourne	1983-84
217 for 4th	G. S. Chappell and G. N. Yallop at Faisalabad	1979-80
171 for 5th	G. S. Chappell and G. J. Cosier at Melbourne	1976-77
	A. R. Border and G. S. Chappell at Brisbane	1983-84
139 for 6th	R. M. Cowper and T. R. Veivers at Melbourne	1964-65
185 for 7th	G. N. Yallop and G. R. J. Matthews at Melbourne	1983-84
117 for 8th	G. J. Cosier and K. J. O'Keeffe at Melbourne	1976-77
83 for 9th	J. R. Watkins and R. A. L. Massie at Sydney	1972-73
52 for 10th	D. K. Lillee and M. H. N. Walker at Sydney	1976-77
	G. F. Lawson and T. M. Alderman at Lahore	1982-83

For Pakistan

249 for 1st†	Khalid Ibadulla and Abdul Kadir at Karachi	1964-65
233 for 2nd	Mohsin Khan and Qasim Omar at Adelaide	1983-84
223* for 3rd	Taslim Arif and Javed Miandad at Faisalabad	1979-80
155 for 4th	Mansoor Akhtar and Zaheer Abbas at Faisalabad	1982-83
186 for 5th	Javed Miandad and Salim Malik at Adelaide	1983-84
191 for 6th	Imran Khan and Wasim Akram at Adelaide	1989-90
104 for 7th	Intikhab Alam and Wasim Bari at Adelaide	1972-73
111 for 8th	Majid Khan and Imran Khan at Lahore	1979-80
56 for 9th	Intikhab Alam and Afaq Hussain at Melbourne	1964-65
87 for 10th	Asif Iqbal and Iqbal Qasim at Adelaide	1976-77

† *Denotes record partnership against all countries.*

TEN WICKETS OR MORE IN A MATCH

For Australia (3)

10-111 (7-87, 3-24)†	R. J. Bright, Karachi	1979-80
10-135 (6-82, 4-53)	D. K. Lillee, Melbourne	1976-77
11-118 (5-32, 6-86)†	C. G. Rackemann, Perth	1983-84

For Pakistan (6)

11-218 (4-76, 7-142)	Abdul Qadir, Faisalabad	1982-83
13-114 (6-34, 7-80)†	Fazal Mahmood, Karachi	1956-57
12-165 (6-102, 6-63)	Imran Khan, Sydney	1976-77
11-118 (4-69, 7-49)	Iqbal Qasim, Karachi	1979-80
11-125 (2-39, 9-86)	Sarfraz Nawaz, Melbourne	1978-79
11-160 (6-62, 5-98)	Wasim Akram, Melbourne	1989-90

† *Signifies ten wickets or more on first appearance in Australia–Pakistan Tests.*

AUSTRALIA v SRI LANKA

Captains

Season	*Australia*	*Sri Lanka*	*T*	*A*	*SL*	*D*
1982-83*SL*	G. S. Chappell	L. R. D. Mendis	1	1	0	0
1987-88*A*	A. R. Border	R. S. Madugalle	1	1	0	0
1989-90*A*	A. R. Border	A. Ranatunga	2	1	0	1
	In Australia		3	2	0	1
	In Sri Lanka		1	1	0	0
	Totals		4	3	0	1

A Played in Australia. SL Played in Sri Lanka.

INNINGS TOTALS

Highest innings total for Australia: 514-4 dec. at Kandy 1982-83
for Sri Lanka: 418 at Brisbane 1989-90

Lowest innings total for Australia: 224 at Hobart 1989-90
for Sri Lanka: 153 at Perth 1987-88

INDIVIDUAL HUNDREDS

For Australia (8)

D. W. Hookes (1)
143*† Kandy 1982-83
D. M. Jones (2)
102† Perth 1987-88
118* Hobart 1989-90

T. M. Moody (1)
106† Brisbane 1989-90
M. A. Taylor (2)
164† Brisbane 1989-90
108 Hobart 1989-90

S. R. Waugh (1)
134* Hobart 1989-90
K. C. Wessels (1)
141† Kandy 1982-83

For Sri Lanka (1)

P. A. de Silva (1)
167 Brisbane 1989-90

† *Signifies hundred on first appearance in Australia–Sri Lanka Tests.*

BEST BOWLING

Best bowling in an innings for Australia: 5-66 by T. G. Hogan at Kandy 1982-83
for Sri Lanka: 6-66 by R. J. Ratnayake at Hobart ... 1989-90

PARTNERSHIPS

Best wicket partnership for Australia: 260* for 6th by D. M. Jones and S. R. Waugh at Hobart 1989-90
for Sri Lanka: 144 for 7th† by P. A. de Silva and J. R. Ratnayeke at Brisbane 1989-90

† *Denotes record partnership against all countries.*

SOUTH AFRICA v NEW ZEALAND

	Captains					
Season	*South Africa*	*New Zealand*	*T*	*SA*	*NZ*	*D*
1931-32*N*	H. B. Cameron	M. L. Page	2	2	0	0
1952-53*N*	J. E. Cheetham	W. M. Wallace	2	1	0	1
1953-54*S*	J. E. Cheetham	G. O. Rabone[1]	5	4	0	1
1961-62*S*	D. J. McGlew	J. R. Reid	5	2	2	1
1963-64*N*	T. L. Goddard	J. R. Reid	3	0	0	3
	In New Zealand		7	3	0	4
	In South Africa		10	6	2	2
	Totals		17	9	2	6

N Played in New Zealand. S Played in South Africa.

Note: The following deputised for the official touring captain:
[1]B. Sutcliffe (Fourth and Fifth).

HIGHEST INNINGS TOTALS

For South Africa	in South Africa: 464 at Johannesburg	1961-62
	in New Zealand: 524-8 at Wellington	1952-53
For New Zealand	in South Africa: 505 at Cape Town	1953-54
	in New Zealand: 364 at Wellington	1931-32

LOWEST INNINGS TOTALS

For South Africa	in South Africa: 148 at Johannesburg	1953-54
	in New Zealand: 223 at Dunedin	1963-64
For New Zealand	in South Africa: 79 at Johannesburg	1953-54
	in New Zealand: 138 at Dunedin	1963-64

INDIVIDUAL HUNDREDS

For South Africa (11)

X. C. Balaskas (1)
122* Wellington .. 1931-32
J. A. J. Christy (1)
103† Christchurch. 1931-32
W. R. Endean (1)
116 Auckland ... 1952-53
D. J. McGlew (3)
255*† Wellington .. 1952-53
127*‡ Durban 1961-62
120 Johannesburg 1961-62
R. A. McLean (2)
101 Durban 1953-54
113 Cape Town . 1961-62
B. Mitchell (1)
113† Christchurch. 1931-32
A. R. A. Murray (1)
109† Wellington .. 1952-53
J. H. B. Waite (1)
101 Johannesburg 1961-62

For New Zealand (7)

P. T. Barton (1)
109 Pt Elizabeth . 1961-62
P. G. Z. Harris (1)
101 Cape Town . 1961-62
G. O. Rabone (1)
107 Durban 1953-54
J. R. Reid (2)
135 Cape Town . 1953-54
142 Johannesburg 1961-62
B. W. Sinclair (1)
138 Auckland ... 1963-64
H. G. Vivian (1)
100† Wellington .. 1931-32

† *Signifies hundred on first appearance in South Africa–New Zealand Tests.*
‡ *Carried his bat.*

RECORD PARTNERSHIPS FOR EACH WICKET

For South Africa

196 for 1st	J. A. J. Christy and B. Mitchell at Christchurch	1931-32
76 for 2nd	J. A. J. Christy and H. B. Cameron at Wellington	1931-32
112 for 3rd	D. J. McGlew and R. A. McLean at Johannesburg	1961-62
135 for 4th	K. J. Funston and R. A. McLean at Durban	1953-54
130 for 5th	W. R. Endean and J. E. Cheetham at Auckland	1952-53
83 for 6th	K. C. Bland and D. T. Lindsay at Auckland	1963-64
246 for 7th†	D. J. McGlew and A. R. A. Murray at Wellington	1952-53
95 for 8th	J. E. Cheetham and H. J. Tayfield at Cape Town	1953-54
60 for 9th	P. M. Pollock and N. A. T. Adcock at Port Elizabeth	1961-62
47 for 10th	D. J. McGlew and H. D. Bromfield at Port Elizabeth	1961-62

For New Zealand

126 for 1st	G. O. Rabone and M. E. Chapple at Cape Town	1953-54
51 for 2nd	W. P. Bradburn and B. W. Sinclair at Dunedin	1963-64
94 for 3rd	M. B. Poore and B. Sutcliffe at Cape Town	1953-54
171 for 4th	B. W. Sinclair and S. N. McGregor at Auckland	1963-64
174 for 5th	J. R. Reid and J. E. F. Beck at Cape Town	1953-54
100 for 6th	H. G. Vivian and F. T. Badcock at Wellington	1931-32
84 for 7th	J. R. Reid and G. A. Bartlett at Johannesburg	1961-62
73 for 8th	P. G. Z. Harris and G. A. Bartlett at Durban	1961-62
69 for 9th	C. F. W. Allcott and I. B. Cromb at Wellington	1931-32
49* for 10th	A. E. Dick and F. J. Cameron at Cape Town	1961-62

† *Denotes record partnership against all countries.*

TEN WICKETS OR MORE IN A MATCH

For South Africa (1)

11-196 (6-128, 5-68)† S. F. Burke, Cape Town 1961-62

† *Signifies ten wickets or more on first appearance in South Africa–New Zealand Tests.*

Note: The best match figures by a New Zealand bowler are 8-180 (4-61, 4-119), J. C. Alabaster at Cape Town, 1961-62.

WEST INDIES v NEW ZEALAND

	Captains					
Season	*West Indies*	*New Zealand*	*T*	*WI*	*NZ*	*D*
1951-52*N*	J. D. C. Goddard	B. Sutcliffe	2	1	0	1
1955-56*N*	D. St E. Atkinson	J. R. Reid[1]	4	3	1	0
1968-69*N*	G. S. Sobers	G. T. Dowling	3	1	1	1
1971-72*W*	G. S. Sobers	G. T. Dowling[2]	5	0	0	5
1979-80*N*	C. H. Lloyd	G. P. Howarth	3	0	1	2
1984-85*W*	I. V. A. Richards	G. P. Howarth	4	2	0	2
1986-87*N*	I. V. A. Richards	J. V. Coney	3	1	1	1
	In New Zealand		15	6	4	5
	In West Indies		9	2	0	7
	Totals		24	8	4	12

N Played in New Zealand. *W Played in West Indies.*

Notes: The following deputised for the official touring captain or were appointed by the home authority for only a minor proportion of the series:

[1]H. B. Cave (First). [2]B. E. Congdon (Third, Fourth and Fifth).

HIGHEST INNINGS TOTALS

For West Indies in West Indies: 564-8 at Bridgetown		1971-72
in New Zealand: 546-6 dec. at Auckland		1951-52
For New Zealand in West Indies: 543-3 dec. at Georgetown		1971-72
in New Zealand: 460 at Christchurch		1979-80

LOWEST INNINGS TOTALS

For West Indies in West Indies: 133 at Bridgetown		1971-72
in New Zealand: 77 at Auckland		1955-56
For New Zealand in West Indies: 94 at Bridgetown		1984-85
in New Zealand: 74 at Dunedin		1955-56

INDIVIDUAL HUNDREDS

By West Indies (25)

M. C. Carew (1)
109† Auckland ... 1968-69
C. A. Davis (1)
183 Bridgetown . 1971-72
R. C. Fredericks (1)
163 Kingston ... 1971-72
C. G. Greenidge (2)
100 Port-of-Spain 1984-85
213 Auckland ... 1986-87
D. L. Haynes (3)
105† Dunedin 1979-80
122 Christchurch. 1979-80
121 Wellington .. 1986-87
A. I. Kallicharran (2)
100*† Georgetown . 1971-72
101 Port-of-Spain 1971-72
C. L. King (1)
100* Christchurch. 1979-80
S. M. Nurse (2)
168† Auckland .. 1968-69
258 Christchurch. 1968-69
I. V. A. Richards (1)
105 Bridgetown . 1984-85
R. B. Richardson (1)
185 Georgetown . 1984-85
L. G. Rowe (3)
214 }
100* } †Kingston .. 1971-72
100 Christchurch. 1979-80
G. S. Sobers (1)
142 Bridgetown . 1971-72
J. B. Stollmeyer (1)
152 Auckland ... 1951-52
C. L. Walcott (1)
115 Auckland ... 1951-52
E. D. Weekes (3)
123 Dunedin 1955-56
103 Christchurch. 1955-56
156 Wellington .. 1955-56
F. M. M. Worrell (1)
100 Auckland ... 1951-52

By New Zealand (17)

M. G. Burgess (1)
101 Kingston ... 1971-72
B. E. Congdon (2)
166* Port-of-Spain 1971-72
126 Bridgetown . 1971-72
J. J. Crowe (1)
112 Kingston ... 1984-85
M. D. Crowe (3)
188 Georgetown . 1984-85
119 Wellington .. 1986-87
104 Auckland ... 1986-87
B. A. Edgar (1)
127 Auckland ... 1979-80
R. J. Hadlee (1)
103 Christchurch. 1979-80
B. F. Hastings (2)
117* Christchurch. 1968-69
105 Bridgetown . 1971-72
G. P. Howarth (1)
147 Christchurch. 1979-80
T. W. Jarvis (1)
182 Georgetown . 1971-72
B. R. Taylor (1)
124† Auckland ... 1968-69
G. M. Turner (2)
223*‡ Kingston ... 1971-72
259 Georgetown . 1971-72
J. G. Wright (1)
138 Wellington .. 1986-87

† *Signifies hundred on first appearance in West Indies–New Zealand Tests.*
‡ *Carried his bat.*

Notes: E. D. Weekes in 1955-56 made three hundreds in consecutive innings.

L. G. Rowe and A. I. Kallicharran each scored hundreds in their first two innings in Test cricket, Rowe being the only batsman to do so in his first match.

RECORD PARTNERSHIPS FOR EACH WICKET

For West Indies

225 for 1st	C. G. Greenidge and D. L. Haynes at Christchurch	1979-80
269 for 2nd	R. C. Fredericks and L. G. Rowe at Kingston	1971-72
185 for 3rd	C. G. Greenidge and R. B. Richardson at Port-of-Spain	1984-85
162 for 4th	E. D. Weekes and O. G. Smith at Dunedin	1955-56
	C. G. Greenidge and A. I. Kallicharran at Christchurch	1979-80
189 for 5th	F. M. M. Worrell and C. L. Walcott at Auckland	1951-52
254 for 6th	C. A. Davis and G. S. Sobers at Bridgetown	1971-72
143 for 7th	D. St E. Atkinson and J. D. C. Goddard at Christchurch	1955-56
83 for 8th	I. V. A. Richards and M. D. Marshall at Bridgetown	1984-85
70 for 9th	M. D. Marshall and J. Garner at Bridgetown	1984-85
31 for 10th	T. M. Findlay and G. C. Shillingford at Bridgetown	1971-72

For New Zealand

387 for 1st†	G. M. Turner and T. W. Jarvis at Georgetown	1971-72
210 for 2nd†	G. P. Howarth and J. J. Crowe at Kingston	1984-85
241 for 3rd†	J. G. Wright and M. D. Crowe at Wellington	1986-87
175 for 4th	B. E. Congdon and B. F. Hastings at Bridgetown	1971-72
142 for 5th	M. D. Crowe and J. V. Coney at Georgetown	1984-85
220 for 6th	G. M. Turner and K. J. Wadsworth at Kingston	1971-72
143 for 7th	M. D. Crowe and I. D. S. Smith at Georgetown	1984-85
136 for 8th†	B. E. Congdon and R. S. Cunis at Port-of-Spain	1971-72
62* for 9th	V. Pollard and R. S. Cunis at Auckland	1968-69
41 for 10th	B. E. Congdon and J. C. Alabaster at Port-of-Spain	1971-72

† *Denotes record partnership against all countries.*

TEN WICKETS OR MORE IN A MATCH

For West Indies (1)

11-120 (4-40, 7-80)	M. D. Marshall, Bridgetown	1984-85

For New Zealand (3)

10-124 (4-51, 6-73)†	E. J. Chatfield, Port-of-Spain	1984-85
11-102 (5-34, 6-68)†	R. J. Hadlee, Dunedin	1979-80
10-166 (4-71, 6-95)	G. B. Troup, Auckland	1979-80

† *Signifies ten wickets or more on first appearance in West Indies–New Zealand Tests.*

WEST INDIES v INDIA

Season	*Captains* *West Indies*	*India*	*T*	*WI*	*I*	*D*
1948-49*I*	J. D. C. Goddard	L. Amarnath	5	1	0	4
1952-53*W*	J. B. Stollmeyer	V. S. Hazare	5	1	0	4
1958-59*I*	F. C. M. Alexander	Ghulam Ahmed[1]	5	3	0	2
1961-62*W*	F. M. M. Worrell	N. J. Contractor[2]	5	5	0	0
1966-67*I*	G. S. Sobers	Nawab of Pataudi jun.	3	2	0	1
1970-71*W*	G. S. Sobers	A. L. Wadekar	5	0	1	4
1974-75*I*	C. H. Lloyd	Nawab of Pataudi jun.[3]	5	3	2	0
1975-76*W*	C. H. Lloyd	B. S. Bedi	4	2	1	1
1978-79*I*	A. I. Kallicharran	S. M. Gavaskar	6	0	1	5
1982-83*W*	C. H. Lloyd	Kapil Dev	5	2	0	3
1983-84*I*	C. H. Lloyd	Kapil Dev	6	3	0	3
1987-88*I*	I. V. A. Richards	D. B. Vengsarkar[4]	4	1	1	2
1988-89*W*	I. V. A. Richards	D. B. Vengsarkar	4	3	0	1
	In India		34	13	4	17
	In West Indies		28	13	2	13
	Totals		62	26	6	30

I Played in India. W Played in West Indies.

Notes: The following deputised for the official touring captain or were appointed by the home authority for only a minor proportion of the series:

[1]P. R. Umrigar (First), V. Mankad (Fourth), H. R. Adhikari (Fifth). [2]Nawab of Pataudi jun. (Third, Fourth and Fifth). [3]S. Venkataraghavan (Second). [4]R. J. Shastri (Fourth).

HIGHEST INNINGS TOTALS

For West Indies	in West Indies: 631-8 dec. at Kingston	1961-62
	in India: 644-8 dec. at Delhi	1958-59
For India	in West Indies: 469-7 at Port-of-Spain	1982-83
	in India: 644-7 dec. at Kanpur	1978-79

LOWEST INNINGS TOTALS

For West Indies	in West Indies: 214 at Port-of-Spain	1970-71
	in India: 127 at Delhi	1987-88
For India	in West Indies: 97† at Kingston	1975-76
	in India: 75 at Delhi	1987-88

† *Five men absent hurt. The lowest with eleven men batting is 98 at Port-of-Spain, 1961-62.*

INDIVIDUAL HUNDREDS

For West Indies (76)

S. F. A. F. Bacchus (1)		
250	Kanpur	1978-79
B. F. Butcher (2)		
103	Calcutta	1958-59
142	Madras	1958-59
R. J. Christiani (1)		
107†	Delhi	1948-49
C. A. Davis (2)		
125*	Georgetown	1970-71
105	Port-of-Spain	1970-71
P. J. L. Dujon (1)		
110	St John's	1982-83
R. C. Fredericks (2)		
100	Calcutta	1974-75
104	Bombay	1974-75
H. A. Gomes (1)		
123	Port-of-Spain	1982-83
G. E. Gomez (1)		
101†	Delhi	1948-49
C. G. Greenidge (5)		
107†	Bangalore	1974-75
154*	St John's	1982-83
194	Kanpur	1983-84
141	Calcutta	1987-88
117	Bridgetown	1988-89
D. L. Haynes (2)		
136	St John's	1982-83
112*	Bridgetown	1988-89
J. K. Holt (1)		
123	Delhi	1958-59
C. L. Hooper (1)		
100*	Calcutta	1987-88
C. C. Hunte (1)		
101	Bombay	1966-67
A. I. Kallicharran (3)		
124†	Bangalore	1974-75
103*	Port-of-Spain	1975-76
187	Bombay	1978-79
R. B. Kanhai (4)		
256	Calcutta	1958-59
138	Kingston	1961-62
139	Port-of-Spain	1961-62
158*	Kingston	1970-71
C. H. Lloyd (7)		
163	Bangalore	1974-75
242*	Bombay	1974-75
102	Bridgetown	1975-76
143	Port-of-Spain	1982-83
106	St John's	1982-83
103	Delhi	1983-84
161*	Calcutta	1983-84
A. L. Logie (2)		
130	Bridgetown	1982-83
101	Calcutta	1987-88
E. D. A. McMorris (1)		
125†	Kingston	1961-62
B. H. Pairaudeau (1)		
115†	Port-of-Spain	1952-53
A. F. Rae (2)		
104	Bombay	1948-49
109	Madras	1948-49
I. V. A. Richards (8)		
192*	Delhi	1974-75
142	Bridgetown	1975-76
130	Port-of-Spain	1975-76
177	Port-of-Spain	1975-76
109	Georgetown	1982-83
120	Bombay	1983-84
109*	Delhi	1987-88
110	Kingston	1988-89
R. B. Richardson (2)		
194	Georgetown	1988-89
156	Kingston	1988-89
O. G. Smith (1)		
100	Delhi	1958-59
G. S. Sobers (8)		
142*†	Bombay	1958-59
198	Kanpur	1958-59
106*	Calcutta	1958-59
153	Kingston	1961-62
104	Kingston	1961-62
108*	Georgetown	1970-71
178*	Bridgetown	1970-71
132	Port-of-Spain	1970-71
J. S. Solomon (1)		
100*	Delhi	1958-59
J. B. Stollmeyer (2)		
160	Madras	1948-49
104*	Port-of-Spain	1952-53
C. L. Walcott (4)		
152†	Delhi	1948-49
108	Calcutta	1948-49
125	Georgetown	1952-53
118	Kingston	1952-53
E. D. Weekes (7)		
128†	Delhi	1948-49
194	Bombay	1948-49
162 } 101 }	Calcutta	1948-49
207	Port-of-Spain	1952-53
161	Port-of-Spain	1952-53
109	Kingston	1952-53
A. B. Williams (1)		
111	Calcutta	1978-79
F. M. M. Worrell (1)		
237	Kingston	1952-53

For India (55)

H. R. Adhikari (1)
114*† Delhi 1948-49
M. Amarnath (3)
101* Kanpur 1978-79
117 Port-of-Spain 1982-83
116 St John's 1982-83
M. L. Apte (1)
163* Port-of-Spain 1952-53
C. G. Borde (3)
109 Delhi 1958-59
121 Bombay 1966-67
125 Madras 1966-67
S. A. Durani (1)
104 Port-of-Spain 1961-62
F. M. Engineer (1)
109 Madras 1966-67
A. D. Gaekwad (1)
102 Kanpur 1978-79
S. M. Gavaskar (13)
116 Georgetown . 1970-71
117* Bridgetown . 1970-71
124 } Port-of-Spain 1970-71
220 }
156 Port-of-Spain 1975-76
102 Port-of-Spain 1975-76
205 Bombay 1978-79
107 } Calcutta 1978-79
182* }
120 Delhi 1978-79
147* Georgetown . 1982-83
121 Delhi 1983-84
236* Madras 1983-84
V. S. Hazare (2)
134* Bombay 1948-49
122 Bombay 1948-49
Kapil Dev (3)
126* Delhi 1978-79
100* Port-of-Spain 1982-83
109 Madras 1987-88
S. V. Manjrekar (1)
108 Bridgetown . 1988-89
V. L. Manjrekar (1)
118 Kingston ... 1952-53
R. S. Modi (1)
112 Bombay 1948-49
Mushtaq Ali (1)
106† Calcutta 1948-49
B. P. Patel (1)
115* Port-of-Spain 1975-76
Pankaj Roy (1)
150 Kingston ... 1952-53
D. N. Sardesai (3)
212 Kingston ... 1970-71
112 Port-of-Spain 1970-71
150 Bridgetown . 1970-71
R. J. Shastri (2)
102 St John's 1982-83
107 Bridgetown . 1988-89
N. S. Sidhu (1)
116 Kingston ... 1988-89
E. D. Solkar (1)
102 Bombay 1974-75
P. R. Umrigar (3)
130 Port-of-Spain 1952-53
117 Kingston ... 1952-53
172* Port-of-Spain 1961-62
D. B. Vengsarkar (6)
157* Calcutta 1978-79
109 Delhi 1978-79
159 Delhi 1983-84
100 Bombay 1983-84
102 Delhi 1987-88
102* Calcutta 1987-88
G. R. Viswanath (4)
139 Calcutta 1974-75
112 Port-of-Spain 1975-76
124 Madras 1978-79
179 Kanpur 1978-79

† *Signifies hundred on first appearance in West Indies–India Tests.*

RECORD PARTNERSHIPS FOR EACH WICKET

For West Indies

296 for 1st	C. G. Greenidge and D. L. Haynes at St John's	1982-83
255 for 2nd	E. D. A. McMorris and R. B. Kanhai at Kingston	1961-62
220 for 3rd	I. V. A. Richards and A. I. Kallicharran at Bridgetown	1975-76
267 for 4th	C. L. Walcott and G. E. Gomez at Delhi	1948-49
219 for 5th	E. D. Weekes and B. H. Pairaudeau at Port-of-Spain	1952-53
250 for 6th	C. H. Lloyd and D. L. Murray at Bombay	1974-75
130 for 7th	C. G. Greenidge and M. D. Marshall at Kanpur	1983-84
124 for 8th†	I. V. A. Richards and K. D. Boyce at Delhi	1974-75
161 for 9th†	C. H. Lloyd and A. M. E. Roberts at Calcutta	1983-84
98* for 10th†	F. M. M. Worrell and W. W. Hall at Port-of-Spain	1961-62

For India

153 for 1st	S. M. Gavaskar and C. P. S. Chauhan at Bombay	1978-79
344* for 2nd†	S. M. Gavaskar and D. B. Vengsarkar at Calcutta	1978-79
159 for 3rd	M. Amarnath and G. R. Viswanath at Port-of-Spain	1975-76
172 for 4th	G. R. Viswanath and A. D. Gaekwad at Kanpur	1978-79
204 for 5th	S. M. Gavaskar and B. P. Patel at Port-of-Spain	1975-76
170 for 6th	S. M. Gavaskar and R. J. Shastri at Madras	1983-84
186 for 7th	D. N. Sardesai and E. D. Solkar at Bridgetown	1970-71
107 for 8th	Yashpal Sharma and B. S. Sandhu at Kingston	1982-83
143* for 9th	S. M. Gavaskar and S. M. H. Kirmani at Madras	1983-84
62 for 10th	D. N. Sardesai and B. S. Bedi at Bridgetown	1970-71

† *Denotes record partnership against all countries.*

TEN WICKETS OR MORE IN A MATCH

For West Indies (4)

11-126 (6-50, 5-76)	W. W. Hall, Kanpur	1958-59
11-89 (5-34, 6-55)	M. D. Marshall, Port-of-Spain	1988-89
12-121 (7-64, 5-57)	A. M. E. Roberts, Madras	1974-75
10-101 (6-62, 4-39)	C. A. Walsh, Kingston	1988-89

For India (4)

11-235 (7-157, 4-78)†	B. S. Chandrasekhar, Bombay	1966-67
10-223 (9-102, 1-121)	S. P. Gupte, Kanpur	1958-59
16-136 (8-61, 8-75)†	N. D. Hirwani, Madras	1987-88
10-135 (1-52, 9-83)	Kapil Dev, Ahmedabad	1983-84

† *Signifies ten wickets or more on first appearance in West Indies–India Tests.*

WEST INDIES v PAKISTAN

Season	Captains: West Indies	Pakistan	T	WI	P	D
1957-58*W*	F. C. M. Alexander	A. H. Kardar	5	3	1	1
1958-59*P*	F. C. M. Alexander	Fazal Mahmood	3	1	2	0
1974-75*P*	C. H. Lloyd	Intikhab Alam	2	0	0	2
1976-77*W*	C. H. Lloyd	Mushtaq Mohammad	5	2	1	2
1980-81*P*	C. H. Lloyd	Javed Miandad	4	1	0	3
1986-87*P*	I. V. A. Richards	Imran Khan	3	1	1	1
1987-88*W*	I. V. A. Richards[1]	Imran Khan	3	1	1	1
	In West Indies		13	6	3	4
	In Pakistan		12	3	3	6
	Totals		25	9	6	10

P Played in Pakistan. W Played in West Indies.

Note: The following was appointed by the home authority for only a minor proportion of the series:

[1]C. G. Greenidge (First).

HIGHEST INNINGS TOTALS

For West Indies in West Indies: 790-3 dec. at Kingston		1957-58
in Pakistan: 493 at Karachi		1974-75
For Pakistan in West Indies: 657-8 dec. at Bridgetown		1957-58
in Pakistan: 406-8 dec. at Karachi		1974-75

LOWEST INNINGS TOTALS

For West Indies in West Indies: 154 at Port-of-Spain		1976-77
in Pakistan: 53 at Faisalabad		1986-87
For Pakistan in West Indies: 106 at Bridgetown		1957-58
in Pakistan: 77 at Lahore		1986-87

INDIVIDUAL HUNDREDS

For West Indies (19)

L. Baichan (1)
105*† Lahore 1974-75
P. J. L. Dujon (1)
106* Port-of-Spain 1987-88
R. C. Fredericks (1)
120 Port-of-Spain 1976-77
C. G. Greenidge (1)
100 Kingston ... 1976-77
C. C. Hunte (3)
142† Bridgetown . 1957-58
260 Kingston ... 1957-58
114 Georgetown . 1957-58
B. D. Julien (1)
101 Karachi 1974-75
A. I. Kallicharran (1)
115 Karachi 1974-75
R. B. Kanhai (1)
217 Lahore 1958-59
C. H. Lloyd (1)
157 Bridgetown . 1976-77
I. V. A. Richards (2)
120* Multan 1980-81
123 Port-of-Spain 1987-88
I. T. Shillingford (1)
120 Georgetown . 1976-77
G. S. Sobers (3)
365* Kingston ... 1957-58
125, 109* } Georgetown . 1957-58
C. L. Walcott (1)
145 Georgetown . 1957-58
E. D. Weekes (1)
197† Bridgetown . 1957-58

For Pakistan (16)

Asif Iqbal (1)
135 Kingston ... 1976-77
Hanif Mohammad (2)
337† Bridgetown . 1957-58
103 Karachi 1958-59
Imtiaz Ahmed (1)
122 Kingston ... 1957-58
Imran Khan (1)
123 Lahore 1980-81
Javed Miandad (2)
114 Georgetown . 1987-88
102 Port-of-Spain 1987-88
Majid Khan (2)
100 Karachi 1974-75
167 Georgetown . 1976-77
Mushtaq Mohammad (2)
123 Lahore 1974-75
121 Port-of-Spain 1976-77
Saeed Ahmed (1)
150 Georgetown . 1957-58
Wasim Raja (2)
107* Karachi 1974-75
117* Bridgetown . 1976-77
Wazir Mohammad (2)
106 Kingston ... 1957-58
189 Port-of-Spain 1957-58

† *Signifies hundred on first appearance in West Indies–Pakistan Tests.*

RECORD PARTNERSHIPS FOR EACH WICKET

For West Indies

182 for 1st	R. C. Fredericks and C. G. Greenidge at Kingston	1976-77
446 for 2nd†	C. C. Hunte and G. S. Sobers at Kingston	1957-58
162 for 3rd	R. B. Kanhai and G. S. Sobers at Lahore	1958-59
188* for 4th	G. S. Sobers and C. L. Walcott at Kingston	1957-58
185 for 5th	E. D. Weekes and O. G. Smith at Bridgetown	1957-58
151 for 6th	C. H. Lloyd and D. L. Murray at Bridgetown	1976-77
70 for 7th	C. H. Lloyd and J. Garner at Bridgetown	1976-77
50 for 8th	B. D. Julien and V. A. Holder at Karachi	1974-75
61* for 9th	P. J. L. Dujon and W. K. M. Benjamin at Bridgetown	1987-88
44 for 10th	R. Nanan and S. T. Clarke at Faisalabad	1980-81

For Pakistan

159 for 1st‡	Majid Khan and Zaheer Abbas at Georgetown	1976-77
178 for 2nd	Hanif Mohammad and Saeed Ahmed at Karachi	1958-59
169 for 3rd	Saeed Ahmed and Wazir Mohammad at Port-of-Spain	1957-58
154 for 4th	Wazir Mohammad and Hanif Mohammad at Port-of-Spain	1957-58
87 for 5th	Mushtaq Mohammad and Asif Iqbal at Kingston	1976-77
166 for 6th	Wazir Mohammad and A. H. Kardar at Kingston	1957-58
128 for 7th	Wasim Raja and Wasim Bari at Karachi	1974-75
94 for 8th	Salim Malik and Salim Yousuf at Port-of-Spain	1987-88
73 for 9th	Wasim Raja and Sarfraz Nawaz at Bridgetown	1976-77
133 for 10th†	Wasim Raja and Wasim Bari at Bridgetown	1976-77

† *Denotes record partnership against all countries.*

‡ *219 runs were added for this wicket in two separate partnerships: Sadiq Mohammad retired hurt and was replaced by Zaheer Abbas when 60 had been added. The highest partnership by two opening batsmen is 152 by Hanif Mohammad and Imtiaz Ahmed at Bridgetown, 1957-58.*

TEN WICKETS OR MORE IN A MATCH

For Pakistan (2)

12-100 (6-34, 6-66)	Fazal Mahmood, Dacca	1958-59
11-121 (7-80, 4-41)	Imran Khan, Georgetown	1987-88

Note: The best match figures by a West Indian bowler are 9-95 (8-29, 1-66) by C. E. H. Croft at Port-of-Spain, 1976-77.

NEW ZEALAND v INDIA

	Captains					
Season	*New Zealand*	*India*	*T*	*NZ*	*I*	*D*
1955-56*I*	H. B. Cave	P. R. Umrigar[1]	5	0	2	3
1964-65*I*	J. R. Reid	Nawab of Pataudi jun.	4	0	1	3
1967-68*N*	G. T. Dowling[2]	Nawab of Pataudi jun.	4	1	3	0
1969-70*I*	G. T. Dowling	Nawab of Pataudi jun.	3	1	1	1
1975-76*N*	G. M. Turner	B. S. Bedi[3]	3	1	1	1
1976-77*I*	G. M. Turner	B. S. Bedi	3	0	2	1
1980-81*N*	G. P. Howarth	S. M. Gavaskar	3	1	0	2
1988-89*I*	J. G. Wright	D. B. Vengsarkar	3	1	2	0
1989-90*N*	J. G. Wright	M. Azharuddin	3	1	0	2
	In India		18	2	8	8
	In New Zealand		13	4	4	5
	Totals		31	6	12	13

I Played in India. N Played in New Zealand.

Notes: The following deputised for the official touring captain or were appointed by the home authority for a minor proportion of the series:

[1]Ghulam Ahmed (First). [2]B. W. Sinclair (First). [3]S. M. Gavaskar (First).

HIGHEST INNINGS TOTALS

For New Zealand in New Zealand: 502 at Christchurch	1967-68
in India: 462-9 dec. at Calcutta	1964-65
For India in New Zealand: 482 at Auckland	1989-90
in India: 537-3 dec. at Madras	1955-56

LOWEST INNINGS TOTALS

For New Zealand in New Zealand: 100 at Wellington	1980-81
in India: 124 at Hyderabad	1988-89
For India in New Zealand: 81 at Wellington	1975-76
in India: 88 at Bombay	1964-65

INDIVIDUAL HUNDREDS

For New Zealand (21)

M. D. Crowe (1)
113 Auckland ... 1989-90

G. T. Dowling (3)
120 Bombay 1964-65
143 Dunedin 1967-68
239 Christchurch. 1967-68

J. W. Guy (1)
102† Hyderabad .. 1955-56

G. P. Howarth (1)
137* Wellington .. 1980-81

A. H. Jones (1)
170* Auckland ... 1989-90

J. M. Parker (1)
104 Bombay 1976-77

J. F. Reid (1)
123* Christchurch. 1980-81

J. R. Reid (2)
119* Delhi 1955-56
120 Calcutta 1955-56

I. D. S. Smith (1)
173 Auckland ... 1989-90

B. Sutcliffe (3)
137*† Hyderabad .. 1955-56
230* Delhi 1955-56
151* Calcutta 1964-65

B. R. Taylor (1)
105† Calcutta 1964-65

G. M. Turner (2)
117 Christchurch. 1975-76
113 Kanpur 1976-77

J. G. Wright (3)
110 Auckland ... 1980-81
185 Christchurch. 1989-90
113* Napier 1989-90

For India (22)

S. Amarnath (1)
124† Auckland ... 1975-76

M. Azharuddin (1)
192 Auckland ... 1989-90

C. G. Borde (1)
109 Bombay 1964-65

S. M. Gavaskar (2)
116† Auckland ... 1975-76
119 Bombay 1976-77

A. G. Kripal Singh (1)
100*† Hyderabad .. 1955-56

V. L. Manjrekar (3)
118† Hyderabad .. 1955-56
177 Delhi 1955-56
102* Madras 1964-65

V. Mankad (2)
223 Bombay 1955-56
231 Madras 1955-56

Nawab of Pataudi jun. (2)
153 Calcutta 1964-65
113 Delhi 1964-65

G. S. Ramchand (1)
106* Calcutta 1955-56

Pankaj Roy (2)
100 Calcutta 1955-56
173 Madras 1955-56

D. N. Sardesai (2)
200* Bombay 1964-65
106 Delhi 1964-65

N. S. Sidhu (1)
116† Bangalore ... 1988-89

P. R. Umrigar (1)
223† Hyderabad .. 1955-56

G. R. Viswanath (1)
103* Kanpur 1976-77

A. L. Wadekar (1)
143 Wellington .. 1967-68

† *Signifies hundred on first appearance in New Zealand–India Tests. B. R. Taylor provides the only instance for New Zealand of a player scoring his maiden hundred in first-class cricket in his first Test.*

RECORD PARTNERSHIPS FOR EACH WICKET

For New Zealand

149 for 1st	T. J. Franklin and J. G. Wright at Napier	1989-90
155 for 2nd	G. T. Dowling and B. E. Congdon at Dunedin	1967-68
222* for 3rd	B. Sutcliffe and J. R. Reid at Delhi	1955-56
125 for 4th	J. G. Wright and M. J. Greatbatch at Christchurch	1989-90
119 for 5th	G. T. Dowling and K. Thomson at Christchurch	1967-68
87 for 6th	J. W. Guy and A. R. MacGibbon at Hyderabad	1955-56
163 for 7th	B. Sutcliffe and B. R. Taylor at Calcutta	1964-65
103 for 8th	R. J. Hadlee and I. D. S. Smith at Auckland	1989-90
136 for 9th†	I. D. S. Smith and M. C. Snedden at Auckland	1989-90
61 for 10th	J. T. Ward and R. O. Collinge at Madras	1964-65

For India

413 for 1st†	V. Mankad and Pankaj Roy at Madras	1955-56
204 for 2nd	S. M. Gavaskar and S. Amarnath at Auckland	1975-76
238 for 3rd	P. R. Umrigar and V. L. Manjrekar at Hyderabad	1955-56
171 for 4th	P. R. Umrigar and A. G. Kripal Singh at Hyderabad	1955-56
127 for 5th	V. L. Manjrekar and G. S. Ramchand at Delhi	1955-56
193* for 6th	D. N. Sardesai and Hanumant Singh at Bombay	1964-65
128 for 7th	S. R. Tendulkar and K. S. More at Napier	1989-90
143 for 8th†	R. G. Nadkarni and F. M. Engineer at Madras	1964-65
105 for 9th	S. M. H. Kirmani and B. S. Bedi at Bombay	1976-77
	S. M. H. Kirmani and N. S. Yadav at Auckland	1980-81
57 for 10th	R. B. Desai and B. S. Bedi at Dunedin	1967-68

† *Denotes record partnership against all countries.*

TEN WICKETS OR MORE IN A MATCH

For New Zealand (2)

11-58 (4-35, 7-23) R. J. Hadlee, Wellington 1975-76
10-88 (6-49, 4-39) R. J. Hadlee, Bombay 1988-89

For India (2)

11-140 (3-64, 8-76) E. A. S. Prasanna, Auckland 1975-76
12-152 (8-72, 4-80) S. Venkataraghavan, Delhi 1964-65

NEW ZEALAND v PAKISTAN

	Captains					
Season	*New Zealand*	*Pakistan*	*T*	*NZ*	*P*	*D*
1955-56*P*	H. B. Cave	A. H. Kardar	3	0	2	1
1964-65*N*	J. R. Reid	Hanif Mohammad	3	0	0	3
1964-65*P*	J. R. Reid	Hanif Mohammad	3	0	2	1
1969-70*P*	G. T. Dowling	Intikhab Alam	3	1	0	2
1972-73*N*	B. E. Congdon	Intikhab Alam	3	0	1	2
1976-77*P*	G. M. Turner[1]	Mushtaq Mohammad	3	0	2	1
1978-79*N*	M. G. Burgess	Mushtaq Mohammad	3	0	1	2
1984-85*P*	J. V. Coney	Zaheer Abbas	3	0	2	1
1984-85*N*	G. P. Howarth	Javed Miandad	3	2	0	1
1988-89*N*†	J. G. Wright	Imran Khan	2	0	0	2
	In Pakistan		15	1	8	6
	In New Zealand		14	2	2	10
	Totals		29	3	10	16

N Played in New Zealand. P Played in Pakistan.
† The First Test at Dunedin was abandoned without a ball being bowled and is excluded.

Note: The following deputised for the official touring captain:
[1]J. M. Parker (Third).

HIGHEST INNINGS TOTALS

For New Zealand in New Zealand 492 at Wellington 1984-85
in Pakistan: 482-6 dec. at Lahore 1964-65

For Pakistan in New Zealand: 616-5 dec. at Auckland 1988-89
in Pakistan: 565-9 dec. at Karachi 1976-77

LOWEST INNINGS TOTALS

For New Zealand in New Zealand: 156 at Dunedin 1972-73
in Pakistan: 70 at Dacca 1955-56

For Pakistan in New Zealand: 169 at Auckland 1984-85
in Pakistan: 114 at Lahore 1969-70

INDIVIDUAL HUNDREDS

For New Zealand (17)

M. G. Burgess (2)
119* Dacca 1969-70
111 Lahore 1976-77
J. V. Coney (1)
111* Dunedin 1984-85
M. D. Crowe (1)
174 Wellington .. 1988-89
B. A. Edgar (1)
129† Christchurch. 1978-79
B. F. Hastings (1)
110 Auckland ... 1972-73
G. P. Howarth (1)
114 Napier 1978-79
W. K. Lees (1)
152 Karachi 1976-77
S. N. McGregor (1)
111 Lahore 1955-56
R. E. Redmond (1)
107† Auckland ... 1972-73
J. F. Reid (3)
106 Hyderabad .. 1984-85
148 Wellington .. 1984-85
158* Auckland ... 1984-85
J. R. Reid (1)
128 Karachi 1964-65
B. W. Sinclair (1)
130 Lahore 1964-65
G. M. Turner (1)
110† Dacca 1969-70
J. G. Wright (1)
107 Karachi 1984-85

For Pakistan (30)

Asif Iqbal (3)
175 Dunedin 1972-73
166 Lahore 1976-77
104 Napier 1978-79
Hanif Mohammad (3)
103 Dacca 1955-56
100* Christchurch. 1964-65
203* Lahore 1964-65
Imtiaz Ahmed (1)
209 Lahore 1955-56
Javed Miandad (7)
163† Lahore 1976-77
206 Karachi 1976-77
160* Christchurch. 1978-79
104 } Hyderabad .. 1984-85
103* }
118 Wellington .. 1988-89
271 Auckland ... 1988-89
Majid Khan (3)
110 Auckland ... 1972-73
112 Karachi 1976-77
119* Napier 1978-79
Mohammad Ilyas (1)
126 Karachi 1964-65
Mudassar Nazar (1)
106 Hyderabad .. 1984-85
Mushtaq Mohammad (3)
201 Dunedin 1972-73
101 Hyderabad .. 1976-77
107 Karachi 1976-77
Sadiq Mohammad (2)
166 Wellington .. 1972-73
103* Hyderabad .. 1976-77
Saeed Ahmed (1)
172 Karachi 1964-65
Salim Malik (1)
119* Karachi 1984-85
Shoaib Mohammad (2)
163 Wellington .. 1988-89
112 Auckland ... 1988-89
Waqar Hassan (1)
189 Lahore 1955-56
Zaheer Abbas (1)
135 Auckland ... 1978-79

† *Signifies hundred on first appearance in New Zealand–Pakistan Tests.*

Note: Mushtaq and Sadiq Mohammad, at Hyderabad in 1976-77, provide the fourth instance in Test matches, after the Chappells (thrice), of brothers each scoring hundreds in the same innings.

RECORD PARTNERSHIPS FOR EACH WICKET

For New Zealand

159 for 1st	R. E. Redmond and G. M. Turner at Auckland	1972-73
195 for 2nd	J. G. Wright and G. P. Howarth at Napier	1978-79
178 for 3rd	B. W. Sinclair and J. R. Reid at Lahore	1964-65
128 for 4th	B. F. Hastings and M. G. Burgess at Wellington	1972-73
183 for 5th†	M. G. Burgess and R. W. Anderson at Lahore	1976-77
145 for 6th	J. F. Reid and R. J. Hadlee at Wellington	1984-85
186 for 7th†	W. K. Lees and R. J. Hadlee at Karachi	1976-77
100 for 8th	B. W. Yuile and D. R. Hadlee at Karachi	1969-70
96 for 9th	M. G. Burgess and R. S. Cunis at Dacca	1969-70
151 for 10th†	B. F. Hastings and R. O. Collinge at Auckland	1972-73

For Pakistan

147 for 1st‡	Sadiq Mohammad and Majid Khan at Karachi	1976-77
114 for 2nd	Mohammad Ilyas and Saeed Ahmed at Rawalpindi	1964-65
248 for 3rd	Shoaib Mohammad and Javed Miandad at Auckland	1988-89
350 for 4th†	Mushtaq Mohammad and Asif Iqbal at Dunedin	1972-73

281 for 5th†	Javed Miandad and Asif Iqbal at Lahore	1976-77
217 for 6th†	Hanif Mohammad and Majid Khan at Lahore	1964-65
308 for 7th†	Waqar Hassan and Imtiaz Ahmed at Lahore	1955-56
89 for 8th	Anil Dalpat and Iqbal Qasim at Karachi	1984-85
52 for 9th	Intikhab Alam and Arif Butt at Auckland	1964-65
65 for 10th	Salah-ud-Din and Mohammad Farooq at Rawalpindi	1964-65

† *Denotes record partnership against all countries.*

‡ *In the preceding Test of this series, at Hyderabad, 164 runs were added for this wicket by Sadiq Mohammad, Majid Khan and Zaheer Abbas. Sadiq Mohammad retired hurt after 136 had been scored.*

TEN WICKETS OR MORE IN A MATCH

For Pakistan (4)

10-182 (5-91, 5-91)	Intikhab Alam, Dacca	1969-70
11-130 (7-52, 4-78)	Intikhab Alam, Dunedin	1972-73
10-128 (5-56, 5-72)	Wasim Akram, Dunedin	1984-85
11-79 (5-37, 6-42)†	Zulfiqar Ahmed, Karachi	1955-56

† *Signifies ten wickets or more on first appearance in New Zealand–Pakistan Tests.*

Note: The best match figures by a New Zealand bowler are 9-70 (4-36, 5-34), F. J. Cameron at Auckland, 1964-65.

NEW ZEALAND v SRI LANKA

	Captains					
Season	*New Zealand*	*Sri Lanka*	*T*	*NZ*	*SL*	*D*
1982-83*N*	G. P. Howarth	D. S. de Silva	2	2	0	0
1983-84*S*	G. P. Howarth	L. R. D. Mendis	3	2	0	1
1986-87*S*†	J. J. Crowe	L. R. D. Mendis	1	0	0	1
	In New Zealand		2	2	0	0
	In Sri Lanka		4	2	0	2
	Totals		6	4	0	2

N Played in New Zealand. S Played in Sri Lanka.

† *The Second and Third Tests were cancelled owing to civil disturbances.*

HIGHEST INNINGS TOTALS

For New Zealand in New Zealand: 344 at Christchurch ... 1982-83
in Sri Lanka: 459 at Colombo (CCC) ... 1983-84

For Sri Lanka in New Zealand: 240 at Wellington ... 1982-83
in Sri Lanka: 397-9 dec. at Colombo (CCC) ... 1986-87

LOWEST INNINGS TOTALS

For New Zealand in New Zealand: 201 at Wellington ... 1982-83
in Sri Lanka: 198 at Colombo (SSC) ... 1983-84

For Sri Lanka in New Zealand: 93 at Wellington ... 1982-83
in Sri Lanka: 97 at Kandy ... 1983-84

INDIVIDUAL HUNDREDS

For New Zealand (3)

J. J. Crowe (1)	**R. J. Hadlee** (1)	**J. F. Reid** (1)
120* Colombo (CCC) 1986-87	151* Colombo (CCC) 1986-87	180 Colombo (CCC) 1983-84

For Sri Lanka (2)

R. L. Dias (1)	**D. S. B. P. Kuruppu** (1)
108† Colombo (SSC) 1983-84	201*† Colombo (CCC) 1986-87

† *Signifies hundred on first appearance in New Zealand–Sri Lanka Tests.*

PARTNERSHIPS

Best wicket partnership for New Zealand: 246* for the 6th† by J. J. Crowe and R. J. Hadlee at Colombo (CCC) 1986-87
for Sri Lanka: 159* for the 3rd†‡ by S. Wettimuny and R. L. Dias at Colombo (SSC) 1983-84

† *Denotes record partnership against all countries.*
‡ *163 runs were added for this wicket in two separate partnerships: S. Wettimuny retired hurt and was replaced by L. R. D. Mendis when 159 had been added.*

TEN WICKETS OR MORE IN A MATCH

For New Zealand (1)

10-102 (5-73, 5-29) R. J. Hadlee, Colombo (CCC) 1983-84

Note: The best match figures by a Sri Lankan bowler are 8-159 (5-86, 3-73), V. B. John at Kandy, 1983-84.

INDIA v PAKISTAN

	Captains					
Season *India*	*Pakistan*	*T*	*I*	*P*	*D*
1952-53*I* L. Amarnath	A. H. Kardar	5	2	1	2
1954-55*P* V. Mankad	A. H. Kardar	5	0	0	5
1960-61*I* N. J. Contractor	Fazal Mahmood	5	0	0	5
1978-79*P* B. S. Bedi	Mushtaq Mohammad	3	0	2	1
1979-80*I* S. M. Gavaskar[1]	Asif Iqbal	6	2	0	4
1982-83*P* S. M. Gavaskar	Imran Khan	6	0	3	3
1983-84*I* Kapil Dev	Zaheer Abbas	3	0	0	3
1984-85*P* S. M. Gavaskar	Zaheer Abbas	2	0	0	2
1986-87*I* Kapil Dev	Imran Khan	5	0	1	4
1989-90*P* K. Srikkanth	Imran Khan	4	0	0	4
In India		24	4	2	18
In Pakistan		20	0	5	15
Totals		44	4	7	33

I Played in India. P Played in Pakistan.

Note: The following was appointed by the home authority for only a minor proportion of the series:

[1]G. R. Viswanath (Sixth).

HIGHEST INNINGS TOTALS

For India in India: 539-9 dec. at Madras 1960-61
in Pakistan: 509 at Lahore 1989-90

For Pakistan in India: 487-9 dec. at Madras 1986-87
in Pakistan: 699-5 at Lahore 1989-90

LOWEST INNINGS TOTALS

For India in India: 106 at Lucknow 1952-53
in Pakistan: 145 at Karachi 1954-55

For Pakistan in India: 116 at Bangalore 1986-87
in Pakistan: 158 at Dacca 1954-55

INDIVIDUAL HUNDREDS

For India (31)

M. Amarnath (4)
109* Lahore 1982-83
120 Lahore 1982-83
103* Karachi 1982-83
101* Lahore 1984-85
M. Azharuddin (3)
141 Calcutta 1986-87
110 Jaipur 1986-87
109 Faisalabad .. 1989-90
C. G. Borde (1)
177* Madras 1960-61
A. D. Gaekwad (1)
201 Jullundur ... 1983-84
S. M. Gavaskar (5)
111 }
137 } Karachi 1978-79
166 Madras 1979-80
127*‡ Faisalabad .. 1982-83
103* Bangalore ... 1983-84
V. S. Hazare (1)
146* Bombay 1952-53
S. V. Manjrekar (2)
113*† Karachi 1989-90
218 Lahore 1989-90
S. M. Patil (1)
127 Faisalabad .. 1984-85
R. J. Shastri (3)
128 Karachi 1982-83
139 Faisalabad .. 1984-85
125 Jaipur 1986-87
R. H. Shodhan (1)
110† Calcutta 1952-53
K. Srikkanth (1)
123 Madras 1986-87
P. R. Umrigar (5)
102 Bombay 1952-53
108 Peshawar ... 1954-55
115 Kanpur 1960-61
117 Madras 1960-61
112 Delhi 1960-61
D. B. Vengsarkar (2)
146* Delhi 1979-80
109 Ahmedabad . 1986-87
G. R. Viswanath (1)
145† Faisalabad .. 1978-79

For Pakistan (41)

Aamer Malik (2)
117 Faisalabad .. 1989-90
113 Lahore 1989-90
Alim-ud-Din (1)
103* Karachi 1954-55
Asif Iqbal (1)
104† Faisalabad .. 1978-79
Hanif Mohammad (2)
142 Bahawalpur . 1954-55
160 Bombay 1960-61
Ijaz Faqih (1)
105† Ahmedabad . 1986-87
Imtiaz Ahmed (1)
135 Madras 1960-61
Imran Khan (3)
117 Faisalabad .. 1982-83
135* Madras 1986-87
109* Karachi 1989-90
Javed Miandad (5)
154*† Faisalabad .. 1978-79
100 Karachi 1978-79
126 Faisalabad .. 1982-83
280* Hyderabad .. 1982-83
145 Lahore 1989-90
Mohsin Khan (1)
101*† Lahore 1982-83
Mudassar Nazar (6)
126 Bangalore ... 1979-80
119 Karachi 1982-83
231 Hyderabad .. 1982-83
152*‡ Lahore 1982-83
152 Karachi 1982-83
199 Faisalabad .. 1984-85
Mushtaq Mohammad (1)
101 Delhi 1960-61
Nazar Mohammad (1)
124*‡ Lucknow ... 1952-53
Qasim Omar (1)
210 Faisalabad .. 1984-85
Ramiz Raja (1)
114 Jaipur 1986-87
Saeed Ahmed (2)
121† Bombay 1960-61
103 Madras 1960-61
Salim Malik (3)
107 Faisalabad .. 1982-83
102* Faisalabad .. 1984-85
102* Karachi 1989-90
Shoaib Mohammad (2)
101 Madras 1986-87
203* Lahore 1989-90
Wasim Raja (1)
125 Jullundur ... 1983-84
Zaheer Abbas (6)
176† Faisalabad .. 1978-79
235* Lahore 1978-79
215 Lahore 1982-83
186 Karachi 1982-83
168 Faisalabad .. 1982-83
168* Lahore 1984-85

† *Signifies hundred on first appearance in India–Pakistan Tests.*
‡ *Carried his bat.*

RECORD PARTNERSHIPS FOR EACH WICKET

For India

200 for 1st	S. M. Gavaskar and K. Srikkanth at Madras	1986-87
135 for 2nd	N. S. Sidhu and S. V. Manjrekar at Karachi	1989-90
190 for 3rd	M. Amarnath and Yashpal Sharma at Lahore	1982-83
186 for 4th	S. V. Manjrekar and R. J. Shastri at Lahore	1989-90
200 for 5th	S. M. Patil and R. J. Shastri at Faisalabad	1984-85
143 for 6th	M. Azharuddin and Kapil Dev at Calcutta	1986-87
155 for 7th	R. M. H. Binny and Madan Lal at Bangalore	1983-84
122 for 8th	S. M. H. Kirmani and Madan Lal at Faisalabad	1982-83
149 for 9th†	P. G. Joshi and R. B. Desai at Bombay	1960-61
109 for 10th†	H. R. Adhikari and Ghulam Ahmed at Delhi	1952-53

For Pakistan

162 for 1st	Hanif Mohammad and Imtiaz Ahmed at Madras	1960-61
250 for 2nd	Mudassar Nazar and Qasim Omar at Faisalabad	1984-85
451 for 3rd†	Mudassar Nazar and Javed Miandad at Hyderabad	1982-83
287 for 4th	Javed Miandad and Zaheer Abbas at Faisalabad	1982-83
213 for 5th	Zaheer Abbas and Mudassar Nazar at Karachi	1982-83
207 for 6th	Salim Malik and Imran Khan at Faisalabad	1982-83
154 for 7th	Imran Khan and Ijaz Faqih at Ahmedabad	1986-87
112 for 8th	Imran Khan and Wasim Akram at Madras	1986-87
60 for 9th	Wasim Bari and Iqbal Qasim at Bangalore	1979-80
104 for 10th	Zulfiqar Ahmed and Amir Elahi at Madras	1952-53

† *Denotes record partnership against all countries.*

TEN WICKETS OR MORE IN A MATCH

For India (3)

11-146 (4-90, 7-56)	Kapil Dev, Madras	1979-80
10-126 (7-27, 3-99)	Maninder Singh, Bangalore	1986-87
13-131 (8-52, 5-79)†	V. Mankad, Delhi	1952-53

For Pakistan (5)

12-94 (5-52, 7-42)	Fazal Mahmood, Lucknow	1952-53
11-79 (3-19, 8-60)	Imran Khan, Karachi	1982-83
11-180 (6-98, 5-82)	Imran Khan, Faisalabad	1982-83
10-175 (4-135, 6-40)	Iqbal Qasim, Bombay	1979-80
11-190 (8-69, 3-121)	Sikander Bakht, Delhi	1979-80

† *Signifies ten wickets or more on first appearance in India–Pakistan Tests.*

INDIA v SRI LANKA

	Captains					
Season	*India*	*Sri Lanka*	*T*	*I*	*SL*	*D*
1982-83*I*	S. M. Gavaskar	B. Warnapura	1	0	0	1
1985-86*S*	Kapil Dev	L. R. D. Mendis	3	0	1	2
1986-87*I*	Kapil Dev	L. R. D. Mendis	3	2	0	1
	In India		4	2	0	2
	In Sri Lanka		3	0	1	2
	Totals		7	2	1	4

I Played in India. *S Played in Sri Lanka.*

HIGHEST INNINGS TOTALS

For India in India: 676-7 at Kanpur 1986-87
in Sri Lanka: 325-5 dec. at Kandy 1985-86

For Sri Lanka in India: 420 at Kanpur 1986-87
in Sri Lanka: 385 at Colombo (PSS) 1985-86

LOWEST INNINGS TOTALS

For India in India: 400 at Cuttack 1986-87
in Sri Lanka: 198 at Colombo (PSS) 1985-86

For Sri Lanka in India: 141 at Nagpur 1986-87
in Sri Lanka: 198 at Kandy 1985-86

INDIVIDUAL HUNDREDS

For India (9)

M. Amarnath (2)
116* Kandy 1985-86
131 Nagpur 1986-87
M. Azharuddin (1)
199 Kanpur 1986-87

S. M. Gavaskar (2)
155† Madras 1982-83
176 Kanpur 1986-87
Kapil Dev (1)
163 Kanpur 1986-87

S. M. Patil (1)
114*† Madras 1982-83
D. B. Vengsarkar (2)
153 Nagpur 1986-87
166 Cuttack 1986-87

For Sri Lanka (7)

R. L. Dias (1)
106 Kandy 1985-86
R. S. Madugalle (1)
103 Colombo (SSC) 1985-86
L. R. D. Mendis (3)
105 } †Madras 1982-83
105 }
124 Kandy 1985-86

A. Ranatunga (1)
111 Colombo (SSC) 1985-86
S. A. R. Silva (1)
111 Colombo (PSS) 1985-86

† *Signifies hundred on first appearance in India–Sri Lanka Tests.*

RECORD PARTNERSHIPS FOR EACH WICKET

For India

156 for 1st	S. M. Gavaskar and Arun Lal at Madras	1982-83
173 for 2nd	S. M. Gavaskar and D. B. Vengsarkar at Madras	1982-83
173 for 3rd	M. Amarnath and D. B. Vengsarkar at Nagpur	1986-87
163 for 4th	S. M. Gavaskar and M. Azharuddin at Kanpur	1986-87
78 for 5th	M. Amarnath and M. Azharuddin at Kandy	1985-86
272 for 6th	M. Azharuddin and Kapil Dev at Kanpur	1986-87
78* for 7th	S. M. Patil and Madan Lal at Madras	1982-83
70 for 8th	Kapil Dev and L. Sivaramakrishnan at Colombo (PSS)	1985-86
16 for 9th	S. M. Gavaskar and Gopal Sharma at Colombo (SSC)	1985-86
29 for 10th	Kapil Dev and Chetan Sharma at Colombo (PSS)	1985-86

For Sri Lanka

159 for 1st†	S. Wettimuny and J. R. Ratnayeke at Kanpur	1986-87
95 for 2nd	S. A. R. Silva and R. S. Madugalle at Colombo (PSS)	1985-86
153 for 3rd	R. L. Dias and L. R. D. Mendis at Madras	1982-83
216 for 4th	R. L. Dias and L. R. D. Mendis at Kandy	1985-86
144 for 5th	R. S. Madugalle and A. Ranatunga at Colombo (SSC)	1985-86
89 for 6th	L. R. D. Mendis and A. N. Ranasinghe at Madras	1982-83
77 for 7th	R. S. Madugalle and D. S. de Silva at Madras	1982-83
40* for 8th	P. A. de Silva and A. L. F. de Mel at Kandy	1985-86
42 for 9th	J. R. Ratnayeke and A. L. F. de Mel at Madras	1982-83
44 for 10th	R. J. Ratnayake and E. A. R. de Silva at Nagpur	1986-87

† Denotes record partnership against all countries.

TEN WICKETS OR MORE IN A MATCH

For India (1)

10-107 (3-56, 7-51)	Maninder Singh, Nagpur	1986-87

Note: The best match figures by a Sri Lankan bowler are 9-125 (4-76, 5-49) by R. J. Ratnayake against India at Colombo (PSS), 1985-86.

PAKISTAN v SRI LANKA

Captains

Season	*Pakistan*	*Sri Lanka*	*T*	*P*	*SL*	*D*
1981-82*P*	Javed Miandad	B. Warnapura[1]	3	2	0	1
1985-86*P*	Javed Miandad	L. R. D. Mendis	3	2	0	1
1985-86*S*	Imran Khan	L. R. D. Mendis	3	1	1	1
	In Pakistan		6	4	0	2
	In Sri Lanka		3	1	1	1
	Totals		9	5	1	3

P Played in Pakistan. S Played in Sri Lanka.

Note: The following deputised for the official touring captain:
[1]L. R. D. Mendis (Second).

HIGHEST INNINGS TOTALS

For Pakistan in Pakistan: 555-3 at Faisalabad ... 1985-86
in Sri Lanka: 318 at Colombo (PSS) ... 1985-86

For Sri Lanka in Pakistan: 479 at Faisalabad ... 1985-86
in Sri Lanka: 323-3 at Colombo (PSS) ... 1985-86

LOWEST INNINGS TOTALS

For Pakistan in Pakistan: 259 at Sialkot ... 1985-86
in Sri Lanka: 132 at Colombo (CCC) ... 1985-86

For Sri Lanka in Pakistan: 149 at Karachi ... 1981-82
in Sri Lanka: 101 at Kandy ... 1985-86

INDIVIDUAL HUNDREDS

For Pakistan (7)

Haroon Rashid (1)
153† Karachi 1981-82
Javed Miandad (1)
203* Faisalabad .. 1985-86
Mohsin Khan (1)
129 Lahore 1981-82
Qasim Omar (1)
206† Faisalabad .. 1985-86
Ramiz Raja (1)
122 Colombo (PSS) 1985-86
Salim Malik (1)
100*† Karachi 1981-82
Zaheer Abbas (1)
134† Lahore 1981-82

For Sri Lanka (6)

P. A. de Silva (2)
122† Faisalabad .. 1985-86
105 Karachi 1985-86
R. L. Dias (1)
109 Lahore 1981-82
A. P. Gurusinha (1)
116* Colombo (PSS) 1985-86
A. Ranatunga (1)
135* Colombo (PSS) 1985-86
S. Wettimuny (1)
157 Faisalabad .. 1981-82

† *Signifies hundred on first appearance in Pakistan–Sri Lanka Tests.*

RECORD PARTNERSHIPS FOR EACH WICKET

For Pakistan

98* for 1st	Mudassar Nazar and Mohsin Khan at Karachi	1985-86
151 for 2nd	Mohsin Khan and Majid Khan at Lahore	1981-82
397 for 3rd	Qasim Omar and Javed Miandad at Faisalabad	1985-86
162 for 4th	Salim Malik and Javed Miandad at Karachi	1981-82
102 for 5th	Mudassar Nazar and Salim Malik at Kandy	1985-86
100 for 6th	Zaheer Abbas and Imran Khan at Lahore	1981-82
104 for 7th	Haroon Rashid and Tahir Naqqash at Karachi	1981-82
29 for 8th	Ashraf Ali and Iqbal Qasim at Faisalabad	1981-82
	Salim Yousuf and Abdul Qadir at Sialkot	1985-86
	Salim Yousuf and Abdul Qadir at Karachi	1985-86
127 for 9th	Haroon Rashid and Rashid Khan at Karachi	1981-82
48 for 10th	Rashid Khan and Tauseef Ahmed at Faisalabad	1981-82

For Sri Lanka

77 for 1st	S. Wettimuny and H. M. Goonatillake at Faisalabad	1981-82
217 for 2nd†	S. Wettimuny and R. L. Dias at Faisalabad	1981-82
85 for 3rd	S. Wettimuny and R. L. Dias at Faisalabad	1985-86
240* for 4th†	A. P. Gurusinha and A. Ranatunga at Colombo (PSS)	1985-86
58 for 5th	R. L. Dias and L. R. D. Mendis at Lahore	1981-82
121 for 6th	A. Ranatunga and P. A. de Silva at Faisalabad	1985-86
66 for 7th	P. A. de Silva and J. R. Ratnayeke at Faisalabad	1985-86
61 for 8th†	R. S. Madugalle and D. S. de Silva at Faisalabad	1981-82
52 for 9th†	P. A. de Silva and R. J. Ratnayake at Faisalabad	1985-86
36 for 10th	R. J. Ratnayake and R. G. C. E. Wijesuriya at Faisalabad	1985-86

† *Denotes record partnership against all countries.*

TEN WICKETS OR MORE IN A MATCH

For Pakistan (1)

14-116 (8-58, 6-58) Imran Khan, Lahore 1981-82

Note: The best match figures by a Sri Lankan bowler are 9-162 (4-103, 5-59), D. S. de Silva at Faisalabad, 1981-82.

TEST MATCH GROUNDS

In Chronological Sequence

	City and Ground	*Date of First Test*	*Match*
1.	Melbourne, Melbourne Cricket Ground	March 15, 1877	Australia v England
2.	London, Kennington Oval	September 6, 1880	England v Australia
3.	Sydney, Sydney Cricket Ground (No. 1)	February 17, 1882	Australia v England
4.	Manchester, Old Trafford	July 11, 1884	England v Australia

This match was due to have started on July 10, but rain prevented any play.

5.	London, Lord's	July 21, 1884	England v Australia
6.	Adelaide, Adelaide Oval	December 12, 1884	Australia v England
7.	Port Elizabeth, St George's Park	March 12, 1889	South Africa v England
8.	Cape Town, Newlands	March 25, 1889	South Africa v England
9.	Johannesburg, Old Wanderers*	March 2, 1896	South Africa v England
10.	Nottingham, Trent Bridge	June 1, 1899	England v Australia
11.	Leeds, Headingley	June 29, 1899	England v Australia
12.	Birmingham, Edgbaston	May 29, 1902	England v Australia
13.	Sheffield, Bramall Lane*	July 3, 1902	England v Australia
14.	Durban, Lord's*	January 21, 1910	South Africa v England
15.	Durban, Kingsmead	January 18, 1923	South Africa v England
16.	Brisbane, Exhibition Ground*	November 30, 1928	Australia v England
17.	Christchurch, Lancaster Park	January 10, 1930	New Zealand v England
18.	Bridgetown, Kensington Oval	January 11, 1930	West Indies v England
19.	Wellington, Basin Reserve	January 24, 1930	New Zealand v England
20.	Port-of-Spain, Queen's Park Oval	February 1, 1930	West Indies v England
21.	Auckland, Eden Park	February 17, 1930	New Zealand v England

This match was due to have started on February 14, but rain prevented any play on the first two days. February 16 was a Sunday.

22.	Georgetown, Bourda	February 21, 1930	West Indies v England
23.	Kingston, Sabina Park	April 3, 1930	West Indies v England
24.	Brisbane, Woolloongabba	November 27, 1931	Australia v South Africa
25.	Bombay, Gymkhana Ground*	December 15, 1933	India v England
26.	Calcutta, Eden Gardens	January 5, 1934	India v England
27.	Madras, Chepauk (Chidambaram Stadium)	February 10, 1934	India v England
28.	Delhi, Feroz Shah Kotla	November 10, 1948	India v West Indies
29.	Bombay, Brabourne Stadium*	December 9, 1948	India v West Indies
30.	Johannesburg, Ellis Park*	December 27, 1948	South Africa v England
31.	Kanpur, Green Park (Modi Stadium)	January 12, 1952	India v England
32.	Lucknow, University Ground*	October 25, 1952	India v Pakistan
33.	Dacca, Dacca Stadium*	January 1, 1955	Pakistan v India
34.	Bahawalpur, Dring Stadium	January 15, 1955	Pakistan v India
35.	Lahore, Lawrence Gardens (Bagh-i-Jinnah)*	January 29, 1955	Pakistan v India
36.	Peshawar, Services Club Ground	February 13, 1955	Pakistan v India
37.	Karachi, National Stadium	February 26, 1955	Pakistan v India
38.	Dunedin, Carisbrook	March 11, 1955	New Zealand v England
39.	Hyderabad, Fateh Maidan (Lal Bahadur Stadium)	November 19, 1955	India v New Zealand

	City and Ground	*Date of First Test*	*Match*
40.	Madras, Corporation Stadium*	January 6, 1956	India v New Zealand
41.	Johannesburg, New Wanderers	December 24, 1956	South Africa v England
42.	Lahore, Gaddafi Stadium	November 21, 1959	Pakistan v Australia
43.	Rawalpindi, Pindi Club Ground	March 27, 1965	Pakistan v New Zealand
44.	Nagpur, Vidarbha Cricket Association Ground	October 3, 1969	India v New Zealand
45.	Perth, Western Australian Cricket Association Ground	December 11, 1970	Australia v England
46.	Hyderabad, Niaz Stadium	March 16, 1973	Pakistan v England
47.	Bangalore, Karnataka State Cricket Association Ground (Chinnaswamy Stadium)	November 22, 1974	India v West Indies
48.	Bombay, Wankhede Stadium	January 23, 1975	India v West Indies
49.	Faisalabad, Iqbal Stadium	October 16, 1978	Pakistan v India
50.	Napier, McLean Park	February 16, 1979	New Zealand v Pakistan
51.	Multan, Ibn-e-Qasim Bagh Stadium	December 30, 1980	Pakistan v West Indies
52.	St John's (Antigua), Recreation Ground	March 27, 1981	West Indies v England
53.	Colombo, P. Saravanamuttu Stadium	February 17, 1982	Sri Lanka v England
54.	Kandy, Asgiriya Stadium	April 22, 1983	Sri Lanka v Australia
55.	Jullundur, Burlton Park	September 24, 1983	India v Pakistan
56.	Ahmedabad, Gujarat Stadium	November 12, 1983	India v West Indies
57.	Colombo, Sinhalese Sports Club Ground	March 16, 1984	Sri Lanka v New Zealand
58.	Colombo, Colombo Cricket Club Ground	March 24, 1984	Sri Lanka v New Zealand
59.	Sialkot, Jinnah Stadium	October 27, 1985	Pakistan v Sri Lanka
60.	Cuttack, Barabati Stadium	January 4, 1987	India v Sri Lanka
61.	Jaipur, Sawai Mansingh Stadium	February 21, 1987	India v Pakistan
62.	Hobart, Bellerive Oval	December 16, 1989	Australia v Sri Lanka

* *Denotes no longer used for Test matches. In some instances the ground is no longer in existence.*

FAMILIES IN TEST CRICKET

FATHERS AND SONS

England

M. C. Cowdrey (114 Tests, 1954-55–1974-75) and C. S. Cowdrey (6 Tests, 1984-85–1988).
J. Hardstaff (5 Tests, 1907-08) and J. Hardstaff jun. (23 Tests, 1935–1948).
L. Hutton (79 Tests, 1937–1954-55) and R. A. Hutton (5 Tests, 1971).
F. T. Mann (5 Tests, 1922-23) and F. G. Mann (7 Tests, 1948-49–1949).
J. H. Parks (1 Test, 1937) and J. M. Parks (46 Tests, 1954–1967-68).
M. J. Stewart (8 Tests, 1962–1963-64) and A. J. Stewart (7 Tests, 1989-90–1990).
F. W. Tate (1 Test, 1902) and M. W. Tate (39 Tests, 1924–1935).
C. L. Townsend (2 Tests, 1899) and D. C. H. Townsend (3 Tests, 1934-35).

Australia

E. J. Gregory (1 Test, 1876-77) and S. E. Gregory (58 Tests, 1890–1912).

South Africa

F. Hearne (4 Tests, 1891-92–1895-96) and G. A. L. Hearne (3 Tests, 1922-23–1924).
F. Hearne also played 2 Tests for England in 1888-89.
J. D. Lindsay (3 Tests, 1947) and D. T. Lindsay (19 Tests, 1963-64–1969-70).
A. W. Nourse (45 Tests, 1902-03–1924) and A. D. Nourse (34 Tests, 1935–1951).
L. R. Tuckett (1 Test, 1913-14) and L. Tuckett (9 Tests, 1947–1948-49).

West Indies

G. A. Headley (22 Tests, 1929-30–1953-54) and R. G. A. Headley (2 Tests, 1973).
O. C. Scott (8 Tests, 1928–1930-31) and A. P. H. Scott (1 Test, 1952-53).

New Zealand

W. M. Anderson (1 Test, 1945-46) and R. W. Anderson (9 Tests, 1976-77–1978).
B. L. Cairns (43 Tests, 1973-74–1985-86) and C. L. Cairns (1 Test, 1989-90).
W. A. Hadlee (11 Tests, 1937–1950-51) and D. R. Hadlee (26 Tests, 1969–1977-78); Sir R. J. Hadlee (86 Tests, 1972-73–1990).
H. G. Vivian (7 Tests, 1931–1937) and G. E. Vivian (5 Tests, 1964-65–1971-72).

India

L. Amarnath (24 Tests, 1933-34–1952-53) and M. Amarnath (69 Tests, 1969-70–1987-88); S. Amarnath (10 Tests, 1975-76–1978-79).
D. K. Gaekwad (11 Tests, 1952–1960-61) and A. D. Gaekwad (40 Tests, 1974-75–1984-85).
Nawab of Pataudi (Iftikhar Ali Khan) (3 Tests, 1946) and Nawab of Pataudi (Mansur Ali Khan) (46 Tests, 1961-62–1974-75).
Nawab of Pataudi sen. also played 3 Tests for England, 1932-33–1934.
V. L. Manjrekar (55 Tests, 1951-52–1964-65) and S. V. Manjrekar (15 Tests, 1987-88–1990).
V. Mankad (44 Tests, 1946–1958-59) and A. V. Mankad (22 Tests, 1969-70–1977-78).
Pankaj Roy (43 Tests, 1951-52–1960-61) and Pranab Roy (2 Tests, 1981-82).

India and Pakistan

M. Jahangir Khan (4 Tests, 1932–1936) and Majid Khan (63 Tests, 1964-65–1982-83).
S. Wazir Ali (7 Tests, 1932–1936) and Khalid Wazir (2 Tests, 1954).

Pakistan

Hanif Mohammad (55 Tests, 1954–1969-70) and Shoaib Mohammad (29 Tests, 1983-84–1989-90).
Nazar Mohammad (5 Tests, 1952-53) and Mudassar Nazar (76 Tests, 1976-77–1988-89).

GRANDFATHERS AND GRANDSONS

Australia

V. Y. Richardson (19 Tests, 1924-25–1935-36) and G. S. Chappell (87 Tests, 1970-71–1983-84); I. M. Chappell (75 Tests, 1964-65–1979-80); T. M. Chappell (3 Tests, 1981).

GREAT-GRANDFATHER AND GREAT-GRANDSON

Australia

W. H. Cooper (2 Tests, 1881-82 and 1884-85) and A. P. Sheahan (31 Tests, 1967-68–1973-74).

BROTHERS IN SAME TEST TEAM

England

E. M., G. F. and W. G. Grace: 1 Test, 1880.
C. T. and G. B. Studd: 4 Tests, 1882-83.
A. and G. G. Hearne: 1 Test, 1891-92.
F. Hearne, their brother, played in this match for South Africa.
D. W. and P. E. Richardson: 1 Test, 1957.

Australia

E. J. and D. W. Gregory: 1 Test, 1876-77.
C. and A. C. Bannerman: 1 Test, 1878-79.
G. and W. F. Giffen: 2 Tests, 1891-92.
G. H. S. and A. E. Trott: 3 Tests, 1894-95.
I. M. and G. S. Chappell: 43 Tests, 1970-71–1979-80.

South Africa
S. J. and S. D. Snooke: 1 Test, 1907.
D. and H. W. Taylor: 2 Tests, 1913-14.
R. H. M. and P. A. M. Hands: 1 Test, 1913-14.
E. A. B. and A. M. B. Rowan: 9 Tests, 1948-49–1951.
P. M. and R. G. Pollock: 23 Tests, 1963-64–1969-70.
A. J. and D. B. Pithey: 5 Tests, 1963-64.

West Indies
G. C. and R. S. Grant: 4 Tests, 1934-35.
J. B. and V. H. Stollmeyer: 1 Test, 1939.
D. St E. and E. St E. Atkinson: 1 Test, 1957-58.

New Zealand
J. J. and M. D. Crowe: 34 Tests, 1983–1989-90.
D. R. and R. J. Hadlee: 10 Tests, 1973–1977-78.
H. J. and G. P. Howarth: 4 Tests, 1974-75–1976-77.
J. M. and N. M. Parker: 3 Tests, 1976-77.
B. P. and J. G. Bracewell: 1 Test, 1980-81.

India
S. Wazir Ali and S. Nazir Ali: 2 Tests, 1932–1933-34.
L. Ramji and Amar Singh: 1 Test, 1933-34.
C. K. and C. S. Nayudu: 4 Tests, 1933-34–1936.
A. G. Kripal Singh and A. G. Milkha Singh: 1 Test, 1961-62.
S. and M. Amarnath: 8 Tests, 1975-76–1978-79.

Pakistan
Wazir and Hanif Mohammad: 18 Tests, 1952-53–1959-60.
Wazir and Mushtaq Mohammad: 1 Test, 1958-59.
Hanif and Mushtaq Mohammad: 19 Tests, 1960-61–1969-70.
Hanif, Mushtaq and Sadiq Mohammad: 1 Test, 1969-70.
Mushtaq and Sadiq Mohammad: 26 Tests, 1969-70–1978–79.
Wasim and Ramiz Raja: 2 Tests, 1983-84.

Sri Lanka
A. and D. Ranatunga: 2 Tests, 1989-90.
M. D. and S. Wettimuny: 2 Tests, 1982-83.

THE ASHES

"In affectionate remembrance of English cricket which died at The Oval, 29th August, 1882. Deeply lamented by a large circle of sorrowing friends and acquaintances, R.I.P. N.B. The body will be cremated and the Ashes taken to Australia."

Australia's first victory on English soil over the full strength of England, on August 29, 1882, inspired a young London journalist, Reginald Shirley Brooks, to write this mock "obituary". It appeared in the *Sporting Times*.

Before England's defeat at The Oval, by 7 runs, arrangements had already been made for the Hon. Ivo Bligh, afterwards Lord Darnley, to lead a team to Australia. Three weeks later they set out, now with the popular objective of recovering the Ashes. In the event, Australia won the First Test by nine wickets, but with England winning the next two it became generally accepted that they brought back the Ashes.

It was long accepted that the real Ashes – a small urn believed to contain the ashes of a bail used in the third match – were presented to Bligh by a group of Melbourne women. At the time of the 1982 centenary of The Oval Test match, however, evidence was produced which suggested that these ashes were the remains of a ball and that they were given to the England captain by Sir William Clarke, the presentation taking place before the Test matches in Australia in 1883. The certain origin of the Ashes, therefore, is the subject of some dispute.

After Lord Darnley's death in 1927, the urn was given to MCC by Lord Darnley's Australian-born widow, Florence. It can be seen in the cricket museum at Lord's, together with a red and gold velvet bag, made specially for it, and the scorecard of the 1882 match.

LIMITED-OVERS INTERNATIONAL RECORDS

Note: Limited-overs international matches do not have first-class status.

SUMMARY OF ALL LIMITED-OVERS INTERNATIONALS

To November 1, 1990

		Matches	*Won by*											*Tied*	*NR*
			E	*A*	*I*	*NZ*	*P*	*SL*	*WI*	*B*	*C*	*EA*	*Z*		
England	v Aust.	47	24	21	–	–	–	–	–	–	–	–	–	1	1
	v India	22	12	–	10	–	–	–	–	–	–	–	–	–	–
	v NZ	29	14	–	–	12	–	–	–	–	–	–	–	–	3
	v Pak.	29	19	–	–	–	10	–	–	–	–	–	–	–	–
	v SL	8	7	–	–	–	–	1	–	–	–	–	–	–	–
	v WI	39	14	–	–	–	–	–	23	–	–	–	–	–	2
	v Canada	1	1	–	–	–	–	–	–	–	0	–	–	–	–
	v E. Africa	1	1	–	–	–	–	–	–	–	–	0	–	–	–
Australia	v India	33	–	18	12	–	–	–	–	–	–	–	–	–	3
	v NZ	43	–	29	–	12	–	–	–	–	–	–	–	–	2
	v Pak.	33	–	15	–	–	16	–	–	–	–	–	–	–	2
	v SL	20	–	15	–	–	–	3	–	–	–	–	–	–	2
	v WI	53	–	17	–	–	–	–	35	–	–	–	–	1	–
	v Bangl.	1	–	1	–	–	–	–	–	0	–	–	–	–	–
	v Canada	1	–	1	–	–	–	–	–	–	0	–	–	–	–
	v Zimb.	4	–	3	–	–	–	–	–	–	–	–	1	–	–
India	v NZ	28	–	–	16	12	–	–	–	–	–	–	–	–	–
	v Pak.	34	–	–	10	–	22	–	–	–	–	–	–	–	2
	v SL	20	–	–	14	–	–	5	–	–	–	–	–	–	1
	v WI	33	–	–	6	–	–	–	27	–	–	–	–	–	–
	v Bangl.	1	–	–	1	–	–	–	–	0	–	–	–	–	–
	v E. Africa	1	–	–	1	–	–	–	–	–	–	0	–	–	–
	v Zimb.	4	–	–	4	–	–	–	–	–	–	–	0	–	–
New Zealand	v Pak.	20	–	–	–	11	8	–	–	–	–	–	–	–	1
	v SL	19	–	–	–	15	–	4	–	–	–	–	–	–	–
	v WI	13	–	–	–	1	–	–	11	–	–	–	–	–	1
	v Bangl.	1	–	–	–	1	–	–	–	0	–	–	–	–	–
	v E. Africa	1	–	–	–	1	–	–	–	–	–	0	–	–	–
	v Zimb.	2	–	–	–	2	–	–	–	–	–	–	0	–	–
Pakistan	v SL	28	–	–	–	–	22	5	–	–	–	–	–	–	1
	v WI	48	–	–	–	–	13	–	35	–	–	–	–	–	–
	v Bangl.	2	–	–	–	–	2	–	–	0	–	–	–	–	–
	v Canada	1	–	–	–	–	1	–	–	–	0	–	–	–	–
Sri Lanka	v WI	11	–	–	–	–	–	1	10	–	–	–	–	–	–
	v Bangl.	2	–	–	–	–	–	2	–	0	–	–	–	–	–
West Indies	v Zimb.	2	–	–	–	–	–	–	2	–	–	–	0	–	–
		635	92	120	74	67	94	21	143	0	0	0	1	2	21

	Matches	*Won*	*Lost*	*Tied*	*No Result*
England	176	92	77	1	6
Australia	235	120	103	2	10
India	176	74	96	–	6
New Zealand	156	67	82	–	7
Pakistan	195	94	95	–	6
Sri Lanka	108	21	83	–	4
West Indies	199	143	52	1	3
Bangladesh	7	–	7	–	–
Canada	3	–	3	–	–
East Africa	3	–	3	–	–
Zimbabwe	12	1	11	–	–

3,500 OR MORE RUNS

	M	*I*	*NO*	*R*	*HI*	*100s*	*Avge*
I. V. A. Richards (West Indies) ...	179	160	24	6,501	189*	11	47.80
D. L. Haynes (West Indies)	174	173	23	6,471	152*	16	43.14
Javed Miandad (Pakistan)	169	162	32	5,610	119*	6	43.15
A. R. Border (Australia)	210	195	29	5,263	127*	3	31.70
C. G. Greenidge (West Indies)	120	119	12	4,981	133*	11	46.55
D. M. Jones (Australia)	100	98	19	3,857	121	6	48.82
R. B. Richardson (West Indies) ...	126	123	17	3,795	110	3	35.80
K. Srikkanth (India)	126	125	3	3,541	123	4	29.02
D. B. Vengsarkar (India)	128	120	19	3,508	105	1	34.73

The leading aggregates for the countries not mentioned above are:

	M	*I*	*NO*	*R*	*HI*	*100s*	*Avge*
J. G. Wright (New Zealand)	127	126	1	3,416	101	1	27.32
A. J. Lamb (England)	99	95	16	3,306	118	4	41.84
A. Ranatunga (Sri Lanka)	88	85	15	2,173	86*	0	31.04

HIGHEST INDIVIDUAL SCORE FOR EACH COUNTRY

189*	I. V. A. Richards	**West Indies** v England at Manchester	1984
175*	Kapil Dev	**India** v Zimbabwe at Tunbridge Wells	1983
171*	G. M. Turner	**New Zealand** v East Africa at Birmingham	1975
158	D. I. Gower	**England** v New Zealand at Brisbane	1982-83
138*	G. S. Chappell	**Australia** v New Zealand at Sydney	1980-81
126*	Shoaib Mohammad	**Pakistan** v New Zealand at Wellington	1988-89
121	R. L. Dias	**Sri Lanka** v India at Bangalore	1982-83

SEVEN OR MORE HUNDREDS

Total		*E*	*A*	*WI*	*NZ*	*I*	*P*	*SL*	*Others*
16	D. L. Haynes (West Indies)	1	6	–	2	2	4	1	0
11	C. G. Greenidge (West Indies) ..	0	1	–	3	3	2	1	1
11	I. V. A. Richards (West Indies) .	3	3	–	1	3	0	1	0
8	G. A. Gooch (England)	–	4	1	1	1	1	0	0
7	D. I. Gower (England)	–	2	0	3	0	1	1	0
7	G. R. Marsh (Australia)	1	–	0	2	3	1	0	0
7	Zaheer Abbas (Pakistan)	0	2	0	1	3	–	1	0

HIGHEST PARTNERSHIP FOR EACH WICKET

212 for 1st	G. R. Marsh (104) and D. C. Boon (111), Australia v India at Jaipur	1986-87
221 for 2nd	C. G. Greenidge (115) and I. V. A. Richards (149), West Indies v India at Jamshedpur	1983-84
224* for 3rd	D. M. Jones (99*) and A. R. Border (118*), Australia v Sri Lanka at Adelaide	1984-85
173 for 4th	D. M. Jones (121) and S. R. Waugh (82), Australia v Pakistan at Perth	1986-87
152 for 5th	I. V. A. Richards (98) and C. H. Lloyd (89*), West Indies v Sri Lanka at Brisbane	1984-85
144 for 6th	Imran Khan (102*) and Shahid Mahboob (77), Pakistan v Sri Lanka at Leeds	1983
115 for 7th	P. J. L. Dujon (57*) and M. D. Marshall (66), West Indies v Pakistan at Gujranwala	1986-87
117 for 8th	D. L. Houghton (141) and I. P. Butchart (54), Zimbabwe v New Zealand at Hyderabad (India)	1987-88
126* for 9th	Kapil Dev (175*) and S. M. H. Kirmani (24*), India v Zimbabwe at Tunbridge Wells	1983
106* for 10th	I. V. A. Richards (189*) and M. A. Holding (12*), West Indies v England at Manchester	1984

100 OR MORE WICKETS

	M	Balls	R	W	BB	4W/i	Avge
Kapil Dev (India)	157	7,941	4,977	185	5-43	2	26.90
Imran Khan (Pakistan)	149	6,337	4,063	165	6-14	4	24.62
R. J. Hadlee (New Zealand)	115	6,182	3,407	158	5-25	6	21.56
J. Garner (West Indies)	98	5,330	2,752	146	5-31	5	18.84
M. A. Holding (West Indies)	102	5,473	3,034	142	5-26	6	21.36
E. J. Chatfield (New Zealand)	114	6,065	3,621	140	5-34	3	25.86
M. D. Marshall (West Indies)	113	5,993	3,412	137	4-23	5	24.90
Abdul Qadir (Pakistan)	101	4,948	3,340	131	5-44	6	25.49
Wasim Akram (Pakistan)	97	4,833	3,072	130	5-21	5	23.63
I. T. Botham (England)	98	5,269	3,511	118	4-56	1	29.75
I. V. A. Richards (West Indies)	179	5,542	4,144	118	6-41	3	35.11
M. C. Snedden (New Zealand)	93	4,519	3,235	114	4-34	1	28.37
R. J. Shastri (India)	123	5,756	4,025	114	4-38	2	35.30
Mudassar Nazar (Pakistan)	122	4,855	3,431	111	5-28	2	30.90
D. K. Lillee (Australia)	63	3,593	2,145	103	5-34	6	20.82
C. A. Walsh (West Indies)	88	4,659	2,977	101	5-1	5	29.47
The leading aggregate for Sri Lanka is:							
J. R. Ratnayeke	78	3,573	2,865	85	4-23	1	33.70

BEST BOWLING FOR EACH COUNTRY

7-51	W. W. Davis	**West Indies** v Australia at Leeds	1983
6-14	G. J. Gilmour	**Australia** v England at Leeds	1975
6-14	Imran Khan	**Pakistan** v India at Sharjah	1984-85
5-20	V. J. Marks	**England** v New Zealand at Wellington	1983-84
5-21	Arshad Ayub	**India** v Pakistan at Dhaka	1988-89
5-23	R. O. Collinge	**New Zealand** v India at Christchurch	1975-76
5-26	S. H. U. Karnain	**Sri Lanka** v New Zealand at Moratuwa	1983-84

HAT-TRICKS

Jalal-ud-Din	Pakistan v Australia at Hyderabad	1982-83
B. A. Reid	Australia v New Zealand at Sydney	1985-86
Chetan Sharma	India v New Zealand at Nagpur	1987-88
Wasim Akram	Pakistan v West Indies at Sharjah	1989-90
Wasim Akram	Pakistan v Australia at Sharjah	1989-90

MOST DISMISSALS IN A MATCH

5 (all ct)	R. W. Marsh	Australia v England at Leeds	1981
5 (all ct)	R. G. de Alwis	Sri Lanka v Australia at Colombo (PSS)	1982-83
5 (all ct)	S. M. H. Kirmani	India v Zimbabwe at Leicester	1983
5 (3 ct, 2 st)	S. Viswanath	India v England at Sydney	1984-85
5 (3 ct, 2 st)	K. S. More	India v New Zealand at Sharjah	1987-88

50 OR MORE DISMISSALS

	M	Ct	St	Total
P. J. L. Dujon (West Indies)	155	170	18	188
R. W. Marsh (Australia)	92	120	4	124
Salim Yousuf (Pakistan)	79	73	18	91
I. D. S. Smith (New Zealand)	73	60	5	65
Wasim Bari (Pakistan)	51	52	10	62
K. S. More (India)	58	32	24	56
I. A. Healy (Australia)	38	45	6	51

MOST CATCHES IN A MATCH

(Excluding wicket-keepers)

4	Salim Malik	Pakistan v New Zealand at Sialkot	1984-85
4	S. M. Gavaskar	India v Pakistan at Sharjah	1984-85

Note: While fielding as substitute, J. G. Bracewell held 4 catches for New Zealand v Australia at Adelaide, 1980-81.

50 OR MORE CATCHES

	M	*Ct*		*M*	*Ct*
I. V. A. Richards (WI)	179	99	Javed Miandad (P)	169	58
A. R. Border (A)	210	96	Kapil Dev (I)	157	57

ALL-ROUND

1,000 Runs and 100 Wickets

	M	*R*	*W*
I. T. Botham (England)	98	1,730	118
R. J. Hadlee (New Zealand)	115	1,749	158
Imran Khan (Pakistan)	149	3,051	165
Kapil Dev (India)	157	3,087	185
Mudassar Nazar (Pakistan)	122	2,654	111
I. V. A. Richards (West Indies)	179	6,501	118
R. J. Shastri (India)	123	2,391	114

1,000 Runs and 100 Dismissals

	M	*R*	*D*
P. J. L. Dujon (West Indies)	155	1,785	188
R. W. Marsh (Australia)	92	1,225	124

HIGHEST INNINGS TOTALS

360-4	(50 overs)	**West Indies** v Sri Lanka at Karachi	1987-88
338-4	(50 overs)	**New Zealand** v Bangladesh at Sharjah	1989-90
338-5	(60 overs)	**Pakistan** v Sri Lanka at Swansea	1983
334-4	(60 overs)	**England** v India at Lord's	1975
333-8	(45 overs)	West Indies v India at Jamshedpur	1983-84
333-9	(60 overs)	England v Sri Lanka at Taunton	1983
332-3	(50 overs)	**Australia** v Sri Lanka at Sharjah	1989-90
330-6	(60 overs)	Pakistan v Sri Lanka at Nottingham	1975

Note: The highest score by **India** is 299-4 (40 overs) v Sri Lanka at Bombay, 1986-87, and the highest by **Sri Lanka** is 289-7 (40 overs) v India at Bombay, 1986-87.

HIGHEST TOTALS BATTING SECOND

Winning

298-6	(54.5 overs)	New Zealand v England at Leeds	1990
297-6	(48.5 overs)	New Zealand v England at Adelaide	1982-83

Losing

289-7	(40 overs)	Sri Lanka v India at Bombay	1986-87
288-9	(60 overs)	Sri Lanka v Pakistan at Swansea	1983

HIGHEST MATCH AGGREGATES

626-14	(120 overs)	Pakistan v Sri Lanka at Swansea	1983
619-19	(118 overs)	England v Sri Lanka at Taunton	1983
604-9	(120 overs)	Australia v Sri Lanka at The Oval	1975
603-11	(100 overs)	Pakistan v Sri Lanka at Adelaide	1989-90

LOWEST INNINGS TOTALS

45	(40.3 overs)	Canada v England at Manchester	1979
55	(28.3 overs)	**Sri Lanka** v West Indies at Sharjah	1986-87
63	(25.5 overs)	**India** v Australia at Sydney	1980-81
64	(35.5 overs)	**New Zealand** v Pakistan at Sharjah	1985-86
70	(25.2 overs)	**Australia** v England at Birmingham	1977
70	(26.3 overs)	Australia v New Zealand at Adelaide	1985-86
74	(29 overs)	New Zealand v Australia at Wellington	1981-82
74	(31.1 overs)	New Zealand v Pakistan at Sharjah	1989-90
78	(24.1 overs)	India v Sri Lanka at Kanpur	1986-87
79	(34.2 overs)	India v Pakistan at Sialkot	1978-79
85	(47 overs)	**Pakistan** v England at Manchester	1978

Notes: This section does not take into account those matches in which the number of overs was reduced.

The lowest innings total by **England** is 93 (36.2 overs) v Australia at Leeds, 1975, and the lowest by **West Indies** is 111 (41.4 overs) v Pakistan at Melbourne, 1983-84.

LARGEST VICTORIES

232 runs	Australia (323-2 in 50 overs) v Sri Lanka (91 in 35.5 overs) at Adelaide	1984-85
206 runs	New Zealand (276-7 in 50 overs) v Australia (70 in 26.3 overs) at Adelaide	1985-86
202 runs	England (334-4 in 60 overs) v India (132-3 in 60 overs) at Lord's	1975

By ten wickets: There have been seven instances of victory by ten wickets.

TIED MATCHES

West Indies 222-5 (50 overs), Australia 222-9 (50 overs) at Melbourne	1983-84
England 226-5 (55 overs), Australia 226-8 (55 overs) at Nottingham	1989

WORLD CUP FINALS

1975 (60 overs) West Indies (291-8) beat Australia (274) by 17 runs at Lord's.
1979 (60 overs) West Indies (286-9) beat England (194) by 92 runs at Lord's.
1983 (60 overs) India (183) beat West Indies (140) by 43 runs at Lord's.
1987 (50 overs) Australia (253-5) beat England (246-8) by 7 runs at Calcutta.

MISCELLANEOUS

LARGE ATTENDANCES

Test Series

943,000	Australia v England (5 Tests)	1936-37
In England		
549,650	England v Australia (5 Tests)	1953

Test Match

†350,534	Australia v England, Melbourne (Third Test)	1936-37
325,000+	India v England, Calcutta (Second Test)	1972-73
In England		
158,000+	England v Australia, Leeds (Fourth Test)	1948
137,915	England v Australia, Lord's (Second Test)	1953

Test Match Day

90,800	Australia v West Indies, Melbourne (Fifth Test, 2nd day)	1960-61

Other First-Class Matches in England

80,000+	Surrey v Yorkshire, The Oval (3 days)	1906
78,792	Yorkshire v Lancashire, Leeds (3 days)	1904
76,617	Lancashire v Yorkshire, Manchester (3 days)	1926

One-day International

86,133‡	Australia v West Indies, Melbourne	1983-84

† *Although no official figures are available, the attendance at the Fourth Test between India and England at Calcutta, 1981-82, was thought to have exceeded this figure.*

‡ *It is estimated that a crowd of more than 90,000 attended the one-day international between India and Pakistan at Calcutta, 1986-87. However, this figure has not been confirmed.*

LORD'S CRICKET GROUND

Lord's and the MCC were founded in 1787. The Club has enjoyed an uninterrupted career since that date, but there have been three grounds known as Lord's. The first (1787-1810) was situated where Dorset Square now is; the second (1809-13), at North Bank, had to be abandoned owing to the cutting of the Regent's Canal; and the third, opened in 1814, is the present one at St John's Wood. It was not until 1866 that the freehold of Lord's was secured by the MCC. The present pavilion was erected in 1890 at a cost of £21,000.

HIGHEST INDIVIDUAL SCORES MADE AT LORD'S

333	G. A. Gooch	England v India	1990
316*	J. B. Hobbs	Surrey v Middlesex	1926
315*	P. Holmes	Yorkshire v Middlesex	1925
281*	W. H. Ponsford	Australians v MCC	1934
278	W. Ward	MCC v Norfolk (with E. H. Budd, T. Vigne and F. Ladbroke)	1820
278	D. G. Bradman	Australians v MCC	1938
277*	E. H. Hendren	Middlesex v Kent	1922

Note: The longest innings in a first-class match at Lord's was played by S. Wettimuny (636 minutes, 190 runs) for Sri Lanka v England, 1984.

HIGHEST TOTALS OBTAINED AT LORD'S

First-Class Matches

729-6 dec.	Australia v England	1930
665	West Indians v Middlesex	1939
653-4 dec.	England v India	1990
652-8 dec.	West Indies v England	1973
629	England v India	1974
612-8 dec.	Middlesex v Nottinghamshire	1921
610-5 dec.	Australians v Gentlemen	1948
609-8 dec.	Cambridge University v MCC and Ground	1913
608-7 dec.	Middlesex v Hampshire	1919
607	MCC and Ground v Cambridge University	1902

Minor Match

735-9 dec.	MCC and Ground v Wiltshire	1888

BIGGEST HIT AT LORD'S

The only known instance of a batsman hitting a ball over the present pavilion at Lord's occurred when A. E. Trott, appearing for MCC against Australians on July 31, August 1, 2, 1899, drove M. A. Noble so far and high that the ball struck a chimney pot and fell behind the building.

HIGHEST SCORE IN A MINOR COUNTY MATCH

323*	F. E. Lacey	Hampshire v Norfolk at Southampton	1887

HIGHEST SCORE IN MINOR COUNTIES CHAMPIONSHIP

282	E. Garnett	Berkshire v Wiltshire at Reading	1908
254	H. E. Morgan	Glamorgan v Monmouthshire at Cardiff	1901
253*	G. J. Whittaker	Surrey II v Gloucestershire II at The Oval	1950
253	A. Booth	Lancashire II v Lincolnshire at Grimsby	1950
252	J. A. Deed	Kent II v Surrey II at The Oval (on début)	1924

HIGHEST SCORE FOR ENGLISH PUBLIC SCHOOL

278	J. L. Guise	Winchester v Eton at Eton	1921

HIGHEST SCORES IN OTHER MATCHES

628*	A. E. J. Collins, Clark's House v North Town at Clifton College. (A Junior House match. His innings of 6 hours 50 minutes was spread over four afternoons.)	1899
566	C. J. Eady, Break-o'-Day v Wellington at Hobart	1901-02
515	D. R. Havewalla, B.B. and C.I. Rly v St Xavier's at Bombay	1933-34
506*	J. C. Sharp, Melbourne GS v Geelong College at Melbourne	1914-15
502*	Chaman Lal, Mehandra Coll., Patiala v Government Coll., Rupar at Patiala	1956-57
485	A. E. Stoddart, Hampstead v Stoics at Hampstead	1886
475*	Mohammad Iqbal, Muslim Model HS v Islamia HS, Sialkot at Lahore	1958-59
466*	G. T. S. Stevens, Beta v Lambda (University College School House match) at Neasden	1919
459	J. A. Prout, Wesley College v Geelong College at Geelong	1908-09

HIGHEST PARTNERSHIP IN MINOR CRICKET

664* for 3rd V. G. Kambli and S. R. Tendulkar, Sharadashram Vidyamandir School v St Xavier's High School at Bombay 1987-88

RECORD HIT

The Rev. W. Fellows, while at practice on the Christ Church ground at Oxford in 1856, drove a ball bowled by Charles Rogers 175 yards from hit to pitch.

THROWING THE CRICKET BALL

140 yards 2 feet, Robert Percival, on the Durham Sands, Co. Durham Racecourse c1882
140 yards 9 inches, Ross Mackenzie, at Toronto 1872

Notes: W. F. Forbes, on March 16, 1876, threw 132 yards at the Eton College sports. He was then eighteen years of age.

Onochie Onuorah, on June 5, 1987, threw a $4\frac{3}{4}$oz ball 100 yards 1 foot $8\frac{1}{2}$ inches (91.94 metres) at The Abbey School, Westgate, sports. He was then thirteen years of age.

William Yardley, while a boy at Rugby, threw 100 yards with his right hand and 78 yards with his left .

Charles Arnold, of Cambridge, once threw 112 yards with the wind and 108 against.

W. H. Game, at The Oval in 1875, threw the ball 111 yards and then back the same distance. W. G. Grace threw 109 yards one way and back 105, and George Millyard 108 with the wind and 103 against. At The Oval in 1868, W. G. Grace made three successive throws of 116, 117 and 118 yards, and then threw back over 100 yards. D. G. Foster (Warwickshire) threw 133 yards, and in 1930 he made a Danish record with 120.1 metres – about 130 yards.

DATES OF FORMATION OF COUNTY CLUBS NOW FIRST-CLASS

County	*First known county organisation*	*Present Club Original date*	*Present Club Reorganisation, if substantial*
Derbyshire	November 4, 1870	November 4, 1870	—
Essex	By May, 1790	January 14, 1876	—
Glamorgan	1863	July 6, 1888	—
Gloucestershire	November 3, 1863	1871	—
Hampshire	April 3, 1849	August 12, 1863	July, 1879
Kent	August 6, 1842	March 1, 1859	December 6, 1870
Lancashire	January 12, 1864	January 12, 1864	—
Leicestershire	By August, 1820	March 25, 1879	—
Middlesex	December 15, 1863	February 2, 1864	—
Northamptonshire ..	1820	1820	July 31, 1878
Nottinghamshire	March/April, 1841	March/April, 1841	December 11, 1866
Somerset	October 15, 1864	August 18, 1875	—
Surrey	August 22, 1845	August 22, 1845	—
Sussex	June 16, 1836	March 1, 1839	August, 1857
Warwickshire	May, 1826	1882	—
Worcestershire	1844	March 5, 1865	—
Yorkshire	March 7, 1861	January 8, 1863	December 10, 1891

DATES OF FORMATION OF CLUBS IN THE CURRENT MINOR COUNTIES CHAMPIONSHIP

County	*First known county organisation*	*Present Club*
Bedfordshire	May, 1847	November 3, 1899
Berkshire	By May, 1841	March 17, 1895
Buckinghamshire	November, 1864	January 15, 1891
Cambridgeshire	March 13, 1844	June 6, 1891
Cheshire	1819	September 29, 1908
Cornwall	1813	November 12, 1894
Cumberland	January 2, 1884	April 10, 1948
Devon	1824	November 26, 1899
Dorset	1862 *or* 1871	February 5, 1896
Durham	January 24, 1874	May 10, 1882
Hertfordshire	1838	March 8, 1876
Lincolnshire	1853	September 28, 1906
Norfolk	January 11, 1827	October 14, 1876
Northumberland	1834	December, 1895
Oxfordshire	1787	December 14, 1921
Shropshire	1819 or 1829	June 28, 1956
Staffordshire	November 24, 1871	November 24, 1871
Suffolk	July 27, 1864	August, 1932
Wiltshire	February 24, 1881	January, 1893

CONSTITUTION OF COUNTY CHAMPIONSHIP

There are references in the sporting press to a champion county as early as 1825, but the list is not continuous and in some years only two counties contested the title. The earliest reference in any cricket publication is from 1864, and at this time there were eight leading counties who have come to be regarded as first-class from that date – Cambridgeshire, Hampshire, Kent, Middlesex, Nottinghamshire, Surrey, Sussex and Yorkshire. The newly formed Lancashire club began playing inter-county matches in 1865, Gloucestershire in 1870 and Derbyshire in 1871, and they are therefore regarded as first-class from these respective dates. Cambridgeshire dropped out after 1871, Hampshire, who had not played inter-county matches in certain seasons, after 1885, and Derbyshire after 1887. Somerset, who had played matches against the first-class counties since 1879, were regarded as first-class from 1882 to 1885, and were admitted formally to the Championship in 1891. In 1894, Derbyshire, Essex, Leicestershire and Warwickshire were granted first-class status, but did not compete in the Championship until 1895 when Hampshire returned. Worcestershire, Northamptonshire and Glamorgan were admitted to the Championship in 1899, 1905 and 1921 respectively and are regarded as first-class from these dates. An invitation in 1921 to Buckinghamshire to enter the Championship was declined, owing to the lack of necessary playing facilities, and an application by Devon in 1948 was unsuccessful.

MOST COUNTY CHAMPIONSHIP APPEARANCES

763	W. Rhodes	Yorkshire	1898-1930
707	F. E. Woolley	Kent	1906-38
665	C. P. Mead	Hampshire	1906-36

MOST CONSECUTIVE COUNTY CHAMPIONSHIP APPEARANCES

423	K. G. Suttle	Sussex	1954-69
412	J. G. Binks	Yorkshire	1955-69
399	J. Vine	Sussex	1899-1914
344	E. H. Killick	Sussex	1898-1912
326	C. N. Woolley	Northamptonshire	1913-31
305	A. H. Dyson	Glamorgan	1930-47
301	B. Taylor	Essex	1961-72

Notes: J. Vine made 417 consecutive appearances for Sussex in all first-class matches between July 1900 and September 1914.

J. G. Binks did not miss a Championship match for Yorkshire between making his début in June 1955 and retiring at the end of the 1969 season.

FEATURES OF 1990

Double-Hundreds (32)

M. W. Alleyne	256	Gloucestershire v Northamptonshire at Northampton.
R. J. Bailey	204*	Northamptonshire v Sussex at Northampton.
P. D. Bowler	210	Derbyshire v Kent at Chesterfield.
B. C. Broad	227*	Nottinghamshire v Kent at Tunbridge Wells.
K. R. Brown	200*	Middlesex v Nottinghamshire at Lord's.
S. J. Cook	313*	Somerset v Glamorgan at Cardiff.
P. A. de Silva	221*	Sri Lankans v Hampshire at Southampton.
N. H. Fairbrother (2)	366†	Lancashire v Surrey at The Oval. The second-highest first-class score by an Englishman.
	203*	Lancashire v Warwickshire at Coventry.
A. Fordham	206*	Northamptonshire v Yorkshire at Leeds.
G. A. Gooch (2)	215	Essex v Leicestershire at Chelmsford.
	333†	England v India (First Test) at Lord's.
I. A. Greig	291	Surrey v Lancashire at The Oval.
D. L. Haynes (2)	220*	Middlesex v Essex at Ilford.
	255*	Middlesex v Sussex at Lord's.
G. A. Hick	252*	Worcestershire v Glamorgan at Abergavenny.
S. G. Hinks	234	Kent v Middlesex at Canterbury.
A. J. Lamb	235	Northamptonshire v Yorkshire at Leeds.
W. Larkins	207	Northamptonshire v Essex at Northampton.
A. J. Moles	224*	Warwickshire v Glamorgan at Swansea.
M. D. Moxon	218*	Yorkshire v Sussex at Eastbourne.
P. J. Prichard	245	Essex v Leicestershire at Chelmsford.
D. A. Reeve	202*	Warwickshire v Northamptonshire at Northampton.
R. T. Robinson	220*	Nottinghamshire v Yorkshire at Nottingham.
P. M. Roebuck	201*	Somerset v Worcestershire at Worcester.
J. P. Stephenson	202*	Essex v Somerset at Bath.
C. J. Tavaré	219	Somerset v Sussex at Hove.
N. R. Taylor	204	Kent v Surrey at Canterbury.
D. M. Ward (2)	263	Surrey v Kent at Canterbury.
	208	Surrey v Essex at The Oval.
M. E. Waugh (2)	204	Essex v Gloucestershire at Ilford.
	207*	Essex v Yorkshire at Middlesbrough.

† *Ground record for all matches.*

Note: The three triple-hundreds in 1990 equal the record number in an English season (1899 and 1934).

Hundred on First-Class Début

J. J. B. Lewis	116*	Essex v Surrey at The Oval.

Three Hundreds in Successive Innings

K. J. Barnett (Derbyshire)	107, 123 and 109.
G. A. Gooch (Essex and England)	177, 333 and 123.
M. R. Ramprakash (Middlesex)	146*, 100* and 125.
I. V. A. Richards (Glamorgan)	111, 118* and 127.

Hundred in Each Innings of a Match (12)

C. W. J. Athey	108*	122	Gloucestershire v Warwickshire at Bristol.
G. A. Gooch (2)	333	123	England v India (First Test) at Lord's.
	The record individual aggregate in a Test match.		
	174	126	Essex v Northamptonshire at Northampton.
M. J. Greatbatch	168*	128*	Michael Parkinson's World XI v Indians at Scarborough.
D. L. Haynes	181	129	Middlesex v New Zealanders at Lord's.
G. A. Hick	252*	100*	Worcestershire v Glamorgan at Abergavenny.
A. A. Metcalfe	194*	107	Yorkshire v Nottinghamshire at Nottingham.
H. Morris	110	102*	Glamorgan v Nottinghamshire at Worksop.
J. E. Morris	122	109	Derbyshire v Somerset at Taunton.
M. R. Ramprakash	100*	125	Middlesex v Kent at Canterbury.
I. V. A. Richards	111	118*	Glamorgan v Essex at Southend.
N. R. Taylor	204	142	Kent v Surrey at Canterbury.

Fastest Hundred

(*For the Walter Lawrence Trophy*)

T. M. Moody ...... 36 balls Warwickshire v Glamorgan at Swansea.

In 26 minutes and including seven sixes and eleven fours. The fastest hundred in first-class cricket but achieved against "soft" bowling used to expedite a declaration.

300 Runs in a Day

N. H. Fairbrother .. 311* Lancashire v Surrey at The Oval (3rd day).

Hundred Before Lunch

B. C. Broad	101*	Nottinghamshire v Kent at Tunbridge Wells (1st day).
N. H. Fairbrother	100*†	Lancashire v Surrey at The Oval (3rd day).
I. A. Greig	145*	Surrey v Lancashire at The Oval (2nd day).
D. L. Haynes (2)	102*	Middlesex v Sussex at Lord's (1st day).
	110*	Middlesex v Yorkshire at Leeds (1st day).
A. A. Metcalfe	107*	Yorkshire v Gloucestershire at Cheltenham (1st day).
D. A. Reeve	102*	Warwickshire v Cambridge University at Cambridge (2nd day).
R. A. Smith	127*	Hampshire v Sussex at Southampton (2nd day).

† *N. H. Fairbrother scored 100 or more in each session – 100, 108, 103.*

Hundred Entirely with the Aid of a Runner

M. P. Speight .... 131 Sussex v Glamorgan at Hove.

500 Runs Without Being Dismissed

G. A. Hick (Worcestershire)..... 645: 171*, 69*, 252*, 100* and 53.

Hick scored seven successive fifties (also twelve in thirteen consecutive innings).

Fifty Boundaries in an Innings

N. H. Fairbrother. . . . . 52 (5 sixes, 47 fours) Lancashire v Surrey at The Oval.

Most Sixes off Successive Balls

4. . . . . Kapil Dev (off E. E. Hemmings) India v England (First Test) at Lord's. The first instance in Test matches.

3. . . . . M. R. Ramprakash (off C. J. Tavaré) Middlesex v Somerset at Uxbridge.

First to 1,000 Runs

S. J. Cook (Somerset) on June 7.

First to 2,000 Runs

S. J. Cook (Somerset) on August 4.

Carrying Bat Through Completed Innings

N. E. Briers . . . . 157*† Leicestershire (359) v Nottinghamshire at Leicester.
P. M. Roebuck . . . . . 114* Somerset (270) v Warwickshire at Taunton.

† *One man retired hurt.*

Most Successive First-Class Innings Without Scoring

12. . . . . M. A. Robinson (Northamptonshire): 0, 0*, 0*, 0*, 0*, 0*, 0, 0, 0, 0*, 0*, 0.

First-Wicket Partnership of 200 in Each Innings

227 220 G. A. Gooch/J. P. Stephenson, Essex v Northamptonshire at Northampton. Only the third instance in all first-class cricket.

First-Wicket Partnership of 100 in Each Innings

145 170 T. J. Boon/N. E. Briers, Leicestershire v Essex at Chelmsford.
140 256 A. R. Butcher/H. Morris, Glamorgan v Worcestershire at Abergavenny.

Other Notable Partnerships

First Wicket
321 D. J. Bicknell/G. S. Clinton, Surrey v Northamptonshire at The Oval.
306 D. L. Haynes/M. A. Roseberry, Middlesex v Essex at Ilford.
292 V. P. Terry/T. C. Middleton, Hampshire v Northamptonshire at Bournemouth.
264 V. P. Terry/C. L. Smith, Hampshire v Oxford University at Oxford.
256 D. J. Bicknell/D. M. Ward, Surrey v Oxford University at Oxford.
256 A. R. Butcher/H. Morris, Glamorgan v Worcestershire at Abergavenny.
255* A. R. Butcher/H. Morris, Glamorgan v Kent at Swansea.
251 R. J. Shastri/N. S. Sidhu, Indians v Gloucestershire at Bristol.

Second Wicket

403† G. A. Gooch/P. J. Prichard, Essex v Leicestershire at Chelmsford.
366† S. G. Hinks/N. R. Taylor, Kent v Middlesex at Canterbury.
264 T. S. Curtis/G. A. Hick, Worcestershire v Somerset at Taunton.
258 P. M. Roebuck/A. N. Hayhurst, Somerset v Worcestershire at Worcester.

Third Wicket

413† D. J. Bicknell/D. M. Ward, Surrey v Kent at Canterbury.
393† A. Fordham/A. J. Lamb, Northamptonshire v Yorkshire at Leeds.
364† M. A. Atherton/N. H. Fairbrother, Lancashire v Surrey at The Oval.
308 G. A. Gooch/A. J. Lamb, England v India (First Test) at Lord's.
293* A. A. Metcalfe/P. E. Robinson, Yorkshire v Derbyshire at Scarborough.
285* S. J. Cook/C. J. Tavaré, Somerset v Glamorgan at Cardiff.
268 M. R. Benson/G. R. Cowdrey, Kent v Essex at Maidstone.
264 G. A. Hick/D. B. D'Oliveira, Worcestershire v Glamorgan at Abergavenny.
256 D. I. Gower/R. A. Smith, Hampshire v Sussex at Southampton.

Fourth Wicket

285 B. C. Broad/D. W. Randall, Nottinghamshire v Kent at Tunbridge Wells.
263 P. A. de Silva/H. P. Tillekeratne, Sri Lankans v Hampshire at Southampton.
258 S. G. Hinks/G. R. Cowdrey, Kent v Leicestershire at Leicester.
256 C. J. Tavaré/R. J. Harden, Somerset v New Zealanders at Taunton.

Sixth Wicket

226 D. B. D'Oliveira/S. J. Rhodes, Worcestershire v Lancashire at Manchester.

Seventh Wicket

229 K. M. Curran/R. C. Russell, Gloucestershire v Somerset at Bristol.

Eighth Wicket

205† I. A. Greig/M. P. Bicknell, Surrey v Lancashire at The Oval.

Ninth Wicket

183† C. J. Tavaré/N. A. Mallender, Somerset v Sussex at Hove.

Tenth Wicket

116 G. Yates/P. J. W. Allott, Lancashire v Nottinghamshire at Nottingham.
107 G. Miller/S. J. Base, Derbyshire v Yorkshire at Chesterfield.

* *Unbroken partnership.* † *County record.*

Twelve Wickets in a Match

C. E. L. Ambrose . . . 12-155 Northamptonshire v Leicestershire at Leicester.
J. G. Bracewell . . . . . 12-227 New Zealanders v Oxford & Cambridge Universities at Cambridge.

Eight Wickets in an Innings

G. D. Harrison . . . . . 9-113 Ireland v Scotland at Edinburgh.
C. A. Walsh . . . . 8-58 Gloucestershire v Northamptonshire at Cheltenham.

Hat-Tricks

D. V. Lawrence . . . . Gloucestershire v Nottinghamshire at Nottingham.
S. M. McEwan . . . . . Worcestershire v Leicestershire at Leicester.
P. A. Smith . . . . Warwickshire v Sussex at Eastbourne.

Wicket with First Ball in First-Class Cricket

J. E. R. Gallian .... Lancashire v Oxford University at Oxford.

100 Wickets

For the second season in succession no bowler took 100 wickets. The highest aggregate was 94 by N. A. Foster (Essex).

1,000 Runs and 50 Wickets

K. M. Curran (Gloucestershire) ... 1,267 runs and 64 wickets.
A. I. C. Dodemaide (Sussex) ...... 1,001 runs and 61 wickets.
G. D. Rose (Somerset) .... 1,000 runs and 53 wickets.

Nine Wicket-Keeping Dismissals in a Match

R. J. Blakey (9 ct) .... Yorkshire v Sussex at Eastbourne.

Six Wicket-Keeping Dismissals in an Innings

R. J. Blakey (6 ct) .... Yorkshire v Sussex at Eastbourne.
C. P. Metson (2) (6 ct) ...... Glamorgan v Hampshire at Southampton.
(6 ct) ...... Glamorgan v Warwickshire at Birmingham.
P. A. Nixon (5 ct, 1 st) ..... Leicestershire v Glamorgan at Hinckley.
K. J. Piper (5 ct, 1 st) ..... Warwickshire v Somerset at Taunton.

Highest Innings Totals

(28 of 500 or more)

863† .... Lancashire v Surrey at The Oval.
761-6 dec. ... Essex v Leicestershire at Chelmsford.
707-9 dec. ... Surrey v Lancashire at The Oval.
653-4 dec. ... England v India (First Test) at Lord's.
648 .... Surrey v Kent at Canterbury.
636-6 dec. ... Northamptonshire v Essex at Chelmsford.
613-6 dec. ... Surrey v Essex at The Oval.
606-9 dec. ... India v England (Third Test) at The Oval.
600-8 dec. ... Hampshire v Sussex at Southampton.
592-6 dec. ... Northamptonshire v Essex at Northampton.
574 .... Gloucestershire v Yorkshire at Cheltenham.
558-6 dec. ... Lancashire v Oxford University at Oxford.
551-8 dec. ... Gloucestershire v Worcestershire at Bristol.
539 .... Essex v Surrey at The Oval.
535-2 dec. ... Somerset v Glamorgan at Cardiff.
525-9 dec. ... Somerset v Sussex at Hove.
521 .... Gloucestershire v Northamptonshire at Northampton.
520-9 dec. ... Worcestershire v Somerset at Taunton.
520 .... Leicestershire v Essex at Chelmsford.
519 .... England v India (Second Test) at Manchester.
517 .... Surrey v Hampshire at Southampton.
514-4 dec. ... Worcestershire v Glamorgan at Abergavenny.
514-5 dec. ... Derbyshire v Kent at Chesterfield.
512-6 dec. ... Indians v Minor Counties at Trowbridge.
510-5 dec. ... Middlesex v Nottinghamshire at Lord's.
508-9 dec. ... Essex v Kent at Chelmsford.
506-7 dec. ... Sri Lankans v Hampshire at Southampton.
500-5 dec. ... Somerset v Sussex at Taunton.

† *The second-highest total in County Championship matches.*

Highest Fourth-Innings Totals

493-6 .... Glamorgan v Worcestershire at Abergavenny (set 495).
446-8 .... Hampshire v Gloucestershire at Southampton (set 445).

Lowest Innings Totals

50† ...... Northamptonshire v Derbyshire at Northampton.
72 .... Derbyshire v Gloucestershire at Derby.
96 .... Warwickshire v Worcestershire at Worcester.
99 .... Middlesex v Derbyshire at Derby.

† *Three men absent.*

Match Aggregates of 1,400 Runs

Runs-Wkts
1,650-19 .. Surrey v Lancashire at The Oval.
1,641-16 .. Glamorgan v Worcestershire at Abergavenny.
1,614-30 .. England v India (Second Test) at Manchester.
1,603-28 .. England v India (First Test) at Lord's.
1,530-19 .. Essex v Leicestershire at Chelmsford.
1,509-36 .. Somerset v Worcestershire at Taunton.
1,451-29 .. Kent v Surrey at Canterbury.
1,430-17 .. Glamorgan v Somerset at Cardiff.
1,423-23 .. England v India (Third Test) at The Oval.

Fifty Extras in an Innings

	b	l-b	w	n-b	
71	33	26	2	10	Nottinghamshire v Leicestershire at Leicester.
56	15	26	11	4	Nottinghamshire v Worcestershire at Worcester.
55	16	22	5	12	England v India (Third Test) at The Oval.
54	10	29	2	13	Northamptonshire v Essex at Chelmsford.
50	11	12	9	18	Kent v Leicestershire at Leicester.

Career Aggregate Milestones†

30,000 runs .... G. A. Gooch
20,000 runs .... A. R. Butcher, C. J. Tavaré.
10,000 runs .... R. J. Bailey, N. H. Fairbrother, R. A. Smith, V. P. Terry.

† *Achieved since September 1989.*

FIRST-CLASS AVERAGES, 1990

BATTING

(Qualification: 8 innings, average 10.00)

** Signifies not out.* *† Denotes a left-handed batsman.*

	M	I	NO	R	HI	100s	50s	Avge
G. A. Gooch (*Essex*)	18	30	3	2,746	333	12	8	101.70
G. A. Hick (*Worcs.*)	21	35	9	2,347	252*	8	14	90.26
T. M. Moody (*Warwicks.*)	9	15	2	1,163	168	7	1	89.46
A. N. Aymes (*Hants*)	5	8	4	317	75*	0	3	79.25
M. E. Waugh (*Essex*)	22	33	6	2,072	207*	8	8	76.74
D. M. Ward (*Surrey*)	24	34	7	2,072	263	7	3	76.74
S. J. Cook (*Somerset*)	24	41	7	2,608	313*	9	11	76.70
B. R. Hardie (*Essex*)	12	17	7	728	125	2	4	72.80
M. A. Atherton (*Lancs.*)	20	31	4	1,924	191	7	12	71.25
†N. H. Fairbrother (*Lancs.*)	22	32	7	1,740	366	4	9	69.60
†D. J. Bicknell (*Surrey*)	15	23	4	1,317	186	5	6	69.31
M. A. Crawley (*OUCC & Lancs.*)	11	14	3	762	105*	2	5	69.27
D. L. Haynes (*Middx*)	23	39	5	2,346	255*	8	7	69.00
R. A. Smith (*Hants*)	18	30	8	1,454	181	6	7	66.09
R. J. Bailey (*Northants*)	23	39	8	1,987	204*	7	9	64.09
A. J. Lamb (*Northants*)	17	29	4	1,596	235	6	5	63.84
I. V. A. Richards (*Glam.*)	18	28	5	1,425	164*	7	3	61.95
N. R. Taylor (*Kent*)	22	37	5	1,979	204	7	10	61.84
C. L. Smith (*Hants*)	22	38	7	1,886	148	4	12	60.83
R. J. Harden (*Somerset*)	24	31	7	1,460	104*	3	12	60.83
†A. R. Butcher (*Glam.*)	23	41	5	2,116	151*	6	15	58.77
C. J. Tavaré (*Somerset*)	24	32	4	1,638	219	3	12	58.50
A. N. Hayhurst (*Somerset*)	22	35	8	1,559	170	4	8	57.74
†M. J. Greatbatch (*New Zealanders & M. Parkinson's World XI*)	11	16	3	744	168*	2	4	57.23
J. P. Stephenson (*Essex*)	25	41	8	1,887	202*	4	13	57.18
M. W. Gatting (*Middx*)	23	37	7	1,704	170*	4	9	56.80
T. S. Curtis (*Worcs.*)	22	39	8	1,731	197*	4	7	55.83
G. D. Rose (*Somerset*)	24	29	11	1,000	97*	0	8	55.55
†H. Morris (*Glam.*)	25	46	5	2,276	160*	10	10	55.51
I. A. Greig (*Surrey*)	24	29	6	1,259	291	2	5	54.73
D. A. Reeve (*Warwicks.*)	25	38	12	1,412	202*	3	5	54.30
†B. C. Broad (*Notts.*)	22	43	2	2,226	227*	9	3	54.29
J. E. Morris (*Derbys.*)	21	33	6	1,459	157*	6	6	54.03
K. R. Brown (*Middx*)	24	36	8	1,505	200*	5	8	53.75
G. D. Mendis (*Lancs.*)	21	35	6	1,551	180	4	8	53.48
C. W. J. Athey (*Glos.*)	23	35	7	1,474	131	3	9	52.64
R. I. Alikhan (*Surrey*)	11	16	2	726	138	2	4	51.85
†W. M. van der Merwe (*OUCC*)	8	9	3	310	84	0	3	51.66
A. A. Metcalfe (*Yorks.*)	23	44	4	2,047	194*	6	7	51.17
K. M. Curran (*Glos.*)	23	33	8	1,267	144*	3	5	50.68
K. J. Barnett (*Derbys.*)	24	39	6	1,648	141	5	9	49.93
N. E. Briers (*Leics.*)	24	44	4	1,996	176	5	11	49.90
P. M. Roebuck (*Somerset*)	18	28	5	1,134	201*	2	6	49.30
†M. R. Benson (*Kent*)	16	25	1	1,171	159	5	5	48.79
A. J. Moles (*Warwicks.*)	24	46	8	1,854	224*	4	10	48.78
P. J. Prichard (*Essex*)	22	32	3	1,407	245	5	4	48.51
M. R. Ramprakash (*Middx*)	24	42	10	1,541	146*	5	6	48.15
M. D. Moxon (*Yorks.*)	22	40	6	1,633	218*	3	7	48.02
G. R. Cowdrey (*Kent*)	22	39	6	1,576	135	3	8	47.75
T. C. Middleton (*Hants*)	18	29	3	1,238	127	5	5	47.61

	M	I	NO	R	HI	100s	50s	Avge
D. J. Capel (*Northants*)	18	29	6	1,092	123	3	7	47.47
P. W. G. Parker (*Sussex*)	15	25	4	985	107	2	6	46.90
†D. I. Gower (*Hants*)	20	32	5	1,263	157*	3	3	46.77
†G. R. Dilley (*Worcs.*)	10	8	4	185	45*	0	0	46.25
†G. S. Clinton (*Surrey*)	20	32	4	1,292	146	1	8	46.14
K. P. Evans (*Notts.*)	15	25	9	738	100*	1	4	46.12
J. R. Ayling (*Hants*)	9	11	3	368	62*	0	3	46.00
M. D. Marshall (*Hants*)	18	24	3	962	117	2	6	45.80
†G. J. Lord (*Worcs.*)	13	24	2	1,003	190	3	5	45.59
N. Shahid (*Essex*)	19	29	7	1,003	125	1	6	45.59
M. A. Lynch (*Surrey*)	24	32	5	1,227	104	1	9	45.44
N. J. Speak (*Lancs.*)	6	9	0	409	138	1	3	45.44
J. J. Whitaker (*Leics.*)	24	45	6	1,767	124*	4	8	45.30
R. E. Morris (*OUCC*)	9	12	1	498	96	0	6	45.27
S. J. Rhodes (*Worcs.*)	22	25	10	672	96	0	5	44.80
R. D. B. Croft (*Glam.*)	16	26	11	672	91*	0	4	44.80
P. A. Neale (*Worcs.*)	21	32	10	976	122	2	3	44.36
P. Bainbridge (*Glos.*)	20	28	3	1,107	152	2	5	44.28
G. D. Lloyd (*Lancs.*)	14	20	2	796	96	0	8	44.22
A. Fordham (*Northants*)	24	42	2	1,767	206*	4	9	44.17
M. P. Maynard (*Glam.*)	23	41	7	1,501	125*	2	11	44.14
M. J. Kilborn (*OUCC*)	6	8	1	309	95	0	2	44.14
P. E. Robinson (*Yorks.*)	23	39	7	1,402	150*	1	12	43.81
R. T. Robinson (*Notts.*)	23	45	5	1,747	220*	4	8	43.67
T. E. Jesty (*Lancs.*)	17	24	6	785	98	0	7	43.61
A. P. Wells (*Sussex*)	24	44	7	1,611	144*	4	7	43.54
A. J. Stewart (*Surrey*)	17	29	6	984	100*	1	9	42.78
G. C. Holmes (*Glam.*)	10	15	4	465	125*	1	2	42.27
W. K. Hegg (*Lancs.*)	21	22	6	674	100*	1	3	42.12
P. D. Bowler (*Derbys.*)	22	39	5	1,428	210	3	7	42.00
V. P. Terry (*Hants*)	22	35	3	1,332	165	5	4	41.62
N. J. Lenham (*Sussex*)	22	41	1	1,663	123	4	9	41.57
†N. A. Felton (*Northants*)	22	39	2	1,538	122	4	9	41.56
A. M. Brown (*Derbys.*)	8	12	2	413	139*	1	1	41.30
N. G. Cowley (*Glam.*)	14	17	4	536	76	0	6	41.23
I. Smith (*Glam.*)	7	10	2	328	112*	1	2	41.00
C. S. Cowdrey (*Kent*)	13	24	6	733	107*	3	2	40.72
T. J. G. O'Gorman (*Derbys.*)	7	12	1	448	100	1	4	40.72
M. W. Alleyne (*Glos.*)	13	21	0	854	256	2	3	40.66
M. P. Speight (*Sussex*)	23	41	7	1,375	131	2	11	40.44
M. A. Roseberry (*Middx*)	24	44	4	1,593	135	3	11	39.82
†K. Sharp (*Yorks.*)	9	13	5	318	53*	0	1	39.75
†N. D. Burns (*Somerset*)	24	34	10	951	166	1	5	39.62
†R. M. Ellison (*Kent*)	15	19	7	473	81	0	3	39.41
G. Miller (*Derbys.*)	14	14	8	233	47*	0	0	38.83
P. A. J. DeFreitas (*Lancs.*)	18	20	3	660	102	2	2	38.82
M. P. Bicknell (*Surrey*)	21	16	8	310	50*	0	1	38.75
D. B. D'Oliveira (*Worcs.*)	23	35	2	1,263	155	2	7	38.27
†J. W. Lloyds (*Glos.*)	24	34	12	839	93	0	4	38.13
P. Johnson (*Notts.*)	23	43	3	1,518	165*	3	9	37.95
†R. C. Russell (*Glos.*)	17	23	2	794	120	2	3	37.80
M. V. Fleming (*Kent*)	19	32	6	980	102	1	5	37.69
N. Hussain (*Essex*)	16	23	3	752	197	1	2	37.60
T. J. Boon (*Leics.*)	24	45	4	1,539	138	2	11	37.53
†S. G. Hinks (*Kent*)	24	43	0	1,588	234	4	6	36.93
G. D. Hodgson (*Glos.*)	24	40	4	1,320	126	2	10	36.66
D. W. Randall (*Notts.*)	15	28	1	987	178	2	5	36.55
A. P. Grayson (*Yorks.*)	5	8	4	145	44*	0	0	36.25
M. Watkinson (*Lancs.*)	19	23	2	754	138	1	4	35.90
M. C. J. Nicholas (*Hants*)	23	35	10	895	104	1	5	35.80
B. Roberts (*Derbys.*)	24	38	7	1,108	124*	2	4	35.74

	M	I	NO	R	HI	100s	50s	Avge
P. J. Newport (*Worcs.*)	21	18	6	424	98	0	3	35.33
I. T. Botham (*Worcs.*)	13	18	1	595	113	1	4	35.00
G. W. Humpage (*Warwicks.*)	13	22	4	628	74	0	5	34.88
J. D. R. Benson (*Leics.*)	18	27	6	725	106	1	3	34.52
S. P. James (*CUCC & Glam.*)	16	31	2	1,000	131*	4	5	34.48
I. P. Butcher (*Glos.*)	12	19	4	513	102	1	2	34.20
C. S. Pickles (*Yorks.*)	16	22	8	478	57*	0	3	34.14
D. R. Pringle (*Essex*)	17	15	2	443	84	0	3	34.07
M. Newell (*Notts.*)	15	27	2	851	112	1	6	34.04
P. Willey (*Leics.*)	22	40	6	1,150	177	2	5	33.82
S. A. Marsh (*Kent*)	24	35	8	911	114*	1	5	33.74
W. K. M. Benjamin (*Leics.*)	12	15	2	437	101*	1	4	33.61
P. A. Cottey (*Glam.*)	20	35	5	1,001	156	3	4	33.36
A. I. C. Dodemaide (*Sussex*)	24	38	8	1,001	112	2	4	33.36
C. M. Wells (*Sussex*)	20	33	5	933	113*	2	4	33.32
R. K. Illingworth (*Worcs.*)	23	22	6	532	117	1	3	33.25
C. C. Lewis (*Leics.*)	17	26	5	697	189*	1	2	33.19
†R. C. J. Williams (*Glos.*)	8	8	4	132	50*	0	1	33.00
†J. J. E. Hardy (*Somerset*)	9	16	5	361	91	0	1	32.81
P. W. Romaines (*Glos.*)	7	11	2	295	95	0	2	32.77
L. Potter (*Leics.*)	23	38	5	1,080	109*	1	7	32.72
J. W. Hall (*Sussex*)	20	37	2	1,140	125	2	5	32.57
P. A. Smith (*Warwicks.*)	12	20	4	520	117	1	3	32.50
†G. Fowler (*Lancs.*)	21	35	6	938	126	2	2	32.34
T. R. Ward (*Kent*)	15	28	1	863	175	2	5	31.96
†A. L. Penberthy (*Northants*)	12	17	3	435	101*	1	3	31.07
C. J. Adams (*Derbys.*)	23	34	4	932	111*	2	5	31.06
S. A. Kellett (*Yorks.*)	16	28	3	774	75*	0	6	30.96
N. M. K. Smith (*Warwicks.*)	10	14	2	370	83*	0	1	30.83
P. N. Hepworth (*Leics.*)	4	8	2	185	55*	0	1	30.83
P. D. Lunn (*OUCC*)	8	10	4	184	44*	0	0	30.66
†I. D. Austin (*Lancs.*)	13	15	6	276	58	0	1	30.66
†M. Saxelby (*Notts.*)	8	15	4	335	73	0	2	30.45
R. J. Blakey (*Yorks.*)	25	43	9	1,033	111	1	6	30.38
B. T. P. Donelan (*Sussex*)	11	13	6	211	53	0	1	30.14
D. J. R. Martindale (*Notts.*)	17	28	3	751	138	2	2	30.04
D. P. Ostler (*Warwicks.*)	11	19	2	510	71	0	5	30.00
D. Ripley (*Northants*)	21	28	6	656	109*	1	2	29.81
M. A. Garnham (*Essex*)	24	28	7	615	84*	0	2	29.28
M. A. Feltham (*Surrey*)	15	16	3	379	101	1	2	29.15
R. J. Maru (*Hants*)	25	20	2	520	59	0	3	28.88
P. Bent (*Worcs.*)	7	12	0	346	79	0	2	28.83
F. D. Stephenson (*Notts.*)	20	35	7	807	121	1	4	28.82
†D. Byas (*Yorks.*)	19	29	4	704	83	0	5	28.16
J. E. Emburey (*Middx*)	23	32	7	702	111*	1	2	28.08
W. Larkins (*Northants*)	15	25	0	701	207	2	2	28.04
Waqar Younis (*Surrey*)	14	9	7	56	14	0	0	28.00
J. D. Ratcliffe (*Warwicks.*)	16	31	3	780	81*	0	3	27.85
Asif Din (*Warwicks.*)	22	39	4	974	100*	1	5	27.82
I. R. Bishop (*Derbys.*)	13	16	4	333	103*	1	0	27.75
†G. P. Thorpe (*Surrey*)	18	28	6	608	86	0	3	27.63
†P. A. Nixon (*Leics.*)	19	23	8	411	46	0	0	27.40
C. A. Walsh (*Glos.*)	20	20	3	464	63*	0	3	27.29
R. G. Williams (*Northants*)	17	26	5	566	96	0	4	26.95
J. E. Benjamin (*Warwicks.*)	15	14	7	188	41	0	0	26.85
†R. G. Twose (*Warwicks.*)	6	10	1	241	64*	0	3	26.77
P. R. Downton (*Middx*)	16	24	2	587	63	0	4	26.68
N. A. Foster (*Essex*)	22	22	2	530	101	1	2	26.50
G. Cook (*Northants*)	9	12	1	287	87	0	1	26.09
A. J. Wright (*Glos.*)	23	38	3	911	112	1	5	26.02
P. Carrick (*Yorks.*)	18	22	2	515	64	0	3	25.75

	M	I	NO	R	HI	100s	50s	Avge
K. T. Medlycott (*Surrey*)	23	25	9	410	44	0	0	25.62
N. A. Mallender (*Somerset*)	20	10	3	177	87*	0	1	25.28
†D. M. Smith (*Sussex*)	9	16	2	353	71	0	2	25.21
†A. N. Jones (*Somerset*)	22	9	5	100	41	0	0	25.00
†T. A. Lloyd (*Warwicks.*)	15	27	1	646	101	1	4	24.84
†G. J. Turner (*OUCC*)	9	12	0	298	59	0	2	24.83
C. A. Connor (*Hants*)	22	10	4	148	46	0	0	24.66
†A. I. Kallicharran (*Warwicks.*)	7	10	1	221	72	0	2	24.55
I. D. K. Salisbury (*Sussex*)	20	23	10	313	68	0	1	24.07
A. P. Kuiper (*Derbys.*)	12	17	0	407	68	0	2	23.94
D. P. Hughes (*Lancs.*)	18	17	7	237	57	0	1	23.70
†I. J. Gould (*Sussex*)	8	12	2	235	73	0	2	23.50
V. J. Wells (*Kent*)	8	15	0	352	58	0	2	23.46
S. M. McEwan (*Worcs.*)	15	12	5	164	54	0	1	23.42
K. J. Piper (*Warwicks.*)	16	21	1	461	111	1	1	23.05
M. J. Lowrey (*CUCC*)	10	18	2	363	72	0	2	22.68
E. E. Hemmings (*Notts.*)	17	20	5	333	83	0	2	22.20
R. Heap (*CUCC*)	10	19	2	376	63	0	2	22.11
P. S. de Villiers (*Kent*)	12	15	3	264	37	0	0	22.00
P. C. R. Tufnell (*Middx*)	23	22	9	283	37	0	0	21.76
P. Moores (*Sussex*)	25	36	4	694	106*	1	2	21.68
N. F. Williams (*Middx*)	21	24	3	448	55*	0	2	21.33
†P. R. Pollard (*Notts.*)	7	13	0	277	72	0	1	21.30
P. Farbrace (*Middx*)	8	8	2	124	79	0	1	20.66
†M. J. Cann (*Glam.*)	6	10	0	206	64	0	2	20.60
†R. A. Pick (*Notts.*)	17	16	6	204	35	0	0	20.40
B. N. French (*Notts.*)	22	34	9	506	105*	1	0	20.24
D. H. Shufflebotham (*CUCC*)	8	9	3	121	29	0	0	20.16
J. C. M. Atkinson (*CUCC*)	11	21	2	374	72	0	2	19.68
R. J. Parks (*Hants*)	20	21	10	216	36*	0	0	19.63
S. J. Base (*Derbys.*)	13	13	2	215	58	0	2	19.54
A. R. C. Fraser (*Middx*)	15	13	2	214	92	0	1	19.45
P. J. Bakker (*Hants*)	16	9	4	95	20	0	0	19.00
R. J. Turner (*CUCC*)	9	16	0	302	38	0	0	18.87
A. C. S. Pigott (*Sussex*)	21	29	5	451	64*	0	4	18.79
S. R. Lampitt (*Worcs.*)	23	24	5	356	45*	0	0	18.73
I. G. Swallow (*Somerset*)	23	17	7	187	32	0	0	18.70
K. M. Krikken (*Derbys.*)	22	29	2	488	77*	0	2	18.07
†R. J. Scott (*Hants*)	6	10	2	144	71	0	1	18.00
G. B. A. Dyer (*CUCC*)	4	8	2	107	23	0	0	17.83
P. W. Jarvis (*Yorks.*)	15	16	4	212	43*	0	0	17.66
†J. D. Robinson (*Surrey*)	8	10	0	175	72	0	1	17.50
R. P. Davis (*Kent*)	24	32	3	504	59	0	2	17.37
†P. A. Booth (*Warwicks.*)	10	16	2	240	60	0	2	17.14
N. V. Radford (*Worcs.*)	12	8	1	118	43*	0	0	16.85
S. C. Goldsmith (*Derbys.*)	12	17	1	267	51	0	1	16.68
†J. D. Fitton (*Lancs.*)	15	13	5	133	25*	0	0	16.62
R. P. Lefebvre (*Somerset*)	17	16	3	214	53	0	1	16.46
G. C. Small (*Warwicks.*)	15	22	4	296	55	0	1	16.44
A. Dale (*Glam.*)	9	14	0	229	92	0	1	16.35
C. P. Metson (*Glam.*)	23	27	5	352	50*	0	1	16.00
H. A. G. Anthony (*Glam.*)	6	8	0	127	39	0	0	15.87
†C. E. L. Ambrose (*Northants*)	15	18	5	203	55*	0	1	15.61
P. J. Hartley (*Yorks.*)	17	15	1	218	75	0	1	15.57
N. M. Kendrick (*Surrey*)	13	12	4	124	52*	0	1	15.50
†M. C. Ilott (*Essex*)	9	10	2	123	42*	0	0	15.37
J. G. Thomas (*Northants*)	12	13	3	152	48	0	0	15.20
M. M. Patel (*Kent*)	9	12	5	104	41*	0	0	14.85
M. J. Morris (*CUCC*)	10	17	3	206	45	0	0	14.71
D. A. Hagan (*OUCC*)	9	12	0	175	47	0	0	14.58
A. R. K. Pierson (*Warwicks.*)	11	9	5	57	16*	0	0	14.25

	M	I	NO	R	HI	100s	50s	Avge
C. White (*Yorks.*)	10	11	2	127	38	0	0	14.11
M. Jean-Jacques (*Derbys.*)	12	13	5	107	25	0	0	13.37
S. J. W. Andrew (*Essex*)	18	16	7	119	35	0	0	13.22
A. P. Igglesden (*Kent*)	14	17	9	105	24	0	0	13.12
N. G. B. Cook (*Northants*)	19	19	8	143	30	0	0	13.00
N. G. Cowans (*Middx*)	18	17	7	127	46*	0	0	12.70
D. J. M. Kelleher (*Kent*)	5	8	0	101	44	0	0	12.62
†Wasim Akram (*Lancs.*)	8	11	0	135	32	0	0	12.27
J. P. Agnew (*Leics.*)	22	26	5	257	46*	0	0	12.23
D. A. Graveney (*Glos.*)	13	13	4	107	46*	0	0	11.88
†K. E. Cooper (*Notts.*)	21	26	6	227	35*	0	0	11.35
P. S. Gerrans (*OUCC*)	9	9	0	102	39	0	0	11.33
†G. J. Parsons (*Leics.*)	10	13	3	112	20	0	0	11.20
†J. H. Childs (*Essex*)	23	16	5	123	26	0	0	11.18
D. Gough (*Yorks.*)	14	17	6	123	24	0	0	11.18
S. L. Watkin (*Glam.*)	24	25	8	187	25*	0	0	11.00
T. A. Merrick (*Kent*)	7	8	2	66	35	0	0	11.00
R. A. Bunting (*Sussex*)	15	13	5	85	24*	0	0	10.62
M. J. Weston (*Worcs.*)	6	10	1	90	38*	0	0	10.00
O. H. Mortensen (*Derbys.*)	12	11	9	20	5*	0	0	10.00

BOWLING

(Qualification: 10 wickets in 10 innings)

† *Denotes a left-arm bowler.*

	O	M	R	W	BB	5W/i	Avge
I. R. Bishop (*Derbys.*)	407.3	94	1,124	59	6-71	3	19.05
M. D. Marshall (*Hants*)	554.2	142	1,381	72	7-47	4	19.18
D. J. Millns (*Leics.*)	206.4	36	662	31	6-63	2	21.35
O. H. Mortensen (*Derbys.*)	316.2	91	785	35	4-22	0	22.42
C. E. L. Ambrose (*Northants*)	503.4	127	1,413	61	7-89	5	23.16
Waqar Younis (*Surrey*)	422	70	1,357	57	7-73	3	23.80
M. W. Alleyne (*Glos.*)	112	29	391	16	3-23	0	24.43
P. A. Smith (*Warwicks.*)	148.5	34	497	20	5-48	1	24.85
N. A. Foster (*Essex*)	819.2	175	2,502	94	6-32	6	26.61
A. R. C. Fraser (*Middx*)	596	144	1,533	57	6-30	4	26.89
M. P. Bicknell (*Surrey*)	671.1	157	1,827	67	5-34	1	27.26
G. J. Parsons (*Leics.*)	304.5	77	963	35	6-75	2	27.51
J. E. Benjamin (*Warwicks.*)	388.3	68	1,205	43	5-29	4	28.02
C. A. Walsh (*Glos.*)	612.1	107	2,022	72	8-58	3	28.08
†R. K. Illingworth (*Worcs.*)	875.5	280	2,122	75	5-59	1	28.29
D. J. Capel (*Northants*)	234	51	711	25	5-74	1	28.44
D. A. Reeve (*Warwicks.*)	377.4	111	940	33	4-42	0	28.48
T. A. Merrick (*Kent*)	184.3	45	488	17	4-66	0	28.70
M. A. Feltham (*Surrey*)	349.4	61	1,150	40	6-53	2	28.75
T. A. Munton (*Warwicks.*)	827.1	199	2,254	78	5-33	2	28.89
K. J. Barnett (*Derbys.*)	293.3	54	757	26	4-28	0	29.11
D. R. Pringle (*Essex*)	358.3	91	994	34	5-66	1	29.23
I. T. Botham (*Worcs.*)	194.4	38	614	21	4-65	0	29.23
N. F. Williams (*Middx*)	530.1	98	1,618	54	7-61	2	29.96
C. C. Lewis (*Leics.*)	536.2	102	1,697	56	6-55	2	30.30
S. Bastien (*Glam.*)	317.1	57	1,187	39	6-75	2	30.43
K. M. Curran (*Glos.*)	598.3	111	1,961	64	5-63	1	30.64
W. K. M. Benjamin (*Leics.*)	284.3	63	858	28	5-73	2	30.64
M. A. Atherton (*Lancs.*)	433.3	104	1,398	45	6-78	3	31.06
N. A. Mallender (*Somerset*)	553.2	116	1,585	51	5-46	2	31.07

	O	M	R	W	BB	5W/i	Avge
S. M. McEwan (*Worcs.*)	375.2	75	1,189	38	3-31	0	31.28
P. J. Newport (*Worcs.*)	626.2	116	2,001	63	6-54	4	31.76
N. G. Cowans (*Middx*)	460	124	1,247	39	5-67	1	31.97
J. E. Emburey (*Middx*)	942.3	275	1,957	61	5-32	2	32.08
G. A. Hick (*Worcs.*)	208.5	41	645	20	5-37	1	32.25
T. D. Topley (*Essex*)	223	34	713	22	4-67	0	32.40
D. E. Malcolm (*Derbys.*)	518.2	99	1,688	52	5-46	2	32.46
R. A. Pick (*Notts.*)	494.5	83	1,657	51	7-128	1	32.49
S. R. Lampitt (*Worcs.*)	565.3	98	1,889	58	5-34	2	32.56
A. P. Kuiper (*Derbys.*)	125.3	29	393	12	4-69	0	32.75
†M. C. Ilott (*Essex*)	322.1	65	1,036	31	5-34	2	33.41
M. Watkinson (*Lancs.*)	508.2	122	1,578	47	5-65	3	33.57
G. R. Dilley (*Worcs.*)	224.2	30	818	24	5-62	2	34.08
†N. G. B. Cook (*Northants*)	527.1	167	1,364	40	5-44	2	34.10
D. V. Lawrence (*Glos.*)	497.3	53	1,979	58	5-51	2	34.12
†P. Carrick (*Yorks.*)	601	173	1,570	46	5-49	3	34.13
P. J. Hartley (*Yorks.*)	491	80	1,781	52	6-57	2	34.25
M. Frost (*Glam.*)	557.1	74	2,047	59	5-40	2	34.69
B. P. Patterson (*Lancs.*)	281.4	45	1,015	29	4-52	0	35.00
A. H. Gray (*Surrey*)	239.5	43	666	19	4-83	0	35.05
†P. C. R. Tufnell (*Middx*)	1,036.5	281	2,635	74	6-79	2	35.60
S. D. Fletcher (*Yorks.*)	292.5	60	1,035	29	5-94	1	35.68
P. M. Such (*Essex*)	272.4	67	715	20	3-34	0	35.75
A. P. Igglesden (*Kent*)	326	47	1,150	32	4-79	0	35.93
A. L. Penberthy (*Northants*)	207.4	29	791	22	4-91	0	35.95
P. A. J. DeFreitas (*Lancs.*)	489.3	109	1,440	40	6-39	2	36.00
E. E. Hemmings (*Notts.*)	688.2	197	1,844	51	6-58	2	36.15
K. P. Evans (*Notts.*)	356	78	1,232	34	4-50	0	36.23
†R. J. Maru (*Hants*)	851.1	219	2,420	66	6-97	2	36.66
A. N. Jones (*Somerset*)	572.4	92	2,055	56	6-75	2	36.69
G. D. Rose (*Somerset*)	571.4	99	1,951	53	5-52	1	36.81
A. C. S. Pigott (*Sussex*)	541	94	1,997	54	5-52	3	36.98
D. Gough (*Yorks.*)	279.4	49	1,037	28	4-68	0	37.03
G. C. Small (*Warwicks.*)	425.4	105	1,190	32	6-94	2	37.18
J. P. Agnew (*Leics.*)	612	108	2,196	59	5-54	5	37.22
G. Miller (*Derbys.*)	461	114	1,308	35	6-45	1	37.37
M. A. Crawley (*OUCC & Lancs.*)	224.5	38	750	20	6-92	1	37.50
A. A. Donald (*Warwicks.*)	391	89	1,089	29	3-28	0	37.55
S. N. Barnes (*Glos.*)	207	45	602	16	4-51	0	37.62
P. W. Jarvis (*Yorks.*)	405.2	68	1,393	37	4-53	0	37.64
†A. D. Mullally (*Leics.*)	487.2	117	1,446	38	4-59	0	38.05
C. A. Connor (*Hants*)	510.1	88	1,789	47	5-96	1	38.06
†D. P. Hughes (*Lancs.*)	280.4	61	918	24	4-25	0	38.25
†D. A. Graveney (*Glos.*)	485.4	136	1,189	31	5-45	3	38.35
A. R. K. Pierson (*Warwicks.*)	302.4	55	965	25	5-101	1	38.60
R. G. Williams (*Northants*)	432.3	119	1,204	31	4-94	0	38.83
F. D. Stephenson (*Notts.*)	610.4	94	2,098	54	6-84	2	38.85
P. J. Bakker (*Hants*)	436.2	90	1,439	37	5-101	1	38.89
†R. P. Davis (*Kent*)	908.1	221	2,844	73	6-40	5	38.95
S. P. Hughes (*Middx*)	386.2	73	1,287	33	5-101	1	39.00
†K. T. Medlycott (*Surrey*)	748.5	170	2,382	61	7-92	3	39.04
S. L. Watkin (*Glam.*)	796.1	137	2,712	69	5-100	1	39.30
T. M. Tremlett (*Hants*)	120.5	30	393	10	3-33	0	39.30
K. J. Shine (*Hants*)	156.4	30	552	14	4-52	0	39.42
P. J. Martin (*Lancs.*)	275.3	52	868	22	4-68	0	39.45
P. S. de Villiers (*Kent*)	304.5	58	992	25	6-70	1	39.68
†Wasim Akram (*Lancs.*)	204	44	640	16	3-76	0	40.00
S. J. Base (*Derbys.*)	414.3	68	1,402	35	6-105	2	40.05
G. J. F. Ferris (*Leics.*)	138.2	29	482	12	4-44	0	40.16
A. I. C. Dodemaide (*Sussex*)	763.1	130	2,457	61	6-106	1	40.27
A. E. Warner (*Derbys.*)	393.3	67	1,330	33	3-56	0	40.30

	O	M	R	W	BB	5W/i	Avge
J. G. Thomas (*Northants*)	305.2	51	1,171	29	7-75	1	40.37
P. J. W. Allott (*Lancs.*)	266	77	730	18	4-23	0	40.55
K. E. Cooper (*Notts.*)	703.4	153	2,203	54	5-56	3	40.79
S. D. Udal (*Hants*)	238.3	46	900	22	4-139	0	40.90
S. J. W. Andrew (*Essex*)	503	75	1,897	46	5-55	1	41.23
R. P. Lefebvre (*Somerset*)	506.1	137	1,281	31	5-30	1	41.32
C. S. Pickles (*Yorks.*)	325.1	72	1,163	28	3-56	0	41.53
†M. M. Patel (*Kent*)	297.5	72	836	20	6-57	2	41.80
M. Jean-Jacques (*Derbys.*)	300	42	1,106	25	6-60	1	44.24
A. J. Murphy (*Surrey*)	404.2	76	1,367	30	5-67	2	45.56
†J. A. Afford (*Notts.*)	688	209	1,944	42	4-137	0	46.28
C. White (*Yorks.*)	159	23	608	13	5-74	1	46.76
P. Bainbridge (*Glos.*)	162.4	30	515	11	3-23	0	46.81
†A. J. Buzza (*CUCC*)	287	47	1,086	23	4-87	0	47.21
M. A. Robinson (*Northants*)	559.1	104	1,889	40	3-47	0	47.22
P. Willey (*Leics.*)	421.4	119	1,091	23	2-7	0	47.43
R. D. B. Croft (*Glam.*)	397.1	83	1,335	28	3-10	0	47.67
†N. M. Kendrick (*Surrey*)	348	66	1,194	25	4-110	0	47.76
M. J. Lowrey (*CUCC*)	151.2	33	483	10	2-13	0	48.30
†S. J. Dennis (*Glam.*)	322	61	1,071	22	5-76	1	48.68
M. V. Fleming (*Kent*)	394.5	94	1,072	22	3-65	0	48.72
†P. A. Booth (*Warwicks.*)	250.5	75	636	13	4-55	0	48.92
I. D. K. Salisbury (*Sussex*)	601.1	113	2,075	42	5-32	2	49.40
B. T. P. Donelan (*Sussex*)	304.4	56	1,000	20	3-79	0	50.00
R. A. Bunting (*Sussex*)	360	62	1,314	26	2-36	0	50.53
R. M. Ellison (*Kent*)	291.5	51	963	19	4-76	0	50.68
J. R. Ayling (*Hants*)	181.2	46	572	11	2-48	0	52.00
R. J. Bailey (*Northants*)	168.2	29	604	11	3-82	0	54.90
I. D. Austin (*Lancs.*)	245	76	662	12	3-42	0	55.16
J. W. Lloyds (*Glos.*)	382.5	60	1,429	25	4-11	0	57.16
C. Penn (*Kent*)	186	35	636	11	3-45	0	57.81
P. S. Gerrans (*OUCC*)	208	40	695	12	3-86	0	57.91
†J. H. Childs (*Essex*)	655.5	211	1,590	27	4-56	0	58.88
J. D. Batty (*Yorks.*)	195	29	722	12	4-76	0	60.16
W. W. Davis (*Northants*)	237.5	28	812	13	3-28	0	62.46
R. A. Pyman (*CUCC*)	308.4	81	938	15	2-29	0	62.53
Asif Din (*Warwicks.*)	159.1	30	635	10	3-17	0	63.50
R. H. J. Jenkins (*CUCC*)	281.4	41	959	15	5-100	1	63.93
I. G. Swallow (*Somerset*)	689.1	161	2,174	34	3-88	0	63.94
A. N. Hayhurst (*Somerset*)	321.2	50	1,087	17	3-58	0	63.94
M. E. Waugh (*Essex*)	191	33	771	12	5-37	1	64.25
I. A. Greig (*Surrey*)	216.1	21	858	13	3-60	0	66.00
N. V. Radford (*Worcs.*)	302	49	1,195	18	4-55	0	66.38
C. M. Wells (*Sussex*)	374	68	1,237	17	3-48	0	72.76
N. G. Cowley (*Glam.*)	316.3	64	900	12	3-84	0	75.00
G. J. Turner (*OUCC*)	212.2	39	819	10	3-100	0	81.90
J. D. Fitton (*Lancs.*)	454.4	91	1,447	14	3-69	0	103.35

The following bowlers took ten wickets but bowled in fewer than ten innings:

	O	M	R	W	BB	5W/i	Avge
V. J. Wells (*Kent*)	85	19	257	12	5-43	1	21.41
H. A. G. Anthony (*Glam.*)	142.4	32	466	12	3-95	0	38.83
C. Pringle (*New Zealanders & M. Parkinson's World XI*)	149	32	483	10	2-49	0	48.30

INDIVIDUAL SCORES OF 100 AND OVER

There were 428 three-figure innings in first-class cricket in 1990, 180 more than in 1989 and fourteen more than in any other season. The total passed the previous record of 414 hundreds scored in 1928, of which 329 were scored in the County Championship and 75 in other matches. In 1990 there were three triple-hundreds, a record equalled only in 1899 and 1934, and 29 other double-hundreds. The record number of double-hundreds is 34 in 1933. In 1928, when 312 first-class matches were played, compared with 241 in 1990, there was one triple-hundred with 28 double-hundreds. In that year, 139 batsmen recorded three-figure innings, compared with 156 in 1990, and thirteen each were played by E. H. Hendren, C. P. Mead and H. Sutcliffe, while the most in 1990 was twelve by G. A. Gooch. The following list includes 327 hit in the County Championship, two by the Zimbabwean touring team and 71 in other first-class games, but not the fifteen scored by the Indian touring team, the seven scored by the Sri Lankan touring team, nor the six scored by the New Zealand touring team, which may be found in their respective sections.

Note: Players' hundreds are listed in chronological order. Previously they have been listed in descending order.

* *Signifies not out.*

G. A. Gooch (12)

137 Essex v Middx, Lord's
215 Essex v Leics., Chelmsford
121 Essex v Worcs., Worcester
120 Essex v Middx, Ilford
102* Essex v New Zealanders, Chelmsford
154 England v New Zealand, Birmingham
177 Essex v Lancs., Colchester
333 } 123 } England v India, Lord's
116 England v India, Manchester
174 } 126 } Essex v Northants, Northampton

H. Morris (10)

103 Glam. v Oxford U., Oxford
100* Glam. v Kent, Swansea
102 Glam. v Yorks., Cardiff
119 Glam. v Worcs., Abergavenny
106 Glam. v Warwicks., Swansea
100 Glam. v Middx, Lord's
110 } 102* } Glam. v Notts., Worksop
126 Glam. v Sri Lankans, Ebbw Vale
160* Glam. v Derbys., Cardiff

B. C. Broad (9)

180 Notts. v Derbys., Nottingham
119 Notts. v Warwicks., Birmingham
227* Notts. v Kent, Tunbridge Wells
112* Notts. v Leics., Nottingham
126 Notts. v Yorks., Scarborough
122 Notts. v Lancs., Southport
140 Notts. v Middx, Nottingham
156 Notts. v Worcs., Nottingham
122 Notts. v Lancs., Nottingham

S. J. Cook (9)

313* Somerset v Glam., Cardiff
117* Somerset v New Zealanders, Taunton
197 Somerset v Sussex, Taunton
112* Somerset v Northants, Taunton
137 Somerset v Warwicks., Taunton
152 Somerset v Middx, Uxbridge
116* Somerset v Surrey, Weston-super-Mare
114 Somerset v Hants, Taunton
143 Somerset v Worcs., Taunton

D. L. Haynes (8)

116 Middx v Essex, Lord's
181 } 129 } Middx v New Zealanders, Lord's
220* Middx v Essex, Ilford
108 Middx v Somerset, Uxbridge
173 Middx v Glam., Lord's
255* Middx v Sussex, Lord's
131 Middx v Yorks., Leeds

G. A. Hick (8)

106* Worcs. v Lancs., Manchester
171* Worcs. v Somerset, Worcester
252* } 100* } Worcs. v Glam., Abergavenny
102 Worcs. v Leics., Leicester
110 Worcs. v Glos., Bristol
154 Worcs. v Somerset, Taunton
138* Worcs. v Glam., Worcester

M. E. Waugh (8)

166* Essex v Worcs., Worcester
125 Essex v Hants, Southampton
204 Essex v Glos., Ilford
103 Essex v Warwicks., Birmingham
126 Essex v Derbys., Colchester
103* Essex v Sussex, Chelmsford
207* Essex v Yorks., Middlesbrough
169 Essex v Kent, Chelmsford

M. A. Atherton (7)
191 Lancs. v Surrey, The Oval
151 England v New Zealand, Nottingham
117 Lancs. v Oxford U., Oxford
101 Lancs. v Kent, Maidstone
108* Lancs. v Essex, Colchester
131 England v India, Manchester
108 Lancs. v Yorks., Manchester

R. J. Bailey (7)
101 Northants v Somerset, Taunton
138* Northants v Kent, Northampton
204* Northants v Sussex, Northampton
134* Northants v Derbys., Chesterfield
105 Northants v Glos., Northampton
108 Northants v Essex, Northampton
107 Northants v Essex, Chelmsford

T. M. Moody (7)
147 Warwicks. v Cambridge U., Cambridge
106 Warwicks. v New Zealanders, Birmingham
168 Warwicks. v Derbys., Derby
103* Warwicks. v Glam., Swansea
101* Warwicks. v Hants, Birmingham
110 Warwicks. v Sussex, Eastbourne
117 Warwicks. v Leics., Birmingham

I. V. A. Richards (7)
119 Glam. v Leics., Cardiff
118* Glam. v Sussex, Hove
109 Glam. v Northants, Northampton
164* Glam. v Hants, Southampton
111 }
118* } Glam. v Essex, Southend
127 Glam. v Notts., Worksop

N. R. Taylor (7)
106 Kent v Glam., Swansea
124* Kent v Yorks., Tunbridge Wells
120 Kent v Cambridge U., Cambridge
107* Kent v Indians, Canterbury
152* Kent v Middx, Canterbury
204 }
142 } Kent v Surrey, Canterbury

D. M. Ward (7)
181 Surrey v Oxford U., Oxford
129* Surrey v Hants, The Oval
154* Surrey v Notts., Nottingham
126 Surrey v Warwicks., The Oval
191 Surrey v Hants, Southampton
263 Surrey v Kent, Canterbury
208 Surrey v Essex, The Oval

A. R. Butcher (6)
139 Glam. v Sussex, Hove
151* Glam. v Kent, Swansea
115 Glam. v Leics., Hinckley
130 Glam. v Worcs., Abergavenny
116 Glam. v Warwicks., Swansea
121* Glam. v Notts., Worksop

A. J. Lamb (6)
235 Northants v Yorks., Leeds
135* Northants v Sussex, Northampton
139 England v India, Lord's
109 England v India, Manchester
134 Northants v Essex, Northampton
165 Northants v Essex, Chelmsford

A. A. Metcalfe (6)
162 Yorks. v Glos., Cheltenham
102 Yorks. v Somerset, Scarborough
146 Yorks. v Lancs., Leeds
150* Yorks. v Derbys., Scarborough
194* }
107 } Yorks. v Notts., Nottingham

J. E. Morris (6)
122 }
109 } Derbys. v Somerset, Taunton
103 Derbys. v Notts., Derby
103* Derbys. v Warwicks., Derby
157* Derbys. v Hants, Portsmouth
109 Derbys. v Yorks., Scarborough

R. A. Smith (6)
181 Hants v Sussex, Southampton
114* Hants v Surrey, The Oval
153 Hants v Glam., Southampton
100* England v India, Lord's
121* England v India, Manchester
124 Hants v Glos., Southampton

K. J. Barnett (5)
141 Derbys. v Yorks., Chesterfield
131 Derbys. v Warwicks., Derby
107 Derbys. v Glos., Derby
123 Derbys. v Sussex, Hove
109 Derbys. v Lancs., Liverpool

M. R. Benson (5)
109 Kent v Sussex, Folkestone
116 Kent v Somerset, Canterbury
159 Kent v Essex, Maidstone
107 Kent v Leics., Dartford
115* Kent v Sussex, Hove

D. J. Bicknell (5)
169 Surrey v Northants, The Oval
143 Surrey v Sussex, Guildford
111 Surrey v Leics., The Oval
186 Surrey v Kent, Canterbury
114 Surrey v Middx, The Oval

N. E. Briers (5)
104 Leics. v Essex, Chelmsford
157* Leics. v Notts., Leicester
150* Leics. v Indians, Leicester
111 Leics. v Worcs., Leicester
176 Leics. v Northants, Leicester

K. R. Brown (5)
141 Middx v Essex, Lord's
109* Middx v Yorks., Uxbridge
120 Middx v Glam., Lord's
200* Middx v Notts., Lord's
116* Middx v Sussex, Hove

T. C. Middleton (5)
127 Hants v Kent, Canterbury
104* Hants v Essex, Southampton
123 Hants v Northants, Bournemouth
117* Hants v Worcs., Worcester
104 Hants v Kent, Bournemouth

P. J. Prichard (5)
245 Essex v Leics., Chelmsford
116 Essex v Cambridge U., Cambridge
115 Essex v Somerset, Bath
103 Essex v Derbys., Derby
102 Essex v Kent, Chelmsford

M. R. Ramprakash (5)
118* Middx v Cambridge U., Cambridge
146* Middx v Somerset, Uxbridge
100* } Middx v Kent, Canterbury
125 }
132 Middx v Notts., Lord's

V. P. Terry (5)
107 Hants v Kent, Canterbury
112 Hants v Oxford U., Oxford
119* Hants v Warwicks., Birmingham
165 Hants v Northants, Bournemouth
120 Hants v Sri Lankans, Southampton

T. S. Curtis (4)
111* Worcs. v Glam., Abergavenny
151* Worcs. v Leics., Leicester
197* Worcs. v Warwicks., Worcester
156 Worcs. v Somerset, Taunton

N. H. Fairbrother (4)
366 Lancs. v Surrey, The Oval
105 Lancs. v Oxford U., Oxford
203* Lancs. v Warwicks., Coventry
109* Lancs. v Essex, Colchester

N. A. Felton (4)
119* Northants v Notts., Nottingham
122 Northants v Glam., Northampton
101 Northants v Somerset, Taunton
106 Northants v Yorks., Northampton

A. Fordham (4)
206* Northants v Yorks., Leeds
128 Northants v Somerset, Taunton
172 Northants v Lancs., Northampton
159 Northants v Essex, Chelmsford

M. W. Gatting (4)
170* Middx v Somerset, Uxbridge
101 Middx v Kent, Canterbury
169* Middx v Notts., Nottingham
119* Middx v Derbys., Derby

A. N. Hayhurst (4)
110* Somerset v Glam., Cardiff
170 Somerset v Sussex, Taunton
119 Somerset v Worcs., Worcester
170 Somerset v Yorks., Scarborough

S. G. Hinks (4)
107 Kent v Glam., Swansea
120 Kent v Surrey, Guildford
234 Kent v Middx, Canterbury
163 Kent v Leics., Leicester

S. P. James (4)
116 Cambridge U. v Glos., Cambridge
104* Cambridge U. v Notts., Cambridge
131* Oxford & Camb. Univs v New Zealanders, Cambridge
102 Cambridge U. v Sussex, Hove

N. J. Lenham (4)
121 Sussex v Hants, Southampton
108 Sussex v Somerset, Taunton
109* Sussex v Surrey, Guildford
123 Sussex v Somerset, Hove

G. D. Mendis (4)
102 Lancs. v Surrey, The Oval
113 Lancs. v Leics., Manchester
114 Lancs. v Middx, Manchester
180 Lancs. v Notts., Southport

A. J. Moles (4)
128* Warwicks. v Middx, Lord's
100* Warwicks. v Lancs., Coventry
224* Warwicks. v Glam., Swansea
117 Warwicks. v Sri Lankans, Birmingham

R. T. Robinson (4)
125* Notts. v Somerset, Weston-super-Mare
123 Notts. v Glos., Nottingham
105 Notts. v Middx, Lord's
220* Notts. v Yorks., Nottingham

C. L. Smith (4)
148 Hants v Oxford U., Oxford
128 Hants v Essex, Southampton
132* Hants v Sussex, Arundel
111 Hants v Surrey, Southampton

J. P. Stephenson (4)
202* Essex v Somerset, Bath
147 Essex v New Zealanders, Chelmsford
131* Essex v Leics., Leicester
116 TCCB Under-25 XI v Indians, Birmingham

A. P. Wells (4)
137 Sussex v Cambridge U., Hove
102* Sussex v Northants, Northampton
144* Sussex v Warwicks., Eastbourne
109* Sussex v Leics., Leicester

J. J. Whitaker (4)
107* Leics. v Lancs., Manchester
124* Leics. v Oxford U., Oxford
116 Leics. v Derbys., Leicester
100 Leics. v Kent, Leicester

C. W. J. Athey (3)
131 Glos. v Sussex, Hove
108* } Glos. v Warwicks., Bristol
122 }

P. D. Bowler (3)
120 Derbys. v Warwicks., Derby
115* Derbys. v Lancs., Liverpool
210 Derbys. v Kent, Chesterfield

D. J. Capel (3)
113 Northants v Glam., Northampton
123 Northants v New Zealanders, Northampton
103* Northants v Derbys., Chesterfield

P. A. Cottey (3)
156 Glam. v Oxford U., Oxford
125 Glam. v Leics., Hinckley
100* Glam. v Worcs., Abergavenny

C. S. Cowdrey (3)
107 Kent v Hants, Canterbury
102* Kent v Cambridge U., Cambridge
107* Kent v Northants, Northampton

G. R. Cowdrey (3)
116 Kent v Essex, Maidstone
119* Kent v Surrey, Guildford
135 Kent v Leics., Leicester

K. M. Curran (3)
103* Glos. v Somerset, Bristol
144* Glos. v Sussex, Bristol
101* Glos. v Hants, Southampton

D. I. Gower (3)
145 Hants v Sussex, Southampton
126* Hants v Indians, Southampton
157* England v India, The Oval

R. J. Harden (3)
104 Somerset v New Zealanders, Taunton
101 Somerset v Yorks., Scarborough
104* Somerset v Surrey, Weston-super-Mare

P. Johnson (3)
165* Notts. v Northants, Nottingham
112* Notts. v Oxford U., Oxford
149 Notts. v Yorks., Scarborough

G. J. Lord (3)
101 Worcs. v Lancs., Kidderminster
190 Worcs. v Hants, Worcester
127 Worcs. v Glam., Worcester

M. D. Moxon (3)
130 Yorks. v Zimbabweans, Leeds
123 Yorks. v Notts., Scarborough
218* Yorks. v Sussex, Eastbourne

D. A. Reeve (3)
102* Warwicks. v Cambridge U., Cambridge
202* Warwicks. v Northants, Northampton
121* Warwicks. v Lancs., Manchester

M. A. Roseberry (3)
122 Middx v Surrey, Lord's
135 Middx v Essex, Ilford
115 Middx v Northants, Luton

C. J. Tavaré (3)
120* Somerset v Glam., Cardiff
156 Somerset v New Zealanders, Taunton
219 Somerset v Sussex, Hove

C. J. Adams (2)
111* Derbys. v Cambridge U., Cambridge
101 Derbys. v Yorks., Scarborough

R. I. Alikhan (2)
119 Surrey v Middx, The Oval
138 Surrey v Essex, The Oval

M. W. Alleyne (2)
118 Glos. v Surrey, Cheltenham
256 Glos. v Northants, Northampton

P. Bainbridge (2)
152 Glos. v Yorks., Cheltenham
129 Glos. v Worcs., Bristol

T. J. Boon (2)
128 Leics. v Somerset, Leicester
138 Leics. v Glos., Gloucester

M. A. Crawley (2)
103* Oxford U. v Glam., Oxford
105* Oxford U. v Leics., Oxford

P. A. J. DeFreitas (2)
102 Lancs. v Oxford U., Oxford
100* Lancs. v Northants, Northampton

A. I. C. Dodemaide (2)
110* Sussex v New Zealanders, Hove
112 Sussex v Somerset, Hove

D. B. D'Oliveira (2)
155 Worcs. v Lancs., Manchester
121 Worcs. v Glam., Abergavenny

G. Fowler (2)
115* Lancs. v Leics., Manchester
126 Lancs. v Glos., Manchester

M. J. Greatbatch (2)
168* } M. Parkinson's World XI v Indians, Scarborough
128* }

I. A. Greig (2)
291 Surrey v Lancs., The Oval
123* Surrey v Somerset, Weston-super-Mare

J. W. Hall (2)
120* Sussex v New Zealanders, Hove
125 Sussex v Notts., Nottingham

B. R. Hardie (2)
125 Essex v Hants, Southampton
110* Essex v Glos., Ilford

G. D. Hodgson (2)
126 Glos. v Zimbabweans, Bristol
109 Glos. v Worcs., Bristol

W. Larkins (2)
107 Northants v Surrey, The Oval
207 Northants v Essex, Northampton

M. D. Marshall (2)
117 Hants v Yorks., Leeds
112 Hants v Leics., Leicester

D. J. R. Martindale (2)
108* Notts. v Northants, Nottingham
138 Notts. v Cambridge U., Cambridge

M. P. Maynard (2)
125* Glam. v Northants, Northampton
115 Glam. v Notts., Worksop

P. A. Neale (2)
122 Worcs. v Notts., Worcester
119* Worcs. v Kent, Canterbury

P. W. G. Parker (2)
100 Sussex v Surrey, Hove
107 Sussex v Kent, Folkestone

D. W. Randall (2)
120 Notts. v Leics., Leicester
178 Notts. v Kent, Tunbridge Wells

B. Roberts (2)
124* Derbys. v Yorks., Chesterfield
100* Derbys. v Kent, Chesterfield

P. M. Roebuck (2)
114* Somerset v Warwicks., Taunton
201* Somerset v Worcs., Worcester

R. C. Russell (2)
120 Glos. v Somerset, Bristol
103* Glos. v Notts., Nottingham

M. P. Speight (2)
131 Sussex v Glam., Hove
108 Sussex v Surrey, Guildford

T. R. Ward (2)
124 Kent v Derbys., Chesterfield
175 Kent v Hants, Bournemouth

C. M. Wells (2)
113* Sussex v New Zealanders, Hove
107 Sussex v Hants, Arundel

P. Willey (2)
177 Leics. v Oxford U., Oxford
112 Leics. v Sussex, Leicester

The following each played one three-figure innings:

Asif Din, 100*, Warwicks. v Cambridge U., Cambridge.

W. K. M. Benjamin, 101*, Leics. v Derbys., Leicester; J. D. R. Benson, 106, Leics. v Indians, Leicester; I. R. Bishop, 103*, Derbys. v Yorks., Scarborough; R. J. Blakey, 111, Yorks. v Somerset, Scarborough; I. T. Botham, 113, Worcs. v Surrey, The Oval; A. M. Brown, 139*, Derbys. v Northants, Chesterfield; G. K. Brown, 103, Minor Counties v Indians, Trowbridge; N. D. Burns, 166, Somerset v Glos., Taunton; I. P. Butcher, 102, Glos. v Middx, Lord's.

G. S. Clinton, 146, Surrey v Northants, The Oval; R. M. F. Cox, 104*, Hants v Worcs., Worcester.

J. E. Emburey, 111*, Middx v Hants, Bournemouth; K. P. Evans, 100*, Notts. v Somerset, Weston-super-Mare.

M. A. Feltham, 101, Surrey v Middx, The Oval; M. V. Fleming, 102, Kent v Notts., Tunbridge Wells; N. A. Foster, 101, Essex v Leics., Chelmsford; B. N. French, 105*, Notts. v Derbys., Derby.

K. Greenfield, 102*, Sussex v Cambridge U., Hove.

W. K. Hegg, 100*, Lancs. v Essex, Colchester; G. C. Holmes, 125*, Glam. v Somerset, Cardiff; N. Hussain, 197, Essex v Surrey, The Oval.

R. K. Illingworth, 117, Worcs. v Notts., Worcester.

K. D. James, 104*, Hants v Kent, Canterbury.

C. C. Lewis, 189*, Leics. v Essex, Chelmsford; J. J. B. Lewis, 116*, Essex v Surrey, The Oval; T. A. Lloyd, 101, Warwicks. v Glam., Swansea; M. A. Lynch, 104, Surrey v Somerset, Weston-super-Mare.

S. A. Marsh, 114*, Kent v Notts., Tunbridge Wells; P. Moores, 106*, Sussex v Glam., Hove; Mudassar Nazar, 107*, M. Parkinson's World XI v Indians, Scarborough.
M. Newell, 112, Notts. v Sri Lankans, Cleethorpes; M. C. J. Nicholas, 104, Hants v Indians, Southampton.
T. J. G. O'Gorman, 100, Derbys. v Leics., Derby.
A. L. Penberthy, 101*, Northants v Cambridge U., Cambridge; I. L. Philip, 100, Scotland v Ireland, Edinburgh (Myreside); K. J. Piper, 111, Warwicks. v Somerset, Birmingham; L. Potter, 109*, Leics. v Yorks., Sheffield.
D. Ripley, 109*, Northants v Leics., Leicester; C. M. Robertson, 125, Zimbabweans v Lancs., Manchester; P. E. Robinson, 150*, Yorks. v Derbys., Scarborough.
A. H. Shah, 185, Zimbabweans v Glos., Bristol; N. Shahid, 125, Essex v Lancs., Colchester; I. Smith, 112*, Glam. v Lancs., Colwyn Bay; P. A. Smith, 117, Warwicks. v Glam., Birmingham; N. J. Speak, 138, Lancs. v Zimbabweans, Manchester; F. D. Stephenson, 121, Notts. v Leics., Nottingham; A. J. Stewart, 100*, Surrey v Hants, The Oval.
S. J. S. Warke, 100*, Ireland v Scotland, Edinburgh (Myreside); M. Watkinson, 138, Lancs. v Yorks., Manchester; A. J. Wright, 112, Glos. v Northants, Cheltenham.
G. Yates, 106, Lancs. v Notts., Nottingham.

TEN WICKETS IN A MATCH

There were thirteen instances of bowlers taking ten or more wickets in a match in first-class cricket in 1990, seventeen fewer than in 1989. The list includes twelve in the County Championship and one by the New Zealand touring team. Two of the instances occurred in the same match and for the same side, when R. P. Davis and M. M. Patel shared all twenty wickets for Kent against Leicestershire at Dartford.

M. D. Marshall (2): 10-107, Hants v Derbys., Portsmouth; 11-92, Hants v Glam., Pontypridd.

The following each took ten wickets in a match on one occasion:

C. E. L. Ambrose, 12-155, Northants v Leics., Leicester.
J. G. Bracewell, 12-227, New Zealanders v Oxford & Cambridge Univs, Cambridge.
R. P. Davis, 10-142, Kent v Leics., Dartford.
N. A. Foster, 11-76, Essex v Surrey, Chelmsford; M. Frost, 10-82, Glam. v Glos., Bristol.
D. A. Graveney, 10-104, Glos. v Sussex, Bristol.
C. C. Lewis, 10-119, Leics. v Glam., Cardiff.
M. M. Patel, 10-148, Kent v Leics., Dartford; R. A. Pick, 10-184, Notts. v Leics., Leicester.
C. A. Walsh, 11-99, Glos. v Northants, Cheltenham.
Waqar Younis, 11-128, Surrey v Warwicks., The Oval.

COUNTY BENEFITS AWARDED IN 1991

Essex	D. E. East.
Glamorgan	G. C. Holmes.
Gloucestershire	P. W. Romaines.
Hampshire	M. C. J. Nicholas.
Kent	M. R. Benson.
Lancashire	G. Fowler.
Middlesex	S. P. Hughes.
Nottinghamshire	B. N. French.
Surrey	M. A. Lynch.
Sussex	A. C. S. Pigott.
Yorkshire	K. Sharp.

No benefit was awarded by Derbyshire, Leicestershire, Northamptonshire, Somerset, Warwickshire or Worcestershire.

THE CRICKET COUNCIL

The Cricket Council, which was set up in 1968 and reconstituted in 1974 and 1983, acts as the governing body for cricket in the British Isles. It comprises the following, the officers listed being those for 1989-90.

Chairman: R. Subba Row.
Vice-Chairman: J. D. Robson.
8 Representatives of the Test and County Cricket Board: R. Subba Row, C. R. M. Atkinson, D. J. Insole, F. G. Mann, M. P. Murray, D. N. Perry, H. J. Pocock, F. M. Turner.
5 Representatives of the National Cricket Association: J. D. Robson, F. R. Brown, F. H. Elliott, E. K. Ingman, J. G. Overy.
3 Representatives of the Marylebone Cricket Club: G. H. G. Doggart, N. E. J. Pocock, Sir Denys Roberts.
1 Representative (non-voting) of the Minor Counties Cricket Association: G. L. B. August.
1 Representative (non-voting) of the Irish Cricket Union: D. Scott.
1 Representative (non-voting) of the Scottish Cricket Union: R. W. Barclay.

Secretary: A. C. Smith.

THE TEST AND COUNTY CRICKET BOARD

The TCCB was set up in 1968 to be responsible for Test matches, official tours, and first-class and minor county competitions. It is composed of representatives of the seventeen first-class counties; Marylebone Cricket Club; Minor Counties Cricket Association; Oxford University Cricket Club, Cambridge University Cricket Club, the Irish Cricket Union and the Scottish Cricket Union.

Officers 1989-90

Chairman: R. Subba Row.

Chairmen of Committees: R. Subba Row (Executive); D. B. Carr (County Pitches); O. S. Wheatley (Cricket), D. J. Insole (Overseas Tours); P. R. Bromage (Discipline); M. P. Murray (Finance); C. R. M. Atkinson (PR and Marketing); D. R. W. Silk (Registration); E. R. Dexter (England Committee); A. C. Smith (Umpires); Revd M. D. Vockins (Under-25 and Second XI Competitions).

Chief Executive: A. C. Smith. *Cricket Secretary:* T. M. Lamb. *Assistant Secretary (Administration):* A. S. Brown. *Accountant:* C. A. Barker. *England Tour Manager:* P. M. Lush. *England Team Manager:* M. J. Stewart. *Media Relations Manager:* P. W. Smith.

THE NATIONAL CRICKET ASSOCIATION

With the setting up of the Cricket Council in 1968 it was necessary to form a separate organisation to represent the interests of all cricket below the first-class game, and it is the National Cricket Association that carries out this function. It comprises representatives from 51 county cricket associations and seventeen national cricketing organisations.

Officers 1989-90

President: F. R. Brown.
Chairman: J. D. Robson.
Vice-Chairman: F. H. Elliott.
Chief Executive: K. V. Andrew.
General Secretary: B. J. Aspital.
Hon. Treasurer: D. W. Carter.

THE NEW ZEALANDERS IN ENGLAND, 1990

New Zealand arrived for their twelfth tour of England with realistic hopes of winning their second successive Test series there. When they left, having lost the three-match series 1-0, there was a distinct feeling among their supporters that the side had played below their potential. Certainly, through no particular fault, the tour fell somewhat flat. In a summer as memorable for high temperatures as high scores, it was blighted at crucial stages by poor weather, and the succeeding tour by India, with its dazzling batting, did the New Zealanders no favours in comparison. Moreover, they came up against an England side with a significantly stiffer backbone than that of a year earlier.

The touring team, spearheaded by their amiable captain, John Wright, and their greatest player, Richard Hadlee, was one of considerable talent and vast experience, with, in addition to their traditional doughty fighters, a clutch of players selected with an eye to the future. Although losing the one-day fixture against MCC, they made a promising start. Inspired perhaps by an enterprising sponsorship of the eight three-day matches against the counties, their cricket was entertaining, even if at times it was, through necessity, contrived at the business end.

However, there was a school of thought which, with the benefit of hindsight, held that the emphasis of the tour should have changed once the tourists were no longer eligible for the Tetley Challenge bonus for winning all the county matches. At least one senior player believed that, rather than continuing to play positive, spectator-pleasing cricket, the New Zealanders should have approached the remaining county games with the Test matches in mind. If that meant batting for the first day and a half of a three-day match, it was suggested, then so be it.

By the final Test, at Edgbaston early in July, the touring team had had wins over Worcestershire – on the liveliest pitch of the tour – Somerset, Sussex and Derbyshire, and had drawn with England twice, Middlesex, Warwickshire, Northamptonshire and Essex. Their one first-class defeat had been to the combined Oxford & Cambridge Universities – whose first win it was over a touring side – and they had shared the two-match one-day series, though failing on run-rate to win the Texaco Trophy. It was suggested by Wright that the success of the tour would be judged by the result of the final Test, for the Test matches are history's criteria. In the event England won, deservedly, by 114 runs after the New Zealand captain had erred badly by putting them in.

The Birmingham Test brought down the curtain on Hadlee's remarkable career. With his impeccable sense of occasion, he took his 431st and final wicket with his last ball in a Test. Although past his finest days, he showed he could still severely embarrass the world's top batsmen. Before the Lord's Test Hadlee had been awarded a knighthood for his services to the game, the first New Zealander so honoured, and if there was criticism of the timing of the announcement, there was precious little doubt about the worthiness of the recipient. Hadlee's knighthood also made the Lord's Test scorecard a unique modern-day sporting document.

Before the tour began, it was felt that run-scoring would not be a problem, but bowling out the opposition would. That suspicion was well founded, especially when the Test and County Cricket Board's edicts on the summer's pitches and the ball's seam were added to the equation. The New Zealanders simply did not have sufficient penetration. Even Sussex, destined to finish last in the 1990 County Championship, managed 570 runs against them for the loss of only six wickets. The most successful bowler was the experienced off-spinner, John Bracewell, who was making his third tour of England. He missed eight matches with a finger injury at the start but, always competitive, he finished with 34 first-class wickets, having, despite his absences, bowled the most overs. His four dismissals in the second innings at Birmingham gave him 102 Test wickets and, after he had passed 1,000 Test runs in the first innings, made him only the second New Zealander, after Hadlee, to complete such a double. By then he had also proved himself to be the world's best attacking off-spinner.

Martin Snedden, another to retire from international cricket at the end of the visit, bowled his nagging medium pace as well as ever for much of the tour. But the sustained aggression expected from Danny Morrison was seen all too infrequently. Nor did injuries help. Chris Pringle and the former Test player, Willie Watson, both just above medium pace, were called into the side from the Bradford and Northern Leagues respectively to cover during a time when the tour party had just one fit fast bowler, the gangling Jonathan Millmow. Misfortune eventually caught up with him at Northampton, with shin splints ending his first senior tour.

Although all the batsmen had their moments, only the tall opener, Trevor Franklin, was able to look back with any real satisfaction. Unspectacular but effective, he arrived in England as a batsman still trying to establish a regular Test place. He finished the tour having topped the Test and first-class aggregates, and only the England opening pair, Graham Gooch and Michael Atherton, bettered his average of 56.75 in the Tests. With Wright he set a New Zealand first-wicket record for Tests in England, putting on 185 at Lord's, and he went on to his maiden Test hundred. Wright, however, fell 2 runs short of his eleventh Test century, a personal disappointment on his final overseas tour. He scored fewer runs than he would have liked, but he proved himself to be perhaps New Zealand's most popular captain ever, even if his Test leadership tended towards a safety-first approach.

New Zealand's premier batsman, Martin Crowe, had a disappointing tour. Runmaking appeared to come all too easily in the county matches, but he passed 50 only once in the Tests. Mark Greatbatch's centuries in the one-day internationals, innings of clean, powerful strokeplay, were probably the finest of the tour. However, impetuosity was his downfall more than once, and he did not really do himself justice. Nor did Andrew Jones, another of whom much was expected. Jones did as well as anyone against the counties, but England found a technical weakness against the short ball and capitalised on it in the Tests. Ken Rutherford did not recover fully from a nasty blow above the left eyebrow in the second one-day international, while Jeff Crowe was always battling for a Test place.

Of the younger players, none did better than the wicket-keeper, Adam Parore, and the left-arm spinner, Mark Priest. Parore, aged nineteen, made his Test début at Edgbaston when injury ruled out the experienced Ian Smith, and although showing that some fine tuning of his glovework was needed, he revealed that he was a technically sound batsman of whom much more should be heard. Priest worked hard at his game, played in one Test and should have had a second chance. He struggled for wickets but fielded well and performed tidily with the bat. – David Leggat.

NEW ZEALAND TOUR RESULTS

Test matches – Played 3: Lost 1, Drawn 2.
First-class matches – Played 12: Won 4, Lost 2, Drawn 6.
Wins – Derbyshire, Somerset, Sussex, Worcestershire.
Losses – England, Oxford & Cambridge Universities.
Draws – England (2), Essex, Middlesex, Northamptonshire, Warwickshire.
One-day internationals – Played 2: Won 1, Lost 1.
Other non first-class matches – Played 5: Won 3, Lost 2. *Wins* – Ireland (2), Lavinia Duchess of Norfolk's XI. *Losses* – Leicestershire, MCC.

TEST MATCH AVERAGES

ENGLAND – BATTING

	T	*I*	*NO*	*R*	*HI*	*100s*	*Avge*
M. A. Atherton	3	5	0	357	151	1	71.40
G. A. Gooch	3	5	0	306	154	1	61.20
G. C. Small	3	4	2	84	44*	0	42.00
A. J. Lamb	3	5	1	129	84*	0	32.25
R. A. Smith	3	5	0	152	64	0	30.40
A. J. Stewart	3	5	0	147	54	0	29.40
P. A. J. DeFreitas	2	2	0	52	38	0	26.00
R. C. Russell	3	4	0	84	43	0	21.00
N. H. Fairbrother	3	5	1	59	33*	0	14.75
E. E. Hemmings	3	4	1	33	20	0	11.00
D. E. Malcolm	3	4	2	4	4*	0	2.00

Played in one Test: C. C. Lewis 32, 1.

* *Signifies not out.*

BOWLING

	O	*M*	*R*	*W*	*BB*	*5W/i*	*Avge*
D. E. Malcolm	118.4	38	269	15	5-46	2	17.93
E. E. Hemmings	107.3	44	215	10	6-58	1	21.50
P. A. J. DeFreitas	59.4	9	175	6	5-53	1	29.16
G. C. Small	104	27	290	5	2-49	0	58.00

Also bowled: M. A. Atherton 10–6–17–0; G. A. Gooch 13–7–25–0; C. C. Lewis 41–8–127–4.

NEW ZEALAND – BATTING

	T	*I*	*NO*	*R*	*HI*	*100s*	*Avge*
T. J. Franklin	3	5	1	227	101	1	56.75
J. G. Wright	3	5	0	177	98	0	35.40
I. D. S. Smith	2	2	1	29	27	0	29.00
M. J. Greatbatch	3	4	0	115	47	0	28.75
A. H. Jones	3	5	0	143	49	0	28.60
Sir R. J. Hadlee	3	4	0	107	86	0	26.75
M. D. Crowe	3	4	0	96	59	0	24.00
M. C. Snedden	3	4	2	36	21*	0	18.00
K. R. Rutherford	2	3	0	47	29	0	15.66
J. G. Bracewell	3	4	0	57	28	0	14.25
D. K. Morrison	3	5	2	9	6	0	3.00

Played in one Test: A. C. Parore 12*, 20; M. W. Priest 26.

* *Signifies not out.*

BOWLING

	O	M	R	W	BB	5W/i	Avge
Sir R. J. Hadlee	133.5	24	384	16	5-53	1	24.00
J. G. Bracewell	148	41	400	12	4-38	0	33.33
M. C. Snedden	101	30	264	6	3-106	0	44.00
D. K. Morrison	85.4	15	351	7	4-64	0	50.14

Also bowled: A. H. Jones 13–3–42–1; M. W. Priest 12–4–26–1; K. R. Rutherford 3–0–18–0.

NEW ZEALAND AVERAGES – FIRST-CLASS MATCHES

BATTING

	M	I	NO	R	HI	100s	Avge
M. D. Crowe	9	13	3	537	123*	1	53.70
A. H. Jones	10	16	3	692	121*	1	53.23
J. G. Wright	9	15	2	653	121	1	50.23
K. R. Rutherford	8	13	5	376	68*	0	47.00
T. J. Franklin	11	17	1	731	103	2	45.68
J. J. Crowe	8	15	4	493	132	1	44.81
M. W. Priest	9	11	3	345	72	0	43.12
M. J. Greatbatch	10	14	1	448	85	0	34.46
Sir R. J. Hadlee	5	6	0	204	90	0	34.00
J. G. Bracewell	8	8	3	169	40*	0	33.80
S. A. Thomson	5	5	4	32	20	0	32.00
A. C. Parore	7	6	1	131	43	0	26.20
I. D. S. Smith	6	4	1	65	34	0	21.66
M. C. Snedden	7	6	3	38	21*	0	12.66
C. Pringle	4	1	0	6	6	0	6.00
D. K. Morrison	9	6	2	14	6	0	3.50

Played in five matches: J. P. Millmow 2*. Played in two matches: W. Watson 17*.

* *Signifies not out.*

BOWLING

	O	M	R	W	BB	5W/i	Avge
Sir R. J. Hadlee	201.5	39	586	24	5-27	2	24.41
M. C. Snedden	231.5	56	633	23	5-63	1	27.52
J. G. Bracewell	383.3	102	1,120	34	7-120	2	32.94
J. P. Millmow	105	14	391	11	3-66	0	35.54
D. K. Morrison	234.4	36	889	21	4-64	0	42.33
C. Pringle	130	31	398	8	2-67	0	49.75
M. W. Priest	312.4	90	907	14	3-35	0	64.78
S. A. Thomson	106.2	18	435	5	2-84	0	87.00

Also bowled: M. D. Crowe 8–3–20–0; A. H. Jones 26–4–87–3; K. R. Rutherford 42–3–196–0; W. Watson 54–10–177–3.

FIELDING

15 – A. C. Parore (14 ct, 1 st); 7 – K. R. Rutherford; 6 – J. J. Crowe, M. W. Priest; 5 – J. G. Bracewell, M. D. Crowe, M. J. Greatbatch, I. D. S. Smith, S. A. Thomson; 4 – Sir R. J. Hadlee; 3 – T. J. Franklin, A. H. Jones, D. K. Morrison, M. C. Snedden, Substitutes; 2 – J. P. Millmow, C. Pringle, J. G. Wright.

HUNDREDS FOR NEW ZEALANDERS

The following eight three-figure innings were played for the New Zealanders, six in first-class matches and two in non first-class matches.

T. J. Franklin (2)
103 v Somerset, Taunton
101 v England, Lord's (Second Test)

M. J. Greatbatch (2)
†102* v England, Leeds (First Texaco Trophy)
†111 v England, The Oval (Second Texaco Trophy)

J. J. Crowe (1)
132 v Oxford & Cambridge Univs, Cambridge

M. D. Crowe (1)
123* v Essex, Chelmsford

A. H. Jones (1)
121* v Derbys., Derby

J. G. Wright (1)
121 v Essex, Chelmsford

* *Signifies not out.* † *Not first-class.*

Note: Those matches which follow which were not first-class are signified by the use of a dagger.

†LAVINIA, DUCHESS OF NORFOLK'S XI v NEW ZEALANDERS

At Arundel, May 6. New Zealanders won by seven wickets. Toss: Lavinia, Duchess of Norfolk's XI. A crowd of 8,000 saw acting-captain Martin Crowe and Rutherford run up 96 in ten overs to win the tourists' opening fixture with nearly three overs to spare. Crowe's 89 not out came from 58 deliveries, and included two sixes and ten fours, six of them in the last sixteen balls, which brought him 39 runs. Earlier his brother, Jeff, and Franklin had given the team a solid start with 81 from 21 overs for the first wicket, Franklin hitting powerfully for his 82. The highlight of the invitation team's innings was Dodemaide's century. Sussex's Australian all-rounder took 143 balls to make 131, and put on 180 with Parker, his county captain, against an attack which was missing Hadlee.

Lavinia, Duchess of Norfolk's XI

I. J. F. Hutchinson b Priest	19
A. I. C. Dodemaide c sub b Snedden	131
*P. W. G. Parker c Priest b Millmow	90
A. P. Wells c M. D. Crowe b Millmow	16
M. P. Speight lbw b Snedden	0
C. M. Wells run out	2
†I. J. Gould not out	1
L-b 16, w 1, n-b 1	18
1/59 2/239 3/262 4/263 5/274 6/277 (6 wkts, 50 overs)	277

V. J. Marks, J. K. Lever, A. R. Hansford and J. Boiling did not bat.

Bowling: Millmow 10–2–55–2; Thomson 10–2–58–0; Priest 10–1–42–1; Snedden 10–1–42–2; Bracewell 9–0–57–0; Rutherford 1–0–7–0.

New Zealanders

J. J. Crowe b Hansford	43
T. J. Franklin b Lever	82
M. J. Greatbatch c Hansford b Boiling	20
*M. D. Crowe not out	89
K. R. Rutherford not out	32
B 1, l-b 11	12
1/81 2/114 3/182 (3 wkts, 47.2 overs)	278

S. A. Thomson, M. W. Priest, J. G. Bracewell, †A. C. Parore, M. C. Snedden and J. P. Millmow did not bat.

Bowling: Lever 9–1–48–1; C. M. Wells 10–1–39–0; Marks 10–0–63–0; Boiling 9–0–57–1; Hansford 9–0–58–1; Parker 0.2–0–1–0.

Umpires: C. Cook and J. G. Langridge.

†MCC v NEW ZEALANDERS

At Lord's, May 7. MCC won by six wickets. Toss: MCC. Gower's fluent 97 in 104 balls provided handsome entertainment for a good Bank Holiday crowd, whose appetite had earlier been whetted by the powerful strokeplay of Greatbatch and enjoyable cameos from Jones and Martin Crowe. The former Essex and England left-armer, Lever, playing in his second match against the tourists, had accounted for the elder Crowe with a breathtaking caught and bowled, low and to his right, in the opening overs. Gower, captaining an MCC side made up otherwise of players from Gloucestershire, Hampshire and Middlesex, drove his first ball to the cover boundary and, helped by 17 runs in one over from Morrison, went to 52 off 47 balls with the fifth of his eleven fours. He also hit two sixes. Brown, who added 109 with Gower, reached his fifty from 70 balls and stayed to see MCC to victory with four overs in hand. For the New Zealanders, Snedden bowled well and Parore's wicket-keeping again made a good impression.

Man of the Match: K. R. Brown.

New Zealanders

T. J. Franklin c Tufnell b Tremlett 29
J. J. Crowe c and b Lever 1
A. H. Jones st Parks b Bainbridge 49
M. J. Greatbatch c Wright b Jarvis ... 52
S. A. Thomson b Bainbridge 5
*M. D. Crowe c Parks b Tremlett 26
M. W. Priest c Bainbridge b Jarvis 28
†A. C. Parore run out 6
M. C. Snedden not out 8
B 1, l-b 2, w 15 18

1/8 2/44 3/129 4/135 5/164 6/178 7/206 8/222 (8 wkts, 55 overs) 222

D. K. Morrison and J. P. Millmow did not bat.

Bowling: Jarvis 11–1–49–2; Lever 11–1–45–1; Tufnell 11–1–42–0; Tremlett 11–0–50–2; Bainbridge 11–1–33–2.

MCC

V. P. Terry b Millmow 4
A. J. Wright c Parore b Snedden 8
*D. I. Gower c Parore b Snedden 97
M. R. Ramprakash c M. D. Crowe b Snedden . 6
K. R. Brown not out 79
P. Bainbridge not out 19
B 4, l-b 3, w 4 11

1/8 2/46 3/62 4/171 (4 wkts, 50.5 overs) 224

T. M. Tremlett, †R. J. Parks, J. K. Lever, P. C. R. Tufnell and K. B. S. Jarvis did not bat.

Bowling: Morrison 5–1–33–0; Millmow 10–0–43–1; Snedden 10–3–28–3; Thomson 9.5–1–40–0; Priest 11–0–40–0; Jones 5–0–33–0.

Umpires: J. D. Bond and R. Julian.

†IRELAND v NEW ZEALANDERS

At Downpatrick, May 9. New Zealanders won by seven wickets. Toss: New Zealanders. The first New Zealand touring team to visit Ireland since 1965, when a first-class match was played in Belfast, had no difficulty winning the first of two one-day matches sponsored by Gilbey's Ulster Games. Only Lamba, the Indian Test cricketer, playing his first game as Ireland's professional, really came to terms with the New Zealanders' bowling, adding 69 for the third wicket with Warke. Wright, in his first game of the tour, set the New Zealanders on their way with a brisk 49 in an opening stand of 71, and Crowe hit three sixes and a four in a rapid 48 before the visitors won with eighteen overs to spare.

Ireland

M. F. Cohen c Hadlee b Millmow 8
R. Lamba c Smith b Hadlee 52
M. A. F. Nulty c Franklin b Millmow . 1
S. J. S. Warke c Smith b Hadlee 23
G. D. Harrison lbw b Millmow 6
D. A. Lewis b Snedden 19
T. J. T. Patterson run out 9
N. E. Thompson b Snedden 2
*†P. B. Jackson b Hadlee 6
P. McCrum not out 1
P. O'Reilly not out 1
B 2, l-b 8, w 4, n-b 9 23

1/25 2/30 3/99 4/100 5/120 6/138 7/138 8/149 9/149 (9 wkts, 55 overs) 151

Bowling: Hadlee 11–1–25–3; Millmow 11–1–28–3; Snedden 11–1–27–2; Thomson 11–3–30–0; Priest 11–1–31–0.

New Zealanders

T. J. Franklin c O'Reilly b Thompson . 26
*J. G. Wright run out 49
M. D. Crowe c Jackson b McCrum . . . 48
K. R. Rutherford not out 13
S. A. Thomson not out 1
L-b 3, w 8, n-b 4 15

1/71 2/89 3/150 (3 wkts, 36.3 overs) 152

A. H. Jones, R. J. Hadlee, †I. D. S. Smith, M. W. Priest, M. C. Snedden and J. P. Millmow did not bat.

Bowling: McCrum 7.3–2–26–1; O'Reilly 4–0–22–0; Thompson 7–0–23–1; Harrison 11–3–42–0; Lamba 6–1–27–0; Lewis 1–0–9–0.

Umpires: L. Hogan and M. Moore.

†IRELAND v NEW ZEALANDERS

At Ormeau, Belfast, May 10. New Zealanders won by 40 runs. Toss: Ireland. Although Ireland's bowlers, off-spinner Harrison in particular, did well to hold the New Zealanders to 203, their batsmen quickly fell behind the asking-rate on a slow pitch of low bounce once Hadlee had removed Cohen and Nulty in his first three overs. Water had seeped under the covers at one end, and Hadlee was a distinctly unpleasant prospect for the Irish so soon in their season.

New Zealanders

*J. G. Wright c Thompson b Harrison . 44
J. J. Crowe st Jackson b Harrison 19
A. H. Jones b Thompson 32
M. J. Greatbatch b O'Reilly 32
K. R. Rutherford c Lamba b O'Reilly . 2
R. J. Hadlee b McCrum 20
I. D. S. Smith c Patterson b Lamba . . . 19
M. W. Priest not out 18
†A. C. Parore not out 4
B 1, l-b 4, w 2, n-b 6 13

1/61 2/72 3/135 (7 wkts, 50 overs) 203
4/139 5/142
6/173 7/191

M. C. Snedden and D. K. Morrison did not bat.

Bowling: McCrum 10–0–42–1; Lamba 10–1–40–1; Harrison 10–2–25–2; O'Reilly 10–0–56–2; Thompson 10–0–35–1.

Ireland

M. F. Cohen b Hadlee 2
R. Lamba c Hadlee b Snedden 5
M. A. F. Nulty lbw b Hadlee 6
S. J. S. Warke run out 44
G. D. Harrison c Hadlee b Priest 17
D. A. Lewis c Crowe b Rutherford 18
T. J. T. Patterson b Rutherford 23
N. E. Thompson b Rutherford 8
*†P. B. Jackson st Parore b Smith 17
P. McCrum not out 9
P. O'Reilly not out 2
B 9, l-b 2, w 1 12

1/2 2/12 3/20 (9 wkts, 50 overs) 163
4/57 5/104 6/104
7/112 8/143 9/160

Bowling: Hadlee 6–2–13–2; Morrison 8–1–20–0; Snedden 5–2–4–1; Priest 10–1–39–1; Rutherford 10–1–38–3; Jones 8–1–27–0; Smith 2–0–8–1; Greatbatch 1–0–3–0.

Umpires: B. Arlow and H. Henderson.

WORCESTERSHIRE v NEW ZEALANDERS

At Worcester, May 12, 13, 14. New Zealanders won by six wickets. Toss: New Zealanders. A game of fluctuating fortunes finally swung the tourists' way through a captain's innings from Wright, who was only 1 run short of a century when he stepped back on his wicket. Set 245 to win from a minimum of 81 overs, the New Zealanders achieved the target with 7.1 overs to spare. The injury-hit county champions, without Botham, Curtis, Dilley and Rhodes, were further handicapped by the early loss of Hick, when the index finger of his left hand was broken by a rising delivery from Morrison. Yet a magnificent all-round performance from Newport gave them a scent of victory. His five for 18 in 14.2 immaculate overs left the tourists in dire straits at 113 for eight at the end of the first day, after Hadlee, with five for 27, had hurried Worcestershire out for 171. Next morning, however, Hadlee added 67 out of 74 runs off the bat to engineer a lead of 30. The New Zealanders strengthened their position by reducing Worcestershire to 59 for four – effectively five without Hick – only to meet resistance from Newport and Illingworth, who added 179 in 50 overs. Newport was just 2 runs short of a maiden century when his career-best innings, laced with eighteen fours, came to an end after 190 minutes. Wright and Franklin then provided the platform for victory with an opening stand of 163, broken when Franklin, for the second time in the match, was caught at slip off McEwan by S. Herzberg, one of several substitute fielders.

Close of play: First day, New Zealanders 113-8 (R. J. Hadlee 23*); Second day, Worcestershire 248-7 (S. R. Lampitt 5*, S. R. Bevins 1*).

Worcestershire

P. Bent b Morrison	22	– lbw b Hadlee	9
M. J. Weston c Rutherford b Hadlee	3	– c Priest b Morrison	7
G. A. Hick retired hurt	2	– absent injured	
D. B. D'Oliveira c Greatbatch b Hadlee	48	– (3) c Morrison b Hadlee	24
*P. A. Neale b Millmow	5	– (4) lbw b Millmow	15
S. R. Lampitt b Hadlee	40	– (7) b Millmow	30
R. K. Illingworth c Rutherford b Hadlee	0	– (5) c Crowe b Morrison	74
P. J. Newport c Greatbatch b Morrison	7	– (6) c Rutherford b Priest	98
N. V. Radford c Priest b Millmow	13	– (8) c and b Morrison	1
†S. R. Bevins lbw b Hadlee	10	– (9) lbw b Millmow	1
S. M. McEwan not out	1	– (10) not out	0
L-b 12, w 1, n-b 7	20	B 1, l-b 8, n-b 6	15
1/11 2/46 3/90 4/102 5/102 6/109 7/133 8/170 9/171	171	1/9 2/21 3/55 4/59 5/238 6/238 7/241 8/269 9/274	274

In the first innings G. A. Hick retired hurt at 23.

Bowling: *First Innings*—Hadlee 15–7–27–5; Morrison 20–5–46–2; Millmow 16–2–59–2; Rutherford 8–2–25–0; Priest 2–1–2–0. *Second Innings*—Morrison 16–2–60–3; Hadlee 20–3–72–2; Millmow 20.2–3–66–3; Priest 22–7–40–1; Rutherford 7–0–27–0.

New Zealanders

T. J. Franklin c sub b McEwan	28	– c sub b McEwan	50
*J. G. Wright lbw b Newport	8	– hit wkt b Illingworth	99
A. H. Jones c Bevins b Newport	1	– c Radford b Illingworth	9
M. J. Greatbatch c sub b Newport	1	– c Radford b Illingworth	19
K. R. Rutherford lbw b Weston	4	– not out	26
J. J. Crowe c Bevins b McEwan	13		
M. W. Priest c sub b Newport	13	– (6) not out	16
R. J. Hadlee c Bevins b McEwan	90		
†I. D. S. Smith c sub b Newport	2		
D. K. Morrison lbw b Newport	5		
J. P. Millmow not out	2		
B 8, l-b 12, w 10, n-b 4	34	B 4, l-b 15, w 4, n-b 3	26
1/16 2/20 3/25 4/29 5/68 6/69 7/111 8/113 9/152	201	1/163 2/172 3/196 4/203	(4 wkts) 245

Bowling: *First Innings*—Newport 26–8–54–6; McEwan 16.3–2–49–3; Weston 7–1–32–1; Illingworth 12–6–13–0; Radford 10–1–33–0. *Second Innings*—Radford 13–3–47–0; McEwan 17.5–3–69–1; Newport 19–4–56–0; Illingworth 17–5–35–3; Weston 7–1–19–0.

Umpires: J. H. Hampshire and B. J. Meyer.

SOMERSET v NEW ZEALANDERS

At Taunton, May 16, 17, 18. New Zealanders won by five wickets. Toss: Somerset. The bat dominated after Somerset's faltering start. From being 70 for three, they recovered thanks to centuries from Tavaré, whose 156 took 217 balls and included 28 fours, and Harden. Together they put on 256 in 62 overs, and Somerset were able to declare in time to snatch a wicket before the close. Franklin, who needed 219 balls for his 103 (thirteen fours), and night-watchman Parore responded with a second-wicket stand of 113 in 43 overs, and when Jones and Martin Crowe had added half-centuries the New Zealanders declared 65 runs behind. Again Somerset lost their first three wickets quickly, but Cook stayed for a hundred that took him to 567 first-class runs for the season to date; Burns and Rose provided the support, the latter hitting three sixes and six fours in 59 from 63 balls. Another declaration left the New Zealanders needing 322 from 65 overs. Runs came crisply throughout their effort, with the highlights and impetus supplied by Martin Crowe's fifty and Greatbatch, whose 85 from 81 balls featured six fours and two sixes, one into the River Tone. After them, the steady Rutherford saw the tourists home with three balls to spare.

Close of play: First day, New Zealanders 22-1 (T. J. Franklin 11*, A. C. Parore 1*); Second day, Somerset 113-3 (S. J. Cook 51*, N. D. Burns 43*).

Somerset

S. J. Cook c Parore b Thomson	31	– not out	117
P. M. Roebuck lbw b Snedden	17	– lbw b Snedden	6
J. J. E. Hardy c Parore b Snedden	13	– c Parore b Millmow	5
*C. J. Tavaré b Snedden	156		
R. J. Harden c Millmow b Priest	104		
†N. D. Burns c Parore b Snedden	1	– (5) c J. J. Crowe b Priest	59
A. N. Hayhurst not out	3	– (4) run out	2
G. D. Rose not out	12	– (6) not out	59
L-b 5, n-b 1	6	L-b 6, n-b 2	8
1/44 2/48 3/70 4/326 5/328 6/329 (6 wkts dec.)	343	1/23 2/34 3/48 4/148 (4 wkts dec.)	256

I. G. Swallow, J. C. Hallett and A. N. Jones did not bat.

Bowling: *First Innings*—Millmow 16–4–55–0; Snedden 30–7–79–4; Thomson 17–2–104–1; Priest 27–8–79–1; Rutherford 3–0–13–0; Jones 2–0–8–0. *Second Innings*—Millmow 8–1–35–1; Snedden 18–3–49–1; Rutherford 10–1–62–0; Priest 28.3–11–80–1; Jones 4–0–8–0; M. D. Crowe 5–1–16–0.

New Zealanders

T. J. Franklin lbw b Swallow	103	– (2) lbw b Hallett	30
J. J. Crowe c and b Jones	0	– (1) c Hardy b Hallett	30
†A. C. Parore c Jones b Swallow	43		
A. H. Jones not out	57	– (3) c Tavaré b Roebuck	53
*M. D. Crowe not out	55	– (4) b Jones	64
M. J. Greatbatch (did not bat)		– (5) b Rose	85
K. R. Rutherford (did not bat)		– (6) not out	46
S. A. Thomson (did not bat)		– (7) not out	4
B 9, l-b 9, w 1, n-b 1	20	B 4, l-b 4, w 1, n-b 1	10
1/9 2/122 3/201 (3 wkts dec.)	278	1/57 2/64 3/174 4/201 5/312 (5 wkts)	322

M. W. Priest, M. C. Snedden and J. P. Millmow did not bat.

Bowling: *First Innings*—Jones 9–2–20–1; Rose 16–4–33–0; Hayhurst 17–3–55–0; Hallett 14–2–52–0; Swallow 19–5–52–2; Roebuck 11–3–26–0; Harden 3–0–22–0. *Second Innings*—Jones 8–1–28–1; Rose 11–0–74–1; Hayhurst 13–1–58–0; Swallow 15–0–68–0; Hallett 11.3–0–51–2; Roebuck 6–0–35–1.

Umpires: D. J. Constant and D. R. Shepherd.

MIDDLESEX v NEW ZEALANDERS

At Lord's, May 19, 20, 21. Drawn. Toss: Middlesex. Haynes, continuing his prolific form, was the dominant figure on the first day, with 146 of his 181 runs resulting from boundaries; he took fourteen fours off Morrison and twelve off Priest. Hadlee was less hostile than usual, but the accurate Snedden sniped away at the other batsmen. Although Middlesex fielded an under-strength attack – Thursfield and Weekes were making their first-class débuts – the bowlers were not mastered until Rutherford and Priest shared a fluent stand of 114. In the second innings a more restrained Haynes hit two sixes and sixteen fours in his 129, his two hundreds for Middlesex against a touring team emulating P. H. Parfitt's feat in 1962 against the Pakistanis. Set a target of 300 in 51 overs, the New Zealanders were eager to keep alive their prospects of the bonus for winning all county games. Jones and Greatbatch added 103 from eighteen overs, but when Tufnell's four wickets put Middlesex in sight of victory, Martin Crowe, who had avoided batting because of hamstring trouble, was required to come in and secure the draw.

Close of play: First day, New Zealanders 13-0 (J. J. Crowe 8*, J. G. Wright 5*); Second day, Middlesex 64-1 (D. L. Haynes 25*, M. R. Ramprakash 36*).

Middlesex

D. L. Haynes lbw b Hadlee	181	– c and b Jones	129
M. A. Roseberry c Rutherford b Snedden	9	– c Hadlee b Morrison	0
M. R. Ramprakash c Hadlee b Snedden	21	– c Priest b Snedden	62
K. R. Brown lbw b Snedden	23	– not out	24
R. O. Butcher lbw b Snedden	0	– not out	22
*†P. R. Downton not out	57		
P. N. Weekes lbw b Snedden	22		
L-b 14, n-b 5	19	B 1, l-b 9, n-b 4	14
1/48 2/96 3/159 4/161 5/286 6/332 (6 wkts dec.)	332	1/4 2/143 3/226 (3 wkts dec.)	251

M. J. Thursfield, S. P. Hughes, N. G. Cowans and P. C. R. Tufnell did not bat.

Bowling: *First Innings*—Hadlee 22–3–78–1; Morrison 22–1–100–0; Snedden 27.5–7–63–5; Priest 22–7–77–0. *Second Innings*—Hadlee 11–2–25–0; Morrison 17–1–67–1; Priest 19–3–73–0; Jones 5–0–28–1; Snedden 8–2–22–1; Rutherford 6–0–26–0.

New Zealanders

J. J. Crowe c Downton b Cowans	14	– lbw b Cowans	20
*J. G. Wright c Weekes b Hughes	54	– c Butcher b Thursfield	18
A. H. Jones lbw b Hughes	41	– run out	70
M. D. Crowe c Downton b Tufnell	13	– (9) not out	13
M. J. Greatbatch b Hughes	34	– (4) b Weekes	52
K. R. Rutherford not out	68	– (5) st Downton b Tufnell	2
M. W. Priest not out	51	– b Tufnell	19
†I. D. S. Smith (did not bat)		– (6) c Weekes b Tufnell	34
R. J. Hadlee (did not bat)		– (8) c Roseberry b Tufnell	7
M. C. Snedden (did not bat)		– not out	0
B 7, l-b 1, n-b 1	9	B 4, l-b 3, w 1	8
1/44 2/77 3/103 4/148 5/170 (5 wkts dec.)	284	1/34 2/40 3/143 4/150 5/173 6/213 7/223 8/242 (8 wkts)	243

D. K. Morrison did not bat.

Bowling: *First Innings*—Cowans 21–4–56–1; Hughes 23.2–6–87–3; Tufnell 20–5–64–1; Thursfield 16–7–41–0; Weekes 13–6–28–0. *Second Innings*—Cowans 6–0–25–1; Hughes 6–0–38–0; Thursfield 9–0–44–1; Tufnell 17–3–76–4; Weekes 13–3–53–1.

Umpires: J. C. Balderstone and N. T. Plews.

†ENGLAND v NEW ZEALAND

First Texaco Trophy Match

At Leeds, May 23. New Zealand won by four wickets. Toss: New Zealand. With Snedden troubled by a stomach strain, the New Zealanders recruited Pringle from the Bradford League, and he it was who made the vital breakthrough, on the point of lunch, after Gooch (88 balls) and Smith had put on 113 in 27 overs. Smith, dropped when 16 off a return catch to Morrison, went on impressively to his first one-day hundred for England and had hit sixteen fours in his 128 (168 balls) when he was fifth out. Stewart's 33 from 25 balls helped the scoring-rate, and England's Pringle reached 30 from seventeen balls by hitting Hadlee's last four deliveries to the boundary. Wright and Jones gave New Zealand a sound start, averaging more than 4 an over while putting on 97, and when Gooch dismissed them both, Crowe and the left-handed Greatbatch added 118 in twenty overs. With twelve overs remaining and eight wickets in hand the target was 72. But three wickets by Lewis and a brilliant catch by Gower at short mid-wicket left them needing 37 at approximately 9 runs an over. Smith, however, responded to the crisis ebulliently, and with Greatbatch saw his side to a dramatic win. Greatbatch reached his first one-day international hundred in the final over, having hit two sixes and nine fours in 104 deliveries.

Man of the Match: M. J. Greatbatch. *Attendance:* 12,000 (est.); *receipts* £179,007.

England

*G. A. Gooch c Millmow b Pringle ... 55
D. I. Gower c Priest b Hadlee 1
R. A. Smith c Crowe b Hadlee 128
A. J. Lamb run out 18
A. J. Stewart lbw b Morrison 33
D. R. Pringle not out 30
†R. C. Russell c Crowe b Pringle 13
P. A. J. DeFreitas not out 1
L-b 10, w 1, n-b 5 16

1/5 (2) 2/118 (1) 3/168 (4) 4/225 (5) 5/261 (3) 6/274 (7) (6 wkts, 55 overs) 295

C. C. Lewis, G. C. Small and E. E. Hemmings did not bat.

Bowling: Hadlee 11–4–46–2; Pringle 11–2–45–2; Morrison 11–0–70–1; Millmow 11–0–65–0; Priest 11–0–59–0.

New Zealand

*J. G. Wright c Stewart b Gooch 52
A. H. Jones st Russell b Gooch 51
M. D. Crowe c Russell b Lewis 46
M. J. Greatbatch not out 102
K. R. Rutherford lbw b Lewis 0
R. J. Hadlee c Lamb b Lewis 12
M. W. Priest c Gower b Small 2
†I. D. S. Smith not out 17
B 5, l-b 7, w 3, n-b 1 16

1/97 (2) 2/106 (1) 3/224 (3) 4/224 (5) 5/254 (6) 6/259 (7) (6 wkts, 54.5 overs) 298

C. Pringle, J. P. Millmow and D. K. Morrison did not bat.

Bowling: Small 11–1–43–1; DeFreitas 10.5–0–70–0; Pringle 7–0–45–0; Lewis 11–0–54–3; Hemmings 11–0–51–0; Gooch 4–0–23–2.

Umpires: B. J. Meyer and N. T. Plews.

†ENGLAND v NEW ZEALAND

Second Texaco Trophy Match

At The Oval, May 25. England won by six wickets. Toss: England. Some fine fast bowling by Malcolm and Lewis, on a pitch providing pace and bounce, had New Zealand in all kinds of trouble. Wright, Jones and Crowe were out with only 53 on the board, and they then lost Rutherford and Hadlee to injuries before the fourth wicket fell. Rutherford was hit above the left eye, trying to hook Lewis early in his innings; Hadlee, struck on the right hand by Lewis, did not resume after lunch and X-rays revealed a broken bone below the knuckle. Greatbatch held the innings together, advancing defiantly to his second hundred of the series. Priest helped him add 81 and Smith 28 before Greatbatch sliced Malcolm to third man in the 54th over. His 111, from 130 balls, contained a six and ten fours. New Zealand's target hardly looked enough, but when Hadlee, despite his injured hand, removed Gower and Smith in a lovely opening spell, and Pringle trapped Lamb in the sixth over, England were themselves struggling. Gooch saw off the openers and then weathered a dangerous spell by Morrison. He lost Stewart straight after tea, having added 75 for the fourth wicket in 80 minutes, but Russell then joined him in a match-winning stand producing 109 runs in 97 minutes. Gooch hit fifteen fours in his 112 not out (152 balls), and ensured that England not only squared the series but, by winning with 5.3 overs to spare, took the Texaco Trophy on run-rate.

Man of the Match: D. E. Malcolm. *Attendance:* 13,909; *receipts* £238,490.

Men of the Series: England – G. A. Gooch; New Zealand – M. J. Greatbatch.

New Zealand

*J. G. Wright c Small b Malcolm	15
A. H. Jones run out	15
M. D. Crowe c Russell b Lewis	7
M. J. Greatbatch c Smith b Malcolm	111
K. R. Rutherford retired hurt	0
R. J. Hadlee retired hurt	9
M. W. Priest c Smith b DeFreitas	24
†I. D. S. Smith not out	25
C. Pringle b Small	1
L-b 2, w 3	5
1/25 (1) 2/34 (2) 3/53 (3) 4/174 (7) 5/202 (4) 6/212 (9) (6 wkts, 55 overs)	212

J. P. Millmow and D. K. Morrison did not bat.

K. R. Rutherford retired hurt at 53; R. J. Hadlee retired hurt at 93.

Bowling: DeFreitas 11–1–47–1; Malcolm 11–5–19–2; Lewis 11–1–51–1; Small 11–0–59–1; Hemmings 11–2–34–0.

England

*G. A. Gooch not out	112
D. I. Gower b Hadlee	4
R. A. Smith c Smith b Hadlee	5
A. J. Lamb lbw b Pringle	4
A. J. Stewart c Morrison b Priest	28
†R. C. Russell not out	47
L-b 7, w 5, n-b 1	13
1/5 (2) 2/15 (3) 3/29 (4) 4/104 (5) (4 wkts, 49.3 overs)	213

C. C. Lewis, P. A. J. DeFreitas, G. C. Small, E. E. Hemmings and D. E. Malcolm did not bat.

Bowling: Hadlee 11–2–34–2; Pringle 9.3–0–53–1; Millmow 9–1–47–0; Morrison 9–0–38–0; Priest 11–2–34–1.

Umpires: D. J. Constant and J. H. Hampshire.

SUSSEX v NEW ZEALANDERS

At Hove, May 26, 27, 28. New Zealanders won by seven wickets. Toss: Sussex. The New Zealanders won an entertaining game with fourteen balls to spare after their captain, Wright, had given them an ideal start with a fluent 82. He put on 147 with Franklin, who, having been stuck on 0 until the tenth over, eventually hit thirteen fours in his 78, and as the innings gained momentum, Jeff Crowe and Greatbatch provided belligerent half-centuries. Nevertheless Sussex, who had lost just six wickets in the match, emerged with great credit. Hall, whose previous four innings in County Championship cricket had all been in single figures, scored his maiden first-class hundred in just under six hours (322 balls), and in their second innings Dodemaide also made a maiden first-class century, his unbeaten 110 including fourteen fours and a six. Dodemaide added 188 in 49 overs with acting-captain Colin Wells, who reached 113 not out in 141 deliveries (four sixes, fourteen fours) before asking the tourists to score 341 from 71 overs.

Close of play: First day, New Zealanders 22-1 (J. J. Crowe 7*, M. W. Priest 15*); Second day, Sussex 144-2 (A. I. C. Dodemaide 52*, C. M. Wells 45*).

Sussex

	First innings		Second innings	
N. J. Lenham b Morrison	64	–	c Parore b Pringle	6
J. W. Hall not out	120	–	run out	40
A. I. C. Dodemaide b Morrison	4	–	not out	110
A. P. Wells c Parore b Thomson	86			
*C. M. Wells c Greatbatch b Pringle	8	–	(4) not out	113
I. J. Gould not out	6			
B 1, l-b 5, w 1, n-b 5	12		L-b 1	1
1/99 2/103 3/269 4/294 (4 wkts dec.)	300		1/12 2/82 (2 wkts dec.)	270

†P. Moores, I. D. K. Salisbury, B. T. P. Donelan, R. A. Bunting and A. M. Babington did not bat.

Bowling: *First Innings*—Morrison 10–2–35–2; Pringle 19–3–66–1; Thomson 18.4–6–52–1; Bracewell 34.2–9–99–0; Priest 16–4–42–0. *Second Innings*—Pringle 25–5–61–1; M. D. Crowe 3–2–4–0; Bracewell 34–5–138–0; Priest 20–3–66–0.

New Zealanders

	First innings		Second innings	
T. J. Franklin b Dodemaide	0	–	b Bunting	78
J. J. Crowe b Salisbury	48	–	(3) not out	81
M. W. Priest c Moores b Donelan	72			
M. J. Greatbatch c C. M. Wells b Bunting	26	–	(5) not out	51
M. D. Crowe c Donelan b Babington	65	–	(4) c Gould b Salisbury	24
*J. G. Wright not out	10	–	(2) c C. M. Wells b Dodemaide	82
S. A. Thomson not out	3			
B 3, l-b 1, n-b 2	6		B 15, l-b 7, n-b 3	25
1/0 2/114 3/139 4/193 5/223 (5 wkts dec.)	230		1/147 2/204 3/268 (3 wkts)	341

J. G. Bracewell, †A. C. Parore, C. Pringle and D. K. Morrison did not bat.

Bowling: *First Innings*—Dodemaide 14–2–56–1; Bunting 14–3–42–1; C. M. Wells 5–1–22–0; Babington 9–0–36–1; Salisbury 16–2–55–1; Donelan 9–3–15–1. *Second Innings*—Dodemaide 19–6–57–1; Babington 11–0–54–0; C. M. Wells 3–0–20–0; Bunting 7–0–45–1; Salisbury 14–0–80–1; Donelan 14–0–62–0; Gould 0.4–0–1–0.

Umpires: B. Hassan and D. R. Shepherd.

WARWICKSHIRE v NEW ZEALANDERS

At Birmingham, May 30, 31, June 1. Drawn. Toss: New Zealanders. Rain on the third day put paid to the possibility of an interesting finish, after a fine hundred from Moody had enabled Warwickshire to leave the tourists a target of 326 in 73 overs. The Australian's batting in both innings showed his immense power off the front foot, and he hit three sixes and fifteen fours in his 106. There were also promising performances from Warwickshire's youngsters. Ratcliffe and Twose, the latter making his highest first-class score, gave both innings a good start; Booth hit his maiden first-class fifty from 59 balls, with ten fours; and Smith hurried to 41 in 36 balls as the county looked to their second declaration. The New Zealanders' bowling, with Pringle and Watson drafted in in the absence of Hadlee and Morrison, lacked penetration, but half-centuries on the second day from Wright, Jones and Martin Crowe (47 balls) underlined the strength of their batting.

Close of play: First day, New Zealanders 12-1 (J. G. Wright 6*, M. C. Snedden 2*); Second day, Warwickshire 141-2 (T. M. Moody 42*, G. W. Humpage 30*).

Warwickshire

First innings		Second innings	
J. D. Ratcliffe c J. J. Crowe b Watson	29	c and b Bracewell	43
R. G. Twose c Pringle b Watson	64	c Wright b Millmow	21
T. M. Moody c Jones b Snedden	44	b Bracewell	106
A. I. Kallicharran c Smith b Millmow	3		
*†G. W. Humpage c Smith b Pringle	9	(4) b Pringle	46
D. P. Ostler c and b Snedden	19	(5) b Pringle	0
N. M. K. Smith c Franklin b Bracewell	24	(6) c Pringle b Bracewell	41
P. A. Booth not out	51		
A. A. Donald not out	25	(7) b Millmow	1
J. E. Benjamin (did not bat)		(8) not out	3
T. A. Munton (did not bat)		(9) b Bracewell	4
B 4, l-b 9, w 2, n-b 14	29	L-b 5, n-b 4	9
1/69 2/133 3/154 4/167 5/171 6/218 7/218 (7 wkts dec.)	297	1/52 2/93 3/186 4/200 5/259 6/267 7/269 8/274 (8 wkts dec.)	274

Bowling: *First Innings*—Millmow 18–2–64–1; Pringle 13–1–57–1; Snedden 24–3–69–2; Watson 22–6–67–2; Bracewell 17–5–27–1. *Second Innings*—Millmow 11–1–47–2; Pringle 15–3–67–2; Snedden 5–0–32–0; Bracewell 10.2–1–66–4; Watson 12–0–57–0.

New Zealanders

First innings		Second innings	
T. J. Franklin b Benjamin	2		
*J. G. Wright c sub b Twose	51	not out	2
M. C. Snedden b Benjamin	2		
A. H. Jones b Benjamin	82		
M. D. Crowe c sub b Smith	52		
J. J. Crowe not out	9	(1) not out	10
J. G. Bracewell not out	31		
B 3, l-b 6, w 6, n-b 2	17	W 3	3
1/7 2/25 3/109 4/203 5/207 (5 wkts dec.)	246	(no wkt)	15

†I. D. S. Smith, C. Pringle, W. Watson and J. P. Millmow did not bat.

Bowling: *First Innings*—Donald 13–3–24–0; Benjamin 18–4–45–3; Munton 15–3–33–0; Twose 14–6–44–1; Smith 24–8–63–1; Moody 3–0–28–0. *Second Innings*—Donald 2–0–9–0; Benjamin 1–0–2–0; Munton 2.4–0–3–0; Humpage 2–1–1–0.

Umpires: M. J. Kitchen and R. C. Tolchard.

DERBYSHIRE v NEW ZEALANDERS

At Derby, June 2, 3, 4. New Zealanders won by 82 runs. Toss: Derbyshire. Rain nearly ruined the match, although the captains were able to make something of it through declarations. There was little more than half an hour's play on the first day and none before lunch on the second, after which Jones dominated the New Zealanders' innings with an exciting 121 not out from 144 balls. Making great use of his bottom hand to place his cover drives, he hit fourteen fours, and was given lively support by Bracewell. Cork, making his first-class début, dismissed Franklin with his third ball, and the opener also became a first victim for Adams in the second innings. Derbyshire declared at their overnight total of 30 without loss and fed the tourists cheap runs before setting out to chase a target of 333 in 80 overs. Barnett was out to the first ball of the innings, and only Kuiper and Krikken diverted attention from Hadlee, practising in the nets, or threatened the New Zealanders, who won with all but two balls of the last twenty overs to spare.

Close of play: First day, New Zealanders 9-0 (T. J. Franklin 5*, J. J. Crowe 1*); Second day, Derbyshire 30-0 (K. J. Barnett 14*, P. D. Bowler 11*).

New Zealanders

T. J. Franklin c Bowler b Cork	19	– (2) c and b Adams	9
J. J. Crowe lbw b Jean-Jacques	1	– (1) c Morris b Roberts	47
A. H. Jones not out	121		
*M. D. Crowe c Krikken b Kuiper	32		
M. J. Greatbatch c and b Kuiper	3		
M. W. Priest c Bowler b Jean-Jacques	20	– (4) c Krikken b Cork	10
J. G. Bracewell not out	40	– (5) not out	3
†A. C. Parore (did not bat)		– (3) lbw b Jean-Jacques	37
L-b 11, w 1, n-b 4	16	L-b 2, w 1, n-b 1	4
1/11 2/55 3/123 4/132 5/191 (5 wkts dec.)	252	1/20 2/83 3/104 4/110 (4 wkts dec.)	110

M. C. Snedden, D. K. Morrison and J. P. Millmow did not bat.

Bowling: *First Innings*—Bishop 12–3–37–0; Malcolm 12–1–36–0; Jean-Jacques 14–2–67–2; Cork 14–2–49–1; Kuiper 10–2–52–2. *Second Innings*—Morris 7–0–47–0; Adams 6–1–20–1; Bowler 3–0–25–0; Roberts 3–0–10–1; Cork 1–0–4–1; Jean-Jacques 0.4–0–2–1.

Derbyshire

*K. J. Barnett not out	14	– lbw b Morrison	0
P. D. Bowler not out	11	– lbw b Snedden	9
J. E. Morris (did not bat)		– b Millmow	20
B. Roberts (did not bat)		– c M. D. Crowe b Morrison	25
A. P. Kuiper (did not bat)		– lbw b Bracewell	68
C. J. Adams (did not bat)		– c J. J. Crowe b Priest	21
†K. M. Krikken (did not bat)		– c M. D. Crowe b Snedden	62
M. Jean-Jacques (did not bat)		– b Snedden	14
I. R. Bishop (did not bat)		– c Greatbatch b Bracewell	7
D. E. Malcolm (did not bat)		– lbw b Snedden	0
D. G. Cork (did not bat)		– not out	2
L-b 1, n-b 4	5	L-b 15, n-b 7	22
(no wkt dec.)	30	1/0 2/24 3/36 4/79 5/159 6/169 7/233 8/248 9/248	250

Bowling: *First Innings*—Morrison 4–0–16–0; Millmow 4–1–13–0. *Second Innings*—Morrison 9–2–40–2; Millmow 8–0–36–1; Snedden 18–4–55–4; Priest 10–1–46–1; Bracewell 15.2–3–58–2.

Umpires: M. J. Kitchen and R. A. White.

ENGLAND v NEW ZEALAND

First Cornhill Test

At Nottingham, June 7, 8, 9, 11, 12. Drawn. Toss: New Zealand. Pre-series prognostication indicated general expectation of three high-scoring draws, given that batting strength on both sides appeared rather more solid than bowling, and pitches were to be hard and true. In the event, the weather proved the decisive factor in the First Test, curtailing play to a degree which made a positive result impossible and shifting the emphasis to seam bowling. More than two hours were lost on the first day, when New Zealand scored 171 runs and lost five wickets. Only 23 minutes of play were possible on the second day, the tourists adding 18 runs for another wicket, and the innings was duly completed, a disappointing 208, before noon on Saturday.

The outstanding batting came from Martin Crowe, who hit five fours and a six in his 94-ball innings, which was of a higher class than anything else offered by New Zealand. Uncharacteristically, he was hitting across the line when he was bowled by DeFreitas. Although the conditions did not help England's fastest bowler, Malcolm, DeFreitas found them very much to his liking, and he bowled a consistently better line and length than on any previous occasion in his Test career. His reward was five wickets for 53 and the figures were well deserved. The one statistical curio was provided by Snedden, whose runless innings was spread over three days.

Hadlee received a warm and sentimental reception from the crowd when he emerged to play his last innings at Trent Bridge, his former county ground, but was unable to acknowledge it as he would have liked; he played on when trying to withdraw his bat before he had scored. He compensated, however, in suitably dramatic style by dismissing the England captain, Gooch, with the first delivery of the innings – his 416th Test wicket, to which he added three more before England declared at 345 for nine on Tuesday afternoon.

In terms of England's Test future the most significant event of the match was Atherton's innings of 151, in his first appearance as an opening bat at that level of cricket. His admirable temperament was illustrated by the way he assumed heavy responsibilities after seeing his captain depart so abruptly, to be followed – after a dashing little knock from Stewart – by the vice-captain, Lamb, who also failed to score.

There had been a certain inevitability about Atherton's progress, from his early days at Manchester Grammar School, through three years at Cambridge and late-summer appearances in the Lancashire side. His patience, concentration and selectivity of strokeplay were almost Boycott-like in his stay of 494 minutes, during which he faced 382 balls and struck sixteen boundaries. His choice as a partner to Gooch was to some extent forced upon the selectors by injury to Larkins, but it proved inspired. Together with the bonus of his leg-spin bowling (which Lancashire had not been afraid to use extensively in their earlier games) it provided the England Committee with a welcome number of new options.

In conditions which at one time or another helped swing and seam bowling, Hadlee showed that, even though his 39th birthday was less than a month away, he remained a dangerous practitioner with new ball or old. Snedden bowled with magnificent accuracy, Bracewell with more of a loop than most English spinners, and the slow left-arm débutant, Priest, with commendable economy to add to his sprightly fielding. Morrison alone would have been disappointed with his figures, probably the result of striving too hard on a pitch which suited him no better than it had Malcolm. – Don Mosey.

Man of the Match: M. A. Atherton. *Attendance:* 17,886; *receipts* £272,693.

Close of play: First day, New Zealand 171-5 (M. W. Priest 23*, M. C. Snedden 0*); Second day, New Zealand 189-6 (M. C. Snedden 0*, J. G. Bracewell 15*); Third day, England 4-1 (M. A. Atherton 3*, A. J. Stewart 1*); Fourth day, England 187-5 (M. A. Atherton 78*, R. C. Russell 4*).

New Zealand

	First innings		Second innings	
T. J. Franklin b Malcolm	33	–	not out	22
*J. G. Wright c Stewart b Small	8	–	c Russell b Small	1
A. H. Jones c Stewart b Malcolm	39	–	c Russell b DeFreitas	13
M. D. Crowe b DeFreitas	59			
M. J. Greatbatch b Hemmings	1			
M. W. Priest c Russell b DeFreitas	26			
M. C. Snedden c Gooch b DeFreitas	0			
J. G. Bracewell c Gooch b Small	28			
R. J. Hadlee b DeFreitas	0			
†I. D. S. Smith not out	2			
D. K. Morrison lbw b DeFreitas	0	–	(4) not out	0
B 1, l-b 10, w 1	12			
1/16 (2) 2/75 (1) 3/110 (3) 4/121 (5) 5/170 (4) 6/174 (6) 7/191 (7) 8/191 (9) 9/203 (8) 10/208 (11)	208		1/8 (2) 2/36 (3) (2 wkts)	36

Bowling: *First Innings*—Small 29–9–49–2; Malcolm 19–7–48–2; Hemmings 19–6–47–1; DeFreitas 22–6–53–5. *Second Innings*—Malcolm 7–2–22–0; Small 6–2–14–1; DeFreitas 2–2–0–1; Hemmings 2–2–0–0.

England

*G. A. Gooch lbw b Hadlee	0
M. A. Atherton c Snedden b Priest	151
A. J. Stewart c Smith b Hadlee	27
A. J. Lamb lbw b Hadlee	0
R. A. Smith c Smith b Bracewell	55
N. H. Fairbrother c Franklin b Snedden	19
†R. C. Russell c Snedden b Morrison	28
P. A. J. DeFreitas lbw b Bracewell	14
G. C. Small c Crowe b Hadlee	26
E. E. Hemmings not out	13
D. E. Malcolm not out	4
B 2, l-b 3, n-b 3	8
1/0 (1) 2/43 (3) 3/45 (4) 4/141 (5) 5/168 (6) 6/260 (7) 7/302 (2) 8/306 (8) 9/340 (9) (9 wkts dec.)	345

Bowling: Hadlee 33–6–89–4; Morrison 22–3–96–1; Snedden 36–17–54–1; Bracewell 35–8–75–2; Priest 12–4–26–1.

Umpires: H. D. Bird and J. H. Hampshire.

†LEICESTERSHIRE v NEW ZEALANDERS

At Leicester, June 14. Leicestershire won by four wickets. Toss: Leicestershire. Put in by Leicestershire on a slow pitch, the tourists delivered one of their poorer batting performances, finishing their 55 overs with a paltry 165 for nine. Only their captain, Wright, played with much conviction. After taking Jeff Crowe's wicket with his loosener, Mullally went from strength to strength to return impressive figures of six for 38 from his eleven overs. Lewis was unusually expensive, conceding 57 runs, but the young England prospect achieved much more success with the bat. Leicestershire had begun unconvincingly, losing three wickets for 29, but Lewis's calmly authoritative 51, made over 90 minutes, and his fourth-wicket partnership of 86 with the opener, Boon, ensured that the home side completed a comfortable victory with fourteen balls to spare.

New Zealanders

*J. G. Wright c Potter b Mullally 62
J. J. Crowe b Mullally 7
M. J. Greatbatch b Mullally 0
K. R. Rutherford b Mullally 19
M. D. Crowe b Agnew 20
S. A. Thomson c Nixon b Benjamin . . . 25
M. W. Priest c Lewis b Mullally 1
†A. C. Parore not out 19
M. C. Snedden c Potter b Mullally 1
D. K. Morrison lbw b Willey 2
J. P. Millmow not out 2
L-b 1, w 3, n-b 3 7

1/23 2/23 3/50 4/76 5/128 6/139 7/141 8/142 9/149 (9 wkts, 55 overs) 165

Bowling: Benjamin 11–1–27–1; Agnew 11–1–21–1; Lewis 11–1–57–0; Mullally 11–3–38–6; Willey 11–3–21–1.

Leicestershire

T. J. Boon c M. D. Crowe b Priest 40
*N. E. Briers b Morrison 7
J. J. Whitaker c Rutherford b Millmow 9
P. Willey c Parore b Snedden 4
C. C. Lewis c J. J. Crowe b Thomson . 51
L. Potter not out 27
J. D. R. Benson run out 19
W. K. M. Benjamin not out 0
L-b 10, w 3, n-b 1 14

1/8 2/23 3/29 4/115 5/119 6/165 (6 wkts, 52.4 overs) 171

†P. A. Nixon, J. P. Agnew and A. D. Mullally did not bat.

Bowling: Morrison 11–1–27–1; Millmow 11–4–28–1; Snedden 9–2–32–1; Thomson 10–0–42–1; Priest 11–3–26–1; M. D. Crowe 0.4–0–6–0.

Umpires: A. A. Jones and V. A. Holder.

NORTHAMPTONSHIRE v NEW ZEALANDERS

At Northampton, June 16, 17, 18. Drawn. Toss: Northamptonshire. In the absence of Hadlee, whose knighthood was announced on the eve of the match, the headlines were stolen by Capel. He registered Northamptonshire's first hundred against the New Zealanders since D. W. Barrick's 147 in 1949, and hit a six and sixteen fours during his 232-minute innings, adding 167 in 59 overs with Williams. This followed an eventful opening session in which Millmow held a return catch to dismiss Bailey after the ball rebounded off the fielder at silly mid-off. The same bowler limped from the field shortly afterwards, with the shin injury which was to finish his tour, but Bracewell, completing Millmow's over, trapped Fordham with his first ball. Lamb also enlivened the proceedings by striking five boundaries in his 21. New Zealand's reply featured a fine display from Franklin, whose 92 took 201 minutes and included three sixes and ten fours, before he became one of three victims for Ambrose in the space of thirteen deliveries. Wright kept the match alive by declaring 14 runs behind, but an uninterrupted final day would have been necessary to secure a result. In the event only 36 overs could be bowled, and Capel again took centre stage with his unbeaten 65.

Close of play: First day, New Zealanders 28-0 (T. J. Franklin 16*, J. G. Wright 9*); Second day, Northamptonshire 71-2 (R. J. Bailey 12*, A. J. Lamb 6*).

Northamptonshire

	First innings		Second innings	
A. Fordham lbw b Bracewell	20	– run out	23
N. A. Felton c Rutherford b Morrison	3	– c sub b Bracewell	22
R. J. Bailey c and b Millmow	0	– lbw b Morrison	22
*A. J. Lamb lbw b Morrison	21	– c Parore b Thomson	42
D. J. Capel c and b Priest	123	– not out	65
R. G. Williams c Wright b Priest	73	– not out	11
†W. M. Noon lbw b Morrison	2		
N. G. B. Cook b Priest	10		
W. W. Davis not out	5		
C. E. L. Ambrose lbw b Bracewell	0		
B 13, l-b 4, w 1, n-b 4	22	B 2, l-b 6, w 1, n-b 2	11
1/22 2/23 3/33 4/73 5/240 6/253 7/267 8/274 9/279	(9 wkts dec.) 279	1/45 2/50 3/92 4/139	(4 wkts) 196

M. A. Robinson did not bat.

Bowling: *First Innings*—Morrison 21–4–68–3; Millmow 3.4–0–16–1; Bracewell 30–9–78–2; Thomson 13–0–65–0; Priest 27–10–35–3. *Second Innings*—Morrison 11–2–49–1; Thomson 21–3–97–1; Bracewell 23–13–27–1; Priest 7.5–1–14–0; Rutherford 1–0–1–0.

New Zealanders

T. J. Franklin c Noon b Ambrose	92
*J. G. Wright b Davis	31
A. H. Jones lbw b Ambrose	46
M. J. Greatbatch c Capel b Ambrose	0
K. R. Rutherford not out	42
M. W. Priest run out	32
S. A. Thomson not out	4
B 1, l-b 5, w 2, n-b 10	18
1/67 2/176 3/182 4/186 5/249	(5 wkts dec.) 265

†A. C. Parore, J. G. Bracewell, J. P. Millmow and D. K. Morrison did not bat.

Bowling: Davis 21–2–65–1; Ambrose 20–3–60–3; Robinson 17–1–53–0; Williams 15–3–39–0; Cook 16–5–42–0.

Umpires: B. Dudleston and D. S. Thompsett.

ENGLAND v NEW ZEALAND

Second Cornhill Test

At Lord's, June 21, 22, 23, 25, 26. Drawn. Toss: New Zealand. A number of factors combined to make this a less than remarkable Test. The pitch was too easy-paced, the bowling was not good enough to dismiss batsmen intent on survival, and the weather intervened.

There were some memorable features, however, the first of which came before the match started. Hadlee had received a knighthood in the Queen's Birthday Honours and there was much discussion as to how he should be designated on the scoreboard. In the event, "Sir R. Hadlee" was settled on, but not everyone was pleased. One senior statistician wrote to MCC complaining, mistakenly as it happened, that Hadlee could not use the title until his official investiture. But most cricket devotees were delighted by the honour and anxious that it should be used. So, fifteen minutes late because of damp conditions, Sir Richard Hadlee led New Zealand on to the field and was warmly received.

It was Morrison, however, who struck first for the visitors when Atherton was bowled in the second over, following his Trent Bridge century with a Lord's duck. This seemed to support Wright's decision to put England in, but it was the only incident of note on the first day, as rain drove the players off after only 50 minutes. The main statistical feature of the 11.3 overs bowled had been eight no-balls, four of them from Morrison. Extras continued to make a valuable contribution the next morning, adding 16 of the 74 runs scored after another late start.

The England captain, Gooch, completed his half-century soon after lunch. It had taken 142 minutes and contained six fours, which increased to twelve fours as he advanced to 85. Stewart's fifty took twenty minutes longer and he was out in the next over, lbw to Hadlee for 54. Lamb, on the other hand, started as though the fastest century of the season was in his sights. His first scoring stroke was an edged four to third man, but he handsomely off-drove Hadlee next delivery and 36 of his 39 runs, made in 46 balls, came in boundaries. Only 7 runs were scored by Smith in a fourth-wicket partnership of 38, which ended when Lamb was lbw to Snedden. Fairbrother, still looking for a big Test score, was missed at second slip off his third ball, and a halt for rain brought him no benefit; he made only 2 before giving Morrison a straightforward catch at mid-on off Bracewell. When Russell was bowled by Hadlee for 13, England were unhealthily placed at 255 for six, but DeFreitas joined Smith and they repaired some of the damage. Smith passed 1,000 runs in Test cricket and completed a half-century in 113 minutes, only to go 14 runs later to a fine catch from Bracewell at deep mid-on. With their last three wickets falling for 12 runs in 22 balls, England's total was a disappointing 334.

As New Zealand replied, none of the bowlers troubled Wright and Franklin. They gleaned runs at their own pace, interrupted only by a delay of nearly three hours caused by rain, which extended play until seven o'clock on Saturday. The openers had put on 185 in four and a half hours when Wright, 2 short of his hundred, was well caught at forward short leg, left-handed, by Stewart off Small. Jones helped Franklin add 93 in two hours before he gave Stewart a second catch, at cover point, 1 short of his half-century.

The wait for Franklin's maiden Test hundred was proving a long one. Missed at second slip by Gooch when 88, he spent threequarters of an hour on 98 before reaching three figures with a two from Malcolm. It had taken him seven hours eleven minutes, and in 309 balls he had hit just eight fours. Next ball he edged Malcolm to Russell and was gone. With Crowe and Rutherford then managing 1 run between them, the New Zealanders had lost four wickets for 7 runs and their innings was losing momentum when Hadlee strode to the middle for his last Test innings at Lord's. His second scoring stroke was a six over long-on off Hemmings, and two overs later he despatched Small over long-off, inspiring Greatbatch to flick Malcolm into the Grand Stand at square leg. Hadlee's fifty came in an hour from only 42 deliveries, and included six fours as well as the two sixes. He had put on 123 for the sixth wicket with Greatbatch, and struck another six fours, when he swung at Hemmings once too often and was bowled. There were many who wished they were saluting his hundred as the great New Zealand all-rounder paused before climbing the pavilion steps and lifted his bat high to acknowledge the applause all round the ground.

Wright declared at 462 for nine, after Malcolm had taken five wickets in a Test innings for the second time. But with less than a day remaining, the match drifted towards a draw. For England, Gooch confirmed his excellent form with 37 unforced runs before losing his off stump to Hadlee, while Atherton made up for his first-innings failure with 54, becoming Jones's first Test victim. An opportunity to move Fairbrother up the order was not taken, but when Smith trod on his wicket without having scored, he came in with just over an hour remaining to advantage himself of batting practice at Test level without excessive pressure. He added 97 with Lamb, whose unbeaten 84 from 99 balls contained fourteen fours and a six, but by this stage of the match Hadlee had returned to the dressing-room – where Snedden was already nursing his shoulder injury – to rest a strained hamstring. – Norman de Mesquita.

Man of the Match: Sir R. J. Hadlee. *Attendance:* 58,047; *receipts* £891,983.

Close of play: First day, England 27-1 (G. A. Gooch 16*, A. J. Stewart 3*); Second day, England 329-8 (P. A. J. DeFreitas 33*, E. E. Hemmings 0*); Third day, New Zealand 156-0 (T. J. Franklin 60*, J. G. Wright 84*); Fourth day, New Zealand 440-8 (I. D. S. Smith 20*, M. C. Snedden 0*).

England

*G. A. Gooch c and b Bracewell	85	– b Hadlee	37
M. A. Atherton b Morrison	0	– c Bracewell b Jones	54
A. J. Stewart lbw b Hadlee	54	– c sub (M. W. Priest) b Bracewell	42
A. J. Lamb lbw b Snedden	39	– not out	84
R. A. Smith c Bracewell b Morrison	64	– hit wkt b Bracewell	0
N. H. Fairbrother c Morrison b Bracewell	2	– not out	33
†R. C. Russell b Hadlee	13		
P. A. J. DeFreitas c Franklin b Morrison	38		
G. C. Small b Morrison	3		
E. E. Hemmings b Hadlee	0		
D. E. Malcolm not out	0		
L-b 13, w 1, n-b 22	36	B 8, l-b 8, n-b 6	22
1/3 (2) 2/151 (3) 3/178 (1) 4/216 (4) 5/226 (6) 6/255 (7) 7/319 (5) 8/322 (9) 9/332 (10) 10/334 (8)	334	1/68 (1) 2/135 (2) 3/171 (3) 4/175 (5) (4 wkts dec.)	272

Bowling: *First Innings*—Hadlee 29–5–113–3; Morrison 18.4–4–64–4; Snedden 21–4–72–1; Bracewell 21–3–72–2. *Second Innings*—Hadlee 13–2–32–1; Morrison 16–0–81–0; Bracewell 34–13–85–2; Jones 12–3–40–1; Rutherford 3–0–18–0.

New Zealand

T. J. Franklin c Russell b Malcolm	101
*J. G. Wright c Stewart b Small	98
A. H. Jones c Stewart b Malcolm	49
M. D. Crowe c Russell b Hemmings	1
M. J. Greatbatch b Malcolm	47
K. R. Rutherford c Fairbrother b Malcolm	0
Sir R. J. Hadlee b Hemmings	86
J. G. Bracewell run out	4
†I. D. S. Smith c Small b Malcolm	27
M. C. Snedden not out	13
D. K. Morrison not out	2
B 12, l-b 15, w 2, n-b 5	34
1/185 (2) 2/278 (3) 3/281 (1) 4/284 (4) 5/285 (6) 6/408 (7) 7/415 (8) 8/425 (5) 9/448 (9)	(9 wkts dec.) 462

Bowling: Malcolm 43–14–94–5; Small 35–4–127–1; DeFreitas 35.4–1–122–0; Hemmings 30–13–67–2; Gooch 13–7–25–0; Atherton 1–1–0–0.

Umpires: M. J. Kitchen and D. R. Shepherd.

OXFORD & CAMBRIDGE UNIVERSITIES v NEW ZEALANDERS

At Cambridge, June 27, 28, 29. Oxford & Cambridge Universities won by two wickets. Toss: Oxford & Cambridge Universities. Chasing 263 in a minimum of 71 overs, the Universities batted with flair and determination to win with ten balls to spare and inflict on the touring side their first defeat in first-class fixtures. The first New Zealand team to tour England, that of 1927, had also lost at Fenner's, to Cambridge University. Perhaps, then, it was fitting that the innings which accomplished defeat on the same ground in 1990 came from the Cambridge opener, James. On a pitch providing helpful turn for off-spinner Bracewell, he batted with great skill for his unbeaten 131, facing 224 balls and winning the match with his sixteenth four. He and Morris, heroes of the Universities' first innings, had taken up the tourists' challenge by putting on 93 at 4 runs an over until Morris, the Oxford captain, became the first of seven wickets for Bracewell. The previous day, Morris had batted for three hours before he was last out for 75, giving Thomson his third catch at short leg and Bracewell his fifth wicket of the Universities' first innings. On the opening day, Crowe underpinned the New Zealanders' batting, hitting 23 fours in his 132. However, both he and Greatbatch were dropped off Pyman (when 11 and 10 respectively), and Crowe spent an hour in the 90s before reaching his hundred in 281 minutes from 246 balls. He played with greater freedom on the second afternoon as the tourists built on a lead of just 24.

Close of play: First day, Oxford & Cambridge Universities 37-1 (S. P. James 30*, M. J. Kilborn 7*); Second day, New Zealanders 125-2 (K. R. Rutherford 33*, A. C. Parore 0*).

New Zealanders

J. J. Crowe c Crawley b Gerrans	132	– c G. J. Turner b Crawley	64
T. J. Franklin c Kilborn b Gerrans	19		
M. J. Greatbatch c van der Merwe b Crawley	62		
K. R. Rutherford c van der Merwe b Buzza	21	– (3) c and b Buzza	38
M. W. Priest not out	55	– (6) c Gerrans b Buzza	31
S. A. Thomson not out	1	– (2) b Gerrans	20
†A. C. Parore (did not bat)		– (4) c R. J. Turner b Buzza	15
J. G. Bracewell (did not bat)		– (5) c R. J. Turner b Buzza	38
W. Watson (did not bat)		– (7) not out	17
C. Pringle (did not bat)		– (8) c Atkinson b Crawley	6
L-b 8, w 1, n-b 2	11	B 4, l-b 2, n-b 3	9
1/33 2/130 3/199 4/297 (4 wkts dec.)	301	1/47 2/124 3/145 4/146 5/205 6/224 7/238 (7 wkts dec.)	238

*I. D. S. Smith did not bat.

Bowling: *First Innings*—van der Merwe 11–3–28–0; Gerrans 18–6–59–2; Pyman 17–3–56–0; G. J. Turner 21–3–76–0; Buzza 13–5–44–1; Crawley 14–5–30–1. *Second Innings*—van der Merwe 8–1–30–0; Gerrans 9–3–18–1; G. J. Turner 14–0–63–0; Buzza 17–0–87–4; Pyman 6–2–12–0; Crawley 6.3–0–22–2.

Oxford & Cambridge Universities

	First Innings		Second Innings	
S. P. James c Thomson b Bracewell	67	– not out	131
P. S. Gerrans c Parore b Pringle	0	– (8) b Bracewell	7
M. J. Kilborn c Parore b Watson	27	– run out	3
M. A. Crawley c Smith b Bracewell	47	– (5) lbw b Bracewell	5
R. E. Morris c Thomson b Bracewell	75	– (2) c Greatbatch b Bracewell	53
*J. C. M. Atkinson c Bracewell b Priest	10	– b Bracewell	4
G. J. Turner c Crowe b Priest	14	– (4) c Crowe b Bracewell	26
W. M. van der Merwe b Priest	24	– (7) c Parore b Bracewell	14
†R. J. Turner b Bracewell	5	– b Bracewell	10
R. A. Pyman c Thomson b Bracewell	4	– not out	0
A. J. Buzza not out	0		
L-b 4	4	B 2, l-b 8, n-b 3	13
1/5 2/74 3/121 4/154 5/177 6/199 7/237 8/264 9/276	277	1/93 2/106 3/164 4/178 5/184 6/220 7/230 8/262 (8 wkts)	266

Bowling: *First Innings*—Pringle 10–2–28–1; Watson 13–3–26–1; Priest 36–16–93–3; Bracewell 38.3–10–107–5; Thomson 6–0–19–0. *Second Innings*—Thomson 5–1–14–0; Watson 7–1–27–0; Bracewell 33–6–120–7; Priest 25.2–7–79–0; Pringle 6–2–16–0.

Umpires: G. I. Burgess and R. Palmer.

ESSEX v NEW ZEALANDERS

At Chelmsford, June 30, July 1, 2. Drawn. Toss: New Zealanders. The game ended in a dull draw after Gooch decided to bat on during the final day, apparently because the tourists were not interested in manufacturing a finish. Ideal batting conditions enabled Wright, who hit 21 fours in his 121, and Martin Crowe, whose unbeaten 123 contained seventeen fours and two sixes, to prosper with ease. And when the home team replied, Gooch and Stephenson also reached three figures. The Essex captain had hit sixteen boundaries by the time he limped out of the action with a jarred knee, immediately after completing his hundred. His fellow-opener went on to 147, which spanned 426 minutes and 332 balls. Gooch's was not the only injury in the run-up to the Birmingham Test; Franklin dislocated his right-hand index finger while attempting to catch Gooch at second slip, and Martin Crowe needed stitches when he was hit in the face by a ball deflected by Parore off Stephenson's bat. Neither took part in the New Zealanders' second innings, which gave Jones and Rutherford some useful practice before Edgbaston.

Close of play: First day, New Zealanders 388-4 (M. D. Crowe 123*, J. J. Crowe 9*); Second day, Essex 306-2 (J. P. Stephenson 107*, M. E. Waugh 55*).

New Zealanders

	First Innings	Second Innings	
T. J. Franklin c Gooch b Topley	74		
*J. G. Wright lbw b Childs	121		
A. H. Jones c Garnham b Topley	3	– not out	66
M. D. Crowe not out	123		
K. R. Rutherford st Garnham b Stephenson	42	– (4) not out	40
J. J. Crowe not out	9	– (1) c Hussain b Topley	15
†A. C. Parore (did not bat)		– (2) lbw b Pringle	4
B 2, l-b 3, w 1, n-b 10	16	L-b 2, w 2, n-b 12	16
1/169 2/180 3/205 4/322 (4 wkts dec.)	388	1/9 2/53 (2 wkts)	141

M. W. Priest, S. A. Thomson, C. Pringle and D. K. Morrison did not bat.

Bowling: *First Innings*—Andrew 14–3–45–0; Pringle 9–4–25–0; Thomas 16–3–76–0; Topley 12–2–57–2; Childs 23–6–76–1; Hussain 7–1–28–0; Waugh 5–0–24–0; Stephenson 8–0–52–1. *Second Innings*—Andrew 8–1–16–0; Pringle 6–0–15–1; Topley 10–0–45–1; Thomas 2.2–0–5–0; Childs 5.4–0–22–0; Stephenson 5–1–15–0; Waugh 3–0–16–0; Hussain 1–0–5–0.

Essex

*G. A. Gooch retired hurt	102
J. P. Stephenson c Thomson b Priest	147
P. J. Prichard c M. D. Crowe b Priest	15
N. Hussain c M. D. Crowe b Jones	1
M. E. Waugh c Priest b Pringle	63
D. R. Pringle c Thomson b Priest	67
†M. A. Garnham lbw b Pringle	0
T. D. Topley not out	23
K. O. Thomas c Priest b Thomson	2
S. J. W. Andrew b Thomson	0
L-b 25, w 1, n-b 3	29
1/209 2/218 3/315 4/404 5/408 6/438 7/449 8/449 (8 wkts dec.)	449

J. H. Childs did not bat.

G. A. Gooch retired hurt at 168.

Bowling: Morrison 19–2–57–0; Pringle 42–15–103–2; Thomson 25.4–6–84–2; Priest 38–7–155–3; Jones 2–1–1–1; Rutherford 4–0–24–0.

Umpires: P. J. Eele and K. E. Palmer.

ENGLAND v NEW ZEALAND

Third Cornhill Test

At Birmingham, July 5, 6, 7, 9, 10. England won by 114 runs. Toss: New Zealand. Even the relief of seeing Sir Richard Hadlee bound up the pavilion steps in a Test for the last time failed to match England's delight at saying goodbye to their worst-ever run in Tests at home. In nearly five years, England had beaten only Sri Lanka, in a one-off Test at Lord's in 1988; their previous success in a series had been in 1985, when Gower's side regained the Ashes. Since then, the Ashes had been retained in Australia and lost at home, and England had failed to win any of their subsequent 24 home Tests in six series. This victory at Edgbaston was also England's first win over New Zealand for seven years, and it provided an exciting finale to a dull Cornhill series which had been disrupted by the weather.

Hadlee's departure and the Test were not the only losses suffered by the tourists. Snedden announced his retirement prior to the match, and the New Zealand captain, Wright, confirmed that this was his final tour. Wright also confessed to his part in New Zealand's first defeat in ten Tests. "I was wrong to put England in. No two ways about it. It was a bad decision." Gooch, England's captain, could have faced two decisions as the home team searched for that elusive win. But he was excused both. Wright won the toss; then, with Gooch pondering on when to declare on the fourth day, England collapsed to their lowest total against the Kiwis in England. That gave New Zealand more time to score fewer runs than Gooch had planned, yet ultimately England's batting failure may have eased their path to victory. Hadlee bowed out with an inspired spell after lunch on the fourth day to open up the contest, and those wickets took his final Test tally to 431 as he claimed five wickets in an innings for a record 36th time. Malcolm provided the final breakthrough for England's success, but Hemmings, Gooch and Atherton all played a crucial part in the victory.

Gooch had been reappointed as captain for the India series after the Lord's Test, and England named an unchanged twelve for Edgbaston. Fraser, as Middlesex had no game, was added to the squad to give him practice following the rib injury which had caused him to withdraw from the Fourth Test in Barbados three months earlier. And when DeFreitas left Wednesday's practice feeling feverish, then eventually dropped out with hamstring trouble, there was speculation that he might make an early return. In the event Lewis, although in some doubt earlier because of knee trouble – as was Stewart, with an ankle problem – came in to make his Test début. England's traditional pre-match dinner was abandoned in favour of a buffet so that the players could watch the soccer World Cup semi-final between England and

West Germany. For New Zealand, Franklin had recovered from a dislocated finger, but Smith was ruled out with a sore hamstring, giving a chance to the promising nineteen-year-old wicket-keeper, Parore, who had been brought on the tour to prepare him as Smith's successor. New Zealand's last Edgbaston Test had been in 1965, when they lost by nine wickets, but the Birmingham ground had become England's favourite Test venue. They went into this match with fourteen wins and just two defeats in 26 matches at Warwickshire's headquarters.

Rain delayed the start on the first day until 2.45 p.m.; and although play might not have been possible so soon without the Brumbrella covering, this was damaged while being removed and was put out of action for the rest of the match. England responded positively to Wright's insertion and finished the day at 191 for one. The three-and-a-half-hour opening partnership of 170 between Gooch and Atherton was England's best since Broad and Athey's stand of 223 at Perth in 1986-87, and as well as Gooch becoming the eleventh Englishman to reach 5,000 Test runs, both openers passed 1,000 first-class runs for the season. Gooch took the first 40 minutes of the second morning to add the 5 runs he needed for his ninth Test hundred, his first in 26 innings, and his 394-minute 154 (281 balls) held the innings together as England's middle order failed to capitalise on the good start. It was left to Lewis, Russell, Hemmings and Small to help England to their first total of 400 in eleven Tests. New Zealand's attack was made to work hard, but there was consolation in Parore's display behind the stumps, despite his dropping Lewis.

Saturday belonged to Hemmings. The 41-year-old off-spinner entered the match with an eight-year, eleven-Test record that had yielded only nineteen wickets. In the space of 90 deliveries and two hours, Hemmings induced a New Zealand collapse from 163 for four to 249 all out with his spell of six for 33, finishing with the best figures by an England spinner since J. E. Emburey's seven for 78 at Sydney in 1986-87. Hemmings, who had started his county career at Edgbaston 24 years earlier, was helped by slick close catching, a receptive pitch, and his captain's attacking policy; it was the first time he had played three consecutive Tests and the first time he had taken more than four wickets in a Test innings. Malcolm made the early breakthrough as the tourists' front-line batsmen paid for their positive approach, and Lewis took his first Test wicket when Crowe was adjudged lbw. Crowe initially refused to look at umpire Meyer's response to England's appeal, and the umpire had to raise his finger a second time before Crowe, who later apologised, departed. Franklin was again the most difficult to dislodge, his 66 taking four and a half hours and 207 balls, and New Zealand's innings disintegrated just before tea when he and Greatbatch were dismissed. However, despite Hemmings, New Zealand managed to escape the follow-on by 13 runs before the close.

England, with a lead of 186, started positively on Monday, posting 50 in 49 minutes, but the quest for quick runs was exploited by Hadlee and Bracewell. The last seven wickets fell for 29 runs, with only Atherton keeping his nerve in a stay of almost three and a quarter hours. England's four middle-order batsmen had a disastrous Test, managing just 68 runs between them, and while it put Stewart's Test future in doubt, Fairbrother seemed certain to pay the penalty for failing to reproduce his county form for his country. The talented Lancashire left-hander had scored 64 runs in seven Tests and, apart from his undefeated 33 at Lord's, had never looked comfortable in this three-match series. Bracewell became the second New Zealander to complete the Test double of 1,000 runs and 100 wickets. The first was, of course, Hadlee, who signed off in style with an eight-over spell of five for 17. Malcolm was just as proud of being Hadlee's 431st and last Test victim as he was of dismissing cricket's latest knight in his final Test innings.

With New Zealand wanting 345 runs for victory in eight and a half hours, Monday's evening session was crucial to both sides. The tourists were 101 runs nearer their target by the close, but England settled for that as they had the wickets of Wright and Franklin. On Tuesday, however, Jones, Greatbatch and Crowe were all denied the big innings needed to give their side a platform for victory, and even the New Zealand romantics had to concede defeat when Hadlee had his stumps splattered by Malcolm. England's fast bowler received good support from Lewis and the England fielders, especially Gooch and Atherton in the slips. Atherton was named England's Man of the Series, while Hadlee picked up the New Zealand award. That was no sentimental gesture; the world's leading Test wicket-taker had called it a day at the peak of his powers. – David Norrie.

Man of the Match: D. E. Malcolm. *Attendance:* 33,963; *receipts* £402,962.

Close of play: First day, England 191-1 (G. A. Gooch 95*, A. J. Stewart 8*); Second day, New Zealand 9-0 (T. J. Franklin 8*, J. G. Wright 1*); Third day, New Zealand 249; Fourth day, New Zealand 101-2 (A. H. Jones 37*, M. D. Crowe 10*).

England

	First innings		Second innings	
*G. A. Gooch c Hadlee b Morrison	154	– b Snedden	30
M. A. Atherton lbw b Snedden	82	– c Rutherford b Bracewell	70
A. J. Stewart c Parore b Morrison	9	– lbw b Bracewell	15
A. J. Lamb c Parore b Hadlee	2	– st Parore b Bracewell	4
R. A. Smith c Jones b Bracewell	19	– c and b Hadlee	14
N. H. Fairbrother lbw b Snedden	2	– lbw b Bracewell	3
†R. C. Russell b Snedden	43	– c sub (J. J. Crowe) b Hadlee	0
C. C. Lewis c Rutherford b Bracewell	32	– c Parore b Hadlee	1
G. C. Small not out	44	– not out	11
E. E. Hemmings c Parore b Hadlee	20	– b Hadlee	0
D. E. Malcolm b Hadlee	0	– lbw b Hadlee	0
B 4, l-b 15, n-b 9	28	L-b 6, n-b 4	10
1/170 (2) 2/193 (3) 3/198 (4) 4/245 (5) 5/254 (6) 6/316 (1) 7/351 (7) 8/381 (8) 9/435 (10) 10/435 (11)	435	1/50 (1) 2/87 (3) 3/99 (4) 4/129 (5) 5/136 (6) 6/141 (7) 7/146 (8) 8/157 (2) 9/158 (10) 10/158 (11)	158

Bowling: *First Innings*—Hadlee 37.5–8–97–3; Morrison 26–7–81–2; Snedden 35–9–106–3; Bracewell 42–12–130–2; Jones 1–0–2–0. *Second Innings*—Hadlee 21–3–53–5; Morrison 3–1–29–0; Snedden 9–0–32–1; Bracewell 16–5–38–4.

New Zealand

	First innings	Second innings	
T. J. Franklin c Smith b Hemmings	66	– lbw b Malcolm	5
*J. G. Wright c Russell b Malcolm	24	– c Smith b Lewis	46
A. H. Jones c Russell b Malcolm	2	– c Gooch b Small	40
M. D. Crowe lbw b Lewis	11	– lbw b Malcolm	25
M. J. Greatbatch b Malcolm	45	– c Atherton b Hemmings	22
K. R. Rutherford c Stewart b Hemmings	29	– c Lamb b Lewis	18
Sir R. J. Hadlee c Atherton b Hemmings	8	– b Malcolm	13
J. G. Bracewell b Hemmings	25	– (9) c Atherton b Malcolm	0
†A. C. Parore not out	12	– (8) c Lamb b Lewis	20
M. C. Snedden lbw b Hemmings	2	– not out	21
D. K. Morrison b Hemmings	1	– b Malcolm	6
B 9, l-b 11, w 2, n-b 2	24	L-b 9, w 1, n-b 4	14
1/45 (2) 2/67 (3) 3/90 (4) 4/161 (5) 5/163 (1) 6/185 (7) 7/223 (8) 8/230 (6) 9/243 (10) 10/249 (11)	249	1/25 (1) 2/85 (2) 3/111 (3) 4/125 (4) 5/155 (5) 6/163 (6) 7/180 (7) 8/180 (9) 9/203 (8) 10/230 (11)	230

Bowling: *First Innings*—Small 18–7–44–0; Malcolm 25–7–59–3; Lewis 19–5–51–1; Hemmings 27.3–10–58–6; Atherton 9–5–17–0. *Second Innings*—Malcolm 24.4–8–46–5; Small 16–5–56–1; Lewis 22–3–76–3; Hemmings 29–13–43–1.

Umpires: J. W. Holder and B. J. Meyer.

THE INDIANS IN ENGLAND, 1990

The theatrical impresarios of London's West End would have been proud to have put on a spectacle like this. The sporting plot was played out on arenas larger than any stage along Shaftesbury Avenue, and it fascinated by its natural twists and turns, supported by bravura performances. Most importantly, the patrons went away delighted by what they had seen. The show was a winner.

The supremacy of cricket as England's summer sport was in question. The preceding Tests against New Zealand had struggled to compete against the circus of soccer's quadrennial showpiece, the World Cup, and neither the knighting of Richard Hadlee nor England's first win in a home series for five years made the impact of the Indian summer which followed.

A certain amateur spirit was needed if cricket was to recapture its glory, and the Indian tourists, led by Mohammad Azharuddin, had that spirit. The fear of losing has often been responsible for dull Test cricket, but India, accustomed to winning abroad once in a blue moon, had none of that fear. Moreover, with conditions so dry that hosepipe bans were being imposed in Britain, the Indian batsmen found themselves in their element. They scored heavily from their earliest games, making fifteen first-class hundreds, six of them in Tests, and their double victory in the Texaco Trophy one-day internationals suggested how attractively they could perform. The Tests would revolve around their success in using these batting skills to support the notoriously weak bowling.

The fate of the series lay in the toss at Lord's. With so many batsmen among the runs, most captains would have grabbed first strike the moment the coin came down in their favour. This is where captaincy may have let India down. Graham Gooch, soon to make this summer his *annus mirabilis*, may not have believed his ears or his luck when England were asked to bat. For while the mild cloud cover at the time of the toss was contrary to the forecast, any moisture in the pitch could only have been imagined. Not without reason did the sagacious Mike Brearley write that the decision was pusillanimous. Moreover, the divisions in Indian cricket were soon emphasised as the team's cricket manager, Bishan Bedi, was reported to have disassociated himself from the decision to put England in, though he made a belated attempt to assuage the players' feelings by denying the words attributed to him.

The die had been cast for a glorious display of batting, and record books were constantly open as the unflappable Gooch piled on the runs to achieve the first Test triple-hundred since L. G. Rowe's 302 for West Indies against England at Bridgetown in 1973-74. The England captain was to score a second century in his next innings, giving him the record Test match aggregate of 456 runs, and another at Old Trafford. All in all, in eleven Test innings during the summer he made 1,058 runs for an average of 96.18, batting with the voracity of a Bradman, whose record of 974 Test runs in an English season he passed at The Oval. Gooch's understanding of Indian bowling, easily tamed by patience and a straight bat, was perfect, and his opening partnership with Mike Atherton went from strength to strength. They confirmed its efficacy at Lord's as they compiled a record opening stand against India of 204, and again as they beat it by 21 runs the next time they walked out together, in Manchester, where Atherton became only the second Lancastrian, after G. Pullar, to make a Test hundred for England at Old Trafford. Their stand of 176 at The Oval was their fourth century partnership in as many Tests; yet opening was an unaccustomed role for Atherton, used to batting at No. 3 for his county.

Although they sometimes seemed to be reduced to supporting players, the contributions of Robin Smith and Allan Lamb, both of whom scored centuries at Lord's and Old Trafford, should not be forgotten. The competent Smith must have put himself among the world's top ten batsmen. Over the series he was only twice out in making 361 runs, and his refreshingly orthodox technique, coupled with amazing power through the off side, gave him ample command of the Indian bowlers, whether pace or spin. No believer in the bat-behind-pad and forward-prod school of batting, he gave an object lesson with his handling of spin when the ball was turning on the second day at Old Trafford. In that innings Lamb's performance against spin was much criticised, but he overcame his supposed weakness later in the match to steer his team away from trouble and towards the chance of victory.

Until the last Test, India's batsmen were always left to battle against the odds, chasing one massive England total after another, but their talented line-up, and especially the brilliant Azharuddin, did much to re-establish the virtues of positive batting. The Indian captain's breathtakingly audacious hundred at Lord's signified the difference between the English straight bat, wielded with control rather than subtlety, and oriental wristiness, which lends itself to innovation. There were also solid and professional innings from Ravi Shastri and Sanjay Manjrekar, but the most spectacular effort came from Kapil Dev at Lord's. With the last man in and 24 needed to save the follow-on, he lifted four sixes in as many deliveries into the uncompleted stands of the Nursery End – just in time, for Narendra Hirwani was to fall next ball.

Despite such heroics, India were let down by their lack of cold-blooded professionalism, most obvious when they failed in the task of batting just under four sessions for the draw at Lord's. Under the pressure of having to remain at the wicket, rather than being able to bat with uninhibited aggression, they succumbed more easily than one would have imagined, while at the same time continuing their spectacular strokeplay. It was after the senior batsmen had displayed the same lack of commitment on the final day at Old Trafford that Sachin Tendulkar completed his conquest of English hearts, saving his side from defeat and scoring the sixth century of the match *en route*. There should be many more Test hundreds for Tendulkar; what made his first so special were the circumstances in which he made it, as a seventeen-year-old coming to the rescue of his country. Yet those who had seen him stand up to a barrage of bouncers from the Pakistani fast bowlers at Sialkot the previous winter would have had no doubts about his genius, or his capacity to set an example to colleagues old enough to be father figures. He had already shown his character in the first innings at Manchester when, after waiting nearly an hour for his first run, he went on to regain his one-day touch, and he had dazzled the crowd at Lord's with an unbelievably athletic catch of the sort that only players of his age can attempt.

How different the series might have been was suggested by the way India performed when they batted first in the final Test, on a parched Oval pitch as close to their native conditions as they were likely to find. They made the most of it with their highest score against England, who came to appreciate the difference now that it was their turn to bat after the opposition had ground out a huge total. The ball was spinning on the third day, and when England followed on before lunch on Monday, conditions pointed to India's first victory in an overseas Test since Leeds in 1986. But their bowling was exposed yet again. Inflexible tactics and lack of penetration led the Indians to accept the draw long before England could relax to enjoy their first summer without a defeat since 1979.

Throughout the tour the Indian bowlers had been expensive and rarely looked better than club class, although leg-spinner Hirwani may have been handicapped by a bleeding index finger, which troubled him all summer. Additionally, their wicket-keeper, Kiran More, was generally agreed to have had a poor tour behind the stumps. Nor was there any relief in the county fixtures. The tourists drew all but two of these, beating Kent and losing to Hampshire, with whom they shared the financial rewards provided by the sponsorship of Tetley Bitter. But it was not a summer for bowlers, and England's Angus Fraser was the only one in the series who rose above mediocrity. Getting lift from closer to a length than the quicker Malcolm, he bowled the off-stump line designed to bring out the worst in Indian batsmen. At 28.75 his average was half that of the most economical of his opponents, Anil Kumble, the second of the leg-spinners, who played in only one Test.

But it was the batting which made the series such a success, and one of the finest examples came on its last day at The Oval, with the elegant century of David Gower. The former England captain, if his critics were to be believed, had spent the series inventing ways of getting out, but the threat of having to go to Australia as a tour host rather than as a member of the England team seemed to bring out the best in him. The timing of his strokes was impeccable in a charming 157 not out, and with England not yet out of the woods, so was the timing of the innings. A lot was at stake, for Gower and for his team; he did not disappoint himself or the crowd.

The happy ending for England brought down the curtain on a popular show. The Indians had been model tourists, ever willing to please the spectators and never once questioning the umpiring, the crowded itinerary (twice they went straight from a Test into six days of first-class cricket), the long coach rides in a criss-cross programme, or even some hotels with less than adequate service. Relations between the teams were excellent. Neither two poor umpiring decisions in successive overs at Old Trafford, when India were poised to match England's total, nor the couple of warnings for attempting to interfere with the ball were allowed to dampen the good cheer.

The Indians left England happier for their visit, convinced that the future would be brighter and that a nucleus of players had been found to serve them for some time to come. In the Texaco series they had also rediscovered their talent in the one-day game. Their hosts were similarly pleased. The triumphs in two Test series confirmed that English cricket had emerged from the shadows, and that the brave performances in the Caribbean in the spring had been no flash in the pan. The fact that only twelve players were used in the series against India, as opposed to the 29 who appeared against Australia in 1989, reflected a settled look and greater wisdom among the selectors. Most of all, the series did more for the game than many recent ones, and that in itself was cause for celebration. – R. Mohan.

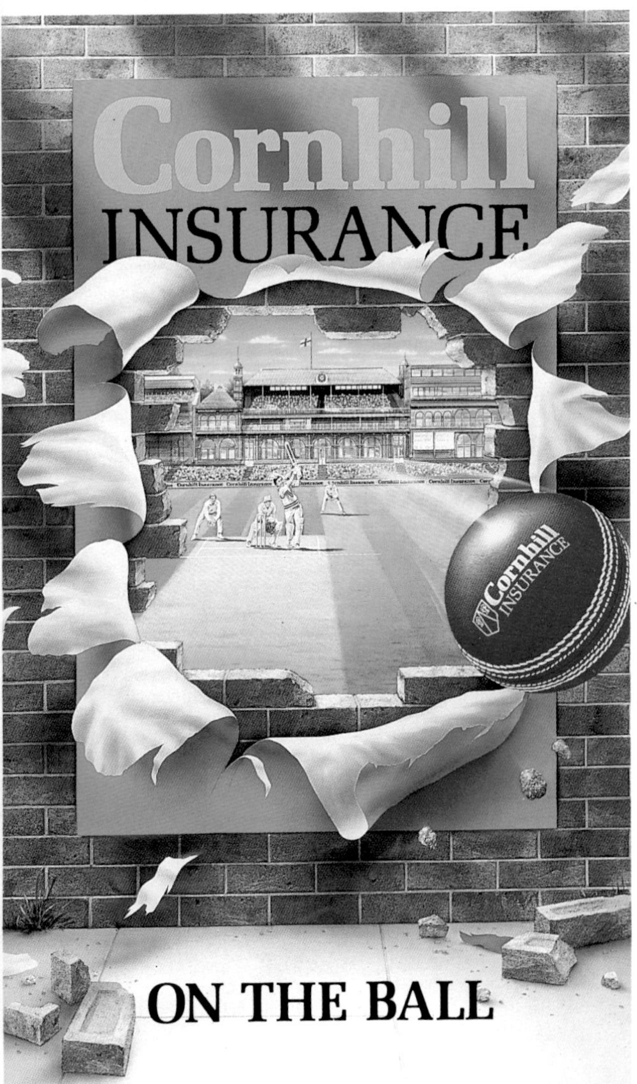

Cornhill
INSURANCE
Cornhill
INSURANCE
ON THE BALL

WELL HELD.

Brewed in th

INDIAN TOUR RESULTS

Test matches – Played 3: Lost 1, Drawn 2.
First-class matches – Played 13: Won 1, Lost 2, Drawn 10.
Win – Kent.
Losses – England, Hampshire.
Draws – England (2), Glamorgan, Gloucestershire, Leicestershire, Michael Parkinson's World XI, Minor Counties, Surrey, TCCB Under-25 XI, Yorkshire.
One-day internationals – Played 2: Won 2.
Other non first-class matches – Played 3: Won 3. *Wins* – Derbyshire, League Cricket Conference, Scotland.

TEST MATCH AVERAGES

ENGLAND – BATTING

	T	*I*	*NO*	*R*	*HI*	*100s*	*Avge*
R. A. Smith	3	6	4	361	121*	2	180.50
G. A. Gooch	3	6	0	752	333	3	125.33
D. I. Gower	3	6	2	291	157*	1	72.75
M. A. Atherton	3	6	0	378	131	1	63.00
A. J. Lamb	3	6	0	364	139	2	60.66
E. E. Hemmings	3	2	0	70	51	0	35.00
R. C. Russell	3	3	1	59	35	0	29.50
D. E. Malcolm	3	2	1	28	15*	0	28.00
J. E. Morris	3	5	2	71	32	0	23.66

Played in three Tests: A. R. C. Fraser 1, 0. Played in two Tests: C. C. Lewis 3. Played in one Test: N. F. Williams 38.

* *Signifies not out.*

BOWLING

	O	*M*	*R*	*W*	*BB*	*5W/i*	*Avge*
A. R. C. Fraser	159.1	41	460	16	5-104	2	28.75
E. E. Hemmings	137.2	26	454	11	3-75	0	41.27
C. C. Lewis	65	8	281	5	2-26	0	56.20
D. E. Malcolm	110	16	436	7	2-65	0	62.28

Also bowled: M. A. Atherton 28–3–161–1; G. A. Gooch 18–4–70–1; N. F. Williams 41–5–148–2.

INDIA – BATTING

	T	*I*	*NO*	*R*	*HI*	*100s*	*Avge*
M. Azharuddin	3	5	0	426	179	2	85.20
R. J. Shastri	3	5	0	336	187	2	67.20
S. R. Tendulkar	3	5	1	245	119*	1	61.25
Kapil Dev	3	5	1	220	110	1	55.00
S. V. Manjrekar	3	5	0	216	93	0	43.20
M. Prabhakar	3	5	1	132	67*	0	33.00
D. B. Vengsarkar	3	5	0	158	52	0	31.60
K. S. More	3	4	1	91	61*	0	30.33
N. D. Hirwani	3	4	3	17	15*	0	17.00
N. S. Sidhu	3	5	0	56	30	0	11.20

Played in one Test: A. Kumble 2; S. K. Sharma 0, 38; A. S. Wassan 15.

* *Signifies not out.*

BOWLING

	O	M	R	W	BB	5W/i	Avge
A. Kumble	60	10	170	3	3-105	0	56.66
A. S. Wassan	37	5	173	3	2-79	0	57.66
Kapil Dev	128	23	445	7	2-66	0	63.57
N. D. Hirwani	212	41	586	9	4-174	0	65.11
S. K. Sharma	48	5	197	3	2-75	0	65.66
M. Prabhakar	155	28	554	8	4-74	0	69.25
R. J. Shastri	95.5	6	341	2	1-29	0	170.50

INDIAN AVERAGES – FIRST-CLASS MATCHES

BATTING

	M	I	NO	R	HI	100s	Avge
M. Azharuddin	9	11	1	770	179	3	77.00
R. J. Shastri	9	11	1	644	187	4	64.40
S. R. Tendulkar	11	19	4	945	119*	2	63.00
S. V. Manjrekar	11	17	3	814	158*	2	58.14
D. B. Vengsarkar	10	14	4	576	83*	0	57.60
W. V. Raman	8	15	2	623	127	1	47.92
N. S. Sidhu	9	17	3	639	142	2	45.64
N. R. Mongia	8	11	4	269	63*	0	38.42
Kapil Dev	9	12	2	377	110	1	37.70
S. K. Sharma	9	7	3	132	38	0	33.00
K. S. More	9	11	2	295	95	0	32.77
M. Prabhakar	10	14	3	296	76	0	26.90
S. L. V. Raju	6	6	2	105	40*	0	26.25
A. S. Wassan	9	3	1	47	24	0	23.50
A. Kumble	7	5	2	63	35*	0	21.00
N. D. Hirwani	9	5	3	17	15*	0	8.50

* *Signifies not out.*

BOWLING

	O	M	R	W	BB	5W/i	Avge
N. D. Hirwani	399.2	59	1,280	31	5-117	1	41.29
A. Kumble	212	40	660	14	6-49	1	47.14
A. S. Wassan	207.3	24	886	18	6-89	1	49.22
Kapil Dev	246.4	59	744	13	2-28	0	57.23
S. L. V. Raju	182.3	41	528	9	4-73	0	58.66
M. Prabhakar	281	47	994	16	4-74	0	62.12
S. K. Sharma	229	36	873	13	2-53	0	67.15
R. J. Shastri	199.2	30	607	7	2-80	0	86.71

Also bowled: K. S. More 8–0–54–0; W. V. Raman 15–2–72–1; S. R. Tendulkar 79–12–268–3.

FIELDING

18 – K. S. More (17 ct, 1 st); 12 – N. R. Mongia (9 ct, 3 st); 6 – S. V. Manjrekar, W. V. Raman, R. J. Shastri; 5 – S. R. Tendulkar; 4 – M. Prabhakar, D. B. Vengsarkar; 3 – M. Azharuddin, N. D. Hirwani, Kapil Dev; 2 – S. K. Sharma; 1 – A. Kumble, N. S. Sidhu, Substitute.

HUNDREDS FOR INDIANS

The following sixteen three-figure innings were played for the Indians, fifteen in first-class matches and one in a non first-class match.

R. J. Shastri (4)
105 v Minor Counties, Trowbridge
100 v England, Lord's (First Test)
133 v Glos., Bristol
187 v England, The Oval (Third Test)

M. Azharuddin (3)
105 v Minor Counties, Trowbridge
121 v England, Lord's (First Test)
179 v England, Manchester (Second Test)

S. R. Tendulkar (3)
†105* v Derbys., Chesterfield
119* v England, Manchester (Second Test)
108 v Michael Parkinson's World XI, Scarborough

S. V. Manjrekar (2)
158* v Yorks., Leeds
116 v TCCB Under-25 XI, Birmingham

N. S. Sidhu (2)
142 v Glos., Bristol
108* v TCCB Under-25 XI, Birmingham

Kapil Dev (1)
110 v England, The Oval (Third Test)

W. V. Raman (1)
127 v Surrey, The Oval

* *Signifies not out.* † *Not first-class.*

Note: Those matches which follow which were not first-class are signified by the use of a dagger.

†LEAGUE CRICKET CONFERENCE v INDIANS

At Sunderland, June 28. Indians won by 40 runs. Toss: Indians. Although the Indians began their tour with a win, it was hard earned, and they would have been harder pressed had there been more support for McLeod. The West Indian all-rounder and Radcliffe professional hit two sixes and four fours in his late assault before running out of overs just 4 runs short of his half-century. Holmes, a 21-year-old medium-pace bowler from Kearsley in the Bolton League, was the pick of the Conference attack, which was promising to embarrass the touring team until More and Raju added 67 for the seventh wicket.

Indians

W. V. Raman b Walcott	0
N. S. Sidhu b Day	17
S. R. Tendulkar c Wundke b Holmes	19
D. B. Vengsarkar c Borthwick b Day	28
*M. Azharuddin b Wundke	20
Kapil Dev c Tuckwell b Wundke	0
†K. S. More b Wundke	58
S. L. V. Raju not out	34
S. K. Sharma c Lambert b Walcott	5
A. S. Wassan c Ingham b McLeod	10
A. Kumble not out	1
B 7, l-b 9, w 19, n-b 4	39
1/1 2/51 3/51 4/87 5/89 6/128 7/195 8/216 9/227 (9 wkts, 55 overs)	231

Bowling: McLeod 11–1–44–1; Walcott 11–2–37–2; Holmes 11–3–20–1; Day 11–1–73–2; Wundke 11–0–41–3.

League Cricket Conference

Batsman	Runs
C. B. Lambert c Kapil Dev b Sharma	22
D. Lampitt c Vengsarkar b Sharma	15
D. A. Tuckwell c Vengsarkar b Wassan	17
*N. J. Heaton st More b Kumble	41
M. J. Ingham lbw b Sharma	26
S. C. Wundke c More b Kumble	3
K. W. McLeod not out	46
†D. Borthwick lbw b Kapil Dev	1
V. D. Walcott b Kapil Dev	0
A. C. Day c More b Sharma	1
B. L. Holmes not out	0
B 10, w 3, n-b 6	19
1/41 2/48 3/82 4/119 5/127 6/189 7/190 8/190 9/191 (9 wkts, 55 overs)	191

Bowling: Kapil Dev 10–3–29–2; Sharma 10–2–25–4; Wassan 7–0–39–1; Tendulkar 6–1–16–0; Kumble 11–4–32–2; Raju 11–0–40–0.

Umpires: J. Atkinson and B. Johnson.

YORKSHIRE v INDIANS

At Leeds, June 30, July 1, 2. Drawn. Toss: Indians. The tourists took full advantage of a favourable pitch and a weakened Yorkshire attack, in which left-arm spinner Doidge was making his début, to score at more than 4 runs an over. Manjrekar led the way, striking his unbeaten 158 from 181 balls, and sharing partnerships of 110 in 24 overs with Sidhu and 159 from 35 overs with Vengsarkar. Bad light and rain reduced the first day to 69.5 overs and the second to 24, but both sides declared at their overnight totals to create a competitive situation, Moxon and Metcalfe having scored briskly in the time available on the second day. The high standards of batting were maintained by Shastri and Azharuddin, who finally set a target of 343 in 75 overs, five of which were lost to a brief shower. Taking up the challenge, Moxon and Metcalfe put on 152 in 33 overs, and the Yorkshire captain's fluent strokeplay brought him 93 runs from 111 balls, including one six and fifteen fours. The momentum could not be maintained, however, and Yorkshire, whose highest fourth-innings total to win a match was 331 for eight against Middlesex at Lord's in 1910, settled for a draw. For the Indians, Kapil Dev and Hirwani bowled with restraint under pressure.

Close of play: First day, Indians 294-2 (S. V. Manjrekar 158*, D. B. Vengsarkar 47*); Second day, Yorkshire 88-0 (M. D. Moxon 45*, A. A. Metcalfe 40*).

Indians

Batsman	First innings		Second innings	
W. V. Raman c Byas b Fletcher		12	b Houseman	0
N. S. Sidhu c Blakey b Fletcher		61	c Blakey b Houseman	3
S. V. Manjrekar not out		158		
D. B. Vengsarkar not out		47		
R. J. Shastri (did not bat)		–	(3) not out	53
*M. Azharuddin (did not bat)		–	(4) not out	75
L-b 3, n-b 13		16	L-b 2, n-b 3	5
1/25 2/135	(2 wkts dec.)	294	1/0 2/12 (2 wkts dec.)	136

Kapil Dev, †K. S. More, M. Prabhakar, A. S. Wassan and N. D. Hirwani did not bat.

Bowling: *First Innings*—Houseman 13–2–43–0; Sidebottom 12.5–1–46–0; Fletcher 18–2–82–2; Byas 5–0–29–0; White 7–2–37–0; Doidge 14–2–54–0. *Second Innings*—Houseman 7–1–26–2; Sidebottom 4–1–23–0; Doidge 10–3–52–0; Fletcher 6–0–17–0; Byas 3–0–16–0.

Yorkshire

Batsman	First innings		Second innings	
*M. D. Moxon not out		45	c Kapil Dev b Hirwani	93
A. A. Metcalfe not out		40	b Shastri	74
K. Sharp (did not bat)		–	c Shastri b Hirwani	2
S. A. Kellett (did not bat)		–	not out	36
†R. J. Blakey (did not bat)		–	b Kapil Dev	2
D. Byas (did not bat)		–	not out	8
L-b 1, n-b 2		3	B 1, l-b 8, w 1	10
	(no wkt dec.)	88	1/152 2/161 3/192 4/208 (4 wkts)	225

M. J. Doidge, C. White, A. Sidebottom, I. J. Houseman and S. D. Fletcher did not bat.

Bowling: *First Innings*—Kapil Dev 8–2–13–0; Prabhakar 8–1–38–0; Wassan 5–0–31–0; Shastri 3–2–5–0. *Second Innings*—Kapil Dev 10–3–37–1; Prabhakar 8–0–48–0; Shastri 16–2–54–1; Wassan 6–2–24–0; Hirwani 13–1–45–2; Raman 3–1–8–0.

Umpires: H. D. Bird and J. H. Hampshire.

HAMPSHIRE v INDIANS

At Southampton, July 4, 5, 6. Hampshire won by seven wickets. Toss: Indians. Azharuddin's willingness to contribute to a genuine contest, rather than to seek batting practice after the first day had been lost to the weather, provided Hampshire with a chance to defeat a touring side for the first time for eight years. The Indian captain's second declaration challenged them to score 305 in a minimum of 62 overs, and after the early loss of Terry and Smith, Nicholas played with characteristic power and authority. With Gower, also at his best, he added 155 in 30 overs, mostly of spin, before being bowled for 104. His only first-class century of the summer, it came from 133 balls and included fourteen boundaries. Gower was undefeated at the close with 126, his second first-class hundred for his new county, having hit two sixes and fourteen fours to secure Hampshire's win with three overs to spare. As well as a victory to savour, the match also gave the Hampshire public the opportunity to assess the exciting potential of Tendulkar, and the seventeen-year-old did not disappoint them in two innings of considerable maturity.

Close of play: First day, No play; Second day, Hampshire 117-2 (M. C. J. Nicholas 37*, D. I. Gower 44*).

Indians

First innings	Second innings
W. V. Raman c Terry b Joseph . . . 26	c Maru b Connor . . . 22
N. S. Sidhu c Terry b Joseph . . . 6	not out . . . 58
S. R. Tendulkar c Terry b Bakker . . . 32	not out . . . 58
D. B. Vengsarkar c Parks b Connor . . . 21	
*M. Azharuddin b Ayling . . . 74	
M. Prabhakar c and b Maru . . . 76	
†N. R. Mongia not out . . . 14	
S. L. V. Raju c Parks b Maru . . . 18	
B 6, l-b 3, w 2 . . . 11	B 1, l-b 3, n-b 1 . . . 5
1/22 2/39 3/78 4/92 5/240 6/246 7/278 (7 wkts dec.) 278	1/38 (1 wkt dec.) 143

S. K. Sharma, A. Kumble and N. D. Hirwani did not bat.

Bowling: *First Innings*—Bakker 22–1–84–1; Joseph 10–2–28–2; Connor 14–4–43–1; Ayling 15–2–45–1; Maru 16.4–1–69–2. *Second Innings*—Connor 8–3–28–1; Bakker 13–2–37–0; Ayling 8–1–26–0; Maru 6–0–31–0; Nicholas 4–0–17–0.

Hampshire

First innings	Second innings
V. P. Terry c Raman b Prabhakar . . . 5	lbw b Sharma . . . 11
C. L. Smith c Raman b Hirwani . . . 24	lbw b Prabhakar . . . 36
*M. C. J. Nicholas not out . . . 37	b Prabhakar . . . 104
D. I. Gower not out . . . 44	not out . . . 126
J. R. Ayling (did not bat) . . . –	not out . . . 21
L-b 1, n-b 6 . . . 7	B 2, l-b 7, n-b 1 . . . 10
1/13 2/55 (2 wkts dec.) 117	1/26 2/85 3/240 (3 wkts) 308

T. C. Middleton, L. A. Joseph, †R. J. Parks, R. J. Maru, C. A. Connor and P. J. Bakker did not bat.

Bowling: *First Innings*—Prabhakar 8–1–20–1; Sharma 8–0–34–0; Hirwani 7–1–25–1; Raju 9–2–28–0; Kumble 2–0–9–0. *Second Innings*—Prabhakar 19–0–102–2; Sharma 16–3–79–1; Raju 13–1–56–0; Hirwani 8–0–39–0; Kumble 5–0–23–0.

Umpires: N. T. Plews and D. R. Shepherd.

KENT v INDIANS

At Canterbury, July 7, 8, 9. Indians won by seven wickets. Toss: Kent. Hinks and Benson gave Kent a solid start, which Taylor built on with an unbeaten 107, hitting seventeen fours in a stay of 241 minutes before Chris Cowdrey declared. Opening the innings because of sickness in the Indian team, Tendulkar stroked fourteen fours as he made 92 of the first 154 runs, facing 156 balls. The tourists declared well behind and were rewarded with a target of 265 to win in a minimum of 62 overs. After another fine performance from Tendulkar, who this time scored his 70 runs in 99 balls with eight fours, Vengsarkar (105 balls, thirteen fours) and Kapil Dev (72 balls) applied the finishing touches, adding 137 in 25 overs to win the game convincingly with three overs to spare. This was to be the Indians' only victory in the county games.

Close of play: First day, Kent 257-2 (N. R. Taylor 58*, G. R. Cowdrey 24*); Second day, Kent 25-0 (S. A. Marsh 16*, M. V. Fleming 8*).

Kent

S. G. Hinks b Raju	62			
M. R. Benson b Hirwani	90			
N. R. Taylor not out	107			
G. R. Cowdrey c More b Wassan	44	–	(6) not out	27
*C. S. Cowdrey not out	20	–	(4) c Tendulkar b Hirwani	12
†S. A. Marsh (did not bat)		–	(1) c Sharma b Raju	44
M. V. Fleming (did not bat)		–	(2) c Hirwani b Wassan	21
R. M. Ellison (did not bat)		–	(3) not out	29
T. A. Merrick (did not bat)		–	(5) b Hirwani	6
B 7, l-b 8, w 2, n-b 10	27		B 4, l-b 5	9
1/126 2/196 3/295 (3 wkts dec.)	350		1/44 2/82 3/96 4/104 (4 wkts dec.)	148

C. Penn and R. P. Davis did not bat.

Bowling: *First Innings*—Kapil Dev 21–6–58–0; Prabhakar 10–1–34–0; Sharma 11–3–37–0; Wassan 24–3–101–1; Shastri 10–2–37–0; Hirwani 14–2–41–1; Raju 14–7–27–1. *Second Innings*—Kapil Dev 8–3–20–0; Sharma 3–0–11–0; Raju 17.3–5–41–1; Hirwani 16–4–48–2; Wassan 3–0–19–1.

Indians

†K. S. More c Taylor b Fleming	32	–	c Penn b Fleming	27
S. R. Tendulkar c Davis b Merrick	92	–	st Marsh b Davis	70
S. V. Manjrekar c Davis b Penn	20	–	c Marsh b Fleming	9
D. B. Vengsarkar not out	50	–	not out	83
Kapil Dev c Ellison b Davis	17	–	not out	59
S. L. V. Raju lbw b Penn	4			
S. K. Sharma not out	13			
L-b 3, n-b 3	6		B 8, l-b 9, n-b 2	19
1/75 2/125 3/154 4/189 5/204 (5 wkts dec.)	234		1/66 2/96 3/130 (3 wkts)	267

*R. J. Shastri, M. Prabhakar, A. S. Wassan and N. D. Hirwani did not bat.

Bowling: *First Innings*—Merrick 17–2–75–1; Penn 16–2–40–2; Davis 23–4–66–1; G. R. Cowdrey 1–1–0–0; Ellison 11–2–27–0; Fleming 8.3–2–23–1. *Second Innings*—Merrick 4.1–1–17–0; Penn 12–0–61–0; Davis 17.5–0–90–1; Ellison 8–1–23–0; Fleming 11–5–28–2; C. S. Cowdrey 4–0–19–0; G. R. Cowdrey 2–0–12–0.

Umpires: M. J. Kitchen and N. T. Plews.

MINOR COUNTIES v INDIANS

At Trowbridge, July 11, 12, 13. Drawn. Toss: Minor Counties. On a pitch perfect for batting, both sides laid out a feast of runs as the Minor Counties entertained a touring side at Trowbridge for the third year in succession. Brown of Durham, brother of the Middlesex middle-order batsman, and Buckinghamshire's Roberts were the principal beneficiaries on the opening day before Kumble changed the emphasis with six for 27 in nine overs after tea.

Roberts posted his fifty in 78 balls in their partnership of 178 in 64 overs, and Brown was still savouring his maiden first-class hundred, which included a six off Raju and eleven fours, when he was smartly stumped off Kumble in the first over after tea. Three balls later the leg-spinner had the left-handed Folland lbw as he attempted to sweep, and the Minor Counties went into a decline. Next day, with the sun blazing down, Raman hit eleven boundaries while racing to his fifty, and Shastri revealed his aptitude as an opening bat. Stuck in the 90s for thirteen overs, he danced to three figures by straight-driving the steady, 46-year-old medium-pacer, Greensword, for six. Azharuddin stroked fifteen fours in his hundred, two and a half hours of great charm, and Tendulkar and Kapil Dev (four sixes in 47 from 39 balls) made sure the entertainment matched the temperature. A lead of 219 offered the Indians a prospect of victory. Instead, Brown and Folland added 157 in 44 overs, and with play scheduled to finish at four o'clock to accommodate their travel arrangements, the tourists settled for a draw. However, the decision to draw stumps after only eight of the last twenty overs robbed Brown of the chance to record two hundreds in the match, leaving him unbeaten with 89 after 4 hours 21 minutes (215 balls, fourteen fours). The first-class status of the match, uncertain at the time, was later confirmed by the TCCB.

Close of play: First day, Indians 24-0 (R. J. Shastri 15*, W. V. Raman 5*); Second day, Indians 512-6 dec.

Minor Counties

G. K. Brown st Mongia b Kumble	103	– not out	89
M. J. Roberts b Shastri	85	– c Azharuddin b Sharma	1
P. Burn c Mongia b Sharma	0	– (4) not out	47
N. A. Folland lbw b Kumble	26	– (3) b Raju	82
T. A. Lester c Raman b Kumble	4		
D. R. Thomas c Shastri b Kumble	27		
*S. Greensword c Mongia b Kapil Dev	1		
†A. R. Fothergill b Kumble	3		
R. A. Evans not out	4		
N. R. Taylor b Kumble	0		
B 8, l-b 17, w 6, n-b 9	40	B 20, l-b 2, n-b 2	24
1/178 2/183 3/245 4/246 5/250 6/253 7/264 8/293 9/293 (9 wkts dec.)	293	1/6 2/163 (2 wkts)	243

K. A. Arnold did not bat.

Bowling: *First Innings*—Kapil Dev 14–6–27–1; Sharma 15–4–43–1; Wassan 9–1–36–0; Raju 21–4–67–0; Kumble 18–3–49–6; Shastri 20–4–43–1; Tendulkar 1–0–3–0. *Second Innings*—Kapil Dev 16–9–20–0; Sharma 15–4–47–1; Wassan 9–0–42–0; Kumble 16–4–54–0; Raju 18–4–58–1.

Indians

R. J. Shastri b Evans	105	†N. R. Mongia not out	43
W. V. Raman c Greensword b Arnold	55	S. L. V. Raju not out	33
S. V. Manjrekar run out	40	B 5, l-b 4, w 3, n-b 7	19
*M. Azharuddin c Arnold b Taylor	105		
Kapil Dev c Arnold b Evans	47	1/102 2/201 3/238 (6 wkts dec.)	512
S. R. Tendulkar lbw b Brown	65	4/312 5/426 6/449	

S. K. Sharma, A. S. Wassan and A. Kumble did not bat.

Bowling: Taylor 23–2–87–1; Arnold 28–6–113–1; Evans 28–1–147–2; Thomas 15–1–65–0; Greensword 19–6–52–0; Brown 9–1–39–1.

Umpires: D. J. Halfyard and G. A. Stickley.

†SCOTLAND v INDIANS

At Titwood, Glasgow, July 14. Indians won by seven wickets. Toss: Indians. Put in on a pitch containing some moisture and with cloud overhead, Scotland struggled to 89 for five at lunch, with the slow left-armer, Raju, taking three wickets courtesy of catches by the bat-pad fieldsmen. Patterson and Salmond, the latter in his first match for Scotland, were out to successive balls. The afternoon brought sunshine and something of a recovery as Henry, who hit a six and eight fours in his 74, and Russell took their sixth-wicket stand to 122 in 81 minutes together. In reply, the Indians batted attractively but well within themselves, and neither the Scottish bowling nor a bomb alert could disturb their serenity.

Scotland

I. L. Philip run out	14	D. Cowan not out	1
C. G. Greenidge lbw b Sharma	34	A. Bee not out	2
B. M. W. Patterson c Manjrekar b Raju	0	L-b 13, w 3, n-b 1	17
G. Salmond c Manjrekar b Raju	0		—
*O. Henry c Raman b Kapil Dev	74	1/44 2/45 3/45 (7 wkts, 55 overs)	196
†D. J. Haggo c Tendulkar b Raju	6	4/56 5/71	
A. B. Russell c and b Kapil Dev	48	6/193 7/194	

C. T. McKnight and J. D. Moir did not bat.

Bowling: Kapil Dev 10–2–25–2; Prabhakar 10–2–43–0; Sharma 11–1–27–1; Tendulkar 3–1–9–0; Raju 11–3–22–3; Kumble 10–0–57–0.

Indians

N. S. Sidhu c McKnight b Henry	50	Kapil Dev not out	11
W. V. Raman c Haggo b Bee	89	B 2, l-b 2, w 1, n-b 4	9
S. V. Manjrekar c Greenidge b Bee	31		—
S. R. Tendulkar not out	10	1/98 2/160 3/183 (3 wkts, 51.3 overs)	200

*M. Azharuddin, M. Prabhakar, S. L. V. Raju, †K. S. More, S. K. Sharma and A. Kumble did not bat.

Bowling: Moir 9–1–34–0; Cowan 9.3–0–48–0; Bee 11–1–35–2; McKnight 11–2–29–0; Henry 11–0–50–1.

Umpires: J. van Geloven and A. Wood.

†DERBYSHIRE v INDIANS

At Chesterfield, July 16. Indians won by two wickets. Toss: Derbyshire. Barnett's fine hundred, scored freely against undemanding bowling, was capped by an exquisite innings from Tendulkar. The Derbyshire captain began in rich form, though he was dropped by More on 10, and his 115 took his total of runs in July to 784. His century included a six and ten fours, and the opening stand of 137 with Bowler was their seventh hundred partnership in all cricket during the season. While the experienced batsmen failed in the Indians' reply, Tendulkar shaped the innings as he wished, impressing the Derbyshire crowd and players not so much by his obvious quality as by his astonishing maturity. He completed his hundred from 147 balls, by hooking Bishop over the trees at square leg, and he clinched the game with his seventh four. But Derbyshire's undisciplined bowling also helped the Indians; they gave away 17 runs in wides and 16 in no-balls.

Derbyshire

*K. J. Barnett c Sidhu b Kapil Dev	115	†K. M. Krikken not out	0
P. D. Bowler b Raju	59		
J. E. Morris c sub b Kapil Dev	37	L-b 7, w 4, n-b 2	13
B. Roberts c Azharuddin b Kapil Dev	8		—
C. J. Adams run out	0	1/137 2/208 3/223 (6 wkts, 55 overs)	235
S. C. Goldsmith run out	3	4/224 5/235 6/235	

G. Miller, I. R. Bishop, S. J. Base and O. H. Mortensen did not bat.

Bowling: Kapil Dev 11–1–76–3; Prabhakar 11–2–29–0; Sharma 11–0–51–0; Kumble 11–1–26–0; Raju 11–0–46–1.

Indians

W. V. Raman b Base	17	S. L. V. Raju c Roberts b Miller	1
N. S. Sidhu lbw b Bishop	0	S. K. Sharma not out	8
S. R. Tendulkar not out	105		
*M. Azharuddin lbw b Miller	7	L-b 2, w 17, n-b 16	35
Kapil Dev c Barnett b Mortensen	1		—
M. Prabhakar run out	31	1/5 2/59 3/80 (8 wkts, 54.4 overs)	239
†K. S. More c Barnett b Miller	6	4/81 5/134 6/144	
D. B. Vengsarkar st Krikken b Miller	28	7/210 8/212	

A. Kumble did not bat.

Bowling: Mortensen 11–1–31–1; Bishop 11–2–44–1; Base 11–0–45–1; Goldsmith 10.4–0–71–0; Miller 11–0–46–4.

Umpires: H. D. Bird and M. J. Kitchen.

†ENGLAND v INDIA

First Texaco Trophy Match

At Leeds, July 18. India won by six wickets. Toss: India. The touring side won comfortably after their bowlers, under-rated in the pre-match forecasts, had dismissed England for 229 inside 55 overs. Such a total seemed unlikely as Gooch and Gower were putting on 64 untroubled runs for the second wicket. But when Gooch was beaten by cleverly disguised flight in Shastri's fifth over and Kumble bowled Gower with a ball that turned a long way, then undid Smith with bounce in his next over, England found themselves 142 for four with thirteen overs remaining. Their next six wickets managed 87, with the last four falling in fifteen deliveries. Although the pitch was on the slow side for one-day batting, all credit was due to the Indian bowlers. Kumble, a leg-spinner, did not concede a boundary in taking two for 29, and he and Shastri bowled their overs straight through. India lost Raman to the first legitimate ball of their innings, DeFreitas having begun with a no-ball. Thereafter they coasted along. Sidhu was out just before tea; afterwards Tendulkar roused the crowd by driving Hemmings straight for six, Manjrekar (133 balls) and Azharuddin (50 balls) added 68 in ten overs, and finally Shastri hit four fours in his 23 to hurry India to victory with two overs to spare.

Man of the Match: A. Kumble. *Attendance:* 16,000 est.; *receipts* £229,819.

England

*G. A. Gooch c and b Shastri	45	A. R. C. Fraser not out	4
M. A. Atherton lbw b Prabhakar	7	D. E. Malcolm c Kapil Dev b Prabhakar	4
D. I. Gower b Kumble	50		
A. J. Lamb c Prabhakar b Kapil Dev	56	B 6, l-b 8, w 9	23
R. A. Smith c More b Kumble	6		—
†R. C. Russell c Manjrekar b Kapil Dev	14	1/22 (2) 2/86 (1) 3/134 (3) (54.3 overs)	229
P. A. J. DeFreitas b Sharma	11	4/142 (5) 5/186 (6) 6/196 (4)	
C. C. Lewis lbw b Prabhakar	6	7/211 (8) 8/221 (9)	
E. E. Hemmings b Sharma	3	9/224 (7) 10/229 (11)	

Bowling: Kapil Dev 11–1–49–2; Prabhakar 10.3–1–40–3; Sharma 11–1–57–2; Shastri 11–0–40–1; Kumble 11–2–29–2.

India

W. V. Raman c Atherton b DeFreitas	0	R. J. Shastri not out	23
N. S. Sidhu lbw b Lewis	39	L-b 5, w 9, n-b 1	15
S. V. Manjrekar c Gower b Lewis	82		—
S. R. Tendulkar b Malcolm	19	1/1 (1) 2/76 (2) (4 wkts, 53 overs)	233
*M. Azharuddin not out	55	3/115 (4) 4/183 (3)	

†K. S. More, Kapil Dev, M. Prabhakar, S. K. Sharma and A. Kumble did not bat.

Bowling: DeFreitas 10–1–40–1; Malcolm 11–0–57–1; Fraser 11–3–37–0; Lewis 10–0–58–2; Hemmings 11–0–36–0.

Umpires: J. H. Hampshire and J. W. Holder.

†ENGLAND v INDIA

Second Texaco Trophy Match

At Nottingham, July 20. India won by five wickets. Toss: India. The Indian batsmen revelled gloriously in ideal batting conditions; England's failed to do them, or themselves, justice. Gooch lost his off stump in the fourth over, offering no stroke to an in-swinger, and Gower and Lamb had been run out by the twentieth over. Having hit 24 of his 25 runs in boundaries, Gower was a victim of his own inattentiveness and the quick thinking of wicket-keeper More, whose throw hit the stumps at the non-striker's end. Smith gave the innings its purpose, reaching fifty from 42 balls and thumping most of the eleven fours in his 103 (105 balls). He added 111 in eighteen overs with the admirable Atherton (95 balls), and then 73 in twelve overs with Russell (50 balls); but when he was bowled in the 49th over, England's next five wickets realised just 35 runs. Small gave the Indians a flying start, conceding 12 runs in his first over, and when later he bowled Sidhu, Manjrekar held the innings together with 59 in 94 balls. By the time he was stumped he had caught the infectious mood of Vengsarkar's batting. India required 145 from the last twenty overs, and Tendulkar (26 balls) played some outrageous shots while adding 63 in seven overs with the felicitous Azharuddin, who went on to score 63 from 44 balls as India again won with two overs in hand. The defeat was England's tenth in their last eleven completed one-day internationals.

Man of the Match: R. A. Smith. *Attendance:* 11,996; *receipts* £217,631.
Men of the Series: England – R. C. Russell; India – M. Azharuddin.

England

*G. A. Gooch b Prabhakar 7
M. A. Atherton c More b Prabhakar .. 59
D. I. Gower run out 25
A. J. Lamb run out 3
R. A. Smith b Shastri 103
†R. C. Russell c Azharuddin b Kapil Dev . 50
P. A. J. DeFreitas c Vengsarkar b Sharma . 1
C. C. Lewis lbw b Prabhakar 7
G. C. Small c Azharuddin b Kapil Dev. 4
E. E. Hemmings run out 0
A. R. C. Fraser not out 0
B 1, l-b 12, w 8, n-b 1 22

1/12 (1) 2/47 (3) 3/62 (4) 4/173 (2) 5/246 (5) 6/254 (7) 7/275 (8) 8/280 (9) 9/281 (10) 10/281 (6) (55 overs) 281

Bowling: Kapil Dev 11–2–40–2; Prabhakar 11–0–58–3; Sharma 10–0–50–1; Shastri 11–0–52–1; Kumble 11–1–58–0; Tendulkar 1–0–10–0.

India

R. J. Shastri c Atherton b Hemmings .. 33
N. S. Sidhu b Small 23
S. V. Manjrekar st Russell b Hemmings 59
D. B. Vengsarkar b Lewis 54
*M. Azharuddin not out 63
S. R. Tendulkar b Fraser 31
Kapil Dev not out 5
L-b 5, w 9 14

1/42 (2) 2/69 (1) 3/166 (3) 4/186 (4) 5/249 (6) (5 wkts, 53 overs) 282

†K. S. More, M. Prabhakar, S. K. Sharma and A. Kumble did not bat.

Bowling: Small 10–0–73–1; DeFreitas 11–0–59–0; Fraser 11–1–38–1; Hemmings 11–1–53–2; Lewis 10–0–54–1.

Umpires: M. J. Kitchen and D. R. Shepherd.

LEICESTERSHIRE v INDIANS

At Leicester, July 21, 22, 23. Drawn. Toss: Leicestershire. Noisily supported by members of Leicester's large Indian community, the visitors found an opportunity to practise their strokes for the Lord's Test in their first innings, averaging 4 runs an over. Leicestershire's batsmen were also among the runs, however, and their captain, Briers, dominated the first day with his unbeaten 150. Having survived a chance when 42, he went on to bat for six hours, hitting seventeen fours and passing 1,000 first-class runs for the season. Whitaker helped him put on 131 for the second wicket and later he added 86 for the seventh with Benjamin, who struck three sixes in his 55. The West Indian fast bowler removed Prabhakar on the first evening, but the Leicestershire attack, already missing the injured Agnew, was weakened the next day when Lewis withdrew because of a headache. Manjrekar, Vengsarkar and Mongia made the most of it, and the Indians' reserve wicket-keeper hit seven fours and a six in his 63 not out. The match was destined to drift towards a draw once Azharuddin chose to bat on for almost an hour after tea on the second day, but Benson enlivened the final day's play by striking twelve fours and three sixes in his maiden first-class hundred. Leicestershire's declaration left the tourists to score an unrealistic 248 from a minimum of 31 overs, only nineteen of which were bowled.

Close of play: First day, Indians 23-1 (N. S. Sidhu 8*, S. V. Manjrekar 8*); Second day, Leicestershire 35-1 (L. Potter 10*, J. D. R. Benson 8*).

Leicestershire

Batsman	First innings		Second innings	
T. J. Boon	b Sharma	1	c Hirwani b Wassan	16
*N. E. Briers	not out	150		
J. J. Whitaker	b Hirwani	61	(9) not out	7
P. Willey	c Tendulkar b Hirwani	5	b Raju	76
L. Potter	b Wassan	22	(2) b Hirwani	30
C. C. Lewis	c Manjrekar b Raju	1	(5) c Prabhakar b Raju	28
J. D. R. Benson	c Sharma b Wassan	0	(3) c Prabhakar b Hirwani	106
W. K. M. Benjamin	c Mongia b Wassan	55	(7) b Raju	0
†P. A. Nixon	not out	3	(6) hit wkt b Raju	13
G. J. Parsons	(did not bat)	–	(8) not out	11
	B 8, w 1, n-b 3	12	L-b 8, w 1, n-b 2	11
	1/1 2/132 3/150 4/199 5/216 6/217 7/303	(7 wkts dec.) 310	1/25 2/108 3/181 4/234 5/274 6/274 7/281	(7 wkts dec.) 298

A. D. Mullally did not bat.

Bowling: *First Innings*—Prabhakar 10–1–35–0; Sharma 16–5–41–1; Tendulkar 1–0–9–0; Wassan 17–1–76–3; Raju 30–7–62–1; Hirwani 22–1–79–2. *Second Innings*—Prabhakar 5–3–6–0; Sharma 13–2–52–0; Wassan 15–0–56–1; Raju 28–6–73–4; Hirwani 21–0–103–2.

Indians

Batsman	First innings		Second innings	
M. Prabhakar	c Potter b Benjamin	2	c Nixon b Lewis	13
N. S. Sidhu	c Nixon b Lewis	25	lbw b Lewis	6
S. V. Manjrekar	c Nixon b Mullally	66	not out	3
S. R. Tendulkar	c Benson b Parsons	30	not out	25
D. B. Vengsarkar	c Whitaker b Potter	80		
*M. Azharuddin	c Mullally b Willey	46		
†N. R. Mongia	not out	63		
S. L. V. Raju	run out	3		
S. K. Sharma	not out	23		
	B 10, l-b 9, n-b 4	23	L-b 6, n-b 1	7
	1/8 2/76 3/131 4/135 5/227 6/285 7/302	(7 wkts dec.) 361	1/20 2/25	(2 wkts) 54

A. S. Wassan and N. D. Hirwani did not bat.

Bowling: *First Innings*—Benjamin 20–2–81–1; Lewis 11–3–28–1; Parsons 16–2–73–1; Mullally 18–1–78–1; Willey 17–5–42–1; Potter 12–1–40–1. *Second Innings*—Lewis 8–3–23–2; Benjamin 4–1–8–0; Mullally 5–0–17–0; Parsons 2–2–0–0.

Umpires: J. H. Harris and J. W. Holder.

ENGLAND v INDIA

First Cornhill Test

At Lord's, July 26, 27, 28, 30, 31. England won by 247 runs. Toss: India. The Indians, and especially their captain, Azharuddin, had small reason to think so by the end, but the First Test was as brilliant a match as the players could hope to take part in, or spectators to watch. England's winning margin made it look one-sided; and no-one would dispute that, from lunch on the first day, when they were 82 for one after being put in, England were in control until the end. Certainly England's win, inspired by Gooch's historic innings of 333 and 123, which broke all kinds of records, was the result of a powerful performance by his team, and following the victory over New Zealand in the last Test of the previous series, it provided the first instance of England winning successive Tests since 1985. Yet it would not have been the match it was without the vibrant batting of the tourists. Shastri and Azharuddin made splendid hundreds of contrasting styles, and Kapil Dev struck a high-velocity 77 not out, jauntily rounded off with four successive sixes to limit England's lead to 199 and thus save the follow-on. Each was straight-driven off Hemmings's off-spin into the building works that throughout the season masqueraded as the Nursery End. When India were challenged by Gooch's second declaration to make 472 to win, or bat seven hours on a crusting pitch to draw, it was possible retrospectively to see that they were fighting a losing battle once Fraser and Malcolm had dismissed their openers in eight overs on the fourth evening.

Such was the depth of their batting, however, and the dash and artistry with which Vengsarkar and Azharuddin batted on the last morning as they put on 51 at 4 an over, that it was not until the former was caught at the wicket, trying not to play an off-break, that it became obvious there could be only one result. When Azharuddin followed twenty minutes later, superbly caught at third slip as he tried to turn a straight ball into the leg side, India's spirit cracked, and the score, at one stage 114 for three, was eroded to 181 for eight. A flourish by the last two wickets added 43 and so raised the match aggregate to 1,603, 2 runs more than the previous record for the ground, established in England's 1930 classic with Australia.

In similar conditions of pitch and outfield, true and fast respectively, Bradman had scored 254 in that Test, Woodfull 155, Duleepsinhji 173 and Chapman 121. What, if anything, could be inferred from the fact that in 1990 the average scoring-rate was 4.08 per over, whereas in the four-day Test of 1930 it had been 3.16? A different lbw Law, favouring the modern bowler, and the swing to heavier bats, supposedly favouring the batsmen – Gooch hit seven sixes with a three-pound Stuart Surridge Grand Prix Turbo – left too many imponderables for the question to be answered.

Of England's winning team against New Zealand at Edgbaston, Fairbrother and Small were dropped, while Stewart was put out of the reckoning by an injured back. They were replaced by Gower, returning after seven Tests, Morris of Derbyshire, a new cap, and Fraser, recovered at last from a rib injury suffered while in the Caribbean. Gower, debatably given out caught at point in the first innings, was outshone, while through no fault of his own, Morris faced only 21 balls. The 6ft 5in Fraser, however, played a leading part. Figures of five for 104 and three for 39 were due reward for his accuracy, bounce and movement at a lively pace. By using Shastri to open the batting, India made room to play the seventeen-year-old Bombay student, Tendulkar, who in England's second innings brought off as wonderful an outfield catch as Lord's has seen, holding Lamb's straight drive one-handed at knee height after hurtling more than 30 yards from wide long-off to a point behind the bowler.

At close of play on the first day, when England were 359 for two, Azharuddin tried to justify his decision to field by pointing out that had More, the wicket-keeper, held a routine chance when Gooch was 36, the score would have been 61 for two after 90 minutes' play. But 653 for four declared, with hundreds also from Lamb (in 276 minutes and 187 balls) and Smith (194 minutes, 155 balls), painted the picture truly. Azharuddin had made a bad misjudgement, and England made the most of it. Gooch, sharing with his vice-captain, Lamb, an all-wicket England v India record of 308, went on to make in 627 minutes (485 balls, three sixes, 43 fours) the highest score at Lord's, the third highest by an Englishman in Tests, and the sixth highest Test score overall before being bowled by medium-pacer Prabhakar, missing an off-drive. He was just 32 runs short of the world record of 365 not out, scored by Sir Garfield Sobers for West Indies against Pakistan in 1957-58.

Shastri, who made his hundred in 246 minutes and 184 balls, absorbed England's fast bowling like a born Test opener, only to mistime an on-drive off Hemmings. By contrast, Azharuddin dazzled. Not a few strokes early in his innings would have been hard to excuse had they cost him his wicket; but his luck held, and a capacity Saturday crowd was treated to a rare exhibition of audacious, wristy strokeplay which, with twenty fours, took him into three figures off only 88 balls. At close of play that day, when he was 117 not out, a draw looked the likeliest result. In Monday's third over, however, Azharuddin was bowled by Hemmings with an off-break that turned up the slope to hit leg stump as he was framing an expansive back-foot stroke through extra cover. Just 40 minutes later, when Fraser dismissed More and Sharma in three balls, India were 430 for nine, needing 24 to save the follow-on. Kapil Dev watched Hirwani survive the last ball of Fraser's over, played the first two of Hemmings's defensively, then ripped into the next four and drove each one for six. Three of them were enormous, clattering the scaffolding, one was simply big; all were magnificent. With the very next delivery, Fraser had Hirwani lbw. India had scored 78 in 15.1 overs, and the devil-may-care Kapil had become the first man to hit four sixes running in a Test. It was an unexpected way to save a follow-on.

Gooch, flicking Kapil Dev off his toes to the 65-yard Tavern boundary, at once set the tempo of England's 218-minute second innings, in which runs came at 5 an over. When he was out with the score 204, caught at extra cover after hitting four sixes and thirteen fours in 148 minutes and 113 balls, he had beaten G. S. Chappell's previous aggregate record for a Test by 76 runs. With Atherton, he had established a new record for England's first wicket against India. Answering in kind, India reached 57 for two in 56 minutes by the close and, despite the early loss of Manjrekar on the last morning, they were still batting as though they believed they had a winning chance at noon. Then, from the Nursery End, Hemmings caught Vengsarkar in two minds with a ball that pitched narrowly outside off stump. At the last moment the batsman decided not to play it, but it hurried through and brushed his gloves, heralding the final chapter of a memorable Test. Fittingly, it was Gooch who brought proceedings to a close midway through the sun-baked afternoon, flattening the middle stump at the bowler's end to run out Sharma from mid-on. – John Thicknesse.

Man of the Match: G. A. Gooch. *Attendance:* 60,924; *receipts* £919,500.

Close of play: First day, England 359-2 (G. A. Gooch 194*, A. J. Lamb 104*); Second day, India 48-0 (R. J. Shastri 27*, N. S. Sidhu 20*); Third day, India 376-6 (M. Azharuddin 117*, Kapil Dev 14*); Fourth day, India 57-2 (S. V. Manjrekar 29*, D. B. Vengsarkar 14*).

England

First innings		Second innings	
*G. A. Gooch b Prabhakar	333	– c Azharuddin b Sharma	123
M. A. Atherton b Kapil Dev	8	– c Vengsarkar b Sharma	72
D. I. Gower c Manjrekar b Hirwani	40	– not out	32
A. J. Lamb c Manjrekar b Sharma	139	– c Tendulkar b Hirwani	19
R. A. Smith not out	100	– b Prabhakar	15
J. E. Morris not out	4		
B 2, l-b 21, w 2, n-b 4	29	L-b 11	11
1/14 (2) 2/141 (3) 3/449 (4) 4/641 (1) (4 wkts dec.)	653	1/204 (1) 2/207 (2) 3/250 (4) 4/272 (5) (4 wkts dec.)	272

†R. C. Russell, C. C. Lewis, E. E. Hemmings, A. R. C. Fraser and D. E. Malcolm did not bat.

Bowling: *First Innings*—Kapil Dev 34–5–120–1; Prabhakar 43–6–187–1; Sharma 33–5–122–1; Shastri 22–0–99–0; Hirwani 30–1–102–1. *Second Innings*—Kapil Dev 10–0–53–0; Prabhakar 11.2–2–45–1; Shastri 7–0–38–0; Sharma 15–0–75–2; Hirwani 11–0–50–1.

India

First innings		Second innings	
R. J. Shastri c Gooch b Hemmings	100	– c Russell b Malcolm	12
N. S. Sidhu c Morris b Fraser	30	– c Morris b Fraser	1
S. V. Manjrekar c Russell b Gooch	18	– c Russell b Malcolm	33
D. B. Vengsarkar c Russell b Fraser	52	– c Russell b Hemmings	35
*M. Azharuddin b Hemmings	121	– c Atherton b Lewis	37
S. R. Tendulkar b Lewis	10	– c Gooch b Fraser	27
M. Prabhakar c Lewis b Malcolm	25	– lbw b Lewis	8
Kapil Dev not out	77	– c Lewis b Hemmings	7
†K. S. More c Morris b Fraser	8	– lbw b Fraser	16
S. K. Sharma c Russell b Fraser	0	– run out	38
N. D. Hirwani lbw b Fraser	0	– not out	0
L-b 1, w 4, n-b 8	13	B 3, l-b 1, n-b 6	10
1/63 (2) 2/102 (3) 3/191 (1) 4/241 (4) 5/288 (6) 6/348 (7) 7/393 (5) 8/430 (9) 9/430 (10) 10/454 (11)	454	1/9 (2) 2/23 (1) 3/63 (3) 4/114 (4) 5/127 (5) 6/140 (7) 7/158 (8) 8/181 (6) 9/206 (9) 10/224 (10)	224

Bowling: *First Innings*—Malcolm 25–1–106–1; Fraser 39.1–9–104–5; Lewis 24–3–108–1; Gooch 6–3–26–1; Hemmings 20–3–109–2. *Second Innings*—Fraser 22–7–39–3; Malcolm 10–0–65–2; Hemmings 21–2–79–2; Atherton 1–0–11–0; Lewis 8–1–26–2.

Umpires: H. D. Bird and N. T. Plews.

SURREY v INDIANS

At The Oval, August 1, 2, 3. Drawn. Toss: Surrey. The Indians had a poor day in the field in the aftermath of their Test defeat at Lord's, not being helped by a spate of dropped catches and some erratic bowling by the lively seamer, Wassan. The bespectacled leg-spinner, Hirwani, suffered most from his team-mates' errors. A studious 97 from Clinton, 82 from Stewart, with three sixes and six fours, and Lynch's robust 94 were the major contributions as Surrey ran up 384 for seven in 90 overs. Next day, however, the touring team were lifted by a smoothly assembled century from the tall left-hander, Raman, augmented by Vengsarkar's meticulous half-century, and Shastri kept the game open by declaring 95 runs in arrears. Before the close Clinton had passed 50 for the second time in the match, in 61 balls, and next day Greig, having hit five sixes and five fours to revive Surrey's stuttering innings, invited the Indians to chase 351 in 65 overs for victory. This was probably a stiffer target than Shastri had been hoping for, given that the Indians were resting some of their top batsmen, and they settled instead for batting practice.

Close of play: First day, Indians 35-1 (W. V. Raman 21*, S. V. Manjrekar 3*); Second day, Surrey 96-1 (G. S. Clinton 53*, A. J. Stewart 22*).

Surrey

D. J. Bicknell b Wassan	22		
G. S. Clinton c Shastri b Kumble	97	– c sub b Shastri	74
A. J. Stewart b Hirwani	82	– lbw b Shastri	22
D. M. Ward c Mongia b Kumble	20	– b Hirwani	28
M. A. Lynch c Raman b Hirwani	94	– c Manjrekar b Hirwani	3
*I. A. Greig st More b Hirwani	36	– not out	76
M. A. Feltham c Mongia b Raju	1	– c Vengsarkar b Hirwani	5
K. T. Medlycott not out	2	– not out	15
†N. F. Sargeant (did not bat)		– (1) c Raman b Hirwani	18
B 5, l-b 8, w 9, n-b 8	30	B 2, l-b 9, n-b 3	14
1/34 2/189 3/233 4/282 5/351 6/352 7/384	(7 wkts dec.) 384	1/57 2/96 3/149 4/149 5/170 6/190	(6 wkts dec.) 255

N. M. Kendrick and A. H. Gray did not bat.

Bowling: *First Innings*—Sharma 10–0–29–0; Wassan 13–1–81–1; Raju 22–4–64–1; Hirwani 24.2–0–122–3; Kumble 21–1–75–2. *Second Innings*—Sharma 3–0–7–0; Wassan 4–0–19–0; Shastri 27.3–5–80–2; Hirwani 15–0–71–4; Kumble 3–0–15–0; Raju 10–1–52–0.

Indians

W. V. Raman c Gray b Kendrick	127	– c sub b Kendrick	58
N. R. Mongia c Kendrick b Feltham	10	– c Feltham b Kendrick	41
S. V. Manjrekar c Kendrick b Gray	9	– not out	52
D. B. Vengsarkar c Stewart b Gray	55		
*R. J. Shastri st Sargeant b Medlycott	8		
†K. S. More c Sargeant b Medlycott	12	– (4) not out	12
S. L. V. Raju c and b Medlycott	7		
S. K. Sharma c Gray b Kendrick	15		
A. Kumble c Kendrick b Gray	19		
A. S. Wassan not out	8		
B 5, l-b 7, n-b 7	19	L-b 1, n-b 3	4
1/18 2/46 3/183 4/209 5/237 6/242 7/261 8/261 9/289	(9 wkts dec.) 289	1/94 2/111	(2 wkts) 167

N. D. Hirwani did not bat.

Bowling: *First Innings*—Gray 18.1–0–69–3; Feltham 11–2–48–1; Medlycott 35–8–102–3; Kendrick 20–4–58–2. *Second Innings*—Gray 9–0–41–0; Feltham 4–0–20–0; Medlycott 24–7–55–0; Kendrick 20–5–50–2.

Umpires: A. G. T. Whitehead and P. B. Wight.

GLOUCESTERSHIRE v INDIANS

At Bristol, August 4, 5, 6. Drawn. Toss: Indians. Although fifteen wickets fell on the first day, it was hard to perceive much malice in the pitch or bowling; many batsmen were out through careless strokes. More and Raju pulled the touring side round after Walsh, captaining Gloucestershire for the first time, had juggled his limited bowling resources to such effect that eight wickets went for 112. The ninth-wicket pair added 127, but Raju's brave innings was his last of the tour. His left hand was broken by a ball from Walsh. Milburn and Williams, with his maiden first-class fifty, helped Athey earn Gloucestershire a lead of 67, which proved insignificant as openers Shastri and Sidhu thrilled their Indian supporters in a partnership of 251. The second highest for any wicket by an Indian side in England, it ended shortly before lunch on the final day when Sidhu was caught going for his seventh six. He also hit sixteen fours, while Shastri hit nineteen. The Indians' declaration, when the lead was 324 and only 38 overs remained, seemed no more than a token until Kapil Dev and Prabhakar, swinging the ball about, caused Gloucestershire further embarrassment by taking four cheap wickets before the game was given up.

Close of play: First day, Gloucestershire 90-5 (C. W. J. Athey 11*, E. T. Milburn 0*); Second day, Indians 140-0 (R. J. Shastri 70*, N. S. Sidhu 69*).

Indians

	First innings		Second innings	
R. J. Shastri b Walsh	5	– b Alleyne	133
N. S. Sidhu c Williams b Lawrence	31	– c Barnes b Lloyds	142
W. V. Raman c Williams b Walsh	0	– not out	56
S. R. Tendulkar c Williams b Milburn	13	– c Lawrence b Romaines	47
*M. Azharuddin b Alleyne	23		
M. Prabhakar c Hodgson b Alleyne	12	– (5) not out	11
Kapil Dev c Butcher b Alleyne	12		
K. S. More c Williams b Milburn	95		
†N. R. Mongia c Alleyne b Lawrence	1		
S. L. V. Raju not out	40		
N. D. Hirwani c Williams b Milburn	0		
L-b 1, n-b 6	7	L-b 1, n-b 1	2
1/13 2/19 3/42 4/54 5/79 6/86 7/103 8/112 9/239	239	1/251 2/301 3/374 (3 wkts dec.)	391

Bowling: *First Innings*—Walsh 17–4–45–2; Lawrence 12–1–65–2; Barnes 5–1–18–0; Milburn 14.3–3–43–3; Alleyne 10–3–41–3; Lloyds 9–1–24–0; Athey 1–0–2–0. *Second Innings*—Lawrence 13–1–42–0; Walsh 11–5–16–0; Alleyne 15–1–54–1; Milburn 11–0–73–0; Lloyds 21–0–136–1; Athey 13–1–39–0; Romaines 6–0–30–1.

Gloucestershire

	First innings		Second innings	
G. D. Hodgson c Hirwani b Tendulkar	16	– not out	23
I. P. Butcher b Hirwani	41	– b Prabhakar	1
P. W. Romaines c Mongia b Tendulkar	2	– c More b Prabhakar	6
C. W. J. Athey c Azharuddin b Hirwani	80		
M. W. Alleyne c Shastri b Tendulkar	0	– (4) c More b Kapil Dev	0
J. W. Lloyds c Kapil Dev b Hirwani	8	– (5) c More b Kapil Dev	21
E. T. Milburn c Mongia b Hirwani	35	– (6) not out	11
†R. C. J. Williams not out	50		
*C. A. Walsh c Prabhakar b Hirwani	0		
D. V. Lawrence c Mongia b Prabhakar	35		
S. N. Barnes not out	12		
B 7, l-b 7, w 1, n-b 12	27	L-b 1, n-b 3	4
1/54 2/66 3/71 4/73 5/89 6/188 7/211 8/219 9/266 (9 wkts dec.)	306	1/2 2/14 3/15 4/42 (4 wkts)	66

Bowling: *First Innings*—Prabhakar 18–4–53–1; Tendulkar 32–6–79–3; Hirwani 43–9–117–5; Shastri 22–6–36–0; Raman 1–0–7–0. *Second Innings*—Kapil Dev 11–1–28–2; Prabhakar 11–2–26–2; Tendulkar 5–1–6–0; Hirwani 4–0–4–0; Raman 1–0–1–0.

Umpires: B. Dudleston and D. S. Thompsett.

ENGLAND v INDIA

Second Cornhill Test

At Manchester, August 9, 10, 11, 13, 14. Drawn. Toss: England. Of the six individual centuries scored in this fascinating contest, none was more outstanding than Tendulkar's, which rescued India on the final afternoon. At 17 years and 112 days, he was only 30 days older than Mushtaq Mohammad was when, against India at Delhi in 1960-61, he became the youngest player to score a Test hundred. More significantly, after several of his colleagues had fallen to reckless strokes, Tendulkar held the England attack at bay with a disciplined display of immense maturity.

India were placed on the defensive once Gooch chose to bat first. The Old Trafford groundsman, Peter Marron, wrong-footed by a cold change in the weather after watering, had predicted even bounce but little pace, and England quickly grasped the opportunity. Leading an unchanged side, Gooch put on 73 untroubled runs with Atherton in the first hour, and India soon resorted to their leg-spinners, Hirwani and Kumble, the latter replacing seamer Sharma from the team at Lord's. They slowed down England's progress, but could do little to prevent a 225-run opening partnership, which overtook by 21 runs the record Gooch and Atherton had set at Lord's a fortnight earlier. In scoring 116, Gooch became the first English batsman for nineteen years to record centuries in three successive Test innings, but on the day he was eclipsed by his junior partner. In five and a half hours, Atherton carefully constructed 131, exactly matching the feat of G. Pullar, the only other Lancastrian to score a Test century for England at Old Trafford, against India 31 years earlier. Smith batted for just over four hours, passing his century during a last-wicket partnership of 60 with Malcolm, an unexpectedly supportive ally, as England reached 519.

The loss of three quick wickets for 57 to the seam movement of Fraser, in the final hour of the second day, placed India in immediate peril. On Saturday, however, they were rescued in style by their captain, Azharuddin, and Manjrekar, whose fourth-wicket stand of 189 set the pace for an entertaining day's play in which 355 runs were scored. Manjrekar made 93 in three and threequarter hours before falling to a bat-pad catch at silly point off the tireless Hemmings, but Azharuddin could not be stopped so easily. In a breathtaking 281-minute stay for 179, he hit 21 fours and a six, and between lunch and tea he became the first player to score 100 runs for India in a Test session. After he had miscued a drive off Fraser to Atherton, the second new ball accounted for most of the remaining Indian batting, although Tendulkar, after taking 54 minutes to get off the mark, gave warning of his talents in scoring 68 from 136 balls to reduce the England lead to just 87.

As England's second innings began on the fourth morning, Gooch suffered a rare failure in a rich summer, departing for 7. But Atherton added a further 74 to his first-innings hundred, and a winning position was achieved through the efforts of Lamb. Earlier in the game he had looked out of his depth against the Indian spinners, but, relishing the challenge, he hit Hirwani for two successive sixes early on, and his 109 from 141 balls, followed by Smith's unbeaten 61, allowed Gooch to declare 25 minutes into the final day.

To win and square the series, India were offered a minimum of 88 overs in which to score 408, 2 runs more than their own record for the highest winning total by a side batting second in a Test. From the seventh ball of their innings, when Sidhu was brilliantly caught off Fraser by the substitute, Adams, at short leg, it looked a tall order. On a slowly wearing pitch Hemmings produced just enough deviation to have both Manjrekar and Azharuddin caught in the leg trap – but it was the gay abandon of three senior Indian batsmen which might have set Tendulkar a bad example. Shastri dragged a wide ball on to his stumps, Vengsarkar offered no stroke to Lewis, and Kapil Dev sallied down the pitch to Hemmings.

When the all-rounder, Prabhakar, joined Tendulkar, India were 183 for six and there were two and a half hours of the match remaining. Gooch crowded the bat and shuffled his bowlers like a croupier, but England were to be denied by their own mistakes. Hemmings put down a simple return catch when Tendulkar was 10, and Gooch failed to get a hand at second slip to a chance offered by Prabhakar. England could ill afford such lapses, and the pair had seen India to safety when the game was halted with two of the final twenty overs still to be bowled.

Tendulkar remained undefeated on 119, having batted for 224 minutes and hit seventeen fours. He looked the embodiment of India's famous opener, Gavaskar, and indeed was wearing a pair of his pads. While he displayed a full repertoire of strokes in compiling his maiden Test hundred, most remarkable were his off-side shots from the back foot. Though only 5ft 5in tall, he was still able to control without difficulty short deliveries from the English pacemen. – Graham Otway.

Man of the Match: S. R. Tendulkar. *Attendance:* 42,424; *receipts* £521,100.

Close of play: First day, England 322-3 (A. J. Lamb 20*, R. C. Russell 7*); Second day, India 77-3 (S. V. Manjrekar 21*, M. Azharuddin 4*); Third day, India 432; Fourth day, England 290-4 (R. A. Smith 49*, J. E. Morris 15*).

England

*G. A. Gooch c More b Prabhakar	116	– c More b Prabhakar	7
M. A. Atherton c More b Hirwani	131	– lbw b Kapil Dev	74
D. I. Gower c Tendulkar b Kapil Dev	38	– b Hirwani	16
A. J. Lamb c Manjrekar b Kumble	38	– b Kapil Dev	109
†R. C. Russell c More b Hirwani	8	– (7) not out	16
R. A. Smith not out	121	– (5) not out	61
J. E. Morris b Kumble	13	– (6) retired hurt	15
C. C. Lewis b Hirwani	3		
E. E. Hemmings lbw b Hirwani	19		
A. R. C. Fraser c Tendulkar b Kumble	1		
D. E. Malcolm b Shastri	13		
B 2, l-b 9, w 1, n-b 6	18	L-b 15, n-b 7	22
1/225 (1) 2/292 (3) 3/312 (2) 4/324 (5) 5/366 (4) 6/392 (7) 7/404 (8) 8/434 (9) 9/459 (10) 10/519 (11)	519	1/15 (1) 2/46 (3) 3/180 (2) 4/248 (4)	(4 wkts dec.) 320

In the second innings J. E. Morris retired hurt at 290.

Bowling: *First Innings*—Kapil Dev 13–2–67–1; Prabhakar 25–2–112–1; Kumble 43–7–105–3; Hirwani 62–10–174–4; Shastri 17.5–2–50–1. *Second Innings*—Kapil Dev 22–4–69–2; Prabhakar 18–1–80–1; Hirwani 15–0–52–1; Kumble 17–3–65–0; Shastri 9–0–39–0.

India

R. J. Shastri c Gooch b Fraser	25	– b Malcolm	12
N. S. Sidhu c Gooch b Fraser	13	– c sub (C. J. Adams) b Fraser	0
S. V. Manjrekar c Smith b Hemmings	93	– c sub (C. J. Adams) b Hemmings	50
D. B. Vengsarkar c Russell b Fraser	6	– b Lewis	32
*M. Azharuddin c Atherton b Fraser	179	– c Lewis b Hemmings	11
S. R. Tendulkar c Lewis b Hemmings	68	– not out	119
M. Prabhakar c Russell b Malcolm	4	– (8) not out	67
Kapil Dev lbw b Lewis	0	– (7) b Hemmings	26
†K. S. More b Fraser	6		
A. Kumble run out	2		
N. D. Hirwani not out	15		
B 5, l-b 4, n-b 12	21	B 17, l-b 3, n-b 6	26
1/26 (2) 2/48 (1) 3/57 (4) 4/246 (3) 5/358 (5) 6/364 (7) 7/365 (8) 8/396 (9) 9/401 (10) 10/432 (6)	432	1/4 (2) 2/35 (1) 3/109 (3) 4/109 (4) 5/127 (5) 6/183 (7)	(6 wkts) 343

Bowling: *First Innings*—Malcolm 26–3–96–1; Fraser 35–5–124–5; Hemmings 29.2–8–74–2; Lewis 13–1–61–1; Atherton 16–3–68–0. *Second Innings*—Malcolm 14–5–59–1; Fraser 21–3–81–1; Hemmings 31–10–75–3; Atherton 4–0–22–0; Lewis 20–3–86–1.

Umpires: J. H. Hampshire and J. W. Holder.

TCCB UNDER-25 XI v INDIANS

At Birmingham, August 15, 16, 17. Drawn. Toss: TCCB Under-25 XI. A slow pitch, and the inhibitions young batsmen invariably feel under the eye of an England selector, made a draw the likeliest outcome, even though Stephenson declared 61 runs in arrears in the hope of being set a target. However, Shastri, captaining the touring team, made it a difficult one – 300 in 56 overs. Shastri himself was unable to bowl because of an injured hand, and having been put in on a pitch which promised to help the seam bowlers, but subsequently reneged, he probably felt he owed few favours. On the opening day, Bicknell enjoyed some success with the second new ball, taking three for 20 in nine overs. But by then Raman and Manjrekar had captivated with a partnership of 85 in 80 minutes, and Manjrekar and Vengsarkar had consolidated the innings with a century stand in 114. Manjrekar, with dancing footwork and supple wrists, was always quick to show up any weakness in line and length, hitting fourteen fours in his three-and-a-quarter-hour stay (197 balls). Sidhu, who missed out in the first innings, took his chance in the second and hit an unbeaten 108 from 189 balls (three sixes, thirteen fours), while Raman hit ten boundaries in his 56 as they opened with 134 in 151 minutes. Stephenson batted soundly for almost four hours in the Under-25s' first innings, his 116 from 242 balls including seventeen fours, and when his side lost three second-innings wickets in the first nine overs, he and Blakey ensured there was no further collapse.

Close of play: First day, Indians 293-6 (M. Prabhakar 2*, N. R. Mongia 1*); Second day, Indians 87-0 (N. S. Sidhu 48*, W. V. Raman 36*).

Indians

W. V. Raman lbw b Stephenson	61	– (2) lbw b Munton	56
N. S. Sidhu c Blakey b Lampitt	13	– (1) not out	108
S. V. Manjrekar c Stephenson b Medlycott	116		
D. B. Vengsarkar c Hussain b Bicknell	54		
S. R. Tendulkar c Lampitt b Bicknell	39	– not out	30
*R. J. Shastri lbw b Bicknell	4		
M. Prabhakar not out	2	– (4) st Blakey b Medlycott	23
†N. R. Mongia not out	1	– (3) b Illingworth	11
L-b 2, n-b 1	3	B 3, l-b 6, n-b 1	10
1/33 2/118 3/220 4/278 5/287 6/290 (6 wkts dec.)	293	1/134 2/167 3/194 (3 wkts dec.)	238

S. K. Sharma, A. Kumble and A. S. Wassan did not bat.

Bowling: *First Innings*—Munton 23–9–49–0; Bicknell 22–6–50–3; Lampitt 18–2–62–1; Medlycott 9–1–46–1; Stephenson 6–2–18–1; Illingworth 24–5–66–0. *Second Innings*—Bicknell 9–2–26–0; Lampitt 8–0–33–0; Shahid 5–0–41–0; Munton 14–6–26–1; Stephenson 6–2–16–0; Illingworth 17–3–58–1; Medlycott 5–0–29–1.

TCCB Under-25 XI

*J. P. Stephenson c Mongia b Kumble	116	– not out	41
N. Shahid st Mongia b Shastri	39	– lbw b Prabhakar	0
G. P. Thorpe b Sharma	18	– lbw b Sharma	5
N. Hussain not out	37		
P. Johnson b Wassan	3	– (4) lbw b Prabhakar	1
†R. J. Blakey (did not bat)		– (5) not out	40
B 8, l-b 1, n-b 10	19	B 7, l-b 15, n-b 1	23
1/118 2/175 3/214 4/232 (4 wkts dec.)	232	1/1 2/12 3/19 (3 wkts)	110

K. T. Medlycott, R. K. Illingworth, S. R. Lampitt, M. P. Bicknell and T. A. Munton did not bat.

Bowling: *First Innings*—Prabhakar 5–0–13–0; Sharma 18–1–57–1; Wassan 19.3–1–74–1; Tendulkar 14–3–40–0; Shastri 5–3–11–1; Kumble 19–8–28–1. *Second Innings*—Prabhakar 7–3–13–2; Sharma 10–3–24–1; Wassan 14–6–18–0; Kumble 5–1–9–0; Tendulkar 6–1–24–0.

Umpires: M. J. Harris and D. O. Oslear.

GLAMORGAN v INDIANS

At Swansea, August 18, 19, 20. Drawn. Toss: Indians. Although the loss of the second day spoiled the match as a contest, the spectators were treated to some spectacular strokeplay by Raman, Sidhu and Tendulkar on the first day, and later in the game only the staunch resistance of Croft and Metson denied the touring team a second victory over county opposition. The Indian openers put on 115 in even time, and after four wickets had fallen for just 13 runs, Tendulkar hit three sixes as he launched the recovery with some quality strokes. Even so, the Indians needed a ninth-wicket partnership of 90 between Mongia and Kumble to see them past 300. Glamorgan lost two quick wickets in the evening, and after Sunday's rain Butcher declared at the overnight 39 for two to help set up an interesting finish. The Indians then batted for an hour before leaving the home county the formidable task of scoring 390 from 79 overs. Despite another fluent innings from Morris, in pursuit of his county's record of nine hundreds in a season, Glamorgan seemed to be facing defeat when they were 170 for seven in the first over after tea, having just lost four wickets for 3 runs. However, Croft and Metson defied the tourists for 33 overs and put on 103, a county record for that wicket against the Indians. Both completed half-centuries, while figures of six for 89 from the medium-pacer, Wassan, ensured him of a place in India's team for the final Test at The Oval.

Close of play: First day, Glamorgan 39-2 (H. Morris 23*, M. P. Maynard 4*); Second day, No play.

Indians

N. S. Sidhu c James b Dale	54	– not out	76
W. V. Raman b Dale	59	– not out	20
S. V. Manjrekar lbw b Anthony	4		
Kapil Dev b Anthony	0		
*M. Azharuddin c Maynard b Anthony	21		
S. R. Tendulkar c Cottey b Croft	68		
K. S. More c Metson b Croft	8		
†N. R. Mongia b Dale	60		
S. K. Sharma c Morris b Croft	9		
A. Kumble not out	35		
L-b 8, w 3, n-b 1	12	W 2	2
1/115 2/126 3/126 4/128 5/168 6/210 7/227 8/240 9/330 (9 wkts dec.)	330	(no wkt dec.)	98

A. S. Wassan did not bat.

Bowling: *First Innings*—Anthony 25–3–95–3; Bastien 22–7–61–0; Dennis 15–2–63–0; Croft 17–3–82–3; Dale 8.3–1–21–3. *Second Innings*—Maynard 9–1–34–0; Dale 9–0–62–0; Anthony 1–0–2–0.

Glamorgan

S. P. James c More b Sharma	7	– c More b Wassan	15
H. Morris not out	23	– c Sidhu b Wassan	73
P. A. Cottey lbw b Kapil Dev	0	– c More b Wassan	29
M. P. Maynard not out	4	– b Wassan	26
*A. R. Butcher (did not bat)		– lbw b Wassan	12
A. Dale (did not bat)		– c More b Kumble	0
R. D. B. Croft (did not bat)		– not out	50
H. A. G. Anthony (did not bat)		– c More b Wassan	0
†C. P. Metson (did not bat)		– not out	50
L-b 1, n-b 4	5	B 8, l-b 2, n-b 8	18
1/14 2/31 (2 wkts dec.)	39	1/63 2/116 3/132 4/167 5/168 6/170 7/170 (7 wkts)	273

S. J. Dennis and S. Bastien did not bat.

Bowling: *First Innings*—Kapil Dev 6–3–8–1; Sharma 5–1–23–1; Wassan 1–0–5–0; Kumble 1–0–2–0. *Second Innings*—Kapil Dev 19–3–58–0; Sharma 9–2–48–0; Wassan 23–3–89–6; Tendulkar 1–0–5–0; Kumble 21–8–51–1; Raman 2–0–12–0.

Umpires: A. A. Jones and K. J. Lyons.

ENGLAND v INDIA

Third Cornhill Test

At The Oval, August 23, 24, 25, 27, 28. Drawn. Toss: India. Gower's sublime strokeplay, unwavering determination and considerable stamina throughout the final day erased India's chances of squaring the series, though their hopes were high when they enforced the follow-on after scoring their third-best score of all time. England thus won 1-0 to complete their first unbeaten Test season at home since 1979, having beaten New Zealand by the same margin earlier in the summer. The six-hour *tour de force* was Gower's sixteenth hundred in Tests and his fourth on the Kennington ground; with Shastri and Kapil Dev he brought the tally of centuries scored by the two teams to fifteen, a record for a three-match series. But while Gower's innings was conclusive in saving the game, Gooch had also continued his record-breaking summer, unchecked by a lightweight Indian attack never capable of marrying its industry to quality and penetration.

This time when Azharuddin won the toss, he needed no persuasion to take first use of an outstanding batting pitch. India had decided against the attacking option of an extra bowler, and at the same time preferred the lively Wassan to Kumble's sharp leg-spin. Just before the toss Lewis suffered a migraine attack during outfield practice, and Williams, the Middlesex seamer, was thrust into his first Test after being named twelfth man.

While Lewis sought rest and aspirin in the plush dressing-rooms of the new stand flanking the pavilion, Shastri settled in to give England their own headache. Gooch, who had lost the toss for the fifth time in six Tests, went through his tactical repertoire but found the tall, upright opener moulding a solid percentage game: playing permanently straight, waiting to punish the wayward delivery, and progressing to his tenth Test hundred and highest Test score. England's main strike bowler, Malcolm, looked jaded, but Williams moved the ball more than anyone else and was rewarded with Azharuddin's wicket just as the Indian captain was threatening to post his fourth hundred in as many Tests. The dependable Fraser was once more England's prime bowler on a day which began with Russell claiming two acrobatic catches in little more than an hour, and ended with India in undisputed command at 324 for four; Shastri 135 not out. It was a neat reversal of fortunes from Lord's and Old Trafford, where the touring team had been completely overrun in the field on the first day.

England had to keep India to a score of 450 or less to retain any hope of victory. But by tea on the second day, their concern was to salvage the match. India had already passed their previous highest total of 510 in England, made at Leeds in 1967, and they marched on to their biggest score against England in either country. The campaign was carried on by Kapil Dev, who added 110 with Shastri until Malcolm had the vice-captain caught at first slip for 187, after 561 minutes and 435 balls, including 23 fours. Kapil, meanwhile, used the wide open space of the playing area to his advantage and resisted the risky shots in the air which England might have expected. After the slowest of his seven Test hundreds – taking 130 balls – he was stumped off Hemmings twelve balls later, having struck sixteen fours, and a late flourish from the pugnacious More enabled India to declare at 606 for nine.

The target of 407 to avoid the follow-on was ultimately beyond England. A rare failure from Atherton that evening brought in Williams as night-watchman, but after he had contributed a useful 38 in 72 minutes, the rock-solid Gooch, understandably unadventurous, then had to watch his middle order being summarily despatched. However, Smith's resourceful half-century and spirited batting from Russell promised a lifeline until Gooch was caught, mis-sweeping Hirwani, for 85 after five and a half hours. His first 5 runs had taken him past Zaheer Abbas's record aggregate of 583 in a three-match series, but he was still 4 short of D. G. Bradman's total of 974 in an English summer. Once Russell had been wastefully run out by a direct hit from Wassan on the fourth morning, England were prepared for the worst, although Hemmings, helped in a last-wicket stand of 41 by Malcolm, seized the opportunity to score his second Test fifty before England were dismissed for 340.

When Gooch and Atherton returned to centre stage, India were soon to regret their lack of firepower. Azharuddin limped off with a sore heel and Shastri, taking over the reins, was to spurn the second new ball, instead keeping Hirwani's leg-breaks probing away into the footmarks in a marathon – and largely unrewarded – 59 consecutive overs from the Vauxhall End. Gooch quickly scored the 5 runs he needed to pass Bradman (though he had taken four more innings) and the opening pair collected their third stand of a hundred in as many Tests. They were poised to make it a third double-century partnership when Gooch, after 225 minutes, was superbly caught, one-handed at backward short leg by Vengsarkar, off the bowling of Hirwani. Joined now by Gower, who was soon displaying some dazzling shots, Atherton advanced to 86, surviving a chance to backward square leg only to fall lbw to Kapil Dev after 5 hours 40 minutes of defensive endeavour. Morris failed to capitalise on a chance to impress the selectors, but for two hours Lamb was under little pressure in making 52 and England saved the match comfortably. Thanks to Gower's elegant, day-long guidance, they finished 211 ahead with six wickets in reserve. His unbeaten 157, from 271 balls and graced with 21 boundaries, provided a satisfying climax to his 109th Test, and convinced spectators that the former captain would, after all, be in the England team to tour Australia. – David Field.

Man of the Match: R. J. Shastri. *Attendance:* 55,405; *receipts* £681,400.

Men of the Series: England – G. A. Gooch; India – M. Azharuddin.

Close of play: First day, India 324-4 (R. J. Shastri 135*, M. Prabhakar 20*); Second day, England 36-1 (G. A. Gooch 5*, N. F. Williams 15*); Third day, England 293-7 (R. C. Russell 34*, E. E. Hemmings 26*); Fourth day, England 215-1 (M. A. Atherton 71*, D. I. Gower 32*).

India

R. J. Shastri c Lamb b Malcolm	187
N. S. Sidhu c Russell b Fraser	12
S. V. Manjrekar c Russell b Malcolm	22
D. B. Vengsarkar c and b Atherton	33
*M. Azharuddin c Russell b Williams	78
M. Prabhakar lbw b Fraser	28
S. R. Tendulkar c Lamb b Williams	21
Kapil Dev st Russell b Hemmings	110
†K. S. More not out	61
A. S. Wassan b Hemmings	15
N. D. Hirwani not out	2
B 7, l-b 8, w 6, n-b 16	37
1/16 (2) 2/61 (3) 3/150 (4) 4/289 (5) 5/335 (6) 6/368 (7) 7/478 (1) 8/552 (8) 9/576 (10)	(9 wkts dec.) 606

Bowling: Malcolm 35–7–110–2; Fraser 42–17–112–2; Williams 41–5–148–2; Gooch 12–1–44–0; Hemmings 36–3–117–2; Atherton 7–0–60–1.

England

Batting	First innings	Second innings
*G. A. Gooch c Shastri b Hirwani	85	– c Vengsarkar b Hirwani 88
M. A. Atherton c More b Prabhakar	7	– lbw b Kapil Dev 86
N. F. Williams lbw b Prabhakar	38	
D. I. Gower lbw b Wassan	8	– (3) not out 157
J. E. Morris c More b Wassan	7	– (4) c More b Wassan 32
A. J. Lamb b Kapil Dev	7	– (5) c Shastri b Kapil Dev 52
R. A. Smith c Manjrekar b Shastri	57	– (6) not out 7
†R. C. Russell run out	35	
E. E. Hemmings c Vengsarkar b Prabhakar	51	
A. R. C. Fraser c More b Prabhakar	0	
D. E. Malcolm not out	15	
B 8, l-b 9, w 4, n-b 9	30	B 16, l-b 22, w 5, n-b 12 55
	340	(4 wkts dec.) 477

First innings fall of wickets: 1/18 (2) 2/92 (3) 3/111 (4) 4/120 (5) 5/139 (6) 6/231 (7) 7/233 (1) 8/295 (8) 9/299 (10) 10/340 (9)

Second innings fall of wickets: 1/176 (1) 2/251 (2) 3/334 (4) 4/463 (5)

Bowling: *First Innings*—Kapil Dev 25–7–70–1; Prabhakar 32.4–9–74–4; Wassan 19–3–79–2; Hirwani 35–12–71–1; Shastri 12–2–29–1. *Second Innings*—Prabhakar 25–8–56–0; Kapil Dev 24–5–66–2; Wassan 18–2–94–1; Hirwani 59–18–137–1; Shastri 28–2–86–0.

Umpires: N. T. Plews and D. R. Shepherd.

MICHAEL PARKINSON'S WORLD XI v INDIANS

At Scarborough, August 29, 30, 31. Drawn. Toss: Michael Parkinson's World XI. Their official matches behind them, the Indians ended their tour in the festival atmosphere of Scarborough with a privately arranged, first-class fixture against Michael Parkinson's invitation side. Conditions typically favoured the batsmen, and the Indians were not helped by the loss of Wassan early in the match with an ankle injury. However, their batsmen provided rich entertainment with their elegant strokeplay, and on the final day, when they were invited to chase 388 in four and a half hours, they were seen towards the safety of a draw by the precocious skills of Tendulkar. The seventeen-year-old hit seventeen fours in reaching his third hundred of the tour from 131 balls. Greatbatch, who had missed out on a first-class century for the New Zealanders earlier in the summer, made amends with two powerful three-figure innings, his 168 not out on the first day coming off 162 balls and containing two sixes and 25 fours. During the match, Bairstow took his tally of dismissals to 1,099 and moved into fourteenth place above G. Duckworth on the all-time list of wicket-keepers.

Close of play: First day, Indians 7-0 (W. V. Raman 3*, N. R. Mongia 0*); Second day, Michael Parkinson's World XI 172-2 (Mudassar Nazar 61*, M. J. Greatbatch 50*).

Michael Parkinson's World XI

Mudassar Nazar c Kapil Dev b Wassan	29	– not out		107
*C. G. Greenidge lbw b Sharma	23	– b Sharma		0
R. B. Richardson c Prabhakar b Kumble	65	– c Raman b Sharma		42
M. J. Greatbatch not out	168	– not out		128
R. A. Harper st Mongia b Raman	17			
P. R. Sleep c Kumble b Kapil Dev	42			
B 2, l-b 18, n-b 15	35	B 1, l-b 15, n-b 7		23
1/44 2/72 3/189 4/252 5/379 (5 wkts dec.)	379	1/6 2/77	(2 wkts dec.)	300

†D. L. Bairstow, E. A. Moseley, Chetan Sharma, M. R. Whitney and C. Pringle did not bat.

Bowling: *First Innings*—Sharma 20–3–91–1; Prabhakar 4–0–7–0; Wassan 8–1–42–1; Tendulkar 12–1–70–0; Kumble 24–4–103–1; Raman 8–1–44–1; Kapil Dev 0.4–0–2–1. *Second Innings*—Prabhakar 13–3–45–0; Sharma 9–0–53–2; Tendulkar 7–0–32–0; Kumble 17–1–72–0; More 8–0–54–0; Kapil Dev 5–0–28–0.

Indians

W. V. Raman c Greenidge b Pringle	58	– b Whitney		13
†N. R. Mongia c Bairstow b Whitney	10	– c Bairstow b Moseley		15
*S. V. Manjrekar c Whitney b Sleep	59	– (5) c Bairstow b Whitney		62
S. R. Tendulkar c Pringle b Harper	23	– c Pringle b Sleep		108
D. B. Vengsarkar c Greatbatch b Whitney	3	– (6) not out		25
M. Prabhakar b Harper	15	– (7) c Greatbatch b Harper		10
Kapil Dev c Harper b Pringle	19	– (3) c Richardson b Whitney		3
A. Kumble lbw b Harper	2	– not out		5
K. S. More c Bairstow b Sleep	18			
S. K. Sharma not out	34			
A. S. Wassan b Harper	24			
B 8, l-b 8, w 4, n-b 7	27	L-b 6, n-b 6		12
1/59 2/114 3/154 4/168 5/169 6/199 7/206 8/229 9/245	292	1/34 2/34 3/43 4/198 5/225 6/243	(6 wkts)	253

Bowling: *First Innings*—Moseley 9–2–22–0; Whitney 14–4–51–2; Pringle 12–0–49–2; C. Sharma 8–0–39–0; Harper 17.4–4–68–4; Sleep 7–0–47–2. *Second Innings*—Moseley 12–1–36–1; Whitney 13–1–46–3; Pringle 7–1–36–0; C. Sharma 5–0–30–0; Harper 16–4–36–1; Sleep 12–1–63–1.

Umpires: J. H. Hampshire and B. Leadbeater.

THE SRI LANKANS IN ENGLAND, 1990

Towards the end of a busy English summer, a young Sri Lankan team made a five-week tour, with matches against eight first-class counties. From the Sri Lankan viewpoint, the purpose of the visit was threefold: to allow some of their cricketers to gain first-class experience abroad before the Asia Cup tournament and the tour of New Zealand in 1990-91; secondly, to accustom them to English conditions in preparation for the tour in 1991 by the full-strength Sri Lankan side, which was to play a Test match at Lord's; and thirdly, to impress on the English public the ability of Sri Lankan cricketers to hold their own against county sides.

All of these objectives were obtained, and if a record of one win and five draws in the first-class games does not in itself reflect the positive attitude shown by Aravinda de Silva's team, the draws against Sussex and Lancashire came when the counties were well short of not unrealistic targets with more than half their batting gone. Moreover, the win against Warwickshire provided Sri Lanka with a win over an English county to accompany the victories of the 1979 team over Oxford University and the 1981 team over a TCCB XI.

The decision of the Sri Lankan Board not to select five of their front-line players, including the current captain and vice-captain, plus injuries during the tour to two experienced players – Saliya Ahangama and Asanka Gurusinha – put considerable responsibility on the remaining players, four of whom were teenagers. That their only defeats came in the two one-day games was a reflection of the depth of playing strength in Sri Lanka. The captain, de Silva, set a good example by the positive way he went about his batting and his declarations, and his chanceless double-hundred to save the match against Hampshire was a gem of an innings. He played in every game and averaged 70.37 in his first-class innings.

In a further indication of their playing strength, the team included two fine wicket-keeper-batsmen, and so could enjoy the advantage of playing seven specialist batsmen. Hashan Tillekeratne hit two hundreds and, like his fellow-keeper, Brendon Kuruppu, was capable of batting anywhere in the order. Both performed their duties behind the stumps well. Roshan Mahanama and Chandika Hathurusinghe put on 210 the first time they opened together, against Nottinghamshire, and generally gave the side a sound start. In the middle order, Sanath Jayasuriya, a left-hander who had hit successive unbeaten double-hundreds against Pakistan B in 1988-89, and Marvan Atapattu, who averaged 60 on the tour, provided solidity or attractive strokeplay according to the team's needs.

The brunt of the bowling was borne by four players. Ranjith Madurasinghe had improved immensely since he toured England in 1988, and with 21 wickets at 26.66 in four games, he showed himself to be an off-spinner of some class. At the same time, the slow left-armer, Piyal Wijetunge, the youngster of the side, suggested that he could become a very good bowler with more experience. Of the faster bowlers, Graeme Labrooy, though at times beset by injury, reminded English spectators that he could trouble the best of batsmen, and Champaka Ramanayake also proved his effectiveness in the batsmen's conditions of 1990.

The team was managed excellently by Mumtaz Yusuf, who had toured England with the 1984 team, and his assistant manager, Jansa Severatne. Like their predecessors, the Sri Lankans were a credit to the game, both in their behaviour and their approach to their cricket. – Pat Culpan.

SRI LANKAN TOUR RESULTS

First-class matches – Played 6: Won 1, Drawn 5.
Win – Warwickshire.
Draws – Glamorgan, Hampshire, Lancashire, Nottinghamshire, Sussex.
Non first-class matches – Played 2: Lost 2. *Losses* – Somerset, Surrey.

SRI LANKAN AVERAGES – FIRST CLASS MATCHES

BATTING

	M	*I*	*NO*	*R*	*HI*	*100s*	*Avge*
P. A. de Silva	6	12	4	563	221*	1	70.37
M. S. Atapattu	6	8	4	241	74*	0	60.25
H. P. Tillekeratne	5	9	2	349	109*	2	49.85
R. S. Mahanama	6	10	0	494	114	2	49.40
S. T. Jayasuriya	6	9	2	345	105*	1	49.28
A. P. Gurusinha	3	6	3	138	58	0	46.00
U. C. Hathurusinghe	5	10	0	385	136	1	38.50
D. S. B. P. Kuruppu	5	10	1	259	56*	0	28.77
A. W. R. Madurasinghe	4	3	1	43	28*	0	21.50
G. F. Labrooy	4	6	0	121	69	0	20.16
G. P. Wickremansinghe	3	2	0	17	17	0	8.50

Played in four matches: C. P. H. Ramanayake 8*, 3*, 5*, 9*; K. I. W. Wijegunawardene 0; P. K. Wijetunge 5*. Played in one match: F. S. Ahangama did not bat.

* *Signifies not out.*

BOWLING

	O	*M*	*R*	*W*	*BB*	*5W/i*	*Avge*
A. P. Gurusinha	40	8	113	5	3-38	0	22.60
A. W. R. Madurasinghe	176.2	28	560	21	5-108	1	26.66
G. F. Labrooy	111	13	440	16	5-97	1	27.50
K. I. W. Wijegunawardene	87.3	13	318	9	2-30	0	35.33
P. K. Wijetunge	129.4	24	438	12	4-133	0	36.50
G. P. Wickremansinghe	79	17	251	6	3-95	0	41.83
C. P. H. Ramanayake	133	12	510	12	3-96	0	42.50

Also bowled: F. S. Ahangama 1.3–0–4–0; M. S. Atapattu 4–0–21–0; P. A. de Silva 25–3–81–2; U. C. Hathurusinghe 21.1–8–58–3; S. T. Jayasuriya 7–1–18–1.

FIELDING

10 – P. A. de Silva, R. S. Mahanama; 9 – H. P. Tillekeratne (7 ct, 2 st); 8 – D. S. B. P. Kuruppu (7ct, 1 st); 7 – M. S. Atapattu; 5 – S. T. Jayasuriya, K. I. W. Wijegunawardene; 3 – P. K. Wijetunge; 1 – U. C. Hathurusinghe, G. F. Labrooy, A. W. R. Madurasinghe, Substitute.

HUNDREDS FOR SRI LANKANS

The following seven three-figure innings were played for the Sri Lankans.

R. S. Mahanama (2)
114 v Notts., Cleethorpes
103 v Lancs., Manchester

H. P. Tillekeratne (2)
109* v Warwicks., Birmingham
100 v Hants, Southampton

P. A. de Silva (1)
221* v Hants, Southampton

U. C. Hathurusinghe (1)
136 v Sussex, Hove

S. T. Jayasuriya (1)
105* v Lancs., Manchester

* *Signifies not out.*

GLAMORGAN v SRI LANKANS

At Ebbw Vale, August 22, 23, 24. Drawn. Toss: Glamorgan. The Sri Lankans began their short, eight-match tour by contributing to an enjoyable three days, the highlight of which for Glamorgan supporters was Morris's ninth hundred of the season. Morris, captaining Glamorgan in Butcher's absence, passed the county record for a season, established by Javed Miandad in 1981, as he scored 126 in the second innings. Labrooy, bowling effectively at medium pace on a pitch which helped the quicker bowlers, claimed five Glamorgan wickets in the first innings, though he was the most prodigal of the Sri Lankan bowlers when it came to no-balls. James, in his second match of the season for the county, batted for four hours after remaining in single figures for nineteen overs. Gurusinha struck a forceful half-century as the visitors provided an attractive reply, and after declaring 23 runs ahead they soon had Glamorgan in trouble at 33 for three. However, a partnership of 191 between Morris and Holmes saved the innings and enabled Morris to set a target of 333 in 66 overs. At 109 for six, defeat for the Sri Lankans appeared imminent, but they were rescued by an attacking stand of 112 in sixteen overs between Atapattu and Labrooy. Labrooy struck Croft for 20 in one over which included three sixes, but when he departed, caught off a ball that lifted, the tourists settled for a draw.

Close of play: First day, Sri Lankans 78-1 (D. S. B. P. Kuruppu 38*, A. P. Gurusinha 29*); Second day, Glamorgan 227-4 (H. Morris 101*, A. Dale 0*).

Glamorgan

Batsman	First innings	Runs	Second innings	Runs
S. P. James	c Mahanama b Wijegunawardene	47	c Mahanama b Labrooy	0
*H. Morris	c Tillekeratne b Labrooy	37	c Mahanama b Wijegunawardene	126
P. A. Cottey	lbw b Wijegunawardene	0	c Atapattu b Ramanayake	0
M. P. Maynard	c Atapattu b Labrooy	20	b Labrooy	14
G. C. Holmes	c Jayasuriya b Labrooy	0	c Wijegunawardene b Labrooy	92
A. Dale	b Wijetunge	36	c Kuruppu b Gurusinha	14
R. D. B. Croft	b Labrooy	20	c de Silva b Wijegunawardene	32
†M. L. Roberts	lbw b Labrooy	25	c Mahanama b Wijetunge	22
H. A. G. Anthony	c Atapattu b Wijetunge	12	st Tillekeratne b Wijetunge	14
S. L. Watkin	lbw b Ramanayake	1	not out	2
M. Frost	not out	2		
	B 1, l-b 6, w 1, n-b 27	35	B 2, l-b 10, w 3, n-b 24	39
	1/53 2/54 3/86 4/90 5/154 6/165 7/190 8/208 9/214	235	1/0 2/8 3/33 4/224 5/260 6/287 7/327 8/336 9/355 (9 wkts dec.)	355

Bowling: *First Innings*—Labrooy 21–2–97–5; Ramanayake 14–1–61–1; Wijegunawardene 13–2–30–2; Wijetunge 24–6–40–2. *Second Innings*—Labrooy 23–5–84–3; Ramanayake 15–0–64–1; Wijegunawardene 15–1–79–2; Gurusinha 15–6–31–1; Wijetunge 18.4–1–85–2.

Sri Lankans

R. S. Mahanama lbw b Anthony	9 – lbw b Frost	35
D. S. B. P. Kuruppu lbw b Watkin	45 – c Watkin b Dale	15
A. P. Gurusinha c Roberts b Watkin	58 – c Morris b Frost	23
*P. A. de Silva b Croft	45 – lbw b Holmes	2
†H. P. Tillekeratne c Cottey b Dale	30 – c Roberts b Frost	5
S. T. Jayasuriya lbw b Watkin	24 – c James b Croft	19
M. S. Atapattu c Roberts b Dale	23 – not out	71
G. F. Labrooy c Roberts b Dale	7 – c Maynard b Watkin	69
C. P. H. Ramanayake not out	8 – not out	3
L-b 5, w 1, n-b 3	9 B 4, l-b 2, w 1, n-b 1	8
1/21 2/99 3/152 4/186 5/207 6/225 7/238 8/258	(8 wkts dec.) 258 1/34 2/74 3/81 4/81 5/87 6/109 7/221	(7 wkts) 250

K. I. W. Wijegunawardene and P. K. Wijetunge did not bat.

Bowling: *First Innings*—Watkin 21–5–92–3; Anthony 12–2–47–1; Frost 14–3–51–0; Croft 10–3–38–1; Dale 9.3–3–25–3. *Second Innings*—Anthony 4–2–14–0; Watkin 15–7–48–1; Frost 14–3–44–3; Croft 13–1–89–1; Dale 12–1–43–1; Holmes 6–1–6–1.

Umpires: M. J. Harris and R. Palmer.

NOTTINGHAMSHIRE v SRI LANKANS

At Cleethorpes, August 25, 26, 27. Drawn. Toss: Nottinghamshire. Leaving the county and going off to the seaside for the Bank Holiday, Nottinghamshire found the weather most pleasant. However, they lost three wickets rather cheaply, and only a dour innings by Newell, 112 off 261 balls, and Evans's fifty made much of an impact on some modest bowling. The Nottinghamshire bowlers then failed to disturb the Sri Lankan opening pair before the close, and on Sunday Mahanama and Hathurusinghe took the score on to 210 before they were parted. The former hit seventeen fours and faced 231 balls for his 114. Although de Silva kept the game alive by declaring behind, Nottinghamshire failed to score at a reasonable rate on the last day until Stephenson hit out. The result was that the tourists felt a target of 274 off 59 overs was too high, and the game meandered to a draw.

Close of play: First day, Sri Lankans 43-0 (R. S. Mahanama 16*, U. C. Hathurusinghe 19*); Second day, Nottinghamshire 73-2 (R. T. Robinson 21*, P. Johnson 37*).

Nottinghamshire

P. R. Pollard b Ramanayake	5 – c Jayasuriya b Labrooy	5
M. Newell c Tillekeratne b Gurusinha	112 – c Atapattu b Labrooy	6
R. T. Robinson c Mahanama b Gurusinha	18 – run out	36
*P. Johnson c Mahanama b Gurusinha	1 – c Mahanama b Wickremansinghe	54
D. J. R. Martindale c Tillekeratne b Labrooy	26 – c Mahanama b Ramanayake	13
K. P. Evans c Jayasuriya b Wickremansinghe	55 – (7) run out	2
F. D. Stephenson not out	27 – (6) c Labrooy b Wickremansinghe	65
†C. W. Scott not out	13 – b Wickremansinghe	31
K. E. Cooper (did not bat)	– not out	10
R. A. Pick (did not bat)	– b Labrooy	5
J. A. Afford (did not bat)	– c sub b Labrooy	2
B 9, l-b 17, n-b 20	46 B 1, l-b 7, w 1, n-b 13	22
1/13 2/55 3/60 4/139 5/259 6/261	(6 wkts dec.) 303 1/13 2/22 3/101 4/117 5/129 6/145 7/232 8/234 9/239	251

Bowling: *First Innings*—Labrooy 19.4–2–68–1; Ramanayake 14–0–60–1; Wickremansinghe 24–9–63–1; Gurusinha 15–2–38–3; Hathurusinghe 3–3–0–0; Wijetunge 9–1–29–0; de Silva 6–1–19–0. *Second Innings*—Labrooy 14.2–3–60–4; Wickremansinghe 26–3–95–3; Ramanayake 15–0–70–1; de Silva 2–1–5–0; Wijetunge 1–0–13–0.

Sri Lankans

R. S. Mahanama lbw b Stephenson	114		
U. C. Hathurusinghe lbw b Cooper	84	(1) lbw b Pick	44
A. P. Gurusinha not out	37	(4) not out	17
*P. A. de Silva c Pollard b Cooper	1	(3) not out	14
†H. P. Tillekeratne c Evans b Pick	0	(2) lbw b Cooper	22
S. T. Jayasuriya c Johnson b Afford	15		
M. S. Atapattu not out	9		
B 4, l-b 10, n-b 7	21	B 2, l-b 8, n-b 3	13
1/210 2/221 3/223 4/224 5/250 (5 wkts dec.)	281	1/69 2/81 (2 wkts)	110

G. F. Labrooy, C. P. H. Ramanayake, P. K. Wijetunge and G. P. Wickremansinghe did not bat.

Bowling: *First Innings*—Pick 19–3–54–1; Cooper 25–10–67–2; Afford 22–5–74–1; Evans 14–0–38–0; Stephenson 12–3–34–1; Newell 1–1–0–0. *Second Innings*—Pick 11–3–33–1; Evans 6–0–19–0; Stephenson 6–1–17–0; Cooper 11–2–31–1.

Umpires: B. Leadbeater and H. J. Rhodes.

WARWICKSHIRE v SRI LANKANS

At Birmingham, August 29, 30, 31. Sri Lankans won by eight wickets. Toss: Warwickshire. While Warwickshire became the first county to lose a first-class match to the Sri Lankans in their five tours of England since 1979, the visitors did well to achieve victory on a typical slow-paced Edgbaston pitch after the home side had scored 349 for nine on the opening day. Moles was five hours over his 117, and he received good support from Ostler, Green and Twose, all young players. The Sri Lankans were unlucky in losing Ahangama so early in the day with a groin injury, but they were well served by their off-spinner, Madurasinghe, who finished the match with eight wickets. The tourists kept the game open by declaring 22 runs in arrears, the left-handed Tillekeratne and Jayasuriya having put on 163 in an unbroken fifth-wicket partnership. Earlier de Silva, the captain, had hit four sixes, as well as six fours, in his 67. Warwickshire, already in some trouble overnight at 37 for three, collapsed unaccountably on the final day and were bowled out for 133 in 57 overs and one ball by an attack which was accurate but not penetrative. With de Silva hitting his second attractive half-century of the match, the Sri Lankans won easily with more than twenty overs in hand.

Close of play: First day, Warwickshire 349-9 (R. G. Twose 64*, A. A. Donald 4*); Second day, Warwickshire 37-3 (A. J. Moles 15*, D. A. Reeve 0*).

Warwickshire

A. J. Moles b Wijegunawardene	117	c Atapattu b Madurasinghe	38
J. D. Ratcliffe c Atapattu b Ramanayake	5	c Tillekeratne b Wijegunawardene	14
D. P. Ostler c Wijegunawardene b Madurasinghe	56	lbw b Ramanayake	3
S. J. Green c Jayasuriya b Madurasinghe	44	c Kuruppu b Wijegunawardene	0
R. G. Twose not out	64	(6) c Atapattu b Madurasinghe	4
*D. A. Reeve lbw b Madurasinghe	5	(5) lbw b Ramanayake	1
N. M. K. Smith b Ramanayake	1	c de Silva b Hathurusinghe	43
†K. J. Piper lbw b Ramanayake	19	b Madurasinghe	0
J. E. Benjamin b Madurasinghe	2	(10) b Hathurusinghe	14
P. A. Booth b Wijegunawardene	8	(9) lbw b Madurasinghe	1
A. A. Donald not out	4	not out	0
L-b 8, n-b 16	24	B 4, l-b 7, n-b 4	15
1/10 2/142 3/209 4/270 5/281 6/293 7/321 8/324 9/345 (9 wkts dec.)	349	1/23 2/30 3/33 4/46 5/57 6/83 7/83 8/101 9/132	133

Bowling: *First Innings*—Ramanayake 27–4–96–3; Ahangama 1.3–0–4–0; Wijegunawardene 19.3–4–82–2; Hathurusinghe 6–2–14–0; Madurasinghe 40–6–120–4; de Silva 9–1–25–0. *Second Innings*—Ramanayake 22–5–53–2; Wijegunawardene 15–3–31–2; Madurasinghe 17–6–35–4; Hathurusinghe 3.1–1–3–2.

Sri Lankans

R. S. Mahanama lbw b Benjamin 30
U. C. Hathurusinghe b Twose .... 19 – lbw b Donald 19
D. S. B. P. Kuruppu c sub b Reeve .... 1 – (1) c Piper b Booth 40
*P. A. de Silva lbw b Reeve .... 67 – (3) not out 54
†H. P. Tillekeratne not out ....109 – (4) not out 29
S. T. Jayasuriya not out 78
B 4, l-b 8, w 1, n-b 10 23   B 5, l-b 6, n-b 4 15

1/42 2/44 3/58 4/164 (4 wkts dec.) 327   1/59 2/107 (2 wkts) 157

C. P. H. Ramanayake, M. S. Atapattu, K. I. W. Wijegunawardene, A. W. R. Madurasinghe and F. S. Ahangama did not bat.

Bowling: *First Innings*—Donald 11.5–4–33–0; Benjamin 12–0–59–1; Reeve 14–3–46–2; Twose 13–4–40–1; Booth 17–1–77–0; Smith 22–3–60–0. *Second Innings*—Donald 9–1–35–1; Benjamin 5–0–22–0; Reeve 6–1–29–0; Booth 11.3–3–41–1; Smith 2–0–19–0.

Umpires: M. J. Harris and R. Julian.

†SURREY v SRI LANKANS

At The Oval, September 2. Surrey won by 14 runs. Toss: Sri Lankans. Although Labrooy kept pulses racing in the closing stages with 28 from nineteen balls, before being caught at extra cover in the 54th over, Surrey had looked to have the match won through some excellent work in the field. Victory was much less certain during the morning as Labrooy, Gurusinha and Madurasinghe held them to 125 for one from 38 overs. However, Thorpe went on to 63 from 82 balls and Bicknell to 86 as Surrey set about the bowling in order to achieve a defendable total.

Surrey

D. J. Bicknell c and b de Silva 86
R. I. Alikhan b Gurusinha 22
*G. P. Thorpe c Atapattu b de Silva .. 63
J. D. Robinson c Wickremansinghe b de Silva . 33
A. D. Brown c Wickremansinghe b de Silva . 2
K. T. Medlycott c Tillekeratne b Labrooy 20
C. K. Bullen not out 1
B 2, l-b 10, w 14 26

1/70 2/164 3/200 4/205 5/239 6/253 (6 wkts, 55 overs) 253

†N. F. Sargeant, N. M. Kendrick, A. H. Gray and A. J. Murphy did not bat.

Bowling: Labrooy 11–2–49–1; Wickremansinghe 8–1–45–0; Gurusinha 8–2–20–1; Madurasinghe 11–1–33–0; Wijegunawardene 9–1–39–0; de Silva 8–0–55–4.

Sri Lankans

D. S. B. P. Kuruppu c Murphy b Bullen 33
†H. P. Tillekeratne c Bullen b Murphy . 45
A. P. Gurusinha lbw b Bullen 4
*P. A. de Silva c Robinson b Kendrick. 35
S. T. Jayasuriya c Bicknell b Kendrick . 32
R. S. Mahanama hit wkt b Kendrick .. 24
M. S. Atapattu b Gray 19
G. F. Labrooy c Bullen b Murphy 28
G. P. Wickremansinghe b Gray 12
A. W. R. Madurasinghe not out 1
K. I. W. Wijegunawardene c Medlycott b Murphy . 1
L-b 3, w 2 5

1/64 2/77 3/97 4/145 5/169 6/191 7/207 8/237 9/237 (53.5 overs) 239

Bowling: Gray 10–1–35–2; Murphy 10.5–0–61–3; Thorpe 3–1–15–0; Robinson 5–0–25–0; Bullen 11–1–37–2; Medlycott 8–0–42–0; Kendrick 6–0–21–3.

Umpires: B. Hassan and R. Julian.

†SOMERSET v SRI LANKANS

At Taunton, September 3. Somerset won by 71 runs. Toss: Sri Lankans. Roebuck (106 balls) and Townsend (112 balls) added 170 in 32 overs after Somerset were put in on a cloudy morning, with the pitch rather fresh. Three wickets fell quickly, but Burns and Harden then added 51 in five overs. The Sri Lankans never recovered from an opening spell of four for 15 in 25 deliveries from Rose. With the result not in doubt, Atapattu and Wickremansinghe put on 72 in the final fourteen overs, largely against the change bowlers.

Somerset

S. J. Cook c Mahanama b Ramanayake 13
G. T. J. Townsend run out 77
P. M. Roebuck c and b Madurasinghe . 95
G. D. Rose c Wickremansinghe b Gurusinha . 2
R. J. Harden c Kuruppu b Ramanayake 25
†N. D. Burns not out 29
*C. J. Tavaré not out 5
L-b 14, n-b 2 16

1/23 2/193 3/198 4/200 5/251 (5 wkts, 48 overs) 262

M. Lathwell, P. J. Rendell, A. R. Kaddick and A. N. Jones did not bat.

Bowling: Ramanayake 8–0–47–2; Wickremansinghe 10–1–45–0; Gurusinha 11–0–59–1; Wijegunawardene 9–0–50–0; Madurasinghe 10–0–47–1.

Sri Lankans

†D. S. B. P. Kuruppu lbw b Rose 1
H. P. Tillekeratne c Cook b Rose 23
A. P. Gurusinha c Burns b Rose 1
*P. A. de Silva c Burns b Rendell 33
S. T. Jayasuriya c Rendell b Rose 6
R. S. Mahanama c and b Rendell 11
M. S. Atapattu not out 63
C. P. H. Ramanayake lbw b Roebuck . 12
G. P. Wickremansinghe not out 24
L-b 7, w 7, n-b 3 17

1/4 2/21 3/31 4/47 5/72 6/88 7/119 (7 wkts, 48 overs) 191

K. I. W. Wijegunawardene and A. W. R. Madurasinghe did not bat.

Bowling: Jones 6–0–31–0; Rose 6–1–16–4; Rendell 11–1–46–2; Kaddick 6–1–19–0; Roebuck 11–0–30–1; Lathwell 7–1–35–0; Harden 1–0–7–0.

Umpires: A. A. Jones and P. B. Wight.

SUSSEX v SRI LANKANS

At Hove, September 5, 6, 7. Drawn. Toss: Sussex. An uninspiring game, affected by rain, ended with Sussex holding out for a draw after some reckless batting had given the touring team a chance of victory. Hathurusinghe was the cornerstone of the Sri Lankans' first innings, revealing great promise in a maiden first-class hundred which included 22 fours, and when he was out de Silva and Atapattu put on 72 in fifteen overs. Sussex, to help make up the time lost to rain on the first day, declared 108 behind. Parker hastened the declaration with three sixes off Madurasinghe as he made a vigorous return to the side after a five-week absence because of injury. Threlfall sparked a potential crisis when he took two cheap wickets before the close, but Atapattu again batted with determination and the home team were left needing 297 from 47 overs to win. They went for the runs early on, but when six wickets had gone for 102, they shut up shop. Dodemaide and Moores, scoring only 45 runs off the final twenty overs, ensured that those members not at Eastbourne, watching the championship-winning Second Eleven, had departed long before the end.

Close of play: First day, Sri Lankans 229-2 (U. C. Hathurusinghe 114*, S. T. Jayasuriya 32*); Second day, Sri Lankans 28-3 (U. C. Hathurusinghe 8*, M. S. Atapattu 2*).

Sri Lankans

†D. S. B. P. Kuruppu b Threlfall	51	– (4) lbw b Threlfall	4
U. C. Hathurusinghe c Moores b Dodemaide	136	– run out	31
A. P. Gurusinha not out	3	– c Moores b Threlfall	0
R. S. Mahanama run out	8	– (1) b Dodemaide	14
S. T. Jayasuriya c Moores b Threlfall	32	– (7) c Parker b Lenham	0
*P. A. de Silva c Wells b Pigott	43	– c Hall b Threlfall	5
M. S. Atapattu not out	49	– (5) not out	74
G. F. Labrooy c Hall b Pigott	0	– (9) b Dodemaide	22
A. W. R. Madurasinghe (did not bat)		– (8) run out	11
G. P. Wickremansinghe (did not bat)		– c Wells b Pigott	17
P. K. Wijetunge (did not bat)		– not out	5
B 2, l-b 20, n-b 3	25	L-b 1, w 3, n-b 1	5
1/99 2/164 3/234 4/268 5/340 6/341 (6 wkts dec.)	347	1/20 2/21 3/25 4/62 5/85 6/94 7/118 8/148 9/182 (9 wkts dec.)	188

A. P. Gurusinha, when 3, retired hurt at 123 and resumed at 341.

Bowling: *First Innings*—Dodemaide 23–6–73–1; Threlfall 14–3–44–2; Pigott 20.5–5–74–2; Lenham 14.1–4–31–0; Salisbury 25–5–103–0. *Second Innings*—Dodemaide 26–4–65–2; Threlfall 16–5–45–3; Pigott 4–1–7–1; Lenham 11–3–29–1; Salisbury 11–3–41–0.

Sussex

N. J. Lenham c Kuruppu b Labrooy	1	– c Kuruppu b Labrooy	1
J. W. Hall c Jayasuriya b Wijetunge	40	– (7) c de Silva b Madurasinghe	0
D. M. Smith lbw b Labrooy	0	– (2) c Wijetunge b Gurusinha	29
A. P. Wells c Kuruppu b Madurasinghe	96	– c de Silva b Wickremansinghe	20
*P. W. G. Parker not out	83	– (3) b Wickremansinghe	21
M. P. Speight not out	5	– (5) c de Silva b Wijetunge	21
A. I. C. Dodemaide (did not bat)		– (6) not out	33
†P. Moores (did not bat)		– not out	14
B 1, l-b 7, n-b 6	14	L-b 1, n-b 7	8
1/11 2/11 3/104 4/197 (4 wkts dec.)	239	1/7 2/49 3/67 4/84 5/101 6/102 (6 wkts)	147

A. C. S. Pigott, I. D. K. Salisbury and P. W. Threlfall did not bat.

Bowling: *First Innings*—Labrooy 12–0–38–2; Wickremansinghe 13–3–41–0; Wijetunge 7–0–40–1; Hathurusinghe 2–0–12–0; Madurasinghe 16.5–1–92–1; Gurusinha 3–0–8–0. *Second Innings*—Labrooy 9–0–40–1; Wickremansinghe 12–2–30–2; Gurusinha 7–0–36–1; Madurasinghe 9–1–17–1; Wijetunge 9–4–15–1; Jayasuriya 1–0–4–0; Atapattu 1–0–4–0.

Umpires: G. I. Burgess and J. H. Harris.

LANCASHIRE v SRI LANKANS

At Manchester, September 8, 9, 10. Drawn. Toss: Sri Lankans. Lancashire fielded a virtual second team, playing only three capped players in Fairbrother, Folley and Austin, and giving a début to Crawley, the former Oxford University captain. Mahanama and de Silva led the Sri Lankans' recovery after two early wickets had fallen to Martin, and on the second morning de Silva allowed Jayasuriya to complete his century before declaring. An eighth-wicket stand between Yates and Folley made certain that Lancashire avoided the follow-on, after the middle order had failed to build on a century opening partnership from Lloyd, who faced only 87 balls for his 96, and Speak. On the final day, Mahanama missed his second century of the match by only 7 runs, being bowled by a full toss to become Speak's maiden first-class victim, and Lancashire were set a victory target of 293 in 58 overs. They made a creditable attempt but gave up at the fall of the eighth wicket, six overs from the end.

Close of play: First day, Sri Lankans 342-7 (S. T. Jayasuriya 60*, A. W. R. Madurasinghe 12*); Second day, Sri Lankans 28-0 (R. S. Mahanama 16*, U. C. Hathurusinghe 11*).

Sri Lankans

R. S. Mahanama c Bramhall b Yates	103	– b Speak	93
U. C. Hathurusinghe c Lloyd b Martin	15	– run out	31
D. S. B. P. Kuruppu c Fitton b Martin	2	– not out	56
*P. A. de Silva c Fairbrother b Yates	95	– not out	14
†H. P. Tillekeratne lbw b Folley	44		
M. S. Atapattu c and b Yates	6		
S. T. Jayasuriya not out	105		
G. P. Wickremansinghe b Yates	0		
A. W. R. Madurasinghe not out	28		
B 3, l-b 3, n-b 2	8	L-b 5	5
1/31 2/35 3/203 4/224 5/248 6/274 7/277 (7 wkts dec.)	406	1/75 2/179 (2 wkts dec.)	199

K. I. W. Wijegunawardene and P. K. Wijetunge did not bat.

Bowling: *First Innings*—Martin 23–2–84–2; Austin 9.5–3–23–0; Crawley 8–1–9–0; Folley 35.1–4–126–1; Fitton 19–4–64–0; Yates 38–9–94–4. *Second Innings*—Martin 12–4–34–0; Crawley 6–2–16–0; Yates 8–0–39–0; Fitton 7–1–18–0; Folley 7–0–25–0; Fairbrother 7–0–29–0; Speak 5–0–26–1; Lloyd 1–0–7–0.

Lancashire

G. D. Lloyd st Tillekeratne b Wijetunge	96	– st Kuruppu b Madurasinghe	34
N. J. Speak b Madurasinghe	43	– c Tillekeratne b Madurasinghe	52
S. P. Titchard lbw b Madurasinghe	11	– c de Silva b Madurasinghe	1
*N. H. Fairbrother c Mahanama b Wijetunge	6	– c Kuruppu b Wijetunge	26
M. A. Crawley c de Silva b Wijetunge	42	– b de Silva	48
I. D. Austin c Wijetunge b Madurasinghe	3	– (7) c Wijegunawardene b de Silva	24
J. D. Fitton c Hathurusinghe b Madurasinghe	13	– (6) c and b Wijetunge	6
G. Yates c de Silva b Jayasuriya	42	– not out	15
I. Folley not out	47	– run out	5
†S. Bramhall c Tillekeratne b Wijetunge	0	– not out	1
P. J. Martin c de Silva b Madurasinghe	2		
B 3, l-b 4, n-b 1	8	B 6, l-b 8, n-b 1	15
1/115 2/143 3/155 4/160 5/178 6/204 7/221 8/298 9/303	313	1/51 2/61 3/113 4/130 5/141 6/191 7/207 8/225 (8 wkts)	227

Bowling: *First Innings*—Wickremansinghe 3–0–11–0; Wijegunawardene 3–1–16–0; Wijetunge 38–6–133–4; Madurasinghe 37.3–7–108–5; de Silva 2–0–7–0; Jayasuriya 5–0–14–1; Atapattu 3–0–17–0. *Second Innings*—Wickremansinghe 1–0–11–0; Wijegunawardene 1–0–5–0; Wijetunge 23–6–83–2; Madurasinghe 26–3–89–3; de Silva 6–0–25–2; Jayasuriya 1–1–0–0.

Umpires: J. C. Balderstone and R. A. White.

HAMPSHIRE v SRI LANKANS

At Southampton, September 12, 13, 14. Drawn. Toss: Hampshire. The Sri Lankan captain, de Silva, put paid to Hampshire's hopes of becoming the only county to beat his side in a three-day match. After the Sri Lankans had struggled against the left-arm spin of Maru in their first innings and been made to follow on, de Silva, 59 not out overnight, kept Hampshire at bay throughout the final day to finish unbeaten with 221. He batted in all for 443 minutes, facing 399 deliveries, hit three sixes and 38 fours, and shared a partnership of 263 in 74 overs with Tillekeratne for the fourth wicket. Hampshire's innings had been dominated by Terry, who hit eighteen fours in a typically applied century, and enlivened by flourishes from Ayling and Aymes.

Close of play: First day, Sri Lankans 4-0 (R. S. Mahanama 2*, U. C. Hathurusinghe 1*); Second day, Sri Lankans 213-3 (P. A. de Silva 59*, H. P. Tillekeratne 60*).

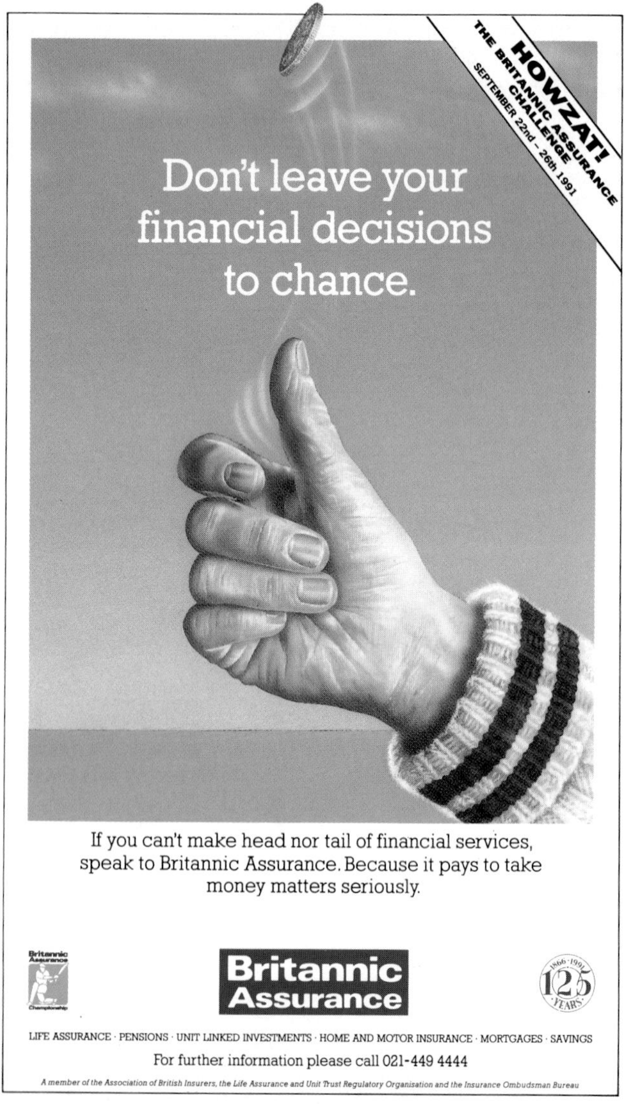

Advertisement

Hampshire

V. P. Terry c Wijegunawardene b Madurasinghe	120
T. C. Middleton c Kuruppu b Ramanayake	22
*M. C. J. Nicholas c Mahanama b Ramanayake	0
J. R. Ayling c Wijegunawardene b Madurasinghe	59
D. I. Gower c and b Madurasinghe	0
R. M. F. Cox b Wijegunawardene	34
†A. N. Aymes not out	62
R. J. Maru c Tillekeratne b Hathurusinghe	6
S. D. Udal c de Silva b Ramanayake	14
C. A. Connor not out	29
L-b 5, w 2, n-b 14	21
1/45 2/45 3/151 4/151 5/242 6/260 7/290 8/325 (8 wkts dec.)	367

P. J. Bakker did not bat.

Bowling: Labrooy 12–1–53–0; Ramanayake 26–2–106–3; Madurasinghe 30–4–99–3; Wijegunawardene 21–2–75–1; Hathurusinghe 7–2–29–1.

Sri Lankans

R. S. Mahanama c Aymes b Bakker	32	– lbw b Udal	56
U. C. Hathurusinghe c Maru b Connor	1	– c Nicholas b Bakker	5
D. S. B. P. Kuruppu lbw b Maru	24	– c Gower b Maru	21
*P. A. de Silva lbw b Bakker	2	– not out	221
†H. P. Tillekeratne st Aymes b Maru	10	– b Maru	100
S. T. Jayasuriya c Middleton b Maru	18	– c Aymes b Udal	54
M. S. Atapattu c Gower b Udal	9	– st Aymes b Udal	0
G. F. Labrooy c Connor b Udal	5	– st Aymes b Udal	18
C. P. H. Ramanayake not out	5	– not out	9
A. W. R. Madurasinghe c Cox b Maru	4		
K. I. W. Wijegunawardene c Cox b Maru	0		
L-b 1, n-b 7	8	B 5, l-b 6, w 3, n-b 8	22
1/4 2/53 3/55 4/76 5/88 6/103 7/108 8/109 9/118	118	1/7 2/84 3/94 4/357 5/457 6/459 7/491 (7 wkts dec.)	506

Bowling: *First Innings*—Bakker 13–1–36–2; Connor 10–2–32–1; Ayling 7–4–9–0; Maru 11.5–4–25–5; Udal 7–2–15–2. *Second Innings*—Bakker 17–0–87–1; Connor 16–2–63–0; Maru 50–20–119–2; Udal 40–9–139–4; Ayling 16–4–38–0; Nicholas 4–0–29–0; Middleton 4–0–19–0; Cox 1–0–1–0.

Umpires: K. E. Palmer and R. C. Tolchard.

THE UNIBIND ICC TROPHY, 1990

By DAVID HARDY

The fourth tournament for the ICC Trophy, following the 1979, 1982 and 1986 events, which were all held in England, was for the first time staged in one of the Associate Member countries competing for it, The Netherlands. For the first time, too, a sponsor's name was attached to the event, that of the Dutch book-binding firm, Unibind. It was indeed a new departure, which had demanded three years of thorough preparation by the ICC Management Committee – under the chairmanship of Gibraltarian Joe Buzaglo, himself a participant in the 1986 tournament – and the Royal Dutch Cricket Association committee, led by the former national wicket-keeper and national association chairman, Henk van Eck.

This was also the first ICC Trophy not to be played on grass pitches, which theoretically should have given an advantage to those countries, such as the host country and Denmark, who habitually play on matting or artificial surfaces. With no grass pitches in The Netherlands, the organising committee was faced with the choice, in the interests of standardisation, of choosing venues with coconut matting wickets, laid over a gravel base, or artificial grass. The former surface was chosen and ten clubs were selected to stage the 58 matches. The majority were located in the west of the country, the heart of Dutch cricket: three in The Hague, two in the Amsterdam area, two in the Rotterdam area and one in Haarlem. The other two venues were at Nijmegen and Deventer, in the east but no more than two hours' drive from the Bel Air Hotel in The Hague, the nerve centre of the tournament for three weeks. Both semi-finals and the final were scheduled for the beautiful HCC ground in The Hague.

It was hoped that all eighteen Associate Members would participate, but at the eleventh hour West Africa pulled out. The only differences from 1986 were the participation this time of Singapore and the expansion of the East Africa team to embrace East and Central Africa (representing Malawi, Tanzania, Uganda and Zambia). However, the arrangement of the qualifying groups was certainly different from the previous tournament. The seventeen teams initially played in four qualifying groups: three of four teams (Groups A, B and C) and one of five (Group D). The first two teams from each group then went forward to two second-round groups (E and F), the first two teams of which qualified for the knockout semi-finals. In order to ensure that all teams played roughly the same number of matches over the three weeks, two additional groups (G and H) were formed by the teams which did not qualify for Groups E and F.

A curiosity of the playing conditions was that group matches not completed because of the weather had to be replayed in their entirety the following day. (In fact, the weather was so kind that only one group match was so affected.) However, this regulation did not apply to the semi-finals or final. These, it was ruled, would be resumed at the score when the game was interrupted, as happened in the Zimbabwe-Bangladesh semi-final. In the event of teams finishing level in groups, run-rate was decisive. Papua New Guinea, although aware of this, failed to realise that in the event of a team being dismissed the run-rate would be decided by the total divided by 60 overs, and not by the actual overs batted. In their last Group E match, chasing the USA's 190, they were all out for 123 in 25.2 overs and failed in the end by 0.28 to reach the semi-finals.

It was thought by many that The Netherlands, with the advantage of playing on home grounds, would never have a better chance of qualifying for the World Cup. They failed by just 25 runs to beat Zimbabwe in 1986; this time, surely, they could go one better. Zimbabwe returned in 1990, however, as favourites with the nucleus of their 1986 team. Moreover, their captain, David Houghton, as the professional for Quick CC of The Hague, had ample experience of Dutch conditions. The Netherlands had two English county cricketers to call on, Paul-Jan Bakker of Hampshire and Roland Lefebvre of Somerset, and selected three foreign-born players – Rupert Gomes, the Trinidadian who played in their 1986 team, Sri Lankan Flavian Aponso, and Nolan Clarke, the 41-year-old prolific six-hitter from Barbados, who a few days before the start of the tournament had broken the all-time Dutch record by scoring 265 not out in a league match. Holland's best all-rounder, Ron Elferink, unfortunately missed the tournament through injury.

The final was duly a repeat of the 1986 Lord's contest. But in front of thousands of enthusiastic Dutch supporters, The Netherlands performed less creditably than in 1986 and lost comfortably to a polished, professional Zimbabwe team. For Zimbabwe, who had never lost an ICC match, the Flower brothers, Andy (who also kept wicket excellently) and Grant, were outstanding with the bat, Andy finishing with the best average of the tournament, 77.75, and Grant third in the list with 63.25. The Zimbabwean pace attack of Eddo Brandes, Malcolm Jarvis, Kevin Duers and Ali Shah, supported by the 43-year-old off-spinner, John Traicos, the meanest bowler in the tournament (1.81 runs per over), was too good for everyone. Houghton himself had scored just 4 runs in three innings before the semi-finals, in which his masterly 91 rescued his side when they were 37 for four against Bangladesh. The Netherlands, despite having the heaviest run-scorer of the tournament in Clarke (523 runs) and the "player of the tournament" in Lefebvre (315 runs at 45 and fourteen wickets at 9.43), failed to achieve what they dearly wanted, principally through a careless batting display in the final.

Although Kenya and Bangladesh reached the semi-finals, their places could have been filled by two of several teams. Kenya, curiously, won only two of their six group matches, qualifying from Group B in the first round with a run-rate 0.14 better than Fiji's, and from Group E in the second round by virtue of that 0.28 runs per over superiority over Papua New Guinea. Bangladesh won all three matches in the initial phase, beating Kenya along the way, and finished level with The Netherlands in Group F in the second stage with two wins out of three. Another 0.07 runs per over from Bangladesh would, in fact, have pitted Zimbabwe and The Netherlands, clearly the two best teams, against each other in the semi-finals. Kenya, with many locally born players in the party, including four Odumbe brothers (the most successful was Maurice with 289 runs at 48.17) and two Tikolos, showed a refreshing advance since 1986. Bangladesh, the only ICC Associate Member with a Test ground, possessed an accomplished opening batsman in Nurul Abedin (235 runs at 47) and an outstanding wicket-keeper in Nasir Nasu, who recorded 22 dismissals.

Canada were the only team to beat The Netherlands before the final, but their batting was too inconsistent. Denmark, with Ole Mortensen, the Derbyshire professional, could not emulate their 1986 performance of reaching the semi-finals and once again lost the "European championship final" against The Netherlands in a decisive Group F match. The other two teams to reach the second stage, Papua New Guinea and USA, were eased out of a semi-final place by Kenya on run-rate.

Of the weaker nations, Fiji emerged as an improved force, pulling off the surprise of the first-round matches by beating Bermuda on the first day of the tournament. Hong Kong had little chance to progress from the five-team Group D – J. Marsden was, however, one of only four batsmen in the tournament to score more than 300 runs – and Singapore were similarly outclassed in Group A. Neither Malaysia nor East and Central Africa managed a win in the first round. Argentina failed as well, but Israel and Gibraltar, the two nations with the smallest reservoir of clubs, both went home happy after winning a qualifying match. Israel, with largely home-grown players, beat Argentina (Israel's star player in that match, with the good cricketing name of Alan Moss, scored 42 and took five for 37), while Gibraltar beat East and Central Africa to register their second-ever win in the ICC Trophy.

The organisation of the tournament, whereby the non-qualifiers for the second stage played in Groups G and H, gave the lesser teams full value for their long trip to The Netherlands, and contributed considerably to the now traditional, extremely sociable atmosphere amongst the players and officials of the Associate Members. The decision to move the tournament away from England proved a great success, and it was hoped that this success would be repeated when the Associate Member countries came together for the 1994 ICC Trophy.

GROUP A

At KZKC, The Hague, June 4. Canada won by eight wickets. Singapore 108 (57 overs) (M. Prashad four for 21); Canada 110 for two (30.5 overs) (G. Budhoo 41 not out, F. Kirmani 31 not out).

At HBS, The Hague, June 4. Zimbabwe won by nine wickets. Malaysia 80 (38.4 overs) (A. J. Traicos four for 10); Zimbabwe 81 for one (23.4 overs) (A. Flower 56 not out).

At Koninklijke UD, Deventer, June 6. Canada won by eight wickets. Malaysia 148 (57.5 overs) (A. Stephens 56; B. Seebaran four for 34, T. Gardner three for 21); Canada 153 for two (39 overs) (P. Prashad 52 not out, I. Lyburd 41, F. Kirmani 33).

At Quick, Nijmegen, June 6. Zimbabwe won by ten wickets. Singapore 108 (50.1 overs) (M. P. Jarvis four for 21, E. A. Brandes three for 30); Zimbabwe 109 for no wkt (24.5 overs) (G. W. Flower 53 not out, G. A. Paterson 52 not out).

At VRA, Amstelveen, June 10. Singapore won by four wickets. Malaysia 147 (51.1 overs) (R. Chander 34; T. Seal three for 16, S. Muruthi three for 26); Singapore 151 for six (58.2 overs) (B. Bala 55 not out).

At Rood en Wit, Haarlem, June 10. Zimbabwe won by 68 runs. Zimbabwe 215 (59.4 overs) (G. W. Flower 70, A. H. Shah 39; D. Joseph three for 27, T. Gardner three for 47); Canada 147 (51.4 overs) (A. Dornellas 33, M. Prashad 32 not out; A. J. Traicos three for 16, A. H. Shah three for 37).

	Played	*Won*	*Lost*	*Points*	*Run-rate*
Zimbabwe	3	3	0	12	3.79
Canada	3	2	1	8	3.18
Singapore	3	1	2	4	2.06
Malaysia	3	0	3	0	2.08

GROUP B

At VRA, Amstelveen, June 4. Bangladesh won by three wickets. Kenya 189 for nine (60 overs) (Maurice Odumbe 41, A. Njoroge 33 not out, I. Tariq Iqbal 31; Minhaz-ul-Abedin three for 29); Bangladesh 190 for seven (58.1 overs) (C. A. Hossain 40, M. A. Khan 39 not out).

At Hermes DVS, Schiedam, June 4. Fiji won by 58 runs. Fiji 206 for nine (60 overs) (S. Campbell 55, J. Sorovakatini 37; K. Lightbourne three for 38); Bermuda 148 (43 overs).

At HBS, The Hague, June 6. Kenya won by four wickets. Fiji 168 for eight (50 overs) (C. Browne 66, A. Browne 36; Martin Odumbe three for 21, B. Odumbe three for 24); Kenya 169 for six (46.2 overs) (A. Njoroge 43 not out, D. McDonald 35, Maurice Odumbe 31; N. Maxwell three for 20).

At KZKC, The Hague, June 6. Bangladesh won by 36 runs. Bangladesh 175 (56.5 overs) (Minhaz-ul-Abedin 47, M. Islam 30; A. Edwards three for 22); Bermuda 139 (53.5 overs) (R. Hill 49; Minhaz-ul-Abedin three for 23).

At VOC, Rotterdam, June 10. Bangladesh won by three wickets. Fiji 189 (59.5 overs) (J. Sorovakatini 43, C. Browne 36, N. Maxwell 36; M. E. Hoque Moni three for 26); Bangladesh 193 for seven (58.4 overs) (M. A. Khan 42 not out; S. Campbell three for 45).

At ACC, Amstelveen, June 10. Bermuda won by 66 runs. Bermuda 280 (58.3 overs) (W. Smith 57, T. Smith 54, O. Jones 44; A. Njoroge three for 58); Kenya 214 for nine (60 overs) (T. Tikolo 44, Maurice Odumbe 41).

	Played	*Won*	*Lost*	*Points*	*Run-rate*
Bangladesh	3	3	0	12	3.17
Kenya	3	1	2	4	3.45
Fiji	3	1	2	4	3.31
Bermuda	3	1	2	4	3.15

GROUP C

At Rood en Wit, Haarlem, June 4. USA won by 95 runs. USA 198 for seven (50 overs) (Z. Amin 53, S. Shivnarine 43, T. Mills 31 not out); Gibraltar 103 (42 overs) (T. Buzaglo 35; K. Khan four for 11, Z. Amin four for 29).

At Hermes DVS, Schiedam, June 6. Denmark won by 103 runs. Denmark 197 for nine (60 overs) (S. Mikkelsen 54 not out, O. Stoustrup 39); East and Central Africa 94 (43.5 overs) (O. H. Mortensen four for 30).

At Koninklijke UD, Deventer, June 8. Denmark won by seven wickets. Gibraltar 128 (46.5 overs) (B. Chinappa 31, A. Raikes 30; O. H. Mortensen four for 27, J. Bredo three for 22, S. Henriksen three for 32); Denmark 129 for three (36 overs) (T. Jensen 36 not out).

At Quick, Nijmegen, June 8. No result; match declared null and replayed on June 11. USA 404 for nine (60 overs) (E. Peart 101, H. Blackman 100, R. R. Winter 44 not out, N. Lashkari 34, S. Shivnarine 32; F. Sarigat four for 76); East and Central Africa 41 for two (20 overs).

At HBS, The Hague, June 10. Gibraltar won by eight wickets. East and Central Africa 123 (42.4 overs) (H. Patadia 55; R. Brooks four for 18, B. Chinappa three for 17); Gibraltar 124 for two (31.3 overs) (T. Buzaglo 40 not out, R. Buzaglo 39).

At Quick, Nijmegen, June 11. USA won by five wickets. East and Central Africa 184 (59.3 overs) (P. Desai 51, H. Bagas 34, Y. Wanakabulo 34; R. Benjamin five for 27, K. Khan three for 41); USA 186 for five (39.5 overs) (H. Blackman 63, S. Smith 45; B. Bouri four for 44).

At ACC, Amstelveen, June 12. USA won by 12 runs. USA 224 for eight (60 overs) (E. Peart 59, K. Khan 38, S. Shivnarine 32; N. Bindsley four for 53); Denmark 212 (58.5 overs) (J. Jensen 57, P. Jensen 48, O. H. Mortensen 35 not out; Z. Amin three for 34).

	Played	*Won*	*Lost*	*Points*	*Run-rate*
USA	3	3	0	12	4.08
Denmark	3	2	1	8	3.45
Gibraltar	3	1	2	4	2.52
East and Central Africa	3	0	3	0	2.23

GROUP D

At Quick, Nijmegen, June 4. Papua New Guinea won by 167 runs. Papua New Guinea 265 for seven (60 overs) (T. Ao 88, T. Raka 59 not out, V. Pala 36; H. Pereyra three for 29); Argentina 98 (44.3 overs) (G. Ravu three for 16, T. Raka three for 28).

At ACC, Amstelveen, June 4. The Netherlands won by 338 runs. The Netherlands 402 for four (60 overs) (R. Gomes 169 not out, N. E. Clarke 154, R. P. Lefebvre 46); Israel 64 (38.1 overs) (S. W. Lubbers four for 13).

At HCC, The Hague, June 6. Israel won by one wicket. Argentina 127 (54.2 overs) (C. Nino 35; A. Moss five for 37, M. Jacob three for 29); Israel 129 for nine (51 overs) (A. Moss 42, S. Perlman 31; D. Annand three for 29, H. Pereyra three for 37).

At VOC, Rotterdam, June 6. The Netherlands won by seven wickets. Hong Kong 178 for seven (60 overs) (K. Kumar 43, M. Sabine 40; R. P. Lefebvre three for 24); The Netherlands 184 for three (25.3 overs) (N. E. Clarke 116 not out, R. Gomes 40).

At Rood en Wit, Haarlem, June 8. Papua New Guinea won by 36 runs. Papua New Guinea 220 for seven (60 overs) (R. Ila 56, C. Amini 50; G. Davies three for 28); Hong Kong 184 (56.5 overs) (D. A. Jones 71, N. Perera 43, J. Marsden 31; K. Loi five for 34).

At KZKC, The Hague, June 8. The Netherlands won by 223 runs. The Netherlands 302 for seven (60 overs) (R. P. Lefebvre 109 not out, N. E. Clarke 61, R. van Oosterom 43, G. J. A. F. Aponso 38); Argentina 79 (40.4 overs) (F. Jansen three for 13).

At Hermes DVS, Schiedam, June 10. Papua New Guinea won by 57 runs. Papua New Guinea 190 (48.4 overs) (T. Ao 59, W. Maha 35; C. Callendar three for 36); Israel 133 for nine (60 overs) (S. Perlman 49; C. Amini three for 21).

At Koninklijke UD, Deventer, June 10. Hong Kong won by 63 runs. Hong Kong 230 for nine (60 overs) (N. Stearns 57, D. A. Jones 30; A. Morris four for 38); Argentina 167 (54.3 overs) (T. Ferguson 57; D. Paull five for 27, S. Tariq four for 34).

At Rood en Wit, Haarlem, June 12. The Netherlands won by 160 runs. The Netherlands 237 (59.5 overs) (T. de Leede 50, S. W. Lubbers 46, N. E. Clarke 40); Papua New Guinea 77 (38.1 overs) (A. van Troost three for 11).

At VRA, Amstelveen, June 12. Hong Kong won by 144 runs. Hong Kong 323 for four (60 overs) (J. Marsden 150, M. Sabine 60 not out, K. Kumar 58); Israel 179 (50 overs) (S. Erulkar 46, C. Callendar 37, A. Moss 31; D. N. Brettell four for 53).

	Played	*Won*	*Lost*	*Points*	*Run-rate*
The Netherlands	4	4	0	16	5.49
Papua New Guinea	4	3	1	12	3.27
Hong Kong	4	2	2	8	3.81
Israel	4	1	3	4	2.29
Argentina	4	0	4	0	1.96

GROUP E

At Rood en Wit, Haarlem, June 14. Zimbabwe won by nine wickets. Papua New Guinea 133 (47.3 overs) (K. Ila 34; K. G. Duers three for 19, J. P. Brent three for 40); Zimbabwe 134 for one (35.4 overs) (A. Flower 80 not out, G. W. Flower 49 not out).

At ACC, Amstelveen, June 14. Kenya won by six wickets. USA 162 (58.5 overs) (S. Shivnarine 30; Maurice Odumbe three for 36); Kenya 163 for four (42 overs) (Maurice Odumbe 79 not out).

At Quick, Nijmegen, June 16. Zimbabwe won by seven wickets. USA 131 (59.3 overs) (K. Khan 32; E. A. Brandes five for 22, K. G. Duers three for 23); Zimbabwe 132 for three (46 overs) (G. W. Flower 52 not out, A. Flower 32).

At HBS, The Hague, June 16. Papua New Guinea won by 37 runs. Papua New Guinea 230 (59.4 overs) (C. Amini 55; E. Odumbe three for 42); Kenya 193 (57.2 overs) (Maurice Odumbe 64; T. Raka three for 29, G. Ravu three for 37, K. Loi three for 37).

At VRA, Amstelveen, June 18. USA won by 67 runs. USA 190 (51.2 overs) (K. Khan 52; V. Pala three for 21, T. Raka three for 31); Papua New Guinea 123 (25.2 overs) (W. Maha 34; E. Daley four for 35, R. R. Winter three for 30).

At ACC, Amstelveen, June 18. Zimbabwe won by 133 runs. Zimbabwe 259 for nine (60 overs) (A. H. Shah 69, G. A. Briant 48, A. Flower 44, A. J. Pycroft 34; M. Suji three for 47); Kenya 126 for six (60 overs) (I. Tariq Iqbal 36, S. Gupta 30 not out; E. A. Brandes three for 39).

	Played	*Won*	*Lost*	*Points*	*Run-rate*
Zimbabwe	3	3	0	12	3.72
Kenya	3	1	2	4	2.98
Papua New Guinea	3	1	2	4	2.70
USA	3	1	2	4	2.68

GROUP F

At VOC, Rotterdam, June 14. Bangladesh won by three wickets. Denmark 233 for nine (60 overs) (A. From Hansen 57, J. Jensen 50, Aftab Ahmed 34; M. J. Alam three for 27); Bangladesh 235 for seven (59.4 overs) (Nurul Abedin 85, M. A. Khan 50, Minhaz-ul-Abedin 37; S. Sorensen three for 32).

At Koninklijke UD, Deventer, June 14. Canada won by 21 runs. Canada 199 (57.2 overs) (D. Singh 64, T. Gardner 46, A. Dornellas 36; E. Dulfer five for 38, A. van Troost three for 25); The Netherlands 178 for eight (60 overs) (T. Gardner three for 40).

At KZKC, The Hague, June 16. Denmark won by six wickets. Canada 142 (54 overs) (M. Prashad 39, T. Gardner 37; O. H. Mortensen three for 15, S. Sorensen three for 32); Denmark 143 for four (50.5 overs) (P. Jensen 32).

At VRA, Amstelveen, June 16. The Netherlands won by 161 runs. The Netherlands 309 for seven (60 overs) (N. E. Clarke 83, R. P. Lefebvre 75, T. de Leede 46, C. Ruskamp 38); Bangladesh 148 (47.4 overs) (Minhaz-ul-Abedin 38; R. P. Lefebvre three for 16, G. J. A. F. Aponso three for 26).

At Rood en Wit, Haarlem, June 18. Bangladesh won by 117 runs. Bangladesh 265 for six (60 overs) (Nurul Abedin 105, Faruq Ahmed 56); Canada 148 (44.4 overs) (I. Lyburd 60).

At Hermes DVS, Schiedam, June 18. The Netherlands won by 54 runs. The Netherlands 176 (59.3 overs) (G. J. A. F. Aponso 54, R. P. Lefebvre 35; S. Sorensen four for 43, S. Mikkelsen three for 15); Denmark 122 (53.4 overs) (O. Stoustrup 31, S. Mikkelsen 30).

	Played	*Won*	*Lost*	*Points*	*Run-rate*
The Netherlands	3	2	1	8	3.68
Bangladesh	3	2	1	8	3.62
Denmark	3	1	2	4	2.93
Canada	3	1	2	4	2.72

GROUP G

At VRA, Amstelveen, June 14. Singapore won by seven wickets. Israel 111 (34.5 overs) (T. Seal three for 20, Srimal three for 28); Singapore 112 for three (30.2 overs) (B. Bala 38, B. Muruga 37 not out).

At Quick, Nijmegen, June 15. Bermuda won by 180 runs. Bermuda 320 for nine (60 overs) (R. Hill 100, A. Douglas 63 not out, T. Smith 48, A. R. Manders 40; R. Brooks four for 42); Gibraltar 140 (49.3 overs) (B. Chinappa 53; G. Brangman three for 18, K. Lightbourne three for 40).

At Hermes DVS, Schiedam, June 16. Gibraltar won by six wickets. Singapore 144 (54.5 overs) (B. Bala 60 not out; A. Raikes four for 30); Gibraltar 146 for four (45.3 overs) (B. Chinappa 51 not out).

At VOC, Rotterdam, June 18. Gibraltar won by five wickets. Israel 269 for nine (60 overs) (H. Awaskar 66, S. Erulkar 54); Gibraltar 270 for five (54.4 overs) (C. Robinson 79, A. Raikes 43 not out, R. Buzaglo 42).

At KZKC, The Hague, June 18. Bermuda won by 208 runs. Bermuda 291 for seven (60 overs) (N. Gibbons 68 not out, D. Lewis 48, A. Amory 41, A. N. Manders 41); Singapore 83 (49.1 overs) (R. Leverock four for 14).

At VOC, Rotterdam, June 19. Bermuda won by seven wickets. Israel 84 (26.3 overs) (G. Brangman four for 9); Bermuda 85 for three (14.3 overs) (A. N. Manders 52 not out).

	Played	*Won*	*Lost*	*Points*	*Run-rate*
Bermuda	3	3	0	12	5.19
Gibraltar	3	2	1	8	3.48
Singapore	3	1	2	4	2.26
Israel	3	0	3	0	2.58

GROUP H

At KZKC, The Hague, June 14. Fiji won by 68 runs. Fiji 288 for eight (60 overs) (J. Sorovakatini 63, C. Browne 52; L. Alonso three for 48, D. Forrester three for 66); Argentina 220 (56.4 overs) (M. Morris 61, G. Kirschbaum 32; A. Tawatatau three for 26).

At Hermes DVS, Schiedam, June 14. East and Central Africa won by 49 runs. East and Central Africa 180 for eight (50 overs) (B. Bouri 41, S. Walusimbi 38 not out); Malaysia 131 (44.4 overs) (S. W. Hong 33; B. Bouri three for 15, S. Lakha three for 19).

At HCC, The Hague, June 15. Argentina won by three wickets. East and Central Africa 184 (59.2 overs) (G. R. Shariff 42); Argentina 188 for seven (54.5 overs) (M. Ryan 76 not out).

At Hermes DVS, Schiedam, June 15. Hong Kong won by three wickets. Malaysia 168 (60 overs) (S. Bell 61; G. Davies three for 27); Hong Kong 169 for seven (58.2 overs) (N. Stearns 34; A. Stephens three for 28).

At VOC, Rotterdam, June 16. Fiji won by six wickets. Hong Kong 182 (60 overs) (K. Kumar 46, N. Stearns 32, J. Marsden 30; N. Maxwell four for 30); Fiji 185 for four (37.3 overs) (C. Browne 65, J. Sorovakatini 57, N. Maxwell 41 not out).

At Koninklijke UD, Deventer, June 16. Malaysia won by 155 runs. Malaysia 246 for nine (60 overs) (A. Stephens 102, M. Saat Jalil 53); Argentina 91 (42.4 overs) (C. Nino 30; S. Muniandy four for 17, R. Chander three for 23).

At HBS, The Hague, June 18. Hong Kong won by three wickets. East and Central Africa 203 (50 overs) (G. R. Shariff 42, H. Patadia 34, H. Tejani 33; S. Tariq four for 46, D. N. Brettell three for 33); Hong Kong 204 for seven (58.2 overs) (J. Marsden 38, D. N. Brettell 32 not out, N. Stearns 32).

At Quick, Nijmegen, June 18. Fiji won by eight wickets. Malaysia 146 (57.2 overs) (R. Chander 31; K. Batina three for 15, J. Mateyawa three for 30); Fiji 147 for two (27.4 overs) (N. Maxwell 84, S. Campbell 34).

At ACC, Amstelveen, June 19. Fiji won by 95 runs. Fiji 214 for nine (50 overs) (J. Sorovakatini 42; S. Lakha three for 35, S. Naik three for 44); East and Central Africa 119 (32 overs) (F. Sarigat 30; J. Mateyawa three for 12, A. Waqa three for 34).

	Played	*Won*	*Lost*	*Points*	*Run-rate*
Fiji	4	4	0	16	4.77
Hong Kong	4	3	1	12	3.33
East and Central Africa	4	1	3	4	3.12
Malaysia	4	1	3	4	3.00
Argentina	4	1	3	4	2.85

Note: Argentina and Hong Kong did not play each other in Group H. However, for the purpose of the table, the result of their Group D game on June 10 was included in the above figures.

SEMI-FINALS

KENYA v THE NETHERLANDS

At HCC, The Hague, June 20. The Netherlands won by five wickets. Toss: Kenya.
Man of the Match: T. de Leede.

Kenya

I. Tariq Iqbal c Ruskamp b Bakker ... 14
D. Chudasama lbw b Bakker ... 6
S. Gupta run out ... 1
Maurice Odumbe b Lefebvre ... 21
L. Tikolo b Bakker ... 0
A. V. Karim c Clarke b Lefebvre ... 53
†M. Kanji c van Oosterom b Lefebvre . 52
Martin Odumbe c de Leede b Bakker .. 24
E. Odumbe c Ruskamp b Bakker ... 1
*T. Tikolo c Gomes b Bakker ... 8
A. Njoroge not out ... 1
B 4, l-b 4, w 13 ... 21

1/9 2/17 3/35 4/36 5/52 6/167 7/168 8/175 9/199 (59.4 overs) 202

Bowling: van Troost 12–2–49–0; Bakker 11.4–2–41–6; Lefebvre 12–2–39–3; Dulfer 11–1–38–0; Aponso 7–3–9–0; Lubbers 6–0–18–0.

The Netherlands

G. J. A. F. Aponso c Karim b E. Odumbe . 9
†C. Ruskamp c Maurice Odumbe b Karim . 37
R. Gomes c Kanji b E. Odumbe ... 4
N. E. Clarke b E. Odumbe ... 32
R. P. Lefebvre lbw b Maurice Odumbe. 20
T. de Leede not out ... 56
*S. W. Lubbers not out ... 26
B 1, l-b 1, w 18, n-b 1 ... 21

1/9 2/15 3/62 4/108 5/120 (5 wkts, 56.2 overs) 205

R. van Oosterom, P. J. Bakker, A. van Troost and E. Dulfer did not bat.

Bowling: Martin Odumbe 8–0–29–0; E. Odumbe 11.2–2–39–3; Njoroge 9–0–45–0; Karim 12–0–33–1; L. Tikolo 10–2–34–0; Maurice Odumbe 6–2–23–1.

Umpires: S. A. Ahad (Bangladesh) and J. D. Robinson (Zimbabwe).

BANGLADESH v ZIMBABWE

At HCC, The Hague, June 21, 22. Zimbabwe won by 84 runs. Toss: Bangladesh.
Man of the Match: D. L. Houghton.

Zimbabwe

G. W. Flower c Chowdhury b Nawsher 7
A. H. Shah c Faruq Ahmed b Nawsher 5
†A. Flower run out 1
*D. L. Houghton c Minhaz-ul-Abedin b Chowdhury . 91
G. A. Paterson c Hoque Moni b Nawsher . 4
K. J. Arnott c Nurul Abedin b Hoque Moni . 29
G. A. Briant st Nasir Nasu b Hoque Moni . 0
E. A. Brandes not out 66
A. J. Traicos not out 1
L-b 7, w 10, n-b 10 27

1/7 2/21 3/23 4/37 5/134 6/135 7/196 (7 wkts, 60 overs) 231

K. G. Duers and M. P. Jarvis did not bat.

Bowling: Nawsher 12–2–47–3; Alam 12–0–42–0; Chowdhury 10–0–51–1; M. A. Hossain 12–1–37–0; Hoque Moni 12–1–35–2; Minhaz-ul-Abedin 2–0–12–0.

Bangladesh

M. A. Hossain c and b Jarvis 9
Nurul Abedin c Jarvis b Duers 9
*C. A. Hossain b Duers 4
Faruq Ahmed c Houghton b Duers 6
A. Karim c A. Flower b Duers 6
Minhaz-ul-Abedin c and b Jarvis 57
M. E. Hoque Moni run out 28
G. Chowdhury c A. Flower b Jarvis 2
M. J. Alam b Jarvis 5
†Nasir Nasu not out 3
G. M. Nawsher b Brandes 0
L-b 8, w 8, n-b 2 18

1/13 2/23 3/31 4/32 5/45 6/128 7/137 8/137 9/147 (53.1 overs) 147

Bowling: Jarvis 9–2–22–4; Duers 12–2–25–4; Traicos 12–2–32–0; Brandes 8.1–1–36–1; Shah 12–2–24–0.

Umpires: W. Molenaar (The Netherlands) and A. Sarkar (Kenya).

FINAL

THE NETHERLANDS v ZIMBABWE

At HCC, The Hague, June 23. Zimbabwe won by six wickets. Toss: The Netherlands. Aponso and Ruskamp provided a solid start for The Netherlands. But an irresponsible innings from Clarke, who holed out on the boundary off Shah, having already hit him for two sixes in the same over – and all this just before lunch – sowed seeds of panic in the Dutch batting. Gomes, Lefebvre, de Leede and van Oosterom all played careless shots before they had settled, and it was left to the captain, Lubbers, to give the home team some sort of chance with a masterly 47 (he was run out in the last over). However, a total of 197 was never going to be enough against the experienced Zimbabwe batting. Lefebvre captured two early wickets (and finished with two for 12 in eleven overs), but Bakker could make no impression and the Dutch attack looked unbalanced with three off-spinners. Andy Flower played a superbly controlled innings and was well supported by Pycroft in a match-winning third-wicket stand of 93. Houghton, on his 33rd birthday, hurried his side to victory with a whirlwind 28, including four sixes.

Man of the Match: A. Flower.

The Netherlands

G. J. A. F. Aponso c A. Flower b Shah 36
†C. Ruskamp c A. Flower b Brandes 21
R. Gomes c Jarvis b Traicos 16
N. E. Clarke c Paterson b Shah 14
R. P. Lefebvre c Houghton b Shah 8
T. de Leede c Jarvis b Duers 9
*S. W. Lubbers run out 47
R. van Oosterom c Arnott b Shah 2
P. J. Bakker c A. Flower b Brandes 7
A. van Troost not out 9
E. Dulfer not out 0
B 2, l-b 4, w 19, n-b 3 28

1/49 2/77 3/100 4/100 5/117 6/125 7/139 8/166 9/195 (9 wkts, 60 overs) 197

Bowling: Jarvis 12–2–32–0; Duers 12–1–39–1; Traicos 12–2–19–1; Shah 12–2–56–4; Brandes 12–1–45–2.

Zimbabwe

G. A. Paterson c Aponso b Lefebvre	20	A. H. Shah not out	11
G. W. Flower b Lefebvre	10		
†A. Flower not out	69	L-b 8, w 7	15
A. J. Pycroft c Ruskamp b van Troost	45		—
*D. L. Houghton c Lefebvre b van Troost	28	1/25 2/41 3/134 4/180 (4 wkts, 54.2 overs)	198

K. J. Arnott, E. A. Brandes, A. J. Traicos, K. G. Duers and M. P. Jarvis did not bat.

Bowling: van Troost 12–1–43–2; Bakker 10.2–2–35–0; Lefebvre 11–3–12–2; Dulfer 12–1–52–0; Aponso 5–0–23–0; Lubbers 2–0–10–0; de Leede 2–0–15–0.

Umpires: J. W. Holder (England) and R. G. Singh (Canada).

PREVIOUS ICC TROPHY FINALS

1979 SRI LANKA beat Canada by 60 runs at Worcester.
1982 ZIMBABWE beat Bermuda by five wickets at Leicester.
1986 ZIMBABWE beat The Netherlands by 25 runs at Lord's.

FUTURE TOURS

1991
West Indians to England
Sri Lankans to England

1991-92
Indians* and West Indians to Australia
Sri Lankans to Pakistan
England to New Zealand
World Cup in Australia and New Zealand
Sri Lankans to India

1992
Pakistanis to England
Australians to Sri Lanka*

1992-93
West Indians to Australia
England to India and *Sri Lanka
Pakistanis to Australia*
Australians to New Zealand
Indians to West Indies
Pakistanis to West Indies

1993
Australians to England
New Zealanders to Sri Lanka*

1993-94
England to West Indies*
Indians to Pakistan
New Zealanders to Australia
Sri Lankans to Australia
Pakistanis to New Zealand
Indians to Sri Lanka
Australians to Pakistan*

1994
Indians to England*
New Zealanders to England

1994-95
England to Australia
West Indians to India*
Pakistanis to India
West Indians to New Zealand
Australians to West Indies*

1995-96
Pakistanis and West Indians to Australia*
Sri Lankans to India
England to New Zealand
New Zealanders to West Indies

* *Signifies unconfirmed.*

Note: The following tours were scheduled for 1990-91: New Zealanders to Pakistan, West Indians to Pakistan, Sri Lankans to India, England to Australia and New Zealand, New Zealanders to Australia, Pakistanis to India (cancelled), Sri Lankans to New Zealand, Australians to West Indies.

THE MARYLEBONE CRICKET CLUB, 1990

Patron – HER MAJESTY THE QUEEN

President – THE HON. SIR DENYS ROBERTS

President Designate – THE RT HON. THE LORD GRIFFITHS

Treasurer – G. H. G. DOGGART

Chairman of Finance – SIR ANTHONY TUKE

*Trustees – D. J. INSOLE, F. G. MANN, SIR OLIVER POPPLEWELL

Hon. Life Vice-Presidents – SIR DONALD BRADMAN, F. R. BROWN, J. G. W. DAVIES, S. C. GRIFFITH, F. G. MANN, C. G. A. PARIS, E. W. SWANTON

Secretary – LT-COL. J. R. STEPHENSON
(Lord's Cricket Ground, London, NW8 8QN)

ASSISTANT SECRETARIES – M. R. BLOW (Finance), J. R. SMITH (Administration), J. A. JAMESON (Cricket)

Curator – S. E. A. GREEN

ICC Administrator – MISS S. A. LAWRENCE

Ground Administrator – A. W. P. FLEMING

MCC Committee for 1989-90: The Hon. Sir Denys Roberts (President), Field-Marshal The Lord Bramall, R. H. Burton, G. H. G. Doggart, C. A. Fry, D. L. Hudd, R. A. Hutton, R. D. V. Knight, M. D. T. Loup, D. R. Male, P. B. H. May, N. E. J. Pocock, D. R. W. Silk, M. J. K. Smith, D. G. Trelford, Sir Anthony Tuke, J. A. F. Vallance, J. C. Woodcock, H. M. Wyndham.

* *Trustees retire annually in rotation but are eligible for re-election. In their capacity as Trustees they are entitled to attend MCC Committee meetings but are ineligible to vote.*

Although their posts do not involve membership of the MCC Committee, the following were chairmen of current MCC Standing Sub-Committees: A. J. B. Mason (Tennis & Squash), M. C. Cowdrey (Indoor School), T. M. B. Sissons (Arts & Library).

Members' concern at the delay in the completion of the Compton and Edrich Stands was voiced at the 203rd Annual General Meeting of MCC, held in the Club's Indoor Cricket School on May 2, 1990, with the President, The Hon. Sir Denys Roberts, in the chair. In January the Secretary of the Club had written to members advising of the delay, and the President in his statement to members expressed regret that this should have been necessary. The committee had originally hoped the stands would be officially opened on the first day of the Lord's Test match between England and New Zealand in June; as it transpired, work on the stands had not been completed by the end of the 1990 season.

The President also drew to the members' attention the Club's good fortune in its staff, some 90 of whom were full-time employees. These were supported by more than 300 part-time assistants during the summer, many of whom received less than the full market-rate for their services, yet provided them cheerfully and willingly because they loved Lord's and what it represented. He warned of the need for more accommodation for MCC and TCCB staff at Lord's, adding that in due course members may have to be consulted on further expansion.

In presenting the Club's accounts, the chairman of the finance sub-committee, Sir Anthony Tuke, said that in the past seven years the club had spent £3 million on improvements to the ground, in addition to which some £750,000 had been spent on safety work to comply with current legislation. In this respect, the public address system had been completely rewired and lightning conductors had been fitted to the Pavilion within the previous year; and further expenditure was expected following the publication of Lord Justice Taylor's report on the Hillsborough disaster. Maintenance costs in 1989 had run at approximately the same level as in 1988, but with income showing an increase, and taking into account major contributions to the National Coaching Scheme, The Cricket Foundation and ICC, the Club had an excess of income over expenditure against a deficit the previous year. The surplus for the year, after taxation, was £240,000 compared with a surplus of £508,000 in 1988. Members were informed that the Club had signed a four-year Deed of Covenant for £50,000 per annum in favour of The Cricket Foundation, a trust fund for the development of youth cricket.

Following Sir Anthony's decision to retire as chairman of finance on September 30, 1990, the meeting approved the appointment of D. L. Hudd as his successor. Similarly J. J. Warr was appointed a Trustee to succeed F. G. Mann when he retired in accordance with Rule 23 on September 30. Following a ballot, there being five nominations and four vacancies, J. R. T. Barclay, Sir Ian MacLaurin, S. G. Metcalfe and M. O. C. Sturt were elected to join the committee on October 1, 1990, to replace C. A. Fry, D. L. Hudd, N. E. J. Pocock and D. R. W. Silk, all of whom were to retire by rotation as elected members on September 30.

The President named The Rt Hon. The Lord Griffiths, a Lord of Appeal in Ordinary, to succeed him on October 1. As W. H. Griffiths, he was in the Charterhouse XI in 1940 and, after wartime service in the Welsh Guards, went up to Cambridge and opened the bowling at Lord's in 1946, 1947 and 1948. During these years he also played eight times for Glamorgan.

The membership of the Club on December 31, 1989 was 19,264, made up of 17,048 full members, 1,970 associate members and 246 honorary members. These comprised the following: 10,375 full and 1,594 associate town members, 2,275 full and 248 associate country members, 3,451 at the over-65 rate, 75 full and 83 associate members at the under-25 rate, 279 full and 20 associate members at the special schoolmasters' rate, 540 full and 25 associate members on the abroad list, 7 life vice-presidents, 53 life members, 16 60-year life members, 41 honorary England cricketers and 182 honorary life members. In 1989, 603 vacancies occurred, owing to 262 deaths, 248 resignations and 93 lapsed memberships.

At a Special General Meeting immediately following the Annual General Meeting, members approved by postal vote or in person the updated and revised Rules of the Club.

MCC v WORCESTERSHIRE

At Lord's, April 17, 18, 19, 20. Drawn. Toss: Worcestershire. England's series in the West Indies had finished only the previous day – a day ahead of schedule at that – and so the opening match of the Lord's season offered an opportunity to a selection of players hoping to catch the selectors' eye. But if either captain was thinking of ways to conjure a result, his plans were ruined by the weather, which cut the third day to 28.1 overs and prevented any play at all on the fourth. Throughout, conditions were cold; neither the weather nor the closeness of the pitch to the Mound and Tavern boundary favoured the bowlers, but with the ball moving about, the batsmen did not have everything their own way. Parker, dropped at slip by Botham off Newport after reaching his fifty, was prevented by his earlier benefactor from starting his season with a century, while the left-handed Benson played and missed a number of times, as well as giving further evidence of his judgement of line. On the second day, Cowans lent some humour, as well as runs, to the end of MCC's innings by hitting two sixes and six fours in 23 balls. Curtis and Lord gave the champion county a solid start, but on the stroke of tea the left-hander's middle stump was plucked out by Lawrence, one of few joyous moments for the Gloucestershire fast bowler. He was no-balled 27 times for over-stepping, recalling the problem he had encountered on the England A team's tour of Zimbabwe. Hick, who had chosen to winter there and take a rest from first-class cricket, enjoyed a less traumatic return to English cricket, even if, on occasions, his strokeplay looked in need of some fine tuning.

Close of play: First day, MCC 285-5 (D. A. Reeve 39*, W. K. Hegg 36*); Second day, Worcestershire 181-3 (G. A. Hick 53*); Third day, Worcestershire 289-7 (P. A. Neale 22*, P. J. Newport 1*).

MCC

M. D. Moxon c Rhodes b McEwan	12	S. L. Watkin c Hick b McEwan	14
M. R. Benson c Newport b Radford	52	N. G. Cowans not out	46
*P. W. G. Parker b Botham	93	P. C. R. Tufnell b Botham	12
M. A. Atherton lbw b Botham	19		
J. E. Morris lbw b Botham	15	L-b 11, w 3, n-b 8	22
D. A. Reeve c Hick b Radford	39		—
†W. K. Hegg c Rhodes b Radford	57	1/13 2/151 3/184 4/191	385
D. V. Lawrence c McEwan b Radford	4	5/216 6/285 7/299 8/319 9/349	

Bowling: Radford 34–7–116–4; McEwan 31–9–101–2; Botham 20–4–68–4; Newport 18–0–85–0; Illingworth 1–0–4–0.

Worcestershire

T. S. Curtis lbw b Watkin	81	†S. J. Rhodes c Hegg b Watkin	19
G. J. Lord b Lawrence	20	P. J. Newport not out	1
G. A. Hick c Parker b Lawrence	72		
R. K. Illingworth c Atherton b Watkin	6	B 4, l-b 5, w 1, n-b 27	37
I. T. Botham c Hegg b Cowans	19		—
*P. A. Neale not out	22	1/81 2/165 3/181 4/213 (7 wkts)	289
D. B. D'Oliveira b Watkin	12	5/237 6/258 7/288	

S. M. McEwan and N. V. Radford did not bat.

Bowling: Lawrence 25.1–1–105–2; Cowans 18–5–39–1; Reeve 13–3–40–0; Watkin 29–7–83–4; Tufnell 7–2–13–0.

Umpires: B. Dudleston and K. J. Lyons.

†At Lord's, May 2. Drawn. Toss: MCC. MCC 248 for five dec. (R. T. Virgin 42, I. J. F. Hutchinson 31, R. O. Butcher 80, J. R. T. Barclay 31 not out; M. J. Thursfield three for 34); MCC Young Cricketers 162 for six (T. K. Chadwick 45, M. N. Lathwell 70; J. R. T. Barclay four for 52).

At Lord's, May 7. MCC beat NEW ZEALANDERS by six wickets (See New Zealand tour section).

At Oxford, May 30, 31, June 1. MCC drew with OXFORD UNIVERSITY (See Oxford University section).

At Cambridge, June 11, 12, 13. MCC drew with CAMBRIDGE UNIVERSITY (See Cambridge University section).

At Durham, June 14, 15. MCC lost to DURHAM UNIVERSITY by six wickets (See Other Matches, 1990).

At Coleraine, June 16, 17, 18. MCC lost to IRELAND by 6 runs (See Other Matches, 1990).

†MCC v MCC SCHOOLS

At Lord's, July 18. MCC Schools won by two wickets. Toss: MCC Schools. A disciplined 54 not out by Walton, of Leeds Grammar School, helped MCC Schools to victory over the parent club, Walton hitting the winning runs from the penultimate ball of the final over. However, just as important in the thrust for victory was a fighting 73 from Wasim Khan, of Mason Sixth Form College in Warwick, who added 94 for the second wicket with Fulton, of Judd School. MCC, put in by Richards, lost Downton at 15, but Nurton and Goldsmith steadied the innings, and Goldsmith and Bainbridge established it with a third-wicket partnership of 104. Goldsmith, from the Chobham club, reached his century in 173 minutes and hit thirteen boundaries, and when he was caught at cover in the 60th over, a third wicket for the well-flighted leg-spin of Hodgson, MCC declared.

MCC

P. R. Downton lbw b Laudat 10
M. D. Nurton c Richards b Hodgson . . 17
A. J. Goldsmith b Laney b Hodgson . . . 103
P. Bainbridge b Hodgson 60
*R. D. V. Knight not out 0
B 4, l-b 9, w 2, n-b 1 16

1/15 2/89 3/193 4/206 (4 wkts dec.) 206

G. J. Toogood, M. Hart, †D. J. Goldsmith, S. Welch, A. T. Crouch and C. Hodgkins did not bat.

Bowling: Weston 8–0–28–0; Laudat 7–0–19–1; Walton 8–2–17–0; Richards 22–6–64–0; Hodgson 14.1–1–65–3.

MCC Schools

Wasim Khan (*Josiah Mason SFC*) b Welch . 73
G. Archer (*Stafford CFE*) c and b Hodgkins . 7
D. P. Fulton (*Judd*) lbw b Crouch 39
J. Laney (*St John's, Marlborough*) c A. J. Goldsmith b Crouch . 12
T. C. Walton (*Leeds GS*) not out 54
R. Murray (*Brigshaw*) c Nurton b Crouch 2
*A. C. Richards (*Forest*) b Bainbridge . . 8
S. V. Laudat (*Oxford CFE*) run out 0
†M. A. Khan (*Aylesbury CFE*) run out . 2
W. P. C. Weston (*Durham*) not out 0
B 4, l-b 6, w 1, n-b 1 12

1/26 2/120 3/132 4/159 5/177 6/195 7/195 8/205 (8 wkts) 209

J. Hodgson (*Ranelagh*) did not bat.

Bowling: Toogood 8–3–19–0; Hodgkins 6–2–20–1; Welch 12–3–52–1; Crouch 21–5–62–3; Bainbridge 10.5–1–46–1.

Umpires: E. G. Burston and A. R. Smith.

†At Lord's, August 22, 23. Scotland won by seven wickets. Toss: MCC. MCC 198 (G. D. Mendis 57; C. L. Parfitt six for 57) and 218 for six dec. (S. C. Wundke 101 not out; C. L. Parfitt three for 71); Scotland 190 for eight dec. (D. J. Haggo 33; M. R. Whitney three for 14, G. Stead three for 68) and 227 for three (I. L. Philip 83, A. C. Storie 37, G. Salmond 56 not out, A. B. Russell 38 not out).

At Swansea, August 27, 28. MCC drew with WALES (See Other Matches, 1990).

MCC HONORARY ENGLAND CRICKETERS

C. J. Barnett
H. Larwood
D. C. S. Compton, CBE
D. V. P. Wright
T. G. Evans, CBE
C. Washbrook
A. V. Bedser, CBE
P. B. H. May, CBE
W. Watson
P. E. Richardson
T. E. Bailey
M. J. K. Smith, OBE
J. B. Statham, CBE
F. S. Trueman, OBE
T. W. Graveney, OBE
G. A. R. Lock
D. A. Allen
R. W. Barber
E. R. Dexter
P. H. Parfitt
F. H. Tyson
M. C. Cowdrey, CBE
J. T. Murray, MBE
J. M. Parks
D. B. Close, CBE
B. L. D'Oliveira, OBE
R. Illingworth, CBE
G. Pullar
F. J. Titmus, MBE
D. J. Brown
M. H. Denness
J. M. Brearley, OBE
R. W. Taylor, MBE
R. G. D. Willis, MBE
J. H. Edrich, MBE
A. P. E. Knott
C. M. Old
J. A. Snow
D. L. Amiss, MBE
K. W. R. Fletcher, OBE

STATUS OF MATCHES IN THE UK

(*a*) **Automatic First-Class Matches**

The following matches of three or more days' duration should automatically be considered first-class:

(i) County Championship matches.
(ii) Official representative tourist matches from Full Member Countries, unless specifically excluded.
(iii) MCC v any First-Class County.
(iv) Oxford v Cambridge and either University against First-Class Counties.
(v) Scotland v Ireland.

(*b*) **Excluded from First-Class Status**

The following matches of three or more days' duration should not normally be accorded first-class status:

(i) County "friendly" matches.
(ii) Matches played by Scotland or Ireland, other than their annual match against each other.
(iii) Unofficial tourist matches, unless circumstances are exceptional.
(iv) MCC v Oxford/Cambridge.
(v) Matches involving privately raised teams, unless included officially in a touring team's itinerary.

(*c*) **Consideration of Doubtful Status**

Matches played by unofficial touring teams of exceptional ability can be considered in advance and decisions taken accordingly.

Certain other matches comprising 22 recognised first-class cricketers might also be considered in advance.

OTHER MATCHES AT LORD'S, 1990

†ETON v HARROW

June 9. Eton won by seven wickets. Toss: Eton. Eton ended the sequence of drawn games since their 1985 victory, winning the 155th match between the two schools with four balls to spare. Although it was their batsmen who provided the victory by successfully chasing a target of 220 in 153 minutes, Eton owed as much to their bowlers who, assisted by some excellent fielding, held Harrow to 219 for eight from 237 minutes' batting. Aldous and Holyoake occupied 32.3 overs while putting on 77 for Harrow's first wicket, and the other major partnership, 57 between Guillebaud and Hewens for the fifth wicket, took almost 21 overs. Whittington employed flight and accuracy effectively in a long and tidy stint of slow left-arm bowling, and when Chetwood, their captain and off-spinner, strained a calf muscle, Eton were well served by Ssennyamantono just as Harrow were looking to accelerate. In reply, Eton first put down a good foundation, then set off in serious pursuit. Eastwood (95 balls) and Sellar added 50 for the second wicket in 38 minutes, and as Eton went into the final twenty overs, needing 121, Sellar (64 balls) and Hagen put on 70 in 46 minutes. Finally, Hagen (68 balls) and Strickland hit off the remaining 54 runs in the last half-hour, with the latter's unbeaten 23 coming from just twenty deliveries.

Harrow

S. H. Aldous c Eastwood b Whittington 26
M. A. Holyoake b Whittington 47
C. E. Williams c Strickland b Lewis . . . 11
S. M. Guillebaud lbw b Ssennyamantono 34
*M. E. D. Jarrett c Sellar b Lewis 10
E. M. S. Hewens b Lewis 43
J. L. Pool lbw b Whittington 1
F. S. J. Yates b Ssennyamantono 19
†H. D. Duncan not out 1
R. E. Sexton not out 2
B 7, l-b 6, w 6, n-b 6 25

1/77 2/98 3/98 4/111 5/168 6/173 7/214 8/214 (8 wkts dec.) 219

W. J. D. Hewitt did not bat.

Bowling: Lewis 17–5–50–3; Ulvert 7–4–7–0; Ssennyamantono 17–2–46–2; Chetwood 10–1–25–0; Whittington 25–4–78–3.

Eton

T. A. J. Jenkins c Hewitt b Hewens . . . 19
P. M. Eastwood c Duncan b Hewitt . . . 53
W. R. G. Sellar c Guillebaud b Pool . . 57
N. R. J. Hagen not out 53
S. C. E. Strickland not out 23
B 3, l-b 8, w 4, n-b 1 16

1/47 2/97 3/167 (3 wkts) 221

*H. J. P. Chetwood, J. M. S. Whittington, †T. J. Stanley, B. K. Ssennyamantono, C. N. Ulvert and G. H. B. Lewis did not bat.

Bowling: Pool 10.2–1–40–1; Hewitt 12–1–52–1; Sexton 10–1–41–0; Hewens 4–0–26–1; Williams 5–0–19–0; Jarrett 7–0–32–0.

Umpires: P. Adams and D. J. Dennis.

ETON v HARROW, RESULTS AND HUNDREDS

Of the 155 matches played Eton have won 51, Harrow 44 and 60 have been drawn. This is the generally published record, but Harrow men object strongly to the first game in 1805 being treated as a regular contest between the two schools, contending that it is no more correct to count that one than the fixture of 1857 which has been rejected.

The matches played during the war years 1915-18 and 1940-45 are not reckoned as belonging to the regular series.

Results since 1950:

1950	Drawn	1971	Drawn
1951	Drawn	1972	Drawn
1952	Harrow won by seven wickets	1973	Drawn
1953	Eton won by ten wickets	1974	Harrow won by eight wickets
1954	Harrow won by nine wickets	1975	Harrow won by an innings and 151 runs
1955	Eton won by 38 runs	1976	Drawn
1956	Drawn	1977	Eton won by six wickets
1957	Drawn	1978	Drawn
1958	Drawn	1979	Drawn
1959	Drawn	1980	Drawn
1960	Harrow won by 124 runs	1981	Drawn
1961	Harrow won by an innings and 12 runs	1982	Drawn
1962	Drawn	1983	Drawn
1963	Drawn	1984	Drawn
1964	Eton won by eight wickets	1985	Eton won by 3 runs
1965	Harrow won by 48 runs	1986	Drawn
1966	Drawn	1987	Drawn
1967	Drawn	1988	Drawn
1968	Harrow won by seven wickets	1989	Drawn
1969	Drawn	1990	Eton won by seven wickets
1970	Eton won by 97 runs		

Forty-five three-figure innings have been played in matches between these two schools. Those since 1918:

161*	M. K. Fosh	1975 Harrow	106	D. M. Smith	1966 Eton
159	E. W. Dawson	1923 Eton	104	R. Pulbrook	1932 Harrow
158	I. S. Akers-Douglas	1928 Eton	103	L. G. Crawley	1921 Harrow
153	N. S. Hotchkin	1931 Eton	103	T. Hare	1947 Eton
151	R. M. Tindall	1976 Harrow	102*	P. H. Stewart-Brown	1923 Harrow
135	J. C. Atkinson-Clark	1930 Eton	102	R. V. C. Robins	1953 Eton
115	E. Crutchley	1939 Harrow	100	R. H. Cobbold	1923 Eton
112	A. W. Allen	1931 Eton	100*	P. V. F. Cazalet	1926 Eton
112*	T. M. H. James	1978 Harrow	100	A. N. A. Boyd	1934 Eton
111	R. A. A. Holt	1937 Harrow	100*	P. M. Studd	1935 Harrow
109	K. F. H. Hale	1929 Eton	100	S. D. D. Sainsbury	1947 Eton
109	N. S. Hotchkin	1932 Eton	100	M. J. J. Faber	1968 Eton
107	W. N. Coles	1946 Eton			

* *Signifies not out.*

In 1904, D. C. Boles of Eton, making 183, set a record for the match, beating the 152 obtained for Eton in 1841 by Emilius Bayley, afterwards the Rev. Sir John Robert Laurie Emilius Bayley Laurie. M. C. Bird, Harrow, in 1907, scored 100 not out and 131, the only batsman who has made two 100s in the match. N. S. Hotchkin, Eton, played the following innings: 1931, 153; 1932, 109 and 96; 1933, 88 and 12.

June 21, 22, 23, 25, 26. Second Cornhill Test. ENGLAND drew with NEW ZEALAND (See New Zealand tour section).

OXFORD UNIVERSITY v CAMBRIDGE UNIVERSITY

July 4, 5, 6. Drawn. Toss: Cambridge University. With no play possible on the first day owing to rain, and the second limited to 42 overs because of interruptions from the weather, not even the decision of the captains to forfeit innings could prevent the match being drawn. Cambridge, commencing their innings almost half an hour after lunch on the final day, needed to score 270 in 61 overs for victory, but at tea, 85 without loss from 26 overs, they had already fallen behind the run-rate. Heap was bowled by Crawley ten minutes after the resumption; and when James gave the former Oxford captain his second wicket, having batted 2 hours 25 minutes (125 balls) for 56, and Turner was run out soon afterwards, the prospect of Cambridge then scoring 159 from the last twenty overs was negligible. Crawley was moving the ball disconcertingly in the air and off the seam at medium pace, but time was not on Oxford's side either, and in the end the match was called off with ten overs remaining. In the morning, Oxford had gone for runs positively and entertainingly, putting on 153 in the session. Crawley's solid half-century was the springboard for van der Merwe's assault which, with eight fours and a six among the workmen on the Nursery End stands, took him to 50 from 45 balls.

Close of play: First day, No play; Second day, Oxford University 108-4 (M. A. Crawley 5*, D. M. Curtis 0*).

Oxford University

D. A. Hagan (*Trinity, Leamington Spa and Linacre*) c James b Jenkins 8
*R. E. Morris (*Dyffryn Conwy, Llanrwst and Oriel*) c Turner b Jenkins 21
P. D. Lunn (*Abingdon and New*) b Shufflebotham 35
G. J. Turner (*St Stithian's, Cape Town U. and St Anne's*) c Jenkins b Shufflebotham . . . 36
M. A. Crawley (*Manchester GS and Keble*) c Johnson b Buzza 55
D. M. Curtis (*Falcon Coll., Harare, Cape Town U. and St Anne's*) run out 27
W. M. van der Merwe (*Grey, OFS U., Cape Town U. and St Anne's*) st Turner b Buzza . 50
P. S. Gerrans (*Daramalau Coll., Aust. Nat. U. and Worcester*) c James b Shufflebotham . 16
S. D. Weale (*Westminster City and Keble*) not out 4
I. M. Henderson (*Laxton and Pembroke*) not out 0
B 3, l-b 12, n-b 2 17

1/13 2/41 3/95 4/108 5/175 6/238 7/263 8/265 (8 wkts dec.) 269

†R. W. D. Trevelyan (*Marlborough and Pembroke*) did not bat.

Bowling: Johnson 16–1–48–0; Jenkins 20–2–68–2; Pyman 18–7–63–0; Shufflebotham 19–5–60–3; Buzza 8–1–15–2.

Oxford University forfeited their second innings.

Cambridge University

Cambridge University forfeited their first innings.

S. P. James (*Monmouth and Hughes Hall*) c Hagan b Crawley 56
R. Heap (*Ipswich and Magdalene*) b Crawley 37
†R. J. Turner (*Millfield and Magdalene*) run out 7
*J. C. M. Atkinson (*Millfield and Downing*) b Crawley 7
M. J. Lowrey (*Radley and Homerton*) not out 18
M. J. Morris (*Cherwell and Pembroke*) not out 9
B 3, l-b 7, n-b 2 12

1/87 2/110 3/111 4/118 (4 wkts) 146

R. A. Pyman (*Harrow and Pembroke*), D. H. Shufflebotham (*Neath GS and Magdalene*), R. H. J. Jenkins (*Oundle and Downing*), A. J. Buzza (*Redruth CS and Hughes Hall*) and S. W. Johnson (*Royal GS, Newcastle and Magdalene*) did not bat.

Bowling: van der Merwe 14–2–23–0; Henderson 5–0–21–0; Gerrans 13–0–37–0; Crawley 17–4–46–3; Lunn 2–1–9–0.

Umpires: D. J. Constant and K. E. Palmer.

OXFORD v CAMBRIDGE, RESULTS AND HUNDREDS

The University match dates back to 1827. Altogether there have been 145 official matches, Cambridge winning 54 and Oxford 46, with 45 drawn. The 1988 match was abandoned without a ball bowled. Results since 1950:

1950	Drawn	1971	Drawn
1951	Oxford won by 21 runs	1972	Cambridge won by an innings and 25 runs
1952	Drawn	1973	Drawn
1953	Cambridge won by two wickets	1974	Drawn
1954	Drawn	1975	Drawn
1955	Drawn	1976	Oxford won by ten wickets
1956	Drawn	1977	Drawn
1957	Cambridge won by an innings and 186 runs	1978	Drawn
1958	Cambridge won by 99 runs	1979	Cambridge won by an innings and 52 runs
1959	Oxford won by 85 runs	1980	Drawn
1960	Drawn	1981	Drawn
1961	Drawn	1982	Cambridge won by seven wickets
1962	Drawn	1983	Drawn
1963	Drawn	1984	Oxford won by five wickets
1964	Drawn	1985	Drawn
1965	Drawn	1986	Cambridge won by five wickets
1966	Oxford won by an innings and 9 runs	1987	Drawn
1967	Drawn	1988	Abandoned
1968	Drawn	1989	Drawn
1969	Drawn	1990	Drawn
1970	Drawn		

Ninety-three three-figure innings have been played in the University matches. For those scored before 1919 see 1940 *Wisden*. Those subsequent to 1919 include the seven highest:

238*	Nawab of Pataudi, sen.	1931	Oxford	121	J. N. Grover	1937	Oxford
211	G. Goonesena	1957	Cam.	119	J. M. Brearley	1964	Cam.
201*	M. J. K. Smith	1954	Oxford	118	H. Ashton	1921	Cam.
201	A. Ratcliffe	1931	Cam.	118	D. R. W. Silk	1954	Cam.
200	Majid Khan	1970	Cam.	117	M. J. K. Smith	1956	Oxford
193	D. C. H. Townsend	1934	Oxford	116*	D. R. W. Silk	1953	Cam.
174	P. A. C. Bail	1986	Cam.	116	M. C. Cowdrey	1953	Oxford
170	M. Howell	1919	Oxford	115	A. W. Allen	1934	Cam.
167	B. W. Hone	1932	Oxford	114*	D. R. Owen-Thomas	1972	Cam.
158	P. M. Roebuck	1975	Cam.	114	J. F. Pretlove	1955	Cam.
157	D. R. Wilcox	1932	Cam.	113*	J. M. Brearley	1962	Cam.
155	F. S. Goldstein	1968	Oxford	113	E. R. T. Holmes	1927	Oxford
149	J. T. Morgan	1929	Cam.	112*	E. D. Fursdon	1975	Oxford
149	G. J. Toogood	1985	Oxford	111*	G. W. Cook	1957	Cam.
146	R. O'Brien	1956	Cam.	109	C. H. Taylor	1923	Oxford
146	D. R. Owen-Thomas	1971	Cam.	109	G. J. Toogood	1984	Oxford
145*	H. E. Webb	1948	Oxford	108	F. G. H. Chalk	1934	Oxford
145	D. P. Toft	1967	Oxford	106	Nawab of Pataudi, sen.	1929	Oxford
142	M. P. Donnelly	1946	Oxford	105	E. J. Craig	1961	Cam.
140	M. A. Crawley	1987	Oxford	104*	D. A. Thorne	1986	Oxford
139	R. J. Boyd-Moss	1983	Cam.	104	H. J. Enthoven	1924	Cam.
136	E. T. Killick	1930	Cam.	104	M. J. K. Smith	1955	Oxford
135	H. A. Pawson	1947	Oxford	103*	A. R. Lewis	1962	Cam.
131	Nawab of Pataudi, jun.	1960	Oxford	103*	D. R. Pringle	1979	Cam.
129	H. J. Enthoven	1925	Cam.	102*	A. P. F. Chapman	1922	Cam.
128*	A. J. T. Miller	1984	Oxford	101*	R. W. V. Robins	1928	Cam.
127	D. S. Sheppard	1952	Cam.	101	N. W. D. Yardley	1937	Cam.
124	A. K. Judd	1927	Cam.	100*	M. Manasseh	1964	Oxford
124	A. Ratcliffe	1932	Cam.	100	P. J. Dickinson	1939	Cam.
124	R. J. Boyd-Moss	1983	Cam.	100	N. J. Cosh	1967	Cam.
122	P. A. Gibb	1938	Cam.	100	R. J. Boyd-Moss	1982	Cam.

* *Signifies not out.*

Highest Totals

503	Oxford	1900	432-9	Cambridge	1936
457	Oxford	1947	431	Cambridge	1932
453-8	Oxford	1931	425	Cambridge	1938

Lowest Totals

32	Oxford	1878	42	Oxford	1890
39	Cambridge	1858	47	Cambridge	1838

Notes: A. P. F. Chapman and M. P. Donnelly enjoy the following distinction: Chapman scored a century at Lord's in the University match (102*, 1922); for Gentlemen v Players (160, 1922), (108, 1926); and for England v Australia (121, 1930). Donnelly scored a century at Lord's in the University match (142, 1946); for Gentlemen v Players (162*, 1947); and for New Zealand v England (206, 1949).

A. Ratcliffe's 201 for Cambridge in 1931 remained a record for the match for only one day, being beaten by the Nawab of Pataudi's 238* for Oxford next day.

M. J. K. Smith (Oxford) and R. J. Boyd-Moss (Cambridge) are the only players who have scored three hundreds. Smith scored 201* in 1954, 104 in 1955, and 117 in 1956; Boyd-Moss scored 100 in 1982 and 139 and 124 in 1983. His aggregate of 489 surpassed Smith's previous record of 477.

The following players have scored two hundreds: W. Yardley (Cambridge) 100 in 1870 and 130 in 1872; H. J. Enthoven (Cambridge) 104 in 1924 and 129 in 1925; Nawab of Pataudi (Oxford) 106 in 1929 and 238* in 1931; A. Ratcliffe (Cambridge) 201 in 1931 and 124 in 1932; D. R. W. Silk (Cambridge) 116* in 1953 and 118 in 1954; J. M. Brearley (Cambridge) 113* in 1962 and 119 in 1964; D. R. Owen-Thomas (Cambridge) 146 in 1971 and 114* in 1972; G. J. Toogood (Oxford) 109 in 1984 and 149 in 1985.

F. C. Cobden, in the Oxford v Cambridge match in 1870, performed the hat-trick by taking the last three wickets and won an extraordinary game for Cambridge by 2 runs. The feat is without parallel in first-class cricket. Other hat-tricks, all for Cambridge, have been credited to A. G. Steel (1879), P. H. Morton (1880), J. F. Ireland (1911), and R. G. H. Lowe (1926).

S. E. Butler, in the 1871 match, took all the wickets in the Cambridge first innings. The feat is unique in University matches. He bowled 24.1 overs. In the follow-on he took five wickets for 57, giving him match figures of fifteen for 95 runs.

The best all-round performances in the history of the match have come from P. R. Le Couteur, who scored 160 and took eleven Cambridge wickets for 66 runs in 1910, and G. J. Toogood, who in 1985 scored 149 and took ten Cambridge wickets for 93.

D. W. Jarrett (Oxford 1975, Cambridge 1976), S. M. Wookey (Cambridge 1975-76, Oxford 1978) and G. Pathmanathan (Oxford 1975-78, Cambridge 1983) are alone in gaining cricket Blues for both Universities.

July 14. Benson and Hedges Cup final. LANCASHIRE beat WORCESTERSHIRE by 69 runs (See Benson and Hedges Cup section).

July 18. MCC SCHOOLS beat MCC by two wickets (See MCC section).

†MCC SCHOOLS v NATIONAL ASSOCIATION OF YOUNG CRICKETERS

July 19. Drawn. Toss: National Association of Young Cricketers. MCC Schools fell 35 runs short of achieving a double on their annual visit to Lord's, having beaten MCC the previous day. The Schools had enjoyed a fair run of success in this match in recent years, through such outstanding young players as Hugh Morris, Roseberry, Atherton and Ramprakash, and while the 1990 crop was not quite of that class, Wasim Khan, Fulton and Walton all showed promise over the two days at Lord's. When Archer of Stafford CFE was claimed by NAYC to open their batting, although in the original Schools selection, Snape of Denstone came in as his replacement. However, Archer was soon despatched by his former team-mate, Weston, after NAYC had won the toss and elected to bat. Williams and Simmonite, both of Lancashire, added 48 for the second wicket, and Dessaur and Shephard 54 for the sixth, but in batting for 62 overs, NAYC left time for only 48 overs for the Schools' innings. Hodgson again flighted the ball well and deserved his four wickets. Needing 4.5 runs an over for victory, MCC Schools were greatly dependent on Wasim Khan. He made an attacking 61, with support from Laney, but as wickets began to fall and the overs ran out, a draw became inevitable.

National Association of Young Cricketers

G. Archer (*Staffs.*) b Weston 3
A. Williams (*Lancs.*) c Fulton b Hodgson 64
P. C. P. Simmonite (*Lancs.*) c M. A. Khan b Walton . 35
A. R. Cornford (*Sussex*) b Walton 4
*R. Bates (*Lincs.*) b Hodgson 10
W. A. Dessaur (*Notts.*) c and b Hodgson 37
G. F. Shephard (*Warwicks.*) not out . . . 32
†I. Gill (*Yorks.*) c Snape b Hodgson . . . 0
A. Hollioake (*Surrey*) not out 16
B 6, l-b 4, w 2, n-b 2 14

1/4 2/52 3/60 4/104 5/135 6/189 7/195 (7 wkts dec.) 215

L. Slater (*Staffs.*) and J. Mann (*Hunts. and Peterborough*) did not bat.

Bowling: Weston 11–2–32–1; Laudat 6–0–21–0; Walton 13–1–56–2; Richards 16–4–53–0; Hodgson 16–5–43–4.

MCC Schools

Wasim Khan (*Josiah Mason SFC*) st Gill b Mann . 61
D. P. Fulton (*Judd*) c Gill b Hollioake . 13
J. N. Snape (*Denstone*) c Gill b Mann . 9
J. Laney (*St John's, Marlborough*) c Archer b Dessaur . 46
T. C. Walton (*Leeds GS*) c Bates b Dessaur . 12
R. Murray (*Brigshaw*) c Simmonite b Shephard . 11
*A. C. Richards (*Forest*) not out 14
S. V. Laudat (*Oxford CFE*) not out 4
B 3, l-b 6, w 2 11

1/55 2/66 3/99 4/133 5/152 6/158 (6 wkts) 181

†M. A. Khan (*Aylesbury CFE*), W. P. C. Weston (*Durham*) and J. Hodgson (*Ranelagh*) did not bat.

Bowling: Slater 5–0–25–0; Hollioake 10–1–33–1; Mann 13–1–44–2; Bates 3–1–16–0; Shephard 11–5–27–1; Dessaur 6–0–27–2.

Umpires: K. Hopley and J. F. Jarvis.

The National Cricket Association selected the following to play for NCA Young Cricketers against Combined Services: Wasim Khan (Warwicks.), A. Williams (Lancs.), T. C. Walton (Yorks.), P. C. P. Simmonite (Lancs.), J. Laney (Wilts.), *A. C. Richards (Essex), G. F. Shephard (Warwicks.), †M. A. Khan (Oxon.), W. P. C. Weston (Worcs.), A. Hollioake (Surrey) and J. Mann (Hunts. and Peterborough).

†July 20. NCA Young Cricketers won by eight wickets. Toss: Combined Services. Combined Services 231 (2nd Lt R. J. Greatorex 31, Capt. P. J. Presland 88, Extras 32; W. P. C. Weston three for 41, T. C. Walton three for 48); NCA Young Cricketers 233 for two (Wasim Khan 80, A. Williams 75, T. C. Walton 67 not out).

July 26, 27, 28, 30, 31. First Cornhill Test. ENGLAND beat INDIA by 247 runs (See Indian tour section).

August 8. ENGLAND YOUNG CRICKETERS beat PAKISTAN YOUNG CRICKETERS by 76 runs (See Pakistan Young Cricketers tour section).

August 19, 20. Holt Cup Knockout final. BUCKINGHAMSHIRE beat LINCOLNSHIRE by 16 runs (See Minor Counties section).

†BLACKPOOL v CHEAM

Cockspur Cup Final

August 24. Blackpool won by three wickets. Toss: Cheam. After successive washouts at headquarters in the two previous years, the final of the National Club Championship, the last under the sponsorship of Cockspur Rum, was played in glorious weather. Indeed, it was so hot that drinks were taken after the first 45 minutes. Neither Blackpool, the north section champions, nor Cheam, the south champions, had won the title before, although Blackpool had been finalists fifteen years earlier, and both were strongly supported. Cheam chose to bat, and after the openers were back in the Pavilion, Butcher, eighteen-year-old son of Glamorgan's captain, enlivened proceedings with two sixes, one of them taking Cheam past 100 in the 29th over. Falconer, the captain, held the innings together, but from 173 for four Cheam lost wickets in the pursuit of runs. Blackpool saw Lawton run out in the first over by Butcher, and were in deeper trouble when Pickles was bowled with the score 10. However, Hesketh, playing almost a lone hand, lifted his side to victory. He and Ashton added 70 for the sixth wicket to rescue Blackpool from a parlous position at 95 for five and leave them needing 40 from the last six overs. The Cheam seam bowlers gave little away, but Hesketh kept the runs coming until 6 were required from the final over. He scored them off the first two balls.

Man of the Match: R. J. Falconer.

Cheam

G. R. E. Martin b Cole	17	C. M. Cornell run out	6
N. B. Driscoll c Mathers b Cole	20	S. F. Travers not out	4
A. W. Smith st Mathers b Lawton	35	B 1, l-b 9, w 4, n-b 1	15
M. A. Butcher c Sanders b Cresswell	27		
*R. J. Falconer b Rayton	53	1/32 2/64 3/97 (8 wkts, 45 overs)	193
†M. A. Rowland c and b Cresswell	13	4/121 5/173 6/183	
P. M. James b Rayton	3	7/187 8/193	

D. J. Allen and D. J. Morgan did not bat.

Bowling: Cross 9–2–24–0; Rayton 9–1–32–2; Cole 9–1–27–2; Lawton 9–0–51–1; Cresswell 9–0–49–2.

Blackpool

M. Pickles b Travers	8	*†D. Mathers b Travers	9
S. Lawton run out	0	D. Rayton not out	7
A. Hesketh not out	86	L-b 7, w 2, n-b 1	10
D. Horn c Driscoll b Cornell	15		
G. Sanders run out	23	1/2 2/10 3/45 (7 wkts, 44.2 overs)	194
P. Cole b Allen	8	4/84 5/95	
M. Ashton lbw b Butcher	28	6/165 7/178	

D. Cresswell and G. Cross did not bat.

Bowling: Butcher 8.2–0–37–1; Travers 9–1–32–2; Allen 9–2–27–1; Cornell 9–1–30–1; Morgan 3–0–26–0; Smith 5–0–29–0; Falconer 1–0–6–0.

Umpires: A. Tayler and B. Wilson.

NATIONAL CLUB CHAMPIONSHIP WINNERS 1969-90

1969 HAMPSTEAD beat Pocklington Pixies by 14 runs.
1970 CHELTENHAM beat Stockport by three wickets.
1971 BLACKHEATH beat Ealing by eight wickets.
1972 SCARBOROUGH beat Brentham by six wickets.
1973 WOLVERHAMPTON beat The Mote by five wickets.
1974 SUNBURY beat Tunbridge Wells by seven wickets.
1975 YORK beat Blackpool by six wickets.
1976 SCARBOROUGH beat Dulwich by five wickets.
1977 SOUTHGATE beat Bowdon by six wickets.
1978 CHELTENHAM beat Bishop's Stortford by 15 runs.
1979 SCARBOROUGH beat Reading by two wickets.
1980 MOSELEY beat Gosport Borough by nine wickets.
1981 SCARBOROUGH beat Blackheath by 57 runs.
1982 SCARBOROUGH beat Finchley by 4 runs.
1983 SHREWSBURY beat Hastings and St Leonards Priory by 2 runs.
1984 OLD HILL beat Bishop's Stortford by five wickets.
1985 OLD HILL beat Reading by nine wickets.
1986 STOURBRIDGE beat Weston-super-Mare by four wickets.
1987 OLD HILL beat Teddington by five wickets.
1988 ENFIELD beat Wolverhampton by nine wickets.
1989 TEDDINGTON beat Old Hill by 11 runs.
1990 BLACKPOOL beat Cheam by three wickets.

From 1969 to 1975, the Championship was contested for the D. H. Robins Trophy, from 1976 to 1982 for the John Haig Trophy, from 1983 to 1986 for the William Younger Cup, and from 1987 to 1990 for the Cockspur Cup.

†DUNSTALL v GOATACRE

National Village Championship Final

August 25. Goatacre won by 50 runs. Toss: Goatacre. Iles, grandson of the Wiltshire village club's founder, played one of the finest innings seen at Lord's for many a day, and by virtually monopolising this nineteenth village final he gave Goatacre their second title. The first was in 1988, when the match was washed out at Lord's and replayed elsewhere. This August Saturday, though, was a glorious day and Iles was its worthy hero. Having won the toss and decided to bat, he saw Leavey out to the first ball of the morning, Spencer at 23 and the punishing Turner at 100 before he joined Hunt. After that it was all Iles. His hundred took only 45 minutes and included seven sixes – four in succession off Shipton – and six fours in 39 balls received. He added two more sixes and a four in his total of 123 (49 balls) and came to the Pavilion to a standing ovation from MCC members and the supporters of both clubs. Iles's hundred was the first, and Goatacre's total the highest, in a village championship final. Dunstall, a tiny Staffordshire village, who had done their share of giant-killing *en route* to Lord's, faced a near-impossible target but stuck bravely to the task. Wallbank, the captain, and Shilton opened with 67, but after 40 overs Dunstall were still 50 runs behind with two wickets in hand. Iles employed nine bowlers, and at the end Ali struck the bowling with gusto. Without a sponsor, the *Cricketer* shouldered the entire responsibility for the organisation, and in doing so they made possible a day of spectacular cricket.

Man of the Match: K. M. Iles.

Goatacre

P. J. Leavey b Shipton	0	†J. Wilkins not out	3
M. A. Hunt b Crossland	39		
A. J. Spencer c Higgott b Shipton	12	L-b 12, w 10, n-b 3	25
J. B. Turner c Crossland b Scrimshaw	53		
*K. M. Iles c Boulton b Shipton	123	1/0 2/23 3/100 (5 wkts, 40 overs)	267
A. Dawson not out	12	4/220 5/260	

P. D. Rose, J. I. N. Angell, J. C. Haines and P. Dolman did not bat.

Bowling: Shipton 9–0–83–3; Crossland 9–1–54–1; Scrimshaw 9–2–35–1; Boulton 5–0–17–0; Ali 6–0–41–0; Wallbank 2–0–25–0.

Dunstall

G. M. Shilton c Leavey b Rose	35	A. Ali not out	31
*P. H. Wallbank c Haines b Angell	51	S. N. J. Scrimshaw not out	7
R. J. Cooper b Turner	1		
V. K. A. Shilton b Angell	23	B 1, l-b 3, w 6, n-b 3	13
C. D. Boulton run out	21		
C. E. Crossland b Angell	2	1/67 2/73 3/114 (8 wkts, 40 overs)	217
R. J. Ingles b Dawson	24	4/125 5/141 6/143	
†A. Higgott c Dawson b Angell	9	7/163 8/188	

D. K. Shipton did not bat.

Bowling: Dawson 6–0–41–1; Spencer 5–0–16–0; Rose 7–0–37–1; Turner 4–1–8–1; Dolman 6–0–41–0; Angell 6–0–18–4; Iles 2–0–15–0; Haines 3–0–31–0; Leavey 1–0–6–0.

Umpires: P. S. G. Stevens and W. A. U. Wickremasinghe.

VILLAGE CHAMPIONSHIP WINNERS 1972-90

1972 TROON (Cornwall) beat Astwood Bank (Worcestershire) by seven wickets.
1973 TROON (Cornwall) beat Gowerton (Glamorgan) by 12 runs.
1974 BOMARSUND (Northumberland) beat Collingham (Nottinghamshire) by three wickets.
1975 GOWERTON (Glamorgan) beat Isleham (Cambridgeshire) by six wickets.
1976 TROON (Cornwall) beat Sessay (Yorkshire) by 18 runs.
1977 COOKLEY (Worcestershire) beat Lindal Moor (Cumbria) by 28 runs.
1978 LINTON PARK (Kent) beat Toft (Cheshire) by four wickets.
1979 EAST BIERLEY (Yorkshire) beat Ynysygerwn (Glamorgan) by 92 runs.
1980 MARCHWIEL (Clwyd) beat Longparish (Hampshire) by 79 runs.
1981 ST FAGANS (Glamorgan) beat Broad Oak (Yorkshire) by 22 runs.
1982 ST FAGANS (Glamorgan) beat Collingham (Nottinghamshire) by six wickets.
1983 QUARNDON (Derbyshire) beat Troon (Cornwall) by eight wickets.
1984 MARCHWIEL (Clwyd) beat Hursley Park (Hampshire) by 8 runs.
1985 FREUCHIE (Fife) beat Rowledge (Surrey) by virtue of fewer wickets lost with the scores level.
1986 FORGE VALLEY (Yorkshire) beat Ynysygerwn (Glamorgan) by 5 runs.
1987 LONGPARISH (Hampshire) beat Treeton Welfare (Yorkshire) by 76 runs.
1988 GOATACRE (Wiltshire) beat Himley (West Midlands) by four wickets.
1989 TOFT (Cheshire) beat Hambledon (Hampshire) by six wickets.
1990 GOATACRE (Wiltshire) beat Dunstall (Staffordshire) by 50 runs.

From 1972 to 1977, the Village Championship was sponsored by John Haig Ltd, in 1978 and 1990 by the Cricketer, *from 1979 to 1984 by Samuel Whitbread and Co. Ltd, and 1986 to 1989 by Hydro Fertilizers. There was no sponsor in 1985.*

September 1. NatWest Bank Trophy final. LANCASHIRE beat NORTHAMPTONSHIRE by seven wickets (See NatWest Bank Trophy section).

BRITANNIC ASSURANCE COUNTY CHAMPIONSHIP, 1990

Middlesex won the County Championship outright for the tenth time, having also shared the title twice, and for the fourth time in eleven seasons. That they deserved to win the pennant is not open to dispute. Middlesex won more games than any other county – two more than their nearest rivals, Essex and Hampshire – and suffered their only defeat on a pitch at Derby which cost the home county 25 points after an inspection by the TCCB. Only runners-up Essex and fifteenth-placed Somerset recorded as many batting bonus points, and while a number of counties had more bowling points, Middlesex could point to the fact that, in eight of their ten victories, they bowled out their opponents in the second innings. Only once, discounting their rain-affected match at Manchester, did they win as a result of being set a target, beating Somerset at Uxbridge by scoring 371 in 69 overs. Middlesex went to the top of the table in June after successive away wins over Leicestershire, Lancashire and Northamptonshire and, but for a ten-day period when they had no game, they were never dislodged. Under Mike Gatting's enterprising captaincy they played positive cricket, fielded well-balanced sides and, in Desmond Haynes, had the Britannic Assurance Player of the Year.

Boosted by three wins in May, Nottinghamshire led the field as the three-day part of the competition settled down in June. But they came back after a fortnight's absence from Championship cricket to find themselves pushed down into fourth place. After that, there was only a win over Yorkshire at Scarborough as they rode the snakes rather than the ladders. Warwickshire, top of the table between Nottinghamshire's brief tenure and Middlesex's long

BRITANNIC ASSURANCE CHAMPIONSHIP

	Win = 16 points	*Played*	*Won*	*Lost*	*Drawn*	*Bonus points Batting*	*Bonus points Bowling*	*Points*
1	Middlesex (3)	22	10	1	11	73	55	288
2	Essex (2)	22	8	2	12	73	56	257
3	Hampshire (6)	22	8	4	10	67	48	243
4	Worcestershire (1)	22	7	1	14	70	58	240
5	Warwickshire (8)	22	7	7	8	55	64	231
6	Lancashire (4)	22	6	3	13	65	56	217
7	Leicestershire (13)	22	6	7	9	61	53	210
8	Glamorgan (17)	22	5	6	11	64	48	192
9	Surrey (12)	22	4	3	15	54	64	190†
10	Yorkshire (16)	22	5	9	8	52	55	187
11	Northamptonshire (5)	22	4	9	9	61	60	185
12	Derbyshire (6)	22	6	7	9	58	52	181*
13	Gloucestershire (9)	22	4	7	11	51	58	173
13	Nottinghamshire (11)	22	4	8	10	51	58	173
15	Somerset (14)	22	3	4	15	73	45	166
16	Kent (15)	22	3	6	13	69	35	152
17	Sussex (10)	22	3	9	10	51	44	143

1989 positions are shown in brackets.

* *Derbyshire had 25 points deducted during the season as a penalty for a sub-standard pitch at Derby.*

† *The total for Surrey includes 8 points for levelling the scores in a drawn game.*

one, filled second or third place throughout August, despite three successive defeats, and a late victory over Glamorgan ensured they held enough points for fifth-place prizemoney. Hampshire's third place was well earned, for they were rarely out of the top four from mid-May.

Worcestershire and Essex, winners and runners-up in 1989, were both slow to start in 1990 yet finished strongly to suggest they would again be among the challengers in 1991. Five of the defending champions' seven wins came in August and September to lift them from thirteenth to fourth, and with four victories in their six four-day fixtures, Worcestershire reinforced the view that they are ideally suited to the extended game. Essex, who finished in the top three for the third year running, once more found their challenge for the title governed by the "if" factor: if Essex picked up points here and Middlesex dropped them elsewhere, it was suggested, Essex would be champions. Three successive wins in July had taken them from fourteenth to seventh, and within a month they were hard on Middlesex's heels. However, Northamptonshire arrested their momentum, as they had the previous season, and after winning at Derby by an innings in two days, Essex failed to win any of their last four games.

Lancashire could have been, should have been, contenders. Like Middlesex, they had a balanced side, if lacking the new champions' resources in spin bowling, but along the way they were sidetracked by the glamour and the big money of the Lord's finals. A ten-wicket defeat by Worcestershire at Kidderminster early in August removed them from the top three for only the second time since June, and this time they did not come back. They finished just out of the money, still to prove themselves capable of staying over the distance.

Yorkshire and Glamorgan, with five wins apiece, had every reason to be satisfied with their seasons, climbing to the middle of the table from sixteenth and seventeenth respectively in 1989. While the Welsh county benefited from the influence of their new overseas player, Viv Richards, Yorkshire's improvement was all their own work, despite the gathering murmurings that the county should look beyond its Ridings for a saviour. The presence of Bobby Simpson, the Australian manager, at Grace Road may have had something to do with Leicestershire's move up six places to seventh, while neighbours Derbyshire would have finished a place behind them but for the deduction of 25 points for that unsatisfactory pitch in the Middlesex match. Instead, they were twelfth, one place behind the enigmatic Northamptonshire, whose talented line-up only occasionally played to its potential.

Activities off the field, as much as those on it, occupied the attentions of Gloucestershire and Kent as they struggled in the lower reaches. Gloucestershire spent most of the season alternating with Sussex between sixteenth and seventeenth, only to escape in the last month with convincing wins over Northamptonshire and Sussex which showed what they could have been capable of. Sussex, on the other hand, rarely looked more than ordinary. They had been rooted at the bottom of the table for more than a month when Middlesex beat them with a day and an innings in hand to clinch the Championship.

REGULATIONS FOR BRITANNIC ASSURANCE CHAMPIONSHIP

(As applied in 1990)

1. Prizemoney

First (Middlesex)	£40,000
Second (Essex)	£20,000
Third (Hampshire)	£11,500
Fourth (Worcestershire)	£5,750
Fifth (Warwickshire)	£3,000
Winner of each match	£225
Championship Player of the Year (D. L. Haynes)	£1,000
County of the Month	£1,000
Player of the Month	£300

2. Scoring of Points

(*a*) For a win, sixteen points, plus any points scored in the first innings.

(*b*) In a tie, each side to score eight points, plus any points scored in the first innings.

(*c*) If the scores are equal in a drawn match, the side batting in the fourth innings to score eight points, plus any points scored in the first innings.

(*d*) **First-innings points** (awarded only for performances *in the first 100 overs* of each first innings and retained whatever the result of the match).

(i) A maximum of four batting points to be available as under:
150 to 199 runs – 1 point; 200 to 249 runs – 2 points; 250 to 299 runs – 3 points; 300 runs or over – 4 points.

(ii) A maximum of four bowling points to be available as under:
3 to 4 wickets taken – 1 point; 5 to 6 wickets taken – 2 points; 7 to 8 wickets taken – 3 points; 9 to 10 wickets taken – 4 points.

(*e*) If play starts when less than eight hours' playing time remains and a one-innings match is played, no first-innings points shall be scored. The side winning on the one innings to score twelve points.

(*f*) A county which is adjudged to have prepared a pitch unsuitable for first-class cricket shall be liable to have 25 points deducted from its aggregate of points.

(*g*) The side which has the highest aggregate of points gained at the end of the season shall be the Champion County. Should any sides in the Championship table be equal on points the side with most wins will have priority.

3. Hours of Play

1st, 2nd [3rd] days ...	11.00 a.m. to 6.30 p.m. or after 110 overs, whichever is the later. (For Sunday play, the home county may decide to play from 12 noon to 7.30 p.m.)
Final day	11.00 a.m. to 6.00 p.m. or after 102 overs, whichever is the later.

Note: The hours of play, including intervals, were brought forward by half an hour for matches in September.

(*a*) If play is suspended (including any interval between innings) the minimum number of overs to be bowled in a day to be reduced by one over for each 3½ minutes or part thereof of such suspension or suspensions in aggregate.

(*b*) If at 5.00 p.m. on the final day, nineteen overs or less remain to be bowled, the umpires shall indicate that play shall continue until a minimum of a further twenty overs has been bowled, or until 6.00 p.m., whichever is the later. Play may cease on the final day at any time between 5.30 p.m. and 6.00 p.m. by mutual agreement of the captains. Should an innings end between 4.50 p.m. and 5.00 p.m., the time at the end of the ten-minute interval to replace 5.00 p.m.

(*c*) The captains may agree or, in the event of disagreement, the umpires may decide to play 30 minutes (or minimum ten overs) extra time at the end of the first and/or second day's play (and/or the third day of four) if, in their opinion, it would bring about a definite result on that day. In the event of the possibility of a finish disappearing before the full period has expired, the whole period must be played out. Any time so claimed does not affect the timing for cessation of play on the final day.

(*d*) If an innings ends during the course of an over, that part shall count as a full over so far as the minimum number of overs per day is concerned.

(*e*) If play is suspended for the day in the middle of an over, that over must be completed next day in addition to the minimum overs required that day.

Intervals

Lunch: 1.15 p.m. to 1.55 p.m. (1st, 2nd [3rd] days), 2.15 p.m. to 2.55 p.m. on Sundays when play commences at 12 noon
1.00 p.m. to 1.40 p.m. (final day)

Tea: 4.10 p.m. to 4.30 p.m. (1st, 2nd [3rd] days), 5.10 p.m. to 5.30 p.m. on Sundays when play commences at 12 noon; or when 40 overs remain to be bowled, whichever is the later.
3.40 p.m. to 4.00 p.m. (final day), or when 40 overs remain to be bowled, whichever is the later.

4. Substitutes

Law 2.1 will apply, but in addition:

A substitute shall be allowed as of right in the event of a cricketer currently playing in a Championship match being required to join the England team for a Test match (or one-day international). Such a substitute may be permitted to bat or bowl in that match, subject to the approval of the TCCB. The player who is substituted may not take further part in the match, even though he might not be required by England. If batting at the time, the player substituted shall be retired "not out" and his substitute may be permitted to bat later in that innings subject to the approval of the TCCB.

The opposing captain shall have no right of objection to any player acting as substitute in the field, nor as to where he shall field. However, no substitute may act as wicket-keeper.

No substitute may take the field until the player for whom he is to substitute has been absent from the field for five consecutive complete overs, with the exception that if a fieldsman sustains an obvious, serious injury, a substitute shall be allowed immediately. If a player leaves the field during an over, the remainder of that over shall not count in the calculation of five complete overs.

5. Fieldsman Leaving the Field

No fieldsman shall leave the field or return during a session of play without the consent of the umpire at the bowler's end. The umpire's consent is also necessary at the start of play or when his side returns to the field after an interval.

If a member of the fielding side does not take the field at the start of play, leaves the field, or fails to return after an interval and is absent longer than fifteen minutes, he shall not bowl in that innings after his return until he has been on the field for at least the length of playing time for which he was absent; nor shall he be permitted to bat unless or until, in the aggregate, he has returned to the field and/or his side's innings has been in progress for at least the length of playing time for which he was absent or, if earlier, when his side has lost five wickets. The restrictions shall not apply if he has been absent for exceptional and acceptable reasons (other than injury or illness) and consent for a substitute has been granted by the opposing captain.

6. New ball

The captain of the fielding side shall have the choice of taking the new ball after 100 overs have been bowled with the old one.

7. Covering of Pitches and Bowler's Run-up

The whole pitch shall be covered:

(*a*) The night before a match and, if necessary, until the first ball is bowled.

(*b*) On each night of a match and, if necessary, throughout Sunday.

(*c*) In the event of play being suspended because of bad light or rain, during the hours of play.

The bowler's run-up shall be covered to a distance of at least ten yards, with a width of four yards.

8. Declarations

Law 14 will apply, but, in addition, a captain may also forfeit his first innings, subject to the provisions set out in Law 14.2. If, owing to weather conditions, the match has not started when fewer than eight hours of playing time remain, the first innings of each side shall automatically be forfeited and a one-innings match played.

CHAMPION COUNTY SINCE 1864

Note: The earliest county champions were decided usually by the fewest matches lost, but in 1888 an unofficial points system was introduced. In 1890, the Championship was constituted officially. From 1977 to 1983 it was sponsored by Schweppes, and since 1984 by Britannic Assurance.

1864	Surrey
1865	Nottinghamshire
1866	Middlesex
1867	Yorkshire
1868	Nottinghamshire
1869	Nottinghamshire
	Yorkshire
1870	Yorkshire
1871	Nottinghamshire
1872	Nottinghamshire
1873	Gloucestershire
	Nottinghamshire
1874	Gloucestershire
1875	Nottinghamshire
1876	Gloucestershire
1877	Gloucestershire
1878	Undecided
1879	Nottinghamshire
	Lancashire
1880	Nottinghamshire
1881	Lancashire
1882	Nottinghamshire
	Lancashire
1883	Nottinghamshire
1884	Nottinghamshire
1885	Nottinghamshire
1886	Nottinghamshire
1887	Surrey
1888	Surrey
1889	Surrey
	Lancashire
	Nottinghamshire
1890	Surrey
1891	Surrey
1892	Surrey
1893	Yorkshire
1894	Surrey
1895	Surrey
1896	Yorkshire
1897	Lancashire
1898	Yorkshire
1899	Surrey
1900	Yorkshire
1901	Yorkshire
1902	Yorkshire
1903	Middlesex
1904	Lancashire
1905	Yorkshire
1906	Kent
1907	Nottinghamshire
1908	Yorkshire
1909	Kent
1910	Kent
1911	Warwickshire
1912	Yorkshire
1913	Kent
1914	Surrey
1919	Yorkshire
1920	Middlesex
1921	Middlesex
1922	Yorkshire
1923	Yorkshire
1924	Yorkshire
1925	Yorkshire
1926	Lancashire
1927	Lancashire
1928	Lancashire
1929	Nottinghamshire
1930	Lancashire
1931	Yorkshire
1932	Yorkshire
1933	Yorkshire
1934	Lancashire
1935	Yorkshire
1936	Derbyshire
1937	Yorkshire
1938	Yorkshire
1939	Yorkshire
1946	Yorkshire
1947	Middlesex
1948	Glamorgan
1949	Middlesex
	Yorkshire
1950	Lancashire
	Surrey
1951	Warwickshire
1952	Surrey
1953	Surrey
1954	Surrey
1955	Surrey
1956	Surrey
1957	Surrey
1958	Surrey
1959	Yorkshire
1960	Yorkshire
1961	Hampshire
1962	Yorkshire
1963	Yorkshire
1964	Worcestershire
1965	Worcestershire
1966	Yorkshire
1967	Yorkshire
1968	Yorkshire
1969	Glamorgan
1970	Kent
1971	Surrey
1972	Warwickshire
1973	Hampshire
1974	Worcestershire
1975	Leicestershire
1976	Middlesex
1977	Middlesex
	Kent
1978	Kent
1979	Essex
1980	Middlesex
1981	Nottinghamshire
1982	Middlesex
1983	Essex
1984	Essex
1985	Middlesex
1986	Essex
1987	Nottinghamshire
1988	Worcestershire
1989	Worcestershire
1990	Middlesex

Notes: The title has been won outright as follows: Yorkshire 31 times, Surrey 18, Nottinghamshire 14, Middlesex 10, Lancashire 8, Kent 6, Worcestershire 5, Essex 4, Gloucestershire 3, Warwickshire 3, Glamorgan 2, Hampshire 2, Derbyshire 1, Leicestershire 1.

Eight times the title has been shared as follows: Nottinghamshire 5, Lancashire 4, Middlesex 2, Surrey 2, Yorkshire 2, Gloucestershire 1, Kent 1.

The earliest date the Championship has been won in any season since it was expanded in 1895 was August 12, 1910, by Kent.

BRITANNIC ASSURANCE CHAMPIONSHIP STATISTICS FOR 1990

	For			*Against*		
County	*Runs*	*Wickets*	*Avge*	*Runs*	*Wickets*	*Avge*
Derbyshire	9,475	280	33.83	9,960	289	34.46
Essex	11,341	232	48.88	10,907	283	38.54
Glamorgan	10,792	276	39.10	10,858	230	47.20
Gloucestershire	9,643	273	35.32	9,942	277	35.89
Hampshire	9,985	228	43.79	10,035	282	35.58
Kent	11,700	326	35.88	10,630	248	42.86
Lancashire	9,725	220	44.20	10,465	269	38.90
Leicestershire	10,380	308	33.70	9,901	265	37.36
Middlesex	10,905	270	40.38	10,486	306	34.26
Northamptonshire	10,742	284	37.82	11,018	286	38.52
Nottinghamshire	11,298	336	33.62	10,953	265	41.33
Somerset	11,277	217	51.96	11,609	264	43.97
Surrey	10,307	220	46.85	11,102	300	37.00
Sussex	10,673	330	32.34	10,735	230	46.67
Warwickshire	9,944	299	33.25	9,709	280	34.67
Worcestershire	11,070	240	46.12	10,513	309	34.02
Yorkshire	10,103	293	34.48	10,537	249	42.31
	179,360	4,632	38.72	179,360	4,632	38.72

COUNTY CHAMPIONSHIP – MATCH RESULTS, 1864-1990

County	*Years of Play*	*Played*	*Won*	*Lost*	*Tied*	*Drawn*
Derbyshire	1871-87; 1895-1990	2,112	517	769	1	825
Essex	1895-1990	2,075	585	596	5	889
Glamorgan	1921-1990	1,609	346	554	0	709
Gloucestershire	1870-1990	2,350	694	867	2	787
Hampshire	1864-85; 1895-1990	2,184	572	752	4	856
Kent	1864-1990	2,472	895	751	4	822
Lancashire	1865-1990	2,550	951	517	3	1,079
Leicestershire	1895-1990	2,042	441	761	1	839
Middlesex	1864-1990	2,252	842	570	5	835
Northamptonshire	1905-1990	1,809	429	643	3	734
Nottinghamshire	1864-1990	2,381	723	624	0	1,034
Somerset	1882-85; 1891-1990	2,082	485	851	3	743
Surrey	1864-1990	2,629	1,042	574	4	1,009
Sussex	1864-1990	2,521	702	870	5	944
Warwickshire	1895-1990	2,056	535	603	1	917
Worcestershire	1899-1990	1,997	493	703	1	800
Yorkshire	1864-1990	2,650	1,194	441	2	1,013
Cambridgeshire	1864-69; 1871	19	8	8	0	3
		18,895	11,454	11,454	22	7,419

Notes: Matches abandoned without a ball bowled are wholly excluded.

Counties participated in the years shown, except that there were no matches in the years 1915-18 and 1940-45; Hampshire did not play inter-county matches in 1868-69, 1871-74 and 1879; Worcestershire did not take part in the Championship in 1919.

COUNTY CHAMPIONSHIP – FINAL POSITIONS, 1890-1990

	Derbyshire	Essex	Glamorgan	Gloucestershire	Hampshire	Kent	Lancashire	Leicestershire	Middlesex	Northamptonshire	Nottinghamshire	Somerset	Surrey	Sussex	Warwickshire	Worcestershire	Yorkshire
1890	—	—	—	6	—	3	2	—	7	—	5	—	1	8	—	—	3
1891	—	—	—	9	—	5	2	—	3	—	4	5	1	7	—	—	8
1892	—	—	—	7	—	7	4	—	5	—	2	3	1	9	—	—	6
1893	—	—	—	9	—	4	2	—	3	—	6	8	5	7	—	—	1
1894	—	—	—	9	—	4	4	—	3	—	7	6	1	8	—	—	2
1895	5	9	—	4	10	14	2	12	6	—	12	8	1	11	6	—	3
1896	7	5	—	10	8	9	2	13	3	—	6	11	4	14	12	—	1
1897	14	3	—	5	9	12	1	13	8	—	10	11	2	6	7	—	4
1898	9	5	—	3	12	7	6	13	2	—	8	13	4	9	9	—	1
1899	15	6	—	9	10	8	4	13	2	—	10	13	1	5	7	12	3
1900	13	10	—	7	15	3	2	14	7	—	5	11	7	3	6	12	1
1901	15	10	—	14	7	7	3	12	2	—	9	12	6	4	5	11	1
1902	10	13	—	14	15	7	5	11	12	—	3	7	4	2	6	9	1
1903	12	8	—	13	14	8	4	14	1	—	5	10	11	2	7	6	3
1904	10	14	—	9	15	3	1	7	4	—	5	12	11	6	7	13	2
1905	14	12	—	8	16	6	2	5	11	13	10	15	4	3	7	8	1
1906	16	7	—	9	8	1	4	15	11	11	5	11	3	10	6	14	2
1907	16	7	—	10	12	8	6	11	5	15	1	14	4	13	9	2	2
1908	14	11	—	10	9	2	7	13	4	15	8	16	3	5	12	6	1
1909	15	14	—	16	8	1	2	13	6	7	10	11	5	4	12	8	3
1910	15	11	—	12	6	1	4	10	3	9	5	16	2	7	14	13	8
1911	14	6	—	12	11	2	4	15	3	10	8	16	5	13	1	9	7
1912	12	15	—	11	6	3	4	13	5	2	8	14	7	10	9	16	1
1913	13	15	—	9	10	1	8	14	6	4	5	16	3	7	11	12	2
1914	12	8	—	16	5	3	11	13	2	9	10	15	1	6	7	14	4
1919	9	14	—	8	7	2	5	9	13	12	3	5	4	11	15	—	1
1920	16	9	—	8	11	5	2	13	1	14	7	10	3	6	12	15	4
1921	12	15	17	7	6	4	5	11	1	13	8	10	2	9	16	14	3
1922	11	8	16	13	6	4	5	14	7	15	2	10	3	9	12	17	1
1923	10	13	16	11	7	5	3	14	8	17	2	9	4	6	12	15	1
1924	17	15	13	6	12	5	4	11	2	16	6	8	3	10	9	14	1
1925	14	7	17	10	9	5	3	12	6	11	4	15	2	13	8	16	1
1926	11	9	8	15	7	3	1	13	6	16	4	14	5	10	12	17	2
1927	5	8	15	12	13	4	1	7	9	16	2	14	6	10	11	17	3
1928	10	16	15	5	12	2	1	9	8	13	3	14	6	7	11	17	4
1929	7	12	17	4	11	8	2	9	6	13	1	15	10	4	14	16	2
1930	9	6	11	2	13	5	1	12	16	17	4	13	8	7	15	10	3
1931	7	10	15	2	12	3	6	16	11	17	5	13	8	4	9	14	1
1932	10	14	15	13	8	3	6	12	10	16	4	7	5	2	9	17	1
1933	6	4	16	10	14	3	5	17	12	13	8	11	9	2	7	15	1
1934	3	8	13	7	14	5	1	12	10	17	9	15	11	2	4	16	5
1935	2	9	13	15	16	10	4	6	3	17	5	14	11	7	8	12	1
1936	1	9	16	4	10	8	11	15	2	17	5	7	6	14	13	12	3
1937	3	6	7	4	14	12	9	16	2	17	10	13	8	5	11	15	1
1938	5	6	16	10	14	9	4	15	2	17	12	7	3	8	13	11	1
1939	9	4	13	3	15	5	6	17	2	16	12	14	8	10	11	7	1
1946	15	8	6	5	10	6	3	11	2	16	13	4	11	17	14	8	1
1947	5	11	9	2	16	4	3	14	1	17	11	11	6	9	15	7	7
1948	6	13	1	8	9	15	5	11	3	17	14	12	2	16	7	10	4
1949	15	9	8	7	16	13	11	17	1	6	11	9	5	13	4	3	1

	Derbyshire	Essex	Glamorgan	Gloucestershire	Hampshire	Kent	Lancashire	Leicestershire	Middlesex	Northamptonshire	Nottinghamshire	Somerset	Surrey	Sussex	Warwickshire	Worcestershire	Yorkshire
1950	5	17	11	7	12	9	1	16	14	10	15	7	1	13	4	6	3
1951	11	8	5	12	9	16	3	15	7	13	17	14	6	10	1	4	2
1952	4	10	7	9	12	15	3	6	5	8	16	17	1	13	10	14	2
1953	6	12	10	6	14	16	3	3	5	11	8	17	1	2	9	15	12
1954	3	15	4	13	14	11	10	16	7	7	5	17	1	9	6	11	2
1955	8	14	16	12	3	13	9	6	5	7	11	17	1	4	9	15	2
1956	12	11	13	3	6	16	2	17	5	4	8	15	1	9	14	9	7
1957	4	5	9	12	13	14	6	17	7	2	15	8	1	9	11	16	3
1958	5	6	15	14	2	8	7	12	10	4	17	3	1	13	16	9	11
1959	7	9	6	2	8	13	5	16	10	11	17	12	3	15	4	14	1
1960	5	6	11	8	12	10	2	17	3	9	16	14	7	4	15	13	1
1961	7	6	14	5	1	11	13	9	3	16	17	10	15	8	12	4	2
1962	7	9	14	4	10	11	16	17	13	8	15	6	5	12	3	2	1
1963	17	12	2	8	10	13	15	16	6	7	9	3	11	4	4	14	1
1964	12	10	11	17	12	7	14	16	6	3	15	8	4	9	2	1	5
1965	9	15	3	10	12	5	13	14	6	2	17	7	8	16	11	1	4
1966	9	16	14	15	11	4	12	8	12	5	17	3	7	10	6	2	1
1967	6	15	14	17	12	2	11	2	7	9	15	8	4	13	10	5	1
1968	8	14	3	16	5	2	6	9	10	13	4	12	15	17	11	7	1
1969	16	6	1	2	5	10	15	14	11	9	8	17	3	7	4	12	13
1970	7	12	2	17	10	1	3	15	16	14	11	13	5	9	7	6	4
1971	17	10	16	8	9	4	3	5	6	14	12	7	1	11	2	15	13
1972	17	5	13	3	9	2	15	6	8	4	14	11	12	16	1	7	10
1973	16	8	11	5	1	4	12	9	13	3	17	10	2	15	7	6	14
1974	17	12	16	14	2	10	8	4	6	3	15	5	7	13	9	1	11
1975	15	7	9	16	3	5	4	1	11	8	13	12	6	17	14	10	2
1976	15	6	17	3	12	14	16	4	1	2	13	7	9	10	5	11	8
1977	7	6	14	3	11	1	16	5	1	9	17	4	14	8	10	13	12
1978	14	2	13	10	8	1	12	6	3	17	7	5	16	9	11	15	4
1979	16	1	17	10	12	5	13	6	14	11	9	8	3	4	15	2	7
1980	9	8	13	7	17	16	15	10	1	12	3	5	2	4	14	11	6
1981	12	5	14	13	7	9	16	8	4	15	1	3	6	2	17	11	10
1982	11	7	16	15	3	13	12	2	1	9	4	6	5	8	17	14	10
1983	9	1	15	12	3	7	12	4	2	6	14	10	8	11	5	16	17
1984	12	1	13	17	15	5	16	4	3	11	2	7	8	6	9	10	14
1985	13	4	12	3	2	9	14	16	1	10	8	17	6	7	15	5	11
1986	11	1	17	2	6	8	15	7	12	9	4	16	3	14	12	5	10
1987	6	12	13	10	5	14	2	3	16	7	1	11	4	17	15	9	8
1988	14	3	17	10	15	2	9	8	7	12	5	11	4	16	6	1	13
1989	6	2	17	9	6	15	4	13	3	5	11	14	12	10	8	1	16
1990	12	2	8	13	3	16	6	7	1	11	13	15	9	17	5	4	10

Note: From 1969 onwards, positions have been given in accordance with the Championship regulations which state that "Should *any* sides in the table be equal on points the side with most wins will have priority".

DERBYSHIRE

President: The Duke of Devonshire
Chairman: C. N. Middleton
Chairman, Cricket Committee: B. Holling
Chief Executive: R. J. Lark
County Ground, Nottingham Road, Derby DE2 6DA (Telephone: 0332-383211)
Captain: K. J. Barnett
Coach: P. E. Russell

Winning the Refuge Assurance League gave Derbyshire their first success for nine years and, significantly, they avoided the mistakes which had made their victory in the 1981 NatWest Bank Trophy final an end rather than a beginning. The team which won at Lord's under Barry Wood started to break up in a matter of days and, against a background of the smallest membership among the first-class counties, Derbyshire spent most of the 1980s in patient rebuilding. Three people were chiefly responsible for recreating a team: Kim Barnett, 22 when he was appointed captain in 1983, coach Philip Russell, and Guy Willatt, a former captain, who stepped down as cricket committee chairman before the 1990 season. His successor, Brian Holling, was insistent that the credit belonged, at committee level, to Willatt.

After completing their Sunday League season with an exciting victory over Essex, Derbyshire announced an intelligent retained list, designed to keep a nucleus of eight players on long-term contracts to the end of 1994. They also demonstrated their ambition by announcing a £10 million redevelopment of the County Ground at Derby, and by engaging India's captain, Mohammad Azharuddin, as their overseas player for 1991 on the assumption that Ian Bishop would be on tour with the West Indians. Adrian Kuiper, as disappointing in the Britannic Assurance Championship as he was successful in one-day cricket, decided not to return from South Africa.

In the other one-day competitions, Derbyshire wasted good positions, thus failing to reach the knockout stages of the Benson and Hedges Cup and allowing Lancashire to escape in the NatWest Trophy. They lost the final of the Refuge Assurance Cup on a depressingly sluggish pitch at Edgbaston.

In addition to his forthright captaincy, Barnett set a Derbyshire record when he passed Denis Smith's total of 30 hundreds for the county, a mark which had stood for 40 years. There were 21 first-class hundreds in the season, another Derbyshire record, but there was also an underlying inconsistency, despite important individual improvements. Bruce Roberts had a better year, and in his first full summer Chris Adams was close to 1,000 runs. Adams also proved himself to be a fine fielder, as he showed a wider audience when he acted as England's substitute against India at Old Trafford. In addition, Bishop, who scored a maiden century against Yorkshire at Scarborough, suggested he had sufficient quality to emerge as a genuine all-rounder.

The Championship batting, however, relied to an unhealthy extent on Barnett, John Morris and Peter Bowler. Spectacular collapses were never far away and certain opponents, notably Essex and Hampshire, could be forgiven for wondering how Derbyshire ever won a game. Bowler completed three notably consistent seasons, and there was much pleasure in the county when Morris, considered unlucky to miss a tour in 1989-90, made his England début against India. Only at The Oval did he have the chance to play a long innings, and failure to do so meant an anxious wait before he was chosen to tour Australia.

Devon Malcolm's selection was in less doubt. He was an unknown quantity when he went to the West Indies, but he was England's leading wicket-taker there and in the home series against New Zealand. Although fatigue was setting in during the second half of the summer, he had by then established himself as fast enough to unsettle the best batsmen in the world. For a variety of reasons – including international calls, the county's system of rotating their fast bowlers, and despair about slow pitches at Derby – Malcolm and Bishop played together in only six Championship games. Yet even when the odds were loaded heavily in favour of batsmen, Bishop, capped in 1990 along with Simon Base, compelled respect and he took his wickets at less than 20 each.

Concern about the pitches culminated in the deduction of 25 points for an unacceptable surface in the Championship match against Middlesex in August. The loss of the points pushed Derbyshire from eighth to twelfth in the final table and knocked on the head any last, lingering hopes of the title or prizemoney. While Derbyshire accepted the decision, they expressed concern about the circumstances leading to it. In May, a Derby pitch which had provided a satisfactory game against Nottinghamshire was reported, not because of its behaviour but because it was too green. Having been ordered to shave the pitches, Derbyshire followed instructions with a sense of impending disaster. They relaid two strips in the autumn, a long-term rather than an immediate solution.

Derbyshire hope that some of their younger players will develop. Andrew Brown, taken back on the staff, scored a maiden century against Northamptonshire, but ended that innings with a broken hand. Dominic Cork, picked as a bowler for England Young Cricketers, saved the series against their Pakistani counterparts with a century as night-watchman, and Tim O'Gorman should be available regularly after a year at Law School. However, Geoff Miller, having made major contributions to two Championship victories and to the balance of the Sunday team on his return after three years with Essex, left when offered a match contract for 1991, rather than a longer-term one.

The memories of 1990 will be of Sunday games, especially the successful pursuits of steep targets at Taunton, where Morris scored four centuries in three competitions, and against Kent at Chesterfield. Kuiper's savage hitting gave Derbyshire a good start and an exciting climax, while Barnett fell only 1 run short of his 1986 record of 700 Sunday runs. It was on Sundays that Ole Mortensen, always the most reliable of Derbyshire's bowlers, Base and Allan Warner were at their most influential. Derbyshire earned their moments of good fortune and believed that more success was on the way. – Gerald Mortimer.

DERBYSHIRE 1990

[*Bill Smith*

Back row: F. A. Griffith, A. M. Brown, D. G. Cork, T. J. G. O'Gorman, C. J. Adams, S. C. Goldsmith, K. M. Krikken. *Middle row:* B. Roberts, A. E. Warner, S. J. Base, P. D. Bowler, M. Jean-Jacques, S. W. Tacey (*scorer*). *Front row:* O. H. Mortensen, J. E. Morris, R. J. Lark (*chief executive*), K. J. Barnett (*captain*), P. E. Russell (*coach*), G. Miller, B. J. M. Maher. *Insets:* D. E. Malcolm, I. R. Bishop, A. P. Kuiper.

DERBYSHIRE RESULTS

All first-class matches – Played 24: Won 7, Lost 8, Drawn 9.

County Championship matches – Played 22: Won 6, Lost 7, Drawn 9.

Bonus points – Batting 58, Bowling 52.

Competition placings – Britannic Assurance County Championship, 12th; NatWest Bank Trophy, 2nd round; Benson and Hedges Cup, 3rd in Group B; Refuge Assurance League, winners; Refuge Assurance Cup, finalists.

BRITANNIC ASSURANCE CHAMPIONSHIP AVERAGES

BATTING

	Birthplace	*M*	*I*	*NO*	*R*	*HI*	*Avge*
‡J. E. Morris	*Crewe*	16	26	4	1,353	157*	61.50
‡K. J. Barnett	*Stoke-on-Trent*	22	36	5	1,572	141	50.70
‡P. D. Bowler	*Plymouth*	21	37	4	1,408	210	42.66
T. J. G. O'Gorman	*Woking*	6	11	1	393	100	39.30
A. M. Brown	*Heanor*	7	11	1	379	139*	37.90
‡B. Roberts	*Lusaka, N. Rhodesia*	22	35	7	1,038	124*	37.07
‡G. Miller	*Chesterfield*	13	13	7	208	47*	34.66
‡I. R. Bishop	*Port-of Spain, Trinidad*	12	15	4	326	103*	29.63
C. J. Adams	*Whitwell*	21	32	3	800	101	27.58
‡S. J. Base	*Maidstone*	13	13	2	215	58	19.54
A. P. Kuiper	*Johannesburg, SA*	10	15	0	288	48	19.20
K. M. Krikken	*Bolton*	21	28	2	426	77*	16.38
S. C. Goldsmith	*Ashford, Kent*	11	16	1	216	34	14.40
M. Jean-Jacques	*Soufrière, Dominica*	10	11	4	80	25	11.42
‡D. E. Malcolm	*Kingston, Jamaica*	9	6	2	44	20*	11.00
‡O. H. Mortensen	*Vejle, Denmark*	11	11	9	20	5*	10.00
‡A. E. Warner	*Birmingham*	14	19	2	160	59	9.41

Also batted: D. G. Cork (*Newcastle-under-Lyme*) (1 match) 7; F. A. Griffith (*Whipps Cross, London*) (1 match) 1; Z. A. Sadiq (*Nairobi, Kenya*) (1 match) 0.

* *Signifies not out.* ‡ *Denotes county cap.*

The following played a total of twenty three-figure innings for Derbyshire in County Championship matches – J. E. Morris 6, K. J. Barnett 5, P. D. Bowler 3, B. Roberts 2, C. J. Adams 1, I. R. Bishop 1, A. M. Brown 1, T. J. G. O'Gorman 1.

BOWLING

	O	*M*	*R*	*W*	*BB*	*5W/i*	*Avge*
I. R. Bishop	395.3	91	1,087	59	6-71	3	18.42
O. H. Mortensen	301.2	88	764	32	4-22	0	23.87
D. E. Malcolm	277.4	44	947	30	4-63	0	31.56
K. J. Barnett	267.1	42	720	19	3-49	0	37.89
S. J. Base	414.3	68	1,402	35	6-105	2	40.05
A. E. Warner	393.3	67	1,330	33	3-56	0	40.30
G. Miller	427.2	94	1,285	31	6-45	1	41.45
M. Jean-Jacques	261.2	33	983	19	6-60	1	51.73

Also bowled: C. J. Adams 8–0–36–1; P. D. Bowler 8–0–56–1; D. G. Cork 24–6–70–0; S. C. Goldsmith 112–19–347–7; F. A. Griffith 11–2–20–1; A. P. Kuiper 108.3–25–325–9; J. E. Morris 20–0–123–1; B. Roberts 7–0–26–0.

Wicket-keepers: K. M. Krikken 58 ct, 3 st; P. D. Bowler 4 ct.

Leading Fielders: B. Roberts 23, C. J. Adams 22.

At Cambridge, April 18, 19, 20. DERBYSHIRE beat CAMBRIDGE UNIVERSITY by 243 runs.

At Nottingham, April 26, 27, 28, 30. DERBYSHIRE drew with NOTTINGHAMSHIRE.

At Northampton, May 3, 4. DERBYSHIRE beat NORTHAMPTONSHIRE by an innings and 51 runs.

DERBYSHIRE v LANCASHIRE

At Derby, May 15, 16, 17, 18. Lancashire won by 60 runs. Lancashire 21 pts, Derbyshire 3 pts. Toss: Lancashire. A lifeless pitch contributed to some dull cricket, but the match ended satisfactorily for Lancashire when Miller was lbw to DeFreitas to give them victory with five balls to spare. Lancashire batted until tea on the second day, having lost 87 minutes because of a thunderstorm on the first, and only DeFreitas, with 79 from 107 balls, interrupted the pattern of steady accumulation. Although Barnett also showed that it was possible to play strokes, Lancashire's policy was justified by Atherton's excellent leg-spin bowling. He took five for 95, the best figures of his career, and Lancashire led by 136. Their second declaration set Derbyshire to score 309 off what proved to be 87 overs but, after a bright start by Barnett and Morris, only Bowler played an innings of substance. Hughes, a bowling recluse in recent seasons, was much the most effective of the spinners.

Close of play: First day, Lancashire 223-2 (M. A. Atherton 69*, N. H. Fairbrother 23*); Second day, Derbyshire 105-2 (S. J. Base 9*, M. Jean-Jacques 0*); Third day, Lancashire 81-2 (M. A. Atherton 28*, N. H. Fairbrother 22*).

Lancashire

First Innings		Second Innings	
G. D. Mendis c Roberts b Miller	90	c and b Jean-Jacques	4
G. Fowler b Barnett	25	c Roberts b Jean-Jacques	23
M. A. Atherton b Barnett	93	run out	51
N. H. Fairbrother c Kuiper b Jean-Jacques	63	not out	65
T. E. Jesty not out	55	not out	15
P. A. J. DeFreitas st Krikken b Barnett	79		
B 17, l-b 18, w 1, n-b 4	40	B 3, l-b 11	14
1/79 2/171 3/267 4/325 5/445 (5 wkts dec.)	445	1/10 2/45 3/141 (3 wkts dec.)	172

J. D. Fitton, *D. P. Hughes, P. J. W. Allott, †W. K. Hegg and P. J. Martin did not bat.

Bonus points – Lancashire 2 (Score at 100 overs: 225-2).

Bowling: *First Innings*—Base 39–8–67–0; Jean-Jacques 34–5–112–1; Miller 59–17–111–1; Goldsmith 11–2–39–0; Barnett 33.3–4–81–3. *Second Innings*—Jean-Jacques 19–2–55–2; Base 8–1–30–0; Miller 19–5–45–0; Barnett 8–0–28–0.

Derbyshire

First Innings		Second Innings	
*K. J. Barnett c Hegg b Fitton	69	c Allott b Fitton	33
J. E. Morris c Hegg b Atherton	27	b Fitton	52
S. J. Base c Fitton b Atherton	54	(9) not out	16
M. Jean-Jacques b Martin	18	(10) c Jesty b Hughes	2
A. P. Kuiper c Fowler b Fitton	48	(3) b Atherton	13
C. J. Adams c Fairbrother b Atherton	9	(5) lbw b Hughes	36
B. Roberts lbw b Atherton	8	(6) b Atherton	0
S. C. Goldsmith b Atherton	24	(7) c Mendis b Hughes	4
P. D. Bowler c Mendis b DeFreitas	24	(4) c Fairbrother b Fitton	54
†K. M. Krikken b Allott	11	(8) b Hughes	26
G. Miller not out	3	lbw b DeFreitas	1
B 4, l-b 8, n-b 2	14	B 4, l-b 6, n-b 1	11
1/93 2/105 3/155 4/183 5/206 6/216 7/255 8/275 9/301	309	1/64 2/99 3/103 4/154 5/155 6/160 7/223 8/229 9/243	248

Bonus points – Derbyshire 3, Lancashire 3 (Score at 100 overs: 275-8).

Bowling: *First Innings*—DeFreitas 24.3–4–70–1; Allott 13–3–40–1; Fitton 36–10–82–2; Atherton 38–11–95–5; Martin 8–4–10–1. *Second Innings*—DeFreitas 7.1–1–36–1; Allott 7–0–26–0; Fitton 24–4–69–3; Atherton 24–5–82–2; Hughes 24–12–25–4.

Umpires: H. D. Bird and R. Palmer.

At Taunton, May 19, 21, 22. DERBYSHIRE beat SOMERSET by 146 runs.

DERBYSHIRE v YORKSHIRE

At Chesterfield, May 23, 24, 25. Derbyshire won by 144 runs. Derbyshire 24 pts, Yorkshire 8 pts. Toss: Derbyshire. A Derbyshire collapse, in which six first-innings wickets fell for the addition of 9 runs, was redeemed by Miller and Base in a last-wicket partnership of 107, 25 short of the county record, also against Yorkshire, set in 1986. Base scored his second half-century, and the stand was one of the crucial phases in an entertaining match. Byas and the hard-hitting Hartley, who added 140 for the seventh wicket in 24 overs, were largely responsible for Yorkshire's lead, but any slight advantage disappeared as Barnett attacked fiercely. The Derbyshire captain and Roberts scored centuries in a partnership of 249, Derbyshire's highest against Yorkshire. Barnett scored 100 from 104 balls with fifteen fours, and went on to 141 from 150 balls. Roberts reached his century from 131 balls, with sixteen fours. Yorkshire, set 307 in 72 overs, were unpicked by Miller's high-class off-spin. Back after three years with Essex, Miller returned his best figures since 1987.

Close of play: First day, Yorkshire 33-0 (M. D. Moxon 9*, A. A. Metcalfe 19*); Second day, Derbyshire 148-1 (K. J. Barnett 93*, B. Roberts 43*).

Derbyshire

*K. J. Barnett c Byas b Fletcher	38	– c Blakey b Hartley 141
J. E. Morris c Byas b Hartley	60	– c Blakey b Fletcher 5
B. Roberts c Byas b Jarvis	49	– not out 124
P. D. Bowler lbw b Fletcher	29	
C. J. Adams run out	12	– c Metcalfe b Byas 10
S. C. Goldsmith c Byas b Hartley	0	– c Moxon b Byas 8
†K. M. Krikken c Bairstow b Hartley	0	
G. Miller not out	47	
I. R. Bishop c Berry b Fletcher	0	
A. E. Warner c Moxon b Jarvis	1	– (4) c Blakey b Hartley 10
S. J. Base c Hartley b Berry	58	– (7) c Robinson b Byas 7
L-b 16, w 1, n-b 6	23	B 1, l-b 9, w 3, n-b 3 16
1/44 2/119 3/180 4/201 5/201 6/201 7/207 8/207 9/210	317	1/10 2/259 3/272 4/292 5/308 6/321 (6 wkts dec.) 321

Bonus points – Derbyshire 4, Yorkshire 4.

Bowling: *First Innings*—Jarvis 29–5–88–2; Hartley 23–4–80–3; Fletcher 24–9–57–3; Byas 8–3–28–0; Berry 13.4–1–48–1. *Second Innings*—Jarvis 12–0–59–0; Fletcher 14–1–100–1; Hartley 14–0–74–2; Berry 9–2–23–0; Byas 11–1–55–3.

Yorkshire

*M. D. Moxon b Warner	45	– c Krikken b Warner 15
A. A. Metcalfe c Krikken b Bishop	32	– c Roberts b Bishop 5
R. J. Blakey c Bowler b Goldsmith	9	– c Goldsmith b Miller 25
S. A. Kellett b Barnett	22	– lbw b Miller 55
P. E. Robinson c Roberts b Base	12	– lbw b Miller 1
†D. L. Bairstow lbw b Base	19	– b Miller 21
D. Byas c Krikken b Bishop	67	– c Goldsmith b Bishop 6
P. J. Hartley c Goldsmith b Warner	75	– c Bowler b Miller 11
P. W. Jarvis c Base b Bishop	15	– c Adams b Bishop 8
P. J. Berry not out	6	– not out 4
S. D. Fletcher c Bowler b Bishop	2	– b Miller 0
L-b 12, w 3, n-b 13	28	L-b 2, w 2, n-b 7 11
1/64 2/80 3/118 4/131 5/143 6/157 7/297 8/308 9/319	332	1/16 2/26 3/78 4/82 5/114 6/135 7/141 8/158 9/158 162

Bonus points – Yorkshire 4, Derbyshire 4.

Bowling: *First Innings*—Bishop 21.2–6–62–4; Base 15–0–72–2; Warner 22–1–90–2; Barnett 9–1–37–1; Goldsmith 7–1–21–1; Miller 11–2–38–0. *Second Innings*—Bishop 18–3–42–3; Warner 10–4–32–1; Base 7–1–29–0; Miller 20.3–6–45–6; Barnett 6–1–12–0.

Umpires: P. J. Eele and A. A. Jones.

DERBYSHIRE v NOTTINGHAMSHIRE

At Derby, May 26, 27, 28. Drawn. Derbyshire 7 pts, Nottinghamshire 6 pts. Toss: Derbyshire. Mortensen gained least reward in Nottinghamshire's first innings, although he was the outstanding bowler. Only Robinson held the visitors together. However, Derbyshire also lost their way after a fine 103 by Morris, whose century came from 193 balls and included seventeen fours. Krikken's 31 was the next highest score. Cooper's consistent accuracy was rewarded by five wickets, limiting Derbyshire's lead to 52, and on the final day Nottinghamshire were steered to safety by French's maiden century. He was struck on the helmet three times but batted with courage and application to achieve three figures from 154 balls, hitting a six and seventeen fours. Randall also batted with determination, and Robinson's declaration was little more than a gesture. The evident ill-feeling in the match reflected no credit on the teams, who ended it as joint leaders of the Championship.

Close of play: First day, Derbyshire 71-2 (J. E. Morris 20*, B. Roberts 12*); Second day, Nottinghamshire 143-4 (D. W. Randall 39*, M. Saxelby 14*).

Nottinghamshire

B. C. Broad c Adams b Warner	45	– lbw b Mortensen	50
D. J. R. Martindale lbw b Mortensen	12	– c Krikken b Malcolm	2
*R. T. Robinson c Adams b Malcolm	69	– lbw b Bishop	15
P. Johnson c Mortensen b Bishop	20	– c Roberts b Malcolm	2
D. W. Randall c Krikken b Bishop	12	– c Roberts b Mortensen	88
M. Saxelby c Krikken b Warner	6	– c Roberts b Bishop	14
†B. N. French c Krikken b Malcolm	9	– not out	105
G. W. Mike c Krikken b Warner	11	– b Barnett	7
K. E. Cooper c Warner b Bishop	16	– not out	35
R. A. Pick not out	1		
J. A. Afford c Roberts b Malcolm	0		
B 4, l-b 12, w 3, n-b 2	21	B 12, l-b 21, w 12, n-b 6	51
1/53 2/77 3/120 4/134 5/147 6/162 7/179 8/216 9/222	222	1/10 2/46 3/55 4/99 5/145 6/234 7/287 (7 wkts dec.)	369

Bonus points – Nottinghamshire 2, Derbyshire 4.

Bowling: *First Innings*—Bishop 18–3–60–3; Malcolm 16.2–2–46–3; Warner 23–4–64–3; Mortensen 24–12–36–1. *Second Innings*—Bishop 24–7–57–2; Malcolm 31–3–106–2; Warner 20–3–72–0; Mortensen 19–5–73–2; Barnett 6–0–28–1.

Derbyshire

*K. J. Barnett c Randall b Cooper	29	– not out	46
P. D. Bowler c Randall b Pick	8	– (4) c French b Cooper	23
J. E. Morris c French b Saxelby	103	– (2) c and b Cooper	7
B. Roberts b Pick	15	– (5) c French b Afford	7
C. J. Adams c Randall b Mike	14	– (6) not out	4
S. C. Goldsmith c French b Cooper	30		
†K. M. Krikken b Cooper	31		
I. R. Bishop lbw b Cooper	8		
A. E. Warner run out	8	– (3) c Mike b Pick	1
O. H. Mortensen not out	0		
D. E. Malcolm b Cooper	12		
L-b 4, w 1, n-b 11	16	B 4, l-b 3, n-b 8	15
1/32 2/42 3/97 4/141 5/191 6/235 7/243 8/258 9/262	274	1/8 2/21 3/73 4/91 (4 wkts)	103

Bonus points – Derbyshire 3, Nottinghamshire 4.

Bowling: *First Innings*—Pick 24–3–97–2; Cooper 25–6–72–5; Mike 14–2–59–1; Afford 18–9–21–0; Saxelby 3–0–21–1. *Second Innings*—Pick 11–1–38–1; Cooper 12–4–36–2; Afford 11–7–13–1; Mike 4–1–9–0.

Umpires: P. J. Eele and A. A. Jones.

At Derby, June 2, 3, 4. DERBYSHIRE lost to NEW ZEALANDERS by 82 runs (See New Zealand tour section).

At The Oval, June 6, 7, 8. DERBYSHIRE drew with SURREY.

DERBYSHIRE v WARWICKSHIRE

At Derby, June 16, 18, 19. Warwickshire won by two wickets. Warwickshire 16 pts, Derbyshire 4 pts. Toss: Warwickshire. The pitch was so obviously bland that Reeve, Warwickshire's captain, sent for Moody, a batsman, to replace Donald, a bowler, as the county's overseas player. Barnett and Bowler scored centuries in Derbyshire's highest opening stand against Warwickshire, and there was a chance of the first four in the order reaching three figures, something not achieved in Championship cricket since Middlesex did it in 1923. Rain prevented play until five o'clock on the second day, after which Morris completed his century but Roberts fell 14 runs short. It was only the fourth time in Derbyshire's history that three or more players had scored centuries in an innings. After negotiations and a forfeiture, Warwickshire were set 350 in what would have been 83 overs. Moody, in his first Championship innings, batted magnificently to win a game in which the opposition had lost only four wickets, reaching his hundred with two consecutive sixes off Miller. When caught at third man, he had made 168 from 173 balls with six sixes and nineteen fours. Ostler then saw Warwickshire to victory with an over to spare.

Close of play: First day, Derbyshire 408-2 (J. E. Morris 70*, B. Roberts 70*); Second day, Warwickshire 25-0 (A. J. Moles 11*, J. D. Ratcliffe 14*).

Derbyshire

*K. J. Barnett c Small b Munton	131
P. D. Bowler c Reeve b Moody	120
J. E. Morris not out	103
B. Roberts c Reeve b Twose	86
A. P. Kuiper c Reeve b Munton	11
C. J. Adams not out	6
B 5, l-b 8, w 2, n-b 3	18
1/249 2/281 3/437 4/452	(4 wkts dec.) 475

†K. M. Krikken, G. Miller, S. J. Base, D. E. Malcolm and A. E. Warner did not bat.

Bonus points – Derbyshire 4 (Score at 100 overs: 340-2).

Bowling: Small 14–3–44–0; Munton 29.2–4–105–2; Pierson 37–9–84–0; Twose 17–1–82–1; Moody 7–0–43–1; Asif Din 19–1–85–0; Moles 7–2–19–0.

Derbyshire forfeited their second innings.

Warwickshire

A. J. Moles not out	70	– c Krikken b Malcolm	4
J. D. Ratcliffe c and b Bowler	38	– c Roberts b Base	25
Asif Din not out	17	– c Miller b Base	30
T. M. Moody (did not bat)		– c Base b Malcolm	168
†G. W. Humpage (did not bat)		– b Barnett	34
*D. A. Reeve (did not bat)		– c Krikken b Malcolm	25
R. G. Twose (did not bat)		– lbw b Malcolm	1
D. P. Ostler (did not bat)		– not out	42
G. C. Small (did not bat)		– run out	8
T. A. Munton (did not bat)		– not out	0
L-b 1	1	L-b 8, w 3, n-b 5	16
1/74	(1 wkt dec.) 126	1/9 2/54 3/80 4/152 5/261 6/271 7/334 8/349	(8 wkts) 353

A. R. K. Pierson did not bat.

Bowling: *First Innings*—Miller 7–4–11–0; Warner 3–1–9–0; Barnett 4–2–5–0; Morris 6–0–52–0; Bowler 6–0–48–1. *Second Innings*—Malcolm 19–1–63–4; Warner 17–4–66–0; Base 18–2–88–2; Kuiper 6–1–18–0; Miller 12–0–71–0; Barnett 10–1–39–1.

Umpires: J. H. Hampshire and A. G. T. Whitehead.

At Leicester, June 20, 21, 22. DERBYSHIRE lost to LEICESTERSHIRE by 140 runs.

DERBYSHIRE v GLOUCESTERSHIRE

At Derby, June 30, July 2, 3. Drawn. Derbyshire 4 pts, Gloucestershire 4 pts. Toss: Derbyshire. Barnett scored his 30th century for Derbyshire to equal the record set by Denis Smith in 1950. It was the first of three hundreds in consecutive Championship innings by Barnett, followed by an unbeaten 90 against Lancashire. There was no substance in either first innings, good bowling and poor batting combining as the first twenty wickets fell for 186. On a first day in which 56 overs were lost, Derbyshire collapsed against Walsh and Lawrence, and then Malcolm and Bishop made inroads into the Gloucestershire innings. With help from Mortensen, they completed the rout next day. Derbyshire batted freely in the second innings and Barnett reached his century from 181 balls, hitting twelve fours. It was his 387th innings for Derbyshire, whereas Smith batted 711 times for the county. Umpire Holder intervened as an argument followed the bowling of a beamer by Walsh to Bowler. Gloucestershire were set 305 in 70 overs but, despite a good start by Wright and Hodgson, they found the chase too demanding and concentrated on saving the game.

Close of play: First day, Gloucestershire 39-4 (P. Bainbridge 3*, K. M. Curran 3*); Second day, Derbyshire 233-3 (B. Roberts 10*, C. J. Adams 5*).

Derbyshire

*K. J. Barnett b Lawrence	7	– c Curran b Walsh	107
P. D. Bowler b Walsh	5	– lbw b Walsh	23
J. E. Morris c Athey b Walsh	9	– c Athey b Lloyds	66
B. Roberts c Barnes b Lawrence	2	– b Barnes	59
C. J. Adams b Barnes	7	– lbw b Barnes	48
S. C. Goldsmith lbw b Lawrence	5	– not out	7
†K. M. Krikken c Lloyds b Barnes	9	– c Russell b Curran	1
M. Jean-Jacques b Lawrence	7	– not out	3
I. R. Bishop b Walsh	10		
D. E. Malcolm not out	0		
O. H. Mortensen b Walsh	4		
N-b 7	7	B 3, l-b 13, w 1, n-b 15	32
1/11 2/13 3/23 4/26 5/31 6/44 7/49 8/68 9/68	72	1/74 2/202 3/213 4/328 5/337 6/338 (6 wkts dec.)	346

Bonus points – Gloucestershire 4.

Bowling: *First Innings*—Walsh 14–2–32–4; Lawrence 10–1–27–4; Curran 3–1–3–0; Barnes 6–2–10–2. *Second Innings*—Walsh 26.4–2–86–2; Lawrence 3–0–20–0; Curran 20.2–2–75–1; Lloyds 29–6–74–1; Barnes 23–2–75–2.

Gloucestershire

G. D. Hodgson c Morris b Bishop	13	– c Krikken b Bishop	52
*A. J. Wright c Morris b Malcolm	3	– c Krikken b Jean-Jacques	44
I. P. Butcher c Krikken b Malcolm	0	– (8) not out	0
C. W. J. Athey lbw b Bishop	12	– (3) b Bishop	21
P. Bainbridge lbw b Bishop	6	– (4) lbw b Barnett	40
K. M. Curran b Bishop	24	– (5) c Morris b Jean-Jacques	3
J. W. Lloyds not out	28	– (6) not out	25
†R. C. Russell b Mortensen	2	– (7) c Krikken b Barnett	15
C. A. Walsh b Mortensen	1		
D. V. Lawrence c Krikken b Mortensen	8		
S. N. Barnes lbw b Mortensen	6		
B 3, l-b 5, w 3	11	B 1, l-b 3	4
1/7 2/7 3/33 4/34 5/43 6/71 7/74 8/78 9/96	114	1/81 2/116 3/137 4/146 5/170 6/198 (6 wkts)	204

Bonus points – Derbyshire 4.

Bowling: *First Innings*—Bishop 19–4–38–4; Malcolm 18–5–46–2; Mortensen 15–7–22–4. *Second Innings*—Bishop 14–1–44–2; Malcolm 17–4–49–0; Mortensen 17–2–52–0; Jean-Jacques 8–0–26–2; Barnett 11–6–19–2; Morris 1–0–10–0.

Umpires: J. W. Holder and B. Leadbeater.

At Hove, July 4, 5, 6. DERBYSHIRE beat SUSSEX by 18 runs.

At Liverpool, July 7, 9, 10. DERBYSHIRE drew with LANCASHIRE.

At Chesterfield, July 16. DERBYSHIRE lost to INDIANS by two wickets (See Indian tour section).

At Colchester, July 18, 19, 20. DERBYSHIRE lost to ESSEX by nine wickets.

At Portsmouth, July 21, 23, 24. DERBYSHIRE lost to HAMPSHIRE by 48 runs.

DERBYSHIRE v WORCESTERSHIRE

At Derby, July 25, 26, 27. Drawn. Derbyshire 2 pts, Worcestershire 7 pts. Toss: Worcestershire. Hick arrived with 592 runs since his last dismissal and needed a further 118 to pass the first-class record set by K. C. Ibrahim in India in 1947-48. He made 53 before falling to a spectacular slip catch by Adams. On an uncertain pitch, Worcestershire concentrated on building a big total, and Derbyshire's bowling was stretched when Mortensen withdrew with a calf injury, even though Base filled the breach with his best return of the season. Worcestershire's decision to bat into the second day was justified when they were able to enforce the follow-on. Derbyshire's batting lacked resolution against Illingworth and Lampitt, who shared the wickets. However, Adams and Brown batted well in the second innings as Derbyshire fought to save the game, and rain, coming ten minutes before the start of the last hour, denied an intriguing finish. Illingworth's sustained effort was reflected in match figures of 91–50–111–8.

Close of play: First day, Worcestershire 332-9 (S. R. Lampitt 10*, N. V. Radford 5*); Second day, Derbyshire 39-1 (A. M. Brown 11*, T. J. G. O'Gorman 8*).

Worcestershire

T. S. Curtis c Krikken b Base	17	P. J. Newport c Barnett b Base	2
C. M. Tolley lbw b Base	16	S. R. Lampitt not out	16
G. A. Hick c Adams b Warner	53	N. V. Radford c Krikken b Base	14
D. B. D'Oliveira b Warner	87		
I. T. Botham c Brown b Barnett	27	B 12, l-b 15, w 5, n-b 13	45
*P. A. Neale c Roberts b Warner	65		——
†S. J. Rhodes c Krikken b Base	0	1/35 2/44 3/136 4/173	348
R. K. Illingworth c Adams b Base	6	5/275 6/277 7/295 8/310 9/323	

Bonus points – Worcestershire 3, Derbyshire 1 (Score at 100 overs: 269-4).

Bowling: Mortensen 3–2–4–0; Base 39.3–3–105–6; Kuiper 19–8–42–0; Barnett 32–8–61–1; Warner 30–5–109–3.

Derbyshire

P. D. Bowler c Botham b Illingworth	36	– c Rhodes b Newport	18
A. M. Brown lbw b Illingworth	32	– c Rhodes b Hick	42
T. J. G. O'Gorman c Radford b Illingworth	0	– c Neale b Lampitt	9
C. J. Adams c Rhodes b Illingworth	32	– st Rhodes b Illingworth	63
A. P. Kuiper c Hick b Lampitt	38	– b Hick	41
B. Roberts c Hick b Lampitt	18	– c Rhodes b Illingworth	0
*K. J. Barnett b Lampitt	9	– c Rhodes b Illingworth	23
†K. M. Krikken lbw b Lampitt	4	– c Neale b Newport	13
A. E. Warner lbw b Lampitt	4	– not out	5
S. J. Base b Illingworth	14	– not out	0
O. H. Mortensen not out	0		
L-b 2, n-b 3	5	B 9, l-b 12	21
1/61 2/61 3/76 4/121 5/147 6/164 7/171 8/175 9/192	192	1/24 2/50 3/119 4/181 5/181 6/201 7/229 8/235	(8 wkts) 235

Bonus points – Derbyshire 1, Worcestershire 4.

Bowling: *First Innings*—Newport 8–1–23–0; Radford 5–0–23–0; Botham 7–2–12–0; Illingworth 38–19–59–5; Hick 14–2–39–0; Lampitt 19.4–6–34–5. *Second Innings*—Newport 7–1–29–2; Radford 4–2–10–0; Illingworth 53–31–52–3; Hick 25–9–45–2; Lampitt 19–3–52–1; Botham 6–1–26–0.

Umpires: P. J. Eele and K. J. Lyons.

DERBYSHIRE v KENT

At Chesterfield, August 4, 6, 7. Derbyshire won by ten wickets. Derbyshire 24 pts, Kent 5 pts. Toss: Kent. Bishop gave Derbyshire an early advantage by dismissing the openers in his first two overs and went on to take six wickets. The support, however, was poor and Ward, who had missed two months of the season with an ankle injury, played powerful and attractive strokes in a career-best 124 from 152 balls, with a six and twenty fours. Bowler scored his first double-century, the county's highest against Kent, and Derbyshire passed 500 for the first time since 1952, against Nottinghamshire at Ilkeston. Kent were weakened by injuries to Ellison and de Villiers as Bowler shared three century partnerships, reached 200 from 353 balls with a five and 25 fours, and batted for 412 minutes. Roberts took full advantage of the situation to hit an unbeaten 100 from 117 balls (four sixes, ten fours). Kent's top batting showed little resolution in the second innings as Jean-Jacques produced his best figures for four years, but Ellison organised more determined resistance. Derbyshire awarded caps to Bishop and Base on the second morning.

Close of play: First day, Derbyshire 110-0 (K. J. Barnett 49*, P. D. Bowler 57*); Second day, Derbyshire 514-5 (B. Roberts 100*, K. M. Krikken 27*).

Kent

S. G. Hinks c Krikken b Bishop	0	– c Roberts b Jean-Jacques	9
*M. R. Benson c Morris b Bishop	0	– b Malcolm	15
N. R. Taylor c Krikken b Base	18	– c Bowler b Jean-Jacques	12
G. R. Cowdrey c Krikken b Malcolm	6	– c Bowler b Jean-Jacques	21
T. R. Ward lbw b Base	124	– c Krikken b Base	5
†S. A. Marsh c Adams b Bishop	38	– c Krikken b Jean-Jacques	4
R. M. Ellison c Roberts b Base	41	– c Krikken b Jean-Jacques	62
R. P. Davis c Krikken b Bishop	41	– c Brown b Malcolm	26
P. S. de Villiers c Roberts b Bishop	5	– c Base b Bishop	30
M. M. Patel c Roberts b Bishop	7	– not out	25
A. P. Igglesden not out	1	– b Jean-Jacques	2
L-b 3, w 5, n-b 14	22	B 4, l-b 4, w 1, n-b 12	21
1/2 2/3 3/15 4/40 5/133 6/231 7/245 8/259 9/293	303	1/29 2/35 3/46 4/58 5/70 6/89 7/134 8/187 9/214	232

Bonus points – Kent 4, Derbyshire 4.

Bowling: *First Innings*—Bishop 22.1–3–71–6; Malcolm 18–7–58–1; Base 21–3–85–3; Jean-Jacques 21–2–84–0; Barnett 2–1–2–0. *Second Innings*—Bishop 15–4–45–1; Malcolm 17–0–57–2; Jean-Jacques 20.4–5–60–6; Base 19–3–59–1; Barnett 1–0–3–0.

Derbyshire

*K. J. Barnett c Davis b de Villiers	64	– not out	10
P. D. Bowler c Cowdrey b Patel	210	– not out	13
J. E. Morris c de Villiers b Davis	32		
A. M. Brown lbw b Igglesden	6		
C. J. Adams c Taylor b Patel	52		
B. Roberts not out	100		
†K. M. Krikken not out	27		
B 2, l-b 20, w 1	23	W 1	1
1/138 2/179 3/191 4/304 5/449	(5 wkts dec.) 514		(no wkt) 24

I. R. Bishop, M. Jean-Jacques, S. J. Base and D. E. Malcolm did not bat.

Bonus points – Derbyshire 4, Kent 1 (Score at 100 overs: 376-4).

Bowling: *First Innings*—de Villiers 21–3–75–1; Igglesden 25–4–113–1; Ellison 6–0–26–0; Davis 39–8–152–1; Patel 27–6–97–2; Hinks 7–0–29–0. *Second Innings*—Marsh 3.4–0–16–0; Taylor 3–0–8–0.

Umpires: J. H. Hampshire and B. Hassan.

DERBYSHIRE v NORTHAMPTONSHIRE

At Chesterfield, August 8, 9, 10. Drawn. Derbyshire 6 pts, Northamptonshire 7 pts. Toss: Northamptonshire. Brown, released by Derbyshire in 1987 and re-engaged for 1990, held an uneven innings together with his maiden century. After spending eight increasingly fretful overs on 99, he reached three figures in 306 minutes from 294 balls. On the second day, he was hit on the left hand by a ball from Ambrose and forced to retire with a broken knuckle, which put him out for the rest of the season. Northamptonshire replied enterprisingly, and Capel, off 79 balls, hit a remarkable century which included eight sixes, a five and eight fours. Larkins declared behind and, after Northamptonshire's bowling changes had encouraged free scoring, Barnett set them 269 in what became 51 overs. Everything depended on Bailey, although Capel (50 from 40 balls) again batted excitingly. Bailey hit four sixes and fourteen fours in a fine display as an ultimately entertaining match ended in a draw, Northamptonshire finishing 19 runs short of victory with two wickets standing.

Close of play: First day, Derbyshire 282-7 (A. M. Brown 122*, G. Miller 11*); Second day, Derbyshire 6-0 (K. J. Barnett 2*, P. D. Bowler 4*).

Derbyshire

*K. J. Barnett b Robinson	20	– c Ripley b Robinson	3
P. D. Bowler c Ripley b Robinson	22	– b Hughes	40
A. M. Brown retired hurt	139		
T. J. G. O'Gorman c Ripley b Hughes	19	– (3) c Bailey b Felton	82
C. J. Adams c Larkins b Robinson	5	– (4) c Fordham b Bailey	12
B. Roberts c Felton b Ambrose	34	– (5) not out	56
†K. M. Krikken c Capel b Ambrose	0	– (6) c Robinson b Cook	24
I. R. Bishop b Williams	34	– (7) c and b Cook	0
G. Miller b Hughes	36	– (8) not out	6
A. E. Warner run out	24		
O. H. Mortensen not out	0		
L-b 9, n-b 6	15	L-b 10, n-b 1	11
1/45 2/46 3/99 4/118 5/181 6/181 7/248 8/344 9/348	348	1/9 2/73 3/109 4/153 5/204 6/206	(6 wkts dec.) 234

Bonus points – Derbyshire 3, Northamptonshire 3 (Score at 100 overs: 251-7).

In the first innings A. M. Brown retired hurt at 320.

Bowling: *First Innings*—Ambrose 33–8–90–2; Robinson 26–9–96–3; Williams 35–19–41–1; Hughes 15–2–57–2; Cook 19–2–55–0. *Second Innings*—Ambrose 9–2–20–0; Robinson 7–1–24–1; Hughes 8–1–36–1; Bailey 17–4–44–1; Larkins 4–0–24–0; Felton 6–0–48–1; Cook 4–1–19–2; Williams 3–0–9–0.

Northamptonshire

A. Fordham c and b Miller	74	– c Krikken b Bishop	4
N. A. Felton c O'Gorman b Mortensen	5	– c Warner b Miller	42
*W. Larkins c sub b Mortensen	16	– c O'Gorman b Miller	5
R. J. Bailey run out	79	– not out	134
D. J. Capel not out	103	– c Krikken b Warner	50
R. G. Williams lbw b Bishop	9	– c Adams b Warner	4
†D. Ripley c Barnett b Warner	12	– hit wkt b Bishop	0
J. G. Hughes b Warner	0	– (9) run out	0
N. G. B. Cook not out	0	– (8) run out	4
C. E. L. Ambrose (did not bat)		– not out	0
L-b 13, n-b 3	16	B 1, l-b 6	7
1/16 2/38 3/185 4/186 5/221 6/310 7/310 (7 wkts dec.)	314	1/4 2/18 3/91 4/188 5/211 6/211 7/235 8/246 (8 wkts)	250

M. A. Robinson did not bat.

Bonus points – Northamptonshire 4, Derbyshire 3.

Bowling: *First Innings*—Bishop 15–6–27–1; Mortensen 13–1–43–2; Warner 21–4–68–2; Miller 19.2–2–108–1; Barnett 12–2–32–0; Roberts 5–0–23–0. *Second Innings*—Bishop 13.5–2–43–2; Mortensen 13–2–42–0; Miller 12–0–62–2; Warner 12–0–96–2.

Umpires: H. D. Bird and B. Hassan.

DERBYSHIRE v MIDDLESEX

At Derby, August 18, 20, 21. Derbyshire won by 171 runs. Derbyshire 22 pts, Middlesex 6 pts. Toss: Derbyshire. Derbyshire became the first county to beat Middlesex in the 1990 Championship, but it was obvious from the first day that the pitch was unsatisfactory. The umpires reported it and, after inspection by Donald Carr (chairman of the TCCB Pitches Committee), Tim Lamb (TCCB Cricket Secretary), Doug Lucas (Northamptonshire) and Old Trafford groundsman Peter Marron, the deputy Inspector of Pitches, Derbyshire had 25 points deducted. "The pitch was clearly unsuitable for first-class cricket", said the TCCB. There was, however, some interesting cricket. After Morris and O'Gorman batted well for Derbyshire, Gatting compiled a magnificent century from 217 balls, hitting fifteen fours in his innings. His display was the more commendable because weekend rain had forced its way under the covers, and Derbyshire's chairman, Chris Middleton, wrote to Middlesex thanking Gatting for his attitude in an embarrassing situation for the home county. Roberts and Miller suggested that sensible application would bring its rewards, but Middlesex, set 271 in a minimum of 54 overs, responded feebly. Base wrecked their innings and bowled well, perhaps too well for Derbyshire's ultimate good.

Close of play: First day, Middlesex 68-3 (M. W. Gatting 31*, D. L. Haynes 8*); Second day, Derbyshire 116-3 (T. J. G. O'Gorman 10*, A. P. Kuiper 20*).

Derbyshire

*K. J. Barnett c Downton b Fraser	3	– c Gatting b Emburey	7
P. D. Bowler b Emburey	38	– c Gatting b Emburey	56
J. E. Morris b Emburey	67	– c Roseberry b Tufnell	12
T. J. G. O'Gorman c Brown b Emburey	55	– c Brown b Fraser	20
A. P. Kuiper b Fraser	0	– c Downton b Emburey	30
B. Roberts c Haynes b Williams	27	– not out	48
†K. M. Krikken c Brown b Emburey	3	– c Roseberry b Emburey	0
G. Miller lbw b Cowans	1	– not out	32
M. Jean-Jacques not out	17		
S. J. Base lbw b Emburey	0		
O. H. Mortensen c Brown b Fraser	1		
B 10, l-b 24, w 1, n-b 2	37	L-b 16, n-b 9	25
1/4 2/112 3/119 4/126 5/176 6/203 7/204 8/236 9/236	249	1/36 2/70 3/91 4/131 5/137 6/143 (6 wkts dec.)	230

Bonus points – Derbyshire 2, Middlesex 4.

Bowling: *First Innings*—Fraser 19.1–4–49–3; Williams 16–2–56–1; Cowans 12–3–40–1; Tufnell 16–6–38–0; Emburey 18–4–32–5. *Second Innings*—Fraser 19–5–46–1; Williams 10–1–39–0; Emburey 36–8–71–4; Cowans 4–0–14–0; Tufnell 16–3–29–1; Ramprakash 2–0–15–0.

Middlesex

M. A. Roseberry c Bowler b Mortensen	7	– (2) b Base	2
N. F. Williams lbw b Base	5	– (8) c Bowler b Miller	3
*M. W. Gatting not out	119	– (5) c Kuiper b Base	4
M. R. Ramprakash lbw b Base	1	– (3) lbw b Base	8
D. L. Haynes b Mortensen	12	– (1) c Kuiper b Mortensen	8
K. R. Brown c Krikken b Mortensen	7	– (4) c Kuiper b Base	12
†P. R. Downton c and b Mortensen	4	– (6) c Barnett b Base	3
J. E. Emburey b Miller	14	– (7) c Bowler b Jean-Jacques	12
A. R. C. Fraser b Base	8	– st Krikken b Miller	26
P. C. R. Tufnell c O'Gorman b Miller	10	– lbw b Miller	5
N. G. Cowans c Jean-Jacques b Miller	0	– not out	5
B 10, l-b 7, n-b 5	22	B 8, l-b 2, n-b 1	11
1/13 2/17 3/28 4/79 5/89 6/97 7/155 8/166 9/205	209	1/4 2/18 3/22 4/28 5/37 6/38 7/41 8/88 9/94	99

Bonus points – Middlesex 2, Derbyshire 4.

Bowling: *First Innings*—Base 27–4–92–3; Mortensen 22–11–29–4; Miller 14.5–3–31–3; Jean-Jacques 15–2–40–0. *Second Innings*—Mortensen 10–4–21–1; Base 14–3–28–5; Miller 9.5–3–21–3; Jean-Jacques 5–0–19–1.

Umpires: J. C. Balderstone and P. B. Wight.

DERBYSHIRE v ESSEX

At Derby, August 23, 24. Essex won by an innings and 94 runs. Essex 24 pts, Derbyshire 3 pts. Toss: Derbyshire. For the second time in five weeks, Derbyshire were totally outplayed by Essex. After the deduction of 25 points earlier in the week, more grass was left on to hold the Derby pitch together, but it was woefully inadequate batting, rather than the green tinge, which caused the collapse against Foster and Ilott. Only Bishop gave evidence of sound technique as Ilott returned the best figures of his career to date. Prichard, who completed his fourth century of the season from 201 balls with eleven fours, and Waugh shared a stand of 126 in 38 overs, and although Essex did not make the most of their position, a lead of 221 was more than adequate. The impressive Ilott dismissed Barnett cheaply for a second time and, despite some hectic counter-attacking by Adams and Goldsmith, Derbyshire collapsed again. They batted for fewer than 80 overs in the match and nothing impeded Essex as they emphasised their challenge for the Championship.

Close of play: First day, Essex 207-3 (P. J. Prichard 65*, M. C. Ilott 2*).

Derbyshire

*K. J. Barnett lbw b Ilott	4	– b Ilott	3
P. D. Bowler c Waugh b Ilott	11	– b Foster	5
T. J. G. O'Gorman c Garnham b Foster	1	– c Garnham b Foster	4
C. J. Adams c Garnham b Foster	0	– c Garnham b Andrew	41
B. Roberts b Ilott	13	– c and b Foster	7
S. C. Goldsmith c Shahid b Foster	11	– lbw b Andrew	32
†K. M. Krikken b Ilott	2	– c Hussain b Ilott	14
G. Miller c Garnham b Foster	19	– absent ill	
I. R. Bishop not out	39	– (8) lbw b Andrew	17
A. E. Warner c Garnham b Foster	4	– (9) lbw b Andrew	0
M. Jean-Jacques lbw b Ilott	0	– (10) not out	0
L-b 6	6	L-b 4	4
1/5 2/16 3/16 4/17 5/41 6/41 7/47 8/91 9/101	110	1/8 2/12 3/12 4/22 5/84 6/99 7/125 8/125 9/127	127

Bonus points – Essex 4.

Bowling: *First Innings*—Foster 16–6–39–5; Ilott 18.4–8–34–5; Andrew 6–2–18–0; Pringle 3–0–13–0. *Second Innings*—Ilott 10.4–3–34–2; Foster 11–1–57–3; Andrew 11–2–30–4; Childs 3–2–2–0.

Essex

N. Shahid c Krikken b Warner	55	N. A. Foster c Adams b Bishop	25
J. P. Stephenson c Adams b Warner	11	J. H. Childs c Krikken b Bishop	8
P. J. Prichard run out	103	S. J. W. Andrew not out	6
M. E. Waugh c Barnett b Jean-Jacques	61		
M. C. Ilott c Adams b Bishop	6	L-b 6, w 3, n-b 11	20
N. Hussain c Adams b Goldsmith	28		
†M. A. Garnham c Roberts b Warner	8	1/59 2/79 3/205 4/234	331
*D. R. Pringle b Goldsmith	0	5/274 6/284 7/284 8/294 9/316	

Bonus points – Essex 4, Derbyshire 3 (Score at 100 overs: 306-8).

Bowling: Bishop 23.5–7–57–3; Warner 24–7–56–3; Jean-Jacques 24–3–105–1; Goldsmith 33–6–105–2; Barnett 1–0–2–0.

Umpires: D. J. Constant and R. Julian.

At Cardiff, August 29, 30, 31. DERBYSHIRE drew with GLAMORGAN.

At Scarborough, September 7, 8, 9, 10. DERBYSHIRE lost to YORKSHIRE by four wickets.

DERBYSHIRE v LEICESTERSHIRE

At Derby, September 18, 19, 20, 21. Drawn. Derbyshire 6 pts, Leicestershire 6 pts. Toss: Derbyshire. After a good start, Leicestershire lost their last nine wickets while adding 60 on a bleakly cold first day which set the tone for a cheerless match. Briers and Whitaker added 133 in 39 overs before Bishop took four for 3 in 21 balls, Briers falling 1 run short of his sixth century of the season. Mortensen finished the innings with three for 1 in fourteen balls. Fewer than two hours of play were possible on the second day, but on the third O'Gorman, who spent much of the summer at Law School, reached 100 from 185 balls, with thirteen fours. It was Derbyshire's 21st first-class century of the season, a county record, but there was little assistance for O'Gorman as Lewis took five for 4 in 36 balls. Briers was 4 short of 2,000 runs when Leicestershire collapsed to 9 for three before the close, leaving themselves to bat through for survival on the final day.

Close of play: First day, Derbyshire 19-1 (T. J. G. O'Gorman 9*, K. M. Krikken 1*); Second day, Derbyshire 124-3 (T. J. G. O'Gorman 64*, C. J. Adams 29*); Third day, Leicestershire 9-3 (J. J. Whitaker 0*, L. Potter 0*).

Leicestershire

T. J. Boon c Barnett b Base	15	– lbw b Base	7
*N. E. Briers b Bishop	99	– b Bishop	2
J. J. Whitaker c Barnett b Base	65	– c Barnett b Bishop	20
P. Willey b Bishop	1	– b Base	0
L. Potter c Krikken b Bishop	2	– lbw b Barnett	65
C. C. Lewis lbw b Bishop	0	– (7) c Adams b Base	54
P. N. Hepworth not out	14	– (6) not out	55
†P. A. Nixon c Roberts b Bishop	17		
C. J. Hawkes c Krikken b Mortensen	3	– (8) not out	2
J. P. Agnew c Krikken b Mortensen	6		
A. D. Mullally lbw b Mortensen	0		
B 5, l-b 10, w 2, n-b 8	25	B 1, l-b 9, n-b 1	11
1/54 2/187 3/196 4/197 5/197 6/200 7/221 8/233 9/247	247	1/9 2/9 3/9 4/48 5/136 6/209 (6 wkts)	216

Bonus points – Leicestershire 2, Derbyshire 4.

Bowling: *First Innings*—Bishop 26–8–62–5; Mortensen 22.3–8–40–3; Base 18–6–51–2; Cork 10–1–39–0; Goldsmith 14–2–40–0. *Second Innings*—Bishop 14–4–39–2; Base 18–7–51–3; Cork 14–5–31–0; Mortensen 12–2–43–0; Adams 3–0–12–0; Barnett 20–6–30–1.

Derbyshire

*K. J. Barnett b Lewis 4
T. J. G. O'Gorman c Hawkes b Mullally .100
†K. M. Krikken b Mullally 1
B. Roberts b Agnew 15
C. J. Adams b Lewis 54
Z. A. Sadiq b Lewis 0
S. C. Goldsmith b Lewis 0
I. R. Bishop c Nixon b Lewis 3
S. J. Base b Lewis 2
D. G. Cork c Briers b Mullally 7
O. H. Mortensen not out 5
L-b 12, n-b 5 17

1/18 2/19 3/77 4/175 5/181 6/181 7/189 8/195 9/195 — 208

Bonus points – Derbyshire 2, Leicestershire 4.

Bowling: Lewis 24–4–58–6; Mullally 20–7–56–3; Agnew 10–1–42–1; Hawkes 14–3–40–0.

Umpires: H. D. Bird and R. A. White.

OVERS BOWLED AND RUNS SCORED IN THE BRITANNIC ASSURANCE CHAMPIONSHIP, 1990

	Over-rate per hour			*Run-rate per 100 balls*		
	1st half	*2nd half*	*Total*	*1st half*	*2nd half*	*Total*
Derbyshire (12)	18.0979	17.8088*	17.9533	53.6269	53.5073	53.5702
Essex (2)	18.2686	18.2253	18.2453	62.4260	65.2450	63.8246
Glamorgan (8)	18.3779	18.3022	18.3408	54.2284	60.1199	57.2519
Gloucestershire (13=)	17.7610*	18.1417	17.9718	49.7259	51.6533	50.9107
Hampshire (3)	18.0425	18.1264	18.0887	56.4806	54.3076	55.2756
Kent (16)	18.2448	18.5674	18.4175	49.7421	57.0352	53.6008
Lancashire (6)	18.1837	18.1257	18.1550	54.3865	58.7860	56.4164
Leicestershire (7)	17.8532*	18.0865	17.9879	50.6758	51.2370	50.9597
Middlesex (1)	18.9109	18.2565	18.5390	54.6164	61.1399	58.0269
Northamptonshire (11)	17.8331*	18.1644	18.0078	54.6617	62.5912	58.9522
Nottinghamshire (13=)	18.1004	18.0883	18.0944	57.6759	51.1340	54.1506
Somerset (15)	18.1044	18.1669	18.1359	59.5397	57.8061	58.5453
Surrey (9)	17.4340†	17.9146*	17.6866	54.4643	57.8941	56.2931
Sussex (17)	18.0586	18.0742	18.0668	54.2411	48.3362	51.1698
Warwickshire (5)	18.1984	17.6749*	17.9211	55.8116	54.9363	55.3335
Worcestershire (4)	18.2891	18.4505	18.3768	54.9120	55.5606	55.2643
Yorkshire (10)	18.1824	18.1315	18.1537	51.6132	55.9143	53.9978
1990	average rate		18.1260			55.5025
1989	average rate		18.3621			50.6788
1988	average rate		18.9202			49.9340
1987	average rate		18.64			51.79
1986	average rate		18.49			52.22
1985	average rate		18.43			52.61

1990 Championship positions are shown in brackets.
* £2,000 fine. † £3,000 fine.

ESSEX

President: T. N. Pearce
Chairman: D. J. Insole
Chairman, Cricket Committee: G. J. Saville
Secretary/General Manager: P. J. Edwards
County Ground, New Writtle Street,
Chelmsford CM2 0PG
(Telephone: 0245-252420)
Captain: G. A. Gooch

In finishing runners-up in the Britannic Assurance Championship for the second successive year, Essex again ended the season nursing acute pangs of disappointment. Yet their achievement represented something of a success, for in the second week of July they were only three places off the foot of the table. A surge in August, during which they won four matches, saw them emerge as title contenders; but failure to win any of their four final games, when dropped catches cost them dearly, kept them in second place behind Middlesex. In the limited-overs competitions, however, Essex were never seen as a potent force. Defeat in the opening four games of the Refuge Assurance League soon relegated them to "also-rans", and they failed to make home advantage count in the quest to reach a Lord's final. Nottinghamshire beat them by six wickets in their Benson and Hedges Cup quarter-final, while in the second round of the NatWest Bank Trophy, Hampshire won because they lost fewer wickets in equalling the Essex total of 307 for six.

It was through no fault of Graham Gooch that Essex failed to land any of the domestic honours. His deeds at Test level, highlighted by his 333 at Lord's, are well chronicled elsewhere, and he also maintained a phenomenal level of consistency for his county. In the eleven first-class matches in which he batted for them, he never once failed to record at least 50, and only a broken thumb, suffered while fielding against Kent in the penultimate fixture, cost him the opportunity of becoming the first batsman since W. E. Alley in 1961 to register 3,000 runs in a season. No doubt he was satisfied with a golden harvest of 2,746 for a first-class average of 101.70 and a total of eighteen hundreds in all forms of cricket.

Mark Waugh, with an elegant ease bordering on arrogance, displayed a rich talent, and even when confronted with the occasional pitch giving encouragement to bowlers, he showed an ability to gather runs fluently. He contributed eight Championship centuries, including double-hundreds against Gloucestershire and Yorkshire, and an aggregate in excess of 2,000 runs. That landmark was one which narrowly eluded John Stephenson, who showed great character in overcoming a wretched start to the season. By early June he had scored just 265 runs in twelve innings, but in twelve of his remaining eighteen first-class games he collected eleven half-centuries and four centuries, including a career-best 202 not out against Somerset. Paul Prichard was another to record a personal best, scoring 245 in only the second Championship match of the summer, against Leicestershire, on a sweltering Chelmsford day. With Gooch he shared a record-breaking second-wicket partnership of 403, the highest stand for any Essex wicket, and Essex's eventual 761 for six declared was the biggest total in the county's history. Neil Foster reached three figures for the first time before Gooch called off the assault on the Leicestershire bowlers.

Nasser Hussain, on the other hand, could not look back on the summer with any real degree of satisfaction. His inspired form the previous season had earned him a place in the England team to the West Indies, but while there he had fractured his wrist. That injury kept him out of first-class cricket until June 30, and his lack of form on his return, combined with an erosion of confidence, was such that he passed 50 only twice in thirteen Championship matches before, in the final game of the season, scoring 197 against Surrey. By then, however, his hopes of regaining a place in the England side had long disappeared, although selection for the A tour provided an opportunity for him to rediscover his touch.

Foster was easily the pick of the bowlers. There were fears at the outset that his knees would not stand up to the rigours of a gruelling summer, especially on hard grounds. But he swept those aside by displaying remarkable resilience and stamina to send down more than 800 overs in the Championship and emerge as the country's leading wicket-taker with 94 victims, six times claiming five or more wickets in an innings. Unfortunately, the attack lacked anyone with the same degree of penetration at the other end. Derek Pringle missed several matches with a troublesome back, while Steve Andrew, despite the occasional match-winning performance, struggled for consistency. There were no rich pickings for the spinners, having to bowl on unhelpful pitches. John Childs, although missing only the opening game, managed just 27 first-class wickets at an average of 58.88, and Peter Such's eleven matches produced a mere twenty dismissals.

Probably the most pleasing aspect was the performance of the younger players. Nadeem Shahid grasped the opportunity to prove himself a fluent batsman and was rewarded with just over 1,000 runs, including a maiden century against Lancashire at Colchester. In addition, he demonstrated a fearlessness in the bat-pad position, where he held several fine catches. Mark Ilott, a left-arm seam bowler, impressed sufficiently to suggest that Essex have quickly found a successor to John Lever, while twenty-year-old Jonathan Lewis, brought into the side for the final fixture against Surrey, marked his first-class dèbut with an unbeaten 116 in his only innings.

One familiar face which will be missing in the months ahead is that of Brian Hardie, the Scot whose ready quip and smile were features of the county circuit for almost two decades. Although his style often defied the coaching manuals, there was never any doubt as to the success of his methods, or to his fierce determination and tremendous value to the side. Following a playing career which brought him 18,103 first-class runs, and well over 400 catches in all competitions, many of them at short leg, he left to take up a post as coach at Brentwood School. Another departure was that of Ray East, the county's youth development officer, an appointment now entrusted to Alan Lilley. East also moved to a school, in Ipswich, and Essex will be pleased that he and Hardie have pursued careers from which the county will undoubtedly benefit in the years ahead. – Nigel Fuller.

ESSEX 1990

[*Bill Smith*

Back row: M. A. Garnham, P. M. Such, M. E. Waugh, K. O. Thomas, A. C. Seymour, A. G. J. Fraser, J. J. B. Lewis, K. A. Butler, N. Shahid. *Middle row:* R. Cole (*physiotherapist*), D. J. P. Boden, T. D. Topley, J. P. Stephenson, A. W. Lilley, A. T. Van-Lint, N. V. Knight, M. C. Ilott, S. J. W. Andrew. *Front row:* P. J. Prichard, J. H. Childs, D. E. East, D. R. Pringle, G. A. Gooch (*captain*), K. W. R. Fletcher, N. A. Foster, B. R. Hardie, N. Hussain.

ESSEX RESULTS

All first-class matches – Played 24: Won 9, Lost 2, Drawn 13.

County Championship matches – Played 22: Won 8, Lost 2, Drawn 12.

Bonus points – Batting 73, Bowling 56.

Competition placings – Britannic Assurance County Championship, 2nd; NatWest Bank Trophy, 2nd round; Benson and Hedges Cup, q-f; Refuge Assurance League, 12th.

BRITANNIC ASSURANCE CHAMPIONSHIP AVERAGES

BATTING

	Birthplace	*M*	*I*	*NO*	*R*	*HI*	*Avge*
‡G. A. Gooch	*Leytonstone*	11	18	2	1,586	215	99.12
‡M. E. Waugh	*Sydney, Australia*	21	32	6	2,009	207*	77.26
‡B. R. Hardie	*Stenhousemuir*	11	15	5	650	125	65.00
‡J. P. Stephenson	*Stebbing*	22	37	7	1,525	202*	50.83
N. Shahid	*Karachi, Pakistan*	18	27	7	964	125	48.20
‡P. J. Prichard	*Billericay*	20	30	3	1,276	245	47.25
‡N. Hussain	*Madras, India*	14	21	2	714	197	37.57
‡M. A. Garnham	*Johannesburg, SA*	22	26	7	589	84*	31.00
‡D. R. Pringle	*Nairobi, Kenya*	15	13	2	318	84	28.90
‡N. A. Foster	*Colchester*	22	22	2	530	101	26.50
P. M. Such	*Helensburgh*	10	5	3	44	27	22.00
‡T. D. Topley	*Canterbury*	7	4	1	55	23	18.33
M. C. Ilott	*Watford*	8	10	2	123	42*	15.37
S. J. W. Andrew	*London*	16	15	7	119	35	14.87
‡J. H. Childs	*Plymouth*	21	16	5	123	26	11.18

Also batted: J. J. B. Lewis (*Isleworth*) (1 match) 116*; ‡A. W. Lilley (*Ilford*) (1 match) 1; A. C. Seymour (*Royston*) (2 matches) 10*, 0, 4*.

* *Signifies not out.* ‡ *Denotes county cap.*

The following played a total of 27 three-figure innings for Essex in County Championship matches – M. E. Waugh 8, G. A. Gooch 7, P. J. Prichard 4, B. R. Hardie 2, J. P. Stephenson 2, N. A. Foster 1, N. Hussain 1, J. J. B. Lewis 1, N. Shahid 1.

BOWLING

	O	*M*	*R*	*W*	*BB*	*5W/i*	*Avge*
N. A. Foster	819.2	175	2,502	94	6-32	6	26.61
D. R. Pringle	325.3	82	927	29	5-66	1	31.96
T. D. Topley	178	26	557	16	4-67	0	34.81
P. M. Such	252.3	58	682	18	3-34	0	37.88
M. C. Ilott	289.1	60	951	25	5-34	1	38.04
S. J. W. Andrew	449	67	1,763	43	5-55	1	41.00
J. H. Childs	595.1	189	1,435	25	4-56	0	57.40
M. E. Waugh	183	33	731	12	5-37	1	60.91

Also bowled: G. A. Gooch 35–8–125–0; B. R. Hardie 1–0–16–0; N. Hussain 4–1–29–0; A. W. Lilley 1–0–7–0; P. J. Prichard 1.4–0–11–0; N. Shahid 106.2–18–413–7; J. P. Stephenson 96–22–383–3.

Wicket-keeper: M. A. Garnham 45 ct, 1 st.

Leading Fielders: N. Shahid 22, M. E. Waugh 18.

At Lord's, April 26, 27, 28, 30. ESSEX drew with MIDDLESEX.

ESSEX v LEICESTERSHIRE

At Chelmsford, May 3, 4, 5, 7. Drawn. Essex 5 pts, Leicestershire 3 pts. Toss: Leicestershire. Gooch and Prichard, the latter recording the highest score of his career, both hit double-hundreds and shared in a second-wicket stand of 403. This was the highest for any wicket by an Essex pair and helped take the county to the highest score in their history, beating their 692 against Somerset at Taunton in 1895. Gooch struck 28 fours and a six in his 215 and Prichard 31 fours and two 6s in his 245. Later Foster raced to his maiden century from just 79 balls, five of which he hit for six. Earlier Lewis had taken full advantage of the docile pitch to collect his first century, and there were five sixes among his 21 boundaries in a stay of six hours. Briers joined the list of century-makers when Leicestershire batted a second time, and with Briers and Boon putting on their second century opening partnership, Leicestershire had no difficulty in saving the match after trailing by 241 on first innings.

Close of play: First day, Leicestershire 323-6 (C. C. Lewis 57*, M. I. Gidley 2*); Second day, Essex 158-1 (G. A. Gooch 73*, P. J. Prichard 38*); Third day, Essex 712-5 (B. R. Hardie 52*, N. A. Foster 83*).

Leicestershire

T. J. Boon lbw b Such	90	– c Waugh b Childs	89
*N. E. Briers c Garnham b Such	65	– c Garnham b Such	104
J. J. Whitaker c and b Such	31	– b Stephenson	15
L. Potter c Prichard b Waugh	62	– not out	16
J. D. R. Benson c Shahid b Foster	8	– not out	10
C. C. Lewis not out	189		
†P. Whitticase lbw b Waugh	0		
M. I. Gidley c and b Shahid	9		
J. P. Agnew lbw b Shahid	37		
G. J. F. Ferris c Waugh b Foster	11		
A. D. Mullally b Foster	3		
B 1, l-b 9, w 4, n-b 1	15	B 5, l-b 3, w 1, n-b 6	15
1/145 2/178 3/197 4/214 5/303 6/309 7/458 8/460 9/498	520	1/170 2/205 3/236 (3 wkts)	249

Bonus points – Leicestershire 3, Essex 1 (Score at 100 overs: 294-4).

In the first innings M. I. Gidley, when 9, retired hurt at 371 and resumed at 458.

Bowling: *First Innings*—Foster 41–8–102–3; Andrew 20–3–72–0; Waugh 23–5–76–2; Childs 41–14–88–0; Such 43–7–118–3; Shahid 13–1–54–2. *Second Innings*—Foster 8–2–30–0; Andrew 9–1–31–0; Childs 33–10–93–1; Shahid 11–3–42–0; Such 19–9–29–1; Stephenson 9–5–16–1.

Essex

*G. A. Gooch c Whitticase b Lewis	215
J. P. Stephenson c Lewis b Mullally	35
P. J. Prichard c Briers b Mullally	245
M. E. Waugh b Lewis	43
B. R. Hardie not out	74
†M. A. Garnham b Lewis	0
N. A. Foster run out	101
B 9, l-b 20, w 3, n-b 16	48
1/82 2/485 3/551 4/587 5/589 6/761 (6 wkts dec.)	761

N. Shahid, J. H. Childs, S. J. W. Andrew and P. M. Such did not bat.

Bonus points – Essex 4 (Score at 100 overs: 435-1).

Bowling: Mullally 31–3–124–2; Agnew 35.5–4–170–0; Ferris 23–2–100–0; Lewis 28–3–115–3; Potter 14–0–91–0; Gidley 25–3–121–0; Benson 2–0–11–0.

Umpires: K. E. Palmer and D. R. Shepherd.

†ESSEX v ZIMBABWEANS

At Chelmsford, May 14. Essex won by 71 runs. Toss: Essex. Having dropped himself down the order, Gooch watched his early batsmen struggle to 83 for four before he emerged in the 27th over of this 55-over contest to stamp his authority on the innings. He did so with a century off only 78 balls, his batting contrasting with Stephenson's laboured effort of 163 deliveries. Only Pycroft provided prolonged resistance when the Zimbabweans replied, but he could not prevent Essex from winning with ease.

Essex

J. P. Stephenson c Arnott b Jarvis	105	P. J. Prichard not out	3
A. C. Seymour lbw b Brandes	6	N. A. Foster not out	4
A. W. Lilley run out	12	L-b 12, n-b 4	16
M. E. Waugh b Duers	0		
†M. A. Garnham c Robertson b Duers	14	1/7 2/49 3/50 (6 wkts, 55 overs)	265
*G. A. Gooch c Briant b Jarvis	105	4/83 5/258 6/258	

T. D. Topley, J. H. Childs and S. J. W. Andrew did not bat.

Bowling: Brandes 11–2–58–1; Jarvis 10–2–44–2; Shah 6–0–20–0; Duers 11–0–52–2; Traicos 11–0–45–0; Brent 6–0–34–0.

Zimbabweans

K. J. Arnott c Garnham b Andrew	6	M. P. Jarvis c Waugh b Foster	5
A. H. Shah c Garnham b Andrew	0	A. J. Traicos not out	8
†W. R. James b Andrew	27	K. G. Duers b Foster	1
*A. J. Pycroft c Prichard b Stephenson	62	L-b 8, w 12, n-b 6	26
C. M. Robertson c Seymour b Andrew	3		
G. A. Briant b Childs	17	1/1 2/21 3/46 (51.1 overs)	194
J. P. Brent lbw b Stephenson	32	4/60 5/95 6/170	
E. A. Brandes c Prichard b Stephenson	7	7/173 8/180 9/184	

Bowling: Foster 8.1–2–19–2; Andrew 11–1–36–4; Gooch 7–1–17–0; Topley 5–0–29–0; Childs 11–1–37–1; Waugh 5–0–22–0; Stephenson 4–0–26–3.

Umpires: P. J. Eele and A. G. T. Whitehead.

At Cambridge, May 16, 17, 18. ESSEX beat CAMBRIDGE UNIVERSITY by 120 runs.

At Worcester, May 19, 21, 22. ESSEX beat WORCESTERSHIRE by ten wickets.

At Southampton, May 23, 24, 25. ESSEX drew with HAMPSHIRE.

ESSEX v MIDDLESEX

At Ilford, June 2, 4, 5. Drawn. Essex 3 pts, Middlesex 8 pts. Toss: Middlesex. Essex had to wait until after tea on the opening day for their first success, by which time Roseberry had registered a career-best 135, which featured 23 fours and a six. The immaculate Haynes continued to accumulate his runs with superb timing on either side of the wicket, and he never looked in the slightest trouble while gathering 33 fours in a day-long effort which also produced a career best. His unbeaten 220 at the close was only the second double-hundred of his distinguished career. Essex never recovered from the early loss of Gooch, despite the fighting qualities of Hardie, but the Essex and England captain was at his imperious best as Essex easily saved the match after being asked to follow on 185 behind. Gooch hit nineteen boundaries, including two sixes, and following his departure, Prichard and Waugh further frustrated the visitors.

Close of play: First day, Middlesex 442-2 (D. L. Haynes 220*, M. R. Ramprakash 30*); Second day, Essex 91-1 (G. A. Gooch 57*, N. A. Foster 2*).

Middlesex

D. L. Haynes not out	220
M. A. Roseberry c Prichard b Foster	135
*M. W. Gatting b Pringle	34
M. R. Ramprakash not out	30
B 4, l-b 11, w 3, n-b 5	23
1/306 2/369 (2 wkts dec.)	442

K. R. Brown, †P. R. Downton, N. F. Williams, J. E. Emburey, S. P. Hughes, M. J. Thursfield and P. C. R. Tufnell did not bat.

Bonus points – Middlesex 4 (Score at 100 overs: 377-2).

Bowling: Foster 18–6–60–1; Pringle 22–8–66–1; Andrew 14–3–61–0; Gooch 9–2–36–0; Childs 17–1–58–0; Stephenson 10–2–36–0; Such 9–2–41–0; Waugh 15–2–69–0.

Essex

*G. A. Gooch c Downton b Hughes	0	– c Brown b Tufnell	120
J. P. Stephenson c Downton b Williams	16	– c Brown b Tufnell	31
P. J. Prichard c Downton b Thursfield	7	– (4) not out	56
M. E. Waugh c Haynes b Emburey	39	– (5) not out	59
B. R. Hardie c Downton b Hughes	74		
†M. A. Garnham lbw b Emburey	36		
D. R. Pringle c Downton b Emburey	8		
N. A. Foster c Brown b Emburey	0	– (3) c Gatting b Williams	13
S. J. W. Andrew c Roseberry b Emburey	15		
J. H. Childs not out	10		
P. M. Such b Williams	27		
L-b 17, n-b 8	25	B 8, l-b 8, n-b 10	26
1/2 2/19 3/31 4/83 5/153 6/168 7/170 8/205 9/213	257	1/88 2/112 3/201 (3 wkts)	305

Bonus points – Essex 3, Middlesex 4.

Bowling: *First Innings*—Williams 19.5–4–58–2; Hughes 14–2–43–2; Thursfield 8–2–24–1; Tufnell 27–7–54–0; Emburey 24–7–61–5. *Second Innings*—Hughes 12–2–58–0; Williams 18–4–57–1; Thursfield 9–2–21–0; Emburey 32–9–80–0; Tufnell 33–12–73–2.

Umpires: B. Leadbeater and B. J. Meyer.

ESSEX v GLOUCESTERSHIRE

At Ilford, June 6, 7, 8. Drawn. Essex 6 pts, Gloucestershire 4 pts. Toss: Essex. Rain was the only winner, restricting the final day's play to fewer than 90 minutes. When Seymour, deputising for Gooch, was forced to retire with a broken hand after being struck by Walsh, Waugh took full advantage of an easy-paced pitch to post his first double-hundred. His 204 contained 92 in boundaries and spanned 291 minutes and 267 deliveries. Hardie, whose second century of the season was a subdued affair, containing just half-a-dozen boundaries, gave the Australian fine support as they added 242 for the third wicket. Essex's overnight declaration left Gloucestershire with a draw as the height of their ambitions. A dour 92 from Wright, plus a more aggressive half-century by Bainbridge, ensured that the follow-on was avoided, but in the end the weather had the final say.

Close of play: First day, Essex 425-4 (B. R. Hardie 110*, M. A. Garnham 20*); Second day, Gloucestershire 289-6 (J. W. Lloyds 29*, G. A. Tedstone 9*).

Essex

J. P. Stephenson b Lawrence	1	– (2) not out	35
A. C. Seymour retired hurt	4		
P. J. Prichard c Curran b Bainbridge	45		
M. E. Waugh b Graveney	204		
B. R. Hardie not out	110	– (1) c Tedstone b Walsh	13
N. Shahid c Lawrence b Curran	15	– (3) not out	14
†M. A. Garnham not out	20		
B 8, l-b 6, w 1, n-b 11	26	L-b 1, w 3, n-b 1	5
1/2 2/105 3/347 4/388 (4 wkts dec.)	425	1/23 (1 wkt)	67

*D. R. Pringle, N. A. Foster, J. H. Childs and P. M. Such did not bat.

Bonus points – Essex 4, Gloucestershire 1 (Score at 100 overs: 411-4).

In the first innings A. C. Seymour retired hurt at 16.

Bowling: *First Innings*—Walsh 16–2–60–0; Lawrence 11–0–57–1; Curran 19–2–93–1; Graveney 27–2–101–1; Bainbridge 18–2–65–1; Lloyds 11–1–35–0. *Second Innings*—Bainbridge 4–0–11–0; Athey 7–1–25–0; Lawrence 6–1–17–0; Walsh 9–6–8–1; Lloyds 2–1–4–0; Tedstone 2–1–1–0.

Gloucestershire

*A. J. Wright b Foster	92
G. D. Hodgson c sub b Foster	27
I. P. Butcher c Waugh b Foster	5
C. W. J. Athey run out	9
P. Bainbridge run out	64
K. M. Curran c Garnham b Childs	39
J. W. Lloyds not out	29
†G. A. Tedstone c Garnham b Foster	13
D. A. Graveney not out	0
B 6, l-b 4, n-b 10	20
1/58 2/88 3/111 4/170 5/235 6/264 7/298 (7 wkts dec.)	298

C. A. Walsh and D. V. Lawrence did not bat.

Bonus points – Gloucestershire 3, Essex 2 (Score at 100 overs: 283-6).

Bowling: Foster 32.4–5–104–4; Pringle 18–3–52–0; Childs 32–16–48–1; Such 9–2–34–0; Waugh 7–3–17–0; Stephenson 7–1–33–0.

Umpires: B. Leadbeater and B. J. Meyer.

At Birmingham, June 9, 11, 12. ESSEX lost to WARWICKSHIRE by five wickets.

At Bath, June 16, 18, 19. ESSEX drew with SOMERSET.

At Chelmsford, June 30, July 1, 2. ESSEX drew with NEW ZEALANDERS (See New Zealand tour section).

At Maidstone, July 4, 5, 6. ESSEX beat KENT by four wickets.

ESSEX v DERBYSHIRE

At Colchester, July 18, 19, 20. Essex won by nine wickets. Essex 24 pts, Derbyshire 7 pts. Toss: Derbyshire. The match swung decisively in Essex's favour after tea on the second day as Derbyshire set out to clear a first-innings deficit of 98. Foster removed Barnett and Brown in his opening over and, underlining the virtue of line and length on a pitch affording generous bounce, went on to take six for 49 as the visitors surrendered meekly. Only brave resistance from Krikken took the match into the third day, when just 45 minutes were needed. Roberts batted spiritedly in Derbyshire's first innings, while Waugh, with his fifth Championship century of the summer, one containing sixteen fours and two sixes, displayed great authority and excellent timing in the Essex reply. Hussain also batted attractively while he and Waugh shared the only three-figure partnership of the match.

Close of play: First day, Essex 62-1 (B. R. Hardie 15*, N. Shahid 29*); Second day, Essex 5-0 (B. R. Hardie 4*, J. P. Stephenson 0*).

Derbyshire

*K. J. Barnett c Stephenson b Foster	38	– c Shahid b Foster	0
P. D. Bowler b Childs	33	– b Foster	4
A. M. Brown c Garnham b Foster	3	– c Garnham b Foster	0
B. Roberts c Shahid b Andrew	56	– c Hardie b Andrew	26
C. J. Adams c Hussain b Andrew	33	– lbw b Foster	7
S. C. Goldsmith c Hardie b Such	11	– lbw b Foster	24
†K. M. Krikken c Hardie b Andrew	4	– b Childs	43
I. R. Bishop lbw b Foster	26	– c Such b Foster	9
A. E. Warner c Shahid b Such	0	– lbw b Andrew	2
G. Miller not out	24	– not out	18
S. J. Base c Garnham b Andrew	26	– b Such	4
B 1, l-b 8, n-b 5	14	L-b 2, w 4, n-b 2	8
1/67 2/71 3/85 4/170 5/176 6/188 7/198 8/203 9/231	268	1/1 2/1 3/26 4/34 5/53 6/66 7/84 8/94 9/132	145

Bonus points – Derbyshire 3, Essex 4.

Bowling: *First Innings*—Foster 24–4–75–3; Andrew 15.5–4–60–4; Childs 19–7–57–1; Pringle 6–1–31–0; Such 17–3–36–2. *Second Innings*—Foster 15–2–49–6; Andrew 9–2–49–2; Pringle 8–1–31–0; Childs 7–4–7–1; Such 2–0–7–1.

Essex

B. R. Hardie c Brown b Warner	24	– not out	41
J. P. Stephenson c Krikken b Bishop	1	– c Krikken b Bishop	4
N. Shahid c Krikken b Goldsmith	42	– not out	4
M. E. Waugh c Krikken b Miller	126		
N. Hussain c Krikken b Bishop	60		
†M. A. Garnham c Krikken b Bishop	16		
*D. R. Pringle b Miller	30		
N. A. Foster b Barnett	32		
J. H. Childs c Base b Barnett	2		
S. J. W. Andrew c Roberts b Miller	1		
P. M. Such not out	0		
L-b 9, w 6, n-b 17	32	L-b 1, w 1	2
1/5 2/72 3/109 4/237 5/267 6/310 7/359 8/363 9/366	366	1/32	(1 wkt) 51

Bonus points – Essex 4, Derbyshire 4.

Bowling: *First Innings*—Bishop 23–7–41–3; Warner 24–2–76–1; Base 17–2–90–0; Miller 25–0–113–3; Goldsmith 7–0–25–1; Barnett 4–0–12–2. *Second Innings*—Bishop 5–2–21–1; Base 4.3–0–29–0.

Umpires: P. J. Eele and N. T. Plews.

ESSEX v LANCASHIRE

At Colchester, July 21, 23, 24. Essex won by six wickets. Essex 24 pts, Lancashire 8 pts. Toss: Lancashire. Gooch led Essex to a spectacular victory with an over to spare after they had been set the daunting task of making 348 in 54 overs. He scored 177 from 152 balls, 21 of which he despatched to the boundary, to inspire his county's third successive Championship win. On a benign pitch, Stephenson and Waugh provided the chief support with brisk half-centuries. Atherton and Fairbrother, who included three sixes among his nineteen boundaries, had hit unbeaten hundreds in a stand of 220 to set up Lancashire's declaration. Hegg rescued Lancashire on the first day with 100 not out off 150 deliveries, while for Essex 21-year-old Shahid played with maturity and style in making 125, his maiden first-class century, which included 21 fours. Having moved from fifteenth place in the Championship to seventh in two games, Essex could look back on their week at Colchester with considerable satisfaction.

Close of play: First day, Essex 24-0 (G. A. Gooch 3*, J. P. Stephenson 20*); Second day, Lancashire 104-2 (M. A. Atherton 20*, N. H. Fairbrother 51*).

Lancashire

G. D. Mendis c Shahid b Andrew	9	– lbw b Childs	20
G. Fowler b Foster	12	– c Pringle b Foster	9
M. A. Atherton c Shahid b Pringle	11	– not out	108
N. H. Fairbrother c Gooch b Pringle	24	– not out	109
T. E. Jesty c Garnham b Childs	66		
M. Watkinson c Garnham b Pringle	45		
Wasim Akram b Pringle	0		
P. A. J. DeFreitas c Foster b Such	41		
†W. K. Hegg not out	100		
*D. P. Hughes run out	57		
P. J. W. Allott not out	10		
B 4, l-b 6, w 1, n-b 9	20	B 1, l-b 2, n-b 3	6
1/24 2/24 3/38 4/70 5/161 6/162 7/190 8/262 9/375	(9 wkts dec.) 395	1/24 2/32	(2 wkts dec.) 252

Bonus points – Lancashire 4, Essex 4 (Score at 100 overs: 389-9).

Bowling: *First Innings*—Foster 20–1–98–1; Andrew 20–2–81–1; Pringle 17–3–47–4; Such 16–4–57–1; Stephenson 2–0–11–0; Childs 19.4–3–63–1; Shahid 6–2–28–0. *Second Innings*—Foster 11–3–30–1; Andrew 7–0–51–0; Childs 23–7–45–1; Such 15–3–24–0; Pringle 8–0–38–0; Shahid 10–0–46–0; Hussain 2–0–15–0.

Essex

*G. A. Gooch c Hegg b DeFreitas	17	– lbw b Atherton	177
J. P. Stephenson run out	21	– c Watkinson b Atherton	60
N. Shahid c and b Atherton	125	– run out	26
M. E. Waugh c Hegg b DeFreitas	0	– c sub b Atherton	58
N. Hussain c Hegg b Atherton	40	– not out	9
†M. A. Garnham lbw b Allott	17		
D. R. Pringle c Mendis b Hughes	45	– (6) not out	6
N. A. Foster c and b Atherton	4		
J. H. Childs not out	13		
S. J. W. Andrew b Hughes	0		
P. M. Such not out	13		
L-b 2, n-b 3	5	B 3, l-b 7, w 2, n-b 3	15
1/39 2/39 3/39 4/130 5/158 6/268 7/270 8/274 9/276	(9 wkts dec.) 300	1/158 2/214 3/331 4/336	(4 wkts) 351

Bonus points – Essex 4, Lancashire 4.

Bowling: *First Innings*—Wasim Akram 3–0–19–0; DeFreitas 22.1–4–68–2; Allott 17–2–76–1; Watkinson 6–0–19–0; Atherton 22–3–73–3; Hughes 14–4–43–2. *Second Innings*—DeFreitas 12–0–69–0; Allott 12–1–59–0; Watkinson 10–0–64–0; Hughes 5–0–43–0; Atherton 14–0–106–3.

Umpires: P. J. Eele and N. T. Plews.

At Leicester, July 25, 26, 27. ESSEX drew with LEICESTERSHIRE.

ESSEX v SUSSEX

At Chelmsford, July 28, 30, 31. Drawn. Essex 7 pts, Sussex 6 pts. Toss: Essex. In a thrilling finish, both sides were tantalisingly close to victory after Essex had been set to score 302 in a minimum of 43 overs. They finished 4 runs short with their last pair together, a fine 89 from 67 balls by Shahid providing the inspiration for their challenge. In contrast, dour half-centuries from Hall were the sheet-anchor for both Sussex innings, and Gould's 122-ball 73 on the opening day, containing twelve fours, was more pleasing to the eye. Waugh also hit twelve fours, as well as a six, as he flowed to his sixth Championship century of the summer from 120 deliveries. Essex then declared, 101 adrift, but Sussex consumed 72.5 overs in adding a further 200 and were able to set a demanding target.

Close of play: First day, Sussex 274-8 (A. I. C. Dodemaide 37*, B. T. P. Donelan 9*); Second day, Sussex 46-1 (J. W. Hall 9*, P. Moores 20*).

Sussex

D. M. Smith c Pringle b Andrew	3	– b Andrew	15
J. W. Hall c Pringle b Childs	62	– c Garnham b Topley	50
*P. W. G. Parker lbw b Foster	20	– (9) c Andrew b Childs	14
A. P. Wells c Garnham b Topley	19	– lbw b Pringle	14
I. J. Gould c Waugh b Topley	73	– c and b Childs	0
C. M. Wells c Stephenson b Topley	0	– lbw b Topley	21
A. I. C. Dodemaide not out	79	– not out	35
†P. Moores c Stephenson b Childs	27	– (3) c Topley b Childs	28
A. C. S. Pigott c Garnham b Andrew	0	– (8) c Prichard b Childs	1
B. T. P. Donelan b Childs	31	– not out	12
R. A. Bunting not out	11		
B 4, l-b 9, n-b 13	26	N-b 10	10
1/3 2/47 3/78 4/190 5/190 6/207 7/247 8/254 9/337 (9 wkts dec.)	351	1/26 2/69 3/101 4/102 5/131 6/143 7/145 8/171 (8 wkts dec.)	200

Bonus points – Sussex 4, Essex 4 (Score at 100 overs: 337-9).

Bowling: *First Innings*—Foster 26–2–102–1; Andrew 25–4–108–2; Topley 14–2–36–3; Pringle 10–2–29–0; Waugh 2–0–12–0; Childs 25–11–51–3. *Second Innings*—Foster 11–3–23–0; Andrew 13–0–60–1; Childs 30–13–56–4; Shahid 3.5–0–15–0; Pringle 4–2–12–1; Topley 10–1–34–2; Waugh 1–1–0–0.

Essex

N. Shahid c Moores b Bunting	55	– b Donelan	89
J. P. Stephenson c A. P. Wells b Pigott	14	– c Gould b Pigott	45
P. J. Prichard lbw b Bunting	11	– (4) b Donelan	22
M. E. Waugh not out	103	– (3) b Pigott	11
N. Hussain lbw b Dodemaide	21	– c Moores b Pigott	21
†M. A. Garnham run out	8	– (7) c Dodemaide b Bunting	20
*D. R. Pringle lbw b C. M. Wells	21	– (6) c Smith b Donelan	39
N. A. Foster not out	2	– c Pigott b Bunting	30
T. D. Topley (did not bat)		– not out	7
J. H. Childs (did not bat)		– run out	0
S. J. W. Andrew (did not bat)		– not out	0
B 10, l-b 2, w 1, n-b 2	15	B 9, l-b 5	14
1/37 2/65 3/100 4/171 5/196 6/244 (6 wkts dec.)	250	1/137 2/137 3/168 4/176 5/226 6/236 7/282 8/292 9/294 (9 wkts)	298

Bonus points – Essex 3, Sussex 2.

Bowling: *First Innings*—Pigott 16–2–67–1; Dodemaide 13–2–41–1; Bunting 12–1–53–2; Donelan 4–0–33–0; C. M. Wells 14.3–2–44–1. *Second Innings*—Pigott 14–1–79–3; Dodemaide 8–1–46–0; Bunting 8–2–36–2; C. M. Wells 4–0–37–0; Donelan 11–0–86–3.

Umpires: D. O. Oslear and K. E. Palmer.

ESSEX v NOTTINGHAMSHIRE

At Southend, August 4, 6, 7. Essex won by ten wickets. Essex 24 pts, Nottinghamshire 4 pts. Toss: Nottinghamshire. Any fears over the pitch at Southchurch Park, scene of so much controversy twelve months earlier when Essex received a 25-point penalty, which cost them the Championship, were swept aside as Gooch and his men gained an easy victory after scoring 400 in the second innings of the match. A resolute half-century by Evans saw Nottinghamshire achieve respectability in the first innings, and Broad and Johnson batted attractively in their second. However, none was able to score with the freedom of Gooch, whose first-innings 87 arrived from 99 deliveries with a dozen boundaries. With Prichard and Hussain also compiling stylish fifties, Essex forged a substantial lead, which Nottinghamshire cleared only with difficulty. They did succeed in keeping Essex in the field until after tea, but Gooch and Stephenson knocked off the 99 needed for victory with nearly seven overs to spare.

Close of play: First day, Essex 140-2 (P. J. Prichard 0*, M. C. Ilott 4*); Second day, Nottinghamshire 80-3 (B. C. Broad 44*).

Nottinghamshire

B. C. Broad c Stephenson b Ilott	19	– c Garnham b Ilott	84
P. R. Pollard c Waugh b Foster	12	– c Gooch b Foster	10
*R. T. Robinson c Waugh b Pringle	6	– c and b Childs	26
P. Johnson run out	34	– (5) b Childs	60
D. W. Randall c Pringle b Ilott	34	– (6) not out	36
F. D. Stephenson c Prichard b Foster	2	– (7) c Prichard b Childs	4
K. P. Evans c Gooch b Foster	51	– (8) c sub b Foster	31
†B. N. French run out	25	– (4) b Such	0
E. E. Hemmings lbw b Foster	32	– c Childs b Ilott	12
K. E. Cooper not out	10	– b Childs	4
J. A. Afford lbw b Such	1	– lbw b Ilott	0
B 1, l-b 1, n-b 3	5	L-b 3	3
1/26 2/38 3/38 4/90 5/100 6/126 7/158 8/219 9/222	231	1/19 2/73 3/80 4/175 5/183 6/194 7/235 8/255 9/270	270

Bonus points – Nottinghamshire 2, Essex 4.

Bowling: *First Innings*—Foster 25–5–73–4; Ilott 15–2–63–2; Pringle 15–2–74–1; Gooch 1–0–4–0; Childs 8–3–10–0; Such 4.3–1–5–1. *Second Innings*—Foster 30–12–59–2; Ilott 19.5–9–48–3; Such 20–4–56–1; Childs 41–13–104–4.

Essex

*G. A. Gooch c Johnson b Hemmings	87	– not out	65
J. P. Stephenson b Hemmings	46	– not out	32
P. J. Prichard b Hemmings	60		
M. C. Ilott b Cooper	37		
M. E. Waugh c Robinson b Hemmings	30		
N. Hussain c French b Stephenson	64		
†M. A. Garnham c French b Hemmings	22		
N. A. Foster b Evans	22		
D. R. Pringle c French b Evans	15		
J. H. Childs c French b Stephenson	2		
P. M. Such not out	2		
B 3, l-b 8, w 1, n-b 4	16	B 1, n-b 2	3
1/135 2/135 3/190 4/261 5/266 6/336 7/379 8/383 9/401	403	(no wkt)	100

Bonus points – Essex 4, Nottinghamshire 2 (Score at 100 overs: 328-5).

Bowling: *First Innings*—Stephenson 27.2–2–105–2; Cooper 17–3–76–1; Evans 15–3–53–2; Hemmings 39–15–99–5; Afford 25–7–59–0. *Second Innings*—Stephenson 6–0–30–0; Hemmings 5–0–32–0; Afford 4–0–18–0; Cooper 3.1–1–19–0.

Umpires: J. C. Balderstone and J. H. Harris.

ESSEX v GLAMORGAN

At Southend, August 8, 9, 10. Drawn. Essex 7 pts, Glamorgan 7 pts. Toss: Glamorgan. An exciting finish ended with Essex, despite 94 in 73 balls by Prichard, 8 runs short of a victory target of 333 in 55 overs. The feature of the match was the batting of Richards, who hit a hundred in each innings for the second time in his career, the previous occasion being for the West Indians against Tasmania in 1975-76. His first-innings 111, containing three sixes and thirteen fours, came off 136 deliveries and was followed by an unbeaten 118 from as many balls in the second. His chief support on that occasion came from Cottey, the pair sharing an unbroken partnership of 206 for the fourth wicket. Dale enjoyed a substantial fifth-wicket stand of 160 with Richards on the opening day while putting together a career-best 92. Garnham, Waugh and Stephenson were others to take advantage of a good pitch, helping Essex get within 31 runs on first innings before Foster, captaining them for the first time in the absence of Gooch and Pringle, declared.

Close of play: First day, Essex 10-1 (J. P. Stephenson 1*, M. C. Ilott 8*); Second day, Glamorgan 85-0 (A. R. Butcher 59*, H. Morris 24*).

Glamorgan

*A. R. Butcher c Foster b Ilott	0	– c Garnham b Andrew	59
H. Morris c Childs b Foster	9	– b Such	28
P. A. Cottey c Garnham b Foster	51	– not out	85
M. P. Maynard c Childs b Such	46	– c Shahid b Andrew	0
I. V. A. Richards c Stephenson b Ilott	111	– not out	118
A. Dale c Waugh b Andrew	92		
R. D. B. Croft c Hussain b Foster	6		
†C. P. Metson not out	15		
S. L. Watkin c Foster b Andrew	7		
S. Bastien not out	3		
L-b 11, w 1, n-b 4	16	L-b 9, n-b 2	11
1/5 2/15 3/103 4/121 5/281 6/297 7/337 8/345 (8 wkts dec.)	356	1/86 2/94 3/95 (3 wkts dec.)	301

M. Frost did not bat.

Bonus points – Glamorgan 4, Essex 3 (Score at 100 overs: 346-8).

Bowling: *First Innings*—Foster 23–6–71–3; Ilott 17–4–62–2; Andrew 16–1–66–2; Childs 19–4–69–0; Such 20–7–43–1; Waugh 3–0–11–0; Shahid 4–1–23–0. *Second Innings*—Foster 7–0–46–0; Ilott 6–0–22–0; Andrew 18–1–67–2; Such 21–4–73–1; Childs 9–2–35–0; Waugh 6–1–40–0; Prichard 1–0–9–0.

Essex

N. Shahid hit wkt b Bastien	1	– c Cottey b Bastien	46
J. P. Stephenson b Watkin	63	– c Metson b Bastien	65
M. C. Ilott c Metson b Frost	9	– (8) b Watkin	17
P. J. Prichard c Metson b Bastien	34	– (3) c Metson b Richards	94
M. E. Waugh c Richards b Watkin	66	– (4) lbw b Frost	14
N. Hussain lbw b Frost	33	– (5) c Morris b Richards	29
†M. A. Garnham not out	84	– (6) b Watkin	19
*N. A. Foster c Cottey b Watkin	18	– (7) run out	16
J. H. Childs not out	8	– (10) not out	1
S. J. W. Andrew (did not bat)		– (9) not out	12
B 4, l-b 3, n-b 2	9	B 4, l-b 6, w 1, n-b 1	12
1/1 2/20 3/66 4/178 5/181 6/230 7/311 (7 wkts dec.)	325	1/97 2/154 3/200 4/252 5/257 6/292 7/294 8/317 (8 wkts)	325

P. M. Such did not bat.

Bonus points – Essex 4, Glamorgan 3.

Bowling: *First Innings*—Watkin 22–2–72–3; Bastien 20–6–60–2; Frost 20–4–73–2; Croft 12–0–63–0; Dale 3–0–18–0; Richards 11–3–32–0. *Second Innings*—Watkin 18–0–102–2; Bastien 14–0–75–2; Croft 5–0–24–0; Frost 8–1–51–1; Richards 10–0–63–2.

Umpires: J. C. Balderstone and J. H. Harris.

At Middlesbrough, August 11, 13. ESSEX beat YORKSHIRE by an innings and 11 runs.

ESSEX v SURREY

At Chelmsford, August 18, 20, 21. Essex won by 283 runs. Essex 22 pts, Surrey 4 pts. Toss: Surrey. Foster emerged as the match-winner as Essex added momentum to their title challenge. His 58 was the major contribution in the first innings and he went on to exploit a Chelmsford pitch containing pace and bounce to collect match figures of eleven for 76. Only Stewart, hitting eight boundaries in his half-century, offered any real resistance as Surrey were bowled out for their lowest score of the season in the first innings. The lively Andrew inflicted the early damage. Gooch, Waugh and Shahid all batted attractively on the second afternoon, and Essex's declaration at their overnight score left their opponents to score 404 for victory on the final day. Surrey never looked like making a fight of it and lost their last six wickets for 30 runs after lunch.

Close of play: First day, Surrey 17-1 (A. J. Stewart 3*, N. M. Kendrick 4*); Second day, Essex 281-5 (M. E. Waugh 79*, N. Shahid 55*).

Essex

*G. A. Gooch c Greig b Waqar Younis	9	– c Clinton b Robinson	53
J. P. Stephenson c Greig b Waqar Younis	7	– b Murphy	36
P. J. Prichard c Medlycott b Murphy	27	– c Ward b Greig	42
M. E. Waugh c Ward b Waqar Younis	0	– not out	79
N. Hussain b Murphy	29	– c Kendrick b Greig	8
N. Shahid lbw b Murphy	27	– (7) not out	55
†M. A. Garnham c Thorpe b Murphy	32		
N. A. Foster c Medlycott b Murphy	58	– (6) c Ward b Greig	0
M. C. Ilott lbw b Robinson	7		
J. H. Childs run out	4		
S. J. W. Andrew not out	9		
B 12, l-b 14, w 1	27	B 4, l-b 2, w 2	8
1/9 2/28 3/28 4/79 5/82 6/142 7/156 8/209 9/218	236	1/80 2/98 3/168 4/186 5/186 (5 wkts dec.)	281

Bonus points – Essex 2, Surrey 4.

Bowling: *First Innings*—Waqar Younis 18.3–4–51–3; Murphy 26.1–4–67–5; Robinson 21.3–5–49–1; Greig 4–0–16–0; Medlycott 3–0–27–0. *Second Innings*—Waqar Younis 11–2–64–0; Murphy 18–0–73–1; Robinson 15–4–39–1; Greig 15–0–60–3; Kendrick 8–0–39–0.

Surrey

G. S. Clinton c Gooch b Ilott	10	– c Garnham b Andrew	32
A. J. Stewart lbw b Andrew	53	– c Ilott b Foster	11
N. M. Kendrick b Andrew	12	– (9) c Hussain b Ilott	3
G. P. Thorpe c Garnham b Andrew	0	– (3) c Garnham b Foster	0
†D. M. Ward c Shahid b Andrew	0	– (4) c Shahid b Andrew	11
M. A. Lynch b Foster	4	– (5) b Childs	25
J. D. Robinson hit wkt b Foster	0	– (6) b Foster	18
*I. A. Greig c Garnham b Foster	0	– (7) c Gooch b Foster	4
K. T. Medlycott c Hussain b Foster	20	– (8) not out	11
Waqar Younis not out	11	– b Foster	1
A. J. Murphy b Foster	1	– c Waugh b Foster	0
L-b 2, n-b 1	3	L-b 4	4
1/13 2/47 3/57 4/70 5/78 6/78 7/78 8/96 9/110	114	1/27 2/27 3/58 4/59 5/99 6/101 7/112 8/115 9/120	120

Bonus points – Essex 4.

Bowling: *First Innings*—Foster 19.2–4–44–5; Ilott 17–5–41–1; Andrew 11–3–27–4. *Second Innings*—Foster 18–6–32–6; Ilott 14–2–40–1; Andrew 9–2–34–2; Childs 6–2–10–1.

Umpires: H. D. Bird and J. H. Hampshire.

At Derby, August 23, 24. ESSEX beat DERBYSHIRE by an innings and 94 runs.

At Northampton, August 29, 30, 31. ESSEX drew with NORTHAMPTONSHIRE.

ESSEX v NORTHAMPTONSHIRE

At Chelmsford, September 7, 8, 9, 10. Northamptonshire won by 276 runs. Northamptonshire 21 pts, Essex 6 pts. Toss: Essex. Northamptonshire hurried to victory before lunch on the final day after Essex, resuming at 134 for four in pursuit of a target of 589, never threatened to stave off their second Championship defeat of the summer. Only Stephenson, with a gritty 76 spread over nearly three hours, put up prolonged resistance. The course of the match was decided by the visitors' second innings, in which they improved on their highest-ever score, made only nine days earlier against Essex at Northampton. Fordham showed the way on Saturday, batting for four hours twenty minutes and hitting a six and twenty fours while sharing century partnerships with Felton and Bailey. Bailey, with a six and nine fours, Lamb (26 fours) and Penberthy then drove home the advantage as the Essex bowlers toiled on a pitch which had become increasingly bland. A series of rash strokes contributed to Northamptonshire's downfall in the first innings as Waugh returned career-best figures with his medium-paced, swinging deliveries. In reply, however, Essex also collapsed ignominiously following a stylish, commanding innings from Gooch, who hit fifteen fours before becoming Robinson's first victim. Earlier in the day the Northamptonshire fast bowler had made history with his eleventh successive scoreless innings in first-class matches.

Close of play: First day, Essex 185-5 (N. Hussain 12*, M. A. Garnham 3*); Second day, Northamptonshire 330-3 (R. J. Bailey 76*, A. J. Lamb 13*); Third day, Essex 134-4 (J. P. Stephenson 49*, N. Hussain 0*).

Northamptonshire

A. Fordham c Garnham b Andrew	23	– c Foster b Ilott	159
N. A. Felton c Waugh b Foster	25	– b Foster	56
W. Larkins c Prichard b Ilott	37	– c Hussain b Foster	0
R. J. Bailey c Garnham b Waugh	28	– lbw b Foster	107
*A. J. Lamb c and b Waugh	22	– c sub b Childs	165
A. L. Penberthy c Foster b Waugh	0	– c Hussain b Andrew	83
R. G. Williams lbw b Waugh	0	– not out	12
†D. Ripley c Shahid b Waugh	18		
C. E. L. Ambrose lbw b Foster	9		
J. G. Thomas c and b Foster	15		
M. A. Robinson not out	0		
L-b 6, w 1, n-b 12	19	B 10, l-b 29, w 2, n-b 13	54
1/42 2/53 3/117 4/121 5/122 6/122 7/151 8/176 9/196	196	1/157 2/175 3/286 4/434 5/584 6/636 (6 wkts dec.)	636

Bonus points – Northamptonshire 1, Essex 4.

Bowling: *First Innings*—Foster 19.2–4–67–3; Ilott 11–3–28–1; Andrew 9–0–58–1; Waugh 12–3–37–5. *Second Innings*—Foster 29–7–79–3; Ilott 26–4–120–1; Childs 37–5–119–1; Andrew 23–1–132–1; Waugh 24–4–87–0; Stephenson 2–0–17–0; Gooch 18–5–43–0.

Essex

*G. A. Gooch c Penberthy b Robinson	92 – c Felton b Robinson	40
J. P. Stephenson c Thomas b Ambrose	0 – b Ambrose	76
P. J. Prichard c Ripley b Ambrose	7 – c Williams b Penberthy	5
N. Shahid b Thomas	26 – (7) c Thomas b Williams	43
M. E. Waugh c Bailey b Ambrose	44 – (4) c Lamb b Ambrose	36
N. Hussain b Robinson	17 – c Ripley b Thomas	24
†M. A. Garnham c and b Ambrose	34 – (8) c Penberthy b Robinson	10
N. A. Foster c Larkins b Thomas	11 – (9) b Robinson	12
M. C. Ilott c Felton b Robinson	0 – (5) c Thomas b Ambrose	0
J. H. Childs c Williams b Thomas	4 – not out	21
S. J. W. Andrew not out	1 – c Thomas b Williams	35
L-b 6, w 1, n-b 1	8 L-b 8, n-b 2	10
1/3 2/29 3/81 4/170 5/170 6/192 7/221 8/225 9/238	244 1/83 2/94 3/134 4/134 5/173 6/199 7/221 8/256 9/263	312

Bonus points – Essex 2, Northamptonshire 4.

Bowling: *First Innings*—Ambrose 23.4–3–67–4; Robinson 22–5–73–3; Penberthy 9–1–34–0; Thomas 13–0–64–3. *Second Innings*—Ambrose 19–6–52–3; Thomas 11–0–72–1; Robinson 15–2–89–3; Penberthy 6–0–27–1; Williams 12.1–2–64–2.

Umpires: B. J. Meyer and R. Palmer.

ESSEX v KENT

At Chelmsford, September 12, 13, 14, 15. Drawn. Essex 6 pts, Kent 6 pts. Toss: Essex. Ellison was the key figure in denying Essex the victory they needed to remain in contention for the Championship. He resisted for nearly three and a quarter hours while scoring an unbeaten 44 in the first innings, and his 68 not out in the second was spread over more than four hours. On the final day Ellison received stubborn match-saving support from Davis after Kent had gone to lunch less than 200 runs ahead with only three wickets remaining. Missed catches cost Essex dearly, and they were handicapped by the absence of Gooch, who broke his left thumb in two places attempting to catch Ward in the first hour of the match. Essex were also frustrated by Taylor, who compiled two half-centuries but failed by 21 runs to complete his 2,000 runs for the season. Waugh, with his eighth Championship hundred of the summer, provided the most entertaining batting of the match, his 169 containing 98 in boundaries and taking him past 2,000 runs. Prichard, with whom he put on 239 for the third wicket, also stroked the ball around elegantly.

Close of play: First day, Kent 358-6 (S. A. Marsh 69*, R. M. Ellison 13*); Second day, Essex 335-3 (M. E. Waugh 152*, N. Hussain 32*); Third day, Kent 185-4 (N. R. Taylor 54*, M. V. Fleming 18*).

Kent

S. G. Hinks c and b Childs	43 – b Andrew	16
T. R. Ward c Garnham b Foster	79 – c Hussain b Ilott	7
V. J. Wells c Waugh b Andrew	34 – lbw b Ilott	46
G. R. Cowdrey c Hussain b Childs	0 – c Garnham b Waugh	33
*N. R. Taylor c Garnham b Foster	56 – c Garnham b Foster	86
M. V. Fleming c Foster b Ilott	36 – c Hussain b Childs	36
†S. A. Marsh b Foster	70 – b Foster	47
R. M. Ellison not out	44 – not out	68
D. J. M. Kelleher c Garnham b Ilott	1 – lbw b Foster	6
R. P. Davis c Shahid b Ilott	0 – b Foster	52
T. N. Wren c Foster b Shahid	16 – c sub b Foster	0
B 5, l-b 5, w 6, n-b 14	30 B 7, l-b 10, w 1, n-b 9	27
1/115 2/155 3/156 4/187 5/253 6/271 7/363 8/366 9/366	409 1/8 2/38 3/97 4/129 5/221 6/251 7/293 8/309 9/424	424

Bonus points – Kent 4, Essex 2 (Score at 100 overs: 323-6).

Bowling: *First Innings*—Foster 37–8–108–3; Ilott 31–7–73–3; Andrew 21–0–99–1; Waugh 5–1–21–0; Childs 37–14–79–2; Stephenson 4–0–18–0; Shahid 2.3–1–1–1. *Second Innings*—Foster 41.3–9–94–5; Ilott 26–4–72–2; Andrew 24–3–78–1; Childs 31–10–60–1; Shahid 17–5–43–0; Waugh 14–4–37–1; Hussain 2–1–14–0; Stephenson 3–1–9–0.

Essex

J. P. Stephenson c Marsh b Ellison	11		
N. Shahid b Ellison	20	– (1) c Ellison b Kelleher	0
P. J. Prichard c Marsh b Fleming	102		
M. E. Waugh c Davis b Wren	169		
N. Hussain c Marsh b Wren	45		
†M. A. Garnham c Marsh b Kelleher	33		
N. A. Foster b Fleming	14		
M. C. Ilott not out	42	– (2) not out	0
J. H. Childs c Taylor b Ellison	26		
S. J. W. Andrew c and b Ellison	11	– (3) not out	8
L-b 8, w 8, n-b 19	35	W 1, n-b 1	2
1/26 2/41 3/280 4/357 5/375 6/398 7/429 8/495 9/508 (9 wkts dec.)	508	1/2 (1 wkt)	10

*G. A. Gooch did not bat.

Bonus points – Essex 4, Kent 2 (Score at 100 overs: 415-6).

Bowling: *First Innings*—Wren 28–1–135–2; Ellison 24.4–2–76–4; Fleming 25–1–87–2; Wells 3–0–22–0; Kelleher 12–1–68–1; Davis 26–3–112–0. *Second Innings*—Kelleher 1–0–10–1.

Umpires: J. C. Balderstone and A. G. T. Whitehead.

At The Oval, September 18, 19, 20, 21. ESSEX drew with SURREY.

UMPIRES FOR 1991

FIRST-CLASS UMPIRES

G. I. Burgess, the former Somerset all-rounder, and R. C. Tolchard, who played for Devon and whose brothers, J.G. and R.W., played for Leicestershire, have been promoted from the Reserve list to join the first-class list for 1991. The full list is: J. C. Balderstone, H. D. Bird, J. D. Bond, G. I. Burgess, D. J. Constant, B. Dudleston, J. H. Hampshire, J. H. Harris, B. Hassan, J. W. Holder, A. A. Jones, R. Julian, M. J. Kitchen, B. Leadbeater, K. J. Lyons, B. J. Meyer, D. O. Oslear, K. E. Palmer, R. Palmer, N. T. Plews, D. R. Shepherd, R. C. Tolchard, R. A. White, A. G. T. Whitehead and P. B. Wight. *Reserves:* Dr D. Fawkner-Corbett, M. J. Harris, V. A. Holder, H. J. Rhodes and G. A. Stickley.

Note: The panel of umpires for the Test matches and one-day internationals was not available at the time *Wisden* went to press.

MINOR COUNTIES UMPIRES

P. Adams, N. P. Atkins, R. Bell, K. Bray, P. Brown, C. J. Chapman, R. K. Curtis, Dr D. Fawkner-Corbett, J. B. Foulkes, P. Gray, D. J. Halfyard, M. A. Johnson, B. Knight, G. I. McLean, T. G. A. Morley, D. Norton, M. K. Reed, K. S. Shenton, C. Smith, C. T. Spencer, G. A. Stickley, J. Stobart, R. Walker, T. V. Wilkins and T. G. Wilson. *Reserves:* D. L. Burden, K. Coburn, H. Cohen, H. W. Cook, R. M. Davison, R. F. Elliott, R. E. Elvidge, A. G. Forster, R. F. Harriott, S. W. Kuhlmann, M. P. Moran, W. Morgan, B. J. Orton, C. T. Puckett, J. M. Tythcott, J. Waite, T. J. White, B. H. Willey and R. Wood.

GLAMORGAN

Patron: HRH The Prince of Wales
President: His Honour Rowe Harding
Chairman: A. R. Lewis
Chairman, Cricket Committee: A. R. Lewis
Chief Executive: 1990 – P. G. Carling
Secretary: 1990 – A. P. Dilloway
1991 – G. Stone
Sophia Gardens, Cardiff CF1 9XR
(Telephone: 0222-343478)
Captain: A. R. Butcher
Senior Coach: A. Jones

It was not a coincidence that the arrival of Viv Richards in Wales led to Glamorgan's most successful season for twenty years, with the club rising from bottom place in the Britannic Assurance Championship, where they had languished for two years, to eighth position. They also reached the quarter-finals of the Benson and Hedges Cup and NatWest Bank Trophy, and the only major disappointment was in the Sunday League, in which they fell away after a promising start. Richards provided inspiration from the moment he helped his adopted county win their first Benson and Hedges tie by trapping Reeve of Warwickshire leg-before with the game's final delivery.

The encouraging early-season form was maintained in the Championship, and they gained a resounding victory at Bristol in the third game of the season. It was achieved without any substantial contribution from Richards, and with Matthew Maynard and Geoff Holmes absent in the second innings, having suffered fractured fingers. However, Richards had already tuned up with a hundred against Leicestershire, and another soon followed against Sussex at Hove. His presence brought out the best in others, notably Maynard, who looked a far more disciplined batsman than in previous years. At Northampton in June, the pair hammered the home attack for 227 in 41 overs, which enabled Glamorgan to win with six wickets and nine overs in hand; and in the following game Richards played one of the greatest innings seen at Southampton. Glamorgan, set 364 by Hampshire, looked to be out of contention at 139 for five, but Richards, in partnership with Cowley, initiated a remarkable recovery and Glamorgan won with two deliveries to spare. The West Indies captain's imperious 164 not out included five sixes and seventeen fours.

Richards hit seven Championship hundreds, but even his outstanding deeds were overshadowed by those of Alan Butcher and Hugh Morris, both of whom exceeded 2,000 runs for the season and broke a number of Glamorgan batting records. The two left-handers proved themselves the most consistent opening pair in the country, sharing ten century partnerships, and allied to Butcher's prolific batting was his positive and thoughtful captaincy. For the second successive season he reached 1,000 runs before any other English-born player, and he fully deserved the accolade of becoming one of *Wisden's* Five Cricketers of the Year. Welsh anger at Morris's omission from the team for Australia was tempered by his appointment as captain of the England A team selected to tour Pakistan. Morris had an outstanding season. His ten hundreds beat by two the previous Glamorgan record, set by Javed Miandad in 1981, and his aggregate of 2,276 runs surpassed by 193 another of Miandad's county records.

Maynard played a number of entertaining innings, scoring 1,501 runs, and this gifted, naturally talented batsman would be capable of even better things if he could curb his impetuosity. Tony Cottey passed 1,000 runs for the first time in his career, fluctuating between No. 3 and No. 6, while Nigel Cowley, in his first season with Glamorgan, played some useful innings in the middle order before his injury in August. There were, however, some disappointments. Holmes, suffering from a troublesome eye infection, played only occasionally, and Ian Smith's form, despite an unbeaten century against Lancashire, fell away. The former Young England player has yet to confirm his early promise.

Steve Watkin was again Glamorgan's willing workhorse, bowling 767 overs in the first-class games, and while his wickets were more expensive than the previous year, he was again the county's leading wicket-taker. The averages, however, were headed by Steve Bastien, a product of Haringey Cricket College, who grasped the opportunity of an extended run in the first team from the end of July and, bowling at a brisk medium pace, finished with 39 wickets at a shade over 30. He took five for 31 as Nottinghamshire were dismissed between lunch and tea on the final day, and he closed his season at Worcester with a match return of nine wickets. Mark Frost, discarded by Surrey, made an immediate impact when he bowled Graeme Hick for 0 in a Benson and Hedges match early in the season, and he ended with 59 first-class wickets at 34.69. There was less joy, though, for Stephen Barwick, who was injured for much of the season and played in only three Championship games. His control over lengthy spells on unresponsive pitches, and his ability to switch from seam to off-cutters, were assets the county could ill afford to lose in a batsman's summer.

The emergence of Glamorgan's younger brigade epitomised the club's policy of promoting Welsh-born players. ASW Holdings, the county's main sponsors, have ensured that any aspiring young cricketer in the Principality is given every opportunity, and through the efforts of Alan Jones, the chief coach, promising young talent has been emerging. Robert Croft, in his first full season, struck 672 runs at 44.80, including an innings of 91 not out when Glamorgan failed by only 2 runs to reach an improbable 495 to beat Worcestershire at Abergavenny. He also emerged as an off-spinner of considerable promise, prompting Bishan Bedi to single him out as the best young spinner he had seen during India's tour. Although Steve James scored almost 1,000 runs in the short Cambridge season, he failed to maintain his form on his return to Glamorgan in July. None the less, he has the ability to succeed, and with Adrian Dale he should be available full-time in 1991. Once again Colin Metson's wicket-keeping was of the highest class; yet in spite of his being rated by most umpires and players as the best in the country, he was denied a tour with the England teams because of his modest batting.

A disappointing feature was the comprehensive defeat sustained in each of the final three games, when Richards was absent owing to a virus. However, Glamorgan's players have to realise that life without him has to go on, and the confidence which he instilled in them must be renewed and the resurgence continued. – Edward Bevan.

GLAMORGAN 1990

[*Bill Smith*

Back row: M. Davies, R. N. Pook, S. Bastien, R. Nancarrow, M. Frost, H. A. G. Anthony, K. A. Somaia, P. A. Cottey, R. D. B. Croft. *Middle row:* D. Conway (*physiotherapist*), M. J. Cann, N. G. Cowley, S. J. Dennis, I. Smith, M. L. Roberts, D. J. Shepherd (*assistant coach*), G. Lewis (*scorer*). *Front row:* J. F. Steele, C. P. Metson, G. C. Holmes, H. Morris, P. G. Carling (*chief executive*), A. R. Butcher (*captain*), S. R. Barwick, M. P. Maynard, J. Derrick, A. Jones (*senior coach*). *Insets:* I. V. A. Richards, S. L. Watkin, S. P. James, D. L. Hemp.

GLAMORGAN RESULTS

All first-class matches – Played 26: Won 5, Lost 6, Drawn 15.

County Championship matches – Played 22: Won 5, Lost 6, Drawn 11.

Bonus points – Batting 64, Bowling 48.

Competition placings – Britannic Assurance County Championship, 8th; NatWest Bank Trophy, q-f; Benson and Hedges Cup, q-f; Refuge Assurance League, 15th equal.

BRITANNIC ASSURANCE CHAMPIONSHIP AVERAGES

BATTING

	Birthplace	*M*	*I*	*NO*	*R*	*HI*	*Avge*
‡I. V. A. Richards	*St John's, Antigua*	18	28	5	1,425	164*	61.95
‡A. R. Butcher	*Croydon*	21	39	5	2,044	151*	60.11
‡H. Morris	*Cardiff*	22	41	4	1,914	160*	51.72
‡M. P. Maynard	*Oldham*	19	34	5	1,306	125*	45.03
R. D. B. Croft	*Morriston*	14	23	10	570	91*	43.84
N. G. Cowley	*Shaftesbury*	13	16	4	523	76	43.58
I. Smith	*Chopwell*	6	8	1	293	112*	41.85
‡G. C. Holmes	*Newcastle-upon-Tyne*	7	10	3	260	125*	37.14
P. A. Cottey	*Swansea*	17	30	5	816	125	32.64
M. J. Cann	*Cardiff*	5	8	0	180	64	22.50
A. Dale	*Germiston, SA*	7	11	0	179	92	16.27
‡C. P. Metson	*Goffs Oak*	22	26	4	302	34	13.72
‡S. L. Watkin	*Maesteg*	22	22	7	170	25*	11.33
S. Bastien	*Stepney, London*	10	9	3	47	12	7.83
M. Frost	*Barking*	18	17	7	40	12	4.00
S. J. Dennis	*Scarborough*	12	8	1	23	6	3.28
S. P. James	*Lydney*	3	6	0	10	7	1.66

Also batted: H. A. G. Anthony (*Urlings Village, Antigua*) (2 matches) 39, 0, 13; ‡S. R. Barwick (*Neath*) (3 matches) 0*, 2*; M. L. Roberts (*Mullion*) (1 match) 13.

* *Signifies not out.* ‡ *Denotes county cap.*

The following played a total of 27 three-figure innings for Glamorgan in County Championship matches – H. Morris 8, I. V. A. Richards 7, A. R. Butcher 6, P. A. Cottey 2, M. P. Maynard 2, G. C. Holmes 1, I. Smith 1.

BOWLING

	O	*M*	*R*	*W*	*BB*	*5W/i*	*Avge*
S. Bastien	274.5	47	1,075	35	6-75	2	30.71
M. Frost	509.1	63	1,919	56	5-40	2	34.26
S. L. Watkin	731.1	118	2,489	61	5-100	1	40.80
S. J. Dennis	283	53	957	20	5-76	1	47.85
R. D. B. Croft	357.1	76	1,126	23	3-10	0	48.95
N. G. Cowley	296.3	58	851	11	3-84	0	77.36

Also bowled: H. A. G. Anthony 62–13–207–5; S. R. Barwick 124.4–27–396–5; A. R. Butcher 25.3–2–153–1; M. J. Cann 35–3–162–1; P. A. Cottey 18–0–116–1; A. Dale 51–8–187–0; G. C. Holmes 21–3–85–1; M. P. Maynard 20–1–150–0; H. Morris 6–0–62–0; I. V. A. Richards 137–26–426–5; I. Smith 33–3–157–1.

Wicket-keeper: C. P. Metson 58 ct.

Leading Fielder: M. P. Maynard 13.

At Oxford, April 14, 16, 17. GLAMORGAN drew with OXFORD UNIVERSITY.

GLAMORGAN v LEICESTERSHIRE

At Cardiff, April 26, 27, 28, 30. Leicestershire won by nine wickets. Leicestershire 24 pts, Glamorgan 3 pts. Toss: Glamorgan. Despite Richards's first century for Glamorgan in their second innings, Leicestershire always looked to have control of a match which began with the weather allowing only 36 overs on the first day. Consistent batting in their first innings and some hostile bowling by Lewis, who took ten wickets in a match for the first time, enabled the visitors to collect maximum points. After Glamorgan's capitulation in the first innings, Richards and Maynard gave them hope with a partnership of 186 when they followed on, but Maynard was run out late on the third day to open the way for Leicestershire. With only 106 needed for victory, Boon led the way with his second half-century of the match.

Close of play: First day, Leicestershire 113-2 (T. J. Boon 52*, L. Potter 4*); Second day, Glamorgan 68-4 (H. Morris 25*, M. J. Cann 6*); Third day, Glamorgan 283-4 (I. V. A. Richards 118*, M. J. Cann 7*).

Leicestershire

First innings		Second innings	
T. J. Boon c Holmes b Dennis	72	– not out	61
*N. E. Briers c Maynard b Frost	21	– c Maynard b Watkin	10
J. J. Whitaker b Dennis	32	– not out	31
L. Potter lbw b Frost	50		
J. D. R. Benson lbw b Frost	9		
C. C. Lewis lbw b Dennis	39		
†P. Whitticase c Metson b Dennis	11		
M. I. Gidley c Dennis b Croft	73		
G. J. F. Ferris lbw b Frost	24		
J. P. Agnew c Metson b Dennis	0		
A. D. Mullally not out	16		
L-b 9, w 3, n-b 2	14	L-b 4, n-b 3	7
1/57 2/109 3/135 4/150 5/230 6/230 7/252 8/320 9/322	361	1/26	(1 wkt) 109

Bonus points – Leicestershire 4, Glamorgan 3 (Score at 100 overs: 302-7).

Bowling: *First Innings*—Watkin 30–3–94–0; Frost 33–3–117–4; Dennis 37–15–76–5; Croft 9.3–0–42–1; Richards 5–2–9–0; Holmes 5–2–14–0. *Second Innings*—Watkin 10.4–0–60–1; Frost 7–0–26–0; Dennis 3–0–16–0; Croft 3–2–3–0.

Glamorgan

First innings		Second innings	
*A. R. Butcher b Lewis	10	– c Agnew b Ferris	4
H. Morris c Whitticase b Lewis	33	– c Whitticase b Agnew	32
G. C. Holmes lbw b Ferris	14	– c Gidley b Mullally	11
M. P. Maynard c Gidley b Ferris	6	– run out	92
I. V. A. Richards b Lewis	3	– lbw b Lewis	119
M. J. Cann c Whitticase b Lewis	11	– c Potter b Ferris	17
R. D. B. Croft c Whitticase b Ferris	5	– not out	27
†C. P. Metson c Boon b Lewis	8	– c Benson b Lewis	5
S. J. Dennis c Whitticase b Lewis	3	– c Whitticase b Lewis	2
S. L. Watkin not out	21	– c Briers b Lewis	5
M. Frost c Boon b Ferris	1	– lbw b Agnew	0
L-b 5, n-b 7	12	L-b 7, w 3, n-b 15	25
1/14 2/34 3/45 4/48 5/86 6/87 7/101 8/101 9/116	127	1/7 2/51 3/53 4/239 5/287 6/309 7/320 8/330 9/336	339

Bonus points – Leicestershire 4.

Bowling: *First Innings*—Lewis 24–7–55–6; Ferris 11.2–1–44–4; Mullally 4–2–10–0; Gidley 2–1–1–0; Agnew 10–5–12–0. *Second Innings*—Lewis 25–3–64–4; Ferris 16–3–57–2; Mullally 24–6–67–1; Agnew 23.5–3–92–2; Gidley 14–7–31–0; Potter 5–2–21–0.

Umpires: M. J. Kitchen and B. Leadbeater.

GLAMORGAN v SOMERSET

At Cardiff, May 3, 4, 5, 6. Drawn. Glamorgan 3 pts, Somerset 5 pts. Toss: Somerset. A match which produced an aggregate of 1,430 runs for the loss of seventeen wickets will be remembered for Cook's mammoth innings of 313 not out, his first triple-hundred. Taking advantage of a benign pitch under a cloudless sky, Cook batted for eight and a half hours, struck 43 fours, and was only 9 runs short of I. V. A. Richards's Somerset record of 322 – achieved against Warwickshire in 1985 – when his captain, Tavaré, declared. His innings was the highest recorded in Wales and also the highest against Glamorgan. Four Glamorgan batsmen hit half-centuries, with Holmes going on to an unbeaten 125, as Glamorgan comfortably avoided the follow-on, and when Somerset batted again, Hayhurst, the former Lancashire all-rounder, scored a century on his Championship début for his new county. Tavaré set Glamorgan the stiff task of scoring 368 at almost 5 an over, but they gave up the chase once Maynard and Richards were dismissed.

Close of play: First day, Somerset 361-2 (S. J. Cook 236*, C. J. Tavaré 33*); Second day, Glamorgan 198-3 (G. C. Holmes 23*, I. Smith 23*); Third day, Somerset 138-1 (A. N. Hayhurst 66*, R. J. Harden 64*).

Somerset

S. J. Cook not out	313		
P. M. Roebuck lbw b Dennis	69		
J. J. E. Hardy b Holmes	7	– (2) lbw b Dennis	0
*C. J. Tavaré not out	120		
A. N. Hayhurst (did not bat)		– (1) not out	110
R. J. Harden (did not bat)		– (3) c Richards b Smith	64
†N. D. Burns (did not bat)		– (4) c sub b Barwick	28
I. G. Swallow (did not bat)		– (5) not out	31
B 8, l-b 16, n-b 2	26	L-b 6, w 1, n-b 4	11
1/210 2/250 (2 wkts dec.)	535	1/4 2/138 3/181 (3 wkts dec.)	244

G. D. Rose, R. P. Lefebvre and A. N. Jones did not bat.

Bonus points – Somerset 4 (Score at 100 overs: 306-2).

Bowling: *First Innings*—Watkin 27–6–84–0; Dennis 27–3–125–1; Barwick 29–7–107–0; Cowley 41–5–88–0; Smith 3–0–19–0; Richards 9–1–22–0; Holmes 12–1–44–1; Cann 6–1–22–0. *Second Innings*—Barwick 16–1–56–1; Dennis 7–1–16–1; Smith 11–1–43–1; Richards 22–2–68–0; Cann 15–2–44–0; Maynard 3–0–11–0.

Glamorgan

M. J. Cann c Harden b Jones	64	– c Swallow b Hayhurst	54
H. Morris c Hardy b Jones	52	– b Lefebvre	19
G. C. Holmes not out	125	– c Burns b Lefebvre	44
M. P. Maynard c Roebuck b Swallow	19	– c Cook b Lefebvre	64
I. Smith c Jones b Swallow	56	– (6) c Cook b Roebuck	16
I. V. A. Richards c Burns b Rose	16	– (5) c Swallow b Roebuck	16
N. G. Cowley run out	43	– not out	8
†C. P. Metson (did not bat)		– not out	4
B 6, l-b 22, w 4, n-b 5	37	B 3, l-b 7, w 3, n-b 1	14
1/120 2/127 3/159 4/270 5/296 6/412 (6 wkts dec.)	412	1/61 2/80 3/188 4/205 5/218 6/227 (6 wkts)	239

S. J. Dennis, *S. R. Barwick and S. L. Watkin did not bat.

Bonus points – Glamorgan 3, Somerset 1 (Score at 100 overs: 263-3).

Bowling: *First Innings*—Jones 18–1–80–2; Rose 22–6–50–1; Swallow 45–11–117–2; Lefebvre 26–8–45–0; Hayhurst 16–2–37–0; Roebuck 20–6–33–0; Harden 7–1–21–0; Tavaré 0.3–0–1–0. *Second Innings*—Jones 7–0–24–0; Rose 9–4–23–0; Lefebvre 17–2–52–3; Hayhurst 8–0–39–1; Swallow 21–6–57–0; Roebuck 14.3–5–34–2.

Umpires: P. J. Eele and J. W. Holder.

At Bristol, May 15, 16, 17. GLAMORGAN beat GLOUCESTERSHIRE by 145 runs.

At Hove, May 19, 21, 22. GLAMORGAN drew with SUSSEX.

GLAMORGAN v KENT

At Swansea, May 23, 24, 25. Kent won by 6 runs. Kent 19 pts, Glamorgan 4 pts. Toss: Kent. The game provided an exciting finish, with Kent winning in the penultimate over after Benson, deputising for Chris Cowdrey, had kept proceedings open by feeding some easy runs to revive Glamorgan's interest. Kent had laboured in the first innings, Taylor taking 351 minutes to score 106 (eleven fours) and sharing a partnership of 161 for the second wicket with the more enterprising Hinks, whose 107 contained sixteen boundaries. After Kent had batted on during the second morning, Glamorgan's openers scored briskly, putting on 255 without being parted before Butcher declared 73 runs behind in the final session. Butcher hit twenty fours in his 151, which included a century between lunch and tea, and there were ten in Morris's first Championship hundred of the season. Kent's declaration, helped along by Cottey and Cann, left Glamorgan to score 321 from a minimum of 63 overs, and the match appeared to be heading for a draw before Cowley and Smith plundered 122 in 56 minutes, with encouragement from some friendly bowling. When Cowley went at 267, Smith took Glamorgan to within 13 runs of victory before he was run out by de Villiers with three overs remaining. Glamorgan's hopes finally evaporated when the South African fast bowler had Watkin caught at long-off and, next ball, trapped Dennis leg-before to give Kent an unlikely victory.

Close of play: First day, Kent 291-3 (N. R. Taylor 101*, G. R. Cowdrey 46*); Second day, Kent 46-1 (M. R. Benson 40*, R. P. Davis 2*).

Kent

S. G. Hinks b Watkin	107	– c Morris b Dennis	4
*M. R. Benson lbw b Watkin	17	– c Morris b Dennis	96
N. R. Taylor lbw b Watkin	106		
T. R. Ward c Cann b Watkin	3	– b Cowley	7
G. R. Cowdrey not out	68	– not out	80
M. V. Fleming not out	10	– not out	45
R. P. Davis (did not bat)		– (3) run out	12
B 6, l-b 7, w 3, n-b 1	17	B 1, l-b 2	3
1/33 2/194 3/210 4/297 (4 wkts dec.)	328	1/23 2/92 3/112 4/132 (4 wkts dec.)	247

†S. A. Marsh, M. A. Ealham, C. Penn and P. S. de Villiers did not bat.

Bonus points – Kent 3, Glamorgan 1 (Score at 100 overs: 263-3).

Bowling: *First Innings*—Watkin 28–5–77–4; Dennis 11–0–39–0; Barwick 28.2–9–72–0; Richards 13–4–34–0; Cowley 33–7–75–0; Cann 1–0–1–0; Butcher 3–1–17–0. *Second Innings*—Watkin 10–1–27–0; Dennis 12–0–53–2; Cowley 22–4–67–1; Barwick 8–3–18–0; Cann 6–0–56–0; Cottey 3–0–23–0.

Glamorgan

*A. R. Butcher not out	151	– b Davis	50
H. Morris not out	100	– c and b Davis	29
I. V. A. Richards (did not bat)		– c Cowdrey b Davis	21
M. J. Cann (did not bat)		– c Fleming b Davis	10
P. A. Cottey (did not bat)		– c sub b Ward	21
I. Smith (did not bat)		– run out	66
N. G. Cowley (did not bat)		– b de Villiers	76
†C. P. Metson (did not bat)		– b de Villiers	21
S. J. Dennis (did not bat)		– lbw b de Villiers	6
S. L. Watkin (did not bat)		– c Davis b de Villiers	1
S. R. Barwick (did not bat)		– not out	0
L-b 2, n-b 2	4	B 8, l-b 1, n-b 4	13
(no wkt dec.)	255	1/60 2/87 3/108 4/139 5/145 6/267 7/297 8/308 9/314	314

Bonus points – Glamorgan 3.

Bowling: *First Innings*—de Villiers 17–5–39–0; Penn 14–5–44–0; Fleming 16–1–48–0; Ealham 12.2–2–48–0; Davis 24–4–74–0. *Second Innings*—de Villiers 15.3–3–69–4; Penn 7–0–39–0; Davis 25–5–97–4; Ward 9–0–52–1; Benson 3–0–28–0; Fleming 3–0–20–0.

Umpires: J. H. Harris and P. B. Wight.

GLAMORGAN v LANCASHIRE

At Colwyn Bay, May 26, 28, 29. Drawn. Glamorgan 5 pts, Lancashire 8 pts. Toss: Glamorgan. Glamorgan returned to Colwyn Bay after an absence of sixteen years, with the team flying from Swansea airport instead of undergoing a tiring 190-mile road journey. On the other hand, the attractive venue on the North Wales coast was an ideal one for Lancashire's supporters, many of whom were only an hour's drive away. Two days of glorious sunshine were followed by a miserable final day when Glamorgan, through the efforts of Butcher and Smith, fought back after being in danger of an innings defeat. Lancashire were indebted to Mendis, Fairbrother and Hegg, who enabled them to declare at 399 for seven with a lead of 194 and almost a day and a half remaining. The home county were vulnerable at 29 for three in their second innings but Smith, whose aggressive century included two sixes and nine fours, and Butcher, batting at No. 4, staved off defeat. When the rain set in, Glamorgan had a slender lead of 9 runs with the new ball due in eighteen overs. Their first innings also owed much to Butcher, while Anthony's spectacular 39 from 32 balls, including two sixes and five fours, on his Championship début prompted resistance from the lower order.

Close of play: First day, Lancashire 187-3 (G. D. Mendis 80*, T. E. Jesty 7*); Second day, Glamorgan 97-3 (A. R. Butcher 31*, I. Smith 41*).

Glamorgan

M. J. Cann c Hughes b DeFreitas	4	– c Hegg b DeFreitas	7
H. Morris lbw b Patterson	3	– lbw b Patterson	1
P. A. Cottey c Hegg b Allott	8	– c Mendis b DeFreitas	13
*A. R. Butcher c Hegg b Patterson	46	– not out	66
I. Smith c Atherton b DeFreitas	10	– not out	112
M. L. Roberts c Jesty b Allott	13		
N. G. Cowley c Allott b Patterson	4		
H. A. G. Anthony c Fairbrother b DeFreitas	39		
†C. P. Metson c and b Allott	34		
S. L. Watkin not out	25		
M. Frost c Hegg b Allott	0		
B 9, l-b 4, n-b 6	19	L-b 3, n-b 1	4
1/5 2/11 3/26 4/39 5/60 6/68 7/114 8/139 9/205	205	1/5 2/22 3/29 (3 wkts)	203

Bonus points – Glamorgan 2, Lancashire 4.

Bowling: *First Innings*—Patterson 19–4–88–3; DeFreitas 24–7–53–3; Allott 15–8–23–4; Fitton 4–1–17–0; Atherton 5–1–11–0. *Second Innings*—Patterson 17–5–41–1; DeFreitas 22–6–61–2; Allott 20–6–54–0; Fitton 15–6–25–0; Atherton 8–5–19–0.

Lancashire

G. D. Mendis c Metson b Watkin	90	*D. P. Hughes b Cowley	33
G. Fowler c Butcher b Watkin	22	J. D. Fitton not out	25
M. A. Atherton lbw b Cowley	15	B 4, l-b 11, n-b 6	21
N. H. Fairbrother c and b Cowley	60		
T. E. Jesty b Anthony	30	1/60 2/92 3/169 (7 wkts dec.)	399
P. A. J. DeFreitas lbw b Anthony	21	4/210 5/237	
†W. K. Hegg not out	82	6/252 7/345	

B. P. Patterson and P. J. W. Allott did not bat.

Bonus points – Lancashire 4, Glamorgan 3.

Bowling: Frost 21–3–81–0; Anthony 20–2–99–2; Watkin 25–4–84–2; Cowley 28–8–84–3; Butcher 3–1–17–0; Smith 3–0–19–0.

Umpires: J. H. Harris and P. B. Wight.

At Oxford, June 2, 4, 5. GLAMORGAN drew with OXFORD UNIVERSITY.

At Northampton, June 9, 11, 12. GLAMORGAN beat NORTHAMPTONSHIRE by six wickets.

At Southampton, June 16, 18, 19. GLAMORGAN beat HAMPSHIRE by four wickets.

At Bath, June 20, 21, 22. GLAMORGAN drew with SOMERSET.

GLAMORGAN v YORKSHIRE

At Cardiff, June 23, 25, 26. Yorkshire won by five wickets. Yorkshire 19 pts, Glamorgan 5 pts. Toss: Yorkshire. Yorkshire, having won their previous game following a generous declaration by the opposing captain, repeated the exercise after Butcher had set them a target of 271 in 72 overs. Although four wickets fell for 102, a partnership of 121 between the aggressive Byas and Blakey ensured Yorkshire of a second successive victory with 6.1 overs to spare. Morris's second Championship century of the season was the counterpoint to Maynard's 54 from 80 balls, and with Richards hitting 38 off 47 balls, Glamorgan were able to declare on Saturday evening with four batting points. However, rain allowed only 36 overs on the second day. Butcher's second declaration was based on Yorkshire's poor batting displays earlier in the season, but Blakey, who had scored only 30 runs in his eight previous Championship innings, and Byas corrected this impression. Robinson then returned after a blow on the chin from Watkin to see Yorkshire home.

Close of play: First day, Yorkshire 8-0 (M. D. Moxon 4*, A. A. Metcalfe 4*); Second day, Yorkshire 152-3 (K. Sharp 53*, P. E. Robinson 53*).

Glamorgan

*A. R. Butcher c Kellett b Carrick	50	– c Robinson b Hartley	17
H. Morris c Blakey b Hartley	102	– c Blakey b Moxon	28
P. A. Cottey c Kellett b Hartley	18	– not out	36
M. P. Maynard c and b Hartley	54	– not out	26
I. V. A. Richards b Gough	38		
G. C. Holmes not out	30		
†C. P. Metson b Gough	14		
W 1, n-b 2	3	L-b 1, n-b 5	6
1/107 2/196 3/209 4/255 5/276 6/309 (6 wkts dec.)	309	1/31 2/75 (2 wkts dec.)	113

M. Frost, S. J. Dennis, S. L. Watkin and S. Bastien did not bat.

Bonus points – Glamorgan 4, Yorkshire 2.

In the first innings P. A. Cottey, when 0, retired hurt at 112 and resumed at 255.

Bowling: *First Innings*—Jarvis 20–3–83–0; Hartley 24–7–51–3; Moxon 13–4–36–0; Gough 21–2–72–2; Carrick 22–6–67–1. *Second Innings*—Hartley 10–1–35–1; Gough 7–0–44–0; Moxon 5–0–10–1; Byas 8–4–23–0.

Yorkshire

*M. D. Moxon c Cottey b Dennis	27	– b Frost	10
A. A. Metcalfe c Morris b Bastien	5	– c Dennis b Watkin	37
S. A. Kellett b Bastien	2	– c Butcher b Bastien	8
K. Sharp not out	53	– b Dennis	24
P. E. Robinson not out	53	– not out	21
†R. J. Blakey (did not bat)		– not out	71
D. Byas (did not bat)		– c Metson b Frost	79
B 4, l-b 4, w 4	12	B 9, l-b 8, w 2, n-b 2	21
1/12 2/18 3/76	(3 wkts dec.) 152	1/28 2/40 3/70 4/102 5/223	(5 wkts) 271

P. J. Hartley, P. Carrick, P. W. Jarvis and D. Gough did not bat.

Bonus points – Yorkshire 1, Glamorgan 1.

In the second innings P. E. Robinson, when 11, retired hurt at 102-3 and resumed at 223.

Bowling: *First Innings*—Frost 13–2–23–0; Watkin 13–2–38–0; Bastien 11–1–49–2; Dennis 7–0–34–1. *Second Innings*—Frost 15.5–1–64–2; Bastien 16–0–67–1; Watkin 14–1–46–1; Dennis 15–2–58–1; Richards 5–0–19–0.

Umpires: D. J. Constant and R. Julian.

GLAMORGAN v SURREY

At Cardiff, June 30, July 2, 3. Drawn. Glamorgan 3 pts, Surrey 5 pts. Toss: Surrey. Surrey, seeking their first Championship win of the season, were content to hold out for a draw on the final afternoon, having been asked to score 277 in 60 overs. On a truncated first day of 48 overs, Morris and Butcher again laid the foundation of a substantial total with an opening partnership of 136 – their seventh century partnership of the summer in all matches. In the course of it, the 36-year-old Butcher, for the second successive season, became the first England-qualified player to reach 1,000 runs. However, Glamorgan failed by 1 run to achieve maximum batting points, losing their last two wickets in the 100th over. Surrey declared 149 runs behind, and while at first glance Butcher's target-setting declaration appeared generous, Surrey had only nine fit players. Alikhan had broken a bone in his foot while fielding on the first day and Darren Bicknell was suffering from an infected hand, although he was prepared to bat in an emergency. At 68 for four Surrey were in trouble, but Greig, with a defiant innings of 25 which occupied the same number of overs, saved his team from defeat. Croft, Glamorgan's twenty-year-old off-spinner, bowled an admirable spell of 24 overs, taking a career-best three for 46.

Close of play: First day, Glamorgan 148-1 (H. Morris 62*, P. A. Cottey 4*); Second day, Surrey 150-1 dec.

Glamorgan

*A. R. Butcher c and b Medlycott	67	– c sub b Feltham	21
H. Morris lbw b M. P. Bicknell	62	– c sub b Gray	8
P. A. Cottey c Ward b M. P. Bicknell	19	– not out	35
M. P. Maynard c Ward b Feltham	22	– c Thorpe b Feltham	5
I. V. A. Richards lbw b Feltham	0	– lbw b M. P. Bicknell	14
A. Dale lbw b M. P. Bicknell	25	– lbw b M. P. Bicknell	4
R. D. B. Croft c Lynch b Medlycott	35	– not out	20
†C. P. Metson st Ward b Medlycott	21		
S. J. Dennis c Gray b M. P. Bicknell	2		
S. L. Watkin not out	3		
M. Frost c Clinton b Medlycott	0		
B 10, l-b 9, w 4, n-b 20	43	B 4, l-b 7, n-b 9	20
1/136 2/148 3/188 4/192 5/192 6/252 7/291 8/296 9/299	299	1/37 2/37 3/45 4/70 5/84	(5 wkts dec.) 127

Bonus points – Glamorgan 3, Surrey 4.

Bowling: *First Innings*—Gray 21–5–42–0; M. P. Bicknell 28–4–87–4; Feltham 21–5–60–2; Medlycott 26.5–3–77–4; Greig 3–1–14–0. *Second Innings*—Gray 11–2–29–1; M. P. Bicknell 10–0–36–2; Feltham 7–1–32–2; Medlycott 7–3–19–0.

Surrey

D. J. Bicknell not out	59		
G. S. Clinton b Watkin	41	– c Morris b Croft	22
G. P. Thorpe not out	40	– c Watkin b Croft	4
K. T. Medlycott (did not bat)		– (1) lbw b Frost	4
†D. M. Ward (did not bat)		– (4) c Butcher b Frost	29
M. A. Lynch (did not bat)		– (5) c Metson b Watkin	7
*I. A. Greig (did not bat)		– (6) c Dale b Croft	25
M. A. Feltham (did not bat)		– (7) not out	30
M. P. Bicknell (did not bat)		– (8) not out	0
L-b 9, n-b 1	10	B 6, l-b 6, w 2, n-b 4	18
1/90 (1 wkt dec.)	150	1/6 2/20 3/68 4/68 5/84 6/117 (6 wkts)	139

R. I. Alikhan and A. H. Gray did not bat.

Bonus points – Surrey 1.

Bowling: *First Innings*—Frost 13–2–48–0; Watkin 14–3–36–1; Croft 20.1–6–46–0; Dennis 8–1–11–0. *Second Innings*—Frost 14–2–33–2; Watkin 17–3–33–1; Croft 24–7–46–3; Dennis 2–0–5–0; Richards 2–1–10–0.

Umpires: R. A. White and A. G. T. Whitehead.

GLAMORGAN v GLOUCESTERSHIRE

At Swansea, July 4, 5, 6. Drawn. Glamorgan 4 pts, Gloucestershire 3 pts. Toss: Glamorgan. The rain, which had prevented any play on the first day, relented on Thursday but returned again on the final afternoon as Gloucestershire were making a spirited effort to achieve their first Championship win after a dismal start to the season. Glamorgan took advantage of an inexperienced Gloucestershire attack, which was without the injured Walsh and Lawrence, to obtain maximum batting points. Croft, with 68, again confirmed his all-round potential, while Maynard, Richards and Cowley all batted consistently. Predictably the two captains forfeited an innings, and Gloucestershire were left with a maximum of 102 overs in which to reach their target. Butcher, brother of the Glamorgan captain, and Athey consolidated with a useful third-wicket partnership, and when play was eventually abandoned in mid-afternoon, the game was interestingly poised.

Close of play: First day, No play; Second day, Glamorgan 334-8 dec.

Glamorgan

*A. R. Butcher b Bell	19	†C. P. Metson b Barnes	30
H. Morris c Williams b Curran	21	S. L. Watkin not out	19
P. A. Cottey lbw b Curran	12	S. J. Dennis not out	4
M. P. Maynard c and b Curran	63	B 5, l-b 7, n-b 1	13
I. V. A. Richards run out	41		
R. D. B. Croft b Curran	68	1/39 2/45 3/55 4/134 (8 wkts dec.)	334
N. G. Cowley b Lloyds	44	5/182 6/262 7/302 8/314	

M. Frost did not bat.

Bonus points – Glamorgan 4, Gloucestershire 3 (Score at 100 overs: 306-7).

Bowling: Curran 30–4–92–4; Barnes 21–4–47–1; Bell 27–3–76–1; Bainbridge 3–0–17–0; Alleyne 2–0–14–0; Lloyds 25–6–76–1.

Glamorgan forfeited their second innings.

Gloucestershire

Gloucestershire forfeited their first innings.

G. D. Hodgson lbw b Watkin	23
*A. J. Wright lbw b Dennis	19
I. P. Butcher not out	25
C. W. J. Athey not out	35
L-b 2, w 2, n-b 2	6
1/44 2/44 (2 wkts)	108

P. Bainbridge, K. M. Curran, M. W. Alleyne, †R. C. J. Williams, J. W. Lloyds, R. M. Bell and S. N. Barnes did not bat.

Bowling: Frost 8–1–31–0; Dennis 12–4–23–1; Watkin 6–1–23–1; Croft 8–2–23–0; Cowley 5–2–6–0.

Umpires: R. A. White and A. G. T. Whitehead.

At Hinckley, July 7, 8, 9. GLAMORGAN drew with LEICESTERSHIRE.

GLAMORGAN v WORCESTERSHIRE

At Abergavenny, July 21, 23, 24. Drawn. Glamorgan 5 pts, Worcestershire 6 pts. Toss: Glamorgan. A remarkable game in which a number of records were broken ended with Glamorgan failing by just 2 runs to score 495 for victory. On a perfect pitch and a parched outfield, 1,641 runs were scored, a record aggregate for a three-day county match and only 9 runs less than the record established for a Championship match by Surrey and Lancashire, over four days, earlier in the season. Hick, the first to hit a double-century and century in a match since 1984, became at 24 the youngest batsman to score 50 first-class hundreds, that record having previously been held by Sir Donald Bradman, when 26. He hit five sixes and 38 fours in the course of his unbeaten 252, and his 79-minute hundred in the second innings, off 71 balls (four sixes, eleven fours), was the fastest so far in the 1990 Championship, in addition to being his 50th. Hick's two innings took his aggregate of runs without being dismissed to 592, beating E. D. Weekes's record for first-class cricket in England (575 runs in 1950). Cottey hit sixteen fours in his unbeaten hundred, at which Glamorgan declared in arrears. Next day they were given 88 overs in which to reach their mammoth target. Butcher and Morris began with 256, their ninth century stand of the summer and the best for Glamorgan against Worcestershire, but the loss of four wickets for 32 runs was a setback. Richards struck 43 from only eighteen deliveries, and when Glamorgan required 169 from twenty overs, Neale kept them interested by using occasional bowlers, who were plundered for 69 in six overs. Cowley and Croft put on 124 in fifteen overs, and at the start of the last over 15 runs were needed. Croft hit a six from the fourth ball, but with 3 required from the final delivery, Illingworth conceded no more than a leg-bye. During the game, sixteen sixes and 249 fours were struck on one of the smallest yet loveliest grounds on the County Championship circuit.

Close of play: First day, Glamorgan 50-0 (A. R. Butcher 16*, H. Morris 31*); Second day, Worcestershire 215-1 (T. S. Curtis 81*, G. A. Hick 48*).

Worcestershire

T. S. Curtis b Watkin	23	– not out	111
P. Bent c Cowley b Croft	69	– c Metson b Watkin	79
G. A. Hick not out	252	– not out	100
D. B. D'Oliveira c Maynard b Cowley	121		
I. T. Botham c Morris b Bastien	29		
B 9, l-b 10, n-b 1	20	L-b 9, w 4, n-b 4	17
1/53 2/157 3/421 4/514 (4 wkts dec.)	514	1/132 (1 wkt dec.)	307

*P. A. Neale, †S. J. Rhodes, R. K. Illingworth, P. J. Newport, S. R. Lampitt and N. V. Radford did not bat.

Bonus points – Worcestershire 4, Glamorgan 1.

Bowling: *First Innings*—Frost 18–0–109–0; Watkin 23–3–93–1; Bastien 15.2–2–90–1; Croft 12–0–71–1; Cowley 22–3–101–1; Richards 7–0–31–0. *Second Innings*—Watkin 19–1–109–1; Frost 11–0–38–0; Cowley 1–0–1–0; Bastien 12.3–2–61–0; Croft 10–0–61–0; Butcher 4–0–28–0.

Glamorgan

*A. R. Butcher b Lampitt	79	– c Neale b Illingworth 130
H. Morris lbw b Botham	57	– c Lampitt b Newport 119
P. A. Cottey not out	100	– (5) c D'Oliveira b Newport 1
M. P. Maynard c Lampitt b Botham	15	– (3) c Hick b Newport 1
I. V. A. Richards c Rhodes b Radford	41	– (4) c and b Illingworth 43
R. D. B. Croft c D'Oliveira b Illingworth	28	– (7) not out 91
N. G. Cowley not out	2	– (6) c Rhodes b Botham 63
†C. P. Metson (did not bat)		– not out 12
L-b 1, n-b 4	5	B 10, l-b 21, n-b 2 33
1/140 2/144 3/178 4/248 5/317 (5 wkts dec.)	327	1/256 2/257 3/272 4/288 (6 wkts) 493 5/326 6/450

S. Bastien, S. L. Watkin and M. Frost did not bat.

Bonus points – Glamorgan 4, Worcestershire 2.

Bowling: *First Innings*—Newport 15–0–72–0; Radford 15–1–79–1; Illingworth 15.1–2–80–1; Lampitt 11–2–40–1; Botham 12–1–55–2; Hick 1–1–0–0. *Second Innings*—Newport 19–4–87–3; Radford 12–1–67–0; Lampitt 3–1–14–0; Hick 12–3–61–0; Botham 12–2–40–1; Illingworth 24–2–124–2; Curtis 3–0–30–0; D'Oliveira 3–0–39–0.

Umpires: D. R. Shepherd and D. S. Thompsett.

GLAMORGAN v WARWICKSHIRE

At Swansea, July 25, 26, 27. Glamorgan won by five wickets. Glamorgan 20 pts, Warwickshire 7 pts. Toss: Warwickshire. Glamorgan achieved their fourth Championship win of the season and their first in Wales, and once again they were involved in a game producing an assault on the record books. Moody, Warwickshire's Australian all-rounder, hit the fastest first-class hundred ever in terms of time, reaching 100 in 26 minutes from only 36 balls with his seventh six. He also hit eleven fours, and went to 50 in eleven minutes from sixteen balls. The record, however, was achieved in farcical proceedings. Maynard and Cottey, who were bowling to hasten the declaration, tossed up a succession of donkey-drops which were struck for four or six. Warwickshire had amassed 443 for the loss of three wickets on the first day, with Moles hitting his highest score in Championship cricket. Glamorgan declared 70 runs behind after Morris had made his fifth century of the season and Croft had played another cultured innings. Rain prevented any play for the first hour of the final day, and after the easy runs had been taken, Glamorgan were set 283 to win from 55 overs. Butcher gave them a splendid start with his fifth hundred of the summer, and after Maynard had struck a breezy 56, Richards, hitting an unbeaten 65 from 43 deliveries, took his team to victory with 2 balls remaining.

Close of play: First day, Warwickshire 443-3 (A. J. Moles 224*, P. A. Smith 14*); Second day, Warwickshire 16-2 (A. J. Moles 9*, T. A. Munton 0*).

Warwickshire

A. J. Moles not out	224	– not out 83
*T. A. Lloyd c Watkin b Croft	101	– c Maynard b Bastien 0
Asif Din c Metson b Watkin	47	– lbw b Bastien 6
T. M. Moody c Dennis b Cowley	40	– (5) not out 103
P. A. Smith not out	14	
T. A. Munton (did not bat)		– (4) c Butcher b Cottey 14
L-b 12, w 2, n-b 3	17	L-b 6 6
1/220 2/327 3/394 (3 wkts dec.)	443	1/4 2/15 3/81 (3 wkts dec.) 212

D. A. Reeve, †K. J. Piper, G. C. Small, J. E. Benjamin and A. R. K. Pierson did not bat.

Bonus points – Warwickshire 4 (Score at 100 overs: 381-2).

Bowling: *First Innings*—Watkin 22–2–94–1; Dennis 25–3–91–0; Bastien 17–1–81–0; Cowley 30–2–111–1; Croft 16–2–54–1. *Second Innings*—Watkin 8–1–36–0; Bastien 6–1–11–2; Croft 7–4–12–0; Cowley 4–2–9–0; Maynard 6–0–89–0; Cottey 6–0–49–1.

Glamorgan

*A. R. Butcher c Piper b Munton	33	– c Piper b Pierson	116
H. Morris c Reeve b Pierson	106	– c Munton b Small	15
P. A. Cottey lbw b Pierson	50	– run out	2
M. P. Maynard b Pierson	27	– c Piper b Asif Din	56
I. V. A. Richards c and b Munton	11	– not out	65
R. D. B. Croft not out	74	– (7) not out	12
N. G. Cowley c Moody b Pierson	30	– (6) c Moody b Pierson	10
†C. P. Metson st Piper b Pierson	7		
S. L. Watkin not out	10		
B 6, l-b 14, w 2, n-b 3	25	L-b 3, w 1, n-b 3	7
1/47 2/163 3/201 4/218 5/267 6/347 7/355 (7 wkts dec.)	373	1/42 2/70 3/167 4/206 5/232 (5 wkts)	283

S. Bastien and S. J. Dennis did not bat.

Bonus points – Glamorgan 4, Warwickshire 3.

Bowling: *First Innings*—Small 12–3–47–0; Munton 17–2–65–2; Benjamin 10–1–45–0; Smith 3–0–17–0; Pierson 35–6–101–5; Asif Din 13–2–50–0; Reeve 7–2–28–0. *Second Innings*—Small 12.4–2–62–1; Munton 15–1–77–0; Pierson 15–2–78–2; Benjamin 6–2–24–0; Asif Din 6–0–39–1.

Umpires: D. R. Shepherd and D. S. Thompsett.

At Lord's, August 4, 6, 7. GLAMORGAN drew with MIDDLESEX.

At Southend, August 8, 9, 10. GLAMORGAN drew with ESSEX.

At Worksop, August 11, 13, 14. GLAMORGAN beat NOTTINGHAMSHIRE by 238 runs.

At Swansea, August 18, 19, 20. GLAMORGAN drew with INDIANS (See Indian tour section).

At Ebbw Vale, August 22, 23, 24. GLAMORGAN drew with SRI LANKANS (See Sri Lankan tour section).

GLAMORGAN v DERBYSHIRE

At Cardiff, August 29, 30, 31. Drawn. Glamorgan 8 pts, Derbyshire 4 pts. Toss: Derbyshire. Rain permitted only 25.4 overs on the first day and prevented any play on the final day until 3.30 p.m. Derbyshire made early inroads and reduced Glamorgan to 90 for four on the opening day, but another outstanding contribution from Morris, with useful support from the middle-order and tail-end batsmen, enabled Glamorgan to obtain maximum batting points. Morris's 160 not out, a career-best score, contained twenty fours and was his tenth first-class hundred of the summer. Derbyshire collapsed dramatically in the 31 remaining overs of the second day, losing five wickets for only 5 runs in six overs as they failed to cope with Frost's seam bowling and the spin of young Croft. The latter claimed his three wickets in the space of fifteen balls at a cost of 1 run. However, on the final afternoon Barnett, who had come in at

No. 7, and Warner played more purposefully. They added 73 in fifteen overs, with Warner hitting an attractive 59 from 44 deliveries. After Derbyshire were dismissed there was enough time for Morris to score the 16 he needed to reach 2,000 runs for the season, but when 4 he was unaccountably out to a long-hop from his Derbyshire namesake, a very occasional bowler.

Close of play: First day, Glamorgan 90-4 (H. Morris 47*, A. Dale 2*); Second day, Derbyshire 97-7 (K. J. Barnett 2*, A. E. Warner 3*).

Glamorgan

*A. R. Butcher b Base	4	– not out	13
H. Morris not out	160	– c Mortensen b Morris	4
P. A. Cottey c Adams b Malcolm	8	– b Adams	3
M. P. Maynard c Barnett b Warner	20	– not out	11
I. V. A. Richards c Roberts b Mortensen	0		
A. Dale lbw b Mortensen	16		
R. D. B. Croft c and b Barnett	31		
†C. P. Metson c Bowler b Barnett	22		
S. L. Watkin c Krikken b Warner	8		
S. Bastien not out	9		
L-b 10, w 3, n-b 10	23	B 4, l-b 1, w 1, n-b 4	10
1/6 2/40 3/79 4/80 5/123 6/206 7/262 8/285 (8 wkts dec.)	301	1/8 2/30 (2 wkts)	41

M. Frost did not bat.

Bonus points – Glamorgan 4, Derbyshire 3.

Bowling: *First Innings*—Malcolm 16–4–61–1; Base 18–3–73–1; Mortensen 18–6–48–2; Warner 16–2–53–2; Barnett 21.4–2–56–2. *Second Innings*—Base 2–0–14–0; Morris 4–0–17–1; Adams 2–0–5–1.

Derbyshire

P. D. Bowler b Croft	28	A. E. Warner b Watkin	59
C. J. Adams c Butcher b Watkin	14	D. E. Malcolm b Frost	2
J. E. Morris b Croft	40	O. H. Mortensen not out	1
B. Roberts lbw b Frost	5		
S. J. Base c Morris b Croft	0	B 4, l-b 5	9
A. P. Kuiper b Frost	0		
*K. J. Barnett c Metson b Watkin	30	1/23 2/81 3/92 4/92 5/92	188
†K. M. Krikken lbw b Frost	0	6/92 7/94 8/167 9/170	

Bonus points – Derbyshire 1, Glamorgan 4.

Bowling: Watkin 14.4–0–39–3; Bastien 7–0–41–0; Frost 18–3–80–4; Croft 10–4–10–3; Dale 2–0–9–0.

Umpires: A. A. Jones and R. Palmer.

GLAMORGAN v HAMPSHIRE

At Pontypridd, September 7, 8, 9. Hampshire won by eight wickets. Hampshire 24 pts, Glamorgan 6 pts. Toss: Glamorgan. Hampshire outplayed Glamorgan to secure an emphatic victory shortly after lunch on the third of the scheduled four days. Without Richards, who withdrew at the last minute because of flu, Glamorgan struggled after Morris and Butcher had given them their customary good start. Maynard put together a disciplined half-century, but Marshall demolished the middle- and lower-order batting, taking five for 23 in a spell of twelve overs. Marshall also contributed with the bat, striking a rapid 51, but Hampshire were themselves struggling at 160 for seven before Aymes, with a career-best 75 not out, and in partnership with Tremlett and Udal, changed the course of the match. Hampshire's last three wickets added an invaluable 153 runs to give them a lead of 103. Glamorgan's opening pair again laid the foundation with a partnership of 77, but the later batsmen wilted as Marshall emulated his first-innings onslaught. On the third morning seven wickets fell for 53 runs in 21.4 overs, Marshall finishing with six for 47 and a match aggregate of eleven for 92.

Close of play: First day, Hampshire 92-3 (R. A. Smith 33*, R. J. Maru 4*); Second day, Glamorgan 116-3 (M. P. Maynard 26*, P. A. Cottey 5*).

Glamorgan

First innings		Second innings	
*A. R. Butcher b Udal	58	– c Terry b Tremlett	33
H. Morris lbw b Udal	29	– lbw b Tremlett	45
P. A. Cottey lbw b Maru	13	– (5) c Aymes b Marshall	23
M. P. Maynard c Maru b Marshall	50	– c Terry b Marshall	27
A. Dale c R. A. Smith b Maru	14	– (6) c Aymes b Marshall	0
S. P. James c Gower b Maru	1	– (3) run out	2
R. D. B. Croft not out	27	– c Terry b Marshall	10
†C. P. Metson b Marshall	0	– c R. A. Smith b Marshall	15
S. L. Watkin c R. A. Smith b Marshall	5	– b Udal	3
S. Bastien c Maru b Marshall	2	– c Gower b Marshall	0
M. Frost c Aymes b Marshall	0	– not out	4
B 6, l-b 1, w 1, n-b 3	11	B 1, l-b 7, w 1, n-b 1	10
1/63 2/95 3/118 4/168 5/174 6/174 7/174 8/194 9/200	210	1/77 2/79 3/84 4/119 5/121 6/150 7/151 8/156 9/157	172

Bonus points – Glamorgan 2, Hampshire 4.

Bowling: *First Innings*—Bakker 17–4–51–0; Marshall 22.4–6–45–5; Tremlett 8–2–29–0; Udal 19–5–56–2; Maru 15–8–22–3. *Second Innings*—Bakker 11–0–46–0; Marshall 22.4–8–47–6; Udal 17–7–34–1; Maru 8–4–22–0; Tremlett 7–3–15–2.

Hampshire

First innings		Second innings	
V. P. Terry c Dale b Croft	36	– b Frost	8
C. L. Smith lbw b Frost	1	– not out	25
D. I. Gower c Metson b Watkin	17	– c Cottey b Frost	23
R. A. Smith b Watkin	42	– not out	14
R. J. Maru lbw b Bastien	5		
M. D. Marshall c Croft b Frost	51		
*M. C. J. Nicholas run out	5		
†A. N. Aymes not out	75		
T. M. Tremlett c Maynard b Croft	23		
S. D. Udal c Metson b Bastien	28		
P. J. Bakker c James b Bastien	12		
B 4, l-b 11, n-b 3	18	B 1, n-b 1	2
1/15 2/48 3/87 4/101 5/105 6/158 7/160 8/230 9/295	313	1/11 2/52	(2 wkts) 72

Bonus points – Hampshire 4, Glamorgan 4.

Bowling: *First Innings*—Frost 19–3–59–2; Watkin 22–3–100–2; Bastien 23.4–5–70–3; Croft 26–8–69–2. *Second Innings*—Watkin 6–1–18–0; Frost 6–1–25–2; Croft 5.2–1–28–0.

Umpires: R. Julian and K. E. Palmer.

At Birmingham, September 12, 13, 14, 15. GLAMORGAN lost to WARWICKSHIRE by 170 runs.

At Worcester, September 18, 19, 20, 21. GLAMORGAN lost to WORCESTERSHIRE by 261 runs.

GLOUCESTERSHIRE

Patron: HRH The Princess of Wales
President: F. J. Twisleton
Chairman: R. W. Rossiter
Chairman, Cricket Committee: D. A. Allen
Secretary: P. G. M. August
Phoenix County Ground, Nevil Road, Bristol BS7 9EJ (Telephone: 0272-245216)
Captain: A. J. Wright
Senior Coach: E. J. Barlow
Youth Coach: G. G. M. Wiltshire

Gloucestershire finished the season in such good style, winning four of their last nine Championship matches, that in normal circumstances it would have been possible to look forward to 1991 with a degree of optimism. Unhappily, however, the season again ended on a note of discord, following the decision to dispense with the services of Kevin Curran, one of the best all-rounders in the county game. The first official announcement, after some weeks of rumour, said that Curran was leaving by "mutual consent". But a day or two later, Dickie Rossiter, the club chairman, revealed that the decision had been taken because Curran was perceived to be a disruptive influence. Eddie Barlow, coming to the end of his first season of a three-year contract as chief coach, said: "It was a difficult decision, but one we felt had to be made in the interests of the club."

Curran certainly presented impressive playing credentials to potential employers in the two remaining games of the season, with scores of 144 not out, 78 and 101 not out, as well as capturing nine wickets. In the same two games David Graveney, who had said earlier in the season that he would be ending his long association with the county, took fifteen wickets. Then, at the end of September, Phil Bainbridge announced his retirement to concentrate on his business interests.

These three departures, allied to the near certainty that Courtney Walsh would be touring with the West Indians in 1991, left a daunting task of rebuilding facing Barlow and the captain, Tony Wright, who had joined forces at the start of the summer. They had made no promises of early success, but with the talent available they must have hoped for a good season. Things soon began to go wrong; there were defeats in three different competitions in the first eight days. They finished bottom of their group in the Benson and Hedges Cup, without a win; and with no Championship wins either, they were soon bottom of the table. The weather was unkind for much of June, the Gloucester week being badly affected by rain, and Wright was quite unable to win the toss. Following defeat at Worcester, when both Walsh and David Lawrence were absent through injury, Gloucestershire arrived at Cheltenham in a parlous state, adrift at the foot of the Championship table with no more than 49 points to show from twelve matches.

However, the players seemed to take heart from the more intimate atmosphere of the College ground and its pitches, which encouraged strokemaking and the quick bowlers. The elusive first victory came when

Northamptonshire were routed in their second innings by some high-class fast bowling from Walsh, whose return of eight for 58 proved to be the best in the Championship during the season. After that, although weaknesses were still apparent, the team began to play with much more confidence, and there was a string of outstanding personal performances. Bill Athey's two centuries against Warwickshire were largely responsible for another win, Jack Russell played two fine innings against Nottinghamshire, and Lawrence achieved his first hat-trick in the same match. Mark Alleyne played a truly remarkable innings in the return game against Northamptonshire, his 256 being the highest for the county since 1939, and Dean Hodgson made his first Championship hundred, with 109 against Worcestershire at Bristol.

The ignominy of bottom place was safely avoided and Alleyne, having been overlooked earlier in the season, was awarded his county cap for playing a full part in the revival. Hodgson could also look back with satisfaction, having scored 1,320 first-class runs in his first full season, a deserved reward for his perseverance and the hard work he had put into improving his game. It has to be said, however, that he and Wright were among the weaker opening pairs around the counties. Wright passed 50 only five times in Championship games, and fears that the captaincy might affect his own form proved to be only too well founded. Gloucestershire's low total of batting points, when conditions were more in favour of batsmen than for many years, must be put down, to a large extent, to the lack of a reliable opening partnership. A total of fifteen Championship centuries, although three more than in 1989, was below par, and Athey would assuredly have scored more heavily had his primary task been more one of consolidation than damage limitation.

The middle order was much stronger when Russell was not required by England; he scored his first two centuries in the Championship with the confidence of a player his country has come to rely on. In fact, Russell was missed more for his batting than his peerless wicket-keeping, for Gloucestershire's discovery of the season was his new deputy, Richard "Reggie" Williams, a club cricketer who, with limited Second Eleven experience, made the transition to the first-class game in splendid style. He not only pulled off some spectacular dismissals but also showed promise as a batsman. Little, however, was seen of Martyn Ball, who had looked so promising in 1989, and Graveney gave as one of the reasons for his own departure a desire not to stand in the young off-spinner's path.

There were fewer Championship hundreds – eleven – scored against Gloucestershire than any other county, which reflected well on an attack which was handicapped by Graveney's absence for a lengthy period, while he recovered from a hand operation, and was not as well supported in the field as in previous years. The team showed improved form in the Refuge Assurance League, without being able to mount a prolonged challenge for a place in the top four, while the NatWest Bank Trophy campaign ended in a defeat of record proportions at Old Trafford in the quarter-finals.

The announcement that Andy Babington, from Sussex, and Jonathan Hardy, from Somerset, would be joining the staff for 1991 hardly assuaged understandable anxieties among members and supporters about the immediate outlook. All were keenly interested to see what Barlow, never a man to shirk a challenge, had come up with in the winter months. – Geoffrey Wheeler.

GLOUCESTERSHIRE 1990

[*Bill Smith*

Back row: G. A. Tedstone, E. T. Milburn, S. N. Barnes, K. B. S. Jarvis, G. D. Hodgson, N. M. A. Pritchard, R. C. J. Williams. *Middle row:* G. G. M. Wiltshire (*youth coach*), K. M. Curran, P. W. Romaines, I. P. Butcher, J. W. Lloyds, M. W. Alleyne, M. W. Pooley, M. C. J. Ball. *Front row:* A. W. Stovold, P. Bainbridge, A. J. Wright (*captain*), E. J. Barlow (*senior coach*), C. W. J. Athey, D. A. Graveney. *Insets:* D. V. Lawrence, C. A. Walsh, R. C. Russell.

GLOUCESTERSHIRE RESULTS

All first-class matches – Played 25: Won 5, Lost 7, Drawn 13.

County Championship matches – Played 22: Won 4, Lost 7, Drawn 11.

Bonus points – Batting 51, Bowling 58.

Competition placings – Britannic Assurance County Championship, 13th equal; NatWest Bank Trophy, q-f; Benson and Hedges Cup, 5th in Group A; Refuge Assurance League, 8th equal.

BRITANNIC ASSURANCE CHAMPIONSHIP AVERAGES

BATTING

	Birthplace	*M*	*I*	*NO*	*R*	*HI*	*Avge*
‡C. W. J. Athey	*Middlesbrough*	21	32	6	1,384	131	53.23
‡K. M. Curran	*Rusape, S. Rhodesia*	22	32	8	1,261	144*	52.54
‡M. W. Alleyne	*Tottenham, London*	11	17	0	763	256	44.88
‡P. Bainbridge	*Stoke-on-Trent*	18	25	2	1,019	152	44.30
‡R. C. Russell	*Stroud*	11	16	1	651	120	43.40
‡J. W. Lloyds	*Penang, Malaya*	21	29	10	704	93	37.05
G. D. Hodgson	*Carlisle*	21	34	2	1,059	109	33.09
‡P. W. Romaines	*Bishop Auckland*	5	7	1	177	61	29.50
‡C. A. Walsh	*Kingston, Jamaica*	19	19	3	464	63*	29.00
I. P. Butcher	*Farnborough, Kent*	9	13	3	280	102	28.00
‡A. W. Stovold	*Bristol*	2	4	0	104	74	26.00
‡A. J. Wright	*Stevenage*	22	36	3	809	112	24.51
R. C. J. Williams ...	*Bristol*	7	7	3	82	44*	20.50
‡D. A. Graveney	*Bristol*	12	12	4	100	46*	12.50
M. C. J. Ball	*Bristol*	3	5	0	39	15	7.80
‡D. V. Lawrence	*Gloucester*	20	21	3	124	29	6.88
S. N. Barnes	*Bath*	7	7	1	11	6	1.83

Also batted: R. M. Bell (*St Mary's, Isles of Scilly*) (2 matches) 0, 0*; K. B. S. Jarvis (*Dartford*) (1 match) 0*, 1*; E. T. Milburn (*Nuneaton*) (1 match) 0, 3*; P. A. Owen (*Regina, Canada*) (3 matches) 1, 1; G. A. Tedstone (*Southport*) (4 matches) 13, 6, 23.

* *Signifies not out.* ‡ *Denotes county cap.*

The following played a total of fifteen three-figure innings for Gloucestershire in County Championship matches – C. W. J. Athey 3, K. M. Curran 3, M. W. Alleyne 2, P. Bainbridge 2, R. C. Russell 2, I. P. Butcher 1, G. D. Hodgson 1, A. J. Wright 1.

BOWLING

	O	*M*	*R*	*W*	*BB*	*5W/i*	*Avge*
M. W. Alleyne	77	23	254	11	3-23	0	23.09
C. A. Walsh	584.1	98	1,961	70	8-58	3	28.01
K. M. Curran	561.3	105	1,839	60	5-63	1	30.65
D. V. Lawrence	418.3	45	1,679	50	5-51	2	33.58
D. A. Graveney	462.4	125	1,145	29	5-45	3	39.48
J. W. Lloyds	314.5	52	1,175	24	4-11	0	48.95

Also bowled: C. W. J. Athey 36.5–9–104–2; P. Bainbridge 137.4–24–426–9; M. C. J. Ball 34–7–114–0; S. N. Barnes 138–25–388–8; R. M. Bell 44–7–114–3; K. B. S. Jarvis 12–1–61–1; E. T. Milburn 7–1–34–0; P. A. Owen 57–7–239–4; G. A. Tedstone 2–1–1–0; A. J. Wright 0.5–0–7–0

Wicket-keepers: R. C. Russell 27 ct; R. C. J. Williams 22 ct, 4 st; G. A. Tedstone 3 ct.

Leading Fielders: A. J. Wright 21, C. W. J. Athey 18, K. M. Curran 15, J. W. Lloyds 15.

At Taunton, April 26, 27, 28, 29. GLOUCESTERSHIRE lost to SOMERSET by ten wickets.

GLOUCESTERSHIRE v GLAMORGAN

At Bristol, May 15, 16, 17. Glamorgan won by 145 runs. Glamorgan 23 pts, Gloucestershire 4 pts. Toss: Glamorgan. Glamorgan overcame the handicap of losing two leading batsmen with broken fingers on the first day to gain a thoroughly deserved victory with more than a day to spare. Maynard batted splendidly, hitting ten fours in his 55, before he retired hurt following a blow from a ball from Lawrence – Holmes was the other casualty, a victim of Walsh – and Butcher grafted for some five and a half hours to ensure a reasonable total. The Gloucestershire bowlers fell into the trap of pitching too short, whereas on the second day Glamorgan's attack, with Frost outstanding, showed the merit of bowling to a fuller length. They also benefited from some slipshod batting. Although Butcher and Cowley again played well in Glamorgan's second innings, Gloucestershire were left with nearly two days in which to get 291. Once more, however, they batted poorly, losing three wickets in four balls with the score at 29. Two of these went to the eager Frost, who completed a match haul of ten wickets for the first time.

Close of play: First day, Gloucestershire 0-0 (M. C. J. Ball 0*, A. J. Wright 0*); Second day, Glamorgan 137-4 (N. G. Cowley 50*, C. P. Metson 0*).

Glamorgan

First innings		Second innings	
*A. R. Butcher c Wright b Alleyne	83	– c Wright b Lloyds	53
H. Morris c Athey b Walsh	7	– c Russell b Lawrence	1
G. C. Holmes c Lawrence b Walsh	12	– absent injured	
M. P. Maynard retired hurt	55	– absent injured	
I. V. A. Richards c and b Bainbridge	32	– (3) lbw b Walsh	1
I. Smith c Russell b Curran	19	– (4) c Athey b Lawrence	14
N. G. Cowley not out	51	– (5) c Athey b Walsh	61
†C. P. Metson lbw b Alleyne	0	– (6) b Walsh	4
S. J. Dennis c Ball b Alleyne	6	– (7) b Walsh	0
S. L. Watkin c Athey b Walsh	1	– (8) c Curran b Walsh	10
M. Frost lbw b Walsh	1	– (9) not out	4
B 1, l-b 7, w 2, n-b 14	24	B 4, l-b 5, n-b 13	22
1/20 2/47 3/170 4/203 5/253 6/253 7/275 8/283 9/291	291	1/4 2/11 3/51 4/136 5/153 6/156 7/157 8/170	170

Bonus points – Glamorgan 3, Gloucestershire 3 (Score at 100 overs: 290-8).

In the first innings M. P. Maynard retired hurt at 120.

Bowling: *First Innings*—Walsh 22.4–4–62–4; Lawrence 17–0–65–0; Bainbridge 17–7–36–1; Curran 16–5–39–1; Ball 12–3–34–0; Alleyne 16–5–47–3. *Second Innings*—Walsh 17.2–3–48–5; Lawrence 10–0–40–2; Curran 13–0–35–0; Bainbridge 3–1–12–0; Alleyne 4–3–9–0; Ball 3–2–4–0; Athey 3–2–4–0; Lloyds 5–3–9–1.

Gloucestershire

First innings		Second innings	
M. C. J. Ball c Richards b Frost	5	– (10) lbw b Cowley	15
*A. J. Wright b Frost	3	– (1) lbw b Frost	5
A. W. Stovold c Metson b Frost	7	– (2) c Metson b Watkin	19
P. Bainbridge b Watkin	35	– (3) b Frost	1
C. W. J. Athey c Smith b Dennis	8	– (4) b Frost	0
K. M. Curran c Metson b Watkin	47	– (5) c Richards b Watkin	44
J. W. Lloyds c Metson b Frost	9	– (6) c Metson b Frost	14
M. W. Alleyne b Frost	0	– c Metson b Frost	6
†R. C. Russell c Metson b Dennis	33	– (7) b Dennis	0
C. A. Walsh not out	19	– (9) b Watkin	31
D. V. Lawrence lbw b Cowley	1	– not out	1
B 1, l-b 2, n-b 1	4	L-b 5, w 2, n-b 2	9
1/3 2/11 3/28 4/43 5/75 6/98 7/98 8/134 9/168	171	1/17 2/29 3/29 4/29 5/50 6/51 7/61 8/124 9/129	145

Bonus points – Gloucestershire 1, Glamorgan 4.

Bowling: *First Innings*—Frost 14–4–42–5; Watkin 18–5–55–2; Dennis 15–5–46–2; Cowley 14.3–6–25–1. *Second Innings*—Frost 14–2–40–5; Watkin 13–3–51–3; Dennis 11–3–35–1; Cowley 5.5–2–14–1.

Umpires: J. D. Bond and K. E. Palmer.

GLOUCESTERSHIRE v ZIMBABWEANS

At Bristol, May 19, 21, 22. Drawn. Toss: Gloucestershire. Curran and Lawrence had to pull out all the stops to deny the touring side a notable victory after they had needed no more than 106 runs from what proved to be 21 overs. It would have been Zimbabwe's first first-class win over a county side in England. Gloucestershire's first-innings declaration, after Hodgson had completed a maiden century in just over four hours, was not reciprocated by the visitors, who decided to let an innings dominated by Shah's seven-hour 185 run its course. Shah, missed three times off Lawrence, ground down the attack during a partnership of 178 in 50 overs with Briant. Providing some extrovert moments amid periods of solid defence, he hit 24 fours and had one five. Gloucestershire, looking forward to second-innings batting practice, were undermined by the artful Traicos and finished off by Brandes, but not quite quickly enough for the Zimbabweans to press home their advantage.

Close of play: First day, Zimbabweans 45-0 (W. R. James 24*, A. H. Shah 21*); Second day, Zimbabweans 366-7 (E. A. Brandes 10*, A. J. Traicos 1*).

Gloucestershire

First innings		Second innings	
I. P. Butcher c Robertson b Brent	78	(6) not out	26
G. D. Hodgson c Traicos b Brent	126	(7) c James b Traicos	6
M. W. Alleyne b Shah	37	(4) b Traicos	54
*C. W. J. Athey not out	8	(9) lbw b Brandes	2
P. Bainbridge not out	4	(1) b Traicos	23
J. W. Lloyds (did not bat)		(2) b Jarvis	31
K. M. Curran (did not bat)		(3) c Briant b Jarvis	6
†G. A. Tedstone (did not bat)		(5) c Traicos b Dolphin	23
D. A. Graveney (did not bat)		(8) b Brandes	7
D. V. Lawrence (did not bat)		b Brandes	0
S. N. Barnes (did not bat)		b Brandes	0
B 4, l-b 8, n-b 2	14	B 10, l-b 15, n-b 3	28
1/170 2/255 3/255 (3 wkts dec.)	267	1/52 2/60 3/90 4/138 5/158 6/175 7/188 8/198 9/202	206

Bowling: *First Innings*—Brandes 12–3–32–0; Jarvis 9–1–40–0; Butchart 7–1–23–0; Dolphin 13–2–58–0; Traicos 17–8–30–0; Shah 15–4–44–1; Brent 13–2–28–2. *Second Innings*—Brandes 10.2–3–35–4; Jarvis 21–6–61–2; Traicos 25–10–43–3; Dolphin 16–7–29–1; Brent 5–3–13–0.

Zimbabweans

First innings		Second innings	
W. R. James c Graveney b Lawrence	36	lbw b Curran	23
A. H. Shah c Alleyne b Graveney	185		
C. M. Robertson c Tedstone b Curran	4	(2) c Tedstone b Lawrence	6
*A. J. Pycroft st Tedstone b Graveney	9	retired hurt	15
†G. A. Briant c Graveney b Curran	69		
J. P. Brent b Alleyne	23	(3) not out	27
I. P. Butchart lbw b Curran	6	(5) run out	5
E. A. Brandes lbw b Lawrence	10	(6) not out	8
A. J. Traicos lbw b Lawrence	1		
M. P. Jarvis not out	1		
B 10, l-b 12, w 1, n-b 1	24	B 3, l-b 1, n-b 1	5
1/60 2/78 3/103 4/281 5/340 6/351 7/359 8/366 9/368 (9 wkts dec.)	368	1/14 2/36 3/78 (3 wkts)	89

D. F. Dolphin did not bat.

Bowling: *First Innings*—Lawrence 18.1–5–45–3; Barnes 26–8–80–0; Curran 27–4–80–3; Graveney 23–11–44–2; Alleyne 10–2–42–1; Bainbridge 5–0–29–0; Lloyds 5–0–26–0. *Second Innings*—Lawrence 10.4–0–43–1; Curran 10–2–42–1.

Umpires: J. D. Bond and R. Julian.

At Cambridge, May 23, 24, 25. GLOUCESTERSHIRE beat CAMBRIDGE UNIVERSITY by 70 runs.

At Lord's, May 26, 28, 29. GLOUCESTERSHIRE lost to MIDDLESEX by 10 runs.

GLOUCESTERSHIRE v SOMERSET

At Bristol, June 2, 4, 5. Drawn. Gloucestershire 7 pts, Somerset 4 pts. Toss: Somerset. Rain took some three hours out of the third day and put an end to Gloucestershire's already fading hopes of avenging their defeat in the opening match of the season. The bowlers had been on top until Curran and Russell joined together on the second day in a seventh-wicket partnership which produced 229 runs and put Gloucestershire in a useful position. Russell, welcoming the opportunity of batting with time on his side, made his first Championship century, which included seventeen fours and came from 179 balls in 205 minutes. Curran's hundred took half an hour longer. Wright was able to declare with a lead of 156, but Cook and Burns played out the day's remaining overs with comparative ease. On the shortened final day, a draw soon became the inevitable outcome.

Close of play: First day, Gloucestershire 69-2 (I. P. Butcher 17*, C. W. J. Athey 24*); Second day, Somerset 53-0 (S. J. Cook 19*, N. D. Burns 28*).

Somerset

S. J. Cook c Wright b Lawrence	40	– lbw b Lawrence	81
P. M. Roebuck c Russell b Walsh	3		
A. N. Hayhurst b Curran	15	– not out	17
*C. J. Tavaré c Lloyds b Graveney	30	– not out	1
R. J. Harden c Lawrence b Curran	81		
†N. D. Burns c Russell b Graveney	16	– (2) c Athey b Walsh	38
G. D. Rose c Athey b Lawrence	0		
I. G. Swallow lbw b Graveney	10		
N. A. Mallender b Walsh	8		
J. C. Hallett c Athey b Graveney	0		
A. N. Jones not out	0		
B 3, l-b 11, n-b 8	22	L-b 10, n-b 11	21
1/37 2/58 3/70 4/143 5/174 6/175 7/197 8/215 9/221	225	1/111 2/148	(2 wkts) 158

Bonus points – Somerset 2, Gloucestershire 4.

Bowling: *First Innings*—Walsh 14.5–1–43–2; Lawrence 14–2–65–2; Curran 16–4–41–2; Graveney 27–7–53–4; Athey 1–0–9–0. *Second Innings*—Walsh 17–3–53–1; Lawrence 12–1–41–1; Graveney 18–7–38–0; Curran 4–2–14–0; Athey 0.5–0–2–0.

Gloucestershire

*A. J. Wright c Roebuck b Mallender	4
G. D. Hodgson b Jones	24
I. P. Butcher c Harden b Hallett	41
C. W. J. Athey c Cook b Rose	37
P. Bainbridge c Burns b Rose	29
K. M. Curran not out	103
J. W. Lloyds c and b Rose	3
†R. C. Russell c Burns b Rose	120
B 6, l-b 8, w 2, n-b 4	20
1/9 2/31 3/134 4/142 5/149 6/152 7/381	(7 wkts dec.) 381

D. A. Graveney, C. A. Walsh and D. V. Lawrence did not bat.

Bonus points – Gloucestershire 3, Somerset 2 (Score at 100 overs: 289-6).

C. W. J. Athey, when 27, retired hurt at 76 and resumed at 134.

Bowling: Jones 25–2–96–1; Mallender 26–7–69–1; Rose 24.3–7–78–4; Swallow 19–5–43–0; Hallett 21–3–63–1; Hayhurst 7–1–18–0.

Umpires: J. C. Balderstone and N. T. Plews.

At Ilford, June 6, 7, 8. GLOUCESTERSHIRE drew with ESSEX.

At Manchester, June 9, 11, 12. GLOUCESTERSHIRE lost to LANCASHIRE by five wickets.

At Hove, June 16, 18, 19. GLOUCESTERSHIRE drew with SUSSEX.

GLOUCESTERSHIRE v HAMPSHIRE

At Gloucester, June 20, 21, 22. Drawn. Toss: Hampshire. Although the game began on time, only twenty overs were bowled before the forecast rain arrived. Subsequently the ground took such a soaking that no further play was possible. There were hopes of play on the final afternoon, but the umpires found that the wicket surrounds were still too wet.

Close of play: First day, Gloucestershire 54-2 (G. D. Hodgson 22*, C. W. J. Athey 14*); Second day, No play.

Gloucestershire

*A. J. Wright c Connor b Marshall		9
G. D. Hodgson not out		22
I. P. Butcher b Connor		4
C. W. J. Athey not out		14
L-b 2, w 1, n-b 2		5
1/19 2/25	(2 wkts)	54

K. M. Curran, M. W. Alleyne, J. W. Lloyds, †G. A. Tedstone, D. A. Graveney, C. A. Walsh and D. V. Lawrence did not bat.

Bowling: Marshall 6–0–20–1; Connor 6–1–17–1; Tremlett 4.1–0–9–0; Shine 3–1–6–0; Maru 1–1–0–0.

Hampshire

V. P. Terry, C. L. Smith, T. C. Middleton, D. I. Gower, *M. C. J. Nicholas, M. D. Marshall, †R. J. Parks, R. J. Maru, T. M. Tremlett, C. A. Connor and K. J. Shine.

Umpires: A. A. Jones and D. S. Thompsett.

GLOUCESTERSHIRE v LEICESTERSHIRE

At Gloucester, June 23, 25, 26. Leicestershire won by 111 runs. Leicestershire 20 pts, Gloucestershire 3 pts. Toss: Gloucestershire. Agnew literally swung the game in Leicestershire's favour on the third morning when he took full advantage of a fortuitous change in conditions to wreck the start of Gloucestershire's second innings. There was only an hour's play on the first day, when Boon and Briers began an opening partnership of 146 in 42 overs which put their side in a position to dictate terms. Boon went on to his second Championship century of the summer, hitting eighteen fours in a stay of 322 minutes. Following Wright's declaration and Leicestershire's forfeiture of their second innings, Gloucestershire were left with all of the final day in which to score 352. However, the weather, which had been cold and blustery, was now sultry, and Agnew, swinging the Reader ball in alarming fashion, took four wickets in 28 balls at a cost of 6 runs. Gloucestershire could find no way back from 13 for five, although as conditions eased Bainbridge rode his luck and the later batsmen, showing commendable determination, kept Leicestershire in the field until 70 minutes after tea.

Close of play: First day, Leicestershire 59-0 (T. J. Boon 27*, N. E. Briers 25*); Second day, Gloucestershire 75-0 (G. D. Hodgson 23*, A. J. Wright 51*).

Leicestershire

T. J. Boon b Lloyds 138	†P. A. Nixon not out 24
*N. E. Briers b Lawrence 67	J. P. Agnew not out 46
J. J. Whitaker c Lloyds b Curran 37	
P. Willey c Tedstone b Curran 8	B 1, l-b 11, w 1, n-b 15 28
L. Potter b Walsh 11	
J. D. R. Benson c Graveney b Curran . 45	1/146 2/209 3/217 (8 wkts dec.) 426
C. C. Lewis lbw b Lloyds 6	4/267 5/289 6/314
W. K. M. Benjamin c Athey b Curran . 16	7/342 8/361

A. D. Mullally did not bat.

Bonus points – Leicestershire 4, Gloucestershire 3 (Score at 100 overs: 357-7).

Bowling: Walsh 21–2–97–1; Curran 28–3–100–4; Lawrence 19–1–84–1; Bainbridge 7–4–16–0; Graveney 28–6–96–0; Lloyds 7–1–21–2.

Leicestershire forfeited their second innings.

Gloucestershire

G. D. Hodgson not out	23	– b Agnew 4
*A. J. Wright not out	51	– lbw b Agnew 2
I. P. Butcher (did not bat)		– c Potter b Benjamin 0
C. W. J. Athey (did not bat)		– c Potter b Agnew 5
P. Bainbridge (did not bat)		– c Nixon b Mullally 74
K. M. Curran (did not bat)		– c Nixon b Agnew 0
J. W. Lloyds (did not bat)		– c Whitaker b Benjamin 26
†G. A. Tedstone (did not bat)		– c Benjamin b Lewis 23
D. A. Graveney (did not bat)		– not out 46
C. A. Walsh (did not bat)		– b Mullally 12
D. V. Lawrence (did not bat)		– c Whitaker b Agnew 29
L-b 1	1	B 5, l-b 9, w 3, n-b 2 19
(no wkt dec.)	75	1/6 2/7 3/11 4/13 5/13 240 6/102 7/135 8/173 9/187

Bowling: *First Innings*—Willey 7–0–25–0; Potter 7–0–49–0. *Second Innings*—Benjamin 23–11–44–2; Agnew 25.5–10–70–5; Mullally 16–5–37–2; Lewis 17–3–73–1; Willey 2–1–2–0.

Umpires: A. A. Jones and D. S. Thompsett.

At Derby, June 30, July 2, 3. GLOUCESTERSHIRE drew with DERBYSHIRE.

At Swansea, July 4, 5, 6. GLOUCESTERSHIRE drew with GLAMORGAN.

At Worcester, July 7, 9, 10. GLOUCESTERSHIRE lost to WORCESTERSHIRE by 148 runs.

GLOUCESTERSHIRE v YORKSHIRE

At Cheltenham, July 21, 23, 24. Drawn. Gloucestershire 6 pts, Yorkshire 5 pts. Toss: Yorkshire. It was surprising that there were no more than two individual hundreds in a match of 1,244 runs. Gloucestershire's innings of 574 was their highest against Yorkshire, and the total against that county had been exceeded only by Somerset, on two occasions. Metcalfe set the tone with a brilliant century before lunch on the opening day, needing only 108 deliveries to reach three figures as the ball was sent racing over the parched outfield, and he finished with 27 fours and two sixes in his 162 made from 172 balls. Moxon was a very junior partner in an opening stand of 204. Gloucestershire, faced with some good off-spin bowling by young

Batty, batted more soberly until the follow-on had been saved. Bainbridge then cut loose and made his first hundred for a year, hitting a six and 21 fours in all. Wright, bravely, decided to try to force a win rather than declare behind, and after Walsh had slogged four sixes and six fours to reach 63 from 42 balls, Yorkshire went in again facing arrears of 123. They had no trouble saving the game.

Close of play: First day, Gloucestershire 42-0 (G. D. Hodgson 26*, A. J. Wright 15*); Second day, Gloucestershire 458-6 (P. Bainbridge 132*, R. C. Russell 4*).

Yorkshire

*M. D. Moxon b Walsh	66	– c and b Lloyds	18
A. A. Metcalfe c and b Lawrence	162	– c Wright b Lawrence	26
†R. J. Blakey c Russell b Curran	9	– c Curran b Lloyds	94
K. Sharp c Russell b Lawrence	38		
P. E. Robinson lbw b Walsh	49	– (4) not out	70
D. Byas not out	63	– (5) not out	0
P. Carrick c Russell b Curran	17		
C. S. Pickles not out	28		
B 4, l-b 4, w 1, n-b 10	19	L-b 1, w 2, n-b 8	11
1/204 2/224 3/286 4/297 5/362 6/409 (6 wkts dec.)	451	1/45 2/51 3/213 (3 wkts dec.)	219

P. J. Hartley, J. D. Batty and S. D. Fletcher did not bat.

Bonus points – Yorkshire 4, Gloucestershire 2.

Bowling: *First Innings*—Walsh 22–5–70–2; Lawrence 14–0–94–2; Curran 22–4–84–2; Bainbridge 7–0–37–0; Lloyds 14–1–73–0; Owen 16–1–72–0; Athey 4–0–13–0. *Second Innings*—Walsh 11–1–46–0; Curran 10–4–30–0; Lawrence 8–0–34–1; Lloyds 14–3–61–2; Owen 16–3–47–0.

Gloucestershire

G. D. Hodgson b Batty	65
*A. J. Wright c Robinson b Batty	78
P. W. Romaines c Byas b Fletcher	46
C. W. J. Athey b Batty	68
P. Bainbridge c Blakey b Hartley	152
K. M. Curran c Moxon b Hartley	8
J. W. Lloyds b Batty	38
†R. C. Russell b Hartley	16
C. A. Walsh not out	63
D. V. Lawrence c Blakey b Fletcher	6
P. A. Owen run out	1
B 8, l-b 17, w 1, n-b 7	33
1/126 2/163 3/227 4/309 5/350 6/452 7/489 8/499 9/554	574

Bonus points – Gloucestershire 4, Yorkshire 1 (Score at 100 overs: 309-4).

Bowling: Hartley 28–5–111–3; Fletcher 28.1–5–98–2; Carrick 50–16–144–0; Pickles 8–0–45–0; Batty 38–6–137–4; Byas 1–0–14–0.

Umpires: J. H. Hampshire and R. A. White.

GLOUCESTERSHIRE v NORTHAMPTONSHIRE

At Cheltenham, July 25, 26, 27. Gloucestershire won by an innings and 128 runs. Gloucestershire 24 pts, Northamptonshire 3 pts. Toss: Northamptonshire. Although every player in the Gloucestershire side made a valuable contribution to their first Championship victory of the season, it might not have been achieved without the fine bowling of Walsh, who dealt Northamptonshire a series of hammer blows. On the first morning his spell of three for 11 in 25 balls began a collapse that was completed by Curran and Lawrence. Ambrose could strike no such sparks from the pitch when Gloucestershire batted, and Wright's first century of the season was well supported all down the order. Walsh knocked the heart out of the Northamptonshire second innings by the sheer pace and variety of his attack, capturing five wickets for 9 runs in 27 balls. Nevertheless Gloucestershire, unable to finish the match in two days, experienced some anxious hours of waiting on the Friday. Three of the remaining four wickets were taken in the 55 minutes of play possible before lunch, but the defiant Felton refused to be moved. Rain then prevented any play until four o'clock when Walsh, fittingly, immediately dismissed Robinson to complete match figures of eleven for 99.

Close of play: First day, Gloucestershire 181-2 (A. J. Wright 94*, C. W. J. Athey 0*); Second day, Northamptonshire 113-6 (N. A. Felton 34*, D. Ripley 25*).

Northamptonshire

A. Fordham c Wright b Curran	13	– c Williams b Walsh	1
*W. Larkins c Williams b Walsh	16	– b Walsh	30
N. A. Felton c Williams b Walsh	6	– not out	82
R. J. Bailey b Curran	36	– c Hodgson b Owen	3
D. J. Capel b Walsh	10	– (6) c Romaines b Walsh	4
R. G. Williams c Williams b Curran	47	– (7) b Walsh	0
†D. Ripley c Williams b Lawrence	6	– (8) b Walsh	31
A. R. Roberts c Lloyds b Curran	0	– (9) b Walsh	0
J. G. Hughes c Williams b Lawrence	1	– (5) hit wkt b Walsh	0
C. E. L. Ambrose c Wright b Lawrence	8	– lbw b Curran	6
M. A. Robinson not out	0	– c Williams b Walsh	0
L-b 1, n-b 6	7	B 8, l-b 4, n-b 8	20
1/20 2/34 3/39 4/61 5/123 6/136 7/140 8/142 9/142	150	1/40 2/41 3/53 4/60 5/72 6/72 7/127 8/127 9/141	177

Bonus points – Northamptonshire 1, Gloucestershire 4.

Bowling: *First Innings*—Walsh 12–0–41–3; Curran 13–4–37–4; Lawrence 13.4–1–52–3; Owen 5–0–12–0; Athey 2–1–7–0. *Second Innings*—Walsh 19.2–6–58–8; Curran 16–1–58–1; Lloyds 5–3–16–0; Owen 4–1–13–1; Lawrence 6–2–20–0.

Gloucestershire

G. D. Hodgson c Fordham b Robinson	50
*A. J. Wright c Ripley b Ambrose	112
P. W. Romaines b Williams	28
C. W. J. Athey b Bailey	27
P. Bainbridge c Capel b Roberts	34
K. M. Curran c and b Roberts	86
J. W. Lloyds c Ripley b Ambrose	34
C. A. Walsh c Larkins b Robinson	12
†R. C. J. Williams not out	44
D. V. Lawrence b Williams	0
L-b 13, w 5, n-b 10	28
1/97 2/159 3/203 4/271 5/271 6/315 7/343 8/454 9/455 (9 wkts dec.)	455

P. A. Owen did not bat.

Bonus points – Gloucestershire 4, Northamptonshire 2 (Score at 100 overs: 310-5).

Bowling: Ambrose 22–7–53–2; Robinson 36–5–119–2; Roberts 39–6–123–2; Hughes 17–4–69–0; Williams 19.2–7–42–2; Bailey 9–1–36–1.

Umpires: J. H. Hampshire and R. A. White.

GLOUCESTERSHIRE v SURREY

At Cheltenham, July 28, 30, 31. Drawn. Gloucestershire 5 pts, Surrey 5 pts. Toss: Surrey. With any one of four results possible off the final ball, the Cheltenham Festival came to a thrilling conclusion. Waqar Younis, Surrey's last man, needing 3 to win the game, swung wildly at Lawrence and edged the ball uppishly. But although Williams, the Gloucestershire wicket-keeper, just got his right hand to it, he could not complete the catch and the batsmen crossed for a single. From Lawrence's previous delivery, Williams had held a fine catch to send back Martin Bicknell and end a ninth-wicket partnership with Medlycott which had taken Surrey to the brink of victory. They had been set a target of 304 in 59 overs. On the opening day, Alleyne batted for five hours for his highest first-class score to date, and in doing so he dashed Greig's hopes of dismissing Gloucestershire cheaply. Bainbridge, who had retired hurt after being hit on the hand by a ball from Younis, returned at the fall of the seventh wicket to see the score past 300. There was an accomplished 83 not out from Darren Bicknell in the Surrey first innings, and he laid a secure foundation for the second-innings run-chase. Explosive batting by Lynch put Surrey in command, but Lawrence, bowling genuinely fast, brought Gloucestershire back into contention.

Close of play: First day, Surrey 9-0 (D. J. Bicknell 1*, G. S. Clinton 8*); Second day, Gloucestershire 44-1 (G. D. Hodgson 25*, C. W. J. Athey 3*).

Gloucestershire

G. D. Hodgson c Medlycott b M. P. Bicknell . . 54 – c M. P. Bicknell b Medlycott . . . 44
*A. J. Wright c Greig b M. P. Bicknell . . . . 2 – c Waqar Younis b M. P. Bicknell 12
P. Bainbridge not out 37
C. W. J. Athey c Thorpe b M. P. Bicknell . . . . . 0 – (3) not out 86
M. W. Alleyne c and b Feltham . . . . .118 – (4) c Lynch b Greig 15
K. M. Curran lbw b Medlycott . . . . 46 – (5) c Feltham b Greig 25
J. W. Lloyds b Medlycott . . . . 23 – (6) not out 8
†R. C. J. Williams c Sargeant b Waqar Younis . 0
D. V. Lawrence c Sargeant b Waqar Younis . . . 2
S. N. Barnes c Thorpe b M. P. Bicknell 2
P. A. Owen c and b Feltham 1
B 1, l-b 7, n-b 8 16   B 2, l-b 6, w 4 12

1/14 2/27 3/86 4/169 5/217 6/218 7/222 8/283 9/291   301   1/28 2/96 3/129 4/183   (4 wkts dec.) 202

Bonus points – Gloucestershire 3, Surrey 3 (Score at 100 overs: 284-8).

In the first innings P. Bainbridge, when 3, retired hurt at 23 and resumed at 222.

Bowling: *First Innings*—Waqar Younis 23–4–69–2; M. P. Bicknell 24–4–63–4; Feltham 19.4–2–73–2; Greig 2–0–6–0; Medlycott 35–10–82–2. *Second Innings*—Waqar Younis 13–4–36–0; M. P. Bicknell 3–0–17–1; Medlycott 25.3–7–97–1; Feltham 6–1–17–0; Greig 10–2–27–2.

Surrey

D. J. Bicknell not out . . . . 83 – c sub b Lloyds 81
G. S. Clinton c Williams b Lloyds . . . . 38 – c Williams b Owen 13
G. P. Thorpe b Lloyds . . . . 0 – (4) c Williams b Lawrence 0
D. M. Ward c Hodgson b Barnes . . . . 5 – (3) c Williams b Lawrence 45
M. A. Lynch c Lloyds b Owen . . . . 33 – b Curran 77
*I. A. Greig st Williams b Owen . . . . 1 – c Curran b Lawrence 34
M. A. Feltham c Hodgson b Lloyds . . . . 14 – b Lawrence 1
K. T. Medlycott not out . . . . 14 – not out 18
†N. F. Sargeant (did not bat) . . . . – c Wright b Curran 1
M. P. Bicknell (did not bat) . . . . – c Williams b Lawrence 7
Waqar Younis (did not bat) . . . . – not out 1
B 3, l-b 7, w 1, n-b 1 12   B 6, l-b 16, n-b 2 24

1/83 2/83 3/90 4/138 5/140 6/161   (6 wkts dec.) 200   1/45 2/124 3/124 4/194 5/259 6/262 7/273 8/278 9/301   (9 wkts) 302

Bonus points – Surrey 2, Gloucestershire 2.

Bowling: *First Innings*—Lawrence 7–1–28–0; Curran 10–2–26–0; Alleyne 5–1–15–0; Barnes 12–4–19–1; Lloyds 19.3–5–65–3; Owen 9–2–37–2. *Second Innings*—Lawrence 15–3–54–5; Curran 14–1–59–2; Lloyds 15–0–80–1; Owen 7–0–58–1; Barnes 8–1–29–0.

Umpires: J. C. Balderstone and B. Leadbeater.

At Bristol, August 4, 5, 6. GLOUCESTERSHIRE drew with INDIANS (See Indian tour section).

GLOUCESTERSHIRE v WARWICKSHIRE

At Bristol, August 8, 9, 10. Gloucestershire won by 66 runs. Gloucestershire 21 pts, Warwickshire 7 pts. Toss: Warwickshire. Nothing looked less likely at the start of the final day than a win for Gloucestershire, who were still 53 runs behind with two second-innings wickets already gone. However, for the second time in the match, Athey stood firmly in

Warwickshire's path. Romaines was a stout partner in a stand of 155 for the third wicket, and by the time Athey had completed his second century of the game, having played almost a lone hand in the first innings, Gloucestershire were out of danger. Curran benefited from the cheap runs then offered before Wright invited his opponents to attempt a target of 243 in 33 overs. While Asif Din was applying his wristy skills, Warwickshire were in with a chance. But he and Reeve both fell in the same over to Lawrence, and when Warwickshire turned to saving the game, Lloyds swept through the tail. Warwickshire were left regretting their inability to capitalise on Small's fine bowling in Gloucestershire's first innings and on the opening partnership of 131 between Moles and Ratcliffe in their own.

Close of play: First day, Warwickshire 59-0 (A. J. Moles 19*, J. D. Ratcliffe 34*); Second day, Gloucestershire 39-2 (P. W. Romaines 16*, C. W. J. Athey 9*).

Gloucestershire

G. D. Hodgson c Ostler b Munton	8	– b Small 8
*A. J. Wright c Lloyd b Small	4	– c Reeve b Munton 4
P. W. Romaines c Ostler b Munton	1	– c Smith b Pierson 61
C. W. J. Athey not out	108	– c Piper b Lloyd 122
M. W. Alleyne c Ratcliffe b Small	34	– b Pierson 13
K. M. Curran c Ratcliffe b Small	15	– not out 83
J. W. Lloyds c Piper b Reeve	14	– not out 18
†R. C. J. Williams c Piper b Reeve	2	
C. A. Walsh lbw b Reeve	8	
D. V. Lawrence b Small	7	
S. N. Barnes c Ostler b Small	0	
L-b 10, w 2	12	B 14, l-b 10, n-b 1 25
1/11 2/13 3/13 4/94 5/114 6/160 7/174 8/184 9/207	213	1/10 2/24 3/179 4/196 5/254 (5 wkts dec.) 334

Bonus points – Gloucestershire 2, Warwickshire 4.

Bowling: *First Innings*—Small 23–5–57–5; Munton 23–5–69–2; Reeve 25–4–46–3; Smith 10–1–31–0. *Second Innings*—Small 16–6–39–1; Munton 22–4–40–1; Pierson 18–4–69–2; Reeve 6–3–9–0; Smith 8–2–26–0; Asif Din 5–2–17–0; Lloyd 9–1–58–1; Moles 6–0–52–0.

Warwickshire

A. J. Moles c Lloyds b Curran	94	– c Athey b Walsh 12
J. D. Ratcliffe b Lloyds	75	– c Athey b Curran 7
*T. A. Lloyd c Williams b Lloyds	11	– (5) c Lloyds b Curran 5
Asif Din b Walsh	0	– (3) c Williams b Lawrence 65
P. A. Smith run out	4	– (4) c Curran b Walsh 21
D. A. Reeve lbw b Walsh	1	– c Williams b Lawrence 20
D. P. Ostler c Romaines b Curran	54	– b Lloyds 23
†K. J. Piper c Wright b Lawrence	0	– (9) b Lloyds 9
G. C. Small c Curran b Alleyne	24	– (8) st Williams b Lloyds 5
A. R. K. Pierson not out	16	– not out 0
T. A. Munton c Hodgson b Curran	2	– c Curran b Lloyds 0
B 3, l-b 17, n-b 4	24	B 1, l-b 6, n-b 2 9
1/131 2/147 3/148 4/164 5/171 6/203 7/211 8/257 9/302	305	1/21 2/23 3/51 4/90 5/139 6/140 7/151 8/171 9/176 176

Bonus points – Warwickshire 3, Gloucestershire 3 (Score at 100 overs: 258-8).

Bowling: *First Innings*—Walsh 32–10–86–2; Curran 27.1–9–50–3; Lawrence 16–2–56–1; Barnes 15–2–38–0; Lloyds 19–5–51–2; Alleyne 2–1–4–1. *Second Innings*—Walsh 11–0–51–2; Curran 9–0–70–2; Lawrence 6–0–37–2; Lloyds 3.4–0–11–4.

Umpires: D. R. Shepherd and P. B. Wight.

GLOUCESTERSHIRE v KENT

At Bristol, August 11, 13, 14. Drawn. Gloucestershire 4 pts, Kent 6 pts. Toss: Kent. Kent's domination was disturbed when the weather broke on the third morning, ruling out a resumption until 40 minutes after lunch. Gloucestershire had finished the second day five wickets down and still needing 128 to avoid the follow-on. But after the rain, with time pressing, they declared, Kent forfeited their second innings, and Gloucestershire set off in pursuit of 278 in 57 overs. Athey, having repaired a poor start to the first innings, batting for four and a half hours, was called upon to do the same in the second. Walsh, enjoying his promotion to No. 5, hit 55 from 38 balls, including five sixes, but Gloucestershire were never really on terms with the required rate. When Athey was sixth out at 237, they were out of the hunt. Davis, who bowled shrewdly for Kent, was well supported in the field. Gloucestershire, on the other hand, dropped too many catches on the opening day when, in splendid batting conditions, runs flowed freely for Kent and Ward, in particular, played with great purpose.

Close of play: First day, Kent 452-7 (S. A. Marsh 54*, R. P. Davis 2*); Second day, Gloucestershire 221-5 (K. M. Curran 45*, J. W. Lloyds 0*).

Kent

S. G. Hinks c Hodgson b Alleyne 53
*M. R. Benson c Williams b Walsh ... 65
N. R. Taylor c Alleyne b Walsh 22
G. R. Cowdrey c Walsh b Alleyne 80
T. R. Ward c Walsh b Curran 82
M. V. Fleming c Athey b Curran 45
†S. A. Marsh c Hodgson b Walsh 54
D. J. M. Kelleher c Williams b Walsh . 35
R. P. Davis c sub b Curran 20
C. Penn not out 23
B 1, l-b 8, w 1, n-b 9 19

1/98 2/145 3/150 4/293 5/350 6/362 7/448 8/454 9/498 (9 wkts dec.) 498

M. M. Patel did not bat.

Bonus points – Kent 4, Gloucestershire 2 (Score at 100 overs: 379-6).

Bowling: Walsh 24–2–117–4; Curran 22–4–97–3; Lawrence 14–4–69–0; Barnes 17–1–51–0; Lloyds 30–6–114–0; Alleyne 13–3–41–2.

Kent forfeited their second innings.

Gloucestershire

	First innings		Second innings	
G. D. Hodgson c Marsh b Penn	2	– c Benson b Davis	17
*A. J. Wright b Davis	16	– run out	9
P. W. Romaines c Hinks b Penn	8	– c Cowdrey b Davis	21
C. W. J. Athey c Marsh b Fleming	83	– c and b Penn	71
M. W. Alleyne c Davis b Patel	47	– (6) c Ward b Davis	40
K. M. Curran not out	45	– (7) c and b Davis	13
J. W. Lloyds not out	0	– (8) not out	6
C. A. Walsh (did not bat)		– (5) b Davis	55
D. V. Lawrence (did not bat)		– st Marsh b Davis	0
†R. C. J. Williams (did not bat)		– not out	0
B 2, l-b 7, w 1, n-b 10	20	B 7, l-b 13, n-b 4	24
1/2 2/32 3/33 4/127 5/221 (5 wkts dec.)	221	1/20 2/53 3/56 4/134 5/214 6/237 7/256 8/256 (8 wkts)	256

S. N. Barnes did not bat.

Bonus points – Gloucestershire 2, Kent 2.

Bowling: *First Innings*—Penn 20–5–44–2; Kelleher 20–7–35–0; Davis 19–6–59–1; Patel 17–4–38–1; Fleming 18–5–36–1. *Second Innings*—Penn 13–0–59–1; Kelleher 9–1–18–0; Davis 22.5–1–111–6; Patel 5–1–30–0; Fleming 7–0–18–0.

Umpires: D. R. Shepherd and P. B. Wight.

At Nottingham, August 18, 20, 21. GLOUCESTERSHIRE drew with NOTTINGHAMSHIRE.

At Northampton, August 23, 24, 25, 27. GLOUCESTERSHIRE beat NORTHAMPTONSHIRE by 157 runs.

GLOUCESTERSHIRE v WORCESTERSHIRE

At Bristol, September 7, 8, 9, 10. Drawn. Gloucestershire 5 pts, Worcestershire 5 pts. Toss: Gloucestershire. A slow pitch dictated the course of the match from the outset. The bowlers had a heartbreaking task, although Illingworth bowled impressively on the first day when Hodgson, who reached his maiden Championship century, and Bainbridge, whose own hundred came at a much livelier tempo, put on 182 in 42 overs. That Hick would achieve the 52nd hundred of his career was almost a foregone conclusion, although he took more than four hours over it as Worcestershire carefully removed the threat of the follow-on. Gloucestershire, meanwhile, improved their over-rate by giving Graveney a long bowl. Neale declared 101 behind, but with Athey in a painfully slow mode on the final day, Gloucestershire's declaration was delayed until only 55 overs remained for Worcestershire to score 321. Hit on the helmet by a delivery from Lawrence, Hick recovered to pose a brief threat. When he was brilliantly caught in the deep, Worcestershire were content to coast to the draw.

Close of play: First day, Gloucestershire 376-5 (M. W. Alleyne 47*, R. C. Russell 2*); Second day, Worcestershire 185-1 (T. S. Curtis 81*, G. A. Hick 28*); Third day, Gloucestershire 72-2 (A. J. Wright 48*).

Gloucestershire

G. D. Hodgson c Rhodes b Illingworth	109	– lbw b Newport	22
*A. J. Wright b Newport	21	– st Rhodes b Illingworth	72
P. Bainbridge c Rhodes b Illingworth	129	– (4) lbw b Illingworth	39
C. W. J. Athey c Lord b Illingworth	18	– (5) not out	34
M. W. Alleyne c and b Radford	52	– (6) c and b Illingworth	8
K. M. Curran c Rhodes b Illingworth	18	– (7) not out	35
†R. C. Russell c Curtis b D'Oliveira	76		
J. W. Lloyds not out	71		
C. A. Walsh c Curtis b D'Oliveira	18		
D. V. Lawrence not out	6	– (3) lbw b Newport	0
B 1, l-b 22, n-b 10	33	B 2, l-b 3, n-b 4	9
1/52 2/234 3/284 4/323 5/365 6/381 7/526 8/544 (8 wkts dec.)	551	1/67 2/72 3/115 4/150 5/164 (5 wkts dec.)	219

D. A. Graveney did not bat.

Bonus points – Gloucestershire 4, Worcestershire 1 (Score at 100 overs: 358-4).

Bowling: *First Innings*—Dilley 21–3–54–0; Radford 25–6–98–1; Newport 29–7–80–1; Lampitt 25–2–103–0; Illingworth 46–12–121–4; Hick 13–1–49–0; D'Oliveira 2.3–0–23–2. *Second Innings*—Dilley 10–0–43–0; Radford 12–1–45–0; Illingworth 27–7–91–3; Newport 10–3–19–2; Lampitt 4–0–16–0.

Worcestershire

T. S. Curtis lbw b Graveney	96	– lbw b Lawrence	8
G. J. Lord b Lloyds	64	– not out	70
G. A. Hick c Alleyne b Bainbridge	110	– c Wright b Graveney	38
D. B. D'Oliveira c Alleyne b Graveney	5	– b Graveney	0
*P. A. Neale c Alleyne b Bainbridge	95	– b Walsh	3
S. R. Lampitt not out	45	– not out	20
†S. J. Rhodes not out	7		
B 7, l-b 8, w 1, n-b 12	28	L-b 6, n-b 3	9
1/114 2/219 3/245 4/343 5/431 (5 wkts dec.)	450	1/23 2/88 3/88 4/103 (4 wkts)	148

N. V. Radford, P. J. Newport, R. K. Illingworth and G. R. Dilley did not bat.

Bonus points – Worcestershire 4, Gloucestershire 1 (Score at 100 overs: 301-3).

Bowling: *First Innings*—Walsh 28–8–83–0; Lawrence 15–0–55–0; Curran 15–8–25–0; Graveney 53–15–96–2; Lloyds 23–1–97–1; Alleyne 4–1–26–0; Bainbridge 16.4–4–39–2; Athey 6–1–14–0. *Second Innings*—Lawrence 7–0–30–1; Curran 8–1–21–0; Graveney 19–3–58–2; Walsh 10–2–24–1; Lloyds 6–0–9–0.

Umpires: D. R. Shepherd and P. B. Wight.

GLOUCESTERSHIRE v SUSSEX

At Bristol, September 12, 13, 14. Gloucestershire won by an innings and 86 runs. Gloucestershire 24 pts, Sussex 4 pts. Toss: Gloucestershire. Graveney led Gloucestershire from the field after taking the final Sussex wicket on his last home appearance for the county he had served for nineteen seasons. Ironically, Gloucestershire's victory, which ensured that they would escape bottom place, where they had spent much of the season, was founded on the efforts of Graveney, who took ten wickets, and Curran, another departure. Curran's adieu was marked by the completion of the modern double of 1,000 runs and 50 wickets during the course of the century which condemned Sussex to defeat. Sussex, who had the worst of the conditions, had struggled against keen Gloucestershire bowling on the opening day, but Pigott put them back in the match. At 82 for five early on the second day, Gloucestershire had lost their advantage. However, Bainbridge attacked while Curran, after being all but bowled by the first ball he received from Salisbury, dropped anchor. When Bainbridge went, Curran in unhurried fashion – he took four and a half hours (233 balls) to reach his hundred – built a match-winning advantage with support from Russell, Lloyds and Walsh. Although Sussex failed to take the match into the fourth day, Moores played with great spirit to delay the end.

Close of play: First day, Gloucestershire 59-4 (P. Bainbridge 30*, D. V. Lawrence 4*); Second day, Gloucestershire 435-8 (K. M. Curran 133*, C. A. Walsh 46*).

Sussex

N. J. Lenham b Curran	11	– lbw b Walsh	33
D. M. Smith c Lloyds b Graveney	52	– c Curran b Lawrence	0
*P. W. G. Parker c Graveney b Curran	0	– c Wright b Graveney	8
A. P. Wells c Wright b Curran	5	– c and b Graveney	27
M. P. Speight c and b Graveney	34	– c Athey b Graveney	13
A. I. C. Dodemaide c Curran b Walsh	17	– c Curran b Lawrence	20
†P. Moores c Lloyds b Graveney	0	– b Walsh	72
A. C. S. Pigott c Russell b Graveney	1	– lbw b Lawrence	0
I. D. K. Salisbury b Walsh	0	– c Alleyne b Graveney	0
B. T. P. Donelan not out	37	– b Graveney	15
R. A. Bunting c Athey b Graveney	4	– not out	0
L-b 10, n-b 8	18	B 2, l-b 5, n-b 7	14
1/22 2/53 3/103 4/110 5/110 6/112 7/113 8/140 9/155	179	1/7 2/29 3/55 4/83 5/88 6/132 7/136 8/150 9/198	202

Bonus points – Sussex 1, Gloucestershire 4.

In the first innings N. J. Lenham, when 4, retired hurt at 22-0 and resumed at 140.

Bowling: *First Innings*—Walsh 17–2–45–2; Lawrence 12–4–17–0; Curran 15–6–24–3; Bainbridge 6–1–7–0; Athey 4–1–15–0; Alleyne 5–1–16–0; Graveney 23.4–7–45–5. *Second Innings*—Lawrence 15–3–59–3; Curran 11–5–20–0; Graveney 37.2–15–59–5; Walsh 15–3–46–2; Lloyds 5–1–11–0.

Gloucestershire

G. D. Hodgson c Salisbury b Pigott	1
*A. J. Wright c Salisbury b Pigott	3
P. Bainbridge c Moores b Bunting	97
C. W. J. Athey c Moores b Pigott	4
M. W. Alleyne c Donelan b Dodemaide	15
D. V. Lawrence lbw b Salisbury	13
K. M. Curran not out	144
†R. C. Russell c Moores b Donelan	31
J. W. Lloyds b Dodemaide	50
C. A. Walsh b Pigott	63
D. A. Graveney c Moores b Pigott	3
B 21, l-b 17, w 1, n-b 4	43
1/4 2/5 3/19 4/52 5/82 6/173 7/244 8/331 9/453	467

Bonus points – Gloucestershire 4, Sussex 3 (Score at 100 overs: 308-7).

Bowling: Dodemaide 28–6–83–2; Pigott 37.3–7–87–5; Bunting 22–4–67–1; Salisbury 29–6–103–1; Donelan 31–8–89–1.

Umpires: P. J. Eele and K. J. Lyons.

At Southampton, September 18, 19, 20, 21. GLOUCESTERSHIRE lost to HAMPSHIRE by two wickets.

HAMPSHIRE

President: W. J. Weld
Chairman: D. Rich
Chairman, Cricket Committee: J. R. Gray
Chief Executive: A. F. Baker
Northlands Road, Southampton SO9 2TY
(Telephone: 0703-333788)
Captain: M. C. J. Nicholas
Coaches: P. J. Sainsbury and T. M. Tremlett

Optimism was tempered with a strong thread of realism when Hampshire began their season in April. The realism was their knowledge that they were short of one top-quality bowler to make a genuine challenge for the supreme prize, the Britannic Assurance Championship. And when the curtain was lowered in mid-September, the truth of that analysis was borne out. Only a dramatic last-afternoon scramble to the highest fourth-innings winning total in their history, reaching 446 for eight against Gloucestershire, took them into third place. Most, possibly, would have settled for that at the outset.

When the early assessments were being made, Hampshire considered that their best chance of a trophy lay in the one-day competitions. They argued that the recruitment of David Gower's supreme skill would tip the balance and make their batting sufficiently powerful to offset the absence of a bowler to complement Malcolm Marshall. But it was not to be. The Benson and Hedges Cup was a disaster for them: a mauling by Yorkshire, an even heavier defeat by Surrey and a wash-out at Old Trafford. The only victory was over the Combined Universities. The NatWest Bank Trophy, however, offered the possibility of consolation and provided great drama. Leicestershire were beaten by a single run, and Essex by virtue of fewer wickets lost when the scores were tied. After that, Yorkshire were destroyed by Marshall's pace in the quarter-final at Southampton, and for the third summer in succession Hampshire were through to the semi-finals. But even though Gower played his most disciplined innings of the season for Hampshire, and Marshall batted with typical flamboyance, Northamptonshire, despite an embarrassment of dropped catches, emerged as the victors by 1 run.

That left the Refuge Assurance League. Six successive victories, making up for an inconsistent beginning, left them needing to win their final match to finish in fourth place and so qualify for the Refuge Cup. Instead they lost by just 4 runs to Surrey.

Curiously, in a summer when batsmen fed themselves insatiably, 1990 was not a vintage year for a side reckoned to have more talent than most. Only three men scored 1,000 runs for Hampshire in all first-class matches, let alone in the Championship, and two of those were predictable. Chris Smith, despite the distractions of his benefit and the problem of suspect knees, had set himself a pre-season target of 1,800 runs, and achieved it with three matches to spare. His aggregate of 1,886 was 554 more than that of Paul Terry, Hampshire's second-highest scorer. It was the third man to attain four figures who was the major surprise. Tony Middleton's continued presence on the staff had been a question of some debate the previous autumn, and when Gower was signed it seemed inevitable that his chances would be limited. However, injuries and England calls decreed otherwise, and the 26-year-old from Winchester made the most of his opportunity. He hit his maiden first-class hundred in the opening match, at Canterbury, and went on to finish with five hundreds, a Championship aggregate of 1,216 and a county cap. In addition, he scored five centuries for the Second Eleven. Not a flamboyant character, nor a prodigious striker of the ball, Middleton nevertheless offered a superb temperament, sound technique and neat placement of shot.

Three other batsmen were within touching distance of their thousand for the county. Robin Smith's regular selection for England allowed him just eleven Championship matches, in which he scored 897 runs; Gower's 972 runs in seventeen matches included 684 in fourteen Britannic appearances; and Marshall, whose first-class innings were restricted to the Championship, finished 38 runs short of the milestone. Gower, perhaps not surprisingly, became a cause of frustration among the county's supporters. Occasionally he batted with almost ethereal skill, as when hitting his lone Championship century against Sussex, but at other times he fell to shots of seemingly careless disdain.

Almost inevitably, Hampshire's bowlers paled in comparison with Marshall. Some felt the West Indian might freewheel a trifle in what was initially intended to be his farewell season, a decision reversed in September. Instead he missed only four Championship matches, bowled 554 overs – a total surpassed only by the left-arm spinner, Raj Maru, the one ever-present in the side – and took 72 wickets at an impressive 19.18. Four times he took five wickets in an innings, twice ten in a match, and it was his blistering pace and controlled swing which brought Hampshire their most dramatic Britannic victory of the season. Derbyshire were 140 for one in pursuit of 235 runs at Portsmouth, yet finished 49 runs short of their target as Marshall took seven for 47.

While Marshall was Hampshire's player of the season, with Middleton not far behind, possibly the most intriguing performances came from 26-year-old Adrian Aymes, who late in the summer ousted Bob Parks as first-choice wicket-keeper. He laid claims to filling the position on a long-term basis with a combination of effective wicket-keeping and impressive batting that brought him three half-centuries in an aggregate of 317 runs from five matches.

For Mark Nicholas, the captain, it was a traumatic and demanding season. The malaria which he contracted while leading the England A tour of Kenya and Zimbabwe was severely debilitating, and his stamina, understandably, was drained. In spite of that, and often against well-meaning advice, he missed only two matches. His form with the bat certainly suffered, but it was a fitting reward for his selfless dedication that he was at the crease, having completed his fifth Championship fifty, when Hampshire claimed third place on the last afternoon of the season. For no-one, though, was the summer more frustrating than for Kevan James. He began with 104 not out at Canterbury, then fell victim to a serious back condition and played no more. In contrast, Jon Ayling, who had not hit or bowled a ball the previous summer because of a serious knee injury, resumed his career. Although still some way short of his peak of 1988, he did enough to suggest that his future remains bright. – Mike Neasom.

HAMPSHIRE 1990

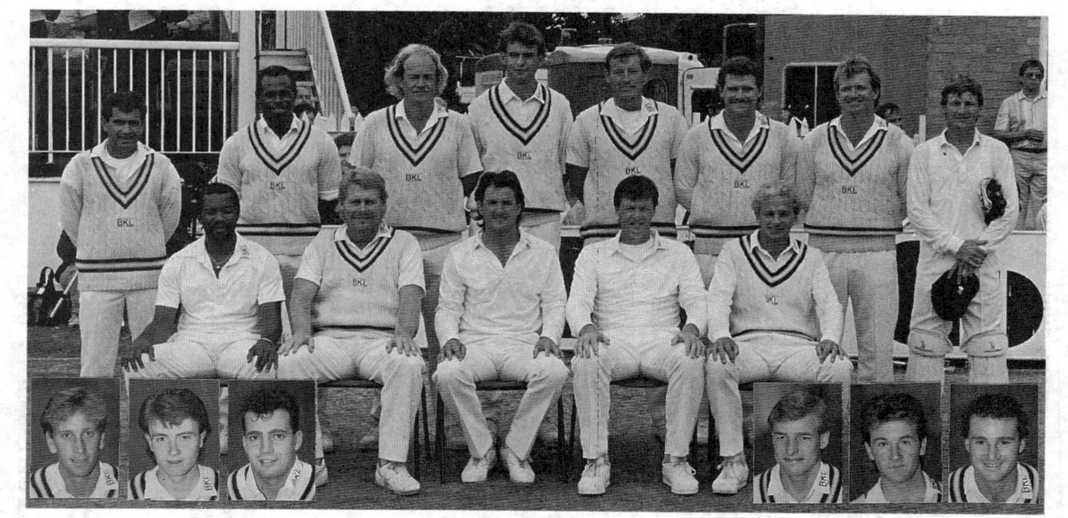

[*Bill Smith*

Back row: R. J. Maru, C. A. Connor, P. J. Bakker, J. R. Ayling, T. M. Tremlett (*coach*), R. A. Smith, R. J. Scott, R. J. Parks. *Front row:* M. D. Marshall, C. L. Smith, M. C. J. Nicholas (*captain*), V. P. Terry, D. I. Gower. *Insets:* K. D. James, S. D. Udal, J. R. Wood, A. N. Aymes, K. J. Shine, T. C. Middleton.

HAMPSHIRE RESULTS

All first-class matches – Played 25: Won 9, Lost 4, Drawn 12.

County Championship matches – Played 22: Won 8, Lost 4, Drawn 10.

Bonus points – Batting 67, Bowling 48.

Competition placings – Britannic Assurance County Championship, 3rd; NatWest Bank Trophy, s-f; Benson and Hedges Cup, 4th in Group C; Refuge Assurance League, 5th.

BRITANNIC ASSURANCE CHAMPIONSHIP AVERAGES

BATTING

	Birthplace	*M*	*I*	*NO*	*R*	*HI*	*Avge*
L. A. Joseph	*Georgetown, Guyana*	4	4	3	83	43*	83.00
‡T. M. Tremlett	*Wellington, Somerset*	8	5	3	143	78	71.50
‡R. A. Smith	*Durban, SA*	11	18	4	897	181	64.07
A. N. Aymes	*Southampton*	4	7	3	255	75*	63.75
‡C. L. Smith	*Durban, SA*	20	35	7	1,678	132*	59.92
‡T. C. Middleton	*Winchester*	16	28	3	1,216	127	48.64
R. M. F. Cox	*Guildford*	3	6	2	186	104*	46.50
‡M. D. Marshall	*St Michael, Barbados*	18	24	3	962	117	45.80
J. R. Ayling	*Portsmouth*	7	9	2	288	62*	41.14
‡V. P. Terry	*Osnabruck, WG*	19	31	3	1,084	165	38.71
‡D. I. Gower	*Tunbridge Wells*	14	21	1	684	145	34.20
‡R. J. Maru	*Nairobi, Kenya*	22	18	2	513	59	32.06
‡M. C. J. Nicholas	*London*	20	30	8	670	78*	30.45
S. D. Udal	*Farnborough, Hants*	6	5	2	65	28*	21.66
‡R. J. Parks	*Cuckfield*	18	19	9	203	36*	20.30
‡C. A. Connor	*The Valley, Anguilla*	19	9	3	119	46	19.83
‡P. J. Bakker	*Vlaardingen, Netherlands*	14	9	4	95	20	19.00
R. J. Scott	*Bournemouth*	6	10	2	144	71	18.00

Also batted: ‡K. D. James (*Lambeth, London*) (1 match) 50, 104*; I. J. Turner (*Denmead*) (4 matches) 1, 0*; J. R. Wood (*Winchester*) (2 matches) 17, 11. K. J. Shine (*Bracknell*) (6 matches) did not bat.

* *Signifies not out.* ‡ *Denotes county cap.*

The following played a total of twenty three-figure innings for Hampshire in County Championship matches – T. C. Middleton 5, R. A. Smith 4, C. L. Smith 3, V. P. Terry 3, M. D. Marshall 2, R. M. F. Cox 1, D. I. Gower 1, K. D. James 1.

BOWLING

	O	*M*	*R*	*W*	*BB*	*5W/i*	*Avge*
M. D. Marshall	554.2	142	1,381	72	7-47	4	19.18
P. J. Bakker	371.2	86	1,195	33	5-101	1	36.21
C. A. Connor	462.1	77	1,623	44	5-96	1	36.88
T. M. Tremlett	120.5	30	393	10	3-33	0	39.30
R. J. Maru	720.1	178	2,087	53	6-97	1	39.37
K. J. Shine	129.4	17	501	12	4-52	0	41.75
J. R. Ayling	135.2	35	454	10	2-48	0	45.40
S. D. Udal	191.3	35	746	16	4-144	0	46.62

Also bowled: K. D. James 28–8–74–1; L. A. Joseph 82–12–406–5; T. C. Middleton 1–0–10–0; M. C. J. Nicholas 54.2–7–209–2; R. J. Scott 36.4–5–165–5; C. L. Smith 22–8–76–3; R. A. Smith 0.3–0–5–0; V. P. Terry 1–0–19–0; I. J. Turner 108.2–28–326–7.

Wicket-keepers: R. J. Parks 46 ct, 4 st; A. N. Aymes 7 ct; R. J. Maru 2 ct.

Leading Fielders: R. J. Maru 23, V. P. Terry 21.

At Canterbury, April 26, 27, 28, 30. HAMPSHIRE beat KENT by 6 runs.

At Oxford, May 3, 4, 5. HAMPSHIRE drew with OXFORD UNIVERSITY.

HAMPSHIRE v SUSSEX

At Southampton, May 15, 16, 17. Hampshire won by an innings and 157 runs. Hampshire 24 pts, Sussex 2 pts. Toss: Sussex. Injuries played a decisive part as Hampshire won conclusively with a day to spare. Early in the Sussex first innings, a ball from Marshall struck Smith's hand, reopening the fracture in his left thumb which he suffered in the West Indies, and he took no further part in the match. In their second innings, Alan Wells's right thumb was broken by Marshall and he, too, retired hurt. To round off the Sussex casualty list, late in their vain bid to make Hampshire bat a second time, Hansford was struck on the forearm by Marshall and, although he batted on, was later found to have a fractured bone. The loss of Smith was a key factor in the collapse of the Sussex first innings, which would have been a disaster had it not been for a 76-run partnership between Pigott and Salisbury. Hampshire's innings was dominated by Gower's first century for his new county, a serene 145 containing 22 fours and two sixes. His third-wicket partnership of 256 in 48 overs with Robin Smith, whose 181 in 188 balls had four sixes and 23 fours, laid the basis for an eventual total of 600 for eight declared. In the Sussex second innings, Lenham batted defiantly, hitting eighteen boundaries in a career-best 121, and with Salisbury, the night-watchman, he added 120 for the second wicket. Once they were parted, however, the absence of Smith and the loss of Alan Wells made the outcome a formality.

Close of play: First day, Hampshire 184-2 (D. I. Gower 87*, R. A. Smith 20*); Second day, Sussex 24-1 (N. J. Lenham 11*, I. D. K. Salisbury 3*).

Sussex

First innings		Second innings	
N. J. Lenham c Gower b Marshall	0	b Maru	121
D. M. Smith retired hurt	5	absent injured	
†P. Moores c Nicholas b Bakker	7	(2) c C. L. Smith b Bakker	5
A. P. Wells lbw b Bakker	0	retired hurt	22
M. P. Speight c Gower b Bakker	7	c Parks b Maru	3
*C. M. Wells c Turner b Connor	22	c Maru b Turner	25
I. J. Gould c C. L. Smith b Marshall	6	c Marshall b Turner	1
A. I. C. Dodemaide c Parks b Bakker	10	not out	37
A. C. S. Pigott c Parks b Turner	50	c Marshall b Maru	3
I. D. K. Salisbury c Terry b Maru	37	(3) c Parks b Connor	19
A. R. Hansford not out	3	(10) b Connor	29
N-b 5	5	B 1, l-b 14, w 2, n-b 9	26
1/0 2/7 3/7 4/21 5/29 6/48 7/66 8/142 9/152	152	1/20 2/140 3/192 4/207 5/219 6/222 7/225 8/291	291

Bonus points – Sussex 1, Hampshire 4.

In the first innings D. M. Smith retired hurt at 15; in the second innings A. P. Wells retired hurt at 190.

Bowling: *First Innings*—Marshall 15–3–26–2; Bakker 20–4–51–4; Connor 12–3–52–1; Turner 5–1–13–1; Maru 7.2–3–10–1. *Second Innings*—Marshall 24–10–66–0; Bakker 16–9–21–1; Turner 27–10–60–2; Connor 21–3–80–2; Maru 22–11–49–3; C. L. Smith 2–2–0–0.

Hampshire

V. P. Terry c Moores b Dodemaide	40
C. L. Smith b Salisbury	35
D. I. Gower c A. P. Wells b Dodemaide	145
R. A. Smith c Moores b C. M. Wells	181
M. D. Marshall c Gould b Hansford	85
*M. C. J. Nicholas c Gould b Hansford	12
†R. J. Parks c Speight b C. M. Wells	36
R. J. Maru not out	54
I. J. Turner st Moores b Salisbury	1
B 1, l-b 8, n-b 2	11
1/68 2/112 3/368 4/453 5/496 6/507 7/593 8/600 (8 wkts dec.)	600

C. A. Connor and P. J. Bakker did not bat.

Bonus points – Hampshire 4, Sussex 1 (Score at 100 overs: 458-4).

Bowling: Pigott 20–2–87–0; Dodemaide 37–6–161–2; Salisbury 28.3–2–159–2; Hansford 26–2–102–2; C. M. Wells 25–1–73–2; Lenham 3–1–9–0.

Umpires: J. C. Balderstone and A. A. Jones.

At The Oval, May 19, 21, 22. HAMPSHIRE drew with SURREY.

HAMPSHIRE v ESSEX

At Southampton, May 23, 24, 25. Drawn. Hampshire 4 pts, Essex 4 pts. Toss: Essex. Two major partnerships dictated the pattern of a match played on a benign wicket. First Hardie, leading Essex in the absence of Gooch, and Waugh frustrated Hampshire after Shine had struck two early blows. They put on 203 for the third wicket in 51 overs before Hardie was dismissed for a patient 125 (thirteen fours). Waugh hit a six and sixteen fours in his 125. Essex declared after 100 overs, and next morning Foster quickly removed Terry. This, however, brought Smith in to join Middleton, and they were not parted for 75 overs, when Smith, having hit twenty fours in his 128, edged a catch to the wicket-keeper. They added 237, and Middleton completed his second first-class century, extending a remarkable sequence in which he had scored five successive Second XI Championship centuries since his maiden first-class hundred at Canterbury in the opening Britannic fixture. Hampshire declared 55 runs behind in the hope of breathing life into the game, and when Essex were 126 for six, it seemed that Nicholas's gamble might pay off. Instead, Garnham and Foster added 75 in sixteen overs and Hardie's challenge to score 266 in 58 overs was too steep.

Close of play: First day, Hampshire 20-0 (V. P. Terry 14*, T. C. Middleton 6*); Second day, Essex 78-2 (M. E. Waugh 37*, T. D. Topley 0*).

Essex

*B. R. Hardie b Connor	125	– c Parks b Maru	31
J. P. Stephenson c Parks b Shine	2	– retired hurt	4
P. J. Prichard c Maru b Shine	23	– b Connor	4
M. E. Waugh c Parks b Marshall	125	– c Maru b Shine	39
N. Shahid not out	19	– (6) b Marshall	0
A. C. Seymour not out	10	– (7) c Parks b Marshall	0
T. D. Topley (did not bat)		– (5) c Parks b Shine	23
†M. A. Garnham (did not bat)		– not out	62
N. A. Foster (did not bat)		– b Maru	40
J. H. Childs (did not bat)		– c Connor b Maru	0
S. J. W. Andrew (did not bat)		– c Turner b Maru	0
B 4, l-b 5, n-b 2	11	B 2, l-b 2, w 1, n-b 2	7
1/16 2/67 3/270 4/294 (4 wkts dec.)	315	1/18 2/78 3/81 4/82 5/86 6/126 7/201 8/208 9/210	210

Bonus points – Essex 4, Hampshire 1.

In the second innings J. P. Stephenson retired hurt at 11.

Bowling: *First Innings*—Marshall 21–3–49–1; Shine 15–1–56–2; Connor 28–6–95–1; Turner 14–2–48–0; Maru 20–5–45–0; Scott 2–0–13–0. *Second Innings*—Marshall 15–5–18–2; Shine 16–6–52–2; Connor 17–1–71–1; Maru 18.3–2–47–4; Turner 9–3–18–0.

Hampshire

V. P. Terry c Stephenson b Foster	14	– c Topley b Andrew	12
T. C. Middleton not out	104	– (3) b Childs	11
C. L. Smith c Garnham b Waugh	128	– (2) st Garnham b Childs	31
†R. J. Parks not out	3		
*M. C. J. Nicholas (did not bat)		– (4) not out	32
M. D. Marshall (did not bat)		– (5) b Foster	9
R. J. Scott (did not bat)		– (6) not out	7
B 4, l-b 3, n-b 4	11		
1/20 2/257 (2 wkts dec.)	260	1/27 2/42 3/59 4/88 (4 wkts)	102

R. J. Maru, I. J. Turner, C. A. Connor and K. J. Shine did not bat.

Bonus points – Hampshire 3.

Bowling: *First Innings*—Foster 19–5–43–1; Andrew 15–5–50–0; Topley 15–3–53–0; Childs 23–6–49–0; Waugh 9–0–33–1; Shahid 5–1–25–0. *Second Innings*—Foster 15–4–33–1; Andrew 13–4–42–1; Childs 17–10–24–2; Topley 2–0–3–0.

Umpires: R. Julian and M. J. Kitchen.

At Leeds, May 26, 28, 29. HAMPSHIRE beat YORKSHIRE by five wickets.

At Leicester, June 2, 4, 5. HAMPSHIRE drew with LEICESTERSHIRE.

HAMPSHIRE v SOMERSET

At Basingstoke, June 6, 7, 8. Drawn. Hampshire 3 pts, Somerset 2 pts. Toss: Hampshire. Somerset's opening batsman, Cook, provided the only memorable moments of a match ruined by persistent rain. Late on the second day, Hampshire declared their first innings at 257 for six after a tea-time conference between Nicholas and Tavaré which aimed to make good the loss of 85 overs. Hampshire's total had been built on a solid but unspectacular innings of 90 by Middleton. The agreement was that Cook would have a chance to score the 59 runs he needed to become the first batsman to reach 1,000 first-class runs for the summer, whereupon Somerset would declare. Cook's pursuit of the target was out of keeping with much of the batting the chilled spectators had earlier suffered. His first 50 was immaculately crafted from 36 deliveries, with Bakker and Joseph the principal sufferers, but he then became circumspect and the remaining 9 runs took 30 deliveries. By the close Hampshire had extended their lead to 202, but on the final morning they found run-scoring difficult. Chris Smith batted with typical determination for his eighth half-century. Somerset were challenged to score 321 in 62 overs, only for the return of the rain to render the equation academic.

Close of play: First day, Hampshire 83-1 (V. P. Terry 50*, T. C. Middleton 6*); Second day, Hampshire 34-2 (C. L. Smith 6*, D. I. Gower 16*).

Hampshire

V. P. Terry lbw b Mallender	64	– lbw b Rose	6
C. L. Smith lbw b Rose	25	– not out	73
T. C. Middleton c Burns b Rose	90	– c Swallow b Rose	1
D. I. Gower lbw b Jones	1	– c and b Swallow	26
*M. C. J. Nicholas retired ill	23	– b Swallow	23
†R. J. Parks c Mallender b Rose	11	– not out	15
L. A. Joseph lbw b Hayhurst	13		
R. J. Maru not out	17		
T. M. Tremlett not out	3		
B 4, l-b 3, w 2, n-b 1	10	B 4, w 1, n-b 3	8
1/69 2/117 3/118 4/218 5/233 6/254 (6 wkts dec.)	257	1/6 2/12 3/50 4/99 (4 wkts dec.)	152

C. A. Connor and P. J. Bakker did not bat.

Bonus points – Hampshire 3, Somerset 2.

In the first innings M. C. J. Nicholas retired ill at 189.

Bowling: *First Innings*—Jones 20–2–56–1; Mallender 26–7–50–1; Rose 25–1–84–3; Swallow 8–2–24–0; Hayhurst 11–5–12–1; Trump 8–1–24–0. *Second Innings*—Rose 9–4–21–2; Hayhurst 6–2–18–0; Swallow 25–8–54–2; Mallender 5–1–9–0; Trump 9.2–0–46–0.

Somerset

S. J. Cook not out .... 59 – c Parks b Connor 29
J. J. E. Hardy not out .... 30 – not out 23
A. N. Hayhurst (did not bat) .... – not out 31
N-b 1 1

(no wkt dec.) 89 1/36 (1 wkt) 84

*C. J. Tavaré, R. J. Harden, †N. D. Burns, G. D. Rose, I. G. Swallow, H. R. J. Trump, N. A. Mallender and A. N. Jones did not bat.

Bowling: *First Innings*—Bakker 4–1–24–0; Joseph 5–1–40–0; Connor 5.2–1–23–0; Maru 4–2–2–0. *Second Innings*—Connor 7–1–20–1; Bakker 6–1–35–0; Middleton 1–0–10–0; Terry 1–0–19–0.

Umpires: D. R. Shepherd and A. G. T. Whitehead.

HAMPSHIRE v GLAMORGAN

At Southampton, June 16, 18, 19. Glamorgan won by four wickets. Glamorgan 19 pts, Hampshire 4 pts. Toss: Hampshire. Richards produced a masterpiece of aggression and timing to steer Glamorgan to a second successive Championship victory, successful negotiations between the captains having overcome the weather's earlier interference. Hampshire's first innings had been dominated by a magnificent 153 from Robin Smith off 155 deliveries. He hit three sixes and 23 fours. Glamorgan were then thwarted by rain, which claimed 86 overs of the second day, and declared 292 behind, which Hampshire quickly extended to 363. A second declaration left Glamorgan with 102 overs to better that, and when they lost half their wickets for 139, Nicholas's boldness seemed likely to be rewarded. However, the former Hampshire all-rounder, Cowley, provided the support Richards needed to play an innings of enormous quality. When the last hour was called with 112 still required, it seemed Richards might have miscalculated, but a four, six and four in Marshall's last over saw Glamorgan home with two balls to spare. Richards faced only 155 deliveries for his 164 and hit five sixes – none of them exploiting a short boundary on the pavilion side – and seventeen fours.

Close of play: First day, Glamorgan 31-1 (H. Morris 20*); Second day, Hampshire 71-0 dec.

Hampshire

V. P. Terry c Metson b Richards .... 52 – not out 25
C. L. Smith c Metson b Watkin .... 48 – not out 39
D. I. Gower c Metson b Watkin 41
R. A. Smith c Metson b Frost 153
M. D. Marshall c Metson b Dennis 4
*M. C. J. Nicholas c Cowley b Watkin 30
†R. J. Parks c Metson b Watkin 0
R. J. Maru c Maynard b Cowley 9
T. M. Tremlett not out 14
L-b 10, w 1, n-b 1 .... 12 L-b 5, w 1, n-b 1 7

1/73 2/127 3/177 4/182 5/336 (8 wkts dec.) 363 (no wkt dec.) 71
6/340 7/341 8/363

C. A. Connor and P. J. Bakker did not bat.

Bonus points – Hampshire 4, Glamorgan 3.

Bowling: *First Innings*—Frost 24–4–107–1; Watkin 30–9–84–4; Dennis 20–5–83–1; Cowley 17.5–6–47–1; Richards 8–3–32–1. *Second Innings*—Smith 8–2–27–0; Maynard 6–1–22–0; Butcher 1.5–0–17–0.

Glamorgan

*A. R. Butcher c Terry b Bakker	7	– c Connor b Maru	51
H. Morris not out	38	– c Maru b Connor	44
M. P. Maynard not out	20	– (4) c Gower b Connor	1
G. C. Holmes (did not bat)		– (3) c Terry b Marshall	14
I. V. A. Richards (did not bat)		– not out	164
I. Smith (did not bat)		– c Parks b Marshall	0
N. G. Cowley (did not bat)		– c and b Maru	58
†C. P. Metson (did not bat)		– not out	14
B 1, l-b 1, w 1, n-b 3	6	B 5, l-b 11, n-b 5	21
1/31 (1 wkt dec.)	71	1/90 2/104 3/106 4/135 5/139 6/306 (6 wkts)	367

S. J. Dennis, S. L. Watkin and M. Frost did not bat.

Bowling: *First Innings*—Marshall 3–1–9–0; Bakker 4–0–14–1; Tremlett 5–2–19–0; Nicholas 4.1–0–27–0. *Second Innings*—Bakker 23–6–54–0; Marshall 22.4–7–63–2; Tremlett 24–7–80–0; Connor 18–1–86–2; Maru 14–2–68–2.

Umpires: J. W. Holder and B. J. Meyer.

At Gloucester, June 20, 21, 22. HAMPSHIRE drew with GLOUCESTERSHIRE.

At Manchester, June 23, 25, 26. HAMPSHIRE drew with LANCASHIRE.

At Southampton, July 4, 5, 6. HAMPSHIRE beat INDIANS by seven wickets (See Indian tour section).

HAMPSHIRE v NOTTINGHAMSHIRE

At Portsmouth, July 18, 19, 20. Hampshire won by eight wickets. Hampshire 24 pts, Nottinghamshire 4 pts. Toss: Hampshire. On a United Services ground known for the encouragement it has offered the faster bowlers, Marshall's pace and control were decisive in sweeping Hampshire to a comfortable victory. The only check on his depredations was provided by a stubborn sixth-wicket partnership of 58 between Saxelby and Stephenson after Nottinghamshire had followed on 191 behind. Once Saxelby was dismissed by Bakker after a patient half-century, Stephenson's aggression, which brought him fourteen boundaries, ensured that Nottinghamshire avoided an innings defeat. Hampshire had claimed maximum batting points in the 100th over, largely through a typically applied innings by Smith, a solid 70 from Nicholas, who at last showed signs of shaking off the effects of his bout of malaria, and some delightful driving by Ayling, a local product.

Close of play: First day, Nottinghamshire 10-1 (P. R. Pollard 2*, K. P. Evans 0*); Second day, Nottinghamshire 177-6 (F. D. Stephenson 32*, B. N. French 1*).

Hampshire

First Innings		Second Innings	
V. P. Terry c Cooper b Stephenson	0		
C. L. Smith c Pollard b Stephenson	85	– not out	46
T. C. Middleton c Evans b Saxelby	37	– (1) b Afford	5
*M. C. J. Nicholas c Robinson b Cooper	70	– (3) c Afford b Cooper	9
M. D. Marshall c Newell b Afford	5	– (4) not out	23
J. R. Wood c French b Evans	11		
J. R. Ayling lbw b Evans	61		
†R. J. Parks c Evans b Cooper	0		
R. J. Maru c Robinson b Evans	19		
C. A. Connor not out	2		
P. J. Bakker not out	1		
L-b 9, w 1	10	L-b 1	1
1/0 2/109 3/149 4/170 5/198 6/257 7/257 8/285 9/298 (9 wkts dec.)	301	1/25 2/50 (2 wkts)	84

Bonus points – Hampshire 4, Nottinghamshire 4.

Bowling: *First Innings*—Stephenson 23–6–78–2; Cooper 24–7–49–2; Evans 21–3–76–3; Afford 21–6–58–1; Saxelby 11–3–31–1. *Second Innings*—Stephenson 8–1–26–0; Cooper 8–3–15–1; Afford 9–3–38–1; Saxelby 1–0–4–0.

Nottinghamshire

First Innings		Second Innings	
B. C. Broad b Maru	8	– c Parks b Connor	13
P. R. Pollard b Bakker	21	– c Wood b Maru	21
K. P. Evans c Terry b Marshall	8	– (9) c Parks b Marshall	7
M. Newell run out	13	– (3) c Parks b Marshall	34
*R. T. Robinson c Maru b Connor	3	– (4) c Marshall b Ayling	7
P. Johnson c Terry b Maru	34	– (5) b Maru	8
M. Saxelby b Connor	0	– (6) c Smith b Bakker	51
F. D. Stephenson lbw b Marshall	10	– (7) not out	88
†B. N. French lbw b Marshall	0	– (8) lbw b Marshall	21
K. E. Cooper b Marshall	6	– c Maru b Marshall	7
J. A. Afford not out	0	– c Parks b Marshall	1
B 4, l-b 2, w 1	7	B 4, l-b 7, w 2, n-b 3	16
1/10 2/41 3/47 4/55 5/63 6/63 7/99 8/104 9/110	110	1/27 2/43 3/54 4/63 5/118 6/176 7/216 8/228 9/259	274

Bonus points – Hampshire 4.

Bowling: *First Innings*—Bakker 9–4–28–1; Marshall 16.1–4–30–4; Maru 8–6–5–2; Ayling 7–3–12–0; Connor 7–2–29–2. *Second Innings*—Bakker 18–3–57–1; Marshall 21.1–4–64–5; Connor 14–3–41–1; Maru 30–6–87–2; Ayling 9–4–14–1.

Umpires: J. C. Balderstone and D. J. Constant.

HAMPSHIRE v DERBYSHIRE

At Portsmouth, July 21, 23, 24. Hampshire won by 48 runs. Hampshire 22 pts, Derbyshire 8 pts. Toss: Hampshire. Among Marshall's many astonishing pieces of fast bowling for Hampshire, few could have bettered that which fashioned this improbable victory. On the opening day, stretched to 7.33 p.m. by Derbyshire's slow over-rate, Hampshire had been dismissed for 307, an innings illuminated by a delightful 45-ball 48 from Gower at his most elegant. Derbyshire had closed at 83 for one, and on Monday Morris's aggressive, unbeaten 157 off 226 deliveries (one six, 28 fours) allowed Barnett to declare at 300 for six after 83.2 overs. As the Derbyshire pace and seam attack dismissed Hampshire for a second time, the only real resistance came from Middleton and Marshall in a fourth-wicket partnership of 94 which Mortensen broke just before the close. The pitch was still playing well on the final day, and when Barnett raced to 63 in under an hour, Derbyshire's target of 235 seemed comfortably attainable. It still seemed so when they lost their second wicket, Bowler, to Marshall at 140, but the great West Indian then gave such a master-class in control and swing that in 16.3 overs Derbyshire lost their remaining wickets for 46 runs. Marshall finished with seven for 47.

Close of play: First day, Derbyshire 83-1 (P. D. Bowler 45*, J. E. Morris 13*); Second day, Hampshire 173-5 (T. C. Middleton 54*, M. C. J. Nicholas 1*).

Hampshire

T. C. Middleton c Barnett b Malcolm	6	– c Krikken b Warner	59
C. L. Smith b Malcolm	57	– c Krikken b Mortensen	2
D. I. Gower run out	48	– b Bishop	3
R. A. Smith c Morris b Mortensen	2	– c Brown b Bishop	37
M. D. Marshall c Adams b Bishop	32	– c Barnett b Mortensen	60
*M. C. J. Nicholas c Krikken b Warner	7	– (7) c Krikken b Warner	15
J. R. Ayling c Krikken b Mortensen	31	– (8) c Morris b Malcolm	5
R. J. Maru c Krikken b Bishop	44	– (6) c Krikken b Mortensen	0
†R. J. Parks run out	0	– not out	8
C. A. Connor b Bishop	46	– c Barnett b Malcolm	6
P. J. Bakker not out	16	– c Krikken b Warner	10
B 4, l-b 11, w 2, n-b 1	18	B 6, l-b 9, w 2, n-b 5	22
1/11 2/85 3/93 4/150 5/159 6/167 7/207 8/208 9/267	307	1/2 2/15 3/78 4/172 5/172 6/196 7/199 8/201 9/212	227

Bonus points – Hampshire 4, Derbyshire 4.

Bowling: *First Innings*—Bishop 23.2–6–72–3; Malcolm 19–1–90–2; Mortensen 18–6–64–2; Warner 16–2–63–1; Roberts 2–0–3–0. *Second Innings*—Bishop 15–4–32–2; Mortensen 17–3–47–3; Malcolm 15–2–39–2; Warner 22.4–4–75–3; Barnett 4–0–19–0.

Derbyshire

P. D. Bowler c Parks b Ayling	58	– (2) b Marshall	56
A. M. Brown lbw b Connor	24	– (3) b Connor	15
J. E. Morris not out	157	– (4) c and b Marshall	10
B. Roberts c Parks b Marshall	7	– (5) c Parks b Marshall	0
C. J. Adams c Parks b Marshall	4	– (6) c Parks b Marshall	1
†K. M. Krikken c Nicholas b Bakker	0	– (7) lbw b Marshall	0
*K. J. Barnett b Marshall	13	– (1) c Parks b Ayling	63
I. R. Bishop not out	27	– b Connor	31
A. E. Warner (did not bat)		– c Parks b Marshall	0
D. E. Malcolm (did not bat)		– b Marshall	0
O. H. Mortensen (did not bat)		– not out	0
B 6, n-b 4	10	L-b 10	10
1/46 2/153 3/179 4/195 5/200 6/230 (6 wkts dec.)	300	1/91 2/140 3/150 4/150 5/151 6/151 7/156 8/160 9/186	186

Bonus points – Derbyshire 4, Hampshire 2.

Bowling: *First Innings*—Bakker 13–1–45–1; Marshall 21–7–60–3; Connor 15–7–58–1; Maru 22–5–70–0; Ayling 12.2–1–61–1. *Second Innings*—Bakker 3–0–24–0; Marshall 15–4–47–7; Maru 12–2–33–0; Connor 12.1–2–49–2; Ayling 6–1–23–1.

Umpires: J. C. Balderstone and D. J. Constant.

At Arundel, July 25, 26, 27. HAMPSHIRE drew with SUSSEX.

At Birmingham, July 28, 30, 31. HAMPSHIRE lost to WARWICKSHIRE by six wickets.

HAMPSHIRE v NORTHAMPTONSHIRE

At Bournemouth, August 4, 6. Hampshire won by an innings and 22 runs. Hampshire 24 pts, Northamptonshire 1 pts. Toss: Hampshire. Northamptonshire, without the pace of Ambrose and the all-round competitiveness of Capel, were swept to defeat in two days on a slow Dean Park pitch. Hampshire's Terry and Middleton built an opening partnership of 292 in 87 overs – the highest stand on the ground – before Middleton became the first of three wickets for off-spinner Williams. He had faced 268 deliveries and hit fifteen fours. Although Robin Smith failed, Hampshire collected maximum points before Terry was stumped, having batted for almost six hours and hit two sixes and twenty fours. Fordham's dogged half-century provided the only resistance to Hampshire's attack, in which left-arm spinner Maru was as effective as Marshall, and Northamptonshire were required to follow on 219 behind. In their second innings Felton played with great composure and, in a lively partnership with Davis, which produced 95 runs in thirteen overs, lent comparative respectability to Northamptonshire's effort. He was ninth out, falling to a spectacular one-handed catch by Ayling at mid-off just 1 run short of a richly deserved century.

Close of play: First day, Northamptonshire 11-1 (A. Fordham 6*).

Hampshire

V. P. Terry st Ripley b Williams 165
T. C. Middleton b Williams 123
R. A. Smith lbw b Williams 0
D. I. Gower not out 28
*M. C. J. Nicholas not out 19
B 6, l-b 10, w 2, n-b 7 25

1/292 2/294 3/331 (3 wkts dec.) 360

M. D. Marshall, J. R. Ayling, R. J. Maru, †R. J. Parks, C. A. Connor and P. J. Bakker did not bat.

Bonus points – Hampshire 4, Northamptonshire 1 (Score at 100 overs: 335-3).

Bowling: Davis 21–3–61–0; Robinson 20–0–60–0; Cook 24–5–73–0; Hughes 14–5–47–0; Williams 19–1–82–3; Bailey 6–1–21–0.

Northamptonshire

A. Fordham c Parks b Marshall	58 – c Parks b Marshall	1
W. Larkins c Bakker b Maru	5 – lbw b Marshall	1
N. A. Felton c and b Connor	26 – c Ayling b Bakker	99
R. J. Bailey c Parks b Connor	5 – lbw b Marshall	6
*A. J. Lamb c Parks b Maru	9 – lbw b Bakker	15
R. G. Williams b Maru	16 – c Gower b Maru	13
†D. Ripley c Terry b Marshall	0 – c Parks b Ayling	5
J. G. Hughes c Maru b Marshall	0 – c Parks b Ayling	2
N. G. B. Cook not out	2 – (10) not out	7
W. W. Davis c Gower b Maru	13 – (9) c Smith b Maru	47
M. A. Robinson b Marshall	0 – b Bakker	0
L-b 5, n-b 2	7 L-b 1	1
1/11 2/62 3/78 4/95 5/121 6/121 7/125 8/125 9/140	141 1/1 2/8 3/24 4/43 5/57 6/70 7/72 8/167 9/197	197

Bonus points – Hampshire 4.

Bowling: *First Innings*—Bakker 9–0–26–0; Marshall 17–4–37–4; Maru 12–3–37–4; Connor 7–0–21–2; Ayling 3–1–15–0. *Second Innings*—Bakker 9.2–0–38–3; Marshall 10–4–24–3; Connor 10–2–22–0; Maru 17–3–64–2; Ayling 6–0–48–2.

Umpires: B. J. Meyer and D. O. Oslear.

HAMPSHIRE v MIDDLESEX

At Bournemouth, August 8, 9, 10. Drawn. Hampshire 4 pts, Middlesex 5 pts. Toss: Middlesex. Having won the toss, Gatting gambled all on bowling Hampshire out twice, delaying his declaration until shortly before lunch on the second day. Tufnell raised his captain's hopes by taking five consecutive wickets to reduce Hampshire to 199 for six, but

Ayling and Maru frustrated the game-plan with a stubborn seventh-wicket partnership which virtually ensured that the follow-on would be avoided. Once that was achieved, the match was consigned to a stalemate. Middlesex had scored only 255 for five in 100 overs and owed their eventual healthy total to a typically improvised and entertaining century by Emburey, whose 111 not out off 127 balls included four sixes and twelve fours.

Close of play: First day, Middlesex 288-5 (P. R. Downton 27*, J. E. Emburey 19*); Second day, Hampshire 183-4 (C. L. Smith 27*, M. C. J. Nicholas 2*).

Middlesex

D. L. Haynes c Scott b Bakker	75	– c Parks b Bakker	0
M. A. Roseberry c Maru b Marshall	84	– c Terry b Bakker	6
*M. W. Gatting b Bakker	3	– (5) c Parks b Maru	35
M. R. Ramprakash c Parks b Marshall	47	– (3) lbw b Marshall	0
K. R. Brown c Maru b Bakker	23	– (4) lbw b Marshall	12
†P. R. Downton c Parks b Bakker	38	– c Smith b Scott	38
J. E. Emburey not out	111	– st Parks b Smith	36
S. P. Hughes c Scott b Bakker	6	– b Smith	0
P. C. R. Tufnell not out	28	– c Parks b Smith	12
N. R. Taylor (did not bat)		– lbw b Scott	0
N. G. Cowans (did not bat)		– not out	4
L-b 12, w 1, n-b 2	15	B 2, l-b 2, n-b 4	8
1/139 2/143 3/179 4/219 5/253 6/320 7/370 (7 wkts dec.)	430	1/0 2/1 3/11 4/23 5/72 6/126 7/134 8/143 9/147	151

Bonus points – Middlesex 3, Hampshire 2 (Score at 100 overs: 255-5).

Bowling: *First Innings*—Bakker 35–8–101–5; Marshall 25–5–54–2; Maru 40–5–153–0; Connor 3–0–15–0; Ayling 25–5–63–0; Smith 1–1–0–0; Scott 7–1–24–0; Nicholas 1–0–8–0. *Second Innings*—Bakker 6–1–19–2; Marshall 11–2–28–2; Ayling 5–1–12–0; Maru 9–3–40–1; Smith 10–2–35–3; Nicholas 6–2–8–0; Scott 2–1–5–2.

Hampshire

T. C. Middleton run out	31
R. J. Scott c and b Tufnell	71
C. L. Smith c Emburey b Tufnell	31
V. P. Terry c Hughes b Tufnell	31
M. D. Marshall lbw b Tufnell	9
*M. C. J. Nicholas c Brown b Tufnell	7
J. R. Ayling c Taylor b Tufnell	41
R. J. Maru c Ramprakash b Taylor	43
†R. J. Parks lbw b Taylor	4
C. A. Connor c Gatting b Taylor	2
P. J. Bakker not out	7
B 4, l-b 6, n-b 9	19
1/104 2/104 3/163 4/179 5/187 6/199 7/271 8/281 9/285	296

Bonus points – Hampshire 2, Middlesex 2 (Score at 100 overs: 239-6).

Bowling: Cowans 17–5–49–0; Hughes 18–4–51–0; Taylor 14–5–44–3; Emburey 34–8–63–0; Tufnell 38–11–79–6.

Umpires: B. J. Meyer and D. O. Oslear.

At Worcester, August 11, 13, 14. HAMPSHIRE drew with WORCESTERSHIRE.

At Taunton, August 18, 19, 20, 21. HAMPSHIRE lost to SOMERSET by five wickets.

HAMPSHIRE v SURREY

At Southampton, August 23, 24, 25, 27. Surrey won by nine wickets. Surrey 23 pts, Hampshire 2 pts. Toss: Hampshire. Hampshire's first encounter with Surrey's new fast bowler, Waqar Younis, was a painful one, the young Pakistani Test cricketer wrecking their first innings with six wickets for 66. He took three wickets in four balls as they plunged from a promising 72 without loss to 143 for eight. Nicholas and fast bowlers Connor and Bakker then added a defiant 54. For Surrey, Ward played an innings of majestic authority, hitting three sixes and 24 fours in his 191, and the visitors built a lead of 320. Chris Smith's fourth century of the season ensured the match would go beyond the weekend, and on Monday Aymes, who kept wicket in preference to Parks, and Maru prevented an innings defeat. Surrey, needing 74 for victory, scored the runs at almost 10 an over.

Close of play: First day, Surrey 106-1 (R. I. Alikhan 30*, A. J. Stewart 34*); Second day, Surrey 467-7 (D. M. Ward 175*, M. P. Bicknell 28*); Third day, Hampshire 263-6 (A. N. Aymes 19*, R. J. Maru 1*).

Hampshire

First innings		Second innings	
T. C. Middleton b Waqar Younis	25	b Feltham	33
C. L. Smith b Waqar Younis	43	c Greig b Bicknell	111
*M. C. J. Nicholas c Lynch b Bicknell	70	b Waqar Younis	19
V. P. Terry c Waqar Younis b Bicknell	8	lbw b Bicknell	6
M. D. Marshall lbw b Feltham	6	c Stewart b Medlycott	31
R. M. F. Cox c Stewart b Feltham	0	lbw b Feltham	23
†A. N. Aymes lbw b Waqar Younis	6	lbw b Feltham	48
R. J. Maru c Lynch b Waqar Younis	0	c Lynch b Waqar Younis	36
S. D. Udal b Waqar Younis	0	not out	28
C. A. Connor b Waqar Younis	12	c Bicknell b Feltham	20
P. J. Bakker not out	12	b Feltham	10
B 6, w 2, n-b 7	15	B 9, l-b 5, w 3, n-b 11	28
1/72 2/77 3/104 4/115 5/115 6/143 7/143 8/143 9/158	197	1/106 2/156 3/184 4/190 5/227 6/251 7/330 8/335 9/369	393

Bonus points – Hampshire 1, Surrey 4.

Bowling: *First Innings*—Waqar Younis 21–5–66–6; Bicknell 18–4–46–2; Feltham 17–1–64–2; Greig 8–2–15–0. *Second Innings*—Waqar Younis 36–4–132–2; Bicknell 32–9–75–2; Feltham 30.5–2–109–5; Medlycott 25–4–63–1.

Surrey

First innings		Second innings	
R. I. Alikhan b Connor	72	lbw b Bakker	0
G. S. Clinton c and b Maru	21		
†A. J. Stewart c Nicholas b Maru	72	not out	27
D. M. Ward c Nicholas b Connor	191		
M. A. Lynch c Nicholas b Maru	13		
*I. A. Greig c Terry b Bakker	11	(2) not out	45
M. A. Feltham c Marshall b Udal	30		
K. T. Medlycott run out	15		
M. P. Bicknell c Udal b Connor	40		
N. M. Kendrick c Middleton b Connor	7		
Waqar Younis not out	13		
B 1, l-b 16, n-b 15	32	B 2, l-b 1	3
1/42 2/175 3/217 4/238 5/273 6/374 7/408 8/494 9/502	517	1/0	(1 wkt) 75

Bonus points – Surrey 3, Hampshire 1 (Score at 100 overs: 262-4).

Bowling: *First Innings*—Bakker 25–8–65–1; Marshall 32–12–64–0; Maru 54–13–129–3; Connor 27.3–3–112–4; Udal 21–6–87–1; Nicholas 12–2–43–0. *Second Innings*—Bakker 3–1–18–1; Connor 3–0–29–0; Udal 1–0–9–0; Nicholas 0.3–0–16–0.

Umpires: J. D. Bond and A. A. Jones.

HAMPSHIRE v KENT

At Bournemouth, August 29, 30, 31. Drawn. Hampshire 4 pts, Kent 6 pts. Toss: Hampshire. Kent's last pair played out the final fourteen deliveries to deny Hampshire victory. Yet the first two days had been the visitors'. On a slow pitch they had reduced Hampshire to 108 for five before being baulked by Aymes and Tremlett's 102-run partnership. Then, after Hinks had fallen to the first ball of Kent's innings, Ward and Wells regained the initiative with a partnership of 131, and Kent waited until Ward was dismissed for an impressive 175 before declaring. His boundaries, three sixes and 27 fours, included a six and four fours in one over from Joseph. Middleton produced another of his invaluable innings of patience and technique for Hampshire, and Robin Smith hit a six and twelve fours in a rapid 74 to enable Nicholas to set a target of 249 in two and threequarter hours, or a minimum of 35 overs. Despite Fleming's belligerent 76, with 50 in boundaries, a draw always seemed the most likely outcome until Bakker induced the sudden collapse which left Patel and Merrick to survive the last overs.

Close of play: First day, Hampshire 215-6 (T. M. Tremlett 42*, R. J. Maru 5*); Second day, Hampshire 56-0 (T. C. Middleton 25*, C. L. Smith 25*).

Hampshire

T. C. Middleton lbw b Kelleher	4	– c Taylor b Patel	104
C. L. Smith c Davis b Merrick	32	– c Marsh b Fleming	53
D. I. Gower c Marsh b Wells	44	– c Davis b Wells	3
R. A. Smith c Patel b Davis	9	– c sub b Davis	74
*M. C. J. Nicholas c Fleming b Wells	1	– not out	42
†A. N. Aymes c Davis b Merrick	70	– not out	10
T. M. Tremlett c Davis b Fleming	78		
R. J. Maru c Cowdrey b Fleming	34		
L. A. Joseph not out	2		
L-b 4, w 1, n-b 3	8	B 1, l-b 9, n-b 1	11
1/14 2/71 3/80 4/85 5/108 6/210 7/275 8/282 (8 wkts dec.)	282	1/137 2/156 3/192 4/266 (4 wkts dec.)	297

S. D. Udal and P. J. Bakker did not bat.

Bonus points – Hampshire 2, Kent 2 (Score at 100 overs: 216-6).

Bowling: *First Innings*—Merrick 28–8–62–2; Kelleher 16–4–54–1; Davis 14–4–31–1; Wells 13–3–29–2; Fleming 30.5–9–75–2; Patel 16–4–27–0. *Second Innings*—Merrick 5.2–3–8–0; Kelleher 6–2–14–0; Davis 30.5–2–127–1; Patel 29.4–6–112–1; Ward 1–1–0–0; Wells 8–4–8–1; Fleming 6–0–18–1.

Kent

S. G. Hinks c C. L. Smith b Bakker	0	– run out	27
T. R. Ward c R. A. Smith b Tremlett	175	– c C. L. Smith b Joseph	8
V. J. Wells c Middleton b Maru	58	– lbw b Udal	9
G. R. Cowdrey c and b Maru	47	– c sub b Udal	41
†S. A. Marsh c Bakker b Joseph	3	– (7) b Bakker	34
M. V. Fleming not out	45	– b Udal	76
*N. R. Taylor (did not bat)		– (5) lbw b Tremlett	0
D. J. M. Kelleher (did not bat)		– c Nicholas b Bakker	9
R. P. Davis (did not bat)		– lbw b Bakker	0
M. M. Patel (did not bat)		– not out	0
T. A. Merrick (did not bat)		– not out	0
L-b 3	3	B 1, l-b 5, n-b 1	7
1/0 2/131 3/215 4/227 5/331 (5 wkts dec.)	331	1/18 2/49 3/55 4/55 5/145 6/173 7/202 8/210 9/211 (9 wkts)	211

Bonus points – Kent 4, Hampshire 2.

Bowling: *First Innings*—Bakker 14–1–73–1; Joseph 10–1–76–1; Tremlett 7.4–1–46–1; Maru 18.3–6–48–2; Udal 16–2–80–0; R. A. Smith 0.3–0–5–0. *Second Innings*—Bakker 11–3–24–3; Joseph 12–1–67–1; Tremlett 6–0–44–1; Udal 18–4–70–3.

Umpires: J. H. Harris and B. Hassan.

At Pontypridd, September 7, 8, 9. HAMPSHIRE beat GLAMORGAN by eight wickets.

At Southampton, September 12, 13, 14. HAMPSHIRE drew with SRI LANKANS (See Sri Lankan tour section).

HAMPSHIRE v GLOUCESTERSHIRE

At Southampton, September 18, 19, 20, 21. Hampshire won by two wickets. Hampshire 21 pts, Gloucestershire 7 pts. Toss: Gloucestershire. Hampshire closed their season spectacularly by chasing a target of 445 throughout the final day and achieving it with an over to spare. In doing so they eclipsed their previous-highest winning fourth-innings total by 36 runs. The first three days had belonged to Gloucestershire, and in particular to Curran. He top-scored in their first innings with 78, and then returned five for 63 to earn his county a first-innings lead of 94. Only another determined display by Aymes prevented Gloucestershire from gaining a greater advantage. Finally, Curran marked his last appearance for the West Country county by hitting an unbeaten century after going in at No. 7, facing 219 balls and hitting thirteen fours. Hampshire's chances of reaching their daunting target wavered when Gower threw away his wicket, but Robin Smith and Middleton gave the innings its base with a partnership of 155 in 30 overs. Smith and Marshall maintained the momentum with 68 in ten overs, and when Smith was brilliantly caught down the leg side by Russell off Walsh, having hit a six and 23 fours in his 124 off 113 balls, Hampshire required 133 from 35 overs. However, the next three wickets managed just 50 in seventeen overs, and it fell to Nicholas to play the decisive innings. His half-century, allied to Maru's 42, ended on a triumphant note a season in which the Hampshire captain had laboured against ill health.

Close of play: First day, Hampshire 2-0 (V. P. Terry 0*, T. C. Middleton 0*); Second day, Gloucestershire 98-3 (G. D. Hodgson 40*, D. A. Graveney 1*); Third day, Hampshire 5-0 (V. P. Terry 5*, T. C. Middleton 0*).

Gloucestershire

G. D. Hodgson c Aymes b Bakker	58	– c and b Maru	76
*A. J. Wright c Terry b Marshall	19	– c Aymes b Maru	19
P. Bainbridge c Aymes b Connor	16	– c Nicholas b Maru	30
M. W. Alleyne c Aymes b Bakker	18	– (6) c Gower b Maru	33
K. M. Curran c Bakker b Maru	78	– (7) not out	101
†R. C. Russell b Ayling	23	– (8) c Smith b Connor	24
J. W. Lloyds b Maru	0	– (9) c Smith b Maru	24
E. T. Milburn c Middleton b Maru	0	– (10) not out	3
C. A. Walsh c Terry b Ayling	20		
D. V. Lawrence b Marshall	18	– (4) lbw b Maru	0
D. A. Graveney not out	1	– (5) c Marshall b Ayling	20
L-b 5, n-b 7	12	B 6, l-b 6, n-b 8	20
1/35 2/62 3/114 4/121 5/172 6/177 7/177 8/210 9/239	263	1/39 2/93 3/93 4/135 5/172 6/228 7/278 8/333 (8 wkts dec.)	350

Bonus points – Gloucestershire 3, Hampshire 4.

Bowling: *First Innings*—Marshall 21–4–54–2; Bakker 21–8–51–2; Connor 17–4–56–1; Ayling 16–5–57–2; Maru 14–4–40–3. *Second Innings*—Marshall 27–7–70–0; Bakker 18–4–61–0; Connor 24–5–55–1; Maru 53.4–18–97–6; Ayling 21–6–55–1.

Hampshire

V. P. Terry c Alleyne b Curran	1	– c Russell b Graveney	46
T. C. Middleton c Russell b Curran	5	– c Russell b Curran	82
D. I. Gower c Lawrence b Curran	14	– b Graveney	4
R. A. Smith b Walsh	8	– c Russell b Walsh	124
M. D. Marshall c Russell b Lawrence	21	– c Walsh b Graveney	46
*M. C. J. Nicholas c Wright b Lawrence	4	– not out	54
J. R. Ayling b Walsh	28	– c Wright b Graveney	10
†A. N. Aymes not out	44	– c Russell b Graveney	2
R. J. Maru c Lloyds b Curran	20	– run out	42
C. A. Connor b Walsh	2	– not out	0
P. J. Bakker c and b Curran	7		
B 4, l-b 3, n-b 8	15	B 5, l-b 16, n-b 15	36
1/3 2/24 3/33 4/40 5/51 6/64 7/128 8/155 9/158	169	1/80 2/89 3/244 4/312 5/339 6/358 7/362 8/442	(8 wkts) 446

Bonus points – Hampshire 1, Gloucestershire 4.

Bowling: *First Innings*—Walsh 18–3–51–3; Lawrence 9–2–30–2; Curran 17.2–3–63–5; Milburn 4–1–10–0; Graveney 9–5–8–0. *Second Innings*—Curran 18–2–86–1; Walsh 25–4–93–1; Lawrence 19–1–64–0; Graveney 35–5–140–5; Milburn 3–0–24–0; Bainbridge 4–0–18–0.

Umpires: J. H. Harris and R. Palmer.

YOUNG CRICKETER OF THE YEAR

(*Elected by the Cricket Writers Club*)

1950	R. Tattersall	1971	J. Whitehouse
1951	P. B. H. May	1972	D. R. Owen-Thomas
1952	F. S. Trueman	1973	M. Hendrick
1953	M. C. Cowdrey	1974	P. H. Edmonds
1954	P. J. Loader	1975	A. Kennedy
1955	K. F. Barrington	1976	G. Miller
1956	B. Taylor	1977	I. T. Botham
1957	M. J. Stewart	1978	D. I. Gower
1958	A. C. D. Ingleby-Mackenzie	1979	P. W. G. Parker
1959	G. Pullar	1980	G. R. Dilley
1960	D. A. Allen	1981	M. W. Gatting
1961	P. H. Parfitt	1982	N. G. Cowans
1962	P. J. Sharpe	1983	N. A. Foster
1963	G. Boycott	1984	R. J. Bailey
1964	J. M. Brearley	1985	D. V. Lawrence
1965	A. P. E. Knott	1986	A. A. Metcalfe
1966	D. L. Underwood	1986	J. J. Whitaker
1967	A. W. Greig	1987	R. J. Blakey
1968	R. M. H. Cottam	1988	M. P. Maynard
1969	A. Ward	1989	N. Hussain
1970	C. M. Old	1990	M. A. Atherton

An additional award, in memory of Norman Preston, Editor of *Wisden* from 1952 to 1980, was made to C. W. J. Athey in 1980.

KENT

Patron: HRH The Duke of Kent
President: 1990 – D. G. Clark
1991 – P. G. Foster
Chairman: P. H. Edgley
Chairman, Cricket Committee:
A. J. P. Woodhouse
Secretary: 1990 – D. B. Dalby
1991 – S. T. W. Anderson
St Lawrence Ground, Old Dover Road,
Canterbury CT1 3NZ
(Telephone: 0227-456886)
Captain: 1990 – C. S. Cowdrey
1991 – M. R. Benson
Cricket Administrator: B. W. Luckhurst

Once again Kent flattered to deceive. It is beginning to sound like the old gramophone record with the worn needle, but the facts have to be relayed – and they add up to yet another disappointing season. Take into account all the injury problems, often to key players; it was still a poor summer, which for the second year in succession ended with the county involved in a struggle to avoid finishing last in the Britannic Assurance Championship. That possibility continued until the final game of the season, when Kent, their programme finished, had to hope that Middlesex would beat Sussex to keep them off the bottom rung. They did, and so it was sixteenth place in the table for Kent; a bitter pill, none the less, for supporters, team and club officials to swallow.

It was not only the Championship that proved disappointing. The side failed to qualify for the Benson and Hedges Cup quarter-finals, fell at the second hurdle in the NatWest Bank Trophy, and, after a promising start, could improve only one position on the previous season's eleventh in the Refuge Assurance League. They had led the Sunday League from early in the summer until late June, encouraging themselves and Kent's success-starved members to think that they could finish in the top four and so qualify for the Refuge Assurance Cup play-offs. The way they subsequently faded was disconcerting, particularly as it was felt that this was the competition which presented them with their best chance of success.

As the season was drifting towards another unsuccessful conclusion, Kent were shocked by the sudden resignation of the captain, Christopher Cowdrey. His decision was made known just before the start of the game against Leicestershire at Dartford on August 8. Ironically, it was a game which Kent then won, on a pitch reported by the umpires on the third day. The surface was not dangerous, but the spin bowlers had been delighted to find their cause assisted from before lunch on the opening day. Cowdrey, unavailable because of injury at that stage, indicated that he would continue until the end of the season and remain as a player for the following summer, as he was contracted to. It must have been a hard decision for the son of a former captain, M. C. Cowdrey, but he had clearly had enough. His own form was suffering, and he was finding it difficult to motivate his side. He played in only thirteen of Kent's 24 first-class games, and while he achieved a batting average of 40.72, his bowling at first-class level fell away and was confined to just 61 overs.

Mark Benson and Neil Taylor performed the captain's duties when Cowdrey was not available, Taylor taking over when Benson was out of action at the end of the season with a broken thumb. Benson had led Kent to that important victory over Leicestershire at Dartford, which provided the escape route from the bottom rung, and his first-innings century represented easily the most accomplished batting of the match. He now succeeds Cowdrey as captain and will need the best possible support from his dressing- and committee-rooms if Kent are to see a revival of their fortunes soon.

In 1990, during a summer dominated by good batting pitches, the Kent bowlers struggled more than most in the Championship, finishing with the fewest bonus points of all the counties. Tony Merrick, newly signed from Warwickshire, and Alan Igglesden were heralded as a fast-bowling duo which could bring better days to Kent cricket. Unfortunately, they were in harness only twice in the Championship, injury reducing Igglesden's first-class appearances to fourteen and Merrick's to seven. As a result, Fanie de Villiers, brought over from South Africa as an additional fast bowler, found himself playing rather more cricket than he might have expected. Chris Penn played in only seven first-class games and Richard Ellison in fifteen as injury and loss of form took their toll, and Ellison's all-round ability was sorely missed by a struggling side.

Fortunately Richard Davis, with his left-arm spin, prospered in his best season yet, taking 73 first-class wickets and scoring more than 500 very useful runs to help shore up a batting order that did not always perform as soundly in the middle as it promised on paper. Midway through the season Davis was joined by another left-arm spinner, twenty-year-old Minal Patel, whose potential came to the fore in the win at Dartford, where he and Davis took all twenty Leicestershire wickets.

Towards the end of the summer, Kent were without seven first-team players, including both their overseas fast bowlers, and with so many injuries there were chances for young players. Vince Wells, with bat and ball, finally revealed some form, and Matthew Fleming, who was awarded his county cap, consolidated his all-round promise by scoring 980 runs and taking 22 wickets. Trevor Ward had a good season with the bat once he had recovered from an early-season injury, and there were more than 900 runs from the bat of wicket-keeper Steven Marsh. None of the side's leading batsmen was in the mood to waste the opportunities provided by the good pitches, and four of them cruised past the thousand mark. Taylor, only 21 runs short of 2,000, and the left-handed Simon Hinks had their best seasons, as did Graham Cowdrey, who benefited from having a regular place in the side.

The county retained all their players for 1991, except for de Villiers, and if fitness could be guaranteed, team selection might cause some headaches for the new captain; but ones he would probably welcome. To put Kent on the upward path will require much dedication from all concerned, on the field and off. At the end of the year, David Dalby retired as secretary and was succeeded by Stuart Anderson, a former army brigadier. Like the players, he will be aware that the club and the supporters will be looking for better results in 1991. – Dudley Moore.

KENT 1990

[Bill Smith

Back row: J. I. Longley, V. J. Wells, M. C. Dobson, N. J. Llong, T. N. Wren, M. A. Ealham, M. M. Patel, G. J. Kersey. *Middle row:* F. Errington (*physiotherapist*), J. Foley (*scorer*), M. V. Fleming, T. R. Ward, C. Penn, R. P. Davis, A. P. Igglesden, D. J. M. Kelleher, T. A. Merrick, A. G. E. Ealham (*coach*), J. C. T. Page (*director of coaching*). *Front row:* S. G. Hinks, S. A. Marsh, M. R. Benson, C. S. Cowdrey (*captain*), N. R. Taylor, R. M. Ellison, G. R. Cowdrey.

KENT RESULTS

All first-class matches – Played 24: Won 4, Lost 7, Drawn 13.
County Championship matches – Played 22: Won 3, Lost 6, Drawn 13.
Bonus points – Batting 69, Bowling 35.
Competition placings – Britannic Assurance County Championship, 16th; NatWest Bank Trophy, 2nd round; Benson and Hedges Cup, 3rd in Group A; Refuge Assurance League, 10th equal.

BRITANNIC ASSURANCE CHAMPIONSHIP AVERAGES

BATTING

	Birthplace	*M*	*I*	*NO*	*R*	*HI*	*Avge*
‡N. R. Taylor	*Orpington*	20	35	4	1,752	204	56.51
‡G. R. Cowdrey	*Farnborough, Kent*	20	36	5	1,471	135	47.45
‡M. R. Benson	*Shoreham*	14	23	1	1,029	159	46.77
‡M. V. Fleming	*Macclesfield*	17	30	5	940	102	37.60
‡R. M. Ellison	*Ashford, Kent*	13	18	6	444	81	37.00
‡S. G. Hinks	*Northfleet*	22	41	0	1,484	234	36.19
‡C. S. Cowdrey	*Farnborough, Kent*	11	21	4	599	107*	35.23
‡S. A. Marsh	*Westminster, London*	22	34	8	867	114*	33.34
‡T. R. Ward	*Farningham*	15	28	1	863	175	31.96
V. J. Wells	*Dartford*	8	15	0	352	58	23.46
P. S. de Villiers	*Vereeniging, SA*	12	15	3	264	37	22.00
‡R. P. Davis	*Margate*	22	32	3	504	59	17.37
‡C. Penn	*Dover*	6	6	2	66	23*	16.50
M. M. Patel	*Bombay, India*	9	12	5	104	41*	14.85
‡A. P. Igglesden	*Farnborough, Kent*	13	17	9	105	24	13.12
D. J. M. Kelleher ..	*Southwark, London*	5	8	0	101	44	12.62
T. A. Merrick	*St John's, Antigua*	5	7	2	60	35	12.00
T. N. Wren	*Folkestone*	5	5	2	23	16	7.66

Also batted: M. C. Dobson (*Canterbury*) (1 match) 0, 6; M. A. Ealham (*Willesborough*) (2 matches) 0, 13*.

** Signifies not out. ‡ Denotes county cap.*

The following played a total of 23 three-figure innings for Kent in County Championship matches – M. R. Benson 5, N. R. Taylor 5, S. G. Hinks 4, G. R. Cowdrey 3, C. S. Cowdrey 2, T. R. Ward 2, M. V. Fleming 1, S. A. Marsh 1.

BOWLING

	O	*M*	*R*	*W*	*BB*	*5W/i*	*Avge*
V. J. Wells	85	19	257	12	5-43	1	21.41
T. A. Merrick	146.2	31	376	13	4-66	0	28.92
A. P. Igglesden	306	42	1,093	30	4-79	0	36.43
P. S. de Villiers	304.5	58	992	25	6-70	1	39.68
R. P. Davis	839.1	202	2,648	65	6-59	4	40.73
M. M. Patel	297.5	72	836	20	6-57	2	41.80
R. M. Ellison	260.5	45	869	19	4-76	0	45.73
M. V. Fleming	360.5	81	994	18	3-65	0	55.22

Also bowled: M. R. Benson 8–2–46–1; C. S. Cowdrey 57–12–173–4; G. R. Cowdrey 3.3–0–32–0; M. C. Dobson 3.1–1–7–0; M. A. Ealham 34.2–5–120–3; S. G. Hinks 15–2–60–2; D. J. M. Kelleher 112.5–20–398–7; S. A. Marsh 8.4–0–36–2; C. Penn 158–33–535–9; N. R. Taylor 21–5–57–1; T. R. Ward 53–6–225–4; T. N. Wren 122–14–489–6.

Wicket-keeper: S. A. Marsh 46 ct, 4 st.

Leading Fielder: R. P. Davis 24.

KENT v HAMPSHIRE

At Canterbury, April 26, 27, 28, 30. Hampshire won by 6 runs. Hampshire 21 pts, Kent 4 pts. Toss: Hampshire. Only 37 overs were bowled on the first day, and from then on Hampshire's batsmen dominated. Terry reached 102 out of 176 in 242 minutes with a six and fifteen fours, and shared an opening stand of 183 off 75 overs with Middleton, whose maiden first-class century, containing nine fours, took him 345 minutes. After losing Taylor in Joseph's first Championship over, Kent were launched on the road to recovery by a century stand for the fourth wicket from the Cowdrey brothers. Hampshire responded to their declaration by gathering quick runs, James following his first-innings half-century with a hundred in which he hit sixteen fours as well as the six with which he achieved three figures. Set a victory target of 278 in 65 overs, Kent developed the run-chase through a third-wicket partnership of 162 between Hinks and Chris Cowdrey, but when the captain was out at 222, with ten overs remaining, the innings lost its impetus. The last five wickets tumbled for 18 runs, leaving Hampshire the winners with five balls to spare.

Close of play: First day, Hampshire 76-0 (V. P. Terry 39*, T. C. Middleton 34*); Second day, Kent 29-1 (S. G. Hinks 14*, T. R. Ward 12*); Third day, Hampshire 55-1 (V. P. Terry 16*, K. D. James 14*).

Hampshire

*V. P. Terry c Ward b Fleming	107	– c Hinks b Merrick	17
T. C. Middleton lbw b Penn	127	– b Fleming	23
K. D. James b Penn	50	– not out	104
C. L. Smith c and b Davis	16	– c C. S. Cowdrey b Hinks	52
R. J. Scott lbw b Penn	0	– not out	1
J. R. Wood c Ellison b Merrick	17		
†R. J. Parks not out	19		
L. A. Joseph not out	25		
B 1, l-b 14, w 1, n-b 2	18	B 1, w 1, n-b 1	3
1/183 2/289 3/300 4/300 5/325 6/337	(6 wkts dec.) 379	1/32 2/57 3/179	(3 wkts dec.) 200

R. J. Maru, C. A. Connor and K. J. Shine did not bat.

Bonus points – Hampshire 3 (Score at 100 overs: 252-1).

Bowling: *First Innings*—Merrick 29–4–83–1; Penn 28–8–79–3; Fleming 20–3–50–1; Ellison 22–6–43–0; Davis 31–8–96–1; C. S. Cowdrey 2–0–13–0. *Second Innings*—Merrick 13–3–24–1; Penn 6–2–6–0; Fleming 7–3–23–1; Ellison 4–1–12–0; Davis 21–3–63–0; Ward 10–3–41–0; C. S. Cowdrey 5–2–14–0; Hinks 3–1–16–1.

Kent

S. G. Hinks c Middleton b Shine	31	– c Maru b James	82
N. R. Taylor c Terry b Joseph	0	– c Terry b Shine	6
T. R. Ward c Parks b Connor	21	– c Middleton b Connor	11
*C. S. Cowdrey b Connor	79	– c Connor b Scott	107
G. R. Cowdrey b Scott	87	– st Parks b Scott	30
†S. A. Marsh not out	61	– b Shine	4
M. V. Fleming not out	6	– b Maru	20
R. M. Ellison (did not bat)		– c Smith b Connor	0
T. A. Merrick (did not bat)		– b Connor	0
C. Penn (did not bat)		– not out	0
R. P. Davis (did not bat)		– run out	1
B 3, l-b 5, w 6, n-b 3	17	L-b 8, w 1, n-b 1	10
1/2 2/45 3/74 4/197 5/290	(5 wkts dec.) 302	1/11 2/25 3/187 4/222 5/237 6/253 7/258 8/258 9/270	271

Bonus points – Kent 4, Hampshire 2.

Bowling: *First Innings*—Shine 19–4–70–1; Joseph 17–3–76–1; Connor 19–5–38–2; James 17–6–31–0; Maru 17–2–64–0; Scott 5–1–15–1. *Second Innings*—Shine 13–1–48–2; Connor 12.1–2–44–3; Maru 20–5–87–1; James 11–2–43–1; Scott 8–1–41–2.

Umpires: J. W. Holder and K. J. Lyons.

KENT v SUSSEX

At Folkestone, May 3, 4, 5, 7. Kent won by five wickets. Kent 20 pts, Sussex 4 pts. Toss: Sussex. Superb batting by Parker dominated the opening day. Hitting fourteen fours, he scored his century in 246 minutes, but Sussex's hopes of a really big score when they resumed on the second day were dashed by Igglesden, who took three of the last four wickets to fall. Benson's third first-class century against Sussex, his native county, was reached in 234 minutes with thirteen boundaries, and with Fleming making a maiden first-class fifty and Ellison 81, Kent obtained a lead of 109. On the final day Sussex fared badly against the left-arm spin of Davis, whose career-best figures included a spell of three wickets in twelve balls without conceding a run and prompted the award of his county cap. Kent, with 21 overs in which to score 81 to win, made a nervous start and later lost three more wickets when in sight of their target. Dodemaide made life as difficult as he could for them, taking four of the five wickets, but Kent won with two overs to spare.

Close of play: First day, Sussex 277-6 (C. M. Wells 7*, I. D. K. Salisbury 2*); Second day, Kent 192-1 (M. R. Benson 105*, N. R. Taylor 29*); Third day, Kent 465-9 (R. M. Ellison 81*, A. P. Igglesden 2*).

Sussex

N. J. Lenham c Fleming b de Villiers	63	– c Ward b Igglesden	18
†P. Moores c Marsh b Igglesden	0	– c Benson b Davis	46
*P. W. G. Parker c Ward b Davis	107	– c Ward b Davis	19
A. P. Wells b Ellison	69	– lbw b Davis	13
M. P. Speight b Davis	12	– lbw b Davis	22
C. M. Wells c Ward b Igglesden	14	– c Marsh b Davis	0
I. J. Gould c Marsh b Ellison	0	– c de Villiers b Ward	33
I. D. K. Salisbury not out	30	– (10) not out	5
A. I. C. Dodemaide c Cowdrey b Igglesden	9	– (8) c and b Davis	13
J. A. North b Igglesden	9	– (9) b de Villiers	6
A. R. Hansford c Marsh b Ellison	19	– lbw b de Villiers	2
B 5, l-b 16, w 1, n-b 2	24	B 6, l-b 6	12
1/4 2/133 3/225 4/257 5/269 6/274 7/286 8/296 9/318	356	1/35 2/64 3/102 4/105 5/105 6/160 7/160 8/175 9/187	189

Bonus points – Sussex 3, Kent 1 (Score at 100 overs: 268-4).

Bowling: *First Innings*—de Villiers 29–4–84–1; Igglesden 31–9–86–4; Ellison 24.4–8–70–3; Davis 42–14–75–2; Fleming 14–8–20–0. *Second Innings*—Igglesden 17–1–44–1; de Villiers 12.1–4–37–2; Ellison 6–4–10–0; Davis 26–10–59–6; Fleming 11–5–21–0; Ward 2–0–6–1.

Kent

S. G. Hinks c North b C. M. Wells	48	– c Moores b Dodemaide	4
M. R. Benson c Speight b Dodemaide	109	– c Moores b Dodemaide	13
N. R. Taylor c Speight b Hansford	57	– (4) c Speight b Dodemaide	20
T. R. Ward c Moores b Hansford	13	– (5) lbw b Dodemaide	0
*C. S. Cowdrey lbw b Dodemaide	24	– (6) not out	0
†S. A. Marsh b Dodemaide	10	– (7) not out	4
M. V. Fleming c Moores b Hansford	53	– (3) b Salisbury	39
R. M. Ellison b Dodemaide	81		
P. S. de Villiers c Dodemaide b C. M. Wells	37		
R. P. Davis run out	3		
A. P. Igglesden not out	2		
B 2, l-b 19, w 1, n-b 6	28	L-b 4	4
1/115 2/210 3/236 4/265 5/268 6/297 7/348 8/412 9/436	465	1/4 2/23 3/79 4/79 5/80	(5 wkts) 84

Bonus points – Kent 3, Sussex 1 (Score at 100 overs: 253-3).

Bowling: *First Innings*—Dodemaide 43.1–10–105–4; Hansford 35–11–91–3; C. M. Wells 30–9–67–2; Salisbury 60–15–135–0; North 15–6–30–0; Gould 2–0–8–0; Lenham 2–1–8–0. *Second Innings*—Dodemaide 7–1–29–4; Hansford 7–0–31–0; Salisbury 5–1–20–1.

Umpires: D. J. Constant and N. T. Plews.

At Lord's, May 15, 16, 17. KENT lost to MIDDLESEX by eight wickets.

At Swansea, May 23, 24, 25. KENT beat GLAMORGAN by 6 runs.

KENT v NOTTINGHAMSHIRE

At Tunbridge Wells, June 2, 4, 5. Drawn. Kent 4 pts, Nottinghamshire 8 pts. Toss: Nottinghamshire. Broad's first double-century and an exciting, vastly entertaining innings by Randall were the highlights on the Saturday. Broad's early dominance was reflected by his reaching 100 (out of 129) off 123 balls with an over to spare before lunch. Randall scored his 178 out of a fourth-wicket stand of 285 in 51 overs with Broad, hitting three sixes and thirteen fours during his 191-minute stay (162 balls). Broad's unbeaten 227 was made off 296 balls in 339 minutes and contained two sixes and 23 fours. Kent lost half their side for 72 before Marsh came to their rescue with 114 not out, made in 217 minutes with a six and twelve fours, but not even his century and his ninth-wicket stand of 94 with Merrick could save Kent from following on. They made another disastrous start, but this time Fleming was the saviour with a maiden first-class century in 175 minutes (one six, thirteen fours) to thwart some good fast bowling by Stephenson. Needing 75 to win off nine overs, Nottinghamshire abandoned the chase with four overs left.

Close of play: First day, Nottinghamshire 477-6 dec.; Second day, Kent 37-2 (N. R. Taylor 16*, R. P. Davis 6*).

Nottinghamshire

B. C. Broad not out	227	– c Marsh b Merrick	1
D. J. R. Martindale lbw b Davis	23		
*R. T. Robinson b Davis	2	– (5) not out	1
P. Johnson c Wells b Davis	25	– (3) c Davis b Merrick	3
D. W. Randall c Benson b Merrick	178	– (2) c Marsh b Merrick	6
†B. N. French c Marsh b Igglesden	0		
F. D. Stephenson c Fleming b Igglesden	4	– (4) not out	1
B 5, l-b 12, w 1	18	L-b 3, w 2	5
1/115 2/121 3/177 4/462 5/467 6/477 (6 wkts dec.)	477	1/3 2/11 3/16 (3 wkts)	17

E. E. Hemmings, K. E. Cooper, R. A. Pick and J. A. Afford did not bat.

Bonus points – Nottinghamshire 4, Kent 1 (Score at 100 overs: 421-3).

Bowling: *First Innings*—Merrick 23–2–60–1; Igglesden 20.3–2–62–2; Penn 19–1–105–0; Davis 37–3–155–3; Fleming 10–0–78–0. *Second Innings*—Merrick 3–0–10–3; Igglesden 2–0–4–0.

Kent

S. G. Hinks b Stephenson	6	– c Afford b Pick	14
*M. R. Benson c French b Cooper	34	– lbw b Stephenson	1
N. R. Taylor c Stephenson b Pick	1	– c Martindale b Hemmings	21
G. R. Cowdrey c French b Stephenson	27	– (5) c French b Stephenson	51
V. J. Wells c French b Pick	2	– (6) c Hemmings b Stephenson	20
M. V. Fleming c Broad b Cooper	1	– (7) b Stephenson	102
†S. A. Marsh not out	114	– (8) c French b Stephenson	4
R. P. Davis lbw b Afford	9	– (4) c French b Pick	13
C. Penn b Pick	23	– b Pick	17
T. A. Merrick c Martindale b Afford	35	– c Martindale b Stephenson	15
A. P. Igglesden c Johnson b Afford	0	– not out	1
B 2, l-b 17, n-b 4	23	B 4, l-b 4, w 1, n-b 8	17
1/19 2/20 3/52 4/65 5/72 6/103 7/129 8/171 9/265	275	1/4 2/28 3/50 4/50 5/104 6/142 7/185 8/210 9/258	276

Bonus points – Kent 3, Nottinghamshire 4.

Bowling: *First Innings*—Pick 22–7–57–3; Stephenson 24–5–77–2; Cooper 20–9–40–2; Hemmings 12–2–52–0; Afford 13–4–30–3. *Second Innings*—Pick 28–6–91–3; Stephenson 21–3–84–6; Hemmings 18–12–15–1; Afford 10–3–21–0; Cooper 18–1–57–0.

Umpires: D. O. Oslear and R. Palmer.

KENT v YORKSHIRE

At Tunbridge Wells, June 6, 7, 8. Drawn. Kent 4 pts, Yorkshire 2 pts. Toss: Kent. The weather ruined this game, virtually washing out the first and last days. On the second, an unbeaten 124 in 342 minutes (eight fours) by Taylor took Kent to maximum batting points, Benson having earlier hit 51 out of 75 off 70 balls. With two early declarations on the last morning, the stage was set for Yorkshire to chase 301 in a minimum of 95 overs, but the weather had the final say. The only result of the negotiations was that Metcalfe, the Yorkshire opener, found himself dismissed twice in the space of 44 minutes.

Close of play: First day, Kent 53-1 (M. R. Benson 37*, N. R. Taylor 2*); Second day, Kent 333-5 (N. R. Taylor 124*, S. A. Marsh 41*).

Kent

S. G. Hinks c Bairstow b Jarvis 6
*M. R. Benson c Metcalfe b Hartley .. 57
N. R. Taylor not out 124
G. R. Cowdrey c Kellett b Moxon 67
V. J. Wells c Bairstow b Hartley 4
M. V. Fleming c Kellett b Hartley 18
†S. A. Marsh not out 41
B 4, l-b 12 16

1/42 2/84 3/230 4/243 5/277 (5 wkts dec.) 333

R. M. Ellison, P. S. de Villiers, R. P. Davis and A. P. Igglesden did not bat.

Bonus points – Kent 4, Yorkshire 2 (Score at 100 overs: 303-5).

Bowling: Jarvis 8–4–16–1; Hartley 36–8–105–3; Gough 23–3–94–0; Carrick 25–9–40–0; White 10–0–33–0; Moxon 10–2–29–1.

Kent forfeited their second innings.

Yorkshire

*M. D. Moxon not out .... 24 – not out 6
A. A. Metcalfe c Davis b Benson .... 0 – c Marsh b de Villiers 14
R. J. Blakey not out .... 9 – not out 1
L-b 2 2

1/1 (1 wkt dec.) 33 1/21 (1 wkt) 23

S. A. Kellett, P. E. Robinson, †D. L. Bairstow, P. Carrick, C. White, P. J. Hartley, P. W. Jarvis and D. Gough did not bat.

Bowling: *First Innings*—Benson 2–0–14–1; Cowdrey 1.3–0–19–0. *Second Innings*—de Villiers 4.1–0–10–1; Igglesden 4–1–11–0.

Umpires: D. O. Oslear and R. Palmer.

KENT v SOMERSET

At Canterbury, June 9, 11, 12. Drawn. Kent 4 pts, Somerset 8 pts. Toss: Somerset. Tavaré, the former Kent captain and now leading Somerset, made a happy return to the St Lawrence Ground, reaching his half-century out of 71 off 64 balls and hitting eleven fours before being caught on the second morning, 18 runs short of his century. Rain had delayed the start on the opening day until after lunch. Kent, 114 for five after 49 overs, found themselves 130 for eight on the final morning when Rose took three wickets in four balls. However, Ellison and the tailenders managed something of a recovery, and when Cowdrey declared well in arrears,

Tavaré's response was to set Kent a target of 270 in a minimum of 45 overs. With Hinks and Benson scoring 121 for the first wicket, and Benson's 116 coming from 115 balls with twelve fours and a six, they were in with a chance. But when they lost five wickets for 26 runs, four of them to Rose in seventeen balls, they were forced to hold on to draw the game.

Close of play: First day, Somerset 200-2 (A. N. Hayhurst 36*, C. J. Tavaré 77*); Second day, Kent 121-5 (M. V. Fleming 31*, S. A. Marsh 3*).

Somerset

S. J. Cook c and b Davis	36		
J. J. E. Hardy c Marsh b Hinks	42	– not out	47
A. N. Hayhurst lbw b Igglesden	55	– c Benson b Igglesden	9
*C. J. Tavaré c Hinks b Igglesden	82		
R. J. Harden not out	52	– (4) not out	50
†N. D. Burns c Ellison b Davis	31	– (1) run out	40
G. D. Rose not out	8		
L-b 15, w 1	16	L-b 3, w 1	4
1/85 2/85 3/211 4/230 5/299 (5 wkts dec.)	322	1/50 2/59 (2 wkts dec.)	150

J. C. Hallett, N. A. Mallender, A. N. Jones and I. G. Swallow did not bat.

Bonus points – Somerset 4, Kent 2.

Bowling: *First Innings*—Igglesden 20–2–85–2; de Villiers 23–7–51–0; Ellison 25–2–101–0; Hinks 5–1–15–1; Davis 19–7–50–2; Fleming 4–0–5–0. *Second Innings*—de Villiers 2–0–7–0; Igglesden 7–1–42–1; C. S. Cowdrey 4–2–9–0; Ellison 7–0–38–0; Taylor 6–1–29–0; Davis 5–0–18–0; Benson 3–2–4–0.

Kent

S. G. Hinks lbw b Hallett	30	– b Swallow	55
M. R. Benson b Jones	0	– c Burns b Rose	116
N. R. Taylor c Hardy b Mallender	9	– c Hardy b Swallow	5
G. R. Cowdrey b Hayhurst	42	– c Cook b Mallender	10
*C. S. Cowdrey b Hallett	0	– b Rose	14
M. V. Fleming c Swallow b Rose	37	– b Rose	6
†S. A. Marsh c Burns b Rose	5	– c Tavaré b Hallett	8
R. M. Ellison not out	31	– not out	6
R. P. Davis lbw b Rose	0	– (10) not out	8
P. S. de Villiers c Burns b Rose	15	– (9) lbw b Rose	0
A. P. Igglesden not out	19		
B 1, l-b 11, w 1, n-b 2	15	L-b 4	4
1/1 2/12 3/61 4/61 5/114 6/129 7/130 8/130 9/153 (9 wkts dec.)	203	1/121 2/135 3/162 4/198 5/209 6/210 7/222 8/224 (8 wkts)	232

Bonus points – Kent 2, Somerset 4.

Bowling: *First Innings*—Jones 8.4–1–24–1; Mallender 19–6–32–1; Rose 19–4–59–4; Hallett 12.2–4–40–2; Hayhurst 14–1–36–1. *Second Innings*—Mallender 10–2–34–1; Rose 10.5–0–55–4; Hayhurst 8–0–48–0; Hallett 7–0–32–1; Swallow 9–1–59–2.

Umpires: D. J. Constant and B. J. Meyer.

At Cambridge, June 20, 21, 22. KENT beat CAMBRIDGE UNIVERSITY by 92 runs.

At Birmingham, June 23, 25, 26. KENT drew with WARWICKSHIRE.

KENT v LANCASHIRE

At Maidstone, June 30, July 2, 3. Lancashire won by three wickets. Lancashire 22 pts, Kent 6 pts. Toss: Kent. After losing half their side for 72 runs in 32 overs, Kent were boosted by the resistance of Graham Cowdrey, but it was Ellison and Davis who rescued them when they were 126 for eight. Lancashire lost Fowler and their night-watchman on Saturday evening, but on Monday Jesty played superbly in a stand of 168 off 50 overs with Atherton, hitting sixteen fours in his highest innings for Lancashire. Atherton, who hit ten boundaries, reached his century amid a collapse in which eight wickets fell for 75 in 23 overs. Batting a second time, Kent found that Atherton's leg-spin presented problems, and they left Lancashire needing to score 190 at less than 3 runs an over for victory. Atherton and Fairbrother established the innings with a stand of 60 in eighteen overs for the third wicket, and then Watkinson really stamped his side's authority on the game, racing to 66 off 60 balls with two sixes and ten fours. The left-arm spin of Davis again caused Lancashire some concern before they won with 14.5 overs in hand.

Close of play: First day, Lancashire 16-2 (M. A. Atherton 5*, T. E. Jesty 7*); Second day, Kent 109-4 (C. S. Cowdrey 15*, R. P. Davis 6*).

Kent

S. G. Hinks c Atherton b DeFreitas	29	– c Fowler b Atherton	49
M. C. Dobson run out	0	– b Allott	6
V. J. Wells lbw b Wasim Akram	9	– lbw b Watkinson	11
G. R. Cowdrey c Fowler b Allott	40	– b Atherton	14
*C. S. Cowdrey b Watkinson	6	– c Hegg b DeFreitas	28
†S. A. Marsh run out	11	– (7) c and b DeFreitas	8
D. J. M. Kelleher b Wasim Akram	0	– (9) lbw b Wasim Akram	0
R. M. Ellison c Hegg b DeFreitas	41	– not out	12
P. S. de Villiers b Allott	0	– (10) lbw b Atherton	33
R. P. Davis c Allott b Wasim Akram	59	– (6) c Hegg b Wasim Akram	19
A. P. Igglesden not out	16	– c Fowler b Atherton	0
L-b 14, n-b 12	26	B 5, l-b 12, w 1, n-b 3	21
1/11 2/34 3/45 4/54 5/72 6/76 7/125 8/126 9/194	237	1/38 2/53 3/83 4/98 5/139 6/152 7/154 8/154 9/201	201

Bonus points – Kent 2, Lancashire 4.

Bowling: *First Innings*—Wasim Akram 22–6–86–3; Allott 23–10–55–2; DeFreitas 19–6–43–2; Watkinson 18–6–38–1; Atherton 1–0–1–0. *Second Innings*—Wasim Akram 21–6–58–2; DeFreitas 23–7–55–2; Allott 9–5–16–1; Watkinson 11–3–32–1; Atherton 10.3–3–23–4.

Lancashire

G. Fowler c and b de Villiers	3	– c sub b de Villiers	13
M. A. Atherton lbw b Kelleher	101	– c Marsh b Davis	44
J. D. Fitton c Kelleher b Igglesden	0		
T. E. Jesty b C. S. Cowdrey	98	– (3) b Ellison	4
N. H. Fairbrother c G. R. Cowdrey b Davis	6	– (4) c Marsh b de Villiers	47
M. Watkinson b Davis	0	– (5) c Marsh b Davis	66
Wasim Akram st Marsh b C. S. Cowdrey	1	– (6) c and b Davis	9
P. A. J. DeFreitas c and b de Villiers	6	– (7) not out	7
†W. K. Hegg not out	20	– (8) lbw b Davis	0
*D. P. Hughes c C. S. Cowdrey b Davis	1	– (9) not out	0
P. J. W. Allott b Davis	0		
B 2, l-b 8, w 1, n-b 2	13	L-b 2, w 1	3
1/5 2/6 3/174 4/185 5/185 6/188 7/210 8/247 9/249	249	1/28 2/37 3/97 4/151 5/174 6/189 7/189	(7 wkts) 193

Bonus points – Lancashire 2, Kent 4.

Bowling: *First Innings*—Igglesden 8–2–29–1; de Villiers 19–6–73–2; Davis 23–7–49–4; Kelleher 8–2–30–1; Ellison 8–1–38–0; C. S. Cowdrey 12–3–20–2. *Second Innings*—de Villiers 11–0–58–2; Ellison 12–1–41–1; Kelleher 6–1–21–0; Davis 17–6–54–4; Dobson 3.1–1–7–0; C. S. Cowdrey 1–0–10–0.

Umpires: J. C. Balderstone and B. Dudleston.

KENT v ESSEX

At Maidstone, July 4, 5, 6. Essex won by four wickets. Essex 17 pts, Kent 4 pts. Toss: Essex. After the first day had been lost to rain, a good finish was achieved by Kent declaring and then forfeiting their second innings, and Essex forfeiting their first. An excellent stand of 268 off 85 overs by Benson and Graham Cowdrey dominated Kent's innings, with Benson hitting eighteen fours in a stay of 345 minutes and Cowdrey eighteen fours in an innings of 320 minutes. Needing 309 off a minimum of 84 overs, Essex paced their effort well. They looked in trouble when three wickets fell for 16 runs in ten overs, but Hussain and Shahid restored their advantage, adding 98 in 24 overs. Pringle then hit six fours in scoring 40 off 34 balls, and with two reverse sweeps for four in the closing stages he hustled Essex home with three overs to spare.

Close of play: First day, No play; Second day, Kent 269-2 (M. R. Benson 141*, G. R. Cowdrey 104*).

Kent

S. G. Hinks c Topley b Pringle 1
M. R. Benson lbw b Pringle 159
N. R. Taylor c Hardie b Pringle 6
G. R. Cowdrey run out 116
*C. S. Cowdrey not out 3
M. V. Fleming not out 0
L-b 8, n-b 15 23

1/4 2/30 3/298 4/308 (4 wkts dec.) 308

†S. A. Marsh, R. M. Ellison, P. S. de Villiers, C. Penn and R. P. Davis did not bat.

Bonus points – Kent 4, Essex 1 (Score at 100 overs: 300-3).

Bowling: Foster 33–2–107–0; Pringle 31–9–54–3; Topley 25–4–60–0; Childs 10–1–41–0; Stephenson 7–1–38–0.

Kent forfeited their second innings.

Essex

Essex forfeited their first innings.

B. R. Hardie c Hinks b de Villiers 12
J. P. Stephenson b Davis 67
P. J. Prichard c Marsh b Fleming 55
M. E. Waugh c Marsh b Davis 3
N. Hussain c C. S. Cowdrey b de Villiers 41
N. Shahid run out 63
*D. R. Pringle not out 40
†M. A. Garnham not out 17
B 2, l-b 6, n-b 3 11

1/18 2/124 3/140 4/140 5/238 6/269 (6 wkts) 309

N. A. Foster, T. D. Topley and J. H. Childs did not bat.

Bowling: de Villiers 19–2–84–2; Penn 22–6–68–0; Davis 18–5–76–2; Ellison 12–0–46–0; Fleming 10–1–23–1; C. S. Cowdrey 2–0–4–0.

Umpires: J. C. Balderstone and B. Dudleston.

At Canterbury, July 7, 8, 9. KENT lost to INDIANS by seven wickets (See Indian tour section).

At Northampton, July 18, 19, 20. KENT drew with NORTHAMPTONSHIRE.

At Guildford, July 21, 23, 24. KENT drew with SURREY.

KENT v MIDDLESEX

At Canterbury, July 25, 26, 27. Drawn. Kent 5 pts, Middlesex 4 pts. Toss: Middlesex. A record Kent second-wicket partnership, in which Hinks scored his first double-century, lasted 101 overs and realised 366 runs. That beat the previous best of 352 between W. H. Ashdown and F. E. Woolley, against Essex at Brentwood in 1934. Hinks hit thirty fours in a stay of 441 minutes, while Taylor, who survived a "catch" by Brown at short leg because the ball first touched the fielder's helmet, batted for 346 minutes and hit eighteen fours. Roseberry and Gatting added 109 in 23 overs, and as Middlesex raced to a declaration Ramprakash hit an unbeaten century off 169 balls in 185 minutes with two sixes and twelve fours. Kent promptly lost five wickets for 53 in nineteen overs, but Marsh batted with resolution and Middlesex were left to score 282 to win in a minimum of 58 overs. At 23 for two they were in trouble, with de Villiers bowling well, but Gatting and Ramprakash put them in sight of victory by adding 198 from 37 overs. Gatting made his 101 off 131 balls with fifteen fours, and Ramprakash's second century of the match – his third in consecutive innings – came off 109 balls with four sixes and seven fours. However, de Villiers and Igglesden struck back, and by keeping Ramprakash away from the strike Kent denied Middlesex victory with a good all-round performance in the field.

Close of play: First day, Kent 392-1 (S. G. Hinks 209*, N. R. Taylor 121*); Second day, Kent 30-3 (G. R. Cowdrey 13*, R. P. Davis 0*).

Kent

S. G. Hinks c Farbrace b Hughes	234	– b Cowans	2
*M. R. Benson c Farbrace b Haynes	45	– b Emburey	10
N. R. Taylor not out	152	– (8) c Roseberry b Cowans	3
G. R. Cowdrey (did not bat)		– (3) lbw b Williams	22
T. R. Ward (did not bat)		– (4) c Williams b Emburey	0
†S. A. Marsh (did not bat)		– c Emburey b Williams	61
R. M. Ellison (did not bat)		– c Brown b Tufnell	9
P. S. de Villiers (did not bat)		– (9) c Haynes b Emburey	9
R. P. Davis (did not bat)		– (5) c Farbrace b Cowans	12
M. M. Patel (did not bat)		– not out	1
A. P. Igglesden (did not bat)		– b Williams	1
L-b 6, w 1, n-b 11	18	B 1, l-b 2, n-b 7	10
1/83 2/449 (2 wkts dec.)	449	1/15 2/30 3/30 4/43 5/53 6/75 7/86 8/126 9/138	140

Bonus points – Kent 4 (Score at 100 overs: 344-1).

Bowling: *First Innings*—Williams 15–2–49–0; Cowans 23–5–57–0; Hughes 16.1–1–87–1; Haynes 10–1–47–1; Emburey 28–4–93–0; Tufnell 22–2–69–0; Ramprakash 9–0–41–0. *Second Innings*—Williams 19.5–1–65–3; Cowans 10–2–20–3; Tufnell 14–5–35–1; Emburey 7–4–3–3; Hughes 2–0–14–0.

Middlesex

D. L. Haynes b Igglesden	9	– b de Villiers	0
M. A. Roseberry c Igglesden b Ellison	82	– lbw b de Villiers	14
*M. W. Gatting c Igglesden b Davis	52	– b Igglesden	101
M. R. Ramprakash not out	100	– b de Villiers	125
K. R. Brown not out	57	– c Hinks b Igglesden	5
J. E. Emburey (did not bat)		– c Marsh b de Villiers	0
N. F. Williams (did not bat)		– c Marsh b de Villiers	8
†P. Farbrace (did not bat)		– lbw b de Villiers	3
S. P. Hughes (did not bat)		– not out	6
N. G. Cowans (did not bat)		– not out	2
B 5, l-b 1, n-b 2	8	B 2, l-b 10	12
1/12 2/121 3/155 (3 wkts dec.)	308	1/0 2/23 3/221 4/231 5/232 6/240 7/250 8/271 (8 wkts)	276

P. C. R. Tufnell did not bat.

Bonus points – Middlesex 4, Kent 1.

Bowling: *First Innings*—Igglesden 10–1–53–1; de Villiers 11–1–32–0; Ellison 9–0–37–1; Davis 30–8–104–1; Patel 16.2–4–54–0; Ward 5–0–22–0. *Second Innings*—de Villiers 21–3–70–6; Igglesden 20–0–93–2; Ellison 9–0–45–0; Davis 8–1–56–0.

Umpires: A. A. Jones and R. Julian.

KENT v WORCESTERSHIRE

At Canterbury, July 28, 30, 31. Drawn. Kent 5 pts, Worcestershire 7 pts. Toss: Worcestershire. For the first time in its 148-year history, Canterbury's Festival Week was completed by the end of July, rather than in August. Despite an assured innings from Hick, who reached 50 off 63 balls, Worcestershire were struggling until Neale and Rhodes embarked on their rescue operation with a sixth-wicket stand of 185. Neale reached 100 in 270 minutes with fourteen boundaries. Newport soon had Kent in trouble, taking five quick wickets as half the side went for 46, but Fleming inspired a recovery which was continued by the injured Taylor and the indisposed Cowdrey, both batting lower down the order. Responding to Kent's declaration in arrears, Worcestershire went for and achieved quick runs and left Kent to chase 272 in a minimum of 57 overs. Never really in touch with the target, they required 124 from the last twenty overs and were forced to hang on grimly when the left-arm spin of Illingworth made a telling contribution. During the luncheon interval on the second day the teams had been presented to the Duke of Kent, the home county's patron.

Close of play: First day, Worcestershire 302-5 (P. A. Neale 101*, S. J. Rhodes 85*); Second day, Kent 236-8 (N. R. Taylor 57*, A. P. Igglesden 7*).

Worcestershire

First innings		Second innings	
G. J. Lord c Benson b Wren	14	c and b Ward	81
C. M. Tolley c Taylor b Ellison	4	lbw b Ellison	0
G. A. Hick c Marsh b Ellison	66	c and b Wren	22
D. B. D'Oliveira c Marsh b Igglesden	21	c Davis b Ward	4
I. T. Botham c Marsh b Igglesden	4	b Davis	46
*P. A. Neale not out	119	not out	14
†S. J. Rhodes c Igglesden b Wren	94	not out	0
R. K. Illingworth lbw b Igglesden	15		
P. J. Newport not out	5		
L-b 5, w 3, n-b 1	9	L-b 3	3
1/12 2/40 3/71 4/75 5/132 6/317 7/341 (7 wkts dec.)	351	1/16 2/82 3/88 4/133 5/162 (5 wkts dec.)	170

S. R. Lampitt and N. V. Radford did not bat.

Bonus points – Worcestershire 4, Kent 2 (Score at 100 overs: 305-5).

Bowling: *First Innings*—Igglesden 21–1–97–3; Ellison 21–4–65–2; Wren 24–4–78–2; Fleming 18–3–46–0; Davis 22–8–54–0; Ward 3–1–6–0. *Second Innings*—Igglesden 6–1–23–0; Ellison 5–1–33–1; Wren 2–0–17–1; Davis 11–1–46–1; Ward 9.3–0–48–2.

Kent

First innings		Second innings	
S. G. Hinks b Newport	32	hit wkt b Botham	25
*M. R. Benson c Rhodes b Newport	10	c Rhodes b Newport	8
†S. A. Marsh c Hick b Newport	0	(7) lbw b Newport	8
T. R. Ward c D'Oliveira b Newport	1	(5) c D'Oliveira b Tolley	18
M. V. Fleming b Radford	59	(6) b Illingworth	42
R. M. Ellison c Hick b Newport	0	(8) c Radford b Illingworth	1
G. R. Cowdrey lbw b Newport	57	(4) lbw b Radford	9
N. R. Taylor not out	64	(3) st Rhodes b Illingworth	73
R. P. Davis c Rhodes b Botham	8	not out	2
A. P. Igglesden not out	13	not out	0
L-b 4, w 1, n-b 1	6	B 4, l-b 3, n-b 1	8
1/15 2/17 3/19 4/46 5/46 6/132 7/197 8/218 (8 wkts dec.)	250	1/23 2/33 3/64 4/107 5/161 6/184 7/189 8/192 (8 wkts)	194

T. N. Wren did not bat.

Bonus points – Kent 3, Worcestershire 3.

Bowling: *First Innings*—Newport 27.1–11–73–6; Botham 13–2–44–1; Lampitt 21–7–42–0; Illingworth 7–3–19–0; Radford 10–2–33–1; Tolley 8–1–29–0; Hick 2–0–6–0. *Second Innings*—Newport 14.5–2–27–2; Botham 6–2–29–1; Lampitt 11–1–45–0; Radford 9–2–41–1; Tolley 10–3–25–1; Illingworth 10–3–20–3.

Umpires: A. A. Jones and R. Julian.

At Chesterfield, August 4, 6, 7. KENT lost to DERBYSHIRE by ten wickets.

KENT v LEICESTERSHIRE

At Dartford, August 8, 9, 10. Kent won by seven wickets. Kent 21 pts, Leicestershire 4 pts. Toss: Leicestershire. With the wicket taking spin early on the first day, Kent's left-arm pair, Davis and Patel, were soon causing all kinds of problems for the Leicestershire batsmen. Ironically, given that Kent bowled only fifteen overs of pace, it was the medium pace of Parsons that accounted for Kent, but not before Benson had put together a fine century, batting for 220 minutes and hitting eighteen fours. When Leicestershire batted a second time, Patel and Davis again shared the wickets, causing a search through the record books to discover when two left-arm spinners had last taken all twenty wickets in a match for Kent. The answer was 1912, at Canterbury, when C. Blythe and F. E. Woolley, taking eleven and nine wickets respectively, bowled unchanged throughout the match against Nottinghamshire. Needing 112 to win, Kent cruised home after Hinks had taken 28 off the first two overs from Agnew. Although the pitch was reported to the TCCB by the umpires, no penalty was imposed.

Close of play: First day, Kent 50-0 (S. G. Hinks 8*, M. R. Benson 39*); Second day, Leicestershire 46-1 (N. E. Briers 16*, J. D. R. Benson 2*).

Leicestershire

T. J. Boon c Ward b Davis	18	– lbw b Patel	21
*N. E. Briers c Fleming b Patel	55	– b Davis	35
J. J. Whitaker c Cowdrey b Patel	6	– (7) b Patel	0
P. Willey c Marsh b Davis	61	– c sub b Davis	10
G. J. Parsons st Marsh b Davis	15	– (6) c Marsh b Patel	13
L. Potter c Marsh b Patel	7	– (5) c Marsh b Davis	0
J. D. R. Benson b Davis	9	– (3) c and b Davis	25
†P. A. Nixon lbw b Davis	17	– b Patel	14
J. P. Agnew c Wren b Patel	0	– b Patel	12
A. D. Mullally c Hinks b Davis	7	– b Patel	21
D. J. Millns not out	0	– not out	10
L-b 5, n-b 1	6	B 6, l-b 12, n-b 1	19
1/41 2/68 3/115 4/136 5/149 6/162 7/185 8/190 9/200	201	1/36 2/95 3/100 4/100 5/119 6/121 7/121 8/135 9/163	180

Bonus points – Leicestershire 1, Kent 3 (Score at 100 overs: 193-8).

Bowling: *First Innings*—Igglesden 8–3–19–0; Wren 7–2–18–0; Davis 44.2–18–63–6; Patel 44–13–91–4; Ward 1–0–5–0. *Second Innings*—Fleming 3–0–20–0; Igglesden 2–0–6–0; Davis 39–9–79–4; Patel 37.5–15–57–6.

Kent

S. G. Hinks c Boon b Willey	14	– b Willey	37
*M. R. Benson c Millns b Potter	107	– b Potter	18
N. R. Taylor b Willey	18	– c Boon b Parsons	32
G. R. Cowdrey c Millns b Parsons	39	– not out	17
T. R. Ward b Parsons	14	– not out	0
M. V. Fleming c Benson b Parsons	31		
†S. A. Marsh b Mullally	0		
R. P. Davis lbw b Mullally	0		
M. M. Patel b Parsons	17		
T. N. Wren b Parsons	1		
A. P. Igglesden not out	0		
B 19, l-b 6, n-b 4	29	B 5, l-b 3	8
1/62 2/159 3/173 4/213 5/230 6/231 7/231 8/259 9/261	270	1/43 2/67 3/106	(3 wkts) 112

Bonus points – Kent 2, Leicestershire 3 (Score at 100 overs: 231-7).

Bowling: *First Innings*—Agnew 11–3–44–0; Willey 39–12–94–2; Mullally 15–6–31–2; Potter 33–15–45–1; Parsons 15–5–31–5. *Second Innings*—Agnew 2–0–28–0; Willey 12–3–29–1; Potter 15–4–29–1; Parsons 5.5–0–18–1.

Umpires: D. S. Thompsett and A. G. T. Whitehead.

At Bristol, August 11, 13, 14. KENT drew with GLOUCESTERSHIRE.

At Hove, August 18, 20, 21. KENT drew with SUSSEX.

At Leicester, August 23, 24, 25, 27. KENT lost to LEICESTERSHIRE by two wickets.

At Bournemouth, August 29, 30, 31. KENT drew with HAMPSHIRE.

KENT v SURREY

At Canterbury, September 7, 8, 9, 10. Drawn. Kent 4 pts, Surrey 6 pts. Toss: Kent. A match which proved remarkable for personal achievement and county records rarely looked like producing a result. Taylor dominated both Kent innings. On the first day he reached his hundred off 99 balls in 106 minutes between lunch and tea, and he continued to his first double-century, batting for 322 minutes (240 balls) and hitting four sixes and 23 fours. Surrey took a substantial first-innings lead after Ward and Darren Bicknell had made career-best scores in a Surrey record third-wicket partnership of 413, which beat the previous best of 353 in 1919 by A. Ducat and E. G. Hayes against Hampshire at Southampton. Bicknell batted for a minute over eight hours and hit 21 fours, while Ward's more fluent strokes produced three sixes and 37 fours. Their stand was the highest for any wicket by any county against Kent; Ward's 263 was the highest by a Surrey batsman against Kent; and Surrey's 648 was the highest total by a county side against Kent. Follow that? Taylor did. He batted for another 263 minutes, hitting 22 fours in his 142, and apart from A. E. Fagg, who scored a double-century in each innings against Essex in 1938, became only the second Kent player after H. T. W. Hardinge (1921) to score a double-hundred and hundred in a match.

Close of play: First day, Kent 367-6 (N. R. Taylor 162*, D. J. M. Kelleher 42*); Second day, Surrey 315-2 (D. J. Bicknell 103*, D. M. Ward 147*); Third day, Kent 67-3 (V. J. Wells 11*, R. P. Davis 6*).

Kent

S. G. Hinks c Lynch b Robinson	16	– c Gray b Robinson	19
T. R. Ward c Kendrick b Murphy	55	– c and b Gray	10
V. J. Wells lbw b Gray	50	– b Murphy	11
G. R. Cowdrey b Gray	8	– c Lynch b Murphy	9
*N. R. Taylor c Robinson b Murphy	204	– (6) c Stewart b Gray	142
M. V. Fleming c Stewart b Greig	9	– (7) b Murphy	80
†S. A. Marsh c Kendrick b Murphy	17	– (8) not out	25
D. J. M. Kelleher c sub b Gray	44	– (9) lbw b Gray	6
R. P. Davis c Stewart b Murphy	5	– (5) lbw b Robinson	46
M. M. Patel c Lynch b Murphy	3	– b Gray	0
T. N. Wren not out	5	– not out	1
B 1, l-b 5, w 1, n-b 2	9	B 6, l-b 17, n-b 6	29
1/62 2/74 3/90 4/252 5/266 6/293 7/385 8/392 9/402	425	1/31 2/37 3/52 4/68 5/185 6/339 7/345 8/358 9/358	(9 wkts) 378

Bonus points – Kent 4, Surrey 2 (Score at 100 overs: 377-6).

Bowling: *First Innings*—Gray 35–7–80–3; M. P. Bicknell 3.3–1–12–0; Murphy 32.1–6–99–5; Robinson 21–3–95–1; Kendrick 12–1–73–0; Greig 14–0–60–1. *Second Innings*—Gray 32.4–9–83–4; Murphy 33–4–112–3; Robinson 24–5–84–2; Greig 10–0–57–0; Kendrick 7–1–19–0.

Surrey

D. J. Bicknell c and b Wells	186	A. H. Gray c Hinks b Kelleher	11
G. S. Clinton c Marsh b Wren	57	M. P. Bicknell b Kelleher	28
†A. J. Stewart c Taylor b Wells	1	A. J. Murphy run out	1
D. M. Ward c Kelleher b Wells	263		
M. A. Lynch not out	73	B 2, l-b 4, w 1, n-b 5	12
*I. A. Greig c and b Wells	0		
J. D. Robinson c Marsh b Fleming	16	1/99 2/100 3/513 4/530	648
N. M. Kendrick c Wells b Kelleher	0	5/531 6/566 7/571 8/607 9/646	

Bonus points – Surrey 4 (Score at 100 overs: 341-2).

Bowling: Kelleher 34.5–2–148–3; Wren 33–3–128–1; Davis 11–1–49–0; Wells 35–4–126–4; Fleming 37–4–127–1; Patel 24–4–64–0.

Umpires: M. J. Kitchen and D. S. Thompsett.

At Chelmsford, September 12, 13, 14, 15. KENT drew with ESSEX.

LANCASHIRE

Patron: HM The Queen
President: A. J. Leggat
Chairman: R. Bennett
Secretary: C. D. Hassell
County Cricket Ground, Old Trafford,
Manchester M16 0PX
(Telephone: 061-848 7021)
Captain: D. P. Hughes
Coach: J. A. Ormrod

Lancashire had a marvellous summer. They became the first county to win both Lord's finals, finished runners-up in the Refuge Assurance League, and were sixth in the Britannic Assurance Championship. The Second Eleven won the 55-overs Bain Clarkson Trophy, but like their seniors they were unable to make their mark in Championship cricket.

Lancashire were virtually invincible in all forms of the limited-overs game, losing only four out of 28 matches. The formidable line-up of batting was enough to carry them to victory on most days, and high among the list of Sunday wins was the seven-wicket victory, with eleven balls to spare, when set to score 268 in 39 overs at The Oval. But the most crushing win of the season was their 241-run victory over Gloucestershire in the quarter-finals of the NatWest Bank Trophy. Lancashire's 372 for five was the highest in any limited-overs game between first-class counties. Another record was denied Lancashire when the weather forced their Benson and Hedges Cup tie against Hampshire to be expunged after they had scored 352 for six, following a third-wicket partnership of 244 between Neil Fairbrother and Mike Atherton.

Lancashire stayed in the running for all the trophies right through to the closing stages of the season. They would have won the Refuge Assurance League if Derbyshire had slipped up in their final game with Essex, and they went into the last eight matches of the Championship handily placed in second position behind Middlesex. However, they won only one of those games, and there is no doubt that success in all the competitions up to the beginning of August took its mental and physical toll on the players. Even while Lancashire managed to stay among the leaders in the Championship, their minds always seemed to be rather more on the next important limited-overs match.

The turning-point came at Northampton in the middle of August, a game which ended the day before the NatWest semi-final against Middlesex. Lancashire, at least one game ahead of the other contenders, had to beat Northamptonshire to stay in the race. Atherton was already absent because of the Old Trafford Test match, and five other key players were rested. All five, nevertheless, returned for the Sunday League match the same weekend, and for the NatWest Trophy semi-final. The Championship was effectively surrendered in that game at Northampton as Lancashire continued their triumphant march in the one-day competitions.

By winning the finals of the Benson and Hedges Cup and the NatWest Bank Trophy Lancashire took to four their total of trophies won in the four years of David Hughes's captaincy. His batting and bowling contributions continued to be modest in 1990, but his fielding was as alert as ever and his enthusiasm for the game and for Lancashire cricket never flagged. Not surprisingly, he was asked to captain the county again in 1991 in his 25th season. Fairbrother, who captained the team whenever Hughes was absent, was appointed vice-captain for the first time, a clear pointer to the day when Hughes decides to retire. He had his best-ever season for Lancashire with 1,681 runs and an average of 80.04, blazing his way through the summer with a series of confident, swash-buckling innings to delight spectators all over the country. But the Fairbrothers of Lancashire and of England looked like two different people, one assured and convincing, the other diffident and uncertain. He was dropped by England after five innings against New Zealand had brought him only 59 runs, but his continuing good form for Lancashire earned him a place in England's A team to Pakistan. His 366 against Surrey at The Oval was the third-highest innings in England after fellow-Lancastrian A. C. MacLaren's 424 and G. A. Hick's 405 not out.

Atherton, too, had an outstanding summer, playing in all six Tests, in which he scored two centuries, and falling just 76 runs short of 2,000 in his first full season since completing his studies at Cambridge. He scored seven hundreds and twelve fifties to finish ninth in the national averages, and although opening the innings for England, he provided the back-bone that Lancashire have long needed at No. 3. He is unquestionably Lancashire's best batting find since Cyril Washbrook was discovered nearly 60 years ago. Atherton also proved to be Lancashire's best bowler, his leg-spin bringing him 44 wickets at a respectable cost of 27 runs each, including three five-wicket returns.

Gehan Mendis was as reliable as ever, his 1,551 runs taking his total to 7,035 in his five seasons with Lancashire since leaving Sussex. But Graeme Fowler had another eccentric summer. Although failing to reach 1,000 first-class runs despite playing in 21 of the 22 Championship matches, he beat Harry Pilling's record of 625 runs in the Sunday game by scoring 773. Lancashire's persistence with Fowler, and preference for Trevor Jesty in the middle of the order meant that Graham Lloyd's opportunities were limited to eleven Championship games, though he played in all but one of the Refuge games.

Mike Watkinson took 47 first-class wickets to go with his 754 runs, while Phillip DeFreitas had a season of mixed fortune. He took only 40 first-class wickets, with just two five-wicket returns, yet he destroyed the Northamptonshire batting in the NatWest final with an opening spell of 8–4–19–5, and he also scored two first-class hundreds.

All in all, the bowling was disappointing, with no-one taking even 50 first-class wickets: the two overseas players, Patrick Patterson – who was released at the end of the season – and Wasim Akram, managed only 45 between them. Wasim had a frustrating year, beset by injury; playing in just seven Championship matches, he took fifteen expensive wickets and scored 117 runs. However, Warren Hegg enhanced his wicket-keeping reputation to win a place on the England A tour and showed his merit as a batsman with 674 first-class runs. Off-spinner Dexter Fitton had a miserable summer on a succession of perfect pitches, and left-arm spinner Ian Folley, unable to regain the form of 1987, was released at the end of the season. – Brian Bearshaw.

LANCASHIRE 1990

[*Bill Smith*

Back row: I. Folley, I. D. Austin, N. J. Speak, B. P. Patterson, P. J. Martin, Wasim Akram, P. A. J. DeFreitas, W. K. Hegg, G. D. Lloyd, J. A. Ormrod (*coach*). *Front row*: S. Bramhall, G. D. Mendis, T. E. Jesty, N. H. Fairbrother, D. P. Hughes (*captain*), P. J. W. Allott, G. Fowler, M. Watkinson. *Inset*: M. A. Atherton.

LANCASHIRE RESULTS

All first-class matches – Played 25: Won 6, Lost 3, Drawn 16.
County Championship matches – Played 22: Won 6, Lost 3, Drawn 13.
Bonus points – Batting 65, Bowling 56.
Competition placings – Britannic Assurance County Championship, 6th; NatWest Bank Trophy, winners; Benson and Hedges Cup, winners; Refuge Assurance League, 2nd; Refuge Assurance Cup, s-f.

BRITANNIC ASSURANCE CHAMPIONSHIP AVERAGES

BATTING

	Birthplace	*M*	*I*	*NO*	*R*	*HI*	*Avge*
‡N. H. Fairbrother . .	*Warrington*	17	24	6	1,544	366	85.77
‡M. A. Atherton	*Manchester*	12	18	4	1,053	191	75.21
‡G. D. Mendis	*Colombo, Ceylon*	21	35	6	1,551	180	53.48
‡T. E. Jesty	*Gosport*	17	24	6	785	98	43.61
‡W. K. Hegg	*Whitefield*	20	21	6	617	100*	41.13
‡P. A. J. DeFreitas . .	*Scotts Head, Dominica*	15	17	3	506	100*	36.14
‡M. Watkinson	*Westhoughton*	18	22	2	706	138	35.30
‡I. D. Austin	*Haslingden*	11	12	5	238	58	34.00
‡G. Fowler	*Accrington*	21	35	6	938	126	32.34
G. D. Lloyd	*Accrington*	11	15	1	434	70	31.00
‡P. J. W. Allott	*Altrincham*	13	6	2	114	55*	28.50
‡D. P. Hughes	*Newton-le-Willows*	18	17	7	237	57	23.70
J. D. Fitton	*Littleborough*	14	11	5	114	25*	19.00
P. J. Martin	*Accrington*	9	6	3	42	21	14.00
‡Wasim Akram	*Lahore, Pakistan*	7	10	0	117	32	11.70
N. J. Speak	*Manchester*	3	4	0	41	30	10.25
‡B. P. Patterson	*Portland, Jamaica*	10	4	1	5	4*	1.66

Also batted: S. Bramhall (*Warrington*) (1 match) 0*; S. N. V. Waterton (*Dartford*) (1 match) 3; G. Yates (*Ashton-under-Lyne*) (2 matches) 106. J. P. Crawley (*Maldon*) (1 match) did not bat.

* *Signifies not out.* ‡ *Denotes county cap.*

The following played a total of seventeen three-figure innings for Lancashire in County Championship matches – M. A. Atherton 4, G. D. Mendis 4, N. H. Fairbrother 3, G. Fowler 2, P. A. J. DeFreitas 1, W. K. Hegg 1, M. Watkinson 1, G. Yates 1.

BOWLING

	O	*M*	*R*	*W*	*BB*	*5W/i*	*Avge*
M. A. Atherton	356.3	85	1,111	42	6-78	3	26.45
M. Watkinson	503.2	120	1,572	47	5-65	3	33.44
B. P. Patterson	281.4	45	1,015	29	4-52	0	35.00
P. A. J. DeFreitas	408.5	96	1,219	33	6-39	1	36.93
P. J. Martin	240.3	46	750	20	4-68	0	37.50
D. P. Hughes	280.4	61	918	24	4-25	0	38.25
Wasim Akram	191	43	594	15	3-76	0	39.60
P. J. W. Allott	266	77	730	18	4-23	0	40.55
I. D. Austin	208.1	64	536	10	3-42	0	53.60
J. D. Fitton	428.4	86	1,365	14	3-69	0	97.50

Also bowled: G. Fowler 4.1–2–33–1; T. E. Jesty 8–3–27–1; G. D. Lloyd 2.1–0–22–0; G. Yates 51–12–117–3.

Wicket-keepers: W. K. Hegg 47 ct, 2 st; S. N. V. Waterton 4 ct; S. Bramhall 1 ct, 1 st.

Leading Fielders: N. H. Fairbrother 18, M. A. Atherton 16, G. D. Mendis 16.

LANCASHIRE v WORCESTERSHIRE

At Manchester, April 26, 27, 28, 30. Drawn. Lancashire 7 pts, Worcestershire 5 pts. Toss: Worcestershire. The combination of a good pitch and two strong contenders for the Championship forced the match to a dull, inconclusive finish. After the first day had been washed out, Lancashire took advantage of what little help the pitch offered bowlers by reducing Worcestershire to 86 for five on the second morning. But D'Oliveira, with his first century in three seasons – a career-best 155 in 257 minutes (205 balls), with two sixes and 24 fours – shared in a stand of 226 in 65 overs with Rhodes. Hick was allowed to reach his century on the final day – he batted for 161 minutes (123 balls) and hit three sixes and ten fours – before Lancashire were set to score 292 in 46 overs, a target they never entertained.

Close of play: First day, No play; Second day, Worcestershire 360-7 (R. K. Illingworth 35*, P. J. Newport 5*); Third day, Worcestershire 22-0 (T. S. Curtis 16*, G. J. Lord 4*).

Worcestershire

T. S. Curtis c DeFreitas b Patterson	7	– b Patterson	37
G. J. Lord c Hegg b Patterson	9	– c Hegg b Jesty	19
G. A. Hick b Watkinson	23	– not out	106
I. T. Botham c Hegg b DeFreitas	17	– not out	50
*P. A. Neale lbw b DeFreitas	10		
D. B. D'Oliveira c Fairbrother b Hughes	155		
†S. J. Rhodes b Hughes	72		
R. K. Illingworth not out	35		
P. J. Newport not out	5		
B 8, l-b 6, n-b 13	27	B 3, l-b 5, w 1, n-b 10	19
1/17 2/25 3/49 4/65 5/86 6/312 7/341 (7 wkts dec.)	360	1/48 2/114 (2 wkts dec.)	231

N. V. Radford and G. R. Dilley did not bat.

Bonus points – Worcestershire 4, Lancashire 3 (Score at 100 overs: 348-7).

Bowling: *First Innings*—Patterson 22.1–5–55–2; DeFreitas 26–11–62–2; Watkinson 21–1–96–1; Atherton 6–0–32–0; Fitton 21–2–79–0; Hughes 8–1–22–2. *Second Innings*—Patterson 10–0–27–1; DeFreitas 15–5–51–0; Watkinson 9–3–19–0; Jesty 5–1–20–1; Fitton 14–1–70–0; Atherton 8–0–36–0.

Lancashire

G. D. Mendis b Illingworth	80	– not out	35
G. Fowler c Botham b Illingworth	16	– not out	35
M. A. Atherton b Illingworth	50		
N. H. Fairbrother not out	74		
T. E. Jesty b Illingworth	54		
M. Watkinson not out	0		
L-b 17, w 5, n-b 4	26	B 1, l-b 6, n-b 1	8
1/47 2/155 3/160 4/296 (4 wkts dec.)	300	(no wkt)	78

*D. P. Hughes, †W. K. Hegg, P. A. J. DeFreitas, J. D. Fitton and B. P. Patterson did not bat.

Bonus points – Lancashire 4, Worcestershire 1.

Bowling: *First Innings*—Dilley 16–1–80–0; Radford 19–6–66–0; Newport 19–3–61–0; Illingworth 35.3–17–46–4; Botham 7–1–24–0; Hick 1–0–6–0. *Second Innings*—Dilley 3–0–9–0; Radford 6–0–15–0; Newport 5–2–14–0; Illingworth 6–2–5–0; Hick 12–4–11–0; D'Oliveira 5–1–12–0; Curtis 2–1–5–0.

Umpires: J. C. Balderstone and H. D. Bird.

At The Oval, May 3, 4, 5, 7. LANCASHIRE drew with SURREY.

At Derby, May 15, 16, 17, 18. LANCASHIRE beat DERBYSHIRE by 60 runs.

LANCASHIRE v LEICESTERSHIRE

At Manchester, May 19, 21, 22. Drawn. Lancashire 6 pts, Leicestershire 3 pts. Toss: Leicestershire. A target of 316 in 61 overs proved too stiff for Lancashire after declarations had been necessary to set up a run-chase on another perfect wicket. Leicestershire recovered from losing two wickets to the new ball on the first morning, and Lancashire declared 86 behind after their first double-century opening stand in sixteen years. Fowler's century, containing a six and twelve fours, was his second in successive days, following his 108 in the Refuge League match. Neither Patterson nor DeFreitas bowled on the final morning as Leicestershire headed for the declaration, a fair one on a still-firm, unmarked pitch that had yielded 479 runs for the loss of two wickets – one of them a run-out – in the previous eight hours. Mendis and Fowler took 62 off the first eleven overs, Mendis and Fairbrother quickly put on 70 for the third wicket, but the loss of four batsmen in six overs left Lancashire blocking out the overs.

Close of play: First day, Leicestershire 318-7 (W. K. M. Benjamin 65*, P. A. Nixon 23*); Second day, Leicestershire 66-1 (N. E. Briers 26*, J. J. Whitaker 3*).

Leicestershire

T. J. Boon c and b Atherton	84	– run out	30
*N. E. Briers c Hegg b DeFreitas	0	– not out	81
J. J. Whitaker c Mendis b Patterson	8	– not out	107
P. Willey c Hegg b Fitton	43		
L. Potter c and b Atherton	55		
C. C. Lewis c Hegg b Atherton	32		
M. I. Gidley st Hegg b Atherton	2		
W. K. M. Benjamin run out	65		
†P. A. Nixon not out	33		
J. P. Agnew c Fairbrother b Patterson	6		
A. D. Mullally c sub b Patterson	2		
L-b 2, n-b 4	6	B 2, l-b 5, n-b 4	11
1/4 2/17 3/113 4/158 5/227 6/228 7/251 8/319 9/326	336	1/49 (1 wkt dec.)	229

Bonus points – Leicestershire 3, Lancashire 3 (Score at 100 overs: 265-7).

Bowling: *First Innings*—Patterson 21–2–68–3; DeFreitas 26–3–78–1; Martin 19–4–45–0; Fitton 22–8–54–1; Atherton 27–5–89–4. *Second Innings*—Patterson 6–2–27–0; DeFreitas 7–0–23–0; Fitton 24–4–54–0; Atherton 15–3–55–0; Martin 5–0–17–0; Hughes 13–1–46–0.

Lancashire

G. D. Mendis c Boon b Willey	113	– c and b Agnew	82
G. Fowler not out	115	– b Willey	22
M. A. Atherton not out	10	– c Briers b Willey	3
N. H. Fairbrother (did not bat)		– c Mullally b Agnew	46
T. E. Jesty (did not bat)		– b Lewis	0
P. A. J. DeFreitas (did not bat)		– not out	19
†W. K. Hegg (did not bat)		– c and b Lewis	1
*D. P. Hughes (did not bat)		– c sub b Potter	6
J. D. Fitton (did not bat)		– not out	0
L-b 7, w 1, n-b 4	12	B 5, l-b 10, w 4, n-b 3	22
1/231 (1 wkt dec.)	250	1/78 2/88 3/158 4/159 5/163 6/167 7/189 (7 wkts)	201

P. J. Martin and B. P. Patterson did not bat.

Bonus points – Lancashire 3.

Bowling: *First Innings*—Lewis 6–0–21–0; Agnew 18–3–76–0; Mullally 22.2–5–60–0; Willey 19–6–43–1; Gidley 9–0–43–0. *Second Innings*—Mullally 17–1–61–0; Agnew 11–1–43–2; Lewis 17–8–20–2; Willey 11–1–54–2; Potter 4.4–3–8–1.

Umpires: B. Hassan and R. Palmer.

LANCASHIRE v ZIMBABWEANS

At Manchester, May 23, 24, 25. Drawn. Toss: Lancashire. Speak hit fifteen boundaries in a maiden first-class hundred as he and Lloyd shared in two opening century partnerships for a Lancashire team mostly made up of second-team players. P. J. Martin was originally named in Lancashire's team, but withdrew injured at the end of the opening day before taking the field. Irani was allowed to play instead and so made his first-class début. Wasim Akram and Watkinson also withdrew injured, which led to Martin fielding as a substitute. For the tourists, Robertson scored a sparkling century, hitting two sixes and twelve fours, and with Flower he put on 188 for the third wicket. The Zimbabweans declared 50 ahead but later refused to take up Lancashire's challenge to score 261 at about 6 runs an over.

Close of play: First day, Zimbabweans 17-1 (G. W. Flower 4*, D. F. Dolphin 6*); Second day, Lancashire 70-0 (G. D. Lloyd 38*, N. J. Speak 31*).

Lancashire

G. D. Lloyd c Traicos b Butchart	78	– c Flower b Shah	76
N. J. Speak c and b Traicos	138	– c sub b Duers	74
S. P. Titchard c Flower b Duers	15	– b Flower	80
J. P. Crawley run out	1	– not out	76
M. Watkinson c Traicos b Shah	48		
Wasim Akram c James b Duers	18		
I. D. Austin not out	11		
G. Yates not out	2		
L-b 5, w 6, n-b 4	15	B 1, l-b 3	4
1/154 2/188 3/204 4/284 5/294 6/320 (6 wkts dec.)	326	1/133 2/165 3/310 (3 wkts dec.)	310

I. Folley, R. Irani and *†J. Stanworth did not bat.

Bowling: *First Innings*—Dube 11–1–48–0; Duers 23–5–96–2; Traicos 15–0–44–1; Butchart 12–3–48–1; Dolphin 8–1–28–0; Shah 23–7–57–1. *Second Innings*—Dube 4–1–18–0; Duers 20–4–59–1; Traicos 27–4–69–0; Dolphin 2–0–19–0; Flower 13.5–0–68–1; Shah 11–1–46–1; Butchart 5–1–27–0.

Zimbabweans

K. J. Arnott c Stanworth b Wasim Akram	0	– (2) lbw b Irani	2
G. W. Flower c Crawley b Folley	65	– (1) not out	20
D. F. Dolphin c Lloyd b Austin	25		
C. M. Robertson c sub b Yates	125	– not out	0
I. P. Butchart c Speak b Irani	71		
*A. J. Pycroft b Austin	55		
†W. R. James not out	16	– (3) lbw b Folley	52
L-b 4, w 1, n-b 14	19	W 2, n-b 2	4
1/0 2/39 3/227 4/228 5/342 6/376 (6 wkts dec.)	376	1/6 2/76 (2 wkts)	78

A. H. Shah, A. J. Traicos, K. G. Duers and L. E. Dube did not bat.

Bowling: *First Innings*—Wasim Akram 13–1–46–1; Watkinson 5–2–6–0; Irani 15–3–61–1; Austin 19–5–93–2; Yates 28–5–88–1; Folley 27–7–78–1. *Second Innings*—Austin 8–4–10–0; Irani 7–4–12–1; Folley 11–3–30–1; Yates 11–3–26–0.

Umpires: G. I. Burgess and D. O. Oslear.

At Colwyn Bay, May 26, 28, 29. LANCASHIRE drew with GLAMORGAN.

At Horsham, June 2, 4, 5. LANCASHIRE beat SUSSEX by nine wickets.

LANCASHIRE v GLOUCESTERSHIRE

At Manchester, June 9, 11, 12. Lancashire won by five wickets. Lancashire 18 pts, Gloucestershire 3 pts. Toss: Lancashire. After the first day had been washed out, both teams forfeited an innings on the final day to leave Lancashire with a victory target of 322 in at least 90 overs. Fowler gave the innings the right base, batting for four and a half hours and hitting sixteen fours in his 126, and Jesty saw Lancashire home, and to the top of the Championship table, with five overs to spare.

Close of play: First day, No play; Second day, Gloucestershire 280-7 (D. A. Graveney 10*, C. A. Walsh 2*).

Gloucestershire

*A. J. Wright c Hegg b Patterson 15
G. D. Hodgson c and b Hughes 72
P. W. Romaines retired hurt 12
C. W. J. Athey c Hegg b Patterson 33
P. Bainbridge b Austin 72
K. M. Curran c Allott b Fitton 48
J. W. Lloyds lbw b Austin 0
†G. A. Tedstone b Austin 6
D. A. Graveney not out 19
C. A. Walsh not out 33
B 2, l-b 8, n-b 1 11

1/26 2/127 3/161 4/236 5/236 6/240 7/273 (7 wkts dec.) 321

D. V. Lawrence did not bat.

Bonus points – Gloucestershire 3, Lancashire 2 (Score at 100 overs: 254-6).

P. W. Romaines retired hurt at 52.

Bowling: Patterson 18–4–43–2; Allott 16–2–39–0; Austin 21–3–42–3; Watkinson 12–3–33–0; Fitton 36–7–111–1; Hughes 17.5–5–43–1.

Gloucestershire forfeited their second innings.

Lancashire

Lancashire forfeited their first innings.

G. Fowler c Lloyds b Curran 126
G. D. Mendis c Hodgson b Graveney . 23
N. J. Speak c Tedstone b Lawrence ... 30
T. E. Jesty not out 84
M. Watkinson b Lawrence 4
†W. K. Hegg lbw b Lawrence 0
I. D. Austin not out 26
B 5, l-b 14, w 1, n-b 11 31

1/94 2/146 3/247 4/277 5/277 (5 wkts) 324

*D. P. Hughes, J. D. Fitton, P. J. W. Allott and B. P. Patterson did not bat.

Bowling: Walsh 20–1–66–0; Lawrence 18–2–86–3; Bainbridge 11–1–32–0; Curran 14–0–68–1; Graveney 19–3–39–1; Lloyds 2–0–7–0; Wright 0.5–0–7–0.

Umpires: M. J. Kitchen and K. J. Lyons.

At Oxford, June 16, 18, 19. LANCASHIRE drew with OXFORD UNIVERSITY.

LANCASHIRE v MIDDLESEX

At Manchester, June 20, 21, 22. Middlesex won by five wickets. Middlesex 18 pts, Lancashire 2 pts. Toss: Middlesex. After only 40 overs had been possible on the opening day and 57 on the second, the second successive double forfeiture of innings at Old Trafford left Middlesex with a minimum of 73 overs in which to score 302 for victory. This they did comfortably with fourteen overs to spare after century stands for the first two wickets involving Haynes, Roseberry and Gatting. For Lancashire, Mendis had scored his third century of the season, occupying more than six hours and spread over three days.

Close of play: First day, Lancashire 91-2 (G. D. Mendis 34*, T. E. Jesty 3*); Second day, Lancashire 222-5 (G. D. Mendis 92*, I. D. Austin 2*).

Lancashire

G. D. Mendis b Emburey	114	I. D. Austin not out	45
G. Fowler b Williams	24	J. D. Fitton not out	13
G. D. Lloyd c Emburey b Fraser	21	B 3, l-b 5, n-b 20	28
T. E. Jesty c Emburey b Tufnell	5		
M. Watkinson c Roseberry b Tufnell	37	1/41 2/77 3/104	(6 wkts dec.) 301
†W. K. Hegg c Haynes b Tufnell	14	4/182 5/219 6/262	

*D. P. Hughes, P. J. W. Allott and B. P. Patterson did not bat.

Bonus points – Lancashire 2, Middlesex 2 (Score at 100 overs: 224-5).

Bowling: Williams 15–4–53–1; Fraser 24–5–52–1; Hughes 13–4–32–0; Tufnell 44–12–90–3; Emburey 18–4–35–1; Ramprakash 2–0–17–0; Roseberry 1–0–14–0.

Lancashire forfeited their second innings.

Middlesex

Middlesex forfeited their first innings.

D. L. Haynes c Mendis b Watkinson	49	†P. Farbrace not out	17
M. A. Roseberry hit wkt b Patterson	79		
*M. W. Gatting c Hegg b Watkinson	95	B 8, l-b 11, n-b 9	28
M. R. Ramprakash c Hegg b Watkinson	8		
K. R. Brown not out	21	1/100 2/216 3/255	(5 wkts) 303
J. E. Emburey c Hegg b Watkinson	6	4/258 5/282	

P. C. R. Tufnell, N. F. Williams, S. P. Hughes and A. R. C. Fraser did not bat.

Bowling: Patterson 13–0–74–1; Allott 7–0–32–0; Austin 13.1–1–58–0; Watkinson 13–0–61–4; Fitton 8–0–35–0; Hughes 5–0–24–0.

Umpires: H. D. Bird and P. J. Eele.

LANCASHIRE v HAMPSHIRE

At Manchester, June 23, 25, 26. Drawn. Lancashire 2 pts, Hampshire 4 pts. Toss: Lancashire. Rain and bad light severely hit the third successive match at Old Trafford, producing another contrived finish. Left to score 330 in at least 70 overs, Lancashire, without Atherton, Fairbrother and DeFreitas, who were playing in the Test match at Lord's, gave up hope after losing their top four batsmen for 60 runs. On the second day, Marshall had put the distractions of several stoppages behind him to ensure that Hampshire achieved four batting points.

Close of play: First day, Hampshire 155-3 (D. I. Gower 43*, M. D. Marshall 27*); Second day, Lancashire 58-0 (G. D. Mendis 37*, G. Fowler 15*).

Hampshire

V. P. Terry lbw b Watkinson	15	– c Hegg b Wasim Akram	0
C. L. Smith c Jesty b Wasim Akram	25	– not out	53
T. C. Middleton b Watkinson	20	– not out	34
D. I. Gower c Speak b Wasim Akram	49		
M. D. Marshall c Mendis b Watkinson	86		
*M. C. J. Nicholas not out	58		
†R. J. Parks not out	14		
B 11, l-b 10, w 1, n-b 11	33		
1/32 2/64 3/104 4/168 5/247	(5 wkts dec.) 300	1/0	(1 wkt dec.) 87

R. J. Maru, T. M. Tremlett, C. A. Connor and K. J. Shine did not bat.

Bonus points – Hampshire 4, Lancashire 2.

Bowling: *First Innings*—Wasim Akram 29–3–106–2; Allott 17–8–26–0; Watkinson 22–8–54–3; Fitton 21.4–5–75–0; Austin 10–5–18–0. *Second Innings*—Wasim Akram 4–0–5–1; Allott 5–1–10–0; Watkinson 4–0–10–0; Fitton 11–1–34–0; Austin 8–1–28–0.

Lancashire

G. D. Mendis not out	37	– c Parks b Marshall	23
G. Fowler not out	15	– c Middleton b Maru	17
G. D. Lloyd (did not bat)		– c Tremlett b Maru	6
N. J. Speak (did not bat)		– b Marshall	6
T. E. Jesty (did not bat)		– not out	26
M. Watkinson (did not bat)		– not out	41
L-b 1, n-b 5	6	B 6, l-b 2, n-b 4	12
(no wkt dec.)	58	1/31 2/47 3/50 4/60 (4 wkts)	131

†W. K. Hegg, I. D. Austin, J. D. Fitton, *P. J. W. Allott and Wasim Akram did not bat.

Bowling: *First Innings*—Marshall 5–0–28–0; Shine 5–0–22–0; Connor 1–0–1–0; Tremlett 1–0–6–0. *Second Innings*—Connor 5.2–1–12–0; Maru 20–12–22–2; Marshall 14–2–42–2; Shine 6.4–0–15–0; Tremlett 5–1–13–0; Nicholas 5–0–11–0; Smith 5–3–8–0.

Umpires: H. D. Bird and P. J. Eele.

At Maidstone, June 30, July 2, 3. LANCASHIRE beat KENT by three wickets.

LANCASHIRE v DERBYSHIRE

At Liverpool, July 7, 9, 10. Drawn. Lancashire 4 pts, Derbyshire 6 pts. Toss: Lancashire. After Lancashire had declared at their Saturday night score, Barnett led his side's reply with his third successive Championship hundred to equal a Derbyshire record shared by W. Storer, L. G. Wright and P. N. Kirsten. He hit seventeen fours while putting on 200 with Bowler for the first wicket. Following Barnett's declaration, half an hour before tea and 51 runs behind, Derbyshire retained the ascendancy by taking five wickets before the close. However, Lancashire rallied on the final morning to leave them with a daunting victory target of 326 in 58 overs, which was way beyond them. Barnett, though hitting fifteen fours in his unbeaten 90, declined the chance of pursuing his fourth successive century.

Close of play: First day, Lancashire 301-8 (D. P. Hughes 25*, J. D. Fitton 6*); Second day, Lancashire 129-5 (M. Watkinson 25*, P. A. J. DeFreitas 6*).

Lancashire

G. D. Mendis c Kuiper b Base	7	– b Kuiper	25
G. Fowler c Roberts b Jean-Jacques	19	– (8) c Goldsmith b Jean-Jacques	31
G. D. Lloyd lbw b Kuiper	62	– (5) c Krikken b Kuiper	26
T. E. Jesty c Krikken b Base	27	– c Adams b Base	4
M. Watkinson b Kuiper	4	– (6) c Goldsmith b Jean-Jacques	63
P. A. J. DeFreitas c Goldsmith b Kuiper	16	– (7) c Kuiper b Base	11
†W. K. Hegg lbw b Miller	83	– (3) c Krikken b Kuiper	34
I. D. Austin c Roberts b Miller	29	– (9) not out	27
*D. P. Hughes not out	25	– (10) not out	36
J. D. Fitton not out	6	– (2) b Kuiper	4
L-b 11, w 4, n-b 8	23	L-b 2, w 1, n-b 10	13
1/10 2/53 3/111 4/122 5/138 6/146 7/234 8/284 (8 wkts dec.)	301	1/12 2/58 3/71 4/84 5/112 6/139 7/206 8/207 (8 wkts dec.)	274

P. J. W. Allott did not bat.

Bonus points – Lancashire 4, Derbyshire 3.

Bowling: *First Innings*—Base 24–2–79–2; Jean-Jacques 25–3–104–1; Goldsmith 6–1–24–0; Kuiper 19–6–42–3; Barnett 1–0–9–0; Miller 18–5–32–2. *Second Innings*—Jean-Jacques 16.3–0–90–2; Kuiper 24–4–69–4; Base 24–5–79–2; Miller 11–4–26–0; Goldsmith 2–0–8–0.

Derbyshire

*K. J. Barnett c Hegg b Watkinson	109	– not out	90
P. D. Bowler not out	115	– (5) c sub b Watkinson	30
J. E. Morris c sub b Hughes	14	– (2) c Hegg b Austin	22
B. Roberts not out	4	– (6) not out	1
A. P. Kuiper (did not bat)		– (3) c Lloyd b DeFreitas	8
S. C. Goldsmith (did not bat)		– (4) lbw b DeFreitas	7
B 2, l-b 4, n-b 2	8	B 8, l-b 3	11
1/200 2/240 (2 wkts dec.)	250	1/55 2/81 3/89 4/152 (4 wkts)	169

C. J. Adams, †K. M. Krikken, M. Jean-Jacques, S. J. Base and G. Miller did not bat.

Bonus points – Derbyshire 3.

Bowling: *First Innings*—DeFreitas 13–1–44–0; Watkinson 14.2–0–56–1; Austin 12–0–33–0; Fitton 23–5–66–0; Hughes 15–3–45–1. *Second Innings*—DeFreitas 10–2–35–2; Watkinson 13–5–47–1; Austin 7–2–18–1; Fitton 11–3–43–0; Hughes 7–1–15–0.

Umpires: R. Julian and D. O. Oslear.

At Coventry, July 18, 19, 20. LANCASHIRE drew with WARWICKSHIRE.

At Colchester, July 21, 23, 24. LANCASHIRE lost to ESSEX by six wickets.

LANCASHIRE v NOTTINGHAMSHIRE

At Southport, July 25, 26, 27. Lancashire won by seven wickets. Lancashire 24 pts, Nottinghamshire 4 pts. Toss: Lancashire. Mendis ended a lean period in the Championship with his fourth century of the season, hitting a six and 26 fours before he was fourth out at 378. Fairbrother's entertaining 93 contained four sixes and twelve fours, and Watkinson hit five sixes before becoming one of the last six wickets to fall for 20 runs. Nottinghamshire followed on 247 behind, despite a fine innings of 122 off 159 balls (22 fours) from Broad. His only support, however, came from Evans in an eighth-wicket partnership of 84. Nottinghamshire were only 18 runs in arrears with seven wickets standing at the end of the second day, but Lancashire cleaned up the remaining batsmen for 144 runs. Rain delayed Lancashire's response, but a requirement of 127 runs in 34 overs was easily reached with seven overs to spare. Waterton, a wicket-keeper formerly with Kent and Northamptonshire, made his Lancashire début as replacement for Hegg, who was injured, and held four catches on the second day.

Close of play: First day, Lancashire 452; Second day, Nottinghamshire 229-3 (P. Johnson 69*, D. W. Randall 34*).

Lancashire

G. D. Mendis c Robinson b Stephenson	180	– c Evans b Stephenson	21
G. Fowler c Stephenson b Evans	18	– c Robinson b Afford	6
G. D. Lloyd c Johnson b Afford	39	– not out	59
N. H. Fairbrother c Robinson b Cooper	93	– c Johnson b Afford	10
T. E. Jesty c and b Evans	38	– not out	30
M. Watkinson st French b Afford	47		
J. D. Fitton c French b Evans	3		
*D. P. Hughes b Evans	7		
†S. N. V. Waterton c Broad b Afford	3		
P. J. W. Allott st French b Afford	5		
P. J. Martin not out	1		
B 2, l-b 5, n-b 11	18	L-b 2, w 1, n-b 1	4
1/54 2/155 3/318 4/378 5/432 6/434 7/441 8/442 9/449	452	1/26 2/39 3/53 (3 wkts)	130

Bonus points – Lancashire 4, Nottinghamshire 2 (Score at 100 overs: 434-5).

Bowling: *First Innings*—Stephenson 23–4–127–1; Cooper 23–1–94–1; Evans 25–10–57–4; Afford 34–5–137–4; Saxelby 3–0–30–0. *Second Innings*—Stephenson 9–0–44–1; Cooper 2–1–11–0; Afford 11–2–58–2; Evans 4.4–1–15–0.

Nottinghamshire

Batsman – First innings		Second innings	
B. C. Broad c Mendis b Allott	122	lbw b Allott	46
P. R. Pollard lbw b Allott	0	c Waterton b Martin	27
*R. T. Robinson c Waterton b Martin	0	c Waterton b Hughes	41
P. Johnson c Mendis b Martin	4	b Allott	82
D. W. Randall lbw b Allott	0	c and b Martin	68
M. Saxelby c Waterton b Fitton	13	c Fairbrother b Martin	8
F. D. Stephenson c Hughes b Fitton	8	run out	18
†B. N. French lbw b Martin	6	run out	1
K. P. Evans not out	48	not out	34
K. E. Cooper b Allott	0	c Fitton b Watkinson	24
J. A. Afford c Watkinson b Hughes	0	run out	0
L-b 2, w 1, n-b 1	4	B 1, l-b 18, w 3, n-b 2	24
1/16 2/17 3/37 4/38 5/77 6/97 7/112 8/196 9/202	205	1/58 2/98 3/172 4/251 5/284 6/295 7/313 8/314 9/367	373

Bonus points – Nottinghamshire 2, Lancashire 4.

Bowling: *First Innings*—Martin 14–1–57–3; Allott 16–5–37–4; Watkinson 7–0–36–0; Fitton 12–1–61–2; Hughes 5–1–12–1. *Second Innings*—Martin 27–2–110–3; Watkinson 34.3–7–129–1; Fitton 6–0–33–0; Allott 14–2–52–2; Hughes 10–3–30–1.

Umpires: J. W. Holder and A. G. T. Whitehead.

LANCASHIRE v SOMERSET

At Manchester, July 28, 30, 31. Drawn. Lancashire 8 pts, Somerset 5 pts. Toss: Lancashire. When the second day ended, Lancashire were in total control. Somerset, in their second innings, were only 35 ahead with five wickets standing after Watkinson had followed his 96 (three sixes, seven fours) by taking four wickets. Lancashire's hopes of a second successive 24-point win could hardly have been higher, but they were thwarted by a remarkable innings from Tavaré, who batted through an uninterrupted final day to add 65 to his overnight 19. He scored 26 in the first session, 25 in the second and 14 in the third, batting for 345 minutes in all and receiving stout support from Rose in a three-hour stand worth 131.

Close of play: First day, Lancashire 95-3 (N. H. Fairbrother 35*, T. E. Jesty 9*); Second day, Somerset 137-5 (C. J. Tavaré 19*, N. D. Burns 0*).

Somerset

Batsman – First innings		Second innings	
S. J. Cook lbw b Martin	49	c Fairbrother b Watkinson	64
P. M. Roebuck lbw b Watkinson	26	c Hegg b Patterson	12
A. N. Hayhurst c Hegg b Watkinson	6	c Hegg b Watkinson	30
*C. J. Tavaré c Fairbrother b Patterson	17	not out	84
R. J. Harden b Martin	60	(6) c Jesty b Watkinson	2
†N. D. Burns c Hegg b Patterson	7	(7) c Fowler b Watkinson	10
G. D. Rose c Mendis b Austin	27	(8) c Lloyd b Martin	76
R. P. Lefebvre lbw b Austin	0	(9) lbw b Austin	2
I. G. Swallow c Lloyd b Watkinson	16	(5) b Watkinson	0
N. A. Mallender not out	3	c Lloyd b Austin	7
H. R. J. Trump b Patterson	1	not out	4
B 8, l-b 8, w 1, n-b 8	25	B 13, l-b 12, w 3, n-b 5	33
1/74 2/86 3/96 4/138 5/163 6/206 7/206 8/212 9/230	237	1/53 2/108 3/133 4/133 5/137 6/166 7/297 8/300 9/312 (9 wkts dec.)	324

Bonus points – Somerset 2, Lancashire 4.

Bowling: *First Innings*—Patterson 13.5–2–76–3; Martin 17–5–55–2; Watkinson 18–12–29–3; Fitton 4–0–17–0; Austin 16–8–44–2. *Second Innings*—Patterson 23–7–68–1; Martin 18–4–50–1; Fitton 26–7–65–0; Watkinson 35–7–97–5; Austin 23–14–19–2; Fowler 2–2–0–0.

Lancashire

G. D. Mendis c and b Swallow 29
G. Fowler c Burns b Swallow 10
G. D. Lloyd lbw b Swallow 0
*N. H. Fairbrother c Burns b Rose 91
T. E. Jesty b Mallender 30
M. Watkinson c Cook b Trump 96
†W. K. Hegg c Rose b Trump 33
I. D. Austin c Swallow b Trump 1
J. D. Fitton not out 25
P. J. Martin c Trump b Rose 9
B. P. Patterson b Mallender 1
B 5, l-b 3, w 1, n-b 5 14

1/42 2/42 3/68 4/141 5/212 6/301 7/302 8/307 9/334 — 339

Bonus points – Lancashire 4, Somerset 3 (Score at 100 overs: 307-7).

Bowling: Mallender 18–5–63–2; Rose 18–0–77–2; Lefebvre 14–5–22–0; Swallow 28–11–88–3; Trump 26–10–58–3; Roebuck 6–0–17–0; Hayhurst 1–0–6–0.

Umpires: J. W. Holder and A. G. T. Whitehead.

At Leeds, August 4, 6, 7. LANCASHIRE drew with YORKSHIRE.

At Kidderminster, August 8, 9, 10. LANCASHIRE lost to WORCESTERSHIRE by ten wickets.

At Northampton, August 11, 13, 14. LANCASHIRE drew with NORTHAMPTONSHIRE.

LANCASHIRE v YORKSHIRE

At Manchester, August 18, 19, 20, 21. Drawn. Lancashire 5 pts, Yorkshire 4 pts. Toss: Lancashire. Lancashire took up a strong position on the opening day through Atherton's seventh century of the season, Watkinson's second of his career, and a near-miss by Fairbrother. The free-scoring left-hander faced only 86 balls for his 99, having reached 50 in 29. After the second day had been washed out, and 35 overs had been lost on the third, two declarations on the fourth morning brought Yorkshire into the game and gave them 95 overs in which to score 317 for victory. In the end it was Lancashire who almost squeezed home. Watkinson, who bowled off-breaks and delivered 44 of the 47 overs from the Warwick Road end, captured five wickets in another big-hearted all-round performance. Sharp, whose right thumb was broken in the first innings by a ball from Wasim Akram, defied Lancashire for thirteen overs, and he and Batty held out for the last 32 deliveries to save the match.

Close of play: First day, Lancashire 417-8 (I. D. Austin 11*, D. P. Hughes 14*); Second day, No play; Third day, Yorkshire 190-3 (M. D. Moxon 90*, D. Byas 2*).

Lancashire

	First innings		Second innings	
G. D. Mendis c Batty b Hartley	13	– (3) not out	15
G. Fowler c Batty b Hartley	7	– not out	50
M. A. Atherton c Byas b Carrick	108		
N. H. Fairbrother c Moxon b Hartley	99		
M. Watkinson c Robinson b Carrick	138		
Wasim Akram c Hartley b Carrick	8	– (1) c Blakey b Jarvis	6
P. A. J. DeFreitas b Batty	4		
†W. K. Hegg c Byas b Carrick	3		
I. D. Austin not out	21		
*D. P. Hughes c Byas b Hartley	16		
P. J. W. Allott st Blakey b Carrick	2		
B 10, l-b 2, n-b 2	14	W 1, n-b 1	2
1/18 2/29 3/164 4/335 5/349 6/354 7/365 8/392 9/422	433	1/11	(1 wkt dec.) 73

Bonus points – Lancashire 4, Yorkshire 3 (Score at 100 overs: 392-8).

Bowling: *First Innings*—Jarvis 20–3–73–0; Hartley 22–1–109–4; Pickles 12–0–57–0; Carrick 40–11–98–5; Batty 22–1–84–1. *Second Innings*—Jarvis 3–2–2–1; Hartley 2.1–0–10–0; Metcalfe 5.4–0–44–0; Pickles 5–1–17–0.

Yorkshire

*M. D. Moxon not out	90	– c Fowler b Atherton	50
A. A. Metcalfe lbw b DeFreitas	2	– c Allott b Watkinson	39
K. Sharp retired hurt	5	– (10) not out	9
P. E. Robinson c Hughes b Watkinson	70	– (3) c Hughes b Watkinson	9
†R. J. Blakey c Allott b Watkinson	1	– (4) c Hegg b Atherton	4
D. Byas not out	2	– (5) c Allott b Atherton	39
P. Carrick (did not bat)		– (6) lbw b Watkinson	57
C. S. Pickles (did not bat)		– (7) c Hegg b Watkinson	16
P. J. Hartley (did not bat)		– (8) lbw b Wasim Akram	0
P. W. Jarvis (did not bat)		– (9) b Watkinson	11
J. D. Batty (did not bat)		– not out	7
B 8, l-b 1, w 2, n-b 9	20	B 10, l-b 6, n-b 9	25
1/3 2/171 3/177 (3 wkts dec.)	190	1/77 2/107 3/109 4/116 5/178 6/223 7/224 8/237 9/258 (9 wkts)	266

Bonus points – Yorkshire 1, Lancashire 1.

In the first innings K. Sharp retired hurt at 24.

Bowling: *First Innings*—Wasim Akram 16–1–47–0; DeFreitas 12–1–44–1; Austin 4–2–5–0; Allott 4–1–10–0; Atherton 12–3–42–0; Watkinson 10–3–24–2; Hughes 8–5–9–0. *Second Innings*—Wasim Akram 21–8–46–1; DeFreitas 5–0–30–0; Watkinson 44–12–105–5; Atherton 25–6–69–3.

Umpires: R. A. White and A. G. T. Whitehead.

LANCASHIRE v SURREY

At Blackpool, August 29, 30, 31. Drawn. Lancashire 3 pts, Surrey 3 pts. Toss: Lancashire. Lancashire's first Championship match at the Stanley Park ground since 1984 was ruined by rain. There was no play on the first day, and with only 71 overs on the second and 29 on the third, there was never any chance of even a concocted finish. Mendis grafted for 245 minutes after the match got under way half an hour before lunch on the second day. Play could not start until 1.40 p.m. on the final afternoon, and Surrey used the remaining time for batting practice.

Close of play: First day, No play; Second day, Lancashire 261-8 (W. K. Hegg 34*, I. D. Austin 6*).

Lancashire

G. D. Mendis c Lynch b M. P. Bicknell	94
G. Fowler lbw b Murphy	42
G. D. Lloyd lbw b Medlycott	1
N. H. Fairbrother c Stewart b Murphy	8
T. E. Jesty b Waqar Younis	25
M. Watkinson lbw b Waqar Younis	0
Wasim Akram c D. J. Bicknell b Feltham	17
P. A. J. DeFreitas b M. P. Bicknell	13
†W. K. Hegg not out	34
I. D. Austin not out	6
B 3, l-b 6, w 2, n-b 10	21
1/97 2/100 3/112 4/170 5/170 6/198 7/217 8/218 (8 wkts dec.)	261

*D. P. Hughes did not bat.

Bonus points – Lancashire 3, Surrey 3.

Bowling: Waqar Younis 18–4–65–2; M. P. Bicknell 18–3–65–2; Feltham 13–4–40–1; Murphy 17–1–73–2; Medlycott 5–1–9–1.

Surrey

D. J. Bicknell lbw b Wasim Akram . . . 25
R. I. Alikhan c Hegg b DeFreitas 9
†A. J. Stewart not out 23
D. M. Ward not out 16
B 1, l-b 2, n-b 6 9

1/40 2/48 (2 wkts dec.) 82

M. A. Lynch, *I. A. Greig, M. A. Feltham, K. T. Medlycott, M. P. Bicknell, A. J. Murphy and Waqar Younis did not bat.

Bowling: Wasim Akram 11–2–32–1; DeFreitas 8–4–31–1; Watkinson 6–3–13–0; Austin 4–2–3–0.

Umpires: B. J. Meyer and R. A. White.

At Manchester, September 8, 9, 10. LANCASHIRE drew with SRI LANKANS (See Sri Lankan tour section).

At Nottingham, September 12, 13, 14, 15. LANCASHIRE beat NOTTINGHAMSHIRE by ten wickets.

LANCASHIRE v WARWICKSHIRE

At Manchester, September 18, 19, 20, 21. Drawn. Lancashire 3 pts, Warwickshire 2 pts. Toss: Lancashire. Only 126.3 overs were possible in a game which lost the final day of the season to the weather. Reeve went in to bat when Warwickshire were 79 for five on the second day and overcame the handicap of a bitterly cold, blustery wind to score 121 of the 201 runs added in nearly four hours for the last five wickets. He hit a six and fourteen fours in his unbeaten innings. John Crawley, younger brother of Mark, made his Championship début before going to Cambridge, but did not have an opportunity to bat.

Close of play: First day, Warwickshire 78-4 (T. A. Lloyd 24*, P. A. Smith 0*); Second day, Warwickshire 271-9 (D. A. Reeve 117*, A. A. Donald 3*); Third day, Lancashire 48-0 (G. D. Mendis 22*, M. A. Atherton 22*).

Warwickshire

A. J. Moles c Fairbrother b Watkinson . 9
J. D. Ratcliffe c Hegg b Atherton 17
Asif Din c DeFreitas b Watkinson 24
*T. A. Lloyd c Atherton b Martin 35
P. A. Booth c Lloyd b Yates 0
P. A. Smith c Watkinson b Martin 1
D. A. Reeve not out 121
†K. J. Piper c Hegg b Watkinson 23
G. C. Small c Hegg b Atherton 30
T. A. Munton c Atherton b Watkinson . 8
A. A. Donald c and b Watkinson 8
L-b 4 4

1/14 2/50 3/73 4/78 5/79 280
6/92 7/154 8/188 9/231

Bonus points – Warwickshire 2, Lancashire 3 (Score at 100 overs: 217-8).

Bowling: DeFreitas 4–0–6–0; Martin 29–6–88–2; Watkinson 24.3–6–65–5; Austin 13–8–23–0; Atherton 23–6–52–2; Yates 21–6–42–1.

Lancashire

G. D. Mendis not out 22
M. A. Atherton not out 22
L-b 4 4

(no wkt) 48

J. P. Crawley, *N. H. Fairbrother, G. D. Lloyd, M. Watkinson, P. A. J. DeFreitas, †W. K. Hegg, G. Yates, I. D. Austin and P. J. Martin did not bat.

Bowling: Donald 6–0–24–0; Munton 3–0–16–0; Booth 3–1–4–0.

Umpires: D. J. Constant and B. Leadbeater.

LEICESTERSHIRE

President: C. H. Palmer
Chairman: J. M. Josephs
Chairman, Cricket Committee: P. R. Haywood
Chief Executive: F. M. Turner
County Cricket Ground, Grace Road,
Leicester LE2 8AD
(Telephone: 0533-831880/832128)
Cricket Manager: R. B. Simpson
Captain: N. E. Briers
Coach: 1990 – K. Higgs

After the disappointments of 1989, when Leicestershire were able only to reinforce a reputation for under-achievement, it was essential from the county committee's point of view that something be done to provide fresh impetus, to generate renewed enthusiasm in the dressing-room, and to maintain an air of optimism in an unfavourable commercial climate. Guided by the club's chief executive, Mike Turner, they decided to appoint a manager: someone with both an unquestionable pedigree and a high media profile. The man they sought initially was Ray Illingworth, who had been Leicestershire's captain during the county's most successful era, in the 1970s, but Illingworth resisted several attempts to lure him back to Grace Road.

Undeterred, the county continued to pitch high and were successful in tempting Bobby Simpson, the Australian national coach, to try his hand in the English domestic game. Coming so soon after Simpson had masterminded England's humiliating surrender of the Ashes, the appointment could not have been matched for prestige. Leicestershire also appointed a new captain, the experienced and enthusiastic Nigel Briers, to take over from David Gower, who had resigned to concentrate on rebuilding his international career.

Against the background of these changes, Leicestershire looked sure to embark on the 1990 season with burgeoning hopes, and so they did, despite the further decision by Gower to join Hampshire. To lose their one batsman of true international class was unquestionably a blow to Leicestershire, but it is reasonable to speculate that Gower's temperament may have made it difficult for him to feel comfortable in a dressing-room run by someone with such a high regard for discipline and punctuality as Simpson. The Australian's arrival was not greeted without scepticism among the players, some of whom held the view that a strong captain was as much leadership as a team required. None the less, within a few days of taking up his duties Simpson had introduced a more organised, professional approach to pre-season preparations than had been customary.

Once the new campaign began, however, it was difficult to distinguish the new Leicestershire from the old model. Although they convincingly defeated Glamorgan in their opening Britannic Assurance Championship fixture, they began badly in the Refuge Assurance League and failed again to qualify for the knockout rounds of the Benson and Hedges Cup, in which they had not progressed beyond the group stage since winning the trophy in 1985. Nor did their fortunes in the limited-overs game improve, in spite of predictions to the contrary made by the manager. The Sunday League soon became a hopelessly lost cause, and the 1-run defeat by Hampshire in the first round of the NatWest Bank Trophy merely emphasised all the failings that Simpson needed to put right.

Leicestershire finished next to bottom of the Refuge table, but their form in the Championship was a contradiction. During August, they were strong contenders for a top-five position in the Britannic table, and they won six matches in total, an improvement of two on 1989. Had they been able to press home clear advantages gained in three or four other games, they might have mounted a strong challenge for the title itself. Sometimes, on these occasions, Briers could have been less cautious in his tactics, but culpability largely rested with individuals for performing below their best. A Championship position of seventh, however, was six places up on 1989.

Briers combined captaincy with supervising a benefit campaign, as well as opening the innings, and he appeared to thrive on multiple responsibility. His aggregate in first-class cricket was 1,996, surpassing his previous highest aggregate by 661 and quashing suggestions that his batting would be impaired by such a heavy workload. He scored five centuries, also a personal best, and in a summer less devalued by the sheer weight of runs made, his innings of 176 against Northamptonshire on a bouncy, awkward pitch at Grace Road might have been regarded as one of the outstanding performances.

The much improved nature of pitches, at Grace Road and elsewhere, helped James Whitaker and Tim Boon to set revised marks, Boon passing 1,500 for the first time in his career and Whitaker totalling 1,767, including four hundreds. Chris Lewis, awarded his county cap on the opening day of the campaign, posted his maiden century in spectacular style when he contributed 189 not out to a high-scoring contest at Chelmsford in May. But while producing regular glimpses of his exceptional all-round talent, he made a smaller contribution in terms of runs and wickets than had been hoped for, although a series of minor fitness and health problems did not help his progress.

Jon Agnew was the busiest Leicestershire bowler, shouldering the heaviest workload and returning the most wickets, 59. David Millns, signed from Nottinghamshire during the close season, and Gordon Parsons made a late impact, the former demonstrating that he possessed genuine pace during a purple patch which placed him third in the national averages with 31 wickets at 21.35 runs apiece. Alan Mullally, a lanky left-arm seam bowler raised in Perth, Western Australia, but English by birth, had an impressive début season, bowling rather better than a first-class average of 38.05 might suggest. Spin was notable only for the modest contribution made by Peter Willey, Laurie Potter and Martyn Gidley.

The season ended with the county in transition, some would say facing a crisis. Two former England bowlers, Agnew and Les Taylor, retired, Agnew to begin a full-time career in journalism. George Ferris, anticipating that he would be surplus to requirements in 1991, decided to take a contract with a Lancashire League club, only for Winston Benjamin, his fellow-Antiguan, to announce that he was giving up county cricket after a summer disrupted by knee trouble. It left Simpson, returning home to Sydney, and Leicestershire to contemplate a winter of major rebuilding. – Jon Culley.

LEICESTERSHIRE 1990

[*Bill Smith*

Back row: J. P. Agnew, G. J. Parsons, J. D. R. Benson, L. Potter, D. J. Millns, C. C. Lewis, P. A. Nixon, P. N. Hepworth. *Front row:* T. J. Boon, R. B. Simpson (*cricket manager*), N. E. Briers (*captain*), J. J. Whitaker, P. Willey. *Insets:* W. K. M. Benjamin, R. A. Cobb, G. J. F. Ferris, L. B. Taylor, P. Whitticase.

LEICESTERSHIRE RESULTS

All first-class matches – Played 24: Won 6, Lost 7, Drawn 11.

County Championship matches – Played 22: Won 6, Lost 7, Drawn 9.

Bonus points – Batting 61, Bowling 53.

Competition placings – Britannic Assurance County Championship, 7th; NatWest Bank Trophy, 1st round; Benson and Hedges Cup, 3rd in Group D; Refuge Assurance League, 15th equal.

BRITANNIC ASSURANCE CHAMPIONSHIP AVERAGES

BATTING

	Birthplace	*M*	*I*	*NO*	*R*	*HI*	*Avge*
‡N. E. Briers	*Leicester*	22	43	3	1,846	176	46.15
‡J. J. Whitaker	*Skipton*	22	42	4	1,575	116	41.44
‡C. C. Lewis	*Georgetown, Guyana*	13	21	5	632	189*	39.50
‡T. J. Boon	*Doncaster*	22	43	4	1,522	138	39.02
‡W. K. M. Benjamin	*St John's, Antigua*	11	13	2	382	101*	34.72
‡L. Potter	*Bexleyheath*	22	36	5	1,028	109*	33.16
P. N. Hepworth	*Ackworth*	4	8	2	185	55*	30.83
J. D. R. Benson	*Dublin, Ireland*	16	24	6	525	86	29.16
‡P. Willey	*Sedgefield*	20	37	6	892	112	28.77
M. I. Gidley	*Leicester*	4	5	1	113	73	28.25
P. A. Nixon	*Carlisle*	17	20	6	379	46	27.07
‡G. J. F. Ferris	*Urlings Village, Antigua*	5	6	0	104	35	17.33
‡J. P. Agnew	*Macclesfield*	22	26	5	257	46*	12.23
‡G. J. Parsons	*Slough*	8	12	2	101	20	10.10
A. D. Mullally	*Southend-on-Sea*	18	18	6	113	29	9.41
‡P. Whitticase	*Solihull*	5	7	2	39	11*	7.80
D. J. Millns	*Clipstone*	8	10	5	23	10*	4.60

Also batted: C. J. Hawkes (*Loughborough*) (1 match) 3, 2*; B. F. Smith (*Corby*) (1 match) 15*. ‡L. B. Taylor (*Earl Shilton*) (1 match) did not bat.

* *Signifies not out.* ‡ *Denotes county cap.*

The following played a total of thirteen three-figure innings for Leicestershire in County Championship matches – N. E. Briers 4, J. J. Whitaker 3, T. J. Boon 2, W. K. M. Benjamin 1, C. C. Lewis 1, L. Potter 1, P. Willey 1.

BOWLING

	O	*M*	*R*	*W*	*BB*	*5W/i*	*Avge*
D. J. Millns	164.1	20	568	25	6-63	1	22.72
G. J. Parsons	247.5	56	821	31	6-75	2	26.48
C. C. Lewis	411.2	80	1,238	44	6-55	2	28.13
W. K. M. Benjamin	260.3	60	769	27	5-73	2	28.48
A. D. Mullally	464.2	116	1,351	37	4-59	0	36.51
J. P. Agnew	612	108	2,196	59	5-54	5	37.22
P. Willey	377.4	101	1,016	20	2-7	0	50.80

Also bowled: J. D. R. Benson 35.5–1–145–1; T. J. Boon 3.5–0–25–0; G. J. F. Ferris 101.2–16–404–9; M. I. Gidley 61–15–228–0; C. J. Hawkes 14–3–40–0; L. Potter 169–39–583–6; L. B. Taylor 9–1–34–0.

Wicket-keepers: P. A. Nixon 44 ct, 1 st; P. Whitticase 13 ct.

Leading Fielder: L. Potter 22.

At Cardiff, April 26, 27, 28, 30. LEICESTERSHIRE beat GLAMORGAN by nine wickets.

At Chelmsford, May 3, 4, 5, 7. LEICESTERSHIRE drew with ESSEX.

LEICESTERSHIRE v NOTTINGHAMSHIRE

At Leicester, May 15, 16, 17. Nottinghamshire won by five wickets. Nottinghamshire 22 pts, Leicestershire 7 pts. Toss: Leicestershire. The match began well for the Leicestershire captain, Briers, who carried his bat for 157, having batted for 6 hours 47 minutes (324 balls) and hit eighteen fours. It was a mark he had bettered only once in his career. In the meantime, Whitticase, Leicestershire's wicket-keeper, had suffered a badly broken finger batting against the quickish medium pace of Pick, whose analysis of seven for 128 was a career best. Boon took over behind the stumps when the visitors batted, which partially accounted for the 71 extras conceded. Nottinghamshire, reduced by Agnew and Lewis to 43 for six in reply, eventually totalled 361, 318 runs having been added in 59 overs in an astonishing recovery led by Randall (197 balls, two sixes, eleven fours) and Hemmings (90 balls, one six, eleven fours). The two put on 163 in 27 overs for the eighth wicket. Leicestershire collapsed in the second innings, losing their last eight wickets for 58 runs, and Nottinghamshire claimed the extra half-hour to win with a day to spare.

Close of play: First day, Leicestershire 301-7 (N. E. Briers 139*); Second day, Leicestershire 33-0 (L. Potter 13*, N. E. Briers 19*).

Leicestershire

First innings		Second innings	
T. J. Boon c Randall b Pick	1	(3) c Randall b Stephenson	27
*N. E. Briers not out	157	b Pick	22
J. J. Whitaker lbw b Pick	43	(4) lbw b Pick	13
P. Willey c Robinson b Hemmings	30	(5) c Randall b Hemmings	1
L. Potter b Pick	24	(1) c French b Stephenson	50
C. C. Lewis lbw b Pick	1	c Hemmings b Pick	2
†P. Whitticase retired hurt	2	absent injured	
M. I. Gidley st French b Afford	8	(7) not out	21
J. P. Agnew c Afford b Pick	36	b Stephenson	4
G. J. F. Ferris lbw b Pick	35	(8) b Hemmings	0
A. D. Mullally c French b Pick	0	(10) b Stephenson	0
B 2, l-b 6, w 3, n-b 11	22	B 4, l-b 5, w 2, n-b 7	18
1/3 2/67 3/107 4/171 5/173 6/185 7/301 8/357 9/359	359	1/55 2/100 3/119 4/120 5/126 6/133 7/134 8/158 9/158	158

Bonus points – Leicestershire 3, Nottinghamshire 2 (Score at 100 overs: 269-6).

In the first innings P. Whitticase retired hurt at 176.

Bowling: *First Innings*—Stephenson 27–4–98–0; Pick 34.5–5–128–7; Saxelby 10–2–39–0; Hemmings 22–6–58–1; Afford 29–17–28–1. *Second Innings*—Stephenson 20.5–4–33–4; Pick 17–2–56–3; Afford 13–5–27–0; Saxelby 6–0–30–0; Hemmings 12–9–3–2.

Nottinghamshire

First innings		Second innings	
B. C. Broad c Boon b Agnew	3	lbw b Willey	23
D. J. R. Martindale c sub b Lewis	9	c Whitaker b Mullally	43
*R. T. Robinson lbw b Agnew	0	lbw b Mullally	8
P. Johnson c sub b Lewis	4	lbw b Mullally	11
D. W. Randall c Whitaker b Ferris	120	c Mullally b Willey	11
M. Saxelby b Agnew	11	not out	18
F. D. Stephenson c Boon b Agnew	0	not out	13
†B. N. French b Mullally	37		
E. E. Hemmings c Whitaker b Agnew	83		
R. A. Pick b Ferris	22		
J. A. Afford not out	1		
B 33, l-b 26, w 2, n-b 10	71	B 21, l-b 7, n-b 2	30
1/11 2/11 3/21 4/22 5/39 6/43 7/99 8/262 9/358	361	1/49 2/66 3/98 4/101 5/139	(5 wkts) 157

Bonus points – Nottinghamshire 4, Leicestershire 4.

Bowling: *First Innings*—Lewis 22–1–92–2; Agnew 22–4–85–5; Mullally 14–2–65–1; Ferris 11–1–37–2; Gidley 5–1–23–0; Willey 1–1–0–0. *Second Innings*—Lewis 10–2–34–0; Ferris 5–0–19–0; Willey 18–4–40–2; Mullally 17.2–5–27–3; Gidley 6–3–9–0.

Umpires: B. J. Meyer and N. T. Plews.

At Manchester, May 19, 21, 22. LEICESTERSHIRE drew with LANCASHIRE.

At Oxford, May 23, 24, 25. LEICESTERSHIRE drew with OXFORD UNIVERSITY.

LEICESTERSHIRE v SOMERSET

At Leicester, May 26, 28, 29. Drawn. Leicestershire 6 pts, Somerset 5 pts. Toss: Leicestershire. Forceful batting on a pitch of easy pace enabled Leicestershire to dominate the opening day, Boon making 128 in five and a half hours, his first century of the season. Whitaker, with whom he shared a second-wicket stand of 161 in 53 overs, failed by 11 runs to record a third consecutive first-class hundred. Leicestershire declared overnight and conditions appeared as good as could be for Cook, Somerset's prolific opening batsman, to attempt the unlikely task of scoring 230 to total 1,000 first-class runs before the end of May. The chance effectively disappeared when he was caught behind off Mullally for 42, but Somerset comfortably collected full batting points before declaring 52 runs behind. They then picked off both Leicestershire openers in the fifteen overs to the close and enjoyed the best of the final morning, having the home side 66 for five. In doing so, however, they committed themselves to bowling Leicestershire out, which, although Rose bowled well, they could not quite manage. Leicestershire's declaration left Somerset to score 253 in 36 overs, little more than a gesture on a pitch becoming erratic, and they declined the challenge as soon as Cook was caught off the glove in the first over.

Close of play: First day, Leicestershire 352-4 (L. Potter 41*, J. D. R. Benson 29*); Second day, Leicestershire 32-2 (J. J. Whitaker 8*, P. Willey 9*).

Leicestershire

	First innings		Second innings	
T. J. Boon c Harden b Swallow	128	–	lbw b Mallender	10
*N. E. Briers lbw b Hayhurst	39	–	c Harden b Jones	5
J. J. Whitaker c Burns b Lefebvre	89	–	lbw b Mallender	18
P. Willey c Rose b Lefebvre	15	–	lbw b Rose	29
L. Potter not out	41	–	c Harden b Rose	2
J. D. R. Benson not out	29	–	c Tavaré b Rose	13
†P. A. Nixon (did not bat)		–	c Cook b Rose	33
J. P. Agnew (did not bat)		–	b Rose	36
G. J. F. Ferris (did not bat)		–	lbw b Swallow	33
A. D. Mullally (did not bat)		–	not out	12
D. J. Millns (did not bat)		–	not out	1
B 4, l-b 3, w 2, n-b 2	11		B 5, l-b 2, n-b 1	8
1/97 2/258 3/272 4/284 (4 wkts dec.)	352		1/11 2/15 3/61 4/65 5/66 6/103 7/122 8/167 9/193 (9 wkts dec.)	200

Bonus points – Leicestershire 4, Somerset 1 (Score at 100 overs: 301-4).

Bowling: *First Innings*—Jones 9–3–34–0; Mallender 19–2–51–0; Rose 17–0–85–0; Lefebvre 24–3–61–2; Hayhurst 14–2–35–1; Swallow 17–2–47–1; Roebuck 10–3–32–0. *Second Innings*—Jones 12–6–26–1; Mallender 21–8–62–2; Swallow 10–3–16–1; Roebuck 4–3–1–0; Rose 20–6–52–5; Lefebvre 10–5–26–0; Hayhurst 4–1–10–0.

Somerset

S. J. Cook c Nixon b Mullally	42	– c Benson b Agnew	8
P. M. Roebuck c Potter b Willey	63	– not out	23
A. N. Hayhurst c Whitaker b Mullally	34	– not out	22
*C. J. Tavaré c Willey b Millns	88		
R. J. Harden c Nixon b Millns	44		
†N. D. Burns not out	2		
G. D. Rose not out	3		
B 2, l-b 6, w 1, n-b 15	24	B 1, l-b 3, w 2, n-b 3	9
1/64 2/121 3/170 4/293 5/296 (5 wkts dec.)	300	1/9 (1 wkt)	62

R. P. Lefebvre, I. G. Swallow, N. A. Mallender and A. N. Jones did not bat.

Bonus points – Somerset 4, Leicestershire 2.

Bowling: *First Innings*—Agnew 24–6–84–0; Ferris 15–4–55–0; Mullally 23–6–57–2; Millns 15.1–1–57–2; Willey 11–5–23–1; Potter 3–1–16–0. *Second Innings*—Agnew 7–3–18–1; Ferris 4–1–15–0; Mullally 4–1–9–0; Willey 4–1–4–0; Potter 7–3–5–0; Benson 4.5–1–7–0.

Umpires: D. J. Constant and B. Dudleston.

LEICESTERSHIRE v HAMPSHIRE

At Leicester, June 2, 4, 5. Drawn. Leicestershire 4 pts, Hampshire 8 pts. Toss: Hampshire. Rain washed out the whole of the last day, to the relief of the home side, who were facing defeat. Gower, the former Leicestershire captain, returned to Grace Road at a time when he needed to reassert his credentials as a current international player, rather than a former one. After a breezy start, though, he was dismissed playing loosely outside off stump, and Hampshire slid to 144 for five. They were rescued superbly by Marshall's second Championship hundred (eighteen fours) in successive matches. Chris Smith came back after retiring with a hand injury, and with him Maru raced to 59 in a seventh-wicket stand which produced 75 runs in 24 overs. Bakker reduced Leicestershire to 7 for two by the close, from which they never properly recovered. By lunch on the second day they were 123 for eight, three of the wickets having fallen to Tremlett, restored to the Hampshire side after postponing his retirement. Lewis shrugged off doubts over his fitness for the First Test against New Zealand by sharing a spirited last-wicket stand of 54 with Mullally, but this failed to save the follow-on. Although Whitaker played well for 62 when Leicestershire batted again, their fortunes did not substantially improve. Had the weather not intervened, they would have begun the final day effectively 18 for five.

Close of play: First day, Leicestershire 7-2 (T. J. Boon 6*, J. J. Whitaker 0*); Second day, Leicestershire 189-5 (J. D. R. Benson 29*, C. C. Lewis 40*).

Hampshire

V. P. Terry c Nixon b Ferris	7
C. L. Smith not out	80
D. I. Gower c Whitaker b Lewis	25
R. A. Smith c Potter b Mullally	1
M. D. Marshall b Mullally	112
*M. C. J. Nicholas b Mullally	13
†R. J. Parks c Willey b Agnew	2
R. J. Maru c Boon b Agnew	59
T. M. Tremlett not out	25
L-b 8, w 1, n-b 16	25
1/21 2/69 3/73 4/119 5/144 6/220 7/295 (7 wkts dec.)	349

C. A. Connor and P. J. Bakker did not bat.

Bonus points – Hampshire 4, Leicestershire 3.

C. L. Smith, when 37, retired hurt at 69-1 and resumed at 220.

Bowling: Agnew 32–2–115–2; Ferris 16–4–77–1; Lewis 14–2–56–1; Mullally 20–4–68–3; Willey 12–3–25–0.

Leicestershire

T. J. Boon c Connor b Marshall	6	– lbw b Bakker	1
*N. E. Briers c sub b Bakker	0	– c Terry b Connor	29
†P. A. Nixon b Bakker	0		
J. J. Whitaker b Bakker	6	– (3) b Marshall	62
P. Willey c Connor b Marshall	42	– (4) c Terry b Marshall	23
L. Potter b Tremlett	43	– (5) b Marshall	0
J. D. R. Benson lbw b Tremlett	11	– (6) not out	29
C. C. Lewis not out	36	– (7) not out	40
J. P. Agnew c Parks b Tremlett	0		
G. J. F. Ferris c Marshall b Bakker	1		
A. D. Mullally b Connor	29		
L-b 4	4	L-b 3, n-b 2	5
1/2 2/2 3/8 4/26 5/87 6/111 7/111 8/123 9/124	178	1/2 2/81 3/111 4/111 5/130	(5 wkts) 189

Bonus points – Leicestershire 1, Hampshire 4.

Bowling: *First Innings*—Marshall 13–2–44–2; Bakker 15–4–51–4; Connor 10.5–2–46–1; Tremlett 15–4–33–3. *Second Innings*—Bakker 10–2–46–1; Marshall 15–4–44–3; Connor 17–4–54–1; Maru 7–1–26–0; Tremlett 9–4–16–0.

Umpires: J. H. Hampshire and P. B. Wight.

At Northampton, June 6, 7, 8. LEICESTERSHIRE drew with NORTHAMPTONSHIRE.

At Leicester, June 14. LEICESTERSHIRE beat NEW ZEALANDERS by four wickets (See New Zealand tour section).

LEICESTERSHIRE v MIDDLESEX

At Leicester, June 16, 18, 19. Middlesex won by 103 runs. Middlesex 19 pts, Leicestershire 4 pts. Toss: Middlesex. Having gained momentum from a fine innings by Haynes, Middlesex collapsed from 129 for two to 174 for seven, which would have been 174 for eight had Benson caught Tufnell first ball at short leg. They were rescued by Ramprakash, who batted almost five hours for 87 and shared a valuable partnership of 79 for the eighth wicket with the fortunate Tufnell. Leicestershire's first innings, which began on the first day, could not resume until four o'clock on the second because of rain, which cost 69 overs. This necessitated some careful manoeuvring by the captains. Leicestershire declared 204 behind and then Middlesex, encouraged to a certain extent by friendly bowling, but with Haynes again in majestic form, declared at close of play, leaving Leicestershire to chase 321 from 102 overs on the last day. Boon and Briers gave the home side a useful start, but after an interruption for rain Fraser and Williams made the necessary breakthrough. Emburey and Tufnell then took advantage of a dry, wearing pitch to dismiss Leicestershire with seventeen overs to spare.

Close of play: First day, Leicestershire 38-1 (N. E. Briers 16*, J. J. Whitaker 8*); Second day, Middlesex 116-1 dec.

Middlesex

D. L. Haynes b Benjamin	85	– not out	68
M. A. Roseberry c Lewis b Benjamin	15	– b Lewis	0
*M. W. Gatting lbw b Lewis	4	– not out	41
M. R. Ramprakash not out	87		
K. R. Brown lbw b Benjamin	0		
J. E. Emburey c Nixon b Mullally	16		
†P. Farbrace c Potter b Agnew	5		
N. F. Williams c and b Lewis	1		
P. C. R. Tufnell b Lewis	37		
S. P. Hughes c Benson b Benjamin	4		
A. R. C. Fraser c Potter b Benjamin	12		
B 4, l-b 10, n-b 15	29	L-b 1, n-b 6	7
1/38 2/60 3/129 4/129 5/148 6/173 7/174 8/253 9/264	295	1/2 (1 wkt dec.)	116

Bonus points – Middlesex 3, Leicestershire 4.

Bowling: *First Innings*—Benjamin 24.1–10–73–5; Agnew 15–2–60–1; Mullally 19–6–34–1; Lewis 21–3–98–3; Willey 8–0–14–0; Potter 1–0–2–0. *Second Innings*—Lewis 6–0–11–1; Agnew 11–1–62–0; Potter 5.2–0–42–0.

Leicestershire

T. J. Boon c Farbrace b Hughes	10	– c Brown b Fraser	51
*N. E. Briers c Farbrace b Fraser	23	– c Farbrace b Tufnell	34
J. J. Whitaker not out	42	– lbw b Fraser	0
P. Willey not out	5	– lbw b Williams	11
L. Potter (did not bat)		– c Brown b Emburey	7
J. D. R. Benson (did not bat)		– b Williams	45
C. C. Lewis (did not bat)		– b Tufnell	21
W. K. M. Benjamin (did not bat)		– c Roseberry b Emburey	1
†P. A. Nixon (did not bat)		– c Gatting b Emburey	22
J. P. Agnew (did not bat)		– c Roseberry b Emburey	0
A. D. Mullally (did not bat)		– not out	0
L-b 1, n-b 10	11	L-b 4, n-b 21	25
1/25 2/65 (2 wkts dec.)	91	1/82 2/82 3/113 4/113 5/126 6/159 7/162 8/210 9/212	217

Bowling: *First Innings*—Williams 12–1–34–0; Fraser 13–1–34–1; Emburey 2–1–2–0; Hughes 3–1–5–1; Tufnell 6–2–15–0. *Second Innings*—Fraser 20–2–45–2; Williams 12.4–2–49–2; Hughes 7–1–23–0; Emburey 26–7–57–4; Tufnell 16–5–39–2.

Umpires: B. Hassan and K. E. Palmer.

LEICESTERSHIRE v DERBYSHIRE

At Leicester, June 20, 21, 22. Leicestershire won by 140 runs. Leicestershire 20 pts, Derbyshire 2 pts. Toss: Leicestershire. A century of increasing confidence from Whitaker, his third of the season, provided the mainstay of Leicestershire's batting on a first day restricted by rain to 86 overs. Only 34 overs were possible on the second day, with no play after lunch. However, enterprising batting, first from Benjamin, who raced from 46 overnight to a 141-ball maiden first-class century in sixteen overs, then from Barnett and Bowler, the Derbyshire openers, sustained the possibility of a positive finish on the last day. Benjamin hit three sixes and eleven fours in his unbeaten 101. More rain caused the first session on the third day to be lost, but declarations by both captains left Derbyshire with a target of 271 from 63 overs. This became meaningless when Derbyshire lost both openers without scoring and stumbled to 43 for six in seventeen overs. Only Morris and, to a lesser extent, Krikken defied a fashion for rash or feeble shots as Derbyshire were dismissed for a miserable 130 runs.

Close of play: First day, Leicestershire 244-5 (J. J. Whitaker 115*, W. K. M. Benjamin 46*); Second day, Derbyshire 70-0 (K. J. Barnett 31*, P. D. Bowler 36*).

Leicestershire

T. J. Boon b Warner	8	– not out 5
*N. E. Briers c Krikken b Jean-Jacques	29	– not out 14
J. J. Whitaker b Warner	116	
P. Willey c Miller b Goldsmith	4	
L. Potter lbw b Miller	16	
J. D. R. Benson c Adams b Miller	9	
W. K. M. Benjamin not out	101	
†P. A. Nixon not out	20	
B 3, l-b 5, n-b 9	17	N-b 1 1
1/22 2/67 3/73 4/148 5/163 6/249	(6 wkts dec.) 320	(no wkt dec.) 20

J. P. Agnew, A. D. Mullally and L. B. Taylor did not bat.

Bonus points – Leicestershire 4, Derbyshire 2 (Score at 100 overs: 315-6).

Bowling: *First Innings*—Warner 28.5–8–72–2; Jean-Jacques 21–3–93–1; Goldsmith 13–5–24–1; Barnett 8–0–25–0; Miller 32–10–98–2. *Second Innings*—Bowler 2–0–8–0; Adams 1.2–0–12–0.

Derbyshire

*K. J. Barnett not out	31	– c Potter b Benjamin 0
P. D. Bowler not out	36	– c Potter b Agnew 0
J. E. Morris (did not bat)		– not out 63
B. Roberts (did not bat)		– c Nixon b Agnew 1
A. P. Kuiper (did not bat)		– c and b Agnew 3
C. J. Adams (did not bat)		– c Nixon b Mullally 5
S. C. Goldsmith (did not bat)		– lbw b Mullally 8
†K. M. Krikken (did not bat)		– b Willey 30
G. Miller (did not bat)		– c Nixon b Benjamin 1
M. Jean-Jacques (did not bat)		– lbw b Benjamin 4
A. E. Warner (did not bat)		– c Whitaker b Willey 2
N-b 3	3	B 2, l-b 9, n-b 2 13
	(no wkt dec.) 70	1/0 2/0 3/2 4/12 5/29 6/43 7/110 8/113 9/117 130

Bowling: *First Innings*—Benjamin 4–0–17–0; Agnew 4–0–25–0; Taylor 4–0–18–0; Mullally 4–2–10–0; Willey 2–2–0–0. *Second Innings*—Benjamin 16–5–35–3; Agnew 9–2–33–3; Mullally 12–3–28–2; Willey 8–4–7–2; Taylor 5–1–16–0.

Umpires: B. Hassan and K. E. Palmer.

At Gloucester, June 23, 25, 26. LEICESTERSHIRE beat GLOUCESTERSHIRE by 111 runs.

At Nottingham, June 30, July 2, 3. LEICESTERSHIRE drew with NOTTINGHAMSHIRE.

LEICESTERSHIRE v GLAMORGAN

At Hinckley, July 7, 8, 9. Drawn. Leicestershire 6 pts, Glamorgan 6 pts. Toss: Glamorgan. Butcher and Morris put on 112 inside 39 overs for the first wicket, their sixth partnership of 100 or more in the Championship in 1990, and Butcher completed his third century of the summer, made off 171 balls, during a 91-run stand with Maynard for the third wicket. With his dismissal, however, the Glamorgan innings tailed off. Nixon, the nineteen-year-old Leicestershire reserve wicket-keeper, held five catches and made one stumping, which equalled the county record for dismissals in an innings, held jointly by P. Corrall and R. W.

Tolchard. The second day's pattern almost repeated that of the first, with Leicestershire's opening pair sharing a century partnership before lunch. Briers and Whitaker added 81 for the second wicket, but both fell short of their centuries and the innings began to lose its way. On the final morning, their bowlers unable to make much headway, Leicestershire resorted to feeding cheap runs to encourage a declaration. The chief beneficiary was Cottey, who struck a maiden Championship century off 166 balls. When Leicestershire set out to score 289 from a minimum of 58 overs, Boon completed his 1,000 runs for the season, as Whitaker had the previous day, and looked in commanding form, but with 137 needed from 21 overs, rain thwarted Leicestershire's bid.

Close of play: First day, Glamorgan 312-9 (R. D. B. Croft 25*, M. Frost 0*); Second day, Glamorgan 33-1 (A. R. Butcher 13*, P. A. Cottey 18*).

Glamorgan

*A. R. Butcher c Nixon b Benjamin	115	– c Mullally b Willey 30
H. Morris c Potter b Agnew	53	– c Nixon b Benjamin 0
P. A. Cottey c Nixon b Agnew	3	– c Smith b Willey 125
M. P. Maynard c Nixon b Agnew	59	– c Potter b Benson 47
I. V. A. Richards c Nixon b Agnew	14	– not out 68
R. D. B. Croft not out	25	– not out 0
N. G. Cowley c Nixon b Agnew	13	
†C. P. Metson c Potter b Willey	2	
S. L. Watkin c and b Potter	2	
S. J. Dennis st Nixon b Potter	0	
M. Frost not out	0	
B 6, l-b 11, w 1, n-b 8	26	L-b 6, w 1 7
1/112 2/127 3/218 4/258 5/261 6/292 7/304 8/307 9/309	(9 wkts dec.) 312	1/3 2/71 3/150 4/272 (4 wkts dec.) 277

Bonus points – Glamorgan 4, Leicestershire 2 (Score at 100 overs: 303-6).

Bowling: *First Innings*—Benjamin 25–6–59–1; Agnew 29–4–89–5; Mullally 29–8–84–0; Willey 19–4–60–1; Benson 1–0–1–0; Potter 2–0–2–2. *Second Innings*—Benjamin 5–0–17–1; Agnew 3–0–8–0; Mullally 10–2–26–0; Willey 16–3–69–2; Benson 17–0–83–1; Potter 7–0–48–0; Boon 3–0–20–0.

Leicestershire

T. J. Boon c Cowley b Watkin	51	– not out 75
*N. E. Briers c Richards b Frost	80	– b Croft 22
J. J. Whitaker c Cowley b Watkin	94	– c Cottey b Cowley 45
P. Willey c and b Frost	4	– not out 0
L. Potter c Butcher b Croft	13	
J. D. R. Benson not out	35	
B. F. Smith not out	15	
B 1, l-b 7, n-b 1	9	L-b 7, n-b 3 10
1/105 2/186 3/196 4/228 5/271	(5 wkts dec.) 301	1/60 2/152 (2 wkts) 152

W. K. M. Benjamin, †P. A. Nixon, J. P. Agnew and A. D. Mullally did not bat.

Bonus points – Leicestershire 4, Glamorgan 2.

Bowling: *First Innings*—Frost 16–5–56–2; Watkin 22.5–6–53–2; Dennis 19–4–79–0; Richards 4–1–13–0; Cowley 18–3–46–0; Croft 13–3–46–1. *Second Innings*—Watkin 10–1–34–0; Dennis 8–1–28–0; Croft 10–2–33–1; Frost 6–0–31–0; Cowley 4.4–0–19–1.

Umpires: J. H. Hampshire and K. J. Lyons.

At Leicester, July 21, 22, 23. LEICESTERSHIRE drew with INDIANS (See Indian tour section).

LEICESTERSHIRE v ESSEX

At Leicester, July 25, 26, 27. Drawn. Leicestershire 7 pts, Essex 5 pts. Toss: Essex. Captained by Pringle in Gooch's absence, Essex chose to bat first in search of a fourth consecutive Championship victory but were dismissed for 197, their lowest total of the season. It might have been lower had Leicestershire not dropped four catches, although the Essex cause was not helped by an injury to Stephenson, who was struck on the helmet by Benjamin and had to play his innings in two parts. With Briers providing stability and Potter and Benjamin lending good support, the home side established a useful first-innings lead of 104. Despite dropping Stephenson at 23 and 66, Leicestershire had Essex in trouble at 176 for six on the final morning. However, bold batting by Pringle, hitting 84 off 80 balls, rescued his side, he and Stephenson (332 minutes) adding 132 in 28 overs before he declared with a lead of 245. Leicestershire began with 59 overs in which to reach their target, but four stoppages for rain reduced this crucially by thirteen overs, more to the disadvantage of Essex, who had taken the first five Leicestershire wickets for 96.

Close of play: First day, Leicestershire 124-3 (N. E. Briers 52*, L. Potter 31*); Second day, Essex 154-4 (J. P. Stephenson 62*, N. Hussain 0*).

Essex

J. P. Stephenson c Nixon b Agnew	7	– not out	131
N. Shahid b Agnew	2	– hit wkt b Agnew	48
P. J. Prichard lbw b Benjamin	2	– c Potter b Agnew	0
M. E. Waugh c Boon b Benjamin	69	– c Willey b Mullally	31
N. Hussain c Nixon b Agnew	9	– (6) c Nixon b Agnew	0
†M. A. Garnham c Benjamin b Parsons	8	– (7) b Mullally	7
*D. R. Pringle c Willey b Benjamin	20	– (8) c Nixon b Mullally	84
N. A. Foster lbw b Benjamin	23	– (9) not out	32
T. D. Topley b Agnew	23	– (5) c Nixon b Mullally	2
J. H. Childs run out	13		
S. J. W. Andrew not out	3		
B 6, l-b 8, w 2, n-b 2	18	B 7, l-b 3, w 1, n-b 3	14
1/10 2/13 3/38 4/58 5/127 6/136 7/159 8/191 9/197	197	1/74 2/76 3/150 4/154 5/159 6/176 7/308 (7 wkts dec.)	349

Bonus points – Essex 1, Leicestershire 4.

In the first innings J. P. Stephenson, when 7, retired hurt at 10-1 and resumed at 197.

Bowling: *First Innings*—Benjamin 21–5–51–4; Agnew 21.3–3–73–4; Mullally 17–6–37–0; Parsons 7–2–22–1. *Second Innings*—Agnew 24–4–106–3; Benjamin 11–1–48–0; Mullally 32–11–131–4; Parsons 18–6–54–0; Willey 2–2–0–0.

Leicestershire

T. J. Boon c Pringle b Andrew	13	– c Waugh b Andrew	20
*N. E. Briers run out	92	– lbw b Foster	1
J. J. Whitaker c Topley b Foster	8	– c Hussain b Foster	34
P. Willey c Shahid b Pringle	7	– c Stephenson b Foster	1
L. Potter c Shahid b Andrew	48	– c Stephenson b Andrew	23
J. D. R. Benson b Pringle	12	– not out	34
W. K. M. Benjamin c Foster b Topley	54	– not out	9
†P. A. Nixon c Garnham b Topley	11		
G. J. Parsons not out	19		
J. P. Agnew c Hussain b Topley	5		
A. D. Mullally b Pringle	0		
B 1, l-b 17, n-b 14	32	B 8, l-b 2, n-b 9	19
1/33 2/51 3/71 4/150 5/178 6/228 7/272 8/277 9/294	301	1/11 2/40 3/48 4/79 5/96 (5 wkts)	141

Bonus points – Leicestershire 3, Essex 4 (Score at 100 overs: 294-9).

Bowling: *First Innings*—Foster 22–3–70–1; Andrew 24–4–62–2; Topley 22–3–69–3; Pringle 20.2–3–51–3; Childs 14–3–31–0. *Second Innings*—Foster 21–9–47–3; Pringle 8–3–19–0; Andrew 9–1–39–2; Topley 3–0–22–0; Waugh 1–0–4–0.

Umpires: D. J. Constant and B. J. Meyer.

At Sheffield, July 28, 30, 31. LEICESTERSHIRE beat YORKSHIRE by eight wickets.

LEICESTERSHIRE v WORCESTERSHIRE

At Leicester, August 4, 6, 7. Worcestershire won by 1 run. Worcestershire 23 pts, Leicestershire 4 pts. Toss: Worcestershire. In sweltering heat, Hick completed his 51st first-class century, which left Derbyshire the only Championship county, apart from his own, against whom he had not made a three-figure score. Although he struck seventeen fours, the innings was not among Hick's most impressive, and he showed a fallibility when hooking which eventually cost him his wicket. Nevertheless, with Curtis overcoming early uncertainty to reach 151 not out, passing the milestone of 10,000 runs for Worcestershire in the process, the visitors declared handsomely placed at 365 for four. The second day was packed with incident. Lampitt, a promising seam bowler, was banished from the attack after warnings from umpire Holder for damaging the pitch with his follow-through stride; Illingworth bowled 41 consecutive overs of testing left-arm spin; and McEwan achieved the first hat-trick of his career to end the Leicestershire innings. Briers's fourth century of the summer, a personal best tally of hundreds, was Leicestershire's salvation. Curtis, captaining Worcestershire in the absence of the injured Neale, left the home side to score 265 in 56 overs, a target they looked sure to reach until, after needing 23 off 27 balls, they lost their last five wickets for 21 runs. Nixon was run out off the final delivery trying to level the scores.

Close of play: First day, Leicestershire 20-0 (T. J. Boon 7*, N. E. Briers 13*); Second day, Worcestershire 22-1 (G. J. Lord 9*, S. R. Lampitt 2*).

Worcestershire

T. S. Curtis not out	151	lbw b Lewis	6
G. J. Lord lbw b Agnew	19	b Mullally	35
G. A. Hick c Boon b Agnew	102	(4) not out	88
D. B. D'Oliveira c Potter b Willey	5	(5) not out	44
I. T. Botham run out	26		
*P. A. Neale not out	20		
S. R. Lampitt (did not bat)		(3) b Lewis	6
B 6, l-b 15, n-b 21	42	B 4, l-b 6, w 1, n-b 10	21
1/33 2/226 3/235 4/288 (4 wkts dec.)	365	1/7 2/30 3/105 (3 wkts dec.)	200

†S. J. Rhodes, R. K. Illingworth, P. J. Newport and S. M. McEwan did not bat.

Bonus points – Worcestershire 4, Leicestershire 1.

Bowling: *First Innings*—Benjamin 9–1–31–0; Agnew 18–2–73–2; Lewis 22–2–76–0; Mullally 19.4–6–56–0; Willey 28–5–96–1; Potter 3–0–12–0. *Second Innings*—Lewis 13–2–31–2; Mullally 16–3–78–1; Willey 16–2–59–0; Potter 7–3–22–0.

Leicestershire

T. J. Boon c D'Oliveira b Lampitt	42	st Rhodes b Illingworth	40
*N. E. Briers c D'Oliveira b Lampitt	111	c and b Newport	17
J. J. Whitaker c Hick b Illingworth	16	c sub b Newport	62
P. Willey c Curtis b Illingworth	7	b Lampitt	79
L. Potter c Newport b Illingworth	20	c Rhodes b McEwan	27
C. C. Lewis c Neale b Illingworth	27	c sub b Lampitt	16
J. D. R. Benson not out	28	st Rhodes b Illingworth	2
W. K. M. Benjamin c D'Oliveira b Newport	10	b Illingworth	6
†P. A. Nixon c Hick b McEwan	5	run out	3
J. P. Agnew b McEwan	0	run out	1
A. D. Mullally lbw b McEwan	0	not out	3
B 10, l-b 17, w 4, n-b 4	35	L-b 4, n-b 3	7
1/104 2/162 3/180 4/198 5/248 6/256 7/282 8/301 9/301	301	1/35 2/120 3/125 4/178 5/242 6/248 7/250 8/258 9/260	263

Bonus points – Leicestershire 3, Worcestershire 3 (Score at 100 overs: 291-7).

Bowling: *First Innings*—Newport 26.1–2–84–1; McEwan 20–4–62–3; Illingworth 42–16–85–4; Lampitt 17.5–4–43–2. *Second Innings*—Newport 15–4–56–2; McEwan 13–5–37–1; Lampitt 11–0–68–2; Illingworth 21–5–98–3.

Umpires: J. W. Holder and R. Palmer.

At Dartford, August 8, 9, 10. LEICESTERSHIRE lost to KENT by seven wickets.

At The Oval, August 11, 13, 14. LEICESTERSHIRE lost to SURREY by an innings and 5 runs.

At Birmingham, August 18, 20, 21. LEICESTERSHIRE beat WARWICKSHIRE by six wickets.

LEICESTERSHIRE v KENT

At Leicester, August 23, 24, 25, 27. Leicestershire won by two wickets. Leicestershire 22 pts, Kent 3 pts. Toss: Kent. Parsons and Millns, thrust into Leicestershire's front-line attack with Mullally injured and Lewis on Test duty, combined with Benjamin to dismiss Kent for 169 in only 52.3 overs. Boon and Briers set up Leicestershire's reply by compiling their seventh opening stand of 100 or more. They were parted at 133 by Wells, Kent's reserve wicket-keeper, whose sharpish medium pace in a depleted attack prompted alarms for Leicestershire when he took three wickets in eighteen balls without conceding a run. He ended with five for 43, a career best. Still, Leicestershire led by 135 on first innings and looked to be in a position to win comfortably when they had Kent 136 for three. This reckoned without a splendid effort by Graham Cowdrey, who struck a century in less than three hours and shared with Hinks a partnership of 258 in 68 overs for the fourth wicket. Hinks went on to reach 163 in 442 minutes with 24 fours, making Leicestershire deeply regret dropping him twice at 14. The declaration left Leicestershire to score a formidable 347 in 87 overs, but they succeeded with three balls to spare. Briers and Whitaker (nineteen fours) provided early impetus with a partnership of 164, and Benjamin hammered a breathtaking 53 off 21 balls, with five sixes and three fours.

Close of play: First day, Leicestershire 64-0 (T. J. Boon 18*, N. E. Briers 38*); Second day, Kent 51-1 (S. G. Hinks 14*, R. P. Davis 1*); Third day, Kent 419-5 (M. V. Fleming 14*, M. M. Patel 0*).

Kent

S. G. Hinks c Nixon b Benjamin	6	– b Millns	163
T. R. Ward c Parsons b Agnew	14	– b Benjamin	29
V. J. Wells c Nixon b Parsons	40	– (4) c Boon b Parsons	28
G. R. Cowdrey b Millns	16	– (5) b Millns	135
M. V. Fleming b Millns	0	– (6) c Briers b Millns	14
*C. S. Cowdrey c Willey b Parsons	15	– (8) c Whitaker b Parsons	2
†S. A. Marsh c Nixon b Parsons	5	– (9) not out	31
R. P. Davis c Hepworth b Benjamin	36	– (3) c Nixon b Agnew	4
P. S. de Villiers c Nixon b Millns	21	– (10) not out	20
M. M. Patel not out	3	– (7) c Nixon b Parsons	5
A. P. Igglesden b Benjamin	0		
L-b 1, w 1, n-b 11	13	B 11, l-b 12, w 9, n-b 18	50
1/15 2/26 3/61 4/62 5/98 6/104 7/109 8/156 9/169	169	1/48 2/65 3/136 4/394 5/418 6/420 7/423 8/440 (8 wkts dec.)	481

Bonus points – Kent 1, Leicestershire 4.

Bowling: *First Innings*—Benjamin 14.3–2–52–3; Agnew 15–4–39–1; Millns 11–1–37–3; Parsons 12–3–40–3. *Second Innings*—Benjamin 27–4–70–1; Agnew 23–5–69–1; Millns 30–7–88–3; Parsons 27–8–104–3; Willey 19–5–84–0; Potter 15–4–43–0.

Leicestershire

First innings		Second innings	
T. J. Boon c Marsh b Wells	66	– c Marsh b Fleming	20
*N. E. Briers b Wells	62	– c G. R. Cowdrey b Patel	75
J. J. Whitaker c Davis b Wells	0	– b Patel	100
P. Willey c Davis b de Villiers	14	– c Ward b Davis	25
L. Potter lbw b Wells	30	– c Wells b Patel	27
P. N. Hepworth lbw b Wells	43	– (8) c sub b Davis	7
W. K. M. Benjamin c de Villiers b Fleming	18	– c Fleming b Patel	53
†P. A. Nixon c Marsh b Igglesden	21	– (9) not out	11
G. J. Parsons c Hinks b Igglesden	20	– (6) c sub b Patel	2
J. P. Agnew b Fleming	6	– not out	3
D. J. Millns not out	0		
B 4, l-b 15, w 1, n-b 4	24	B 13, l-b 11	24
1/133 2/139 3/144 4/177 5/190 6/229 7/272 8/287 9/294	304	1/30 2/194 3/210 4/250 5/258 6/291 7/328 8/338	(8 wkts) 347

Bonus points – Leicestershire 2, Kent 2 (Score at 100 overs: 242-6).

Bowling: *First Innings*—de Villiers 24–9–57–1; Igglesden 30–7–84–2; Davis 19–7–47–0; Fleming 18–5–25–2; Patel 10–3–29–0; Wells 18–7–43–5. *Second Innings*—Igglesden 2–0–11–0; de Villiers 7–0–31–0; Fleming 14–4–36–1; Davis 27.3–4–120–2; Patel 27–3–96–5; C. S. Cowdrey 1–1–0–0; Wells 8–1–29–0.

Umpires: B. Dudleston and D. O. Oslear.

LEICESTERSHIRE v SUSSEX

At Leicester, August 29, 30, 31. Sussex won by 29 runs. Sussex 23 pts, Leicestershire 4 pts. Toss: Leicestershire. Sussex took advantage of Leicestershire's decision to field first by achieving full batting bonus points on a placid pitch. Alan Wells, captain of Sussex for the first time, dominated the innings with a carefully constructed 109 not out. A marathon spell of Salisbury's leg-spin was a feature of the second day, but Willey's first Championship century for two years, combined with the doughty support of Potter, enabled Leicestershire to recover from 34 for three and declare just 62 runs in arrears. The final day was a triumph for Wells's tactical leadership. The cavalier approach to batting he prescribed brought Sussex 210 runs from 62 overs, to which he contributed 43 and Speight 53 off 53 balls. Then, as Leicestershire chased 273 in 57 overs to secure a third consecutive win, Wells boldly employed Salisbury as his chief weapon of attack. The policy paid handsome dividends. The home side came to the final twenty overs needing 122 with eight wickets in hand, but Salisbury then took the wickets of Briers, Willey and Potter in three overs, added that of Whitticase and, critically, had Lewis stumped for the second time in the match after the England all-rounder had raced to 54 off 42 balls (one six, nine fours). Salisbury finished with an impressive five for 79 in a Sussex triumph achieved with seventeen balls remaining.

Close of play: First day, Leicestershire 24-2 (J. J. Whitaker 12*, P. Willey 6*); Second day, Sussex 58-1 (J. W. Hall 9*, I. D. K. Salisbury 6*).

Sussex

First innings		Second innings	
N. J. Lenham lbw b Parsons	58	– c Whitticase b Parsons	40
J. W. Hall lbw b Willey	34	– c Whitticase b Lewis	17
K. Greenfield c sub b Millns	38	– (4) b Willey	20
*A. P. Wells not out	109	– (5) c Parsons b Millns	43
M. P. Speight c Potter b Millns	45	– (7) lbw b Millns	53
A. I. C. Dodemaide not out	17	– lbw b Lewis	0
I. D. K. Salisbury (did not bat)		– (3) c Potter b Parsons	6
J. A. North (did not bat)		– c Willey b Millns	0
†P. Moores (did not bat)		– c Lewis b Millns	18
A. C. S. Pigott (did not bat)		– not out	6
R. A. Bunting (did not bat)		– c Lewis b Parsons	0
L-b 6, w 1, n-b 6	13	L-b 6, n-b 1	7
1/90 2/98 3/186 4/277	(4 wkts dec.) 314	1/49 2/59 3/82 4/96 5/96 6/166 7/166 8/192 9/205	210

Bonus points – Sussex 4, Leicestershire 1.

Bowling: *First Innings*—Agnew 9–2–35–0; Lewis 23–9–62–0; Millns 16–1–67–2; Parsons 17–5–53–1; Willey 27–10–61–1; Potter 8–1–30–0. *Second Innings*—Lewis 14–1–36–2; Millns 11–3–48–4; Parsons 20–2–90–3; Willey 17–9–30–1.

Leicestershire

T. J. Boon lbw b Pigott	6	– run out	14
*N. E. Briers c Dodemaide b Pigott	0	– c Moores b Salisbury	78
J. J. Whitaker c Bunting b Pigott	16	– b Dodemaide	42
P. Willey c Wells b North	112	– c Lenham b Salisbury	35
L. Potter b Pigott	51	– c Greenfield b Salisbury	4
C. C. Lewis st Moores b Salisbury	20	– st Moores b Salisbury	54
P. N. Hepworth c Moores b Pigott	17	– run out	0
†P. Whitticase not out	11	– c Wells b Salisbury	4
G. J. Parsons not out	1	– b Pigott	1
J. P. Agnew (did not bat)		– not out	2
D. J. Millns (did not bat)		– b Pigott	1
B 9, l-b 5, w 2, n-b 2	18	L-b 6, n-b 2	8
1/1 2/6 3/34 4/135 5/174 6/234 7/247 (7 wkts dec.)	252	1/34 2/114 3/156 4/160 5/183 6/187 7/212 8/224 9/240	243

Bonus points – Leicestershire 3, Sussex 3.

Bowling: *First Innings*—Pigott 17–5–52–5; Dodemaide 20–4–30–0; Bunting 15–7–21–0; North 14–0–48–1; Salisbury 33.4–9–87–1. *Second Innings*—Pigott 10.1–2–41–2; Dodemaide 18–1–64–1; Bunting 5–0–27–0; Salisbury 17–1–79–5; North 4–0–26–0.

Umpires: M. J. Kitchen and A. G. T. Whitehead.

LEICESTERSHIRE v NORTHAMPTONSHIRE

At Leicester, September 12, 13, 14, 15. Northamptonshire won by 171 runs. Northamptonshire 22 pts, Leicestershire 7 pts. Toss: Northamptonshire. Steep bounce at one end enabled Millns, bowling with genuine pace, to return career-best figures, but with Ambrose and Cook making 84 for the ninth wicket, Northamptonshire still accumulated a useful total. The tall Ambrose then employed the awkward end to his advantage, taking the first five Leicestershire wickets. Only a brave and wholly admirable innings from their captain, Briers, who batted for five hours for his 176, kept Leicestershire in the game. Briers shared a stand of 101 for the sixth wicket with the promising Hepworth, but Ambrose came back to return his best figures for Northamptonshire. Having conceded a lead of 31, Northamptonshire lost Fordham and Larkins for 2 runs, and when Agnew, on his farewell appearance at Grace Road, removed Bailey and Felton, they looked in trouble at 66 for four. But as Leicestershire failed to press home their advantage, Lamb, Williams and Ripley plundered runs against an attack deprived of Millns, who had an injured knee. Lamb's declaration gave Leicestershire 75 overs to score 337, a task which always looked too steep once both openers had fallen for 3 runs. Whitaker made a forceful 92 off 99 balls, but when Ambrose had him caught behind, Leicestershire subsided rapidly, losing six wickets for 15 runs. Ambrose returned match figures of twelve for 155.

Close of play: First day, Northamptonshire 342-8 (C. E. L. Ambrose 49*, N. G. B. Cook 25*); Second day, Leicestershire 341-7 (P. Whitticase 9*); Third day, Northamptonshire 300-8 (D. Ripley 58*, N. G. B. Cook 4*).

Northamptonshire

A. Fordham c Whitticase b Millns	85	– c Potter b Millns	0
N. A. Felton c Potter b Lewis	5	– b Agnew	13
W. Larkins b Millns	27	– c Millns b Lewis	0
R. J. Bailey lbw b Parsons	77	– lbw b Agnew	33
*A. J. Lamb c Whitticase b Millns	0	– b Willey	67
A. L. Penberthy c Whitticase b Millns	52	– c Lewis b Parsons	10
R. G. Williams b Millns	1	– b Lewis	89
†D. Ripley c Agnew b Lewis	6	– not out	109
C. E. L. Ambrose not out	55	– c Whitticase b Lewis	0
N. G. B. Cook b Millns	28	– b Agnew	13
M. A. Robinson lbw b Lewis	0	– not out	1
L-b 6, w 1, n-b 8	15	B 11, l-b 9, w 1, n-b 11	32
1/26 2/102 3/128 4/128 5/218 6/230 7/263 8/266 9/350	351	1/0 2/2 3/50 4/66 5/103 6/172 7/288 8/295 9/363 (9 wkts dec.)	367

Bonus points – Northamptonshire 4, Leicestershire 3 (Score at 100 overs: 337-8).

Bowling: *First Innings*—Agnew 26–5–96–0; Lewis 33.3–8–83–3; Parsons 19–2–91–1; Millns 22–3–63–6; Willey 6–0–12–0. *Second Innings*—Millns 11–0–31–1; Lewis 30–6–84–3; Agnew 26–4–69–3; Parsons 20–1–88–1; Willey 20–4–56–1; Potter 4–1–19–0.

Leicestershire

T. J. Boon c Larkins b Ambrose	13	– c Ripley b Robinson	0
*N. E. Briers c and b Bailey	176	– c Fordham b Ambrose	0
J. J. Whitaker c Robinson b Ambrose	28	– c Ripley b Ambrose	92
P. Willey c Bailey b Ambrose	0	– c Larkins b Cook	30
L. Potter b Ambrose	45	– not out	31
C. C. Lewis b Ambrose	1	– c Cook b Ambrose	0
P. N. Hepworth c Penberthy b Williams	49	– lbw b Ambrose	0
†P. Whitticase b Ambrose	11	– b Ambrose	0
G. J. Parsons c Bailey b Ambrose	8	– run out	0
J. P. Agnew c Cook b Penberthy	24	– c Fordham b Williams	6
D. J. Millns not out	1	– absent injured	
B 8, l-b 15, w 1, n-b 2	26	B 6	6
1/36 2/115 3/120 4/213 5/215 6/316 7/341 8/351 9/380	382	1/1 2/3 3/98 4/150 5/150 6/158 7/158 8/158 9/165	165

Bonus points – Leicestershire 4, Northamptonshire 2 (Score at 100 overs: 328-6).

Bowling: *First Innings*—Ambrose 28–5–89–7; Robinson 23–3–117–0; Penberthy 15.5–3–57–1; Cook 37–18–56–0; Williams 6–1–27–1; Bailey 8–2–13–1. *Second Innings*—Ambrose 15–4–66–5; Robinson 8–2–23–1; Penberthy 7–0–26–0; Cook 8–2–37–1; Williams 5–4–7–1.

Umpires: J. D. Bond and B. Leadbeater.

At Derby, September 18, 19, 20, 21. LEICESTERSHIRE drew with DERBYSHIRE.

MIDDLESEX

Patron: HRH The Duke of Edinburgh
President: F. G. Mann
Chairman: M. P. Murray
Chairman, Cricket Committee: R. A. Gale
Secretary: J. Hardstaff
Lord's Cricket Ground, St John's Wood, London NW8 8QN (Telephone: 071-289 1300)
Captain: M. W. Gatting
Coach: D. Bennett

Two unconnected decisions taken in 1989 were decisive factors in Middlesex winning the 1990 Britannic Assurance Championship. Firstly, Mike Gatting and John Emburey committed themselves to a tour of South Africa, which carried a five-year suspension from Test cricket and meant that they would be available for their county throughout the season. Gatting especially had been such a focal-point of Middlesex's success in the 1980s that they automatically became favourites for the title, outweighing the claims of recent winners. When it was pointed out to him that supporters would look forward to a Championship or two during their suspension, Gatting asked, "Why not five?"

His self-belief was reinforced by the second decision. This was taken by the TCCB, who, having finally begun to penalise counties for poor pitches, also legislated for a reduced seam on the ball. The policy on pitches and the ball ensured that only attacking bowlers would earn regular reward, and proved advantageous to Middlesex, whose attack was not made up of trundling medium-pacers. Their bowlers knew that even if they were destined for hard work, some bowlers in other counties were due for even harder toil. Moreover, as the hot summer kept pitches hard and guaranteed long spells for spinners, Middlesex benefited from their policy over two decades of invariably choosing two spinners. Where once Edmonds and Titmus, and then Edmonds and Emburey had held sway, now another left- and right-arm alliance, Tufnell and Emburey emerged as a match-winner. "They bowled nearly 2,000 overs between them and took plenty of wickets", said a grateful Gatting. "They were comforting alternatives, because the pace-bowling strength was sometimes worryingly near breaking-point with Test calls and injuries."

Even before the season began, the potential of the new-ball attack was jeopardised when it was discovered, in the West Indies, that Ricardo Ellcock needed a back operation. Happily, Neil Williams, who had endured back problems himself, remained active all season, and his sharp pace and out-swing won him an unexpected England call. This brought to seven the number of Test players in the team – in 1981 there were eleven – and Philip Tufnell was given the opportunity to achieve that status when he was chosen to tour Australia. Angus Fraser recovering from a side injury and then wanted by England, Norman Cowans and Simon Hughes all made a limited impact until they began taking wickets in the last four fixtures.

Although the bowlers varied from match to match, the top five in the batting remained constant. In a particularly rare occurrence in the County Championship, Desmond Haynes, Mike Roseberry, Gatting

Mark Ramprakash and Keith Brown played in all 22 games. Roseberry could hardly fail to profit from opening with Haynes, and they launched the innings with such commanding strokeplay that the opposition was forced into premature defence. Brown was the near-perfect No. 5, capable of stabilising the innings when it became necessary, or consolidating a thriving start, as he demonstrated when making an unbeaten double-hundred against Nottinghamshire. Middlesex expected much of Haynes when he joined them in 1989, and he fulfilled their expectations in both Championship and limited-overs cricket.

Gatting had averaged 58 in all Championship games in the 1980s, and with the best batting conditions of his career he would surely have backed himself to surpass that mark last summer. His average, however, remained in the late 50s. He had ankle trouble at the start of the season, and never shook off a hamstring problem, but he enjoyed himself in the last eleven days of July, when he amassed 534 runs, including two big centuries, and in August he showed his team what bad-pitch technique is with a brave, unbeaten 119 against Derbyshire. While Gatting's injuries were an occupational hazard, Paul Downton had a career-threatening wound when a bail struck him in the eye during a Sunday League game at Basingstoke. He showed admirable dedication in returning successfully to his twin tasks as wicket-keeper and batsman.

Middlesex went top of the Championship following three consecutive wins in late June. By this time, undisciplined batting in their quarter-final at Taunton had ended their interest in the Benson and Hedges Cup; but the Championship match against Somerset at Uxbridge in July introduced a run of three centuries from Ramprakash. A Middlesex victory there depended on whether Ramprakash could score 12 runs from the final over, and his nerve and skill stood the test. He developed significantly in 1990 and at twenty established himself as Middlesex's No. 4.

A sequence of draws led up to the only defeat, at Derby, on a pitch which cost the hosts 25 points. Yorkshire were again beaten, and between then and their next Championship match Middlesex had a ten-day respite. Even though it allowed Essex to go to the top of the table, the break could not have come at a better time. In the week of the Derby setback, they had been eliminated from the NatWest Bank Trophy in a high-scoring semi-final at Old Trafford and had seen their Refuge Assurance League hopes badly damaged when the no result at Derby followed a surprise defeat by Sussex.

Refreshed, Middlesex found the run-in for the Championship unexpectedly easy. They won twice, Essex lost and then drew twice, and the winning margin was an emphatic 31 points. The title was made certain when Sussex were bowled out twice, the sixth time Middlesex had managed the feat in a batsman's summer.

They had tuned up for the last lap of the Championship by winning their Refuge Cup semi-final at Old Trafford, and when they returned to the top of the table, with one game left, they expressed their confident mood by winning the Refuge Cup final. Of the longer-standing competitions, Gatting has now won the Championship, Benson and Hedges Cup and NatWest Bank Trophy twice each in his eight years as captain, and has gone only two summers without a trophy. It is a record to compare with J. M. Brearley's four Championship and two Gillette Cup titles in his last seven years in charge. – Terry Cooper.

MIDDLESEX 1990

[*Bill Smith*

Back row: P. Farbrace, M. A. Roseberry, J. C. Pooley, P. N. Weekes, K. R. Brown, A. Habib. *Middle row:* H. P. H. Sharp (*scorer*), D. Bennett (*coach*), M. Keech, J. D. Carr, A. A. Barnett, J. R. Hemstock, I. J. F. Hutchinson, P. C. R. Tufnell, M. R. Ramprakash, J. Davis (*physiotherapist*), C. T. Radley (*assistant coach*), A. Jones (*2nd XI scorer*). *Front row:* S. P. Hughes, N. G. Cowans, P. R. Downton, J. E. Emburey, M. W. Gatting (*captain*), R. O. Butcher, N. F. Williams, D. L. Haynes. *Insets:* A. R. C. Fraser, R. M. Ellcock, T. A. Radford.

MIDDLESEX RESULTS

All first-class matches – Played 24: Won 10, Lost 1, Drawn 13.
County Championship matches – Played 22: Won 10, Lost 1, Drawn 11.
Bonus points – Batting 73, Bowling 55.
Competition placings – Britannic Assurance County Championship, winners; NatWest Bank Trophy, s-f; Benson and Hedges Cup, q-f; Refuge Assurance League, 3rd; Refuge Assurance Cup, winners.

BRITANNIC ASSURANCE CHAMPIONSHIP AVERAGES

BATTING

	Birthplace	*M*	*I*	*NO*	*R*	*HI*	*Avge*
‡D. L. Haynes	*Holders Hill, Barbados*	22	37	5	2,036	255*	63.62
‡M. W. Gatting	*Kingsbury*	22	36	7	1,685	170*	58.10
‡K. R. Brown	*Edmonton*	22	33	7	1,416	200*	54.46
‡M. R. Ramprakash	*Bushey*	22	38	8	1,327	146*	44.23
‡M. A. Roseberry	*Houghton-le-Spring*	22	40	3	1,497	135	40.45
‡J. E. Emburey	*Peckham*	22	31	7	698	111*	29.08
‡P. R. Downton	*Farnborough, Kent*	15	23	1	530	63	24.09
‡A. R. C. Fraser	*Billinge*	12	11	2	213	92	23.66
‡P. C. R. Tufnell	*Barnet*	20	20	9	235	37	21.36
‡N. F. Williams	*Hope Well, St Vincent*	19	22	3	390	55*	20.52
‡S. P. Hughes	*Kingston-upon-Thames*	15	17	5	109	23*	9.08
P. Farbrace	*Ash, Kent*	7	7	2	45	17*	9.00
‡N. G. Cowans	*Enfield St Mary, Jamaica*	16	16	6	81	31	8.10

Also batted: C. W. Taylor (*Banbury*) (2 matches) 13, 0*; N. R. Taylor (*Boscombe*) (1 match) 0; P. N. Weekes (*Hackney, London*) (2 matches) 51, 2. M. J. Thursfield (*South Shields*) (1 match) did not bat.

** Signifies not out. ‡ Denotes county cap.*

The following played a total of 23 three-figure innings for Middlesex in County Championship matches – D. L. Haynes 6, K. R. Brown 5, M. W. Gatting 4, M. R. Ramprakash 4, M. A. Roseberry 3, J. E. Emburey 1.

BOWLING

	O	*M*	*R*	*W*	*BB*	*5W/i*	*Avge*
A. R. C. Fraser	436.5	103	1,073	41	6-30	2	26.17
N. F. Williams	469.1	88	1,430	49	7-61	2	29.18
N. G. Cowans	415	115	1,127	36	5-67	1	31.30
J. E. Emburey	902	254	1,911	57	5-32	2	33.52
P. C. R. Tufnell	948.5	254	2,389	65	6-79	2	36.75
S. P. Hughes	333	60	1,121	28	5-101	1	40.03

Also bowled: K. R. Brown 6–2–49–0; P. R. Downton 1.1–0–4–1; M. W. Gatting 45–18–113–7; D. L. Haynes 35–7–113–2; M. R. Ramprakash 34–5–147–2; M. A. Roseberry 11–3–74–1; C. W. Taylor 47.5–7–139–6; N. R. Taylor 14–5–44–3; M. J. Thursfield 17–4–45–1; P. N. Weekes 54–8–183–3.

Wicket-keepers: P. R. Downton 40 ct, 2 st; P. Farbrace 15 ct, 2 st.

Leading Fielders: J. E. Emburey 31, K. R. Brown 27, M. A. Roseberry 21, M. W. Gatting 19.

MIDDLESEX v ESSEX

At Lord's, April 26, 27, 28, 30. Drawn. Middlesex 5 pts, Essex 6 pts. Toss: Essex. There were only 33 overs on the first day and, with two cautious counties, this militated against a win. Brown was the only Middlesex batsman to develop a first innings, staying for six hours, hitting twenty fours and a six, and being rewarded with his county cap when he returned to the dressing-room. Inevitably, Gooch was the more authoritative and faster of the first-innings century-makers. He batted two hours less than Brown and struck nineteen fours and a six. Essex declared 76 behind, whereupon Middlesex doubled their lead by the end of the third day. Although they began the fourth day without Gatting, who injured an ankle in the Sunday League game, Haynes swept them to a declaration with 116 off 185 balls, including 21 boundaries. Essex's target was 313 in a minimum of 55 overs, but only when Gooch was hitting six fours and a six in 41 balls did it look other than hopeless.

Close of play: First day, Middlesex 76-3 (M. W. Gatting 19*, K. R. Brown 8*); Second day, Essex 24-0 (G. A. Gooch 14*, J. P. Stephenson 8*); Third day, Middlesex 82-1 (D. L. Haynes 47*, M. W. Gatting 32*).

Middlesex

D. L. Haynes c Garnham b Foster	24	– c Foster b Shahid	116
M. A. Roseberry c Waugh b Andrew	12	– c Stephenson b Foster	1
*M. W. Gatting b Andrew	41	– retired hurt	32
M. R. Ramprakash c Topley b Pringle	12	– c Garnham b Foster	1
K. R. Brown lbw b Topley	141	– c Waugh b Andrew	12
†P. R. Downton lbw b Topley	47	– not out	42
J. E. Emburey b Andrew	41	– not out	21
N. F. Williams c Garnham b Waugh	26		
N. G. Cowans b Waugh	2		
S. P. Hughes not out	14		
P. C. R. Tufnell not out	7		
L-b 6, n-b 3	9	B 2, l-b 5, n-b 4	11
1/36 2/36 3/61 4/111 5/217 6/296 7/346 8/349 9/356 (9 wkts dec.)	376	1/11 2/88 3/126 4/210 (4 wkts dec.)	236

Bonus points – Middlesex 3, Essex 2 (Score at 100 overs: 277-5).

Bowling: *First Innings*—Foster 30–7–86–1; Pringle 30–10–79–1; Andrew 29–5–93–3; Topley 36–4–79–2; Shahid 1–0–12–0; Waugh 8–1–21–2. *Second Innings*—Foster 17–4–39–2; Pringle 5–3–12–0; Topley 10–2–42–0; Andrew 20–2–79–1; Waugh 3–1–17–0; Shahid 8–0–33–1; Gooch 1–1–0–0; Stephenson 2–0–7–0.

Essex

*G. A. Gooch c Downton b Williams	137	– c Downton b Williams	39
J. P. Stephenson c Downton b Hughes	14	– c Roseberry b Tufnell	59
P. J. Prichard c Downton b Williams	10	– not out	49
M. E. Waugh b Tufnell	34	– run out	0
B. R. Hardie c Emburey b Williams	21	– not out	0
N. Shahid not out	34		
†M. A. Garnham not out	36		
B 1, l-b 6, w 1, n-b 6	14	B 4, l-b 6, n-b 6	16
1/44 2/75 3/146 4/223 5/227 (5 wkts dec.)	300	1/67 2/141 3/141 (3 wkts)	163

D. R. Pringle, T. D. Topley, N. A. Foster and S. J. W. Andrew did not bat.

Bonus points – Essex 4, Middlesex 2.

Bowling: *First Innings*—Williams 18–4–69–3; Cowans 17–3–43–0; Hughes 16–3–60–1; Emburey 19–3–53–0; Tufnell 21.5–5–68–1. *Second Innings*—Cowans 5–1–32–0; Hughes 7–0–29–0; Williams 6–0–26–1; Emburey 16–7–23–0; Tufnell 13–4–35–1; Ramprakash 1–0–8–0.

Umpires: B. Hassan and A. G. T. Whitehead.

At Cambridge, May 3, 4, 5. MIDDLESEX drew with CAMBRIDGE UNIVERSITY.

MIDDLESEX v KENT

At Lord's, May 15, 16, 17. Middlesex won by eight wickets. Middlesex 23 pts, Kent 4 pts. Toss: Middlesex. Williams confirmed his return to match-winning form after back injuries by bowling at a fast-medium pace which at times became genuinely fast. His seven wickets included two bowled, two caught behind and one caught at slip – an illustration of his straightness – and provided his best figures for Middlesex. Middlesex batted as though a long lead were a formality, and several of their batsmen were out to loose strokes. However, the Middlesex bowlers did not allow Kent to escape, despite Taylor's defiance for more than five hours. Gatting enjoyed a purple patch by taking the last four Kent wickets in a seven-ball span and then winning the match with a day to spare with the disdainful, powerful strokeplay that has been his hallmark against county attacks.

Close of play: First day, Middlesex 71-0 (D. L. Haynes 32*, M. A. Roseberry 38*); Second day, Kent 118-3 (N. R. Taylor 55*, C. S. Cowdrey 19*).

Kent

S. G. Hinks b Williams	16	– c Haynes b Fraser	5
M. R. Benson b Cowans	0	– c Emburey b Williams	24
N. R. Taylor c Emburey b Williams	12	– c Emburey b Hughes	91
T. R. Ward b Williams	0	– lbw b Fraser	13
*C. S. Cowdrey c Haynes b Williams	47	– c Gatting b Fraser	44
M. V. Fleming c Downton b Cowans	69	– b Williams	12
†S. A. Marsh c Downton b Williams	15	– b Gatting	38
M. A. Ealham c Downton b Williams	0	– not out	13
C. Penn c Ramprakash b Williams	3	– b Gatting	0
T. A. Merrick c Emburey b Hughes	10	– c Ramprakash b Gatting	0
R. P. Davis not out	6	– lbw b Gatting	0
B 4, l-b 3, n-b 11	18	B 11, l-b 8, n-b 6	25
1/0 2/20 3/20 4/33 5/155 6/166 7/166 8/174 9/183	196	1/24 2/63 3/83 4/172 5/198 6/220 7/265 8/265 9/265	265

Bonus points – Kent 1, Middlesex 4.

Bowling: *First Innings*—Fraser 17–3–30–0; Cowans 16–6–41–2; Williams 22–4–61–7; Hughes 19.3–5–50–1; Emburey 3–2–7–0. *Second Innings*—Fraser 26–4–79–3; Cowans 11–4–39–0; Williams 20–0–67–2; Hughes 17–4–43–1; Emburey 14–6–16–0; Gatting 2–1–2–4.

Middlesex

D. L. Haynes st Marsh b Cowdrey	36	– lbw b Ealham	25
M. A. Roseberry c Ward b Merrick	50	– c Marsh b Ealham	37
*M. W. Gatting b Merrick	58	– not out	87
M. R. Ramprakash c Ward b Penn	9	– not out	36
K. R. Brown c Taylor b Davis	58		
†P. R. Downton c Marsh b Ealham	19		
N. F. Williams c Taylor b Penn	18		
J. E. Emburey c Marsh b Merrick	3		
S. P. Hughes c Davis b Penn	4		
A. R. C. Fraser lbw b Merrick	0		
N. G. Cowans not out	0		
B 1, l-b 6, n-b 10	17	B 4, l-b 3, n-b 1	8
1/86 2/96 3/145 4/202 5/247 6/247 7/267 8/272 9/272	272	1/60 2/79	(2 wkts) 193

Bonus points – Middlesex 3, Kent 3 (Score at 100 overs: 269-7).

Bowling: *First Innings*—Merrick 26–7–66–4; Penn 22–5–45–3; Fleming 21–7–49–0; Ealham 11–2–39–1; Davis 12–4–25–1; Cowdrey 12–2–41–1. *Second Innings*—Merrick 10–2–44–0; Penn 7–1–46–0; Ealham 11–1–33–2; Cowdrey 2–1–2–0; Fleming 7–1–23–0; Davis 7–2–23–0; Ward 4.3–1–15–0.

Umpires: J. H. Hampshire and M. J. Kitchen.

At Lord's, May 19, 20, 21. MIDDLESEX drew with NEW ZEALANDERS (See New Zealand tour section).

MIDDLESEX v SURREY

At Lord's, May 23, 24, 25. Drawn. Middlesex 7 pts, Surrey 6 pts. Toss: Middlesex. Roseberry underpinned the Middlesex first innings, making his best score, and hit two sixes and seventeen fours in a responsible balance between consolidation and attack. Surrey's batsmen struggled in reply against an attack that presented no unusual menace, and only two batting points were taken before Bicknell and Kendrick batted briskly for an hour. However, when Bicknell and Murphy dismissed both Middlesex openers without scoring before the close, and Bicknell claimed two more wickets early on the third morning, Middlesex were obliged to bat for most of the day to avoid defeat. Brown and Downton supplied the necessary defensive innings.

Close of play: First day, Surrey 17-0 (R. I. Alikhan 10*, P. D. Atkins 7*); Second day, Middlesex 8-2 (J. E. Emburey 8*, M. W. Gatting 0*).

Middlesex

D. L. Haynes c Lynch b Gray	33	– b Bicknell	0
M. A. Roseberry c Greig b Murphy	122	– c Ward b Murphy	0
*M. W. Gatting c Ward b Gray	20	– (4) c Medlycott b Bicknell	13
M. R. Ramprakash c Alikhan b Kendrick	30	– (5) b Medlycott	10
K. R. Brown c Murphy b Medlycott	16	– (6) c and b Medlycott	56
†P. R. Downton b Murphy	3	– (7) st Ward b Kendrick	55
N. F. Williams c Alikhan b Medlycott	40	– (8) c Kendrick b Medlycott	18
J. E. Emburey c Ward b Medlycott	10	– (3) b Bicknell	17
N. G. Cowans c Kendrick b Medlycott	6	– (10) c Bicknell b Kendrick	5
S. P. Hughes c Greig b Bicknell	0	– (9) not out	23
P. C. R. Tufnell not out	14	– b Medlycott	1
B 4, l-b 8, w 1, n-b 3	16	B 16, l-b 8, n-b 2	26
1/75 2/103 3/165 4/206 5/220 6/241 7/258 8/266 9/275	310	1/0 2/4 3/24 4/31 5/85 6/137 7/167 8/201 9/221	224

Bonus points – Middlesex 4, Surrey 4 (Score at 100 overs: 310-9).

Bowling: *First Innings*—Gray 22–3–68–2; Bicknell 25–7–72–1; Murphy 22–8–50–2; Greig 1–0–5–0; Medlycott 26.1–5–91–4; Kendrick 4–0–12–1. *Second Innings*—Bicknell 25–14–25–3; Murphy 25–7–75–1; Medlycott 32–14–65–4; Greig 3–0–8–0; Kendrick 14–4–25–2; Alikhan 1–0–2–0.

Surrey

R. I. Alikhan b Hughes	20	– not out	0
P. D. Atkins c Gatting b Hughes	23	– not out	0
G. P. Thorpe c Tufnell b Emburey	16		
†D. M. Ward c Downton b Hughes	46		
M. A. Lynch b Tufnell	46		
*I. A. Greig b Williams	44		
K. T. Medlycott c Downton b Williams	0		
M. P. Bicknell not out	26		
N. M. Kendrick not out	52		
L-b 11, n-b 2	13		
1/42 2/53 3/77 4/124 5/206 6/206 7/208	(7 wkts dec.) 286	(no wkt)	0

A. H. Gray and A. J. Murphy did not bat.

Bonus points – Surrey 2, Middlesex 3 (Score at 100 overs: 227-7).

Bowling: *First Innings*—Williams 22–5–57–2; Cowans 21–8–36–0; Tufnell 24–11–57–1; Emburey 24.1–8–58–1; Hughes 16–2–57–3; Gatting 2–0–6–0; Haynes 1–0–4–0. *Second Innings*—Haynes 3–3–0–0; Tufnell 2–2–0–0.

Umpires: K. J. Lyons and R. A. White.

MIDDLESEX v GLOUCESTERSHIRE

At Lord's, May 26, 28, 29. Middlesex won by 10 runs. Middlesex 21 pts, Gloucestershire 6 pts. Toss: Middlesex. Curran ended Middlesex's promising start with three wickets in nine overs, after which the innings maintained an uneven course. However, Ramprakash showed enterprise, and Emburey hit effectively to ensure full batting points. Williams, who forced Wright to retire after a blow on the elbow, had both Gloucestershire's chief scorers dropped early on, and, having survived, Hodgson and Butcher played watchfully against the Middlesex spinners. Butcher, batting for four hours, hit his county's first Championship hundred of the season, but the innings was so laboured that Gloucestershire had to scramble to record a third batting point. Middlesex lost wickets dangerously before Brown, Downton, Williams and Emburey saw them to a declaration which set 272 in 66 overs. When Gloucestershire were 232 for eight with just four overs remaining, Gatting ordered Brown to concede runs. Curran took 18 off the over and subsequently hit Tufnell for six to make the target 13 off ten balls. But Tufnell then had Graveney caught at slip, and when Lawrence sliced Emburey to cover, Curran was left stranded. Gatting had presented Gloucestershire with a slog or block dilemma, and his tactics brought a win with two balls to spare.

Close of play: First day, Gloucestershire 25-0 (A. J. Wright 15*, G. D. Hodgson 8*); Second day, Middlesex 44-2 (D. L. Haynes 31*, M. R. Ramprakash 0*).

Middlesex

D. L. Haynes c Wright b Curran	24	– c Bainbridge b Lloyds	49
M. A. Roseberry c Russell b Curran	50	– lbw b Lawrence	1
*M. W. Gatting c and b Curran	16	– lbw b Walsh	4
M. R. Ramprakash c Bainbridge b Graveney	64	– b Lloyds	0
K. R. Brown b Graveney	5	– c Russell b Athey	60
†P. R. Downton lbw b Curran	63	– c Russell b Athey	25
N. F. Williams b Lloyds	0	– not out	50
J. E. Emburey not out	38	– not out	30
S. P. Hughes not out	12		
B 1, l-b 14, n-b 14	29	L-b 9, n-b 2	11
1/61 2/94 3/97 4/124 5/210 6/211 7/261 (7 wkts dec.)	301	1/30 2/39 3/44 4/77 5/136 6/157 (6 wkts dec.)	230

N. G. Cowans and P. C. R. Tufnell did not bat.

Bonus points – Middlesex 4, Gloucestershire 3.

Bowling: *First Innings*—Walsh 17–6–59–0; Lawrence 16–4–46–0; Curran 22.4–7–64–4; Graveney 32–7–89–2; Bainbridge 5–2–9–0; Lloyds 5–0–19–1. *Second Innings*—Walsh 5–2–25–1; Lawrence 4–0–13–1; Lloyds 20.2–3–109–2; Graveney 27–6–61–0; Athey 7–2–13–2.

Gloucestershire

*A. J. Wright retired hurt	24	– b Cowans	8
G. D. Hodgson c Emburey b Tufnell	65	– b Hughes	25
I. P. Butcher c Roseberry b Emburey	102	– st Downton b Tufnell	31
C. W. J. Athey c Gatting b Tufnell	31	– c Ramprakash b Emburey	69
P. Bainbridge st Downton b Tufnell	2	– (6) c Roseberry b Emburey	22
K. M. Curran not out	9	– (7) not out	53
J. W. Lloyds not out	10	– (5) c Roseberry b Tufnell	19
C. A. Walsh (did not bat)		– b Emburey	16
†R. C. Russell (did not bat)		– c and b Tufnell	1
D. A. Graveney (did not bat)		– c Emburey b Tufnell	3
D. V. Lawrence (did not bat)		– c Hughes b Emburey	0
B 1, l-b 10, n-b 6	17	B 9, l-b 4, n-b 1	14
1/155 2/231 3/241 4/241 (4 wkts dec.)	260	1/27 2/33 3/87 4/127 5/169 6/194 7/229 8/232 9/260	261

Bonus points – Gloucestershire 3, Middlesex 1 (Score at 100 overs: 250-4).

In the first innings A. J. Wright retired hurt at 45.

Bowling: *First Innings*—Williams 17–5–32–0; Cowans 16–5–36–0; Emburey 32–10–63–1; Tufnell 27–6–68–3; Hughes 10–2–37–0; Gatting 4–1–13–0. *Second Innings*—Williams 5–2–10–0; Cowans 9–4–24–1; Hughes 6–3–16–1; Tufnell 22–0–111–4; Emburey 22.4–4–69–4; Brown 1–0–18–0.

Umpires: K. J. Lyons and R. A. White.

At Ilford, June 2, 4, 5. MIDDLESEX drew with ESSEX.

MIDDLESEX v WARWICKSHIRE

At Lord's, June 6, 7, 8. Drawn. Middlesex 2 pts, Warwickshire 8 pts. Toss: Middlesex. Warwickshire outplayed Middlesex all the way, building on a massive double-century start which involved Moles, Lloyd and Asif Din. Lloyd had batted fluently before aggravating a hamstring injury and retiring during lunch. Moles, 22 at that stage, accelerated in the next two sessions and at the close had faced 354 balls and hit two sixes and eleven fours in his 128 not out. Humpage cut loose towards the end with 73 from 57 balls, including two sixes and nine fours. In contrast, Middlesex failed to profit from an excellent opening which saw them 142 for one at lunch on the second day. Gatting batted on after being cracked on the back of the helmet by Donald, but he was dismissed in a collapse so sharp that it needed the last pair to get Middlesex past the follow-on. Benjamin's attacking bowling brought him his best Championship figures. With Moles maintaining his good form, Warwickshire eventually set Middlesex a target of 273 in 49 overs, but with Haynes out first ball, and Gatting prevented from batting until No. 7 because he had not fielded, this was never a prospect. By the time rain washed out the final hour, Warwickshire's bowlers again had Middlesex in disarray.

Close of play: First day, Warwickshire 372-4 (A. J. Moles 128*, P. A. Smith 0*); Second day, Middlesex 243.

Warwickshire

A. J. Moles not out	128	– not out	65
*T. A. Lloyd retired hurt	70		
Asif Din c Emburey b Tufnell	49	– (2) c Williams b Roseberry	44
A. I. Kallicharran c Emburey b Tufnell	10		
†G. W. Humpage c Gatting b Emburey	73		
D. A. Reeve b Hughes	12	– (3) not out	31
P. A. Smith not out	0		
B 11, l-b 16, w 1, n-b 2	30	B 1, l-b 1, n-b 1	3
1/206 2/222 3/351 4/371 (4 wkts dec.)	372	1/94 (1 wkt dec.)	143

N. M. K. Smith, A. A. Donald, J. E. Benjamin and T. A. Munton did not bat.

Bonus points – Warwickshire 4 (Score at 100 overs: 305-2).

In the first innings T. A. Lloyd retired hurt at 106.

Bowling: *First Innings*—Williams 22–2–77–0; Fraser 19–9–18–0; Hughes 16–5–48–1; Gatting 11–3–43–0; Tufnell 28–4–111–2; Emburey 14–3–48–1. *Second Innings*—Fraser 8–1–23–0; Williams 5–2–12–0; Hughes 4–1–20–0; Roseberry 6–0–58–1; Ramprakash 4–0–28–0.

Middlesex

D. L. Haynes c Humpage b Donald .... 67 – b Donald 0
M. A. Roseberry lbw b Benjamin .... 64 – retired hurt 19
*M. W. Gatting c sub b P. A. Smith 23
M. R. Ramprakash lbw b Benjamin .... 0 – (3) c Reeve b Munton 38
K. R. Brown c Reeve b Benjamin .... 15 – (4) not out 41
†P. R. Downton lbw b P. A. Smith .... 4 – (5) lbw b Munton 11
N. F. Williams c Humpage b Donald 17
J. E. Emburey c Benjamin b Donald .... 18 – (6) not out 5
S. P. Hughes c sub b Benjamin 2
P. C. R. Tufnell not out 11
A. R. C. Fraser b Benjamin 7
B 8, l-b 7 .... 15 B 4, l-b 4 8

1/130 2/142 3/142 4/178 5/178 6/191 7/204 8/219 9/221 — 243 1/0 2/90 3/116 (3 wkts) 122

Bonus points – Middlesex 2, Warwickshire 4.

In the second innings M. A. Roseberry retired hurt at 46.

Bowling: *First Innings*—Donald 25–5–60–3; Benjamin 22.5–5–71–5; Munton 18–7–36–0; P. A. Smith 11–3–46–2; N. M. K. Smith 5–1–15–0. *Second Innings*—Donald 7–3–26–1; Benjamin 7–0–30–0; Munton 8–1–21–2; Reeve 7.4–1–37–0.

Umpires: D. J. Constant and R. Julian.

At Leicester, June 16, 18, 19. MIDDLESEX beat LEICESTERSHIRE by 103 runs.

At Manchester, June 20, 21, 22. MIDDLESEX beat LANCASHIRE by five wickets.

At Luton, June 23, 25, 26. MIDDLESEX beat NORTHAMPTONSHIRE by 79 runs.

MIDDLESEX v WORCESTERSHIRE

At Lord's, June 30, July 2, 3. Drawn. Middlesex 8 pts, Worcestershire 4 pts. Toss: Middlesex. After McEwan had removed Haynes and Gatting when they were in full flow, Illingworth, in 32 consecutive overs, prevented the Middlesex batting from establishing control. Roseberry and Ramprakash both had prolonged passive patches, with Ramprakash remaining on 27 for 57 balls. The first day was shortened by the weather, forcing Middlesex to bat on into the second, but an impressive all-round bowling performance made up for lost time by making Worcestershire follow on. On the final day, the spinners worked tirelessly, but in a situation in which inactivity was a virtue for batsmen, their only reward came when Tufnell gained Hick's wicket. Although Botham went instantly to Fraser, D'Oliveira, who batted just over four and a half hours, and Neale saw that the match was saved.

Close of play: First day, Middlesex 276-7 (N. F. Williams 7*, P. C. R. Tufnell 2*); Second day, Worcestershire 2-1 (P. Bent 1*, S. M. McEwan 1*).

Middlesex

D. L. Haynes b McEwan 40
M. A. Roseberry c Botham b Illingworth 43
*M. W. Gatting c Rhodes b McEwan . 26
M. R. Ramprakash c D'Oliveira b Lampitt . 69
K. R. Brown c Rhodes b Illingworth .. 52
†P. Farbrace c Curtis b Illingworth 14
J. E. Emburey lbw b Lampitt 9
N. F. Williams not out 49
P. C. R. Tufnell b Lampitt 3
A. R. C. Fraser b Botham 27
N. G. Cowans c Hick b Botham 1
B 4, l-b 10, n-b 1 15

1/57 2/85 3/130 4/201 5/225 6/256 7/269 8/281 9/344 — 348

Bonus points – Middlesex 4, Worcestershire 3 (Score at 100 overs: 301-8).

Bowling: Botham 18.1–3–71–2; Lampitt 32–1–119–3; McEwan 14–1–51–2; Illingworth 37–12–65–3; Hick 8–1–28–0.

Worcestershire

First Innings		Second Innings	
T. S. Curtis c Emburey b Williams	30	lbw b Cowans	0
P. Bent b Cowans	7	b Fraser	13
G. A. Hick b Cowans	0	(4) c Roseberry b Tufnell	80
D. B. D'Oliveira st Farbrace b Emburey	13	(5) not out	87
I. T. Botham c Haynes b Williams	4	(6) c Emburey b Fraser	0
*P. A. Neale c Farbrace b Fraser	16	(7) not out	41
M. J. Weston c and b Emburey	2		
†S. J. Rhodes c Emburey b Cowans	26		
R. K. Illingworth lbw b Fraser	0		
S. R. Lampitt lbw b Williams	5		
S. M. McEwan not out	27	(3) b Fraser	7
B 3, l-b 25, n-b 12	40	B 1, l-b 7, n-b 9	17
	170	(5 wkts dec.)	245
1/21 2/21 3/48 4/68 5/70 6/77 7/95 8/95 9/122		1/0 2/11 3/30 4/153 5/154	

Bonus points – Worcestershire 1, Middlesex 4.

Bowling: *First Innings*—Fraser 22–7–40–2; Cowans 10–5–23–3; Williams 17–4–27–3; Emburey 19–9–27–2; Tufnell 14–7–25–0. *Second Innings*—Cowans 15–6–36–1; Fraser 23–6–53–3; Williams 11–3–28–0; Emburey 22–6–52–0; Tufnell 31–12–68–1.

Umpires: R. Palmer and D. R. Shepherd.

MIDDLESEX v YORKSHIRE

At Uxbridge, July 18, 19, 20. Middlesex won by seven wickets. Middlesex 24 pts, Yorkshire 5 pts. Toss: Yorkshire. Middlesex began their annual visit to Uxbridge in a business-like manner. Yorkshire's top batting failed on a pitch which had always rewarded determined effort by bowlers and they never caught up. Byas, clipping ten neat fours and one six, effected a partial repair with help from White and Carrick. When Middlesex batted, Gatting exploited the ground's accessible boundaries to hit 60 of his 86 in fours, and when he was out the stalwart Brown, initially in partnership with Emburey, ensured that Middlesex's lead would be a worthwhile one. Carrick efficiently worked his way through the tail, leaving Brown unbeaten with 109 from 175 balls, including fourteen fours. On the final day Williams removed Yorkshire's overnight pair in a hostile early burst, after which Emburey and Tufnell found there was just enough turn and bounce in the pitch for their contrasting spin attack. Brown continued to have an influence on the match by taking four catches at short leg, and he was at the crease when Middlesex won before the last hour.

Close of play: First day, Middlesex 48-1 (M. A. Roseberry 16*, M. W. Gatting 9*); Second day, Yorkshire 59-1 (M. D. Moxon 21*, R. J. Blakey 27*).

Yorkshire

First Innings		Second Innings	
*M. D. Moxon c Roseberry b Williams	12	c Gatting b Williams	23
C. A. Chapman c Farbrace b Emburey	20	lbw b Emburey	5
†R. J. Blakey c Farbrace b Williams	0	c Farbrace b Williams	42
P. E. Robinson c Emburey b Hughes	3	c Emburey b Williams	40
D. Byas c Gatting b Emburey	83	c Brown b Tufnell	17
C. White c Haynes b Williams	12	c Brown b Emburey	0
P. Carrick b Emburey	52	c and b Emburey	10
C. S. Pickles c Roseberry b Tufnell	17	c Brown b Tufnell	18
P. J. Hartley c Farbrace b Tufnell	11	not out	9
D. Gough b Emburey	11	c Brown b Tufnell	2
S. D. Fletcher not out	0	b Williams	0
B 6, l-b 5, n-b 11	22	B 10, l-b 8, w 1, n-b 7	26
	243		192
1/31 2/31 3/39 4/56 5/106 6/195 7/204 8/229 9/239		1/20 2/77 3/84 4/122 5/123 6/140 7/161 8/187 9/191	

Bonus points – Yorkshire 2, Middlesex 4.

Bowling: *First Innings*—Williams 19–5–55–3; Cowans 11–3–21–0; Emburey 27–10–51–4; Hughes 9–3–38–1; Tufnell 24–7–67–2. *Second Innings*—Williams 18.5–2–43–4; Cowans 3–1–7–0; Emburey 27–8–62–3; Tufnell 24–7–49–3; Haynes 1–0–4–0; Hughes 5–1–9–0.

Middlesex

D. L. Haynes c Robinson b Hartley	18 – c Hartley b Carrick	26
M. A. Roseberry c Blakey b Gough	36 – c Moxon b Hartley	9
*M. W. Gatting c Carrick b Fletcher	86 – b White	28
M. R. Ramprakash c Chapman b Hartley	9 – not out	15
K. R. Brown not out	109 – not out	12
J. E. Emburey st Blakey b Carrick	45	
N. F. Williams b Pickles	2	
†P. Farbrace c Chapman b Carrick	2	
P. C. R. Tufnell c White b Carrick	10	
S. P. Hughes st Blakey b Carrick	4	
N. G. Cowans c Pickles b Carrick	2	
L-b 7, n-b 10	17	L-b 2, n-b 4 — 6
1/30 2/104 3/125 4/180 5/266 6/281 7/290 8/318 9/338	340	1/13 2/60 3/76 (3 wkts) 96

Bonus points – Middlesex 4, Yorkshire 3 (Score at 100 overs: 319-8).

Bowling: *First Innings*—Hartley 20–3–76–2; Fletcher 17–7–29–1; Gough 13–5–40–1; Carrick 31–4–99–5; White 12–1–59–0; Pickles 10–3–30–1. *Second Innings*—Hartley 5–0–24–1; Fletcher 4–0–10–0; Carrick 10.3–2–22–1; White 9–0–38–1.

Umpires: J. D. Bond and B. Dudleston.

MIDDLESEX v SOMERSET

At Uxbridge, July 21, 23, 24. Middlesex won by four wickets. Middlesex 20 pts, Somerset 4 pts. Toss: Somerset. Despite their large opening stand, Somerset came nowhere near obtaining full batting points, but they did leave Middlesex without a single bowling point. Cook stroked eight of his first 65 balls for four, but then he and Roebuck and their successors submitted to the trio of spinners, Middlesex having given Weekes, an off-spinner, his Championship début. Cook was 305 balls over his 152, which contained 21 fours, and it needed Rose to galvanise Somerset. On the second morning he struck four fours and four sixes in his 38-ball 57, taking 26 off one over from Weekes. Gatting's belligerence was the focus as Middlesex hurried the match along by taking maximum batting points in the 68th over and immediately declaring. He opened his score with a six, hit three more, made 100 in fours and required only 188 balls for his unbeaten 170. Somerset's second declaration set Middlesex to score 369 in what proved to be 69 overs. Haynes made a crisp century, but the last twenty overs began with 149 wanted and wickets falling. In an attempt to collect more wickets, Tavaré fed Ramprakash with soft bowling. His gamble was seized upon. Ramprakash hit him for three sixes in an over, hit Trump for two more and, with 12 wanted from the last over, stroked three twos and then two fours for a Middlesex victory. His 146 not out had come from 133 balls and, in addition to the five sixes, contained twelve fours.

Close of play: First day, Somerset 340-4 (C. J. Tavaré 53*, N. D. Burns 6*); Second day, Somerset 63-1 (S. J. Cook 29*, R. J. Harden 20*).

Somerset

S. J. Cook c Farbrace b Tufnell	152 – lbw b Ramprakash	85
P. M. Roebuck b Tufnell	70 – b Fraser	9
A. N. Hayhurst c and b Weekes	15	
*C. J. Tavaré c Haynes b Weekes	57 – c Emburey b Tufnell	61
R. J. Harden c Brown b Tufnell	17 – (3) c Farbrace b Emburey	38
†N. D. Burns not out	37 – not out	4
G. D. Rose b Fraser	57 – (5) not out	10
I. G. Swallow not out	11	
L-b 22, n-b 7	29	B 10, l-b 2, n-b 9 — 21
1/189 2/234 3/274 4/302 5/349 6/426	(6 wkts dec.) 445	1/27 2/100 3/210 4/218 (4 wkts dec.) 228

H. R. J. Trump, A. N. Jones and N. A. Mallender did not bat.

Bonus points – Somerset 3 (Score at 100 overs: 273-2).

Bowling: *First Innings*—Fraser 23–3–66–1; Williams 10–0–45–0; Emburey 35–11–57–0; Tufnell 51–11–140–3; Weekes 28–2–115–2. *Second Innings*—Fraser 6–1–11–1; Williams 5–0–38–0; Emburey 20–4–52–1; Tufnell 24–4–96–1; Ramprakash 5–1–19–1.

Middlesex

D. L. Haynes c Cook b Swallow	41	– c Harden b Mallender	108
M. A. Roseberry c Burns b Mallender	25	– lbw b Rose	7
*M. W. Gatting not out	170	– b Mallender	36
M. R. Ramprakash c Tavaré b Mallender	2	– not out	146
K. R. Brown c and b Trump	46	– c Burns b Mallender	9
J. E. Emburey not out	1	– b Mallender	11
N. F. Williams (did not bat)		– b Jones	22
†P. Farbrace (did not bat)		– not out	4
B 6, l-b 4, n-b 10	20	B 10, l-b 14, n-b 4	28
1/67 2/117 3/142 4/296 (4 wkts dec.)	305	1/40 2/110 3/215 4/238 5/260 6/353 (6 wkts)	371

A. R. C. Fraser, P. N. Weekes and P. C. R. Tufnell did not bat.

Bonus points – Middlesex 4, Somerset 1.

Bowling: *First Innings*—Jones 10–1–47–0; Mallender 11–2–46–2; Trump 20.4–3–91–1; Swallow 19–2–100–1; Rose 7–3–11–0. *Second Innings*—Jones 14–2–69–1; Mallender 16.5–1–60–4; Rose 10–1–43–1; Swallow 12–0–66–0; Trump 15–1–89–0; Tavaré 1–0–20–0.

Umpires: J. D. Bond and B. Dudleston.

At Canterbury, July 25, 26, 27. MIDDLESEX drew with KENT.

At Nottingham, July 28, 30, 31. MIDDLESEX drew with NOTTINGHAMSHIRE.

MIDDLESEX v GLAMORGAN

At Lord's, August 4, 6, 7. Drawn. Middlesex 7 pts, Glamorgan 7 pts. Toss: Middlesex. Only three days after their bowlers had suffered at the hands of Haynes and Gatting in the NatWest Trophy quarter-finals, Glamorgan endured similar treatment. The pair added 171 in 37 overs, and later Brown assisted Haynes while 134 came in 35 overs. Helped by the proximity of the Tavern boundary, most of the batsmen in the match plundered runs. Haynes hit 24 fours in his 244-ball innings. Brown increased his pace dramatically after taking 95 balls over his first fifty; his next fifty came from 54 balls, and in his penultimate over he hit Frost for 20 to finish with three sixes and twelve fours in his 120. Glamorgan had their own century-maker in Morris (fourteen fours), and with Richards gracing one of his favourite settings, they took full batting points, declared and then forced Middlesex to struggle towards a declaration. Only when Butcher and Cottey were scoring 79 in 21 overs did Glamorgan hint that 251 in 53 overs was possible. Fraser captured wickets regularly as Glamorgan went into defensive mode, but Watkin and Frost fended off the last 34 balls to save the match.

Close of play: First day, Glamorgan 10-0 (A. R. Butcher 9*, H. Morris 1*); Second day, Glamorgan 360-9 (N. G. Cowley 52*, M. Frost 4*).

Middlesex

D. L. Haynes b Croft	173		
M. A. Roseberry c Metson b Bastien	0	(1) b Croft	62
*M. W. Gatting b Bastien	89	(2) b Watkin	21
M. R. Ramprakash lbw b Watkin	8	(3) c Metson b Frost	18
K. R. Brown c Metson b Croft	120	(4) c Morris b Frost	4
†P. R. Downton c Watkin b Croft	4	(5) c Maynard b Bastien	6
J. E. Emburey c Butcher b Frost	23	(6) c Metson b Watkin	7
N. F. Williams c Morris b Frost	17	(7) c Cowley b Bastien	1
A. R. C. Fraser not out	4	(8) c Metson b Frost	23
P. C. R. Tufnell (did not bat)	–	(9) not out	4
N. G. Cowans (did not bat)	–	(10) not out	12
L-b 7, n-b 2	9	L-b 4, n-b 1	5
1/0 2/171 3/196 4/330 5/344 6/413 7/431 8/447	(8 wkts dec.) 447	1/33 2/63 3/72 4/83 5/93 6/98 7/147 8/151	(8 wkts dec.) 163

Bonus points – Middlesex 4, Glamorgan 3 (Score at 100 overs: 434-7).

Bowling: *First Innings*—Watkin 24–2–85–1; Bastien 15.2–1–81–2; Frost 19.4–1–110–2; Croft 24–4–100–3; Cowley 9–1–29–0; Richards 6–0–22–0; Butcher 3.4–0–13–0. *Second Innings*—Watkin 15–4–47–2; Bastien 21–4–72–2; Frost 8–0–24–3; Croft 2–0–16–1.

Glamorgan

*A. R. Butcher c Brown b Williams	34	lbw b Fraser	54
H. Morris c Downton b Cowans	100	lbw b Williams	4
P. A. Cottey c Gatting b Williams	0	b Fraser	33
M. P. Maynard c Downton b Tufnell	27	c Cowans b Tufnell	20
I. V. A. Richards c Haynes b Emburey	80	b Fraser	9
R. D. B. Croft c Brown b Cowans	15	b Tufnell	13
N. G. Cowley not out	52	c Downton b Fraser	8
†C. P. Metson lbw b Williams	4	c Gatting b Fraser	0
S. L. Watkin c Gatting b Williams	9	not out	0
S. Bastien c and b Williams	11	lbw b Fraser	0
M. Frost not out	4	not out	0
B 9, l-b 11, w 1, n-b 3	24	L-b 2, n-b 3	5
1/71 2/71 3/117 4/255 5/266 6/280 7/294 8/324 9/346	(9 wkts dec.) 360	1/7 2/86 3/101 4/125 5/125 6/146 7/146 8/146 9/146	(9 wkts) 146

Bonus points – Glamorgan 4, Middlesex 3 (Score at 100 overs: 311-7).

Bowling: *First Innings*—Fraser 21–2–76–0; Williams 23–6–59–5; Emburey 32–10–88–1; Cowans 15–2–50–2; Tufnell 24–4–67–1. *Second Innings*—Fraser 14–7–30–6; Williams 7–2–30–1; Cowans 2–1–8–0; Emburey 16–7–28–0; Tufnell 14–5–48–2.

Umpires: D. J. Constant and K. J. Lyons.

At Bournemouth, August 8, 9, 10. MIDDLESEX drew with HAMPSHIRE.

MIDDLESEX v SUSSEX

At Lord's, August 11, 13, 14. Drawn. Middlesex 7 pts, Sussex 4 pts. Toss: Middlesex. For the second consecutive Saturday Haynes played the outstanding innings, recording his second double-century of the summer after scoring his first hundred before lunch, and he batted with easy command into the second day. He faced 353 balls for his unbeaten 255 and hit 30 fours and a six. However, the failure of the other main batsmen to produce a big innings forced Middlesex to take extra time to build their total. Sussex set their sights on saving the follow-on and they managed it in an innings that lurched erratically. Hall and Smith gave a promise of the later defiance when they battled for 40 overs, but at 129 for five, with the ball turning for their three spinners, Middlesex looked winners. Instead, Speight and Dodemaide ground out runs on the second day, and Moores and Pigott emulated them on the third with a partnership of 97 which saw the follow-on saved before lunch. Salisbury prolonged the Sussex innings, and Middlesex's hopes of bowling Sussex out twice were put in perspective when they failed to do so once.

Close of play: First day, Middlesex 385-6 (D. L. Haynes 222*, P. N. Weekes 34*); Second day, Sussex 217-7 (P. Moores 8*, A. C. S. Pigott 7*).

Middlesex

D. L. Haynes not out	255		
M. A. Roseberry b Donelan	22	– (1) lbw b Salisbury	37
*M. W. Gatting b Dodemaide	28		
M. R. Ramprakash c Dodemaide b Salisbury	28	– (2) c C. M. Wells b Donelan	5
K. R. Brown st Moores b Donelan	2		
†P. R. Downton c and b Salisbury	3		
J. E. Emburey c Moores b Salisbury	14		
P. N. Weekes b Pigott	51	– (3) lbw b Donelan	2
N. F. Williams lbw b Dodemaide	9	– (4) not out	55
P. C. R. Tufnell not out	3	– (5) not out	0
B 8, l-b 16, n-b 10	34	B 5, l-b 2, n-b 1	8
1/99 2/188 3/251 4/270 5/279 6/331 7/427 8/444 (8 wkts dec.)	449	1/17 2/27 3/103 (3 wkts)	107

N. G. Cowans did not bat.

Bonus points – Middlesex 4, Sussex 2 (Score at 100 overs: 341-6).

Bowling: *First Innings*—Pigott 23–2–105–1; Dodemaide 32–6–75–2; Donelan 37–5–116–2; Salisbury 31–3–115–3; C. M. Wells 2–0–14–0. *Second Innings*—C. M. Wells 2–0–2–0; Donelan 22–7–38–2; Salisbury 20–4–60–1.

Sussex

N. J. Lenham c Downton b Williams	5
J. W. Hall c Roseberry b Emburey	49
D. M. Smith c Downton b Weekes	42
A. P. Wells lbw b Emburey	9
M. P. Speight lbw b Cowans	52
*C. M. Wells c Brown b Tufnell	1
A. I. C. Dodemaide c Brown b Tufnell	26
†P. Moores c Brown b Haynes	49
A. C. S. Pigott c Gatting b Tufnell	58
I. D. K. Salisbury not out	40
B. T. P. Donelan not out	8
B 18, l-b 14, w 3, n-b 13	48
1/9 2/93 3/113 4/126 5/129 6/196 7/203 8/300 9/363 (9 wkts dec.)	387

Bonus points – Sussex 2, Middlesex 3 (Score at 100 overs: 209-7).

Bowling: Cowans 11–2–30–1; Williams 20–4–69–1; Tufnell 54–20–85–3; Emburey 51–17–85–2; Weekes 26–6–68–1; Haynes 7–1–18–1.

Umpires: B. J. Meyer and A. G. T. Whitehead.

At Derby, August 18, 20, 21. MIDDLESEX lost to DERBYSHIRE by 171 runs.

At Leeds, August 23, 24, 25, 27. MIDDLESEX beat YORKSHIRE by 64 runs.

MIDDLESEX v NOTTINGHAMSHIRE

At Lord's, September 7, 8, 9, 10. Middlesex won by ten wickets. Middlesex 24 pts, Nottinghamshire 3 pts. Toss: Middlesex. Having slipped to second place in the Championship since they last played, Middlesex were in some anxiety when their top three were prised out without making a significant score. Ramprakash and Brown eased all tension with their excellently judged stand of 188 in 58 overs. Ramprakash faced 253 balls and hit 21 fours in his

132. Brown's strokeplay and authority developed on the second morning, and he enabled Middlesex to declare on schedule, having batted for six hours for his maiden double-hundred (309 balls, 23 fours). Nottinghamshire produced two contrasting days of batting. There were occasional pockets of resistance in the first innings, but only when the last two wickets held out for 95 minutes on the third morning did Middlesex realise that a concerted defensive action had begun. Fraser dug out Broad, but for the rest of the day Newell and Robinson batted Middlesex to a standstill. On the last day, however, Fraser ran out Robinson and Cowans, having earlier broken Johnson's finger, finally bowled Newell after the opener had battled for six and a half hours (319 balls). The rest of the innings folded in time for Middlesex to hit off the winning runs after tea and return to the top of the Championship table.

Close of play: First day, Middlesex 358-4 (K. R. Brown 127*, P. R. Downton 12*); Second day, Nottinghamshire 179-8 (B. N. French 10*, R. A. Pick 16*); Third day, Nottinghamshire 185-1 (M. Newell 61*, R. T. Robinson 87*).

Middlesex

D. L. Haynes b Stephenson	29	– not out	44
M. A. Roseberry lbw b Pick	11	– not out	20
*M. W. Gatting c French b Stephenson	30		
M. R. Ramprakash c Martindale b Hemmings	132		
K. R. Brown not out	200		
†P. R. Downton c Stephenson b Cooper	63		
J. E. Emburey not out	22		
B 5, l-b 10, n-b 8	23		
1/38 2/42 3/108 4/296 5/464 (5 wkts dec.)	510	(no wkt)	64

N. F. Williams, A. R. C. Fraser, P. C. R. Tufnell and N. G. Cowans did not bat.

Bonus points – Middlesex 4, Nottinghamshire 1 (Score at 100 overs: 304-4).

Bowling: *First Innings*—Stephenson 33–5–89–2; Cooper 31–3–134–1; Pick 22–3–79–1; Afford 29–10–76–0; Hemmings 29.3–2–117–1. *Second Innings*—Cooper 5–1–10–0; Hemmings 7–0–31–0; Afford 3–1–23–0.

Nottinghamshire

B. C. Broad b Tufnell	38	– b Fraser	20
M. Newell lbw b Williams	6	– b Cowans	80
*R. T. Robinson lbw b Cowans	57	– run out	105
P. Johnson c Williams b Tufnell	2	– retired hurt	12
D. J. R. Martindale c Brown b Tufnell	32	– c Gatting b Fraser	11
F. D. Stephenson c Downton b Cowans	7	– c Downton b Cowans	20
†B. N. French not out	40	– c Downton b Cowans	1
E. E. Hemmings c Tufnell b Williams	3	– c Brown b Emburey	6
K. E. Cooper lbw b Fraser	5	– (10) b Cowans	21
R. A. Pick b Williams	35	– (9) lbw b Emburey	26
J. A. Afford b Tufnell	3	– not out	0
L-b 3, w 1, n-b 3	7	B 9, l-b 10, w 1, n-b 13	33
1/8 2/71 3/87 4/130 5/142 6/144 7/150 8/155 9/220	235	1/32 2/211 3/240 4/273 5/277 6/285 7/297 8/335 9/335	335

Bonus points – Nottinghamshire 2, Middlesex 4 (Score at 100 overs: 229-9).

In the second innings P. Johnson retired hurt at 232.

Bowling: *First Innings*—Fraser 23–5–63–1; Williams 13–4–41–3; Cowans 14–2–26–2; Emburey 25–7–33–0; Tufnell 26.5–6–69–4. *Second Innings*—Fraser 34–9–84–2; Cowans 24–11–46–4; Emburey 43–14–85–2; Tufnell 47–16–93–0; Haynes 2–1–8–0.

Umpires: D. J. Constant and A. G. T. Whitehead.

At The Oval, September 12, 13, 14, 15. MIDDLESEX drew with SURREY.

At Hove, September 18, 19, 20. MIDDLESEX beat SUSSEX by an innings and 57 runs.

NORTHAMPTONSHIRE

Patron: The Earl of Dalkeith
President: W. R. F. Chamberlain
Chairman: L. A. Wilson
Chairman, Cricket Committee: A. P. Arnold
Secretary: S. P. Coverdale
County Ground, Wantage Road,
Northampton NN1 4TJ
(Telephone: 0604-32917)
Captain: A. J. Lamb
Coach: R. M. Carter
Cricket Development Officer: B. L. Reynolds

Northamptonshire retained the unwanted title of the county circuit's principal under-achievers after failing, for the tenth season running, to capture a major honour. By reaching the NatWest Bank Trophy final, they gave themselves a chance to erase at least some of the earlier disappointments, but an emphatic seven-wicket defeat at the hands of Lancashire served only to expose to a wider public many of the shortcomings apparent to regular followers throughout the season.

The Britannic Assurance Championship campaign began promisingly enough, Alan Fordham and Allan Lamb hitting double-centuries in an innings win at Headingley, and ended with victories against Essex, contenders for the title, and Leicestershire in the last two games. The intervening period, however, featured a solitary win in a run-chase against Somerset at Taunton; and much of the cricket played by the team was, at best, mediocre. For the first time since 1951, Northamptonshire did not win a single Championship match at their own headquarters, and although the late rally enabled them to finish eleventh, this was still a drop of six places on 1989. All this, together with another wretched showing to take the Refuge Assurance League wooden spoon, and the early exit from the Benson and Hedges Cup, prompted understandable consternation among supporters. Lamb had already attended a "clear the air" meeting with a group of them in mid-season.

Much discussion centred around the on-field leadership, particularly the lack of continuity brought about by Lamb's frequent absences on international duty. Injuries at various times to the vice-captain, Wayne Larkins, and the senior cricketer, Nick Cook, did not help the situation, and as early as May 12 Northamptonshire were being led by the fourth choice, Robert Bailey, who displayed a level-headed approach during his short spell in charge. By September, Lamb himself was supporting the appointment of a cricket manager to be in attendance with the team.

Few excuses could legitimately be offered for the succession of poor performances, although the club's inability to field the strongest eleven on more than a handful of occasions was a source of intense frustration. All the recognised bowlers were sidelined with fitness problems at some stage, and the back injury suffered by the key all-rounder, David Capel, led to a reappraisal of his long-term role in the side. Physiotherapist Richie Norman was frequently the man most in demand at the County Ground, never more so than during the traumatic and portentous Championship game with Derbyshire in early May. Northamptonshire, batting three men short in the second innings, lost inside two days by an innings, and from that low point the season never completely recovered.

The majority of outstanding individual performances came from the batsmen. Bailey failed by just 13 runs to achieve 2,000 for the county, and his tally of seven hundreds was one short of R. A. Haywood's 69-year-old Northamptonshire record. He blossomed in the second half of the summer, whereas Capel shone most brightly in June and July, his purple patch producing three memorable centuries in a week. Lamb was also at his best, when available, and comfortably headed Northamptonshire's first-class averages.

The new opening partnership of Fordham and Nigel Felton replaced the "old firm" of Larkins and Geoff Cook. Fordham built impressively on the foundations laid during the previous year to score 1,767 runs in his first full season, while Felton, often thriving in adversity, played many valuable innings. They formed an excellent understanding and ran well between the wickets to capitalise on the advantages enjoyed by a left- and right-hand combination. In contrast, Larkins, his newly revived international career jeopardised again by a badly broken finger, which caused a seven-week lay-off, struggled to find consistent form. A timely 207 against Gooch's Essex secured his place on England's winter tour to Australia.

Geoff Cook announced in June his intention to retire at the end of the season, and immediately drifted out of the side. There were occasions when one yearned for Cook's batting experience and determination, and it was pleasing to witness the warm reception afforded him by the Northampton crowd when he and Larkins opened together for the last time in the Refuge game against Gloucestershire.

In a summer heavy with prolific run-scoring around the country, only Curtly Ambrose exceeded 50 wickets for Northamptonshire, saving his best effort – twelve for 155 – until the final Championship fixture at Leicester. The club hope he will return in 1992, after the West Indies tour of England this summer. However, his overseas colleague, Winston Davis, was not retained at the end of a season which had offered him few opportunities, with the consequent decline in his confidence.

Mark Robinson was promoted to take the new ball in the absence of the injured Capel and Greg Thomas, and while his first-class figures did not always do him justice, he could never be faulted for lack of effort. He enjoyed some well-deserved success in the NatWest quarter- and semi-final matches, in which he twice kept his head during the hectic closing overs to secure victory for his side. Like so many others in the squad, Nick Cook fought a year-long battle for full fitness, and neither he nor fellow-spinner Richard Williams could look back on the summer with a great deal of satisfaction. In mitigation, the bowlers did not always receive adequate fielding support. Important catches were missed, and David Ripley was generally a little below his best behind the stumps.

Despite Northamptonshire's immediate problems, the quality of their rising generation offered genuine hope for the future. Tony Penberthy, Wayne Noon, Andy Roberts and John Hughes have all sampled life in the first team, and it should not be long before a trio of talented young batsmen – Russell Warren, Malachy Loye and Richard Montgomerie – do likewise. The kind of cricketing environment they inherit at Northampton, though, depends on the club's response to the tribulations of 1990. – Andrew Radd.

NORTHAMPTONSHIRE 1990

[*Bill Smith*

Back row: J. W. Govan, J. G. Hughes, A. L. Penberthy, A. Walker, W. W. Davis, D. J. Wild, D. Ripley, R. J. Warren, P. J. Berry, A. R. Roberts. *Middle row:* R. Norman (*physiotherapist*), R. R. Montgomerie, M. B. Loye, S. J. Brown, M. A. Robinson, C. E. L. Ambrose, J. G. Thomas, A. Fordham, W. M. Noon, N. A. Felton, R. M. Carter (*coach*). *Front row:* D. J. Capel, G. Cook, W. Larkins, A. J. Lamb (*captain*), N. G. B. Cook, R. J. Bailey, R. G. Williams.

NORTHAMPTONSHIRE RESULTS

All first-class matches – Played 24: Won 4, Lost 9, Drawn 11.
County Championship matches – Played 22: Won 4, Lost 9, Drawn 9.

Bonus points – Batting 61, Bowling 60.

Competition placings – Britannic Assurance County Championship, 11th; NatWest Bank Trophy, finalists; Benson and Hedges Cup, 5th in Group D; Refuge Assurance League, 17th.

BRITANNIC ASSURANCE CHAMPIONSHIP AVERAGES

BATTING

	Birthplace	M	I	NO	R	HI	Avge
‡A. J. Lamb	*Langebaanweg, SA*	10	16	3	1,040	235	80.00
‡R. J. Bailey	*Biddulph*	22	37	8	1,965	204*	67.75
‡A. Fordham	*Bedford*	22	38	2	1,653	206*	45.91
‡N. A. Felton	*Guildford*	20	35	2	1,484	122	44.96
‡D. J. Capel	*Northampton*	17	27	5	904	113	41.09
‡D. Ripley	*Leeds*	20	27	6	634	109*	30.19
‡W. Larkins	*Roxton*	15	25	0	701	207	28.04
‡R. G. Williams	*Bangor*	16	24	4	482	96	24.10
A. L. Penberthy	*Troon*	11	16	2	334	83	23.85
‡G. Cook	*Middlesbrough*	8	11	1	200	49	20.00
‡C. E. L. Ambrose	*Swetes Village, Antigua*	14	17	5	203	55*	16.91
‡W. W. Davis	*Sion Hill, St Vincent*	8	6	0	96	47	16.00
J. G. Thomas	*Trebanos*	11	11	2	131	48	14.55
‡N. G. B. Cook	*Leicester*	17	17	7	133	30	13.30
J. G. Hughes	*Wellingborough*	4	7	0	4	2	0.57
‡M. A. Robinson	*Hull*	17	16	10	3	1*	0.50

Also batted: S. J. Brown (*Cleadon*) (3 matches) 2, 4*; J. W. Govan (*Dunfermline*) (2 matches) 17, 4, 17; W. M. Noon (*Grimsby*) (2 matches) 2, 2; A. R. Roberts (*Kettering*) (2 matches) 5, 0, 0; ‡D. J. Wild (*Northampton*) (1 match) 17, 0.

* *Signifies not out.* ‡ *Denotes county cap.*

The following played a total of 24 three-figure innings for Northamptonshire in County Championship matches – R. J. Bailey 7, N. A. Felton 4, A. Fordham 4, A. J. Lamb 4, D. J. Capel 2, W. Larkins 2, D. Ripley 1.

BOWLING

	O	M	R	W	BB	5W/i	Avge
C. E. L. Ambrose	483.4	124	1,353	58	7-89	5	23.32
D. J. Capel	234	51	711	25	5-74	1	28.44
N. G. B. Cook	507.1	159	1,320	40	5-44	2	33.00
R. G. Williams	417.3	116	1,165	31	4-94	0	37.58
J. G. Thomas	288.2	49	1,098	28	7-75	1	39.21
A. L. Penberthy	196	23	768	19	4-91	0	40.42
M. A. Robinson	520.1	97	1,794	38	3-47	0	47.21
R. J. Bailey	168.2	29	604	11	3-82	0	54.90
W. W. Davis	216.5	26	747	12	3-28	0	62.25

Also bowled: S. J. Brown 52–7–221–4; N. A. Felton 19–1–113–1; A. Fordham 9–0–39–1; J. W. Govan 33–5–120–3; J. G. Hughes 66–12–293–3; W. Larkins 10–1–45–0; A. R. Roberts 63–14–207–3; D. J. Wild 12.5–4–42–0.

Wicket-keepers: D. Ripley 28 ct, 6 st; W. M. Noon 4 ct, 1 st.

Leading Fielders: A. Fordham 22, N. A. Felton 18, R. J. Bailey 16, D. J. Capel 15.

At Cambridge, April 14, 15, 16. NORTHAMPTONSHIRE drew with CAMBRIDGE UNIVERSITY.

At Leeds, April 26, 27, 28, 30. NORTHAMPTONSHIRE beat YORKSHIRE by an innings and 50 runs.

NORTHAMPTONSHIRE v DERBYSHIRE

At Northampton, May 3, 4. Derbyshire won by an innings and 51 runs. Derbyshire 23 pts, Northamptonshire 6 pts. Toss: Northamptonshire. Beset by injuries and faced with hostile fast bowling from Bishop and Malcolm, Northamptonshire capitulated inside two of the scheduled four days to give Derbyshire a most emphatic victory. The home side's problems began on the first morning, when Lamb tore a hamstring and was unable to take any further part in the match. Later in the day Nick Cook suffered a fractured knuckle from a blow on the hand off Malcolm, and Ripley could not take the field on the second day owing to a stomach ailment. With these three absent, Northamptonshire were dismissed in seventeen overs for their lowest first-class total since 1946; only Fordham, last out, offered any serious resistance. First time around Geoff Cook held the innings together during a 170-minute stay, but solid Derbyshire batting earned a lead of 101, which proved more than sufficient. Northamptonshire's substitute fielders included two members of the county's colts team, one of whom, Jonathan Swann, held a good catch to dismiss Griffith.

Close of play: First day, Derbyshire 55-1 (A. M. Brown 15*, C. J. Adams 9*).

Northamptonshire

A. Fordham c Krikken b Bishop	10	– (2) c and b Bishop	32
W. Larkins c Krikken b Malcolm	1	– (1) b Bishop	0
R. J. Bailey c Adams b Griffith	30	– b Malcolm	8
*A. J. Lamb retired hurt	14	– absent injured	
D. J. Capel c Roberts b Jean-Jacques	11	– lbw b Bishop	2
G. Cook run out	44	– (4) b Bishop	3
†D. Ripley c Roberts b Malcolm	17	– absent ill	
J. W. Govan lbw b Goldsmith	17	– (6) c Adams b Malcolm	4
W. W. Davis c Barnett b Malcolm	23	– (7) b Malcolm	0
N. G. B. Cook retired hurt	9	– absent injured	
M. A. Robinson not out	1	– (8) not out	0
B 4, l-b 9, w 6, n-b 6	25	W 1	1
1/5 2/24 3/62 4/79 5/119 6/161 7/166 8/202	202	1/0 2/9 3/20 4/40 5/48 6/48 7/50	50

Bonus points – Northamptonshire 2, Derbyshire 3.

In the first innings A. J. Lamb retired hurt at 53 and N. G. B. Cook at 186.

Bowling: *First Innings*—Bishop 17–2–48–1; Malcolm 22.4–5–60–3; Jean-Jacques 17–2–39–1; Griffith 11–2–20–1; Goldsmith 11–2–21–1; Barnett 3–2–1–0. *Second Innings*—Bishop 9–2–25–4; Malcolm 8–2–25–3.

Derbyshire

P. D. Bowler lbw b Robinson	24
A. M. Brown c Fordham b Govan	44
C. J. Adams c Larkins b Capel	24
*K. J. Barnett c and b Capel	58
B. Roberts lbw b Robinson	44
S. C. Goldsmith b Robinson	34
F. A. Griffith c sub b Capel	1
†K. M. Krikken lbw b Capel	0
I. R. Bishop b Davis	19
M. Jean-Jacques run out	4
D. E. Malcolm not out	20
B 5, l-b 19, n-b 7	31
1/37 2/71 3/142 4/183 5/234 6/253 7/253 8/254 9/258	303

Bonus points – Derbyshire 4, Northamptonshire 4.

Bowling: Davis 24.3–3–85–1; Capel 27–7–83–4; Robinson 28–8–80–3; Govan 14–5–19–1; Bailey 5–2–12–0.

Umpires: J. H. Harris and R. A. White.

NORTHAMPTONSHIRE v WARWICKSHIRE

At Northampton, May 15, 16, 17, 18. Warwickshire won by an innings and 30 runs. Warwickshire 23 pts, Northamptonshire 4 pts. Toss: Northamptonshire. A match in which controversy was no stranger ended in victory for Warwickshire 35 minutes into the fourth day. After a poor start the visitors, put in to bat by Bailey, recovered magnificently, initially through Kallicharran, who batted carefully for more than three hours, and then Reeve, the vice-captain. Reeve's unbeaten 202 (405 minutes, 355 balls, 4 sixes, 25 fours) was the highest individual innings for Warwickshire against Northamptonshire, beating F. R. Santall's 57-year-old record, and with Small and Donald helping him in century stands for the seventh and eighth wickets, Warwickshire built up an unassailable position. In the course of his innings Reeve, who survived a confident appeal for a catch behind when 103, received three "beamers" in quick succession from Ambrose. The bowler was duly warned by umpire Dudleston, and the following day Northamptonshire issued a statement, condemning such deliveries and promising strong disciplinary action in the event of any repetition. Dudleston was also instrumental in the removal of Robinson from the Northamptonshire attack for running on the pitch. After all these problems, the home team appeared to have little stomach for the fight and twice fell to Munton, who returned the best match figures of his career.

Close of play: First day, Warwickshire 286-6 (D. A. Reeve 82*, G. C. Small 42*); Second day, Northamptonshire 136-6 (G. Cook 32*, D. Ripley 23*); Third day, Northamptonshire 192-7 (D. Ripley 5*, J. G. Thomas 0*).

Warwickshire

A. J. Moles lbw b Thomas	13
*T. A. Lloyd c Ripley b Ambrose	21
Asif Din lbw b Penberthy	3
A. I. Kallicharran c and b Penberthy	72
†G. W. Humpage c Ripley b Thomas	13
D. A. Reeve not out	202
N. M. K. Smith b Penberthy	8
G. C. Small c Felton b Robinson	55
A. A. Donald c Felton b Robinson	24
J. E. Benjamin b Penberthy	14
T. A. Munton not out	1
B 4, l-b 28, w 7, n-b 8	47
1/29 2/38 3/47 4/75 5/174 6/198 7/317 8/419 9/458 (9 wkts dec.)	473

Bonus points – Warwickshire 3, Northamptonshire 2 (Score at 100 overs: 276-6).

Bowling: Ambrose 30–8–80–1; Thomas 28–5–84–2; Robinson 35.1–9–91–2; Penberthy 29.5–5–91–4; Wild 12.5–4–42–0; Williams 5–1–38–0; Bailey 8–1–15–0.

Northamptonshire

A. Fordham c Kallicharran b Munton	37	– c Humpage b Munton	18
N. A. Felton c Moles b Small	8	– c Small b Asif Din	75
*R. J. Bailey c Kallicharran b Small	0	– c Humpage b Munton	31
A. L. Penberthy run out	0	– lbw b Reeve	12
G. Cook lbw b Munton	33	– c Humpage b Reeve	13
R. G. Williams c Smith b Donald	8	– b Smith	9
D. J. Wild c Humpage b Small	17	– b Reeve	0
†D. Ripley c Humpage b Munton	36	– c Reeve b Munton	6
J. G. Thomas c Asif Din b Munton	30	– not out	14
C. E. L. Ambrose not out	11	– c Moles b Donald	16
M. A. Robinson c Kallicharran b Munton	1	– lbw b Munton	0
B 17, l-b 8, w 8, n-b 5	38	B 8, l-b 9, w 9, n-b 4	30
1/18 2/18 3/29 4/46 5/58 6/94 7/140 8/184 9/198	219	1/43 2/127 3/160 4/169 5/181 6/181 7/187 8/193 9/223	224

Bonus points – Northamptonshire 2, Warwickshire 4.

Bowling: *First Innings*—Donald 20–5–51–1; Small 20–3–72–3; Munton 25.1–10–33–5; Benjamin 12–2–16–0; Smith 13–4–17–0; Asif Din 2–1–5–0. *Second Innings*—Munton 19.5–7–44–4; Small 7–1–34–0; Donald 14–2–45–1; Benjamin 9–2–23–0; Reeve 17–7–26–3; Smith 12–7–22–1; Asif Din 4–1–13–1.

Umpires: B. Dudleston and D. O. Oslear.

At Nottingham, May 23, 24, 25. NORTHAMPTONSHIRE lost to NOTTINGHAMSHIRE by eight wickets.

At Birmingham, June 2, 4, 5. NORTHAMPTONSHIRE drew with WARWICKSHIRE.

NORTHAMPTONSHIRE v LEICESTERSHIRE

At Northampton, June 6, 7, 8. Drawn. Northamptonshire 4 pts, Leicestershire 3 pts. Toss: Northamptonshire. Rain, which docked 78 overs from the first two days, prevented any play at all on the third, dashing hopes of a positive outcome which had been raised by Nick Cook's enterprising declaration, 166 runs behind, on the second afternoon. Benson (209 minutes, eleven fours) scored a maiden Championship half-century and received good support from Benjamin in a sixth-wicket stand worth 70 in fourteen overs. Northamptonshire made a purposeful reply, Fordham striking the ball handsomely on his way to 59 off 76 balls before the declaration.

Close of play: First day, Leicestershire 210-6 (J. D. R. Benson 57*, P. A. Nixon 20*); Second day, Leicestershire 46-2 (T. J. Boon 18*, P. Willey 20*).

Leicestershire

T. J. Boon c Capel b Thomas	4	– not out	18
*N. E. Briers b Thomas	6	– b Capel	5
J. J. Whitaker c N. G. B. Cook b Penberthy	35	– c and b Capel	3
P. Willey c Noon b Ambrose	34	– not out	20
L. Potter c Noon b Ambrose	14		
J. D. R. Benson c Capel b Penberthy	86		
W. K. M. Benjamin b Capel	33		
†P. A. Nixon b Ambrose	27		
J. P. Agnew c Noon b Capel	8		
A. D. Mullally not out	1		
D. J. Millns c Capel b Penberthy	1		
B 3, l-b 3, w 3, n-b 3	12		
1/6 2/13 3/81 4/83 5/112 6/182 7/223 8/259 9/259	261	1/13 2/17	(2 wkts) 46

Bonus points – Leicestershire 3, Northamptonshire 4.

Bowling: *First Innings*—Ambrose 23–6–54–3; Thomas 22–5–74–2; Capel 22–7–49–2; N. G. B. Cook 6–1–17–0; Penberthy 15.2–2–61–3. *Second Innings*—Capel 6–3–4–2; Thomas 4–0–12–0; Williams 9–3–19–0; N. G. B. Cook 7–3–11–0.

Northamptonshire

A. Fordham not out	59
N. A. Felton c Benjamin b Mullally	22
G. Cook not out	8
L-b 2, w 2, n-b 2	6
1/44	(1 wkt dec.) 95

R. J. Bailey, D. J. Capel, R. G. Williams, A. L. Penberthy, †W. M. Noon, J. G. Thomas, C. E. L. Ambrose and *N. G. B. Cook did not bat.

Bowling: Benjamin 11–2–33–0; Agnew 7–1–23–0; Mullally 5–0–17–1; Willey 1–0–1–0; Millns 2–0–19–0.

Umpires: J. D. Bond and P. B. Wight.

NORTHAMPTONSHIRE v GLAMORGAN

At Northampton, June 9, 11, 12. Glamorgan won by six wickets. Glamorgan 22 pts, Northamptonshire 8 pts. Toss: Northamptonshire. Batting of the highest calibre from Maynard and Richards guided Glamorgan to a first Championship victory at Northampton since their title-winning year of 1969. Set 307 to win in 72 overs, the visitors lost three wickets for 71 before their fourth-wicket pair took charge, adding 227 in 41 overs and totally dominating the home attack. Maynard batted for 169 minutes (150 balls) and hit a six and nineteen fours; Richards's 109 came off 111 balls in 164 minutes and contained four sixes and twelve fours. Northamptonshire, however, had only themselves to blame. Richards survived two chances before reaching 20, while Maynard was dropped in the slips when 19. The first day belonged to Capel, who unveiled his full range of strokes, hitting three sixes and sixteen fours during his two and a half hours (120 balls) at the crease. His brilliance tended to overshadow Felton's worthy effort which, although not chanceless, laid a solid foundation on which Capel could build. After a century opening stand between Morris and Butcher, Glamorgan ran into trouble against Thomas, who produced a career-best performance against his former county to earn Northamptonshire a lead of 91. With Capel again in sparkling form, the home side made good progress on the final morning after Frost had claimed three wickets in an over that spanned two days.

Close of play: First day, Glamorgan 16-0 (A. R. Butcher 2*, H. Morris 14*); Second day, Northamptonshire 91-2 (A. Fordham 37*, G. Cook 0*).

Northamptonshire

A. Fordham lbw b Frost	27	– lbw b Barwick	45
N. A. Felton c Richards b Barwick	122	– c Metson b Frost	44
G. Cook lbw b Frost	7	– (4) c Metson b Frost	0
R. J. Bailey c Metson b Barwick	38	– (5) not out	47
D. J. Capel c Metson b Frost	113	– (6) not out	64
A. L. Penberthy c Watkin b Barwick	1		
R. G. Williams c Metson b Frost	34		
†W. M. Noon run out	2	– (3) lbw b Frost	2
J. G. Thomas not out	0		
L-b 4, n-b 2	6	B 6, l-b 4, w 3	13
1/50 2/62 3/149 4/267 5/283 6/342 7/350 8/350	(8 wkts dec.) 350	1/89 2/91 3/91 4/124	(4 wkts dec.) 215

C. E. L. Ambrose and *N. G. B. Cook did not bat.

Bonus points – Northamptonshire 4, Glamorgan 3.

Bowling: *First Innings*—Frost 23.2–6–82–4; Watkin 26–2–93–0; Barwick 24–4–76–3; Cowley 12–1–65–0; Richards 11–3–30–0. *Second Innings*—Frost 13–0–58–3; Watkin 13–1–66–0; Barwick 19.2–3–67–1; Cowley 6–0–14–0.

Glamorgan

*A. R. Butcher b Williams	43	– st Noon b Williams	36
H. Morris lbw b Thomas	80	– c Noon b Williams	24
P. A. Cottey c Bailey b N. G. B. Cook	11	– lbw b Capel	2
I. V. A. Richards lbw b Thomas	25	– (5) c Fordham b Williams	109
N. G. Cowley lbw b Thomas	0		
†C. P. Metson b Thomas	0		
M. P. Maynard lbw b Thomas	74	– (4) not out	125
G. C. Holmes c Bailey b N. G. B. Cook	9	– (6) not out	0
S. L. Watkin b Thomas	3		
S.R. Barwick not out	2		
M. Frost c Capel b Thomas	4		
B 2, l-b 5, n-b 1	8	B 3, l-b 4, w 5, n-b 1	13
1/102 2/131 3/137 4/137 5/145 6/178 7/208 8/248 9/253	259	1/58 2/61 3/71 4/298	(4 wkts) 309

Bonus points – Glamorgan 3, Northamptonshire 4.

Bowling: *First Innings*—Ambrose 20–4–65–0; Thomas 25–7–75–7; Penberthy 5–0–33–0; Williams 19–5–42–1; Capel 6–0–20–0; N. G. B. Cook 11–2–17–2. *Second Innings*—Ambrose 14–4–58–0; Thomas 10–0–68–0; Williams 13–2–51–3; Capel 7–2–17–1; N. G. B. Cook 19.4–1–108–0.

Umpires: J. D. Bond and P. B. Wight (B. Leadbeater deputised for P. B. Wight on 3rd day).

At Northampton, June 16, 17, 18. NORTHAMPTONSHIRE drew with NEW ZEALANDERS (See New Zealand tour section).

NORTHAMPTONSHIRE v MIDDLESEX

At Luton, June 23, 25, 26. Middlesex won by 79 runs. Middlesex 23 pts, Northamptonshire 3 pts. Toss: Middlesex. The two Middlesex spinners, Emburey and Tufnell, claimed fifteen wickets between them to clinch victory with 7.5 overs remaining, despite two skilful and disciplined innings from Bailey. Although rain caused the loss of 26 overs on Saturday, Middlesex took the initiative as Roseberry and Gatting added 130. Roseberry, who hit three sixes and eight fours in an innings of 322 minutes, completed his century early on the second morning before Williams and Nick Cook took the last seven wickets for 67. It was then clear that the slow men would hold sway for the rest of the game, and although Bailey managed to avoid the follow-on for Northamptonshire with a single off the last ball of the day, the home side trailed by 144. Haynes and Roseberry then attacked seamers and spinners alike, giving Gatting the opportunity to set a generous target of 252 in 81 overs. Once the fourth-wicket stand between Bailey and Capel was broken, however, a Middlesex win always looked likely. Bailey was again last out, having batted for more than seven and a half hours in the match with minimal support, no-one else reaching 20 in either innings.

Close of play: First day, Middlesex 252-3 (M. A. Roseberry 98*, K. R. Brown 35*); Second day, Northamptonshire 195-9 (R. J. Bailey 68*, M. A. Robinson 0*).

Middlesex

	First innings		Second innings	
D. L. Haynes c G. Cook b Ambrose	9	– not out	69
M. A. Roseberry c and b N. G. B. Cook	115	– c Fordham b Ambrose	36
*M. W. Gatting c Felton b Ambrose	62	– c Ripley b Ambrose	0
M. R. Ramprakash b Williams	26	– not out	0
K. R. Brown b N. G. B. Cook	69		
†P. Farbrace c Robinson b Williams	0		
J. E. Emburey st Ripley b Williams	13		
N. F. Williams st Ripley b Williams	14		
P. C. R. Tufnell c Williams b N. G. B. Cook	8		
A. R. C. Fraser not out	1		
S. P. Hughes c G. Cook b N. G. B. Cook	1		
B 2, l-b 9, n-b 15	26	W 1, n-b 1	2
1/17 2/147 3/191 4/277 5/278 6/302 7/328 8/339 9/342	344	1/107 2/107	(2 wkts dec.) 107

Bonus points – Middlesex 3, Northamptonshire 2 (Score at 100 overs: 294-5).

Bowling: *First Innings*—Ambrose 18–4–53–2; Thomas 17–3–40–0; Robinson 19–6–46–0; N. G. B. Cook 28.4–4–79–4; Capel 6–0–21–0; Williams 35–6–94–4. *Second Innings*—Ambrose 11–2–38–2; Thomas 6–0–38–0; N. G. B. Cook 4–0–31–0; Robinson 0.3–0–0–0.

Northamptonshire

	First innings		Second innings	
A. Fordham	c Farbrace b Williams	4	c and b Fraser	7
N. A. Felton	lbw b Williams	19	c Brown b Tufnell	11
G. Cook	c Roseberry b Emburey	8	c Farbrace b Fraser	1
R. J. Bailey	c Roseberry b Emburey	73	b Tufnell	87
D. J. Capel	c Gatting b Tufnell	12	st Farbrace b Tufnell	15
R. G. Williams	c Roseberry b Emburey	4	c Gatting b Emburey	11
†D. Ripley	run out	17	c Roseberry b Emburey	5
J. G. Thomas	lbw b Emburey	0	b Emburey	5
*N. G. B. Cook	c Roseberry b Tufnell	18	c Brown b Tufnell	0
C. E. L. Ambrose	b Tufnell	6	c and b Tufnell	3
M. A. Robinson	not out	0	not out	0
	B 10, l-b 8, w 1, n-b 20	39	B 6, l-b 6, n-b 15	27
	1/5 2/34 3/40 4/72 5/86 6/113 7/126 8/178 9/194	200	1/7 2/9 3/36 4/94 5/118 6/133 7/150 8/155 9/166	172

Bonus points – Northamptonshire 1, Middlesex 4 (Score at 100 overs: 198-9).

Bowling: *First Innings*—Williams 9–1–23–2; Fraser 10–1–22–0; Emburey 44.1–17–55–4; Tufnell 38–8–80–3; Ramprakash 1–0–2–0. *Second Innings*—Williams 5–1–12–0; Fraser 5–2–11–2; Emburey 33–5–80–3; Tufnell 30.1–7–57–5.

Umpires: N. T. Plews and R. A. White.

At Taunton, June 30, July 2, 3. NORTHAMPTONSHIRE beat SOMERSET by seven wickets.

At The Oval, July 4, 5, 6. NORTHAMPTONSHIRE lost to SURREY by 147 runs.

NORTHAMPTONSHIRE v YORKSHIRE

At Northampton, July 7, 9, 10. Drawn. Northamptonshire 6 pts, Yorkshire 7 pts. Toss: Yorkshire. Cook played out the last over from Carrick to earn the home side a draw in a match which came to life on the final afternoon. Set 314 for victory in 55 overs, Northamptonshire prospered thanks to an opening partnership of 115 before Felton (170 minutes, one six, ten fours) and Capel added 127 at 7 runs per over to bring the target down to 62. The charge was halted, however, by the departure of both batsmen in consecutive overs, and with Carrick and Fletcher sharing another five wickets in quick succession, Yorkshire were closer to victory at the end. The first two days saw each side collect maximum batting points, Yorkshire achieving them when Hartley hit the last two balls of the 100th over, from Williams, for six. Overall, though, the most memorable feature of the game was the strokeplay of Capel, whose 83 in the second innings came in just 60 deliveries with two sixes and ten fours.

Close of play: First day, Yorkshire 318; Second day, Yorkshire 62-0 (R. J. Blakey 18*, A. A. Metcalfe 39*).

Yorkshire

	First innings		Second innings	
†R. J. Blakey	c Felton b Ambrose	17	c Bailey b Cook	57
*A. A. Metcalfe	b Cook	48	c and b Bailey	79
K. Sharp	retired hurt	40		
P. E. Robinson	b Cook	58	not out	76
D. Byas	lbw b Cook	28	c Ripley b Fordham	35
C. A. Chapman	c Felton b Williams	5	(3) c Fordham b Bailey	17
C. White	c Felton b Cook	38	(6) not out	29
P. Carrick	c Capel b Robinson	27		
P. J. Hartley	c Fordham b Williams	40		
S. D. Fletcher	lbw b Cook	0		
I. J. Houseman	not out	0		
	B 2, l-b 8, w 1, n-b 6	17	L-b 4, w 1, n-b 4	9
	1/50 2/97 3/203 4/204 5/222 6/263 7/318 8/318 9/318	318	1/143 2/143 3/187 4/260 (4 wkts dec.)	302

Bonus points – Yorkshire 4, Northamptonshire 2 (Score at 100 overs: 304-6).

In the first innings K. Sharp retired hurt at 129.

Bowling: *First Innings*—Ambrose 12–0–42–1; Capel 5–0–24–0; Robinson 22–3–67–1; Cook 25–10–44–5; Penberthy 12–2–32–0; Williams 27.2–5–99–2. *Second Innings*—Robinson 12–2–50–0; Capel 6–1–17–0; Cook 14–6–25–1; Williams 4–1–6–0; Penberthy 6–0–29–0; Bailey 24.2–3–81–2; Felton 12–0–65–0; Fordham 5–0–25–1.

Northamptonshire

A. Fordham c Blakey b Hartley	12	– c Metcalfe b Fletcher	59
N. A. Felton c Fletcher b Carrick	66	– b Carrick	106
R. J. Bailey b Hartley	0	– c and b Carrick	6
D. J. Capel c Metcalfe b Fletcher	64	– b Fletcher	83
*W. Larkins c Hartley b Fletcher	15	– c and b Carrick	4
R. G. Williams run out	69	– st Blakey b Carrick	2
A. L. Penberthy c and b Carrick	8	– c and b Fletcher	1
†D. Ripley not out	34	– c Blakey b Fletcher	16
N. G. B. Cook run out	30	– (10) not out	1
C. E. L. Ambrose (did not bat)		– (9) b Fletcher	14
M. A. Robinson (did not bat)		– not out	0
L-b 5, n-b 4	9	B 2, l-b 4, n-b 2	8
1/52 2/52 3/107 4/156 5/169 6/200 7/257 8/307 (8 wkts dec.)	307	1/115 2/125 3/252 4/264 5/268 6/269 7/271 8/299 9/300 (9 wkts)	300

Bonus points – Northamptonshire 4, Yorkshire 3 (Score at 100 overs: 306-7).

Bowling: *First Innings*—Hartley 15.2–2–56–2; Fletcher 17–6–44–2; Houseman 12–1–53–0; Carrick 37–9–91–2; White 10–1–39–0; Byas 9–1–19–0. *Second Innings*—Hartley 11–0–66–0; Fletcher 18–0–94–5; Houseman 6–0–36–0; Carrick 20–1–98–4.

Umpires: J. C. Balderstone and A. A. Jones.

NORTHAMPTONSHIRE v KENT

At Northampton, July 18, 19, 20. Drawn. Northamptonshire 8 pts, Kent 4 pts. Toss: Northamptonshire. Northamptonshire recovered from the early loss of both openers to equal their highest Championship total against Kent, benefiting from two significant middle-order partnerships. First Felton and Capel posted 146 for the third wicket, and then Bailey (228 minutes three sixes, twelve fours) was assisted by Williams in a fifth-wicket stand worth 187 in 51 overs. Capel hit 74 of his 85 runs in boundaries, three sixes among them. Kent's reply owed much to Taylor who, alone of the early batsmen, came to terms with the hostility of Ambrose. The West Indian claimed four for 10 in 24 balls, and despite Taylor's three-and-a-half-hour stay, followed by stubborn efforts from Davis, Patel and Igglesden, Kent followed on 162 behind late on the second day. With the pitch becoming progressively easier, they encountered few problems in saving the match. Davis, promoted to open in the absence of the injured Benson, and Hinks put on 131, and Chris Cowdrey (148 minutes) brightened the closing overs with some attractive strokes as he reached a century containing a six and seventeen fours.

Close of play: First day, Northamptonshire 445-8 (R. J. Bailey 138*, C. E. L. Ambrose 0*); Second day, Kent 21-0 (S. G. Hinks 10*, R. P. Davis 10*).

Northamptonshire

A. Fordham c Marsh b Igglesden	2
*W. Larkins c Marsh b de Villiers	12
N. A. Felton b Patel	90
D. J. Capel c Taylor b Igglesden	85
R. J. Bailey not out	138
R. G. Williams c Ellison b de Villiers	96
†D. Ripley b Ellison	7
S. J. Brown b Ellison	2
N. G. B. Cook c C. S. Cowdrey b Ellison	1
C. E. L. Ambrose not out	0
L-b 12	12
1/5 2/29 3/175 4/207 5/394 6/409 7/419 8/441 (8 wkts dec.)	445

M. A. Robinson did not bat.

Bonus points – Northamptonshire 4, Kent 1 (Score at 100 overs: 378-4).

Bowling: de Villiers 20–2–78–2; Igglesden 14–2–41–2; Ellison 21–1–85–3; C. S. Cowdrey 9–0–39–0; Davis 24–4–109–0; Patel 22–4–81–1.

Kent

S. G. Hinks c Capel b Ambrose	5	– b Cook	83
M. R. Benson c Ripley b Ambrose	10		
N. R. Taylor c Fordham b Cook	97	– b Bailey	36
G. R. Cowdrey c Larkins b Ambrose	0	– c Felton b Ambrose	4
*C. S. Cowdrey c Fordham b Ambrose	0	– not out	107
†S. A. Marsh c Felton b Brown	29	– not out	25
R. M. Ellison c Ripley b Robinson	24		
R. P. Davis c Capel b Bailey	43	– (2) c Bailey b Cook	41
P. S. de Villiers c and b Williams	0		
M. M. Patel not out	41		
A. P. Igglesden b Ambrose	24		
L-b 2, w 1, n-b 7	10	B 4, l-b 2, n-b 3	9
1/15 2/42 3/45 4/49 5/94 6/143 7/202 8/203 9/230	283	1/131 2/132 3/151 4/210 (4 wkts dec.)	305

Bonus points – Kent 3, Northamptonshire 4.

Bowling: *First Innings*—Ambrose 19–4–59–5; Brown 15–1–81–1; Robinson 19–3–75–1; Cook 25–17–33–1; Williams 18–7–28–1; Bailey 3–2–5–1. *Second Innings*—Ambrose 18–7–47–1; Robinson 10–2–19–0; Williams 22–8–67–0; Brown 8–2–22–0; Cook 28–13–59–2; Bailey 19–3–71–1; Fordham 4–0–14–0.

Umpires: B. Hassan and B. Leadbeater.

NORTHAMPTONSHIRE v SUSSEX

At Northampton, July 21, 23, 24. Drawn. Northamptonshire 7 pts, Sussex 5 pts. Toss: Sussex. Even on an easy-paced pitch and with a depleted attack, Northamptonshire erred on the side of caution in setting Sussex 389 to win in 64 overs. In the event, some indiscreet batting allowed the home side a glimpse of victory, but a level-headed century from Alan Wells ensured a draw. This, once Northamptonshire had weathered some testing new-ball bowling on the first morning, had always appeared the most likely result. Lamb was at his brutal best, hitting a six and 22 fours in a 158-ball innings of great power and dominating an unbroken fifth-wicket partnership of 105 with Bailey. Sussex responded with an even display in which Parker was outstanding, but events on the last day bordered on the farcical when the visitors, having reduced Northamptonshire to 183 for five – just 210 ahead – opted to feed runs to Bailey. He duly helped himself to the third double-century of his career, featuring five sixes and 27 fours, before Lamb's guarded declaration.

Close of play: First day, Sussex 35-0 (N. J. Lenham 27*, J. W. Hall 7*); Second day, Northamptonshire 110-2 (N. A. Felton 37*, R. J. Bailey 34*).

Northamptonshire

A. Fordham c C. M. Wells b Pigott	9	– c Lenham b Bunting	26
W. Larkins b Pigott	61	– lbw b Pigott	11
N. A. Felton c Moores b Dodemaide	78	– c Speight b Dodemaide	42
*A. J. Lamb not out	135	– (6) b A. P. Wells	1
D. J. Capel c Speight b Bunting	12	– b Lenham	29
R. J. Bailey not out	24	– (4) not out	204
†D. Ripley (did not bat)		– not out	44
B 4, l-b 6	10	B 1, l-b 3	4
1/11 2/136 3/179 4/224 (4 wkts dec.)	329	1/30 2/42 3/118 4/178 5/183 (5 wkts dec.)	361

S. J. Brown, W. W. Davis, N. G. B. Cook and M. A. Robinson did not bat.

Bonus points – Northamptonshire 4, Sussex 1.

Bowling: *First Innings*—Dodemaide 21–4–55–1; Pigott 19–2–83–2; C. M. Wells 20–6–42–0; Bunting 23–6–79–1; Salisbury 7–1–36–0; Lenham 8–3–24–0. *Second Innings*—Dodemaide 12–1–26–1; Pigott 5–0–28–1; Bunting 15–1–68–1; C. M. Wells 4–2–10–0; Lenham 13.5–1–78–1; A. P. Wells 16–4–88–1; Parker 8–0–59–0.

Sussex

N. J. Lenham c Felton b Davis	41	– lbw b Robinson	38
J. W. Hall lbw b Cook	42	– b Brown	7
*P. W. G. Parker lbw b Davis	90	– lbw b Robinson	38
A. P. Wells c Bailey b Brown	21	– not out	102
M. P. Speight c Bailey b Cook	2	– b Bailey	13
C. M. Wells b Cook	42	– c Lamb b Bailey	6
A. I. C. Dodemaide c Ripley b Robinson	26	– c Fordham b Bailey	14
†P. Moores b Cook	10	– c Cook b Robinson	8
A. C. S. Pigott not out	5	– not out	17
I. D. K. Salisbury not out	0		
L-b 9, w 2, n-b 12	23	B 4, l-b 1, n-b 3	8
1/61 2/120 3/163 4/166 5/239 6/264 7/295 8/299	(8 wkts dec.) 302	1/25 2/78 3/89 4/111 5/131 6/174 7/209	(7 wkts) 251

R. A. Bunting did not bat.

Bonus points – Sussex 4, Northamptonshire 3.

Bowling: *First Innings*—Davis 21–5–75–2; Robinson 17.1–3–61–1; Cook 31–9–89–4; Brown 14–3–46–1; Bailey 3–0–22–0. *Second Innings*—Brown 7–0–41–1; Robinson 17–2–68–3; Cook 13–4–21–0; Bailey 20–2–82–3; Larkins 6–1–21–0; Capel 1–0–13–0.

Umpires: B. Hassan and B. Leadbeater.

At Cheltenham, July 25, 26, 27. NORTHAMPTONSHIRE lost to GLOUCESTERSHIRE by an innings and 128 runs.

At Bournemouth, August 4, 6. NORTHAMPTONSHIRE lost to HAMPSHIRE by an innings and 22 runs.

At Chesterfield, August 8, 9, 10. NORTHAMPTONSHIRE drew with DERBYSHIRE.

NORTHAMPTONSHIRE v LANCASHIRE

At Northampton, August 11, 13, 14. Drawn. Northamptonshire 6 pts, Lancashire 5 pts. Toss: Northamptonshire. In fourth place and still in contention for the Championship title, Lancashire chose to rest several players and nearly came unstuck after being set 253 to win. With Davis producing his best spell of the season, they lost wickets at regular intervals and were grateful for Fowler's two and a quarter hours of defence. Northamptonshire enjoyed a highly successful first day as Fordham took complete command, batting for 272 minutes and hitting three sixes and 25 fours. Felton, Larkins and Bailey all lent excellent support. Lloyd batted beautifully for the visitors before throwing away a most promising start when he tried to charge Cook. Nevertheless, progress was generally sound rather than spectacular until DeFreitas launched a thrilling assault, completing a superb hundred off 94 deliveries with four sixes and eleven fours. Hughes declared 88 behind and Northamptonshire, although faltering briefly when three wickets went for 20 on the last morning, were able to issue a realistic challenge after Ripley had cashed in against the occasional bowlers.

Close of play: First day, Lancashire 23-0 (G. D. Mendis 15*, G. Fowler 8*); Second day, Northamptonshire 14-0 (A. Fordham 3*, N. A. Felton 11*).

Northamptonshire

A. Fordham c Bramhall b Patterson	172	– lbw b DeFreitas	24
N. A. Felton c DeFreitas b Hughes	66	– c Hughes b DeFreitas	51
*W. Larkins b Hughes	56		
R. J. Bailey not out	62	– (3) st Bramhall b Hughes	30
D. J. Capel c DeFreitas b Hughes	19	– (4) c Jesty b Hughes	9
R. G. Williams not out	11	– (5) not out	10
†D. Ripley (did not bat)		– (6) c Speak b Fowler	34
S. J. Brown (did not bat)		– (7) not out	4
B 14, l-b 14, n-b 7	35	L-b 2	2
1/179 2/294 3/325 4/365 (4 wkts dec.)	421	1/47 2/94 3/109 4/114 5/155 (5 wkts dec.)	164

W. W. Davis, N. G. B. Cook and M. A. Robinson did not bat.

Bonus points – Northamptonshire 4, Lancashire 1.

Bowling: *First Innings*—Patterson 14–2–54–1; DeFreitas 15–3–59–0; Martin 17–3–64–0; Austin 24–5–73–0; Hughes 30–1–143–3. *Second Innings*—Patterson 6–0–32–0; Martin 5–0–15–0; DeFreitas 11–3–23–2; Hughes 13–4–45–2; Jesty 2–2–0–0; Fowler 2.1–0–33–1; Lloyd 2–0–14–0.

Lancashire

G. D. Mendis b Brown	50	– c Capel b Davis	5
G. Fowler c Felton b Davis	30	– c Williams b Davis	47
G. D. Lloyd st Ripley b Cook	59	– c Ripley b Robinson	8
T. E. Jesty c Capel b Robinson	56	– lbw b Cook	8
N. J. Speak c Cook b Williams	5	– b Capel	0
P. A. J. DeFreitas not out	100	– st Ripley b Cook	15
I. D. Austin run out	5	– c Bailey b Davis	11
*D. P. Hughes not out	1	– not out	1
†S. Bramhall (did not bat)		– not out	0
B 4, l-b 12, w 1, n-b 10	27	L-b 6, w 1, n-b 8	15
1/79 2/84 3/180 4/199 5/294 6/331 (6 wkts dec.)	333	1/10 2/36 3/58 4/59 5/84 6/95 7/108 (7 wkts)	110

P. J. Martin and B. P. Patterson did not bat.

Bonus points – Lancashire 4, Northamptonshire 2.

Bowling: *First Innings*—Davis 25–2–85–1; Robinson 18.2–1–81–1; Cook 21–12–53–1; Capel 6–2–10–0; Brown 8–1–31–1; Williams 19–7–57–1. *Second Innings*—Davis 14.4–2–28–3; Robinson 6–1–19–1; Williams 9–4–16–0; Capel 8–1–22–1; Cook 7–2–19–2.

Umpires: J. H. Harris and D. S. Thompsett.

At Worcester, August 18, 20, 21. NORTHAMPTONSHIRE drew with WORCESTERSHIRE.

NORTHAMPTONSHIRE v GLOUCESTERSHIRE

At Northampton, August 23, 24, 25, 27. Gloucestershire won by 157 runs. Gloucestershire 22 pts, Northamptonshire 5 pts. Toss: Gloucestershire. The batting of Alleyne was the feature of a match which Gloucestershire won with virtually 25 overs to spare, completing their first double over Northamptonshire since 1961. The 22-year-old hit 38 fours and displayed remarkable powers of concentration, as well as a full range of strokes, during his 439-minute stay. He became the county's youngest double-centurion in the Championship – D. N. Moore was nineteen when he scored 206 against Oxford University in 1930 – and his was the highest score recorded by any Gloucestershire batsman since W. R. Hammond's 302 against Glamorgan at Newport in 1939. Northamptonshire were left needing 372 to avoid the follow-on and achieved this task for the loss of six wickets. Bailey (184 minutes, fourteen fours) passed 10,000 first-class runs for his county on the way to a responsible century. The visitors built purposefully on their lead of 119 to set a victory target of 366 in 72 overs, and although Ripley offered late resistance, a four-wicket burst from Walsh decided the outcome. His victims included Capel, who suffered a broken finger when he gloved a catch to silly point.

Close of play: First day, Gloucestershire 271-4 (M. W. Alleyne 132*, K. M. Curran 9*); Second day, Northamptonshire 169-2 (W. Larkins 32*, R. J. Bailey 18*); Third day, Gloucestershire 143-3 (C. W. J. Athey 34*, M. W. Alleyne 30*).

Gloucestershire

G. D. Hodgson c Ripley b Ambrose	4	– lbw b Ambrose	22
*A. J. Wright c Felton b Capel	11	– c Felton b Thomas	4
P. Bainbridge c Ripley b Penberthy	19	– c Felton b Capel	45
C. W. J. Athey lbw b Capel	79	– not out	88
M. W. Alleyne c Cook b Penberthy	256	– lbw b Ambrose	38
K. M. Curran c Ripley b Williams	19	– b Penberthy	19
J. W. Lloyds b Cook	35	– not out	16
†R. C. J. Williams not out	35		
C. A. Walsh c Penberthy b Cook	31		
D. V. Lawrence c Bailey b Penberthy	3		
M. C. J. Ball c and b Cook	4		
B 2, l-b 21, w 1, n-b 1	25	B 5, l-b 9	14
1/10 2/33 3/47 4/246 5/297 6/390 7/472 8/511 9/517	521	1/10 2/54 3/75 4/163 5/220 (5 wkts dec.)	246

Bonus points – Gloucestershire 3, Northamptonshire 1 (Score at 100 overs: 289-4).

Bowling: *First Innings*—Ambrose 27–5–77–1; Thomas 19–6–58–0; Capel 28–5–90–2; Penberthy 20–1–83–3; Cook 28–5–97–3; Williams 33–5–73–1; Bailey 3–0–20–0. *Second Innings*—Ambrose 16–7–35–2; Thomas 13–2–59–1; Penberthy 11–1–51–1; Capel 8–2–16–1; Cook 17–1–58–0; Williams 5–0–13–0.

Northamptonshire

A. Fordham st Williams b Bainbridge	64	– lbw b Lawrence	41
N. A. Felton b Bainbridge	41	– c Lloyds b Walsh	15
*W. Larkins c Williams b Lawrence	36	– b Walsh	1
R. J. Bailey c Hodgson b Lawrence	105	– c Wright b Walsh	4
D. J. Capel b Lawrence	38	– c Ball b Walsh	2
R. G. Williams b Walsh	1	– b Curran	15
A. L. Penberthy c Hodgson b Alleyne	28	– c Williams b Curran	18
†D. Ripley lbw b Curran	34	– not out	41
J. G. Thomas b Curran	0	– b Lloyds	5
C. E. L. Ambrose lbw b Lawrence	10	– st Williams b Lloyds	18
N. G. B. Cook not out	0	– c Wright b Lawrence	11
B 11, l-b 8, w 6, n-b 20	45	B 8, l-b 8, w 4, n-b 17	37
1/99 2/133 3/174 4/318 5/320 6/320 7/385 8/385 9/388	402	1/53 2/54 3/63 4/71 5/71 6/101 7/114 8/123 9/179	208

Bonus points – Northamptonshire 4, Gloucestershire 3 (Score at 100 overs: 385-7).

Bowling: *First Innings*—Walsh 18–3–63–1; Lawrence 24.5–2–90–4; Curran 22–2–68–2; Ball 6–1–35–0; Bainbridge 12–1–38–2; Alleyne 11–4–36–1; Lloyds 12–2–53–0. *Second Innings*—Walsh 19–3–101–4; Curran 7–1–17–2; Lawrence 13.1–1–53–2; Lloyds 8–1–21–2.

Umpires: P. J. Eele and K. E. Palmer.

NORTHAMPTONSHIRE v ESSEX

At Northampton, August 29, 30, 31. Drawn. Northamptonshire 7 pts, Essex 5 pts. Toss: Essex. Anxious for a victory in their quest for Championship honours, Essex were thwarted by another docile Northampton pitch on which 1,285 runs were scored in three innings for the loss of only seventeen wickets. The match began in controversial fashion, with Davis showing blatant dissent at umpire Lyons's decision when his appeal for leg-before against Gooch was turned down in the first over. The West Indian bowler was subsequently fined heavily by the club, and Gooch went on to dominate the home attack for four and a half hours (225 balls), hitting a six and 31 fours. However, this achievement was put in the shade as Northamptonshire beat their 76-year-old county record total in first-class cricket, only to surpass the new figure nine days later at Chelmsford. Larkins, in five and a half hours, survived four chances to register two sixes and 27 fours in his third double-hundred, while both Bailey (three sixes, ten fours) and Lamb (one six, 26 fours) completed centuries before the declaration came with five hours left for play. Any possibility of a result was soon discounted as Gooch (25 fours) passed the three-figure mark for the second time in the match, he and Stephenson becoming only the third pair ever to post a double-hundred opening stand in each innings of a first-class game.

Close of play: First day, Northamptonshire 18-1 (A. Fordham 11*, D. Ripley 5*); Second day, Northamptonshire 515-5 (A. J. Lamb 101*, R. G. Williams 1*).

Essex

*G. A. Gooch c and b Williams	174	– c Lamb b Bailey	126
J. P. Stephenson b Penberthy	76	– c Davis b Thomas	82
P. J. Prichard c Fordham b Williams	22	– not out	29
M. E. Waugh b Davis	1	– b Penberthy	16
N. Hussain not out	30	– b Penberthy	3
†M. A. Garnham lbw b Davis	1	– not out	23
D. R. Pringle lbw b Williams	1		
N. A. Foster c Fordham b Williams	50		
B 5, l-b 12, w 1, n-b 17	35	L-b 14, w 1, n-b 9	24
1/227 2/300 3/301 4/308 5/310 6/313 7/390 (7 wkts dec.)	390	1/220 2/231 3/254 4/258 (4 wkts dec.)	303

M. C. Ilott, P. M. Such and J. H. Childs did not bat.

Bonus points – Essex 4, Northamptonshire 3.

Bowling: *First Innings*—Davis 24–1–76–2; Robinson 14–0–75–0; Thomas 13–2–60–0; Penberthy 20–4–59–1; Williams 26.4–8–99–4; Bailey 1–0–4–0. *Second Innings*—Davis 5–0–37–0; Robinson 15–0–69–0; Thomas 14–3–49–1; Penberthy 14–1–67–2; Bailey 16–4–59–1; Williams 4–1–8–0; Felton 1–1–0–0.

Northamptonshire

A. Fordham lbw b Foster	16
N. A. Felton c Stephenson b Foster	0
†D. Ripley c Garnham b Waugh	50
W. Larkins c Waugh b Stephenson	207
R. J. Bailey lbw b Pringle	108
*A. J. Lamb c Prichard b Such	134
R. G. Williams not out	21
A. L. Penberthy not out	15
B 14, l-b 21, n-b 6	41
1/9 2/45 3/94 4/303 5/514 6/561 (6 wkts dec.)	592

J. G. Thomas, W. W. Davis and M. A. Robinson did not bat.

Bonus points – Northamptonshire 4, Essex 1 (Score at 100 overs: 392-4).

Bowling: Foster 31–6–115–2; Ilott 27–4–115–0; Pringle 14–2–46–1; Waugh 19–1–96–1; Childs 14–4–46–0; Such 15–1–57–1; Stephenson 9–1–40–1; Gooch 6–0–42–0.

Umpires: D. J. Constant and K. J. Lyons.

At Chelmsford, September 7, 8, 9, 10. NORTHAMPTONSHIRE beat ESSEX by 276 runs.

At Leicester, September 12, 13, 14, 15. NORTHAMPTONSHIRE beat LEICESTERSHIRE by 171 runs.

NOTTINGHAMSHIRE

President: 1990 – J. W. Baddiley
Chairman: C. W. Gillott
Chairman, Cricket Committee: R. T. Simpson
General Manager/Secretary: B. Robson
County Cricket Ground, Trent Bridge,
Nottingham NG2 6AG
(Telephone: 0602-821525)
Cricket Manager: 1990 – K. A. Taylor
1991 – J. D. Birch
Captain: R. T. Robinson

Nottinghamshire's fortunes underwent such a dramatic about-turn during 1990 that a season for which expectations were so high at one point ended in bitter disappointment. Where only a few months earlier there had been optimism, and talk of building on the 1989 Benson and Hedges Cup success, despondency settled on Trent Bridge. Only a top-four place in the Refuge Assurance League, to qualify for the Refuge Assurance Cup, held back the gloom as Nottinghamshire suffered seven defeats in their last eleven Britannic Assurance Championship games and plummeted to thirteenth, their lowest position for seven years.

At the beginning of June, however, the story had been quite different. Nottinghamshire, with three consecutive wins behind them, sat proudly atop the Championship table and were within one step of carrying their defence of the Benson and Hedges trophy back to Lord's. They were bubbling with confidence after eight wins in their last nine games in all cricket. Even more encouraging, in a summer in which a high proportion of Championship victories would be achieved by teams successfully chasing targets – an aspect of their game for which they had not previously been noted – Nottinghamshire had indicated that they were capable of meeting such challenges.

Yet it was the frailty of the Nottinghamshire batting that was responsible for the complexion of their season changing so drastically. All too often, a lack of application and consistency in the first innings gave their opponents the opportunity to seize the initiative, and only occasionally were Nottinghamshire able to regain it. Paul Pollard, who had made such an impression in 1989, experienced a traumatic time in 1990 and played just fourteen games of first-team cricket, while Derek Randall was hampered by injury all summer: this had an unsettling effect on a batting line-up which, on paper at least, looked particularly strong. Both Chris Broad and Tim Robinson, the captain, were available throughout the season, and Paul Johnson began the season as though determined to prove a point.

Broad, without any doubt, had an outstanding summer. He hit the first double-hundred of his career, 227 not out against Kent at Tunbridge Wells, passed 2,000 runs in a season for the first time, despite playing only in Championship matches, and his nine hundreds equalled the county record shared by W. W. Whysall and M. J. Harris, who accomplished the feat in 1928 and 1971 respectively. Rarely did a bad ball go unpunished; though considering Broad's reputation as a strong leg-side player, it was astonishing how many bowlers fed his strength with inviting deliveries. Robinson also hit a double-hundred, against Yorkshire, and finished the season with a flourish after experiencing a remarkable series of first-innings failures. Including the match in which Nottinghamshire forfeited, he did not reach double figures in nine successive first innings. Happily, the introduction of the Second Eleven captain, John Birch, to help with the running of the side towards the end of the season took a lot of weight off the captain's shoulders, and the benefit was seen in the form Robinson produced late on.

Johnson was anxious to show that he had matured from being merely a promising young player to an established middle-order batsman. For a time he succeeded, especially with his match-winning hundreds against Northamptonshire and Yorkshire. But old habits die hard, and there were too many occasions later in the season when he failed to turn sparkling cameos into more substantial contributions.

Nottinghamshire were no different from many other counties in that their bowlers, having been pampered for so long with "result" pitches, found the going considerably tougher as the balance swung in favour of batsmen. Given the change in conditions, the form of Andy Pick was most pleasing. Had his season been less disrupted by injury, the fast bowler might easily have figured among the country's leading wicket-takers. As it was, he made a good enough impression to earn selection for the England A tour to Pakistan in the winter. Franklyn Stephenson was troubled by fitness problems and never looked like reproducing his bowling form of the previous two summers. But his batting showed signs of greater consistency after a disappointing season in 1989.

An all-rounder who did excel was Kevin Evans. The 26-year-old's development into a reliable performer with bat and ball was rewarded when he was presented with his county cap, an honour also bestowed upon the left-arm spinner, Andy Afford. In Afford's case, the recognition was based on previous success rather than current performances, for his 38 Championship wickets cost him more than 47 runs apiece. With the county's most experienced bowler, Eddie Hemmings, required by England throughout the summer, Kevin Cooper, the other senior bowler, had to carry the heaviest workload – and this in his benefit year.

On the whole, Nottinghamshire could be satisfied with their record in the limited-overs competitions, despite going out in the second round of the NatWest Bank Trophy to the eventual finalists, Northamptonshire. In the Sunday League and especially the Benson and Hedges Cup, the excellent batting of Robinson was the chief reason for their progressing so far, but the side could not rise to the occasion in the semi-finals of the Benson and Hedges and Refuge Assurance cups.

As for resolving what went wrong in the Championship, Nottinghamshire wasted no time in taking steps towards an improvement. Birch was appointed cricket manager as successor to the long-serving Ken Taylor, and the club looked to strengthen the staff with players of proven calibre. Just how much Nottinghamshire owe Taylor for leading them out of the doldrums in his thirteen years as manager is incalculable: they were seventeenth in the Championship when he took over and had never won a limited-overs trophy. All that has changed, and now Birch has to try to retain the club's hard-won status at the forefront of English cricket. – Nick Lucy.

NOTTINGHAMSHIRE 1990

[*Bill Smith*

Back row: P. Johnson, R. A. Pick, M. Newell, J. A. Afford, K. E. Cooper, D. J. R. Martindale, B. C. Broad. *Front row:* E. E. Hemmings, R. T. Robinson (*captain*), B. N. French, F. D. Stephenson. *Insets:* P. R. Pollard, C. W. Scott, D. W. Randall, K. Saxelby, M. Saxelby, J. D. Birch, K. P. Evans.

NOTTINGHAMSHIRE RESULTS

All first-class matches – Played 25: Won 4, Lost 8, Drawn 13.
County Championship matches – Played 22: Won 4, Lost 8, Drawn 10.
Bonus points – Batting 51, Bowling 58.
Competition placings – Britannic Assurance County Championship, 13th equal; NatWest Bank Trophy, 2nd round; Benson and Hedges Cup, s-f; Refuge Assurance League, 4th; Refuge Assurance Cup, s-f.

BRITANNIC ASSURANCE CHAMPIONSHIP AVERAGES

BATTING

	Birthplace	*M*	*I*	*NO*	*R*	*HI*	*Avge*
‡B. C. Broad	*Bristol*	22	43	2	2,226	227*	54.29
‡K. P. Evans	*Calverton*	12	22	8	638	100*	45.57
‡R. T. Robinson	*Sutton-in-Ashfield*	22	43	5	1,693	220*	44.55
‡P. Johnson	*Newark*	19	36	2	1,294	165*	38.05
‡D. W. Randall	*Retford*	15	28	1	987	178	36.55
‡M. Newell	*Blackburn*	12	23	1	653	89*	29.68
D. J. R. Martindale	*Harrogate*	14	24	3	559	108*	26.61
‡F. D. Stephenson	*St James, Barbados*	19	33	6	715	121	26.48
P. R. Pollard	*Nottingham*	5	10	0	254	72	25.40
M. Saxelby	*Worksop*	7	13	3	232	51	23.20
‡E. E. Hemmings	*Leamington Spa*	11	14	4	230	83	23.00
‡R. A. Pick	*Nottingham*	14	15	6	199	35	22.11
‡B. N. French	*Warsop*	22	34	9	506	105*	20.24
G. W. Mike	*Nottingham*	3	5	1	45	18*	11.25
‡K. E. Cooper	*Hucknall*	20	25	5	217	35*	10.85
‡K. Saxelby	*Worksop*	4	6	0	42	20	7.00
‡J. A. Afford	*Crowland*	19	21	7	14	5	1.00

Also batted: R. J. Evans (*Calverton*) (1 match) 11, 4; M. G. Field-Buss (*Mtarfa, Malta*) (1 match) 0, 0.

* *Signifies not out.* ‡ *Denotes county cap.*

The following played a total of 21 three-figure innings for Nottinghamshire in County Championship matches – B. C. Broad 9, R. T. Robinson 4, P. Johnson 2, D. W. Randall 2, K. P. Evans 1, B. N. French 1, D. J. R. Martindale 1, F. D. Stephenson 1.

BOWLING

	O	*M*	*R*	*W*	*BB*	*5W/i*	*Avge*
R. A. Pick	443.5	70	1,507	48	7-128	1	31.39
F. D. Stephenson	592.4	90	2,047	53	6-84	2	38.62
E. E. Hemmings	443.3	127	1,175	30	5-99	1	39.16
K. P. Evans	292	60	1,085	27	4-57	0	40.18
K. E. Cooper	667.4	141	2,105	51	5-56	3	41.27
J. A. Afford	627	186	1,804	38	4-137	0	47.47

Also bowled: M. G. Field-Buss 10–2–43–0; G. W. Mike 54.2–9–230–2; M. Newell 2.2–0–13–0; K. Saxelby 89–19–309–7; M. Saxelby 56.4–8–260–3.

Wicket-keeper: B. N. French 46 ct, 11 st.

Leading Fielder: D. W. Randall 14.

NOTTINGHAMSHIRE v DERBYSHIRE

At Nottingham, April 26, 27, 28, 30. Drawn. Nottinghamshire 5 pts, Derbyshire 3 pts. Toss: Nottinghamshire. Broad dominated a showery first day, on which there were four breaks for rain, and remained undefeated at the close after giving a sound display. On the second morning however, he looked less comfortable and soon lost his wicket, having faced 349 balls and having hit 22 fours in his highest score. Runs came slowly in Derbyshire's reply. They had managed only 123 in 54 overs by the close, and good bowling by Hemmings and Afford kept the run-rate low on the Saturday. With just 41 runs between the two sides after the first innings, it looked as if Monday's play would be of little consequence, and so it turned out. Robinson set the visitors 267 off a minimum of 52 overs, but once the openers were out, no attempt was made to chase the target.

Close of play: First day, Nottinghamshire 295-4 (B. C. Broad 171*, F. D. Stephenson 2*); Second day, Derbyshire 123-2 (J. E. Morris 45*, A. P. Kuiper 0*); Third day, Nottinghamshire 47-1 (P. R. Pollard 25*, R. T. Robinson 13*).

Nottinghamshire

B. C. Broad c Miller b Base	180	– c Bowler b Base	5
P. R. Pollard c Bowler b Mortensen	40	– lbw b Mortensen	27
*R. T. Robinson b Kuiper	11	– b Barnett	86
P. Johnson c Bowler b Warner	45	– b Barnett	54
D. W. Randall c Brown b Barnett	6	– c and b Barnett	23
F. D. Stephenson c sub b Warner	18	– b Miller	12
†B. N. French c Brown b Mortensen	25	– not out	1
E. E. Hemmings c Adams b Mortensen	15		
K. E. Cooper b Miller	12		
R. A. Pick not out	14		
J. A. Afford c Bowler b Mortensen	2		
B 4, l-b 12, w 4, n-b 13	33	B 5, l-b 7, w 3, n-b 2	17
1/127 2/153 3/266 4/293 5/308 6/323 7/366 8/378 9/384	401	1/12 2/62 3/180 4/195 5/221 6/225 (6 wkts dec.)	225

Bonus points – Nottinghamshire 3, Derbyshire 1 (Score at 100 overs: 282-3).

Bowling: *First Innings*—Mortensen 26.5–6–67–4; Base 28–5–89–1; Warner 30–6–78–2; Kuiper 13–2–60–1; Miller 45–16–84–1; Barnett 2–0–7–1. *Second Innings*—Base 12.3–2–56–1; Warner 4–1–14–0; Miller 18–3–60–1; Barnett 17–2–49–3; Kuiper 7–2–20–0; Mortensen 7–3–14–1.

Derbyshire

†P. D. Bowler c Broad b Pick	20	– lbw b Afford	11
A. M. Brown c Johnson b Cooper	54	– c Cooper b Hemmings	20
J. E. Morris lbw b Cooper	66	– not out	16
A. P. Kuiper c Randall b Afford	25	– c Pollard b Afford	10
C. J. Adams c French b Cooper	3	– not out	11
B. Roberts st French b Hemmings	46		
*K. J. Barnett c Johnson b Hemmings	73		
G. Miller b Hemmings	10		
A. E. Warner lbw b Pick	11		
S. J. Base st French b Afford	34		
O. H. Mortensen not out	5		
L-b 9, n-b 4	13	B 2, l-b 4, n-b 1	7
1/50 2/122 3/170 4/170 5/175 6/280 7/299 8/320 9/326	360	1/32 2/34 3/53 (3 wkts)	75

Bonus points – Derbyshire 2, Nottinghamshire 2 (Score at 100 overs: 224-5).

Bowling: *First Innings*—Stephenson 27–7–92–0; Cooper 35–9–75–3; Pick 25–4–81–2; Hemmings 39–17–64–3; Afford 19.5–8–39–2. *Second Innings*—Stephenson 4–0–9–0; Cooper 6–1–17–0; Afford 22–17–21–2; Hemmings 21–12–22–1.

Umpires: B. J. Meyer and D. O. Oslear.

At Worcester, May 3, 4, 5, 7. NOTTINGHAMSHIRE lost to WORCESTERSHIRE by an innings and 6 runs.

At Leicester, May 15, 16, 17. NOTTINGHAMSHIRE beat LEICESTERSHIRE by five wickets.

At Birmingham, May 19, 21, 22. NOTTINGHAMSHIRE beat WARWICKSHIRE by 5 runs.

NOTTINGHAMSHIRE v NORTHAMPTONSHIRE

At Nottingham, May 23, 24, 25. Nottinghamshire won by eight wickets. Nottinghamshire 22 pts, Northamptonshire 8 pts. Toss: Northamptonshire. The Northamptonshire first innings occupied the whole of the first day, with Penberthy putting the run-out of Bailey and an early chance to second slip behind him to remain unbeaten at the close. He and the more adventurous Ripley added 95 for the seventh wicket, and were instrumental in Northamptonshire's achieving four batting points. Despite losing Martindale cheaply, Nottinghamshire reached 150 by lunch on the second morning, but with wickets falling regularly, they only just obtained three batting points. In the evening Fordham and Felton hit up a century partnership for Northamptonshire's first wicket, and when the declaration came at lunch next day Felton, with nine fours and a six in 214 balls, had gone on to his best score for his new county. As Nottinghamshire set out to get 341 in a minimum of 70 overs, Broad was run out off the first ball. By tea, however, they were 102 for two off 32 overs, and in the last session Johnson attacked the bowlers with increasing confidence, reaching 100 in 88 minutes. His career-best 165 not out from 120 balls contained 24 fours and a six, and his unbroken partnership of 249 with Martindale, occupying 35 overs, saw Nottinghamshire to victory with 5.2 overs in hand.

Close of play: First day, Northamptonshire 325; Second day, Northamptonshire 117-0 (A. Fordham 60*, N. A. Felton 47*).

Northamptonshire

	First innings		Second innings	
A. Fordham c Johnson b Pick	21	–	c French b Pick	74
N. A. Felton lbw b Pick	11	–	not out	119
*R. J. Bailey run out	65	–	not out	54
G. Cook b Pick	49			
D. J. Capel c Randall b Cooper	4			
A. L. Penberthy not out	67			
J. G. Thomas c French b Afford	5			
†D. Ripley st French b Afford	55			
W. W. Davis b Cooper	4			
A. R. Roberts b Afford	5			
J. W. Govan b Saxelby	17			
L-b 12, n-b 10	22		B 6, l-b 11, n-b 1	18
1/24 2/47 3/150 4/157 5/170 6/178 7/273 8/278 9/301	325		1/147 (1 wkt dec.)	265

Bonus points – Northamptonshire 4, Nottinghamshire 3 (Score at 100 overs: 300-8).

Bowling: *First Innings*—Stephenson 16–5–23–0; Cooper 25–6–65–2; Pick 19–1–64–3; Saxelby 13.4–1–71–1; Afford 33–6–90–3. *Second Innings*—Pick 17–4–40–1; Cooper 22–1–59–0; Stephenson 13–0–52–0; Afford 17–4–74–0; Saxelby 5–1–23–0.

Nottinghamshire

B. C. Broad b Govan	49	– run out	0
D. J. R. Martindale c Fordham b Thomas	0	– not out	108
*R. T. Robinson b Capel	30	– lbw b Davis	56
P. Johnson c Thomas b Govan	27	– not out	165
D. W. Randall run out	37		
M. Saxelby b Penberthy	42		
F. D. Stephenson b Roberts	11		
†B. N. French c and b Penberthy	33		
K. E. Cooper c Ripley b Penberthy	4		
R. A. Pick c Penberthy b Davis	3		
J. A. Afford not out	0		
L-b 3, w 2, n-b 9	14	B 4, l-b 4, w 1, n-b 6	15
1/6 2/82 3/94 4/150 5/153 6/176 7/233 8/237 9/246	250	1/0 2/95	(2 wkts) 344

Bonus points – Nottinghamshire 3, Northamptonshire 4.

Bowling: *First Innings*—Davis 13–1–50–1; Thomas 7–1–41–1; Govan 13–0–56–2; Capel 14–2–45–1; Penberthy 6–0–28–3; Roberts 15–8–27–1. *Second Innings*—Davis 14.4–1–63–1; Thomas 12–1–54–0; Capel 13–1–60–0; Penberthy 10–1–57–0; Roberts 9–0–57–0; Govan 6–0–45–0.

Umpires: J. W. Holder and A. G. T. Whitehead.

At Derby, May 26, 27, 28. NOTTINGHAMSHIRE drew with DERBYSHIRE.

At Tunbridge Wells, June 2, 4, 5. NOTTINGHAMSHIRE drew with KENT.

At Oxford, June 6, 7, 8. NOTTINGHAMSHIRE drew with OXFORD UNIVERSITY.

At Cambridge, June 16, 18, 19. NOTTINGHAMSHIRE drew with CAMBRIDGE UNIVERSITY.

NOTTINGHAMSHIRE v SURREY

At Nottingham, June 20, 21, 22. Drawn. Nottinghamshire 1 pt, Surrey 8 pts. Toss: Surrey. The miserable conditions which were a feature of June continued on the first day, when Nottinghamshire, put in to bat, collapsed to 87 for seven by lunch. Only Randall of the specialist batsmen remained, and with his dismissal soon after the resumption, adjudged caught behind much to the batsman's displeasure, went Nottinghamshire's resistance. Bicknell was the chief destroyer, his five wickets including four for 7 in 24 balls and first-ball dismissals for Martindale, Field-Buss and Saxelby. Surrey lost two cheap wickets, but by the time the bad weather ended play they had already moved ahead. Next morning Ward hit 95 runs before lunch, and his Championship-best 154 not out, coming in 245 minutes and containing four sixes and nineteen fours, put Surrey in a strong position, despite the loss of half the second day to rain. Nottinghamshire batted much better on the final day, however, with Robinson and Johnson adding 141 for the third wicket, and although wickets fell quickly at the end, Surrey were left with only six overs in which to score 105. It was a challenge they declined.

Close of play: First day, Surrey 102-2 (R. I. Alikhan 39*, D. M. Ward 28*); Second day, Surrey 303-3 (D. M. Ward 154*, M. A. Lynch 18*).

Nottinghamshire

B. C. Broad c Thorpe b Robinson	30 – b Medlycott	30
D. J. R. Martindale lbw b Bicknell	0 – b Medlycott	33
*R. T. Robinson lbw b Waqar Younis	5 – lbw b Medlycott	72
P. Johnson b Murphy	10 – b Medlycott	78
D. W. Randall c Ward b Bicknell	24 – c Ward b Bicknell	26
F. D. Stephenson b Waqar Younis	9 – c and b Medlycott	2
†B. N. French b Waqar Younis	0 – not out	14
M. G. Field-Buss lbw b Bicknell	0 – c Alikhan b Medlycott	0
K. E. Cooper c Ward b Bicknell	7 – lbw b Bicknell	1
K. Saxelby c Thorpe b Bicknell	0 – lbw b Medlycott	8
J. A. Afford not out	0 – lbw b Bicknell	0
B 1, l-b 13, w 1	15 B 26, l-b 14, w 3	43
1/5 2/22 3/54 4/54 5/73 6/79 7/80 8/97 9/97	100 1/76 2/77 3/218 4/263 5/269 6/287 7/292 8/293 9/306	307

Bonus points – Surrey 4.

Bowling: *First Innings*—Waqar Younis 15–3–29–3; Bicknell 14.2–4–34–5; Murphy 4–1–9–1; Robinson 4–2–14–1. *Second Innings*—Waqar Younis 22–3–86–0; Bicknell 19.3–6–46–3; Murphy 9–2–34–0; Medlycott 33–4–92–7; Greig 1–0–9–0.

Surrey

R. I. Alikhan c Robinson b Stephenson	88
G. S. Clinton lbw b Stephenson	1
G. P. Thorpe c Randall b Afford	20
†D. M. Ward not out	154
M. A. Lynch not out	18
B 5, l-b 11, n-b 6	22
1/3 2/40 3/262 (3 wkts dec.)	303

*I. A. Greig, K. T. Medlycott, J. D. Robinson, M. P. Bicknell, Waqar Younis and A. J. Murphy did not bat.

Bonus points – Surrey 4, Nottinghamshire 1.

Bowling: Stephenson 27.5–7–66–2; Cooper 25–8–52–0; Saxelby 14–5–42–0; Afford 22–3–84–1; Field-Buss 10–2–43–0.

Umpires: J. C. Balderstone and J. H. Hampshire.

NOTTINGHAMSHIRE v LEICESTERSHIRE

At Nottingham, June 30, July 2, 3. Drawn. Nottinghamshire 5 pts, Leicestershire 6 pts. Toss: Leicestershire. The same damp conditions prevailed as in the previous match, and again Nottinghamshire, invited to bat, fell apart. In between two stoppages for rain, aggressive bowling by Benjamin and Agnew reduced them to 109 for six before French joined Stephenson and 77 runs were added for the seventh wicket. Stephenson, batting responsibly but without inhibition, reached his hundred before the close, and on Monday he went on to his highest score for the county, batting in all for 245 minutes and hitting sixteen fours. With Leicestershire's runs coming too slowly, Briers declared in arrears and on the final morning fed Nottinghamshire runs until Robinson set a target of 271 off a minimum of 48 overs. Leicestershire began badly, but some vigorous batting by Whitaker, Potter and Benson left them needing 76 off eleven overs. However, Cooper and Stephenson took four wickets, and Leicestershire's last pair had 21 balls to face to save the match. Owing to a dropped catch, they survived.

Close of play: First day, Nottinghamshire 241-8 (F. D. Stephenson 105*, R. A. Pick 0*); Second day, Nottinghamshire 21-0 (B. C. Broad 14*, M. Newell 6*).

Nottinghamshire

B. C. Broad lbw b Benjamin	40	– not out	112
M. Newell lbw b Benjamin	7	– lbw b Potter	26
*R. T. Robinson lbw b Agnew	0	– not out	69
P. Johnson c Benson b Benjamin	4		
D. J. R. Martindale c Nixon b Benjamin	7		
F. D. Stephenson c Lewis b Willey	121		
E. E. Hemmings c Nixon b Agnew	17		
†B. N. French c Nixon b Mullally	27		
K. E. Cooper c Benson b Benjamin	29		
R. A. Pick c Nixon b Mullally	34		
J. A. Afford not out	0		
L-b 5, w 1	6	B 3, l-b 4	7
1/13 2/16 3/27 4/47 5/64 6/109 7/186 8/230 9/292	292	1/79	(1 wkt dec.) 214

Bonus points – Nottinghamshire 3, Leicestershire 4.

Bowling: *First Innings*—Benjamin 32–5–109–5; Agnew 27–5–97–2; Lewis 6–1–23–0; Mullally 17–1–43–2; Willey 8.4–3–15–1. *Second Innings*—Lewis 14–5–28–0; Benjamin 3–0–12–0; Willey 10–3–24–0; Mullally 7–1–17–0; Potter 18–0–78–1; Benson 11–0–43–0; Boon 0.5–0–5–0.

Leicestershire

T. J. Boon st French b Afford	40	– lbw b Cooper	8
*N. E. Briers c French b Stephenson	30	– c Johnson b Cooper	8
J. J. Whitaker c Cooper b Hemmings	43	– c French b Stephenson	83
P. Willey not out	73	– c Broad b Afford	2
L. Potter lbw b Cooper	0	– (6) c and b Cooper	48
J. D. R. Benson c Afford b Cooper	11	– (7) c French b Cooper	62
C. C. Lewis not out	28	– (5) run out	3
W. K. M. Benjamin (did not bat)		– lbw b Cooper	0
†P. A. Nixon (did not bat)		– lbw b Stephenson	0
J. P. Agnew (did not bat)		– not out	8
A. D. Mullally (did not bat)		– not out	2
B 3, l-b 6, n-b 2	11	B 10, l-b 6, n-b 2	18
1/56 2/94 3/146 4/150 5/170	(5 wkts dec.) 236	1/17 2/20 3/42 4/49 5/195 6/230 7/232 8/232 9/232	(9 wkts) 242

Bonus points – Leicestershire 2, Nottinghamshire 2.

In the second innings J. J. Whitaker, when 66, retired hurt at 118 and resumed at 195.

Bowling: *First Innings*—Stephenson 16–4–53–1; Pick 14–1–52–0; Cooper 21–6–47–2; Hemmings 13–3–52–1; Afford 11–4–23–1. *Second Innings*—Stephenson 15–5–36–2; Pick 2–0–12–0; Cooper 15–2–56–5; Afford 15–4–62–1; Hemmings 14–1–60–0.

Umpires: R. Julian and D. S. Thompsett.

At Scarborough, July 4, 5, 6. NOTTINGHAMSHIRE beat YORKSHIRE by five wickets.

NOTTINGHAMSHIRE v SUSSEX

At Nottingham, July 7, 9, 10. Drawn. Nottinghamshire 5 pts, Sussex 8 pts. Toss: Nottinghamshire. Pick quickly removed Lenham and Gould when Sussex were put in on an overcast day. Hall, however, batted soundly and was nearing his century when rain arrived to end Saturday's play. On Monday he went on to reach 125, his innings of 267 minutes containing eighteen fours, and Sussex collected full batting points. Although the weather was much improved, Nottinghamshire fared poorly, the only landmark being Randall's 20,000th first-class run for his county, and they narrowly avoided the follow-on. Sussex batted until lunch on the third day, then set Nottinghamshire 347 off 68 overs. Newell, who batted for 166 minutes, helped Robinson to add 111 for the second wicket; later Evans and French were content to bat out time.

Close of play: First day, Sussex 219-5 (J. W. Hall 96*, A. I. C. Dodemaide 25*); Second day, Sussex 36-0 (N. J. Lenham 24*, J. W. Hall 11*).

Sussex

First innings		Second innings	
N. J. Lenham c French b Pick	0	– c French b Pick	27
J. W. Hall b Cooper	125	– not out	59
I. J. Gould c Newell b Pick	4		
A. P. Wells c French b Evans	23	– (3) c and b Saxelby	25
M. P. Speight lbw b Pick	55	– (4) c Broad b Afford	30
*C. M. Wells c Evans b Saxelby	5	– (5) c Saxelby b Afford	44
A. I. C. Dodemaide c French b Evans	72	– (6) c and b Pick	7
†P. Moores c Johnson b Evans	22	– (7) not out	7
A. C. S. Pigott lbw b Cooper	3		
I. D. K. Salisbury not out	0		
L-b 9, w 1, n-b 3	13	L-b 9, n-b 1	10
1/0 2/4 3/48 4/135 5/146 6/279 7/311 8/320 9/322 (9 wkts dec.)	322	1/43 2/80 3/136 4/190 5/197 (5 wkts dec.)	209

R. A. Bunting did not bat.

Bonus points – Sussex 4, Nottinghamshire 4.

Bowling: *First Innings*—Pick 21–5–49–3; Saxelby 14–3–44–1; Cooper 19.4–2–79–2; Evans 13–2–69–3; Afford 19–2–72–0. *Second Innings*—Pick 13–1–40–2; Cooper 10–1–37–0; Evans 8–2–47–0; Afford 9–2–47–2; Saxelby 10–2–29–1.

Nottinghamshire

First innings		Second innings	
B. C. Broad c Moores b Pigott	12	– b Dodemaide	34
M. Newell c Salisbury b Pigott	8	– b C. M. Wells	85
*R. T. Robinson c Gould b Pigott	6	– c Pigott b C. M. Wells	52
P. Johnson c Salisbury b Dodemaide	68	– c Speight b C. M. Wells	14
D. W. Randall c Moores b C. M. Wells	34	– lbw b Salisbury	9
K. P. Evans c Salisbury b Dodemaide	29	– not out	21
†B. N. French c Moores b Dodemaide	5	– not out	17
K. E. Cooper c Gould b Salisbury	0		
R. A. Pick not out	13		
K. Saxelby b Bunting	5		
J. A. Afford b Bunting	0		
L-b 4, w 1	5	L-b 7, w 4, n-b 1	12
1/14 2/23 3/34 4/111 5/147 6/166 7/166 8/166 9/185	185	1/64 2/175 3/186 4/201 5/201 (5 wkts)	244

Bonus points – Nottinghamshire 1, Sussex 4.

Bowling: *First Innings*—Pigott 14–4–47–3; Dodemaide 15–4–44–3; Bunting 13–3–42–2; C. M. Wells 9–1–20–1; Salisbury 9–2–28–1. *Second Innings*—Pigott 9–2–18–0; Dodemaide 14–4–39–1; Bunting 9–0–46–0; Salisbury 23–6–86–1; C. M. Wells 14–3–48–3.

Umpires: H. D. Bird and K. E. Palmer.

At Portsmouth, July 18, 19, 20. NOTTINGHAMSHIRE lost to HAMPSHIRE by eight wickets.

At Southport, July 25, 26, 27. NOTTINGHAMSHIRE lost to LANCASHIRE by seven wickets.

NOTTINGHAMSHIRE v MIDDLESEX

At Nottingham, July 28, 30, 31. Drawn. Nottinghamshire 7 pts, Middlesex 4 pts. Toss: Nottinghamshire. Only Broad and Randall of the Nottinghamshire batsmen took advantage of Robinson's decision to bat first. But while Broad hit fourteen fours in his 140 (264 balls), Randall was more subdued over approximately three hours. Nevertheless, with Middlesex struggling against the seam bowlers on the second day, the home side gathered a substantial lead. Stephenson and Evans hit out before lunch on the last morning, and Robinson's declaration set Middlesex 354 in a minimum of 70 overs. They made a dreadful start, but Gatting was in fine form, and helped first by Ramprakash and then Brown he took the total to 244. At this point Stephenson bowled Brown, and he then bowled so accurately that the remaining batsmen were unable to maintain the scoring-rate. Gatting was unbeaten at the end with 169, having faced 205 balls in four and a quarter hours and hit fifteen fours and a six.

Close of play: First day, Nottinghamshire 336-8 (K. P. Evans 28*, K. E. Cooper 3*); Second day, Nottinghamshire 87-3 (P. R. Pollard 34*, D. W. Randall 17*).

Nottinghamshire

B. C. Broad	lbw b Cowans	140	b Tufnell	25
P. R. Pollard	c Brown b Emburey	24	c Haynes b Tufnell	72
*R. T. Robinson	lbw b Cowans	5	(4) c Downton b Williams	2
P. Johnson	c Emburey b Cowans	30	(3) c and b Tufnell	5
D. W. Randall	b Emburey	70	b Cowans	56
F. D. Stephenson	c Downton b Tufnell	8	not out	44
K. P. Evans	not out	28	not out	24
†B. N. French	c Cowans b Emburey	4		
G. W. Mike	c Downton b Tufnell	9		
K. E. Cooper	not out	3		
	B 2, l-b 10, n-b 3	15	L-b 7, w 4, n-b 1	12
1/58 2/63 3/116 4/254 5/271 6/291 7/309 8/331	(8 wkts dec.)	336	1/57 2/63 3/66 4/156 5/171 (5 wkts dec.)	240

J. A. Afford did not bat.

Bonus points – Nottinghamshire 3, Middlesex 2 (Score at 100 overs: 296-6).

Bowling: *First Innings*—Williams 18–6–34–0; Cowans 22–3–80–3; Taylor 13–1–45–0; Emburey 18–0–61–3; Tufnell 39–5–104–2. *Second Innings*—Williams 15–4–46–1; Cowans 17–1–70–1; Taylor 6–0–15–0; Emburey 8–2–16–0; Tufnell 26–6–86–3.

Middlesex

D. L. Haynes	c Pollard b Cooper	21	c French b Cooper	0
M. A. Roseberry	c Mike b Evans	74	c Cooper b Stephenson	0
*M. W. Gatting	c French b Cooper	6	not out	169
M. R. Ramprakash	lbw b Stephenson	46	c Randall b Afford	52
K. R. Brown	c Johnson b Stephenson	4	b Stephenson	55
†P. R. Downton	b Cooper	16	(7) b Evans	20
J. E. Emburey	c Johnson b Cooper	0	(8) b Stephenson	10
N. F. Williams	lbw b Evans	14	(9) lbw b Stephenson	3
P. C. R. Tufnell	c Pollard b Evans	12	(10) not out	5
C. W. Taylor	b Cooper	13		
N. G. Cowans	not out	11	(6) lbw b Stephenson	0
	L-b 5, n-b 1	6	L-b 13, n-b 2	15
1/27 2/39 3/129 4/133 5/164 6/173 7/178 8/198 9/201		223	1/0 2/7 3/99 4/244 5/244 6/293 7/310 8/318 (8 wkts)	329

Bonus points – Middlesex 2, Nottinghamshire 4.

Bowling: *First Innings*—Stephenson 16–6–33–2; Cooper 25–6–108–5; Evans 18–4–54–3; Mike 6–3–12–0; Afford 5–1–11–0. *Second Innings*—Cooper 14–2–41–1; Stephenson 20.5–1–82–5; Evans 12–2–72–1; Afford 14–1–75–1; Mike 9–0–46–0.

Umpires: J. H. Hampshire and M. J. Kitchen.

At Southend, August 4, 6, 7. NOTTINGHAMSHIRE lost to ESSEX by ten wickets.

At Weston-super-Mare, August 8, 9, 10. NOTTINGHAMSHIRE drew with SOMERSET.

NOTTINGHAMSHIRE v GLAMORGAN

At Worksop, August 11, 13, 14. Glamorgan won by 238 runs. Glamorgan 22 pts, Nottinghamshire 7 pts. Toss: Glamorgan. The visiting batsmen enjoyed themselves on the first day. Morris (one six, fourteen fours) and Maynard added 164 for the third wicket, with Maynard needing just 112 balls for his 115 (one six, 21 fours), having hit 46 of his first fifty in boundaries. Then came Richards. The West Indian captain hit 127 off 136 balls, his third consecutive hundred, with fourteen fours and five sixes. Several of his strokes cleared the ground and landed in either the river or the canal. Broad (thirteen fours) and Robinson shared a century stand on Monday, and Martindale and Evans ensured full batting points for Nottinghamshire. However, the final day was one of humiliation for the home team. Unbeaten hundreds by Butcher (twenty fours) and Morris (a six and fourteen fours) left Nottinghamshire needing 351 off a minimum of 65 overs. Their batting fell apart, and though Newell fought against the tide until he was seventh out, the Welshmen strolled to victory with 35 overs to spare.

Close of play: First day, Nottinghamshire 1-0 (R. A. Pick 1*, M. Newell 0*); Second day, Glamorgan 76-0 (A. R. Butcher 41*, H. Morris 32*).

Glamorgan

*A. R. Butcher c Evans b Saxelby	13	– not out	121
H. Morris c French b Afford	110	– not out	102
P. A. Cottey c Broad b Pick	5		
M. P. Maynard b Afford	115		
I. V. A. Richards c Pick b Saxelby	127		
A. Dale c Johnson b Evans	7		
R. D. B. Croft run out	1		
†C. P. Metson c Cooper b Saxelby	29		
S. L. Watkin lbw b Saxelby	0		
S. Bastien not out	10		
M. Frost lbw b Cooper	0		
L-b 6, n-b 4	10	B 4, l-b 6, w 1, n-b 2	13
1/33 2/57 3/221 4/274 5/309 6/315 7/399 8/399 9/427	427	(no wkt dec.)	236

Bonus points – Glamorgan 4, Nottinghamshire 3 (Score at 100 overs: 399-8).

Bowling: *First Innings*—Pick 13–1–65–1; Saxelby 23–4–92–4; Cooper 21.2–4–95–1; Evans 18–3–69–1; Afford 29–4–100–2. *Second Innings*—Pick 13–1–55–0; Saxelby 12–1–47–0; Cooper 9–1–40–0; Afford 16–4–47–0; Evans 7–1–37–0.

Nottinghamshire

R. A. Pick b Bastien	11	– (9) c Cottey b Bastien	2
M. Newell c Metson b Bastien	10	– c Cottey b Bastien	42
B. C. Broad c Metson b Croft	98	– (1) c Metson b Watkin	10
*R. T. Robinson c Metson b Watkin	46	– (3) c Maynard b Frost	8
P. Johnson c Metson b Bastien	44	– (4) c Dale b Frost	12
D. J. R. Martindale not out	35	– (5) c Metson b Bastien	1
K. P. Evans not out	60	– (6) lbw b Bastien	26
†B. N. French (did not bat)		– (7) c Maynard b Croft	1
K. E. Cooper (did not bat)		– (8) b Bastien	2
K. Saxelby (did not bat)		– c Dale b Watkin	3
J. A. Afford (did not bat)		– not out	1
L-b 3, w 3, n-b 3	9	L-b 2, w 1, n-b 1	4
1/19 2/39 3/152 4/216 5/216 (5 wkts dec.)	313	1/18 2/28 3/42 4/55 5/99 6/100 7/102 8/104 9/107	112

Bonus points – Nottinghamshire 4, Glamorgan 2.

Bowling: *First Innings*—Watkin 19–2–79–1; Bastien 20–5–71–3; Frost 22–2–79–0; Croft 22–5–65–1; Dale 7–0–16–0. *Second Innings*—Watkin 10–1–45–2; Frost 7–0–32–2; Bastien 10–2–31–5; Croft 3–1–2–1.

Umpires: D. J. Constant and D. O. Oslear.

NOTTINGHAMSHIRE v GLOUCESTERSHIRE

At Nottingham, August 18, 20, 21. Drawn. Nottinghamshire 7 pts, Gloucestershire 6 pts. Toss: Gloucestershire. Stephenson and Pick gave the home side an excellent start, sending back the first four Gloucestershire batsmen for 16, but Russell held the lower order together and the total was not as low as expected. On the second day Newell and Robinson increased their partnership to 203, and a large lead seemed in the offing until Lawrence transformed the innings by taking five wickets in fifteen balls, including those of Robinson, Evans and Stephenson with successive deliveries. The captain's 123 lasted 225 balls and included thirteen fours and a six. Nottinghamshire, missing the injured Randall, lost nine wickets for 30 runs in the afternoon session. Gloucestershire again began badly, and again Russell came to the rescue, remaining unbeaten with 103 (233 balls, one six, twelve fours). Left with 42 overs, Nottinghamshire never looked like scoring 236 for victory, and if Martindale had not defended stoutly, the match might have ended in defeat.

Close of play: First day, Nottinghamshire 109-1 (M. Newell 30*, R. T. Robinson 52*); Second day, Gloucestershire 115-5 (M. W. Alleyne 65*, R. C. Russell 10*).

Gloucestershire

*A. J. Wright lbw b Pick	2	– (2) b Pick	0
G. D. Hodgson b Stephenson	4	– (1) c French b Stephenson	0
P. Bainbridge b Stephenson	6	– c French b Stephenson	29
C. W. J. Athey lbw b Pick	37	– c Newell b Pick	0
M. W. Alleyne lbw b Pick	1	– lbw b Pick	69
K. M. Curran lbw b Stephenson	54	– b Stephenson	7
†R. C. Russell b Afford	79	– not out	103
C. A. Walsh lbw b Pick	29	– (9) c Saxelby b Hemmings	18
M. C. J. Ball c Robinson b Hemmings	14	– (8) c Stephenson b Hemmings	1
D. V. Lawrence st French b Afford	0	– c Evans b Afford	18
S. N. Barnes not out	0	– b Pick	3
L-b 5, w 1, n-b 7	13	B 2, n-b 5	7
1/4 2/6 3/15 4/16 5/104 6/117 7/161 8/222 9/238	239	1/0 2/2 3/2 4/61 5/79 6/121 7/137 8/168 9/231	255

Bonus points – Gloucestershire 2, Nottinghamshire 4.

Bowling: *First Innings*—Stephenson 18–0–66–3; Pick 18–2–70–4; Evans 13–3–51–0; Afford 13.1–4–28–2; Hemmings 9–3–19–1. *Second Innings*—Stephenson 27–4–94–3; Pick 21.1–10–45–4; Evans 9–1–38–0; Hemmings 29–7–48–2; Afford 17–8–28–1.

Nottinghamshire

B. C. Broad c Russell b Walsh	13	– c Russell b Alleyne	35
M. Newell c Alleyne b Lawrence	78	– c Russell b Walsh	6
*R. T. Robinson lbw b Lawrence	123	– c Hodgson b Walsh	13
D. J. R. Martindale lbw b Lawrence	0	– not out	66
M. Saxelby not out	11	– c Walsh b Curran	13
K. P. Evans lbw b Lawrence	0	– (7) c Russell b Curran	0
F. D. Stephenson c Alleyne b Lawrence	0	– (6) c Bainbridge b Curran	0
†B. N. French b Alleyne	5	– lbw b Lawrence	4
E. E. Hemmings b Alleyne	0	– c Curran b Lawrence	0
R. A. Pick c and b Alleyne	3	– not out	4
J. A. Afford b Walsh	0		
B 4, l-b 10, w 1, n-b 11	26	B 1, l-b 5, w 1, n-b 7	14
1/26 2/229 3/231 4/234 5/234 6/234 7/250 8/250 9/258	259	1/20 2/42 3/85 4/109 5/110 6/111 7/140 8/147	(8 wkts) 155

Bonus points – Nottinghamshire 3, Gloucestershire 4.

Bowling: *First Innings*—Walsh 23.1–6–44–2; Curran 15–3–36–0; Lawrence 18–1–51–5; Barnes 13–5–39–0; Alleyne 9–3–23–3; Athey 2–1–2–0; Ball 11–1–32–0; Bainbridge 5–0–18–0. *Second Innings*—Walsh 14–0–41–2; Lawrence 10.5–2–41–2; Alleyne 6–1–23–1; Curran 9–0–35–3; Ball 2–0–9–0.

Umpires: J. D. Bond and N. T. Plews.

At Cleethorpes, August 25, 26, 27. NOTTINGHAMSHIRE drew with SRI LANKANS (See Sri Lankan tour section).

NOTTINGHAMSHIRE v WORCESTERSHIRE

At Nottingham, August 29, 30, 31. Drawn. Nottinghamshire 7 pts, Worcestershire 8 pts. Toss: Nottinghamshire. A marvellous third-wicket partnership between Broad and Johnson produced 183 runs at 5 an over on the first day. Broad scored 91 before lunch and hit 23 fours and a six in his 156; Johnson's 98 came off 108 balls with sixteen fours and a six. Bad light ended play early after the visitors had lost Lord. Stephenson took three quick wickets on the second morning, but Curtis soldiered on and, with help from the lower order, full batting points were achieved. Neale then closed the innings, but with the Nottinghamshire batsmen unable to score at a fast rate on Friday morning, and Neale not resorting to joke bowling, Robinson in the end set a demanding target of 266 off a minimum of 49 overs. Hick failed, and with fifteen overs unbowled the players went home.

Close of play: First day, Worcestershire 28-1 (T. S. Curtis 13*, S. M. McEwan 0*); Second day, Nottinghamshire 18-1 (M. Newell 9*, D. J. R. Martindale 0*).

Nottinghamshire

Batsman	First innings		Second innings	
B. C. Broad c Illingworth b Hick	156	–	c Hick b Newport	7
M. Newell c Rhodes b Newport	1	–	run out	16
D. J. R. Martindale c Newport b Lampitt	37	–	c Rhodes b Newport	14
P. Johnson c Neale b Hick	98	–	c Neale b McEwan	13
*R. T. Robinson b Lampitt	39	–	c Rhodes b Illingworth	45
K. P. Evans c Neale b Illingworth	12	–	c Hick b Newport	0
F. D. Stephenson b Newport	25	–	c Rhodes b Illingworth	30
†B. N. French b Newport	3	–	c Hick b Illingworth	25
E. E. Hemmings not out	12	–	not out	6
K. E. Cooper b Newport	7	–	not out	1
R. A. Pick not out	4			
B 2, l-b 3, n-b 3	8		L-b 1, w 2, n-b 4	7
1/2 2/107 3/290 4/303 5/336 6/368 7/375 8/382 9/390 (9 wkts dec.)	402		1/16 2/41 3/55 4/59 5/59 6/106 7/142 8/161 (8 wkts dec.)	164

Bonus points – Nottinghamshire 4, Worcestershire 4.

Bowling: *First Innings*—Dilley 12–3–47–0; Newport 18.4–2–75–4; McEwan 14–1–76–0; Lampitt 22–2–90–2; Illingworth 22–5–79–1; Hick 8–0–30–2. *Second Innings*—Newport 23–7–50–3; McEwan 13–4–41–1; Illingworth 18–9–34–3; Lampitt 10–1–38–0.

Worcestershire

Batsman	First innings		Second innings	
T. S. Curtis b Evans	82	–	not out	84
G. J. Lord b Pick	13	–	c Pick b Hemmings	12
S. M. McEwan b Stephenson	6			
G. A. Hick c French b Stephenson	4	–	(3) c Broad b Hemmings	18
D. A. Leatherdale c French b Stephenson	2	–	(4) lbw b Cooper	10
*P. A. Neale lbw b Cooper	74	–	(5) not out	5
S. R. Lampitt lbw b Hemmings	40			
†S. J. Rhodes not out	50			
R. K. Illingworth not out	15			
L-b 6, n-b 9	15		B 1, l-b 5, n-b 1	7
1/22 2/49 3/53 4/57 5/153 6/197 7/251 (7 wkts dec.)	301		1/57 2/89 3/119 (3 wkts)	136

P. J. Newport and G. R. Dilley did not bat.

Bonus points – Worcestershire 4, Nottinghamshire 3.

Bowling: *First Innings*—Stephenson 21.2–3–72–3; Pick 18–2–72–1; Cooper 16–6–48–1; Hemmings 25–7–54–1; Evans 17–2–49–1. *Second Innings*—Stephenson 12–1–51–0; Pick 3–0–21–0; Cooper 7–0–28–1; Evans 1–0–3–0; Hemmings 12–1–27–2.

Umpires: H. D. Bird and J. D. Bond.

At Lord's, September 7, 8, 9, 10. NOTTINGHAMSHIRE lost to MIDDLESEX by ten wickets.

NOTTINGHAMSHIRE v LANCASHIRE

At Nottingham, September 12, 13, 14, 15. Lancashire won by ten wickets. Lancashire 24 pts, Nottinghamshire 5 pts. Toss: Nottinghamshire. Put in to bat, Lancashire reached 148 for one by lunch, Mendis and Atherton batting well. After the interval Nottinghamshire seemed to gain control, the total slipping to 216 for six, but DeFreitas, Hegg and Yates changed the picture. The second morning was one of embarrassment for the home side as Yates, making his Championship début, completed his maiden first-class hundred off 188 balls, hitting twenty fours, and with Allott added 116 for the last wicket. Martin then removed Newell, Robinson and Randall in quick succession, and although Broad and Evans made useful scores, Lancashire enforced the follow-on early on the third day, during which 56 former Nottinghamshire players attended a reunion on the ground. Broad's 122 second time round, with seventeen fours and off 218 balls, was his ninth century for the county in 1990, equalling the record held by W. W. Whysall (1928) and M. J. Harris (1971). On the final day 9 runs were still required to avoid an innings defeat, and though this was achieved with comfort, Atherton's leg-spin put paid to any prolonged resistance. His six-wicket return was a career best, and Lancashire won the match half an hour before lunch.

Close of play: First day, Lancashire 382-8 (G. Yates 45*, P. J. Martin 21*); Second day, Nottinghamshire 168-7 (B. N. French 10*, G. W. Mike 3*); Third day, Nottinghamshire 288-6 (F. D. Stephenson 15*, B. N. French 12*).

Lancashire

G. D. Mendis b Evans	85	– not out	23
G. Fowler c French b Cooper	1	– not out	20
M. A. Atherton c Randall b Stephenson	81		
*N. H. Fairbrother lbw b Evans	0		
G. D. Lloyd c Mike b Afford	31		
M. Watkinson c Stephenson b Afford	4		
P. A. J. DeFreitas c French b Evans	49		
†W. K. Hegg c French b Afford	48		
G. Yates c Cooper b Mike	106		
P. J. Martin c French b Evans	21		
P. J. W. Allott not out	55		
L-b 7, w 5, n-b 6	18	L-b 7, n-b 1	8
1/8 2/151 3/151 4/194 5/211 6/216 7/299 8/320 9/383	499		(no wkt) 51

Bonus points – Lancashire 4, Nottinghamshire 3 (Score at 100 overs: 363-8).

Bowling: *First Innings*—Stephenson 29–3–131–1; Cooper 30–8–93–1; Mike 17.2–3–80–1; Evans 28–4–95–4; Afford 29–5–93–3. *Second Innings*—Evans 4–1–20–0; Mike 4–0–24–0.

Nottinghamshire

B. C. Broad c Mendis b Watkinson	42 – c Martin b Yates	122
M. Newell c Allott b Martin	0 – c Atherton b DeFreitas	12
*R. T. Robinson c Lloyd b Martin	8 – lbw b Watkinson	23
D. W. Randall lbw b Martin	0 – c Fairbrother b Atherton	24
D. J. R. Martindale c Fairbrother b DeFreitas	22 – c Hegg b Atherton	6
K. P. Evans c Fowler b Watkinson	49 – b Yates	55
F. D. Stephenson c Martin b Watkinson	24 – c Watkinson b Atherton	51
†B. N. French c Fowler b DeFreitas	16 – c Fairbrother b Atherton	19
G. W. Mike not out	18 – c Hegg b Atherton	0
K. E. Cooper c Mendis b DeFreitas	5 – not out	9
J. A. Afford c Atherton b Martin	5 – c Martin b Atherton	0
B 4, l-b 9	13 B 9, l-b 13, w 1, n-b 2	25
1/20 2/34 3/34 4/65 5/97 6/144 7/165 8/181 9/197	202 1/20 2/63 3/147 4/161 5/247 6/258 7/323 8/323 9/346	346

Bonus points – Nottinghamshire 2, Lancashire 4.

Bowling: *First Innings*—DeFreitas 25–7–63–3; Martin 20.3–4–68–4; Watkinson 16–3–34–3; Allott 14–8–18–0; Yates 2–0–6–0. *Second Innings*—DeFreitas 14–5–33–1; Martin 10–3–30–0; Allott 15–7–41–0; Watkinson 17–1–73–1; Yates 28–6–69–2; Atherton 21.3–4–78–6.

Umpires: J. H. Hampshire and B. J. Meyer.

NOTTINGHAMSHIRE v YORKSHIRE

At Nottingham, September 18, 19, 20, 21. Yorkshire won by four wickets. Yorkshire 21 pts, Nottinghamshire 3 pts. Toss: Nottinghamshire. On the first day, reduced by bad light and showers to 88 overs, Robinson reached his hundred in 213 minutes. Resuming next day, he not only improved his career best but also made the highest individual score for Nottinghamshire against Yorkshire. He hit 28 fours and faced 370 balls for his 220 not out. Stephenson enjoyed himself, hitting 95 off 109 balls as he and his captain put on 197 for the sixth wicket. The pitch was still perfect when Yorkshire batted, and Metcalfe hit 30 fours in his 194, missing his double-hundred when Moxon declared as soon as the follow-on was avoided. The weather remained miserable on the last day, and Robinson generously declared at lunch, leaving Yorkshire to score 324 from a minimum of 66 overs. Stephenson, who strained his side in the first innings, was unable to bowl properly, which further eased Yorkshire's task on such a bland pitch. Moxon and Metcalfe put on 143 for the first wicket, and Metcalfe again reached three figures, as well as completing 2,000 runs for the season, the first to do so for Yorkshire since G. Boycott in 1971. His 107 came from 155 balls and contained thirteen fours. Yorkshire won off the penultimate ball.

Close of play: First day, Nottinghamshire 241-4 (R. T. Robinson 101*, K. P. Evans 29*); Second day, Yorkshire 51-0 (M. D. Moxon 25*, A. A. Metcalfe 26*); Third day, Nottinghamshire 0-0 (B. C. Broad 0*, M. Newell 0*).

Nottinghamshire

B. C. Broad lbw b Hartley	40 – st Blakey b Grayson	43
M. Newell b Hartley	38 – not out	89
*R. T. Robinson not out	220 – not out	36
D. W. Randall lbw b Hartley	10	
D. J. R. Martindale c Byas b Pickles	11	
K. P. Evans b Pickles	43	
F. D. Stephenson c Byas b Jarvis	95	
†B. N. French not out	2	
B 3, l-b 14, w 1, n-b 5	23 B 3, l-b 4	7
1/62 2/109 3/125 4/175 5/272 6/469	(6 wkts dec.) 482 1/93	(1 wkt dec.) 175

E. E. Hemmings, K. E. Cooper and J. A. Afford did not bat.

Bonus points – Nottinghamshire 3, Yorkshire 2 (Score at 100 overs: 284-5).

Bowling: *First Innings*—Jarvis 27–1–106–1; Hartley 35–7–95–3; Pickles 32–9–120–2; White 17–2–66–0; Grayson 28–6–78–0. *Second Innings*—Jarvis 2–0–9–0; Hartley 6–0–23–0; Pickles 7–3–16–0; Grayson 13–4–55–1; White 11–1–65–0.

Yorkshire

*M. D. Moxon c French b Cooper	42	– c Martindale b Stephenson	83
A. A. Metcalfe not out	194	– c and b Evans	107
S. A. Kellett c Evans b Hemmings	27	– (6) c and b Cooper	20
P. E. Robinson not out	62	– (3) lbw b Cooper	5
†R. J. Blakey (did not bat)		– (4) c Afford b Cooper	64
D. Byas (did not bat)		– (5) lbw b Evans	8
A. P. Grayson (did not bat)		– not out	6
C. S. Pickles (did not bat)		– not out	23
L-b 6, n-b 3	9	B 1, l-b 7, n-b 3	11
1/89 2/163 (2 wkts dec.)	334	1/143 2/152 3/246 4/260 5/298 6/299 (6 wkts)	327

P. J. Hartley, P. W. Jarvis and C. White did not bat.

Bonus points – Yorkshire 3 (Score at 100 overs: 254-2).

Bowling: *First Innings*—Stephenson 0.2–0–4–0; Cooper 27.4–9–70–1; Evans 25.2–9–71–0; Hemmings 27–5–102–1; Afford 35–12–81–0. *Second Innings*—Cooper 29.5–3–128–3; Evans 16–0–79–2; Afford 4–0–33–0; Stephenson 5–0–30–1; Hemmings 11–1–49–0.

Umpires: J. W. Holder and M. J. Kitchen.

THE CRICKETER CUP WINNERS, 1967-1990

1967	REPTON PILGRIMS	beat Radley Rangers by 96 runs.
1968	OLD MALVERNIANS	beat Harrow Wanderers by five wickets.
1969	OLD BRIGHTONIANS	beat Stowe Templars by 156 runs.
1970	OLD WYKEHAMISTS	beat Old Tonbridgians by 94 runs.
1971	OLD TONBRIDGIANS	beat Charterhouse Friars on faster scoring-rate.
1972	OLD TONBRIDGIANS	beat Old Malvernians by 114 runs.
1973	RUGBY METEORS	beat Old Tonbridgians by five wickets.
1974	OLD WYKEHAMISTS	beat Old Alleynians on faster scoring-rate.
1975	OLD MALVERNIANS	beat Harrow Wanderers by 97 runs.
1976	OLD TONBRIDGIANS	beat Old Blundellians by 170 runs.
1977	SHREWSBURY SARACENS	beat Oundle Rovers by nine wickets.
1978	CHARTERHOUSE FRIARS	beat Oundle Rovers by nine wickets.
1979	OLD TONBRIDGIANS	beat Uppingham Rovers by 5 runs.
1980	MARLBOROUGH BLUES	beat Old Wellingtonians by 31 runs.
1981	CHARTERHOUSE FRIARS	beat Old Wykehamists by nine wickets.
1982	OLD WYKEHAMISTS	beat Old Malvernians on faster scoring-rate.
1983	REPTON PILGRIMS	beat Haileybury Hermits by seven wickets.
1984	OLD TONBRIDGIANS	beat Old Malvernians by seven wickets.
1985	OUNDLE ROVERS	beat Repton Pilgrims by three wickets.
1986	OLD MALVERNIANS	beat Downside Wanderers by six wickets.
1987	SHREWSBURY SARACENS	beat Old Cliftonians by 58 runs.
1988	OUNDLE ROVERS	beat Shrewsbury Saracens by 19 runs.
1989	OUNDLE ROVERS	beat Shrewsbury Saracens by 9 runs.
1990	OLD MALVERNIANS	beat Harrow Wanderers by four wickets.

From 1967 to 1983 the final was played at Burton Court, Chelsea. Since then, it has been played at Vincent Square, Westminster.

SOMERSET

President: C. R. M. Atkinson
Chairman: R. Parsons
Chairman, Cricket Committee: R. E. Marshall
Chief Executive: P. W. Anderson
The County Ground, St James's Street,
Taunton TA1 1JT
(Telephone: 0823-272946/253666)
Cricket Manager: 1990 – J. Birkenshaw
Captain: C. J. Tavaré
Coach: P. J. Robinson

In an unusual season memorable mostly for high scores, flat seams, flatter pitches and contrived run-chases, Somerset, despite a number of changes in personnel, finished with a playing record remarkably similar to that of 1989. After a promising start, with a ten-wicket win over Gloucestershire, they endured some sterile periods which produced little reward. Two wins in their last four Championship games helped them do no more than finish one position lower in the Britannic Assurance table than in 1989, and a rise of two places to eighth in the Refuge Assurance League constituted a marginal improvement. A good win over Middlesex at Taunton took them to the semi-finals of the Benson and Hedges Cup for the second year in succession, but no farther, and they again failed to get beyond the second round in the NatWest Bank Trophy, being beaten decisively by Worcestershire. All in all, it added up to a disappointing return.

It was a curious commentary on the Championship system, none the less, that Somerset should be fifteenth, and yet have gained more bonus points than nine counties, and have lost fewer matches than all but six counties. They collected as many batting bonus points as Middlesex and Essex, the champions and runners-up.

In general terms, Somerset's was a happy team. They usually fielded excellently, often played interesting cricket, and they reacted well to adversity. The batting rarely failed, and occasionally it rose to great heights. Jimmy Cook, the prolific South African opener, again played in every match, despite suffering a bruising blow on the arm from a fierce drive by Richard Harden in the Championship game against Northamptonshire at Taunton. Once more he was the first to reach 1,000 runs, getting there at exactly the same stage of the season as the previous year, and the first to 2,000, finishing with 2,608 runs in first-class cricket. Added to that were his new Sunday League record of 902 runs and the excellent work he did as vice-captain. At the age of 37, Cook always gave an enthusiastic display in the field and continued to provide an outstanding example.

Chris Tavaré proved to be a popular captain and enjoyed another fine year with the bat, scoring more than 2,500 runs in all cricket at an average of 53. Harden, returning to his best form, notched just over 2,000 runs at 51.51 in all cricket, while Peter Roebuck, although standing down from some games in his benefit year, averaged 54 in the Championship as a result of a golden mid-season spell.

For some years the No. 3 position in the batting order had caused Somerset problems, but last summer these were solved by one of the new recruits. Andy Hayhurst, released by Lancashire in 1989, scored 1,559 first-class runs for an average of 57.74 and made some useful contributions with bat and ball in the one-day games. Wicket-keeper Neil Burns had a good season, almost getting his thousand runs for the first time, a feat which was accomplished by Graham Rose, the county's most improved player. Given the encouragement to play his powerful strokes, Rose produced some startling innings, particularly in limited-overs games, and he gave evidence of his worth as an all-round cricketer by taking 53 first-class wickets, as well as making himself into a reliable slip fielder. An excellent fitness record allowed him to be one of those ever present for Somerset throughout the season.

Behind such a weight of batting, there were few chances for Ian Swallow, an off-spinner from Yorkshire, and Roland Lefebvre, two cricketers with plenty of all-round ability. Both, however, had to do a lot of bowling in first-class cricket for the first time, and they could look back on some rewarding days. In a season less affected by the radical changes introduced by the TCCB, the willing Lefebvre, the first Dutchman to play regularly for Somerset, would certainly have produced better results. As in the previous two seasons, Adrian Jones and Neil Mallender each took 50 wickets as the opening attack, and Mallender enjoyed more consistent fitness than in some years.

Indeed, with injuries at a minimum and the side more settled, there were not so many opportunities for the younger players. Harvey Trump's development was a shade slower than hoped for, but Ricky Bartlett, the Second Eleven Player of the Year, performed usefully in his eight Sunday League outings and one Championship appearance. Jeremy Hallett, who the year before had been opening the bowling for Millfield School, began the difficult transition to county cricket and represented England Young Cricketers against the visiting Pakistanis, his five wickets in the second innings of the Headingley "Test" setting up the decisive victory for England. Another heavy Second Eleven scorer, Gareth Townsend, had two Championship games towards the end of the season, and though he did little of note in either game, his 77 was an essential ingredient of Somerset's 71-run victory over the Sri Lankan touring team. The released list included Jonathan Hardy and Jonathon Atkinson, neither of whom, unhappily, had quite lived up to the rich promise of his early Somerset days.

For this summer, the county have signed Ken MacLeay, a 32-year-old, English-born all-rounder from Australia, who has strong one-day international credentials. However, there are clearly still some openings, notably for a slow left-arm bowler, and Somerset, with a small population, will continue to look for recruits from other counties, as they have always had to. But with the Second Eleven reaching the final of the Bain Clarkson competition, and junior teams excelling in national competitions, there are also hopes that more places will be filled by local players in the future. – Eric Hill.

SOMERSET 1990

[*Bill Smith*

Back row: A. N. Hayhurst, M. W. Cleal, P. J. Rendell, S. M. Priscott. *Middle row:* R. J. Harden, I. Fletcher, D. M. Kutner, R. P. Lefebvre, N. J. Pringle, G. T. J. Townsend, R. J. Bartlett, I. G. Swallow. *Front row:* P. J. Robinson (*coach*), N. A. Mallender, N. D. Burns, S. J. Cook, C. J. Tavaré (*captain*), R. Parsons (*chairman*), J. Birkenshaw (*cricket manager*), T. Gard, A. N. Jones, J. J. E. Hardy, G. D. Rose, P. M. Roebuck. *Inset:* H. R. J. Trump.

SOMERSET RESULTS

All first-class matches – Played 24: Won 3, Lost 5, Drawn 16.

County Championship matches – Played 22: Won 3, Lost 4, Drawn 15.

Bonus points – Batting 73, Bowling 45.

Competition placings – Britannic Assurance County Championship, 15th; NatWest Bank Trophy, 2nd round; Benson and Hedges Cup, s-f; Refuge Assurance League, 8th equal.

BRITANNIC ASSURANCE CHAMPIONSHIP AVERAGES

BATTING

	Birthplace	*M*	*I*	*NO*	*R*	*HI*	*Avge*
‡S. J. Cook	*Johannesburg, SA*	22	38	6	2,432	313*	76.00
‡A. N. Hayhurst	*Manchester*	21	33	7	1,554	170	59.76
‡R. J. Harden	*Bridgwater*	22	29	7	1,257	104*	57.13
‡P. M. Roebuck	*Oxford*	16	25	5	1,085	201*	54.25
‡C. J. Tavaré	*Orpington*	22	30	4	1,399	219	53.80
‡G. D. Rose	*Tottenham, London*	22	26	9	897	97*	52.76
‡J. J. E. Hardy	*Nakaru, Kenya*	7	13	5	343	91	42.87
‡N. D. Burns	*Chelmsford*	22	31	9	863	166	39.22
‡N. A. Mallender	*Kirk Sandall*	19	10	3	177	87*	25.28
‡A. N. Jones	*Woking*	20	9	5	100	41	25.00
I. G. Swallow	*Barnsley*	21	17	7	187	32	18.70
R. P. Lefebvre	*Rotterdam, Netherlands*	16	16	3	214	53	16.46
G. T. J. Townsend	*Tiverton*	2	4	1	21	15	7.00
H. R. J. Trump	*Taunton*	7	5	1	11	4*	2.75

Also batted: R. J. Bartlett (*Ash Priors*) (1 match) 73, 12; J. C. Hallett (*Yeovil*) (2 matches) 0.

* *Signifies not out.* ‡ *Denotes county cap.*

The following played a total of nineteen three-figure innings for Somerset in County Championship matches – S. J. Cook 8, A. N. Hayhurst 4, R. J. Harden 2, P. M. Roebuck 2, C. J. Tavaré 2, N. D. Burns 1.

BOWLING

	O	*M*	*R*	*W*	*BB*	*5W/i*	*Avge*
N. A. Mallender	537.2	114	1,555	51	5-46	2	30.49
G. D. Rose	530.4	93	1,807	51	5-52	1	35.43
A. N. Jones	539.4	81	1,990	52	6-75	2	38.26
R. P. Lefebvre	493.1	132	1,258	30	5-30	1	41.93
A. N. Hayhurst	291.2	46	974	17	3-58	0	57.29
I. G. Swallow	642.1	150	2,042	31	3-88	0	65.87

Also bowled: N. D. Burns 0.3–0–8–0; S. J. Cook 8–0–42–2; J. C. Hallett 40.2–7–135–4; R. J. Harden 64–6–254–6; P. M. Roebuck 160.3–37–460–7; C. J. Tavaré 17.2–0–162–0; H. R. J. Trump 164–41–520–9.

Wicket-keeper: N. D. Burns 43 ct, 1 st.

Leading Fielders: R. J. Harden 18, C. J. Tavaré 15.

At Oxford, April 18, 19, 20. SOMERSET drew with OXFORD UNIVERSITY.

SOMERSET v GLOUCESTERSHIRE

At Taunton, April 26, 27, 28, 29. Somerset won by ten wickets. Somerset 24 pts, Gloucestershire 5 pts. Toss: Somerset. Rain reduced the first day to 35.3 overs, but after that the weather was ideal. Lefebvre, in his first Championship match, and Mallender supported their captain's decision to put Gloucestershire in, and on a good pitch only Athey (146 balls), Curran and Walsh made any significant progress. Building on the determined batting of Roebuck and Harden when Somerset replied, Burns hit one six and nineteen fours in a career-best 166 from 182 balls, and Rose splendidly helped him put on a brilliant, decisive 213 in 37 overs for the sixth wicket as the bowling wilted. Although Gloucestershire trailed by 241, Stovold led a crisp response with 74 in 119 balls. However, the Somerset bowlers, and in particular Jones, whittled away at the innings until all that stood between their team and victory was the former Somerset player, Lloyds. When, finally, he hooked Jones to square leg to bring his defiant, 221-ball innings to an end, Somerset required just 99 runs with 52 overs remaining.

Close of play: First day, Gloucestershire 114-3 (C. W. J. Athey 46*, K. M. Curran 25*); Second day, Somerset 382-5 (N. D. Burns 148*, G. D. Rose 75*); Third day, Gloucestershire 239-5 (J. W. Lloyds 32*, D. V. Lawrence 7*).

Gloucestershire

*A. J. Wright c Tavaré b Lefebvre	25	– c Hardy b Rose	37
A. W. Stovold b Mallender	4	– st Burns b Swallow	74
G. D. Hodgson lbw b Lefebvre	8	– lbw b Jones	25
C. W. J. Athey c Rose b Lefebvre	68	– b Jones	39
K. M. Curran c Burns b Lefebvre	41	– c Burns b Rose	13
J. W. Lloyds b Mallender	0	– c Lefebvre b Jones	93
†R. C. Russell lbw b Rose	12	– (8) c Tavaré b Jones	18
C. A. Walsh c Burns b Mallender	26	– (9) c Harden b Jones	0
D. V. Lawrence lbw b Mallender	3	– (7) c Lefebvre b Rose	9
D. A. Graveney b Lefebvre	2	– c Rose b Jones	5
K. B. S. Jarvis not out	0	– not out	1
L-b 6, n-b 2	8	B 1, l-b 21, n-b 3	25
1/16 2/38 3/39 4/133 5/134 6/148 7/192 8/192 9/197	197	1/84 2/141 3/149 4/178 5/228 6/250 7/301 8/305 9/338	339

Bonus points – Gloucestershire 1, Somerset 4.

Bowling: *First Innings*—Jones 14–1–68–0; Mallender 19–4–46–4; Rose 15–5–46–1; Lefebvre 15.1–7–30–5; Swallow 1–0–1–0. *Second Innings*—Jones 27.1–5–75–6; Mallender 26–6–55–0; Lefebvre 24–6–66–0; Rose 25–5–64–3; Swallow 34–13–57–1.

Somerset

S. J. Cook c Russell b Walsh	16	– not out	62
P. M. Roebuck c Graveney b Curran	40		
J. J. E. Hardy c Walsh b Lawrence	4	– (2) not out	30
*C. J. Tavaré c Lloyds b Jarvis	18		
R. J. Harden c Athey b Walsh	46		
†N. D. Burns c Athey b Curran	166		
G. D. Rose c Russell b Walsh	85		
R. P. Lefebvre lbw b Walsh	3		
I. G. Swallow not out	7		
N. A. Mallender c Russell b Walsh	0		
A. N. Jones c Wright b Walsh	9		
B 3, l-b 15, w 4, n-b 22	44	B 4, l-b 1, n-b 2	7
1/30 2/38 3/75 4/101 5/196 6/409 7/419 8/419 9/420	438	(no wkt)	99

Bonus points – Somerset 4, Gloucestershire 4.

Bowling: *First Innings*—Lawrence 14–1–77–1; Walsh 26.1–2–112–6; Jarvis 12–1–61–1; Curran 18–3–91–2; Graveney 19–3–62–0; Lloyds 5–1–17–0. *Second Innings*—Walsh 5–0–31–0; Curran 2–0–8–0; Graveney 11–4–12–0; Lawrence 2–0–21–0; Lloyds 6.2–0–22–0.

Umpires: K. E. Palmer and N. T. Plews.

At Cardiff, May 3, 4, 5, 6. SOMERSET drew with GLAMORGAN.

At Taunton, May 16, 17, 18. SOMERSET lost to NEW ZEALANDERS by five wickets (See New Zealand tour section).

SOMERSET v DERBYSHIRE

At Taunton, May 19, 21, 22. Derbyshire won by 146 runs. Derbyshire 21 pts, Somerset 5 pts. Toss: Somerset. Barnett, in 152 balls, and Morris, hitting 22 fours in 216 balls, took full advantage of an easy pitch and some early wayward bowling. Adams, with a half-century in 147 balls, led the support. After early inroads by Warner, Somerset's response rested with Hayhurst (226 balls), Tavaré and Harden before Tavaré declared 100 runs behind. The extensive use of occasional bowlers helped Morris to his second century of the match, and his fourth on the ground in 21 days, and Krikken achieved a career-best 77 not out before the declaration left Somerset to score 366 in four hours. Malcolm and Mortensen put a Derbyshire victory on the cards with three wickets, but there was a fine counter-attack from Hardy, with 91 in 134 balls and Harden, followed by defiance from Rose and Lefebvre. Eventually, however, Malcolm and Miller assured the win with eleven overs to spare.

Close of play: First day, Derbyshire 372-9 (O. H. Mortensen 2*); Second day, Derbyshire 93-2 (J. E. Morris 59*, K. M. Krikken 3*).

Derbyshire

*K. J. Barnett c Hayhurst b Jones	94		
P. D. Bowler c Harden b Rose	6	– (7) lbw b Swallow	25
J. E. Morris c Burns b Lefebvre	122	– (1) b Harden	109
A. P. Kuiper b Jones	5	– (5) c Hayhurst b Cook	19
C. J. Adams c Roebuck b Swallow	58	– (2) c Burns b Rose	23
B. Roberts lbw b Jones	37	– (3) lbw b Roebuck	4
†K. M. Krikken lbw b Lefebvre	24	– (4) not out	77
A. E. Warner lbw b Swallow	1	– (6) lbw b Cook	1
D. E. Malcolm lbw b Swallow	10		
O. H. Mortensen not out	2	– (8) not out	2
B 1, l-b 9, n-b 3	13	N-b 5	5
1/18 2/189 3/217 4/237 5/317 6/335 7/338 8/360 9/372 (9 wkts dec.)	372	1/52 2/81 3/178 4/201 5/204 6/249 (6 wkts dec.)	265

G. Miller did not bat.

Bonus points – Derbyshire 4, Somerset 2 (Score at 100 overs: 335-6).

Bowling: *First Innings*—Jones 17–1–85–3; Rose 16–0–75–1; Lefebvre 24.3–6–67–2; Hayhurst 16–5–42–0; Swallow 40–7–89–3; Roebuck 3–2–4–0. *Second Innings*—Jones 4–0–26–0; Rose 5–1–24–1; Lefebvre 3–1–5–0; Swallow 20–4–51–1; Roebuck 12–3–23–1; Harden 16–2–60–1; Tavaré 5–0–43–0; Cook 5–0–25–2; Burns 0.3–0–8–0.

Somerset

S. J. Cook c Kuiper b Warner	1	– c Adams b Malcolm	5
J. J. E. Hardy c Krikken b Warner	4	– c sub b Malcolm	91
A. N. Hayhurst c Mortensen b Miller	90	– lbw b Mortensen	0
*C. J. Tavaré b Kuiper	64	– c Kuiper b Malcolm	9
R. J. Harden not out	69	– c Mortensen b Warner	42
P. M. Roebuck not out	34	– lbw b Miller	6
†N. D. Burns (did not bat)		– c Kuiper b Barnett	10
G. D. Rose (did not bat)		– c Krikken b Malcolm	31
R. P. Lefebvre (did not bat)		– st Krikken b Miller	13
I. G. Swallow (did not bat)		– lbw b Miller	0
A. N. Jones (did not bat)		– not out	8
B 1, l-b 6, n-b 3	10	B 1, w 1, n-b 2	4
1/3 2/25 3/152 4/189 (4 wkts dec.)	272	1/6 2/7 3/25 4/118 5/138 6/153 7/174 8/201 9/211	219

Bonus points – Somerset 3, Derbyshire 1.

Bowling: *First Innings*—Malcolm 12.4–4–20–0; Warner 11–3–30–2; Mortensen 10–3–17–0; Kuiper 12–1–46–1; Miller 19–3–69–1; Barnett 25–3–83–0. *Second Innings*—Mortensen 7–0–25–1; Malcolm 17–2–88–4; Miller 23.5–5–57–3; Warner 9–1–34–1; Barnett 4–0–14–1.

Umpires: K. E. Palmer and D. S. Thompsett.

SOMERSET v SUSSEX

At Taunton, May 23, 24, 25. Drawn. Somerset 7 pts, Sussex 4 pts. Toss: Somerset. A magnificent innings by Cook, lasting 258 minutes and comprising 197 balls, one six and 30 fours, was well supported by a career-best 170 off 277 balls from Hayhurst (one six, 23 fours). Together they added 243 in 54 overs for the second wicket and effectively gave Somerset's bowlers two days in which to dismiss Sussex twice. They made a useful start, having Sussex 108 for four despite a defiant 166-ball half-century from Lenham. But Colin Wells, after an escape when 7, batted through 185 balls in a determined rearguard action. He hit two sixes and eleven fours in his 99 not out, and had he not turned down many singles at the end, he would have had a deserved century. Speight, with 73 from 131 balls, and Gould also profited from escapes. Following on 187 behind, Sussex were again forced on to the defensive by an early wicket, but the patient Lenham (252 balls, eleven fours) found equally determined partners in Dodemaide and Alan Wells, and by the time Speight had ensured the draw with his second half-century, Somerset had had recourse to ten bowlers.

Close of play: First day, Somerset 500-5 (N. D. Burns 14*, G. D. Rose 4*); Second day, Sussex 304-9 (C. M. Wells 92*, A. M. Babington 8*).

Somerset

S. J. Cook c Gould b C. M. Wells	197
P. M. Roebuck c Moores b Babington	27
A. N. Hayhurst c Babington b Dodemaide	170
*C. J. Tavaré c and b Babington	28
R. J. Harden c and b Pigott	51
†N. D. Burns not out	14
G. D. Rose not out	4
B 1, l-b 3, w 1, n-b 4	9
1/76 2/319 3/364 4/477 5/487 (5 wkts dec.)	500

R. P. Lefebvre, I. G. Swallow, N. A. Mallender and A. N. Jones did not bat.

Bonus points – Somerset 4, Sussex 1 (Score at 100 overs: 453-3).

Bowling: Pigott 22–2–117–1; Dodemaide 25–2–115–1; Babington 23–2–109–2; C. M. Wells 21–1–72–1; Salisbury 17–4–66–0; Lenham 2–0–17–0.

Sussex

First innings		Second innings	
N. J. Lenham lbw b Roebuck	51	run out	108
J. W. Hall lbw b Mallender	6	c Tavaré b Jones	1
A. I. C. Dodemaide lbw b Rose	0	b Lefebvre	20
A. P. Wells c Burns b Roebuck	18	b Mallender	23
M. P. Speight c Rose b Lefebvre	73	not out	83
*C. M. Wells not out	99	not out	6
I. J. Gould c sub b Rose	30		
†P. Moores b Rose	1		
A. C. S. Pigott c Rose b Swallow	2		
I. D. K. Salisbury c Harden b Jones	5		
A. M. Babington c Burns b Jones	8		
B 4, l-b 2, n-b 14	20	B 5, l-b 7, w 3	15
1/30 2/30 3/64 4/108 5/206 6/268 7/270 8/277 9/291	313	1/4 2/45 3/107 4/219 (4 wkts dec.)	256

Bonus points – Sussex 3, Somerset 3 (Score at 100 overs: 280-8).

Bowling: *First Innings*—Jones 18.5–1–71–2; Mallender 16–6–21–1; Swallow 24–8–62–1; Rose 17–4–52–3; Roebuck 21–4–63–2; Lefebvre 18–4–38–1. *Second Innings*—Jones 8–5–11–1; Rose 8–2–21–0; Lefebvre 12–2–33–1; Mallender 13–2–24–1; Swallow 14–4–28–0; Roebuck 12–1–38–0; Harden 11–1–43–0; Hayhurst 5–0–22–0; Tavaré 3–0–12–0; Cook 2–0–12–0.

Umpires: K. E. Palmer and D. S. Thompsett.

At Leicester, May 26, 28, 29. SOMERSET drew with LEICESTERSHIRE.

At Bristol, June 2, 4, 5. SOMERSET drew with GLOUCESTERSHIRE.

At Basingstoke, June 6, 7, 8. SOMERSET drew with HAMPSHIRE.

At Canterbury, June 9, 11, 12. SOMERSET drew with KENT.

SOMERSET v ESSEX

At Bath, June 16, 18, 19. Drawn. Somerset 3 pts, Essex 4 pts. Toss: Essex. Stephenson's maiden double-century, coming from 343 balls and containing three sixes and 24 fours, set Essex up on a slow pitch. Having shared a century opening stand with Gooch, Stephenson then added 225 for the second wicket with Prichard, whose appreciation of an escape before scoring came in the form of 115 from 188 balls, his third hundred of the summer to date. Rain took the first 40 overs of the second day, after which Hayhurst, in 175 balls, and Tavaré built on a fair start. Somerset declared 200 runs behind, and then fed Essex with easy runs until Gooch set a target of 353 in five hours. A thunderstorm ended any prospect of a good finish.

Close of play: First day, Essex 431-3 (J. P. Stephenson 202*, B. R. Hardie 22*); Second day, Somerset 231-2 (A. N. Hayhurst 65*, C. J. Tavaré 78*).

Essex

*G. A. Gooch c Hardy b Swallow	72		
J. P. Stephenson not out	202	– not out	63
P. J. Prichard c Burns b Mallender	115	– c Hayhurst b Harden	4
M. E. Waugh c Burns b Mallender	0	– not out	73
B. R. Hardie not out	22		
†M. A. Garnham (did not bat)		– (1) c Hayhurst b Harden	10
B 1, l-b 14, n-b 5	20	L-b 1, n-b 1	2
1/106 2/331 3/331 (3 wkts dec.)	431	1/13 2/17 (2 wkts dec.)	152

D. R. Pringle, T. D. Topley, N. A. Foster, J. H. Childs and P. M. Such did not bat.

Bonus points – Essex 4, Somerset 1 (Score at 100 overs: 349-3).

Bowling: *First Innings*—Jones 17–2–59–0; Mallender 20–2–74–2; Rose 18–1–78–0; Swallow 35–8–140–1; Hayhurst 12–1–39–0; Roebuck 8–2–26–0. *Second Innings*—Hayhurst 2–0–11–0; Harden 9–1–54–2; Tavaré 7.5–0–86–0.

Somerset

S. J. Cook c Childs b Foster	32	– not out	19
J. J. E. Hardy lbw b Topley	42	– not out	13
A. N. Hayhurst not out	65		
*C. J. Tavaré not out	78		
B 1, l-b 10, n-b 3	14		
1/52 2/100 (2 wkts dec.)	231	(no wkt)	32

P. M. Roebuck, R. J. Harden, †N. D. Burns, G. D. Rose, I. G. Swallow, N. A. Mallender and A. N. Jones did not bat.

Bonus points – Somerset 2.

Bowling: *First Innings*—Pringle 15–6–28–0; Foster 14–2–56–1; Topley 14–1–48–1; Childs 16–8–21–0; Such 12–2–29–0; Waugh 6–0–38–0. *Second Innings*—Foster 6.5–2–25–0; Pringle 6–3–7–0.

Umpires: R. Julian and K. J. Lyons.

SOMERSET v GLAMORGAN

At Bath, June 20, 21, 22. Drawn. Somerset 4 pts, Glamorgan 1 pt. Toss: Somerset. Having reduced play on the first two days to a total of 45.1 overs, rain then removed 45 minutes at a critical stage on the last day as Glamorgan were pursuing a target of 302 in four hours. On a pitch generally slow but providing some variations, Cook (163 balls) and Hayhurst put on 86 in 31 overs against a searching attack, while on the final day, largely against the occasional bowlers, Rose (87 balls, six sixes, eight fours) and Burns took 160 off 26 overs. Each side then forfeited an innings. Glamorgan lost two early wickets, but Butcher (152 balls) and Maynard added 60 in fourteen overs either side of a thunderstorm. This interruption, followed by the loss of Maynard and Richards, put paid to the run-chase, leaving Croft to support his captain through the final 21 overs.

Close of play: First day, Somerset 95-1 (S. J. Cook 40*, A. N. Hayhurst 38*); Second day, Somerset 104-1 (S. J. Cook 42*, A. N. Hayhurst 44*).

Somerset

S. J. Cook c Metson b Watkin 61
J. J. E. Hardy lbw b Bastien 10
A. N. Hayhurst c Butcher b Watkin ... 48
†N. D. Burns not out 71
G. D. Rose not out 97
L-b 7, w 2, n-b 5 14

1/22 2/108 3/141 (3 wkts dec.) 301

*C. J. Tavaré, R. J. Harden, I. G. Swallow, N. A. Mallender, H. R. J. Trump and A. N. Jones did not bat.

Bonus points – Somerset 4, Glamorgan 1.

Bowling: Watkin 26–9–53–2; Bastien 25–9–64–1; Dennis 8–1–20–0; Cowley 1–0–4–0; Croft 4–1–12–0; Holmes 4–0–27–0; Morris 3–0–41–0; Butcher 7–0–45–0; Maynard 5–0–28–0.

Somerset forfeited their second innings.

Glamorgan

Glamorgan forfeited their first innings.

*A. R. Butcher not out 83
H. Morris c Harden b Jones 2
G. C. Holmes lbw b Mallender 1
M. P. Maynard c Harden b Swallow ... 33
I. V. A. Richards b Swallow 21
R. D. B. Croft not out 17
L-b 2, n-b 6 8

1/8 2/27 3/87 4/113 (4 wkts) 165

N. G. Cowley, †C. P. Metson, S. J. Dennis, S. L. Watkin and S. Bastien did not bat.

Bowling: Jones 7–3–15–1; Mallender 9–1–27–1; Swallow 19–3–63–2; Rose 9–0–35–0; Trump 4–2–11–0; Harden 3–0–12–0.

Umpires: R. Julian and N. T. Plews.

SOMERSET v NORTHAMPTONSHIRE

At Taunton, June 30, July 2, 3. Northamptonshire won by seven wickets. Northamptonshire 21 pts, Somerset 5 pts. Toss: Somerset. On a pitch which played easily after starting slightly damp, the batsmen dominated throughout and it needed three declarations before Northamptonshire were left to score 329 in four hours. Cook and Roebuck opened for Somerset with more than 100 in each innings, and Lefebvre's maiden first-class fifty in the second came from just 44 balls against the spinners. Cook's retirement in the second innings resulted from a blow on the arm from Harden's fierce straight drive. Felton, in 158 balls, hit a six and thirteen fours to register a hundred against his former county and received steady support throughout, although night-watchman Thomas's 48 was at the cost of a broken hand. In Northamptonshire's second innings, Fordham (169 balls) and Bailey (108 balls) redressed a slow start to the run-chase by adding 185 in 34 overs, after which Lamb, with 64 from 51 balls, steered his side home with fifteen balls to spare.

Close of play: First day, Northamptonshire 14-1 (N. A. Felton 7*, J. G. Thomas 0*); Second day, Somerset 124-0 (S. J. Cook 71*, P. M. Roebuck 42*).

Somerset

S. J. Cook c Fordham b Williams	65	– retired hurt	112
P. M. Roebuck c Ripley b Thomas	60	– lbw b Davis	44
A. N. Hayhurst c Davis b Cook	81	– (7) not out	28
*C. J. Tavaré c Felton b Williams	39		
R. J. Harden b Williams	23	– (3) b Robinson	28
G. D. Rose not out	33	– (4) c sub b Robinson	8
†N. D. Burns b Thomas	0	– (6) c Bailey b Cook	7
R. P. Lefebvre not out	0	– (5) c Bailey b Cook	53
I. G. Swallow (did not bat)		– (8) run out	9
L-b 8, w 1, n-b 14	23	L-b 3, n-b 13	16
1/128 2/134 3/254 4/278 5/309 6/317 (6 wkts dec.)	324	1/126 2/196 3/211 4/254 5/279 6/305 (6 wkts dec.)	305

N. A. Mallender and A. N. Jones did not bat.

Bonus points – Somerset 4, Northamptonshire 1 (Score at 100 overs: 302-4).

In the second innings S. J. Cook retired hurt at 184.

Bowling: *First Innings*—Davis 18–1–45–0; Thomas 20–5–76–2; Cook 25–8–69–1; Robinson 18–1–62–0; Williams 22–6–64–3. *Second Innings*—Davis 14–2–72–1; Robinson 15–1–76–2; Cook 20–3–63–2; Williams 21–5–54–0; Bailey 4–0–37–0.

Northamptonshire

A. Fordham c Tavaré b Mallender	6	– c Burns b Rose	128
N. A. Felton c Rose b Jones	101	– c Rose b Lefebvre	7
J. G. Thomas c Roebuck b Rose	48		
R. J. Bailey not out	80	– (3) b Jones	101
*A. J. Lamb c Mallender b Swallow	40	– (4) not out	64
D. J. Capel not out	13	– (5) not out	21
B 1, l-b 5, w 1, n-b 6	13	B 5, l-b 3, n-b 3	11
1/13 2/92 3/215 4/263 (4 wkts dec.)	301	1/26 2/211 3/287 (3 wkts)	332

R. G. Williams, †D. Ripley, W. W. Davis, N. G. B. Cook and M. A. Robinson did not bat.

Bonus points – Northamptonshire 4, Somerset 1.

Bowling: *First Innings*—Jones 14–0–48–1; Mallender 14–1–70–1; Lefebvre 14–4–49–0; Rose 7–1–15–1; Swallow 21–5–84–1; Roebuck 6–2–17–0; Hayhurst 5–0–12–0. *Second Innings*—Jones 12–2–63–1; Mallender 12–2–33–0; Lefebvre 10–2–41–1; Rose 13–0–77–1; Swallow 13.3–0–76–0; Roebuck 4–0–21–0; Hayhurst 1–0–13–0.

Umpires: K. J. Lyons and D. O. Oslear.

SOMERSET v WARWICKSHIRE

At Taunton, July 4, 5, 6. Drawn. Somerset 4 pts, Warwickshire 5 pts. Toss: Warwickshire. A gritty, patient first century of the season by Roebuck, who hit thirteen fours in 269 balls while carrying his bat for the third time in his career, held the Somerset innings together after they had been put in on a pitch giving some encouragement to bowlers. Rain reduced the first day to 54 overs, and the second was marked by gale-force winds, although these did not hamper Asif Din and Humpage as they shaped a brisk response, which allowed Reeve to make an enterprising declaration. Next day, in the best batting conditions of the match, and given some help by the use of occasional bowlers, Cook and Roebuck put on 223 in 54 overs. Cook hit two sixes and nineteen fours in his 137 from 170 balls, while Roebuck's unbeaten 90 came from 160 balls. Warwickshire, chasing a target of 357 in 210 minutes, received a setback when Mallender took two wickets in his fourth over, but rain three overs later banished any hopes of a win for either side by bringing the game to a premature conclusion.

Close of play: First day, Somerset 173-6 (P. M. Roebuck 75*, N. A. Mallender 0*); Second day, Somerset 15-0 (S. J. Cook 10*, P. M. Roebuck 5*).

Somerset

S. J. Cook c Piper b Reeve	35	– c Ostler b Moles	137
P. M. Roebuck not out	114	– not out	90
A. N. Hayhurst c Humpage b Reeve	6	– c Reeve b Moles	3
*C. J. Tavaré c Piper b Benjamin	23		
R. J. Harden lbw b Benjamin	9		
†N. D. Burns c Piper b Benjamin	0	– (4) not out	3
G. D. Rose c Piper b Donald	14		
N. A. Mallender c Piper b Benjamin	0		
R. P. Lefebvre c Humpage b Reeve	22		
I. G. Swallow c Reeve b Pierson	32		
A. N. Jones st Piper b Pierson	0		
L-b 3, w 1, n-b 11	15	B 1, l-b 2, w 1, n-b 1	5
1/77 2/97 3/129 4/146 5/152 6/173 7/181 8/226 9/268	270	1/223 2/231 (2 wkts dec.)	238

Bonus points – Somerset 3, Warwickshire 4.

Bowling: *First Innings*—Donald 23–9–58–1; Benjamin 27–3–86–4; Munton 21–2–65–0; Reeve 20–8–47–3; Pierson 1.5–0–11–2. *Second Innings*—Donald 8–1–27–0; Benjamin 8–1–31–0; Pierson 9–2–23–0; Reeve 5–0–19–0; Munton 6–0–35–0; Asif Din 10–0–41–0; Moles 8–0–56–2; Humpage 2–1–3–0.

Warwickshire

A. J. Moles c Harden b Jones	14	– c Burns b Mallender	6
J. D. Ratcliffe lbw b Rose	7	– not out	16
Asif Din c Rose b Lefebvre	45	– lbw b Mallender	0
G. W. Humpage not out	67	– not out	0
*D. A. Reeve b Jones	4		
D. P. Ostler not out	11		
L-b 2, n-b 2	4	L-b 1, n-b 1	2
1/16 2/46 3/106 4/117 (4 wkts dec.)	152	1/22 2/22 (2 wkts)	24

†K. J. Piper, A. A. Donald, J. E. Benjamin, A. R. K. Pierson and T. A. Munton did not bat.

Bonus points – Warwickshire 1, Somerset 1.

Bowling: *First Innings*—Jones 11–3–38–2; Mallender 10.2–2–24–0; Lefebvre 11–5–31–1; Rose 9–0–57–1. *Second Innings*—Jones 6–1–19–0; Mallender 5–4–4–2.

Umpires: K. J. Lyons and D. O. Oslear.

At Worcester, July 18, 19, 20. SOMERSET drew with WORCESTERSHIRE.

At Uxbridge, July 21, 23, 24. SOMERSET lost to MIDDLESEX by four wickets.

At Scarborough, July 25, 26, 27. SOMERSET drew with YORKSHIRE.

At Manchester, July 28, 30, 31. SOMERSET drew with LANCASHIRE.

SOMERSET v SURREY

At Weston-super-Mare, August 4, 6, 7. Drawn. Somerset 6 pts, Surrey 6 pts. Toss: Surrey. After Cook had, for the second season in succession, become the first player to 2,000 first-class runs, Somerset batted productively. The high points were Harden's unbeaten 117-ball century and the mighty innings of Rose, whose 85 from 55 balls contained eight sixes and five fours.

In one over Medlycott was struck for 29 runs. As the pitch continued to play easily, Surrey recovered handsomely from 39 for four through a fifth-wicket partnership of 188 between Greig (220 balls) and Lynch (155 balls, eighteen fours). Greig declared 139 behind, and Cook's seventh first-class century of the summer set up a target of 369 in 250 minutes. Thorpe (136 balls) and Ward, before he was brilliantly caught on the boundary, put on 105 in 28 overs to launch the charge, and Lynch, with a superb 104 from 83 balls, including five sixes and nine fours, propelled Surrey to 325 for five with six overs left. However, Lynch, Medlycott and Stewart all went in four balls, and it fell to the ninth-wicket pair to play out the final 27 deliveries.

Close of play: First day, Somerset 441-8 (R. J. Harden 104*); Second day, Somerset 58-0 (S. J. Cook 29*, P. M. Roebuck 18*).

Somerset

S. J. Cook c Stewart b Waqar Younis	52	– not out	116
P. M. Roebuck c Lynch b Bicknell	49	– lbw b Kendrick	39
A. N. Hayhurst c Stewart b Waqar Younis	40		
*C. J. Tavaré b Kendrick	38	– (3) b Kendrick	4
R. J. Harden not out	104	– (4) not out	55
†N. D. Burns b Waqar Younis	25		
G. D. Rose b Bicknell	85		
R. P. Lefebvre c Stewart b Bicknell	8		
I. G. Swallow c Stewart b Bicknell	11		
B 8, l-b 9, w 3, n-b 9	29	B 1, l-b 10, n-b 4	15
1/99 2/110 3/194 4/194 5/277 6/401 7/415 8/441	(8 wkts dec.) 441	1/110 2/118	(2 wkts dec.) 229

N. A. Mallender and A. N. Jones did not bat.

Bonus points – Somerset 4, Surrey 2 (Score at 100 overs: 392-5).

Bowling: *First Innings*—Waqar Younis 23–2–80–3; Bicknell 23–3–79–4; Feltham 6–0–23–0; Medlycott 25–8–100–0; Kendrick 21–3–87–1; Greig 12–0–55–0. *Second Innings*—Waqar Younis 8–1–31–0; Bicknell 8–1–15–0; Kendrick 21–4–73–2; Medlycott 21–3–99–0; Greig 0.1–0–0–0.

Surrey

G. S. Clinton c Roebuck b Jones	8	– (2) c Burns b Jones	16
M. A. Feltham c Harden b Jones	0	– (1) b Jones	0
G. P. Thorpe run out	9	– lbw b Swallow	86
†D. M. Ward b Lefebvre	18	– c Lefebvre b Swallow	43
M. A. Lynch b Swallow	97	– b Hayhurst	104
*I. A. Greig not out	123	– lbw b Lefebvre	24
A. J. Stewart not out	24	– (8) lbw b Rose	0
K. T. Medlycott (did not bat)		– (7) c sub b Rose	38
M. P. Bicknell (did not bat)		– not out	2
N. M. Kendrick (did not bat)		– not out	0
B 4, l-b 6, w 4, n-b 9	23	L-b 13, w 1	14
1/1 2/13 3/25 4/39 5/227	(5 wkts dec.) 302	1/0 2/37 3/142 4/179 5/245 6/325 7/325 8/325	(8 wkts) 327

Waqar Younis did not bat.

Bonus points – Surrey 4, Somerset 2.

Bowling: *First Innings*—Jones 16–4–62–2; Mallender 13–2–49–0; Lefebvre 17–4–47–1; Rose 13–1–40–0; Hayhurst 6–2–11–0; Swallow 20.5–3–83–1. *Second Innings*—Jones 9–1–36–2; Mallender 14–1–47–0; Lefebvre 14.5–0–72–1; Rose 9–3–26–2; Hayhurst 13–0–59–1; Swallow 11–0–74–2.

Umpires: P. J. Eele and R. A. White.

SOMERSET v NOTTINGHAMSHIRE

At Weston-super-Mare, August 8, 9, 10. Drawn. Somerset 8 pts, Nottinghamshire 5 pts. Toss: Nottinghamshire. In good weather, on a gradually slowing pitch, Trump's spell of three for 4 in eight balls arrested a useful start initiated by Robinson (236 balls) and Newell, who added 104 in 41 overs. Stephenson helped his captain add 69, but Mallender swept the tail aside to complete a fine bowl. Somerset's poor start was redressed by Tavaré (167 balls, sixteen fours) and Hayhurst, who put on 164 in 55 overs for the third wicket. Crisp half-centuries from Burns and Rose helped produce a lead of 150. Nottinghamshire also began badly, and when Mallender reduced them to 96 for five, still 54 behind with 160 minutes remaining, they seemed doomed. However, Robinson kept doggedly on, remaining unbeaten for close on five hours (281 balls), and Evans, soon settling, registered his maiden century from 167 balls, a timely and sterling effort in a partnership of 196 which saved the match.

Close of play: First day, Somerset 38-2 (A. N. Hayhurst 21*, C. J. Tavaré 4*); Second day, Nottinghamshire 11-1 (M. Newell 3*, K. Saxelby 0*).

Nottinghamshire

B. C. Broad c Burns b Mallender	4	– c Burns b Mallender	7
M. Newell c Burns b Trump	59	– c Hayhurst b Lefebvre	7
*R. T. Robinson b Lefebvre	79	– (4) not out	125
P. Johnson c Mallender b Trump	4	– (5) b Mallender	12
D. W. Randall b Trump	0	– (6) c Burns b Mallender	0
K. P. Evans lbw b Mallender	0	– (7) not out	100
F. D. Stephenson b Swallow	34		
†B. N. French not out	24		
K. E. Cooper c Tavaré b Mallender	7		
K. Saxelby lbw b Mallender	6	– (3) c Cook b Trump	20
J. A. Afford lbw b Mallender	0		
B 4, l-b 13, w 3, n-b 1	21	B 10, l-b 6, n-b 5	21
1/12 2/116 3/120 4/120 5/121 6/190 7/201 8/220 9/230	238	1/11 2/19 3/64 4/96 5/96 (5 wkts dec.)	292

Bonus points – Nottinghamshire 2, Somerset 4.

Bowling: *First Innings*—Mallender 20.1–6–46–5; Rose 13–4–37–0; Lefebvre 13–6–20–1; Hayhurst 8–2–24–0; Swallow 15–6–33–1; Trump 21–5–61–3. *Second Innings*—Mallender 26–6–69–3; Rose 13–4–26–0; Trump 19–5–56–1; Lefebvre 13–5–24–1; Hayhurst 4–0–15–0; Roebuck 8–1–22–0; Swallow 16–5–46–0; Harden 6–1–13–0; Cook 1–0–5–0.

Somerset

S. J. Cook lbw b Cooper	6
P. M. Roebuck c French b Cooper	0
A. N. Hayhurst c and b Saxelby	79
*C. J. Tavaré b Stephenson	96
R. J. Harden c Afford b Stephenson	0
†N. D. Burns c and b Afford	56
G. D. Rose b Afford	60
R. P. Lefebvre lbw b Evans	0
I. G. Swallow c Johnson b Cooper	27
N. A. Mallender not out	17
H. R. J. Trump st French b Afford	4
B 4, l-b 24, w 1, n-b 14	43
1/1 2/17 3/181 4/185 5/258 6/288 7/289 8/355 9/365	388

Bonus points – Somerset 4, Nottinghamshire 3 (Score at 100 overs: 318-7).

Bowling: Stephenson 27–2–89–2; Cooper 20–1–57–3; Saxelby 16–4–55–1; Afford 38–11–102–3; Evans 15–5–57–1.

Umpires: P. J. Eele and R. A. White.

SOMERSET v HAMPSHIRE

At Taunton, August 18, 19, 20, 21. Somerset won by five wickets. Somerset 22 pts, Hampshire 8 pts. Toss: Hampshire. Terry's 224-ball vigil held Hampshire together after a poor start, and he received excellent help from Robin Smith and Marshall, although Ayling and Maru put together the highest stand of the innings – 105 in 29 overs. Mallender bowled steadily, and was responsible for Ayling's retirement shortly before the close. Only six overs were possible on the second day, owing to bad light and rain, but on the third day Cook gave Somerset a fine start with his eighth hundred of the season (181 balls, sixteen fours). The patient Tavaré, with 66 from 206 balls, kept them going after a mid-innings slump, getting spirited assistance from Lefebvre. Terry and Chris Smith put Hampshire on the way to a declaration which set a target of 302 in 205 minutes (53 overs minimum). Cook again starred, making his 77 from 103 balls, and after healthy contributions from Hayhurst, Tavaré (67 balls) and Harden, Rose and Burns were left to score 30 from four overs. Rose, hitting three sixes in his nineteen-ball 33, steered his side home with four balls to spare.

Close of play: First day, Hampshire 359-8 (C. A. Connor 8*, P. J. Bakker 3*); Second day, Hampshire 401-9 (J. R. Ayling 62*, C. A. Connor 29*); Third day, Hampshire 21-0 (V. P. Terry 10*, C. L. Smith 9*).

Hampshire

V. P. Terry c Jones b Rose	96	– c and b Harden	59
C. L. Smith lbw b Mallender	1	– c and b Harden	88
D. I. Gower c Burns b Jones	14	– c Harden b Lefebvre	29
R. A. Smith c Burns b Mallender	58	– not out	13
M. D. Marshall lbw b Swallow	58		
*M. C. J. Nicholas lbw b Jones	0	– (5) not out	6
J. R. Ayling not out	62		
R. J. Maru c Lefebvre b Mallender	46		
†R. J. Parks lbw b Mallender	1		
C. A. Connor not out	29		
P. J. Bakker b Mallender	20		
L-b 11, n-b 5	16	L-b 4, n-b 2	6
1/4 2/26 3/129 4/221 5/222 6/242 7/347 8/356 9/401	(9 wkts dec.) 401	1/135 2/182 3/182	(3 wkts dec.) 201

Bonus points – Hampshire 4, Somerset 2 (Score at 100 overs: 314-6).

In the first innings J. R. Ayling, when 62, retired hurt at 347 and resumed at 401.

Bowling: *First Innings*—Jones 22–3–87–2; Mallender 27–3–102–5; Lefebvre 19–6–59–0; Rose 15–2–48–1; Hayhurst 12–2–40–0; Swallow 17–7–37–1; Roebuck 4–0–17–0. *Second Innings*—Jones 9–1–21–0; Mallender 8–1–23–0; Rose 3–2–2–0; Lefebvre 12.4–1–40–1; Roebuck 8–0–34–0; Hayhurst 6–0–38–0; Harden 8–0–39–2.

Somerset

S. J. Cook c Parks b Maru	114	– lbw b Marshall	77
P. M. Roebuck c Connor b Bakker	0	– c Parks b Nicholas	19
A. N. Hayhurst c Parks b Connor	28	– st Parks b Maru	47
*C. J. Tavaré c Parks b Maru	66	– run out	64
R. J. Harden lbw b Marshall	0	– c Gower b Connor	36
†N. D. Burns c and b Maru	1	– (7) not out	8
G. D. Rose c C. L. Smith b Marshall	13	– (6) not out	33
R. P. Lefebvre c Parks b Maru	37		
N. A. Mallender b Marshall	17		
A. N. Jones not out	8		
I. G. Swallow not out	0		
L-b 11, n-b 6	17	B 10, l-b 8, w 1, n-b 1	20
1/1 2/65 3/179 4/180 5/181 6/194 7/273 8/284 9/292	(9 wkts dec.) 301	1/84 2/147 3/155 4/246 5/272	(5 wkts) 304

Bonus points – Somerset 4, Hampshire 4.

Bowling: *First Innings*—Bakker 22–6–58–1; Marshall 16–3–43–3; Connor 17–2–75–1; Maru 37.3–5–103–4; Nicholas 6–2–11–0. *Second Innings*—Marshall 11–2–34–1; Bakker 11–0–53–0; Maru 24.2–2–123–1; Connor 8–0–45–1; Nicholas 2–0–7–1; C. L. Smith 1–0–2–0; Ayling 3–0–22–0.

Umpires: J. H. Harris and B. Hassan.

At Hove, August 23, 24, 25, 27. SOMERSET beat SUSSEX by ten wickets.

At Taunton, September 3. SOMERSET beat SRI LANKANS by 71 runs (See Sri Lankan tour section).

At Birmingham, September 7, 8, 9, 10. SOMERSET drew with WARWICKSHIRE.

SOMERSET v WORCESTERSHIRE

At Taunton, September 12, 13, 14, 15. Worcestershire won by 173 runs. Worcestershire 23 pts, Somerset 5 pts. Toss: Worcestershire. A second-wicket stand of 264 in 68 overs between Hick and Curtis established the Worcestershire innings, and after a second-morning slump the last-wicket pair of Newport and McEwan added an unbroken 88 in seventeen overs. Curtis hit 100 of his 156 (280 balls) in boundaries, while Hick, having reached 2,000 runs with a six off the last ball before lunch, scored 109 in the second session and had 27 fours in his 154 from 195 balls. Cook (165 balls, 24 fours) responded in kind for Somerset, including 100 runs between lunch and tea, and after another morning collapse Harden and Jones put on 70 in eighteen overs for Somerset's last wicket. Newport was warned by stand-in umpire Harris after bowling four bouncers in one over to Jones. Lord, Hick and D'Oliveira added briskly to Worcestershire's lead of 78, and after another quick fall of wickets the target was set at 400 in 85 overs. Radford, getting more out of the slightly wearing pitch, set Somerset back with a spell of three for 16 in 33 balls, and with Newport chipping in they were reduced to 57 for five. Harden defiantly and positively hit seventeen fours in 90 from 111 balls, but safe slip catching took the visitors home with 30 overs to spare.

Close of play: First day, Worcestershire 378-4 (P. A. Neale 31*, S. R. Lampitt 10*); Second day, Somerset 287-2 (R. J. Bartlett 69*, C. J. Tavaré 14*); Third day, Worcestershire 267-4 (D. B. D'Oliveira 59*, S. R. Lampitt 2*).

Worcestershire

T. S. Curtis c Tavaré b Jones	156	– c Swallow b Jones 10
G. J. Lord c Tavaré b Jones	6	– lbw b Mallender 80
G. A. Hick c Tavaré b Mallender	154	– lbw b Jones 81
D. B. D'Oliveira b Jones	14	– c Burns b Jones 60
*P. A. Neale lbw b Mallender	40	– lbw b Mallender 12
S. R. Lampitt lbw b Mallender	16	– c Burns b Jones 10
†S. J. Rhodes c Harden b Mallender	6	– not out 34
R. K. Illingworth c Lefebvre b Jones	8	– b Jones 3
P. J. Newport not out	65	– not out 7
N. V. Radford c Lefebvre b Hayhurst	14	
S. M. McEwan not out	30	
L-b 9, n-b 2	11	B 12, l-b 10, n-b 2 24
1/43 2/307 3/331 4/346 5/386 6/398 7/411 8/411 9/432	(9 wkts dec.) 520	1/28 2/166 3/198 4/252 5/268 6/279 7/284 (7 wkts dec.) 321

Bonus points – Worcestershire 4, Somerset 1 (Score at 100 overs: 356-4).

Bowling: *First Innings*—Jones 35–6–154–4; Mallender 32–7–100–4; Rose 6–1–15–0; Lefebvre 30–9–67–0; Hayhurst 22–2–87–1; Swallow 24–5–88–0. *Second Innings*—Jones 21–2–76–5; Mallender 24–4–75–2; Hayhurst 8–1–43–0; Rose 9–1–51–0; Swallow 9–0–51–0; Lefebvre 4–2–3–0.

Somerset

A. N. Hayhurst c Rhodes b Lampitt	50	– c Hick b Newport	22
S. J. Cook c Neale b Illingworth	143	– c Hick b Radford	13
R. J. Bartlett c D'Oliveira b Newport	73	– c Rhodes b Radford	12
*C. J. Tavaré c Rhodes b Newport	18	– b Radford	5
R. J. Harden not out	51	– c D'Oliveira b Radford	90
†N. D. Burns b Newport	0	– c Hick b Newport	0
G. D. Rose b Lampitt	29	– lbw b Lampitt	36
R. P. Lefebvre c Hick b Lampitt	0	– c D'Oliveira b McEwan	15
I. G. Swallow run out	4	– b Illingworth	0
N. A. Mallender c Hick b Lampitt	15	– c Hick b Lampitt	23
A. N. Jones b Illingworth	41	– not out	2
B 1, l-b 3, w 3, n-b 11	18	L-b 1, w 1, n-b 6	8
1/132 2/252 3/295 4/296 5/296 6/345 7/345 8/352 9/372	442	1/23 2/50 3/52 4/56 5/57 6/119 7/172 8/173 9/212	226

Bonus points – Somerset 4, Worcestershire 3 (Score at 100 overs: 372-8).

Bowling: *First Innings*—Newport 28–4–95–3; McEwan 26–1–116–0; Lampitt 24–3–97–4; Radford 18–6–75–0; Illingworth 22.5–5–55–2; Hick 1–1–0–0. *Second Innings*—Newport 13–1–74–2; Radford 13–2–55–4; Lampitt 10.5–1–43–2; McEwan 8–0–39–1; Illingworth 8–3–10–1; Hick 2–0–4–0.

Umpires: R. Julian and D. R. Shepherd
(J. H. Harris deputised for D. R. Shepherd on 2nd, 3rd and 4th days).

FIELDING IN 1990

(Qualification: 20 dismissals)

69	S. J. Rhodes (61 ct, 8 st)	30	G. W. Humpage (all ct)
63	K. M. Krikken (60 ct, 3 st)	30	M. A. Lynch
63	P. Moores (53 ct, 10 st)	30	R. J. Maru
59	C. P. Metson (all ct)	27	R. P. Davis
57	B. N. French (46 ct, 11 st)	26	G. A. Hick
54	R. J. Blakey (45 ct, 9 st)	26	D. A. Reeve
54	S. A. Marsh (49 ct, 5 st)	25	C. J. Adams
53	R. J. Parks (49 ct, 4 st)	24	M. A. Atherton
51	W. K. Hegg (49 ct, 2 st)	24	A. J. Stewart
50	M. A. Garnham (48 ct, 2 st)	24	V. P. Terry
50	P. A. Nixon (49 ct, 1 st)	23	L. Potter
46	R. C. Russell (45 ct, 1 st)	23	B. Roberts
45	P. R. Downton (42 ct, 3 st)	23	M. A. Roseberry
44	N. D. Burns (43 ct, 1 st)	23	A. J. Wright
44	K. J. Piper (40 ct, 4 st)	22	A. Fordham
35	D. M. Ward (32 ct, 3 st)	22	N. Shahid
34	D. Ripley (28 ct, 6 st)	21	D. Byas
33	D. B. D'Oliveira	20	N. H. Fairbrother
33	J. E. Emburey	20	M. W. Gatting
31	R. C. J. Williams (27 ct, 4 st)	20	P. E. Robinson
30	K. R. Brown		

SURREY

SURREY COUNTY CRICKET CLUB

ICH DIEN

Patron: HM The Queen
President: 1990 – E. A. Bedser
1991 – B. Coleman
Chairman: D. H. Newton
Chairman, Cricket Committee: J. A. Fulford
Secretary: D. G. Seward
The Oval, London SE11 5SS
(Telephone: 071-582 6660)
Captain: I. A. Greig
County Coach: G. G. Arnold
Assistant County Coach: C. E. Waller

In a year when batsmen reigned supreme, Surrey spent much of the summer of 1990 admiring their unexpected and rare gift from the Orient, the teenage Pakistani fast bowler, Waqar Younis. Club coach Geoff Arnold polished the magic lamp provided by the great all-rounder, Imran Khan, the genie Waqar appeared, and, granting three wishes in one, he provided a treasure chest of 95 wickets in all cricket.

Imran could hardly have recommended his latest pace protégé to Surrey at a more propitious time. Tony Gray, the West Indian fast bowler, whom they had re-engaged after a year's absence, was experiencing fitness problems, and Arnold, himself a fine purveyor of swing bowling, saw enough of Younis in a brief net trial to thrust him straight into a Benson and Hedges Cup quarter-final at Old Trafford at a few hours' notice. That was late May, and Younis was there to stay for the season. Initially, that is. The Surrey committee prudently recognised the benefits of such a special talent and granted him a five-year contract. The compactly built Younis, of the two-way swing and devastating yorker, was Surrey's most effective Championship bowler, with 57 wickets at just under 24 apiece. Of these, 29 were bowled and eight lbw; the other twenty were all caught behind the wicket, twelve by the wicket-keeper or first slip. In the Refuge Assurance League, he was top of the national averages and the leading wicket-taker with 31 at 12.77.

Indeed, Surrey's season was highlighted by Waqar and Ward, a cricketing double-act with an entrepreneurial ring which produced its most profitable business in the middle. David Ward, hitherto regarded as a useful county professional, became one of ten players in the country to pass 2,000 runs in a prosperous summer for strokemakers. In his previous five years at The Oval, he had made only three hundreds, but now he rubbed shoulders with such international "heavyweights" as Gooch, Cook, Hick and Haynes. Of his seven hundreds, two were doubles, including a career-best 263 against Kent at Canterbury, and he became the first Surrey player since J. H. Edrich in 1962, and the thirteenth in all, to score 2,000 for the county alone. Greats such as Hayward, Hobbs, Sandham and May had achieved the same feat, but in the days when more matches were played.

Although the final Britannic Assurance Championship placing of ninth was an improvement of three places on 1989, the Surrey members doubtless expected better. However, the committee and the backroom staff were largely content to be patient and await the harvest of their expansive youth scheme within the next few years. Furthermore, while The Oval pitches, with all their excellence and reliability, were an outstanding example to the rest of English cricket, they were a two-edged sword for Surrey. They won only three matches at The Oval, albeit going undefeated there. Their preference for four-day cricket, therefore, is not surprising, for it would offer them the opportunity to enjoy more winning options; in theory, anyway, if not always in practice.

The second of Surrey's six four-day matches last summer, against Lancashire, became a record-breaking bonanza which produced a new Championship mark of 1,650 runs for nineteen wickets. Ian Greig's 291 was the highest Championship score by a Surrey player at The Oval since A. Sandham's 292 not out against Northamptonshire in 1921. The Surrey captain was, however, upstaged by Neil Fairbrother's 366 in a Lancashire total of 863, the second highest in the Championship and the ninth biggest in all first-class cricket. It set the trend for the glut of run-getting around the country and left Martin Bicknell, with just one wicket for 305 in the opening two matches, fearing for his Surrey place. But by allying a deft change of pace to his natural away-swing, Bicknell claimed 67 wickets in first-class games and earned a place in England's side to tour Australia, along with team-mate Alec Stewart. Bicknell and Waqar Younis helped Surrey collect 64 bowling bonus points, joint best in the country, although their total of 54 for batting was of a low order.

Darren Bicknell made five first-class hundreds, all in the Championship, to win selection for the England A tour, for which he was joined by Keith Medlycott and Graham Thorpe. Left-arm spinner Medlycott had a chequered season after touring the West Indies with the England senior side early in 1990, while Thorpe, after a splendid first full season in 1989, had a lean time as others broke the run bank. However, his phlegmatic temperament and undoubted class once more won the selectors' confidence, whereas Ward, in spite of his feats, went unrecognised. In the coming summer, Surrey will be without one of their other left-handers, Grahame Clinton, who signed off not only by passing 1,000 runs for the seventh time in twelve seasons at The Oval but by achieving his highest aggregate in seventeen years of first-class cricket.

The one-day game produced nothing special in terms of results. After reaching the last eight of the Benson and Hedges Cup, Surrey were drawn against the eventual winners, Lancashire, while they did not progress beyond a meeting with Middlesex in round two of the NatWest Bank Trophy. Sixth place in the Refuge Assurance League mirrored their Sabbath performances of the previous summer. As the season unfolded, the impressive West Side stand was nearing completion, and apart from finishing touches, it was ready for spectators, sponsors and scribes during the traditional final Test, against India, in late August. – David Field.

SURREY 1990

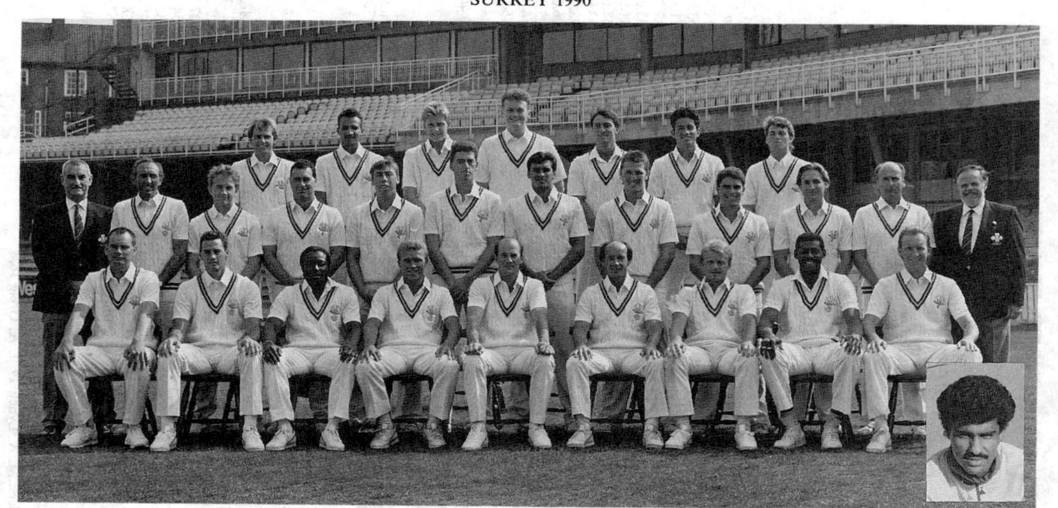

[*Bill Smith*

Back row: A. W. Smith, M. A. Butcher, A. G. Robson, J. Boiling, G. P. Thorpe, A. Hollioake, N. F. Sargeant. *Middle row:* J. Deary (*physiotherapist*), G. G. Arnold (*county coach*), A. D. Brown, A. J. Murphy, D. M. Ward, D. J. Bicknell, R. I. Alikhan, P. D. Atkins, J. D. Robinson, N. M. Kendrick, C. E. Waller (*assistant county coach*), M. R. L. W. Ayers (*scorer*). *Front row:* C. K. Bullen, M. P. Bicknell, M. A. Lynch, A. J. Stewart, I. A. Greig (*captain*), G. S. Clinton, K. T. Medlycott, A. H. Gray, M. A. Feltham. *Inset:* Waqar Younis.

SURREY RESULTS

All first-class matches – Played 24: Won 4, Lost 3, Drawn 17.

County Championship matches – Played 22: Won 4, Lost 3, Drawn 15.

Bonus points – Batting 54, Bowling 64.

Competition placings – Britannic Assurance County Championship, 9th; NatWest Bank Trophy, 2nd round; Benson and Hedges Cup, q-f; Refuge Assurance League, 6th equal.

BRITANNIC ASSURANCE CHAMPIONSHIP AVERAGES

BATTING

	Birthplace	*M*	*I*	*NO*	*R*	*HI*	*Avge*
‡D. M. Ward	*Croydon*	22	31	7	1,843	263	76.79
‡D. J. Bicknell	*Guildford*	13	20	4	1,199	186	74.93
‡I. A. Greig	*Queenstown, SA*	22	26	5	1,130	291	53.80
R. I. Alikhan	*Westminster*	11	16	2	726	138	51.85
‡A. J. Stewart	*Merton*	12	21	6	709	100*	47.26
‡G. S. Clinton	*Sidcup*	18	29	4	1,092	146	43.68
‡M. A. Lynch	*Georgetown, BG*	22	29	4	1,049	104	41.96
‡M. P. Bicknell	*Guildford*	19	15	7	309	50*	38.62
‡M. A. Feltham	*St John's Wood*	14	14	3	373	101	33.90
‡Waqar Younis	*Vehari, Pakistan*	14	9	7	56	14	28.00
G. P. Thorpe	*Farnham*	16	24	4	537	86	26.85
‡K. T. Medlycott	*Whitechapel*	20	22	7	389	44	25.93
J. D. Robinson	*Epsom*	7	9	0	151	72	16.77
N. M. Kendrick	*Bromley*	11	12	4	124	52*	15.50
A. J. Murphy	*Manchester*	12	6	3	6	4*	2.00

Also batted: P. D. Atkins (*Aylesbury*) (1 match) 23, 0*; ‡A. H. Gray (*Port-of-Spain, Trinidad*) (6 matches) 11, 11; N. F. Sargeant (*Hammersmith*) (2 matches) 1.

* *Signifies not out.* ‡ *Denotes county cap.*

The following played a total of nineteen three-figure innings for Surrey in County Championship matches – D. M. Ward 6, D. J. Bicknell 5, R. I. Alikhan 2, I. A. Greig 2, G. S. Clinton 1, M. A. Feltham 1, M. A. Lynch 1, A. J. Stewart 1.

BOWLING

	O	*M*	*R*	*W*	*BB*	*5W/i*	*Avge*
Waqar Younis	422	70	1,357	57	7-73	3	23.80
M. P. Bicknell	597.5	137	1,653	60	5-34	1	27.55
M. A. Feltham	334.4	59	1,082	39	6-53	2	27.74
A. H. Gray	212.4	43	556	16	4-83	0	34.75
K. T. Medlycott	617.5	134	2,020	53	7-92	3	38.11
A. J. Murphy	404.2	76	1,367	30	5-67	2	45.56
N. M. Kendrick	273	50	987	17	4-110	0	58.05
I. A. Greig	199.1	19	805	12	3-60	0	67.08

Also bowled: R. I. Alikhan 20–1–83–1; D. J. Bicknell 9–1–20–0; M. A. Lynch 27–5–130–1; J. D. Robinson 118.3–21–393–6; A. J. Stewart 5–0–32–0; G. P. Thorpe 9–1–69–0.

Wicket-keepers: D. M. Ward 25 ct, 2 st; A. J. Stewart 10 ct; N. F. Sargeant 5 ct.

Leading Fielders: M. A. Lynch 29, I. A. Greig 16.

At Hove, April 26, 27, 28, 30. SURREY lost to SUSSEX by five wickets.

SURREY v LANCASHIRE

At The Oval, May 3, 4, 5, 7. Drawn. Surrey 4 pts, Lancashire 6 pts. Toss: Surrey. This record-breaking match will long be remembered and chronicled for its quite phenomenal feats of scoring on a pitch exemplifying the tougher standards laid down by the Test and County Cricket Board. Greig, the Surrey captain, drove an extremely hard tactical bargain by amassing 707 for nine declared in the hope that his bowlers could take twenty wickets for an innings victory. However, it presented Lancashire with a *fait accompli.* Needing 558 to avoid the follow-on, and realising that victory for them was out of the question, they settled down to revel in the sumptuous batting conditions. The home bowling was savaged for a colossal 863, the highest Championship total of the century and second only to Yorkshire's 887 against Warwickshire at Birmingham in 1896. Lancashire's dapper left-hander, Fairbrother, was unstoppable in the run-glut, thrashing 366 to pass by 2 runs the previous best score at The Oval – 364 by Sir Leonard Hutton in the 1938 Test match against Australia. Greig, who, coming in at No. 7, had made the highest Championship innings by a Surrey player since 1926 and by one on the ground since 1921, could hardly have envisaged his career-best 291 off 251 balls being bettered the next day.

Although Surrey enjoyed a bountiful first day, reaching 396 for six, with Lynch falling just short of three figures, there was no reason to suspect such a wholesale assault on the pages of this Almanack. Greig's stand of 205 with Bicknell next day was a Surrey best for the eighth wicket, surpassing their oldest record partnership which had stood since 1898: 204 by T. W. Hayward and L. C. Braund, also against Lancashire at The Oval. In his first Championship hundred for Surrey, Greig hit 145 runs before lunch and was the prime contributor to the 101 runs which came in twelve overs after the interval as Surrey powered on to the highest total conceded by Lancashire. He batted in all for 277 minutes and hit nine sixes and 25 fours.

Lancashire, having responded with 179 for one from 55 overs by the close, took over inexorably on day three. Mendis, 97 overnight, was out soon after reaching his hundred, but Atherton eased to a personal top score of 191 and Fairbrother strode on to 311. By lunch Fairbrother had reached 100 from 102 balls (125 minutes), and in the next two sessions he scored 108 from 109 balls (135 minutes) and 103 from 110 balls (120 minutes), leaving the statisticians with Sunday to wonder if he might beat the English record of 424, set by another famous Lancastrian, A. C. MacLaren. Already the Atherton–Fairbrother alliance of 364 had eclipsed the county's third-wicket record of 306 by E. Paynter and N. Oldfield against Hampshire at Southampton in 1938. Lancashire's captain, Hughes, gave Fairbrother the chance of batting throughout the final day to pass MacLaren, but fatigue had its way. He eventually departed to his 407th ball, having batted for 500 minutes and struck five sixes and 47 fours, the eighth highest number in the list of boundary hits. His 366 was the third highest in the Championship after MacLaren's 424 and G. A. Hick's 405 not out. Surrey reached 80 for one in the remaining time, with Stewart passing 50 for the second time and the aggregate for the match soaring to 1,650 runs, a new mark in Championship cricket and the second highest for a match in England.

Close of play: First day, Surrey 396-6 (I. A. Greig 56*, K. T. Medlycott 33*); Second day, Lancashire 179-1 (G. D. Mendis 97*, M. A. Atherton 56*); Third day, Lancashire 665-3 (N. H. Fairbrother 311*, T. E. Jesty 18*).

Surrey

R. I. Alikhan st Hegg b Fitton	55		
G. S. Clinton c Patterson b DeFreitas	8	(1) c Watkinson b Atherton	15
A. J. Stewart c Fowler b Patterson	70	(2) not out	54
M. A. Lynch c and b Watkinson	95	(3) not out	6
G. P. Thorpe c Atherton b Fitton	27		
†D. M. Ward c Hughes b Fitton	36		
*I. A. Greig c Jesty b Hughes	291		
K. T. Medlycott c Fairbrother b Patterson	33		
M. P. Bicknell c Hegg b Hughes	42		
N. M. Kendrick not out	18		
B 6, l-b 16, n-b 10	32	B 2, l-b 1, n-b 2	5
1/10 2/118 3/187 4/261 5/275 6/316 7/401 8/606 9/707	(9 wkts dec.) 707	1/57	(1 wkt) 80

A. J. Murphy did not bat.

Bonus points – Surrey 4, Lancashire 2 (Score at 100 overs: 335-6).

Bowling: *First Innings*—Patterson 27–4–108–2; DeFreitas 26–4–99–1; Watkinson 23–2–113–1; Fitton 45–6–185–3; Atherton 22–5–75–0; Hughes 22.1–0–105–2. *Second Innings*—DeFreitas 4–0–10–0; Fitton 16–4–42–0; Atherton 13–5–25–1.

Lancashire

G. D. Mendis run out	102
G. Fowler run out	20
M. A. Atherton c Greig b Kendrick	191
N. H. Fairbrother c Kendrick b Greig	366
T. E. Jesty retired hurt	18
M. Watkinson b Greig	46
†W. K. Hegg c Ward b Bicknell	45
P. A. J. DeFreitas b Murphy	31
*D. P. Hughes not out	8
J. D. Fitton c Stewart b Murphy	3
B. P. Patterson c Greig b Medlycott	0
B 8, l-b 15, w 1, n-b 9	33
1/45 2/184 3/548 4/745 5/774 6/844 7/848 8/862 9/863	863

Bonus points – Lancashire 4 (Score at 100 overs: 401-2).

T. E. Jesty retired hurt at 665.

Bowling: Murphy 44–6–160–2; Bicknell 43–2–175–1; Kendrick 56–10–192–1; Medlycott 50.5–4–177–1; Lynch 5–2–17–0; Greig 19–3–73–2; Thorpe 7–1–46–0.

Umpires: B. Dudleston and A. A. Jones.

At Oxford, May 16, 17, 18. SURREY drew with OXFORD UNIVERSITY.

SURREY v HAMPSHIRE

At The Oval, May 19, 21, 22. Drawn. Surrey 5 pts, Hampshire 5 pts. Toss: Hampshire. Not even three declarations and a target which required Hampshire to score 329 in a minimum of 62 overs could produce a positive conclusion on another top-rate Oval pitch. On the opening day Surrey's Ward, with only the fifth hundred of his five-year career, but his second in successive innings, destroyed the Hampshire change bowlers with an explosive 129 not out off 144 balls (23 fours) and lifted Surrey from 173 for four to 374 for five. Left-arm spinner Maru was his main opponent, bowling an unchanged spell of 36 overs lasting four hours. Next morning the Smith brothers also found the conditions to their liking, Chris making a solid 71 and Robin clubbing fourteen fours in an unbeaten 114 before Hampshire conceded a lead of 124 runs. Stewart then hit the game's third century to set up the final declaration. Hampshire's hopes were high during a stand of 158 between Chris Smith and Gower, Smith making 84 off 117 balls and Gower 69 from 83. But when they lost their top order, Hampshire abandoned the chase and Marshall saw them to a draw with his second solid innings of the match.

Close of play: First day, Surrey 374-5 (D. M. Ward 129*, K. T. Medlycott 30*); Second day, Surrey 59-0 (A. J. Stewart 21*, G. S. Clinton 35*).

Surrey

First innings		Second innings	
D. J. Bicknell retired hurt	41		
G. S. Clinton c Maru b Connor	73	– retired hurt	37
A. J. Stewart c Maru b Connor	17	– (1) not out	100
M. A. Lynch c Gower b Marshall	11	– (3) c Gower b Shine	2
G. P. Thorpe c Parks b Marshall	2	– (4) lbw b Maru	18
†D. M. Ward not out	129	– (5) b Turner	23
*I. A. Greig c Terry b Marshall	34	– (6) c Maru b Turner	4
K. T. Medlycott not out	30	– (7) c Parks b Maru	8
M. A. Feltham (did not bat)		– (8) not out	3
B 4, l-b 15, w 2, n-b 16	37	B 2, l-b 4, w 1, n-b 2	9
1/148 2/151 3/166 4/173 5/308 (5 wkts dec.)	374	1/73 2/111 3/154 4/158 5/187 (5 wkts dec.)	204

M. P. Bicknell and A. J. Murphy did not bat.

Bonus points – Surrey 4, Hampshire 2 (Score at 100 overs: 321-5).

In the first innings D. J. Bicknell retired hurt at 117; in the second innings G. S. Clinton retired hurt at 70.

Bowling: *First Innings*—Marshall 20–4–65–3; Shine 16–2–75–0; Connor 25–4–84–2; Turner 13–0–45–0; Maru 36–12–86–0. *Second Innings*—Marshall 7–1–14–0; Shine 9–0–55–1; Connor 5–0–13–0; Maru 21–5–47–2; Turner 14.3–4–60–2; C. L. Smith 1–0–9–0.

Hampshire

	First Innings		Second Innings	
V. P. Terry lbw b Murphy	8	c Medlycott b M. P. Bicknell	0
*C. L. Smith run out	71	c Medlycott b Murphy	84
D. I. Gower b Feltham	4	c sub b M. P. Bicknell	69
R. A. Smith not out	114	c Feltham b M. P. Bicknell	1
T. C. Middleton lbw b Greig	1	(6) b Medlycott	20
M. D. Marshall not out	47	(5) not out	51
†R. J. Parks (did not bat)		not out	5
B 2, l-b 2, n-b 1	5	B 6, l-b 1, w 1	8
1/19 2/26 3/163 4/179	(4 wkts dec.) 250	1/0 2/158 3/161 4/167 5/197	(5 wkts) 238

R. J. Maru, C. A. Connor, I. J. Turner and K. J. Shine did not bat.

Bonus points – Hampshire 3, Surrey 1.

Bowling: *First Innings*—M. P. Bicknell 15–5–43–0; Murphy 22–6–65–1; Feltham 19–7–51–1; Greig 8–1–40–1; Medlycott 21.1–8–47–0. *Second Innings*—M. P. Bicknell 16–5–39–3; Murphy 12–1–65–1; Feltham 8–0–31–0; Medlycott 20–3–84–1; Lynch 3–0–12–0.

Umpires: P. J. Eele and J. W. Holder.

At Lord's, May 23, 24, 25. SURREY drew with MIDDLESEX.

SURREY v DERBYSHIRE

At The Oval, June 6, 7, 8. Drawn. Surrey 5 pts, Derbyshire 3 pts. Toss: Surrey. Alikhan, after 71 first-class appearances without a hundred, was 18 runs short when a heavy downpour swept in at the start of the last hour, with Surrey needing another 107 in seventeen overs for victory and all their wickets intact. On an opening day when 44 overs were lost to rain, Waqar Younis, the young Pakistani fast bowler, registered a week earlier, claimed the wickets of Barnett, Morris and Kuiper as the ball swung consistently. Bowler, 75 overnight, became his fourth victim first thing next morning, and the visitors had to settle for a total of 275 when Medlycott produced his own four-wicket flourish. Thorpe's first half-century of the season saw Surrey to an expected declaration, although there was little urgency to their batting until Ward arrived to reel off six fours in quick succession. Derbyshire's second innings took on a more familiar look as Barnett and Bowler moved solidly to 144 before the first of the last day's stoppages. This advanced a declaration which left Surrey to make 268 in just over three hours, but the threat of a further interruption was always evident in the slate-grey skies. The pitch had become depressingly slow, as indicated by the lack of a single wicket while 304 runs were scored on the abbreviated final day.

Close of play: First day, Derbyshire 183-5 (P. D. Bowler 75*, K. M. Krikken 7*); Second day, Derbyshire 1-0 (K. J. Barnett 1*, P. D. Bowler 0*).

Derbyshire

	First Innings		Second Innings	
*K. J. Barnett c Greig b Waqar Younis	1	not out	51
P. D. Bowler c Ward b Waqar Younis	75	not out	85
J. E. Morris lbw b Waqar Younis	25		
B. Roberts c Clinton b Feltham	17		
A. P. Kuiper lbw b Waqar Younis	37		
C. J. Adams lbw b Feltham	3		
†K. M. Krikken c Feltham b Medlycott	35		
M. Jean-Jacques c Greig b Medlycott	25		
A. E. Warner c sub b Medlycott	17		
S. J. Base b Medlycott	0		
G. Miller not out	10		
B 6, l-b 14, w 6, n-b 4	30	B 4, l-b 4	8
1/9 2/57 3/95 4/163 5/168 6/186 7/239 8/242 9/242	275		(no wkt dec.) 144

Bonus points – Derbyshire 3, Surrey 4 (Score at 100 overs: 271-9).

Bowling: *First Innings*—Waqar Younis 30–4–77–4; Bicknell 20–4–64–0; Murphy 22–4–59–0; Feltham 19–7–40–2; Medlycott 10.1–4–14–4; Alikhan 1–0–1–0. *Second Innings*—Waqar Younis 4–0–16–0; Murphy 4–2–7–0; Medlycott 11–2–21–0; Greig 9–1–36–0; Alikhan 5–0–29–0; Lynch 4–0–27–0.

Surrey

R. I. Alikhan c Bowler b Miller	39	– not out	82
K. T. Medlycott run out	6		
G. P. Thorpe not out	58		
†D. M. Ward not out	37		
G. S. Clinton (did not bat)		– (2) not out	70
L-b 3, w 2, n-b 7	12	L-b 6, w 2, n-b 1	9
1/9 2/88	(2 wkts dec.) 152		(no wkt) 161

M. A. Lynch, *I. A. Greig, M. A. Feltham, M. P. Bicknell, Waqar Younis and A. J. Murphy did not bat.

Bonus points – Surrey 1.

Bowling: *First Innings*—Jean-Jacques 14.1–3–47–0; Base 12–1–38–0; Warner 11–2–36–0; Kuiper 7–1–15–0; Miller 8–2–13–1. *Second Innings*—Jean-Jacques 8–0–49–0; Base 9–2–33–0; Warner 9–0–30–0; Miller 9–2–30–0; Kuiper 1.3–0–13–0.

Umpires: J. H. Harris and J. W. Holder.

At Harrogate, June 9, 11, 12. SURREY drew with YORKSHIRE.

SURREY v WORCESTERSHIRE

At The Oval, June 16, 18, 19. Drawn. Surrey 4 pts, Worcestershire 4 pts. Toss: Surrey. A resolute century from Botham, his first for three seasons in the Championship, helped Worcestershire recover from 94 for four. He cast off his attacking instincts and batted for more than four hours (198 balls), hitting two sixes and eleven fours in his 113. The value of his innings was fully realised next morning when the defending county champions were able to declare with maximum batting points. Surrey, for their part, were rewarded with four bowling points, and that proved to be the high point of a second day restricted by rain after lunch to 38 overs. Surrey declared immediately on the third morning, and when Worcestershire closed their second innings, somewhat generously, at 84, the home county were left to score 318 in 77 overs. Worcestershire squandered three chances as Clinton and Stewart added 113 for the second wicket, but when McEwan dismissed Stewart and Thorpe in successive balls, Surrey faltered. With 146 required from the final twenty overs, Neale gambled with the spin of Stemp and Hick, and the strategy almost worked. Surrey lost three wickets for 47 and Medlycott and Bicknell were obliged to play out the final twelve overs encircled by close fielders.

Close of play: First day, Worcestershire 263-7 (P. J. Newport 28*, S. R. Lampitt 0*); Second day, Surrey 67-1 (G. S. Clinton 33*, A. J. Stewart 7*).

Worcestershire

T. S. Curtis c Ward b Bicknell	0	– not out	31
M. J. Weston c Gray b Bicknell	6	– not out	38
G. A. Hick c Ward b Bicknell	59		
D. B. D'Oliveira c Lynch b Bicknell	0		
I. T. Botham c Stewart b Medlycott	113		
*P. A. Neale b Gray	36		
P. J. Newport c Ward b Medlycott	41		
†S. J. Rhodes c Lynch b Medlycott	4		
S. R. Lampitt not out	21		
S. M. McEwan c Bicknell b Medlycott	2		
R. D. Stemp not out	0		
B 5, l-b 11, w 1, n-b 1	18	B 4, l-b 9, w 2	15
1/11 2/16 3/22 4/94 5/187 6/257 7/263 8/282 9/284	(9 wkts dec.) 300		(no wkt dec.) 84

Bonus points – Worcestershire 4, Surrey 4.

Bowling: *First Innings*—Gray 26–8–41–1; Bicknell 22–4–70–4; Murphy 19–4–64–0; Medlycott 29–8–92–4; Greig 4–0–17–0. *Second Innings*—Gray 6–3–8–0; Bicknell 5–0–15–0; Murphy 5–1–12–0; Medlycott 5–1–19–0; Alikhan 1–0–17–0.

Surrey

R. I. Alikhan run out	23	– c Rhodes b Lampitt	21
G. S. Clinton not out	33	– c Lampitt b Newport	80
A. J. Stewart not out	7	– c Rhodes b McEwan	55
G. P. Thorpe (did not bat)		– c D'Oliveira b McEwan	0
†D. M. Ward (did not bat)		– c Curtis b Hick	21
M. A. Lynch (did not bat)		– c Botham b Hick	21
*I. A. Greig (did not bat)		– c Lampitt b Hick	6
K. T. Medlycott (did not bat)		– not out	16
M. P. Bicknell (did not bat)		– not out	15
L-b 2, n-b 2	4	L-b 7, w 1, n-b 1	9
1/46	(1 wkt dec.) 67	1/42 2/155 3/155 4/163 5/199 6/212 7/219	(7 wkts) 244

A. H. Gray and A. J. Murphy did not bat.

Bowling: *First Innings*—Newport 9–7–6–0; McEwan 6–2–26–0; Stemp 9–3–13–0; Lampitt 6.2–1–20–0. *Second Innings*—Newport 13–1–35–1; McEwan 17–4–40–2; Lampitt 13–4–40–1; Botham 10.4–2–24–0; Stemp 17–5–78–0; Hick 6–1–20–3.

Umpires: H. D. Bird and J. H. Harris.

At Nottingham, June 20, 21, 22. SURREY drew with NOTTINGHAMSHIRE.

At Cardiff, June 30, July 2, 3. SURREY drew with GLAMORGAN.

SURREY v NORTHAMPTONSHIRE

At The Oval, July 4, 5, 6. Surrey won by 147 runs. Surrey 20 pts. Toss: Northamptonshire. Following the loss of the opening day's play, Surrey won their first Championship match of the season. Two forfeitures on the final day left Northamptonshire needing 348 from 76 overs, but they never came close and Surrey eased home with 12.4 overs in hand. The initial work was done by Darren Bicknell and Clinton who, on the second day after 45 overs had been lost to heavy morning rain, put on 251 without being parted. Next morning, when Surrey batted on for another 23 overs, they stretched their opening stand to 321, the county's highest since J. B. Hobbs and T. W. Hayward compiled 352 against Warwickshire in 1909. Bicknell's 169 was easily a career best. His brother, Martin, quickly made inroads into Northamptonshire's innings, and then Waqar Younis, with his swinging, skidding deliveries, accounted for the middle order. Only Larkins, batting in the unaccustomed position of No. 5 on his return after seven weeks off through injury, stood in their way. Though made in a lost cause, his hundred in 165 minutes, resplendent with two sixes and eighteen fours, was a resounding effort.

Close of play: First day, No play; Second day, Surrey 251-0 (D. J. Bicknell 131*, G. S. Clinton 108*).

Surrey

D. J. Bicknell b Williams 169
G. S. Clinton b Robinson 146
G. P. Thorpe not out 15
†D. M. Ward not out 4
L-b 3, n-b 10 13

1/321 2/331 (2 wkts dec.) 347

M. A. Lynch, *I. A. Greig, J. D. Robinson, M. A. Feltham, K. T. Medlycott, M. P. Bicknell and Waqar Younis did not bat.

Bonus points – Surrey 4.

Bowling: Davis 22–5–70–0; Robinson 20–4–57–1; Hughes 12–0–84–0; Williams 25–8–65–1; Cook 9–2–34–0; Bailey 7–1–34–0.

Surrey forfeited their second innings.

Northamptonshire

Northamptonshire forfeited their first innings.

A. Fordham c Greig b M. P. Bicknell . 3
N. A. Felton lbw b M. P. Bicknell 2
R. J. Bailey c Ward b Waqar Younis .. 33
D. J. Capel b Waqar Younis 19
*W. Larkins b Waqar Younis 107
R. G. Williams b Waqar Younis 0
†D. Ripley b M. P. Bicknell 9
J. G. Hughes c Ward b M. P. Bicknell . 1
W. W. Davis b Waqar Younis 9
N. G. B. Cook b Waqar Younis 0
M. A. Robinson not out 0
B 4, l-b 6, n-b 7 17

1/3 2/6 3/58 4/83 5/83 200
6/107 7/153 8/187 9/199

Bowling: Waqar Younis 18.2–9–36–6; M. P. Bicknell 16–3–58–4; Feltham 13–1–42–0; Medlycott 16–4–54–0.

Umpires: M. J. Kitchen and R. Palmer.

SURREY v WARWICKSHIRE

At The Oval, July 7, 9, 10. Surrey won by 168 runs. Surrey 24 pts, Warwickshire 3 pts. Toss: Warwickshire. Ward's consistent middle-order batting, mirrored in his fourth first-class hundred in eleven innings, gave Surrey an advantage they never conceded. It was driven home by Waqar Younis, whose seven for 73 was the best return of his brief career. Ultimately he finished with match figures of eleven for 128. Ward arrived with Surrey 13 for two; at 47 for three, Warwickshire's decision to put them in was looking a sound one. However, Lynch shed his natural exuberance and joined Ward in a vital stand of 208. He was out 8 runs short of a century after facing 199 balls. Ward's 126 contained three sixes and eleven fours in 220 deliveries. On the second day, Younis scythed through the Warwickshire innings, illustrating his pace by hitting the stumps five times and having an lbw and a caught behind in his impressive tally. Warwickshire were nine wickets down when they avoided the follow-on, Benjamin being dropped in the gully with a single needed, but Surrey purposefully extended their lead to 317 by the close of play. To some extent they were helped by the back strain which prevented Donald from bowling. Next morning Surrey added 45 in 35 minutes and set a target of 363. Apart from Ostler and Benjamin, Warwickshire had no consistent answer to Younis, who was well supported by Feltham.

Close of play: First day, Warwickshire 18-0 (A. J. Moles 5*, J. D. Ratcliffe 11*); Second day, Surrey 191-7 (K. T. Medlycott 9*, M. A. Feltham 1*).

Surrey

D. J. Bicknell c Ratcliffe b Benjamin	1	– lbw b Benjamin	9
G. S. Clinton c Humpage b Munton	18	– b Benjamin	33
G. P. Thorpe c Humpage b Donald	9	– c Piper b Munton	3
†D. M. Ward c Ostler b Reeve	126	– c Benjamin b Munton	15
M. A. Lynch c Piper b Munton	92	– c Piper b Benjamin	46
J. D. Robinson c Piper b Reeve	11	– (7) b Benjamin	27
*I. A. Greig not out	30	– (6) b Munton	34
K. T. Medlycott not out	4	– c sub b Benjamin	23
M. A. Feltham (did not bat)		– not out	22
M. P. Bicknell (did not bat)		– not out	6
B 2, l-b 8, w 1, n-b 1	12	L-b 14, n-b 4	18
1/2 2/13 3/47 4/255 5/255 6/293 (6 wkts dec.)	303	1/22 2/31 3/55 4/100 5/115 6/173 7/185 8/210 (8 wkts dec.)	236

Waqar Younis did not bat.

Bonus points – Surrey 4, Warwickshire 2.

Bowling: *First Innings*—Donald 12–1–31–1; Benjamin 17–4–37–1; Munton 33–4–85–2; Reeve 24–6–64–2; Pierson 7–0–39–0; Asif Din 2–0–6–0; Humpage 5–1–31–0. *Second Innings*—Benjamin 24–2–72–5; Munton 27–3–107–3; Reeve 12–3–43–0.

Warwickshire

A. J. Moles b Waqar Younis	16	– b Waqar Younis	1
J. D. Ratcliffe lbw b Waqar Younis	15	– (7) lbw b M. P. Bicknell	19
Asif Din c Lynch b M. P. Bicknell	22	– (2) c Lynch b Waqar Younis	4
G. W. Humpage b Waqar Younis	0	– c sub b Waqar Younis	4
D. P. Ostler b Waqar Younis	30	– (3) b Medlycott	59
†K. J. Piper c Clinton b M. P. Bicknell	28	– (5) b Feltham	14
*D. A. Reeve c Medlycott b M. P. Bicknell	11	– (6) lbw b Waqar Younis	17
A. R. K. Pierson c Ward b Waqar Younis	0	– not out	10
J. E. Benjamin not out	28	– c M. P. Bicknell b Feltham	41
A. A. Donald b Waqar Younis	0	– c Lynch b Feltham	3
T. A. Munton b Waqar Younis	6	– c Thorpe b Feltham	3
B 3, l-b 11, w 7	21	B 9, l-b 3, w 1, n-b 6	19
1/34 2/44 3/44 4/74 5/124 6/138 7/141 8/143 9/151	177	1/9 2/10 3/21 4/56 5/78 6/128 7/128 8/185 9/188	194

Bonus points – Warwickshire 1, Surrey 4.

Bowling: *First Innings*—Waqar Younis 21.1–2–73–7; M. P. Bicknell 24–7–56–3; Feltham 10–3–15–0; Robinson 2–0–9–0; Medlycott 2–0–10–0. *Second Innings*—Waqar Younis 14–0–55–4; M. P. Bicknell 16–7–32–1; Feltham 15.4–2–59–4; Medlycott 8–0–36–1.

Umpires: D. J. Constant and R. Palmer.

SURREY v SUSSEX

At Guildford, July 18, 19, 20. Sussex won by seven wickets. Sussex 21 pts, Surrey 7 pts. Toss: Surrey. Sussex, languishing near the foot of the Championship table, raced to their second win of the season against Surrey after Lenham had fashioned an aggressive, unbeaten 109 off 127 deliveries. They won with two balls remaining after being asked to make an improbable 254 in a minimum of 43 overs. On the first day, Surrey looked to be establishing control as Darren Bicknell, handicapped by ribs painfully bruised by Pigott, spent five and a half hours (98 overs) compiling a century on a pitch prompting suspicion and caution. Salisbury's leg-breaks spun generously, although a belligerent 52 from Lynch in 75 minutes raised the tenor. Bicknell progressed to 143 on the second day, when Sussex, after a collapse from 76 for one to 80 for five, were spared the follow-on by a more spectacular century from Speight. He reached 100 off 105 balls and had hit six sixes and eight fours when he was caught behind by Greig, Surrey's third wicket-keeper of the innings after Ward had damaged a thumb and Lynch had proved untidy. Sussex trailed by 32, but with Clinton taking 56 overs for his 93, and no easy runs offered, it was three o'clock before Surrey set out their demands. However, the fast-scoring Guildford ground proved to the liking of Lenham and his captain, Parker, and with quick running and attacking batting they upset Greig's calculations in their second-wicket partnership of 90.

Close of play: First day, Surrey 305-6 (D. J. Bicknell 123*, K. T. Medlycott 8*); Second day, Surrey 7-0 (D. J. Bicknell 6*, G. S. Clinton 1*).

Surrey

D. J. Bicknell b Pigott	143	– b Donelan	6
G. S. Clinton c Parker b Dodemaide	1	– b Dodemaide	93
G. P. Thorpe c Speight b C. M. Wells	33	– c and b Salisbury	79
†D. M. Ward b Salisbury	40	– not out	36
M. A. Lynch c Dodemaide b Salisbury	52	– not out	1
*I. A. Greig run out	37		
M. A. Feltham lbw b Dodemaide	0		
K. T. Medlycott c A. P. Wells b Dodemaide	16		
M. P. Bicknell c and b Pigott	8		
N. M. Kendrick c Parker b Dodemaide	2		
Waqar Younis not out	1		
B 2, l-b 9, w 1	12	L-b 4, w 1, n-b 1	6
1/2 2/67 3/152 4/228 5/293 6/296 7/314 8/340 9/343	345	1/9 2/140 3/220 (3 wkts dec.)	221

Bonus points – Surrey 3, Sussex 1 (Score at 100 overs: 250-4).

Bowling: *First Innings*—Pigott 22.3–0–68–2; Dodemaide 27–2–84–4; C. M. Wells 22–10–47–1; Donelan 21–7–42–0; Salisbury 26–4–84–2; Lenham 2–0–9–0. *Second Innings*—Dodemaide 10–3–23–1; Pigott 7–1–26–0; Donelan 22–3–70–1; Salisbury 15–0–77–1; C. M. Wells 6.3–0–21–0.

Sussex

N. J. Lenham run out	46	– not out	109
J. W. Hall c and b Medlycott	16	– c M. P. Bicknell b Medlycott	21
*P. W. G. Parker b Waqar Younis	11	– c Ward b Feltham	64
A. P. Wells c Kendrick b Medlycott	0	– c Kendrick b Medlycott	42
M. P. Speight c Greig b Waqar Younis	108	– not out	0
C. M. Wells c Ward b Waqar Younis	0		
A. I. C. Dodemaide b Medlycott	11		
†P. Moores lbw b Feltham	24		
A. C. S. Pigott c Feltham b Medlycott	33		
I. D. K. Salisbury b Medlycott	21		
B. T. P. Donelan not out	11		
B 19, l-b 9, w 1, n-b 3	32	B 7, l-b 10, n-b 1	18
1/54 2/76 3/76 4/80 5/80 6/111 7/193 8/263 9/290	313	1/69 2/159 3/251 (3 wkts)	254

Bonus points – Sussex 4, Surrey 4.

Bowling: *First Innings*—Waqar Younis 21–4–65–3; M. P. Bicknell 18–5–32–0; Feltham 17–5–44–1; Medlycott 27.1–3–121–5; Kendrick 8–2–23–0. *Second Innings*—Waqar Younis 8–0–45–0; M. P. Bicknell 12.4–3–52–0; Medlycott 14–3–61–2; Kendrick 5–0–43–0; Feltham 4–0–36–1.

Umpires: B. J. Meyer and K. E. Palmer.

SURREY v KENT

At Guildford, July 21, 23, 24. Drawn. Surrey 8 pts, Kent 6 pts. Toss: Surrey. Hinks, Taylor and Graham Cowdrey all flourished on a docile pitch, with Hinks's second Championship hundred of the season the basis of Kent's secure 372. Surrey lost Darren Bicknell on Saturday evening, and on Monday were 181 in arrears with five wickets down before Greig's unbeaten 89 in 112 balls and Feltham's first half-century of the season saw them to a declaration only 28 behind. An interesting finish looked in prospect when Kent lost three top wickets before the close, but Ward's 88 and Graham Cowdrey's 119 not out in 205 minutes thwarted Surrey. When they claimed an eighth wicket with 107 minutes left, and Kent 262 ahead, Surrey still entertained the possibility of a run-chase, but the Cowdrey brothers stayed together for 90 minutes to deny them. The outcome might have been different had Chris, batting with a fractured toe, inflicted by Waqar Younis in the Sunday League game, not been missed at silly point when 2.

Close of play: First day, Surrey 35-1 (G. S. Clinton 20*, G. P. Thorpe 10*); Second day, Kent 62-3 (T. R. Ward 18*, P. S. de Villiers 6*).

Kent

S. G. Hinks c Clinton b Gray	120	– c and b Feltham	1
R. P. Davis c Lynch b Feltham	0	– b Gray	4
N. R. Taylor c Gray b Kendrick	69	– (4) lbw b Gray	26
G. R. Cowdrey c Lynch b Feltham	71	– (6) not out	119
T. R. Ward lbw b Feltham	10	– (3) c Thorpe b Medlycott	88
*C. S. Cowdrey c Greig b Gray	20	– (10) lbw b Medlycott	27
†S. A. Marsh c Sargeant b Kendrick	7	– c Sargeant b Medlycott	11
R. M. Ellison c and b Kendrick	10	– c Sargeant b Medlycott	0
P. S. de Villiers lbw b Kendrick	32	– (5) b Kendrick	28
M. M. Patel c Lynch b Feltham	2	– (9) c Lynch b Medlycott	0
A. P. Igglesden not out	15	– c Ward b Kendrick	6
B 2, l-b 2, n-b 12	16	B 1, l-b 2, w 2, n-b 14	19
1/4 2/118 3/243 4/257 5/298 6/301 7/314 8/328 9/335	372	1/4 2/10 3/48 4/125 5/187 6/228 7/234 8/234 9/310	329

Bonus points – Kent 4, Surrey 4.

Bowling: *First Innings*—Gray 20–4–54–2; Feltham 22–1–86–4; Greig 6–0–36–0; Thorpe 2–0–23–0; Medlycott 7–0–59–0; Kendrick 33.2–8–110–4. *Second Innings*—Gray 24–2–93–2; Feltham 11–1–32–1; Medlycott 41–13–99–5; Kendrick 29.4–7–102–2; Lynch 1–1–0–0.

Surrey

D. J. Bicknell c Patel b Igglesden	4	– not out	9
G. S. Clinton c Marsh b Igglesden	38	– not out	8
G. P. Thorpe lbw b Igglesden	42		
D. M. Ward c Marsh b Igglesden	48		
M. A. Lynch b de Villiers	20		
M. A. Feltham b Ellison	55		
*I. A. Greig not out	89		
K. T. Medlycott b Ellison	28		
B 1, l-b 11, w 4, n-b 4	20		
1/4 2/85 3/114 4/148 5/191 6/249 7/344	(7 wkts dec.) 344		(no wkt) 17

N. M. Kendrick, A. H. Gray and †N. F. Sargeant did not bat.

Bonus points – Surrey 4, Kent 2 (Score at 100 overs: 310-6).

Bowling: *First Innings*—Igglesden 25–1–88–4; de Villiers 21–5–57–1; Davis 24–3–89–0; Patel 17–3–54–0; Ellison 19.3–4–44–2. *Second Innings*—Davis 6–2–9–0; Patel 5–2–6–0; Ward 1–0–1–0; Taylor 1–0–1–0.

Umpires: B. J. Meyer and K. E. Palmer.

At Cheltenham, July 28, 30, 31. SURREY drew with GLOUCESTERSHIRE.

At The Oval, August 1, 2, 3. SURREY drew with INDIANS (See Indian tour section).

At Weston-super-Mare, August 4, 6, 7. SURREY drew with SOMERSET.

SURREY v LEICESTERSHIRE

At The Oval, August 11, 13, 14. Surrey won by an innings and 5 runs. Surrey 24 pts, Leicestershire 4 pts. Toss: Leicestershire. Feltham's career-best six for 53 triggered Surrey's third win of a disappointing Championship campaign and hastened Leicestershire's third defeat in as many matches. On the opening day, the visiting county did not benefit from taking first use of the pitch, or from a sound start by Boon and Briers, the penetrative Waqar Younis doing the initial damage with four wickets in 26 balls in his second spell. Only Potter and Nixon, adding 93 for the sixth wicket, stood in Surrey's way. With Darren Bicknell providing the foundation over five and a half hours, Surrey built heavily on their advantage in the hope of bowling Leicestershire out a second time. Already without Lewis and Benjamin, the Leicestershire bowling was further weakened when Mullally was forced off with a strained hip. However, Parsons responded well to the extra responsibility and finished with six for 75. Leicestershire again passed 50 without loss, but with Feltham gaining extra lift to go with his swing, the match was over twenty minutes before tea. Boon's 56 from 78 balls was little consolation as the last nine wickets fell for 72.

Close of play: First day, Surrey 58-2 (D. J. Bicknell 14*, N. M. Kendrick 0*); Second day, Leicestershire 32-0 (T. J. Boon 16*, N. E. Briers 13*).

Leicestershire

First innings		Second innings	
T. J. Boon b Waqar Younis	32	c Ward b M. P. Bicknell	56
*N. E. Briers c Greig b M. P. Bicknell	22	b Waqar Younis	16
J. J. Whitaker b Waqar Younis	20	b Feltham	23
P. Willey b Waqar Younis	1	lbw b Feltham	3
L. Potter not out	52	c Greig b Feltham	19
J. D. R. Benson c Kendrick b Waqar Younis	7	c Lynch b M. P. Bicknell	5
†P. A. Nixon c and b Medlycott	46	not out	17
G. J. Parsons run out	14	lbw b Feltham	7
J. P. Agnew b M. P. Bicknell	4	b Waqar Younis	3
A. D. Mullally c Ward b M. P. Bicknell	9	c and b Feltham	8
D. J. Millns b M. P. Bicknell	1	b Feltham	4
B 15, l-b 12, w 2, n-b 7	36	B 6, l-b 2, w 1, n-b 1	10
1/55 2/80 3/84 4/89 5/99 6/192 7/212 8/225 9/237	244	1/53 2/99 3/104 4/107 5/118 6/138 7/146 8/155 9/164	171

Bonus points – Leicestershire 2, Surrey 4.

Bowling: *First Innings*—Waqar Younis 23–2–72–4; M. P. Bicknell 22–3–42–4; Feltham 15–4–40–0; Medlycott 20–6–44–1; Greig 2–0–16–0; Kendrick 4–1–3–0. *Second Innings*—Waqar Younis 17–3–41–2; M. P. Bicknell 22–3–69–2; Feltham 18.5–4–53–6.

Surrey

D. J. Bicknell c Whitaker b Millns	111
G. S. Clinton c Nixon b Parsons	34
A. J. Stewart c Nixon b Mullally	3
†D. M. Ward c Benson b Parsons	33
N. M. Kendrick c Potter b Millns	9
M. A. Lynch c Nixon b Parsons	12
*I. A. Greig c and b Parsons	84
M. A. Feltham c Whitaker b Parsons	38
K. T. Medlycott not out	21
M. P. Bicknell c Whitaker b Parsons	23
Waqar Younis not out	10
B 6, l-b 26, w 1, n-b 9	42
1/14 2/57 3/97 4/178 5/194 6/274 7/355 8/362 9/400 (9 wkts dec.)	420

Bonus points – Surrey 4, Leicestershire 2 (Score at 100 overs: 330-6).

G. S. Clinton, when 2, retired hurt at 6 and resumed at 97.

Bowling: Agnew 30–2–126–0; Mullally 9–3–14–1; Millns 25–1–97–2; Parsons 31–8–75–6; Willey 18–4–60–0; Potter 6–0–16–0.

Umpires: J. D. Bond and B. Leadbeater.

At Chelmsford, August 18, 20, 21. SURREY lost to ESSEX by 283 runs.

At Southampton, August 23, 24, 25, 27. SURREY beat HAMPSHIRE by nine wickets.

At Blackpool, August 29, 30, 31. SURREY drew with LANCASHIRE.

At The Oval, September 2. SURREY beat SRI LANKANS by 14 runs (See Sri Lankan tour section).

At Canterbury, September 7, 8, 9, 10. SURREY drew with KENT.

SURREY v MIDDLESEX

At The Oval, September 12, 13, 14, 15. Drawn. Surrey 5 pts, Middlesex 6 pts. Toss: Surrey. Middlesex, entertaining ambitions of winning the County Championship six days before the end of the season, received early indications that victory would be a feat in itself on the country's most reliable batting surface. Alikhan compiled his maiden hundred in his 79th first-class match, a whimsical innings in which his first 60 runs came in the opening session and the next 59 took more than five hours. Ward's magnificent season was reflected in a robust 75 off as many balls in a stand of 102, and he was the only player to master Fraser's quality fast bowling. On the second day, Feltham stretched Surrey's innings to 480 for nine with his maiden century (one six, thirteen fours), and by the close Middlesex were in some difficulty after fierce fast bowling from Waqar Younis. He beat Haynes for pace, had Roseberry taken at slip and, worse still for Middlesex, hit Gatting below the left elbow first ball and put him out of the match. Ramprakash passed 50 on the third morning before departing to the refreshed Waqar Younis, but Downton, Emburey and Fraser saw Middlesex avoid the follow-on. Fraser's astonishing, career-best 92 included five sixes off Kendrick in the space of twelve balls as 90 raced up in ten overs before Gatting declared 55 behind. An earlier closure might have encouraged Greig to be more expansive in his outlook, but with three bowlers incapacitated the Surrey captain found it beyond his means to set a target. Bicknell's fifth hundred of the season, containing a six and fourteen fours, and solid lower-middle-order batting against non-recognised bowling made the draw a certainty.

Close of play: First day, Surrey 302-5 (R. I. Alikhan 116*, J. D. Robinson 15*); Second day, Middlesex 182-3 (M. R. Ramprakash 46*, P. R. Downton 11*); Third day, Surrey 132-3 (D. J. Bicknell 61*, A. J. Stewart 33*).

Surrey

D. J. Bicknell c Gatting b Fraser	41	– b Hughes	114
R. I. Alikhan c Haynes b Cowans	119	– c Roseberry b Fraser	13
†A. J. Stewart b Fraser	0	– (5) c Emburey b Tufnell	47
D. M. Ward c Haynes b Tufnell	75	– (6) c Downton b Tufnell	6
M. A. Lynch c Emburey b Fraser	17	– (4) c Downton b Hughes	22
*I. A. Greig c Ramprakash b Emburey	31	– (7) lbw b Hughes	30
J. D. Robinson c Haynes b Emburey	72	– (3) c Ramprakash b Fraser	0
M. A. Feltham c Emburey b Fraser	101	– c Fraser b Ramprakash	58
K. T. Medlycott c Downton b Fraser	5	– b Emburey	44
N. M. Kendrick not out	6	– lbw b Downton	14
Waqar Younis (did not bat)		– not out	4
B 1, l-b 3, n-b 9	13	B 8, l-b 10, w 1, n-b 2	21
1/106 2/108 3/210 4/238 5/282 6/320 7/444 8/453 9/480	(9 wkts dec.) 480	1/29 2/29 3/71 4/184 5/194 6/236 7/237 8/344 9/365	373

Bonus points – Surrey 3, Middlesex 2 (Score at 100 overs: 284-5).

Bowling: *First Innings*—Fraser 32.4–9–95–5; Cowans 24–6–76–1; Hughes 21–1–89–0; Emburey 45–10–96–2; Haynes 4–0–17–0; Tufnell 35–10–103–1. *Second Innings*—Cowans 15–5–49–0; Fraser 20–9–44–2; Tufnell 30–8–90–2; Hughes 16–1–56–3; Emburey 23–5–49–1; Ramprakash 10–4–17–1; Haynes 4–0–13–0; Brown 5–2–31–0; Roseberry 4–3–2–0; Downton 1.1–0–4–1.

Middlesex

D. L. Haynes b Waqar Younis	69		
M. A. Roseberry c Greig b Waqar Younis	28	– (4) not out	27
*M. W. Gatting retired hurt	0		
M. R. Ramprakash c Stewart b Waqar Younis	54	– (3) not out	40
K. R. Brown c Feltham b Kendrick	21		
†P. R. Downton c Waqar Younis b Kendrick	48		
J. E. Emburey c Kendrick b Feltham	66		
A. R. C. Fraser b Feltham	92		
S. P. Hughes c Medlycott b Feltham	15	– (1) c Stewart b Alikhan	4
P. C. R. Tufnell not out	23		
N. G. Cowans (did not bat)		– (2) c Feltham b Lynch	31
B 2, l-b 6, w 1	9		
1/100 2/108 3/145 4/197 5/267 6/354 7/389 8/425 (8 wkts dec.)	425	1/6 2/45 (2 wkts)	102

Bonus points – Middlesex 4, Surrey 2 (Score at 100 overs: 335-5).

In the first innings M. W. Gatting retired hurt at 101.

Bowling: *First Innings*—Waqar Younis 28–4–91–3; Feltham 20.4–4–69–3; Greig 11–1–41–0; Robinson 17–2–59–0; Medlycott 8–1–35–0; Kendrick 30–8–122–2. *Second Innings*—Alikhan 7–1–12–1; Bicknell 7–1–15–0; Lynch 5–0–43–1; Stewart 5–0–32–0.

Umpires: B. Dudleston and B. Hassan.

SURREY v ESSEX

At The Oval, September 18, 19, 20, 21. Drawn. Surrey 2 pts, Essex 7 pts. Toss: Essex. Surrey comfortably preserved their unbeaten record at The Oval after following on, thanks principally to Ward's second double-hundred and seventh three-figure innings of the season. In the course of his 208 from 182 balls, during which he struck three sixes and 33 fours, Ward became the first Surrey batsman to score 2,000 runs in a season for the county since J. H. Edrich in 1962. After Essex had won the toss and batted, Hussain compensated for the absence of Gooch and Waugh, through injury, with a pugnacious hundred. Even so, they had to forego one batting point, despite Waqar Younis managing only one spell because of elbow trouble. Hussain fell 3 runs short of a maiden double-century on the second day after batting for 5 hours 38 minutes, and Lewis, with whom he put on 194 for the sixth wicket, marked his first-class début with an unbeaten hundred. For all the batting excellence of the pitch, Foster buckled Surrey with figures of six for 72 and they followed on 399 behind. By the end of the third day, however, the home county had entrenched themselves defiantly at 177 for one, and the news had come through that Middlesex had won at Hove to secure the Championship, consigning Essex to second place. Alikhan duly progressed to his second hundred in successive matches, batting for almost seven and a half hours, but Ward, hitting powerfully through the line, monopolised the glory as they added 239 for the third wicket.

Close of play: First day, Essex 328-5 (N. Hussain 124*, J. J. B. Lewis 25*); Second day, Surrey 124-8 (M. P. Bicknell 7*, Waqar Younis 4*); Third day, Surrey 177-1 (R. I. Alikhan 61*, A. J. Stewart 50*).

Essex

J. P. Stephenson c Lynch b Greig 51
N. Shahid c Lynch b Greig 42
P. J. Prichard c Stewart b Murphy 28
N. Hussain run out 197
B. R. Hardie c sub b Kendrick 42
†M. A. Garnham c Lynch b Greig 5
J. J. B. Lewis not out 116
*N. A. Foster c D. J. Bicknell b Murphy . 19
M. C. Ilott c Waqar Younis b Kendrick . 5
J. H. Childs c Stewart b M. P. Bicknell . 0
S. J. W. Andrew c sub b M. P. Bicknell . 18
B 4, l-b 11, n-b 1 16

1/96 2/103 3/133 4/262 5/275 6/469 7/496 8/515 9/519 — 539

Bonus points – Essex 3, Surrey 2 (Score at 100 overs: 291-5).

Bowling: M. P. Bicknell 30.5–8–64–2; Waqar Younis 5–0–21–0; Murphy 41–9–154–2; Robinson 14–0–44–0; Greig 42–6–150–3; Kendrick 20–1–64–2; Alikhan 5–0–22–0; D. J. Bicknell 2–0–5–0.

Surrey

	First innings		Second innings	
D. J. Bicknell b Foster	0	– c and b Foster	50
R. I. Alikhan lbw b Foster	16	– c Hardie b Shahid	138
D. M. Ward c Shahid b Andrew	58	– (4) b Stephenson	208
†A. J. Stewart c Shahid b Foster	2	– (3) c Garnham b Foster	51
M. A. Lynch c Garnham b Ilott	12	– b Shahid	16
*I. A. Greig c Garnham b Foster	11	– not out	57
J. D. Robinson run out	7	– b Shahid	0
M. P. Bicknell c Hussain b Foster	13	– not out	49
N. M. Kendrick lbw b Ilott	1		
Waqar Younis c Lewis b Foster	14		
A. J. Murphy not out	0		
L-b 2, w 1, n-b 3	6	B 9, l-b 20, w 1, n-b 14	44
1/0 2/76 3/78 4/80 5/96 6/112 7/113 8/120 9/135	140	1/80 2/184 3/423 4/455 5/511 6/514 (6 wkts dec.)	613

Bonus points – Essex 4.

Bowling: *First Innings*—Foster 17.3–2–72–6; Ilott 16–3–42–2; Andrew 9–4–24–1. *Second Innings*—Foster 29–10–88–2; Ilott 34–2–157–0; Childs 21–3–51–0; Andrew 18–4–65–0; Shahid 25–4–91–3; Stephenson 29–7–116–1; Hardie 1–0–16–0.

Umpires: A. A. Jones and P. B. Wight.

HONOURS' LIST, 1990

In 1990, the following were decorated for their services to cricket:

New Year's Honours: E. J. Chatfield (New Zealand) MBE, T. Jones (Merseyside cricket) BEM, J. Simmons (Lancashire) MBE.

Queen's Birthday Honours: B. Coleman (Surrey and TCCB committees) OBE, Sir Richard Hadlee (New Zealand) Kt, J. K. Lever (England) MBE, P. J. Mansfield (services to groundsmanship) BEM.

SUSSEX

President: The Marquess of Abergavenny
Chairman: A. M. Caffyn
Secretary: N. Bett
County Ground, Eaton Road,
Hove BN3 3AN
(Telephone: 0273-732161)
Captain: P. W. G. Parker
Coach: N. Gifford

Not surprisingly, Sussex, finishing bottom of the Britannic Assurance Championship for the second time in four years, derived most satisfaction from the performance of their Second Eleven. While the senior side recorded only twelve victories in all cricket during 1990, the second team capped a splendid summer by capturing the Second Eleven Championship for the second time, winning nine of their sixteen games and losing only once. This heartening display went some way towards rescuing a forgettable, depressing season in which Sussex managed only three Championship victories and flopped in limited-overs cricket. Their low point came with a dramatic collapse when they were well placed to beat Glamorgan in the second round of the NatWest Bank Trophy. After that defeat in Cardiff Sussex won only four games in the remaining ten weeks of the season.

Sussex's dive to the depths of the Championship followed the optimism of the previous season, when a final placing of tenth was their best position since they finished seventh in 1985. The coach, Norman Gifford, having completed his second year at Hove, warned that, although some supporters would be demanding changes, Sussex might not be able to strengthen the side and might have to go into 1991 with the same players.

The county's major weakness – the lack of a fast bowler to provide back-up for the Tony Pigott-Tony Dodemaide new-ball attack – was in evidence throughout the season. Of Sussex's three Championship victories, only one was achieved by bowling a side out. Nevertheless, Pigott and Dodemaide stuck to an uphill task manfully to take 107 Championship wickets between them, and the Australian all-rounder, in his second season with Sussex, again proved himself a splendid team man. He played in all Championship games and, in addition to his bowling, scored 1,001 runs in first-class cricket. Pigott, leading wicket-taker the previous season, ended with 54 first-class wickets, seven fewer than Dodemaide, and with thirteen years of loyal service behind him he takes a deserved benefit in 1991.

The fine form of Neil Lenham, after his unlucky run of finger injuries, was a major plus for the batting; he passed 1,000 runs for the first time, heading the club's Championship averages with 1,499 at 44.08, and hit four hundreds. Batting with a specially designed glove to protect his right index finger, broken no fewer than five times, Lenham displayed a new confidence and was rewarded with his county cap in June. He also led the way for Sussex in the Sunday League, with 444 runs at 40.36, but neither he nor any Sussex player scored a century in the 40-overs competition, in which Sussex finished thirteenth – a drop of two places. A troublesome thumb injury limited David Smith to only eight Championship appearances, and Sussex lost no time in drafting in Jamie Hall, a promising 22-year-old batsman from Chichester. Hall failed to make double figures in his first four innings, but he never looked back after scoring his maiden first-class century against the New Zealanders in his fifth and finished with 1,140 runs from twenty first-class matches.

Martin Speight emerged as a dependable middle-order batsman in his first full season since leaving Durham University, scoring 1,349 Championship runs, including two hundreds, and he was followed closely in the averages by Alan Wells, who like Speight missed only one Championship game. While Wells completed 1,000 first-class runs for the fifth time, his elder brother, Colin, was handicapped by a hernia problem, which required an operation. This restricted his usual haul of runs and limited his success as a bowler. Colin gave way as on-field captain to his brother late in a season which had seen the club captain, Paul Parker, suffering from severe hamstring problems for the second successive year. Parker missed ten Championship matches, yet finished the season just 15 runs short of his first-class 1,000, having hit two hundreds. Ian Gould was another troubled by injury and, dropped midway through the summer, he appeared in only eight first-class games in his benefit season.

The selection of Ian Salisbury for the England A tour in the winter gave Sussex supporters a welcome lift and came as a complete surprise to the gifted twenty-year-old leg-spinner, who had not even received a letter from Lord's asking about his availability. Salisbury, after an early interest in soccer, was fourteen before he started to play cricket, and following a spell on Northamptonshire's books he joined the Lord's groundstaff. He was spotted by Sussex when playing against them for MCC Young Cricketers, and they wasted no time in offering him a contract. Salisbury, who claimed 42 first-class wickets in his second season, was quick to acknowledge the help he had received from Gifford, especially on the way he should bowl on certain pitches, and his tour place emphasised the value of his coach's vast experience. Sussex also have high hopes of Bradleigh Donelan, a promising off-spinner, who took 25 wickets for the first team and 59 for the Second Eleven.

As Sussex turned to Salisbury and Donelan, leg-spinner Andy Clarke was again out of favour, and he played only in limited-overs cricket. Clarke had appeared in just five first-class matches the previous year, after taking 42 Championship wickets in his début season, 1988, and he was not retained at the end of the season. Nor was seam bowler Andy Babington, who promptly joined Gloucestershire.

Sussex had good cause to look back on a successful first Championship fixture at the picturesque Arundel Castle ground, where a crowd of more than 3,500 watched the first day's play against Hampshire and gate receipts topped £11,000. Meanwhile, plans are under way to redevelop completely the Hove County Ground, at an estimated cost of five to seven million pounds. The rebuilding programme will take ten years and will include the construction of a new pavilion, function and conference facilities, and terraced seating to increase the ground capacity to some 6,500. – Jack Arlidge.

SUSSEX 1990

[*Bill Smith*

Back row: A. R. Clarke, C. C. Remy, A. R. Hansford, A. M. Babington, K. Greenfield, B. T. P. Donelan. *Middle row:* L. V. Chandler (*scorer*), C. P. Cale (*assistant coach*), A. R. Cornford, I. D. K. Salisbury, P. W. Threlfall, R. A. Bunting, J. W. Hall, A. I. C. Dodemaide, N. J. Lenham, I. C. Waring (*assistant coach*), B. Turner (*physiotherapist*), N. Gifford (*coach*). *Front row:* J. A. North, P. Moores, A. C. S. Pigott, C. M. Wells, P. W. G. Parker (*captain*), I. J. Gould, A. P. Wells, M. P. Speight. *Inset:* D. M. Smith.

SUSSEX RESULTS

All first-class matches – Played 25: Won 3, Lost 11, Drawn 11.

County Championship matches – Played 22: Won 3, Lost 9, Drawn 10.

Bonus points – Batting 51, Bowling 44.

Competition placings – Britannic Assurance County Championship, 17th; NatWest Bank Trophy, 2nd round; Benson and Hedges Cup, 4th in Group B; Refuge Assurance League, 13th.

BRITANNIC ASSURANCE CHAMPIONSHIP AVERAGES

BATTING

	Birthplace	*M*	*I*	*NO*	*R*	*HI*	*Avge*
‡N. J. Lenham	*Worthing*	19	35	1	1,499	123	44.08
‡P. W. G. Parker	*Bulawayo, S. Rhodesia*	12	21	2	778	107	40.94
M. P. Speight	*Walsall*	21	39	6	1,349	131	40.87
‡A. P. Wells	*Newhaven*	21	39	6	1,245	144*	37.72
B. T. P. Donelan	*Park Royal, London*	9	13	6	211	53	30.14
‡C. M. Wells	*Newhaven*	19	31	4	812	107	30.07
J. W. Hall	*Chichester*	17	31	1	888	125	29.60
‡A. I. C. Dodemaide	*Melbourne, Australia*	22	35	6	854	112	29.44
‡D. M. Smith	*Balham, London*	8	14	2	324	71	27.00
I. D. K. Salisbury	*Northampton*	18	23	10	313	68	24.07
‡I. J. Gould	*Slough*	7	11	1	229	73	22.90
‡P. Moores	*Macclesfield*	22	35	3	680	106*	21.25
‡A. C. S. Pigott	*London*	20	29	5	451	64*	18.79
K. Greenfield	*Brighton*	2	4	0	74	38	18.50
A. R. Hansford	*Burgess Hill*	4	6	1	55	29	11.00
R. A. Bunting	*East Winch*	13	13	5	85	24*	10.62
J. A. North	*Slindon*	3	5	1	41	19*	10.25
R. Hanley	*Tonbridge*	2	4	0	32	28	8.00

Also batted: A. M. Babington (*London*) (2 matches) 20, 8; C. C. Remy (*Castries, St Lucia*) (1 match) 4*.

* *Signifies not out.* ‡ *Denotes county cap.*

The following played a total of fifteen three-figure innings for Sussex in County Championship matches – N. J. Lenham 4, A. P. Wells 3, P. W. G. Parker 2, M. P. Speight 2, A. I. C. Dodemaide 1, J. W. Hall 1, P. Moores 1, C. M. Wells 1.

BOWLING

	O	*M*	*R*	*W*	*BB*	*5W/i*	*Avge*
A. C. S. Pigott	516.1	88	1,916	51	5-52	3	37.56
A. I. C. Dodemaide	681.1	112	2,206	56	6-106	1	39.39
B. T. P. Donelan	258.4	50	853	19	3-79	0	44.89
I. D. K. Salisbury	535.1	103	1,796	40	5-32	2	44.90
R. A. Bunting	298	55	1,113	21	2-36	0	53.00
C. M. Wells	366	67	1,195	17	3-48	0	70.29

Also bowled: A. M. Babington 43–7–166–2; I. J. Gould 5–0–18–0; K. Greenfield 0.3–0–8–0; A. R. Hansford 123.5–21–425–7; N. J. Lenham 62.5–11–231–2; J. A. North 49.2–10–147–3; P. W. G. Parker 8–0–59–0; C. C. Remy 17–0–91–1; A. P. Wells 29–4–144–1.

Wicket-keeper: P. Moores 46 ct, 10 st.

Leading Fielders: I. D. K. Salisbury 13, M. P. Speight 13.

SUSSEX v SURREY

At Hove, April 26, 27, 28, 30. Sussex won by five wickets. Sussex 21 pts, Surrey 4 pts. Toss: Sussex. Speight, starting his first full season of first-class cricket, and Gould, in his benefit year, put on 122 in thirteen overs to take Sussex to victory with sixteen balls remaining after the Surrey captain, Greig, had set them to score 335 in 220 minutes. Only 40 overs were possible on the first day, but consistent batting, with Bicknell and Stewart establishing the innings with 136 in 44 overs for the second wicket, enabled Surrey to control the game's path. Parker, with eight fours and a five in the only century of the match, declared 125 behind on the third afternoon in expectation of a target, but the easy nature of the pitch persuaded Greig to delay his declaration until after lunch on the final day. However, with Medlycott's left-arm spin proving costly, Sussex began the season with an impressive win.

Close of play: First day, Surrey 118-1 (D. J. Bicknell 36*, A. J. Stewart 31*); Second day, Sussex 29-1 (N. J. Lenham 11*, P. W. G. Parker 12*); Third day, Surrey 64-2 (G. S. Clinton 17*, M. A. Lynch 26*).

Surrey

First innings		Second innings	
D. J. Bicknell lbw b Dodemaide	65	– c Speight b Dodemaide	2
G. S. Clinton b Hansford	43	– run out	98
A. J. Stewart c A. P. Wells b Salisbury	77	– c Speight b Hansford	15
M. A. Lynch c Lenham b C. M. Wells	70	– b C. M. Wells	46
G. P. Thorpe c Gould b Salisbury	9	– not out	23
†D. M. Ward c Parker b Pigott	38	– not out	18
*I. A. Greig c Salisbury b Pigott	9		
K. T. Medlycott c Lenham b Salisbury	29		
M. P. Bicknell not out	50		
A. H. Gray run out	11		
A. J. Murphy not out	4		
B 5, l-b 15	20	L-b 6, w 1	7
1/57 2/193 3/201 4/221 5/282 6/304 7/355 8/367 9/393	(9 wkts dec.) 425	1/9 2/37 3/110 4/180	(4 wkts dec.) 209

Bonus points – Surrey 3, Sussex 1 (Score at 100 overs: 274-4).

Bowling: *First Innings*—Pigott 30–8–77–2; Dodemaide 26–3–96–1; C. M. Wells 27–8–59–1; Hansford 25.5–3–84–1; Salisbury 32–7–89–3. *Second Innings*—Pigott 5–1–17–0; Dodemaide 13–3–38–1; Hansford 10–2–41–1; Salisbury 11–0–26–0; C. M. Wells 9–2–16–1; A. P. Wells 9–0–39–0; Lenham 4–0–16–0; Gould 3–0–10–0.

Sussex

First innings		Second innings	
N. J. Lenham c Lynch b Murphy	85	– run out	44
†P. Moores b Gray	1	– c Stewart b Medlycott	30
*P. W. G. Parker b Murphy	100	– b Murphy	42
A. P. Wells not out	44	– c Ward b Murphy	16
M. P. Speight not out	50	– not out	75
C. M. Wells (did not bat)		– c Lynch b Medlycott	37
I. J. Gould (did not bat)		– not out	62
B 5, l-b 8, n-b 7	20	B 8, l-b 21, w 1, n-b 1	31
1/9 2/197 3/198	(3 wkts dec.) 300	1/52 2/123 3/130 4/154 5/215	(5 wkts) 337

A. I. C. Dodemaide, A. C. S. Pigott, I. D. K. Salisbury and A. R. Hansford did not bat.

Bonus points – Sussex 4, Surrey 1.

Bowling: *First Innings*—Gray 15–0–58–1; M. P. Bicknell 24–5–71–0; Murphy 19–4–68–2; Medlycott 29–9–67–0; Greig 5–0–19–0; Lynch 2–1–4–0. *Second Innings*—M. P. Bicknell 15–2–59–0; Murphy 17–2–76–2; Greig 10–2–45–0; Medlycott 14.2–1–101–2; Lynch 7–1–27–0.

Umpires: D. J. Constant and D. S. Thompsett.

At Folkestone, May 3, 4, 5, 7. SUSSEX lost to KENT by five wickets.

†SUSSEX v ZIMBABWEANS

At Hove, May 13. Sussex won by 95 runs. Toss: Zimbabweans. Hall celebrated his first-team début with a half-century and a share in a century partnership for the third wicket with Speight. Speight's 76 came off 100 balls and included twelve fours.

Sussex

N. J. Lenham b Jarvis	1	R. A. Bunting lbw b Traicos	6
J. W. Hall c Briant b Brandes	53	P. W. Threlfall not out	17
K. Greenfield b Jarvis	10		
M. P. Speight c Butchart b Traicos	76	B 7, l-b 6, w 3, n-b 5	21
C. C. Remy not out	0		
*P. W. G. Parker lbw b Shah	10	1/1 2/23 3/145 (8 wkts, 55 overs)	233
†P. Moores c Robertson b Brandes	39	4/158 5/177 6/182	
I. D. K. Salisbury run out	0	7/190 8/232	

A. M. Babington did not bat.

C. C. Remy retired hurt at 155 and resumed at 232.

Bowling: Brandes 11–0–39–2; Jarvis 9–3–30–2; Dube 8–0–43–0; Shah 11–1–36–1; Traicos 11–0–42–2; Butchart 5–0–30–0.

Zimbabweans

K. J. Arnott lbw b Threlfall	11	A. J. Traicos b Salisbury	0
G. A. Paterson b Salisbury	18	M. P. Jarvis b Threlfall	4
C. M. Robertson b Threlfall	0	L. E. Dube not out	0
*A. J. Pycroft run out	10	L-b 10, w 7, n-b 3	20
†G. A. Briant run out	7		
A. H. Shah b Salisbury	21	1/32 2/38 3/50 (40.3 overs)	138
I. P. Butchart lbw b Babington	24	4/55 5/106 6/108	
E. A. Brandes c Bunting b Salisbury	23	7/108 8/114 9/127	

Bowling: Babington 9–2–20–1; Threlfall 10–0–40–3; Lenham 7–0–13–0; Bunting 7–1–30–0; Salisbury 7.3–2–25–4.

Umpires: B. Dudleston and P. B. Wight.

At Southampton, May 15, 16, 17, 18. SUSSEX lost to HAMPSHIRE by an innings and 157 runs.

SUSSEX v GLAMORGAN

At Hove, May 19, 21, 22. Drawn. Sussex 3 pts, Glamorgan 8 pts. Toss: Glamorgan. Sussex batted throughout the final day for a draw after being forced to follow on 180 behind. Speight, although batting with a runner because of blood poisoning in his leg, registered his maiden first-class century, hitting twenty fours, while Moores faced 125 deliveries for his second first-class hundred. On another excellent batting pitch, Glamorgan scored at nearly 4 an over on the Saturday, Butcher and Morris giving them a perfect start with 188 in 59 overs. Butcher had seventeen fours and three sixes in his 139, but he was overshadowed by a scintillating innings from Richards, whose hundred came from just 73 balls. In all he faced 87 deliveries, cracking sixteen fours and four sixes, before Glamorgan declared. Sussex lost Hall that evening and on Monday, despite Speight's 60 with ten fours, collapsed against persistent Glamorgan bowling to 157 for nine in 47 overs. Parker, batting at No. 9 because of a torn hamstring, then added 65 for the last wicket with Babington, but Sussex were still 31 short of avoiding the follow-on when Cowley caught and bowled Babington.

Close of play: First day, Sussex 12-1 (N. J. Lenham 3*); Second day, Sussex 120-2 (A. I. C. Dodemaide 26*, M. P. Speight 62*).

Glamorgan

*A. R. Butcher c Moores b Pigott 139	P. A. Cottey not out 43
H. Morris c Moores b Dodemaide 73	B 6, l-b 7, n-b 3 16
M. J. Cann c Moores b Wells 13	——
I. V. A. Richards not out 118	1/188 2/241 3/241 (3 wkts dec.) 402

I. Smith, N. G. Cowley, †C. P. Metson, S. J. Dennis, S. L. Watkin and M. Frost did not bat.

Bonus points – Glamorgan 4, Sussex 1 (Score at 100 overs: 386-3).

Bowling: Pigott 17–1–86–1; Dodemaide 24–4–81–1; Babington 20–5–57–0; Wells 22–2–90–1; Lenham 6–1–18–0; Salisbury 13–2–57–0.

Sussex

N. J. Lenham lbw b Dennis 34	– c Cowley b Watkin	18
J. W. Hall lbw b Frost 8	– c Metson b Dennis	7
A. I. C. Dodemaide c Cottey b Watkin 3	– c Richards b Dennis	45
M. P. Speight c Richards b Frost 60	– c Cann b Dennis	131
C. M. Wells c and b Watkin 1	– c Frost b Watkin	94
I. J. Gould lbw b Frost 9	– c Morris b Butcher	11
†P. Moores lbw b Richards 3	– not out	106
A. C. S. Pigott c Metson b Richards 8	– c Morris b Cann	54
*P. W. G. Parker not out 57		
I. D. K. Salisbury c Metson b Frost 3	– (9) not out	10
A. M. Babington c and b Cowley 20		
B 10, l-b 3, n-b 3 16	B 4, l-b 4, w 5, n-b 3	16
1/12 2/29 3/76 4/91 5/118 6/121 7/121 8/138 9/157 222	1/15 2/27 3/163 4/279 5/295 6/350 7/443 (7 wkts dec.)	492

Bonus points – Sussex 2, Glamorgan 4.

Bowling: *First Innings*—Frost 18–2–62–4; Watkin 19–2–66–2; Dennis 11–2–36–1; Richards 15–4–27–2; Cowley 8.4–1–18–1. *Second Innings*—Frost 24–0–96–0; Watkin 30–4–94–2; Cowley 13–5–28–0; Dennis 25–3–83–3; Richards 9–2–14–0; Smith 8–0–49–0; Cottey 9–0–44–0; Cann 7–0–39–1; Butcher 3–0–16–1; Morris 3–0–21–0.

Umpires: M. J. Kitchen and R. A. White.

At Taunton, May 23, 24, 25. SUSSEX drew with SOMERSET.

At Hove, May 26, 27, 28. SUSSEX lost to NEW ZEALANDERS by seven wickets (See New Zealand tour section).

SUSSEX v LANCASHIRE

At Horsham, June 2, 4, 5. Lancashire won by nine wickets. Lancashire 24 pts, Sussex 6 pts. Toss: Sussex. Devastating fast bowling from DeFreitas, in poor light on the final morning, set up a straightforward victory that brought Lancashire maximum points. Almost as important was the ninth-wicket partnership of 100 in Lancashire's first innings between Fowler and Allott which, in addition to ensuring their third and fourth batting points, gave the visitors a crucial lead of 89 as the pitch began to wear. Fowler had gone in as low as No. 9 because of an injury to his lip, suffered while fielding at slip on the opening day. Sussex, after winning the toss, had been unable to dominate the Lancashire bowling, with Dodemaide lingering some four and a quarter hours while scoring 70. However, Lancashire, apart from Atherton's 76 in 64 overs, and Watkinson's violent 51 from 74 balls, also struggled as Dodemaide exploited the increasingly varied bounce. They were 11 runs behind when their eighth wicket fell, but Allott then joined Fowler and they wrested the initiative. Next day, after DeFreitas had demolished the Sussex top- and middle-order batting, Patterson, bowling at great speed, ripped out the tail with three wickets in four balls.

Close of play: First day, Lancashire 47-1 (M. A. Atherton 12*, J. D. Fitton 25*); Second day, Sussex 57-1 (N. J. Lenham 22*, A. I. C. Dodemaide 13*).

Sussex

N. J. Lenham c Mendis b Watkinson	8	– c Hughes b DeFreitas	24
J. W. Hall c Watkinson b Allott	24	– c Allott b Patterson	15
A. I. C. Dodemaide c Hegg b Watkinson	70	– c Hughes b DeFreitas	14
A. P. Wells c Fairbrother b Fitton	33	– lbw b DeFreitas	0
M. P. Speight c Hughes b Patterson	11	– lbw b DeFreitas	21
*C. M. Wells c Hegg b Patterson	0	– (8) c Atherton b DeFreitas	13
†P. Moores c Fairbrother b Allott	28	– (6) c Mendis b DeFreitas	2
A. C. S. Pigott c Fairbrother b Atherton	14	– (7) c Hegg b Patterson	6
I. D. K. Salisbury c Hughes b Atherton	15	– not out	0
B. T. P. Donelan c Atherton b Watkinson	8	– b Patterson	0
R. A. Bunting not out	10	– c Hegg b Patterson	0
B 3, l-b 9, n-b 2	14	B 1, l-b 2, n-b 10	13
1/21 2/47 3/108 4/127 5/127 6/161 7/197 8/207 9/219	235	1/21 2/58 3/58 4/62 5/72 6/87 7/106 8/108 9/108	108

Bonus points – Sussex 2, Lancashire 4.

Bowling: *First Innings*—Patterson 17–3–37–2; DeFreitas 13–4–27–0; Watkinson 14–8–26–3; Allott 14–4–30–2; Fitton 19–6–56–1; Atherton 20.1–8–47–2. *Second Innings*—Patterson 18.4–2–52–4; DeFreitas 19–8–39–6; Allott 4–2–10–0; Atherton 3–2–4–0.

Lancashire

G. D. Mendis lbw b Dodemaide	9	– c Moores b Bunting	11
M. A. Atherton c Pigott b Dodemaide	76	– not out	0
J. D. Fitton c Pigott b Dodemaide	25		
N. H. Fairbrother c A. P. Wells b Bunting	22	– (3) not out	10
M. Watkinson c Donelan b Salisbury	51		
P. A. J. DeFreitas c Moores b Pigott	26		
†W. K. Hegg c Dodemaide b Salisbury	10		
*D. P. Hughes c Moores b Dodemaide	0		
G. Fowler not out	54		
P. J. W. Allott b Dodemaide	42		
B. P. Patterson b Dodemaide	0		
B 4, l-b 4, n-b 1	9	L-b 1	1
1/11 2/54 3/111 4/185 5/187 6/224 7/224 8/224 9/324	324	1/12	(1 wkt) 22

Bonus points – Lancashire 4, Sussex 4.

Bowling: *First Innings*—Pigott 14–2–60–1; Dodemaide 28.4–2–106–6; Salisbury 24–7–46–2; C. M. Wells 7–1–16–0; Bunting 13–1–61–1; Donelan 5–1–27–0. *Second Innings*—Bunting 3–0–20–1; Donelan 2–1–1–0.

Umpires: B. Hassan and D. R. Shepherd.

SUSSEX v GLOUCESTERSHIRE

At Hove, June 16, 18, 19. Drawn. Sussex 4 pts, Gloucestershire 5 pts. Toss: Sussex. Sussex finished 17 runs short of victory with two wickets standing after both captains had reacted positively to the loss of more than five hours' play on the second day. Set 342 to win in at least 84 overs, they needed just 47 from the last eight overs after Colin Wells and Speight had put on 105 in seventeen overs. Instead, disciplined bowling from Walsh and Curran enabled Gloucestershire not only to avoid defeat but to come close to seizing victory. After putting Gloucestershire in, Sussex had reduced them to 177 for six before Athey, whose 131 included 22 fours, and Russell (98 from 140 balls) put on 169. On the second day, Parker, scoring 36 of his 48 in boundaries, had taken his side to 120 for three before rain and bad light drove the players from the field after 31 overs.

Close of play: First day, Sussex 30-0 (N. J. Lenham 15*, J. W. Hall 11*); Second day, Sussex 120-3 (P. W. G. Parker 48*, M. P. Speight 0*).

Gloucestershire

*A. J. Wright c Moores b Dodemaide	17	– not out	45
G. D. Hodgson c Salisbury b Dodemaide	0	– b Remy	33
I. P. Butcher c Speight b C. M. Wells	42	– not out	3
C. W. J. Athey st Moores b Salisbury	131		
P. Bainbridge c Salisbury b C. M. Wells	3		
K. M. Curran c and b Bunting	15		
J. W. Lloyds b Bunting	43		
†R. C. Russell c Moores b Dodemaide	98		
C. A. Walsh c and b Salisbury	9		
D. A. Graveney c Dodemaide b Salisbury	0		
D. V. Lawrence not out	0		
B 4, l-b 9, w 1, n-b 2	16	L-b 6	6
1/3 2/49 3/69 4/73 5/117 6/177 7/346 8/368 9/368	374	1/73 (1 wkt dec.)	87

Bonus points – Gloucestershire 4, Sussex 4.

Bowling: *First Innings*—Dodemaide 22–3–95–3; Bunting 23–6–91–2; C. M. Wells 20–3–59–2; Remy 12–0–54–0; Salisbury 20–6–62–3. *Second Innings*—Dodemaide 3–0–6–0; Bunting 4–0–21–0; Remy 5–0–37–1; A. P. Wells 4–0–17–0.

Sussex

N. J. Lenham c Russell b Lawrence	37	– c Wright b Curran	84
J. W. Hall b Walsh	19	– c Russell b Walsh	17
*P. W. G. Parker not out	48	– c Wright b Lloyds	53
A. P. Wells b Walsh	8	– c Lloyds b Curran	22
M. P. Speight not out	0	– run out	59
C. M. Wells (did not bat)		– c Walsh b Curran	55
†P. Moores (did not bat)		– run out	6
A. I. C. Dodemaide (did not bat)		– c Lawrence b Walsh	11
C. C. Remy (did not bat)		– not out	4
I. D. K. Salisbury (did not bat)		– not out	3
L-b 2, n-b 6	8	L-b 8, n-b 3	11
1/57 2/69 3/117 (3 wkts dec.)	120	1/35 2/132 3/183 4/190 5/295 6/306 7/314 8/321 (8 wkts)	325

R. A. Bunting did not bat.

Bonus point – Gloucestershire 1.

Bowling: *First Innings*—Lawrence 9–3–30–1; Walsh 13–3–40–2; Graveney 4.4–2–9–0; Curran 11–1–33–0; Bainbridge 3–0–6–0. *Second Innings*—Lawrence 10–0–56–0; Walsh 21–1–79–2; Curran 19–3–64–3; Graveney 16–3–48–0; Lloyds 18–2–70–1.

Umpires: J. D. Bond and R. Palmer.

At Worcester, June 20, 21, 22. SUSSEX drew with WORCESTERSHIRE.

SUSSEX v CAMBRIDGE UNIVERSITY

At Hove, June 30, July 2, 3. Cambridge University won by three wickets. Toss: Cambridge University. On the eve of the University Match at Lord's, Cambridge recorded their first victory over a county since 1982, when Lancashire were beaten by seven wickets. Set 256 to win in a minimum of 61 overs, they reached their target with seven balls to spare, thanks principally to James, an opening batsman under contract to Glamorgan. His 102, containing eleven fours, came in only 158 minutes, and as they added 142 in 35 overs for the second wicket, he and Lowrey exploited an inexperienced Sussex attack with attacking flair. James fell with 27 still needed, but a huge six from Heap settled the issue in Cambridge's favour. Sussex fielded seven uncapped players and one, Greenfield, the Second XI captain, went on to a maiden first-class hundred after Wells had hit twenty fours and two sixes in his 137. Remy returned a career-best four for 63 in Cambridge's first innings, when James and Heap both scored worthy half-centuries.

Close of play: First day, Sussex 318-3 (K. Greenfield 92*, P. W. G. Parker 2*); Second day, Cambridge University 248-9 (R. H. J. Jenkins 19*, S. W. Johnson 8*).

Sussex

N. J. Lenham b Shufflebotham	70	– b Pyman	22
J. W. Hall c Heap b Jenkins	3	– c Turner b Buzza	49
K. Greenfield not out	102	– not out	54
A. P. Wells c Shufflebotham b Pyman	137	– not out	27
*P. W. G. Parker not out	10		
B 5, l-b 1, n-b 11	17	B 1, l-b 9, n-b 2	12
1/15 2/124 3/316 (3 wkts dec.)	339	1/40 2/114 (2 wkts dec.)	164

M. P. Speight, C. C. Remy, J. A. North, †P. Moores, B. T. P. Donelan and R. A. Bunting did not bat.

Bowling: *First Innings*—Johnson 12–1–48–0; Jenkins 22.2–5–94–1; Pyman 26–7–60–1; Shufflebotham 12–2–36–1; Buzza 12–2–65–0; Lowrey 4–0–30–0. *Second Innings*—Johnson 6–1–18–0; Jenkins 4–0–18–0; Pyman 14–1–59–1; Shufflebotham 6–1–25–0; Buzza 7.5–1–34–1.

Cambridge University

S. P. James c Wells b Remy	61	– c Speight b North	102
R. Heap b Bunting	63	– (7) not out	20
†R. J. Turner c Moores b Wells	38	– (2) c Moores b Bunting	14
*J. C. M. Atkinson c Parker b Wells	2	– run out	0
M. J. Lowrey lbw b North	6	– (3) lbw b Lenham	72
M. J. Morris c Hall b Remy	12	– (5) lbw b Lenham	7
R. A. Pyman b Remy	0	– (6) run out	8
D. H. Shufflebotham b Remy	0	– b North	6
R. H. J. Jenkins not out	19	– not out	4
A. J. Buzza c Moores b Bunting	10		
S. W. Johnson not out	8		
B 8, l-b 20, w 1	29	B 9, l-b 12, w 1, n-b 3	25
1/88 2/171 3/181 4/185 5/202 6/202 7/202 8/205 9/238 (9 wkts dec.)	248	1/28 2/170 3/178 4/206 5/223 6/229 7/245 (7 wkts)	258

Bowling: *First Innings*—Bunting 27–4–60–2; North 22–5–46–1; Remy 22–6–63–4; Donelan 11–2–26–0; Wells 10–4–25–2. *Second Innings*—Bunting 14–0–54–1; North 11.5–2–43–2; Remy 15–0–70–0; Donelan 12–1–44–0; Lenham 7–1–26–2.

Umpires: J. H. Harris and A. A. Jones.

SUSSEX v DERBYSHIRE

At Hove, July 4, 5, 6. Derbyshire won by 18 runs. Derbyshire 20 pts, Sussex 3 pts. Toss: Sussex. Two forfeitures compensated for the loss of 136 overs, including the whole of the first day, to rain and opened the way for a dramatic finish in which a last-wicket partnership of 89 between two uncapped bowlers, Salisbury and Bunting, took Sussex to within 19 runs of victory. Derbyshire had scored 363 for seven in the 84.1 overs available on the second day, with Barnett hitting 123, including sixteen fours, in three and a half hours. He needed just 39 balls to move from 50 to 100, and when he reached three figures he passed the Derbyshire record of 30 centuries established by opener Denis Smith in a career that went from 1927 to

1952. Adams, with a six and twelve fours in his 91, was the other major contributor. The weather on the final day was excellent as Sussex embarked on the task of scoring 364 to win in 102 overs. Despite 51 from Colin Wells, they were rarely in contention and looked to have lost when their ninth wicket fell at 256. However, Salisbury, hitting nine fours in a career-best 68, and Bunting batted with such confidence that they were within 18 runs of Derbyshire, with more than six overs left, when Salisbury was taken at second slip off the shoulder of the bat to give Bishop his fifth wicket.

Close of play: First day, No play; Second day, Derbyshire 363-7 dec.

Derbyshire

*K. J. Barnett c Salisbury b Pigott 123
P. D. Bowler b Bunting 50
J. E. Morris c Hall b Pigott 21
B. Roberts c Moores b Pigott 47
C. J. Adams st Moores b Salisbury 91
S. C. Goldsmith c Moores b Pigott 11
†K. M. Krikken c Lenham b Salisbury . 12
M. Jean-Jacques not out 0
I. R. Bishop not out 0
L-b 6, w 2 8

1/126 2/185 3/214 4/265 5/291 6/338 7/361 (7 wkts dec.) 363

S. J. Base and O. H. Mortensen did not bat.

Bonus points – Derbyshire 4, Sussex 3.

Bowling: Dodemaide 22.1–1–81–0; Pigott 18–4–69–4; Bunting 20–1–100–1; C. M. Wells 13–1–58–0; Salisbury 11–4–49–2.

Derbyshire forfeited their second innings.

Sussex

Sussex forfeited their first innings.

N. J. Lenham lbw b Mortensen 12
J. W. Hall c Morris b Bishop 6
†P. Moores c Goldsmith b Mortensen .. 13
A. P. Wells c sub b Jean-Jacques 18
M. P. Speight lbw b Base 43
C. M. Wells c Morris b Goldsmith 51
A. I. C. Dodemaide c and b Bishop 33
A. C. S. Pigott c Roberts b Bishop 12
*P. W. G. Parker c Krikken b Bishop . 35
I. D. K. Salisbury c Adams b Bishop .. 68
R. A. Bunting not out 24
B 5, l-b 8, w 2, n-b 15 30

1/16 2/33 3/47 4/68 5/152 6/166 7/185 8/243 9/256 345

Bowling: Bishop 27.1–6–90–5; Mortensen 27–5–77–2; Jean-Jacques 13–3–60–1; Base 20–5–65–1; Goldsmith 8–0–40–1.

Umpires: J. H. Harris and A. A. Jones.

At Nottingham, July 7, 9, 10. SUSSEX drew with NOTTINGHAMSHIRE.

At Guildford, July 18, 19, 20. SUSSEX beat SURREY by seven wickets.

At Northampton, July 21, 23, 24. SUSSEX drew with NORTHAMPTONSHIRE.

SUSSEX v HAMPSHIRE

At Arundel, July 25, 26, 27. Drawn. Sussex 5 pts, Hampshire 6 pts. Toss: Sussex. The first County Championship match at Arundel Castle was blessed with fine weather. And although it petered out into a draw, it was nevertheless a financial success for Sussex, with more than 3,500 spectators present on the first day. The pitch proved slow, which enabled the home side to recover from 28 for three to a declaration on the second day at 383 for nine. Colin Wells's first Championship hundred of the season came from 133 balls and included fifteen fours and three sixes, while there were four wickets for the Hampshire off-spinner, Udal, on his Championship début. Hampshire batted carefully to secure a third bonus point and then declared, 129 behind, at their overnight score. Smith, unbeaten from the start, hit sixteen fours in his 132. Sussex lost wickets rapidly as they attempted to set a realistic target and eventually declared at lunch, leaving 70 overs for Hampshire to score 274 runs. But once Smith (87 balls) and Marshall had gone, Hampshire struggled to maintain the momentum, and with ten overs to go they abandoned the chase.

Close of play: First day, Sussex 342-9 (A. C. S. Pigott 30*, B. T. P. Donelan 6*); Second day, Hampshire 254-5 (C. L. Smith 132*, J. R. Ayling 28*).

Sussex

First innings		Second innings	
N. J. Lenham c Maru b Ayling	15	b Connor	15
J. W. Hall lbw b Marshall	4	run out	36
*P. W. G. Parker b Marshall	0	b Ayling	18
A. P. Wells c Scott b Udal	53	b Maru	32
M. P. Speight c and b Udal	37	run out	24
C. M. Wells c Ayling b Udal	107	c Cox b Udal	6
A. I. C. Dodemaide lbw b Marshall	2	(8) not out	2
†P. Moores c Smith b Udal	61		
A. C. S. Pigott not out	64	(7) b Udal	5
I. D. K. Salisbury run out	0		
B. T. P. Donelan not out	11		
B 1, l-b 21, w 4, n-b 3	29	L-b 4, n-b 2	6
1/13 2/13 3/28 4/105 5/134 6/137 7/276 8/319 9/324 (9 wkts dec.)	383	1/27 2/51 3/90 4/123 5/129 6/141 7/144 (7 wkts dec.)	144

Bonus points – Sussex 3, Hampshire 3 (Score at 100 overs: 289-7).

Bowling: *First Innings*—Connor 12–4–20–0; Marshall 16–4–35–3; Ayling 15.4–8–36–1; Maru 32.2–5–105–0; Udal 43–7–144–4; Scott 4–1–21–0. *Second Innings*—Connor 8–1–23–1; Marshall 9–4–18–0; Maru 6–0–51–1; Ayling 6.2–0–36–1; Udal 2–0–12–2.

Hampshire

First innings		Second innings	
T. C. Middleton b Pigott	50	b Donelan	28
C. L. Smith not out	132	st Moores b Donelan	61
R. J. Scott c Dodemaide b Salisbury	13	st Moores b Donelan	16
*M. C. J. Nicholas run out	0	c Moores b Pigott	1
M. D. Marshall c Dodemaide b Salisbury	11	c Donelan b Salisbury	34
R. M. F. Cox c Moores b Dodemaide	9	(7) not out	35
J. R. Ayling not out	28	(6) c Hall b Salisbury	22
†R. J. Parks (did not bat)	–	not out	15
B 6, l-b 4, n-b 1	11	B 6, n-b 2	8
1/96 2/131 3/144 4/157 5/192 (5 wkts dec.)	254	1/76 2/93 3/94 4/141 5/143 6/189 (6 wkts)	220

R. J. Maru, S. D. Udal and C. A. Connor did not bat.

Bonus points – Hampshire 3, Sussex 2.

Bowling: *First Innings*—Dodemaide 20–9–31–1; Pigott 18–7–43–1; C. M. Wells 5–0–18–0; Donelan 19–5–44–0; Salisbury 36–5–108–2. *Second Innings*—Dodemaide 10–2–23–0; Pigott 8–3–12–1; C. M. Wells 11–1–31–0; Salisbury 16–1–69–2; Donelan 19.4–4–79–3.

Umpires: B. Dudleston and B. Leadbeater.

At Chelmsford, July 28, 30, 31. SUSSEX drew with ESSEX.

SUSSEX v WARWICKSHIRE

At Eastbourne, August 4, 6, 7. Warwickshire won by six wickets. Warwickshire 24 pts, Sussex 4 pts. Toss: Sussex. A remarkable hat-trick by Paul Smith, wearing odd boots, set up a comfortable victory for Warwickshire. Smith went off to borrow a spare from Munton, which was two sizes too big, after his had split. He returned, promptly bowled Dodemaide, and immediately had Moores caught at short leg and Pigott snapped up by wicket-keeper Piper. It was the second hat-trick of his career and left Warwickshire needing 99 to win. Smith had earlier played his part in the first innings as Warwickshire bowled accurately on a lifeless pitch, and in sweltering heat, to dismiss Sussex cheaply. Then, after Moles and Ratcliffe had begun with 113 for the first wicket, Moody ensured Warwickshire of a substantial first-innings lead by hitting thirteen fours and a six in his 110. Sussex, batting again 196 in arrears, were given some hope of saving the match by Alan Wells's unbeaten 144, his highest score of the season, which included 24 fours and two sixes. Donelan chipped in with a career-best 53 as the pair added 112 for the sixth wicket, but the other batting was generally poor. Hanley, a 22-year-old making his first-class début on his home ground, showed promise in his 28.

Close of play: First day, Warwickshire 96-0 (A. J. Moles 52*, J. D. Ratcliffe 38*); Second day, Sussex 130-5 (A. P. Wells 61*, B. T. P. Donelan 0*).

Sussex

First innings		Second innings	
D. M. Smith c Piper b Munton	18	– b G. Smith	4
J. W. Hall b Moody	30	– lbw b Munton	12
R. Hanley lbw b P. A. Smith	2	– c and b Munton	28
A. P. Wells lbw b P. A. Smith	0	– not out	144
M. P. Speight c Piper b G. Smith	22	– b Pierson	11
*C. M. Wells run out	40	– (8) c G. Smith b Reeve	19
A. I. C. Dodemaide b Munton	4	– (9) b P. A. Smith	1
†P. Moores lbw b Munton	10	– (10) c Asif Din b P. A. Smith	0
A. C. S. Pigott lbw b G. Smith	32	– (11) c Piper b P. A. Smith	0
B. T. P. Donelan c Reeve b G. Smith	6	– (7) c Piper b Munton	53
R. A. Bunting not out	1	– (6) c Asif Din b Pierson	2
B 4, l-b 3, w 1, n-b 6	14	B 10, l-b 6, w 2, n-b 2	20
1/33 2/48 3/48 4/79 5/79 6/93 7/109 8/162 9/170	179	1/9 2/23 3/73 4/120 5/130 6/242 7/277 8/294 9/294	294

Bonus points – Sussex 1, Warwickshire 4.

Bowling: *First Innings*—Munton 20–7–46–3; G. Smith 15.5–2–36–3; P. A. Smith 13–3–30–2; Reeve 14–5–28–0; Pierson 3–0–8–0; Moody 8–5–7–1; Asif Din 4–1–17–0. *Second Innings*—Munton 28–7–63–3; G. Smith 11–1–45–1; P. A. Smith 11.5–2–45–3; Reeve 11–1–31–1; Pierson 14–3–65–2; Asif Din 9–5–29–0.

Warwickshire

First innings		Second innings	
A. J. Moles b Dodemaide	58	– c Moores b Donelan	39
J. D. Ratcliffe c Moores b Bunting	61	– c Moores b Dodemaide	8
T. M. Moody c Hall b Donelan	110		
*T. A. Lloyd b Bunting	1	– (3) c Moores b Donelan	28
P. A. Smith b Dodemaide	2	– (4) lbw b Dodemaide	13
D. A. Reeve c and b Pigott	30	– (5) not out	7
Asif Din not out	57	– (6) not out	0
†K. J. Piper lbw b Pigott	5		
A. R. K. Pierson b Pigott	9		
G. Smith b Dodemaide	30		
B 1, l-b 11	12	B 4, l-b 3	7
1/113 2/131 3/143 4/183 5/271 6/273 7/279 8/297 9/375	(9 wkts dec.) 375	1/24 2/73 3/88 4/98	(4 wkts) 102

T. A. Munton did not bat.

Bonus points – Warwickshire 4, Sussex 3 (Score at 100 overs: 334-8).

Bowling: *First Innings*—Pigott 30–4–101–3; Dodemaide 28.2–6–84–3; Bunting 21–3–89–2; Donelan 12–3–46–1; C. M. Wells 17–5–43–0. *Second Innings*—Pigott 3–0–21–0; Dodemaide 11.2–0–45–2; Bunting 3–0–10–0; Donelan 6–1–19–2.

Umpires: J. D. Bond and M. J. Kitchen.

SUSSEX v YORKSHIRE

At Eastbourne, August 8, 9, 10. Yorkshire won by an innings and 5 runs. Yorkshire 23 pts, Sussex 2 pts. Toss: Yorkshire. Outstanding performances by Moxon and Carrick sentenced Sussex to a crushing innings defeat and brought a sorry end to Eastbourne week, where both Championship matches and the Sunday League game were lost. Moxon, the Yorkshire captain, applied himself superbly in wilting heat to hit his county's highest individual score since Boycott's 233 against Essex in 1971. His unbeaten 218, from 318 balls in exactly six hours, included 28 fours and a six, and he shared century partnerships with Metcalfe and Robinson. When Sussex replied, Smith and Hall put on 60 for the opening wicket before Carrick took charge, ripping out the heart of the innings with his left-arm spin on a turning pitch. Sussex began the final day needing 160 to avoid an innings defeat, with all wickets standing, but once the openers were parted for 62 only Speight, with a defiant 53, offered much resistance. Carrick increased his match return to nine for 86; Jarvis was the best fast bowler on view, taking six wickets; and Blakey gave a fine display behind the stumps to hold nine catches.

Close of play: First day, Sussex 9-0 (D. M. Smith 2*, J. W. Hall 5*); Second day, Sussex 13-0 (D. M. Smith 5*, J. W. Hall 8*).

Yorkshire

*M. D. Moxon not out 218	†R. J. Blakey not out 2
A. A. Metcalfe b Donelan 53	B 12, l-b 6, n-b 8 26
K. Sharp c Moores b C. M. Wells 42	
P. E. Robinson c Hansford b Donelan . 59	1/120 2/213 3/375 (3 wkts dec.) 400

D. Byas, P. Carrick, C. S. Pickles, P. J. Hartley, P. W. Jarvis and J. D. Batty did not bat.

Bonus points – Yorkshire 4, Sussex 1 (Score at 100 overs: 378-3).

Bowling: Dodemaide 20–3–57–0; Pigott 21–7–76–0; Hansford 20–3–76–0; C. M. Wells 14–3–76–1; Donelan 28–1–97–2.

Sussex

D. M. Smith c Blakey b Pickles	29	– c Blakey b Pickles	37
J. W. Hall c Blakey b Carrick	32	– c Hartley b Jarvis	38
R. Hanley b Jarvis	2	– c Metcalfe b Pickles	0
A. P. Wells c Blakey b Carrick	42	– c Blakey b Carrick	4
M. P. Speight lbw b Jarvis	14	– c Blakey b Jarvis	53
*C. M. Wells c Blakey b Carrick	0	– b Carrick	15
A. I. C. Dodemaide c Byas b Pickles	40	– lbw b Hartley	0
†P. Moores c Blakey b Carrick	10	– c and b Carrick	2
A. C. S. Pigott not out	29	– lbw b Carrick	0
B. T. P. Donelan c Blakey b Carrick	9	– not out	10
A. R. Hansford b Jarvis	2	– b Jarvis	0
B 14, l-b 4	18	B 9	9
1/60 2/70 3/70 4/85 5/92 6/158 7/181 8/197 9/218	227	1/62 2/62 3/69 4/91 5/124 6/131 7/140 8/148 9/160	168

Bonus points – Sussex 1, Yorkshire 3 (Score at 100 overs: 197-8).

Bowling: *First Innings*—Jarvis 21.4–7–56–3; Hartley 19–7–50–0; Carrick 44–22–49–5; Pickles 15–5–28–2; Batty 9–1–26–0. *Second Innings*—Jarvis 14.1–4–39–3; Hartley 16–2–60–1; Pickles 6–2–23–2; Carrick 20–6–37–4.

Umpires: J. D. Bond and M. J. Kitchen.

At Lord's, August 11, 13, 14. SUSSEX drew with MIDDLESEX.

SUSSEX v KENT

At Hove, August 18, 20, 21. Drawn. Sussex 5 pts, Kent 6 pts. Toss: Sussex. An exciting finish to an absorbing struggle looked likely when Kent asked Sussex to score 312 off at least 71 overs on the final afternoon. The second-wicket pair, Hall and Smith, put on 82 in good time, but Sussex's push for victory was undermined by the Kent left-arm spinner, Davis, in a marathon spell. When Pigott became his sixth victim – his fifth in seven overs – Sussex called off the chase with 65 needed from the last six overs. A rain-affected first day had been dominated by Kent's left-handed opener, Benson, who hit his fifth century of the season, including fourteen fours and a six, before his right thumb was broken by a rising delivery from Dodemaide. He and Taylor added 113 for the second wicket before his injury. Dodemaide and Pigott bowled well without enjoying a great deal of luck. Kent's hopes of bowling their hosts out twice were dashed by the defiance of Lenham, but things might have been different had Wren held a chance at fine leg when Lenham was 11. Sussex declared 150 behind on the second evening, but Pigott checked Kent's bid for quick runs on the final morning by taking four wickets during a hundred-minute spell.

Close of play: First day, Kent 449-7 (S. A. Marsh 70*, P. S. de Villiers 15*); Second day, Kent 31-2 (N. R. Taylor 8*, G. R. Cowdrey 18*).

Kent

S. G. Hinks b Dodemaide	7	– b Dodemaide	4
M. R. Benson retired hurt	115		
N. R. Taylor c Pigott b Dodemaide	61	– (2) not out	70
G. R. Cowdrey b Dodemaide	29	– lbw b Pigott	34
T. R. Ward lbw b Donelan	64	– c Moores b Pigott	12
M. V. Fleming b Pigott	30	– b Pigott	16
*C. S. Cowdrey c Lenham b Donelan	20	– b Pigott	0
†S. A. Marsh not out	70		
R. P. Davis c Speight b Pigott	29	– (3) c Moores b Pigott	0
P. S. de Villiers not out	15	– (8) not out	19
B 3, l-b 3, w 2, n-b 1	9	B 5, l-b 1	6
1/60 2/212 3/227 4/311 5/311 6/365 7/418 (7 wkts dec.)	449	1/5 2/6 3/54 4/72 5/116 6/116 (6 wkts dec.)	161

T. N. Wren did not bat.

Bonus points – Kent 4, Sussex 2 (Score at 100 overs: 393-6).

In the first innings M. R. Benson retired hurt at 173.

Bowling: *First Innings*—Pigott 22–5–93–2; Dodemaide 31–4–123–3; Bunting 22–5–88–0; C. M. Wells 19–5–80–0; Donelan 16–4–59–2. *Second Innings*—Pigott 18–2–77–5; Dodemaide 12.4–2–43–1; Bunting 7–1–28–0; Donelan 3–0–7–0.

Sussex

N. J. Lenham b Fleming	86	– c C. S. Cowdrey b Fleming	20
J. W. Hall b Fleming	24	– c sub b Davis	52
†P. Moores run out	23	– (9) not out	1
A. P. Wells c Ward b Davis	78	– c and b Davis	36
M. P. Speight c C. S. Cowdrey b Fleming	14	– lbw b Davis	1
*C. M. Wells not out	41	– not out	42
D. M. Smith not out	6	– (3) c Ward b Davis	71
A. I. C. Dodemaide (did not bat)		– (7) c de Villiers b Davis	13
A. C. S. Pigott (did not bat)		– (8) c Ward b Davis	10
B 14, l-b 4, w 6, n-b 3	27	B 14, l-b 5	19
1/53 2/129 3/180 4/202 5/293 (5 wkts dec.)	299	1/50 2/132 3/193 4/198 5/201 6/221 7/247 (7 wkts)	265

R. A. Bunting and B. T. P. Donelan did not bat.

Bonus points – Sussex 3, Kent 2.

Bowling: *First Innings*—de Villiers 14–1–34–0; Wren 21–4–74–0; Fleming 27–10–65–3; C. S. Cowdrey 5–0–16–0; Davis 31–11–89–1; Ward 2–0–3–0. *Second Innings*—de Villiers 14–3–46–0; Wren 7–0–39–0; Davis 31.4–10–97–6; Fleming 14–3–38–1; Ward 5–0–26–0.

Umpires: P. J. Eele and R. Julian.

SUSSEX v SOMERSET

At Hove, August 23, 24, 25, 27. Somerset won by ten wickets. Somerset 23 pts, Sussex 3 pts. Toss: Somerset. Somerset were always in control after they had dismissed Sussex cheaply on the first day. Their lively seam attack found little resistance, apart from Lenham and the determined Dodemaide, and although Sussex briefly threatened to bowl themselves back into contention, reducing Somerset to 30 for three, Tavaré ensured there was no way back. His career-best 219, a maiden double-hundred, was an innings full of glorious shots which, in 413 deliveries, included 29 fours. Having shared in century stands with Harden and Rose, he equalled the county's ninth-wicket record of 183, set 27 years earlier, in partnership with Mallender, whose Somerset-best 87 was made with the aid of a runner. Tavaré declared 372 ahead first thing on the third morning, and although Lenham and Dodemaide again led a spirited rearguard action, Somerset's victory was never in much doubt. Lenham's 123 featured twenty fours, and Dodemaide took the match into the final day, hitting thirteen fours in his maiden Championship century.

Close of play: First day, Somerset 136-4 (C. J. Tavaré 45*, H. R. J. Trump 0*); Second day, Somerset 525-9 (N. A. Mallender 87*, A. N. Jones 24*); Third day, Sussex 331-8 (A. I. C. Dodemaide 86*, I. D. K. Salisbury 13*).

Sussex

N. J. Lenham c Burns b Lefebvre	45	– c Trump b Hayhurst	123
J. W. Hall c Townsend b Jones	1	– c Townsend b Rose	2
K. Greenfield c Burns b Mallender	5	– c and b Hayhurst	11
A. P. Wells lbw b Mallender	2	– b Rose	14
M. P. Speight c Hayhurst b Jones	2	– c Burns b Jones	11
*C. M. Wells c Burns b Rose	4	– c Burns b Lefebvre	2
A. I. C. Dodemaide not out	57	– c and b Jones	112
†P. Moores c Tavaré b Lefebvre	8	– c Tavaré b Trump	38
A. C. S. Pigott lbw b Rose	2	– c Cook b Harden	23
I. D. K. Salisbury c Burns b Lefebvre	3	– not out	30
R. A. Bunting c Burns b Hayhurst	14	– c Tavaré b Hayhurst	8
L-b 4, w 1, n-b 5	10	L-b 3, n-b 5	8
1/19 2/43 3/45 4/51 5/68 6/78 7/108 8/111 9/122	153	1/14 2/69 3/105 4/119 5/148 6/183 7/258 8/290 9/365	382

Bonus points – Sussex 1, Somerset 4.

Bowling: *First Innings*—Jones 11–2–47–2; Mallender 13–5–31–2; Rose 11–4–22–2; Lefebvre 17–4–46–3; Hayhurst 3.4–2–3–1. *Second Innings*—Jones 34–5–117–2; Rose 26–5–95–2; Hayhurst 23–6–58–3; Lefebvre 24–9–48–1; Trump 23–9–49–1; Harden 4–0–12–1.

Somerset

S. J. Cook c Moores b Pigott	13		
G. T. J. Townsend c Moores b Dodemaide	0	– not out	0
A. N. Hayhurst c Moores b Dodemaide	11		
*C. J. Tavaré c Speight b Pigott	219		
R. J. Harden c Moores b Pigott	59		
H. R. J. Trump c Moores b Dodemaide	0		
†N. D. Burns c C. M. Wells b Bunting	28	– (1) not out	13
G. D. Rose b Dodemaide	54		
R. P. Lefebvre b Pigott	6		
N. A. Mallender not out	87		
A. N. Jones not out	24		
B 8, l-b 9, n-b 7	24		
1/2 2/20 3/30 4/132 5/137 6/176 7/292 8/301 9/484 (9 wkts dec.)	525	(no wkt)	13

Bonus points – Somerset 3, Sussex 2 (Score at 100 overs: 282-6).

Bowling: *First Innings*—Pigott 37–6–119–4; Dodemaide 36–5–117–4; Bunting 33–8–77–1; C. M. Wells 23–1–111–0; Salisbury 29–9–80–0; Lenham 3–0–4–0. *Second Innings*—Salisbury 1–0–5–0; Greenfield 0.3–0–8–0.

Umpires: J. C. Balderstone and R. A. White.

At Leicester, August 29, 30, 31. SUSSEX beat LEICESTERSHIRE by 29 runs.

At Hove, September 5, 6, 7. SUSSEX drew with SRI LANKANS (See Sri Lankan tour section).

At Bristol, September 12, 13, 14. SUSSEX lost to GLOUCESTERSHIRE by an innings and 86 runs.

SUSSEX v MIDDLESEX

At Hove, September 18, 19, 20. Middlesex won by an innings and 57 runs. Middlesex 24 pts, Sussex 3 pts. Toss: Middlesex. Any hope Sussex had of denying Middlesex the Championship was effectively over on the first of the four scheduled days. Middlesex, inspired by Hughes's nagging accuracy and Gatting's important two-wicket contribution, bowled their hosts out cheaply on a good pitch, despite brave innings from the dependable Smith and Speight. The visitors then batted steadily rather than spectacularly. Haynes and Roseberry provided the perfect platform by putting on 133 for the first wicket, and Brown produced the highlight of the innings with an undefeated 116 which included thirteen boundaries. However, Haynes hardly endeared himself to the spectators with a display of bad temper when he was caught by wicket-keeper Moores after being distracted by a cameraman's movements behind the bowler's arm. Gatting and Emburey both chipped in with useful runs, and Middlesex were 224 ahead when they were dismissed at the end of the second day. The weather, rather than Sussex's batting, was their main worry, but the rain stayed away long enough to ensure a fifth Championship title, plus one shared, in fifteen seasons. Fraser bowled beautifully to take four wickets, and Hughes, who finished with match figures of seven for 89, signalled great celebrations among the large contingent of Middlesex supporters by claiming the last two wickets with successive balls.

Close of play: First day, Middlesex 88-0 (D. L. Haynes 34*, M. A. Roseberry 51*); Second day, Middlesex 411.

Sussex

N. J. Lenham c Emburey b Williams	9	lbw b Fraser	5
D. M. Smith c Downton b Cowans	32	lbw b Cowans	10
*P. W. G. Parker c Brown b Hughes	24	b Cowans	16
A. P. Wells lbw b Gatting	6	c Downton b Fraser	50
M. P. Speight c Downton b Hughes	33	b Fraser	12
A. I. C. Dodemaide b Fraser	18	c Downton b Fraser	16
†P. Moores c sub b Hughes	4	lbw b Hughes	10
J. A. North lbw b Cowans	7	not out	19
A. C. S. Pigott c Fraser b Gatting	4	c sub b Gatting	9
I. D. K. Salisbury not out	18	b Hughes	0
R. A. Bunting c Emburey b Hughes	11	lbw b Hughes	0
B 10, l-b 6, n-b 5	21	B 8, l-b 4, w 1, n-b 7	20
1/19 2/42 3/78 4/103 5/130 6/136 7/151 8/151 9/170	187	1/10 2/17 3/46 4/74 5/119 6/126 7/158 8/167 9/167	167

Bonus points – Sussex 1, Middlesex 4.

Bowling: *First Innings*—Fraser 21–4–55–1; Williams 3–1–9–1; Cowans 12–5–19–2; Hughes 17.1–4–34–4; Gatting 18–8–42–2; Emburey 10–5–12–0; Haynes 1–1–0–0. *Second Innings*—Fraser 17–4–47–4; Cowans 16–4–33–2; Hughes 16.5–3–55–3; Gatting 8–5–7–1; Emburey 3–0–13–0.

Middlesex

D. L. Haynes c Moores b Bunting 46
M. A. Roseberry run out 83
*M. W. Gatting c Parker b Lenham ... 51
M. R. Ramprakash lbw b Bunting 13
K. R. Brown not out 116
†P. R. Downton lbw b North 5
J. E. Emburey c Smith b Dodemaide .. 48
N. F. Williams c Wells b Dodemaide .. 18
A. R. C. Fraser b Salisbury 13
S. P. Hughes lbw b Salisbury 0
N. G. Cowans c Pigott b North 0
B 1, l-b 12, w 1, n-b 4 18

1/133 2/135 3/168 4/225 5/244 411
6/352 7/389 8/410 9/410

Bonus points – Middlesex 4, Sussex 2 (Score at 100 overs: 362-6).

Bowling: Dodemaide 28–2–128–2; Pigott 24–4–92–0; Bunting 17–4–49–2; North 16.2–4–43–2; Lenham 19–4–48–1; Salisbury 11–2–38–2.

Umpires: K. E. Palmer and D. S. Thompsett.

I ZINGARI RESULTS, 1990

Matches – 22: Won 9, Lost 4, Drawn 8, Abandoned 1.

April 24	Eton College	Drawn
May 12	Honourable Artillery Company	Won by 128 runs
May 20	Staff College, Camberley	Drawn
May 26	Eton Ramblers	Drawn
May 31	Harrow School	Drawn
June 9	Hurlingham CC	Drawn
June 10	Earl of Carnarvon's XI	Won by 53 runs
June 16	Charterhouse School	Lost by four wickets
June 23	Guards CC	Abandoned
July 7	Bradfield Waifs	Won by 102 runs
July 8	Hagley CC	Won by four wickets
July 14	Green Jackets Club	Drawn
July 15	Rickling Green CC	Lost by two wickets
July 21	Leicester Gentlemen	Won by five wickets
July 22	Sir John Starkey's XI	Won by eight wickets
July 29	Royal Armoured Corps	Won by 60 runs
August 4	R. Leigh-Pemberton's XI	Drawn
August 5	Band of Brothers	Lost by seven wickets
August 11, 12	South Wales Hunts XI	Lost by six wickets
September 2	Captain R. H. Hawkins' XI	Won by 127 runs
September 8	Hampshire Hogs	Drawn
September 9	J. H. Pawle's XI	Won by 102 runs

WARWICKSHIRE

President: The Earl of Aylesford
Chairman: R. J. Evans
Chairman, Cricket Committee: W. N. Houghton
Secretary: D. M. W. Heath
County Ground, Edgbaston,
Birmingham B5 7QU
(Telephone: 021-446 4422)
Cricket Manager/Coach: 1990 – R. M. H. Cottam
Captain: T. A. Lloyd

Given that Warwickshire's 64 bowling bonus points in the Britannic Assurance Championship were more than those obtained by any county other than Surrey (64 also), their seemingly satisfactory advance from eighth to fifth in the final table was, in fact, a slight disappointment. The summer produced the biggest swing of balance between bat and ball for many years. Yet only five counties secured fewer batting points than Warwickshire's 55, and the side suffered from a shortage of runs far too often to be realistic title contenders.

Even so, a win in their last, rain-ruined game at Old Trafford would still have earned Warwickshire third place, a remarkable effort considering that injury and a decline in form restricted Allan Donald and Gladstone Small to only 55 wickets between them at 34 apiece, compared with 137 at just under 19 in the 1989 Championship. It was fortunate for the club that this shortfall was more than made up for by the advance of Tim Munton and the breakthrough made by Joey Benjamin, together with supportive performances from Dermot Reeve and Paul Smith.

The consistency of the bowlers, however, was not matched by the top batsmen. Only Andy Moles, with his best-ever aggregate of 1,854 runs, and the prolific Australian, Tom Moody, took advantage of the most favourable batting conditions for many summers. Moody's 1,000 runs were recorded in fewer innings, twelve, than anyone had previously taken for the county, and his seven hundreds came in his first eight games. He hit the fastest hundred of the season, off 36 balls against Glamorgan at Swansea, but his best hundred was a brilliant 168 from 173 balls to win the Championship game at Derby. Nevertheless, it was ironic that, having been signed on a one-year contract to play in the limited-overs matches, Moody should help the side into the place money in the Championship. Warwickshire's performances in the three one-day competitions were unmitigated disasters.

The county's policy resulted in Donald, one of the most successful bowlers in limited-overs cricket the previous year, playing only one such game, because of the legislation governing overseas players, while Moody played in all but one of the rest. Twice forced, as a result, to chase targets in excess of 250 in the Benson and Hedges Cup group games, the county failed to qualify for the knockout stage; and after winning three of their first four games in the Refuge Assurance League, they managed only two more wins in the next twelve matches and finished fourteenth as in 1989. In the NatWest Bank Trophy, Yorkshire handed out a ten-wicket thrashing at Headingley in the second round to underline the difference a fit and in-form Donald might have made.

The South African fast bowler sustained a back injury halfway through the season, and this enabled Moody to come into the side and score so consistently that it was far from automatic which player would return to Edgbaston in 1991. In the end the committee unanimously decided to honour their contractual obligations to Donald, and Moody eventually signed for Worcestershire. In addition to his 1,163 runs in first-class cricket at an average of 89.46, the big Western Australian scored 581 runs in limited-overs cricket from twenty games. To illustrate his powerful strokeplay, which included the ability to drive in a wide "V" and square cut with great ferocity, he passed 1,000 runs off only 1,200 deliveries.

As well as Donald's back, the side had other injuries to contend with, among them the hamstring problem which kept Andy Lloyd, the captain, out of action for a third of the season. Lloyd's overall form was disappointing, not an unusual occurrence in a player's benefit year, but with Alvin Kallicharran and Geoff Humpage stepping down from the first team midway through their farewell season, much depended on Asif Din. He had a splendid season in one-day cricket, scoring 792 runs in 21 games, but a first-class record of 974 runs for an average of 27.82 was well below both his capabilities and the needs of the team. To some degree the middle order compensated, with Reeve in particular having his best season with the bat, his three first-class hundreds including his maiden double-century. As well as his 1,412 runs at an average of 54.30, he took 33 wickets, held 26 catches, many of them at slip, and led the side in Lloyd's absence.

All-rounder Paul Smith bounced back after a serious knee operation, and although he played in only twelve first-class and ten one-day games, for the second season in succession he averaged more than 30 with the bat and less than 30 with the ball in the Championship to emphasise his importance to the side's balance. Twenty-year-old Keith Piper performed well as wicket-keeper when he took over from Humpage, and in addition to his 43 dismissals he scored 432 useful runs in the Championship, including his maiden first-class hundred. He looked set for a long and successful career. Other youngsters to make their mark were Jason Ratcliffe and Dominic Ostler, both of whom batted well enough to show that a first-class career is within their capabilities.

Even though Humpage was omitted after thirteen games, he still averaged 34.88 to finish fourth in Warwickshire's first-class averages. He announced his retirement to go into business, and left Edgbaston after a distinguished career of seventeen years, having been one of the best wicket-keeper-batsmen of the 1980s. His 29 first-class hundreds enabled him to finish with a county average of 36.41, which has been bettered for Warwickshire by only six players, while his 704 dismissals for the county are exceeded only by E. J. "Tiger" Smith. Kallicharran, one of the best batsmen to play for the county, scored in excess of 18,000 runs at an average of more than 40 for Warwickshire, including 52 of his 87 hundreds.

An unexpected departure was that of the cricket manager and coach, Bob Cottam, who resigned in late October over policy differences with the cricket committee. In spite of this, however, the 1991 season promises much, provided the playing staff steer clear of injuries – and assuming that the bowlers receive better support from the batsmen than they did in 1990. – Jack Bannister.

WARWICKSHIRE 1990

[*Bill Smith*

Back row: K. J. Piper, R. G. Twose, N. M. K. Smith, J. E. Benjamin, S. J. Green, G. Welch, I. G. S. Steer. *Middle row:* T. L. Penney, G. Smith, D. P. Ostler, A. R. K. Pierson, T. A. Munton, J. D. Ratcliffe, A. A. Donald, A. J. Moles, P. A. Booth. *Front row:* R. N. Abberley (*coach*), G. C. Small, G. W. Humpage, R. M. H. Cottam (*cricket manager/coach*), T. A. Lloyd (*captain*), A. I. Kallicharran, Asif Din, P. A. Smith. *Insets:* T. M. Moody, D. A. Reeve, P. C. L. Holloway.

WARWICKSHIRE RESULTS

All first-class matches – Played 25: Won 7, Lost 8, Drawn 10.

County Championship matches – Played 22: Won 7, Lost 7, Drawn 8.

Bonus points – Batting 55, Bowling 64.

Competition placings – Britannic Assurance County Championship, 5th; NatWest Bank Trophy, 2nd round; Benson and Hedges Cup, 4th in Group A; Refuge Assurance League, 14th.

BRITANNIC ASSURANCE CHAMPIONSHIP AVERAGES

BATTING

	Birthplace	*M*	*I*	*NO*	*R*	*HI*	*Avge*
‡T. M. Moody	*Adelaide, Australia*	7	12	2	866	168	86.60
‡D. A. Reeve	*Kowloon, Hong Kong*	22	34	11	1,265	202*	55.00
‡A. J. Moles	*Solihull*	22	42	8	1,669	224*	49.08
‡G. W. Humpage	*Birmingham*	11	18	3	552	74	36.80
J. E. Benjamin	*Christ Church, St Kitts*	12	11	6	169	41	33.80
D. P. Ostler	*Solihull*	9	15	2	432	71	33.23
‡P. A. Smith	*Jesmond*	12	20	4	520	117	32.50
N. M. K. Smith	*Birmingham*	7	9	2	214	83*	30.57
J. D. Ratcliffe	*Solihull*	14	27	3	689	81*	28.70
‡Asif Din	*Kampala, Uganda*	21	37	3	874	70	25.70
K. J. Piper	*Leicester*	14	18	1	432	111	25.41
‡A. I. Kallicharran	*Paidama, BG*	5	8	1	175	72	25.00
‡T. A. Lloyd	*Oswestry*	15	27	1	646	101	24.84
P. A. Booth	*Huddersfield*	7	12	0	177	60	14.75
R. G. Twose	*Torquay*	4	6	0	88	51	14.66
A. R. K. Pierson	*Enfield*	11	9	5	57	16*	14.25
‡G. C. Small	*St George, Barbados*	12	18	2	212	55	13.25
‡T. A. Munton	*Melton Mowbray*	22	23	9	121	29*	8.64
‡A. A. Donald	*Bloemfontein, SA*	14	18	3	118	24*	7.86

Also batted: G. Smith (*Jarrow*) (1 match) 30.

* *Signifies not out.* ‡ *Denotes county cap.*

The following played a total of thirteen three-figure innings for Warwickshire in County Championship matches – T. M. Moody 5, A. J. Moles 3, D. A. Reeve 2, T. A. Lloyd 1, K. J. Piper 1, P. A. Smith 1.

BOWLING

	O	*M*	*R*	*W*	*BB*	*5W/i*	*Avge*
P. A. Smith	148.5	34	497	20	5-48	1	24.85
T. A. Munton	748.3	174	2,086	75	5-33	2	27.81
D. A. Reeve	319.4	94	782	28	4-42	0	27.92
J. E. Benjamin	322.3	51	1,036	34	5-71	3	30.47
G. C. Small	321.4	78	900	27	6-94	2	33.33
A. A. Donald	355.1	81	988	28	3-28	0	35.28
A. R. K. Pierson	302.4	55	965	25	5-101	1	38.60
P. A. Booth	214.2	70	495	12	4-55	0	41.25

Also bowled: Asif Din 133.2–24–569–6; G. W. Humpage 7–2–34–0; T. A. Lloyd 9–1–58–1; A. J. Moles 22–2–133–2; T. M. Moody 38–7–145–3; G. Smith 26.5–3–81–4; N. M. K. Smith 109.5–20–350–5; R. G. Twose 26–2–101–2.

Wicket-keepers: K. J. Piper 39 ct, 4 st; G. W. Humpage 22 ct.

Leading Fielder: D. A. Reeve 23.

At Cambridge, April 26, 27, 28. WARWICKSHIRE drew with CAMBRIDGE UNIVERSITY.

WARWICKSHIRE v YORKSHIRE

At Birmingham, May 3, 4, 5. Warwickshire won by seven wickets. Warwickshire 23 pts, Yorkshire 5 pts. Toss: Yorkshire. With Small, Donald and Munton bowling with great penetration on a slow, seaming pitch, Yorkshire had to rely on Sidebottom's 38, top score of the innings, to gain a single batting point. In turn, Sidebottom and Fletcher, in particular, disconcerted Warwickshire on the first evening and second morning, and it took an unbeaten, hard-hitting 83 from Smith to rescue them from a parlous position at 162 for eight and put them 92 ahead. Smith hit a six and twelve fours, and in partnership with Donald added 80 for the ninth wicket. Only Robinson, batting for three and threequarter hours, showed the necessary application when Yorkshire batted a second time. Booth, the former Yorkshire left-arm spinner, bowled well for his four wickets on the second evening and left his home county facing defeat inside three of the scheduled four days. Reeve finished with a freakish match analysis of 22–15–8–3.

Close of play: First day, Warwickshire 111-4 (G. W. Humpage 40*, D. A. Reeve 24*); Second day, Yorkshire 139-5 (P. E. Robinson 21*, P. Carrick 13*).

Yorkshire

*M. D. Moxon c Humpage b Small	12	(5) c Kallicharran b Booth	0
A. A. Metcalfe c Reeve b Donald	33	b Smith	24
†R. J. Blakey c Booth b Reeve	6	c Moles b Booth	24
S. A. Kellett lbw b Small	31	(1) c Humpage b Booth	31
P. E. Robinson run out	1	(4) lbw b Reeve	59
C. White b Small	1	c Asif Din b Booth	6
P. Carrick c Reeve b Munton	7	b Small	14
A. Sidebottom c Asif Din b Munton	38	c Moles b Munton	19
P. W. Jarvis c Humpage b Small	0	c Humpage b Reeve	6
D. Gough c Humpage b Donald	4	not out	3
S. D. Fletcher not out	11	b Donald	0
B 9, l-b 11, w 2, n-b 1	23	B 17, l-b 12, w 2, n-b 2	33
1/35 2/60 3/74 4/102 5/104 6/105 7/119 8/121 9/139	167	1/57 2/61 3/100 4/104 5/120 6/149 7/199 8/213 9/216	219

Bonus points – Yorkshire 1, Warwickshire 4.

Bowling: *First Innings*—Donald 19–5–56–2; Small 18–5–40–4; Munton 15.5–3–41–2; Reeve 17–12–6–1; Booth 2–1–4–0. *Second Innings*—Donald 17.4–4–41–1; Small 19–9–29–1; Munton 8–3–21–1; Booth 33–9–55–4; Smith 12–2–36–1; Asif Din 2–1–6–0; Reeve 5–3–2–2.

Warwickshire

A. J. Moles lbw b Sidebottom	6	(2) c Blakey b White	32
*T. A. Lloyd b Fletcher	31	(1) b Carrick	30
Asif Din c Blakey b Sidebottom	0	c Blakey b Carrick	23
A. I. Kallicharran lbw b Fletcher	2	not out	11
†G. W. Humpage lbw b Sidebottom	52	not out	19
D. A. Reeve c Moxon b Fletcher	29		
N. M. K. Smith not out	83		
P. A. Booth lbw b Jarvis	15		
G. C. Small b Jarvis	0		
A. A. Donald c Sidebottom b Carrick	16		
T. A. Munton lbw b Fletcher	0		
B 10, l-b 6, w 5, n-b 4	25	B 8, l-b 5	13
1/11 2/11 3/38 4/43 5/127 6/134 7/162 8/162 9/242	259	1/60 2/96 3/102	(3 wkts) 128

Bonus points – Warwickshire 3, Yorkshire 4.

Bowling: *First Innings*—Jarvis 16–1–52–2; Sidebottom 18–4–54–3; Fletcher 20.5–6–47–4; Gough 14–1–53–0; Carrick 10–3–31–1; White 2–0–6–0. *Second Innings*—Jarvis 6–2–22–0; Fletcher 4–0–18–0; Carrick 12.2–2–35–2; White 11–2–40–1.

Umpires: R. Palmer and P. B. Wight.

At Northampton, May 15, 16, 17, 18. WARWICKSHIRE beat NORTHAMPTONSHIRE by an innings and 30 runs.

WARWICKSHIRE v NOTTINGHAMSHIRE

At Birmingham, May 19, 21, 22. Nottinghamshire won by 5 runs. Nottinghamshire 24 pts, Warwickshire 5 pts. Toss: Nottinghamshire. A thrilling finale, which brought victory to the visitors, saw Stephenson take the last three wickets in eight deliveries, including two with consecutive balls in the last over. Set to score 304 off a minimum of 64 overs, Warwickshire at one stage were 259 for four, with time on their side. And though in retrospect the run-out of Humpage for 62 from 68 balls was to prove the turning-point, Warwickshire looked certain to win when they needed just 20 from the last four overs with five wickets in hand. However, the run-out of Lloyd, who was batting with a runner, and the first-ball dismissal of Small tipped the scales. Nottinghamshire deserved their win, having batted solidly in both innings and declared twice. Broad hit nineteen fours in his first-innings 119 and his opening partnership of 176 in 63 overs with Martindale provided his side with an excellent start. Humpage, with 74 from 88 balls, gave substance to Warwickshire's reply, and while on the final day Asif Din and Kallicharran seemingly set the home side on course for victory, the bowling of Hemmings and later Stephenson proved conclusive.

Close of play: First day, Warwickshire 17-1 (A. J. Moles 8*, T. A. Munton 5*); Second day, Nottinghamshire 126-2 (R. T. Robinson 38*, P. Johnson 43*).

Nottinghamshire

B. C. Broad b Smith	119	– c Reeve b Benjamin	30
D. J. R. Martindale c Humpage b Munton	73	– lbw b Munton	10
*R. T. Robinson c Smith b Small	41	– lbw b Small	47
P. Johnson c sub b Munton	2	– c Benjamin b Munton	73
D. W. Randall c Humpage b Small	5	– lbw b Benjamin	17
M. Saxelby not out	32	– c Asif Din b Smith	13
F. D. Stephenson c Munton b Donald	15	– c Moles b Smith	12
†B. N. French not out	1	– not out	25
E. E. Hemmings (did not bat)		– not out	16
L-b 14, n-b 1	15	L-b 5, w 2, n-b 2	9
1/176 2/247 3/247 4/254 5/255 6/295 (6 wkts dec.)	303	1/30 2/54 3/135 4/176 5/195 6/197 7/217 (7 wkts dec.)	252

K. E. Cooper and R. A. Pick did not bat.

Bonus points – Nottinghamshire 4, Warwickshire 2.

Bowling: *First Innings*—Donald 16–5–38–1; Small 19–3–34–2; Munton 25–5–85–2; Smith 23.5–0–82–1; Benjamin 14–2–41–0; Asif Din 2–1–9–0. *Second Innings*—Small 12–12–1–39–1; Munton 18–3–57–2; Donald 3–0–5–0; Smith 17–1–76–2; Benjamin 18–1–55–2; Asif Din 2–0–15–0.

Warwickshire

A. J. Moles b Cooper	13	– lbw b Cooper	35
*T. A. Lloyd lbw b Stephenson	4	– (7) run out	10
T. A. Munton lbw b Cooper	13	– (11) b Stephenson	0
Asif Din c Randall b Hemmings	41	– (2) lbw b Hemmings	61
A. I. Kallicharran st French b Hemmings	20	– (3) c Saxelby b Hemmings	58
†G. W. Humpage c Randall b Pick	74	– (4) run out	62
D. A. Reeve c French b Stephenson	34	– (5) c Saxelby b Hemmings	26
N. M. K. Smith c French b Pick	6	– (6) c Robinson b Stephenson	14
G. C. Small c Randall b Cooper	0	– (8) c French b Pick	0
A. A. Donald not out	24	– (9) not out	9
J. E. Benjamin b Stephenson	14	– (10) b Stephenson	1
B 1, l-b 7, n-b 1	9	B 4, l-b 18	22
1/8 2/28 3/45 4/79 5/134 6/178 7/190 8/198 9/234	252	1/88 2/120 3/185 4/253 5/259 6/284 7/285 8/287 9/298	298

Bonus points – Warwickshire 3, Nottinghamshire 4.

Bowling: *First Innings*—Pick 20–4–46–2; Stephenson 19.3–1–69–3; Hemmings 15–3–46–2; Cooper 23–6–72–3; Saxelby 4–1–11–0. *Second Innings*—Pick 11–0–56–1; Cooper 16–3–43–1; Stephenson 14.4–2–69–3; Hemmings 23–0–108–3.

Umpires: J. H. Hampshire and A. A. Jones.

WARWICKSHIRE v WORCESTERSHIRE

At Birmingham, May 26, 28, 29. Drawn. Warwickshire 6 pts, Worcestershire 5 pts. Toss: Warwickshire. Rain on the final afternoon prevented any tangible reward coming from the three earlier declarations. Lloyd, with understandable caution on such a good pitch, had asked Worcestershire to score 244 in a minimum of 46 overs and then challenged them to chase the target by employing his spin bowlers. In Warwickshire's first innings, a second-wicket stand of 151 in 174 minutes between Moles and Asif Din (134 balls) was the major contribution to a batting effort that struggled at times against Botham's swing bowling and the negative tactics of Illingworth, bowling over the wicket into the rough to the right-handers. This line of attack was later emulated by Booth, earning the disapprobation of Botham, one of four wickets for Munton in a six-over spell which left Worcestershire much in need of the entertaining ninth-wicket partnership of 89 in 29 overs between Radford and Dilley. On the last day, as Warwickshire extended their lead of 42 on first innings, Moles hit his second half-century of the game and Booth underlined his increasing value to the side with a career-best 43 as night-watchman.

Close of play: First day, Worcestershire 11-0 (T. S. Curtis 4*, M. J. Weston 6*); Second day, Warwickshire 20-1 (A. J. Moles 11*, P. A. Booth 0*).

Warwickshire

A. J. Moles c Rhodes b Illingworth	76	– c Rhodes b Illingworth	56
*T. A. Lloyd c Illingworth b Dilley	9	– lbw b Newport	9
Asif Din c D'Oliveira b Botham	70	– (7) c Radford b Illingworth	1
†G. W. Humpage c Curtis b Illingworth	9	– c Weston b Illingworth	12
D. A. Reeve lbw b Botham	21	– not out	49
D. P. Ostler c Rhodes b Lampitt	26	– b Lampitt	14
N. M. K. Smith c Dilley b Lampitt	33	– (8) c D'Oliveira b Lampitt	0
P. A. Booth lbw b Lampitt	3	– (3) c Rhodes b Radford	43
A. A. Donald not out	10	– b Lampitt	0
J. E. Benjamin not out	12	– not out	12
B 2, l-b 16, w 4, n-b 4	26	L-b 4, n-b 1	5
1/18 2/169 3/169 4/193 5/203 6/251 7/257 8/281 (8 wkts dec.)	295	1/16 2/109 3/118 4/129 5/168 6/169 7/169 8/169 (8 wkts dec.)	201

T. A. Munton did not bat.

Bonus points – Warwickshire 3, Worcestershire 3 (Score at 100 overs: 291-8).

Bowling: *First Innings*—Dilley 10–2–34–1; Radford 12–2–49–0; Newport 11–2–38–0; Botham 22–6–46–2; Lampitt 14–3–44–3; Illingworth 33–9–66–2. *Second Innings*—Dilley 11–3–33–0; Radford 8–1–32–1; Newport 7–1–26–1; Lampitt 10.1–1–39–3; Illingworth 22–4–67–3.

Worcestershire

T. S. Curtis lbw b Benjamin	34	– not out	47
M. J. Weston c Humpage b Donald	6	– c Reeve b Booth	11
*P. A. Neale c Humpage b Donald	29	– not out	39
I. T. Botham b Munton	48		
D. B. D'Oliveira c Humpage b Munton	29		
S. R. Lampitt c Humpage b Munton	0		
P. J. Newport lbw b Munton	9		
†S. J. Rhodes c Reeve b Booth	2		
N. V. Radford not out	43		
G. R. Dilley not out	32		
B 2, l-b 12, w 4, n-b 3	21	L-b 8, n-b 1	9
1/12 2/60 3/87 4/151 5/152 6/153 7/162 8/164 (8 wkts dec.)	253	1/29 (1 wkt)	106

R. K. Illingworth did not bat.

Bonus points – Worcestershire 2, Warwickshire 3 (Score at 100 overs: 213-8).

Bowling: *First Innings*—Donald 21–4–54–2; Benjamin 19–5–52–1; Munton 21.5–6–45–4; Booth 38–18–67–1; Smith 1–1–0–0; Reeve 10–4–21–0. *Second Innings*—Donald 4–2–10–0; Benjamin 3–1–6–0; Munton 2.3–0–12–0; Booth 11–2–36–1; Smith 8–2–34–0.

Umpires: B. Leadbeater and N. T. Plews.

At Birmingham, May 30, 31, June 1. WARWICKSHIRE drew with NEW ZEALANDERS (See New Zealand tour section).

WARWICKSHIRE v NORTHAMPTONSHIRE

At Birmingham, June 2, 4, 5. Drawn. Warwickshire 5 pts, Northamptonshire 8 pts. Toss: Northamptonshire. Rain, which had already cost 30 overs on the opening day, cut 285 minutes from the final day's play, but Northamptonshire made a brave bid for victory in the hour and a half possible that evening. They were thwarted by Pierson and Munton, the last-wicket pair, who came together in the fifteenth of the final twenty overs, with Warwickshire just 16 runs ahead, and made sure that there would be no improbable win to avenge the innings defeat handed out by Warwickshire at Northampton in May. Warwickshire, put in on another slow, seaming pitch, had been on the defensive since Capel, on the first day, had removed Lloyd, Asif Din and Kallicharran at a cost of 5 runs in 31 balls to set himself up for a five-wicket haul. On the second day Capel batted brilliantly for 89 off 85 deliveries, hitting three sixes and twelve fours. For Warwickshire, there was some consolation in the return after injury of Paul Smith, who brought stability to the middle of the order.

Close of play: First day, Northamptonshire 57-2 (R. J. Bailey 14*); Second day, Warwickshire 88-5 (G. W. Humpage 25*, P. A. Smith 25*).

Warwickshire

A. J. Moles lbw b Ambrose	40	– lbw b Ambrose	13
*T. A. Lloyd lbw b Capel	65	– b Thomas	10
Asif Din b Capel	5	– c Fordham b Thomas	9
A. I. Kallicharran b Capel	2	– lbw b Thomas	0
†G. W. Humpage c Fordham b Ambrose	13	– b Ambrose	42
D. A. Reeve c Fordham b Capel	5	– lbw b Ambrose	0
P. A. Smith b Ambrose	23	– run out	41
G. C. Small lbw b Capel	24	– c and b Thomas	0
A. A. Donald c Capel b Ambrose	0	– (10) run out	1
A. R. K. Pierson not out	5	– (9) not out	9
T. A. Munton b Ambrose	0	– not out	10
B 11, l-b 8, w 1	20	L-b 7	7
1/104 2/113 3/123 4/140 5/141 6/153 7/171 8/171 9/201	202	1/20 2/30 3/32 4/42 5/42 6/115 7/118 8/122 9/132	(9 wkts) 142

Bonus points – Warwickshire 2, Northamptonshire 4.

Bowling: *First Innings*—Ambrose 21–8–53–5; Thomas 6–0–29–0; Capel 21–5–74–5; Penberthy 7–2–27–0. *Second Innings*—Ambrose 25–6–55–3; Thomas 23–6–53–4; Capel 7–3–21–0; N. G. B. Cook 4–4–0–0; Penberthy 2–0–6–0.

Northamptonshire

A. Fordham c Lloyd b Munton	33
N. A. Felton c Kallicharran b Small	8
R. J. Bailey c Humpage b Munton	40
*A. J. Lamb run out	48
D. J. Capel lbw b Smith	89
G. Cook b Munton	34
A. L. Penberthy c Humpage b Donald	17
J. G. Thomas c Asif Din b Pierson	9
C. E. L. Ambrose not out	23
†D. Ripley not out	2
B 1, l-b 13, w 1	15
1/14 2/57 3/134 4/134 5/263 6/267 7/289 8/304	(8 wkts dec.) 318

N. G. B. Cook did not bat.

Bonus points – Northamptonshire 4, Warwickshire 3.

Bowling: Donald 23–5–56–1; Small 17–2–44–1; Munton 33–8–92–3; Smith 15–4–63–1; Pierson 8–1–49–1.

Umpires: D. J. Constant and B. Dudleston.

At Lord's, June 6, 7, 8. WARWICKSHIRE drew with MIDDLESEX.

WARWICKSHIRE v ESSEX

At Birmingham, June 9, 11, 12. Warwickshire won by five wickets. Warwickshire 18 pts, Essex 3 pts. Toss: Essex. With six hours lost to rain, mostly on the first day, only agreement between the captains made a result possible. Warwickshire were given a target of 291 in a minimum of 85 overs, which could have become 89 had they not scored the runs with 8.3 overs to spare. A solid 97 by Moles anchored the run-chase and enabled the free-scoring Asif Din (56 balls) and Humpage (46 balls) to make the win possible. The feature of the Essex innings was a splendid 103 off 164 balls by Waugh, his fourth Championship hundred in seven innings and containing a six and nine fours. Stephenson, who contributed just 29 runs to their third-wicket partnership of 134, was altogether more circumspect over his 85, taking 274 balls against a steady attack on a good pitch, while Shahid's unbeaten 75 was a career best.

Close of play: First day, Essex 57-1 (J. P. Stephenson 26*, P. J. Prichard 27*); Second day, Essex 331-5 dec.

Essex

B. R. Hardie lbw b Benjamin	2	†M. A. Garnham not out	26
J. P. Stephenson c Humpage b Benjamin	85		
P. J. Prichard c and b Munton	29	B 6, w 1, n-b 3	10
M. E. Waugh c Humpage b Munton	103		
A. W. Lilley lbw b Donald	1	1/11 2/60 3/194	(5 wkts dec.) 331
N. Shahid not out	75	4/197 5/244	

*D. R. Pringle, N. A. Foster, J. H. Childs and S. J. W. Andrew did not bat.

Bonus points – Essex 3, Warwickshire 2 (Score at 100 overs: 268-5).

Bowling: Donald 25–7–53–1; Benjamin 22–2–79–2; Munton 35–8–72–2; Pierson 26.1–2–86–0; N. M. K. Smith 12–2–35–0.

Essex forfeited their second innings.

Warwickshire

A. J. Moles not out	14	– lbw b Pringle	97
J. D. Ratcliffe not out	27	– run out	22
Asif Din (did not bat)		– run out	42
†G. W. Humpage (did not bat)		– run out	43
*D. A. Reeve (did not bat)		– not out	33
P. A. Smith (did not bat)		– lbw b Pringle	2
N. M. K. Smith (did not bat)		– not out	30
		B 1, l-b 12, w 1, n-b 11	25
(no wkt dec.)	41	1/56 2/148 3/212 4/245 5/253	(5 wkts) 294

A. R. K. Pierson, A. A. Donald, J. E. Benjamin and T. A. Munton did not bat.

Bowling: *First Innings*—Waugh 6–2–7–0; Stephenson 6–2–25–0; Lilley 1–0–7–0; Prichard 0.4–0–2–0. *Second Innings*—Foster 14–2–68–0; Pringle 23–6–72–2; Childs 25.3–7–66–0; Stephenson 3–1–7–0; Andrew 12–1–44–0; Waugh 3–0–24–0.

Umpires: B. Dudleston and R. A. White.

At Derby, June 16, 18, 19. WARWICKSHIRE beat DERBYSHIRE by two wickets.

At Sheffield, June 20, 21, 22. WARWICKSHIRE lost to YORKSHIRE by two wickets.

WARWICKSHIRE v KENT

At Birmingham, June 23, 25, 26. Drawn. Warwickshire 6 pts, Kent 6 pts. Toss: Warwickshire. A declaration from each side was not enough to make up for the three hours lost to rain on the first two days, and a slow pitch also helped defeat their efforts to obtain a positive result. The promising Ostler again impressed as he compiled a career-best 71, the top score in a match which contained five half-centuries. Kent, who collected four bowling bonus points for the first time in 1990, were eventually invited to score 233 in just under two and a half hours, but three wickets by Donald in the fourth over of the final twenty ended their interest.

Close of play: First day, Warwickshire 208-6 (D. P. Ostler 49*, A. R. K. Pierson 0*); Second day, Kent 177-8 (C. S. Cowdrey 38*, A. P. Igglesden 0*).

Warwickshire

A. J. Moles b Merrick	12 – run out	11
J. D. Ratcliffe c Marsh b Ellison	28 – b Davis	43
Asif Din c and b Igglesden	19 – c Davis b Fleming	14
R. G. Twose c C. S. Cowdrey b Ellison	51 – c G. R. Cowdrey b Davis	12
*D. A. Reeve c Marsh b Igglesden	30 – not out	59
D. P. Ostler c and b Davis	71 – b Taylor	8
†K. J. Piper c Wells b C. S. Cowdrey	9 – c Wells b Davis	10
A. R. K. Pierson c Marsh b Igglesden	2 – lbw b Marsh	6
A. A. Donald c Wells b Davis	0 – c Igglesden b Marsh	1
J. E. Benjamin not out	3 – not out	15
T. A. Munton c C. S. Cowdrey b Igglesden	4	
B 4, l-b 7, w 1, n-b 1	13	B 4, l-b 6, w 1 ... 11
1/14 2/51 3/68 4/127 5/166 6/202 7/223 8/224 9/237	242	1/17 2/51 3/70 4/84 5/105 6/118 7/155 8/173 (8 wkts dec.) 190

Bonus points – Warwickshire 2, Kent 4.

Bowling: *First Innings*—Merrick 9–2–19–1; Igglesden 27.3–4–79–4; Fleming 13–7–22–0; Ellison 18–7–36–2; Davis 26–8–70–2; C. S. Cowdrey 2–1–5–1. *Second Innings*—Igglesden 6–0–23–0; Ellison 7–3–23–0; Davis 26–5–61–3; Fleming 7–1–21–1; Taylor 11–4–19–1; G. R. Cowdrey 2–0–13–0; Marsh 5–0–20–2.

Kent

S. G. Hinks lbw b Donald	66 – lbw b Benjamin	15
V. J. Wells c Twose b Benjamin	5 – lbw b Pierson	25
N. R. Taylor lbw b Pierson	25 – b Donald	28
G. R. Cowdrey c Reeve b Munton	20 – not out	22
*C. S. Cowdrey not out	56 – lbw b Donald	0
M. V. Fleming lbw b Reeve	3 – b Donald	0
†S. A. Marsh c Reeve b Benjamin	5	
R. M. Ellison lbw b Benjamin	6 – (7) not out	8
R. P. Davis c Twose b Pierson	5	
A. P. Igglesden c Munton b Asif Din	5	
T. A. Merrick not out	0	
L-b 2, w 2	4	L-b 1, n-b 3 ... 4
1/10 2/47 3/90 4/133 5/136 6/154 7/160 8/177 9/192	(9 wkts dec.) 200	1/19 2/68 3/76 4/76 5/76 (5 wkts) 102

Bonus points – Kent 2, Warwickshire 4.

Bowling: *First Innings*—Donald 14–5–19–1; Benjamin 16–4–31–3; Munton 13–4–46–1; Pierson 21–5–68–2; Reeve 7–3–16–1; Asif Din 1.5–0–18–1. *Second Innings*—Donald 10.5–2–28–3; Benjamin 8–1–34–1; Pierson 14–5–19–1; Asif Din 3–0–14–0; Munton 7–4–6–0.

Umpires: J. D. Bond and K. E. Palmer.

At Taunton, July 4, 5, 6. WARWICKSHIRE drew with SOMERSET.

At The Oval, July 7, 9, 10. WARWICKSHIRE lost to SURREY by 168 runs.

WARWICKSHIRE v LANCASHIRE

At Coventry, July 18, 19, 20. Drawn. Warwickshire 7 pts, Lancashire 7 pts. Toss: Warwickshire. The first first-class match at the Binley Road ground since 1919 was dominated by a staggering performance from the Lancashire left-hander, Fairbrother, who rescued his side from a disastrous position at 116 for six with a brilliant, unbeaten double-century in 299 minutes. He faced 223 balls and hit two sixes and 35 fours with strokeplay that annihilated an otherwise successful Warwickshire attack and made a mockery of his disappointing Test-match batting for England. A pitch with welcome pace had also enabled the home batsmen to strike form, and Reeve and Smith both played well while adding 130 in even time for the sixth wicket on the opening day. In Warwickshire's second innings, not even the impressive Wasim Akram troubled Moles as he scored 100 not out off 276 balls, and Moody was superb, hitting eighteen fours in his 96 off 149 balls. He and Moles put on 158 for the third wicket as Warwickshire looked to set Lancashire a target. It was a stiff one, 299 off only 39 overs, but while Fairbrother was cracking 50 he briefly raised their hopes. Once he was out, a draw was inevitable.

Close of play: First day, Lancashire 12-1 (G. D. Mendis 5*, J. D. Fitton 4*); Second day, Warwickshire 51-2 (A. J. Moles 24*, T. M. Moody 6*).

Warwickshire

A. J. Moles b Wasim Akram	31	– not out	100
*T. A. Lloyd lbw b Allott	1	– b Wasim Akram	8
Asif Din c Mendis b Watkinson	45	– lbw b Wasim Akram	1
T. M. Moody c Hegg b Wasim Akram	30	– c Hegg b Hughes	96
D. P. Ostler lbw b Wasim Akram	3	– c Mendis b Hughes	18
D. A. Reeve run out	78		
P. A. Smith c Hughes b Fitton	82	– (6) not out	7
†K. J. Piper not out	40		
J. E. Benjamin not out	28		
B 13, l-b 18, w 2, n-b 3	36	B 5, l-b 7, n-b 14	26
1/2 2/71 3/105 4/114 5/117 6/247 7/332 (7 wkts dec.)	374	1/29 2/31 3/189 4/235 (4 wkts dec.)	256

A. R. K. Pierson and T. A. Munton did not bat.

Bonus points – Warwickshire 4, Lancashire 3 (Score at 100 overs: 339-7).

Bowling: *First Innings*—Wasim Akram 26–6–76–3; Allott 14–1–45–1; Austin 16–5–48–0; Watkinson 15–3–53–1; Hughes 17–0–73–0; Fitton 15–3–48–1. *Second Innings*—Allott 10–1–31–0; Watkinson 17–3–38–0; Wasim Akram 18–7–51–2; Austin 10–3–19–0; Fitton 15–2–44–0; Hughes 15.4–2–54–2; Jesty 1–0–7–0.

Lancashire

G. D. Mendis c Piper b Munton	5	– (6) not out	20
G. Fowler c Piper b Munton	0	– (1) c sub b Pierson	30
J. D. Fitton c Ostler b Benjamin	10		
T. E. Jesty c Ostler b Benjamin	17	– (5) lbw b Asif Din	6
N. H. Fairbrother not out	203	– (4) b Pierson	50
M. Watkinson lbw b Smith	14	– (2) lbw b Benjamin	5
Wasim Akram c Ostler b Smith	7	– (3) c sub b Pierson	32
†W. K. Hegg c Pierson b Benjamin	9	– (7) not out	20
I. D. Austin lbw b Munton	9		
*D. P. Hughes not out	29		
B 12, l-b 5, w 3, n-b 9	29	B 1, l-b 7, n-b 2	10
1/7 2/12 3/26 4/49 5/107 6/116 7/181 8/203 (8 wkts dec.)	332	1/25 2/44 3/86 4/107 5/131 (5 wkts)	173

P. J. W. Allott did not bat.

Bonus points – Lancashire 4, Warwickshire 3.

Bowling: *First Innings*—Munton 22–7–75–3; Benjamin 21–4–97–3; Pierson 24–8–70–0; Smith 10–2–37–2; Moody 5–0–25–0; Asif Din 4.3–2–11–0. *Second Innings*—Munton 3–0–30–0; Benjamin 7–0–42–1; Pierson 14–1–56–3; Asif Din 10–3–37–1.

Umpires: R. Palmer and R. A. White.

At Swansea, July 25, 26, 27. WARWICKSHIRE lost to GLAMORGAN by five wickets.

WARWICKSHIRE v HAMPSHIRE

At Birmingham, July 28, 30, 31. Warwickshire won by six wickets. Warwickshire 21 pts, Hampshire 3 pts. Toss: Hampshire. Only nineteen wickets fell on a good batting pitch which provided some turn, albeit slowly, but Warwickshire revived their title challenge with a successful run-chase. Set to score 271 in a minimum of 56 overs, and with Nicholas admirably keeping the game open by his generous use of spin, they won in the final over thanks to a well-paced, unbeaten 101 off 100 balls by Moody. On the opening day, Terry and Maru had put Hampshire on the road to recovery with 118 for the sixth wicket after Reeve, on a humid morning, had reduced them to 81 for four at lunch. Terry marked his return to form, following illness, with 119 not out in 281 minutes. Contrasting innings from Ratcliffe (228 minutes) and Smith (101 balls) were the basis of Warwickshire's first innings, the pair adding 143 in 31 overs before Lloyd declared 54 in arrears to make up for time lost to rain in the morning. Nicholas hit 78 from 73 balls as Hampshire set up the third declaration of the match.

Close of play: First day, Hampshire 287-6 (V. P. Terry 113*, R. J. Parks 29*); Second day, Hampshire 40-0 (T. C. Middleton 21*, C. L. Smith 11*).

Hampshire

	First innings		Second innings	
T. C. Middleton c Asif Din b Reeve	10	– c Reeve b Asif Din	64
C. L. Smith c Ratcliffe b Reeve	18	– b Smith	29
R. J. Scott lbw b Reeve	4	– c Reeve b Pierson	0
*M. C. J. Nicholas b Munton	16	– not out	78
M. D. Marshall c Reeve b Pierson	26	– c Moody b Pierson	10
V. P. Terry not out	119	– not out	19
R. J. Maru run out	53		
†R. J. Parks c Asif Din b Pierson	33		
S. D. Udal b Pierson	9		
B 4, l-b 7, n-b 8	19	B 11, l-b 1, n-b 4	16
1/28 2/34 3/37 4/80 5/90 6/208 7/291 8/307 (8 wkts dec.)	307	1/82 2/92 3/123 4/150 (4 wkts dec.)	216

C. A. Connor and P. J. Bakker did not bat.

Bonus points – Hampshire 2, Warwickshire 2 (Score at 100 overs: 236-6).

Bowling: *First Innings*—Benjamin 12–3–37–0; Munton 27–9–50–1; Reeve 29–11–58–3; Smith 7–3–11–0; Pierson 30.4–2–73–3; Asif Din 14–0–67–0. *Second Innings*—Munton 8–1–24–0; Benjamin 3–0–7–0; Pierson 25–5–66–2; Asif Din 11–2–62–1; Smith 6–1–16–1; Moody 3–0–23–0; Moles 1–0–6–0.

Warwickshire

	First innings		Second innings	
A. J. Moles b Connor	24	– b Udal	36
J. D. Ratcliffe not out	81	– st Parks b Maru	46
*T. A. Lloyd c Terry b Connor	1	– b Udal	61
T. M. Moody c Middleton b Maru	48	– not out	101
P. A. Smith not out	85	– c Smith b Maru	5
D. A. Reeve (did not bat)		– not out	12
B 4, l-b 8, n-b 2	14	L-b 8, n-b 5	13
1/32 2/38 3/110 (3 wkts dec.)	253	1/79 2/103 3/234 4/251 (4 wkts)	274

Asif Din, †K. J. Piper, A. R. K. Pierson, J. E. Benjamin and T. A. Munton did not bat.

Bonus points – Warwickshire 3, Hampshire 1.

Bowling: *First Innings*—Bakker 14–6–44–0; Marshall 8–3–17–0; Maru 22–2–67–1; Connor 10–2–23–2; Udal 13–0–66–0; Nicholas 2.4–0–24–0. *Second Innings*—Bakker 4–1–17–0; Marshall 8–1–27–0; Maru 24–1–90–2; Connor 9–0–39–0; Udal 17.3–0–93–2.

Umpires: D. R. Shepherd and R. A. White.

At Eastbourne, August 4, 6, 7. WARWICKSHIRE beat SUSSEX by six wickets.

At Bristol, August 8, 9, 10. WARWICKSHIRE lost to GLOUCESTERSHIRE by 66 runs.

WARWICKSHIRE v LEICESTERSHIRE

At Birmingham, August 18, 20, 21. Leicestershire won by six wickets. Leicestershire 22 pts, Warwickshire 5 pts. Toss: Leicestershire. Warwickshire never recovered from being put in on a slow, seaming pitch and being bowled out for 154. Agnew made the early inroads, and just when wicket-keeper Piper was leading Warwickshire to a relative recovery from 81 for seven, Parsons returned to finish with four well-earned wickets. The loss of 58 overs on Monday, to wet ground conditions in the morning and poor light in the evening, kept the game in Leicestershire's grasp, even though they lost their last seven wickets for 95. On the final day Agnew and Lewis, the latter ending Warwickshire's innings with three wickets in fourteen balls, ensured that Leicestershire needed only 162 to win at less than 4 an over, which they achieved with sixteen balls to spare. Victory would have come sooner but for Moody's seventh hundred in eight first-class matches; his fourth in successive games. His 117, made out of 161 runs scored in three partnerships, came from 151 deliveries and included a six and eighteen fours. In the first innings, when 7, he had set a Warwickshire record by reaching 1,000 runs for the season in twelve innings, five fewer than R. B. Kanhai in 1970.

Close of play: First day, Leicestershire 147-3 (P. Willey 38*, L. Potter 4*); Second day, Warwickshire 38-1 (A. J. Moles 19*, T. A. Lloyd 0*).

Warwickshire

A. J. Moles c Nixon b Agnew	5	– c Willey b Lewis	30
J. D. Ratcliffe c Lewis b Agnew	15	– lbw b Parsons	14
*T. A. Lloyd c Lewis b Agnew	0	– lbw b Agnew	4
T. M. Moody c Willey b Parsons	26	– c Willey b Agnew	117
P. A. Smith b Millns	22	– c Lewis b Agnew	2
D. A. Reeve c Nixon b Millns	1	– c Boon b Agnew	31
Asif Din lbw b Parsons	0	– c Briers b Agnew	1
†K. J. Piper c Agnew b Parsons	36	– b Lewis	11
G. C. Small b Lewis	16	– not out	10
P. A. Booth c sub b Parsons	14	– c Potter b Lewis	10
T. A. Munton not out	0	– b Lewis	0
L-b 12, w 2, n-b 5	19	B 8, l-b 4, n-b 7	19
1/20 2/20 3/27 4/72 5/73 6/76 7/81 8/122 9/154	154	1/38 2/47 3/60 4/71 5/208 6/217 7/222 8/232 9/249	249

Bonus points – Warwickshire 1, Leicestershire 4.

Bowling: *First Innings*—Agnew 18–5–51–3; Lewis 17–4–48–1; Parsons 10–2–21–4; Millns 10–1–22–2. *Second Innings*—Agnew 21–4–75–5; Lewis 24.5–6–70–4; Parsons 16–3–53–1; Millns 11–2–39–0.

Leicestershire

T. J. Boon c Moles b Reeve	40	– c Lloyd b Munton	5
*N. E. Briers lbw b Reeve	33	– c sub b Reeve	55
J. J. Whitaker b Moody	16	– c Small b Munton	13
P. Willey c Piper b Munton	46	– not out	51
L. Potter c Piper b Small	13	– lbw b Reeve	3
C. C. Lewis c Munton b Smith	38	– not out	25
J. D. R. Benson c Moles b Munton	1		
†P. A. Nixon not out	25		
G. J. Parsons b Reeve	1		
J. P. Agnew c Moody b Reeve	0		
D. J. Millns run out	4		
B 5, l-b 19, w 1	25	L-b 9, w 1	10
1/78 2/101 3/109 4/156 5/170 6/171 7/224 8/229 9/231	242	1/17 2/43 3/107 4/121	(4 wkts) 162

Bonus points – Leicestershire 2, Warwickshire 4.

Bowling: *First Innings*—Small 20–8–34–1; Munton 22–5–74–2; Booth 5–1–7–0; Smith 10–1–25–1; Moody 12–2–36–1; Reeve 20–7–42–4. *Second Innings*—Small 9–2–36–0; Munton 11–2–21–2; Reeve 14–1–51–2; Smith 2–0–11–0; Booth 5.2–0–34–0.

Umpires: J. W. Holder and K. E. Palmer.

At Worcester, August 23, 24, 25, 27. WARWICKSHIRE lost to WORCESTERSHIRE by 323 runs.

At Birmingham, August 29, 30, 31. WARWICKSHIRE lost to SRI LANKANS by eight wickets (See Sri Lankan tour section).

WARWICKSHIRE v SOMERSET

At Birmingham, September 7, 8, 9, 10. Drawn. Warwickshire 6 pts, Somerset 6 pts. Toss: Warwickshire. Two top-order collapses illustrated perfectly why Warwickshire's challenge for Championship honours was not a realistic one. The middle-order batsmen had to work hard to achieve recoveries, rather than use their talents to build on a solid platform. On the first day, Piper underlined his potential by reaching 50 for the first time and going on to a maiden first-class hundred by the close, having hit fifteen boundaries, and half-centuries from Reeve and Booth helped the young wicket-keeper add 112 for both the sixth and eighth wickets. Somerset, batting solidly, established a lead of 37, Smith finishing the innings with a career-best return of five for 48. But with Warwickshire batting for 118 overs in their second innings, the visitors were left with a minimum of 50 overs in which to score 254 to win. When three wickets fell, their thoughts turned to saving the match. Warwickshire's second recovery had been underpinned by Smith, who with 75 completed a good all-round match, and Reeve, who remained unbeaten for four and a half hours.

Close of play: First day, Warwickshire 321-7 (K. J. Piper 100*, P. A. Booth 59*); Second day, Somerset 264-5 (N. D. Burns 42*, G. D. Rose 33*); Third day, Warwickshire 152-4 (P. A. Smith 60*, D. A. Reeve 22*).

Warwickshire

A. J. Moles c Rose b Jones	2	– c Burns b Jones	44
J. D. Ratcliffe lbw b Jones	6	– lbw b Hayhurst	20
Asif Din lbw b Hayhurst	55	– c Tavaré b Hayhurst	0
D. P. Ostler lbw b Hayhurst	11	– c Hayhurst b Lefebvre	1
P. A. Smith c Harden b Hayhurst	4	– lbw b Jones	75
*D. A. Reeve run out	58	– not out	81
†K. J. Piper b Rose	111	– c Townsend b Jones	0
G. C. Small lbw b Lefebvre	7	– b Lefebvre	10
P. A. Booth c Swallow b Rose	60	– c Rose b Jones	15
A. A. Donald b Rose	7	– b Lefebvre	1
T. A. Munton not out	0	– not out	29
B 4, l-b 9, w 4, n-b 2	19	L-b 6, w 4, n-b 4	14
1/10 2/17 3/56 4/60 5/91 6/203 7/215 8/327 9/335	340	1/43 2/45 3/52 (9 wkts dec.) 4/75 5/178 6/178 7/192 8/210 9/215	290

Bonus points – Warwickshire 4, Somerset 3 (Score at 100 overs: 318-7).

Bowling: *First Innings*—Jones 27–2–110–2; Rose 19.2–3–49–3; Hayhurst 21–1–82–3; Lefebvre 21–6–44–1; Swallow 12–4–26–0; Trump 9–3–16–0. *Second Innings*—Jones 33–8–72–4; Rose 12–2–54–0; Hayhurst 26–8–68–2; Lefebvre 26–7–48–3; Swallow 12–4–23–0; Trump 9–2–19–0.

Somerset

Batsman	First innings		Second innings	
S. J. Cook c Moles b Smith	52	–	c Moles b Munton	27
G. T. J. Townsend c Piper b Munton	15	–	c Piper b Small	6
A. N. Hayhurst c Ostler b Munton	57	–	not out	56
*C. J. Tavaré lbw b Donald	10	–	c Reeve b Munton	2
R. J. Harden lbw b Munton	32			
†N. D. Burns b Smith	88	–	(5) b Booth	28
G. D. Rose c Ratcliffe b Munton	41	–	(6) not out	14
R. P. Lefebvre b Smith	27			
I. G. Swallow not out	14			
H. R. J. Trump b Smith	2			
A. N. Jones c Booth b Smith	8			
B 7, l-b 19, w 3, n-b 2	31		B 4, l-b 1	5
1/57 2/84 3/102 4/176 5/185 6/278 7/340 8/351 9/359	377		1/12 2/43 3/57 4/114 (4 wkts)	138

Bonus points – Somerset 3, Warwickshire 2 (Score at 100 overs: 271-5).

Bowling: *First Innings*—Donald 27–5–91–1; Small 24–5–58–0; Munton 33–11–66–4; Smith 16.1–5–48–5; Reeve 12–2–26–0; Booth 23–4–57–0; Asif Din 2–1–5–0. *Second Innings*—Donald 10–2–36–0; Small 6–0–18–1; Munton 9–5–7–2; Booth 8–0–37–1; Asif Din 4–0–18–0; Smith 3.5–0–17–0.

Umpires: J. H. Hampshire and D. O. Oslear.

WARWICKSHIRE v GLAMORGAN

At Birmingham, September 12, 13, 14, 15. Warwickshire won by 170 runs. Warwickshire 24 pts, Glamorgan 5 pts. Toss: Glamorgan. Maximum points kept alive Warwickshire's hopes of finishing in the first three in the Championship. There were splendid batting performances from Smith, Lloyd and Reeve in the first innings, while Piper's 65, and his seventh-wicket partnership with Reeve, steadied the home side's second innings when good bowling by Watkin and Frost had threatened to let Glamorgan into the game. Smith's first-innings 117, in 211 minutes, underlined how much his all-round talents had been missed earlier in the season, owing to a knee injury. He hit a six and eighteen fours and shared a fourth-wicket stand of 187 in 53 overs with his captain. Glamorgan's first innings began well, with Butcher and Morris putting up a hundred for the tenth time in 1990, but then fell away surprisingly. Morris passed Javed Miandad's Glamorgan record of 2,083 runs in a season, while Butcher reached 2,000 runs for the first time. But once Smith dismissed them both, only Cottey resisted the keen home attack. Lloyd's decision not to enforce the follow-on seemed curious at the time, but his bowlers proved him right by dismissing Glamorgan a second time with half a day to spare. Donald, ripping through the lower order, showed that, in form and fully fit, he was still one of the most penetrative fast bowlers in the game, which was why the Warwickshire committee had decided to retain him and release Moody as their overseas player.

Close of play: First day, Warwickshire 351-9 (D. A. Reeve 37*, T. A. Munton 1*); Second day, Warwickshire 13-2 (P. A. Booth 5*, Asif Din 0*); Third day, Glamorgan 67-3 (M. P. Maynard 36*, P. A. Cottey 7*).

Warwickshire

Batsman	First innings		Second innings	
A. J. Moles c Metson b Frost	0	–	c Dale b Croft	8
J. D. Ratcliffe b Anthony	41	–	lbw b Frost	0
Asif Din lbw b Watkin	40	–	(4) b Frost	34
*T. A. Lloyd c Metson b Frost	78	–	(5) lbw b Watkin	39
P. A. Smith c Dale b Watkin	117	–	(6) lbw b Watkin	0
D. A. Reeve not out	68	–	(7) c Croft b Watkin	45
†K. J. Piper c Metson b Anthony	8	–	(8) b Croft	65
G. C. Small c Metson b Watkin	2	–	(9) c Maynard b Croft	4
P. A. Booth c Metson b Watkin	0	–	(3) c Metson b Watkin	10
A. A. Donald b Watkin	7	–	b Anthony	3
T. A. Munton c Metson b Frost	23	–	not out	1
L-b 8, w 3, n-b 10	21		B 1, l-b 5	6
1/1 2/78 3/94 4/281 5/296 6/327 7/342 8/342 9/350	405		1/1 2/13 3/26 4/91 5/91 6/102 7/191 8/196 9/207	215

Bonus points – Warwickshire 4, Glamorgan 2 (Score at 100 overs: 327-6).

Bowling: *First Innings*—Anthony 26–9–70–2; Frost 23.2–4–78–3; Watkin 36–9–100–5; Dale 14–1–64–0; Croft 28–3–85–0. *Second Innings*—Frost 17–2–49–2; Anthony 16–2–38–1; Croft 35.1–13–64–3; Watkin 19–4–48–4; Dale 4–1–10–0.

Glamorgan

*A. R. Butcher c Asif Din b Smith	71	– c Ratcliffe b Munton	3
H. Morris c Lloyd b Smith	73	– lbw b Munton	20
S. P. James lbw b Smith	0	– lbw b Munton	0
M. P. Maynard st Piper b Booth	8	– lbw b Munton	79
P. A. Cottey c Lloyd b Munton	52	– c Moles b Booth	22
A. Dale c Piper b Donald	5	– c Piper b Munton	9
R. D. B. Croft lbw b Donald	0	– c Piper b Donald	12
H. A. G. Anthony st Piper b Booth	0	– c Piper b Booth	13
†C. P. Metson c Piper b Munton	23	– lbw b Donald	4
S. L. Watkin b Munton	0	– not out	15
M. Frost not out	6	– c Reeve b Donald	12
B 6, l-b 6, n-b 1	13	B 6, l-b 3, n-b 1	10
1/141 2/146 3/151 4/161 5/168 6/168 7/169 8/214 9/214	251	1/13 2/13 3/27 4/101 5/124 6/151 7/154 8/158 9/170	199

Bonus points – Glamorgan 3, Warwickshire 4.

Bowling: *First Innings*—Small 10–0–44–0; Munton 13.3–1–44–3; Donald 14–4–51–2; Booth 25–11–44–2; Reeve 3–0–13–0; Smith 13–4–43–3. *Second Innings*—Donald 10.4–2–33–3; Munton 18–3–64–5; Small 9–3–14–0; Smith 9–3–31–0; Booth 18–8–48–2.

Umpires: N. T. Plews and P. B. Wight.

At Manchester, September 18, 19, 20, 21. WARWICKSHIRE drew with LANCASHIRE.

COUNTY CAPS AWARDED IN 1990

Derbyshire	S. J. Base, I. R. Bishop.
Essex	M. A. Garnham.
Glamorgan	I. V. A. Richards.
Gloucestershire	M. W. Alleyne.
Hampshire	D. I. Gower, T. C. Middleton.
Kent	R. P. Davis, M. V. Fleming.
Lancashire	I. D. Austin.
Leicestershire	C. C. Lewis.
Middlesex	K. R. Brown, M. R. Ramprakash, M. A. Roseberry, P. C. R. Tufnell.
Northamptonshire	C. E. L. Ambrose, N. A. Felton, A. Fordham, M. A. Robinson.
Nottinghamshire	J. A. Afford, K. P. Evans.
Somerset	A. N. Hayhurst.
Surrey	D. J. Bicknell, C. K. Bullen, M. A. Feltham, Waqar Younis, D. M. Ward.
Sussex	N. J. Lenham.
Warwickshire	T. M. Moody.
Worcestershire	G. J. Lord.

No cap was awarded by Yorkshire.

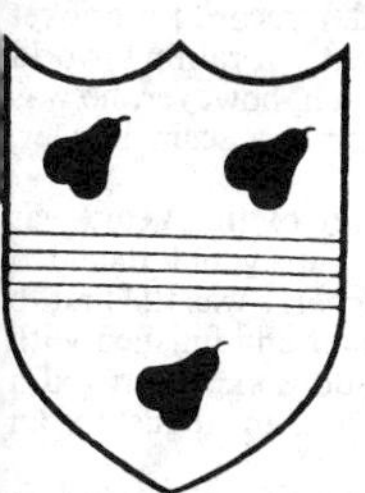

WORCESTERSHIRE

Patron: The Duke of Westminster
President: G. H. Chesterton
Chairman: C. D. Fearnley
Chairman, Cricket Committee: M. G. Jones
Secretary: The Revd Michael Vockins
County Ground, New Road, Worcester
WR2 4QQ (Telephone: 0905-748474)
Captain: P. A. Neale
Coach: B. L. D'Oliveira

Few counties can have suffered quite as much from injuries in one season as Worcestershire did in 1990: not one of their first-team squad avoided some period of inactivity. The catalogue of casualties contained five players needing surgery, while Curtis, Hick, Illingworth and Rhodes were among five others out at some stage with broken fingers or thumbs. By mid-July, when the injury crisis was at its worst, the Britannic Assurance champions of 1988 and 1989 were second from bottom after ten matches. Yet by winning five of their last twelve Championship fixtures they managed to finish with a share of the prizemoney, only three points behind third-placed Hampshire. Most impressive was the fact that in all but one of their nineteen Championship victories in 1989 and 1990, Worcestershire bowled out their opponents in both innings.

There was also the disappointment of their failure, at the third attempt, to win a Benson and Hedges Cup final. Defeat by Lancashire sent them away from Lord's for the sixth time without a trophy and meant that Worcestershire and Glamorgan remained the only counties not to have won a final there. In the other competitions, Northamptonshire beat them by 4 runs in a thrilling finish to their quarter-final of the NatWest Bank Trophy, while a record of only seven wins in the Refuge Assurance League left them in tenth place, after being Sunday champions in 1987 and 1988 and runners-up in 1989.

Worcestershire, however, wasted little time in setting out their stall for 1991 and, barring a similar series of setbacks through injuries, there seemed little to suggest they would not be a side to reckon with. No sooner had Warwickshire announced that they were retaining Allan Donald as their overseas player, in preference to Tom Moody, than Worcestershire had signed up the record-breaking Australian as their overseas player for 1991, when Graeme Hick became eligible for England.

As for Hick, second to Gooch in the national averages with 2,347 runs at 90.26, he hit eight hundreds to increase his career count to 54, and his unbeaten century in the second innings at Abergavenny made him the youngest player, at 24 years and 62 days, to compile 50 first-class hundreds. The previous record had been held by Sir Donald Bradman, who was 26 years and eight days old when he reached the landmark. When Hick had scored 147 of his unbeaten 252 in the first innings of that game, he became the youngest player to complete 10,000 first-class runs for the county, in his 179th innings, and he was the first Worcestershire player to record a hundred and double-hundred in the same match. By its end he had scored 592 runs without being dismissed, a record for cricket in England, and he needed another 118 to beat K. C. Ibrahim's world record of 709 for Bombay in 1947-48. In his next match, however, he was dismissed for 53 at Derby by the former Worcestershire seam bowler, Allan Warner.

Tim Curtis, the Worcestershire supporters' Player of the Year, was second to Hick with a career-best aggregate of 1,731 runs which included 197 not out against Warwickshire, his highest innings. He was the first to reach 1,000 runs in one-day cricket during the summer and finished with a county-best 784 runs in the Sunday League. In addition, he proved a most capable deputy when Phil Neale went into hospital in August for an operation on his left thigh.

The Dick Lygon award for the best team man went to Curtis's opening partner, Gordon Lord. The left-hander, emerging from a three-month spell in the second team, during which his future with the county was in doubt, hit a century against Lancashire and followed it with 190 against Hampshire in the next game. He sealed a new contract, and won his county cap, by scoring 127 and 57 in the final match of the season to complete 1,000 runs for the first time. Damian D'Oliveira also enjoyed his most successful season, finishing with 1,263 runs, including a career-best 155 against Lancashire, and 33 catches in the Championship.

Ian Botham's appearances were restricted first by an early-season knee operation and towards the end by a hamstring strain. His 138 not out against Gloucestershire was a personal best in the Benson and Hedges Cup, while his 113 against Surrey was his first Championship hundred since July 1987. Graham Dilley, who in July underwent the fourth operation in two years on his right knee, made only ten Championship appearances, and did not play in the Sunday League, and Neal Radford was out of action for six weeks after an operation on a torn stomach muscle. Radford returned for the Benson and Hedges final, whereas Martin Weston had delayed surgery on his right knee until after Lord's, having hit an unbeaten 99 in the semi-final victory over holders Nottinghamshire to win his first Gold Award.

Richard Illingworth, Steve Rhodes and Phil Newport were named for the winter's England A team. Illingworth had his best wicket-taking season to date with 75 first-class wickets, as well as hitting his third first-class century, while Rhodes's 61 catches and eight stumpings put him on top of the wicket-keepers' list, and he twice went close to achieving an elusive maiden first-class hundred. Newport had a similar experience, following a career-best 98 against the New Zealanders with 96 against Essex, and he showed a welcome recovery after his misfortunes in 1989 to finish with 63 wickets.

Stuart Lampitt and Steve McEwan, meanwhile, further enhanced their reputations. Only Illingworth and Newport bowled more overs than Lampitt, and McEwan, against Leicestershire, became the first Worcestershire bowler since H. L. Alleyne in 1981 to take a hat-trick in the Championship. David Leatherdale's appearances were reserved in the main for the one-day competitions, while the injury position provided opportunities for all-rounder Chris Tolley, left-arm spinner Richard Stemp, reserve wicket-keeper Stuart Bevins and off-spinner Steve Herzberg to experience first-team cricket. – Chris Moore.

WORCESTERSHIRE 1990

[*Bill Smith*

Back row: R. P. Gofton, R. D. Stemp, G. J. Lord, G. R. Haynes, D. A. Leatherdale. *Middle row:* S. R. Bevins, S. M. McEwan, I. T. Botham, G. R. Dilley, B. L. D'Oliveira (*coach*), S. R. Lampitt, P. Bent, W. P. C. Weston, M. S. Scott. *Front row:* P. J. Newport, S. J. Rhodes, N. V. Radford, T. S. Curtis, P. A. Neale (*captain*), D. B. D'Oliveira, G. A. Hick, R. K. Illingworth, M. J. Weston.

WORCESTERSHIRE RESULTS

All first-class matches – Played 24: Won 7, Lost 2, Drawn 15.

County Championship matches – Played 22: Won 7, Lost 1, Drawn 14.

Bonus points – Batting 70, Bowling 58.

Competition placings – Britannic Assurance County Championship, 4th; NatWest Bank Trophy, q-f; Benson and Hedges Cup, finalists; Refuge Assurance League, 10th equal.

BRITANNIC ASSURANCE CHAMPIONSHIP AVERAGES

BATTING

	Birthplace	*M*	*I*	*NO*	*R*	*HI*	*Avge*
‡G. A. Hick	*Salisbury, Rhodesia*	19	33	8	2,273	252*	90.92
‡T. S. Curtis	*Chislehurst*	21	38	8	1,650	197*	55.00
‡G. J. Lord	*Birmingham*	12	23	2	983	190	46.80
‡P. A. Neale	*Scunthorpe*	19	29	9	934	122	46.70
‡S. J. Rhodes	*Bradford*	21	24	10	653	96	46.64
‡G. R. Dilley	*Dartford*	10	8	4	185	45*	46.25
‡D. B. D'Oliveira	*Cape Town, SA*	21	32	2	1,179	155	39.30
‡I. T. Botham	*Heswall*	12	17	1	576	113	36.00
‡R. K. Illingworth	*Bradford*	20	19	6	452	117	34.76
‡P. J. Newport	*High Wycombe*	19	15	5	318	96	31.80
P. Bent	*Worcester*	6	10	0	315	79	31.50
D. A. Leatherdale	*Bradford*	4	6	0	154	70	25.66
‡S. M. McEwan	*Worcester*	13	10	3	163	54	23.28
‡N. V. Radford	*Luanshya, N. Rhodesia*	10	6	1	104	43*	20.80
‡S. R. Lampitt	*Wolverhampton*	21	22	5	286	45*	16.82
C. M. Tolley	*Kidderminster*	6	6	1	79	29	15.80
‡M. J. Weston	*Worcester*	5	8	1	80	38*	11.42

Also batted: S. R. Bevins (*Solihull*) (1 match) 6*; R. D. Stemp (*Erdington*) (2 matches) 3*, 0*.

* *Signifies not out.* ‡ *Denotes county cap.*

The following played a total of 21 three-figure innings for Worcestershire in County Championship matches – G. A. Hick 8, T. S. Curtis 4, G. J. Lord 3, D. B. D'Oliveira 2, P. A. Neale 2, I. T. Botham 1, R. K. Illingworth 1.

BOWLING

	O	*M*	*R*	*W*	*BB*	*5W/i*	*Avge*
R. K. Illingworth	804.5	261	1,946	71	5-59	1	27.40
S. M. McEwan	310	61	970	32	3-31	0	30.31
S. R. Lampitt	539.3	96	1,794	57	5-34	2	31.47
P. J. Newport	563.2	104	1,806	57	6-73	3	31.68
I. T. Botham	174.4	34	546	17	4-65	0	32.11
G. A. Hick	208.5	41	645	20	5-37	1	32.25
G. R. Dilley	224.2	30	818	24	5-62	2	34.08
N. V. Radford	245	38	999	14	4-55	0	71.35

Also bowled: T. S. Curtis 5.3–1–43–0; D. B. D'Oliveira 11.3–1–80–2; R. D. Stemp 45–14–123–1; C. M. Tolley 88–14–326–5; M. J. Weston 7–1–23–0.

Wicket-keepers: S. J. Rhodes 59 ct, 8 st; S. R. Bevins 3 ct.

Leading Fielders: D. B. D'Oliveira 33, G. A. Hick 24.

At Lord's, April 17, 18, 19, 20. WORCESTERSHIRE drew with MCC.

At Manchester, April 26, 27, 28, 30. WORCESTERSHIRE drew with LANCASHIRE.

WORCESTERSHIRE v NOTTINGHAMSHIRE

At Worcester, May 3, 4, 5, 7. Worcestershire won by an innings and 6 runs. Worcestershire 23 pts, Nottinghamshire 2 pts. Toss: Worcestershire. Even without the injured Botham, Radford and Rhodes, Worcestershire secured their first Championship win of the season with more than two sessions to spare. Following on 347 in arrears, Nottinghamshire were indebted to a fifth-wicket stand of 187 between Randall and Johnson which took play into the fourth day. But on the last morning the visitors lost their remaining wickets in 75 minutes, with Dilley's swing bringing him four for 16 in 8.2 overs. Hick had reached another milestone on the first day, in passing 13,000 runs in his 150th first-class game before departing to a low delivery from Stephenson when only 3 short of his 48th century. Neale, with twenty boundaries in his 122, then added 220 for the sixth wicket with Illingworth, who batted four hours for his 117. By the close on the second day, Nottinghamshire were 110 for nine, with Newport having taken four for 32 in sixteen overs, his first Championship wickets since suffering an Achilles' tendon injury in the First Test of the Ashes series the previous year.

Close of play: First day, Worcestershire 292-5 (P. A. Neale 72*, R. K. Illingworth 35*); Second day, Nottinghamshire 110-9 (E. E. Hemmings 7*, R. A. Pick 20*); Third day, Nottinghamshire 302-4 (P. Johnson 77*, D. W. Randall 86*).

Worcestershire

T. S. Curtis c French b Cooper	46	G. R. Dilley b Hemmings	8
G. J. Lord b Pick	12	†S. R. Bevins not out	6
G. A. Hick b Stephenson	97	S. M. McEwan lbw b Pick	0
D. B. D'Oliveira c Evans b Pick	9		
*P. A. Neale b Hemmings	122	B 10, l-b 9, w 2, n-b 7	28
S. R. Lampitt st French b Hemmings	1		
R. K. Illingworth b Stephenson	117	1/24 2/133 3/154 4/193 5/206	481
P. J. Newport c Newell b Pick	35	6/426 7/432 8/451 9/481	

Bonus points – Worcestershire 3, Nottinghamshire 2 (Score at 100 overs: 265-5).

Bowling: Stephenson 35–4–112–2; Cooper 37–11–113–1; Pick 36.5–5–119–4; Hemmings 61–21–117–3; Newell 1–0–1–0.

Nottinghamshire

B. C. Broad c Newport b Dilley	2	– c Hick b Dilley	16
M. Newell c Curtis b Lampitt	6	– c Curtis b Lampitt	30
R. J. Evans c Lampitt b Newport	11	– (4) lbw b McEwan	4
*R. T. Robinson c Bevins b Newport	15	– (3) c Lampitt b McEwan	48
P. Johnson c Dilley b Newport	3	– lbw b McEwan	83
D. W. Randall b Lampitt	6	– c Bevins b Dilley	87
†B. N. French b Newport	10	– (8) c Bevins b Dilley	0
F. D. Stephenson lbw b McEwan	13	– (7) not out	12
E. E. Hemmings lbw b Lampitt	24	– retired hurt	4
K. E. Cooper c and b McEwan	1	– b Dilley	1
R. A. Pick not out	27	– b Dilley	0
B 8, l-b 3, w 4, n-b 1	16	B 15, l-b 26, w 11, n-b 4	56
1/3 2/24 3/24 4/27 5/36	134	1/22 2/99 3/121 4/122 5/309	341
6/49 7/77 8/77 9/79		6/309 7/309 8/341 9/341	

Bonus points – Worcestershire 4.

In the second innings E. E. Hemmings retired hurt at 327.

Bowling: *First Innings*—Dilley 8–2–13–1; McEwan 13–2–26–2; Newport 18–4–44–4; Illingworth 1–1–0–0; Lampitt 11.2–2–40–3. *Second Innings*—Dilley 23.2–4–62–5; McEwan 23–5–57–3; Newport 16–3–42–0; Illingworth 30–15–47–0; Lampitt 19–6–60–1; Hick 8–1–32–0.

Umpires: B. Leadbeater and K. J. Lyons.

At Worcester, May 12, 13, 14. WORCESTERSHIRE lost to NEW ZEALANDERS by six wickets (See New Zealand tour section).

WORCESTERSHIRE v ESSEX

At Worcester, May 19, 21, 22. Essex won by ten wickets. Essex 24 pts, Worcestershire 4 pts. Toss: Essex. Worcestershire, outplayed in all departments, suffered their first defeat in eleven Championship games, and Neale, their captain, admitted afterwards that he doubted his team would ever bowl as badly as on the first day. Gooch needed just 126 balls for his third Championship century in four innings and hit 22 boundaries in his 121. Waugh's unbeaten 166, including 27 fours, was his highest score to date for Essex, who declared when they had amassed 447 for four in 100 overs. Despite 89 runs from night-watchman Illingworth, Worcestershire were forced to follow on, only to be reduced to 32 for five in the first eleven overs from Foster and Pringle. Six dropped catches and a ninth-wicket partnership of 120 between Newport and Dilley saved them from an innings defeat in two days, but Essex were left needing only 45 for victory. Newport fell just short of his maiden first-class century for the second time in ten days.

Close of play: First day, Worcestershire 26-1 (T. S. Curtis 9*, R. K. Illingworth 15*); Second day, Worcestershire 165-8 (P. J. Newport 71*, G. R. Dilley 18*).

Essex

*G. A. Gooch c Rhodes b Newport	121	– not out	42
J. P. Stephenson c Curtis b Radford	4	– not out	6
P. J. Prichard run out	45		
M. E. Waugh not out	166		
B. R. Hardie c D'Oliveira b Botham	59		
N. Shahid not out	35		
L-b 7, n-b 10	17		
1/37 2/135 3/226 4/392 (4 wkts dec.)	447	(no wkt)	48

D. R. Pringle, †M. A. Garnham, N. A. Foster, T. D. Topley and J. H. Childs did not bat.

Bonus points – Essex 4, Worcestershire 1.

Bowling: *First Innings*—Dilley 10–1–76–0; Radford 16–1–95–1; Newport 19–2–88–1; Lampitt 15–5–55–0; Botham 19–2–58–1; Illingworth 14–3–45–0; Weston 7–1–23–0. *Second Innings*—Dilley 5–1–33–0; Newport 5–1–7–0; Curtis 0.3–0–8–0.

Worcestershire

T. S. Curtis c Shahid b Pringle	48	– lbw b Foster	2
M. J. Weston c Gooch b Foster	0	– c Gooch b Foster	14
R. K. Illingworth b Pringle	89	– (7) c Gooch b Topley	9
*P. A. Neale b Pringle	9	– (3) c Hardie b Pringle	4
I. T. Botham c Foster b Topley	53	– (4) lbw b Pringle	5
D. B. D'Oliveira c Hardie b Topley	32	– (5) c Stephenson b Pringle	25
S. R. Lampitt lbw b Topley	0	– (6) c Stephenson b Foster	1
†S. J. Rhodes b Foster	1	– (11) not out	5
P. J. Newport c Waugh b Topley	18	– (8) c and b Pringle	96
N. V. Radford b Foster	10	– (9) lbw b Pringle	10
G. R. Dilley not out	0	– (10) c Garnham b Foster	40
L-b 6, w 2, n-b 5	13	L-b 4, n-b 3	7
1/5 2/104 3/152 4/163 5/223 6/223 7/226 8/254 9/267	273	1/12 2/19 3/21 4/25 5/32 6/58 7/66 8/82 9/202	218

Bonus points – Worcestershire 3, Essex 4.

Bowling: *First Innings*—Foster 22.1–5–70–3; Pringle 21–2–67–3; Topley 19–5–67–4; Waugh 13–4–63–0. *Second Innings*—Foster 23–5–64–4; Pringle 24.1–6–66–5; Topley 8–1–44–1; Childs 8–6–9–0; Waugh 3–0–21–0; Stephenson 3–1–10–0.

Umpires: B. Dudleston and P. B. Wight.

At Birmingham, May 26, 28, 29. WORCESTERSHIRE drew with WARWICKSHIRE.

WORCESTERSHIRE v YORKSHIRE

At Worcester, June 2, 4, 5. Drawn. Worcestershire 7 pts, Yorkshire 6 pts. Toss: Yorkshire. Worcestershire were left with mixed feelings as the final day's play was lost to the weather. Yorkshire had begun badly, sliding from 44 without loss to 45 for four, but injuries deprived Worcestershire of the bowling of Botham and Newport in the second innings; they were already without Dilley, Radford and Illingworth. Botham made light of a hamstring strain on the second morning, when he reached 86, his highest score in the County Championship for three years, and shared a fifth-wicket stand of 125 in 32 overs with night-watchman McEwan, who contributed a career-best 54. Yorkshire wiped out their deficit of 66 in the evening session, notable mostly for newcomer Stemp's first first-class wicket.

Close of play: First day, Worcestershire 108-4 (I. T. Botham 11*, S. M. McEwan 0*); Second day, Yorkshire 106-2 (A. A. Metcalfe 56*, S. A. Kellett 4*).

Yorkshire

*M. D. Moxon c Botham b Lampitt	23	– c D'Oliveira b McEwan	28
A. A. Metcalfe c Rhodes b Lampitt	20	– not out	56
R. J. Blakey lbw b Botham	0	– c McEwan b Stemp	8
S. A. Kellett c Rhodes b Lampitt	0	– not out	4
P. E. Robinson c Rhodes b Botham	28		
†D. L. Bairstow c D'Oliveira b Lampitt	61		
P. Carrick c D'Oliveira b Botham	2		
C. S. Pickles c D'Oliveira b Newport	30		
P. J. Hartley b Lampitt	36		
P. W. Jarvis c Stemp b Botham	17		
S. D. Fletcher not out	0		
L-b 1, n-b 4	5	B 2, l-b 3, w 3, n-b 2	10
1/44 2/45 3/45 4/45 5/85 6/87 7/127 8/197 9/216	222	1/78 2/95	(2 wkts) 106

Bonus points – Yorkshire 2, Worcestershire 4.

Bowling: *First Innings*—Newport 17–2–55–1; McEwan 13–3–47–0; Botham 16.5–3–65–4; Lampitt 20–5–54–5. *Second Innings*—McEwan 15–4–35–1; Lampitt 17–6–34–0; Stemp 19–6–32–1.

Worcestershire

T. S. Curtis lbw b Fletcher	13	†S. J. Rhodes c Bairstow b Hartley	13
P. Bent c Blakey b Jarvis	39	S. R. Lampitt b Hartley	10
*P. A. Neale c Jarvis b Fletcher	1	R. D. Stemp not out	3
D. B. D'Oliveira c Hartley b Pickles	41		
I. T. Botham lbw b Carrick	86	L-b 6, n-b 2	8
S. M. McEwan c Bairstow b Jarvis	54		
M. J. Weston lbw b Jarvis	3	1/19 2/27 3/95 4/108 5/233	288
P. J. Newport c Bairstow b Carrick	17	6/245 7/246 8/266 9/276	

Bonus points – Worcestershire 3, Yorkshire 4 (Score at 100 overs: 288-9).

Bowling: Jarvis 25–5–59–3; Hartley 20.1–4–92–2; Fletcher 11–2–31–2; Carrick 36–12–70–2; Pickles 8–3–30–1.

Umpires: J. H. Harris and K. J. Lyons.

At The Oval, June 16, 18, 19. WORCESTERSHIRE drew with SURREY.

WORCESTERSHIRE v SUSSEX

At Worcester, June 20, 21, 22. Drawn. Worcestershire 1 pt, Sussex 3 pts. Toss: Sussex. Rain restricted play on the first two days to 40 overs and both sides forfeited an innings in a bid to fashion a finish. Sussex began the final day at 85 without loss, and their declaration left Worcestershire a target of 291 from a minimum of 53 overs after Hall, with 72, and Lenham had put on 126 for the first wicket. Worcestershire were on course as Botham and D'Oliveira added 122 in eighteen overs for the fourth wicket. But fortunes changed dramatically after Botham, having completed his fifth half-century in eight Championship innings, holed out next ball from leg-spinner Salisbury, who went on to take four wickets in thirteen deliveries and finished with career-best figures of five for 32. It was left to Rhodes and Illingworth to play out the last three overs to deny Sussex the spoils.

Close of play: First day, Sussex 55-0 (N. J. Lenham 27*, J. W. Hall 23*); Second day, Sussex 85-0 (N. J. Lenham 42*, J. W. Hall 36*).

Sussex

N. J. Lenham b Illingworth	66
J. W. Hall lbw b Botham	72
*P. W. G. Parker c Hick b Botham	14
A. P. Wells not out	59
M. P. Speight not out	60
L-b 8, w 2, n-b 9	19
1/126 2/155 3/183 (3 wkts dec.)	290

C. M. Wells, A. I. C. Dodemaide, A. C. S. Pigott, †P. Moores, R. A. Bunting and I. D. K. Salisbury did not bat.

Bonus points – Sussex 3, Worcestershire 1.

Bowling: Newport 22–3–64–0; McEwan 6–2–12–0; Lampitt 14–2–55–0; Botham 15–4–32–2; Illingworth 23–6–82–1; Hick 6–0–37–0.

Sussex forfeited their second innings.

Worcestershire

Worcestershire forfeited their first innings.

T. S. Curtis c Parker b Bunting	27
P. Bent b Bunting	5
G. A. Hick c Moores b Pigott	28
D. B. D'Oliveira st Moores b Salisbury	79
I. T. Botham c A. P. Wells b Salisbury	50
*P. A. Neale c Pigott b Salisbury	8
P. J. Newport st Moores b Salisbury	2
†S. J. Rhodes not out	9
S. R. Lampitt c and b Salisbury	3
R. K. Illingworth not out	0
L-b 6, w 1, n-b 1	8
1/21 2/43 3/71 4/193 5/197 6/207 7/210 8/217 (8 wkts)	219

S. M. McEwan did not bat.

Bowling: Dodemaide 14.5–6–32–0; Pigott 15–2–68–1; Bunting 10–2–40–2; C. M. Wells 5–0–41–0; Salisbury 10–2–32–5.

Umpires: D. J. Constant and J. W. Holder.

At Lord's, June 30, July 2, 3. WORCESTERSHIRE drew with MIDDLESEX.

WORCESTERSHIRE v GLOUCESTERSHIRE

At Worcester, July 7, 9, 10. Worcestershire won by 148 runs. Worcestershire 22 pts, Gloucestershire 5 pts. Toss: Worcestershire. Hick, dismissed without scoring on the opening morning, had the final say with bat and ball to seal what was only Worcestershire's second win in their nine Championship matches to date. His 79 off 45 balls, as the home batsmen plundered 165 runs from the final morning session, left Gloucestershire a target of 276 from a minimum of 75 overs on a worn wicket conducive to spin. After Dilley, playing his first match for five weeks, had sent back the top three Gloucestershire batsmen, Hick followed up his best bowling figures of five for 37 in the first innings with four for 43, returning nine for 80 in the match. The previous day only Hodgson, with 77, had offered prolonged resistance against Hick and Illingworth, and Gloucestershire trailed by 99; in the visitors' second innings their last five wickets went for 7 runs.

Close of play: First day, Worcestershire 265-7 (R. K. Illingworth 41*, C. M. Tolley 26*); Second day, Worcestershire 11-0 (T. S. Curtis 4*, P. Bent 6*).

Worcestershire

T. S. Curtis lbw b Curran	4	– b Graveney	21
P. Bent c Athey b Barnes	44	– b Curran	22
G. A. Hick c Williams b Bell	0	– b Bainbridge	79
D. B. D'Oliveira c Williams b Bell	69	– b Bainbridge	26
I. T. Botham c Wright b Barnes	2	– c Barnes b Bainbridge	16
*P. A. Neale c Wright b Curran	14	– not out	3
†S. J. Rhodes b Graveney	55		
R. K. Illingworth run out	50		
C. M. Tolley b Curran	29		
S. R. Lampitt not out	20		
G. R. Dilley not out	17		
B 1, l-b 11, w 1, n-b 2	15	L-b 6, n-b 3	9
1/16 2/17 3/60 4/62 5/94 6/168 7/214 8/274 9/279 (9 wkts dec.)	319	1/46 2/46 3/126 4/173 5/176 (5 wkts dec.)	176

Bonus points – Worcestershire 2, Gloucestershire 3 (Score at 100 overs: 225-7).

Bowling: *First Innings*—Curran 33–6–76–3; Barnes 22–4–74–2; Bell 17–4–38–2; Graveney 46–24–64–1; Bainbridge 13–1–42–0; Lloyds 2–0–13–0. *Second Innings*—Curran 12–2–37–1; Barnes 1–0–6–0; Graveney 11–1–67–1; Lloyds 3–0–37–0; Bainbridge 3–0–23–3.

Gloucestershire

G. D. Hodgson lbw b Hick	77	– c D'Oliveira b Dilley	22
*A. J. Wright lbw b Botham	13	– (3) lbw b Dilley	5
I. P. Butcher b Dilley	27	– (2) c D'Oliveira b Dilley	0
C. W. J. Athey c D'Oliveira b Hick	15	– c Botham b Illingworth	32
P. Bainbridge not out	31	– c Botham b Illingworth	7
K. M. Curran b Illingworth	7	– b Hick	19
J. W. Lloyds c Rhodes b Hick	28	– st Rhodes b Hick	40
D. A. Graveney c and b Illingworth	1	– b Hick	0
†R. C. J. Williams c Curtis b Illingworth	0	– st Rhodes b Hick	1
S. N. Barnes b Hick	0	– c D'Oliveira b Illingworth	0
R. M. Bell c Curtis b Hick	0	– not out	0
B 10, l-b 7, w 3, n-b 1	21	B 1	1
1/44 2/96 3/133 4/140 5/155 6/208 7/215 8/215 9/218	220	1/15 2/26 3/27 4/49 5/80 6/120 7/121 8/126 9/127	127

Bonus points – Gloucestershire 2, Worcestershire 4.

Bowling: *First Innings*—Dilley 9–1–26–1; Lampitt 11–0–38–0; Tolley 3–1–7–0; Botham 10–3–20–1; Illingworth 32–10–75–3; Hick 16.3–5–37–5. *Second Innings*—Dilley 7–2–16–3; Tolley 2–0–20–0; Illingworth 18–4–47–3; Hick 14.3–1–43–4.

Umpires: P. J. Eele and P. B. Wight.

WORCESTERSHIRE v SOMERSET

At Worcester, July 18, 19, 20. Drawn. Worcestershire 4 pts, Somerset 5 pts. Toss: Somerset. There was never any possibility of either side forcing victory on the most benign of pitches and in searing heat. The first two days produced 764 runs while only six wickets fell. Memories of the way Worcestershire, through Hick, had scored 300 in 57 overs to win the corresponding game the year before ensured that Tavaré would be less generous in his declaration. In the event, Worcestershire never seriously contemplated the challenge of 340 in 60 overs, calling a halt with twelve of the final twenty remaining. Roebuck dominated the first day in reaching the second double-hundred of his career, a chanceless innings bearing witness to his concentration. He completed his hundred in 187 balls and scored 26 boundaries in all, sharing a second-wicket stand of 258 in 79 overs with Hayhurst. Somerset's 66-year-old record of 290 for the second wicket was under threat before Hayhurst was needlessly run out, having reached his century in 240 balls, with one six and thirteen fours. Inevitably, the second day belonged to Hick, whose unbeaten 171, including 29 fours and one six, was his fifth Championship century against Somerset in six seasons. In seventeen first-class innings against them he had scored a total of 1,389, at an average of 126.27. Hick added 139 in 46 overs with D'Oliveira and 148 in 32 overs with Neale before Worcestershire declared 98 runs behind. At the close the following day he was unbeaten again with 69.

Close of play: First day, Somerset 398-3 (P. M. Roebuck 201*, R. J. Harden 0*); Second day, Somerset 66-0 (S. J. Cook 37*, P. M. Roebuck 28*).

Somerset

S. J. Cook c and b Tolley	6	– c Neale b Tolley	39
P. M. Roebuck not out	201	– lbw b Lampitt	68
A. N. Hayhurst run out	119	– (5) c Rhodes b Tolley	16
*C. J. Tavaré c and b Newport	54	– b Lampitt	10
R. J. Harden not out	0	– (3) c Rhodes b Lampitt	29
†N. D. Burns (did not bat)		– not out	27
G. D. Rose (did not bat)		– not out	44
B 5, l-b 7, w 1, n-b 5	18	B 2, l-b 4, n-b 2	8
1/9 2/267 3/398 (3 wkts dec.)	398	1/85 2/137 3/144 4/152 5/189 (5 wkts dec.)	241

R. P. Lefebvre, I. G. Swallow, N. A. Mallender and A. N. Jones did not bat.

Bonus points – Somerset 4 (Score at 100 overs: 324-2).

Bowling: *First Innings*—Newport 19–1–70–1; Tolley 24–4–84–1; Radford 18–0–78–0; Lampitt 16–2–70–0; Illingworth 30–8–72–0; Hick 3–0–12–0. *Second Innings*—Newport 11–2–46–0; Tolley 18–2–66–2; Lampitt 13.2–1–46–3; Radford 12–0–49–0; Illingworth 7–1–28–0.

Worcestershire

T. S. Curtis lbw b Mallender	6	– lbw b Mallender	24
P. Bent c Rose b Jones	1	– c and b Lefebvre	36
G. A. Hick not out	171	– not out	69
D. B. D'Oliveira c sub b Swallow	55	– c and b Swallow	24
*P. A. Neale not out	49	– not out	22
B 7, l-b 10, w 1	18	L-b 4, n-b 2	6
1/3 2/13 3/152 (3 wkts dec.)	300	1/40 2/94 3/127 (3 wkts)	181

C. M. Tolley, †S. J. Rhodes, R. K. Illingworth, P. J. Newport, S. R. Lampitt and N. V. Radford did not bat.

Bonus points – Worcestershire 4, Somerset 1.

Bowling: *First Innings*—Jones 8–3–17–1; Mallender 13–5–35–1; Rose 13–1–49–0; Lefebvre 17–4–49–0; Swallow 23–5–84–1; Roebuck 5–1–20–0; Hayhurst 5.4–0–29–0. *Second Innings*—Jones 5–0–25–0; Mallender 5–1–13–1; Rose 10–1–29–0; Lefebvre 11–2–33–1; Swallow 15–0–69–1; Roebuck 2–1–8–0.

Umpires: A. A. Jones and D. S. Thompsett.

At Abergavenny, July 21, 23, 24. WORCESTERSHIRE drew with GLAMORGAN.

At Derby, July 25, 26, 27. WORCESTERSHIRE drew with DERBYSHIRE.

At Canterbury, July 28, 30, 31. WORCESTERSHIRE drew with KENT.

At Leicester, August 4, 6, 7. WORCESTERSHIRE beat LEICESTERSHIRE by 1 run.

WORCESTERSHIRE v LANCASHIRE

At Kidderminster, August 8, 9, 10. Worcestershire won by ten wickets. Worcestershire 24 pts, Lancashire 2 pts. Toss: Worcestershire. Worcestershire completed their fourth Championship win of the season, and their second of the week under the captaincy of Curtis, deputising for the injured Neale. Curtis and Lord, scoring his first Championship century for two seasons, provided the platform for their formidable first-innings total of 451 for six declared. Hick passed 50 for the tenth time in eleven Championship innings, adding 90 in 24 overs with D'Oliveira, and there was little respite for the Lancashire attack as Leatherdale hit his highest score of 70. Newport pressed home Worcestershire's advantage with five wickets for 59 as the visitors were dismissed for 160 in 47.1 overs, their last three wickets falling to Illingworth in 25 deliveries. Following on 291 behind, they fared little better, slumping to 162 for six at the end of the second day. Fairbrother, batting down the order after being hit on the jaw by McEwan in the first innings, added 123 in 31 overs with Austin in a defiant eighth-wicket stand. But it still left Worcestershire needing just 7 runs for victory, which they achieved with almost two sessions to spare.

Close of play: First day, Worcestershire 395-4 (D. A. Leatherdale 68*, C. M. Tolley 15*); Second day, Lancashire 162-6 (T. E. Jesty 50*, I. D. Austin 1*).

Worcestershire

*T. S. Curtis lbw b Austin	56	– not out	4
G. J. Lord c Martin b Hughes	101	– not out	0
G. A. Hick c Lloyd b Hughes	67		
D. B. D'Oliveira run out	59		
D. A. Leatherdale c Fairbrother b Hughes	70		
C. M. Tolley not out	28		
†S. J. Rhodes b Austin	22		
R. K. Illingworth not out	19		
B 10, l-b 9, n-b 10	29	W 4	4
1/152 2/189 3/279 4/336 5/398 6/424	(6 wkts dec.) 451		(no wkt) 8

P. J. Newport, S. R. Lampitt and S. M. McEwan did not bat.

Bonus points – Worcestershire 4, Lancashire 1 (Score at 100 overs: 335-3).

Bowling: *First Innings*—Wasim Akram 20–4–68–0; Martin 17–7–39–0; Watkinson 20–3–85–0; Austin 27–5–105–2; Hughes 42–12–135–3. *Second Innings*—Lloyd 0.1–0–8–0.

Lancashire

G. D. Mendis b Newport	15	– c D'Oliveira b Lampitt	36
G. Fowler c Rhodes b Newport	9	– lbw b Lampitt	18
G. D. Lloyd b McEwan	2	– b Tolley	14
N. H. Fairbrother c Rhodes b Newport	22	– (9) not out	64
T. E. Jesty b Lampitt	35	– (4) b Illingworth	54
M. Watkinson lbw b Newport	4	– (5) c Rhodes b Lampitt	7
Wasim Akram c Hick b Newport	14	– (6) c D'Oliveira b McEwan	23
†W. K. Hegg c Lord b Illingworth	47	– (7) lbw b McEwan	5
I. D. Austin c D'Oliveira b Illingworth	0	– (8) c Lampitt b Hick	58
*D. P. Hughes lbw b Illingworth	2	– c Leatherdale b Hick	1
P. J. Martin not out	1	– b Illingworth	0
L-b 5, w 2, n-b 2	9	B 12, l-b 4, n-b 1	17
1/19 2/23 3/35 4/51 5/55 6/89 7/144 8/149 9/151	160	1/41 2/68 3/72 4/99 5/133 6/157 7/167 8/290 9/296	297

Bonus points – Lancashire 1, Worcestershire 4.

Bowling: *First Innings*—Newport 18–1–59–5; McEwan 10–1–31–1; Tolley 9–1–41–0; Lampitt 6–1–16–1; Illingworth 4.1–0–8–3. *Second Innings*—Newport 10–0–48–0; McEwan 14–3–25–2; Lampitt 16–4–58–3; Tolley 10–2–39–1; Illingworth 25.3–3–92–2; Hick 6–2–19–2.

Umpires: B. Dudleston and K. E. Palmer.

WORCESTERSHIRE v HAMPSHIRE

At Worcester, August 11, 13, 14. Drawn. Worcestershire 5 pts, Hampshire 5 pts. Toss: Worcestershire. Worcestershire failed by two wickets to force a third successive Championship victory, which would have kept alive their aspirations of retaining the title. Set a target of 266 in 61 overs, Hampshire were rescued by an unbeaten 43 from Joseph, after they had started the final twenty overs precariously placed at 126 for five. Worcestershire had run up 413 for six against the visitors' second-string attack on the opening day. Lord struck 29 fours and two sixes in his five-and-a-half-hour innings before being caught 9 runs short of his career-best 199. He put on 167 with Curtis for the first wicket and 164 in 35 overs with Hick, and completed his second Championship hundred in four days, in 159 balls. Hampshire's target of 300 to avoid the follow-on looked a long way off when Newport reduced them to 26 for two. But Middleton, with his fourth Championship century of the season, and Cox, who reached his maiden hundred in 133 balls during his second first-class game, added 161 for the fifth wicket, steering Hampshire to 302 for four at the close on the second day.

Close of play: First day, Worcestershire 413-6 (S. J. Rhodes 8*, R. K. Illingworth 1*); Second day, Hampshire 302-4 (T. C. Middleton 117*, R. M. F. Cox 104*).

Worcestershire

*T. S. Curtis c Scott b Joseph	71	– not out	38
G. J. Lord c Middleton b Udal	190	– c Joseph b Maru	19
G. A. Hick c Parks b Joseph	72	– not out	50
D. B. D'Oliveira lbw b Tremlett	30		
D. A. Leatherdale c Maru b Tremlett	13		
C. M. Tolley c Parks b Tremlett	2		
†S. J. Rhodes not out	33		
R. K. Illingworth not out	9		
B 7, l-b 15, w 1, n-b 6	29	B 2, l-b 5, n-b 4	11
1/167 2/331 3/375 4/388 5/403 6/404 (6 wkts dec.)	449	1/40 (1 wkt dec.)	118

P. J. Newport, S. R. Lampitt and S. M. McEwan did not bat.

Bonus points – Worcestershire 4, Hampshire 1 (Score at 100 overs: 388-3).

Bowling: *First Innings*—Joseph 30–4–128–2; Scott 7–0–38–0; Tremlett 23–4–61–3; Maru 29–5–92–0; Udal 24–4–95–1; Nicholas 4–0–13–0. *Second Innings*—Joseph 8–2–19–0; Tremlett 6–2–22–0; Maru 3–0–13–1; Nicholas 5–0–27–0; Smith 2–0–22–0; Scott 1.4–0–8–0.

Hampshire

R. J. Scott c Rhodes b Newport	17	– c D'Oliveira b McEwan	15
C. L. Smith c Rhodes b Newport	5	– c Leatherdale b McEwan	12
T. C. Middleton not out	117	– c D'Oliveira b McEwan	2
V. P. Terry c Rhodes b Illingworth	40	– c D'Oliveira b Illingworth	42
*M. C. J. Nicholas lbw b Lampitt	6	– c and b Lampitt	35
R. M. F. Cox not out	104	– run out	15
L. A. Joseph (did not bat)		– not out	43
R. J. Maru (did not bat)		– c Tolley b Illingworth	7
†R. J. Parks (did not bat)		– c Hick b Illingworth	0
S. D. Udal (did not bat)		– not out	0
L-b 6, w 1, n-b 6	13	L-b 3, w 2, n-b 4	9
1/9 2/26 3/120 4/141 (4 wkts dec.)	302	1/20 2/27 3/34 4/101 5/120 6/130 7/167 8/179 (8 wkts)	180

T. M. Tremlett did not bat.

Bonus points – Hampshire 4, Worcestershire 1.

Bowling: *First Innings*—Newport 16–6–23–2; McEwan 12–1–40–0; Lampitt 18–2–39–1; Illingworth 32–6–99–1; Tolley 4–0–15–0; Hick 17–1–74–0; D'Oliveira 1–0–6–0. *Second Innings*—Newport 18–2–61–0; McEwan 11–1–38–3; Illingworth 21–8–44–3; Lampitt 9–0–29–1; Hick 1.5–0–5–0.

Umpires: B. Dudleston and K. E. Palmer.

WORCESTERSHIRE v NORTHAMPTONSHIRE

At Worcester, August 18, 20, 21. Drawn. Worcestershire 6 pts, Northamptonshire 6 pts. Toss: Northamptonshire. The most absorbing contest of the season at New Road, dominated by the spinners, ended with Rhodes and Newport batting out the last eleven overs to stave off defeat. With the ball turning appreciably and lifting from the Diglis End, Cook and Illingworth finished with respective match figures of nine for 137 and seven for 92. In his first appearance for six weeks, after a fourth knee operation, Dilley quickly accounted for Felton, and Fordham and Lamb were the only Northamptonshire batsmen to make significant contributions on the opening day. Curtis anchored Worcestershire's reply, staying 64 overs for his 48, while Rhodes and Dilley added 35 for the last wicket to reduce the deficit to 9. Worcestershire looked to have regained the initiative when the visitors were 78 for four on the final morning, but Bailey's defiant 66 enabled Northamptonshire to set a demanding target of 241 in 51 overs. Cook ran through the middle order with four wickets in seven overs, including Hick's after his thirteenth half-century in fifteen innings, but Worcestershire's eighth-wicket pair held firm to the finish.

Close of play: First day, Worcestershire 39-1 (T. S. Curtis 11*, S. M. McEwan 10*); Second day, Northamptonshire 77-2 (W. Larkins 26*, R. J. Bailey 11*).

Northamptonshire

	First innings		Second innings	
A. Fordham	c Hick b Lampitt	81	c Rhodes b Newport	19
N. A. Felton	c Rhodes b Dilley	10	c Rhodes b McEwan	11
W. Larkins	c D'Oliveira b Newport	27	c Rhodes b Illingworth	26
R. J. Bailey	c McEwan b Lampitt	7	run out	66
D. J. Capel	st Rhodes b Illingworth	12	lbw b Dilley	0
*A. J. Lamb	c Illingworth b McEwan	63	c Rhodes b Illingworth	28
A. L. Penberthy	c Rhodes b Hick	1	c Lampitt b Hick	21
†D. Ripley	c Hick b Illingworth	14	not out	26
C. E. L. Ambrose	b Illingworth	12	b Illingworth	12
N. G. B. Cook	b Illingworth	2	not out	7
M. A. Robinson	not out	0		
	B 1, l-b 5, w 1, n-b 6	13	B 2, l-b 12, n-b 1	15
1/27 2/114 3/132 4/132 5/167 6/182 7/223 8/233 9/241		242	1/19 2/51 3/77 4/78 5/121 6/184 7/190 8/221 (8 wkts dec.)	231

Bonus points – Northamptonshire 2, Worcestershire 4.

Bowling: *First Innings*—Dilley 16–3–36–1; Newport 17–2–67–1; McEwan 11–1–39–1; Lampitt 17–7–44–2; Illingworth 17.4–6–29–4; Hick 7–0–21–1. *Second Innings*—Dilley 10–0–48–1; McEwan 5–2–11–1; Illingworth 38–12–63–3; Newport 6–1–11–1; Hick 24–8–66–1; Lampitt 4–0–18–0.

Worcestershire

	First innings		Second innings	
*T. S. Curtis	lbw b Ambrose	48	lbw b Ambrose	12
G. J. Lord	c Ripley b Capel	17	lbw b Robinson	6
S. M. McEwan	b Cook	14		
G. A. Hick	c Ripley b Cook	34	(3) st Ripley b Cook	50
D. B. D'Oliveira	c Penberthy b Cook	0	(4) c and b Robinson	21
D. A. Leatherdale	c Capel b Cook	52	(5) c Felton b Cook	7
S. R. Lampitt	lbw b Ambrose	0	(6) c Lamb b Cook	16
†S. J. Rhodes	not out	44	(7) not out	28
R. K. Illingworth	lbw b Robinson	9	(8) lbw b Cook	0
P. J. Newport	c Larkins b Robinson	1	(9) not out	8
G. R. Dilley	b Cook	8		
	L-b 2, n-b 4	6	B 4, l-b 2, n-b 3	9
1/25 2/44 3/88 4/92 5/153 6/153 7/171 8/196 9/198		233	1/19 2/20 3/70 4/85 5/111 6/132 7/132 (7 wkts)	157

Bonus points – Worcestershire 2, Northamptonshire 4 (Score at 100 overs: 233-9).

Bowling: *First Innings*—Ambrose 26–7–53–2; Robinson 22–3–63–2; Capel 4–0–13–1; Cook 40.1–17–80–5; Bailey 8–1–22–0. *Second Innings*—Ambrose 11–3–28–1; Robinson 13–4–40–2; Cook 19.4–3–57–4; Bailey 7–2–26–0.

Umpires: D. J. Constant and B. Leadbeater.

WORCESTERSHIRE v WARWICKSHIRE

At Worcester, August 23, 24, 25, 27. Worcestershire won by 323 runs. Worcestershire 23 pts, Warwickshire 6 pts. Toss: Worcestershire. Rarely can a side have made a more complete recovery to win by such a large margin. Neale's decision to bat first, on a relaid pitch not used before, was in question when Small took five wickets for 13 in 25 balls, reducing the home side to 57 for five on the first morning. Rhodes and Neale held up the slide by adding 88 in 25 overs, but Warwickshire regained the initiative the following day when they reached 101 for 1, only to lose their last nine wickets for 121 and trail by 43 on first innings. Thereafter Worcestershire assumed total control. Curtis's unbeaten 197 was his highest first-class score and his third century of the summer. He occupied the crease for seven and a quarter hours, hitting two sixes and 25 fours. Needing 420 for their first Championship win over their neighbours for ten years, Warwickshire were bowled out in just 29.3 overs for 96, Newport taking five for 37 in 14.3 overs.

Close of play: First day, Worcestershire 228-9 (G. R. Dilley 11*, S. M. McEwan 0*); Second day, Worcestershire 47-0 (T. S. Curtis 25*, G. J. Lord 13*); Third day, Worcestershire 376-5 (T. S. Curtis 197*, S. J. Rhodes 30*).

Worcestershire

T. S. Curtis c Lloyd b Small	27	– not out	197
G. J. Lord lbw b Small	7	– c Piper b Munton	25
G. A. Hick c Piper b Small	14	– b Reeve	42
D. B. D'Oliveira c Piper b Small	0	– c Moles b Booth	30
*P. A. Neale c Twose b Reeve	46	– c Piper b Twose	17
S. R. Lampitt c Piper b Small	0	– c and b Munton	4
†S. J. Rhodes b Reeve	96	– not out	30
R. K. Illingworth lbw b Munton	13		
P. J. Newport c Piper b Munton	7		
G. R. Dilley c Lloyd b Small	35		
S. M. McEwan not out	12		
L-b 7, w 1	8	B 8, l-b 20, w 2, n-b 1	31
1/35 2/40 3/40 4/57 5/57 6/145 7/169 8/183 9/217	265	1/78 2/155 3/204 4/258 5/273 (5 wkts dec.)	376

Bonus points – Worcestershire 3, Warwickshire 4.

Bowling: *First Innings*—Small 29–5–94–6; Munton 27–6–84–2; Reeve 23–3–60–2; Moody 3–0–11–0; Booth 7–5–9–0. *Second Innings*—Small 25–12–61–0; Munton 27–9–66–2; Reeve 25–8–85–1; Booth 36–10–93–1; Smith 6–0–33–0; Twose 5–1–10–1.

Warwickshire

A. J. Moles c Neale b Dilley	59	– b Dilley	8
J. D. Ratcliffe c Lampitt b Newport	29	– lbw b Newport	4
*T. A. Lloyd c Neale b Lampitt	12	– lbw b Newport	2
T. M. Moody c Rhodes b McEwan	21	– c Rhodes b Dilley	6
R. G. Twose b Newport	9	– lbw b Dilley	0
D. A. Reeve c D'Oliveira b Lampitt	27	– b McEwan	25
N. M. K. Smith c D'Oliveira b Newport	20	– b Newport	20
†K. J. Piper b Dilley	14	– c Rhodes b Newport	0
G. C. Small not out	5	– c Illingworth b Newport	12
P. A. Booth c Rhodes b Lampitt	2	– c Rhodes b McEwan	5
T. A. Munton c Curtis b Lampitt	1	– not out	5
B 1, l-b 7, w 2, n-b 13	23	L-b 3, w 1, n-b 5	9
1/66 2/101 3/123 4/146 5/150 6/182 7/209 8/212 9/214	222	1/14 2/16 3/16 4/19 5/45 6/71 7/71 8/82 9/88	96

Bonus points – Warwickshire 2, Worcestershire 4.

Bowling: *First Innings*—Dilley 16–2–56–2; Newport 19–5–60–3; McEwan 14–2–49–1; Illingworth 1–0–2–0; Lampitt 14–1–47–4. *Second Innings*—Dilley 10–0–45–3; Newport 14.3–4–37–5; McEwan 5–2–11–2.

Umpires: J. H. Harris and B. Hassan.

At Nottingham, August 29, 30, 31. WORCESTERSHIRE drew with NOTTINGHAMSHIRE.

At Bristol, September 7, 8, 9, 10. WORCESTERSHIRE drew with GLOUCESTERSHIRE.

At Taunton, September 12, 13, 14, 15. WORCESTERSHIRE beat SOMERSET by 173 runs.

WORCESTERSHIRE v GLAMORGAN

At Worcester, September 18, 19, 20, 21. Worcestershire won by 261 runs. Worcestershire 24 pts, Glamorgan 6 pts. Toss: Worcestershire. Worcestershire, who two months earlier had been next to bottom in the County Championship table, fashioned their fifth win in their last twelve games to finish fourth. Hick signed off with his eighth hundred of the summer on his way to passing 15,000 first-class runs, hitting sixteen fours and one six in an unbeaten 138 off 155 balls. But Lord could feel no less satisfied. His 127 on the first day was rated one of the most entertaining innings of the year at New Road, and he was later awarded his county cap. By adding 57 runs in the second innings he completed 1,000 runs in a season for the first time. For the visitors, a spell of three for 0 in seven balls had helped Bastien to return his best bowling figures, six for 75, in the first innings. On the final day, when Glamorgan were chasing 477 for victory, Morris made his twentieth first-class score of 50 or more and brought his total runs for the season to 2,276, a record for his county. Butcher helped him delay the inevitable, but Dilley bowled Morris and took the last two wickets to finish with five for 72.

Close of play: First day, Glamorgan 14-0 (S. P. James 6*, H. Morris 8*); Second day, Worcestershire 10-0 (T. S. Curtis 4*, G. J. Lord 6*); Third day, Glamorgan 27-2 (H. Morris 19*, M. P. Maynard 2*).

Worcestershire

T. S. Curtis lbw b Frost	16	– c James b Watkin	60
G. J. Lord c Maynard b Bastien	127	– c Maynard b Croft	57
G. A. Hick c Metson b Watkin	6	– not out	138
D. B. D'Oliveira c Metson b Bastien	22	– b Bastien	12
*P. A. Neale b Bastien	4	– c Morris b Bastien	17
S. R. Lampitt lbw b Bastien	34	– c Metson b Watkin	18
†S. J. Rhodes c Cottey b Bastien	0	– c Maynard b Bastien	22
R. K. Illingworth c Metson b Watkin	48	– not out	7
N. V. Radford lbw b Watkin	13		
G. R. Dilley not out	45		
S. M. McEwan b Bastien	11		
B 4, l-b 4, n-b 1	9	L-b 12	12
1/24 2/43 3/95 4/107 5/212 6/212 7/213 8/239 9/307	335	1/117 2/138 3/168 4/198 5/248 6/314 (6 wkts dec.)	343

Bonus points – Worcestershire 4, Glamorgan 4 (Score at 100 overs: 313-9).

Bowling: *First Innings*—Frost 23–2–71–1; Watkin 31–7–124–3; Bastien 24–8–75–6; Croft 20–5–41–0; Dale 10–5–16–0. *Second Innings*—Frost 12–3–44–0; Watkin 20–5–47–2; Bastien 17–0–76–3; Dale 11–1–54–0; Croft 28–3–110–1.

Glamorgan

S. P. James lbw b Dilley	7	– c D'Oliveira b Dilley	0
H. Morris c Rhodes b McEwan	71	– b Dilley	50
P. A. Cottey c Rhodes b Lampitt	19	– c Curtis b Dilley	3
M. P. Maynard b Radford	4	– c Rhodes b McEwan	35
*A. R. Butcher c Hick b McEwan	21	– c Lord b Illingworth	61
A. Dale lbw b McEwan	7	– c Rhodes b McEwan	0
R. D. B. Croft not out	26	– c Neale b Lampitt	27
†C. P. Metson c Rhodes b Lampitt	10	– lbw b Lampitt	4
S. L. Watkin c McEwan b Radford	19	– b Dilley	4
S. Bastien c Rhodes b Radford	0	– c Lord b Dilley	12
M. Frost lbw b Radford	0	– not out	4
B 5, l-b 6, n-b 7	18	L-b 8, w 1, n-b 6	15
1/20 2/86 3/91 4/123 5/142 6/145 7/177 8/198 9/200	202	1/1 2/18 3/68 4/102 5/107 6/152 7/156 8/191 9/199	215

Bonus points – Glamorgan 2, Worcestershire 4.

Bowling: *First Innings*—Dilley 13–1–35–1; Radford 20–4–58–4; McEwan 18–6–31–3; Lampitt 22–7–52–2; Illingworth 14–7–15–0. *Second Innings*—Dilley 14–1–72–5; Radford 11–1–31–0; McEwan 9–4–30–2; Lampitt 12–2–52–2; Illingworth 9–5–22–1.

Umpires: P. J. Eele and R. Julian.

NATIONAL POWER AWARDS, 1990

The National Power Awards, of £1,000 each, went to the leading run-scorer, wicket-taker and six-hitter in first-class matches during the English season. A special bonus of £10,000 was available to be shared by batsmen scoring 2,500 runs and bowlers taking 125 wickets, while those players hitting twenty or more sixes received £10 per six. G. A. Gooch, the leading run-scorer, received an additional £1,000 for being the first to reach a bonus target. As part of their sponsorship, National Power presented the winners' counties with a similar sum to that won by the players. The Awards were run with the cooperation of *Wisden Cricket Monthly*.

Batting Awards

£7,000 G. A. Gooch (Essex) 2,746 runs. £5,000 S. J. Cook (Somerset) 2,608 runs.

Bowling Award

£1,000 N. A. Foster (Essex) 94 wickets.

Six-hit Awards

£1,400 I. V. A. Richards (Glamorgan) ... 40 sixes.

The following received £10 per six:

N. H. Fairbrother (Lancashire)	32	D. M. Ward (Surrey)	23
G. D. Rose (Somerset)	30	C. A. Walsh (Gloucestershire)	22
G. A. Hick (Worcestershire)	28	M. A. Roseberry (Middlesex)	21
D. J. Capel (Northamptonshire)	27	M. E. Waugh (Essex)	21
R. J. Bailey (Northamptonshire)	25	I. A. Greig (Surrey)	20
T. M. Moody (Warwickshire)	23		

YORKSHIRE

Patron: HRH The Duchess of Kent
President: 1990 – Sir Leonard Hutton
1991 – Sir Lawrence Byford
Chairman: B. Walsh
Chairman, Cricket Committee: D. B. Close
Secretary: J. Lister
Headingley Cricket Ground, Leeds LS6 3BU
(Telephone: 0532-787394)
Cricket Manager: S. Oldham
Captain: M. D. Moxon

Yorkshire cricket was a mass of contradictions at the end of yet another worrying season. On the one hand, leading officials took public comfort from an overall statistical improvement reflected in the county's rise from sixteenth to tenth in the Britannic Assurance Championship and from eleventh to sixth in the Refuge Assurance League, arguing that important strides had been made in the right direction. In contrast, however, other members of the committee were so concerned at the poor quality of the cricket that they echoed the dressing-room plea from the previous year for outside assistance. And the loss of around 1,000 members caused the overseas-player issue to be debated once more. The outcome was that in November, by 18-1, the committee voted to relax the county's "Yorkshire born" policy and make eligible those cricketers who, although not born in Yorkshire, had grown up there.

Martyn Moxon and manager Steve Oldham, the new partnership in charge of the team, adopted some positive attitudes, and Yorkshire were always ready to run the risk of defeat in pursuit of victory. But as the season developed, all concerned became rather too keen to set up a last-afternoon run-chase, forgetting, it appeared, that the object in the Championship should be to bowl out the opposition twice. Yorkshire managed this just once – against bottom-of-the-table Sussex – yet conceded all twenty wickets themselves on eight occasions.

The bowling proved dreadfully poor, and for the first time in a full Championship season no-one took 50 wickets. Peter Hartley, with 48, was the most successful, but his form remained erratic. Arnie Sidebottom was restricted to two Championship games and sixteen appearances in the national one-day competitions by a knee injury for which he twice had surgery, while Paul Jarvis, the other seamer capable of upsetting batsmen on good pitches, rarely hit an effective rhythm. Jarvis suffered the indignity of being dropped at the end of May, for the Hampshire game, and he subsequently missed most of July with a stress fracture of the shin. Even so, it was disappointing and significant that he did not take five wickets in any first-class innings.

Stuart Fletcher fell out of favour for the second successive year and was not offered an extension of his contract, due to expire at the end of 1991, and Darren Gough did little to justify the high hopes held for him. The absence of Sidebottom gave Chris Pickles another chance to press his claims, but while he showed an unfailing enthusiasm, his tidy medium pace never threatened to take wickets on a match-winning basis. His brightest moments concerned his batting. Phil Carrick headed the bowling averages and, after a rather shaky start, enjoyed one of his better summers. However, off-spinner Jeremy Batty, when brought into the side, lacked the control to avoid fairly heavy punishment, and it was an indictment of Yorkshire's failure to encourage younger exponents of an almost lost art that at 38 Carrick was Yorkshire's only reliable spinner.

The county expressed great faith in the Academy venture at Bradford, and in a scheme to develop fast bowlers with the aid of specialised athletic coaching, but neither of these ventures looked like solving the immediate problem. Certainly there is no-one with an excess of pace at the Academy, which no doubt was why a keen interest was displayed in the plans of Yorkshire exiles with other first-class counties.

Overall, the batting was patchy and could not be relied on under pressure. Moxon scored steadily without quite fulfilling his potential, and Ashley Metcalfe had the satisfaction of becoming the first batsman since Geoff Boycott in 1971 to score 2,000 first-class runs. Richard Blakey, however, endured a miserable sequence early on, averaging only 17.46 in the Championship at the end of June. Although he scored fluently in the Sunday League, he continued to be hesitant at the higher level and eventually dropped down the order. This was a sensible move, for he was establishing himself as first-choice wicket-keeper in succession to David Bairstow, who featured briefly in his testimonial year before being informed that his services would no longer be required.

Moxon, Metcalfe and Phil Robinson all compiled career-best first-class aggregates, the last-mentioned managing just one Championship century while maintaining a steady consistency. But miserable luck with injuries meant that Kevin Sharp had little opportunity to approach his benefit season in style, though he took some advantage of favourable conditions when he did get to the middle. Given that Yorkshire's prospects were not helped by a collective inability to hold reasonable chances, notably at slip, it was an indication of how things went for them that their most reliable catcher, David Byas, suffered a lean time with the bat. Indeed, with Simon Kellett emerging as a leading candidate for regular inclusion, the tall left-hander's future became distinctly clouded.

Another player to make an interesting mark was Craig White, a young all-rounder born in Morley, near Leeds, who learned his cricket in Australia. Arriving to join the Academy, he immediately impressed Oldham sufficiently to be included in the senior squad. In the event, he did little either as a batsman or with his off-spin, but he looked very much the part and Yorkshire were convinced that, after another winter in Australia, he would figure prominently in their plans.

The team made a disastrous start, losing their first four Championship fixtures and four of the opening five games in the Sunday League. Losing to the Combined Universities – at Headingley – put them out of the Benson and Hedges Cup at the qualifying stages for the third time in a row. They followed on in three out of four Championship matches in late July and August, but four generous declarations subsequently enabled them to pick up useful points, and they also won seven of their last nine Sunday games to finish with a much needed flourish. In the NatWest Bank Trophy, Yorkshire became the first side to reach the last eight without losing a wicket, only to collapse miserably against Hampshire at Southampton. The consequent defeat merely reinforced the doubts about their temperament. – John Callaghan.

YORKSHIRE 1990

[*Bill Smith*

Back row: D. Gough, P. J. Berry, M. K. Bore (*Academy coach*), C. Shaw, D. Byas, C. S. Pickles, S. A. Kellett, N. G. Nicholson, I. J. Houseman. *Middle row:* W. P. Morton (*physiotherapist*), R. J. Blakey, P. W. Jarvis, S. D. Fletcher, P. J. Hartley, P. E. Robinson, S. N. Hartley, J. D. Batty, A. P. Grayson, M. J. Doidge. *Front row:* A. Sidebottom, D. L. Bairstow, D. E. V. Padgett (*coach*), S. Oldham (*cricket manager*), M. D. Moxon (*captain*), A. A. Metcalfe, P. Carrick, K. Sharp.

YORKSHIRE RESULTS

All first-class matches – Played 24: Won 5, Lost 9, Drawn 10.

County Championship matches – Played 22: Won 5, Lost 9, Drawn 8.

Bonus points – Batting 52, Bowling 55.

Competition placings – Britannic Assurance County Championship, 10th; NatWest Bank Trophy, q-f; Benson and Hedges Cup, 3rd in Group C; Refuge Assurance League, 6th equal.

BRITANNIC ASSURANCE CHAMPIONSHIP AVERAGES

BATTING

	Birthplace	*M*	*I*	*NO*	*R*	*HI*	*Avge*
‡A. A. Metcalfe	*Horsforth*	21	40	3	1,854	194*	50.10
‡K. Sharp	*Leeds*	8	12	5	316	53*	45.14
A. P. Grayson	*Ripon*	4	7	4	135	44*	45.00
‡P. E. Robinson	*Keighley*	22	38	7	1,389	150*	44.80
‡M. D. Moxon	*Barnsley*	19	36	5	1,353	218*	43.64
S. A. Kellett	*Mirfield*	14	25	2	699	75*	30.39
C. S. Pickles	*Mirfield*	15	21	7	424	57*	30.28
‡D. L. Bairstow	*Bradford*	5	6	0	179	61	29.83
‡R. J. Blakey	*Huddersfield*	22	39	7	928	111	29.00
D. Byas	*Kilham*	17	27	3	693	83	28.87
‡A. Sidebottom	*Barnsley*	2	4	0	104	38	26.00
‡P. Carrick	*Armley*	18	22	2	515	64	25.75
‡P. W. Jarvis	*Redcar*	15	16	4	212	43*	17.66
‡P. J. Hartley	*Keighley*	16	14	1	215	75	16.53
C. White	*Morley Hall*	8	9	1	106	38	13.25
C. A. Chapman	*Bradford*	2	4	0	47	20	11.75
D. Gough	*Barnsley*	13	16	5	116	24	10.54
J. D. Batty	*Bradford*	7	5	2	30	21	10.00
‡S. D. Fletcher	*Keighley*	10	13	3	39	19	3.90
P. J. Berry	*Saltburn*	2	4	4	45	31*	–

Also batted: I. J. Houseman (*Harrogate*) (2 matches) 0*.

* *Signifies not out.* ‡ *Denotes county cap.*

The following played a total of ten three-figure innings for Yorkshire in County Championship matches – A. A. Metcalfe 6, M. D. Moxon 2, R. J. Blakey 1, P. E. Robinson 1.

BOWLING

	O	*M*	*R*	*W*	*BB*	*5W/i*	*Avge*
P. Carrick	601	173	1,570	46	5-49	3	34.13
S. D. Fletcher	268.5	58	936	27	5-94	1	34.66
P. J. Hartley	481.1	79	1,754	48	6-57	2	36.54
P. W. Jarvis	405.2	68	1,393	37	4-53	0	37.64
D. Gough	256.4	43	984	24	4-68	0	41.00
C. S. Pickles	296.1	59	1,107	25	3-56	0	44.28
J. D. Batty	195	29	722	12	4-76	0	60.16

Also bowled: P. J. Berry 44.3–4–172–2; D. Byas 69–14–253–3; A. P. Grayson 63–13–227–1; I. J. Houseman 30–6–129–0; A. A. Metcalfe 9.1–0–88–0; M. D. Moxon 57–9–175–3; P. E. Robinson 3.3–0–28–1; A. Sidebottom 44–9–121–4; C. White 122–12–519–9.

Wicket-keepers: R. J. Blakey 34 ct, 8 st; D. L. Bairstow 9 ct; C. White 1 ct.

Leading Fielders: D. Byas 19, P. E. Robinson 18.

YORKSHIRE v NORTHAMPTONSHIRE

At Leeds, April 26, 27, 28, 30. Northamptonshire won by an innings and 50 runs. Northamptonshire 24 pts, Yorkshire 1 pt. Toss: Northamptonshire. Put in on a pitch from which Ambrose made the occasional delivery lift sharply, Yorkshire collapsed. And though their bowlers claimed two early wickets in their turn, Fordham and Lamb took complete command, adding 393 in 100 overs, the highest partnership for any Northamptonshire wicket. The previous best was 376 for the sixth wicket between R. Subba Row and A. Lightfoot at The Oval in 1958. Lamb made his runs in 342 minutes, from 301 balls, hitting three sixes and 31 fours. Fordham's career-best, unbeaten 206 took 446 minutes, and in 378 deliveries he hit a six as well as 28 fours. Both batsmen took full advantage as Yorkshire stood back and waited for the declaration. Lamb's 235, his best for the county, was the highest innings by a Northamptonshire batsman against Yorkshire, and the total of 498 for three was the biggest for the county at Yorkshire's expense. Yorkshire did slightly better at the second attempt, Kellett completing his maiden first-class half-century as he resisted for 142 balls and hit five fours. Thomas, however, took three wickets without cost in eleven balls on the final morning to expose the middle order. Blakey, who came in at No. 10, had fallen ill during Northamptonshire's innings and White had taken over as wicket-keeper, subsequently catching Lamb.

Close of play: First day, Yorkshire 119-5 (C. White 9*, P. Carrick 10*); Second day, Northamptonshire 241-2 (A. Fordham 87*, A. J. Lamb 126*); Third day, Yorkshire 125-2 (S. A. Kellett 55*, P. E. Robinson 14*).

Yorkshire

First innings		Second innings	
S. A. Kellett c Fordham b Ambrose	0	lbw b Thomas	63
*A. A. Metcalfe c Fordham b Robinson	38	lbw b Capel	45
†R. J. Blakey b Ambrose	25	(10) b Robinson	0
P. E. Robinson c Ripley b Ambrose	30	b Thomas	22
C. White c Thomas b Ambrose	9	(3) lbw b Ambrose	9
D. Byas b Robinson	0	(5) c Ripley b Thomas	0
P. Carrick b Capel	37	(6) c Lamb b Robinson	23
A. Sidebottom c Fordham b Ambrose	16	(7) c Ripley b Capel	31
P. W. Jarvis b Capel	29	(8) c Ripley b Robinson	0
P. J. Berry not out	4	(9) not out	31
S. D. Fletcher c Robinson b Thomas	1	b Capel	19
B 4, l-b 5	9	B 4, l-b 2, w 1	7
1/0 2/44 3/98 4/98 5/98 6/124 7/144 8/188 9/197	198	1/69 2/93 3/136 4/138 5/141 6/191 7/191 8/201 9/201	250

Bonus points – Yorkshire 1, Northamptonshire 4.

Bowling: *First Innings*—Ambrose 22–9–49–5; Thomas 12.2–2–45–1; Capel 16–4–40–2; Robinson 22–12–47–2; N. G. B. Cook 5–2–8–0. *Second Innings*—Ambrose 21–5–70–1; Thomas 13–1–47–3; Capel 23–6–72–3; Robinson 20–5–47–3; N. G. B. Cook 7–2–8–0.

Northamptonshire

W. Larkins b Jarvis	0
A. Fordham not out	206
R. J. Bailey c Byas b Sidebottom	16
*A. J. Lamb c White b Berry	235
D. J. Capel not out	21
B 3, l-b 16, n-b 1	20
1/0 2/41 3/434 (3 wkts dec.)	498

G. Cook, †D. Ripley, J. G. Thomas, C. E. L. Ambrose, N. G. B. Cook and M. A. Robinson did not bat.

Bonus points – Northamptonshire 4 (Score at 100 overs: 337-2).

Bowling: Jarvis 23–3–90–1; Sidebottom 26–5–67–1; Fletcher 28–6–109–0; Byas 8–2–23–0; Carrick 23–4–89–0; Berry 21.5–1–101–1.

Umpires: J. H. Hampshire and D. R. Shepherd.

At Birmingham, May 3, 4, 5. YORKSHIRE lost to WARWICKSHIRE by seven wickets.

YORKSHIRE v ZIMBABWEANS

At Leeds, May 16, 17, 18. Drawn. Toss: Zimbabweans. Moxon, making his runs from 211 balls and hitting twenty boundaries, had the satisfaction of recording Yorkshire's first century of the season in the course of a patchy batting performance on a slow pitch. Once Metcalfe had fallen to a superb catch, the innings fell apart in the face of steady seam bowling. Pickles, however, saved Yorkshire's potential embarrassment by hammering eleven fours in a 45-ball half-century. After a long delay because of rain on the second day, Hartley had the visitors in trouble, gaining extra pace and bounce, and although Brandes followed his useful bowling with a determined defensive display, they were spared the indignity of the follow-on only because Moxon wanted to give some of his batsmen practice. Kellett had the unusual experience of being "retired out" by the umpires when he made way for White during this exercise. The Zimbabweans were finally set a victory target of 299, but, more realistically, Yorkshire left themselves with 67 overs in which to try to win the game. Brent frustrated them as he battled through the last 28 overs after Gough, taking three wickets in five balls, had initiated a collapse to 84 for five.

Close of play: First day, Zimbabweans 8-1 (A. H. Shah 2*, W. R. James 6*); Second day, Yorkshire 7-0 (S. A. Kellett 2*, A. A. Metcalfe 5*).

Yorkshire

*M. D. Moxon c Pycroft b Shah	130		
A. A. Metcalfe c Brandes b Duers	49	– c Pycroft b Butchart	30
†R. J. Blakey c James b Brandes	5	– not out	58
S. A. Kellett lbw b Brandes	0	– (1) retired out	39
P. E. Robinson b Flower	13		
C. White c and b Flower	9	– (4) not out	12
D. Byas c Flower b Shah	3		
A. P. Grayson c James b Brandes	10		
C. S. Pickles not out	54		
P. J. Hartley b Duers	3		
D. Gough not out	7		
B 6, l-b 8, w 1	15	B 5, l-b 1, n-b 2	8
1/93 2/126 3/126 4/188 5/218 6/220 7/225 8/261 9/290 (9 wkts dec.)	298	1/57 2/93 (2 wkts dec.)	147

Bowling: *First Innings*—Brandes 21–5–75–3; Dube 4–1–19–0; Butchart 7–1–19–0; Duers 18–5–63–2; Shah 26–7–46–2; Brent 6–1–29–0; Flower 16–4–33–2. *Second Innings*—Brandes 6–1–23–0; Dube 6–1–22–0; Duers 13–3–48–0; Butchart 10–1–39–1; Brent 2–0–9–0.

Zimbabweans

G. W. Flower c Robinson b Hartley	0	– c Hartley b Gough	12
A. H. Shah c Blakey b Hartley	10	– lbw b Gough	20
†W. R. James b Hartley	16	– lbw b Gough	0
*A. J. Pycroft lbw b Byas	18	– (6) b White	23
C. M. Robertson lbw b White	18	– c Kellett b White	15
G. A. Briant c Byas b Pickles	5	– (4) c Moxon b Pickles	35
J. P. Brent b White	17	– not out	34
I. P. Butchart c White b Pickles	18	– not out	15
E. A. Brandes b Gough	22		
K. G. Duers not out	11		
L. E. Dube c Robinson b Hartley	1		
B 2, l-b 8, w 1	11	L-b 5	5
1/0 2/20 3/31 4/59 5/64 6/74 7/85 8/114 9/146	147	1/28 2/32 3/33 4/82 5/84 6/134 (6 wkts)	159

Bowling: *First Innings*—Hartley 9.5–1–27–4; Gough 10–1–21–1; Pickles 17–6–29–2; Byas 12–4–40–1; White 8–2–12–2; Grayson 4–2–8–0. *Second Innings*—Pickles 12–7–27–1; Gough 13–5–32–3; Byas 7–1–20–0; White 22–7–40–2; Grayson 13–4–35–0.

Umpires: B. Leadbeater and K. J. Lyons.

At Chesterfield, May 23, 24, 25. YORKSHIRE lost to DERBYSHIRE by 144 runs.

YORKSHIRE v HAMPSHIRE

At Leeds, May 26, 28, 29. Hampshire won by five wickets. Hampshire 23 pts, Yorkshire 7 pts. Toss: Yorkshire. Yorkshire batted carefully on an easy-paced pitch, Robinson leading the way with 60 from 147 balls. Maru bowled his slow left-arm spin accurately, until he was called on to keep wicket for the rest of the match when Parks injured a finger in the 76th over, and Shine gained reward for keeping a full length, but Yorkshire plundered 21 from the last two overs to gain the maximum batting points. Marshall held the Hampshire reply together with a workmanlike century, batting for almost four hours as he received 193 deliveries and hit one six and eighteen fours. The declaration by Nicholas, with a lead of 37, appeared to have left the game in no-man's-land, but Connor, finding some uneven bounce, suddenly broke the back of the Yorkshire second innings, taking three for 8 in the space of nineteen balls. Carrick and Pickles, the latter launching a furious counter-attack to make 57 from 65 balls with ten fours, rescued the situation, and Hampshire were left to make 215 from 47 overs. Yorkshire did not help themselves by setting defensive fields, which often allowed a single from every ball, and Robinson, at slip, missed Chris Smith on 30 and 34. Smith's 58 came from 88 deliveries and set the stage for his brother, Robin, to win the game with an unbeaten 51 from only 39 balls. Hampshire had seven balls to spare at the end.

Close of play: First day, Hampshire 28-0 (V. P. Terry 11*, C. L. Smith 14*); Second day, Yorkshire 83-1 (A. A. Metcalfe 35*, R. J. Blakey 15*).

Yorkshire

First innings		Second innings	
S. A. Kellett c Gower b Connor	56	– c sub b Turner	26
*A. A. Metcalfe c Maru b Connor	22	– c C. L. Smith b Connor	35
R. J. Blakey c Parks b Shine	17	– b Connor	20
P. E. Robinson lbw b Shine	60	– b Connor	24
D. Byas b Shine	29	– c Maru b Connor	0
†D. L. Bairstow c Connor b Turner	37	– lbw b Marshall	9
P. Carrick c Maru b Marshall	23	– c Gower b Marshall	32
P. J. Hartley c Terry b Shine	3	– c Terry b Nicholas	5
C. S. Pickles not out	13	– not out	57
D. Gough not out	7	– c Shine b Marshall	8
S. D. Fletcher (did not bat)		– c Gower b Connor	6
L-b 19, w 1, n-b 13	33	B 10, l-b 11, w 1, n-b 7	29
1/56 2/93 3/130 4/200 5/225 6/259 7/279 8/288 (8 wkts dec.)	300	1/45 2/84 3/100 4/100 5/113 6/138 7/153 8/186 9/230	251

Bonus points – Yorkshire 4, Hampshire 3.

Bowling: *First Innings*—Marshall 22–7–44–1; Shine 19–2–52–4; Maru 21–9–43–0; Connor 21–2–79–2; Turner 16.5–3–63–1. *Second Innings*—Shine 8–0–50–0; Marshall 22–5–51–3; Connor 27.5–3–96–5; Turner 9–5–19–1; Nicholas 6–1–14–1.

Hampshire

First innings		Second innings	
V. P. Terry lbw b Pickles	23	– b Fletcher	18
C. L. Smith c Kellett b Hartley	28	– c Bairstow b Gough	58
D. I. Gower lbw b Hartley	64	– c Robinson b Gough	33
R. A. Smith b Pickles	15	– not out	51
M. D. Marshall c Blakey b Carrick	117	– b Gough	28
*M. C. J. Nicholas lbw b Fletcher	0	– c Gough b Hartley	15
R. J. Maru c Bairstow b Gough	25		
†R. J. Parks not out	36	– (7) not out	1
I. J. Turner not out	0		
B 3, l-b 19, w 1, n-b 6	29	L-b 11	11
1/53 2/61 3/99 4/178 5/182 6/281 7/337 (7 wkts dec.)	337	1/37 2/103 3/113 4/181 5/206 (5 wkts)	215

C. A. Connor and K. J. Shine did not bat.

Bonus points – Hampshire 4, Yorkshire 3.

Bowling: *First Innings*—Hartley 23–6–68–2; Fletcher 20–5–57–1; Carrick 15.4–6–46–1; Pickles 14–1–64–2; Gough 13–3–67–1; Byas 7–1–13–0. *Second Innings*—Hartley 15–3–52–1; Fletcher 14–1–66–1; Pickles 4–0–25–0; Gough 12.5–1–61–3.

Umpires: D. O. Oslear and A. G. T. Whitehead.

At Worcester, June 2, 4, 5. YORKSHIRE drew with WORCESTERSHIRE.

At Tunbridge Wells, June 6, 7, 8. YORKSHIRE drew with KENT.

YORKSHIRE v SURREY

At Harrogate, June 9, 11, 12. Drawn. Yorkshire 3 pts, Surrey 12 pts. Toss: Surrey. Surrey received eight extra points as the side batting last in a drawn game in which the scores finished level. The two captains came to an agreement after the first day had been washed out by rain. Bicknell put Yorkshire under pressure on a good pitch which had enough pace to interest the quicker bowlers, his first fifteen overs bringing him two wickets for 9 runs. Robinson, with 85 from 211 balls, began the recovery, and Carrick, with nine boundaries, also played well in an eighth-wicket stand worth 131 from 37 overs. Surrey were finally set a target of 281 in what became 73 overs and were hurried along by Ward, whose 71 needed only 96 balls as he hit eleven fours. Greig was even more forceful, racing to 72 from 71 deliveries with nine fours. He survived a difficult chance when 2 to backward short leg off White, who took career-best figures of five for 74 with his off-spin. In a hectic finish, Bicknell was run out attempting a bye to wicket-keeper Bairstow, whose throw from the final ball missed the stumps as Waqar Younis scrambled home for the bye which levelled the scores.

Close of play: First day, No play; Second day, Yorkshire 200-7 (P. E. Robinson 71*, P. Carrick 36*).

Yorkshire

*M. D. Moxon lbw b Waqar Younis	10	– not out	23
A. A. Metcalfe c Lynch b Bicknell	6	– c Lynch b Medlycott	1
R. J. Blakey b Waqar Younis	1	– not out	2
S. A. Kellett lbw b Feltham	24		
P. E. Robinson c Lynch b Medlycott	85		
†D. L. Bairstow c Ward b Bicknell	32		
C. White b Waqar Younis	2		
C. S. Pickles c and b Bicknell	0		
P. Carrick c Bicknell b Medlycott	64		
P. W. Jarvis b Feltham	7		
D. Gough not out	1		
B 7, l-b 8, w 7	22		
1/14 2/19 3/29 4/55 5/101 6/110 7/114 8/245 9/252	254	1/9	(1 wkt dec.) 26

Bonus points – Yorkshire 3, Surrey 4.

Bowling: *First Innings*—Waqar Younis 24–6–56–3; Bicknell 25–11–40–3; Feltham 18–4–45–2; Murphy 13–4–45–0; Medlycott 16–0–53–2. *Second Innings*—Medlycott 3.4–2–5–1; Feltham 3–0–21–0.

Surrey

Surrey forfeited their first innings.

R. I. Alikhan lbw b Pickles	31
G. S. Clinton c Robinson b White	5
G. P. Thorpe c Blakey b White	44
†D. M. Ward c Blakey b Pickles	71
M. A. Lynch c Bairstow b Jarvis	11
*I. A. Greig c Pickles b White	72
K. T. Medlycott b White	6
M. A. Feltham c Jarvis b White	21
M. P. Bicknell run out	0
Waqar Younis not out	1
A. J. Murphy not out	0
B 6, l-b 6, w 6	18
1/41 2/45 3/147 4/166 5/183 6/204 7/270 8/270 9/279 (9 wkts)	280

Bowling: Jarvis 17–4–60–1; Gough 6–1–24–0; Pickles 12–2–45–2; White 18–2–74–5; Carrick 20–6–65–0.

Umpires: J. C. Balderstone and D. S. Thompsett.

YORKSHIRE v WARWICKSHIRE

At Sheffield, June 20, 21, 22. Yorkshire won by two wickets. Yorkshire 20 pts, Warwickshire 4 pts. Toss: Yorkshire. Rain on all three days encouraged a series of declarations to set up a positive finish. Warwickshire were in trouble at 118 for six, but Ostler and Piper both achieved career-best first-class scores in a partnership worth 81 in 27 overs. Ostler played particularly well, his 61 coming from 114 balls and including ten fours. Hartley's return of six for 57 was also his best at this level. Only Metcalfe played with any assurance in the first innings for Yorkshire, who survived with a good deal of luck a very hostile spell from Donald. In contrast, Moles and Reeve scored readily in Warwickshire's second innings before the declaration set a target of 243 in 55 overs. Yorkshire took some time to get the run-chase under way, Moxon being in for 39 overs for his 46. Kellett, however, played extremely well. Although he needed some fortune after completing his half-century, being missed twice in the 50s off reasonably straightforward chances, he finished unbeaten with 75 from 83 deliveries, having hit two sixes and three fours. Benjamin bowled a long and persistent spell, but Robinson's 28 from seventeen balls turned the game Yorkshire's way, and when Jarvis hit his second ball for six over cover, they had scrambled home with two balls to spare. The match was contested in a very good spirit, both Moles and Moxon walking without hesitation for the thinnest of edges.

Close of play: First day, Warwickshire 207-7 (K. J. Piper 31*, A. A. Donald 2*); Second day, Yorkshire 123-5 (K. Sharp 22*, P. Carrick 1*).

Warwickshire

A. J. Moles c Blakey b Hartley	21	– not out 60
J. D. Ratcliffe b Gough	9	– run out 16
Asif Din lbw b Hartley	0	– lbw b Jarvis 0
G. W. Humpage lbw b Gough	23	– b Jarvis 12
*D. A. Reeve lbw b Moxon	30	– not out 42
R. G. Twose c Blakey b Hartley	15	
D. P. Ostler c Carrick b Gough	61	
†K. J. Piper c Moxon b Hartley	49	
A. A. Donald c Blakey b Hartley	4	
J. E. Benjamin c Moxon b Hartley	1	
T. A. Munton not out	1	
L-b 8, w 2, n-b 7	17	L-b 2, w 1, n-b 1 4
1/33 2/33 3/33 4/88 5/97 6/118 7/199 8/212 9/222	231	1/36 2/38 3/52 (3 wkts dec.) 134

Bonus points – Warwickshire 2, Yorkshire 4.

Bowling: *First Innings*—Jarvis 22–6–52–0; Hartley 21.3–3–57–6; Gough 18–5–36–3; Pickles 9–5–33–0; Moxon 8–2–16–1; Carrick 13–5–29–0. *Second Innings*—Jarvis 8–0–43–2; Hartley 6–1–21–0; Pickles 9.3–0–34–0; Gough 8–0–34–0.

Yorkshire

Batsman	First innings		Second innings	
*M. D. Moxon	c Ratcliffe b Donald	3	c Piper b Benjamin	46
A. A. Metcalfe	c and b Munton	53	c Moles b Benjamin	45
S. A. Kellett	c Benjamin b Asif Din	18	not out	75
†R. J. Blakey	b Munton	1	(5) c Piper b Benjamin	8
P. E. Robinson	c Piper b Benjamin	14	(6) c Humpage b Benjamin	28
K. Sharp	not out	22	(4) c Humpage b Munton	8
P. Carrick	not out	1	(8) run out	3
P. J. Hartley	(did not bat)		(7) b Donald	13
C. S. Pickles	(did not bat)		b Benjamin	1
P. W. Jarvis	(did not bat)		not out	7
	L-b 8, n-b 3	11	B 3, l-b 5, n-b 1	9
1/14 2/64 3/75 4/88 5/105	(5 wkts dec.)	123	1/70 2/135 3/148 4/161 5/197 6/219 7/234 8/235 (8 wkts)	243

D. Gough did not bat.

Bonus points – Warwickshire 2.

Bowling: *First Innings*—Donald 12–3–30–1; Benjamin 16–4–37–1; Munton 18.3–6–34–2; Twose 4–0–9–0; Asif Din 3–1–5–1. *Second Innings*—Donald 13–0–65–1; Benjamin 20.4–2–83–5; Munton 15–1–63–1; Reeve 6–0–24–0.

Umpires: B. Leadbeater and D. O. Oslear.

At Cardiff, June 23, 25, 26. YORKSHIRE beat GLAMORGAN by five wickets.

At Leeds, June 30, July 1, 2. YORKSHIRE drew with INDIANS (See Indian tour section).

YORKSHIRE v NOTTINGHAMSHIRE

At Scarborough, July 4, 5, 6. Nottinghamshire won by five wickets. Nottinghamshire 17 pts, Yorkshire 4 pts. Toss: Nottinghamshire. After the first day had been lost to rain, both sides forfeited an innings. Yorkshire, put in on a typical Scarborough pitch which heavily favoured the batsmen, scored readily. Moxon, enjoying most of the strike for long spells, registered the county's first Championship hundred of the season, reaching three figures in less than three hours, having hit fifteen fours. His 123 came out of an opening stand of 175 in 52 overs with Metcalfe, who also batted well. Nottinghamshire were clearly happy to wait on events and had little trouble in meeting a target of 352 in 94 overs, although only once before had a bigger total been made in the last innings to beat Yorkshire – by Gloucestershire, who compiled 392 for four at Bristol in 1948. Yorkshire, fielding a weakened attack, paid a heavy price for missing Broad, who was 15 when Byas put him down at slip off Hartley. The left-hander completed his fifth century of the season from 165 balls, while Johnson made his 149 at a run a ball, hitting 21 fours. The Broad-Johnson partnership, which put on 187 in 37 overs, effectively settled the contest, and Nottinghamshire won with five wickets and 6.3 overs to spare.

Close of play: First day, No play; Second day, Yorkshire 304-3 (P. E. Robinson 47*, R. J. Blakey 26*).

Yorkshire

*M. D. Moxon	c Robinson b Evans	123
A. A. Metcalfe	c Pick b Evans	75
K. Sharp	c Robinson b Afford	17
P. E. Robinson	not out	73
†R. J. Blakey	not out	46
	L-b 13, n-b 4	17
1/175 2/223 3/223	(3 wkts dec.)	351

D. Byas, C. White, P. Carrick, P. J. Hartley, D. Gough and I. J. Houseman did not bat.

Bonus points – Yorkshire 4, Nottinghamshire 1 (Score at 100 overs: 325-3).

Bowling: Stephenson 6–1–23–0; Cooper 25–5–69–0; Pick 20–2–74–0; Evans 22–4–73–2; Afford 29–7–87–1; Newell 1.2–0–12–0.

Yorkshire forfeited their second innings.

Nottinghamshire

Nottinghamshire forfeited their first innings.

B. C. Broad c Robinson b White	126	K. P. Evans not out	12
M. Newell b Hartley	0		
*R. T. Robinson c Sharp b Carrick	43	B 8, l-b 2, n-b 6	16
P. Johnson c and b White	149		
D. J. R. Martindale b Carrick	4	1/15 2/111 3/298	(5 wkts) 354
F. D. Stephenson not out	4	4/334 5/334	

†B. N. French, K. E. Cooper, R. A. Pick and J. A. Afford did not bat.

Bowling: Hartley 18–2–75–1; Houseman 12–5–40–0; Carrick 23.3–4–69–2; Gough 8–0–46–0; White 22–3–99–2; Byas 4–0–15–0.

Umpires: H. D. Bird and R. Julian.

At Northampton, July 7, 9, 10. YORKSHIRE drew with NORTHAMPTONSHIRE.

At Uxbridge, July 18, 19, 20. YORKSHIRE lost to MIDDLESEX by seven wickets.

At Cheltenham, July 21, 23, 24. YORKSHIRE drew with GLOUCESTERSHIRE.

YORKSHIRE v SOMERSET

At Scarborough, July 25, 26, 27. Drawn. Yorkshire 6 pts, Somerset 6 pts. Toss: Somerset. Yorkshire, still with a much weakened attack, made an impressive start on a pitch offering the bowlers no hint of assistance. However, Hayhurst and Harden then shared in a partnership of 174 in 48 overs for the fourth wicket. Harden's 101 came from 145 balls and included fifteen fours; Hayhurst made his 170 from 285 deliveries with one six and 29 fours. Metcalfe, with 102 from 214 balls as he collected fourteen boundaries, led a solid Yorkshire reply, while Swallow bowled a good spell of off-spin, without luck, against his former county. Somerset recovered from a minor second-innings collapse through some robust hitting from Burns, which ended when Robinson claimed his first wicket in county cricket as Yorkshire assisted in the timing of the declaration. The target was 320 in what became 65 overs and Blakey, hitting two sixes and fifteen fours in 111 from only 155 deliveries, kept Yorkshire in touch. With Blakey and Kellett adding 116 in 28 overs, Yorkshire needed 152 from the last twenty overs, which became 85 from ten. Rose bowled an accurate spell for Somerset, and in an exciting finish Grayson tried to hit the last ball – a yorker from Mallender – for the necessary six. Instead he managed only 2.

Close of play: First day, Yorkshire 25-0 (M. D. Moxon 14*, A. A. Metcalfe 10*); Second day, Somerset 49-1 (S. J. Cook 30*, A. N. Hayhurst 11*).

Somerset

S. J. Cook b Fletcher	21	– c Blakey b Gough	53
P. M. Roebuck b Pickles	11	– c Byas b Fletcher	8
A. N. Hayhurst c Blakey b Gough	170	– c Byas b Pickles	24
*C. J. Tavaré c Robinson b Gough	14	– b Gough	0
R. J. Harden c Pickles b Batty	101	– b Pickles	24
†N. D. Burns c Moxon b Pickles	33	– c Metcalfe b Robinson	72
G. D. Rose c Batty b Gough	35	– c Blakey b Pickles	0
R. P. Lefebvre not out	3	– not out	25
I. G. Swallow not out	3	– not out	12
B 1, l-b 6, w 1, n-b 2	10	L-b 2, n-b 1	3
1/33 2/33 3/77 4/251 5/302 6/376 7/396	(7 wkts dec.) 401	1/21 2/85 3/85 4/85 5/126 6/126 7/206	(7 wkts dec.) 221

A. N. Jones and N. A. Mallender did not bat.

Bonus points – Somerset 4, Yorkshire 2 (Score at 100 overs: 367-5).

Bowling: *First Innings*—Fletcher 22.5–6–47–1; Gough 15–3–77–3; Pickles 20–1–82–2; Batty 22–3–83–1; Moxon 6–0–24–0; Grayson 17–2–66–0; Byas 2–0–15–0. *Second Innings*—Fletcher 5–1–12–1; Gough 13–3–47–2; Pickles 15–1–56–3; Batty 8–2–41–0; Grayson 4–1–23–0; Byas 5–2–14–0; Moxon 3–1–6–0; Metcalfe 1.3–0–10–0; Robinson 1–0–10–1.

Yorkshire

First innings		Second innings	
*M. D. Moxon c Burns b Mallender	23	lbw b Jones	4
A. A. Metcalfe c Jones b Roebuck	102	b Rose	23
†R. J. Blakey c Hayhurst b Swallow	29	c Swallow b Roebuck	111
S. A. Kellett c Roebuck b Swallow	15	c Cook b Rose	57
P. E. Robinson c Burns b Rose	31	c Lefebvre b Hayhurst	44
D. Byas b Jones	36	b Hayhurst	32
A. P. Grayson not out	44	(8) not out	16
C. S. Pickles not out	9	(7) b Mallender	1
D. Gough (did not bat)		not out	7
B 1, l-b 5, n-b 8	14	B 8, l-b 13	21
1/36 2/118 3/159 4/202 5/210 6/277 (6 wkts dec.)	303	1/4 2/57 3/173 4/244 5/274 6/280 7/298 (7 wkts)	316

J. D. Batty and S. D. Fletcher did not bat.

Bonus points – Yorkshire 4, Somerset 2.

Bowling: *First Innings*—Jones 18–1–78–1; Mallender 11–2–42–1; Lefebvre 15–2–40–0; Rose 15–2–41–1; Swallow 25.5–6–71–2; Roebuck 11–3–25–1. *Second Innings*—Jones 12–1–54–1; Mallender 15–0–69–1; Lefebvre 16–5–52–0; Rose 10–2–41–2; Swallow 7–2–35–0; Roebuck 2–0–25–1; Hayhurst 3–0–19–2.

Umpires: M. J. Kitchen and P. B. Wight.

YORKSHIRE v LEICESTERSHIRE

At Sheffield, July 28, 30, 31. Leicestershire won by eight wickets. Leicestershire 24 pts, Yorkshire 5 pts. Toss: Leicestershire. Boon, missed by Hartley from a hard return chance when 6, and Briers provided the visitors with a sound platform on a good pitch with plenty of pace. Potter also took full advantage of an inexperienced attack, his unbeaten 109 coming from 192 balls with two sixes and eight fours. Only Hartley, the sole capped bowler, threatened the Leicestershire batsmen's security. When Yorkshire replied, Agnew swept through some feeble resistance to record his best figures of the season. Despite an unbeaten 36 by Grayson, who displayed a sound batting technique in his second Championship match, Yorkshire had to follow on for the first time in four years. They did little better at the second attempt, until Byas and Kellett put on 83 in 36 overs for the fifth wicket. Even so, only a late flourish from Pickles stretched Yorkshire's innings into the third afternoon. Wicket-keeper Nixon equalled the Leicestershire record for catches in a match with eight, and Mullally bowled accurately for his career-best four for 59.

Close of play: First day, Yorkshire 18-1 (M. D. Moxon 12*, S. A. Kellett 5*); Second day, Yorkshire 116-4 (S. A. Kellett 53*, D. Byas 23*).

Leicestershire

First innings		Second innings	
T. J. Boon lbw b Hartley	76	c Moxon b Pickles	11
*N. E. Briers c Batty b Hartley	45	b Hartley	21
J. J. Whitaker c Byas b Hartley	23	not out	38
P. Willey c Blakey b Hartley	47	not out	18
L. Potter not out	109		
J. D. R. Benson lbw b Hartley	0		
W. K. M. Benjamin c Kellett b Batty	16		
†P. A. Nixon b Batty	33		
J. P. Agnew not out	4		
B 1, l-b 10, w 2, n-b 10	23	N-b 2	2
1/121 2/152 3/161 4/271 5/271 6/294 7/372 (7 wkts dec.)	376	1/27 2/35 (2 wkts)	90

G. J. Parsons and A. D. Mullally did not bat.

Bonus points – Leicestershire 4, Yorkshire 3.

Bowling: *First Innings*—Hartley 26–2–106–5; Gough 15–3–53–0; Pickles 20–7–65–0; Batty 32–4–124–2; Moxon 5–0–12–0; Grayson 1–0–5–0. *Second Innings*—Hartley 7–1–20–1; Gough 7–1–34–0; Pickles 4–0–9–1; Byas 4–0–20–0; Moxon 2–0–7–0.

Yorkshire

*M. D. Moxon c Nixon b Benjamin	21	– b Mullally	17
A. A. Metcalfe c Benson b Agnew	1	– c Benson b Agnew	1
S. A. Kellett c Nixon b Mullally	47	– (4) c Nixon b Mullally	54
†R. J. Blakey c Nixon b Agnew	36	– (3) c Nixon b Mullally	12
P. E. Robinson c Potter b Mullally	7	– c Nixon b Mullally	4
D. Byas run out	5	– b Willey	81
A. P. Grayson not out	36	– c Nixon b Parsons	11
C. S. Pickles lbw b Agnew	14	– not out	56
P. J. Hartley c Nixon b Agnew	0	– c Willey b Agnew	7
D. Gough lbw b Agnew	24	– c Briers b Agnew	2
J. D. Batty b Benjamin	2	– run out	0
B 1, l-b 2, w 1, n-b 3	7	B 7, l-b 7, n-b 3	17
1/6 2/34 3/107 4/107 5/118 6/130 7/158 8/158 9/193	200	1/1 2/33 3/38 4/50 5/133 6/156 7/218 8/247 9/249	262

Bonus points – Yorkshire 2, Leicestershire 4.

Bowling: *First Innings*—Benjamin 19.5–3–78–2; Agnew 21–4–54–5; Parsons 7–2–20–0; Mullally 15–2–45–2. *Second Innings*—Agnew 22–4–54–3; Benjamin 15–5–40–0; Parsons 23–7–61–1; Mullally 25–9–59–4; Willey 16–4–29–1; Potter 4–2–5–0.

Umpires: K. J. Lyons and P. B. Wight.

YORKSHIRE v LANCASHIRE

At Leeds, August 4, 6, 7. Drawn. Yorkshire 5 pts, Lancashire 8 pts. Toss: Lancashire. A solid batting performance on an easy-paced pitch put Lancashire in control of the match. Mendis, Fowler and Atherton made sure of a substantial total, and DeFreitas added impetus with 66 from 85 balls, hitting three sixes and six fours. Carrick bowled his 36 overs straight through, with breaks for only lunch and tea, and gained some slow turn. Despite the absence of DeFreitas, who had bruised his left big toe while batting, Lancashire brought about a remarkable Yorkshire collapse. Atherton's leg-spin claimed five for 26, his best bowling figures to date, and only a vigorous effort by the tail prevented total disaster. When Yorkshire followed on, Metcalfe, whose 146 came from 325 balls and included sixteen fours, organised a revival, to which Pickles added substance after another middle-order failure. Lancashire were left needing 148 in thirteen overs. They made a brave effort as Lloyd struck a superb 70 from 38 balls, hitting four sixes and two fours, and adding 74 in six overs with Atherton. Yorkshire had eight men on the boundary, and while this tactic allowed a number of twos, the target proved just too stiff. As wickets fell Lancashire, who had bowled their overs slowly throughout, settled for a draw.

Close of play: First day, Yorkshire 26-1 (A. A. Metcalfe 12*, D. Gough 0*); Second day, Yorkshire 90-0 (M. D. Moxon 32*, A. A. Metcalfe 50*).

Lancashire

G. D. Mendis c Metcalfe b Gough	54	– lbw b Fletcher	10
G. Fowler c Moxon b Carrick	43	– c Moxon b Fletcher	6
M. A. Atherton c Kellett b Jarvis	64	– (6) st Blakey b Fletcher	25
N. H. Fairbrother c Fletcher b Carrick	5	– c Blakey b Jarvis	7
G. D. Lloyd c Blakey b Pickles	36	– (3) c Pickles b Jarvis	70
M. Watkinson b Jarvis	33	– (5) run out	1
P. A. J. DeFreitas st Blakey b Carrick	66	– b Jarvis	2
†W. K. Hegg st Blakey b Carrick	29	– not out	0
*D. P. Hughes b Jarvis	14		
P. J. Martin not out	10		
B. P. Patterson not out	4		
L-b 10, n-b 1	11	B 1, l-b 11	12
1/94 2/116 3/123 4/195 5/230 6/253 7/328 8/349 9/355	(9 wkts dec.) 369	1/15 2/26 3/49 4/55 5/129 6/131 7/133	(7 wkts) 133

Bonus points – Lancashire 4, Yorkshire 4.

Bowling: *First Innings*—Jarvis 21–2–91–3; Fletcher 15–3–55–0; Pickles 16–4–69–1; Gough 12–3–37–1; Carrick 36–10–107–4. *Second Innings*—Jarvis 6.4–0–59–3; Fletcher 6–0–62–3.

Yorkshire

First innings		Second innings	
*M. D. Moxon c Fowler b Atherton	14	– b Patterson	39
A. A. Metcalfe c Atherton b Patterson	31	– c Atherton b Watkinson	146
D. Gough lbw b Patterson	3	– (10) c Fowler b Atherton	13
†R. J. Blakey c Fairbrother b Atherton	22	– (3) b Watkinson	3
S. A. Kellett b Watkinson	25	– (8) run out	15
P. E. Robinson c Atherton b Watkinson	2	– (4) b Martin	11
D. Byas c Hughes b Atherton	0	– (5) c Hegg b Martin	9
P. Carrick not out	34	– (6) b Martin	5
C. S. Pickles b Martin	21	– (7) c Fowler b Watkinson	39
P. W. Jarvis c Fowler b Atherton	27	– (9) not out	20
S. D. Fletcher c Hegg b Atherton	0	– c Patterson b Atherton	0
B 1, l-b 1, n-b 7	9	B 3, l-b 11, n-b 14	28
1/23 2/41 3/50 4/94 5/98 6/100 7/100 8/154 9/188	188	1/115 2/118 3/155 4/167 5/197 6/262 7/283 8/296 9/328	328

Bonus points – Yorkshire 1, Lancashire 4.

Bowling: *First Innings*—Patterson 18–3–77–2; Martin 16–2–54–1; Atherton 11–5–26–5; Watkinson 11–4–29–2. *Second Innings*—Patterson 18–0–88–1; Watkinson 38–14–94–3; Atherton 27.2–5–71–2; Hughes 9–6–6–0; Martin 18–1–48–3; DeFreitas 2–0–7–0.

Umpires: B. Leadbeater and N. T. Plews.

At Eastbourne, August 8, 9, 10. YORKSHIRE beat SUSSEX by an innings and 5 runs.

YORKSHIRE v ESSEX

At Middlesbrough, August 11, 13. Essex won by an innings and 11 runs. Essex 24 pts, Yorkshire 4 pts. Toss: Yorkshire. Nothing went right for Yorkshire from the moment Moxon elected to field first. The pitch, which looked slightly green and hard, did not play as expected. Still, Essex would have been in trouble had Waugh not struck a career-best 207 not out, the highest score on the ground since first-class cricket was introduced there in 1956. The Australian batted for 346 minutes, faced 288 balls and hit four sixes and 26 fours. He shared two crucial partnerships, 123 with Stephenson and 92 with Garnham. Although Metcalfe and Sharp gave Yorkshire a solid start with a second-wicket stand worth 91 in 27 overs, they were forced to follow on for the third time in four matches. There was some uneven bounce, and Such achieved slow turn with his off-spin, but the conditions did not explain why Yorkshire lost nineteen wickets for 239 runs in 67 overs. The failure of Moxon, who received two balls which lifted sharply, appeared to unsettle his colleagues, and Essex held some fine catches as Foster, Pringle and Andrew made the most of Yorkshire's uncertainty. With Essex claiming the extra half-hour, the match ended on the second day.

Close of play: First day, Essex 308-8 (M. E. Waugh 178*, J. H. Childs 0*).

Essex

N. Shahid c Robinson b Jarvis	3
J. P. Stephenson b Gough	62
P. J. Prichard b Jarvis	1
M. E. Waugh not out	207
N. Hussain c Blakey b Pickles	6
†M. A. Garnham c Robinson b Gough	35
*D. R. Pringle c Byas b Pickles	9
N. A. Foster c Robinson b Carrick	8
S. J. W. Andrew c Robinson b Carrick	0
J. H. Childs c Byas b Jarvis	11
P. M. Such b Jarvis	2
L-b 5, w 1, n-b 1	7
1/20 2/22 3/145 4/160 5/252 6/279 7/306 8/308 9/343	351

Bonus points – Essex 4, Yorkshire 3 (Score at 100 overs: 343-8).

Bowling: Jarvis 23.5–4–53–4; Hartley 20–2–71–0; Pickles 20–5–68–2; Gough 14–1–54–2; Carrick 22–6–88–2; Moxon 3–0–12–0.

Yorkshire

*M. D. Moxon c Stephenson b Foster	1	– c Waugh b Pringle	27
A. A. Metcalfe c Shahid b Pringle	60	– c Garnham b Andrew	0
K. Sharp b Such	42	– c Pringle b Foster	16
P. E. Robinson b Pringle	3	– c Stephenson b Andrew	39
†R. J. Blakey c Prichard b Pringle	5	– c Garnham b Andrew	26
D. Byas lbw b Foster	7	– c Shahid b Childs	6
P. Carrick b Such	19	– c Shahid b Andrew	3
C. S. Pickles c Hussain b Such	20	– c Shahid b Such	19
P. J. Hartley lbw b Foster	0	– c Garnham b Andrew	5
P. W. Jarvis not out	8	– b Such	0
D. Gough lbw b Foster	1	– not out	0
L-b 14	14	B 8, l-b 9, n-b 2	19
1/10 2/101 3/104 4/119 5/120 6/143 7/151 8/151 9/171	180	1/2 2/30 3/57 4/109 5/124 6/126 7/154 8/160 9/160	160

Bonus points – Yorkshire 1, Essex 4.

Bowling: *First Innings*—Foster 16–3–63–4; Andrew 6–1–28–0; Pringle 11–6–15–3; Childs 5–0–26–0; Such 19–6–34–3. *Second Innings*—Foster 6–0–14–1; Andrew 13.1–2–55–5; Such 11–3–39–2; Pringle 6–1–18–1; Childs 4–0–17–1.

Umpires: B. Hassan and A. A. Jones.

At Manchester, August 18, 19, 20, 21. YORKSHIRE drew with LANCASHIRE.

YORKSHIRE v MIDDLESEX

At Leeds, August 23, 24, 25, 27. Middlesex won by 64 runs. Middlesex 23 pts, Yorkshire 5 pts. Toss: Middlesex. Haynes, who achieved 2,000 first-class runs for the season when 30, plundered a weakened Yorkshire attack on an easy-paced pitch, making his first 51 runs out of a total of 61 and going on to hit a hundred before lunch. His 131 took only 145 balls and included 26 boundaries. Gatting, despite a hamstring strain, made sure that the tempo did not slacken while Gough was rewarded for his persistence with career-best bowling figures of four for 68. Moxon held the Yorkshire reply together, but Hughes, during a long spell, broke through the batting, taking three for 8 in 22 balls. The pressure was kept up by the accurate Tufnell. Moxon's 95, which included one six and fourteen fours, came from 206 deliveries, and there was some spirited resistance from the bottom half of the order. Haynes and Roseberry tightened Middlesex's grip with an opening partnership of 104, while Emburey hammered a brisk 51 from 84 balls. Yorkshire had little chance of making the 331 needed for victory and Cowans, claiming two wickets for no runs in less than two overs, soon had them in trouble. Robinson battled defiantly in a lost cause, but the inexperienced Taylor, bowling an effective line, cut through the middle order and took five wickets in an innings for the first time.

Close of play: First day, Middlesex 377; Second day, Yorkshire 229-6 (P. Carrick 33*, C. S. Pickles 7*); Third day, Yorkshire 13-0 (M. D. Moxon 5*, A. A. Metcalfe 7*).

Middlesex

D. L. Haynes lbw b Pickles	131	– b Batty	57
M. A. Roseberry c Blakey b Gough	2	– c Grayson b Gough	80
M. R. Ramprakash c Blakey b Jarvis	29	– c Robinson b Batty	29
K. R. Brown c Byas b Jarvis	56	– c Pickles b Batty	0
*M. W. Gatting c Robinson b Carrick	91	– (7) lbw b Gough	10
†P. R. Downton b Pickles	12	– (5) b Jarvis	1
J. E. Emburey lbw b Gough	0	– (6) c Metcalfe b Jarvis	51
S. P. Hughes c Moxon b Jarvis	4	– (9) not out	10
P. C. R. Tufnell c Grayson b Gough	37	– (8) c Robinson b Batty	5
C. W. Taylor not out	0		
N. G. Cowans c Metcalfe b Gough	0		
B 1, l-b 14	15	B 5, l-b 2, w 1	8
1/10 2/116 3/182 4/270 5/304 6/305 7/328 8/373 9/377	377	1/104 2/156 3/158 (8 wkts dec.) 4/159 5/190 6/208 7/219 8/251	251

Bonus points – Middlesex 4, Yorkshire 3 (Score at 100 overs: 355-7).

Bowling: *First Innings*—Jarvis 23–4–74–3; Gough 17.5–2–68–4; Pickles 20–2–80–2; Moxon 2–0–23–0; Byas 2–0–14–0; Carrick 29–8–61–1; Batty 13–3–42–0. *Second Innings*—Jarvis 16–3–51–2; Gough 19–6–43–2; Carrick 14–5–35–0; Pickles 9–1–39–0; Batty 23–4–76–4.

Yorkshire

*M. D. Moxon c Downton b Tufnell	95	– c Hughes b Cowans	7
A. A. Metcalfe c Downton b Hughes	26	– lbw b Cowans	26
A. P. Grayson b Hughes	4	– c sub b Cowans	18
P. E. Robinson c Downton b Hughes	0	– c Downton b Taylor	72
†R. J. Blakey c and b Tufnell	14	– c Emburey b Taylor	16
D. Byas c Emburey b Taylor	36	– lbw b Cowans	12
P. Carrick c Emburey b Hughes	34	– c Downton b Taylor	20
C. S. Pickles c and b Cowans	37	– c Emburey b Taylor	1
P. W. Jarvis b Cowans	14	– not out	43
D. Gough lbw b Hughes	21	– lbw b Cowans	9
J. D. Batty not out	0	– c Downton b Taylor	21
B 1, l-b 9, w 1, n-b 6	17	B 10, l-b 8, w 1, n-b 2	21
1/63 2/73 3/81 4/108 5/158 6/206 7/238 8/266 9/294	298	1/34 2/34 3/60 4/97 5/125 6/172 7/176 8/192 9/233	266

Bonus points – Yorkshire 2, Middlesex 3 (Score at 100 overs: 244-7).

Bowling: *First Innings*—Cowans 22–6–55–2; Hughes 28.2–5–101–5; Taylor 14–2–46–1; Emburey 19–6–43–0; Tufnell 26–9–41–2; Haynes 2–0–2–0. *Second Innings*—Cowans 21–6–67–5; Hughes 23–2–66–0; Emburey 12–2–32–0; Tufnell 21–5–50–0; Taylor 14.5–4–33–5.

Umpires: J. W. Holder and D. S. Thompsett.

At Scarborough, September 1. YORKSHIRE lost to MICHAEL PARKINSON'S WORLD XI by 7 runs (See Other Matches, 1990).

At Scarborough, September 6. YORKSHIRE beat THE YORKSHIREMEN by eight wickets (See Other Matches, 1990).

YORKSHIRE v DERBYSHIRE

At Scarborough, September 7, 8, 9, 10. Yorkshire won by four wickets. Yorkshire 22 pts, Derbyshire 4 pts. Toss: Derbyshire. Much of the first day was washed out by rain, but next day Derbyshire scored freely in ideal batting conditions, with Yorkshire conceding three centuries in an innings for the first time since 1986 against Nottinghamshire at Worksop. Bishop struck some lusty blows in reaching his maiden hundred from 99 deliveries. Derbyshire were equally vulnerable in the field as Metcalfe and Robinson shared a partnership of 293 in 70 overs – the best for the county's third wicket since 1939. Yorkshire declared 98 behind and were content to sit back and wait for a target, helping the visitors along with some gentle bowling which O'Gorman and Roberts cheerfully despatched in a stand worth 109 in 23 overs. Yorkshire required 300 in 59 overs, and Moxon gave them a splendid start with 94 from 122 balls, hitting a six and eleven fours. Blakey maintained the momentum with an unbeaten 91 from 88 deliveries, putting on 70 in eleven overs with Carrick for the sixth wicket. For Derbyshire, Bishop and Malcolm bowled too short on a slow pitch and were inevitably expensive, although Yorkshire had only one ball to spare in the end. Carrick became the eighth Yorkshire player to complete the double of 9,000 first-class runs and 900 wickets for the county.

Close of play: First day, Derbyshire 114-2 (J. E. Morris 88*, C. J. Adams 0*); Second day, Yorkshire 8-0 (M. D. Moxon 6*, A. A. Metcalfe 1*); Third day, Derbyshire 13-0 (J. E. Morris 8*, P. D. Bowler 1*).

Derbyshire

P. D. Bowler c Blakey b Jarvis	4	(2) c Blakey b Jarvis	13
J. E. Morris c and b Carrick	109	(1) c Byas b Hartley	36
T. J. G. O'Gorman b Pickles	21	not out	82
C. J. Adams c Metcalfe b Carrick	101	c Robinson b Hartley	17
B. Roberts b Pickles	31	not out	44
*K. J. Barnett c Robinson b Carrick	47		
†K. M. Krikken c Pickles b Carrick	35		
I. R. Bishop not out	103		
A. E. Warner not out	10		
L-b 13, n-b 1	14	B 2, l-b 5, n-b 2	9
1/4 2/95 3/158 4/229 5/323 6/326 7/411 (7 wkts dec.)	475	1/47 2/61 3/92 (3 wkts dec.)	201

D. E. Malcolm and G. Miller did not bat.

Bonus points – Derbyshire 4, Yorkshire 2 (Score at 100 overs: 337-6).

Bowling: *First Innings*—Jarvis 29–1–124–1; Hartley 23–2–109–0; Pickles 20.4–4–72–2; Carrick 39–14–90–4; Batty 17–3–67–0. *Second Innings*—Jarvis 12–4–32–1; Hartley 15–6–58–2; Batty 11–2–42–0; Carrick 8–2–10–0; Robinson 2.3–0–18–0; Metcalfe 2–0–34–0.

Yorkshire

*M. D. Moxon b Bishop	14	c Adams b Miller	94
A. A. Metcalfe not out	150	lbw b Warner	32
S. A. Kellett b Warner	22	b Warner	2
P. E. Robinson not out	150	run out	14
†R. J. Blakey (did not bat)		not out	91
D. Byas (did not bat)		c Krikken b Malcolm	13
P. Carrick (did not bat)		b Bishop	31
C. S. Pickles (did not bat)		not out	4
B 9, l-b 18, w 7, n-b 7	41	B 9, l-b 7, n-b 3	19
1/34 2/84 (2 wkts dec.)	377	1/83 2/109 3/148 4/178 5/225 6/295 (6 wkts)	300

P. J. Hartley, P. W. Jarvis and J. D. Batty did not bat.

Bonus points – Yorkshire 4 (Score at 100 overs: 372-2).

Bowling: *First Innings*—Bishop 15–3–50–1; Malcolm 15–1–56–0; Warner 14–3–43–1; Miller 25–2–92–0; Barnett 21–1–58–0; Morris 9–0–44–0; Adams 1.4–0–7–0. *Second Innings*—Bishop 16.5–1–61–1; Malcolm 16–1–83–1; Warner 16–0–64–2; Barnett 1–0–8–0; Miller 9–0–68–1.

Umpires: H. D. Bird and J. D. Bond.

At Nottingham, September 18, 19, 20, 21. YORKSHIRE beat NOTTINGHAMSHIRE by four wickets.

OXFORD UNIVERSITY 1990

[*Bill Smith*

Back row: L. J. Lenham (*coach*), R. W. D. Trevelyan, P. S. Gerrans, W. M. van der Merwe, G. J. Turner, P. D. Lunn, D. M. Curtis, M. J. Russell.
Front row: I. M. Henderson, S. D. Weale, R. E. Morris (*captain*), D. A. Hagan, M. A. Crawley.

THE UNIVERSITIES IN 1990

OXFORD

President: M. J. K. Smith (St Edmund Hall)
Hon. Treasurer: Dr S. R. Porter (Nuffield College)

Captain: R. E. Morris (Dyffryn Conwy, Llanrwst and Oriel)
Secretary: S. A. Almaer (Ilford County HS and St Catherine's)

Captain for 1991: G. J. Turner (St Stithian's, University of Cape Town and St Anne's)
Secretary: M. J. Russell (Medina HS, Isle of Wight, and Pembroke)

The season heralded the revival, long overdue, of Oxford University as respected opponents in English first-class cricket. The excellent pitches prepared at The Parks by head groundsman Richard Sula and the controversial new ball played their part, but there were other factors, too. Not the least were the willingness of St Anne's to admit sportsmen of high academic ability, the return of several old Blues as post-graduates, and the use of a full-time coach, Les Lenham, who instilled a more positive and professional attitude. It was at his suggestion that all players wore sweaters resembling those awarded to Blues, and although some spectators regretted the loss of a multicoloured array, the uniformity was accepted by the team.

The 1990 captain, Russell Morris, had eight Blues at his disposal, four of them post-graduates, while the new intake included Willem van der Merwe and Graeme Turner, both of whom had played for Western Province in South Africa. This provided Morris with a well-balanced side little affected by the demands of examiners.

Thanks to their strongest batting for many years, Oxford were unbeaten by a first-class side, a feat they had not achieved since the Second World War. The line-up was headed by the 1989 captain, Mark Crawley, who enjoyed an outstanding season with an average of more than 94 in his games at The Parks, where he hit the University's two centuries – against Glamorgan and Leicestershire – and 91 not out against Lancashire. Mike Kilborn's 83 against Glamorgan and 95 against Lancashire were his highest first-class scores, Morris's 96 against Surrey was his best in senior cricket, and van der Merwe, a powerful left-hander, gave the counties the sort of punishment more often inflicted on university bowlers. One result of this strength was that Morris began to bat when he won the toss, a shock to opponents accustomed to batting first. Their score of 289 for seven declared in the opening match was Oxford's highest in first-class games in The Parks for five years, and they passed 300 on three occasions. An average of 35 runs scored for each wicket lost, against 17 the previous year, underlined the improvement.

The bowling was more hostile and varied than in 1989. The new ball was shared by van der Merwe, Iain Henderson and Phil Gerrans, backed by Crawley who, having taken just one wicket in the previous two seasons, emerged as the leading wicket-taker with seventeen. The bulk of the slow bowling was shared by the off-spinners, Turner and Henry Davies, and Simon Weale (slow left-arm). With conditions so much in favour of batsmen, the almost identical haul of wickets to that of 1989, at a similar cost, was a real achievement. There was also an improvement in the Oxford out-cricket, though wicket-keeping remained weak.

In 1991 Turner, the new captain, will be without Crawley, van der Merwe (winner of the Gold Award in the Benson and Hedges match against Yorkshire), and Henderson, who have completed their studies. However, several Freshmen with outstanding credentials will be in residence, and there are high hopes that the renaissance will continue. – Paton Fenton.

OXFORD UNIVERSITY RESULTS

First-class matches – Played 9: Drawn 9.

FIRST-CLASS AVERAGES

BATTING AND FIELDING

	Birthplace	*M*	*I*	*NO*	*R*	*HI*	*Avge*	*Ct/St*
M. A. Crawley	*Newton-le-Willows*	9	10	3	620	105*	88.57	8
W. M. van der Merwe	*Rustenburg, SA*	7	7	3	272	84	68.00	4
M. J. Kilborn	*Gunnedah, Australia*	5	6	1	279	95	55.80	4
I. M. Henderson	*Glapthorn*	6	4	3	46	44	46.00	2
R. E. Morris	*St Asaph*	8	10	1	370	96	41.11	1
P. D. Lunn	*Oxford*	8	10	4	184	44*	30.66	1
G. J. Turner	*Bulawayo, Rhodesia*	8	10	0	258	59	25.80	4
D. M. Curtis	*Salisbury, Rhodesia*	4	4	0	89	43	22.25	0
H. R. Davies		4	4	2	36	24	18.00	0
D. A. Hagan	*Wide Open*	9	12	0	175	47	14.58	2
P. S. Gerrans	*Melbourne, Australia*	8	7	0	95	39	13.57	3
S. D. Weale	*Knightsbridge*	5	4	2	24	13	12.00	0

Also batted: S. A. Almaer (*Wanstead*) (1 match) 4 (2 ct); S. Chauhan (*Delhi, India*) (3 matches) 25, 4; J. E. McGrady (*Ryton, Co. Durham*) (6 matches) 14, 1 (2 st); M. J. Russell (*Lincoln*) (4 matches) 4, 4, 2 (1 ct); R. W. D. Trevelyan (*Folkestone*) (3 matches) 0 (2 ct); A. L. C. Winchester (1 match) 0*.

* *Signifies not out.*

M. A. Crawley played the two three-figure innings for Oxford University.

BOWLING

	O	*M*	*R*	*W*	*BB*	*Avge*
M. A. Crawley	190.2	30	673	17	6-92	39.58
G. J. Turner	177.2	36	680	10	3-100	68.00
P. S. Gerrans	181	31	618	9	3-86	68.66
I. M. Henderson	105.2	9	469	6	3-102	78.16

Also bowled: S. Chauhan 15–1–58–1; D. M. Curtis 1–0–8–0; H. R. Davies 54–6–261–3; P. D. Lunn 23–4–92–2; W. M. van der Merwe 112–23–341–3; S. D. Weale 50–8–251–1; A. L. C. Winchester 13–0–81–0.

OXFORD UNIVERSITY v GLAMORGAN

At Oxford, April 14, 16, 17. Drawn. Toss: Oxford University. Glamorgan responded to the invitation to bat with two century stands in succession. Morris put on 123 with Butcher and then 103 with Holmes, completing his own hundred in 298 minutes and striking fifteen fours. Crawley, bowling at a steady medium pace, took six of the seven wickets which fell before the county's declaration at 352, and before the second day was over he had begun the game's next hundred partnership, in company with Kilborn. He next added 74 with Hagan, who returned at the fall of the third wicket after being hit on the hand by the first ball of the innings. Crawley's unbeaten century, which took nearly five and a half hours, contained ten fours and helped his team to their highest first-class score in The Parks for five years. When Oxford declared Glamorgan made 55 without loss in the remaining half-hour of play.

Close of play: First day, Glamorgan 188-1 (H. Morris 73*, G. C. Holmes 36*); Second day, Oxford University 90-2 (M. J. Kilborn 45*, M. A. Crawley 16*).

Glamorgan

*A. R. Butcher c Lunn b Crawley	60		
H. Morris c and b Crawley	103		
G. C. Holmes c van der Merwe b Turner	62		
M. P. Maynard b Crawley	40	(2) not out	32
I. Smith c van der Merwe b Crawley	17	(1) not out	18
H. A. G. Anthony c Gerrans b Crawley	19		
N. G. Cowley c and b Crawley	13		
†M. L. Roberts not out	5		
B 9, l-b 9, w 5, n-b 10	33	L-b 2, n-b 3	5
1/123 2/226 3/278 4/301 5/325 6/337 7/352 (7 wkts dec.)	352	(no wkt)	55

S. J. Dennis, M. Frost and S. R. Barwick did not bat.

Bowling: *First Innings*—van der Merwe 15–3–43–0; Henderson 9–2–36–0; Gerrans 27–7–80–0; Crawley 27.3–4–92–6; Turner 16–3–52–1; Weale 10–3–31–0. *Second Innings*—Henderson 4–1–8–0; van der Merwe 2–0–24–0; Turner 2–0–21–0.

Oxford University

D. A. Hagan c Holmes b Cowley	47
*R. E. Morris c Cowley b Dennis	16
M. J. Kilborn c Roberts b Holmes	83
G. J. Turner lbw b Barwick	5
M. A. Crawley not out	103
P. D. Lunn lbw b Dennis	5
W. M. van der Merwe lbw b Anthony	1
P. S. Gerrans b Anthony	0
S. D. Weale not out	7
B 2, l-b 9, w 2, n-b 9	22
1/41 2/54 3/165 4/239 5/262 6/263 7/263 (7 wkts dec.)	289

I. M. Henderson and †J. E. McGrady did not bat.

D. A. Hagan, when 0, retired hurt at 0 and resumed at 165.

Bowling: Anthony 20.4–5–72–2; Frost 20–5–33–0; Cowley 20–6–49–1; Barwick 15–6–16–1; Dennis 24–6–51–2; Smith 6–0–24–0; Holmes 8–2–33–1.

Umpires: J. D. Bond and A. G. T. Whitehead.

OXFORD UNIVERSITY v SOMERSET

At Oxford, April 18, 19, 20. Drawn. Toss: Oxford University. Rain restricted play to fewer than five hours on the last two days of this match, which had begun promisingly for Oxford when they took three wickets for 1 run, reducing Somerset to 58 for three. But their bowlers' success was put in perspective by former Blue Tavaré and Harden, who put on 188 for the next wicket. Replying to a total of 328 for six declared, Oxford also lost three early wickets, for 14 runs, before their former captains, Kilborn and Crawley, came to the rescue with a stand of 69. Lunn and van der Merwe increased the score to 144 in the time left by rain.

Close of play: First day, Oxford University 6-0 (D. A. Hagan 0*, S. A. Almaer 4*); Second day, Oxford University 60-3 (M. J. Kilborn 27*, M. A. Crawley 18*).

Somerset

S. J. Cook lbw b Gerrans	28	†N. D. Burns not out	28
P. M. Roebuck c Crawley b van der Merwe	26	G. D. Rose c Crawley b Turner	32
J. J. E. Hardy c Almaer b Gerrans	0	B 10, l-b 8, w 3, n-b 11	32
*C. J. Tavaré c Almaer b Henderson	83	1/57 2/57 3/58 (6 wkts dec.)	328
R. J. Harden c and b Henderson	99	4/246 5/277 6/328	

R. P. Lefebvre, I. G. Swallow, N. A. Mallender and A. N. Jones did not bat.

Bowling: van der Merwe 17–5–44–1; Henderson 17–1–92–2; Gerrans 24–8–56–2; Turner 11.2–4–41–1; Crawley 13–0–63–0; Weale 4–1–14–0.

Oxford University

D. A. Hagan c Roebuck b Jones	7	W. M. van der Merwe not out	18
S. A. Almaer b Rose	4		
M. J. Kilborn c and b Swallow	37	B 2, l-b 15, w 1, n-b 8	26
G. J. Turner b Jones	0		
*M. A. Crawley b Lefebvre	33	1/8 2/14 3/14 (5 wkts)	144
P. D. Lunn not out	19	4/83 5/95	

S. D. Weale, I. M. Henderson, †J. E. McGrady and P. S. Gerrans did not bat.

Bowling: Jones 16–8–17–2; Mallender 16–2–30–0; Rose 14–2–37–1; Lefebvre 13–5–23–1; Swallow 13–6–12–1; Roebuck 5–2–8–0.

Umpires: J. D. Bond and A. G. T. Whitehead.

†At Oxford, April 24, 25. Drawn. Berkshire 205 for nine dec. (M. L. Simmons 67; G. J. Turner five for 57) and 218 for six dec. (J. Barrett 77, D. J. M. Mercer 100 not out); Oxford University 209 for five dec. (W. M. van der Merwe 90 not out, G. J. Turner 81) and 179 for seven (M. J. Russell 57 not out).

OXFORD UNIVERSITY v HAMPSHIRE

At Oxford, May 3, 4, 5. Drawn. Toss: Hampshire. Oxford's bowling was ravaged as Terry and Chris Smith ran up 264 for the first wicket. After reaching a hundred which included fourteen fours, Smith threw caution to the wind and thrashed five sixes and three fours in fifteen balls before being stumped for 148. Terry hit two sixes and twelve fours in his 112, and Gower and Robin Smith kept up the pace with 108 from 22 overs for the third wicket. Hampshire passed 400 before declaring, but Oxford replied with 324, their highest total against a first-class county since 1982, when they made 332 for five declared against Northamptonshire, and their first first-class score over 300 for five years. The captain, Morris, completed his first half-century of the season, and Turner his maiden fifty for the University. The latter's fellow South African, van der Merwe, then took full advantage of an attack which had been reduced to a seamer and two slow left-arm bowlers, hitting two sixes and thirteen fours in his 84. Such was the authority of his batting that Russell contributed only 4 as they added 46 for the seventh wicket. Hampshire's second innings was dominated by an unbeaten 69 from their West Indian bowler, Joseph.

Close of play: First day, Hampshire 437-4 (M. C. J. Nicholas 37*, R. J. Parks 5*); Second day, Oxford University 225-6 (W. M. van der Merwe 38*, M. J. Russell 0*).

Hampshire

V. P. Terry c and b Turner	112		
C. L. Smith st McGrady b Turner	148		
D. I. Gower c and b Crawley	72	(1) c van der Merwe b Turner	46
R. A. Smith c van der Merwe b Lunn	44		
*M. C. J. Nicholas not out	37	(2) c Kilborn b Davies	47
†R. J. Parks not out	5	(3) c Kilborn b Davies	8
R. J. Maru (did not bat)	–	(4) b Davies	1
L. A. Joseph (did not bat)	–	(5) not out	69
I. J. Turner (did not bat)	–	(6) c Russell b Turner	14
K. J. Shine (did not bat)	–	(7) not out	24
B 9, l-b 4, n-b 6	19	B 1, l-b 4, n-b 1	6
1/264 2/275 3/383 4/427 (4 wkts dec.)	437	1/57 2/82 3/86 4/125 5/164 (5 wkts dec.)	215

C. A. Connor did not bat.

Bowling: *First Innings*—van der Merwe 22–5–77–0; Winchester 10–0–50–0; Crawley 20–1–100–1; Turner 32–4–148–2; Lunn 13–2–49–1. *Second Innings*—van der Merwe 6–2–9–0; Winchester 3–0–31–0; Crawley 3–0–16–0; Turner 23–5–61–2; Davies 23–4–93–3.

Oxford University

D. A. Hagan c R. A. Smith b Maru	14
*R. E. Morris c Parks b Shine	61
M. J. Kilborn c C. L. Smith b Turner	17
G. J. Turner c and b C. L. Smith	59
M. A. Crawley c and b Maru	9
P. D. Lunn c Maru b Turner	16
W. M. van der Merwe c C. L. Smith b Maru	84
M. J. Russell b Shine	4
H. R. Davies c Nicholas b C. L. Smith	24
†J. E. McGrady c Gower b Maru	14
A. L. C. Winchester not out	0
B 4, l-b 12, n-b 6	22
1/39 2/80 3/104 4/142 5/171 6/197 7/243 8/302 9/324	324

Bowling: Shine 27–13–51–2; Joseph 10–2–28–0; Maru 46.3–16–89–4; Turner 40–11–98–2; Nicholas 7–2–21–0; C. L. Smith 6–1–21–2.

Umpires: H. D. Bird and R. Julian.

†At Oxford, May 14, 15. Oxfordshire won by three wickets. Oxford University 201 for three dec. (R. E. Morris 111) and 184 for two dec. (R. E. Morris 78, P. D. Lunn 55 not out); Oxfordshire 137 for four dec. and 249 for seven (D. Woods 75).

OXFORD UNIVERSITY v SURREY

At Oxford, May 16, 17, 18. Drawn. Toss: Oxford University. For the first time in several years Oxford elected to bat after winning the toss, and Morris's decision proved justified. He provided the backbone of his team's innings of 322 for eight, batting for four and a quarter hours and missing a maiden first-class century by only 4 runs. After his dismissal, Crawley and Lunn put on 84 for the fifth wicket, and Lunn stayed to see Oxford to the declaration. Surrey's batsmen all scored freely, and when Lynch and Thorpe had added an unbeaten 123, Greig declared 100 runs behind. In Oxford's second innings, opening bowler Henderson hit a career-best 44 after going in as night-watchman when Hagan was injured, and Morris, Kilborn and Crawley all made useful contributions before Oxford's second declaration set Surrey to score 308 in 100 minutes plus twenty overs. Ward and Darren Bicknell put them in sight of victory with an opening partnership of 256, of which Ward made a magnificent 181 in 152 minutes, passing his previous highest score of 145, against the same opponents in 1989, and scoring 100 of his runs in fours, as well as hitting two sixes. Late in the innings, however, Oxford held three vital catches and Surrey finished 3 runs short.

Close of play: First day, Oxford University 258-4 (M. A. Crawley 54*, P. D. Lunn 21*); Second day, Oxford University 15-0 (R. E. Morris 0*, I. M. Henderson 4*).

Oxford University

D. A. Hagan c Thorpe b Greig	17	– c Ward b Medlycott	12
*R. E. Morris c Ward b M. P. Bicknell	96	– c Stewart b Kendrick	31
M. J. Kilborn c Ward b Thorpe	11	– (7) not out	36
G. J. Turner c Clinton b Kendrick	34	– b Medlycott	3
M. A. Crawley c Lynch b M. P. Bicknell	60	– c Ward b Kendrick	47
P. D. Lunn not out	44	– st Ward b Kendrick	20
H. R. Davies lbw b M. P. Bicknell	2	– (8) not out	1
P. S. Gerrans b Robinson	0		
S. D. Weale c Ward b M. P. Bicknell	13		
I. M. Henderson (did not bat)		– (3) c Ward b Medlycott	44
B 9, l-b 15, w 16, n-b 5	45	B 7, l-b 5, n-b 1	13
1/33 2/81 3/158 4/187 5/271 6/280 7/285 8/322 (8 wkts dec.)	322	1/55 2/62 3/72 4/141 5/151 6/196 (6 wkts dec.)	207

†J. E. McGrady did not bat.

In the second innings D. A. Hagan, when 11, retired hurt at 11 and resumed at 62.

Bowling: *First Innings*—M. P. Bicknell 35.2–11–80–4; Robinson 26–7–69–1; Greig 12–1–38–1; Thorpe 14–6–30–1; Medlycott 33–13–61–0; Kendrick 10–3–20–1. *Second Innings*—M. P. Bicknell 7–1–18–0; Robinson 2–0–14–0; Greig 5–1–15–0; Medlycott 25–7–69–3; Kendrick 25–4–79–3.

Surrey

D. J. Bicknell b Crawley	33	– b Gerrans	63
G. S. Clinton c and b Turner	29		
A. J. Stewart c Crawley b Gerrans	24		
M. A. Lynch not out	81		
G. P. Thorpe not out	46	– (7) not out	2
†D. M. Ward (did not bat)		– (2) c Turner b Crawley	181
J. D. Robinson (did not bat)		– (3) c and b Crawley	24
*I. A. Greig (did not bat)		– (4) c Crawley b Gerrans	17
K. T. Medlycott (did not bat)		– (5) c Kilborn b Gerrans	4
M. P. Bicknell (did not bat)		– (6) not out	1
B 1, l-b 3, w 5	9	B 4, l-b 5, w 1, n-b 3	13
1/64 2/64 3/99 (3 wkts dec.)	222	1/256 2/256 3/278 4/289 5/302 (5 wkts)	305

N. M. Kendrick did not bat.

Bowling: *First Innings*—Henderson 9–1–24–0; Gerrans 13–1–50–1; Crawley 19–5–29–1; Turner 16–4–54–1; Davies 7–1–25–0; Weale 5–0–36–0. *Second Innings*—Henderson 4–1–23–0; Gerrans 15–1–86–3; Turner 10–2–53–0; Crawley 13–0–83–2; Weale 6–0–51–0.

Umpires: P. J. Eele and V. A. Holder.

OXFORD UNIVERSITY v LEICESTERSHIRE

At Oxford, May 23, 24, 25. Drawn. Toss: Oxford University. Oxford's decision to bat first backfired spectacularly when Hagan, Morris and Curtis were dismissed for 1 run, but Turner and Crawley halted the collapse with a stand of 105. When both fell in the fifties, the visitors faced further resistance from van der Merwe and Chauhan. The last wicket gave Millns his best bowling figures, on his first-class début for Leicestershire. It was then the University bowlers' turn to suffer, at the hands of Benson and Willey, who put on 165 before Benson was out 6 short of a century. Willey continued, making his highest score for Leicestershire in a third-wicket partnership of 191 with Whitaker, who was unbeaten on 124 when his captain declared at the overnight score, leaving Oxford needing 268 to avoid an innings defeat. Their cause seemed lost when four wickets fell for 71, but Leicestershire were punished by the later batsmen. After the Zimbabwean, Curtis, had batted nearly two hours for his 19, Crawley put on 67 with Gerrans and an unbeaten 81 with van der Merwe. He had hit sixteen fours in his 105 not out when Briers settled for a draw with ten overs remaining.

Close of play: First day, Leicestershire 17-0 (J. D. R. Benson 8*, P. Willey 7*); Second day, Leicestershire 447-3 (J. J. Whitaker 124*, P. A. Nixon 16*).

Oxford University

	First innings		Second innings	
D. A. Hagan b Millns	0	c Parsons b Ferris	6
*R. E. Morris lbw b Ferris	0	c Whitaker b Ferris	11
D. M. Curtis lbw b Millns	0	c Benson b Willey	19
G. J. Turner c Ferris b Willey	51	lbw b Gidley	9
M. A. Crawley c Nixon b Millns	50	not out	105
P. S. Gerrans c Nixon b Millns	0	lbw b Millns	22
W. M. van der Merwe lbw b Parsons	24	not out	39
S. Chauhan c Boon b Parsons	25		
M. J. Russell c Benson b Parsons	4		
H. R. Davies not out	9		
†J. E. McGrady lbw b Millns	1		
B 6, l-b 4, w 5	15	L-b 7, n-b 1	8
1/0 2/0 3/1 4/106 5/107 6/114 7/154 8/165 9/170	179	1/16 2/17 3/33 4/71 5/138	(5 wkts) 219

Bowling: *First Innings*—Millns 22.3–8–47–5; Ferris 20–6–45–1; Parsons 24–11–34–3; Gidley 14–4–27–0; Willey 5–4–4–1; Benson 4–2–12–0. *Second Innings*—Millns 20–8–47–1; Ferris 17–7–33–2; Parsons 15–6–35–0; Gidley 19–8–54–1; Willey 22–9–29–1; Boon 3–0–14–0.

Leicestershire

J. D. R. Benson b van der Merwe	94
P. Willey b Chauhan	177
B. F. Smith lbw b Crawley	4
J. J. Whitaker not out	124
†P. A. Nixon not out	16
B 12, l-b 10, w 5, n-b 5	32
1/165 2/189 3/380	(3 wkts dec.) 447

T. J. Boon, *N. E. Briers, G. J. Parsons, M. I. Gidley, D. J. Millns and G. J. F. Ferris did not bat.

Bowling: van der Merwe 16–1–52–1; Gerrans 19–3–73–0; Crawley 19–4–50–1; Turner 21–3–72–0; Davies 20–1–112–0; Chauhan 15–1–58–1; Curtis 1–0–8–0.

Umpires: R. Palmer and H. J. Rhodes.

†At Oxford, May 26, 28, 29. Oxford University won by two wickets with three balls to spare. Free Foresters 276 (E. D. Fursdon 65 not out, C. J. C. Rowe 59) and 244 for six dec. (J. R. Kilbee 59 retired; D. M. Curtis four for 53); Oxford University 241 for six dec. (R. E. Morris 62) and 280 for eight (R. E. Morris 102, D. A. Hagan 63; C. J. C. Rowe four for 71).

†At Oxford, May 30, 31, June 1. Drawn. Toss: Oxford University. Oxford University 229 for nine dec. (R. E. Morris 40, P. D. Lunn 80) and 323 for eight dec. (R. E. Morris 30, M. J. Russell 51, P. D. Lunn 52, W. M. van der Merwe 59, S. D. Weale 33, I. M. Henderson 33 not out); MCC 279 for seven dec. (S. G. Plumb 34, S. C. Wundke 54, R. M. Wight 40 not out, M. Hart 48 not out; I. M. Henderson three for 77, W. M. van der Merwe four for 67) and 76 for no wkt (D. C. Briance 38 not out).

OXFORD UNIVERSITY v GLAMORGAN

At Oxford, June 2, 4, 5. Drawn. Toss: Oxford University. Paying their second visit of the season to The Parks, Glamorgan made another score of more than 300 after Oxford's gamble of putting them in on a rain-affected pitch had not paid off. Cottey completed a maiden century after adding 104 with Holmes. Oxford lost four wickets for 77, but Crawley, who had hit an unbeaten 103 on the county's first visit, put on 75 in ten overs with Gerrans, and Curtis hit a career-best 43. Although leading by 170, Glamorgan did not enforce the follow-on; but any hopes of a result were spoiled by rain, which restricted play on the third day to 5.2 overs before lunch.

Close of play: First day, Glamorgan 388-7 (J. Derrick 28*, M. Davies 5*); Second day, Glamorgan 10-0 (M. J. Cann 0*, G. C. Holmes 8*).

Glamorgan

M. J. Cann c Gerrans b Henderson	19	– c Trevelyan b Henderson	7
P. A. Cottey run out	156		
G. C. Holmes b Henderson	39	– (2) not out	12
M. P. Maynard c Turner b Gerrans	59		
R. N. Pook lbw b Gerrans	0	– (3) not out	0
†M. L. Roberts c Trevelyan b Henderson	14		
H. A. G. Anthony c Gerrans b Crawley	30		
J. Derrick not out	28		
M. Davies not out	5		
B 6, l-b 14, w 2, n-b 16	38	L-b 3, n-b 2	5
1/37 2/141 3/233 4/233 5/284 6/343 7/369 (7 wkts dec.)	388	1/21 (1 wkt)	24

S. Bastien and *S. R. Barwick did not bat.

Bowling: *First Innings*—Henderson 28–1–102–3; Gerrans 26–3–94–2; Crawley 26–6–94–1; Turner 19–4–78–0. *Second Innings*—Gerrans 5–3–4–0; Henderson 4.2–0–17–1.

Oxford University

D. A. Hagan c Cottey b Barwick	43
*R. E. Morris c Roberts b Bastien	0
P. D. Lunn c Roberts b Bastien	11
G. J. Turner b Bastien	13
M. A. Crawley c Davies b Anthony	67
P. S. Gerrans c Roberts b Barwick	18
D. M. Curtis lbw b Holmes	43
M. J. Russell c Roberts b Barwick	2
S. Chauhan run out	4
I. M. Henderson not out	1
†R. W. D. Trevelyan c Roberts b Bastien	0
L-b 8, w 3, n-b 5	16
1/2 2/31 3/66 4/77 5/152 6/187 7/204 8/212 9/217	218

Bowling: Anthony 18–7–29–1; Bastien 20.2–3–51–4; Barwick 19–10–29–3; Derrick 9–2–58–0; Davies 8–1–16–0; Pook 8–3–19–0; Holmes 7–4–8–1.

Umpires: P. J. Eele and A. A. Jones.

OXFORD UNIVERSITY v NOTTINGHAMSHIRE

At Oxford, June 6, 7, 8. Drawn. Toss: Nottinghamshire. An unusual feature of this match was that Nottinghamshire used twelve players. Wicket-keeper Scott had been omitted because of illness, and Newell, their opening batsman, was to have kept wicket in his place. However, at the end of the first day, when he was 20 not out, Newell was summoned to Trent Bridge to act as twelfth man for England in the Test match against New Zealand. After calls to the TCCB, Scott, now recovered, was reinstated, although the TCCB's Playing Conditions for first-class matches made provision for the introduction of a substitute player only in the case of County Championship matches, and Lenham, the Oxford coach, was rightly critical of the whole incident. In the play between showers – only five and a half hours were possible on the first two days and the third was washed out – Johnson hit an unbeaten 112, containing a six and thirteen fours, and the Oxford captain, Morris, was 73 not out in his team's reply.

Close of play: First day, Nottinghamshire 84-2 (M. Newell 20*, P. Johnson 42*); Second day, Oxford University 118-1 (R. E. Morris 73*, P. D. Lunn 22*).

Nottinghamshire

†M. Newell retired not out	20
D. J. R. Martindale c Morris b Crawley	15
R. J. Evans c sub b Gerrans	1
*P. Johnson not out	112
D. R. Laing b van der Merwe	2
K. P. Evans not out	43
B 4, l-b 3, n-b 1	8
1/27 2/32 3/92 (3 wkts dec.)	201

G. W. Mike, M. G. Field-Buss, R. A. Pick, K. Saxelby, †C. W. Scott and J. A. Afford did not bat.

Bowling: van der Merwe 20–5–69–1; Gerrans 19–4–58–1; Crawley 15.5–4–36–1; Davies 4–0–31–0.

Oxford University

D. A. Hagan c Mike b K. P. Evans	15
*R. E. Morris not out	73
P. D. Lunn not out	22
B 2, l-b 5, w 1	8
1/33 (1 wkt dec.)	118

D. M. Curtis, M. J. Russell, M. A. Crawley, W. M. van der Merwe, H. R. Davies, S. Chauhan, P. S. Gerrans and †R. W. D. Trevelyan did not bat.

Bowling: Pick 3–0–20–0; Saxelby 2–0–10–0; Mike 6–1–33–0; K. P. Evans 6–4–13–1; Afford 8–4–9–0; Laing 5–1–21–0; Field-Buss 2.1–1–5–0.

Umpires: K. J. Lyons and H. J. Rhodes.

†At Oxford, June 13, 14, 15. Drawn. Oxford University 279 for nine dec. (J. Morris 103) and 325 for five dec. (D. A. Hagan 167 not out, P. D. Lunn 82, R. E. Morris 57); Combined Services 376 (Sgt G. S. Lumb 94, 2nd Lt R. J. Greatorex 83) and 207 for six.

OXFORD UNIVERSITY v LANCASHIRE

At Oxford, June 16, 18, 19. Drawn. Toss: Oxford University. Oxford produced their best batting of the season, and their biggest total against a first-class county since their 413 for nine against Warwickshire in 1969. After Gallian, an eighteen-year-old Australian, dismissed Hagan with his first ball in first-class cricket, Kilborn came in to make his highest score, 95, sharing stands which put on a total of 254 runs with Morris, Turner and Crawley. Later Crawley added 86 in twelve overs with van der Merwe, whose unbeaten 56 came from 35 balls, but Oxford's declaration at their overnight score, after rain had delayed the start on the second morning, deprived him of the chance of a hundred against his native county – who were playing his younger brother. Lancashire's reply was even more spectacular, with their three England players, appearing between the Trent Bridge and Lord's Tests, all hitting centuries. Atherton struck nineteen fours and a six in his 117, acting-captain Fairbrother made 105, and on the third day DeFreitas raced to the fastest hundred of the season to date, from 69 balls in 79 minutes. His seven sixes and eleven fours included four sixes and a four in one over from Turner.

Close of play: First day, Oxford University 366-5 (M. A. Crawley 91*, W. M. van der Merwe 56*); Second day, Lancashire 260-2 (N. H. Fairbrother 52*, P. A. J. DeFreitas 12*).

Oxford University

D. A. Hagan c Atherton b Gallian	1	– c Stanworth b Folley	5
*R. E. Morris lbw b DeFreitas	61		
M. J. Kilborn c DeFreitas b Atherton	95		
G. J. Turner run out	48		
M. A. Crawley not out	91		
P. D. Lunn c Stanworth b Folley	3	– (3) not out	9
W. M. van der Merwe not out	56		
P. S. Gerrans (did not bat)		– (2) c DeFreitas b Folley	39
S. D. Weale (did not bat)		– (4) lbw b Atherton	0
I. M. Henderson (did not bat)		– (5) not out	1
B 1, l-b 5, w 1, n-b 4	11	B 1, l-b 9	10
1/3 2/118 3/189 4/257 5/280 (5 wkts dec.)	366	1/28 2/58 3/58 (3 wkts)	64

†J. E. McGrady did not bat.

Bowling: *First Innings*—DeFreitas 17–3–39–1; Gallian 18–8–50–1; Folley 24–1–120–1; Yates 27–7–52–0; Atherton 31–5–99–1. *Second Innings*—DeFreitas 4–1–7–0; Gallian 3–0–15–0; Atherton 8–5–10–1; Folley 10–3–18–2; Yates 4–2–4–0.

Lancashire

N. J. Speak c Hagan b Turner	61	G. D. Lloyd not out	78
M. A. Atherton c Henderson b Weale	117	J. E. R. Gallian not out	17
*N. H. Fairbrother c Kilborn b Turner	105		
P. A. J. DeFreitas st McGrady b Turner	102	B 12, l-b 3, w 2, n-b 13	30
S. P. Titchard b Crawley	22	1/115 2/248 3/383 4/416 5/446 6/474	(6 wkts dec.) 558
J. P. Crawley b Lunn	26		

G. Yates, I. Folley and †J. Stanworth did not bat.

Bowling: Henderson 25–2–146–0; Gerrans 20–1–80–0; Crawley 17–2–64–1; Turner 27–7–100–3; Weale 25–4–119–1; Lunn 8–1–34–1.

Umpires: G. I. Burgess and N. T. Plews.

†At Oxford, June 20, 21, 22. Drawn. Wiltshire 325 for five dec. (S. Perrin 117 not out) and second innings forfeited; Oxford University first innings forfeited and 283 for seven (P. D. Lunn 125 not out, R. E. Morris 55; N. Prigent four for 63).

At Lord's, July 4, 5, 6. OXFORD UNIVERSITY drew with CAMBRIDGE UNIVERSITY (See Other Matches at Lord's, 1990).

CAMBRIDGE

President: Lord Butterfield (Downing)

Captain: J. C. M. Atkinson (Millfield and Downing)
Secretary: R. A. Pyman (Harrow and Pembroke)

Captain for 1991: R. J. Turner (Millfield and Magdalene)
Secretary: M. J. Morris (Cherwell, Oxford, Pembroke and Downing)

A glorious finish to the term, when the combined Oxford & Cambridge side beat the New Zealanders, followed immediately by Cambridge's victory over Sussex at Hove – their first win against a county since 1982 – disguised what was, on the whole, a disappointing season at Fenner's.

Much had been expected of the side Jonathon Atkinson was to lead, for there was considerable experience in batting and bowling. Yet for most of the season, one of the driest at Fenner's in living memory, little happened to realise those hopes. The highlights were provided more often than not by Steve James, the Glamorgan batsman, who had given notice of his considerable ability when heading the Cambridge averages the previous season. In eleven matches, including Oxford & Cambridge Universities against the tourists, he scored 921 runs. Only the rain that ruined the University Match at Lord's denied him the chance to become the first Cambridge batsman since J. M. Brearley to score 1,000 first-class runs in a university season, although he did reach the milestone on his return to Glamorgan. Of his four centuries, all scored in the later half of the term, the unbeaten match-winning 131 against the New Zealanders was his best, and was followed by a hundred that proved to be the corner-stone of the victory at Hove. In the same innings he shared in one of only two century partnerships made by the University, putting on 142 with Mark Lowrey as Cambridge chased 256 in 148 minutes plus twenty overs.

CAMBRIDGE UNIVERSITY 1990

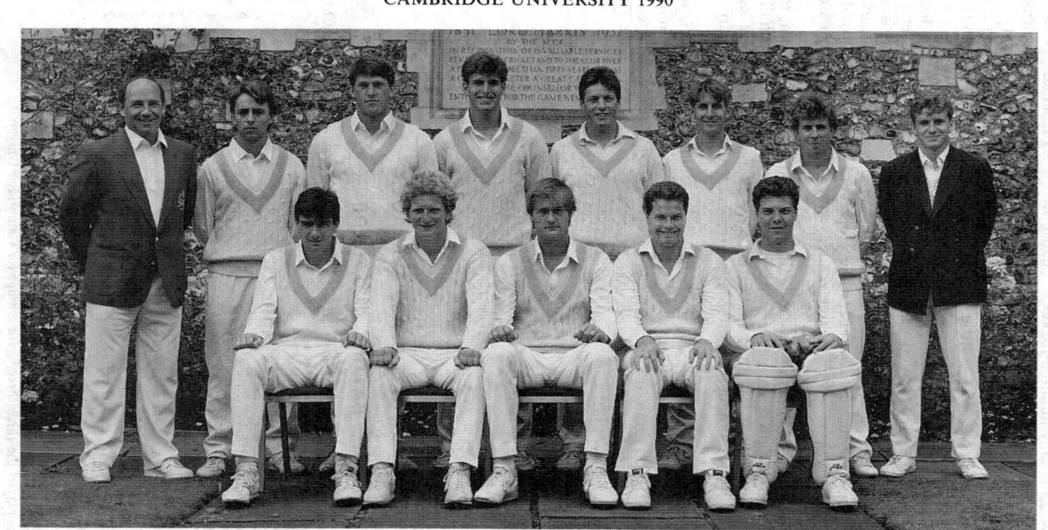

[*Bill Smith*

Back row: G. J. Saville (*coach*), D. H. Shufflebotham, R. H. J. Jenkins, S. W. Johnson, A. J. Buzza, M. J. Morris, M. J. Lowrey, G. B. A. Dyer. *Front row:* S. P. James, R. A. Pyman, J. C. M. Atkinson (*captain*), R. Heap, R. J. Turner.

James was the only hundred-maker, though Lowrey, a Freshman, showed skills that should stand the University in good stead. He was one of only three other batsmen who passed 50, despite the considerable improvement in the Fenner's pitches. Much work had been carried out on the square during the winter, and the result was a little more bounce and pace to encourage batsmen and bowlers alike.

Alan Buzza was again the top bowler, earning 23 wickets, including five against the New Zealanders, with his left-arm spin, although he was never as effective as he had been the previous season, when bowling at the opposite end to Mike Atherton's leg-spin. Lowrey, an off-spinner, headed Cambridge's averages with ten wickets, while Rory Jenkins, a strongly built Freshman, used the new ball willingly and, along with Richard Pyman, finished with fifteen wickets.

The biggest disappointment was the failure of Atkinson, the captain, to realise fully his potential. He showed what he was capable of in his two half-centuries but innings of sustained application were all too infrequent. He led his side cheerfully, although he often appeared content to let things drift, waiting for declarations by the visitors.

Despite going into the University Match as the underdogs, Cambridge arrived at Lord's in confident mood. But in a match ruined again by rain, they revealed their limitations, failing to grasp the opportunity provided when both captains forfeited an innings and they were required to score 270 to win in a minimum of 61 overs. – David Hallett.

CAMBRIDGE UNIVERSITY RESULTS

First-class matches – Played 10: Won 1, Lost 4, Drawn 5.

FIRST-CLASS AVERAGES

BATTING AND FIELDING

	Birthplace	*M*	*I*	*NO*	*R*	*HI*	*Avge*	*Ct/St*
S. P. James	*Lydney*	10	19	1	723	116	40.16	7
J. P. Arscott	*Tooting*	2	4	1	75	43*	25.00	0/2
M. J. Lowrey	*Hampstead*	10	18	2	363	72	22.68	1
R. Heap	*Leeds*	10	19	2	376	63	22.11	3
J. C. M. Atkinson	*Butleigh*	10	19	2	360	72	21.17	6
R. J. Turner	*Malvern*	8	14	0	287	38	20.50	6/4
D. H. Shufflebotham	*Neath*	8	9	3	121	29	20.16	1
G. B. A. Dyer	*Glasgow*	4	8	2	107	23	17.83	0
S. W. Johnson	*Newcastle-upon-Tyne*	6	6	4	35	14*	17.50	2
M. J. Morris	*Melbourne, Australia*	10	17	3	206	45	14.71	4
R. A. Pyman	*Changi, Singapore*	9	12	1	94	23*	8.54	2
R. H. J. Jenkins	*Leicester*	9	12	5	58	19*	8.28	1
A. J. Buzza	*Beverley*	9	11	2	49	21	5.44	2

Also batted: A. M. Hooper (*Perivale*) (2 matches) 0, 0, 5 (1 ct); G. M. Hutchinson (*Welshpool*) (2 matches) 29, 2; G. A. Pointer (*Lewisham*) (1 match) 7, 9.

* *Signifies not out.*

S. P. James played the three three-figure innings for Cambridge University.

BOWLING

	O	*M*	*R*	*W*	*BB*	*Avge*
M. J. Lowrey	151.2	33	483	10	2-13	48.30
A. J. Buzza	257	42	955	18	4-108	53.05
R. A. Pyman	285.4	76	870	15	2-29	58.00
R. H. J. Jenkins	281.4	41	959	15	5-100	63.93
D. H. Shufflebotham	139	20	538	6	3-60	89.66

Also bowled: J. C. M. Atkinson 23–3–101–1; S. W. Johnson 113–14–452–3; G. A. Pointer 17–3–67–0.

†At Cambridge, April 11. Middlesex won by 68 runs. Middlesex 187 for eight (50 overs); Cambridge University 119 for five (50 overs) (R. Heap 54).

†At Cambridge, April 12. Cambridge University won on faster scoring-rate in a rain-affected match. Loughborough University 216 for five (55 overs) (N. V. Knight 113 not out, C. M. Tolley 53); Cambridge University 138 for four (33 overs).

CAMBRIDGE UNIVERSITY v NORTHAMPTONSHIRE

At Cambridge, April 14, 15, 16. Drawn. Toss: Cambridge University. From the outset the University bowlers toiled as the county made steady progress on a cold, occasionally showery opening day. With Geoff Cook taking 164 balls to reach 50, the best batting came from the left-handed Penberthy, who completed his fifty by the close and on the second day went on to his maiden hundred and the first century of the season, hitting thirteen fours and a six in 196 deliveries. Later in the day the young all-rounder came back to wrap up the Cambridge innings with an impressive spell of medium-pace bowling. Nick Cook, captaining Northamptonshire in the absence of Lamb and Larkins – playing in the Test match in Antigua, along with county team-mates Bailey, Capel and Ambrose – chose not to enforce the follow-on and eventually set Cambridge a target of 281 in four and a half hours. This time, however, the University batted more confidently and, helped by an interruption for rain, had no trouble saving the match.

Close of play: First day, Northamptonshire 228-4 (A. L. Penberthy 56*, D. Ripley 11*); Second day, Northamptonshire 26-1 (A. Fordham 23*).

Northamptonshire

G. Cook c James b Johnson	87		
A. Fordham c Morris b Johnson	17	– (1) c Johnson b Pyman	54
N. A. Felton b Pyman	26	– (2) lbw b Jenkins	3
D. J. Wild c Hooper b Lowrey	20	– (3) c Turner b Lowrey	43
A. L. Penberthy not out	101		
†D. Ripley lbw b Pyman	22		
J. G. Thomas not out	13	– (6) c James b Lowrey	8
J. W. Govan (did not bat)		– (4) lbw b Pyman	3
*N. G. B. Cook (did not bat)		– (5) not out	0
L-b 6, n-b 5	11		
1/37 2/79 3/110 4/197 5/254 (5 wkts dec.)	297	1/26 2/88 3/103 4/103 5/111 (5 wkts dec.)	111

S. J. Brown and M. A. Robinson did not bat.

Bowling: *First Innings*—Johnson 21–2–86–2; Jenkins 23.5–2–59–0; Pyman 36–12–62–2; Shufflebotham 5–0–26–0; Lowrey 24–7–58–1. *Second Innings*—Johnson 4–0–17–0; Jenkins 11–1–52–1; Pyman 12–6–29–2; Lowrey 4.1–1–13–2.

Cambridge University

S. P. James lbw b Thomas	39	– lbw b Brown	6
R. Heap c Felton b Govan	18	– c Thomas b Wild	37
M. J. Lowrey run out	8	– not out	23
*J. C. M. Atkinson c N. G. B. Cook b Robinson	2	– not out	47
M. J. Morris b Brown	5		
A. M. Hooper c Thomas b Robinson	0		
R. A. Pyman b Govan	4		
†R. J. Turner c Brown b Penberthy	21		
D. H. Shufflebotham not out	16		
R. H. J. Jenkins lbw b Penberthy	0		
S. W. Johnson c Brown b Penberthy	0		
B 1, l-b 13, w 1	15	L-b 3	3
1/54 2/66 3/74 4/74 5/75 6/88 7/90 8/123 9/126	128	1/28 2/46	(2 wkts) 116

Bowling: *First Innings*—Brown 12–6–18–1; Thomas 10–1–47–1; Govan 11–7–12–2; Robinson 16–6–24–2; N. G. B. Cook 2–1–2–0; Penberthy 8.4–5–11–3. *Second Innings*—Brown 9–4–11–1; Thomas 7–1–26–0; Wild 9–2–32–1; N. G. B. Cook 2–2–0–0; Robinson 6–0–18–0; Govan 3–2–10–0; Penberthy 3–1–12–0; Fordham 1–0–4–0.

Umpires: B. Hassan and R. Julian.

CAMBRIDGE UNIVERSITY v DERBYSHIRE

At Cambridge, April 18, 19, 20. Derbyshire won by 243 runs. Toss: Cambridge University. Derbyshire were in control from the start, when they were asked to bat and enjoyed some gentle practice. Adams completed a maiden century in 206 minutes, hitting twelve fours from 187 deliveries, and the South African, Kuiper, marked his first appearance for the county with a half-century. The visitors tightened their grip on the match on the second day as Cambridge limped to three figures; then Barnett, lending variety to the attack with his leg-spinners, took the last three wickets in eight balls without conceding a run. However, he declined to enforce the follow-on, and after some more Derbyshire batsmen had taken practice he declared a second time, leaving the University a target of 354. That was quite beyond Cambridge, as was batting throughout the final day to save the game; only two batsmen reached double figures. Barnett added another four wickets and Miller, back with his home county after three years with Essex, took three for 14.

Close of play: First day, Cambridge University 16-0 (S. P. James 11*, R. Heap 3*); Second day, Cambridge University 3-1 (S. P. James 3*, M. J. Lowrey 0*).

Derbyshire

*K. J. Barnett c Atkinson b Buzza	62		
T. J. G. O'Gorman c Heap b Pyman	55		
C. J. Adams not out	111		
A. P. Kuiper lbw b Pyman	51		
B. Roberts b Buzza	12	– (1) c Lowrey b Buzza	33
A. M. Brown not out	34		
S. C. Goldsmith (did not bat)		– (2) lbw b Atkinson	51
G. Miller (did not bat)		– (3) not out	25
M. Jean-Jacques (did not bat)		– (4) not out	13
B 3, l-b 4	7	L-b 2, w 3	5
1/78 2/156 3/241 4/268	(4 wkts dec.) 332	1/86 2/86	(2 wkts dec.) 127

†B. J. M. Maher and O. H. Mortensen did not bat.

Bowling: *First Innings*—Jenkins 13–3–47–0; Pointer 8–0–35–0; Pyman 28–3–94–2; Buzza 32–5–117–2; Lowrey 9–1–32–0. *Second Innings*—Jenkins 8–2–37–0; Pointer 9–3–32–0; Atkinson 7–1–27–1; Buzza 10–2–27–1; Pyman 4.3–2–2–0.

Cambridge University

S. P. James b Jean-Jacques	21	– c Adams b Kuiper 7
R. Heap lbw b Mortensen	4	– c Brown b Miller 0
M. J. Lowrey c Adams b Mortensen	4	– lbw b Jean-Jacques 1
*J. C. M. Atkinson lbw b Miller	36	– b Roberts 23
M. J. Morris c Miller b Jean-Jacques	2	– c Miller b Barnett 45
A. M. Hooper lbw b Mortensen	0	– b Barnett 5
R. A. Pyman c O'Gorman b Roberts	5	– b Miller 2
†R. J. Turner c Miller b Barnett	18	– c Goldsmith b Barnett 0
G. A. Pointer lbw b Barnett	7	– b Barnett 9
A. J. Buzza c Goldsmith b Barnett	0	– not out 9
R. H. J. Jenkins not out	0	– lbw b Miller 1
L-b 5, w 3, n-b 1	9	B 5, l-b 3 8
1/22 2/32 3/32 4/36 5/39 6/58 7/90 8/105 9/105	106	1/1 2/8 3/8 4/70 5/82 6/89 7/89 8/92 9/103 110

Bowling: *First Innings*—Mortensen 15–3–21–3; Jean-Jacques 14–4–31–2; Miller 10–4–9–1; Barnett 8.2–5–9–3; Goldsmith 7–2–15–0; Roberts 6–2–16–1. *Second Innings*—Miller 23.4–16–14–3; Barnett 18–7–28–4; Kuiper 7–2–16–1; Jean-Jacques 10–3–23–1; Goldsmith [illegible]–1–21–0; Roberts 3–3–0–1.

Umpires: B. Hassan and R. Julian.

CAMBRIDGE UNIVERSITY v WARWICKSHIRE

At Cambridge, April 26, 27, 28. Drawn. Toss: Cambridge University. Warwickshire's batsmen picked up three centuries, and Moody celebrated his county début by giving a foretaste of feats to follow. On a first day reduced by rain to two and a half hours, the tall Australian needed only 125 balls to reach his hundred, hitting ten fours and six sixes; next day he went on to 147, from 147 balls, with 100 of his runs coming in boundaries (six sixes, sixteen fours). Reeve was even faster, scoring a hundred before lunch from 109 deliveries with three sixes and ten fours. When Cambridge batted, Atkinson, aided by the tail, limited the damage done by Benjamin, who finished with five wickets for the first time. Then, as Reeve opted to bat again, it was the turn of the Cambridge bowlers to suffer once more. Asif Din rode his luck somewhat with a flourish of strokes which brought him three sixes and thirteen fours, and he reached his hundred in 76 minutes from 70 balls. Cambridge ignored a target of 359 but batted with sufficient determination to save the game.

Close of play: First day, Warwickshire 168-2 (T. M. Moody 105*, A. I. Kallicharran 42*); Second day, Warwickshire 10-0 (A. J. Moles 5*, Asif Din 5*).

Warwickshire

A. J. Moles c Atkinson b Johnson	1	– lbw b Shufflebotham 29
T. M. Moody b Buzza	147	
†G. W. Humpage c Turner b Pyman	17	– not out 4
A. I. Kallicharran c James b Buzza	43	
*D. A. Reeve not out	102	
Asif Din c Turner b Buzza	0	– (2) not out 100
K. J. Piper run out	10	
N. M. K. Smith b Buzza	47	
P. A. Booth not out	3	
L-b 2, n-b 6	8	L-b 8, n-b 2 10
1/2 2/41 3/188 4/214 5/214 6/231 7/366	(7 wkts dec.) 378	1/105 (1 wkt dec.) 143

T. A. Munton and J. E. Benjamin did not bat.

Bowling: *First Innings*—Johnson 9–2–43–1; Pyman 20–4–109–1; Shufflebotham 17–1–76–0; Buzza 22–1–108–4; Atkinson 8–1–40–0. *Second Innings*—Johnson 6–0–41–0; Pyman [illegible]–1–43–0; Buzza 1–0–4–0; Shufflebotham 5–0–29–1; Lowrey 3.1–0–18–0.

Cambridge University

S. P. James c Humpage b Benjamin	19	– (7) c Smith b Munton	8
R. Heap lbw b Benjamin	0	– (1) c Humpage b Munton	17
M. J. Lowrey b Benjamin	1	– c Smith b Reeve	24
*J. C. M. Atkinson c Reeve b Smith	41	– c Reeve b Asif Din	17
M. J. Morris lbw b Benjamin	0	– lbw b Reeve	19
G. B. A. Dyer b Asif Din	19	– not out	20
†R. J. Turner c Booth b Asif Din	12	– (2) lbw b Reeve	28
R. A. Pyman run out	21	– not out	23
D. H. Shufflebotham c Reeve b Asif Din	24		
A. J. Buzza b Benjamin	1		
S. W. Johnson not out	14		
L-b 10, w 1	11	B 13, l-b 9, n-b 3	25
1/2 2/6 3/44 4/44 5/72 6/95 7/106 8/135 9/142	163	1/19 2/74 3/95 4/101 5/122 6/133	(6 wkts) 181

Bowling: *First Innings*—Munton 8–3–17–0; Benjamin 18–8–29–5; Moody 8–1–33–0; Smith 10–4–25–1; Asif Din 10.5–3–17–3; Booth 8–1–23–0; Reeve 6–3–9–0. *Second Innings*—Benjamin 12–5–12–0; Munton 16–4–40–2; Smith 10–2–18–0; Asif Din 15–3–49–1; Reeve 19–7–34–3; Moody 10–7–6–0.

Umpires: B. Dudleston and P. J. Eele.

CAMBRIDGE UNIVERSITY v MIDDLESEX

At Cambridge, May 3, 4, 5. Drawn. Toss: Middlesex. Ramprakash dominated the first day, putting on 90 with Roseberry and 98 with Brown, to complete his hundred in 206 minutes, having faced 176 deliveries and hit nine fours and two sixes. A half-century by James, recapturing his form of the previous year, failed to take the University past the follow-on target, but once again the visiting county preferred to give their other batsmen some practice. Jenkins claimed the first five-wicket haul of the season by a Cambridge bowler as Middlesex increased their lead to 362, then left the University with four hours' batting. In this time the Middlesex players also had some bowling practice; every man was given at least two overs, except wicket-keeper Farbrace, a recent recruit from Kent, who had earlier made his highest first-class score.

Close of play: First day, Cambridge University 15-0 (S. P. James 5*, R. Heap 9*); Second day, Middlesex 112-4 (P. Farbrace 52*, N. F. Williams 8*).

Middlesex

M. A. Roseberry st Turner b Buzza	85	– (9) not out	2
J. C. Pooley b Pyman	8	– b Jenkins	13
*M. W. Gatting c Morris b Buzza	19		
M. R. Ramprakash not out	118	– (8) not out	13
K. R. Brown b Jenkins	42		
R. O. Butcher not out	29	– (1) c Buzza b Jenkins	32
†P. Farbrace (did not bat)		– (3) c Pyman b Buzza	79
S. P. Hughes (did not bat)		– (4) b Jenkins	2
J. E. Emburey (did not bat)		– (5) lbw b Jenkins	4
N. F. Williams (did not bat)		– (6) c Turner b Jenkins	20
P. C. R. Tufnell (did not bat)		– (7) c James b Buzza	36
L-b 7, w 5, n-b 7	19	L-b 2, n-b 1	3
1/26 2/76 3/166 4/264	(4 wkts dec.) 320	1/35 2/52 3/58 4/70 5/132 6/183 7/200	(7 wkts dec.) 204

Bowling: *First Innings*—Jenkins 20–1–96–1; Pyman 20–8–54–1; Shufflebotham 14–3–50–0; Buzza 26–5–55–2; Lowrey 16–1–58–0. *Second Innings*—Jenkins 26–3–100–5; Pyman 7–2–31–0; Buzza 11.1–2–25–2; Lowrey 9–2–29–0; Shufflebotham 9–1–17–0.

Cambridge University

	First innings		Second innings	
S. P. James c Butcher b Hughes	54	–	c Roseberry b Tufnell	46
R. Heap c Emburey b Williams	15	–	b Tufnell	23
M. J. Lowrey c Brown b Williams	6	–	(5) c Emburey b Tufnell	12
*J. C. M. Atkinson c Farbrace b Hughes	6	–	c Butcher b Brown	17
M. J. Morris lbw b Emburey	9	–	(6) not out	32
G. B. A. Dyer c Farbrace b Williams	23	–	(7) not out	9
†R. J. Turner c Tufnell b Emburey	26	–	(3) c Pooley b Roseberry	34
R. A. Pyman c Brown b Emburey	10			
D. H. Shufflebotham c Brown b Tufnell	1			
A. J. Buzza c Gatting b Emburey	0			
R. H. J. Jenkins not out	0			
B 4, l-b 5, w 3	12		B 4, l-b 17, w 6	27
1/24 2/30 3/38 4/61 5/95 6/135 7/153 8/162 9/162	162		1/43 2/91 3/126 4/138 5/157 (5 wkts)	200

Bowling: *First Innings*—Williams 18–5–35–3; Hughes 20–5–30–2; Emburey 26.3–13–33–4; Tufnell 17–6–36–1; Gatting 8–3–19–0. *Second Innings*—Williams 2–0–5–0; Hughes 4–2–11–0; Tufnell 27–11–57–3; Emburey 14–8–13–0; Ramprakash 7–2–17–0; Brown 10–2–16–1; Roseberry 11–2–41–1; Gatting 3–0–6–0; Pooley 2–0–11–0; Butcher 2–0–2–0.

Umpires: V. A. Holder and M. J. Kitchen.

†At Cambridge, May 13. Cambridge University won by 11 runs. Cambridge University 289 for four dec. (R. A. Pyman 110 not out, S. P. James 102); Cryptics 278 (R. Sethi 68; A. J. Buzza five for 103).

†At Cambridge, May 15. Cambridgeshire won by six wickets. Cambridge University 189 (A. Akhtar five for 42); Cambridgeshire 190 for four (N. T. Gadsby 80, N. J. Adams 67).

CAMBRIDGE UNIVERSITY v ESSEX

At Cambridge, May 16, 17, 18. Essex won by 120 runs. Toss: Essex. Fifties from Heap and Atkinson enabled Cambridge to pass 200 for the first time in the season, in reply to Essex's 319 for five declared. It was also the first time they had compelled a visiting team to bat again, but it was not enough to save the game. Earlier Prichard had batted freely, hitting fifteen fours and a six in his 117-ball hundred, while Stephenson compiled a less fluent half-century. In the county's second innings, the promising Seymour, making a career-best 89, and the experienced Hardie put on 155 for the first wicket before Pringle declared, setting his former university 274 to win at almost a run a minute. Any thoughts of victory were quickly dispelled when Ilott took the first four wickets at a personal cost of 10 runs, and Buzza's dismissal later gave him five in an innings for the first time. Only Lowrey stood in Essex's way. Batting for 206 minutes, and reaching his maiden half-century in a ninth-wicket stand with Jenkins worth 50 in 71 minutes, he was so close to staving off defeat that just 8.5 overs remained when he was last out.

Close of play: First day, Cambridge University 23-2 (R. Heap 6*, A. J. Buzza 4*); Second day, Essex 102-0 (A. C. Seymour 62*, B. R. Hardie 31*).

Essex

	First innings		Second innings	
J. P. Stephenson c Buzza b Lowrey	58			
A. C. Seymour lbw b Jenkins	28	–	(1) b Pyman	89
P. J. Prichard c Heap b Pyman	116			
†M. A. Garnham c James b Jenkins	26			
B. R. Hardie not out	22	–	(2) not out	56
*D. R. Pringle c Morris b Pyman	58			
T. D. Topley (did not bat)		–	(3) lbw b Pyman	0
L-b 7, n-b 4	11		B 5, l-b 4, w 1	10
1/36 2/197 3/235 4/239 5/319 (5 wkts dec.)	319		1/155 2/155 (2 wkts dec.)	155

M. C. Ilott, J. H. Childs, S. J. W. Andrew and P. M. Such did not bat.

Bowling: *First Innings*—Johnson 8–0–59–0; Jenkins 25–7–68–2; Pyman 22.1–7–46–2; Buzz 21–2–90–0; Atkinson 2–0–23–0; Lowrey 9–1–26–1. *Second Innings*—Jenkins 14–3–48–0 Johnson 4–1–23–0; Pyman 16–5–36–2; Lowrey 6–0–22–0; Buzza 5–1–17–0.

Cambridge University

S. P. James c Topley b Andrew	5	– lbw b Ilott	1
R. Heap c Seymour b Pringle	50	– lbw b Ilott	2
R. A. Pyman c Stephenson b Andrew	0	– b Ilott	1
A. J. Buzza b Ilott	21	– (9) c Hardie b Ilott	0
*J. C. M. Atkinson run out	51	– (4) c Pringle b Ilott	0
M. J. Lowrey c Hardie b Pringle	6	– (5) lbw b Such	6
M. J. Morris c Prichard b Pringle	2	– (6) c Garnham b Andrew	1
G. B. A. Dyer c Hardie b Topley	17	– (7) c Pringle b Topley	1
†J. P. Arscott lbw b Childs	9	– (8) c Hardie b Pringle	1
R. H. J. Jenkins c Garnham b Topley	6	– lbw b Such	1
S. W. Johnson not out	10	– not out	
B 7, l-b 5, w 2, n-b 10	24	B 4, l-b 8, w 3, n-b 7	2
1/13 2/17 3/53 4/137 5/146 6/148 7/153 8/173 9/188	201	1/13 2/23 3/24 4/30 5/32 6/76 7/97 8/100 9/150	15

Bowling: *First Innings*—Andrew 20–3–39–2; Ilott 17–3–42–1; Childs 16–7–39–1; Tople 12–4–25–2; Such 12–4–27–0; Pringle 9–2–16–3; Stephenson 2–1–1–0. *Second Innings*—Andrew 12–1–34–1; Ilott 16–2–43–5; Topley 11–2–29–1; Childs 16–9–18–0; Such 8.1–5–6–2 Pringle 9–3–11–1.

Umpires: G. I. Burgess and J. W. Holder.

CAMBRIDGE UNIVERSITY v GLOUCESTERSHIRE

At Cambridge, May 23, 24, 25. Gloucestershire won by 70 runs. Toss: Gloucestershire. Agai the Cambridge bowling struggled on a flat pitch, with four of the first five county batsme hitting half-centuries, but a first hundred of the season from James led a solid reply by th University batsmen. The Cambridge opener reached three figures in 282 minutes (233 balls) with eleven fours, and shared a 75-minute century partnership for the third wicket with hi captain, Atkinson, who struck twelve fours and a six in his 72. When Atkinson eventuall declared at 314 for eight, the University's total was their highest against a first-class count since 1982, when they made 380 for six against Middlesex. Gloucestershire had little difficult in setting a target of 270 in 153 minutes plus twenty overs, but Cambridge made a disastrou start. They were quickly 13 for three, and although they kept up with the required rate, the continued to lose batsmen steadily. Barnes, the Gloucestershire opening bowler, gained fou wickets for the second time in the match.

Close of play: First day, Cambridge University 38-1 (S. P. James 18*, A. J. Buzza 6*) Second day, Gloucestershire 73-0 (A. J. Wright 33*, P. W. Romaines 38*).

Gloucestershire

*A. J. Wright st Arscott b Buzza	44	– run out	5
G. D. Hodgson lbw b Shufflebotham	51	– (4) not out	3
I. P. Butcher c Atkinson b Lowrey	79	– (5) b Jenkins	
P. Bainbridge st Arscott b Lowrey	61		
J. W. Lloyds not out	73	– (6) not out	
P. W. Romaines not out	15	– (2) c Atkinson b Buzza	9
†G. A. Tedstone (did not bat)		– (3) c Morris b Buzza	2
B 7, l-b 11, w 2, n-b 10	30	L-b 3, w 1, n-b 1	
1/107 2/107 3/198 4/312	(4 wkts dec.) 353	1/103 2/179 3/198 4/220	(4 wkts dec.) 23

M. W. Pooley, S. N. Barnes, M. C. J. Ball and K. B. S. Jarvis did not bat.

Bowling: *First Innings*—Jenkins 20–3–61–0; Johnson 14–1–44–0; Shufflebotha 17–2–65–1; Buzza 27–6–97–1; Atkinson 4–1–9–0; Lowrey 14–2–59–2. *Second Innings*—Jenkins 23.3–3–68–1; Johnson 13–5–25–0; Shufflebotham 11–3–37–0; Buzza 20–1–91–2 Lowrey 2–0–6–0.

Cambridge University

S. P. James c Tedstone b Pooley	116	– lbw b Jarvis	6
R. Heap c Butcher b Barnes	11	– c Wright b Barnes	0
A. J. Buzza c Ball b Pooley	6	– (9) b Barnes	1
*J. C. M. Atkinson c Hodgson b Ball	72	– b Ball	34
M. J. Lowrey c Tedstone b Bainbridge	20	– run out	45
M. J. Morris c Butcher b Barnes	18	– lbw b Bainbridge	17
G. B. A. Dyer c Ball b Barnes	1	– (3) c Tedstone b Jarvis	4
†J. P. Arscott c Lloyds b Barnes	13	– (7) not out	43
D. H. Shufflebotham not out	25	– (8) c Tedstone b Barnes	29
R. H. J. Jenkins not out	3	– c Butcher b Barnes	1
S. W. Johnson (did not bat)		– c Wright b Ball	1
B 12, l-b 9, n-b 8	29	B 6, l-b 7, w 1, n-b 4	18
1/23 2/38 3/146 4/190 5/226 6/241 7/257 8/304 (8 wkts dec.)	314	1/7 2/12 3/13 4/81 5/116 6/121 7/173 8/184 9/186	199

Bowling: *First Innings*—Barnes 24–9–65–4; Jarvis 15–2–50–0; Ball 15–4–50–1; Pooley 13–1–51–2; Bainbridge 12–3–33–1; Lloyds 22–5–44–0. *Second Innings*—Barnes 14–2–51–4; Jarvis 7–0–31–2; Pooley 3–0–16–0; Ball 13–4–37–2; Lloyds 11–2–24–0; Bainbridge 8–3–27–1.

Umpires: D. R. Shepherd and R. C. Tolchard.

†At Cambridge, June 10. Cambridge University won by 72 runs. Cambridge University 176 (A. R. Wingfield Digby five for 41); Free Foresters 104 (R. A. Pyman five for 32).

†At Cambridge, June 11, 12, 13. Drawn. Toss: MCC. MCC 317 for five dec. (J. F. Short 105, A. J. Goldsmith 32, R. J. Robinson 45, P. J. Mir 104) and 21 for three; Cambridge University 134 (R. J. Turner 53; P. J. Mir three for 18, M. Halliday three for 21) and 391 for nine dec. (S. P. James 99, J. C. M. Atkinson 56, R. A. Pyman 65, R. H. J. Jenkins 50 not out; M. J. Robinson three for 50).

†At Cambridge, June 14. Cambridge University won by eight wickets. Club Cricket Conference Under-25 96; Cambridge University 97 for two.

CAMBRIDGE UNIVERSITY v NOTTINGHAMSHIRE

At Cambridge, June 16, 18, 19. Drawn. Toss: Nottinghamshire. A second-innings century by James, who hit fifteen fours to reach three figures from 199 balls in 211 minutes, meant Cambridge were never in danger of defeat, but nor was there ever any prospect of victory. On the opening day, Martindale hit nineteen fours in his career-best 138, from 243 deliveries in 274 minutes, and dominated a 183-run partnership with Newell for Nottinghamshire's second wicket. However, with almost two hours lost to rain on the second day, and prevented by Hutchinson, a Freshman in his first match, from making Cambridge follow on, Nottinghamshire needed runs quickly if they were to press for victory. In the event, they batted until lunch, leaving the University 180 minutes plus twenty overs to chase 340. As James and Heap occupied 33 overs while putting on 63 for the first wicket, Nottinghamshire's prospects began to recede.

Close of play: First day, Cambridge University 9-2 (R. H. J. Jenkins 0*); Second day, Nottinghamshire 46-0 (P. Johnson 35*, M. Saxelby 10*).

Nottinghamshire

P. R. Pollard lbw b Jenkins	13		
D. J. R. Martindale st Turner b Lowrey	138		
M. Newell c Atkinson b Jenkins	60		
*P. Johnson lbw b Pyman	4	(1) run out	49
M. Saxelby not out	30	(2) c Atkinson b Lowrey	73
R. J. Evans not out	21	(4) not out	0
†C. W. Scott (did not bat)		(3) not out	67
B 2, l-b 2, n-b 6	10	B 4, l-b 3, n-b 2	9
1/29 2/212 3/220 4/226	(4 wkts dec.) 276	1/79 2/172	(2 wkts dec.) 198

K. P. Evans, R. A. Pick, J. A. Afford and M. G. Field-Buss did not bat.

Bowling: *First Innings*—Jenkins 21–1–51–2; Pyman 21–3–72–1; Shufflebotham 11–2–38–0; Lowrey 20–6–55–1; Buzza 18–5–54–0; Atkinson 2–0–2–0. *Second Innings*—Jenkins 11–0–49–0; Pyman 9–0–50–0; Buzza 10–1–50–0; Shufflebotham 5–0–37–0; Lowrey 3–0–5–1.

Cambridge University

S. P. James b Pick	1	not out	104
R. Heap c K. P. Evans b Field-Buss	4	lbw b K. P. Evans	31
R. H. J. Jenkins lbw b K. P. Evans	12		
†R. J. Turner c K. P. Evans b Afford	32	(3) c Scott b K. P. Evans	0
*J. C. M. Atkinson c K. P. Evans b Afford	0	(4) c Pick b Afford	5
M. J. Lowrey c Pick b K. P. Evans	19	(5) b Newell	25
M. J. Morris b K. P. Evans	4	(6) not out	0
G. M. Hutchinson b K. P. Evans	29		
R. A. Pyman b Field-Buss	11		
D. H. Shufflebotham not out	4		
A. J. Buzza b Field-Buss	0		
B 4, l-b 13, n-b 2	19	B 3, l-b 4, w 1, n-b 1	9
1/5 2/9 3/43 4/44 5/57 6/75 7/88 8/112 9/130	135	1/63 2/67 3/80 4/173	(4 wkts) 174

Bowling: *First Innings*—Pick 13–6–31–1; K. P. Evans 23–8–50–4; Afford 14–8–13–2; Field-Buss 15.4–9–14–3; Saxelby 5–1–10–0. *Second Innings*—Pick 5–1–12–0; K. P. Evans 15–6–27–2; Field-Buss 21–4–37–0; Afford 17–6–44–1; Newell 5–2–22–1; R. J. Evans 6–1–24–0; Johnson 1–0–1–0.

Umpires: B. Leadbeater and R. A. White.

†At Cambridge, June 17. Cambridge University won by two wickets. Quidnuncs 184 for seven dec. (D. J. Fell 67); Cambridge University 186 for eight.

CAMBRIDGE UNIVERSITY v KENT

At Cambridge, June 20, 21, 22. Kent won by 92 runs. Toss: Cambridge University. The captains' willingness to achieve a result defeated the weather. Contrasting hundreds from Taylor, hitting fifteen fours from 276 deliveries in 283 minutes, and Chris Cowdrey, with three fours and seven sixes from 104 balls in 137 minutes, had enabled Kent to pass 300 with only three wickets down, but rain and bad light ruled out most of the second day. Cambridge declared their first innings at 57 for two and Kent forfeited their second, to leave the University needing 273 in the entire third day's play. A half-century by James and solid support from Turner saw them to 122 for one by early afternoon. But Merrick then took three wickets in eleven balls and Davis's left-arm spin brought him career-best figures of six for 40 as Cambridge lost nine wickets for 58 runs.

Close of play: First day, Kent 329-3 (C. S. Cowdrey 102*, M. V. Fleming 19*); Second day, Cambridge University 57-2 (R. Heap 27*, J. C. M. Atkinson 0*).

Kent

S. G. Hinks lbw b Lowrey 42	M. V. Fleming not out 19
N. R. Taylor c Pyman b Buzza 120	B 1, l-b 5, w 5, n-b 1 12
G. R. Cowdrey st Turner b Lowrey ... 34	
*C. S. Cowdrey not out 102	1/91 2/144 3/225 (3 wkts dec.) 329

†S. A. Marsh, R. M. Ellison, R. P. Davis, T. A. Merrick, N. J. Llong and A. P. Igglesden did not bat.

Bowling: Jenkins 19–5–43–0; Pyman 26–8–60–0; Shufflebotham 8–0–42–0; Buzza 26–7–106–1; Lowrey 28–12–72–2.

Kent forfeited their second innings.

Cambridge University

S. P. James c Marsh b Igglesden	3	– b Merrick 57
R. Heap not out	27	– b Davis 17
†R. J. Turner b Fleming	22	– c and b Merrick 35
*J. C. M. Atkinson not out	0	– b Merrick 0
M. J. Lowrey (did not bat)		– b Davis 4
M. J. Morris (did not bat)		– b Davis 24
G. M. Hutchinson (did not bat)		– c and b Davis 2
R. A. Pyman (did not bat)		– c G. R. Cowdrey b Davis 0
D. H. Shufflebotham (did not bat)		– c Marsh b Igglesden 16
R. H. J. Jenkins (did not bat)		– c Llong b Davis 1
A. J. Buzza (did not bat)		– not out 1
L-b 5	5	B 12, l-b 8, w 1, n-b 2 23
1/3 2/53 (2 wkts dec.)	57	1/27 2/122 3/122 4/125 5/129 6/137 7/141 8/172 9/175 180

Bowling: *First Innings*—Merrick 7–5–7–0; Igglesden 6–2–12–1; Fleming 5.3–1–13–1; Ellison 5–0–20–0. *Second Innings*—Merrick 10–6–13–3; Igglesden 14–3–45–1; Davis 28.1–15–40–6; Ellison 7–3–24–0; Llong 7–1–24–0; Fleming 9–5–14–0.

Umpires: G. I. Burgess and B. J. Meyer.

†At Portsmouth, June 23, 24, 25. Cambridge University won by one wicket. Combined Services 314 for three dec. (SAC A. Jones 105 not out, 2nd Lt R. J. Greatorex 79, Cpl G. J. P. Richards 55 not out) and 239 for five dec. (SAC A. Jones 92, Capt. P. S. Germain 57 not out); Cambridge University 206 for six dec. (R. Heap 62) and 349 for nine (G. M. Hutchinson 75, M. J. Lowrey 68, R. A. Pyman 63; Sgt M. W. Ings five for 101).

At Hove, June 30, July 2, 3. CAMBRIDGE UNIVERSITY beat SUSSEX by three wickets.

At Lord's, July 4, 5, 6. CAMBRIDGE UNIVERSITY drew with OXFORD UNIVERSITY (See Other Matches at Lord's, 1990).

OXFORD AND CAMBRIDGE BLUES

From 1946 to 1990, and some others

A full list of Blues from 1837 may be found in all *Wisdens* published between 1923 and 1939. Between 1948 and 1972 the list was confined to all those who had won Blues after 1880, plus some of "special interest for personal or family reasons". Between 1972 and 1982 the list was restricted to those who had won Blues since 1919. Such adjustments have been necessary owing to the exigencies of space.

OXFORD

Aamer Hameed (Central Model HS and Punjab U.) 1979
Abell, G. E. B. (Marlborough) 1924, 1926-27
Allan, J. M. (Edinburgh Academy) 1953-56
Allerton, J. W. O. (Stowe) 1969
Allison, D. F. (Greenmore Coll.) 1970
Almaer, S. A. (Ilford County HS) 1988-89
Altham, H. S. (Repton) 1911-12
Arenhold, J. A. (Diocesan Coll., SA) 1954

Baig, A. A. (Aliya and Osmania U., India) 1959-62
Baig, M. A. (Osmania U., India) 1962-64
Bailey, J. A. (Christ's Hospital) (Capt. in 1958) 1956-58
Barber, A. T. (Shrewsbury) (Capt. in 1929) 1927-29
Barker, A. H. (Charterhouse) 1964-65, 1967
Bartlett, J. H. (Chichester) 1946, 1951
Beech, A. R. (John XXIII Coll., Perth and Univ. of Western Australia) 1987
Bettington, R. H. B. (The King's School, Parramatta) (Capt. in 1923) 1920-23
Bird, W. S. (Malvern) (Capt. in 1906) 1904-06
Birrell, H. B. (St Andrews, SA) 1953-54
Blake, P. D. S. (Eton) (Capt. in 1952) 1950-52
Bloy, N. C. F. (Dover) 1946-47
Boobbyer, B. (Uppingham) 1949-52
Bosanquet, B. J. T. (Eton) 1898-1900
Botton, N. D. (King Edward's, Bath) 1974
Bowman, R. C. (Fettes) 1957
Brettell, D. N. (Cheltenham) 1977
Bristowe, W. R. (Charterhouse) 1984-85
Brooks, R. A. (Quintin and Bristol U.) 1967
Brown, M. E. O. (Diocesan Coll. and Univ. of Cape Town) 1988
Burchnall, R. L. (Winchester) 1970-71
Burki, J. (St Mary's, Rawalpindi and Punjab U.) 1958-60
Burton, M. St J. W. (Umtali HS, Rhodesia and Rhodes U.) (Capt. in 1970) 1969-71
Bury, T. E. O. (Charterhouse) 1980
Bush, J. E. (Magdalen Coll. Sch.) 1952

Campbell, A. N. (Berkhamsted) 1970
Campbell, I. P. (Canford) 1949-50
Campbell, I. P. F. (Repton) (Capt. in 1913) 1911-13
Cantlay, C. P. T. (Radley) 1975
Carr, D. B. (Repton) (Capt. in 1950) 1949-51
Carr, J. D. (Repton) 1983-85
Carroll, P. R. (Newington Coll. and Sydney U.) 1971
Chalk, F. G. H. (Uppingham) (Capt. in 1934) 1931-34
Chesterton, G. H. (Malvern) 1949
Claughton, J. A. (King Edward's, Birmingham) (Capt. in 1978) 1976-79
Clements, S. M. (Ipswich) (Capt. in 1979) 1976, 1979
Clube, S. V. M. (St John's, Leatherhead) 1956
Cope, J. E. B. (St John's, Leatherhead) 1986-87
Corlett, S. C. (Worksop) 1971-72
Corran, A. J. (Gresham's) 1958-60
Coutts, I. D. F. (Dulwich) 1952
Cowan, R. S. (Lewes Priory CS) 1980-82
Cowdrey, M. C. (Tonbridge) (Capt. in 1954) 1952-54
Coxon, A. J. (Harrow CS) 1952
Crawley, A. M. (Harrow) 1927-30
Crawley, M. A. (Manchester GS) (Capt. in 1989) 1987-90
Crutchley, G. E. V. (Harrow) 1912
Cullinan, M. R. (Hilton Coll., SA) 1983-84
Curtis, D. M. (Falcon Coll., Harare and Cape Town U.) 1990
Curtis, I. J. (Whitgift) 1980, 1982
Cushing, V. G. B. (KCS Wimbledon) 1973
Cuthbertson, J. L. (Rugby) 1962-63

Davidson, W. W. (Brighton) 1947-48
Davis, F. J. (Blundell's) 1963
Dawson, T. A. J. (Mill Hill) 1986
Delisle, G. P. S. (Stonyhurst) 1955-56
de Saram, F. C. (Royal Coll., Colombo) 1934-35
Divecha, R. V. (Podar HS and Bombay U.) 1950-51
Dixon, E. J. H. (St Edward's, Oxford) (Capt. in 1939) 1937-39
Donnelly, M. P. (New Plymouth BHS and Canterbury U., NZ) (Capt. in 1947) 1946-47

Dowding, A. L. (St Peter's, Adelaide) (Capt. in 1953) 1952-53
Drybrough, C. D. (Highgate) (Capt. in 1961-62) 1960-62
Duff, A. R. (Radley) 1960-61
Dyer, A. W. (Mill Hill) 1965-66
Dyson, E. M. (QEGS, Wakefield) 1958

Eagar, M. A. (Rugby) 1956-59
Easter, J. N. C. (St Edward's, Oxford) 1967-68
Edbrooke, R. M. (Queen Elizabeth's Hospital) 1984
Edwards, P. G. (Canford) 1987-89
Ellis, R. G. P. (Haileybury) (Capt. in 1982) 1981-83
Elviss, R. W. (Leeds GS) 1966-67
Ezekowitz, R. A. B. (Westville BHS, Durban and Cape Town U., SA) 1980-81

Faber, M. J. J. (Eton) 1972
Fane, F. L. (Charterhouse) 1897-98
Fasken, D. K. (Wellington) 1953-55
Fellows-Smith, J. P. (Durban HS, SA) 1953-55
Fillary, E. W. J. (St Lawrence) 1963-65
Findlay, W. (Eton) (Capt. in 1903) 1901-03
Firth, T. (Stockport GS) 1987
Fisher, P. B. (St Ignatius, Enfield) 1975-78
Foster, G. N. (Malvern) 1905-08
Foster, H. K. (Malvern) 1894-96
Foster, R. E. (Malvern) (Capt. in 1900) 1897-1900
Franks, J. G. (Stamford) 1984-85
Fry, C. A. (Repton) 1959-61
Fry, C. B. (Repton) (Capt. in 1894) 1892-95
Fursdon, E. D. (Sherborne) 1974-75

Gamble, N. W. (Stockport GS) 1967
Garofall, A. R. (Latymer Upper) 1967-68
Gerrans, P. S. (Daramalau Coll. and Aust. Nat. U.) 1990
Gibbs, P. J. K. (Hanley GS) 1964-66
Gibson, I. (Manchester GS) 1955-58
Gilliat, R. M. C. (Charterhouse) (Capt. in 1966) 1964-67
Gilligan, F. W. (Dulwich) (Capt. in 1920) 1919-20
Glover, T. R. (Lancaster RGS) (Capt. in 1975) 1973-75
Goldstein, F. S. (Falcon Coll., Bulawayo) (Capt. in 1968-69) 1966-69
Green, D. M. (Manchester GS) 1959-61
Grover, J. N. (Winchester) (Capt. in 1938) 1936-38
Groves, M. G. M. (Diocesan Coll., SA) 1964-66
Guest, M. R. J. (Rugby) 1964-66
Guise, J. L. (Winchester) (Capt. in 1925) 1924-25
Gurr, D. R. (Aylesbury GS) 1976-77

Hagan, D. A. (Trinity, Leamington Spa) 1986, 1988-90
Halliday, S. J. (Downside) 1980
Hamblin, C. B. (King's, Canterbury) 1971-73
Hamilton, A. C. (Charterhouse) 1975
Hampton, A. N. S. (Reading) 1989
Harris, C. R. (Buckingham RLS) 1964
Harris, Hon. G. R. C. (Lord Harris) (Eton) 1871-72, 1874
Hayes, K. A. (QEGS, Blackburn) (Capt. in 1984) 1981-84
Heal, M. G. (St Brendan's, Bristol) 1970, 1972
Heard, H. (QE Hosp.) 1969-70
Henderson, D. (St Edward's, Oxford) 1950
Henderson, I. M. (Laxton) 1987, 1989-90
Henley, D. F. (Harrow) 1947
Heseltine, P. J. (Holgate GS) 1983
Hester, E. D. (Thornleigh Salesian Coll.) 1989
Hiller, R. B. (Bec) 1966
Hobbs, J. A. D. (Liverpool Coll.) 1957
Hofmeyr, M. B. (Pretoria, SA) (Capt. in 1951) 1949-51
Holmes, E. R. T. (Malvern) (Capt. in 1927) 1925-27
Hone, B. W. (Adelaide U.) (Capt. in 1933) 1931-33
Howell, M. (Repton) (Capt. in 1919) 1914, 1919
Huxford, P. N. (Richard Hale) 1981

Imran Khan (Aitchison Coll., Lahore and Worcester RGS) (Capt. in 1974) 1973-75

Jack, T. B. (Aquinas Coll. and Univ. of WA) 1988
Jakobson, T. R. (Charterhouse) 1961
Jardine, D. R. (Winchester) 1920-21, 1923
Jardine, M. R. (Fettes) (Capt. in 1891) 1889-92
Jarrett, D. W. (Wellington) 1975
Johns, R. L. (St Albans and Keele U.) 1970
Jones, A. K. C. (Solihull) (Capt. in 1973) 1971-73
Jones, P. C. H. (Milton HS, Rhodesia and Rhodes U.) (Capt. in 1972) 1971-72
Jose, A. D. (Adelaide U.) 1950-51
Jowett, D. C. P. R. (Sherborne) 1952-55
Jowett, R. L. (Bradford GS) 1957-59

Kamm, A. (Charterhouse) 1954
Kardar, A. H. (Islamia Coll. and Punjab U.) 1947-49
Kayum, D. A. (Selhurst GS and Chatham House GS) 1977-78
Keighley, W. G. (Eton) 1947-48
Kentish, E. S. M. (Cornwall Coll., Jamaica) 1956
Khan, A. J. (Aitchison Coll., Lahore and Punjab U.) 1968-69
Kilborn, M. J. (Farrer Agric. HS and Univ. of NSW) (Capt. in 1988) 1986-88
Kingsley, P. G. T. (Winchester) (Capt. in 1930) 1928-30

Kinkead-Weekes, R. C. (Eton) 1972
Knight, D. J. (Malvern) 1914, 1919
Knight, J. M. (Oundle) 1979
Knott, C. H. (Tonbridge) (Capt. in 1924) 1922-24
Knott, F. H. (Tonbridge) (Capt. in 1914) 1912-14
Knox, F. P. (Dulwich) (Capt. in 1901) 1899-1901

Lamb, Hon. T. M. (Shrewsbury) 1973-74
Lawrence, M. P. (Manchester GS) 1984-86
Lee, R. J. (Church of England GS and Sydney U.) 1972-74
Legge, G. B. (Malvern) (Capt. in 1926) 1925-26
L'Estrange, M. G. (St Aloysius Coll. and Sydney U.) 1977, 1979
Leveson Gower, H. D. G. (Winchester) (Capt. in 1896) 1893-96
Lewis, D. J. (Cape Town U.) 1951
Lloyd, M. F. D. (Magdalen Coll. Sch.) 1974
Luddington, R. S. (KCS, Wimbledon) 1982
Lunn, P. D. (Abingdon) 1989-90

McCanlis, M. A. (Cranleigh) (Capt. in 1928) 1926-28
Macindoe, D. H. (Eton) (Capt. in 1946) 1937-39, 1946
McKinna, G. H. (Manchester GS) 1953
MacLarnon, P. C. (Loughborough GS) 1985
Majendie, N. L. (Winchester) 1962-63
Mallett, A. W. H. (Dulwich) 1947-48
Mallett, N. V. H. (St Andrew's Coll. and Cape Town U.) 1981
Manasseh, M. (Epsom) 1964
Marie, G. V. (Western Australia U. and Reading U.) (Capt. in 1979, but injury prevented him playing v Cambridge) 1978
Marks, V. J. (Blundell's) (Capt. in 1976-77) 1975-78
Marsden, R. (Merchant Taylors', Northwood) 1982
Marshall, J. C. (Rugby) 1953
Marsham, C. D. B. (Private) (Capt. in 1857-58) 1854-58
Marsham, C. H. B. (Eton) (Capt. in 1902) 1900-02
Marsham, C. J. B. (Private) 1851
Marsham, R. H. B. (Private) 1856
Marsland, G. P. (Rossall) 1954
Martin, J. D. (Magdalen Coll. Sch.) (Capt. in 1965) 1962-63, 1965
Maudsley, R. H. (Malvern) 1946-47
May, B. (Prince Edward's, Salisbury and Cape Town U.) (Capt. in 1971) 1970-72
Mee, A. A. G. (Merchant Taylors', Northwood) 1986
Melville, A. (Michaelhouse, SA) (Capt. in 1931-32) 1930-33
Melville, C. D. M. (Michaelhouse, SA) 1957
Metcalfe, S. G. (Leeds GS) 1956
Millener, D. J. (Auckland GS and Auckland U.) 1969-70
Miller, A. J. T. (Haileybury) (Capt. in 1985) 1983-85
Minns, R. E. F. (King's, Canterbury) 1962-63
Mitchell, W. M. (Dulwich) 1951-52
Mitchell-Innes, N. S. (Sedbergh) (Capt. in 1936) 1934-37
Moore, D. N. (Shrewsbury) (Capt. in 1931, when he did not play v Cambridge owing to illness) 1930
Morgan, A. H. (Hastings GS) 1969
Morrill, N. D. (Sandown GS and Millfield) 1979
Morris, R. E. (Dyffryn Conwy, Llanrwst) (Capt. in 1990) 1987, 1989-90
Moulding, R. P. (Haberdashers' Aske's) (Capt. in 1981) 1978-83
Mountford, P. N. G. (Bromsgrove) 1963

Neate, F. W. (St Paul's) 1961-62
Newton-Thompson, J. O. (Diocesan Coll., SA) 1946
Niven, R. A. (Berkhamsted) 1968-69, 1973
Nuttall, J. D. (Pocklington) 1988-89

O'Brien, T. C. (St Charles' College, Notting Hill) 1884-85
Orders, J. O. D. (Winchester) 1978-81
Owen-Smith, H. G. (Diocesan College, SA) 1931-33

Palairet, L. C. H. (Repton) (Capt. in 1892-93) 1890-93
Pataudi, Nawab of (Chief's College, Lahore) 1929-31
Pataudi, Nawab of (Winchester) (Capt. in 1961, when he did not play v Cambridge owing to a car accident, and 1963) 1960, 1963
Pathmanathan, G. (Royal Coll., Colombo and Sri Lanka U.) 1975-78
Paver, R. G. L. (Fort Victoria HS and Rhodes U.) 1973-74
Pawson, A. C. (Winchester) 1903
Pawson, A. G. (Winchester) (Capt. in 1910) 1908-11
Pawson, H. A. (Winchester) (Capt. in 1948) 1947-48
Pearce, J. P. (Ampleforth) 1979
Peebles, I. A. R. (Glasgow Academy) 1930
Petchey, M. D. (Latymer Upper) 1983
Phillips, J. B. M. (King's, Canterbury) 1955
Piachaud, J. D. (St Thomas's, Colombo) 1958-61
Pithey, D. B. (Plumtree HS and Cape Town U.) 1961-62
Porter, S. R. (Peers School) 1973
Potter, I. C. (King's, Canterbury) 1961-62
Potts, H. J. (Stand GS) 1950

Price, V. R. (Bishop's Stortford) (Capt. in 1921) 1919-22
Pycroft, J. (Bath) 1836

Quinlan, J. D. (Sherborne) 1985

Rawlinson, H. T. (Eton) 1983-84
Raybould, J. G. (Leeds GS) 1959
Reynolds, G. D. (Wellington Coll.) 1988-89
Ridge, S. P. (Dr Challenor's GS) 1982
Ridley, G. N. S. (Milton HS, Rhodesia) (Capt. in 1967) 1965-68
Ridley, R. M. (Clifton) 1968-70
Robertson-Glasgow, R. C. (Charterhouse) 1920-23
Robinson, G. A. (Preston Cath. Coll.) 1971
Robinson, H. B. O. (North Shore Coll., Vancouver) 1947-48
Rogers, J. J. (Sedbergh) 1979-81
Ross, C. J. (Wanganui CS and Wellington U., NZ) (Capt. in 1980) 1978-80
Rudd, C. R. D. (Eton) 1949
Rumbold, J. S. (St Andrew's Coll., NZ) 1946
Rutnagur, R. S. (Westminster) 1985-86
Rydon, R. A. (Sherborne) 1986

Sabine, P. N. B. (Marlborough) 1963
Sale, R. (Repton) 1910
Sale, R. (Repton) 1939, 1946
Salvi, N. V. (Rossall) 1986
Sanderson, J. F. W. (Westminster) 1980
Sardesai, R. D. (St Xavier's Coll., Bombay and Univ. of Bombay) 1987
Saunders, C. J. (Lancing) 1964
Savage, R. Le Q. (Marlborough) 1976-78
Sayer, D. M. (Maidstone GS) 1958-60
Scott, M. D. (Winchester) 1957
Singleton, A. P. (Shrewsbury) (Capt. in 1937) 1934-37
Siviter, K. (Liverpool) 1976
Smith, A. C. (King Edward's, Birmingham) (Capt. in 1959-60) 1958-60
Smith, G. O. (Charterhouse) 1895-96
Smith, M. J. K. (Stamford) (Capt. in 1956) 1954-56
Stallibrass, M. J. D. (Lancing) 1974
Stevens, G. T. S. (UCS) (Capt. in 1922) 1920-23
Sutcliffe, S. P. (King George V GS, Southport) 1980-81
Sutton, M. A. (Ampleforth) 1946
Sygrove, M. R. (Lutterworth GS) 1988

Tavaré, C. J. (Sevenoaks) 1975-77
Taylor, C. H. (Westminster) 1923-26
Taylor, T. J. (Stockport GS) 1981-82
Thackeray, P. R. (St Edward's, Oxford and Exeter U.) 1974
Thomas, R. J. A. (Radley) 1965
Thorne, D. A. (Bablake) (Capt. in 1986) 1984-86
Toft, D. P. (Tonbridge) 1966-67
Toogood, G. J. (N. Bromsgrove HS) (Capt. in 1983) 1982-85
Tooley, C. D. M. (St Dunstan's) (Capt. in 1987) 1985-87
Topham, R. D. N. (Shrewsbury and Australian National U., Canberra) 1976
Travers, B. H. (Sydney U.) 1946, 1948
Trevelyan, R. W. D. (Marlborough) 1990
Turner, G. J. (St Stithian's and Cape Town U.) 1990
Twining, R. H. (Eton) (Capt. in 1912) 1910-13

van der Bijl, P. G. (Diocesan Coll., SA) 1932
van der Merwe, W. M. (Grey, OFS U. and Cape Town U.) 1990
Van Ryneveld, C. B. (Diocesan Coll., SA) (Capt. in 1949) 1948-50
Varey, J. G. (Birkenhead) 1982-83

Wagstaffe, M. C. (Rossall and Exeter U.) 1972
Walford, M. M. (Rugby) 1936, 1938
Walker, D. F. (Uppingham) (Capt. in 1935) 1933-35
Waller, G. de W. (Hurstpierpoint) 1974
Walsh, D. R. (Marlborough) 1967-69
Walshe, A. P. (Milton HS, Rhodesia) 1953, 1955-56
Walton, A. C. (Radley) (Capt. in 1957) 1955-57
Ward, J. M. (Newcastle-under-Lyme HS) 1971-73
Warner, P. F. (Rugby) 1895-96
Watson, A. G. M. (St Lawrence) 1965-66, 1968
Weale, S. D. (Westminster City) 1987-88, 1990
Webb, H. E. (Winchester) 1948
Webbe, A. J. (Harrow) (Capt. in 1877-78) 1875-78
Wellings, E. M. (Cheltenham) 1929, 1931
Westley, S. A. (Lancaster RGS) 1968-69
Wheatley, G. A. (Uppingham) 1946
Whitcombe, P. A. (Winchester) 1947-49
Whitcombe, P. J. (Worcester RGS) 1951-52
Wiley, W. G. A. (Diocesan Coll., SA) 1952
Williams, C. C. P. (Westminster) (Capt. in 1955) 1953-55
Wilson, P. R. B. (Milton HS, Rhodesia and Cape Town U.) 1968, 1970
Wilson, R. W. (Warwick) 1957
Wingfield Digby, A. R. (Sherborne) 1971, 1975-77
Winn, C. E. (KCS, Wimbledon) 1948-51
Woodcock, R. G. (Worcester RGS) 1957-58
Wookey, S. M. (Malvern and Cambridge U.) 1978
Wordsworth, Chas. (Harrow) (Capt. both years, first Oxford Capt.) 1827, 1829
Worsley, D. R. (Bolton) (Capt. in 1964) 1961-64
Wrigley, M. H. (Harrow) 1949

CAMBRIDGE

Acfield, D. L. (Brentwood) 1967-68
Aers, D. R. (Tonbridge) 1967
Ahluwalia, M. S. (Latymer Upper) 1986
Aird, R. (Eton) 1923
Alban, M. T. (Sedbergh) 1989
Alexander, F. C. M. (Wolmer's Coll., Jamaica) 1952-53
Allbrook, M. E. (Tonbridge) 1975-78
Allen, G. O. (Eton) 1922-23
Allom, M. J. C. (Wellington) 1927-28
Andrew, C. R. (Barnard Castle) (Capt. in 1985) 1984-85
Ashton, C. T. (Winchester) (Capt. in 1923) 1921-23
Ashton, G. (Winchester) (Capt. in 1921) 1919-21
Ashton, H. (Winchester) (Capt. in 1922) 1920-22
Atherton, M. A. (Capt. in 1988-89) (Manchester GS) 1987-89
Atkins, G. (Dr Challenor's GS) 1960
Atkinson, J. C. M. (Millfield) (Capt. in 1990) 1988-90
Aworth, C. J. (Tiffin) (Capt. in 1975) 1973-75

Bail, P. A. C. (Millfield) 1986-88
Bailey, T. E. (Dulwich) 1947-48
Baker, R. K. (Brentwood) 1973-74
Bannister, C. S. (Caterham) 1976
Barber, R. W. (Ruthin) 1956-57
Barford, M. T. (Eastbourne) 1970-71
Barrington, W. E. J. (Lancing) 1982
Bartlett, H. T. (Dulwich) (Capt. in 1936) 1934-36
Bate, R. (Haberdashers' Aske's) 1988
Beaumont, D. J. (West Bridgford GS and Bramshill Coll.) 1978
Benke, A. F. (Cheltenham) 1962
Bennett, B. W. P. (Welbeck and RMA Sandhurst) 1979
Bennett, C. T. (Harrow) (Capt. in 1925) 1923, 1925
Bernard, J. R. (Clifton) 1958-60
Bhatia, A. N. (Doon School, India) 1969
Bligh, Hon. Ivo F. W. (Lord Darnley) (Eton) (Capt. in 1881) 1878-81
Blofeld, H. C. (Eton) 1959
Bodkin, P. E. (Bradfield) (Capt. in 1946) 1946
Boyd-Moss, R. J. (Bedford) 1980-83
Brearley, J. M. (City of London) (Capt. in 1963-64) 1961-64
Breddy, M. N. (Cheltenham GS) 1984
Brodie, J. B. (Union HS, SA) 1960
Brodrick, P. D. (Royal GS, Newcastle) 1961
Bromley, R. C. (Christ's Coll. and Canterbury U., NZ) 1970
Brooker, M. E. W. (Lancaster RGS and Burnley GS) 1976
Brown, A. D. (Clacton HS) 1986
Brown, F. R. (The Leys) 1930-31
Browne, D. W. (Stamford) 1986
Burnett, A. C. (Lancing) 1949
Burnley, I. D. (Queen Elizabeth, Darlington) 1984
Bush, D. J. (King Edward VI, Fiveways) 1989
Bushby, M. H. (Dulwich) (Capt. in 1954) 1952-54
Buzza, A. J. (Redruth CS) 1989-90

Calthorpe, Hon. F. S. G. (Repton) 1912-14, 1919
Cameron, J. H. (Taunton) 1935-37
Cangley, B. G. M. (Felsted) 1947
Carling, P. G. (Kingston GS) 1968, 1970
Chambers, R. E. J. (Forest) 1966
Chapman, A. P. F. (Oakham and Uppingham) 1920-22
Close, P. A. (Haileybury) 1965
Cobden, F. C. (Harrow) 1870-72
Cockett, J. A. (Aldenham) 1951
Coghlan, T. B. L. (Rugby) 1960
Conradi, E. R. (Oundle) 1946
Cook, G. W. (Dulwich) 1957-58
Cooper, N. H. C. (St Brendan's, Bristol and East Anglia U.) 1979
Cosh, N. J. (Dulwich) 1966-68
Cotterell, T. A. (Downside) 1983-85
Cottrell, G. A. (Kingston GS) (Capt. in 1968) 1966-68
Cottrell, P. R. (Chislehurst and Sidcup GS) 1979
Coverdale, S. P. (St Peter's, York) 1974-77
Craig, E. J. (Charterhouse) 1961-63
Crawford, N. C. (Shrewsbury) 1979-80
Crawley, E. (Harrow) 1887-89
Crawley, L. G. (Harrow) 1923-25
Croft, P. D. (Gresham's) 1955
Crookes, D. V. (Michaelhouse, SA) 1953
Curtis, T. S. (Worcester RGS) 1983

Daniell, J. (Clifton) 1899-1901
Daniels, D. M. (Rutlish) 1964-65
Datta, P. B. (Asutosh Coll., Calcutta) 1947
Davies, A. G. (Birkenhead) 1984-85
Davies, J. G. W. (Tonbridge) 1933-34
Davidson, J. E. (Penglais) 1985-86
Dawson, E. W. (Eton) (Capt. in 1927) 1924-27
Day, S. H. (Malvern) (Capt. in 1901) 1899-1902
Dewes, A. R. (Dulwich) 1978
Dewes, J. G. (Aldenham) 1948-50
Dexter, E. R. (Radley) (Capt. in 1958) 1956-58
Dickinson, D. C. (Clifton) 1953
Doggart, A. G. (Bishop's Stortford) 1921-22
Doggart, G. H. G. (Winchester) (Capt. in 1950) 1948-50

Doggart, S. J. G. (Winchester) 1980-83
Douglas-Pennant, S. (Eton) 1959
Duleepsinhji, K. S. (Cheltenham) 1925-26, 1928

Edmonds, P. H. (Gilbert Rennie HS, Lusaka, Skinner's and Cranbrook) (Capt. in 1973) 1971-73
Edwards, T. D. W. (Sherborne) 1981
Elgood, B. C. (Bradfield) 1948
Ellison, C. C. (Tonbridge) 1982-83, 1985-86
Enthoven, H. J. (Harrow) (Capt. in 1926) 1923-26
Estcourt, N. S. D. (Plumtree, Southern Rhodesia) 1954

Falcon, M. (Harrow) (Capt. in 1910) 1908-11
Farnes, K. (Royal Liberty School, Romford) 1931-33
Fell, D. J. (John Lyon) 1985-87
Fenton, N. C. W. (Rugby) 1988
Field, M. N. (Bablake) 1974
Fitzgerald, J. F. (St Brendan's, Bristol) 1968
Ford, A. F. J. (Repton) 1878-81
Ford, F. G. J. (Repton) (Capt. in 1889) 1887-90
Ford, W. J. (Repton) 1873
Fosh, M. K. (Harrow) 1977-78

Gardiner, S. J. (St Andrew's, Bloemfontein) 1978
Garlick, P. L. (Sherborne) 1984
Gibb, P. A. (St Edward's, Oxford) 1935-38
Gibson, C. H. (Eton) 1920-21
Gilligan, A. E. R. (Dulwich) 1919-20
Goldie, C. F. E. (St Paul's) 1981-82
Golding, A. K. (Colchester GS) 1986
Goodfellow, A. (Marlborough) 1961-62
Goonesena, G. (Royal Coll., Colombo) (Capt. in 1957) 1954-57
Gorman, S. R. (St Peter's, York) 1985, 1987
Grace, W. G., jun. (Clifton) 1895-96
Grant, G. C. (Trinidad) 1929-30
Grant, R. S. (Trinidad) 1933
Green, D. J. (Burton GS) (Capt. in 1959) 1957-59
Greig, I. A. (Queen's Coll., SA) (Capt. in 1979) 1977-79
Grierson, H. (Bedford GS) 1911
Grimes, A. D. H. (Tonbridge) 1984
Griffith, M. G. (Marlborough) 1963-65
Griffith, S. C. (Dulwich) 1935
Griffiths, W. H. (Charterhouse) 1946-48

Hadley, R. J. (Sanfields CS) 1971-73
Hall, J. E. (Ardingly) 1969
Hall, P. J. (Geelong) 1949
Harvey, J. R. W. (Marlborough) 1965
Hawke, Hon. M. B. (Eton) (Capt. in 1885) 1882-83, 1885
Hayes, P. J. (Brighton) 1974-75, 1977
Hays, D. L. (Highgate) 1966, 1968
Hayward, W. I. D. (St Peter's Coll., Adelaide) 1950-51, 1953
Haywood, D. C. (Nottingham HS) 1968
Hazelrigg, A. G. (Eton) (Capt. in 1932) 1930-32
Heap, R. (Ipswich) 1989-90
Heath, S. D. (King Edward's, Birmingham) 1988
Henderson, S. P. (Downside and Durham U.) (Capt. in 1983) 1982-83
Hewitt, S. G. P. (Bradford GS) 1983
Hignell, A. J. (Denstone) (Capt. in 1977-78) 1975-78
Hobson, B. S. (Taunton) 1946
Hodgson, K. I. (Oundle) 1981-83
Hodson, R. P. (QEGS, Wakefield) 1972-73
Holliday, D. C. (Oundle) 1979-81
Hooper, A. M. (Latymer Upper) 1987
Howat, M. G. (Abingdon) 1977, 1980
Howland, C. B. (Dulwich) (Capt. in 1960) 1958-60
Hughes, G. (Cardiff HS) 1965
Human, J. H. (Repton) (Capt. in 1934) 1932-34
Hurd, A. (Chigwell) 1958-60
Hutton, R. A. (Repton) 1962-64
Huxter, R. J. A. (Magdalen Coll. Sch.) 1981

Insole, D. J. (Monoux, Walthamstow) (Capt. in 1949) 1947-49

Jackson, E. J. W. (Winchester) 1974-76
Jackson, F. S. (Harrow) (Capt. in 1892-93) 1890-93
Jahangir Khan (Lahore), 1933-36
James, R. M. (St John's, Leatherhead) 1956-58
James, S. P. (Monmouth) 1989-90
Jameson, T. E. N. (Taunton and Durham U.) 1970
Jarrett, D. W. (Wellington and Oxford U.) 1976
Jefferson, R. I. (Winchester) 1961
Jenkins, R. H. J. (Oundle) 1990
Jenner, Herbert (Eton) (Capt. in 1827, First Cambridge Capt.) 1827
Jessop, G. L. (Cheltenham GS) (Capt. in 1899) 1896-99
Johnson, P. D. (Nottingham HS) 1970-72
Johnson, S. W. (Royal GS, Newcastle) 1990
Jones, A. O. (Bedford Modern) 1893
Jorden, A. M. (Monmouth) (Capt. in 1969-70) 1968-70

Kelland, P. A. (Repton) 1950
Kemp-Welch, G. D. (Charterhouse) (Capt. in 1931) 1929-31
Kendall, M. P. (Gillingham GS) 1972
Kenny, C. J. M. (Ampleforth) 1952
Kerslake, R. C. (Kingswood) 1963-64
Killick, E. T. (St Paul's) 1928-30
Kirby, D. (St Peter's, York) (Capt. in 1961) 1959-61
Kirkman, M. C. (Dulwich) 1963
Knight, R. D. V. (Dulwich) 1967-70
Knightley-Smith, W. (Highgate) 1953

Lacey, F. E. (Sherborne) 1882
Lacy-Scott, D. G. (Marlborough) 1946
Lea, A. E. (High Arcal GS) 1984-86
Lewis, A. R. (Neath GS) (Capt. in 1962) 1960-62
Lewis, L. K. (Taunton) 1953
Littlewood, D. J. (Enfield GS) 1978
Lowrey, M. J. (Radley) 1990
Lowry, T. C. (Christ's College, NZ) (Capt. in 1924) 1923-24
Lumsden, V. R. (Munro College, Jamaica) 1953-55
Lyttelton, 4th Lord (Eton) 1838
Lyttelton, Hon. Alfred (Eton) (Capt. in 1879) 1876-79
Lyttelton, Hon. C. F. (Eton) 1908-09
Lyttelton, Hon. C. G. (Lord Cobham) (Eton) 1861-64
Lyttelton, Hon. Edward (Eton) (Capt. in 1878) 1875-78
Lyttelton, Hon. G. W. S. (Eton) 1866-67

McAdam, K. P. W. J. (Prince of Wales, Nairobi and Millfield) 1965-66
MacBryan, J. C. W. (Exeter) 1920
McCarthy, C. N. (Maritzburg Coll., SA) 1952
McDowall, J. I. (Rugby) 1969
MacGregor, G. (Uppingham) (Capt. in 1891) 1888-91
McLachlan, A. A. (St Peter's, Adelaide) 1964-65
McLachlan, I. M. (St Peter's, Adelaide) 1957-58
Majid Khan (Aitchison Coll., Lahore and Punjab U.) (Capt. in 1971-72) 1970-72
Malalasekera, V. P. (Royal Coll., Colombo) 1966-67
Mann, E. W. (Harrow) (Capt. in 1905) 1903-05
Mann, F. G. (Eton) 1938-39
Mann, F. T. (Malvern) 1909-11
Marlar, R. G. (Harrow) (Capt. in 1953) 1951-53
Marriott, C. S. (St Columba's) 1920-21
Mathews, K. P. A. (Felsted) 1951
May, P. B. H. (Charterhouse) 1950-52
Melluish, M. E. L. (Rossall) (Capt. in 1956) 1954-56
Meyer, R. J. O. (Haileybury) 1924-26
Middleton, M. R. (Harrow) 1987
Miller, M. E. (Prince Henry GS, Hohne, WG) 1963
Mills, J. M. (Oundle) (Capt. in 1948) 1946-48
Mills, J. P. C. (Oundle) (Capt. in 1982) 1979-82
Mischler, N. M. (St Paul's) 1946-47
Mitchell, F. (St Peter's, York) (Capt. in 1896) 1894-97
Morgan, J. T. (Charterhouse) (Capt. in 1930) 1928-30
Morgan, M. N. (Marlborough) 1954
Morris, M. J. (Cherwell) 1990
Morris, R. J. (Blundell's) 1949
Morrison, J. S. F. (Charterhouse) (Capt. in 1919) 1912, 1914, 1919
Moses, G. H. (Ystalyfera GS) 1974
Moylan, A. C. D. (Clifton) 1977
Mubarak, A. M. (Royal Coll., Colombo and Sri Lanka U.) 1978-80
Murray, D. L. (Queen's RC, Trinidad) (Capt. in 1966) 1965-66
Murrills, T. J. (The Leys) (Capt. in 1976) 1973-74, 1976

Nevin, M. R. S. (Winchester) 1969
Norris, D. W. W. (Harrow) 1967-68
Noyes, S. J. (Royal GS, High Wycombe) 1988

O'Brien, R. P. (Wellington) 1955-56
Odendaal, A. (Queen's Coll. and Stellenbosch U., SA) 1980
Owen-Thomas, D. R. (KCS, Wimbledon) 1969-72

Palfreman, A. B. (Nottingham HS) 1966
Palmer, R. W. M. (Bedford) 1982
Parker, G. W. (Crypt, Gloucester) (Capt. in 1935) 1934-35
Parker, P. W. G. (Collyer's GS) 1976-78
Parsons, A. B. D. (Brighton) 1954-55
Pathmanathan, G. (Royal Coll., Colombo, Sri Lanka U. and Oxford U.) 1983
Paull, R. K. (Millfield) 1967
Payne, M. W. (Wellington) (Capt. in 1907) 1904-07
Pearman, H. (King Alfred's and St Andrew's U.) 1969
Pearson, A. J. G. (Downside) 1961-63
Peck, I. G. (Bedford) (Capt. in 1980-81) 1980-81
Pepper, J. (The Leys) 1946-48
Perry, J. N. (Ampleforth) 1987-88
Pieris, P. I. (St Thomas's, Colombo) 1957-58
Pointer, G. A. (St Dunstan's) 1987-88
Pollock, A. J. (Shrewsbury) (Capt. in 1984) 1982-84
Ponniah, C. E. M. (St Thomas's, Colombo) 1967-69
Ponsonby, Hon. F. G. B. (Lord Bessborough) (Harrow) 1836
Popplewell, N. F. M. (Radley) 1977-79
Popplewell, O. B. (Charterhouse) 1949-51
Pretlove, J. F. (Alleyn's) 1954-56
Price, D. G. (Haberdashers' Aske's) (Capt. in 1986-87) 1984-87
Prideaux, R. M. (Tonbridge) 1958-60
Pringle, D. R. (Felsted) (Capt. in 1982, when he did not play v Oxford owing to Test selection) 1979-81
Pritchard, G. C. (King's, Canterbury) 1964
Pryer, B. J. K. (City of London) 1948
Pyemont, C. P. (Marlborough) 1967
Pyman, R. A. (Harrow) 1989-90

Ranjitsinhji, K. S. (Rajkumar Coll., India) 1893
Ratcliffe, A. (Rydal) 1930-32
Reddy, N. S. K. (Doon School, India) 1959-61
Rimell, A. G. J. (Charterhouse) 1949-50
Robins, R. W. V. (Highgate) 1926-28
Roebuck, P. G. P. (Millfield) 1984-85
Roebuck, P. M. (Millfield) 1975-77
Roopnaraine, R. (Queen's RC, BG) 1965-66
Rose, M. H. (Pocklington) 1963-64
Ross, N. P. G. (Marlborough) 1969
Roundell, J. (Winchester) 1973
Russell, D. P. (West Park GS, St Helens) 1974-75
Russell, S. G. (Tiffin) (Capt. in 1967) 1965-67
Russom, N. (Huish's GS) 1980-81

Scott, A. M. G. (Seaford Head) 1985-87
Seabrook, F. J. (Haileybury) (Capt. in 1928) 1926-28
Seager, C. P. (Peterhouse, Rhodesia) 1971
Selvey, M. W. W. (Battersea GS and Manchester U.) 1971
Sheppard, D. S. (Sherborne) (Capt. in 1952) 1950-52
Short, R. L. (Denstone) 1969
Shufflebotham, D. H. (Neath GS) 1989-90
Shuttleworth, G. M. (Blackburn GS) 1946-48
Silk, D. R. W. (Christ's Hospital) (Capt. in 1955) 1953-55
Singh, S. (Khalsa Coll. and Punjab U.) 1955-56
Sinker, N. D. (Winchester) 1966
Slack, J. K. E. (UCS) 1954
Smith, C. S. (William Hulme's GS) 1954-57
Smith, D. J. (Stockport GS) 1955-56
Smyth, R. I. (Sedbergh) 1973-75
Snowden, W. (Merchant Taylors', Crosby) (Capt. in 1974) 1972-75
Spencer, J. (Brighton and Hove GS) 1970-72
Steele, H. K. (King's Coll., NZ) 1971-72
Stevenson, M. H. (Rydal) 1949-52
Studd, C. T. (Eton) (Capt. in 1883) 1880-83
Studd, G. B. (Eton) (Capt. in 1882) 1879-82
Studd, J. E. K. (Eton) (Capt. in 1884) 1881-84
Studd, P. M. (Harrow) (Capt. in 1939) 1937-39
Studd, R. A. (Eton) 1895
Subba Row, R. (Whitgift) 1951-53
Surridge, D. (Richard Hale and Southampton U.) 1979
Swift, B. T. (St Peter's, Adelaide) 1957

Taylor, C. R. V. (Birkenhead) 1971-73
Thomson, R. H. (Bexhill) 1961-62
Thwaites, I. G. (Eastbourne) 1964
Tindall, M. (Harrow) (Capt. in 1937) 1935-37
Tordoff, G. G. (Normanton GS) 1952
Trapnell, B. M. W. (UCS) 1946
Tremellen, J. M. (Bradfield) 1987-88
Turnbull, M. J. (Downside) (Capt. in 1929) 1926, 1928-29
Turner, R. J. (Millfield) 1988-90

Urquhart, J. R. (King Edward VI School, Chelmsford) 1948

Valentine, B. H. (Repton) 1929
Varey, D. W. (Birkenhead) 1982-83

Wait, O. J. (Dulwich) 1949, 1951
Warr, J. J. (Ealing County GS) (Capt. in 1951) 1949-52
Watts, H. E. (Downside) 1947
Webster, W. H. (Highgate) 1932
Weedon, M. J. H. (Harrow) 1962
Wells, T. U. (King's Coll., NZ) 1950
Wheatley, O. S. (King Edward's, Birmingham) 1957-58
Wheelhouse, A. (Nottingham HS) 1959
White, R. C. (Hilton Coll., SA) (Capt. in 1965) 1962-65
Wilcox, D. R. (Dulwich) (Capt. in 1933) 1931-33
Wilenkin, B. C. G. (Harrow) 1956
Wilkin, C. L. A. (St Kitts GS) 1970
Willard, M. J. L. (Judd) 1959-61
Willatt, G. L. (Repton) (Capt. in 1947) 1946-47
Willatt, J. M. G. (Repton) 1989
Windows, A. R. (Clifton) 1962-64
Wood, G. E. C. (Cheltenham) (Capt. in 1920) 1914, 1919-20
Wookey, S. M. (Malvern) 1975-76
Wooller, W. (Rydal) 1935-36
Wright, S. (Mill Hill) 1973

Yardley, N. W. D. (St Peter's, York) (Capt. in 1938) 1935-38
Young, R. A. (Repton) (Capt. in 1908) 1905-08

OTHER MATCHES, 1990

TILCON TROPHY

†SURREY v WARWICKSHIRE

At Harrogate, June 13. Warwickshire won by two wickets. Toss: Warwickshire. Warwickshire were permitted to include three overseas players – Donald of South Africa, Moody of Australia and Penney of Zimbabwe.

Man of the Match: T. M. Moody.

Surrey

G. S. Clinton c Asif Din b Moody 32
M. A. Feltham c Moody b Donald 10
A. J. Stewart c Reeve b Benjamin 20
†D. M. Ward c Asif Din b Moody 40
G. P. Thorpe c Reeve b Smith 0
*I. A. Greig run out 39
K. T. Medlycott c Benjamin b Munton . 1
C. K. Bullen run out 22
M. P. Bicknell c Donald b Moody 10
A. H. Gray not out 9
A. J. Murphy not out 6
B 5, l-b 10, w 8 23

1/16 2/47 3/75 4/77 5/127 6/132 7/173 8/193 9/197 (9 wkts, 55 overs) 212

Bowling: Donald 11–0–41–1; Benjamin 11–2–25–1; Munton 11–1–36–1; Moody 11–3–49–3; Smith 11–2–46–1.

Warwickshire

A. J. Moles c and b Medlycott 51
Asif Din c Ward b Gray 0
T. M. Moody lbw b Feltham 31
†G. W. Humpage b Gray 2
*D. A. Reeve c and b Murphy 13
T. L. Penney b Bicknell 36
R. G. Twose not out 36
N. M. K. Smith c Ward b Bicknell 23
A. A. Donald c Medlycott b Bicknell .. 0
J. E. Benjamin not out 7
B 6, l-b 1, w 7 14

1/15 2/58 3/62 4/78 5/121 6/159 7/197 8/197 (8 wkts, 54 overs) 213

T. A. Munton did not bat.

Bowling: Gray 11–1–55–2; Bicknell 9–0–48–3; Feltham 3–0–16–1; Murphy 9–0–23–1; Medlycott 11–0–40–1; Bullen 11–1–24–0.

Umpires: J. C. Balderstone and D. S. Thompsett.

†YORKSHIRE v SUSSEX

At Harrogate, June 14. Yorkshire won by seven wickets. Toss: Yorkshire.

Man of the Match: A. A. Metcalfe.

Sussex

N. J. Lenham c Jarvis b Carrick 52
K. Greenfield c Robinson b Jarvis 10
*P. W. G. Parker c Bairstow b Jarvis .. 0
A. P. Wells c Byas b Moxon 5
M. P. Speight c White b Carrick 30
C. C. Remy c Robinson b White 3
†P. Moores c Moxon b Pickles 40
J. A. North c Byas b Carrick 6
I. D. K. Salisbury not out 14
B. T. P. Donelan c White b Pickles ... 4
R. A. Bunting not out 5
L-b 7 7

1/19 2/19 3/27 4/68 5/81 6/135 7/151 8/157 9/162 (9 wkts, 55 overs) 176

Bowling: Jarvis 11–4–29–2; Pickles 11–2–26–2; Moxon 11–4–26–1; White 9–1–42–1; Carrick 11–1–39–3; Byas 2–0–7–0.

Yorkshire

*M. D. Moxon c Wells b Lenham 22
A. A. Metcalfe c Parker b Remy 64
R. J. Blakey run out 21
K. Sharp not out 37
P. E. Robinson not out 24
B 2, l-b 6, w 4 12

1/56 2/111 3/119 (3 wkts, 53.3 overs) 180

†D. L. Bairstow, D. Byas, P. Carrick, C. White, C. S. Pickles and P. W. Jarvis did not bat.

Bowling: Remy 11–2–38–1; Bunting 10.3–1–28–0; Donelan 11–2–25–0; Salisbury 11–1–44–0; Lenham 5–2–16–1; North 4–0–17–0; Parker 1–0–4–0.

Umpires: J. C. Balderstone and D. S. Thompsett.

FINAL

†YORKSHIRE v WARWICKSHIRE

At Harrogate, June 15. Warwickshire won by 4 runs. Toss: Warwickshire. Moles faced 139 balls, seven of which he hit for four.

Man of the Match: A. J. Moles.

Warwickshire

A. J. Moles not out 102
Asif Din c Metcalfe b Pickles 10
T. M. Moody c Moxon b Carrick 67
†G. W. Humpage c Bairstow b Carrick 11
*D. A. Reeve lbw b Carrick 2
R. G. Twose b Pickles 2
T. L. Penney not out 64
B 4, l-b 6, w 4 14

1/20 2/126 3/142 4/152 5/156 (5 wkts, 55 overs) 272

N. M. K. Smith, A. A. Donald, J. E. Benjamin and T. A. Munton did not bat.

Bowling: Jarvis 11–1–53–0; Pickles 11–1–51–2; Fletcher 10–0–59–0; Carrick 11–1–41–3; Byas 11–0–55–0; Moxon 1–0–3–0.

Yorkshire

*M. D. Moxon c Smith b Asif Din 77
A. A. Metcalfe c Moody b Asif Din ... 76
R. J. Blakey run out 54
K. Sharp c Reeve b Smith 34
P. E. Robinson c Moody b Smith 3
†D. L. Bairstow c Reeve b Donald 1
D. Byas not out 4
P. Carrick not out 7
B 4, l-b 2, w 5, n-b 1 12

1/133 2/194 3/240 4/254 5/254 6/257 (6 wkts, 55 overs) 268

C. S. Pickles, S. D. Fletcher and P. W. Jarvis did not bat.

Bowling: Donald 11–0–53–1; Benjamin 11–2–35–0; Munton 11–0–49–0; Smith 10–0–52–2; Moody 2–0–15–0; Asif Din 10–0–58–2.

Umpires: J. C. Balderstone and D. S. Thompsett.

†At Durham, June 14, 15. Durham University won by six wickets. Toss: Durham University. MCC 207 for nine dec. (S. P. Henderson 41, S. C. Wundke 95; R. H. Macdonald three for 59, J. R. C. Dakin four for 67) and 214 for three dec. (M. F. Richardson 68 not out, R. M. O. Cooke 120; J. Boiling three for 64); Durham University 193 for five dec. (R. S. M. Morris 58, B. G. Evans 47, J. S. Hodgson 47 not out) and 231 for four (R. S. M. Morris 110 not out, B. G. Evans 59, J. I. Longley 31).

†At Coleraine, June 16, 17, 18. Ireland won by 6 runs. Toss: Ireland. Ireland 275 for eight dec. (A. R. Dunlop 69, S. J. S. Warke 81, Extras 34; W. G. Merry three for 54) and 99 (M. P. Rea 32, D. A. Lewis 34; M. J. Thursfield five for 15); MCC 243 (A. J. Goldsmith 76, T. Smith 48, M. J. Thursfield 32; P. McCrum three for 57, G. D. Harrison three for 46) and 125 (G. D. Mendis 49, G. J. Toogood 30; G. D. Harrison three for 13, P. O'Reilly three for 36).

CALLERS-PEGASUS FESTIVAL

†ENGLAND XI v REST OF THE WORLD XI

At Jesmond, August 2. England XI won by nine wickets. Toss: England XI. After some fine containing work by the England XI seam bowlers, Broad anchored the reply with his unbeaten 84 from 156 balls, hitting a six and ten fours. Gooch (72 balls) had thirteen fours in his 62, and Morris (91 balls) the same number plus a six in his most entertaining 87 not out.

Man of the Match: T. A. Munton.

Rest of the World XI

*C. G. Greenidge lbw b Munton	27
S. J. Cook c Hussain b Munton	39
M. D. Crowe lbw b Munton	16
T. M. Moody c Stephenson b Hemmings	27
M. J. Greatbatch c Hussain b Cowans	57
A. I. C. Dodemaide b Barnett	36
P. R. Sleep not out	35
F. D. Stephenson c Munton b Cowans	0
†A. C. Parore c Munton b Cowans	5
W. K. M. Benjamin b Munton	1
I. R. Bishop not out	1
B 4, l-b 6, w 7, n-b 3	20
1/54 2/80 3/91 4/121 5/193 6/240 7/240 8/252 9/259 (9 wkts, 55 overs)	264

Bowling: Cowans 10–0–44–3; Igglesden 10–0–44–0; Munton 11–1–38–4; Stephenson 4–0–20–0; Hemmings 11–1–50–1; Barnett 9–0–58–1.

England XI

*G. A. Gooch c Sleep b Stephenson	62
B. C. Broad not out	84
J. E. Morris not out	87
L-b 13, w 18, n-b 3	34
1/107 (1 wkt, 52.4 overs)	267

J. P. Stephenson, N. Hussain, K. J. Barnett, †B. N. French, N. G. Cowans, E. E. Hemmings, A. P. Igglesden and T. A. Munton did not bat.

Bowling: Bishop 11–1–40–0; Stephenson 9.4–1–41–1; Benjamin 11–1–40–0; Dodemaide 10–1–67–0; Sleep 6–0–38–0; Moody 5–0–28–0.

Umpires: S. Levison and G. I. McLean.

†ENGLAND XI v REST OF THE WORLD XI

At Jesmond, August 3. Rest of the World XI won by ten wickets. Toss: Rest of the World XI. This match brought to an end the sponsorship of the Jesmond matches by Callers-Pegasus, under whose patronage the event had attracted 119 of the world's leading players in the past decade. Crowe hit six sixes and thirteen fours in his unbeaten 112, finishing the match with three successive sixes, while Cook had eleven fours in his 70 not out.

Man of the Match: P. R. Sleep.

England XI

B. C. Broad b Sleep	55
J. P. Stephenson b Benjamin	7
J. E. Morris c Parore b Dodemaide	5
N. Hussain b Moody	26
*A. J. Lamb c Dodemaide b Sleep	20
K. J. Barnett b Moody	10
†B. N. French c Moody b Greenidge	30
E. E. Hemmings c Parore b Sleep	0
N. G. Cowans c Crowe b Sleep	1
A. P. Igglesden c Benjamin b Greenidge	11
T. A. Munton not out	0
B 4, l-b 6, w 4	14
1/27 2/36 3/82 4/118 5/126 6/137 7/138 8/146 9/179 (50.2 overs)	179

Bowling: Benjamin 5–1–21–1; Bishop 4–0–7–0; Dodemaide 7–1–32–1; Stephenson 6–2–17–0; Sleep 10–0–34–4; Moody 8–1–23–2; Crowe 6–0–26–0; Greatbatch 4–0–9–0; Greenidge 0.2–0–0–2.

Rest of the World XI

S. J. Cook not out 70
M. D. Crowe not out 112
L-b 2, w 1 3

(no wkt, 25.4 overs) 185

*C. G. Greenidge, T. M. Moody, M. J. Greatbatch, A. I. C. Dodemaide, †A. C. Parore, F. D. Stephenson, P. R. Sleep, W. K. M. Benjamin and I. R. Bishop did not bat.

Bowling: Cowans 5–1–22–0; Munton 7–0–33–0; Hemmings 6–0–53–0; Igglesden 3–1–26–0; Barnett 2–0–10–0; Stephenson 2–0–21–0; Hussain 0.4–0–18–0.

Umpires: S. Levison and G. I. McLean.

SCOTLAND v IRELAND

At Myreside, Edinburgh, August 11, 12, 13. Drawn. Toss: Ireland. With Scotland extending their first innings into the third morning, and rain in prospect if only once in evidence, there was little possibility of a result other than the draw. Play had commenced at 10.30 a.m., and stumps were drawn shortly after three o'clock as soon as Warke, with his ninth four, reached 100 (140 minutes, 145 balls). He had been missed at silly point before scoring and again, by the wicket-keeper, when 17. The game's other century-maker, Philip, also benefited from fielding lapses, enjoying three lives as he and Patterson put on 147 for Scotland's first wicket in three and a quarter hours. Philip batted for 216 minutes (175 balls) for his hundred, hitting a six and eight fours, only to become the second of Harrison's nine wickets four balls later. The Irish off-spinner bowled 27 overs unchanged on the second afternoon to take his first five wickets for 72 runs; that evening and the following morning he took a further four for 26 in 9.2 overs to record the best innings figures of the 1990 first-class season.

Close of play: First day, Scotland 22-0 (I. L. Phillip 11*, B. M. W. Patterson 11*); Second day, Scotland 333-8 (A. Bee 7*, J. D. Moir 5*).

Ireland

M. F. Cohen b McKnight	60	– (2) b Mahmood	15
M. P. Rea st Haggo b Russell	22	– (3) not out	21
A. R. Dunlop c and b Mahmood	56		
*S. J. S. Warke c Storie b Mahmood	4	– (1) not out	100
D. A. Lewis c Patterson b McKnight	6		
T. J. T. Patterson c Patterson b Henry	84		
G. D. Harrison c Patterson b Mahmood	1		
†P. B. Jackson st Haggo b Moir	59		
N. Nelson c Moir b McKnight	0		
P. McCrum c McKnight b Henry	0		
A. N. Nelson not out	23		
B 6, l-b 4, w 2	12	B 2	2
1/44 2/129 3/137 4/155 5/156 6/179 7/289 8/291 9/292	327	1/51	(1 wkt) 138

Bowling: *First Innings*—Moir 26.3–8–76–1; Bee 19–7–53–0; Russell 6–1–23–1; Henry 18–0–54–2; Mahmood 18–5–63–3; McKnight 16–5–48–3. *Second Innings*—Bee 9–4–20–0; Mahmood 13–4–40–1; Henry 14.4–3–52–0; McKnight 7–0–24–0.

Scotland

I. L. Philip b Harrison 100
B. M. W. Patterson b Harrison 60
A. C. Storie b Harrison 32
*R. G. Swan c sub b Harrison 9
O. Henry st Jackson b Harrison 23
A. B. Russell c N. Nelson b A. N. Nelson 47
†D. J. Haggo lbw b Harrison 34
C. T. McKnight c Warke b Harrison .. 0
A. Bee not out 29
J. D. Moir c Dunlop b Harrison 12
M. Mahmood c Patterson b Harrison .. 3
L-b 8, w 2, n-b 7 17

1/147 2/175 3/193 4/209 5/241 6/316 7/316 8/324 9/353 366

Bowling: McCrum 12–3–28–0; A. N. Nelson 33–8–74–1; N. Nelson 15–0–51–0; Harrison 43.2–11–113–9; Lewis 11–0–55–0; Dunlop 10–0–37–0.

Umpires: J. Breslin and D. N. Herd.

†At Swansea, August 27, 28. Drawn. Toss: MCC. MCC 166 for seven dec. (D. B. Storer 47, K. G. G. Brooks 42; B. J. Lloyd three for 44) and 197 (A. Needham 32, D. B. Storer 33, K. G. G. Brooks 50; B. J. Lloyd five for 43); Wales 181 for five dec. (S. Evans 56, A. Harris 45 not out) and 165 for seven (J. Bishop 66, Extras 30; M. Hart four for 22).

At Scarborough, August 29, 30, 31. MICHAEL PARKINSON'S WORLD XI drew with INDIANS (See Indian tour section).

†At Scarborough, September 1. Michael Parkinson's World XI won by 7 runs. Toss: Michael Parkinson's World XI. Michael Parkinson's World XI 278 for eight (50 overs) (J. E. Morris 60, C. L. Hooper 62, N. Hussain 30, B. C. Lara 34; P. J. Hartley three for 68); Yorkshire 271 for eight (50 overs) (S. A. Kellett 57, P. E. Robinson 114).

SCARBOROUGH FESTIVAL TROPHY

†HAMPSHIRE v WORCESTERSHIRE

At Scarborough, September 2. Hampshire won by 81 runs. Toss: Worcestershire. Terry faced 155 balls and hit six boundaries.

Man of the Match: V. P. Terry.

Hampshire

V. P. Terry st Rhodes b Illingworth	95	†A. N. Aymes not out	11
T. C. Middleton b Botham	39	S. D. Udal not out	0
R. A. Smith b Botham	6	B 4, l-b 17, w 6	27
*M. C. J. Nicholas b Hick	6		
R. M. F. Cox c and b Hick	43	1/96 2/107 3/135 (6 wkts, 50 overs)	249
J. R. Ayling c Botham b Illingworth	22	4/208 5/226 6/247	

T. M. Tremlett, C. A. Connor and P. J. Bakker did not bat.

Bowling: McEwan 8–0–35–0; Weston 6–1–18–0; Radford 9–0–40–0; Illingworth 10–0–62–2; Botham 7–0–30–2; Hick 10–0–43–2.

Worcestershire

T. S. Curtis c Smith b Tremlett	16	R. K. Illingworth b Nicholas	29
G. J. Lord b Bakker	1	N. V. Radford not out	39
D. A. Leatherdale c Terry b Connor	5	S. M. McEwan b Nicholas	0
I. T. Botham b Connor	1	B 2, l-b 9, w 4	15
G. A. Hick b Udal	20		
*P. A. Neale run out	1	1/8 2/13 3/16 (45 overs)	168
M. J. Weston lbw b Nicholas	19	4/45 5/46 6/46	
†S. J. Rhodes c Terry b Tremlett	22	7/82 8/97 9/166	

Bowling: Connor 6–2–14–2; Bakker 7–0–21–1; Tremlett 10–1–24–2; Udal 9–0–42–1; Ayling 6–0–28–0; Nicholas 7–0–28–3.

Umpires: B. Leadbeater and D. O. Oslear.

†YORKSHIRE v ESSEX

At Scarborough, September 3. Essex won by 82 runs. Toss: Essex.
Man of the Match: P. J. Prichard.

Essex

J. P. Stephenson st Bairstow b Carrick 57
N. Shahid lbw b Jarvis 16
M. E. Waugh b Jarvis 0
P. J. Prichard c Hartley b Pickles 86
N. Hussain c Byas b Pickles 31
*M. A. Garnham c and b Pickles 37
A. G. J. Fraser run out 0
T. D. Topley not out 0
M. C. Ilott not out 6
L-b 3, w 8, n-b 3 14

1/20 2/20 3/163 4/178 5/239 6/239 7/241 (7 wkts, 50 overs) 247

S. J. W. Andrew and P. M. Such did not bat.

Bowling: Jarvis 10–1–48–2; Hartley 10–0–52–0; Pickles 9–0–40–3; Batty 9–0–40–0; Carrick 10–0–54–1; Byas 2–0–10–0.

Yorkshire

*M. D. Moxon c Garnham b Andrew 4
S. A. Kellett b Such 28
R. J. Blakey c Garnham b Andrew 0
P. E. Robinson c Prichard b Topley 26
D. Byas c Waugh b Such 22
†D. L. Bairstow b Stephenson 36
P. Carrick b Stephenson 12
C. S. Pickles b Waugh 1
P. J. Hartley c Topley b Shahid 16
P. W. Jarvis b Stephenson 3
J. D. Batty not out 5
B 1, w 5, n-b 6 12

1/6 2/6 3/50 4/73 5/112 6/132 7/135 8/141 9/147 (47.2 overs) 165

Bowling: Andrew 4–0–35–2; Ilott 7–4–11–0; Topley 6–0–15–1; Such 10–0–32–2; Fraser 4–0–16–0; Stephenson 10–0–42–3; Waugh 6–0–9–1; Shahid 0.2–0–4–1.

Umpires: B. Leadbeater and D. O. Oslear.

FINAL

†HAMPSHIRE v ESSEX

At Scarborough, September 4. Hampshire won by five wickets. Toss: Essex.
Man of the Match: M. C. J. Nicholas.

Essex

*J. P. Stephenson c Smith b Ayling 18
N. Shahid c Middleton b Connor 10
M. E. Waugh c Connor b Turner 30
P. J. Prichard st Aymes b Udal 21
N. Hussain c Nicholas b Tremlett 39
†M. A. Garnham c Turner b Nicholas 4
A. G. J. Fraser run out 0
T. D. Topley b Turner 1
M. C. Ilott b Nicholas 17
S. J. W. Andrew b Nicholas 0
P. M. Such not out 6
B 2, l-b 3, w 12, n-b 2 19

1/19 2/33 3/72 4/89 5/106 6/109 7/118 8/144 9/144 (49.5 overs) 165

Bowling: Connor 7–0–21–1; Tremlett 7.5–2–16–1; Udal 10–0–25–1; Ayling 7–0–26–1; Turner 8–0–44–2; Nicholas 10–1–28–3.

Hampshire

*M. C. J. Nicholas run out 57
T. C. Middleton c sub b Fraser 53
R. M. F. Cox b Stephenson 4
J. R. Ayling c and b Fraser 25
R. A. Smith not out 14
V. P. Terry c Ilott b Topley 1
†A. N. Aymes not out 1
L-b 3, w 7, n-b 1 11

1/96 2/101 3/140 4/163 5/164 (5 wkts, 45.1 overs) 166

T. M. Tremlett, S. D. Udal, C. A. Connor and I. J. Turner did not bat.

Bowling: Topley 7–1–19–1; Ilott 7–1–20–0; Such 10–1–22–0; Andrew 5–0–29–0; Shahid 2–0–6–0; Stephenson 7–0–31–1; Waugh 4–0–11–0; Fraser 3–0–24–2; Prichard 0.1–0–1–0.

Umpires: B. Leadbeater and D. O. Oslear.

SEEBOARD TROPHY

†SUSSEX v KENT

At Hove, September 2. Kent won by 45 runs. Toss: Kent.
Man of the Match: M. V. Fleming.

Kent

T. R. Ward c Greenfield b Donelan . . . 67
V. J. Wells b Threlfall 18
J. I. Longley c Moores b Dodemaide . . 3
G. R. Cowdrey st Moores b Salisbury . . 43
*N. R. Taylor c Smith b Lenham 30
M. V. Fleming st Moores b Salisbury . . 6
†S. A. Marsh st Moores b Donelan 52
D. J. M. Kelleher c Greenfield b Donelan . 2
M. A. Ealham c Moores b Salisbury . . . 4
M. M. Patel c Salisbury b Dodemaide . 1
T. N. Wren not out 0
B 1, l-b 3, w 3 7

1/20 2/29 3/133 4/133 5/143 6/220 7/223 8/229 9/233 (48.1 overs) 233

Bowling: Dodemaide 9–2–20–2; Threlfall 10–0–55–1; Remy 4–0–32–0; Donelan 10–2–34–3; Salisbury 10–0–59–3; Lenham 5.1–0–29–1.

Sussex

N. J. Lenham b Fleming 47
D. M. Smith lbw b Wren 14
K. Greenfield c and b Taylor 34
*A. P. Wells run out 5
I. J. Gould c Longley b Ward 9
A. I. C. Dodemaide c Marsh b Fleming 40
C. C. Remy c Ealham b Fleming 16
†P. Moores run out 2
I. D. K. Salisbury c Marsh b Fleming . 0
B. T. P. Donelan c Wells b Wren 10
P. W. Threlfall not out 0
L-b 6, w 3, n-b 2 11

1/51 2/75 3/89 4/113 5/133 6/162 7/165 8/167 9/184 (45.4 overs) 188

Bowling: Wren 7–1–18–2; Kelleher 2–0–19–0; Patel 10–0–48–0; Ward 10–0–23–1; Fleming 7.4–0–30–4; Ealham 3–0–14–0; Taylor 6–0–30–1.

Umpires: D. J. Constant and A. G. T. Whitehead.

†SURREY v WARWICKSHIRE

At Hove, September 3. Surrey won by four wickets. Toss: Surrey.
Man of the Match: M. A. Lynch.

Warwickshire

Asif Din c D. J. Bicknell b Greig 51
†K. J. Piper lbw b Bullen 44
D. P. Ostler c Lynch b Bullen 6
S. J. Green b Waqar Younis 21
P. A. Smith c Stewart b Waqar Younis . 6
*D. A. Reeve lbw b Waqar Younis 42
N. M. K. Smith c Stewart b M. P. Bicknell . 13
R. G. Twose not out 8
A. A. Donald not out 16
B 2, l-b 17, w 2 21

1/86 2/104 3/133 4/134 5/161 6/202 7/204 (7 wkts, 50 overs) 228

G. Smith and T. A. Munton did not bat.

Bowling: M. P. Bicknell 10–1–38–1; Murphy 10–0–47–0; Greig 6–0–26–1; Thorpe 4–0–21–0; Waqar Younis 10–1–31–3; Bullen 10–0–46–2.

Surrey

D. J. Bicknell c Twose b Reeve 33	*I. A. Greig run out 2
G. S. Clinton c Piper b Munton 8	C. K. Bullen not out 11
G. P. Thorpe c Twose b Donald 30	L-b 9, w 7, n-b 2 18
†A. J. Stewart c N. M. K. Smith b Reeve 36	
D. M. Ward c Piper b G. Smith 27	1/24 2/68 3/104 (6 wkts, 49.1 overs) 230
M. A. Lynch not out 65	4/133 5/165 6/168

A. J. Murphy, M. P. Bicknell and Waqar Younis did not bat.

Bowling: Donald 10–3–24–1; Munton 10–0–64–1; G. Smith 9.1–2–38–1; Reeve 10–0–53–2; P. A. Smith 10–0–42–0.

Umpires: D. J. Constant and A. G. T. Whitehead.

FINAL

†KENT v SURREY

At Hove, September 4. Kent won by 35 runs. Toss: Kent. Ealham's return of eight for 49 included a spell of seven for 24 in 4.4 overs. Wells hit eleven fours in his 107.

Man of the Match: M. A. Ealham.

Kent

T. R. Ward b Robinson 41	D. J. M. Kelleher not out 20
V. J. Wells run out 107	
J. I. Longley lbw b Waqar Younis 0	
G. R. Cowdrey b Murphy 78	B 4, l-b 10, w 8 22
*N. R. Taylor b Greig 25	
M. V. Fleming not out 43	1/78 2/79 3/223 (6 wkts, 50 overs) 338
†S. A. Marsh c D. J. Bicknell b M. P. Bicknell . 2	4/256 5/277 6/286

M. A. Ealham, M. M. Patel and T. N. Wren did not bat.

Bowling: M. P. Bicknell 10–1–43–1; Murphy 10–1–71–1; Waqar Younis 10–1–57–1; Robinson 10–1–54–1; Bullen 4–0–49–0; Greig 6–0–50–1.

Surrey

D. J. Bicknell c Marsh b Ealham 2	M. P. Bicknell b Ealham 2
J. D. Robinson b Ealham 98	Waqar Younis not out 13
G. P. Thorpe c Marsh b Patel 78	A. J. Murphy c and b Ealham 2
†A. J. Stewart c Wren b Ealham 52	L-b 3, w 14, n-b 3 20
D. M. Ward b Wren 26	
M. A. Lynch b Ealham 0	1/18 2/166 3/244 (48.4 overs) 303
*I. A. Greig c Cowdrey b Ealham 4	4/255 5/256 6/266
C. K. Bullen c Fleming b Ealham 6	7/281 8/286 9/301

Bowling: Wren 10–0–49–1; Ealham 9.4–0–49–8; Patel 8–0–50–1; Ward 4–0–20–0; Fleming 7–0–64–0; Kelleher 10–0–68–0.

Umpires: D. J. Constant and A. G. T. Whitehead.

†At Scarborough, September 6. Yorkshire won by eight wickets. Toss: The Yorkshiremen. The Yorkshiremen 229 for five (50 overs) (T. J. Boon 82, S. J. Rhodes 66 not out); Yorkshire 235 for two (37.5 overs) (A. A. Metcalfe 65, D. Byas 59, R. J. Blakey 69 not out).

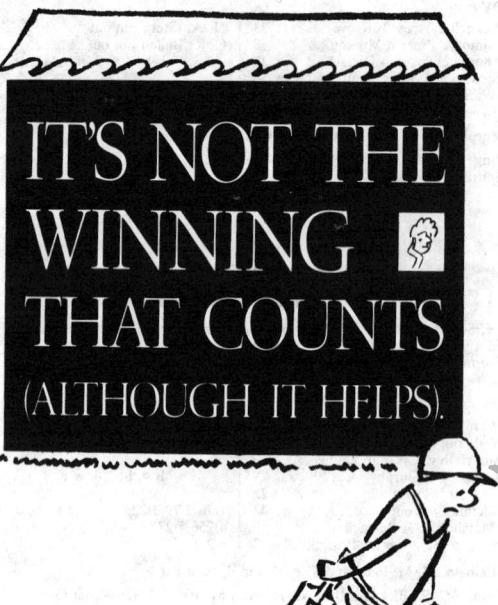

NATWEST BANK TROPHY, 1990

Lancashire, by defeating Northamptonshire convincingly by seven wickets on the first day of September, not only won the NatWest Bank Trophy for the first time but became the only county to win both Lord's finals in the same season. It was their fifth victory in eight finals of the 60-overs competition, putting them ahead of Middlesex and Sussex, each with four wins.

In addition to the NatWest Bank Trophy, held for a year, Lancashire won £24,000 in prizemoney, while Northamptonshire received £12,000. The losing semi-finalists, Hampshire and Middlesex, each received £6,000, and the losing quarter-finalists, Glamorgan, Gloucestershire, Worcestershire and Yorkshire, £3,000 each. The total prizemoney for the competition in 1990, including the Man of the Match awards, was £64,500, an increase of £6,000 over 1989.

Phillip DeFreitas, nominated as Man of the Match in the final by Fred Trueman for his match-winning bowling in the morning session, received a cheque for £550. The awards in the earlier rounds were: first round, £100 each; second round, £125 each; quarter-finals, £200 each; semi-finals, £275 each. Graham Gooch (Essex) and Chris Smith (Hampshire) each won an award in 1990 to increase his total in the competition to seven, a mark also reached by Imran Khan (Worcestershire and Sussex), Peter Willey (Northamptonshire and Leicestershire) and Barry Wood (Lancashire and Cheshire). Only Clive Lloyd, the former Lancashire captain, with eight awards, had been named Man of the Match more times.

FIRST ROUND

BUCKINGHAMSHIRE v NOTTINGHAMSHIRE

At Marlow, June 27. Nottinghamshire won by 192 runs. Toss: Buckinghamshire. Broad's century, his first in the competition, came off 149 balls, and his 115 included a six and fifteen fours. Nottinghamshire's total was their highest in limited-overs competition.

Man of the Match: B. C. Broad.

Nottinghamshire

B. C. Broad b Black	115	K. E. Cooper c Percy b Barry	10
M. Newell b Scriven	35	R. A. Pick not out	4
F. D. Stephenson c Harwood b Burrow	29	J. A. Afford not out	2
*R. T. Robinson c and b Percy	30	B 4, l-b 10, w 6, n-b 2	22
P. Johnson c Harwood b Lynch	14		
M. Saxelby c Lynch b Black	41	1/97 2/140 3/187 (9 wkts, 60 overs)	312
†B. N. French c Black b Barry	7	4/206 5/277 6/288	
E. E. Hemmings b Barry	3	7/293 8/305 9/308	

Bowling: Barry 12–2–49–3; Black 11–2–52–2; Burrow 12–1–42–1; Scriven 12–0–73–1; Lynch 7–0–52–1; Percy 6–0–30–1.

Buckinghamshire

A. R. Harwood c French b Cooper	13	S. G. Lynch c Newell b Hemmings	46
M. J. Roberts retired hurt	17	T. J. Barry c Saxelby b Hemmings	5
T. Butler c Johnson b Cooper	5	†D. J. Goldsmith not out	0
S. Burrow c Hemmings b Pick	19	L-b 2, w 2	4
T. J. A. Scriven c Robinson b Cooper	1		
*N. G. Hames c French b Hemmings	4	1/32 2/42 3/44 (40.3 overs)	120
B. S. Percy b Pick	0	4/55 5/56 6/63	
G. R. Black lbw b Pick	6	7/70 8/95 9/120	

M. J. Roberts retired hurt at 30.

Bowling: Stephenson 5–2–12–0; Pick 9–2–22–3; Cooper 8–3–16–3; Afford 11–6–26–0; Hemmings 7.3–2–42–3.

Umpires: P. J. Eele and D. S. Thompsett.

DERBYSHIRE v SHROPSHIRE

At Chesterfield, June 27. Derbyshire won by seven wickets. Toss: Derbyshire. The start of play was delayed by 40 minutes while the match balls were brought to the ground from the county ground at Derby, and the lunch interval was reduced by ten minutes. The third-wicket partnership of 117 between Morris and Kuiper was a record for Derbyshire in the competition.

Man of the Match: J. E. Morris.

Shropshire

*J. Foster lbw b Kuiper 20
J. B. R. Jones c Bowler b Warner 26
J. Abrahams b Mortensen 47
T. Parton lbw b Mortensen 2
M. R. Davies c Bowler b Warner 20
†J. R. Weaver lbw b Mortensen 0
P. B. Wormald b Warner 16
D. B. K. Page b Warner 0
A. B. Byram not out 20
B. K. Shantry not out 4
L-b 11, w 18 29

1/33 2/97 3/112 4/114 5/114 6/147 7/149 8/169 (8 wkts, 60 overs) 184

A. S. Barnard did not bat.

Bowling: Malcolm 12–3–31–0; Mortensen 11–2–29–3; Warner 12–1–39–4; Goldsmith 5–0–23–0; Miller 10–0–31–0; Kuiper 10–0–20–1.

Derbyshire

*K. J. Barnett c Weaver b Shantry 1
†P. D. Bowler c Weaver b Shantry 14
J. E. Morris not out 94
A. P. Kuiper c Parton b Wormald 49
B. Roberts not out 14
L-b 6, w 5, n-b 3 14

1/9 2/45 3/162 (3 wkts, 38.1 overs) 186

C. J. Adams, S. C. Goldsmith, A. E. Warner, G. Miller, D. E. Malcolm and O. H. Mortensen did not bat.

Bowling: Page 5–0–24–0; Shantry 10–1–47–2; Barnard 6–1–19–0; Wormald 5.1–1–24–1; Byram 6–0–35–0; Abrahams 6–0–31–0.

Umpires: J. D. Bond and J. W. Holder.

DEVON v SOMERSET

At Torquay, June 27. Somerset won by 346 runs. Toss: Devon. In a match of record breaking, not only was Somerset's total the highest in a major limited-overs competition in England, but their margin of victory was also the largest. Both these records were previously held by Worcestershire, who scored 404 for three when beating Devon by 299 runs in the first round of the NatWest Bank Trophy at Worcester in 1987. Rose, while scoring 110 from 40 balls, hit the fastest hundred in the 60-overs competition, reaching his century from 36 balls and hitting seven sixes and ten fours. Tavaré's unbeaten 162, the highest innings for Somerset in the competition, came off 130 balls and contained four sixes and 26 fours. When Devon replied, Lefebvre also recorded best figures for the county as he equalled the third-best return in the Gillette Cup/NatWest Bank Trophy.

Man of the Match: C. J. Tavaré.

Somerset

S. J. Cook run out 42
P. M. Roebuck c and b Woodman 43
A. N. Hayhurst c Pugh b Folland 51
*C. J. Tavaré not out 162
G. D. Rose c Pugh b Dawson 110
W 5 5

1/79 2/88 3/224 4/413 (4 wkts, 60 overs) 413

R. J. Harden, †N. D. Burns, I. G. Swallow, R. P. Lefebvre, N. A. Mallender and A. N. Jones did not bat.

Bowling: Donohue 12–2–101–0; Woodman 12–3–50–1; Tierney 11–2–62–0; Yeabsley 12–0–77–0; Rice 6–0–34–0; Dawson 4–0–37–1; Folland 3–0–52–1.

Devon

*J. H. Edwards lbw b Jones	4	J. K. Tierney b Lefebvre	0
K. G. Rice b Mallender	0	M. C. Woodman b Lefebvre	1
N. A. Folland c Burns b Mallender	0	R. S. Yeabsley lbw b Lefebvre	2
A. J. Pugh b Lefebvre	12	L-b 5, w 9	14
P. A. Brown lbw b Lefebvre	12		
†R. C. Turpin c Rose b Lefebvre	4	1/4 2/4 3/11 (30.3 overs)	67
R. I. Dawson lbw b Lefebvre	0	4/35 5/41 6/41	
K. Donohue not out	18	7/44 8/44 9/63	

Bowling: Jones 6–1–20–1; Mallender 6–3–4–2; Rose 5–1–11–0; Lefebvre 9.3–6–15–7; Swallow 4–0–12–0.

Umpires: D. J. Halfyard and R. Julian.

ESSEX v SCOTLAND

At Chelmsford, June 27. Essex won by nine wickets. Toss: Scotland. Gooch's unbeaten 103, which featured eighteen fours, was scored from 109 deliveries.

Man of the Match: G. A. Gooch.

Scotland

†I. L. Philip c Waugh b Andrew	1	J. D. Moir not out	4
C. G. Greenidge b Foster	15	A. Bee run out	14
B. M. W. Patterson b Andrew	19	C. L. Parfitt b Pringle	0
*R. G. Swan c Pringle b Childs	26	B 2, l-b 15, w 9	26
A. B. Russell run out	37		
O. Henry c Hardie b Pringle	53	1/5 2/33 3/37 (59.3 overs)	200
W. Morton c Garnham b Foster	5	4/82 5/164 6/170	
P. G. Duthie lbw b Foster	0	7/176 8/180 9/199	

Bowling: Andrew 12–2–34–2; Foster 12–4–26–3; Topley 7–0–32–0; Pringle 11.3–2–30–2; Childs 12–1–44–1; Waugh 5–1–17–0.

Essex

*G. A. Gooch not out	103
B. R. Hardie b Bee	31
P. J. Prichard not out	37
B 2, l-b 17, w 11, n-b 1	31
1/105 (1 wkt, 42.4 overs)	202

M. E. Waugh, D. R. Pringle, J. P. Stephenson, †M. A. Garnham, N. A. Foster, T. D. Topley, J. H. Childs and S. J. W. Andrew did not bat.

Bowling: Moir 10–3–34–0; Duthie 8–0–37–0; Parfitt 9.4–3–29–0; Bee 10–4–27–1; Henry 3–0–21–0; Morton 2–0–35–0.

Umpires: J. H. Hampshire and H. J. Rhodes.

GLAMORGAN v DORSET

At Swansea, June 27, 28. Glamorgan won by 34 runs. Toss: Dorset. Dorset's total was the highest by a Minor County in the competition, beating by 5 runs Oxfordshire's 256 against Warwickshire at Birmingham in 1983. Morris (188 balls, sixteen fours) and Richards (80 balls, six sixes, eleven fours) provided the first instance for Glamorgan of two players scoring hundreds in a limited-overs game. Close of play: Glamorgan 207-2 (51 overs) (H. Morris 91*, I. V. A. Richards 64*).

Man of the Match: I. V. A. Richards.

Glamorgan

*A. R. Butcher st Fitzgerald b Stone .. 41
H. Morris c Calway b Merriman 116
M. P. Maynard st Fitzgerald b Stone .. 8
I. V. A. Richards c Hall b Merriman ..118
P. A. Cottey not out 2
A. Dale not out 4
L-b 2, w 4 6

1/76 2/90 3/266 4/288 (4 wkts, 60 overs) 295

N. G. Cowley, †C. P. Metson, S. J. Dennis, S. L. Watkin and M. Frost did not bat.

Bowling: Taylor 10–0–55–0; Shackleton 12–1–44–0; Hall 6–2–26–0; Stone 12–2–44–2; Wingfield Digby 12–0–60–0; Calway 4–0–29–0; Merriman 3–0–32–2; Graham-Brown 1–0–3–0.

Dorset

R. P. Merriman c Cottey b Frost 25
G. D. Reynolds c Dennis b Watkin ... 60
J. M. H. Graham-Brown c Metson b Richards . 58
G. S. Calway c Butcher b Frost 32
V. B. Lewis b Watkin 0
C. Stone b Richards 25
J. R. Hall c Metson b Frost 12
N. R. Taylor run out 7
*A. R. Wingfield Digby not out 23
†S. M. Fitzgerald not out 2
B 2, l-b 11, w 4 17

1/35 2/127 3/165 4/166 5/211 6/215 7/225 8/252 (8 wkts, 60 overs) 261

J. H. Shackleton did not bat.

Bowling: Frost 12–3–50–3; Watkin 12–0–56–2; Cowley 12–2–31–0; Dennis 6–0–28–0; Dale 6–1–28–0; Richards 12–0–55–2.

Umpires: D. J. Dennis and A. A. Jones.

GLOUCESTERSHIRE v LINCOLNSHIRE

At Gloucester, June 27. Gloucestershire won by 195 runs. Toss: Gloucestershire. Gloucestershire's total fell just 2 runs short of their highest in the competition: 327 for seven against Berkshire at Reading in 1966.

Man of the Match: A. J. Wright.

Gloucestershire

G. D. Hodgson c McKeown b Airey .. 42
*A. J. Wright st Priestley b Marshall .. 92
P. Bainbridge lbw b Marshall 13
C. W. J. Athey not out 81
K. M. Curran b Pont 2
J. W. Lloyds not out 73
L-b 13, w 5, n-b 4 22

1/113 2/142 3/173 4/178 (4 wkts, 60 overs) 325

M. W. Alleyne, †R. C. Russell, C. A. Walsh, D. A. Graveney and D. V. Lawrence did not bat.

Bowling: Pont 12–0–52–1; French 12–1–42–0; McKeown 12–1–84–0; Airey 10–0–60–1; Marshall 12–0–63–2; Love 2–0–11–0.

Lincolnshire

*†N. Priestley c Graveney b Alleyne .. 54
D. B. Storer lbw b Walsh 0
J. D. Love b Walsh 1
N. J. C. Gandon b Alleyne 31
I. L. Pont b Graveney 1
R. T. Bates b Graveney 5
S. N. Warman lbw b Alleyne 3
N. French c Wright b Alleyne 7
J. R. Airey st Russell b Alleyne 0
P. D. McKeown not out 3
D. Marshall b Lloyds 5
B 5, l-b 6, w 7, n-b 2 20

1/6 2/17 3/79 4/80 5/98 6/108 7/112 8/112 9/117 (49 overs) 130

Bowling: Walsh 7–1–16–2; Curran 8–3–11–0; Lawrence 5–0–15–0; Bainbridge 6–0–15–0; Graveney 12–0–26–2; Alleyne 10–2–30–5; Lloyds 1–0–6–1.

Umpires: J. H. Harris and C. T. Spencer.

HERTFORDSHIRE v WARWICKSHIRE

At St Albans, June 27. Warwickshire won by 128 runs. Toss: Hertfordshire.
Man of the Match: Asif Din.

Warwickshire

A. J. Moles b Surridge 60	G. C. Small c Surridge b Merry 0
Asif Din c Evans b Needham 66	J. E. Benjamin not out 1
T. M. Moody c T. S. Smith b Needham 58	
A. I. Kallicharran c MacLaurin b Surridge . 41	B 5, l-b 22, w 3 30
†G. W. Humpage b Surridge 43	1/133 2/147 3/229 (7 wkts, 60 overs) 336
*D. A. Reeve not out 36	4/292 5/304
R. G. Twose c Vartan b Merry 1	6/321 7/321

A. R. K. Pierson and T. A. Munton did not bat.

Bowling: Harris 12–0–67–0; Surridge 12–0–61–3; T. S. Smith 12–1–57–0; Merry 11–0–62–2; Needham 12–0–50–2; D. M. Smith 1–0–12–0.

Hertfordshire

B. G. Evans b Munton 27	W. G. Merry c Moody b Asif Din 11
N. P. G. Wright run out 17	G. A. R. Harris c Moles b Asif Din . . . 0
†R. N. R. Vartan c Moody b Munton . 10	*D. Surridge not out 3
A. Needham c Benjamin b Asif Din . . . 35	B 4, l-b 12, w 13 29
N. R. C. MacLaurin c Moles b Munton 21	
I. Fletcher c and b Asif Din 1	1/52 2/65 3/74 (53.1 overs) 208
D. M. Smith st Humpage b Moody 39	4/106 5/125 6/134
T. S. Smith c Twose b Asif Din 15	7/163 8/189 9/189

Bowling: Small 6–0–21–0; Benjamin 6–1–9–0; Reeve 8–1–20–0; Munton 12–1–46–3; Pierson 12–1–49–0; Asif Din 8–2–40–5; Moody 1.1–0–7–1.

Umpires: V. A. Holder and A. G. T. Whitehead.

IRELAND v SUSSEX

At Downpatrick, June 27. Sussex won by nine wickets. Toss: Ireland. Dodemaide's figures were the best for Sussex in the 60-overs competition.
Man of the Match: A. I. C. Dodemaide.

Ireland

A. R. Dunlop b Dodemaide 1	†P. B. Jackson b Dodemaide 0
R. Lamba b Dodemaide 5	A. N. Nelson b Dodemaide 3
M. P. Rea c Moores b Pigott 5	A. Johnston b Dodemaide 0
*S. J. S. Warke c Speight b Dodemaide 22	B 3, l-b 3, w 7 13
D. A. Lewis b C. M. Wells 1	
S. G. Smyth c Clarke b Lenham 15	1/1 2/10 3/18 (49 overs) 72
G. D. Harrison c Moores b Lenham . . . 3	4/19 5/47 6/58
P. McCrum not out 4	7/61 8/64 9/72

Bowling: Pigott 8–1–14–1; Dodemaide 11–7–9–6; C. M. Wells 9–6–6–1; Salisbury 5–2–19–0; Clarke 10–7–6–0; Lenham 6–0–12–2.

Sussex

N. J. Lenham not out 41
I. J. Gould c Lamba b Nelson 26
*P. W. G. Parker not out 4
W 2 2

1/58 (1 wkt, 15.1 overs) 73

A. P. Wells, M. P. Speight, C. M. Wells, A. I. C. Dodemaide, †P. Moores, A. C. S. Pigott, I. D. K. Salisbury and A. R. Clarke did not bat.

Bowling: McCrum 3–0–16–0; Johnston 4–0–21–0; Nelson 5–0–27–1; Harrison 3.1–0–9–0.

Umpires: J. C. Balderstone and B. Dudleston.

LANCASHIRE v DURHAM

At Manchester, June 27. Lancashire won by eight wickets. Toss: Lancashire.
Man of the Match: N. H. Fairbrother.

Durham

G. K. Brown lbw b Wasim Akram 42
J. D. Glendenen b Allott 14
P. Burn c Wasim Akram b Atherton .. 26
P. V. Simmons c Hegg b Austin 14
J. F. Sykes lbw b DeFreitas 4
A. S. Patel not out 31
*N. A. Riddell b Austin 16
S. Greensword lbw b Allott 0
P. G. Newman lbw b Allott 0
†A. R. Fothergill b Austin 2
I. Young b Wasim Akram 0
L-b 11, w 1, n-b 3 15

1/17 2/76 3/108 4/114 5/116 6/157 7/160 8/160 9/163 (55.2 overs) 164

Bowling: Allott 10–4–24–3; DeFreitas 10–2–22–1; Wasim Akram 9.2–1–19–2; Watkinson 12–1–45–0; Austin 12–0–36–3; Atherton 2–1–7–1.

Lancashire

G. D. Mendis not out 62
G. Fowler b Newman 31
M. A. Atherton c Burn b Sykes 4
N. H. Fairbrother not out 50
B 5, l-b 4, w 8, n-b 1 18

1/70 2/90 (2 wkts, 34.1 overs) 165

M. Watkinson, *D. P. Hughes, P. A. J. DeFreitas, Wasim Akram, I. D. Austin, †W. K. Hegg and P. J. W. Allott did not bat.

Bowling: Newman 10–0–30–1; Young 6.1–0–47–0; Simmons 4–0–28–0; Sykes 6–0–16–1; Greensword 6–1–23–0; Patel 2–0–12–0.

Umpires: D. B. Harrison and B. Leadbeater.

LEICESTERSHIRE v HAMPSHIRE

At Leicester, June 27. Hampshire won by 1 run. Toss: Leicestershire. Having required 49 runs from the last ten overs, Leicestershire began the final over still needing 9 for victory. Connor conceded just 6 off the first five balls, and off the sixth Nixon was run out attempting a second run.
Man of the Match: P. Willey.

Hampshire

V. P. Terry c Lewis b Willey 21
C. L. Smith c Willey b Benjamin 52
R. A. Smith c Nixon b Lewis 35
D. I. Gower c Willey b Mullally 28
M. D. Marshall c Briers b Agnew 6
*M. C. J. Nicholas b Mullally 19
J. R. Ayling b Agnew 29
†R. J. Parks not out 14
R. J. Maru not out 6
L-b 4, w 8, n-b 4 16

1/65 2/91 3/129 4/151 5/151 6/188 7/213 (7 wkts, 60 overs) 226

C. A. Connor and P. J. Bakker did not bat.

Bowling: Benjamin 12–4–34–1; Agnew 12–1–44–2; Lewis 12–1–35–1; Willey 12–2–54–1; Mullally 12–0–55–2.

Leicestershire

T. J. Boon c Parks b Maru 19
*N. E. Briers b Bakker 8
J. J. Whitaker c R. A. Smith b Maru .. 24
P. Willey not out 72
C. C. Lewis lbw b Maru 32
L. Potter run out 19
J. D. R. Benson c Nicholas b Ayling .. 11
W. K. M. Benjamin c Gower b Ayling . 7
†P. A. Nixon run out 12
B 1, l-b 12, w 6, n-b 2 21

1/16 2/55 3/56 4/118 5/157 6/185 7/195 8/225 (8 wkts, 60 overs) 225

J. P. Agnew and A. D. Mullally did not bat.

Bowling: Marshall 12–2–32–0; Bakker 12–0–51–1; Connor 12–1–49–0; Ayling 12–3–34–2; Maru 12–1–46–3.

Umpires: H. D. Bird and B. Hassan.

MIDDLESEX v BERKSHIRE

At Lord's, June 27. Middlesex won by four wickets. Toss: Middlesex. Berkshire reached 200 for the first time since they began competing in the 60-overs competition in 1965.
Man of the Match: M. W. Gatting.

Berkshire

G. E. Loveday c Roseberry b Gatting . 36
M. G. Lickley lbw b Cowans 12
*M. L. Simmons c Haynes b Cowans .. 30
G. T. Headley c Butcher b Emburey ... 13
D. Shaw run out 36
B. S. Jackson c Farbrace b Fraser 10
P. J. Oxley not out 33
M. G. Stear not out 5
L-b 9, w 8, n-b 12 29

1/24 2/68 3/99 4/114 5/135 6/178 (6 wkts, 60 overs) 204

†M. E. Stevens, J. H. Jones and D. J. B. Hartley did not bat.

Bowling: Cowans 10–3–25–2; Williams 12–1–67–0; Fraser 12–0–37–1; Gatting 6–0–31–1; Haynes 8–3–18–0; Emburey 12–2–17–1.

Middlesex

D. L. Haynes b Headley 50
M. A. Roseberry lbw b Jones 3
*M. W. Gatting not out 79
M. R. Ramprakash run out 3
K. R. Brown lbw b Stear 16
R. O. Butcher c Jackson b Hartley 22
†P. Farbrace b Hartley 17
J. E. Emburey not out 4
B 2, l-b 6, w 5, n-b 1 14

1/3 2/100 3/117 4/149 5/186 6/204 (6 wkts, 50.3 overs) 208

N. F. Williams, A. R. C. Fraser and N. G. Cowans did not bat.

Bowling: Jones 9–2–32–1; Jackson 10–1–46–0; Headley 12–1–35–1; Stear 9–0–39–1; Lickley 1–0–13–0; Hartley 9.3–1–35–2.

Umpires: J. A. Jameson and K. E. Palmer.

NORTHAMPTONSHIRE v STAFFORDSHIRE

At Northampton, June 27. Northamptonshire won by 216 runs. Toss: Staffordshire. Northamptonshire's total was their highest in the Gillette Cup/NatWest Bank Trophy, while Fordham, who hit a six and fifteen fours in 130 from 143 balls, equalled G. Cook's county record for the competition. Lamb, scoring 68 not out from 35 balls, hit four sixes and three fours.
Man of the Match: A. Fordham.

Northamptonshire

A. Fordham c Cartledge b Blank 130
N. A. Felton c Humphries b Blank 70
R. J. Bailey not out 72
*A. J. Lamb not out 68
L-b 14, w 6 20

1/166 2/242 (2 wkts, 60 overs) 360

D. J. Capel, R. G. Williams, †D. Ripley, J. G. Thomas, C. E. L. Ambrose, N. G. B. Cook and M. A. Robinson did not bat.

Bowling: Taylor 12–0–92–0; Grant 12–2–56–0; Blank 12–0–74–2; Dyer 8–0–49–0; Dutton 12–1–52–0; Cartledge 4–0–23–0.

Staffordshire

S. J. Dean c Williams b Ambrose 8
D. Cartledge run out 19
J. P. Addison c Thomas b Robinson ... 10
P. R. Oliver lbw b Thomas 28
*N. J. Archer b Williams 26
A. J. Dutton c Lamb b Cook 32
†M. I. Humphries not out 5
J. P. Taylor c Capel b Bailey 5
D. C. Blank not out 1
L-b 1, w 6, n-b 3 10

1/29 2/30 3/66 4/73 5/133 6/133 7/142 (7 wkts, 60 overs) 144

R. J. Dyer and R. J. Grant did not bat.

Bowling: Ambrose 10–2–15–1; Thomas 10–2–21–1; Cook 12–4–31–1; Robinson 12–1–39–1; Williams 12–3–32–1; Fordham 2–1–3–0; Bailey 2–1–2–1.

Umpires: D. Fawkner-Corbett and N. T. Plews.

OXFORDSHIRE v KENT

At Christ Church, Oxford, June 27. Kent won by 102 runs. Toss: Oxfordshire. Wells, promoted to open because of injuries to senior players, batted throughout the Kent innings, facing 160 deliveries and reaching his maiden century for the county off the final ball. He then kept wicket as Oxfordshire were bowled out for 132.

Man of the Match: V. J. Wells.

Kent

S. G. Hinks c Garner b Hartley 43
†V. J. Wells not out 100
N. R. Taylor retired hurt 13
G. R. Cowdrey c Hartley b Curtis 3
*C. S. Cowdrey c Jobson b Evans 6
M. V. Fleming b Evans 7
D. J. M. Kelleher c Evans b Curtis ... 21
P. S. de Villiers st Waterton b Evans .. 10
A. P. Igglesden not out 12
B 2, l-b 9, w 8 19

1/70 2/110 3/124 4/140 5/188 6/206 (6 wkts, 60 overs) 234

M. M. Patel and R. P. Davis did not bat.

N. R. Taylor retired hurt at 95.

Bowling: Hale 4–0–15–0; Arnold 12–3–48–0; Savin 12–0–35–0; Hartley 8–1–26–1; Curtis 12–0–53–2; Evans 12–1–46–3.

Oxfordshire

G. C. Ford b Davis ... 26
†S. N. V. Waterton c C. S. Cowdrey b Igglesden . 0
J. S. Hartley lbw b Igglesden ... 7
T. A. Lester lbw b Kelleher ... 13
*P. J. Garner lbw b Patel ... 4
P. M. Jobson b Patel ... 7
G. P. Savin lbw b Fleming ... 23
R. A. Evans b Fleming ... 24
D. A. Hale lbw b Kelleher ... 6
K. A. Arnold b Kelleher ... 2
I. J. Curtis not out ... 0
B 4, l-b 11, w 5 ... 20

1/8 2/22 3/41 4/58 5/66 6/66 7/119 8/120 9/131 (49 overs) 132

Bowling: de Villiers 7–3–28–0; Igglesden 6–1–13–2; Kelleher 9–3–16–3; Patel 12–6–29–2; Davis 12–3–27–1; Fleming 3–1–4–2.

Umpires: D. J. Constant and S. Cook.

SUFFOLK v WORCESTERSHIRE

At Bury St Edmunds, June 27. Worcestershire won by eight wickets. Toss: Worcestershire. *Man of the Match:* S. R. Lampitt.

Suffolk

M. S. A. McEvoy c Illingworth b Lampitt . 55
C. Gladwin c and b Lampitt ... 5
J. W. Edrich c Rhodes b D'Oliveira ... 52
P. J. Caley not out ... 39
S. M. Clements c Weston b D'Oliveira . 11
M. J. Peck b Botham ... 0
I. D. Graham lbw b Lampitt ... 3
A. K. Golding c Neale b Botham ... 0
†A. D. Brown b Lampitt ... 4
*M. D. Bailey b Botham ... 0
R. C. Green lbw b Lampitt ... 0
L-b 3, w 3, n-b 2 ... 8

1/10 2/117 3/121 4/138 5/146 6/163 7/164 8/169 9/176 (59.4 overs) 177

Bowling: Botham 12–2–44–3; Lampitt 11.4–1–22–5; Illingworth 12–5–26–0; Hick 12–2–30–0; D'Oliveira 5–0–17–2; McEwan 3–0–15–0; Weston 4–0–20–0.

Worcestershire

T. S. Curtis b Golding ... 16
M. J. Weston c and b Golding ... 40
G. A. Hick not out ... 78
D. B. D'Oliveira not out ... 33
B 2, l-b 2, w 7, n-b 3 ... 14

1/38 2/97 (2 wkts, 48 overs) 181

I. T. Botham, *P. A. Neale, D. A. Leatherdale, †S. J. Rhodes, S. R. Lampitt, R. K. Illingworth and S. M. McEwan did not bat.

Bowling: Green 11–1–38–0; Graham 9–1–37–0; Golding 12–4–29–2; Bailey 6–0–18–0; Caley 9–0–49–0; Gladwin 1–0–6–0.

Umpires: D. O. Oslear and R. A. White.

WILTSHIRE v SURREY

At Trowbridge, June 27. Surrey won by nine wickets. Toss: Surrey. Bullen, called on to open the innings after Stewart had twisted an ankle while fielding, hit two sixes and sixteen fours in his unbeaten 93.
Man of the Match: C. K. Bullen.

Wiltshire

*B. H. White c Lynch b Waqar Younis 0
P. A. C. Bail run out 66
D. R. Turner c Ward b Bullen 18
K. N. Foyle b Waqar Younis 16
S. Williams b Murphy 11
D. P. Simpkins c Thorpe b Bicknell 18
J. Thompson run out 7
†N. Shardlow b Waqar Younis 6
A. Mildenhall run out 3
S. J. Malone not out 5
M. Holland not out 0
B 3, l-b 9, w 4 16

1/0 2/55 3/102 4/116 5/131 6/148 7/158 8/159 9/161 (9 wkts, 60 overs) 166

Bowling: Waqar Younis 12–3–23–3; Bicknell 12–3–16–1; Murphy 12–1–46–1; Medlycott 12–1–27–0; Bullen 12–1–42–1.

Surrey

G. S. Clinton c Shardlow b Mildenhall 50
C. K. Bullen not out 93
G. P. Thorpe not out 15
L-b 5, w 6, n-b 1 12

1/111 (1 wkt, 36.1 overs) 170

A. J. Stewart, †D. M. Ward, M. A. Lynch, *I. A. Greig, K. T. Medlycott, M. P. Bicknell, Waqar Younis and A. J. Murphy did not bat.

Bowling: Malone 9.1–0–54–0; Thompson 8–0–40–0; Simpkins 6–2–29–0; Mildenhall 8–2–32–1; Holland 5–2–10–0.

Umpires: K. J. Lyons and R. C. Tolchard.

YORKSHIRE v NORFOLK

At Leeds, June 27. Yorkshire won by ten wickets. Toss: Yorkshire.
Man of the Match: P. Carrick.

Norfolk

*S. G. Plumb c Byas b Hartley 20
F. L. Q. Handley c Sharp b Hartley 0
D. M. Stamp lbw b Moxon 18
R. J. Finney c Blakey b Moxon 25
S. B. Dixon c Sharp b Gough 1
D. R. Thomas b Carrick 5
N. S. Taylor b Carrick 0
J. C. M. Lewis c Blakey b Carrick 9
R. Kingshott b Gough 9
†D. E. Mattocks lbw b Hartley 2
M. T. Ellis not out 0
B 5, l-b 1, w 5, n-b 4 15

1/7 2/29 3/55 4/72 5/81 6/81 7/81 8/92 9/103 (47.5 overs) 104

Bowling: Hartley 8.5–1–28–3; Sidebottom 10–1–21–0; Moxon 7–2–19–2; Gough 10–2–22–2; Carrick 12–9–8–3.

Yorkshire

*M. D. Moxon not out 56
A. A. Metcalfe not out 46
L-b 1, w 3 4

(no wkt, 20.2 overs) 106

S. A. Kellett, K. Sharp, P. E. Robinson, †R. J. Blakey, D. Byas, P. Carrick, P. J. Hartley, A. Sidebottom and D. Gough did not bat.

Bowling: Lewis 8–2–37–0; Taylor 4–0–32–0; Kingshott 6–2–24–0; Ellis 2.2–0–12–0.

Umpires: B. J. Meyer and T. G. Wilson.

SECOND ROUND

DERBYSHIRE v LANCASHIRE

At Derby, July 11. Lancashire won by three wickets. Toss: Lancashire. Derbyshire established a good position when Barnett and Morris shared a partnership of 105 for the second wicket. However, Morris suffered from a lapse of concentration before lunch, when he drove Atherton to extra cover, and the later batting collapsed spectacularly as DeFreitas and Wasim Akram took the last five wickets in ten balls. Lancashire were well in control until Malcolm and Goldsmith took three wickets in two overs, and Austin and Hegg had to bat carefully to steer Lancashire through with four balls to spare.

Man of the Match: M. A. Atherton.

Derbyshire

*K. J. Barnett b Wasim Akram	59	A. E. Warner not out	1
†P. D. Bowler b Wasim Akram	2	D. E. Malcolm b Wasim Akram	0
J. E. Morris c Fairbrother b Atherton	74	O. H. Mortensen b Wasim Akram	0
A. P. Kuiper c Atherton b Austin	25		
B. Roberts b DeFreitas	31	L-b 12, w 12, n-b 4	28
C. J. Adams c Hegg b Austin	0		
S. C. Goldsmith c Watkinson b DeFreitas	21	1/18 2/123 3/161 4/180 5/180 6/239 7/239 8/240 9/241	(56.5 overs) 241
G. Miller b DeFreitas	0		

Bowling: Wasim Akram 10.5–0–34–4; DeFreitas 11–4–34–3; Watkinson 5–0–31–0; Martin 5–0–28–0; Austin 10–0–46–2; Atherton 12–0–37–1; Hughes 3–0–19–0.

Lancashire

G. D. Mendis c Bowler b Mortensen	42	I. D. Austin not out	13
M. A. Atherton b Miller	55	†W. K. Hegg not out	13
G. D. Lloyd c Adams b Warner	36	B 6, l-b 14, w 6, n-b 3	29
N. H. Fairbrother c Miller b Malcolm	39		
M. Watkinson b Malcolm	5	1/64 2/134 3/184 4/194 5/209 6/214 7/215	(7 wkts, 59.2 overs) 242
Wasim Akram b Goldsmith	9		
P. A. J. DeFreitas c Roberts b Malcolm	1		

*D. P. Hughes and P. J. Martin did not bat.

Bowling: Malcolm 12–1–54–3; Mortensen 12–4–22–1; Warner 12–1–45–1; Miller 12–1–56–1; Kuiper 6–1–25–0; Goldsmith 5.2–0–20–1.

Umpires: M. J. Kitchen and K. E. Palmer.

ESSEX v HAMPSHIRE

At Chelmsford, July 11. Hampshire won, having lost fewer wickets with the scores level. Toss: Hampshire. Nicholas and Ayling took 6 runs off the first five balls of the last over, whereupon the Hampshire captain played the sixth defensively rather than risk losing a wicket going for the winning run. A start of 14 off the first ten overs by Chris Smith and Terry scarcely hinted at their partnership of 173 which launched Hampshire towards the highest total in the competition by a team batting second and winning. When 75 were needed from eleven overs following Gower's dismissal, Robin Smith's powerful fifty was as vital as his brother's century. Had Chris Smith been run out when 79, Gooch's eleventh hundred of the summer might not have been in vain. Gooch batted for 227 minutes without giving a chance, putting on 93 for the first wicket with Stephenson and 97 in sixteen overs with Waugh.

Man of the Match: C. L. Smith.

Essex

*G. A. Gooch b Connor 144
J. P. Stephenson run out 44
P. J. Prichard c Gower b Marshall 21
M. E. Waugh c Parks b Marshall 47
D. R. Pringle c Nicholas b Bakker 33
N. A. Foster c Gower b Connor 0
N. Hussain not out 2
†M. A. Garnham not out 1
B 5, l-b 3, w 3, n-b 4 15

1/93 2/143 3/240 4/304 5/304 6/304 (6 wkts, 60 overs) 307

T. D. Topley, J. H. Childs and M. C. Ilott did not bat.

Bowling: Marshall 12–0–45–2; Bakker 12–3–60–1; Connor 12–0–71–2; Ayling 12–0–57–0; Maru 12–0–66–0.

Hampshire

V. P. Terry c Gooch b Ilott 76
C. L. Smith c Gooch b Stephenson 106
D. I. Gower c Topley b Foster 19
R. A. Smith c Topley b Pringle 59
M. D. Marshall b Pringle 9
*M. C. J. Nicholas not out 9
J. R. Ayling not out 10
L-b 13, w 6 19

1/173 2/195 3/233 4/253 5/289 (5 wkts, 60 overs) 307

†R. J. Parks, R. J. Maru, C. A. Connor and P. J. Bakker did not bat.

Bowling: Foster 12–4–35–1; Ilott 9–0–45–1; Pringle 12–1–64–2; Topley 11–0–66–0; Childs 12–0–60–0; Stephenson 4–0–24–1.

Umpires: J. D. Bond and J. H. Harris.

GLAMORGAN v SUSSEX

At Cardiff, July 11. Glamorgan won by 34 runs. Toss: Sussex. Put in on a slow pitch, Glamorgan had Richards to thank for a winning total. He and Cowley took 77 off the last seven overs, and his unbeaten 74 from 50 balls included two straight sixes as Dodemaide went for 21 runs in the final over. Morris, in contrast, anchored the innings with 58 in 44 overs. While Wells and Parker were adding 128 in 21 overs, Sussex were in control. When Wells was caught, having hit two sixes and eight fours in his 85, their target was 55 from ten overs. Instead, they lost their remaining seven wickets for 20 runs in 38 deliveries.

Man of the Match: I. V. A. Richards.

Glamorgan

*A. R. Butcher c Pigott b Dodemaide . 30
H. Morris c Salisbury b Dodemaide ... 58
P. A. Cottey lbw b Clarke 27
M. P. Maynard c Speight b Lenham ... 24
I. V. A. Richards not out 74
I. Smith st Moores b Clarke 22
N. G. Cowley not out 32
B 2, l-b 12, w 2 16

1/33 2/97 3/144 4/160 5/206 (5 wkts, 60 overs) 283

†C. P. Metson, S. J. Dennis, S. L. Watkin and M. Frost did not bat.

Bowling: Clarke 12–0–53–2; Pigott 11–1–56–0; Dodemaide 12–1–70–2; Remy 10–1–30–0; Salisbury 12–1–47–0; Lenham 3–0–13–1.

Sussex

N. J. Lenham lbw b Smith 47
J. W. Hall run out.................. 0
*P. W. G. Parker b Richards 83
A. P. Wells c Smith b Cowley 85
M. P. Speight c Butcher b Cowley 4
A. I. C. Dodemaide lbw b Richards ... 1
A. C. S. Pigott b Watkin 1
†P. Moores run out 0
C. C. Remy b Watkin 1
I. D. K. Salisbury not out 2
A. R. Clarke lbw b Watkin 0
B 1, l-b 18, w 5, n-b 1 25

1/2 2/101 3/229 4/233 5/236 6/243 7/243 8/247 9/249 (55.5 overs) 249

Bowling: Cowley 12–0–71–2; Frost 10–1–34–0; Watkin 11.5–5–18–3; Dennis 8–0–44–0; Richards 10–0–43–2; Smith 4–0–20–1.

Umpires: P. J. Eele and R. Palmer.

GLOUCESTERSHIRE v KENT

At Bristol, July 11. Gloucestershire won by six wickets. Toss: Kent. High-class fast bowling by Walsh quickly made Chris Cowdrey regret his decision to bat. And when Kent hinted at a recovery through Graham Cowdrey and Ward, his three quick wickets after lunch cut the heart out of the innings. Although Ellison and the tailenders nudged the score up to 181, this never seemed enough on what was basically a good batting pitch. Kent's new-ball bowlers were handled comfortably by Wright and Hodgson, and Bainbridge produced some crisp strokes to see Gloucestershire home with nearly twelve overs to spare.

Man of the Match: C. A. Walsh.

Kent

M. R. Benson c Russell b Walsh 7
S. G. Hinks c Graveney b Curran 15
N. R. Taylor b Walsh 0
G. R. Cowdrey c Bainbridge b Alleyne . 37
T. R. Ward lbw b Walsh 47
*C. S. Cowdrey b Walsh 5
†S. A. Marsh b Walsh 0
R. M. Ellison not out 27
P. S. de Villiers b Curran 14
R. P. Davis c Russell b Walsh 12
A. P. Igglesden not out 2
L-b 9, w 4, n-b 2 15

1/11 2/13 3/30 4/93 5/120 6/123 7/124 8/156 9/175 (9 wkts, 60 overs) 181

Bowling: Walsh 12–3–21–6; Curran 12–2–30–2; Barnes 6–0–29–0; Bainbridge 11.1–1–38–0; Graveney 6.5–0–21–0; Alleyne 12–2–33–1.

Gloucestershire

G. D. Hodgson c Davis b de Villiers .. 39
*A. J. Wright c Ellison b Davis 45
P. Bainbridge not out 56
C. W. J. Athey c Marsh b Ellison 22
K. M. Curran c Taylor b G. R. Cowdrey 1
J. W. Lloyds not out 4
L-b 3, w 11, n-b 1 15

1/88 2/94 3/175 4/178 (4 wkts, 48.3 overs) 182

M. W. Alleyne, †R. C. Russell, C. A. Walsh, D. A. Graveney and S. N. Barnes did not bat.

Bowling: de Villiers 9–1–29–1; Igglesden 8–0–34–0; Ellison 12–6–18–1; C. S. Cowdrey 5–0–29–0; Davis 9–0–33–1; Hinks 3–0–23–0; G. R. Cowdrey 2.3–0–13–1.

Umpires: B. Hassan and K. J. Lyons.

MIDDLESEX v SURREY

At Uxbridge, July 11. Middlesex won by five wickets. Toss: Middlesex. Though no Surrey batsman did excessive damage, their total was nevertheless more than Middlesex had previously scored in the 60-overs competition. Middlesex were especially pleased to run out Lynch, who had noted the square-leg boundary with two consecutive sixes off Emburey in his 59 from 74 balls. With Haynes out in the first over and Gatting injured, Middlesex needed major innings from Roseberry, Ramprakash and Brown, who obliged gloriously. Roseberry laid the foundation with Ramprakash, who then added 126 in 26 overs with Brown. Ramprakash faced 142 balls for his 104, but it was necessary for Brown to go even faster. His winning hit, with two balls left, brought his century from just 113 balls.

Man of the Match: K. R. Brown.

Surrey

D. J. Bicknell b Cowans 12
G. S. Clinton lbw b Fraser 33
*A. J. Stewart c Farbrace b Fraser 48
M. A. Lynch run out 59
†D. M. Ward c Brown b Haynes 11
G. P. Thorpe c Cowans b Fraser 16
M. A. Feltham c Farbrace b Fraser ... 5
K. T. Medlycott c Farbrace b Cowans . 38
C. K. Bullen not out 20
M. P. Bicknell not out 4
B 1, l-b 19, w 16, n-b 6 42

1/18 2/113 3/114 4/175 5/215 6/221 7/221 8/274 (8 wkts, 60 overs) 288

Waqar Younis did not bat.

Bowling: Cowans 11–2–45–2; Williams 11–2–42–0; Haynes 12–0–41–1; Gatting 2–0–20–0; Fraser 12–1–44–4; Emburey 12–0–76–0.

Middlesex

D. L. Haynes c Ward b Waqar Younis . 0
M. A. Roseberry c M. P. Bicknell b Waqar Younis . 48
M. R. Ramprakash c Ward b M. P. Bicknell . 104
K. R. Brown not out . 103
R. O. Butcher c Stewart b Medlycott . 1
*M. W. Gatting c Ward b Feltham . 3
J. E. Emburey not out . 15
B 8, l-b 6, w 1, n-b 2 . 17

1/0 2/94 3/220 4/223 5/241 (5 wkts, 59.4 overs) 291

†P. Farbrace, N. F. Williams, A. R. C. Fraser and N. G. Cowans did not bat.

Bowling: Waqar Younis 12–2–39–2; M. P. Bicknell 12–0–63–1; Feltham 11.4–0–65–1; Medlycott 12–0–64–1; Bullen 12–0–46–0.

Umpires: N. T. Plews and D. S. Thompsett.

NORTHAMPTONSHIRE v NOTTINGHAMSHIRE

At Northampton, July 11. Northamptonshire won by 24 runs. Toss: Nottinghamshire. A magnificent innings from Capel, whose 101 runs came off as many balls with five sixes and seven fours, paved the way for a Northamptonshire total far more formidable than had looked likely when they lost their first three wickets for 72. Lamb, for once content to play the secondary role, helped Capel add 154 in 30 overs. Nottinghamshire were unlucky in that two of their key batsmen, Broad (ricked neck) and Johnson (hit on the head by Ambrose) were forced to retire hurt. Although both later returned, the innings lost its momentum for a time. Randall and French regained the initiative in a brisk 64-run stand, but Randall became a third victim of Bailey's occasional off-spin, and with Evans and Cooper succumbing to suicidal run-outs, French was left with too much to do.

Man of the Match: D. J. Capel.

Northamptonshire

A. Fordham c French b Cooper . 23
N. A. Felton b Hemmings . 32
R. J. Bailey c French b Evans . 7
*A. J. Lamb c Evans b Stephenson . 61
D. J. Capel b Evans . 101
W. Larkins c French b Stephenson . 21
R. G. Williams not out . 9
†D. Ripley not out . 1
B 1, l-b 14, w 3, n-b 1 . 19

1/33 2/66 3/72 4/226 5/258 6/264 (6 wkts, 60 overs) 274

C. E. L. Ambrose, N. G. B. Cook and M. A. Robinson did not bat.

Bowling: Stephenson 12–1–40–2; Cooper 12–0–49–1; Pick 12–1–64–0; Evans 12–3–53–2; Hemmings 12–2–53–1.

Nottinghamshire

B. C. Broad c Robinson b Williams . 13
M. Newell run out . 4
*R. T. Robinson b Bailey . 61
P. Johnson b Robinson . 48
D. W. Randall c Ambrose b Bailey . 56
F. D. Stephenson c Ambrose b Bailey . 4
†B. N. French c Fordham b Ambrose . 35
K. P. Evans run out . 0
E. E. Hemmings c and b Cook . 0
K. E. Cooper run out . 0
R. A. Pick not out . 5
L-b 3, w 10, n-b 11 . 24

1/24 2/119 3/149 4/163 5/171 6/235 7/239 8/240 9/240 (57.1 overs) 250

B. C. Broad, when 13, retired hurt at 22 and resumed at 117; P. Johnson, when 41, retired hurt at 117 and resumed at 149.

Bowling: Ambrose 10.1–1–30–1; Robinson 11–0–46–1; Cook 12–1–42–1; Capel 6–0–43–0; Williams 8–1–39–1; Bailey 10–1–47–3.

Umpires: J. H. Hampshire and P. B. Wight.

SOMERSET v WORCESTERSHIRE

At Taunton, July 11. Worcestershire won by seven wickets. Toss: Somerset. Accurate bowling by Illingworth and Lampitt slowed Somerset after a brisk start, with Hayhurst and Tavaré needing 28 overs to add 100. And although 76 runs came from the last ten overs, with Tavaré (122 balls) helped notably by Burns, in splendid weather and good conditions for run-scoring a total of 283 hardly looked sufficient. Curtis and Weston, who batted for 147 balls for 98 despite receiving a nasty blow under the heart, put on 188 in 41 overs. Lefebvre then took two quick wickets, but Curtis, reaching 100 in 124 balls, and D'Oliveira ensured Worcestershire won with sixteen balls to spare.

Man of the Match: T. S. Curtis.

Somerset

S. J. Cook lbw b Lampitt	45	†N. D. Burns not out	25
P. M. Roebuck b Lampitt	20		
A. N. Hayhurst c Lampitt b Newport	46	B 6, l-b 7, w 6, n-b 1	20
*C. J. Tavaré not out	99		
G. D. Rose c Neale b Botham	16	1/64 2/71 3/171 (5 wkts, 60 overs)	283
R. J. Harden b Botham	12	4/200 5/230	

R. P. Lefebvre, I. G. Swallow, N. A. Mallender and A. N. Jones did not bat.

Bowling: Botham 12–0–65–2; Newport 10–0–54–1; Lampitt 12–1–48–2; Illingworth 12–3–22–0; Tolley 6–0–32–0; Hick 8–0–49–0.

Worcestershire

T. S. Curtis c Swallow b Rose	112	I. T. Botham not out	0
M. J. Weston c Cook b Lefebvre	98	L-b 12, w 7, n-b 2	21
G. A. Hick c Burns b Lefebvre	2		
D. B. D'Oliveira not out	51	1/188 2/195 3/279 (3 wkts, 57.2 overs)	284

*P. A. Neale, †S. J. Rhodes, R. K. Illingworth, P. J. Newport, S. R. Lampitt and C. M. Tolley did not bat.

Bowling: Jones 10–0–64–0; Mallender 10–2–29–0; Lefebvre 12–0–46–2; Rose 9–0–40–1; Hayhurst 2–0–14–0; Swallow 9–0–57–0; Roebuck 5.2–0–22–0.

Umpires: B. Dudleston and D. R. Shepherd.

YORKSHIRE v WARWICKSHIRE

At Leeds, July 11. Yorkshire won by ten wickets. Toss: Yorkshire. Warwickshire were always struggling against accurate bowling on a good one-day pitch. Gough claimed two wickets for 1 run in six balls to upset them after a reasonable start, and Carrick won a significant duel with the free-scoring Moody. Asif Din, missed when 22 off Hartley, made his 58 from 80 balls, while Smith's 52 came from 46 deliveries. When Yorkshire batted, Moxon and Metcalfe took complete control, the latter racing to his half-century off 63 balls. The Warwickshire bowlers had no answer as the Yorkshire pair established a new record opening stand for the competition. Moxon's 107 came from 168 balls (nine fours) and Metcalfe's 127 from 165 (fifteen fours).

Man of the Match: M. D. Moxon.

Warwickshire

A. J. Moles c Blakey b Gough	27	G. C. Small b Hartley	8
*T. A. Lloyd c Byas b Sidebottom	15	J. E. Benjamin not out	2
T. M. Moody c Metcalfe b Carrick	51	T. A. Munton not out	1
†G. W. Humpage c Sidebottom b Gough	2	L-b 9, w 7, n-b 5	21
D. A. Reeve c Robinson b Carrick	0		
D. P. Ostler c Blakey b Carrick	4	1/33 2/79 3/85 (9 wkts, 60 overs)	241
Asif Din c Gough b Byas	58	4/86 5/97 6/138	
N. M. K. Smith c Robinson b Hartley	52	7/211 8/236 9/236	

Bowling: Hartley 12–0–62–2; Sidebottom 12–4–20–1; Fletcher 12–1–56–0; Carrick 12–0–26–3; Gough 9–1–45–2; Byas 3–0–23–1.

Yorkshire

*M. D. Moxon not out	107
A. A. Metcalfe not out	127
L-b 3, w 3, n-b 2	8
(no wkt, 55 overs)	242

S. A. Kellett, P. E. Robinson, †R. J. Blakey, D. Byas, P. Carrick, P. J. Hartley, A. Sidebottom, D. Gough and S. D. Fletcher did not bat.

Bowling: Benjamin 8–1–40–0; Small 9–1–37–0; Reeve 12–1–42–0; Munton 6–0–31–0; Smith 8–0–41–0; Moody 9–0–34–0; Asif Din 3–0–14–0.

Umpires: H. D. Bird and R. A. White.

QUARTER-FINALS

HAMPSHIRE v YORKSHIRE

At Southampton, August 1. Hampshire won by 111 runs. Toss: Yorkshire. Hampshire's often underrated attack bowled them to an unexpected victory. After Hampshire had been restricted to 229 for nine, with Nicholas's vigilant 50 providing the backbone, Yorkshire were clear favourites for a place in the semi-finals. Yet within seven overs their hopes lay in ruins. Moxon was needlessly run out in the first over, and Metcalfe and Kellett fell in Marshall's fourth over with the total 9. After that, only Hartley and Carrick delayed the inevitable with a stand of 34 for the seventh wicket. Hartley hit two sixes and six fours in his lively half-century.

Man of the Match: P. J. Hartley.

Hampshire

V. P. Terry c Byas b Hartley	16
C. L. Smith c Blakey b Hartley	30
D. I. Gower c Moxon b Hartley	26
R. A. Smith c Byas b Sidebottom	27
M. D. Marshall c Sidebottom b Hartley	4
*M. C. J. Nicholas b Hartley	50
J. R. Ayling st Blakey b Carrick	7
†R. J. Parks not out	27
R. J. Maru c Blakey b Fletcher	22
C. A. Connor c Blakey b Fletcher	13
P. J. Bakker not out	3
L-b 3, w 1	4
1/28 2/63 3/76 4/80 5/121 6/154 7/168 8/199 9/223 (9 wkts, 60 overs)	229

Bowling: Jarvis 12–1–58–0; Sidebottom 12–3–35–1; Hartley 12–2–46–5; Fletcher 12–0–53–2; Carrick 12–0–34–1.

Yorkshire

*M. D. Moxon run out	1
A. A. Metcalfe c Maru b Marshall	2
†R. J. Blakey b Ayling	21
S. A. Kellett b Marshall	0
P. E. Robinson c Terry b Connor	7
D. Byas b Maru	4
P. Carrick c R. A. Smith b Ayling	14
P. J. Hartley c C. L. Smith b Ayling	52
P. W. Jarvis c Connor b Marshall	6
A. Sidebottom c Parks b Marshall	1
S. D. Fletcher not out	6
L-b 1, w 2, n-b 1	4
1/1 2/9 3/9 4/34 5/34 6/40 7/74 8/105 9/107 (39 overs)	118

Bowling: Marshall 8–1–17–4; Bakker 7–1–12–0; Connor 6–2–10–1; Ayling 9–2–30–3; Maru 9–0–48–1.

Umpires: R. Julian and R. Palmer.

LANCASHIRE v GLOUCESTERSHIRE

At Manchester, August 1. Lancashire won by 241 runs. Toss: Gloucestershire. Lancashire followed the highest total in any limited-overs game between first-class counties with the highest victory margin. It was Watkinson's 29th birthday and he celebrated with the biggest innings (90 from 58 balls) and the best bowling return in the match. Gloucestershire were never in the game after Mendis and Fowler had given Lancashire a 124-run start at 5 runs an over. Watkinson hit six fours and four sixes, and he and Fairbrother put on 169 in twenty overs.

Man of the Match: M. Watkinson.

Lancashire

G. D. Mendis run out 88
G. Fowler c Russell b Lawrence 52
M. A. Atherton c and b Barnes 25
N. H. Fairbrother b Walsh 86
M. Watkinson c Wright b Walsh 90
Wasim Akram not out 5
L-b 5, w 20, n-b 1 26

1/124 2/176 3/180 4/349 5/372 (5 wkts, 60 overs) 372

*D. P. Hughes, P. A. J. DeFreitas, I. D. Austin, †W. K. Hegg and P. J. Martin did not bat.

Bowling: Walsh 12–0–69–2; Curran 12–2–63–0; Barnes 12–1–64–1; Lawrence 9–0–62–1; Alleyne 7–0–51–0; Lloyds 5–0–44–0; Athey 3–0–14–0.

Gloucestershire

*A. J. Wright c Atherton b DeFreitas . 4
G. D. Hodgson c and b Atherton 52
P. W. Romaines b Austin 20
C. W. J. Athey c and b Wasim Akram. 8
†R. C. Russell c and b Atherton 12
K. M. Curran c Hegg b Watkinson ... 1
J. W. Lloyds c Hegg b Watkinson 2
M. W. Alleyne not out 9
C. A. Walsh c Hegg b Watkinson 7
D. V. Lawrence b Wasim Akram 0
S. N. Barnes b Wasim Akram 0
B 4, w 12 16

1/21 2/59 3/90 4/106 5/107 6/113 7/115 8/123 9/131 (30 overs) 131

Bowling: Martin 3–0–25–0; DeFreitas 5–1–22–1; Austin 7–0–22–1; Wasim Akram 6–0–29–3; Watkinson 5–0–14–3; Atherton 4–0–15–2.

Umpires: B. Leadbeater and K. J. Lyons.

MIDDLESEX v GLAMORGAN

At Lord's, August 1. Middlesex won by nine wickets. Toss: Glamorgan. This was an unusual limited-overs match, with spin bowlers playing an attacking role on a pitch which assisted them extravagantly. As the Middlesex spin attack was superior to Glamorgan's, there was an inevitability about the result once it became clear that nobody would emulate Butcher's fighting effort. The Glamorgan captain reached his century in the penultimate over and hit ten fours in an innings of 177 balls. Cowley and Croft demanded a degree of watchfulness, but none of the three Middlesex batsmen was anything but forceful as they progressed comfortably towards their target.

Man of the Match: A. R. Butcher.

Glamorgan

*A. R. Butcher not out 104
H. Morris b Tufnell 26
M. P. Maynard c Cowans b Emburey .. 1
I. V. A. Richards c Gatting b Emburey 9
A. Dale c Emburey b Tufnell......... 3
R. D. B. Croft run out 26
N. G. Cowley b Cowans 5
†C. P. Metson c Gatting b Emburey ... 9
S. L. Watkin not out 6
B 10, l-b 7, w 1, n-b 6 24

1/49 2/50 3/76 4/86 5/150 6/162 7/187 (7 wkts, 60 overs) 213

S. J. Dennis and M. Frost did not bat.

Bowling: Cowans 12–2–48–1; Fraser 12–2–47–0; Williams 8–0–38–0; Emburey 12–5–27–3; Tufnell 12–2–22–2; Ramprakash 4–1–14–0.

Middlesex

D. L. Haynes not out 75
M. A. Roseberry lbw b Dale 48
*M. W. Gatting not out 70
L-b 15, w 8 23

1/84 (1 wkt, 50.1 overs) 216

M. R. Ramprakash, K. R. Brown, †P. R. Downton, J. E. Emburey, N. F. Williams, P. C. R. Tufnell, A. R. C. Fraser and N. G. Cowans did not bat.

Bowling: Frost 9–1–39–0; Watkin 11.1–1–28–0; Dennis 5–0–27–0; Cowley 8–1–33–0; Croft 10–0–44–0; Dale 3–0–14–1; Richards 4–0–16–0.

Umpires: A. A. Jones and D. O. Oslear.

NORTHAMPTONSHIRE v WORCESTERSHIRE

At Northampton, August 1. Northamptonshire won by 4 runs. Toss: Worcestershire. Robinson was Northamptonshire's hero in an absorbing match of fluctuating fortunes, and although Botham was preferred for the Man of the Match award, the young fast bowler enjoyed the greater satisfaction of seeing his side into the semi-finals. Botham (80 balls, four sixes, five fours) had put Worcestershire into a winning position, adding 85 in fourteen overs with Neale and, when Neale and Rhodes departed in quick succession to Williams, exacting revenge by hitting the off-spinner for three sixes in an over. However, with Botham frustratingly losing the strike, Robinson tilted the match back in Northamptonshire's favour by bowling Radford and Newport, and the task of scoring 10 off his final over proved beyond Botham and the last man, Lampitt. Earlier, Northamptonshire's innings had been given a solid foundation by Fordham (143 balls, eleven fours), Larkins and Capel, but Newport bowled impressively at the end as the last five wickets tumbled in three overs.

Man of the Match: I. T. Botham.

Northamptonshire

A. Fordham lbw b Lampitt 96
N. A. Felton c Curtis b Newport 12
W. Larkins b Illingworth 52
*A. J. Lamb c Rhodes b Illingworth 0
D. J. Capel c Rhodes b Newport 53
R. J. Bailey c Weston b Botham 29
R. G. Williams b Newport 6
†D. Ripley run out 2
C. E. L. Ambrose lbw b Newport 0
N. G. B. Cook run out 1
M. A. Robinson not out 0
L-b 11, w 1 12

1/46 2/138 3/140 (59.1 overs) 263
4/205 5/231 6/251
7/259 8/261 9/263

Bowling: Newport 12–0–46–4; Radford 4–0–23–0; Botham 7.1–0–42–1; Lampitt 12–0–58–1; Illingworth 12–1–44–2; Hick 12–0–39–0.

Worcestershire

T. S. Curtis b Cook 30
M. J. Weston c Fordham b Robinson 14
G. A. Hick c Cook b Williams 49
D. B. D'Oliveira b Cook 2
I. T. Botham not out 86
*P. A. Neale c Larkins b Williams 43
†S. J. Rhodes c and b Williams 2
R. K. Illingworth b Ambrose 7
N. V. Radford b Robinson 0
P. J. Newport b Robinson 0
S. R. Lampitt not out 3
B 2, l-b 14, w 7 23

1/28 2/56 3/72 (9 wkts, 60 overs) 259
4/107 5/192 6/195
7/243 8/244 9/246

Bowling: Ambrose 12–3–39–1; Robinson 12–1–33–3; Capel 12–0–51–0; Cook 12–2–34–2; Williams 12–0–86–3.

Umpires: J. C. Balderstone and M. J. Kitchen.

SEMI-FINALS

HAMPSHIRE v NORTHAMPTONSHIRE

At Southampton, August 15. Northamptonshire won by 1 run. Toss: Hampshire. Twelve months after missing out on their first appearance in a 60-overs final by 4 runs, Hampshire came even closer. This time they needed 2 off the final delivery, from Robinson to Bakker, and managed only a single. After choosing to field first, Hampshire did well to contain Northamptonshire to 284, even though they had lost their early initiative when Lamb and Capel hit 66 in eleven overs for the fourth wicket. Their reply began badly, with Chris Smith falling in the fourth over, and when Hampshire were 55 for three, Northamptonshire were clear favourites. However, Gower, playing his most disciplined innings of the summer for Hampshire, and Marshall, profiting from missed catches, then added 141 in 26 overs to take them to the threshold of victory. Gower, having hit eleven fours in his 86, was caught in the deep, and when Marshall (one six, six fours) drove a return catch to Cook, the pendulum swung back towards Northamptonshire.

Man of the Match: M. D. Marshall.

Northamptonshire

A. Fordham c Ayling b Bakker 1
N. A. Felton c Gower b Connor 31
W. Larkins c Parks b Ayling 48
*A. J. Lamb c C. L. Smith b Maru ... 58
D. J. Capel c Nicholas b Maru 43
R. J. Bailey c Parks b Connor 8
R. G. Williams b Connor 44
†D. Ripley c Maru b Marshall 7
C. E. L. Ambrose st Parks b Ayling ... 22
N. G. B. Cook not out 6
M. A. Robinson b Connor 0
L-b 6, w 9, n-b 1 16

1/6 2/70 3/111 4/177 5/205 6/205 7/230 8/272 9/284 (60 overs) 284

Bowling: Marshall 12–3–37–1; Bakker 12–2–41–1; Connor 12–1–73–4; Ayling 12–0–76–2; Maru 12–0–51–2.

Hampshire

V. P. Terry c Robinson b Cook 24
C. L. Smith c Felton b Robinson 0
R. A. Smith c Ripley b Capel 20
D. I. Gower c Capel b Williams 86
M. D. Marshall c and b Cook 77
*M. C. J. Nicholas c Lamb b Cook ... 29
J. R. Ayling c Williams b Robinson ... 8
†R. J. Parks c Felton b Ambrose 4
R. J. Maru c Capel b Robinson 14
C. A. Connor not out 3
P. J. Bakker run out 2
L-b 12, w 4 16

1/6 2/37 3/55 4/196 5/246 6/253 7/259 8/269 9/280 (60 overs) 283

Bowling: Ambrose 12–4–29–1; Robinson 12–1–62–3; Cook 12–3–52–3; Capel 12–1–67–1; Williams 12–1–61–1.

Umpires: K. J. Lyons and A. G. T. Whitehead.

LANCASHIRE v MIDDLESEX

At Manchester, August 15, 16, 17. Lancashire won by five wickets. Toss: Lancashire. Only 49 overs were possible on the opening day, when in front of a near-capacity crowd of 18,000 Middlesex reached 199 for two (D. L. Haynes 95*, M. R. Ramprakash 17*). The second day was washed out, and it was still raining on the third morning when play should have started. Happily, all suggestions of bowling at stumps to get a result, or replaying the match the following week, were abandoned when the game resumed at 1.45 p.m. Middlesex added 97 runs in the remaining eleven overs to reach their highest total in the competition, with Haynes batting through the innings, facing 177 balls and hitting eleven fours. Mendis responded with his first century for Lancashire in limited-overs games, and he received sound support from Atherton, followed by sharp acceleration from Fairbrother (48 in 42 balls) and Watkinson (43 in 40 balls, including three huge sixes). As word of the match's progress spread through Manchester, the crowd of about 500 at the start built to 5,000 by the end.

Man of the Match: G. D. Mendis.

Middlesex

D. L. Haynes not out 149
M. A. Roseberry lbw b Allott 16
*M. W. Gatting b Watkinson 53
M. R. Ramprakash run out 45
K. R. Brown c Hegg b Wasim Akram . 1
†P. R. Downton not out 4
B 6, l-b 11, w 8, n-b 3 28

1/23 2/147 3/269 4/271 (4 wkts, 60 overs) 296

J. E. Emburey, N. F. Williams, A. R. C. Fraser, S. P. Hughes and N. G. Cowans did not bat.

Bowling: Allott 12–3–40–1; DeFreitas 12–0–52–0; Wasim Akram 12–2–65–1; Watkinson 12–1–62–1; Austin 12–1–60–0.

Lancashire

G. D. Mendis not out 121
G. Fowler b Cowans 8
M. A. Atherton b Hughes 34
N. H. Fairbrother c Downton b Hughes 48
M. Watkinson c Downton b Fraser 43
Wasim Akram b Fraser 14
P. A. J. DeFreitas not out 2
B 1, l-b 21, w 3, n-b 4 29

1/23 2/83 3/185 4/269 5/293 (5 wkts, 55.5 overs) 299

†W. K. Hegg, I. D. Austin, *D. P. Hughes and P. J. W. Allott did not bat.

Bowling: Cowans 12–1–40–1; Fraser 11.5–0–43–2; Williams 10–0–72–0; Hughes 12–0–68–2; Emburey 10–0–54–0.

Umpires: D. J. Constant and B. J. Meyer.

FINAL

LANCASHIRE v NORTHAMPTONSHIRE

At Lord's, September 1. Lancashire won by seven wickets. Toss: Lancashire. DeFreitas, with wickets in the second, sixth, eighth, twelfth and fourteenth overs of the morning, determined the course of the final in an opening spell of 8–4–19–5. Only Hughes's good fortune in winning the toss and being able to put Northamptonshire in on a pitch containing some moisture could be said to be more influential. In seaming the ball both ways, DeFreitas exposed technical weaknesses in the Northamptonshire top-order batting. Capel and Ambrose showed what could be achieved by getting properly forward on the front foot whenever possible; both were unlucky in being run out at the non-striker's end by deflections from the bowler, Allott and Wasim Akram being the respective agents. The irony was that it was Ambrose's straight drive which brought Capel's dismissal.

To have a chance of winning, Northamptonshire needed to keep Lancashire's batsmen under pressure from the start. Fowler was soon caught off a leading edge; Mendis was caught behind off a thin one to leave Lancashire 28 for two in the sixteenth over. Ambrose should have caught Fairbrother at mid-on off Cook when he was 6. He didn't, and the left-hander provided the batting entertainment of the day. His cavalier innings of 81 from 68 balls included two sixes and nine fours, and he walked off to a standing ovation. Watkinson, hitting two sixes while scoring 24 from eighteen balls, and the steady Atherton then took Lancashire to the victory which made them the first county to win both Lord's finals in the same season.

Man of the Match: P. A. J. DeFreitas.

Attendance: 13,500 (excl. members); *receipts* £330,000.

Northamptonshire

A. Fordham lbw b DeFreitas 5
N. A. Felton c Allott b DeFreitas 4
W. Larkins c Hegg b DeFreitas 7
*A. J. Lamb lbw b DeFreitas 8
R. J. Bailey c Hegg b DeFreitas 7
D. J. Capel run out 36
R. G. Williams b Watkinson 9
†D. Ripley b Watkinson 13
C. E. L. Ambrose run out 48
N. G. B. Cook b Austin 9
M. A. Robinson not out 3
B 1, l-b 10, w 9, n-b 2 22

1/8 (2) 2/19 (1) 3/20 (3) 4/38 (5) 5/39 (4) 6/56 (7) 7/87 (8) 8/126 (6) 9/166 (9) 10/171 (10) (60 overs) 171

Bowling: Allott 12–3–29–0; DeFreitas 12–5–26–5; Wasim Akram 12–0–35–0; Watkinson 12–1–29–2; Austin 12–4–41–1.

Lancashire

G. D. Mendis c Ripley b Capel 14
G. Fowler c Cook b Robinson 7
M. A. Atherton not out 38
N. H. Fairbrother c Ambrose b Williams 81
M. Watkinson not out 24
L-b 4, w 2, n-b 3 9

1/16 (2) 2/28 (1) (3 wkts, 45.4 overs) 173
3/142 (4)

*D. P. Hughes, Wasim Akram, P. A. J. DeFreitas, †W. K. Hegg, I. D. Austin and P. J. W. Allott did not bat.

Bowling: Ambrose 10–1–23–0; Robinson 9–2–26–1; Cook 10.4–2–50–0; Capel 9–0–44–1; Williams 7–0–26–1.

Umpires: J. W. Holder and D. R. Shepherd.

NATWEST BANK TROPHY RECORDS

(Including Gillette Cup, 1963-80)

Batting

Highest individual scores: 206, A. I. Kallicharran, Warwickshire v Oxfordshire, Birmingham, 1984; 177, C. G. Greenidge, Hampshire v Glamorgan, Southampton, 1975; 172 not out, G. A. Hick, Worcestershire v Devon, Worcester, 1987; 165 not out, V. P. Terry, Hampshire v Berkshire, Southampton, 1985; 162 not out, C. J. Tavaré, Somerset v Devon, Torquay, 1990; 159, C. L. Smith, Hampshire v Cheshire, Chester, 1989; 158, G. D. Barlow, Middlesex v Lancashire, Lord's, 1984; 158, Zaheer Abbas, Gloucestershire v Leicestershire, Leicester, 1983; 156, D. I. Gower, Leicestershire v Derbyshire, Leicester, 1984; 155, J. J. Whitaker, Leicestershire v Wiltshire, Swindon, 1984; 154 not out, H. Morris, Glamorgan v Staffordshire, Cardiff, 1989; 154, P. Willey, Leicestershire v Hampshire, Leicester, 1987; 153, A. Hill, Derbyshire v Cornwall, Derby, 1986. (93 hundreds were scored in the Gillette Cup; 98 hundreds have been scored in the NatWest Bank Trophy.)

Most runs: 1,950, D. L. Amiss.

Fastest hundred: G. D. Rose off 36 balls, Somerset v Devon, Torquay, 1990.

Most hundreds: 6, C. L. Smith; 5, D. I. Gower and G. M. Turner.

Highest innings totals (off 60 overs): 413 for four, Somerset v Devon, Torquay, 1990; 404 for three, Worcestershire v Devon, Worcester, 1987; 392 for five, Warwickshire v Oxfordshire, Birmingham, 1984; 386 for five, Essex v Wiltshire, Chelmsford, 1988; 372 for five, Lancashire v Gloucestershire, Manchester, 1990; 371 for four, Hampshire v Glamorgan, Southampton, 1975; 365 for three, Derbyshire v Cornwall, Derby, 1986; 360 for two, Northamptonshire v Staffordshire, Northampton, 1990; 359 for four, Kent v Dorset, Canterbury, 1989; 354 for seven, Leicestershire v Wiltshire, Swindon, 1984; 349 for six, Lancashire v Gloucestershire, Bristol, 1984; 341 for six, Leicestershire v Hampshire, Leicester, 1987; 339 for four, Hampshire v Berkshire, Southampton, 1985; 336 for five, Worcestershire v Cumberland, Worcester, 1988; 336 for seven, Warwickshire v Hertfordshire, St Albans, 1990; 330 for four, Somerset v Glamorgan, Cardiff, 1978. *In the final:* 317 for four, Yorkshire v Surrey, 1965.

Highest innings total by a minor county: 261 for eight (60 overs), Dorset v Glamorgan, Swansea, 1990.

Highest innings by a side batting first and losing: 307 for six (60 overs), Essex v Hampshire, Chelmsford, 1990. *In the final:* 242 for eight (60 overs), Lancashire v Sussex, 1986.

Highest totals by a side batting second: 326 for nine (60 overs), Hampshire v Leicestershire, Leicester, 1987; 307 for five (60 overs), Hampshire v Essex, Chelmsford, 1990; 306 for six (59.3 overs), Gloucestershire v Leicestershire, Leicester, 1983; 298 (59 overs), Lancashire v Worcestershire, Manchester, 1985; 297 for four (57.1 overs), Somerset v Warwickshire, Taunton, 1978; 296 for four (58 overs), Kent v Surrey, Canterbury, 1985; 290 for seven (59.3 overs), Yorkshire v Worcestershire, Leeds, 1982; 287 for six (59 overs), Warwickshire v Glamorgan, Birmingham, 1976; 287 (60 overs), Essex v Somerset, Taunton, 1978; 282 for nine (60 overs), Leicestershire v Gloucestershire, Leicester, 1975. *In the final:* 279 for five (60 overs), Nottinghamshire v Essex, 1985.

Highest total by a side batting second and winning: 307 for five (60 overs), Hampshire v Essex, Chelmsford, 1990. *In the final:* 243 for three (58.2 overs), Sussex v Lancashire, 1986.

Highest total by a side batting second and losing: 326 for nine (60 overs), Hampshire v Leicestershire, Leicester, 1987.

Lowest innings in the final at Lord's: 118 (60 overs), Lancashire v Kent, 1974.

Lowest completed innings totals: 39 (26.4 overs), Ireland v Sussex, Hove, 1985; 41 (20 overs), Cambridgeshire v Buckinghamshire, Cambridge, 1972; 41 (19.4 overs), Middlesex v Essex, Westcliff, 1972; 41 (36.1 overs), Shropshire v Essex, Wellington, 1974.

Lowest total by a side batting first and winning: 98 (56.2 overs), Worcestershire v Durham, Chester-le-Street, 1968.

Shortest innings: 10.1 overs (60 for one), Worcestershire v Lancashire, Worcester, 1963.

Matches re-arranged on a reduced number of overs are excluded from the above.

Record partnerships for each wicket

242* for 1st	M. D. Moxon and A. A. Metcalfe, Yorkshire v Warwickshire at Leeds	1990
286 for 2nd	I. S. Anderson and A. Hill, Derbyshire v Cornwall at Derby	1986
209 for 3rd	P. Willey and D. I. Gower, Leicestershire v Ireland at Leicester	1986
234* for 4th	D. Lloyd and C. H. Lloyd, Lancashire v Gloucestershire at Manchester	1978
166 for 5th	M. A. Lynch and G. R. J. Roope, Surrey v Durham at The Oval ..	1982
105 for 6th	G. S. Sobers and R. A. White, Nottinghamshire v Worcestershire at Worcester	1974
160* for 7th	C. J. Richards and I. R. Payne, Surrey v Lincolnshire at Sleaford ..	1983
83 for 8th	S. N. V. Waterton and D. A. Hale, Oxfordshire v Gloucestershire at Oxford	1989
87 for 9th	M. A. Nash and A. E. Cordle, Glamorgan v Lincolnshire at Swansea	1974
81 for 10th	S. Turner and R. E. East, Essex v Yorkshire at Leeds	1982

Bowling

Most wickets: 81, G. G. Arnold; 79, J. Simmons.

Hat-tricks (7): J. D. F. Larter, Northamptonshire v Sussex, Northampton, 1963; D. A. D. Sydenham, Surrey v Cheshire, Hoylake, 1964; R. N. S. Hobbs, Essex v Middlesex, Lord's, 1968; N. M. McVicker, Warwickshire v Lincolnshire, Birmingham, 1971; G. S. le Roux, Sussex v Ireland, Hove, 1985; M. Jean-Jacques, Derbyshire v Nottinghamshire, Derby, 1987; J. F. M. O'Brien, Cheshire v Derbyshire, Chester, 1988.

Four wickets in five balls: D. A. D. Sydenham, Surrey v Cheshire, Hoylake, 1964.

Best bowling (12 overs unless stated): eight for 21 (10.1 overs), M. A. Holding, Derbyshire v Sussex, Hove, 1988; eight for 31 (11.1 overs), D. L. Underwood, Kent v Scotland, Edinburgh, 1987; seven for 15, A. L. Dixon, Kent v Surrey, The Oval, 1967; seven for 15 (9.3 overs), R. P. Lefebvre, Somerset v Devon, Torquay, 1990; seven for 30, P. J. Sainsbury, Hampshire v Norfolk, Southampton, 1965; seven for 32, S. P. Davis, Durham v Lancashire, Chester-le-Street, 1983; seven for 33, R. D. Jackman, Surrey v Yorkshire, Harrogate, 1970; seven for 37, N. A. Mallender, Northamptonshire v Worcestershire, Northampton, 1984.

Most economical analysis: 12–9–3–1, J. Simmons, Lancashire v Suffolk, Bury St Edmunds, 1985.

Most expensive analysis: 12–0–106–2, D. A. Gallop, Oxfordshire v Warwickshire, Birmingham, 1984.

Wicket-keeping and Fielding

Most dismissals: 66, R. W. Taylor; 65, A. P. E. Knott.

Most dismissals in an innings: 6 (5 ct, 1 st), R. W. Taylor, Derbyshire v Essex, Derby, 1981; 6 (4 ct, 2 st), T. Davies, Glamorgan v Staffordshire, Stone, 1986.

Most catches by a fielder: 25, J. Simmons; 24, G. Cook and P. J. Sharpe.

Most catches by a fielder in an innings: 4 – A. S. Brown, Gloucestershire v Middlesex, Bristol, 1963; G. Cook, Northamptonshire v Glamorgan, Northampton, 1972; C. G. Greenidge, Hampshire v Cheshire, Southampton, 1981; D. C. Jackson, Durham v Northamptonshire, Darlington, 1984; T. S. Smith, Hertfordshire v Somerset, St Albans, 1984; H. Morris, Glamorgan v Scotland, Edinburgh, 1988.

Results

Largest victories in runs: Somerset by 346 runs v Devon, Torquay, 1990; Worcestershire by 299 runs v Devon, Worcester, 1987; Essex by 291 runs v Wiltshire, Chelmsford, 1988; Sussex by 244 runs v Ireland, Hove, 1985; Lancashire by 241 runs v Gloucestershire, Manchester, 1990; Warwickshire by 227 runs v Oxfordshire, Birmingham, 1984; Essex by 226 runs v Oxfordshire, Chelmsford, 1985; Northamptonshire by 216 runs v Staffordshire, Northampton, 1990; Leicestershire by 214 runs v Staffordshire, Longton, 1975; Hampshire by 209 runs v Dorset, Southampton, 1987; Derbyshire by 204 runs v Cornwall, Derby, 1986; Warwickshire by 201 runs v Buckinghamshire, Birmingham, 1987; Sussex by 200 runs v Durham, Hove, 1964. *In the final:* 175 runs, Yorkshire v Surrey, Lord's, 1965.

Victories by ten wickets (9): Northamptonshire v Leicestershire, Leicester, 1964; Warwickshire v Cambridgeshire, Birmingham, 1965; Sussex v Derbyshire, Hove, 1968; Hampshire v Nottinghamshire, Southampton, 1977; Middlesex v Worcestershire, Worcester, 1980; Yorkshire v Cheshire, Birkenhead, 1985; Yorkshire v Berkshire, Finchampstead, 1988; Yorkshire v Norfolk, Leeds, 1990; Yorkshire v Warwickshire, Leeds, 1990.

Earliest finishes: both at 2.20 p.m. Worcestershire beat Lancashire by nine wickets at Worcester, 1963; Essex beat Middlesex by eight wickets at Westcliff, 1972.

Scores level (9): Nottinghamshire 215, Somerset 215 for nine at Taunton, 1964; Surrey 196, Sussex 196 for eight at The Oval, 1970; Somerset 287 for six, Essex 287 at Taunton, 1978; Surrey 195 for seven, Essex 195 at Chelmsford, 1980; Essex 149, Derbyshire 149 for eight at Derby, 1981; Northamptonshire 235 for nine, Derbyshire 235 for six in the final at Lord's, 1981; Middlesex 222 for nine, Somerset 222 for eight at Lord's, 1983; Hampshire 224 for eight, Essex 224 for seven at Southampton, 1985; Essex 307 for six, Hampshire 307 for five at Chelmsford, 1990. Under the rules the side which lost fewer wickets won.

Wins by a minor county over a first-class county (7): Durham v Yorkshire (by five wickets), Harrogate, 1973; Lincolnshire v Glamorgan (by six wickets), Swansea, 1974; Hertfordshire v Essex (by 33 runs), 2nd round, Hitchin, 1976; Shropshire v Yorkshire (by 37 runs), Telford, 1984; Durham v Derbyshire (by seven wickets), Derby, 1985; Buckinghamshire v Somerset (by 7 runs), High Wycombe, 1987; Cheshire v Northamptonshire (by one wicket), Chester, 1988.

WINNERS

Gillette Cup

1963 SUSSEX beat Worcestershire by 14 runs.
1964 SUSSEX beat Warwickshire by eight wickets.
1965 YORKSHIRE beat Surrey by 175 runs.
1966 WARWICKSHIRE beat Worcestershire by five wickets.
1967 KENT beat Somerset by 32 runs.
1968 WARWICKSHIRE beat Sussex by four wickets.
1969 YORKSHIRE beat Derbyshire by 69 runs.
1970 LANCASHIRE beat Sussex by six wickets.
1971 LANCASHIRE beat Kent by 24 runs.
1972 LANCASHIRE beat Warwickshire by four wickets.
1973 GLOUCESTERSHIRE beat Sussex by 40 runs.
1974 KENT beat Lancashire by four wickets.
1975 LANCASHIRE beat Middlesex by seven wickets.
1976 NORTHAMPTONSHIRE beat Lancashire by four wickets.
1977 MIDDLESEX beat Glamorgan by five wickets.
1978 SUSSEX beat Somerset by five wickets.
1979 SOMERSET beat Northamptonshire by 45 runs.
1980 MIDDLESEX beat Surrey by seven wickets.

NatWest Bank Trophy

1981 DERBYSHIRE beat Northamptonshire by losing fewer wickets with the scores level.
1982 SURREY beat Warwickshire by nine wickets.
1983 SOMERSET beat Kent by 24 runs.
1984 MIDDLESEX beat Kent by four wickets.
1985 ESSEX beat Nottinghamshire by 1 run.
1986 SUSSEX beat Lancashire by seven wickets.
1987 NOTTINGHAMSHIRE beat Northamptonshire by three wickets.
1988 MIDDLESEX beat Worcestershire by three wickets.
1989 WARWICKSHIRE beat Middlesex by four wickets.
1990 LANCASHIRE beat Northamptonshire by seven wickets.

BENSON AND HEDGES CUP, 1990

Lancashire, playing in their ninth Lord's final, emerged as convincing winners of the Benson and Hedges Cup, which they had won previously in 1984. Their victory also proved to be the first leg of a historic double, for in September they returned to take the NatWest Bank Trophy, becoming the first county to win both Lord's finals in the same season. For their opponents, Worcestershire, it was their sixth final at Lord's and for the sixth time they left runners-up. This was their third defeat in the final of the Benson and Hedges Cup.

The total prizemoney for the competition in 1990 was £96,900, an increase of £6,000 from 1989. Of this, Lancashire won £24,000 and Worcestershire £12,000. Nottinghamshire and Somerset, the losing semi-finalists, each received £6,000, while the losing quarter-finalists, Essex, Glamorgan, Middlesex and Surrey, received £3,000 each. In addition, the winners of each group match won £750. The prizemoney for the Gold Award winners was £125 in the group matches, £200 in the quarter-finals, £275 in the semi-finals and £550 in the final.

Benson and Hedges increased their total sponsorship to the TCCB in 1990 by £39,070 to £521,031, and following the final at Lord's on July 14 it was announced that the company had signed a new five-year contract with the Board for the 1991 to 1995 seasons.

FINAL GROUP TABLE

	Played	*Won*	*Lost*	*No Result*	*Pts*	*Run-rate*
Group A						
WORCESTERSHIRE	4	3	1	0	6	72.77
GLAMORGAN	4	3	1	0	6	69.46
Kent	4	2	1	1	5	71.71
Warwickshire	4	1	3	0	2	63.58
Gloucestershire	4	0	3	1	1	67.77
Group B						
SOMERSET	4	3	1	0	6	85.46
MIDDLESEX	4	3	1	0	6	74.86
Derbyshire	4	2	2	0	4	77.34
Sussex	4	2	2	0	4	78.94
Minor Counties	4	0	4	0	0	66.43
Group C						
LANCASHIRE	4	3	0	1	7	67.84
SURREY	4	2	2	0	4	75.30
Yorkshire	4	2	2	0	4	62.08
Hampshire	4	1	2	1	3	75.45
Combined Universities	4	1	3	0	2	61.91
Group D						
ESSEX	4	3	0	1	7	82.35
NOTTINGHAMSHIRE	4	3	1	0	6	63.44
Leicestershire	4	1	2	1	3	62.33
Scotland	4	1	3	0	2	66.66
Northamptonshire	4	1	3	0	2	60.60

The top two teams in each group qualified for the quarter-finals.

Where two or more teams finished with the same number of points, the position in the group was based on run-rate.

GROUP A

GLOUCESTERSHIRE v WORCESTERSHIRE

At Bristol, April 24. Worcestershire won by three wickets. Toss: Gloucestershire. In his first three-figure innings since July 1987, Botham faced 145 balls, of which he hit six for six and nine for four.

Gold Award: I. T. Botham.

Gloucestershire

*A. J. Wright c Newport b Botham	97
A. W. Stovold c D'Oliveira b Dilley	8
G. D. Hodgson c Botham b Illingworth	1
C. W. J. Athey c Neale b Radford	49
K. M. Curran c Rhodes b Dilley	55
†R. C. Russell c Hick b Dilley	10
M. W. Alleyne not out	23
P. Bainbridge not out	0
L-b 6, w 3, n-b 2	11
1/34 2/37 3/148 4/185 5/206 6/250 (6 wkts, 55 overs)	254

D. A. Graveney, E. T. Milburn and D. V. Lawrence did not bat.

Bowling: Dilley 11–0–43–3; Radford 11–1–45–1; Newport 7–0–23–0; Illingworth 10–0–43–1; Hick 5–0–25–0; Botham 11–0–69–1.

Worcestershire

T. S. Curtis c Lawrence b Curran	2
G. J. Lord c Athey b Graveney	26
G. A. Hick c Lawrence b Milburn	2
I. T. Botham not out	138
*P. A. Neale c and b Curran	30
D. B. D'Oliveira b Lawrence	2
†S. J. Rhodes run out	1
R. K. Illingworth c Alleyne b Curran	5
P. J. Newport not out	22
B 1, l-b 7, w 14, n-b 6	28
1/3 2/20 3/87 4/184 5/187 6/190 7/220 (7 wkts, 54.1 overs)	256

N. V. Radford and G. R. Dilley did not bat.

Bowling: Curran 11–0–53–3; Lawrence 11–3–36–1; Milburn 5–1–23–1; Bainbridge 8–0–37–0; Graveney 11–0–40–1; Alleyne 8.1–0–59–0.

Umpires: A. A. Jones and M. J. Kitchen.

WARWICKSHIRE v GLAMORGAN

At Birmingham, April 24. Glamorgan won by 3 runs. Toss: Warwickshire.

Gold Award: M. P. Maynard.

Glamorgan

*A. R. Butcher c Humpage b Munton	11
H. Morris c Humpage b Small	1
G. C. Holmes c Asif Din b Munton	11
M. P. Maynard c Lloyd b Small	77
I. V. A. Richards b Booth	21
P. A. Cottey lbw b Booth	2
N. G. Cowley b Donald	19
†C. P. Metson c Booth b Small	20
S. J. Dennis c Lloyd b Small	2
S. L. Watkin not out	2
B 4, l-b 20, w 4, n-b 2	30
1/2 2/21 3/28 4/97 5/111 6/139 7/175 8/182 9/196 (9 wkts, 55 overs)	196

S. R. Barwick did not bat.

Bowling: Donald 11–1–42–1; Small 11–2–22–4; Munton 7–0–28–2; Reeve 10–0–26–0; Smith 5–0–15–0; Booth 11–1–39–2.

Warwickshire

*T. A. Lloyd c Richards b Barwick	10	G. C. Small run out	1
A. J. Moles run out	52	P. A. Booth not out	13
Asif Din b Cowley	50	L-b 5, w 7	12
A. I. Kallicharran c Holmes b Richards	13		
P. A. Smith lbw b Richards	13	1/20 2/117 3/123 (8 wkts, 55 overs)	193
†G. W. Humpage c Butcher b Barwick	15	4/143 5/162 6/164	
D. A. Reeve lbw b Richards	14	7/165 8/193	

A. A. Donald and T. A. Munton did not bat.

Bowling: Watkin 11–2–35–0; Dennis 6–0–20–0; Barwick 11–0–44–2; Richards 11–1–38–3; Cowley 11–0–23–1; Holmes 5–0–28–0.

Umpires: B. Hassan and B. Leadbeater.

GLAMORGAN v GLOUCESTERSHIRE

At Cardiff, May 1. Glamorgan won by 9 runs. Toss: Glamorgan.
Gold Award: A. R. Butcher.

Glamorgan

*A. R. Butcher c Russell b Curran	95	S. J. Dennis not out	2
H. Morris lbw b Curran	23	S. R. Barwick b Walsh	1
M. P. Maynard c Graveney b Alleyne	33		
I. V. A. Richards c Russell b Alleyne	28	L-b 10, w 1, n-b 2	13
G. C. Holmes c Russell b Walsh	9		
I. Smith c Russell b Alleyne	0	1/65 2/115 3/157 (9 wkts, 55 overs)	219
N. G. Cowley lbw b Alleyne	1	4/172 5/173 6/181	
†C. P. Metson c Athey b Curran	14	7/215 8/215 9/219	

M. Frost did not bat.

Bowling: Jarvis 10–1–32–0; Walsh 11–1–32–2; Curran 9–1–29–3; Graveney 11–1–55–0; Bainbridge 3–0–19–0; Alleyne 11–1–42–4.

Gloucestershire

*A. J. Wright c Holmes b Barwick	10	C. A. Walsh lbw b Cowley	1
A. W. Stovold b Frost	1	D. A. Graveney not out	12
P. Bainbridge b Dennis	55		
C. W. J. Athey b Holmes	20	B 4, l-b 9, w 1, n-b 1	15
K. M. Curran b Holmes	14		
J. W. Lloyds lbw b Richards	6	1/5 2/17 3/65 (8 wkts, 55 overs)	210
M. W. Alleyne b Frost	30	4/87 5/104 6/129	
†R. C. Russell not out	46	7/159 8/164	

K. B. S. Jarvis did not bat.

Bowling: Frost 8–4–14–2; Barwick 9–1–37–1; Dennis 10–2–38–1; Cowley 11–0–40–1; Holmes 8–0–27–2; Richards 9–0–41–1.

Umpires: P. J. Eele and R. Julian.

WORCESTERSHIRE v KENT

At Worcester, May 1. Worcestershire won by 27 runs. Toss: Kent. Rhodes suffered a broken thumb when he was hit by a ball from Merrick but nevertheless kept wicket in Kent's innings.
Gold Award: T. R. Ward.

Worcestershire

T. S. Curtis lbw b Ealham 11
†S. J. Rhodes c G. R. Cowdrey b Ealham 8
G. A. Hick c Marsh b Ealham 41
I. T. Botham c Ellison b C. S. Cowdrey 37
*P. A. Neale c Hinks b C. S. Cowdrey . 13
D. B. D'Oliveira c Marsh b Davis 7
S. R. Lampitt c Ward b Fleming 6
R. K. Illingworth not out 36
P. J. Newport c Ward b Ealham 28
N. V. Radford not out 1
L-b 8, w 4, n-b 7 19

1/19 2/32 3/91 (8 wkts, 55 overs) 207
4/117 5/130 6/134
7/147 8/203

G. R. Dilley did not bat.

Bowling: Merrick 11–0–46–0; Ellison 6–2–14–0; Ealham 11–1–57–4; Fleming 9–1–27–1; Davis 11–1–36–1; C. S. Cowdrey 7–1–19–2.

Kent

S. G. Hinks c Hick b Dilley 1
N. R. Taylor c D'Oliveira b Dilley 8
T. R. Ward c Hick b Newport 94
*C. S. Cowdrey c Hick b Newport 6
G. R. Cowdrey c Rhodes b Newport . . 0
†S. A. Marsh run out 17
R. M. Ellison lbw b Dilley 12
M. V. Fleming c Radford b Lampitt . . . 6
M. A. Ealham c Hick b Dilley 5
T. A. Merrick b Newport 14
R. P. Davis not out 0
L-b 5, w 6, n-b 6 17

1/11 2/12 3/40 (49 overs) 180
4/46 5/86 6/120
7/132 8/141 9/176

Bowling: Dilley 9–1–48–4; Radford 7–3–13–0; Newport 8–0–25–4; Lampitt 11–1–47–1; Illingworth 8–1–23–0; Botham 6–2–19–0.

Umpires: M. J. Kitchen and R. A. White.

KENT v WARWICKSHIRE

At Canterbury, May 8. Kent won by 70 runs. Toss: Kent. Hinks kept wicket after tea in place of the injured Marsh.

Gold Award: C. S. Cowdrey.

Kent

S. G. Hinks c Humpage b Small 2
M. R. Benson c Reeve b Smith 85
N. R. Taylor b Small 90
T. R. Ward lbw b Small 1
*C. S. Cowdrey c Humpage b Reeve . . 64
M. V. Fleming c Twose b Small 0
†S. A. Marsh c and b Munton 9
M. A. Ealham run out 0
T. A. Merrick not out 1
A. P. Igglesden not out 0
B 2, l-b 4, w 6, n-b 1 13

1/14 2/142 3/147 (8 wkts, 55 overs) 265
4/235 5/235 6/259
7/263 8/264

R. P. Davis did not bat.

Bowling: Small 11–0–38–4; Munton 10–2–39–1; Moody 9–1–50–0; Reeve 9–0–52–1; Smith 10–0–43–1; Booth 4–0–33–0; Twose 2–0–4–0.

Warwickshire

*T. A. Lloyd lbw b Cowdrey 72
Asif Din c Marsh b Ealham 9
T. M. Moody c Ealham b Davis 33
A. I. Kallicharran c sub b Ealham 11
†G. W. Humpage lbw b Merrick 1
D. A. Reeve c Hinks b Cowdrey 12
R. G. Twose run out 2
N. M. K. Smith c sub b Davis 11
P. A. Booth c Merrick b Cowdrey 5
G. C. Small lbw b Merrick 22
T. A. Munton not out 1
B 6, l-b 8, w 2 16

1/26 2/78 3/111 (44.4 overs) 195
4/120 5/150 6/152
7/153 8/163 9/186

Bowling: Merrick 8.4–2–30–2; Igglesden 5–0–31–0; Ealham 8–0–37–2; Davis 11–0–40–2; Fleming 6–1–14–0; Cowdrey 6–1–29–3.

Umpires: D. J. Constant and N. T. Plews.

WORCESTERSHIRE v GLAMORGAN

At Worcester, May 8. Glamorgan won by 16 runs. Toss: Glamorgan.
Gold Award: M. Frost.

Glamorgan

*A. R. Butcher b Hick	57	†C. P. Metson not out	14
H. Morris c D'Oliveira b Lampitt	57	S. L. Watkin not out	1
M. P. Maynard b Radford	36	L-b 18, w 4, n-b 3	25
I. V. A. Richards c and b Radford	25		—
G. C. Holmes c and b Newport	8	1/121 2/134 3/176 (7 wkts, 55 overs)	255
I. Smith c Radford b Dilley	21	4/185 5/223	
N. G. Cowley c Lampitt b Dilley	11	6/229 7/248	

M. Frost and S. R. Barwick did not bat.

Bowling: Dilley 11–3–45–2; Radford 11–0–52–2; Lampitt 6–0–43–1; Newport 11–1–28–1; Illingworth 8–0–33–0; Hick 8–0–36–1.

Worcestershire

T. S. Curtis c Metson b Cowley	36	N. V. Radford c Holmes b Barwick	40
G. J. Lord c Morris b Frost	0	G. R. Dilley not out	5
G. A. Hick b Frost	0	†S. R. Bevins not out	0
D. B. D'Oliveira c Smith b Frost	57	L-b 10, w 9	19
*P. A. Neale b Barwick	31		—
S. R. Lampitt c Metson b Barwick	41	1/15 2/17 3/77 (9 wkts, 55 overs)	239
R. K. Illingworth c Morris b Frost	6	4/112 5/152 6/170	
P. J. Newport c Butcher b Barwick	4	7/175 8/229 9/239	

Bowling: Barwick 11–0–67–4; Watkin 11–1–45–0; Frost 11–3–25–4; Cowley 11–0–33–1; Richards 11–0–59–0.

Umpires: H. D. Bird and P. B. Wight.

WARWICKSHIRE v WORCESTERSHIRE

At Birmingham, May 10. Worcestershire won by 32 runs. Toss: Worcestershire.
Gold Award: G. A. Hick.

Worcestershire

T. S. Curtis c Lloyd b Benjamin	97	S. R. Lampitt not out	1
M. J. Weston b Reeve	36		
G. A. Hick c Twose b Small	64	L-b 13, w 5	18
N. V. Radford run out	31		—
D. B. D'Oliveira c Benjamin b Small	3	1/78 2/206 3/217 (5 wkts, 55 overs)	255
*P. A. Neale not out	5	4/239 5/250	

R. K. Illingworth, P. J. Newport, G. R. Dilley and †S. R. Bevins did not bat.

Bowling: Small 11–1–36–2; Benjamin 11–4–40–1; Moody 5–0–29–0; Munton 11–0–35–0; Reeve 11–1–70–1; Smith 5–0–20–0; Twose 1–0–12–0.

Warwickshire

*T. A. Lloyd b Radford	8	G. C. Small c Radford b Illingworth	5
Asif Din c Bevins b Hick	37	J. E. Benjamin run out	20
T. M. Moody lbw b Hick	41	T. A. Munton c Lampitt b Dilley	0
A. I. Kallicharran c Neale b Lampitt	32	L-b 12, w 7, n-b 2	21
†G. W. Humpage st Bevins b Hick	6		—
D. A. Reeve c Bevins b Radford	6	1/16 2/87 3/109 (51.5 overs)	223
R. G. Twose c Weston b Radford	17	4/120 5/136 6/151	
N. M. K. Smith not out	30	7/166 8/173 9/219	

Bowling: Dilley 8.5–0–36–1; Radford 9–1–41–3; Newport 3–0–21–0; Illingworth 9–0–42–1; Hick 11–0–36–3; Lampitt 11–0–35–1.

Umpires: D. O. Oslear and D. S. Thompsett.

KENT v GLOUCESTERSHIRE

At Canterbury, May 10, 11. No result. Toss: Kent. This match, of thirteen overs a side, was begun after rain from before lunch on the second day until after tea had forced the abandonment of the game which started on the first day. Further rain, however, prevented a result. In the original 55-overs match Gloucestershire, 180 for three overnight after 42.2 overs, made 268 for seven (A. J. Wright 134 off 176 balls including fourteen fours, A. W. Stovold 42) and Kent were 49 for two from nineteen overs when rain stopped play. Wright's hundred, which ceased to count when the match became void, was his first in limited-overs competition.

Kent

S. G. Hinks c Bainbridge b Jarvis 3
T. R. Ward not out 60
*C. S. Cowdrey not out 67
L-b 2, w 3, n-b 3 8

1/7 (1 wkt, 10 overs) 138

M. R. Benson, N. R. Taylor, †S. A. Marsh, M. V. Fleming, R. P. Davis, M. A. Ealham, T. A. Merrick and C. Penn did not bat.

Bowling: Bainbridge 2–0–21–0; Jarvis 2–0–30–1; Ball 2–0–28–0; Alleyne 1–0–22–0; Curran 2–0–23–0; Walsh 1–0–12–0.

Gloucestershire

*A. J. Wright, A. W. Stovold, P. Bainbridge, C. W. J. Athey, K. M. Curran, M. W. Alleyne, †R. C. Russell, J. W. Lloyds, M. C. J. Ball, C. A. Walsh and K. B. S. Jarvis.

Umpires: B. Dudleston and J. H. Harris.

GLAMORGAN v KENT

At Swansea, May 12. Kent won by 18 runs. Toss: Kent.
Gold Award: M. R. Benson.

Kent

S. G. Hinks c Morris b Frost 1
M. R. Benson c Richards b Frost 118
N. R. Taylor c Metson b Dennis 19
T. R. Ward c Morris b Cowley 36
G. R. Cowdrey c Cowley b Frost 12
*C. S. Cowdrey c Morris b Watkin 35
†S. A. Marsh c Morris b Holmes 9
M. A. Ealham not out 17
P. S. de Villiers run out 0
C. Penn not out 8
B 1, l-b 5, w 4 10

1/8 2/48 3/103 (8 wkts, 55 overs) 265
4/135 5/195 6/215
7/243 8/243

R. P. Davis did not bat.

Bowling: Frost 11–1–56–3; Dennis 9–1–37–1; Watkin 11–2–51–1; Cowley 9–0–55–1; Richards 11–0–30–0; Holmes 4–0–30–1.

;lamorgan

'A. R. Butcher b de Villiers 6
I. Morris run out 16
;. C. Holmes c G. R. Cowdrey
b C. S. Cowdrey . 62
M. P. Maynard c Davis b de Villiers . . 84
. V. A. Richards c sub b Ealham 27
. Smith c Hinks b Ealham 9
N. G. Cowley c G. R. Cowdrey
b C. S. Cowdrey . 4
†C. P. Metson b Penn 23
S. J. Dennis c de Villiers b C. S. Cowdrey 1
S. L. Watkin b Penn 6
M. Frost not out 1
B 3, w 4, n-b 1 8

1/8 2/36 3/161 4/202 5/204 6/214 7/219 8/228 9/246 (53.5 overs) 247

Bowling: de Villiers 10–0–37–2; Penn 10.5–1–40–2; Davis 8–0–45–0; Ealham 11–0–47–2; :. S. Cowdrey 9–0–52–3; G. R. Cowdrey 5–0–23–0.

Umpires: J. C. Balderstone and K. J. Lyons.

GLOUCESTERSHIRE v WARWICKSHIRE

At Bristol, May 12. Warwickshire won by six wickets. Toss: Warwickshire.
Gold Award: C. W. J. Athey.

Gloucestershire

*A. J. Wright c Small b Reeve 15
A. W. Stovold c Humpage b Benjamin . 5
P. Bainbridge c Humpage b Reeve 10
C. W. J. Athey not out 83
K. M. Curran c Humpage b Munton . . 0
M. W. Alleyne c Smith b Small 11
†R. C. Russell c Humpage b Benjamin . 20
J. W. Lloyds not out 53
L-b 7, w 3 10

1/14 2/31 3/34 4/36 5/69 6/99 (6 wkts, 55 overs) 207

M. C. J. Ball, C. A. Walsh and K. B. S. Jarvis did not bat.

Bowling: Small 11–1–27–1; Benjamin 11–2–32–2; Reeve 11–3–27–2; Munton 11–1–41–1; Moody 11–0–73–0.

Warwickshire

A. J. Moles run out 57
Asif Din c Alleyne b Curran 27
T. M. Moody c Alleyne b Bainbridge . . 16
A. I. Kallicharran c and b Bainbridge . 21
†G. W. Humpage not out 30
*D. A. Reeve not out 29
B 4, l-b 14, w 7, n-b 3 28

1/77 2/109 3/141 4/141 (4 wkts, 49.4 overs) 208

R. G. Twose, N. M. K. Smith, G. C. Small, J. E. Benjamin and T. A. Munton did not bat.

Bowling: Walsh 11–1–30–0; Jarvis 5–0–25–0; Curran 10–1–36–1; Alleyne 4.4–0–28–0; Ball 8–0–40–0; Bainbridge 11–3–31–2.

Umpires: A. A. Jones and B. Leadbeater.

GROUP B

DERBYSHIRE v SUSSEX

At Derby, April 24. Sussex won by five wickets. Toss: Sussex. The opening partnership of 169 in 44 overs between Barnett and Bowler was a record for Derbyshire's first wicket in the Benson and Hedges Cup.
Gold Award: M. P. Speight.

Derbyshire

*K. J. Barnett run out	94	C. J. Adams not out	2
†P. D. Bowler st Moores b Lenham	61	L-b 8, w 11, n-b 1	20
J. E. Morris b Dodemaide	23		
A. P. Kuiper not out	41	1/169 2/169 3/206 (4 wkts, 55 overs)	249
T. J. G. O'Gorman b Pigott	8	4/238	

B. Roberts, G. Miller, A. E. Warner, O. H. Mortensen and S. J. Base did not bat.

Bowling: Pigott 11–2–38–1; Dodemaide 11–3–37–1; C. M. Wells 11–0–44–0; Hansford 11–0–58–0; Salisbury 6–0–32–0; Lenham 5–0–32–1.

Sussex

N. J. Lenham c Bowler b Warner	22	A. C. S. Pigott not out	38
*P. W. G. Parker c Mortensen b Base	8		
A. P. Wells c and b Warner	53	B 1, l-b 7, w 5, n-b 2	15
M. P. Speight c Adams b Mortensen	71		
C. M. Wells not out	36	1/17 2/59 3/142 (5 wkts, 53.4 overs)	250
I. J. Gould c Miller b Warner	7	4/167 5/178	

A. I. C. Dodemaide, †P. Moores, A. R. Hansford and I. D. K. Salisbury did not bat.

Bowling: Base 10–3–46–1; Mortensen 11–1–43–1; Kuiper 10.4–0–64–0; Warner 11–0–47–3; Miller 11–0–42–0.

Umpires: D. O. Oslear and D. R. Shepherd.

MIDDLESEX v MINOR COUNTIES

At Lord's, April 24. Middlesex won by four wickets. Toss: Minor Counties.
Gold Award: D. L. Haynes.

Minor Counties

M. J. Roberts c Emburey b Tufnell	57	S. Greensword b Emburey	3
†S. N. V. Waterton c Haynes b Hemstock	6	R. A. Evans not out	5
G. K. Brown lbw b Emburey	32	L-b 10, w 13, n-b 1	24
N. A. Folland not out	53		
*S. G. Plumb c Downton b Williams	5	1/16 2/96 3/125 (6 wkts, 55 overs)	189
T. A. Lester b Hemstock	4	4/145 5/160 6/176	

N. R. Taylor, R. C. Green and A. J. Mack did not bat.

Bowling: Hemstock 10–1–37–2; Williams 11–2–27–1; Haynes 5–0–19–0; Weekes 7–1–27–0; Tufnell 11–0–42–1; Emburey 11–0–27–2.

Middlesex

D. L. Haynes c Waterton b Taylor	80	*J. E. Emburey b Green	0
M. A. Roseberry b Taylor	4	N. F. Williams not out	1
M. R. Ramprakash c Brown b Mack	2	L-b 5, w 2, n-b 3	10
K. R. Brown b Mack	56		
R. O. Butcher c Roberts b Evans	23	1/16 2/37 3/129 (6 wkts, 49.5 overs)	193
†P. R. Downton not out	17	4/157 5/188 6/188	

P. N. Weekes, P. C. R. Tufnell and J. R. Hemstock did not bat.

Bowling: Taylor 11–2–26–2; Green 10.5–1–49–1; Mack 11–2–47–2; Greensword 7–2–30–0; Evans 10–1–36–1.

Umpires: J. W. Holder and K. J. Lyons.

MINOR COUNTIES v SUSSEX

At Marlow, May 1. Sussex won by five wickets. Toss: Sussex. Minor Counties' total was the highest by a non-county side in the Benson and Hedges Cup, while Roberts's 121 was the highest score by a Minor Counties batsman. Playing in only his second match for the side, he faced 151 balls, hitting one six and twelve fours.

Gold Award: M. J. Roberts.

Minor Counties

M. J. Roberts c Dodemaide b Clarke . . 121
G. K. Brown c Speight b Lenham 46
N. A. Folland not out 78
S. Sharp not out 11
B 4, l-b 7, w 6 17

1/118 2/252 (2 wkts, 55 overs) 273

*S. G. Plumb, T. A. Lester, S. Greensword, †A. R. Fothergill, N. R. Taylor, R. C. Green and A. J. Mack did not bat.

Bowling: Pigott 9–2–38–0; Dodemaide 11–0–52–0; C. M. Wells 9–1–30–0; Clarke 11–1–53–1; Hansford 11–0–70–0; Gould 3–0–16–0; Lenham 1–0–3–1.

Sussex

N. J. Lenham b Mack 37
†P. Moores c Brown b Greensword 41
*P. W. G. Parker not out 86
A. P. Wells c Fothergill b Mack 0
M. P. Speight run out 40
C. M. Wells c Taylor b Green 33
I. J. Gould not out 15
L-b 17, w 3, n-b 2 22

1/70 2/106 3/106 4/177 5/232 (5 wkts, 51.4 overs) 274

A. I. C. Dodemaide, A. C. S. Pigott, A. R. Clarke and A. R. Hansford did not bat.

Bowling: Taylor 9–1–37–0; Green 10.4–0–51–1; Mack 11–2–36–2; Greensword 9–0–53–1; Plumb 9–0–54–0; Sharp 3–0–26–0.

Umpires: J. W. Holder and A. A. Jones.

SOMERSET v DERBYSHIRE

At Taunton, May 1. Somerset won by 7 runs. Toss: Somerset. The match aggregate of 613 runs passed by 12 the previous record, set at the same ground in 1982, while Derbyshire's total was their highest in the competition and the highest by a side batting second and losing. The second-wicket partnership of 210 between Bowler (158 balls, three fours) and Morris (119 balls, fourteen fours) was a record for any Derbyshire wicket in the competition, and Morris's score of 123 was also a Derbyshire record. Hardy faced 147 balls and hit nine fours in his 109 for Somerset.

Gold Award: G. D. Rose.

Somerset

S. J. Cook st Bowler b Miller 66
J. J. E. Hardy b Mortensen 109
G. D. Rose c Morris b Base 64
*C. J. Tavaré not out 47
R. J. Harden not out 3
L-b 12, w 9 21

1/126 2/234 3/298 (3 wkts, 55 overs) 310

P. M. Roebuck, A. N. Hayhurst, †N. D. Burns, R. P. Lefebvre, I. G. Swallow and J. C. Hallett did not bat.

Bowling: Malcolm 11–1–54–0; Base 11–1–54–1; Mortensen 10–0–55–1; Miller 11–0–46–1; Kuiper 11–0–80–0; Barnett 1–0–9–0.

Derbyshire

*K. J. Barnett c Hardy b Rose 0
†P. D. Bowler b Hayhurst 109
J. E. Morris c Harden b Hallett 123
A. P. Kuiper run out 22
C. J. Adams b Lefebvre 8
B. Roberts c Hardy b Hayhurst 4
S. C. Goldsmith c Cook b Rose 4
S. J. Base not out 15
D. E. Malcolm not out 0
L-b 13, w 4, n-b 1 18

1/0 2/210 3/250 4/270 5/275 6/285 7/291 (7 wkts, 55 overs) 303

G. Miller and O. H. Mortensen did not bat.

Bowling: Rose 11–0–58–2; Hallett 9–0–52–1; Lefebvre 11–1–55–1; Swallow 11–0–45–0; Roebuck 8–0–57–0; Hayhurst 5–0–23–2.

Umpires: B. Leadbeater and R. Palmer.

SOMERSET v MINOR COUNTIES

At Taunton, May 8. Somerset won by six wickets. Toss: Minor Counties.
Gold Award: A. N. Hayhurst.

Minor Counties

G. K. Brown c Tavaré b Rose 4
M. J. Roberts lbw b Jones 7
N. A. Folland lbw b Hayhurst 16
*S. G. Plumb st Burns b Swallow 63
T. A. Lester c Burns b Lefebvre 14
S. Greensword c Cook b Swallow 10
D. R. Thomas not out 49
†A. R. Fothergill not out 45
B 5, l-b 11, w 16 32

1/9 2/17 3/51 4/77 5/102 6/160 (6 wkts, 55 overs) 240

N. R. Taylor, R. C. Green and A. J. Mack did not bat.

Bowling: Jones 11–1–63–1; Rose 11–2–31–1; Hallett 2–0–18–0; Lefebvre 11–0–44–1; Hayhurst 11–0–36–1; Swallow 9–0–32–2.

Somerset

S. J. Cook b Mack 27
P. M. Roebuck c Fothergill b Taylor . . 13
A. N. Hayhurst lbw b Taylor 76
*C. J. Tavaré c Fothergill b Mack 29
R. J. Harden not out 53
G. D. Rose not out 26
L-b 6, w 6, n-b 5 17

1/41 2/45 3/107 4/192 (4 wkts, 51.4 overs) 241

†N. D. Burns, R. P. Lefebvre, A. N. Jones, I. G. Swallow and J. C. Hallett did not bat.

Bowling: Taylor 11–2–50–2; Green 10.4–0–57–0; Mack 9–0–22–2; Thomas 5–0–29–0; Greensword 7–0–34–0; Plumb 9–0–43–0.

Umpires: B. Hassan and K. E. Palmer.

SUSSEX v MIDDLESEX

At Hove, May 8. Middlesex won on faster scoring-rate over the first 30 overs, having tied the scores with the same number of wickets lost. After 30 overs, Sussex had been 99 for three and Middlesex 125 for two. Toss: Middlesex. Haynes faced a total of 155 balls, hitting thirteen fours.
Gold Award: D. L. Haynes.

Sussex

N. J. Lenham c Emburey b Williams .. 3
†P. Moores b Haynes 76
*P. W. G. Parker c Downton b Gatting 7
A. P. Wells c Ramprakash b Williams . 74
M. P. Speight c Roseberry b Hughes .. 43
C. M. Wells c Butcher b Emburey 59
I. J. Gould not out 12
B 1, l-b 2, w 1, n-b 4 8

1/39 2/64 3/98 4/197 5/249 6/282 (6 wkts, 55 overs) 282

A. I. C. Dodemaide, J. A. North, A. R. Hansford and A. R. Clarke did not bat.

Bowling: Cowans 11–0–66–0; Williams 10–1–45–2; Gatting 8–0–41–1; Hughes 11–0–47–1; Emburey 11–0–57–1; Haynes 4–0–23–1.

Middlesex

D. L. Haynes c A. P. Wells b Hansford .131
M. A. Roseberry c Gould b C. M. Wells 1
*M. W. Gatting c Parker b Hansford .. 54
M. R. Ramprakash c Moores b Dodemaide . 44
K. R. Brown b North 12
R. O. Butcher b Dodemaide 5
†P. R. Downton not out 15
J. E. Emburey not out 4
B 1, l-b 11, w 2, n-b 2 16

1/14 2/110 3/210 4/229 5/254 6/269 (6 wkts, 55 overs) 282

N. F. Williams, S. P. Hughes and N. G. Cowans did not bat.

Bowling: Dodemaide 11–0–36–2; C. M. Wells 11–2–45–1; North 8–0–48–1; Hansford 11–0–55–2; Clarke 11–0–70–0; Lenham 3–0–16–0.

Umpires: J. D. Bond and J. H. Hampshire.

MIDDLESEX v SOMERSET

At Lord's, May 10, 11. Middlesex won by 8 runs. Toss: Somerset. Close of play: Middlesex 183-6 (48 overs) (P. R. Downton 2*, J. E. Emburey 1*).
Gold Award: M. W. Gatting.

Middlesex

D. L. Haynes lbw b Mallender 28
M. A. Roseberry b Mallender 30
*M. W. Gatting run out 66
M. R. Ramprakash c Burns b Hayhurst 4
K. R. Brown b Hayhurst 31
R. O. Butcher run out 3
†P. R. Downton c Mallender b Jones .. 15
J. E. Emburey c Roebuck b Rose 12
N. F. Williams not out 22
N. G. Cowans not out 10
B 6, l-b 15, w 5 26

1/56 2/95 3/115 4/160 5/175 6/181 7/205 8/226 (8 wkts, 55 overs) 247

S. P. Hughes did not bat.

Bowling: Jones 11–0–49–1; Rose 11–4–47–1; Mallender 11–2–32–2; Lefebvre 11–1–46–0; Swallow 1–0–9–0; Hayhurst 10–0–43–2.

Somerset

S. J. Cook c Downton b Cowans 6
P. M. Roebuck c Butcher b Hughes ... 8
A. N. Hayhurst c Emburey b Gatting .. 20
*C. J. Tavaré c Downton b Gatting ... 93
R. J. Harden c Haynes b Williams 5
†N. D. Burns c Butcher b Cowans 21
G. D. Rose c sub b Williams 15
I. G. Swallow b Emburey 0
R. P. Lefebvre run out 37
A. N. Jones c Brown b Gatting 7
N. A. Mallender not out 3
L-b 11, w 13 24

1/13 2/17 3/78 4/108 5/153 6/178 7/178 8/197 9/226 (54.2 overs) 239

Bowling: Hughes 11–0–39–1; Cowans 11–0–35–2; Williams 11–0–52–2; Emburey 10.2–2–37–1; Gatting 11–0–65–3.

Umpires: J. D. Bond and J. H. Hampshire.

MINOR COUNTIES v DERBYSHIRE

At Wellington, May 10. Derbyshire won by 43 runs. Toss: Minor Counties.
Gold Award: S. C. Goldsmith.

Derbyshire

*K. J. Barnett b Taylor 8
†P. D. Bowler c Folland b Thomas 16
J. E. Morris lbw b Mack 6
A. P. Kuiper c Fothergill b Taylor 16
C. J. Adams c Fothergill b Greensword 44
B. Roberts c Plumb b Greensword 46
S. J. Base lbw b Greensword 0
S. C. Goldsmith not out 45
A. E. Warner c Sharp b Mack 16
D. E. Malcolm b Taylor 5
O. H. Mortensen not out 2
L-b 6, w 3, n-b 5 14

1/9 2/15 3/42 (9 wkts, 55 overs) 218
4/74 5/131 6/134
7/165 8/192 9/207

Bowling: Taylor 10–0–52–3; Mack 10–1–49–2; Green 8–1–26–0; Thomas 11–3–24–1; Greensword 11–0–38–3; Plumb 5–0–23–0.

Minor Counties

M. J. Roberts lbw b Goldsmith 31
G. K. Brown c Barnett b Warner 16
N. A. Folland c Bowler b Goldsmith . . 25
S. Sharp b Goldsmith 0
*S. G. Plumb c Kuiper b Malcolm 16
S. Greensword b Base 28
D. R. Thomas b Warner 14
†A. R. Fothergill b Base 3
N. R. Taylor b Warner 3
R. C. Green not out 5
A. J. Mack b Base 6
L-b 16, w 7, n-b 5 28

1/43 2/79 3/79 (50.4 overs) 175
4/99 5/115 6/146
7/151 8/164 9/164

Bowling: Mortensen 8–3–15–0; Malcolm 8–1–22–1; Warner 11–1–31–3; Base 8.4–0–33–3; Kuiper 5–0–20–0; Goldsmith 10–0–38–3.

Umpires: P. J. Eele and K. E. Palmer.

DERBYSHIRE v MIDDLESEX

At Derby, May 12. Derbyshire won by 8 runs. Toss: Derbyshire. The partnership of 158 between Bowler and Kuiper was a Derbyshire record for the third wicket in all limited-overs cricket. Kuiper's hundred came off 120 balls, with twelve fours.
Gold Award: A. P. Kuiper.

Derbyshire

*K. J. Barnett c Downton b Williams . . 22
†P. D. Bowler c Haynes b Hughes 77
J. E. Morris c Downton b Williams . . . 0
A. P. Kuiper not out 106
C. J. Adams b Williams 26
A. E. Warner b Emburey 7
B. Roberts not out 5
L-b 1, w 4, n-b 3 8

1/29 2/29 3/187 (5 wkts, 55 overs) 251
4/227 5/236

S. C. Goldsmith, S. J. Base, D. E. Malcolm and O. H. Mortensen did not bat.

Bowling: Williams 11–3–37–3; Cowans 11–2–48–0; Tufnell 7–0–36–0; Hughes 11–0–64–1; Emburey 9–0–41–1; Gatting 6–0–24–0.

Middlesex

D. L. Haynes c Mortensen b Kuiper . . . 64
M. R. Ramprakash c Bowler b Malcolm 7
*M. W. Gatting b Malcolm 6
K. R. Brown b Kuiper 34
R. O. Butcher c Barnett b Warner 9
†P. R. Downton c Adams b Base 40
J. E. Emburey c Roberts b Kuiper 1
N. F. Williams b Warner 28
S. P. Hughes b Base 22
N. G. Cowans b Malcolm 12
P. C. R. Tufnell not out 7
B 1, l-b 7, w 4, n-b 1 13

1/16 2/26 3/89 (54.2 overs) 243
4/110 5/138 6/141
7/186 8/204 9/230

Bowling: Malcolm 11–0–55–3; Mortensen 11–5–18–0; Base 10.2–0–43–2; Kuiper 11–0–71–3; Warner 11–1–48–2.

Umpires: H. D. Bird and R. Palmer.

SUSSEX v SOMERSET

At Hove, May 12. Somerset won by 107 runs. Toss: Somerset. Somerset's total was their highest in the competition, while Cook's innings was a record for Somerset and the second-highest by any batsman in the Benson and Hedges Cup. His hundred came off 113 balls and in all he faced 158 deliveries, hitting one six and 22 fours. C. M. Wells hit two sixes and eleven fours off 100 balls.

Gold Award: S. J. Cook.

Somerset

S. J. Cook c Smith b Dodemaide 177
P. M. Roebuck b Pigott 91
G. D. Rose b Salisbury 14
*C. J. Tavaré b Pigott 5
R. J. Harden b Dodemaide 15
A. N. Hayhurst not out 5
†N. D. Burns not out 6
B 1, l-b 6, n-b 1 8

1/194 2/222 3/280 (5 wkts, 55 overs) 321
4/309 5/310

R. P. Lefebvre, A. N. Jones, I. G. Swallow and N. A. Mallender did not bat.

Bowling: Pigott 11–1–33–2; Dodemaide 11–1–68–2; C. M. Wells 11–0–71–0; Hansford 11–0–82–0; Salisbury 11–0–60–1.

Sussex

D. M. Smith c Burns b Jones 3
†P. Moores c Mallender b Rose 13
*P. W. G. Parker lbw b Jones 1
A. P. Wells c Tavaré b Swallow 23
M. P. Speight b Rose 6
C. M. Wells c Mallender b Rose 101
I. J. Gould c Swallow b Hayhurst 6
A. I. C. Dodemaide c Cook b Rose ... 32
A. C. S. Pigott b Lefebvre 12
I. D. K. Salisbury lbw b Lefebvre 2
A. R. Hansford not out 2
B 1, l-b 4, w 8 13

1/17 2/20 3/23 (46.2 overs) 214
4/40 5/87 6/96
7/194 8/206 9/211

Bowling: Jones 7–2–22–2; Rose 9–0–37–4; Lefebvre 9.2–0–39–2; Mallender 6–0–14–0; Hayhurst 8–0–42–1; Swallow 7–0–55–1.

Umpires: B. Dudleston and P. B. Wight.

GROUP C

The Combined Universities' squad of twelve named for the competition was: M. A. Crawley (Oxford) (*captain*), J. C. M. Atkinson (Cambridge), J. Boiling (Durham), A. Dale (Swansea), S. P. James (Cambridge), N. V. Knight (Loughborough), J. I. Longley (Durham), T. M. Orrell (Salford), A. M. Smith (Exeter), C. M. Tolley (Loughborough), R. J. Turner (Cambridge) and W. M. van der Merwe (Oxford).

HAMPSHIRE v YORKSHIRE

At Southampton, April 24. Yorkshire won by seven wickets. Toss: Yorkshire.

Gold Award: P. E. Robinson.

Hampshire

*V. P. Terry c Metcalfe b Byas	15	J. R. Ayling b Fletcher	14
R. J. Scott c Metcalfe b Carrick	47	†R. J. Parks not out	6
K. D. James run out	2	L-b 7, w 4	11
C. L. Smith b Fletcher	44		
M. D. Marshall run out	24	1/28 2/41 3/106 (6 wkts, 55 overs)	206
J. R. Wood not out	43	4/121 5/149 6/189	

R. J. Maru, C. A. Connor and K. J. Shine did not bat.

Bowling: Jarvis 11–2–48–0; Sidebottom 11–4–37–0; Fletcher 11–0–42–2; Byas 6–1–13–1; Carrick 11–1–31–1; Berry 5–0–28–0.

Yorkshire

*M. D. Moxon c Parks b James	11	C. White not out	17
A. A. Metcalfe c Parks b Ayling	36	L-b 4, n-b 1	5
†R. J. Blakey b Connor	66		
P. E. Robinson not out	73	1/37 2/49 3/179 (3 wkts, 53.2 overs)	208

D. Byas, P. Carrick, A. Sidebottom, P. W. Jarvis, S. D. Fletcher and P. J. Berry did not bat.

Bowling: Marshall 10–0–28–0; Shine 9.2–1–53–0; Connor 11–1–25–1; James 11–3–34–1; Ayling 7–0–41–1; Maru 5–0–23–0.

Umpires: A. G. T. Whitehead and P. B. Wight.

LANCASHIRE v SURREY

At Manchester, April 24. Lancashire won by 76 runs. Toss: Surrey.
Gold Award: N. H. Fairbrother.

Lancashire

G. D. Mendis c and b Bullen	40	I. D. Austin not out	1
G. Fowler c and b M. P. Bicknell	9		
M. A. Atherton c M. P. Bicknell b Bullen	44		
N. H. Fairbrother not out	95	L-b 4, w 4, n-b 2	10
M. Watkinson b Thorpe	23		
P. A. J. DeFreitas c Lynch b M. P. Bicknell	20	1/10 2/71 3/124 (5 wkts, 55 overs)	242
		4/188 5/231	

*D. P. Hughes, P. J. W. Allott, †W. K. Hegg and B. P. Patterson did not bat.

Bowling: Gray 11–1–52–0; M. P. Bicknell 11–4–48–2; Feltham 6–0–28–0; Greig 11–0–45–0; Bullen 11–1–35–2; Thorpe 5–0–30–1.

Surrey

D. J. Bicknell c Hegg b Patterson	9	C. K. Bullen not out	17
G. S. Clinton c Hegg b Austin	40	M. P. Bicknell not out	27
A. J. Stewart c Hegg b Atherton	31		
M. A. Lynch b Austin	0	L-b 4, w 3, n-b 4	11
G. P. Thorpe c Hegg b Austin	8		
†D. M. Ward st Hegg b Atherton	18	1/11 2/78 3/78 (8 wkts, 55 overs)	166
*I. A. Greig c and b Atherton	1	4/89 5/100 6/101	
M. A. Feltham b Austin	4	7/117 8/121	

A. H. Gray did not bat.

Bowling: Patterson 8–2–6–1; Allott 10–1–35–0; DeFreitas 9–0–33–0; Watkinson 6–0–31–0; Atherton 11–1–32–3; Austin 11–3–25–4.

Umpires: J. C. Balderstone and B. J. Meyer.

COMBINED UNIVERSITIES v LANCASHIRE

At Cambridge, May 1. Lancashire won by 22 runs. Toss: Combined Universities.
Gold Award: C. M. Tolley.

Lancashire

G. D. Mendis c James b van der Merwe	6	I. D. Austin not out	61
G. Fowler c Turner b van der Merwe	18	L-b 8, w 7	15
M. A. Atherton not out	69		
N. H. Fairbrother c Turner b Dale	25		
M. Watkinson lbw b Crawley	3	1/23 2/26 3/65 (5 wkts, 55 overs)	209
P. A. J. DeFreitas c and b Boiling	12	4/74 5/96	

*D. P. Hughes, †W. K. Hegg, P. J. W. Allott and B. P. Patterson did not bat.

Bowling: van der Merwe 10–4–42–2; Tolley 8–1–26–0; Crawley 11–3–18–1; Dale 8–1–21–1; Boiling 8–0–37–1; Smith 10–0–57–0.

Combined Universities

S. P. James c Allott b Patterson	0	W. M. van der Merwe b DeFreitas	10
N. V. Knight c Hegg b Austin	9	†R. J. Turner not out	12
*M. A. Crawley c Fairbrother b Watkinson	46	A. M. Smith not out	4
C. M. Tolley lbw b Allott	77	B 1, l-b 8, w 4	13
J. I. Longley run out	4	1/0 2/22 3/114 (8 wkts, 55 overs)	187
J. C. M. Atkinson c Hughes b Allott	10	4/126 5/154 6/159	
A. Dale c Mendis b Watkinson	2	7/161 8/180	

J. Boiling did not bat.

Bowling: Patterson 11–3–24–1; Allott 11–3–23–2; Austin 11–1–42–1; DeFreitas 11–0–38–1; Watkinson 11–0–51–2.

Umpires: D. J. Constant and K. J. Lyons.

SURREY v HAMPSHIRE

At The Oval, May 1. Surrey won by 87 runs. Toss: Hampshire. Surrey's total, their highest and the third-highest by any county in the competition, was also the highest in a Benson and Hedges Cup match involving two first-class counties. Darren Bicknell faced 137 balls, hitting twelve fours, for his 119; Robin Smith hit four sixes and fourteen fours in 132 off 118 balls.
Gold Award: D. J. Bicknell.

Surrey

D. J. Bicknell c Gower b Shine	119	*I. A. Greig not out	9
G. S. Clinton c Terry b James	9	L-b 8, w 6, n-b 8	22
A. J. Stewart c Parks b Shine	76		
M. A. Lynch c Terry b Shine	8		
G. P. Thorpe not out	50	1/20 2/164 3/174 (5 wkts, 55 overs)	331
†D. M. Ward c Parks b Shine	38	4/262 5/322	

K. T. Medlycott, M. A. Feltham, M. P. Bicknell and A. J. Murphy did not bat.

Bowling: Marshall 11–1–52–0; Shine 10–0–68–4; James 5–0–36–1; Connor 11–0–71–0; Maru 7–0–40–0; Scott 11–0–56–0.

Hampshire

*V. P. Terry st Ward b Medlycott	24	R. J. Maru c and b Greig	9
D. I. Gower c and b M. P. Bicknell	6	C. A. Connor c Ward b Murphy	3
R. A. Smith c Greig b Murphy	132	K. J. Shine run out	0
C. L. Smith c Ward b Greig	3	L-b 5, w 2	7
K. D. James b Medlycott	2		
R. J. Scott run out	7	1/9 2/68 3/75 (46.2 overs)	244
M. D. Marshall c Ward b M. P. Bicknell	31	4/82 5/101 6/161	
†R. J. Parks not out	20	7/222 8/233 9/239	

Bowling: M. P. Bicknell 8–1–48–2; Murphy 9–3–36–2; Feltham 3–0–24–0; Medlycott 11–0–44–2; Greig 6.2–0–35–2; Lynch 9–0–52–0.

Umpires: N. T. Plews and D. S. Thompsett.

LANCASHIRE v HAMPSHIRE

At Manchester, May 8, 9. No result. Toss: Hampshire. After rain and bad light had interrupted Hampshire's reply to Lancashire's 352 for six on the second day, the umpires ruled that there was not sufficient time to complete the match under the playing conditions and another of eighteen overs a side was started. However, torrential rain and bad light again intervened and at 7.15 p.m. this game, too, was called off.

Lancashire

G. D. Mendis c Parks b Connor	9	I. D. Austin not out	9
G. Fowler c Nicholas b Connor	1		
N. H. Fairbrother c Terry b Ayling	8	L-b 1, w 1, n-b 1	3
M. A. Atherton c C. L. Smith b Ayling	2		
M. Watkinson st Parks b Maru	40	1/4 2/20 3/22 (5 wkts, 18 overs)	147
P. A. J. DeFreitas not out	75	4/23 5/106	

*D. P. Hughes, P. J. W. Allott, †W. K. Hegg and B. P. Patterson did not bat.

Bowling: Marshall 4–0–45–0; Shine 4–0–13–0; Connor 3–0–26–2; Ayling 3–0–22–2; Maru 4–0–40–1.

Hampshire

V. P. Terry c Fairbrother b DeFreitas	7
D. I. Gower not out	44
R. A. Smith not out	45
W 2, n-b 1	3
1/24 (1 wkt, 12 overs)	99

C. L. Smith, *M. C. J. Nicholas, K. J. Shine, M. D. Marshall, J. R. Ayling, †R. J. Parks, R. J. Maru and C. A. Connor did not bat.

Bowling: Patterson 2–0–10–0; Allott 3–0–29–0; DeFreitas 2–0–14–1; Austin 3–0–26–0; Watkinson 2–0–20–0.

Umpires: D. O. Oslear and D. S. Thompsett.

In the original match, which was subsequently declared void, Lancashire's total would have been a record for the competition and a county record in limited-overs cricket. Fairbrother's 145, off 119 balls and containing three sixes and eleven fours, was a limited-overs record for Lancashire, and his third-wicket partnership of 244 with Atherton was a county record for any wicket in limited-overs competition. Because the match was abandoned, however, and a new one started, none of these records stood. Just as unsatisfactory was Hampshire's slow over-rate, with eight overs still to be bowled when the allotted playing time for 55 overs had elapsed. On the first day, at the close of which Lancashire were 142 for two off 27 overs (M. A. Atherton 43*, N. H. Fairbrother 82*), some six hours had been lost to the weather.

Lancashire

G. D. Mendis c R. A. Smith b Shine	4	I. D. Austin b Maru	2
G. Fowler c Nicholas b Shine	1	†W. K. Hegg not out	1
M. A. Atherton b Shine	100	L-b 14, w 6, n-b 4	24
N. H. Fairbrother c Shine b Ayling	145		
M. Watkinson not out	40	1/3 2/16 3/260 (6 wkts, 55 overs)	352
P. A. J. DeFreitas c Parks b Connor	35	4/276 5/344 6/347	

*D. P. Hughes, P. J. W. Allott and B. P. Patterson did not bat.

Bowling: Marshall 11–1–48–0; Shine 11–0–73–3; Connor 11–0–72–1; Ayling 11–0–75–1; Maru 11–1–70–1.

Hampshire

V. P. Terry c Allott b Patterson 16
C. L. Smith not out 16
R. A. Smith not out 1
N-b 2 2

1/32 (1 wkt, 7 overs) 35

D. I. Gower, *M. C. J. Nicholas, K. J. Shine, M. D. Marshall, J. R. Ayling, †R. J. Parks, R. J. Maru and C. A. Connor did not bat.

Bowling: Patterson 4–0–23–1; Allott 3–1–12–0.

Umpires: D. O. Oslear and D. S. Thompsett.

YORKSHIRE v COMBINED UNIVERSITIES

At Leeds, May 8, 9. Combined Universities won by two wickets. Toss: Combined Universities. Close of play: Yorkshire 197-8 (55 overs).
Gold Award: W. M. van der Merwe.

Yorkshire

*M. D. Moxon run out 4
A. A. Metcalfe c Boiling b Crawley ... 11
†R. J. Blakey run out 65
S. A. Kellett c Boiling b Smith 29
P. E. Robinson c Tolley b van der Merwe 57
C. White run out 1
P. Carrick c James b Smith 8
A. Sidebottom not out 9
P. J. Hartley c Orrell b van der Merwe . 0
P. W. Jarvis not out 2
L-b 9, w 2 11

1/14 2/17 3/76 4/166 5/167 6/180 7/190 8/190 (8 wkts, 55 overs) 197

S. D. Fletcher did not bat.

Bowling: van der Merwe 11–3–34–2; Tolley 11–3–38–0; Crawley 11–2–21–1; Dale 8–1–38–0; Smith 11–0–46–2; Boiling 3–0–11–0.

Combined Universities

S. P. James b Sidebottom 63
*M. A. Crawley c Blakey b Jarvis 9
A. Dale c Sidebottom b Hartley 16
C. M. Tolley c Sidebottom b Hartley .. 6
J. C. M. Atkinson lbw b Hartley 16
J. I. Longley c Blakey b Jarvis 14
T. M. Orrell run out 15
W. M. van der Merwe run out 27
†R. J. Turner not out 12
A. M. Smith not out 4
B 1, l-b 11, w 3, n-b 3 18

1/17 2/50 3/65 4/85 5/121 6/145 7/176 8/195 (8 wkts, 53.5 overs) 200

J. Boiling did not bat.

Bowling: Jarvis 10–0–29–2; Sidebottom 11–1–41–1; Fletcher 10.5–1–44–0; Hartley 11–2–34–3; Carrick 11–0–40–0.

Umpires: J. C. Balderstone and B. J. Meyer.

COMBINED UNIVERSITIES v SURREY

At Oxford, May 10. Surrey won by six wickets. Toss: Surrey.
Gold Award: A. J. Stewart.

Combined Universities

*M. A. Crawley c Lynch b M. P. Bicknell . 9
S. P. James b Medlycott 59
A. Dale c Clinton b Greig 40
J. C. M. Atkinson c M. P. Bicknell b Bullen . 9
C. M. Tolley run out 14
W. M. van der Merwe c Stewart b Medlycott . 14
J. I. Longley st Ward b Medlycott 9
T. M. Orrell c Ward b M. P. Bicknell . 0
†R. J. Turner not out 25
A. M. Smith not out 15
B 8, l-b 11, w 10, n-b 5 34

1/17 2/120 3/133 4/144 5/162 6/178 7/179 8/179 (8 wkts, 55 overs) 228

J. Boiling did not bat.

Bowling: Gray 10–1–20–0; M. P. Bicknell 11–2–27–2; Greig 10–0–51–1; Thorpe 2–0–15–0; Bullen 11–1–48–1; Medlycott 11–0–48–3.

Surrey

D. J. Bicknell st Turner b Crawley 32
G. S. Clinton lbw b van der Merwe . . . 61
A. J. Stewart not out 84
M. A. Lynch lbw b van der Merwe . . . 1
G. P. Thorpe run out 8
†D. M. Ward not out 33
L-b 3, w 4, n-b 3 10

1/56 2/137 3/149 4/165 (4 wkts, 53.4 overs) 229

*I. A. Greig, K. T. Medlycott, C. K. Bullen, M. P. Bicknell and A. H. Gray did not bat.

Bowling: van der Merwe 10.4–0–50–2; Tolley 11–2–43–0; Crawley 11–1–34–1; Boiling 11–1–33–0; Smith 8–0–53–0; Dale 2–0–13–0.

Umpires: B. Hassan and A. G. T. Whitehead.

YORKSHIRE v LANCASHIRE

At Leeds, May 10. Lancashire won by five wickets. Toss: Yorkshire.
Gold Award: M. Watkinson.

Yorkshire

*M. D. Moxon c Hegg b Allott 9
S. A. Kellett lbw b DeFreitas 22
R. J. Blakey b Austin 2
A. A. Metcalfe lbw b DeFreitas 28
P. E. Robinson c Allott b DeFreitas . . . 0
†D. L. Bairstow c Hegg b Watkinson . . 9
P. Carrick b Watkinson 3
A. Sidebottom run out 2
P. J. Hartley c Fowler b Watkinson . . . 1
P. W. Jarvis b Patterson 42
S. D. Fletcher not out 15
L-b 5, w 3 8

1/22 2/31 3/35 4/35 5/49 6/68 7/77 8/80 9/88 (53.1 overs) 141

Bowling: Allott 11–2–22–1; Patterson 10.1–4–33–1; Austin 11–6–14–1; DeFreitas 10–1–36–3; Watkinson 11–1–31–3.

Lancashire

G. D. Mendis run out 25
G. Fowler c Jarvis b Fletcher 36
M. A. Atherton lbw b Sidebottom 3
N. H. Fairbrother lbw b Fletcher 12
M. Watkinson not out 43
P. A. J. DeFreitas b Jarvis 10
I. D. Austin not out 0
B 1, l-b 5, w 6, n-b 3 15

1/49 2/68 3/86 4/88 5/138 (5 wkts, 36.1 overs) 144

*D. P. Hughes, †W. K. Hegg, P. J. W. Allott and B. P. Patterson did not bat.

Bowling: Jarvis 11–1–51–1; Sidebottom 7.1–0–35–1; Fletcher 9–3–23–2; Hartley 9–1–29–0.

Umpires: B. J. Meyer and R. A. White.

HAMPSHIRE v COMBINED UNIVERSITIES

At Southampton, May 12. Hampshire won by 99 runs. Toss: Hampshire. The opening partnership of 252 in 165 minutes between Terry and Chris Smith was a record for the first wicket in all limited-overs cricket in England. Terry faced 146 balls for his 134, hitting one six and ten fours, while Smith's unbeaten 154 came off 170 balls, fifteen of which produced fours.
Gold Award: C. L. Smith.

Hampshire

V. P. Terry c van der Merwe b Smith .134
C. L. Smith not out 154
D. I. Gower c Smith b van der Merwe . 0
R. A. Smith not out 8
L-b 1 1

1/252 2/252 (2 wkts, 55 overs) 297

*M. C. J. Nicholas, †R. J. Parks, L. A. Joseph, R. J. Maru, C. A. Connor, K. J. Shine and P. J. Bakker did not bat.

Bowling: Smith 11–2–49–1; van der Merwe 11–0–53–1; Crawley 11–1–40–0; Boiling 11–0–71–0; Dale 3–0–21–0; Tolley 8–0–62–0.

Combined Universities

S. P. James b Maru 46
N. V. Knight c Parks b Bakker 16
A. Dale c Maru b Connor 2
C. M. Tolley c C. L. Smith b Connor .. 74
*M. A. Crawley b Maru 26
J. C. M. Atkinson lbw b Connor 0
J. I. Longley run out 1
W. M. van der Merwe run out 4
†R. J. Turner b Maru 0
A. M. Smith not out 7
J. Boiling lbw b Nicholas 2
L-b 16, w 4 20

1/33 2/38 3/104 (52 overs) 198
4/171 5/172 6/179
7/184 8/184 9/190

Bowling: Shine 9–0–33–0; Bakker 10–3–21–1; Joseph 11–1–38–0; Connor 9–0–40–3; Maru 11–2–46–3; C. L. Smith 1–0–2–0; Nicholas 1–0–2–1.

Umpires: R. Julian and D. R. Shepherd.

SURREY v YORKSHIRE

At The Oval, May 12. Yorkshire won by six wickets. Toss: Yorkshire.
Gold Award: R. J. Blakey.

Surrey

D. J. Bicknell lbw b Sidebottom 55
G. S. Clinton run out 30
A. J. Stewart b Fletcher 76
M. A. Lynch c Bairstow b Jarvis 0
G. P. Thorpe lbw b White 14
†D. M. Ward not out 46
*I. A. Greig c White b Jarvis 15
J. D. Robinson not out 2
B 5, l-b 8, w 9, n-b 2 24

1/71 2/116 3/117 (6 wkts, 55 overs) 262
4/157 5/222 6/242

K. T. Medlycott, M. P. Bicknell and A. J. Murphy did not bat.

Bowling: Jarvis 11–0–58–2; Sidebottom 11–2–43–1; Fletcher 11–0–53–1; Gough 6–0–27–0; Byas 7–0–37–0; White 9–0–31–1.

Yorkshire

S. A. Kellett b Robinson 45
*A. A. Metcalfe c Medlycott b Robinson 38
R. J. Blakey c D. J. Bicknell
b M. P. Bicknell . 79
D. Byas c Robinson b M. P. Bicknell .. 36
P. E. Robinson not out 43
†D. L. Bairstow not out 1
B 6, l-b 10, w 2, n-b 3 21

1/82 2/104 3/178 (4 wkts, 53.5 overs) 263
4/258

C. White, A. Sidebottom, D. Gough, P. W. Jarvis and S. D. Fletcher did not bat.

Bowling: M. P. Bicknell 10.5–0–53–2; Murphy 9–1–41–0; Greig 9–0–45–0; Robinso 11–0–41–2; Medlycott 11–0–53–0; Lynch 3–0–14–0.

Umpires: J. H. Harris and D. O. Oslear.

GROUP D

ESSEX v NOTTINGHAMSHIRE

At Chelmsford, April 24. Essex won by four wickets. Toss: Essex. Johnson faced 125 balls hitting twelve fours and reaching his hundred with a six. Gooch scored his century off 13 balls, with nine fours. Randall took his total of runs in the competition to 2,339, becoming th second most prolific batsman after Gooch.

Gold Award: G. A. Gooch.

Nottinghamshire

B. C. Broad b Topley 22
P. R. Pollard c Garnham b Pringle 5
*R. T. Robinson c Childs b Waugh . . . 56
P. Johnson not out 104
D. W. Randall c Garnham b Foster . . . 25
F. D. Stephenson not out 2
B 1, l-b 3, w 2, n-b 1 . . . .

1/8 2/51 3/103 4/194 (4 wkts, 55 overs) 24

†B. N. French, E. E. Hemmings, R. A. Pick, K. E. Cooper and J. A. Afford did not bat.

Bowling: Foster 11–0–46–1; Pringle 11–0–57–1; Gooch 11–2–51–0; Topley 6–1–16–1; Child 10–0–42–0; Waugh 6–0–25–1.

Essex

*G. A. Gooch c Hemmings b Stephenson.102
B. R. Hardie c Robinson b Cooper 20
P. J. Prichard run out 17
M. E. Waugh c Johnson b Afford 16
D. R. Pringle not out 55
J. P. Stephenson b Hemmings 0
A. W. Lilley b Pick . . . .
†M. A. Garnham not out 1
L-b 7, w 4, n-b 2 1

1/48 2/80 3/131 4/207 5/210 6/229 (6 wkts, 52 overs) 24

N. A. Foster, T. D. Topley and J. H. Childs did not bat.

Bowling: Stephenson 11–1–49–1; Cooper 10–2–37–1; Pick 9–0–37–1; Hemming 11–0–49–1; Afford 11–1–63–1.

Umpires: B. Dudleston and D. S. Thompsett.

LEICESTERSHIRE v NORTHAMPTONSHIRE

At Leicester, April 24. Northamptonshire won by 5 runs. Toss: Leicestershire.

Gold Award: R. J. Bailey.

Northamptonshire

G. Cook run out 6
W. Larkins c Lewis b Taylor 46
R. J. Bailey not out 92
*A. J. Lamb b Mullally 34
D. J. Capel b Lewis 33
D. J. Wild c Whitticase b Lewis 0
†D. Ripley not out . . . .
B 1, l-b 11, w 1, n-b 1 . . . .

1/14 2/81 3/155 4/218 5/218 (5 wkts, 55 overs) 22

J. G. Thomas, C. E. L. Ambrose, N. G. B. Cook and M. A. Robinson did not bat.

Bowling: Lewis 11–2–42–2; Mullally 10–2–47–1; Taylor 9–1–32–1; Agnew 11–1–49–(Willey 11–0–36–0; Potter 3–0–8–0.

Leicestershire

T. J. Boon c G. Cook b Thomas 84
*N. E. Briers b Ambrose 7
J. J. Whitaker b Capel 46
P. Willey b Ambrose 49
L. Potter c N. G. B. Cook b Ambrose . 6
C. C. Lewis run out 5
J. D. R. Benson b Thomas 1
†P. Whitticase not out 7
L-b 13, w 2, n-b 1 16

1/9 2/138 3/171 4/195 5/206 6/211 7/221 (7 wkts, 55 overs) 221

J. P. Agnew, A. D. Mullally and L. B. Taylor did not bat.

Bowling: Ambrose 11–4–19–3; Capel 11–1–38–1; Thomas 11–0–59–2; Robinson 11–0–47–0; N. G. B. Cook 11–1–45–0.

Umpires: P. J. Eele and R. Palmer.

NOTTINGHAMSHIRE v LEICESTERSHIRE

At Nottingham, May 1. Nottinghamshire won by four wickets. Toss: Nottinghamshire.
Gold Award: K. E. Cooper.

Leicestershire

T. J. Boon c French b Cooper 4
*N. E. Briers c Randall b Pick 10
J. J. Whitaker c Johnson b Cooper 7
L. Potter c French b Cooper 0
J. D. R. Benson c Cooper b Pick 43
C. C. Lewis b Afford 23
†P. Whitticase c Broad b Pick 45
M. I. Gidley not out 20
W. K. M. Benjamin c Cooper b Stephenson . 2
J. P. Agnew not out 1
B 2, l-b 1, w 6 9

1/10 2/19 3/23 4/23 5/79 6/103 7/157 8/163 (8 wkts, 55 overs) 164

L. B. Taylor did not bat.

Bowling: Stephenson 11–1–39–1; Cooper 11–2–25–3; Pick 11–0–50–3; Hemmings 11–5–10–0; Afford 11–3–37–1.

Nottinghamshire

B. C. Broad run out 49
M. Newell lbw b Agnew 13
P. Johnson c Lewis b Potter 39
D. W. Randall c Whitaker b Taylor . . . 6
F. D. Stephenson c Whitticase b Benjamin . 10
†B. N. French not out 14
E. E. Hemmings b Benjamin 5
*R. T. Robinson not out 25
B 1, w 2, n-b 4 7

1/46 2/66 3/83 4/119 5/126 6/136 (6 wkts, 46.4 overs) 168

K. E. Cooper, R. A. Pick and J. A. Afford did not bat.

Bowling: Benjamin 9–3–29–2; Lewis 9–2–28–0; Agnew 6–0–34–1; Taylor 9.4–0–34–1; Gidley 5–0–16–0; Potter 8–1–26–1.

Umpires: H. D. Bird and D. R. Shepherd.

SCOTLAND v ESSEX

At Glasgow, May 1. Essex won by 83 runs. Toss: Essex. Pringle's 77 came off 38 balls, with four sixes and six fours, while Prichard faced 131 balls for his first hundred in the competition and hit one six and thirteen fours.
Gold Award: P. J. Prichard.

Essex

*G. A. Gooch run out	2
B. R. Hardie c Henry b Parfitt	34
P. J. Prichard run out	107
M. E. Waugh b Bee	62
D. R. Pringle not out	77
†M. A. Garnham run out	5
J. P. Stephenson not out	4
B 1, l-b 7, w 5, n-b 5	18
1/2 2/105 3/185 4/250 5/304 (5 wkts, 55 overs)	309

T. D. Topley, N. A. Foster, J. H. Childs and A. W. Lilley did not bat.

Bowling: Moir 11–2–50–0; Cowan 11–0–80–0; Bee 10–0–67–1; Parfitt 11–1–41–1; Henry 10–1–54–0; Russell 2–0–9–0.

Scotland

I. L. Philip c Garnham b Pringle	29
C. G. Greenidge b Childs	50
O. Henry c Childs b Foster	24
B. M. W. Patterson b Gooch	42
*R. G. Swan b Childs	11
A. B. Russell b Foster	9
A. Bee lbw b Childs	0
D. Cowan b Stephenson	7
†D. J. Haggo not out	18
J. D. Moir lbw b Stephenson	5
C. L. Parfitt not out	1
B 4, l-b 13, w 11, n-b 2	30
1/93 2/101 3/131 4/179 5/188 6/188 7/195 8/213 9/223 (9 wkts, 55 overs)	226

Bowling: Foster 11–1–44–2; Pringle 8–3–28–1; Topley 11–0–35–0; Gooch 9–0–44–1; Childs 11–1–37–3; Stephenson 3–0–14–2; Lilley 2–0–7–0.

Umpires: B. Hassan and A. G. T. Whitehead.

NORTHAMPTONSHIRE v ESSEX

At Northampton, May 8. Essex won by eight wickets to qualify for the quarter-finals. Toss: Essex.

Gold Award: G. A. Gooch.

Northamptonshire

*W. Larkins lbw b Pringle	20
A. Fordham c Topley b Foster	9
G. Cook b Childs	28
R. J. Bailey c Prichard b Stephenson	29
D. J. Capel c Waugh b Stephenson	12
D. J. Wild b Stephenson	0
†D. Ripley c Garnham b Foster	27
J. G. Thomas c Waugh b Pringle	3
J. W. Govan c Gooch b Foster	11
C. E. L. Ambrose run out	12
M. A. Robinson not out	0
L-b 10, w 6	16
1/17 2/43 3/79 4/100 5/107 6/108 7/116 8/146 9/161 (53.3 overs)	167

Bowling: Foster 10–2–18–3; Ilott 9–1–39–0; Topley 11–1–25–0; Pringle 10.3–1–28–2; Childs 6–0–25–1; Stephenson 7–0–22–3.

Essex

*G. A. Gooch not out	94
B. R. Hardie c Larkins b Robinson	27
P. J. Prichard b Larkins b Ambrose	26
M. E. Waugh not out	8
B 1, l-b 2, w 5, n-b 5	13
1/82 2/151 (2 wkts, 38.3 overs)	168

J. P. Stephenson, †M. A. Garnham, D. R. Pringle, T. D. Topley, N. A. Foster, J. H. Childs and M. C. Ilott did not bat.

Bowling: Ambrose 11–0–35–1; Capel 6–0–24–0; Robinson 7.3–0–35–1; Thomas 8–0–48–0 Govan 1–0–3–0; Wild 5–2–20–0.

Umpires: J. H. Harris and R. A. White.

SCOTLAND v NOTTINGHAMSHIRE

At Glasgow, May 8, 9. Nottinghamshire won by four wickets. Toss: Nottinghamshire. Close of play: Scotland 115-4 (37 overs) (R. G. Swan 42*, O. Henry 14*). Parfitt's return of four for 16 was the best by any bowler for Scotland in the competition.
Gold Award: R. T. Robinson.

Scotland

I. L. Philip lbw b Pick	16
C. G. Greenidge c Cooper b Stephenson	1
B. M. W. Patterson run out	22
*R. G. Swan c Pick b Saxelby	53
M. J. Smith lbw b Saxelby	7
O. Henry not out	62
D. R. Brown b Stephenson	24
†D. J. Haggo not out	2
B 1, l-b 10, w 9, n-b 1	21
1/7 2/46 3/46 4/61 5/151 6/204 (6 wkts, 55 overs)	208

D. Cowan, J. D. Moir and C. L. Parfitt did not bat.

Bowling: Stephenson 11–0–49–2; Cooper 11–1–33–0; Pick 11–0–45–1; Saxelby 11–3–39–2; Afford 11–2–31–0.

Nottinghamshire

B. C. Broad b Cowan	14
P. R. Pollard c Greenidge b Moir	5
*R. T. Robinson not out	70
P. Johnson b Parfitt	52
D. W. Randall lbw b Parfitt	7
F. D. Stephenson b Parfitt	5
†B. N. French c Brown b Parfitt	25
K. E. Cooper not out	11
B 3, l-b 5, w 14	22
1/20 2/20 3/95 4/114 5/133 6/173 (6 wkts, 54.2 overs)	211

R. A. Pick, J. A. Afford and K. Saxelby did not bat.

Bowling: Cowan 10.2–0–51–1; Moir 11–2–43–1; Brown 11–0–43–0; Henry 1–0–5–0; Smith 10–0–45–0; Parfitt 11–3–16–4.

Umpires: B. Leadbeater and K. J. Lyons.

ESSEX v LEICESTERSHIRE

At Chelmsford, May 10, 11. No result. Toss: Essex. When rain interrupted play after only four overs on the second day, the match was abandoned and a game of nineteen overs a side scheduled. The captains tossed and Essex elected to bat, but continuing drizzle led to the new game being called off at 5.35 without a ball having been bowled. In the void game, Leicestershire, 153 for four from 41 overs overnight after being put in, were 162 for four, L. Potter 46 not out, when rain drove the players from the field.

Essex

*G. A. Gooch, J. P. Stephenson, M. E. Waugh, P. J. Prichard, B. R. Hardie, A. W. Lilley, D. R. Pringle, †M. A. Garnham, N. A. Foster, T. D. Topley and M. C. Ilott.

Leicestershire

*N. E. Briers, T. J. Boon, J. J. Whitaker, L. Potter, C. C. Lewis, †P. Whitticase, G. J. Parsons, M. I. Gidley, J. P. Agnew, A. D. Mullally and L. B. Taylor.

Umpires: D. J. Constant and N. T. Plews.

NORTHAMPTONSHIRE v SCOTLAND

At Northampton, May 10. Scotland won by 2 runs. Toss: Northamptonshire. Scotland's highest total in the Benson and Hedges Cup brought them their second victory in the competition. The first was against Lancashire at Perth in 1986. Larkins hit one six and thirteen fours, and Philip struck two sixes and seven fours as he compiled the highest innings by a Scotland player in the competition.
Gold Award: I. L. Philip.

Scotland

†I. L. Philip lbw b Ambrose 95
C. G. Greenidge lbw b Capel 32
B. M. W. Patterson b Govan 8
*R. G. Swan c Ripley b Ambrose 44
A. C. Storie c Larkins b Robinson 8
A. B. Russell b Robinson 0
D. R. Brown b Capel 16
A. Bee b Ambrose 0
D. Cowan not out . . . .
J. D. Moir not out . . . .
B 2, l-b 7, w 12 2

1/54 2/81 3/166 (8 wkts, 55 overs) 23
4/195 5/195 6/213
7/213 8/221

C. L. Parfitt did not bat.

Bowling: Ambrose 11–3–26–3; Thomas 9–0–52–0; Robinson 10–0–47–2; Capel 11–0–29–2 Govan 11–2–55–1; Wild 3–0–13–0.

Northamptonshire

*W. Larkins c Bee b Moir 111
A. Fordham lbw b Moir 0
G. Cook lbw b Cowan 6
R. J. Bailey b Cowan 1
D. J. Capel b Brown 0
D. J. Wild c Parfitt b Brown 15
†D. Ripley b Brown 9
J. G. Thomas c Patterson b Cowan . . . 32
J. W. Govan run out 3
C. E. L. Ambrose not out 1
M. A. Robinson not out . . . .
B 1, l-b 7, w 4, n-b 2 1

1/11 2/55 3/57 (9 wkts, 55 overs) 22
4/76 5/105 6/137
7/159 8/212 9/226

Bowling: Moir 11–0–51–2; Bee 11–1–58–0; Parfitt 11–1–26–0; Cowan 11–1–36–3; Brown 11–2–50–3.

Umpires: H. D. Bird and P. B. Wight.

LEICESTERSHIRE v SCOTLAND

At Leicester, May 12. Leicestershire won by seven wickets. Toss: Leicestershire. *Gold Award:* N. E. Briers.

Scotland

†I. L. Philip c Whitticase b Agnew 29
C. G. Greenidge c Whitticase b Taylor . 34
B. M. W. Patterson c Lewis b Agnew . 4
*R. G. Swan c Potter b Agnew 40
A. C. Storie b Mullally 19
O. Henry run out 48
D. R. Brown c Potter b Taylor 17
A. Bee b Taylor . . . .
J. D. Moir not out . . . .
L-b 4, w 8, n-b 2 1

1/43 2/70 3/72 (8 wkts, 55 overs) 21
4/128 5/134 6/184
7/189 8/215

D. Cowan and C. L. Parfitt did not bat.

Bowling: Lewis 11–0–49–0; Parsons 4–1–26–0; Agnew 11–3–20–3; Taylor 11–0–65–3 Mullally 11–3–28–1; Gidley 7–1–23–0.

Leicestershire

T. J. Boon run out 39
*N. E. Briers not out 93
J. J. Whitaker c Henry b Moir 46
L. Potter c Philip b Cowan 10
C. C. Lewis not out 2
B 1, l-b 2, w 7, n-b 1 1

1/75 2/159 3/182 (3 wkts, 51.3 overs) 21

†P. Whitticase, M. I. Gidley, G. J. Parsons, J. P. Agnew, A. D. Mullally and L. B. Taylor did not bat.

Bowling: Bee 3–0–21–0; Moir 11–3–35–1; Brown 8.3–0–47–0; Cowan 7–0–45–1; Parfitt 11–1–39–0; Henry 11–1–29–0.

Umpires: J. D. Bond and K. E. Palmer.

NOTTINGHAMSHIRE v NORTHAMPTONSHIRE

At Nottingham, May 12. Nottinghamshire won by three wickets. Toss: Nottinghamshire. Robinson hit two sixes and eight fours in his unbeaten 106.

Gold Award: R. T. Robinson.

Northamptonshire

A. Fordham c Johnson b Pick 67
N. A. Felton c Pollard b Hemmings . . . 16
*R. J. Bailey st French b Afford 18
R. G. Williams b Stephenson 17
A. L. Penberthy run out 10
†D. Ripley c French b Cooper 7
J. G. Thomas c French b Stephenson . . 0
J. W. Govan b Cooper 1
C. E. L. Ambrose not out 11
A. Walker b Stephenson 5
M. A. Robinson b Pick 1
B 8, w 17 25

1/64 2/113 3/114 4/137 5/146 6/146 7/156 8/157 9/166 (54.4 overs) 178

Bowling: Cooper 11–1–41–2; Stephenson 11–1–33–3; Pick 10.4–1–47–2; Hemmings 11–2–30–1; Afford 11–3–19–1.

Nottinghamshire

B. C. Broad c Bailey b Thomas 8
P. R. Pollard c Ambrose b Thomas . . . 5
*R. T. Robinson not out 106
P. Johnson lbw b Thomas 9
F. D. Stephenson c Ambrose b Thomas 2
D. W. Randall c Thomas b Ambrose . . 2
†B. N. French c Ripley b Ambrose 24
E. E. Hemmings c Ambrose b Robinson 6
K. E. Cooper not out 8
L-b 2, w 8 10

1/11 2/16 3/34 4/40 5/54 6/127 7/159 (7 wkts, 54.1 overs) 180

R. A. Pick and J. A. Afford did not bat.

Bowling: Ambrose 11–2–20–2; Walker 11–1–39–0; Thomas 11–0–45–4; Robinson 10.1–1–47–1; Govan 11–2–27–0.

Umpires: J. W. Holder and M. J. Kitchen.

QUARTER-FINALS

ESSEX v NOTTINGHAMSHIRE

At Chelmsford, May 30. Nottinghamshire won by six wickets. Toss: Nottinghamshire. Johnson, having taken six overs to score a run, put Nottinghamshire on the way to a comfortable win with 50 off 66 balls in a partnership of 92 from 21 overs with his captain, Robinson. Essex had never managed to break free of Nottinghamshire's control in the field after being put in. At lunch they were 134 for five after 37 overs, and the loss of Gooch in the afternoon prevented the final flourish that might have inconvenienced their visitors.

Gold Award: P. Johnson.

Essex

*G. A. Gooch c French b Cooper 87
B. R. Hardie b Pick 0
P. J. Prichard lbw b Afford 25
M. E. Waugh st French b Hemmings . . 4
D. R. Pringle b Afford 19
J. P. Stephenson c and b Hemmings . . . 4
A. W. Lilley b Stephenson 23
†M. A. Garnham not out 21
N. A. Foster run out 8
T. D. Topley not out 10
L-b 8, w 5, n-b 2 15

1/2 2/65 3/84 4/117 5/132 6/169 7/172 8/184 (8 wkts, 55 overs) 216

J. H. Childs did not bat.

Bowling: Pick 11–0–60–1; Cooper 11–4–34–1; Afford 11–0–47–2; Stephenson 11–1–34–1; Hemmings 11–1–33–2.

Nottinghamshire

B. C. Broad c Garnham b Gooch 38
D. W. Randall c Hardie b Childs 16
*R. T. Robinson not out 72
P. Johnson c and b Stephenson 50
M. Saxelby st Garnham b Stephenson . 0
F. D. Stephenson not out 25
L-b 11, w 7 18

1/51 2/73 3/165 4/165 (4 wkts, 52.1 overs) 219

†B. N. French, E. E. Hemmings, K. E. Cooper, R. A. Pick and J. A. Afford did not bat.

Bowling: Foster 11–3–37–0; Pringle 9.1–0–35–0; Gooch 8–1–27–1; Childs 11–2–40–1; Topley 3–0–25–0; Stephenson 10–0–44–2.

Umpires: J. C. Balderstone and D. J. Constant.

LANCASHIRE v SURREY

At Manchester, May 30. Lancashire won by 46 runs. Toss: Surrey. A record second-wicket partnership of 172 for Lancashire between Fowler and Atherton was followed by a 36-ball innings from Fairbrother, who took his total of runs in four innings against Surrey to 573. It also earned him his second Gold Award against Surrey in five weeks, following the qualifying group game in which he scored 95 not out. Surrey, too, were boosted by a second-wicket partnership, 123 between Clinton and Stewart, but once they were separated by Watkinson, Surrey collapsed. The last eight wickets fell in nine overs for 48 runs.

Gold Award: N. H. Fairbrother.

Lancashire

G. D. Mendis c and b Bicknell 9
G. Fowler c Bullen b Waqar Younis ... 96
M. A. Atherton c Lynch b Murphy 74
N. H. Fairbrother not out 61
M. Watkinson c Lynch b Murphy 4
Wasim Akram c Lynch b Waqar Younis 2
P. A. J. DeFreitas run out 0
†W. K. Hegg not out 10
B 4, l-b 8, w 6, n-b 5 23

1/26 2/198 3/203 4/235 5/246 6/249 (6 wkts, 55 overs) 279

*D. P. Hughes, I. D. Austin and P. J. W. Allott did not bat.

Bowling: Bicknell 11–2–61–1; Waqar Younis 11–0–55–2; Bullen 11–2–37–0; Murphy 11–1–61–2; Medlycott 11–0–53–0.

Surrey

M. A. Lynch c Fowler b Allott 24
G. S. Clinton c Atherton b DeFreitas .. 77
A. J. Stewart b Watkinson 67
†D. M. Ward b Austin 10
*I. A. Greig b DeFreitas 9
G. P. Thorpe c Fairbrother b Allott ... 9
K. T. Medlycott b DeFreitas 1
C. K. Bullen b Watkinson 10
M. P. Bicknell c Allott b Watkinson ... 8
Waqar Younis c Mendis b Watkinson . 4
A. J. Murphy not out 0
B 1, l-b 5, w 7, n-b 1 14

1/37 2/160 3/185 4/190 5/203 6/207 7/208 8/219 9/233 (51.4 overs) 233

Bowling: DeFreitas 11–2–40–3; Allott 11–3–25–2; Wasim Akram 9–0–39–0; Watkinson 10.4–1–58–4; Atherton 3–0–20–0; Austin 7–0–45–1.

Umpires: J. H. Harris and A. G. T. Whitehead.

SOMERSET v MIDDLESEX

At Taunton, May 30. Somerset won by 22 runs. Toss: Middlesex. On an unexpectedly slow pitch, in cloudy weather, Somerset never really came to terms with tight bowling and keen fielding. Of seven players to reach double figures, only Tavaré (82 balls) and Harden put together a partnership, adding 50 in eleven overs. After a racing start, the Middlesex innings plotted a similar course. Some good catches, excellent holding spells by Lefebvre and Swallow, and sharp fielding – which brought two run-outs – gradually whittled away the batting. Mallender, Jones and Roebuck took the last six wickets for 39 runs in twelve overs.

Gold Award: A. N. Jones.

Somerset

S. J. Cook c Downton b Williams 4
P. M. Roebuck b Cowans 17
A. N. Hayhurst b Hughes 17
*C. J. Tavaré c Gatting b Hughes 49
R. J. Harden c Downton b Emburey . . 23
†N. D. Burns c Haynes b Cowans 12
G. D. Rose b Emburey 12
R. P. Lefebvre c Downton b Williams . 8
I. G. Swallow c Emburey b Hughes . . . 18
A. N. Jones b Williams 3
N. A. Mallender not out 6
L-b 5, w 6, n-b 3 14

1/9 2/35 3/53 4/103 5/123 6/142 7/146 8/154 9/160 (53.5 overs) 183

Bowling: Williams 11–1–40–3; Cowans 11–3–22–2; Hughes 10.5–0–37–3; Gatting 8–1–28–0; Emburey 10–1–36–2; Haynes 3–0–15–0.

Middlesex

D. L. Haynes c Roebuck b Jones 23
M. A. Roseberry run out 38
*M. W. Gatting b Lefebvre 16
M. R. Ramprakash lbw b Mallender . . 21
K. R. Brown run out 8
R. O. Butcher c Roebuck b Jones 22
†P. R. Downton lbw b Jones 15
N. F. Williams lbw b Roebuck 4
J. E. Emburey not out 6
S. P. Hughes b Roebuck 2
N. G. Cowans b Jones 1
L-b 2, w 1, n-b 2 5

1/34 2/60 3/87 4/100 5/122 6/144 7/150 8/153 9/158 (51.5 overs) 161

Bowling: Mallender 9–1–25–1; Jones 8.5–0–41–4; Lefebvre 8–1–15–1; Rose 3–0–23–0; Swallow 11–2–26–0; Hayhurst 6–0–16–0; Roebuck 6–0–13–2.

Umpires: K. J. Lyons and B. J. Meyer.

WORCESTERSHIRE v GLAMORGAN

At Worcester, May 30. Worcestershire won by seven wickets. Toss: Glamorgan. Glamorgan, losing nine wickets for 72, squandered a good base laid down by Morris and Holmes in a second-wicket partnership of 89. Both had been dropped by Botham at slip, Morris when 18 and Holmes when 7, but Botham made amends by dismissing Holmes and Maynard in the first four balls of his second spell. His first five overs had conceded just 8 runs. Morris was eighth out, his 106 coming from 137 balls with twelve fours. Worcestershire's batting was much more of a team performance, built around Curtis's unbeaten 76 off 150 balls.

Gold Award: H. Morris.

Glamorgan

H. Morris c D'Oliveira b Newport 106
*A. R. Butcher c D'Oliveira b Dilley . . 16
G. C. Holmes c Rhodes b Botham 19
M. P. Maynard c Rhodes b Botham . . . 0
I. V. A. Richards lbw b Radford 3
I. Smith b Radford 2
N. G. Cowley c Newport b Weston . . . 0
†C. P. Metson c Lampitt b Newport . . 7
S. L. Watkin c Rhodes b Radford 5
S. R. Barwick not out 13
M. Frost c Curtis b Radford 3
L-b 7, w 5, n-b 5 17

1/30 2/119 3/119 4/132 5/138 6/139 7/158 8/168 9/181 (54.3 overs) 191

Bowling: Dilley 11–0–39–1; Radford 10.3–4–26–4; Newport 11–3–34–2; Botham 11–3–29–2; Lampitt 5–0–35–0; Weston 6–1–21–1.

Worcestershire

T. S. Curtis not out 76
M. J. Weston lbw b Barwick 25
*P. A. Neale lbw b Watkin 50
I. T. Botham b Richards 22
D. B. D'Oliveira not out 12
L-b 6, w 3, n-b 1 10

1/48 2/146 3/176 (3 wkts, 52.2 overs) 195

D. A. Leatherdale, S. R. Lampitt, P. J. Newport, †S. J. Rhodes, N. V. Radford and G. R. Dilley did not bat.

Bowling: Frost 9.2–0–51–0; Watkin 11–2–32–1; Barwick 10–2–45–1; Cowley 11–2–22–0; Richards 9–0–32–1; Holmes 2–0–7–0.

Umpires: R. Julian and K. E. Palmer.

SEMI-FINALS

LANCASHIRE v SOMERSET

At Manchester, June 13. Lancashire won by six wickets. Toss: Lancashire. Fairbrother, Gold Award winner in Lancashire's quarter-final, received his second award in succession after a devastating round of strokeplay which, including three sixes and eight fours, produced 78 runs off 53 balls. He and the undefeated Atherton added 111 in just eighteen overs for the third wicket to set Lancashire up for victory with ten overs to spare. Somerset, put in under cloud cover that helped the bowlers in the morning, made a solid start but were never given the freedom to accelerate by Lancashire's accurate bowling, backed by keen fielding.

Gold Award: N. H. Fairbrother.

Somerset

S. J. Cook c Hegg b Austin 49
J. J. E. Hardy c Allott b Wasim Akram 19
A. N. Hayhurst c Hegg b Wasim Akram 1
*C. J. Tavaré c Hughes b Austin 10
R. J. Harden c Hegg b DeFreitas 16
†N. D. Burns c Hughes b Watkinson .. 21
G. D. Rose run out 32
R. P. Lefebvre not out 25
I. G. Swallow b Wasim Akram 8
N. A. Mallender run out 3
A. N. Jones not out 1
B 5, l-b 12, w 6, n-b 4 27

1/50 2/55 3/81 4/109 5/113 6/163 7/174 8/202 9/207 (9 wkts, 55 overs) 212

Bowling: Allott 11–2–34–0; DeFreitas 11–0–51–1; Wasim Akram 11–0–29–3; Watkinson 11–1–33–1; Austin 11–0–48–2.

Lancashire

G. D. Mendis c and b Swallow 37
G. Fowler b Jones 14
M. A. Atherton not out 56
N. H. Fairbrother c Burns b Rose 78
M. Watkinson c Harden b Rose 11
Wasim Akram not out 8
L-b 4, w 5, n-b 1 10

1/34 2/74 3/185 4/203 (4 wkts, 44.5 overs) 214

*D. P. Hughes, P. A. J. DeFreitas, I. D. Austin, †W. K. Hegg and P. J. W. Allott did not bat.

Bowling: Jones 9–0–48–1; Mallender 9–3–31–0; Rose 10–0–44–2; Lefebvre 8–1–31–0; Swallow 6.5–1–40–1; Hayhurst 2–0–16–0.

Umpires: B. Dudleston and J. W. Holder.

NOTTINGHAMSHIRE v WORCESTERSHIRE

At Nottingham, June 13. Worcestershire won by nine wickets. Toss: Worcestershire. Put in to bat, Nottinghamshire made a poor start against the moving ball, and only when Stephenson joined Randall did the runs begin to flow. Stephenson's attack on McEwan's last over produced 21 runs but left him 2 runs short of his century, his 98 having come from 92 balls. As the pitch eased in the late afternoon – it was that used for the Test match – Worcestershire, despite poor light, had no difficulty in winning. Curtis and Weston put on 141 by the 35th over, and Weston became the second player in the match to miss out narrowly on a hundred when Hick's seventh four sent Worcestershire to Lord's.

Gold Award: M. J. Weston.

Nottinghamshire

B. C. Broad c Lampitt b Botham 32
D. J. R. Martindale b McEwan 0
*R. T. Robinson c D'Oliveira b Lampitt 26
P. Johnson c Hick b Botham 4
D. W. Randall c Rhodes b McEwan ... 39
F. D. Stephenson not out 98
†B. N. French run out 4
E. E. Hemmings not out 12
L-b 9, w 5, n-b 1 15

1/5 2/56 3/65 4/70 5/162 6/171 (6 wkts, 55 overs) 230

K. E. Cooper, R. A. Pick and J. A. Afford did not bat.

Bowling: Newport 11–3–28–0; McEwan 11–0–53–2; Lampitt 11–0–47–1; Botham 11–2–43–2; Stemp 8–1–38–0; Hick 3–0–12–0.

Worcestershire

*T. S. Curtis b Stephenson 61
M. J. Weston not out 99
G. A. Hick not out 57
L-b 10, w 3, n-b 2 15

1/141 (1 wkt, 53.2 overs) 232

I. T. Botham, S. R. Lampitt, D. B. D'Oliveira, †S. J. Rhodes, P. J. Newport, R. D. Stemp, S. M. McEwan and D. A. Leatherdale did not bat.

Bowling: Pick 11–1–45–0; Cooper 10.2–1–29–0; Stephenson 11–0–45–1; Afford 11–0–43–0; Hemmings 10–0–60–0.

Umpires: D. O. Oslear and R. Palmer.

FINAL

LANCASHIRE v WORCESTERSHIRE

At Lord's, July 14. Lancashire won by 69 runs. Toss: Worcestershire. Thoughts that Lancashire's 241 would not be enough on a dry pitch on a hot midsummer's day had been dispelled by tea, when Worcestershire were 56 for three after 25 overs. The turning point had been the introduction of Wasim Akram to the attack after thirteen overs. His second ball was too fast for Curtis, prompting an involuntary flick as the ball lifted and left him. In Akram's third over, a similar delivery but with not so much movement off the pitch found Hick's defence wanting and Hegg, diving to his right, held his second catch. Botham's reputation meant that Worcestershire always had a chance, but Watkinson, bowling unchanged, permitted few liberties and punished indiscretions. Moreover Hughes, captaining Lancashire with a deft touch, could always recall Akram. Botham batted for 92 minutes and hit three fours before, in the 42nd over, he tried to pull a ball from DeFreitas and was bowled when it did not bounce as much as he expected.

Earlier in the day, Akram had helped wrest the match from Worcestershire's grip, adding 55 in eight overs with DeFreitas after Lancashire had been 136 for five in the 42nd over. The left-arm all-rounder hit two sixes in one over off Radford, scarcely more than a waft depositing the ball over square leg and then a full swing of the bat threatening the top balcony of the Pavilion. His 28 came from 21 balls, and towards the end Hegg improvised a splendid 31 not out off seventeen balls. Like Akram he could have won the Gold Award, for he also kept with great panache; instead R. B. Simpson, the adjudicator, chose Watkinson, whose 50 from 79 balls and partnership of 88 with Atherton provided the platform for the strokeplay that followed.

Gold Award: M. Watkinson. *Attendance:* 14,618 (excl. members); *receipts* £369,799.

Lancashire

G. D. Mendis c Neale b Botham 19
G. Fowler c Neale b Newport 11
M. A. Atherton run out 40
N. H. Fairbrother b Lampitt 11
M. Watkinson c and b Botham 50
Wasim Akram c Radford b Newport . . 28
P. A. J. DeFreitas b Lampitt 28
I. D. Austin run out 17
†W. K. Hegg not out 31
*D. P. Hughes not out 1
L-b 4, n-b 1 5

1/25 (2) 2/33 (1) 3/47 (4) 4/135 (3) 5/136 (5) 6/191 (6) 7/199 (7) 8/231 (8) (8 wkts, 55 overs) 241

P. J. W. Allott did not bat.

Bowling: Newport 11–1–47–2; Botham 11–0–49–2; Lampitt 11–3–43–2; Radford 8–1–41–0; Illingworth 11–0–41–0; Hick 3–0–16–0.

Worcestershire

T. S. Curtis c Hegg c Wasim Akram	16	P. J. Newport b Wasim Akram	3
M. J. Weston b Watkinson	19	S. R. Lampitt b Austin	4
G. A. Hick c Hegg b Wasim Akram	1		
D. B. D'Oliveira b Watkinson	23	L-b 9, w 8, n-b 4	21
I. T. Botham b DeFreitas	38		
*P. A. Neale c Hegg b Austin	0	1/27 (1) 2/38 (3) 3/41 (2) (54 overs)	172
†S. J. Rhodes lbw b Allott	5	4/82 (4) 5/87 (6) 6/112 (7)	
N. V. Radford not out	26	7/114 (5) 8/154 (9)	
R. K. Illingworth lbw b DeFreitas	16	9/164 (10) 10/172 (11)	

Bowling: Allott 10–1–22–1; DeFreitas 11–2–30–2; Wasim Akram 11–0–30–3; Watkinson 11–0–37–2; Austin 11–1–44–2.

Umpires: J. H. Hampshire and N. T. Plews.

BENSON AND HEDGES CUP RECORDS

Highest individual scores: 198 not out, G. A. Gooch, Essex v Sussex, Hove, 1982; 177, S. J. Cook, Somerset v Sussex, Hove, 1990; 173 not out, C. G. Greenidge, Hampshire v Minor Counties (South), Amersham, 1973; 158 not out, B. F. Davison, Leicestershire v Warwickshire, Coventry, 1972; 155 not out, M. D. Crowe, Somerset v Hampshire, Southampton, 1987; 155 not out, R. A. Smith, Hampshire v Glamorgan, Southampton, 1989; 154 not out, M. J. Procter, Gloucestershire v Somerset, Taunton, 1972; 154 not out, C. L. Smith, Hampshire v Combined Universities, Southampton, 1990. (188 hundreds have been scored in the competition. The most hundreds in one season is 20 in 1990.)

Fastest hundred: M. A. Nash in 62 minutes, Glamorgan v Hampshire at Swansea, 1976.

Highest totals in 55 overs: 350 for three, Essex v Oxford & Cambridge Univs, Chelmsford, 1979; 333 for four, Essex v Oxford & Cambridge Univs, Chelmsford, 1985; 331 for five, Surrey v Hampshire, The Oval, 1990; 327 for four, Leicestershire v Warwickshire, Coventry, 1972; 327 for two, Essex v Sussex, Hove, 1982; 321 for one, Hampshire v Minor Counties (South), Amersham, 1973; 321 for five, Somerset v Sussex, Hove, 1990. *In the final:* 290 for six, Essex v Surrey, 1979.

Highest total by a side batting second and winning: 291 for five (53.5 overs), Warwickshire v Lancashire (288 for nine), Manchester, 1981. *In the final:* 244 for six (55 overs), Yorkshire v Northamptonshire (244 for seven), 1987; 244 for seven (55 overs), Nottinghamshire v Essex (243 for seven), 1989.

Highest total by a side batting second and losing: 303 for seven (55 overs) Derbyshire v Somerset (310 for three), Taunton, 1990. *In the final:* 255 (51.4 overs), Surrey v Essex (290 for six), 1979.

Highest match aggregate: 613 for ten wickets, Somerset (310-3) v Derbyshire (303-7), Taunton, 1990.

Lowest totals: 56 in 26.2 overs, Leicestershire v Minor Counties, Wellington, 1982; 59 in 34 overs, Oxford & Cambridge Univs v Glamorgan, Cambridge, 1983; 60 in 26 overs, Sussex v Middlesex, Hove, 1978; 62 in 26.5 overs, Gloucestershire v Hampshire, Bristol, 1975. *In the final:* 117 in 46.3 overs, Derbyshire v Hampshire, 1988.

Shortest completed innings: 21.4 overs (156), Surrey v Sussex, Hove, 1988.

Record partnership for each wicket

252 for 1st	V. P. Terry and C. L. Smith, Hampshire v Combined Universities at Southampton	1990
285* for 2nd	C. G. Greenidge and D. R. Turner, Hampshire v Minor Counties (South) at Amersham	1973
269* for 3rd	P. M. Roebuck and M. D. Crowe, Somerset v Hampshire at Southampton	1987
184* for 4th	D. Lloyd and B. W. Reidy, Lancashire v Derbyshire at Chesterfield.	1980
160 for 5th	A. J. Lamb and D. J. Capel, Northamptonshire v Leicestershire at Northampton	1986
121 for 6th	P. A. Neale and S. J. Rhodes, Worcestershire v Yorkshire at Worcester	1988
149* for 7th	J. D. Love and C. M. Old, Yorkshire v Scotland at Bradford	1981
109 for 8th	R. E. East and N. Smith, Essex v Northamptonshire at Chelmsford.	1977
83 for 9th	P. G. Newman and M. A. Holding, Derbyshire v Nottinghamshire at Nottingham	1985
80* for 10th	D. L. Bairstow and M. Johnson, Yorkshire v Derbyshire at Derby	1981

Best bowling: Seven for 12, W. W. Daniel, Middlesex v Minor Counties (East), Ipswich, 1978; seven for 22, J. R. Thomson, Middlesex v Hampshire, Lord's, 1981; seven for 32, R. G. D. Willis, Warwickshire v Yorkshire, Birmingham, 1981. *In the final:* Five for 13, S. T. Jefferies, Hampshire v Derbyshire, 1988.

Hat-tricks (10): G. D. McKenzie, Leicestershire v Worcestershire, Worcester, 1972; K. Higgs, Leicestershire v Surrey in the final, Lord's, 1974; A. A. Jones, Middlesex v Essex, Lord's, 1977; M. J. Procter, Gloucestershire v Hampshire, Southampton, 1977; W. Larkins, Northamptonshire v Oxford & Cambridge Univs, Northampton, 1980; E. A. Moseley, Glamorgan v Kent, Cardiff, 1981; G. C. Small, Warwickshire v Leicestershire, Leicester, 1984; N. A. Mallender, Somerset v Combined Univs, Taunton, 1987; W. K. M. Benjamin, Leicestershire v Nottinghamshire, Leicester, 1987; A. R. C. Fraser, Middlesex v Sussex, Lord's, 1988.

Largest victories in runs: Essex by 214 runs v Combined Universities, Chelmsford, 1979; Sussex by 186 runs v Cambridge University, Hove, 1974.

Victories by ten wickets (14): By Derbyshire, Essex (twice), Glamorgan, Hampshire, Kent, Lancashire, Leicestershire, Northamptonshire, Somerset, Warwickshire, Worcestershire, Yorkshire (twice).

WINNERS 1972-90

1972 LEICESTERSHIRE beat Yorkshire by five wickets.
1973 KENT beat Worcestershire by 39 runs.
1974 SURREY beat Leicestershire by 27 runs.
1975 LEICESTERSHIRE beat Middlesex by five wickets.
1976 KENT beat Worcestershire by 43 runs.
1977 GLOUCESTERSHIRE beat Kent by 64 runs.
1978 KENT beat Derbyshire by six wickets.
1979 ESSEX beat Surrey by 35 runs.
1980 NORTHAMPTONSHIRE beat Essex by 6 runs.
1981 SOMERSET beat Surrey by seven wickets.
1982 SOMERSET beat Nottinghamshire by nine wickets.
1983 MIDDLESEX beat Essex by 4 runs.
1984 LANCASHIRE beat Warwickshire by six wickets.
1985 LEICESTERSHIRE beat Essex by five wickets.
1986 MIDDLESEX beat Kent by 2 runs.
1987 YORKSHIRE beat Northamptonshire, having taken more wickets with the scores tied.
1988 HAMPSHIRE beat Derbyshire by seven wickets.
1989 NOTTINGHAMSHIRE beat Essex by three wickets.
1990 LANCASHIRE beat Worcestershire by 69 runs.

WINS BY UNIVERSITIES

1973 OXFORD beat Northamptonshire at Northampton by two wickets.
1975 { OXFORD & CAMBRIDGE beat Worcestershire at Cambridge by 66 runs.
OXFORD & CAMBRIDGE beat Northamptonshire at Oxford by three wickets. }
1976 OXFORD & CAMBRIDGE beat Yorkshire at Barnsley by seven wickets.
1984 OXFORD & CAMBRIDGE beat Gloucestershire at Bristol by 27 runs.
1989 { COMBINED UNIVERSITIES beat Surrey at Cambridge by 9 runs.
COMBINED UNIVERSITIES beat Worcestershire at Worcester by five wickets. }
1990 COMBINED UNIVERSITIES beat Yorkshire at Leeds by two wickets.

WINS BY MINOR COUNTIES AND SCOTLAND

1980 MINOR COUNTIES beat Gloucestershire at Chippenham by 3 runs.
1981 MINOR COUNTIES beat Hampshire at Southampton by 3 runs.
1982 MINOR COUNTIES beat Leicestershire at Wellington by 131 runs.
1986 SCOTLAND beat Lancashire at Perth by 3 runs.
1987 MINOR COUNTIES beat Glamorgan at Oxford (Christ Church) by seven wickets.
1990 SCOTLAND beat Northamptonshire at Northampton by 2 runs.

REFUGE ASSURANCE LEAGUE, 1990

Derbyshire, putting behind them defeat in two days in the County Championship by Essex on the preceding Thursday and Friday, and also the fact that they had not beaten Essex in any competition since 1982, beat them by five wickets at Derby on the last day of the Sunday League season to win the Refuge Assurance Trophy. It was only their third trophy in 120 years, following the County Championship in 1936 and the NatWest Bank Trophy in 1981, and they became the eleventh county to win the Sunday title.

Having begun with four victories in their first five games, Derbyshire had shared the early lead with Kent and Middlesex and, with games in hand, had returned to the top of the table, alongside Middlesex, in mid-July. So closely contested was the competition that if Derbyshire had not taken all four points from their last game, Lancashire would have won the title on away wins by beating Warwickshire. Had Derbyshire and Lancashire both lost on August 26, and Middlesex beaten Yorkshire, Middlesex would have been champions on run-rate. Instead Middlesex, who won nine of their first ten games, lost at Scarborough, their fourth defeat in six games, one of which failed to produce a result.

Lancashire, who began the season by losing to Middlesex, could reflect on two matches lost to the weather. Victory in either would have won them the trophy. Their only other defeats were at the hands of Gloucestershire, when Michael Atherton, Neil Fairbrother and Phillip DeFreitas were away on England duty, and Derbyshire, when they were without the first two.

Continued over

REFUGE ASSURANCE LEAGUE

	P	*W*	*L*	*T*	*NR*	*Pts*	*Away Wins*	*Run-Rate*
1 – Derbyshire (5)	16	12	3	0	1	50	6	87.354
2 – Lancashire (1)	15	11	3	0	2	48	7	100.186
3 – Middlesex (9)	16	10	5	0	1	42	5	95.400
4 – Nottinghamshire (4)	16	10	5	0	1	42	4	89.312
5 – Hampshire (6)	16	9	5	0	2	40	4	88.827
6 { Yorkshire (11)	15	9	6	0	1	38	4	83.607
Surrey (6)	15	9	6	0	1	38	3	90.393
8 { Somerset (10)	16	8	8	0	0	32	4	91.254
Gloucestershire (16)	16	7	7	0	2	32	2	87.807
10 { Worcestershire (2)	16	7	8	0	1	30	4	84.964
Kent (11)	15	7	8	0	1	30	3	85.949
12 – Essex (3)	15	6	9	0	1	26	3	90.560
13 – Sussex (11)	14	5	9	0	2	24	2	85.906
14 – Warwickshire (14)	16	5	10	0	1	22	2	80.694
15 { Glamorgan (16)	15	4	11	0	1	18	2	84.208
Leicestershire (14)	16	4	11	0	1	18	1	76.590
17 – Northamptonshire (6)	16	3	12	0	1	14	1	86.406

1989 positions in brackets.

When two or more counties finish with an equal number of points for any of the first four places, the positions are decided by a) most wins, b) most away wins, c) runs per 100 balls.

No play was possible in the following four matches: June 3 – Sussex v Lancashire at Horsham; June 24 – Glamorgan v Yorkshire at Newport; August 19 – Essex v Surrey at Chelmsford, Kent v Sussex at Canterbury.

Derbyshire, it should be added, were without Devon Malcolm and John Morris, with the England team at The Oval, for the crucial match against Essex.

Kent's position in the final table hides the fact that in mid-season they were the front-runners alongside Derbyshire and Middlesex, boasting seven wins from eight games. But defeat by Warwickshire on June 24 began a downhill run that produced just two more points from eight games. Surrey and Yorkshire, on the other hand, operated in a reverse fashion. Yorkshire, taking 30 points from their last nine games, and Surrey 26 from their last eight, could look back from joint sixth to early-season occupation of the bottom rungs. Essex, third in 1989, also made a poor start, losing their first four games. Nottinghamshire, inconsistent in midsummer, found winning form in the last fortnight of July to finish fourth in the table and qualify for the Refuge Assurance Cup.

Derbyshire's captain, Kim Barnett, led from the front, scoring 699 runs at 43.68, but he was the only Derbyshire batsman to reach 500. With Simon Base and Adrian Kuiper their leading wicket-takers with nineteen apiece, theirs was very much a team effort. In contrast, Middlesex and Nottinghamshire each had three batsmen with more than 500 runs: Desmond Haynes (632), Mark Ramprakash (615) and Mike Roseberry (575); Paul Johnson (666), Chris Broad (558) and Tim Robinson (514). Graeme Fowler and Graham Lloyd topped Lancashire's batting with 773, a county record, and 512 runs respectively.

The season's leading batsman, however, was the prolific Somerset opener, Jimmy Cook, who with 902 runs at 64.42 set a new aggregate for a Sunday League season, comfortably passing C. E. B. Rice's record of 814 in 1977. Tim Curtis of Worcestershire was the next highest with 784 runs at 60.30. The top wicket-taker was the young Pakistani fast bowler, Waqar Younis, who in his first season of county cricket claimed 31 wickets at 12.77 in twelve games for Surrey, including a best of five for 26 against Kent at The Oval. His strike-rate was a wicket every sixteen balls. After him came Middlesex's John Emburey with 30 at 19.60 apiece. Peter Bowler held 22 catches and made one stumping in thirteen games as Derbyshire's wicket-keeper, while the Gloucestershire captain, Tony Wright (13), and Hampshire's Paul Terry (11) held the most catches, other than those by the wicket-keepers.

After a season when it was 22 yards, the limit on the bowler's run-up in League matches returned to 15 yards in 1990.

DISTRIBUTION OF PRIZEMONEY

Team awards

£24,000 and Refuge Assurance Trophy: DERBYSHIRE.
£12,000 to runners-up: LANCASHIRE.
£6,000 for third place: MIDDLESEX.
£3,000 for fourth place: NOTTINGHAMSHIRE.
£275 each match to the winner – shared if tied or no result.

Individual awards

£300 for highest innings: G. D. Rose (Somerset), 148 v Glamorgan at Neath.
£300 for best bowling: shared by P. W. Jarvis (Yorkshire), five for 18 v Derbyshire at Leeds, and D. V. Lawrence (Gloucestershire) five for 18 v Somerset at Bristol.

DERBYSHIRE

At Hove, April 22. DERBYSHIRE beat SUSSEX by six wickets.

DERBYSHIRE v WORCESTERSHIRE

At Derby, April 29. Derbyshire won by 35 runs. Toss: Worcestershire.

Derbyshire

*K. J. Barnett st Rhodes b Illingworth	66	A. E. Warner run out	5
†P. D. Bowler lbw b Illingworth	40	D. E. Malcolm not out	0
J. E. Morris run out	3	L-b 5, w 8	13
A. P. Kuiper c Leatherdale b Newport	17		
C. J. Adams b Illingworth	26	1/97 2/117 3/117 (7 wkts, 40 overs)	193
B. Roberts b Radford	9	4/162 5/166	
G. Miller not out	14	6/178 7/189	

S. J. Base and O. H. Mortensen did not bat.

Bowling: Newport 8–0–30–1; Botham 8–0–27–0; Radford 6–0–26–1; Illingworth 8–0–41–3; McEwan 8–0–42–0; Hick 2–0–22–0.

Worcestershire

T. S. Curtis c Morris b Mortensen	7	R. K. Illingworth c Bowler b Base	8
I. T. Botham c Bowler b Mortensen	15	P. J. Newport not out	12
G. A. Hick c Adams b Kuiper	46	S. M. McEwan b Base	5
D. B. D'Oliveira c Adams b Base	10	L-b 6, w 5	11
*P. A. Neale c Warner b Base	40		
D. A. Leatherdale lbw b Warner	2	1/11 2/40 3/57 (37.5 overs)	158
†S. J. Rhodes c Roberts b Miller	2	4/95 5/98 6/105	
N. V. Radford c Adams b Miller	0	7/105 8/141 9/144	

Bowling: Malcolm 7–0–32–0; Mortensen 8–3–15–2; Warner 8–0–28–1; Base 5.5–0–32–4; Kuiper 4–0–23–1; Miller 5–2–22–2.

Umpires: J. H. Hampshire and B. J. Meyer.

At Northampton, May 6. DERBYSHIRE beat NORTHAMPTONSHIRE by four wickets.

At Leeds, May 13. DERBYSHIRE lost to YORKSHIRE by six wickets.

At Taunton, May 20. DERBYSHIRE beat SOMERSET by seven wickets.

DERBYSHIRE v NOTTINGHAMSHIRE

At Derby, June 10. Nottinghamshire won by four wickets. Toss: Nottinghamshire. Following a brief stoppage for bad light, Nottinghamshire were set a revised target of 216 off 38 overs. Robinson's 116 came off 110 balls and contained two sixes and five fours.

Derbyshire

*K. J. Barnett c French b Evans 63
†P. D. Bowler b M. Saxelby 45
J. E. Morris c Evans b K. Saxelby 32
A. P. Kuiper c French b Stephenson . . 46
B. Roberts not out 26
C. J. Adams b Stephenson 0
S. C. Goldsmith not out 0
L-b 13, w 2 15

1/112 2/116 3/189 4/214 5/216 (5 wkts, 40 overs) 227

A. E. Warner, G. Miller, M. Jean-Jacques and S. J. Base did not bat.

Bowling: K. Saxelby 8–0–53–1; Cooper 8–1–29–0; Stephenson 8–0–43–2; Evans 8–0–39–1; Afford 3–0–26–0; M. Saxelby 5–0–24–1.

Nottinghamshire

B. C. Broad c Bowler b Jean-Jacques . . 11
D. W. Randall c Kuiper b Warner 21
P. Johnson c Bowler b Base 0
*R. T. Robinson run out 116
M. Saxelby c Kuiper b Jean-Jacques . . . 34
F. D. Stephenson c Kuiper b Jean-Jacques . 6
†B. N. French not out 17
K. E. Cooper not out 1
L-b 7, w 6 13

1/23 2/25 3/50 4/151 5/158 6/214 (6 wkts, 38 overs) 219

K. Saxelby, K. P. Evans and J. A. Afford did not bat.

Bowling: Jean-Jacques 8–0–47–3; Base 8–0–52–1; Warner 6–0–39–1; Miller 8–0–34–0; Barnett 8–0–40–0.

Umpires: J. W. Holder and N. T. Plews.

DERBYSHIRE v WARWICKSHIRE

At Derby, June 17. Derbyshire won by 1 run. Toss: Warwickshire. Small, needing to hit the last ball for six to win the match, could manage only a four.

Derbyshire

*K. J. Barnett c Asif Din b Pierson . . . 19
†P. D. Bowler c Pierson b Twose 0
J. E. Morris c Ostler b Twose 4
A. P. Kuiper c Ostler b Pierson 37
B. Roberts lbw b Small 9
C. J. Adams not out 58
S. C. Goldsmith b Smith 50
A. E. Warner c Munton b Smith 6
D. E. Malcolm c Moles b Moody 0
S. J. Base not out 0
L-b 15, w 4, n-b 1 20

1/2 2/10 3/36 4/58 5/77 6/184 7/191 8/191 (8 wkts, 40 overs) 203

G. Miller did not bat.

Bowling: Munton 8–0–25–0; Twose 8–2–11–2; Pierson 8–0–24–2; Small 8–1–53–1; Smith 4–0–37–2; Moody 4–0–38–1.

Warwickshire

A. J. Moles b Malcolm 81
Asif Din c Bowler b Base 11
T. M. Moody run out 45
†G. W. Humpage c Bowler b Kuiper . . 0
*D. A. Reeve b Base 31
D. P. Ostler not out 7
R. G. Twose c Bowler b Kuiper 9
G. C. Small not out 4
B 2, l-b 9, w 3 14

1/27 2/129 3/130 4/181 5/181 6/198 (6 wkts, 40 overs) 202

G. Smith, A. R. K. Pierson and T. A. Munton did not bat.

Bowling: Base 8–1–32–2; Malcolm 8–0–33–1; Miller 8–0–38–0; Warner 8–0–35–0; Kuiper 8–0–53–2.

Umpires: J. H. Hampshire and A. G. T. Whitehead.

At The Oval, June 24. DERBYSHIRE beat SURREY by three wickets.

DERBYSHIRE v GLOUCESTERSHIRE

At Derby, July 1. Derbyshire won by six wickets. Toss: Derbyshire. With no play possible until 3.30, the match was reduced to 27 overs a side.

Gloucestershire

†R. C. Russell c Roberts b Mortensen . 5
C. W. J. Athey c Bowler b Mortensen . 17
*A. J. Wright c Goldsmith b Mortensen 17
P. Bainbridge run out 21
K. M. Curran run out 4
P. W. Romaines run out 2
J. W. Lloyds c and b Kuiper 21
M. W. Alleyne lbw b Base 7
G. D. Hodgson not out 5
C. A. Walsh not out 15
B 5, l-b 10, w 4 19

1/12 2/42 3/48 4/55 5/59 6/89 7/105 8/106 (8 wkts, 27 overs) 133

D. V. Lawrence did not bat.

Bowling: Malcolm 5–0–16–0; Mortensen 6–0–16–3; Miller 5–0–26–0; Base 6–0–25–1; Kuiper 5–1–35–1.

Derbyshire

*K. J. Barnett c Hodgson b Lloyds 57
†P. D. Bowler c Lawrence b Curran . . . 5
J. E. Morris run out 57
A. P. Kuiper c Hodgson b Lloyds 0
B. Roberts not out 5
C. J. Adams not out 2
B 1, l-b 4, w 3 8

1/18 2/125 3/125 4/125 (4 wkts, 26.3 overs) 134

S. C. Goldsmith, S. J. Base, G. Miller, D. E. Malcolm and O. H. Mortensen did not bat.

Bowling: Walsh 6–0–19–0; Lawrence 2–0–18–0; Curran 6–0–20–1; Bainbridge 5–0–27–0; Alleyne 5–0–32–0; Lloyds 2.3–0–13–2.

Umpires: J. W. Holder and B. Leadbeater.

At Manchester, July 8. DERBYSHIRE beat LANCASHIRE by 5 runs.

DERBYSHIRE v LEICESTERSHIRE

At Knypersley, July 15. Derbyshire won by 118 runs. Toss: Derbyshire. Derbyshire's victory took them back to first place in the League, equal with Middlesex but with a game in hand.

Derbyshire

*K. J. Barnett c Nixon b Mullally 39
†P. D. Bowler c Nixon b Benjamin 4
J. E. Morris c Nixon b Lewis 21
A. P. Kuiper c Benjamin b Agnew 42
B. Roberts not out 77
C. J. Adams b Benjamin 9
S. C. Goldsmith not out 4
L-b 13, w 10, n-b 3 26

1/16 2/66 3/71 4/158 5/206 (5 wkts, 40 overs) 222

D. E. Malcolm, S. J. Base, A. E. Warner and O. H. Mortensen did not bat.

Bowling: Benjamin 8–0–32–2; Agnew 8–1–52–1; Lewis 8–0–43–1; Mullally 8–1–37–1; Willey 8–0–45–0.

Leicestershire

T. J. Boon c Bowler b Base	2
*N. E. Briers lbw b Warner	29
J. J. Whitaker c Roberts b Malcolm	12
P. Willey c Bowler b Malcolm	24
C. C. Lewis run out	0
L. Potter b Barnett	6
J. D. R. Benson c Morris b Warner	1
W. K. M. Benjamin b Malcolm	11
†P. A. Nixon c Adams b Warner	4
J. P. Agnew b Malcolm	0
A. D. Mullally not out	5
L-b 4, w 5, n-b 1	10
1/6 2/33 3/55 4/58 5/79 6/81 7/83 8/98 9/98	(28 overs) 104

Bowling: Base 5–0–20–1; Mortensen 6–0–18–0; Malcolm 6–0–21–4; Warner 5–0–18–3; Goldsmith 3–0–14–0; Barnett 3–0–9–1.

Umpires: D. O. Oslear and R. A. White.

At Portsmouth, July 22. DERBYSHIRE lost to HAMPSHIRE by 189 runs.

At Swansea, July 29. DERBYSHIRE beat GLAMORGAN by six wickets.

DERBYSHIRE v KENT

At Chesterfield, August 5. Derbyshire won by six wickets. Toss: Derbyshire. Barnett's 127 came off 101 balls and contained two sixes and thirteen fours.

Kent

S. G. Hinks c Morris b Miller	50
M. R. Benson run out	4
N. R. Taylor c Roberts b Kuiper	78
T. R. Ward c Warner b Kuiper	80
G. R. Cowdrey not out	36
M. V. Fleming not out	15
L-b 6, w 7	13
1/8 2/80 3/210 4/249	(4 wkts, 40 overs) 276

*C. S. Cowdrey, †S. A. Marsh, T. A. Merrick, R. P. Davis and A. P. Igglesden did not bat.

Bowling: Warner 8–0–59–0; Mortensen 8–2–23–0; Malcolm 8–0–55–0; Miller 8–0–59–1; Kuiper 8–0–74–2.

Derbyshire

*K. J. Barnett run out	127
†P. D. Bowler b Fleming	54
J. E. Morris c C. S. Cowdrey b Igglesden	45
A. P. Kuiper not out	22
T. J. G. O'Gorman b Davis	11
B. Roberts not out	11
B 4, l-b 2, w 1	7
1/146 2/232 3/234 4/259	(4 wkts, 38.2 overs) 27[illegible]

C. J. Adams, A. E. Warner, G. Miller, O. H. Mortensen and D. E. Malcolm did not bat.

Bowling: Igglesden 7.2–0–54–1; Merrick 7–0–43–0; C. S. Cowdrey 8–0–50–0; Fleming 8–0–60–1; Davis 8–0–64–1.

Umpires: J. H. Hampshire and B. Hassan.

DERBYSHIRE v MIDDLESEX

At Derby, August 19. No result. Toss: Middlesex. Rain, which had reduced the match to fourteen overs a side, ended play before a result could be achieved.

Derbyshire

*K. J. Barnett c Haynes b Williams	5	T. J. G. O'Gorman not out	0
†P. D. Bowler b Fraser	50	B 3, n-b 1	4
J. E. Morris c Roseberry b Cowans	48		
A. P. Kuiper lbw b Emburey	18	1/29 2/100 3/116 (5 wkts, 14 overs)	128
C. J. Adams run out	3	4/128 5/128	

B. Roberts, A. E. Warner, S. J. Base, D. E. Malcolm and O. H. Mortensen did not bat.

Bowling: Cowans 2–0–26–1; Williams 3–0–27–1; Hughes 3–0–18–0; Emburey 3–0–30–1; Fraser 3–0–24–1.

Middlesex

D. L. Haynes not out	48
M. A. Roseberry c Bowler b Warner	0
*M. W. Gatting run out	7
M. R. Ramprakash not out	26
L-b 1, w 2, n-b 1	4
1/1 2/10 (2 wkts, 9.2 overs)	85

K. R. Brown, †P. R. Downton, J. E. Emburey, N. F. Williams, S. P. Hughes, A. R. C. Fraser and N. G. Cowans did not bat.

Bowling: Warner 3–0–20–1; Mortensen 3–0–22–0; Malcolm 2–0–17–0; Kuiper 1–0–15–0; Base 0.2–0–10–0.

Umpires: J. C. Balderstone and P. B. Wight.

DERBYSHIRE v ESSEX

At Derby, August 26. Derbyshire won by five wickets. Toss: Essex. Derbyshire won the Refuge Assurance League when they beat Essex for the first time in any competition since 1982. Kuiper's half-century came off 31 balls and included a six and six fours.

Essex

*B. R. Hardie b Warner	76	N. Shahid not out	9
J. P. Stephenson c Barnett b Mortensen	3	B 1, l-b 11, w 7	19
M. E. Waugh c Adams b Kuiper	59		
P. J. Prichard c Mortensen b Kuiper	25	1/7 2/133 3/177 (4 wkts, 40 overs)	203
N. Hussain not out	12	4/185	

P. M. Such, †M. A. Garnham, J. H. Childs, M. C. Ilott and S. J. W. Andrew did not bat.

Bowling: Mortensen 8–2–10–1; Warner 8–0–36–1; Base 8–0–33–0; Jean-Jacques 6–0–47–0; Goldsmith 4–0–25–0; Kuiper 6–0–40–2.

Derbyshire

*K. J. Barnett c Garnham b Ilott	7	S. C. Goldsmith not out	5
†P. D. Bowler c Stephenson b Childs	43		
B. Roberts lbw b Waugh	45	B 1, l-b 6, w 5	12
A. P. Kuiper c Prichard b Waugh	56		
T. J. G. O'Gorman c Such b Ilott	12	1/19 2/98 3/116 (5 wkts, 39.3 overs)	207
C. J. Adams not out	27	4/168 5/179	

M. Jean-Jacques, A. E. Warner, S. J. Base and O. H. Mortensen did not bat.

Bowling: Andrew 8–0–53–0; Ilott 7.3–0–41–2; Such 8–0–28–0; Childs 8–0–38–1; Waugh 8–0–40–2.

Umpires: D. J. Constant and R. Julian.

ESSEX

ESSEX v KENT

At Chelmsford, April 22. Kent won by 27 runs. Toss: Essex. In the Kent innings, Foster captured his four wickets in eight balls while conceding just 1 run.

Kent

S. G. Hinks b Childs	50	M. V. Fleming not out	24
N. R. Taylor c Pringle b Childs	58	†S. A. Marsh not out	27
T. R. Ward c Garnham b Foster	13	B 1, l-b 14, w 8, n-b 3	26
*C. S. Cowdrey b Foster	11		—
G. R. Cowdrey c Garnham b Foster	6	1/98 2/122 3/145 (6 wkts, 40 overs)	215
R. M. Ellison b Foster	0	4/153 5/153 6/154	

M. A. Ealham, C. Penn and T. A. Merrick did not bat.

Bowling: Foster 8–1–21–4; Topley 8–0–38–0; Waugh 5–0–32–0; Gooch 5–0–28–0; Pringle 8–0–43–0; Childs 6–0–38–2.

Essex

*G. A. Gooch c Ealham b Merrick	3	N. A. Foster c Ellison b Merrick	6
B. R. Hardie run out	56	T. D. Topley not out	3
M. E. Waugh c Taylor b Fleming	50	J. H. Childs b Penn	2
P. J. Prichard c Ealham b Ellison	18	L-b 8, w 2	10
D. R. Pringle b Ellison	15		—
J. P. Stephenson b Penn	5	1/5 2/116 3/121 (39 overs)	188
A. W. Lilley b Merrick	10	4/151 5/152 6/159	
†M. A. Garnham b Merrick	10	7/171 8/181 9/183	

Bowling: Penn 8–1–30–2; Merrick 7–0–24–4; Ealham 8–0–29–0; Fleming 8–0–43–1; C. S. Cowdrey 1–0–9–0; Ellison 7–0–45–2.

Umpires: D. O. Oslear and N. T. Plews.

At Lord's, April 29. ESSEX lost to MIDDLESEX by 12 runs.

At Leicester, May 6. ESSEX lost to LEICESTERSHIRE by five wickets.

ESSEX v GLOUCESTERSHIRE

At Chelmsford, May 13. Gloucestershire won by seven wickets. Toss: Gloucestershire. For their first victory of the season in any competition, Gloucestershire were indebted to Athey, whose century came off 132 balls.

Essex

*G. A. Gooch lbw b Bainbridge	56	†M. A. Garnham not out	24
B. R. Hardie st Russell b Alleyne	42	N. A. Foster not out	11
M. E. Waugh b Bainbridge	1	B 1, l-b 6, w 5	12
P. J. Prichard c Wright b Alleyne	21		—
D. R. Pringle c Romaines b Alleyne	21	1/94 2/97 3/120 (6 wkts, 40 overs)	211
J. P. Stephenson run out	23	4/144 5/153 6/182	

T. D. Topley, J. H. Childs and M. C. Ilott did not bat.

Bowling: Walsh 8–0–42–0; Jarvis 6–0–30–0; Curran 8–0–43–0; Alleyne 6–1–25–3; Bainbridge 8–0–46–2; Ball 4–0–18–0.

Gloucestershire

R. C. Russell c Topley b Foster 62
C. W. J. Athey not out 101
. W. Lloyds c and b Foster 10
*A. J. Wright c Prichard b Pringle 20
K. M. Curran not out 5
L-b 9, w 5, n-b 3 17

1/137 2/158 3/208 (3 wkts, 39.1 overs) 215

. W. Romaines, P. Bainbridge, M. W. Alleyne, C. A. Walsh, K. B. S. Jarvis and M. C. J. Ball did not bat.

Bowling: Ilott 8–0–34–0; Foster 8–0–22–2; Pringle 7.1–0–49–1; Topley 8–0–51–0; Childs –0–35–0; Stephenson 2–0–15–0.

Umpires: P. J. Eele and A. G. T. Whitehead.

At Worcester, May 20. ESSEX beat WORCESTERSHIRE by two wickets.

ESSEX v GLAMORGAN

At Ilford, June 3. Essex won by six wickets. Toss: Essex. The match was reduced to fifteen overs a side after rain had delayed the start until 5.05 p.m. Prichard won it for Essex with a four off the last ball.

Glamorgan

M. P. Maynard b Topley 75
H. Morris c and b Pringle 18
I. V. A. Richards c and b Topley 0
I. Smith c Gooch b Pringle 8
*A. R. Butcher c Stephenson b Foster . 1
G. C. Holmes not out 14
†C. P. Metson b Waugh 1
S. J. Dennis b Waugh 3
S. L. Watkin not out 1
W 4, n-b 6 10

1/95 2/95 3/104 4/111 5/115 6/119 7/123 (7 wkts, 15 overs) 131

S. R. Barwick and M. Frost did not bat.

Bowling: Andrew 3–0–38–0; Foster 3–0–33–1; Topley 3–0–23–2; Waugh 3–0–19–2; Pringle 3–0–18–2.

Essex

*G. A. Gooch run out 58
B. R. Hardie c Butcher b Barwick 30
M. E. Waugh b Frost 12
P. J. Prichard not out 23
D. R. Pringle run out 9
N. A. Foster not out 0
L-b 2, w 1 3

1/75 2/97 3/106 4/129 (4 wkts, 15 overs) 135

J. P. Stephenson, A. W. Lilley, †M. A. Garnham, T. D. Topley and S. J. W. Andrew did not bat.

Bowling: Frost 3–0–26–1; Watkin 3–0–19–0; Dennis 3–0–23–0; Richards 3–0–31–0; Barwick 3–0–34–1.

Umpires: B. Leadbeater and B. J. Meyer.

At Birmingham, June 10. ESSEX beat WARWICKSHIRE by seven wickets.

At Bath, June 17. ESSEX beat SOMERSET by 101 runs.

At Southampton, July 8. ESSEX lost to HAMPSHIRE by seven wickets.

ESSEX v NORTHAMPTONSHIRE

At Chelmsford, July 15. Essex won by six wickets. Toss: Essex. Fourteen deliveries were hit out of the ground during the match, including three in succession by Bailey off Topley.

Northamptonshire

A. Fordham run out	74	†D. Ripley not out	3
W. Larkins c Gooch b Foster	6		
D. J. Capel c Garnham b Ilott	56	L-b 7, w 5	12
*A. J. Lamb c Prichard b Pringle	34		
R. J. Bailey c Hussain b Topley	26	1/15 2/141 3/147 (7 wkts, 40 overs)	233
D. J. Wild c and b Pringle	20	4/188 5/226	
W. W. Davis c Ilott b Waugh	2	6/227 7/233	

N. G. B. Cook, M. A. Robinson and S. J. Brown did not bat.

Bowling: Foster 8–1–36–1; Ilott 8–0–17–1; Topley 5–0–34–1; Childs 6–0–38–0; Pringle 8–0–59–2; Waugh 5–0–42–1.

Essex

*G. A. Gooch run out	0	†M. A. Garnham not out	29
J. P. Stephenson c Fordham b Wild	66	L-b 7, w 1	8
M. E. Waugh b Cook	53		
N. Hussain b Bailey	22	1/0 2/111 3/139 (4 wkts, 38.2 overs)	239
D. R. Pringle not out	61	4/158	

P. J. Prichard, N. A. Foster, T. D. Topley, J. H. Childs and M. C. Ilott did not bat.

Bowling: Robinson 7–1–46–0; Davis 8–0–38–0; Cook 8–0–42–1; Brown 5.2–0–39–0; Wild 5–0–36–1; Bailey 5–0–31–1.

Umpires: M. J. Kitchen and D. S. Thompsett.

ESSEX v LANCASHIRE

At Colchester, July 22. Lancashire won by two wickets. Toss: Lancashire. Stephenson, who a week earlier had scored his maiden Sunday League fifty, made 109 off 122 balls, including one six and six fours. He put on 214 for the second wicket with Waugh, who struck a total of twelve fours and reached his hundred off 79 balls. Atherton's hundred, also his first in the competition, featured one six and ten fours.

Essex

*G. A. Gooch lbw b Allott	1	B. R. Hardie not out	2
J. P. Stephenson c Hughes b Austin	109		
M. E. Waugh b DeFreitas	111	L-b 2, w 3, n-b 2	7
D. R. Pringle run out	1		
N. Hussain b Wasim Akram	12	1/8 2/222 3/225 (5 wkts, 40 overs)	247
N. A. Foster not out	4	4/234 5/245	

N. Shahid, †M. A. Garnham, M. C. Ilott and J. H. Childs did not bat.

Bowling: DeFreitas 8–0–38–1; Allott 8–0–40–1; Watkinson 8–0–47–0; Wasim Akram 8–0–53–1; Austin 8–0–67–1.

Lancashire

G. Fowler c Hardie b Ilott	5	†W. K. Hegg not out	24
M. A. Atherton b Pringle	111	*D. P. Hughes not out	8
G. D. Lloyd c Shahid b Pringle	30		
N. H. Fairbrother run out	23	L-b 10, w 6	16
M. Watkinson c Garnham b Foster	1		
Wasim Akram b Ilott	3	1/9 2/84 3/145 (8 wkts, 39.5 overs)	249
P. A. J. DeFreitas c Pringle b Foster	18	4/156 5/169 6/198	
I. D. Austin c Hussain b Pringle	10	7/212 8/221	

P. J. W. Allott did not bat.

Bowling: Foster 8–0–42–2; Ilott 8–0–44–2; Gooch 3–0–24–0; Childs 8–0–37–0; Pringle 7.5–0–47–3; Waugh 5–0–45–0.

Umpires: P. J. Eele and N. T. Plews.

ESSEX v SUSSEX

At Chelmsford, July 29. Essex won by two wickets. Toss: Sussex. Essex, needing 8 runs off the last over with four wickets in hand, lost Garnham and Topley to Hansford in five balls. Childs, however, drove the final delivery past the bowler for four to win the match.

Sussex

D. M. Smith b Topley	0	A. C. S. Pigott lbw b Pringle	30
J. J. Gould c and b Such	56	†P. Moores not out	2
*P. W. G. Parker c Such b Topley	72	B 2, l-b 7, w 3, n-b 6	18
A. P. Wells c Foster b Such	6		
C. M. Wells c Hussain b Childs	28	1/8 2/103 3/124 (6 wkts, 39 overs)	238
A. I. C. Dodemaide not out	26	4/172 5/187 6/233	

R. A. Bunting, A. R. Hansford and B. T. P. Donelan did not bat.

Bowling: Foster 8–0–43–0; Topley 8–0–43–2; Childs 8–2–47–1; Such 8–0–43–2; Pringle 7–0–53–1.

Essex

B. R. Hardie run out	44	T. D. Topley b Hansford	0
N. Shahid c Parker b Pigott	31	J. H. Childs not out	4
M. E. Waugh b Pigott	28		
P. J. Prichard run out	64		
*D. R. Pringle c Moores b Donelan	15	L-b 4, w 6, n-b 2	12
N. Hussain not out	32		
N. A. Foster c Smith b Dodemaide	5	1/76 2/93 3/130 (8 wkts, 39 overs)	241
†M. A. Garnham c Dodemaide b Hansford	6	4/171 5/214 6/225 7/234 8/237	

P. M. Such did not bat.

Bowling: Dodemaide 8–0–51–1; C. M. Wells 6–1–27–0; Hansford 8–0–62–2; Donelan 8–0–43–1; Pigott 8–0–42–2; Bunting 1–0–12–0.

Umpires: D. O. Oslear and K. E. Palmer.

ESSEX v NOTTINGHAMSHIRE

At Southend, August 5. Nottinghamshire won by six wickets. Toss: Nottinghamshire. Gooch faced just 106 balls for his 136, which contained fifteen fours. Newell's unbeaten hundred, which anchored Nottinghamshire to victory, was his first in the competition.

Essex

*G. A. Gooch c Johnson b Cooper	136	T. D. Topley b Evans	2
J. P. Stephenson c Randall b Hemmings	50	M. C. Ilott run out	3
M. E. Waugh c Newell b Hemmings	7	J. H. Childs not out	1
P. J. Prichard c Johnson b Stephenson	4	L-b 6, w 1, n-b 1	8
N. Hussain c French b Mike	5		
N. Shahid c Mike b Stephenson	8	1/147 2/158 3/178 (38.4 overs)	239
N. A. Foster c Newell b Stephenson	10	4/192 5/212 6/221	
†M. A. Garnham b Evans	5	7/229 8/233 9/238	

Bowling: Cooper 8–0–49–1; Stephenson 8–0–28–3; Evans 7.4–0–52–2; Mike 7–0–68–1; Hemmings 8–0–36–2.

Nottinghamshire

B. C. Broad b Gooch 35
M. Newell not out 109
P. Johnson c Hussain b Topley 48
*R. T. Robinson c and b Foster 4
D. W. Randall run out 9
F. D. Stephenson not out 26
L-b 7, w 1, n-b 1 9

1/61 2/154 3/160 4/184 (4 wkts, 38.3 overs) 240

K. P. Evans, †B. N. French, E. E. Hemmings, K. E. Cooper and G. W. Mike did not bat.

Bowling: Ilott 7.3–0–41–0; Foster 8–0–50–1; Gooch 8–0–34–1; Childs 6–0–43–0; Topley 7–0–45–1; Waugh 2–0–20–0.

Umpires: J. C. Balderstone and J. H. Harris.

At Middlesbrough, August 12. ESSEX lost to YORKSHIRE by 59 runs.

ESSEX v SURREY

At Chelmsford, August 19. No result.

At Derby, August 26. ESSEX lost to DERBYSHIRE by five wickets.

GLAMORGAN

At Bristol, April 22. GLAMORGAN beat GLOUCESTERSHIRE by 5 runs.

GLAMORGAN v LEICESTERSHIRE

At Cardiff, April 29. Glamorgan won by 32 runs. Toss: Leicestershire.

Glamorgan

A. Dale b Benjamin 3
H. Morris c Boon b Benjamin 13
M. P. Maynard c Whitticase b Taylor . 22
I. V. A. Richards b Taylor 59
*A. R. Butcher c Potter b Agnew 17
I. Smith run out 35
N. G. Cowley c Whitticase b Taylor ... 0
†C. P. Metson c Briers b Mullally 11
S. J. Dennis run out 7
M. Frost not out 0
S. R. Barwick not out 0
L-b 8, w 5, n-b 2 15

1/15 2/39 3/43 4/90 5/131 6/131 7/165 8/180 9/182 (9 wkts, 40 overs) 182

Bowling: Parsons 8–0–53–0; Benjamin 8–1–26–2; Taylor 8–0–34–3; Agnew 8–1–20–1; Mullally 8–0–41–1.

Leicestershire

T. J. Boon c Smith b Frost 2
*N. E. Briers c Richards b Cowley 37
J. J. Whitaker c Morris b Frost 72
L. Potter lbw b Cowley 6
J. D. R. Benson c Richards b Barwick . 3
†P. Whitticase run out 2
W. K. M. Benjamin c Morris b Dale .. 5
G. J. Parsons c Richards b Barwick ... 12
J. P. Agnew c Barwick b Frost 1
A. D. Mullally c and b Richards 2
L. B. Taylor not out 0
L-b 6, w 2 8

1/2 2/79 3/87 4/96 5/114 6/121 7/138 8/142 9/145 (38.1 overs) 150

Bowling: Frost 8–0–30–3; Dennis 6–0–13–0; Barwick 6.1–0–30–2; Cowley 8–0–26–2; Dale 4–0–22–1; Richards 6–1–23–1.

Umpires: M. J. Kitchen and B. Leadbeater.

GLAMORGAN v KENT

At Llanelli, May 13. Kent won by two wickets. Toss: Glamorgan. Needing to score 20 runs from the last over, bowled by Watkin, Kent made 23 from five deliveries. Ealham hit the first for six, a single followed, and then Penn hit two sixes and a four to win the match with a ball to spare. Glamorgan's innings had also finished with a flourish when Smith hit Chris Cowdrey for 20 in the final over.

Glamorgan

H. Morris c Marsh b Penn	0	I. Smith not out	39
G. C. Holmes c Merrick b Fleming	57	N. G. Cowley not out	0
M. P. Maynard c G. R. Cowdrey b Fleming	20	B 5, l-b 2, w 4	11
I. V. A. Richards c Ealham b Fleming	55	1/1 2/41 3/132 (5 wkts, 40 overs)	220
*A. R. Butcher c Taylor b C. S. Cowdrey	38	4/132 5/200	

†C. P. Metson, S. J. Dennis, S. L. Watkin and M. Frost did not bat.

Bowling: Penn 8–0–51–1; Merrick 8–1–32–0; Davis 4–0–27–0; Fleming 7–0–30–3; Ealham 7–1–37–0; C. S. Cowdrey 6–0–36–1.

Kent

S. G. Hinks c Metson b Watkin	74	T. A. Merrick b Frost	8
N. R. Taylor c Metson b Richards	27	C. Penn not out	20
T. R. Ward b Richards	0		
*C. S. Cowdrey c Holmes b Cowley	3	B 1, l-b 15, w 10	26
G. R. Cowdrey c Dennis b Holmes	5		
M. V. Fleming run out	18	1/65 2/65 3/77 (8 wkts, 39.5 overs)	224
†S. A. Marsh b Frost	14	4/124 5/131 6/162	
M. A. Ealham not out	29	7/164 8/177	

R. P. Davis did not bat.

Bowling: Watkin 7.5–1–48–1; Richards 8–0–28–2; Dennis 8–0–28–0; Frost 8–0–45–2; Cowley 3–0–27–1; Holmes 5–0–32–1.

Umpires: J. C. Balderstone and K. J. Lyons.

At Hove, May 20. GLAMORGAN lost to SUSSEX by six wickets.

GLAMORGAN v LANCASHIRE

At Colwyn Bay, May 27. Lancashire won by four wickets. Toss: Lancashire. Maynard, whose partnership with Richards produced 143 runs in eighteen overs, hit eleven fours in his 102-ball century. But even Glamorgan's third-wicket pair were overshadowed by the hitting of Wasim Akram in Lancashire's innings. He hit three sixes and four fours in reaching his half-century off 31 balls.

Glamorgan

H. Morris c Austin b DeFreitas	6	†C. P. Metson not out	5
*A. R. Butcher b Wasim Akram	38	N. G. Cowley b Austin	1
M. P. Maynard c Austin b Wasim Akram	100	L-b 5, w 3, n-b 1	9
I. V. A. Richards c Fairbrother b Austin	77	1/26 2/73 3/216 (6 wkts, 40 overs)	242
I. Smith b Hughes	6	4/224 5/227 6/242	

S. J. Dennis, J. Derrick, S. R. Barwick and M. Frost did not bat.

Bowling: Allott 8–1–28–0; DeFreitas 8–0–42–1; Atherton 7–0–66–0; Wasim Akram 8–0–46–2; Austin 8–0–51–2; Hughes 1–0–4–1.

Lancashire

G. Fowler c Metson b Dennis 2
M. A. Atherton c Maynard b Richards . 74
G. D. Lloyd c Metson b Frost 3
N. H. Fairbrother run out 27
T. E. Jesty c Butcher b Barwick 25
Wasim Akram c Cowley b Frost 50
P. A. J. DeFreitas not out 35
I. D. Austin not out 10
B 5, l-b 7, w 8 20

1/5 2/20 3/113 (6 wkts, 37.5 overs) 246
4/114 5/183 6/211

†W. K. Hegg, *D. P. Hughes and P. J. W. Allott did not bat.

Bowling: Frost 8–0–39–2; Dennis 8–0–38–1; Barwick 8–1–54–1; Derrick 3–0–26–0; Richards 6.5–0–42–1; Cowley 4–0–35–0.

Umpires: J. H. Harris and P. B. Wight.

At Ilford, June 3. GLAMORGAN lost to ESSEX by six wickets.

At Northampton, June 10. GLAMORGAN lost to NORTHAMPTONSHIRE by 10 runs.

At Bournemouth, June 17. GLAMORGAN lost to HAMPSHIRE by 64 runs.

GLAMORGAN v YORKSHIRE

At Newport, June 24. No result. There was no play in the last county match scheduled for the Newport ground, on which it was planned to build a school.

GLAMORGAN v SURREY

At Cardiff, July 1. Glamorgan won by eight wickets. Toss: Glamorgan. The first game having been interrupted by rain after eight deliveries, a second match of ten overs a side was started at 4.57 p.m. In the abandoned match, Surrey were 4 for one, having been put in.

Surrey

M. A. Feltham c and b Watkin 12
†D. M. Ward c Butcher b Watkin 5
M. A. Lynch c Cottey b Frost 38
*I. A. Greig c Richards b Dennis 23
D. J. Bicknell c Richards b Frost 6
G. P. Thorpe not out 11
L-b 2, w 1 3

1/18 2/21 3/73 (5 wkts, 10 overs) 98
4/86 5/98

G. S. Clinton, C. K. Bullen, Waqar Younis, M. P. Bicknell and A. J. Murphy did not bat.

Bowling: Derrick 1–0–12–0; Watkin 2–0–18–2; Dale 2–0–16–0; Richards 1–0–14–0; Dennis 2–0–14–1; Frost 2–0–22–2.

Glamorgan

H. Morris b Waqar Younis 48
M. P. Maynard b Bullen 11
I. V. A. Richards not out 34
*A. R. Butcher not out 0
B 2, l-b 2, w 2 6

1/29 2/94 (2 wkts, 9.5 overs) 99

P. A. Cottey, A. Dale, J. Derrick, †C. P. Metson, S. J. Dennis, S. L. Watkin and M. Frost did not bat.

Bowling: Murphy 2–0–9–0; M. P. Bicknell 2–0–16–0; Feltham 2–0–25–0; Bullen 2–0–28–1; Waqar Younis 1.5–0–17–1.

Umpires: R. A. White and A. G. T. Whitehead.

At Birmingham, July 15. GLAMORGAN beat WARWICKSHIRE by seven wickets.

GLAMORGAN v SOMERSET

At Neath, July 22. Somerset won by 220 runs. Toss: Somerset. Somerset's total passed by 50 runs the previous Sunday League record, achieved by Essex, also against Glamorgan, at Southend in 1983. Their margin of victory was also a record, being 30 runs greater than Kent's 190-run victory over Northamptonshire at Brackley in 1973. Rose, who a month earlier had struck the fastest century in the NatWest Bank Trophy, also set new Sunday League records with the fastest century – off 46 balls – and the fastest fifty – off sixteen. When 54 he was well held by Butcher on the mid-wicket boundary, but in completing the catch the Glamorgan captain stepped on the boundary rope. Rose went on to make 148 off only 69 balls, including eight sixes and seventeen fours, and in nineteen overs he and Cook put on 223 for the third wicket, another record for the competition. Cook, during his highest Refuge League innings (110 balls, two sixes, fifteen fours), passed I. V. A. Richards's Somerset record, set in 1975, of 579 runs in a Sunday League season.

Somerset

S. J. Cook not out ... 136
R. J. Bartlett c Dale b Cowley ... 11
*C. J. Tavaré c Maynard b Dale ... 10
G. D. Rose c Smith b Richards ... 148
R. J. Harden not out ... 32
L-b 5, w 17, n-b 1 ... 23

1/35 2/62 3/285 (3 wkts, 40 overs) 360

†N. D. Burns, A. N. Hayhurst, R. P. Lefebvre, I. G. Swallow, N. A. Mallender and J. C. Hallett did not bat.

Bowling: Watkin 8–0–71–0; Frost 8–0–46–0; Dennis 8–0–67–0; Cowley 5–0–44–1; Dale 3–0–28–1; Richards 7–0–76–1; Maynard 1–0–23–0.

Glamorgan

M. P. Maynard c Swallow b Mallender. 0
H. Morris c Lefebvre b Rose ... 3
I. V. A. Richards b Hallett ... 36
I. Smith run out ... 6
*A. R. Butcher c Tavaré b Hayhurst .. 18
A. Dale c Tavaré b Hallett ... 14
N. G. Cowley c Harden b Hallett ... 10
†C. P. Metson b Hayhurst ... 10
S. L. Watkin b Lefebvre ... 28
S. J. Dennis run out ... 5
M. Frost not out ... 2
L-b 6, w 2 ... 8

1/0 2/6 3/19 4/50 5/81 6/85 7/96 8/108 9/127 (28.5 overs) 140

Bowling: Mallender 5–0–19–1; Rose 5–1–24–1; Hallett 8–0–41–3; Lefebvre 5.5–0–26–1; Hayhurst 5–0–24–2.

Umpires: D. R. Shepherd and D. S. Thompsett.

GLAMORGAN v DERBYSHIRE

At Swansea, July 29. Derbyshire won by six wickets. Toss: Derbyshire. The game was reduced to 34 overs a side after rain interrupted Glamorgan's innings for 50 minutes. At the time they were 55 for one off fifteen overs.

Glamorgan

H. Morris c Bowler b Mortensen ... 16
M. P. Maynard b Warner ... 30
I. V. A. Richards c Bowler b Warner .. 22
*A. R. Butcher c Barnett b Base ... 28
G. C. Holmes c Base b Kuiper ... 21
A. Dale not out ... 13
†C. P. Metson st Bowler b Kuiper ... 9
S. L. Watkin not out ... 2
L-b 3, w 8, n-b 2 ... 13

1/41 2/62 3/80 4/125 5/143 6/152 (6 wkts, 34 overs) 154

S. Bastien, S. J. Dennis and M. Frost did not bat.

Bowling: Base 8–0–40–1; Mortensen 8–0–17–1; Jean-Jacques 8–0–35–0; Goldsmith 1–0–6–0; Kuiper 4–0–27–2; Warner 5–0–26–2.

Derbyshire

*K. J. Barnett c Metson b Bastien	14	C. J. Adams not out	9
†P. D. Bowler not out	52	L-b 10, w 4	14
B. Roberts lbw b Watkin	23		
A. P. Kuiper b Watkin	12	1/19 2/55 3/80 (4 wkts, 32.4 overs)	156
T. J. G. O'Gorman c and b Richards	32	4/141	

S. C. Goldsmith, S. J. Base, A. E. Warner, O. H. Mortensen and M. Jean-Jacques did not bat.

Bowling: Frost 7–2–26–0; Bastien 4–0–21–1; Watkin 8–0–29–2; Dennis 6.4–0–26–0; Dale 3–0–17–0; Richards 4–0–27–1.

Umpires: B. Dudleston and B. Hassan.

At Lord's, August 5. GLAMORGAN lost to MIDDLESEX by 84 runs.

At Nottingham, August 12. GLAMORGAN lost to NOTTINGHAMSHIRE by eight wickets.

GLAMORGAN v WORCESTERSHIRE

At Swansea, August 26. Worcestershire won by 34 runs. Toss: Glamorgan. Curtis's 95 took him to a total of 784 runs in the Sunday League season, a record for Worcestershire. The previous record of 668, scored by Younis Ahmed in 1979, had been passed two weeks earlier by Hick, who finished the season with 751.

Worcestershire

T. S. Curtis c Richards b Dale	95	P. J. Newport st Metson b Dale	0
G. J. Lord lbw b Watkin	7	S. R. Lampitt run out	6
G. A. Hick st Metson b Croft	31		
D. B. D'Oliveira b Richards	14	L-b 15, w 11	26
I. T. Botham b Dale	4		
*P. A. Neale c Croft b Watkin	7	1/17 2/97 3/126 (9 wkts, 40 overs)	214
†S. J. Rhodes not out	23	4/153 5/172 6/188	
R. K. Illingworth run out	1	7/206 8/207 9/214	

S. M. McEwan did not bat.

Bowling: Frost 6–0–32–0; Watkin 7–1–33–2; Dennis 8–0–42–0; Croft 8–0–39–1; Richards 3–0–18–1; Dale 8–0–35–3.

Glamorgan

H. Morris c Illingworth b Newport	7	S. L. Watkin b Lampitt	0
M. P. Maynard c and b Lampitt	36	S. J. Dennis c Neale b Newport	14
I. V. A. Richards c and b Newport	3	M. Frost not out	1
*A. R. Butcher c and b Illingworth	30	L-b 9, w 14, n-b 1	24
P. A. Cottey st Rhodes b Illingworth	8		
A. Dale c D'Oliveira b Hick	34	1/17 2/23 3/85 (37.2 overs)	180
R. D. B. Croft c Hick b McEwan	13	4/87 5/107 6/137	
†C. P. Metson run out	10	7/162 8/162 9/164	

Bowling: McEwan 8–0–52–1; Newport 6.2–1–19–3; Lampitt 7–0–28–2; Illingworth 8–1–19–2; Hick 8–0–53–1.

Umpires: R. Palmer and A. G. T. Whitehead.

GLOUCESTERSHIRE

GLOUCESTERSHIRE v GLAMORGAN

At Bristol, April 22. Glamorgan won by 5 runs. Toss: Gloucestershire.

Glamorgan

G. C. Holmes c Russell b Curran	8	†C. P. Metson not out	0
H. Morris st Russell b Graveney	46		
A. Dale c Wright b Alleyne	42	L-b 5, w 2, n-b 3	10
M. P. Maynard c Athey b Alleyne	11		
*A. R. Butcher b Lawrence	8	1/10 2/82 3/114 (7 wkts, 40 overs)	188
I. Smith b Lawrence	46	4/116 5/133	
N. G. Cowley c Russell b Lawrence	17	6/180 7/188	

S. J. Dennis, S. L. Watkin and S. R. Barwick did not bat.

Bowling: Curran 8–0–22–1; Jarvis 8–1–45–0; Milburn 2–0–11–0; Lawrence 7–0–40–3; Graveney 8–1–20–1; Alleyne 7–0–45–2.

Gloucestershire

*A. J. Wright c Maynard b Cowley	30	E. T. Milburn not out	5
C. W. J. Athey c Butcher b Dale	15		
G. D. Hodgson c Dale b Cowley	28	L-b 6, w 1	7
K. M. Curran run out	37		
P. W. Romaines c Holmes b Watkin	22	1/33 2/58 3/84 (7 wkts, 40 overs)	183
M. W. Alleyne c Maynard b Dennis	11	4/134 5/145	
†R. C. Russell c Watkin b Barwick	28	6/151 7/183	

D. A. Graveney, D. V. Lawrence and K. B. S. Jarvis did not bat.

Bowling: Dennis 8–1–35–1; Watkin 8–2–24–1; Barwick 8–2–24–1; Dale 6–0–41–1; Cowley 8–1–36–2; Smith 2–0–17–0.

Umpires: B. Hassan and R. Palmer.

At Southampton, May 6. HAMPSHIRE v GLOUCESTERSHIRE. No result.

At Chelmsford, May 13. GLOUCESTERSHIRE beat ESSEX by seven wickets.

GLOUCESTERSHIRE v WARWICKSHIRE

At Moreton-in-Marsh, May 20. Gloucestershire won by 48 runs. Toss: Gloucestershire.

Gloucestershire

†R. C. Russell c Humpage b Munton	7	P. W. Romaines c Humpage b Munton	5
C. W. J. Athey lbw b Benjamin	4	M. W. Alleyne not out	13
*A. J. Wright b Munton	40	L-b 15, w 2	17
K. M. Curran c Smith b Munton	75		
J. W. Lloyds c Twose b Munton	0	1/13 2/21 3/127 (6 wkts, 40 overs)	202
P. Bainbridge not out	41	4/127 5/159 6/176	

M. W. Pooley, C. A. Walsh and M. C. J. Ball did not bat.

Bowling: Benjamin 8–1–21–1; Munton 8–1–23–5; Moody 8–1–33–0; Small 8–0–50–0; Twose 2–0–14–0; Smith 6–0–46–0.

Warwickshire

Asif Din c Athey b Walsh	59	G. C. Small lbw b Pooley	1
A. I. Kallicharran c Wright b Pooley	0	J. E. Benjamin c Russell b Alleyne	1
T. M. Moody b Walsh	1	T. A. Munton lbw b Curran	3
†G. W. Humpage c Wright b Alleyne	11	B 3, l-b 5, w 14, n-b 1	23
*T. A. Lloyd c and b Bainbridge	13		
N. M. K. Smith c Alleyne b Ball	5	1/1 2/6 3/39 (34.2 overs)	154
R. G. Twose b Alleyne	13	4/71 5/83 6/116	
D. P. Ostler not out	24	7/127 8/132 9/141	

Bowling: Walsh 6–1–14–2; Pooley 7–0–29–2; Curran 5.2–0–22–1; Alleyne 7–0–40–3; Bainbridge 5–0–24–1; Ball 4–0–17–1.

Umpires: J. D. Bond and R. Julian.

At Lord's, May 27. GLOUCESTERSHIRE lost to MIDDLESEX by seven wickets.

GLOUCESTERSHIRE v SOMERSET

At Bristol, June 3. Gloucestershire won by eight wickets. Toss: Gloucestershire. Lawrence's return of five for 18 included a spell of four for 4 in seventeen balls.

Somerset

S. J. Cook c Walsh b Lawrence	10	I. G. Swallow c Wright b Bainbridge	19
P. M. Roebuck b Curran	4	N. A. Mallender b Bainbridge	24
A. N. Hayhurst c Russell b Lawrence	4	J. C. Hallett not out	4
*C. J. Tavaré c Wright b Lawrence	4	B 1, l-b 4, w 6, n-b 1	12
R. J. Harden c Wright b Lawrence	3		
†N. D. Burns c Lloyds b Walsh	20	1/12 2/21 3/21 (39.3 overs)	118
G. D. Rose c Bainbridge b Lawrence	14	4/25 5/32 6/61	
M. W. Cleal c Wright b Alleyne	0	7/63 8/69 9/103	

Bowling: Walsh 8–1–14–1; Curran 8–0–22–1; Lawrence 8–1–18–5; Barnes 5–0–26–0; Alleyne 8–0–26–1; Bainbridge 2.3–0–7–2.

Gloucestershire

†R. C. Russell b Cleal	13
C. W. J. Athey not out	53
*A. J. Wright c Rose b Hayhurst	17
K. M. Curran not out	29
L-b 5, w 2	7
1/39 2/67 (2 wkts, 25.5 overs)	119

P. Bainbridge, J. W. Lloyds, P. W. Romaines, M. W. Alleyne, C. A. Walsh, D. V. Lawrence and S. N. Barnes did not bat.

Bowling: Mallender 8–0–25–0; Hallett 5.5–1–28–0; Rose 5–0–34–0; Cleal 3–0–14–1; Hayhurst 4–0–13–1.

Umpires: J. C. Balderstone and N. T. Plews.

At Manchester, June 10. GLOUCESTERSHIRE beat LANCASHIRE by two wickets.

GLOUCESTERSHIRE v LEICESTERSHIRE

At Gloucester, June 24. Leicestershire won on scoring-rate. Toss: Gloucestershire. Two stoppages for rain reduced Gloucestershire's target first to 173 from 37 overs, and then to 159 from 34 overs.

Leicestershire

T. J. Boon c Wright b Bainbridge 15
*N. E. Briers not out 90
J. J. Whitaker c Lloyds b Alleyne 31
P. Willey c Lloyds b Lawrence 1
C. C. Lewis c Hodgson b Curran 30
L. Potter b Curran 2
J. D. R. Benson not out 8
B 7, w 2, n-b 1 10

1/26 2/95 3/98 4/153 5/166 (5 wkts, 40 overs) 187

†P. A. Nixon, W. K. M. Benjamin, J. P. Agnew and A. D. Mullally did not bat.

Bowling: Curran 8–0–38–2; Walsh 8–1–38–0; Bainbridge 8–0–21–1; Lawrence 8–0–47–1; Alleyne 8–0–36–1.

Gloucestershire

*A. J. Wright c Nixon b Agnew 0
J. W. Lloyds c Nixon b Benjamin 10
P. Bainbridge b Benjamin 20
K. M. Curran c Willey b Lewis 14
C. W. J. Athey b Willey 15
P. W. Romaines c Briers b Benjamin . . 13
M. W. Alleyne run out 14
C. A. Walsh b Willey 0
G. D. Hodgson lbw b Mullally 12
†G. A. Tedstone c Willey b Mullally . . 25
D. V. Lawrence not out 1
B 4, l-b 4, w 7 15

1/0 2/27 3/32 4/53 5/83 6/85 7/85 8/102 9/134 (31 overs) 139

Bowling: Agnew 6–0–22–1; Benjamin 7–0–36–3; Lewis 8–0–41–1; Mullally 7–0–20–2; Willey 3–0–12–2.

Umpires: A. A. Jones and D. S. Thompsett.

At Derby, July 1. GLOUCESTERSHIRE lost to DERBYSHIRE by six wickets.

At Worcester, July 8. GLOUCESTERSHIRE lost to WORCESTERSHIRE by eight wickets.

GLOUCESTERSHIRE v SUSSEX

At Swindon, July 15. Gloucestershire won by one wicket. Toss: Gloucestershire. With Gloucestershire needing 9 runs off the last over, Clarke's third-ball dismissal of Hodgson was followed by a leg-bye and five wides which levelled the scores. Lloyds then hit his final delivery for four to win the match.

Sussex

N. J. Lenham run out 65
*P. W. G. Parker b Curran 7
A. P. Wells c Russell b Barnes 17
M. P. Speight c Romaines b Barnes . . . 60
C. M. Wells b Bainbridge 9
A. I. C. Dodemaide c Alleyne b Curran 23
A. C. S. Pigott run out 10
J. A. North run out 1
†P. Moores not out 4
C. C. Remy run out 2
A. R. Clarke b Walsh 0
B 4, l-b 5, w 1, n-b 2 12

1/26 2/60 3/136 4/163 5/175 6/198 7/199 8/205 9/210 (34.5 overs) 210

Bowling: Walsh 5.5–0–33–1; Curran 5–0–21–2; Bainbridge 8–0–52–1; Barnes 8–0–46–2; Alleyne 8–0–49–0.

Gloucestershire

†R. C. Russell c Moores b Dodemaide . 2
C. W. J. Athey c C. M. Wells b Pigott . 23
*A. J. Wright c Remy b Dodemaide . . . 3
K. M. Curran b Pigott 52
P. Bainbridge c Speight b Pigott 0
P. W. Romaines c Parker b Lenham . . 47
J. W. Lloyds not out 38
M. W. Alleyne st Moores b Clarke 20
C. A. Walsh c North b Lenham 11
G. D. Hodgson st Moores b Clarke 1
S. N. Barnes not out 0
B 1, l-b 4, w 12 17

1/10 2/16 3/32 4/32 5/130 6/146 7/179 8/202 9/204 (9 wkts, 40 overs) 214

Bowling: Dodemaide 8–0–22–2; C. M. Wells 8–0–17–0; Pigott 8–2–35–3; Remy 2–0–23–0; Clarke 7–0–58–2; Lenham 7–0–54–2.

Umpires: D. J. Constant and R. Palmer.

GLOUCESTERSHIRE v YORKSHIRE

At Cheltenham, July 22. Yorkshire won by seven wickets. Toss: Yorkshire.

Gloucestershire

*A. J. Wright c Sharp b Carrick 57
C. W. J. Athey c Blakey b Moxon 80
J. W. Lloyds c Metcalfe b Carrick 0
P. Bainbridge c and b Moxon 11
K. M. Curran not out 31
P. W. Romaines run out 9
†R. C. Russell c Sharp b Moxon 12
M. W. Alleyne not out 14
L-b 7, w 3, n-b 2 12

1/104 2/123 3/145 4/165 5/183 6/203 (6 wkts, 40 overs) 226

C. A. Walsh, R. M. Bell and S. N. Barnes did not bat.

Bowling: Hartley 5–0–36–0; Sidebottom 8–1–27–0; Fletcher 8–0–36–0; Carrick 8–0–47–2; Pickles 4–0–21–0; Moxon 7–0–52–3.

Yorkshire

*M. D. Moxon run out 68
A. A. Metcalfe c Russell b Curran 0
†R. J. Blakey not out 100
P. E. Robinson c Romaines b Alleyne . 33
K. Sharp not out 9
L-b 4, w 11, n-b 2 17

1/1 2/132 3/204 (3 wkts, 35.5 overs) 227

D. Byas, P. J. Hartley, P. Carrick, C. S. Pickles, A. Sidebottom and S. D. Fletcher did not bat.

Bowling: Curran 8–0–31–1; Walsh 6–0–16–0; Bell 4–0–38–0; Barnes 6–0–53–0; Alleyne 5.5–0–38–1; Lloyds 6–0–47–0.

Umpires: J. H. Hampshire and R. A. White.

GLOUCESTERSHIRE v SURREY

At Cheltenham, July 29. Gloucestershire won by five wickets. Toss: Gloucestershire. Athey struck a six and twelve fours in his 113.

Surrey

A. J. Stewart c Williams b Barnes 3
M. A. Feltham c Hodgson b Barnes . . . 47
G. P. Thorpe c Wright b Barnes 11
D. M. Ward c Wright b Milburn 51
M. A. Lynch c Williams b Walsh 3
*I. A. Greig c Walsh b Alleyne 14
K. T. Medlycott c Williams b Milburn . 2
C. K. Bullen c Barnes b Curran 25
†N. F. Sargeant c Romaines b Walsh . . 22
M. P. Bicknell not out 4
Waqar Younis not out 0
B 1, l-b 4, w 3, n-b 2 10

1/10 2/49 3/70 4/85 5/113 6/118 7/157 8/176 9/191 (9 wkts, 40 overs) 192

Bowling: Barnes 8–1–39–3; Walsh 8–0–29–2; Curran 8–0–50–1; Alleyne 8–1–35–1; Milburn 8–0–34–2.

Gloucestershire

G. D. Hodgson c Ward b Medlycott	28	M. W. Alleyne not out	1
C. W. J. Athey c Ward b Waqar Younis	113	L-b 2, w 3	5
*A. J. Wright c Ward b Bullen	21		
K. M. Curran c and b Medlycott	23		
P. W. Romaines c and b Medlycott	0	1/71 2/118 3/185 (5 wkts, 39.5 overs)	196
J. W. Lloyds not out	5	4/185 5/190	

C. A. Walsh, †R. C. J. Williams, E. T. Milburn and S. N. Barnes did not bat.

Bowling: Bicknell 8–0–24–0; Feltham 8–0–44–0; Medlycott 8–0–47–3; Bullen 8–1–41–1; Waqar Younis 7.5–0–38–1.

Umpires: J. C. Balderstone and B. Leadbeater.

GLOUCESTERSHIRE v KENT

At Bristol, August 12. Gloucestershire won by six wickets. Toss: Gloucestershire.

Kent

S. G. Hinks b Barnes	13	P. S. de Villiers run out	4
N. R. Taylor c Athey b Alleyne	37	C. Penn c Williams b Walsh	0
T. R. Ward c Alleyne b Barnes	3	R. P. Davis not out	0
G. R. Cowdrey lbw b Walsh	24	L-b 3, w 1	4
M. V. Fleming c Alleyne b Bainbridge	10		
†S. A. Marsh c Athey b Curran	24	1/18 2/22 3/75 (39.2 overs)	148
*C. S. Cowdrey run out	27	4/90 5/96 6/137	
D. J. M. Kelleher b Walsh	2	7/140 8/148 9/148	

Bowling: Barnes 8–0–25–2; Walsh 7.2–0–28–3; Curran 8–2–24–1; Alleyne 8–0–33–1; Milburn 4–0–24–0; Bainbridge 4–0–11–1.

Gloucestershire

G. D. Hodgson b Fleming	27	M. W. Alleyne not out	39
C. W. J. Athey c and b Kelleher	3	L-b 4, w 1, n-b 1	6
P. Bainbridge not out	59		
K. M. Curran b Fleming	12	1/20 2/65 3/86 (4 wkts, 35.5 overs)	149
*A. J. Wright run out	3	4/89	

P. W. Romaines, C. A. Walsh, E. T. Milburn, †R. C. J. Williams and S. N. Barnes did not bat.

Bowling: Kelleher 8–2–20–1; de Villiers 6.5–2–25–0; C. S. Cowdrey 3–0–20–0; Fleming 8–1–20–2; Penn 7–0–44–0; Davis 3–0–16–0.

Umpires: D. R. Shepherd and P. B. Wight.

At Nottingham, August 19. NOTTINGHAMSHIRE v GLOUCESTERSHIRE. No result.

At Northampton, August 26. GLOUCESTERSHIRE lost to NORTHAMPTONSHIRE by 2 runs.

HAMPSHIRE

At Canterbury, April 29. HAMPSHIRE lost to KENT by 53 runs.

HAMPSHIRE v GLOUCESTERSHIRE

At Southampton, May 6. No result, the match having been ended by a thunderstorm during tea. Toss: Gloucestershire.

Hampshire

V. P. Terry c Lloyds b Walsh	6
D. I. Gower c Lloyds b Walsh	0
R. A. Smith c Ball b Bainbridge	85
C. L. Smith run out	89
*M. C. J. Nicholas lbw b Bainbridge	15
R. J. Scott c Ball b Walsh	12
M. D. Marshall not out	6
J. R. Ayling not out	2
B 1, l-b 3, w 3, n-b 2	9
1/1 2/20 3/165 4/201 5/209 6/221 (6 wkts, 40 overs)	224

†R. J. Parks, R. J. Maru and C. A. Connor did not bat.

Bowling: Walsh 8–1–30–3; Curran 8–0–41–0; Alleyne 7–0–41–0; Milburn 4–0–25–0; Ball 6–0–31–0; Bainbridge 7–0–52–2.

Gloucestershire

*A. J. Wright, P. W. Romaines, P. Bainbridge, C. W. J. Athey, J. W. Lloyds, M. W. Alleyne, †R. C. Russell, E. T. Milburn, C. A. Walsh, M. C. J. Ball and K. M. Curran.

Umpires: H. D. Bird and D. S. Thompsett.

At Taunton, May 13. HAMPSHIRE lost to SOMERSET by five wickets.

At Leeds, May 27. HAMPSHIRE beat YORKSHIRE by 36 runs.

At Leicester, June 3. HAMPSHIRE beat LEICESTERSHIRE by five wickets.

HAMPSHIRE v MIDDLESEX

At Basingstoke, June 10. Middlesex won by seven wickets. Toss: Middlesex. Downton, keeping wicket for Middlesex, was hit in the left eye by a bail when Emburey bowled Wood, and was later admitted to hospital.

Hampshire

R. J. Scott c Haynes b Hughes	0
V. P. Terry c Downton b Williams	4
D. I. Gower c Hughes b Fraser	23
M. D. Marshall c Butcher b Hughes	46
J. R. Wood b Emburey	18
*M. C. J. Nicholas b Emburey	1
J. R. Ayling c Brown b Williams	9
†R. J. Parks b Fraser	11
R. J. Maru c Gatting b Hughes	9
C. A. Connor b Hughes	3
P. J. Bakker not out	0
L-b 6, w 6, n-b 4	16
1/2 2/12 3/47 4/101 5/102 6/112 7/118 8/134 9/137 (39.5 overs)	140

Bowling: Hughes 6.5–1–19–4; Williams 8–0–29–2; Fraser 8–1–26–2; Gatting 3–0–20–0; Haynes 6–1–21–0; Emburey 8–2–19–2.

Middlesex

D. L. Haynes b Ayling 19
M. A. Roseberry b Connor 17
*M. W. Gatting c and b Maru 27
M. R. Ramprakash not out 52
K. R. Brown not out 13
B 5, l-b 5, w 5, n-b 1 16

1/41 2/41 3/93 (3 wkts, 37.5 overs) 144

R. O. Butcher, †P. R. Downton, N. F. Williams, J. E. Emburey, S. P. Hughes and A. R. C. Fraser did not bat.

Bowling: Marshall 8–0–19–0; Bakker 4–0–23–0; Connor 8–1–18–1; Ayling 7–0–27–1; Maru 7.5–0–40–1; Scott 3–0–7–0.

Umpires: K. E. Palmer and R. Palmer.

HAMPSHIRE v GLAMORGAN

At Bournemouth, June 17. Hampshire won by 64 runs in a match reduced to 37 overs a side. Toss: Glamorgan. Robin Smith's century came off 89 balls, and in all he faced 104 balls, hitting two sixes and thirteen fours. Butcher, when 48, passed 5,000 runs in the Sunday League.

Hampshire

V. P. Terry lbw b Watkin 2
R. J. Scott c Dennis b Cowley 61
R. A. Smith c Maynard b Frost 122
D. I. Gower lbw b Richards 1
M. D. Marshall c Metson b Watkin . . . 1
*M. C. J. Nicholas b Frost 16
J. R. Ayling not out 5
R. J. Maru not out 4
B 1, l-b 14, w 7 22

1/6 2/165 3/181 (6 wkts, 37 overs) 234
4/184 5/215 6/228

†R. J. Parks, C. A. Connor and P. J. Bakker did not bat.

Bowling: Frost 8–0–49–2; Watkin 8–0–46–2; Dennis 8–0–43–0; Cowley 8–0–43–1; Richards 5–0–38–1.

Glamorgan

*A. R. Butcher c Nicholas b Ayling . . . 52
H. Morris c Smith b Bakker 7
M. P. Maynard c Nicholas b Maru 34
I. V. A. Richards c Terry b Maru 8
I. Smith c Terry b Maru 2
N. G. Cowley b Bakker 7
†C. P. Metson not out 30
J. Derrick c sub b Bakker 19
S. J. Dennis not out 1
L-b 8, w 2 10

1/12 2/82 3/98 (7 wkts, 37 overs) 170
4/104 5/113
6/116 7/166

S. L. Watkin and M. Frost did not bat.

Bowling: Connor 6–0–26–0; Bakker 8–1–33–3; Marshall 5–0–23–0; Ayling 8–0–39–1; Maru 8–0–38–3; Nicholas 2–0–3–0.

Umpires: J. W. Holder and B. J. Meyer.

At Manchester, June 24. LANCASHIRE v HAMPSHIRE. No result.

At Hove, July 1. HAMPSHIRE lost to SUSSEX on scoring-rate.

HAMPSHIRE v ESSEX

At Southampton, July 8. Hampshire won by seven wickets. Toss: Essex.

Essex

B. R. Hardie c Parks b Marshall 4
J. P. Stephenson c Gower b Tremlett .. 28
M. E. Waugh c Gower b Ayling 17
P. J. Prichard c Parks b Maru 12
*D. R. Pringle c Gower b Tremlett 63
N. Hussain b Ayling 12
†M. A. Garnham not out 40
N. A. Foster c Gower b Marshall 4
T. D. Topley c Terry b Bakker 2
M. C. Ilott not out 1
B 1, l-b 8, w 4 13

1/7 2/49 3/53 4/75 5/120 6/161 7/179 8/186 (8 wkts, 40 overs) 196

J. H. Childs did not bat.

Bowling: Bakker 8–2–30–1; Marshall 8–0–33–2; Ayling 8–0–40–2; Tremlett 8–1–43–2; Maru 8–0–41–1.

Hampshire

V. P. Terry c Hardie b Foster 52
R. J. Scott lbw b Foster 7
*D. I. Gower c Childs b Topley 66
M. D. Marshall not out 43
C. L. Smith not out 22
B 2, l-b 4, w 2, n-b 2 10

1/23 2/130 3/132 (3 wkts, 39 overs) 200

J. R. Ayling, T. C. Middleton, †R. J. Parks, T. M. Tremlett, R. J. Maru and P. J. Bakker did not bat.

Bowling: Foster 8–0–43–2; Ilott 7–1–34–0; Childs 8–2–36–0; Topley 8–0–32–1; Pringle 7–0–42–0; Waugh 1–0–7–0.

Umpires: B. Hassan and D. R. Shepherd.

HAMPSHIRE v NOTTINGHAMSHIRE

At Southampton, July 15. Hampshire won by 7 runs. Toss: Nottinghamshire.

Hampshire

V. P. Terry c Robinson b Cooper 3
R. J. Scott b Saxelby 55
R. A. Smith c Newell b Afford 77
D. I. Gower not out 66
M. D. Marshall run out 7
*M. C. J. Nicholas not out 46
L-b 5, w 7, n-b 1 13

1/15 2/134 3/154 4/162 (4 wkts, 40 overs) 267

J. R. Ayling, †R. J. Parks, R. J. Maru, C. A. Connor and P. J. Bakker did not bat.

Bowling: Cooper 8–0–44–1; Stephenson 8–1–43–0; Hemmings 7–0–36–0; Mike 4–0–26–0; Afford 8–0–74–1; Saxelby 5–0–39–1.

Nottinghamshire

B. C. Broad b Connor 86
P. Johnson c Parks b Marshall 9
*R. T. Robinson b Maru 44
M. Saxelby b Ayling 24
F. D. Stephenson c Nicholas b Ayling . 14
G. W. Mike c Scott b Ayling 10
†B. N. French c Terry b Ayling 9
K. E. Cooper b Marshall 1
M. Newell not out 11
E. E. Hemmings not out 32
B 5, l-b 9, w 3, n-b 3 20

1/34 2/142 3/155 4/182 5/196 6/205 7/213 8/214 (8 wkts, 40 overs) 260

J. A. Afford did not bat.

Bowling: Bakker 7–0–52–0; Marshall 8–0–36–2; Connor 7–0–49–1; Ayling 8–0–37–4; Maru 5–0–38–1; Scott 5–0–34–0.

Umpires: J. H. Harris and A. G. T. Whitehead.

HAMPSHIRE v DERBYSHIRE

At Portsmouth, July 22. Hampshire won by 189 runs. Toss: Derbyshire. Derbyshire's total was their lowest in the Sunday League, while the margin of 189 runs was Hampshire's largest and Derbyshire's worst in the competition.

Hampshire

*M. C. J. Nicholas c Malcolm b Mortensen	4	C. L. Smith run out	30
R. J. Scott c Roberts b Malcolm	76	J. R. Ayling not out	0
R. A. Smith c Kuiper b Malcolm	83	L-b 4, w 5	9
D. I. Gower not out	47	1/8 2/155 3/178 (5 wkts, 38 overs)	250
M. D. Marshall run out	1	4/180 5/245	

†R. J. Parks, R. J. Maru, C. A. Connor and P. J. Bakker did not bat.

Bowling: Base 7–0–37–0; Mortensen 7–0–35–1; Malcolm 8–0–50–2; Miller 8–0–54–0; Goldsmith 4–0–42–0; Kuiper 4–0–28–0.

Derbyshire

*K. J. Barnett c Nicholas b Bakker	5	D. E. Malcolm b Connor	9
J. E. Morris c Parks b Marshall	1	O. H. Mortensen not out	2
B. Roberts c Parks b Connor	10	G. Miller absent injured	
A. P. Kuiper c C. L. Smith b Bakker	1	L-b 3, w 3	6
C. J. Adams c Parks b Connor	21		
S. C. Goldsmith c C. L. Smith b Bakker	4	1/6 2/6 3/14 (19.1 overs)	61
†K. M. Krikken b Connor	0	4/22 5/37 6/38	
S. J. Base b Ayling	2	7/42 8/50 9/61	

Bowling: Bakker 6–1–31–3; Marshall 4–2–4–1; Connor 5.1–0–11–4; Ayling 3–0–9–1; Scott 1–0–3–0.

Umpires: J. C. Balderstone and D. J. Constant.

At Birmingham, July 29. HAMPSHIRE beat WARWICKSHIRE by three wickets.

HAMPSHIRE v NORTHAMPTONSHIRE

At Bournemouth, August 5. Hampshire won by six wickets. Toss: Northamptonshire.

Northamptonshire

A. Fordham c Scott b Marshall	63	D. J. Wild not out	16
W. Larkins c Scott b Bakker	7	B 1, l-b 2, w 2, n-b 5	10
R. J. Bailey c Marshall b Maru	33		
*A. J. Lamb b Connor	45	1/19 2/109 3/111 (4 wkts, 40 overs)	208
R. G. Williams not out	34	4/180	

J. W. Govan, †D. Ripley, N. G. B. Cook, M. A. Robinson and S. J. Brown did not bat.

Bowling: Bakker 7–0–36–1; Marshall 8–1–33–1; Connor 8–0–51–1; Ayling 8–0–44–0; Maru 8–0–28–1; Scott 1–0–13–0.

Hampshire

V. P. Terry c Robinson b Brown	84	*M. C. J. Nicholas not out	0
R. J. Scott c Ripley b Brown	70	L-b 9, w 2, n-b 1	12
R. A. Smith c and b Cook	9		
D. I. Gower c Bailey b Cook	18	1/127 2/140 (4 wkts, 37.5 overs)	210
M. D. Marshall not out	17	3/188 4/200	

J. R. Ayling, †R. J. Parks, R. J. Maru, C. A. Connor and P. J. Bakker did not bat.

Bowling: Robinson 7–1–21–0; Brown 6.5–0–37–2; Wild 4–0–23–0; Cook 8–1–42–2; Govan 3–0–23–0; Larkins 4–0–26–0; Williams 5–0–29–0.

Umpires: B. J. Meyer and D. O. Oslear.

At Worcester, August 12. HAMPSHIRE beat WORCESTERSHIRE by 20 runs.

HAMPSHIRE v SURREY

At Southampton, August 26. Surrey won by 4 runs. Toss: Hampshire. Hampshire, needing to win to qualify for the Refuge Assurance Cup, were well placed at 192 for one before losing Middleton, Marshall, Smith, Ayling and Nicholas in the space of twelve deliveries. In dismissing Marshall, Waqar Younis passed I. A. Greig's Surrey record of 28 wickets in a season in 1988. Surrey's winning total was built around a century off 71 balls by Ward.

Surrey

A. J. Stewart c Nicholas b Connor 36
A. D. Brown b Tremlett 24
G. P. Thorpe lbw b Tremlett 26
†D. M. Ward not out 102
M. A. Lynch b Maru 26
J. D. Robinson c Middleton b Maru ... 7
*I. A. Greig not out 16
B 1, l-b 3, w 4, n-b 3 11

1/44 2/69 3/103 4/154 5/186 (5 wkts, 38 overs) 248

K. T. Medlycott, C. K. Bullen, A. J. Murphy and Waqar Younis did not bat.

Bowling: Bakker 5–0–35–0; Marshall 8–0–50–0; Tremlett 8–0–33–2; Connor 7–0–45–1; Maru 5–0–31–2; Ayling 5–0–50–0.

Hampshire

V. P. Terry run out 56
T. C. Middleton run out 72
*M. C. J. Nicholas b Waqar Younis ... 59
M. D. Marshall lbw b Waqar Younis .. 0
C. L. Smith c Stewart b Murphy 0
J. R. Ayling run out 3
†R. J. Parks b Waqar Younis 10
R. J. Maru c Stewart b Murphy 1
T. M. Tremlett c Brown b Greig 21
C. A. Connor not out 4
P. J. Bakker not out 2
B 4, l-b 8, w 4 16

1/100 2/192 3/192 4/193 5/196 6/200 7/203 8/223 9/235 (9 wkts, 38 overs) 244

Bowling: Murphy 8–0–41–2; Robinson 5–0–22–0; Greig 5–0–37–1; Medlycott 7–0–49–0; Bullen 5–0–43–0; Waqar Younis 8–0–40–3.

Umpires: J. D. Bond and A. A. Jones.

KENT

At Chelmsford, April 22. KENT beat ESSEX by 27 runs.

KENT v HAMPSHIRE

At Canterbury, April 29. Kent won by 53 runs. Toss: Kent.

Kent

S. G. Hinks c Terry b James 1
N. R. Taylor st Parks b Scott 95
T. R. Ward c Connor b Maru 24
*C. S. Cowdrey c Connor b Tremlett .. 18
G. R. Cowdrey st Parks b Scott 22
†S. A. Marsh c Terry b Connor 15
M. V. Fleming not out 29
R. M. Ellison not out 3
L-b 3, w 3 6

1/3 2/51 3/87 4/134 5/173 6/186 (6 wkts, 40 overs) 213

M. A. Ealham, R. P. Davis and T. A. Merrick did not bat.

Bowling: James 8–0–33–1; Connor 8–2–49–1; Tremlett 5–0–22–1; Maru 6–0–29–1; Marshall 8–0–41–0; Scott 5–0–36–2.

Hampshire

*V. P. Terry b Ellison	9	T. M. Tremlett c C. S. Cowdrey b Fleming	18
R. J. Scott lbw b Merrick	0	R. J. Maru not out	12
R. A. Smith c C. S. Cowdrey b Fleming	22	L-b 6, w 2, n-b 1	9
D. I. Gower c Fleming b Davis	32		
C. L. Smith not out	47		
K. D. James c Marsh b Davis	4	1/12 2/12 3/61 (8 wkts, 40 overs)	160
M. D. Marshall c Fleming b Davis	3	4/71 5/78 6/93	
†R. J. Parks b Davis	4	7/98 8/133	

C. A. Connor did not bat.

Bowling: Ellison 8–0–23–1; Merrick 8–0–32–1; Ealham 8–0–35–0; Davis 8–0–25–4; Fleming 8–0–39–2.

Umpires: J. W. Holder and K. J. Lyons.

KENT v MIDDLESEX

At Folkestone, May 6. Middlesex won by six wickets. Toss: Middlesex.

Kent

S. G. Hinks run out	86	R. M. Ellison not out	11
N. R. Taylor b Emburey	28	T. A. Merrick not out	1
T. R. Ward lbw b Taylor	24	L-b 8	8
*C. S. Cowdrey c Roseberry b Cowans	20		
G. R. Cowdrey st Downton b Gatting	28	1/72 2/129 3/155 (6 wkts, 40 overs)	224
†S. A. Marsh st Downton b Emburey	18	4/170 5/202 6/222	

R. P. Davis, M. A. Ealham and C. Penn did not bat.

Bowling: Williams 7–0–51–0; Cowans 8–2–29–1; Taylor 8–0–47–1; Emburey 8–1–36–2; Gatting 7–0–41–1; Haynes 2–0–12–0.

Middlesex

D. L. Haynes c G. R. Cowdrey b Davis	67	†P. R. Downton not out	9
M. A. Roseberry lbw b Ealham	52	L-b 15, w 3	18
M. R. Ramprakash c Ealham b Ellison	32		
K. R. Brown c Marsh b Ward	20	1/112 2/134 (4 wkts, 37.5 overs)	225
R. O. Butcher not out	27	3/180 4/204	

*M. W. Gatting, J. E. Emburey, N. F. Williams, N. R. Taylor and N. G. Cowans did not bat.

Bowling: Penn 3–0–22–0; Merrick 7.5–0–39–0; Ellison 7–0–32–1; Davis 8–0–29–1; Ealham 7–0–47–1; C. S. Cowdrey 3–0–24–0; Ward 2–0–17–1.

Umpires: D. J. Constant and N. T. Plews.

At Llanelli, May 13. KENT beat GLAMORGAN by two wickets.

KENT v YORKSHIRE

At Canterbury, May 20. Kent won by 69 runs. Toss: Kent. Merrick took three wickets in five balls for no runs, and later forced Yorkshire's White to retire from a blow to the face.

Kent

S. G. Hinks b Fletcher 89
N. R. Taylor c Gough b White 35
T. R. Ward c Gough b White 37
*C. S. Cowdrey c sub b Gough 18
G. R. Cowdrey not out 31
M. V. Fleming b Fletcher 13
†S. A. Marsh not out 2
B 1, l-b 11, w 8 20

1/74 2/156 3/195 4/196 5/229 (5 wkts, 40 overs) 245

M. A. Ealham, C. Penn, R. P. Davis and T. A. Merrick did not bat.

Bowling: Pickles 8–0–42–0; Jarvis 8–0–37–0; Fletcher 8–1–32–2; Gough 8–0–54–1; White 6–0–49–2; Byas 2–0–19–0.

Yorkshire

*M. D. Moxon c Davis b Fleming 43
A. A. Metcalfe b Davis 32
R. J. Blakey b Davis 9
D. Byas c Ward b Ealham 25
P. E. Robinson c Taylor b Ealham 17
†D. L. Bairstow c Marsh b Merrick ... 10
C. White retired hurt 20
C. S. Pickles c C. S. Cowdrey b Merrick 0
P. W. Jarvis c Marsh b Merrick 1
D. Gough b Penn 4
S. D. Fletcher not out 1
B 4, l-b 8, w 2 14

1/59 2/75 3/105 4/122 5/135 6/152 7/152 8/156 9/176 (36.3 overs) 176

C. White retired hurt at 170-8.

Bowling: Penn 6.3–0–28–1; Merrick 7–0–22–3; Fleming 8–1–47–1; Ealham 4–0–25–2; Davis 8–0–30–2; C. S. Cowdrey 3–0–12–0.

Umpires: P. J. Eele and J. W. Holder.

At Northampton, May 27. KENT beat NORTHAMPTONSHIRE by 55 runs.

KENT v SOMERSET

At Canterbury, June 10. Kent won by six wickets. Toss: Kent.

Somerset

S. J. Cook c C. S. Cowdrey b Fleming . 50
P. M. Roebuck c Benson b C. S. Cowdrey . 29
G. D. Rose b Merrick 29
*C. J. Tavaré c Benson b C. S. Cowdrey 11
R. J. Harden not out 21
†N. D. Burns b Igglesden 14
A. N. Hayhurst b Merrick 3
M. W. Cleal run out 0
I. G. Swallow not out 0
L-b 6, w 2 8

1/80 2/89 3/125 4/127 5/156 6/163 7/163 (7 wkts, 40 overs) 165

N. A. Mallender and A. N. Jones did not bat.

Bowling: Igglesden 8–0–27–1; Merrick 8–2–26–2; Fleming 8–0–27–1; Ealham 8–0–42–0; Davis 3–0–17–0; C. S. Cowdrey 5–0–20–2.

Kent

S. G. Hinks c Cook b Mallender 1
M. R. Benson c Roebuck b Rose 55
N. R. Taylor c Cook b Jones 59
*C. S. Cowdrey not out 26
G. R. Cowdrey c Cook b Jones 6
M. V. Fleming not out 11
B 1, l-b 6, w 4 11

1/1 2/121 3/127 4/150 (4 wkts, 37.5 overs) 169

†S. A. Marsh, M. A. Ealham, A. P. Igglesden, T. A. Merrick and R. P. Davis did not bat.

Bowling: Jones 8–0–25–2; Mallender 7.5–0–29–1; Rose 8–0–29–1; Cleal 2–0–9–0; Hayhurst 5–0–34–0; Swallow 3–0–12–0; Roebuck 4–0–24–0.

Umpires: D. J. Constant and B. J. Meyer.

KENT v NOTTINGHAMSHIRE

At Canterbury, June 17. Kent won by 24 runs. Toss: Kent. Igglesden hurried his side to victory by taking three wickets in five balls.

Kent

S. G. Hinks c Saxelby b Stephenson	12	T. A. Merrick not out	12
M. A. Ealham c Evans b Stephenson	2	A. P. Igglesden run out	0
N. R. Taylor c and b Hemmings	28	R. P. Davis not out	0
*C. S. Cowdrey c Broad b Saxelby	13	L-b 6, w 6, n-b 3	15
G. R. Cowdrey c Broad b Stephenson	46		
M. V. Fleming b Saxelby	21	1/10 2/17 3/54 (9 wkts, 40 overs)	178
†S. A. Marsh run out	20	4/73 5/124 6/148	
R. M. Ellison b Stephenson	9	7/154 8/171 9/171	

Bowling: Stephenson 8–0–28–4; Cooper 8–1–33–0; Saxelby 8–0–48–2; Evans 7–1–34–0; Afford 4–1–12–0; Hemmings 5–0–17–1.

Nottinghamshire

B. C. Broad c Marsh b Igglesden	8	E. E. Hemmings c Ealham b Igglesden	15
D. W. Randall run out	49	K. E. Cooper c Taylor b Igglesden	1
P. Johnson c Marsh b Merrick	3	J. A. Afford not out	0
*R. T. Robinson b Fleming	3	L-b 7, w 4	11
M. Saxelby c G. R. Cowdrey b Davis	25		
†B. N. French c and b Davis	0	1/20 2/23 3/28 (38.3 overs)	154
F. D. Stephenson lbw b C. S. Cowdrey	9	4/93 5/93 6/97	
K. P. Evans c Ellison b Igglesden	30	7/111 8/144 9/154	

Bowling: Igglesden 6.3–1–24–4; Merrick 7–0–26–1; Fleming 8–0–21–1; Ellison 2–0–18–0; Ealham 3–0–18–0; Davis 8–0–25–2; C. S. Cowdrey 4–0–15–1.

Umpires: B. Leadbeater and R. A. White.

At Birmingham, June 24. KENT lost to WARWICKSHIRE by three wickets.

KENT v LANCASHIRE

At Maidstone, July 1. Lancashire won by 77 runs. Toss: Kent. Lloyd, on his 21st birthday, completed his first Sunday League hundred in the final over, having faced 88 balls, of which twelve went for four. He had been dropped by Fleming off Ellison when 10.

Lancashire

G. Fowler c Wells b C. S. Cowdrey	59	M. Watkinson not out	33
M. A. Atherton c Marsh b Fleming	13	L-b 3, w 6	9
G. D. Lloyd not out	100		
N. H. Fairbrother c Ealham b de Villiers	45	1/33 2/112 3/201 (3 wkts, 40 overs)	259

Wasim Akram, *D. P. Hughes, I. D. Austin, P. A. J. DeFreitas, †W. K. Hegg and P. J. W. Allott did not bat.

Bowling: Igglesden 8–0–39–0; de Villiers 8–0–53–1; Ellison 4–0–24–0; Fleming 8–0–51–1; Ealham 3–0–21–0; Davis 5–0–33–0; C. S. Cowdrey 4–0–35–1.

Kent

S. G. Hinks b Allott	17	P. S. de Villiers c Watkinson b DeFreitas	1
M. A. Ealham lbw b Allott	3	R. P. Davis b Austin	14
V. J. Wells c Fowler b DeFreitas	13	A. P. Igglesden not out	0
*C. S. Cowdrey b Watkinson	33		
G. R. Cowdrey c Hegg b Allott	0	B 2, l-b 9, w 1	12
M. V. Fleming c Fairbrother b Wasim Akram	8	1/11 2/34 3/36 (37.1 overs)	182
†S. A. Marsh c Hughes b Watkinson	38	4/38 5/69 6/90	
R. M. Ellison b Wasim Akram	43	7/148 8/151 9/182	

Bowling: Allott 7–1–28–3; DeFreitas 8–0–48–2; Watkinson 8–0–37–2; Wasim Akram 7.1–0–31–2; Austin 7–0–27–1.

Umpires: J. C. Balderstone and B. Dudleston.

At The Oval, July 22. KENT lost to SURREY by five wickets.

KENT v WORCESTERSHIRE

At Canterbury, July 29. Worcestershire won by five wickets. Toss: Worcestershire.

Kent

S. G. Hinks c Botham b Lampitt 51
M. R. Benson lbw b Newport 24
V. J. Wells c Radford b Botham 16
T. R. Ward c Lampitt b Botham 45
*C. S. Cowdrey c D'Oliveira b Illingworth . 4
M. V. Fleming b Illingworth 8
†S. A. Marsh b Illingworth 7
R. M. Ellison not out 9
T. A. Merrick c Rhodes b Botham 11
L-b 5, w 3, n-b 1 9

1/34 2/85 3/113 4/123 5/141 6/159 7/165 8/184 (8 wkts, 40 overs) 184

R. P. Davis and A. P. Igglesden did not bat.

Bowling: Weston 6–0–26–0; Newport 8–1–18–1; Botham 7–0–54–3; Radford 3–0–24–0; Lampitt 8–0–38–1; Illingworth 8–1–19–3.

Worcestershire

I. T. Botham b Davis 45
M. J. Weston c Merrick b Fleming 6
G. A. Hick b Davis 25
D. B. D'Oliveira c Merrick b Ellison .. 35
*P. A. Neale c Marsh b Merrick 39
D. A. Leatherdale not out 20
†S. J. Rhodes not out 1
B 2, l-b 13, w 1 16

1/31 2/83 3/84 4/148 5/178 (5 wkts, 38 overs) 187

N. V. Radford, P. J. Newport, R. K. Illingworth and S. R. Lampitt did not bat.

Bowling: Igglesden 7–1–26–0; Merrick 7–0–38–1; Fleming 8–0–32–1; Ellison 8–0–37–1; Davis 5–0–30–2; Cowdrey 3–0–9–0.

Umpires: A. A. Jones and R. Julian.

At Chesterfield, August 5. KENT lost to DERBYSHIRE by six wickets.

At Bristol, August 12. KENT lost to GLOUCESTERSHIRE by six wickets.

KENT v SUSSEX

At Canterbury, August 19. No result.

At Leicester, August 26. KENT lost to LEICESTERSHIRE by six wickets.

LANCASHIRE

LANCASHIRE v MIDDLESEX

At Manchester, April 22. Middlesex won by eight wickets. Toss: Middlesex. Haynes reached his hundred off 97 balls, with three sixes and eight fours, while Fowler's century had come off 118 balls, including ten fours. The Middlesex opening partnership of 176 between Haynes and Roseberry was a record for any wicket against Lancashire in the Sunday League.

Lancashire

G. Fowler lbw b Williams ... 101
M. A. Atherton b Emburey ... 63
N. H. Fairbrother run out ... 1
G. D. Lloyd run out ... 7
M. Watkinson c Emburey b Williams ... 7
P. A. J. DeFreitas c Brown b Williams ... 6
T. E. Jesty lbw b Williams ... 10
I. D. Austin not out ... 8
L-b 6, w 5, n-b 1 ... 12

1/141 2/148 3/181 4/187 5/190 6/196 7/215 (7 wkts, 40 overs) 215

*D. P. Hughes, P. J. W. Allott and †W. K. Hegg did not bat.

Bowling: Williams 8–0–49–4; Hemstock 8–0–43–0; Emburey 8–1–35–1; Carr 3.4–0–20–0; Weekes 4–0–21–0; Haynes 7.2–0–34–0; Ramprakash 1–0–7–0.

Middlesex

D. L. Haynes not out ... 107
M. A. Roseberry lbw b Watkinson ... 73
M. R. Ramprakash run out ... 22
K. R. Brown not out ... 2
L-b 9, w 4, n-b 2 ... 15

1/176 2/213 (2 wkts, 38.2 overs) 219

J. R. Hemstock, *M. W. Gatting, †P. R. Downton, J. E. Emburey, P. N. Weekes, J. D. Carr and N. F. Williams did not bat.

Bowling: DeFreitas 8–0–35–0; Allott 8–1–20–0; Austin 6–0–45–0; Watkinson 7.2–0–50–1; Jesty 2–0–16–0; Atherton 4–0–24–0; Hughes 3–0–20–0.

Umpires: J. H. Hampshire and R. A. White.

At Nottingham, April 29. LANCASHIRE beat NOTTINGHAMSHIRE by five wickets.

At The Oval, May 6. LANCASHIRE beat SURREY by seven wickets.

LANCASHIRE v LEICESTERSHIRE

At Manchester, May 20. Lancashire won by 23 runs. Toss: Leicestershire. Fowler faced 110 balls for his 108, hitting one six and twelve fours.

Lancashire

G. Fowler c Boon b Taylor ... 108
M. A. Atherton b Willey ... 33
N. H. Fairbrother c and b Willey ... 27
G. D. Lloyd c Nixon b Lewis ... 10
T. E. Jesty b Lewis ... 19
Wasim Akram b Benson ... 5
P. A. J. DeFreitas b Lewis ... 7
I. D. Austin c Whitaker b Agnew ... 2
†W. K. Hegg lbw b Lewis ... 0
*D. P. Hughes not out ... 0
L-b 9, w 5 ... 14

1/117 2/157 3/173 4/186 5/200 6/212 7/217 8/224 9/225 (9 wkts, 39 overs) 225

P. J. W. Allott did not bat.

Bowling: Benjamin 5–0–23–0; Lewis 8–1–34–4; Agnew 7–0–39–1; Taylor 8–0–65–1; Willey 8–0–39–2; Benson 3–0–16–1.

Leicestershire

T. J. Boon c Hegg b Austin	46	J. D. R. Benson b DeFreitas	21
*N. E. Briers run out	26	†P. A. Nixon not out	1
J. J. Whitaker c Allott b Austin	34	B 1, l-b 10, w 2, n-b 1	14
P. Willey c Atherton b Austin	18		
C. C. Lewis c Hughes b DeFreitas	10	1/66 2/94 3/131 (6 wkts, 39 overs)	202
L. Potter not out	32	4/143 5/145 6/197	

W. K. M. Benjamin, J. P. Agnew and L. B. Taylor did not bat.

Bowling: DeFreitas 7–0–40–2; Allott 8–0–46–0; Atherton 8–0–40–0; Wasim Akram 8–0–32–0; Austin 8–0–33–3.

Umpires: B. Hassan and R. Palmer.

At Colwyn Bay, May 27. LANCASHIRE beat GLAMORGAN by four wickets.

At Horsham, June 3. SUSSEX v LANCASHIRE. No result.

LANCASHIRE v GLOUCESTERSHIRE

At Manchester, June 10. Gloucestershire won by two wickets. Toss: Gloucestershire.

Lancashire

G. D. Mendis c and b Lawrence	32	†W. K. Hegg not out	2
G. Fowler run out	6	I. D. Austin not out	1
G. D. Lloyd run out	85	B 2, l-b 11, w 9	22
T. E. Jesty c Lawrence b Alleyne	22		
M. Watkinson c Bainbridge b Alleyne	23	1/22 2/68 3/109 (6 wkts, 40 overs)	230
Wasim Akram b Walsh	37	4/162 5/220 6/229	

*D. P. Hughes, J. D. Fitton and P. J. W. Allott did not bat.

Bowling: Walsh 8–0–46–1; Curran 8–0–52–0; Bainbridge 8–0–39–0; Lawrence 8–0–38–1; Alleyne 8–0–42–2.

Gloucestershire

I. P. Butcher c Fowler b Watkinson	13	C. A. Walsh b Wasim Akram	12
C. W. J. Athey c Hegg b Watkinson	6	†G. A. Tedstone not out	1
*A. J. Wright c Mendis b Watkinson	68		
K. M. Curran c Hegg b Wasim Akram	7	L-b 14, w 7, n-b 1	22
P. Bainbridge b Wasim Akram	39		
J. W. Lloyds lbw b Wasim Akram	0	1/15 2/30 3/49 (8 wkts, 39.4 overs)	231
P. W. Romaines not out	45	4/139 5/139 6/166	
M. W. Alleyne st Hegg b Fitton	18	7/188 8/225	

D. V. Lawrence did not bat.

Bowling: Watkinson 8–0–22–3; Allott 8–0–46–0; Wasim Akram 8–0–39–4; Fitton 8–0–53–1; Austin 7.4–0–57–0.

Umpires: M. J. Kitchen and K. J. Lyons.

LANCASHIRE v HAMPSHIRE

At Manchester, June 24. No result. Toss: Hampshire. The match, already reduced to 23 overs a side, was abandoned after only one over.

Lancashire

G. D. Mendis not out 1
G. Fowler not out 1
W 1 1

(no wkt, 1 over) 3

G. D. Lloyd, T. E. Jesty, M. Watkinson, Wasim Akram, I. D. Austin, *D. P. Hughes, J. D. Fitton, †J. Stanworth and P. J. W. Allott did not bat.

Bowling: Marshall 1–0–3–0.

Hampshire

V. P. Terry, R. J. Scott, C. L. Smith, D. I. Gower, M. D. Marshall, *M. C. J. Nicholas, J. R. Ayling, R. J. Maru, †R. J. Parks, C. A. Connor and T. M. Tremlett.

Umpires: H. D. Bird and P. J. Eele.

At Maidstone, July 1. LANCASHIRE beat KENT by 77 runs.

LANCASHIRE v DERBYSHIRE

At Manchester, July 8. Derbyshire won by 5 runs. Toss: Lancashire.

Derbyshire

*K. J. Barnett c Wasim Akram b Watkinson . 85
†P. D. Bowler c Allott b Watkinson . . . 40
J. E. Morris c Lloyd b DeFreitas 55
A. P. Kuiper c Allott b DeFreitas 7
B. Roberts b Allott 28
C. J. Adams b Wasim Akram 14
S. C. Goldsmith not out 7
L-b 8, w 3, n-b 2 13

1/108 2/175 3/198 4/198 5/230 6/249 (6 wkts, 40 overs) 249

S. J. Base, G. Miller, A. E. Warner and O. H. Mortensen did not bat.

Bowling: Allott 8–0–34–1; DeFreitas 8–0–53–2; Watkinson 8–0–42–2; Wasim Akram 8–0–59–1; Austin 8–0–53–0.

Lancashire

G. D. Mendis c Barnett b Kuiper 71
G. D. Lloyd c Bowler b Base 1
†W. K. Hegg run out 10
T. E. Jesty b Miller 20
G. Fowler lbw b Warner 57
M. Watkinson c and b Base 8
Wasim Akram c Adams b Kuiper 7
P. A. J. DeFreitas c Kuiper b Base . . . 17
I. D. Austin c Bowler b Kuiper 3
*D. P. Hughes not out 21
P. J. W. Allott run out 12
B 1, l-b 12, w 4 17

1/6 2/30 3/81 4/134 5/147 6/158 7/189 8/203 9/207 (39.5 overs) 244

Bowling: Mortensen 8–1–25–0; Base 7.5–0–49–3; Miller 8–0–50–1; Warner 8–0–57–1; Kuiper 8–0–50–3.

Umpires: R. Julian and D. O. Oslear.

LANCASHIRE v WORCESTERSHIRE

At Manchester, July 15. Lancashire won by seven wickets. Toss: Lancashire.

Worcestershire

*T. S. Curtis lbw b Watkinson	32	P. J. Newport not out	16
M. J. Weston c Fowler b Watkinson	31	S. R. Lampitt c DeFreitas b Austin	0
G. A. Hick b Wasim Akram	42	C. M. Tolley not out	1
D. B. D'Oliveira c Hegg b Watkinson	3	L-b 8, w 6	14
D. A. Leatherdale c Hughes b Watkinson	4		
†S. J. Rhodes b Austin	12	1/68 2/68 3/80 (8 wkts, 40 overs)	157
N. V. Radford c Atherton b Wasim Akram	2	4/92 5/117 6/125 7/148 8/149	

S. M. McEwan did not bat.

Bowling: Allott 8–0–31–0; DeFreitas 8–1–28–0; Watkinson 8–0–30–4; Wasim Akram 8–0–34–2; Austin 8–1–26–2.

Lancashire

G. Fowler c Curtis b Lampitt	33	M. Watkinson not out	15
M. A. Atherton c Rhodes b Tolley	1	L-b 5, w 4, n-b 1	10
G. D. Lloyd not out	65		
N. H. Fairbrother run out	36	1/4 2/71 3/125 (3 wkts, 30.1 overs)	160

Wasim Akram, †W. K. Hegg, *D. P. Hughes, P. A. J. DeFreitas, I. D. Austin and P. J. W. Allott did not bat.

Bowling: Newport 7–0–31–0; Tolley 6–0–20–1; Radford 4–0–24–0; Lampitt 7.1–0–34–1; McEwan 3–0–23–0; Hick 2–0–17–0; Leatherdale 1–0–6–0.

Umpires: B. Hassan and J. W. Holder.

At Colchester, July 22. LANCASHIRE beat ESSEX by two wickets.

LANCASHIRE v SOMERSET

At Manchester, July 29. Lancashire won by six wickets. Toss: Somerset.

Somerset

S. J. Cook c Martin b Wasim Akram	41	R. P. Lefebvre not out	14
R. J. Bartlett c Lloyd b Watkinson	55	I. G. Swallow not out	7
*C. J. Tavaré c Mendis b Austin	17	L-b 2, w 4, n-b 5	11
R. J. Harden b Wasim Akram	32		
G. D. Rose b Austin	1	1/73 2/110 3/122 (7 wkts, 40 overs)	203
†N. D. Burns b Watkinson	8	4/124 5/140	
A. N. Hayhurst c Fowler b Austin	17	6/174 7/188	

N. A. Mallender and J. C. Hallett did not bat.

Bowling: DeFreitas 8–0–36–0; Martin 8–0–38–0; Wasim Akram 8–0–36–2; Watkinson 8–0–57–2; Austin 8–1–34–3.

Lancashire

G. Fowler c Rose b Swallow	60	M. Watkinson not out	11
G. D. Mendis c Burns b Mallender	7	L-b 7, w 3, n-b 2	12
G. D. Lloyd c Hayhurst b Rose	57		
*N. H. Fairbrother c Rose b Hallett	47	1/12 2/103 3/171 (4 wkts, 37.4 overs)	207
T. E. Jesty not out	13	4/186	

Wasim Akram, P. A. J. DeFreitas, I. D. Austin, †W. K. Hegg and P. J. Martin did not bat.

Bowling: Mallender 8–1–37–1; Rose 8–0–24–1; Hallett 4.4–0–31–1; Hayhurst 4–0–23–0; Swallow 7–0–41–1; Lefebvre 6–0–44–0.

Umpires: J. W. Holder and A. G. T. Whitehead.

At Scarborough, August 5. LANCASHIRE beat YORKSHIRE by 78 runs.

At Northampton, August 12. LANCASHIRE beat NORTHAMPTONSHIRE by seven wickets.

LANCASHIRE v WARWICKSHIRE

At Manchester, August 26. Lancashire won by 49 runs. Toss: Warwickshire. Fowler's tenth Sunday League fifty in 1990 increased his Lancashire record aggregate for a Sunday League season to 773 runs at 55.21.

Lancashire

G. D. Mendis lbw b Munton 9
G. Fowler b Smith 69
G. D. Lloyd c Asif Din b Twose 31
N. H. Fairbrother c Asif Din b Twose . 20
M. Watkinson b Smith 22
Wasim Akram b Reeve 31
P. A. J. DeFreitas c Moody b Benjamin 32
†W. K. Hegg not out 10
I. D. Austin not out 2
B 1, l-b 7, w 6, n-b 1 15

1/17 2/100 3/138 4/143 5/172 6/226 7/231 (7 wkts, 39 overs) 241

*D. P. Hughes and P. J. W. Allott did not bat.

Bowling: Small 0.3–0–3–0; Moody 3.3–0–32–0; Munton 7–0–45–1; Benjamin 8–0–41–1; Reeve 6–0–31–1; Twose 6–0–38–2; Smith 8–2–43–2.

Warwickshire

A. J. Moles b DeFreitas 70
Asif Din c Hegg b Allott 1
T. M. Moody b Allott 17
*T. A. Lloyd b Wasim Akram 16
D. A. Reeve lbw b Watkinson 0
R. G. Twose c Fowler b Watkinson 6
N. M. K. Smith c Lloyd b Watkinson . 10
†K. J. Piper b Watkinson 30
J. E. Benjamin c Austin b Watkinson .. 24
T. A. Munton not out 4
G. C. Small absent injured
B 1, l-b 8, w 4, n-b 1 14

1/3 2/45 3/78 4/79 5/99 6/116 7/136 8/178 9/192 (35.4 overs) 192

Bowling: DeFreitas 8–0–34–1; Allott 8–0–51–2; Wasim Akram 6–0–21–1; Watkinson 7.4–0–46–5; Austin 6–0–31–0.

Umpires: J. H. Harris and B. Hassan.

LEICESTERSHIRE

LEICESTERSHIRE v NORTHAMPTONSHIRE

At Leicester, April 22. Northamptonshire won by six wickets. Toss: Northamptonshire. Robinson's figures were the most economical for Northamptonshire since Sarfraz Nawaz's 8–4–7–2 against Worcestershire at Worcester in 1977.

Leicestershire

T. J. Boon b Capel 9
*N. E. Briers c Lamb b Cook 10
J. J. Whitaker c Ripley b Robinson ... 32
P. Willey c Bailey b Cook 5
J. D. R. Benson b Thomas 8
C. C. Lewis b Thomas 9
†P. Whitticase c Lamb b Thomas 38
M. I. Gidley c Capel b Brown 10
J. P. Agnew b Brown 1
A. D. Mullally not out 0
L. B. Taylor lbw b Brown 0
L-b 9, w 6, n-b 2 17

1/20 2/35 3/43 4/66 5/80 6/97 7/134 8/137 9/138 (38 overs) 139

Bowling: Capel 6–2–18–1; Brown 6–0–26–3; Robinson 8–4–8–1; Cook 8–1–31–2; Thomas 7–1–27–3; Penberthy 3–0–20–0.

Northamptonshire

W. Larkins c Whitticase b Lewis	17	A. L. Penberthy not out	0
R. J. Bailey c Lewis b Gidley	70	W 5	5
*A. J. Lamb c Whitaker b Lewis	4		
D. J. Capel not out	47	1/39 2/53 3/138 (4 wkts, 37.1 overs)	143
D. J. Wild lbw b Lewis	0	4/139	

†D. Ripley, J. G. Thomas, N. G. B. Cook, M. A. Robinson and S. J. Brown did not bat.

Bowling: Taylor 7–1–34–0; Mullally 6–0–33–0; Lewis 8–0–18–3; Agnew 8–1–25–0; Gidley 6.1–0–28–1; Willey 2–0–5–0.

Umpires: J. W. Holder and B. J. Meyer.

At Cardiff, April 29. LEICESTERSHIRE lost to GLAMORGAN by 32 runs.

LEICESTERSHIRE v ESSEX

At Leicester, May 6. Leicestershire won by five wickets. Toss: Essex. Gooch became the eighth to pass 6,000 runs in the Sunday League. In Leicestershire's reply, Lewis's 93 not out came off 58 balls and contained four sixes and six fours.

Essex

*G. A. Gooch c Nixon b Mullally	65	A. W. Lilley c Boon b Agnew	2
B. R. Hardie c Potter b Mullally	2	T. D. Topley not out	1
M. E. Waugh st Nixon b Benson	84	B 1, l-b 4, w 5, n-b 1	11
P. J. Prichard c Boon b Gidley	8		
J. P. Stephenson not out	38	1/5 2/131 3/140 (7 wkts, 40 overs)	223
N. A. Foster c Potter b Agnew	8	4/186 5/197	
†M. A. Garnham c Briers b Lewis	4	6/214 7/220	

M. C. Ilott and J. H. Childs did not bat.

Bowling: Lewis 8–0–42–1; Mullally 8–0–32–2; Agnew 8–0–39–2; Taylor 8–0–41–0; Gidley 6–0–51–1; Benson 2–0–13–1.

Leicestershire

T. J. Boon b Ilott	56	M. I. Gidley not out	6
*N. E. Briers c Garnham b Foster	5		
J. J. Whitaker c Topley b Gooch	44	L-b 3, w 2	5
C. C. Lewis not out	93		
L. Potter run out	4	1/14 2/80 3/131 (5 wkts, 38.3 overs)	225
J. D. R. Benson b Ilott	12	4/157 5/186	

†P. A. Nixon, A. D. Mullally, J. P. Agnew and L. B. Taylor did not bat.

Bowling: Foster 7.3–0–37–1; Ilott 8–0–41–2; Topley 8–0–49–0; Childs 8–0–29–0; Gooch 7–0–66–1.

Umpires: K. E. Palmer and D. R. Shepherd.

At Manchester, May 20. LEICESTERSHIRE lost to LANCASHIRE by 23 runs.

LEICESTERSHIRE v SOMERSET

At Leicester, May 27. Somerset won by three wickets. Toss: Somerset.

Leicestershire

T. J. Boon c Burns b Cleal	18	†P. A. Nixon not out	9
*N. E. Briers c Lefebvre b Rose	6		
J. J. Whitaker c Tavaré b Rose	83	L-b 5	5
P. Willey c Cook b Rose	52		
L. Potter run out	1	1/17 2/31 3/156 (5 wkts, 40 overs)	191
J. D. R. Benson not out	17	4/163 5/166	

J. P. Agnew, G. J. F. Ferris, A. D. Mullally and D. J. Millns did not bat.

Bowling: Rose 8–0–36–3; Cleal 5–0–27–1; Lefebvre 8–0–42–0; Mallender 8–0–28–0; Swallow 5–0–20–0; Hayhurst 6–0–33–0.

Somerset

S. J. Cook b Millns	60	R. P. Lefebvre lbw b Willey	0
P. M. Roebuck b Ferris	28	M. W. Cleal not out	8
A. N. Hayhurst lbw b Ferris	1	B 1, l-b 4, w 11	16
*C. J. Tavaré b Agnew	26		
R. J. Harden not out	31	1/54 2/62 3/124 (7 wkts, 38.3 overs)	193
†N. D. Burns b Willey	3	4/126 5/131	
G. D. Rose c Briers b Millns	20	6/166 7/169	

N. A. Mallender and I. G. Swallow did not bat.

Bowling: Agnew 7–2–20–1; Millns 8–1–71–2; Mullally 7.3–1–36–0; Ferris 8–1–28–2; Willey 8–0–33–2.

Umpires: D. J. Constant and B. Dudleston.

LEICESTERSHIRE v HAMPSHIRE

At Leicester, June 3. Hampshire won by five wickets. Toss: Hampshire.

Leicestershire

T. J. Boon c Parks b Ayling	6	G. J. F. Ferris lbw b Marshall	6
*N. E. Briers run out	9	A. D. Mullally not out	10
J. J. Whitaker b Connor	0		
P. Willey not out	68	B 5, l-b 2, w 12, n-b 3	22
L. Potter lbw b Tremlett	23		
J. D. R. Benson c Maru b Tremlett	7	1/13 2/13 3/17 (8 wkts, 40 overs)	166
†P. A. Nixon c Maru b Ayling	10	4/75 5/86 6/114	
J. P. Agnew b Connor	5	7/129 8/138	

L. B. Taylor did not bat.

Bowling: Marshall 8–1–23–1; Connor 8–1–35–2; Ayling 8–1–28–2; Tremlett 8–1–28–2; Maru 2–0–14–0; Scott 6–0–31–0.

Hampshire

V. P. Terry c Briers b Agnew	2	J. R. Ayling not out	23
R. J. Scott b Mullally	4		
R. A. Smith c Nixon b Mullally	0	L-b 4, w 9, n-b 2	15
D. I. Gower c Nixon b Taylor	53		
M. D. Marshall c Mullally b Benson	44	1/8 2/8 3/8 (5 wkts, 38.2 overs)	169
*M. C. J. Nicholas not out	28	4/104 5/118	

†R. J. Parks, C. A. Connor, T. M. Tremlett and R. J. Maru did not bat.

Bowling: Agnew 7.2–1–35–1; Mullally 8–0–27–2; Taylor 8–1–35–1; Ferris 5–0–27–0; Willey 8–0–25–0; Benson 2–0–16–1.

Umpires: J. H. Hampshire and P. B. Wight.

LEICESTERSHIRE v SUSSEX

At Leicester, June 10. Leicestershire won by seven wickets. Toss: Leicestershire.

Sussex

N. J. Lenham c Benson b Willey 32
I. J. Gould c Potter b Agnew 8
*P. W. G. Parker c Nixon b Lewis 2
A. P. Wells c Willey b Lewis 2
M. P. Speight c Lewis b Mullally 21
C. M. Wells c Nixon b Lewis 16
A. I. C. Dodemaide c Briers b Benjamin 26
C. C. Remy not out 12
†P. Moores not out 17
L-b 6, w 5, n-b 5 16

1/8 2/21 3/26 4/70 5/86 6/95 7/126 (7 wkts, 40 overs) 152

A. R. Clarke and I. D. K. Salisbury did not bat.

Bowling: Benjamin 8–3–13–1; Agnew 8–1–25–1; Lewis 8–0–36–3; Mullally 8–0–28–1; Willey 8–0–44–1.

Leicestershire

T. J. Boon c Lenham b Dodemaide ... 29
*N. E. Briers c Speight b Salisbury 31
J. J. Whitaker not out 53
P. Willey c Moores b Salisbury 4
C. C. Lewis not out 25
B 4, l-b 7, w 1, n-b 2 14

1/65 2/87 3/91 (3 wkts, 37.4 overs) 156

L. Potter, J. D. R. Benson, †P. A. Nixon, W. K. M. Benjamin, J. P. Agnew and A. D. Mullally did not bat.

Bowling: C. M. Wells 7–0–30–0; Dodemaide 8–3–20–1; Remy 6.4–0–34–0; Clarke 8–0–40–0; Salisbury 8–1–21–2.

Umpires: P. J. Eele and D. O. Oslear.

LEICESTERSHIRE v MIDDLESEX

At Leicester, June 17. Middlesex won by 16 runs. Toss: Leicestershire. Gatting's 124 not out, his highest in the Sunday League, came off 93 balls and contained one six and seventeen fours.

Middlesex

D. L. Haynes c and b Lewis 49
M. A. Roseberry lbw b Agnew 18
*M. W. Gatting not out 124
M. R. Ramprakash c and b Willey 22
K. R. Brown c Nixon b Willey 8
R. O. Butcher lbw b Agnew 22
J. E. Emburey not out 5
B 1, l-b 6, w 3, n-b 1 11

1/34 2/88 3/125 4/164 5/226 (5 wkts, 40 overs) 259

†P. Farbrace, N. F. Williams, S. P. Hughes and A. R. C. Fraser did not bat.

Bowling: Benjamin 8–0–59–0; Agnew 8–3–35–2; Lewis 8–0–64–1; Mullally 8–0–36–0; Willey 8–0–58–2.

Leicestershire

T. J. Boon st Farbrace b Emburey 84
*N. E. Briers c Farbrace b Hughes 46
J. J. Whitaker c Gatting b Haynes 4
C. C. Lewis c Roseberry b Fraser 14
P. Willey c Butcher b Williams 39
L. Potter c and b Williams 8
J. D. R. Benson not out 36
W. K. M. Benjamin not out 2
L-b 3, w 3, n-b 4 10

1/119 2/128 3/148 4/168 5/191 6/227 (6 wkts, 40 overs) 243

†P. A. Nixon, J. P. Agnew and A. D. Mullally did not bat.

Bowling: Fraser 8–0–34–1; Williams 8–1–55–2; Haynes 5–0–29–1; Gatting 3–0–18–0; Hughes 8–0–52–1; Emburey 8–0–52–1.

Umpires: B. Hassan and K. E. Palmer.

At Gloucester, June 24. LEICESTERSHIRE beat GLOUCESTERSHIRE on faster scoring-rate.

At Nottingham, July 1. LEICESTERSHIRE lost to NOTTINGHAMSHIRE by eight wickets.

At Knypersley, July 15. LEICESTERSHIRE lost to DERBYSHIRE by 118 runs.

At Sheffield, July 29. LEICESTERSHIRE lost to YORKSHIRE by eight wickets.

LEICESTERSHIRE v WORCESTERSHIRE

At Leicester, August 5. Worcestershire won by seven wickets. Toss: Worcestershire. Hick, having hit thirteen fours, missed his century when, with the scores level, a short-pitched delivery from Lewis flew over his head and was called a wide by umpire Palmer.

Leicestershire

T. J. Boon c Lampitt b Weston 16
*N. E. Briers b Newport 42
B. F. Smith c Curtis b McEwan 10
C. C. Lewis c Neale b Lampitt 13
J. D. R. Benson b Illingworth 15
L. Potter c Lampitt b McEwan 33
M. I. Gidley not out 14
†P. A. Nixon c Rhodes b McEwan 0
G. J. Parsons not out 19
L-b 14, w 9 23

1/34 2/49 3/81 4/100 5/132 6/156 7/157 (7 wkts, 40 overs) 185

D. J. Millns and A. D. Mullally did not bat.

Bowling: Newport 8–0–36–1; Weston 8–0–27–1; McEwan 8–0–38–3; Lampitt 8–1–38–1; Illingworth 8–0–32–1.

Worcestershire

I. T. Botham c Lewis b Millns 1
T. S. Curtis b Mullally 19
G. A. Hick not out 98
D. B. D'Oliveira b Lewis 24
*P. A. Neale not out 34
B 1, l-b 1, w 7, n-b 1 10

1/3 2/74 3/121 (3 wkts, 36.3 overs) 186

†S. J. Rhodes, M. J. Weston, P. J. Newport, R. K. Illingworth, S. R. Lampitt and S. M. McEwan did not bat.

Bowling: Lewis 7.3–0–34–1; Millns 5–1–22–1; Parsons 5–0–27–0; Mullally 7–0–35–1; Gidley 8–0–40–0; Benson 4–0–26–0.

Umpires: J. W. Holder and R. Palmer.

At The Oval, August 12. LEICESTERSHIRE lost to SURREY by 69 runs.

At Birmingham, August 19. WARWICKSHIRE v LEICESTERSHIRE. No result.

LEICESTERSHIRE v KENT

At Leicester, August 26. Leicestershire won by six wickets. Toss: Leicestershire.

Kent

S. G. Hinks c and b Benson 60
N. R. Taylor c Whitaker b Parsons . . . 52
T. R. Ward c Whitaker b Parsons 0
G. R. Cowdrey c Benson b Millns 43
*C. S. Cowdrey c Nixon b Millns 6
M. V. Fleming b Benson 9
†S. A. Marsh not out 18
V. J. Wells not out 7
L-b 5, w 9 14

1/110 2/117 3/122 4/164 5/175 6/188 (6 wkts, 39 overs) 209

D. J. M. Kelleher, R. P. Davis and T. N. Wren did not bat.

Bowling: Benjamin 7–0–40–0; Parsons 8–0–37–2; Lewis 8–0–23–0; Millns 8–0–47–2; Gidley 3–0–24–0; Benson 5–0–33–2.

Leicestershire

T. J. Boon run out 97
*N. E. Briers c Hinks b Wren 16
B. F. Smith lbw b Davis 6
J. J. Whitaker c and b Fleming 20
C. C. Lewis not out 58
J. D. R. Benson not out 1
L-b 4, w 7, n-b 1 12

1/42 2/55 3/109 4/202 (4 wkts, 38.5 overs) 210

W. K. M. Benjamin, †P. A. Nixon, G. J. Parsons, D. J. Millns and M. I. Gidley did not bat.

Bowling: Kelleher 7.5–0–50–0; Wren 6–0–31–1; Davis 8–1–29–1; Ward 8–0–44–0; Fleming 8–0–47–1; Wells 1–0–5–0.

Umpires: B. Dudleston and D. O. Oslear.

MIDDLESEX

At Manchester, April 22. MIDDLESEX beat LANCASHIRE by eight wickets.

MIDDLESEX v ESSEX

At Lord's, April 29. Middlesex won by 12 runs. Toss: Essex.

Middlesex

D. L. Haynes b Pringle 31
M. A. Roseberry c Foster b Pringle . . . 16
*M. W. Gatting c Garnham b Pringle . 7
M. R. Ramprakash c Waugh b Topley . 40
K. R. Brown c Garnham b Topley 50
R. O. Butcher not out 44
†P. R. Downton c Garnham b Pringle . 6
J. E. Emburey not out 10
L-b 12, w 2, n-b 2 16

1/42 2/58 3/59 4/145 5/156 6/202 (6 wkts, 40 overs) 220

N. F. Williams, S. P. Hughes and N. G. Cowans did not bat.

Bowling: Foster 8–0–51–0; Topley 8–0–37–2; Pringle 8–3–27–4; Gooch 8–0–44–0; Waugh 4–0–25–0; Childs 4–0–24–0.

Essex

*G. A. Gooch c Downton b Williams . . 3
B. R. Hardie c and b Emburey 16
M. E. Waugh c Brown b Williams 44
P. J. Prichard run out 35
D. R. Pringle b Hughes 18
J. P. Stephenson st Downton b Emburey 5
A. W. Lilley c Butcher b Emburey 10
†M. A. Garnham run out 26
N. A. Foster c Roseberry b Cowans . . . 19
T. D. Topley c Downton b Cowans . . . 10
J. H. Childs not out 3
L-b 11, w 4, n-b 4 19

1/4 2/54 3/91 4/129 5/133 6/140 7/157 8/185 9/200 (39.5 overs) 208

Bowling: Hughes 8–1–37–1; Williams 8–0–33–2; Cowans 8–1–40–2; Emburey 7.5–1–49–3; Gatting 8–0–38–0.

Umpires: B. Hassan and A. G. T. Whitehead.

At Folkestone, May 6. MIDDLESEX beat KENT by six wickets.

MIDDLESEX v NOTTINGHAMSHIRE

At Lord's, May 13. Nottinghamshire won by 12 runs. Toss: Middlesex. Johnson reached his first Sunday League hundred off 97 balls with fifteen boundaries.

Nottinghamshire

B. C. Broad c Emburey b Cowans 72
*R. T. Robinson run out 6
P. Johnson c Ramprakash b Williams . .100
D. W. Randall not out 30
M. Saxelby c Taylor b Haynes 20
F. D. Stephenson not out 5
L-b 13, w 5 18

1/15 2/183 3/192 4/244 (4 wkts, 40 overs) 251

†B. N. French, E. E. Hemmings, K. E. Cooper, K. Saxelby and J. A. Afford did not bat.

Bowling: Taylor 8–0–34–0; Williams 8–1–30–1; Cowans 8–1–52–1; Emburey 8–0–53–0; Gatting 5–0–52–0; Haynes 3–0–17–1.

Middlesex

D. L. Haynes lbw b Stephenson 10
M. A. Roseberry lbw b Hemmings 80
*M. W. Gatting c Hemmings b Stephenson . 0
M. R. Ramprakash st French b Afford . 17
K. R. Brown lbw b Hemmings 56
R. O. Butcher c Randall b Hemmings . 7
†P. R. Downton b Hemmings 10
N. F. Williams c and b Stephenson ... 3
J. E. Emburey st French b Hemmings . 4
N. G. Cowans c Afford b K. Saxelby .. 27
N. R. Taylor not out 4
B 4, l-b 8, w 7, n-b 2 21

1/24 2/25 3/80 4/171 5/180 6/187 7/199 8/207 9/208 (37.5 overs) 239

Bowling: Stephenson 7–0–29–3; Cooper 8–0–40–0; K. Saxelby 4.5–0–51–1; Afford 6–0–41–1; M. Saxelby 4–0–33–0; Hemmings 8–0–33–5.

Umpires: J. H. Harris and D. O. Oslear.

MIDDLESEX v GLOUCESTERSHIRE

At Lord's, May 27. Middlesex won by seven wickets. Toss: Gloucestershire. When Emburey dismissed Alleyne, he passed T. E. Jesty's total of 248 wickets in the Sunday League to become the seventh most successful bowler in the competition.

Gloucestershire

†R. C. Russell b Cowans 17
C. W. J. Athey c Gatting b Emburey .. 29
*A. J. Wright run out 58
K. M. Curran c Roseberry b Gatting .. 13
P. Bainbridge b Gatting 18
J. W. Lloyds not out 36
P. W. Romaines c Downton b Cowans . 11
M. W. Alleyne b Emburey 1
C. A. Walsh b Williams 1
D. V. Lawrence b Hughes 1
M. C. J. Ball run out 1
L-b 9, w 6 15

1/29 2/80 3/115 4/137 5/152 6/179 7/186 8/195 9/198 (40 overs) 201

Bowling: Cowans 8–2–27–2; Hughes 8–0–43–1; Gatting 8–0–48–2; Williams 8–0–44–1; Emburey 8–1–30–2.

Middlesex

D. L. Haynes lbw b Alleyne 50
M. A. Roseberry b Lawrence 0
*M. W. Gatting c Wright b Walsh 5
M. R. Ramprakash not out 88
K. R. Brown not out 39
L-b 10, w 11 21

1/4 2/17 3/105 (3 wkts, 37.4 overs) 203

R. O. Butcher, †P. R. Downton, J. E. Emburey, N. F. Williams, S. P. Hughes and N. G. Cowans did not bat.

Bowling: Walsh 7.4–2–22–1; Lawrence 8–0–39–1; Curran 7–0–37–0; Bainbridge 7–0–40–0; Ball 2–0–20–0; Alleyne 6–0–35–1.

Umpires: K. J. Lyons and R. A. White.

MIDDLESEX v WARWICKSHIRE

At Lord's, June 3. Middlesex won by nine wickets in a match reduced by rain to seventeen overs a side. Toss: Middlesex.

Warwickshire

T. M. Moody b Taylor	17
P. A. Smith b Williams	2
A. I. Kallicharran not out	41
†G. W. Humpage c Haynes b Hughes	13
D. A. Reeve c Ramprakash b Emburey	5
Asif Din run out	17
N. M. K. Smith c Williams b Emburey	10
*T. A. Lloyd not out	0
L-b 3, w 7	10
1/13 2/29 3/53 4/62 5/91 6/112 (6 wkts, 17 overs)	115

G. C. Small, J. E. Benjamin and T. A. Munton did not bat.

Bowling: Taylor 4–0–16–1; Williams 4–0–22–1; Gatting 1–0–13–0; Hughes 3–0–32–1; Emburey 3–0–21–2; Haynes 2–0–8–0.

Middlesex

D. L. Haynes c Asif Din b Benjamin	50
M. A. Roseberry not out	51
*M. W. Gatting not out	6
W 3, n-b 6	9
1/107 (1 wkt, 13 overs)	116

M. R. Ramprakash, K. R. Brown, †P. R. Downton, N. F. Williams, J. E. Emburey, S. P. Hughes, R. O. Butcher and N. R. Taylor did not bat.

Bowling: Munton 3–0–19–0; Benjamin 3–0–31–1; Small 2–0–28–0; N. M. K. Smith 3–0–26–0; P. A. Smith 2–0–12–0.

Umpires: P. J. Eele and A. A. Jones.

At Basingstoke, June 10. MIDDLESEX beat HAMPSHIRE by seven wickets.

At Leicester, June 17. MIDDLESEX beat LEICESTERSHIRE by 16 runs.

At Luton, June 24. MIDDLESEX beat NORTHAMPTONSHIRE by nine wickets.

MIDDLESEX v WORCESTERSHIRE

At Lord's, July 1. Middlesex won by 99 runs. Toss: Worcestershire. Both Middlesex's total of 290 for six and Ramprakash's unbeaten 147, his maiden hundred in the competition, were records for the county in the Sunday League. Ramprakash, who put on 132 in 51 minutes for the third wicket with Roseberry, scored his runs from only 90 balls, hitting eight sixes and ten fours.

Middlesex

D. L. Haynes c Neale b Lampitt 11
M. A. Roseberry lbw b Botham 73
*M. W. Gatting b Lampitt 9
M. R. Ramprakash not out 147
K. R. Brown c and b Lampitt 14
R. O. Butcher c and b Lampitt 1
†P. Farbrace b Lampitt 3
J. E. Emburey not out 8
L-b 19, w 5 24

1/43 2/64 3/196 4/230 5/232 6/238 (6 wkts, 40 overs) 290

N. F. Williams, A. R. C. Fraser and N. G. Cowans did not bat.

Bowling: Botham 8–1–42–1; Weston 4–0–30–0; Illingworth 8–1–28–0; Lampitt 8–1–67–5; McEwan 3–0–33–0; Hick 3–0–31–0; Leatherdale 6–0–40–0.

Worcestershire

T. S. Curtis st Farbrace b Gatting 16
M. J. Weston c Williams b Gatting ... 7
G. A. Hick c Haynes b Cowans 45
I. T. Botham c Williams b Emburey ... 35
D. B. D'Oliveira c Williams b Cowans . 2
*P. A. Neale c Williams b Emburey ... 13
D. A. Leatherdale b Emburey 0
†S. J. Rhodes st Farbrace b Emburey .. 16
R. K. Illingworth not out 16
S. R. Lampitt not out 25
L-b 14, w 1, n-b 1 16

1/28 2/33 3/86 4/98 5/125 6/126 7/137 8/152 (8 wkts, 40 overs) 191

S. M. McEwan did not bat.

Bowling: Fraser 5–1–15–0; Williams 4–0–17–0; Haynes 4–0–21–0; Gatting 8–0–29–2; Emburey 8–1–39–4; Cowans 8–0–43–2; Ramprakash 2–0–9–0; Brown 1–0–4–0.

Umpires: R. Palmer and D. R. Shepherd.

MIDDLESEX v SOMERSET

At Lord's, July 8. Somerset won by 24 runs. Toss: Middlesex. Tavaré and Harden put on 105 in twelve overs for the third wicket.

Somerset

S. J. Cook b Williams 58
R. J. Bartlett c Gatting b Emburey 54
*C. J. Tavaré not out 72
R. J. Harden not out 41
B 2, l-b 7, w 11, n-b 3 23

1/116 2/143 (2 wkts, 40 overs) 248

A. N. Hayhurst, G. D. Rose, †N. D. Burns, R. P. Lefebvre, I. G. Swallow, J. C. Hallett and N. A. Mallender did not bat.

Bowling: Williams 8–0–39–1; Fraser 8–0–49–0; Haynes 7–0–41–0; Gatting 2–0–11–0; Cowans 7–0–59–0; Emburey 8–1–40–1.

Middlesex

D. L. Haynes c Harden b Mallender ... 82
M. A. Roseberry b Mallender 16
*M. W. Gatting b Hayhurst 24
M. R. Ramprakash b Hayhurst 9
K. R. Brown c Harden b Mallender ... 15
R. O. Butcher c Lefebvre b Swallow ... 12
†P. Farbrace b Mallender 0
N. F. Williams c Bartlett b Swallow ... 12
J. E. Emburey c and b Rose 32
A. R. C. Fraser b Lefebvre 6
N. G. Cowans not out 0
B 4, l-b 12 16

1/32 2/87 3/107 4/141 5/166 6/166 7/170 8/190 9/204 (39.3 overs) 224

Bowling: Rose 5.3–0–42–1; Mallender 8–1–32–4; Lefebvre 7–0–37–1; Hallett 5–0–23–0; Hayhurst 6–0–30–2; Swallow 8–0–44–2.

Umpires: J. H. Harris and D. S. Thompsett.

At The Oval, July 15. MIDDLESEX lost to SURREY by 68 runs.

MIDDLESEX v GLAMORGAN

At Lord's, August 5. Middlesex won by 84 runs. Toss: Middlesex. When Emburey dismissed Dennis, he passed J. N. Shepherd to become the sixth most successful bowler in the Sunday League.

Middlesex

D. L. Haynes c Cottey b Dale	37
M. A. Roseberry c Frost b Butcher	68
*M. W. Gatting b Dennis	99
M. R. Ramprakash b Watkin	47
K. R. Brown run out	5
J. E. Emburey not out	6
N. F. Williams not out	9
B 2, l-b 14	16
1/61 2/154 3/264 4/270 5/272 (5 wkts, 40 overs)	287

†P. R. Downton, P. C. R. Tufnell, A. R. C. Fraser and N. G. Cowans did not bat.

Bowling: Watkin 8–1–67–1; Frost 5–0–40–0; Dennis 7–0–54–1; Dale 8–0–38–1; Croft 8–0–52–0; Butcher 4–0–20–1.

Glamorgan

M. P. Maynard b Fraser	59
H. Morris c Haynes b Williams	11
I. V. A. Richards b Emburey	35
*A. R. Butcher st Downton b Emburey	52
P. A. Cottey b Fraser	28
R. D. B. Croft b Fraser	6
A. Dale c Ramprakash b Fraser	0
†C. P. Metson not out	2
S. L. Watkin b Emburey	1
S. J. Dennis b Emburey	0
M. Frost c Roseberry b Ramprakash	6
B 1, l-b 1, w 1	3
1/30 2/83 3/136 4/176 5/194 6/194 7/195 8/196 9/196 (39.3 overs)	203

Bowling: Williams 6–0–33–1; Cowans 8–0–46–0; Tufnell 8–0–45–0; Emburey 8–2–32–4; Fraser 8–0–28–4; Haynes 1–0–12–0; Ramprakash 0.3–0–5–1.

Umpires: D. J. Constant and K. J. Lyons.

MIDDLESEX v SUSSEX

At Lord's, August 12. Sussex won by seven wickets. Toss: Middlesex.

Middlesex

D. L. Haynes b C. M. Wells	7
M. A. Roseberry run out	4
*M. W. Gatting run out	5
M. R. Ramprakash b Pigott	11
K. R. Brown c Pigott b Hansford	68
†P. R. Downton b Donelan	23
J. E. Emburey c Hanley b Dodemaide	27
N. F. Williams not out	11
P. C. R. Tufnell not out	0
L-b 4, w 4	8
1/9 2/15 3/27 4/31 5/93 6/149 7/162 (7 wkts, 40 overs)	164

N. R. Taylor and N. G. Cowans did not bat.

Bowling: Dodemaide 8–1–24–1; C. M. Wells 8–0–28–1; Pigott 8–0–20–1; Donelan 8–2–23–1; Hansford 5–0–46–1; Salisbury 3–0–19–0.

Sussex

N. J. Lenham b Tufnell	78	A. I. C. Dodemaide not out	19
*C. M. Wells c Emburey b Taylor	10	L-b 2, w 6, n-b 4	12
A. P. Wells c Gatting b Williams	30		—
M. P. Speight not out	16	1/36 2/129 3/135 (3 wkts, 34.5 overs)	165

R. Hanley, †P. Moores, A. C. S. Pigott, B. T. P. Donelan, A. R. Hansford and I. D. K. Salisbury did not bat.

Bowling: Taylor 6.5–0–38–1; Williams 8–0–32–1; Cowans 8–0–23–0; Tufnell 7–0–40–1; Emburey 5–0–30–0.

Umpires: B. J. Meyer and A. G. T. Whitehead.

At Derby, August 19. DERBYSHIRE v MIDDLESEX. No result.

At Scarborough, August 26. MIDDLESEX lost to YORKSHIRE by 44 runs.

NORTHAMPTONSHIRE

At Leicester, April 22. NORTHAMPTONSHIRE beat LEICESTERSHIRE by six wickets.

At Birmingham, April 29. NORTHAMPTONSHIRE lost to WARWICKSHIRE by seven wickets.

NORTHAMPTONSHIRE v DERBYSHIRE

At Northampton, May 6. Derbyshire won by four wickets. Toss: Derbyshire.

Northamptonshire

*W. Larkins c Adams b Malcolm	13	J. W. Govan c Adams b Malcolm	5
A. Fordham c Kuiper b Malcolm	0	W. W. Davis not out	4
R. J. Bailey c Bowler b Kuiper	29		
D. J. Capel c Bowler b Warner	39	B 1, l-b 6, w 6	13
N. A. Felton run out	19		—
D. J. Wild not out	48	1/2 2/13 3/76 (8 wkts, 40 overs)	180
†W. M. Noon run out	1	4/88 5/123 6/126	
J. G. Thomas c Barnett b Warner	9	7/155 8/175	

M. A. Robinson did not bat.

Bowling: Mortensen 8–1–19–0; Malcolm 8–1–34–3; Base 8–0–40–0; Warner 8–0–34–2; Kuiper 8–0–46–1.

Derbyshire

*K. J. Barnett b Robinson	23	S. C. Goldsmith run out	13
†P. D. Bowler b Thomas	30	A. E. Warner not out	13
J. E. Morris b Govan	12	L-b 4, w 3, n-b 1	8
A. P. Kuiper not out	62		—
C. J. Adams b Robinson	5	1/57 2/57 3/79 (6 wkts, 38.5 overs)	181
B. Roberts c Govan b Capel	15	4/92 5/122 6/152	

S. J. Base, O. H. Mortensen and D. E. Malcolm did not bat.

Bowling: Capel 7.5–0–46–1; Davis 7–1–42–0; Thomas 8–1–39–1; Robinson 8–1–23–2; Govan 8–0–27–1.

Umpires: J. H. Harris and R. A. White.

NORTHAMPTONSHIRE v KENT

At Northampton, May 27. Kent won by 55 runs. Toss: Kent. Kent's total of 287 for three was the highest by any county in the Sunday League against Northamptonshire, who suffered their ninth successive defeat of the season in all competitions. Graham Cowdrey hit 70 off 39 balls and shared in an unbroken fourth-wicket partnership of 115 in ten overs with his brother, Chris, whose 45 came off 27 balls.

Kent

S. G. Hinks c Penberthy b Capel 11
N. R. Taylor c Capel b Robinson 73
T. R. Ward c Felton b Penberthy 71
*C. S. Cowdrey not out 45
G. R. Cowdrey not out 70
B 1, l-b 10, w 6 17

1/17 2/137 3/172 (3 wkts, 40 overs) 287

†S. A. Marsh, M. V. Fleming, M. A. Ealham, C. Penn, R. P. Davis and T. A. Merrick did not bat.

Bowling: Davis 8–1–49–0; Capel 8–1–40–1; Thomas 8–1–46–0; Govan 4–0–28–0; Robinson 8–0–73–1; Penberthy 4–0–40–1.

Northamptonshire

A. Fordham run out 28
N. A. Felton c Marsh b C. S. Cowdrey. 64
*A. J. Lamb c Penn b C. S. Cowdrey . . 27
R. J. Bailey lbw b Fleming 11
D. J. Capel c Davis b C. S. Cowdrey . . 38
A. L. Penberthy c Ealham b C. S. Cowdrey . 6
J. G. Thomas c C. S. Cowdrey b Merrick 1
†D. Ripley c Taylor b Merrick 6
J. W. Govan not out 9
W. W. Davis c C. S. Cowdrey b Penn . 19
M. A. Robinson b Merrick 0
B 2, l-b 16, w 5 23

1/67 2/116 3/135 4/145 5/161 6/178 7/189 8/196 9/223 (37.4 overs) 232

Bowling: Penn 7–1–33–1; Merrick 7.4–0–37–3; Ealham 5–0–33–0; Davis 4–0–29–0; Fleming 6–0–25–1; C. S. Cowdrey 8–0–57–4.

Umpires: B. J. Meyer and D. S. Thompsett.

At The Oval, June 3. NORTHAMPTONSHIRE lost to SURREY by four wickets.

NORTHAMPTONSHIRE v GLAMORGAN

At Northampton, June 10. Northamptonshire won by 10 runs. Toss: Northamptonshire. Capel, playing in his 100th Sunday League match, reached his first hundred in the competition off 88 deliveries. In all he faced 100 balls, hit three sixes and ten fours, and shared with Bailey in a third-wicket partnership of 191 in 29 overs. Richards, when 33, reached 5,000 runs in the Sunday League.

Northamptonshire

A. Fordham c Metson b Frost 0
N. A. Felton c Cowley b Watkin 21
R. J. Bailey b Frost 71
D. J. Capel c Morris b Frost 121
D. J. Wild c Metson b Frost 4
R. G. Williams not out 1
†W. M. Noon c Morris b Dennis 11
J. G. Thomas not out 0
B 2, l-b 6, w 7 15

1/0 2/27 3/218 4/228 5/232 6/243 (6 wkts, 40 overs) 244

*N. G. B. Cook, W. W. Davis and M. A. Robinson did not bat.

Bowling: Frost 8–1–30–4; Watkin 8–0–37–1; Cowley 7–0–43–0; Dennis 8–0–63–1; Richards 7–0–45–0; Holmes 2–0–18–0.

Glamorgan

*A. R. Butcher b Williams 40
H. Morris lbw b Cook 40
M. P. Maynard c Williams b Cook 13
I. V. A. Richards c Cook b Robinson .. 45
G. C. Holmes not out 50
P. A. Cottey c Noon b Davis 28
N. G. Cowley not out 2
B 1, l-b 10, w 5 16

1/77 2/102 3/105 4/172 5/218 (5 wkts, 40 overs) 234

†C. P. Metson, S. J. Dennis, S. L. Watkin and M. Frost did not bat.

Bowling: Capel 6–0–34–0; Davis 8–1–39–1; Thomas 8–0–42–0; Williams 8–0–34–1; Cook 6–1–40–2; Robinson 4–0–34–1.

Umpires: J. D. Bond and P. B. Wight.

NORTHAMPTONSHIRE v MIDDLESEX

At Luton, June 24. Middlesex won by nine wickets. Toss: Middlesex.

Northamptonshire

A. Fordham c Hughes b Williams 4
N. A. Felton c Haynes b Gatting 10
R. J. Bailey c Butcher b Emburey 60
D. J. Capel st Farbrace b Emburey ... 46
D. J. Wild run out 8
R. G. Williams run out 1
†D. Ripley st Farbrace b Emburey 3
J. G. Thomas c Ramprakash b Fraser . 2
W. W. Davis c Ramprakash b Hughes . 7
*N. G. B. Cook b Emburey 1
M. A. Robinson not out 0
L-b 1, w 3, n-b 5 9

1/8 2/32 3/113 4/127 5/131 6/137 7/140 8/143 9/151 (37.2 overs) 151

Bowling: Fraser 7–2–16–1; Williams 8–1–39–1; Gatting 8–1–34–1; Hughes 7–0–35–1; Emburey 7.2–0–26–4.

Middlesex

*M. W. Gatting not out 76
M. A. Roseberry run out 50
M. R. Ramprakash not out 8
L-b 7, w 8, n-b 4 19

1/112 (1 wkt, 27.4 overs) 153

D. L. Haynes, K. R. Brown, R. O. Butcher, J. E. Emburey, †P. Farbrace, N. F. Williams, S. P. Hughes and A. R. C. Fraser did not bat.

Bowling: Davis 5–0–19–0; Capel 4–0–31–0; Thomas 2–0–20–0; Robinson 7–0–32–0; Cook 3–0–13–0; Wild 4.4–0–31–0; Williams 2–2–0–0.

Umpires: N. T. Plews and R. A. White.

At Taunton, July 1. NORTHAMPTONSHIRE lost to SOMERSET by seven wickets.

NORTHAMPTONSHIRE v YORKSHIRE

At Tring, July 8. Yorkshire won by 61 runs. Toss: Northamptonshire.

Yorkshire

S. A. Kellett run out 10
*A. A. Metcalfe lbw b Wild 55
†R. J. Blakey st Ripley b Wild 42
P. E. Robinson not out 58
P. J. Hartley b Davis 51
D. Byas not out 18
B 5, l-b 7, w 4, n-b 1 17

1/18 2/113 3/118 4/200 (4 wkts, 40 overs) 251

C. White, C. A. Chapman, P. Carrick, A. Sidebottom and S. D. Fletcher did not bat.

Bowling: Davis 8–1–38–1; Capel 8–0–26–0; Cook 8–0–60–0; Robinson 6–0–53–0; Williams 4–0–36–0; Wild 6–0–26–2.

Northamptonshire

A. Fordham b Sidebottom	28	†D. Ripley c Chapman b Hartley	17
*W. Larkins c Hartley b Sidebottom	12	N. G. B. Cook b White	1
R. J. Bailey b Hartley	18	M. A. Robinson not out	0
D. J. Capel c Robinson b Carrick	25	B 1, l-b 2, w 1, n-b 2	6
N. A. Felton st Blakey b Carrick	9		
D. J. Wild c Fletcher b White	19	1/40 2/53 3/72 (37.1 overs)	190
R. G. Williams b Hartley	35	4/94 5/97 6/124	
W. W. Davis c Carrick b Byas	20	7/146 8/187 9/190	

Bowling: Sidebottom 8–1–21–2; Hartley 7–0–37–3; Fletcher 5–0–34–0; Carrick 8–2–22–2; White 7.1–0–56–2; Byas 2–0–17–1.

Umpires: J. C. Balderstone and A. A. Jones.

At Chelmsford, July 15. NORTHAMPTONSHIRE lost to ESSEX by six wickets.

NORTHAMPTONSHIRE v SUSSEX

At Wellingborough School, July 22. Sussex won by 21 runs. Toss: Northamptonshire. Capel reached his hundred off 77 balls, and hit four sixes and eleven fours in his 115.

Sussex

N. J. Lenham c Larkins b Robinson	25	J. A. North not out	15
I. J. Gould c Bailey b Cook	55	†P. Moores not out	6
*P. W. G. Parker lbw b Williams	34		
A. P. Wells lbw b Cook	2	B 1, l-b 14, w 6, n-b 1	22
M. P. Speight b Cook	32		
C. M. Wells c Williams b Davis	6	1/55 2/113 3/121 (8 wkts, 40 overs)	253
A. I. C. Dodemaide c and b Davis	19	4/127 5/140 6/177	
A. C. S. Pigott c Cook b Robinson	37	7/226 8/239	

I. D. K. Salisbury did not bat.

Bowling: Davis 8–1–32–2; Brown 8–0–48–0; Robinson 8–0–59–2; Williams 8–0–63–1; Cook 8–1–36–3.

Northamptonshire

A. Fordham lbw b North	21	S. J. Brown not out	3
W. Larkins lbw b Dodemaide	7	N. G. B. Cook not out	0
*A. J. Lamb c Parker b Pigott	17		
D. J. Capel c Salisbury b Lenham	115	L-b 2, w 7	9
R. J. Bailey c Speight b Pigott	4		
R. G. Williams c Gould b North	6	1/22 2/39 3/61 (8 wkts, 40 overs)	232
†D. Ripley c C. M. Wells b Pigott	26	4/67 5/88 6/149	
W. W. Davis b Lenham	24	7/204 8/231	

M. A. Robinson did not bat.

Bowling: C. M. Wells 8–0–28–0; Dodemaide 8–0–38–1; Pigott 8–0–60–3; North 8–0–45–2; Lenham 8–0–59–2.

Umpires: B. Hassan and B. Leadbeater.

At Nottingham, July 29. NORTHAMPTONSHIRE lost to NOTTINGHAMSHIRE by 5 runs.

At Bournemouth, August 5. NORTHAMPTONSHIRE lost to HAMPSHIRE by six wickets.

NORTHAMPTONSHIRE v LANCASHIRE

At Northampton, August 12. Lancashire won by seven wickets as Northamptonshire recorded their eighth successive defeat. Toss: Lancashire. Larkins faced a total of 97 balls, needing only 31 for his second fifty, and hit twelve fours. Fowler began Lancashire's reply needing 3 runs to pass H. Pilling's Lancashire record, set in 1970, of 625 runs in a Sunday League season.

Northamptonshire

A. Fordham c Mendis b Watkinson ... 44
N. A. Felton run out ... 8
*W. Larkins c Lloyd b DeFreitas ... 104
R. J. Bailey c Allott b DeFreitas ... 47
D. J. Capel c Allott b DeFreitas ... 4
D. J. Wild c Lloyd b DeFreitas ... 0
R. G. Williams not out ... 1
†D. Ripley not out ... 6
B 2, l-b 6, w 1 ... 9

1/13 2/71 3/203 4/214 5/214 6/215 (6 wkts, 40 overs) 223

N. G. B. Cook, S. J. Brown and M. A. Robinson did not bat.

Bowling: Allott 6–1–19–0; DeFreitas 8–1–22–4; Watkinson 6–0–32–1; Wasim Akram 8–0–50–0; Hughes 6–0–49–0; Austin 6–0–43–0.

Lancashire

G. D. Mendis c Felton b Wild ... 37
G. Fowler c Cook b Robinson ... 81
G. D. Lloyd c Ripley b Wild ... 0
N. H. Fairbrother not out ... 86
M. Watkinson not out ... 6
L-b 10, w 5 ... 15

1/67 2/68 3/209 (3 wkts, 36.5 overs) 225

Wasim Akram, P. A. J. DeFreitas, I. D. Austin, †W. K. Hegg, *D. P. Hughes and P. J. W. Allott did not bat.

Bowling: Brown 4.5–0–21–0; Robinson 7–0–56–1; Cook 6–0–42–0; Wild 8–0–31–2; Williams 8–0–45–0; Bailey 3–0–20–0.

Umpires: J. H. Harris and D. S. Thompsett.

At Worcester, August 19. WORCESTERSHIRE v NORTHAMPTONSHIRE. No result.

NORTHAMPTONSHIRE v GLOUCESTERSHIRE

At Northampton, August 26. Northamptonshire won by 2 runs. Toss: Gloucestershire. Larkins faced 77 balls, hitting seven sixes and seven fours.

Northamptonshire

G. Cook b Curran ... 16
*W. Larkins c Alleyne b Milburn ... 109
A. Fordham c Wright b Bainbridge ... 50
R. J. Bailey c Milburn b Alleyne ... 20
D. J. Capel c Barnes b Alleyne ... 16
N. A. Felton b Walsh ... 24
D. J. Wild b Walsh ... 15
W. W. Davis c Barnes b Curran ... 9
†W. M. Noon c and b Curran ... 0
J. G. Thomas c and b Walsh ... 4
N. G. B. Cook not out ... 0
B 1, l-b 5, w 4, n-b 1 ... 11

1/28 2/111 3/200 4/201 5/225 6/245 7/268 8/268 9/273 (40 overs) 274

Bowling: Barnes 6–0–22–0; Walsh 8–0–36–3; Curran 8–0–45–3; Milburn 5–0–54–1; Alleyne 7–0–49–2; Bainbridge 6–0–62–1.

Gloucestershire

C. W. J. Athey c and b Thomas	22	G. D. Hodgson not out	2
M. W. Alleyne c N. G. B. Cook b Wild	38	E. T. Milburn not out	4
P. Bainbridge c Felton b Wild	2	L-b 10, w 6, n-b 1	17
K. M. Curran c Capel b Thomas	92		
*A. J. Wright b Capel	50	1/44 2/58 3/105 (7 wkts, 40 overs)	272
P. W. Romaines b Davis	31	4/208 5/245	
C. A. Walsh b Davis	14	6/265 7/266	

†R. C. J. Williams and S. N. Barnes did not bat.

Bowling: Thomas 8–0–43–2; Davis 8–0–40–2; Capel 8–0–62–1; Wild 8–0–58–2; N. G. B. Cook 8–0–59–0.

Umpires: P. J. Eele and K. E. Palmer.

NOTTINGHAMSHIRE

NOTTINGHAMSHIRE v YORKSHIRE

At Nottingham, April 22. Nottinghamshire won by five wickets. Toss: Nottinghamshire.

Yorkshire

*M. D. Moxon lbw b Pick	37	A. Sidebottom c French b Stephenson	1
A. A. Metcalfe lbw b Saxelby	11	P. W. Jarvis not out	28
†R. J. Blakey b Hemmings	30	L-b 9, w 6, n-b 1	16
P. E. Robinson c Robinson b Hemmings	4		
D. Byas c French b Saxelby	7	1/38 2/61 3/76 (7 wkts, 40 overs)	161
C. White not out	26	4/96 5/102	
P. Carrick run out	1	6/104 7/107	

D. Gough and S. D. Fletcher did not bat.

Bowling: Stephenson 8–2–28–1; Cooper 8–2–24–0; Saxelby 8–0–49–2; Hemmings 8–0–28–2; Pick 8–0–23–1.

Nottinghamshire

B. C. Broad c Blakey b Jarvis	4	†B. N. French not out	15
P. R. Pollard b Jarvis	3		
*R. T. Robinson lbw b Sidebottom	1	B 1, l-b 3	4
P. Johnson c Blakey b Carrick	39		
D. W. Randall not out	54	1/8 2/9 3/9 (5 wkts, 39.1 overs)	162
F. D. Stephenson c Blakey b Gough	42	4/67 5/129	

E. E. Hemmings, K. E. Cooper, R. A. Pick and K. Saxelby did not bat.

Bowling: Jarvis 8–1–26–2; Sidebottom 8–3–22–1; Fletcher 7.1–0–31–0; Gough 5–0–29–1; Carrick 6–0–27–1; Byas 5–0–23–0.

Umpires: J. D. Bond and B. Leadbeater.

NOTTINGHAMSHIRE v LANCASHIRE

At Nottingham, April 29. Lancashire won by five wickets. Toss: Lancashire.

Nottinghamshire

B. C. Broad lbw b Allott	13	E. E. Hemmings c Fowler b DeFreitas	12
P. R. Pollard lbw b DeFreitas	8	K. E. Cooper c Jesty b DeFreitas	21
*R. T. Robinson c Fairbrother b Atherton	61	R. A. Pick not out	0
P. Johnson c Atherton b Jesty	15	B 1, l-b 6, w 7, n-b 1	15
D. W. Randall b Austin	14		
F. D. Stephenson c Fowler b Allott	23	1/14 2/28 3/54 (39.3 overs)	193
†B. N. French c Watkinson b Atherton	11	4/107 5/128 6/148	
K. P. Evans st Hegg b Atherton	0	7/149 8/162 9/186	

Bowling: Allott 8–0–29–2; DeFreitas 7.3–0–36–3; Watkinson 7–0–41–0; Jesty 2–0–9–1; Austin 8–0–38–1; Atherton 7–0–33–3.

Lancashire

G. Fowler c Robinson b Hemmings ... 52
M. A. Atherton c Robinson b Pick 5
G. D. Lloyd b Hemmings 47
N. H. Fairbrother c French b Evans .. 19
T. E. Jesty c Broad b Stephenson 15
M. Watkinson not out 33
P. A. J. DeFreitas not out 7
B 1, l-b 10, w 4, n-b 1 16

1/14 2/100 3/126 4/139 5/166 (5 wkts, 38.4 overs) 194

I. D. Austin, *D. P. Hughes, †W. K. Hegg and P. J. W. Allott did not bat.

Bowling: Cooper 8–0–32–0; Pick 8–0–43–1; Evans 7–0–42–1; Stephenson 7.4–1–48–1; Hemmings 8–2–18–2.

Umpires: D. O. Oslear and D. R. Shepherd.

At Worcester, May 6. NOTTINGHAMSHIRE lost to WORCESTERSHIRE by 61 runs.

At Lord's, May 13. NOTTINGHAMSHIRE beat MIDDLESEX by 12 runs.

NOTTINGHAMSHIRE v SURREY

At Nottingham, May 20. Nottinghamshire won by eight wickets. Toss: Nottinghamshire. Broad's 106 not out, his highest in the Sunday League, came off 125 balls and contained a six and eight fours.

Surrey

G. S. Clinton c Broad b Afford 40
A. J. Stewart lbw b K. Saxelby 10
M. A. Lynch b Hemmings 20
G. P. Thorpe c Afford b Hemmings ... 0
†D. M. Ward c Afford b M. Saxelby .. 34
*I. A. Greig b Hemmings 12
K. T. Medlycott c M. Saxelby b Hemmings . 2
M. A. Feltham c Hemmings b K. Saxelby . 14
C. K. Bullen not out 23
M. P. Bicknell not out 11
B 1, l-b 9, w 5 15

1/32 2/64 3/68 4/84 5/107 6/130 7/132 8/154 (8 wkts, 40 overs) 181

A. J. Murphy did not bat.

Bowling: Stephenson 8–1–21–0; Cooper 6–0–19–0; K. Saxelby 6–0–44–2; Afford 8–1–24–1; Hemmings 8–0–48–4; M. Saxelby 4–0–15–1.

Nottinghamshire

B. C. Broad not out 106
*R. T. Robinson c Ward b Bicknell ... 2
P. Johnson b Bicknell 63
D. W. Randall not out 9
L-b 3, w 2 5

1/5 2/144 (2 wkts, 38.1 overs) 185

M. Saxelby, F. D. Stephenson, †B. N. French, E. E. Hemmings, K. E. Cooper, J. A. Afford and K. Saxelby did not bat.

Bowling: Bicknell 8–1–23–2; Murphy 8–0–41–0; Feltham 8–1–34–0; Medlycott 4–0–35–0; Bullen 8–0–36–0; Lynch 2–0–9–0; Stewart 0.1–0–4–0.

Umpires: J. H. Hampshire and A. A. Jones.

At Derby, June 10. NOTTINGHAMSHIRE beat DERBYSHIRE by four wickets.

At Canterbury, June 17. NOTTINGHAMSHIRE lost to KENT by 24 runs.

At Bath, June 24. NOTTINGHAMSHIRE lost to SOMERSET by 29 runs.

NOTTINGHAMSHIRE v LEICESTERSHIRE

At Nottingham, July 1. Nottinghamshire won by eight wickets. Toss: Nottinghamshire. The match was reduced to 38 overs a side after rain had delayed the start.

Leicestershire

T. J. Boon c French b Evans 13
*N. E. Briers c and b K. Saxelby 33
J. J. Whitaker c Cooper b Evans 4
P. Willey b Evans 41
C. C. Lewis c and b Stephenson 36
J. D. R. Benson b Stephenson 2
G. J. Parsons not out 11
†P. A. Nixon b Evans 6
J. P. Agnew c M. Saxelby b Stephenson 1
A. D. Mullally run out 4
L-b 3, w 1 4

1/28 2/38 3/72 4/127 5/131 6/136 7/145 8/148 9/155 (9 wkts, 38 overs) 155

L. B. Taylor did not bat.

Bowling: Stephenson 8–1–21–3; Cooper 8–2–21–0; Evans 8–0–30–4; Hemmings 7–0–33–0; K. Saxelby 5–0–27–1; M. Saxelby 2–0–20–0.

Nottinghamshire

B. C. Broad c Whitaker b Mullally 57
M. Newell not out 60
P. Johnson c Nixon b Taylor 35
*R. T. Robinson not out 0
L-b 4, w 1 5

1/104 2/144 (2 wkts, 31.4 overs) 157

M. Saxelby, F. D. Stephenson, †B. N. French, K. P. Evans, E. E. Hemmings, K. Saxelby and K. E. Cooper did not bat.

Bowling: Agnew 5–0–25–0; Mullally 6.4–1–25–1; Lewis 5–1–27–0; Taylor 7–0–35–1; Willey 2–0–17–0; Parsons 6–1–24–0.

Umpires: R. Julian and D. S. Thompsett.

NOTTINGHAMSHIRE v SUSSEX

At Nottingham, July 8. Nottinghamshire won by 8 runs. Toss: Sussex. Johnson's century came off only 71 balls, with eight fours.

Nottinghamshire

B. C. Broad c Salisbury b Pigott 61
M. Newell c Moores b Lenham 15
P. Johnson lbw b Clarke 104
F. D. Stephenson b Pigott 32
G. W. Mike lbw b Pigott 13
*R. T. Robinson not out 15
K. P. Evans not out 7
B 1, l-b 10, w 5 16

1/51 2/128 3/202 4/224 5/245 (5 wkts, 40 overs) 263

†B. N. French, K. E. Cooper, K. Saxelby and J. A. Afford did not bat.

Bowling: C. M. Wells 8–0–45–0; Dodemaide 6–0–46–0; Clarke 7–0–37–1; Lenham 8–0–36–1; Pigott 8–0–55–3; Salisbury 3–0–33–0.

Sussex

N. J. Lenham b Afford	60	C. C. Remy run out	1
I. J. Gould c French b Cooper	6	I. D. K. Salisbury b Stephenson	0
A. P. Wells run out	98	A. R. Clarke not out	0
M. P. Speight run out	2	L-b 12, w 2	14
*C. M. Wells b Mike	25		
A. I. C. Dodemaide lbw b Mike	22	1/34 2/93 3/98	(39.2 overs) 255
A. C. S. Pigott c Johnson b Mike	17	4/150 5/201 6/229	
†P. Moores run out	10	7/251 8/254 9/254	

Bowling: Saxelby 6–0–49–0; Cooper 4–0–18–1; Stephenson 7.2–0–48–1; Afford 6–0–40–1; Evans 8–0–46–0; Mike 8–0–42–3.

Umpires: H. D. Bird and K. E. Palmer.

At Southampton, July 15. NOTTINGHAMSHIRE lost to HAMPSHIRE by 7 runs.

At Birmingham, July 22. NOTTINGHAMSHIRE beat WARWICKSHIRE by 10 runs.

NOTTINGHAMSHIRE v NORTHAMPTONSHIRE

At Nottingham, July 29. Nottinghamshire won by 5 runs. Toss: Northamptonshire.

Nottinghamshire

B. C. Broad lbw b Capel	38	K. P. Evans not out	28
M. Newell lbw b Capel	16		
P. Johnson c Capel b Larkins	29	L-b 4, w 6	10
*R. T. Robinson not out	74		
M. Saxelby b Larkins	5	1/50 2/70 3/115	(5 wkts, 40 overs) 202
F. D. Stephenson b Williams	2	4/125 5/136	

†B. N. French, K. E. Cooper, G. W. Mike and J. A. Afford did not bat.

Bowling: Robinson 6–0–34–0; Hughes 4–0–16–0; Capel 8–0–34–2; Cook 5–0–21–0; Wild 5–0–24–0; Larkins 6–0–34–2; Williams 6–0–35–1.

Northamptonshire

A. Fordham c Robinson b Mike	59	†D. Ripley run out	0
*W. Larkins b Afford	58	J. G. Hughes not out	1
D. J. Capel run out	4	L-b 9, w 7	16
R. J. Bailey b Cooper	4		
N. A. Felton not out	33	1/113 2/123 3/136	(7 wkts, 40 overs) 197
R. G. Williams c Newell b Mike	20	4/138 5/190	
D. J. Wild b Evans	2	6/195 7/196	

N. G. B. Cook and M. A. Robinson did not bat.

Bowling: Cooper 8–0–62–1; Stephenson 8–2–19–0; Evans 8–0–42–1; Mike 8–0–41–2; Afford 8–0–24–1.

Umpires: J. H. Hampshire and M. J. Kitchen.

At Southend, August 5. NOTTINGHAMSHIRE beat ESSEX by six wickets.

NOTTINGHAMSHIRE v GLAMORGAN

At Nottingham, August 12. Nottinghamshire won by eight wickets. Toss: Nottinghamshire. Robinson celebrated the birth of his second son in the morning with an unbeaten century, reaching three figures off 111 balls. His innings of 107 not out contained twelve fours.

Glamorgan

M. P. Maynard lbw b Cooper 7
H. Morris c Evans b Mike 9
I. V. A. Richards c and b Afford 54
*A. R. Butcher c French b Mike 11
P. A. Cottey not out 50
A. Dale c Saxelby b Afford 7
R. D. B. Croft c Robinson b Stephenson 31
†C. P. Metson not out 17
B 1, l-b 4, w 2, n-b 1 8

1/15 2/28 3/85 4/87 5/101 6/151 (6 wkts, 40 overs) 194

S. L. Watkin, S. J. Dennis and M. Frost did not bat.

Bowling: Cooper 8–1–25–1; Stephenson 8–1–40–1; Evans 8–0–47–0; Mike 8–1–38–2; Afford 8–0–39–2.

Nottinghamshire

B. C. Broad b Richards 26
*R. T. Robinson not out 107
P. Johnson c Metson b Richards 23
M. Saxelby not out 28
L-b 4, w 10 14

1/95 2/154 (2 wkts, 37 overs) 198

M. Newell, F. D. Stephenson, †B. N. French, K. P. Evans, G. W. Mike, K. E. Cooper and J. A. Afford did not bat.

Bowling: Watkin 7–0–27–0; Frost 8–0–48–0; Croft 8–0–40–0; Dennis 5–0–32–0; Richards 8–0–32–2; Dale 1–0–15–0.

Umpires: D. J. Constant and D. O. Oslear.

NOTTINGHAMSHIRE v GLOUCESTERSHIRE

At Nottingham, August 19. No result. Toss: Nottinghamshire. Rain ended the match, which had already been reduced to twenty overs a side.

Gloucestershire

C. W. J. Athey lbw b Cooper 2
K. M. Curran b Cooper 15
P. Bainbridge c French b Mike 2
†R. C. Russell c French b Mike 45
M. W. Alleyne c Stephenson b Mike . . 19
C. A. Walsh c Saxelby b Stephenson . . 23
*A. J. Wright not out 21
P. W. Romaines not out 15
L-b 6, w 2, n-b 2 10

1/6 2/11 3/45 4/79 5/109 6/120 (6 wkts, 20 overs) 152

G. D. Hodgson, D. V. Lawrence and E. T. Milburn did not bat.

Bowling: Mike 4–0–30–3; Cooper 4–0–21–2; Evans 4–0–27–0; Stephenson 4–0–28–1; Hemmings 3–0–30–0; Saxelby 1–0–10–0.

Nottinghamshire

B. C. Broad c Athey b Alleyne 22
*R. T. Robinson c Hodgson b Lawrence 6
P. Johnson not out 25
M. Saxelby not out 24
B 1, l-b 2, w 3 6

1/18 2/37 (2 wkts, 11.4 overs) 83

M. Newell, F. D. Stephenson, †B. N. French, K. P. Evans, E. E. Hemmings, G. W. Mike and K. E. Cooper did not bat.

Bowling: Lawrence 4–0–23–1; Curran 2–0–11–0; Alleyne 2–0–12–1; Walsh 2–0–15–0; Milburn 1–0–15–0; Bainbridge 0.4–0–4–0.

Umpires: J. D. Bond and N. T. Plews.

SOMERSET

SOMERSET v WORCESTERSHIRE

At Taunton, April 22. Worcestershire won by 33 runs. Toss: Somerset. Curtis, whose 124 came from 143 balls, and Hick added 150 for Worcestershire's second wicket in just eighteen overs. The six dismissals by Rhodes were a record for Worcestershire in all one-day competitions.

Worcestershire

T. S. Curtis c Cook b Roebuck 124
I. T. Botham st Burns b Swallow 24
G. A. Hick not out 78
D. B. D'Oliveira not out 0
L-b 6, w 5 11

1/86 2/236 (2 wkts, 40 overs) 237

*P. A. Neale, M. J. Weston, †S. J. Rhodes, R. K. Illingworth, P. J. Newport, N. V. Radford and S. M. McEwan did not bat.

Bowling: Jones 8–0–40–0; Mallender 8–1–26–0; Rose 8–0–54–0; Swallow 7–0–47–1; Lefebvre 8–0–54–0; Roebuck 1–0–10–1.

Somerset

S. J. Cook c Rhodes b Newport 18
P. M. Roebuck c Rhodes b McEwan .. 39
R. J. Bartlett c Rhodes b Newport 2
*C. J. Tavaré c Rhodes b Botham 3
R. J. Harden c Rhodes b Botham 35
†N. D. Burns run out 19
G. D. Rose not out 41
R. P. Lefebvre c and b Illingworth 11
A. N. Jones st Rhodes b Illingworth ... 10
I. G. Swallow not out 6
L-b 11, w 6, n-b 3 20

1/30 2/35 3/45 4/102 5/121 6/139 7/175 8/197 (8 wkts, 40 overs) 204

N. A. Mallender did not bat.

Bowling: Newport 8–1–17–2; Weston 3–0–22–0; Botham 8–0–39–2; McEwan 8–0–49–1; Radford 5–0–20–0; Illingworth 8–0–46–2.

Umpires: K. E. Palmer and D. R. Shepherd.

SOMERSET v HAMPSHIRE

At Taunton, May 13. Somerset won by five wickets. Toss: Hampshire. Cook faced 87 balls, hitting three sixes and fifteen fours in his second three-figure innings of the weekend. His second fifty came off just 23 balls.

Hampshire

D. I. Gower c Tavaré b Jones	12	*M. C. J. Nicholas not out	33
V. P. Terry not out	113	B 1, l-b 6, w 5	12
R. A. Smith c Hayhurst b Cleal	51		
C. L. Smith b Lefebvre	25	1/23 2/125 3/181 (3 wkts, 40 overs)	246

J. R. Ayling, M. D. Marshall, †R. J. Parks, R. J. Maru, C. A. Connor and P. J. Bakker did not bat.

Bowling: Jones 6–1–40–1; Rose 8–0–49–0; Lefebvre 8–0–50–1; Hayhurst 8–0–35–0; Swallow 4–0–24–0; Cleal 6–0–41–1.

Somerset

S. J. Cook c R. A. Smith b Bakker	132	†N. D. Burns not out	13
P. M. Roebuck b Bakker	1		
A. N. Hayhurst c and b Maru	38	B 4, l-b 2, w 1, n-b 2	9
G. D. Rose c Terry b Marshall	32		
*C. J. Tavaré c Parks b Marshall	9	1/2 2/130 3/195 (5 wkts, 37 overs)	247
R. J. Harden not out	13	4/211 5/220	

R. P. Lefebvre, A. N. Jones, I. G. Swallow and M. W. Cleal did not bat.

Bowling: Marshall 8–0–53–2; Bakker 6–1–42–2; Connor 8–0–48–0; Ayling 5–0–38–0; Maru 8–0–38–1; Nicholas 2–0–22–0.

Umpires: A. A. Jones and B. Leadbeater.

SOMERSET v DERBYSHIRE

At Taunton, May 20. Derbyshire won by seven wickets. Toss: Derbyshire. The first-wicket partnership of 232 between Barnett and Morris was a Derbyshire record for any wicket in the Sunday League and was also the highest opening partnership for the county in one-day competitions. Barnett reached his hundred off 105 balls, while Morris's 134, a record for Derbyshire in the Sunday League, came off 116 balls and contained two sixes and eleven fours. This was Morris's third of four hundreds against Somerset in the month. The previous day he had scored 122 in the County Championship, and he went on to make his second of the match on the third day. On May 1 he had hit 123 in the Benson and Hedges Cup. In Somerset's innings Cook, when 7, became the first batsman to score 1,000 runs in all competitive matches in the season.

Somerset

S. J. Cook b Malcolm	53	R. P. Lefebvre not out	16
P. M. Roebuck b Barnett	85	M. W. Cleal not out	13
A. N. Hayhurst lbw b Miller	13	L-b 2, w 4	6
G. D. Rose c Goldsmith b Kuiper	5		
*C. J. Tavaré run out	7	1/91 2/119 3/124 (7 wkts, 40 overs)	258
R. J. Harden c Barnett b Malcolm	30	4/135 5/183	
†N. D. Burns run out	30	6/210 7/230	

I. G. Swallow and A. N. Jones did not bat.

Bowling: Mortensen 8–0–42–0; Miller 8–0–37–1; Warner 2–0–26–0; Malcolm 8–0–48–2; Kuiper 8–0–48–1; Barnett 6–0–55–1.

Derbyshire

*K. J. Barnett b Lefebvre	100	C. J. Adams not out	0
J. E. Morris b Rose	134	L-b 3, w 2	5
A. P. Kuiper not out	21		
A. E. Warner c Harden b Jones	4	1/232 2/240 3/258 (3 wkts, 40 overs)	264

B. Roberts, S. C. Goldsmith, G. Miller, D. E. Malcolm, O. H. Mortensen and †K. M. Krikken did not bat.

Bowling: Jones 6–0–38–1; Rose 8–0–45–1; Hayhurst 8–0–47–0; Lefebvre 8–0–44–1; Swallow 5–0–38–0; Cleal 3–0–27–0; Roebuck 2–0–22–0.

Umpires: K. E. Palmer and D. S. Thompsett.

At Leicester, May 27. SOMERSET beat LEICESTERSHIRE by three wickets.

At Bristol, June 3. SOMERSET lost to GLOUCESTERSHIRE by eight wickets.

At Canterbury, June 10. SOMERSET lost to KENT by six wickets.

SOMERSET v ESSEX

At Bath, June 17. Essex won by 101 runs. Toss: Somerset.

Essex

*G. A. Gooch b Hayhurst	34	N. A. Foster not out	39
B. R. Hardie b Mallender	7	†M. A. Garnham not out	12
M. E. Waugh b Rose	3	B 5, l-b 2, w 3	10
P. J. Prichard c and b Rose	64		
D. R. Pringle b Mallender	37	1/32 2/38 3/79 (7 wkts, 40 overs)	217
J. P. Stephenson b Rose	1	4/149 5/150	
A. W. Lilley c Bartlett b Jones	10	6/159 7/179	

T. D. Topley and J. H. Childs did not bat.

Bowling: Jones 7–0–47–1; Mallender 8–0–30–2; Rose 8–0–33–3; Swallow 5–0–32–0; Hayhurst 7–0–41–1; Roebuck 5–0–27–0.

Somerset

S. J. Cook lbw b Pringle	23	I. G. Swallow c Gooch b Topley	3
P. M. Roebuck c Hardie b Foster	0	A. N. Jones b Stephenson	0
R. J. Bartlett run out	16	N. A. Mallender not out	7
*C. J. Tavaré b Childs	5	L-b 6, w 3	9
R. J. Harden run out	13		
A. N. Hayhurst run out	20	1/3 2/33 3/48 (34.5 overs)	116
G. D. Rose b Topley	20	4/48 5/80 6/104	
†N. D. Burns b Foster	0	7/104 8/106 9/108	

Bowling: Topley 7.5–1–22–2; Foster 6–0–16–2; Childs 8–2–14–1; Pringle 6–0–23–1; Waugh 6–1–32–0; Stephenson 1–0–3–1.

Umpires: R. Julian and K. J. Lyons.

SOMERSET v NOTTINGHAMSHIRE

At Bath, June 24. Somerset won by 29 runs. Toss: Nottinghamshire.

Somerset

S. J. Cook lbw b Stephenson	3	M. W. Cleal not out	12
R. J. Bartlett run out	50	I. G. Swallow not out	3
*C. J. Tavaré b Cooper	86	B 4, l-b 14, w 8	26
†N. D. Burns b K. Saxelby	10		
G. D. Rose b Stephenson	45	1/11 2/120 3/145 (7 wkts, 40 overs)	245
R. J. Harden c Cooper b Evans	2	4/202 5/218	
A. N. Hayhurst run out	8	6/224 7/236	

J. C. Hallett and N. A. Mallender did not bat.

Bowling: Cooper 8–0–32–1; Stephenson 8–0–34–2; K. Saxelby 8–0–51–1; Evans 6–0–40–1; Afford 4–0–25–0; M. Saxelby 6–0–45–0.

Nottinghamshire

B. C. Broad c Burns b Mallender	18	K. E. Cooper b Hayhurst	9
M. Newell c Cleal b Hayhurst	85	K. Saxelby not out	6
P. Johnson c Burns b Hallett	1		
*R. T. Robinson c Tavaré b Swallow	12	B 4, l-b 5, w 4	13
M. Saxelby c Burns b Rose	19		
F. D. Stephenson c Rose b Hallett	34	1/26 2/27 3/60 (8 wkts, 40 overs)	216
†B. N. French c Bartlett b Rose	1	4/93 5/155 6/170	
K. P. Evans not out	18	7/180 8/207	

J. A. Afford did not bat.

Bowling: Mallender 8–0–34–1; Hallett 8–0–39–2; Swallow 8–0–35–1; Cleal 4–0–17–0; Rose 8–0–61–2; Hayhurst 4–0–21–2.

Umpires: K. J. Lyons and R. Palmer.

SOMERSET v NORTHAMPTONSHIRE

At Taunton, July 1. Somerset won by seven wickets. Toss: Somerset.

Northamptonshire

A. Fordham b Lefebvre	53	W. W. Davis b Lefebvre	3
N. A. Felton b Swallow	41	S. J. Brown c Burns b Rose	0
R. J. Bailey run out	6	N. G. B. Cook c Burns b Lefebvre	5
*A. J. Lamb c Lefebvre b Hayhurst	41	L-b 6, w 4	10
D. J. Capel c and b Mallender	11		
R. G. Williams c Burns b Lefebvre	1	1/75 2/89 3/118 (40 overs)	193
J. G. Thomas not out	19	4/154 5/158 6/163	
†D. Ripley c Burns b Rose	3	7/170 8/178 9/183	

Bowling: Mallender 8–1–24–1; Hallett 3–0–27–0; Lefebvre 8–0–35–4; Rose 6–0–40–2; Swallow 8–1–19–1; Hayhurst 7–1–42–1.

Somerset

S. J. Cook run out	88	G. D. Rose not out	22
N. J. Pringle c Ripley b Thomas	1	L-b 3, w 2	5
*C. J. Tavaré c Felton b Williams	56		
R. J. Harden not out	22	1/10 2/124 3/161 (3 wkts, 37.4 overs)	194

A. N. Hayhurst, †N. D. Burns, I. G. Swallow, R. P. Lefebvre, N. A. Mallender and J. C. Hallett did not bat.

Bowling: Davis 6.4–0–25–0; Thomas 7–0–38–1; Cook 8–0–42–0; Brown 8–0–55–0; Williams 8–0–31–1.

Umpires: K. J. Lyons and D. O. Oslear.

At Lord's, July 8. SOMERSET beat MIDDLESEX by 24 runs.

At Scarborough, July 15. SOMERSET lost to YORKSHIRE by 16 runs.

At Neath, July 22. SOMERSET beat GLAMORGAN by 220 runs.

At Manchester, July 29. SOMERSET lost to LANCASHIRE by six wickets.

SOMERSET v SURREY

At Weston-super-Mare, August 5. Surrey won by six wickets. Toss: Surrey.

Somerset

S. J. Cook c Stewart b Feltham	21
*C. J. Tavaré c Brown b Waqar Younis	41
R. J. Harden b Bicknell	53
J. C. M. Atkinson b Waqar Younis	8
G. D. Rose run out	3
R. P. Lefebvre lbw b Feltham	10
†N. D. Burns c Brown b Waqar Younis	26
A. N. Hayhurst b Bicknell	2
I. G. Swallow not out	8
N. A. Mallender not out	10
B 7, l-b 4, w 6	17
1/41 2/98 3/113 4/119 5/144 6/161 7/177 8/179 (8 wkts, 40 overs)	199

A. N. Jones did not bat.

Bowling: Bicknell 8–1–38–2; Feltham 8–0–40–2; Bullen 8–0–37–0; Medlycott 8–0–34–0; Waqar Younis 8–0–39–3.

Surrey

M. A. Feltham b Rose	24
A. D. Brown c Hayhurst b Jones	32
G. P. Thorpe run out	42
†D. M. Ward c Burns b Hayhurst	27
M. A. Lynch not out	32
*I. A. Greig not out	27
L-b 8, w 11	19
1/37 2/76 3/120 4/150 (4 wkts, 38.2 overs)	203

A. J. Stewart, K. T. Medlycott, C. K. Bullen, M. P. Bicknell and Waqar Younis did not bat.

Bowling: Mallender 8–0–44–0; Rose 7–0–41–1; Lefebvre 3.2–0–19–0; Jones 8–0–33–1; Swallow 5–1–28–0; Hayhurst 7–0–30–1.

Umpires: P. J. Eele and R. A. White.

SOMERSET v WARWICKSHIRE

At Weston-super-Mare, August 12. Somerset won by seven wickets. Toss: Warwickshire. Cook's unbeaten 112, scored off 100 balls with ten fours, took him to 857 runs for the season with one possible innings to play. He thus surpassed C. E. B. Rice's record for the competition of 814 runs in 1977. Asif Din faced 109 balls, twelve of which he hit for four.

Warwickshire

A. J. Moles c Cook b Lefebvre	37
Asif Din c Tavaré b Mallender	113
S. J. Green b Roebuck	25
P. A. Smith c Pringle b Rose	33
N. M. K. Smith c Cook b Roebuck	21
*T. A. Lloyd not out	12
D. A. Reeve not out	18
B 1, l-b 4, w 6	11
1/70 2/130 3/200 4/237 5/240 (5 wkts, 40 overs)	270

†G. W. Humpage, R. G. Twose, J. E. Benjamin and T. A. Munton did not bat.

Bowling: Mallender 8–0–57–1; Rose 8–0–41–1; Hallett 2–0–16–0; Trump 7–0–43–0; Lefebvre 8–0–60–1; Roebuck 7–1–48–2.

Somerset

S. J. Cook not out 112
P. M. Roebuck c Humpage b Benjamin 9
*C. J. Tavaré b P. A. Smith 54
G. D. Rose c Benjamin b N. M. K. Smith . 37
R. J. Harden not out 41
B 2, l-b 8, w 8 18

1/16 2/114 3/176 (3 wkts, 37.4 overs) 271

N. J. Pringle, †N. D. Burns, R. P. Lefebvre, N. A. Mallender, H. R. J. Trump and J. C. Hallett did not bat.

Bowling: Munton 7.4–0–42–0; Benjamin 8–0–46–1; Reeve 7–0–55–0; P. A. Smith 5–0–38–1; N. M. K. Smith 8–0–59–1; Twose 2–0–21–0.

Umpires: R. Julian and K. J. Lyons.

At Hove, August 26. SOMERSET beat SUSSEX by 60 runs.

SURREY

At Hove, April 29. SURREY lost to SUSSEX by three wickets.

SURREY v LANCASHIRE

At The Oval, May 6. Lancashire won by seven wickets. Toss: Lancashire. Lancashire's total was their highest in the Sunday League. Stewart faced 101 balls, hitting four sixes and seven fours.

Surrey

G. S. Clinton c Fairbrother b DeFreitas . 26
A. J. Stewart c Atherton b DeFreitas ..125
M. A. Lynch c Mendis b Watkinson .. 58
G. P. Thorpe c Allott b DeFreitas 11
†D. M. Ward not out 17
*I. A. Greig not out 21
B 1, l-b 6, w 1, n-b 1 9

1/75 2/190 3/213 4/232 (4 wkts, 39 overs) 267

K. T. Medlycott, M. A. Feltham, C. K. Bullen, M. P. Bicknell and A. J. Murphy did not bat.

Bowling: Patterson 8–0–55–0; Allott 8–0–40–0; DeFreitas 8–0–48–3; Austin 7–0–56–0; Watkinson 8–0–61–1.

Lancashire

G. D. Mendis c and b Medlycott 45
†G. Fowler c and b Bicknell 84
M. A. Atherton not out 76
N. H. Fairbrother c Stewart b Bicknell 51
M. Watkinson not out 3
L-b 4, w 5 9

1/79 2/194 3/265 (3 wkts, 37.1 overs) 268

G. D. Lloyd, P. A. J. DeFreitas, *D. P. Hughes, I. D. Austin, P. J. W. Allott and B. P. Patterson did not bat.

Bowling: Bicknell 7–0–48–2; Murphy 7.1–0–63–0; Bullen 8–0–46–0; Medlycott 8–0–39–1; Lynch 4–0–40–0; Feltham 3–0–28–0.

Umpires: B. Dudleston and A. A. Jones.

At Nottingham, May 20. SURREY lost to NOTTINGHAMSHIRE by eight wickets.

SURREY v NORTHAMPTONSHIRE

At The Oval, June 3. Surrey won by four wickets. Toss: Surrey. The match was reduced to nineteen overs a side after a heavy rainstorm delayed the start until 4.40 p.m. Surrey's victory was their first of the season in the Sunday League.

Northamptonshire

A. Fordham c and b Bicknell 7
N. A. Felton c Waqar Younis b Feltham 10
*A. J. Lamb b Murphy 0
R. J. Bailey lbw b Bullen 20
D. J. Capel c and b Feltham 0
D. J. Wild c Greig b Bullen 10
†W. M. Noon c Feltham b Waqar Younis . 21
J. G. Thomas c and b Bullen 0
A. L. Penberthy c Bullen b Waqar Younis . 4
W. W. Davis c Bicknell b Murphy 9
N. G. B. Cook not out 7
B 2, l-b 4, w 6, n-b 1 13

1/11 2/14 3/43 4/46 5/50 6/72 7/72 8/84 9/84 (18.4 overs) 101

Bowling: Bicknell 4–0–21–1; Murphy 3.4–0–15–2; Feltham 3–0–23–2; Bullen 4–0–13–3; Waqar Younis 4–1–23–2.

Surrey

A. J. Stewart c Penberthy b Thomas . . 20
M. A. Lynch c Davis b Wild 37
G. P. Thorpe c Noon b Wild 2
†D. M. Ward c Fordham b Wild 7
*I. A. Greig c Cook b Thomas 19
J. D. Robinson c Capel b Thomas 4
M. A. Feltham not out 1
C. K. Bullen not out 1
L-b 8, w 2, n-b 1 11

1/32 2/56 3/72 4/77 5/100 6/101 (6 wkts, 18.1 overs) 102

M. P. Bicknell, Waqar Younis and A. J. Murphy did not bat.

Bowling: Davis 3.1–0–13–0; Capel 4–0–22–0; Thomas 4–0–21–3; Penberthy 3–0–19–0; Cook 1–0–11–0; Wild 3–0–8–3.

Umpires: D. O. Oslear and R. Palmer.

At Hull, June 10. SURREY beat YORKSHIRE by six wickets.

SURREY v WORCESTERSHIRE

At The Oval, June 17. Surrey won by seven wickets. Toss: Surrey.

Worcestershire

T. S. Curtis c Ward b Bicknell 0
M. J. Weston c Ward b Murphy 5
G. A. Hick c Stewart b Murphy 16
I. T. Botham b Waqar Younis 27
D. B. D'Oliveira c and b Medlycott . . . 53
*P. A. Neale run out 3
P. J. Newport c Waqar Younis b Medlycott . 3
†S. J. Rhodes not out 35
S. R. Lampitt b Waqar Younis 11
S. M. McEwan b Waqar Younis 0
R. D. Stemp not out 3
B 2, l-b 10, w 8, n-b 1 21

1/0 2/23 3/23 4/81 5/90 6/103 7/131 8/164 9/166 (9 wkts, 40 overs) 177

Bowling: Bicknell 6–0–19–1; Murphy 7–0–38–2; Feltham 3–0–19–0; Bullen 8–1–29–0; Waqar Younis 8–0–27–3; Medlycott 8–0–33–2.

Surrey

A. J. Stewart lbw b Newport	0	M. A. Lynch not out	21
M. A. Feltham c Stemp b Hick	56	L-b 6, w 15	21
G. P. Thorpe c and b Hick	55		
†D. M. Ward not out	27	1/0 2/120 3/133 (3 wkts, 38.5 overs)	180

*I. A. Greig, K. T. Medlycott, C. K. Bullen, M. P. Bicknell, Waqar Younis and A. J. Murphy did not bat.

Bowling: Newport 8–2–31–1; Weston 3–0–15–0; McEwan 4–0–15–0; Botham 7–0–32–0; Stemp 8–0–37–0; Lampitt 2–0–15–0; Hick 6.5–1–29–2.

Umpires: H. D. Bird and J. H. Harris.

SURREY v DERBYSHIRE

At The Oval, June 24. Derbyshire won by three wickets. Toss: Derbyshire.

Surrey

G. S. Clinton c Bowler b Kuiper	45	K. T. Medlycott not out	4
M. A. Feltham lbw b Miller	42		
G. P. Thorpe c and b Kuiper	27	L-b 5, w 6	11
†D. M. Ward b Jean-Jacques	25		
M. A. Lynch c Miller b Jean-Jacques	48	1/64 2/113 3/130 (5 wkts, 40 overs)	210
*I. A. Greig not out	8	4/167 5/204	

C. K. Bullen, A. G. Robson, Waqar Younis and A. J. Murphy did not bat.

Bowling: Jean-Jacques 8–0–51–2; Mortensen 8–0–27–0; Warner 8–0–56–0; Miller 8–0–39–1; Kuiper 8–0–32–2.

Derbyshire

*K. J. Barnett c Ward b Murphy	0	G. Miller c Ward b Robson	2
†P. D. Bowler run out	50	A. E. Warner not out	11
J. E. Morris b Waqar Younis	45	B 5, l-b 14, w 3, n-b 3	25
A. P. Kuiper c Bullen b Medlycott	34		
B. Roberts b Waqar Younis	13	1/0 2/77 3/136 (7 wkts, 38.3 overs)	213
C. J. Adams b Waqar Younis	19	4/143 5/173	
S. C. Goldsmith not out	14	6/178 7/186	

O. H. Mortensen and M. Jean-Jacques did not bat.

Bowling: Murphy 7–0–26–1; Robson 7.3–0–37–1; Feltham 3–0–15–0; Bullen 8–0–38–0; Waqar Younis 7–0–41–3; Medlycott 6–0–37–1.

Umpires: J. H. Harris and B. J. Meyer.

At Cardiff, July 1. SURREY lost to GLAMORGAN by eight wickets.

SURREY v WARWICKSHIRE

At The Oval, July 8. Surrey won by 15 runs. Toss: Warwickshire. The match was reduced to 37 overs a side following a delay during the twelfth over of Surrey's innings. This occurred when Feltham was treated for a blow on the hand, suffered in the previous over.

Surrey

D. J. Bicknell c Piper b Twose	0	M. P. Bicknell b Benjamin	0
M. A. Feltham b Reeve	61	N. M. Kendrick not out	2
G. P. Thorpe c Moody b Munton	35	Waqar Younis not out	1
†D. M. Ward c and b Reeve	0	B 1, l-b 6, w 4	11
M. A. Lynch c Reeve b P. A. Smith	25		
*I. A. Greig c Humpage b Reeve	43	1/0 2/90 3/93 (9 wkts, 37 overs)	205
K. T. Medlycott run out	27	4/114 5/142 6/191	
C. K. Bullen c and b Reeve	0	7/192 8/193 9/200	

Bowling: Twose 4–0–29–1; Benjamin 8–0–38–1; Moody 3–0–27–0; N. M. K. Smith 6–0–35–0; Munton 6–1–25–1; Reeve 8–0–36–4; P. A. Smith 2–1–8–1.

Warwickshire

*T. A. Lloyd run out	5	†K. J. Piper b Waqar Younis	2
P. A. Smith c Waqar Younis b Feltham	9	J. E. Benjamin not out	8
T. M. Moody b M. P. Bicknell	3	T. A. Munton not out	6
G. W. Humpage b Medlycott	33	B 4, l-b 3, w 10	17
D. A. Reeve st Ward b Medlycott	25		
N. M. K. Smith c Greig b Medlycott	12	1/8 2/11 3/27 (9 wkts, 37 overs)	190
R. G. Twose c and b Feltham	40	4/76 5/90 6/91	
D. P. Ostler run out	30	7/162 8/172 9/175	

Bowling: M. P. Bicknell 8–0–34–1; Feltham 8–1–23–2; Bullen 4–0–22–0; Waqar Younis 8–0–41–1; Medlycott 6–0–43–3; Kendrick 3–0–20–0.

Umpires: D. J. Constant (replaced by G. G. Arnold, who stood at square leg) and R. Palmer.

SURREY v MIDDLESEX

At The Oval, July 15. Surrey won by 68 runs. Toss: Middlesex. Waqar Younis took his four wickets for 3 runs in a spell of twelve balls.

Surrey

D. J. Bicknell b Emburey	75	A. D. Brown run out	2
M. A. Feltham c Brown b Williams	4	K. T. Medlycott not out	0
G. P. Thorpe c Gatting b Haynes	41	L-b 6, w 10, n-b 1	17
†D. M. Ward c Haynes b Cowans	60		
M. A. Lynch lbw b Emburey	25	1/6 2/77 3/182 (6 wkts, 40 overs)	228
*I. A. Greig not out	4	4/215 5/222 6/224	

C. K. Bullen, M. P. Bicknell and Waqar Younis did not bat.

Bowling: Cowans 8–0–46–1; Williams 8–1–42–1; Emburey 8–1–39–2; Brown 2–0–16–0; Fraser 8–0–40–0; Haynes 6–0–39–1.

Middlesex

D. L. Haynes c Ward b M. P. Bicknell	4	N. F. Williams lbw b Waqar Younis	1
M. A. Roseberry b Medlycott	48	A. R. C. Fraser not out	4
*M. W. Gatting b M. P. Bicknell	2	N. G. Cowans c and b M. P. Bicknell	0
M. R. Ramprakash c Thorpe b Waqar Younis	60	L-b 3, w 5, n-b 1	9
K. R. Brown c Greig b Medlycott	12		
R. O. Butcher b Waqar Younis	3	1/4 2/18 3/99 (33.2 overs)	160
J. E. Emburey c Bullen b M. P. Bicknell	15	4/125 5/134 6/136	
†P. Farbrace b Waqar Younis	2	7/142 8/156 9/160	

Bowling: M. P. Bicknell 4.2–0–14–4; Feltham 4–0–23–0; Greig 3–0–16–0; Bullen 8–0–38–0; Waqar Younis 6–0–27–4; Medlycott 8–0–39–2.

Umpires: P. J. Eele and D. R. Shepherd.

SURREY v KENT

At The Oval, July 22. Surrey won by five wickets. Toss: Surrey.

Kent

S. G. Hinks run out ... 41
N. R. Taylor c Ward b Medlycott ... 26
T. R. Ward b Waqar Younis ... 14
*C. S. Cowdrey c Sargeant b Waqar Younis . 7
G. R. Cowdrey c Sargeant b Medlycott. 14
M. V. Fleming b Waqar Younis ... 4
†S. A. Marsh c Bullen b Waqar Younis 35
R. M. Ellison c Robinson b Bullen ... 0
P. S. de Villiers b Waqar Younis ... 6
R. P. Davis c Sargeant b Feltham ... 0
A. P. Igglesden not out ... 3
L-b 6, w 8 ... 14

1/54 2/80 3/93 4/98 5/107 6/122 7/123 8/153 9/157 (37.4 overs) 164

Bowling: Feltham 7–0–26–1; Robinson 3–0–19–0; Medlycott 8–0–40–2; Greig 4–0–22–0; Bullen 8–0–25–1; Waqar Younis 7.4–0–26–5.

Surrey

D. J. Bicknell b Davis ... 26
M. A. Feltham b de Villiers ... 9
G. P. Thorpe not out ... 69
D. M. Ward b Fleming ... 4
M. A. Lynch lbw b Ward ... 26
J. D. Robinson c Igglesden b Ellison .. 16
*I. A. Greig not out ... 0
L-b 11, w 6 ... 17

1/16 2/53 3/64 4/118 5/162 (5 wkts, 37.1 overs) 167

K. T. Medlycott, C. K. Bullen, †N. F. Sargeant and Waqar Younis did not bat.

Bowling: Igglesden 8–0–29–0; de Villiers 6.1–1–26–1; Davis 8–0–30–1; Ellison 8–0–33–1; Fleming 3–0–21–1; Ward 4–0–17–1.

Umpires: B. J. Meyer and K. E. Palmer.

At Cheltenham, July 29. SURREY lost to GLOUCESTERSHIRE by five wickets.

At Weston-super-Mare, August 5. SURREY beat SOMERSET by six wickets.

SURREY v LEICESTERSHIRE

At The Oval, August 12. Surrey won by 69 runs. Toss: Surrey. Surrey's total of 278 for seven was the highest conceded by Leicestershire in the Sunday League.

Surrey

M. A. Feltham c Nixon b Parsons ... 0
A. D. Brown c Mullally b Gidley ... 56
G. P. Thorpe c Millns b Mullally ... 85
†D. M. Ward b Gidley ... 6
M. A. Lynch c Millns b Gidley ... 23
*I. A. Greig c Boon b Benson ... 26
J. D. Robinson c Benson b Millns ... 13
K. T. Medlycott not out ... 44
C. K. Bullen not out ... 12
B 2, l-b 3, w 3, n-b 5 ... 13

1/0 2/112 3/121 4/163 5/185 6/213 7/216 (7 wkts, 40 overs) 278

M. P. Bicknell and Waqar Younis did not bat.

Bowling: Parsons 8–0–70–1; Millns 8–0–47–1; Mullally 8–0–57–1; Gidley 8–0–45–3; Benson 8–1–54–1.

Leicestershire

J. J. Whitaker c Bullen b Bicknell 8
*N. E. Briers c Bullen b Bicknell 5
B. F. Smith c Bullen b Bicknell 10
T. J. Boon c Thorpe b Bullen 59
L. Potter run out 6
J. D. R. Benson c Brown b Bicknell ... 67
G. J. Parsons c sub b Waqar Younis .. 18
†P. A. Nixon b Waqar Younis 1
M. I. Gidley not out 5
A. D. Mullally c Bicknell b Feltham ... 5
D. J. Millns b Waqar Younis 0
B 5, l-b 10, w 10 25

1/15 2/26 3/29 4/45 5/160 6/193 7/196 8/196 9/208 (40 overs) 209

Bowling: Bicknell 8–0–26–4; Feltham 7–0–29–1; Bullen 8–0–35–1; Medlycott 6–0–39–0; Waqar Younis 8–0–43–3; Robinson 3–0–22–0.

Umpires: J. D. Bond and B. Leadbeater.

At Chelmsford, August 19. ESSEX v SURREY. No result.

At Southampton, August 26. SURREY beat HAMPSHIRE by 4 runs.

SUSSEX

SUSSEX v DERBYSHIRE

At Hove, April 22. Derbyshire won by six wickets. Toss: Derbyshire.

Sussex

N. J. Lenham c Bowler b Base 0
*P. W. G. Parker lbw b Mortensen ... 0
A. P. Wells c Kuiper b Malcolm 57
M. P. Speight c Bowler b Base 77
C. M. Wells c Mortensen b Kuiper 8
I. J. Gould b Kuiper 0
A. C. S. Pigott c Bowler b Base 11
A. I. C. Dodemaide not out 24
†P. Moores c Bowler b Base 0
A. R. Hansford not out 5
L-b 17, w 2, n-b 4 23

1/1 2/3 3/140 4/153 5/160 6/164 7/183 8/183 (8 wkts, 40 overs) 205

I. D. K. Salisbury did not bat.

Bowling: Mortensen 8–0–23–1; Base 8–0–28–4; Miller 6–0–38–0; Malcolm 8–0–47–1; Kuiper 6–0–30–2; Barnett 4–0–22–0.

Derbyshire

*K. J. Barnett c Moores b Pigott 60
†P. D. Bowler c and b Salisbury 51
J. E. Morris run out 5
A. P. Kuiper not out 53
T. J. G. O'Gorman lbw b Pigott 0
C. J. Adams not out 30
L-b 6, w 2, n-b 2 10

1/117 2/125 3/128 4/128 (4 wkts, 38.5 overs) 209

B. Roberts, G. Miller, D. E. Malcolm, S. J. Base and O. H. Mortensen did not bat.

Bowling: C. M. Wells 7.5–1–41–0; Dodemaide 8–0–38–0; Salisbury 8–1–29–1; Hansford 7–0–35–0; Pigott 8–0–60–2.

Umpires: A. G. T. Whitehead and P. B. Wight.

SUSSEX v SURREY

At Hove, April 29. Sussex won by three wickets. Toss: Surrey.

Surrey

D. J. Bicknell c Moores b Clarke	21	C. K. Bullen b Hansford	3
A. J. Stewart b Salisbury	64	M. P. Bicknell not out	4
M. A. Lynch lbw b Clarke	9		
G. P. Thorpe run out	53	L-b 6, w 1	7
†D. M. Ward b Salisbury	7		
*I. A. Greig c Moores b Salisbury	2	1/50 2/64 3/131 (8 wkts, 40 overs)	194
K. T. Medlycott b Hansford	17	4/141 5/145 6/169	
M. A. Feltham not out	7	7/183 8/187	

A. J. Murphy did not bat.

Bowling: C. M. Wells 8–1–34–0; Dodemaide 8–0–43–0; Clarke 8–0–23–2; Hansford 8–0–48–2; Salisbury 8–0–40–3.

Sussex

N. J. Lenham run out	12	†P. Moores b Lynch	0
I. J. Gould run out	9	A. R. Clarke not out	0
A. P. Wells not out	86	B 8, l-b 14, w 1	23
M. P. Speight c Ward b Feltham	18		
C. M. Wells b Bullen	5	1/31 2/51 3/89 (7 wkts, 39.4 overs)	198
*P. W. G. Parker b Murphy	28	4/107 5/165	
A. I. C. Dodemaide b Lynch	17	6/190 7/190	

I. D. K. Salisbury and A. R. Hansford did not bat.

Bowling: M. P. Bicknell 7–0–33–0; Murphy 7.4–0–41–1; Bullen 8–0–40–1; Medlycott 8–0–30–0; Feltham 8–0–30–1; Lynch 1–0–2–2.

Umpires: D. J. Constant and D. S. Thompsett.

SUSSEX v GLAMORGAN

At Hove, May 20. Sussex won by six wickets. Toss: Sussex.

Glamorgan

H. Morris c Pigott b Salisbury	68	†M. L. Roberts not out	12
P. A. Cottey lbw b Clarke	36	L-b 9, w 3	12
I. V. A. Richards c Pigott b Salisbury	31		
*A. R. Butcher c Dodemaide b Salisbury	6	1/76 2/126 3/140 (4 wkts, 40 overs)	198
I. Smith not out	33	4/156	

N. G. Cowley, M. Frost, S. J. Dennis, S. R. Barwick and S. L. Watkin did not bat.

Bowling: Wells 8–0–21–0; Babington 4–0–21–0; Pigott 8–1–32–0; Clarke 8–0–47–1; Dodemaide 7–0–32–0; Salisbury 5–0–36–3.

Sussex

N. J. Lenham b Richards	62	A. C. S. Pigott not out	24
I. J. Gould c Butcher b Dennis	41	L-b 5, w 3, n-b 1	9
M. P. Speight b Richards	26		
C. M. Wells c Butcher b Richards	14	1/71 2/120 3/150 (4 wkts, 38.4 overs)	201
A. I. C. Dodemaide not out	25	4/153	

†P. Moores, *P. W. G. Parker, A. R. Clarke, I. D. K. Salisbury and A. M. Babington did not bat.

Bowling: Watkin 6–0–28–0; Frost 7.4–0–51–0; Dennis 8–0–25–1; Cowley 3–0–15–0; Barwick 7–0–40–0; Richards 7–0–37–3.

Umpires: M. J. Kitchen and R. A. White.

SUSSEX v LANCASHIRE

At Horsham, June 3. No result. This was the first Sunday League game of the season to be abandoned without a ball bowled.

At Leicester, June 10. SUSSEX lost to LEICESTERSHIRE by seven wickets.

SUSSEX v YORKSHIRE

At Hove, June 17. Yorkshire won by 40 runs. Toss: Sussex.

Yorkshire

K. Sharp b Pigott 34
A. A. Metcalfe c Moores b C. M. Wells 16
R. J. Blakey c Moores b Lenham 23
D. Byas c Parker b Remy 26
*M. D. Moxon c Dodemaide b Remy .. 39
P. E. Robinson c Moores b Dodemaide 1
†D. L. Bairstow c A. P. Wells b Pigott 14
P. Carrick not out 24
P. J. Hartley not out 5
L-b 6, w 4 10

1/33 2/77 3/79 4/132 5/133 6/157 7/175 (7 wkts, 40 overs) 192

C. S. Pickles and P. W. Jarvis did not bat.

Bowling: C. M. Wells 8–1–17–1; Remy 8–0–45–2; Dodemaide 8–2–32–1; Salisbury 4–0–36–0; Pigott 8–0–35–2; Lenham 4–0–21–1.

Sussex

N. J. Lenham c Robinson b Jarvis 16
I. J. Gould run out 0
*P. W. G. Parker lbw b Moxon 36
A. P. Wells c Blakey b Moxon 6
M. P. Speight b Moxon 24
C. M. Wells c and b Carrick 2
A. I. C. Dodemaide c Pickles b Carrick 20
A. C. S. Pigott st Bairstow b Carrick .. 19
†P. Moores c Byas b Jarvis 8
C. C. Remy c Moxon b Hartley 7
I. D. K. Salisbury not out 3
B 4, l-b 6, w 1 11

1/1 2/24 3/38 4/76 5/83 6/93 7/122 8/131 9/143 (36.5 overs) 152

Bowling: Pickles 7–0–24–0; Jarvis 5–0–19–2; Hartley 6.5–0–26–1; Moxon 8–0–29–3; Byas 2–0–16–0; Carrick 8–2–28–3.

Umpires: J. D. Bond and R. Palmer.

At Worcester, June 24. SUSSEX lost to WORCESTERSHIRE by 2 runs.

SUSSEX v HAMPSHIRE

At Hove, July 1. Sussex won on scoring-rate. Toss: Hampshire. Rain, which delayed the start for 30 minutes, caused the match to be reduced to 36 overs a side, although Hampshire managed to bowl only 33. When Hampshire were 78 for two off sixteen overs in reply, rain again intervened and they were set a revised target of 208 off 28 overs.

Sussex

N. J. Lenham c Connor b Maru 72
I. J. Gould c R. A. Smith b Nicholas .. 68
*P. W. G. Parker c Nicholas b Bakker. 12
A. P. Wells not out 44
M. P. Speight c R. A. Smith b Ayling . 21
C. M. Wells b Marshall 1
A. I. C. Dodemaide not out 1
B 1, l-b 13, w 9, n-b 2 25

1/135 2/172 3/176 4/217 5/228 (5 wkts, 33 overs) 244

A. C. S. Pigott, †P. Moores, C. C. Remy and A. R. Clarke did not bat.

Bowling: Marshall 7–0–50–1; Bakker 7–0–48–1; Connor 5–0–18–0; Ayling 7–0–52–1; Maru 5–0–39–1; Nicholas 2–0–23–1.

Hampshire

V. P. Terry c Lenham b C. M. Wells	25	R. J. Maru c Clarke b Dodemaide	2
M. D. Marshall c Lenham b C. M. Wells	19	C. A. Connor c Lenham b Pigott	4
R. A. Smith b Dodemaide	24	P. J. Bakker st Moores b Clarke	9
D. I. Gower c Speight b Pigott	10	L-b 3, w 4	7
C. L. Smith c Moores b Pigott	3		
*M. C. J. Nicholas b Dodemaide	27	1/37 2/53 3/79 (27.3 overs)	151
J. R. Ayling not out	17	4/82 5/88 6/114	
†R. J. Parks c C. M. Wells b Pigott	4	7/119 8/123 9/133	

Bowling: C. M. Wells 7–0–30–2; Dodemaide 8–0–50–3; Clarke 5.3–0–26–1; Pigott 7–0–42–4.

Umpires: J. H. Harris and A. A. Jones.

At Nottingham, July 8. SUSSEX lost to NOTTINGHAMSHIRE by 8 runs.

At Swindon, July 15. SUSSEX lost to GLOUCESTERSHIRE by one wicket.

At Wellingborough School, July 22. SUSSEX beat NORTHAMPTONSHIRE by 21 runs.

At Chelmsford, July 29. SUSSEX lost to ESSEX by two wickets.

SUSSEX v WARWICKSHIRE

At Eastbourne, August 5. Warwickshire won by 2 runs. Toss: Sussex.

Warwickshire

A. J. Moles c Moores b Dodemaide	3	R. G. Twose not out	1
Asif Din c Smith b Dodemaide	6	†K. J. Piper not out	3
T. M. Moody b Pigott	64	L-b 4, w 1	5
D. A. Reeve lbw b Clarke	22		
P. A. Smith c Hansford b Pigott	11	1/7 2/9 3/65 (7 wkts, 40 overs)	179
*T. A. Lloyd c Remy b Clarke	48	4/82 5/144	
N. M. K. Smith st Moores b Hansford	16	6/174 7/174	

G. Smith and T. A. Munton did not bat.

Bowling: Pigott 8–0–46–2; Dodemaide 8–1–21–2; C. M. Wells 8–1–17–0; Hansford 8–1–49–1; Clarke 8–0–42–2.

Sussex

M. P. Speight b Munton	20	A. C. S. Pigott not out	29
D. M. Smith b Moody	18	†P. Moores b Munton	6
A. P. Wells c Piper b Munton	0	A. R. Hansford c Asif Din b P. A. Smith	2
*C. M. Wells c N. M. K. Smith b P. A. Smith	64	A. R. Clarke not out	4
		B 1, l-b 6, w 2	9
R. Hanley b N. M. K. Smith	11		
C. C. Remy b N. M. K. Smith	11	1/30 2/30 3/53 (9 wkts, 40 overs)	177
A. I. C. Dodemaide c N. M. K. Smith b P. A. Smith	3	4/101 5/121 6/134	
		7/134 8/146 9/155	

Bowling: Munton 8–1–36–3; G. Smith 2–0–8–0; Reeve 8–1–20–0; Moody 7–0–31–1; N. M. K. Smith 7–0–41–2; P. A. Smith 8–0–34–3.

Umpires: J. D. Bond and M. J. Kitchen.

At Lord's, August 12. SUSSEX beat MIDDLESEX by seven wickets.

At Canterbury, August 19. KENT v SUSSEX. No result.

SUSSEX v SOMERSET

At Hove, August 26. Somerset won by 60 runs. Toss: Sussex. Cook took his record number of runs for a Sunday League season to 902.

Somerset

S. J. Cook c Pigott b Lenham	45	A. N. Jones c Lenham b Dodemaide	2
R. J. Bartlett c Moores b Dodemaide	2	H. R. J. Trump b Dodemaide	0
*C. J. Tavaré b C. M. Wells	12	J. C. Hallett not out	3
R. J. Harden c Moores b C. M. Wells	0	B 1, l-b 1, w 14	16
G. D. Rose c Gould b Pigott	7		
A. N. Hayhurst not out	70	1/14 2/38 3/38 (9 wkts, 40 overs)	222
†N. D. Burns c and b Dodemaide	58	4/61 5/99 6/182	
R. P. Lefebvre b Pigott	7	7/193 8/197 9/198	

Bowling: Dodemaide 8–0–40–4; C. M. Wells 7–1–28–2; Pigott 8–0–39–2; Salisbury 6–0–32–0; Donelan 6–0–37–0; Lenham 5–0–44–1.

Sussex

N. J. Lenham c Burns b Jones	19	†P. Moores b Hayhurst	1
I. J. Gould b Jones	5	I. D. K. Salisbury run out	7
A. P. Wells c Jones b Trump	31	B. T. P. Donelan b Lefebvre	4
M. P. Speight c Burns b Hayhurst	21	B 1, l-b 11, w 10, n-b 2	24
*C. M. Wells c Jones b Hayhurst	3		
K. Greenfield b Hayhurst	2	1/12 2/37 3/79 (35.4 overs)	162
A. I. C. Dodemaide not out	31	4/85 5/91 6/98	
A. C. S. Pigott c Hayhurst b Trump	14	7/120 8/122 9/145	

Bowling: Jones 7–0–31–2; Rose 5–0–12–0; Hallett 4–1–18–0; Lefebvre 4.4–0–22–1; Hayhurst 8–0–37–4; Trump 7–0–30–2.

Umpires: J. C. Balderstone and R. A. White.

WARWICKSHIRE

WARWICKSHIRE v NORTHAMPTONSHIRE

At Birmingham, April 29. Warwickshire won by seven wickets. Toss: Warwickshire.

Northamptonshire

R. J. Bailey c Reeve b N. M. K. Smith	58	†D. Ripley not out	3
W. Larkins c N. M. K. Smith b Munton	0		
*A. J. Lamb b Moody	70	L-b 9, w 7	16
D. J. Capel c Small b Moody	20		
A. Fordham not out	29	1/0 2/128 3/145 (5 wkts, 40 overs)	196
D. J. Wild c sub b Reeve	0	4/177 5/177	

J. G. Thomas, N. G. B. Cook, C. E. L. Ambrose and M. A. Robinson did not bat.

Bowling: Small 8–1–27–0; Munton 6–1–22–1; Reeve 8–1–45–1; N. M. K. Smith 7–0–34–1; P. A. Smith 3–0–17–0; Moody 8–0–42–2.

Warwickshire

Asif Din hit wkt b Capel 23
A. I. Kallicharran b Robinson 76
T. M. Moody b Cook 56
†G. W. Humpage not out 22
D. A. Reeve not out 17
L-b 4, w 2 6

1/39 2/153 3/171 (3 wkts, 37.3 overs) 200

*T. A. Lloyd, P. A. Smith, G. C. Small, N. M. K. Smith, R. G. Twose and T. A. Munton did not bat.

Bowling: Ambrose 7–1–31–0; Robinson 7.3–0–53–1; Capel 8–0–35–1; Thomas 7–0–37–0; Cook 8–0–40–1.

Umpires: J. C. Balderstone and H. D. Bird.

WARWICKSHIRE v YORKSHIRE

At Birmingham, May 6. Warwickshire won by eight wickets. Toss: Yorkshire.

Yorkshire

S. A. Kellett b Reeve 21
*A. A. Metcalfe b Moody 56
†R. J. Blakey b Reeve 9
P. E. Robinson c Reeve b Booth 22
D. Byas run out 7
C. White not out 30
P. Carrick c Munton b Reeve 22
P. J. Hartley not out 3
L-b 8, w 7 15

1/47 2/62 3/96 4/116 5/129 6/171 (6 wkts, 40 overs) 185

P. W. Jarvis, S. D. Fletcher and D. Gough did not bat.

Bowling: Small 8–0–41–0; Munton 8–2–23–0; Reeve 8–1–29–3; Booth 8–0–46–1; Moody 8–0–38–1.

Warwickshire

A. I. Kallicharran c Fletcher b Carrick . 65
Asif Din b Byas 40
T. M. Moody not out 51
†G. W. Humpage not out 16
L-b 13, w 3, n-b 1 17

1/73 2/140 (2 wkts, 37.1 overs) 189

D. A. Reeve, *T. A. Lloyd, P. A. Booth, G. C. Small, R. G. Twose, N. M. K. Smith and T. A. Munton did not bat.

Bowling: Jarvis 8–1–21–0; Fletcher 5.1–0–27–0; Hartley 4–0–16–0; Gough 3–0–20–0 Carrick 7–0–39–1; Byas 5–0–27–1; White 5–0–26–0.

Umpires: R. Palmer and P. B. Wight.

At Moreton-in-Marsh, May 20. WARWICKSHIRE lost to GLOUCESTERSHIRE by 4 runs.

At Worcester, May 27. WARWICKSHIRE beat WORCESTERSHIRE by six wickets.

At Lord's, June 3. WARWICKSHIRE lost to MIDDLESEX by nine wickets.

WARWICKSHIRE v ESSEX

At Birmingham, June 10. Essex won by seven wickets. Toss: Essex.

Warwickshire

Asif Din lbw b Foster 4	J. E. Benjamin not out 10
T. M. Moody c Shahid b Childs 54	G. Smith b Pringle 5
P. A. Smith lbw b Topley 2	T. A. Munton not out 2
†G. W. Humpage c Stephenson b Pringle 5	L-b 7, w 3, n-b 3 13
R. G. Twose st Garnham b Stephenson. 4	—
*D. A. Reeve b Foster 28	1/19 2/29 3/43 (9 wkts, 40 overs) 155
D. P. Ostler b Waugh 18	4/64 5/82 6/118
N. M. K. Smith c Stephenson b Pringle 10	7/135 8/137 9/153

Bowling: Topley 8–1–27–1; Foster 8–0–35–2; Childs 8–0–19–1; Pringle 8–1–29–3; Stephenson 3–0–20–1; Waugh 5–0–18–1.

Essex

B. R. Hardie b G. Smith 54	A. W. Lilley not out 9
P. J. Prichard lbw b Benjamin 8	L-b 4, w 3, n-b 3 10
M. E. Waugh b G. Smith 60	—
*D. R. Pringle not out 17	1/19 2/121 3/149 (3 wkts, 35.3 overs) 158

J. P. Stephenson, N. Shahid, †M. A. Garnham, N. A. Foster, T. D. Topley and J. H. Childs did not bat.

Bowling: Munton 8–1–23–0; Benjamin 6–1–18–1; Moody 4–1–18–0; Reeve 3–0–12–0; N. M. K. Smith 6.3–0–40–0; G. Smith 5–0–20–2; P. A. Smith 1–0–6–0; Asif Din 2–0–17–0.

Umpires: B. Dudleston and R. A. White.

At Derby, June 17. WARWICKSHIRE lost to DERBYSHIRE by 1 run.

WARWICKSHIRE v KENT

At Birmingham, June 24. Warwickshire won by three wickets. Toss: Warwickshire. Kallicharran's innings brought him his 5,000th run in the Sunday League.

Kent

S. G. Hinks c Moody b Munton 6	P. S. de Villiers b Benjamin 10
M. A. Ealham b Twose 25	R. P. Davis not out 2
N. R. Taylor st Piper b Pierson 18	A. P. Igglesden c Piper b Reeve 1
*C. S. Cowdrey b Benjamin 46	B 6, l-b 3, w 4, n-b 3 16
G. R. Cowdrey run out 16	—
M. V. Fleming lbw b Moody 2	1/11 2/45 3/68 (39.1 overs) 159
†S. A. Marsh run out 9	4/89 5/95 6/128
R. M. Ellison run out 8	7/137 8/152 9/158

Bowling: Munton 6–0–9–1; Twose 8–1–35–1; Benjamin 8–0–29–2; Pierson 5–2–18–1; Moody 6–0–27–1; Reeve 6.1–0–32–1.

Warwickshire

A. J. Moles c Ealham b C. S. Cowdrey. 24	†K. J. Piper run out 4
A. I. Kallicharran c Ealham b C. S. Cowdrey . 23	J. E. Benjamin not out 14
T. M. Moody c and b Davis 29	B 4, l-b 6, w 4 14
*D. A. Reeve b C. S. Cowdrey 25	—
Asif Din not out 19	1/46 2/58 3/107 (7 wkts, 39 overs) 160
R. G. Twose c Igglesden b Davis 5	4/115 5/122
D. P. Ostler c Davis b de Villiers 3	6/127 7/137

A. R. K. Pierson and T. A. Munton did not bat.

Bowling: Igglesden 8–0–37–0; de Villiers 7–1–17–1; Fleming 8–0–39–0; Ellison 8–0–27–0; C. S. Cowdrey 4–0–19–3; Davis 4–0–11–2.

Umpires: J. D. Bond and K. E. Palmer.

At The Oval, July 8. WARWICKSHIRE lost to SURREY by 15 runs.

WARWICKSHIRE v GLAMORGAN

At Birmingham, July 15. Glamorgan won by seven wickets. Toss: Warwickshire.

Warwickshire

*T. A. Lloyd c Dale b Watkin 12
Asif Din run out 46
T. M. Moody b Dale 4
G. W. Humpage c Watkin b Cowley . . 11
D. P. Ostler b Cowley 15
D. A. Reeve b Watkin 28
†K. J. Piper b Richards 1
G. C. Small b Watkin 4
J. E. Benjamin b Watkin 5
A. R. K. Pierson c Metson b Watkin . . 1
T. A. Munton not out 2
B 1, l-b 6, w 5 12

1/19 2/32 3/63 4/93 5/95 6/97 7/118 8/130 9/133 (39.4 overs) 141

Bowling: Frost 6–0–21–0; Watkin 7.4–0–23–5; Dale 8–0–29–1; Dennis 6–0–24–0; Cowley 8–1–17–2; Richards 4–0–20–1.

Glamorgan

M. P. Maynard not out 61
H. Morris b Benjamin 19
I. V. A. Richards c Pierson b Reeve . . . 31
I. Smith c Moody b Pierson 10
*A. R. Butcher not out 6
B 1, l-b 4, w 10 15

1/45 2/92 3/125 (3 wkts, 34 overs) 142

A. Dale, N. G. Cowley, †C. P. Metson, S. J. Dennis, S. L. Watkin and M. Frost did not bat.

Bowling: Small 8–1–17–0; Munton 6–2–14–0; Benjamin 6–1–34–1; Reeve 6–0–28–1; Pierson 7–1–38–1; Moody 1–0–6–0.

Umpires: A. A. Jones and B. J. Meyer.

WARWICKSHIRE v NOTTINGHAMSHIRE

At Birmingham, July 22. Nottinghamshire won by 10 runs. Toss: Nottinghamshire. Johnson reached his third Sunday League hundred of the season off 82 balls, with three sixes and twelve fours, but then added only 14 from the next nineteen balls he received.

Nottinghamshire

B. C. Broad c Piper b Munton 1
P. R. Pollard b Benjamin 3
P. Johnson c Munton b Twose 114
*R. T. Robinson c Moody b Twose . . . 63
F. D. Stephenson b Munton 4
M. Newell run out 6
G. W. Mike run out 4
†B. N. French not out 34
K. P. Evans run out 1
E. E. Hemmings not out 2
L-b 6, w 3 9

1/1 2/7 3/176 4/186 5/196 6/199 7/222 8/239 (8 wkts, 40 overs) 241

K. E. Cooper did not bat.

Bowling: Benjamin 8–0–20–1; Munton 8–2–45–2; Pierson 3–0–27–0; Reeve 7–0–43–0; Small 4–0–29–0; Smith 2–0–21–0; Twose 8–0–50–2.

Warwickshire

*T. A. Lloyd c Pollard b Evans	63	J. E. Benjamin not out	3
Asif Din lbw b Hemmings	43		
T. M. Moody lbw b Mike	7	L-b 7, w 14, n-b 4	25
P. A. Smith st French b Hemmings	19		
D. A. Reeve run out	41	1/99 2/115 3/133 (5 wkts, 40 overs)	231
R. G. Twose not out	30	4/154 5/224	

†K. J. Piper, G. C. Small, A. R. K. Pierson and T. A. Munton did not bat.

Bowling: Cooper 8–0–50–0; Stephenson 8–0–29–0; Mike 8–0–54–1; Evans 8–0–57–1; Hemmings 8–1–34–2.

Umpires: J. D. Bond and B. Dudleston.

WARWICKSHIRE v HAMPSHIRE

At Birmingham, July 29. Hampshire won by three wickets. Toss: Hampshire.

Warwickshire

A. J. Moles c Parks b Marshall	14	R. G. Twose b Udal	5
*T. A. Lloyd lbw b Bakker	4	N. M. K. Smith not out	38
T. M. Moody b Marshall	5	L-b 6, w 2, n-b 1	9
P. A. Smith c Parks b Ayling	26		
D. A. Reeve b Bakker	1	1/6 2/23 3/24 (6 wkts, 40 overs)	179
Asif Din not out	77	4/25 5/74 6/102	

†K. J. Piper, J. E. Benjamin and T. A. Munton did not bat.

Bowling: Marshall 8–0–36–2; Bakker 7–1–33–2; Connor 8–0–45–0; Ayling 8–0–27–1; Udal 8–0–20–1; Maru 1–0–12–0.

Hampshire

V. P. Terry c Munton b N. M. K. Smith	53	†R. J. Parks not out	23
R. J. Scott st Piper b N. M. K. Smith	47	S. D. Udal not out	2
*M. C. J. Nicholas b Benjamin	0	B 1, l-b 5, w 2	8
M. D. Marshall run out	24		
C. L. Smith run out	0	1/88 2/89 3/127 (7 wkts, 39.4 overs)	183
J. R. Ayling c Lloyd b Munton	25	4/127 5/139	
R. J. Maru st Piper b N. M. K. Smith	1	6/149 7/165	

C. A. Connor and P. J. Bakker did not bat.

Bowling: Twose 7.4–0–47–0; Munton 8–1–29–1; Benjamin 8–1–29–1; Reeve 8–0–36–0; N. M. K. Smith 8–0–36–3.

Umpires: D. R. Shepherd and R. A. White.

At Eastbourne, August 5. WARWICKSHIRE beat SUSSEX by 2 runs.

At Weston-super-Mare, August 12. WARWICKSHIRE lost to SOMERSET by seven wickets.

WARWICKSHIRE v LEICESTERSHIRE

At Birmingham, August 19. No result, rain having stopped play. Toss: Warwickshire.

Leicestershire

T. J. Boon b Small 5
*N. E. Briers b Munton 2
B. F. Smith st Piper b Booth 29
C. C. Lewis lbw b Small 43
J. D. R. Benson b Small 14
L. Potter not out 7
M. I. Gidley not out 2
B 1, l-b 10, w 8 19

1/5 2/15 3/81 4/109 5/118 (5 wkts, 28.1 overs) 121

G. J. Parsons, †P. A. Nixon, A. D. Mullally and D. J. Millns did not bat.

Bowling: Small 8–0–20–3; Munton 6.1–1–8–1; Moody 3–0–23–0; Booth 5–0–33–1; P. A. Smith 6–0–26–0.

Warwickshire

A. J. Moles, Asif Din, T. M. Moody, P. A. Smith, S. J. Green, *T. A. Lloyd, N. M. K. Smith, †K. J. Piper, P. A. Booth, G. C. Small and T. A. Munton.

Umpires: J. W. Holder and K. E. Palmer.

At Manchester, August 26. WARWICKSHIRE lost to LANCASHIRE by 49 runs.

WORCESTERSHIRE

At Taunton, April 22. WORCESTERSHIRE beat SOMERSET by 33 runs.

At Derby, April 29. WORCESTERSHIRE lost to DERBYSHIRE by 35 runs.

WORCESTERSHIRE v NOTTINGHAMSHIRE

At Worcester, May 6. Worcestershire won by 61 runs. Toss: Nottinghamshire. Hick faced 105 balls and hit two sixes and eight fours in his highest score in the Sunday League.

Worcestershire

T. S. Curtis lbw b Pick 73
R. K. Illingworth c French b Cooper . . 3
G. A. Hick not out 114
D. B. D'Oliveira b Stephenson 6
*P. A. Neale b Saxelby 11
S. R. Lampitt not out 4
L-b 6, w 3, n-b 1 10

1/19 2/161 3/182 4/217 (4 wkts, 40 overs) 221

D. A. Leatherdale, †S. R. Bevins, P. J. Newport, N. V. Radford and S. M. McEwan did not bat.

Bowling: Stephenson 8–1–41–1; Cooper 8–1–32–1; Saxelby 8–0–54–1; Pick 8–0–47–1; Hemmings 8–0–41–0.

Nottinghamshire

B. C. Broad c Bevins b Newport 0
*R. T. Robinson run out 0
P. R. Pollard c Leatherdale b Lampitt . 13
P. Johnson c Bevins b McEwan 58
D. W. Randall c Hick b Radford 12
F. D. Stephenson c Bevins b McEwan . 3
†B. N. French c Illingworth b Newport 9
E. E. Hemmings st Bevins b Illingworth 24
K. E. Cooper c Hick b Newport 4
R. A. Pick b Lampitt 12
K. Saxelby not out 6
L-b 13, w 6 19

1/0 2/1 3/35 4/66 5/76 6/99 7/115 8/129 9/138 (39.2 overs) 160

Bowling: Newport 8–0–37–3; McEwan 8–0–32–2; Lampitt 7.2–0–22–2; Radford 8–0–30–1; Illingworth 8–0–26–1.

Umpires: B. Leadbeater and K. J. Lyons.

WORCESTERSHIRE v ESSEX

At Worcester, May 20. Essex won by two wickets. Toss: Worcestershire. Essex achieved their first Sunday League victory of the season in their fifth match.

Worcestershire

T. S. Curtis c Prichard b Topley	34
M. J. Weston b Pringle	90
I. T. Botham c Garnham b Foster	5
D. B. D'Oliveira c Hardie b Pringle	41
N. V. Radford not out	26
*P. A. Neale run out	1
B 2, l-b 11, w 5	18
1/78 2/116 3/164 4/209 5/215 (5 wkts, 40 overs)	215

S. R. Lampitt, †S. J. Rhodes, P. J. Newport, R. K. Illingworth and S. M. McEwan did not bat.

Bowling: Foster 8–1–38–1; Ilott 8–0–28–0; Gooch 6–0–35–0; Topley 8–0–39–1; Pringle 8–0–48–2; Childs 2–0–14–0.

Essex

*G. A. Gooch b Weston	30
B. R. Hardie c Newport b Illingworth	54
M. E. Waugh c and b Weston	4
P. J. Prichard c Neale b Botham	47
D. R. Pringle not out	48
J. P. Stephenson c McEwan b Botham	9
†M. A. Garnham c Weston b Botham	5
N. A. Foster run out	0
T. D. Topley lbw b Botham	0
J. H. Childs not out	5
L-b 12, w 2	14
1/50 2/55 3/148 4/148 5/172 6/181 7/181 8/188 (8 wkts, 39.3 overs)	216

M. C. Ilott did not bat.

Bowling: Newport 6–0–33–0; Weston 8–0–33–2; Radford 7–0–39–0; Illingworth 8–0–41–1; Lampitt 4.3–0–33–0; Botham 6–1–25–4.

Umpires: B. Dudleston and P. B. Wight.

WORCESTERSHIRE v WARWICKSHIRE

At Worcester, May 27. Warwickshire won by six wickets. Toss: Worcestershire. Warwickshire's win was their first at New Road in 22 seasons of the Sunday League.

Worcestershire

T. S. Curtis run out	61
M. J. Weston c Humpage b Reeve	15
I. T. Botham c Ostler b Smith	29
D. B. D'Oliveira b Smith	3
*P. A. Neale run out	23
D. A. Leatherdale run out	3
S. R. Lampitt not out	16
N. V. Radford c Munton b Small	4
P. J. Newport run out	8
L-b 13, w 7	20
1/42 2/111 3/115 4/135 5/139 6/163 7/169 8/182 (8 wkts, 40 overs)	182

†S. J. Rhodes and S. M. McEwan did not bat.

Bowling: Munton 8–0–36–0; Benjamin 8–0–27–0; Reeve 8–2–45–1; Smith 8–1–39–2; Small 8–0–22–1.

Warwickshire

Asif Din not out	86
*T. A. Lloyd c Rhodes b Weston	0
T. M. Moody c Rhodes b Radford	29
A. I. Kallicharran lbw b McEwan	5
D. A. Reeve c Botham b Lampitt	11
†G. W. Humpage not out	40
B 2, l-b 2, w 7, n-b 3	14
1/2 2/45 3/67 4/104 (4 wkts, 39.4 overs)	185

N. M. K. Smith, D. P. Ostler, J. E. Benjamin, G. C. Small and T. A. Munton did not bat.

Bowling: Newport 8–2–20–0; Weston 3–0–12–1; Radford 8–0–34–1; Botham 6–0–43–0; McEwan 6.4–0–39–1; Lampitt 8–0–33–1.

Umpires: B. Leadbeater and N. T. Plews.

WORCESTERSHIRE v YORKSHIRE

At Worcester, June 3. Yorkshire won by 16 runs. Toss: Worcestershire.

Yorkshire

K. Sharp run out 71
*A. A. Metcalfe c D'Oliveira b Newport 0
R. J. Blakey c Rhodes b McEwan 79
P. E. Robinson c Rhodes b McEwan .. 13
D. Byas b Lampitt 14
†D. L. Bairstow not out 5
C. S. Pickles c Rhodes b McEwan 0
P. J. Hartley run out 7
P. Carrick not out 0
L-b 8, w 8 16

1/4 2/161 3/177 4/193 5/193 6/193 7/204 (7 wkts, 37 overs) 205

P. W. Jarvis and S. D. Fletcher did not bat.

Bowling: Newport 8–0–32–1; Weston 8–0–36–0; Botham 1–0–4–0; McEwan 8–0–44–3; Lampitt 8–0–53–1; Stemp 4–0–28–0.

Worcestershire

T. S. Curtis b Hartley 76
M. J. Weston c Jarvis b Hartley 4
*P. A. Neale c Sharp b Hartley 18
D. B. D'Oliveira c Jarvis b Carrick ... 1
D. A. Leatherdale c Blakey b Pickles .. 35
†S. J. Rhodes c Metcalfe b Jarvis 2
I. T. Botham c Jarvis b Hartley 12
P. J. Newport c Carrick b Hartley 8
S. R. Lampitt c Hartley b Jarvis 8
R. D. Stemp b Fletcher 1
S. M. McEwan not out 18
L-b 6 6

1/6 2/34 3/37 4/106 5/109 6/137 7/152 8/164 9/165 (36.1 overs) 189

Bowling: Jarvis 7.1–0–26–2; Hartley 8–0–38–5; Carrick 8–0–34–1; Fletcher 7–0–42–1; Pickles 6–0–43–1.

Umpires: J. H. Harris and K. J. Lyons.

At The Oval, June 17. WORCESTERSHIRE lost to SURREY by seven wickets.

WORCESTERSHIRE v SUSSEX

At Worcester, June 24. Worcestershire won by 2 runs. Toss: Sussex.

Worcestershire

T. S. Curtis c and b Pigott 58
I. T. Botham b C. M. Wells 19
G. A. Hick c Pigott b Dodemaide 75
D. B. D'Oliveira b Clarke 16
*P. A. Neale c Pigott b Lenham 8
D. A. Leatherdale run out 6
P. J. Newport c Salisbury b Dodemaide 3
†S. J. Rhodes c and b Dodemaide 0
S. R. Lampitt not out 0
L-b 12, w 3 15

1/46 2/153 3/177 4/182 5/195 6/200 7/200 8/200 (8 wkts, 40 overs) 200

R. K. Illingworth and S. M. McEwan did not bat.

Bowling: C. M. Wells 8–0–21–1; Dodemaide 8–0–27–3; Clarke 8–0–42–1; Pigott 8–0–43–1; Salisbury 7–0–50–0; Lenham 1–0–5–1.

Sussex

*P. W. G. Parker lbw b McEwan 42
I. J. Gould b Lampitt 12
A. P. Wells c Illingworth b Newport .. 34
M. P. Speight lbw b Illingworth 15
C. M. Wells c Neale b Botham 29
A. C. S. Pigott b Botham 4
A. I. C. Dodemaide run out 24
†P. Moores c and b Botham 13
N. J. Lenham not out 3
I. D. K. Salisbury c Rhodes b Lampitt . 0
A. R. Clarke not out 1
L-b 11, w 5, n-b 5 21

1/48 2/83 3/111 4/130 5/155 6/155 7/171 8/196 9/197 (9 wkts, 40 overs) 198

Bowling: Newport 8–0–33–1; McEwan 8–0–55–1; Botham 8–0–40–3; Lampitt 8–1–24–2; Illingworth 8–0–35–1.

Umpires: B. Hassan and A. G. T. Whitehead.

At Lord's, July 1. WORCESTERSHIRE lost to MIDDLESEX by 99 runs.

WORCESTERSHIRE v GLOUCESTERSHIRE

At Worcester, July 8. Worcestershire won by eight wickets. Toss: Worcestershire.

Gloucestershire

G. D. Hodgson c Leatherdale b Weston . 10
C. W. J. Athey c Leatherdale b Lampitt 63
*A. J. Wright c Leatherdale b Tolley . . 24
K. M. Curran c Curtis b Botham 56
P. Bainbridge lbw b Lampitt 15
P. W. Romaines not out 27
J. W. Lloyds b Botham 2
M. W. Alleyne not out 8
L-b 9, w 6 15

1/19 2/53 3/155 4/171 5/198 6/205 (6 wkts, 40 overs) 220

†R. C. J. Williams, C. A. Walsh and D. A. Graveney did not bat.

Bowling: Weston 7–0–26–1; Tolley 8–0–26–1; Botham 8–0–40–2; Lampitt 6–0–56–2; Hick 4–0–23–0; Herzberg 5–0–28–0; Leatherdale 2–0–12–0.

Worcestershire

T. S. Curtis not out 93
M. J. Weston b Walsh 4
G. A. Hick c Williams b Alleyne 67
I. T. Botham not out 41
L-b 8, w 7, n-b 1 16

1/20 2/146 (2 wkts, 38.4 overs) 221

*P. A. Neale, D. B. D'Oliveira, †S. J. Rhodes, D. A. Leatherdale, S. R. Lampitt, C. M. Tolley and S. Herzberg did not bat.

Bowling: Curran 7.4–0–39–0; Walsh 7–0–28–1; Bainbridge 5–0–25–0; Graveney 8–0–42–0; Alleyne 7–0–51–1; Lloyds 4–0–28–0.

Umpires: P. J. Eele and P. B. Wight.

At Manchester, July 15. WORCESTERSHIRE lost to LANCASHIRE by seven wickets.

At Canterbury, July 29. WORCESTERSHIRE beat KENT by five wickets.

At Leicester, August 5. WORCESTERSHIRE beat LEICESTERSHIRE by seven wickets.

WORCESTERSHIRE v HAMPSHIRE

At Worcester, August 12. Hampshire won by 20 runs. Toss: Worcestershire. Hick took his total of Sunday League runs for the season to 694, passing Younis Ahmed's Worcestershire record of 668 scored in 1979.

Hampshire

V. P. Terry run out 17
R. J. Scott c McEwan b Hick 53
*M. C. J. Nicholas c Illingworth b McEwan . 17
C. L. Smith c Lampitt b Hick 21
M. D. Marshall c Newport b Lampitt . 38
J. R. Ayling not out 47
†R. J. Parks b Hick 4
R. M. F. Cox not out 2
B 4, l-b 2, w 2 8

1/42 2/81 3/115 4/115 5/191 6/200 (6 wkts, 40 overs) 207

R. J. Maru, T. M. Tremlett and S. D. Udal did not bat.

Bowling: Newport 6–1–33–0; Weston 8–0–32–0; Illingworth 8–0–24–0; McEwan 3–0–15–1; Hick 8–0–47–3; Lampitt 7–0–50–1.

Worcestershire

*T. S. Curtis b Tremlett 13
G. J. Lord c Terry b Tremlett 17
G. A. Hick c Terry b Scott 88
D. A. Leatherdale lbw b Tremlett 0
M. J. Weston c Terry b Udal 6
C. M. Tolley c Terry b Udal 1
†S. J. Rhodes c Udal b Ayling 26
R. K. Illingworth b Marshall 7
P. J. Newport run out 7
S. R. Lampitt b Scott 8
S. M. McEwan not out 3
L-b 10, n-b 1 11

1/32 2/35 3/35 4/44 5/46 6/125 7/165 8/171 9/184 (39.4 overs) 187

Bowling: Marshall 8–0–22–1; Tremlett 8–0–22–3; Ayling 8–0–43–1; Udal 7–0–36–2; Maru 7–0–46–0; Scott 1.4–0–8–2.

Umpires: B. Dudleston and K. E. Palmer.

WORCESTERSHIRE v NORTHAMPTONSHIRE

At Worcester, August 19. No result. Toss: Northamptonshire. Rain ended the match, which had already been reduced to 35 overs a side. D'Oliveira's 58 came off 38 balls, including two sixes and two fours in one over bowled by Davis.

Worcestershire

*T. S. Curtis not out 83
G. J. Lord c Ripley b Penberthy 78
G. A. Hick c Penberthy b Cook 26
D. B. D'Oliveira c Wild b Robinson ... 58
D. A. Leatherdale b Robinson 0
M. J. Weston not out 3
L-b 11, w 3, n-b 3 17

1/116 2/151 3/248 4/251 (4 wkts, 35 overs) 265

†S. J. Rhodes, R. K. Illingworth, P. J. Newport, S. R. Lampitt and S. M. McEwan did not bat.

Bowling: Davis 8–0–58–0; Robinson 5–0–36–2; Larkins 3–0–20–0; Capel 5–0–35–0; Cook 8–0–54–1; Penberthy 5–0–45–1; Wild 1–0–6–0.

Northamptonshire

A. Fordham c McEwan b Weston 21
W. Larkins c Curtis b Newport 1
*A. J. Lamb c Leatherdale b Newport . 10
D. J. Capel not out 1
R. J. Bailey not out 0
W 2 2

1/7 2/33 3/35 (3 wkts, 8.4 overs) 35

D. J. Wild, A. L. Penberthy, †D. Ripley, N. G. B. Cook, W. W. Davis and M. A. Robinson did not bat.

Bowling: Newport 4.4–0–15–2; Weston 4–0–20–1.

Umpires: D. J. Constant and B. Leadbeater.

At Swansea, August 26. WORCESTERSHIRE beat GLAMORGAN by 34 runs.

YORKSHIRE

At Nottingham, April 22. YORKSHIRE lost to NOTTINGHAMSHIRE by five wickets.

At Birmingham, May 6. YORKSHIRE lost to WARWICKSHIRE by eight wickets.

YORKSHIRE v DERBYSHIRE

At Leeds, May 13. Yorkshire won by six wickets. Toss: Yorkshire. Jarvis took three of the last four Derbyshire wickets in his seventh over, a maiden.

Derbyshire

*K. J. Barnett c White b Byas	29	S. J. Base b Fletcher	0
P. D. Bowler c Bairstow b Sidebottom	5	D. E. Malcolm b Jarvis	0
B. Roberts c Sidebottom b Jarvis	53	O. H. Mortensen not out	0
A. P. Kuiper c Blakey b Jarvis	5	L-b 11, w 5, n-b 2	18
C. J. Adams c Bairstow b Byas	7		
S. C. Goldsmith c Byas b Sidebottom	7	1/14 2/71 3/79 (38.1 overs)	143
†K. M. Krikken b Jarvis	14	4/106 5/121 6/122	
A. E. Warner c Kellett b Jarvis	5	7/143 8/143 9/143	

Bowling: Sidebottom 8–0–18–2; Jarvis 7–1–18–5; Fletcher 7.1–0–37–1; Gough 8–0–26–0; Byas 8–0–33–2.

Yorkshire

S. A. Kellett run out	32	†D. L. Bairstow not out	1
*A. A. Metcalfe b Base	41	B 1, l-b 9, w 11	21
R. J. Blakey c Krikken b Base	1		
D. Byas not out	30	1/71 2/78 3/85 (4 wkts, 39 overs)	147
P. E. Robinson c Krikken b Barnett	21	4/140	

C. White, A. Sidebottom, P. W. Jarvis, D. Gough and S. D. Fletcher did not bat.

Bowling: Mortensen 8–0–26–0; Malcolm 8–1–28–0; Warner 8–0–28–0; Base 8–2–33–2; Goldsmith 3–0–10–0; Barnett 4–0–12–1.

Umpires: H. D. Bird and R. Palmer.

At Canterbury, May 20. YORKSHIRE lost to KENT by 69 runs.

YORKSHIRE v HAMPSHIRE

At Leeds, May 27. Hampshire won by 36 runs. Toss: Yorkshire.

Hampshire

V. P. Terry b Byas	56	†A. N. Aymes not out	15
D. I. Gower c Byas b Hartley	12	T. M. Tremlett not out	2
R. A. Smith b Hartley	44	L-b 14, w 8, n-b 1	23
M. D. Marshall b Byas	10		
R. J. Scott c Robinson b Carrick	1	1/34 2/113 3/129 (7 wkts, 40 overs)	184
*M. C. J. Nicholas c Blakey b Byas	8	4/131 5/146	
J. R. Ayling b Fletcher	13	6/149 7/180	

C. A. Connor and R. J. Maru did not bat.

Bowling: Fletcher 8–0–34–1; Pickles 8–0–30–0; Hartley 8–1–24–2; Carrick 8–1–39–1; Gough 2–0–17–0; Byas 6–0–26–3.

Yorkshire

C. S. Pickles c Maru b Marshall	6	P. J. Hartley b Connor	14
*A. A. Metcalfe b Connor	0	D. Gough not out	17
S. A. Kellett run out	7	S. D. Fletcher c Nicholas b Connor	6
R. J. Blakey c Gower b Tremlett	22	B 1, l-b 10, n-b 2	13
P. E. Robinson c Maru b Scott	26		
D. Byas lbw b Tremlett	2	1/7 2/7 3/23 (39 overs)	148
†D. L. Bairstow c Smith b Scott	21	4/49 5/55 6/71	
P. Carrick c Nicholas b Ayling	14	7/100 8/116 9/125	

Bowling: Connor 8–1–31–3; Marshall 7–1–32–1; Tremlett 8–0–19–2; Ayling 8–2–16–1; Scott 8–0–39–2.

Umpires: D. O. Oslear and A. G. T. Whitehead.

At Worcester, June 3. YORKSHIRE beat WORCESTERSHIRE by 16 runs.

YORKSHIRE v SURREY

At Hull, June 10. Surrey won by six wickets. Toss: Surrey.

Yorkshire

K. Sharp c Ward b Bicknell	0	P. J. Hartley b Waqar Younis	8
A. A. Metcalfe lbw b Feltham	16	P. W. Jarvis c Bicknell b Murphy	3
R. J. Blakey b Medlycott	38	A. Sidebottom not out	3
P. E. Robinson b Medlycott	22	L-b 10, w 5	15
*M. D. Moxon c Ward b Medlycott	9		
D. Byas b Waqar Younis	2	1/0 2/39 3/78 (9 wkts, 40 overs)	144
†D. L. Bairstow not out	21	4/91 5/92 6/102	
P. Carrick b Murphy	7	7/114 8/131 9/136	

Bowling: Bicknell 6–1–20–1; Murphy 8–1–29–2; Feltham 4–0–10–1; Bullen 6–0–21–0; Medlycott 8–1–20–3; Waqar Younis 8–0–34–2.

Surrey

G. S. Clinton c Metcalfe b Byas	28	*I. A. Greig not out	2
M. A. Feltham c Sharp b Sidebottom	16	B 3, l-b 13, w 3, n-b 4	23
G. P. Thorpe not out	46		
†D. M. Ward b Hartley	22	1/39 2/68 3/112 (4 wkts, 37.5 overs)	145
M. A. Lynch c Metcalfe b Jarvis	8	4/131	

C. K. Bullen, K. T. Medlycott, M. P. Bicknell, Waqar Younis and A. J. Murphy did not bat.

Bowling: Jarvis 8–1–19–1; Sidebottom 8–1–29–1; Hartley 8–2–22–1; Byas 6–0–22–1; Carrick 4–0–22–0; Moxon 3.5–0–15–0.

Umpires: J. C. Balderstone and D. S. Thompsett.

At Hove, June 17. YORKSHIRE beat SUSSEX by 40 runs.

At Newport, June 24. GLAMORGAN v YORKSHIRE. No result.

At Tring, July 8. YORKSHIRE beat NORTHAMPTONSHIRE by 61 runs.

YORKSHIRE v SOMERSET

At Scarborough, July 15. Yorkshire won by 16 runs. Toss: Somerset. Moxon's 105, his first Sunday League century, came off 124 balls with nine fours.

Yorkshire

*M. D. Moxon c Tavaré b Mallender . . 105
A. A. Metcalfe c Harden b Hallett 14
†R. J. Blakey c Harden b Rose 52
P. J. Hartley c Burns b Lefebvre 27
P. E. Robinson b Hayhurst 15
D. Byas not out 6
C. S. Pickles not out 1
B 1, l-b 4, w 2 7

1/46 2/157 3/198 4/217 5/226 (5 wkts, 40 overs) 227

C. White, P. Carrick, A. Sidebottom and S. D. Fletcher did not bat.

Bowling: Mallender 8–0–51–1; Rose 8–0–45–1; Lefebvre 8–0–35–1; Hallett 5–0–23–1; Hayhurst 7–0–43–1; Swallow 4–0–25–0.

Somerset

S. J. Cook c Blakey b Carrick 52
R. J. Bartlett c Robinson b Pickles 21
*C. J. Tavaré c and b Pickles 8
R. J. Harden c White b Pickles 28
G. D. Rose c Moxon b White 6
†N. D. Burns run out 1
A. N. Hayhurst b Pickles 16
R. P. Lefebvre b Fletcher 28
I. G. Swallow c Carrick b Fletcher 31
N. A. Mallender b Hartley 3
J. C. Hallett not out 0
L-b 16, n-b 1 17

1/55 2/69 3/95 4/110 5/119 6/147 7/147 8/194 9/205 (39.4 overs) 211

Bowling: Hartley 7–0–42–1; Sidebottom 5–0–25–0; Fletcher 7.4–0–40–2; Pickles 6–0–36–4; Carrick 8–0–18–1; White 6–0–34–1.

Umpires: H. D. Bird and J. D. Bond.

At Cheltenham, July 22. YORKSHIRE beat GLOUCESTERSHIRE by seven wickets.

YORKSHIRE v LEICESTERSHIRE

At Sheffield, July 29. Yorkshire won by eight wickets. Toss: Leicestershire.

Leicestershire

T. J. Boon c Carrick b Hartley 88
*N. E. Briers st Blakey b Carrick 37
J. J. Whitaker c Metcalfe b Carrick . . . 25
P. Willey b Jarvis 7
L. Potter c Sharp b Hartley 0
J. D. R. Benson not out 18
W. K. M. Benjamin c Blakey b Jarvis . 3
†P. A. Nixon not out 8
B 6, l-b 12, w 3 21

1/104 2/165 3/177 4/177 5/177 6/183 (6 wkts, 40 overs) 207

G. J. Parsons, J. P. Agnew and A. D. Mullally did not bat.

Bowling: Jarvis 8–0–25–2; Pickles 3–0–21–0; Fletcher 7–0–40–0; Hartley 8–0–42–2; Carrick 8–0–29–2; Moxon 6–0–32–0.

Yorkshire

*M. D. Moxon c Whitaker b Potter . . . 73
A. A. Metcalfe c Willey b Parsons 71
†R. J. Blakey not out 30
K. Sharp not out 26
L-b 4, w 3, n-b 1 8

1/134 2/155 (2 wkts, 35.5 overs) 208

P. E. Robinson, D. Byas, P. J. Hartley, P. Carrick, C. S. Pickles, P. W. Jarvis and S. D. Fletcher did not bat.

Bowling: Benjamin 6–1–35–0; Agnew 7.5–0–33–0; Mullally 7–0–24–0; Parsons 5–0–36–1; Willey 3–0–25–0; Potter 7–0–51–1.

Umpires: K. J. Lyons and P. B. Wight.

YORKSHIRE v LANCASHIRE

At Scarborough, August 5. Lancashire won by 78 runs. Toss: Yorkshire.

Lancashire

G. Fowler c Sidebottom b Fletcher 55
M. A. Atherton b Fletcher 53
G. D. Lloyd c and b Fletcher 76
N. H. Fairbrother lbw b Fletcher 3
M. Watkinson run out 31
Wasim Akram not out 35
†W. K. Hegg not out 1
L-b 6, n-b 3 9

1/106 2/115 3/127 4/210 5/253 (5 wkts, 40 overs) 263

P. J. Martin, I. D. Austin, *D. P. Hughes and P. J. W. Allott did not bat.

Bowling: Jarvis 8–0–69–0; Sidebottom 8–0–33–0; Hartley 8–1–44–0; Carrick 8–0–48–0; Fletcher 8–0–63–4.

Yorkshire

*M. D. Moxon c Watkinson b Allott . . 31
A. A. Metcalfe c Fairbrother b Allott . . 6
†R. J. Blakey c Hegg b Wasim Akram . 35
K. Sharp c Martin b Atherton 37
P. E. Robinson b Wasim Akram 0
D. Byas not out 35
P. J. Hartley c Watkinson b Atherton . 18
P. Carrick c Hughes b Austin 1
P. W. Jarvis b Wasim Akram 3
A. Sidebottom b Wasim Akram 2
S. D. Fletcher lbw b Austin 2
L-b 9, w 5, n-b 1 15

1/26 2/59 3/105 4/105 5/138 6/161 7/169 8/176 9/182 (35.3 overs) 185

Bowling: Allott 8–1–21–2; Martin 6–0–41–0; Watkinson 8–0–47–0; Wasim Akram 6–0–19–4; Austin 4.3–0–21–2; Atherton 3–0–27–2.

Umpires: B. Leadbeater and N. T. Plews.

YORKSHIRE v ESSEX

At Middlesbrough, August 12. Yorkshire won by 59 runs. Toss: Essex.

Yorkshire

*M. D. Moxon c Garnham b Ilott 12
A. A. Metcalfe run out 1
†R. J. Blakey c Stephenson b Waugh . . 76
K. Sharp c Hussain b Waugh 30
P. E. Robinson c Waugh b Stephenson . 14
D. Byas c Hussain b Ilott 18
P. Carrick c Hussain b Andrew 30
C. S. Pickles b Andrew 0
P. J. Hartley not out 9
P. W. Jarvis b Waugh 7
A. Sidebottom not out 8
L-b 12, w 4 16

1/3 2/23 3/124 4/131 5/149 6/193 7/194 8/194 9/208 (9 wkts, 40 overs) 221

Bowling: Ilott 8–2–24–2; Andrew 8–2–30–2; Such 4–0–35–0; Topley 7–0–48–0; Waugh 8–0–37–3; Stephenson 5–0–35–1.

Essex

*B. R. Hardie c Sidebottom b Jarvis	5	M. C. Ilott run out	6
J. P. Stephenson b Sidebottom	4	S. J. W. Andrew c Metcalfe b Pickles	5
M. E. Waugh c Pickles b Hartley	19	P. M. Such c Metcalfe b Jarvis	5
P. J. Prichard c Byas b Jarvis	2	B 5, l-b 8, w 1, n-b 1	15
N. Hussain not out	66		
N. Shahid b Carrick	31	1/11 2/11 3/15 (34.4 overs)	162
†M. A. Garnham c Blakey b Carrick	0	4/39 5/105 6/105	
T. D. Topley c Pickles b Carrick	4	7/124 8/131 9/145	

Bowling: Jarvis 5.4–0–16–3; Sidebottom 8–1–22–1; Hartley 6–0–27–1; Carrick 8–0–46–3; Pickles 7–0–38–1.

Umpires: B. Hassan and A. A. Jones.

YORKSHIRE v MIDDLESEX

At Scarborough, August 26. Yorkshire won by 44 runs. Toss: Yorkshire. Yorkshire's total was their highest in the Sunday League. Haynes took his season's total of runs in the Sunday League to 632, passing C. T. Radley's record for Middlesex of 618 in 1974. Emburey's 30th Sunday League wicket of the season passed by one W. W. Daniel's county record set in 1984.

Yorkshire

*M. D. Moxon run out	38	P. Carrick run out	7
A. A. Metcalfe c Carr b Cowans	84		
†R. J. Blakey c Ramprakash b Cowans	63	L-b 6, w 3	9
P. E. Robinson c Weekes b Cowans	11		
D. Byas run out	22	1/60 2/169 3/192 (7 wkts, 40 overs)	271
C. A. Chapman not out	36	4/204 5/249	
P. J. Hartley b Emburey	1	6/264 7/271	

P. W. Jarvis, A. Sidebottom and C. S. Pickles did not bat.

Bowling: Cowans 8–0–43–3; Taylor 8–0–46–0; Hughes 8–1–52–0; Emburey 8–0–57–1; Weekes 4–0–36–0; Haynes 4–0–31–0.

Middlesex

D. L. Haynes lbw b Carrick	60	N. G. Cowans c Blakey b Hartley	0
M. A. Roseberry lbw b Jarvis	9	S. P. Hughes b Jarvis	14
M. R. Ramprakash c Hartley b Carrick	34	N. R. Taylor not out	5
K. R. Brown c Robinson b Hartley	16	L-b 8, w 1	9
J. D. Carr run out	9		
*J. E. Emburey c Metcalfe b Carrick	14	1/19 2/106 3/123 (9 wkts, 40 overs)	227
†P. R. Downton c and b Pickles	28	4/135 5/137 6/152	
P. N. Weekes not out	29	7/190 8/193 9/218	

Bowling: Jarvis 8–0–41–2; Sidebottom 8–0–33–0; Hartley 8–0–51–2; Pickles 8–0–50–1; Carrick 8–0–44–3.

Umpires: J. W. Holder and D. S. Thompsett.

SUNDAY LEAGUE RECORDS

Batting

Highest score: 176 – G. A. Gooch, Essex v Glamorgan (Southend), 1983.

Most hundreds: 11 – C. G. Greenidge; 10 – G. A. Gooch; 9 – W. Larkins, K. S. McEwan and B. A. Richards. 368 hundreds have been scored in the League. The most in one season is 40 in 1990.

Most runs: D. L. Amiss 7,040; C. T. Radley 6,650; D. R. Turner 6,639; P. Willey 6,353; C. G. Greenidge 6,344; G. A. Gooch 6,324; C. E. B. Rice 6,265; G. M. Turner 6,144.

Most runs in a season: 902 – S. J. Cook (Somerset), 1990.

Most sixes in an innings: 13 – I. T. Botham, Somerset v Northamptonshire (Wellingborough School), 1986.

Most sixes by a team in an innings: 18 – Derbyshire v Worcestershire (Knypersley), 1985.

Most sixes in a season: 26 – I. V. A. Richards (Somerset), 1977.

Highest total: 360 for three – Somerset v Glamorgan (Neath), 1990.

Highest total – batting second: 301 for six – Warwickshire v Essex (Colchester), 1982.

Highest match aggregate: 604 – Surrey (304) v Warwickshire (300 for nine) (The Oval), 1985.

Lowest total: 23 (19.4 overs) – Middlesex v Yorkshire (Leeds), 1974.

Shortest completed innings: 16 overs – Northamptonshire 59 v Middlesex (Tring), 1974.

Shortest match: 2 hr 13 min (40.3 overs) – Essex v Northamptonshire (Ilford), 1971.

Biggest victories: 220 runs, Somerset beat Glamorgan (Neath), 1990.
There have been 21 instances of victory by ten wickets – by Derbyshire, Essex (twice), Glamorgan, Hampshire, Leicestershire (twice), Middlesex (twice), Northamptonshire, Nottinghamshire, Somerset (twice), Surrey (twice), Warwickshire, Worcestershire (twice) and Yorkshire (three times). This does not include those matches in which the side batting second was set a reduced target.

Ties (30): Nottinghamshire v Kent (Nottingham), 1969, in a match reduced to twenty overs.
Gloucestershire v Hampshire (Bristol), 1972; Gloucestershire v Northamptonshire (Bristol), 1972.
Surrey v Worcestershire (Byfleet), 1973.
Middlesex v Lancashire (Lord's), 1974; Sussex v Leicestershire (Hove), 1974.
Lancashire v Worcestershire (Manchester), 1975; Somerset v Glamorgan (Taunton), 1975.
Warwickshire v Kent (Birmingham), 1980.
Kent v Lancashire (Maidstone), 1981.
Yorkshire v Nottinghamshire (Hull), 1982; Hampshire v Lancashire (Southampton), 1982; Surrey v Hampshire (The Oval), 1982.
Worcestershire v Nottinghamshire (Hereford), 1983; Lancashire v Worcestershire (Manchester), 1983, in a match reduced to nineteen overs; Warwickshire v Worcestershire (Birmingham), 1983, Warwickshire's innings having been reduced to ten overs.
Middlesex v Essex (Lord's), 1984.
Essex v Leicestershire (Chelmsford), 1985; Northamptonshire v Lancashire (Northampton), 1985; Lancashire v Glamorgan (Manchester), 1985.
Kent v Surrey (Canterbury), 1986; Middlesex v Warwickshire (Lord's), 1986; Yorkshire v Warwickshire (Leeds), 1986.
Hampshire v Gloucestershire (Southampton), 1987; Hampshire v Derbyshire (Southampton), 1987.
Essex v Sussex (Ilford), 1988; Surrey v Derbyshire (The Oval), 1988; Sussex v Glamorgan (Eastbourne), 1988.
Middlesex v Hampshire (Lord's), 1989; Somerset v Sussex (Taunton), 1989.

Record partnerships for each wicket

239 for 1st	G. A. Gooch and B. R. Hardie, Essex v Nottinghamshire at Nottingham	1985
273 for 2nd	G. A. Gooch and K. S. McEwan, Essex v Nottinghamshire at Nottingham	1983
223 for 3rd	S. J. Cook and G. D. Rose, Somerset v Glamorgan at Neath	1990
219 for 4th	C. G. Greenidge and C. L. Smith, Hampshire v Surrey at Southampton	1987
185* for 5th	B. M. McMillan and Asif Din, Warwickshire v Essex at Chelmsford.	1986
121 for 6th	C. P. Wilkins and A. J. Borrington, Derbyshire v Warwickshire at Chesterfield	1972

132 for 7th	K. R. Brown and N. F. Williams, Middlesex v Somerset at Lord's . . .	1988
95* for 8th	D. Breakwell and K. F. Jennings, Somerset v Nottinghamshire at Nottingham . . .	1976
105 for 9th	D. G. Moir and R. W. Taylor, Derbyshire v Kent at Derby . . .	1984
57 for 10th	D. A. Graveney and J. B. Mortimore, Gloucestershire v Lancashire at Tewkesbury . . .	1973

Bowling

Best analyses: eight for 26, K. D. Boyce, Essex v Lancashire (Manchester), 1971; seven for 15, R. A. Hutton, Yorkshire v Worcestershire (Leeds), 1969; seven for 39, A. Hodgson, Northamptonshire v Somerset (Northampton), 1976; seven for 41, A. N. Jones, Sussex v Nottinghamshire (Nottingham), 1986; six for 6, R. W. Hooker, Middlesex v Surrey (Lord's), 1969; six for 7, M. Hendrick, Derbyshire v Nottinghamshire (Nottingham), 1972.

Four wickets in four balls: A. Ward, Derbyshire v Sussex (Derby), 1970.

Hat-tricks (19): A. Ward, Derbyshire v Sussex (Derby), 1970; R. Palmer, Somerset v Gloucestershire (Bristol), 1970; K. D. Boyce, Essex v Somerset (Westcliff), 1971; G. D. McKenzie, Leicestershire v Essex (Leicester), 1972; R. G. D. Willis, Warwickshire v Yorkshire (Birmingham), 1973; W. Blenkiron, Warwickshire v Derbyshire (Buxton), 1974; A. Buss, Sussex v Worcestershire (Hastings), 1974; J. M. Rice, Hampshire v Northamptonshire (Southampton), 1975; M. A. Nash, Glamorgan v Worcestershire (Worcester), 1975; A. Hodgson, Northamptonshire v Somerset (Northampton), 1976; A. E. Cordle, Glamorgan v Hampshire (Portsmouth), 1979; C. J. Tunnicliffe, Derbyshire v Worcestershire (Derby), 1979; M. D. Marshall, Hampshire v Surrey (Southampton), 1981; I. V. A. Richards, Somerset v Essex (Chelmsford), 1982; P. W. Jarvis, Yorkshire v Derbyshire (Derby), 1982; R. M. Ellison, Kent v Hampshire (Canterbury), 1983; G. C. Holmes, Glamorgan v Nottinghamshire (Ebbw Vale), 1987; K. Saxelby, Nottinghamshire v Worcestershire (Nottingham), 1987; K. M. Curran, Gloucestershire v Warwickshire (Birmingham), 1989.

Most economical analysis: 8–8–0–0, B. A. Langford, Somerset v Essex (Yeovil), 1969.

Most expensive analyses: 7.5–0–89–3, G. Miller, Derbyshire v Gloucestershire (Gloucester), 1984; 8–0–88–1, E. E. Hemmings, Nottinghamshire v Somerset (Nottingham), 1983.

Most wickets in a season: 34 – R. J. Clapp (Somerset), 1974, and C. E. B. Rice (Nottinghamshire), 1986.

Most wickets: J. K. Lever 386; D. L. Underwood 346; J. Simmons 307; S. Turner 303; N. Gifford 284; J. E. Emburey 270; J. N. Shepherd 267; E. E. Hemmings 258; T. E. Jesty 249; R. D. Jackman 234.

Wicket-keeping and Fielding

Most dismissals: D. L. Bairstow 255 (231 ct, 24 st); R. W. Taylor 236 (187 ct, 49 st); E. W. Jones 223 (184 ct, 39 st).

Most dismissals in a season: 29 (26 ct, 3 st) – S. J. Rhodes (Worcestershire), 1988.

Most dismissals in an innings: 7 (6 ct, 1 st) – R. W. Taylor, Derbyshire v Lancashire (Manchester), 1975.

Most catches in an innings: 6 – K. Goodwin, Lancashire v Worcestershire (Worcester), 1969, and R. W. Taylor, Derbyshire v Lancashire (Manchester), 1975.

Most stumpings in an innings: 4 – S. J. Rhodes, Worcestershire v Warwickshire (Birmingham), 1986.

Most catches by a fielder (not a wicket-keeper): J. F. Steele 101; G. Cook and D. P. Hughes 94; C. T. Radley 90.

Most catches in a season: 16 – J. M. Rice (Hampshire), 1978.

Most catches in an innings: 5 – J. M. Rice, Hampshire v Warwickshire (Southampton), 1978.

CHAMPIONS 1969-90

John Player League			
1969	Lancashire	1980	Warwickshire
1970	Lancashire	1981	Essex
1971	Worcestershire	1982	Sussex
1972	Kent	1983	Yorkshire
1973	Kent	1984	Essex
1974	Leicestershire	1985	Essex
1975	Hampshire	1986	Hampshire
1976	Kent	*Refuge Assurance League*	
1977	Leicestershire	1987	Worcestershire
1978	Hampshire	1988	Worcestershire
1979	Somerset	1989	Lancashire
		1990	Derbyshire

REFUGE ASSURANCE CUP

Middlesex, only one game away from winning the 1990 County Championship, collected their first 40-overs trophy when they beat Derbyshire in the Refuge Assurance Cup final at Edgbaston in September. Previously the closest they had come to success in a 40-overs competition was second to Sussex in the Sunday League in 1982 and the knockout round of the Cup in 1988. In addition to receiving the Refuge Assurance Cup, Middlesex won £6,000, while runners-up Derbyshire received £3,000 to compensate in part for failing to become the first county to achieve the League and Cup double. Lancashire and Nottinghamshire, the losing semi-finalists, each received £1,500. The Man of the Match award was worth £350 in the final and £175 in the semi-finals.

DERBYSHIRE v NOTTINGHAMSHIRE

At Derby, September 5. Derbyshire won by 22 runs. Toss: Nottinghamshire. After two early interruptions because of rain, Barnett and Bowler gave Derbyshire a steady start with an opening partnership of 118. Barnett scored 83 from 89 balls but, as in the final Sunday game, the crucial innings came from Kuiper. He hit 74 from 45 balls, with three sixes and seven fours, helping Derbyshire to add 96 in the last ten overs. At 87 for five in the 23rd over, Nottinghamshire were in trouble, but Robinson and Evans added 112 in thirteen overs to revive their hopes. Robinson's 96 came from 90 balls and contained eight fours. When he was caught at mid-on, Derbyshire regained control in poor light.

Man of the Match: R. T. Robinson.

Derbyshire

*K. J. Barnett c Johnson b Saxelby . . . 83
†P. D. Bowler c Evans b Cooper 59
J. E. Morris c Robinson b Evans 0
A. P. Kuiper c Mike b Stephenson 74
T. J. G. O'Gorman not out 20
L-b 12, w 7 19

1/118 2/134 3/168 (4 wkts, 40 overs) 255
4/255

B. Roberts, C. J. Adams, D. E. Malcolm, O. H. Mortensen, A. E. Warner and S. J. Base did not bat.

Bowling: Cooper 8–0–40–1; Stephenson 8–1–49–1; Evans 8–0–58–1; Mike 8–0–48–0; Hemmings 3–0–23–0; Saxelby 5–0–25–1.

Nottinghamshire

B. C. Broad c Barnett b Mortensen	28	†B. N. French b Kuiper	0
M. Newell b Warner	10	E. E. Hemmings not out	6
P. Johnson b Warner	2		
*R. T. Robinson c Warner b Malcolm	96	L-b 5, w 6, n-b 3	14
M. Saxelby lbw b Base	9		
F. D. Stephenson run out	7	1/16 2/22 3/48 (8 wkts, 40 overs)	233
K. P. Evans not out	55	4/69 5/87 6/199	
G. W. Mike run out	6	7/207 8/207	

K. E. Cooper did not bat.

Bowling: Mortensen 8–0–27–1; Warner 8–0–41–2; Malcolm 8–0–45–1; Base 8–0–65–1; Kuiper 8–0–50–1.

Umpires: B. Dudleston and R. Palmer.

LANCASHIRE v MIDDLESEX

At Manchester, September 5. Middlesex won by 45 runs. Toss: Lancashire. Middlesex, beginning with 81 from the first ten overs and finishing with 77 from the last ten, made Lancashire pay for a generally shoddy showing in the field. Haynes and Roseberry (88 balls) both had lives against Watkinson as they put on 153 in 21 overs. In contrast to Allott, whose four overs at the start cost 33 runs, and DeFreitas, 24 from three, Fraser conceded just 6 in his first four overs, and Lancashire had only 28 runs on the board after ten overs. When Fairbrother, after a typically aggressive half-century, was very well caught by Brown at long-off in the 29th over, the possibility of a Lancashire victory faded faster than the light.

Man of the Match: M. A. Roseberry.

Middlesex

D. L. Haynes c Atherton b Hughes	72	*J. E. Emburey run out	0
M. A. Roseberry c Allott b Hughes	86	N. F. Williams not out	10
M. R. Ramprakash c Lloyd b Austin	22	B 5, l-b 6, w 3	14
K. R. Brown not out	48		
J. C. Pooley c Hegg b DeFreitas	6	1/153 2/191 3/192 (6 wkts, 40 overs)	272
†P. R. Downton b Watkinson	14	4/216 5/245 6/246	

S. P. Hughes, A. R. C. Fraser and P. C. R. Tufnell did not bat.

Bowling: Allott 4–0–33–0; DeFreitas 8–0–71–1; Wasim Akram 5–0–27–0; Watkinson 7–0–50–1; Austin 8–0–40–1; Hughes 8–0–40–2.

Lancashire

G. Fowler b Emburey	20	†W. K. Hegg not out	19
M. A. Atherton run out	33	I. D. Austin not out	0
G. D. Lloyd c Downton b Fraser	65	B 2, l-b 9, w 1, n-b 3	15
N. H. Fairbrother c Brown b Hughes	56		
M. Watkinson c Hughes b Emburey	10	1/59 2/66 3/147 (7 wkts, 40 overs)	227
Wasim Akram st Downton b Emburey	7	4/167 5/186	
P. A. J. DeFreitas c Hughes b Emburey	2	6/190 7/227	

*D. P. Hughes and P. J. W. Allott did not bat.

Bowling: Fraser 8–3–28–1; Williams 8–0–32–0; Tufnell 8–0–57–0; Emburey 8–1–39–4; Hughes 8–0–60–1.

Umpires: H. D. Bird and A. G. T. Whitehead.

FINAL

DERBYSHIRE v MIDDLESEX

At Birmingham, September 16. Middlesex won by five wickets. Toss: Middlesex. Accurate Middlesex bowling, with a noteworthy performance from their 21-year-old off-spinner, Weekes, in the team for the injured Williams, contained Derbyshire on a slow pitch. Only Warner's late burst of hitting saw them reach 197 from 151 for six after 35 overs. Haynes and Gatting, whose fitness had been in doubt after he was struck on the elbow three days earlier at The Oval, established the Middlesex reply with 92 in eighteen overs. However, the return of Malcolm and Warner saw three wickets fall in twelve balls, and Middlesex needed 62 from ten overs, 30 from five and finally 7 from the last. Emburey could have been run out as the scores were levelled off the third ball, and Downton hit the next to the mid-wicket boundary for the victory his steady batting had helped secure.

Man of the Match: P. R. Downton. *Attendance:* 7,212; *receipts* £52,985.

Derbyshire

*K. J. Barnett b Weekes	42	A. E. Warner not out	28
†P. D. Bowler b Hughes	11	S. J. Base not out	1
J. E. Morris c Weekes b Haynes	46	B 1, l-b 9, w 5, n-b 1	16
A. P. Kuiper c Fraser b Weekes	9		
T. J. G. O'Gorman b Fraser	10	1/32 2/81 3/113 (7 wkts, 40 overs)	197
B. Roberts b Hughes	21	4/116 5/145	
C. J. Adams run out	13	6/151 7/196	

O. H. Mortensen and D. E. Malcolm did not bat.

Bowling: Fraser 8–0–32–1; Cowans 6–0–22–0; Hughes 8–0–45–2; Emburey 7–0–37–0; Weekes 8–1–35–2; Haynes 3–0–16–1.

Middlesex

D. L. Haynes b Malcolm	49	J. E. Emburey not out	5
M. A. Roseberry b Warner	17		
*M. W. Gatting b Malcolm	44	B 1, l-b 5, w 4, n-b 1	11
M. R. Ramprakash c Bowler b Warner	1		
K. R. Brown c Barnett b Malcolm	40	1/23 2/115 3/120 (5 wkts, 39.4 overs)	201
†P. R. Downton not out	34	4/120 5/191	

P. N. Weekes, S. P. Hughes, A. R. C. Fraser and N. G. Cowans did not bat.

Bowling: Warner 8–0–35–2; Mortensen 8–0–19–0; Malcolm 8–0–41–3; Base 8–0–53–0; Kuiper 7.4–0–47–0.

Umpires: D. J. Constant and M. J. Kitchen.

WINNERS 1988-90

1988 LANCASHIRE beat Worcestershire by 52 runs.
1989 ESSEX beat Nottinghamshire by 5 runs.
1990 MIDDLESEX beat Derbyshire by five wickets.

MINOR COUNTIES CHAMPIONSHIP, 1990

By MICHAEL BERRY and ROBERT BROOKE

The summer of 1990 took on an experimental look for Minor Counties cricket, following the implementation of a reshaped points-scoring system. After years of discussion, bowling bonus points were introduced – one for every two wickets taken in the first innings – and the limitation by which first-innings points were obtained only from the first 55 overs was abolished. It was, inevitably, a curate's egg of a change. The bowling bonus points proved a welcome addition; but from the moment that Berkshire and Oxfordshire extended the first innings of their opening game into the second, and final, afternoon, the absence of the 55-overs yardstick, first used in 1974, fostered much distrust. Agreements between the captains to restrict the length of their first innings served only to reinforce the doubts over the new legislation.

Continued over

MINOR COUNTIES CHAMPIONSHIP, 1990

Eastern Division	P	W	L	Drawn W 1st Inns	Drawn L 1st Inns	Drawn T 1st Inns	NR	Bonus Pts	Total Pts
Hertfordshire^NW	9	3	2*	3	1	0	0	34	77
Lincolnshire^NW	9	2	2*	2	3	0	0	36	68
Staffordshire^NW	8	3	1	2	2	0	1	24	65
Bedfordshire^NW	8	3	1	2	2	0	1	22	63
Durham^NW	9	1	0	6	2	0	0	33	63
Norfolk^NW	9	2	1	1	5	0	0	33	61
Cambridgeshire^NW	9	1	2*	3	2	1	0	31	57
Suffolk	9	2	3*	1	3	0	0	24	53
Cumberland	9	0	2	5	1	1	0	30	48
Northumberland	9	0	3*	1	5	0	0	23	34

Western Division	P	W	L	Drawn W 1st Inns	Drawn L 1st Inns	Drawn T 1st Inns	NR	Bonus Pts	Total Pts
Berkshire^NW	9	3	1‡	3	2	0	0	26	69
Oxfordshire^NW	9	2	1*	4	2	0	0	26	63
Shropshire^NW	9	2	0	4	3	0	0	25	60
Buckinghamshire^NW	9	2	0	4	3	0	0	25	60
Dorset^NW	9	2	3†	0	4	0	0	27	57
Devon^NW	9	0	1*	7	1	0	0	32	57
Wiltshire	9	1	3†	3	1	0	1	24	53
Wales	9	1	2	1	5	0	0	28	46
Cheshire	9	1	0	2	5	0	1	16	40
Cornwall	9	1	4	1	3	0	0	17	33

* *Denotes first-innings points (3) in one match lost.*
† *Denotes first-innings points (3) in two matches lost.*
‡ *Denotes tie on first innings (2 pts) in one match lost.*
NW *Denotes qualified for NatWest Bank Trophy in 1991.*

Win = 10 pts, Tie = 5 pts, First-innings win = 3 pts, First-innings tie = 2 pts, First-innings loss = 1 pt, No result = 3 pts.

Note: Where points are equal, priority is given to the county winning the greater number of completed matches. Where this number also is equal, priority is decided according to the nett batting averages.

The modifications, while providing extra interest, did little to alter the formbook. **Hertfordshire** were again at the forefront of the championship, and this time won the title to make up for their double disappointment in 1989. Beaten in both finals then, Hertfordshire took the 1990 championship with a seven-wicket victory over Berkshire in the September final at Luton. Their successful defence of the Eastern Division title revolved largely around the contributions of Andy Needham, John Carr and David Surridge, their shrewd captain. Needham scored 750 runs and took eighteen wickets, Carr scored 365 runs in only four games, and Surridge claimed 29 wickets. Although losing to Staffordshire and Bedfordshire in mid-season, Hertfordshire showed their true worth with a ten-wicket win over Suffolk in their final divisional fixture.

Runners-up in the Eastern Division were **Lincolnshire**, who enjoyed their best season for twenty years. They also reached the final of the Holt Cup at Lord's, but the subsequent dismissal of Neil Priestley, their captain, showed that, despite the success, all was not well behind the scenes. Jim Love, the former Yorkshire stalwart, who made his début in 1990, was chosen to succeed Priestley as captain. Love's 537 championship runs included centuries in both innings against Staffordshire, while Austin Jelfs, a 40-year-old newcomer from the same Harrogate club as Love, took 25 wickets in six games. Ian Pont, having switched from Northumberland, finished with 26 wickets, while Nigel Illingworth performed the season's only hat-trick, in Lincolnshire's Holt Cup semi-final win over Devon.

Staffordshire again just missed out and will rarely have a better chance of reaching the championship play-off. They went into their final fixture, against Lincolnshire, clear at the top of the table. But the batting fell apart in the first innings, and they took only one point from an eight-wicket defeat, while Hertfordshire were closing the gap with eight points from a draw with Durham. David Cartledge and Steve Dean, their swashbuckling openers, both scored in excess of 500 runs, and fast bowler Paul Taylor captured 32 wickets. Had rain not washed out their home games with Bedfordshire – abandoned without a ball being bowled – and Norfolk, Staffordshire could well have been regional winners. However, by beating Shropshire in the qualifying round they did manage to open their account in the Holt Cup, after seven successive unsuccessful years.

Bedfordshire, in beating Cumberland and Hertfordshire in consecutive games, achieved their highest Eastern Division placing of fourth. They gambled with three spinners to beat Cumberland, and successfully chased a target of 302 against Hertfordshire, having begun their campaign in May with victory over Lincolnshire. Mark Briers, an all-rounder who bowled leg-breaks, scored 451 runs and took seventeen wickets in five appearances, while Ray Swann furthered his reputation with 584 runs. Another newcomer in addition to Briers was Gary Palmer, formerly of Somerset.

A last-match triumph over Lincolnshire salvaged **Durham's** season by ensuring them a place in the NatWest Bank Trophy (or Gillette Cup) for the fifteenth successive season. Neil Riddell's final year in charge was especially notable for the return of Peter Kippax, the 49-year-old leg-spinner, after two seasons' absence because of injury. Kippax played in eight of the nine championship games and his 26 wickets included a career-best five for 23 against Cambridgeshire. Paul Burn made 582 runs, Ashok Patel 512, and Gary Brown, a prolific run-scorer for the Minor Counties representative side, would also have passed 500 had he not missed three championship games. Paul Newman of Derbyshire was a Durham newcomer.

The loss of Andy Mack, owing to a heel injury, was a handicap which **Norfolk** could not overcome. The big seam bowler was their major success of 1989, and Norfolk never filled the void. Their captain, Steve Plumb, resigned from the post at the end of the season. Ray Kingshott, the venerable slow left-armer, took 35 wickets, including the season's best analysis of eight for 47, against Northumberland, and Jimmy Lewis established himself with 27. The batting was led by two up-and-coming youngsters in Danny Stamp and Carl Rogers.

Cambridgeshire completed the seven-strong contingent of Eastern Division qualifiers for the NatWest Trophy. Another serious injury to Nigel Gadsby, this time a shattered forearm, blighted their programme, but Stuart Turner again excelled. The 47-year-old former Essex man, bowling off-breaks in the second half of the season, increased his tally of championship wickets in four years to 175, while John Lever, in his first season away from the first-class game, revealed his own versatility by bowling slow left-arm. He managed only twenty wickets, but another newcomer, Ajaz Akhtar, collected 23. Giles Ecclestone, a stylish left-hander destined for greater things, was the leading run-maker with 487 at an average of 60.87.

Suffolk's season started well, but ended disastrously. Chris Gladwin (171 not out) and Mike McEvoy (113 not out) shared a record-breaking unbroken stand of 295 in just 38.5 overs to spearhead a memorable ten-wicket win over Northumberland at Jesmond, and a second win soon followed against Cambridgeshire. But they lost three of their last five games, surrendering miserably to Staffordshire and Hertfordshire. They were not helped by the fact that Gladwin played in only two championship games, or that McEvoy's form deserted him. Andrew Golding, the former Essex and Cambridge University slow left-armer, was their only bowling success, with 28 wickets, but at 34.50 apiece they were not cheap.

Neither Cumberland nor Northumberland managed a single championship victory. It was the second successive season that **Cumberland** had failed to win, and they had to look back to August 1988 for their last taste of championship success. The all-round displays of David Makinson complemented the performances of Chris Stockdale (508 runs) and Malcolm Woods (30 wickets), while there were encouraging late-season débuts by David Pearson and Dipak Patel. Steve O'Shaughnessy's first appearance for **Northumberland** aptly summed up their summer. He registered a pair, did not bowl a ball, and was never seen again. Injury forced Mike Younger to hand over the captaincy to Graeme Morris halfway through the season, and although Northumberland had several consistent run-scorers, their bowling was woefully limited. Jonathon Benn, an opening batsman, had four hundreds in an impressive aggregate of 760 runs.

After finishing as runners-up in the Western Division in the previous three seasons, **Berkshire** finally found the right formula to claim the regional crown. Such was the depth of their bowling that six bowlers collected fourteen or more wickets. David Hartley, a leg-spinner, took the most, but Peter Lewington, their normally productive off-spinner, made only four championship appearances owing to injury. Martin Lickley (838 runs) and Gary Loveday (626) were as dependable as ever as opening batsmen, with Lickley scoring three centuries.

Oxfordshire, the 1989 champions, were runners-up, and had the honour of their captain, 44-year-old Phil Garner, being chosen as the first captain of the newly formed NCA England Amateur XI. A bout of food poisoning afflicted the side in the penultimate game, against Buckinghamshire, as a consequence of which they slumped to an ultimately crucial defeat by 88 runs. Stuart Waterton amassed 883 runs, and Keith Arnold (33 wickets) and Rupert Evans (31) were again greatly influential with the ball. John Abrahams, the former Lancashire captain, had another richly rewarding season for **Shropshire**. His 765 runs and 23 wickets were backed up by Mark Davies, captain John Foster and Tony Parton, all of whom scored in excess of 500 runs, and by Geoff Edmunds, whose slow left-arm bowling resulted in 36 wickets.

Buckinghamshire, who lifted the Holt Cup at Lord's when they beat Lincolnshire, will remember 1990 for their one-day achievements. Paul Atkins was their match-winner, hitting 97 not out and then running out Jim Love with a direct throw from long-on. In the championship Malcolm Roberts, with a Benson and Hedges Cup century at Marlow against Sussex to his name, compiled 921 runs; and Steve Burrow, despite failing to pass three figures in any of his seventeen innings, ran up 743. Burrow, a highly respected all-rounder, also took 27 wickets, while left-arm spinner Tim Scriven was close behind with 24.

Dorset and **Devon** finished on the same number of points, and qualified for the NatWest Bank Trophy, but Devon, without a win, owed their position to their ability to secure both first-innings points and a healthy number of bowling points. For Dorset, Graeme Calway totalled 721 runs, while Julian Shackleton, son of Derek, marked his first full season for the county with 33 wickets. Andy Pugh, Kevin Rice and Nick Folland led the Devon batting with aggregates of more than 500, and Mark Woodman, a tireless and accurate seam bowler, deserved his 29 wickets.

David Turner returned to Minor Counties cricket after 24 years with Hampshire and hit 887 runs, including three hundreds, for his native **Wiltshire**. Paul Bail made 437 in six games, but although Matthew Holland, a teenage slow left-armer, took 21 wickets, their bowling lacked penetration. **Wales** celebrated their first Minor Counties home win when they beat Wiltshire by four wickets at Colwyn Bay in their final match, only their second victory in three seasons in the championship. Andy Puddle captained the side for the first time and led by example with 512 runs, while Tudor Hughes made 454 and Tony Smith, a slow left-armer, collected 23 wickets at a reasonable cost of 25.39 each.

Cheshire, for so long a force in the Western Division, again languished down in the lower reaches. John Hitchmough, a resounding success in 1989, struggled for runs in 1990, with the result that the batting relied heavily on the hard-hitting Steve Crawley and the experienced Ian Cockbain. Andy Greasley, an off-spinner new to Minor Counties cricket, took 22 wickets in just four appearances. **Cornwall**, though recipients of the wooden spoon for the seventh time in eight seasons, did show signs of improvement with a last-match victory over Dorset. A pre-season fitness course and an early Holt Cup win against Wiltshire had sharpened their resolve, but the unavailability of Steve Williams, a batsman of immense quality, for all but one championship game was a substantial loss. Ed Nicolson and Kevin Thomas gave the batting some backbone but, Chris Lovell apart, the bowling was inadequate.

CHAMPIONSHIP FINAL

BERKSHIRE v HERTFORDSHIRE

At Luton, September 9. Hertfordshire won by seven wickets. Toss: Hertfordshire. MacLaurin's unbeaten 52 saw Hertfordshire to victory with thirteen balls to spare. Berkshire, put in, had lost their way from 88 for one, when Loveday and Mercer succumbed to the first two balls of Smith's flighted slow left-arm spin. Headley grafted his way to an unbeaten 50 in 45 overs, but Hertfordshire in reply always seemed to have plenty in reserve. MacLaurin settled it by twice lifting Lewington, the off-spinner, for six in his final over.

Berkshire

M. G. Lickley c Ligertwood b Merry	15	T. P. J. Dodd not out	3
G. E. Loveday c Ligertwood b Smith	42		
G. T. Headley not out	50	B 1, l-b 16, w 5, n-b 2	24
D. J. M. Mercer c and b Smith	0		—
*M. L. Simmons run out	6	1/25 2/88 3/88 (5 wkts, 55 overs)	171
P. J. Oxley c MacLaurin b Surridge	31	4/97 5/167	

M. G. Stear, †M. E. Stevens, J. H. Jones and P. J. Lewington did not bat.

Bowling: Harris 10–1–36–0; Merry 11–2–36–1; Neal 2–0–12–0; Surridge 10–1–31–1; Needham 11–3–24–0; Smith 11–3–15–2.

Hertfordshire

N. P. G. Wright c Stevens b Jones	45	B. G. Evans not out	18
J. D. Carr c Simmons b Jones	16	B 4, l-b 5, w 2, n-b 1	12
A. Needham c Oxley b Lewington	29		—
N. R. C. MacLaurin not out	52	1/23 2/81 3/118 (3 wkts, 52.5 overs)	172

†D. G. C. Ligertwood, D. M. Smith, E. P. Neal, W. G. Merry, *D. Surridge and G. A. R. Harris did not bat.

Bowling: Jones 10.5–3–35–2; Headley 5–3–10–0; Stear 10–2–31–0; Dodd 7–1–30–0; Lewington 11–3–30–1; Oxley 9–0–27–0.

Umpires: P. Adams and T. V. Wilkins.

HOLT CUP KNOCKOUT FINAL

BUCKINGHAMSHIRE v LINCOLNSHIRE

At Lord's, August 20. Buckinghamshire won by 16 runs. Toss: Buckinghamshire. Atkins, a 24-year-old batsman on the Surrey staff, proved the key to Buckinghamshire's victory. His 97 not out, which began in a second-wicket stand of 88 with Harwood, was largely responsible for Buckinghamshire's reaching 227 on a slow, unresponsive pitch. Then, when Lincolnshire appeared to be staging a recovery after losing Priestley in the first over, Atkins ran out Love for 47 with a direct throw from long-on. Hibbitt fell to the next ball and Lincolnshire, 116 for four in the 38th over, were suddenly 117 for six. Thereafter they were fighting a lost cause, despite a brave effort from the tail.

Buckinghamshire

A. R. Harwood st Priestley b Fell 52
M. J. Roberts c Priestley b Pont 7
P. D. Atkins not out 97
T. J. A. Scriven c Hibbitt b Love 23
S. Burrow b Love 1
*N. G. Hames b Love 7
B. S. Percy b Illingworth 8
S. G. Lynch lbw b Love 0
T. J. Barry not out 10
L-b 18, w 2, n-b 2 22

1/23 2/111 3/163 4/165 5/175 6/197 7/198 (7 wkts, 55 overs) 227

†D. J. Goldsmith and C. D. Booden did not bat.

Bowling: Pont 7–3–9–1; Illingworth 10–1–54–1; Jelfs 6–1–30–0; Christmas 11–1–31–0; Fell 11–1–41–1; Love 10–1–44–4.

Lincolnshire

*†N. Priestley c Goldsmith b Barry ... 2
D. B. Storer b Scriven 23
N. J. C. Gandon b Barry 7
J. D. Love run out 47
M. A. Fell c Harwood b Scriven 13
R. C. Hibbitt b Percy 13
I. L. Pont b Percy 5
J. H. T. Bramhill c Roberts b Burrow . 21
N. J. B. Illingworth b Barry 31
D. A. Christmas not out 29
A. C. Jelfs not out 1
B 4, l-b 8, w 4, n-b 3 19

1/2 2/19 3/50 4/76 5/117 6/117 7/130 8/154 9/196 (9 wkts, 55 overs) 211

Bowling: Barry 11–3–39–3; Booden 11–3–24–0; Burrow 11–5–33–1; Lynch 6–0–32–0; Scriven 7–0–34–2; Percy 9–0–37–2.

Umpires: P. Adams and T. V. Wilkins.

*In the averages that follow, * against a score signifies not out, * against a name signifies the captain and † signifies a wicket-keeper.*

BEDFORDSHIRE

Secretary – A. J. PEARCE, 15 Dene Way, Upper Caldecote, Biggleswade SG18 8DL

Matches 8: Won – Cumberland, Hertfordshire, Lincolnshire. Lost – Norfolk. Won on first innings – Cambridgeshire, Suffolk. Lost on first innings – Durham, Northumberland. Abandoned (No result) – Staffordshire.

Batting Averages

	M	*I*	*NO*	*R*	*HI*	*100s*	*50s*	*Avge*
R. Swann	7	14	2	584	135*	2	2	48.66
M. P. Briers	5	10	0	451	124	1	2	45.10
S. J. Renshaw	5	7	5	90	34*	0	0	45.00
M. R. Gouldstone	8	16	2	438	60*	0	2	31.28
G. V. Palmer	7	13	2	312	59*	0	2	28.36
P. D. B. Hoare	8	14	2	340	97	0	2	28.33
A. Dean	4	6	2	112	33	0	0	28.00
*J. R. Wake	8	10	2	162	50	0	1	20.25
S. J. Lines	3	6	1	83	47	0	0	16.60
T. C. Thomas	5	6	1	71	42	0	0	14.20
N. G. Folland	3	6	0	61	39	0	0	10.16

Played in seven matches: B. C. Banks 0, 24*, 6, 12*, 0. Played in six matches: †G. D. Sandford 3*, 5, 2, 0*. Played in four matches: P. D. Thomas 22, 15, 0. Played in two matches: K. Gentle 29*, 31, 0. Played in one match: R. G. Blair 6, 2; †G. Conway 0, 0; S. D. L. Davis 7, 17*; R. W. Morris 22, 15; M. R. White 0*; †E. R. Osborn did not bat.

Bowling Averages

	O	M	R	W	BB	5W/i	Avge
M. P. Briers	95	12	405	17	6-45	2	23.82
P. D. Thomas	104.3	17	347	11	3-35	0	31.54
J. R. Wake	194.3	44	620	17	5-51	1	36.47
G. V. Palmer	165	28	595	16	4-32	0	37.18

Also bowled: B. C. Banks 116–23–370–8; A. Dean 37.1–9–131–3; S. J. Renshaw 92–18–300–6; R. Swann 100–25–282–8; M. R. White 15–2–58–2.

BERKSHIRE

Secretary – C. M. S. CROMBIE, Orchard Cottage, Waltham St Lawrence

Matches 9: Won – Cornwall, Devon, Wiltshire. Lost – Dorset. Won on first innings – Cheshire, Oxfordshire, Shropshire. Lost on first innings – Buckinghamshire, Wales.

Batting Averages

	M	I	NO	R	HI	100s	50s	Avge
M. G. Lickley	9	16	3	838	122*	3	4	64.46
G. E. Loveday	9	16	0	626	110	1	6	39.12
P. J. Oxley	9	14	7	258	63*	0	2	36.85
D. J. M. Mercer	9	16	3	470	146*	1	2	36.15
*M. L. Simmons	9	15	4	322	58*	0	1	29.27
G. T. Headley	7	12	1	238	100	1	0	21.63
†M. E. Stevens	9	7	3	43	33	0	0	10.75
M. G. Stear	8	9	4	51	24	0	0	10.20

Played in nine matches: J. H. Jones 2*. Played in five matches: N. B. Fusedale 9*, 17, 2, 9*. Played in four matches: D. J. B. Hartley 2, 0, 1; P. J. Lewington did not bat. Played in three matches: T. P. J. Dodd 37, 94, 0; B. S. Jackson 52, 86, 0*, 9. Played in one match: D. Shaw 61; J. Barrow did not bat.

Bowling Averages

	O	M	R	W	BB	5W/i	Avge
D. J. B. Hartley	84	12	392	18	4-51	0	21.77
P. J. Lewington	139	49	375	15	4-20	0	25.00
G. T. Headley	86.3	15	363	14	3-45	0	25.92
N. B. Fusedale	140	42	389	15	4-36	0	25.93
J. H. Jones ...	165.1	37	536	15	4-41	0	35.73
M. G. Stear ...	144.5	15	544	14	4-59	0	38.85

Also bowled: J. Barrow 12–1–31–0; T. P. J. Dodd 37–5–139–6; B. S. Jackson 50–6–180–3; M. G. Lickley 51.5–13–199–3; D. J. M. Mercer 8.2–2–41–3; P. J. Oxley 73–15–282–6; D. Shaw 9–3–23–2; M. L. Simmons 12–1–76–4.

BUCKINGHAMSHIRE

Secretary – S. J. TOMLIN, Orchardleigh Cottage, Bigfrith Lane, Cookham Dean SL6 9PH

Matches 9: Won – Cornwall, Oxfordshire. Won on first innings – Berkshire, Cheshire, Dorset Wales. Lost on first innings – Devon, Shropshire, Wiltshire.

Batting Averages

	M	I	NO	R	HI	100s	50s	Avge
M. J. Roberts	9	18	1	921	124	2	5	54.17
S. Burrow	9	17	1	743	86	0	7	46.43
T. J. A. Scriven	8	16	4	445	79*	0	4	37.08
P. D. Atkins	5	10	0	303	63	0	2	30.30
A. R. Harwood	5	10	0	280	83	0	2	28.00
*N. G. Hames	8	15	1	315	53	0	2	22.50
S. G. Lynch	9	13	4	176	38	0	0	19.55
S. M. Shearman	3	6	2	68	35	0	0	17.00
T. J. Barry	9	10	4	94	30	0	0	15.66
G. R. Black	6	10	2	122	45	0	0	15.25

Played in nine matches: C. D. Booden 0*, 2. Played in five matches: †D. J. Goldsmith 0, 3*, 0, 0. Played in three matches: J. N. B. Bovill 3, 4*, 7, 2*; N. Farrow 18, 14, 2, 32*; †C. J. Tungate 4*, 0, 0. Played in two matches: T. Butler 1, 35, 32, 10. Played in one match: P. D. Dolphin 39*, 37; †G. Fryer 3*, 4*; B. S. Percy 1, 15.

Bowling Averages

	O	M	R	W	BB	5W/i	Avge
G. R. Black	73.2	12	248	11	4-43	0	22.54
S. Burrow	194	34	648	27	6-30	1	24.00
T. J. A. Scriven	200	45	706	24	5-23	1	29.41
C. D. Booden	182	39	586	14	4-57	0	41.85
T. J. Barry	221.2	29	862	20	3-42	0	43.10

Also bowled: J. N. B. Bovill 40–3–174–5; S. G. Lynch 102.5–11–425–7; B. S. Percy 14–3–52–3; M. J. Roberts 5–3–9–1.

CAMBRIDGESHIRE

Secretary – P. W. GOODEN, The Redlands, Oakington Road, Cottenham, Cambridge CB4 4TW

Matches 9: Won – Northumberland. Lost – Hertfordshire, Suffolk. Won on first innings – Durham, Norfolk, Staffordshire. Lost on first innings – Bedfordshire, Lincolnshire. Tied on first innings – Cumberland.

Batting Averages

	M	I	NO	R	HI	100s	50s	Avge
G. W. Ecclestone	5	10	2	487	111	1	5	60.87
R. A. Milne	6	11	1	421	134*	1	2	42.10
N. J. Adams	8	15	3	429	102	1	2	35.75
A. M. Cade	7	12	6	206	70*	0	1	34.33
*N. T. Gadsby	4	8	1	239	104*	1	0	34.14
†R. J. Turner	6	11	3	271	52*	0	1	33.87
I. S. Lawrence	8	16	0	393	65	0	3	24.56
Ajaz Akhtar	9	13	2	188	54*	0	1	17.09
S. K. Thomas	5	10	2	123	55	0	1	15.37
S. Turner	8	13	4	130	35*	0	0	14.44
D. P. Norman	5	9	0	126	40	0	0	14.00
S. W. Ecclestone	4	8	1	76	28	0	0	10.85

Played in six matches: J. K. Lever 1, 3, 6, 1, 18*. Played in four matches: M. G. Stephenson 6*. Played in three matches: D. C. Collard 0; A. Howorth 9*, 7, 25. Played in two matches: †M. S. L. Rollinson 0; M. W. Taylor 8*, 4. Played in one match: P. J. Dicks 28, 0; C. R. F. Green 0*, 5; P. A. Redfarn 21; D. M. Cousins did not bat.

Bowling Averages

	O	*M*	*R*	*W*	*BB*	*5W/i*	*Avge*
S. Turner	286.5	79	727	40	7-86	2	18.17
M. G. Stephenson	100.4	34	303	14	5-40	1	21.64
Ajaz Akhtar	208.3	55	579	23	4-16	0	25.17
J. K. Lever	231.1	49	725	20	3-35	0	36.25

Also bowled: N. J. Adams 18–0–71–1; A. M. Cade 3.5–0–25–0; D. C. Collard 68–22–215–4; D. M. Cousins 5.3–1–24–1; N. T. Gadsby 8–3–22–0; C. R. F. Green 1–0–5–0; A. Howorth 63.2–18–182–5; M. W. Taylor 29–8–95–2.

CHESHIRE

Secretary – J. B. PICKUP, 2 Castle Street, Northwich CW8 1AB

Matches 9: Won – Cornwall. Won on first innings – Dorset, Wales. Lost on first innings – Berkshire, Buckinghamshire, Devon, Oxfordshire, Shropshire. No result – Wiltshire.

Batting Averages

	M	*I*	*NO*	*R*	*HI*	*100s*	*50s*	*Avge*
S. T. Crawley	9	17	4	671	107	2	4	51.61
I. Cockbain	7	12	0	590	106	1	6	49.16
J. Bean	9	15	3	397	58	0	2	33.08
I. J. Tansley	4	8	1	217	78	0	2	31.00
P. A. Davis	4	8	1	188	63	0	1	26.85
J. J. Hitchmough	8	14	1	305	77	0	1	23.46
*N. T. O'Brien	9	15	2	279	63	0	1	21.46
†S. Bramhall	9	11	4	65	21*	0	0	9.28

Played in nine matches: N. D. Peel 0*, 3*. Played in four matches: G. J. Blackburn 0, 14, 8*, 12, 4*; M. G. Boocock 0*, 4*, 11*, 50*; E. McCray 47, 20, 11*, 6, 16; A. D. Greasley did not bat. Played in three matches: J. G. Bacon 8, 1, 27; A. Fox 0*, 0. Played in two matches: J. D. Gray 9*, 1, 18; J. F. M. O'Brien 4, 8, 50*; K. Teasdale 19, 3, 1*; P. Wakefield 4*, 16*, 0, 6. Played in one match: P. H. de Prez 10.

Bowling Averages

	O	*M*	*R*	*W*	*BB*	*5W/i*	*Avge*
A. D. Greasley	138.1	37	471	22	5-96	1	21.40
N. D. Peel	183.1	41	524	15	8-62	1	34.93
S. T. Crawley	111.2	11	375	10	3-46	0	37.50

Also bowled: J. G. Bacon 41–12–140–3; G. J. Blackburn 91.3–27–262–7; M. G. Boocock 79–17–330–7; I. Cockbain 15–5–47–0; P. H. de Prez 34.2–8–129–7; A. Fox 59.3–17–175–6; E. McCray 80.2–20–269–6; J. F. M. O'Brien 48–11–174–5; N. T. O'Brien 27–4–116–1; P. Wakefield 26–5–106–5.

CORNWALL

Secretary – T. D. MENEER, Falbridge, Penvale Cross, Penryn

Matches 9: Won – Dorset. Lost – Berkshire, Buckinghamshire, Cheshire, Shropshire. Won on first innings – Wales. Lost on first innings – Devon, Oxfordshire, Wiltshire.

atting Averages

	M	*I*	*NO*	*R*	*HI*	*100s*	*50s*	*Avge*
. J. C. Thomas ...	6	12	1	414	108*	1	2	37.63
Nicolson	9	18	1	615	77	0	4	36.17
Hooper	6	12	1	348	103*	1	1	31.63
. T. Walton	6	12	0	324	69	0	3	27.00
. C. Lovell	8	15	2	335	54*	0	1	25.76
. G. Furse	8	14	3	276	46	0	0	25.09
Moyle	4	6	2	85	47*	0	0	21.25
. A. Coombe	4	7	2	101	34	0	0	20.20
. P. Eva	9	14	7	137	27*	0	0	19.57
Wherry	8	16	0	298	75	0	2	18.62
Turner	5	9	3	97	27*	0	0	16.16
F. T. Willetts	9	13	2	122	42	0	0	11.09

Played in four matches: M. Bell 4*, 0*, 0, 8*; A. J. Buzza 1*, 5*, 8*. Played in three atches: D. A. Toseland 0*, 2, 1, 1. Played in two matches: S. Lonsdale 7; S. Pedlar 1, 37, 7. Played in one match: G. G. Watts 1, 19; S. M. Williams 15, 71.

owling Averages

	O	*M*	*R*	*W*	*BB*	*5W/i*	*Avge*
. G. Furse	87.4	11	303	12	4-38	0	25.25
. C. Lovell	175.3	18	732	25	6-65	1	29.28
. Bell	106	17	378	11	5-72	1	34.36

Also bowled: A. J. Buzza 94–11–380–3; P. A. Coombe 77–15–244–4; S. Lonsdale .4–5–161–3; S. Moyle 67.1–6–283–7; S. Pedlar 7–0–38–2; D. A. Toseland 87.2–16–282–6; Turner 94–8–412–6; R. T. Walton 7–1–34–0; G. G. Watts 18–4–90–2; F. T. Willetts -0–25–1.

CUMBERLAND

Secretary – M. BEATY, 9 Abbey Drive, Natland, Kendal, Cumbria LA9 7QN

latches 9: Lost – Bedfordshire, Staffordshire. Won on first innings – Hertfordshire, Lincolnshire, orfolk, Northumberland, Suffolk. Lost on first innings – Durham. Tied on first innings – ambridgeshire.

atting Averages

	M	*I*	*NO*	*R*	*HI*	*100s*	*50s*	*Avge*
J. R. Moyes	9	13	3	437	137	1	1	43.70
. W. Reidy	7	11	1	339	104*	1	1	33.90
. J. Stockdale	9	15	0	508	87	0	5	33.86
James	6	8	5	98	36*	0	0	32.66
. J. Makinson	8	13	3	291	97	0	2	29.10
M. Burns	7	11	3	180	52*	0	1	22.50
. J. Clarke	4	6	1	98	35	0	0	19.60
1. D. Woods	9	6	2	13	7	0	0	3.25

Played in six matches: R. Ellwood 7, 0. Played in five matches: S. Wall 10*, 8, 27, 19; . M. Wheatman 3, 2*, 0. Played in four matches: S. Sharp 15, 31, 32, 9, 29. Played in three atches: †S. M. Dutton 3, 30, 26, 6*; D. Patel 48, 11, 62*, 55, 74; S. D. Philbrook 1, 25*, 1, *. Played in two matches: D. Halliwell 4, 2; D. Pearson 8, 18, 18, 131*. Played in one match: . I. Cooper 0, 17; C. R. Knight 18, 8*; N. Maxwell 19, 1; S. D. Myles 0; N. Pattinson 21, 15; 1. G. Scothern 19*, 7; G. Bolton did not bat.

Bowling Averages

	O	*M*	*R*	*W*	*BB*	*5W/i*	*Avg*
B. W. Reidy	94	25	289	13	3-28	0	22.2
M. D. Woods	242.1	83	704	30	6-47	2	23.4
D. J. Makinson	267.2	69	700	29	5-43	1	24.1
R. Ellwood	105.3	34	281	10	2-28	0	28.1

Also bowled: G. Bolton 36–6–77–5; M. Burns 2–0–7–0; D. Halliwell 39–5–152–2; S. Jam 8–3–32–0; S. D. Myles 14–2–42–2; M. G. Scothern 13–2–52–0; S. Sharp 8–3–27–1; C. Stockdale 1–0–1–0; S. Wall 92.2–20–315–6; D. M. Wheatman 70.5–10–250–5.

DEVON

Secretary – G. R. EVANS, Blueberry Haven, 20 Boucher Road, Budleigh Salterton EX9 6JF

Matches 9: Lost – Berkshire. Won on first innings – Buckinghamshire, Cheshire, Cornwall, Dorse Shropshire, Wales, Wiltshire. Lost on first innings – Oxfordshire.

Batting Averages

	M	*I*	*NO*	*R*	*HI*	*100s*	*50s*	*Avg*
A. J. Pugh	9	16	3	582	100*	1	3	44.7
K. G. Rice	7	14	2	528	93*	0	4	44.0
N. A. Folland	8	16	3	562	109*	1	3	43.2
K. Donohue	4	7	3	111	40*	0	0	27.7
J. K. Tierney	4	7	3	109	46	0	0	27.2
G. P. Randall-Johnson	7	14	4	256	42	0	0	25.6
*J. H. Edwards	9	18	1	395	66	0	3	23.2
R. I. Dawson	9	16	1	343	85	0	2	22.8
†C. S. Pritchard	7	8	5	45	26*	0	0	15.0

Played in nine matches: M. C. Woodman 6*, 4. Played in five matches: J. Rhodes 0* Played in four matches: R. H. J. Jenkins 0*, 23*, 4, 5, 12*. Played in three matches: N. R Gaywood 4, 2, 41*, 1, 26; M. J. Record 5, 6*, 2*. Played in two matches: G. Wallen 9, 3, 1 A. C. Cottam did not bat. Played in one match: S. Cockram 0*; L. R. Hart 13, 4; S. Lott 9* S. A. Moore 2, 28; †R. C. Turpin 17; †P. J. Lucketti and G. W. White did not bat.

Bowling Averages

	O	*M*	*R*	*W*	*BB*	*5W/i*	*Avge*
M. J. Record	62	7	245	16	6-54	1	15.3
M. C. Woodman	286	67	785	29	4-40	0	27.0
J. K. Tierney	91.1	22	338	11	4-57	0	30.7

Also bowled: S. Cockram 12–2–38–0; A. C. Cottam 44.1–7–187–6; R. I. Dawsor 41–1–243–5; K. Donohue 112–26–304–9; N. A. Folland 25–3–142–4; N. R. Gaywoo 8.1–2–32–2; L. R. Hart 10–0–47–1; R. H. J. Jenkins 56.2–7–248–9; S. Lott 24–4–89–5; S. A Moore 26.1–7–73–3; J. Rhodes 112–21–443–9; K. G. Rice 44–3–182–5.

DORSET

Secretary – D. J. W. BRIDGE, Long Acre, Tinney's Lane, Sherborne DT9 3DY

Matches 9: Won – Berkshire, Wales. Lost – Cornwall, Shropshire, Wiltshire. Lost on first innings – Buckinghamshire, Cheshire, Devon, Oxfordshire.

Batting Averages

	M	I	NO	R	HI	100s	50s	Avge
J. A. Claughton	5	10	4	283	81	0	3	47.16
G. S. Calway	9	18	0	721	121	2	4	40.05
J. M. H. Graham-Brown	6	12	1	368	78	0	3	33.45
G. D. Reynolds	7	13	3	318	101*	1	1	31.80
R. A. Pyman	6	8	2	173	71	0	2	28.83
V. B. Lewis	3	6	1	129	75	0	1	25.80
R. P. Merriman	9	18	0	443	77	0	3	24.61
A. Willows	7	13	2	254	59	0	1	23.09
†S. M. Fitzgerald	8	6	4	45	15*	0	0	22.50
J. H. Shackleton	9	7	3	75	33	0	0	18.75
C. Stone	9	17	1	271	67	0	2	16.93
N. R. Taylor	6	9	1	77	24	0	0	9.62
*A. R. Wingfield Digby	9	11	2	67	19	0	0	7.44

Played in one match: J. M. Blackburn 4, 6; R. V. J. Coombs 43; S. J. Legg 11, 39; †N. Lynn 0*; S. W. D. Rintoul 13, 36*; S. Sawney 6*, 0.

Bowling Averages

	O	M	R	W	BB	5W/i	Avge
N. R. Taylor	165	39	497	24	5-38	1	20.70
J. H. Shackleton	290.3	79	759	33	6-67	2	23.00
R. A. Pyman	93.1	16	365	15	4-29	0	24.33
C. Stone	221.5	46	666	26	5-59	1	25.61
A. R. Wingfield Digby	175.2	42	604	12	2-38	0	50.33

Also bowled: J. M. Blackburn 5–0–29–1; G. S. Calway 74.3–17–265–6; R. V. J. Coombs 22–5–103–0; J. M. H. Graham-Brown 2–1–1–0; R. P. Merriman 2–0–9–0; S. Sawney 9–0–62–0; A. Willows 25–4–96–2.

DURHAM

Secretary – J. ILEY, Roselea, Springwell Avenue, Durham DH1 4LY

Matches 9: Won – Lincolnshire. Won on first innings – Bedfordshire, Cumberland, Norfolk, Northumberland, Staffordshire, Suffolk. Lost on first innings – Cambridgeshire, Hertfordshire.

Batting Averages

	M	I	NO	R	HI	100s	50s	Avge
P. Burn	7	13	4	582	105	2	4	64.66
A. S. Patel	8	12	4	512	103*	1	4	64.00
G. K. Brown	6	11	4	417	110*	2	0	59.57
*N. A. Riddell	8	9	2	314	92	0	3	44.85
J. D. Glendenen	9	16	1	413	130	2	1	27.53

Played in eight matches: P. J. Kippax 19, 23, 4*, 7, 58. Played in seven matches: †A. R. Fothergill 12, 10*, 8*, 3, 0. Played in six matches: P. G. Newman 4, 5, 44*, 14, 6; S. Peel 44, 7, 5*, 0. Played in five matches: I. E. Conn 4*, 11, 6*. Played in four matches: G. Clennell 5*; S. Greensword 4, 46*, 26. Played in three matches: P. J. Barnes 50, 34*, 43*, 10, 67; A. Birbeck 15, 9, 1, 1*; J. Tindale 44, 10, 17, 19, 4*; I. Young 2. Played in two matches: †D. Playfor 2, 12; J. F. Sykes 5, 11*; A. C. Day did not bat. Played in one match: S. Ball 2, 0; I. Robson 0; J. Johnston did not bat.

Bowling Averages

	O	M	R	W	BB	5W/i	Avge
A. S. Patel	119.5	35	318	21	5-80	1	15.14
P. J. Kippax	220.4	75	531	26	5-23	1	20.42
I. E. Conn	144.1	30	452	19	3-19	0	23.78
S. Peel	122	25	391	14	4-38	0	27.92
P. G. Newman	175.1	49	519	17	4-65	0	30.52

Also bowled: G. K. Brown 39–7–117–1; P. Burn 6–0–34–1; G. Clennell 77–24–224–2; A. C. Day 37–5–147–3; J. D. Glendenen 6–0–33–0; S. Greensword 43–10–133–5; J. Johnston 29–13–45–5; N. A. Riddell 2–0–21–0; J. F. Sykes 15–1–58–1; I. Young 59–7–278–4.

HERTFORDSHIRE

Secretary – D. DREDGE, 38 Santers Lane, Potters Bar EN6 2BX

Matches 9: Won – Cambridgeshire, Norfolk, Suffolk. Lost – Bedfordshire, Staffordshire. Won on first innings – Durham, Lincolnshire, Northumberland. Lost on first innings – Cumberland.

Batting Averages

	M	I	NO	R	HI	100s	50s	Avge
A. Needham	8	13	2	750	130*	3	4	68.18
J. D. Carr	4	7	1	365	92	0	4	60.83
†D. G. C. Ligertwood	5	7	3	232	81	0	2	58.00
B. G. Evans	5	9	3	292	113*	1	2	48.66
N. P. G. Wright	7	13	2	486	113	1	3	44.18
P. A. Waterman	6	6	2	113	52	0	1	28.25
N. R. C. MacLaurin	4	7	0	173	46	0	0	24.71
M. D. Dale	5	7	2	102	21*	0	0	20.40

Played in eight matches: *D. Surridge 6*, 6*, 9*. Played in six matches: G. A. R. Harris 8, 0, 6. Played in five matches: W. G. Merry 11, 15; D. M. Smith 38*, 8*, 1, 7*. Played in four matches: T. S. Smith 7*, 8, 27, 32, 1. Played in three matches: C. N. Cavenor 24, 4*, 7, 19*; I. Fletcher 15, 5*, 24, 3, 0; E. P. Neal 20, 12, 11, 2*; †M. W. C. Olley 35, 0, 0; D. G. Price 2, 1*, 1*. Played in two matches: N. J. Ilott 4, 53; D. M. Robinson 12*, 7, 10; C. Thomas 2, 47, 0; †M. C. G. Wright 9, 11, 1*. Played in one match: J. G. Franks 28, 10; G. Herath 21, 20; †S. March 1; R. S. Shakespeare 8, 21.

Bowling Averages

	O	M	R	W	BB	5W/i	Avge
D. M. Smith	93.3	35	215	16	3-31	0	13.43
D. Surridge	224.2	69	488	29	5-24	1	16.82
W. G. Merry	115	27	271	14	4-20	0	19.35
A. Needham	192.1	74	417	18	4-26	0	23.16
G. A. R. Harris	146	30	502	16	3-59	0	31.37

Also bowled: C. N. Cavenor 38–11–130–3; G. Herath 2–1–5–0; N. R. C. MacLaurin 2–1–5–0; E. P. Neal 42–8–151–5; D. G. Price 22.3–1–106–4; R. S. Shakespeare 2–0–10–0; T. S. Smith 56.2–20–129–7; P. A. Waterman 87–11–388–8; N. P. G. Wright 1–0–1–0.

LINCOLNSHIRE

Secretary – D. H. WRIGHT, 18 Spencers Road, Ketton, Stamford

Matches 9: Won – Staffordshire, Suffolk. Lost – Bedfordshire, Durham. Won on first innings – Cambridgeshire, Northumberland. Lost on first innings – Cumberland, Hertfordshire, Norfolk.

Batting Averages

	M	I	NO	R	HI	100s	50s	Avge
N. J. C. Gandon	8	14	4	476	103*	1	1	47.60
J. D. Love	7	14	1	537	103*	2	4	41.30
D. B. Storer	8	15	2	497	100	1	4	38.23
†N. Priestley	9	17	1	512	83*	0	2	32.00
M. A. Fell	7	13	2	335	130*	1	0	30.45
. N. Warman	7	10	1	226	84	0	1	25.11
R. C. Hibbitt	7	11	3	189	47*	0	0	23.62
L. Pont	7	9	0	170	81	0	1	18.88
N. French	5	7	0	79	23	0	0	11.28
D. Marshall	7	8	7	9	6*	0	0	9.00
D. A. Christmas	8	6	1	30	10	0	0	6.00

Played in six matches: A. C. Jelfs 17*, 3, 6, 9, 8. Played in four matches: N. J. B. Illingworth 0*, 17, 1, 41, 1. Played in two matches: J. R. Airey 28*, 15*; R. T. Bates 16, 1, 6, 1; J. H. T. Bramhill 0, 30; P. D. McKeown 6, 3, 9*. Played in one match: P. A. Houghton 4, 14.

Bowling Averages

	O	M	R	W	BB	5W/i	Avge
M. A. Fell	90	20	257	15	4-35	0	17.13
A. C. Jelfs	158.5	36	488	25	5-61	1	19.52
N. J. B. Illingworth	91	18	298	14	5-38	1	21.28
. L. Pont	150.5	26	569	26	6-34	1	21.88
N. French	94	20	298	11	3-33	0	27.09
D. Marshall	197.2	57	527	17	4-54	0	31.00

Also bowled: J. R. Airey 38–10–77–2; R. T. Bates 11–1–40–0; D. A. Christmas 35.5–15–331–8; N. J. C. Gandon 2–1–1–1; R. C. Hibbitt 1–0–2–0; J. D. Love 75–18–256–7; P. D. McKeown 21–0–133–1; D. B. Storer 3–0–27–0.

NORFOLK

Secretary – S. J. SKINNER, 27 Colkett Drive, Old Catton, Norwich NR6 7ND

Matches 9: Won – Bedfordshire, Northumberland. Lost – Hertfordshire. Won on first innings – Lincolnshire. Lost on first innings – Cambridgeshire, Cumberland, Durham, Staffordshire, Suffolk.

Batting Averages

	M	I	NO	R	HI	100s	50s	Avge
C. J. Rogers	8	15	2	487	75	0	5	37.46
D. M. Stamp	9	17	2	505	81	0	3	33.66
R. J. Finney	9	15	3	395	101*	1	2	32.91
J. Whitehead	5	8	2	158	33*	0	0	26.33
S. B. Dixon	5	7	1	141	49	0	0	23.50
*S. G. Plumb	8	13	1	261	58	0	2	21.75
F. L. Q. Handley	6	12	0	232	56	0	1	19.33
J. C. M. Lewis	9	10	1	157	88	0	1	17.44
D. R. Thomas	9	11	2	135	42	0	0	15.00
R. Kingshott	9	10	3	77	22	0	0	11.00
†D. E. Mattocks	5	6	3	29	13	0	0	9.66
M. T. Ellis	7	6	3	7	4	0	0	2.33

Played in four matches: †M. M. Jervis 6, 13, 14*, 8. Played in three matches: N. S. Taylor 6, 17, 4, 46. Played in two matches: B. J. Goodfellow 0*, 0*. Played in one match: D. G. Savage 3, 0.

Bowling Averages

	O	M	R	W	BB	5W/i	Avge
S. G. Plumb	125.5	42	358	17	3-39	0	21.0
D. R. Thomas	72.5	12	232	10	4-36	0	23.2
R. Kingshott	279.4	69	878	35	8-47	2	25.0
J. C. M. Lewis ...	189	30	703	27	6-62	1	26.0
M. T. Ellis	101.2	19	348	11	6-60	1	31.6

Also bowled: B. J. Goodfellow 31–5–98–3; D. M. Stamp 5–2–10–0; N. S. Taylo 33–5–144–5.

NORTHUMBERLAND

Secretary – F. J. FARMER, Northumberland County Cricket Ground, Osborne Avenue, Jesmond, Newcastle upon Tyne NE2 1JS

Matches 9: Lost – Cambridgeshire, Norfolk, Suffolk. Won on first innings – Bedfordshire. Lost o first innings – Cumberland, Durham, Hertfordshire, Lincolnshire, Staffordshire.

Batting Averages

	M	I	NO	R	HI	100s	50s	Avge
J. A. Benn	9	18	1	760	129	4	3	44.7
G. R. Morris	8	16	2	486	118*	1	3	34.7
*M. E. Younger	4	6	0	186	75	0	2	31.0
P. N. S. Dutton	8	16	2	405	111	1	2	28.9
P. G. Cormack	5	10	1	214	110	1	0	23.7
S. C. Dunsford	7	14	2	254	91	0	1	21.1
†M. S. Tiffin	6	11	2	170	40	0	0	18.8
T. A. S. Brown	5	9	0	156	48	0	0	17.3
N. B. Campbell	6	9	5	60	27*	0	0	15.0
J. R. Purvis	9	13	4	124	38*	0	0	13.7
R. Perry	5	9	0	108	36	0	0	12.0
P. G. Clark	5	10	1	82	22*	0	0	9.1
P. C. Graham	8	11	4	29	9	0	0	4.1

Played in three matches: †N. H. G. Bates 6*; M. Shepherd 0, 11*; †H. M. Sidney-Wilmo 10, 39, 20, 12*, 37. Played in one match: M. D. Abbott 22; C. S. Gott 4; M. J. Green 0, 6 P. Nicholson 3*, 4; S. J. O'Shaughnessy 0, 0.

Bowling Averages

	O	M	R	W	BB	5W/i	Avge
J. R. Purvis	169.4	22	685	20	5-54	1	34.2
P. C. Graham	233.4	51	779	17	3-85	0	45.8
N. B. Campbell	148	22	559	11	2-48	0	50.8

Also bowled: M. D. Abbott 25–4–110–0; J. A. Benn 10–0–74–0; T. A. S. Brown 7–0–37–2 P. G. Cormack 11–1–52–1; S. C. Dunsford 1–0–8–0; P. N. S. Dutton 92–9–454–5; C. S. Got 13.5–3–53–0; G. R. Morris 2–0–17–0; R. Perry 45.1–7–192–8; M. Shepherd 40–1–277–0 H. M. Sidney-Wilmot 5.5–0–50–0; M. E. Younger 64–11–261–3.

OXFORDSHIRE

Secretary – J. E. O. SMITH, 2 The Green, Horton-cum-Studley OX9 1AE

Matches 9: Won – Wales, Wiltshire. Lost – Buckinghamshire. Won on first innings – Cheshire Cornwall, Devon, Dorset. Lost on first innings – Berkshire, Shropshire.

Batting Averages

	M	I	NO	R	HI	100s	50s	Avge
†S. N. V. Waterton	9	17	3	883	123*	1	9	63.07
T. A. Lester	8	16	5	471	98*	0	4	42.81
D. C. Woods	4	8	0	269	83	0	1	33.62
D. A. J. Wise	3	6	2	129	58*	0	1	32.25
G. C. Ford	5	10	0	280	96	0	2	28.00
*P. J. Garner	9	17	0	474	69	0	3	27.88
T. H. C. Hancock	7	13	6	149	51*	0	1	21.28
J. S. Hartley	9	16	4	235	93*	0	1	19.58
G. P. Savin	9	11	5	77	16*	0	0	12.83
R. A. Evans	9	7	1	41	18	0	0	6.83

Played in nine matches: K. A. Arnold 1, 2*, 4, 5*; I. J. Curtis 0*, 0*. Played in three matches: D. A. Hale 5*, 13*; P. M. Jobson 0, 16*, 1, 9. Played in two matches: M. D. Nurton 39, 36, 27. Played in one match: S. V. Laudat did not bat.

Bowling Averages

	O	M	R	W	BB	5W/i	Avge
R. A. Evans	258.5	71	713	31	5-85	1	23.00
K. A. Arnold	267.1	57	767	33	5-40	2	23.24
I. J. Curtis	197.1	48	641	23	5-33	2	27.86
G. P. Savin	151	30	479	10	4-42	0	47.90

Also bowled: P. J. Garner 8–3–19–0; D. A. Hale 40–7–204–2; J. S. Hartley 61.5–8–243–4; S. V. Laudat 24–5–88–1.

SHROPSHIRE

Secretary – N. H. BIRCH, 8 Port Hill Close, Copthorne, Shrewsbury SY3 8RR

Matches 9: Won – Cornwall, Dorset. Won on first innings – Buckinghamshire, Cheshire, Oxfordshire, Wales. Lost on first innings – Berkshire, Devon, Wiltshire.

Batting Averages

	M	I	NO	R	HI	100s	50s	Avge
J. Abrahams	7	13	4	765	113*	4	3	85.00
M. R. Davies	9	15	7	628	114*	2	2	78.50
*J. Foster	9	14	2	533	123*	1	2	44.41
T. Parton	9	16	4	506	119	1	2	42.16
†J. R. Weaver	7	12	3	256	66	0	2	28.44
J. B. R. Jones	8	13	1	335	84*	0	3	27.91
P. B. Wormald ...	7	6	2	68	21	0	0	17.00
A. B. Byram	8	7	2	76	26	0	0	15.20

Played in nine matches: G. Edmunds 2*, 2. Played in eight matches: A. S. Barnard 3*, 4, 0*. Played in five matches: B. K. Shantry 25, 6, 14*, 9, 0. Played in four matches: J. T. Aspinall 0*. Played in three matches: J. S. Johnson 3, 30, 12, 37, 31. Played in two matches: †D. J. Ashley 9*; A. N. Johnson 41, 5, 27*; D. B. K. Page did not bat.

Bowling Averages

	O	M	R	W	BB	5W/i	Avge
G. Edmunds	270.4	68	807	36	8-60	2	22.41
J. Abrahams	168.5	35	610	23	5-103	1	26.52
B. K. Shantry	110	20	365	13	4-59	0	28.07
P. B. Wormald	115.5	26	368	10	3-32	0	36.80
A. S. Barnard	176	41	557	11	4-83	0	50.63

Also bowled: J. T. Aspinall 43–4–169–3; A. B. Byram 114–24–422–9; J. B. R. Jones [illegible]5–1–104–3; D. B. K. Page 26–3–103–3.

STAFFORDSHIRE

Secretary – W. S. BOURNE, 10 The Pavement, Brewood ST19 9BZ

Matches 8: Won – Cumberland, Hertfordshire, Suffolk. Lost – Lincolnshire. Won on first innings – Norfolk, Northumberland. Lost on first innings – Cambridgeshire, Durham. Abandoned (No result) – Bedfordshire.

Batting Averages

	M	*I*	*NO*	*R*	*HI*	*100s*	*50s*	*Avge*
D. Cartledge	7	13	2	626	141*	2	4	56.90
S. J. Dean	8	14	2	587	101*	2	2	48.91
D. A. Banks	4	7	3	181	91	0	1	45.25
*N. J. Archer	8	8	3	224	58*	0	2	44.80
J. P. Addison	8	13	2	398	104*	1	0	36.18
P. R. Oliver	8	13	3	358	123*	1	0	35.80
A. J. Dutton	6	6	3	105	28*	0	0	35.00

Played in eight matches: J. P. Taylor 35, 1*, 23*, 0. Played in six matches: †M. I. Humphries 17, 0*, 14*, 0. Played in five matches: D. W. Headley 1. Played in four matches: D. C. Blank 1*; G. D. Williams 14*, 18. Played in two matches: A. D. Hobson 12, 19, 0; †A. N. Mackelworth 15; A. Butler and R. J. Dyer did not bat. Played in one match: G. Archer 7; G. Carr 5; N. M. Podmore 1*; J. A. Waterhouse 6.

Bowling Averages

	O	*M*	*R*	*W*	*BB*	*5W/i*	*Avge*
J. P. Taylor	280.3	66	811	32	6-46	1	25.34
D. C. Blank	104.3	22	326	12	3-31	0	27.16
D. W. Headley	135.4	17	465	17	4-38	0	27.35

Also bowled: J. P. Addison 8–0–48–0; G. Archer 2–0–5–0; N. J. Archer 6–2–13–1; A. Butler 7–0–25–0; G. Carr 18–3–73–3; D. Cartledge 62.2–11–228–5; S. J. Dean 1–0–1–0; A. J. Dutton 80–19–198–8; R. J. Dyer 29–11–65–2; N. M. Podmore 25–2–121–1; G. D. Williams 64–12–161–5.

SUFFOLK

Secretary – P. HOLLAND, 22 Ashmere Grove, Ipswich IP4 2RE

Matches 9: Won – Cambridgeshire, Northumberland. Lost – Hertfordshire, Lincolnshire, Staffordshire. Won on first innings – Norfolk. Lost on first innings – Bedfordshire, Cumberland, Durham.

Batting Averages

	M	*I*	*NO*	*R*	*HI*	*100s*	*50s*	*Avge*
S. M. Clements	8	14	2	483	137	1	3	40.25
M. S. A. McEvoy	9	17	3	497	113*	1	3	35.50
J. W. Edrich	5	8	2	191	66*	0	2	31.83
A. J. Squire	4	8	0	245	62	0	3	30.62
P. J. Caley	9	15	1	398	101	1	1	28.42
H. J. W. Wright	5	7	2	139	48	0	0	27.80
M. J. Peck	9	15	2	317	80	0	2	24.38
S. J. Halliday	5	10	2	168	39	0	0	21.00
A. K. Golding	8	12	2	186	79	0	1	18.60
*M. D. Bailey	7	8	1	101	24	0	0	14.42
I. D. Graham	6	8	0	107	26	0	0	13.37
†A. D. Brown	9	13	3	112	24	0	0	11.20
R. C. Green	6	6	3	7	5	0	0	2.33

Played in three matches: R. M. Edgeley 1*, 4*. Played in two matches: C. Gladwin 52, 171*, 13, 17; P. J. Hayes 1, 20; R. A. Pybus 2*.

Bowling Averages

	O	M	R	W	BB	5W/i	Avge
H. J. W. Wright	111	16	371	13	5-27	1	28.53
A. K. Golding	260.4	45	966	28	6-44	1	34.50
M. D. Bailey	129	25	443	12	4-31	0	36.91
I. D. Graham	108.5	20	392	10	3-37	0	39.20

Also bowled: P. J. Caley 43.4–8–137–3; R. M. Edgeley 80–19–256–4; J. W. Edrich 2–1–4–0; C. Gladwin 7–1–15–0; R. C. Green 162–34–551–9; P. J. Hayes 45.5–8–125–3; R. A. Pybus 47–3–179–8.

WALES MINOR COUNTIES

Secretary – BILL EDWARDS, 59a King Edward Road, Swansea SA1 4LN

Matches 9: Won – Wiltshire. Lost – Dorset, Oxfordshire. Won on first innings – Berkshire. Lost on first innings – Buckinghamshire, Cheshire, Cornwall, Devon, Shropshire.

Batting Averages

	M	I	NO	R	HI	100s	50s	Avge
*A. C. Puddle	9	18	5	512	100*	1	1	39.38
A. W. Harris	4	7	2	181	99	0	1	36.20
T. C. Hughes	7	14	1	454	129*	1	4	34.92
N. G. Roberts	6	12	1	381	95*	0	2	34.63
B. J. Lloyd	4	6	2	121	72*	0	1	30.25
S. W. Evans	5	10	0	269	86	0	2	26.90
S. A. Williams	6	12	0	254	55	0	2	21.16
J. D. Hughes	4	8	1	145	50	0	1	20.71
M. A. G. Jones	4	7	0	83	30	0	0	11.85
A. C. Smith	6	8	1	76	47	0	0	10.85
C. Williams	8	6	2	13	11	0	0	3.25

Played in five matches: H. G. Rogers 3, 4*, 2. Played in four matches: †M. H. Davies 13, 2, 0; †P. Lloyd 7*, 18, 0*, 1; A. Williams 6, 13*, 8*. Played in three matches: G. Edwards 23, 11*, 3, 21. Played in two matches: D. A. Francis 18, 60, 4, 95; M. Kear 48, 2, 4, 3*; R. Morris 8, 36, 56, 34; P. D. North 15, 11, 61*, 4; J. Roach 5, 7*; S. G. Watkins 4, 91, 36, 30. Played in one match: A. R. Davies 1; †A. Shaw 10*, 38; C. Stephens 1*; D. R. Williams 6, 5*.

Bowling Averages

	O	M	R	W	BB	5W/i	Avge
N. G. Roberts	100.5	17	337	15	4-64	0	22.46
A. C. Smith	187.2	46	584	23	5-54	1	25.39
B. J. Lloyd	142.3	45	441	15	4-62	0	29.40
H. G. Rogers	123	30	435	13	3-43	0	33.46
C. Williams	155.1	20	555	11	4-47	0	50.45

Also bowled: A. R. Davies 12–1–49–1; G. Edwards 62–13–210–4; P. D. North 51–16–140–2; J. Roach 75–13–235–4; C. Stephens 18–2–61–1; S. G. Watkins 36.2–6–147–2; A. Williams 85–19–269–7; D. R. Williams 19.4–1–83–4.

WILTSHIRE

Secretary – C. R. SHEPPARD, 45 Ipswich Street, Swindon SN2 1DB

Matches 9: Won – Dorset. Lost – Berkshire, Oxfordshire, Wales. Won on first innings – Buckinghamshire, Cornwall, Shropshire. Lost on first innings – Devon. No result – Cheshire.

Batting Averages

	M	*I*	*NO*	*R*	*HI*	*100s*	*50s*	*Avge*
D. R. Turner	9	17	3	887	125*	3	5	63.35
D. R. Parry	3	6	2	244	56*	0	3	61.00
K. N. Foyle	6	11	4	373	87*	0	3	53.28
P. A. C. Bail	6	11	0	437	119	1	4	39.72
C. R. Trembath	4	7	1	204	91	0	1	34.00
D. P. Simpkins	9	14	3	299	100*	1	0	27.18
S. Williams	9	17	1	428	96	0	2	26.75
*B. H. White	8	15	0	356	66	0	2	23.73
A. Mildenhall	4	6	3	59	33*	0	0	19.66
†S. M. Perrin	7	7	1	59	25*	0	0	9.83
S. J. Malone	8	6	1	41	20	0	0	8.20

Played in seven matches: M. Holland 3*, 1, 2. Played in five matches: I. G. Osborne 1*, 3*, 0. Played in four matches: D. R. Pike 41, 21, 25*, 33, 32. Played in three matches: N. Prigent 1*, 7*, 18, 8*. Played in two matches: R. R. Savage 4, 16, 21*; †N. Shardlow 1, 7, 0. Played in one match: M. J. Beel 1; J. J. Newman 49, 27; G. Sheppard 0*.

Bowling Averages

	O	*M*	*R*	*W*	*BB*	*5W/i*	*Avge*
C. R. Trembath	129	23	412	17	4-51	0	24.23
M. Holland	145.2	20	632	21	4-106	0	30.09
D. P. Simpkins	189	33	667	17	5-31	2	39.23
S. J. Malone	159.5	12	640	14	4-55	0	45.71

Also bowled: P. A. C. Bail 5–2–10–0; M. J. Beel 7–3–34–1; K. N. Foyle 2–1–5–0; A. Mildenhall 96–12–361–9; I. G. Osborne 79–13–260–7; D. R. Pike 51–14–152–6; N. Prigent 37–4–155–5; G. Sheppard 22–2–77–2; B. H. White 2–1–9–0.

TOP TEN MINOR COUNTIES CHAMPIONSHIP AVERAGES, 1990

BATTING

(Qualification: 8 innings)

	M	*I*	*NO*	*R*	*HI*	*100s*	*Avge*
J. Abrahams (*Shropshire*)	7	13	4	765	113*	4	85.00
M. R. Davies (*Shropshire*)	9	15	7	628	114*	2	78.50
A. Needham (*Hertfordshire*)	8	13	2	750	130*	3	68.18
P. Burn (*Durham*)	7	13	4	582	105	2	64.66
M. G. Lickley (*Berkshire*)	9	16	3	838	122*	3	64.46
A. S. Patel (*Durham*)	8	12	4	512	103*	1	64.00
D. R. Turner (*Wiltshire*)	9	17	3	887	125*	3	63.35
S. N. V. Waterton (*Oxfordshire*)	9	17	3	883	123*	1	63.07
G. W. Ecclestone (*Cambridgeshire*)	5	10	2	487	111	1	60.87
G. K. Brown (*Durham*)	6	11	4	417	110*	2	59.57

BOWLING

(Qualification: 20 wickets)

	O	*M*	*R*	*W*	*BB*	*Avge*
A. S. Patel (*Durham*)	119.5	35	318	21	5-80	15.14
D. Surridge (*Hertfordshire*)	224.2	69	488	29	5-24	16.82
S. Turner (*Cambridgeshire*)	286.5	79	727	40	7-86	18.17
A. C. Jelfs (*Lincolnshire*)	158.5	36	488	25	5-61	19.52
P. J. Kippax (*Durham*)	220.4	75	531	26	5-23	20.42
N. R. Taylor (*Dorset*)	165	39	497	24	5-38	20.70
A. D. Greasley (*Cheshire*)	138.1	37	471	22	5-96	21.40
I. L. Pont (*Lincolnshire*)	150.5	26	569	26	6-34	21.88
G. Edmunds (*Shropshire*)	270.4	68	807	36	8-60	22.41
J. H. Shackleton (*Dorset*)	290.3	79	759	33	6-67	23.00
R. A. Evans (*Oxfordshire*)	258.5	71	713	31	5-85	23.00

THE MINOR COUNTIES CHAMPIONS

1895	Norfolk / Durham / Worcestershire	1925	Buckinghamshire	1961	Somerset II
1896	Worcestershire	1926	Durham	1962	Warwickshire II
1897	Worcestershire	1927	Staffordshire	1963	Cambridgeshire
1898	Worcestershire	1928	Berkshire	1964	Lancashire II
1899	Northamptonshire / Buckinghamshire	1929	Oxfordshire	1965	Somerset II
1900	Glamorgan / Durham / Northamptonshire	1930	Durham	1966	Lincolnshire
1901	Durham	1931	Leicestershire II	1967	Cheshire
1902	Wiltshire	1932	Buckinghamshire	1968	Yorkshire II
1903	Northamptonshire	1933	Undecided	1969	Buckinghamshire
1904	Northamptonshire	1934	Lancashire II	1970	Bedfordshire
1905	Norfolk	1935	Middlesex II	1971	Yorkshire II
1906	Staffordshire	1936	Hertfordshire	1972	Bedfordshire
1907	Lancashire II	1937	Lancashire II	1973	Shropshire
1908	Staffordshire	1938	Buckinghamshire	1974	Oxfordshire
1909	Wiltshire	1939	Surrey II	1975	Hertfordshire
1910	Norfolk	1946	Suffolk	1976	Durham
1911	Staffordshire	1947	Yorkshire	1977	Suffolk
1912	In abeyance	1948	Lancashire II	1978	Devon
1913	Norfolk	1949	Lancashire II	1979	Suffolk
1914	Staffordshire	1950	Surrey II	1980	Durham
1920	Staffordshire	1951	Kent II	1981	Durham
1921	Staffordshire	1952	Buckinghamshire	1982	Oxfordshire
1922	Buckinghamshire	1953	Berkshire	1983	Hertfordshire
1923	Buckinghamshire	1954	Surrey II	1984	Durham
1924	Berkshire	1955	Surrey II	1985	Cheshire
		1956	Kent II	1986	Cumberland
		1957	Yorkshire II	1987	Buckinghamshire
		1958	Yorkshire II	1988	Cheshire
		1959	Warwickshire II	1989	Oxfordshire
		1960	Lancashire II	1990	Hertfordshire

RAPID CRICKETLINE SECOND ELEVEN CHAMPIONSHIP, 1990

Sussex were comfortable winners of the Second Eleven Championship, finishing with a 26-point lead over Glamorgan, the runners-up, to take the title for the second time, having won it previously in 1978. They did not feature in the knockout rounds of the 55-overs Bain Clarkson Trophy, though, that competition being won by Lancashire, who beat Somerset by eight wickets in the final.

There was consolation for Somerset in the nomination of their leading batsman, Ricky Bartlett, as the Rapid Cricketline Player of the Year. His 1,393 runs were the second highest aggregate of a season in which a record ten batsmen passed 1,000 runs in the championship; nine had done so in 1989, when twelve more matches were played. Sussex's New Zealander, Graham Burnett, recorded the highest aggregate (1,432) since S. Jayasinghe's 1,485 for Leicestershire in 1961, achieved in four more innings. In a batsman's season in which only six bowlers took 50 wickets, the Middlesex slow left-armer, Alex Barnett, captured 71, sixteen more than anyone else.

Widespread approval was expressed by players and officials alike for the new format of the championship, whereby all the counties played each other once. It was agreed that this produced a more satisfactory and realistic competition.

As expected, 1990 proved to be a difficult year for **Derbyshire**, who returned to the lower reaches of the table. Often fielding non-contract players, lacking the experience of many opponents, they managed only two wins. Of their eight defeats, three came in the final overs. There were some useful bowling performances from the Young England seamer, Dominic Cork, and from Ewan McCray, a spin bowler whose 50 wickets included six for 122 at Cardiff. McCray also scored 748 runs, with a highest score of 104 at Southampton. He shared the batting honours with Steve Goldsmith, who hit 109 and 163 against Kent at Chesterfield, and Zahid Sadiq, whose aggregate of 892 included 103 at Watford, 106 at Southampton and 112 at Taunton. Of the numerous local players who appeared, Neil Sparham and Paul Shaw played some fine innings.

SECOND ELEVEN CHAMPIONSHIP, 1990

						Bonus points		
Win = 16 points	*P*	*W*	*L*	*D*	*T*	*Batting*	*Bowling*	*Points*
1 – Sussex (14)	16	9	1	6	0	45	39	228
2 – Glamorgan (10)	16	7	3	6	0	34	56	202
3 – Surrey (16)	16	5	1	9	1	40	54	182
4 – Nottinghamshire (7)	16	6	4	6	0	32	53	181
5 – Kent (3)	16	5	2	9	0	43	46	169
6 – Middlesex (1)	16	4	3	9	0	45	43	152
7 – Warwickshire (2)	16	4	3	9	0	39	46	149
8 – Lancashire (15)	16	3	5	8	0	43	48	139
9 – Essex (12)	16	3	3	10	0	39	49	136
10 – Worcestershire (17)	16	2	3	10	1	43	51	134
11 – Hampshire (6)	16	2	5	9	0	45	44	129
12 – Northamptonshire (5)	16	3	4	9	0	40	35	123
13 – Derbyshire (4)	16	2	8	6	0	33	44	109
14 – Gloucestershire (11)	16	2	5	9	0	33	36	101
15 – Somerset (13)	16	1	2	13	0	41	40	97
16 – Leicestershire (8)	16	0	1	15	0	43	47	90
17 – Yorkshire (9)	16	1	6	9	0	33	40	89

1989 positions in brackets.
The totals for Surrey and Worcestershire each include 8 points for a tied match.
The total for Hampshire includes 8 points for levelling the scores in a drawn game.

Essex, once Mark Ilott had been promoted to the first team, generally struggled to bowl sides out twice. His 36 wickets contained match figures of fifteen for 147 from 44.4 overs at Lytham. Still, the slow left-arm bowling of Guy Lovell, an early-season recruit from Cumberland, provided 52 wickets, including returns of eight for 48 against Nottinghamshire and six for 58 against Yorkshire, both at Chelmsford. The batting was again reliable, with Nick Knight and Jon Lewis the leading run-scorers, despite their unavailability early in the season owing to university and college commitments. Lewis followed his 135 against Surrey at Chelmsford in July with 116 not out against them on his first-class début at The Oval at the end of the season. Three centuries each were scored by Keith Butler and the left-handed Knight, the latter's 108 not out at Derby, 141 at Weston-super-Mare and 108 against Yorkshire at Chelmsford coming in successive matches. Adam Seymour overcame the interruption of a broken hand, sustained on his County Championship début, to score 648 runs, and Alastair Fraser also batted well, although his bowling form was inconsistent.

At the end of their best season since they won the championship ten years earlier, runners-up **Glamorgan** could reflect on the crucial defeat in August by the eventual champions, Sussex. While the enterprising captaincy of John Steele was essential to their success, they owed as much to their bowlers, who earned them 56 bonus points – more than any other county. Hamesh Anthony, Steve Bastien, Simon Dennis and Steve Barwick all made significant contributions, particularly in helping win the last three games. In the first and second of these, Dennis returned seven for 46 against Derbyshire at Cardiff and six for 65 at Southampton; in June, Bastien, the team's player of the year, took seven for 67 against Lancashire at Cardiff. John Derrick hit two unbeaten hundreds to top the averages, and seven other players contributed three-figure innings, the highest of which was Robert Croft's 149 against Essex at Swansea. Martin Roberts had another good season, effecting 36 dismissals to set beside his 598 runs, including 120 not out at Guildford.

Gloucestershire were another county to find the majority of their opponents were considerably more experienced. This handicap led to three defeats by an innings in August – by Hampshire, Surrey and Warwickshire – although after the first two they in turn inflicted an innings defeat on Derbyshire. Of the 37 players used, Paul Romaines was by far the most successful of the batsmen, his 778 runs in nine matches featuring two centuries, while at the other end of the experience scale promise was shown by sixteen-year-old Darren Blenkiron and Bob Dawson, with maiden centuries respectively at Canterbury and against Middlesex at Bristol. David Graham also hit his maiden hundred at Bristol, against Leicestershire. It was the bowling that gave most cause for concern, with opponents averaging more than 40 runs per wicket and scoring sixteen hundreds. However, seventeen-year-old Jason de la Pena showed potential as an opening bowler, and Ed Milburn took a hat-trick against Lancashire at Bristol, only a dropped catch preventing four wickets in four balls. "Reggie" Williams caught the eye behind the stumps and made the most of his opportunities when deputising in the first team for Jack Russell. Part way through the season, Andy Stovold took over as captain/coach, and later it was announced that this successful arrangement would continue in 1991.

At **Hampshire**, individual batting performances dominated an otherwise indifferent season, in which a team weakened through injuries managed only two wins and dropped to eleventh place. Tony Middleton was exceptional. He made his maiden first-class hundred, against Kent, on April 27 and then, in his first five innings for the Second Eleven, scored 104 and 144 against Somerset at Southampton, 121 at Bingley, and 100 and 124 against Leicestershire at Bournemouth before returning to the first team on May 19 and scoring 104 not out against Essex five days later. Rupert Cox was hardly less impressive, his aggregate of 1,162 runs also containing five hundreds – 135 against Lancashire at Bournemouth, 134 not out against Derbyshire at Southampton, 128 at Maidstone, 127 at Kidderminster and 102 at Gloucester. Sean Morris, an opening batsman and captain of Durham University, headed the averages with 812 runs at 81.20, including four hundreds: 115 not out against Warwickshire at Southampton, 104 retired hurt at Gloucester, 103 not out at Wellingborough School and 102 against Glamorgan at Southampton. It was not surprising, given such batting strength, that Hampshire gained the most batting bonus points, along with Middlesex and Sussex. Linden Joseph, from Guyana, occasionally bowled with genuine pace and was the leading wicket-taker, just ahead of off-spinner Shaun Udal, whose form improved considerably during the second half of the season.

Kent, the only side to beat the eventual champions, Sussex, doing so by an innings at Eastbourne, finished fifth after an encouraging campaign which saw the emergence of several promising youngsters. Matthew Brimson, David Fulton, Nick Preston and Graham Kersey, all products of the county's youth coaching system, came through with distinction, with Kersey, in particular, developing from a schoolboy wicket-keeper into a capable understudy to Steve Marsh. The Ashford all-rounder, Nigel Llong, progressed as a batsman, with innings of 101 at Marske and 104 not out at Clevedon to accompany a string of fifties. Vince Wells benefited from an extended run in the first team, while Mark Ealham, having had an unsettled start to the season as he moved in and out of the senior side, made a major contribution to the Second Eleven in the last month and finished with 802 runs, including 161 not out against Gloucestershire at Canterbury. Two others to earn first-team calls were the left-arm bowlers, Tim Wren and Min Patel; Wren, at medium-pace, took the most wickets, including seven for 34 against Glamorgan at Sittingbourne, and spinner Patel continued his advance on his return from university.

Lancashire, emulating their seniors, challenged the leaders in the championship for two-thirds of the season, only to lose four of their last five games and finish eighth, and won the limited-overs Bain Clarkson Trophy. Nick Speak, who took over the captaincy after John Stanworth severed tendons in his hand, again scored the most runs, his 1,274 including 171 against Warwickshire and 119 against Worcestershire, both at Manchester, and 105 at Northampton. Close behind him came Stephen Titchard, whose aggregate of 1,137 contained 139 against Middlesex at Crosby, followed by 117 and 150 without being dismissed at The Oval. John Crawley displayed his rich talent in compiling 870 runs, including 101 at Leicester, 100 not out at Northampton and 117 at Shireoaks. Of the bowlers only Ian Folley, with 55 wickets, made much impression, although Peter Martin took seven for 31 at Bristol, Ian Austin six for 54 at Leicester and Wasim Akram five in each innings, for 76, against Derbyshire at Liverpool. The Australian Under-19 captain, Jason Gallian, outstanding for Werneth in the Central Lancashire League, also made a significant all-round contribution.

Beaten by Sussex in their first match, **Leicestershire** drew the rest and were the only side without a win. That they managed to edge into sixteenth ahead of Yorkshire at the bottom of the table was due to their 90 bonus points, the fourth-highest total in the championship. There were maiden centuries for Ben Smith, who headed the batting averages, Andrew Roseberry, who scored the most runs, and the Loughborough schoolboy, Chris Hawkes. Smith began the season with 101 not out against Sussex at Leicester, and two weeks later hit 125 not out at Bournemouth; Roseberry made his unbeaten 113 at The Oval, and 110 against Worcestershire at Leicester; and Hawkes hit 122 against Middlesex at Market Harborough. Les Taylor took 36 economical wickets, including seven for 34 at Bournemouth and six for 45 at Canterbury in consecutive matches, and although Lloyd Tennant's tally was three higher, he was 11 runs a wicket more expensive. Paul Nixon had fifteen dismissals in his five matches, and Justin Benson held ten catches in three appearances.

Middlesex, champions and favourites when the season began, were beaten for the first time in four years and dropped to sixth place. This was perhaps inevitable following the promotion of Keith Brown and Mike Roseberry, coupled with first-team demands on the seam bowling resources. Nevertheless they remained a powerful batting side. The left-handed Jason Pooley again passed 1,000 runs, scoring 111 and 201 not out against Somerset at Enfield to follow innings of 158 against Derbyshire at Watford and 100 against Warwickshire at Uxbridge. Matthew Keech found his second season more difficult, but Toby Radford looked sound and Aftab Habib compiled his maiden hundred – 104 at Bristol – in the last match, a promising advance for a player who was too often out for a spectacular thirty. Ian Hutchinson, frequently affected by injuries, had a disappointing season by his standards but scored most runs after Pooley and John Carr, whose three hundreds included 120 and 116 against Derbyshire at Watford. Slow bowling was the side's other strength. Before joining the Young England side, Alex Barnett captured 71 wickets, taking five in an innings five times, including a match return of eleven for 103 against Somerset. Off-spinner Paul Weekes made an ideal partner, and with 641 runs to set alongside his 51 wickets he demonstrated his potential to become a valuable all-rounder. Chas Taylor, an Oxfordshire farmer, was a valuable find whose left-arm fast-medium bowling brought him 21 wickets in seven games, while in Paul Farbrace, who joined the county from Kent, Middlesex had a first-rate wicket-keeper-batsman in the tradition of Paul Downton.

Northamptonshire, hampered by injuries throughout the playing staff, called on 41 players in their sixteen championship games. Although they slipped to twelfth, there was consolation in the performances of some young players, notably Richard Montgomerie, Malachy Loye and Russell Warren, each in his first year on the staff. Montgomerie passed 1,000 runs, with scores of 123 against Middlesex at Bedford School and 104 at Canterbury; Loye hit 165 at Southend; and Warren, available for only ten matches owing to school commitments, scored 121 at York, 157 at Shireoaks and 200 not out at Canterbury. Wayne Noon, the Young England captain, kept wicket to a high standard and had an unbeaten 160 at Southend among his batting successes. John Hughes, a lively medium-paced all-rounder, looked promising, and leg-spinner Andy Roberts fully deserved his selection for Young England.

Nottinghamshire began well, playing some fine competitive cricket, but as injuries and first-team calls disrupted the side, they ceased to function as a unit and fell away towards the end. None the less, the progress of some younger players into the senior side was a bonus. Duncan Martindale was the outstanding batsman, his 866 runs at 86.60 including 171 not out at Elland, 140 not out against Warwickshire at Worksop College and 101 not out at Taunton. The fast-scoring Steve Brogan was close behind him with 848 runs, including six fifties and 135 at Heanor. The bowlers, too, did well, with only Glamorgan and Surrey gaining more bowling bonus points. The most wickets were taken by the fast bowlers, Greg Mike and the South African, Dean Laing: Mike's 47 included seven for 41 at Elland and six for 65 against Northamptonshire at Shireoaks, while Laing's best was seven for 64 at Heanor. The younger of the Saxelby brothers, Mark, took four for 1 at Worcester, and several weeks later scored 109 not out at Taunton.

Though involved in a number of close finishes, **Somerset** could manage only one championship win, which left them in fifteenth place. On the other hand, the side went as far as the final in the limited-overs competition. Ricky Bartlett had an outstanding season, scoring 1,393 runs in the three-day games and being named Rapid Cricketline Player of the Year. He hit six hundreds: 134 and 113 not out at Southampton, 153 against Surrey at Yeovil, 109 at Manchester, plus 175 against Derbyshire and 105 against Northamptonshire, both at Taunton. Nick Pringle also passed 1,000 runs, helped by four hundreds, two of them – 130 not out and 111 not out – against Gloucestershire. In that same game, at Bristol, sixteen-year-old Andrew Cottam, a promising slow left-arm bowler, took a hat-trick. The Young England opening bowler, Jeremy Hallett, did well on occasions, but Andrew Caddick, a New Zealander hoping to be qualified for the 1992 season, looked the pick of the seam bowlers. He took six for 42 at Enfield, while another medium-pacer, Daryn Kutner, produced a return of five for 6 at Manchester in Somerset's only victory. Gareth Townsend, who was particularly successful at Taunton, fell just 11 runs short of four figures, and Ian Fletcher, like Harvey Trump and Hallett a product of Millfield School, had a sound first full season.

Surrey climbed from sixteenth in 1989 to third and were able to look back on five wins and some memorable matches. The last fixture, at Worcester, was tied when Surrey were dismissed for 319, having declared at 300 for five in the first innings with Steve Cooper 103 not out in only his second match. Jonathan Robinson's unbeaten 214 not out, in a total of 400 for three declared against Gloucestershire at Guildford, was a personal best, and in the two-wicket defeat of Lancashire at The Oval, five hundreds were scored, three for Surrey. Paul Atkins and Rehan Alikhan made 149 and 103 not out respectively before Surrey declared at 262 for one, and Graham Thorpe made 126 not out in the second innings. Earlier in the season Alikhan had made 151 not out against Leicestershire at The Oval, and Atkins 116 not out at Canterbury. Although spending almost half the season with the first team, Neil Kendrick took 36 wickets, including eleven for 107 in the defeat of Hampshire at The Oval, and Tony Murphy took 28 wickets in his six games. Tony Gray took six for 20 in the rain-affected match at Ilkeston, and all the bowlers benefited from the wicket-keeping of Neil Sargeant, who effected 40 dismissals.

Captained by Keith Greenfield, **Sussex** leapt from fourteenth place to win the title for the first time since 1978. This was particularly encouraging in view of their first team having languished at the foot of the County Championship table for most of the season. Losing only to Kent, they won their first four and last four matches, plus one in July. The key to their success was a settled and varied attack, in which the leg-spin of Andy Clarke complemented the off-breaks of Bradleigh Donelan. Donelan returned match figures of fifteen for 142 as Middlesex were beaten at Hove, and Andy Babington, who, with Clarke, was released at the end of the season, had seven for 52 in the ten-wicket win over challengers Glamorgan at Swansea. The batting was dominated by a New Zealander from Wellington, Graham Burnett, whose aggregate of 1,432 was the highest in the championship in 1990. He struck four hundreds, including 212 against Derbyshire at Hove and 201 at Northampton. Also among the runs was Robin Hanley, whose three hundreds at Hove – 161 against Essex, 139 not out against Derbyshire and 103 against Middlesex – earned him his first-team début in his first season.

A mid-table position accurately reflected the performance of **Warwickshire**, the runners-up in 1989. A young, less experienced side tended to be inconsistent, but there were four hundreds from Jason Ratcliffe – 107 at Worksop, 101 not out at Hinckley, 151 at Southampton and 118 against Derbyshire at Walmley – and two each from Dominic Ostler, Simon Green and the Zimbabwean, Trevor Penney. The leading wicket-takers, with 36 apiece, were off-spinner Adrian Pierson and Gareth Smith, a left-arm seam bowler from Northamptonshire whose match figures of eleven for 97 were instrumental in the innings defeat of Derbyshire. Roger Twose had a good all-round season, highlights of which were his 102 at Swansea and a return of six for 103 against Yorkshire at Moseley. There was recognition for Keith Piper's wicket-keeping with his promotion to the first team, and Warwickshire were fortunate in having as his replacement Piran Holloway, the Young England representative.

Worcestershire moved up from the bottom of the table to tenth place; although they won just twice, with Surrey they accumulated more bonus points (94) than any other side. Both Paul Bent and Gavin Haynes passed 1,000 runs, the first time two Worcestershire players had done so in a championship season, and the first time anyone had reached four figures for the county since J. Robson in 1979. Bent was remarkably consistent, with 174 against Hampshire at Kidderminster, 113 at Manchester, and ten fifties. Martin Weston and Haynes also hit two hundreds each, and there were three from David Leatherdale – 119 not out against Hampshire at Kidderminster, 118 at Colchester and 101 not out at Derby. Stuart Lampitt made a fine all-round contribution to the defeat of Hampshire, hitting an unbeaten century and taking six for 57. In his first season, Steve Herzberg, an English-born all-rounder who grew up in Australia, scored 743 runs as a mid-order batsman, and his 50 wickets, from 505 overs of off-spin, were the most for Worcestershire since J. A. Standen took the same number in 1966. Neal Radford produced the best innings return of the championship with nine for 98 against Northamptonshire at Halesowen, while another fast-medium bowler, Nick Hitchings, took six for 39 against Gloucestershire at Stourbridge.

It was a disappointing season for **Yorkshire**, joint winners in 1987, who finished last. They could manage only one win – over Northamptonshire at York – and were beaten six times; only Derbyshire lost more. Yet there were encouraging individual performances from several of the 30 players used. Craig White, the Yorkshire-born and Australian-bred all-rounder, was soon enlisted in the first team, having made his presence felt with seven for 55 against Leicestershire at Bradford and innings of 209 and 115 without being dismissed at Worcester. In that match wicket-keeper Colin Chapman also reached three figures, and he later followed White into the senior side. Another double-century came from Kevin Sharp, whose 221 not out against Gloucestershire at Todmorden was the season's highest by any batsman in the championship. Bowling was not Yorkshire's strong suit. The left-arm spinner, Matthew Doidge, took the most wickets (24), but with an average of 39.29, and off-spinners Philip Berry and Jeremy Batty, the only others to take twenty, were hardly less expensive.

*In the averages that follow, * against a score signifies not out, * against a name signifies the captain and † signifies a wicket-keeper.*

DERBYSHIRE SECOND ELEVEN

Matches 16: Won – Kent, Yorkshire. Lost – Glamorgan, Gloucestershire, Hampshire, Lancashire, Middlesex, Northamptonshire, Nottinghamshire, Warwickshire. Drawn – Essex, Leicestershire, Somerset, Surrey, Sussex, Worcestershire.

Batting Averages

	M	*I*	*NO*	*R*	*HI*	*100s*	*Avge*
*†B. J. M. Maher	15	23	18	242	61*	0	48.40
S. C. Goldsmith	8	14	1	558	163	2	42.92
G. T. Headley	2	4	0	165	110	1	41.25
A. M. Brown	4	7	0	288	84	0	41.14
G. A. Smith	3	6	0	218	106	1	36.33
T. A. Tweats	3	5	2	109	40*	0	36.33
Z. A. Sadiq	14	27	0	892	112	3	33.03
N. Sparham	5	10	0	328	101	1	32.80
P. F. Shaw	10	20	0	614	86	0	30.70
T. J. G. O'Gorman	2	4	0	120	51	0	30.00
S. Peall	4	8	1	189	74	0	27.00
E. McCray	16	29	1	748	104	1	26.71
D. G. Cork	9	15	3	244	46	0	20.33
F. A. Griffith	11	20	0	340	60	0	17.00
M. R. May	6	11	0	185	33	0	16.81
D. J. Adams	10	19	4	239	40	0	15.93
R. W. Sladdin	10	17	4	207	34	0	15.92
A. M. A. Aduhene	6	12	3	124	33	0	13.77
R. C. Williams	2	4	0	52	33	0	13.00
D. N. Weston	3	5	0	64	36	0	12.80
I. Ahmed	3	6	0	55	28	0	9.16
C. E. Wall	2	3	0	26	21	0	8.66
L. J. Slater	9	14	3	87	29	0	7.90
P. A. Mestecky	2	3	0	11	9	0	3.66
C. G. Smith	2	3	1	7	4*	0	3.50
M. R. Spencer	3	5	0	14	9	0	2.80

Played in two matches: S. J. Base 28, 0. Played in one match: G. F. Archer 1, 4; D. R. Eyre 0*; D. J. Foster 15, 0; †A. A. D. Gillgrass 31*, 0; L. J. Henshaw 1*; M. Jean-Jacques 2, 12; N. Kingham 0, 15; A. J. McCulloch 20, 17*; R. P. Marsh 11, 6; S. Mohammad 15, 4; P. F. Ridgeway 11, 0*; P. C. P. Simmonite 13, 23; J. F. Trueman 6, 2.

Note: After the first innings of the match v Northamptonshire at Derby, Cork, Goldsmith and Griffith were replaced by Henshaw, McCray and Weston, owing to injuries to first-team players.

Bowling Averages

	O	*M*	*R*	*W*	*BB*	*Avge*
F. A. Griffith	101	26	334	12	5-26	27.83
R. W. Sladdin	259.2	65	770	26	4-42	29.61
E. McCray	481.2	108	1,511	50	6-122	30.22
S. J. Base	41	7	158	5	3-70	31.60
D. J. Adams	224.1	57	703	19	5-44	37.00
S. C. Goldsmith	113	33	305	8	2-43	38.12
A. M. A. Aduhene	118.5	17	518	12	5-119	43.16
D. G. Cork	181.5	44	672	15	4-95	44.80
S. Peall	60	10	226	5	2-57	45.20
L. J. Slater	125.2	16	483	8	2-43	60.37

Also bowled: I. Ahmed 20–4–55–1; D. R. Eyre 7–0–35–1; D. J. Foster 18–3–64–1; G. T. Headley 19–2–57–2; L. J. Henshaw 11–0–61–0; M. Jean-Jacques 24–2–119–1; A. J. McCulloch 16–3–55–0; B. J. M. Maher 11–0–96–2; M. R. May 2.5–0–20–0; P. A. Mestecky 40–7–140–0; P. F. Ridgeway 16–6–66–0; C. G. Smith 37–3–128–0; G. A. Smith 8–0–69–0; M. R. Spencer 39–6–150–2; R. C. Williams 35–6–127–2.

ESSEX SECOND ELEVEN

Matches 16: Won – Lancashire, Northamptonshire, Yorkshire. Lost – Kent, Surrey, Sussex. Drawn – Derbyshire, Glamorgan, Gloucestershire, Hampshire, Leicestershire, Middlesex, Nottinghamshire, Somerset, Warwickshire, Worcestershire.

Batting Averages

	M	*I*	*NO*	*R*	*HI*	*100s*	*Avge*
N. V. Knight	12	20	5	790	141	3	52.66
J. J. B. Lewis	12	21	3	906	135	1	50.33
K. A. Butler	11	18	3	723	116*	3	48.20
A. C. Seymour	9	18	1	648	70	0	38.11
*K. W. R. Fletcher	10	11	4	255	76	0	36.42
G. W. Ecclestone	2	4	0	137	62	0	34.25
N. Shahid	5	9	0	288	59	0	32.00
M. C. Ilott	8	11	6	154	58	0	30.80
A. W. Lilley	10	17	0	521	191	1	30.64
A. G. J. Fraser	13	23	5	530	85*	0	29.44
B. R. Hardie	3	4	1	83	51	0	27.66
C. A. Miller	7	13	5	212	47	0	26.50
T. D. Topley	5	6	0	134	57	0	22.33
†D. E. East	16	25	3	485	86	0	22.04
A. T. Van-Lint	9	14	0	288	103	1	20.57
D. J. P. Boden	7	11	2	166	81	0	18.44
K. O. Thomas	9	10	2	133	33	0	16.62
P. M. Such	5	6	2	40	32	0	10.00
W. G. Lovell	13	11	4	45	14*	0	6.42
S. J. W. Andrew	4	5	0	24	19	0	4.80

Played in one match: A. Churchill, 28, 47*; N. Hussain 4; I. A. Kidd 2, 15; D. Muneeb 2, 0; P. J. Prichard 12, 51*; A. C. Richards 28, 3.

Bowling Averages

	O	*M*	*R*	*W*	*BB*	*Avge*
S. J. W. Andrew	86.1	6	303	16	7-57	18.93
M. C. Ilott	234.1	59	708	36	8-81	19.66
W. G. Lovell	468.2	121	1,438	52	8-48	27.65
T. D. Topley	109	26	315	10	5-32	31.50
C. A. Miller	131	22	475	15	4-53	31.66
K. O. Thomas	202.1	42	623	18	5-50	34.61
A. T. Van-Lint	168.5	33	610	15	3-46	40.66
N. Shahid	91.3	15	306	6	4-60	51.00
A. G. J. Fraser	177.4	24	710	13	3-86	54.61
P. M. Such	184	56	474	8	2-52	59.25
D. J. P. Boden	119	23	452	4	1-13	113.00

Also bowled: K. A. Butler 0.3–0–11–1; A. Churchill 8–2–28–2; N. V. Knight 3–0–9–0; A. W. Lilley 2–0–16–1; A. C. Richards 15.3–3–70–2; A. C. Seymour 0.2–0–4–0.

GLAMORGAN SECOND ELEVEN

Matches 16: Won – Derbyshire, Gloucestershire, Hampshire, Middlesex, Nottinghamshire, Somerset, Surrey. Lost – Kent, Lancashire, Sussex. Drawn – Essex, Leicestershire, Northamptonshire, Warwickshire, Worcestershire, Yorkshire.

Batting Averages

	M	*I*	*NO*	*R*	*HI*	*100s*	*Avge*
J. Derrick	11	16	3	621	114*	2	47.76
S. P. James	5	10	2	342	105*	1	42.75
P. A. Cottey	7	12	0	512	111	1	42.66
†M. L. Roberts	14	20	4	598	120*	1	37.37
D. L. Hemp	7	11	2	328	67	0	36.44
J. B. Bishop	3	4	1	103	56	0	34.33
S. J. Dennis	5	7	3	136	84	0	34.00
I. Smith	7	11	0	372	118	1	33.81

	M	*I*	*NO*	*R*	*HI*	*100s*	*Avge*
G. C. Holmes	4	7	0	227	125	1	32.42
M. J. Cann	14	24	3	664	84	0	31.61
H. A. G. Anthony	13	17	2	373	73	0	24.86
R. N. Pook	9	16	3	313	100*	1	24.07
K. A. Somaia	12	16	3	296	62	0	22.76
M. Davies	16	16	6	121	31	0	12.10
*J. F. Steele	11	10	6	42	16*	0	10.50
S. Bastien	10	8	2	33	19	0	5.50

Also batted: S. R. Barwick 0*, 9, 1, 4; M. R. J. Brugnoli 1*; M. Burns 5*, 9*; G. M. Charlesworth 15, 0*; R. D. B. Croft 149, 47; A. Dale 0, 71; G. T. Headley 27; S. Kirnon 8, 0; S. D. Lerigo 8, 10; S. Mohammad 65, 6; R. Nancarrow 1*, 0; †A. D. Shaw 2, 15; G. Winterbourne 12. M. J. Newbold and S. Vestegaad did not bat.

Bowling Averages

	O	*M*	*R*	*W*	*BB*	*Avge*
S. J. Dennis	175.2	50	513	31	7-46	16.54
S. R. Barwick	251.4	96	522	31	5-35	16.83
I. Smith	76.1	23	191	10	3-16	19.10
S. Kirnon	57	17	149	6	3-36	24.83
S. Bastien	313.2	96	862	34	7-67	25.35
H. A. G. Anthony	365.4	84	1,014	38	6-90	26.68
R. D. B. Croft	111	42	330	11	4-100	30.00
M. Davies	250.1	80	629	20	3-33	31.45
K. A. Somaia	139	41	345	10	3-36	34.50
J. Derrick	143	30	583	15	3-49	38.86

Also bowled: M. R. J. Brugnoli 11–0–53–1; M. J. Cann 6–1–38–1; P. A. Cottey 5–3–6–0; A. Dale 2–0–2–0; G. T. Headley 19–2–63–1; G. C. Holmes 9–1–28–0; S. D. Lerigo 14–3–57–0; R. Nancarrow 7–1–24–0; R. N. Pook 39–15–89–2; S. Vestegaad 15–0–70–1; G. Winterbourne 10–3–27–0.

GLOUCESTERSHIRE SECOND ELEVEN

Matches 16: Won – Derbyshire, Worcestershire. Lost – Glamorgan, Hampshire, Nottinghamshire, Surrey, Warwickshire. Drawn – Essex, Kent, Lancashire, Leicestershire, Middlesex, Northamptonshire, Somerset, Sussex, Yorkshire.

Batting Averages

	M	*I*	*NO*	*R*	*HI*	*100s*	*Avge*
P. W. Romaines	9	15	4	778	172	2	70.72
D. A. Graham	4	6	1	261	101*	1	52.20
M. W. Alleyne	5	8	2	283	120*	1	47.16
D. A. Blenkiron	4	7	1	260	136	1	43.33
G. D. Hodgson	4	8	1	286	80	0	40.85
*A. W. Stovold	13	18	3	497	88	0	33.13
†G. A. Tedstone	7	9	1	241	64	0	30.12
B. G. Evans	3	4	1	82	76*	0	27.33
M. W. Pooley	12	14	3	299	74*	0	27.18
E. T. Milburn	12	17	4	345	85	0	26.53
O. C. K. Smith	9	12	0	296	88	0	24.66
N. M. A. Pritchard	12	22	1	489	73	0	23.28
*†I. P. Butcher	8	14	0	292	69	0	20.85
M. C. J. Ball	12	11	2	140	45*	0	15.55
J. R. Mann	2	4	0	57	19	0	14.25
†R. C. J. Williams	6	6	0	85	47	0	14.16
A. D. A. Chidgey	2	4	0	49	19	0	12.25
S. N. Barnes	7	9	2	62	16*	0	8.85

	M	I	NO	R	HI	100s	Avge
J. M. de la Pena	6	7	3	31	14	0	7.75
K. B. S. Jarvis	5	5	2	19	9	0	6.33
N. J. Pitts	6	7	1	37	16*	0	6.16
A. M. Smith	6	9	3	31	17*	0	5.16
P. A. Owen	2	4	1	15	6	0	5.00

Played in five matches: R. M. Bell 0*, 0, 0. Played in two matches: R. I. Dawson 23, 33, 100*; M. J. Rawlings 17. Played in one match: P. Bainbridge 106; D. R. Brown 0*, 11*; G. S. Calway 4; O. S. Chagar 24*, 5; D. A. Graveney 12*, 11; I. A. Kidd 24; J. W. Lloyds 0, 40; P. C. P. Simmonite 8, 6; B. St A. Browne, B. L. Holmes and D. V. Lawrence did not bat.

Bowling Averages

	O	M	R	W	BB	Avge
K. B. S. Jarvis	107.3	37	236	11	4-20	21.45
A. M. Smith	125	24	364	12	3-29	30.33
J. M. de la Pena	100.1	14	373	11	4-47	33.90
E. T. Milburn	212	37	739	20	4-29	36.95
M. C. J. Ball	271.5	49	937	23	5-57	40.73
N. J. Pitts	112	27	372	9	3-83	41.33
S. N. Barnes	188.3	40	614	13	4-70	47.23
M. W. Pooley	209.5	28	807	14	3-46	57.64
R. M. Bell	97	27	220	3	3-48	73.33
M. W. Alleyne	103	20	317	4	2-35	79.25

Also bowled: P. Bainbridge 6.3–0–23–1; D. R. Brown 11–1–51–2; B. St A. Browne 29–7–73–3; G. S. Calway 18–1–64–0; O. S. Chagar 26–9–64–3; D. A. Graveney 57–16–145–4; G. D. Hodgson 1–0–24–0; B. L. Holmes 43–22–73–2; D. V. Lawrence 37.2–5–118–5; J. W. Lloyds 13.5–2–34–0; J. R. Mann 55–13–193–5; P. A. Owen 40–6–138–0; M. J. Rawlings 16–3–64–4; P. W. Romaines 30.5–4–172–4; O. C. K. Smith 64.1–7–246–2.

HAMPSHIRE SECOND ELEVEN

Matches 16: Won – Derbyshire, Gloucestershire. Lost – Glamorgan, Northamptonshire, Surrey, Warwickshire, Worcestershire. Drawn – Essex, Kent, Lancashire, Leicestershire, Middlesex, Nottinghamshire (levelled scores when batting fourth), Somerset, Sussex, Yorkshire.

Batting Averages

	M	I	NO	R	HI	100s	Avge
R. S. M. Morris	8	14	4	812	115*	4	81.20
T. C. Middleton	8	13	0	837	144	5	64.38
*R. M. F. Cox	15	24	3	1,162	135	5	55.33
T. M. Tremlett	11	10	6	217	59*	0	54.25
†A. N. Aymes	15	21	7	689	105*	2	49.21
J. R. Ayling	7	11	2	381	73	0	42.33
I. J. Turner	12	9	5	157	38*	0	39.25
J. R. Wood	10	15	1	513	100*	1	36.64
C. H. Forward	6	8	1	237	63	0	33.85
S. D. Udal	14	17	3	451	100*	1	32.21
R. J. Scott	10	16	1	464	103	1	30.93
W. J. Holdsworth	3	5	1	109	33*	0	27.25
M. J. Russell	3	6	0	144	48	0	24.00
L. A. Joseph	10	12	4	149	43*	0	18.62
D. P. J. Flint	16	12	4	33	15*	0	4.12
K. J. Shine	5	5	0	18	9	0	3.60

Also batted: R. D. Allen 8, 9; P. J. Bakker 8, 7, 0; L. Bryden 0, 8; A. J. Collins 0, 7; D. B. M. Fox 0*; M. Garaway 1, 5; E. S. H. Giddins 17; M. M. King 0, 8, 7*, 3; I. K. Maynard 12; J. P. Osborne 6; †R. J. Parks 4, 2; R. M. Peterson 0, 11; D. J. Skidmore 9, 82*. K. Bird played in one match but did not bat.

Bowling Averages

	O	*M*	*R*	*W*	*BB*	*Avge*
P. J. Bakker	91	22	226	13	5-60	17.38
W. J. Holdsworth	101	16	320	16	5-68	20.00
L. A. Joseph	279	54	837	32	5-21	26.15
K. J. Shine	80.1	28	196	7	5-34	28.00
I. J. Turner	274.3	81	745	24	4-113	31.04
T. M. Tremlett	90.5	24	226	7	1-2	32.28
M. M. King	109.3	18	427	13	3-36	32.84
R. J. Scott	118.1	32	313	9	3-24	34.77
S. D. Udal	369.5	97	1,184	30	4-83	39.46
J. R. Ayling	149	37	407	8	2-32	50.87
D. P. J. Flint	318.5	79	1,018	14	3-103	72.71

Also bowled: K. Bird 15–0–67–1; L. Bryden 15–1–58–1; A. J. Collins 22–7–62–2; D. B. M. Fox 23–4–77–1; E. S. H. Giddins 30–5–125–2; T. C. Middleton 3–0–28–0; R. S. M. Morris 1–0–3–0; R. M. Peterson 44–6–156–4; J. R. Wood 4–0–23–0.

KENT SECOND ELEVEN

Matches 16: Won – Essex, Glamorgan, Nottinghamshire, Sussex, Yorkshire. Lost – Derbyshire, Northamptonshire. Drawn – Gloucestershire, Hampshire, Lancashire, Leicestershire, Middlesex, Somerset, Surrey, Warwickshire, Worcestershire.

Batting Averages

	M	*I*	*NO*	*R*	*HI*	*Avge*
T. R. Ward	4	8	1	397	201*	56.71
R. M. Ellison	4	7	2	275	105	55.00
N. J. Llong	14	22	5	757	104*	44.52
M. A. Ealham	13	25	4	802	161*	38.19
J. Creed	6	8	4	138	67	34.50
*D. J. M. Kelleher	11	18	1	566	86	33.29
V. J. Wells	12	22	1	698	121	33.23
M. J. Walker	3	4	1	95	47	31.66
D. P. Fulton	5	9	1	249	69	31.12
J. I. Longley	9	17	3	400	77	28.57
M. C. Dobson	15	28	1	683	108	25.29
C. Penn	6	7	1	123	43	20.50
D. R. Penfold	3	5	0	99	43	19.80
†G. J. Kersey	16	24	7	296	51*	17.41
P. S. de Villiers	3	6	0	82	67	13.66
M. M. Patel	4	5	1	42	33	10.50
M. T. Brimson	16	15	2	126	29	9.69
G. D. Myers	3	4	0	38	17	9.50
C. J. Hollins	3	4	0	25	10	6.25
T. N. Wren	10	9	4	23	13*	4.60
N. W. Preston	3	3	1	4	3	2.00

Played in two matches: A. G. E. Ealham 5, 7*, 61*; M. V. Fleming 37*, 50, 136; K. D. Masters 6*, 11*; T. A. Merrick 3, 62, 1. Played in one match: G. R. Cowdrey 69, 6; A. P. Igglesden 0; M. Librizzi 32; S. G. Milroy 0, 7; S. C. Willis 8.

Bowling Averages

	O	*M*	*R*	*W*	*BB*	*Avge*
P. S. de Villiers	73	19	168	9	3-60	18.66
T. N. Wren	208.4	43	713	34	7-34	20.97
M. C. Dobson	185.2	57	451	20	3-18	22.55
T. A. Merrick	81	14	235	9	4-90	26.11
M. M. Patel	99.5	38	235	9	4-48	26.11
M. A. Ealham	214.2	37	694	25	3-32	27.76

	O	M	R	W	BB	Avge
C. Penn	159.4	37	494	16	5-89	30.87
R. M. Ellison	85.5	21	255	8	3-93	31.87
N. J. Llong	169.5	30	582	18	3-6	32.33
M. T. Brimson	359.1	89	1,061	32	5-67	33.15
D. J. M. Kelleher	252	63	748	20	5-36	37.40
V. J. Wells	113	20	372	9	2-39	41.33

Also bowled: G. R. Cowdrey 8–3–24–0; M. V. Fleming 24–8–58–3; A. P. Igglesden 26–5–74–2; J. I. Longley 1–0–17–0; K. D. Masters 18–4–64–0; G. D. Myers 3–2–4–0; N. W. Preston 34–8–106–3; T. R. Ward 5–2–3–0.

LANCASHIRE SECOND ELEVEN

Matches 16: Won – Derbyshire, Glamorgan, Warwickshire. Lost – Essex, Middlesex, Somerset, Surrey, Sussex. Drawn – Gloucestershire, Hampshire, Kent, Leicestershire, Northamptonshire, Nottinghamshire, Worcestershire, Yorkshire.

Batting Averages

	M	I	NO	R	HI	100s	Avge
M. A. Crawley	7	13	4	552	103	2	61.33
J. P. Crawley	11	20	3	870	117	3	51.17
D. T. Foy	2	3	2	51	45*	0	51.00
S. P. Titchard	16	30	6	1,137	150*	3	47.37
*N. J. Speak	16	31	2	1,274	171	3	43.93
J. F. Hurst	3	4	2	74	28	0	37.00
J. E. R. Gallian	9	14	2	411	60	0	34.25
G. D. Lloyd	9	17	0	556	101	1	32.70
*†J. Stanworth	8	6	3	97	36	0	32.33
T. M. Orrell	10	17	1	446	89	0	27.87
G. Yates	16	23	11	330	58*	0	27.50
I. Folley	16	15	4	302	78	0	27.45
R. Irani	12	20	3	322	63	0	18.94
J. D. Fitton	7	11	0	177	47	0	16.09
S. J. Speak	2	3	1	18	10	0	9.00
N. A. Derbyshire	4	4	3	7	5*	0	7.00
†S. Bramhall	4	3	0	17	8	0	5.66

Played in seven matches: P. J. Martin 24*, 18. Played in five matches: M. A. Sharp 2, 0. Played in three matches: †T. Wallwork 0, 0. Played in one match: I. D. Austin 20*, 1; S. Clarkson 15, 5; J. Fielding 6; D. Gandy 5; M. E. Parkinson 5*; Wasim Akram 4; G. Chapple, †J. D. Harvey and S. J. Rimmer did not bat.

Bowling Averages

	O	M	R	W	BB	Avge
Wasim Akram	37.2	10	76	10	5-36	7.60
I. D. Austin	22.3	8	54	6	6-54	9.00
S. J. Speak	23	4	79	5	4-60	15.80
D. T. Foy	30	9	67	4	2-21	16.75
P. J. Martin	216	54	501	25	7-31	20.04
M. A. Crawley	45	11	132	5	4-58	26.40
J. E. R. Gallian	198.4	53	591	19	5-62	31.10
I. Folley	584	130	1,723	55	4-39	31.32
R. Irani	277.4	54	799	25	5-41	31.96
M. A. Sharp	92	24	242	7	3-34	34.57
J. D. Fitton	244	61	663	18	4-100	36.83
N. A. Derbyshire	54.3	5	228	5	3-7	45.60
G. Yates	450.5	101	1,439	29	4-88	49.62

Also bowled: G. Chapple 4–3–4–0; J. Fielding 10–2–27–1; G. D. Lloyd 8–0–46–0; T. M. Orrell 10–0–70–0; M. E. Parkinson 11–0–79–0; S. J. Rimmer 12–2–38–0; N. J. Speak 14–1–89–1; S. P. Titchard 10–0–54–2.

LEICESTERSHIRE SECOND ELEVEN

Matches 16: Lost – Sussex. Drawn – Derbyshire, Essex, Glamorgan, Gloucestershire, Hampshire, Kent, Lancashire, Middlesex, Northamptonshire, Nottinghamshire, Somerset, Surrey, Warwickshire, Worcestershire, Yorkshire.

Batting Averages

	M	*I*	*NO*	*R*	*HI*	*100s*	*Avge*
B. F. Smith	14	19	5	701	125*	2	50.07
†P. A. Nixon	5	7	3	200	50*	0	50.00
P. N. Hepworth	12	20	5	663	125*	1	44.20
M. I. Gidley	12	15	6	395	92	0	43.88
A. Roseberry	16	23	2	829	113*	2	39.47
*R. A. Cobb	15	25	3	759	108	1	34.50
J. D. R. Benson	3	6	0	179	86	0	29.83
C. J. Hawkes	7	8	0	227	122	1	28.37
†P. Whitticase	3	4	0	105	43	0	26.25
G. J. F. Ferris	6	6	3	76	32*	0	25.33
M. A. Gilliver	7	10	1	222	44	0	24.66
I. F. Plender	14	21	1	492	75	0	24.60
D. J. Millns	9	7	4	73	32*	0	24.33
G. J. Parsons	9	13	2	238	52*	0	21.63
L. Tennant	14	14	4	145	26	0	14.50
W. K. M. Benjamin	3	3	0	41	22	0	13.66
I. H. Bell	2	3	0	38	29	0	12.66
L. B. Taylor	9	7	3	5	4*	0	1.25

Played in five matches: †C. Bloor 7, 2. Played in two matches: N. Pretorius 0*, 0; R. W. Sladdin 14; G. B. Wilson 0. Played in one match: M. P. Briers 7; C. Griffiths 3; W. Matthews 4; L. Potter 59, 43; P. Willey 75.

Bowling Averages

	O	*M*	*R*	*W*	*BB*	*Avge*
L. B. Taylor	270	59	691	36	7-34	19.19
C. J. Hawkes	194.3	65	485	19	5-102	25.52
J. D. R. Benson	63	20	160	6	2-56	26.66
N. Pretorius	77	18	232	8	4-70	29.00
L. Tennant	373.4	76	1,181	39	5-72	30.28
G. J. Parsons	271.4	59	793	26	4-39	30.50
W. K. M. Benjamin	76	11	249	8	3-93	31.12
G. J. F. Ferris	121	29	314	10	3-20	31.40
I. F. Plender	96.4	16	374	10	3-55	37.40
M. I. Gidley	319.5	112	775	20	3-35	38.75
D. J. Millns	212.4	50	579	7	2-50	82.71

Also bowled: M. P. Briers 10–2–34–0; M. A. Gilliver 51.3–7–188–2; C. Griffiths 18–5–78–1; P. N. Hepworth 2–0–8–1; W. Matthews 33–6–101–0; L. Potter 17.4–10–22–1; R. W. Sladdin 44–7–144–1; P. Willey 19.4–7–45–0.

MIDDLESEX SECOND ELEVEN

Matches 16: Won – Derbyshire, Lancashire, Nottinghamshire, Somerset. Lost – Glamorgan, Sussex, Worcestershire. Drawn – Essex, Gloucestershire, Hampshire, Kent, Leicestershire, Northamptonshire, Surrey, Warwickshire, Yorkshire.

Batting Averages

	M	*I*	*NO*	*R*	*HI*	*Avge*
J. D. Carr	7	10	0	765	179	76.50
*C. T. Radley	9	10	6	270	67*	67.50
J. C. Pooley	14	23	3	1,021	201*	51.05
R. O. Butcher	10	16	1	602	110	40.13
I. J. F. Hutchinson	13	22	2	644	95	32.20
P. N. Weekes	15	22	2	641	65	32.05
A. Habib	13	21	3	563	104	31.27
†P. Farbrace	10	17	0	529	125	31.11
M. Keech	12	19	4	394	74*	26.26
T. A. Radford	10	15	3	273	74	22.75
R. C. Williams	3	4	0	87	76	21.75
†R. J. Sims	5	8	2	124	44	20.66
C. W. Taylor	7	10	3	129	21*	18.42
M. J. Lowrey	2	4	1	49	28*	16.33
A. A. Barnett	13	15	4	160	54*	14.54
M. J. Thursfield	5	5	1	43	18*	10.75
A. F. Haye	2	3	1	13	13	6.50
J. R. Hemstock	12	11	4	18	6*	2.57

Played in two matches: D. J. Bowett 1, 0*. Played in one match: †P. R. Downton 68; †J. D. Harvey 42; S. Joshi 5, 21; J. W. D. Lishman 0, 7; J. C. Makin 7*; G. R. Mason 0; C. Patel 31*; G. M. Pooley 7; P. C. R. Tufnell 11*; R. S. Yeabsley 1; G. E. Brown and S. P. Hughes did not bat.

Bowling Averages

	O	*M*	*R*	*W*	*Avge*
J. C. Pooley	17	6	54	4	13.50
S. Joshi	37	10	85	5	17.00
A. A. Barnett	642.4	261	1,404	71	19.77
J. D. Carr	76.2	33	145	7	20.71
P. C. R. Tufnell	63.2	10	166	6	27.66
P. N. Weekes	628.3	204	1,472	51	28.86
C. W. Taylor	197	40	641	21	30.52
R. C. Williams	63.3	14	172	4	43.00
A. F. Haye	43	2	219	4	54.75
M. J. Thursfield	162.3	33	496	9	55.11
J. R. Hemstock	147	33	469	5	93.80

Also bowled: D. J. Bowett 35–13–79–1; R. O. Butcher 4–0–18–0; P. Farbrace 1–0–9–0; A. Habib 4–0–14–0; J. D. Harvey 1–0–2–0; S. P. Hughes 22–6–96–1; I. J. F. Hutchinson 24.5–5–69–1; M. Keech 16–6–48–1; J. W. D. Lishman 22–6–96–1; M. J. Lowrey 21–0–105–0; J. C. Makin 17–4–41–3; G. R. Mason 17–1–80–1; C. Patel 17–0–26–0; T. A. Radford 9–1–58–0; C. T. Radley 1–0–10–0; R. S. Yeabsley 20–4–52–2.

NORTHAMPTONSHIRE SECOND ELEVEN

Matches 16: Won – Derbyshire, Hampshire, Kent. Lost – Essex, Nottinghamshire, Sussex, Yorkshire. Drawn – Glamorgan, Gloucestershire, Lancashire, Leicestershire, Middlesex, Somerset, Surrey, Warwickshire, Worcestershire.

Batting Averages

	M	*I*	*NO*	*R*	*HI*	*Avge*
G. Cook	2	4	1	181	92	60.33
J. N. Snape	2	4	1	175	68*	58.33
R. R. Montgomerie	15	26	3	1,013	123	44.04
M. B. Loye	7	11	3	347	165	43.37
R. J. Warren	10	17	1	668	200*	41.75

	M	*I*	*NO*	*R*	*HI*	*Avge*
A. L. Penberthy	5	10	2	318	71	39.75
†W. M. Noon	10	13	2	402	160*	36.54
*D. J. Wild	11	16	1	531	107	35.40
A. R. Roberts	11	19	4	507	102	33.80
P. J. Berry	14	23	2	699	88	33.28
J. W. Govan	12	16	3	423	73*	32.53
J. G. Hughes	12	15	7	259	56	32.37
L. Howell	11	15	2	385	77	29.61
*R. M. Carter	10	8	5	70	23	23.33
R. G. Williams	3	5	0	113	39	22.60
S. J. Brown	7	9	2	90	36	12.85
S. L. Munday	3	3	0	24	21	8.00

Played in three matches: V. Johnson 3, 0*. Played in two matches: W. W. Davis 5, 0; †D. Ripley 26, 49; M. A. Robinson 0; J. Swann 9, 0*; C. Wigham 42, 1*, 14*. Played in one match: I. Ahmed 3, 28; C. Atkins 44; M. P. Briers 7; D. M. Cousins 0; T. de Leede 6, 16; N. A. Felton 59, 125*; H. Hall 3; T. Hancock 35; M. Hunt 5, 0; K. Innes 18, 0; †M. A. Khan 24, 0*; S. Mahboob 2, 0; T. K. Marriott 42*, 1*; C. Rogers 0, 24; M. Sagheer 22, 0*; R. Storr 0*; J. G. Thomas 27; A. Walker did not bat.

Bowling Averages

	O	*M*	*R*	*W*	*Avge*
R. G. Williams	50	16	84	5	16.80
W. W. Davis	43	11	110	4	27.50
M. A. Robinson	50.5	18	114	4	28.50
J. G. Hughes	250.5	53	770	26	29.61
S. J. Brown	183.2	33	592	19	31.15
A. L. Penberthy	102	29	286	9	31.77
A. R. Roberts	345.4	92	1,077	31	34.74
J. W. Govan	483	118	1,517	36	42.13
V. Johnson	89	21	280	6	46.66

Also bowled: I. Ahmed 8–3–24–1; C. Atkins 23–5–94–2; M. P. Briers 5–1–27–0; G. Cook 1–0–12–0; D. M. Cousins 10–2–41–0; T. de Leede 42–5–131–1; H. Hall 15–4–39–1; T. Hancock 4–0–25–0; L. Howell 16.5–2–71–1; K. Innes 11–1–55–0; S. Mahboob 38–8–93–4; T. K. Marriott 12–4–52–0; R. R. Montgomerie 6–4–8–1; S. L. Munday 60.3–13–195–3; M. Sagheer 14–0–69–1; J. Swann 28–1–166–1; J. G. Thomas 7–2–16–1; A. Walker 34–10–71–0; C. Wigham 41.5–2–184–0; D. J. Wild 160.5–35–593–5.

NOTTINGHAMSHIRE SECOND ELEVEN

Matches 16: Won – Derbyshire, Gloucestershire, Northamptonshire, Warwickshire, Worcestershire, Yorkshire. Lost – Glamorgan, Kent, Middlesex, Sussex. Drawn – Essex, Hampshire, Lancashire, Leicestershire, Somerset, Surrey.

Batting Averages

	M	*I*	*NO*	*R*	*HI*	*100s*	*Avge*
D. J. R. Martindale	8	16	6	866	171*	3	86.60
G. F. Archer	3	5	1	230	99	0	57.50
†C. W. Scott	16	23	7	758	96	0	47.37
M. Saxelby	7	12	1	438	109*	1	39.81
M. Newell	6	11	2	321	64	0	35.66
S. M. Brogan	15	29	3	848	135	1	32.61
R. J. Evans	13	22	3	589	76	0	31.00
M. G. Field-Buss	7	10	2	225	71	0	28.12
P. R. Pollard	9	16	1	393	82*	0	26.20
D. R. Laing	16	26	2	529	72	0	22.04
*J. D. Birch	11	10	3	113	28*	0	16.14
R. T. Bates	5	4	1	48	25*	0	16.00

	M	*I*	*NO*	*R*	*HI*	*100s*	*Avge*
K. P. Evans	6	7	2	76	26*	0	15.20
C. T. McKnight	2	3	1	30	25	0	15.00
G. W. Mike	13	19	0	274	63	0	14.42
W. A. Dessaur	8	12	3	124	39	0	13.77
K. Saxelby	12	14	4	125	36*	0	12.50
R. J. Chapman	4	6	3	32	13	0	10.66
N. A. Hunt	2	4	0	24	12	0	6.00
J. E. Hindson	2	3	0	14	14	0	4.66

Played in one match: J. A. Afford 2, 2; M. A. Fell 33, 15; J. E. Haynes 31, 3; P. Johnson 16*, 11; S. N. Neal 2*, 0; S. Patel 11*; R. A. Pick 35; D. W. Randall 27, 5; D. B. Storer 21, 0; K. Thomas 5; J. F. Trueman 25, 10.

Bowling Averages

	O	*M*	*R*	*W*	*BB*	*Avge*
M. Saxelby	70.2	16	237	12	4-1	19.75
K. P. Evans	209.2	53	575	28	5-33	20.53
J. A. Afford	60	21	174	8	5-66	21.75
W. A. Dessaur	69	23	167	7	3-47	23.85
K. Saxelby	344.5	88	1,025	39	5-56	26.28
M. G. Field-Buss	301.5	107	639	24	5-57	26.62
D. R. Laing	394.1	96	1,274	46	7-64	27.69
G. W. Mike	435	96	1,328	47	7-41	28.25
J. D. Birch	31.3	7	151	5	4-54	30.20
R. T. Bates	59.4	14	201	6	2-44	33.50
R. J. Chapman	79	18	261	7	3-73	37.28

Also bowled: R. J. Evans 12–3–40–2; M. A. Fell 42–10–82–2; J. E. Hindson 32–10–73–0; C. T. McKnight 64–17–210–2; M. Newell 5–1–11–0; S. Patel 28–10–82–1; R. A. Pick 32–1–109–1; P. R. Pollard 4–0–49–0; K. Thomas 4–1–20–0.

SOMERSET SECOND ELEVEN

Matches 16: Won – Lancashire. Lost – Glamorgan, Middlesex. Drawn – Derbyshire, Essex, Gloucestershire, Hampshire, Kent, Leicestershire, Northamptonshire, Nottinghamshire, Surrey, Sussex, Warwickshire, Worcestershire, Yorkshire.

Batting Averages

	I	*NO*	*R*	*HI*	*Avge*
†R. J. Turner	5	3	130	45*	65.00
R. J. Bartlett	24	2	1,393	175	63.31
N. J. Pringle	26	5	1,187	130*	56.52
M. Lathwell	6	1	271	168*	54.20
Keith Parsons	4	2	92	52*	46.00
G. T. J. Townsend	26	4	989	152*	44.95
H. R. J. Trump	8	5	110	63*	36.66
I. Fletcher	27	1	824	137	31.69
J. C. M. Atkinson	13	0	399	97	30.69
M. W. Cleal	12	1	315	57*	28.63
D. M. Kutner	13	3	269	65*	26.90
J. C. Hallett	13	4	225	61	25.00
S. Toogood	3	0	75	53	25.00
S. D. Myles	5	0	111	61	22.20
*†T. Gard	13	6	144	51*	20.57
A. R. Caddick	6	3	60	27	20.00
M. A. Harris	7	0	107	42	15.28
P. J. Rendell	5	0	65	42	13.00
A. C. Cottam	6	2	40	18	10.00

Also batted: P. Bradbury 53*; S. Brodrick 4*, 0; G. Brown 38*, 9; S. Bryan 1; J. J. E. Hardy 104; J. D. Harvey 39, 1; K. Martin 10; K. Moyse 0*, 0*; Kevin Parsons 37, 9; S. M. Priscott 8*, 6; R. A. Pyman 9, 6*; D. Read 4, 0; P. J. Robinson 5, 3*; A. P. van Troost 0; M. Wakefield 12. M. Copping and E. Robinson each played in one match but did not bat.

Bowling Averages

	O	*M*	*R*	*W*	*BB*	*Avge*
P. Bradbury	16	0	70	4	2-25	17.50
M. W. Cleal	165	29	477	17	4-49	28.05
A. R. Caddick	241	45	713	24	6-42	29.70
H. R. J. Trump	354.4	91	913	29	5-80	31.48
D. M. Kutner	72.3	12	302	9	5-6	33.55
J. C. Hallett	285.4	46	1,006	28	4-68	35.92
A. C. Cottam	277	62	998	26	5-100	38.38
M. A. Harris	71	9	255	4	1-27	63.75
A. P. van Troost	91	10	392	6	2-80	65.33
P. J. Rendell	99	7	396	4	3-65	99.00

Also bowled: J. C. M. Atkinson 22.1–3–82–3; R. J. Bartlett 6–0–29–0; S. Brodrick 12.5–3–56–2; M. Copping 29–3–96–2; M. Lathwell 25–8–78–1; K. Martin 22–0–90–1; K. Moyse 22.1–3–89–2; S. D. Myles 45.4–4–144–2; Keith Parsons 5–1–14–3; S. M. Priscott 66–7–307–2; R. A. Pyman 29–11–50–1; D. Read 23–3–93–2; E. Robinson 45–14–140–3; P. J. Robinson 18–5–34–3; S. Toogood 64.1–6–305–3; G. T. J. Townsend 1–0–18–0; M. Wakefield 9–3–28–0.

SURREY SECOND ELEVEN

Matches 16: Won – Essex, Gloucestershire, Hampshire, Lancashire, Yorkshire. Lost – Glamorgan. Drawn – Derbyshire, Kent, Leicestershire, Middlesex, Northamptonshire, Nottinghamshire, Somerset, Sussex, Warwickshire. Tied – Worcestershire.

Batting Averages

	M	*I*	*NO*	*R*	*HI*	*100s*	*Avge*
R. I. Alikhan	8	11	4	497	151*	2	71.00
G. P. Thorpe	4	6	1	301	126*	1	60.20
J. D. Robinson	10	16	3	627	214*	1	48.23
*P. D. Atkins	14	21	4	756	149	2	44.47
C. K. Bullen	10	14	4	438	93	0	43.80
A. D. Brown	15	20	1	712	152	1	37.47
A. W. Smith	14	20	3	571	80	0	33.58
M. A. Butcher	15	23	3	627	127	1	31.35
†N. F. Sargeant	14	15	4	308	81	0	28.00
A. Hodgson	4	6	1	136	70	0	27.20
N. M. Kendrick	9	8	2	159	53*	0	26.50
M. A. Feltham	4	5	0	104	61	0	20.80
A. H. Gray	5	3	1	41	24*	0	20.50
D. J. Bicknell	3	4	0	63	35	0	15.75
A. Hollioake	5	6	2	45	16*	0	11.25
N. H. Peters	8	7	1	53	32	0	8.83
A. G. Robson	9	5	1	24	9	0	6.00
J. Boiling	6	5	3	9	4*	0	4.50

Played in six matches: A. J. Murphy 9; C. E. Waller 1*, 2*, 7*. Played in two matches: S. J. Cooper 3*, 103*, 0; D. Foster 6*. Played in one match: M. R. J. Brugnoli 0, 1; M. A. Lynch 56; A. T. Van-Lint 6; A. Giles did not bat.

Bowling Averages

	O	*M*	*R*	*W*	*BB*	*Avge*
M. A. Feltham	125.2	33	272	16	6-34	17.00
A. H. Gray	154.4	38	406	22	6-20	18.45
A. J. Murphy	204	52	530	28	5-41	18.92
N. M. Kendrick	345.1	118	694	36	6-56	19.27
C. K. Bullen	312.2	119	577	21	4-63	27.47
J. Boiling	182.3	63	426	14	4-44	30.42
J. D. Robinson	148.3	31	464	15	3-52	30.93
A. G. Robson	272	48	827	22	4-34	37.59
N. H. Peters	153.1	31	543	14	4-36	38.78
S. J. Cooper	89.3	20	273	7	3-96	39.00
A. Hollioake	90	14	357	8	3-46	44.62

Also bowled: P. D. Atkins 17–3–43–0; A. D. Brown 24.3–1–150–1; M. R. J. Brugnoli 12–2–36–1; M. A. Butcher 19–4–62–0; D. Foster 48.4–9–125–4; A. Giles 18–5–42–1; M. A. Lynch 10–3–30–0; N. F. Sargeant 1–0–14–0; A. W. Smith 54–16–170–3; G. P. Thorpe 35–7–148–2; A. T. Van-Lint 39.2–6–135–4; C. E. Waller 29–6–67–1.

SUSSEX SECOND ELEVEN

Matches 16: Won – Essex, Glamorgan, Lancashire, Leicestershire, Middlesex, Northamptonshire, Nottinghamshire, Warwickshire, Yorkshire. Lost – Kent. Drawn – Derbyshire, Gloucestershire, Hampshire, Somerset, Surrey, Worcestershire.

Batting Averages

	M	*I*	*NO*	*R*	*HI*	*100s*	*Avge*
R. Hanley	13	20	3	992	161	3	58.35
G. P. Burnett	16	28	3	1,432	212	4	57.28
*K. Greenfield	14	21	5	840	129	2	52.50
J. W. Hall	6	11	1	433	126*	2	43.30
*D. M. Smith	2	3	0	98	91	0	32.66
†C. H. H. Pegg	4	5	1	125	79*	0	31.25
B. T. P. Donelan	13	19	7	341	66	0	28.41
*†I. J. Gould	4	5	0	141	42	0	28.20
J. A. North	10	14	2	324	117	1	27.00
†D. J. Pepperell	4	5	3	54	25*	0	27.00
C. C. Remy	12	19	1	404	48	0	22.44
J. W. Dean	11	13	3	170	36	0	17.00
A. R. Hansford	3	5	2	33	12	0	11.00
A. R. Clarke	13	11	1	105	24	0	10.50
K. Newell	4	5	0	52	23	0	10.40
A. M. Babington	10	9	4	50	15	0	10.00
A. R. Cornford	8	11	2	85	23	0	9.44
R. A. Bunting	8	7	0	40	14	0	5.71

Played in five matches: P. W. Threlfall 14, 0. Played in four matches: E. S. H. Giddins 4*. Played in two matches: A. M. A. Aduhene 4*. Played in one match: T. Chadwick 9; T. de Leede 54, 33; †J. Finch 4*; I. A. Kidd 42; †P. Moores 5; H. Nankivell 14, 0*; †J. Smith 2, 1; †M. P. Speight 43; I. C. Waring 0; C. M. Wells 38.

Bowling Averages

	O	*M*	*R*	*W*	*BB*	*Avge*
A. R. Clarke	337.3	128	772	42	5-29	18.38
B. T. P. Donelan	363	114	919	46	8-40	19.97
R. A. Bunting	216.3	50	551	27	4-24	20.40
C. C. Remy	163.2	37	388	19	4-44	20.42
E. S. H. Giddins	49	8	198	9	3-20	22.00
A. R. Hansford	36	8	92	4	3-57	23.00
A. M. Babington	208.3	45	590	23	7-52	25.65
J. W. Dean	246	98	607	21	5-63	28.90
P. W. Threlfall	111	25	295	10	3-47	29.50
J. A. North	157.3	36	462	13	5-57	35.53

Also bowled: A. M. A. Aduhene 47–7–157–0; A. R. Cornford 11–4–29–0; T. de Leede 6–4–6–0; K. Greenfield 28–6–64–2; J. W. Hall 2–0–18–0; H. Nankivell 7–2–14–0; D. M. Smith 1–0–3–0; I. C. Waring 4–2–5–0.

WARWICKSHIRE SECOND ELEVEN

Matches 16: Won – Derbyshire, Gloucestershire, Hampshire, Worcestershire. Lost – Lancashire, Nottinghamshire, Sussex. Drawn – Essex, Glamorgan, Kent, Leicestershire, Middlesex, Northamptonshire, Somerset, Surrey, Yorkshire.

Batting Averages

	M	*I*	*NO*	*R*	*HI*	*100s*	*Avge*
Wasim Khan	4	5	1	234	171*	1	58.50
J. D. Ratcliffe	10	18	1	964	151	4	56.70
G. W. Humpage	4	6	0	334	122	2	55.66
D. P. Ostler	9	14	1	707	149	2	54.38
N. M. K. Smith	2	3	1	97	74	0	48.50
S. J. Green	11	15	2	538	122	2	41.38
R. G. Twose	9	14	1	480	102	1	36.92
*T. L. Penney	11	15	3	441	113	2	36.75
†P. C. L. Holloway	8	13	2	383	82	0	34.81
I. G. S. Steer	14	24	5	608	73*	0	32.00
†K. J. Piper	8	13	2	326	64	0	29.63
D. R. Brown	11	13	2	312	60*	0	28.36
A. R. K. Pierson	9	11	5	132	43*	0	22.00
G. J. P. B. Williamson	5	9	1	153	38	0	19.12
O. S. Chagar	10	12	2	156	40	0	15.60
G. Welch	12	15	6	118	22	0	13.11
P. A. Smith	4	7	0	89	34	0	12.71
G. Smith	12	10	3	45	19	0	6.42
P. A. Booth	3	3	0	15	13	0	5.00

Played in three matches: M. P. Clewley 7*, 0*; A. A. Donald 10*, 0. Played in two matches: A. J. Hunt 41, 0; T. A. Lloyd 61, 40; P. Mirza did not bat. Played in one match: Asif Din 54; M. A. V. Bell 3; †M. Burns 22; A. B. Byram 46, 0; D. B. M. Fox 1; A. J. Moles 93, 16; M. J. Pidgeon 5*; G. F. Shephard 38*.

Bowling Averages

	O	*M*	*R*	*W*	*BB*	*Avge*
A. A. Donald	88	33	175	13	6-56	13.46
P. A. Booth	101	35	211	11	4-56	19.18
P. A. Smith	92.5	21	228	10	3-29	22.80
N. M. K. Smith	54.1	18	161	7	6-48	23.00
D. B. M. Fox	34	10	97	4	4-54	24.25
A. R. K. Pierson	383.1	123	878	36	4-51	24.38
G. Smith	321	61	931	36	6-53	25.86
R. G. Twose	186.4	41	529	17	6-103	31.11
D. R. Brown	256.2	40	962	24	4-63	40.08
G. Welch	154	35	492	11	5-40	44.72
O. S. Chagar	250	58	713	15	3-60	47.53
M. P. Clewley	63.5	6	264	4	2-38	66.00

Also bowled: Asif Din 11–4–24–2; M. A. V. Bell 21–4–53–2; A. B. Byram 43–7–153–2; S. J. Green 11–1–56–1; P. Mirza 3–0–14–0; D. P. Ostler 7–4–19–1; T. L. Penney 0.4–0–0–0; M. J. Pidgeon 19–6–57–0; K. J. Piper 1–0–8–0; J. D. Ratcliffe 14–3–35–1; I. G. S. Steer 25–5–64–2.

WORCESTERSHIRE SECOND ELEVEN

Matches 16: Won – Hampshire, Middlesex. Lost – Gloucestershire, Nottinghamshire, Warwickshire. Drawn – Derbyshire, Essex, Glamorgan, Kent, Lancashire, Leicestershire, Northamptonshire, Somerset, Sussex, Yorkshire. Tied – Surrey.

Batting Averages

	M	*I*	*NO*	*R*	*HI*	*100s*	*Avge*
M. J. Weston	4	8	1	414	161	2	59.14
N. Davey	2	4	1	172	120	1	57.33
S. R. Lampitt	3	5	1	219	100*	1	54.75
*M. S. Scott	16	10	7	159	70*	0	53.00
D. A. Leatherdale	9	16	2	728	119*	3	52.00
P. Bent	12	24	1	1,116	174	2	48.52
G. R. Haynes	14	25	3	1,043	137	2	47.40
C. M. Tolley	4	7	1	252	62*	0	42.00
J. W. D. Leighton	2	3	1	81	58*	0	40.50
N. V. Radford	4	6	0	236	144	1	39.33
S. Herzberg	15	26	5	743	61*	0	35.38
G. J. Lord	11	20	0	590	94	0	29.50
S. M. McEwan	4	5	2	70	39*	0	23.33
†S. R. Froggatt	4	5	1	81	33	0	20.25
R. P. Gofton	12	18	2	318	141	1	19.87
A. Wylie	6	7	5	38	24	0	19.00
W. P. C. Weston	5	8	0	147	39	0	18.37
I. A. Kidd	3	6	0	100	33	0	16.66
R. D. Stemp	11	12	3	137	39	0	15.22
†S. R. Bevins	14	21	6	218	45*	0	14.53
G. R. Dilley	1	2	0	26	15	0	13.00
M. G. Fowles	3	4	0	18	14	0	4.50
I. T. Wood	4	6	0	26	10	0	4.33

Played in four matches: N. A. Hitchings 10, 0. Played in one match: M. S. Bevins 2; D. M. Cox 16*; S. Grant 29*; P. Mirza 22; S. A. Morgan 0; R. A. Pybus 6; S. G. Reape 9, 8; R. M. Wight 8; R. J. Coyle did not bat.

Bowling Averages

	O	*M*	*R*	*W*	*BB*	*Avge*
G. R. Dilley	33.1	6	100	9	6-46	11.11
S. R. Lampitt	52.2	12	162	9	6-57	18.00
D. A. Leatherdale	62	14	188	7	4-63	26.85
P. Bent	77	25	191	7	3-57	27.28
N. A. Hitchings	67.5	11	262	9	6-39	29.11
G. R. Haynes	255.4	65	713	24	4-33	29.70
S. M. McEwan	126	22	432	14	3-21	30.85
S. Herzberg	505	119	1,687	50	5-118	33.74
R. P. Gofton	257.5	50	877	25	3-43	35.08
S. Grant	45	7	178	5	4-78	35.60
N. V. Radford	112.4	21	440	12	9-98	36.66
R. D. Stemp	340.1	110	1,485	35	5-80	42.42
A. Wylie	111.5	14	481	11	2-28	43.72

Also bowled: D. M. Cox 12–1–59–0; M. G. Fowles 21–2–107–2; G. J. Lord 13–4–32–2; P. Mirza 21–6–83–1; R. A. Pybus 19–1–117–0; S. G. Reape 3–0–19–0; C. M. Tolley 44–12–89–1; M. J. Weston 30–8–89–1; W. P. C. Weston 50–9–181–3; R. M. Wight 26–18–28–1.

YORKSHIRE SECOND ELEVEN

Matches 16: Won – Northamptonshire. Lost – Derbyshire, Essex, Kent, Nottinghamshire, Surrey, Sussex. Drawn – Glamorgan, Gloucestershire, Hampshire, Lancashire, Leicestershire, Middlesex, Somerset, Warwickshire, Worcestershire.

Batting Averages

	M	*I*	*NO*	*R*	*HI*	*100s*	*Avge*
C. White	3	6	3	469	209*	2	156.33
K. Sharp	6	11	1	590	221*	2	59.00
*S. N. Hartley	16	24	8	715	105*	2	44.68
C. S. Pickles	5	9	1	309	76	0	38.62
†C. A. Chapman	12	22	0	748	107	1	34.00
B. Parker	5	10	1	270	105	1	30.00
A. P. Grayson	9	17	2	440	90*	0	29.33
S. J. Bartle	6	10	2	230	50	0	28.75
D. Byas	5	9	2	199	79	0	28.42
N. G. Nicholson	14	25	2	583	138	1	25.34
M. J. Doidge	15	27	3	568	81	0	23.66
P. J. Berry	13	17	5	278	119	1	23.16
J. R. Goldthorp	5	8	0	183	59	0	22.87
S. D. Fletcher	6	6	0	132	70	0	22.00
S. Hutton	3	6	0	131	43	0	21.83
M. J. Foster	2	4	0	81	40	0	20.25
S. Bethel	6	10	0	172	96	0	17.20
J. D. Batty	7	7	3	66	29	0	16.50
C. Shaw	13	12	4	85	46*	0	10.62
N. S. Taylor	3	4	0	41	17	0	10.25
I. J. Houseman	8	8	3	23	8*	0	4.60
D. B. Pennett	5	5	1	9	8	0	2.25

Also batted: †D. L. Bairstow 60, 12, 57*; R. J. Blakey 139, 36; D. Gough 0; P. J. Hartley 0, 0; P. W. Jarvis 9; S. A. Kellett 30, 16; D. Mynott 16*, 8*, 17; I. M. Priestley 43.

Note: After the first innings of the match v Hampshire at Bingley, Bairstow was called to Leeds for the Benson and Hedges Cup match v Lancashire and was replaced by Chapman.

Bowling Averages

	O	*M*	*R*	*W*	*BB*	*Avge*
C. White	95	37	235	11	7-55	21.36
N. S. Taylor	75.4	15	231	9	4-65	25.66
S. D. Fletcher	151.3	44	433	16	4-48	27.06
A. P. Grayson	106	19	348	10	3-55	34.80
P. J. Berry	310.5	95	732	21	6-77	34.85
J. D. Batty	206.4	31	716	20	5-61	35.80
I. J. Houseman	164	22	714	19	5-52	37.57
S. J. Bartle	46	4	188	5	4-109	37.60
M. J. Doidge	301.5	64	943	24	3-93	39.29
D. B. Pennett	105	13	374	9	2-19	41.55
C. Shaw	184.1	30	680	16	4-58	42.50
C. S. Pickles	126	22	401	9	3-29	44.55

Also bowled: D. Byas 18–2–45–1; M. J. Foster 18–4–55–1; J. R. Goldthorp 5–0–37–0; D. Gough 32–8–77–1; P. J. Hartley 32–4–93–0; P. W. Jarvis 32–9–80–0; N. G. Nicholson 3–0–8–0; I. M. Priestley 26–4–99–1.

SECOND ELEVEN CHAMPIONS

1959	Gloucestershire	1970	Kent	1981	Hampshire
1960	Northamptonshire	1971	Hampshire	1982	Worcestershire
1961	Kent	1972	Nottinghamshire	1983	Leicestershire
1962	Worcestershire	1973	Essex	1984	Yorkshire
1963	Worcestershire	1974	Middlesex	1985	Nottinghamshire
1964	Lancashire	1975	Surrey	1986	Lancashire
1965	Glamorgan	1976	Kent	1987	Kent Yorkshire
1966	Surrey	1977	Yorkshire		
1967	Hampshire	1978	Sussex	1988	Surrey
1968	Surrey	1979	Warwickshire	1989	Middlesex
1969	Kent	1980	Glamorgan	1990	Sussex

BAIN CLARKSON
INTERNATIONAL INSURANCE BROKERS
BAIN CLARKSON LIMITED
15 Minories
London EC3N 1NJ
AND AT LLOYD'S
Tel: 071-481 3232
BAIN CLARKSON TROPHY
A member of the Inchcape Group

BAIN CLARKSON TROPHY, 1990

orth Zone	*P*	*W*	*L*	*NR*	*Pts*	*Runs/100b*
ancashire	10	7	1	2	16	71.16
orkshire	10	6	4	0	12	68.28
orthamptonshire	10	5	5	0	10	67.83
ottinghamshire	10	4	5	1	9	65.32
eicestershire	10	4	5	1	9	60.37
erbyshire	10	1	7	2	4	62.81

outh-West Zone	*P*	*W*	*L*	*NR*	*Pts*	*Runs/100b*
omerset	8	5	1	2	12	81.47
arwickshire	8	5	2	1	11	68.71
orcestershire	8	3	4	1	7	71.25
lamorgan	8	3	4	1	7	59.89
loucestershire	8	1	6	1	3	62.13

outh-East Zone	*P*	*W*	*L*	*NR*	*Pts*	*Runs/100b*
urrey	10	7	2	1	15	67.51
ussex	10	6	3	1	13	60.81
ent	10	5	4	1	11	66.72
ampshire	10	4	6	0	8	61.49
iddlesex	10	4	6	0	8	60.00
ssex	10	2	7	1	5	51.77

otes: Warwickshire qualified for the semi-finals as the second-placed county with the ighest run-rate.

Counties are restricted to players "qualified for England" (or from a European Community ountry), only two of whom may be capped players. The matches are of 55 overs per side.

SEMI-FINALS

t Guildford, August 13. Somerset won by 27 runs. Somerset 264 for seven (55 overs) (A. N. ayhurst 42, N. J. Pringle 122 not out; G. P. Thorpe three for 41); Surrey 237 (54 overs) (R. I. ikhan 65, P. D. Atkins 32, G. P. Thorpe 47, A. D. Brown 54; A. N. Hayhurst three for 48).

At Great Crosby, August 14. Lancashire won by eight wickets. Warwickshire 159 (51.5 vers) (S. J. Green 33; J. D. Fitton four for 42); Lancashire 160 for two (40.1 overs) (T. M. rrell 71 not out, M. A. Crawley 33 not out).

FINAL

LANCASHIRE v SOMERSET

t Manchester, September 3. Lancashire won by eight wickets. Toss: Lancashire.

omerset

. N. Hayhurst c J. P. Crawley b Fitton 64
Fletcher st Wallwork b Folley 15
J. Bartlett c Folley b Martin 71
C. M. Atkinson run out 2
. J. Pringle lbw b Fitton 1
G. Swallow c Sharp b Austin 10
. P. Lefebvre not out 14
Keith Parsons b Austin 4
J. C. Hallett not out 8
B 5, l-b 4, w 2, n-b 1 12

1/49 2/142 3/151 4/152 5/175 6/175 7/183 (7 wkts, 55 overs) 201

T. Gard and H. R. J. Trump did not bat.

Bowling: Martin 11–2–46–1; Sharp 11–2–34–0; Folley 11–1–35–1; Austin 11–1–33–2; itton 11–0–44–2.

Lancashire

G. D. Lloyd b Hallett 2
*N. J. Speak c Pringle b Swallow 48
J. P. Crawley not out 85
M. A. Crawley not out 54
L-b 7, w 3, n-b 3 13

1/28 2/72 (2 wkts, 51.4 overs) 202

S. P. Titchard, I. D. Austin, J. D. Fitton, I. Folley, P. J. Martin, †T. Wallwork and M. A. Sharp did not bat.

Bowling: Hallett 11–2–54–1; Lefebvre 9–1–30–0; Hayhurst 9.4–0–48–0; Swallow 11–2–30–1; Trump 11–1–33–0.

Umpires: P. J. Eele and J. H. Harris.

WINNERS 1986-90

1986 NORTHAMPTONSHIRE beat Essex by 14 runs at Chelmsford.
1987 DERBYSHIRE beat Hampshire by seven wickets at Southampton.
1988 YORKSHIRE beat Kent by seven wickets at Leeds.
1989 MIDDLESEX beat Kent by six wickets at Canterbury.
1990 LANCASHIRE beat Somerset by eight wickets at Manchester.

UAU CHAMPIONSHIP, 1990

By GRENVILLE HOLLAND

'he 1990 season was another good one for UAU cricket. In the Benson and Hedges Cup, ıe Combined Universities once more demonstrated that university cricketers were a ›rce to be reckoned with; and given a little more experience, they could well have qualified gain for the knockout rounds. The Commercial Union UAU Championship, blessed for ıe most part with fine and sunny weather, also revealed the impressive level of cricket now eing played in the provincial universities, and the season culminated in a final of high uality.

Durham were again outstanding, and reached their seventh consecutive final. Theirs was a ıore mature and balanced team than in previous years, with three post-graduates – Rob 1acdonald, a fast bowler from the University of Cape Town, Brian Evans, the Hertfordshire pener, and Wasim Raja, the former Pakistan Test cricketer – adding depth and strength. 'heir presence, coupled to the abilities of two Combined Universities players, James Boiling ıd Jon Longley, made Durham strong contenders from the outset. Loughborough also looked powerful side, with Nick Knight, Piran Holloway and the gifted Worcestershire all-rounder, 'hris Tolley, providing the main links in a side that was strong throughout. As Loughborough 'ere in the opposite half of the draw to Durham, it might have been anticipated that a repeat f the 1989 final was in store. Exeter, however, had other ideas.

In 1990 the road to the final was a long one. In an arbitrary moment, the UAU executive ommittee decided that the structured draw, which had allowed the competition to progress moothly for many seasons, should be abandoned in favour of an open draw. This proved xpensive on overstretched Athletic Union budgets and took up a great deal of time just when udents are most hard pressed – during their summer examinations. Fortunately, throughout ıe critical period the weather held fine, and expensive cancellations and venue reversals were or the most part avoided. But another season may not be as kind.

On that long road to the final, Durham played only one game at their Racecourse ground. 'his was their first one, a league match against near neighbours, Newcastle. Batting first on a ood pitch, and with their innings anchored by Hampshire's Sean Morris (103), Durham ccumulated 286. Newcastle's response, in the face of the spin attack of Wasim Raja 15–10–14–4) and Boiling (15–7–17–4), realised only 57 runs. The following Saturday Durham isited Hull, who struggled on an unsympathetic pitch to 132 for seven in their 60 overs. The ›ft-arm spinner, Sanjay Patel, on his first outing with Durham, took five for 47 in 23 overs. ;vans's 67 led Durham's cautious reply, which required 46 overs to achieve victory by seven 'ickets.

In the challenge round, Durham were away to Reading, who elected to bat on an uneven nd turning wicket. Macdonald's opening spell was disconcertingly hostile, and the ntroduction of Boiling and Patel did nothing to reduce Reading's woes as they struggled to 71 ll out. The visitors applied themselves diligently to win by seven wickets in the 27th over. In ›und five, Durham were at Southampton, who had headed their league with comfortable 'ictories over Surrey (by 226 runs) and Reading (seven wickets). The previous week, in the hallenge round, they had beaten Hull by 170 runs, and so approached this game with some onfidence. Southampton's captain, Gary Corcoran, decided to bat on a well-prepared wicket, nd in warm sunshine, but Macdonald was again hostile, and Southampton were further estricted by Boiling's off-breaks (23–5–44–5). By lunch they were 66 for five off 39 overs, and took 48 not out in 47 balls from Timothy Butterworth to get them to 124. Morris (67 not out) nd Evans (44 not out) eased Durham into the quarter-finals and a visit to Swansea, the 1988 JAU champions.

Swansea had won through to this stage by heading their league with a narrow, one-wicket 'ictory over UWCC and a more comfortable one, by 94 runs, over UWCM. After a bye in the hallenge round they remained in Wales to visit UCNW (Bangor), whom they defeated by ine wickets. Their encounter with Durham was more taxing. The visitors chose to bat first, nd on a placid pitch runs came slowly as Morris (60) and Evans forged an opening partnerhip of 104. Longley (49) and Wasim Raja (44) then almost doubled the score and paved the vay for a total of 229 for seven. Swansea's innings was even more pedestrian, Paul Duffy's orceful, unbeaten 47 coming too late as they plodded to 182 for seven.

Leeds were also moving towards the semi-finals, although their progress had bee somewhat more chequered. In their Roses league they had been defeated at Lancaster by 3 runs, but had gone on to beat York by 170 runs at home. Run-rate placed Leeds on top of thei group, and after a bye in the challenge round they entertained Bath. Having managed 182 fc six in their 60 overs, they dismissed Bath for 133, with John Hamlin claiming five for 32. I the quarter-finals it was Manchester's turn to visit Leeds, who were dismissed in the 47th ove for 147 (Gavin Black 51). In reply Manchester, despite a tidy 57 from John Dymond, coul manage only 123 as Paul Briggs returned five for 27 and secured Leeds a semi-final agains Durham.

In the opposite half of the draw, Exeter were showing excellent form, thanks in particular t the all-round performances of their captain, Martin Barker, and Marcus Wight. Sustained b good fielding, their attack consistently restricted opposing batsmen, and it was not until th final that any one player scored more than 50 runs against them. Exeter began their seaso with a 110-run victory over Bath. Wight's brisk 55 off 93 balls led the way, and Barker's 52 i 29 balls gave them a distinct edge as they finished with 241 for six. Bath were never up t the task, and with Wight taking seven for 54 they were bowled out for 131 in the 58th ove Barker (19–3–65–5) and Wight (17–4–49–4) then held Bristol to 158 for nine, which Exete needed 50 overs to pass.

After a bye in the challenge round Exeter visited RHBNC and dismissed them in the 46t over for 165. Exeter, like Royal Holloway, lost three wickets early on, but Roger Mould (4 and Peter Baldwin (72) added 104 runs; when the score slipped to 140 for seven, a swift 21 nc out from Barker gave Exeter victory by three wickets. They now travelled to Birminghan where Barker elected to bat first on a green pitch and in hazy sunshine. Steady progres carried them to 153 for eight in the 52nd over, and a late flurry from Danny Clark and Mik Smith took the score to 207 for eight. Birmingham made a sound start, and with ten overs le needed 55. When Rowland Craddock departed for 38 after three of them, Birmingham los momentum and were all out for 190 in the 58th over.

Exeter's semi-final opponents were Loughborough, who in their opening league match ha destroyed a weak Buckingham side. Loughborough had amassed 460 for six, with a centur from Tolley, 74 from Holloway and 65 from Simon Hooper; Buckingham were bowled out fo 64 in 23 overs. Loughborough then demolished Warwick, scoring 238 for nine, Perry Rende 68, in reply to which Warwick managed only 134. In their final league match, a century fron Hooper helped Loughborough to 291 for four against Leicester, who reached 184 for eight i reply, and after a bye in round four Loughborough overwhelmed UWCC by ten wicket Their quarter-final visit to Nottingham should also have passed off without alarm, fo Nottingham were all out for 149 in the 60th over, Tolley taking five for 32. Yet now Lough borough revealed a frailty which was to return in the semi-finals. Although Knight made substantial opening contribution with 58, their other batsmen added little and they scramble through by one wicket in the 55th over.

The semi-finals and finals were played at Liverpool. By mid-June the fine weather ha broken, and outbreaks of heavy rain were crossing the Lancashire coast. Durham and Leed were scheduled to meet at Northern CC, Crosby, where the wicket was covered; but Exete and Loughborough played at Sefton CC, whose wicket was open to the elements. The game a Northern hardly lasted into the afternoon. When morning rain-clouds gave way to brigh sunshine, Leeds chose to bat on a hard, dry wicket and, for fifteen overs, made cautiou progress to 37 without loss. When Macdonald (16–9–22–5) dismissed Briggs for 15, thei innings fell apart, and the introduction of the tall Freshman, James Dakin (8.2–3–6–4), seale Leeds' fate. They were dismissed for 49 before lunch, and a brisk 52 by openers Morris an Evans carried Durham into another final.

The second semi-final was delayed into the afternoon because of morning rain, and th soggy conditions at Sefton reduced the game to 45 overs. An intelligent and penetrativ opening spell from Tolley (13–4–21–4) saw Exeter slip to 42 for five in the seventeenth over and not for the first time Clark and Barker came to the rescue in a timely and match-winnin partnership which more than doubled the score. Even so, Exeter's 138 for eight seemed hardly a daunting target for Loughborough as an opening stand of 30 between Tolley and Knight pu them on course. After 25 overs they had reached 61 for three, but from then on wickets begar to fall regularly. The tight bowling of Smith (14–4–29–3) and Wight (11.4–2–22–3) wa excellently supported in the field, and when Rendell was run out in the 29th over, Lough borough were adrift by 43 runs.

FINAL

DURHAM v EXETER

At Liverpool CC, June 20, 21. Durham won by six wickets. Toss: Durham. Wight and Hill gave Exeter a slow but secure start before being parted in the nineteenth over, but the leg-spin of Wasim Raja brought Durham a second wicket before the threatening rain interrupted play until the afternoon. After the resumption Macdonald had Baldwin caught, and there was time for Boiling to capture the vital wicket of Wight before further heavy rain stopped play a second time, with Exeter 99 for four. With the square rapidly disappearing under a sheet of water, and more rain forecast for the following afternoon, the UAU officials decided that play would recommence at ten o'clock next morning, a bold decision that just paid off. Recognising that time was at a premium, Durham's bowlers approached their task with a sense of urgency. Boiling plied his off-breaks skilfully; at the other end, Macdonald combined genuine pace with meticulous line and length. Five wickets fell for the addition of 19 runs, and despite last-wicket defiance from Snelling and Waters, Exeter lasted less than an hour. Yet as the gloom gathered, Durham in turn faltered. Evans was caught in his first over, Morris was run out by Clark's direct throw after a misunderstanding with Longley, who himself soon went, caught behind, playing at a waspish ball from Smith. Much now depended on Wasim Raja, in his last innings as a university cricketer. A motoring accident the previous December had all but ended his life, and the recovery of his cricketing skills had been a triumph of determination and dedication. At first with caution, he turned those skills on the Exeter bowling; but as lunch approached, he widened his range of strokes and accelerated. After the interval Keey lost patience against Wight, the end of an invaluable, intelligent contribution, but there were no further alarms for Durham as Wasim Raja saw them to victory.

Exeter

R. M. Wight c Ellison b Boiling 48
G. F. Hill c Keey b Macdonald 21
R. Mould b Wasim Raja 0
P. J. A. Baldwin c Longley b Macdonald 13
G. R. S. Scovell c and b Boiling 8
D. J. Clark lbw b Macdonald 12
*M. K. Barker c Longley b Boiling 6
P. Snelling b Macdonald 10
A. M. Smith c Boiling b Macdonald . . . 0
R. K. Brook b Macdonald 0
†J. A. G. Waters not out 10
L-b 4, n-b 2 6

1/39 2/45 3/80 4/90 5/107 6/111 7/114 8/116 9/118 (57.1 overs) 134

Bowling: Macdonald 28.1–5–56–6; Ellison 7–2–10–0; Dakin 2–0–13–0; Wasim Raja 5–0–17–1; Boiling 15–1–34–3.

Durham

*R. S. M. Morris run out 12
B. G. Evans c Barker b Brook 0
J. I. Longley c Waters b Smith 16
Wasim Raja not out 57
C. L. Keey lbw b Wight 32
†W. M. I. Bailey not out 11
B 2, l-b 1, w 1, n-b 5 9

1/6 2/26 3/37 4/112 (4 wkts, 44.3 overs) 137

J. R. C. Dakin, B. C. Ellison, R. H. Macdonald, J. Boiling and S. Patel did not bat.

Bowling: Smith 18–1–59–1; Brook 8–4–13–1; Barker 7–1–30–0; Wight 10.3–4–24–1; Scovell 1–0–8–0.

Umpires: K. Hopley and W. T. Robins.

THE LANCASHIRE LEAGUES, 1990

By CHRIS ASPIN

Batsmen had the best of a season which yielded a rich harvest of runs and records. The leading amateurs were only a little way behind the most successful professionals, though they made far less impact with the ball. As usual, clubs with bowling professionals did best.

East Lancashire won the Lancashire League championship after a gap of six years, thanks largely to Paul Reiffel from Victoria, who took 105 wickets and scored 770 runs. The one other bowler to reach 100 wickets was also an Australian, Colin Miller of South Australia who, playing for Rawtenstall, became only the third man since the league was formed to do the double. The feat had last been accomplished in 1949, by Cec Pepper and Vijay Hazare. Miller was also the match-winner in the Worsley Cup final, taking nine for 25, the season's best return, as Bacup were dismissed for 79 in reply to Rawtenstall's 185 for six.

The decision to replay as many rain-spoiled fixtures as possible helped the record-breakers. These included Miller's fellow-South Australian, Peter Sleep, who scored 1,294 runs for Rishton, and Geoff Parker (Victoria), close behind with 1,250 for Church, both records for their clubs. Craig Smith of Rishton became the fourth amateur in 98 years to score more than 1,000 runs in a season, his total of 1,069 (50.90) including two hundreds and nine fifties. Amateur club records were also set by Paul Simmonite, of Colne, with 970 runs at an average of 44.41, and Chris Bleazard, of Lowerhouse, with 857 (37.26). David Pearson (East Lancashire) scored 968 runs (44.00), and also claimed 53 dismissals to equal the League's 35-year-old wicket-keeping record. Bryan Knowles became the first player to complete 12,000 runs for a single club – he added another 864 for Haslingden at 37.56 – and Peter Wood (Rawtenstall), who made 790 (43.88), passed 10,000. The West Indian, Roger Harper, scored 1,010 runs and took 64 wickets for Bacup. Rishton accumulated a record 4,505 runs, including 323 which Sleep took off the unfortunate Church bowlers. In their first encounter he scored 152 not out and in the second 171 not out.

The leading wicket-takers after Reiffel and Miller were Robert Haynes, the Jamaican leg-spinner, for Accrington and Haslingden's Australian, Mike Whitney. The best amateur returns came from Mark Price (Ramsbottom) with 60 wickets at 19.27, Alan Barnes (Haslingden) with 55 at 20.11, and Jez Hope (Lowerhouse) with 53 at 22.47. Enfield had the dubious distinction of conceding 500 extras during the season.

Rochdale, for whom the South African, David Callaghan, acted as both professional and captain, won the Central Lancashire League championship for the first time since 1956. They ended the season five points ahead of Oldham, who started favourites after signing the West Indian all-rounder, Ezra Moseley. Callaghan was one of four players – three professionals and one amateur – to top 1,000 runs and he was also fifth in the bowling averages. The leading run-maker was an Australian, Geoff Foley, who scored 1,335 for Milnrow, including the season's highest score of 150 against Norden. He was followed by Carl Hooper of Guyana, with 1,118 for Werneth, Nick Hayward, the Stockport amateur, with 1,032 and an average of 39.69, and Callaghan with 1,021. Among fourteen amateurs to score more than 700 runs were Chris Dearden of Littleborough, whose 973 at 32.43 set a new record for the club, and Russell Davies (Norden) with 944 (36.31).

The bowling averages were headed by Cec Wright, the oldest player in the ompetition, who made light of his 56 years to bowl 357 overs for Crompton nd take 67 wickets at 11.78. Two professionals each took 101 wickets – Iiddleton's South African professional, Brad Osborne, and the Barbadian, 'ictor Walcott (Littleborough). Moseley took 94 wickets for Oldham, and iere were similar returns for the Australian Peter Gladigau at Norden nd Barrington Browne, the Guyanese fast bowler, at Unsworth. Among ie amateurs, Imran Adrees (Radcliffe) took 82 wickets at 16.05, Craig Iopkinson (Royton) 71 at 19.38 and Ian Hayward (Stockport) 65 at 12.25. Verneth won the Lees Wood Cup for the tenth time when they beat Norden y 37 runs in an exciting final, Hooper making 136 not out in a total of 269 or eight. The fastest scoring of the season came from Stockport's Australian rofessional, Steve Wundke, who hit the Rochdale spinner, Neil Avery, for ve consecutive sixes and completed his fifty in twelve balls.

MATTHEW BROWN LANCASHIRE LEAGUE

	P	*W*	*L*	*D*	*Pts*	*Professional*	*Runs*	*Avge*	*Wkts*	*Avge*
ast Lancashire	26	21	3	1	102*	P. R. Reiffel	770	45.29	105	11.63
Iaslingden	26	19	4	2	90*	M. R. Whitney	151	11.62	81	17.76
awtenstall	26	19	7	0	85	C. R. Miller	1,078	51.33	100	15.73
ccrington	26	17	8	0	80*	R. C. Haynes	691	46.07	88	13.89
acup	26	16	9	1	72	R. A. Harper	1,010	53.16	64	15.64
ishton	26	13	12	0	60*	P. R. Sleep	1,294	64.70	71	21.54
urnley	26	13	13	0	58	Mudassar Nazar	973	40.54	41	27.27
Ielson	26	13	12	1	56	B. P. Julian	463	46.30	16	38.38
						E. O. Simons	339	48.43	20	20.00
olne	26	11	14	1	50	H. L. Alleyne	323	29.36	49	16.92
amsbottom	26	9	17	0	43	S. Monkhouse	12	3.00	41	25.61
owerhouse	26	9	16	0	41*	D. S. Morgan	803	33.46	53	17.55
odmorden	26	7	16	2	37*	B. Williams	688	31.27	34	29.26
hurch	26	4	22	0	19	G. R. Parker	1,250	48.07	48	32.31
nfield	26	4	22	0	19	C. Killen	663	33.15	50	23.44

** Includes two points awarded in a tied match.*

Note: One point awarded for dismissing the opposition.

BROTHER CENTRAL LANCASHIRE LEAGUE

	P	*W*	*L*	*D*	*Pts*	*Professional*	*Runs*	*Avge*	*Wkts*	*Avge*
ochdale	30	20	4	6	101*	D. J. Callaghan	1,021	40.84	71	14.21
)ldham	30	19	5	6	96	E. A. Moseley	517	28.72	94	13.51
ittleborough	30	19	9	2	86	V. D. Walcott	293	10.85	101	16.17
Verneth	30	18	8	4	84	C. L. Hooper	1,118	43.00	91	16.98
tockport	30	15	9	6	81*	S. C. Wundke	944	36.31	85	15.64
Iiddleton	30	16	9	5	80	B. M. Osborne	704	32.00	101	14.76
Ieywood	30	16	8	6	77	J. Abrahams	913	39.70	40	27.73
Iorden	30	15	10	5	75	P. W. Gladigau	689	23.29	94	14.95
Ailnrow	30	13	12	5	66	G. I. Foley	1,335	55.63	48	21.46
rompton	30	11	13	6	57*	A. Johnston	429	18.65	69	17.94
Iyde	30	10	14	6	52	V. S. Greene	793	36.05	67	17.61
adcliffe	30	9	15	6	48*	K. W. McLeod	398	18.95	63	24.97
shton	30	7	18	5	36	D. Foley	487	21.17	44	24.34
Insworth	30	6	21	3	30	B. St A. Browne	54	4.05	94	19.37
oyton	30	3	22	5	20	D. Tuckwell	892	31.86	23	29.87
Valsden	30	2	22	6	15	A. G. Daley	803	33.46	77	19.35

** Includes two points awarded in a tied match.*

Notes: Five points awarded for an outright win; four for a limited win.
Averages include cup games.

IRISH CRICKET IN 1990

By DEREK SCOTT

After three years of transition, the Ireland team could glimpse a modicum o light at the end of the tunnel in 1990. They celebrated their first victory sinc 1987, and by the end of the season appeared to have a settled team. They di not do well in the five one-day games played in May and June against first class opposition, despite fielding their first non-qualified player in the India Test batsman, Raman Lamba. But these games pitted Saturday amateur against Test cricketers and county professionals. The three-day matches against mostly amateur opposition, provided real hope for the future; after run of 21 matches without a win of any sort, Ireland beat MCC, and thei games against Wales and Scotland were drawn. In these matches the Iris bowlers took 49 of a possible 50 wickets, and at the reasonable cost of 24.5 runs per wicket. P. McCrum was recalled to share the new ball with A. N Nelson, whose brother, Noel, was the third seamer. Off-spinner G. D Harrison had a most successful year, and a leg-spinner, C. Hoey, and slov left-armer, S. Taylor, were waiting in the wings. The batting had becom stable, with a new cap, the left-handed S. G. Smyth, adding variety, and th team seemed to flourish on a change of captaincy. After 25 matches leadin the side, P. B. Jackson handed the job over to S. J. S. Warke. Jackson' wicket-keeping immediately went from very good to excellent, as did Warke' batting, so the selectors were vindicated.

In early May, the New Zealanders visited Ireland for the first time sinc 1965 and won the two one-day matches, sponsored by Gilbey's Ulster Games It was much too soon for the home players to give of their best, but it must b said that these tourists were a pleasure to entertain; and it was a delight fo Irish spectators to watch Richard Hadlee take three for 25 in the first game

Worcestershire were in Dublin in early June for two similar matches sponsored by JMA, at Castle Avenue. The first was much interrupted by rai and reduced to 34 overs a side, but those lucky enough to be there in mid afternoon saw an unforgettable innings from Graeme Hick. Having reache 50 in 67 minutes, with a six and eight fours off 65 balls, he then took only te minutes and eleven balls to get to 101 not out, hitting another three fours an six sixes. When the last over began he was 73, but a final six off the last bal of the innings carried him past his century. Furthermore it was not slogging Next day it was the turn of David Leatherdale, with 76, and Ian Botham who scored 61 in 44 minutes as Worcestershire totalled 304 all out in 55 overs Ireland could not match the run-rate, but Smyth scored a splendid 59 not ou on his début.

A week later, at Coleraine, came the first three-day match of the season and Ireland's first victory for three years. MCC were the visitors for a game sponsored by Allied Irish Banks. Another new cap, A. R. Dunlop (69), anc the recently appointed captain, Warke (81), were the main contributors tc Ireland's first-innings total of 275 for eight declared. When the visitors batted, McCrum and Harrison took three wickets each, but MCC's 243 (A. J Goldsmith 76) represented a recovery from 160 for eight. On the thirc morning Ireland reached 64 for two, but then slumped to 99 all out as M. J. Thursfield took five for 15. Ironically this low score probably turned the match in their favour. Had Ireland batted on, there would have been too little time to bowl out their visitors. Chasing 132, MCC were given a flying start by Gehan Mendis of Lancashire; when Harrison bowled him, he had made 49 of his team's 55 runs. Mendis was the fourth man out, and MCC had lost two more wickets, with 46 still required, when the final hour began. However, eight overs were now lost to rain, raising the rate to 4 an over, and when O'Reilly bowled Giles Toogood for 30 MCC, with four overs to go, were 112 for nine and needed 20 to win. They were still 7 runs short when A. T. Crouch was caught on the mid-wicket boundary with five balls remaining. It was Ireland's first win since they defeated MCC at Lord's in 1987.

Ten days later they had to face county opposition again. Sussex overwhelmed them in a nine-wicket win at Downpatrick, in a NatWest Bank Trophy match which could not start until 3.30 p.m. and finished at 7.45 p.m. Six of Ireland's wickets went to Tony Dodemaide, for 9 runs, a performance which earned him the Man of the Match award.

In late July a new venue, Kimmage in Dublin, hosted the annual three-day match against Wales, sponsored by Mycil Products. A good pitch and sunshine brought plenty of runs. Warke declared Ireland's first innings at 299 for four, of which he had made 65 and D. A. Lewis 136 not out in two and a half hours, his maiden international century and the highest score by an Irish batsman against Wales. Bowling for Ireland for the first time, off-spinner Dunlop took five for 26 to give them a 97-run lead, and more consistent batting in the second innings left Wales to score 268 to win in 193 minutes plus twenty overs. They were 124 for four when A. C. Puddle and B. J. Lloyd put on 109 in 85 minutes, but Harrison, who finished with seven for 91, began to spin his way through the lower order. With 4 runs needed from the last ball, the Welsh No. 10 failed to connect and was bowled, leaving the match drawn.

The annual first-class fixture against Scotland was played at Myreside, Edinburgh, in mid-August. The only memorable features for Ireland were Warke's hundred, his second against Scotland, and Harrison's bowling. In 43.2 overs the off-spinner took nine for 113, becoming the only bowler with nine first-class wickets in an innings in the British Isles during 1990, and the first Irishman to achieve the feat since 1957. Warke and Harrison were also Ireland's leading players over the season. In eight matches Warke scored 368 at 36.80, and reached 2,000 career runs to join I. J. Anderson, S. F. Bergin, J. F. Short and A. J. O'Riordan. He was followed by Lewis, who averaged 34.55 from 311 runs, and Dunlop, with 183 runs at 36.60. Newcomer Smyth averaged 47.00 for his 141 runs. Harrison's 26 wickets came at 17.69 each, well ahead of A. N. Nelson, with 13 wickets at 29.38, and McCrum, with 11 at 37.72. Wicket-keeper Jackson claimed his 100th dismissal during the season, and M. F. Cohen earned his 50th cap.

An Irish Under-23 team spent five days in Scotland in August, playing three Scottish Districts Under-23 sides and a two-day game against Scotland Under-23, though the second day was washed out. M. A. Nulty's performances on this tour forced the selectors to recall him for the team to tour Zimbabwe in March 1991, and leg-spinner Hoey was also named for the tour. The Schools eleven was not strong in 1990, and did well to draw with England over two days at Winchester College, after losing to Wales in their three-day match at Ynysygerwn.

The Ulster Bank-sponsored Interprovincial Cup was played according to a new format, whereby the six teams assembled for a festival weekend in the

Northern area and played the nine North/South matches over three days. The remaining six games were played later on various Sundays. Ulster Country were the winners, their first success since 1979. Needing to win their last match against Ulster Town, they did so handsomely – a relief after two years in which they had not lost a match, but had drawn too often to win the tournament they had dominated in the 1970s. The Under-19 interprovincial tournament was won by North-West, while Leinster and Northern Unions shared the Under-15 tournament in Cork. For Leinster, A. Joyce scored 100 not out, 73 and 106 in three matches.

In the Schweppes Cup, a national competition at senior club level, Lurgan recorded their third win in the Cup's nine-year history, recovering from a bad start against Dublin's Clontarf when Ross McCollum struck 91 off 89 balls. Lurgan have become a force in Northern club cricket. In 1989 they won the Northern Union Cup for only the second time, and one year on they claimed their first title in the league, sponsored by Lombard & Ulster Bank, albeit having to share the honour with North of Ireland, joint title-holders three times since 1986 and outright winners in 1987. In the Cup, however, North of Ireland beat holders Lurgan by three wickets in the two-innings final – their nineteenth win since 1889. For only the third time in 26 seasons, Waringstown failed to win or share any of the competitions. In the North-West, Donemana went back a notch. They did win the Prudential-sponsored league, but only after a play-off with a revitalised Eglinton, who won the Northern Bank Cup to deprive Donemana of their usual league and cup double.

In Dublin the powerful YMCA team won the Belvedere Bond league, without losing a game, and the Sportsgear Cup. Their bid for the treble failed when they lost their semi-final of the Wiggins Teape league to Clontarf, the second-best team in the province, who went on to beat Old Belvedere in the final by ten wickets. Clontarf's D. A. Vincent scored thrilling centuries in this and the Sportsgear final, an unprecedented double. During the year it was announced that in 1993 the fourteen senior clubs in the Dublin area would be divided into two leagues of seven, with results over the intervening two seasons determining who should be in which section. All fourteen, however, will compete in the knockout cup and in the Wiggins Teape league in August. In Munster, Waterford won the cup, but surrendered their league title to Limerick. In 1990 County Galway played in this league, which necessitated a 320-mile round trip for fixtures against Waterford.

Exciting prospects for 1991 included the three-week tour of Zimbabwe in March and home matches against the West Indian tourists and against Middlesex in the NatWest Bank Trophy. Ireland also looked forward to the Under-19 tournament in Winnipeg, hoping to repeat the success of their visit to Canada in 1979 when they reached the final of this tournament for the only time.

SCOTTISH CRICKET IN 1990

By J. WATSON BLAIR

While another excellent summer produced a surfeit of runs throughout Scotland, the national side had their best season for many years with four victories, including a memorable one away to Northamptonshire in the Benson and Hedges Cup in May. Following a close encounter with

Nottinghamshire at Titwood in Glasgow, which did not end until after 7.30 p.m. on the second day, the Scotland players left for Northampton by coach. Arriving at their hotel at 3.30 a.m. was not the best preparation for an important match, but the team shrugged off tiredness to win by 2 runs and record their second success in the Benson and Hedges Cup. Ian Philip failed by just 5 runs to become the first Scot to score a century in the competition.

Although they lost their other three Benson and Hedges matches, Scotland's run-rate of 66.66 per 100 balls was the second-best in Group D after Essex, who headed the table with a scoring-rate of 82.35. In addition to Philip's efforts, there were regular contributions from Gordon Greenidge, a new recruit to Scottish colours, the captain, Richard Swan, and Omar Henry, Scotland's player-coach. Scotland met Essex again in the first round of the NatWest Bank Trophy, but Chelmsford has never been a successful ground for them, and Graham Gooch's century set up a nine-wicket victory for the county.

The visit of the Indian tourists in July attracted a large crowd to Titwood for an entertaining 55-overs game. Despite a stand of 122 runs in 81 minutes for the sixth wicket between Henry (74) and Bruce Russell (48), Scotland reached only 196 for seven, a total which the Indians passed with three and a half overs to spare, for the loss of three wickets. However, the following week the recently formed England Amateur XI were beaten by Scotland in what were loosely described as two amateur one-day internationals. Scotland won by 65 runs at Nunholm, Dumfries, and by 2 runs next day at Hamilton Crescent, Glasgow.

August brought the senior internationals to a close with a drawn match against Ireland at Myreside, Edinburgh, followed by the biennial visit to Lord's to play MCC. The former, the only regular first-class match in the calendar of Ireland or Scotland, was disrupted by rain, but Philip registered exactly 100 in Scotland's innings, his second hundred in this fixture. At Lord's, however, Scotland won for the first time since 1874. Gehan Mendis of Lancashire scored 57 out of MCC's first-innings 198 and Scotland declared at 190 for eight before lunch on the second day. A sparkling unbeaten 101 from Steve Wundke, an Australian, enabled MCC to reply with 218 for six declared, setting a target of 227, but Philip with 83, George Salmond (56 not out) and Russell (38 not out) successfully countered the MCC attack, and the clock, to score the winning runs with seven wickets to spare.

In this match the Scots were led to victory by Henry, as Richard Swan was detained by the pressures of business, and at the conclusion of the season the 38-year-old Swan announced that he was giving up the captaincy. A farmer in the Borders, and a stalwart of the Carlton club in the East League, he was educated at Merchiston Castle School and Durham University and first appeared for Scotland in 1974 against MCC. Since then he has represented his country 82 times, a figure surpassed only by Jimmy Brown of Perthshire, and has captained it on 62 occasions – well ahead of Brown, who led Scotland 53 times, and George Goddard (Heriot's FP), 35 times. To the end of 1990, his aggregate of runs in 97 innings for Scotland was 2,105 with a highest score of 100 and an average of 23.38. That total included 49 appearances in limited-overs competitions with the English counties, against whom he scored 1,128 runs with a highest innings of 64 and an average of 23.50. His first-class bowling figures must be rare: against Ireland in 1983 he returned 0.4–0–0–0 (byes from the fourth delivery gave Ireland victory). Swan received special awards from Famous Grouse and the East League for his invaluable contribution to Scottish cricket.

Scotland B began their season with two one-day matches against Durham University at the Racecourse Ground in June, losing the first and winning the second. At the end of July they travelled to Grace Road for a one-day game against Leicestershire Second Eleven, followed by a three-day match with Nottinghamshire Second Eleven at Trent Bridge. With most of the county's contract players on duty, this second game was an uphill struggle for the young Scots. Nottinghamshire declared twice, at 410 for two and 212 for five, and Scotland B replied with 359 for seven declared and 146 for eight to draw. Bruce Patterson scored 125 and 65 for the visitors. A two-day match at Under-23 level between Scotland and Ireland at Cambusdoon in Ayr petered out in a disappointing draw, washed out by rain after an interesting first day. Earlier the Irish side had beaten the North District and drawn with the East and the West in Scotland's Under-23 District Championship.

Scotland's Young Cricketers had a disappointing season. The Under-19 side lost by six wickets to the Welsh Schools in a three-day match at Titwood in mid-May, while the Welsh Under-16s triumphed by the same margin to complete the double. The subsequent visits to Lancashire to challenge the more experienced English Schools produced slightly better results. The Under-19 match was drawn, but in the Under-16 engagement the Scots were beaten in the final over. Sanjay Patel of Clackmannanshire, son of the local professional, scored 112 on his début in representative cricket and looked like developing into a fine batsman.

In the Area Championship, sponsored by Ryden & Partners, the North again won the league section, but they were beaten in the knockout by Edinburgh, who in turn were beaten in the final at Glenpark by Strathclyde West. This match, as well as avenging Strathclyde West's defeat by Edinburgh in the 1989 final, was a personal triumph for Greenock's Peter Duthie, whose performances with both bat and ball undoubtedly turned the game. Grange, champions of Division 1 in the East League, ahead of Royal High and Stenhousemuir, beat Strathmore County to win the Scottish Cup, and also won the Towry Law Cup (formerly the Masterton Trophy) and the Evening Knockout Cup. Division 2 of the Ryden & Partners East League was headed by Watsonians, with Corstorphine as runners-up, Division 3 by Fauldhouse with Marchmont second, and Division 4 by Dalgety Bay, followed by Largo. The individual awards went to two Carlton players, Hugh Parker for his batting and Allan McLeod for bowling.

The Western Union competition, sponsored by D. M. Hall, was won by West of Scotland, with Greenock and Ferguslie runners-up and third respectively. The Second Eleven champions were Greenock, and Kelburne won both the Third Eleven and Junior titles. Individual awards went to Duthie of Greenock for batting and, for the second year in succession, to Ronald McGregor (Ferguslie) for bowling. In the final of the West League Cup, Ayrshire beat the holders, West of Scotland, who also lost the Rowan Charity Cup final to Greenock. Throughout the Western Union, professionals played an important role in coaching, not only the senior sides but all players and at various levels, and their value was seen in the success of Western Union clubs in the Bank of Scotland's national age-group leagues. Ayr defeated Strathmore in the final of the Under-18 competition, and Clydesdale Under-15s successfully accounted for Freuchie in their league.

The Scottish Counties Championship was won by Ayrshire on the last Saturday of the season when they defeated their nearest challengers, Strathmore County, beaten finalists in the Scottish Cup at the beginning of the week. Aberdeenshire finished some way back in third place. Lack of sponsorship prevented the staging of the cup competition or awards for best performances. Professionals dominated the averages, but the top amateur bowler, with 23 wickets, was Colin Mitchell of Aberdeenshire, while the Ayrshire and Scotland wicket-keeper, David Haggo, was the leading amateur batsman with 428 runs. Haggo also won the Famous Grouse award for being Scotland's top wicket-keeper. Other Famous Grouse awards went to Duthie as best all-rounder, Philip of Stenhousemuir as best batsman, and McLeod of Carlton as best bowler. The achievements of Grange throughout the season deservedly won the Edinburgh club the title Team of the Year. Of their batsmen, Alec Davies and Chris Warner were consistently outstanding, while David Orr was the star of their three cup successes, scoring 493 runs without being dismissed.

Winners of the other leagues and competitions included – *Strathmore Union*: Aberdeen GSFP. *Three Counties Cup*: Aberdeen GSFP. *Two Counties Cup*: Lawside. *Border League*: Kelso, for the seventh season in succession, with a 100 per cent record. *Border Knockout Cup*: Gala. *Nottinghamshire Sports Small Clubs Cup*: Old Grammarians. *Perthshire Cricket League*: Crieff. *Bon Accord Cup*: Mannofield. *Perthshire League Cup*: Crieff. *Glasgow & District League Division 1*: East Kilbride; *Division 2*: Milngavie & Bearsden; *Division 3*: Old Grammarians. *Glasgow & District Knockout Cup*: Glasgow High/Kelvinside. *North of Scotland League*: Ross County. *North of Scotland Reserve League*: Elgin Second Eleven. *North of Scotland Knockout Cup*: Keith. *North of Scotland Reserve League Cup*: Ross County Second Eleven. *Tony Leicester Cup*: Thornliebank. *Cockspur Cup* (Scottish section): Clydesdale. *Glasgow Evening League Division 1*: Weirs; *Division 2*: Glasgow Academicals. *Glasgow Evening League Knockout Cup*: Vale of Leven. *McLays of Alloa Indoor Sixes*: Ayrshire.

The Scottish Cricket Union experienced an eventful year, with Douglas Lawrence (Royal High FP) faithfully and diligently carrying out his duties as president. His successor in 1991, Andy Little, played cricket and rugby for Glasgow High/Kelvinside for many years, and with more than a share of success. Robin Prentice retired from the office of administrator, and from May 1 a new post, general manager, was created. The first incumbent, Peter Wilkinson, was formerly a lieutenant-colonel in the Royal Marines; after a two-year spell as administrator of the Northern Ireland Cricket Association, he appeared well equipped for the job of maintaining an efficient operation as Scottish cricket looked to increase its commitments. However, the AGM of the Union, in Glasgow on December 19, revealed a considerable financial loss on the year, following a substantial profit in 1989. The post of cricket chairman, vacated by Don Haines (Poloc), was filled by Chris Carruthers, of Fettes College, who has been at the forefront of Scottish youth cricket for many years.

The SCU has been making strenuous efforts to set up a national league to commence in 1992. To date, the response has been mixed: late in 1990 the Western Union clubs rejected the idea, and the more senior clubs in the East League were of a similar mind. Discussions will undoubtedly continue throughout 1991, with sponsorship likely to be the deciding factor. Indeed, sponsorship is now essential if the game is to continue and progress, especially as costs in all departments are escalating. The SCU is indebted to the Scottish Sports Council, the Bank of Scotland, the Clydesdale Bank, the Royal Mail and many others who have provided invaluable financial assistance throughout the years.

PAKISTAN YOUNG CRICKETERS IN ENGLAND, 1990

England's Young Cricketers entertained their Pakistani counterparts for the first time – Pakistan were the only major cricketing country they had not met at Under-19 level – and did well in winning the "Test" series and sharing the honours in the two one-day "internationals". The series was sponsored by Bull as part of their commitment to the new TCCB/NCA Development of Excellence programme at Under-15, Under-17 and Under-19 age-groups.

Well captained by Moin Khan, their wicket-keeper-batsman, and managed and coached by the former Test cricketers, Majid Khan and Haroon Rashid, the young Pakistanis were an attractive touring side, with a number of players who had, or were on the brink of, experience of first-class cricket. Indeed, two of the team, Moin Khan and Zahid Fazal, went on to play for Pakistan in the Test series against West Indies. Touring England in 1990, the team had the good fortune of encountering the kindest of English summers, as well as the benefit of playing their main matches under the watchful, and sometimes stern, eyes of first-class umpires. Certainly, the stridence and frequency of their appealing, at times unwarranted, appeared to lessen as the tour progressed.

England's selectors kept faith, in the main, with the players who had wintered, not altogether successfully, in Australia. In Wayne Noon, the Northamptonshire reserve wicket-keeper, they had an ideal captain, and there were promising batting performances from John Crawley of Lancashire, Piran Holloway of Warwickshire and Matthew Keech of Middlesex. Dominic Cork of Derbyshire bowled quickly and accurately, and scored a match-saving hundred in the Third "Test", while Alex Barnett of Middlesex provided some excellent spells of left-arm spin.

The tour party was: Majid Khan (*manager*), Haroon Rashid (*assistant manager and coach*), Moin Khan (Karachi, *captain*), Ataur Rahman (Lahore), Athar Laeeq (Karachi), Masroor Hussain (Multan), Mujahid Jamshed (Lahore Division), Maqsood Rana (Lahore), Mushahid Afridi (Karachi), Naeem Khan (Sargodha), Naseer Ahmed (Rawalpindi), Rashid Mehmood (Karachi/PNSC), Shahid Hussain (Peshawar), Shakeel Ahmed (Gujranwala), Sohail Ahmed Qureshi (Hyderabad), Tariq Mehmood (Lahore), Zahid Fazal (Gujranwala/PACO).

RESULTS

Matches 14: Won 8, Lost 2, Drawn 4.

Note: None of the matches played was first-class.

v England Under-17: at Southgate CC, July 31. Pakistan Young Cricketers won by 213 runs. Pakistan Young Cricketers 312 for six (55 overs) (Mujahid Jamshed 144, Rashid Mehmood 74); England Under-17 99 for eight (55 overs) (Maqsood Rana four for 20).

v Middlesex Young Cricketers: at Ealing CC, August 1. Pakistan Young Cricketers won by 203 runs. Pakistan Young Cricketers 298 for six (55 overs) (Rashid Mehmood 113, Zahid Fazal 78); Middlesex Young Cricketers 95.

v NCA England Amateur XI: at Esher CC, August 2. Pakistan Young Cricketers won by three wickets. NCA England Amateur XI 188 for seven (55 overs) (M. J. Roberts 60, R. J. Leiper 40); Pakistan Young Cricketers 189 for seven (53.3 overs).

v MCC Young Cricketers: at Charterhouse, August 3, 4, 5. Drawn. Pakistan Young Cricketers 309 for seven dec. (Tariq Mehmood 85, Zahid Fazal 81) and 246 (Zahid Fazal 78); MCC Young Cricketers 397 for nine dec. (T. K. Chadwick 209 not out; Sohail Ahmed Qureshi six for 140) and 76 for six.

v English Schools CA: at NatWest Bank Ground, Beckenham, August 6. Pakistan Young Cricketers won by four wickets. English Schools CA 194 for seven (55 overs) (D. P. Fulton 59; Rashid Mehmood three for 47); Pakistan Young Cricketers 195 for six (Tariq Mehmood 54 not out).

v England Young Cricketers (First one-day "international"): at Lord's, August 8. England Young Cricketers won by 76 runs. Toss: England Young Cricketers. England Young Cricketers 218 for nine (55 overs) (P. C. L. Holloway 32, K. A. Butler 77, W. M. Noon 51; Athar Laeeq four for 40); Pakistan Young Cricketers 142 (42.2 overs) (Masroor Hussain 36, Zahid Fazal 39; J. C. Hallett three for 26, D. G. Cork four for 24).

v England Young Cricketers (Second one-day "international"): at The Oval, August 10. Pakistan Young Cricketers won by 23 runs. Toss: England Young Cricketers. Pakistan Young Cricketers 220 for nine (55 overs) (Rashid Mehmood 38, Shakeel Ahmed 39, Naseer Ahmed 77; D. G. Cork three for 68); England Young Cricketers 197 (52.4 overs) (P. C. L. Holloway 60, M. Keech 32, Extras 32; Athar Laeeq four for 33).

v Combined Services: at RAF Vine Lane, Uxbridge, August 11, 12. Pakistan Young Cricketers won by seven wickets. Combined Services 230 for eight dec. (Capt. J. W. F. Cottrell 45, 2nd Lt R. J. Greatorex 43, Pte J. G. Storey 41, J. Tech. A. Elks 46; Shahid Hussain four for 78) and 164 (Flight Lt A. P. Laws 55; Shahid Hussain six for 49); Pakistan Young Cricketers 220 (Shakeel Ahmed 52, Naseer Ahmed 54; L. Seaman R. Learmouth six for 76) and 178 for three (Shakeel Ahmed 78, Rashid Mehmood 55).

v Northamptonshire Second XI: at Oundle School, August 15, 16, 17. Pakistan Young Cricketers won by 236 runs. Pakistan Young Cricketers 340 (Mujahid Jamshed 163, Tariq Mehmood 54, Moin Khan 50 not out) and 252 for five dec. (Tariq Mehmood 56, Masroor Hussain 52 not out); Northamptonshire Second XI 242 (P. J. Berry 150; Shahid Hussain six for 76) and 114 (R. R. Montgomerie 37; Maqsood Rana four for 30, Shahid Hussain four for 38).

ENGLAND YOUNG CRICKETERS v PAKISTAN YOUNG CRICKETERS

First "Test" Match

At Northampton, August 18, 19, 20, 21. Drawn. Toss: Pakistan Young Cricketers. With the start delayed for two hours by overnight rain, and all of the second day washed out, a draw seemed inevitable. Rashid Mehmood and Mujahid Jamshed gave Pakistan a marvellous start with an opening stand of 156, but Barnett and Roberts, the local leg-spinner, used the conditions well and pegged them to 266 for six at the close. Rashid batted for just over three and a half hours before becoming Roberts's third victim. Some rapid scoring on the third morning prefaced Pakistan's declaration, whereupon England, principally through a stand of 155 in 40 overs between Holloway and Crawley, made their position safe, ending the day at 269 for four. Next day Butler and Roberts tried to accelerate, but Athar Laeeq held things in check and the eventual lead was 54 runs. When Pakistan started their second innings badly, losing three wickets before clearing the deficit, there was the faint possibility of the day going England's way. Instead, Zahid Fazal thwarted them with a remarkable innings of 73, twice clearing the pavilion with tremendous sixes. The ball was not returned the second time.

Pakistan Young Cricketers

Rashid Mehmood st Noon b Roberts	76 – (2) c Roberts b Gough	0
Mujahid Jamshed c Holloway b Barnett	98 – (1) c Roberts b Hallett	7
Shakeel Ahmed c Crawley b Roberts	10 – (6) c Noon b Barnett	5
Zahid Fazal b Barnett	7 – b Grayson	73
Tariq Mehmood lbw b Roberts	3 – (3) c Noon b Gough	24
Naseer Ahmed c Grayson b Gough	57 – (5) c Noon b Barnett	4
*†Moin Khan c Crawley b Barnett	1	
Shahid Hussain b Gough	34 – (7) not out	49
Athar Laeeq not out	3 – (8) c Crawley b Grayson	0
Maqsood Rana (did not bat)	– (9) b Gough	2
Ataur Rahman (did not bat)	– (10) not out	1
L-b 7, n-b 2	9 B 4, l-b 2	6
1/156 2/173 3/184 4/189 5/206 6/213 7/280 8/298 (8 wkts dec.)	298 1/1 2/23 3/45 4/68 5/100 6/122 7/122 8/162 (8 wkts)	171

Bowling: *First Innings*—Gough 13.1–3–45–2; Hallett 13–1–64–0; Cork 14–1–59–0; Barnett 34–14–69–3; Roberts 22–6–54–3. *Second Innings*—Gough 13–1–53–3; Hallett 6–1–25–1; Barnett 16–4–25–2; Cork 1–0–5–0; Roberts 11–1–57–0; Grayson 4–4–0–2.

England Young Cricketers

A. P. Grayson b Athar Laeeq	18
P. C. L. Holloway lbw b Athar Laeeq	96
J. P. Crawley lbw b Shahid Hussain	93
M. Keech b Shahid Hussain	10
K. A. Butler c Tariq Mehmood b Athar Laeeq	43
A. R. Roberts st Shakeel Ahmed b Shahid Hussain	33
*†W. M. Noon b Ataur Rahman	16
J. C. Hallett c Shakeel Ahmed b Maqsood Rana	1
D. Gough lbw b Maqsood Rana	8
D. G. Cork c Tariq Mehmood b Shahid Hussain	13
A. A. Barnett not out	4
B 3, l-b 7, w 1, n-b 6	17
1/42 2/197 3/218 4/231 5/300 6/304 7/309 8/321 9/344	352

Bowling: Maqsood Rana 20–2–67–2; Ataur Rahman 19.3–0–72–1; Athar Laeeq 31–8–90–3; Shahid Hussain 49–20–66–4; Rashid Mehmood 18–3–47–0.

Umpires: B. Dudleston and B. J. Meyer.

v English Schools CA: at Worksop College, August 24, 25, 26. Drawn. English Schools CA 188 (J. Hodgson 48 not out; Ataur Rahman four for 34) and 342 (G. Archer 98, R. Murray 61, I. Maynard 64, J. Hodgson 48 not out; Ataur Rahman three for 73); Pakistan 263 (Masroor Hussain 105; S. V. Laudat three for 58, A. C. Richards three for 50) and 207 for six (Shakeel Ahmed 61 not out; J. Hodgson three for 60).

ENGLAND YOUNG CRICKETERS v PAKISTAN YOUNG CRICKETERS

Second "Test" Match

At Leeds, August 28, 29, 30. England Young Cricketers won by nine wickets. Toss: Pakistan Young Cricketers. England's victory, with a day to spare, rewarded the players and selectors alike for much hard work, and provided compensation for some earlier disappointments. A stirring, unbeaten 114 by Moin Khan, who hit two sixes and thirteen fours, held England up on the opening day, the Pakistan captain adding 84 for the last wicket with Ataur Rahman, who kept out 57 balls while contributing 6 runs. Otherwise, the only defiance came early on from Zahid Fazal and Shakeel Ahmed in a fourth-wicket partnership of 69. Gough and Cork did sterling work after Hallett had injured a finger, fielding off his own bowling, and they fully deserved the nine wickets they shared. However, Pakistan's 277 took on a better aspect when Moin crowned his day by catching both England openers and sending the home country to supper at 26 for three. That England managed a first-innings lead of 48 was due to Crawley and the three seam bowlers. The tall, upright Crawley batted for four and a half hours and hit thirteen fours, while Hallett remained unbeaten for four hours, first adding 59 in 30 overs with Gough, following Crawley's dismissal, and then 79 for the last wicket with Cork on a pitch of increasingly variable bounce. Having experienced at first hand the problems of batting, Cork then set about the Pakistanis' second innings, taking the first three wickets in nineteen balls at a cost of 2 runs. Hallett's introduction allowed no possibility of a recovery, and in two and a quarter hours the innings was over, leaving England to score just 31 for victory.

Pakistan Young Cricketers

Mujahid Jamshed lbw b Cork	15	– c Noon b Cork	4
Rashid Mehmood c Noon b Gough	7	– b Cork	3
Tariq Mehmood c Noon b Cork	24	– c Holloway b Hallett	11
Zahid Fazal c Keech b Gough	32	– lbw b Cork	1
Shakeel Ahmed lbw b Cork	64	– c Noon b Hallett	9
Naseer Ahmed lbw b Gough	0	– c Crawley b Cork	0
*†Moin Khan not out	114	– c Noon b Hallett	6
Shahid Hussain c Butler b Cork	0	– lbw b Hallett	29
Athar Laeeq lbw b Gough	1	– c Grayson b Hallett	4
Naeem Khan c Noon b Roberts	5	– b Gough	1
Ataur Rahman c and b Gough	6	– not out	1
B 1, l-b 6, n-b 2	9	B 5, l-b 4	9
1/15 2/37 3/48 4/117 5/117 6/157 7/159 8/182 9/193	277	1/4 2/13 3/15 4/35 5/36 6/38 7/55 8/67 9/76	78

Bowling: *First Innings*—Gough 27.2–4–106–5; Hallett 3–0–21–0; Cork 24–8–73–4; Barnett 20–8–47–0; Roberts 12–4–23–1. *Second Innings*—Gough 12–5–18–1; Cork 15–7–18–4; Hallett 11.3–4–33–5.

England Young Cricketers

A. P. Grayson c Moin Khan b Naeem Khan	11	– c Zahid Fazal b Ataur Rahman	9
P. C. L. Holloway c Moin Khan b Ataur Rahman	8	– not out	20
A. A. Barnett c Rashid Mehmood b Ataur Rahman	0		
J. P. Crawley c Moin Khan b Shahid Hussain	84	– (3) not out	5
K. A. Butler b Naeem Khan	10		
M. Keech lbw b Naeem Khan	22		
A. R. Roberts c Shakeel Ahmed b Athar Laeeq	17		
*†W. M. Noon lbw b Ataur Rahman	25		
J. C. Hallett not out	55		
D. Gough c Moin Khan b Shahid Hussain	36		
D. G. Cork lbw b Zahid Fazal	45		
B 1, l-b 7, n-b 4	12		
1/19 2/19 3/25 4/42 5/99 6/132 7/175 8/187 9/246	325	1/20	(1 wkt) 34

Bowling: *First Innings*—Naeem Khan 39–12–81–3; Ataur Rahman 32–10–79–3; Athar Laeeq 35–7–105–1; Shahid Hussain 29–17–36–2; Rashid Mehmood 1–0–4–0; Zahid Fazal 1.4–0–12–1. *Second Innings*—Ataur Rahman 5–1–19–1; Naeem Khan 4.1–1–15–0.

Umpires: J. W. Holder and D. O. Oslear.

v National Association of Young Cricketers: at Millfield School, September 2, 3, 4. Pakistan Young Cricketers won by an innings and 7 runs. Pakistan Young Cricketers 339 (Mujahid Jamshed 127, Zahid Fazal 61; A. Hollioake four for 92); National Association of Young Cricketers 108 (S. V. Laudat 47 not out; Athar Laeeq four for 26, Shahid Hussain four for 28) and 224 (Wasim Khan 82, A. Hollioake 48).

ENGLAND YOUNG CRICKETERS v PAKISTAN YOUNG CRICKETERS

Third "Test" Match

At Taunton, September 7, 8, 9, 10. Drawn. Toss: Pakistan Young Cricketers. The Pakistanis, winning the toss for the third time in the series, took full advantage of first use of a benign pitch. They lost Mujahid Jamshed in the first over, but Tariq Mehmood and Shakeel Ahmed set them on their way with a partnership of 227 in 63 overs. Tariq hit eighteen fours in his 106, and Shakeel's 190 contained a six and 27 fours; he had batted for six hours when he succumbed to the new ball. Resuming next day at 384 for three, Pakistan progressed without much difficulty to 561 for five, a declaration which left England to score 412 to avoid following on. At stumps they were 123 for two, and on Sunday, after Ataur Rahman had made an early breakthrough, Keech batted determinedly for four and a half hours while scoring 87. Roberts and Noon helped, but by now Shahid Hussain was flighting his left-arm spin into the bowlers' rough and posing endless problems. By the close, England were batting again and had lost their openers. When Cork, the night-watchman, came to the wicket on Sunday evening, they needed 181 to save an innings defeat; on Monday, the final day, he batted for five hours to deny Pakistan the win which would have levelled the series. Although defence was his main object, he none the less hit seventeen fours in his 110. There was a moment, as three wickets fell to the new ball in ten overs, when it seemed Pakistan might still have a chance, but Roberts and Gough saw off the threat.

Pakistan Young Cricketers

Mujahid Jamshed c Noon b Cork	2
Tariq Mehmood c Keech b Hallett	106
Shakeel Ahmed c Hallett b Cork	190
Zahid Fazal c Noon b Barnett	99
Masroor Hussain c Keech b Barnett	74
Naseer Ahmed not out	21
*†Moin Khan not out	52
B 2, l-b 10, w 2, n-b 3	17
1/2 2/229 3/332 4/483 5/494	(5 wkts dec.) 561

Shahid Hussain, Ataur Rahman, Athar Laeeq and Naeem Khan did not bat.

Bowling: Cork 37–8–104–2; Gough 23–2–100–0; Butler 2–0–13–0; Hallett 27–7–101–1; Barnett 35–10–111–2; Roberts 39–6–120–0.

England Young Cricketers

First innings		Second innings	
A. P. Grayson c Moin Khan b Athar Laeeq	43	run out	1
P. C. L. Holloway c Moin Khan b Athar Laeeq	38	c Zahid Fazal b Ataur Rahman	4
J. P. Crawley b Ataur Rahman	41	b Ataur Rahman	34
K. A. Butler c Moin Khan b Ataur Rahman	19	(5) b Athar Laeeq	29
M. Keech c Naseer Ahmed b Shahid Hussain	87	(6) b Shakeel Ahmed b Ataur Rahman	25
A. R. Roberts c and b Naeem Khan	30	(7) not out	24
*†W. M. Noon c Naseer Ahmed b Shahid Hussain	24	(8) lbw b Naeem Khan	1
J. C. Hallett lbw b Shahid Hussain	5	(9) c Shakeel Ahmed b Athar Laeeq	0
D. Gough lbw b Zahid Fazal	3	(10) not out	19
D. G. Cork b Ataur Rahman	9	(4) c Naeem Khan b Athar Laeeq	110
A. A. Barnett not out	20		
B 12, l-b 17, w 6, n-b 10	45	B 10, l-b 9, n-b 3	22
1/91 2/100 3/148 4/173 5/242 6/311 7/323 8/326 9/332	364	1/5 2/16 3/55 4/127 5/204 6/240 7/243 8/244	(8 wkts) 269

Bowling: *First Innings*—Athar Laeeq 31–10–81–2; Naeem Khan 20–1–46–1; Ataur Rahman 31–8–79–3; Shahid Hussain 54–16–113–3; Zahid Fazal 11–4–16–1. *Second Innings*—Ataur Rahman 26–4–71–3; Naeem Khan 21–5–57–1; Shahid Hussain 31–10–55–0; Athar Laeeq 23–10–50–3; Zahid Fazal 5–2–9–0; Moin Khan 2–0–8–0.

Umpires: B. Dudleston and K. J. Lyons.

ESSO/NAYC UNDER-19 COUNTY FESTIVALS, 1990

By JOHN MINSHULL-FOGG

Essex, not unexpectedly, won the final of the fifth Esso/NAYC County Festivals, beating Hertfordshire by 92 runs at Oxford's Christ Church ground. This was the culmination of a week of cricket which had begun the previous Monday, August 13, with 32 counties taking part and playing mainly on the college grounds at Cambridge and Oxford. Gloucestershire and Buckinghamshire joined the tournament for the first time.

The counties at Oxford, in their groups, were: Somerset, Derbyshire, Hertfordshire and Leinster; Kent, Shropshire, Warwickshire and Durham; Buckinghamshire, Hampshire, Worcestershire and Berkshire; and Staffordshire, Glamorgan, Oxfordshire and Gloucestershire. At Cambridge: Middlesex, Lancashire, Surrey and Suffolk; Essex, Sussex, Norfolk and Cheshire; Yorkshire, Leicestershire, Lincolnshire and Bedfordshire; Nottinghamshire, Northamptonshire, Huntingdon & Peterborough, and Cambridgeshire. Of these, Lancashire, Yorkshire and Warwickshire (twice) had won the tournament previously.

In addition to the two new counties, the 1990 tournament introduced some amendments to the playing conditions. The overs limit was raised from 54 overs to 60 a side, and the start of play was moved forward from 10.30 a.m. to 10.45 a.m. This lengthened the hours of play significantly. Provision was made for a reduction of overs in the event of stoppages for poor weather, but only after one hour's play had been lost. It proved to be not the most ideal of changes and gave rise to a number of difficulties, not the least being the need of young cricketers to find somewhere to eat when matches finished well into the evening. At Oxford, the organisers chose to take an independent line by reverting to the original format for some matches, though the area final was played over the full distance. It produced an upset when Warwickshire, strong and confident favourites for a hat-trick of victories, were beaten by Hertfordshire, a minor county. In the Cambridge area final, Essex beat Surrey to become the first holders of the Norman Yardley Trophy, presented by the family of the late England, Yorkshire and Cambridge University captain for the winners of the Cambridge festival. Essex then travelled to Oxford that Friday evening to take on Hertfordshire the following day.

AREA FINALS

At Cambridge, August 17. Essex won by 38 runs. Toss: Essex. Essex 238 for five (60 overs) (D. J. Robinson 65, A. C. Richards 56 not out); Surrey 200 (55.5 overs) (M. Hodgson 65; T. Kemp five for 55, A. C. Richards four for 90).

At Oxford, August 17. Hertfordshire won by 3 runs. Toss: Warwickshire. Hertfordshire 174 for nine (60 overs) (S. Moffat 44; E. Bourke four for 36); Warwickshire 171 (58.5 overs) (E. Bourke 46; D. Hodges four for 38).

FINAL

ESSEX v HERTFORDSHIRE

At Christ Church, Oxford, August 18. Essex won by 92 runs. Toss: Essex. Batting first on a good pitch, Bate and Robinson gave Essex a sound start with 81 for the first wicket in 27 overs. Bate went on to complete a good half-century, and there was another from Churchill of Hornchurch as Essex piled on the pressure in pursuit of a large total. Hertfordshire in reply were quickly in trouble, losing three wickets for 14, all to Carpenter of Chingford. Benyon, the captain, and Smith, both of the Welwyn club, added 50, but that was the only serious resistance before Kemp and Ranawat, the latter spinning the ball tidily, bowled out the minor county inside their allotted 60 overs.

Essex

M. R. Bate run out	50
D. J. Robinson b Wilkins	34
*S. C. Ecclestone c Griffin b Skeggs	25
Gul Abbas c Easterbrook b Yeabsley	22
A. Churchill b Yeabsley	55
A. C. Richards c Chippeck b Wilkins	23
†R. Rollins run out	22
R. Slater run out	0
A. Ranawat not out	0
L-b 17, w 3	20
1/81 2/118 3/144 4/150 5/189 6/246 7/251 8/251 (8 wkts, 60 overs)	251

J. Carpenter and T. Kemp did not bat.

Bowling: Easterbrook 8–2–24–0; Skeggs 14–5–43–1; Wilkins 16–1–77–2; Hodges 7–0–34–0; Yeabsley 15–3–56–2.

Hertfordshire

S. Moffat lbw b Carpenter	2
D. Chippeck b Carpenter	6
S. Crosier c Richards b Carpenter	0
R. Smith c Robinson b Ranawat	24
*D. Benyon c Bate b Ranawat	39
A. Wilkins c Richards b Kemp	5
M. I. Yeabsley c Ecclestone b Kemp	30
T. Skeggs run out	0
†A. Griffin lbw b Ranawat	0
D. Hodges not out	31
S. Easterbrook st Rollins b Ranawat	7
B 4, l-b 3, w 8	15
1/5 2/7 3/14 4/64 5/72 6/101 7/101 8/103 9/137 (56.3 overs)	159

Bowling: Slater 5–0–12–0; Carpenter 7–3–18–3; Ecclestone 4–1–9–0; Kemp 21–2–54–2; Ranawat 19.3–3–59–4.

Umpires: D. O. Oslear and R. Palmer.

SCHOOLS CRICKET IN 1990

Of the players capped for English Schools Under-19 in 1989, only M. A. Khan, T. C. Walton and A. C. Richards were available in 1990, C. J. Hawkes, T. A. Radford and R. J. Warren preferring to play for their county Second Elevens. Including the two matches at Lord's, played under the appellation of MCC Schools, fifteen players appeared for the senior Schools side. They were: G. Archer, D. P. Fulton, N. F. Gibbs, J. Hodgson, M. A. Khan, J. Laney, S. V. Laudat, I. Maynard, R. Murray, M. Rawlings, A. C. Richards (captain), J. N. Snape, T. C. Walton, Wasim Khan and W. P. C. Weston. Their schools may be found in the scorecards of matches played at the MCC Festival, Oxford.

As in other cricket arenas in 1990, the bat was dominant, and it soon became apparent from the regional trials that quality bowlers, particularly fast bowlers, were in short supply; a view confirmed at the Oxford Festival, where the majority of wickets fell to the spinners. This imbalance in the attack led to all four international matches being drawn, which was especially disappointing after MCC Schools' fine victory over a strong MCC side at Lord's and their having the best of a draw against NAYC the next day.

The batting was strong right down the order, although there was a tendency for batsmen to get out when seemingly well set. None the less, Archer, Fulton, Wasim Khan, Murray, Snape, Walton and Laney all made significant contributions, and the batting ability of the lower order was in evidence against Welsh Schools and Pakistan Young Cricketers. The main strike bowlers were Weston and Laudat but, with the exception of the Irish match, they were unable to capitalise on an initial breakthrough. The spinners were the leading wicket-takers, both Richards (off-spin) and Hodgson (leg-spin) bowling for long spells with accuracy and good variation. In a side which at times fielded quite brilliantly, Archer and Walton were outstanding, while Marcel Khan kept wicket competently and Richards captained with authority.

The first international was played against Irish Schools at Winchester College on July 26, 27. English Schools batted first, reaching 270 for nine in the allotted 60 overs with Fulton (82), Archer (50), Laney (31) and Snape (36) the main contributors. Weston's fast left-arm bowling then reduced Ireland to 23 for five, but a brave 51 from Taylor led something of a recovery to 121 all out, Weston finishing with five for 38. Following on, the Irish were 95 for five at the close, still in arrears, but the weather cut into the second day, and Ireland occupied the crease long enough in making 170 to leave English Schools only two overs in which to score 22 for victory. Five deliveries brought no run, and when 6 were needed off the last ball, only a single resulted.

At Pontarddulais on July 30, 31, Wasim Khan (105) and Fulton (68) opened with a partnership of 175 after Welsh Schools had put the English in, but some irresponsible batting further down the order led to a final total of only 228 for eight. The Welsh batting was equally disappointing, only J. R. A. Williams (36) putting up much resistance against steady bowling from Laudat (three for 24 off 15 overs) and Richards (four for 37 from 22.2) as the home side were dismissed for 152. With the exception of a positive 40 from Fulton, English Schools batted unconvincingly until an attractive partnership between Marcel Khan (34) and Laudat (39 not out) enabled

Richards to declare at 190 for nine. A target of 267 in two and a half hours plus twenty overs asked a lot of the Welsh, who mustered only 149 for seven from 59 overs.

Against Scottish Young Cricketers at Aigburth, Liverpool, on August 2, 3, English Schools elected to bat on an excellent pitch in superb weather and totalled 263 for six in 60 overs. Fulton (70) was again in good form and Snape fashioned a class innings of 88. The Scots struggled against the in-swing bowling of Walton, who took six for 17 in 9.4 overs, and were all out for 128 in 46.4 overs. When the Scots followed on, however, the English attack was once again unable to repeat its earlier performance, lacking in determination somewhat, and a century from Patel and fifties from Mudie and Garden allowed the visitors the safety of a declaration at 335 for seven and a fairly academic target of 201 in 100 minutes. English Schools were 148 for four (Snape 48, Laney 51 not out) at the close.

English Schools lost their one-day game against Pakistan Young Cricketers at Beckenham on August 6 by four wickets, despite having put up a good performance against strong opponents. Unfortunately, several first-choice players were not available for the three-day fixture at Worksop College on August 24, 25, 26. Given first use of a fresh pitch by Richards's decision to bat, the Pakistani seam attack reduced English Schools to 78 for six at lunch. Another wicket fell soon after, but the depth of batting showed as the last three wickets put on 100, Marcel Khan (25), Laudat (22), Rawlings (22) and especially Hodgson (48 not out) all batting with skill and application. A total of 188 looked useful when the Pakistanis also struggled against the new ball and slumped to 20 for three. However, Tariq Mehmood and Masroor Hussain steadied the innings, and Masroor went on next day to a fine 105. The English bowlers stuck to the task, though, and the visitors' lead was restricted to 75. Batting again, Maynard (64) and Archer added 106 in fine style, and with two overs of the day remaining a score of 247 for three was just reward for sensible strokeplay. However, Archer was dismissed in the penultimate over, missing by 2 runs a well-deserved century, and when in the last over Murray (61) trod on his wicket, the commanding position was gone. Needing 268 in 56 overs, the Pakistanis found themselves 127 for six, but Shakeel Ahmed (61 not out) guided them to 207 for no further loss to frustrate English hopes of victory. This fine, fluctuating game showed English Schools cricket at its best, especially in terms of sportsmanship and attitudes to opponents and umpires.

The Welsh Schools' season was dominated by the batting of the captain, D. L. Hemp, who scored a century in each innings against both Scottish Young Cricketers and Irish Schools. At Titwood, Glasgow, Scottish Young Cricketers declared at 306 for six (S. Millin 76 not out, N. McRae 54), to which Welsh Schools responded with 289 for four declared (Hemp 104 not out, B. Davies 65). Second time around, Scotland were dismissed for 204 (D. Rigby 48; R. Beaumont five for 40, Davies four for 49), whereupon Hemp struck 101 not out and Davies 41 as Wales made 225 for four for victory. At Ynysygerwn, Irish Schools were beaten by 202 runs. Batting first this time, Welsh Schools amassed 367 (Hemp 120, Williams 43, Davies 43; F. Ward three for 86, S. Taylor three for 87) before dismissing Irish Schools for 226 (S. McCready 76 not out; E. P. M. Holland four for 57) and then racing to 237 for one declared (Hemp 102 not out, A. J. Jones 106 not out). A change of batting order was of no avail to the Irish, who were bowled out for 176 (J. Kennedy 50; Davies four for 37).

HMC SOUTHERN SCHOOLS v THE REST

At Wadham College, July 15, 16. HMC Southern Schools won by three wickets. The Rest made a poor start, with two run-outs in the first half-hour contributing to the loss of four wickets for 44 as Yeabsley and Stevens bowled good opening spells. However, Walton and Kendall initiated a recovery and Murphy hit vigorously at the end. Fulton then played the best innings of the match, receiving useful support from the Southern Schools' middle order, and a significant lead looked in prospect until the off-spin of Chetwood and Snape pegged them back. When the Rest batted again, Janes made a solid 60, and with more vigorous knocks from Brand and Snape, Walton was able to set a target of 215 in 53 overs. Walker anchored the early part of Southern Schools' challenge, and a final flourish from Fulton took them to victory with seven balls to spare. The wicket-keeping was competent, Jaggard held three good catches, and the ground fielding of Fulton, Walton and Kendall stood out.

The Rest

C. M. Jaggard (*Merchant Taylors', Northwood*) run out	9	– c Maddock b Stevens	7
M. J. Brooke (*Batley GS*) lbw b Yeabsley	7	– (3) b Yeabsley	4
A. J. Brand (*Merchant Taylors', Northwood*) run out	9	– (5) c Walker b Richards	57
J. N. Snape (*Denstone*) b Stevens	4	– c Semmence b Richards	39
*T. C. Walton (*Leeds GS*) b Semmence	38	– (6) c Maddock b Semmence	22
J. T. C. Kendall (*Bradfield*) c Inglis b Stevens	44	– (7) b Stevens	0
†S. C. Janes (*Hampton*) lbw b Richards	8	– (2) run out	60
H. J. P. Chetwood (*Eton*) not out	11	– c and b Yeabsley	28
J. M. Windsor (*Repton*) b Richards	7	– not out	1
J. G. H. Murphy (*Barnard Castle*) b Yeabsley	33		
J. G. Slater (*Ellesmere*) c Maddock b Yeabsley	0		
Extras	16	Extras	23
1/19 2/28 3/29 4/44 5/96 6/129 7/130 8/144 9/186	186	1/18 2/30 3/112 4/182 5/197 6/197 7/230 8/241 (8 wkts dec.)	241

Bowling: *First Innings*—Stevens 16–3–32–2; Yeabsley 12–2–55–3; Semmence 9–5–14–1; Salter 10–2–42–0; Richards 11–2–33–2. *Second Innings*—Yeabsley 7–2–15–2; Stevens 17–1–73–2; Salter 15–5–43–0; Semmence 9–0–42–1; Richards 14–2–49–2.

HMC Southern Schools

C. N. Gates (*Brighton*) c and b Murphy	16	– c Murphy b Slater	20
D. P. Fulton (*Judd*) c Windsor b Chetwood	67	– (8) not out	20
*A. C. Richards (*Forest*) c Jaggard b Chetwood	21	– c and b Windsor	0
B. D. Atwell (*Sherborne*) c Jaggard b Windsor	13	– (6) c Janes b Snape	19
M. J. Walker (*King's, Rochester*) c Snape b Chetwood	21	– (2) c Janes b Murphy	63
J. M. A. Inglis (*Solihull*) b Snape	26	– (5) c Jaggard b Snape	38
†A. R. Maddock (*Plymouth*) c Janes b Snape	23	– (4) run out	18
M. J. Semmence (*Hurstpierpoint*) not out	6	– (7) st Janes b Snape	20
R. S. Yeabsley (*Haberdashers' Aske's*) c and b Snape	1	– not out	6
R. M. Salter (*King Edward VI, Southampton*) run out	0		
S. W. Stevens (*Sherborne*) b Chetwood	0		
Extras	19	Extras	14
1/55 2/101 3/117 4/136 5/162 6/206 7/207 8/213 9/213	213	1/51 2/54 3/111 4/118 5/150 6/185 7/204 (7 wkts)	218

Bowling: *First Innings*—Windsor 11–5–17–1; Slater 9–0–47–0; Kendall 3–0–19–0; Murphy 6–1–23–1; Snape 6–1–19–3; Chetwood 15–2–48–4; Walton 7–2–26–0. *Second Innings*—Windsor 7–0–20–1; Slater 10–3–58–1; Chetwood 14–2–48–0; Murphy 8–0–12–1; Snape 9.5–0–46–3; Walton 3–0–20–0.

ESCA NORTH v ESCA SOUTH

At Keble College, July 15, 16. Drawn. Although ESCA North always had the better of the match, they were unable to break through the solid defence of Gibbs and Hodgson to force the win that had looked likely when ESCA South were 37 for five in pursuit of 241. Strokeplay was not easy on the slow and turning wicket, yet it was still surprising that none of the five batsmen who reached 40 in the first three innings could go on to a half-century. Bourke's off-spin and Weston's medium-fast left-arm seam bowling for the North particularly caught the eye, while Hodgson and Jacques both bowled good spells of spin for the South.

ESCA North

Batsman	First innings		Second innings	
*Wasim Khan (*Josiah Mason SFC; Warwicks.*)	b Mirza	2	c Maynard b Bates	40
G. Archer (*Stafford CFE; Staffs.*)	c Morgan b Hodgson	43		
R. Hughes (*Newbold-on-Avon; Warwicks.*)	b Hodgson	42		
S. V. Laudat (*Oxford CFE; Oxon.*)	b Hodgson	12	c Gibbs b Jacques	19
†M. A. Khan (*Aylesbury CFE; Oxon.*)	c Sims b Bates	18	(3) lbw b Mirza	8
R. Murray (*Brigshaw; Yorks.*)	b Mirza	36	c Jacques b Bates	0
R. A. Kettleborough (*Worksop; Yorks.*)	c Bates b Gibbs	35		
E. Bourke (*Archbishop Grimshaw; Warwicks.*)	not out	2	(7) not out	31
W. P. C. Weston (*Durham; Durham*)	not out	0	(5) not out	40
R. Catley (*Ipswich; Suffolk*)	(did not bat)	–	(2) b Mirza	7
Extras		43	Extras	14
1/4 2/96 3/96 4/131 5/139 6/228 7/233	(7 wkts dec.)	233	1/29 2/42 3/77 4/87 5/88 (5 wkts dec.)	159

G. Chapple (*West Craven HS; Lancs.*) did not bat.

Bowling: *First Innings*—Rawlings 8–1–19–0; Mirza 12–1–53–2; Jacques 4–0–24–0; Gibbs 12–6–24–1; Bates 10–4–29–1; Hodgson 14–3–48–3. *Second Innings*—Rawlings 11–1–37–0; Mirza 12–1–46–2; Hodgson 7–3–16–0; Bates 12–6–21–2; Gibbs 4–1–9–0; Jacques 10–5–16–1.

ESCA South

Batsman	First innings		Second innings	
H. Morgan (*Westlands; Devon*)	c Archer b Bourke	40		
I. Maynard (*QMC Basingstoke; Hants*)	b Bourke	23	c Kettleborough b Bourke	28
J. Laney (*St John's; Wilts.*)	lbw b Bourke	0	(1) b Weston	1
P. Sims (*Lowestoft CFE; Suffolk*)	c and b Bourke	7	(3) lbw b Bourke	12
*N. F. Gibbs (*Millfield; Som.*)	b Weston	23	(6) not out	44
J. Hodgson (*Ranelagh; Berks.*)	c Kettleborough b Weston	23	(7) not out	18
M. Rawlings (*Filton; Avon*)	c Wasim Khan b Weston	6		
†M. Garaway (*Medina; IOW*)	not out	16	(4) c Archer b Bourke	0
R. Bates (*Stamford CFE; Lincs.*)	not out	1	(5) c Archer b Catley	0
Extras		13	Extras	6
1/60 2/64 3/67 4/84 5/120 6/136 7/136	(7 wkts dec.)	152	1/6 2/34 3/34 4/35 5/37 (5 wkts)	109

P. Mirza (*E. Birmingham; Warwicks.*) and P. T. Jacques (*Millfield; Som.*) did not bat.

Bowling: *First Innings*—Weston 11–5–24–3; Chapple 8–1–20–0; Catley 19–8–41–0; Bourke 18–8–35–4; Kettleborough 4–1–20–0. *Second Innings*—Chapple 10–2–27–0; Weston 8–3–6–1; Bourke 17–10–18–3; Catley 15–4–39–1; Laudat 10–1–16–0.

At Keble College, July 16. Drawn. A. C. Richards's XI 234 for eight dec. (D. P. Fulton 116, R. Hughes 36, Extras 35; P. T. Jacques three for 42, R. A. Kettleborough three for 16); Wasim Khan's XI 227 for seven (Wasim Khan 66, C. M. Jaggard 35, R. Bates 40; P. Mirza three for 48, A. C. Richards three for 63).

At St Edward's School, July 16. N. F. Gibbs's XI won by 54 runs. N. F. Gibbs's XI 259 for five dec. (G. Archer 169, J. Laney 49); T. C. Walton's XI 205 (I. Maynard 38; W. P. C. Weston three for 48).

At Christ Church, July 17. MCC Schools East won by 71 runs in a twelve-a-side match. MCC Schools East 267 for seven dec. (R. Murray 58, T. C. Walton 88, A. C. Richards 35; N. F. Gibbs three for 36, P. T. Jacques three for 95); MCC Schools West 196 (J. Laney 97, M. A. Khan 33; W. P. C. Weston three for 22, A. C. Richards three for 55).

The match at Lord's between MCC and MCC Schools may be found in the MCC section, and that at Lord's between MCC Schools and the National Association of Young Cricketers may be found in Other Matches at Lord's, 1990.

Reports from the Schools:
In a summer memorable for high scoring in county cricket, school records tumbled also. However, it is interesting to note, at a time when there has been concern over the shortening of the summer term because of exams, that a number of schools seem to be playing more matches, with the result that many schoolboy batsmen are getting more innings than in recent years. Eleven from the schools reviewed here passed 1,000 runs: C. N. Gates of Brighton (1,378 at 72.52), C. M. Jaggard (1,364 at 62.00) and A. J. Brand (1,311 at 72.83), both of Merchant Taylors', Northwood, A. R. Maddock of Plymouth College (1,128 at 86.76), J. M. Attfield of Wellingborough (1,116 at 85.84), D. P. Kerkar of Ardingly (1,102 at 61.22), D. Bowen of Enfield GS (1,089 at 64.05), K. A. Graham of King's, Macclesfield (1,075 at 76.78), G. W. White of Millfield (1,061 at 62.41), G. A. H. Awudu of Bedford Modern (1,009 at 56.05) and G. J. Kennis of Tiffin (1,008 at 72.00). Of these only Maddock played fewer than nineteen innings. No batsman recorded a three-figure average, the highest being 97.50 from 780 runs by J. M. A. Inglis of Solihull.

As runs flowed in conditions favouring batsmen, the bowlers often struggled, and a feature of the season was the high proportion of draws. Although they fared better during the poor weather of June, no bowler took 60 wickets, although twelve collected 50 or more. A. R. C. Gilmour of Merchiston Castle had the highest return with 59 at 9.45, while C. J. Eyers of Royal GS Worcester was the outstanding all-rounder with 932 runs and 51 wickets. Notable individual performances included double-centuries by Brand, S. A. I. Dyer of Campbell College, R. C. Weston of The Leys and G. W. White of Millfield. N. C. L. Sinfield of Monkton Combe took all ten wickets v Dauntsey's, who were also the victims of a hat-trick by S. B. Thomas of Wycliffe. Other hat-tricks were performed by S. C. James of King's, Macclesfield, and D. C. Hindle of King's, Ely, who had two in successive matches.

Alleyn's, Ashville College, Bedford, Bradford GS, Canford and Uppingham all participated in the Sir Garfield Sobers International Schools Festival in Barbados, where Canford and Uppingham were perhaps unfortunate not to reach the final. In their semi-final v Harrison's College, Canford were well placed at 40 for three in pursuit of 93 when rain ended play. They lost the replay. The weather similarly rescued Presentation College, who, on a difficult pitch, had been reduced by Uppingham to 6 for five in reply to 66. The English school could not gain the same advantage the next day, and the Trinidad college qualified for the final, which Harrison's College won by ten wickets.

In a relatively successful season, **Abingdon** lost only to RGS High Wycombe in schools matches, and that after a sporting declaration. Their six wins included those v Magdalen College School, Douai and St Edward's, Oxford early in the season and University College School at the end. Frequently batting second in pursuit of a target, the batsmen had limited chances to score consistently, although the opening pair of D. E. Stanley and J. S. Tilley often provided a sound base. Although there was depth in the bowling, the lack of a top-rate spinner was evident. Highlights for **Aldenham** were S. P. Moffat's unbeaten 131 v Liverpool College and a return of six for 23 by M. Okoro v Mill Hill. Unbeaten in their domestic matches **Alleyn's** enjoyed six wins, their best record for many years, while at the Sir Garfield Sobers festival in Barbados they lost only to the two eventual finalists. The batting of the captain, P. C. Berglund, was the outstanding feature of the summer, especially his 131 not out v Highgate. A. C. Winter, opening the bowling, took 38 wickets in England, plus another twelve in Barbados, and his 116 not out there v Ashville College was the highest score of the tournament. P. Haslam took 24 wickets in his first season as a leg-spinner.

Allhallows managed no wins and were beaten seven times, a disappointing record which they attributed to their batting, bowling and fielding rarely coming good at the same time. The best performance was in the narrow defeat by Exeter School, against whom J. M. Rowe made a splendid unbeaten 122 in a total of 170 for five declared. Rowe, the captain and opening bat, invariably gave the side a good start, and he bowled his off-spin intelligently to take most wickets. R. J. Gilmore was the outstanding bowler at **Ampleforth**, his 51 wickets including a return of seven for 54 v Sedbergh. **Ardingly** won more than half their matches, notably v Lancing, Sevenoaks and St George's, Weybridge, while the only defeats were by Brighton (twice) and Reigate GS. D. P. Kerkar (1,102 runs) and the captain, M. T. E. Peirce (929 runs), both passed the previous record aggregate for the school, as well as taking 38 and 34 wickets respectively. Against Worth, Peirce hit 123 not out in a total of 269 for six, whereupon C. S. Spencer took seven for 12 in eight overs to help dismiss their opponents for 43. **Arnold** were captained by a fifth-former, M. J. Clinning, who was their most successful cricketer, whether as batsman or off-spin bowler. The other top-order batsmen tended to get out in the twenties. I. Best, bowling at medium pace, beat the bat regularly and headed the averages. Victories were recorded v Kirkham GS, Hutton GS, Bangor GS and RGS Clitheroe. A highlight for the unbeaten **Ashville College** XI was an opening partnership of 215 v Bury between the brothers, A. W. and S. R. Alexander.

All fourteen matches played by **Ballymena Academy GS** produced a positive result, ten finishing in their favour. Low-scoring games were the norm on the soft, slow wickets of May and June: Bangor GS were dismissed for 59 (M. McGladdery four for 9) in reply to 80, Antrim GS for 56 in reply to 142, and Larne GS for 85, a total overtaken for the loss of three wickets. In a season of rebuilding, **Bancroft's** results did not reflect accurately the XI's cricket. Fifteen-year-old C. S. Greenhill batted with commendable concentration and determination to total 640 in his first season, just 19 short of the record aggregate, while his opening partner, T. M. Dowling, scored quickly and stylishly, in addition to keeping wicket efficiently. T. C. Dolan, the captain, and T. W. Clark also scored freely, but called on to open the bowling neither was able to produce a match-winning performance. Though somewhat under-bowled, the side's three spinners – J. P. Manning (leg-breaks and googlies), R. Patel (off-breaks) and A. A. Khan (left-arm) – took 67 wickets between them. Under the astute captaincy of M. W. R. McCord, **Bangor GS** enjoyed another profitable season, although inconsistent batting was of continued concern. McCord (slow left-arm) took his wickets for the school to 171 and shared 89 with R. G. Scott, a fast-medium bowler whose aggregate rose to 102. Both players represented Irish Schools.

Barnard Castle failed to live up to expectations; the potentially strong batting performed only moderately, and the bowling tended to lack penetration. Still, they won six matches, notably those v The Edinburgh Academy and St Peter's, York, and enjoyed a successful tour of Denmark. A highlight was the unbeaten hundred v RGS Newcastle by J. G. H. Murphy, who in his final year improved his school figures to 1,684 runs and 137 wickets. **Bedford** beat The Leys, Rugby and Repton and lost to just two schools. R. W. H. Smith scored 578 runs in his second year as captain, with excellent hundreds v MCC and Uppingham, while B. J. A. Miller, as well as keeping wicket tidily, also passed 500 runs. The lower-order also contributed, more than once seeing the side past 200 after a stuttering start. Openers R. J. Stone and M. B. Jenkins toiled manfully, though lacking penetrating pace, but Smith could call on a variety of spin. It was encouraging to see both leg-spinners, A. Focken and D. R. Fossey, operating regularly in tandem. R. M. Pape, an Under-15 fast bowler, marked his début with five for 19 v Repton at the end-of-term festival.

Bedford Modern's excellent season contained victories over Christ's College Cambridge, St Albans, Stamford, The Leys, The Perse, Watford GS, Gentlemen of Bedfordshire and RGS Worcester, who were bowled out for 55 in reply to 224. They lost only to Scots College, from Sydney, in a 40-overs match. The captain, G. A. H. Awudu, scored 1,009 runs with four centuries, his highest being 148 v Nottingham HS, and there were two hundreds from E. R. Osborn. Two promising spinners, A. R. Woodcock (left-arm) and P. D. Brownridge, gave balance and contrast to the three strike bowlers, M. C. Waddingham (left-arm), Awudu and M. J. Rolton, and all five took 25 or more wickets. Among many noteworthy returns, Rolton took eight for 14 v Christ's College, Waddingham six for 13 v Selwyn College, and Awudu seven for 28 v Watford.

Beechen Cliff, who exceeded 200 in seven of their ten innings, finished with five wins, including those v Bristol GS, Kingswood and Lansdown CC's midweek XI. The captain, P. Tisdale, and wicket-keeper S. Bryan hit two hundreds each in four consecutive matches, and among six successive century opening partnerships was a school-record 210 between Tisdale and D. Benton v Wells Cathedral School. Bryan, whose eight innings yielded 604 runs, went on to play for Somerset Second XI. The attack was dominated by A. Piper (fast-medium) and D. Perryman (leg-spin), the only two bowlers to take ten wickets. In schools matches, **Berkhamsted** beat Brentwood, Mill Hill, St Albans, St Lawrence Ramsgate and – having recovered from 18 for six to 124 – Bishop's Stortford. E. P. Shek, the captain, was a consistent left-handed opening bat whose 821 runs included a brilliant 123 v Aldenham, and of the many other batsmen who contributed, D. T. Wotherspoon hit 99 in 80 minutes v Brentwood. A strong attack was spearheaded by R. D. Hilton and M. J. Spooner, with main support coming from medium-pacers J. M. Rennie and R. D. Collett (six for 28 v Kimbolton). B. P. Howard, a young left-arm spinner, gained in confidence during the term and headed the averages. A good season finished with a tour of Holland, where all three matches, played on the mat, were won.

Birkenhead, with a strong side, achieved less than might have been expected, and it was felt that most of the drawn games could have been won. L. C. Parnell, a sensible, positive captain, batted and bowled fast-medium aggressively, and N. D. Cross hit centuries in difficult conditions v King's Macclesfield and Manchester GS; against the latter, Parnell scored 50 not out and then took six for 10 in seventeen overs. The leg-spin of D. A. Allan won two matches, and all the bowlers benefited from the outstanding fielding at short leg of I. G. Berry, who held fourteen catches in eight games. **Bishop's Stortford**, a particularly young side, beat Kimbolton, Dean Close, Wrekin and St Edmund's, Ware, but experienced eight defeats. Unexpectedly brittle batting – an exception being E. M. Peachey's maiden hundred v MCC – and a failure to exploit several commanding positions contributed to their undistinguished record. None the less the bowling was good. R. S. Jayatileke, a Sri Lankan off-spinner, took seven for 6 v Kimbolton, and D. N. Child, the captain, had six-wicket hauls v Berkhamsted and Dean Close. With their Under-17s reaching the South final of the Barclays Bank Cup, and the majority of the First XI expected to return, the college looked to 1991 with optimism.

Bloxham, playing mostly afternoon matches, often found results elusive, particularly on their own excellent pitches, even if batsmen did not always take full advantage of them. Rendcomb, Shiplake, Dean Close and MCC were all beaten. R. D. Beaty performed well both with gloves and bat, proving especially effective in a crisis at No. 7 or No. 8. E. R. H. Wornum (fast-medium in-swing) was the leading bowler, capturing an impressive 41 wickets. With only one win in schools matches and an exciting tie v Taunton, **Blundell's** were left to reflect on their inability either to defend a reasonable total or to score sufficient runs. M. R. N. Hunt, the captain, had a fine season with the bat, but his 524 runs were nearly twice the next aggregate. However, a record of one victory and three defeats in thirteen matches does not do justice to the strong batting side of **Bradfield College**. S. P. Bridgman's 596 runs featured two successive unbeaten hundreds – v Stowe, where he mastered some fiery opening bowling, and v the Old Boys. J. T. C. Kendall, an excellent captain, set a fine example with 25 wickets and 494 runs, his 153 not out v Westminster including a hundred before lunch. His younger brother, W. S. Kendall, also passed 400 runs.

An eventful season for **Bradford GS** culminated in the visit to Barbados for the Sir Garfield Sobers festival in July. The high number of drawn games reflected both a lack of penetration in the bowling and relative inexperience in the batting. Five of the seven victories came in limited-overs games, as did four of the six defeats. The consistent N. J. Gomersall and the captain, D. C. Whitfield, dominated the batting, with the hard-hitting M. J. Savage and the left-handed opener, S. A. W. Davies, also contributing. Slow bowlers D. J. Collinge and M. J. Hannan (left-arm) had encouraging first seasons. **Brentwood**, captained by the Under-19 rugby international, C. J. Wilkins, had a poor summer, with sound batting but a mediocre attack. They were hampered by a crop of injuries to key players, as well as a loss of form by others of whom more had been expected. On the other hand **Brighton College** had an excellent season, winning 14 of their 22 matches and regaining the Langdale Cup when they beat Lancing by 16 runs. C. N. Gates batted superbly, his 1,378 runs being the second-highest in a season by a schoolboy after 1,534 by N. J. Lenham, also of Brighton, in 1984. Fully recovered from a fractured skull, suffered in a road accident at the end of the 1989 season, he hit four hundreds, including 178 not out v Ipswich, and won the *Daily Telegraph* Under-19 batting award. His opening partner and captain, R. D. Oliphant-Callum, made 832 and together they put on 222 unbroken v MCC and 265 v Ipswich. A varied attack was spearheaded by R. I. Lewis, with 45 wickets.

It was a season of rebuilding for **Campbell College**. D. A. Parker, an understanding captain, hit 112 not out v Banbridge Academy, as well as taking 24 economical wickets. Indeed, economy was a feature of the attack, in which four bowlers finished with single-figure averages. S. A. I. Dyer, whose 203 not out v Dungannon Royal School was a record for the college, went on to play for Irish Schools, and there were Ulster Schools honours for R. H. Lucas, the most successful bowler, Parker and C. R. M. Caves. The positive cricket played by **Canford** was apparent from their record of just three draws in sixteen games; Bryanston, Blundell's, the XL Club, Milton Abbey, MCC, RNCC, Wimborne CC and King's, Taunton were all defeated. The captain and opener, J. A. Perry, produced some outstanding performances with the bat, and seam bowler M. W. Forward gave the attack its edge. The real strength of the side, though, lay in the fielding, which was a key factor in their reaching the semi-finals of the Sir Garfield Sobers festival in Barbados.

With eight of **Caterham's** promising 1989 side in the XI again, hopes were high as the season began. However, injury prevented the captain, I. W. Armitage, from bowling, and although S. J. Constantin and S. K. Perera were steady and accurate, they had neither the support nor the penetration to put Caterham in control. K. A. Amaning overshadowed the other batsmen with his strokeplay. Benefiting from a pre-season tour to Southern Spain, a young, rather inexperienced **Cheltenham** XI enjoyed six wins, the most notable being v Haileybury, Pates GS, Free Foresters and St Edward's, Oxford – all achieved when batting second. They were ably led by B. B. Jones, and if his batting was generally disappointing, he did make a fine 102 v Free Foresters. Other hundreds came from two young players, M. C. Cawdron (114 not out v Malvern) and D. R. Hewson (109 v Dean Close). Cawdron, a left-hand opening bat and medium-pace out-swing bowler, collected 578 runs and 23 wickets and with Hewson (412 runs and, with off-breaks, 18 wickets) was selected for West of England Under-15. Hewson later played for England Under-15. D. R. Fulton again took the most wickets with his sharp in-swing, while M. C. Green's seven for 43, bowling left-arm medium, set up the win v St Edward's.

Chigwell's season was built around their Essex Under-19 all-rounders, P. C. Harvey (left-hand bat, right-arm medium) and J. F. Carpenter (right-hand bat, left-arm medium-fast), who provided 1,289 runs and 76 wickets. Harvey hit hundreds v Bancroft's (102 not out off 79 balls), Forest (126) and Wellingborough (119), and had figures of seven for 11 in 6.3 overs v City of London and six for 17 off ten v St Edmund's. Other highlights were a first-ever win v Bishop's Stortford; the defeat of Bancroft's, in which Harvey hit three sixes and fifteen fours in taking his side to 202 from 23 overs in 86 minutes; and the win v Forest, when Chigwell totalled a school-record 292 for seven, to which Harvey and D. R. Evans (96) contributed a record fifth-wicket stand of 182. Other wins were v City of London, Enfield GS, St Edmund's, Latymer and William Hulme's GS, while in schools matches they lost only to Magdalen College School. After a useful start, the **Christ College, Brecon** XI, which had promised so much at Under-17 level, failed to muster the cohesion and determination either to press home an advantage or to save the game. It was felt that the side was too confident and easy-going. Head and shoulders above the rest was the captain, E. P. M. Holland, who again won three caps for Welsh Schools as a fast bowler who can bat.

Clayesmore's young side performed better than anticipated, losing only three schools matches and achieving some excellent wins, in particular those v Allhallows and King Edward VI, Southampton. They owed much to the leadership and example of their captain, P. Bradbury, who headed both averages and was judged best batsman at the Bearwood festival. There were also noteworthy bowling performances from the young off-spinner, L. Coley, especially his six for 41 v the XL Club. **Clifton's** record eight wins included victories v Colston's, Blundell's, Marlborough, Tonbridge and Winchester in schools games. The captain, J. R. A. Williams's aggregate of 935 runs passed C. M. Trembath's record of 767 in 1979 and included hundreds v Rugby, Marlborough, Tonbridge and MCC. Against Rugby, he and J. P. Parish shared a second-wicket partnership of 250. M. G. N. Windows hit 127 v Millfield on his way to an aggregate of 649 runs, while B. M. O. Gibbs, at fast-medium, was the most successful bowler. Williams played for Welsh Schools Under-19 and captained their Under-16s.

Colfe's, an inexperienced side, worked hard and performed creditably. Even so, they depended heavily on three all-rounders: M. Horder, the captain, M. Quilter and wrist-spinner J. Gledhill-Carr. Of the younger players, T. Shoben and A. Hameed showed run-scoring potential, but as yet lacked consistency, while it was hoped that E. Gratwick (fast-medium) and R. Dennis (off-spin) would develop and strengthen the attack. In a moderately successful season **Colston's** beat King Edward's Bath, Prior Park, Bristol Cathedral School, Truro School and Christ College, Brecon. The captain, J. A. Franklin, I. J. Webb and M. J. Sheedy all scored centuries, with Franklin's 144 v Bristol Cathedral School, 136 v Kingswood and 186 v Hutton GS helping him to a school record aggregate of 906 runs. **Cranleigh's** positive approach brought them wins v the Cryptics, Eastbourne, Cranleigh Village, Epsom and Loretto. Defeats were by MCC, Lancing, King's Canterbury, St John's Leatherhead and Merchant Taylors', Northwood. The high standard of ground fielding was especially noteworthy, as were figures of eight for 44 and six for 44 by H. C. Watkinson and seven for 32 v Epsom by G. B. Atkinson. The batsmen were always looking for runs, but there were few dominating innings.

Dauntsey's, building afresh, began the season tentatively and at half-term were still looking for their first win. The XL Club obliged, after A. N. Field (fast-medium) had taken six for 72, and three more victories followed in the last four matches. The batting was strengthened by newcomer I. D. Hardman, a left-hander, whose 103 v King Edward's, Bath was the only hundred. D. P. Atkins (slow left-arm) took six for 52 on a responsive pitch v Kingswood and Field returned seven for 44 v Wycliffe, who won an exciting game by one wicket in the last over. Under the captaincy of G. M. Gaiger, a good spirit was maintained, even during the frustrating early weeks. **Dean Close**, if somewhat disappointing in terms of results, provided some exciting cricket. Neither of their Gloucestershire Under-19 representatives, C. J. Townsend, the captain, and C. S. Knightley, quite lived up to expectations, although Townsend played some good innings and Knightley, batting left-handed and bowling right-arm medium pace, made a useful all-round contribution. J. M. Bowditch, if not yet accurate enough with the new ball, had his moments.

The young **Denstone** XI, unbeaten and never bowled out, should perhaps have achieved more than four victories – v Wrekin, Old Denstonians, Abbot Beyne and King Edward's, Birmingham. While not quite reproducing his form of 1989, the captain, J. N. Snape, did hit an impressive unbeaten 128 v Worksop and provided seven other fifties. He went on to play for Northamptonshire Second XI and English Schools, and also captained England Under-17 against the touring Pakistanis. **Dover College** began with victory over the Duke of York's Royal Military School, but thereafter won only once more. Weak bowling again put undue pressure on the batsmen, among whom A. S. Burrell showed resolution as an opener and S. J. Schilder played some handsome strokes. The captain, D. M. Rouse, though scoring far fewer runs than in 1989, finished his school days with a total of 1,586. It was the opposite at the **Duke of York's Royal Military School** where, with batsmen losing their wickets in a premature attempt to push the score along, they struggled to compile big totals. On the other hand, the bowlers performed with great credit. G. J. Kennett purveyed his leg-spin with commendable enterprise and looked to give the ball air, while D. J. Reynolds's left-arm swing was always threatening. He returned six for 20 as St Edmund's, Canterbury were bowled out in pursuit of a total of 120. Of the batsmen, N. M. Conway demonstrated a sound technique and showed promise as a wicket-keeper, while the captain, C. N. Conway, generated a good team spirit and led by example in the field.

A record of three wins and five defeats for **Dulwich College** is a little misleading, for three of those losses were sustained while four leading players were on a rugby tour of Australia. Highlights were the defeat of King's, Canterbury and J. H. Potter's 115 v Epsom. The left-handed R. S. Sheldon, captain of the XI, headed the batting. **Durham** began the season by winning their first three games, but defeat by Pocklington on a damp wicket was followed by several drawn games which should have been won. The talented Weston brothers were the mainstay of the side: the captain, W. P. C., opening the batting and bowling, contributed 527 runs and 30 wickets, while his younger brother, R. M. S., opening bat and leg-spinner, scored 643 runs and took 22 wickets. Philip Weston played for English Schools and was chosen to tour New Zealand with England Young Cricketers in 1990-91, and Robin, the England Under-15 captain, received the Sir Jack Hobbs England Under-16 all-round award. Highlights were a nine-wicket win v St Peter's, York and the school's appearance for the third time in five years in the final of the Barclays Bank Under-17 Cup; they were beaten by Richard Huish VI Form College, Taunton.

At **Eastbourne College** the skill and good sense of the captain, A. J. T. Halliday, made for a cheerful, well-motivated side. Potentially gifted young cricketers were encouraged to play some exciting cricket, seen noticeably in the wins v Tonbridge, Christ's Hospital and King's, Canterbury. Halliday's 114 v Christ's Hospital and B. H. Miller's unbeaten 100 v St John's, Leatherhead were major batting moments, while the best performance with the ball was E. G. R. Barrett's return of seven for 13 v Stragglers of Asia. Highlight of an erratic season at the **Edinburgh Academy** was the exciting two-wicket win v Glenalmond, and there were interesting games v Barnard Castle and Scots College, Sydney, the latter winning by just 1 run. J. N. K. Godfrey's captaincy became more enterprising as the season developed, while the innings of 152 v Kelvinside by his fellow-opener, R. W. Cairns, was the highest for the Academy in twenty years. In a season of rebuilding, **Elizabeth College, Guernsey** were content with a record of eight wins, those v Malta and Victoria College, Jersey being particular highlights. Notable individual performances came from the captain, P. J. A. Moody, whose 50 wickets included seven for 30 v Latymer and six for 48 v Victoria, and T. Hollyer-Hill, who scored 103 not out v Reed's in an aggregate of 617 runs.

Ellesmere College beat five sides, including a strong MCC XI, and were one wicket away from a comfortable victory in three of their drawn games. G. N. Phillips (fast-medium) returned seven for 41 v Shrewsbury, and his opening partner, J. G. Slater (fast), took five for 12 v Liverpool College. **Eltham's** strong batting line-up was headed by the consistent left-handed opener, J. M. Ramsey, but their bowling, while capable of containment, struggled to bowl sides out. The college were Kent Cup finalists for the second successive season; in the semi-finals, the captain and leading wicket-taker, F. Kavina (leg-spin), took six for 27 v Judd. **Emanuel** enjoyed an outstanding season, their nine victories including the finals of both the London and Surrey Cup competitions. In the former they recovered from 34 for four in rain-affected conditions to pass Alleyn's 101 with an over to spare; in the latter, a boundary in the last over brought a two-wicket win v KCS Wimbledon. J. C. Cole deputised admirably in the absence, for much of the season, of the captain and all-rounder, M. D. Coe.

After losing two of their first three matches, **Enfield** never looked like losing again until late July. Wins v Hampton, Forest and Scots College, Sydney, and the draws v Haberdashers' Aske's and Merchant Taylors', Northwood, were season's highlights. D. Bowen became the first batsman to score 1,000 runs in a season for the school; of his three centuries, his unbeaten 196 v Reigate GS included a hundred before lunch. Other three-figure innings were played by N. Clydesdale and the captain and wicket-keeper, J. King. N. Lutwyche (off-spin) and M. Stevens (left-arm medium) made a contrasting attack and took 56 and 40 wickets respectively. **Epsom College** won six of their ten matches, including those v St George's Weybridge, Christ's Hospital and – scoring 261 with one ball to spare – KCS Wimbledon. T. R. Newton, a left-handed all-rounder, took 33 wickets, including six for 18 v Lancing, and hit out strongly, while P. E. Roche and N. A. Morris provided the backbone of the batting, the latter playing the side's only three-figure innings.

A record of three wins and three defeats does not do full credit to a good **Eton** side, unbeaten against schools in term and losing only to Eton Ramblers and, in the Silk Trophy festival, to hosts Radley and Shrewsbury. The wins were v St Edward's Oxford, Cranbrook and Harrow at Lord's, where Eton's batsmen played to potential and Harrow were outplayed. J. M. S. Whittington, in his first season, took 49 wickets with his left-arm slow bowling and went on to take 22 more for Berkshire Schools and win the *Daily Telegraph* Under-19 bowling award. In his first schools match for the XI he had figures of 7.3–4–3–8 v St Edward's. The XI was led with rare commitment by all-rounder H. J. P. Chetwood, though in part at the expense of his off-spin bowling. **Exeter School** achieved three of their seven wins on an end-of-term tour to Hereford and Brecon. A consistent batting line-up was headed by D. R. Gannon, whose last two innings produced centuries, while the captain, M. J. Stevenson, bore the brunt of the bowling when injury to M. H. T. Jones (medium-fast) disrupted the attack. However, T. R. Price (slow left-arm) returned good figures on the tour.

It was a disappointing season for **Fettes**, who rarely looked like winning and were beaten eight times. One bright spot was the bowling of the captain, J. R. S. Lloyd, who repeatedly took five wickets in an innings, to finish with 43, and looked a fine prospect. **Forest** won six and lost five of their sixteen fixtures. The distraction of A levels possibly affected the performance of their leading players; the captain, A. C. Richards's aggregate was half that of 1989, for example. Even so, he, P. O'Neill (medium) and wicket-keeper A. Heyes all made major contributions, along with the left-arm spinner, J. Dwyer, who emerged as the leading wicket-taker. Richards went on to captain English Schools and was offered a summer contract for 1991 by Essex, having played for their Second XI in 1990. Under the captaincy of B. Smyth, **Foyle and Londonderry College** won fourteen of their eighteen matches and finished the season as joint holders of the Gordon McCullough Memorial Cup. Their strong attack was spearheaded by J. Brown, who took seven for 19 v Coleraine Academical Institution and, with Smyth and J. McFarland, was selected for Ulster Schools. These three, with T. Dougherty, were the essence of the side's batting strength. Six of **Framlingham's** eight wins came in a run that ended with their only loss – to Kimbolton at the St Lawrence, Ramsgate festival. Success came from their all-round strength: N. I. Barker, S. E. Iliffe, the captain, and W. J. Earl scored consistently, while the opening attack of M. J. Rutterford and J. G. C. Townsend was balanced effectively by the slow left-arm bowling of P. Edwards.

Giggleswick beat Hipperholme GS, Oakwood and the Old Boys, but generally struggled to bowl sides out. **Glenalmond's** young, competitive side were moderately successful in an enjoyable season. Highlights were a fine century v Strathallan by S. C. Scott Elliot and his opening partnership of 158 with J. D. Thomson v Fettes. The captain, R. M. Jebb, bowled leg-spin to good effect for 31 wickets, while the medium pace of J. C. Caldwell provided a further 27. With **Gordonstoun's** senior players in particularly lean form, 1990 was not a vintage year. Poor weather in June led to several matches being cancelled, which, combined with the pressure of exams, meant the season ended on an unsatisfactory note. A highlight for **Grenville College** was their win v rivals West Buckland, against whom R. S. Hann took six for 28. The batting was headed by S. Blakers, an Australian, the consistent J. F. T. Pallister and D. R. Ellacott, who had an outstanding season behind the stumps. Seam bowlers took the most wickets, and a newcomer to the XI, M. J. Graham, though erratic, was fast and hostile. **Gresham's**, though not playing to their true potential for much of the season, finished in fine style with resounding victories v Oakham and Bromsgrove. The individual highlight was an innings of 141 by the captain, I. D. Barnett, v The Leys.

Haberdashers' Aske's were unbeaten. B. Moore (the captain), M. I. Yeabsley and R. Thacker, the top three in the order, made 2,121 between them, with Moore and Yeabsley putting on 225 unbroken for the first wicket v Queen Elizabeth's, Barnet, and three days later, in their next match, opening with 171 v Berkhamsted before being parted. Against Queen Elizabeth's, Yeabsley's younger brother, R. S. Yeabsley, returned eight for 29. The bowling honours were shared between the two brothers, Michael bowling off-spin and Richard medium-fast, supported by Moore (medium). Both Yeabsleys represented Hertfordshire Under-19 and Richard played for Middlesex Second XI and for Devon in the NatWest Bank Trophy; Moore played for Middlesex Young Cricketers and Thacker for Middlesex Under-17. **Hampton** enjoyed four successive wins in May, only for a frustrating string of draws to follow. S. C. Janes and J. E. Sudbury blended sound defence with attacking flair in a successful opening partnership, while seamer S. A. H. Cochrane produced match-winning spells v Latymer and RGS Guildford. The hostility of J. A. Scowen with the new ball and the increasing control of left-arm spinner J. E. Saunders promised well for the future. In schools matches, **Harrow** beat Bedford and St Edward's, Oxford, and lost only to Eton and Zimbabwe Schools; otherwise results were hard to come by on the good, dry wickets of 1990. An unbeaten century by C. E. Williams v Radley was the batting highlight, while among the bowlers R. E. Sexton took 40 wickets in his first season.

The Harvey GS recorded fourteen victories and won the Lemon Cup for Kent schools for a record seventh time. They owed much to their opening bowlers, R. J. N. Davis and A. W. Morris (both medium), who took 56 and 50 wickets respectively and were well supported in the field. **Highgate** enjoyed their best season in terms of wins since 1971, thanks particularly to the bowling of T. Gladwin and M. Sylvester, plus some steady batting. Thirteen-year-old E. Gladwin showed much promise with 50 on début, v MCC, and an average of 38.66 from his three innings. The relatively young side of **Hurstpierpoint** beat Seaford, Worth, Whitgift, St John's, Eastbourne and Ellesmere in schools matches, and the Under-17s reached the last four of the Barclays Bank Cup. P. T. Wicker, who hit an unbeaten 100 v St George's, and M. J. Semmence, the captain, were selected for Sussex Young Cricketers. M. J. King, who bowled some brisk spells, took the most wickets, including seven for 35 v Ellesmere; their other three wickets fell for 5 runs to Semmence. **Ipswich** continued their success of 1989, winning five games, losing only once, and finishing the season in style with victory v Dutch Colts at The Hague. The steady batting and leg-spin bowling of R. Catley stood out, while the seam bowling of C. Earley made its mark late on. J. Douglas, in his first season, made hundreds v The Perse and Brighton College, and also headed the bowling averages.

Kelly College, a young side, acquitted themselves well, though occasionally betraying their inexperience. They could bat right down the order – C. P. Insole, the captain, was the most impressive of the batsmen – and only one opposing team exceeded 175 against a steady attack built around J. J. Wood (medium), W. G. Pendrill (left-arm medium) and I. J. Saunders, a promising leg-spinner. Their best victories were v Exeter School and Truro School. **Kimbolton**, disappointing in terms of results, had a successful season in terms of development and attitude, with excellent wins v Berkhamsted and Framlingham providing reward and optimism. The captain, R. J. T. Ramply, a left-hander, headed the batting and forged a useful opening partnership with S. G. Wood, a fine wicket-keeper. The bowling was spearheaded by I. Prideaux (fast-medium), who operated with ideal control and pace. The experienced, well-balanced XI at **King Edward VI College, Stourbridge**, characterised by all-round team effort and fine catching, featured in some exciting finishes. Three of their six wins came in the last over, and close of play in four of the six draws found their opponents' last pair at the crease.

First-ever wins v Canford and St George's, Weybridge were highlights for **King Edward VI, Southampton**, who won eight other matches, retained the Altham Trophy and lost only to Brighton in schools fixtures. B. Quantrill proved to be an able captain, and while his steady batting was well supported by R. T. Markham, it fell to a fourth-form boy, G. R. Treagus, to play the only three-figure innings. The left-arm spinner, R. M. Salter, again exceeded 50 wickets. A difficult season for the young side of **King Edward VII, Lytham** brought no wins, but there were close draws v Arnold and King's, Macclesfield, to suggest the potential for 1991. The captain, P. Macauley, a left-hander, played quality strokes on occasions, and his opening partner, G. Maitland, a promising Under-15 player, headed the averages. P. Young (medium-fast) bowled tirelessly without having much luck or reward. **King Edward's, Birmingham** were pleased to win more matches than they lost at a time when the attack, with the exception of the captain, M. M. Dean, was expected to be only average. The bowling of C. D. Atkin was a bonus. As anticipated, the batting was sound, and an unbroken tenth-wicket stand of 112 v Solihull between N. M. Linehan (81 not out), a colt, and D. A. Bhadri (50 not out) was an unusual highlight.

King's College, Taunton were well captained by W. J. K. Greswell, who had two fine centuries amongst his 625 runs, while the openers, R. E. Berry and C. P. W. Cashell, scored 72 and 93 respectively in a school record opening stand of 178 to beat Blundell's by ten wickets. With most of the XI due to return in 1991, it was an encouraging season. At **King's College School, Wimbledon**, meanwhile, J. Parrish and captain R. Q. Cake formed an opening partnership that few could rival, scoring 833 and 927 runs respectively. H. S. Malik was another to pass 600, while of the bowlers A. M. Denslow (fast-medium) captured 47 wickets in his first season. Cake's sensible but sporting declarations made for some exciting cricket, notably v Epsom (q.v.). **King's, Bruton** beat Taunton School, Canford, Milton Abbey and Queen's, Taunton, losing only to the Old Boys. With seven of the side expected to return in 1991, prospects are good. Five wins were more than might have been expected by **King's Canterbury**. Their inexperienced batting was always likely to be a problem, and indeed several defeats resulted from batting collapses, but their difficulties were compounded by an injury to their opening bowler, M. I. G. Wilkinson. His absence from all but five matches considerably weakened the attack. The well-balanced **King's, Chester** XI recorded ten victories, were unbeaten by schools and lost, in the last over, only to a strong MCC side.

King's, Ely also won ten games, the most memorable of which was the 1-run victory v The Leys in the final of the Cambridgeshire County Cup. They lost to just one school. D. C.

Hindle, their captain, claimed a hat-trick in successive matches – v Woodbridge (all bowled) and v King's, Peterborough – and in taking seven wickets in the final match he equalled the school record of 49 in a season. C. Q. Taylor, an opening bat, hit hundreds in successive matches, and A. M. Gallop's 143 not out v King Edward's (King's Lynn) was Ely's best for some time. Undefeated by schools for the first time in recent memory, **King's, Macclesfield** lost only to MCC and beat Bury GS, the Masters' XI, William Hulme's, Arnold, Bolton School, Bury GS, Ipswich School and Brighton College. Their Australian opening batsman, K. A. Graham, was outstanding, his 1,075 runs passing by 83 the school record set in 1981 by P. Moores, the Sussex wicket-keeper. The attack was led by S. C. James (fast-medium) whose six for 32 v William Hulme's included a hat-trick, and M. R. Palmer, who opened at fast-medium but could also ply off-breaks. The batting of **King's, Rochester** was dominated by M. J. Walker, whose 872 runs included 156 not out v Chatham House, 143 not out v the XL Club, 105 v Maidstone GS and 124 v KCR Common Room. He also took the most wickets (28) and went on to play for Kent Second XI and England Under-17 v Pakistan Young Cricketers. **King's, Worcester** did not play as well as anticipated, injuries and exams affecting the form of at least two senior players. However, R. Tomlinson, captain and wicket-keeper, passed 500 runs for the second successive season, and there was a feeling of satisfaction when A. Thompson, having hitherto struggled for runs, hit an unbeaten century v Reigate on the end-of-season tour to Victoria College, Jersey.

Kingston GS, a young XI, made good progress; they won five games, and three of their eight defeats came in the last over. The captain, E. S. Gratton, batted consistently well, his 120 not out v RGS Guildford lifting the side from 91 for eight. With the ball, M. E. Bendel (fast-medium) began the season in fine form, only to incur a back injury, and the lack of a good spin bowler was a further handicap. **Kingswood's** batsmen hit a record number of three hundreds, with the captain, G. J. B. Williams's 156 not out in 140 minutes v Colston's a school best. Unfortunately, moderate bowling resources meant that batting dominance was only thrice converted into victory. The attack of **King William's College, Isle of Man** had similar limitations, with openers N. C. Capewell and D. R. Norman failing to fulfil earlier promise. However, L. R. Clarke, a young medium-pace bowler, responded well to additional responsibility. The batting relied heavily on a solid start from the openers, M. L. Craine, the captain, and U. A. Nwachuku, an Under-15 colt.

Following a tour to Australia at Easter, **Lancing** had a reasonable season, reaching the final of the Langdale Cup, only to lose to Brighton College. S. Baker dominated with bat and ball, bowling at a lively pace for his 34 wickets and including a fine century v Worth in his 934 runs. For the first time the college were hosts to Malvern, Charterhouse and Rugby in the end-of-term festival. Not surprisingly, the main contributor for unbeaten **Leeds GS** was their captain and all-rounder, T. C. Walton, who scored 545 runs, took 49 wickets and went on to play for English Schools and England Under-17 v the touring Pakistanis. A fourteen-year-old left-hander, I. C. Sutcliffe, developed promisingly as an opening bat, but while R. M. Atkinson bowled his left-arm spin to good effect, Leeds, like many schools, simply could not bowl sides out to exploit winning situations. Pre-eminent at **The Leys** was their left-handed opening bat, R. C. Weston, who set three new school records. His aggregate of 988 runs passed the 977 scored in 1984 by J. D. R. Benson of Leicestershire; his 202 v The Perse (three sixes, 21 fours) overtook Benson's 201 not out in 1983; and he shared in a record opening partnership of 219 with M. C. Donnor (82) v the XL Club, going on to 163 not out. Weston scored 692 runs in June, and missed the opportunity of totalling 1,000 for the season when the school's last match was abandoned. Donnor, a Cambridgeshire Under-16 representative, scored 607 runs and took 23 wickets with his leg-spin. D. J. Woods, the wicket-keeper, captained Cambridgeshire Under-17.

Initial promise tailed off into disappointment for **Liverpool College** as technical weaknesses, to some extent countered earlier in the season by spirit and determination, were exposed by stronger sides. Only J. Q. Harrington, the captain, and the left-handed B. Latto scored consistently. With the ball, J. Rushton (medium) bowled steadily, J. Rylance (fast-medium) showed potential, and Harrington sometimes bowled his leg-breaks to good effect. **Llandovery College**, unbeaten by schools, won half their matches and lost only to Pontyberem CC. Their strength lay in the batting, headed by S. A. Richards, who batted with style and maturity and proved to be an excellent captain. He also led the Welsh Independent Schools. On May's hard wickets, runs flowed, but rain and exams made June a difficult month. B. Rowlands developed encouragingly as an all-rounder, and his left-arm fast-medium bowling was supported by G. D. A. Lyddon-Jones and H. G. Davies (both medium-fast). **Lord Wandsworth College**, with seven wins to set against a solitary defeat, owed their success to the opening attack of N. P. B. Rochford and J. R. Cowles. Both showed genuine pace and hostility and, sharing 71 wickets, contributed to the dismissal of four sides for less than 100. The captain, D. A. Robinson, chipped in with 24 wickets from off-breaks. Though the batting was seldom tested, fifteen-year-old B. A. Hames opened the innings stylishly and scored the first hundred for the school in three years.

Loretto's young side did well on the local circuit, losing only to Merchiston Castle and beating Strathallan (all out for 47), Glenalmond (for 54), Fettes, George Watson's and Stewart's Melville; but their record was dented during their festival when the batting, capable in pursuit of low scores, proved more brittle. Defeats by Bryanston, Cranleigh and Rossall outweighed the win v St Peter's, York. A. C. F. Mason (left-arm fast) bowled consistently well, with figures of six for 31 v Stewart's Melville and four for 9 v Strathallan contributing to the 81 wickets he shared with the captain, J. A. G. Grant (medium). Two left-handers, C. J. Hawkes and G. Leeson, were the outstanding cricketers at **Loughborough GS**. Leeson, opening the batting, hit four hundreds in his 808 runs, while Hawkes contributed 611 runs and 48 wickets. Hawkes played for Leicestershire Second XI and at the end of the season made his County Championship début v Derbyshire. Friars of Derby, Old Loughburians, Leicestershire Gentlemen, the XL Club, King Henry VIII Coventry, and Bablake (bowled out for 48; J. Simpson seven for 13), were all beaten; the one defeat came in the final over v RGS Worcester.

Enterprising cricket earned **Magdalen College School** ten victories. Among the four batsmen who passed 500 runs, M. B. Bixby and fifteen-year-old N. S. Hawken, scoring 110 and 100 respectively, put on 212 unbroken for the second wicket v Reading School. S. D. Stinchcombe (off-spin) again took the most wickets, ably assisted by the wicket-keeping of the captain, T. H. Boyles, whose 34 dismissals included a school record of seventeen stumpings. **Malvern College**, in their second-best season since the war, were unbeaten by schools and defeated Shrewsbury, Marlborough, Dean Close and Cheltenham, against whom they successfully chased 250 in two and a half hours. There were hundreds from P. V. Sykes and J. W. A. Horton, the captain, while a good seam quartet was spearheaded by C. R. Phillips. S. J. C. Ferguson, an able wicket-keeper, could put aside the gloves to bowl leg-breaks when required.

Reservations about the inexperienced batting of **Manchester GS** seemed justified when they were bowled out for 119 by Rossall in their first match. However, revealing fine character, they improved to beat Bradford GS, Liverpool College, Arnold, William Hulme's, Bury GS (twice) and King Edward VII, Lytham, losing again only to Bangor GS and Pocklington. The batting relied heavily on M. J. P. Ward, who followed scores of 96 not out v Shrewsbury and 98 v RGS Lancaster with 106 not out v William Hulme's, 104 v Taunton and 145 not out v Bury to total 962 runs. L. J. Marland, promoted from the Under-14s to open with Ward, possessed a sound technique but as yet lacked the power to dominate. The bowling was opened by N. S. Farmer and M. C. Jones, who was often too fast for opposing batsmen, while Ward and Marland, in their differing styles, provided variety with off-spin. The XI were ably led by A. M. Dodd. For **Marlborough**, 1990 was a disappointing season. Their batting was sound enough, but they bowled just one side out and managed only a single win – v St Edward's, Oxford. The fielding of J. Simkins and the potential all-round talent of M. E. C. Harris were noteworthy.

Merchant Taylors', Crosby reported an unspectacular but enjoyable season in which morale was good under the captaincy of G. S. Glynne-Jones. However, his inability to bowl, owing to injury, weakened the attack. Only three sides were dismissed, and there were heavy defeats at the hands of Leeds GS and RGS Lancaster. Glynne-Jones contributed soundly with the bat though, to head the averages, and the Doggett brothers looked promising prospects. **Merchant Taylors', Northwood** numbered St Albans, Highgate, Watford GS, Aldenham, University College School, Dulwich, Stowe, Mill Hill, Cranleigh and Bryanston among their record twelve wins. A. J. Brand, the captain, passed 1,000 runs for the second successive season, but was beaten to the mark by opener C. M. Jaggard, whose 1,364 runs, including five centuries, fell 33 short of J. E. Raphael's record aggregate of 1,397 in 1901. Brand's 202 not out v Cranleigh in the Loretto festival improved by 1 run the school record he established the previous year. They and R. A. Hawkey, who scored 975 runs, made a formidable top three

Merchiston Castle, under the captaincy of G. C. Wearmouth, were undefeated by Scottish schools and won v Dollar Academy, George Heriot's, Glenalmond, Dundee HS, Loretto, Strathallan, Fettes and the strong Durham XI (by 97 runs after recovering from 41 for six to declare at 199 for nine). The only schools to beat them were Barnard Castle and RGS Newcastle. In a strong seam attack, A. R. C. Gilmour's excellent line-and-length medium pace brought him 59 wickets, including five for 17 and five for 30 in the two-day game v Fettes. His opening partner, A. A. L. Ramsay, B. R. S. Eriksson, able to swing the ball both ways, and D. W. Hodge (in-swing) lent admirable and accurate support. For **Millfield**, G. W. White became only the third player to score 1,000 runs for the school, his 1,061 including 200 not out v Welsh Schools and 104 v Somerset Second XI. He was followed in the batting by the captain, N. F. Gibbs, who headed the bowling and represented English Schools.

Mill Hill's young side were without a win until the end-of-term festival, where they beat Norwich, Warwick and Plymouth. A colt, D. M. J. Kraft, was the most successful batsman, while the bowling again relied heavily on the slow left-arm skills of the captain, G. E. S. Brock. Although they had no outstanding players, **Milton Abbey's** strength in depth helped them beat St John's Southsea, Clayesmore, Allhallows and Portsmouth GS, the last-mentioned victory coming when Portsmouth, chasing 187, collapsed from 166 for three to 184 all out. In contrast, **Monkton Combe's** season was notable more for individual performances. N. C. L. Sinfield took all ten for 39 in 15.1 overs v Dauntsey's, although he never quite bowled his medium-pace in-swing to such good effect again, and T. Simmons, the captain, compiled a school-record aggregate of 630 runs. His 100 not out v the XL Club was the first hundred for the XI since 1971, and S. Lockyer followed it with another unbeaten century in the eight-wicket win v Fettes at the St Paul's festival. The inexperience of **Monmouth's** bowling told in their record of ten draws in fifteen games. A. J. Jones, by far the most successful batsman, scored 136 v Wellingborough School and, along with J. H. Langworth, played for Welsh Schools. P. A. Clitheroe's leading aggregate of 31 wickets included six for 49 in the six-wicket victory v Colston's.

Newcastle-under-Lyme, unbeaten, experienced little difficulty in bowling sides out. L. Bradbury was their most successful bowler, and wicket-keeper R. M. Davis enjoyed another distinguished season. With the bat M. H. Colclough, an England Under-15 representative, and J. N. Britton both averaged over 70, scoring 100 each v Royal Wolverhampton as they put on a record 219 for the third wicket. The excellent attitude and team spirit of **Nottingham HS** made for an enjoyable and moderately successful season; the high proportion of drawn games was attributed to the good batting wickets and some sides setting safe targets. However, there were a number of exciting finishes, none more so than in the 100th fixture v Trent College (Nottingham 174 for eight dec., Trent 174 for nine).

Oakham's disappointing record stemmed from a lack of application among their batsmen, of whom only N. C. Kingham, the captain, and P. M. J. Webb were consistent enough. M. Cullen and Kingham were the pick of the bowlers, invariably bowling a good line and length. Hard work and team spirit brought success to **The Oratory** XI, whose ten wins included those v Magdalen College School, Pangbourne College, St Edmund's, Reading School, Berkshire Gentlemen, the XL Club and Emeriti. J. D. Clarke and D. Olszowski both passed 500 runs, with a century apiece; Clarke hit 125 v Abingdon and Olszowski 101 v Reading in a total of 206 for five from 28 overs. Although the attack lacked the incisive edge of recent years, four bowlers took twenty wickets each. A young **Oundle** side, well led by A. Lee, also played with fine team spirit. They beat The Leys, Oakham, Oundle Rovers, Northamptonshire Amateurs and St Edward's, Oxford, losing only to Felsted (in an overs match) and at the end of the season to Uppingham. A highlight was the fast-medium bowling of A. Richardson v Repton, taking six for 43 in a skilful display.

The Perse again showed themselves capable of scoring prolifically, passing 200 on five occasions, and once going on to 303 for four only to be beaten by The Leys. This illustrates their bowlers' lack of penetration and accuracy; unable to capitalise on their batting strength, the side went without a win. D. Crabb completed three excellent seasons behind the stumps and both E. W. H. Wiseman and R. T. Ragnauth showed promise with the bat. B. J. G. Edgar, an England Under-18 hockey international, scored 158 v Bishop's Stortford – the fourth time in two seasons the school record had been beaten. For their ten victories, set against a single defeat, **Plymouth College** owed much to the magnificent batting of A. R. Maddock, whose 1,128 runs at 86.76 included five centuries. He received sound support from any number of batsmen, all of whom could have scored more runs had the need arisen. T absence for much of the season of S. W. Nicholson and A. Ginster left a gap in the attac although S. D. Hunt and K. J. Willcock bowled well to share 71 wickets. **Portsmouth GS** d not quite live up to expectations, with only five wins in fifteen games. The captain, J. Osborne, and C. J. Ward both passed 500 runs, while opening bowlers J. R. Compton ar H. Rushin took their wickets at a reasonable strike-rate. Inexperience and ill fortune affect **Prior Park**, who had hoped for more than four wins from potentially their best side for decade. They played to a high standard and were captained with maturity by G. Lee, w provided the self-belief missing in some of the younger players. J. Power included the side only hundred in his 744 runs, an aggregate not surpassed in recent years, while Lee twice we close to three figures in compiling 595 runs; he also took 35 wickets with his off-spi J. Smithers's 36 wickets were an excellent return for a seam bowler at the college.

Carried along by a great team spirit, **Queen Elizabeth GS, Wakefield** enjoyed their be season for many years, winning three games and finishing "moral winners" in six of their ni draws. Much depended on the all-rounder, R. J. Ledger, and opening bat P. M. Dickinson; was significant that the only defeat – v Woodhouse Grove – came when neither performed potential. Highlight in a successful season for **Queen Elizabeth's Hospital** was the eight-wick victory v local rivals, Colston's; in other regular schools matches only the powerful Queen' Taunton side beat them. D. C. Taylor, bowling left-arm wrist-spin, captured the most wicket although N. O. McDowell (medium) headed both averages. He was followed in each by tl captain, D. N. Bennett (fast-medium), who took six for 42 v Bristol GS. **Queen's, Taunto** with their outstanding depth in batting, were bowled out only once. Schools beaten in seve victories included Bristol GS, Wycliffe, Queen Elizabeth's Hospital, Bishop Vesey's ar Taunton. N. J. Burke, who headed the batting, made 103 v King's, Bruton.

An unusual feature of **Radley's** season was their drawing two games with the scores level – Free Foresters and St Edward's, Oxford. In both cases Radley were chasing, and it was fe these should have been added to the wins v Cheltenham, Marlborough, Winchester (scoring off the last ball), Eton and Geelong. They lost only to Stowe and, hosting the festival, won tl inaugural Silk Trophy. **Ratcliffe**, with four wins, were unbeaten until the penultimate game, Nottingham HS, and could look back with satisfaction on victory over Mount St Marys ar draws with Oakham, Wellingborough and Loughborough. The bowling relied too heavily c the captain, P. G. Meredith, but the batting, while not really strong enough to chase larg totals with confidence, had a more solid look about it. Fifteen-year-old E. J. Meredith heade the averages for the second year. **Reading**, a young and inexperienced XI, enjoyed the cricket, despite winning only once. **Reed's**, capable of making runs, were handicapped by lack of variety in bowling, with too much being done by the specialist batsmen. One of thes M. R. Neal-Smith, took 31 wickets with his off-spin bowling.

Reigate GS were disappointed to lose nine of their 25 fixtures. Consolation came in tl batting of A. J. Dewson, whose 680 runs included 102 v Emanuel, M. K. Hynard (110 v O Reigatians) and in particular of S. J. Hygate, who had scores of 136 v Victoria College, Jers and 129 v Portsmouth GS in his 873 runs, the second-highest aggregate for the school aft N. J. Falkner's 1,139 in 1980. Opener C. B. Amos and left-armer R. J. Hathaway provided tl bowling support for N. J. Chapman, an outstanding prospect who captured 43 wickets and h 368 runs in his first season. **Rendcomb** began well, winning three of their first four match and drawing with Cheltenham; but only one more match was won. The left-arm spin of tl Gloucestershire Under-19 representative, A. Jones, was the pick of the bowling, whi R. Milner (medium), who took six for 19 v Cheltenham, and R. Hughes (medium awa swing), eight for 42 v Bloxham, led the seam attack. Milner, a left-handed opening bat, ar J. Carroll both passed 600 runs, but no-one else reached 250.

In schools matches **Repton** registered victories v Pocklington, Oakham, Wellington ar King Edward's, Birmingham, and in all games suffered only one defeat. Though eleven gam were drawn, there was much exciting cricket, with several going to the last ball and any c four results possible. The side was led by the opening bowler, J. M. Windsor, who took th most wickets; the batting was headed by A. R. Paulett, who scored 105 not out v Pocklingto and M. D. Murray, son of the former West Indian wicket-keeper, D. L. Murray. **Richar Huish College, Taunton** beat the strong Durham side to become the first state school to win th Barclays Bank Under-17 Cup since its inception in 1982; an encouraging result at a time whe cricket in state schools is said to be in decline. With the last pair together, and chasir urham's 140, Huish's opening bowler, N. Hammacott, hit 2 off the last ball to tie the scores, aking them winners by virtue of fewer wickets lost. For thirteen wins in eighteen matches, ey owed much to a batting line-up headed by Kevin Parsons, whose 886 runs in twelve nings were a school record, his twin brother Keith, the captain, and B. Collins, the last two aking solid all-round contributions. The Parsons, who between them also held 21 catches, ayed for Somerset Second XI, as did the seam bowler, K. Moyse.

Rossall's season was one of the most successful for many years. They began by beating lanchester GS in their first fixture and followed with seven more wins, including those v rnold, Giggleswick, Stonyhurst and King Edward VII, Lytham. The opening attack was specially hostile and quick, with S. D. Holmes in particular worrying many batsmen when e wickets were hard in May. He took six for 28 v King Edward's. While N. H. Crust was ss successful with the bat than in 1989, he still scored the most runs, and his captaincy was n important factor in the team's success. J. Elliott hit their only century, 100 v Cranleigh in e festival at Loretto. Batting and bowling records were broken at **Royal GS, Guildford**. B. C. ay, the captain, compiled a record aggregate of 673 runs, his 141 v RGS Colchester being oted the outstanding individual performance of the RGS festival. He and N. Kent, whose 00 runs included six fifties, dominated the batting, but the middle order rarely seemed able to onsolidate. A. Thomson's ability to move the ball both ways at medium pace brought him 48 ickets, also a record, including a return of eight for 57 v St Dunstan's. The fact that 28 of his ictims were bowled is a testimony to his accuracy. Newcomers G. Morley and T. Fraser put good performances at the festival, taking five for 17 v RGS Worcester and six for 34 v RGS ligh Wycombe respectively.

Royal GS, Worcester continued their winning ways, beating thirteen sides and losing only Bedford Modern in schools games. The batting was dominated by the first three – D. M. Valker, C. J. Eyers and A. V. Powell – all of whom looked set to make 1,000 runs but faltered the end. The captain, M. J. N. Taylor, backed them up with 615 runs. Among the bowlers, I. P. Haddock's left-arm spin accounted for 58 wickets, and Eyers, at fast-medium, captured 1 wickets to go with his 932 runs, an impressive all-round performance. Batsmen prospered **Rugby**, but as a record of twelve draws in fifteen matches suggests, bowlers had to work ard for wickets on the summer's pitches. W. Glazebrook emerged as the leading all-rounder; rong in defence, he also hit hard and straight, and his bowling was tight and tireless. Support ame in both departments from the experienced M. Semmens (fast-medium). **Rydal**, ncouraged by some early-season performances, suffered a setback when they lost control of a ame they should have won, v Liverpool College, and then were completely outplayed by ing's, Chester. However, although Rydal finished without a win, with seven of the side xpected to return in 1991, there was cause for optimism.

What was always going to be a difficult season for **St Albans** looked even bleaker when their aptain and leading all-rounder, B. LeFleming, severed both main tendons in his right palm nly months before summer term began. Yet, despite holding the bat with difficulty, he ollected the second-most runs and wickets, as well as taking a record number of catches. . Cornwell's 649 runs included 104 not out v St George's, but of the bowlers, only . Sherman looked capable of bowling sides out. Even so, his 37 wickets were fewer than ad been expected of him. **St Bees** felt they could have improved on their record of four natches won and seven drawn had they possessed a more incisive attack. P. Hoffman headed ne batting averages, and A. Mawson, a colt, showed great potential in scoring the most runs, ncluding the side's only hundred.

St Edmund's, Canterbury anticipated a lacklustre season, yet by the end a young side had een transformed into a confident, cohesive unit, able to overcome the loss of their first four ames and finish with five victories. St Augustine's, Cranbrook, the XL Club and St dmund's Society were teams beaten. A. Hajilou developed the art of astute captaincy, and is unbeaten 117 v St Edmund's Society was the highlight of his significant all-round ontribution. C. R. M. Whittington demonstrated a rare talent with the ball, achieving many ariations of pace, flight and turn, while P. Walker and T. Wong showed all-round promise. **St Edward's, Oxford**, also a young XI, struggled for much of the season, with only wins v towe and the Cryptics to counter nine defeats. The opening batsman, H. Varney, and C. M. itcher, a fast-medium bowler, carried a heavy responsibility, but with most of the side eturning, and some promising colts coming through, the prospects for 1991 are better.

Another school to win just twice was **St George's, Weybridge**. A powerful batting line-u was headed by S. Marsh, whose 871 runs featured his 126 before lunch v Epsom (ten sixes nine fours), 123 not out v Emeriti (seven sixes, eleven fours) and 182 v KCS Wimbledon (10 minutes, twelve sixes, twenty fours) – the highest for St George's since H. Cannon's 214 i 1901. The bowling, however, lacked the experience needed on good wickets. **St Joseph's Ipswich** recorded eight wins and five defeats, their mixed fortunes reflecting some soun batting and inconsistent bowling. A highlight in a difficult year for **St Lawrence College Ramsgate** was the 79-run victory v Kimbolton. The mainstay of the side was O. G. Morris, left-handed batsman and right-arm medium-pace bowler, with good support coming from th left-handed G. Turner, a fast bowler and useful middle-order bat. **St Paul's** could field a highl competent batting XI, but the bowling struggled, especially on the school's pitches at Barnes B. R. Taberner, captain and wicket-keeper, and T. J. Taberner, his younger brother, playe the two three-figure innings, the elder hitting 130 not out v Highgate in the opening match and the younger 101 not out v The Leys on the final day of the season. J. W. Hill, a leg-spinne who took just nine wickets in eight games, set up the win v Mill Hill with the remarkabl figures of 18–12–18–6 on a good batting pitch.

St Peter's, York were handicapped by the absence for much of the season of some senio players. Although their results were disappointing, there were good individual performances notably J. D. Rigby's unbeaten 102 v Yorkshire Gentleman. **Sevenoaks** were another stron batting side whose bowling failed to reach a similar level, even if T. R. Payton's 21 wicket were not due reward for his efforts. Omar Iqbal, the captain, scored 825 runs, the highes aggregate for the school since C. J. Tavaré's 1,036 in 1973, with the most fluent of his fou hundreds being 107 v Brentwood in the better of the XI's two wins. **Sherborne's** undefeated XI, in winning more games than any of their predecessors, beat Taunton, King's Taunton Clifton, Canford, Downside, Blundell's, Geelong College, Marlborough, Cheltenham, Dorse Rangers, Free Foresters and MCC. Their fast bowler, S. W. Stevens, broke the 67-year-ol school record with 55 wickets, while the steadiness of A. J. Rutherford (fast-medium) an R. H. F. Pugsley (off-spin) was an ingredient in a successful attack. Wicket-keeper C. R. Lev set an outstanding example for an enthusiastic fielding side which held some splendid catches

Shiplake reported eight wins; and the game v Lord Wandsworth College ended in a draw with the scores level. A. J. Hall scored most runs and took 56 wickets: in consecutive matche he took nine for 18 v St Bartholomew's and scored 145 not out v Reading School. After an uncertain start, C. P. J. Abbiss emerged as a solid No. 3 batsman and useful stock bowler while a fourteen-year-old Canadian, P. C. Lefort, showed promise as a left-arm swing bowler While their batsmen struggled to find early form, **Shrewsbury** endured three consecutive defeats in April; after that they lost only once, and among their four wins was that by 50 runs v Eton in the Silk Trophy festival at Radley. D. J. Bowett, who played for Middlesex Second XI, was again to the fore with 34 wickets and 523 runs, including 139 not out v Zimbabwe Schools. P. W. Trimby's leg-breaks and googlies consistently troubled batsmen, and B. R Parfitt, son of P. H. Parfitt, showed his batting potential in his seven games, heading the averages.

In a season of rebuilding, **Simon Langton GS** did well to win six matches. N. Jones headed the batting, and the leading wicket-taker was R. Moulton, who captained the side in the absence through injury of R. Stevens. A highlight was the return of seven for 48 v St Edmund's, Canterbury by fourth-former N. Bielby. Excellently captained by J. M. A. Inglis who was selected for Warwickshire Colts, **Solihull** had six wins to offset their one defeat – in the final of the Birmingham Schools Under-19 competition. Inglis dominated both batting and bowling, but as the season progressed the less-experienced players gained confidence under his guidance. R. A. Kallicharran played some useful innings, as well as moving the ball both ways at medium pace, S. R. Fell brought much-needed steadiness to the middle order and K. A. Mortimer and P. S. Amiss emerged as a sound opening pair. Mortimer's bowling became more hostile as the season progressed, but S. M. Franklin had a disappointing return by his own standards. Of particular note were successive unbeaten centuries v MCC and King's, Worcester, by Inglis, and his six for 43 v Wolverhampton.

Stowe's bowling earned them five wins, notably that by 100 runs v otherwise unbeaten Radley. The fragility of their middle-order batting, though, led to six defeats. The side was captained with enthusiasm by the wicket-keeper, M. C. G. Atkinson, the third member of his family to lead the school. **Strathallan**, too, looked to their bowling, especially with the ball sc dominant in Scottish cricket. Their attack was spearheaded by H. A. D. McKenzie-Wilson (fast), with valuable support from the young M. R. Tench (fast-medium). K. L. Salters (right-hand bat, slow left-arm bowler) headed both averages. Three all-rounders were prominent in the unbeaten XI of **Sutton Valence**: the captain J. F. Barr (right-hand bat, slow left-arm), I. Page (medium) and J. Cowell (fast-medium). Highlights were the win v MCC, with a target of 231 met in the last over; the draw v King's, Rochester, in which Barr made 142 in a total of 235 for three dec.; and Barr's hundred from 73 balls as they achieved 189 for one in 29 overs in reply to Dover College's 208 for five off 81.

Taunton's young side exceeded expectations with seven victories. Memorable were P. Tarr's unbeaten 118 v the XL Club and the tie v Blundell's, in which Taunton lost their last wicket to the final ball of the match. **Tiffin's** formidable batting line-up was seen to advantage chasing runs, the most spectacular wins coming when scoring 249 for six v MCC, 222 for six v Magdalen College School and 283 for seven v Elizabeth College, Guernsey. Opener G. J. Kennis became the first since D. G. Ottley in 1962 to score 1,000 runs for the school, his unbeaten 128 v MCC being the most notable of his three hundreds. The captain and No. 4, R. D. Nash, had an aggregate of 819, despite missing a month with a broken finger, and hit four centuries v schools, the highest being 137 v Hampton. He went on to play for Surrey Young Cricketers. Of the bowlers, only B. J. Walters (left-arm spin) performed with match-winning consistency. The leadership skills of the **Tonbridge** captain, J. F. S. Rowland, fostered an excellent spirit and enthusiasm in the XI, which beat Tonbridge CC, Lancing, Free Foresters, Haileybury and Felsted, and were just one wicket from victory in four drawn games. Four of their five defeats came in the last two weeks, only two being v schools. S. J. Doel, batting with care and concentration, consistently gave the side a good start, but the middle order generally failed to build on it. No-one scored a hundred. The bowling honours were shared by R. P. Ziegler and D. L. Gilbert, who, both medium-fast, troubled batsmen in all matches.

Trent College followed an eleven-match tour of Australia by playing exciting, positive cricket. More than half the eleven draws ended in their favour, three with the opposition nine wickets down. T. A. Ellis's 683 runs included 111 v Bradford GS, and C. M. Winterbottom hit an unbeaten 104 v Pocklington. The bowling was headed by M. T. White and N. D. Johnson, the latter, under sixteen, making a significant impact in his first year in the XI. Another successful season for **Trinity** came as something of a surprise at a time of rebuilding. Capably captained by the wicket-keeper, S. P. Fairchild, they recorded eleven victories, notably v St Dunstan's, Tiffin, Emanuel and Elizabeth College, Guernsey, and lost just twice, bringing the school's results against all opposition over three years to 33 won, 5 lost and 29 drawn. S. S. Prabhu led the batting with 758 runs, well supported by C. H. Maiden and the left-handed R. W. Nowell, while the bowling revolved around two left-arm spinners, P. S. Kember and Nowell, who shared 84 wickets. Nowell, an Under-14, took seven for 16 v Whitgift. The good work of the **Truro** bowlers was not backed up by their batsmen, who tended to get out to injudicious strokes when a steadier, more solid approach was called for.

Warwick, with wins v Bablake, Trent, Bishop Vesey's, MCC, Norwich School and King's, Worcester, looked primarily to their batsmen. Most reliable were D. Dalton, S. Ensall and the England Under-15 representative, C. Mulraine, whose 124 not out v MCC was the only century. Half-centuries from the captain, G. Rawstorne, saw the side to three of their victories. Fifteen-year-old S. Webb headed the bowling averages with 25 wickets. Undefeated, **Wellingborough** beat seven sides, including The Perse, Oakham, Forest, William Hulme's GS and Pocklington. The last two were beaten during the Wellingborough festival, on the final three days of which the captain, J. M. Attfield, hit successive hundreds v Chigwell, Pocklington and Magdalen College School. He dominated the season with a school record of 1,116 runs, overshadowing the excellent all-round contribution of N. J. Haste (441 runs and 39 wickets). **Wellington College** had in A. P. D. Wyke a tactically aware captain who, overcoming an injury, took the most wickets, including six for 33 v Charterhouse. The strength of the XI, however, was the depth of their batting, with A. E. Newman and T. N. Sawrey-Cookson particularly effective. Most of the seven wins by **Wellington School** came at the end of term, the best being v BRNC Dartmouth, Queen's Taunton and Christ College, Brecon. R. Fisher batted consistently well, with sound support from G. Wolfendon and S. Palmer, a positive captain, but the bowlers were not helped by the alarming number of dropped catches.

Whitgift enjoyed their best season for some years. In schools matches they beat St Dunstan's, Brighton, Reigate and Christ's Hospital, losing only to Hurstpierpoint. The left-handed J. D. G. Ufton, son of D. G. Ufton, established a post-war record of 817 runs at 54.46, including 123 not out v St John's, Leatherhead. Hundreds also came from R. Shah, 163 not out, and P. M. Horne, 101 not out, in Whitgift's 404 for two off 45 overs v Excelsior, Rotterdam. Another 36 wickets by R. J. Targett (fast-medium) took his tally for the school to 108 in three years, and he and all the bowlers were backed by sound fielding: wicket-keeper N. W. J. Edwards effected 31 dismissals (26 ct, 5 st). **Winchester** followed a successful ten-match tour of Australia at Easter with their best season for some years. Under the captaincy of R. J. Turnill, the experienced side played positive cricket throughout to win six games, although a sharper attack might have wrought four more victories. Another experienced XI, that of **Woodbridge**, failed to achieve what had been hoped of them. The captain, B. K. Sindell, led from the front, and scored a fine century v St Joseph's College, but otherwise the batting failed to take advantage of good wickets and never totalled 200. Consequently the bowlers, accurate but not particularly incisive, never had the opportunity to apply pressure.

Woodhouse Grove suffered their only defeat by a school in their first match – v Ashville College. Showing greater application thereafter, they beat Giggleswick, Hipperholme and Queen Elizabeth, Wakefield in schools fixtures. Among a team thought to be the most talented at the school for many years, three all-rounders were prominent, S. N. Lee's leg-spin being well supported by the medium pace of R. D. Webster and C. J. Rika. They also scored the most runs, although the captain and opening bat, D. M. Lawson, would have totalled more had he not missed several matches with a rugby injury. A highlight was Lee's return of six for 31 v Batley. Undefeated by schools, **Worksop College** recorded wins v Ampleforth, Bloxham and Nottinghamshire Club and Ground, as well as participating in an exciting draw v Repton. Their two losses were sustained after declaring. A strong batting side, positive in approach, compiled six totals in excess of 200, with hundreds coming from the captain, J. D. Goode, and two left-handers, R. A. Kettleborough and C. J. Walker. Without much variety, the bowling tended to struggle on the firm home pitches.

Wrekin, with a steady opener in M. R. Savage, their wicket-keeper, lacked a reliable batsman to sustain the middle order. The bowling was the stronger suit, with most opposing sides being bowled out. A. J. Holloway (left-arm spin) took five wickets v schools three times, S. R. D. H. Lander was genuinely quick, and S. R. Phillips-Broadhurst, moving the ball about at a lively pace, also registered three five-wicket returns. A highlight was the nine-wicket defeat of Bromsgrove. **Wycliffe** won only twice, but with most of the XI expected to return in 1991, they look forward to an improvement. S. B. Thomas opened the bowling with pace and movement, and took a hat-trick v Dauntsey's, while W. R. Tovey's flighted off-spin troubled many good batsmen and brought him the season's best return of seven for 47 v Bromsgrove. Although some senior batsmen at **Wyggeston & Queen Elizabeth I Sixth Form College** struggled to find form, the depth of batting and the consistent starts provided by S. Kennell ensured that they always scored enough runs. A newcomer to the XI, S. Patel (fast-medium), joined D. Green in constituting a formidable opening attack, but insufficient support meant that advantages gained were not always pressed home.

THE SCHOOLS

(Qualification: Batting 100 runs; Bowling 10 wickets)

* *On name indicates captain.* * *On figures indicates not out.*

Note: The line for batting reads Innings–Not Outs–Runs–Highest Innings–Average; that for bowling reads Overs–Maidens–Runs–Wickets–Average.

ABINGDON SCHOOL

Played 17: Won 6, Lost 3, Drawn 8

Master i/c: A. M. Broadbent

Batting—R. J. Taylor 4–0–169–99–42.25; J. S. Tilley 14–4–355–61*–35.50; D. E. Stanley 17–1–527–83–32.93; *E. J. Tilley 16–1–397–73–26.46; J. S. Taylor 5–1–102–58*–25.50; M. D. Gordon 14–2–234–31*–19.50; J. M. Allen 10–0–173–61–17.30; P. A. B. Page 13–3–144–56–14.40.

Bowling—L. M. Golding 53–10–150–10–15.00; H. E. Wilkinson 70.2–19–246–14–17.57; B. R. Marnane 105.4–24–322–17–18.94; P. A. B. Page 205.2–50–494–25–19.76; J. M. Wallace 147–38–407–18–22.61; J. S. Tilley 46.5–7–229–10–22.90.

ALDENHAM SCHOOL

Played 13: Won 4, Lost 6, Drawn 3

Master i/c: P. K. Smith

Batting—S. P. Moffat 13–3–544–131*–54.40; D. G. Marsh 13–3–389–101*–38.90; R. Robertson 11–3–260–109*–32.50; C. Molyneux 9–2–142–59–20.28; R. Meara 12–0–220–56–18.33; J. Clemow 11–0–196–76–17.81.

Bowling—M. Okoro 134–27–400–27–14.81; R. Robertson 103–21–315–16–19.68; J. Clemow 121–19–384–18–21.33.

ALLEYN'S SCHOOL

Played 15: Won 6, Lost 0, Drawn 9

Master i/c: S. E. Smith

Batting—*P. C. Berglund 15–3–770–131*–64.16; M. Humber 10–6–105–31*–26.25; G. Brook 9–4–119–37–23.80; A. C. Winter 14–2–241–52*–20.08; M. T. Roberts 13–1–219–99*–18.25; R. Ellis 10–1–149–29–16.55; J. Naish 13–2–131–60–11.90.

Bowling—A. C. Winter 166.3–40–395–38–10.39; P. C. Berglund 113–23–278–22–12.63; P. Haslam 118.2–23–333–24–13.87; G. Brook 143–31–360–19–18.94.

ALLHALLOWS SCHOOL

Played 11: Won 0, Lost 7, Drawn 4

Masters i/c: C. G. McNee and M. Hill

Batting—*J. M. Rowe 11–1–279–122*–27.90; J. A. Carstairs 10–0–221–69–22.10; A. C. Boddy 11–0–102–32–9.27.

Bowling—J. M. Rowe 117–20–395–22–17.95; G. D. Moxon 82–17–295–11–26.81.

AMPLEFORTH COLLEGE

Played 17: Won 4, Lost 4, Drawn 9. Abandoned 3

Master i/c: The Revd J. F. Stephens OSB

Batting—A. R. Nesbit 15–2–382–75–29.38; A. J. Finch 14–4–284–39–28.40; R. M. Wilson 17–1–382–84–23.87; T. J. Willcox 16–1–330–57–22.00; T. O. Scrope 17–1–337–71–21.06; G. Finch 12–3–180–95–20.00; R. J. Lamballe 14–1–217–69–16.69; S. B. Pilkington 12–5–102–34*–14.57.

Bowling—D. A. Thompson 77–24–236–15–15.73; R. J. Gilmore 293.4–66–894–51–17.52; R. M. Wilson 69–16–302–10–30.20; S. B. Pilkington 246–55–759–16–47.43.

ARDINGLY COLLEGE

Played 19: Won 10, Lost 3, Drawn 6

Master i/c: T. J. Brooker Cricket professional: S. S. Sawant

Batting—*M. T. E. Peirce 19–4–929–123*–61.93; D. P. Kerkar 19–1–1,102–150–61.22; A. C. C. Slight 19–5–423–76–30.21; T. D. James 10–2–139–62–17.37; M. J. Newcomb 16–0–224–59–14.00; N. Simonin 14–2–145–56–12.08; C. S. Spencer 12–1–129–25–11.72.

Bowling—D. P. Kerkar 156.5–34–491–38–12.92; M. T. E. Peirce 186.1–37–636–34–18.70; C. S. Spencer 141.5–33–508–27–18.81; N. Simonin 112–15–391–19–20.57; M. J. Newcomb 63–10–258–10–25.80; T. D. James 68–5–286–11–26.00; S. Skeel 79–13–314–10–31.40.

ARNOLD SCHOOL

Played 13: Won 4, Lost 5, Drawn 4. Abandoned 2

Master i/c: S. Burnage Cricket professional: J. Simmons MBE

Batting—*M. J. Clinning 12–1–451–96*–41.00; P. N. Bentley 12–2–194–47–19.40; R. Chew 9–0–135–44–15.00; R. Day 10–1–125–24*–13.88; I. Best 12–0–166–49–13.83; C. Outram 10–0–107–50–10.70.

Bowling—I. Best 157.2–30–534–25–21.36; M. J. Clinning 257.2–73–742–33–22.48; R. Chew 124–30–374–13–28.76.

ASHVILLE COLLEGE, HARROGATE

Played 16: Won 6, Lost 0, Drawn 10. Abandoned 2

Master i/c: J. M. Bromley Cricket professional: P. J. Kippax

Batting—A. W. Alexander 15–2–632–135*–48.61; S. R. Alexander 15–1–382–98–27.28; J. J. C. Moorhouse 13–1–297–101*–24.75; T. P. Loveridge 14–5–187–38–20.77; R. A. Neil 11–2–133–47*–14.77; A. J. B. Casey 13–0–190–33–14.61; K. D. Crack 13–3–131–29*–13.10.

Bowling—C. E. Pick 105–20–378–25–15.12; S. R. Alexander 45–11–171–11–15.54; R. A. Neil 81–14–243–13–18.69; A. W. Alexander 116–24–378–19–19.89; K. D. Crack 161–39–452–22–20.54.

BALLYMENA ACADEMY GRAMMAR SCHOOL

Played 14: Won 10, Lost 4, Drawn 0. Abandoned 4

Master i/c: P. G. Davidson

Batting—D. Kennedy 13–0–236–47–18.15; C. Williams 12–0–217–38–18.08; *M. Dunlop 12–1–169–50*–15.36.

Bowling—D. Kennedy 92.4–25–189–29–6.51.

BANCROFT'S SCHOOL

Played 20: Won 4, Lost 9, Drawn 6, Tied 1. Abandoned 1

Master i/c: J. G. Bromfield Cricket professional: J. K. Lever MBE

Batting—C. S. Greenhill 18–5–640–92*–49.23; T. W. Clark 16–1–520–75–34.66; *T. C. Dolan 19–2–514–76–30.23; T. M. Dowling 19–1–438–70–24.33; A. A. Khan 11–3–129–37–16.12; R. Patel 17–3–183–29–13.07; J. Pollard 10–1–100–16–11.11; C. C. Barlow 15–2–123–39–9.46; J. P. Manning 17–1–127–32–7.93.

Bowling—T. C. Dolan 171–39–594–33–18.00; A. A. Khan 91–15–362–18–20.11; J. P. Manning 111.5–13–516–25–20.64; R. Patel 120.3–17–504–24–21.00; T. W. Clark 175.1–56–561–24–23.37.

BANGOR GRAMMAR SCHOOL

Played 21: Won 10, Lost 6, Drawn 5. Abandoned 1

Master i/c: C. C. J. Harte

Batting—P. A. McIlwaine 17–5–316–56*–26.33; M. L. Edwards 9–3–113–68*–18.83; R. G. Scott 19–3–300–103*–18.75; M. N. Wade 17–5–223–51*–18.58; A. J. Irwin 16–2–220–59–15.71; M. S. J. Law 10–2–107–31–13.37; P. J. English 15–2–154–34–11.84; *M. W. R. McCord 16–5–118–29*–10.72.

Bowling—R. G. Scott 147.2–36–340–43–7.90; M. W. R. McCord 198.3–63–454–46–9.86; P. A. Skelly 91.5–31–212–20–10.60; C. P. Escott 101–31–241–21–11.47; J. L. Cunningham 72.5–16–200–10–20.00.

BARNARD CASTLE SCHOOL

Played 20: Won 6, Lost 5, Drawn 9. Abandoned 2

Master i/c: C. P. Johnson

Batting—*J. G. H. Murphy 17–5–611–100*–50.91; S. G. Riddell 19–3–316–60–19.75; J. Simon 17–2–296–70*–19.73; R. J. B. Wearmouth 17–3–221–51*–15.78; J. W. Foster 14–2–183–46–15.25; R. Brewis 17–1–227–46–14.18; K. R. Lowe 16–0–175–36–10.93; A. W. Hutchinson 16–3–106–29–8.15.

Bowling—M. R. Rock 37–6–146–11–13.27; J. G. H. Murphy 242–61–646–39–16.56; J. M. Watson 121–21–421–21–20.04; R. Brewis 318–71–916–41–22.34; R. J. B. Wearmouth 154–25–662–26–25.46.

BEDFORD SCHOOL

Played 17: Won 3, Lost 5, Drawn 9. Abandoned 2

Master i/c: D. W. Jarrett Cricket professional: R. G. Caple

Batting—*R. W. H. Smith 18–3–578–113*–38.53; B. J. A. Miller 19–0–532–88–28.00; D. R. Fossey 10–1–249–61–27.66; A. Focken 19–1–437–54*–24.27; C. S. G. Parke 5–0–119–55–23.80; R. J. Stone 11–3–171–42–21.37; G. I. Green 8–2–112–34*–18.66; P. C. Wynn 17–1–286–99–17.87; N. V. Sinfield 12–1–177–52*–16.09; R. G. Simmonds 14–4–153–36–15.30; M. B. Jenkins 13–0–196–49–15.07.

Bowling—A. Focken 120–35–373–21–17.76; D. G. Stones 131–23–438–21–20.85; M. B. Jenkins 181–36–595–24–24.79; R. J. Stone 146–18–509–17–29.94; R. W. H. Smith 154–26–525–14–37.50.

BEDFORD MODERN SCHOOL

Played 21: Won 8, Lost 1, Drawn 12

Master i/c: N. J. Chinneck

Batting—*G. A. H. Awudu 21–3–1,009–148–56.05; E. R. Osborn 21–3–716–105*–39.77; R. C. Shah 15–4–362–70*–32.90; D. B. Reavill 21–1–446–51–22.30; G. S. Pilgrim 15–5–179–41–17.90; D. E. Jones 11–1–148–52*–14.80; P. A. Wildman 16–2–184–49*–13.14.

Bowling—M. J. Rolton 99.3–24–284–26–10.92; M. C. Waddingham 201.2–50–610–37–16.48; P. D. Brownridge 196.3–58–545–28–19.46; A. R. Woodcock 172.4–38–559–26–21.50; G. A. H. Awudu 203.3–40–646–29–22.27.

BEECHEN CLIFF SCHOOL, BATH

Played 10: Won 5, Lost 1, Drawn 4. Abandoned 2

Master i/c: K. J. L. Mabe Cricket professional: P. J. Colbourne

Batting—S. Bryan 8–0–604–127–75.50; *P. Tisdale 9–1–570–131–71.25; R. Parker 4–2–140–79–70.00; D. Benton 9–0–226–90–25.11; A. Durrans 6–1–103–64–20.60.

Bowling—D. Perryman 99.1–21–308–19–16.21; A. Piper 83.3–21–260–14–18.57.

BERKHAMSTED SCHOOL

Played 19: Won 10, Lost 4, Drawn 5. Abandoned 1

Master i/c: J. G. Tolchard Cricket professional: M. Herring

Batting—*E. P. Shek 19–0–821–123–43.21; D. T. Wotherspoon 18–0–492–99–27.33; T. N. Agius 17–6–291–83*–26.45; N. E. Mawdsley 13–4–230–65*–25.55; A. P. Spooner 16–0–353–76–22.06; A. J. Rigden 19–3–255–42–15.93; M. J. Spooner 13–1–181–61–15.08; R. D. Collett 18–1–250–73–14.70.

Bowling—B. P. Howard 81–11–314–21–14.95; J. M. Rennie 156–44–351–21–16.71; R. D. Collett 103–22–325–17–19.11; R. D. Hilton 237–60–657–31–21.19; M. J. Spooner 213–42–642–29–22.13.

BIRKENHEAD SCHOOL

Played 14: Won 5, Lost 2, Drawn 7

Master i/c: G. Prescott

Batting—N. D. Cross 10–0–490–116–49.00; S. J. Renshaw 7–4–122–78*–40.66; I. G. Berry 7–1–210–84*–35.00; N. J. Corran 10–4–199–43–33.16; *L. C. Parnell 9–1–233–65–29.12; J. L. Cooper 7–1–105–22–17.50; M. G. Roberts 7–1–101–28*–16.83; D. A. Allan 10–0–162–57–16.20.

Bowling—N. D. Cross 95–26–219–17–12.88; N. J. Corran 135.5–37–287–22–13.04; L. C. Parnell 88–31–211–16–13.18; M. G. Roberts 45.3–4–178–12–14.83; D. A. Allan 123.2–30–354–20–17.70; S. J. Renshaw 83.5–25–198–11–18.00.

BISHOP'S STORTFORD COLLEGE

Played 18: Won 4, Lost 8, Drawn 6. Abandoned 1

Master i/c: D. A. Hopper

Batting—E. M. Peachey 13–0–345–100–26.53; L. E. M. Riddell 11–1–243–54–24.30; R. F. Hudson 16–4–286–56*–23.83; O. W. R. Haslam 9–2–136–48–19.42; *D. N. Child 15–0–268–88–17.86; D. F. Gilbert 8–1–116–47–16.57; A. J. P. Brown 14–0–225–71–16.07; R. N. Myers 11–0–120–38–10.90.

Bowling—R. S. Jayatileke 204–71–553–38–14.55; D. N. Child 148.1–27–475–24–19.79; M. J. S. Armitage 81.5–12–261–13–20.07; A. J. P. Brown 88.3–14–341–14–24.35.

BLOXHAM SCHOOL

Played 16: Won 4, Lost 3, Drawn 9. Abandoned 1

Master i/c: J. P. Horton

Batting—R. D. Beaty 15–6–306–62–34.00; S. Hehir 13–1–310–59–25.83; E. R. H. Wornum 15–1–289–86*–20.64; A. W. A. Adejumo 12–0–238–56–19.83; S. P. Johnson 11–0–201–34–18.27; C. T. G. Carr 11–0–181–40–16.45; R. A. F. Whitton 12–5–101–25*–14.42.

Bowling—E. R. H. Wornum 241.5–60–805–41–19.63; *A. R. Channing 116–14–491–16–30.68; R. A. F. Whitton 194–46–690–22–31.36.

BLUNDELL'S SCHOOL

Played 15: Won 3, Lost 9, Drawn 2, Tied 1. Abandoned 1

Master i/c: G. P. Randall Johnson

Batting—*M. R. N. Hunt 15–0–524–119–34.93; S. Bailey 15–1–272–52–19.42; T. V. P. Patidar 14–0–257–85–18.35; M. Grose 15–2–232–54–17.84; E. Whitefield 13–1–205–45–17.08; P. Steward 15–0–230–38–15.33; I. Gompertz 10–0–145–35–14.50; M. Patidar 12–1–158–54–14.36; R. Temple 9–1–110–45–13.75.

Bowling—R. Morris 171–23–500–24–20.83; R. Clayton 139.1–16–271–11–24.63; P. Steward 223.4–51–638–24–26.58.

BRADFIELD COLLEGE

Played 13: Won 1, Lost 3, Drawn 9. Abandoned 1

Master i/c: F. R. Dethridge Cricket professional: J. F. Harvey

Batting—S. P. Bridgman 11–2–596–121*–66.22; *J. T. C. Kendall 12–1–494–153*–44.90; W. S. Kendall 12–1–447–98–40.63; D. A. C. Smith 12–1–195–73–17.72; B. Wyatt 11–2–143–52–15.88; A. Williams 10–1–137–65–15.22.

Bowling—J. T. C. Kendall 156–31–435–25–17.40; B. Maxwell 115–37–268–13–20.61; S. P. Bridgman 135–40–401–19–21.10.

BRADFORD GRAMMAR SCHOOL

Played 24: Won 7, Lost 6, Drawn 11. Abandoned 5

Master i/c: A. G. Smith

Batting—N. J. Gomersall 22–11–534–80*–48.54; M. J. Savage 19–5–380–65–27.14; *D. C. Whitfield 22–0–534–89–24.27; S. A. W. Davies 18–0–332–51–18.44; A. M. Bretherton 11–1–165–59*–16.50; A. J. Brosnan 15–3–186–40–15.50; D. Priestley 20–0–241–46–12.05.

Bowling—D. J. Collinge 166.2–42–546–34–16.05; C. W. A. McIntosh 129.1–33–445–24–18.54; P. R. Booth 201–47–604–31–19.48; M. J. Hannan 146.1–33–532–26–20.46; J. D. Morton 105–13–384–12–32.00.

BRENTWOOD SCHOOL

Played 13: Won 1, Lost 6, Drawn 6

Master i/c: J. C. Wolters Cricket professional: K. C. Preston

Batting—*C. J. Wilkins 7–0–242–70–34.57; A. R. J. Sansom 11–2–230–74–25.55; P. J. Collier 13–1–282–68–23.50; J. Cameron 10–0–223–48–22.30; A. Foch-Heng 13–0–250–38–19.23; A. J. Duke 12–3–166–50*–18.44; S. I. Reeve 10–4–103–30–17.16; G. Fletcher 10–0–154–30–15.40.

Bowling—D. McAllister 164.1–34–487–24–20.29; S. I. Reeve 89.1–28–327–11–29.72; A. R. J. Sansom 101.3–22–360–12–30.00.

BRIGHTON COLLEGE

Played 22: Won 14, Lost 2, Drawn 6. Abandoned 1

Master i/c: J. Spencer Cricket professional: J. D. Morley

Batting—C. N. Gates 22–3–1,378–178*–72.52; *R. D. Oliphant-Callum 22–2–832–124–41.60; R. J. Gibson 20–5–503–81*–33.53; J. Owen 20–4–533–82–33.31; A. J. Sweet 19–6–424–69*–32.61; C. P. Hart 19–5–324–53–23.14; A. Sell 12–6–116–54–19.33.

Bowling—R. J. Gibson 48.2–17–107–10–10.70; R. I. Lewis 283.3–90–671–45–14.91; A. J. Strong 47–14–169–10–16.90; C. N. Gates 190.3–51–547–31–17.64; C. P. Hart 256.3–74–629–34–18.50; A. J. Sweet 131.5–25–290–15–19.33; J. Owen 165.1–29–541–21–25.76.

BROMSGROVE SCHOOL

Played 14: Won 1, Lost 5, Drawn 8. Abandoned 4

Master i/c: D. Langlands Cricket professional: P. G. Newman

Batting—H. W. Humphries 14–5–426–79*–47.33; A. A. Burton 13–0–258–53–19.84; M. P. Birch 13–2–147–43–13.36; J. Court 13–2–127–62–11.54.

Bowling—G. Harrhy 50.5–6–200–11–18.18; A. Bridge 138.2–23–451–22–20.50; A. Wylie 100–21–335–16–20.93; H. W. Humphries 94.3–13–354–14–25.28.

BRYANSTON SCHOOL

Played 17: Won 6, Lost 7, Drawn 4. Abandoned 1

Master i/c: K. T. Ruck

Batting—G. Bucknell 16–3–486–74–37.38; R. Thomas 7–1–189–77*–31.50; M. Davies 8–3–121–52*–24.20; J. Freisenbruch 16–1–362–60–24.13; R. Sadler 8–2–119–45–19.83; J. Singleton 16–1–274–45–18.26; T. Clarke 16–0–253–40–15.81; N. Lind 16–3–177–54–13.61; A. Tapper 12–0–135–24–11.25.

Bowling—N. Lind 28–6–122–11–11.09; T. Clarke 180–30–544–38–14.31; J. Stephens 70–13–248–17–14.58; M. Brewin 213–46–606–33–18.36; J. Singleton 89–19–322–10–32.20.

CAMPBELL COLLEGE

Played 13: Won 7, Lost 4, Drawn 2

Master i/c: E. T. Cooke

Batting—S. A. I. Dyer 12–3–535–203*–59.44; *D. A. Parker 9–2–225–112*–32.14; R. H. Lucas 9–1–140–41–17.50; A. E. Logan 12–2–103–49–10.30.

Bowling—R. H. Lucas 106–29–228–34–6.70; B. J. Mockford 37–4–87–11–7.90; D. A. Parker 98–20–201–24–8.37; S. A. I. Dyer 62–7–121–14–8.64; J. G. N. Lucas 44–11–133–10–13.30.

CANFORD SCHOOL

Played 16: Won 8, Lost 5, Drawn 3

Master i/c: S. J. Turrill Cricket professional: B. Touzel

Batting—*J. A. Perry 16–1–651–112–43.40; D. J. C. Allom 15–4–291–94–26.45; M. Kind 11–0–194–62–17.63; T. R. Murray Walker 15–3–208–51*–17.33; G. Rees 10–3–104–32–14.85; D. Young 14–0–195–36–13.92; J. Blacker 14–1–160–44–12.30.

Bowling—M. W. Forward 231.4–55–610–40–15.25; M. Kind 75.5–20–202–11–18.36; M. J. C. Allom 68.1–15–187–10–18.70; G. Rees 182–42–487–26–18.73; G. Herring 129–19–432–22–19.63.

CATERHAM SCHOOL

Played 14: Won 0, Lost 6, Drawn 8

Master i/c: A. G. Simon Cricket professional: K. Morris

Batting—K. A. Amaning 14–0–492–68–35.14; S. M. Lillicrap 15–2–293–49–22.53; N. A. Green 14–3–195–40–17.72; T. G. W. Bailey 13–1–174–37–14.50; S. J. Constantin 14–0–132–33–9.42; *I. W. Armitage 15–0–136–22–9.06; K. S. Amaning 15–0–129–30–8.60.

Bowling—S. M. Lillicrap 189–15–743–34–21.85; S. K. Perera 95.3–15–323–11–29.36; S. J. Constantin 164.2–29–541–17–31.82.

CHARTERHOUSE

Played 18: Won 5, Lost 4, Drawn 9. Abandoned 1

Master i/c: J. M. Knight Cricket professional: R. V. Lewis

Batting—G. D. Butler 5–1–121–100*–30.25; T. A. Bristowe 14–1–381–95–29.30; B. G. Blyth 18–1–485–110*–28.52; D. N. Shah 15–8–176–26–25.14; T. D. Rowell 15–1–302–105*–21.57; E. L. Green 17–4–280–49–21.53; *W. J. Chignell 17–1–340–53–21.25; C. A. M. Ayres 14–1–233–42–17.92; J. L. Merrick 17–2–246–42–16.40.

Bowling—D. N. Shah 159.4–35–505–33–15.30; J. L. Merrick 162–36–472–23–20.52; T. D. Courtenay-Evans 201.4–37–722–32–22.56; J. F. Wilson 128–25–408–13–31.38; W. J. Chignell 144.3–38–445–12–37.08.

CHELTENHAM COLLEGE

Played 19: Won 6, Lost 4, Drawn 9. Abandoned 1

Master i/c: W. J. Wesson Cricket professional: M. W. Stovold

Batting—M. C. Cawdron 17–3–578–114*–41.28; M. E. Dalton-Morris 6–2–138–44–34.50; J. T. G. Westbrook 8–1–214–80–30.57; B. J. C. Lawrence 11–3–227–48–28.37; D. R. Fulton 17–3–371–80–26.50; D. R. Hewson 18–2–412–109–25.75; S. A. La Rocco 14–3–282–66–25.63; *B. B. Jones 18–1–398–102–23.41; P. M. Evans 18–7–177–34–16.09.

Bowling—M. C. Green 186.4–36–612–29–21.10; M. C. Cawdron 178.4–34–573–23–24.91; D. R. Fulton 280.4–52–858–34–25.23; D. R. Hewson 137.1–27–534–18–29.66.

CHIGWELL SCHOOL

Played 18: Won 8, Lost 4, Drawn 6

Master i/c: D. N. Morrison Cricket professional: A. W. Lilley

Batting—P. C. Harvey 17–2–748–126–49.86; J. F. Carpenter 17–5–541–100*–45.08; *T. B. Tarring 18–1–465–67*–27.35; A. D. N. Kurukulasooriya 15–2–317–83*–24.38; D. C. Pugson 10–4–137–27*–22.83; T. Offen 15–3–245–75*–20.41; D. R. Evans 13–1–179–96–14.91.

Bowling—P. C. Harvey 221–49–729–39–18.69; J. F. Carpenter 250.5–58–710–37–19.18; V. C. Nigam 67.5–11–302–10–30.20.

CHRIST COLLEGE, BRECON

Played 15: Won 3, Lost 5, Drawn 7. Abandoned 1

Master i/c: C. W. Kleiser

Batting—M. Richards 13–1–335–103*–27.91; M. E. Morris 14–2–314–83–26.16; *E. P. M. Holland 12–3–210–62*–23.33; M. Roderick 13–2–250–50*–22.72; J. Hall 12–0–197–52–16.41; C. S. R. Morgan 14–2–168–47–14.00.

Bowling—E. P. M. Holland 179.1–49–424–27–15.70; J. Hall 91.1–16–317–11–28.81; G. A. Powell 76–9–341–11–31.00; M. Roderick 132.3–28–423–12–35.25.

CLAYESMORE SCHOOL

Played 19: Won 6, Lost 6, Drawn 7. Abandoned 2

Master i/c: R. Hammond

Batting—*P. Bradbury 18–2–503–81*–31.43; B. Julyan 16–5–275–59–25.00; J. Brown 10–5–118–30*–23.60; P. Humphreys 15–1–292–67–20.85; J. Dakin 12–5–127–29–18.14; G. J. Latimer 16–0–229–48–14.31; A. Ferguson 14–1–142–26–10.92; A. Gartell 17–0–158–25–9.29.

Bowling—P. Bradbury 171.5–32–560–32–17.50; J. Dakin 92.5–13–321–18–17.83; L. Coley 132.4–23–453–25–18.12; G. J. Latimer 133–32–407–18–22.61; A. Gartell 139–23–448–16–28.00.

CLIFTON COLLEGE

Played 17: Won 8, Lost 3, Drawn 6. Abandoned 2

Master i/c: C. M. E. Colquhoun Cricket professional: F. J. Andrew

Batting—*J. R. A. Williams 17–6–935–136*–85.00; M. G. N. Windows 16–3–649–127–49.92; G. H. J. Rees 13–4–308–98–34.22; J. J. L. Bretten 12–4–261–74*–32.62; J. P. Parish 15–3–294–119*–24.50.

Bowling—N. E. L. Howe 95.2–24–310–20–15.50; B. M. O. Gibbs 175–35–633–32–19.78; M. G. N. Windows 159.2–31–537–22–24.40; J. P. Parish 184–29–594–19–31.26; R. C. Clifford 193.5–40–690–18–38.33.

COLFE'S SCHOOL

Played 12: Won 3, Lost 2, Drawn 7. Abandoned 1

Master i/c: P. Hollingum

Batting—*M. Horder 12–2–574–132*–57.40; M. Quilter 12–2–428–78–42.80; D. Perry 9–2–188–41–26.85; A. Hameed 9–4–129–43–25.80; T. Shoben 12–0–263–38–21.91; J. Gledhill-Carr 12–0–200–47–16.66.

Bowling—M. Quilter 97.4–18–361–20–18.05; J. Gledhill-Carr 165.4–36–494–19–26.00; M. Horder 114.3–18–401–15–26.73.

COLSTON'S SCHOOL

Played 17: Won 5, Lost 4, Drawn 8. Abandoned 2

Master i/c: M. P. B. Tayler

Batting—*J. A. Franklin 16–0–906–186–56.62; I. J. Webb 16–4–413–104*–34.41; A. I. Vickery 7–0–177–67–25.28; M. J. Sheedy 13–3–224–103–22.40; L. A. Collins 14–2–249–62–20.75; M. C. Bryan 13–3–206–37*–20.60; R. J. Pandya 16–2–272–77–19.42.

Bowling—S. W. Brown 134.2–30–523–23–22.73; J. A. Franklin 108.1–28–349–15–23.26; R. J. Pandya 136.2–23–463–19–24.36; M. C. Bryan 127–23–442–14–31.57.

COVENTRY SCHOOL – BABLAKE

Played 13: Won 5, Lost 5, Drawn 3

Master i/c: B. J. Sutton

Batting—G. Dowall 12–3–304–75*–33.77; D. A. Hart 9–3–166–41*–27.66; M. A. Ward 12–0–322–56–26.83; R. J. S. Hill 13–1–257–48–21.41; A. Cronin 10–3–132–33–18.85; *M. G. H. Sutton 11–2–147–40*–16.33.

Bowling—J. Hart 53.1–6–144–10–14.40; Azhar Khan 79.1–9–262–12–21.83; M. G. H. Sutton 71–15–243–11–22.09.

CRANBROOK SCHOOL

Played 12: Won 1, Lost 8, Drawn 3

Master i/c: T. K. Gunn

Batting—J. Lawson 11–1–237–84*–23.70; R. Fishwick 12–0–283–56–23.58; K. Wookey 11–1–206–67–20.60; C. Barrett 12–1–185–55–16.81; J. Barron 12–0–152–35–12.66.

Bowling—J. Thompson 75–15–244–14–17.42; K. Wookey 80–15–303–10–30.30; A. Brooks 105–14–439–14–31.35.

CRANLEIGH SCHOOL

Played 16: Won 5, Lost 5, Drawn 6

Master i/c: R. D. V. Knight

Batting—B. R. Seal 10–3–176–43–25.14; H. C. Watkinson 16–2–348–71*–24.85; S. C. G. Copleston 15–3–274–83*–22.83; R. L. Johnson 12–0–268–68–22.33; *S. J. Bailey 16–0–332–61–20.75; A. C. Baillieu 16–0–270–93–16.87; N. P. F. Swiss 14–0–177–39–12.64; J. R. Tabor 14–0–167–41–11.92; A. R. Kyle 15–4–112–25–10.18.

Bowling—H. C. Watkinson 212.1–53–674–42–16.04; G. B. Atkinson 167–46–498–27–18.44; A. R. Kyle 176.5–45–500–21–23.80.

DAME ALLAN'S SCHOOL

Played 14: Won 9, Lost 2, Drawn 3

Master i/c: J. P. E. Procter

Batting—*R. W. Thompson 14–2–413–102–34.41; M. J. Thompson 12–3–282–52–31.33; C. Harrison 11–5–182–41*–30.33; J. J. Ditchburn 8–2–104–52*–17.33; R. I. P. Hodgson 10–2–135–60*–16.87; P. J. Nicholson 11–2–141–45–15.66; T. P. Ditchburn 13–2–171–50*–15.54.

Bowling—M. J. Thompson 98–25–244–21–11.61; M. Ingram 30–0–128–11–11.63; J. J. Ditchburn 56–11–205–15–13.66; R. I. P. Hodgson 74.1–9–249–12–20.75; R. W. Thompson 80.1–15–297–13–22.84.

DAUNTSEY'S SCHOOL

Played 13: Won 4, Lost 4, Drawn 5

Master i/c: D. C. R. Baker — Cricket professional: P. Knowles

Batting—M. R. Whistler 12–4–399–63–49.87; A. N. Field 12–2–332–64*–33.20; *G. M. Gaiger 13–1–354–55–29.50; I. D. Hardman 13–0–368–103–28.30; S. F. E. Cottle 12–1–138–28–12.54; S. W. C. Gilmour 11–0–126–42–11.45; T. J. Heigl 11–2–102–20–11.33.

Bowling—G. M. Gaiger 72.1–12–280–19–14.73; A. N. Field 134.4–30–430–29–14.82; S. F. E. Cottle 83–8–331–16–20.68; D. P. Atkins 128.3–19–426–16–26.62.

DEAN CLOSE SCHOOL

Played 16: Won 3, Lost 6, Drawn 7. Abandoned 1

Master i/c: C. M. Kenyon — Cricket professional: M. Heath

Batting—*C. J. Townsend 16–2–498–96–35.57; M. Butler 14–1–399–103–30.69; C. S. Knightley 16–2–308–62–22.00; S. H. Odell 12–3–183–47–20.33; G. G. Hunton 14–2–234–53*–19.50; A. M. Egan 10–2–154–51–19.25; A. H. Odell 9–2–112–52–16.00; R. J. Husband 11–0–151–43–13.72.

Bowling—J. M. Bowditch 153.1–28–459–28–16.39; C. S. Knightley 143.1–18–464–21–22.09; A. H. Odell 79–12–327–14–23.35; M. R. James 126–16–500–21–23.80.

DENSTONE COLLEGE

Played 14: Won 4, Lost 0, Drawn 10. Abandoned 3

Master i/c: A. N. James

Batting—*J. N. Snape 13–4–660–128*–73.33; P. J. Barnes 11–2–205–65–22.77; J. J. Mason 11–2–163–70*–18.11; A. S. H. Oyston 14–1–213–33–16.38; T. J. Mason 10–0–129–22–12.90.

Bowling—J. Broughton 111.5–29–270–19–14.21; N. A. Warr 85–17–258–18–14.33; P. J. Barnes 90–24–210–13–16.15; T. J. Mason 73–16–218–11–19.81; J. N. Snape 94.1–18–288–14–20.57; C. C. Tissainayagam 103–20–295–13–22.69.

DOUAI SCHOOL

Played 11: Won 3, Lost 2, Drawn 6. Abandoned 1

Master i/c: J. Shaw

Batting—*M. G. Allen 12–4–466–115–58.25; C. J. Bartlett 12–3–260–77–28.88; I. M. Anison 11–0–197–63–17.90.

Bowling—N. J. Saw 86–16–305–21–14.52; I. M. Anison 96–14–341–18–18.94; S. A. German 60–8–237–11–21.54.

DOVER COLLEGE

Played 13: Won 2, Lost 6, Drawn 5. Abandoned 2

Master i/c: D. C. Butler

Batting—A. S. Burrell 11–2–327–68–36.33; S. J. Schilder 13–0–415–90–31.92; *D. M. Rouse 11–0–304–74–27.63; M. D. Schilder 13–4–169–54*–18.77; A. B. Dandeh-N'Jie 13–1–111–47–9.25.

Bowling—D. A. Cruickshank 113.5–15–439–16–27.43; B. Amedee 76.4–12–360–13–27.69; R. V. Price 84.5–8–316–11–28.72.

DOWNSIDE SCHOOL

Played 13: Won 7, Lost 4, Drawn 2. Abandoned 1

Master i/c: K. J. Burke Cricket professional: B. Bing

Batting—O. B. Ratcliffe 12–4–277–68*–34.62; *J. L. Morgan 13–1–351–59–29.25; M. C. R. Thatcher 13–1–341–103*–28.41; M. F. Fitzgerald 9–2–118–44*–16.85; B. P. N. Ramsay 12–2–167–32–16.70; M. R. Kennedy 13–0–170–55–13.07; T. V. E. Hansom 13–1–130–23–10.83.

Bowling—M. F. Fitzgerald 158.4–49–379–32–11.84; G. J. Bell 50–11–175–10–17.50; B. M. Kennard 71–17–224–12–18.66; O. B. Ratcliffe 131.2–31–408–21–19.42.

DUKE OF YORK'S ROYAL MILITARY SCHOOL

Played 12: Won 3, Lost 5, Drawn 4

Master i/c: S. Salisbury Cricket professional: S. Skeate

Batting—N. M. Conway 5–1–161–76*–40.25; G. J. Kennett 10–1–213–79–23.66; *C. N. Conway 10–0–191–58–19.10; S. P. Neary 7–0–106–31–15.14.

Bowling—J. N. J. Marsh 76–24–173–12–14.41; G. J. Kennett 73–6–293–15–19.53; D. J. Reynolds 88–14–281–11–25.54.

DULWICH COLLEGE

Played 17: Won 3, Lost 5, Drawn 9. Abandoned 1

Master i/c: N. D. Cousins Cricket professionals: A. R. Ranson and W. A. Smith

Batting—*R. S. Sheldon 15–1–449–86–32.07; G. Y. Mohabir 17–2–394–82*–26.26; R. W. Scholar 14–1–313–56–24.07; S. C. Davey 10–1–206–41–22.88; J. H. Potter 17–0–380–115–22.35; S. M. Bottle 12–4–142–39–17.75; P. J. Smith 12–4–121–24–15.12; T. R. Sandars 8–1–104–39*–14.85.

Bowling—R. S. Sharp 88–18–257–17–15.11; E. P. Rusling 135–34–340–20–17.00; R. W. Scholar 94–23–301–11–27.36; P. J. Smith 145–26–444–16–27.75; S. C. Davey 108–21–376–13–28.92.

DURHAM SCHOOL

Played 17: Won 6, Lost 4, Drawn 7. Abandoned 2

Master i/c: N. J. Willings Cricket professional: M. Hirsch

Batting—R. M. S. Weston 17–3–643–100*–45.92; *W. P. C. Weston 17–4–527–80–40.53; J. M. W. Taylor 13–7–230–65*–38.33; M. T. Warkup 11–2–205–46–22.77; P. McCutcheon 13–2–190–51*–17.27; D. Parkin 14–3–104–26–9.45.

Bowling—W. P. C. Weston 238.1–62–469–30–15.63; N. C. F. Taylor 74.3–12–274–17–16.11; N. W. Darling 213.3–48–670–34–19.70; R. M. S. Weston 183.5–34–593–22–26.95.

EASTBOURNE COLLEGE

Played 21: Won 7, Lost 6, Drawn 8

Master i/c: N. L. Wheeler Cricket professional: A. E. James

Batting—D. C. Richards 16–5–388–66*–35.27; B. H. Miller 20–3–533–100*–31.35; *A. J. T. Halliday 20–0–588–114–29.40; W. R. Green 19–0–497–72–26.15; T. J. W. Parker 20–1–453–66–23.84; P. J. Hillman 18–3–357–77–23.80; C. D. Grove 10–2–143–42–17.87; H. A. Skinner 8–0–109–42–13.62; A. C. J. de Mierre 15–3–139–35–11.58.

Bowling—E. G. R. Barrett 90.3–30–213–19–11.21; A. J. T. Halliday 172.2–46–484–27–17.92; H. A. Skinner 93–15–301–13–23.15; C. D. Grove 132–15–513–22–23.31; A. C. J. de Mierre 175–34–550–22–25.00; P. J. Hillman 163.4–31–571–13–43.92.

THE EDINBURGH ACADEMY

Played 16: Won 4, Lost 5, Drawn 7

Master i/c: G. R. Bowe Cricket professional: N. A. Perry

Batting—R. W. Cairns 14–1–399–152–30.69; J. J. Edmond 14–1–248–64–19.07; R. D. J. Wilkinson 14–2–205–56–17.08; *J. N. K. Godfrey 15–0–252–79–16.80; D. J. C. Thomson 13–0–193–47–14.84; W. P. Haslett 13–1–104–23–8.66.

Bowling—R. W. Cairns 159.3–37–490–30–16.33; J. J. Edmond 157.3–28–533–25–21.32; M. J. Anderson 147.2–18–495–15–33.00.

ELIZABETH COLLEGE, GUERNSEY

Played 22: Won 8, Lost 6, Drawn 8. Abandoned 1

Master i/c: M. E. Kinder

Batting—T. Hollyer-Hill 19–6–617–103*–47.46; *P. J. A. Moody 18–4–436–98–31.14; D. B. L. Mackay 19–3–368–65–23.00; S. P. Noyon 19–0–393–83–20.68; J. R. M. Harris 19–2–340–84*–20.00; P. J. le Ray 9–1–113–46*–14.12; A. J. C. Whalley 16–5–155–28–14.09; C. R. Hamon 17–0–217–40–12.76; A. Biggins 14–4–116–23*–11.60.

Bowling—P. J. A. Moody 236–53–796–50–15.92; A. M. Mitchell 156.2–19–541–32–16.90; M. A. Smith 191–32–656–22–29.81; T. Hollyer-Hill 79–5–360–11–32.72.

ELLESMERE COLLEGE

Played 17: Won 5, Lost 4, Drawn 8

Master i/c: E. Marsh Cricket professionals: R. G. Mapp and M. Stone

Batting—*A. C. Barrett 15–1–408–70*–29.14; R. C. Carew 15–2–347–57*–26.69; N. J. B. Allan 12–4–211–76–26.37; D. O. Jenkins 13–1–273–60–22.75; S. R. Montgomery 14–3–189–36–17.18; S. Hussain 12–1–161–64–14.63; J. G. Slater 11–3–113–43*–14.12.

Bowling—G. N. Phillips 131–45–308–33–9.33; J. G. Slater 225–82–468–43–10.88; N. J. B. Allan 74–17–214–13–16.46; D. C. Gervis 137–21–552–22–25.09.

ELTHAM COLLEGE

Played 19: Won 5, Lost 4, Drawn 10. Abandoned 1

Masters i/c: B. M. Withecombe and P. McCartney Cricket professional: R. Winup

Batting—J. M. Ramsey 18–2–688–105–43.00; K. M. Morrell 18–5–419–79*–32.23; S. G. Hughes 16–0–408–58–25.50; R. N. Garnett 9–2–162–34–23.14; *F. Kavina 19–1–409–103–22.72; S. Baksh 16–2–243–65–17.35; A. L. Paterson 14–4–157–30*–15.70; G. B. Tibbs 12–1–104–23–9.45.

Bowling—J. M. Ramsey 46.1–9–173–10–17.30; G. B. Tibbs 100.2–10–392–20–19.60; F. Kavina 130–17–522–25–20.88; R. N. Garnett 120.2–21–423–17–24.88; K. M. Morrell 136–28–505–19–26.57.

EMANUEL SCHOOL

Played 17: Won 9, Lost 2, Drawn 6

Master i/c: R. M. S. Woodall Cricket professional: J. R. Cremer

Batting—N. Saint 12–6–278–79*–46.33; P. Cross 9–3–221–45–36.83; D. J. Legg 17–1–546–140*–34.12; G. Neame 17–2–497–119*–33.13; E. Pullinger 14–1–412–62*–31.69; I. R. Tournès 12–2–301–73–30.10; *M. D. Coe 11–0–323–90–29.36; J. Khan 10–1–198–72–22.00; J. C. Cole 15–5–218–48*–21.80.

Bowling—N. K. Young 134–27–408–25–16.32; P. Chapman 117–13–477–23–20.73; J. C. Cole 151.2–31–564–21–26.85.

ENFIELD GRAMMAR SCHOOL

Played 22: Won 7, Lost 3, Drawn 12. Abandoned 1

Master i/c: J. J. Conroy

Batting—D. Bowen 20–3–1,089–196*–64.05; *J. King 19–2–578–113–34.00; N. Clydesdale 21–2–583–100*–30.68; P. Chapman 12–3–169–45*–18.77; T. Holmes 16–3–242–47–18.61; M. Stevens 17–5–210–25–17.50; I. Cully 12–3–106–26–11.77.

Bowling—N. Lutwyche 283.5–62–834–56–14.89; M. Stevens 227.3–38–690–40–17.25; R. Hore 77–17–232–11–21.09; T. Holmes 186.2–31–719–29–24.79.

EPSOM COLLEGE

Played 10: Won 6, Lost 2, Drawn 2

Master i/c: M. D. Hobbs

Batting—N. A. Morris 9–2–293–100*–41.85; J. C. Harris 5–2–117–55*–39.00; P. E. Roche 9–0–339–80–37.66; A. R. Pym 8–1–175–75–25.00; T. R. Newton 10–4–146–34–24.33; *J. G. Jackson 9–2–122–49*–17.42.

Bowling—T. R. Newton 146.1–43–387–33–11.72; J. R. Rose 109–30–347–15–23.13; A. S. M. Trengove 91.4–20–287–11–26.09.

ETON COLLEGE

Played 15: Won 3, Lost 3, Drawn 9

Master i/c: J. A. Claughton Cricket professional: J. M. Rice

Batting—P. M. Eastwood 13–1–556–98–46.33; N. R. J. Hagen 14–1–517–88–39.76; S. C. E. Strickland 14–3–391–103*–35.54; *H. J. P. Chetwood 13–3–221–66*–22.10; T. A. J. Jenkins 15–0–330–53–22.00; W. R. G. Sellar 14–1–236–57–18.15.

Bowling—J. M. S. Whittington 235.1–34–780–49–15.91; H. J. P. Chetwood 247.3–53–748–29–25.79; G. H. B. Lewis 134.3–30–464–15–30.93.

EXETER SCHOOL

Played 17: Won 7, Lost 3, Drawn 7. Abandoned 1

Master i/c: M. C. Wilcock

Batting—D. R. Gannon 15–1–579–124*–41.35; M. J. Perring 8–3–182–41–36.40; M. W. Evans 13–5–207–53*–25.87; P. B. Hughes 10–1–196–51*–21.77; C. J. Walker 15–1–282–65–20.14; D. D. McNaught 13–1–236–50*–19.66; *M. J. Stevenson 14–2–216–41–18.00; M. D. Keylock 10–3–113–24–16.14; W. D. Clarkson 7–0–111–66–15.85; H. S. V. Thomas 11–2–119–26–13.22.

Bowling—M. H. T. Jones 54.5–13–143–12–11.91; M. D. Keylock 76.4–15–252–18–14.00; J. R. Price 110–18–389–21–18.52; T. P. Quartley 77.3–20–244–13–18.76; M. J. Stevenson 196.2–38–621–30–20.70.

FELSTED SCHOOL

Played 21: Won 7, Lost 4, Drawn 10

Master i/c: M. Surridge Cricket professional: G. O. Barker

Batting—M. J. Crisp 20–5–761–118–50.73; A. C. M. Woods 21–0–839–102–39.95; T. W. H. Bulgin 18–0–648–104–36.00; R. J. Slater 19–1–502–100–27.88; *J. P. Garner 21–5–435–63–27.18; A. J. Martin 10–5–123–58–24.60; D. R. A. Hughes 15–3–293–53–24.41; M. G. Mixer 10–4–142–41–23.66; R. D. Havard-Davies 13–3–146–25–14.60.

Bowling—M. G. Mixer 240–49–726–36–20.16; R. J. Slater 242–63–754–37–20.37; M. J. S. Martin 99–24–272–13–20.92; A. J. Martin 115–21–415–18–23.05; D. G. Rawlinson 216–41–724–28–25.85.

FETTES COLLEGE

Played 13: Won 0, Lost 8, Drawn 5

Master i/c: M. C. G. Peel Cricket professional: J. van Geloven

Batting—A. F. Zulfiqar 13–1–267–89–22.25; J. B. Macpherson 14–2–267–81–22.25; R. A. N. R. Llewellyn 12–4–126–26*–15.75; J. D. Weir 13–0–143–34–11.00; *J. R. S. Lloyd 14–0–138–40–9.85; N. M. Turner 12–0–105–31–8.75.

Bowling—J. R. S. Lloyd 204.1–47–540–43–12.55; J. G. M. Burns 132.2–31–430–11–39.09; J. A. Hammond Chambers 116–13–437–11–39.72.

FOREST SCHOOL

Played 16: Won 6, Lost 5, Drawn 5. Abandoned 2

Master i/c: S. Turner

Batting—P. O'Neill 12–3–425–88–47.22; *A. C. Richards 14–3–479–79–43.54; N. Johnson 11–5–201–45*–33.50; A. Heyes 14–3–357–56–32.45; P. Sharma 11–1–182–39–18.20; J. Moore 10–0–100–20–10.00.

Bowling—A. C. Richards 104–38–280–22–12.72; P. O'Neill 89–25–260–15–17.33; A. Hashmi 130–26–481–19–25.31; J. Dwyer 161–30–627–23–27.26; M. Pike 128–21–404–11–36.72.

FOYLE AND LONDONDERRY COLLEGE

Played 18: Won 14, Lost 2, Drawn 2. Abandoned 1

Masters i/c: G. R. McCarter and I. McCracken

Batting—T. Dougherty 18–4–489–75*–34.92; *B. Smyth 17–3–421–82–30.07; J. McFarland 17–2–396–77–26.40; J. Brown 18–1–380–98–22.35; C. Parke 11–2–148–33–16.44; C. Donaghy 11–4–104–34*–14.85; A. Brown 13–4–107–33*–11.88.

Bowling—J. Brown 153.4–39–319–44–7.25; C. Parke 77–15–244–26–9.38; S. Lapsley 73.5–9–266–24–11.08; R. Martin 119.1–22–305–23–13.26; D. Cooke 119–33–300–22–13.63.

FRAMLINGHAM COLLEGE

Played 17: Won 8, Lost 1, Drawn 8

Master i/c: P. J. Hayes — Cricket professional: C. Rutterford

Batting—N. I. Barker 17–3–599–82–42.78; J. A. Newton 16–7–374–86–41.55; *S. E. Iliffe 17–1–563–106–35.18; W. J. Earl 17–1–526–122*–32.87; M. C. Osborne 9–4–163–71*–32.60; A. J. Thorogood 12–4–238–47–29.75.

Bowling—S. E. Iliffe 69.4–11–227–18–12.61; M. J. Rutterford 232.5–66–548–43–12.74; P. Edwards 189.3–49–483–34–14.20; J. G. C. Townsend 217.5–36–704–29–24.27.

GIGGLESWICK SCHOOL

Played 14: Won 3, Lost 3, Drawn 8. Abandoned 1

Master i/c: D. Seed — Cricket professional: B. Julian

Batting—*A. D. Nesbitt 13–1–323–83*–26.91; A. G. Holmes 11–0–285–71–25.90; A. G. G. Caton 12–2–224–45–22.40; J. J. Knighton 13–2–191–57–17.36; S. J. Taylor 11–0–184–49–16.72; T. J. Bentley 13–1–180–36–15.00.

Bowling—S. M. Burton 47–9–150–11–13.63; T. J. Bentley 107–24–314–17–18.47; A. G. G. Caton 107–13–332–17–19.52; O. P. J. White 90–12–455–21–21.66; A. D. Armstrong 67–8–314–14–22.42; A. D. Nesbitt 97–19–290–12–24.16.

THE GLASGOW ACADEMY

Played 11: Won 0, Lost 6, Drawn 5

Master i/c: D. N. Barrett — Cricket professional: B. M. W. Patterson

Batting—J. M. Gayfer 11–1–286–58–28.60; *K. P. Sandberg 11–2–194–55*–21.55; J. J. Millen 10–1–131–50*–14.55.

Bowling—J. Gardee 115.4–22–343–23–14.91; J. M. Gayfer 135.3–26–413–21–19.66; D. G. Gourlay 75–10–263–13–20.23.

GLENALMOND

Played 14: Won 3, Lost 4, Drawn 7. Abandoned 3

Master i/c: A. James

Batting—C. J. C. Breese 15–3–374–79*–31.16; J. D. Thomson 15–0–402–87–26.80; S. C. Scott Elliot 12–0–317–109–26.41; J. P. Jack 15–1–286–67*–20.42; *R. M. Jebb 14–0–235–70–16.78; E. R. Lindsay 15–1–170–35–12.14; G. J. N. Nardini 12–1–120–30–10.90.

Bowling—J. C. Caldwell 189–46–461–27–17.07; A. R. L. Wager 73.1–15–209–12–17.41; R. M. Jebb 158.2–31–547–31–17.64.

GORDONSTOUN SCHOOL

Played 10: Won 2, Lost 3, Drawn 5

Masters i/c: C. J. Barton and J. E. Lofthouse

Batting—E. Ruane 10–1–269–54–29.88; R. Collett 8–2–144–52–24.00; D. Craven 8–1–164–58*–23.42; A. J. Clark 7–1–125–32–20.83.

Bowling—H. Cliffe-Thompson 93–10–280–20–14.00; D. Craven 65–13–156–10–15.60; A. Assatourian 36–4–240–11–21.81.

GRENVILLE COLLEGE

Played 18: Won 10, Lost 6, Drawn 2

Master i/c: R. J. Davis

Batting—S. Blakers 6–2–182–84*–45.50; J. F. T. Pallister 7–1–192–67–32.00; E. C. Johns 14–5–142–36*–15.77; D. R. Ellacott 15–3–174–24*–14.50; R. S. Hann 13–3–131–27–13.10; A. J. Symons 11–1–119–35–11.90.

Bowling—M. J. Graham 47–9–127–18–7.05; *S. D. Wait 110–22–319–29–11.00; A. J. Symons 47.1–4–228–15–15.20; R. S. Hann 89–14–376–16–23.50.

GRESHAM'S SCHOOL

Played 18: Won 5, Lost 3, Drawn 10

Master i/c: A. M. Ponder

Batting—K. S. C. Tuck 14–3–390–63–35.45; M. V. A. Robins 11–3–254–58–31.75; *I. D. Barnett 17–0–485–141–28.52; D. J. Newton 17–1–420–52–26.25; P. D. Holliday 12–2–248–59–24.80; S. E. Child 8–1–129–34*–18.42; A. J. Evans 17–3–244–33*–17.42.

Bowling—A. J. Ward 68–16–178–17–10.47; I. D. Barnett 172–34–512–26–19.69; S. G. Lind 134–21–376–18–20.88; M. P. Seaman 89.3–7–350–13–26.92; D. A. Jackson 191–27–674–23–29.30.

HABERDASHERS' ASKE'S SCHOOL, ELSTREE

Played 18: Won 8, Lost 0, Drawn 10. Abandoned 1

Master i/c: N. G. Folland

Batting—*B. Moore 18–3–785–147*–52.33; M. I. Yeabsley 17–3–722–123*–51.57; R. Thacker 16–4–614–120*–51.16; S. Liddle 8–3–153–52–30.60; R. S. Yeabsley 13–2–275–49–25.00; B. Arumugam 10–3–126–42–18.00.

Bowling—B. Moore 69.2–19–196–17–11.52; R. S. Yeabsley 265.1–68–678–42–16.14; M. I. Yeabsley 221–78–589–36–16.36.

HAILEYBURY

Played 17: Won 6, Lost 3, Drawn 8. Abandoned 1

Master i/c: M. S. Seymour   Cricket professional: P. M. Ellis

Batting—*W. T. R. Meacock 18–1–495–88–29.11; G. A. Ritchie 18–3–394–118–26.26; J. Malhotra 14–1–333–66–25.61; A. M. W. Lemon 15–3–252–45–21.00; J. W. Holding 9–1–138–68*–17.25; S. J. Ansell 18–1–290–40–17.05; T. C. Roundell 17–2–212–41–14.13.

Bowling—A. M. W. Lemon 213–48–590–47–12.55; R. G. A. Gunn 258–93–567–30–18.90; G. A. Ritchie 182–56–458–23–19.91.

HAMPTON SCHOOL

Played 17: Won 4, Lost 4, Drawn 9

Master i/c: A. J. Cook

Batting—S. C. Janes 12–4–503–76*–62.87; J. E. Sudbury 17–2–610–89–40.66; J. O. Trinder 10–1–311–100*–34.55; M. E. Hurles 12–4–253–92*–31.62; *J. P. Diprose 11–0–307–91–27.90; S. A. H. Cochrane 10–2–185–55–23.12; R. A. F. Hall 8–2–112–51*–18.66; M. H. Chalavatzis 9–0–146–83–16.22.

Bowling—S. R. Caruana 72–17–224–13–17.23; J. E. Saunders 182–47–637–36–17.69; J. A. Scowen 80–20–218–11–19.81; S. A. H. Cochrane 165–49–463–23–20.13; R. A. F. Hall 187–33–792–24–33.00.

HARROW SCHOOL

Played 18: Won 4, Lost 2, Drawn 12

Master i/c: W. Snowden Cricket professional: R. K. Sethi

Batting—C. E. Williams 16–3–521–127*–40.07; S. M. Guillebaud 16–5–439–72*–39.90; S. H. Aldous 18–3–504–69–33.60; M. A. Holyoake 15–1–363–73–25.92; E. M. S. Hewens 11–3–198–47–24.75; F. S. J. Yates 11–3–172–40–21.50; J. L. Pool 10–1–182–38–20.22; *M. E. D. Jarrett 16–1–269–50*–17.93.

Bowling—J. L. Pool 153–40–366–26–14.07; R. E. Sexton 261–72–749–40–18.72; R. A. H. Peasgood 72–14–191–10–19.10; W. J. D. Hewitt 142–18–492–21–23.42.

THE HARVEY GRAMMAR SCHOOL

Played 25: Won 14, Lost 3, Drawn 8

Master i/c: P. J. Harding

Batting—M. R. Fletcher 16–3–447–101*–34.38; P. D. Crocker 23–8–472–80*–31.46; S. F. Hobbs 24–3–520–93–24.76; R. J. N. Davis 14–4–197–59–19.70; G. N. Thompson 16–5–184–52*–16.72; C. K. Crampton 8–0–119–49–14.87; A. W. Morris 12–3–133–42–14.77; *S. Lowe 21–2–276–54–14.52; S. G. Rees 11–2–118–45–13.11.

Bowling—A. W. Morris 181.4–59–478–50–9.56; A. J. Bowers 127.1–30–366–30–12.20; R. J. N. Davis 279.4–74–685–56–12.23; S. G. Rees 103.1–33–308–23–13.39; M. R. Fletcher 91.4–35–212–15–14.13.

HEREFORD CATHEDRAL SCHOOL

Played 15: Won 6, Lost 3, Drawn 6

Master i/c: A. H. Connop

Batting—J. Sparey 9–2–355–109*–50.71; *E. Bottoms 13–4–248–39*–27.55; L. James 8–1–176–51–25.14; R. King 13–0–300–67–23.07; C. Banks 11–2–158–40–17.55; E. Symonds 12–3–145–47–16.11; I. Cathcart 13–0–147–28–11.30.

Bowling—L. James 70.1–19–213–16–13.31; B. Plane 123–36–323–22–14.68; E. Bottoms 196.3–42–579–36–16.08; I. Cathcart 50–7–179–10–17.90.

HIGHGATE SCHOOL

Played 14: Won 7, Lost 4, Drawn 3

Master i/c: C. J. Davies Cricket professional: R. E. O. Jones

Batting—E. Gladwin 3–0–116–50–38.66; A. Shams 14–1–338–46*–26.00; M. Tudor 11–5–150–44*–25.00; T. Gladwin 14–0–324–66–23.14; R. Tillett 11–0–226–51–20.54; K. Jay 10–2–133–36*–16.62; A. Maruf 11–3–132–51–16.50.

Bowling—T. Gladwin 155.4–31–566–37–15.29; R. Grant 87.2–14–386–19–20.31; M. Sylvester 150.4–24–510–23–22.17; R. Parbhoo 74–8–319–12–26.58.

HURSTPIERPOINT COLLEGE

Played 16: Won 7, Lost 3, Drawn 6. Abandoned 1

Master i/c: M. E. Allbrook Cricket professional: D. J. Semmence

Batting—*M. J. Semmence 15–6–492–90*–54.66; P. T. Wicker 15–2–490–100*–37.69; J. M. Kemp-Gee 11–4–248–86*–35.42; H. M. Reid 16–0–379–63–23.68; C. M. Rhodes 12–1–167–39–15.18; N. R. Beacham 10–2–113–38*–14.12; S. L. Lilly 10–2–108–33–13.50; G. W. Budibent 9–1–103–40–12.87.

Bowling—M. J. Semmence 122–36–325–24–13.54; M. J. King 188–43–506–36–14.05; S. R. J. Hall 151.5–47–335–17–19.70; P. T. Wicker 110.5–32–259–12–21.58; C. C. Cheshire 162.4–28–485–19–25.52.

IPSWICH SCHOOL

Played 14: Won 5, Lost 1, Drawn 8

Master i/c: P. Rees Cricket professional: R. E. East

Batting—R. Catley 14–1–476–110–36.61; J. Douglas 13–4–316–104*–35.11; M. Thorndyke 7–0–210–82–30.00; *R. Burgess 14–3–309–68–28.09; O. Magnus 12–5–144–33*–20.57; R. Freeman 13–2–219–66–19.90.

Bowling—J. Douglas 58.4–8–179–24–7.45; P. Douglas 198–58–496–28–17.71; R. Catley 172–53–542–28–19.35; C. Earley 184.1–47–540–19–28.42.

KELLY COLLEGE

Played 13: Won 5, Lost 3, Drawn 5. Abandoned 1

Master i/c: G. C. L. Cooper

Batting—J. J. Wood 11–5–239–51*–39.83; *C. P. Insole 9–1–246–67*–30.75; G. E. M. Baber 13–1–282–72*–23.50; G. J. Down 12–1–196–69–17.81; W. J. Kingwell 12–1–175–42–15.90; J. R. Hurst 12–1–167–44–15.18.

Bowling—A. M. Dakin 40.4–3–170–12–14.16; P. K. Tyrer 60–16–194–13–14.92; I. J. Saunders 78.3–5–397–21–18.90; W. G. Pendrill 117.1–22–378–17–22.23; J. J. Wood 144.2–33–465–20–23.25.

KIMBOLTON SCHOOL

Played 15: Won 3, Lost 9, Drawn 3. Abandoned 1

Master i/c: R. P. Merriman Cricket professional: M. E. Latham

Batting—*R. J. T. Ramply 14–1–572–114*–44.00; S. G. Wood 15–2–415–81*–31.92; T. C. Agnew 13–2–179–65–16.27; N. J. Fuller 15–0–205–51–13.66; T. A. Littlewood 12–0–153–26–12.75; A. W. Ford 14–0–144–25–10.28.

Bowling—I. Prideaux 210.5–31–593–40–14.82; R. J. T. Ramply 114.2–18–421–17–24.76; A. W. Ford 96–14–373–15–24.86; T. A. Littlewood 112.5–22–319–11–29.00.

KING EDWARD VI COLLEGE, STOURBRIDGE

Played 15: Won 6, Lost 3, Drawn 6. Abandoned 4

Masters i/c: D. E. D. Campbell and M. L. Ryan

Batting—G. R. Day 15–2–451–68–34.69; *A. D. Hadley 14–2–394–104*–32.83; M. Fullwood 12–2–235–59*–23.50; J. Allen 12–1–231–80–21.00; E. M. James 9–0–167–54–18.55.

Bowling—M. Fullwood 63–17–133–14–9.50; N. Bell 73–16–178–13–13.69; J. R. T. Burn 76–15–234–14–16.71; A. D. Hadley 110.4–29–305–16–19.06; J. Allen 134.5–45–310–14–22.14.

KING EDWARD VI SCHOOL, SOUTHAMPTON

Played 22: Won 10, Lost 4, Drawn 8. Abandoned 1

Master i/c: R. J. Putt

Batting—*B. Quantrill 20–2–626–83–34.77; M. E. Munro 10–5–170–48–34.00; R. T. Markham 17–0–538–68–31.64; G. R. Treagus 12–2–262–105*–26.20; J. D. Chrispin 21–4–438–61–25.76; R. P. Knights 17–2–380–58–25.33; M. J. Self 14–4–248–35–24.80; A. J. Tidby 20–6–277–52*–19.78; E. L. Godber 10–0–185–78–18.50.

Bowling—R. M. Salter 241–64–717–53–13.52; E. L. Godber 162–25–561–34–16.50; J. D. Chrispin 153–34–568–21–27.04; M. J. Self 106–15–434–15–28.93; B. Quantrill 107–22–411–14–29.35.

KING EDWARD VII SCHOOL, LYTHAM

Played 13: Won 0, Lost 6, Drawn 7

Master i/c: A. Crowther

Batting—G. Maitland 10–0–287–94–28.70; *P. Macauley 15–1–357–88–25.50; M. Dawson 15–4–166–45*–15.09; S. Walton 12–2–142–37*–14.20; B. Martin 15–1–166–50–11.85; T. Shaw 14–0–100–21–7.14.

Bowling—T. Shaw 79–9–335–16–20.93; P. Young 164–51–434–20–21.70; B. Martin 105–9–468–17–27.52.

KING EDWARD'S SCHOOL, BIRMINGHAM

Played 20: Won 6, Lost 5, Drawn 9. Abandoned 3

Master i/c: M. D. Stead — Cricket professional: R. J. Newman

Batting—C. E. R. Meyer 14–4–493–117*–49.30; N. M. Linehan 12–4–321–81*–40.12; *M. M. Dean 17–1–509–79*–31.81; N. S. Ratnam 18–1–462–110–27.17; C. N. Ashton 17–1–398–80–24.87; C. E. Hitchins 16–3–261–70–20.07; D. A. Bhadri 10–4–114–50*–19.00; J. D. T. West 8–0–150–42–18.75; M. R. Dunbar 14–3–193–62–17.54.

Bowling—H. D. Irfan 39–4–143–10–14.30; M. M. Dean 287.2–78–799–50–15.98; C. D. Atkin 214.2–42–816–36–22.66; O. J. Sharp 78–8–334–10–33.40.

KING HENRY VIII SCHOOL, COVENTRY

Played 13: Won 6, Lost 6, Drawn 1. Abandoned 2

Master i/c: G. P. C. Courtois

Batting—P. H. Harrison 11–5–332–89*–55.33; *M. D. Scott 13–3–510–102*–51.00; G. Gascoyne 12–1–305–114–27.72; C. H. Field 10–1–222–101*–24.66; G. O. Thomas 7–2–109–37–21.80; A. Saeed 11–3–158–44*–19.75.

Bowling—A. P. M. Wilson 94.2–18–423–22–19.22; M. D. Scott 79–13–321–16–20.06; P. H. Harrison 51–5–252–12–21.00; G. O. Thomas 42–4–229–10–22.90; R. G. Whitehall 129.4–16–523–19–27.52.

KING'S COLLEGE, TAUNTON

Played 16: Won 6, Lost 4, Drawn 6

Master i/c: R. J. R. Yeates — Cricket professional: D. Breakwell

Batting—*W. J. K. Greswell 13–2–625–108*–56.81; R. E. Berry 15–1–521–84–37.21; C. P. W. Cashell 15–1–495–93*–35.35; M. K. Coley 10–4–175–38*–29.16; M. J. Scott 8–3–131–45–26.20; J. G. M. Ross 13–1–220–46–18.33; D. G. C. Chubb 13–3–154–30*–15.40; M. F. D. Robinson 11–0–164–34–14.90.

Bowling—M. F. D. Robinson 202.1–48–587–29–20.24; M. J. Scott 131–28–440–17–25.88; D. J. G. Dowsett 159–29–487–18–27.05; A. F. Lacy-Smith 120.3–17–455–13–35.00; M. K. Coley 125.1–24–434–11–39.45.

KING'S COLLEGE SCHOOL, WIMBLEDON

Played 23: Won 10, Lost 3, Drawn 10

Master i/c: G. C. McGinn — Cricket professional: L. Moody

Batting—J. Parrish 18–6–833–100*–69.41; A. J. Barnes 4–2–118–53–59.00; *R. Q. Cake 18–2–927–155*–57.93; H. S. Malik 20–5–615–87–41.00; N. J. Stafford 5–1–160–72*–40.00; R. D. Day 8–5–119–34*–39.66; T. P. Howland 18–3–412–63–27.46; B. C. M. Gardner 15–2–330–77–25.38; B. J. D. Cook 16–2–297–81*–21.21.

Bowling—A. M. Denslow 220–39–779–47–16.57; R. Q. Cake 145.4–32–526–28–18.78; I. M. Hepburn 191.1–42–606–26–23.30; S. A. Bayly 107.3–17–436–16–27.25; H. S. Malik 170–32–620–20–31.00; A. C. Fordyce 122–18–440–12–36.66.

KING'S SCHOOL, BRUTON

Played 12: Won 4, Lost 1, Drawn 7. Abandoned 2

Master i/c: P. Platts-Martin Cricket professional: N. J. Lockhart

Batting—F. L. Stewart 8–5–107–48*–35.66; N. I. Paul 11–4–224–61*–32.00; N. J. Gammon 9–1–245–63–30.62; A. R. MacEwen 12–2–304–71*–30.40; J. L. Hayes 9–2–206–80*–29.42; P. K. Harding 9–2–168–39–24.00; D. M. Stewart 12–0–273–65–22.75; *C. M. Squire 11–1–175–39–17.50.

Bowling—N. I. Paul 153–37–437–26–16.80; N. J. Gammon 146–24–518–26–19.92; P. K. Harding 81–12–243–12–20.25.

THE KING'S SCHOOL, CANTERBURY

Played 12: Won 5, Lost 5, Drawn 2. Abandoned 2

Master i/c: A. W. Dyer Cricket professional: D. V. P. Wright

Batting—K. O. O. Sonaike 10–2–294–87–36.75; P. G. Davies 12–0–325–71–27.08; *M. G. Northeast 13–0–340–61–26.15; B. M. Cooper 12–1–148–28*–13.45; S. M. A. C. Satchu 12–1–139–39–12.63; J. J. Rhodes 12–0–101–34–8.41.

Bowling—S. R. Maggs 188.4–56–454–20–22.70; B. M. Cooper 170–36–526–19–27.68.

THE KING'S SCHOOL, CHESTER

Played 18: Won 10, Lost 1, Drawn 7. Abandoned 1

Master i/c: K. H. Mellor

Batting—G. P. Barrett 16–1–540–104*–36.00; *J. R. H. Spencer 17–3–426–60–30.42; J. M. Thomas 12–4–234–73–29.25; B. J. Mitchell 17–3–334–65–23.85; J. Hinkins 14–1–310–57–23.84; A. M. Miln 13–5–161–25–20.12.

Bowling—J. M. Thomas 121–25–346–23–15.04; M. J. Cox 152.3–39–399–22–18.13; S. F. Williams 119.3–29–366–20–18.30; B. J. Mitchell 97–19–275–13–21.15; G. P. Barrett 130.5–42–318–15–21.20.

THE KING'S SCHOOL, ELY

Played 16: Won 10, Lost 2, Drawn 4

Master i/c: R. M. Parsons Cricket professional: T. G. A. Morley

Batting—A. M. Gallop 16–7–665–143*–73.88; *D. C. Hindle 12–5–349–94*–49.85; C. Q. Taylor 15–1–489–118–34.92; A. R. Watts 14–3–349–77*–31.72; M. C. Savage 9–1–220–42–27.50; P. D. Griffiths 9–1–158–42–19.75.

Bowling—A. W. Marshall 24–6–99–13–7.61; D. C. Hindle 201–50–672–49–13.71; R. G. Willis 130–25–447–23–19.43; J. Fuller 79–19–277–10–27.70.

THE KING'S SCHOOL, MACCLESFIELD

Played 19: Won 8, Lost 1, Drawn 10. Abandoned 3

Master i/c: D. M. Harbord Cricket professional: S. Moores

Batting—K. A. Graham 19–5–1,075–128*–76.78; *A. J. Wilson 19–4–418–69*–27.86; M. J. Hammond 12–5–165–42–23.57; B. Cartlidge 16–2–314–50–22.42; A. N. Owens 17–0–310–56–18.23; E. K. Dalboth 14–1–134–28–10.30.

Bowling—M. C. Orchison 52.1–18–133–10–13.30; S. C. James 236.5–47–664–39–17.02; M. R. Palmer 246–50–694–39–17.79; A. M. James 196–50–573–24–23.87.

KING'S SCHOOL, ROCHESTER

Played 15: Won 5, Lost 2, Drawn 8. Abandoned 1

Master i/c: J. Irvine

Batting—*M. J. Walker 15–3–872–156*–72.66; T. J. Mitchell 10–4–243–56–40.50; A. C. Mackenzie 13–3–396–75*–39.60; R. Greer 15–3–370–69–30.83; A. P. R. Lane 13–2–267–69–24.27.

Bowling—R. E. C. Jones 77.4–19–283–20–14.15; D. P. Johnson 164–48–424–27–15.70; A. C. Mackenzie 52–15–158–10–15.80; M. J. Walker 157–26–535–28–19.10; J. Mitchell 113–38–265–10–26.50.

THE KING'S SCHOOL, WORCESTER

Played 20: Won 5, Lost 6, Drawn 9

Master i/c: D. P. Iddon

Batting—*R. Tomlinson 17–0–563–93–33.11; M. Wheeler 15–1–393–95–28.07; J. Richardson 17–4–276–48–21.23; P. O'Neill 16–2–273–39–19.50; D. Hughes 20–1–361–56–19.00; A. Thompson 17–2–279–102*–18.60; J. Rogers 19–4–268–46–17.86; J. Malins 15–3–167–36–13.91.

Bowling—R. Allum 167–47–470–31–15.16; M. Bourne 115–18–453–26–17.42; B. Crabbe 110–17–405–19–21.31; D. Hughes 138–25–469–19–24.68; J. Richardson 135–28–371–13–28.53; J. Malins 129–18–445–15–29.66.

KINGSTON GRAMMAR SCHOOL

Played 17: Won 5, Lost 8, Drawn 4. Abandoned 1

Master i/c: J. A. Royce

Batting—*E. S. Gratton 15–4–602–120*–54.72; J. N. Makepeace-Taylor 4–1–115–70–38.33; D. Spencer 10–2–268–91*–33.50; D. J. Lipscomb 16–3–346–68–26.61; J. M. Wallis 15–2–207–36–15.92; S. J. Grey 13–1–177–59*–14.75.

Bowling—D. Spencer 67.2–10–199–15–13.26; A. M. Allen 145.2–21–516–27–19.11; M. E. Bendel 135–23–472–24–19.66; E. S. Gratton 121.5–13–457–17–26.88; S. J. Temlett 101–19–344–12–28.66.

KINGSWOOD SCHOOL

Played 10: Won 3, Lost 3, Drawn 4

Master i/c: G. Mobley

Batting—N. M. Job 5–1–179–111*–44.75; *G. J. B. Williams 10–2–355–156*–44.37; T. G. R. Gibbs 9–1–299–114*–37.37; N. P. Dowling 7–2–154–54–30.80; D. R. Bowden 9–1–193–46–24.12; D. T. R. Smith 6–0–140–55–23.33; M. T. R. Langstaff 9–2–118–31*–16.85.

Bowling—J. Dyson 96–19–314–21–14.95; N. J. Page 68.2–10–216–10–21.60.

KING WILLIAM'S COLLEGE, ISLE OF MAN

Played 11: Won 2, Lost 5, Drawn 4. Abandoned 2

Master i/c: T. M. Manning Cricket professional: D. Mark

Batting—U. A. Nwachuku 9–2–224–61*–32.00; *M. L. Craine 9–0–234–60–26.00; D. R. Norman 9–0–234–55–26.00; L. R. Clarke 12–4–157–61*–19.62; J. C. D. Hinds 9–0–175–49–19.44; S. G. McNeill 8–0–135–72–16.87.

Bowling—R. C. Turner 48.3–9–148–10–14.80; L. R. Clarke 146.3–36–380–21–18.09; N. C. Capewell 126–32–336–18–18.66; D. R. Norman 124–28–427–17–25.11.

LANCING COLLEGE

Played 18: Won 7, Lost 6, Drawn 5. Abandoned 1

Master i/c: I. Perrins Cricket professional: R. G. Davies

Batting—*S. Baker 17–3–934–111–66.71; R. Spink 17–0–425–66–25.00; J. Rees 13–8–112–25*–22.40; J. Hegan 18–1–363–81*–21.35; J. Annetts 12–2–205–42–20.50; P. Goulstone 15–1–257–44–18.35; A. Lutwyche 13–1–186–54–15.50; T. Fowler 12–1–162–47*–14.72.

Bowling—J. Pattisson 122–26–371–29–12.79; S. Baker 153–33–528–34–15.52; R. Spink 129–39–304–19–16.00; I. Meadows 165–38–498–26–19.15.

LEEDS GRAMMAR SCHOOL

Played 17: Won 2, Lost 0, Drawn 15. Abandoned 1

Master i/c: R. Hill

Batting—*T. C. Walton 16–2–545–88*–38.92; I. C. Sutcliffe 13–1–449–80–37.41; C. G. P. Jackson 12–1–371–102–33.72; G. C. Allman 7–3–100–42–25.00; R. M. Atkinson 10–2–181–66*–22.62; S. M. J. Surrey 10–1–170–43–18.88; R. J. Melville 14–1–232–57–17.84; S. P. Stephens 10–0–177–31–17.70; G. D. Simmons 10–3–112–37–16.00.

Bowling—R. M. Atkinson 171–49–401–42–9.54; T. C. Walton 229.3–70–603–49–12.30; M. P. Walker 57–13–168–10–16.80.

THE LEYS SCHOOL

Played 20: Won 8, Lost 6, Drawn 6. Abandoned 1

Master i/c: P. S. D. Carpenter Cricket professional: D. Gibson

Batting—R. C. Weston 18–2–988–202–61.75; A. S. Brule Ball 14–5–326–77*–36.22; M. C. Donnor 19–1–607–89–33.72; D. J. Woods 18–3–460–79–30.66; T. R. Griffiths 4–0–114–54–28.50; T. E. Hebden 9–2–196–69*–28.00; J. R. Tilbrook 11–3–213–75*–26.62; J. P. Gillham 8–3–124–35*–24.80; *D. D. Spencer 13–2–176–56–16.00.

Bowling—M. C. Donnor 114–7–568–23–24.69; M. S. Khan 129–23–504–17–29.64; D. M. A. Bullen 140–18–514–16–32.12; J. P. Gillham 138.1–28–525–16–32.81; R. P. B. Amar 102–18–370–10–37.00.

LIVERPOOL COLLEGE

Played 12: Won 1, Lost 6, Drawn 5. Abandoned 4

Master i/c: The Revd J. R. Macaulay

Batting—*J. Q. Harrington 12–2–413–107–41.30; B. Latto 11–2–265–50–29.44; A. Williams 11–2–147–48*–16.33; T. Henderson 11–1–125–51–12.50.

Bowling—J. Q. Harrington 82–16–256–17–15.05; J. Rushton 138–23–433–23–18.82; B. Latto 33–2–189–10–18.90; J. Rylance 95–11–300–11–27.27.

LLANDOVERY COLLEGE

Played 14: Won 7, Lost 1, Drawn 6. Abandoned 4

Master i/c: T. G. Marks

Batting—*S. A. Richards 14–5–477–90–53.00; J. L. Evans 6–1–166–70–33.20; B. Rowlands 8–2–126–67*–21.00; I. W. Jones 8–0–167–45–20.87; D. I. Simcock 8–1–132–37–18.85; R. G. Jones 11–2–142–44*–15.77.

Bowling—G. D. A. Lyddon-Jones 116–26–280–23–12.17; H. G. Davies 90–21–275–21–13.09; B. Rowlands 118–18–333–23–14.47; S. A. Richards 46–4–181–11–16.45.

LORD WANDSWORTH COLLEGE

Played 15: Won 7, Lost 1, Drawn 7

Master i/c: G. R. Smith

Batting—B. A. Hames 11-4-356-103*-50.85; G. C. Shoobridge 8-1-255-75-36.42; C. J. Fairley 5-1-107-34-26.75; T. A. Dyson 15-3-268-62-22.33; E. J. Kearney 10-1-173-36-19.22; M. J. F. Middleditch 9-0-154-53-17.11; R. P. Wightman 9-1-135-43*-16.87; *D. A. Robinson 10-3-101-36-14.42.

Bowling—N. P. B. Rochford 124.5-25-420-37-11.35; J. R. Cowles 133.4-25-499-34-14.67; D. A. Robinson 103.5-20-370-24-15.41.

LORETTO SCHOOL

Played 16: Won 6, Lost 4, Drawn 6. Abandoned 2

Master i/c: R. G. Selley

Batting—*J. A. G. Grant 14-2-381-65-31.75; A. G. King 9-2-192-68*-27.42; A. C. F. Mason 11-6-128-38*-25.60; E. Barbour 11-4-172-41*-24.57; A. J. R. Gibb 15-1-328-102*-23.42; S. C. Fraser 14-1-223-43-17.15.

Bowling—A. Allan 66-31-110-11-10.00; A. C. F. Mason 265-96-489-40-12.22; J. A. G. Grant 245-66-569-41-13.87; J. S. Bedi 193-53-529-25-21.16.

LOUGHBOROUGH GRAMMAR SCHOOL

Played 16: Won 6, Lost 1, Drawn 9

Master i/c: E. Thorpe

Batting—G. Leeson 16-6-808-119*-80.80; *C. J. Hawkes 13-0-611-94-47.00; I. Partridge 13-2-421-89-38.27; C. Hill 9-3-146-44-24.33; P. Harris 11-0-239-61-21.72; J. Simpson 11-4-130-35*-18.57.

Bowling—C. J. Hawkes 206.4-79-475-48-9.89; J. Simpson 163.3-39-529-30-17.63; P. Gidley 133.4-27-476-14-34.00.

MAGDALEN COLLEGE SCHOOL

Played 21: Won 10, Lost 5, Drawn 6. Abandoned 1

Master i/c: N. A. Rollings Cricket professional: M. Joyce

Batting—N. S. Hawken 18-4-562-100*-40.14; M. J. Winson 18-2-577-91*-36.06; M. B. Bixby 21-2-624-110*-32.84; J. C. Bobby 18-2-515-88*-32.18; *T. H. Boyles 20-1-457-77-24.05; S. D. Stinchcombe 15-8-127-32-18.14; C. A. Lawrence 13-2-160-63-14.54.

Bowling—N. H. B. Wilson 69.5-14-267-17-15.70; C. A. Lawrence 172.5-44-508-29-17.51; J. C. Bobby 184-41-585-33-17.72; J. A. Brady 196.2-53-577-32-18.03; S. D. Stinchcombe 228.3-53-726-39-18.61.

MALVERN COLLEGE

Played 16: Won 5, Lost 1, Drawn 10. Abandoned 2

Master i/c: R. W. Tolchard

Batting—P. V. Sykes 16-4-499-110-41.58; *J. W. A. Horton 15-0-529-100-35.26; S. J. C. Ferguson 13-5-274-53-34.25; J. H. Verity 17-2-450-82-30.00; J. T. B. Crawley 14-6-237-77*-29.62; N. J. Gaunt 11-3-140-24*-17.50.

Bowling—C. R. Phillips 215.1-41-675-33-20.45; F. E. O. Nyaseme 102.2-20-339-16-21.18; J. H. Verity 145-32-346-14-24.71; J. T. B. Crawley 151-41-393-14-28.07.

MANCHESTER GRAMMAR SCHOOL

Played 20: Won 7, Lost 3, Drawn 10. Abandoned 1

Master i/c: D. Moss

Batting—M. J. P. Ward 19–3–962–145*–60.12; M. C. Jones 19–3–427–70–26.68; L. J. Marland 16–1–310–74–20.66; C. M. Gresty 17–3–175–37–12.50.

Bowling—L. J. Marland 91.3–25–265–17–15.58; M. C. Jones 226.5–58–631–36–17.52; M. J. P. Ward 291.5–90–762–35–21.77; N. S. Farmer 192.3–41–583–24–24.29.

MARLBOROUGH COLLEGE

Played 14: Won 1, Lost 7, Drawn 6. Abandoned 1

Master i/c: R. B. Pick Cricket professional: R. M. Ratcliffe

Batting—*T. C. Oxborrow 15–2–421–90*–32.38; B. G. Harvey 10–1–285–109–31.66; O. P. R. Whitehead 7–2–145–42–29.00; R. R. Brass 8–3–145–56*–29.00; M. E. C. Harris 13–3–262–46–26.20; J. Simkins 11–1–219–65*–21.90; R. A. S. Kikonyogo 10–1–173–39–19.22; J. R. R. Fletcher 12–0–221–68–18.41; D. A. R. Wood 14–0–237–47–16.92; D. M. Del Mar 11–0–110–40–10.00.

Bowling—P. M. Taggart 84–5–400–16–25.00; M. E. C. Harris 213.1–27–704–20–35.20; N. Alonso-McGregor 131.4–29–530–11–48.18.

MERCHANT TAYLORS' SCHOOL, CROSBY

Played 16: Won 2, Lost 4, Drawn 10

Master i/c: The Revd D. A. Smith Cricket professional: M. Chee Quee

Batting—*G. S. Glynne-Jones 14–2–392–77–32.66; M. P. Edwards 16–0–424–99–26.50; I. G. Sutcliffe 14–2–307–45*–25.58; M. G. Doggett 16–2–307–73–21.92; J. M. Pearce 10–0–169–38–16.90.

Bowling—C. E. R. Earlam 125.5–26–329–15–21.93; R. A. Buckels 151.1–30–490–21–23.33; I. G. Sutcliffe 157.2–32–494–20–24.70.

MERCHANT TAYLORS' SCHOOL, NORTHWOOD

Played 25: Won 12, Lost 2, Drawn 11. Abandoned 1

Master i/c: W. M. B. Ritchie Cricket professional: H. C. Latchman

Batting—*A. J. Brand 25–7–1,311–202*–72.83; C. M. Jaggard 25–3–1,364–145–62.00; R. A. Hawkey 25–4–975–101*–46.42; A. E. S. Bartlett 18–4–288–58–20.57; A. J. Powell-Williams 21–5–302–65–18.87; A. I. Macpherson 15–3–125–25*–10.41.

Bowling—A. J. Preston 85–24–188–13–14.46; P. Knowles 225.1–59–512–34–15.05; R. A. Hawkey 193–58–518–32–16.18; A. E. S. Bartlett 246–67–606–30–20.20; P. Parekh 182.2–32–670–30–22.33; A. J. Todd 92.4–18–323–13–24.84; A. J. Brand 155.4–26–581–22–26.40; A. J. Powell-Williams 152–33–467–17–27.47.

MERCHISTON CASTLE SCHOOL

Played 19: Won 9, Lost 5, Drawn 5. Abandoned 1

Master i/c: C. W. Swan Cricket professional: I. Philip

Batting—B. R. S. Eriksson 18–1–376–72–22.11; *G. C. Wearmouth 19–4–303–54–20.20; J. M. Prescott 19–2–290–42–17.05; A. C. Wearmouth 16–8–130–25*–16.25; D. W. Hodge 19–1–289–39–16.05; G. W. Anderson 17–0–238–94–14.00.

Bowling—B. R. S. Eriksson 134–45–263–40–6.57; A. R. C. Gilmour 281–79–558–59–9.45; D. W. Hodge 94–21–224–16–14.00; A. A. L. Ramsay 270–68–605–38–15.92.

MILLFIELD SCHOOL

Played 20: Won 7, Lost 3, Drawn 10

Master i/c: A. D. Curtis Cricket professional: G. C. Wilson

Batting—G. W. White 20–3–1,061–200*–62.41; *N. F. Gibbs 20–3–769–92–45.23; I. J. Ward 20–4–572–62–35.75; R. O. Jones 17–6–300–47*–27.27; A. S. Golder 10–4–135–53*–22.50; J. R. Eccles 7–2–109–48–21.80; A. J. Dalton 15–5–182–35–18.20; B. S. Little 19–1–289–68–16.05.

Bowling—N. F. Gibbs 247.1–56–627–37–16.94; R. J. Ballinger 209.5–46–620–29–21.37; R. O. Jones 126.1–21–416–18–23.11; P. T. Jacques 230.2–72–604–24–25.16; G. W. White 115–29–389–10–38.90.

MILL HILL SCHOOL

Played 16: Won 3, Lost 8, Drawn 5

Master i/c: R. J. Denning Cricket professional: G. A. R. Lock

Batting—D. M. J. Kraft 15–1–370–84–26.42; A. Ismail 10–0–200–75–20.00; J. D. A. Brown 16–4–224–35–18.66; N. C. Propper 15–0–247–73–16.46; S. M. P. Mortali 12–2–138–33–13.80; N. Kamath 13–0–111–48–8.53; *G. E. S. Brock 16–0–135–22–8.43.

Bowling—G. E. S. Brock 222–63–612–37–16.54; A. Ismail 118–36–331–16–20.68; T. J. Petropoulos 121–25–388–14–27.71.

MILTON ABBEY SCHOOL

Played 14: Won 4, Lost 5, Drawn 5. Abandoned 1

Master i/c: S. T. Smail

Batting—M. C. W. Williams 11–1–271–61–27.10; D. C. J. Henderson 11–1–225–76*–22.50; G. E. Bundock 10–3–156–38*–22.28; J. C. Brewer 7–1–126–40–21.00; *T. H. Brassey 13–3–198–67*–19.80; N. J. Smallman 14–2–232–42–19.33; E. J. Pownall 11–1–178–50–17.80; J. G. Hodges 9–2–111–52–15.85; P. le Q. Herbert 14–1–177–45–13.61.

Bowling—N. J. Smallman 88.5–18–299–18–16.61; R. P. R. Coulman 122.1–24–484–27–17.92; T. H. Brassey 149–27–528–27–19.55; D. C. J. Henderson 94.5–17–333–14–23.78.

MONKTON COMBE SCHOOL

Played 16: Won 7, Lost 3, Drawn 6

Masters i/c: P. C. Sibley and N. D. Botton

Batting—*T. Simmons 16–5–630–100*–57.27; N. C. L. Sinfield 15–2–481–75–37.00; R. Johns 16–0–432–65–27.00; J. Ward 12–3–178–72*–19.77; S. Lockyer 13–2–211–100*–19.18; J. Thomas 11–3–143–40*–17.87.

Bowling—N. C. L. Sinfield 134.4–25–409–28–14.60; J. Veitch 158.1–34–473–25–18.92; T. Simmons 182.1–27–631–31–20.35; T. Hannell 139.3–20–463–15–30.86; J. Ward 95–13–386–11–35.09.

MONMOUTH SCHOOL

Played 15: Won 2, Lost 3, Drawn 10. Abandoned 1

Master i/c: D. H. Messenger

Batting—A. J. Jones 15–1–702–136–50.14; J. H. Langworth 12–4–349–79–43.62; M. J. Tamplin 9–2–253–54–36.14; T. M. King 11–2–248–49–27.55; P. A. Clitheroe 9–1–189–68–23.62; R. D. Turner 10–0–103–26–10.30.

Bowling—P. A. Clitheroe 202.3–55–547–31–17.64; D. J. R. Price 139–47–347–19–18.26; M. J. Tamplin 61.4–14–232–10–23.20; R. W. Price 87–21–281–11–25.54.

NEWCASTLE-UNDER-LYME SCHOOL

Played 13: Won 5, Lost 0, Drawn 8. Abandoned 2

Master i/c: S. A. Robson Cricket professional: D. Headley

Batting—M. H. Colclough 11–5–528–100–88.00; *J. N. Britton 7–3–285–100*–71.25; D. M. Gilwhite 10–1–203–42*–22.55; R. A. Spence 11–2–189–63*–21.00; M. H. Foster 8–1–123–42–17.57; S. G. Devaney 10–3–110–24*–15.71.

Bowling—M. A. Smith 25–6–65–10–6.50; I. Bradbury 105.5–24–283–29–9.75; M. H. Colclough 76.1–15–222–14–15.85; P. R. Leverett 78.3–18–267–16–16.68; R. M. Taylor 103.3–26–289–12–24.08.

NOTTINGHAM HIGH SCHOOL

Played 17: Won 3, Lost 3, Drawn 11. Abandoned 3

Master i/c: P. G. Morris Cricket professional: K. J. Poole

Batting—S. H. Ferguson 4–2–143–102*–71.50; *S. A. O'Brien 14–1–558–107*–42.92; S. W. Holliday 10–2–221–76*–27.62; R. I. Howarth 13–2–293–73–26.63; M. J. Bonsall 16–1–395–64–26.33; M. Kennedy 13–3–176–43*–17.60; A. S. Chisholm 10–4–105–27*–17.50; S. D. Goodley 16–0–263–70–16.43.

Bowling—R. I. Howarth 164.2–27–675–33–20.45; J. W. Phillips 124–20–513–15–34.20; A. S. Chisholm 114–22–444–12–37.00; A. E. Brydon 118–15–376–10–37.60.

OAKHAM SCHOOL

Played 16: Won 2, Lost 7, Drawn 7

Master i/c: J. Wills

Batting—*N. C. Kingham 15–5–467–99*–46.70; P. M. J. Webb 13–1–394–94–32.83; J. W. Lewin 9–1–139–34–17.37; M. B. Smith 14–2–196–58*–16.33; A. T. Craig 12–0–193–72–16.08.

Bowling—P. J. R. Smith 65–16–236–12–19.66; M. Cullen 152.4–23–379–19–19.94; J. M. Astill 63–6–259–12–21.58; J. W. Lewin 100–25–352–12–29.33; N. C. Kingham 179.3–32–665–20–33.25.

THE ORATORY SCHOOL

Played 18: Won 10, Lost 3, Drawn 5

Master i/c: P. L. Tomlinson Cricket professional: J. B. K. Howell

Batting—J. D. Clarke 18–4–632–125–45.14; D. Olszowski 18–2–525–101–32.81; J. P. S. Tomlinson 5–0–102–47–20.40; *R. P. Unwin 13–1–243–47–20.25; C. E. Watson 9–1–156–60–19.50; J. A. Keeble 16–2–262–58*–18.71; E. N. Dunseath 8–0–141–38–17.62; D. T. Curran 10–0–163–32–16.30; D. A. Thorne 8–0–103–34–12.87.

Bowling—K. R. Welsh 107–16–336–27–12.44; J. P. S. Tomlinson 38–6–138–10–13.80; R. P. Unwin 172–26–493–26–18.96; R. L. Belgrave 126–16–382–19–20.10; D. A. Thorne 132–14–489–23–21.26; E. N. Dunseath 126–26–462–20–23.10.

OUNDLE SCHOOL

Played 20: Won 5, Lost 2, Drawn 13

Master i/c: V. G. B. Cushing Cricket professional: T. Howorth

Batting—*A. Lee 17–8–343–59–38.11; S. de Morgan 18–1–500–79–29.41; D. Anslow 8–0–466–87–25.88; A. Richardson 19–1–452–62–25.11; N. Delahooke 15–7–197–34–24.62; M. Epton 16–1–356–60–23.73; R. J. C. Harris 17–4–280–50–21.53; C. Herbert 2–2–198–46–19.80.

Bowling—M. Epton 160.4–33–473–28–16.89; A. Richardson 212.4–48–564–27–20.88; M. Simpson 72.3–17–244–11–22.18; N. Delahooke 167.5–33–592–20–29.60; A. Lee 33–48–698–23–30.34.

THE PERSE SCHOOL

Played 15: Won 0, Lost 6, Drawn 9. Abandoned 2

Master i/c: A. W. Billinghurst Cricket professional: D. C. Collard

Batting—E. W. H. Wiseman 13–4–467–102*–51.88; B. J. G. Edgar 14–1–518–158–39.84; D. L. Young 12–1–437–88–39.72; R. T. Ragnauth 11–4–254–70*–36.28; D. M. Johnson 15–0–268–61–17.86; D. R. Sutton 12–2–156–58–15.60.

Bowling—J. A. H. Martin 131–18–603–22–27.40; M. J. Oakman 169–50–514–18–28.55; D. L. Young 114.5–21–458–10–45.80.

PLYMOUTH COLLEGE

Played 19: Won 10, Lost 1, Drawn 8

Master i/c: T. J. Stevens

Batting—A. R. Maddock 17–4–1,128–139*–86.76; J. Osborne 17–6–468–107*–42.54; K. J. Willcock 14–6–301–86*–37.62; J. W. Dadge 13–3–315–84–31.50; *P. E. Stewart 15–3–331–64–27.58; S. W. Nicholson 10–4–153–37–25.50; G. V. Roberts 10–1–143–54–15.88.

Bowling—S. W. Nicholson 114.5–25–321–19–16.89; S. D. Hunt 170.3–43–545–32–17.03; K. J. Willcock 215–55–737–39–18.89; R. M. Powlesland 47–8–196–10–19.60; A. J. Battersby 54–20–223–10–22.30.

PORTSMOUTH GRAMMAR SCHOOL

Played 15: Won 5, Lost 4, Drawn 6

Master i/c: G. D. Payne

Batting—C. J. Ward 13–2–548–79–49.81; *J. P. Osborne 15–0–511–68–34.06; A. M. Small 12–1–258–53–23.45; J. Gold 14–0–322–98–23.00; J. R. Compton 10–5–113–24*–22.60; D. K. Pickup 9–2–105–21*–15.00; S. Patel 13–2–164–23*–14.90.

Bowling—H. Rushin 122–28–334–22–15.18; J. R. Compton 121–33–326–21–15.52; S. Patel 59–16–195–10–19.50; J. R. N. Brooke 93.5–24–371–16–23.18; J. Herman 100–16–363–15–24.20; A. M. Small 57–7–281–10–28.10.

PRIOR PARK COLLEGE

Played 17: Won 4, Lost 5, Drawn 8

Master i/c: P. B. Fisher

Batting—J. Power 17–4–744–101*–57.23; *G. Lee 15–3–595–97–49.58; J. Smithers 14–4–265–49*–26.50; D. Gibney 17–1–236–61–14.75; J. Hemmings 14–2–133–25*–11.08.

Bowling—C. Moan 62.4–10–204–19–10.73; J. Smithers 193.3–57–530–36–14.72; G. Lee 237–62–722–35–20.62.

QUEEN ELIZABETH GRAMMAR SCHOOL, WAKEFIELD

Played 13: Won 3, Lost 1, Drawn 9. Abandoned 2

Master i/c: T. Barker

Batting—P. M. Dickinson 13–2–442–109–40.18; R. J. Ledger 12–0–311–74–25.91; J. Cross 13–4–188–100*–20.88; S. K. Mandal 11–0–125–21–11.36.

Bowling—R. J. Ledger 152.4–53–389–34–11.44; *R. K. Bhagobati 71.1–16–228–16–14.25; A. P. Clegg 92–23–259–16–16.18; S. K. Mandal 87.4–18–261–11–23.72.

QUEEN ELIZABETH'S HOSPITAL

Played 12: Won 5, Lost 3, Drawn 4

Master i/c: M. S. E. Broadley

Batting—N. O. McDowell 12–3–313–70–34.77; *D. N. Bennett 11–2–289–97–32.11; A. Hamid 11–0–248–69–22.54; J. A. E. Brown 10–2–108–29–13.50.

Bowling—N. O. McDowell 46.5–8–167–17–9.82; D. N. Bennett 82.1–16–235–16–14.68; A. Hamid 61.1–12–223–13–17.15; D. C. Taylor 133.3–23–445–22–20.22; W. M. Phelan 104–14–327–16–20.43.

QUEEN'S COLLEGE, TAUNTON

Played 14: Won 7, Lost 2, Drawn 5. Abandoned 1

Master i/c: J. W. Davies

Batting—N. J. Burke 10–4–465–103–77.50; R. Jones 7–2–216–56–43.20; J. Brown 11–4–283–62–40.42; M. Knight 12–2–305–70*–30.50; M. A. Gibson 11–2–267–46*–29.66; J. Tanner 11–2–225–55–25.00; W. Thresher 7–1–126–34–21.00.

Bowling—M. Bashforth 42.5–10–126–13–9.69; S. Holland 30–7–113–10–11.30; D. A. Williams 152.1–32–435–27–16.11; J. Tanner 84.4–15–302–15–20.13; M. Irish 141–40–381–17–22.41; M. Knight 99.2–15–331–14–23.64.

RADLEY COLLEGE

Played 16: Won 5, Lost 1, Drawn 10. Abandoned 1

Master i/c: G. de W. Waller Cricket professionals: A. G. Robinson and A. R. Wagner

Batting—T. P. Robinson 11–0–418–119–38.00; P. L. Hollis 16–2–432–125*–30.85; T. J. Etridge 14–5–244–49*–27.11; J. T. A. Martin-Jenkins 11–2–231–55–25.66; N. O. Hunter 5–2–320–61–24.61; G. E. I. Culley 11–3–149–30–18.62; R. A. MacDowel 5–1–235–52–16.78; J. A. Arbib 11–4–103–20–14.71; *H. C. L. Sinclair 12–0–143–47–11.91.

Bowling—E. R. Cropley 57–17–132–10–13.20; J. A. Arbib 267–87–713–37–19.27; D. R. N. Ely 243–70–670–32–20.93; N. J. Walker 156–42–417–14–29.78.

RATCLIFFE COLLEGE

Played 16: Won 4, Lost 1, Drawn 11

Master i/c: R. M. Hughes Cricket professional: S. G. Peall

Batting—E. J. Meredith 14–6–380–75–47.50; C. P. Bagshaw 15–2–416–77*–32.00; S. M. Hilton 14–2–319–63–26.58; *P. G. Meredith 12–5–148–41*–21.14; A. R. Fernando 2–1–137–37–12.45.

Bowling—P. G. Meredith 188.4–40–622–31–20.06; C. P. Bagshaw 131.1–17–677–24–28.20; . Flynn 123.3–14–443–15–29.53.

READING SCHOOL

Played 13: Won 1, Lost 6, Drawn 5, Tied 1. Abandoned 2

Master i/c: R. G. Owen

Batting—A. J. Cole 11–0–231–63–21.00; S. Gibson 10–3–137–83*–19.57; B. D. Hall –1–176–40–17.60; M. L. Dykes 12–0–203–36–16.91; A. C. Clouting 12–0–194–73–16.16; . P. Bold 11–1–160–49–16.00.

Bowling—B. D. Hall 112.1–21–439–17–25.82; *C. J. Kays 98.4–8–414–11–37.63.

REED'S SCHOOL

Played 19: Won 7, Lost 6, Drawn 6

Master i/c: G. R. Martin

Batting—*C. M. Pole 13–3–342–69*–34.20; M. R. Neal-Smith 17–2–486–82*–32.40; D. J. Manton 5–0–158–81–31.60; P. F. Howgate 19–0–545–141–28.68; A. J. Newton 19–3–423–58*–26.43; M. C. Fradgley 17–3–334–100*–23.85; A. M. Grell 11–1–107–33*–10.70.

Bowling—M. R. Neal-Smith 163.1–18–621–31–20.03; C. M. Pole 227.2–46–648–32–20.25; D. S. Faulkner 181.4–48–589–27–21.81; D. P. Andronicou 104.5–19–412–17–24.23.

REIGATE GRAMMAR SCHOOL

Played 25: Won 5, Lost 9, Drawn 11

Master i/c: D. C. R. Jones — Cricket professional: H. Newton

Batting—S. J. Hygate 25–0–873–136–34.92; A. J. Dewson 25–1–680–102–28.33; M. K. Hynard 17–1–392–110–24.50; *J. R. Munday 23–2–449–75*–21.38; N. J. Chapman 23–4–368–63*–19.36; C. B. Amos 20–7–193–49–14.84; M. C. Pritchard 16–2–197–90*–14.07.

Bowling—N. J. Chapman 274.1–43–949–43–22.06; R. J. Hathaway 151–24–696–28–24.85; C. B. Amos 298–51–984–38–25.89.

RENDCOMB COLLEGE

Played 16: Won 4, Lost 3, Drawn 9

Master i/c: C. Burden — Cricket professional: D. Essenhigh

Batting—R. Milner 16–4–601–77*–50.08; J. Carroll 16–3–612–93*–47.07; N. Smith 5–1–155–49*–38.75; A. Jones 12–4–221–56*–27.62; P. Grimsdale 8–3–102–43*–20.40; K. Holmes 14–2–149–45*–12.41; M. Head 15–0–156–38–10.40.

Bowling—R. Hughes 93.3–24–225–19–11.84; A. Jones 169.2–67–371–30–12.36; W. King 63–15–195–15–13.00; R. Milner 112–31–263–19–13.84; J. Carroll 129–32–246–16–15.37.

REPTON SCHOOL

Played 17: Won 5, Lost 1, Drawn 11. Abandoned 3

Master i/c: M. Stones — Cricket professional: M. K. Kettle

Batting—A. R. Paulett 14–1–505–105*–38.84; M. D. Murray 15–1–416–91–29.71; E. J. Spencer 8–3–120–36*–24.00; G. E. Shipley 5–0–110–44–22.00; D. R. Hand 8–0–107–45–13.37; M. D. Robinson 14–1–173–52*–13.30; N. J. W. Campion 13–1–149–37–12.41; P. G. Hewstone 12–2–113–33–11.30.

Bowling—*J. M. Windsor 161–44–411–30–13.70; E. G. Prince 51–15–160–10–16.00; N. J. W. Campion 139–22–465–26–17.88; D. R. Hand 115–30–346–15–23.06; D. A. Bacon 196–37–601–22–27.31.

RICHARD HUISH COLLEGE, TAUNTON

Played 18: Won 13, Lost 2, Drawn 3

Master i/c: W. J. Maidlow

Batting—Kevin Parsons 12–2–886–107–88.60; *Keith Parsons 14–4–449–86–44.90; S. Pimm 5–2–129–60*–43.00; B. Collins 15–1–452–111–32.28; A. Coupe 13–2–335–72*–30.45; D. Pearcey 10–4–164–58*–27.33; R. Warr 9–3–138–39*–23.00.

Bowling—Keith Parsons 67–14–241–19–12.68; P. Dimond 75.1–6–323–20–16.15; K. Moyse 102–24–252–15–16.80; B. Collins 72.3–5–321–19–16.89; N. Hammacott 96.3–18–296–17–17.41; S. Nelson 72.4–9–299–11–27.18.

ROSSALL SCHOOL

Played 17: Won 8, Lost 1, Drawn 8. Abandoned 2

Master i/c: R. J. Clapp

Batting—S. D. Holmes 12–5–234–36*–33.42; *N. H. Crust 16–2–433–67–30.92; C. A. Mawdsley 8–1–191–73–27.28; S. N. Fretwell 15–1–367–65–26.21; J. Elliott 17–1–377–100–23.56; J. R. Newbold 10–3–125–34–17.85; T. M. Higson 12–3–130–43–14.44; H. M. Parr 14–2–169–33–14.08.

Bowling—J. D. Mathers 54–13–147–13–11.30; N. H. Crust 90–20–301–20–15.05; S. D. Holmes 186–36–563–29–19.41; H. M. Parr 166–39–491–20–24.55; D. M. Gough 101–29–295–12–24.58.

ROYAL GRAMMAR SCHOOL, GUILDFORD

Played 17: Won 8, Lost 5, Drawn 4

Master i/c: S. B. R. Shore

Batting—*B. C. Ray 16–3–673–141–51.76; N. Kent 16–2–500–71–35.71; J. Wydenbach 13–4–223–83–24.77; D. Riddell 15–0–276–49–18.40; S. Eggleston 14–2–181–49–15.08; A. Thomson 11–3–114–39–14.25; R. Gilbert 12–1–109–50–9.90.

Bowling—A. Thomson 249.1–52–776–48–16.16; A. Barlow 74–12–265–12–22.08; B. C. Ray 158.5–44–392–16–24.50.

ROYAL GRAMMAR SCHOOL, NEWCASTLE

Played 14: Won 6, Lost 1, Drawn 7

Master i/c: D. W. Smith

Batting—L. J. Crozier 14–3–639–100*–58.09; *R. S. Papps 13–1–458–118–38.16; J. C. Hammill 10–3–168–45*–24.00; J. D. V. Ryan 13–3–153–23*–15.30; N. R. Gandy ‑0–102–41–14.57.

Bowling—J. D. V. Ryan 164.3–56–385–28–13.75; L. J. Crozier 161.4–50–418–25–16.72; T. J. Wright 151.5–34–421–18–23.38.

ROYAL GRAMMAR SCHOOL, WORCESTER

Played 28: Won 13, Lost 4, Drawn 11

Master i/c: B. M. Rees — Cricket professional: M. J. Horton

Batting—C. J. Eyers 24–5–932–93*–49.05; D. M. Walker 26–5–994–130*–47.33; A. V. Powell 25–1–948–113*–39.50; *M. J. N. Taylor 25–8–615–67–36.17; S. D. C. Haynes 10–2–182–81–22.75; D. B. Berry 8–2–136–49–22.66; M. V. Williams 15–6–150–43–16.66; G. Pilgrim 14–3–159–43*–14.45.

Bowling—A. D. Baker 133.3–30–362–25–14.48; C. J. Eyers 280.3–55–773–51–15.15; N. P. Maddock 336.4–89–998–58–17.20; M. W. Williams 145–36–475–21–22.61.

RUGBY SCHOOL

Played 15: Won 1, Lost 2, Drawn 12

Master i/c: K. Siviter — Cricket professional: W. J. Stewart

Batting—A. Alexander 4–1–108–64*–36.00; W. Glazebrook 13–4–308–80*–34.22; [illegible]. Semmens 14–2–385–68–32.08; P. Carter 15–0–414–82–27.60; *S. P. Corkhill [illegible]5–1–386–71–27.57; F. Fitch 11–6–109–19–21.80; N. Joseph 10–1–190–53–21.11.

Bowling—W. Glazebrook 216–65–568–38–14.94; N. Joseph 70–17–211–11–19.18; [illegible]. Semmens 158.2–45–524–27–19.40.

RYDAL SCHOOL

Played 13: Won 0, Lost 5, Drawn 8

Master i/c: M. T. Leach　　Cricket professional: R. Pitman

Batting—S. M. Ashley 10–1–176–48–19.55; J. C. Davies 12–1–182–40–16.54.

Bowling—M. G. MacDonald 153.4–36–362–27–13.40; S. M. Ashley 67–14–197–11–17.90; *P. J. Acheson 87–7–391–16–24.43; A. J. Jamil 154–44–432–14–30.85.

ST ALBANS SCHOOL

Played 19: Won 5, Lost 6, Drawn 8

Master i/c: I. Jordan

Batting—H. Cornwell 16–6–649–104*–64.90; *B. LeFleming 15–4–365–58*–33.18; H. Sherman 12–4–212–57–26.50; T. Mote 15–3–310–48–25.83; J. Hobson 13–1–272–50–22.66; Julian Baines 12–3–202–88*–22.44; John Baines 10–4–110–20–18.33.

Bowling—H. Sherman 145–24–614–37–16.59; Julian Baines 72–10–238–14–17.00; B. LeFleming 163–37–519–23–22.56.

ST BEES SCHOOL

Played 14: Won 4, Lost 3, Drawn 7. Abandoned 1

Master i/c: P. M. Evans

Batting—P. Hoffman 13–4–276–69–30.66; P. Mawson 14–3–332–52*–30.18; A. Mawson 14–1–387–107*–29.76; D. Ng 14–2–295–54*–24.58; M. Birkett 13–1–206–55–17.16; L. Norman 12–4–128–44–16.00.

Bowling—P. Mawson 140.3–39–319–24–13.29; A. Mawson 88.3–10–336–19–17.68; D. Ng 171–51–445–25–17.80; D. Spires 53.1–9–184–10–18.40; G. Gainford 81–10–259–12–21.58; M. Richardson 97–32–267–10–26.70.

ST EDMUND'S SCHOOL, CANTERBURY

Played 11: Won 5, Lost 5, Drawn 1. Abandoned 1

Master i/c: D. E. Knight

Batting—*A. Hajilou 11–2–423–117*–47.00; C. Bainbridge 10–0–133–44–13.30 A. Gompertz 9–1–100–26–12.50; J. Hutchings 10–0–109–32–10.90.

Bowling—C. R. M. Whittington 122.2–30–379–23–16.47; A. Hajilou 104–23–351–17–20.64 L. Wilkinson 63.2–10–289–10–28.90.

ST EDWARD'S SCHOOL, OXFORD

Played 14: Won 2, Lost 9, Drawn 3. Abandoned 1

Master i/c: M. D. Peregrine　　Cricket professional: G. Fitnes

Batting—H. Varney 13–0–430–86–33.07; *D. E. C. Wethey 13–0–197–48–15.15; A. M. B Goodwin 12–0–181–64–15.08; C. M. Pitcher 14–0–197–52–14.07; P. L. Bur 10–0–136–59–13.60; T. W. T. Stanley 14–1–148–31*–11.38; A. J. Stewa 14–1–137–21*–10.53.

Bowling—C. M. Pitcher 187.3–40–452–28–16.14; L. Siriwardene 191.2–37–669–18–37.16 D. E. C. Wethey 107–19–395–10–39.50.

ST GEORGE'S COLLEGE, WEYBRIDGE

Played 18: Won 2, Lost 7, Drawn 9

Master i/c: B. V. O'Gorman

Batting—S. Marsh 18–1–871–182–51.23; M. D. Miller 17–0–558–91–32.82; M. Boulton 15–5–308–74*–30.80; M. Church 13–0–363–76–27.92; C. Segal 18–1–464–67–27.29; D. Crowley 12–4–128–26–16.00; P. Curtin 16–3–191–63–14.69; R. Hirst 16–1–197–45–13.13.

Bowling—M. D. Miller 142–35–413–15–27.53; P. Crisell 233–63–628–22–28.54; J. Peters 104–9–519–18–28.83; R. Hirst 262–52–901–31–29.06; D. Gurivey 223–42–683–23–29.69.

ST JOSEPH'S COLLEGE, IPSWICH

Played 20: Won 8, Lost 5, Drawn 7. Abandoned 1

Master i/c: A. C. Rutherford Cricket professional: J. Pugh

Batting—J. McLoughlin 19–4–682–98*–45.46; P. Landen 17–1–447–63–27.93; A. Cole 18–2–380–62–23.75; D. White 11–3–165–60*–20.62; R. Farrow 16–2–205–51*–14.64; *S. McGrath 13–3–145–32–14.50; M. McDonough 14–3–145–51*–13.18; D. Ladbrook 14–2–138–41–11.50.

Bowling—A. Cole 204.5–40–594–32–18.56; J. King 68.4–12–262–14–18.71; D. Dellamaestra 196.1–48–549–26–21.11; J. McLoughlin 202.3–41–711–33–21.54; R. Ledwidge 138.1–24–523–19–27.52.

ST LAWRENCE COLLEGE, RAMSGATE

Played 13: Won 3, Lost 5, Drawn 5. Abandoned 3

Master i/c: N. O. S. Jones Cricket professionals: L. A. C. D'Arcy and A. P. E. Knott

Batting—O. G. Morris 13–0–489–96–37.61; D. J. Gear 13–3–218–50*–21.80; G. Turner 13–0–265–68–20.38; W. A. Taylaur 13–0–208–68–16.00; *B. T. Everett 13–0–173–33–13.30; O. D. Olakanpo 11–0–123–38–11.18.

Bowling—O. G. Morris 129.2–34–333–27–12.33; G. Turner 164–41–410–29–14.13.

ST PAUL'S SCHOOL

Played 14: Won 6, Lost 2, Drawn 6. Abandoned 2

Master i/c: G. Hughes Cricket professional: E. W. Whitfield

Batting—T. J. Taberner 13–4–428–101*–47.55; *B. R. Taberner 8–1–290–130*–41.42; S. Patel 14–3–437–85*–39.72; J. E. Gordon-Smith 7–2–156–34–31.20; S. D. S. Kaikini 10–1–247–59–27.44; P. A. Shapiro 12–3–206–69*–22.88; J. M. H. Weldon –2–134–34*–22.33; S. B. Clarke 9–2–108–31–15.42; J. O. Morris 13–1–166–57–13.83.

Bowling—S. D. S. Kaikini 143.9–23–459–25–18.36; S. B. Clarke 184.3–41–555–25–22.20; C. G. O. Burton 85–15–329–12–27.41.

ST PETER'S SCHOOL, YORK

Played 18: Won 2, Lost 7, Drawn 9. Abandoned 2

Master i/c: D. Kirby Cricket professional: K. F. Mohan

Batting—C. H. Metcalfe 9–0–262–83–29.11; M. P. Forrester 16–1–365–79*–24.33; J. D. Rigby 17–1–389–102*–24.31; P. F. Carvosso 16–2–316–65–22.57; G. J. Harding 12–1–195–38–17.72; R. N. Twigg 12–2–174–89–17.40; M. J. Davies 16–3–199–41–15.30.

Bowling—M. P. Forrester 127.2–22–449–23–19.52; A. G. G. Smith 77.4–11–286–13–22.00; R. N. Twigg 143–29–519–18–28.83; D. Bundy 100.2–14–470–15–31.33.

SEDBERGH SCHOOL

Played 13: Won 2, Lost 5, Drawn 6

Master i/c: A. W. McPhail

Batting—D. J. Player 14–1–357–68–27.46; A. F. M. Metcalfe 12–1–271–75*–24.63; P. M. Birkbeck 12–0–248–54–20.66; M. Manson 10–2–159–43–19.87; *W. J. H. Greenwood 12–1–208–51–18.90; D. W. Hudson 10–2–151–86*–18.87; R. C. F. Smailes 14–0–166–32–11.85.

Bowling—W. J. H. Greenwood 169–55–403–29–13.89; M. S. Wrigley 92–21–324–18–18.00; D. J. Player 222.4–63–600–31–19.35.

Note: The Sedbergh averages for 1989 may be found on page 966.

SEVENOAKS SCHOOL

Played 16: Won 2, Lost 1, Drawn 13. Abandoned 2

Master i/c: I. J. B. Walker

Batting—*Omar Iqbal 15–2–825–134*–63.46; L. W. Neil-Dwyer 14–6–476–100*–59.50; Hesham Iqbal 3–1–117–117*–58.50; T. R. Payton 12–3–251–64–27.88; B. C. Milligan 8–2–139–36–23.16; J. D. M. Brearley 13–2–209–72–19.00; J. N. Thomson 15–0–282–62–18.80.

Bowling—J. J. S. Lane 90–16–257–13–19.76; C. J. Peters 107–20–367–14–26.21; T. R. Payton 206–48–638–21–30.38.

SHERBORNE SCHOOL

Played 15: Won 12, Lost 0, Drawn 3

Master i/c: G. C. Allen Cricket professionals: A. Willows and C. Stone

Batting—A. J. Rutherford 7–4–132–43*–44.00; W. F. F. Hughes 6–2–148–64–37.00 M. W. D. Ford 15–1–473–80*–33.78; J. R. Tweedale 15–2–439–70*–33.76; E. J. Sangster 10–6–134–31–33.50; J. L. Pexton 14–2–313–48*–26.08; *B. D. Atwell 15–1–351–67–25.07 R. J. Preston 13–3–176–45–17.60; S. C. G. Watling 9–0–114–27–12.66.

Bowling—A. J. Rutherford 62.2–18–132–16–8.25; S. W. Stevens 329–94–795–55–14.45 R. H. F. Pugsley 148.2–42–342–22–15.54; M. W. D. Ford 138.3–35–342–19–18.00; J. L Pexton 158–30–456–17–26.82.

SHIPLAKE COLLEGE

Played 15: Won 8, Lost 2, Drawn 5

Master i/c: P. M. Davey Cricket professional: M. J. Hobb

Batting—A. J. Hall 14–3–401–145*–36.45; C. P. J. Abbiss 13–0–326–56–25.07; A. S. Kid 10–2–194–63–24.25; R. H. Wilson 8–3–106–34*–21.20; A. E. Rouse 10–1–165–42*–18.33 G. M. Carradine 12–0–198–44–16.50.

Bowling—A. J. Hall 230.4–73–560–56–10.00; P. C. Lefort 60–10–219–12–18.25; G. W. Phil 152–47–338–18–18.77; C. P. J. Abbiss 81–13–274–13–21.07.

SHREWSBURY SCHOOL

Played 18: Won 4, Lost 4, Drawn 10

Master i/c: S. M. Holroyd Cricket professionals: A. P. Pridgeon and P. H. Bromle

Batting—B. R. Parfitt 7–4–125–62*–41.66; D. J. Bowett 16–2–523–139*–37.35; S. J. Clark 18–4–516–63*–36.85; W. A. Hughes 17–2–341–72–22.73; J. J. Clark 16–0–328–84–20.50 A. D. Browne 18–0–286–55–15.88; R. F. Wycherley 18–0–256–32–14.22; P. W. Trimb 15–5–107–24–10.70.

Bowling—D. J. Bowett 208.7–42–455–34–13.38; D. J. Watson 63.5–13–159–11–14.45; P. W Trimby 246–39–771–37–20.83; I. K. Mainwaring 169.1–26–580–20–29.00; T. C. Corfie 94.3–8–381–12–31.75; R. J. Hanson 141.4–9–543–10–54.30.

SIMON LANGTON GRAMMAR SCHOOL

Played 11: Won 6, Lost 5, Drawn 0

Master i/c: A. Raines

Batting—N. Jones 8–2–339–123*–56.50; J. Kember 4–1–149–69*–49.66; P. Livesey 9–0–171–40–19.00; D. Isard 9–2–117–31*–16.71; P. Maxwell 9–0–112–33–12.44.

Bowling—N. Bielby 45.1–15–161–17–9.47; R. Moulton 75.3–14–232–21–11.04; *R. Stevens 40–11–152–10–15.20; D. Clark 67.5–18–185–10–18.50.

SOLIHULL SCHOOL

Played 17: Won 6, Lost 1, Drawn 10

Master i/c: M. R. Brough Cricket professional: S. P. Perryman

Batting—*J. M. A. Inglis 13–5–780–135*–97.50; R. A. Kallicharran 12–3–411–79*–45.66; R. A. Chapman 9–3–253–53*–42.16; S. R. Fell 13–5–204–59–25.50; K. A. Mortimer 13–0–326–68–25.07; M. J. Ketland-Jones 7–1–113–34–18.83; M. A. Jones 10–0–132–27–13.20; P. S. Amiss 13–0–106–21–8.15.

Bowling—J. M. A. Inglis 112.1–18–356–31–11.48; R. A. Kallicharran 88.5–10–378–17–22.23; J. E. Vertigen 116.1–20–438–18–24.33; M. C. Cattell 99.2–9–509–18–28.27; S. M. Franklin 92–16–416–13–32.00.

STAMFORD SCHOOL

Played 15: Won 1, Lost 6, Drawn 8

Master i/c: P. D. McKeown

Batting—S. Holland 13–0–407–73–31.30; *N. L. Boyd 14–2–321–48–26.75; R. E. Grundy 10–1–234–65–26.00; P. Banbury 14–0–317–68–22.64; D. G. Bartle 10–4–125–40–20.83; D. P. M. Herrick 10–4–101–28–16.83; D. M. Palmer 14–0–180–58–12.85.

Bowling—N. L. Boyd 210–39–832–30–27.73; A. Hale 82–9–386–12–32.16; D. P. M. Herrick 70–6–360–11–32.72.

STOWE SCHOOL

Played 17: Won 5, Lost 6, Drawn 6. Abandoned 1

Master i/c: G. A. Cottrell Cricket professional: M. J. Harris

Batting—A. J. Scott-Gall 16–5–409–56–37.18; M. W. Pumfrey 17–1–460–81–28.75; M. J. T. Jefferson 15–3–298–56–24.83; R. J. O. Green 17–0–384–74–22.58; D. E. Hyman 12–0–178–50–14.83; T. H. P. Russell 13–1–134–57–11.16.

Bowling—M. J. T. Jefferson 192–44–551–26–21.19; J. M. de la Pena 213.3–25–725–33–21.96; J. G. Raynor 159.5–33–508–21–24.19; J. C. J. Burrough 180–40–625–21–29.76.

STRATHALLAN SCHOOL

Played 15: Won 6, Lost 6, Drawn 3. Abandoned 1

Master i/c: R. J. W. Proctor

Batting—K. L. Salters 12–3–254–56–28.22; T. S. T. Walker 9–2–159–57*–22.71; H. M. Lochore 10–1–143–67–15.88; *D. G. Thorburn 12–2–153–51–15.30; H. A. D. McKenzie-Wilson 11–3–110–50–13.75; M. G. Vance 13–2–140–39*–12.72; H. A. D. Blanche 10–0–127–48–12.70.

Bowling—K. L. Salters 143.2–35–401–33–12.15; H. A. D. McKenzie-Wilson 206.3–54–488–36–13.55; J. D'Ath 64–12–217–16–13.56; M. R. Tench 137.5–29–435–23–18.91.

SUTTON VALENCE SCHOOL

Played 18: Won 7, Lost 0, Drawn 11

Master i/c: D. Pickard

Batting—*J. F. Barr 17–5–805–142–67.08; J. Page 18–5–584–79–44.92; A. D. Barr 6–2–179–46–44.75; J. Cowell 15–1–445–74–31.78.

Bowling—Y. S. Patel 101–19–265–17–15.58; J. F. Barr 215–80–599–38–15.76; J. Page 143–43–378–21–18.00; J. Cowell 180–39–568–30–18.93.

TAUNTON SCHOOL

Played 16: Won 7, Lost 3, Drawn 5, Tied 1. Abandoned 1

Master i/c: D. Baty Cricket professional: A. Kennedy

Batting—P. Tarr 15–3–561–118*–46.75; G. Crompton 15–3–477–74–39.75; K. Sedgbeer 10–3–266–85–38.00; A. Snow 9–3–209–53*–34.83; N. Smith 15–4–308–50*–28.00; B. Wellington 14–0–280–52–20.00; B. Craddock 15–0–279–60–18.60.

Bowling—E. Little 144–39–442–23–19.21; B. Wellington 207.3–60–559–27–20.70; *J. Hales 211–76–488–23–21.21; T. Joy 76–12–293–12–24.41.

TIFFIN SCHOOL

Played 20: Won 6, Lost 3, Drawn 11. Abandoned 1

Master i/c: M. J. Williams

Batting—G. J. Kennis 19–5–1,008–128*–72.00; *R. D. Nash 14–1–819–137–63.00; T. M. Phillips 15–3–351–86*–29.25; B. J. Walters 16–1–394–64–26.26; M. D. McPherson 14–2–271–43–22.58; N. G. Hodgson 13–5–171–41–21.37; A. P. Currie 16–3–217–42–16.69; S. R. A. Leeds 10–2–115–33*–14.37.

Bowling—B. J. Walters 318.5–129–770–41–18.78; R. D. Nash 80.4–17–323–14–23.07; T. M. Phillips 172.3–24–712–27–26.37; G. J. Kennis 167.4–38–553–19–29.10; S. R. A. Leeds 163.4–31–610–20–30.50.

TONBRIDGE SCHOOL

Played 16: Won 5, Lost 5, Drawn 6. Abandoned 1

Master i/c: G. E. Wynne Cricket professional: Syed Altaf Hossain

Batting—S. J. Doel 17–0–644–92–37.88; S. J. Jobber 16–3–421–52*–32.38; *J. F. S. Rowland 17–1–431–69–26.93; D. L. Gilbert 11–6–133–49*–26.60; M. O. Church 6–1–125–88–25.00; W. R. Tomkins 16–2–316–38*–22.57; P. E. M. Le Marchand 7–0–152–65–21.71; C. S. Madderson 12–0–253–67–21.08; T. R. Crabtree 16–2–276–78–19.71; R. L. Brewster 12–2–136–37*–13.60; R. J. Arthur 12–2–109–27*–10.90.

Bowling—R. P. Ziegler 153–30–542–32–16.93; D. L. Gilbert 210–52–615–32–19.21; W. R. Tomkins 63–14–310–14–22.14; R. L. Brewster 167–32–548–23–23.82; R. J. Arthur 188–33–614–22–27.90.

TRENT COLLEGE

Played 15: Won 1, Lost 3, Drawn 11. Abandoned 4

Master i/c: Dr T. P. Woods Cricket professional: L. Spendlove

Batting—T. A. Ellis 17–1–683–111–42.68; C. M. Winterbottom 13–5–223–104*–27.87; *A. W. Bocking 18–3–349–91–23.26; J. Pavis 14–0–280–57–20.00; J. D. Pratt 15–3–237–45–19.75; N. D. Johnson 13–6–136–47*–19.42; A. J. Vaughan 13–2–201–72*–18.27; M. A. Walker 11–3–138–50*–17.25; M. T. White 13–3–150–30–15.00.

Bowling—N. D. Johnson 186.3–56–437–31–14.09; M. T. White 207–52–604–32–18.87; A. W. Bocking 152.3–46–403–20–20.15; C. M. Winterbottom 126–35–349–10–34.90.

TRINITY SCHOOL

Played 21: Won 11, Lost 2, Drawn 8. Abandoned 1

Masters i/c: B. Widger and I. W. Cheyne

Batting—S. S. Prabhu 20–2–758–101–42.11; R. W. Nowell 14–1–500–88*–38.46; D. O. Dyer 7–1–177–60*–29.50; C. M. Brown 6–1–139–56–27.80; C. H. Maiden 20–0–514–84–25.70; A. Abbot 19–0–455–68–23.94; A. J. Codling 13–3–230–83*–23.00; P. B. Wren 18–6–194–49–16.16; P. S. Kember 16–4–183–43–15.25; M. D. C. Butterworth 15–8–102–51–14.57.

Bowling—R. W. Nowell 224.4–59–602–39–15.43; P. S. Kember 204.3–37–707–45–15.71; S. S. Prabhu 66.5–8–238–10–23.80; M. D. C. Butterworth 161.2–33–504–21–24.00; P. B. Wren 123.1–24–408–10–40.80.

TRURO SCHOOL

Played 12: Won 4, Lost 6, Drawn 2

Master i/c: D. M. Phillips

Batting—T. R. Perkins 12–2–201–38–20.10; *A. Symons 11–0–214–92–19.45; M. R. Thomas 12–0–218–44–18.16; D. P. Griffiths 12–0–175–42–14.58.

Bowling—A. Symons 66.3–16–166–20–8.30; M. R. Thomas 77.1–16–246–24–10.25; R. N. Peters 62–19–173–16–10.81; T. R. Perkins 101.1–20–304–20–15.20.

UNIVERSITY COLLEGE SCHOOL

Played 14: Won 1, Lost 9, Drawn 4

Master i/c: S. M. Bloomfield — Cricket professional: W. G. Jones

Batting—R. J. Ayre 15–3–649–133*–54.08; A. M. Stewart 14–1–529–108*–40.69; S. K. Cattermole 14–1–402–87–30.92; *K. J. Schofield 15–1–304–57–21.71.

Bowling—S. K. Cattermole 236.1–52–562–25–22.48; D. S. Quint 180.4–42–490–20–24.50; K. J. Schofield 218.2–50–759–22–34.50.

WARWICK SCHOOL

Played 15: Won 6, Lost 2, Drawn 7. Abandoned 1

Master i/c: D. C. Elstone

Batting—C. Mulraine 12–1–486–124*–44.18; S. Ensall 14–4–401–68*–40.10; D. Dalton 15–0–432–67–28.80; J. Wilsdon 12–4–213–37–26.62; *G. Rawstorne 16–3–331–57–25.46; T. McCann 15–1–303–70–21.64; C. Harcourt 10–2–115–36–14.37.

Bowling—S. Webb 138.3–30–444–25–17.76; J. Wilsdon 80–14–267–11–24.27; J. Ward 185–33–714–26–27.46; M. Covington 123–16–486–17–28.58.

WELLINGBOROUGH SCHOOL

Played 19: Won 7, Lost 0, Drawn 12. Abandoned 2

Master i/c: M. H. Askham — Cricket professional: J. C. J. Dye

Batting—*J. M. Attfield 19–6–1,116–120*–85.84; N. J. Haste 14–6–441–87*–55.12; S. McMillan 19–3–730–92–45.62; S. Swaroop 12–5–232–83–33.14; R. D. Mann 19–2–532–74–31.29; M. J. Haste 8–3–104–31*–20.80.

Bowling—N. J. Haste 246.4–43–819–39–21.00; R. I. T. Matheson 93.5–21–408–18–22.66; J. M. Attfield 131–22–449–18–24.94; D. W. Hallworth 146–34–470–16–29.37; P. J. Dolman 120–11–612–14–43.71.

WELLINGTON COLLEGE

Played 17: Won 5, Lost 5, Drawn 7. Abandoned 1

Masters i/c: C. M. St G. Potter and R. I. H. B. Dyer Cricket professional: P. J. Lewington

Batting—R. de V. Butland 16–6–498–71–49.80; A. E. Newman 20–1–726–81–38.21; T. N. Sawrey-Cookson 20–1–696–106*–36.63; J. A. D. Wyke 20–2–474–80–26.33; D. P. Bailey 12–6–148–30–24.66; *A. P. D. Wyke 18–3–368–49–24.53; W. P. G. Waugh 7–2–110–46–22.00; A. P. M. Samuel 9–2–107–30–15.28.

Bowling—A. P. D. Wyke 217–33–720–35–20.57; S. Goldsworthy 87.5–13–382–15–25.46; J. W. Maunder-Taylor 83–16–266–10–26.60; A. P. M. Samuel 163–24–510–17–30.00.

WELLINGTON SCHOOL

Played 16: Won 7, Lost 2, Drawn 7

Master i/c: P. M. Pearce

Batting—R. Fisher 15–2–488–91–37.53; *S. Palmer 14–3–305–57–27.72; G. Wolfendon 16–1–354–50–23.60; N. Hutchings 7–2–106–34–21.20; J. Postlethwaite 15–4–195–51–17.72; T. Hughes 8–1–117–36–16.71; D. Hine 15–1–197–47–14.07; B. Kelly 12–0–139–24–11.58.

Bowling—T. Hughes 151.5–34–524–36–14.55; S. Palmer 102–12–392–26–15.07; D. Hine 31.4–3–221–13–17.00; N. Hutchings 162–31–528–26–20.30.

WESTMINSTER SCHOOL

Played 13: Won 4, Lost 4, Drawn 5

Master i/c: D. Cook Cricket professional: R. Gilson

Batting—A. Worthington 9–0–488–92–54.22; C. Luke 11–0–210–52–19.09; T. Hyam 12–0–204–60–17.00; S. Goulden 11–0–179–31–16.27; P. Campbell 8–0–110–34–13.75.

Bowling—C. Ash 126–36–452–27–16.74; T. Hyam 44–16–177–10–17.70; D. Owen 55–20–218–10–21.80; L. Gillam 77–19–277–12–23.08.

WHITGIFT SCHOOL

Played 20: Won 7, Lost 3, Drawn 10

Master i/c: P. C. Fladgate

Batting—J. D. G. Ufton 21–6–817–123*–54.46; R. Shah 21–1–629–163*–31.45; P. M. Horne 20–2–481–101*–26.72; R. W. Milligan 9–3–157–51–26.16; J. S. Harford 17–3–338–61–24.14; R. S. Gibson 9–2–102–33–14.57; *A. R. Biswas 20–1–252–68–13.26; R. J. Targett 12–2–132–44–13.20; P. J. Brown 13–2–134–23*–12.18.

Bowling—S. N. Jackson 54–11–164–12–13.66; A. T. Lark 107–29–308–20–15.40; J. D. G. Ufton 116–25–332–18–18.44; T. J. Colbourn 189.4–26–603–32–18.84; R. J. Targett 240.3–50–728–36–20.22; J. S. Harford 134.2–25–437–21–20.80; R. S. Gibson 169–31–521–14–37.21.

WILLIAM HULME'S GRAMMAR SCHOOL

Played 21: Won 5, Lost 8, Drawn 8. Abandoned 2

Master i/c: I. J. Shaw Cricket professional: B. Wood

Batting—N. T. Wood 11–1–380–106–38.00; A. K. Hollingworth 18–2–458–91–28.62; P. D. Warren 17–1–440–109*–27.50; *A. S. Partington 15–1–256–48–18.28; I. A. Brassell 10–2–146–56–18.25; L. E. Tilston 17–1–274–98–17.12; J. P. Abrahams 14–2–178–51–14.83; M. Ekstein 11–1–109–27–10.90.

Bowling—N. T. Wood 39.3–10–111–10–11.10; L. E. Tilston 101–25–267–17–15.70; A. A. Khan 64.4–7–201–12–16.75; A. J. Edwards 106–17–394–22–17.90; A. K. Hollingworth 145.4–30–441–24–18.37; A. R. Ladd 91.2–19–321–15–21.40; A. S. Partington 98–26–260–11–23.63.

WINCHESTER COLLEGE

Played 19: Won 6, Lost 5, Drawn 8. Abandoned 1

Master i/c: P. J. Metcalfe Cricket professional: K. N. Foyle

Batting—C. E. van der Noot 12–1–478–136*–43.45; J. C. Guise 9–4–169–66*–33.80; J. M. Collier 14–4–335–114*–33.50; *R. J. Turnill 20–4–513–87*–32.06; W. F. Poole-Wilson 19–0–497–80–26.15; A. W. Maclay 11–4–181–37*–25.85; R. Field 14–5–192–33*–21.33; S. J. Beloe 13–1–245–67*–20.41; A. R. Hobson 13–0–188–89–14.46; A. P. McKenna 17–3–160–43*–11.42.

Bowling—R. Field 208–31–738–32–23.06; A. W. Maclay 267–51–844–36–23.44; A. B. Donald 207–33–799–28–28.53; A. P. McKenna 158–19–614–20–30.70.

WOODBRIDGE SCHOOL

Played 13: Won 2, Lost 6, Drawn 5

Master i/c: P. Kesterton

Batting—*B. K. Sindell 12–1–452–109–41.09; N. Waller 9–3–169–50*–28.16; H. P. Turbervill 13–1–272–61–22.66; M. Vipond 12–0–175–32–14.58.

Bowling—H. P. Turbervill 69–13–249–13–19.15; J. M. Percival 107.1–20–361–17–21.23; M. Bettell 109–37–286–12–23.83; N. S. Pagan 137.5–29–422–13–32.46.

WOODHOUSE GROVE SCHOOL

Played 14: Won 4, Lost 2, Drawn 8. Abandoned 2

Master i/c: E. R. Howard Cricket professional: D. M. Stranger

Batting—J. C. M. Dobbs 8–5–173–53*–57.66; S. N. Lee 12–6–252–59–42.00; *D. M. Lawson 9–1–225–96–28.12; C. J. Rika 11–1–269–47*–26.90; R. D. Webster 12–1–269–75–24.45; J. A. Lockwood 8–1–133–69–19.00.

Bowling—S. N. Lee 107.5–22–366–30–12.20; R. D. Webster 128.4–35–360–21–17.14; C. J. Rika 110–23–330–17–19.41.

WORKSOP COLLEGE

Played 15: Won 3, Lost 2, Drawn 10. Abandoned 2

Master i/c: B. Wilks Cricket professional: A. Kettleborough

Batting—*J. D. Goode 14–5–485–107*–53.88; R. A. Kettleborough 9–2–356–100*–50.85; C. J. Walker 14–1–489–107–37.61; J. C. Beardsley 11–2–300–74–33.33; M. L. Morewood 6–2–107–31–26.75; M. A. Hawley 10–4–136–56–22.66; P. W. Milton 11–1–122–32*–12.20.

Bowling—J. D. Goode 115–25–350–20–17.50; J. C. Beardsley 106–21–332–18–18.44; M. L. Morewood 165–38–481–22–21.86; M. A. Hawley 122–15–436–13–33.53.

WREKIN COLLEGE

Played 18: Won 5, Lost 9, Drawn 4. Abandoned 1

Master i/c: T. J. Murphy

Batting—M. R. Savage 19–2–402–91–23.64; C. J. Davies 17–3–266–53*–19.00; J. Taylor 18–2–293–62–18.31; B. Cox 11–3–132–29–16.50; J. D. King 16–0–205–37–12.81; J. A. Brassington 12–1–132–43–12.00; *M. R. Prince 15–2–122–50*–9.38; S. R. D. H. Lander 14–1–121–28*–9.30; A. J. Holloway 14–0–114–28–8.14.

Bowling—C. J. Davies 35–1–132–10–13.20; A. J. Holloway 164–30–482–36–13.38; S. R. Phillips-Broadhurst 148–23–494–31–15.93; M. R. Prince 70–11–285–15–19.00; S. R. D. H. Lander 149–28–476–19–25.05.

WYCLIFFE COLLEGE

Played 18: Won 2, Lost 6, Drawn 10

Master i/c: P. Woolley Cricket professional: K. Biddulph

Batting—I. M. Collins 6–3–110–47–36.66; G. A. McDade 17–1–390–94–24.37; *J. J. Lister 16–0–320–55–20.00; S. P. Collins 18–0–343–61–19.05; M. J. Singer 16–0–273–73–17.06; M. H. Workman 11–4–116–33–16.57; S. T. A. Cady 16–3–192–67–14.76; B. Harding 17–3–191–35–13.64; M. A. House 13–2–130–32–11.81.

Bowling—W. R. Tovey 131.5–16–583–39–14.94; J. J. Lister 144.5–36–459–23–19.95; S. B. Thomas 189.4–38–584–25–23.36; M. A. House 83.5–16–298–12–24.83.

WYGGESTON & QUEEN ELIZABETH I SIXTH FORM COLLEGE

Played 11: Won 3, Lost 2, Drawn 6. Abandoned 1

Master i/c: G. G. Wells

Batting—S. Kennell 9–0–325–69–36.11; D. Green 5–1–104–36–26.00; J. E. Kent 10–1–191–57–21.22; P. N. Green 6–0–122–52–20.33; *D. M. Rodwell 8–0–148–47–18.50.

Bowling—S. Patel 83.2–22–211–23–9.17; D. Green 49.1–11–140–12–11.66; R. Sargent 55–6–210–10–21.00.

SEDBERGH SCHOOL, 1989

Batting—*S. D. Gawthorpe 16–1–805–165*–53.66; D. J. Player 14–5–398–69–42.22; J. N. Ayton 12–2–375–73–37.50; J. E. Gundill 12–3–214–104–23.77; R. C. F. Smailes 6–0–133–55–22.16; M. D. Latham 10–0–175–71–19.50; A. J. Meadows 16–2–258–51–18.42; P. J. T. Nickalls 10–2–107–32*–13.37; A. F. M. Metcalfe 12–2–120–24*–12.00.

Bowling—D. J. Player 265–40–497–32–15.53; M. J. Jameson 99–22–266–15–17.73; W. J. H. Greenwood 136.2–27–498–18–27.66; M. S. Wrigley 177–33–590–17–34.70; J. E. Gundill 173–20–562–13–43.23.

OVERSEAS CRICKET, 1989-90

Note: Throughout this section, matches not first-class are denoted by the use of a dagger.

ENGLAND IN THE WEST INDIES, 1989-90

By ALAN LEE

The essential weakness of any statistical record is that it can reflect neither circumstance nor injustice. A potted summary of England's Test series in the Caribbean, early in 1990, indicates merely that they lost 2-1, with one match drawn and the other abandoned. In years to come, that stark scoreline may be read to mean that England did slightly better than anticipated. The truth of the matter is that at worst they merited a shared series, and at best an unimaginable upset of the world champions of Test cricket.

When the tour began, in late January, England were given no chance. They had been beaten 4-0 by Australia in England in their previous series. The response of the selectors to that had been to dismiss David Gower, as both captain and player, and replace him with Graham Gooch, who, though stoical to his plodding feet, had never been thought to be inspirational leadership material. A touring party had been chosen with express aims in mind. Gower and Botham were banished as redolent of a defeatist era, and in their place came men of less talent and charisma but, the selectors believed, equipped to combat the West Indians in their own aggressive, unrelenting style. "Fighting fire with fire" was the comment of Ted Dexter, chairman of the England Committee, when the squad was announced. Much scoffing and snorting ensued. Yet, fanciful though the theory seemed, given England's slender resources for pace bowling, it was justified in the final analysis.

England's nine-wicket victory in the First Test, at Kingston, unarguably qualified to be one of the most outlandish results in Test-cricket history. West Indies were thoroughly outplayed. Georgetown, venue for the Second Test, was struck by atrocious weather which prevented a ball being bowled, but those who maintained that the Jamaica Test result had been an unrepeatable freak were silenced in Trinidad. England, with the benefit of winning an important toss, set up a second victory, which was cruelly denied them by a persistent downpour on the final afternoon. This, if you like, was a real freak.

The tour was never the same after that. With their strongest side, England might have withstood the travesty and risen again. But for the two remaining Tests they were without Gooch, whose captaincy had become even more crucial than his batting, and Angus Fraser, the most dependable member of a startlingly influential four-man seam attack. It was too much to bear. In Barbados England battled ferociously, losing a dramatic and controversial match with half an hour's daylight remaining on the final evening. In Antigua, for the finale, they had nothing left to offer and were beaten, by an innings, before tea on the fourth day.

When it was over, England's dressing-room was a casualty ward, virtually half the party having suffered injuries in the battle. Two, Robin Smith and Nasser Hussain, batted in Antigua with broken bones. The character of the players was beyond question. As Micky Stewart, the team manager, said: "You have to feel so sorry for them, having nothing to show for it."

Stewart was one of those who gained most from the tour. When it began, his future as manager was being debated, both in the media and among the public. His time in charge had been attended by little other than defeat and controversy, some of it thoroughly unsavoury, and under Gower's captaincy his authority had been seen to diminish. By the end of the 1989 season, it was justifiable for anyone to ask precisely what he had achieved, or was likely to. Perhaps the best thing that could have happened for Stewart was the defection of Mike Gatting to South Africa. This dismissed any possibility of his being brought back as captain, and a pairing being reunited which, latterly, had been distinguished by little more than its blinkered condoning of indefensible on-field conduct.

Gooch acceded to the captaincy in an unfortunate manner, for he was nobody's first choice. But he confounded all preconceived notions about his limitations and emerged as the most influential figure of the tour. He was obsessive about his own physical fitness and his own mental preparation. He believed intensive training vital to the extension of his career, and from his self-motivation came the spur for other, younger and less gifted players to approach their game the same way. Gooch rapidly commanded an unfailing respect among his players, and earned it by his quiet, individual counselling, his caring touch and his thoughtful tactics. In his own way, he was the most impressive England captain since Brearley.

Allan Lamb, his vice-captain, was ideal for the position, but less suited to taking command, which he was obliged to do once Gooch had suffered a broken hand in Trinidad. Gregarious and positive, Lamb had few grey areas in his outlook, which was just what was required as support for the more complex ways of Gooch. His batting, too, once again rose to the peaks against the West Indian fast bowlers, his Test centuries in Jamaica and Barbados being his first overseas.

There were heroes in the ranks, as well. Devon Malcolm was thought to be a wild-card selection during the Australian series of the preceding summer, a bowler of genuine pace but without reliable direction. He had not even played a full season for Derbyshire, and yet when the tour was over he could be held up as the vindication of the management's policies. They made him the weapon they required, and to his credit he was a willing pupil. There were times when he was at least as quick as any of the West Indians. Gladstone Small saw the series through, a pleasant surprise given his injury record, and bowled with dedicated skill and control. Fraser, until his untimely rib injury, was the third seamer to answer a captain's prayers, his probing line unflagging. David Capel, as fourth bowler and seventh batsman, also had his moments, and no-one exuded more commitment.

Robin Smith set out to discard finally the image of a compulsive strokemaker and to occupy the crease against the fast men. He did so to enormous effect, batting for more than fifteen hours in the series. Wayne Larkins, who underwent a similar identity change, and the brave Jack Russell were just as adhesive, but the disappointment was the failure of any of the newer batsmen to establish themselves. Despite everything, there was an enduring suspicion that this would have been a better side with Gower involved from the outset, rather than his being somewhat frivolously shuffled in and out of the squad from his temporary role in the press box whenever an emergency demanded. A third specialist opener was also required, as had always been probable, and it was unsatisfactory to have Alec Stewart doing the job, out of position.

There was no place for spin in the Test series. England remained faithful to their stated policies, and West Indies resisted loud local calls to include the Jamaican leg-break bowler, Robert Haynes, who twice caused England problems in representative matches. If this was predictable, so too was the problem of poor over-rates. The nominal minimum of 90 overs a day was not supported by sanctions of any sort. Consequently, the quota was never completed before dusk. In Trinidad, on the final day, the West Indians' time-wasting tactics were deplorably unscrupulous, particularly the orchestration of Desmond Haynes, deputising as captain for the stricken Viv Richards. England wasted no time in trying to match their hosts for cynicism, Lamb's delaying devices in Barbados being only slightly less overt. Until stern penalties are introduced, which ICC in the past has seemed unable to agree upon, such insulting passages of play will never be prevented.

Considering the preponderance of fast bowling, it is pleasant to recount that intimidation became an aggravated issue only during the final Test in Antigua, when England's Smith was systematically worked over with the short ball, one of which broke a finger. No warnings were issued, yet a plainer case of deliberate intimidation was difficult to imagine. When West Indies batted, Capel, at no more than medium pace, received a caution for two consecutive short balls at a tailender. This was a nonsensical inconsistency.

Umpiring was also at the centre of an explosive situation during the Barbados Test. Rob Bailey, who suffered a wretched tour, was given out on the fourth evening, caught behind down the leg side off Curtly Ambrose. The ball had appeared to make contact only with his hip, but a debatable decision became a major incident owing to interpretations of Richards's startling, finger-flapping rush at the umpire, Lloyd Barker, in the moments before and during the raising of his finger. Some construed this as intimidating the official, and a remark to that effect by the BBC cricket correspondent, Christopher Martin-Jenkins, broadcast on the World Service, prompted a quite hysterical counter-reaction. The implied suggestion was that all such comments were basically racist.

For West Indies, this was a series which looked to have slipped sensationally away from them, only to be recovered by suddenly restored self-belief. Ambrose and Ian Bishop, supported by Courtney Walsh, were an awesome handful in the latter part of the series, and the spell with which Ambrose won the Barbados Test was unforgettable. Malcolm Marshall, however, achieved little in the series and missed two matches through injury, prompting speculation about his future. Richards, still troubled by illness, had a generally unhappy time. He offended Caribbean Asians with comments about his "African" team, and subsequent to the scene involving umpire Barker, he responded so irrationally to criticism by an English journalist that he chose to confront the writer in the Antigua press box instead of leading his players on to the field. His apologies to his Board were accepted only with a strict warning about any future misdemeanours. He emerged with another series won, but it was not one which advanced his reputation as either captain or batsman.

ENGLAND TOUR RESULTS

Test matches – Played 4: Won 1, Lost 2, Drawn 1. Abandoned 1.
First-class matches – Played 9: Won 2, Lost 3, Drawn 4. Abandoned 1.
Wins – West Indies, West Indies Board President's XI.
Losses – West Indies (2), Windward Islands.
Drawn – West Indies, Leeward Islands, Jamaica, Barbados.
Abandoned – West Indies.
One-day internationals – Played 6: Lost 4, No result 2.

TEST MATCH AVERAGES

WEST INDIES – BATTING

	T	*I*	*NO*	*R*	*HI*	*100s*	*Avge*
D. L. Haynes	4	7	0	371	167	2	53.00
C. A. Best	3	5	0	242	164	1	48.40
C. G. Greenidge	4	7	0	308	149	1	44.00
A. L. Logie	3	5	0	212	98	0	42.40
I. V. A. Richards	3	5	0	141	70	0	28.20
R. B. Richardson	4	7	0	195	45	0	27.85
P. J. L. Dujon	4	7	2	109	31	0	21.80
I. R. Bishop	4	7	3	69	16	0	17.25
C. L. Hooper	3	5	0	71	32	0	14.20
C. E. L. Ambrose	3	5	1	51	20*	0	12.75
E. A. Moseley	2	4	0	35	26	0	8.75
M. D. Marshall	2	4	1	19	8*	0	6.33
C. A. Walsh	3	5	1	25	8*	0	6.25

Played in one Test: E. A. E. Baptiste 9; B. P. Patterson 0, 2.

* *Signifies not out.*

BOWLING

	O	*M*	*R*	*W*	*BB*	*5W/i*	*Avge*
C. E. L. Ambrose	132	32	307	20	8-45	1	15.35
I. R. Bishop	162.1	37	419	21	5-84	1	19.95
C. A. Walsh	93.2	14	243	12	5-68	1	20.25
E. A. Moseley	87	13	261	6	2-70	0	43.50
M. D. Marshall	59	17	132	3	2-55	0	44.00

Also bowled: E. A. E. Baptiste 23–5–77–1; C. A. Best 4–0–19–0; C. L. Hooper 24–5–54–0; B. P. Patterson 21–3–85–1; I. V. A. Richards 28–10–47–0; R. B. Richardson 2–1–3–0.

ENGLAND – BATTING

	T	*I*	*NO*	*R*	*HI*	*100s*	*Avge*
A. J. Lamb	4	7	0	390	132	2	55.71
G. A. Gooch	2	4	1	128	84	0	42.66
R. A. Smith	4	7	2	186	62	0	37.20
W. Larkins	4	8	1	176	54	0	25.14
A. J. Stewart	4	8	1	170	45	0	24.28
R. C. Russell	4	7	1	139	55	0	23.16
N. Hussain	3	5	0	100	35	0	20.00
D. J. Capel	4	7	1	81	40	0	13.50
A. R. C. Fraser	2	2	1	13	11	0	13.00
R. J. Bailey	3	6	0	73	42	0	12.16
P. A. J. DeFreitas	2	4	0	45	24	0	11.25
D. E. Malcolm	4	6	3	17	12	0	5.66
G. C. Small	4	6	1	17	8	0	3.4

* *Signifies not out.*

BOWLING

	O	M	R	W	BB	5W/i	Avge
A. R. C. Fraser	71.1	19	161	11	5-28	1	14.63
G. C. Small	161	33	505	17	4-58	0	29.70
D. E. Malcolm	161.4	21	577	19	6-77	1	30.36
P. A. J. DeFreitas	78.5	11	242	6	3-69	0	40.33
D. J. Capel	124	17	436	9	3-88	0	48.44

ENGLAND AVERAGES – FIRST-CLASS MATCHES

BATTING

	M	I	NO	R	HI	100s	Avge
G. A. Gooch	6	11	1	616	239	1	61.60
A. J. Lamb	7	12	0	549	132	2	45.75
W. Larkins	8	16	2	524	124*	2	37.42
R. A. Smith	9	16	3	477	99*	0	36.69
A. J. Stewart	9	18	1	516	125	1	30.35
N. Hussain	6	10	1	260	70*	0	28.88
R. C. Russell	8	15	5	269	55	0	26.90
D. J. Capel	8	15	3	245	65	0	20.41
R. J. Bailey	6	12	1	177	52	0	16.09
P. A. J. DeFreitas	6	11	4	108	24	0	15.42
C. C. Lewis	2	3	0	33	21	0	11.00
K. T. Medlycott	3	3	0	24	21	0	8.00
D. E. Malcolm	7	9	3	29	12	0	4.83
A. R. C. Fraser	4	5	1	17	11	0	4.25
G. C. Small	5	6	1	17	8	0	3.40
E. E. Hemmings	4	6	1	13	6	0	2.60

Played in one match: D. I. Gower 4.

* *Signifies not out.*

BOWLING

	O	M	R	W	BB	5W/i	Avge
E. E. Hemmings	108.1	30	301	15	5-77	1	20.06
A. R. C. Fraser	122.2	28	353	17	5-28	1	20.76
G. C. Small	201	41	644	23	4-58	0	28.00
D. E. Malcolm	258.4	37	948	32	6-77	1	29.62
K. T. Medlycott	100.2	11	425	13	4-36	0	32.69
P. A. J. DeFreitas	196.4	28	697	21	4-54	0	33.19
D. J. Capel	201	26	733	14	3-88	0	52.35

Also bowled: G. A. Gooch 3–0–6–1; C. C. Lewis 35–6–128–2.

FIELDING

26 – R. C. Russell (24 ct, 2 st); 9 – A. J. Lamb; 6 – G. A. Gooch; 5 – D. J. Capel, R. A. Smith, A. J. Stewart; 4 – W. Larkins, G. C. Small; 3 – R. J. Bailey, D. E. Malcolm; 2 – P. A. J. DeFreitas, E. E. Hemmings, N. Hussain; 1 – A. R. C. Fraser, C. C. Lewis, K. T. Medlycott, Substitute (D. L. Bairstow).

LEEWARD ISLANDS v ENGLAND XI

At Basseterre, St Kitts, February 2, 3, 4, 5. Drawn. Toss: England XI. The first three days on this charming ground provided England with encouragement; the fourth gave them a fright as the Red Stripe Cup winners indicated that a target of 402 in a minimum of 64 overs was not beyond them. When the captains called a halt, with 101 needed, five wickets standing, and twelve overs left, Gooch was probably the more relieved. England's bowling had lacked discipline under attack, and while Arthurton was making 86 from 71 balls, a home win looked possible. On an easy-paced pitch, England had batted for almost five sessions after electing to bat first. Larkins reached his century in five hours, and Stewart emulated him the following day. A penetrative new-ball spell by Small was then put into perspective by Richardson, who scored 66 of his 83 in boundaries, and Baptiste nourished the lower order. England, obtaining a lead of 188, preferred further batting practice to enforcing the follow-on, but a patchy second innings was notable mostly for an unacceptable case of dissent by Hussain in his first tour match. He was officially reprimanded by the captain and management. Gooch delayed his declaration until shortly before lunch on the final day, a cautious approach which was vindicated by his wayward bowlers.

Close of play: First day, England XI 244-2 (A. J. Stewart 65*, R. A. Smith 13*); Second day, Leeward Islands 138-3 (R. B. Richardson 81*, R. M. Otto 18*); Third day, England XI 112-4 (R. A. Smith 2*, A. J. Stewart 2*).

England XI

*G. A. Gooch c Harris b W. K. M. Benjamin	46	– c and b Guishard	50
W. Larkins c and b Arthurton	107	– b Guishard	27
A. J. Stewart c sub b Guishard	125	– (6) b Anthony	28
R. A. Smith b Guishard	71	– (5) c sub b Guishard	37
N. Hussain b Guishard	42	– (4) lbw b Arthurton	10
R. J. Bailey lbw b Anthony	1	– (3) c sub b Arthurton	10
†R. C. Russell not out	15	– not out	32
P. A. J. DeFreitas not out	17	– not out	6
B 2, l-b 9, w 5, n-b 4	20	B 5, l-b 7, w 1	13
1/96 2/220 3/364 4/379 5/380 6/424 (6 wkts dec.)	444	1/68 2/91 3/101 4/108 5/156 6/200 (6 wkts dec.)	213

K. T. Medlycott, G. C. Small and D. E. Malcolm did not bat.

Bowling: *First Innings*—K. C. G. Benjamin 6–4–4–0; W. K. M. Benjamin 21–3–62–1; Anthony 32–11–79–1; Baptiste 33–9–76–0; Guishard 53–11–150–3; Arthurton 11–3–23–1; Otto 10–0–39–0. *Second Innings*—Baptiste 6–1–14–0; Anthony 21–3–64–1; Richardson 8–3–21–0; Guishard 29.3–8–71–3; Arthurton 16–6–31–2.

Leeward Islands

R. E. Bassue lbw b Small	21	– (2) c Bailey b Medlycott	57
S. C. Williams b Small	1	– (1) lbw b Small	31
*R. B. Richardson c and b Small	83	– c Russell b Malcolm	5
K. L. T. Arthurton lbw b DeFreitas	7	– b Medlycott	86
R. M. Otto lbw b Malcolm	18	– not out	51
H. A. G. Anthony b Malcolm	0	– c Gooch b Small	4
†L. L. Harris c Malcolm b DeFreitas	19	– not out	54
E. A. E. Baptiste b Malcolm	61		
N. C. Guishard c Russell b Small	21		
W. K. M. Benjamin not out	0		
K. C. G. Benjamin absent injured			
B 3, l-b 8, w 3, n-b 11	25	B 4, l-b 4, w 1, n-b 4	13
1/2 2/60 3/72 4/138 5/138 6/146 7/172 8/248 9/256	256	1/50 2/75 3/140 4/196 5/208 (5 wkts)	301

Bowling: *First Innings*—Malcolm 23–4–86–3; Small 23–5–75–4; DeFreitas 14–5–53–2; Medlycott 5–0–31–0. *Second Innings*—Small 17–3–64–2; Malcolm 13–1–81–1; DeFreitas 7–1–49–0; Medlycott 17–1–99–2.

Umpires: C. Mack and A. E. Weekes.

WINDWARD ISLANDS v ENGLAND XI

At Castries, St Lucia, February 8, 9, 10, 11. Windward Islands won by one wicket. Toss: Windward Islands. England contributed little to the quality of this match until the final evening, when their two spin bowlers all but conjured an improbable victory. Eventually Windward Islands won, their last man, Allen, hitting Medlycott for four, but England emerged in higher spirits than had seemed possible. On a grassless pitch, destined to turn, this was a good toss to win, and the experienced Windwards' opener, John, ensured that it was not wasted. England's seam bowling was again untidy, and there were far too many no-balls. Worse was to follow as England's batting dramatically surrendered, the last six wickets falling for 29 runs in an hour on the third morning. Five were taken by Durand, a left-arm spin bowler who was making his first-class début at the age of 29. Following on, England were in trouble again until Steward and Lamb added 152 for the third wicket. The Windwards needed only 136, in 52 overs, for their second win over consecutive England tour teams, but from 82 for two they almost lost their way, panicking against some fine slow bowling by Medlycott and Hemmings.

Close of play: First day, Windward Islands 264-5 (M. Durand 6*, D. J. Collymore 15*); Second day, England XI 97-4 (R. A. Smith 7*, D. J. Capel 2*); Third day, England XI 217-5 (D. J. Capel 12*, K. T. Medlycott 5*).

Windward Islands

L. D. John b DeFreitas	83	lbw b DeFreitas	6
D. T. Telemaque lbw b Fraser	20	c Stewart b Medlycott	43
D. A. Joseph st Russell b Medlycott	59	b Hemmings	19
J. Eugene c Smith b Fraser	8	c Smith b Medlycott	17
*J. D. Charles c Russell b Capel	39	b Hemmings	10
M. Durand run out	6	b Medlycott	17
D. J. Collymore c Lamb b Hemmings	29	c Gooch b Hemmings	3
†J. R. Murray c Gooch b DeFreitas	1	c Gooch b Medlycott	8
T. Z. Kentish lbw b DeFreitas	9	not out	4
W. L. Thomas st Russell b Hemmings	19	b Hemmings	1
I. B. A. Allen not out	0	not out	4
B 1, l-b 4, w 4, n-b 35	44	L-b 4, n-b 3	7
1/73 2/138 3/154 4/208 5/241 6/264 7/270 8/287 9/317	317	1/12 2/55 3/82 4/101 5/101 6/113 7/126 8/131 9/132	(9 wkts) 139

Bowling: *First Innings*—DeFreitas 22–2–87–3; Fraser 22–3–71–2; Hemmings 17.3–4–64–2; Capel 18–4–46–1; Medlycott 13–1–44–1. *Second Innings*—DeFreitas 5–1–25–1; Fraser 8–2–33–0; Hemmings 17–5–41–4; Medlycott 12.2–0–36–4.

England XI

*G. A. Gooch lbw b Allen	19	c Telemaque b Collymore	7
W. Larkins c Murray b Durand	31	lbw b Allen	0
A. J. Stewart lbw b Collymore	6	b Kentish	77
A. J. Lamb b Durand	20	c Telemaque b Kentish	83
R. A. Smith b Durand	12	c Joseph b Kentish	19
D. J. Capel c Telemaque b Kentish	6	c Telemaque b Allen	65
†R. C. Russell b Durand	7	(8) not out	22
P. A. J. DeFreitas not out	3	(9) c Murray b Thomas	2
K. T. Medlycott c Collymore b Durand	3	(7) run out	21
E. E. Hemmings c Charles b Durand	6	lbw b Allen	1
A. R. C. Fraser c Charles b Durand	0	lbw b Thomas	1
B 1, n-b 12	13	B 7, l-b 3, w 1, n-b 17	28
1/36 2/43 3/87 4/88 5/103 6/111 7/113 8/118 9/124	126	1/3 2/14 3/166 4/193 5/208 6/272 7/308 8/318 9/325	326

Bowling: *First Innings*—Allen 9–3–23–1; Collymore 11–1–35–1; Thomas 7–0–19–0; Kentish 24–8–33–1; Durand 19.4–11–15–7. *Second Innings*—Allen 20–2–55–3; Collymore 19–0–59–1; Kentish 33–6–92–3; Thomas 9.2–1–23–2; Durand 31–10–55–0; Charles 7–0–32–0.

Umpires: M. A. Hippolyte and L. Thomas.

†WEST INDIES v ENGLAND

First One-day International

At Port-of-Spain, Trinidad, February 14. No result. Toss: England. England bowled and fielded with a consistency unrecognisable from their early matches. Gooch directed operations with precision and care, and none of the West Indian batsmen dominated. However, England's batsmen, facing only a moderate target, were already behind the clock against Marshall and Bishop when persistent rain forced an abandonment. Lewis, who had been drafted into the team from the England A tour of Zimbabwe because of injury to Ellcock, found himself playing when DeFreitas twisted a knee while warming up and, like the other England seam bowlers, did himself full justice. The first of Stewart's two catches, to dismiss Greenidge, was a spectacular, leaping clutch at mid-wicket, and the England fielding in general was of a high standard.

West Indies

C. G. Greenidge c Stewart b Capel 21
D. L. Haynes c Russell b Lewis 25
R. B. Richardson c Stewart b Fraser .. 51
C. L. Hooper c Smith b Hemmings ... 17
C. A. Best c and b Gooch 6
*I. V. A. Richards b Small 32
E. A. Moseley c Lewis b Fraser 2
M. D. Marshall b Small 9
†P. J. L. Dujon not out 15
I. R. Bishop not out 18
B 4, l-b 4, w 3, n-b 1 12

1/49 (1) 2/49 (2) 3/89 (4) 4/100 (5) 5/155 (6) 6/162 (7) 7/172 (3) 8/180 (8) (8 wkts, 50 overs) 208

C. A. Walsh did not bat.

Bowling: Small 10–1–41–2; Fraser 10–1–37–2; Capel 6–0–25–1; Lewis 7–1–30–1; Hemmings 9–0–41–1; Gooch 8–0–26–1.

England

*G. A. Gooch not out 13
W. Larkins c Best b Marshall 2
R. A. Smith not out 6
L-b 1, n-b 4 5

1/9 (2) (1 wkt, 13 overs) 26

A. J. Lamb, A. J. Stewart, D. J. Capel, †R. C. Russell, C. C. Lewis, G. C. Small, E. E. Hemmings and A. R. C. Fraser did not bat.

Bowling: Marshall 6–1–12–1; Bishop 5–2–6–0; Walsh 1–0–1–0; Moseley 1–0–6–0.

Umpires: D. M. Archer and C. E. Cumberbatch.

†WEST INDIES v ENGLAND

Second One-day International

At Port-of-Spain, Trinidad, February 17. No result. Toss: England. Play began on time, despite the visible effects of overnight rain, but there was time for only 5.5 overs before further heavy rain precluded any prospect of the match continuing.

West Indies

C. G. Greenidge not out 8
D. L. Haynes not out 4
L-b 1 1

(no wkt, 5.5 overs) 13

R. B. Richardson, C. L. Hooper, C. A. Best, *I. V. A. Richards, †P. J. L. Dujon, M. D. Marshall, E. A. Moseley, I. R. Bishop and C. A. Walsh did not bat.

Bowling: Small 3–1–7–0; Fraser 2.5–0–5–0.

England

*G. A. Gooch, W. Larkins, R. A. Smith, A. J. Lamb, A. J. Stewart, D. J. Capel, †R. C. Russell, C. C. Lewis, G. C. Small, E. E. Hemmings and A. R. C. Fraser.

Umpires: D. M. Archer and C. E. Cumberbatch.

JAMAICA v ENGLAND XI

At Kingston, Jamaica, February 19, 20, 21. Drawn. Toss: England XI. Once Jamaica had withdrawn all three of their West Indies players, two of them fast bowlers, this match, played on a slow pitch of increasingly low bounce, lost any authenticity as Test match preparation. Gooch, however, took the opportunity to demonstrate that he can be a wonderfully destructive batsman when the mood takes him, his highest score on an England tour occupying 286 minutes and including five sixes and 31 fours. Most of his runs came from four Jamaican slow bowlers, who between them delivered 89 of the 114 overs in the England innings. Haynes, much the best of them, figured with the bat, too, his career-best 98 helping Jamaica avoid the follow-on against some variable England seam bowling. Leading by 94, the England XI took leisurely batting practice on the final day, but only Larkins, whose century came in 115 minutes, genuinely impressed. Gooch's token declaration gave his two main bowlers another brief work-out.

Close of play: First day, England XI 405 all out; Second day, Jamaica 259-7 (R. C. Haynes 81*, N. O. Perry 12*).

England XI

*G. A. Gooch c Staple b Perry	239		
W. Larkins c Kennedy b Haynes	45	– retired hurt	124
A. J. Stewart b Haynes	2	– (1) lbw b Perry	39
A. J. Lamb c Morgan b Haynes	31	– (3) b Banton	17
R. A. Smith b Morgan	23	– (4) b Banton	0
N. Hussain run out	14	– (5) b Banton	24
D. J. Capel c Kennedy b Perry	26	– (6) not out	12
†R. C. Russell c Adams b Morgan	3	– (7) not out	10
A. R. C. Fraser lbw b Morgan	3		
E. E. Hemmings not out	2		
D. E. Malcolm b Morgan	0		
B 7, l-b 2, w 1, n-b 7	17	B 9, l-b 4, n-b 9	22
1/145 2/149 3/244 4/341 5/363 6/381 7/383 8/403 9/405	405	1/137 2/180 3/203 4/225 (4 wkts dec.)	248

In the first innings G. A. Gooch, when 222, retired hurt at 337 and resumed at 381. In the second innings W. Larkins retired hurt at 180-1.

Bowling: *First Innings*—Banton 6–1–25–0; Williams 15–3–70–0; Davidson 4–0–17–0; Haynes 43–10–118–3; Perry 19–2–70–2; Carter 10–0–65–0; Morgan 17–6–31–4. *Second Innings*—Banton 18–3–64–3; Williams 14–5–25–0; Perry 18–1–93–1; Carter 13–0–53–0.

Jamaica

*D. S. Morgan c Russell b Fraser	10		
G. R. Samuels b Capel	41	– (1) c Smith b Fraser	5
N. Kennedy c Russell b Capel	22		
†J. C. Adams run out	27	– (3) not out	10
R. Staple c Capel b Malcolm	6	– (2) c Hemmings b Malcolm	25
C. A. Davidson c Hussain b Fraser	14		
R. C. Haynes c Fraser b Gooch	98		
L. Williams b Hemmings	36	– (4) not out	0
N. O. Perry c Stewart b Fraser	35		
C. de L. Carter b Malcolm	12		
C. Banton not out	0		
L-b 5, w 2, n-b 3	10	L-b 4	4
1/17 2/62 3/81 4/88 5/117 6/128 7/217 8/285 9/311	311	1/12 2/44 (2 wkts)	44

Bowling: *First Innings*—Malcolm 24–3–88–2; Fraser 14.1–1–75–3; Capel 22–1–97–2; Hemmings 16–2–40–1; Gooch 3–0–6–1. *Second Innings*—Fraser 7–3–13–1; Malcolm 7–1–27–1.

Umpires: L. U. Bell and A. J. Gaynor.

WEST INDIES v ENGLAND

First Test Match

At Kingston, Jamaica, February 24, 25, 26, 28, March 1. England won by nine wickets, their first victory against West Indies in sixteen years and 30 Tests. Toss: West Indies. Before this match began, it would have been hard to find one person in the Caribbean willing to give England a chance of victory. When it ended, just before lunch on the final day, the game's established order had been so dramatically overturned that even those within the England party were scarcely able to absorb the fact. Among those who witnessed it were two members of the only previous England team to win in Kingston, 36 years earlier, Sir Leonard Hutton and T. G. Evans.

West Indies were without Logie and Ambrose, both unfit, but their team none the less had a familiar appearance. England gave first caps to Stewart and Hussain and opted, controversially, to include only four bowlers, not one of them a spinner. It was a policy vindicated by subsequent events, and none of the chosen quartet can ever have bowled better.

There was no hint of the sensations to come as West Indies' opening pair were putting on 62. However, Greenidge's run-out, as he tried to take a second when Malcolm fumbled at fine leg, was the first of several needlessly sacrificed wickets as all ten went down for the addition of only 102 runs. Not that West Indies' lowest total against England for 21 years, since the Leeds Test of 1969, was entirely due to slapdash batting. Operating rigidly to an off-stump line, England's four bowlers could not be faulted, and after Small, Malcolm and Capel had taken important top-order wickets, Fraser collected the last five at a personal cost of 6 runs. To complete one of their best days' cricket in some years, England navigated to close of play for the loss only of Gooch and Stewart, the latter to a viciously rising ball from Bishop which was a sobering reminder of possible reprisals.

The first two sessions of the second day were decisive, with England losing only one wicket as Larkins, Lamb and Smith applied themselves to five-day disciplines with a will not always evident in recent England displays. Lamb and Smith put on 172 for the fourth wicket, and Lamb went on to his tenth Test century, five of them against West Indies. He had been batting for 364 minutes when he was out, and by the close of play England were 178 on with two wickets remaining.

That lead was stretched to 200 early on the third day, which ended with the game all but decided. Despite approaching their second innings more professionally than their first, the West Indians still found some curious ways of getting out on a pitch on which the increasingly low bounce called for the elimination of certain shots. Malcolm bowled fast, and with unsuspected control, taking the crucial wicket when he dismissed Richards (for the second time in the match) to end a partnership of 80 with Best. That wicket fell with West Indies still 8 runs short of avoiding an innings defeat, and when three more fell in consecutive overs while they clawed a lead of 29 before the close, it seemed that only the weather could deny England.

This being Jamaica, such a thing could not happen – yet it so nearly did. It rained intermittently on the rest day and again, heavily, overnight. The fourth day's play was abandoned, after numerous inspections, but English prayers were answered when the final day dawned sunny and clear. The two outstanding West Indian wickets were taken in twenty balls, their confusion ending, as it had begun, in a run-out. England, needing 41 to win, coasted home for the loss of Gooch, who had waited ten years to beat West Indies and now, as captain, deserved to have been there at the end. This, however, was a match of no logic, and while it paid handsome tribute to the preparation and discipline of the England team, it asked more questions than it answered about West Indies.

Man of the Match: A. J. Lamb.

Close of play: First day, England 80-2 (W. Larkins 28*, A. J. Lamb 10*); Second day, England 342-8 (R. C. Russell 12*, A. R. C. Fraser 1*); Third day, West Indies 229-8 (M. D. Marshall 2*, C. A. Walsh 0*); Fourth day, No play.

West Indies

C. G. Greenidge run out	32	c Hussain b Malcolm	36
D. L. Haynes c and b Small	36	b Malcolm	14
R. B. Richardson c Small b Capel	10	lbw b Fraser	25
C. A. Best c Russell b Capel	4	c Gooch b Small	64
C. L. Hooper c Capel b Fraser	20	c Larkins b Small	8
*I. V. A. Richards lbw b Malcolm	21	b Malcolm	37
†P. J. L. Dujon not out	19	b Malcolm	15
M. D. Marshall b Fraser	0	not out	8
I. R. Bishop c Larkins b Fraser	0	c Larkins b Small	3
C. A. Walsh b Fraser	6	b Small	2
B. P. Patterson b Fraser	0	run out	2
B 9, l-b 3, n-b 4	16	B 14, l-b 10, w 1, n-b 1	26
1/62 (1) 2/81 (3) 3/92 (4) 4/92 (2) 5/124 (6) 6/144 (5) 7/144 (8) 8/150 (9) 9/164 (10) 10/164 (11)	164	1/26 (2) 2/69 (3) 3/87 (1) 4/112 (5) 5/192 (6) 6/222 (4) 7/222 (7) 8/227 (9) 9/237 (10) 10/240 (11)	240

Bowling: *First Innings*—Small 15–6–44–1; Malcolm 16–4–49–1; Fraser 20–8–28–5; Capel 13–4–31–2. *Second Innings*—Small 22–6–58–4; Malcolm 21.3–2–77–4; Capel 15–1–50–0; Fraser 14–5–31–1.

England

*G. A. Gooch c Dujon b Patterson	18	c Greenidge b Bishop	8
W. Larkins lbw b Walsh	46	not out	29
A. J. Stewart c Best b Bishop	13	not out	0
A. J. Lamb c Hooper b Walsh	132		
R. A. Smith c Best b Bishop	57		
N. Hussain c Dujon b Bishop	13		
D. J. Capel c Richardson b Walsh	5		
†R. C. Russell c Patterson b Walsh	26		
G. C. Small lbw b Marshall	4		
A. R. C. Fraser not out	2		
D. E. Malcolm lbw b Walsh	0		
B 23, l-b 12, w 1, n-b 12	48	L-b 1, n-b 3	4
1/40 (1) 2/60 (3) 3/116 (2) 4/288 (5) 5/315 (6) 6/315 (4) 7/325 (7) 8/339 (9) 9/364 (8) 10/364 (11)	364	1/35 (1)	(1 wkt) 41

Bowling: *First Innings*—Patterson 18–2–74–1; Bishop 27–5–72–3; Marshall 18–3–46–1; Walsh 27.2–4–68–5; Hooper 6–0–28–0; Richards 9–1–22–0; Best 4–0–19–0. *Second Innings*—Patterson 3–1–11–0; Bishop 7.3–2–17–1; Walsh 6–0–12–0.

Umpires: L. H. Barker and S. N. Bucknor.

†WEST INDIES v ENGLAND

Third One-day International

At Kingston, Jamaica, March 3. West Indies won by three wickets. Toss: England. As Fraser bowled the final ball of the match, West Indies required 2 runs to bring the scores level and win on the tie-breaker of fewer wickets lost. Bishop left no room for dispute by off-driving mightily for four. This thrilling climax disguised a game of no great distinction, although it doubtless helped replace mislaid confidence in the West Indian camp. Any relief they felt, however, was counteracted by the news that Marshall had broken a bone at the base of his left index finger while trying to take a return catch. As Greenidge had missed the match with a recurrence of back trouble, injury problems were mounting for West Indies. Their match-winners here were Bishop, who not only struck the decisive blow but took four cheap wickets as England were confined to 214, and Richardson, who made his third one-day international hundred. Missed four times, he faced 124 balls for his century and hit three sixes and ten fours.

Man of the Match: R. B. Richardson.

England

*G. A. Gooch b Bishop	2	G. C. Small b Bishop	0
W. Larkins b Walsh	33		
R. A. Smith c Marshall b Hooper	43	B 3, l-b 25, w 6, n-b 3	37
A. J. Lamb b Bishop	66		
A. J. Stewart c Dujon b Hooper	0	1/20 (1) 2/71 (2) (8 wkts, 50 overs)	214
D. J. Capel c Dujon b Bishop	28	3/117 (3) 4/117 (5)	
†R. C. Russell b Marshall	2	5/185 (6) 6/206 (7)	
P. A. J. DeFreitas not out	3	7/212 (4) 8/214 (9)	

E. E. Hemmings and A. R. C. Fraser did not bat.

Bowling: Marshall 10–1–39–1; Bishop 10–1–28–4; Walsh 6–0–38–1; Moseley 6–1–15–0; Richards 9–0–32–0; Hooper 9–0–34–2.

West Indies

D. L. Haynes c Smith b DeFreitas	8	E. A. Moseley c Gooch b Fraser	0
C. A. Best b Small	4	I. R. Bishop not out	6
R. B. Richardson not out	108	B 12, l-b 4, w 1, n-b 1	18
C. L. Hooper b Hemmings	20		
*I. V. A. Richards c Small b Hemmings	25	1/11 (2) 2/33 (1) (7 wkts, 50 overs)	216
K. L. T. Arthurton c Russell b Hemmings	0	3/74 (4) 4/158 (5)	
		5/158 (6) 6/204 (7)	
†P. J. L. Dujon c Smith b Small	27	7/210 (8)	

M. D. Marshall and C. A. Walsh did not bat.

Bowling: Small 9–0–37–2; DeFreitas 10–2–29–1; Capel 9–1–47–0; Fraser 10–0–41–1; Hemmings 10–0–31–3; Gooch 2–0–15–0.

Umpires: L. H. Barker and S. N. Bucknor.

†WEST INDIES v ENGLAND

Fourth One-day International

At Georgetown, Guyana, March 7. West Indies won by six wickets. Toss: West Indies. West Indies took a winning 2-0 lead in the one-day series, and no other outcome looked likely once a lively England first-wicket stand of 71 had been broken. Gooch and Larkins had shown the pitch to be blameless, with a stream of confident shots off front and back foot, but England's middle order collapsed tamely against an under-strength attack. Five wickets were lost for 41, and only Russell made the final total respectable. The match was effectively over when the West Indies openers put on 113. Haynes, the senior partner in Greenidge's absence, was upstaged by fellow-Barbadian Best, who recorded his first international century before running himself out for exactly 100 off 121 balls. Hooper, whose off-spin had earlier been effective, finished the job with sixteen balls to spare.

Man of the Match: C. A. Best.

England

*G. A. Gooch b Moseley	33	G. C. Small not out	18
W. Larkins c Richards b Moseley	34	E. E. Hemmings not out	0
R. A. Smith c Richardson b Walsh	18	B 1, l-b 8, w 7, n-b 7	23
A. J. Lamb c Dujon b Bishop	22		
A. J. Stewart c Dujon b Walsh	0	1/71 (1) 2/88 (2) (8 wkts, 48 overs)	188
D. J. Capel b Hooper	1	3/109 (3) 4/109 (5)	
†R. C. Russell b Bishop	28	5/112 (6) 6/132 (4)	
P. A. J. DeFreitas run out	11	7/156 (8) 8/181 (7)	

A. R. C. Fraser did not bat.

Bowling: Bishop 10–1–41–2; Walsh 10–1–33–2; Baptiste 8–3–21–0; Moseley 10–0–52–2; Hooper 10–0–32–1.

West Indies

D. L. Haynes c DeFreitas b Hemmings 50
C. A. Best run out 100
R. B. Richardson c Russell b Capel ... 19
C. L. Hooper not out 16
*I. V. A. Richards c DeFreitas b Fraser 2
K. L. T. Arthurton not out 0
L-b 2, w 1, n-b 1 4

1/113 (1) 2/155 (3) 3/179 (2) 4/182 (5) (4 wkts, 45.2 overs) 191

†P. J. L. Dujon, E. A. E. Baptiste, E. A. Moseley, I. R. Bishop and C. A. Walsh did not bat.

Bowling: DeFreitas 7–1–32–0; Small 9.2–1–43–0; Capel 9–2–39–1; Fraser 10–1–42–1; Hemmings 10–1–33–1.

Umpires: D. M. Archer and C. Duncan.

WEST INDIES v ENGLAND

Second Test Match

At Georgetown, Guyana, March 10, 11, 12, 14, 15. Abandoned. Torrential rain, falling nightly for five days, left the Bourda ground under water, and a contentiously early decision to abandon the match was taken on the evening of the rest day. It was the first time that a Test match in the West Indies had been abandoned, and the fifth time in Test cricket history. The two teams had announced their twelve players as follows:

West Indies

C. G. Greenidge, D. L. Haynes, R. B. Richardson, C. L. Hooper, C. A. Best, *I. V. A. Richards, †P. J. L. Dujon, I. R. Bishop, C. E. L. Ambrose, C. A. Walsh, B. P. Patterson and K. L. T. Arthurton.

England

*G. A. Gooch, W. Larkins, A. J. Stewart, A. J. Lamb, R. A. Smith, N. Hussain, D. J. Capel, †R. C. Russell, G. C. Small, A. R. C. Fraser, D. E. Malcolm and E. E. Hemmings.

†WEST INDIES v ENGLAND

One-day International

At Georgetown, Guyana, March 15. West Indies won by seven wickets. Toss: West Indies. Played on the scheduled final day of the Test match, this game was approached in a desultory fashion by both teams. England batted as if uncertain whether they should be taking Test match practice or trying to make a winning total; as a result, they achieved neither. Greenidge's 77, aided by 48 from the Guyanese opener, Lambert, playing in his first international, ensured that the outcome was never in doubt. Although it was not part of the one-day series, the match was given the status of an unofficial one-day international.

Man of the Match: C. G. Greenidge.

England

*G. A. Gooch b Hooper 42
W. Larkins c and b Bishop 1
R. A. Smith c Dujon b Bishop 1
A. J. Lamb c Richardson b Moseley ... 9
A. J. Stewart b Hooper 13
R. J. Bailey c and b Ambrose 42
D. J. Capel c Dujon b Ambrose 7
†R. C. Russell c Best b Ambrose 19
G. C. Small c Dujon b Ambrose 0
E. E. Hemmings not out 3
A. R. C. Fraser not out 3
B 2, l-b 9, w 13, n-b 2 26

1/13 (2) 2/18 (3) 3/46 (4) 4/86 (1) 5/88 (5) 6/102 (7) 7/149 (8) 8/150 (9) 9/160 (6) (9 wkts, 49 overs) 166

Bowling: Bishop 7–2–22–2; Ambrose 9–1–18–4; Moseley 10–1–48–1; Baptiste 10–1–31–0; Hooper 10–0–28–2; Best 3–0–8–0.

West Indies

C. G. Greenidge lbw b Fraser 77
C. B. Lambert b Hemmings 48
R. B. Richardson c Capel b Small 7
C. L. Hooper not out 19
C. A. Best not out 7
L-b 2, w 4, n-b 3 9

1/88 (2) 2/105 (3) (3 wkts, 40.2 overs) 167
3/152 (1)

K. L. T. Arthurton, *†P. J. L. Dujon, E. A. E. Baptiste, E. A. Moseley, I. R. Bishop and C. E. L. Ambrose did not bat.

Bowling: Capel 9–1–41–0; Small 7–0–32–1; Fraser 9.2–1–33–1; Gooch 5–1–22–0; Hemmings 10–1–37–1.

Umpires: D. M. Archer and C. Duncan.

WEST INDIES BOARD PRESIDENT'S XI v ENGLAND XI

At Pointe-à-Pierre, Trinidad, March 17, 18, 19, 20. England XI won by 113 runs. Toss: West Indies Board President's XI. The legacy of the lost fortnight in Guyana was evident as the touring team showed every sign of having taken several steps backwards since their win in Kingston. They batted unconvincingly on the first day and bowled scruffily on the second. However, Gooch and Smith batted them back into a competitive position, and, in an extraordinary climax, the President's XI were bowled out in a little more than two hours on the final evening. The game, staged in the oilfield community of southern Trinidad, 40 miles from Port-of-Spain, was as much a Test trial for the President's men – almost exclusively fringe West Indies players – as it was for England. Baptiste, who took four first-innings wickets, and the local left-hander, Lara, who made a brilliant 134, did well enough to win places in the West Indies Test squad, but the leg-spinner, Haynes, was surprisingly omitted, despite match figures of eight for 147. For England, Gooch played two commanding innings, Bailey a significant one, and Smith a reassuring 99 not out before being stranded by the dismissal of the last man, Malcolm. Then, with the ball keeping increasingly low, Malcolm and DeFreitas were largely responsible for the decisive collapse.

Close of play: First day, England XI 225-7 (P. A. J. DeFreitas 6*, C. C. Lewis 13*); Second day, West Indies Board President's XI 286-7 (R. C. Haynes 20*, E. A. E. Baptiste 4*); Third day, England XI 135-6 (R. A. Smith 13*, R. C. Russell 0*).

England XI

*G. A. Gooch c Harris b Haynes . . . . 66 – c and b Haynes 61
W. Larkins c Harris b Patterson . . . . 1 – lbw b Haynes 13
A. J. Stewart c Adams b Benjamin . . . . 6 – b Benjamin 15
R. A. Smith c Morgan b Haynes . . . . 29 – not out 99
R. J. Bailey lbw b Baptiste . . . . 52 – b Haynes 7
D. J. Capel c Harris b Arthurton . . . . 1 – (7) lbw b Benjamin 0
†R. C. Russell c Harris b Baptiste . . . . 25 – (8) c Lambert b Haynes 16
P. A. J. DeFreitas not out . . . . 10 – (9) lbw b Haynes 15
C. C. Lewis lbw b Patterson . . . . 21 – (10) lbw b Haynes 6
E. E. Hemmings b Baptiste . . . . 3 – (6) lbw b Benjamin 1
D. E. Malcolm b Baptiste . . . . 8 – b Patterson 4
L-b 5, w 5, n-b 20 . . . . 30 B 10, l-b 7, w 3, n-b 21 . . 41

1/12 2/36 3/107 4/136 5/150 252 1/38 2/98 3/104 4/131 5/132 278
6/201 7/206 8/239 9/243 6/132 7/166 8/209 9/249

Bowling: *First Innings*—Patterson 9–1–45–2; Benjamin 15–2–34–1; Baptiste 33.1–5–91–4; Haynes 32–12–57–2; Arthurton 5–0–18–1; Morgan 1–0–2–0. *Second Innings*—Patterson 23.5–7–59–1; Benjamin 27–7–70–3; Haynes 40–11–90–6; Baptiste 22–6–42–0.

West Indies Board President's XI

C. B. Lambert b Malcolm	12	– c Capel b Malcolm	0
D. S. Morgan run out	0	– c Bailey b Malcolm	12
K. L. T. Arthurton c Russell b Capel	37	– b DeFreitas	2
B. C. Lara b DeFreitas	134	– lbw b DeFreitas	1
*A. L. Logie c Russell b Hemmings	40	– (6) c and b Hemmings	26
J. C. Adams lbw b DeFreitas	8	– (5) c Russell b DeFreitas	8
†L. L. Harris run out	8	– lbw b Malcolm	0
R. C. Haynes c Russell b Malcolm	20	– b DeFreitas	30
E. A. E. Baptiste c and b Malcolm	9	– lbw b Capel	19
K. C. G. Benjamin c Russell b DeFreitas	2	– not out	6
B. P. Patterson not out	0	– lbw b Hemmings	11
B 3, l-b 5, w 1, n-b 15	24	N-b 8	8
1/16 2/21 3/98 4/229 5/245 6/260 7/271 8/286 9/292	294	1/0 2/3 3/6 4/26 5/26 6/26 7/58 8/106 9/110	123

Bowling: *First Innings*—Malcolm 19–4–60–3; DeFreitas 26.5–1–89–3; Lewis 11–2–47–0; Capel 9–0–42–1; Hemmings 18–5–48–1. *Second Innings*—Malcolm 11–3–29–3; DeFreitas 13–2–54–4; Hemmings 7.4–2–31–2; Capel 5–3–9–1.

Umpires: Mohammed Hosein and Farouk Al.

WEST INDIES v ENGLAND

Third Test Match

At Port-of-Spain, Trinidad, March 23, 24, 25, 27, 28. Drawn. Toss: England. England, who won an important toss, looked likely winners for much of this game, and at lunch on the final day it seemed that nothing could prevent their going 2-0 ahead in the series. Instead, two hours of heavy rain turned a straightforward target into a difficult race against the clock, with imminent darkness and cynical West Indian time-wasting their dual obstacles. The match continued an hour beyond the scheduled close, but thirteen overs remained unbowled when the players came off because the light was so poor as to endanger life and limb. A deflating day for England was then immeasurably worsened by the news that their captain, Gooch, who had retired hurt after being struck twice on the left hand by Moseley, had broken a bone and would almost certainly miss the remainder of the tour.

The pitch was well grassed, and both sides were anxious to bowl first. The events of the morning session, however, defeated even the most alarmist pre-match assessments. Eighty minutes into the game, West Indies were 29 for five, sent into decline by accurate seam bowling on a surface which was uncertain not only of bounce but also of pace. A crowd of some 10,000 was hushed in disbelief as it became evident that the Kingston upset was not the freak result many had believed it to be.

There was a time when West Indies' lowest Test score against England (86 at The Oval in 1957) was seriously threatened – an irony, as that was the last occasion on which England had completed two successive wins over West Indies. Their progress towards a similar feat was now retarded by a familiar foe. Logie, back in the West Indies side after missing the first two Tests with a hand injury, quickly restated his liking for English bowling. In 1988, in England, he averaged 72.80, often rescuing precarious positions. None, though, was as desperate as this. In his singular style, with its minimal backlift, Logie batted through the remainder of the innings, adding 63 for the sixth wicket with Hooper and, to England's weary frustration, 74 for the ninth with Bishop. He was 2 runs short of a third Test century when he cut Fraser to cover, having batted for 250 minutes.

A total of 199 represented relative riches, but Gooch and Larkins put it in perspective by batting through the first 53 overs of England's reply. They put on 112, deliberately circumspect with so much time available, but the expected acceleration never came. A day spent accruing 146 runs was arguably too slow, even allowing for the tardy over-rate. Gooch had been batting six-and-a-half hours for his anchoring 84 when he was out to a lifting ball from Bishop, but his personal tactics were justified when the next five wickets fell for 49. This was West Indian fast bowling of renewed hostility, and Capel's 40, in three and a half hours, was an innings of considerable courage at a vulnerable time.

England's lead of 89 was wiped out early on the fourth day as Greenidge and Haynes put on 96 for the first wicket. This absorbing Test twisted again in the moment that Greenidge, to his visible disgust, was adjudged leg-before to Fraser. Malcolm, untidy earlier in the day, then took three wickets in four balls of a furiously fast over and West Indies were 100 for four. Logie and Richardson hinted at a recovery, and the tailenders all contributed, but by the close West Indies were only 145 ahead with their last pair together. Malcolm completed the innings in the third over of the final day and returned figures of six for 77, and ten for 137 in the match, each a career best. As impressive as his speed was his previously unsuspected stamina, which allowed him to bowl 24 overs in a day, probably for the first time in his life. His selection now seemed a glorious gamble.

Needing 151 to win, with virtually all day in which to get them, England were given a positive launch, 25 coming from six overs. Larkins then fell to Moseley, who struck a more grievous blow by banishing Gooch in agony. The extent of his injury was kept from the England players while they fretted through the rain-ruined afternoon. When play resumed, in barely fit conditions, 78 were required from 30 overs, of which only seventeen were bowled before the light became too dangerous. England had lost wickets at vital times and, just fleetingly, a West Indies win had seemed possible. With delaying tactics of a blatant nature dictating the pace of the play, it was an unsatisfactory finish to an otherwise marvellous match.

Man of the Match: D. E. Malcolm.

Close of play: First day, England 43-0 (G. A. Gooch 19*, W. Larkins 19*); Second day, England 189-2 (G. A. Gooch 83*, A. J. Lamb 20*); Third day, West Indies 11-0 (C. G. Greenidge 6*, D. L. Haynes 0*); Fourth day, West Indies 234-9 (I. R. Bishop 11*, C. A. Walsh 0*).

West Indies

C. G. Greenidge c Stewart b Malcolm	5	lbw b Fraser	42
*D. L. Haynes c Lamb b Small	0	c Lamb b Malcolm	45
R. B. Richardson c Russell b Fraser	8	c Gooch b Small	34
C. A. Best c Lamb b Fraser	10	lbw b Malcolm	0
†P. J. L. Dujon lbw b Small	4	b Malcolm	0
A. L. Logie c Lamb b Fraser	98	c Larkins b Malcolm	20
C. L. Hooper c Russell b Capel	32	run out	10
E. A. Moseley c Russell b Malcolm	0	c Lamb b Malcolm	26
C. E. L. Ambrose c Russell b Malcolm	7	c Russell b Fraser	18
I. R. Bishop b Malcolm	16	not out	15
C. A. Walsh not out	8	lbw b Malcolm	1
L-b 4, n-b 7	11	B 2, l-b 13, w 1, n-b 12	28
1/5 (1) 2/5 (2) 3/22 (3) 4/27 (4) 5/29 (5) 6/92 (7) 7/93 (8) 8/103 (9) 9/177 (10) 10/199 (6)	199	1/96 (1) 2/100 (2) 3/100 (4) 4/100 (5) 5/142 (6) 6/167 (3) 7/200 (8) 8/200 (7) 9/234 (9) 10/239 (11)	239

Bowling: *First Innings*—Small 17–4–41–2; Malcolm 20–2–60–4; Fraser 13.1–2–41–3; Capel 15–2–53–1. *Second Innings*—Malcolm 26.2–4–77–6; Small 21–8–56–1; Capel 13–3–30–0; Fraser 24–4–61–2.

England

*G. A. Gooch c Dujon b Bishop	84	retired hurt	18
W. Larkins c Dujon b Ambrose	54	c Dujon b Moseley	7
A. J. Stewart c Dujon b Ambrose	9	c Bishop b Walsh	31
A. J. Lamb b Bishop	32	lbw b Bishop	25
R. A. Smith c Dujon b Moseley	5	lbw b Walsh	2
R. J. Bailey c Logie b Moseley	0	b Walsh	0
D. J. Capel c Moseley b Ambrose	40	not out	17
†R. C. Russell c Best b Walsh	15	not out	5
G. C. Small lbw b Bishop	0		
A. R. C. Fraser c Hooper b Ambrose	11		
D. E. Malcolm not out	0		
B 6, l-b 13, w 3, n-b 16	38	B 2, l-b 7, n-b 6	15
1/112 (2) 2/152 (3) 3/195 (1) 4/214 (5) 5/214 (6) 6/214 (4) 7/243 (8) 8/244 (9) 9/284 (10) 10/288 (7)	288	1/27 (2) 2/74 (3) 3/79 (5) 4/85 (6) 5/106 (4) (5 wkts)	120

In the second innings G. A. Gooch retired hurt at 37.

Bowling: *First Innings*—Ambrose 36.2–8–59–4; Bishop 31–6–69–3; Walsh 22–5–45–1; Hooper 18–5–26–0; Moseley 30–5–70–2. *Second Innings*—Bishop 10–1–31–1; Ambrose 6–0–20–0; Moseley 10–2–33–1; Walsh 7–0–27–3.

Umpires: L. H. Barker and C. E. Cumberbatch.

BARBADOS v ENGLAND XI

At Bridgetown, Barbados, March 30, 31, April 1. Drawn. Toss: England XI. In the absence of Gooch, Lamb took over as captain and Gower was "borrowed" from his media commitments. With injuries now casting so many shadows, it was thought that Gower could come into the Test side if his form and fitness justified it. Given this possibility, and the fact that the touring side put out a reserve bowling attack, Lamb's decision to insert Barbados was difficult to fathom. Their response was to make light of Haynes's early departure with a second-wicket stand of 215 between Greenidge and Best. England, meanwhile, used three wicket-keepers, a mockery of the decision to rest Russell. Bailey and Stewart both suffered hand injuries, and D. L. Bairstow was eventually recruited from Yorkshire's pre-season tour to act as substitute wicket-keeper, contrary to Experimental Law 2.2 (Objection to Substitutes). He caught Marshall in the second innings. The spinners, Hemmings and Medlycott, took the last six wickets for 27 runs on the second morning, whereupon England were embarrassingly dismissed for 158. Only Hussain, batting bravely on his return after injury, coped with the Barbados seam attack. Gower failed, and his hopes of atoning in the second innings were dashed when Haynes declined to enforce the follow-on and delayed his declaration until the match was dead.

Close of play: First day, Barbados 340-4 (C. G. Greenidge 163*, M. D. Marshall 23*); Second day, Barbados 67-1 (C. G. Greenidge 31*, C. A. Best 12*).

Barbados

	First innings		Second innings	
C. G. Greenidge c and b Medlycott	183	–	c Stewart b Medlycott	51
*D. L. Haynes c Bailey b DeFreitas	9	–	lbw b DeFreitas	13
C. A. Best c DeFreitas b Medlycott	95	–	lbw b Lewis	71
T. R. O. Payne b Medlycott	0	–	(6) lbw b Medlycott	13
R. I. C. Holder lbw b Hemmings	18	–	not out	26
M. D. Marshall c Lewis b Hemmings	24	–	(4) c sub b Lewis	31
†R. L. Hoyte b Hemmings	2	–	not out	4
H. W. D. Springer lbw b Hemmings	2			
A. L. Johnson c Lamb b Hemmings	0			
S. M. Skeete c Capel b Medlycott	1			
V. D. Walcott not out	1			
B 3, l-b 8, n-b 21	32		B 1, l-b 6, n-b 9	16
1/32 2/247 3/250 4/289 5/345 6/359 7/365 8/365 9/365	367		1/24 2/114 3/177 4/186 5/200 (5 wkts dec.)	225

Bowling: *First Innings*—DeFreitas 17–3–60–1; Lewis 11–1–51–0; Capel 10–0–53–0; Hemmings 32–12–77–5; Medlycott 30–3–115–4. *Second Innings*—DeFreitas 13–2–38–1; Capel 13–1–50–0; Lewis 13–3–30–2; Medlycott 23–6–100–2.

England XI

	First innings		Second innings	
A. J. Stewart c Best b Marshall	21	–	hit wkt b Walcott	27
D. J. Capel c Greenidge b Marshall	3	–	not out	51
†R. J. Bailey c sub b Walcott	7	–	not out	27
N. Hussain not out	70			
R. A. Smith lbw b Marshall	1			
D. I. Gower c Holder b Johnson	4			
*A. J. Lamb lbw b Springer	8			
P. A. J. DeFreitas lbw b Springer	10			
C. C. Lewis c Best b Walcott	6			
K. T. Medlycott c Best b Springer	0			
E. E. Hemmings b Walcott	0			
B 8, l-b 5, w 2, n-b 13	28		B 8, l-b 6, w 2, n-b 5	21
1/25 2/36 3/52 4/56 5/87 6/110 7/128 8/156 9/157	158		1/49 (1 wkt)	126

Bowling: *First Innings*—Marshall 16–3–57–3; Skeete 6–1–21–0; Walcott 12.5–4–25–3; Johnson 6–0–21–1; Springer 8–1–21–3. *Second Innings*—Walcott 11–1–30–1; Marshall 5–0–16–0; Johnson 5–2–15–0; Springer 12–3–30–0; Best 3–1–6–0; Haynes 6–0–15–0.

Umpires: N. D. B. Harrison and S. E. Parris.

†WEST INDIES v ENGLAND

Fifth One-day International

At Bridgetown, Barbados, April 3. West Indies won by four wickets. Toss: West Indies. Delayed by rain, and reduced to 38 overs per side, this game was won by West Indies more easily than a result off the third ball of the last over might suggest. England thus lost the one-day series 3-0, but of greater concern to them, with just the final two Tests to play, was their ever-lengthening injury list. Fraser was ruled out of this match with a rib muscle strain, Stewart's injured finger was not risked, and the replacement for Gooch, David Smith, was hit on the thumb by the same bowler who broke Gooch's hand, Moseley. Smith made only 5, but Larkins, Robin Smith and Lamb all played handsomely to give England a useful total. West Indies, required to score at almost 6 an over, were always up with the rate, with Best's 51 from 44 balls being an especially violent innings. They lost four wickets for 22 with the game in their pockets, but Dujon saw them safely home.

Man of the Match: R. B. Richardson.

England

D. M. Smith b Moseley	5
W. Larkins b Walsh	34
R. A. Smith run out	69
*A. J. Lamb not out	55
N. Hussain not out	15
B 2, l-b 8, w 14, n-b 12	36
1/47 (1) 2/98 (2) 3/161 (3) (3 wkts, 38 overs)	214

D. J. Capel, †R. C. Russell, P. A. J. DeFreitas, C. C. Lewis, G. C. Small and E. E. Hemmings did not bat.

Bowling: Ambrose 9–2–31–0; Walsh 8–0–49–1; Moseley 7–0–43–1; Marshall 8–0–50–0; Hooper 6–0–31–0.

West Indies

C. G. Greenidge c Russell b Small	6
*D. L. Haynes c Hussain b Hemmings	45
R. B. Richardson b Small	80
C. A. Best c sub (A. J. Stewart) b Capel	51
A. L. Logie c R. A. Smith b DeFreitas	2
C. L. Hooper c Larkins b Small	12
†P. J. L. Dujon not out	11
E. A. Moseley not out	1
L-b 6, w 1, n-b 2	9
1/39 (1) 2/78 (2) 3/190 (4) 4/193 (5) 5/199 (3) 6/212 (6) (6 wkts, 37.3 overs)	217

M. D. Marshall, C. E. L. Ambrose and C. A. Walsh did not bat.

Bowling: Small 9–0–29–3; DeFreitas 8.3–0–63–1; Lewis 5–0–35–0; Capel 6–0–52–1; Hemmings 9–0–32–1.

Umpires: D. M. Archer and L. H. Barker.

WEST INDIES v ENGLAND

Fourth Test Match

At Bridgetown, Barbados, April 5, 6, 7, 8, 10. West Indies won by 164 runs. Toss: England. This, in its way, was every bit as dramatic and emotional as the two previous Test matches. That it ended in a West Indian win, with perhaps half an hour of daylight to spare, was the right result if the match is viewed in isolation. In the context of what occurred in Trinidad, it was particularly rough on England. They were outclassed here, as West Indies played to their potential at last, but never outfought. The stirring defiance of Russell and Smith on the final day will live in the memory as long as the earlier centuries from Best, Lamb and Haynes.

Amid the great and good, however, there was bad and downright ugly. England indulged in time-wasting every bit as blatant, if not quite so theatrical, as West Indies' efforts in Port-of-Spain. Then, on the fourth evening, with the crowd at fever pitch as England's second innings staggered, came an incident with loud repercussions. Bailey was given out in controversial circumstances by umpire Barker after a charging finger-flapping appeal by Richards which was at best undignified and unsightly. At worst, it was calculated gamesmanship.

England won the toss and Lamb chose to bowl. He was working on the theory that the pitch supported seam on the first day, but he was flying in the face of recent evidence. The previous two England captains in Tests on this ground made the same decision and were beaten by 298 runs and by an innings and 30, respectively. When West Indies reached 311 for five by the end of the opening day, Lamb knew he was not about to reverse the trend. It was a day belonging to Best, a local hero, delighting in the first century of a hitherto frustrating Test career. For England, shorn of Fraser's reliability, it was a day on which Malcolm's inconsistencies were reiterated. Richards deliberately assaulted his bowling, taking 18 in one spectacular over. On a pitch playing well, and without the valuable variety of spin, Lamb was at a loss. This, surely, had been an opportunity to make use of Hemmings, but England persisted with their policy of four fast bowlers.

West Indies, who had won their previous eight Tests on this ground, completed a total of 446 by mid-afternoon on the second day. England then made the worst possible start, Larkins out first ball to Bishop. Stewart, pressed unsatisfactorily into service as an opener, lived dangerously for his 45, and not until Smith and Lamb came together was any authority imposed on the England innings. These two carried a heavy burden in Gooch's absence, and they stayed together for five hours, putting on 193 and raising the genuine hope that England could match West Indies' score. Instead, once Lamb had gone for his second century of the series, an innings of brilliance, and Smith for a six-hour, self-denying 62, the collapse was swift. The last six wickets fell for 61, and West Indies quickly set about building on a lead of 38. This time it was Haynes who fired, for the first time in the series. His century occupied nuch of the fourth day and defied all Lamb's attempts to waste time, tactics which reduced he over-rate to a funereal eleven per hour. Haynes's hundred was his thirteenth in Tests and is fourth against England.

Richards delayed his declaration well beyond most neutral estimates, but before the ustomary curtailment because of the light, 50 minutes into the extra hour, England, needing n improbable 356 to win, had plunged to 15 for three. Larkins lasted one ball more than in he first innings, Bailey appeared to be caught behind off his hip, and the night-watchman, mall, was lbw. A rest day followed, necessary to cool some high emotions and to give ngland time to regroup. What was plain, however, was that either Lamb or Smith, or referably both, had to be at his best to save the game. In the event it was Smith, unbeaten ith 40 and extending his batting time in the game to eleven hours, who held up West Indies, company with the marvellously game Russell. Russell batted five hours for 55 and was not ismissed until the new ball was claimed, more than an hour after tea. England had been 166 r five at the time, but Ambrose, suddenly inspired, took the last five wickets in five overs. ll but one were out lbw, giving Ambrose final figures of eight for 45, the best of his short but estructive career, and levelling the series.

Man of the Match: C. E. L. Ambrose.

Close of play: First day, West Indies 311-5 (C. A. Best 102*, P. J. L. Dujon 2*); Second day, ngland 155-3 (A. J. Lamb 63*, R. A. Smith 17*); Third day, West Indies 19-1 (D. L. Haynes)*, R. B. Richardson 6*); Fourth day, England 15-3 (A. J. Stewart 4*, R. C. Russell 3*).

West Indies

C. G. Greenidge c Russell b DeFreitas	41	– lbw b Small	3
D. L. Haynes c Stewart b Small	0	– c Malcolm b Small	109
R. B. Richardson c Russell b Small	45	– lbw b DeFreitas	39
C. A. Best c Russell b Small	164		
*I. V. A. Richards c Russell b Capel	70	– (4) c Small b Capel	12
A. L. Logie c Russell b Capel	31	– (5) lbw b DeFreitas	48
†P. J. L. Dujon b Capel	31	– (8) not out	15
M. D. Marshall c Lamb b Small	4	– (7) c Smith b Small	7
C. E. L. Ambrose not out	20	– c Capel b DeFreitas	1
I. R. Bishop run out	10	– not out	11
E. A. Moseley b DeFreitas	4	– (6) b Small	5
L-b 8, n-b 18	26	L-b 12, w 1, n-b 4	17
1/6 (2) 2/69 (1) 3/108 (3) 4/227 (5) 5/291 (6) 6/395 (7) 7/406 (8) 8/411 (4) 9/431 (10) 10/446 (11)	446	1/13 (1) 2/80 (3) 3/109 (4) 4/223 (2) 5/228 (5) 6/238 (7) 7/238 (6) 8/239 (9)	(8 wkts dec.) 267

Bowling: *First Innings*—Malcolm 33–6–142–0; Small 35–5–109–4; DeFreitas 29.5–5–99–2; Capel 24–5–88–3. *Second Innings*—Malcolm 10–0–46–0; Small 20–1–74–4; DeFreitas 22–2–69–3; Capel 16–1–66–1.

England

A. J. Stewart c Richards b Moseley	45	– c Richards b Ambrose	37
W. Larkins c Richardson b Bishop	0	– c Dujon b Bishop	0
R. J. Bailey b Bishop	17	– c Dujon b Ambrose	6
*A. J. Lamb lbw b Ambrose	119	– (6) c Dujon b Moseley	10
R. A. Smith b Moseley	62	– (7) not out	40
N. Hussain lbw b Marshall	18	– (8) lbw b Ambrose	0
D. J. Capel c Greenidge b Marshall	2	– (9) lbw b Ambrose	6
†R. C. Russell lbw b Bishop	7	– (5) b Ambrose	55
P. A. J. DeFreitas c and b Ambrose	24	– (10) lbw b Ambrose	0
G. C. Small not out	1	– (4) lbw b Ambrose	0
D. E. Malcolm b Bishop	12	– lbw b Ambrose	4
B 14, l-b 9, w 3, n-b 25	51	B 8, l-b 9, w 1, n-b 15	33
1/1 (2) 2/46 (3) 3/75 (1) 4/268 (4) 5/297 (5) 6/301 (7) 7/308 (6) 8/340 (8) 9/340 (9) 10/358 (11)	358	1/1 (2) 2/10 (3) 3/10 (4) 4/71 (1) 5/97 (6) 6/166 (5) 7/173 (8) 8/181 (9) 9/181 (10) 10/191 (11)	191

Bowling: *First Innings*—Bishop 24.3–8–70–4; Ambrose 25–2–82–2; Moseley 28–3–114–2; Marshall 23–6–55–2; Richards 9–4–14–0. *Second Innings*—Bishop 20–7–40–1; Ambrose 22.4–10–45–8; Marshall 18–8–31–0; Moseley 19–3–44–1; Richards 10–5–11–0; Richardson 2–1–3–0.

Umpires: D. M. Archer and L. H. Barker.

WEST INDIES v ENGLAND

Fifth Test Match

At St John's, Antigua, April 12, 14, 15, 16. West Indies won by an innings and 32 runs. Toss England. A series which had been richly competitive ended with a match which was so one sided as to be anticlimactic. West Indies won before tea on the fourth day; England finishe bruised and deflated, harshly beaten in a series in which they had boldly made much c the running.

If, overall, they could be considered unfortunate, this last game contained all the element that many had predicted for the entire series, most notably fast bowling of a hostile intensity Bishop took eight wickets in the match and Ambrose six, while England's Smith wa subjected to a concerted short-pitched assault which failed to attract umpiring censure. On such ball broke Smith's right forefinger, though this was revealed only after he had bravely attempted to bat in the second innings. When the game was over, the England management also announced that Hussain, who made 35 and 34, had played with a broken wrist and that Lamb had chipped a bone in his elbow.

West Indies were without Marshall, Moseley and Best, all injured. Gooch, Fraser and David Smith were similarly ruled out of the England side, and the inclusion of Gower was this time seriously considered. Lamb won the toss and chose to bat on the quickest, bounciest pitch of the series. Although England lost only one wicket before lunch, and two more before tea, the opening day was dictated by the West Indian bowlers. England's first four were all out to indiscreet strokes when well set, and the middle order made no great impression. Dismissed shortly after lunch on the second day, England then played their worst cricket of the series, allowing the West Indian openers 228 runs in 51 overs. Mightily though Greenidge and Haynes batted, life was made easy for them by England's stray and undisciplined bowling. Both were past 100 by close of play, Greenidge's eighteenth Test hundred being appropriate in his 100th Test. The Antiguan crowd, always among the world's noisiest, celebrated in animated style.

Without a spin bowler for variety, England continued to look stereotyped the following day. However, having finally parted Greenidge and Haynes after a West Indies first-wicket record of 298, they took the next nine wickets for only 148 runs. Greenidge was run out by Small's direct hit from 70 yards, but Haynes extended his stay to nine hours for 167. Richards, who had been involved in an ugly press box scene with an English journalist, was out to the second ball he received. Late in the innings, Capel was cautioned for two consecutive bouncers at Ambrose, a quaint diversion by umpires who had ignored far more overt intimidation on the opening day.

Trailing by 186, England needed to bat for two days to save the game and the series. But they were not in a mental or physical condition for such heroics. They lost Larkins before the close of the third day, the opening batsman failing to sight a ball from Ambrose in confusing, shadowy light. Three more wickets went down in the first hour next morning, and when Smith, such a rock of resistance all series, was reluctantly obliged to retire hurt, it was only a matter of waiting for the end. Lamb counter-attacked spiritedly and Hussain's contribution was undeniably brave, but England were left to rue their inadequate first-innings batting and, particularly, their over-generous bowling.

Man of the Match: D. L. Haynes.

Close of play: First day, England 203-6 (N. Hussain 16*, R. C. Russell 4*); Second day, West Indies 228-0 (C. G. Greenidge 118*, D. L. Haynes 101*); Third day, England 16-1 (A. J. Stewart 4*).

England

A. J. Stewart c Richards b Walsh	27	– c Richardson b Bishop	8
W. Larkins c Hooper b Ambrose	30	– b Ambrose	10
R. J. Bailey c Dujon b Bishop	42	– (4) c Dujon b Bishop	8
*A. J. Lamb c Richards b Ambrose	37	– (5) b Baptiste	35
R. A. Smith lbw b Walsh	12	– (6) retired hurt	8
N. Hussain c Dujon b Bishop	35	– (7) c Dujon b Bishop	34
D. J. Capel c Haynes b Bishop	10	– (8) run out	1
†R. C. Russell c Dujon b Bishop	7	– (9) c Richardson b Ambrose	24
P. A. J. DeFreitas lbw b Bishop	21	– (10) c Greenidge b Ambrose	0
G. C. Small lbw b Walsh	8	– (3) b Ambrose	4
D. E. Malcolm not out	0	– not out	1
B 5, l-b 11, n-b 15	31	B 1, l-b 8, w 1, n-b 11	21
1/42 (1) 2/101 (2) 3/143 (3) 4/167 (5) 5/167 (4) 6/195 (7) 7/212 (8) 8/242 (9) 9/259 (10) 10/260 (6)	260	1/16 (2) 2/20 (1) 3/33 (4) 4/37 (3) 5/86 (5) 6/94 (8) 7/148 (9) 8/148 (10) 9/154 (7)	154

In the second innings R. A. Smith retired hurt at 61.

Bowling: *First Innings*—Bishop 28.1–6–84–5; Ambrose 29–5–79–2; Walsh 21–4–51–3; Baptiste 13–4–30–0. *Second Innings*—Bishop 14–2–36–3; Ambrose 13–7–22–4; Walsh 10–1–40–0; Baptiste 10–1–47–1.

West Indies

C. G. Greenidge run out	149	C. E. L. Ambrose c DeFreitas b Capel	5
D. L. Haynes c Russell b Small	167	I. R. Bishop not out	14
R. B. Richardson c Russell b Malcolm	34	C. A. Walsh b Malcolm	8
C. L. Hooper b Capel	1	L-b 5, n-b 13	18
*I. V. A. Richards c Smith b Malcolm	1		
A. L. Logie c Lamb b DeFreitas	15	1/298 (1) 2/357 (3) 3/358 (4) 4/359 (5)	446
†P. J. L. Dujon run out	25	5/382 (6) 6/384 (2) 7/415 (7)	
E. A. E. Baptiste c Russell b Malcolm	9	8/417 (8) 9/433 (9) 10/446 (11)	

Bowling: Small 31–3–123–1; Malcolm 34.5–3–126–4; Capel 28–1–118–2; DeFreitas 27–4–74–1.

Umpires: D. M. Archer and A. E. Weekes.

THE DELOITTE RATINGS

Introduced in 1987, the Deloitte Ratings rank Test cricketers on a scale from 0 to 1,000 according to their performances in Test matches since 1981. The ratings are calculated by computer and take into account playing conditions, the quality of the opposition and the result of the matches. The value of a player's performance is assessed in relation to the Deloitte Ratings of the opposing players and it also reflects his ability to score match-winning runs or take match-winning wickets. Updated after every Test match, with a player's most recent performances carrying more weight than his earlier ones, the Deloitte Ratings endeavour to provide a current assessment of a Test cricketer's form and his place among his peers.

The leading 30 batsmen and bowlers in the Ratings after the 1990 series between England and India were:

	Batsmen	*Rating*	*Bowlers*	*Rating*
1.	M. A. Taylor (*Aust.*)	813	Sir R. J. Hadlee (*NZ*)	868
2.	Javed Miandad (*Pak.*)	807	M. D. Marshall (*WI*)	836
3.	G. A. Gooch (*Eng.*)	793	I. R. Bishop (*WI*)	766
4.	D. L. Haynes (*WI*)	781	A. R. C. Fraser (*Eng.*)	755
5.	R. A. Smith (*Eng.*)	778	Imran Khan (*Pak.*)	753
6.	R. B. Richardson (*WI*)	774	T. M. Alderman (*Aust.*)	712
7.	A. R. Border (*Aust.*)	758	C. E. L. Ambrose (*WI*)	688
8.	M. Azharuddin (*India*)	721	Wasim Akram (*Pak.*)	688
9.	M. A. Atherton (*Eng.*)	711	M. G. Hughes (*Aust.*)	680
10.	Imran Khan (*Pak.*)	703	C. A. Walsh (*WI*)	644
11.	J. G. Wright (*NZ*)	699	Kapil Dev (*India*)	625
12.	D. M. Jones (*Aust.*)	678	D. E. Malcolm (*Eng.*)	578
13.	I. V. A. Richards (*WI*)	678	G. F. Lawson (*Aust.*)	575
14.	C. G. Greenidge (*WI*)	657	D. K. Morrison (*NZ*)	538
15.	M. D. Crowe (*NZ*)	649	J. R. Ratnayeke (*SL*)	532
16.	M. J. Greatbatch (*NZ*)	631	Chetan Sharma (*India*)	528
17.	A. Ranatunga (*SL*)	627	Abdul Qadir (*Pak.*)	506
18.	Salim Malik (*Pak.*)	621	Tauseef Ahmed (*Pak.*)	473
19.	D. B. Vengsarkar (*India*)	621	G. C. Small (*Eng.*)	472
20.	A. L. Logie (*WI*)	615	N. D. Hirwani (*India*)	462
21.	A. J. Lamb (*Eng.*)	614	J. G. Bracewell (*NZ*)	447
22.	S. R. Waugh (*Aust.*)	605	Saleem Jaffer (*Pak.*)	445
23.	A. H. Jones (*NZ*)	597	C. G. Rackemann (*Aust.*)	431
24.	Shoaib Mohammad (*Pak.*)	579	Arshad Ayub (*India*)	425
25.	S. V. Manjrekar (*India*)	574	S. R. Waugh (*Aust.*)	423
26.	C. A. Best (*WI*)	548	R. J. Shastri (*India*)	421
27.	D. I. Gower (*Eng.*)	539	A. R. Border (*Aust.*)	415
28.	P. A. de Silva (*SL*)	516	R. J. Ratnayake (*SL*)	401
29.	S. R. Tendulkar (*India*)	516	B. P. Patterson (*WI*)	379
30.	R. J. Shastri (*India*)	492	Maninder Singh (*India*)	375

ENGLAND A IN KENYA AND ZIMBABWE, 1989-90

By RICHARD STREETON

A seven-week visit to Kenya and Zimbabwe early in 1990 by an England A team, led by Mark Nicholas, was a tangible step forward for the Test and County Cricket Board's ambition to create a development structure to monitor the progress of potential Test players. England on this occasion also served to help Zimbabwean cricket in its efforts to reach Test match status, though it clearly emerged that this remained some way out of reach. Both on results and in terms of individual promise for the future, the tour proved successful for the English game. Nicholas's players won the unofficial "Test" series 1-0 and had mostly the better of two drawn games; in addition, the one-day "internationals" were won 3-0.

The only reservation about the tour concerned the dreadfully slow run-rate by both teams, who averaged barely 2 runs an over in the "Tests". These were the first five-day matches played by Zimbabwe, and they were mostly a new experience for the England players. The series, therefore, was a learning process for both teams and a cautious approach was understandable in some ways. It did nothing, however, to encourage spectators to attend in a country where limited-overs cricket has always been the staple diet. Attendances, in fact, were usually disappointing at every fixture, including the one-day matches. If occupation of the crease was too often considered the only requisite, there were other factors which also contributed to some dull cricket in most of the fixtures. These included lifeless pitches, which must be improved if Zimbabwe are to find the bowlers they lack. Thick, coarse grass on several outfields cut down the value of many strokes, while defensive bowling also played a part.

None of this should detract from the concentration, hard work and professional efficiency frequently shown by the inexperienced England players still learning their trade. On a short, crowded itinerary, dominated by representative fixtures, everyone contributed at some time or other. The team's character and determination were epitomised from the start when the party arrived in Harare still stricken with Salmonella poisoning after a brief visit to Kenya, where acclimatisation had been the main purpose. Nobody shirked the early practices, and the majority of the players were still struggling when an opening one-day game against Zimbabwe Country Districts was narrowly lost. Overall, too, this was as happy and contented a tour party as it is possible to imagine. An understanding and sympathetic management must be given full credit for an expedition which could bring considerable benefit to English cricket for some years ahead. Nicholas was a selfless leader and a fine ambassador; Keith Fletcher, the former Essex captain, excelled as coach and adviser; and Bob Bennett, the Lancashire chairman, proved an ideal manager. It was not the least of their successes that these three between them also ensured trouble-free relations with the media from start to finish.

Four of the English team finished with the strongest claims to be considered for Test places within the next two years. Michael Atherton was easily the most consistent batsman and scarcely knew what it was to fail. His wrist-spin, particularly early on, had its moments and he was the team's most reliable slip catcher. Richard Blakey, too, showed the temperament and remorseless concentration needed in five-day cricket. Graham Thorpe, a virtually unknown left-handed batsman before the start, did more than hint at an emerging talent of the highest quality. His mental flexibility to adjust his strokeplay to the needs of the moment was remarkable in one so inexperienced. Alan Igglesden was the fourth player to confirm his pedigree in both the one-day and longer matches. He was always a threat with his ability to obtain lift and movement, irrespective of the heat, unhelpful conditions and, near the end of the tour, niggling injuries.

Steve Rhodes had a consistent tour as wicket-keeper, and his batting improved almost match by match. Among the main batsmen, Darren Bicknell, James Whitaker and John Stephenson shared a trait for getting out when they seemed well set. These three, incidentally, were always prominent in the field among a side which made few mistakes generally in this department. Two left-arm spinners in the party, Andy Afford and Richard Illingworth, always gave the selectors a difficult choice, even if they were of contrasting type. There was never anything in the pitches for either: Afford's sharper spin brought him useful wickets; Illingworth's variations of flight were an asset at other times.

On figures, Martin Bicknell, Derek Pringle and Steve Watkin might not appear to have done themselves justice. Bicknell and Pringle, whose tour ended prematurely with a back injury, did not always have the rub of the green, not least in umpiring decisions in a country where local officials tended to be "non-givers". Watkin took a while to come to terms with the Kookaburra ball, but by the time the tour finished, both he and Bicknell had adjusted their line and length to the conditions. They returned home clearly having learned a great deal. David Lawrence, who was summoned when Chris Lewis was called to join England in the West Indies as soon as he reached Nairobi, was easily the most hostile of the England bowlers, though he tended to be erratic. A great trier, he was unlucky to sustain a calf strain in mid-tour, and later he developed technical problems with his approach run.

For Zimbabwe the visit underlined that standards in their cricket had fallen away since their best performances were achieved between 1983 and 1985. Their confidence had already been dented a few months earlier by Young West Indies, and England's one-day successes, in the form of cricket supposedly Zimbabwe's forte, emphasised their decline. It was fortunate that David Houghton, the Zimbabwe captain, found the best batting form of his career, or they would have been even harder pressed. Houghton, recognised for more than a decade as a fine, aggressive player, had at the age of 32 added discretion to his other gifts, knowing that everything depended on him. The outcome was a succession of responsible innings, the best of which was a magnificent 202 in the second "Test" at Bulawayo. John Traicos, the former South African Test off-spinner, who was 42, carried a similar, lone burden in the Zimbabwe attack, as far as consistency and influence were concerned. Among the younger players the Flower brothers, Andy and Grant, hinted that their batting might develop in the years ahead, and it was unfortunate for Zimbabwe that Eddo Brandes, their quickest bowler, was seldom fully fit.

It became quite obvious as England completed their fixtures that there was little depth in Zimbabwean cricket. The same, moderate players were met time and again outside the "Tests", and there was never any question that the three-day games should be given first-class status. While Zimbabwe had not been helped in recent years by the continued exodus abroad of their best players, it was hard nevertheless to see any realistic improvement in their levels of performance for ten years or longer. By then the zealous development schemes now under way at schools and elsewhere might have brought forth the natural talents that must exist among Africans.

Meanwhile, the diminishing white minority deserves every possible help as it struggles to keep cricket alive amid numerous problems. Not least of these is the horrendous cost locally of cricket equipment. Zimbabwean cricket lost a whole generation of players, effectively, during the troubled time around independence and its aftermath, and it was not surprising that an ageing representative side's powers had started to wane.

ENGLAND A TOUR RESULTS

First-class matches – Played 3: Won 1, Drawn 2.
Win – Zimbabwe.
Draws – Zimbabwe (2).
Non first-class matches – Played 9: Won 5, Lost 2, Drawn 2. Cancelled 1. *Wins* – Kenya Cricket Association, Young Zimbabwe, Zimbabwe (3). *Losses* – Kenya Cricket Association, Zimbabwe Country Districts XI. *Drawn* – Zimbabwe B (2). *Cancelled* – Kenya CA Chairman's XI.

ENGLAND A AVERAGES – FIRST-CLASS MATCHES

BATTING

	M	*I*	*NO*	*R*	*HI*	*100s*	*Avge*
R. J. Blakey	3	4	0	337	221	1	84.25
M. A. Atherton	2	3	0	250	122	2	83.33
G. P. Thorpe	2	2	0	142	98	0	71.00
M. C. J. Nicholas	3	4	1	178	53	0	59.33
S. J. Rhodes	3	4	1	153	86	0	51.00
J. P. Stephenson	3	5	1	90	24	0	22.50
A. P. Igglesden	3	3	2	17	10*	0	17.00
D. R. Pringle	2	2	0	34	27	0	17.00
J. J. Whitaker	2	3	0	40	19	0	13.33
D. J. Bicknell	3	5	1	51	26	0	12.75
M. P. Bicknell	2	2	0	10	10	0	5.00

Played in two matches: J. A. Afford 0*; S. L. Watkin 0. Played in one match: R. K. Illingworth 106.

* *Signifies not out.*

BOWLING

	O	*M*	*R*	*W*	*BB*	*5W/i*	*Avge*
. P. Stephenson	28	8	56	4	3-22	0	14.00
M. P. Bicknell	77	26	158	7	4-74	0	22.57
A. P. Igglesden	137.4	35	315	13	5-33	1	24.23
D. R. Pringle	72	26	158	5	3-70	0	31.60
. A. Afford	79	26	134	4	2-18	0	33.50
M. A. Atherton	44.2	15	107	3	3-4	0	35.66
. L. Watkin	99.3	27	233	6	2-35	0	38.83

Also bowled: R. K. Illingworth 66–36–58–2.

FIELDING

6 – S. J. Rhodes; 3 – M. A. Atherton, R. J. Blakey, J. J. Whitaker; 2 – G. P. Thorpe, S. L. Watkin; 1 – J. A. Afford, M. P. Bicknell, A. P. Igglesden, M. C. J. Nicholas, D. R. Pringle, substitute (R. K. Illingworth).

†At Nairobi Club, Nairobi, February 10. England A won by five wickets. Toss: England A. Kenya Cricket Association 180 for eight (55 overs) (D. Tikolo 35; M. P. Bicknell three for 42); England A 186 for five (52.2 overs) (D. J. Bicknell 31, J. P. Stephenson 65, D. R. Pringle 34 not out).

†At Gymkhana Club, Nairobi, February 11. Kenya Cricket Association won by five wickets. Toss: England A. England A 271 for three (55 overs) (D. J. Bicknell 75, M. A. Atherton 96, M. C. J. Nicholas 35); Kenya Cricket Association 275 for five (53.5 overs) (D. Chudasama 32, Tariq Iqbal 41, M. Odumbe 58, S. Kassamali 39, D. Tikolo 45 not out).

†At Aga Khan Club, Nairobi, February 14. Kenya Cricket Association Chairman's XI v England A. Cancelled owing to eight of the England A team being indisposed with food poisoning.

†At Harare South, February 18. Zimbabwe Country Districts won by 9 runs. Toss: England A. Zimbabwe Country Districts 216 for eight (50 overs) (R. D. Brown 65, C. M. Robertson 67; A. P. Igglesden four for 22); England A 207 for nine (50 overs) (J. J. Whitaker 59, R. J. Blakey 46, R. K. Illingworth 34; I. P. Butchart four for 40).

†YOUNG ZIMBABWE v ENGLAND A

At Mutare, February 20, 21, 22. England A won by 138 runs. Toss: England A. Excellent form by Atherton, with both bat and ball, was the highlight for England A as they dominated throughout against inexperienced opponents. On a lifeless pitch there were three declarations before England won with sixteen balls to spare after Young Zimbabwe were left to score 282 for victory in 52 overs. Atherton and Stephenson both drove strongly and avoided serious errors as they launched the England first innings with a stand of 188 in 61 overs. Atherton's wrist-spin brought him five wickets after Young Zimbabwe had lost only one batsman in the first three hours of their first innings. Flower sternly defended for 46 in 62 overs. Whitaker and Thorpe made attractive runs together on the third morning before Whitaker retired with a knee strain. When Young Zimbabwe started their run-chase, Goodwin hit hard for 60, but otherwise England remained in control.

England A 294 for five dec. (J. P. Stephenson 90, M. A. Atherton 91, D. J. Bicknell 50 not out; S. J. Rhodes 32 not out; G. J. Crocker three for 68) and 191 for three dec. (J. J. Whitaker 81 retired hurt, G. P. Thorpe 69); Young Zimbabwe 204 for eight dec. (G. K. Bruk-Jackson 43, G. W. Flower 46, C. N. Evans 35; M. A. Atherton five for 35) and 143 (D. G. Goodwin 60; J. A. Afford three for 25).

†ZIMBABWE v ENGLAND A

First One-day "International"

At Harare, February 24. England A won by six wickets, having been set a revised target of 118 in 44 overs after rain fell between the innings. Toss: England A.

Zimbabwe

C. M. Robertson c Pringle b Igglesden	7	J. P. Brent not out	28
G. A. Paterson c Atherton b Watkin	11	E. A. Brandes not out	33
†A. Flower lbw b Igglesden	0	L-b 3, w 5, n-b 5	13
A. J. Pycroft c Nicholas b Igglesden	0		
*D. L. Houghton c Watkin b Afford	22	1/19 2/19 3/21 (6 wkts, 50 overs)	134
I. P. Butchart st Rhodes b Atherton	20	4/27 5/57 6/79	

K. G. Duers, M. P. Jarvis and A. J. Traicos did not bat.

Bowling: Igglesden 10–2–39–3; Pringle 10–1–26–0; Watkin 10–2–26–1; Afford 10–4–16–1; Atherton 10–2–24–1.

England A

D. J. Bicknell c Flower b Duers	5	J. P. Stephenson not out	19
M. A. Atherton run out	6	L-b 7, w 6, n-b 2	15
R. J. Blakey c Pycroft b Brent	29		
J. J. Whitaker c Flower b Duers	5	1/15 2/29 3/36 (4 wkts, 41.5 overs)	118
*M. C. J. Nicholas not out	39	4/88	

†S. J. Rhodes, D. R. Pringle, A. P. Igglesden, J. A. Afford and S. L. Watkin did not bat.

Bowling: Brandes 6.5–0–24–0; Jarvis 7–3–13–0; Duers 10–2–25–2; Traicos 10–0–26–0; Brent 8–1–23–1.

Umpires: J. H. Hampshire and K. Kanjee.

†ZIMBABWE v ENGLAND A

Second One-day "International"

At Harare, February 25. England A won by 61 runs. Toss: Zimbabwe.

England A

D. J. Bicknell b Coughlan	70	*M. C. J. Nicholas not out	13
M. A. Atherton c Pycroft b Coughlan	20		
R. J. Blakey c Paterson b Traicos	73	L-b 2, w 4	6
G. P. Thorpe not out	50		
J. P. Stephenson c Shah b Butchart	3	1/48 2/130 3/189 (5 wkts, 50 overs)	245
D. R. Pringle c sub b Butchart	10	4/197 5/220	

†S. J. Rhodes, R. K. Illingworth, A. P. Igglesden and J. A. Afford did not bat.

Bowling: Brandes 7–1–36–0; Duers 9–2–38–0; Shah 10–0–47–0; Coughlan 8–0–42–2; Traicos 10–1–37–1; Butchart 6–0–43–2.

Zimbabwe

A. H. Shah c Blakey b Illingworth	20	T. Coughlan not out	3
G. A. Paterson b Igglesden	12	A. J. Traicos not out	1
C. M. Robertson c Rhodes b Atherton	8		
A. J. Pycroft c and b Atherton	4	L-b 5, w 6, n-b 1	12
*D. L. Houghton c Rhodes b Igglesden	88		
†A. Flower c Rhodes b Afford	2	1/36 2/36 3/41 (8 wkts, 50 overs)	184
I. P. Butchart c Blakey b Atherton	6	4/62 5/69 6/84	
E. A. Brandes b Pringle	28	7/170 8/183	

K. G. Duers did not bat.

Bowling: Pringle 10–1–42–1; Igglesden 10–1–37–2; Illingworth 10–2–38–1; Atherton 10–0–23–3; Afford 10–1–39–1.

Umpires: J. H. Hampshire and I. D. Robinson.

†ZIMBABWE B v ENGLAND A

At Harare South, February 27, 28, March 1. Drawn. Toss: Zimbabwe B. The touring team found it impossible to dismiss their opponents a second time on an easy-paced pitch after a calf strain forced Lawrence to retire on the final afternoon. Lawrence had bowled with considerable hostility on the first day as Zimbabwe B were dismissed for 107. Bicknell and Stephenson made 90 together by the close against an attack which was steady rather than threatening. Both were out early the next day, and after this Atherton was the only Englishman to take the chance of practice as the pitch became even slower. He found timing and his best touches elusive but persevered through 75 overs before he declared 3 runs short of his century. Zimbabwe B, 175 runs behind, were 74 for five shortly after lunch on the final afternoon. Hough and the left-handed Brent then thwarted England with a watchful stand of 114 in 49 overs, Hough having survived a hard stumping chance by Rhodes against Illingworth before he had scored. He was eventually caught at second slip early in the final hour. Zimbabwe were 30 runs on, with four wickets in hand, when the game was given up.

Zimbabwe B 107 (D. V. Lawrence six for 35) and 205 for six (N. P. Hough 77, J. P. Brent 46 not out); England A 282 for five dec. (D. J. Bicknell 66, J. P. Stephenson 49, M. A. Atherton 97 not out).

ZIMBABWE v ENGLAND A

First Unofficial "Test"

At Harare, March 3, 4, 5, 7, 8. England A won by ten wickets. Toss: Zimbabwe. In the first five-day representative game played by Zimbabwe, their batsmen, apart from Houghton in the first innings, were unable to summon the determination required for a match of this duration. A more resolute England A side won with 2 hours 40 minutes remaining on the final afternoon. Zimbabwe were doubly unfortunate in that Arnott, a dour opener, had his right index finger broken on the first morning, and in that Brandes, their main new-ball bowler, having gone into the match with an elbow injury to his bowling arm, was unable to reach his fastest pace. Overall, though, they lacked the disciplined approach exemplified by Atherton, with a seven-hour century, and Blakey, who in the England first innings laid the foundation for their team's success by sharing a painfully slow third-wicket stand of 185 in 97 overs. England had excluded Lawrence, their fastest bowler, because of a calf strain and had preferred Thorpe, an extra batsman, to Illingworth, a second left-arm spinner, from their nominated twelve.

A hard, grassless pitch at the Harare Sports Club lasted well, with the bounce becoming slightly variable only late in the match. England's quicker bowlers lacked control on the first day, when Zimbabwe made a solid start by scoring 253 for three. Houghton, restricting his aggressive instincts, and Shah, who took more risks, were mainly responsible. On the second morning, Igglesden led the way in a more purposeful attack and Zimbabwe's last seven wickets fell for a further 37 runs. Houghton was sixth out at 261 when he mistimed a drive to mid-on. Square-cuts, drives and pulls brought him most of his runs, and he batted for five hours ten minutes, faced 247 balls and hit thirteen fours.

England batted with grim efficiency, but their progress at times was unjustifiably slow. When their innings ended for 366, a lead of 76, after lunch on the fourth day, it had been in progress nearly twelve and a quarter hours. Traicos was allowed to bowl 68 overs for 71 runs. Atherton and Blakey eliminated all risks from their strokeplay. Blakey faced 313 balls, with nine fours, before he lifted a catch to extra cover; Atherton received 342 balls, and hit seven fours, before Shah beat his tired defensive stroke. Zimbabwe had already started their second innings shakily when rain permitted only ten overs after tea. And although there was some brief resistance on the final morning, England were left to make just 43 to win.

Close of play: First day, Zimbabwe 253-3 (D. L. Houghton 103*, A. Flower 26*); Second day, England A 115-2 (M. A. Atherton 54*, R. J. Blakey 55*); Third day, England A 294-5 (G. P. Thorpe 29*, S. J. Rhodes 4*); Fourth day, Zimbabwe 64-3 (A. Flower 5*, A. J. Traicos 4*).

Zimbabwe

K. J. Arnott not out	0	– (9) c Thorpe b Atherton	6
A. H. Shah c Rhodes b Pringle	98	– b Afford	15
C. M. Robertson c Blakey b Afford	2	– (1) c Afford b Pringle	23
A. J. Pycroft lbw b Afford	8	– c Atherton b Igglesden	14
*D. L. Houghton c Watkin b Igglesden	108	– (6) c Pringle b Watkin	0
†A. Flower lbw b Igglesden	28	– (3) b Watkin	15
G. A. Paterson c Atherton b Igglesden	0	– lbw b Atherton	23
E. A. Brandes c Rhodes b Watkin	14	– lbw b Afford	0
A. J. Traicos lbw b Pringle	11	– (5) c Atherton b Igglesden	6
M. P. Jarvis run out	3	– not out	12
K. G. Duers c Rhodes b Pringle	0	– c Rhodes b Atherton	0
L-b 7, w 1, n-b 10	18	L-b 3, n-b 1	4
1/35 2/57 3/187 4/260 5/260 6/261 7/279 8/284 9/286	290	1/36 2/40 3/58 4/66 5/67 6/82 7/89 8/105 9/110	118

In the first innings, K. J. Arnott retired hurt at 11 and resumed at 286.

Bowling: *First Innings*—Igglesden 24–8–50–3; Watkin 16.3–3–64–1; Pringle 33–11–70–3; Afford 37–12–58–2; Atherton 15–1–41–0. *Second Innings*—Igglesden 23–7–47–2; Pringle 10–5–11–1; Afford 15–8–18–2; Watkin 19–8–35–2; Atherton 5.2–4–4–3.

England A

D. J. Bicknell lbw b Brandes	0	– not out	22
J. P. Stephenson c Flower b Brandes	2	– not out	21
M. A. Atherton b Shah	103		
R. J. Blakey c Robertson b Jarvis	92		
*M. C. J. Nicholas c sub b Shah	53		
G. P. Thorpe c Flower b Brandes	44		
†S. J. Rhodes c Traicos b Duers	20		
D. R. Pringle b Duers	27		
A. P. Igglesden c Houghton b Duers	7		
S. L. Watkin c Flower b Duers	0		
J. A. Afford not out	0		
B 10, l-b 6, w 2	18		
1/0 2/13 3/198 4/218 5/287 6/321 7/344 8/355 9/365	366		(no wkt) 43

Bowling: *First Innings*—Brandes 36–7–92–3; Jarvis 41–13–99–1; Duers 38.2–8–66–4; Shah 21–10–22–2; Traicos 68–34–71–0. *Second Innings*—Duers 3–1–7–0; Jarvis 6–0–20–0; Traicos 3–0–11–0; Pycroft 1–0–5–0.

Umpires: J. H. Hampshire and I. D. Robinson.

ZIMBABWE v ENGLAND A

Second Unofficial "Test"

At Bulawayo, March 10, 11, 12, 14, 15. Drawn. Toss: England A. Tenacious double-hundreds by Blakey and Houghton set the tone for this match, the pattern of which was decided by a slow pitch at the Bulawayo Athletic Club. For four days, though, the cricket seldom lacked interest for the connoisseur, and it was unfortunate that on the final day, with no chance of a result, England A batted at such a funereal pace that it came close to being a travesty. Zimbabwe exuded more confidence and determination than they had shown in the first "Test".

With Brandes unfit, Zimbabwe went into the match with only three specialist bowlers, preferring to strengthen their batting by giving a first cap to Grant Flower, a promising batsman. It meant that each side included a pair of brothers, as England brought in Martin Bicknell. He and Whitaker took the places of Watkin and Thorpe after a deliberate change of selection policy by the England tour management. It was felt essential, on such a short tour, that everyone be given the chance of regular cricket.

England's first innings lasted until an hour into the third day. Atherton and Blakey again provided the backbone with a patient third-wicket stand, putting on 154 in 67 overs. Atherton excelled with drives on both sides of the wicket before he was held at second slip early on the second day, having batted for 319 minutes (277 balls) and hit twelve fours and a six. Blakey's runs mostly came on the off side, and he did not make a serious mistake as he stayed nearly ten hours, a remarkable feat of concentration in great heat and humidity. He was out first ball on the third morning, caught at second slip as he tried to square cut. He faced 503 balls and hit 23 fours.

Martin Bicknell took three quick wickets when Zimbabwe replied, but Houghton and Paterson stayed together for five hours to add 177 in 77 overs for the fifth wicket. Andy Flower then helped Houghton put on 99 for the sixth wicket, and the follow-on was easily avoided against bowlers who seemed dispirited when several appeals were turned down. Houghton's momentous 202 ended when, having held the Zimbabwean innings together for nine and a quarter hours, he lifted a catch to deep square leg. Eighth out, he had faced 422 balls and hit three sixes and nineteen fours, interspersing a variety of aggressive strokes with watchful defence. Not even the loss of early wickets could justify the meagre 123 runs England scored from 82 overs on the fifth day before the final hour was abandoned.

Close of play: First day, England A 216-2 (M. A. Atherton 112*, R. J. Blakey 55*); Second day, England A 480-5 (R. J. Blakey 221*, S. J. Rhodes 13*); Third day, Zimbabwe 159-4 (D. L. Houghton 63*, G. A. Paterson 52*); Fourth day, England A 10-0 (D. J. Bicknell 3*, J. P. Stephenson 7*).

England A

D. J. Bicknell c Houghton b Traicos	26	– c Paterson b Shah	3
J. P. Stephenson c and b Jarvis	21	– c Paterson b Jarvis	22
M. A. Atherton c Pycroft b Duers	122	– (4) c A. Flower b Duers	25
R. J. Blakey c Pycroft b Jarvis	221	– (5) c Pycroft b G. W. Flower	18
*M. C. J. Nicholas c Jarvis b Traicos	50	– (6) not out	37
J. J. Whitaker c Traicos b Shah	19	– (3) lbw b Jarvis	19
†S. J. Rhodes lbw b Jarvis	41	– not out	6
D. R. Pringle c A. Flower b Jarvis	7		
M. P. Bicknell c Houghton b Jarvis	0		
A. P. Igglesden not out	10		
L-b 10, n-b 2	12	N-b 3	3
1/29 2/80 3/234 4/358 5/435 6/480 7/498 8/498 9/529	(9 wkts dec.) 529	1/15 2/38 3/49 4/76 5/108	(5 wkts) 133

J. A. Afford did not bat.

Bowling: *First Innings*—Jarvis 56.5–20–157–5; Duers 52–8–149–1; Shah 36–14–88–1; Traicos 59–24–93–2; G. W. Flower 9–2–32–0. *Second Innings*—Jarvis 26–15–29–2; Duers 25–10–36–1; Traicos 17–11–10–0; Shah 15–3–28–1; G. W. Flower 8–1–30–1.

Zimbabwe

A. H. Shah lbw b M. P. Bicknell	1
D. G. Goodwin lbw b M. P. Bicknell	15
C. M. Robertson b M. P. Bicknell	0
A. J. Pycroft b Pringle	21
*D. L. Houghton c sub (R. K. Illingworth) b Stephenson	202
G. A. Paterson c Blakey b Stephenson	93
†A. Flower lbw b M. P. Bicknell	37
G. W. Flower c Rhodes b Stephenson	14
A. J. Traicos b Igglesden	1
M. P. Jarvis not out	5
K. G. Duers b Igglesden	0
B 2, l-b 9, w 1, n-b 2	14
1/2 2/2 3/26 4/52 5/229 6/328 7/384 8/397 9/403	403

Bowling: Igglesden 34.4–7–99–2; M. P. Bicknell 32–10–74–4; Atherton 24–10–62–0; Pringle 29–10–77–1; Afford 27–6–58–0; Stephenson 12–4–22–3.

Umpires: E. Gilmour and J. H. Hampshire.

†ZIMBABWE v ENGLAND A

Third One-day "International"

At Bulawayo, March 18. England A won by 28 runs. Toss: Zimbabwe. The tourists made a clean sweep of the one-day series when Zimbabwe failed to match a total owing much to Atherton's 101 off 123 balls (one six, five fours). Thorpe struck a run-a-minute half-century after surviving an early chance to the wicket-keeper, but in Zimbabwe's reply Goodwin was not so fortunate. He had hit two sixes and five fours in 60 when, trying to regain his ground, he overbalanced and was run out by the bowler, Illingworth, as he followed through.

England A

D. J. Bicknell lbw b Traicos 25
M. A. Atherton c Brent b Jarvis 101
R. J. Blakey lbw b Jarvis 24
G. P. Thorpe not out 66
*M. C. J. Nicholas c Pycroft b Duers .. 13
J. P. Stephenson run out 0
†S. J. Rhodes not out 2
B 1, l-b 6, w 5, n-b 4 16

1/54 2/106 3/188 4/225 5/235 (5 wkts, 50 overs) 247

R. K. Illingworth, A. P. Igglesden, M. P. Bicknell and S. L. Watkin did not bat.

Bowling: Brandes 10–2–32–0; Jarvis 10–1–47–2; Traicos 10–0–44–1; Brent 10–1–58–0; Duers 10–0–59–1.

Zimbabwe

†A. Flower b Illingworth 31
D. G. Goodwin run out 60
*D. L. Houghton c Atherton b Stephenson . 37
A. J. Pycroft c Nicholas b Igglesden ... 4
C. M. Robertson c Stephenson b Igglesden . 38
E. A. Brandes c Thorpe b M. P. Bicknell 0
G. A. Paterson c M. P. Bicknell b Watkin . 19
J. P. Brent c Rhodes b Igglesden 4
M. P. Jarvis b Igglesden 6
A. J. Traicos c Thorpe b Watkin 4
K. G. Duers not out 0
B 1, l-b 12, w 3 16

1/76 2/110 3/117 4/175 5/180 6/185 7/196 8/208 9/219 (49.1 overs) 219

Bowling: Igglesden 10–1–34–4; M. P. Bicknell 10–1–26–1; Watkin 6.1–0–31–2; Atherton 6–0–34–0; Stephenson 8–0–40–1; Illingworth 9–0–41–1.

Umpires: E. Gilmour and J. H. Hampshire.

†ZIMBABWE B v ENGLAND A

At Harare, March 20, 21, 22. Drawn. Toss: England A. On a dreadfully slow pitch, even by local standards, there was never any chance of an even contest between bat and ball. Whitaker, who led England A in this match, drove powerfully on the off side to make 186 against a limited attack. He hit two sixes and twenty fours in five and a half hours before he was caught at extra cover shortly before the declaration. Zimbabwe B began shakily but avoided the follow-on after watchful batting by James and Brent. Lawrence, having trouble with his run-up, conceded 22 no-balls and was twice warned for running on the pitch. Darren Bicknell (two sixes, six fours) and Rhodes hit strongly on the final morning to set up England's second declaration, but Zimbabwe B never threatened to achieve a target of 311 in 67 overs. The final act was enlivened by Briant, who reached a confident hundred from 136 balls before the game was given up. Earlier, play had been briefly interrupted when a swarm of bees flew over the cricketers' heads, causing everyone to lie flat on the ground.

England A 329 for five dec. (D. J. Bicknell 49, J. J. Whitaker 186, G. P. Thorpe 55) and 179 for one dec. (D. J. Bicknell 101 not out, S. J. Rhodes 65 not out); Zimbabwe B 198 (W. R. James 78; D. V. Lawrence three for 62, M. P. Bicknell three for 44, S. L. Watkin three for 54) and 207 for five (G. A. Briant 103 not out).

ZIMBABWE v ENGLAND A

Third Unofficial "Test"

At Harare, March 24, 25, 26, 28, 29. Drawn. Toss: Zimbabwe. For most of another slow-scoring match, England A were in the ascendant, but determined resistance in the closing stages earned their opponents a draw. Rain shortened both the third and fifth days, and on the fourth day England's bowlers were adversely affected by a misunderstanding which led to the pitch being mown twice instead of once. Initially the pitch had more bounce than in earlier fixtures, but as the match progressed it became more docile. England were unable to include Atherton and Pringle because of injuries, while Illingworth was preferred to Afford and for the second time in his career scored a hundred after being sent in as night-watchman. Brandes returned to strengthen the Zimbabwe attack, and Grant Flower, who made way for him, was recalled when Shah dropped out with a strained side shortly before the start. Though it was polling day in a general election, President Mugabe found time to visit the ground after the match to meet both teams.

Zimbabwe batted disappointingly after winning the toss and had surrendered the initiative before the first day ended. Their batsmen either concentrated exclusively on defence or got themselves out when they tried to increase the tempo. Igglesden, using his height well to get the ball to lift and swing, finished with five wickets. Throughout the second day Illingworth showed confidence and a full measure of sensible strokes as he reached 102 out of 187 after 5 hours 37 minutes. He hit nine fours and did not give a chance to hand. England were 85 for four at one point, but Nicholas defended sturdily against lively bowling from Brandes and the usual pinpoint accuracy of Traicos.

England's recovery was completed by jaunty strokeplay from Thorpe and Rhodes after Illingworth had been dismissed by the first ball on the third morning. Thorpe was rather unfortunate to miss a century by 2 runs, being stumped, immediately after play resumed following a thunderstorm, when the ball rebounded from the wicket-keeper's pads. England declared 228 runs ahead early on the fourth morning. Goodwin was quickly out, but the Flower brothers began the Zimbabwean rearguard action with a gritty stand which lasted for four and a half hours. Houghton and Pycroft were together at the close, and England were unable to separate them until halfway through the last afternoon. Rain allowed only twelve overs before lunch, and immediately after the interval Pycroft was dropped at slip off Igglesden. At this juncture Zimbabwe still needed 37 to avoid an innings defeat and four hours remained. The dismissal of Houghton, just after the arrears had been cleared, and two run-outs rekindled England hopes, but Pycroft found another staunch ally in Brandes. When Pycroft was yorked after 4 hours 50 minutes of watchful batting, the match was given up with nine overs left and Zimbabwe 68 runs ahead with three wickets in hand.

Close of play: First day, England A 6-1 (J. P. Stephenson 0*, R. K. Illingworth 6*); Second day, England A 197-5 (R. K. Illingworth 106*, G. P. Thorpe 17*); Third day, England A 334-7 (S. J. Rhodes 55*, M. P. Bicknell 1*); Fourth day, Zimbabwe 156-3 (D. L. Houghton 6*, A. J. Pycroft 11*).

Zimbabwe

G. W. Flower c Blakey b Igglesden	21	– c Thorpe b Igglesden	52
D. G. Goodwin c Whitaker b Igglesden	4	– c Watkin b M. P. Bicknell	0
†A. Flower c Whitaker b M. P. Bicknell	36	– lbw b Stephenson	78
A. J. Pycroft c Nicholas b Igglesden	15	– (5) lbw b M. P. Bicknell	70
*D. L. Houghton b Watkin	29	– (4) b Watkin	57
C. M. Robertson c M. P. Bicknell b Illingworth	7	– run out	0
G. A. Paterson c Whitaker b Illingworth	4	– run out	0
E. A. Brandes lbw b Igglesden	12	– not out	23
A. J. Traicos c Rhodes b Watkin	8	– not out	0
M. P. Jarvis not out	1		
K. G. Duers c and b Igglesden	0		
B 1, l-b 3, w 5, n-b 3	12	B 4, l-b 8, w 1, n-b 3	16
1/5 2/60 3/78 4/89 5/109 6/123 7/123 8/146 9/148	149	1/0 2/138 3/138 4/233 5/233 6/239 7/294	(7 wkts) 296

Bowling: *First Innings*—Igglesden 20–7–33–5; M. P. Bicknell 16–4–35–1; Watkin 26–8–43–2; Stephenson 4–1–6–0; Illingworth 23–12–28–2. *Second Innings*—Igglesden 36–6–86–1; M. P. Bicknell 29–12–49–2; Watkin 38–8–91–1; Illingworth 43–24–30–0; Stephenson 12–3–28–1.

England A

D. J. Bicknell c Goodwin b Brandes	0	M. P. Bicknell c Houghton b Jarvis	10
J. P. Stephenson c Brandes b Traicos	24	A. P. Igglesden not out	0
R. K. Illingworth lbw b Jarvis	106		
R. J. Blakey c Pycroft b Brandes	6	L-b 6, w 1	7
J. J. Whitaker c A. Flower b Brandes	2		
*M. C. J. Nicholas c Goodwin b Brandes	38	1/0 2/70 3/81 (9 wkts dec.)	377
G. P. Thorpe st A. Flower b Traicos	98	4/85 5/171 6/197	
†S. J. Rhodes b Traicos	86	7/333 8/367 9/377	

S. L. Watkin did not bat.

Bowling: Brandes 42–9–119–4; Traicos 49–18–81–3; Jarvis 42–7–109–2; Duers 31–12–50–0; G. W. Flower 3–0–12–0.

Umpires: J. H. Hampshire and K. Kanjee.

ENGLAND YOUNG CRICKETERS IN AUSTRALIA, 1989-90

England Young Cricketers toured Australia in January and February 1990, playing twelve games. They won four, lost four and drew four. Australian Young Cricketers won the three-match "Test" series 1-0, with an innings victory at Perth, and the one-day series 3-0. The team comprised: W. M. Noon (Northamptonshire) (*captain*), A. A. Barnett (Middlesex), J. D. Batty (Yorkshire), K. A. Butler (Essex), D. G. Cork (Derbyshire), J. P. Crawley (Lancashire). D. Gough (Yorkshire), A. P. Grayson (Yorkshire), A. Habib (Middlesex), J. C. Hallett (Somerset), P. C. L. Holloway (Warwickshire), R. Irani (Lancashire), M. Keech (Middlesex), T. A. Radford (Middlesex) and A. G. Robson (Surrey). Manager: The Revd M. D. Vockins (Worcestershire). Coach: G. J. Saville (Essex).

First Youth "Test": At North Sydney, January 14, 15, 16, 17. Drawn. Australian Young Cricketers 410 for six dec. (J. E. R. Gallian 158 not out, K. Vowles 40, L. Harper 61, B. Ruddell 64, D. Mann 40 not out; D. Gough three for 93) and 220 for six dec. (J. Young 65, D. Martyn 71 not out; J. C. Hallett three for 54); England Young Cricketers 319 (A. P. Grayson 110, J. P. Crawley 52, W. M. Noon 40; W. Adlam three for 60, J. E. R. Gallian three for 30) and 145 for three (J. P. Crawley 44 not out, K. A. Butler 54 not out).

Second Youth "Test": At Geelong, January 25, 26, 27, 28. Drawn. England Young Cricketers 279 (A. P. Grayson 34, P. C. L. Holloway 40, M. Keech 49, K. A. Butler 37; J. E. R. Gallian four for 46, D. Mann three for 30) and 236 (J. P. Crawley 48, M. Keech 40, W. M. Noon 35, Extras 30; D. Castle four for 44, D. Martyn four for 27); Australian Young Cricketers 288 (J. Young 134, D. Martyn 33, D. Mann 57; J. C. Hallett three for 47, J. D. Batty five for 60) and 64 for three (J. C. Hallett three for 22).

Third Youth "Test": At Perth, February 6, 7, 8. Australian Young Cricketers won by an innings and 2 runs. England Young Cricketers 71 (S. Cottrell six for 40) and 272 (P. C. L. Holloway 44, J. P. Crawley 43, M. Keech 30, T. A. Radford 36, W. M. Noon 30; S. Cottrell four for 60, S. Oliver four for 95); Australian Young Cricketers 345 (J. Young 69, B. Ruddell 68, L. Harper 53, J. Langer 30, D. Mann 40, W. Adlam 46; J. C. Hallett five for 73).

THE INDIANS IN PAKISTAN, 1989-90

By R. MOHAN

Two cricketers made a quiet and yet very effective contribution to the tenth series between India and Pakistan. They were not players. John Hampshire and John Holder, both from England, were the "third country" umpires invited to officiate in the four Test matches, and their presence changed the nature of cricket contests between these two Asian neighbours. The frisson was missing. Events on the field were far less contentious, with both teams accepting the umpires, and their rulings, in good faith. The occasional mistakes, some glaring, did not lead to flare-ups, with the result that the atmosphere was refreshingly free of suspicion. Teams had been touring Pakistan for years without any firm belief that they could, or even would be allowed to, win a Test. In this series, the relations between the two sides were cordial and the cricket, if not spectacular, was highly competitive.

The "neutral" umpires stood only in the Tests, not in the one-day series, and conjecture was that their presence had much to do with the 0-0 result. That line of thinking, however, paid little regard to the splendid manner in which Sanjay Manjrekar held together the Indian batting. Pakistan had the better of the exchanges in the first two Tests but were unable to translate their advantage into victory.

India were treading a beaten path in the sense that they never lent thought to much else except drawing the Tests, which in the old days was considered the equivalent of victory. Their batting effort was a most determined one, while their bowling, orientated towards seam, did not lag behind in this respect. However, in conditions that were, in three Tests, conducive to swing and seam bowling, Pakistan had the more penetrative attack. But fitness, or the lack of it, posed problems which had an unsettling effect on Imran Khan's plans to extend his success against India.

Manjrekar was a steady influence on the Indian batting. He made 569 runs in the series at an average of 94.83 with a double-hundred, a hundred and three half-centuries, several of which were match-saving innings. Moreover, he made his runs with a classicism only too rare in the era of the all-pervasive one-day international. Mohammad Azharuddin and Navjot Sidhu made vital contributions in those Tests in which the bowlers had more going for them, and sixteen-year-old Sachin Tendulkar showed that age is no consideration in Test cricket when a batsman is brimming with talent. The third-youngest Test cricketer, and the youngest Indian, he made runs at critical stages to bolster a fiercely motivated side playing under a new captain in Krish Srikkanth. Srikkanth himself, however, failed with the bat and was to be unceremoniously dropped after the series.

Manoj Prabhakar, fast emerging as India's leading all-rounder, and Kapil Dev, revealing much enthusiasm, were used as a check on the Pakistan batting. They gave little away and, called on to deliver more than half of the overs bowled by India in the series, responded superbly to a captain who commanded such loyalty. Wasim Akram, with eighteen wickets for Pakistan, was the outstanding bowler of the series. His capacity for wicket-taking was, perhaps, at its peak, and time and again he destroyed India's peace of mind with an amazing display of variety, particularly with the new ball. The support bowling was nowhere in his class, even if Imran Khan did take thirteen wickets.

Imran admitted that he had batted better than ever in his career in this series. Salim Malik was another in good form with the bat, Javed Miandad made runs in his own combative way, despite the discomfort of a back problem, and Aamer Malik made two hundreds on the trot. Shoaib Mohammad, like Manjrekar for India, compiled a double-hundred in the ennui-inducing Third Test at Lahore, played on a featherbed of a pitch in contrast to the more lively surfaces at the other centres.

The one-day series never took off, the weather conspiring to deny the thrills associated with the short game. The crowds at these matches were invariably close to capacity – whereas those at the Test matches were not encouraging enough – but trouble caused by a rowdy Karachi crowd led to the abandonment of the third one-day international. This disturbance accentuated undercurrents in the troubled sea of India-Pakistan relations, in which cricket had once been an island of normalcy. Although Pakistan did not win the disrupted one-day series with their customary superiority over India, their two wins nevertheless suggested that little had changed in this form of the game as far as India were concerned.

INDIAN TOUR RESULTS

Test matches – Played 4: Drawn 4.
First-class matches – Played 5: Drawn 5.
Draws – Pakistan (4), BCCP Patron's XI.
One-day internationals – Played 3: Lost 2, No Result 1. Abandoned 1.
Other non first-class matches – Played 2: Lost 2. *Losses* – Pakistan XI (2).

TEST MATCH AVERAGES

PAKISTAN – BATTING

	T	*I*	*NO*	*R*	*HI*	*100s*	*Avge*
Shoaib Mohammad	4	5	1	412	203*	1	103.00
Imran Khan	4	5	2	262	109*	1	87.33
Salim Malik	4	5	1	290	102*	1	72.50
Javed Miandad	4	5	0	279	145	1	55.80
Aamer Malik	4	5	0	254	117	2	50.80
Ramiz Raja	4	5	0	223	63	0	44.60
Abdul Qadir	4	4	2	55	39*	0	27.50
Nadeem Abbasi	3	2	0	46	36	0	23.00
Wasim Akram	4	3	0	58	30	0	19.33
Waqar Younis	2	2	0	4	4	0	2.00

Played in one Test: Naved Anjum 12; Saleem Jaffer 0*; Salim Yousuf 36, 4; Shahid Saeed 12; Zakir Khan 9*. Akram Raza and Shahid Mahboob each played in one Test but did not bat.

* *Signifies not out.*

BOWLING

	O	*M*	*R*	*W*	*BB*	*5W/i*	*Avge*
Wasim Akram	204.4	50	551	18	5-102	1	30.61
Naved Anjum	51	10	149	4	2-57	0	37.25
Imran Khan	185.3	46	504	13	4-45	0	38.76
Waqar Younis	58	4	237	6	4-80	0	39.50
Zakir Khan	29	3	109	2	2-50	0	54.50
Abdul Qadir	109	18	346	6	3-97	0	57.66
Shahid Mahboob	49	12	131	2	2-131	0	65.50

Also bowled: Aamer Malik 3–0–12–0; Akram Raza 18–3–58–0; Saleem Jaffer 17–4–54–1; Salim Malik 1–0–2–0; Shahid Saeed 15–0–43–0; Shoaib Mohammad 4–1–7–0.

INDIA – BATTING

	T	*I*	*NO*	*R*	*HI*	*100s*	*Avge*
S. V. Manjrekar	4	7	1	569	218	2	94.83
K. S. More	4	6	4	122	58*	0	61.00
M. Prabhakar	4	6	3	168	54*	0	56.00
M. Azharuddin	4	7	0	312	109	1	44.57
N. S. Sidhu	4	7	0	269	97	0	38.42
S. R. Tendulkar	4	6	0	215	59	0	35.83
R. J. Shastri	4	7	1	164	61	0	27.33
Kapil Dev	4	6	0	159	55	0	26.50
K. Srikkanth	4	7	0	97	36	0	13.85
V. Razdan	2	2	1	6	6*	0	6.00
Arshad Ayub	2	2	0	11	10	0	5.50
Maninder Singh	3	3	0	11	8	0	3.66

Played in one Test: S. A. Ankola 6.

* *Signifies not out.*

BOWLING

	O	*M*	*R*	*W*	*BB*	*5W/i*	*Avge*
V. Razdan	40	6	141	5	5-79	1	28.20
Kapil Dev	168.4	50	378	12	4-69	0	31.50
M. Prabhakar	181.2	26	542	16	6-132	2	33.87
S. A. Ankola	30	7	128	2	1-35	0	64.00
R. J. Shastri	50.4	3	186	2	2-105	0	93.00
Maninder Singh	83	11	265	2	2-191	0	132.50

Also bowled: Arshad Ayub 86–8–300–0; K. S. More 2–0–12–0; K. Srikkanth 6–0–33–0; S. R. Tendulkar 5–0–25–0.

INDIAN AVERAGES – FIRST-CLASS MATCHES

BATTING

	M	*I*	*NO*	*R*	*HI*	*100s*	*Avge*
S. V. Manjrekar	5	8	1	581	218	2	83.00
M. Prabhakar	4	6	3	168	54*	0	56.00
K. S. More	5	7	4	147	58*	0	49.00
M. Azharuddin	5	8	0	323	109	1	40.37

	M	*I*	*NO*	*R*	*HI*	*100s*	*Avge*
N. S. Sidhu	4	7	0	269	97	0	38.42
S. R. Tendulkar	5	7	0	262	59	0	37.42
R. J. Shastri	5	8	2	223	61	0	37.16
Kapil Dev	4	6	0	159	55	0	26.50
K. Srikkanth	5	8	0	119	36	0	14.87
S. A. Ankola	2	2	0	14	8	0	7.00
Arshad Ayub	2	2	0	11	10	0	5.50
Maninder Singh	4	4	0	15	8	0	3.75
V. Razdan	3	3	1	6	6*	0	3.00

Played in one match: R. Lamba 62; W. V. Raman 1.

* *Signifies not out.*

BOWLING

	O	*M*	*R*	*W*	*BB*	*5W/i*	*Avge*
S. A. Ankola	56	8	251	10	6-77	1	25.10
V. Razdan	64	12	270	9	5-79	1	30.00
Kapil Dev	168.4	50	378	12	4-69	0	31.50
M. Prabhakar	181.2	26	542	16	6-132	2	33.87
R. J. Shastri	67.4	12	219	3	2-105	0	73.00
Maninder Singh	118	17	385	3	2-191	0	128.33

Also bowled: Arshad Ayub 86–8–300–0; K. S. More 2–0–12–0; W. V. Raman 14–1–68–0; K. Srikkanth 9–0–40–0; S. R. Tendulkar 11–0–56–0.

FIELDING

13 – K. S. More; 8 – M. Azharuddin; 3 – S. V. Manjrekar; 2 – R. J. Shastri, S. R. Tendulkar; 1 – Maninder Singh, M. Prabhakar, V. Razdan, K. Srikkanth, substitute (W. V. Raman).

†At Lahore, November 10. Pakistan XI won by 4 runs in a charity match staged to raise funds for a cancer research hospital project to be named after Imran Khan's mother. Pakistan XI 187 for seven (37 overs) (Ramiz Raja 56, Imran Khan 37; V. Razdan three for 42); India XI 183 for seven (37 overs) (N. S. Sidhu 69, S. V. Manjrekar 40; Abdul Qadir three for 39).

BCCP PATRON'S XI v INDIANS

At Rawalpindi, November 11, 12, 13. Drawn. Toss: BCCP Patron's XI. Ankola and Razdan, helped by a pitch of low bounce, gave the Indians' attack the cutting edge it had been lacking in recent times. However, the Patron's XI staged a smart recovery from 74 for six thanks to a fighting, unbeaten 62, including eight boundaries, from Akram Raza. Lamba, hitting ten fours, led the tourists' reply, but it needed the enterprise of Tendulkar, on his first tour, and Shastri, with three sixes and five fours in his half-century, to help the Indians gain the lead. Saeed Anwar, a diminutive left-hander, used the rest of the match to press his case for higher honours, taking three and a half hours over his well-made 150 (two sixes, 22 fours). Mansoor Rana, son of the Test umpire, Shakoor Rana, hit ten boundaries in his unbeaten 70 and was associated in a stand of 121 with Anwar.

Close of play: First day, Indians 40-1 (R. Lamba 17*, S. V. Manjrekar 0*); Second day, BCCP Patron's XI 22-2 (Shahid Saeed 4*, Saeed Anwar 8*).

BCCP Patron's XI

Shahid Saeed c Razdan b Ankola	14	– lbw b Razdan	47
Munir-ul-Haq b Ankola	13	– b Ankola	7
Shaukat Mirza lbw b Ankola	2	– b Ankola	1
Saeed Anwar lbw b Razdan	5	– c and b Maninder	150
Mansoor Rana c Tendulkar b Razdan	27	– not out	70
Shahid Nawaz c More b Shastri	35	– not out	13
†Nadeem Abbasi b Razdan	0		
*Iqbal Qasim c More b Ankola	24		
Akram Raza not out	62		
Zakir Khan c Azharuddin b Ankola	21		
Saleem Jaffer lbw b Ankola	5		
B 2, l-b 13, w 4, n-b 7	26	B 4, l-b 5, n-b 4	13
1/28 2/29 3/39 4/39 5/79 6/80 7/116 8/174 9/214	234	1/12 2/14 3/134 4/255 (4 wkts)	301

Bowling: *First Innings*—Ankola 17–0–77–6; Razdan 9–0–63–3; Tendulkar 1–0–4–0; Maninder 17–6–40–0; Shastri 13–8–24–1; Raman 3–0–4–0; Srikkanth 3–0–7–0. *Second Innings*—Razdan 15–6–66–1; Ankola 9–1–46–2; Maninder 18–0–80–1; Tendulkar 5–0–27–0; Shastri 4–1–9–0; Raman 11–1–64–0.

Indians

*K. Srikkanth lbw b Zakir Khan	22
R. Lamba c Shahid Nawaz b Zakir Khan	62
S. V. Manjrekar lbw b Saleem Jaffer	12
M. Azharuddin st Nadeem Abbasi b Iqbal Qasim	11
S. R. Tendulkar st Nadeem Abbasi b Iqbal Qasim	47
R. J. Shastri not out	59
W. V. Raman c Nadeem Abbasi b Akram Raza	1
†K. S. More lbw b Shahid Saeed	25
V. Razdan c Nadeem Abbasi b Shahid Saeed	0
S. A. Ankola c Nadeem Abbasi b Shahid Saeed	8
Maninder Singh c and b Shahid Saeed	4
B 13, l-b 4, n-b 4	21
1/40 2/80 3/110 4/154 5/175 6/176 7/258 8/258 9/268	272

Bowling: Saleem Jaffer 15–2–67–1; Zakir Khan 14–0–64–2; Akram Raza 20–3–72–1; Iqbal Qasim 23–7–42–2; Shahid Saeed 3.5–0–10–4.

Umpires: Javed Akhtar and Khizar Hayat.

PAKISTAN v INDIA

First Test Match

At Karachi, November 15, 16, 17, 19, 20. Drawn. Toss: India. The intrusion of a zealot who became involved in a scuffle with the Indian captain, Srikkanth, provided a contentious moment on the opening day and led to the strengthening of security at the National Stadium. For Pakistan it was a day of consolidation, with Shoaib Mohammad setting the trend for slow but steady scoring as the Indian new-ball bowlers, Prabhakar and Kapil Dev, established a hold which the Pakistan batsmen never shook off during the series. It was Imran Khan whc injected the dynamism Pakistan were looking for, batting for 201 minutes and hitting a si and seventeen fours in his unbeaten 109, his fifth Test century. India, in desperate trouble a 85 for six against the wiles of Wasim Akram and the pace of the newcomer, Waqar Younis staged a recovery through Kapil Dev and Shastri, who added 78 for the seventh wicket Shastri and More then saw India beyond the follow-on figure in an eighth-wicket partnershi worth 57.

Pakistan were batting again by the third day, but were unable to force the pace agains Kapil, swinging the old ball, and Prabhakar. Shoaib was an hour over 1 run in the fina session, and only when Salim Malik moved into his stride on the fourth day did the home sid make their runs at the desired rate. Malik dominated his 141-run partnership with Shoait and he and Imran then put on 55 in eight overs before the declaration left India to make 45 off 102 overs or bat through four sessions to save the match. Manjrekar, the find of India tour to the West Indies, led their defensive action, reaching his second Test century in five hours nineteen minutes (221 balls, thirteen fours) and batting with utmost competence. He and Sidhu, who battled against an attack which was missing Younis with a strained back, added 135, a record for India's second wicket against Pakistan.

This was Kapil Dev's 100th Test, and with his third wicket he became the fourth bowler to take 350 Test wickets. He also became the first bowler to play in 100 Tests, a singular achievement in a career in which he had missed only one Test match – and that through a controversial disciplinary action by selectors. At the other end of the spectrum, Tendulkar made his début at the age of 16 years 205 days. In Pakistan's first innings, Azharuddin, dropped from the Test side on the eve of the match and playing only because Lamba pulled out owing to a toe injury, equalled the world record by a fielder of five catches in an innings with some brilliant takes in the slips.

Man of the Match: Kapil Dev.

Close of play: First day, Pakistan 259-4 (Javed Miandad 76*, Imran Khan 17*); Second day, India 157-6 (R. J. Shastri 25*, Kapil Dev 49*); Third day, Pakistan 106-3 (Shoaib Mohammad 46*, Salim Yousuf 3*); Fourth day, India 86-1 (N. S. Sidhu 34*, S. V. Manjrekar 14*).

Pakistan

First innings		Second innings	
Aamer Malik c Azharuddin b Kapil Dev	0	– c Manjrekar b Kapil Dev	15
Ramiz Raja c Shastri b Prabhakar	44	– b Prabhakar	2
Shoaib Mohammad c Azharuddin b Kapil Dev	67	– lbw b Kapil Dev	95
Javed Miandad c Azharuddin b Kapil Dev	78	– b Kapil Dev	36
Salim Malik c Azharuddin b Ankola	36	– (6) not out	102
*Imran Khan not out	109	– (7) not out	28
Shahid Saeed c More b Kapil Dev	12		
†Salim Yousuf c More b Prabhakar	36	– (5) c More b Ankola	4
Wasim Akram c Azharuddin b Prabhakar	0		
Abdul Qadir c More b Prabhakar	4		
Waqar Younis c More b Prabhakar	0		
B 4, l-b 9, w 3, n-b 7	23	B 3, l-b 11, n-b 9	23
1/4 2/83 3/158 4/233 5/271 6/307 7/398 8/398 9/409	409	1/2 2/24 3/92 4/109 5/250 (5 wkts dec.)	305

Bowling: *First Innings*—Kapil Dev 24–5–69–4; Prabhakar 34.5–6–104–5; Ankola 19–1–93–1; Shastri 10–1–37–0; Arshad Ayub 27–3–81–0; Srikkanth 1–0–2–0; Tendulkar 1–0–10–0. *Second Innings*—Kapil Dev 36–15–82–3; Prabhakar 30–4–107–1; Ankola 11–6–35–1; Arshad Ayub 10–1–37–0; Shastri 5–0–15–0; Tendulkar 4–0–15–0.

India

First innings		Second innings	
*K. Srikkanth lbw b Wasim Akram	4	– lbw b Wasim Akram	31
N. S. Sidhu b Wasim Akram	0	– c Ramiz Raja b Imran Khan	85
S. V. Manjrekar c Salim Yousuf b Waqar Younis	3	– not out	113
M. Azharuddin lbw b Imran Khan	35	– c Aamer Malik b Abdul Qadir	35
M. Prabhakar b Waqar Younis	9		
S. R. Tendulkar b Waqar Younis	15		
R. J. Shastri c Imran Khan b Abdul Qadir	45	– (5) not out	22
Kapil Dev c Javed Miandad b Waqar Younis	55		
†K. S. More not out	58		
Arshad Ayub lbw b Wasim Akram	1		
S. A. Ankola b Wasim Akram	6		
B 5, l-b 10, w 5, n-b 11	31	B 9, l-b 4, w 1, n-b 3	17
/1 2/13 3/13 4/41 5/73 /85 7/163 8/220 9/241	262	1/43 2/178 3/256 (3 wkts)	303

Bowling: *First Innings*—Wasim Akram 26.2–4–83–4; Waqar Younis 19–1–80–4; Imran Khan 15–4–44–1; Shahid Saeed 2–0–7–0; Abdul Qadir 10–1–33–1. *Second Innings*—Imran Khan 28–10–56–1; Wasim Akram 25–7–68–1; Abdul Qadir 28–3–119–1; Waqar Younis –0–11–0; Shahid Saeed 13–0–36–0.

Umpires: J. H. Hampshire and J. W. Holder.

PAKISTAN v INDIA

Second Test Match

At Faisalabad, November 23, 24, 25, 27, 28. Drawn. Toss: Pakistan. The Pakistanis, troubled by injuries, recalled Saleem Jaffer and, as in the First Test, pressed two newcomers, Naved Anjum and wicket-keeper Nadeem Abbasi, into service. As the wintry conditions of the Punjab province were likely to assist seam bowlers, Imran Khan did not hesitate to insert India on what appeared to be a fast wicket. A bright start of 68, to be India's best of the series, and another classical effort from Manjrekar were not sufficient to keep the Indians entirely out of trouble. The first four wickets fell in the space of 33 runs, and it was only in the course of the 143-run stand between Manjrekar and Tendulkar (165 balls) that India showed any sign of having the measure of the Pakistani attack. Manjrekar batted almost five and a half hours for his 76, but Imran's fiery spell on the second morning enabled Pakistan to make up for time lost to bad light the previous evening.

When Aamer Malik and Ramiz Raja opened Pakistan's account with a century stand, the inadequacy of the Indian total became apparent. Again Kapil Dev and Prabhakar worked tirelessly to contain the batsmen, but Aamer Malik's solid century provided Pakistan with the basis of a reasonable lead. None the less, even though he and Salim Malik had put on 96 in 103 minutes for the fourth wicket, the time and overs consumed during Pakistan's innings were enormous, given the shortness of the days and the tardy over-rate. It was after lunch on the fourth day before Imran could declare with a lead of just 135.

With Wasim Akram now showing a clear dominance over Srikkanth, it was once again up to Sidhu and Manjrekar to provide stability. They responded well, but the deficit was still to be wiped out when Sidhu contributed to his own run-out. However, Azharuddin shed his initial diffidence against the short ball, and his 109 from 175 balls, including ten fours, was the innings that determined the course of the match. He provided some anxious moments as he progressed towards his first Test hundred outside India, running out Tendulkar while trying to go from 99 to 100 and being dropped at slip while on the same score. Before the game was called off after seven of the final twenty overs, Prabhakar and Kapil Dev added 95 runs briskly, with the former hitting his first Test fifty to go with his best Test figures of six for 132. Pakistan's attempt to bowl India out a second time had not been helped by the absence of Saleem Jaffer, who had broken down in the first innings.

Man of the Match: S. V. Manjrekar.

Close of play: First day, India 200-4 (S. V. Manjrekar 58*, S. R. Tendulkar 35*); Second day, Pakistan 82-0 (Aamer Malik 26*, Ramiz Raja 45*); Third day, Pakistan 338-6 (Imran Khan 16*, Nadeem Abbasi 5*); Fourth day, India 164-2 (S. V. Manjrekar 43*, M. Azharuddin 48*).

India

First innings		Second innings	
*K. Srikkanth lbw b Wasim Akram	36	– b Wasim Akram	13
N. S. Sidhu c Nadeem Abbasi b Wasim Akram	20	– run out	51
S. V. Manjrekar c Salim Malik b Naved Anjum	76	– lbw b Naved Anjum	83
M. Azharuddin lbw b Wasim Akram	0	– b Naved Anjum	109
R. J. Shastri c Nadeem Abbasi b Saleem Jaffer	11	– c Nadeem Abbasi b Wasim Akram	5
S. R. Tendulkar lbw b Imran Khan	59	– run out	8
M. Prabhakar not out	24	– not out	54
Kapil Dev lbw b Naved Anjum	0	– c Ramiz Raja b Abdul Qadir	49
†K. S. More lbw b Imran Khan	4	– not out	2
Maninder Singh c Ramiz Raja b Imran Khan	3		
V. Razdan c sub (Ijaz Ahmed) b Imran Khan	0		
B 2, l-b 16, w 15, n-b 22	55	B 7, l-b 7, w 7, n-b 3	24
1/68 2/74 3/85 4/101 5/244 6/252 7/253 8/278 9/284	288	1/33 2/91 3/249 4/258 5/274 6/290 7/385	(7 wkts) 398

Bowling: *First Innings*—Imran Khan 26.1–7–45–4; Wasim Akram 38–4–107–3; Saleem Jaffer 17–4–54–1; Naved Anjum 29–6–57–2; Abdul Qadir 3–1–7–0. *Second Innings*—Imran Khan 27–5–100–0; Wasim Akram 31–6–86–2; Naved Anjum 22–4–92–2; Abdul Qadir 31–3–90–1; Aamer Malik 2–0–9–0; Shoaib Mohammad 3–0–7–0.

Pakistan

Aamer Malik c and b Prabhakar	117	Wasim Akram c Tendulkar b Prabhakar	28
Ramiz Raja c Srikkanth b Prabhakar	58	Abdul Qadir not out	5
Shoaib Mohammad lbw b Kapil Dev	24	Saleem Jaffer not out	0
Javed Miandad lbw b Prabhakar	13	B 2, l-b 9, w 8, n-b 14	33
Salim Malik lbw b Prabhakar	63		
*Imran Khan c Azharuddin b Prabhakar	34	1/105 2/157 3/193 (9 wkts dec.)	423
Naved Anjum c More b Kapil Dev	12	4/289 5/307 6/331	
†Nadeem Abbasi c More b Kapil Dev	36	7/368 8/409 9/419	

Bowling: Kapil Dev 45–11–106–3; Prabhakar 42.3–4–132–6; Razdan 13–1–62–0; Maninder 21–4–70–0; Shastri 9–0–29–0; Srikkanth 2–0–13–0.

Umpires: J. H. Hampshire and J. W. Holder.

PAKISTAN v INDIA

Third Test Match

At Lahore, December 1, 2, 3, 5, 6. Drawn. Toss: Pakistan. A strip devoid of grass stood out in contrast to the lush outfield of the Gaddafi Stadium and caused the Pakistan captain no small amount of annoyance. This was to be a match for batsmen, with the possibility of a result minimal. The twin strike at the start, Srikkanth playing on as he shaped to leave a ball from Akram in the second over and Sidhu leg before to Imran in the third over, soon became irrelevant as Manjrekar and Azharuddin carried on from where they had left off in Faisalabad. Azharuddin, without the short ball to contend with, proved an elegant strokemaker; Manjrekar batted on, steady as a rock. For the third successive Test Pakistan had two new players, and one of them, Shahid Mahboob, was to bowl his medium pace in long spells. Imran shouldered the rest of the burden after Akram had stiffened up and strained his groin on the first day. Manjrekar coasted along serenely to his maiden double-hundred, and when he ran himself out his 218, made in 511 minutes off 401 balls and containing 28 fours, was the highest score by an Indian against Pakistan. His partnership of 186 with Shastri for the fourth wicket was also a record for India against Pakistan, and on the third day India passed 500 to record their highest total in Pakistan.

Miandad, on the ground on which he had marked his Test début with a century, celebrated his 100th Test appearance with another, a unique double. He thus emulated M. C. Cowdrey in scoring a century in his 100th Test, and in all he batted for 369 minutes (291 balls) for 145, his 22nd Test hundred. The previous day Aamer Malik had completed his second successive Test hundred (113 off 276 balls) and later on the final day Shoaib Mohammad achieved his first Test double-century, off 335 balls in 486 minutes with nineteen fours. The Pakistan innings stretched beyond the scheduled close, in the mandatory hour, to accommodate Shoaib's double-hundred. In fact, play had to be restarted after the scoreboard had given Shoaib the landmark prematurely, and the players were already leaving the middle. The Indian seamers had some respite, with their spinners bearing the burden of the attack as Pakistan advanced to their second-highest total in Test matches and their highest against India.

Man of the Match: S. V. Manjrekar.

Close of play: First day, India 255-3 (S. V. Manjrekar 132*, R. J. Shastri 33*); Second day, India 458-5 (M. Prabhakar 44*, S. R. Tendulkar 34*); Third day, Pakistan 159-1 (Aamer Malik 60*, Salim Malik 30*); Fourth day, Pakistan 416-3 (Javed Miandad 84*, Shoaib Mohammad 90*).

India

*K. Srikkanth b Wasim Akram	0	†K. S. More not out	26
N. S. Sidhu lbw b Imran Khan	4	Arshad Ayub c sub (Ijaz Ahmed) b Abdul Qadir	10
S. V. Manjrekar run out	218	Maninder Singh c Akram Raza b Imran Khan	0
M. Azharuddin c Nadeem Abbasi b Shahid Mahboob	77		
R. J. Shastri c Javed Miandad b Shahid Mahboob	61	B 4, l-b 19, w 1, n-b 2	26
M. Prabhakar run out	45		
S. R. Tendulkar b Abdul Qadir	41	1/1 2/5 3/154 4/340 5/375	509
Kapil Dev b Abdul Qadir	1	6/466 7/466 8/469 9/508	

Bowling: Imran Khan 50.2–13–130–2; Wasim Akram 24–6–65–1; Shahid Mahboob 49–12–131–2; Akram Raza 18–3–58–0; Abdul Qadir 35–8–97–3; Salim Malik 1–0–2–0; Aamer Malik 1–0–3–0.

Pakistan

Aamer Malik c sub (W. V. Raman) b Maninder	113
Ramiz Raja c More b Prabhakar	63
Salim Malik c Manjrekar b Maninder	55
Javed Miandad b Shastri	145
Shoaib Mohammad not out	203
*Imran Khan c Manjrekar b Shastri	66
Abdul Qadir not out	39
B 3, l-b 4, n-b 8	15
1/100 2/223 3/248 4/494 5/628	(5 wkts) 699

Wasim Akram, Shahid Mahboob, Akram Raza and †Nadeem Abbasi did not bat.

Bowling: Kapil Dev 28–2–77–0; Prabhakar 34–2–107–1; Maninder 61–7–191–2; Arshad Ayub 49–4–182–0; Srikkanth 3–0–18–0; Shastri 26.4–2–105–2; More 2–0–12–0.

Umpires: J. H. Hampshire and J. W. Holder.

PAKISTAN v INDIA

Fourth Test Match

At Sialkot, December 9, 10, 11, 13, 14. Drawn. Toss: Pakistan. Although a green and seemingly lively pitch held something for the fast bowlers, India were not hard pressed to compile a reasonable total after being put in. The start was delayed until after noon because of early-morning rain. Srikkanth, for the sixth time in the series, and Sidhu were victims of Wasim Akram, but Manjrekar again showed the way with an impeccable innings and Azharuddin stressed his new-found confidence with a half-century full of strokes. Indeed, Pakistan were the side in greater trouble against the moving ball, the Indian bowlers keeping a full length and letting the pitch help the ball seam. Razdan, playing in his second Test, surprised Ramiz Raja, Pakistan's top scorer, and Shoaib Mohammad with his pace and then came back to wind up the innings. India were 74 ahead, which if not promising was an improvement on what had gone before.

On the third day, more time had been lost when those witnessing only the second Test in Sialkot revealed a tendency to pelt the Indian fieldsmen with orange peel and some harder missiles. A draw seemed the obvious result. But on the afternoon of the fourth day the match sprang to life when Akram and Imran reduced India to 38 for four. They were rescued by Sidhu and Tendulkar, who stood firm in a century stand, even though the youngster was bounced repeatedly by the Pakistan pacemen. At one stage umpire Holder had to warn Akram for intimidatory bowling. Tendulkar batted for three and a quarter hours for his second fifty of the series, but Sidhu missed out on what would have been his third Test hundred when he cut a short ball from Zakir Khan to Imran at point. The contest, which had promised much when wickets were falling the previous afternoon, petered out, and the umpires called the match off at tea.

Man of the Match: N. S. Sidhu.

Close of play: First day, India 181-3 (S. V. Manjrekar 72*, R. J. Shastri 5*); Second day, Pakistan 23-1 (Ramiz Raja 9*, Shoaib Mohammad 2*); Third day, Pakistan 181-5 (Imran Khan 21*, Nadeem Abbasi 7*); Fourth day, India 102-4 (N. S. Sidhu 54*, S. R. Tendulkar 33*).

India

First innings		Second innings	
*K. Srikkanth lbw b Wasim Akram	10	c Wasim Akram b Imran Khan	3
N. S. Sidhu c Ramiz Raja b Wasim Akram	12	c Imran Khan b Zakir Khan	97
S. V. Manjrekar lbw b Waqar Younis	72	lbw b Imran Khan	4
M. Azharuddin run out	52	c Shoaib Mohammad b Wasim Akram	4
R. J. Shastri c and b Imran Khan	20	lbw b Wasim Akram	0
S. R. Tendulkar lbw b Wasim Akram	35	c Nadeem Abbasi b Imran Khan	57
Kapil Dev b Wasim Akram	27	lbw b Zakir Khan	27
M. Prabhakar c Shoaib Mohammad b Imran Khan	25	not out	11
†K. S. More c Zakir Khan b Waqar Younis	15	not out	17
Maninder Singh c Nadeem Abbasi b Wasim Akram	8		
V. Razdan not out	6		
B 6, l-b 14, w 8, n-b 14	42	B 5, l-b 7, n-b 2	14
1/20 2/39 3/167 4/181 5/225 6/251 7/270 8/296 9/314	324	1/10 2/33 3/38 4/38 5/139 6/198 7/207	(7 wkts) 234

Bowling: *First Innings*—Wasim Akram 28.2–6–101–5; Waqar Younis 21–2–83–2; Zakir Khan 16–3–59–0; Imran Khan 17–3–61–2; Abdul Qadir 2–2–0–0. *Second Innings*—Wasim Akram 32–17–41–2; Imran Khan 22–4–68–3; Shoaib Mohammad 1–1–0–0; Waqar Younis 16–1–63–0; Zakir Khan 13–0–50–2.

Pakistan

Aamer Malik lbw b Prabhakar	9
Ramiz Raja b Razdan	56
Shoaib Mohammad b Razdan	23
Javed Miandad c More b Kapil Dev	7
Salim Malik c Shastri b Razdan	34
*Imran Khan c More b Prabhakar	25
†Nadeem Abbasi b Prabhakar	10
Wasim Akram b Razdan	30
Abdul Qadir c Azharuddin b Razdan	7
Zakir Khan not out	9
Waqar Younis c More b Kapil Dev	4
B 7, l-b 24, w 1, n-b 4	36
1/11 2/76 3/87 4/133 5/170 6/185 7/194 8/222 9/233	250

Bowling: Kapil Dev 35.4–17–44–2; Prabhakar 40–10–92–3; Razdan 27–5–79–5; Maninder 1–0–4–0.

Umpires: J. H. Hampshire and J. W. Holder.

†PAKISTAN v INDIA

First One-day International

At Peshawar, December 16. Abandoned owing to poor light. In an exhibition match of twenty overs a side which was played in place of the scheduled one-day international, Tendulkar hit an unbeaten half-century off just eighteen balls. His five sixes and two fours included three successive sixes and a four off one over from Abdul Qadir which cost 27 runs. The Pakistanis won the match by 4 runs.

Pakistan XI 157 for four (20 overs) (Mansoor Akhtar 53, Salim Malik 75); India XI 153 for three (20 overs) (W. V. Raman 42, S. R. Tendulkar 53 not out).

†PAKISTAN v INDIA

Second One-day International

At Gujranwala, December 18. Toss: India. Pakistan won by 7 runs. With poor light precluding a start till past lunch, the match was reduced to twenty overs a side, but India bowled only sixteen in the allotted 85 minutes. Saeed Anwar, the young left-hander recalled to the Pakistan side, was the only one of their batsmen to shine, lifting the ball cleanly to hit four fours and two sixes. Although the target was a moderate one, in the swinging and seaming conditions Pakistan's four-man pace attack struck at regular intervals and pushed India behind the asking-rate. Fine catching in the outfield accounted for some of the Indian batsmen as they attempted over-ambitious strokes under pressure.

Man of the Match: Saeed Anwar.

Pakistan

Mansoor Akhtar run out	18
Ramiz Raja c Sidhu b Maninder	10
Salim Malik c Azharuddin b Maninder	0
Wasim Akram run out	2
Saeed Anwar not out	42
Javed Miandad run out	1
*Imran Khan c Srikkanth b Ankola	1
Abdul Qadir lbw b Lamba	0
†Zulqarnain c Prabhakar b Ankola	2
Waqar Younis run out	3
L-b 4, w 2, n-b 2	8
1/20 2/22 3/29 4/52 5/59 6/65 7/68 8/75 9/87 (9 wkts, 16 overs)	87

Aaqib Javed did not bat.

Bowling: Prabhakar 3–0–8–0; Razdan 2–0–9–0; Ankola 4–0–26–2; Maninder 4–0–17–2; Lamba 2–0–9–1; Shastri 1–0–14–0.

India

*K. Srikkanth b Waqar Younis 17
R. Lamba run out 9
N. S. Sidhu c Mansoor Akhtar b Aaqib Javed . 2
M. Azharuddin c Salim Malik b Aaqib Javed . 21
S. R. Tendulkar c Wasim Akram b Waqar Younis . 0
R. J. Shastri b Waqar Younis 1
M. Prabhakar lbw b Imran Khan 10
†K. S. More c Abdul Qadir b Imran Khan . 2
V. Razdan b Imran Khan 1
S. A. Ankola not out 7
Maninder Singh not out 0
B 2, l-b 5, w 2, n-b 1 10

1/26 2/32 3/34 4/36 5/51 6/59 7/68 8/73 9/80 (9 wkts, 16 overs) 80

Bowling: Wasim Akram 4–0–16–0; Imran Khan 4–0–18–3; Waqar Younis 4–0–21–3; Aaqib Javed 4–0–18–2.

Umpires: Feroze Butt and Mian Aslam.

†PAKISTAN v INDIA

Third One-day International

At Karachi, December 20. No result, the match being stopped because of crowd trouble. Toss: India. Put in on a damp pitch, Pakistan were in dire straits when Prabhakar picked up three wickets in his opening spell of five overs. However, the Indian team were forced to leave the field owing to repeated stone-thowing by the huge crowd, particularly from the galleries. The police were still struggling to control the student faction when the Indians, though reluctantly, took the field for the second time. As missiles more deadly than stones kept coming, they walked off again. With a full-scale battle between the police and the students resulting in the use of tear-gas and gun shots outside the National Stadium being heard, the abandonment of the match was a formality.

Pakistan

Ramiz Raja lbw b Prabhakar 0
Shoaib Mohammad not out 13
Salim Malik b Prabhakar 0
Javed Miandad lbw b Prabhakar 2
*Imran Khan not out 9
L-b 2, w 2 4

1/0 2/0 3/11 (3 wkts, 14.2 overs) 28

Saeed Anwar, Wasim Akram, Abdul Qadir, †Zulqarnain, Waqar Younis and Aaqib Javed did not bat.

Bowling: Prabhakar 5–2–5–3; Kapil Dev 7–1–14–0; Ankola 2.2–0–7–0.

India

*K. Srikkanth, R. Lamba, N. S. Sidhu, M. Azharuddin, R. J. Shastri, S. V. Manjrekar, M. Prabhakar, †K. S. More, Kapil Dev, S. A. Ankola and Maninder Singh.

Umpires: Feroze Butt and Salim Badar.

†PAKISTAN v INDIA

Fourth One-day International

At Lahore, December 22. Pakistan won by 38 runs. Toss: India. A match shortened by overnight rain and played on a doubtful wicket saw the home team extend their run of success against India in one-day internationals. The slow pace at which the Pakistani front-line batsmen made their runs was justified by the conditions. India were 70 for five by the 22nd over, with Aaqib Javed bowling his out-swingers intelligently after Imran had picked up the first two wickets. Srikkanth was reprieved twice in making the top score of the match, but it was to no avail. India finished well behind.

Man of the Match: Aaqib Javed.

Pakistan

Shoaib Mohammad run out	26	Abdul Qadir not out	0
Ramiz Raja c Maninder b Shastri	24	Waqar Younis not out	2
Saeed Anwar run out	7		
Salim Malik c Razdan b Ankola	29	L-b 7, w 5, n-b 2	14
Wasim Akram b Maninder	1		
Javed Miandad c Sidhu b Razdan	30	1/45 2/57 3/68 (8 wkts, 37 overs)	150
*Imran Khan c Sidhu b Prabhakar	14	4/72 5/106 6/131	
†Salim Yousuf c Razdan b Prabhakar	3	7/144 8/145	

Aaqib Javed did not bat.

Bowling: Prabhakar 8–0–24–2; Razdan 8–0–37–1; Ankola 4–0–20–1; Lamba 1–0–9–0; Maninder 8–1–24–1; Shastri 8–0–29–1.

India

*K. Srikkanth c Salim Yousuf b Waqar Younis	31	S. A. Ankola c Salim Yousuf b Wasim Akram	0
R. Lamba lbw b Imran Khan	7	V. Razdan st Salim Yousuf b Abdul Qadir	18
N. S. Sidhu c and b Imran Khan	1	Maninder Singh not out	2
S. V. Manjrekar c Salim Yousuf b Aaqib Javed	13		
M. Azharuddin c Saeed Anwar b Aaqib Javed	4	B 4, l-b 5, w 9	18
R. J. Shastri run out	12		
M. Prabhakar b Aaqib Javed	0	1/15 2/18 3/49 (30.2 overs)	112
†K. S. More c Abdul Qadir b Wasim Akram	6	4/66 5/70 6/70 7/82 8/82 9/90	

Bowling: Imran Khan 5–2–10–2; Wasim Akram 7–1–25–2; Aaqib Javed 8–1–28–3; Waqar Younis 7–0–27–1; Abdul Qadir 3.2–0–13–1.

Umpires: Khalid Aziz and Shakoor Rana.

INDIA v SRI LANKA, 1990-91

India and Sri Lanka played one match, which India won by an innings with a day to spare. Sri Lanka recorded their lowest total in Tests when they were dismissed in the first innings for 82, S. L. V. Raju returning figures of 17.5–13–12–6. Kapil Dev finished the match with 376 wickets in Tests, level with I. T. Botham and second only to Sir Richard Hadlee.

At Chandigarh, November 23, 24, 25, 27. India won by an innings and 8 runs. India 288 (R. J. Shastri 88, M. Prabhakar 31, S. V. Manjrekar 39, K. S. More 37 not out, Extras 34; R. J. Ratnayake three for 60, K. P. J. Warnaweera three for 90, A. W. R. Madurasinghe three for 60); Sri Lanka 82 (A. P. Gurusinha 52 not out, S. L. V. Raju six for 12) and 198 (R. S. Mahanama 48, A. Ranatunga 42, H. P. Tillekeratne 55, Extras 30; Kapil Dev four for 36, M. Prabhakar three for 44).

THE NEW ZEALANDERS IN AUSTRALIA, 1989-90

By CHRIS HARTE

The eighteenth New Zealand team to visit Australia undertook a four-match, three-week tour during November 1989. The mainspring for the short tour had come the previous April, when the Australian Cricket Board learned that its proposed itinerary for the 1989-90 season would not be honoured by Pakistan, who had double-booked for the period leading up to Christmas. Pakistan were to be hosts to India for a four-Test series in November and December. After hasty negotiations, Pakistan agreed to a three-Test tour of Australia, starting in the New Year, while Sri Lanka, Australia's other visitors, were awarded two Test matches instead of one, as originally planned.

An approach was made to the New Zealand Cricket Council in early May to fill the remaining scheduled Test date, and even though its senior players were opposed to the idea, the NZCC agreed to the ACB's suggestion. The ACB was not helped in its planning by the insistence of its television and marketing organisation that the New Zealand visit had to be early in the season, because no international cricket could be played while Channel Nine was televising the Commonwealth Games from Auckland. The consequence of this was that John Wright and his team arrived in Perth with, at most, two club games behind them by way of early-season match practice. Moreover Richard Hadlee, their most successful Test bowler, had withdrawn four days before the team's departure with a recurrence of an Achilles' tendon problem. When Brendon Bracewell, Hadlee's replacement, broke down in the first week, and there were also injuries to his off-spinner brother, John, and to Andrew Jones, Mr Gerald Bailey, the New Zealand manager, had to call for Dipak Patel and Chris Cairns as additional replacements. Cairns won his first cap for New Zealand in the Test match at Perth.

Although excellent ambassadors for the game of cricket, the New Zealanders did not attract large crowds to any of their matches. The first of these, a day/night game against Western Australia, saw just under 5,000 present as the New Zealanders were comprehensively outplayed and lost by seven wickets with 15.5 overs remaining. The subsequent four-day match in Perth was drawn, after Wright and Ian Smith, the New Zealand wicket-keeper, had put on 191 runs for the seventh wicket on the last day, and another draw followed against South Australia in Adelaide, where both sides viewed the match as an ideal opportunity for batting practice.

The Test match, in Perth, was poorly attended, with an official attendance of 29,607 for the five days. Of those present, a considerable number were Western Australia Cricket Association members, corporate box ticket-holders, and those who took advantage of offers from Perth's six radio stations, each of whom gave away 250 free tickets a day. Yet the match was a classic Test encounter. Australia built a large first-innings score, after which New Zealand failed to avoid the follow-on and then, led by a marathon innings by Mark Greatbatch, batted courageously to claim a draw.

NEW ZEALAND TOUR RESULTS

Test matches – Played 1: Drawn 1.
First-class matches – Played 3: Drawn 3.
Draws – Australia, Western Australia, South Australia.
Non first-class match – Lost to Western Australia.

NEW ZEALAND AVERAGES – FIRST-CLASS MATCHES

BATTING

	M	*I*	*NO*	*R*	*HI*	*100s*	*Avge*
M. D. Crowe	3	5	0	332	143	1	66.40
M. J. Greatbatch ...	3	5	1	261	146*	1	65.25
J. J. Crowe	3	5	1	195	109*	1	48.75
J. G. Wright	3	5	1	170	107*	1	42.50
I. D. S. Smith	3	5	0	164	123	1	32.80
C. L. Cairns	2	3	0	68	39	0	22.66
R. H. Vance	3	5	0	79	65	0	15.80
D. N. Patel	2	3	0	27	20	0	9.00
D. K. Morrison	3	3	2	3	3	0	3.00
W. Watson	3	2	0	4	4	0	2.00
M. C. Snedden	2	2	2	46	33*	0	—

Played in one match: B. P. Bracewell 8, 9; J. G. Bracewell 86, 18; A. H. Jones 13.

* *Signifies not out.*

BOWLING

	O	*M*	*R*	*W*	*BB*	*5W/i*	*Avge*
J. G. Bracewell ...	34	6	81	4	4-81	0	20.25
M. C. Snedden	79	16	213	7	4-108	0	30.42
D. N. Patel	55.4	13	142	4	3-62	0	35.50
D. K. Morrison ...	91.1	16	318	8	4-71	0	39.75
C. L. Cairns	51	8	190	4	2-22	0	47.50
W. Watson	113	20	355	2	2-103	0	177.50

Also bowled: B. P. Bracewell 32–8–88–1.

FIELDING

4 – J. J. Crowe; 3 – M. J. Greatbatch, J. G. Wright; 2 – B. P. Bracewell, C. L. Cairns, M. D. Crowe; 1 – A. H. Jones, I. D. S. Smith.

†At Perth, November 8 (day/night). Western Australia won by seven wickets. Toss: New Zealanders. New Zealanders 181 for eight (50 overs) (A. H. Jones 84, J. J. Crowe 51 not out; T. M. Alderman three for 33); Western Australia 184 for three (34.1 overs) (G. M. Wood 48, T. M. Moody 94 not out).

WESTERN AUSTRALIA v NEW ZEALANDERS

At Perth, November 10, 11, 12, 13. Drawn. Toss: Western Australia. Put in to bat, the New Zealanders lost two wickets in the first six overs, and their lack of match practice showed as they slumped to 98 for five. However, Martin Crowe spent 287 minutes compiling 87 runs and his sixth-wicket partnership of 135 in 140 minutes with John Bracewell saved the visitors. In reply, Western Australia batted for nine and threequarter hours before Wood declared. Wood's century, his 21st for the state, took exactly 500 minutes and saw his side to a first-innings lead of 91. New Zealand again lost quick wickets, but a defiant seventh-wicket stand between Wright and Smith guaranteed the draw. Wright was six and a half hours over his unbeaten hundred, whereas Smith's 123 came from 120 balls and contained a six and seventeen fours.

Close of play: First day, New Zealanders 271-7 (I. D. S. Smith 23*, B. P. Bracewell 0*); Second day, Western Australia 156-2 (M. R. J. Veletta 71*, G. M. Wood 36*); Third day, New Zealanders 28-3 (J. G. Wright 9*, B. P. Bracewell 0*).

New Zealanders

First innings		Second innings	
R. H. Vance c Moody b Alderman	1	(2) lbw b Mullally	1
*J. G. Wright c Zoehrer b Mullally	3	(1) not out	107
A. H. Jones b Matthews	13		
M. D. Crowe c Mullally b Yardley	87	(3) lbw b Moody	10
M. J. Greatbatch lbw b Matthews	0	(6) c sub b Hogan	3
J. J. Crowe c Veletta b Yardley	25	(4) c sub b Yardley	5
J. G. Bracewell c Andrews b Yardley	86	c Zoehrer b Yardley	18
†I. D. S. Smith b Mullally	26	c Zoehrer b Moody	123
B. P. Bracewell c Matthews b Wood	8	(5) c Marsh b Moody	9
D. K. Morrison not out	0	(9) not out	0
W. Watson run out	0		
B 5, l-b 16, w 8, n-b 5	34	B 8, l-b 7, w 4, n-b 1	20
1/5 2/5 3/47 4/49 5/98 6/233 7/267 8/283 9/283	283	1/3 2/20 3/27 4/44 5/67 6/105 7/296	(7 wkts) 296

Bowling: *First Innings*—Mullally 21–5–48–2; Alderman 9–3–11–1; Moody 16–4–43–0; Matthews 17–2–52–2; Yardley 22–4–76–3; Hogan 10–1–32–0; Wood 0.4–0–0–1. *Second Innings*—Mullally 25–3–74–1; Moody 28.1–11–89–3; Matthews 4.5–0–9–0; Yardley 24–10–56–2; Hogan 17–8–46–1; Andrews 1–0–7–0.

Western Australia

G. R. Marsh c M. D. Crowe b Morrison	2
M. R. J. Veletta c M. D. Crowe b J. G. Bracewell	91
T. M. Moody lbw b Morrison	34
*G. M. Wood not out	125
W. S. Andrews lbw b Morrison	21
†T. J. Zoehrer c B. P. Bracewell b Morrison	3
T. G. Hogan c J. J. Crowe b B. P. Bracewell	47
C. D. Matthews c Jones b J. G. Bracewell	28
B. Yardley c B. P. Bracewell b J. G. Bracewell	3
A. D. Mullally lbw b J. G. Bracewell	0
B 4, l-b 8, w 1, n-b 7	20
1/8 2/65 3/203 4/238 5/242 6/326 7/369 8/373 9/374	(9 wkts dec.) 374

T. M. Alderman did not bat.

Bowling: Morrison 27–4–71–4; Watson 45–9–122–0; B. P. Bracewell 32–8–88–1; J. G. Bracewell 34–6–81–4.

Umpires: P. J. McConnell and T. A. Prue.

SOUTH AUSTRALIA v NEW ZEALANDERS

At Adelaide, November 17, 18, 19, 20. Drawn. Toss: New Zealanders. The visitors' gamble of putting South Australia in to bat on a typically true Adelaide pitch, and hoping for a match of declarations, came to nothing when Hookes allowed the home state's innings to run its full course. South Australia were not dismissed until just before tea on the second day, with the

New Zealanders' bowlers unable to make much headway against batsmen determined to succeed. Bishop, recalled as opener, spent 404 minutes over his 173, but Lehmann was much more positive, scoring his 80 in glorious fashion. Martin Crowe replied for the New Zealanders with his fourth hundred in as many matches on the Adelaide Oval, boosting his aggregate there to 741 in seven innings at an average of 148.20. His 50th first-class century, his 143 took 381 minutes (322 balls), included sixteen fours, and along with his brother's unbeaten 109 (373 minutes, 279 balls) made sure that the New Zealanders were never in danger of embarrassment.

Close of play: First day, South Australia 290-3 (G. A. Bishop 144*, D. S. Lehmann 38*); Second day, New Zealanders 89-1 (R. H. Vance 36*, M. J. Greatbatch 27*); Third day, New Zealanders 303-4 (M. D. Crowe 115*, J. J. Crowe 39*).

South Australia

A. M. J. Hilditch lbw b Snedden	33	– (2) c J. J. Crowe b Cairns	32
G. A. Bishop b Watson	173	– (1) not out	26
P. C. Nobes b Snedden	58	– b Cairns	2
*D. W. Hookes c Greatbatch b Snedden	8	– not out	3
D. S. Lehmann c Cairns b Patel	80		
P. R. Sleep c Cairns b Watson	0		
J. C. Scuderi not out	75		
†D. S. Berry c J. J. Crowe b Cairns	7		
P. W. Gladigau lbw b Cairns	0		
P. J. S. Alley lbw b Patel	1		
D. A. Clarke c Greatbatch b Patel	9		
B 1, l-b 10, n-b 4	15	L-b 1, n-b 3	4
1/72 2/212 3/223 4/343 5/343 6/386 7/402 8/416 9/429	459	1/55 2/59 (2 wkts)	67

Bowling: *First Innings*—Morrison 22–3–90–0; Cairns 31–4–108–2; Watson 25–4–103–2; Snedden 26–3–85–3; Patel 27.4–8–62–3. *Second Innings*—Morrison 3–1–12–0; Watson 6–0–12–0; Snedden 11–3–20–0; Cairns 8–2–22–2.

New Zealanders

R. H. Vance c Hookes b Alley	65
*J. G. Wright lbw b Alley	23
M. J. Greatbatch c Berry b Gladigau	36
M. D. Crowe c Bishop b Alley	143
D. N. Patel c Alley b Sleep	20
J. J. Crowe not out	109
†I. D. S. Smith lbw b Sleep	4
C. L. Cairns b Hilditch	39
L-b 5, n-b 1	6
1/57 2/114 3/141 4/188 5/345 6/350 7/445 (7 wkts dec.)	445

M. C. Snedden, D. K. Morrison and W. Watson did not bat.

Bowling: Gladigau 33–10–82–1; Clarke 33–14–70–0; Scuderi 38–18–67–0; Alley 26–10–78–3; Sleep 49–13–131–2; Hilditch 4–0–12–1.

Umpires: A. R. Crafter and D. J. Harper.

AUSTRALIA v NEW ZEALAND

Test Match

At Perth, November 24, 25, 26, 27, 28. Drawn. Toss: New Zealand. Wright had no hesitation in putting Australia in to bat on a good, bouncy pitch, but with the temperature near the century mark, his fast bowlers were made to toil by Australian batsmen determined to extend their record of first-innings totals over 400 to nine consecutive matches. After the early loss of Taylor, Boon and Moody, playing in his first Test, added 149 in 192 minutes for the second wicket. The next day saw Boon record his first Test double-hundred, and also the first in seventeen Test matches at Perth. Opening the innings again because Marsh had a broken toe, he batted for 7 hours 31 minutes, faced 327 balls and hit 28 fours. Jones continued the assault on the visiting attack, which never gave up despite being weakened by the absence of New Zealand's own newcomer, Cairns, with a back strain after the first day. Border declared on

Jones's dismissal for 99 immediately after a drinks break late on the second day, giving his bowlers three days in which to dismiss New Zealand twice. They almost succeeded and were thwarted only by one of the most valiant rearguard actions in Test history.

Although Wright batted for two and a quarter hours when New Zealand began their reply, the only stand of substance in the first innings was between the left-handed Greatbatch and Martin Crowe, who put on 89 for the third wicket. Greatbatch was three and threequarter hours scoring 76 and Crowe slightly less over his 62, which included ten fours. Hughes, with four for 6 in 24 balls either side of tea, began New Zealand's slump, and from the relative security of 173 for two, they found themselves following on early on the fourth morning. Jeff Crowe had batted 90 minutes for his 7.

In their second innings, New Zealand lost two wickets for 11 runs, Border taking an excellent catch at gully to remove Wright, and at 107 for four a few minutes after the tea interval, they appeared to be heading for defeat. Instead, Greatbatch, in only his seventh Test, saved them. His battling, unbeaten 146 took five minutes under eleven hours, and his stands with Jeff Crowe (155 minutes), Cairns (93 minutes) and finally Snedden (202 minutes) ensured that New Zealand escaped without defeat from a match they had never looked likely to win. Greatbatch was 462 minutes reaching his second Test century, which at the time was the slowest first-class hundred in Australia, and his unbroken partnership of 88 with Snedden was a record for New Zealand's eighth wicket against Australia.

Man of the Match: M. J. Greatbatch. *Attendance:* 29,607.

Close of play: First day, Australia 296-2 (D. C. Boon 169*, A. R. Border 45*); Second day, New Zealand 25-0 (J. G. Wright 12*, R. H. Vance 4*); Third day, New Zealand 218-8 (M. C. Snedden 7*, D. K. Morrison 0*); Fourth day, New Zealand 168-4 (M. J. Greatbatch 69*, J. J. Crowe 42*).

Australia

M. A. Taylor c Wright b Morrison 9	G. F. Lawson b Morrison 1
D. C. Boon c Wright b Snedden 200	C. G. Rackemann not out 15
T. M. Moody c Smith b Snedden 61	
*A. R. Border b Morrison 50	B 1, l-b 9, w 2, n-b 13 25
D. M. Jones lbw b Morrison 99	
S. R. Waugh c Greatbatch b Snedden . 17	1/28 2/177 3/316 (9 wkts dec.) 521
†I. A. Healy c J. J. Crowe b Patel 28	4/361 5/395 6/449
M. G. Hughes c Wright b Snedden 16	7/489 8/490 9/521

T. M. Alderman did not bat.

Bowling: Morrison 39.1–8–145–4; Cairns 12–2–60–0; Snedden 42–10–108–4; Watson 37–7–118–0; Patel 28–5–80–1.

New Zealand

First innings		Second innings	
*J. G. Wright b Rackemann	34	– c Border b Lawson	3
R. H. Vance b Alderman	4	– c Alderman b Rackemann	8
M. J. Greatbatch c Healy b Hughes	76	– not out	146
M. D. Crowe lbw b Alderman	62	– c Taylor b Moody	30
D. N. Patel c Boon b Hughes	0	– lbw b Alderman	7
J. J. Crowe c Healy b Rackemann	7	– lbw b Hughes	49
†I. D. S. Smith c Lawson b Hughes	11	– c Border b Hughes	0
C. L. Cairns c Healy b Hughes	1	– lbw b Hughes	28
M. C. Snedden not out	13	– not out	33
D. K. Morrison c Border b Lawson	3		
W. Watson lbw b Alderman	4		
B 1, l-b 6, w 4, n-b 5	16	L-b 14, n-b 4	18
1/28 2/84 3/173 4/178 5/191 6/204 7/206 8/212 9/226	231	1/11 2/11 3/79 4/107 5/189 6/189 7/234	(7 wkts) 322

Bowling: *First Innings*—Alderman 25.4–7–73–3; Lawson 22–5–54–1; Rackemann 20–4–39–2; Hughes 20–7–51–4; Moody 4–1–6–0; Border 1–0–1–0. *Second Innings*—Alderman 32–14–59–1; Lawson 38–12–88–1; Rackemann 31–21–23–1; Hughes 36–8–92–3; Moody 17–6–23–1; Border 5–2–17–0; Jones 3–2–6–0.

Umpires: R. J. Evans and P. J. McConnell.

THE SRI LANKANS IN AUSTRALIA, 1989-90

By CHRIS HARTE

The fourth Sri Lankan team to visit Australia undertook the longest tour by a side from that country, playing 27 matches in three months. However, of those fixtures, only six were first-class, including two Test matches. It was not a satisfactory situation for a team bereft of sustained competitive cricket at the highest level.

There were problems for the touring team even before it had been selected. According to the country's sports laws, all representative players and officials have to be approved by the Sri Lankan Ministry of Sport, and in this instance the Ministry refused to give its approval to the Sri Lankan Cricket Board's choice of Abu Fuard as manager and Ranjit Fernando as his assistant. For previous Sri Lankan tours, approval had been a formality, but this time three sets of names had been required.

Following the Ministry's rejection of the Board's proposed officials, its president, Ian Pieris, resigned, after only five months in office. In his resignation statement, Pieris said: "In my opinion, and in the best interests of Sri Lankan cricket, we should have complied with the Ministry's directive to submit three names each for the posts of manager and assistant-manager. However, the majority in the committee took another view and I could not in all conscience continue in office." The Board then submitted two further names – Nisal Senaratne as manager and Anuruddha Polonowita as assistant-manager – which the Ministry ratified immediately "in view of the time constraint".

This had not been the only problem prior to the start of the tour. The Sri Lankan Board had been most dissatisfied with the itinerary sent to them by the Australian Cricket Board. With the Australian season being disrupted by the later-than-scheduled arrival of Pakistan, and with the ACB undertaking to Channel Nine television not to programme international cricket while the Commonwealth Games were being broadcast from Auckland, New Zealand, the Sri Lankans were faced with a period of 37 days in which they would play no senior cricket. The Sri Lankan Board put two options to the ACB, the preferred choice being to make a short tour of New Zealand during this period. The other was to return home for a time. The ACB refused to entertain the New Zealand concept and insisted that the Sri Lankans wander aimlessly around Australia, playing mainly at country venues. That the visitors agreed with such good grace to this schedule, which at times meant three flights a day, was a credit to them.

When the sixteen-man Sri Lankan team was announced, the surprise omission was Brendon Kuruppu, a wicket-keeper-batsman, who had been to Australia in 1987-88. The three newcomers were Dhammika Ranatunga – the elder brother of the captain, Arjuna Ranatunga, and an opening batsman – all-rounder Sanath Jayasuriya, and wicket-keeper Gamini Wickremasinghe. As the tour wore on and the list of injured players grew, three replacements joined the party – Nilantha Ratnayake, Ruwan Kalpage and finally Kuruppu, who was flown to Australia for the last three limited-overs internationals.

The tour was a learning process for many of the Sri Lankans. Aravinda de Silva, who had been on two previous tours, in 1984-85 and 1987-88, scored

934 runs at 37.36 in all matches. He was followed by the ever-improving Asanka Gurusinha (849 runs at 28.30), who played in 25 fixtures, and Athula Samarasekera (707 runs at 28.28), whose improvement was marked as the tour progressed. Off-spinner Ranjith Madurasinghe, who had performed so well in local competitions, arrived in Australia as an unknown but soon proved his ability. His 31 wickets at 23.06 in all matches, particularly on the slower country pitches, augured well for his future. However, the loss of Graeme Labrooy and Rumesh Ratnayake through injury was a serious blow to Sri Lankan hopes in both the Test matches and the one-day internationals.

The team was ably led by Arjuna Ranatunga, with Ravi Ratnayeke as his deputy. No matter what the travelling schedules, the players always appeared at the numerous functions laid on for them correctly dressed in the team-issue blazer and trousers. But while the public relations side was exemplary, the fact is that the tour did little to enhance the standard of Sri Lankan cricket. Both Test matches showed the capability of the visitors, and never again should they suffer the indignity of being used in such a way by the Australian Cricket Board. A full fixture list of first-class matches should have been prepared, and it is to be hoped that future visits will reflect this view.

SRI LANKAN TOUR RESULTS

Test matches – Played 2: Lost 1, Drawn 1.
First-class matches – Played 6: Lost 2, Drawn 4.
Losses – Australia, Victoria.
Draws – Australia, New South Wales, South Australia, Tasmania.
One-day internationals – Played 8: Won 1, Lost 7. *Win* – Pakistan. *Losses* – Australia (4), Pakistan (3).
Other non first-class matches – Played 13: Won 5, Lost 5, Drawn 3. *Wins* – South Australian Country XI, New South Wales Country XI, Queensland Country XI, Western Australia, Western Australian Country XI. *Losses* – Victoria, Victorian Country Cricket League, New South Wales, Queensland, Western Australia. *Draws* – Australian Cricket Academy Australian Country XI, Queensland.

TEST MATCH AVERAGES

AUSTRALIA – BATTING

	T	*I*	*NO*	*R*	*HI*	*100s*	*Avge*
S. R. Waugh	2	4	1	267	134*	1	89.0
M. A. Taylor	2	4	0	304	164	2	76.0
A. R. Border	2	3	0	165	85	0	55.0
D. M. Jones	2	4	1	159	118*	1	53.0
T. M. Moody	2	4	0	147	106	1	36.7
M. G. Hughes	2	4	1	105	30	0	35.0
I. A. Healy	2	3	1	64	26*	0	32.0
D. C. Boon	2	4	0	67	41	0	16.7
T. M. Alderman	2	2	0	18	18	0	9.0

Played in one Test: G. D. Campbell 6; G. F. Lawson 22; C. G. Rackemann 5*, 0; P. F Sleep 47*.

* *Signifies not out.*

BOWLING

	O	M	R	W	BB	5W/i	Avge
P. R. Sleep	46	20	99	5	3-26	0	19.80
M. G. Hughes	92.2	22	279	11	5-88	1	25.36
G. D. Campbell	56	17	143	5	3-102	0	28.60
C. G. Rackemann	30.3	6	88	3	3-88	0	29.33
T. M. Alderman	93	27	200	5	3-81	0	40.00
G. F. Lawson	33	10	51	1	1-51	0	51.00

Also bowled: A. R. Border 12–4–38–0; D. M. Jones 5–2–6–0; T. M. Moody 18–8–24–0; S. R. Waugh 6–3–6–0.

SRI LANKA – BATTING

	T	I	NO	R	HI	100s	Avge
P. A. de Silva	2	3	0	314	167	1	104.66
J. R. Ratnayeke	2	3	0	140	75	0	46.66
R. S. Mahanama	2	3	0	95	85	0	31.66
D. Ranatunga	2	3	0	87	45	0	29.00
A. Ranatunga	2	3	0	84	38	0	28.00
E. A. R. de Silva	2	3	0	74	50	0	24.66
A. P. Gurusinha	2	3	0	63	43	0	21.00
G. F. Labrooy	2	3	0	17	11	0	5.66

Played in two Tests: C. P. H. Ramanayake 10*, 4*, 2*. Played in one Test: R. J. Ratnayake , 5; M. A. R. Samarasekera 18; H. P. Tillekeratne 0, 6; A. G. D. Wickremasinghe 2.

** Signifies not out.*

BOWLING

	O	M	R	W	BB	5W/i	Avge
A. P. Gurusinha	24.3	4	88	5	2-31	0	17.60
R. J. Ratnayake	54.4	7	189	8	6-66	1	23.62
. A. de Silva	33	3	110	3	2-65	0	36.66
G. F. Labrooy	96.1	15	363	7	5-133	1	51.85
C. P. H. Ramanayake	68	5	252	4	2-81	0	63.00
. A. R. de Silva	77	17	226	2	1-10	0	113.00
. R. Ratnayeke	42.5	4	142	1	1-39	0	142.00

Also bowled: R. S. Mahanama 1–0–3–0; A. Ranatunga 19–1–74–0.

SRI LANKAN AVERAGES – FIRST-CLASS MATCHES

BATTING

	M	I	NO	R	HI	100s	Avge
A. de Silva	6	10	0	524	167	1	52.40
R. Ratnayeke	5	7	1	244	75	0	40.66
. P. H. Ramanayake	4	5	4	35	16*	0	35.00
T. Jayasuriya	4	7	2	171	37*	0	34.20
. A. R. Samarasekera	4	7	1	201	133	1	33.50
A. R. de Silva	5	7	1	198	66*	0	33.00

	M	*I*	*NO*	*R*	*HI*	*100s*	*Avge*
A. P. Gurusinha	5	9	0	295	109	1	32.77
A. Ranatunga	4	6	0	181	75	0	30.16
R. S. Mahanama	4	7	1	173	85	0	28.83
H. P. Tillekeratne	4	7	1	143	74	0	23.83
D. Ranatunga	5	9	0	197	56	0	21.88
G. F. Labrooy	5	5	1	43	26*	0	10.75
A. G. D. Wickremasinghe	4	7	1	50	24	0	8.33
R. J. Ratnayake	2	4	0	13	5	0	3.25

Played in two matches: A. W. R. Madurasinghe 4*. Played in one match: R. S. Kalpage 10*, 0; K. I. W. Wijegunawardene 5, 1*; N. L. K. Ratnayake did not bat.

* *Signifies not out.*

BOWLING

	O	*M*	*R*	*W*	*BB*	*5W/i*	*Avge*
A. P. Gurusinha	28.3	4	111	5	2-31	0	22.2
R. J. Ratnayake	83.4	7	318	10	6-66	1	31.8
G. F. Labrooy	167.1	23	652	15	5-133	2	43.4
A. W. R. Madurasinghe	60	5	207	4	4-80	0	51.7
A. Ranatunga	51	1	166	3	2-17	0	55.3
C. P. H. Ramanayake	129	13	490	8	2-81	0	61.2
P. A. de Silva	68	7	227	3	2-65	0	75.6
E. A. R. de Silva	160.1	29	486	6	3-121	0	81.0
J. R. Ratnayeke	125.5	13	423	5	2-75	0	84.6

Also bowled: S. T. Jayasuriya 20–3–74–1; R. S. Kalpage 1–0–6–0; R. S. Mahanam 1–0–3–0; N. L. K. Ratnayake 21–3–45–1; M. A. R. Samarasekera 1–0–15–0; H. P Tillekeratne 2–0–10–0; K. I. W. Wijegunawardene 20–1–109–0.

FIELDING

7 – A. P. Gurusinha; 6 – A. G. D. Wickremasinghe (5 ct, 1 st); 5 – H. P. Tillekeratne; 4 E. A. R. de Silva, R. S. Mahanama, A. Ranatunga, J. R. Ratnayeke; 2 – P. A. de Silv A. W. R. Madurasinghe; 1 – R. S. Kalpage, G. F. Labrooy, C. P. H. Ramanayake, I Ranatunga, R. J. Ratnayake, M. A. R. Samarasekera.

NEW SOUTH WALES v SRI LANKANS

At Canberra, November 17, 18, 19, 20. Drawn. Toss: Sri Lankans. Batting first against team which was not only short of match practice but was playing its first first-class match f fourteen months, New South Wales scored freely until Lawson declared at lunch on t second day. Bad weather interrupted the Sri Lankan reply, which finally got going on t third afternoon with Samarasekera scoring a career-best 133. The opening partnership of 1 was the highest for any wicket by Sri Lanka in Australia, passing 140 for the eighth wicket J. R. Ratnayeke and S. Jeganathan against Tasmania at Devonport in 1982-83. A final-d flurry by New South Wales left the Sri Lankans with a target of 238 from 40 overs for victo but after losing their first four wickets for 14, they played out for a draw.

Close of play: First day, New South Wales 335-6 (M. D. O'Neill 38*, G. R. J. Matthews 9 Second day, Sri Lankans 17-0 (D. Ranatunga 11*, M. A. R. Samarasekera 4*); Third day, Lankans 217-3 (P. A. de Silva 18*, A. G. D. Wickremasinghe 0*).

New South Wales

S. M. Small c Ratnayeke b Labrooy	36	– not out	36
M. A. Taylor c Ratnayeke b Labrooy	53	– c Ratnayeke b A. Ranatunga	28
T. H. Bayliss c D. Ranatunga b Labrooy	89	– lbw b A. Ranatunga	2
S. R. Waugh c Gurusinha b Labrooy	57	– not out	11
M. E. Waugh c Gurusinha b Labrooy	42		
M. D. O'Neill run out	65		
P. L. Taylor c Madurasinghe b Ratnayeke	2		
G. R. J. Matthews not out	52		
†P. A. Emery not out	15		
L-b 9, n-b 3	12	W 1, n-b 4	5
/84 2/108 3/223 4/254 5/297 /306 7/385 (7 wkts dec.)	423	1/54 2/58 (2 wkts dec.)	82

'G. F. Lawson and M. R. Whitney did not bat.

Bowling: *First Innings*—Ratnayeke 34–3–111–1; Labrooy 31–2–141–5; Madurasinghe 2–0–83–0; A. Ranatunga 13–0–36–0; Samarasekera 1–0–15–0; Jayasuriya 3–0–14–0; de Silva –2–14–0. *Second Innings*—Ratnayeke 9–2–38–0; Gurusinha 4–0–23–0; A. Ranatunga –0–17–2; Madurasinghe 2–0–4–0.

Sri Lankans

. Ranatunga c Emery b Whitney	56	– lbw b Whitney	0
A. R. Samarasekera c Emery b Matthews	133	– b Whitney	0
. P. Gurusinha c and b O'Neill	8	– c Matthews b P. L. Taylor	45
. A. de Silva c Emery b Whitney	30	– c S. R. Waugh b Whitney	2
A. G. D. Wickremasinghe b Whitney	0	– (9) not out	4
A. Ranatunga lbw b Lawson	4	– c Matthews b P. L. Taylor	18
. P. Tillekeratne lbw b Lawson	0	– (5) lbw b M. E. Waugh	5
T. Jayasuriya lbw b M. E. Waugh	27	– (7) not out	27
R. Ratnayeke lbw b M. E. Waugh	1	– (8) c Emery b O'Neill	12
. W. R. Madurasinghe not out	4		
. F. Labrooy absent injured			
L-b 4, n-b 1	5	L-b 5, n-b 1	6
'159 2/190 3/208 4/218 5/225 '225 7/255 8/258 9/268	268	1/0 2/1 3/9 4/14 5/59 6/98 7/113 (7 wkts)	119

Bowling: *First Innings*—Lawson 25–13–39–2; Whitney 24–7–54–3; M. E. Waugh 3–2–7–2; P. L. Taylor 15–3–40–0; Matthews 23–6–58–1; O'Neill 20–5–66–1. *Second nings*—Whitney 9–2–21–3; M. E. Waugh 6–1–29–1; Matthews 11–4–32–0; P. L. Taylor –3–28–2; O'Neill 3–2–4–1.

Umpires: G. E. Reed and I. S. Thomas.

VICTORIA v SRI LANKANS

: Sale, November 24, 25, 26, 27. Victoria won by an innings and 3 runs. Toss: Victoria. ıstralia's 31st first-class venue had a most entertaining start, with two centuries on the ening day. Phillips and Siddons put on 203 for Victoria's third wicket in even time, with ddons's ninth first-class century taking 191 minutes from 157 balls. Phillips, in comparison, k 299 minutes and faced 202 deliveries. The following morning O'Donnell scored the third ntury of the innings and declared in mid-afternoon. After losing their openers cheaply, the Lankans battled to 318, with four players scoring half-centuries, but they were unable to oid the follow-on. The first session on the final day was bizarre, as Wickremasinghe, 5 not t overnight, faced 121 balls in the two hours with his only scoring shot, at 11.29 a.m., being edge to backward square leg for 2 runs. From that time, he went 111 minutes and 94 liveries without scoring, so breaking the Australian record set by B. Mitchell of South rica at Brisbane in 1931-32. Another twenty minutes and Wickremasinghe would have ıalled Shoaib Mohammad's world record, established in 1983-84. Victoria won the match minutes into the final session.

Close of play: First day, Victoria 315-5 (S. P. O'Donnell 28*, D. W. Fleming 2*); Second day, Sri Lankans 156-4 (A. Ranatunga 39*, E. A. R. de Silva 0*); Third day, Sri Lankans 63-2 (D. Ranatunga 37*, A. G. D. Wickremasinghe 5*).

Victoria

G. M. Watts b Ratnayeke 4
I. D. Frazer c Mahanama b Ratnayeke 0
W. N. Phillips c A. Ranatunga b Jayasuriya .134
J. D. Siddons c Wickremasinghe b Ratnayake .113
G. R. Parker c Mahanama b Ratnayake . 8
*S. P. O'Donnell st Wickremasinghe b A. Ranatunga .121
D. W. Fleming not out 63
†M. G. D. Dimattina not out 32
L-b 8, n-b 24 32

1/4 2/7 3/210 4/233 5/305 6/443 (6 wkts dec.) 507

P. W. Jackson, P. R. Reiffel and P. E. McIntyre did not bat.

Bowling: Ratnayeke 22–2–75–2; Ratnayake 29–0–129–2; Wijegunawardene 20–1–109–0; E. A. R. de Silva 22–3–70–0; P. A. de Silva 17–1–60–0; Jayasuriya 7–2–17–1; A. Ranatunga 12–0–39–1.

Sri Lankans

R. S. Mahanama c Siddons b Fleming . . . . 0 – c Frazer b O'Donnell 12
D. Ranatunga c Dimattina b Fleming . . . . 0 – c Frazer b Jackson 46
A. P. Gurusinha c Frazer b Fleming . . . . 55 – st Dimattina b McIntyre 5
P. A. de Silva c Fleming b O'Donnell . . . . 54 – (5) c Fleming b McIntyre 22
*A. Ranatunga c Dimattina b Fleming . . . . 75 – absent injured
E. A. R. de Silva c O'Donnell b McIntyre . . . . . 9 – (8) c Parker b McIntyre 15
S. T. Jayasuriya run out . . . . 31 – (6) c Dimattina b Jackson 34
J. R. Ratnayeke not out . . . . 65 – (7) run out 26
†A. G. D. Wickremasinghe lbw b Reiffel . . . . . . 6 – (4) st Dimattina b McIntyre 13
R. J. Ratnayake c Dimattina b Reiffel . . . . 4 – (9) b Reiffel 4
K. I. W. Wijegunawardene b Jackson . . . . 5 – (10) not out 1
L-b 5, w 1, n-b 8 . . . . 14 B 3, l-b 3, n-b 2 8

1/0 2/5 3/101 4/150 5/180 6/226 7/236 8/276 9/288 318 1/30 2/47 3/74 4/96 5/114 6/144 7/172 8/184 9/186 18

Bowling: *First Innings*—Reiffel 28–5–61–2; Fleming 23–3–74–4; McIntyre 23–2–104–1; Jackson 20.3–8–43–1; O'Donnell 6–2–13–1; Siddons 1–0–3–0; Parker 5–1–15–0. *Secon[d] Innings*—Reiffel 19.1–9–22–1; Fleming 10–2–22–0; O'Donnell 9–3–13–1; McInty[re] 39–18–56–4; Jackson 31–16–59–2; Siddons 2–1–8–0.

Umpires: D. W. Holt and W. P. Sheahan.

SOUTH AUSTRALIA v SRI LANKANS

At Adelaide, December 1, 2, 3, 4. Drawn. Toss: South Australia. After only 40 minutes' pl[ay] was possible on the first day, owing to rain, the Sri Lankans batted purposefully througho[ut] the second day, even though they found scoring difficult against the leg-spin of Sleep a[nd] Francis. Gurusinha hit his sixth first-class century, his 109 coming in 255 minutes from 2[...] deliveries (eight fours) before he was needlessly run out. Ratnayeke, declaring overnigh[t] clearly expected Hookes to reciprocate and make a game of it. Instead, South Australia batt[ed] until tea on the final day. Bishop, on his return to the side, made 156 from 287 balls, but it w[as] the nineteen-year-old left-hander, Lehmann, who took the honours with 109 from 1[...] deliveries, scoring all round the wicket. Hookes kept wicket in the Sri Lankans' seco[nd] innings, Berry having been injured while batting.

Close of play: First day, Sri Lankans 10-0 (R. S. Mahanama 7*, D. Ranatunga 2*); Second day, Sri Lankans 274-5 (H. P. Tillekeratne 23*, S. T. Jayasuriya 37*); Third day, South Australia 340-3 (G. A. Bishop 145*, D. S. Lehmann 74*).

Sri Lankans

R. S. Mahanama b Miller	10	– not out	56
D. Ranatunga b Miller	8	– lbw b Miller	0
A. P. Gurusinha run out	109	– b Miller	10
P. A. de Silva b Sleep	54	– run out	9
M. A. R. Samarasekera run out	26	– not out	10
†H. P. Tillekeratne not out	23		
S. T. Jayasuriya not out	37		
L-b 2, w 3, n-b 2	7	B 1, l-b 2	3
1/16 2/31 3/155 4/206 5/220 (5 wkts dec.)	274	1/4 2/22 3/50 (3 wkts)	88

*J. R. Ratnayeke, E. A. R. de Silva, G. F. Labrooy and C. P. H. Ramanayake did not bat.

Bowling: *First Innings*—Gladigau 17–3–51–0; Miller 25–7–49–2; Zesers 12–4–30–0; Sleep 33–14–70–1; Francis 20–1–72–0; Hookes 1–1–0–0. *Second Innings*—Gladigau 10–3–17–0; Miller 10–3–30–2; Zesers 8–3–24–0; Sleep 5–2–12–0; Francis 2–0–2–0; Nobes 1–1–0–0.

South Australia

A. M. J. Hilditch c Gurusinha b Ratnayeke	9
G. A. Bishop c P. A. de Silva b Labrooy	156
P. C. Nobes c Gurusinha b E. A. R. de Silva	45
*D. W. Hookes c Ratnayeke b E. A. R. de Silva	50
D. S. Lehmann c E. A. R. de Silva b Ramanayake	109
P. R. Sleep c E. A. R. de Silva b Labrooy	0
†D. S. Berry retired hurt	17
A. K. Zesers not out	25
P. W. Gladigau lbw b Labrooy	0
C. R. Miller b E. A. R. de Silva	34
B 2, l-b 8, n-b 17	27
1/25 2/115 3/221 4/361 5/368 6/414 7/414 8/472 (8 wkts dec.)	472

C. L. Francis did not bat.

D. S. Berry retired hurt at 404.

Bowling: Ratnayeke 18–2–57–1; Labrooy 31–5–116–3; Ramanayake 25–2–103–1; E. A. R. de Silva 35.1–7–121–3; P. A. de Silva 8–0–35–0; Jayasuriya 6–0–30–0.

Umpires: I. R. Berry and A. R. Crafter.

AUSTRALIA v SRI LANKA

First Test Match

At Brisbane, December 8, 9, 10, 11, 12. Drawn. Toss: Sri Lanka. Ranatunga's decision to bowl on winning the toss was vindicated when his pace attack claimed two early wickets on a day of low cloud and high humidity. During the afternoon, however, the mainstay of his bowling, Ratnayeke, left the field with a rib injury, and the balance swung towards the batsmen. No further wickets fell, and Moody initiated a recovery with his maiden Test century, needing 161 balls and hitting twelve fours. His early dismissal the next day, along with that of his captain, Border, set off an Australian batting slump from which only Waugh was immune. Labrooy returned his best Test-match figures as Australia failed to reach 400 for the first time in ten Tests.

Sri Lanka's reply was spirited, although slow. Aravinda de Silva's splendid 167, from 361 deliveries, took 491 minutes and contained seventeen fours as well as a hooked six off Rackemann. His seventh-wicket partnership of 144 in 211 minutes with the injured Ratnayeke, Sri Lanka's best for this wicket, frustrated the Australian bowlers, of whom only Hughes showed any real penetration or guile. de Silva's century was the first by a Sri Lankan batsman against Australia and saw his side to an unexpected first-innings lead of 51. When Australia batted again, Taylor, at 64, became the first player to score 1,000 Test runs in the calendar year of his Test dêbut. His innings of 425 minutes was one of patience and no little skill, containing two sixes and seventeen fours. With Waugh contributing his second half-century of the match, a draw was the only possible result.

Although 160 minutes of play were lost to rain on the first day, the weather was perfect for the other four. Even so, the match attendance, of only 15,461, was the lowest recorded for any Test match in Brisbane.

Man of the Match: P. A. de Silva.

Close of play: First day, Australia 178-2 (T. M. Moody 101*, A. R. Border 54*); Second day, Sri Lanka 81-2 (A. P. Gurusinha 28*, E. A. R. de Silva 1*); Third day, Sri Lanka 275-6 (P. A. de Silva 75*, J. R. Ratnayeke 22*); Fourth day, Australia 94-1 (M. A. Taylor 36*, T. M. Moody 22*).

Australia

D. C. Boon c Samarasekera b Labrooy	0	– (2) lbw b Ramanayake	26
M. A. Taylor c Wickremasinghe b Ramanayake	9	– (1) lbw b Ramanayake	164
T. M. Moody c Wickremasinghe b Labrooy	106	– c A. Ranatunga b E. A. R. de Silva	30
*A. R. Border c A. Ranatunga b Labrooy	56		
D. M. Jones lbw b Labrooy	15	– (4) c Ramanayake b P. A. de Silva	23
S. R. Waugh c A. Ranatunga b Ramanayake	60	– (5) b Gurusinha	57
†I. A. Healy lbw b Gurusinha	21	– (6) not out	26
M. G. Hughes run out	25	– not out	23
G. F. Lawson c Wickremasinghe b Labrooy	22		
C. G. Rackemann not out	5	– (7) b Gurusinha	0
T. M. Alderman c P. A. de Silva b Gurusinha	18		
B 1, l-b 8, n-b 21	30	B 5, l-b 4, n-b 17	26
1/1 2/27 3/185 4/197 5/210 6/247 7/295 8/339 9/339	367	1/60 2/124 3/167 4/316 5/324 6/324	(6 wkts) 375

Bowling: *First Innings*—Ratnayeke 8.5–1–17–0; Labrooy 31.1–5–133–5; Ramanayake 26–2–101–2; A. Ranatunga 13–1–49–0; E. A. R. de Silva 8–1–21–0; Gurusinha 8.3–1–37–2. *Second Innings*—Labrooy 24–4–69–0; Ramanayake 28–3–81–2; E. A. R. de Silva 39–8–112–1; P. A. de Silva 15–2–45–1; Gurusinha 10–3–31–2; A. Ranatunga 6–0–25–0; Mahanama 1–0–3–0.

Sri Lanka

R. S. Mahanama lbw b Alderman	5
D. Ranatunga c Waugh b Lawson	40
A. P. Gurusinha c Healy b Rackemann	43
E. A. R. de Silva b Alderman	22
P. A. de Silva c Lawson b Rackemann	167
*A. Ranatunga lbw b Hughes	25
M. A. R. Samarasekera c Moody b Rackemann	18
J. R. Ratnayeke lbw b Hughes	56
†A. G. D. Wickremasinghe c Boon b Hughes	[illegible]
G. F. Labrooy lbw b Alderman	[illegible]
C. P. H. Ramanayake not out	1[illegible]
L-b 23, w 2, n-b 4	2[illegible]
1/10 2/80 3/114 4/148 5/201 6/238 7/382 8/386 9/391	41[illegible]

Bowling: Alderman 40–13–81–3; Lawson 33–10–51–1; Rackemann 30.3–6–88–3; Hughe[illegible] 39–8–123–3; Moody 16–8–15–0; Border 7–0–36–0; Jones 1–0–1–0.

Umpires: A. R. Crafter and C. D. Timmins.

AUSTRALIA v SRI LANKA

Second Test Match

.t Hobart, December 16, 17, 18, 19, 20. Australia won by 173 runs. Toss: Sri Lanka. Bellerive val, Test cricket's 62nd venue, provided a match of swaying fortunes in a delightful setting n the eastern shores of the Derwent River. A two-year, £1.75 million redevelopment rogramme, conducted by the Tasmanian Cricket Council, had transformed the Clarence 'ricket Club's oval into a ground of Test quality.

Ranatunga asked Australia to bat for the second successive Test, and an hour after tea on ie first day Sri Lanka had dismissed them for 224. Ratnayake bowled splendidly on a pitch 'hich provided assistance for the seam bowlers, his six for 66 being his best figures in his fteen Test matches. Only Sleep, with a three-hour, unbeaten 47, provided any resistance for ustralia. Sri Lanka's reply began disastrously, three wickets falling in a 32-minute spell efore stumps, but the next wicket fell at exactly the halfway mark on the second day, when ravinda de Silva's innings of 75 came to an end. However, his partnership of 128 with lahanama in 190 minutes proved to be the backbone of the visitors' score.

Having gained a first-innings lead of 8 runs, the Australians soon lost Boon and Moody, but ext day Taylor posted his fourth century in his eleventh Test and shared a fourth-wicket artnership of 163 with Border in 187 minutes. The third afternoon and fourth morning howed Australian cricket at its best as Jones and Waugh hammered the Sri Lankan bowling all parts of the ground in an unbroken sixth-wicket stand of 260 in 234 minutes (346 eliveries). Jones's 118 came from 178 balls in 252 minutes, and Waugh's 134 took one ball ss. During Jones's innings, his seventh Test century, he passed 1,000 Test runs for the year, 'hile the total of 513 for five declared was only the seventh time Australia had passed 500 in a econd innings. The Sri Lankan attack held together under the assault.

Needing a nigh-impossible 522 to win, the visiting batsmen none the less made a fine effort bat for ten hours to save the match, Aravinda de Silva leading with way with 72 to cap a ne series. Not until the last four wickets fell for 16 in the final session could Australia be sure f victory. The crowd of 29,122 enjoyed a well-organised Test, although afterwards the Sri ankan captain, Ranatunga, expressed his disappointment at the racial abuse used by certain ustralian players during play.

Man of the Match: P. A. de Silva. *Man of the Series:* P. A. de Silva.

Close of play: First day, Sri Lanka 27-3 (R. S. Mahanama 18*, P. A. de Silva 5*); Second ay, Australia 25-2 (M. A. Taylor 11*, M. G. Hughes 9*); Third day, Australia 387-5). M. Jones 51*, S. R. Waugh 77*); Fourth day, Sri Lanka 166-3 (P. A. de Silva 64*, A. anatunga 25*).

ustralia

). C. Boon c Mahanama b Ratnayake	41	– (2) c Ratnayake b Labrooy	0
1. A. Taylor c Tillekeratne b Ratnayake	23	– (1) c Gurusinha b P. A. de Silva	108
. M. Moody c Gurusinha b Ratnayake	6	– c Tillekeratne b Ratnayake	5
A. R. Border c E. A. R. de Silva b Ratnayeke	24	– (5) b P. A. de Silva	85
). M. Jones c Tillekeratne b Ratnayake	3	– (6) not out	118
. R. Waugh c Tillekeratne b Labrooy	16	– (7) not out	134
. R. Sleep not out	47		
I. A. Healy c Tillekeratne b Gurusinha	17		
1. G. Hughes b E. A. R. de Silva	27	– (4) c Gurusinha b Ratnayake	30
i. D. Campbell c Mahanama b Ratnayake	6		
. M. Alderman b Ratnayake	0		
L-b 7, w 1, n-b 6	14	B 2, l-b 5, w 4, n-b 22	33
'50 2/68 3/83 4/89 5/112 '123 7/166 8/207 9/224	224	1/1 2/10 3/77 4/240 5/253 (5 wkts dec.)	513

Bowling: *First Innings*—Ratnayeke 15–2–39–1; Labrooy 19–3–61–1; Ratnayake).4–2–66–6; Ramanayake 4–0–21–0; Gurusinha 6–0–20–1; E. A. R. de Silva 9–6–10–1. *'econd Innings*—Labrooy 22–3–100–1; Ratnayake 35–5–123–2; Ratnayeke 19–1–86–0; . A. R. de Silva 21–2–83–0; P. A. de Silva 18–1–65–2; Ramanayake 10–0–49–0.

Sri Lanka

R. S. Mahanama c Healy b Sleep	85 – lbw b Campbell	5
D. Ranatunga c Moody b Alderman	2 – c Healy b Hughes	45
A. P. Gurusinha c Taylor b Alderman	0 – c sub (R. J. Tucker) b Hughes	20
E. A. R. de Silva c Border b Campbell	2 – (8) b Campbell	50
P. A. de Silva lbw b Campbell	75 – (4) c Campbell b Sleep	72
*A. Ranatunga c Moody b Sleep	21 – (5) c Jones b Hughes	38
†H. P. Tillekeratne c Taylor b Sleep	0 – (6) c Waugh b Sleep	6
J. R. Ratnayeke c Taylor b Hughes	9 – (7) c Healy b Campbell	75
G. F. Labrooy b Hughes	11 – b Hughes	5
C. P. H. Ramanayake not out	4 – not out	2
R. J. Ratnayake c Border b Hughes	0 – lbw b Hughes	5
L-b 4, n-b 3	7 B 9, l-b 12, n-b 4	25
1/11 2/15 3/18 4/146 5/188 6/192 7/193 8/201 9/216	216 1/6 2/53 3/94 4/187 5/187 6/208 7/332 8/337 9/337	348

Bowling: *First Innings*—Alderman 23–2–71–2; Campbell 23–9–41–2; Hughes 21.4–6–68–3; Sleep 10–4–26–3; Waugh 6–3–6–0. *Second Innings*—Alderman 30–12–48–0; Campbell 33–8–102–3; Sleep 36–16–73–2; Hughes 31.4–8–88–5; Moody 2–0–9–0; Jones 4–2–5–0; Border 5–4–2–0.

Umpires: L. J. King and S. G. Randell.

†At Melbourne, December 22. Victoria won by 109 runs. Toss: Victoria. Victoria 257 for seven (50 overs) (G. M. Watts 111, K. I. W. Wijegunawardene three for 55); Sri Lankans 14[illegible] (42 overs) (A. Ranatunga 45).

†At Hastings, December 23. Victorian Country Cricket League won by three wickets. Toss: Sri Lankans. Sri Lankans 174 (49 overs) (A. G. D. Wickremasinghe 53, R. J. Ratnayake 30, T. Doyle three for 38); Victorian Country Cricket League 176 for seven (49.4 overs) (L. Wu[illegible] 30, R. Bedford 38).

Sri Lanka's matches v Australia and Pakistan in the Benson and Hedges World Series Cup (December 26 – January 4) may be found in that section.

TASMANIA v SRI LANKANS

At Devonport, January 6, 7, 8. Drawn. Toss: Sri Lankans. The injury-hit Sri Lankans suffered on the first afternoon at the hands of Boon, who scored 101 runs in the two hours before tea when Wellham declared. Boon went from 32 at lunch to 133 to become only the second Tasmanian, after A. C. Newton in 1921-22, to score a century in a session. The visitors took up Wellham's challenge and declared after they too had batted for two sessions. A revised second-innings order saw some slowing in the Tasmanian batting, especially following Madurasinghe's three quick wickets late on the second day, and Wellham's eventual declaration left the Sri Lankans 66 overs in which to score 242. Shortly after lunch, with the Sri Lankans making strong inroads into the target, an incident occurred between Aravinda de Silva and the Tasmanian bowler, Tucker. Umpires Clark and Knight separated the pair, and de Silva was charged after the match under the Australian Cricket Board's code of behaviour. He later pleaded guilty and apologised for his actions, but he was not fined. The match faded to a draw following the altercation.

Close of play: First day, Sri Lankans 86-3 (H. P. Tillekeratne 37*, E. A. R. de Silva 7*); Second day, Tasmania 175-6 (G. R. Robertson 17*, D. R. Gilbert 6*).

Tasmania

First innings		Second innings	
R. J. Bennett c E. A. R. de Silva b Ramanayake	9	c Madurasinghe b E. A. R. de Silva	60
G. Shipperd not out	57		
D. C. Boon not out	133	(9) not out	25
†R. E. Soule (did not bat)	–	(2) c Wickremasinghe b Ratnayake	4
J. Cox (did not bat)	–	(3) c Labrooy b Madurasinghe	31
R. J. Tucker (did not bat)	–	(4) b Ramanayake	10
*D. M. Wellham (did not bat)	–	(5) b Madurasinghe	27
G. R. Robertson (did not bat)	–	(6) c Kalpage b Madurasinghe	39
T. J. Cooley (did not bat)	–	(7) lbw b Madurasinghe	10
D. R. Gilbert (did not bat)	–	(8) lbw b Ramanayake	7
G. D. Campbell (did not bat)	–	(10) not out	5
W 4, n-b 7	11	B 6, l-b 4, n-b 10	20
1/18 (1 wkt dec.)	210	1/11 2/61 3/75 4/138 5/138 6/162 7/178 8/216 (8 wkts dec.)	238

Bowling: *First Innings*—Labrooy 9–1–32–0; Ratnayake 12–2–27–0; Ramanayake 11–2–39–1; Kalpage 1–0–6–0; E. A. R. de Silva 13–2–45–0; Madurasinghe 7–0–40–0; Jayasuriya 4–1–13–0; P. A. de Silva 2–1–8–0. *Second Innings*—Ramanayake 25–4–96–2; Ratnayake 9–1–18–1; Tillekeratne 2–0–10–0; Madurasinghe 29–5–80–4; E. A. R. de Silva 13–0–24–1.

Sri Lankans

First innings		Second innings	
M. A. R. Samarasekera c Robertson b Gilbert	3	c Cox b Cooley	11
†A. G. D. Wickremasinghe hit wkt b Gilbert	24	b Gilbert	1
H. P. Tillekeratne b Tucker	74	b Campbell	35
S. T. Jayasuriya c Shipperd b Campbell	2	(8) c Cooley b Robertson	13
E. A. R. de Silva not out	66	lbw b Gilbert	34
C. P. H. Ramanayake c Soule b Tucker	3	(7) not out	16
G. F. Labrooy c Soule b Tucker	0	(9) not out	26
R. S. Kalpage not out	10	(6) c Cooley b Robertson	0
*P. A. de Silva (did not bat)	–	(4) hit wkt b Campbell	39
B 9, l-b 6, n-b 10	25	B 7, l-b 7, w 1, n-b 10	25
1/5 2/61 3/63 4/166 5/172 6/172 (6 wkts dec.)	207	1/14 2/17 3/83 4/121 5/121 6/139 7/156 (7 wkts)	200

A. W. R. Madurasinghe and N. L. K. Ratnayake did not bat.

Bowling: *First Innings*—Gilbert 14–3–52–2; Cooley 11–2–44–0; Campbell 13–3–42–1; Robertson 5–1–6–0; Tucker 9–0–48–3. *Second Innings*—Gilbert 13–1–44–2; Cooley 9–3–45–1; Tucker 8–1–26–0; Campbell 16–4–44–2; Robertson 16–6–27–2.

Umpires: P. T. Clark and B. T. Knight.

†At Adelaide, January 11, 12. Drawn. Toss: Australian Cricket Academy. Sri Lankans 103 (A. W. R. Madurasinghe 35 not out; C. Mack three for 38, B. P. Julian four for 14) and 117 for one (A. P. Gurusinha 66 not out, J. R. Ratnayeke 39 not out); Australian Cricket Academy 348 (M. J. Slater 43, C. White 84, B. P. Julian 32, C. B. Williamson 54, J. M. Williams 39, D. A. Clarke 36; A. W. R. Madurasinghe five for 95, R. S. Kalpage four for 47).

†At Port Lincoln, January 14. Sri Lankans won by 35 runs. Toss: South Australian Country XI. Sri Lankans 170 (49 overs) (R. S. Mahanama 37, C. P. H. Ramanayake 34; S. Fuchs five for 47); South Australian Country XI 135 for nine (50 overs) (D. Jackson 45, J. Mosey 35; A. W. R. Madurasinghe three for 38, S. T. Jayasuriya three for 7).

†At Bendigo, January 17, 18, 19. Drawn. Toss: Australian Country XI. Sri Lankans 234 (M. A. R. Samarasekera 51, A. P. Gurusinha 38, A. Ranatunga 38; E. Nix four for 62) and 175 for nine dec. (M. A. R. Samarasekera 83, A. Ranatunga 54 not out; P. Gerhard three for 42, J. Wrigley three for 51); Australian Country XI 238 for nine dec. (T. Oliver 59, T. Waldron 51 not out; A. W. R. Madurasinghe four for 51) and 100 for five (A. W. R. Madurasinghe three for 24).

†At Coffs Harbour, January 21. New South Wales won by 81 runs. Toss: New South Wales. New South Wales 262 for four (50 overs) (S. M. Small 101, P. A. Emery 31, T. H. Bayliss 97 not out; A. P. Gurusinha three for 38); Sri Lankans 181 (41.4 overs) (M. A. R. Samarasekera 44, A. P. Gurusinha 39, P. A. de Silva 43; G. R. J. Matthews four for 22, M. D. O'Neill three for 36).

†At South Grafton, January 23. Sri Lankans won by three wickets. Toss: New South Wales Country XI. New South Wales Country XI 162 for nine (50 overs) (M. Curry 40; S. T. Jayasuriya four for 36); Sri Lankans 165 for seven (48.1 overs) (H. P. Tillekeratne 46, R. S. Mahanama 44; M. Christie three for 25, J. Frame three for 15).

†At North Rockhampton, January 26, 27. Drawn. Toss: Queensland. Sri Lankans 129 (A. Ranatunga 35; M. S. Kasprowicz five for 29) and 28 for no wkt; Queensland 291 (G. I. Foley 51, P. E. Cantrell 105, S. C. Storey 40; E. A. R. de Silva five for 52).

†At North Rockhampton, January 28. Queensland won by 5 runs. Toss: Queensland. Queensland 195 for seven (49 overs) (G. I. Foley 65, R. B. Kerr 30); Sri Lankans 190 (41 overs) (M. A. R. Samarasekera 36, R. S. Mahanama 67 not out; C. J. McDermott three for 18).

†At Caloundra, January 30. Sri Lankans won by seven wickets. Toss: Sri Lankans. Queensland Country XI 188 for seven (45 overs) (S. Scuderi 44, A. Walsh 44; A. W. R. Madurasinghe three for 32); Sri Lankans 190 for three (35.3 overs) (M. A. R. Samarasekera 75, A. P. Gurusinha 54).

†At Perth, February 2 (day/night). Sri Lankans won by four wickets. Toss: Western Australia. Western Australia 204 for seven (48 overs) (W. S. Andrews 103 not out, T. G. Hogan 33; R. J. Ratnayake three for 37); Sri Lankans 206 for six (46.3 overs) (H. P. Tillekeratne 68, R. S. Mahanama 65).

†At Perth, February 4 (day/night). Western Australia won by 65 runs. Toss: Western Australia. Western Australia 208 for six (48 overs) (M. W. McPhee 68, G. M. Wood 71 not out; E. A. R. de Silva three for 45); Sri Lankans 143 (40.4 overs).

†At Brookton, February 6. Sri Lankans won by 63 runs. Toss: Western Australian Country XI. Sri Lankans 173 (37.1 overs) (P. A. de Silva 96, E. A. R. de Silva 32 not out; R. Menasse three for 53); Western Australian County XI 110 (35.1 overs).

Sri Lanka's matches v Australia and Pakistan in the Benson and Hedges World Series Cup (February 10 – February 18) may be found in that section.

THE PAKISTANIS IN AUSTRALIA, 1989-90

By JOHN WOODCOCK

Pakistan's tour of Australia, comprising three Test matches, three other first-class games and their participation in the triangular World Series Cup, brought them disappointingly little success. Defeat in the first of the three Test matches cost them the series; they lost to Western Australia and Victoria, as well as to the Prime Minister's XI in a one-day game; and they were no match for Australia in the WSC finals.

Although they had had the offer of a full five-Test series, they opted instead for another of their predictable stalemates with India, in Pakistan, before going to Australia just after Christmas. As the two sides were generally considered to be playing for the right to be ranked behind West Indies as the second-strongest Test-playing country, this was a pity. In the three Tests that were played, Australia were emphatically the better side, if not, in theory, the better balanced.

Arriving without two of their established batsmen, Salim Malik and Ramiz Raja, one ill, the other injured, Pakistan were soon further reduced when Abdul Qadir returned home before the Test series started, ostensibly with a damaged finger but at least as much on temperamental grounds. As Qadir had been Pakistan's greatest match-winner of the 1980s, his departure got the touring team off on the wrong foot, though in the event the pitches were better suited to the faster bowlers. Qadir's replacement, Mushtaq Ahmed, was another wrist-spinner, young and highly promising, but without as yet much of a leg-break to go with the googly and top-spinner.

The player of the tour was undoubtedly Wasim Akram, whose brisk and varied left-arm bowling and belligerent left-handed batting soon had him being talked of as the world's best all-rounder. Pakistan's main failing was in their early batting, which left Imran Khan and Javed Miandad with much repair work to do, assisted by Wasim and Ijaz Ahmed, a 21-year-old whose century in the First Test was a brilliant effort. Imran batted exceptionally well. But Pakistan's fielding, especially their catching, was so poor as to give Australia, in this respect, a telling advantage.

For Australia, Terry Alderman, though he missed the Second Test, and Mark Taylor were scarcely less effective than they had been in England a few months earlier. Taylor's dependability contrasted with Pakistan's vain search for someone to anchor their innings. What Australia lacked was variety in their attack, owing to a shortage of good spin bowling. In three of the six Test matches they played during the season, they failed to complete victories which seemed to be there for the taking.

Pakistan were managed by Intikhab Alam, whose popularity was undoubtedly tarnished by an incident in the match against Victoria, when he failed to quell the wholly unreasonable anger of his players after one of Australia's most experienced umpires, Robin Bailhache, had given Mushtaq Ahmed a final warning for following through too straight. When this was ignored, Bailhache notified Ramiz Raja, who was captaining the Pakistanis, that Mushtaq would not be allowed to bowl again in the innings, a ruling which the Pakistanis refused to accept. Having been summoned on to the field, Intikhab then allowed his players to walk off, himself at the head of them. Although a compromise was reached, whereby Mushtaq was allowed to continue bowling, the incident revealed the lack of discipline which has so often prevented Pakistan from making the best use of their natural cricketing ability.

PAKISTANI TOUR RESULTS

Test matches – Played 3: Lost 1, Drawn 2.
First-class matches – Played 6: Lost 3, Drawn 3.
Losses – Australia, Western Australia, Victoria.
Draws – Australia (2), Queensland.
One-day internationals – Played 10: Won 5, Lost 5. *Wins* – Sri Lanka (3), Australia (2). *Losses* – Sri Lanka (1), Australia (4).
Other non first-class match – Lost to Prime Minister's XI.

TEST MATCH AVERAGES

AUSTRALIA – BATTING

	T	*I*	*NO*	*R*	*HI*	*100s*	*Avge*
M. A. Taylor	3	5	1	390	101*	2	97.50
D. M. Jones	3	4	1	247	121*	2	82.33
A. R. Border	3	5	2	134	62*	0	44.66
I. A. Healy	3	4	0	112	48	0	28.00
M. G. Hughes	3	4	2	48	32	0	24.00
G. R. Marsh	2	3	0	67	30	0	22.33
P. L. Taylor	2	2	0	34	33	0	17.00
D. C. Boon	2	4	0	55	29	0	13.75
S. R. Waugh	3	4	0	44	20	0	11.00
T. M. Alderman	2	2	1	1	1*	0	1.00

Played in three Tests: C. G. Rackemann 0*, 0. Played in one Test: G. D. Campbell 0; T. M. Moody 26; P. R. Sleep 23, 0; M. R. J. Veletta 9.

* *Signifies not out.*

BOWLING

	O	*M*	*R*	*W*	*BB*	*5W/i*	*Avge*
T. M. Alderman	86.4	22	200	13	5-65	2	15.38
M. G. Hughes	140	51	357	16	5-111	1	22.31
C. G. Rackemann	139.5	43	257	10	4-40	0	25.70
P. R. Sleep	29	12	70	2	1-6	0	35.00
G. D. Campbell	50.3	7	162	4	3-79	0	40.50
P. L. Taylor	61.5	14	174	2	2-94	0	87.00

Also bowled: A. R. Border 8–0–15–1; S. R. Waugh 3–0–13–1.

PAKISTAN – BATTING

	T	*I*	*NO*	*R*	*HI*	*100s*	*Avge*
Imran Khan	3	5	1	279	136	1	69.75
Wasim Akram	3	5	0	197	123	1	39.40
Javed Miandad	3	5	0	190	65	0	38.00
Ijaz Ahmed	3	5	0	180	121	1	36.00
Salim Yousuf	3	5	0	99	38	0	19.80
Tauseef Ahmed	3	5	2	41	18	0	13.66
Shoaib Mohammad	3	5	0	68	43	0	13.60
Waqar Younis	3	4	1	39	18	0	13.00
Aamer Malik	2	3	0	14	7	0	4.66
Ramiz Raja	2	3	0	11	9	0	3.66

Played in one Test: Aaqib Javed 0, 0; Mansoor Akhtar 5, 14; Mushtaq Ahmed 0, 4; Nadeem Ghauri 0; Salim Malik 11, 65*.

* *Signifies not out.*

BOWLING

	O	*M*	*R*	*W*	*BB*	*5W/i*	*Avge*
Wasim Akram	135.4	37	318	17	6-62	3	18.70
Aaqib Javed	43.1	8	102	3	2-47	0	34.00
Imran Khan	70	16	167	4	2-53	0	41.75
Tauseef Ahmed	89	14	258	5	3-80	0	51.60
Waqar Younis	83	19	224	4	2-66	0	56.00

Also bowled: Ijaz Ahmed 2–0–3–0; Mushtaq Ahmed 48–9–141–1; Nadeem Ghauri 8–1–20–0; Shoaib Mohammad 1–0–7–0.

PAKISTANI AVERAGES – FIRST-CLASS MATCHES

BATTING

	M	*I*	*NO*	*R*	*HI*	*100s*	*Avge*
Javed Miandad	4	7	1	322	77	0	53.66
Imran Khan	4	7	1	320	136	1	53.33
Wasim Akram	3	5	0	197	123	1	39.40
Ijaz Ahmed	6	11	0	349	121	1	31.72
Salim Yousuf	6	11	2	265	78	0	29.44
Saeed Anwar	3	6	0	131	44	0	21.83
Mansoor Akhtar	3	6	0	127	74	0	21.16
Shoaib Mohammad	6	11	0	219	52	0	19.90
Tauseef Ahmed	4	7	2	99	36	0	19.80
Abdul Qadir	2	3	0	51	51	0	17.00
Mushtaq Ahmed	2	4	0	51	32	0	12.75
Aamer Malik	5	9	0	113	53	0	12.55
Waqar Younis	6	9	2	81	23	0	11.57
Nadeem Ghauri	3	5	1	20	19	0	5.00
Ramiz Raja	3	5	0	24	9	0	4.80
Aaqib Javed	4	7	2	10	9*	0	2.00

Played in one match: Maqsood Rana 0, 7; Salim Malik 11, 65*.

* *Signifies not out.*

BOWLING

	O	*M*	*R*	*W*	*BB*	*5W/i*	*Avge*
Wasim Akram	135.4	37	318	17	6-62	3	18.70
Nadeem Ghauri	76	21	194	7	4-59	0	27.71
Tauseef Ahmed	131.5	26	358	10	5-42	1	35.80
Aaqib Javed	121.1	30	327	9	2-47	0	36.33
Mushtaq Ahmed	74	18	212	5	2-17	0	42.40
Waqar Younis	157	26	496	10	3-84	0	49.60
Abdul Qadir	53.2	8	181	3	2-101	0	60.33
Imran Khan	104	22	247	4	2-53	0	61.75

Also bowled: Aamer Malik 14–1–57–2; Ijaz Ahmed 2–0–3–0; Maqsood Rana 15–2–57–2; Saeed Anwar 14.5–1–35–2; Shoaib Mohammad 5–1–26–0.

FIELDING

13 – Salim Yousuf (12 ct, 1 st); 6 – Ijaz Ahmed; 5 – Aamer Malik; 4 – Saeed Anwar; 3 – Shoaib Mohammad, substitutes (Aamer Malik 1, Maqsood Rana 1, Saeed Anwar 1); 2 – Aaqib Javed, Mansoor Akhtar, Mushtaq Ahmed, Wasim Akram; 1 – Abdul Qadir, Imran Khan, Javed Miandad, Maqsood Rana, Nadeem Ghauri, Ramiz Raja.

WESTERN AUSTRALIA v PAKISTANIS

At Perth, December 27, 28, 29. Western Australia won by an innings and 78 runs. Toss: Western Australia. The left-arm swing bowling of Matthews in the first innings and of Capes in the second swept the Pakistanis to defeat with more than a day to spare. They lost their last four wickets in 32 minutes on the third morning, and had it not been for half-centuries from Yousuf and Qadir, they could have been bowled out twice in a day. Matthews, brought into the attack just before noon on the second day, took 72 minutes to run through the first innings. Keeping a full length, he moved the ball into the batsmen and was helped both by the ball which straightened off the pitch and by batsmen who played across the line. The Pakistanis, already without Salim Malik and Ramiz Raja, were weakened further by the decision to rest their captain, Imran Khan, Javed Miandad and Wasim Akram. Matthews took a wicket with his first ball in the second innings but later injured a leg, leaving Capes with the opportunity to return career-best figures of six for 92. On the first day, Moody hit ten fours and a six in his 93 from 108 balls, and Andrews struck Qadir for three fours in an over as he scored 80 in 142 minutes. So slow was the Pakistanis' over-rate that by six o'clock only 78 of the agreed 90 overs had been bowled, and play continued long into the evening.

Close of play: First day, 398-9 (T. G. Hogan 41*, P. A. Capes 7*); Second day, Pakistanis 221-6 (Salim Yousuf 60*, Maqsood Rana 4*).

Western Australia

J. A. Brayshaw c Salim Yousuf b Aaqib Javed	23
M. R. J. Veletta c Salim Yousuf b Abdul Qadir	51
T. M. Moody c Maqsood Rana b Nadeem Ghauri	93
*G. M. Wood c Ijaz Ahmed b Waqar Younis	1
W. S. Andrews c Shoaib Mohammad b Maqsood Rana	80
†T. J. Zoehrer b Maqsood Rana	33
T. G. Hogan not out	41
K. H. MacLeay c Ijaz Ahmed b Nadeem Ghauri	27
R. S. Russell c Saeed Anwar b Nadeem Ghauri	18
C. D. Matthews st Salim Yousuf b Abdul Qadir	1
P. A. Capes not out	7
L-b 9, w 1, n-b 13	23
1/50 2/138 3/145 4/210 5/297 6/305 7/350 8/379 9/380 (9 wkts dec.)	398

Bowling: Aaqib Javed 19–5–50–1; Waqar Younis 15–2–72–1; Maqsood Rana 15–2–57–2; Abdul Qadir 21–2–101–2; Nadeem Ghauri 18–0–94–3; Shoaib Mohammad 2–0–15–0.

Pakistanis

First innings		Second innings	
Aamer Malik c Zoehrer b Matthews	19	– c Veletta b Capes	0
Shoaib Mohammad b Matthews	30	– c sub b Hogan	40
Mansoor Akhtar lbw b Matthews	0	– c Wood b Capes	20
Saeed Anwar c Wood b Russell	0	– c Brayshaw b Capes	11
Ijaz Ahmed lbw b Matthews	3	– lbw b Matthews	27
†Salim Yousuf c Veletta b Russell	18	– c Russell b Capes	78
*Abdul Qadir c MacLeay b Matthews	0	– c Zoehrer b MacLeay	51
Aaqib Javed c Zoehrer b Russell	0	– (11) b Capes	0
Nadeem Ghauri b Matthews	1	– (10) not out	0
Waqar Younis not out	1	– (9) c Zoehrer b MacLeay	3
Maqsood Rana b Matthews	0	– (8) b Capes	7
B 1, l-b 1, w 1	3	L-b 6, n-b 2	8
1/41 2/45 3/46 4/51 5/68 6/68 7/69 8/70 9/74	75	1/0 2/53 3/77 4/79 5/142 6/216 7/234 8/241 9/245	245

Bowling: *First Innings*—Capes 5–2–17–0; MacLeay 6–0–24–0; Matthews 8.3–2–22–7; Russell 7–4–10–3. *Second Innings*—Capes 18–3–92–6; MacLeay 12–7–18–2; Matthews 12.4–1–37–1; Russell 11–2–29–0; Hogan 12–2–54–1; Moody 3–1–7–0; Brayshaw 0.2–0–2–0.

Umpires: G. J. Bibby and T. A. Prue.

Pakistan's matches v Australia and Sri Lanka in the Benson and Hedges World Series Cup (December 31 – January 3) may be found in that section.

QUEENSLAND v PAKISTANIS

At Brisbane, January 6, 7, 8, 9. Drawn. Toss: Queensland. After Queensland had batted for most of the second and third days, the Pakistanis used the final day for batting practice in preparation for the forthcoming Test match. In their first innings, only Javed Miandad of their leading batsmen had played with any kind of fluency. The tourists' bowling also gave cause for concern. Wasim Akram did not play because of a groin strain, and Qadir was withdrawn from the attack on the third morning, ostensibly to prevent further damage to the finger he injured the previous day. Queensland's innings revolved around the 22-year-old left-handed opener, Foley. On his first-class début, and surviving chances at 46 and 83, he reached his maiden hundred in 325 minutes (272 balls) and batted in all for one minute under nine hours, having posted the slowest 150 in Australian first-class cricket. Ritchie's twentieth century, containing a six and eleven fours, provided rather more entertaining fare.

Close of play: First day, Pakistanis 254-8 (Salim Yousuf 34*, Waqar Younis 0*); Second day, Queensland 203-2 (G. I. Foley 101*, G. M. Ritchie 45*); Third day, Pakistanis 8-0 (Aamer Malik 5*, Shoaib Mohammad 3*).

Pakistanis

Aamer Malik c Healy b Polzin	5	– c Ritchie b Polzin	14
Shoaib Mohammad c Foley b Polzin	13	– c Clifford b Polzin	52
Mansoor Akhtar c Healy b Rackemann	14	– b Cantrell	74
Javed Miandad st Healy b Storey	77	– (5) not out	55
Saeed Anwar c Healy b Polzin	28	– (6) c Smart b Carew	25
Ijaz Ahmed c Smart b Storey	44	– (4) c Polzin b Cantrell	35
*Imran Khan c Healy b Carew	20	– c Law b Foley	21
†Salim Yousuf not out	35	– not out	21
Abdul Qadir b Carew	0		
Waqar Younis c Clifford b Polzin	1		
Aaqib Javed c Clifford b Polzin	0		
B 1, l-b 11, n-b 8	20	B 2, l-b 3, n-b 5	10
1/20 2/26 3/57 4/109 5/191 6/192 7/246 8/250 9/257	257	1/28 2/115 3/165 4/194 5/233 6/266	(6 wkts) 307

Bowling: *First Innings*—Polzin 24–8–56–5; Carew 16–5–43–2; Rackemann 21–4–47–1; Storey 17–6–45–2; Cantrell 12–1–40–0; Foley 8–1–14–0. *Second Innings*—Polzin 18–3–60–2; Carew 21–6–65–1; Rackemann 9–2–22–0; Storey 15–4–67–0; Cantrell 14–3–46–2; Foley 10–0–28–1; Law 2–0–13–0; Healy 1–0–1–0.

Queensland

P. E. Cantrell c Abdul Qadir b Waqar Younis	19
G. I. Foley c Salim Yousuf b Aaqib Javed	155
S. G. Law c Imran Khan b Abdul Qadir	30
*G. M. Ritchie c Salim Yousuf b Aamer Malik	123
P. S. Clifford b Aamer Malik	1
C. B. Smart lbw b Aaqib Javed	11
S. C. Storey c Aaqib Javed b Saeed Anwar	54
†I. A. Healy b Saeed Anwar	25
M. A. Polzin not out	0
L-b 12, w 1, n-b 5	18
1/35 2/105 3/330 4/332 5/349 6/356 7/434 8/436	(8 wkts dec.) 436

C. G. Rackemann and P. J. Carew did not bat.

Bowling: Imran Khan 34–6–80–0; Aaqib Javed 34–11–79–2; Waqar Younis 28–4–89–1; Abdul Qadir 32.2–6–80–1; Shoaib Mohammad 2–1–4–0; Aamer Malik 14–1–57–2; Saeed Anwar 14.5–1–35–2.

Umpires: P. D. Parker and C. D. Timmins.

AUSTRALIA v PAKISTAN

First Test Match

At Melbourne, January 12, 13, 14, 15, 16. Australia won by 92 runs. Toss: Pakistan. A match which looked in its earlier stages like being over with ample time to spare was eventually decided with only 22 minutes left on the clock. The playing conditions for the series would have allowed for another over or two to be added at the umpires' discretion, for time-wasting by the batting side (Pakistan) on the last day, and this would almost certainly have happened.

For the first two days, with the ball being well pitched up, the pitch offered the faster bowlers excessive help. But for a straightforward chance going astray, given by Taylor to Miandad at second slip in the fourth over of the match, Australia would have been most unlikely to gain such a vital first-innings lead as 116. In the event, he and Marsh made 90 for Australia's first wicket and batted through half the first day before being separated. In the next day and a half, however, nineteen wickets fell for only 241 runs. Wasim Akram impressed everyone with his pace and movement, achieved off a run of only a dozen paces, and returned his best Test figures. His dismissal of Alderman, as he finished off the Australian innings with a spell of three for 8 in four overs, was his 100th wicket in his 30th Test match. Alderman, Hughes and Rackemann also enjoyed the conditions, and it was not until the pitch lost pace, and the bowlers of both sides began to make the batsmen their target as often as the stumps, that the play changed in character. Towards the end of Pakistan's first innings, Hughes, from round the wicket, bowled five successive bouncers at Tauseef Ahmed without any intervention from the umpire.

Taylor's fifth Test century (322 minutes) in his last eighteen Test innings, and Border's dedicated 62 not out (262 minutes), provided Australia with the runs they needed for a second-innings declaration. It left them with a good ten hours in which to bowl Pakistan out again, and early losses in Pakistan's second innings suggested a quick finish. However, Ijaz Ahmed batted for seven and a half hours for a wonderfully accomplished 121, which was ended only just in time for Australia by a spectacular one-handed catch at cover point by Marsh, diving to his left to hold a full-blooded square-cut.

The fact that six leg-before decisions went Australia's way in Pakistan's second innings, five of them to Alderman, including the last wicket of all (with the batsman on the front foot), brought a good match to a somewhat contentious conclusion. The total attendance was a disappointing 68,865, with a best day of 19,989.

Man of the Match: Wasim Akram.

Close of play: First day, Australia 198-6 (P. R. Sleep 23*, I. A. Healy 33*); Second day, Australia 1-0 (M. A. Taylor 0*, G. R. Marsh 0*); Third day, Australia 260-7 (A. R. Border 51*); Fourth day, Pakistan 159-4 (Ijaz Ahmed 46*, Imran Khan 13*).

Australia

G. R. Marsh c Salim Yousuf b Wasim Akram	30	(2) c Wasim Akram b Aaqib Javed	24
M. A. Taylor c Aaqib Javed b Imran Khan	52	(1) c Aamer Malik b Tauseef Ahmed	101
D. C. Boon lbw b Wasim Akram	0	run out	21
*A. R. Border c Javed Miandad b Wasim Akram	24	not out	62
D. M. Jones c Salim Yousuf b Imran Khan	0	lbw b Wasim Akram	10
S. R. Waugh c Salim Yousuf b Aaqib Javed	20	c Salim Yousuf b Wasim Akram	3
P. R. Sleep lbw b Wasim Akram	23	b Wasim Akram	0
†I. A. Healy c Shoaib Mohammad b Aaqib Javed	48	c Ijaz Ahmed b Wasim Akram	25
M. G. Hughes c Mansoor Akhtar b Wasim Akram	8	c Mansoor Akhtar b Wasim Akram	32
T. M. Alderman c Aamer Malik b Wasim Akram	0	not out	1
C. G. Rackemann not out	0		
L-b 9, n-b 9	18	B 2, l-b 10, w 1, n-b 20	33
1/90 2/90 3/98 4/98 5/131 6/148 7/201 8/223 9/223	223	1/73 2/116 3/204 4/216 5/220 6/220 7/260 8/305 (8 wkts dec.)	312

Bowling: *First Innings*—Imran Khan 18–6–53–2; Wasim Akram 30–9–62–6; Aaqib Javed 22.1–7–47–2; Waqar Younis 12–3–27–0; Tauseef Ahmed 8–1–25–0. *Second Innings*—Wasim Akram 41.4–12–98–5; Imran Khan 8–2–21–0; Aaqib Javed 21–1–55–1; Waqar Younis 22–4–68–0; Tauseef Ahmed 16–3–58–1.

Pakistan

Aamer Malik lbw b Alderman	7	– c Taylor b Hughes	0
Shoaib Mohammad c Healy b Alderman	6	– (3) c Boon b Hughes	10
Mansoor Akhtar c Taylor b Rackemann	5	– (2) lbw b Alderman	14
Javed Miandad c Healy b Alderman	3	– lbw b Waugh	65
Ijaz Ahmed c Taylor b Hughes	19	– c Marsh b Hughes	121
*Imran Khan c Alderman b Rackemann	3	– lbw b Alderman	45
†Salim Yousuf c Taylor b Hughes	16	– lbw b Alderman	38
Wasim Akram c Healy b Hughes	6	– c Taylor b Sleep	6
Tauseef Ahmed not out	9	– not out	14
Waqar Younis lbw b Sleep	18	– lbw b Alderman	4
Aaqib Javed c Healy b Rackemann	0	– lbw b Alderman	0
B 1, l-b 4, n-b 10	15	B 1, l-b 7, w 2, n-b 9	19
1/12 2/20 3/20 4/44 5/44 6/65 7/71 8/71 9/106	107	1/4 2/23 3/31 4/134 5/218 6/291 7/303 8/328 9/333	336

Bowling: *First Innings*—Alderman 19–6–30–3; Rackemann 21.5–8–32–3; Hughes 17–7–34–3; Sleep 8–5–6–1. *Second Innings*—Hughes 42–14–79–3; Rackemann 38–13–67–0; Alderman 33.5–6–105–5; Sleep 21–7–64–1; Waugh 3–0–13–1.

Umpires: R. J. Evans and P. J. McConnell.

AUSTRALIA v PAKISTAN

Second Test Match

At Adelaide, January 19, 20, 21, 22, 23. Drawn. Toss: Pakistan. Pakistan were saved from seemingly imminent defeat, indeed provided with a chance of victory, by a great sixth-wicket second-innings partnership of 191 between Imran Khan and Wasim Akram. It was not the only highlight of an excellent Test match played on a pitch with more life in it than is usual at Adelaide.

Pakistan included in their side three players recently flown in from Karachi – Ramiz Raja and Salim Malik, who had been prevented through injury and illness from being among the original party, and Mushtaq Ahmed, a wrist-spinner. Australia made two changes from the side that won the First Test match, Campbell and Peter Taylor coming in for Alderman (groin strain) and Sleep. Before the start of play on the second day Sir Donald Bradman, looking in good shape in his 82nd year, opened a fine new stand, at the city end, named after him.

After starting with great gusto (91 for one after 22 overs) Pakistan, playing without due care off the back foot, subsided to 187 for six before Wasim made his first contribution towards what was to be a brilliant all-round performance, hitting 52 from 89 balls. He next took five wickets in Australia's first innings, including three in the last over to finish off the innings. Mark Taylor, however, and Jones had ensured Australia a useful lead by then, and when, in their second innings, Pakistan were reduced to 22 for four midway through the third afternoon by an accurately hostile opening spell from Hughes, the match looked to be as good as over. Had Imran not been dropped at short leg off Rackemann, Pakistan would have been 22 for five and virtually beyond recall.

Instead, he and Miandad stayed together for nearly three hours, and then Imran and Wasim each played the innings of his life, Imran's being a model of responsibility and orthodoxy, Wasim's a comparatively carefree exhibition of flair and fine driving. Imran batted for 485 minutes, Wasim for 244 minutes, and no-one else in the match hit the ball with anything like the same power as Wasim. There were eighteen fours and a six in his maiden Test hundred, while Imran hit ten fours.

With Salim Malik catching the mood, despite batting with a broken finger, Imran was able to make a challenging declaration 40 minutes into the last day, leaving Australia 304 to win in a minimum of 78 overs. Except while Mark Taylor and Jones were going well together after lunch, Australia, already one up in the series, always had an eye on the draw. This they achieved without too many alarms. The decisive moment came at 137 for four, when Jones survived a difficult return chance to Mushtaq. Using his feet well to the Pakistani spinners, Jones went on to become the first Australian to score two hundreds in an Adelaide Test match since Arthur Morris in 1946-47, and his unbeaten 121 contained a six and eleven fours. Until now his best score in eight Test innings against Pakistan had been 21 not out. Marsh, who broke his thumb catching Ijaz Ahmed on the first day, did not bat in the second innings.

Man of the Match: Wasim Akram.

Close of play: First day, Australia 10-0 (G. R. Marsh 6*, M. A. Taylor 3*); Second day, Australia 259-5 (D. M. Jones 67*, P. L. Taylor 14*); Third day, Pakistan 73-4 (Imran Khan 43*, Javed Miandad 16*); Fourth day, Pakistan 357-7 (Salim Malik 46*, Tauseef Ahmed 11*).

Pakistan

First innings		Second innings	
Shoaib Mohammad lbw b Hughes	43	– c Healy b Hughes	0
Ramiz Raja c P. L. Taylor b Campbell	9	– c Waugh b Hughes	2
†Salim Yousuf lbw b Rackemann	38	– c M. A. Taylor b Hughes	1
Javed Miandad c Healy b Campbell	52	– (6) c P. L. Taylor b Hughes	21
Ijaz Ahmed c Marsh b Border	28	– (4) c P. L. Taylor b Hughes	4
Salim Malik c Healy b Hughes	11	– (8) not out	65
*Imran Khan c Healy b Rackemann	13	– (5) b P. L. Taylor	136
Wasim Akram c Border b Campbell	52	– (7) b Campbell	123
Tauseef Ahmed c Healy b Rackemann	0	– c Healy b Rackemann	18
Mushtaq Ahmed c Healy b Rackemann	0	– b P. L. Taylor	4
Waqar Younis not out	1		
B 4, l-b 4, w 1, n-b 1	10	B 4, l-b 5, w 1, n-b 3	13
1/27 2/91 3/95 4/166 5/187 6/187 7/241 8/251 9/251	257	1/0 2/2 3/7 4/22 5/90 6/281 7/316 8/380 9/387 (9 wkts dec.)	387

Bowling: *First Innings*—Hughes 18–5–63–2; Campbell 21.3–2–79–3; P. L. Taylor 12–0–57–0; Rackemann 21–3–40–4; Border 4–0–10–1. *Second Innings*—Hughes 32–9–111–5; Campbell 29–5–83–1; Rackemann 37–11–85–1; P. L. Taylor 41.5–13–94–2; Border 4–0–5–0.

Australia

First innings		Second innings	
G. R. Marsh c Salim Yousuf b Wasim Akram	13		
M. A. Taylor lbw b Imran Khan	77	– (1) c sub (Saeed Anwar) b Mushtaq Ahmed	59
D. C. Boon lbw b Wasim Akram	29	– (2) c Ramiz Raja b Wasim Akram	5
*A. R. Border b Waqar Younis	13	– (3) c Salim Yousuf b Waqar Younis	8
D. M. Jones c Wasim Akram b Imran Khan	116	– (4) not out	121
S. R. Waugh lbw b Wasim Akram	17	– (5) b Tauseef Ahmed	4
†I. A. Healy c sub (Maqsood Rana) b Waqar Younis	12	– (6) c sub (Aamer Malik) b Tauseef Ahmed	27
P. L. Taylor run out	33	– (7) c Shoaib Mohammad b Tauseef Ahmed	1
M. G. Hughes not out	6	– (8) not out	2
G. D. Campbell lbw b Wasim Akram	0		
C. G. Rackemann b Wasim Akram	0		
L-b 12, n-b 13	25	L-b 3, n-b 3	6
1/82 2/113 3/156 4/188 5/216 6/328 7/328 8/341 9/341	341	1/9 2/33 3/106 4/129 5/213 6/229 (6 wkts)	233

In the first innings, G. R. Marsh, when 6, retired hurt at 10 and resumed at 328-6.

Bowling: *First Innings*—Wasim Akram 43–10–100–5; Waqar Younis 26–4–66–2; Mushtaq Ahmed 23–4–69–0; Imran Khan 27–6–61–2; Tauseef Ahmed 14–1–33–0. *Second Innings*—Wasim Akram 11–3–29–1; Waqar Younis 14–4–42–1; Tauseef Ahmed 32–6–80–3; Mushtaq Ahmed 25–5–72–1; Shoaib Mohammad 1–0–7–0.

Umpires: A. R. Crafter and L. J. King.

VICTORIA v PAKISTANIS

At Melbourne, January 26, 27, 28, 29. Victoria won by 59 runs. Toss: Victoria. Victoria's victory, with more than three hours to spare, was overshadowed by the shameful incident on the first day which threatened to end the match there and then. It occurred when umpire Bailhache, having twice warned the Pakistani leg-spinner, Mushtaq Ahmed, for following through on the pitch in contravention of Law 42.11 – and having notified his captain, Ramiz Raja, of the warnings – directed Ramiz to take Mushtaq off when he continued to transgress. The Pakistani players refused to accept the umpire's ruling and were supported by their manager, Intikhab Alam, who came on to the ground and then accompanied his players from it. Eventually, so that the match could continue, a compromise was reached, based on Ramiz's contention that he had been unaware of the final warning. Victoria were well served by their left-handed opener, Watts, who followed his first-innings century with 70 in two and a half hours on the third day as Victoria sought to build a winning position on a pitch already taking turn. They lost their last eight second-innings wickets for 63 in seventeen overs after tea. The Pakistanis, with more than a day in which to score 254 to win, lost two wickets cheaply before the close and on the final day could never get the better of the leg-spin of McIntyre, playing in his first full season for the state.

Close of play: First day, Victoria 247-5 (S. P. O'Donnell 60*, A. I. C. Dodemaide 14*); Second day, Pakistanis 177-6 (Mushtaq Ahmed 27*, Tauseef Ahmed 11*); Third day, Pakistanis 23-2 (Tauseef Ahmed 4*, Ramiz Raja 3*).

Victoria

First innings		Second innings	
G. M. Watts lbw b Waqar Younis	102	c Ijaz Ahmed b Tauseef Ahmed	70
S. S. Prescott c Saeed Anwar b Nadeem Ghauri	10	b Waqar Younis	2
W. N. Phillips c Saeed Anwar b Mushtaq Ahmed	4	b Tauseef Ahmed	16
J. D. Siddons c Nadeem Ghauri b Mushtaq Ahmed	17	not out	22
W. G. Ayres b Nadeem Ghauri	24	lbw b Aaqib Javed	9
*S. P. O'Donnell c Ijaz Ahmed b Waqar Younis	69	(7) lbw b Tauseef Ahmed	16
A. I. C. Dodemaide c Aamer Malik b Nadeem Ghauri	16	(8) c Mushtaq Ahmed b Tauseef Ahmed	15
P. R. Reiffel not out	18	(9) c Aamer Malik b Mushtaq Ahmed	0
†M. G. D Dimattina lbw b Waqar Younis	0	(6) c Salim Yousuf b Aaqib Javed	1
D. W. Fleming c Salim Yousuf b Nadeem Ghauri	11	c Ijaz Ahmed b Mushtaq Ahmed	0
P. E. McIntyre c Mushtaq Ahmed b Aaqib Javed	20	c Saeed Anwar b Tauseef Ahmed	6
B 12, l-b 3, n-b 7	22	B 3, l-b 10, n-b 3	16
1/51 2/56 3/91 4/142 5/218 6/257 7/259 8/259 9/280	313	1/21 2/67 3/110 4/113 5/119 6/134 7/141 8/149 9/167	173

In the second innings J. D. Siddons, when 7, retired hurt at 96 and resumed at 149.

Bowling: *First Innings*—Waqar Younis 25–1–84–3; Aaqib Javed 11–3–43–1; Nadeem Ghauri 40–16–59–4; Tauseef Ahmed 24–5–58–0; Mushtaq Ahmed 21–7–54–2. *Second Innings*—Waqar Younis 6–0–27–1; Aaqib Javed 14–3–53–2; Nadeem Ghauri 10–4–21–0; Tauseef Ahmed 18.5–7–42–5; Mushtaq Ahmed 5–2–17–2.

Pakistanis

First innings		Second innings	
*Ramiz Raja c Dimattina b Reiffel	4	(4) c O'Donnell b Reiffel	9
Shoaib Mohammad c Siddons b Reiffel	9	lbw b Fleming	7
†Aamer Malik c Fleming b Reiffel	53	(1) c sub b Reiffel	8
Ijaz Ahmed lbw b Dodemaide	36	(5) c Reiffel b McIntyre	24
Salim Yousuf c Siddons b Reiffel	3	(7) c and b McIntyre	11
Saeed Anwar c Dimattina b Dodemaide	23	c Prescott b O'Donnell	44
Mushtaq Ahmed c Prescott b Dodemaide	32	(8) c Dodemaide b McIntyre	15
Tauseef Ahmed c Prescott b Fleming	36	(3) b McIntyre	22
Waqar Younis b Fleming	23	c Ayres b McIntyre	14
Nadeem Ghauri c Siddons b Fleming	0	c O'Donnell b Dodemaide	19
Aaqib Javed not out	1	not out	9
L-b 6, n-b 7	13	L-b 4, n-b 8	12
1/5 2/36 3/108 4/111 5/114 6/144 7/184 8/224 9/224	233	1/12 2/16 3/31 4/68 5/120 6/133 7/136 8/151 9/174	194

Bowling: *First Innings*—Reiffel 20–5–62–4; Fleming 17.4–4–63–3; O'Donnell 6–0–23–0; McIntyre 12–4–31–0; Dodemaide 19–6–48–3. *Second Innings*—Reiffel 18–4–79–2; Fleming 7–3–21–1; McIntyre 22–7–53–5; O'Donnell 10–2–33–1; Dodemaide 1.5–1–4–1.

Umpires: R. C. Bailhache and W. P. Sheahan.

†At Canberra, January 31. Prime Minister's XI won by 81 runs. Toss: Prime Minister's XI. Prime Minister's XI 266 for eight (50 overs) (J. Cox 66, M. R. J. Veletta 50, M. G. Bevan 74); Pakistanis 185 for seven (50 overs) (Shoaib Mohammad 33, Salim Yousuf 54 not out). Only T. J. Zoehrer, the wicket-keeper, did not bowl in the Pakistanis' innings.

AUSTRALIA v PAKISTAN

Third Test Match

At Sydney, February 3, 4, 5, 6, 7, 8. Drawn. Toss: Australia. What had promised to be another good match was ruined by rain. After the first two days had been washed out an extra day was added, at the request of the New South Wales Cricket Association (the home authority), in the hope of making up the time already lost; but in Sydney's wettest week for more than 100 years (16½ inches of rain fell between the morning of the eve of the match and lunch-time on what should have been the second day) there was little play of any consequence. Australia had Alderman back in place of Campbell, while Marsh and Boon, both injured, were replaced by Veletta and Moody. Pakistan preferred their orthodox left-arm spinner, Nadeem Ghauri, to Mushtaq Ahmed, and Aamer Malik returned for the injured Salim Malik. Altogether there were eleven hours twenty minutes of play, distributed between the third, fourth and sixth days.

The chance to field first gave Australia the initiative on a pitch which had never previously been played on, the whole square and much of the ground having been relaid since the end of the football season. The faster bowlers were soon in their element, none more than Alderman, whose swing took any amount of watching. Batting always with extreme caution, as though they thought the pitch might go to pieces and so render something in the region of 200 a winning total, Pakistan took seven hours to make 199. Miandad took almost four hours for his 49, and Imran, playing another particularly stoical innings, batted for four and threequarter hours.

In the end, though, the loss of the fifth day to rain meant that by the sixth and last day, which Australia spent at the crease, the play was of merely academic interest. Taylor made his sixth hundred for Australia (258 minutes, eight fours), all within a period of nine months. A total attendance for the match of 13,864, for the series of 133,309, and for the season's six Test matches of 206,646, represented a disconcertingly low return.

Man of the Match: T. M. Alderman. *Man of the Series*: Wasim Akram.

Close of play: First day, No play; Second day, No play; Third day, Pakistan 110-5 (Imran Khan 27*, Wasim Akram 4*); Fourth day, Australia 0-0 (M. A. Taylor 0*, M. R. J. Veletta 0*); Fifth day, No play.

Pakistan

Aamer Malik c Healy b Alderman	7
Ramiz Raja c and b Hughes	0
Shoaib Mohammad lbw b Alderman	9
Javed Miandad c Jones b Hughes	49
Ijaz Ahmed c M. A. Taylor b Rackemann	8
*Imran Khan not out	82
Wasim Akram c M. A. Taylor b Alderman	10
†Salim Yousuf c Jones b Rackemann	6
Tauseef Ahmed b Alderman	0
Waqar Younis c Veletta b Hughes	16
Nadeem Ghauri b Alderman	0
B 1, l-b 7, n-b 4	12
1/2 2/15 3/20 4/51 5/106 6/128 7/154 8/160 9/191	199

Bowling: Alderman 33.5–10–65–5; Hughes 31–16–70–3; Rackemann 22–8–33–2; P. L. Taylor 8–1–23–0.

Australia

M. A. Taylor not out 101	*A. R. Border not out 27
M. R. J. Veletta lbw b Waqar Younis . 9	B 4, l-b 5, n-b 4 13
T. M. Moody c Aamer Malik b Tauseef Ahmed . 26	
	1/33 2/106 (2 wkts) 176

D. M. Jones, S. R. Waugh, †I. A. Healy, P. L. Taylor, M. G. Hughes, C. G. Rackemann and T. M. Alderman did not bat.

Bowling: Wasim Akram 10–3–29–0; Imran Khan 17–2–32–0; Tauseef Ahmed 19–3–62–1; Nadeem Ghauri 8–1–20–0; Waqar Younis 9–4–21–1; Ijaz Ahmed 2–0–3–0.

Umpires: A. R. Crafter and P. J. McConnell.

Pakistan's matches v Australia and Sri Lanka in the Benson and Hedges World Series Cup (February 10 – February 25) may be found in that section.

PAKISTAN v WEST INDIES, 1990-91

The series was drawn, with Pakistan winning the first Test by eight wickets, West Indies taking the second by seven wickets in three days, and the third being drawn. When at Faisalabad Waqar Younis took his 50th Test wicket in only his tenth Test, he had reached that landmark faster than any other Pakistani, having needed one match fewer than Khan Mohammad in the 1950s. In the First Test, the fourth-wicket stand of 174 between Shoaib Mohammad and Salim Malik was a record for Pakistan against West Indies.

First Test: At Karachi, November 15, 16, 17, 19, 20. Pakistan won by eight wickets. West Indies 261 (D. L. Haynes 117; Wasim Akram three for 61, Waqar Younis five for 76) and 181 (D. L. Haynes 47, A. L. Logie 58 not out; Wasim Akram three for 39, Waqar Younis four for 44); Pakistan 345 (Shoaib Mohammad 86, Salim Malik 102, Imran Khan 73 not out, Extras 48; C. E. L. Ambrose four for 78, I. R. Bishop three for 81) and 98 for two (Shoaib Mohammad 32 not out, Salim Malik 30 not out).

Second Test: At Faisalabad, November 23, 24, 25. West Indies won by seven wickets. Pakistan 170 (Zahid Fazal 32, Salim Malik 74; I. R. Bishop four for 47) and 154 (Salim Malik 71, Moin Khan 32; M. D. Marshall four for 24); West Indies 195 (R. B. Richardson 44, Extras 39; Wasim Akram three for 63, Waqar Younis five for 46) and 130 for three (R. B. Richardson 70 not out, C. L. Hooper 33 not out; Wasim Akram three for 46).

Third Test: At Lahore, December 6, 7, 8, 10, 11. Drawn. West Indies 294 (B. C. Lara 44, C. L. Hooper 134, Extras 30; Wasim Akram four for 61) and 173 (C. L. Hooper 49, A. L. Logie 59; Wasim Akram five for 28); Pakistan 122 (Wasim Akram 38; C. E. L. Ambrose five for 35, I. R. Bishop five for 41) and 242 for six (Ramiz Raja 41, Shoaib Mohammad 49, Masood Anwar 37, Imran Khan 58 not out).

Full details of the West Indians' tour of Pakistan will appear in the 1992 edition of Wisden.

THE INDIANS IN NEW ZEALAND, 1989-90

By DICK BRITTENDEN

India sent a team tender in years, although not necessarily in experience, to New Zealand for their fourth tour there. Kapil Dev was the only player over 30, and eight were under 25. When Navjot Sidhu was injured in the First Test, his replacement, Dilip Vengsarkar, became the senior member of the side. In addition to Vengsarkar, the Indians had omitted Ravi Shastri, Krish Srikkanth and Arshad Ayub from the original touring party, to the surprise of many in New Zealand.

The cricket manager, Bishan Bedi, said that the Indians proposed to play positive and entertaining cricket. They were, indeed, a highly attractive side, but their commendably positive approach cost them the First Test when too many airy, imaginative shots were played. With the Napier Test ruined by the rain, and the Auckland one ending in an honourable draw, New Zealand extended their run of home series without defeat to eleven years. India's new captain, Mohammad Azharuddin, by far the best of their batsmen in style and in run-scoring, was among those who felt a desperate need to demolish the New Zealand attack in the Christchurch Test. He made 48 and 30, but all the evidence was that he should have batted a lot longer. He played brilliantly at Auckland, where for the second time in his career he narrowly missed the opportunity of scoring a Test double-century.

All the principal batsmen had their successes in New Zealand, although Sanjay Manjrekar had a disappointing series, considering his Test average of 60.30 before the tour began. Wookeri Raman, a left-handed opener, was impressive in defence, while sixteen-year-old Sachin Tendulkar batted with the poise of a player twice his age. At Napier, 80 not out overnight, he seemed destined to become the youngest batsman to score a Test century, but he added only 8 more runs next morning. Kiran More, the vice-captain, gave plenty of vocal encouragement to the leg-spinner, Narendra Hirwani, from his position as wicket-keeper, and he showed what a valuable batsman he was late in the order.

Hirwani, although bowling tidily, found the New Zealand pitches not to his liking. Atul Wassan bowled medium-fast to good effect, and played a whirlwind innings at Auckland. Kapil Dev, however, failed to fire with bat or ball, and the best all-rounder in the side was Manoj Prabhakar. He bowled tightly, without a lot of luck, and when required to open the innings after Sidhu's injury, he scored 234 runs in four innings.

At the end of the Test matches, the Indians competed in a triangular one-day series, with New Zealand and Australia. For so youthful a side, gracious and popular, they did reasonably well in strange conditions. But if neither in the Tests nor in the one-day internationals was the best seen of this side, as tourists they were a delight for their opponents, for administrators and for the public. Not only did they play cricket with zest; as a side they were well disciplined, on the field and beyond it. At the slightest show of dissent – and this happened only once or twice – Azharuddin was quick to soothe the bowler or the fieldsman concerned. The whole tour was a triumph.

John Wright, the New Zealand captain, scored two centuries in the Tests, Andrew Jones, Martin Crowe and Ian Smith one each. Wright, forsaking his usual stance with the bat held at the horizontal, adopted a more natural style which was an immediate success. His hundred at Napier was his ninth in Tests. At Auckland, Smith played one of the most remarkable of New Zealand Test innings. New Zealand, 78 for five at lunch on the first day, were 131 for seven when Smith came in. In 128 balls, he scored an extraordinary 169 runs before the close of play, passing the previous highest score by a No. 9 batsman in Test cricket and equalling another Test record by plundering 24 in an over by Wassan.

When Richard Hadlee bowled Manjrekar in the second innings at Christchurch, he had his 400th Test wicket, a landmark achieved after three injury-ridden seasons. He was presented, on the ground, with 400 roses by a local admirer, and Bedi also came out to congratulate him. Over the series, however, Danny Morrison was the star bowler, taking five wickets in an innings in each of the Tests. While still occasionally wayward, he bowled with genuine pace and New Zealand were looking to him to be their leading strike bowler in the years to come.

INDIAN TOUR RESULTS

Test matches – Played 3: Lost 1, Drawn 2.
First-class matches – Played 6: Won 1, Lost 1, Drawn 4.
Win – NZCC President's XI.
Loss – New Zealand.
Draws – New Zealand (2), Otago, Northern Districts.
One-day internationals – Played 4: Won 1, Lost 3. *Win* – New Zealand. *Losses* – Australia (2), New Zealand.

TEST MATCH AVERAGES

NEW ZEALAND – BATTING

	T	*I*	*NO*	*R*	*HI*	*100s*	*Avge*
J. G. Wright	3	4	1	375	185	2	125.00
A. H. Jones	3	4	2	245	170*	1	122.50
I. D. S. Smith	3	2	0	182	173	1	91.00
R. J. Hadlee	3	2	0	115	87	0	57.50
M. D. Crowe	3	3	0	161	113	1	53.66
K. R. Rutherford	3	3	0	97	69	0	32.33
M. J. Greatbatch	3	3	0	93	46	0	31.00
T. J. Franklin	3	4	0	76	50	0	19.00
M. C. Snedden	3	3	1	26	22	0	13.00

Played in three Tests: D. K. Morrison 1*, 1*, 0*. Played in two Tests: J. G. Bracewell 0. Played in one Test: S. A. Thomson 22, 43*.

* *Signifies not out.*

BOWLING

	O	M	R	W	BB	5W/i	Avge
R. J. Hadlee	105.5	24	319	12	4-69	0	26.58
D. K. Morrison	110	14	446	16	5-75	3	27.87
M. C. Snedden	117.5	24	322	6	2-20	0	53.66
J. G. Bracewell	45	5	109	2	2-45	0	54.50
S. A. Thomson	27.3	4	122	2	2-92	0	61.00

Also bowled: M. J. Greatbatch 1–1–0–0. A. H. Jones 9–1–28–0; K. R. Rutherford 17–0–59–0.

INDIA – BATTING

	T	I	NO	R	HI	100s	Avge
M. Azharuddin	3	4	0	303	192	1	75.75
M. Prabhakar	3	5	1	235	95	0	58.75
W. V. Raman	3	5	1	176	96	0	44.00
K. S. More	3	4	0	135	73	0	33.75
S. R. Tendulkar	3	4	0	117	88	0	29.25
S. L. V. Raju	2	3	1	55	31	0	27.50
A. S. Wassan	3	4	1	79	53	0	26.33
D. B. Vengsarkar	2	2	0	47	47	0	23.50
S. V. Manjrekar	3	4	0	67	42	0	16.75
Kapil Dev	3	4	0	55	25	0	13.75
N. D. Hirwani	3	4	3	2	1*	0	2.00

Played in one Test: Gursharan Singh 18; N. S. Sidhu 51.

** Signifies not out.*

BOWLING

	O	M	R	W	BB	5W/i	Avge
S. L. V. Raju	46	16	113	3	3-86	0	37.66
A. S. Wassan	81.4	11	331	7	4-108	0	47.28
N. D. Hirwani	110	28	309	6	3-143	0	51.50
Kapil Dev	102.5	18	305	5	3-89	0	61.00
M. Prabhakar	119.1	20	382	5	3-123	0	76.40

Also bowled: W. V. Raman 19–10–23–0.

INDIAN AVERAGES – FIRST-CLASS MATCHES

BATTING

	M	I	NO	R	HI	100s	Avge
K. S. More	5	8	4	301	73	0	75.25
Gursharan Singh	3	5	1	274	115	1	68.50
M. Azharuddin	5	8	0	505	192	2	63.12
W. V. Raman	5	9	1	460	123	1	57.50
Ajay Sharma	2	4	1	160	87	0	53.33
M. Prabhakar	4	7	1	260	95	0	43.33
N. S. Sidhu	2	3	0	104	51	0	34.66
V. B. Chandrasekhar	3	6	0	204	92	0	34.00
S. R. Tendulkar	5	8	1	211	88	0	30.14

	M	*I*	*NO*	*R*	*HI*	*100s*	*Avge*
S. V. Manjrekar	5	8	0	240	82	0	30.00
A. S. Wassan	5	5	2	90	53	0	30.00
S. L. V. Raju	5	7	2	122	52*	0	24.40
Kapil Dev	5	7	0	101	25	0	14.42
D. B. Vengsarkar	3	4	0	52	47	0	13.00
V. Razdan	2	2	0	18	18	0	9.00
N. D. Hirwani	5	7	4	15	11	0	5.00

Played in two matches: M. Venkataramana 7.

* *Signifies not out.*

BOWLING

	O	*M*	*R*	*W*	*BB*	*5W/i*	*Avge*
N. D. Hirwani	192	55	480	15	4-31	0	32.00
S. L. V. Raju	211	64	496	13	3-72	0	38.15
A. S. Wassan	167.4	25	601	15	4-108	0	40.06
M. Prabhakar	154.2	28	493	12	4-87	0	41.08
Kapil Dev	148.5	35	398	7	3-89	0	56.85
M. Venkataramana	74.1	12	289	4	2-29	0	72.25

Also bowled: K. S. More 1–0–7–0; W. V. Raman 23–10–44–0; V. Razdan 60–10–227–1; Ajay Sharma 24–6–79–1; S. R. Tendulkar 9–2–23–0.

FIELDING

14 – K. S. More (13 ct, 1 st); 6 – V. B. Chandrasekhar; 3 – Gursharan Singh, M. Prabhakar, W. V. Raman; 2 – M. Azharuddin, Kapil Dev, S. L. V. Raju, M. Venkataramana; 1 – N. D. Hirwani, S. V. Manjrekar, substitute (V. Razdan), S. R. Tendulkar, A. S. Wassan.

NZCC PRESIDENT'S XI v INDIANS

At New Plymouth, January 22, 23, 24, 25. Indians won by 195 runs. Toss: Indians. The Indians made an impressive start, on the most picturesque of New Zealand grounds, scoring 512 off only 119 overs. Chandrasekhar and Manjrekar made light of the bowling in the top order, and Azharuddin, in total command, played delightfully, hitting a six and 25 fours in his 159. Through Rutherford, Bradburn – the son of a former Test player, W. P. Bradburn – and Larsen, the President's XI came within 34 runs of the follow-on figure, before declaring on the understanding that they would not be asked to bat again immediately. As it happened, they were batting before the close, needing 369 to win after bowling the Indians out for 185. A middle-order collapse cost the touring team four wickets in the space of 6 runs. On the final day Prabhakar accounted for the home team's openers, and again only Rutherford, hitting six fours on his way to 30, and Bradburn made much of it. Prabhakar and Hirwani bowled well on a good, placid pitch to start the Indians' tour with a convincing win.

Close of play: First day, Indians 431-6 (Kapil Dev 25*, K. S. More 1*); Second day, NZCC President's XI 214-4 (G. E. Bradburn 62*, G. R. Larsen 41*); Third day, NZCC President's XI 9-0 (K. A. Wealleans 0*, D. J. White 1*).

Indians

V. B. Chandrasekhar c Thomson b Larsen	92	– b Thomson	3
N. S. Sidhu c White b Thomson	23	– c Parore b Snedden	30
S. V. Manjrekar c Parore b Thomson	80	– (4) c Rutherford b Larsen	11
*M. Azharuddin c Bradburn b Thomson	159	– (7) run out	24
S. R. Tendulkar c Richardson b Millmow	13	– (3) c Douglas b Richardson	47
M. Prabhakar c Douglas b Millmow	24	– (5) c Wealleans b Richardson	1
Kapil Dev c Rutherford b Millmow	25	– (6) c Snedden b Richardson	0
†K. S. More not out	45	– not out	59
S. L. V. Raju c Parore b Millmow	3	– c Parore b Thomson	9
V. Razdan c Snedden b Millmow	18	– c Bradburn b Thomson	0
N. D. Hirwani c Rutherford b Thomson	11	– c and b Bradburn	0
B 4, l-b 11, n-b 4	19	L-b 1	1
1/77 2/150 3/268 4/298 5/394 6/430 7/432 8/436 9/475	512	1/23 2/59 3/87 4/88 5/92 6/93 7/143 8/172 9/172	185

Bowling: *First Innings*—Millmow 27–3–127–5; Thomson 29–6–108–4; Rutherford 3–0–29–0; Snedden 12–2–46–0; Larsen 19–6–53–1; Richardson 16–0–61–0; Bradburn 13–1–73–0. *Second Innings*—Millmow 5–0–15–0; Thomson 13–0–56–3; Snedden 8–3–12–1; Larsen 15–3–45–1; Richardson 11–2–47–3; Bradburn 5.5–1–9–1.

NZCC President's XI

K. A. Wealleans lbw b Prabhakar	0	– (2) lbw b Prabhakar	9
D. J. White run out	20	– (1) b Prabhakar	6
K. R. Rutherford c Manjrekar b Kapil Dev	54	– c More b Razdan	30
M. W. Douglas c More b Raju	30	– (5) lbw b Raju	6
G. E. Bradburn c More b Prabhakar	74	– (4) c More b Raju	42
G. R. Larsen lbw b Prabhakar	43	– c Chandrasekhar b Hirwani	26
S. A. Thomson c Azharuddin b Kapil Dev	24	– c Kapil Dev b Hirwani	4
†A. C. Parore c Prabhakar b Hirwani	22	– c Chandrasekhar b Hirwani	4
*M. C. Snedden c More b Prabhakar	16	– b Hirwani	0
M. H. Richardson not out	29	– c More b Prabhakar	18
J. P. Millmow not out	4	– not out	15
L-b 7, n-b 6	13	B 7, l-b 6	13
1/2 2/59 3/93 4/150 5/225 6/234 7/280 8/280 9/319	(9 wkts dec.) 329	1/23 2/24 3/74 4/102 5/103 6/110 7/126 8/126 9/141	173

Bowling: *First Innings*—Kapil Dev 20–6–48–2; Prabhakar 23–4–87–4; Razdan 13–2–76–0; Raju 27–11–68–1; Hirwani 28–12–43–1. *Second Innings*—Prabhakar 12.1–4–24–3; Kapil Dev 8–5–9–0; Razdan 7–0–37–1; Raju 20–5–59–2; Hirwani 17–5–31–4.

Umpires: R. L. McHarg and S. J. Woodward.

OTAGO v INDIANS

At Dunedin, January 27, 28, 29, 30. Drawn. Toss: Otago. Although the third day was almost completely washed out, the match contained plenty of runs and much excitement before ending with India nine wickets down and requiring 5 more runs to win. The first day was dominated by Rutherford, who hit his eighteenth hundred in first-class cricket and was 173 not out at the close. Quick-footed, he drove superbly against the spinners, and in the course of the day he hit 25 fours, off 252 balls. He received sound support from Blair and Mawhinney, who had a particularly good match. Next day Rutherford went on to 226 not out, Mawhinney to 68, but Otago's declaration left the Indians with time to be 274 for three overnight, with Raman and Gursharan Singh compiling attractive centuries. Having lost all but 3.3 overs of the third day, the Indians declared before the start of the final day, and eventually Otago left them with 56 overs to score 261. Chandrasekhar and Sharma, whose 70 came off 88 balls, threatened to win the game themselves, but when Azharuddin went cheaply to the slow-medium left-arm bowling of Mawhinney, there was something of a collapse, occasioned in part by Otago's brilliance in the field. Hirwani survived an lbw appeal off the last ball of the match.

Close of play: First day, Otago 333-4 (K. R. Rutherford 173*, R. E. W. Mawhinney 48*); Second day, Indians 274-3 (Gursharan Singh 115*, S. R. Tendulkar 4*); Third day, Indians 277-4 (S. R. Tendulkar 4*, Ajay Sharma 2*).

Otago

	First innings		Second innings	
P. W. Dobbs c Venkataramana b Wassan	11	–	c Raman b Venkataramana	38
B. Z. Harris lbw b Hirwani	23	–	c Azharuddin b Wassan	3
K. J. Burns c Chandrasekhar b Hirwani	12	–	lbw b Wassan	0
*K. R. Rutherford not out	226	–	c Chandrasekhar b Wassan	0
B. R. Blair c Raju b Hirwani	43	–	c sub b Raju	47
R. E. W. Mawhinney c Raman b Hirwani	68	–	not out	5
†S. A. Robinson not out	18			
P. W. Hills (did not bat)		–	(7) c Raman b Venkataramana	7
B 3, l-b 12, n-b 10	25		B 8, l-b 1, n-b 2	11
1/30 2/59 3/64 4/208 5/374 (5 wkts dec.)	426		1/9 2/9 3/10 4/84 5/100 6/111 (6 wkts dec.)	111

V. F. Johnson, D. J. Hunter and J. K. Lindsay did not bat.

Bowling: *First Innings*—Wassan 28–6–105–1; Kapil Dev 11–2–30–0; Tendulkar 5–0–13–0; Hirwani 37–10–97–4; Raju 34–9–76–0; Venkataramana 18.2–1–71–0; A. Sharma 3–0–19–0. *Second Innings*—Wassan 11–1–25–3; Kapil Dev 7–4–6–0; Tendulkar 4–2–10–0; Venkataramana 8.5–2–29–2; Raju 8–2–25–1; Raman 1–0–7–0.

Indians

	First innings		Second innings	
†V. B. Chandrasekhar b Hunter	3	–	(2) c Dobbs b Johnson	71
W. V. Raman c Robinson b Hunter	123	–	(1) lbw b Hunter	22
Gursharan Singh b Mawhinney	115	–	(7) run out	10
*M. Azharuddin c sub b Lindsay	17	–	(6) c Dobbs b Mawhinney	2
S. R. Tendulkar not out	4	–	(3) b Johnson	30
Ajay Sharma not out	2	–	(4) c Dobbs b Hills	70
Kapil Dev (did not bat)		–	(5) c Hunter b Mawhinney	21
M. Venkataramana (did not bat)		–	(8) c Dobbs b Hills	7
A. S. Wassan (did not bat)		–	(9) not out	11
N. D. Hirwani (did not bat)		–	(11) not out	2
S. L. V. Raju (did not bat)		–	(10) b Mawhinney	3
N-b 13	13		B 1, n-b 6	7
1/17 2/223 3/269 4/274 (4 wkts dec.)	277		1/43 2/110 3/141 4/196 5/199 6/217 7/236 8/240 9/253 (9 wkts)	256

Bowling: *First Innings*—Hills 14–1–68–0; Hunter 15–1–66–2; Johnson 22.3–3–74–0; Mawhinney 9–3–10–1; Lindsay 15–1–59–1. *Second Innings*—Hills 9–2–27–2; Johnson 16–0–77–2; Hunter 10–1–63–1; Lindsay 4–0–19–0; Mawhinney 17–2–69–3.

Umpires: B. L. Aldridge and R. S. Dunne.

NEW ZEALAND v INDIA

First Test Match

At Christchurch, February 2, 3, 4, 5. New Zealand won by ten wickets. Toss: New Zealand. A painstaking century by Wright put New Zealand on their way. Yet on the first morning, when the pitch had a touch of green to help the seam bowlers, Prabhakar in particular beat the New Zealand captain with deliveries which swung away late from the left-hander. Even as the pitch eased in the afternoon Prabhakar persisted, and his figures bore no testimony to his skill. Wright took all day to score an unbeaten 127, his century coming in almost five hours off 242 balls, but he had a confident partner in Jones, who drove handsomely during their second-wicket partnership of 105. Crowe was acquisitive, helping add 51, and Greatbatch, having survived three chances before the close, accompanied Wright in a partnership of 125, New Zealand's best for the fourth wicket against India, as the home side made measured progress on the second day. Wright had been batting for nine and a quarter hours (443 balls) and was well past his previous highest score in Tests when he was fifth out, providing a second wicket for the slow left-armer, Raju. Playing in his first Test, Raju bowled accurately and effectively.

By stumps, India had lost three wickets to Hadlee, among them that of Azharuddin, who made 31 off the first 21 balls he faced. Superb driving, and lithe wrists in his leg-side shots, brought him six fours. He was in only 48 minutes (44 balls) for his 48, and even the most partisan spectator was loath to see him go.

India started the third day in a frenzy, scoring 34 in seven overs. Hadlee was hit out of the attack, but when Morrison took over at Hadlee's end and bowled with the wind behind him, he stole the show. In six overs he took five for 16, and India collapsed dismally from 146 for three to be all out for 164. It was during this fiercely competitive spell of fast bowling that Morrison put Sidhu out of the tour with a wrist injury. Raju, who had been sent in as night-watchman, was last out after 155 minutes of stern battle. The lead, 295, was New Zealand's third largest, and India were asked to follow on.

After lunch, as Raman and Prabhakar put on 80 for the first wicket, the match bore an air of normality. Then, with Hadlee in his second spell, Manjrekar secured a place in history when he dragged an inside edge on to his stumps and became Hadlee's 400th Test victim. Azharuddin played another delightful innings, but again it was too brief. He was bowled recklessly attempting to hit Bracewell out of the ground. Raman earned his best Test score of 96, batting for five and a half hours, but although there were also acts of defiance from Kapil Dev, Raju and Wassan, New Zealand won with a day to spare.

Man of the Match: J. G. Wright.

Close of play: First day, New Zealand 255-3 (J. G. Wright 127*, M. J. Greatbatch 21*); Second day, India 97-3 (N. S. Sidhu 27*, S. L. V. Raju 7*); Third day, India 210-5 (W. V. Raman 85*, Kapil Dev 4*).

New Zealand

*J. G. Wright b Raju	185		
T. J. Franklin c Prabhakar b Kapil Dev	20		
A. H. Jones c Raju b Hirwani	52		
M. D. Crowe lbw b Raju	24		
M. J. Greatbatch b Wassan	46		
K. R. Rutherford b Kapil Dev	69		
J. G. Bracewell b Hirwani	0		
†I. D. S. Smith lbw b Raju	9		
R. J. Hadlee c Hirwani b Prabhakar	28		
M. C. Snedden lbw b Kapil Dev	3	(1) not out	1
D. K. Morrison not out	1	(2) not out	1
B 3, l-b 12, n-b 7	22		
1/26 2/131 3/182 4/307 5/374 6/375 7/394 8/448 9/454	459	(no wkt)	2

Bowling: *First Innings*—Kapil Dev 28.3–4–89–3; Prabhakar 38–8–114–1; Wassan 25–3–95–1; Raju 35–12–86–3; Hirwani 29–9–60–2. *Second Innings*—Prabhakar 0.5–0–2–0.

India

W. V. Raman lbw b Hadlee	0	c Jones b Morrison	96
N. S. Sidhu lbw b Morrison	51	absent injured	
S. V. Manjrekar c Jones b Hadlee	5	b Hadlee	4
*M. Azharuddin lbw b Hadlee	48	b Bracewell	30
S. L. V. Raju c Crowe b Snedden	31	(8) c Smith b Snedden	21
S. R. Tendulkar c Smith b Morrison	0	c Smith b Bracewell	24
M. Prabhakar c Smith b Snedden	1	(2) b Snedden	40
Kapil Dev c Snedden b Morrison	4	(7) lbw b Hadlee	25
†K. S. More c Smith b Morrison	1	(5) b Hadlee	11
A. S. Wassan c Smith b Morrison	2	(9) not out	24
N. D. Hirwani not out	1	(10) c Bracewell b Hadlee	0
B 5, l-b 5, n-b 10	20	B 6, l-b 2, n-b 13	21
1/0 2/27 3/88 4/146 5/146 6/148 7/153 8/158 9/161	164	1/80 2/85 3/135 4/160 5/206 6/242 7/254 8/289 9/296	296

Bowling: *First Innings*—Hadlee 14–1–45–3; Morrison 16–2–75–5; Snedden 12.5–4–20–2; Bracewell 3–0–14–0. *Second Innings*—Hadlee 22.5–3–69–4; Morrison 19–0–94–1; Snedden 25–5–59–2; Rutherford 5–0–21–0; Bracewell 20–3–45–2.

Umpires: R. S. Dunne and S. J. Woodward.

NEW ZEALAND v INDIA

Second Test Match

At Napier, February 9, 10, 11, 12, 13. Drawn. Toss: India. The match was ruined by rain. No play was possible on the first day because of a drenched outfield, and on the second, which started an hour late and finished early because of bad light, only 52 overs were bowled. When the fifth day was abandoned after rain spread under the covers, the game simply slipped into obscurity.

Raman fell to Hadlee without scoring, as he had in the First Test, but Prabhakar and Manjrekar added 92, at 30 runs an hour. On the third day Prabhakar, strong off his legs but hitting only four boundaries in his vigilant innings, carried through to 95, his best Test score. He was out to a doubtful decision. Azharuddin was shackled by the slow pace of the completely grassless pitch and took 90 minutes for his 33; Vengsarkar was out second ball. Tendulkar, however, made the match his own. He looked considerably older than his sixteen years as, with strong driving and deft placements, he reached 80 by the close, off 258 balls. With the perky More, he had added 128 for an Indian seventh-wicket record against New Zealand. More hit eleven fours, distinctly under par for the course, in his best Test score of 73. Tendulkar began the fourth day with the prospect of becoming the youngest Test century-maker. But after a four off Morrison and an all-run four from a superb drive in the next over, he went to the well of Morrison's bowling once too often and offered a straightforward catch to mid-off. When India declared soon afterwards, Morrison, all aggression on a heartless pitch, had again captured five wickets.

Wright and Franklin were studies in concentration in the early stages of their opening partnership, which produced 149 runs, a record for New Zealand against India. Although Franklin hit a lovely straight-driven six off Hirwani, the leg-spinner was in control, conceding only 21 runs from his first fifteen overs. It took New Zealand almost three hours to reach 100, but then Wright took charge. Off the next two Hirwani overs he scored 19, his three fours and a six a welcome light in the Napier gloom. Wright took 172 minutes and 130 balls to score his first 50, but he reached his century in another 75 minutes and 60 balls.

Man of the Match: J. G. Wright.

Close of play: First day, No play; Second day, India 126-2 (M. Prabhakar 54*, M. Azharuddin 19*); Third day, India 348-7 (S. R. Tendulkar 80*, S. L. V. Raju 2*); Fourth day, New Zealand 178-1 (J. G. Wright 113*, A. H. Jones 4*).

India

W. V. Raman lbw b Hadlee	0
M. Prabhakar c Smith b Hadlee	95
S. V. Manjrekar c Smith b Morrison	42
*M. Azharuddin b Morrison	33
D. B. Vengsarkar c Smith b Morrison	0
S. R. Tendulkar c Wright b Morrison	88
Kapil Dev lbw b Hadlee	4
†K. S. More c Franklin b Snedden	73
S. L. V. Raju not out	3
A. S. Wassan b Morrison	0
N. D. Hirwani not out	1
L-b 5, n-b 14	19
1/0 2/92 3/150 4/152 5/210 6/218 7/346 8/356 9/356	(9 wkts dec.) 358

Bowling: Hadlee 35–11–73–3; Morrison 38–8–98–5; Snedden 42–10–104–1; Bracewell 22–2–50–0; Rutherford 9–0–28–0.

New Zealand

T. J. Franklin c Kapil Dev b Wassan	50
*J. G. Wright not out	113
A. H. Jones not out	4
B 5, l-b 3, w 1, n-b 2	11
1/149	(1 wkt) 178

M. D. Crowe, M. J. Greatbatch, K. R. Rutherford, R. J. Hadlee, †I. D. S. Smith, J. G. Bracewell, M. C. Snedden and D. K. Morrison did not bat.

Bowling: Prabhakar 13–3–25–0; Kapil Dev 14–4–30–0; Wassan 15–2–48–1; Hirwani 18–7–40–0; Raju 11–4–27–0.

Umpires: B. L. Aldridge and S. J. Woodward.

NORTHERN DISTRICTS v INDIANS

At Hamilton, February 16, 17, 18, 19. Drawn. Toss: Northern Districts. On a slow, low pitch, only 24 wickets fell over the four days while 1,322 runs were scored. Most of the batsmen profited, a notable exception being Vengsarkar, who was out for 1 and 4. Wealleans, yet to reach his 21st birthday, scored the only century of the match and followed it with 61 in the second innings. He must have gone close to winning a place in the New Zealand team to England. His opening partner, White, on the verge of New Zealand selection for several years, made 55 and 58, and they had century opening stands in both innings. The Indians sportingly declared after the second day with a 16-run lead, and on the fourth they were required to make 346 to win in a minimum of 72 overs. An utterly demoralising match for bowlers was called off with half the mandatory twenty overs still to be bowled.

Close of play: First day, Northern Districts 286-5 (G. E. Bradburn 67*, B. A. Young 0*); Second day, Indians 356-6 (K. S. More 53*, S. L. V. Raju 52*); Third day, Northern Districts 306-6 (B. A. Young 44*, D. A. Beard 1*).

Northern Districts

K. A. Wealleans c More b A. Sharma	101	– c Chandrasekhar b Raju	61
D. J. White b Raju	55	– c and b Venkataramana	58
*C. M. Kuggeleijn c Chandrasekhar b Raju	24	– c Gursharan b Raju	58
G. E. Bradburn st More b Raju	80	– b Raju	16
G. W. McKenzie c More b Wassan	26	– lbw b Wassan	50
M. D. Bailey lbw b Wassan	2	– lbw b Venkataramana	9
†B. A. Young not out	22	– not out	80
D. A. Beard not out	16	– lbw b Wassan	13
B. P. Bracewell (did not bat)		– not out	2
B 1, l-b 8, n-b 5	14	B 5, l-b 8, w 1	14
1/109 2/162 3/237 4/282 5/284 6/309 (6 wkts dec.)	340	1/111 2/145 3/192 4/195 5/217 6/305 7/341 (7 wkts dec.)	361

S. B. Doull and P. S. Neutze did not bat.

Bowling: *First Innings*—Wassan 24–3–72–2; Razdan 22–5–53–0; Raju 41–11–83–3; Venkataramana 16–3–65–0; Raman 3–0–14–0; A. Sharma 17–6–44–1. *Second Innings*—Wassan 23–4–68–2; Razdan 18–3–61–0; Venkataramana 31–6–124–2; Raju 35–10–72–3; A. Sharma 4–0–16–0; More 1–0–7–0.

Indians

V. B. Chandrasekhar c Neutze b Bracewell	17	– (2) run out	18
W. V. Raman lbw b Doull	51	– (1) b Beard	88
Gursharan Singh st Young b Bradburn	80	– (5) not out	51
D. B. Vengsarkar c Young b Doull	1	– c Young b Bracewell	4
Ajay Sharma c McKenzie b Bradburn	87	– (6) c Bradburn b Beard	1
S. V. Manjrekar c McKenzie b Bradburn	0	– (3) c Young b Bracewell	82
*†K. S. More not out	53	– (7) not out	9
S. L. V. Raju not out	52		
B 7, l-b 5, n-b 3	15	B 5, l-b 4, n-b 3	12
1/26 2/102 3/114 4/233 5/233 6/258 (6 wkts dec.)	356	1/60 2/190 3/194 4/201 5/205 (5 wkts)	265

A. S. Wassan, V. Razdan and M. Venkataramana did not bat.

Bowling: *First Innings*—Doull 8–3–32–2; Bracewell 12–1–38–1; Beard 14–1–64–0; Neutze 20–4–59–0; Kuggeleijn 11–1–34–0; Bailey 4–0–22–0; Bradburn 24–2–95–3. *Second Innings*—Beard 13–4–43–2; Bracewell 15–2–46–2; Bradburn 18–2–64–0; Kuggeleijn 13–4–34–0; Neutze 16–3–69–0.

Umpires: J. A. Holland and L. F. Jones.

NEW ZEALAND v INDIA

Third Test Match

At Auckland, February 22, 23, 24, 25, 26. Drawn. Toss: India. The first four days provided the best entertainment for many years in a Test match in New Zealand, with the opening day producing the most dramatic turn-round in the home team's fortunes. Glad to be in the field, India's bowlers made the most of the humid conditions and the lateral movement off the pitch, which seemed like a lawn bowling green after the one at Napier. At lunch New Zealand were five wickets down for 78, most falling to catches behind the wicket, and when Rutherford was out soon after the resumption, New Zealand were in all sorts of trouble. However, Thomson, on his Test début, and Hadlee met fire with fire, adding 46 in 36 minutes, and as the pitch lost its early life, New Zealand staged a remarkable recovery. With Hadlee at his most assertive, hitting his 87 from 108 balls, Smith was virtually a passenger as he contributed 38 to their eight-wicket partnership of 103 in 23 overs, a New Zealand record against India.

But after Hadlee had departed, 1 run short of his 3,000 Test aggregate, Smith was definitely the driver, finishing with 169 not out at the close of play off 128 balls. With Snedden he set a New Zealand ninth-wicket record against all countries, putting on 136, of which the junior partner scored 22. Most of Smith's early runs came from hooks, pulls and on-drives but, true to character, he later played a full measure of cuts, and strokes into the covers. He went to 50 off 56 balls, 100 off 95 and 150 off 118, and by the day's end he had hit three sixes and 23 fours. In taking 24 off an over from Wassan (244266), he equalled the Test record for runs off a six-ball over shared by A. M. E. Roberts, S. M. Patil and I. T. Botham. Smith's eventual 173, off 136 balls, was the highest score by a New Zealander at Eden Park, the highest by a New Zealand wicket-keeper, and the highest by anyone batting at No. 9 in a Test, beating C. Hill's 160 for Australia against England in 1907-08. The savagery of the attack by Hadlee and Smith had the Indian attack reeling. Wassan had taken three for 23 on the first morning; his nine overs in the afternoon cost 85 runs, and New Zealand scored 309 in the last two sessions.

India in reply lost an early wicket, but there was the dour Prabhakar, and Vengsarkar showed the first glimpse of form since reaching New Zealand. He was there while 144 were added for the fourth wicket, but no-one could doubt who the senior partner was. Azharuddin was masterly, treating the New Zealand seam bowlers – and there were no others – with polite contempt. He stroked the ball silkily and with educated wrists, and there was no stopping the eighteen boundaries he hit during the day, many of them coming from fluent drives. He reached his century from 144 balls and next day, in perfect batting conditions, he went on to 192 before being last out. More, making 50 from 58 balls, helped him put on 88 in 84 minutes; Wassan carried the attack further, facing 58 balls also in scoring 53 as he and his captain added 86. The run-rate was staggering. Before lunch, 148 came in the two hours, and the first five overs of the new ball cost New Zealand 50 runs. India finished with their highest total in New Zealand and a lead of 91.

After Franklin had gone quickly, Wright and Jones had the utmost difficulty in keeping out the eager Indian bowling. They survived so well, though, that New Zealand were ahead without further loss by the close of play. But on the fourth day, from a full quota of 90 overs, New Zealand scored just 281 runs, a reminder that this was a Test match. Wright became the first New Zealander to make 4,000 Test runs, Crowe, who had promised a century in every home series, delivered, and Jones and Crowe were associated in a third-wicket partnership of 179. India bowled with such purpose that only 79 runs were scored in the morning, and Raman finished the day with his nineteen overs having cost just 23 runs. The final day was a sad anticlimax. Rain in the morning cost 45 minutes' play, and New Zealand declared shortly before lunch with the addition of 67 to their overnight lead of 325. Jones remained unbeaten with his highest Test score, his 170 in 634 minutes being the longest innings by a New Zealanders in a major home match.

Wright defended his action in declaring so late – India needed 393 at 6.14 an over – by saying that the Indians had scored 4.6 runs an over in the first innings and that New Zealand's only hope of winning in perfect batting conditions was for India's batsmen to self-destruct in a frantic effort to get the runs. Bedi agreed. "If we were one up, I wouldn't have declared. It wasn't a festival game, it was a Test match."

Man of the Match: I. D. S. Smith.

Close of play: First day, New Zealand 387-9 (I. D. S. Smith 169*, D. K. Morrison 0*); Second day, India 316-7 (M. Azharuddin 130*, K. S. More 6*); Third day, New Zealand 135-1 (J. G. Wright 58*, A. H. Jones 62*); Fourth day, New Zealand 416-5 (A. H. Jones 144*, S. A. Thomson 8*).

New Zealand

First innings		Second innings	
T. J. Franklin c Tendulkar b Wassan	4	lbw b Prabhakar	2
*J. G. Wright c Gursharan b Kapil Dev	3	c Wassan b Hirwani	74
A. H. Jones c More b Prabhakar	19	not out	170
M. D. Crowe c More b Wassan	24	lbw b Hirwani	113
M. J. Greatbatch b Wassan	4	c Gursharan b Wassan	43
K. R. Rutherford c Prabhakar b Wassan	20	c More b Hirwani	8
S. A. Thomson c More b Kapil Dev	22	not out	43
R. J. Hadlee b Hirwani	87		
†I. D. S. Smith lbw b Prabhakar	173		
M. C. Snedden c More b Prabhakar	22		
D. K. Morrison not out	0		
L-b 9, n-b 4	13	B 4, l-b 14, n-b 12	30
	391	(5 wkts dec.)	483
1/8 2/29 3/29 4/51 5/64 6/85 7/131 8/234 9/370		1/7 2/155 3/334 4/396 5/406	

Bowling: *First Innings*—Kapil Dev 29.2–6–85–2; Prabhakar 29.2–3–123–3; Wassan 16.4–1–108–4; Hirwani 17–1–66–1. *Second Innings*—Kapil Dev 31–4–101–0; Prabhakar 38–6–118–1; Wassan 25–5–80–1; Hirwani 46–11–143–3; Raman 19–10–23–0.

India

First innings		Second innings	
W. V. Raman c Franklin b Hadlee	8	not out	72
M. Prabhakar lbw b Snedden	36	not out	63
S. V. Manjrekar b Morrison	16		
D. B. Vengsarkar c Smith b Morrison	47		
*M. Azharuddin c Rutherford b Thomson	192		
S. R. Tendulkar c Smith b Morrison	5		
Gursharan Singh c and b Thomson	18		
Kapil Dev c Jones b Hadlee	22		
†K. S. More lbw b Morrison	50		
A. S. Wassan b Morrison	53		
N. D. Hirwani not out	0		
B 1, l-b 11, w 1, n-b 22	35	L-b 9, n-b 5	14
	482	(no wkt)	149
1/15 2/65 3/71 4/215 5/223 6/263 7/308 8/396 9/482			

Bowling: *First Innings*—Hadlee 30–8–123–2; Morrison 30–3–145–5; Snedden 26–4–110–1; Thomson 18.3–3–92–2. *Second Innings*—Hadlee 4–1–9–0; Morrison 7–1–34–0; Snedden 12–1–29–0; Thomson 9–1–30–0; Jones 9–1–28–0; Rutherford 3–0–10–0; Greatbatch 1–1–0–0.

Umpires: B. L. Aldridge and R. S. Dunne.

ROTHMANS CUP TRIANGULAR SERIES

†NEW ZEALAND v INDIA

At Dunedin, March 1. New Zealand won by 108 runs. Toss: India. Early rain reduced th game to 47 overs a side. New Zealand, put in on a pitch of low bounce, might have struggled but Crowe and Rutherford added 152, a New Zealand record for the fourth wicket in one-da internationals. Crowe was full of confidence and Rutherford played a particularly entertainin innings, scoring 78 not out from 75 balls, with five fours and a six. India made a depressin start, due primarily to Morrison, and never recovered. Thomson took three wickets a minimal cost.

Man of the Match: M. D. Crowe.

New Zealand

*J. G. Wright c Kapil Dev b Wassan	23	S. A. Thomson b Prabhakar	3
M. D. Crowe b Prabhakar	104		
A. H. Jones lbw b Wassan	0	B 5, l-b 10, w 5, n-b 1	21
M. J. Greatbatch c A. Sharma b Wassan	13		
K. R. Rutherford not out	78	1/38 2/38 3/66 (6 wkts, 47 overs)	246
†I. D. S. Smith b Kapil Dev	4	4/218 5/233 6/246	

G. R. Larsen, M. C. Snedden, D. K. Morrison and S. J. Roberts did not bat.

Bowling: Kapil Dev 9–0–49–1; Prabhakar 10–1–49–2; Wassan 10–0–45–3; Raju 9–0–38–0; A. Sharma 9–0–50–0.

India

W. V. Raman c Wright b Snedden	32	†K. S. More not out	23
V. B. Chandrasekhar c Smith b Morrison	4	A. S. Wassan b Morrison	16
D. B. Vengsarkar lbw b Morrison	2	S. L. V. Raju run out	4
*M. Azharuddin c Greatbatch b Thomson	12	B 4, l-b 4, w 7, n-b 1	16
S. R. Tendulkar c and b Thomson	0		
Ajay Sharma b Thomson	3	1/19 2/33 3/57 (32.1 overs)	138
Kapil Dev c Smith b Larsen	12	4/57 5/65 6/65	
M. Prabhakar run out	14	7/91 8/97 9/128	

Bowling: Morrison 8.1–2–43–3; Roberts 4–0–26–0; Thomson 6–1–19–3; Snedden 8–1–28–1; Larsen 6–1–14–1.

Umpires: B. L. Aldridge and R. S. Dunne.

†AUSTRALIA v INDIA

At Christchurch, March 3. Australia won by 18 runs. Toss: Australia. India should have won this match. With well-disciplined bowling, and giving their best exhibition of the summer in the field, they restricted Australia to 187 on a pitch of low bounce which helped the seam bowlers. Border's 37 from 49 balls was to prove the highest innings of the match. The loss of the first three Indian wickets for 23 seemed to signal an Australian victory, but Vengsarkar and Azharuddin added 52 for the fourth wicket and put their side ahead of the run-rate. When India were six down for 154, with ample overs in hand, they should have gone on to win comfortably. Instead, in what was almost a reprise of the Christchurch Test, their batsmen threw their wickets away. There were still five overs to be bowled when the match ended.

Man of the Match: T. M. Alderman.

Australia

D. C. Boon run out	22	G. D. Campbell c More b Kapil Dev	0
M. A. Taylor st More b Hirwani	10	C. G. Rackemann c Kapil Dev b Prabhakar	6
D. M. Jones c Manjrekar b Hirwani	32		
*A. R. Border run out	37	L-b 8, w 4, n-b 3	15
S. R. Waugh c Manjrekar b Kapil Dev	10		
S. P. O'Donnell lbw b A. Sharma	12	1/31 2/51 3/92 (9 wkts, 50 overs)	187
†I. A. Healy run out	25	4/119 5/123 6/140	
P. L. Taylor not out	18	7/170 8/172 9/187	

T. M. Alderman did not bat.

Bowling: Kapil Dev 10–0–29–2; Prabhakar 10–3–35–1; Wassan 10–0–36–0; Hirwani 10–2–39–2; A. Sharma 10–0–40–1.

India

V. B. Chandrasekhar c Waugh b Alderman . 8
W. V. Raman c M. A. Taylor b Alderman . 2
S. V. Manjrekar c Healy b Rackemann . 6
D. B. Vengsarkar c Jones b Campbell . 35
*M. Azharuddin c Alderman b P. L. Taylor . 26
Ajay Sharma lbw b O'Donnell 15
Kapil Dev c Jones b Alderman 27
M. Prabhakar c Waugh b Rackemann . 2
†K. S. More c Campbell b Alderman . .
A. S. Wassan b Alderman . . . .
N. D. Hirwani not out . . . .

B 4, l-b 2, w 3, n-b 7 1

1/5 2/14 3/23 4/75 5/98 6/110 7/154 8/155 9/167 (45 overs) 16

Bowling: Alderman 10–2–32–5; Rackemann 9–0–27–2; Campbell 8–0–29–1; O'Donne 8–0–36–1; P. L. Taylor 10–2–39–1.

Umpires: B. L. Aldridge and R. L. McHarg.

†NEW ZEALAND v AUSTRALIA

At Christchurch, March 4. Australia won by 150 runs. Toss: Australia. New Zealand suffere their largest defeat by runs in a one-day international after their last eight wickets fell for 1 runs in 55 balls. A crowd approaching 20,000 saw Jones and Boon put on 145 in 119 minute for Australia's second wicket, a stand marked by the power of their strokes and by their swif instinctive running between the wickets. Boon took 72 balls to reach 50; Jones was at tha mark from 87 balls, but needed only 53 more to complete his century. Between them they hi thirteen of the fourteen fours in the Australian innings. New Zealand in reply were 79 for tw in the seventeenth over. But O'Donnell, mostly with in-swingers, captured five wickets fo 5 runs from his last 28 balls and Campbell claimed three, for just 1 run, from his last eleven Crowe learned of his promotion to captain within half an hour of the start when Wrigh reluctantly pulled out because of influenza.

Man of the Match: D. M. Jones.

Australia

D. C. Boon c Crowe b Larsen 67
G. R. Marsh c Smith b Hadlee 2
D. M. Jones b Hadlee 107
S. R. Waugh run out 3
*A. R. Border c Bracewell b Snedden . . 6
S. P. O'Donnell c Jones b Snedden 20
†I. A. Healy b Snedden 6
P. L. Taylor not out 6
G. D. Campbell b Morrison . . . .
C. G. Rackemann not out . . . .

L-b 17, w 3, n-b 3 2

1/3 2/148 3/153 4/190 5/214 6/229 7/233 8/240 (8 wkts, 50 overs) 24

T. M. Alderman did not bat.

Bowling: Hadlee 10–1–43–2; Morrison 9–0–51–1; Snedden 10–2–32–3; Thomson 8–0–49–0 Larsen 10–0–32–1; Bracewell 3–0–20–0.

New Zealand

*M. D. Crowe c Waugh b Rackemann . 17
A. H. Jones c Border b Campbell 43
M. J. Greatbatch c Healy b Rackemann 0
K. R. Rutherford lbw b O'Donnell 20
S. A. Thomson b O'Donnell 1
G. R. Larsen b O'Donnell 1
†I. D. S. Smith c Border b Campbell . . 3
R. J. Hadlee b Campbell 2
J. G. Bracewell b O'Donnell . . . .
M. C. Snedden c Jones b O'Donnell . . .
D. K. Morrison not out . . . .

L-b 3, w 3, n-b 1 . . . .

1/39 2/39 3/79 4/81 5/87 6/91 7/92 8/93 9/94 (25.2 overs) 9

Bowling: Alderman 7–1–34–0; Rackemann 6–2–27–2; Campbell 6.2–2–17–3; O'Donnel 6–0–13–5.

Umpires: B. L. Aldridge and R. L. McHarg.

†NEW ZEALAND v INDIA

At Wellington, March 6. India won by 1 run. Toss: India. The match was reduced by rain to 49 overs a side. On a murky morning, and batting first in a typical Wellington wind, India profited from a fluent partnership between Prabhakar and Manjrekar, which provided 58 for the second wicket. Azharuddin produced his usual magic, Tendulkar contributed 36 from 39 balls, and Kapil Dev, who had not batted well throughout the tour, was at his best in hitting 46 from 38 deliveries. New Zealand made a laboured start, but Greatbatch and Rutherford put on 80 for the fourth wicket at a rate which argued that New Zealand would win at a canter. The ensuing collapse, however, left Hadlee trying to win the game single-handed. So well did he counter-attack that New Zealand needed 11 runs to win from the last over, with two wickets in hand. Hadlee hit 4, 2, 2, but Snedden was run out off the fourth ball, which produced a single. Kapil Dev then bowled the perfect yorker as Hadlee tried to hit the winning runs.

Man of the Match: Kapil Dev.

India

W. V. Raman run out	0
M. Prabhakar c M. D. Crowe b Morrison	36
S. V. Manjrekar run out	36
D. B. Vengsarkar lbw b Morrison	0
*M. Azharuddin run out	29
S. R. Tendulkar c Smith b Thomson	36
Kapil Dev c Rutherford b Morrison	46
†K. S. More c Rutherford b Thomson	2
Ajay Sharma c Smith b Hadlee	12
A. S. Wassan not out	4
N. D. Hirwani c M. D. Crowe b Hadlee	0
L-b 13, w 7	20
1/8 2/66 3/66 4/93 5/122 6/163 7/173 8/207 9/219 (48.2 overs)	221

Bowling: Hadlee 9.2–2–27–2; Snedden 10–0–50–0; Morrison 9–0–33–3; Thomson 10–0–47–2; Larsen 10–0–51–0.

New Zealand

*M. D. Crowe c More b Kapil Dev	18
J. J. Crowe c More b Hirwani	26
A. H. Jones run out	9
M. J. Greatbatch c Prabhakar b Wassan	53
K. R. Rutherford b Prabhakar	44
R. J. Hadlee b Kapil Dev	46
†I. D. S. Smith c sub (Gursharan Singh) b Wassan	5
S. A. Thomson c Wassan b Prabhakar	2
G. R. Larsen b Prabhakar	0
M. C. Snedden run out	0
D. K. Morrison not out	0
L-b 11, w 6	17
1/33 2/55 3/68 4/148 5/174 6/195 7/210 8/211 9/220 (48.5 overs)	220

Bowling: Prabhakar 10–1–37–3; Kapil Dev 9.5–1–45–2; Wassan 10–0–46–2; Hirwani 10–0–46–1; A. Sharma 9–0–35–0.

Umpires: G. I. J. Cowan and S. J. Woodward.

†AUSTRALIA v INDIA

At Hamilton, March 8. Australia won by seven wickets. Toss: India. Raman, Manjrekar and Azharuddin distinguished themselves as India reached 92 for one. But the off-spin of Peter Taylor, and Alderman's usual meticulous accuracy, kept the final total to 211, even though Kapil Dev swung to good effect. The Australians set about their task in a businesslike fashion, with Marsh (one six, nine fours) and Mark Taylor (eight fours) always in command during a partnership of 112. It was the 42nd over before Australia averaged 4 runs an over, but by then the result was not in doubt. Hirwani was the best of the Indian bowlers, his flight and turn causing problems.

Man of the Match: G. R. Marsh.

India

W. V. Raman c Healy b P. L. Taylor .. 58
M. Prabhakar c M. A. Taylor b Hughes 7
S. V. Manjrekar run out 33
*M. Azharuddin lbw b Hughes 37
V. B. Chandrasekhar c Border
b P. L. Taylor . 3
Gursharan Singh lbw b P. L. Taylor ... 4
Kapil Dev not out 48
Ajay Sharma c Campbell b Hughes ....
†K. S. More run out ....
A. S. Wassan not out ....
L-b 4, n-b 1 ....

1/12 2/92 3/108 4/114 5/123 6/174 7/194 8/200 (8 wkts, 50 overs) 21

N. D. Hirwani did not bat.

Bowling: Alderman 7–0–13–0; Hughes 7–0–36–3; Campbell 8–0–25–0; O'Donne 9–1–62–0; P. L. Taylor 10–2–31–3; Border 9–0–40–0.

Australia

G. R. Marsh c Gursharan b Kapil Dev. 86
M. A. Taylor st More b A. Sharma 56
S. R. Waugh c Prabhakar b Hirwani .. 23
D. C. Boon not out 24
*A. R. Border not out ....
B 4, l-b 5, w 4, n-b 1 1

1/112 2/158 3/203 (3 wkts, 48 overs) 21

S. P. O'Donnell, †I. A. Healy, P. L. Taylor, M. G. Hughes, G. D. Campbell and T. M Alderman did not bat.

Bowling: Kapil Dev 8–0–37–1; Prabhakar 8–1–29–0; Wassan 2–0–12–0; Hirwar 10–2–25–1; Raman 10–1–43–0; A. Sharma 10–0–57–1.

Umpires: G. I. J. Cowan and R. L. McHarg.

†NEW ZEALAND v AUSTRALIA

At Auckland, March 10. Australia won on faster scoring-rate. Toss: New Zealand. Early rai restricted the innings to 47 overs. Jones was in overpowering form for Australia, his 5 coming from only 42 balls, mainly through confident, lofted drives. Waugh and O'Donnell pu on 66 in 49 minutes, O'Donnell hitting two sixes in his 52 from 51 deliveries, and Healy an Peter Taylor added 45 in little over half an hour to take Australia to 239. Wright, restored t the New Zealand team, and Crowe responded with an opening partnership of 99 fron eighteen overs. The New Zealand captain struck the Australian bowlers for nine fours in hi 48 from 53 balls, but after his dismissal the run-rate began to mount appreciably. A stoppag for rain at 115 for one reduced New Zealand's target to 204, but from 40 overs, and whe more wet weather ended play, Australia's run-rate was superior (5.09 to 4.79). New Zealand however, had done enough to shade India and go into the final.

Man of the Match: D. M. Jones.

Australia

M. A. Taylor c Larsen b Thomson 17
*G. R. Marsh c Jones b Snedden 6
D. M. Jones c and b Hadlee 59
D. C. Boon c Rutherford b Morrison .. 9
S. R. Waugh c Smith b Snedden 36
S. P. O'Donnell run out 52
†I. A. Healy not out 3
P. L. Taylor not out 1
B 1, l-b 4, w 7, n-b 1 1

1/12 2/61 3/85 4/118 5/184 6/194 (6 wkts, 47 overs) 23

M. G. Hughes, G. D. Campbell and C. G. Rackemann did not bat.

Bowling: Hadlee 10–1–40–1; Snedden 9–1–45–2; Morrison 9–1–39–1; Thomson 8–0–60–1 Larsen 10–0–45–0; Rutherford 1–0–5–0.

New Zealand

J. G. Wright b P. L. Taylor	48	K. R. Rutherford not out	29
M. D. Crowe retired hurt	51	L-b 3, w 9, n-b 1	13
A. H. Jones not out	26		
M. J. Greatbatch c Healy b Rackemann	0	1/99 2/115 (2 wkts, 34.5 overs)	167

R. J. Hadlee, †I. D. S. Smith, G. R. Larsen, S. A. Thomson, M. C. Snedden and D. K. Morrison did not bat.

M. D. Crowe retired hurt at 115-1.

Bowling: Hughes 4–0–28–0; Campbell 7.5–0–37–0; O'Donnell 6–0–35–0; Rackemann 10–0–37–1; P. L. Taylor 7–0–27–1.

Umpires: R. S. Dunne and S. J. Woodward.

FINAL TABLE

	Played	*Won*	*Lost*	*Points*	*Run-rate*
Australia	4	4	0	8	4.52
New Zealand	4	1	3	2	4.66
India	4	1	3	2	4.21

FINAL

†NEW ZEALAND v AUSTRALIA

At Auckland, March 11. Australia won by eight wickets. Toss: New Zealand. The pitch, early on, was ideal for seam bowling and Australia all but decided the outcome of the match by taking the first five wickets for 33. Hadlee, on his last appearance at Eden Park, where he had enjoyed so many of his triumphs, played a magnificent, almost lone-handed innings. He was with Jeff Crowe while 80 were added for the sixth wicket, but from the point when both were 16 Hadlee made all but 1 of the runs as he advanced his total to 57. He hit 22 off two overs from Taylor. However, New Zealand's total of 162 was not nearly enough, particularly as Jones was again in tremendous form for Australia, hitting his fifth one-day century off 94 balls. Among his five sixes were two off Hadlee, and he also had seven fours in his dazzling display.

Man of the Match: D. M. Jones.

New Zealand

J. G. Wright c Healy b Rackemann	4	J. G. Bracewell c Healy b Campbell	3
A. H. Jones c Boon b Alderman	7	M. C. Snedden c Marsh b Taylor	5
M. J. Greatbatch c Jones b Campbell	11	D. K. Morrison not out	9
K. R. Rutherford c Healy b Rackemann	2	L-b 2, w 2	4
J. J. Crowe c and b Alderman	28		
G. R. Larsen c Healy b O'Donnell	1	1/12 2/15 3/26 (49.2 overs)	162
R. J. Hadlee c Boon b Rackemann	79	4/32 5/33 6/113	
†I. D. S. Smith c Jones b Campbell	9	7/134 8/147 9/147	

Bowling: Alderman 10–2–34–2; Rackemann 10–2–22–3; O'Donnell 8–3–12–1; Campbell 10–0–37–3; Taylor 9.2–0–50–1; Border 2–0–5–0.

Australia

G. R. Marsh b Bracewell	24
D. C. Boon lbw b Morrison	9
D. M. Jones not out	102
*A. R. Border not out	19
L-b 2, w 4, n-b 4	10
1/13 2/81 (2 wkts, 39.1 overs)	164

S. R. Waugh, S. P. O'Donnell, †I. A. Healy, P. L. Taylor, G. D. Campbell, T. M. Alderman and C. G. Rackemann did not bat.

Bowling: Hadlee 9–3–34–0; Morrison 8–0–46–1; Snedden 5–0–13–0; Larsen 7.1–1–27–0; Bracewell 10–0–42–1.

Umpires: R. S. Dunne and S. J. Woodward.

THE AUSTRALIANS IN NEW ZEALAND, 1989-90

By DICK BRITTENDEN

A full-strength Australian side, captained by Allan Border, paid a brief visi to New Zealand in March. Initially they participated in a triangular one-da tournament against New Zealand and India, which concluded India's tou there, and then they played New Zealand in a one-off Test match which wa a reply in kind to the early-season Test in Perth, where New Zealand ha escaped with a draw through a splendid fighting innings by Mark Great batch. Australia went through the one-day series undefeated, but in a low scoring, closely fought match at the Basin Reserve, Wellington, they wer beaten for the first time in fifteen Tests. During this match, Richard Hadle scored his 3,000th run to join I. T. Botham, Kapil Dev and Imran Khan in a élite group of all-rounders with 3,000 runs and 300 wickets in Test cricket.

NEW ZEALAND v AUSTRALIA

Test Match

At Wellington, March 15, 16, 17, 18, 19. New Zealand won by nine wickets. Toss: Australia After recent heavy rain, play did not begin until two o'clock on the first day. Border clearl thought that, while runs would come with difficulty, the pitch would not get better. He electe to bat, and that, for all the excitement of the later days, virtually decided Australia's fate Although the pitch provided generous help for the seam bowlers that afternoon and, befor the close, sufficient turn to interest the most innocuous tweaker, it did improve, grudgingl and marginally, over the next four days.

With the ball generally keeping low as well as seaming dangerously, the condition demanded that the batsmen played forward. This the Australians failed to do, loitering abou the crease as Morrison and Hadlee went enthusiastically about their business. The first fou wickets went for 12, Morrison taking three for 8 in his first five overs. Jones and Waug offered some resistance, and Waugh partnered Peter Taylor in a stand of 26 before Hadle beat him with a ball which pitched on middle and leg and took the off bail. Taylor, on batsman who went forward, played stoutly, but Hadlee cleaned out the tail to finish with hi 35th haul of five wickets in a Test innings, and his 100th in first-class cricket. Australia's 11 was their second-lowest total against New Zealand.

New Zealand, 18 without loss overnight, had to wait until 3.30 p.m. before play got unde way on the second day. Border set only two slips, but had two men in front of the bat on th off side, and two on the on side. Wright and Franklin, who played forward religiously, had stern struggle to get the ball off the square. Wright, having hit his first ball for four, scored jus 9 runs in the next two hours, but the opening partnership of 48 was invaluable. At the clos New Zealand were 17 runs short, having added only 75 runs in the day's 45 overs. And so i was on the third day; 88 overs produced 166 runs. Australian bowling of particular accuracy, pitch still offering plenty for the seamers, and antagonistic fields kept the New Zealanders lead to 92. Wright, top scorer with 36, was there for 221 minutes, and Snedden, sent in at th end of the second day, remained on 6 for 94 minutes and finally was out for 23 scored in 17 minutes. That New Zealand were not further restricted was due to the cheerful last-wicke partnership of 31 between Bracewell and Morrison. Off-spinner Taylor had excellent figures but his lack of flight mystified a number of observers. Bracewell, on the other hand, hinte that giving the ball air was justified when he bowled five maiden overs before the close an had the wicket of Boon.

The fourth day belonged to Peter Taylor, Border and Bracewell. As night-watchman, Taylo went well beyond his brief with an innings of 87, in 197 minutes, marked by splendid drivin and a penchant for hitting over the top. He and Border added 103 for the fourth wicket to giv Australia a lead of 102, but without any addition to the score Jones was given out to questionable lbw decision. Waugh, looking dangerous with his fluent front-foot shots, tempte fate once too often and, at full stretch, played a ball from Hadlee to Greatbatch at cover. Tha was practically the end of Australia's resistance. Bracewell, with ample flight and spinning th ball sharply, took the last four wickets for 3 runs in nineteen balls. New Zealand wanted 178 to win, with every prospect of a nail-biting finish on the final day.

The Australians, basing their optimism particularly on Taylor, were confident of winning, but Franklin and Wright were equal to the demanding task. A lunch score of 70 for one was a sound platform from which to launch a victory bid, and after the break Wright and Jones added 34 in half an hour. First the New Zealand captain took to Taylor, whose occasional efforts at flight cost runs, and then he attacked Border, who had had the batsmen defending. Two fours and a six in one over took him to 99 and the game was over. Wright hit seventeen fours as well as the six, and his second fifty came from 74 balls; he had not played a better innings for New Zealand. Jones, who had taken 40 minutes to score his first run, was also assertive in the closing stages.

Man of the Match: J. G. Wright.

Close of play: First day, New Zealand 18-0 (T. J. Franklin 12*, J. G. Wright 5*); Second day, New Zealand 93-3 (M. C. Snedden 0*, M. J. Greatbatch 4*); Third day, Australia 57-2 (G. R. Marsh 33*, P. L. Taylor 1*); Fourth day, New Zealand 4-0 (T. J. Franklin 2*, J. G. Wright 1*).

Australia

	First innings		Second innings	
M. A. Taylor lbw b Morrison	4	–	(2) lbw b Hadlee	5
G. R. Marsh b Morrison	4	–	(1) c Rutherford b Bracewell	41
D. C. Boon lbw b Hadlee	0	–	c Smith b Bracewell	12
*A. R. Border lbw b Morrison	1	–	(5) not out	78
D. M. Jones c Wright b Snedden	20	–	(6) lbw b Morrison	0
S. R. Waugh b Hadlee	25	–	(7) c Greatbatch b Hadlee	25
†I. A. Healy b Snedden	0	–	(8) c Rutherford b Bracewell	10
P. L. Taylor c Wright b Hadlee	29	–	(4) c Smith b Morrison	87
G. D. Campbell lbw b Hadlee	4	–	b Bracewell	0
C. G. Rackemann not out	6	–	b Bracewell	1
T. M. Alderman b Hadlee	4	–	st Smith b Bracewell	1
L-b 6, n-b 7	13		L-b 6, n-b 3	9
/4 2/9 3/9 4/12 5/38 /44 7/70 8/87 9/103	110		1/27 2/54 3/91 4/194 5/194 6/232 7/261 8/261 9/267	269

Bowling: *First Innings*—Hadlee 16.2–5–39–5; Morrison 10–4–22–3; Snedden 15–2–33–2; Rutherford 2–0–8–0; Bracewell 2–1–2–0. *Second Innings*—Hadlee 25–3–70–2; Morrison 4–8–58–2; Snedden 25–5–46–0; Bracewell 34.2–11–85–6; Jones 1–0–4–0.

New Zealand

	First innings		Second innings	
. J. Franklin c Marsh b P. L. Taylor	28	–	c Healy b Campbell	18
. G. Wright c Healy b Alderman	36	–	not out	117
. H. Jones c and b Border	18	–	not out	33
I. C. Snedden b Alderman	23			
I. J. Greatbatch c Healy b P. L. Taylor	16			
. R. Rutherford c Healy b P. L. Taylor	12			
J. Crowe lbw b Alderman	9			
J. Hadlee lbw b Campbell	18			
. D. S. Smith c M. A. Taylor b Campbell	1			
G. Bracewell not out	19			
. J. Morrison c M. A. Taylor b Alderman	12			
B 2, l-b 5, n-b 3	10		B 2, l-b 10, n-b 1	13
48 2/89 3/89 4/111 5/123 150 7/151 8/152 9/171	202		1/53 (1 wkt)	181

Bowling: *First Innings*—Alderman 29–9–46–4; Rackemann 32–17–42–0; P. L. Taylor -19–44–3; Campbell 21–3–51–2; Border 6–3–12–1. *Second Innings*—Alderman 14–8–27–0; ackemann 15–4–39–0; P. L. Taylor 11–3–39–0; Campbell 7–2–23–1; Jones 6–3–14–0; order 10.4–5–27–0.

Umpires: R. S. Dunne and S. J. Woodward.

stralia's matches v New Zealand and India in the Rothmans Cup (March 3-11) may be found the coverage of the Indian tour of New Zealand.

SHARJAH CHAMPIONS TROPHY, 1989-90

Pakistan, unbeaten in their four games, were accomplished winners of the Cricketers' Benefit Fund Series for the Sharjah Champions Trophy. In addition to his team winning all their matches, Imran Khan could reflect on the successful introduction of new players into the Pakistan squad. Shahid Saeed and Sohail Fazal batted with flair, while Waqar Younis, an eighteen-year-old fast bowler, at times looked quicker than anyone in the round-robin tournament. West Indies, who had won the trophy the previous season by beating Pakistan in the final, were disappointing and finished third behind India on run-rate.

The competition was originally scheduled to start on October 12, but it began a day later following the death in Germany of the United Arab Emirates' Deputy Prime Minister, Sheikh Hamadan Bin Mohammad. The CBFS beneficiaries were Fazal Mahmood and Iqbal Qasim of Pakistan, K. Srikkanth and P. R. Umrigar of India, and the West Indies captain, I. V. A. Richards, each of whom received US$35,000 (£20,000 approx.)

†INDIA v WEST INDIES

At Sharjah, October 13. West Indies won by five wickets. Toss: India. On a pitch slow enough to inhibit confident strokeplay, Richards played the key role. As India struggled to gain momentum, having been contained by the fine bowling of Walsh, the West Indies captain bowled Amarnath, ran out Vengsarkar off his own bowling, removed Azharuddin with a direct hit at the bowler's end from point, and had Shastri caught when he hit across the line. Coming in when West Indies were 31 for three, Richards hit a six and four fours in scoring 34 off 33 balls, 18 of his runs coming in Prabhakar's eighth over. Logie (65 balls) and Arthurton (118 balls), both playing sensibly, then took West Indies towards a comfortable victory.

Man of the Match: I. V. A. Richards.

India

*K. Srikkanth c Dujon b Walsh 11
N. S. Sidhu c and b Walsh 28
M. Amarnath b Richards 20
D. B. Vengsarkar run out 14
M. Azharuddin run out 14
R. J. Shastri c Richardson b Richards . 5
Kapil Dev c Dujon b Walsh 16
Ajay Sharma b Ambrose 17
M. Prabhakar c Dujon b Walsh ......
†K. S. More b Ambrose 1
Arshad Ayub not out ....

B 1, l-b 9, w 10 2

1/43 2/46 3/72 4/91 5/97 (48.1 overs) 16
6/106 7/126 8/126 9/146

Bowling: Ambrose 9.1–1–22–2; Bishop 9–0–45–0; Marshall 10–1–23–0; Walsh 10–1–25–4; Richards 10–0–44–2.

West Indies

D. L. Haynes c More b Arshad Ayub . . 12
P. V. Simmons c Srikkanth b Prabhakar 6
R. B. Richardson c Vengsarkar b Prabhakar . 5
K. L. T. Arthurton c Amarnath b A. Sharma . 48
*I. V. A. Richards c Sidhu b Arshad Ayub . 34
A. L. Logie not out 5
†P. J. L. Dujon not out ....

L-b 3, w 1, n-b 2 ....

1/18 2/23 3/31 (5 wkts, 47.5 overs) 1
4/80 5/165

M. D. Marshall, C. E. L. Ambrose, I. R. Bishop and C. A. Walsh did not bat.

Bowling: Kapil Dev 8–4–16–0; Prabhakar 10–2–45–2; Arshad Ayub 10–2–27–2; Shastri 10–1–41–0; A. Sharma 5–1–14–1; Srikkanth 4.5–0–27–0.

Umpires: H. D. Bird and D. R. Shepherd.

†PAKISTAN v WEST INDIES

t Sharjah, October 14. Pakistan won by 11 runs. Toss: West Indies. Wasim Akram's hat-rick – the fourth in one-day internationals – ended West Indies' challenge just when they oked to have the match under control at 209 for five. Going round the wicket, the left-arm ast bowler hit Dujon and Marshall's leg stump, and, reverting to over the wicket, he finished is eighth over by bowling the left-handed Ambrose. Best and Walsh added 29 for the last vicket, but Akram's fourth wicket in thirteen balls left West Indies 11 runs short. The ifference was exactly the number of wides conceded by the West Indian bowlers in akistan's innings. This was built around a splendid 74 off 83 balls by Salim Malik and tretched to 250 by Imran's powerful hitting at the end, including two sixes and two fours in mbrose's last over.

Man of the Match: Wasim Akram.

akistan

amiz Raja c Richardson b Walsh 17
hoaib Mohammad b Richards 45
hahid Saeed b Bishop 22
alim Malik c Richards b Bishop 74
az Ahmed run out 6
Imran Khan b Ambrose 45
Vasim Akram lbw b Ambrose 0
†Salim Yousuf c and b Bishop 4
Abdul Qadir not out 2
B 4, l-b 14, w 11, n-b 6 35

1/31 2/86 3/139 4/159 5/214 6/221 7/226 8/250 (8 wkts, 50 overs) 250

Iushtaq Ahmed and Waqar Younis did not bat.

Bowling: Ambrose 10–1–58–2; Bishop 10–0–49–3; Walsh 10–0–36–1; Marshall 10–0–41–0; ichards 10–0–48–1.

West Indies

. L. Haynes c Wasim Akram b Imran Khan . 59
. V. Simmons lbw b Wasim Akram .. 16
. B. Richardson b Imran Khan 31
. L. T. Arthurton st Salim Yousuf b Mushtaq Ahmed . 0
I. V. A. Richards c sub (Sohail Fazal) b Shoaib Mohammad . 46
. A. Best not out 53
P. J. L. Dujon b Wasim Akram 6
M. D. Marshall b Wasim Akram 0
C. E. L. Ambrose b Wasim Akram ... 0
I. R. Bishop b Abdul Qadir 0
C. A. Walsh b Wasim Akram 10
L-b 8, w 4, n-b 6 18

1/32 2/117 3/118 4/124 5/195 6/209 7/209 8/209 9/210 (48.4 overs) 239

Bowling: Wasim Akram 9.4–1–38–5; Waqar Younis 4–0–14–0; Abdul Qadir 9–0–45–1; hahid Saeed 3–0–19–0; Imran Khan 10–0–51–2; Mushtaq Ahmed 10–0–47–1; Shoaib Mohammad 3–0–17–1.

Umpires: D. Buultjens and S. Ponnudurai.

†INDIA v PAKISTAN

t Sharjah, October 15. Pakistan won by six wickets. Toss: India. The heat, the noise of the artisans, and a pitch full of runs contributed to an occasion equal to the rivalry between these rotagonists. Once again, albeit less dramatically, Pakistan's hero was Wasim Akram, who ook his 100th one-day international wicket when he dismissed Amarnath. Bowling fast and btaining unexpected bounce, he checked India after Srikkanth (69 balls), Sidhu (117 balls) nd Amarnath had threatened to make Pakistan pay for their fielding lapses. Sidhu hit eight ours and a six in his first one-day international hundred, and with Amarnath he added 161 ff 145 balls. Pakistan were given a good start with 99 coming in twenty overs from Shoaib nd Shahid Saeed, the latter needing just 59 balls for 50 in his second one-day international. kram, promoted to No. 3, then struck four sixes and a four in 37 off 22 balls and prepared he way for Salim Malik's sublime 68 not out from 58 balls. Pakistan needed 40 off the last six vers and won with eight balls to spare.

Man of the Match: N. S. Sidhu.

India

*K. Srikkanth st Salim Yousuf b Mushtaq Ahmed . 51
N. S. Sidhu b Wasim Akram 108
M. Amarnath c Salim Malik b Wasim Akram . 88
Kapil Dev c Shahid Saeed b Wasim Akram . 13
R. J. Shastri not out .... (
M. Azharuddin not out ....
L-b 6, w 3, n-b 2 11

1/92 2/253 3/271 4/271 (4 wkts, 46 overs) 27

D. B. Vengsarkar, †K. S. More, Chetan Sharma, M. Prabhakar and Arshad Ayub did not bat.

Bowling: Wasim Akram 9–0–30–3; Aaqib Javed 8–0–46–0; Shahid Saeed 3–0–24–0; Shoaib Mohammad 2–0–18–0; Mushtaq Ahmed 10–0–47–1; Abdul Qadir 7–0–44–0; Imran Khan 7–0–58–0.

Pakistan

Shoaib Mohammad run out 65
Shahid Saeed b Shastri 50
Wasim Akram c More b Arshad Ayub . 37
Salim Malik not out 68
Javed Miandad st More b Shastri 31
*Imran Khan not out 1
L-b 4, w 1, n-b 1 ....

1/99 2/152 3/169 4/234 (4 wkts, 44.4 overs) 27

Ijaz Ahmed, †Salim Yousuf, Abdul Qadir, Mushtaq Ahmed and Aaqib Javed did not bat.

Bowling: Kapil Dev 8–0–47–0; Prabhakar 10–0–46–0; C. Sharma 5.4–0–35–0; Amarnath 2–0–15–0; Arshad Ayub 10–0–67–1; Shastri 9–0–60–2.

Umpires: H. D. Bird and D. R. Shepherd.

†INDIA v WEST INDIES

At Sharjah, October 16. India won by 37 runs. Toss: West Indies. Kapil Dev's all-round skill brought India an unexpected victory. Coming in at 123 for five in the 31st over, and survivin a chance to mid-wicket when 14, he scored 41 off 50 balls, and later he took two for 19 in 7. overs as the West Indians generally failed to apply themselves with the bat. Marshall (46 balls and the unbeaten Dujon pulled the innings round from 78 for five at the halfway stage, bu Vengsarkar's throw from mid-on to run out Richards proved decisive. The West Indie captain had come in at No. 9 after injuring a finger on his right hand while fielding.

Man of the Match: Kapil Dev.

India

*K. Srikkanth b Walsh 40
R. Lamba c Walsh b Ambrose 18
M. Amarnath c Richards b Benjamin .. 29
D. B. Vengsarkar run out 6
M. Azharuddin b Walsh 28
Ajay Sharma c Richardson b Ambrose . 2
Kapil Dev b Benjamin 41
R. J. Shastri run out 6
M. Prabhakar lbw b Marshall ....
†K. S. More not out ....
Arshad Ayub not out ....
L-b 10, w 11, n-b 3 2

1/37 2/76 3/82 4/115 5/123 6/149 7/164 8/179 9/201 (9 wkts, 50 overs) 21

Bowling: Ambrose 10–1–43–2; Benjamin 10–1–36–2; Walsh 10–1–32–2; Marsha 10–0–50–1; Richards 10–0–40–0.

West Indies

D. L. Haynes b Kapil Dev 3
P. V. Simmons c Vengsarkar b Prabhakar . 3
R. B. Richardson run out 39
K. L. T. Arthurton b Arshad Ayub 16
C. A. Best c Vengsarkar b Arshad Ayub 5
†P. J. L. Dujon not out 37
M. D. Marshall b A. Sharma 40
C. E. L. Ambrose st More b Shastri ... 3
*I. V. A. Richards run out ....
W. K. M. Benjamin st More b A. Sharma 1
C. A. Walsh b Kapil Dev ....
L-b 9, w 1, n-b 2 1

1/5 2/24 3/59 4/71 5/78 6/129 7/146 8/157 9/171 (46.4 overs) 17

Bowling: Kapil Dev 7.4–1–19–2; Prabhakar 7–1–18–1; Arshad Ayub 10–0–29–2; Shastri 10–0–40–1; A. Sharma 10–0–44–2; Srikkanth 2–0–15–0.

Umpires: D. Buultjens and S. Ponnudurai.

†PAKISTAN v WEST INDIES

At Sharjah, October 17. Pakistan won by 57 runs. Toss: Pakistan. Victory gave Pakistan the Champions Trophy with one game still to play. At 86 for four in the 25th over, they were making hard work of batting on a good pitch, but a sparkling half-century from Ijaz (51 balls, seven fours) and Imran's 60 not out off 57 balls improved their position. Even so, a total of 237 looked insufficient when Simmons, driving powerfully and once hitting Imran into the grandstand, was putting on 43 with Haynes. When Waqar Younis removed both openers, however, there followed another uneven batting display as the defending champions surrendered their title.

Man of the Match: Imran Khan.

Pakistan

Shoaib Mohammad c Benjamin b Walsh	21
Ramiz Raja c R. C. Haynes b Ambrose	33
Shahid Saeed b R. C. Haynes	7
Salim Malik c Dujon b Ambrose	16
Ijaz Ahmed b Benjamin	50
*Imran Khan not out	60
Sohail Fazal c R. C. Haynes b Walsh	24
†Salim Yousuf b Bishop	4
Mushtaq Ahmed not out	3
B 8, l-b 8, w 3	19
1/40 2/55 3/85 4/86 5/154 6/207 7/221 (7 wkts, 50 overs)	237

Abdul Qadir and Waqar Younis did not bat.

Bowling: Ambrose 10–0–43–2; Bishop 10–0–31–1; Benjamin 10–0–58–1; R. C. Haynes 10–1–44–1; Walsh 10–1–45–2.

West Indies

*D. L. Haynes c Salim Yousuf b Waqar Younis	15
P. V. Simmons c Sohail Fazal b Waqar Younis	27
R. B. Richardson b Mushtaq Ahmed	6
C. A. Best b Abdul Qadir	44
K. L. T. Arthurton b Abdul Qadir	1
R. C. Haynes lbw b Abdul Qadir	4
†P. J. L. Dujon c Salim Yousuf b Shoaib Mohammad	26
C. E. L. Ambrose not out	26
W. K. M. Benjamin b Waqar Younis	3
I. R. Bishop run out	3
C. A. Walsh b Imran Khan	14
L-b 10, w 1	11
1/43 2/50 3/52 4/53 5/65 6/127 7/135 8/149 9/155 (44.4 overs)	180

Bowling: Imran Khan 5.4–0–21–1; Waqar Younis 9–2–28–3; Abdul Qadir 10–1–31–3; Mushtaq Ahmed 10–0–38–1; Sohail Fazal 1–0–4–0; Shahid Saeed 3–0–19–0; Shoaib Mohammad 6–0–29–1.

Umpires: H. D. Bird and D. R. Shepherd.

†INDIA v PAKISTAN

At Sharjah, October 20. Pakistan won by 38 runs. Toss: India. Even without Imran and Akram, Pakistan were untroubled in maintaining their unbeaten record. A brilliant century by Salim Malik, who featured in entertaining stands with Shoaib, Sohail and Miandad, provided the backbone of a total which India never threatened. With Aaqib Javed and Waqar Younis moving the ball disconcertingly, the Indian batsmen fell further and further behind the run-rate of 5.38 – just as their bowlers had failed to meet the agreed over-rate in an attempt to lessen the effect of Pakistan's attacking strokeplay.

Man of the Match: Salim Malik.

Pakistan

Shahid Saeed lbw b Prabhakar 16
Shoaib Mohammad st More b A. Sharma 51
Salim Malik c Azharuddin b Prabhakar 102
Sohail Fazal c Azharuddin b Arshad Ayub . 32
*Javed Miandad not out 28
Ijaz Ahmed not out 2
B 3, l-b 11, w 5, n-b 2 2
1/33 2/125 3/195 4/248 (4 wkts, 47 overs) 25

†Salim Yousuf, Abdul Qadir, Mushtaq Ahmed, Waqar Younis and Aaqib Javed did not bat

Bowling: C. Sharma 9–0–42–0; Prabhakar 10–0–45–2; Amarnath 8–1–27–0; Arshad Ayu 9–0–51–1; Shastri 4–0–35–0; A. Sharma 7–0–38–1.

India

*K. Srikkanth c Salim Yousuf b Aaqib Javed . 8
N. S. Sidhu c Ijaz Ahmed b Mushtaq Ahmed . 28
M. Azharuddin c Salim Yousuf b Aaqib Javed . 12
D. B. Vengsarkar lbw b Shoaib Mohammad . 35
R. J. Shastri c Salim Malik b Mushtaq Ahmed . 22
Ajay Sharma c Ijaz Ahmed b Shahid Saeed . 6
M. Prabhakar run out 2
M. Amarnath not out 3
†K. S. More st Salim Yousuf b Shoaib Mohammad . 2
Chetan Sharma c and b Aaqib Javed ..
Arshad Ayub not out ....
B 1, l-b 9, w 5 1
1/17 2/42 3/53 4/88 5/100 6/145 7/146 8/187 9/202 (9 wkts, 47 overs) 21

Bowling: Waqar Younis 6–0–18–0; Aaqib Javed 10–0–49–3; Shahid Saeed 10–1–27–1 Mushtaq Ahmed 6–0–33–2; Abdul Qadir 7–0–35–0; Shoaib Mohammad 8–0–42–2.

Umpires: H. D. Bird and D. R. Shepherd.

FINAL TABLE

	Played	*Won*	*Lost*	*Pts*	*Run-rate*
Pakistan	4	4	0	16	5.31
India	4	1	3	4	4.53
West Indies	4	1	3	4	4.08

NEHRU CUP, 1989-90

Staged to celebrate the centenary of the birth of Jawaharlal Nehru, the first Prime Minister of India after Independence, and sponsored by the Madras Rubber Foundry, the MRF World Series for the Jawaharlal Nehru Cup brought together all of the Test-playing countries except New Zealand. The tournament also had a secondary purpose in attracting the attention of the Indian population to Mr Ranjiv Gandhi, the current Prime Minister and grandson of Nehru, in the run-up to the country's elections.

The tournament's true significance, however, is perhaps best gauged by the way in which the various competing countries arrived in India for it. When England and Sri Lanka played the opening match, in Delhi before a crowd of less than 1,000, the hosts, India, were playing Pakistan in a different tournament in Sharjah. Indeed, India and Pakistan did not arrive in India until five days later. There had been a time when it seemed that neither Australia nor West Indies would attend, and it was to accommodate them that the tournament was brought forward, so clashing with the Champions Trophy in Sharjah. West Indies' first priority after Sharjah was an indoor exhibition match in Toronto, Canada, on November 6.

Only England and Sri Lanka could be said to have found any value, other than prizemoney, in yet another one-day competition. For the latter it provided the much-needed stimulus of international competition, while it gave England an opportunity to begin preparations for their forthcoming tour of the West Indies. For Pakistan, the Nehru Cup brought further success to add to their victory in the Champions Trophy. Their defeat of West Indies in the final at Calcutta was their ninth win in eleven one-day internationals, played in the space of nineteen days. By this achievement, in addition to winning the large trophy, they increased their winnings by $US40,000 (£22,850). West Indies received $US25,000 (£14,285) as runners-up, while the losing semi-finalists, England and India, won $US15,000 (£8,570) each. Imran Khan, Pakistan's captain, was the Man of the Series.

†ENGLAND v SRI LANKA

At Delhi, October 15. England won by five wickets. Toss: England. Accomplished batting by Smith, who added 103 in 23 overs with Lamb, eased England to a comfortable victory in the opening match of the competition. Lamb hit three sixes in his 52, and Russell batted perkily at the end after Stewart and Capel had gone quickly. Sri Lanka, put in, had begun badly. Mahanama was run out second ball, failing to beat Stewart's direct hit side-on from square leg as he came back for a second run, and Kuruppu was well caught off an inside edge. The innings was saved by Aravinda de Silva. Dropped when 10 at slip off Capel, he struck 80 from 90 balls, including ten fours, and put on 72 in sixteen overs with Samarasekera. After he was out at 174, the innings collapsed as DeFreitas took three wickets in four overs.

Man of the Match: R. A. Smith.

Sri Lanka

R. S. Mahanama run out 1
†D. S. B. P. Kuruppu c Russell b Fraser 5
A. P. Gurusinha c Lamb b Capel 19
P. A. de Silva lbw b Hemmings 80
*A. Ranatunga b Gooch 7
M. A. R. Samarasekera c Stewart b Gooch . 24
J. R. Ratnayeke c Gooch b DeFreitas . 6
G. F. Labrooy lbw b DeFreitas 0
E. A. R. de Silva b DeFreitas 2
S. D. Anurasiri not out 5
K. I. W. Wijegunawardene b Fraser . . . 3
B 6, l-b 22, w 10, n-b 3 41

1/1 2/17 3/42 4/82 5/154 6/174 7/180 8/180 9/186 (48.3 overs) 193

Bowling: DeFreitas 10–3–38–3; Fraser 8.3–1–25–2; Small 6–0–26–0; Capel 4–0–16–1; Gooch 10–2–26–2; Hemmings 10–1–34–1.

England

*G. A. Gooch c P. A. de Silva b Labrooy . 5
W. Larkins c P. A. de Silva b Ranatunga . 19
R. A. Smith not out 81
A. J. Lamb c P. A. de Silva b Wijegunawardene . 52
A. J. Stewart c Kuruppu b Ranatunga . 4
D. J. Capel lbw b Wijegunawardene . . . 4
†R. C. Russell not out 10
B 1, l-b 8, w 10, n-b 2 21

1/18 2/34 3/137 4/157 5/170 (5 wkts, 48.4 overs) 196

P. A. J. DeFreitas, G. C. Small, E. E. Hemmings and A. R. C. Fraser did not bat.

Bowling: Ratnayeke 7–1–10–0; Labrooy 7–1–34–1; Ranatunga 10–0–39–2; E. A. R. de Silva 10–0–29–0; Anurasiri 3–0–22–0; P. A. de Silva 3–0–16–0; Wijegunawardene 8.4–1–37–2.

Umpires: R. B. Gupta and P. J. McConnell.

†AUSTRALIA v ENGLAND

At Hyderabad, October 19. England won by seven wickets. Toss: Australia. Border's stunning 84 off only 44 balls, and Larkins's century off 126 balls, made memorable what could have been a routine encounter. England's bowlers, having removed Boon in the first over, restricted Marsh and Jones to 108 in 34 overs, but Taylor and Border added 120 in the final twelve overs. The Australian captain struck Small for three successive sixes in an over costing 21 runs; in the next over, again worth 21, he hit Fraser for a six and three fours off consecutive balls. In all, he hit five sixes and eight fours. Larkins's reply, while less savage, was equally commanding, his strokeplay both powerful and subtle. His previous highest in a one-day international was 34 in 1979-80: now he dominated an opening stand of 185 with Gooch, hit two sixes and nineteen fours in his 124, and justified his recall to the England team after an absence of eight years.

Man of the Match: W. Larkins.

Australia

D. C. Boon c Gooch b Fraser 0
G. R. Marsh c Lamb b Small 54
D. M. Jones run out 50
P. L. Taylor not out 36
*A. R. Border not out 84
L-b 6, w 4, n-b 8 18

1/0 2/108 3/122 (3 wkts, 50 overs) 242

S. R. Waugh, S. P. O'Donnell, †I. A. Healy, T. B. A. May, G. F. Lawson and T. M. Alderman did not bat.

Bowling: Fraser 10–2–48–1; Pringle 10–3–42–0; Small 10–0–55–1; Capel 8–0–39–0; Gooch 10–3–35–0; Hemmings 2–0–17–0.

England

*G. A. Gooch lbw b Border 56
W. Larkins c Border b May 124
R. A. Smith not out 24
A. J. Lamb b Lawson 23
A. J. Stewart not out 4
B 1, l-b 9, n-b 2 12

1/185 2/191 3/234 (3 wkts, 47.3 overs) 243

D. J. Capel, †R. C. Russell, D. R. Pringle, G. C. Small, E. E. Hemmings and A. R. C. Fraser did not bat.

Bowling: Alderman 7–1–28–0; Lawson 10–1–51–1; May 10–0–55–1; O'Donnell 7.3–0–27–0; Border 10–0–43–1; Taylor 3–0–29–0.

Umpires: L. H. Barker and Khizar Hayat.

†SRI LANKA v WEST INDIES

At Rajkot, October 19. Sri Lanka won by four wickets. Toss: Sri Lanka. The left-handed Gurusinha, with a solid 66, held Sri Lanka's innings together after the loss of three wickets for 45 had threatened to jeopardise their reply to a jaded performance by West Indies. When he was fifth out, at 146, Sri Lanka's first victory over West Indies – in eleven one-day internationals – was virtually assured. Just two days earlier, the West Indians had been losing to Pakistan in Sharjah, and apart from Haynes and Logie, and to a lesser extent Richards, their batsmen showed little interest in applying themselves against some steady bowling.

Man of the Match: A. P. Gurusinha.

West Indies

D. L. Haynes c Labrooy b P. A. de Silva 42
P. V. Simmons c E. A. R. de Silva b Ratnayeke . 7
R. B. Richardson c Ranatunga b Ratnayeke . 5
*I. V. A. Richards b Wijegunawardene . 24
A. L. Logie not out 54
C. A. Best b E. A. R. de Silva 6
†P. J. L. Dujon c Ratnayeke b E. A. R. de Silva . 4
W. K. M. Benjamin b Wijegunawardene 7
C. E. L. Ambrose c Gurusinha b P. A. de Silva . 2
I. R. Bishop run out 3
C. A. Walsh not out 13
L-b 2, w 7 9

1/12 2/20 3/83 4/86 5/96 6/108 7/141 8/144 9/157 (9 wkts, 50 overs) 176

Bowling: Ratnayeke 10–1–36–2; Labrooy 7–0–27–0; Ranatunga 3–0–14–0; Wijegunawardene 10–0–30–2; E. A. R. de Silva 10–0–30–2; P. A. de Silva 10–0–37–2.

Sri Lanka

R. S. Mahanama c Dujon b Benjamin . 12
†D. S. B. P. Kuruppu c Richards b Bishop . 1
A. P. Gurusinha b Benjamin 66
P. A. de Silva c Dujon b Benjamin 1
J. R. Ratnayeke c and b Richards 18
*A. Ranatunga c Richards b Ambrose . 34
M. A. R. Samarasekera not out 12
H. P. Tillekeratne not out 10
L-b 14, w 7, n-b 5 26

1/6 2/43 3/45 4/80 5/146 6/156 (6 wkts, 47.1 overs) 180

G. F. Labrooy, E. A. R. de Silva and K. I. W. Wijegunawardene did not bat.

Bowling: Ambrose 10–2–27–1; Bishop 10–1–44–1; Walsh 10–0–35–0; Benjamin 9–0–22–3; Richards 6–0–23–1; Simmons 2–0–11–0; Best 0.1–0–4–0.

Umpires: P. J. McConnell and P. D. Reporter.

†AUSTRALIA v WEST INDIES

At Madras, October 21. Australia won by 99 runs. Toss: Australia. From the moment Border won the toss and chose to bat, this was very much his match. He had a role in all departments. Marsh anchored the Australian innings until the 42nd over, by which time Border had helped him put on 112 and Waugh had set out his stall with a mighty six off Ambrose. Waugh's unbeaten 53 from 44 balls (two sixes, four fours) provided a thrilling counter to a tight performance by the West Indians in the field. Their batsmen, however, could not match it. Best failed to score, Haynes was run out by Waugh's throw from deep cover, Logie played on, and Richards swung and missed. Only Richardson, until Border tied him down with accurate slow left-arm bowling, played with any fluency, though the Australians were convinced Border had caught him at slip when he was 3. When Border caught and bowled him for 61 off 101 balls, West Indies tumbled to a heavy defeat with almost ten overs unused.

Man of the Match: A. R. Border.

Australia

D. C. Boon b Benjamin 1
G. R. Marsh c D. L. Haynes b R. C. Haynes . 74
D. M. Jones c Best b Walsh 20
*A. R. Border c Ambrose b R. C. Haynes . 46
S. R. Waugh not out 53
S. P. O'Donnell c R. C. Haynes b Benjamin . 17
†I. A. Healy b Benjamin 2
M. G. Hughes not out 3
B 1, l-b 12, w 7, n-b 5 25

1/2 2/35 3/147 4/169 5/230 6/237 (6 wkts, 50 overs) 241

G. F. Lawson, T. B. A. May and T. M. Alderman did not bat.

Bowling: Ambrose 9–1–37–0; Benjamin 9–2–38–3; Walsh 10–0–50–1; Marshall 10–0–31–0; Richards 6–0–36–0; R. C. Haynes 6–0–36–2.

West Indies

D. L. Haynes run out 5
C. A. Best b Alderman 0
R. B. Richardson c and b Border 61
A. L. Logie b O'Donnell 8
*I. V. A. Richards b Hughes 5
†P. J. L. Dujon b Border 13
R. C. Haynes c Jones b Hughes 18
M. D. Marshall c Alderman b Border .. 12
W. K. M. Benjamin lbw b Jones 2
C. E. L. Ambrose not out 0
C. A. Walsh b Jones 6
B 2, l-b 3, w 4, n-b 3 12

1/2 2/11 3/36 4/59 5/86 6/110 7/122 8/134 9/134 (40.3 overs) 142

Bowling: Alderman 5–0–19–1; Lawson 7–0–18–0; Hughes 6–0–27–2; O'Donnell 6–0–19–1; Border 10–2–20–3; Jones 6.3–0–34–2.

Umpires: S. K. Ghosh and J. W. Holder.

†ENGLAND v PAKISTAN

At Cuttack, October 22. England won by four wickets. Toss: Pakistan. An unsuitable pitch made for an absorbing match. Whether the ball jumped and deviated, or ran along the ground, was a matter of chance, and only Salim Malik of the Pakistan batsmen displayed the necessary skills once Capel had removed their openers. Wasim Akram returned the compliment when England batted, but whereas Gooch had left Capel on to capitalise on a tight opening spell, Imran relieved the pressure by taking Akram off and bringing on Qadir. Lamb took 14 from the leg-spinner's first over, and in partnership with Smith and then Stewart, he gave the innings its impetus. Stewart and Capel took England to within 10 runs of what was never an easy target, and one which would have been more difficult but for the profligate display by Pakistan in the field. It was England's third consecutive win of the tournament and a significant triumph for their captain, Gooch, who completed his ten overs with a two-wicket maiden to return his best figures in a one-day international.

Man of the Match: G. A. Gooch.

Pakistan

Shahid Saeed b Capel 5
Shoaib Mohammad c Cook b Capel ... 3
Ijaz Ahmed b Cook 15
Javed Miandad b Gooch 14
Salim Malik b Small 42
*Imran Khan st Russell b Hemmings .. 19
†Salim Yousuf c Lamb b Gooch 6
Abdul Qadir c Russell b Cook 13
Wasim Akram lbw b Gooch 0
Mushtaq Ahmed not out 9
Waqar Younis not out 4
B 5, l-b 8, w 2, n-b 3 18

1/8 2/16 3/37 4/53 5/107 6/111 7/128 8/128 9/132 (9 wkts, 50 overs) 148

Bowling: Fraser 10–3–15–0; Capel 8–2–16–2; Small 8–2–29–1; Gooch 10–4–19–3; Cook 10–0–43–2; Hemmings 4–0–13–1.

England

*G. A. Gooch b Wasim Akram	7	D. J. Capel run out	23
W. Larkins c Javed Miandad b Wasim Akram	0	†R. C. Russell not out	7
R. A. Smith c Javed Miandad b Mushtaq Ahmed	19	G. C. Small not out	0
A. J. Lamb b Salim Malik	42	B 8, l-b 4, w 8	20
A. J. Stewart c Javed Miandad b Abdul Qadir	31	1/1 2/21 3/68 4/92 5/139 6/148 (6 wkts, 43.2 overs)	149

E. E. Hemmings, A. R. C. Fraser and N. G. B. Cook did not bat.

Bowling: Wasim Akram 10–1–32–2; Waqar Younis 10–1–30–0; Abdul Qadir 9.2–2–29–1; Mushtaq Ahmed 6–2–25–1; Salim Malik 2–0–9–1; Imran Khan 6–1–12–0.

Umpires: R. B. Gupta and V. K. Ramaswamy.

†INDIA v SRI LANKA

At Ahmedabad, October 22. India won by 6 runs. Toss: India. Sri Lanka almost toppled the tournament's hosts, India, another of the late arrivals from Sharjah. The Sri Lankans began their final over needing 8 runs with two wickets in hand, but were thwarted by Kapil Dev. Gurusinha was again their batting strength, recording his highest one-day international score as his team worked convincingly towards an Indian total of 227. This owed much to Sidhu's confident 80. India's third-wicket stand of 61 between Sidhu and Amarnath came to an unexpected end when Sidhu sent back his partner and Amarnath, the striker, was adjudged by umpire Khizar Hayat to have obstructed the field. Amarnath had kicked away the ball as Ratnayeke, the bowler, and Ranatunga were converging on it. This was the second such dismissal in a one-day international – Ramiz Raja, for Pakistan against England at Karachi in 1987-88 provided the first instance – and it gave Amarnath a dubious double. In 1985-86 he had been dismissed handled the ball in a World Series Cup game against Australia at Melbourne.

Man of the Match: N. S. Sidhu.

India

*K. Srikkanth c Ranatunga b Wijegunawardene	16	Ajay Sharma c Gurusinha b Ratnayeke	6
R. Lamba c Ranatunga b Ratnayeke	11	†K. S. More not out	7
N. S. Sidhu run out	80	M. Prabhakar not out	11
M. Amarnath obstructing the field	28	B 4, l-b 5, w 5	14
M. Azharuddin b Ratnayeke	26	1/24 2/34 3/95 4/168 5/176 6/199 7/208 8/209 (8 wkts, 50 overs)	227
Kapil Dev run out	6		
R. J. Shastri c Tillekeratne b Labrooy	22		

Arshad Ayub did not bat.

Bowling: Ratnayeke 10–1–35–3; Labrooy 10–1–35–1; Wijegunawardene 10–0–60–1; Ranatunga 10–0–49–0; E. A. R. de Silva 10–0–39–0.

Sri Lanka

R. S. Mahanama c Sidhu b Prabhakar	12	J. R. Ratnayeke c Lamba b Kapil Dev	20
†D. S. B. P. Kuruppu lbw b Kapil Dev	9	E. A. R. de Silva not out	1
A. P. Gurusinha b Prabhakar	83	K. I. W. Wijegunawardene b Kapil Dev	0
P. A. de Silva c and b Arshad Ayub	20	L-b 7, w 4	11
*A. Ranatunga c Kapil Dev b Shastri	7		
M. A. R. Samarasekera c and b Shastri	22	1/22 2/24 3/72 4/87 5/137 6/161 7/186 8/220 9/220 (49.4 overs)	221
H. P. Tillekeratne run out	11		
G. F. Labrooy b Prabhakar	25		

Bowling: Kapil Dev 8.4–2–26–3; Prabhakar 9–2–34–3; Amarnath 4–0–20–0; A. Sharma 4–0–30–0; Shastri 10–0–47–2; Arshad Ayub 10–2–31–1; Srikkanth 4–0–26–0.

Umpires: Khizar Hayat and P. J. McConnell.

†AUSTRALIA v PAKISTAN

At Bombay, October 23. Pakistan won by 66 runs. Toss: Australia. This was a much more convincing performance in the field by Pakistan. Imran made the crucial strike, sending back the Australian middle order at a time when it needed someone to establish a partnership with Jones. And although Taylor did provide that support, seeing Jones reach his fifty off 78 balls, Qadir trapped Jones lbw and went on to take two more wickets. Pakistan's innings had been held together by Shoaib's chanceless 73 off 121 balls and owed much to his third-wicket stand of 72 with Miandad. Lawson, holding a spectacular diving catch at long-on, ended that. And after Shoaib had become one of three wickets by Alderman in seven balls, Pakistan needed the positive approach of Wasim Akram and Akram Raza to get them a defendable score.

Man of the Match: Imran Khan.

Pakistan

Shoaib Mohammad c Waugh b Alderman	73
Ramiz Raja c Jones b Lawson	2
Shahid Saeed c and b Alderman	6
†Javed Miandad c Lawson b Border	34
Salim Malik c Boon b Alderman	15
Ijaz Ahmed c Border b Alderman	1
*Imran Khan c Healy b Hughes	8
Wasim Akram run out	28
Akram Raza not out	12
Abdul Qadir not out	5
B 2, l-b 11, w 3, n-b 5	21
1/10 2/29 3/101 4/138 5/140 6/153 7/154 8/197 (8 wkts, 50 overs)	205

Waqar Younis did not bat.

Bowling: Alderman 10–3–22–4; Lawson 10–1–34–1; Hughes 9–1–29–1; O'Donnell 10–1–38–0; Taylor 6–0–37–0; Border 5–0–32–1.

Australia

D. C. Boon run out	0
G. R. Marsh c Salim Malik b Waqar Younis	8
D. M. Jones lbw b Abdul Qadir	58
*A. R. Border c Javed Miandad b Imran Khan	4
S. R. Waugh b Imran Khan	0
S. P. O'Donnell lbw b Imran Khan	3
P. L. Taylor not out	31
†I. A. Healy c Ijaz Ahmed b Shoaib Mohammad	7
M. G. Hughes lbw b Abdul Qadir	0
G. F. Lawson b Abdul Qadir	1
T. M. Alderman lbw b Wasim Akram	0
B 4, l-b 11, w 9, n-b 3	27
1/2 2/46 3/58 4/58 5/70 6/104 7/126 8/134 9/136 (43.2 overs)	139

Bowling: Wasim Akram 6.2–0–21–1; Waqar Younis 7–2–27–1; Imran Khan 8–2–13–3; Akram Raza 10–0–26–0; Abdul Qadir 9–0–27–3; Shoaib Mohammad 3–0–10–1.

Umpires: L. H. Barker and P. D. Reporter.

†INDIA v WEST INDIES

At Delhi, October 23. West Indies won by 20 runs. Toss: India. An outstanding all-round display by their captain, Richards, restored West Indies' fortunes after a sequence of five defeats in one-day internationals. First, while adding 66 with Richardson, he struck 44 from 42 balls to ensure West Indies' recovery from an uncertain start. Later, after Lamba had put India in a strong position with 61 from 81 deliveries, Richards dismissed Shastri, Kapil Dev and More in the 38th over to reduce India from 158 for five to 160 for eight. Finally, he bowled Arshad Ayub to return his best figures in a one-day international.

Man of the Match: I. V. A. Richards.

West Indies

D. L. Haynes c More b Prabhakar	6	W. K. M. Benjamin b Kapil Dev	4
C. A. Best c Lamba b C. Sharma	13	C. E. L. Ambrose not out	6
R. B. Richardson c and b Arshad Ayub	57	C. A. Walsh not out	6
A. L. Logie b Amarnath	8	L-b 12, w 5, n-b 1	18
*I. V. A. Richards run out	44		
†P. J. L. Dujon st More b Arshad Ayub.	3	1/11 2/44 3/65 (9 wkts, 45 overs)	196
M. D. Marshall c Amarnath b C. Sharma	27	4/131 5/139 6/168	
R. C. Haynes b C. Sharma	4	7/177 8/183 9/185	

Bowling: Kapil Dev 8–1–23–1; Prabhakar 9–1–26–1; C. Sharma 9–0–46–3; Amarnath 10–0–34–1; Arshad Ayub 9–0–55–2.

India

*K. Srikkanth c Dujon b Marshall	10	†K. S. More lbw b Richards	0
R. Lamba c Dujon b Walsh	61	Chetan Sharma not out	7
N. S. Sidhu c D. L. Haynes b Walsh	9	Arshad Ayub b Richards	5
M. Amarnath c Logie b Richards	23	B 1, l-b 7, w 4, n-b 3	15
M. Azharuddin c and b Richards	18		
R. J. Shastri c R. C. Haynes b Richards	20	1/29 2/74 3/91 (41.4 overs)	176
Kapil Dev c D. L. Haynes b Richards	7	4/115 5/143 6/158	
M. Prabhakar run out	1	7/160 8/160 9/165	

Bowling: Ambrose 7–1–19–0; Benjamin 7–0–31–0; Walsh 9–1–37–2; Marshall 9–0–40–1; Richards 9.4–0–41–6.

Umpires: K. T. Francis and J. W. Holder.

†AUSTRALIA v SRI LANKA

At Margao, October 25. Australia won by 28 runs. Toss: Australia. Jones (101 balls) and Aravinda de Silva (107 balls) shared the batting honours, each hitting two sixes and seven fours. However, whereas de Silva's 92-minute 96 was virtually all Sri Lanka had to offer, Jones followed a sound start by Marsh and Boon and, Labrooy apart, Sri Lanka's bowlers presented few problems as he laid the cornerstone of the Australian innings. There was a time when it looked as if Tillekeratne might lend de Silva the support he needed, but O'Donnell broke their stand of 63, and his three wickets swept aside Sri Lanka's hopes of springing another upset.

Man of the Match: P. A. de Silva.

Australia

G. R. Marsh run out	38	†I. A. Healy run out	3
D. C. Boon lbw b Fernando	19	M. G. Hughes not out	8
D. M. Jones lbw b Labrooy	85	B 4, l-b 10, w 8, n-b 1	23
*A. R. Border b Labrooy	26		
S. R. Waugh run out	2	1/40 2/105 3/160 (7 wkts, 50 overs)	222
T. M. Moody b Labrooy	12	4/165 5/190	
S. P. O'Donnell not out	6	6/205 7/210	

G. F. Lawson and T. M. Alderman did not bat.

Bowling: Ratnayeke 9–1–34–0; Labrooy 10–1–38–3; Wijegunawardene 10–0–40–0; Fernando 3–0–16–1; E. A. R. de Silva 7–0–30–0; P. A. de Silva 9–0–36–0; Ranatunga 2–0–14–0.

Sri Lanka

R. S. Mahanama lbw b Alderman	5	G. F. Labrooy run out	1
†D. S. B. P. Kuruppu b Hughes	13	E. A. R. de Silva not out	7
A. P. Gurusinha c Boon b Lawson	13	K. I. W. Wijegunawardene b Lawson	0
P. A. de Silva b O'Donnell	96	B 2, l-b 2, w 4, n-b 2	10
J. R. Ratnayeke run out	2		
*A. Ranatunga c Waugh b Border	15	1/7 2/21 3/54 (47.1 overs)	194
H. P. Tillekeratne c Boon b O'Donnell	24	4/74 5/103 6/166	
T. L. Fernando c Alderman b O'Donnell	8	7/179 8/182 9/191	

Bowling: Alderman 9–1–41–1; Lawson 8.1–2–23–2; Hughes 10–0–39–1; O'Donnell 10–1–48–3; Border 10–0–39–1.

Umpires: L. H. Barker and P. D. Reporter.

†ENGLAND v INDIA

At Kanpur, October 25. India won by six wickets. Toss: India. An astonishing century by Chetan Sharma, in truth little more than a slog, brought about England's first defeat of the tournament. Promoting Chetan in the order to wrest control from England's bowlers was a gamble. Had Smith caught him on the boundary when he was 3, it would have misfired. As it was, Chetan put on 105 with Sidhu and, surviving the chance of a run-out when 74 and a catch to Gooch moments later, he reached his century and won the match with his eighth four. He faced 96 balls and also hit a six. England, having begun their innings well, rather lost their way for a time. Stewart, who moved to his half-century with a six off Chetan, batted well for his 61, but it was Lamb (109 balls), engineering 55 from the last five overs, who was most responsible for England's setting a challenging target.

Man of the Match: Chetan Sharma.

England

*G. A. Gooch c Azharuddin b C. Sharma 21	†R. C. Russell not out 10
W. Larkins lbw b A. Sharma 42	G. C. Small not out 0
R. A. Smith c Azharuddin b Prabhakar 0	
A. J. Lamb c Srikkanth b C. Sharma 91	L-b 7, w 7, n-b 3 17
A. J. Stewart run out 61	
D. J. Capel b Kapil Dev 2	1/43 2/48 3/80 (7 wkts, 50 overs) 255
P. A. J. DeFreitas c Azharuddin	4/210 5/219
b Kapil Dev 11	6/239 7/251

E. E. Hemmings and A. R. C. Fraser did not bat.

Bowling: Kapil Dev 10–0–56–2; Prabhakar 10–0–50–1; C. Sharma 10–0–78–2; Arshad Ayub 10–0–27–0; A. Sharma 10–1–37–1.

India

*K. Srikkanth st Russell b Hemmings 32	Kapil Dev not out 4
R. Lamba c Russell b Small 16	L-b 6, w 6, n-b 2 14
N. S. Sidhu run out 61	
Chetan Sharma not out 101	1/41 2/65 3/170 (4 wkts, 48.1 overs) 259
D. B. Vengsarkar c Larkins b DeFreitas 31	4/251

M. Azharuddin, Ajay Sharma, †K. S. More, M. Prabhakar and Arshad Ayub did not bat.

Bowling: Fraser 10–2–31–0; DeFreitas 10–0–66–1; Hemmings 10–0–51–1; Small 10–0–44–1; Capel 3–0–24–0; Gooch 5.1–0–37–0.

Umpires: K. T. Francis and Khizar Hayat.

†PAKISTAN v WEST INDIES

At Jullundur, October 25. West Indies won by six wickets. Toss: Pakistan. With Pakistan's top-order batsmen unable to get the better of controlled West Indies bowling, it was the 34th over before their score moved into three figures. Aamer Malik, who had joined the team only the previous day as a replacement for the injured Salim Yousuf, batted responsibly for his 77, and at the end Salim Malik and Imran added 59 in seven overs. When Wasim Akram removed Haynes and Simmons, West Indies were under some pressure. Richardson and Dujon relieved it with a partnership of 94 in 140 balls, and Richards saw his side to victory with an unbeaten 47.

Man of the Match: R. B. Richardson.

Pakistan

Ramiz Raja b Ambrose 14	*Imran Khan c Richards b Benjamin .. 24
Shoaib Mohammad c Richards b Marshall . 12	B 5, l-b 5, w 3 13
†Aamer Malik run out 77	
Javed Miandad c Haynes b Ambrose .. 39	1/23 2/27 3/148 (5 wkts, 50 overs) 223
Salim Malik not out 44	4/164 5/223

Ijaz Ahmed, Wasim Akram, Abdul Qadir, Mushtaq Ahmed and Waqar Younis did not bat.

Bowling: Ambrose 10–0–45–2; Benjamin 10–0–45–1; Walsh 10–2–17–0; Marshall 10–1–51–1; Richards 7–0–38–0; Simmons 3–0–17–0.

West Indies

D. L. Haynes b Wasim Akram 4	*I. V. A. Richards not out 47
P. V. Simmons lbw b Wasim Akram .. 16	A. L. Logie not out 12
R. B. Richardson st Aamer Malik b Abdul Qadir . 80	B 2, l-b 15, w 3, n-b 1 21
†P. J. L. Dujon st Aamer Malik b Abdul Qadir . 46	1/21 2/33 3/127 (4 wkts, 48.3 overs) 226 4/191

K. L. T. Arthurton, M. D. Marshall, W. K. M. Benjamin, C. E. L. Ambrose and C. A. Walsh did not bat.

Bowling: Wasim Akram 9.3–1–38–2; Waqar Younis 10–0–48–0; Mushtaq Ahmed 10–2–33–0; Imran Khan 5–1–22–0; Abdul Qadir 10–0–48–2; Shoaib Mohammad 4–0–20–0.

Umpires: J. W. Holder and V. K. Ramaswamy.

†AUSTRALIA v INDIA

At Bangalore, October 27. India won by three wickets. Toss: Australia. A crowd of more than 50,000 carried India to the win that put them alongside England at the top of the qualifying table. Ajay Sharma was their hero. He took three wickets with his left-arm spin bowling, including those of Jones and Border just when Australia looked capable of building a commanding position, and later he hit three sixes in his 32 while re-establishing India's reply following the loss of Vengsarkar and Azharuddin. The job was finished by Chetan Sharma and Prabhakar, who put on 40 in an unbroken eighth-wicket partnership, with Chetan winning the match by swinging O'Donnell over mid-wicket for six. Just as Boon had given Australia a flying start, scoring all but 10 of their first-wicket 59, so Srikkanth and Lamba set India on the way with a century stand. Both fell to Matthews, who was playing his first and only match after replacing the injured May.

Man of the Match: Ajay Sharma.

Australia

D. C. Boon c Srikkanth b Amarnath .. 49	†I. A. Healy not out 14
G. R. Marsh st More b A. Sharma 27	M. G. Hughes run out 1
D. M. Jones c More b A. Sharma 53	G. F. Lawson not out 3
*A. R. Border b A. Sharma 41	B 1, l-b 7, w 1 9
S. R. Waugh c A. Sharma b Kapil Dev 28	
G. R. J. Matthews lbw b Kapil Dev ... 5	1/59 2/109 3/165 (8 wkts, 50 overs) 247
S. P. O'Donnell c sub (R. J. Shastri) b Prabhakar . 17	4/188 5/203 6/214 7/233 8/236

T. M. Alderman did not bat.

Bowling: Prabhakar 7–1–35–1; Kapil Dev 10–0–49–2; C. Sharma 3–0–22–0; Amarnath 10–0–43–1; Arshad Ayub 10–0–49–0; A. Sharma 10–0–41–3.

India

*K. Srikkanth c O'Donnell b Matthews 58
R. Lamba lbw b Matthews 57
M. Amarnath b Matthews 5
D. B. Vengsarkar c Boon b Lawson ... 25
M. Azharuddin c and b Border 8
Ajay Sharma c Waugh b Border 32
Kapil Dev c Healy b Lawson 9
Chetan Sharma not out 20
M. Prabhakar not out 16
L-b 11, w 7, n-b 1 19

1/115 2/122 3/132 4/141 5/191 6/199 7/209 (7 wkts, 47.1 overs) 249

†K. S. More and Arshad Ayub did not bat.

Bowling: Alderman 6–2–23–0; Lawson 10–1–39–2; Hughes 6–0–27–0; O'Donnell 5.1–0–42–0; Matthews 10–0–56–3; Border 10–0–51–2.

Umpires: L. H. Barker and Khizar Hayat.

†ENGLAND v WEST INDIES

At Gwalior, October 27. West Indies won by 26 runs. Toss: West Indies. England had no-one to equal the brilliance of Haynes and Marshall. Chasing the highest total of the tournament to date – built on Haynes's fifteenth hundred in one-day internationals – they began solidly but were undone by Marshall's decisive spell of three wickets for 14 runs in four overs. Having in his first spell had Larkins caught at cover in the eighteenth over, Marshall returned to remove Gooch and Lamb with consecutive balls (give or take an interruption for drinks) and then Smith, the last of the experienced strokemakers. Haynes, who batted throughout the West Indian innings, faced 164 balls and hit two sixes and twelve fours in his unbeaten 138.

Man of the Match: D. L. Haynes.

West Indies

D. L. Haynes not out 138
P. V. Simmons run out 13
R. B. Richardson run out 44
*I. V. A. Richards c Hemmings b Small 16
A. L. Logie c Stewart b Small 17
M. D. Marshall c Smith b Small 16
R. C. Haynes not out 0
L-b 10, w 9, n-b 2 21

1/31 2/155 3/188 4/236 5/264 (5 wkts, 50 overs) 265

†P. J. L. Dujon, W. K. M. Benjamin, C. E. L. Ambrose and C. A. Walsh did not bat.

Bowling: Fraser 10–1–47–0; DeFreitas 10–1–42–0; Capel 8–0–49–0; Small 10–0–39–3; Hemmings 7–0–44–0; Gooch 5–0–34–0.

England

*G. A. Gooch c Dujon b Marshall 59
W. Larkins c sub (K. L. T. Arthurton) b Marshall . 29
R. A. Smith c Dujon b Marshall 65
A. J. Lamb b Marshall 0
A. J. Stewart c Logie b Simmons 20
D. J. Capel b Benjamin 21
P. A. J. DeFreitas c sub (K. L. T. Arthurton) b Walsh . 7
†R. C. Russell not out 8
G. C. Small b Benjamin 4
E. E. Hemmings not out 1
B 1, l-b 13, w 11 25

1/58 2/150 3/150 4/189 5/191 6/209 7/229 8/238 (8 wkts, 50 overs) 239

A. R. C. Fraser did not bat.

Bowling: Ambrose 10–0–33–0; Benjamin 10–1–46–2; Walsh 10–0–41–1; Marshall 10–0–33–4; R. C. Haynes 4–0–25–0; Richards 5–0–44–0; Simmons 1–0–3–1.

Umpires: S. K. Ghosh and V. K. Ramaswamy.

†PAKISTAN v SRI LANKA

At Lucknow, October 27. Pakistan won by 6 runs. Toss: Pakistan. Yet again the Sri Lankans came so close to causing an upset; yet again they fell at the last. But while Tillekeratne (one six, one four) and Aravinda de Silva (two sixes, three fours) were adding 150 for the third wicket, Pakistan's prospects of a semi-final place looked to be slipping away. Once this pair were separated, though, inexperience told. Needing 8 runs off the last two overs, Sri Lanka lost Ratnayeke and Labrooy to successive balls from Wasim Akram, Asoka de Silva was run out, and Mahanama was bowled by Qadir with four balls remaining. Pakistan's recovery from 70 for four at the halfway stage was due to Imran's unbeaten 84 off 110 balls which contained just three boundaries.

Man of the Match: Imran Khan.

Pakistan

Ramiz Raja run out	17
Shoaib Mohammad b E. A. R. de Silva	11
Ijaz Ahmed c Kuruppu b Wijegunawardene	0
Salim Malik c Ranatunga b P. A. de Silva	27
*Imran Khan not out	84
Abdul Qadir c and b P. A. de Silva	18
Wasim Akram b Labrooy	29
†Aamer Malik not out	19
B 3, l-b 6, w 5	14
1/30 2/30 3/32 4/70 5/115 6/172 (6 wkts, 50 overs)	219

Akram Raza, Mushtaq Ahmed and Waqar Younis did not bat.

Bowling: Ratnayeke 10–2–48–0; Labrooy 10–0–52–1; Wijegunawardene 10–1–36–1; E. A. R. de Silva 10–2–31–1; P. A. de Silva 10–0–43–2.

Sri Lanka

†D. S. B. P. Kuruppu b Waqar Younis	8
H. P. Tillekeratne run out	71
A. P. Gurusinha c and b Akram Raza	8
P. A. de Silva c Salim Malik b Akram Raza	83
M. A. R. Samarasekera b Abdul Qadir	3
*A. Ranatunga run out	5
R. S. Mahanama b Abdul Qadir	11
J. R. Ratnayeke b Wasim Akram	0
G. F. Labrooy b Wasim Akram	0
E. A. R. de Silva run out	0
K. I. W. Wijegunawardene not out	0
B 3, l-b 17, w 4	24
1/18 2/37 3/187 4/194 5/202 6/202 7/212 8/212 9/213 (49.2 overs)	213

Bowling: Waqar Younis 6–2–14–1; Wasim Akram 10–1–30–2; Akram Raza 10–0–34–2; Mushtaq Ahmed 8–1–39–0; Abdul Qadir 7.2–0–36–2; Imran Khan 7–0–29–0; Shoaib Mohammad 1–0–11–0.

Umpires: R. B. Gupta and P. J. McConnell.

†INDIA v PAKISTAN

At Calcutta, October 28. Pakistan won by 77 runs. Toss: India. Pakistan, needing to win to qualify for the semi-finals, handsomely overcame India, whose consolation was in scoring the 175 they needed to head the qualifying table. With that honour, however, came the double-edged privilege of meeting the improved West Indians in the Bombay semi-final. A sparkling 120 in 21 overs by Srikkanth and Lamba gave the Indians the start they needed, but once they were out Pakistan's 279, the highest total of the tournament, was never threatened. Imran set the seal on the Pakistan innings with an unbeaten 47 from 39 balls, taking 19 off Kapil Dev in the 50th over.

Man of the Match: Imran Khan.

Pakistan

†Aamer Malik c A. Sharma b Amarnath	51	Wasim Akram lbw b Prabhakar	1
Ramiz Raja c Kapil Dev b Srikkanth	77	Akram Raza not out	9
Salim Malik c Srikkanth b A. Sharma	14		
Javed Miandad lbw b Arshad Ayub	13	B 4, l-b 11, w 5, n-b 1	21
Abdul Qadir c Vengsarkar b Arshad Ayub	17	1/97 2/125 3/165 (7 wkts, 50 overs)	279
Ijaz Ahmed c Lamba b Kapil Dev	29	4/165 5/196	
*Imran Khan not out	47	6/242 7/243	

Mushtaq Ahmed and Aaqib Javed did not bat.

Bowling: Kapil Dev 10–0–60–1; Prabhakar 9–0–41–1; C. Sharma 5–0–23–0; Amarnath 10–0–45–1; A. Sharma 5–0–38–1; Arshad Ayub 7–1–31–2; Srikkanth 4–0–26–1.

India

*K. Srikkanth run out	65	S. V. Manjrekar run out	1
R. Lamba c Aaqib Javed b Abdul Qadir	57	M. Prabhakar not out	7
M. Amarnath c Abdul Qadir b Mushtaq Ahmed	20	†K. S. More b Aaqib Javed	2
D. B. Vengsarkar c Imran Khan b Akram Raza	10	Arshad Ayub lbw b Wasim Akram	0
Chetan Sharma c sub (Shoaib Mohammad) b Mushtaq Ahmed	10	B 1, l-b 8, w 3	12
Ajay Sharma b Mushtaq Ahmed	1	1/120 2/132 3/155 (42.3 overs)	202
Kapil Dev b Wasim Akram	17	4/166 5/171 6/176	
		7/189 8/196 9/201	

Bowling: Wasim Akram 7.3–0–21–2; Aaqib Javed 7–1–32–1; Akram Raza 10–1–47–1; Mushtaq Ahmed 10–0–51–3; Abdul Qadir 8–0–42–1.

Umpires: K. T. Francis and J. W. Holder.

QUALIFYING TABLE

	Played	*Won*	*Lost*	*Points*	*Run-rate*
India	5	3	2	12	4.637
England	5	3	2	12	4.517
Pakistan	5	3	2	12	4.296
West Indies	5	3	2	12	4.127
Australia	5	2	3	8	4.364
Sri Lanka	5	1	4	4	4.049

SEMI-FINALS

†ENGLAND v PAKISTAN

At Nagpur, October 30. Pakistan won by six wickets. Toss: Pakistan. The match was reduced to 30 overs a side after heavy overnight rain had soaked the outfield. England began briskly, their runs coming at 5 and then 6 an over, and only in the later stages of Pakistan's innings did they concede the initiative. It was swept away from them by Ramiz Raja and Salim Malik, who struck 122 off 77 balls for the fourth wicket. Malik, batting with a runner after straining a hamstring in the field, hit three sixes and six fours in his 66 off 41 balls, including 18 off four successive balls from Fraser. Ramiz faced 82 balls for his unbeaten 85, and hit eight fours. Until then Smith had been the dominant batsman, hitting six fours and two sixes in his half-century. Qadir dismissed Hussain, the indisposed Lamb and Smith in five balls, but Capel and Pringle struck back with 39 off 33 balls. And when DeFreitas sent back Miandad and Ijaz in quick succession, England had looked firmly in control.

Man of the Match: Ramiz Raja.

England

*G. A. Gooch c sub (Shoaib Mohammad) b Waqar Younis	35	D. J. Capel run out	20
W. Larkins c and b Akram Raza	25	D. R. Pringle not out	21
R. A. Smith b Abdul Qadir	55	P. A. J. DeFreitas not out	4
†A. J. Stewart b Waqar Younis	0	B 3, l-b 20, w 3	26
N. Hussain lbw b Abdul Qadir	2	1/44 2/102 3/103 (7 wkts, 30 overs)	194
A. J. Lamb c Aamer Malik b Abdul Qadir	6	4/136 5/144 6/145 7/184	

G. C. Small and A. R. C. Fraser did not bat.

Bowling: Imran Khan 4–0–26–0; Wasim Akram 6–0–28–0; Akram Raza 5–0–28–1; Waqar Younis 6–1–40–2; Mushtaq Ahmed 3–0–19–0; Abdul Qadir 6–0–30–3.

Pakistan

Ramiz Raja not out	85	Wasim Akram not out	0
Javed Miandad b DeFreitas	17	L-b 10	10
Ijaz Ahmed c Smith b DeFreitas	2		
*Imran Khan lbw b Small	15	1/26 2/32 3/69 (4 wkts, 28.3 overs)	195
Salim Malik c Lamb b Fraser	66	4/191	

†Aamer Malik, Abdul Qadir, Akram Raza, Mushtaq Ahmed and Waqar Younis did not bat.

Bowling: Fraser 6–0–58–1; DeFreitas 6–0–40–2; Capel 6–0–24–0; Pringle 5–0–33–0; Small 5.3–0–30–1.

Umpires: R. B. Gupta and V. K. Ramaswamy.

†INDIA v WEST INDIES

At Bombay, October 30. West Indies won by eight wickets. Toss: India. Accurate fast bowling and their own unconvincing batting prevented the Indians from gaining the benefit of first use of a good batting pitch. Indeed, they never really recovered from the run-out of their captain at the start of the innings. Srikkanth, at the non-striker's end, was much too extravagant in his backing-up to be able to regain his ground when Lamba played the ball to Simmons at short square leg. When Lamba and Amarnath hinted at a restoration by taking the score to 50, Walsh removed them both and also Vengsarkar. India's 165 never looked as if it would tax the West Indians. Haynes's 64 off 100 balls included seven boundaries, while Richardson was unbeaten with 58 off 110 balls when West Indies won with more than seven overs to spare.

Man of the Match: I. V. A. Richards.

India

*K. Srikkanth run out	1	Chetan Sharma c Richards b Benjamin	12
R. Lamba c Richardson b Walsh	29	†K. S. More not out	5
M. Amarnath b Walsh	15	Arshad Ayub c Marshall b Ambrose	3
D. B. Vengsarkar c Richards b Walsh	8	B 3, w 11, n-b 2	16
M. Azharuddin c Haynes b Simmons	38		
Kapil Dev lbw b Ambrose	19	1/3 2/50 3/55 (48.5 overs)	165
Ajay Sharma b Benjamin	15	4/76 5/107 6/131	
M. Prabhakar c Richards b Marshall	4	7/141 8/151 9/159	

Bowling: Ambrose 8.5–0–13–2; Benjamin 9–2–34–2; Walsh 10–0–39–3; Marshall 10–2–19–1; Richards 4–0–21–0; Simmons 7–0–36–1.

West Indies

D. L. Haynes lbw b Kapil Dev 64
P. V. Simmons lbw b Kapil Dev 11
R. B. Richardson not out 58
†P. J. L. Dujon not out 20
B 2, l-b 4, w 3, n-b 4 13

1/22 2/139 (2 wkts, 42.1 overs) 166

*I. V. A. Richards, K. L. T. Arthurton, A. L. Logie, M. D. Marshall, W. K. M. Benjamin, C. E. L. Ambrose and C. A. Walsh did not bat.

Bowling: Kapil Dev 8–0–31–2; Prabhakar 4–0–21–0; Arshad Ayub 10–2–29–0; A. Sharma 10–2–30–0; Srikkanth 7–1–30–0; Azharuddin 3–0–17–0; Lamba 0.1–0–2–0.

Umpires: J. W. Holder and P. J. McConnell.

FINAL

†PAKISTAN v WEST INDIES

At Calcutta, November 1. Pakistan won by four wickets. Toss: West Indies. This exciting, entertaining match was brought to a memorable climax by Wasim Akram, who came to the wicket in the final over when Akram Raza was run out by Walsh's direct hit from 35 yards. A single by Imran Khan then reduced Pakistan's target to 3 runs off Richards's last two deliveries, the first of which Wasim swung high over wide mid-wicket for an astonishing six. Richards's earlier decision to bowl out his front-line attack in a bid to stop Pakistan's dynamic advance had left him with no option but to bowl the final over himself. Unlike the West Indians, whose innings took time to develop, Pakistan had quickly overcome the loss of Aamer Malik in the second over. Ramiz hit six fours in his 31-ball 35 as he and Ijaz put on 60; Ijaz (56) and Salim Malik (71) faced 66 and 62 balls respectively, the latter hitting a straight six off Walsh; and Salim and Imran added 93 off 95 balls for the fifth wicket to keep Pakistan up with the run-rate. West Indies' total was built around an unbeaten 107 off 134 balls by Haynes, his sixteenth one-day international hundred. Pakistan fielded aggressively and Imran, bowling his nine overs at the end, kept the final slog in check. Richards, who hit a six and two fours in scoring 21 from eleven balls, was the first of Imran's three wickets in five overs.

Man of the Match: Imran Khan. *Attendance:* 70,000 approx.

West Indies

D. L. Haynes not out 107
P. V. Simmons c Ijaz Ahmed
b Mushtaq Ahmed . 40
R. B. Richardson b Akram Raza 27
*I. V. A. Richards c Mushtaq Ahmed
b Imran Khan . 21
†P. J. L. Dujon c Abdul Qadir
b Imran Khan . 28
A. L. Logie c sub (Shoaib Mohammad)
b Imran Khan . 14
M. D. Marshall not out 10
B 11, l-b 14, w 1 26

1/83 2/144 3/175 4/221 5/244 (5 wkts, 50 overs) 273

R. C. Haynes, W. K. M. Benjamin, C. E. L. Ambrose and C. A. Walsh did not bat.

Bowling: Aaqib Javed 10–2–25–0; Wasim Akram 10–1–46–0; Akram Raza 5–0–26–1; Mushtaq Ahmed 9–0–55–1; Abdul Qadir 7–0–49–0; Imran Khan 9–0–47–3.

Pakistan

†Aamer Malik c Dujon b Benjamin ... 3
Ramiz Raja c Logie b Walsh 35
Ijaz Ahmed run out 56
Javed Miandad c Richards b Benjamin. 17
Salim Malik c Dujon b Ambrose 71
*Imran Khan not out 55
Akram Raza run out 19
Wasim Akram not out 6
L-b 4, w 10, n-b 1 15

1/4 2/64 3/110 4/133 5/226 6/270 (6 wkts, 49.5 overs) 277

Abdul Qadir, Mushtaq Ahmed and Aaqib Javed did not bat.

Bowling: Ambrose 10–0–41–1; Benjamin 10–0–71–2; Marshall 10–0–43–0; Walsh 10–0–55–1; R. C. Haynes 3–0–21–0; Richards 6.5–0–42–0.

Umpires: S. K. Ghosh and P. D. Reporter.

BENSON AND HEDGES WORLD SERIES CUP, 1989-90

By CHRIS HARTE

†AUSTRALIA v SRI LANKA

At Melbourne, December 26. Australia won by 30 runs. Toss: Sri Lanka. Australia made a slow start on a suspect pitch against keen bowling and fielding, but the arrival of Jones in the thirteenth over soon quickened the scoring-rate. When O'Donnell joined him in the 34th over, they added 108 for the sixth wicket in 67 minutes from 98 balls before rain halted the innings. Jones's unbeaten 85 came from 89 balls (one six, four fours) and O'Donnell's 57 not out from 60. Sri Lanka's captain, Ranatunga, who earlier had taken three important wickets for 15 runs in twenty balls, provided the basis of their reply, scoring 55 from 70 balls. It was his dismissal by O'Donnell in the 41st over which put paid to Sri Lanka's victory bid.

Man of the Match: S. P. O'Donnell. *Attendance:* 45,012.

Australia

M. A. Taylor c and b Ratnayeke 11
G. R. Marsh c P. A. de Silva b Ranatunga . 38
D. C. Boon c Jayasuriya b Ratnayake . 11
D. M. Jones not out 85
*A. R. Border c Samarasekera b Ranatunga . 11
S. R. Waugh c Tillekeratne b Ranatunga 5
S. P. O'Donnell not out 57
L-b 6, w 2, n-b 2 10

1/17 2/42 3/88 4/106 5/120 (5 wkts, 48.5 overs) 228

†I. A. Healy, P. L. Taylor, M. G. Hughes and G. D. Campbell did not bat.

Bowling: Labrooy 9–0–40–0; Ratnayeke 9–1–47–1; Ratnayake 9.5–0–43–1; Ranatunga 10–2–41–3; E. A. R. de Silva 10–0–42–0; Gurusinha 1–0–9–0.

Sri Lanka

R. S. Mahanama c Border b Waugh ... 36
M. A. R. Samarasekera c Hughes b O'Donnell . 30
*A. Ranatunga c Healy b O'Donnell ... 55
P. A. de Silva c Border b P. L. Taylor . 9
S. T. Jayasuriya c Campbell b Hughes .. 3
A. P. Gurusinha c O'Donnell b P. L. Taylor . 22
†H. P. Tillekeratne c Healy b O'Donnell 11
J. R. Ratnayeke run out 0
E. A. R. de Silva not out 13
G. F. Labrooy b O'Donnell 6
R. J. Ratnayake c Healy b Hughes 0
L-b 6, w 4, n-b 3 13

1/59 2/85 3/101 4/109 5/161 6/169 7/169 8/190 9/197 (47.2 overs) 198

Bowling: Hughes 9.2–0–41–2; Campbell 10–2–36–0; O'Donnell 9–1–36–4; Waugh 6–0–26–1; P. L. Taylor 10–1–36–2; Border 3–0–17–0.

Umpires: L. J. King and C. D. Timmins.

†AUSTRALIA v SRI LANKA

At Perth, December 30 (day/night). Australia won by nine wickets. Toss: Sri Lanka. Ranatunga's decision to bat on a green pitch rebounded badly as Sri Lanka were reduced to 60 for five in eighteen overs, and they would not have reached 200 had the Australians not dropped eleven catches. Ranatunga, whose unbeaten 71 from 106 balls held the innings together, had lives at 0, 6, 14, 20 and 21. Racing to victory at more than 5 runs an over, Australia's batsmen showed less charity to Sri Lanka's bowlers. Marsh batted throughout the innings, putting on 117 in 106 minutes with Boon and scoring 80 from 136 deliveries. Two overs were lost at the start because the groundstaff had forgotten to mark the fielding circles, and later there was a disquieting delay while Channel Nine TV technicians repaired a sound-effects microphone in a stump. After their efforts, the stump stood taller than the rest, with the result that a replacement had to be found. The crowd did not appreciate the delay.

Man of the Match: G. R. Marsh. *Attendance:* 22,150.

Sri Lanka

R. S. Mahanama lbw b Alderman 27
M. A. R. Samarasekera c Alderman b Hughes . 5
A. P. Gurusinha c Healy b Alderman .. 0
†H. P. Tillekeratne c Jones b O'Donnell 13
P. A. de Silva c Border b Campbell ... 4
*A. Ranatunga not out 71
S. T. Jayasuriya c Healy b O'Donnell .. 13
J. R. Ratnayeke lbw b Alderman 25
G. F. Labrooy b Waugh 1
R. J. Ratnayake c Waugh b O'Donnell . 19
L-b 8, w 15, n-b 2 25

1/8 2/9 3/50 4/56 5/60 6/100 7/162 8/167 9/203 (9 wkts, 48 overs) 203

K. I. W. Wijegunawardene did not bat.

Bowling: Hughes 10–0–35–1; Alderman 10–2–25–3; Campbell 10–2–54–1; O'Donnell 9–1–36–3; Waugh 9–0–45–1.

Australia

G. R. Marsh not out 80
M. A. Taylor c Tillekeratne b Wijegunawardene . 37
D. C. Boon not out 49
L-b 16, w 11, n-b 11 38

1/87 (1 wkt, 38.5 overs) 204

*A. R. Border, D. M. Jones, S. R. Waugh, S. P. O'Donnell, †I. A. Healy, M. G. Hughes, G. D. Campbell and T. M. Alderman did not bat.

Bowling: Labrooy 10–1–46–0; Ratnayeke 7.5–0–51–0; Ratnayake 10–0–37–0; Wijegunawardene 7–0–33–1; Ranatunga 4–0–21–0.

Umpires: A. R. Crafter and R. J. Evans.

†PAKISTAN v SRI LANKA

At Perth, December 31 (day/night). Sri Lanka won by three wickets. Toss: Pakistan. Playing on the ground on which they lost to Western Australia two days earlier, Pakistan nevertheless took time to adjust to the bounce of the pitch and the speed of the ball over the outfield. Three run-outs testified to their misjudgements, with the dismissals of Mansoor in the nineteenth over and Saeed in the 32nd being crucial. When fourth out, Aamer Malik had taken 122 balls over his 69, which left Miandad and Imran to try to raise the run-rate against tight bowling from Labrooy and Ratnayeke. A splendid 60 from 89 balls by Samarasekera against some ineffectual bowling gave Sri Lanka the start they needed, de Silva controlled the innings in its later stages, and finally the injured Mahanama guided his country to their third one-day victory in Australia. Both sides were fined for their slow over-rates.

Man of the Match: M. A. R. Samarasekera. *Attendance:* 4,009.

Pakistan

†Aamer Malik b Ratnayeke 69
Shoaib Mohammad b Ratnayeke 9
Mansoor Akhtar run out 13
Saeed Anwar run out 33
Javed Miandad c Samarasekera b Labrooy . 43
*Imran Khan c and b Labrooy 32
Ijaz Ahmed not out 3
Wasim Akram run out 0
Abdul Qadir not out 0
B 1, l-b 5, w 11, n-b 3 20

1/27 2/51 3/118 4/151 5/206 6/220 7/221 (7 wkts, 47 overs) 222

Waqar Younis and Aaqib Javed did not bat.

Bowling: Labrooy 10–1–43–2; Ratnayeke 10–2–33–2; Wijegunawardene 7–0–27–0; Ratnayake 9–0–54–0; Ranatunga 4–0–18–0; Gurusinha 7–0–41–0.

Sri Lanka

R. S. Mahanama not out 19
M. A. R. Samarasekera c Aaqib Javed b Abdul Qadir . 60
†H. P. Tillekeratne c Aamer Malik b Wasim Akram . 1
A. P. Gurusinha b Waqar Younis 37
P. A. de Silva c Imran Khan b Wasim Akram . 40
*A. Ranatunga run out 0
S. T. Jayasuriya c Aamer Malik b Imran Khan . 24
J. R. Ratnayeke c Saeed Anwar b Imran Khan . 2
R. J. Ratnayake not out 1
B 1, l-b 22, w 10, n-b 6 39

1/8 2/103 3/120 4/124 5/179 6/205 7/211 (7 wkts, 45.3 overs) 223

G. F. Labrooy and K. I. W. Wijegunawardene did not bat.

R. S. Mahanama, when 0, retired hurt at 1 and resumed at 179.

Bowling: Wasim Akram 10–1–37–2; Aaqib Javed 10–0–45–0; Waqar Younis 8–1–44–1; Imran Khan 9.3–1–40–2; Abdul Qadir 8–0–34–1.

Umpires: A. R. Crafter and P. J. McConnell.

†AUSTRALIA v PAKISTAN

At Melbourne, January 3 (day/night). Australia won by seven wickets. Toss: Pakistan. Another disappointing performance by Pakistan followed the loss of both openers to Rackemann in the space of four balls. On a difficult pitch, Mansoor and Imran were the only batsmen to show any aggression, with Imran's 39 from 62 balls in 99 minutes holding the lower-order batting together as the scoring slowed markedly. In reply Australia were 17 for two in the sixth over, and had Boon not been given the benefit on a run-out appeal 1 run later, they could have been in trouble. As it was, Border scored a splendid 69 not out from 103 balls and led Australia to a comfortable victory. Both he and Imran were captaining their countries for the 100th time in one-day international matches.

Man of the Match: A. R. Border. *Attendance:* 52,813.

Pakistan

†Aamer Malik c Healy b Rackemann . . 23
Shoaib Mohammad c Healy b Rackemann . 22
Mansoor Akhtar b Taylor 32
Saeed Anwar c Marsh b Taylor 3
*Imran Khan c Hughes b O'Donnell . . . 39
Ijaz Ahmed run out 3
Wasim Akram c Taylor b Rackemann . 8
Abdul Qadir c Border b Alderman 1
Maqsood Rana run out 5
Nadeem Ghauri not out 7
Aaqib Javed run out 1
L-b 8, w 8, n-b 1 17

1/56 2/59 3/67 4/107 5/115 6/136 7/138 8/148 9/156 (50 overs) 161

Bowling: Hughes 10–3–16–0; Alderman 10–2–31–1; Rackemann 10–2–21–3; O'Donnell 9–0–43–1; Taylor 10–0–36–2; Waugh 1–0–6–0.

Australia

D. C. Boon b Nadeem Ghauri 39
G. R. Marsh c Aamer Malik b Wasim Akram . 3
D. M. Jones b Aaqib Javed 2
*A. R. Border not out 69
S. R. Waugh not out 31
B 7, l-b 8, w 2, n-b 1 18

1/6 2/17 3/81 (3 wkts, 41 overs) 162

S. P. O'Donnell, †I. A. Healy, P. L. Taylor, M. G. Hughes, C. G. Rackemann and T. M. Alderman did not bat.

Bowling: Wasim Akram 10–1–24–1; Aaqib Javed 8–0–30–1; Maqsood Rana 2–0–11–0; Imran Khan 7–0–29–0; Nadeem Ghauri 10–3–30–1; Abdul Qadir 4–0–23–0.

Umpires: L. J. King and S. G. Randell.

†AUSTRALIA v SRI LANKA

At Melbourne, January 4 (day/night). Australia won by 73 runs. Toss: Australia. The first part of the World Series Cup ended with both teams going through the motions on an unpredictable pitch. As Border, the Australian captain, said, "To see the pitch crack as it did was disturbing. The cracks lifted the pitch, which made each ball behave differently." Certainly, winning the toss was to Australia's advantage, but it needed a fifth-wicket stand of 82 in 75 minutes to ensure they could exploit it. Jones batted for 130 minutes and faced 98 balls for his 69. Although the Sri Lankan top-order batting tried valiantly to master the conditions, the dismissal of Gurusinha at 121 opened the way for the Australian bowlers. In all, six wickets fell for 8 runs in 27 minutes from 31 deliveries as Australia claimed their fourth win in a row and, even at this early stage, a place in the finals.

Man of the Match: D. M. Jones. *Attendance:* 33,029.

Australia

M. A. Taylor c Tillekeratne b Ratnayeke 16
G. R. Marsh c Tillekeratne b Labrooy . 9
D. M. Jones run out 69
*A. R. Border c Jayasuriya b Ratnayake 10
S. R. Waugh c Tillekeratne b Ratnayake 0
S. P. O'Donnell c Ranatunga b Ratnayake . 36
†I. A. Healy c and b Labrooy 33
P. L. Taylor not out 16
M. G. Hughes not out 0
B 5, l-b 5, w 3 13

1/28 2/28 3/42 4/46 5/128 6/163 7/201 (7 wkts, 50 overs) 202

C. G. Rackemann and T. M. Alderman did not bat.

Bowling: Labrooy 10–0–46–2; Ratnayeke 8–1–24–1; Ratnayake 10–2–44–3; E. A. R. de Silva 10–0–29–0; Ranatunga 2–0–13–0; P. A. de Silva 10–0–36–0.

Sri Lanka

R. S. Mahanama lbw b Rackemann . . . 27
M. A. R. Samarasekera lbw b Alderman 6
†H. P. Tillekeratne c Healy b Hughes . 38
P. A. de Silva lbw b O'Donnell 4
*A. Ranatunga b P. L. Taylor 39
A. P. Gurusinha st Healy b P. L. Taylor 8
R. J. Ratnayake c Hughes b P. L. Taylor 1
S. T. Jayasuriya b Alderman 0
J. R. Ratnayeke c O'Donnell b Alderman 2
E. A. R. de Silva run out 1
G. F. Labrooy not out 1
L-b 1, w 1 2

1/8 2/49 3/58 4/101 5/121 6/125 7/125 8/125 9/127 (41 overs) 129

Bowling: Hughes 8–1–20–1; Alderman 9–1–29–3; Rackemann 8–0–19–1; O'Donnell 7–1–24–1; P. L. Taylor 9–0–36–3.

Umpires: S. G. Randell and C. D. Timmins.

†PAKISTAN v SRI LANKA

At Brisbane, February 10. Pakistan won by five wickets. Toss: Pakistan. The competition resumed with a splendid exhibition of one-day cricket played in the right spirit on an excellent pitch. Sri Lanka owed their good start to a second-wicket partnership of 138 in 116 minutes between Tillekeratne (127 balls) and Gurusinha (108 balls) which occupied 30 overs. For Pakistan, Ijaz Ahmed scored his second century (101 balls) in his 65th one-day international. Batting with aggression and skill, but without resorting to slogging, he hit nine fours and a six in exactly two and a half hours. Had Salim Yousuf (73 balls) and then Javed Miandad not been affected by the high humidity during their innings, Pakistan's victory would have been achieved sooner.

Man of the Match: Ijaz Ahmed. *Attendance:* 4,697.

Sri Lanka

M. A. R. Samarasekera c Ijaz Ahmed b Aaqib Javed . 10
†H. P. Tillekeratne c Ijaz Ahmed b Mushtaq Ahmed . 61
A. P. Gurusinha st Salim Yousuf b Mushtaq Ahmed . 88
R. J. Ratnayake b Tauseef Ahmed 31
P. A. de Silva c Waqar Younis b Tauseef Ahmed . 32
R. S. Mahanama not out 4
*A. Ranatunga not out 1
B 1, l-b 14, w 7, n-b 4 26

1/25 2/163 3/191 4/236 5/251 (5 wkts, 50 overs) 253

S. T. Jayasuriya, E. A. R. de Silva, C. P. H. Ramanayake and N. L. K. Ratnayake did not bat.

Bowling: Wasim Akram 10–1–39–0; Waqar Younis 5–0–27–0; Aaqib Javed 10–1–39–1; Imran Khan 7–0–30–0; Tauseef Ahmed 10–0–48–2; Mushtaq Ahmed 8–0–55–2.

Pakistan

Ramiz Raja c Gurusinha b Ramanayake . 12
†Salim Yousuf b E. A. R. de Silva 52
Ijaz Ahmed not out 102
Javed Miandad c Jayasuriya b P. A. de Silva . 39
Salim Malik c Tillekeratne b Gurusinha 14
*Imran Khan c Mahanama b N. L. K. Ratnayake . 15
Wasim Akram not out 3
L-b 7, w 9, n-b 1 17

1/45 2/114 3/193 4/228 5/251 (5 wkts, 47 overs) 254

Tauseef Ahmed, Mushtaq Ahmed, Waqar Younis and Aaqib Javed did not bat.

Bowling: R. J. Ratnayake 9–1–39–0; N. L. K. Ratnayake 7–0–39–1; Ramanayake 5.2–0–25–1; Ranatunga 3–0–22–0; E. A. R. de Silva 10–0–47–1; Gurusinha 6.4–0–40–1; P. A. de Silva 6–0–35–1.

Umpires: R. J. Evans and C. D. Timmins.

†AUSTRALIA v PAKISTAN

At Brisbane, February 11. Australia won by 67 runs. Toss: Pakistan. A first-wicket stand of 154 in 28 overs and Moody's 89 in 106 minutes from 82 balls put the Australians into a virtually unbeatable position. One of Moody's four sixes landed in nearby Stanley Street, and another just failed to clear the Wilson Stand. Jones and Border, whose 24th run was his 5,000th in his 197th one-day international, increased the scoring-rate, and Australia moved on to 300, only the third time they had reached this milestone in a WSC match. Pakistan replied in kind, scoring at 6 runs an over, but they also lost wickets regularly. Imran's 82 from 89 balls was a valiant effort, but the dismissal of Salim Malik, run out by Moody's direct hit from the deep mid-wicket boundary, proved to be the turning-point.

Man of the Match: T. M. Moody. *Attendance*: 19,874.

Australia

M. A. Taylor b Tauseef Ahmed 66
T. M. Moody lbw b Mushtaq Ahmed .. 89
D. M. Jones run out 32
*A. R. Border c Salim Yousuf b Wasim Akram . 26
S. R. Waugh c Salim Malik b Mushtaq Ahmed . 13
S. P. O'Donnell not out 31
†I. A. Healy not out 22
B 3, l-b 13, w 4, n-b 1 21

1/154 2/176 3/222 4/241 5/246 (5 wkts, 50 overs) 300

P. L. Taylor, C. G. Rackemann, M. G. Hughes and T. M. Alderman did not bat.

Bowling: Wasim Akram 10–1–43–1; Imran Khan 10–0–54–0; Aaqib Javed 10–0–54–0; Tauseef Ahmed 10–0–57–1; Mushtaq Ahmed 10–0–76–2.

Pakistan

Javed Miandad c Waugh b Alderman . 18
†Salim Yousuf c M. A. Taylor b Hughes . 7
Saeed Anwar c Jones b Rackemann . . . 37
Ramiz Raja c P. L. Taylor b O'Donnell 9
Ijaz Ahmed run out 27
*Imran Khan c Border b Rackemann . . 82
Salim Malik run out 27
Wasim Akram b Rackemann 8
Mushtaq Ahmed c M. A. Taylor b Rackemann . 11
Tauseef Ahmed run out 1
Aaqib Javed not out 0
B 2, l-b 2, w 1, n-b 1 6

1/20 2/37 3/66 4/77 5/132 6/192 7/206 8/228 9/233 (39.1 overs) 233

Bowling: Alderman 5–0–39–1; Hughes 7–0–39–1; Rackemann 8.1–0–44–4; O'Donnell 8–0–43–1; P. L. Taylor 7–0–41–0; Border 4–0–23–0.

Umpires: R. J. Evans and T. A. Prue.

†AUSTRALIA v PAKISTAN

At Sydney, February 13 (day/night). Pakistan won by five wickets. Toss: Pakistan. With 25 inches of rain having fallen in Sydney over the previous twelve days, it was a credit to the curator, Peter Leroy, and his staff that the match was played at all. In the circumstances, Pakistan's decision to ask Australia to bat was a wise one, for only four strokes reached the boundary in their 50 overs. Jones, with 54 from 89 balls, reached his 24th half-century in limited-overs internationals in possibly the worst batting conditions of his career. Nor did umpiring errors improve matters: overs were miscounted and Miandad was adjudged lbw when batting well in front of his crease. Next day the newspapers were unanimous in describing the match as "the farce on grass". Pakistan owed their victory to Imran (106 balls) and Akram (30 balls).

Man of the Match: Imran Khan. *Attendance:* 29,810.

Australia

M. A. Taylor b Imran Khan 23
T. M. Moody b Wasim Akram 3
D. M. Jones run out 54
S. R. Waugh c Javed Miandad b Shoaib Mohammad . 28
S. P. O'Donnell b Imran Khan 3
*A. R. Border run out 22
†I. A. Healy b Wasim Akram 11
P. L. Taylor not out 3
C. J. McDermott run out 0
L-b 13, w 3, n-b 2 18

1/8 2/68 3/110 4/123 5/125 6/153 7/164 8/165 (8 wkts, 50 overs) 165

C. G. Rackemann and T. M. Alderman did not bat.

Bowling: Wasim Akram 10–2–21–2; Waqar Younis 10–1–36–0; Aaqib Javed 7–0–28–0; Nadeem Ghauri 10–1–23–0; Imran Khan 10–1–30–2; Shoaib Mohammad 3–0–14–1.

Pakistan

Saeed Anwar b McDermott 27
Shoaib Mohammad c McDermott b O'Donnell . 9
Ijaz Ahmed b O'Donnell 3
Javed Miandad lbw b Alderman 29
*Imran Khan not out 56
Salim Malik c Border b P. L. Taylor . . 0
Wasim Akram not out 34
B 3, l-b 4, n-b 2 9

1/32 2/38 3/43 4/102 5/111 (5 wkts, 48.3 overs) 167

†Salim Yousuf, Waqar Younis, Aaqib Javed and Nadeem Ghauri did not bat.

Bowling: Alderman 10–2–29–1; McDermott 8–1–35–1; O'Donnell 9.3–1–32–2; Rackemann 8–1–24–0; P. L. Taylor 9–1–26–1; Border 4–0–14–0.

Umpires: R. J. Evans and T. A. Prue.

†PAKISTAN v SRI LANKA

At Hobart, February 15. Pakistan won by six wickets. Toss: Pakistan. In contrast to the previous fixture, Bellerive Oval was in perfect condition for what proved to be a most entertaining match. Waqar Younis claimed early wickets, but a fifth-wicket stand of 72 in 47 minutes between Gurusinha and Ranatunga pulled Sri Lanka out of trouble. Gurusinha, batting in an enterprising manner, scored his 59 from 84 deliveries, but when he was out, the lower order failed to consolidate the innings. Ramiz Raja, in his 101st one-day international, batted throughout the Pakistan reply, reaching his fifty from 60 balls, his hundred from 133, and in all batting for 198 minutes (148 balls). His third-wicket partnership of 105 with Miandad gradually took any initiative away from the Sri Lankan bowlers.

Man of the Match: Ramiz Raja. *Attendance:* 3,323.

Sri Lanka

M. A. R. Samarasekera lbw b Waqar Younis . 7
D. S. B. P. Kuruppu c Salim Yousuf b Waqar Younis . 1
A. P. Gurusinha b Waqar Younis 59
†H. P. Tillekeratne b Imran Khan 19
P. A. de Silva c and b Aaqib Javed . . . 5
*A. Ranatunga c Wasim Akram b Nadeem Ghauri . 42
R. S. Mahanama c Salim Yousuf b Nadeem Ghauri . 24
E. A. R. de Silva b Waqar Younis 1
R. J. Ratnayake c Salim Yousuf b Wasim Akram . 14
G. F. Labrooy c Ramiz Raja b Aaqib Javed . 2
K. I. W. Wijegunawardene not out 0
L-b 10, w 9, n-b 2 21

1/6 2/25 3/62 4/79 5/151 6/152 7/158 8/188 9/193 (47.5 overs) 195

Bowling: Wasim Akram 9–2–23–1; Imran Khan 10–0–28–1; Waqar Younis 10–2–39–4; Aaqib Javed 8.5–0–44–2; Nadeem Ghauri 10–0–51–2.

Pakistan

Ramiz Raja not out 116
Saeed Anwar b Ratnayake 17
Ijaz Ahmed lbw b Wijegunawardene . . . 1
Javed Miandad c E. A. R. de Silva b Wijegunawardene . 42
Salim Malik run out 3
†Salim Yousuf not out 10
B 1, l-b 4, w 4 9

1/46 2/53 3/158 4/166 (4 wkts, 48.3 overs) 198

*Imran Khan, Wasim Akram, Waqar Younis, Aaqib Javed and Nadeem Ghauri did not bat.

Bowling: Labrooy 9–0–41–0; Ratnayake 9.3–0–47–1; Wijegunawardene 10–1–34–2; Ranatunga 10–0–37–0; E. A. R. de Silva 10–0–34–0.

Umpires: L. J. King and S. G. Randell.

†PAKISTAN v SRI LANKA

At Adelaide, February 17. Pakistan won by 27 runs. Toss: Sri Lanka. A WSC record aggregate of 603 runs, with only eleven wickets falling, was the product of a near-perfect Adelaide pitch and a match which, for a long time, was evenly poised. The Pakistan openers, Ramiz and Anwar, were not parted until the 33rd over, by which time they had put on 202 in just 132 minutes and beaten the previous best opening stand (182) in WSC matches. They were just 10 short of the world best for the first wicket in one-day internationals. Anwar, normally a middle-order batsman, hit six sixes and eight fours in his 126 (99 balls), while Ramiz again batted throughout the innings. His unbeaten 107 came from 158 balls and contained three boundaries. Sri Lanka lost wickets at regular intervals before Ranatunga and Mahanama, in a fifth-wicket stand, added 128 in 78 minutes from 120 balls. However, tight bowling by Waqar Younis prevented Sri Lanka's final assault from getting too close to Pakistan's total.

Man of the Match: Saeed Anwar. *Attendance:* 3,854.

Pakistan

Ramiz Raja not out ... 107
Saeed Anwar b E. A. R. de Silva ... 126
Salim Malik c Ratnayake b E. A. R. de Silva . 25
Wasim Akram b Ratnayake ... 34
*Imran Khan not out ... 1
B 5, l-b 10, w 4, n-b 3 ... 22

1/202 2/252 3/314 (3 wkts, 50 overs) 315

Javed Miandad, Ijaz Ahmed, †Salim Yousuf, Waqar Younis, Aaqib Javed and Nadeem Ghauri did not bat.

Bowling: Labrooy 10–0–56–0; Ratnayake 10–1–38–1; Wijegunawardene 4–0–38–0; Ranatunga 10–0–50–0; P. A. de Silva 4–0–30–0; E. A. R. de Silva 9–0–57–2; Gurusinha 3–0–31–0.

Sri Lanka

†D. S. B. P. Kuruppu run out ... 37
M. A. R. Samarasekera c Wasim Akram b Aaqib Javed . 24
P. A. de Silva run out ... 22
*A. Ranatunga c Salim Malik b Aaqib Javed . 64
A. P. Gurusinha c Javed Miandad b Nadeem Ghauri . 16
R. S. Mahanama run out ... 72
R. J. Ratnayake b Waqar Younis ... 3
G. F. Labrooy b Waqar Younis ... 12
E. A. R. de Silva not out ... 3
H. P. Tillekeratne not out ... 5
B 1, l-b 21, w 6, n-b 2 ... 30

1/55 2/90 3/94 4/123 5/251 6/258 7/271 8/280 (8 wkts, 50 overs) 288

K. I. W. Wijegunawardene did not bat.

Bowling: Wasim Akram 10–0–49–0; Waqar Younis 10–1–35–2; Aaqib Javed 10–0–57–2; Nadeem Ghauri 8–0–54–1; Imran Khan 10–0–60–0; Ijaz Ahmed 2–0–11–0.

Umpires: A. R. Crafter and S. G. Randell.

†AUSTRALIA v SRI LANKA

At Adelaide, February 18. Australia won by seven wickets. Toss: Sri Lanka. Ranatunga's decision to bat first was not supported by his top-order batsmen, who fell to unnecessary strokes against a jaded Australian attack. Aravinda de Silva struck 39 from 29 balls, including three sixes and three fours, but it needed an eighth-wicket partnership of 44 between Jayasuriya and Ratnayake to give the total any substance. Jones opened the innings for Australia and was unbeaten at the end with 80, made in 149 minutes from 120 deliveries with five fours.

Man of the Match: D. M. Jones. *Attendance:* 16,827.

Sri Lanka

D. S. B. P. Kuruppu c Alderman b Rackemann . 12
M. A. R. Samarasekera c Healy b Rackemann . 1
A. P. Gurusinha c Healy b Campbell .. 20
P. A. de Silva b Alderman ... 39
*A. Ranatunga c Healy b Campbell ... 1
†H. P. Tillekeratne b Campbell ... 3
S. T. Jayasuriya c M. A. Taylor b Border 31
E. A. R. de Silva b O'Donnell ... 7
R. J. Ratnayake run out ... 31
A. W. R. Madurasinghe c P. L. Taylor b Border . 1
K. I. W. Wijegunawardene not out ... 1
B 1, l-b 5, w 1, n-b 4 ... 11

1/10 2/21 3/68 4/70 5/81 6/88 7/106 8/150 9/155 (40.4 overs) 158

Bowling: Alderman 7–0–30–1; Rackemann 9–0–48–2; Campbell 7–1–31–3; O'Donnell 7–0–19–1; P. L. Taylor 8–1–22–0; Border 2.4–1–2–2.

Australia

M. A. Taylor c Madurasinghe b E. A. R. de Silva . 23
D. M. Jones not out 80
T. M. Moody c Kuruppu b Gurusinha . 5
*A. R. Border b Madurasinghe 29
S. R. Waugh not out 11
B 7, l-b 2, w 2 11

1/67 2/78 3/134 (3 wkts, 40 overs) 159

S. P. O'Donnell, †I. A. Healy, P. L. Taylor, G. D. Campbell, C. G. Rackemann and T. M. Alderman did not bat.

Bowling: Ratnayake 7–1–20–0; Wijegunawardene 7–0–34–0; Gurusinha 7–0–16–1; E. A. R. de Silva 10–0–37–1; Madurasinghe 6–0–27–1; Jayasuriya 3–0–16–0.

Umpires: A. R. Crafter and P. J. McConnell.

†AUSTRALIA v PAKISTAN

At Sydney, February 20 (day/night). Pakistan won by 2 runs. Toss: Pakistan. With the result of no importance to the placings in the qualifying table, both sides provided entertaining cricket in damp conditions. Border, the Australian captain, was playing in his 200th one-day international, becoming the first to reach this milestone. Although the Pakistan innings began under heavy cloud cover and in high humidity, this did not prevent Saeed Anwar from playing some superb attacking strokes, including a six which failed narrowly to clear the roof of the Ladies' Stand. Salim Malik and Imran then added 87 for the third wicket in 75 minutes. Moody anchored the Australian reply, being sixth out after scoring 74 from 109 balls. O'Donnell hit out at the end, but the decisive influence on the result was Imran, who bowled a fourteen-minute maiden over in which three wickets fell. After the match, the five judges of the Man of the Match award stated publicly that they would have given it to Imran had they not been under pressure from Channel Nine to name the player before the match was over. At the time of their early decision, O'Donnell had looked like winning the game for Australia.

Man of the Match: S. P. O'Donnell. *Attendance:* 24,581.

Pakistan

Ramiz Raja c Moody b Alderman 3
Saeed Anwar c Waugh b Campbell 43
Salim Malik c Moody b Rackemann . . . 67
*Imran Khan c M. A. Taylor b Alderman . 56
Ijaz Ahmed c Waugh b O'Donnell 9
†Salim Yousuf lbw b O'Donnell 5
Aamer Malik b Campbell 14
Mushtaq Ahmed not out 17
Waqar Younis run out 0
Tauseef Ahmed not out 1
W 2, n-b 3 5

1/4 2/74 3/161 4/176 5/184 6/196 7/207 8/218 (8 wkts, 49 overs) 220

Aaqib Javed did not bat.

Bowling: Alderman 9–2–46–2; Rackemann 10–0–45–1; Campbell 9–0–46–2; O'Donnell 10–0–32–2; P. L. Taylor 7–0–28–0; Border 4–0–23–0.

Australia

M. A. Taylor c Salim Yousuf b Waqar Younis . 29
T. M. Moody st Salim Yousuf b Saeed Anwar . 74
D. M. Jones c Ijaz Ahmed b Aaqib Javed 10
*A. R. Border b Tauseef Ahmed 26
S. R. Waugh st Salim Yousuf b Mushtaq Ahmed . 3
P. L. Taylor c Imran Khan b Mushtaq Ahmed . 14
S. P. O'Donnell lbw b Imran Khan 39
†I. A. Healy run out 8
G. D. Campbell not out 4
C. G. Rackemann b Imran Khan 0
T. M. Alderman not out 0
L-b 5, w 6 11

1/44 2/58 3/122 4/127 5/159 6/169 7/192 8/218 9/218 (9 wkts, 49 overs) 218

Bowling: Imran Khan 7–1–28–2; Waqar Younis 7–0–40–1; Aaqib Javed 9–0–39–1; Aamer Malik 3–0–12–0; Tauseef Ahmed 10–0–33–1; Mushtaq Ahmed 10–1–46–2; Saeed Anwar 3–0–15–1.

Umpires: L. J. King and P. J. McConnell.

QUALIFYING TABLE

	Played	Won	Lost	Points	Run-rate
Australia	8	6	2	12	4.44
Pakistan	8	5	3	10	4.53
Sri Lanka	8	1	7	2	4.19

†AUSTRALIA v PAKISTAN

First Final Match

At Melbourne, February 23 (day/night). Australia won by seven wickets. Toss: Australia. Following early-morning rain – and the failure of the groundstaff to cover the pitch overnight – the umpires allowed play to start on time only after a number of inspections. In such conditions the toss was crucial, and Pakistan, put in, were reduced to 50 for five by the Australian fast bowlers. They went six overs without scoring, from the twelfth to the seventeenth, as Rackemann embarked on a spell of four consecutive maiden overs. However, Wasim Akram overcame the difficult conditions and a groin injury to make the match something of a contest, hitting three sixes and six fours in 86 from 76 balls before he was ninth out. To the delight of the Melbourne crowd, Jones hit an unbeaten 83 from 135 balls, and in an 87-minute partnership with Border (61 balls) he added 109 to win the match with some ease.

Attendance: 55,205.

Pakistan

Saeed Anwar c and b Alderman	2
Ramiz Raja c Healy b O'Donnell	1
Salim Malik c Alderman b Campbell	39
Javed Miandad c Healy b Rackemann	2
*Imran Khan c Healy b Rackemann	1
Ijaz Ahmed lbw b O'Donnell	7
Wasim Akram c P. L. Taylor b Campbell	86
†Salim Yousuf c Rackemann b P. L. Taylor	4
Tauseef Ahmed c P. L. Taylor b Campbell	10
Waqar Younis b Alderman	0
Nadeem Ghauri not out	3
L-b 3, w 3, n-b 1	7
1/2 2/8 3/46 4/50 5/50 6/77 7/96 8/153 9/159 (47.5 overs)	162

Bowling: Alderman 8.5–2–26–2; O'Donnell 10–2–29–2; Rackemann 10–5–32–2; Campbell 9–1–39–3; P. L. Taylor 10–0–33–1.

Australia

M. A. Taylor c Salim Yousuf b Waqar Younis	13
T. M. Moody c Salim Yousuf b Wasim Akram	4
D. M. Jones not out	83
S. R. Waugh b Wasim Akram	13
*A. R. Border not out	44
L-b 3, w 1, n-b 2	6
1/9 2/23 3/54 (3 wkts, 45.5 overs)	163

S. P. O'Donnell, †I. A. Healy, P. L. Taylor, G. D. Campbell, C. G. Rackemann and T. M. Alderman did not bat.

Bowling: Wasim Akram 10–0–30–2; Imran Khan 9–0–32–0; Waqar Younis 9–0–26–1; Nadeem Ghauri 9–0–27–0; Tauseef Ahmed 8.5–0–45–0.

Umpires: A. R. Crafter and P. J. McConnell.

†AUSTRALIA v PAKISTAN

Second Final Match

At Sydney, February 25. Australia won by 69 runs. Toss: Australia. The Australian selectors omitted Stephen Waugh for the first time in 87 one-day internationals, bringing in his twin, Mark. Moody (63 balls) and Mark Taylor put on 84 in twenty overs for the first wicket, and after Taylor (120 balls) and Jones (53 balls) had added 95 in eighteen overs, the later batsmen gathered runs freely, helped by some appalling fielding. Pakistan's gamble in promoting Wasim Akram up the order was thwarted when, after he had scored 36 from 29 deliveries, Peter Taylor deceived him through the air and Healy made an excellent stumping. Salim Yousuf hit out in the dying stages, scoring 59 from 75 balls, but the loss of Imran for a single had signalled the end for Pakistan much earlier.

Man of the Finals: D. M. Jones. *Attendance:* 34,443.

Australia

M. A. Taylor c Waqar Younis b Mushtaq Ahmed . 76	†I. A. Healy c Saeed Anwar b Mushtaq Ahmed . 15
T. M. Moody st Salim Yousuf b Nadeem Ghauri . 44	P. L. Taylor not out 3
D. M. Jones run out 46	
*A. R. Border not out 34	B 1, l-b 11, w 6, n-b 2 20
M. E. Waugh run out 14	
S. P. O'Donnell c Salim Yousuf b Imran Khan . 3	1/84 2/179 3/183 4/207 5/214 6/231 (6 wkts, 50 overs) 255

G. D. Campbell, C. G. Rackemann and T. M. Alderman did not bat.

Bowling: Wasim Akram 10–0–42–0; Imran Khan 10–0–43–1; Waqar Younis 10–0–48–0; Nadeem Ghauri 10–0–45–1; Mushtaq Ahmed 10–0–65–2.

Pakistan

Saeed Anwar c Healy b O'Donnell 5	Mushtaq Ahmed c Healy b P. L. Taylor 0
Ramiz Raja lbw b Alderman 0	Waqar Younis not out 20
Wasim Akram st Healy b P. L. Taylor . 36	Nadeem Ghauri c Campbell b O'Donnell 4
Salim Malik b Alderman 15	L-b 2, w 2, n-b 2 6
Javed Miandad run out 11	
*Imran Khan c M. A. Taylor b Campbell 1	1/6 2/6 3/52 (47 overs) 186
Ijaz Ahmed b P. L. Taylor 29	4/62 5/72 6/76
†Salim Yousuf c Moody b O'Donnell . . 59	7/132 8/132 9/176

Bowling: Alderman 7–1–28–2; O'Donnell 6–1–38–3; P. L. Taylor 10–1–43–3; Rackemann 8–1–20–0; Campbell 7–0–21–1; Border 9–0–34–0.

Umpires: A. R. Crafter and P. J. McConnell.

AUSTRAL-ASIA CUP, 1989-90

By QAMAR AHMED

Pakistan continued their winning ways in Sharjah tournaments when they beat Australia by 36 runs in the final of the six-nation Austral-Asia Cup early in May 1990. In addition to the trophy, Pakistan won $US30,000 while Australia, as runners-up, received $US20,000 and New Zealand and Sri Lanka, the losing semi-finalists, $US10,000 each. Bangladesh and India were the other countries involved.

For the second time in six months, the Pakistan left-arm all-rounder, Wasim Akram, claimed a hat-trick in Sharjah. This time he did so against Australia in the final. The highlight of the tournament, however, was the fast bowling of his young team-mate, Waqar Younis, whose seventeen wickets brought him the Man of the Series award and $US5,000. In Australia's semi-final against Sri Lanka, Simon O'Donnell hit a half-century off just eighteen deliveries to beat the previous record for the fastest fifty in one-day internationals: off 21 deliveries by B. L. Cairns (New Zealand v Australia at Melbourne, 1982-83) and Salim Malik (Pakistan v India at Calcutta, 1986-87).

The Cricketers' Benefit Fund Series beneficiaries at the Austral-Asia Cup tournament were the Australian captain, A. R. Border, the former Sri Lankan captain, L. R. D. Mendis, Ghulam Ahmed and Madan Lal of India, and Imtiaz Ahmed and Salim Malik of Pakistan.

GROUP A

†AUSTRALIA v NEW ZEALAND

At Sharjah, April 26. Australia won by 63 runs. Toss: New Zealand. Australia, 115 for three when they lost Mark Taylor in the 27th over, built on this good start to set New Zealand a target in excess of 5 an over. Boon and Waugh added 81 for the fourth wicket, and Boon and Border put on 51 off 47 balls for the fifth. New Zealand, 26 for two in the tenth over, partially recovered as Crowe and Greatbatch put on 65 in seventeen overs, but when Border cut through their middle order with a spell of three for 1 in fourteen balls, an Australian victory never looked in doubt.

Man of the Match: D. C. Boon.

Australia

G. R. Marsh c Smith b Snedden 26	S. P. O'Donnell not out 3
M. A. Taylor run out 60	
D. M. Jones c Morrison b Snedden 1	B 2, l-b 4, w 2 8
D. C. Boon not out 92	—
S. R. Waugh run out 34	1/67 2/73 3/115 (5 wkts, 50 overs) 258
*A. R. Border c Bracewell b Morrison . 34	4/196 5/247

†I. A. Healy, P. L. Taylor, C. G. Rackemann and T. M. Alderman did not bat.

Bowling: Morrison 10–1–51–1; Millmow 10–0–57–0; Bracewell 10–0–47–0; Snedden 10–1–31–2; Priest 7–0–43–0; Rutherford 3–0–23–0.

New Zealand

*J. G. Wright c Marsh b Alderman . . . 0
M. D. Crowe b P. L. Taylor 41
A. H. Jones b O'Donnell 15
M. J. Greatbatch b Border 37
K. R. Rutherford c and b Border 20
†I. D. S. Smith c Marsh b Border 2
J. G. Bracewell not out 36
M. W. Priest b Alderman 15
M. C. Snedden not out 13
L-b 11, w 4, n-b 1 16

1/0 2/26 3/91 4/121 5/127 6/129 7/166 (7 wkts, 50 overs) 195

J. P. Millmow and D. K. Morrison did not bat.

Bowling: Alderman 10–0–46–2; Rackemann 7–0–27–0; O'Donnell 10–3–27–1; Waugh 7–0–32–0; P. L. Taylor 10–0–27–1; Border 6–1–25–3.

Umpires: R. B. Gupta and Khizar Hayat.

†BANGLADESH v NEW ZEALAND

At Sharjah, April 28. New Zealand won by 161 runs. Toss: New Zealand. New Zealand took advantage of some mediocre Bangladeshi bowling to reach their highest total in a one-day international, their previous best being 309 for five (off 60 overs) against East Africa in the 1975 World Cup. Wright and Crowe initiated the run spree with a New Zealand record opening stand of 158. Wright hit eight fours in his 93 and Crowe a six and just two fours in his 69. Jones, who also missed his hundred by 7 runs, struck three sixes and five fours in his 73-ball 93.

Man of the Match: A. H. Jones.

New Zealand

M. D. Crowe b Minhaz-ul-Abedin 69
*J. G. Wright c and b Minhaz-ul-Abedin 93
A. H. Jones c Jahangir Shah b Nawsher 93
M. J. Greatbatch c Akram Khan b Golam Faruq . 32
K. R. Rutherford not out 30
S. A. Thomson not out 8
L-b 6, w 5, n-b 2 13

1/158 2/178 3/269 4/321 (4 wkts, 50 overs) 338

†I. D. S. Smith, J. G. Bracewell, M. C. Snedden, J. P. Millmow and D. K. Morrison did not bat.

Bowling: Nawsher 10–0–55–1; Golam Faruq 4.3–0–28–1; Jahangir Shah 9–0–62–0; Enam-ul-Haque 10–0–72–0; Azhar Hussain 7–0–51–0; Minhaz-ul-Abedin 7–0–39–2; Gazi Ashraf 0.3–0–4–0; Amin-ul-Islam 2–0–21–0.

Bangladesh

Azhar Hussain b Rutherford 54
Zahid Razzak lbw b Millmow 4
*Gazi Ashraf b Snedden 8
Akram Khan c and b Bracewell 33
Minhaz-ul-Abedin c Wright b Millmow. 18
Amin-ul-Islam not out 30
Enam-ul-Haque not out 13
B 1, l-b 10, w 6 17

1/11 2/37 3/79 4/115 5/137 (5 wkts, 50 overs) 177

ahangir Shah, †Nasir Nasu, Golam Faruq and G. M. Nawsher did not bat.

Bowling: Morrison 6–0–19–0; Millmow 10–0–41–2; Thomson 10–1–32–0; Snedden -2–18–1; Bracewell 10–0–32–1; Jones 4–1–12–0; Rutherford 3–0–12–1.

Umpires: R. B. Gupta and Khizar Hayat.

†AUSTRALIA v BANGLADESH

t Sharjah, April 30. Australia won by seven wickets. Toss: Bangladesh. Having chosen to at first, Bangladesh were 59 for six in the 39th over before Amin-ul-Islam and Enam-ul-laque put on 48 for the seventh wicket. Islam made his 41 not out off 76 balls, hitting three urs. Australia reached their target in the 26th over, with Peter Taylor remaining undefeated ith 54 scored off 46 balls.

Man of the Match: P. L. Taylor.

Bangladesh

Azhar Hussain c Healy b Hughes 5
Zahid Razzak c Healy b Campbell 4
*Gazi Ashraf b P. L. Taylor 18
Akram Khan c Marsh b O'Donnell 13
Faruq Ahmed lbw b Waugh 6
Minhaz-ul-Abedin c Healy b P. L. Taylor 0
Amin-ul-Islam not out 41
Enam-ul-Haque c Jones b Waugh 18
†Nasir Nasu b O'Donnell 3
Alam Talukdar not out 7
B 2, l-b 7, w 8, n-b 2 19

1/10 2/12 3/33 4/47 5/50 6/59 7/107 8/121 (8 wkts, 50 overs) 134

G. M. Nawsher did not bat.

Bowling: Hughes 10–3–15–1; Campbell 10–1–32–1; Waugh 10–2–22–2; O'Donnell 10–1–34–2; P. L. Taylor 10–2–22–2.

Australia

S. P. O'Donnell c Gazi Ashraf b Minhaz-ul-Abedin . 20
†I. A. Healy c Azhar Hussain b Nawsher 34
D. M. Jones c Faruq Ahmed b Minhaz-ul-Abedin . 19
P. L. Taylor not out 54
M. G. Hughes not out 10
L-b 1, w 1, n-b 1 3

1/50 2/58 3/102 (3 wkts, 25.4 overs) 140

M. A. Taylor, G. R. Marsh, D. C. Boon, *A. R. Border, S. R. Waugh and G. D. Campbell did not bat.

Bowling: Nawsher 6–0–27–1; Alam Talukdar 4–0–20–0; Azhar Hussain 7–1–26–0; Minhaz-ul-Abedin 6–0–43–2; Amin-ul-Islam 1.4–0–16–0; Enam-ul-Haque 1–0–7–0.

Umpires: R. B. Gupta and Khizar Hayat.

GROUP A FINAL TABLE

	Played	*Won*	*Lost*	*Points*	*Run-rate*
Australia	2	2	0	4	5.25
New Zealand	2	1	1	2	5.33
Bangladesh	2	0	2	0	3.11

GROUP B

†INDIA v SRI LANKA

At Sharjah, April 25. Sri Lanka won by three wickets. Toss: Sri Lanka. The Sri Lankans having required 55 off the last five overs, won with four balls remaining, thanks to a spectacular unbeaten 85 off 77 balls by their captain, Ranatunga (three sixes, four fours). A 134 for six in the 36th over, his side's challenge was in the balance, but a seventh-wicke partnership of 69 from 66 balls with Ratnayeke set up a final assault which produced 44 runs in twenty deliveries.

Man of the Match: A. Ranatunga.

India

K. Srikkanth c Samarasekera b Karnain 19
W. V. Raman c Tillekeratne b Ratnayeke . 7
N. S. Sidhu c Ratnayake b Gurusinha . 64
*M. Azharuddin c Madurasinghe b Ratnayeke .108
S. R. Tendulkar run out 10
R. J. Shastri c P. A. de Silva b Karnain 9
Kapil Dev run out 8
†K. S. More c Samarasekera b Ratnayeke .
M. Prabhakar not out ....
Sanjeev Sharma not out ....
L-b 3, w 6, n-b 1 1

1/30 2/35 3/149 4/168 5/190 6/223 7/236 8/238 (8 wkts, 50 overs) 24

A. Kumble did not bat.

Bowling: Ratnayeke 10–0–31–3; Ratnayake 10–0–52–0; Karnain 10–1–43–2; Ranatung 8–0–40–0; E. A. R. de Silva 6–0–38–0; Gurusinha 6–0–34–1.

Sri Lanka

M. A. R. Samarasekera c More b Kapil Dev . 14
†H. P. Tillekeratne b S. Sharma 24
A. P. Gurusinha run out 21
P. A. de Silva b S. Sharma 34
*A. Ranatunga not out 85
S. T. Jayasuriya c Tendulkar b Shastri . 4
S. H. U. Karnain c More b Kumble 1
J. R. Ratnayeke b Prabhakar 22
R. J. Ratnayake not out 15
L-b 12, w 7, n-b 3 22

1/29 2/41 3/97 4/111 5/128 6/134 7/203 (7 wkts, 49.2 overs) 242

E. A. R. de Silva and A. W. R. Madurasinghe did not bat.

Bowling: Kapil Dev 9.2–1–44–1; Prabhakar 10–1–51–1; Kumble 10–0–42–1; S. Sharma 10–1–63–2; Shastri 10–1–30–1.

Umpires: B. L. Aldridge and A. R. Crafter.

†INDIA v PAKISTAN

At Sharjah, April 27. Pakistan won by 26 runs. Toss: India. India's second successive defeat cost them a place in the semi-finals. Needing 236 to win, they were bowled out in the 47th over, having succumbed at vital stages to the pace of Waqar Younis. The only batting of note came from their captain, Azharuddin, whose unbeaten 78 from 98 balls included two sixes. Pakistan's innings was established by Salim Yousuf, who had been promoted to open the batting and hit a calculated 62.

Man of the Match: Waqar Younis.

Pakistan

Saeed Anwar c Kapil Dev b Shastri . . . 37
†Salim Yousuf st More b Kumble 62
Salim Malik b Shastri 7
Javed Miandad run out 37
*Imran Khan c More b Prabhakar 18
Wasim Akram lbw b S. Sharma 11
Ijaz Ahmed c Shastri b Prabhakar 32
Abdul Qadir run out 1
Sajjad Akbar run out 5
Waqar Younis not out 7
Aaqib Javed not out 0
B 4, l-b 6, w 8 18

1/73 2/90 3/130 4/166 5/178 6/193 7/195 8/216 9/235 (9 wkts, 50 overs) 235

Bowling: Kapil Dev 5–0–30–0; Prabhakar 10–0–55–2; S. Sharma 10–0–52–1; Shastri 10–0–36–2; Kumble 10–0–33–1; Srikkanth 5–0–19–0.

India

K. Srikkanth st Salim Yousuf b Sajjad Akbar . 35
M. Prabhakar run out 27
N. S. Sidhu b Waqar Younis 0
M. Azharuddin not out 78
Kapil Dev b Waqar Younis 1
S. V. Manjrekar c Ijaz Ahmed b Sajjad Akbar . 10
S. R. Tendulkar c Saeed Anwar b Imran Khan . 20
R. J. Shastri c Salim Yousuf b Waqar Younis . 3
†K. S. More c Javed Miandad b Wasim Akram . 4
Sanjeev Sharma c Salim Yousuf b Waqar Younis . 5
A. Kumble run out 0
B 2, l-b 6, w 17, n-b 1 26

1/61 2/61 3/88 4/91 5/129 6/165 7/190 8/197 9/208 (46.3 overs) 209

Bowling: Wasim Akram 8.3–0–28–1; Aaqib Javed 8–0–25–0; Waqar Younis 10–0–42–4; Abdul Qadir 7–0–44–0; Sajjad Akbar 10–1–45–2; Imran Khan 3–0–17–1.

Umpires: B. L. Aldridge and A. R. Crafter.

†PAKISTAN v SRI LANKA

At Sharjah, April 29. Pakistan won by 90 runs. Toss: Sri Lanka. After a solid start from Salim Yousuf and the left-handed Saeed Anwar, Javed Miandad and Ijaz Ahmed set about the Sri Lankan bowling in the most thrilling manner. Miandad's 75 came from 85 balls and included five fours, while Ijaz hit three sixes and eight fours in an electrifying 89 off 65 deliveries. Waqar Younis never allowed the Sri Lankan batsmen time to take up the challenge and finished with six for 26 from his ten overs. Ratnayake provided a momentary respite to Pakistan's dominance by hitting three sixes in his nineteen-ball 26.

Man of the Match: Ijaz Ahmed.

Pakistan

Saeed Anwar b Madurasinghe 40
†Salim Yousuf run out 46
Javed Miandad c Gurusinha b Ratnayeke . 75
Salim Malik b P. A. de Silva 26
Ijaz Ahmed c Ranatunga b Ratnayake . 89
*Imran Khan c Tillekeratne b Ratnayeke 8
Mansoor Rana lbw b Ratnayeke 5
Mushtaq Ahmed not out 4
Waqar Younis b Ratnayake 2
Zakir Khan not out 2
B 2, l-b 3, w 7, n-b 2 14

1/82 2/110 3/163 4/246 5/294 6/301 7/302 8/307 (8 wkts, 50 overs) 311

Aaqib Javed did not bat.

Bowling: Ratnayeke 10–0–65–3; Ratnayake 9–0–44–2; Karnain 2–0–18–0; Madurasinghe 10–0–40–1; E. A. R. de Silva 8–0–57–0; P. A. de Silva 10–0–63–1; Ranatunga 1–0–19–0.

Sri Lanka

M. A. R. Samarasekera run out 29
H. P. Tillekeratne lbw b Waqar Younis 19
A. P. Gurusinha c Salim Yousuf b Aaqib Javed . 9
P. A. de Silva b Waqar Younis 0
†D. S. B. P. Kuruppu b Waqar Younis 41
*A. Ranatunga c Saeed Anwar b Mushtaq Ahmed . 38
R. J. Ratnayake b Waqar Younis 26
S. H. U. Karnain b Waqar Younis 14
J. R. Ratnayeke c Salim Yousuf b Zakir Khan . 9
E. A. R. de Silva lbw b Waqar Younis . 0
A. W. R. Madurasinghe not out 1
B 2, l-b 13, w 16, n-b 4 35

1/43 2/60 3/64 4/64 5/132 6/184 7/185 8/214 9/217 (47.4 overs) 221

Bowling: Zakir Khan 9.4–0–41–1; Aaqib Javed 9–2–34–1; Waqar Younis 10–1–26–6; Mushtaq Ahmed 8–0–49–1; Saeed Anwar 10–0–49–0; Mansoor Rana 1–0–7–0.

Umpires: B. L. Aldridge and A. R. Crafter.

GROUP B FINAL TABLE

	Played	*Won*	*Lost*	*Points*	*Run-rate*
Pakistan	2	2	0	4	5.46
Sri Lanka	2	1	1	2	4.77
India	2	0	2	0	4.66

SEMI-FINALS

†NEW ZEALAND v PAKISTAN

At Sharjah, May 1. Pakistan won by eight wickets. Toss: New Zealand. Having elected t bat, the New Zealanders were humiliated by the young Pakistan fast bowler, Waqar Younis who finished with five wickets for 20 in nine overs to assure Pakistan of a place in the fina Pakistan reached their target in the sixteenth over for the loss of only two wickets. Ne Zealand never recovered from being 44 for four by the fifteenth over, and only Jones, who wa last out, came to terms with the struggle. He hit four boundaries in his 47 from 85 deliverie

Man of the Match: Waqar Younis.

New Zealand

M. D. Crowe c Salim Yousuf b Wasim Akram . 5
*J. G. Wright b Aaqib Javed 1
A. H. Jones c Imran Khan b Mushtaq Ahmed . 47
M. J. Greatbatch c sub (Mansoor Rana) b Wasim Akram . 4
K. R. Rutherford c Salim Yousuf b Waqar Younis . 0
S. A. Thomson b Waqar Younis 4
J. G. Bracewell c Aaqib Javed b Mushtaq Ahmed . 4
†I. D. S. Smith c Salim Yousuf b Waqar Younis . 0
M. C. Snedden lbw b Waqar Younis . . 1
D. K. Morrison lbw b Waqar Younis . . 0
J. P. Millmow not out 0
L-b 4, w 3, n-b 1 8

1/7 2/21 3/37 4/44 5/56 6/65 7/70 8/74 9/74 (31.1 overs) 74

Bowling: Wasim Akram 6–1–16–2; Aaqib Javed 6–0–23–1; Waqar Younis 9–2–20–5; Imran Khan 6–2–7–0; Mushtaq Ahmed 4.1–2–4–2.

Pakistan

Saeed Anwar c Thomson b Millmow . . 3
†Salim Yousuf c Crowe b Millmow 25
Salim Malik not out 31
*Imran Khan not out 13
L-b 1, w 3, n-b 1 5

1/19 2/33 (2 wkts, 15.4 overs) 77

Javed Miandad, Ijaz Ahmed, Wasim Akram, Mushtaq Ahmed, Sajjad Akbar, Waqar Younis and Aaqib Javed did not bat.

Bowling: Morrison 4–0–32–0; Millmow 5–0–22–2; Thomson 4–1–9–0; Jones 2–0–8–0; Crowe 0.4–0–5–0.

Umpires: A. R. Crafter and R. B. Gupta.

†AUSTRALIA v SRI LANKA

At Sharjah, May 2. Australia won by 114 runs. Toss: Australia. O'Donnell's whirlwind 74 off just 29 balls, including the fastest half-century in one-day internationals (off eighteen deliveries), virtually sealed Sri Lanka's fate. In all, O'Donnell hit six sixes and four fours, and his 106-run partnership with century-maker Jones, following 137 for the second wicket between Marsh and Jones, put Australia *en route* to their highest total in one-day internationals. Their previous highest, 328 for five off 60 overs, had also been scored against Sri Lanka, at The Oval in the 1975 World Cup.

Man of the Match: S. P. O'Donnell.

Australia

M. A. Taylor st Kuruppu b Madurasinghe . 27
G. R. Marsh c Kuruppu b Ratnayeke . 68
D. M. Jones not out 117
S. P. O'Donnell b Ramanayake 74
D. C. Boon not out 30
B 5, l-b 6, w 5 16

1/35 2/172 3/278 (3 wkts, 50 overs) 332

*A. R. Border, S. R. Waugh, †I. A. Healy, P. L. Taylor, C. G. Rackemann and T. M. Alderman did not bat.

Bowling: Ratnayeke 10–0–70–1; Ratnayake 10–0–55–0; Madurasinghe 10–0–32–1; Ramanayake 10–0–82–1; E. A. R. de Silva 5–0–34–0; Gurusinha 5–0–48–0.

Sri Lanka

†D. S. B. P. Kuruppu c Marsh b Alderman . 14
M. A. R. Samarasekera lbw b Alderman 25
H. P. Tillekeratne st Healy b Border .. 76
P. A. de Silva c Marsh b P. L. Taylor . 19
*A. Ranatunga c Rackemann b Waugh 26
J. R. Ratnayeke run out 4
R. J. Ratnayake c Border b P. L. Taylor 8
E. A. R. de Silva c Healy b Border 9
C. P. H. Ramanayake c Waugh b O'Donnell . 19
A. W. R. Madurasinghe not out 8
A. P. Gurusinha absent injured
B 1, l-b 6, w 3 10

1/26 2/43 3/77 4/126 5/135 6/150 7/174 8/208 9/218 (45.4 overs) 218

Bowling: Alderman 7–0–35–2; Rackemann 10–0–51–0; O'Donnell 5.4–0–19–1; P. L. Taylor 10–1–28–2; Waugh 7–0–36–1; Border 6–0–42–2.

Umpires: B. L. Aldridge and Khizar Hayat.

FINAL

†AUSTRALIA v PAKISTAN

At Sharjah, May 4. Pakistan won by 36 runs. Toss: Pakistan. Pakistan's mercurial all-rounder, Wasim Akram, hitting 49 off 35 deliveries and later finishing the Australian innings with a hat-trick, enabled Pakistan to retain the trophy they won four years earlier when they beat India, with a six by Javed Miandad, off the last ball. With almost four overs left, Australia required 37 to win with three wickets in hand, but Akram dashed any hopes they might have entertained by clean-bowling Hughes, Rackemann and Alderman. The architect of Pakistan's innings was Salim Malik, whose polished 87 from 104 balls contained a six and seven fours. Saeed Anwar got them going with a swashbuckling 40 from 37 balls, but it needed Akram's devastating hitting to bring 60 runs from the last five overs and so set the Australians a challenging target. Two of his three sixes came in the final over, both landing in the stands, as he took 18 runs off O'Donnell. Leg-spinner Mushtaq Ahmed's three wickets put the brake on Australia after Waugh and O'Donnell had added 54 for the fifth wicket.

Man of the Match: Wasim Akram.

Pakistan

Saeed Anwar c Healy b Rackemann ... 40
†Salim Yousuf lbw b Alderman 5
Javed Miandad c Healy b Waugh 14
Salim Malik c Border b P. L. Taylor .. 87
Ijaz Ahmed c Healy b Rackemann 20
*Imran Khan c Healy b Rackemann .. 2
Mansoor Rana run out 10
Wasim Akram not out 49
Mushtaq Ahmed not out 17
B 3, l-b 10, w 9 22

1/40 2/54 3/80 4/109 5/154 6/179 7/207 (7 wkts, 50 overs) 266

Waqar Younis and Aaqib Javed did not bat.

Bowling: Alderman 5–1–22–1; Hughes 10–0–55–0; Rackemann 10–0–49–3; O'Donnell 10–0–66–0; Waugh 5–0–22–1; P. L. Taylor 10–0–39–1.

Australia

D. C. Boon run out 37
M. A. Taylor run out 52
D. M. Jones b Waqar Younis 0
*A. R. Border lbw b Waqar Younis ... 1
S. R. Waugh c Aaqib Javed b Mushtaq Ahmed . 64
S. P. O'Donnell c Ijaz Ahmed b Mushtaq Ahmed . 33
P. L. Taylor c Saeed Anwar b Mushtaq Ahmed . 9
†I. A. Healy not out 1
M. G. Hughes b Wasim Akram ......
C. G. Rackemann b Wasim Akram ...
T. M. Alderman b Wasim Akram .....
L-b 10, w 3 1

1/62 2/62 3/64 4/133 5/187 6/207 7/207 8/230 9/230 (46.5 overs) 23

Bowling: Wasim Akram 8.5–0–45–3; Aaqib Javed 7–0–27–0; Waqar Younis 8–0–38–
Mushtaq Ahmed 10–1–48–3; Imran Khan 7–0–28–0; Saeed Anwar 6–0–34–0.

Umpires: B. L. Aldridge and R. B. Gupta.

CRICKET IN AUSTRALIA, 1989-90

By JOHN MACKINNON

The return of Australia's cricketers from their victorious 1989 tour of England was greeted with almost hysterical fervour. Dinners, breakfasts, street parades, accolades: it was heady wine, but any hopes of it spilling over into the Sheffield Shield competition were soon dashed. In a trice, the team had packed their bags and set off to India for the Nehru Cup. Politically expedient the trip may have been, but with Pakistan reneging on previously agreed commitments for their Australian tour, the domestic season was once again left to wage its own battle for survival.

The summer's schedule made fragmentation look like an art form. After the Nehru Cup visit to India came a one-off Test at home against New Zealand, two Tests with Sri Lanka, three with Pakistan (with a break in the middle to allow television to cover the Commonwealth Games in New Zealand), and finally a tour to New Zealand. Throw in the World Series Cup, which was played either side of the Pakistan series, and the Sheffield Shield could only languish at the bottom of the priority table. Not only was the competition frequently without Australia's much fêted heroes, but when they were available, the opportunity for resting injured limbs was often the preferred option to playing. Allan Border underlined the problem when he resigned the Queensland captaincy and appeared in only two of his state's ten matches prior to the Shield final.

Rather perversely, New South Wales probably benefited from the dilemma. Geoff Lawson played two early Tests, looked thoroughly jaded and was dropped. He spent the rest of the season captaining New South Wales with no little flair, taking a swag of wickets, and leading his state into the final. Indeed, the positive demeanour of the new Shield champions was a revelation. They took risks and they made challenging declarations, and while some of them proved expensive, nevertheless New South Wales achieved three outright wins to Queensland's two. This gave them top position and the vital home ground advantage in the final.

The New South Wales batting boasted some wonderful strokeplayers, and no-one improved more than Trevor Bayliss at No. 3. The selectors gave him his head, and his daring shots ensured that the innings quickly moved into overdrive. Moreover, his efforts often set the stage for Mark Waugh, whose confidence grew and grew as the season progressed. Waugh was dismissed only once for a score between 50 and 100, his five centuries were a worthy reward, and the umpires recognised his supreme talent by voting him Shield Cricketer of the Year. Steve Small's contribution as opener was that of a busy but proficient technician, and no doubt he would have enjoyed Mark Taylor's company for more than five matches. Their combined effect on the course of the Shield final was an inspiration to their colleagues. Taylor continued to demonstrate his appetite for runs, alike in Test, Shield and even one-day matches, and his seven first-class centuries had a classy inevitability about them. His concentration and technique were equally evident in his slip fielding. Other batsmen had their moments, notably Mark O'Neill and Greg

Matthews, but Steve Waugh's big hundred in Hobart was his only significant contribution.

The bowling suffered a cruel blow when Mike Whitney broke his left arm while batting against Queensland at Newcastle in only the second match. Lawson's courageous battle against an arm injury ultimately foundered on the morning of the final, but not before he had borne the full burden of his team's wicket-taking needs. Steve Waugh was unable to bowl a single ball, and the fastest bowler, Wayne Holdsworth, also spent a lot of time with the medicos. Matthews's transformation at the end of the season coincided with three matches on spinners' pitches at the SCG. These yielded him 23 wickets, and another seven in Perth suggested a coming of age for one of Australia's more individualistic characters. The young leg-spinner, Adrian Tucker, also enjoyed the helpful conditions in Sydney, which was bad news for Peter Taylor, whose omission from the final suggested a future restricted to limited-overs cricket. No more gritty cricketer ever played, but the value of Taylor's bowling in the conventional game had diminished by the day. Phil Emery kept wicket tidily in a side whose fielding was always competitive.

Queensland's challenge fell away embarrassingly at the SCG in the final. To capture points in nine out of ten matches was no mean effort, but the failure to translate these successes into more than two outright wins suggested some serious deficiencies. Although Border's absence often left the batting undermanned, Greg Ritchie discovered some tremendous form late in the season, playing two big innings in Melbourne and Adelaide. Yet it was in Melbourne that positive leadership could have secured outright points, which were there for the taking. In Ritchie's defence, his options as captain were not enhanced by Queensland's having a predominance of fast bowling and a virtual absence of spin. Craig McDermott bowled a huge number of overs, mostly with great enthusiasm, and took more wickets than anyone; but his partner, Carl Rackemann, was away half the time. On their day, they were as effective a pair as any in the country. Dirk Tazelaar battled away for form and fitness, and Mick Polzin had the Victorians on their knees in Melbourne, but the contrasting spin of Steve Storey and Peter Cantrell simply was not able to fulfil Queensland's needs. Cantrell's batting, however, looked promising early on. Peter Clifford made a successful comeback, but Robbie Kerr lost form and was dropped. While Queensland had every chance to win their first Shield title, by the same token they could not complain about the final result.

South Australia's fortunes ebbed and flowed. At their best they were irresistible, thanks to a dynamic batting line-up. At other times, their meagre bowling resources caused their downfall. The departure of their coach, Barry Richards, for greener pastures in Queensland was disappointing, as the SACA had done much to facilitate his move to Australia. His successor, Les Stillman, gave his all, but at the end of the season he too decided to leave and accept the coaching position in his native Victoria.

Darren Lehmann, who rejected the offer of a scholarship at the Cricket Academy in Adelaide, became the talk of the town with his simplistic approach to batting, hitting the ball hard and often and impressing friend and foe alike with his wide range of powerful strokes. His cause was helped in no small way by the contributions of Andrew Hilditch, Paul Nobes and David Hookes. Hilditch batted as meticulously as ever but lacked a regular opening partner. Nobes at No. 3 was, if anything, more explosive than his colleagues, and after a series of near misses he reached his first hundred, taking 124 off the Western Australian bowlers in Perth. Hookes, as usual, captained the side with tremendous involvement and in the latter half of the season found his best batting form. The bowling was held together by the medium-pacer, Colin Miller. The former Victorian was a model of persistence, and he enjoyed useful support from Joe Scuderi. Although Scuderi did not quite live up to the promise of the previous year, he will never forget the January afternoon in Adelaide when his six wickets for 6 runs skittled the Western Australians for 41. It was unfortunate for the team that off-spinner Tim May failed to achieve any sort of fitness, while leg-spinner Peter Sleep's few wickets cost him more than 50 runs each.

Tasmania enjoyed their best season since 1983-84. They had outright wins against New South Wales, the 1989-90 Shield winners, and Western Australia, the defending champions, in both instances exploiting declarations by their opponents with a deal of exuberance. For all but two Shield matches they had to make do without their best batsman, David Boon, but the spirit of the side was embodied by the tireless bowling of Dave Gilbert. He and Greg Campbell, for six games, made up a most formidable attack. It was the batting, however, that made Tasmania such competitive opponents. Greg Shipperd was very much the immovable object, even more so than in his most obdurate days with Western Australia. Of the younger players, Jamie Cox played some excellent innings, including two hundreds in the victory over New South Wales, while the two all-rounders, Rod Tucker and Gavin Robertson, were worthy contributors. Dirk Wellham found runs hard to come by – in two seasons for Tasmania he had yet to score a century – but he remained a master of tactics with much to offer his adopted state.

To drop from first, for three years running, to second-last was a traumatic experience for Western Australia. Judging by their end-of-season form, when they enjoyed big wins over Queensland and New South Wales, such a slide should not have happened. Their change of fortune coincided with Graeme Wood's enforced departure from the team. He had lost the captaincy after the innings defeat in Adelaide, and when the team moved on to Launceston and lost again, in spite of Wood's substantial batting contributions, his team-mates voted against his continued presence in the side. Western Australia, now under Wayne Andrews's leadership, then dramatically returned to form with their wins against the two top Shield contenders.

The absence of key players obviously undermined team balance. Terry Alderman played three Shield matches, Geoff Marsh only four. The latter was a victim of a wretched run of injuries, but a memorable 355 not out against South Australia at Perth reminded the national selectors rather forcibly of his value to the Test team. For Mike Veletta, batting was either a feast or a famine, with failures being interspersed with extraordinary feats of concentration and endurance. Of the others, Andrews was always positive, but Tom Moody, in spite of a maiden Test hundred against Sri Lanka, achieved little for his state. Until Chris Matthews found his best form, spurred on by a return of seven for 22 in Western Australia's innings victory over the Pakistani tourists, the bowling was ordinary. Matthews was well supported by his fellow left-arm paceman, Peter Capes, and those faithful stalwarts, Ken MacLeay and Tom Hogan, had their moments. However, the comeback of 42-year-old Bruce Yardley foundered almost as soon as it started.

There was much soul-searching in Melbourne and changes were called for as Victoria occupied last place for the second year running. Ian Redpath resigned as coach and John Chambers was deposed as chairman of selectors. Although the events were not directly related, the MCG curator also resigned, and the demolition work on the old Southern stand, Bay 13 and all, began. The side was never settled, and Dean Jones, Merv Hughes and latterly Simon O'Donnell were sorely missed when away on international duty. It was a bonus when that sturdiest of competitors, Gary Watts, "cancelled" his retirement and played for the whole season with great distinction. Statistically, Jamie Siddons could claim to have had a good year, but too often his talent was wasted by lapses in concentration. Several young players came and went, and given the number of opportunities, more might have been expected of Ian Frazer and Wayne Phillips. Of the bowlers, Paul Reiffel worked up a bit of pace and was the most improved, but Damien Fleming, after a spectacular début against Western Australia, could not keep his place. The leg-spinner, Peter McIntyre, was given every chance, and while he bowled accurately enough, he found wickets elusive. His best return was five for 53 in the victory over the Pakistanis, despite which he was omitted from the side for the next Shield match.

What had been a rather patchy season ended unsatisfactorily, at the end of March in Perth, where Western Australia bowled out South Australia for 87 in the FAI Cup final – an example of instant cricket being far too instant.

The Australian Cricket Board tackled the no-ball issue by doubling the initial penalty, and also adding any further runs, thus making, for example an eight off one ball quite feasible. Not surprisingly, the international visitors decided against the innovation. However, Pakistan and Sri Lanka were prepared to take issue with the umpiring and "sledging". The latter is one of the less attractive elements of many Australian sports, notably football and cricket, where a wholehearted volley of verbal abuse is thought necessary to establish mental, and sometimes physical, superiority over an opponent. The Sri Lankans thought that these exchanges represented racial taunts, but as Australians do it to each other as well, that may have been a misunderstanding. Sadly it seems that no-one has been willing to stop the practice short of legislation; and with a growing number of expert practitioners in other parts of the world, this has become an issue for the game's authorities to settle.

With an Ashes tour the focal point, and the Sheffield Shield restored to some prominence, the 1990-91 season should have seen a vast improvement. Although the radicals are still testing yellow balls and touting first-class cricket under lights, the 1989-90 Sheffield Shield final should have proved a few points, notably that gimmickry is not always the key to gaining public interest. In Sydney, two full-strength teams contesting a five-day match were able to attract record crowds. Of course, it may have helped that the home side quickly established a winning position.

FIRST-CLASS AVERAGES, 1989-90

BATTING

(Qualification: 500 runs)

	M	I	NO	R	HI	100s	Avge
M. E. Waugh (NSW)	12	17	4	1,009	198*	5	77.61
D. M. Jones (Vic.)	10	16	4	868	149	4	72.33
M. A. Taylor (NSW)	12	21	1	1,403	199	7	70.15
D. S. Lehmann (SA)	12	20	0	1,142	228	5	57.10
A. R. Border (Qld)	9	15	4	621	144*	1	56.45
G. Shipperd (Tas.)	11	18	3	845	200*	3	56.33
G. R. Marsh (WA)	7	11	2	501	355*	1	55.66
T. H. Bayliss (NSW)	12	20	2	992	115	2	55.11
D. C. Boon (Tas.)	8	14	2	657	200	3	54.75
G. M. Ritchie (Qld)	12	19	2	928	213*	3	54.58
J. D. Siddons (Vic.)	10	17	2	793	159	3	52.86
G. A. Bishop (SA)	7	12	1	561	173	2	51.00
S. P. O'Donnell (Vic.)	8	13	2	544	121	2	49.45
D. W. Hookes (SA)	11	18	1	823	159	3	48.41
M. R. J. Veletta (WA)	13	20	2	855	228	3	47.50
S. R. Waugh (NSW)	12	19	3	704	196	2	44.00
R. J. Tucker (Tas.)	11	18	1	737	118	1	43.35
G. M. Watts (Vic.)	12	23	1	940	162*	3	42.72
W. S. Andrews (WA)	12	18	0	759	103	1	42.16
M. D. O'Neill (NSW)	11	16	1	621	71	0	41.40
S. M. Small (NSW)	12	21	2	780	86	0	41.05
A. M. J. Hilditch (SA)	12	21	2	737	103	3	38.78
P. C. Nobes (SA)	12	21	0	814	124	1	38.76
J. Cox (Tas.)	11	18	0	693	175	3	38.50
P. E. Cantrell (Qld)	12	20	1	693	125	1	36.47
T. M. Moody (WA)	13	21	1	708	106	1	35.40
W. N. Phillips (Vic.)	12	23	2	735	134	1	35.00

* *Signifies not out.*

BOWLING

(Qualification: 20 wickets)

	O	M	R	W	BB	Avge
C. D. Matthews (WA)	304.3	77	806	42	7-22	19.19
S. P. O'Donnell (Vic.)	179.3	54	410	20	4-38	20.50
C. G. Rackemann (Qld)	508.2	144	1,074	50	4-39	21.48
T. M. Alderman (WA)	336.4	102	784	34	5-62	23.05
G. F. Lawson (NSW)	464.2	142	1,018	44	4-26	23.13
G. R. J. Matthews (NSW)	470.3	166	1,040	44	7-50	23.63
D. R. Gilbert (Tas.)	350.1	70	1,000	42	7-127	23.80
M. A. Polzin (Qld)	260.2	65	682	28	8-51	24.35
G. D. Campbell (Tas.)	354.2	91	866	35	6-80	24.74
D. W. Fleming (Vic.)	234.3	59	693	28	6-37	24.75
C. R. Miller (SA)	402.1	107	1,117	44	6-83	25.38
C. J. McDermott (Qld)	432	100	1,376	54	8-44	25.48
M. R. Whitney (NSW)	220.5	58	639	24	5-125	26.62
M. G. Hughes (Vic.)	428.2	126	1,129	42	5-88	26.88
D. Tazelaar (Qld)	272.4	59	703	22	6-48	31.95

	O	M	R	W	BB	Avge
P. R. Reiffel (*Vic.*)	301.2	57	994	31	4-43	32.06
P. A. Capes (*WA*)	305	64	978	30	6-92	32.60
J. C. Scuderi (*SA*)	363.5	100	915	27	6-6	33.88
W. J. Holdsworth (*NSW*)	196.1	27	736	21	5-71	35.04
A. I. C. Dodemaide (*Vic.*)	285.4	67	750	21	4-54	35.71
P. E. McIntyre (*Vic.*)	451.3	116	1,196	27	5-53	44.29
P. R. Sleep (*SA*)	382.1	95	1,055	22	3-26	47.95

SHEFFIELD SHIELD, 1989-90

	Played	Won	Lost	Drawn	1st Inns Pts	Pts	Quotient
New South Wales	10	3	3*	4	8	26	1.4138
Queensland	10	2	2*	6	14	26	0.9902
South Australia	10	3	3	4	2	20	0.8929
Tasmania	10	2	3	5	4	16	0.8353
Western Australia	10	2	2	6	2	14	0.9807
Victoria	10	1	0	9	8	13.6†	0.9652

* *1 outright loss after leading on first innings.*
† *0.4 penalty points deducted for slow over-rates.*
Outright win = 6 pts; lead on first innings in a drawn or lost game = 2 pts.
***Final:** New South Wales beat Queensland by 345 runs.*

QUEENSLAND v VICTORIA

At Brisbane, October 25, 26, 27, 28. Drawn. Queensland 2 pts. Toss: Queensland. After rain had washed out the first morning's play, Ritchie invited the Victorians to bat. Against Rackemann's speed and movement, they slumped from 162 for three to 235 all out, with Siddons's dashing 71 the only threat to the bowlers' dominance. Queensland's reply rested with the diligent Cantrell, whose career-best 125 included thirteen fours but occupied seven and a half painstaking hours. Reiffel having strained a muscle round the ribs early on, Dodemaide was forced to bowl a marathon spell and he never faltered. Trailing by 82, Victoria reached 98 for four at lunch on the fourth day. Their only hope of survival was with Watts. He had been dropped by Kerr when 21, but thereafter he never offered the semblance of a chance, batting through to the end and hitting seventeen fours in an innings lasting seven hours. Parker gave him faithful support and made his highest score.

Victoria

G. M. Watts c Barsby b McDermott	0	– not out	162
I. D. Frazer c Barsby b Rackemann	5	– c Cantrell b McDermott	7
W. N. Phillips c Law b Polzin	52	– (4) c Anderson b Tazelaar	2
*J. D. Siddons c Law b Inwood	71	– (5) lbw b Rackemann	5
G. R. Parker c Kerr b Rackemann	37	– (6) c Polzin b Cantrell	75
P. W. Young c Anderson b Rackemann	7	– (7) not out	0
A. I. C. Dodemaide c Anderson b Rackemann	9		
†M. G. D. Dimattina b Tazelaar	7	– (3) b Polzin	6
P. R. Reiffel not out	8		
D. J. Hickey c Ritchie b McDermott	2		
P. E. McIntyre b McDermott	2		
L-b 9, n-b 26	35	L-b 5, n-b 22	27
1/0 2/41 3/83 4/162 5/192 6/201 7/214 8/220 9/231	235	1/19 2/69 3/74 4/98 5/284	(5 wkts) 284

Bowling: *First Innings*—McDermott 20.2–7–54–3; Tazelaar 24–7–35–1; Polzin 13–4–27–1 Rackemann 20–4–53–4; Cantrell 10–2–48–0; Inwood 7–3–9–1. *Second Innings*—McDermott 23–3–72–1; Tazelaar 19–5–32–1; Polzin 16–4–41–1; Rackemann 19–5–37–1; Cantrell 22–6–64–1; Inwood 15–7–33–0.

Queensland

T. J. Barsby b Dodemaide	18
P. E. Cantrell c Watts b Parker	125
R. B. Kerr lbw b Hickey	4
*G. M. Ritchie c Dimattina b Young	56
M. A. Polzin c Frazer b McIntyre	29
S. G. Law c McIntyre b Hickey	24
B. P. Inwood lbw b Dodemaide	19
†P. W. Anderson c and b Dodemaide	0
C. J. McDermott b Parker	26
D. Tazelaar c Hickey b Dodemaide	0
C. G. Rackemann not out	1
L-b 5, n-b 10	15
1/29 2/34 3/123 4/183 5/232 6/273 7/273 8/303 9/304	317

Bowling: Hickey 29.3–5–118–2; Dodemaide 45–17–76–4; Reiffel 3.3–1–6–0; McIntyre 20–6–56–1; Young 9–0–26–1; Parker 15.3–4–30–2.

Umpires: P. D. Parker and C. D. Timmins.

WESTERN AUSTRALIA v TASMANIA

At Perth, November 1, 2, 3, 4. Drawn. Tasmania 2 pts. Toss: Western Australia. Tasmania went close to recording their first Shield win in Perth. Wood won the toss, but by lunch on the first day five of his batsmen were out for 51 to some hostile bowling from Gilbert and Campbell. Wood stayed put, however, and with the lower order fashioned a partial recovery. Even so, Western Australia's 215 was their lowest score against Tasmania. Shipperd began his innings on the first evening. By stumps on the second, he had progressed to 91. He took 449 minutes to reach 100 and 708 minutes to reach 200, the slowest times for a century and double-century in Australian cricket, and when Wellham declared he had hit one six and 22 fours in his career-best score. Cox was five and a half hours over his maiden hundred, but Tucker livened things up with 54 in an hour. Tasmania's lead of 263 looked imposing as Gilbert took three quick wickets on the third evening. However, wickets were hard to come by on the last day, when the Tasmanian bowlers toiled in vain for their elusive prize.

Western Australia

G. R. Marsh c Shipperd b Gilbert	5	(2) lbw b Gilbert	9
M. R. J. Veletta c Robertson b Campbell	8	(1) c Soule b Gilbert	4
T. M. Moody b Gilbert	6	c Tucker b Gilbert	41
*G. M. Wood c Boon b de Winter	36	(5) run out	44
W. S. Andrews c de Winter b Campbell	7	(6) lbw b Gilbert	77
†T. J. Zoehrer b Campbell	0	(7) c Wellham b Robertson	23
K. H. MacLeay c Boon b de Winter	27	(8) not out	9
T. G. Hogan not out	58	(9) not out	28
P. A. Capes c de Winter b Campbell	5		
A. D. Mullally c and b Gilbert	34	(4) c sub b Gilbert	0
T. M. Alderman b Tucker	18		
L-b 6, w 3, n-b 2	11	B 9, l-b 6, w 1, n-b 14	30
1/9 2/17 3/35 4/51 5/51 6/77 7/104 8/113 9/184	215	1/4 2/29 3/29 4/80 5/143 6/208 7/228	(7 wkts) 265

Bowling: *First Innings*—Gilbert 24–4–82–3; Campbell 19–5–38–4; Robertson 7–2–16–0; de Winter 21–2–60–2; Tucker 7–2–13–1. *Second Innings*—Gilbert 23–9–47–5; Campbell 23–8–40–0; Robertson 26–6–58–1; de Winter 25–1–100–0; Tucker 6–2–5–0.

Tasmania

S. G. Hookey c Zoehrer b Capes	0
G. Shipperd not out	200
D. R. Gilbert c Zoehrer b Mullally	6
D. C. Boon c Moody b Hogan	63
J. Cox b Alderman	101
R. J. Tucker st Zoehrer b Hogan	54
*D. M. Wellham c and b Alderman	11
G. R. Robertson not out	21
B 7, l-b 6, w 1, n-b 8	22
1/0 2/17 3/110 4/322 5/403 6/438	(6 wkts dec.) 478

†R. E. Soule, A. J. de Winter and G. D. Campbell did not bat.

Bowling: Capes 30–10–71–1; Alderman 38–14–96–2; Mullally 37–10–112–1; MacLeay 31.4–12–70–0; Moody 20–8–37–0; Hogan 27–5–79–2.

Umpires: R. J. Evans and T. A. Prue.

QUEENSLAND v SOUTH AUSTRALIA

At Brisbane, November 3, 4, 5, 6. Queensland won by six wickets. Queensland 6 pts. Toss: Queensland. Splendid bowling by Rackemann, Border's superb batting, and some suicidal strokeplay by the South Australians combined to give Queensland a comfortable victory. South Australia squandered a useful start on the first day as their batsmen succumbed to Queensland's persistent pace attack, whereas Border's innings was in stark contrast. His driving, cutting and pulling brought him sixteen fours, as well as a six which bounced off Alley's hands at deep mid-wicket. South Australia did well to restrict Queensland's lead to 36, but their second innings foundered in mid-stream when Storey, like Alley making his first-class début, claimed two wickets in two balls and Hookes promptly hit the next delivery to mid-on. This left Queensland with a comparatively simple task on the last day. Cantrell played another important innings, Kerr showed a welcome return to form, and Border repelled a late burst by Miller to guide his team to victory.

South Australia

First innings		Second innings	
B. D. Williams c Healy b Rackemann	28	– b Rackemann	17
A. M. J. Hilditch b McDermott	14	– c Border b McDermott	0
P. C. Nobes c Border b Rackemann	46	– c Healy b Rackemann	30
*D. W. Hookes c Healy b Inwood	39	– c McDermott b Rackemann	67
D. S. Lehmann c Ritchie b Tazelaar	15	– lbw b Storey	35
P. R. Sleep lbw b McDermott	52	– c Kerr b Storey	0
J. C. Scuderi c Border b Tazelaar	0	– c Cantrell b McDermott	39
†D. S. Berry c Healy b Rackemann	6	– c Healy b Tazelaar	10
P. W. Gladigau c Border b Rackemann	5	– not out	18
P. J. S. Alley not out	3	– lbw b McDermott	0
C. R. Miller c Kerr b McDermott	4	– lbw b Inwood	7
L-b 5, n-b 22	27	B 4, l-b 1, n-b 20	25
1/35 2/78 3/143 4/145 5/161 6/161 7/194 8/204 9/233	239	1/3 2/56 3/79 4/168 5/168 6/168 7/217 8/221 9/221	248

Bowling: *First Innings*—McDermott 25.3–7–69–3; Tazelaar 28–4–76–2; Rackemann 21–5–39–4; Cantrell 3–0–12–0; Inwood 4–1–14–1; Storey 11–5–24–0. *Second Innings*—McDermott 19–4–69–3; Tazelaar 20–3–72–1; Rackemann 15–5–34–3; Cantrell 4–1–14–0; Inwood 4.1–1–12–1; Storey 7–0–42–2.

Queensland

First innings		Second innings	
P. E. Cantrell c sub b Sleep	51	– (2) c Williams b Miller	85
R. B. Kerr c Sleep b Miller	0	– (1) c Lehmann b Miller	86
S. G. Law lbw b Miller	2	– c Berry b Miller	1
A. R. Border not out	144	– (5) not out	19
*G. M. Ritchie run out	0	– (4) b Miller	2
B. P. Inwood c Nobes b Scuderi	15	– not out	12
†I. A. Healy c Berry b Scuderi	0		
S. C. Storey run out	46		
C. J. McDermott c Sleep b Miller	6		
D. Tazelaar c Berry b Miller	0		
C. G. Rackemann c Berry b Gladigau	1		
L-b 2, n-b 8	10	L-b 6, n-b 2	8
1/4 2/10 3/123 4/123 5/176 6/178 7/256 8/270 9/270	275	1/173 2/175 3/177 4/188	(4 wkts) 213

Bowling: *First Innings*—Gladigau 30–11–70–1; Miller 23–6–67–4; Alley 14–2–48–0; Scuderi 29–10–50–2; Sleep 7–0–38–1. *Second Innings*—Gladigau 16–4–42–0; Miller 20–8–46–4; Alley 7–2–19–0; Scuderi 3–0–12–0; Sleep 17–2–44–0; Williams 4–1–15–0; Hookes 8.1–0–28–0; Hilditch 2–1–1–0.

Umpires: P. D. Parker and C. D. Timmins.

SOUTH AUSTRALIA v NEW SOUTH WALES

At Adelaide, November 10, 11, 12, 13. Drawn. South Australia 2 pts. Toss: South Australia. New South Wales made the most of Hookes's invitation to bat first and declared just after tea on the second day. Taylor and Mark Waugh played with great application in a fourth-wicket partnership of 263 in even time, and Taylor, who had fourteen boundaries in his 199, looked like batting forever until falling to a debatable catch after 502 minutes. Waugh demonstrated his tremendous talent to reach his highest score. South Australia made an indifferent start, but Hookes and Lehmann took to the bowling with a vengeance. The two left-handers added 200 in three hours for the fifth wicket, and Lehmann not only reached his first hundred but went on to hit the winning runs for the first-innings lead. He batted for seven and a half hours and was always in total command. On a pitch that was tailor-made for batting, the two quick left-armers, Alley and Whitney, were by far the best bowlers.

New South Wales

S. M. Small b Alley	23	– st Berry b Sleep	79
M. A. Taylor c Hookes b Sleep	199	– c Berry b Alley	30
T. H. Bayliss c Berry b Gladigau	36	– not out	48
S. R. Waugh c Nobes b Alley	22		
M. E. Waugh c Berry b Gladigau	172		
M. D. O'Neill b Alley	36		
G. R. J. Matthews lbw b Alley	6		
†P. A. Emery not out	6		
W. J. Holdsworth (did not bat)		– (4) not out	16
L-b 10, w 2, n-b 4	16	L-b 4, n-b 2	6
1/50 2/128 3/159 4/422 5/494 6/504 7/516	(7 wkts dec.) 516	1/58 2/153	(2 wkts) 179

*G. F. Lawson and M. R. Whitney did not bat.

Bowling: *First Innings*—Gladigau 27–2–109–2; Miller 33–7–114–0; Alley 31.5–8–98–4; Scuderi 28–6–76–0; Sleep 34–2–109–1. *Second Innings*—Gladigau 17–2–60–0; Alley 11–3–32–1; Sleep 22–5–50–1; Hookes 10–2–24–0; Hilditch 6–2–9–0.

South Australia

B. D. Williams c Taylor b Whitney	9
A. M. J. Hilditch c M. E. Waugh b Whitney	44
P. C. Nobes run out	30
†D. S. Berry c Bayliss b Matthews	4
*D. W. Hookes lbw b Whitney	99
D. S. Lehmann c Whitney b O'Neill	228
P. R. Sleep lbw b M. E. Waugh	31
J. C. Scuderi c Small b Whitney	43
P. W. Gladigau b Whitney	2
P. J. S. Alley not out	5
C. R. Miller c Holdsworth b O'Neill	0
B 2, l-b 12, n-b 10	24
1/27 2/76 3/90 4/90 5/290 6/388 7/474 8/494 9/519	519

Bowling: Lawson 27–3–87–0; Whitney 34–3–125–5; Holdsworth 20–0–93–0; Matthews 35–7–117–1; O'Neill 15.4–1–65–2; M. E. Waugh 5–1–18–1; Bayliss 1–1–0–0.

Umpires: A. R. Crafter and D. J. Harper.

VICTORIA v TASMANIA

At St Kilda, Melbourne, November 10, 11, 12, 13. Drawn. Tasmania 2 pts. Toss: Tasmania. For Tasmania, the match followed an identical course to that in Perth the previous week. Campbell rewarded his captain's decision to bowl with an outstanding spell which produced career-best figures, although the Victorian batsmen had only themselves to blame after Watts and Frazer had given them such a good start. Phillips was unlucky to deflect a high full toss from spinner Robertson on to his face and had to retire hurt when 31. As Tasmania ground out their reply, Cox narrowly missed a second consecutive hundred, having batted for five and a half hours. Dropped by Siddons and Jones, he was latterly handicapped by a blow on the wrist. Tasmania's cause was helped by another inept effort from Victoria's batsmen. Trailing by 122, they were saved from probable defeat by the determination of Dodemaide and Hughes. They batted for 90 minutes, leaving Tasmania with the honours if not the victory.

Victoria

G. M. Watts c Soule b Campbell	67	– c Soule b de Winter	23
I. D. Frazer c Robertson b Campbell	71	– lbw b Gilbert	4
W. N. Phillips c Shipperd b Campbell	32	– c Soule b Tucker	16
J. D. Siddons c de Winter b Robertson	17	– run out	9
D. M. Jones c de Winter b Campbell	5	– c Campbell b Tucker	19
*S. P. O'Donnell c Robertson b Campbell	16	– c Wellham b Campbell	10
A. I. C. Dodemaide c Soule b Gilbert	1	– not out	30
†M. G. D. Dimattina c Soule b Campbell	1	– b Robertson	5
M. G. Hughes c Robertson b Gilbert	20	– not out	22
P. E. McIntyre b Gilbert	6		
D. J. Hickey not out	2		
B 2, l-b 6, n-b 13	21	B 8, l-b 7, w 6, n-b 2	23
1/134 2/163 3/208 4/211 5/218 6/223 7/250 8/250 9/257	259	1/15 2/49 3/49 4/86 5/89 6/103 7/119	(7 wkts) 161

In the first innings W. N. Phillips, when 31, retired hurt at 193 and resumed at 250-7.

Bowling: *First Innings*—Gilbert 26.1–5–71–3; Campbell 33–8–80–6; Robertson 30–9–52–1; de Winter 14–5–23–0; Tucker 9–2–25–0. *Second Innings*—Gilbert 22–6–32–1; Campbell 24–9–41–1; Robertson 15–9–12–1; de Winter 13–4–34–1; Tucker 23–10–27–2.

Tasmania

R. J. Bennett c Watts b McIntyre	35
G. Shipperd b Hickey	29
J. Cox b O'Donnell	99
R. J. Tucker c Dimattina b Hickey	54
*D. M. Wellham c Dimattina b Hughes	5
D. F. G. O'Connor c Dimattina b Hickey	43
G. R. Robertson run out	42
†R. E. Soule c Hughes b McIntyre	4
A. J. de Winter b Hughes	28
G. D. Campbell b Hughes	1
D. R. Gilbert not out	4
B 2, l-b 19, w 4, n-b 12	37
1/78 2/100 3/180 4/197 5/281 6/315 7/325 8/369 9/371	381

Bowling: Hughes 38–13–68–3; Hickey 32–4–89–3; Dodemaide 23–5–59–0; McIntyre 46.5–13–95–2; O'Donnell 18–3–42–1; Jones 4–2–7–0.

Umpires: R. C. Bailhache and L. J. King.

TASMANIA v QUEENSLAND

At Hobart, November 17, 18, 19, 20. Drawn. Queensland 2 pts. Toss: Queensland. When Bennett edged the first ball of the match to Healy, Tasmania adopted their attritional style and scored just 223 on the opening day. However, wickets fell regularly as McDermott and Tazelaar exploited the overcast conditions, and once Tazelaar had finished off the innings next morning, Queensland batted even more sedately, reaching 150 for four off 83 overs. Fortunately for the Sunday crowd of more than 3,000, Healy lifted the tempo with a spirited undefeated 81 in two and a quarter hours. Queensland slipped past the Tasmanian score with their last pair together. Having lost the first-innings points, Tasmania decided that a day and a half was not enough time in which to press for an outright result, whereupon Shipperd and Boon made the most of the opportunity to improve their aggregates. Boon's hundred contained nine fours and came off 217 balls.

Tasmania

Batsman	First innings	Runs	Second innings	Runs
R. J. Bennett	c Healy b McDermott	0	(2) c Trimble b Tazelaar	3
G. Shipperd	c Cantrell b Tazelaar	42	(1) c Ritchie b Tazelaar	72
D. C. Boon	c Kerr b Tazelaar	14	c Trimble b Tazelaar	100
J. Cox	c Healy b Rackemann	18	b Rackemann	1
R. J. Tucker	b Storey	30	(8) not out	9
*D. M. Wellham	lbw b Tazelaar	35	(7) not out	19
G. R. Robertson	lbw b Tazelaar	53	(6) b Storey	7
†R. E. Soule	c Healy b Tazelaar	4		
A. J. de Winter	b McDermott	2	(5) lbw b Rackemann	0
G. D. Campbell	not out	9		
D. R. Gilbert	c Healy b Tazelaar	22		
	B 3, l-b 8, n-b 22	33	B 3, l-b 6, n-b 10	19
1/0 2/17 3/56 4/106 5/125 6/209 7/219 8/224 9/236		262	1/6 2/172 3/177 4/177 5/197 6/204 (6 wkts dec.)	230

Bowling: *First Innings*—McDermott 32–8–93–2; Tazelaar 28.5–11–48–6; Rackemann 19–4–65–1; Inwood 5–2–12–0; Storey 19–6–25–1; Cantrell 2–0–8–0. *Second Innings*—McDermott 17–0–63–0; Tazelaar 25–5–54–3; Rackemann 30–8–50–2; Inwood 10–6–10–0; Storey 15–4–28–1; Cantrell 8–2–16–0.

Queensland

Batsman	First innings	Runs	Second innings	Runs
P. E. Cantrell	c Soule b Tucker	23		
R. B. Kerr	c Boon b Campbell	28		
S. G. Law	lbw b Gilbert	14	(2) not out	13
*G. M. Ritchie	c de Winter b Gilbert	52		
G. S. Trimble	c Soule b Tucker	39		
B. P. Inwood	c Soule b Gilbert	6	(1) not out	18
S. C. Storey	c Soule b Robertson	20		
†I. A. Healy	not out	81		
C. J. McDermott	c sub b Gilbert	15		
D. Tazelaar	lbw b Campbell	0		
C. G. Rackemann	c Robertson b Campbell	9		
	L-b 11, w 3, n-b 2	16		
1/45 2/70 3/72 4/144 5/154 6/183 7/205 8/246 9/261		303	(no wkt)	31

Bowling: *First Innings*—Gilbert 35–8–76–4; Campbell 32–8–74–3; de Winter 19–5–48–0; Tucker 27–10–42–2; Robertson 21–5–52–1. *Second Innings*—de Winter 8–2–17–0; Tucker 5–2–5–0; Robertson 3–1–3–0; Wellham 4–1–6–0; Cox 1–1–0–0.

Umpires: D. R. Close and S. G. Randell.

VICTORIA v WESTERN AUSTRALIA

At St Kilda, Melbourne, November 17, 18, 19, 20. Drawn. Victoria 2 pts. Toss: Victoria. The match provided a memorable début for the nineteen-year-old Victorian fast bowler, Fleming. He bowled throughout the rain-shortened first day to take three wickets for 19 after O'Donnell had given Western Australia first use of an under-prepared pitch, and he continued to exploit the conditions on the second day as Western Australia were dismissed for 133. Only Andrews, with his unique brand of hitting, resisted for long, even in adversity managing to hit Hughes out of the ground. Watts went to the first ball of the Victorian innings, but Frazer held his side together with six hours of defiance. Jones gave good support, and O'Donnell lashed out successfully. When Western Australia's batting crumbled a second time, Andrews again came to the rescue, taking four and a half hours over his century and ensuring that Victoria had only eleven overs in which to get 81 for victory. Their batsmen tried to slog their way to the target when they might have achieved more by pushing for ones and twos against the far-flung fieldsmen.

Western Australia

M. R. J. Veletta c McIntyre b Fleming	2	(2) b Dodemaide	13
G. R. Marsh c Dimattina b Fleming	13	(1) c Dimattina b Fleming	9
T. M. Moody c Dimattina b Fleming	4	c Watts b Fleming	30
K. H. MacLeay c Watts b Fleming	2	(7) c Dodemaide b O'Donnell	13
P. A. Capes c Dodemaide b Fleming	9	(9) c Hughes b Dodemaide	10
*G. M. Wood c Parker b Hughes	20	(4) c Frazer b Hughes	0
W. S. Andrews c Parker b O'Donnell	51	(5) c Dimattina b O'Donnell	103
†T. J. Zoehrer b Fleming	7	(6) run out	27
T. G. Hogan lbw b O'Donnell	10	(8) b Hughes	9
A. D. Mullally c and b O'Donnell	2	not out	2
B. Yardley not out	7	c Watts b O'Donnell	10
B 2, l-b 3, w 1	6	B 3, l-b 10, n-b 5	18
1/3 2/11 3/13 4/34 5/39 6/57 7/66 8/104 9/110	133	1/13 2/56 3/60 4/60 5/114 6/175 7/191 8/230 9/232	244

Bowling: *First Innings*—Hughes 12–5–27–1; Fleming 18–5–37–6; O'Donnell 11–4–40–3; Dodemaide 7–0–24–0. *Second Innings*—Hughes 25–8–72–2; Fleming 25–7–57–2; O'Donnell 18–6–28–3; Dodemaide 17–7–20–2; McIntyre 19–5–53–0; Jones 3–2–1–0.

Victoria

G. M. Watts lbw b Mullally	0	run out	21
I. D. Frazer b Capes	90		
W. N. Phillips c Zoehrer b Moody	18	(2) lbw b Capes	1
D. M. Jones c Marsh b Mullally	49	(3) not out	27
G. R. Parker c Zoehrer b Moody	22		
*S. P. O'Donnell b Mullally	39	(4) not out	5
A. I. C. Dodemaide b Moody	6		
†M. G. D. Dimattina b Hogan	19		
M. G. Hughes not out	19		
D. W. Fleming not out	0		
B 6, l-b 7, n-b 22	35	B 1, l-b 1	2
1/0 2/47 3/162 4/207 5/211 6/254 7/264 8/279	(8 wkts dec.) 297	1/10 2/44	(2 wkts) 56

P. E. McIntyre did not bat.

Bowling: *First Innings*—Mullally 37–12–74–3; MacLeay 22–11–34–0; Capes 23–3–74–1; Moody 24–3–57–3; Yardley 15–4–29–0; Hogan 5–3–16–1. *Second Innings*—Mullally 5.2–0–25–0; Capes 5–0–29–1.

Umpires: R. C. Bailhache and L. J. King.

NEW SOUTH WALES v QUEENSLAND

At Newcastle, December 1, 2, 3, 4. New South Wales won by 32 runs. New South Wales 6 pts, Queensland 2 pts. Toss Queensland. Queensland looked well placed for victory when they started the last day needing 155 with all wickets intact. Furthermore, Whitney was unable to bowl, having had his left arm broken by a ball from McDermott in the first innings, and various other New South Wales players had been struck down by a virus. With umpire Thomas also a virus victim, umpire Reed was involuntarily thrust into the spotlight, being required to officiate throughout the day at the bowler's end while local replacements stood at square leg. As it happened, several Queensland batsmen felt aggrieved by decisions that went against them, which unfortunately took some gloss from the courageous bowling efforts of Lawson, Mark Waugh and Peter Taylor. Bowlers generally held control throughout the match. McDermott and Rackemann were quite outstanding for Queensland, and Holdsworth was equally effective for New South Wales, taking two wickets in the opening over of Queensland's first innings. Healy and O'Neill were the only batsmen to pass 50 in the match.

New South Wales

S. M. Small lbw b Rackemann	48 – b McDermott	2
M. A. Taylor c Healy b McDermott	46 – lbw b Tazelaar	15
T. H. Bayliss c Border b Rackemann	6 – lbw b Rackemann	21
S. R. Waugh lbw b McDermott	2 – c Healy b Rackemann	13
M. E. Waugh c Healy b McDermott	46 – c Tazelaar b Rackemann	18
M. D. O'Neill c Trimble b Rackemann	24 – b McDermott	69
P. L. Taylor c Border b McDermott	5 – c Smart b Rackemann	33
†P. A. Emery not out	11 – c Cantrell b McDermott	1
*G. F. Lawson c Cantrell b McDermott	0 – not out	13
M. R. Whitney retired hurt	0 – absent injured	
W. J. Holdsworth b McDermott	0 – (10) c Healy b Tazelaar	0
L-b 4, n-b 19	23 L-b 4, n-b 22	26
1/81 2/102 3/113 4/118 5/191 6/191 7/205 8/209 9/211	211 1/6 2/46 3/46 4/63 5/88 6/174 7/193 8/198 9/211	211

In the first innings M. R. Whitney retired hurt at 209-8.

Bowling: *First Innings*—McDermott 23.5–7–77–6; Tazelaar 15–4–49–0; Rackemann 20–6–37–3; Storey 10–0–39–0; Cantrell 3–1–5–0. *Second Innings*—McDermott 19–4–65–3; Tazelaar 17.5–1–48–2; Rackemann 17–2–51–4; Storey 2–0–16–0; Cantrell 13–4–22–0; Border 4–2–5–0.

Queensland

P. E. Cantrell b Holdsworth	0 – (2) c Holdsworth b P. L. Taylor	30
R. B. Kerr lbw b Holdsworth	11 – (1) lbw b Holdsworth	12
C. B. Smart c Emery b Holdsworth	0 – lbw b Lawson	3
S. C. Storey c Bayliss b O'Neill	30 – (7) c Emery b P. L. Taylor	20
†I. A. Healy c Emery b M. E. Waugh	66 – (8) c M. E. Waugh b P. L. Taylor	17
A. R. Border c Emery b Holdsworth	34 – (4) lbw b Lawson	5
*G. M. Ritchie c Bayliss b P. L. Taylor	42 – (5) c Emery b M. E. Waugh	7
G. S. Trimble c Emery b Lawson	11 – (6) c sub b M. E. Waugh	0
C. J. McDermott c M. A. Taylor b P. L. Taylor	37 – c and b Lawson	23
D. Tazelaar c Emery b Holdsworth	6 – c M. E. Waugh b P. L. Taylor	1
C. G. Rackemann not out	0 – not out	4
B 4, l-b 14, n-b 4	22 B 1, l-b 6, n-b 2	9
1/0 2/0 3/27 4/117 5/117 6/183 7/205 8/223 9/259	259 1/24 2/37 3/43 4/54 5/54 6/83 7/90 8/107 9/115	131

Bowling: *First Innings*—Holdsworth 18.3–0–71–5; Lawson 24–10–43–1; P. L. Taylor 22–8–53–2; M. E. Waugh 10–1–31–1; O'Neill 12–2–43–1. *Second Innings*—Holdsworth 11–1–40–1; Lawson 12.5–4–21–3; P. L. Taylor 14–4–29–4; M. E. Waugh 15–5–34–2.

Umpires: G. E. Reed and I. S. Thomas.

TASMANIA v VICTORIA

At Launceston, December 1, 2, 3, 4. Drawn. Victoria 2 pts. Toss: Victoria. Rain on the second day consigned the match to a contest for first-innings points, with Victoria already well placed at 313 for four after the first day. Jones, in his best form, batted impeccably for 264 minutes, and his partnership of 192 with O'Donnell occupied only three and a quarter hours. O'Donnell, too, played splendidly, hitting his second consecutive first-class hundred, and his declaration left Tasmania with more than two days for their reply. Shipperd fell easily into his sheet-anchor role and eventually won back his record for the slowest century in Australian cricket, which had been taken from him by the New Zealander, Greatbatch, in the Perth Test match. His new time, eight hours and one minute, was nineteen minutes slower. Tucker, by comparison with his third-wicket partner, was almost carefree; his maiden hundred took 307 minutes. Tasmania were handicapped by the absence through illness of their captain, Wellham, and their depleted forces fell 16 runs short of the Victorian total.

Victoria

G. M. Watts c O'Connor b Campbell	18	– c Tucker b Robertson	11
I. D. Frazer lbw b Gilbert	1	– not out	16
W. N. Phillips c Cox b Robertson	14	– (4) not out	2
J. D. Siddons c Cox b Robertson	57		
D. M. Jones b Gilbert	149		
*S. P. O'Donnell c Bennett b de Winter	104		
†M. G. D. Dimattina lbw b Campbell	19		
M. G. Hughes c Campbell b de Winter	1		
D. W. Fleming c O'Connor b Campbell	1		
P. W. Jackson not out	14		
P. E. McIntyre not out	15	– (3) b de Winter	0
B 4, l-b 4, w 2, n-b 22	32	W 4	4
1/1 2/32 3/48 4/142 5/334 6/392 7/393 8/395 9/395 (9 wkts dec.)	425	1/27 2/28 (2 wkts)	33

Bowling: *First Innings*—Gilbert 27–5–87–2; Campbell 36–7–114–3; Robertson 24–6–66–2; Tucker 22–7–58–0; de Winter 23–4–86–2; O'Connor 2–0–6–0. *Second Innings*—Gilbert 5–2–6–0; Campbell 3–1–7–0; Robertson 9–4–6–1; de Winter 7–2–14–1.

Tasmania

R. J. Bennett c Frazer b Jones	47
G. Shipperd c Dimattina b Jackson	100
J. Cox c McIntyre b Jackson	45
R. J. Tucker b Jackson	118
D. F. G. O'Connor lbw b McIntyre	5
G. R. Robertson lbw b Fleming	13
†R. E. Soule c Watts b McIntyre	22
A. J. de Winter run out	33
G. D. Campbell lbw b O'Donnell	2
D. R. Gilbert not out	0
*D. M. Wellham absent ill	
B 10, l-b 10, n-b 4	24
1/80 2/159 3/268 4/289 5/322 6/357 7/389 8/408 9/409	409

Bowling: Hughes 30–8–50–0; Fleming 25–11–60–1; Jackson 56–16–103–3; McIntyre 53–11–130–2; Jones 7–1–25–1; O'Donnell 8.3–4–21–1.

Umpires: D. R. Close and S. G. Randell.

VICTORIA v SOUTH AUSTRALIA

At Melbourne, December 8, 9, 10, 11. Victoria won by four wickets. Victoria 6 pts. Toss: South Australia. Victoria won off the last ball of the match, Dimattina hooking a bouncer from Miller to Hilditch at fine leg and just beating the return for the vital second run. It was the climax to a run-chase which started with Victoria needing 180 off 53 overs. The pitch was variable, the outfield very slow, and with wickets falling regularly 18 runs were still needed off the last two overs. However, O'Donnell's flair and power enabled him to survive two chances in the deep and to guide his team home. Having won the toss, the South Australian captain, Hookes, experienced dismay – as his team slumped to 58 for five – and pleasure when during his own short innings he passed I. M. Chappell's record aggregate of runs for the state. The burly Lehmann came to the rescue and in four hours of controlled aggression, with good support from Scuderi and May, he set the innings back on track. In Victoria's first innings, the South Australian wicket-keeper, Berry, broke a world record established by K. V. Andrew of Northamptonshire in 1965 – 2,132 runs without conceding a bye.

South Australia

G. A. Bishop c Siddons b Dodemaide	20	– (2) c O'Donnell b McIntyre	69
A. M. J. Hilditch c O'Donnell b Fleming	3	– (1) c Parker b Fleming	14
P. C. Nobes b Fleming	0	– c Dimattina b Dodemaide	37
*D. W. Hookes c Watts b O'Donnell	18	– run out	23
D. S. Lehmann lbw b Dodemaide	128	– c McIntyre b Reiffel	9
P. R. Sleep c Parker b Dodemaide	3	– c Dimattina b Reiffel	13
J. C. Scuderi c Watts b McIntyre	21	– run out	33
†D. S. Berry c Dimattina b McIntyre	0	– c Phillips b Reiffel	17
P. J. S. Alley c Siddons b Dodemaide	0	– (10) b Fleming	0
T. B. A. May not out	35	– (9) lbw b Reiffel	0
C. R. Miller c O'Donnell b Reiffel	5	– not out	0
B 2, l-b 7, n-b 4	13	L-b 3, n-b 8	11
1/6 2/12 3/45 4/51 5/58 6/124 7/136 8/137 9/222	246	1/19 2/115 3/131 4/151 5/176 6/177 7/224 8/226 9/226	226

Bowling: *First Innings*—Reiffel 23.2–7–63–1; Fleming 14–2–32–2; Dodemaide 15–2–54–4; O'Donnell 15–6–35–1; McIntyre 24–9–50–2; Phillips 1–0–3–0. *Second Innings*—Reiffel 20–4–43–4; Fleming 10.5–2–31–2; Dodemaide 24–4–51–1; O'Donnell 12–3–21–0; McIntyre 31–7–77–1.

Victoria

G. M. Watts lbw b Hilditch	55	– lbw b Alley	29
I. D. Frazer c Berry b May	59	– c Berry b Scuderi	6
W. N. Phillips c Bishop b May	5	– c Alley b Sleep	33
J. D. Siddons c Nobes b May	14	– c Bishop b May	33
G. R. Parker lbw b Miller	18	– lbw b May	3
*S. P. O'Donnell c Hilditch b Miller	47	– not out	50
A. I. C. Dodemaide c and b Sleep	38	– lbw b Miller	7
†M. G. D. Dimattina lbw b Miller	0	– not out	8
D. W. Fleming c Berry b Miller	4		
P. R. Reiffel not out	19		
P. E. McIntyre lbw b Sleep	4		
L-b 12, n-b 18	30	L-b 5, n-b 6	11
1/122 2/135 3/142 4/155 5/219 6/236 7/240 8/258 9/283	293	1/30 2/46 3/103 4/106 5/110 6/142	(6 wkts) 180

Bowling: *First Innings*—Alley 13–2–43–0; Miller 28–11–59–4; Scuderi 21–4–54–0; May 42–11–89–3; Sleep 18.2–7–30–2; Hilditch 4–3–5–1; Hookes 3–2–1–0. *Second Innings*—Alley 6–2–12–1; Miller 10–2–50–1; Scuderi 6–1–21–1; May 20–4–62–2; Sleep 11–0–30–1.

Umpires: D. W. Holt and L. J. King.

NEW SOUTH WALES v VICTORIA

At Albury, December 15, 16, 17, 18. Drawn. New South Wales 2 pts. Toss: Victoria. Phillips left his sick-bed to bat for two and threequarter hours and save Victoria from defeat. Lawson had set them a target of 274 off 69 overs, and when Phillips came in at 54 for five, the cause seemed lost. However, with Fleming lasting 51 minutes and Reiffel 80 minutes, the Victorians held out against some fine bowling by Holdsworth, Lawson and Matthews. New South Wales had made most of the running, in spite of their batsmen's inability to capitalise on a number of good starts in the first innings. Victoria pursued a policy of caution in their quest for first-innings points and paid the penalty. O'Neill's leg-breaks caused unusual concern and Holdsworth came back well after an untidy start. Waugh's second-innings hundred (186 balls, one six, seven fours) set up the declaration. During his three and a half hours at the crease, the batting reached a higher plane than at any other stage of the match. But his pleasure with that performance was tempered in the last half hour when he failed to catch a chance offered by Reiffel. It was the last opportunity for the New South Welshmen to force a deserved victory and to make the first match at Albury one to remember.

New South Wales

S. M. Small c Siddons b O'Donnell	47	– b Reiffel 2
G. S. Milliken c Dimattina b O'Donnell	19	– c Dimattina b Reiffel 10
T. H. Bayliss c Reiffel b Fleming	47	– c Watts b Reiffel 56
M. D. O'Neill c Fleming b McIntyre	47	– lbw b Dodemaide 0
M. E. Waugh c O'Donnell b Dodemaide	4	– not out 100
B. E. McNamara c Parker b O'Donnell	11	– (7) not out 11
G. R. J. Matthews b O'Donnell	56	
P. L. Taylor c Siddons b Fleming	15	
†P. A. Emery b McIntyre	16	– (6) b Fleming 29
*G. F. Lawson c Phillips b McIntyre	14	
W. J. Holdsworth not out	0	
L-b 12, w 1, n-b 18	31	L-b 3, w 1, n-b 14 18
1/64 2/105 3/151 4/167 5/191 6/199 7/241 8/293 9/303	307	1/2 2/34 3/49 4/139 5/197 (5 wkts dec.) 226

Bowling: *First Innings*—Reiffel 24–4–67–0; Fleming 23–8–62–2; Dodemaide 33–5–68–1; McIntyre 23.4–5–55–3; O'Donnell 20–7–38–4; Siddons 1–0–5–0. *Second Innings*—Reiffel 15–2–62–3; Fleming 12–3–43–1; Dodemaide 15.5–3–56–1; McIntyre 17–3–48–0; O'Donnell 8–3–14–0.

Victoria

G. M. Watts c Emery b O'Neill	50	– c Matthews b Holdsworth 4
I. D. Frazer lbw b Lawson	8	– lbw b Matthews 31
W. N. Phillips st Emery b O'Neill	44	– (7) not out 78
J. D. Siddons c and b O'Neill	36	– c Milliken b Lawson 0
G. R. Parker lbw b Holdsworth	29	– (3) lbw b Lawson 4
*S. P. O'Donnell c Waugh b Holdsworth	9	– (5) c Lawson b Holdsworth 8
P. R. Reiffel b Matthews	27	– (10) not out 12
A. I. C. Dodemaide c O'Neill b Holdsworth	27	– (6) lbw b Matthews 8
†M. G. D. Dimattina c Small b Holdsworth	14	– (8) b Matthews 0
D. W. Fleming not out	0	– (9) c Waugh b Matthews 11
P. E. McIntyre run out	0	
B 5, l-b 3, n-b 8	16	B 2, l-b 2, w 1 5
1/25 2/75 3/125 4/154 5/171 6/182 7/234 8/258 9/258	260	1/5 2/16 3/16 4/35 5/54 6/73 7/73 8/109 (8 wkts) 161

Bowling: *First Innings*—Lawson 19–7–33–1; Holdsworth 28–7–97–4; Waugh 15–4–39–0; O'Neill 30–9–51–3; Taylor 9–2–13–0; Matthews 8–3–10–1; McNamara 3–0–9–0. *Second Innings*—Lawson 13–3–31–2; Holdsworth 17–1–57–2; Waugh 1–0–1–0; O'Neill 15–3–35–0; Taylor 8–3–20–0; Matthews 18–12–13–4.

Umpires: D. B. Hair and I. S. Thomas.

WESTERN AUSTRALIA v SOUTH AUSTRALIA

At Perth, December 15, 16, 17, 18. Drawn. Western Australia 2 pts. Toss: South Australia. By the time Western Australia lost their first wicket at 431, Hookes had ample reason to regret his decision to field. It was the highest opening stand in Sheffield Shield cricket, and it signalled a massive return to form by Marsh and Veletta. Marsh, who had missed a number of games owing to a broken toe sustained at net practice, batted for 628 minutes, hit 53 fours and two sixes, and never offered a chance until late in his innings. When Western Australia were 71, Berry, the South Australian wicket-keeper, conceded his first bye in first-class cricket to end at 2,446 his world-record sequence of runs scored against his side without his allowing a bye. South Australia in reply struggled initially against some splendid pace bowling by the left-armers, Matthews and Capes. But with the score 63 for five Nobes was joined by Bevan, a recruit from the ACT and the Adelaide Cricket Academy, who was making his début. They put on 221 in four and a quarter hours and both hit maiden hundreds. Bevan played with great maturity but could not save his side from the follow-on. Batting a second time, the South Australians easily avoided defeat as Hilditch defended stubbornly for four hours.

Western Australia

M. R. J. Veletta c Bishop b Hookes . . .150	*G. M. Wood not out 26
G. R. Marsh not out 355	B 1, l-b 10, n-b 10 21
C. D. Matthews b Hookes 2	
D. J. Ramshaw c Berry b Gladigau . . . 11	1/431 2/452 3/489 (3 wkts dec.) 565

J. A. Brayshaw, W. S. Andrews, †T. J. Zoehrer, K. H. MacLeay, P. A. Capes and A. D. Mullally did not bat.

Bowling: Gladigau 42–10–126–1; Miller 28–6–100–0; Scuderi 31–9–103–0; May 38–9–126–0; Hookes 27–5–89–2; Bevan 2–0–10–0.

South Australia

First innings		Second innings	
G. A. Bishop lbw b Matthews	22	(2) c and b MacLeay	27
A. M. J. Hilditch b Capes	20	(1) not out	62
†D. S. Berry lbw b Matthews	0		
P. C. Nobes c Wood b Matthews	124	(3) b Matthews	59
*D. W. Hookes lbw b Capes	0		
D. S. Lehmann b Capes	0	(4) b Matthews	48
M. G. Bevan c Zoehrer b Mullally	114	(5) b Marsh	2
J. C. Scuderi c Zoehrer b Capes	38	(6) not out	0
T. B. A. May c Ramshaw b Mullally	15		
P. W. Gladigau c Brayshaw b Mullally	1		
C. R. Miller not out	3		
B 1, l-b 4, n-b 24	29	L-b 5, n-b 4	9
1/46 2/46 3/59 4/63 5/63 6/284 7/340 8/362 9/363	366	1/50 2/129 3/191 4/207 (4 wkts)	207

Bowling: *First Innings*—Capes 34–7–109–4; MacLeay 40–16–77–0; Matthews 18–3–62–3; Mullally 20.2–2–83–3; Brayshaw 8–4–8–0; Andrews 11–2–22–0. *Second Innings*—Capes 3–0–14–0; MacLeay 15–3–40–1; Matthews 16–4–42–2; Mullally 12–5–31–0; Brayshaw 5–1–23–0; Andrews 11–3–47–0; Zoehrer 3–1–4–0; Marsh 2–1–1–1.

Umpires: R. J. Evans and P. J. McConnell.

QUEENSLAND v NEW SOUTH WALES

At Brisbane, December 29, 30, 31, January 1. Queensland won by five wickets. Queensland 6 pts, New South Wales 2 pts. Toss: New South Wales. New South Wales got away to a flying start, reaching 342 for six on the first day after Bayliss had batted for 229 minutes for his first century. Small and O'Neill helped him in run-a-minute partnerships and Waugh provided 60 in 85 minutes, hitting three sixes and five fours. The cricket was more circumspect on the second day as New South Wales were quickly bowled out by Rackemann. Queensland then lost three wickets for 32, all to the 23-year-old Rowell, who dismissed Kerr with the second ball of his first-class career. As New South Wales sought quick runs in their second innings, Storey's left-arm spin claimed four wickets late on the third day, but splendid batting by O'Neill enabled Lawson to set Queensland a target of 304 in 76 overs. Kerr and Cantrell measured their response perfectly with a second-wicket partnership of 166 in 164 minutes, and Kerr went on to an excellent hundred. After he was run out, Storey hit five huge sixes, and a four, to win the match with three overs to spare. New South Wales were handicapped by the loss of Holdsworth with torn muscles in his side, but Lawson deserved credit for his enterprising captaincy.

New South Wales

S. M. Small c Storey b Rackemann	75	– c Cantrell b Storey	28
G. S. Milliken lbw b McDermott	1	– b Rackemann	11
T. H. Bayliss c Barsby b Cantrell	115	– c Clifford b Tazelaar	47
M. D. O'Neill run out	37	– not out	64
M. E. Waugh b McDermott	60	– c Smart b Storey	4
B. E. McNamara c Cantrell b Storey	18	– c Anderson b Rackemann	2
G. R. J. Matthews lbw b McDermott	23	– st Anderson b Storey	13
†P. A. Emery c Kerr b Rackemann	16	– c Anderson b Storey	2
G. J. Rowell c Ritchie b Rackemann	1	– c Ritchie b McDermott	9
*G. F. Lawson c Clifford b Rackemann	0	– not out	10
W. J. Holdsworth not out	0		
L-b 3, n-b 18	21	B 2, l-b 7, n-b 2	11
1/11 2/167 3/234 4/261 5/312 6/321 7/349 8/357 9/367	367	1/19 2/87 3/100 4/104 5/115 6/132 7/138 8/174 (8 wkts dec.)	201

Bowling: *First Innings*—McDermott 23.2–4–94–3; Tazelaar 20–1–78–0; Rackemann 25–7–69–4; Cantrell 20–6–75–1; Storey 10–3–41–1; Barsby 1–0–7–0. *Second Innings*—McDermott 14–4–54–1; Tazelaar 11–2–32–1; Rackemann 21–5–55–2; Cantrell 8–0–32–0; Storey 10–5–19–4.

Queensland

P. E. Cantrell c Waugh b Rowell	17	– (2) c Matthews b Lawson	81
R. B. Kerr c Waugh b Rowell	5	– (3) run out	123
T. J. Barsby c Milliken b Rowell	6	– (1) c Milliken b Lawson	2
*G. M. Ritchie c Emery b O'Neill	44	– c Emery b Lawson	5
P. S. Clifford c McNamara b Holdsworth	75	– b McNamara	28
C. B. Smart run out	58	– (7) not out	6
S. C. Storey lbw b Holdsworth	3	– (6) not out	53
†P. W. Anderson c and b Lawson	4		
C. J. McDermott b Lawson	0		
D. Tazelaar c Waugh b Matthews	28		
C. G. Rackemann not out	8		
B 1, l-b 9, w 1, n-b 6	17	L-b 6, w 1	7
1/17 2/29 3/32 4/124 5/186 6/192 7/201 8/201 9/246	265	1/9 2/175 3/181 4/224 5/270 (5 wkts)	305

Bowling: *First Innings*—Holdsworth 23–5–72–2; Lawson 27–10–43–2; Rowell 23–9–41–3; Matthews 26–8–57–1; Waugh 9–2–26–0; O'Neill 16–7–16–1. *Second Innings*—Holdsworth 10–2–28–0; Lawson 19–3–67–3; Rowell 8–0–45–0; Matthews 21.5–0–98–0; Waugh 5–0–14–0; O'Neill 5–0–23–0; McNamara 4–0–24–1.

Umpires: C. A. Bertwistle and A. J. McQuillan.

NEW SOUTH WALES v WESTERN AUSTRALIA

At Sydney, January 6, 7, 8, 9. Drawn. New South Wales 2 pts. Toss: Western Australia. Wood took first use of the relaid Sydney pitch, but superb bowling by Lawson had the Western Australians in trouble at 80 for five by lunch. However, Veletta, missed by Mark Waugh when 3, carried his bat to ensure a respectable total, his plucky six-and-a-half-hour effort inspiring the tailenders, particularly Yardley. Mark Taylor and Small launched the New South Wales reply in fine style, and the 6,000-strong crowd warmed to their strokes and to those of the Waugh twins. Yet just when a comfortable first-innings lead seemed a formality, Alderman roduced an outstanding spell to take five for 15 off nine overs. New South Wales, losing their ast seven wickets for 22, were lucky to inch their way ahead. Rain washed out much of the hird and all of the fourth day, but not before Moody had demonstrated his quality in a gritty artnership with Marsh.

Western Australia

	First Innings		Second Innings	
G. R. Marsh lbw b Lawson	5	(2) not out	36
M. R. J. Veletta not out	110	(1) c Emery b Lawson	0
T. M. Moody c Small b Lawson	0	not out	66
G. M. Wood b Lawson	0		
W. S. Andrews c M. A. Taylor b Matthews	34		
†T. J. Zoehrer c and b Matthews	0		
T. G. Hogan c Emery b M. E. Waugh	18		
R. S. Russell c M. E. Waugh b Lawson	7		
P. A. Capes c Emery b Stobo	22		
T. M. Alderman c Lawson b M. E. Waugh	11		
B. Yardley b Stobo	27		
L-b 10, w 2, n-b 16	28	L-b 1, w 1, n-b 2	4
1/16 2/16 3/20 4/78 5/80 6/137 7/150 8/204 9/219	262	1/0	(1 wkt) 106

Bowling: *First Innings*—Lawson 27–12–51–4; Stobo 22.2–6–73–2; M. E. Waugh 11–1–58–2; P. L. Taylor 22–11–35–0; Matthews 20–9–35–2. *Second Innings*—Lawson 14–5–27–1; Stobo 3–4–11–0; M. E. Waugh 0.1–0–0–0; P. L. Taylor 2–0–12–0; Matthews 8–1–27–0; O'Neill 16–9–28–0.

New South Wales

S. M. Small b Hogan	70
M. A. Taylor c and b Russell	67
T. H. Bayliss c Russell b Yardley	28
S. R. Waugh b Hogan	33
M. E. Waugh b Alderman	31
M. D. O'Neill c Veletta b Yardley	0
G. R. J. Matthews not out	16
P. L. Taylor lbw b Alderman	0
†P. A. Emery lbw b Alderman	5
*G. F. Lawson b Alderman	0
R. M. Stobo c Capes b Alderman	0
B 3, l-b 10, w 1	14
1/140 2/150 3/197 4/242 5/242 6/246 7/246 8/264 9/264	264

Bowling: Capes 18–5–48–0; Alderman 26.4–10–62–5; Russell 15–2–55–1; Yardley 14–8–37–2; Hogan 23–5–49–2.

Umpires: D. B. Hair and I. S. Thomas.

SOUTH AUSTRALIA v VICTORIA

At Adelaide, January 6, 7, 8, 9. Drawn. Victoria 2 pts. Toss: Victoria. Much to the chagrin of two captains desperately in need of outright points, the Adelaide pitch was again the winner. Sleep, deputising for the injured Hookes, described it as "the best non-result wicket in Australia". Batsmen on both sides thrived, with Siddons leading the way for Victoria in both innings. In the first, he shared a third-wicket stand of 207 in 229 minutes with Phillips and was especially severe on the spinners. Even Hughes made batting look easy, hitting seven fours and a six in 94 minutes. A crowd of 8,000 watched South Australia make a careful reply until Lehmann's arrival heralded a supreme exhibition of hitting. His 125 took only 141 minutes, with eighteen fours and a six, and he completely dominated a stand of 169 with Hilditch. Hilditch for his part battled away for six hours, but South Australia's innings folded as they lost eight wickets for 102 to some spirited bowling by Reiffel and Hughes. On the last day, O'Donnell's declaration set South Australia to make 313 off 54 overs. Nobes took up the challenge, racing to 89 in 85 minutes (fourteen fours), but when he and Lehmann were out, South Australia gave up the chase.

Victoria

G. M. Watts c Bishop b Miller	0	– lbw b Miller 22
I. D. Frazer c George b Miller	8	– run out 47
W. N. Phillips lbw b Scuderi	73	– lbw b Scuderi 14
J. D. Siddons b Scuderi	159	– (5) not out 78
D. M. Jones c Berry b George	65	– (6) not out 49
*S. P. O'Donnell st Berry b May	50	
P. R. Reiffel c Berry b George	0	
A. I. C. Dodemaide c Lehmann b Sleep	73	
M. G. Hughes not out	60	
†M. G. D. Dimattina (did not bat)		– (4) b Miller 8
B 1, l-b 10, w 1	12	L-b 4 4
1/1 2/14 3/221 4/291 5/311 6/313 7/389 8/500	(8 wkts dec.) 500	1/27 2/48 3/73 4/122 (4 wkts dec.) 222

P. E. McIntyre did not bat.

Bowling: *First Innings*—George 27–7–95–2; Miller 35–6–101–2; Scuderi 30–7–81–2; May 34–3–144–1; Sleep 15–1–67–1; Hilditch 1–0–1–0. *Second Innings*—George 6–1–33–0; Miller 24–6–72–2; Scuderi 18–3–51–1; Sleep 7–0–41–0; Hilditch 5–0–21–0.

South Australia

G. A. Bishop b O'Donnell	35	– (2) c Dimattina b Reiffel 3
A. M. J. Hilditch b Reiffel	102	– (1) c Jones b O'Donnell 37
P. C. Nobes lbw b Reiffel	42	– b O'Donnell 89
D. S. Lehmann c Siddons b Dodemaide	125	– run out 22
M. G. Bevan st Dimattina b McIntyre	6	– not out 8
*P. R. Sleep lbw b Hughes	3	– not out 16
J. C. Scuderi c McIntyre b Reiffel	28	
†D. S. Berry b O'Donnell	6	
T. B. A. May not out	18	
S. P. George c Siddons b Hughes	0	
C. R. Miller b Reiffel	13	
B 6, l-b 10, n-b 16	32	B 2, l-b 3, n-b 6 11
1/81 2/139 3/308 4/322 5/333 6/351 7/367 8/377 9/380	410	1/6 2/127 3/152 4/159 (4 wkts) 186

Bowling: *First Innings*—Hughes 26–2–97–2; Reiffel 22.1–1–78–4; McIntyre 17–3–90–1; O'Donnell 21–5–58–2; Dodemaide 16–4–51–1; Jones 6–2–20–0. *Second Innings*—Hughes 9–2–36–0; Reiffel 4–0–42–1; McIntyre 19–3–65–0; O'Donnell 17–6–31–2; Jones 2–0–7–0.

Umpires: A. R. Crafter and D. J. Harper.

QUEENSLAND v WESTERN AUSTRALIA

At Brisbane, January 19, 20, 21, 22. Drawn. Queensland 2 pts. Toss: Western Australia. A match bereft of merit was doomed to mediocrity once Queensland spent the first day, all 8[illegible] overs of it, scoring 189 runs for the loss of four wickets. Claims of pathetic batting and counter-claims of excessively wide bowling did nothing to enhance the contest. Queensland's bowlers, notably McDermott and Kasprowicz, donated 28 no-balls, worth 56 runs, as Western Australia struggled to avoid the follow-on. Western Australia's declaration, 99 runs behind, evoked no sort of return gesture from Ritchie, who set a target of 293 in 34 overs and then used the time bowling overs as quickly as possible to avert the danger of penalty points from their slow rate in the first innings. Veletta proved his value as a wicket-keeper, taking four catches and conceding no byes when he replaced the injured Zoehrer from tea on the first day.

ueensland

. I. Foley c Zoehrer b Matthews	37	– (2) c Mullally b Matthews 11
. E. Cantrell c Veletta b Matthews	69	– (1) c Hogan b Capes 6
G. M. Ritchie c Zoehrer b Russell	15	– (4) b Matthews 83
. B. Kerr c Veletta b Capes	4	– (3) b Hogan 58
. S. Clifford c sub b Matthews	114	
. B. Smart c sub b Matthews	98	
. C. Storey c Veletta b Russell	0	– (5) not out 11
P. W. Anderson c Mullally b Hogan	44	
. J. McDermott c Veletta b Mullally	20	– (6) not out 6
1. A. Polzin not out	4	
1. S. Kasprowicz lbw b Matthews	0	
L-b 29, w 11, n-b 4	44	B 5, l-b 5, n-b 8 18
/89 2/109 3/130 4/175 5/323 /328 7/392 8/421 9/449	449	1/14 2/35 3/171 4/179 (4 wkts dec.) 193

Bowling: *First Innings*—Capes 31–2–86–1; Mullally 41–8–104–1; Russell 30–7–72–2; 1atthews 40.3–13–72–5; Hogan 30–6–77–1; Moody 3–3–0–0; Andrews 4–1–9–0. *Second nnings*—Capes 10–3–25–1; Mullally 15–3–38–0; Russell 11–3–43–0; Matthews 12–2–43–2; logan 10–1–34–1.

Vestern Australia

1. W. McPhee c Cantrell b Foley	19	– (2) not out 35
1. R. J. Veletta b McDermott	23	
. M. Moody lbw b Polzin	59	
G. M. Wood c sub b Polzin	39	
V. S. Andrews c Anderson b McDermott	31	– (1) c Anderson b Polzin 31
T. J. Zoehrer c sub b Polzin	48	
. G. Hogan c sub b McDermott	0	
. S. Russell c sub b McDermott	6	– (3) not out 14
. D. Matthews b Cantrell	51	
. A. Capes not out	15	
L-b 3, n-b 56	59	L-b 1 1
/45 2/71 3/169 4/176 5/213 /213 7/227 8/297 9/350	(9 wkts dec.) 350	1/48 (1 wkt) 81

. D. Mullally did not bat.

Bowling: *First Innings*—McDermott 27–6–97–4; Polzin 20–3–58–3; Kasprowicz 14–2–71–0; oley 17–7–45–1; Cantrell 8.4–1–36–1; Storey 11–0–40–0. *Second Innings*—Polzin 7–3–13–1; asprowicz 6–2–12–0; Foley 9–1–29–0; Ritchie 8–1–26–0.

Umpires: A. J. McQuillan and C. D. Timmins.

TASMANIA v SOUTH AUSTRALIA

t Devonport, January 19, 20, 21, 22. South Australia won by five wickets. South Australia pts. Toss: Tasmania. Tasmania's first outright loss in the fifteen matches played under Wellham's captaincy came after their batsmen failed to cope with South Australia's steady owling. Hookes's nonchalant century on the second day was also a decisive factor. Both aptains questioned the validity of eleven lbw decisions and May continued to incur the isapproval of the umpires by bowling fourteen no-balls, an indication that the Test off-pinner was still struggling to regain fitness and rhythm. With outright results so scarce, South ustralia's victory was a welcome boost to their Shield hopes.

Tasmania

R. J. Bennett run out	55	– c Lehmann b Miller	
G. Shipperd b Miller	4	– lbw b May	2
J. Cox b Owen	5	– c Berry b Scuderi	2
R. J. Tucker b May	58	– c Berry b Owen	4
*D. M. Wellham c Berry b Scuderi	2	– lbw b May	3
S. G. Hookey c Hookes b May	4	– lbw b Scuderi	4
P. I. Faulkner c Hookes b Miller	0	– lbw b Miller	1
G. R. Robertson run out	0	– b Owen	2
†R. E. Soule b Owen	47	– st Berry b May	
D. R. Gilbert lbw b Scuderi	19	– c Berry b Scuderi	2
T. J. Cooley not out	4	– not out	
B 3, l-b 8, n-b 20	31	L-b 9, n-b 22	3
1/15 2/36 3/112 4/125 5/142 6/147 7/147 8/152 9/225	229	1/8 2/46 3/48 4/144 5/154 6/216 7/220 8/237 9/272	27

Bowling: *First Innings*—Miller 16–3–45–2; Owen 11–1–30–2; Scuderi 25.4–8–55–2; Ma 33–10–77–2; Hookes 3–1–11–0. *Second Innings*—Miller 23–7–71–2; Owen 18–5–49–2; Scude 23.3–7–44–3; May 37–11–99–3.

South Australia

G. A. Bishop lbw b Tucker	19	– (2) lbw b Cooley	
A. M. J. Hilditch c Soule b Gilbert	18	– (1) lbw b Gilbert	2
P. C. Nobes lbw b Robertson	52	– b Tucker	3
*D. W. Hookes c Tucker b Gilbert	139	– lbw b Tucker	
D. S. Lehmann c Soule b Gilbert	34	– b Tucker	1
M. G. Bevan lbw b Gilbert	0	– not out	
J. C. Scuderi c Soule b Gilbert	1	– not out	1
†D. S. Berry b Gilbert	38		
T. B. A. May c Wellham b Gilbert	1		
C. J. Owen c Faulkner b Robertson	16		
C. R. Miller not out	3		
B 9, l-b 5, n-b 46	60	B 1, l-b 6, n-b 14	2
1/54 2/74 3/154 4/215 5/215 6/221 7/319 8/331 9/372	381	1/4 2/76 3/76 4/96 5/96	(5 wkts) 12

Bowling: *First Innings*—Gilbert 33–2–127–7; Faulkner 17–4–37–0; Cooley 20–2–66–0 Tucker 17–2–56–1; Robertson 25.2–7–81–2. *Second Innings*—Gilbert 13–2–40–1; Faulkne 1–0–5–0; Cooley 4–1–16–1; Tucker 14.5–3–36–3; Robertson 7–1–17–0.

Umpires: D. R. Close and S. G. Randell.

SOUTH AUSTRALIA v WESTERN AUSTRALIA

At Adelaide, January 26, 27, 28. South Australia won by an innings and 44 runs. Sout Australia 6 pts. Toss: Western Australia. The fortunes of the defending champions, Wester Australia, sank to their lowest ebb on the second day when they were dismissed in 24.2 over for 41. It was their worst effort in Shield cricket and occurred only six weeks after they ha taken 565 for the loss of three wickets off virtually the same attack in Perth. The first day gav no hint of what was to come as South Australia amassed 331 for four, Hookes provin irresistible as he thrashed ten fours and five sixes in his three-and-a-quarter-hour centur Even Hilditch shed his usual staid approach to help his captain put on 150 in 140 minutes. O the rain-affected second day, however, fifteen wickets fell for only 99 runs. Scuderi and Mille thrived in the conditions and they shared the last seven Western Australian wickets at a cost of only 3 runs. Western Australia fared better in their second innings but, apart from the defiant Andrews, the batsmen appeared to lack the heart to extend the match into the last day. Wood was relieved of the captaincy of the state soon after.

South Australia

G. A. Bishop c and b Alderman	8
A. M. J. Hilditch c Veletta b Yardley	100
P. C. Nobes c Zoehrer b Capes	53
*D. W. Hookes c Zoehrer b Alderman	118
D. S. Lehmann c Zoehrer b Capes	41
P. R. Sleep lbw b Capes	7
J. C. Scuderi lbw b Alderman	2
†D. S. Berry c McPhee b Alderman	0
S. P. George not out	16
C. J. Owen not out	3
L-b 7, n-b 16	23
1/14 2/127 3/277 4/328 5/345 6/352 7/352 8/352	(8 wkts dec.) 371

C. R. Miller did not bat.

Bowling: Alderman 25.4–5–83–4; Capes 23–7–69–3; Matthews 16–3–58–0; Yardley 29–5–105–1; Hogan 15–3–49–0.

Western Australia

M. W. McPhee b Scuderi	10	(2) b Miller	23
M. R. J. Veletta c Miller b George	13	(1) lbw b Miller	7
T. M. Moody b Scuderi	6	lbw b Scuderi	49
*G. M. Wood c Berry b Miller	2	c Berry b Owen	12
W. S. Andrews lbw b Miller	0	b Hookes	89
†T. J. Zoehrer lbw b Scuderi	0	lbw b Scuderi	6
T. G. Hogan c Berry b Miller	2	c Berry b George	52
C. D. Matthews b Scuderi	0	not out	11
P. A. Capes c Berry b Scuderi	1	lbw b George	0
T. M. Alderman c Berry b Scuderi	0	b Miller	0
B. Yardley not out	0	b Miller	11
B 5, n-b 2	7	L-b 5, w 1, n-b 20	26
1/23 2/29 3/34 4/38 5/38 6/40 7/40 8/40 9/40	41	1/18 2/58 3/83 4/111 5/129 6/262 7/263 8/263 9/268	286

Bowling: *First Innings*—George 8–2–16–1; Miller 12–4–14–3; Scuderi 4.2–1–6–6. *Second Innings*—George 18–5–53–2; Miller 17–5–44–4; Scuderi 25–6–70–2; Owen 18–2–71–1; Sleep 8–0–34–0; Hookes 5–1–9–1.

Umpires: M. G. O'Connell and D. P. Rebbeck.

TASMANIA v NEW SOUTH WALES

At Hobart, January 26, 27, 28, 29. Tasmania won by four wickets. Tasmania 6 pts. Toss: Tasmania. Two declarations by Lawson left New South Wales empty-handed after they had made most of the running. They raced to 366 for five on the first day, with Steve Waugh and Matthews in complete control. The sixth-wicket pair helped themselves to 50 off five overs of the second new ball, and on the second day extended their partnership to 271. Led by Cox, whose career-best 175 took seven hours and contained eighteen fours, Tasmania made a strong reply. Cox put on 107 with Tucker and 192 with Wellham, but it still needed Cooley and McPhee, the last pair, surviving 40 minutes, to bring Tasmania the first-innings points. New South Wales had only a day in which to attempt to win, and although strong hitting by Small and Bayliss enabled Lawson to set a target of 219 off 41 overs, realistically he had no chance of victory. Instead, a second and inspired hundred from Cox saw Tasmania home. He batted for just two hours, facing 95 balls and hitting three sixes and nine fours, and although he was twice dropped, his ferocious attack on Peter Taylor revealed batting of high class. Tasmania's win came with one ball remaining.

New South Wales

S. M. Small c Soule b McPhee	33	– c Soule b Robertson	86
M. A. Taylor b McPhee	16	– c Bennett b McPhee	19
T. H. Bayliss c Cooley b Robertson	34	– not out	75
S. R. Waugh c Soule b Robertson	196	– not out	26
M. E. Waugh c Soule b Gilbert	0		
M. D. O'Neill c Robertson b McPhee	19		
G. R. J. Matthews b Robertson	117		
P. L. Taylor not out	2		
†P. A. Emery not out	0		
L-b 13, n-b 24	37	L-b 8, n-b 6	14
1/49 2/72 3/130 4/130 5/181 6/452 7/453	(7 wkts dec.) 454	1/53 2/164	(2 wkts dec.) 220

*G. F. Lawson and W. J. Holdsworth did not bat.

Bowling: *First Innings*—Gilbert 30–5–113–1; Cooley 21–2–111–0; McPhee 20–1–70–3; Robertson 35–4–107–3; Tucker 11–1–40–0. *Second Innings*—Gilbert 8–2–18–0; Cooley 6–1–23–0; McPhee 11–3–29–1; Robertson 20–1–78–1; Tucker 12–0–64–0.

Tasmania

R. J. Bennett c M. E. Waugh b Holdsworth	3	– (8) not out	0
G. Shipperd lbw b Lawson	11	– b P. L. Taylor	64
J. Cox c Small b P. L. Taylor	175	– run out	102
R. J. Tucker c Emery b Holdsworth	49	– b Lawson	2
*D. M. Wellham b O'Neill	90	– c Emery b Lawson	7
S. G. Hookey c M. E. Waugh b P. L. Taylor	8	– (1) c Emery b Holdsworth	4
G. R. Robertson c Holdsworth b Lawson	47	– (6) not out	19
†R. E. Soule st Emery b O'Neill	20	– (7) b M. E. Waugh	6
D. R. Gilbert c P. L. Taylor b Lawson	6		
T. J. Cooley not out	17		
P. T. McPhee not out	5		
L-b 9, n-b 16	25	B 11, l-b 3, w 1	15
1/8 2/22 3/129 4/321 5/359 6/368 7/393 8/431 9/435	(9 wkts dec.) 456	1/23 2/128 3/143 4/189 5/191 6/216	(6 wkts) 219

Bowling: *First Innings*—Holdsworth 24–0–108–2; Lawson 33.1–9–93–3; P. L. Taylor 37–16–53–2; M. E. Waugh 13–0–48–0; Matthews 26–6–60–0; O'Neill 29–11–83–2; Bayliss 1–0–2–0. *Second Innings*—Holdsworth 6–0–27–1; Lawson 13–1–46–2; P. L. Taylor 11–0–71–1; M. E. Waugh 6.5–0–42–1; O'Neill 4–0–19–0.

Umpires: B. T. Knight and S. G. Randell.

QUEENSLAND v TASMANIA

At Brisbane, February 2, 3, 4, 5. Drawn. Queensland 2 pts. Toss: Queensland. Cyclone Nancy washed out nearly five sessions on the first two days and also succeeded in blowing off the covers, thus enabling McDermott to obtain career-best figures in Tasmania's first innings as the damp pitch assisted his efforts. Queensland also found batting difficult, and at 85 for seven, with Gilbert and Campbell exploiting the conditions well, it fell to Storey and McDermott to gain them the lead. As the wicket eased, the result could only be a draw. Hookey played a remarkable innings on the last day, scoring his 116 off 110 balls in a 148-run partnership with Wellham. The Tasmanian left-hander hit three sixes and eleven fours before his captain rather perversely declared.

Tasmania

R. J. Bennett c Ritchie b Polzin	9	– c Polzin b Foley	44
G. Shipperd b McDermott	26	– c Ritchie b McDermott	11
J. Cox c Clifford b McDermott	22	– c Smart b Kasprowicz	1
R. J. Tucker c Anderson b McDermott	17	– c Anderson b Foley	59
*D. M. Wellham c Storey b McDermott	3	– not out	28
S. G. Hookey c Storey b McDermott	6	– not out	116
G. R. Robertson c Storey b McDermott	2		
†R. E. Soule c Anderson b McDermott	4		
G. D. Campbell c Anderson b McDermott	3		
D. R. Gilbert c Ritchie b Kasprowicz	1		
P. T. McPhee not out	0		
L-b 4, n-b 8	12	B 4, l-b 5, n-b 6	15
1/21 2/58 3/69 4/73 5/83 6/89 7/99 8/102 9/105	105	1/17 2/25 3/126 4/126 (4 wkts dec.)	274

Bowling: *First Innings*—McDermott 22–8–44–8; Polzin 20–6–35–1; Kasprowicz 8.5–2–14–1; Foley 4–1–8–0; Cantrell 1–1–0–0. *Second Innings*—McDermott 21–8–51–1; Polzin 14–5–25–0; Kasprowicz 12–4–25–1; Foley 13–2–57–2; Cantrell 10–2–25–0; Storey 22–5–76–0; Ritchie 1–0–6–0.

Queensland

G. I. Foley c Shipperd b Gilbert	35	– (2) not out	6
P. E. Cantrell c Soule b Campbell	8	– (1) not out	1
R. B. Kerr b McPhee	6		
*G. M. Ritchie c Campbell b Gilbert	11		
P. S. Clifford c Robertson b Gilbert	4		
C. B. Smart lbw b Gilbert	1		
S. C. Storey not out	18		
†P. W. Anderson c Hookey c Campbell	5		
C. J. McDermott not out	7		
L-b 6, n-b 8	14	L-b 1, w 1	2
1/11 2/24 3/45 4/53 5/55 6/78 7/85 (7 wkts dec.)	109	(no wkt)	9

M. A. Polzin and M. S. Kasprowicz did not bat.

Bowling: *First Innings*—Gilbert 19–4–46–4; Campbell 12.5–3–24–2; McPhee 12–4–33–1. *Second Innings*—McPhee 7–5–5–0; Robertson 5–4–2–0; Hookey 1–0–1–0.

Umpires: C. A. Bertwistle and P. D. Parker.

TASMANIA v WESTERN AUSTRALIA

At Launceston, February 9, 10, 11, 12. Tasmania won by 85 runs. Tasmania 6 pts. Toss: Tasmania. In an attempt to win outright points, Andrews, Western Australia's new captain, declared his first innings 58 runs in arrears. His strategy looked likely to succeed when Hogan and Matthews had reduced Tasmania's second innings to 119 for nine by stumps on the third day, and even after Robertson and Gilbert had added a precious 25 for the last wicket, Western Australia were well on course when McPhee and Wood took them to 70 for one. At this point, however, Gilbert shrugged off the effects of a sprained ankle and, in tandem with Campbell, produced an inspired spell to bowl Tasmania to victory. On a pitch that was never easy for batsmen, yet another marathon innings – nearly eight hours – by Shipperd was also a deciding factor. Wood batted well for Western Australia, yet soon after the match his invitation to play for his state was revoked. This followed complaints from his team-mates and came only days after he had been relieved of the captaincy.

Tasmania

First Innings		Second Innings	
R. J. Bennett b Mack	1	c Matthews b Hogan	17
G. Shipperd not out	132	c Matthews b Hogan	24
J. Cox c Zoehrer b Matthews	30	b Matthews	6
R. J. Tucker c Zoehrer b Mack	12	b Hogan	36
*D. M. Wellham c Hogan b Julian	57	lbw b Matthews	1
†R. E. Soule c Brayshaw b Mack	5	(8) lbw b Hogan	3
S. G. Hookey b Matthews	12	(6) c Zoehrer b Matthews	0
G. R. Robertson b Hogan	6	(7) not out	33
G. D. Campbell lbw b Matthews	11	b Mack	5
D. R. Gilbert not out	0	(11) b Mack	9
P. T. McPhee (did not bat)		(10) lbw b Hogan	3
B 3, l-b 7, w 1, n-b 10	21	B 2, l-b 2, n-b 2	6
1/4 2/54 3/75 4/187 5/223 6/247 7/258 8/277	(8 wkts dec.) 287	1/36 2/50 3/50 4/60 5/60 6/96 7/102 8/109 9/118	143

Bowling: *First Innings*—Mullally 20–6–42–0; Mack 28–5–70–3; Matthews 27–8–56–3; Julian 11–3–30–1; Hogan 27–10–61–1; Brayshaw 12–4–18–0. *Second Innings*—Mullally 6–1–17–0; Mack 16.5–5–27–2; Matthews 20–8–35–3; Hogan 36–16–60–5.

Western Australia

First Innings		Second Innings	
M. W. McPhee b Robertson	12	(2) lbw b Gilbert	37
M. R. J. Veletta lbw b Gilbert	0	(1) c Soule b McPhee	5
G. M. Wood not out	88	not out	47
*W. S. Andrews b McPhee	48	c Shipperd b Gilbert	8
J. A. Brayshaw c Cox b Tucker	43	c Shipperd b Campbell	4
B. P. Julian not out	6	c Soule b Campbell	1
†T. J. Zoehrer (did not bat)		b Campbell	1
T. G. Hogan (did not bat)		b McPhee	2
C. D. Matthews (did not bat)		b Gilbert	0
A. D. Mullally (did not bat)		lbw b Campbell	0
C. D. Mack (did not bat)		lbw b Gilbert	0
B 11, l-b 12, w 1, n-b 8	32	L-b 3, w 6, n-b 2	11
1/1 2/36 3/116 4/205	(4 wkts dec.) 229	1/5 2/70 3/80 4/91 5/93 6/101 7/104 8/110 9/113	116

Bowling: *First Innings*—Gilbert 15–4–33–1; Campbell 21–7–36–0; McPhee 19–8–29–1; Robertson 26–2–72–1; Tucker 15–3–36–1. *Second Innings*—Gilbert 11–1–30–4; Campbell 15–4–21–4; McPhee 15–5–25–2; Robertson 11–1–37–0.

Umpires: B. T. Knight and S. G. Randell.

VICTORIA v NEW SOUTH WALES

At Melbourne, February 9, 10, 11, 12. Drawn. New South Wales 2 pts. Toss: New South Wales. New South Wales dominated the match until the last day, when they could take only three wickets. After Victoria's poor first innings, Lawson's men had four sessions in which to bowl them out again, but Ayres settled in for 431 minutes, faced 361 balls, and easily surpassed his previous highest score. It was the only bright point for the Victorians, whose bowling and fielding were as pedestrian as their first-innings batting. The New South Wales batsmen, in contrast, made the most of their chances. Bayliss was especially dominant in the early stages, racing to 90 in two and a half hours, and the left-handed Milliken, in only his third Shield match, was an admirable replacement for Mark Taylor. Having given Baylis great support, he then stayed firmly put as O'Neill and Waugh laid about them. Milliken batted for 440 minutes, and when he left, Waugh pressed on to an effortless hundred. None of the bowlers could contain him, and Lawson's declaration came as a merciful relief to the dispirited Victorians.

New South Wales

S. M. Small c Dimattina b Reiffel 6
G. S. Milliken c Dimattina b McCarthy 151
T. H. Bayliss c Siddons b Jackson 90
M. D. O'Neill b Reiffel 70
M. E. Waugh not out 100
G. R. J. Matthews b Dodemaide 39
P. H. Marks not out 2
B 6, l-b 15, n-b 16 37

1/22 2/173 3/328 4/371 5/486 (5 wkts dec.) 495

†P. A. Emery, *G. F. Lawson, M. R. Whitney and W. J. Holdsworth did not bat.

Bowling: Reiffel 27.4–1–120–2; Fleming 23–2–84–0; Dodemaide 28–6–99–1; McCarthy 32–7–90–1; Jackson 38–8–81–1.

Victoria

G. M. Watts c Emery b Lawson . . . . 19 – c Lawson b Matthews 68
I. D. Frazer c Marks b Holdsworth . . . . 1 – (4) c Matthews b Bayliss 61
W. N. Phillips c Small b Matthews . . . . 62 – lbw b Matthews 11
*J. D. Siddons c Holdsworth b Whitney 21
†M. G. D. Dimattina c Waugh b Whitney 5
W. G. Ayres c Waugh b Matthews . . . . 12 – (2) not out 134
A. I. C. Dodemaide c Emery b Whitney 10
R. C. A. M. McCarthy c Marks b O'Neill 28
P. R. Reiffel not out 11
D. W. Fleming lbw b Lawson 11
P. W. Jackson c Waugh b Holdsworth . . . . 1 – (5) not out 0
L-b 1, n-b 10 . . . . 11 B 3, l-b 6, w 1, n-b 13 . . . 23

1/20 2/20 3/72 4/86 5/115 6/126 7/156 8/175 9/189 192 1/118 2/148 3/297 (3 wkts) 297

Bowling: *First Innings*—Lawson 16–2–45–2; Holdsworth 13.4–2–40–2; Waugh 1–0–12–0; Marks 2–0–6–0; Whitney 15–5–31–3; Matthews 33–17–45–2; O'Neill 10–4–12–1. *Second Innings*—Lawson 17–8–25–0; Holdsworth 4–0–17–0; Waugh 4–2–8–0; Marks 2–0–10–0; Whitney 18–4–60–0; Matthews 38–14–95–2; O'Neill 29–11–66–0; Bayliss 4–2–7–1; Small 2–2–0–0.

Umpires: R. C. Bailhache and L. J. King.

NEW SOUTH WALES v SOUTH AUSTRALIA

At Sydney, February 15, 16, 17, 18. New South Wales won by ten wickets. New South Wales 6 pts. Toss: South Australia. A superb all-round performance by New South Wales brought them victory early on the fourth day. Once again their batsmen gave them an excellent start, with Bayliss providing the early fireworks with 59 off 62 balls and then Waugh taking command. Waugh batted for three hours, scored 136 out of a 196-run partnership with Matthews, and dealt harshly with the spinners. He hit two enormous sixes off Sleep in the space of three balls, and he also had thirteen fours in his 137. Miller bowled steadily, and was duly rewarded as the New South Wales tail folded. South Australia's batsmen could make little headway against the New South Wales bowling. The pace of Lawson and Whitney, supported by Matthews's spin, always had their measure, although Bevan battled hard. With the weather doubtful, Lawson enforced the follow-on, and when South Australia lost their last five wickets for 15, New South Wales were left with a simple task.

New South Wales

First innings		Second innings	
S. M. Small c Hilditch b Miller	4	not out	16
G. S. Milliken c Plummer b Miller	33	not out	15
T. H. Bayliss lbw b George	59		
M. E. Waugh c Scuderi b Hilditch	137		
G. R. J. Matthews c Berry b Miller	73		
P. H. Marks lbw b Miller	0		
†P. A. Emery c Berry b George	9		
A. E. Tucker c Berry b Miller	17		
*G. F. Lawson run out	12		
R. M. Stobo b Miller	3		
M. R. Whitney not out	0		
B 3, l-b 14, n-b 12	29	W 2, n-b 2	4
1/15 2/108 3/116 4/312 5/318 6/337 7/351 8/367 9/376	376	(no wkt)	35

Bowling: *First Innings*—George 25–3–95–2; Miller 28.5–7–83–6; Scuderi 21–5–54–0; Plummer 11–3–56–0; Hookes 1–1–0–0; Sleep 10–1–50–0; Hilditch 7–1–21–1. *Second Innings*—George 5–2–16–0; Miller 5–1–13–0; Plummer 1.1–0–4–0; Nobes 1–0–2–0.

South Australia

First innings		Second innings	
A. M. J. Hilditch c Emery b Lawson	9	run out	51
M. G. Bevan c Whitney b Matthews	64	c Matthews b Marks	7
P. C. Nobes c Tucker b Lawson	25	c Emery b Tucker	18
*D. W. Hookes c Marks b Lawson	10	c Whitney b Lawson	20
D. S. Lehmann c Tucker b Stobo	9	c Milliken b Lawson	5
P. R. Sleep b Matthews	14	c Small b Matthews	31
J. C. Scuderi lbw b Matthews	2	c Milliken b Lawson	52
N. R. Plummer not out	29	run out	0
†D. S. Berry c Emery b Whitney	27	not out	3
S. P. George b Whitney	0	(11) b Lawson	2
C. R. Miller c Marks b Whitney	0	(10) lbw b Matthews	4
L-b 9, n-b 6	15	B 3, l-b 2, n-b 8	13
1/18 2/62 3/74 4/91 5/122 6/136 7/149 8/196 9/196	204	1/29 2/68 3/102 4/104 5/121 6/191 7/196 8/196 9/203	206

Bowling: *First Innings*—Lawson 21–10–37–3; Whitney 15.1–7–41–3; Stobo 11–1–49–1; Waugh 3–0–13–0; Matthews 23–9–27–3; Tucker 12–3–28–0. *Second Innings*—Lawson 13.2–5–26–4; Whitney 12–3–37–0; Stobo 5–1–21–0; Matthews 26–11–46–2; Tucker 14–3–47–1; Marks 9–2–24–1.

Umpires: D. B. Hair and I. S. Thomas.

WESTERN AUSTRALIA v QUEENSLAND

At Perth, February 16, 17, 18, 19. Western Australia won by an innings and 177 runs. Western Australia 6 pts. Toss: Western Australia. Western Australia's woes, culminating in Wood's dismissal from the side, were comprehensively resolved as they won their first match of the season at the expense of the competition leaders. Queensland's cause was not enhanced by the late withdrawal of the injured Tazelaar, and it was their bowlers who bore the brunt of Western Australia's resurgence. McPhee, profiting from a dropped catch by Clifford before he had scored, dominated a wonderful opening stand with Veletta. His 113 came in only two and a half hours, whereas Veletta committed himself to one of his longest and most dedicated innings, batting for seven and a quarter hours (323 balls, 28 fours) while his colleagues threw their bats at everything. Queensland were so disheartened that they lost eight second-innings wickets for 67, and although the last two wickets put on 90, they were decisively beaten with three hours of the match left. Their first innings was only marginally better, Clifford being the one player prepared to resist the Western Australian bowlers. His 109 occupied five and a quarter hours and contained sixteen fours.

Queensland

P. E. Cantrell c Veletta b MacLeay	10	– (2) lbw b Matthews	8
G. I. Foley c McPhee b MacLeay	24	– (1) c Zoehrer b Capes	4
R. B. Kerr c Zoehrer b Mack	10	– c Zoehrer b MacLeay	13
*G. M. Ritchie c Zoehrer b Capes	22	– lbw b Matthews	1
P. S. Clifford c Zoehrer b Matthews	109	– c Zoehrer b MacLeay	21
M. V. Tooley c Andrews b Mack	31	– (8) not out	17
S. C. Storey lbw b Matthews	20	– (6) c Veletta b Capes	6
†P. W. Anderson b Mack	7	– (7) lbw b MacLeay	0
M. A. Polzin b Matthews	28	– c McPhee b Capes	0
P. J. Carew c Julian b MacLeay	0	– b Matthews	23
M. S. Kasprowicz not out	0	– c Zoehrer b Julian	49
B 1, l-b 7, n-b 4	12	B 1, l-b 6, w 2, n-b 6	15
1/33 2/40 3/55 4/75 5/151 6/200 7/219 8/273 9/273	273	1/5 2/34 3/34 4/43 5/63 6/65 7/67 8/67 9/97	157

Bowling: *First Innings*—Capes 26–7–74–1; Mack 28–9–81–3; Matthews 22–8–49–3; MacLeay 24.4–10–38–3; Julian 4–1–13–0; Andrews 8–4–10–0; Brayshaw 3–3–0–0. *Second Innings*—Capes 16–6–32–3; Mack 16–8–25–0; Matthews 18–4–54–3; MacLeay 16–5–22–3; Julian 2.3–1–7–1; Andrews 5–1–10–0.

Western Australia

M. W. McPhee st Anderson b Storey	113
M. R. J. Veletta c Ritchie b Polzin	228
D. J. Ramshaw c Ritchie b Carew	44
*W. S. Andrews c Anderson b Polzin	92
J. A. Brayshaw run out	2
B. P. Julian c Ritchie b Polzin	9
†T. J. Zoehrer c Anderson b Polzin	34
K. H. MacLeay not out	18
C. D. Matthews c Ritchie b Carew	40
P. A. Capes not out	1
B 1, l-b 11, w 8, n-b 6	26
1/188 2/347 3/460 4/470 5/481 6/541 7/548 8/596	(8 wkts dec.) 607

C. D. Mack did not bat.

Bowling: Kasprowicz 24.5–4–115–0; Polzin 37–4–133–4; Carew 42–8–181–2; Foley 17–2–68–0; Cantrell 7–0–39–0; Storey 8–2–49–1; Ritchie 1–0–10–0.

Umpires: R. J. Evans and T. A. Prue.

SOUTH AUSTRALIA v TASMANIA

At Adelaide, March 2, 3, 4, 5. South Australia won by 127 runs. South Australia 6 pts. Toss: Tasmania. Two attacking declarations by Hookes were handsomely rewarded as his bowlers dismissed Tasmania twice in effortless fashion. Hilditch batted throughout the first day to ensure a reasonable South Australian total, but Tasmania's reply, in spite of Tucker's determination, was never adequate. McPhee put in a spirited burst of bowling and enjoyed career-best figures when South Australia batted again, but Bevan and Lehmann's century stand enabled Hookes to declare on the third evening. Once again Tucker fought valiantly to prevent a collapse, but when he eventually succumbed to Miller, South Australia's best bowler, Tasmania's demise was complete.

South Australia

A. M. J. Hilditch not out	103	– lbw b McPhee	2
M. G. Bevan c Cooley b Tucker	35	– c Robertson b McPhee	88
P. C. Nobes c Robertson b McPhee	29	– c Shipperd b de Winter	33
*D. W. Hookes lbw b de Winter	27	– c Cooley b McPhee	38
D. S. Lehmann lbw b Cooley	9	– b Tucker	63
J. C. Scuderi c Bennett b Tucker	40	– b Tucker	2
P. R. Sleep not out	23	– c Robertson b McPhee	7
†C. R. Miller (did not bat)		– not out	5
D. S. Berry (did not bat)		– lbw b McPhee	1
C. J. Owen (did not bat)		– run out	0
S. P. George (did not bat)		– not out	7
B 3, l-b 5, w 9, n-b 8	25	B 7, l-b 12, w 1, n-b 18	38
1/62 2/117 3/155 4/180 5/229 (5 wkts dec.)	291	1/8 2/79 3/141 4/245 5/253 6/270 7/272 8/273 9/273 (9 wkts dec.)	284

Bowling: *First Innings*—McPhee 29–11–66–1; Cooley 16–3–62–1; Tucker 14–4–40–2; de Winter 12–1–42–1; Robertson 25–4–67–0; Cox 1–0–6–0. *Second Innings*—McPhee 26–7–73–5; Cooley 16–2–74–0; Tucker 13–1–48–2; de Winter 8–3–24–1; Robertson 20–6–46–0.

Tasmania

R. J. Bennett lbw b Miller	1	– lbw b Miller	14
G. Shipperd c Bevan b Owen	15	– lbw b Owen	36
J. Cox lbw b George	3	– lbw b Scuderi	19
R. J. Tucker c Berry b Miller	71	– b Miller	67
*D. M. Wellham b George	21	– c and b Scuderi	4
S. G. Hookey lbw b Owen	42	– c Berry b Scuderi	0
G. R. Robertson b Scuderi	30	– c Nobes b Scuderi	24
†R. E. Soule c George b Scuderi	12	– b Miller	0
A. J. de Winter c Nobes b Scuderi	2	– c Owen b Sleep	30
T. J. Cooley c Hilditch b Sleep	9	– b Owen	4
P. T. McPhee not out	2	– not out	5
L-b 5, n-b 12	17	B 7, l-b 3, n-b 10	20
1/3 2/6 3/43 4/121 5/121 6/191 7/200 8/204 9/221	225	1/27 2/69 3/83 4/90 5/92 6/124 7/137 8/191 9/199	223

Bowling: *First Innings*—George 16–3–53–2; Miller 18–5–40–2; Owen 18–6–38–2; Scuderi 15.2–2–45–3; Hookes 1–1–0–0; Sleep 16–4–44–1. *Second Innings*—George 14–2–37–0; Miller 22.2–6–59–3; Owen 16–6–28–2; Scuderi 21–8–48–4; Hookes 5–2–12–0; Sleep 13–5–29–1.

Umpires: A. R. Crafter and D. J. Harper.

VICTORIA v QUEENSLAND

At Melbourne, March 2, 3, 4, 5. Drawn. Queensland 2 pts, Victoria minus 0.4 pts. Toss: Queensland. At tea on the third day, a Queensland win seemed a formality. Victoria's second innings was in tatters at 94 for five, giving them a lead of only 8, with Polzin having taken four cheap wickets. But Ritchie unaccountably took him off, whereupon Dodemaide and Harris embarked on a 168-run partnership which extended the innings into the final afternoon. Another devastating spell by Polzin, in which he took three wickets in four balls, left Queensland a feasible target of 200 in 49 overs. Two wickets in Reiffel's second over, three run-outs, and two simple dropped catches led to McDermott and Polzin going into the last over needing 7 runs to win. When McDermott was run out off the penultimate ball, 5 were still wanted, but Tazelaar made no effort to get them as Victoria's fieldsmen crowded the bat. The best batting in Victoria's first innings was a stylish four-hour 93 by Ayres, while for Queensland Ritchie took a relentless toll of the Victorian bowlers in his six-hour stay, which included fourteen fours and a six. He and Law added 125 in just 93 minutes on the third morning.

Victoria

Batsman	First innings		Second innings	
*G. M. Watts c Tazelaar b McDermott	41	– c Ritchie b McDermott	24
W. G. Ayres run out	93	– c McDermott b Polzin	23
W. N. Phillips c Cantrell b Tazelaar	5	– c Drinnen b Polzin	15
C. E. Bradley c Foley b McDermott	46	– c Drinnen b Polzin	0
S. S. Prescott c Cantrell b McDermott	8	– c Drinnen b Polzin	9
D. A. Harris b Cantrell	30	– lbw b Polzin	90
A. I. C. Dodemaide lbw b McDermott	16	– b McDermott	54
R. C. A. M. McCarthy b Tazelaar	0	– c Ritchie b Polzin	1
P. R. Reiffel c Drinnen b Tazelaar	1	– c Clifford b Polzin	0
†M. G. D. Dimattina b McDermott	9	– c Ritchie b Polzin	13
P. E. McIntyre not out	0	– not out	6
L-b 6, w 1, n-b 16	23	B 5, l-b 12, w 1, n-b 32	50
1/87 2/94 3/184 4/207 5/208 6/256 7/257 8/257 9/268	272	1/66 2/72 3/72 4/89 5/94 6/262 7/265 8/265 9/266	285

Bowling: *First Innings*—McDermott 27–5–99–5; Tazelaar 19–9–32–3; Polzin 9–2–21–0; Storey 6–1–36–0; Foley 15–5–25–0; Cantrell 21–6–53–1. *Second Innings*—McDermott 30–7–83–2; Tazelaar 15–3–48–0; Polzin 25.2–12–51–8; Storey 8–2–30–0; Foley 9–6–13–0; Cantrell 19–4–43–0.

Queensland

Batsman	First innings		Second innings	
T. J. Barsby lbw b Reiffel	28	– (2) b Reiffel	0
P. E. Cantrell c Bradley b McCarthy	25	– (1) run out	53
*G. M. Ritchie not out	167	– b Reiffel	0
G. I. Foley c McIntyre b Dodemaide	34	– run out	18
P. S. Clifford b Reiffel	8	– b McCarthy	14
S. G. Law not out	66	– c Dimattina b Dodemaide	25
S. C. Storey (did not bat)		– run out	22
†P. J. Drinnen (did not bat)		– c Dimattina b McCarthy	0
C. J. McDermott (did not bat)		– run out	33
M. A. Polzin (did not bat)		– not out	7
D. Tazelaar (did not bat)		– not out	0
B 4, l-b 10, n-b 16	30	B 1, l-b 18, n-b 4	23
1/45 2/81 3/162 4/179 (4 wkts dec.)	358	1/7 2/7 3/70 4/81 5/107 6/125 7/128 8/177 9/195 (9 wkts)	195

Bowling: *First Innings*—Reiffel 24–3–94–2; McCarthy 27–6–81–1; Dodemaide 26–5–79–1; McIntyre 29–8–83–0; Phillips 3–1–7–0. *Second Innings*—Reiffel 10–2–43–2; McCarthy 15–2–43–2; Dodemaide 15–2–61–1; McIntyre 9–1–29–0.

Umpires: D. W. Holt and W. P. Sheahan.

WESTERN AUSTRALIA v NEW SOUTH WALES

At Perth, March 2, 3, 4, 5. Western Australia won by 156 runs. Western Australia 6 pts. Toss: New South Wales. Lawson's decision to give Western Australia first innings proved unsuccessful and the rejuvenated home side coasted to an easy victory. Lawson himself bowled with great heart, but a shoulder injury put him out of action after he had reduced Western Australia's second innings to 22 for three. Matthews, too, bowled splendidly and his off-spin was never mastered. However, the New South Wales batsmen were unable to come to terms with the Western Australian fast bowlers, notably the left-armers, Matthews in the first innings and Capes in the second. Bayliss was an outstanding exception, hitting a fine century on the second day in three and a quarter hours. His enterprise brought him thirteen fours and two big sixes. Brayshaw and Andrews rescued Western Australia's second innings with a match-winning partnership of 124, and New South Wales, needing 324 on the last day with all wickets intact, were never in the hunt. Zoehrer supported his bowlers with an inspired display behind the stumps.

Western Australia

First Innings		Second Innings	
M. R. J. Veletta c Waugh b Matthews	45	(2) c Emery b Lawson	5
M. W. McPhee c Matthews b Lawson	32	(1) c Emery b Lawson	11
T. M. Moody c Matthews b Lawson	63	c Emery b Lawson	0
*W. S. Andrews b Matthews	21	b Waugh	59
J. A. Brayshaw b Matthews	29	c Whitney b Waugh	69
D. J. Ramshaw c Emery b Lawson	5	lbw b Whitney	1
†T. J. Zoehrer c Stobo b Lawson	8	run out	31
K. H. MacLeay not out	53	c Waugh b Matthews	27
C. D. Matthews c Emery b Stobo	41	c O'Neill b Whitney	10
P. A. Capes c Emery b Matthews	0	c Stobo b Matthews	7
C. D. Mack c Waugh b Matthews	0	not out	1
L-b 5, w 5, n-b 10	20	B 5, l-b 5, w 2, n-b 14	26
1/86 2/88 3/131 4/195 5/205 6/209 7/220 8/314 9/315	317	1/13 2/13 3/22 4/146 5/155 6/159 7/214 8/227 9/244	247

Bowling: *First Innings*—Lawson 29–5–69–4; Whitney 23–5–90–0; Stobo 17–2–58–1; Marks 8–2–23–0; Matthews 37.4–14–70–5; O'Neill 1–0–2–0. *Second Innings*—Lawson 15–3–32–3; Whitney 18.4–4–56–2; Stobo 12–1–47–0; Matthews 25–10–47–2; Waugh 13–1–55–2.

New South Wales

First Innings		Second Innings	
S. M. Small c Moody b Capes	32	c Andrews b MacLeay	24
G. S. Milliken c Zoehrer b Matthews	18	c Veletta b Capes	2
T. H. Bayliss b MacLeay	101	c Zoehrer b Matthews	35
M. D. O'Neill c MacLeay b Matthews	19	c Andrews b Mack	50
M. E. Waugh c Veletta b Matthews	5	c Zoehrer b Capes	11
G. R. J. Matthews c Zoehrer b Matthews	22	c Zoehrer b MacLeay	4
P. H. Marks lbw b Matthews	0	c Moody b Capes	5
†P. A. Emery c Moody b Matthews	5	c Veletta b Capes	4
*G. F. Lawson c Andrews b MacLeay	10	st Zoehrer b Andrews	17
M. R. Whitney not out	1	st Zoehrer b Moody	0
R. M. Stobo c Veletta b MacLeay	0	not out	0
L-b 3, w 5, n-b 15	23	B 1, l-b 5, w 2, n-b 12	20
1/52 2/74 3/106 4/112 5/154 6/154 7/166 8/231 9/236	236	1/7 2/71 3/71 4/83 5/104 6/147 7/147 8/172 9/172	172

Bowling: *First Innings*—Capes 11–1–52–1; Matthews 21–4–81–6; Mack 12–0–39–0; MacLeay 14–4–61–3. *Second Innings*—Capes 15–2–60–4; Matthews 10–2–41–1; Mack 13–1–46–1; MacLeay 8–3–18–2; Andrews 4–3–1–1; Moody 0.2–0–0–1.

Umpires: R. A. Emerson and R. J. Evans.

NEW SOUTH WALES v TASMANIA

At Sydney, March 9, 10, 11. New South Wales won by an innings and 156 runs. New South Wales 6 pts. Toss: Tasmania. On an underprepared pitch, New South Wales took just two and a half days to overwhelm the bemused Tasmanians. Wellham opted to take first innings, but by the end of the first day the home team had secured the lead. Their spinners, Matthews and Tucker, revelled in the conditions, and the classic combination of off- and leg-spin proved too much for the tentative batsmen. Waugh, 36 overnight, batted through the second day to reach his highest score, and his disciplined innings inspired O'Neill and Emery to share partnerships of 122 and 224 respectively. Lawson's declaration left his bowlers with two days to win the match. Matthews again carried all before him with the best figures of his career, and only a fighting 96 off 167 balls by the newcomer, Farrell, held up the bowlers. With six points from the match, New South Wales finished on top of the Shield table.

Tasmania

M. G. Farrell c Whitney b Lawson	5	– b Matthews	96
G. Shipperd b Whitney	1	– lbw b Holdsworth	0
J. Cox lbw b Holdsworth	10	– c Emery b Matthews	4
R. J. Tucker b Tucker	37	– c Holdsworth b Matthews	5
*D. M. Wellham lbw b Tucker	27	– c Bayliss b Matthews	0
S. G. Hookey c Milliken b Matthews	19	– c Waugh b Matthews	0
G. R. Robertson c Small b Matthews	0	– c and b Matthews	10
†R. E. Soule b Matthews	4	– c Whitney b Tucker	2
D. R. Gilbert c Emery b Tucker	9	– not out	23
T. J. Cooley not out	0	– c Whitney b Matthews	8
P. T. McPhee c Bayliss b Tucker	0	– b O'Neill	0
L-b 1, n-b 4	5	B 4, l-b 5	9
1/4 2/12 3/32 4/82 5/95 6/103 7/104 8/113 9/117	117	1/2 2/33 3/41 4/49 5/49 6/77 7/106 8/130 9/146	157

Bowling: *First Innings*—Lawson 6–2–10–1; Whitney 9–3–26–1; Holdsworth 6–1–29–1; Matthews 12–3–26–3; Tucker 9.5–4–25–4. *Second Innings*—Whitney 7–4–8–0; Holdsworth 7–5–24–1; Matthews 25–12–50–7; Tucker 19–6–51–1; O'Neill 5.5–1–15–1.

New South Wales

S. M. Small lbw b Gilbert	0	†P. A. Emery lbw b McPhee	81
G. S. Milliken c Cox b McPhee	0	A. E. Tucker not out	18
T. H. Bayliss b Robertson	20	B 1, l-b 14, n-b 22	37
M. D. O'Neill run out	71		
M. E. Waugh not out	198	1/2 2/4 3/33 (6 wkts dec.)	430
G. R. J. Matthews lbw b Gilbert	5	4/155 5/161 6/385	

*G. F. Lawson, M. R. Whitney and W. J. Holdsworth did not bat.

Bowling: Gilbert 32–7–96–2; McPhee 36–10–83–2; Robertson 44–8–125–1; Cooley 19–1–81–0; Farrell 17–3–30–0.

Umpires: D. B. Hair and I. S. Thomas.

SOUTH AUSTRALIA v QUEENSLAND

At Adelaide, March 9, 10, 11, 12. Drawn. Queensland 2 pts. Toss: South Australia. South Australia's hopes of reaching the Shield final virtually evaporated on the first morning when they lost four wickets for 24, three to a fired-up McDermott. Lehmann surveyed the damage and took to the Queensland bowling. In only 166 minutes, and off 122 balls, he raced to his fifth century, becoming the youngest player (at 20 years 32 days) to score 1,000 runs in an Australian season, and then turned a shoulder-high full toss to Polzin at mid-wicket. Queensland's reply was a triumph for their captain, Ritchie, who batted superbly for seven and a quarter hours and hit 21 fours in reaching his highest score. When Queensland's innings ended just before tea on the third day, South Australia trailed by 194, and they were now committed to batting for a draw. McDermott again cut into the early order, but Hookes played one of his best innings, hitting 24 fours and a six in five hours. With Hilditch and Lehmann also showing great determination, South Australia were never in danger.

South Australia

A. M. J. Hilditch b Kasprowicz	4	– b Cantrell	54
M. G. Bevan c Ritchie b McDermott	5	– c Drinnen b McDermott	0
P. C. Nobes lbw b McDermott	3	– c and b McDermott	0
*D. W. Hookes b McDermott	5	– b Cantrell	159
D. S. Lehmann c Polzin b Storey	100	– c sub b Polzin	72
J. C. Scuderi c Cantrell b Polzin	21	– c Barsby b Kasprowicz	24
P. R. Sleep not out	75	– not out	31
†D. S. Berry run out	19	– c sub b Foley	16
C. R. Miller c Kasprowicz b McDermott	0	– c Polzin b Storey	20
C. J. Owen c Cantrell b McDermott	2	– not out	0
S. P. George c Drinnen b Kasprowicz	10		
L-b 4, w 1, n-b 13	18	B 9, l-b 8, n-b 8	25
1/9 2/9 3/15 4/24 5/81 6/180 7/223 8/233 9/249	262	1/13 2/13 3/179 4/276 5/319 6/340 7/365 8/399	(8 wkts) 401

Bowling: *First Innings*—McDermott 21–5–75–5; Kasprowicz 15.2–0–59–2; Polzin 24–4–82–1; Cantrell 12–4–20–0; Foley 1–0–6–0; Storey 4–1–16–1. *Second Innings*—McDermott 11–4–34–2; Kasprowicz 21–4–74–1; Polzin 33–7–80–1; Cantrell 33–11–92–2; Foley 10–6–17–1; Storey 17–4–76–1; Clifford 3–2–2–0; Ritchie 3–0–9–0.

Queensland

T. J. Barsby c Berry b George	27
P. E. Cantrell b Scuderi	22
G. I. Foley b Owen	20
*G. M. Ritchie not out	213
P. S. Clifford b Miller	30
S. G. Law b Owen	54
S. C. Storey c Berry b George	12
†P. J. Drinnen c and b Sleep	14
C. J. McDermott c Nobes b Sleep	23
M. A. Polzin c Berry b Owen	2
M. S. Kasprowicz c Miller b Sleep	18
B 3, l-b 12, w 4, n-b 2	21
1/56 2/73 3/94 4/129 5/254 6/283 7/317 8/382 9/391	456

Bowling: George 23–4–89–2; Miller 24–7–60–1; Scuderi 24–5–78–1; Owen 19–5–80–3; Sleep 41.5–7–107–3; Hookes 14–3–27–0.

Umpires: A. R. Crafter and D. P. Rebbeck.

WESTERN AUSTRALIA v VICTORIA

At Perth, March 9, 10, 11, 12. Drawn. Victoria 2 pts. Toss: Victoria. Siddons's dashing century did the Victorians proud on the first day after he had won the toss and chosen to bat. His 269-minute innings should have ended when, at 14, he gave a chance to McPhee, but he went on to hit thirteen fours and a six and share a stand of 167 in three hours with Harris. Although Western Australia struggled against the spin of McIntyre and the pace of Fleming, Brayshaw propped up the middle order, and a late burst of hitting by Matthews raised temporary hopes of first-innings points. Enjoying a lead of 44, Victoria then batted steadily enough. Watts hit sixteen fours in his three-and-threequarter-hour stay, and Siddons's declaration left Western Australia to score 353 from 54 overs. They made an exciting start, reaching 100 in only seventeen overs as Zoehrer, promoted to opener, hit out at everything. His own hundred came up in 86 minutes with twenty fours, but predictably the later Western Australian batsmen were unable to sustain this momentum.

ictoria

M. Watts c Moody b Hogan .... 42 – c MacLeay b Matthews 108
. G. Ayres lbw b Capes .... 6 – lbw b MacLeay 9
. N. Phillips c Brayshaw b MacLeay .... 29 – st Zoehrer b Andrews 75
. D. Siddons c Zoehrer b Hogan ....124 – c Brayshaw b Andrews 17
A. Harris c Veletta b Mack .... 50 – c MacLeay b Andrews 19
1. G. D. Dimattina c Veletta b Capes .... 4 – (7) not out 29
E. Bradley c Brayshaw b Mack .... 23 – (6) c Mack b Zoehrer 30
C. A. M. McCarthy c Moody b Capes ..... 0 – not out 13
R. Reiffel not out 5
W. Fleming c Zoehrer b MacLeay 12
E. McIntyre c Moody b Hogan 0
L-b 6, w 6, n-b 16 .... 28 L-b 5, w 1, n-b 2 8

35 2/58 3/102 4/269 5/277 323 1/43 2/187 3/213 (6 wkts dec.) 308
289 7/296 8/306 9/322 4/225 5/242 6/289

Bowling: *First Innings*—Capes 26–4–93–3; Mack 18–4–71–2; Hogan 20.3–3–44–3; atthews 28–10–64–0; MacLeay 21–10–20–2; Brayshaw 6–0–25–0. *Second Innings*—Capes –2–33–0; Mack 16–2–56–0; Hogan 16–7–40–0; Matthews 13–3–29–1; MacLeay 12–2–41–1; ayshaw 6–0–20–0; Moody 11–1–32–0; Andrews 11–2–43–3; Zoehrer 4–1–9–1.

/estern Australia

. R. J. Veletta b Fleming .... 59 – (7) not out 32
. W. McPhee c Siddons b Fleming .... 16 – (1) b Fleming 3
M. Moody c Siddons b McCarthy .... 0 – c Harris b Reiffel 23
/. S. Andrews c Dimattina b Fleming .... 3 – (6) c Siddons b McIntyre 4
A. Brayshaw c Watts b McIntyre .... 80 – (8) not out 41
H. MacLeay lbw b McIntyre 1
. J. Zoehrer b McIntyre .... 6 – (2) b McCarthy 103
G. Hogan c sub b Reiffel 19
D. Matthews not out .... 53 – (5) b McCarthy 22
A. Capes c Reiffel b McCarthy .... 14 – (4) b McIntyre 3
D. Mack c Siddons b Reiffel 8
B 5, l-b 9, n-b 6 .... 20 L-b 5, n-b 12 17

21 2/36 3/45 4/108 5/109 279 1/7 2/98 3/137 4/139 (6 wkts) 248
135 7/180 8/192 9/261 5/154 6/184

Bowling: *First Innings*—Reiffel 27.3–7–77–2; Fleming 18–6–52–3; McCarthy 23–3–70–2; :Intyre 32–9–63–3; Phillips 2–1–3–0. *Second Innings*—Reiffel 15–2–75–1; Fleming 1–55–1; McCarthy 8–0–55–2; McIntyre 15–2–58–2.

Umpires: G. J. Bibby and T. A. Prue.

FINAL

NEW SOUTH WALES v QUEENSLAND

Sydney, March 23, 24, 25, 26, 27. New South Wales won by 345 runs. Toss: Queensland. ıy misgivings Queensland may have had about playing this match on the Sydney Cricket ound were comprehensively realised. They were outplayed virtually from the first ball, and : before the game started it was New South Wales who had the more genuine concern when eir captain and best bowler, Lawson, ruled himself out with an injured shoulder. The home-ıte selectors made two critical decisions, appointing Mark Taylor as captain, ahead of the re experienced Steve Waugh, and then choosing the leg-spinner, Tucker, instead of the st off-spinner Peter Taylor. Put in, New South Wales' left-handed openers, Small and ylor, survived 237 minutes, playing with impeccable judgement and self denial, and Taylor ntinued on into the second day. Queensland's reply foundered from the start. Foley ducked .o a ball from Holdsworth and retired with concussion and double vision; Cantrell played no oke to a straight ball from Whitney. After that, Matthews and Tucker established control and Queensland lurched to 91 for eight by stumps. Though the match was as good as ove 10,295 people turned up for the third day, the biggest Shield crowd at the SCG for 28 year and they received good value. Matthews took Queensland's last two wickets in no time, b Taylor had no reason to enforce the follow-on. Instead, with Rackemann not called on for overs, he and Small raced to their second century opening stand. Taylor went on inevitably his own second hundred and left the ground to a standing ovation. The runs continued to flo from the bats of Bayliss and Mark Waugh, and soon after Waugh had passed 1,000 runs f the season, Taylor declared. Queensland showed more aptitude in their second innings, b they were all out with more than three hours left.

Close of play: First day, New South Wales 231-4 (M. A. Taylor 107*, P. A. Emery 4* Second day, Queensland 91-8 (I. A. Healy 14*, C. G. Rackemann 5*); Third day, New Sou Wales 286-6 (M. E. Waugh 12*, P. A. Emery 0*); Fourth day, Queensland 156-4 (G. M Ritchie 22*, P. S. Clifford 12*).

New South Wales

S. M. Small c Law b Rackemann	75	– b Law ... 5
*M. A. Taylor c Healy b Tazelaar	127	– st Healy b Border ... 1(
T. H. Bayliss lbw b Border	25	– c and b Rackemann ... 5
S. R. Waugh c Healy b McDermott	6	– c Healy b Rackemann ...
M. E. Waugh c Healy b Border	3	– not out ...
†P. A. Emery b McDermott	13	– (8) c Tazelaar b Rackemann ...
M. D. O'Neill c Healy b Rackemann	50	– (6) b Cantrell ...
G. R. J. Matthews lbw b Tazelaar	8	– (7) b Cantrell ...
A. E. Tucker b Border	4	– run out ...
M. R. Whitney not out	15	– c Border b Cantrell ...
W. J. Holdsworth b Kasprowicz	7	
B 2, l-b 7, n-b 18	27	B 13, l-b 13, w 2, n-b 10 . 3
1/160 2/194 3/205 4/220 5/261 6/272 7/286 8/309 9/347	360	1/133 2/205 3/242 4/249 5/254 6/282 7/311 8/372 9/396 (9 wkts dec.) 3

Bowling: *First Innings*—McDermott 38–8–102–2; Rackemann 28–6–72–2; Tazela 18–4–46–2; Kasprowicz 12.3–2–40–1; Cantrell 15–4–39–0; Border 24–5–44–3; Foley 3–1–8– *Second Innings*—McDermott 18–1–81–0; Rackemann 22–7–36–3; Tazelaar 12–0–53– Kasprowicz 12–2–41–0; Cantrell 20.5–5–71–3; Border 16–1–58–1; Clifford 4–1–14–0; La 3–1–16–1.

Queensland

P. E. Cantrell b Whitney	0	– (2) st Emery b Matthews ...
G. I. Foley c and b Matthews	0	– (1) c Emery b M. E. Waugh ...
*G. M. Ritchie c Emery b Matthews	16	– (5) b Matthews ...
A. R. Border b Tucker	36	– c Emery b Tucker ...
P. S. Clifford c Emery b M. E. Waugh	0	– (6) run out ...
S. G. Law b Matthews	8	– (3) c Small b Whitney ...
†I. A. Healy not out	21	– not out ...
C. J. McDermott c and b Tucker	2	– lbw b M. E. Waugh ...
M. S. Kasprowicz c Small b Tucker	0	– b Whitney ...
D. Tazelaar lbw b Matthews	0	– c Emery b Whitney ...
C. G. Rackemann b Matthews	9	– c and b Matthews ...
L-b 7, n-b 4	11	B 2, l-b 5, n-b 10 ...
1/0 2/44 3/49 4/64 5/72 6/76 7/76 8/77 9/95	103	1/33 2/42 3/114 4/122 5/216 6/234 7/256 8/257 9/279 3

In the first innings G. I. Foley retired hurt at 0 and resumed at 95.

Bowling: *First Innings*—Whitney 8–2–24–1; Holdsworth 5–3–16–0; Matthews 16.3–5–31– M. E. Waugh 3–0–8–1; Tucker 11–4–17–3. *Second Innings*—Whitney 28–9–66–3; Holdswor 3–0–17–0; Matthews 37.5–15–96–3; M. E. Waugh 6–0–22–2; Tucker 27–3–92–1; O'Ne 2–0–8–0.

Umpires: A. R. Crafter and P. J. McConnell.

SHEFFIELD SHIELD WINNERS

1892-93	Victoria	1940-46	No competition
1893-94	South Australia	1946-47	Victoria
1894-95	Victoria	1947-48	Western Australia
1895-96	New South Wales	1948-49	New South Wales
1896-97	New South Wales	1949-50	New South Wales
1897-98	Victoria	1950-51	Victoria
1898-99	Victoria	1951-52	New South Wales
1899-1900	New South Wales	1952-53	South Australia
1900-01	Victoria	1953-54	New South Wales
1901-02	New South Wales	1954-55	New South Wales
1902-03	New South Wales	1955-56	New South Wales
1903-04	New South Wales	1956-57	New South Wales
1904-05	New South Wales	1957-58	New South Wales
1905-06	New South Wales	1958-59	New South Wales
1906-07	New South Wales	1959-60	New South Wales
1907-08	Victoria	1960-61	New South Wales
1908-09	New South Wales	1961-62	New South Wales
1909-10	South Australia	1962-63	Victoria
1910-11	New South Wales	1963-64	South Australia
1911-12	New South Wales	1964-65	New South Wales
1912-13	South Australia	1965-66	New South Wales
1913-14	New South Wales	1966-67	Victoria
1914-15	Victoria	1967-68	Western Australia
1915-19	No competition	1968-69	South Australia
1919-20	New South Wales	1969-70	Victoria
1920-21	New South Wales	1970-71	South Australia
1921-22	Victoria	1971-72	Western Australia
1922-23	New South Wales	1972-73	Western Australia
1923-24	Victoria	1973-74	Victoria
1924-25	Victoria	1974-75	Western Australia
1925-26	New South Wales	1975-76	South Australia
1926-27	South Australia	1976-77	Western Australia
1927-28	Victoria	1977-78	Western Australia
1928-29	New South Wales	1978-79	Victoria
1929-30	Victoria	1979-80	Victoria
1930-31	Victoria	1980-81	Western Australia
1931-32	New South Wales	1981-82	South Australia
1932-33	New South Wales	1982-83	New South Wales
1933-34	Victoria	1983-84	Western Australia
1934-35	Victoria	1984-85	New South Wales
1935-36	South Australia	1985-86	New South Wales
1936-37	Victoria	1986-87	Western Australia
1937-38	New South Wales	1987-88	Western Australia
1938-39	South Australia	1988-89	Western Australia
1939-40	New South Wales	1989-90	New South Wales

New South Wales have won the Shield 40 times, Victoria 24, South Australia 12, Western Australia 12, Queensland 0, Tasmania 0.

†FAI CUP

At Adelaide, October 21. South Australia won by five wickets. Toss: Queensland. Queensland 210 for six (50 overs) (G. M. Ritchie 66, P. W. Anderson 63 not out); South Australia 211 for five (48.5 overs) (A. M. J. Hilditch 61, D. S. Lehmann 67, P. R. Sleep 45 not out).

At Adelaide, October 22. Victoria won by 28 runs. Toss: Victoria. Victoria 260 for four (50 overs) (G. M. Watts 67, I. D. Frazer 47, J. D. Siddons 84 not out); South Australia 232 for nine (50 overs) (D. S. Lehmann 33, P. R. Sleep 41, J. C. Scuderi 58).

At Perth, October 22 (day/night). Western Australia won by four wickets. Toss: New South Wales. New South Wales 248 for five (50 overs) (S. M. Small 80, M. E. Waugh 32, T. H. Bayliss 36, P. H. Marks 39 not out); Western Australia 252 for six (49.5 overs) (M. R. J. Veletta 31, G. M. Wood 50, W. S. Andrews 72, T. J. Zoehrer 57 not out).

At North Sydney, October 28. New South Wales won by 83 runs. Toss: New South Wales. New South Wales 183 (50 overs) (S. M. Small 48, G. L. Smith 37); Tasmania 100 (38.5 overs) (D. M. Wellham 32; P. H. Marks four for 30, B. E. McNamara three for 26).

At Brisbane, October 29. Queensland won by seven wickets. Toss: Victoria. Victoria 78 (42.1 overs) (M. G. D. Dimattina 30); Queensland 79 for three (24 overs) (S. G. Law 37).

At Perth, November 5 (day/night). Western Australia won by four wickets. Toss: Tasmania. Tasmania 249 for six (50 overs) (S. G. Hookey 76, R. J. Tucker 54, D. F. G. O'Connor 30); Western Australia 250 for six (47.2 overs) (G. R. Marsh 38, T. M. Moody 102 not out, Extras 37).

Semi-finals

At Perth, March 17 (day/night). Western Australia won by six wickets. Toss: Queensland. Queensland 202 (50 overs) (G. M. Ritchie 39, P. S. Clifford 52 not out; T. M. Moody three for 29, C. D. Matthews three for 38); Western Australia 203 for four (32.5 overs) (M. R. J. Veletta 52, M. W. McPhee 32, T. M. Moody 81).

At Adelaide, March 18. South Australia won by 53 runs. Toss: South Australia. South Australia 234 for nine (50 overs) (A. M. J. Hilditch 31, D. W. Hookes 45, D. S. Lehmann 52, M. G. Bevan 55); New South Wales 181 (48.3 overs) (M. E. Waugh 50, G. R. J. Matthews 38; D. W. Hookes five for 41).

FINAL

WESTERN AUSTRALIA v SOUTH AUSTRALIA

At Perth, March 31 (day/night). Western Australia won by seven wickets. Toss: Western Australia.

Man of the Match: T. M. Alderman.

South Australia

A. M. J. Hilditch b Alderman 0
P. C. Nobes c Veletta b MacLeay 9
J. C. Scuderi c Zoehrer b Alderman . . . 5
*D. W. Hookes c Zoehrer b Alderman 0
D. S. Lehmann lbw b Alderman 11
M. G. Bevan not out 23
D. B. Scott run out 10
†D. S. Berry run out 10
P. W. Gladigau b Matthews 0
C. R. Miller c Veletta b MacLeay 4
T. B. A. May c Moody b Matthews . . . 2
L-b 6, w 7 1

1/0 2/7 3/8 4/28 5/30 6/45 7/61 8/61 9/82 (34.5 overs) 8

Bowling: Alderman 8–3–14–4; Capes 5–0–19–0; MacLeay 8–2–18–2; Matthew 9.5–3–16–2; Moody 4–0–14–0.

Western Australia

M. W. McPhee c Berry b Miller 25
*G. R. Marsh not out 29
T. M. Moody c May b Gladigau 8
W. S. Andrews c Hookes b Miller 8
M. R. J. Veletta not out . . . .
L-b 6, w 8 1

1/46 2/67 3/84 (3 wkts, 19.1 overs) 8

J. A. Brayshaw, †T. J. Zoehrer, K. H. MacLeay, C. D. Matthews, P. A. Capes and T. M Alderman did not bat.

Bowling: Miller 10–0–42–2; Gladigau 9.1–1–40–1.

Umpires: R. J. Evans and T. A. Prue.

CRICKET IN SOUTH AFRICA, 1989-90

By FRANK HEYDENRYCH

Eastern Province, Currie Cup winners the previous season, dominated South African cricket in 1989-90, retaining a share of the Cup after the drawn final against Western Province and winning the two limited-overs trophies. Moreover, from the way that Kepler Wessels, their captain, had reinforced their playing squad with high-quality players, it was difficult to see an immediate end to the golden days (and nights) he had brought to Eastern Province. They lost only two matches in the Currie Cup, to Transvaal and Western Province, and would be quick to point out that neither defeat came when it really mattered. What was most remarkable about their second defeat was Western Province's superiority, given their record of five successive defeats in one-day matches against their Port Elizabeth neighbours.

Eastern Province's strength was that they had no apparent weakness. Philip Amm, in a prolific season, the maturing Mark Rushmere, Wessels, the evergreen Ken McEwan, Dave Callaghan and Dave Richardson comprised a nigh-invincible batting line-up, and Amm's 136 against Western Province at Cape Town was considered the greatest innings yet seen in the Benson and Hedges night series. The bowling was equally well balanced, with the two Australians, Rod McCurdy and John Maguire, the most successful fast-bowling pairing in South Africa since Garth le Roux and Stephen Jefferies spearheaded the Western Province attack. Maguire, in his first season, took 60 wickets in ten first-class games at 15.05, a record for Eastern Province, and McCurdy 45 at 23.40. The former bowled more overs than anyone all season, 430.2, and at fast-medium was seemingly tireless, adding to the timeless virtues of line and length a genuine appetite for bowling and a dedicated approach to fitness. Minutes after a match he would be out jogging. In addition to his bowling, he hit a career-best 65 not out in the Currie Cup to rescue his side after Gerbrand Grobler had sent Eastern Province tumbling to 116 for eight against Northern Transvaal.

In support, Wessels could call on the containing, if often negative, left-arm spin of Tim Shaw, the attacking but wayward leg-spin of Larry Hobson, who took eleven wickets against Orange Free State at Port Elizabeth, Callaghan's useful seamers or the explosive, "wrong-foot" left-arm fast bowling of Brett Schultz, who took six for 72 on début against Natal B and was a valuable support bowler in the closing one-day matches. Brent Robey, in his mid-30s, was a guiding light in the Nissan Shield campaign, showing again that there is no substitute for accuracy and a little variation in a medium-pace bowler.

Western Province's season was the opposite of the previous one. Unable to get past the one-day semi-finals, beaten by Eastern Province each time, they beat Northern Transvaal, Natal and Eastern Province in the Currie Cup and had much the better of their games against Orange Free State and Transvaal. In the final they put the match out of Eastern Province's reach, with the Kirsten brothers, Peter and Gary, laying the foundation for a large total with their second-wicket partnership of 252.

Adrian Kuiper, despite being stricken by meningitis in the middle of the season, was a dominant force, scoring three first-class centuries and frequently holding the batting together. Although at the end of the season he went to England with the reputation of a big hitter, he had shown that there was more to his game than slogging, being as prepared as anyone to battle it out in difficult conditions. Peter and Gary Kirsten scored valuable runs, but Daryll Cullinan's three brilliant centuries were countered by his grotesque failures. Among the bowlers, Meyrick Pringle was the undoubted success, capturing seven wickets in an innings against Natal and taking over the strike role left vacant since le Roux's unexpected retirement the previous season. Dave Rundle, Kuiper, Jefferies and an improving Craig Matthews all chipped in with wickets, but the real threat was Brian McMillan, whose aggression allowed him to get lift even from lifeless pitches. Yet, for all their talent, Western Province remained a side who could go from clinical execution one match to pathetic despair the next. What they lacked was that sheer resistance to defeat which marks great teams.

That quality, once deeply ingrained in Transvaal sides, had begun to elude them as well. Transvaal even lost the Protea Challenge, the one trophy that had been theirs the season before. In the absence of Neal Radford their bowling laboured at times, in spite of the attempts of the Springbok fast bowlers, Richard Snell and Hugh Page. With the bat, Roy Pienaar had a vintage season, being the only batsman to score 1,000 runs, and the Australian, Steve Smith, played some useful innings. Jimmy Cook, however, looked to have left his best form at Taunton, and while the captain, Clive Rice, was as pugnacious as ever, this alone rarely wins tournaments. In the end, Transvaal were a far cry from the champion sides of the 1970s and 1980s.

Natal reserved their best for the Benson and Hedges night series and will long wonder how they lost a final which had appeared to be theirs until the last ball. Beaten by Eastern Province, Northern Transvaal and Western Province in the Currie Cup, and also-rans in the Nissan Shield semi-finals, they were invincible at night until the final, when the unfortunate Dave Norman bowled a series of full tosses which allowed Eastern Province back into contention. Kim Hughes was a disappointment as a batsman, seldom topping 20, but his captaincy was shrewd and he brought out the best in many players, not least leg-spinner Richard McGlashan, who thrived on the extra trust and responsibility given him. Henry Fotheringham, back from the Transvaal, was Natal's best batsman, not surprisingly, while Peter Rawson, down from Zimbabwe, gave full value as an all-rounder and returned some excellent figures in the one-day games. His return of two for 8 in nine overs in the night final deserved to be rewarded with the trophy. Of particular interest, and importance, was the performance in three Currie Cup matches of Rodney Malamba, the first black South African to play first-class cricket in South Africa. He started well enough, taking two cheap wickets against Western Province, but bowling fast-medium he generally struggled at this level. He took good wickets for Natal B, though, and finished the season with twenty at 32.70, including a best of four for 40 against Border at Pietermaritzburg.

Northern Transvaal once again looked a champion side, until they lost Fanie de Villiers, the country's most exciting fast bowler. Without him Tertius Bosch, still learning, and an inconsistent Sylvester Clarke were left with too much to do. Rodney Ontong, in a surprise comeback, took few wickets, and these were expensive, while Anton Ferreira was a spent force as a bowler. An extraordinary run of form brought Vernon du Preez six successive half-centuries, and Mike Haysman scored quick, attractive runs in l competitions. Lee Barnard, after eight successful seasons of captaincy, in hich he led Northern Transvaal to a position of respectability in the Currie up, announced his retirement at the age of 34. Orange Free State fell away, rgely because their much vaunted fast-bowling attack of Allan Donald and orrie van Zyl failed to click. Donald revealed his true worth only in the last atch of the season, taking eight wickets for South Africa against Mike atting's English side at Johannesburg. Left-arm spinner Omar Henry lent iriety to the bowling, and Gordon Parsons, bristling with aggression, imbered some good batsmen among his season's return. Joubert Strydom, e captain, had his best season with the bat, but his top order often let him wn.

Border, the Bowl champions in 1988-89, retained a share of the trophy with estern Province B after drawing the final. They played throughout with a indsome consistency, and in Geoff Holmes, of Glamorgan, and Grant Long ey had the most successful openers in the competition. Simon Base, Kenny 'atson and the left-arm spinner, Hugo Lindenberg, shared the bulk of the ickets. Lindenberg, a top-flight spinner, deserved to have his talents tested a higher level.

The visit by the English XI, initially meant to be the first of two tours, was unhappy episode, dogged by controversy and soured by death threats, iled threats of assorted mayhem, and pitch damage. Its timing, coinciding ith the unbanning of the ANC and the release of Nelson Mandela, was oubly unfortunate. But while the calling off of the tour was widely hailed as e triumph of democracy, it should also be remembered that just as the nial of democratic rights to the bulk of South Africa's population is not ceptable, nor is the use of non-democratic methods to stop a cricket tour. ltimately, however, the ruckus had nothing to do with cricket. The tour was e focus of a power struggle for the sporting high ground, which the ational Sports Congress (NSC) and its leader, Krish Naidoo, clearly won. he morality, or lack thereof, of the cricket tour was not the issue, and a irticularly regrettable aspect was the damage it did to the South African ricket Union's laudable township coaching programme. Coaches, seen as ing part of the "oppressive system", were threatened, and the extensive aching scheme in the townships of Bloemfontein had to be cancelled. It as probably in everyone's best interest that the second tour, scheduled for 90-91, was also cancelled.

The tour itself produced little good cricket, with the Englishmen ismatched and outplayed in the international games. It will be remembered ostly for Rushmere's record-breaking 150 not out and 151 not out for the ivitation XI at Pietermaritzburg, for Kuiper's phenomenal hitting in the ie-day match at Bloemfontein, in which he hit 117 off 67 balls, with eight xes and eight fours, and for Kim Barnett's scintillating hitting in the final ie-day match. Gatting's leadership was excellent throughout. He carried mself well, never rose to provocation and, although he was attacked for his iivety regarding the situation in South Africa, spectators took him to their arts.

FIRST-CLASS AVERAGES, 1989-90

BATTING

(Qualification: 8 innings, average 35.00)

	M	*I*	*NO*	*R*	*HI*	*100s*	*Av*
A. P. Kuiper (*W. Province*)	8	14	5	795	161*	3	88.
G. Kirsten (*W. Province/W. Province B*)	7	12	1	751	175	2	68.
R. F. Pienaar (*Transvaal*)	11	20	4	1,010	152*	3	63.
G. C. Holmes (*Border*)	6	10	1	563	182	2	62.
J. J. E. Hardy (*W. Province/W. Province B*)	8	14	5	550	119	2	61.
J. M. Arthur (*Griqualand West*)	5	10	1	522	131	2	58.
R. V. Jennings (*Transvaal*)	9	13	4	479	120	1	53.
V. F. du Preez (*N. Transvaal*)	7	13	2	562	82*	0	51.
E. N. Trotman (*Border*)	8	12	1	529	143	1	48.
C. E. B. Rice (*Transvaal*)	7	12	1	515	129*	1	46.
M. J. Cann (*OFS B*)	5	8	0	360	138	2	45.
B. W. Lones (*E. Province/E. Province B*)	7	13	6	313	61*	0	44.
H. R. Fotheringham (*Natal*)	7	13	1	510	143*	1	42.
J. M. Truter (*OFS/OFS B*)	8	14	1	549	132	2	42.
M. W. Rushmere (*E. Province*)	11	22	3	795	151*	2	41.
D. J. Cullinan (*W. Province*)	10	17	3	581	137	3	41.
M. Ferreira (*N. Transvaal B*)	4	8	0	329	157	1	41.
P. G. Amm (*E. Province*)	11	21	2	765	116	2	40.
N. E. Wright (*Transvaal/Transvaal B*)	6	12	2	401	107	1	40.
J. J. Strydom (*OFS*)	9	18	2	632	104	1	39.
S. J. Cook (*Transvaal*)	9	16	1	566	111*	1	37.
D. J. Callaghan (*E. Province/E. Province B*)	10	14	3	414	107	1	37.
S. B. Smith (*Transvaal*)	9	16	1	564	115	1	37.
E. O. Simons (*W. Province/W. Province B*)	7	12	2	375	95	0	37.
P. N. Kirsten (*W. Province*)	9	17	1	590	185	2	36
L. J. Wilkinson (*OFS/OFS B*)	7	12	0	431	94	0	35
W. S. Truter (*Boland*)	4	8	0	284	141	1	35.
K. D. Robinson (*Natal/Natal B*)	5	10	0	350	130	1	35.

* *Signifies not out.*

BOWLING

(Qualification: 20 wickets)

	O	*M*	*R*	*W*	*BB*	*Av*
J. N. Maguire (*E. Province*)	430.2	130	903	60	6-48	15
H. C. Lindenberg (*Border*)	329	123	718	42	6-53	17
S. J. Base (*Border*)	198	44	566	31	5-43	18
A. J. McClement (*W. Province/W. Province B*)	243	90	576	31	7-25	18
C. Roelofse (*E. Province/E. Province B*)	184.4	54	402	21	5-71	19.
S. T. Jefferies (*W. Province/W. Province B*)	169	41	444	21	5-63	21.
A. A. Donald (*OFS*)	291.1	62	784	37	5-54	21
P. E. Smith (*Transvaal/Transvaal B*)	176.5	30	490	23	5-50	21.
M. W. Pringle (*W. Province*)	201.1	34	581	25	7-60	23
R. J. McCurdy (*E. Province*)	362.3	65	1,053	45	5-92	23
R. P. Snell (*Transvaal*)	275	70	777	33	5-71	23
S. T. Clarke (*N. Transvaal*)	200	53	471	20	5-46	23
B. M. McMillan (*W. Province*)	193.4	53	528	22	4-28	24
C. R. Matthews (*W. Province*)	205.3	58	509	21	4-52	24
W. K. Watson (*Border*)	215.2	59	511	21	5-37	24
P. S. de Villiers (*N. Transvaal/N. Transvaal B*)	176.5	30	488	20	5-66	24

	O	*M*	*R*	*W*	*BB*	*Avge*
D. B. Rundle (*W. Province*)	371.5	138	736	30	5-32	24.53
G. J. Parsons (*OFS*)	237.5	58	705	27	5-65	26.11
C. J. P. G. van Zyl (*OFS*)	309	74	794	30	5-32	26.46
H. A. Page (*Transvaal*)	189.2	31	621	22	7-38	28.22
C. E. Eksteen (*Transvaal*)	260.1	64	783	27	6-169	29.00
G. Grobler (*N. Transvaal/N. Transvaal B*)	185.3	36	581	20	7-69	29.05
M. Erasmus (*Boland*)	201.3	38	605	20	5-45	30.25
O. Henry (*OFS*)	406	126	1,059	34	5-66	31.14
R. K. McGlashan (*Natal/Natal B*)	351.4	99	1,029	33	5-120	31.18
T. G. Shaw (*E. Province*)	438.3	166	915	28	3-24	32.67
R. L. Malamba (*Natal/Natal B*)	212	41	654	20	4-40	32.70
T. Bosch (*N. Transvaal*)	265	32	893	25	5-60	35.72

CASTLE CURRIE CUP, 1989-90

					Bonus Points		*Total*
Section One	*Played*	*Won*	*Lost*	*Drawn*	*Batting*	*Bowling*	*Pts*
Western Province	7	3	0	4	32	22	99
Transvaal	7	1	0	6	25	21	61
Natal	7	0	3	4	29	21	50

					Bonus Points		*Total*
Section Two	*Played*	*Won*	*Lost*	*Drawn*	*Batting*	*Bowling*	*Pts*
Eastern Province	7	2	2	3	33	23	86
Northern Transvaal	7	2	2	3	30	23	83
Orange Free State	7	1	2	4	23	23	61

Win = 15 pts.

Final: *Eastern Province and Western Province drew to share the Cup.*

*In the following scores, * by the name of a team indicates that they won the toss.*

At Wanderers, Johannesburg, October 13, 14, 15. Transvaal won by six wickets. Eastern Province 336 for nine dec. (P. G. Amm 116, M. Michau 39, K. S. McEwan 43, T. G. Shaw 33 not out, R. E. Bryson 31; S. Jacobs three for 58) and 148 (H. A. Page seven for 38); Transvaal* 266 (M. S. Venter 55, R. V. Jennings 36, S. B. Smith 65; J. N. Maguire six for 39) and 219 for four (S. J. Cook 42, R. V. Jennings 35, R. F. Pienaar 39, L. P. Vorster 54 not out). *Transvaal 23 pts, Eastern Province 9 pts.*

At Kingsmead, Durban, October 13, 14, 15. Drawn. Western Province 142 (A. P. Kuiper 34, B. M. McMillan 44; T. J. Packer three for 31, R. K. McGlashan four for 54) and 338 for six dec. (A. P. Kuiper 161 not out, B. M. McMillan 41, L. F. Bleekers 34, E. O. Simons 51; P. W. E. Rawson four for 83); Natal* 171 (J. N. Rhodes 43, P. W. E. Rawson 47; A. P. Kuiper four for 29) and 192 for four (B. J. Whitfield 46 retired hurt, T. R. Madsen 45 not out, P. W. E. Rawson 60 not out). *Natal 7 pts, Western Province 6 pts.*

At Centurion Park, Verwoerdburg, October 13, 14, 15. Northern Transvaal won by nine wickets. Orange Free State 201 (J. J. Strydom 62, C. J. van Heerden 45, O. Henry 32 not out; P. S. de Villiers four for 56, T. Bosch three for 65) and 204 (C. J. van Heerden 49, O. Henry 78; P. S. de Villiers five for 66); Northern Transvaal* 331 (M. Yachad 50, V. F. du Preez 38, L. J. Barnard 74, A. M. Ferreira 45; G. J. Parsons five for 65) and 75 for one (V. F. du Preez 30 not out). *Northern Transvaal 23 pts, Orange Free State 6 pts.*

At Newlands, Cape Town, October 20, 21, 22. Western Province won by eight wickets. Northern Transvaal* 154 (A. M. Ferreira 33, W. F. Morris 34; B. M. McMillan three for 31) and 203 (V. F. du Preez 37, M. D. Haysman 63; S. T. Jefferies three for 49, C. R. Matthews three for 35); Western Province 255 (D. J. Cullinan 137; P. S. de Villiers three for 52, S. Elworthy three for 78) and 105 for two (P. N. Kirsten 31, A. P. Kuiper 35 not out). *Western Province 24 pts, Northern Transvaal 7 pts.*

At Springbok Park, Bloemfontein, October 20, 21, 22. Drawn. Transvaal* 273 (S. J. Cook 93, R. F. Pienaar 54, Extras 41; C. J. P. G. van Zyl three for 55, O. Henry five for 72) and 150 (H. A. Page 37; A. A. Donald four for 42); Orange Free State 259 for five dec. (P. J. R. Steyn 41, J. J. Strydom 83, G. C. Victor 32, C. J. van Heerden 53 not out) and 85 for eight (C. E. B. Rice three for 17). *Orange Free State 7 pts, Transvaal 5 pts.*

At St George's Park, Port Elizabeth, October 20, 21, 22. Eastern Province won by ten wickets. Natal 170 (T. R. Madsen 30, P. W. E. Rawson 38; R. J. McCurdy four for 54) and 188 (J. N. Rhodes 35; R. J. McCurdy three for 55, J. N. Maguire three for 34, T. G. Shaw three for 71); Eastern Province* 200 for seven dec. (M. W. Rushmere 40, B. W. Lones 61 not out; D. Norman three for 55) and 159 for no wkt (P. G. Amm 83 not out, M. W. Rushmere 70 not out). *Eastern Province 23 pts, Natal 5 pts.*

At St George's Park, Port Elizabeth, December 26, 27, 28. Drawn. Eastern Province* 336 for eight dec. (K. C. Wessels 182, D. J. Richardson 41 not out; S. T. Clarke three for 36) and 225 for five dec. (M. W. Rushmere 73, A. L. Hobson 35, K. S. McEwan 42); Northern Transvaal 288 (M. J. R. Rindel 76, N. T. Day 94 not out; R. J. McCurdy four for 93) and 128 for three (M. D. Haysman 32 not out, L. J. Barnard 56). *Eastern Province 7 pts, Northern Transvaal 6 pts.*

At Newlands, Cape Town, December 26, 27, 28. Drawn. Western Province* 328 for eight dec. (L. Seeff 55, P. N. Kirsten 185, B. M. McMillan 38; C. J. P. G. van Zyl three for 71) and 181 (P. N. Kirsten 44, J. J. E. Hardy 36; A. A. Donald four for 39); Orange Free State 290 for nine dec. (J. J. Strydom 80, L. J. Wilkinson 94; M. W. Pringle three for 60) and 134 for eight (D. B. Rundle three for 45). *Western Province 9 pts, Orange Free State 8 pts.*

At Wanderers, Johannesburg, December 26, 27, 28. Drawn. Transvaal 301 (N. E. Wright 50, C. E. B. Rice 99, P. J. Botha 36; T. J. Packer four for 62, R. K. McGlashan three for 59) and 185 for seven (N. E. Wright 39 retired hurt, P. J. Botha 31, R. V. Jennings 41 not out; P. W. E. Rawson three for 30); Natal* 268 for eight dec. (H. R. Fotheringham 96, R. K. McGlashan 52 not out; R. P. Snell five for 71). *Transvaal 8 pts, Natal 7 pts.*

At Newlands, Cape Town, December 30, January 1, 2. Drawn. Western Province* 387 (P. W. Martin 41, L. Seeff 55, P. N. Kirsten 60, B. M. McMillan 89, C. R. Matthews 34, D. B. Rundle 32 not out; C. E. Eksteen six for 169) and 13 for no wkt; Transvaal 331 (S. B. Smith 55, S. J. Cook 44, C. E. B. Rice 45, D. R. Laing 59, H. A. Page 58; B. M. McMillan three for 54). *Western Province 6 pts, Transvaal 5 pts.*

At Kingsmead, Durban, December 30, January 1, 2. Northern Transvaal won by four wickets. Natal 252 (B. J. Whitfield 66, A. C. Hudson 39, P. W. E. Rawson 30, Extras 39; S. T. Clarke three for 37, T. Bosch five for 60) and 225 (H. R. Fotheringham 64, J. N. Rhodes 60; R. C. Ontong five for 60); Northern Transvaal* 257 (V. F. du Preez 69, M. D. Haysman 50, R. C. Ontong 37; R. K. McGlashan five for 120, D. Norman four for 29) and 221 for six (V. F. du Preez 55, L. J. Barnard 56 not out; R. K. McGlashan four for 132). *Northern Transvaal 23 pts, Natal 9 pts.*

At St George's Park, Port Elizabeth, January 1, 2, 3. Eastern Province won by 135 runs. Eastern Province* 287 for five dec. (M. W. Rushmere 78, P. G. Amm 55, K. C. Wessels 74 not out, K. S. McEwan 46) and 169 for seven dec. (M. W. Rushmere 40, M. Michau 31 not out; O. Henry five for 66); Orange Free State 154 (P. J. R. Steyn 31, R. A. Brown 35, G. J. Parsons 32 not out; C. Roelofse three for 38, A. L. Hobson six for 62) and 167 (R. A. Brown 36, L. J. Wilkinson 47; A. L. Hobson five for 61). *Eastern Province 24 pts, Orange Free State 4 pts.*

At Wanderers, Johannesburg, January 6, 7, 8. Drawn. Western Province* 355 (L. Seeff 35, A. P. Kuiper 40, J. J. E. Hardy 119, B. M. McMillan 38; R. P. Snell five for 84) and 137 for three dec. (L. Seeff 50, A. P. Kuiper 38 not out); Transvaal 207 for eight dec. (R. F. Pienaar 70, C. E. B. Rice 78) and 237 for seven (S. J. Cook 72, R. F. Pienaar 65, C. E. B. Rice 30; C. R. Matthews four for 52). *Transvaal 6 pts, Western Province 7 pts.*

At Harmony Ground, Virginia, January 6, 7, 8. Drawn. Natal* 301 for three dec. (H. R. Fotheringham 143 not out, A. C. Hudson 87, R. M. Bentley 31) and 277 for seven dec. (H. R. Fotheringham 33, A. C. Hudson 94, T. R. Madsen 38, D. Norman 37 not out); Orange Free State 264 (C. J. P. G. van Zyl 50, L. J. Wilkinson 51, C. J. van Heerden 69; T. J. Packer four for 40, R. K. McGlashan four for 74) and 138 for two (P. J. R. Steyn 72 not out, J. J. Strydom 56 not out). *Orange Free State 5 pts, Natal 10 pts.*

At Centurion Park, Verwoerdburg, January 6, 7, 8. Drawn. Northern Transvaal* 253 (V. F. du Preez 79, A. M. Ferreira 61, S. T. Clarke 42 not out; R. J. McCurdy four for 48, J. N. Maguire four for 37) and 223 for eight dec. (V. F. du Preez 78, M. J. R. Rindel 51; T. G. Shaw three for 63); Eastern Province 214 (J. N. Maguire 65 not out; G. Grobler seven for 69) and 162 for four (P. G. Amm 68, B. W. Lones 30). *Northern Transvaal 9 pts, Eastern Province 8 pts.*

At Newlands, Cape Town, January 12, 13, 14. Western Province won by 234 runs. Western Province* 317 for eight dec. (L. Seeff 79, A. P. Kuiper 104 not out, J. J. E. Hardy 40; D. Norman three for 35) and 211 for six dec. (G. Kirsten 80, A. P. Kuiper 56; D. Norman three for 70); Natal 184 (H. R. Fotheringham 50, R. M. Bentley 51, K. J. Hughes 34; M. W. Pringle seven for 60, D. B. Rundle three for 54) and 110 (T. R. Madsen 30; M. W. Pringle three for 36, D. B. Rundle four for 15). *Western Province 24 pts, Natal 6 pts.*

At Springbok Park, Bloemfontein, January 12, 13, 14. Drawn. Orange Free State 265 (P. J. R. Steyn 95, W. J. Cronje 32, C. J. P. G. van Zyl 35, Extras 30; R. J. McCurdy five for 92, J. N. Maguire five for 61) and 161 (L. J. Wilkinson 48; R. J. McCurdy three for 59, J. N. Maguire six for 48); Eastern Province* 237 (D. J. Callaghan 107, Extras 30; A. A. Donald five for 54) and 170 for eight (D. J. Callaghan 47, D. J. Richardson 33; A. A. Donald four for 42). *Orange Free State 8 pts, Eastern Province 8 pts.*

At Centurion Park, Verwoerdburg, January 12, 13, 14. Drawn. Transvaal 280 for eight dec. (R. F. Pienaar 44, R. V. Jennings 57 not out, H. A. Page 31, R. P. Snell 31 not out; T. Bosch three for 66, S. T. Clarke three for 38) and 396 for three dec. (S. B. Smith 62, S. J. Cook 34, R. F. Pienaar 150 not out, C. E. B. Rice 129 not out); Northern Transvaal* 349 for seven dec. (M. Yachad 77, V. F. du Preez 64, M. D. Haysman 44, L. J. Barnard 74, M. J. R. Rindel 61). *Northern Transvaal 9 pts, Transvaal 6 pts.*

At Kingsmead, Durban, January 19, 20, 21. Drawn. Transvaal* 331 for six dec. (S. B. Smith 60, R. F. Pienaar 60, C. E. B. Rice 61, R. V. Jennings 66 not out, H. A. Page 35 not out; R. K. McGlashan four for 98) and 251 for two dec. (S. J. Cook 111 not out, R. F. Pienaar 100 not out); Natal 292 for nine dec. (T. R. Madsen 63, P. W. E. Rawson 95, R. K. McGlashan 32; R. P. Snell four for 50) and 195 for seven (D. Norman 46 not out, P. W. E. Rawson 43; K. J. Kerr four for 59). *Natal 6 pts, Transvaal 8 pts.*

At St George's Park, Port Elizabeth, January 19, 20, 21. Western Province won by 201 runs. Western Province* 264 (G. Kirsten 45, D. J. Cullinan 113; R. J. McCurdy three for 90, J. N. Maguire three for 59) and 217 for four dec. (D. J. Cullinan 40, A. P. Kuiper 103 not out, J. J. E. Hardy 54 not out; R. J. McCurdy three for 46); Eastern Province 155 (M. W. Rushmere 31, T. G. Shaw 32 not out; M. W. Pringle three for 64, B. M. McMillan four for 28) and 125 (K. S. McEwan 78; D. B. Rundle five for 32). *Western Province 23 pts, Eastern Province 7 pts.*

At Springbok Park, Bloemfontein, January 19, 20, 21. Orange Free State won by 51 runs. Orange Free State* 319 for eight dec. (W. J. Cronje 30, J. J. Strydom 104, C. J. van Heerden 46, Extras 36; P. S. de Villiers three for 84) and 156 for eight dec. (W. J. Cronje 82 not out; S. T. Clarke five for 46); Northern Transvaal 207 for nine dec. (M. Yachad 65, V. F. du Preez 82 not out; G. J. Parsons three for 60, C. J. van Heerden four for 27) and 217 (M. D. Haysman 50, G. Grobler 45, P. S. de Villiers 32 not out; A. A. Donald four for 52, C. J. P. G. van Zyl three for 47). *Orange Free State 23 pts, Northern Transvaal 6 pts.*

Final

At St George's Park, Port Elizabeth, January 26, 27, 28, 30, 31. Drawn. Western Province and Eastern Province shared the Cup. Western Province* 507 for nine dec. (L. Seeff 65, G. Kirsten 175, P. N. Kirsten 128, D. J. Cullinan 41, Extras 33; R. J. McCurdy four for 129, J. N. Maguire five for 137) and 166 for six dec. (P. N. Kirsten 42, A. P. Kuiper 31, J. J. E. Hardy 36; T. G. Shaw three for 35); Eastern Province 404 (M. W. Rushmere 81, K. C. Wessels 33, K. S. McEwan 101, T. G. Shaw 36, Extras 39; D. B. Rundle three for 96) and 18 for two.

CURRIE CUP WINNERS

1889-90	Transvaal	1958-59	Transvaal
1890-91	Griqualand West	1959-60	Natal
1892-93	Western Province	1960-61	Natal
1893-94	Western Province	1962-63	Natal
1894-95	Transvaal	1963-64	Natal
1896-97	Western Province	1965-66	Natal/Transvaal (Tied)
1897-98	Western Province	1966-67	Natal
1902-03	Transvaal	1967-68	Natal
1903-04	Transvaal	1968-69	Transvaal
1904-05	Transvaal	1969-70	Transvaal/W. Province (Tied)
1906-07	Transvaal	1970-71	Transvaal
1908-09	Western Province	1971-72	Transvaal
1910-11	Natal	1972-73	Transvaal
1912-13	Natal	1973-74	Natal
1920-21	Western Province	1974-75	Western Province
1921-22	Transvaal/Natal/W. Prov. (Tied)	1975-76	Natal
1923-24	Transvaal	1976-77	Natal
1925-26	Transvaal	1977-78	Western Province
1926-27	Transvaal	1978-79	Transvaal
1929-30	Transvaal	1979-80	Transvaal
1931-32	Western Province	1980-81	Natal
1933-34	Natal	1981-82	Western Province
1934-35	Transvaal	1982-83	Transvaal
1936-37	Natal	1983-84	Transvaal
1937-38	Natal/Transvaal (Tied)	1984-85	Transvaal
1946-47	Natal	1985-86	Western Province
1947-48	Natal	1986-87	Transvaal
1950-51	Transvaal	1987-88	Transvaal
1951-52	Natal	1988-89	Eastern Province
1952-53	Western Province	1989-90	E. Province/W. Province (Drawn)
1954-55	Natal		
1955-56	Western Province		

THE BOWL, 1989-90

Section One	*Played*	*Won*	*Lost*	*Drawn*	*Bonus Points Batting*	*Bonus Points Bowling*	*Total Pts*
Transvaal B	4	2	0	2	13	18	61
Northern Transvaal B	4	1	0	3	14	15	44
Boland	4	0	3	1	10	17	27

Section Two	*Played*	*Won*	*Lost*	*Drawn*	*Bonus Points Batting*	*Bonus Points Bowling*	*Total Pts*
Western Province B	4	2	2	0	17	18	65
Orange Free State B	4	1	1	2	14	17	46
Griqualand West	4	1	1	2	12	13	40

Section Three	*Played*	*Won*	*Lost*	*Drawn*	*Bonus Points Batting*	*Bonus Points Bowling*	*Total Pts*
Border	4	3	0	1	12	20	77
Eastern Province B	4	0	1	3	11	18	29
Natal B	4	0	2	2	10	18	28

Win = 15 pts.

Final: *Border and Western Province B drew to share the Bowl.*

At Wanderers, Johannesburg, November 18, 19, 20. Drawn. Transvaal B* 318 for six dec. (N. E. Wright 107, P. J. Botha 109, K. J. Rule 54; G. W. Symmonds three for 48) and 245 for seven dec. (N. E. Wright 37, M. S. Venter 67, L. P. Vorster 42, D. R. Laing 40; W. F. Morris three for 56); Northern Transvaal B 291 for eight dec. (P. J. A. Visagie 150 not out, R. C. Ontong 71) and 56 for one (D. O. Nosworthy 33 not out). *Transvaal B 7 pts, Northern Transvaal B 6 pts.*

At Harmony Ground, Virginia, November 18, 19, 20. Drawn. Orange Free State B* 505 for eight dec. (M. J. Cann 138, K. Craigen 43, J. M. Truter 74, L. J. Wilkinson 60, F. J. C. Cronje 31, R. E. Cullinan 77; G. P. van Rensburg three for 103); Griqualand West 304 (J. M. Arthur 131, G. C. Abbott 39, H. F. Wilson 45; N. W. Pretorius three for 80, F. J. C. Cronje five for 22) and 294 for five (J. M. Arthur 39, B. I. Stott 94, G. M. Charlesworth 43, G. C. Abbott 62 not out, Extras 35). *Orange Free State B 10 pts, Griqualand West 6 pts.*

At Jan Smuts Stadium, Pietermaritzburg, November 24, 25, 26. Border won by seven wickets. Natal B* 143 (I. B. Hobson 30, A. K. C. Lambert 40 not out, R. K. McGlashan 33; S. J. Base five for 59, H. C. Lindenberg four for 23) and 182 (I. B. Hobson 94; A. W. Schoeman three for 8, H. C. Lindenberg three for 62); Border 160 (G. C. Holmes 45, D. H. Howell 40; R. L. Malamba four for 40, R. K. McGlashan three for 40) and 167 for three (E. N. Trotman 58 not out, C. S. Stirk 82 not out). *Border 22 pts, Natal B 6 pts.*

At Wanderers, Johannesburg, November 24, 25, 26. Transvaal B won by eight wickets. Boland 140 (R. Marais 36; P. E. Smith five for 50, B. A. Matthews four for 43) and 239 (N. M. Snyman 66; P. E. Smith three for 41, B. A. Matthews four for 73); Transvaal B* 285 (N. E. Wright 36, L. P. Vorster 31, K. J. Rule 89, P. E. Smith 37; M. Erasmus three for 45, H. Barnard five for 68) and 96 for two (K. J. Rule 33). *Transvaal B 24 pts, Boland 6 pts.*

At Centurion Park, Verwoerdburg, November 28, 29, 30. Northern Transvaal B won by four wickets. Boland 218 (C. A. Lowe 51, J. S. Justus 39, M. Erasmus 38; D. W. McCosh four for 49, W. F. Morris four for 57) and 172 (N. M. Snyman 51, R. Marais 32; G. Grobler four for 53, I. A. Hoffmann five for 20); Northern Transvaal B* 244 (M. Ferreira 40, A. Geringer 81, P. J. A. Visagie 36; C. A. Lowe four for 42) and 149 for six (S. Vercueil 34, I. A. Hoffmann 37 not out; R. Marais three for 29). *Northern Transvaal B 23 pts, Boland 8 pts.*

At Kemsley Park, Port Elizabeth, December 11, 12, 13. Drawn. Natal B 289 (K. A. Forde 150, J. Payn 66; N. C. Johnson four for 57) and 228 for three dec. (I. B. Hobson 35, K. D. Robinson 130); Eastern Province B* 275 for seven dec. (B. W. Lones 56, T. B. Reid 38, M. B. Billson 49, N. C. Johnson 36 not out, A. L. Hobson 44; R. L. Malamba four for 92) and 94 for three (B. W. Lones 58 not out). *Eastern Province B 8 pts, Natal B 6 pts.*

At SFW Ground, Stellenbosch, December 13, 14, 15. Drawn. Northern Transvaal B* 199 (J. Groenewald 35, M. J. R. Rindel 64, P. A. Tullis 36; M. Erasmus five for 45, J. G. de Villiers four for 30) and 312 for eight dec. (M. Ferreira 157, S. Vercueil 65, I. A. Hoffmann 41; J. G. de Villiers five for 99); Boland 218 (N. M. Snyman 47, K. J. Bridgens 43, J. D. du Toit 33; A. J. Plint four for 82, A. Geringer five for 41) and 198 for five (W. S. Truter 34, K. J. Bridgens 40, J. Barnard 38 not out, J. D. du Toit 38). *Boland 8 pts, Northern Transvaal B 7 pts.*

At De Beers Country Club, Kimberley, December 13, 14, 15. Western Province B won by 118 runs. Western Province B* 348 for six dec. (L. F. Bleekers 72, G. Kirsten 56, J. J. E. Hardy 102 not out, E. O. Simons 46, T. J. Mitchell 32) and 191 for two dec. (L. F. Bleekers 102 not out, J. J. E. Hardy 64 not out); Griqualand West 287 for six dec. (J. M. Arthur 34, G. F. J. Liebenberg 84, G. M. Charlesworth 70, G. C. Abbott 45 not out) and 134 (H. F. Wilson 57; A. J. McClement seven for 25). *Western Province B 23 pts, Griqualand West 6 pts.*

At Springbok Park, Bloemfontein, December 17, 18, 19. Orange Free State B won by four wickets. Western Province B* 197 (G. Kirsten 32, A. M. Kirsten 39; N. W. Pretorius three for 43) and 230 (G. Kirsten 57, T. J. Mitchell 86, A. J. McClement 30 not out; N. W. Pretorius four for 103, P. W. Henning three for 18); Orange Free State B 261 (J. M. Truter 71, D. Ferreira 64, P. J. L. Radley 30; E. O. Simons five for 61, D. G. Payne three for 38) and 168 for six (K. Craigen 35, J. M. Truter 38). *Orange Free State B 23 pts, Western Province B 7 pts.*

At Buffalo Park, East London, December 26, 27, 28. Drawn. Border* 238 (G. L. Long 64, B. M. Osborne 34, I. L. Howell 53, N. R. Boonzaaier 36; C. Roelofse five for 75, D. J. Callaghan three for 29) and 277 for six dec. (G. L. Long 61, G. C. Holmes 69, C. S. Stirk 46, D. H. Howell 52; C. Roelofse three for 91); Eastern Province B 221 (H. H. Donachie 57, D. J. Callaghan 73; H. C. Lindenberg three for 63, I. L. Howell three for 52) and 99 for two (H. H. Donachie 55 not out). *Border 7 pts, Eastern Province B 6 pts.*

At Buffalo Park, East London, December 31, January 1, 2. Border won by nine wickets. Natal B 187 (K. D. Robinson 60, R. M. Bentley 43; S. J. Base four for 64, H. C. Lindenberg four for 40) and 337 (K. A. Forde 33, R. M. Bentley 72, G. M. Walsh 112, J. Payn 44; H. C. Lindenberg four for 81, including a hat-trick); Border* 366 (G. C. Holmes 75, B. M. Osborne 91, E. N. Trotman 91, D. H. Howell 43, I. L. Howell 33; M. D. Clare four for 48, R. L. Malamba four for 98) and 159 for one (G. C. Holmes 67 not out, B. M. Osborne 75 not out). *Border 25 pts, Natal B 7 pts.*

At R. J. E. Burt Oval, Constantia, January 6, 7, 8. Western Province B won by ten wickets. Orange Free State B 136 (S. T. Jefferies five for 77, J. E. Nolte four for 47) and 283 (M. J. Cann 120, R. E. Cullinan 60; S. T. Jefferies five for 63, A. J. McClement four for 75); Western Province B* 406 for five dec. (L. J. Koen 40, A. G. Elgar 66, G. Kirsten 153 not out, L. F. Bleekers 65, A. M. Kirsten 38) and 14 for no wkt. *Western Province B 26 pts, Orange Free State B 3 pts.*

At Kingsmead, Durban, January 6, 7, 8. Drawn. Natal B* 292 (K. D. Robinson 84, J. Payn 94; B. N. Schultz six for 72, H. C. F. Langenberg three for 64) and 213 (I. B. Hobson 46, K. D. Robinson 30, M. R. Woodburn 42, A. G. Small 32 not out; C. Roelofse five for 71); Eastern Province B 279 (P. A. Amm 77, A. L. Hobson 35; K. D. Robinson five for 84) and 124 for four (H. H. Donachie 44 not out, M. B. Billson 45 not out). *Natal B 9 pts, Eastern Province B 8 pts.*

At Kemsley Park, Port Elizabeth, January 12, 13, 14. Border won by four wickets. Eastern Province B* 195 (T. B. Reid 111; S. J. Base five for 43, H. C. Lindenberg three for 54) and 153 (P. A. Amm 37, N. C. Johnson 31; W. K. Watson five for 49, H. C. Lindenberg three for 41); Border 200 (I. L. Howell 60; P. B. du Plessis three for 52, N. C. Johnson three for 41) and 151 for six (G. L. Long 60, C. S. Stirk 31 not out; C. Roelofse three for 31). *Border 23 pts, Eastern Province B 7 pts.*

At De Beers Country Club, Kimberley, January 11, 12, 13. Drawn. Griqualand West* 190 (G. M. Charlesworth 75; P. W. Henning three for 25, F. J. C. Cronje four for 49, D. Ferreira three for 30) and 271 for two (J. M. Arthur 112 not out, G. F. J. Liebenberg 108); Orange Free State B 454 for eight dec. (J. M. Truter 132, G. C. Victor 78, R. E. Cullinan 75, J. F. Venter 51 not out; G. M. Charlesworth three for 109). *Orange Free State B 10 pts, Griqualand West 5 pts.*

At SFW Ground, Stellenbosch, January 12, 13, 14. Transvaal B won by an innings and 36 runs. Transvaal B* 435 for seven dec. (M. S. Venter 33, L. P. Vorster 117, K. J. Rule 103, M. J. Mitchley 51, S. Jacobs 102 not out); Boland 242 (I. G. Richards 54, R. Marais 82; K. J. Kerr four for 73, M. James four for 71) and 157 (J. D. du Toit 37, O. Douglas 31; K. J. Kerr six for 37). *Transvaal B 24 pts, Boland 5 pts.*

At Plumstead, Cape Town, January 19, 20, 21. Griqualand West won by 43 runs. Griqualand West 236 (G. C. Abbott 38, H. F. Wilson 39, P. McLaren 48 not out; A. A. Johnson five for 75, I. R. Solomon five for 56) and 234 (J. M. Arthur 69, G. C. Abbott 35, D. G. Mills 30, G. P. van Rensburg 31; L. J. Ryan five for 79, A. G. Elgar three for 39); Western Province B* 251 (E. O. Simons 95, A. A. Johnson 42; H. F. Wilson three for 38) and 176 (T. N. Lazard 63, A. P. Plantema 45 not out; I. M. Kidson three for 33). *Griqualand West 23 pts, Western Province B 9 pts.*

At Centurion Park, Verwoerdburg, January 26, 27, 28. Drawn. Northern Transvaal B 237 for eight dec. (M. Ferreira 82, A. M. Ferreira 52 not out; G. E. McMillan three for 54) and 158 for six dec. (A. M. Ferreira 45; S. D. Jack three for 50); Transvaal B* 195 (L. P. Vorster 50, K. J. Rule 41, D. R. Laing 54; S. Elworthy six for 37) and 119 for nine (P. S. de Villiers three for 38, S. Elworthy four for 44). *Northern Transvaal B 8 pts, Transvaal B 6 pts.*

Semi-finals

At Centurion Park, Verwoerdburg, February 9, 10, 11, 12. Drawn. Western Province B qualified for the final by virtue of their first-innings lead. Western Province B 325 for seven dec. (P. W. Martin 78, J. B. Commins 100 not out, A. T. Holdstock 45) and 192 (T. N. Lazard 65, A. M. Kirsten 62; P. E. Smith three for 49, D. R. Laing three for 35); Transvaal B* 189 (B. McBride 31, K. J. Kerr 31; A. J. McClement five for 63) and 224 for nine (M. S. Venter 43, B. McBride 50, G. E. McMillan 40 not out; A. J. McClement six for 52).

At Buffalo Park, East London, February 9, 10, 11. Border won by an innings and 199 runs. Orange Free State B* 150 (J. F. Venter 30, F. J. C. Cronje 44; S. J. Base four for 22, I. L. Howell four for 51) and 181 (M. J. Cann 38, J. F. Venter 55, G. C. Victor 34; S. J. Base three for 49, H. C. Lindenberg six for 53); Border 530 for six dec. (G. C. Holmes 103, E. N. Trotman 143, D. H. Howell 98, R. D. Moult 100 not out).

Final

At Buffalo Park, East London, February 23, 24, 25, 26. Drawn. Border and Western Province B shared the Bowl. Border* 506 for nine dec. (G. C. Holmes 182, G. L. Long 156, E. N. Trotman 78; M. B. Minnaar five for 143); Western Province B 273 (T. N. Lazard 54, F. B. Touzel 46, P. W. Martin 68, E. O. Simons 32; H. C. Lindenberg three for 78, N. R. Boonzaaier three for 37) and 179 for nine (F. B. Touzel 38, E. O. Simons 51 not out; H. C. Lindenberg five for 70).

OTHER FIRST-CLASS MATCHES

At Buffalo Park, East London, September 22, 23, 24. Drawn. Western Province* 341 for five dec. (T. N. Lazard 36, G. Kirsten 96, D. J. Cullinan 105, A. P. Kuiper 42; F. D. Toppin three for 70) and 184 for three (L. Seeff 50, L. F. Bleekers 35, J. B. Commins 44); Border 215 for seven dec. (G. L. Long 44, B. M. Osborne 46, E. N. Trotman 75; E. O. Simons three for 35).

At Brackenfell, September 29, 30. October 1. Eastern Province won by 133 runs. Eastern Province* 188 for four dec. (P. G. Amm 40, M. Michau 46, D. J. Callaghan 50 not out) and 186 for four dec. (P. G. Amm 38, K. C. Wessels 87); Boland 121 (S. Nackerdien 37, I. G. Richards 31; J. N. Maguire five for 22, T. G. Shaw three for 24) and 120 (J. G. de Villiers 30, C. A. Lowe 33; J. N. Maguire five for 32, T. G. Shaw three for 38).

At Buffalo Park, East London, October 6, 7, 8. Eastern Province won by ten wickets. Border* 94 (R. J. McCurdy four for 25, J. N. Maguire three for 23) and 267 (B. M. Osborne 80, W. K. Watson 78; R. E. Bryson three for 49, T. G. Shaw three for 58); Eastern Province 320 (P. G. Amm 112, K. S. McEwan 72, D. J. Callaghan 30; W. K. Watson five for 37) and 43 for no wkt (K. C. Wessels 34 not out).

At Dick Fourie Stadium, Vereeniging, October 6, 7, 8. Drawn. Transvaal 318 for two dec. (R. F. Pienaar 152 not out, S. B. Smith 115) and 264 for four dec. (M. S. Venter 49, R. V. Jennings 120); Boland* 300 for six dec. (W. S. Truter 141, N. M. Snyman 31, J. D. du Toit 65 not out) and 135 for seven (C. E. Eksteen three for 45).

At Springbok Park, Bloemfontein, October 7, 8, 9. Drawn. SA Defence Force* 336 (J. M. Truter 127, J. J. Strydom 86, D. O. Nosworthy 34; C. J. P. G. van Zyl three for 61, C. J. van Heerden four for 48, G. J. Parsons three for 66) and 124 for six (J. M. Truter 34 not out, S. Elworthy 36); Orange Free State 436 (P. J. R. Steyn 40, G. A. Hughes 123, G. C. Victor 64, C. J. van Heerden 56; J. J. Strydom three for 23).

At Wanderers, Johannesburg, December 1, 2, 3. Drawn. Transvaal* 195 (P. J. Botha 78, S. B. Smith 42; C. J. P. G. van Zyl five for 32) and 155 (N. E. Wright 63, S. B. Smith 30; A. A. Donald three for 30); Orange Free State 274 (W. J. Cronje 76, C. J. van Heerden 41, O. Henry 53; R. O. Estwick three for 55) and 75 for nine (R. O. Estwick five for 34, C. E. Eksteen three for 21).

NISSAN SHIELD, 1989-90

(55 overs per side)

At SFW Ground, Stellenbosch, October 24. Border won by two wickets. Boland 160 (J. D. du Toit 41; F. D. Toppin three for 27, W. K. Watson three for 28); Border* 162 for eight (G. L. Long 35, B. M. Osborne 40; R. Marais four for 38, M. Erasmus three for 25).

At Recreation Ground, Oudtshoorn, October 25. Eastern Province won by 180 runs. Eastern Province* 282 for five (P. G. Amm 79, K. S. McEwan 57, K. C. Wessels 47, D. J. Callaghan 36, M. Michau 34 not out); Southern Cape 102 (S. Meyer 32; R. E. Bryson three for 16, K. C. Wessels three for 27).

At Empangeni, October 25. Western Province won by 100 runs. Western Province* 258 for six (P. W. Martin 78, P. N. Kirsten 63, D. J. Cullinan 60; C. F. Craven three for 43); Natal Country Districts 158 (A. D. Faure 43; C. R. Matthews three for 21).

At Grahamstown, October 25. Natal won by nine wickets. Eastern Province Country Districts* 130 for six (M. J. P. Ford 66, A. Emslie 31); Natal 133 for one (B. Hobson 60, H. R. Fotheringham 41 not out).

At Barnard Stadium, Kempton Park, October 25. Orange Free State won by six wickets, after being set a revised target of 167 off 53 overs. Eastern Transvaal 173 for eight (C. R. Norris 62, K. Moxham 30); Orange Free State* 171 for four (W. J. Cronje 108 not out).

At Lowveld Country Club, Nelspruit, October 25. Transvaal won by 199 runs. Transvaal* 310 for four (S. J. Cook 38, R. F. Pienaar 135, S. B. Smith 62, C. E. B. Rice 34 not out); Northern Transvaal Country Districts 111 (J. Jameson 33; S. Jacobs five for 26).

At Vereeniging, October 25. Northern Transvaal won by 112 runs. Northern Transvaal 241 for five (M. D. Haysman 71, L. J. Barnard 68, N. T. Day 37 not out); Southern Transvaal Country Districts* 129 for six (A. Spies 45, C. Coutts 31).

At Potchefstroom, October 25. Griqualand West won by nine wickets. Western Transvaal 186 (S. du Plessis 40, A. van Deventer 39, R. van Rooyen 35, D. P. le Roux 33; P. McLaren five for 30); Griqualand West* 188 for one (J. M. Arthur 111 not out, G. M. Charlesworth 36 not out).

Quarter-finals

First leg: At Centurion Park, Verwoerdburg, October 28. Northern Transvaal won by 23 runs. Northern Transvaal* 260 for four (M. Yachad 145, V. F. du Preez 43, M. J. R. Rindel 40); Border 237 for five (G. C. Holmes 36, B. M. Osborne 87, E. N. Trotman 39; S. T. Clarke three for 38).

First leg: At De Beers Country Club, Kimberley, October 28. Natal won by five wickets. Griqualand West 127 (D. G. Mills 38 not out; D. Norman four for 26, R. J. Varner three for 10, T. J. Packer three for 32); Natal* 129 for five (K. J. Hughes 74, J. N. Rhodes 32).

First leg: At St George's Park, Port Elizabeth, October 28. Eastern Province won by seven wickets. Orange Free State 153 (W. J. Cronje 36, P. J. R. Steyn 35; J. N. Maguire three for 37, D. J. Callaghan three for 24); Eastern Province* 154 for three (P. G. Amm 36, K. C. Wessels 65 not out, D. J. Callaghan 44 not out).

First leg: At Wanderers, Johannesburg, October 29. Transvaal won by 159 runs. Transvaal 270 for seven (S. J. Cook 45, R. F. Pienaar 95, C. E. B. Rice 50); Western Province* 111 (D. J. Cullinan 37; S. Jacobs three for 23, P. J. Botha three for 31).

Second leg: At Kingsmead, Durban, November 4. Natal won by ten wickets. Griqualand West 155 (J. M. Arthur 33); Natal* 156 for no wkt (H. R. Fotheringham 93 not out, B. J. Whitfield 59 not out).

Second leg: At Newlands, Cape Town, November 4. Western Province won by three wickets. Transvaal 199 (S. B. Smith 32, C. E. B. Rice 30; C. R. Matthews three for 28, E. O. Simons three for 53); Western Province* 201 for seven (P. N. Kirsten 77).

Second leg: At Victoria Ground, King William's Town, November 4. Abandoned. Northern Transvaal qualified for the semi-finals by virtue of having won the first leg v Border.

Second leg: At Springbok Park, Bloemfontein, November 4. Orange Free State won by 91 runs. Orange Free State* 241 for seven (W. J. Cronje 92, J. J. Strydom 38, G. C. Victor 35); Eastern Province 150 for six (M. Michau 43; O. Henry three for 19).

Third leg: At Springbok Park, Bloemfontein, November 5. Eastern Province won by six wickets. Orange Free State* 242 for six (G. A. Hughes 98, G. C. Victor 41, J. J. Strydom 37, P. J. R. Steyn 33); Eastern Province 245 for four (M. W. Rushmere 71, K. C. Wessels 76, D. J. Callaghan 30 not out).

Third leg: At Newlands, Cape Town, November 5. Western Province won by 63 runs. Western Province* 277 for eight (P. N. Kirsten 126, D. J. Cullinan 74, L. Seeff 54; C. E. B. Rice three for 38); Transvaal 214 (S. J. Cook 77, S. B. Smith 33; P. N. Kirsten three for 39).

Semi-finals

First leg: At Newlands, Cape Town, November 11. Eastern Province won by ten wickets. Western Province* 209 for eight (P. N. Kirsten 52, A. P. Kuiper 45, D. J. Cullinan 39; J. N. Maguire three for 40); Eastern Province 211 for no wkt (P. G. Amm 102 not out, K. C. Wessels 101 not out).

First leg: At Kingsmead, Durban, November 12. Northern Transvaal won by 19 runs. Northern Transvaal 233 for five (M. Yachad 71, L. J. Barnard 59 not out, V. F. du Preez 38); Natal* 214 (H. R. Fotheringham 65, P. W. E. Rawson 35, B. J. Whitfield 31; S. T. Clarke five for 31).

Second leg: At St George's Park, Port Elizabeth, November 18. Eastern Province won by 113 runs. Eastern Province 230 for six (M. W. Rushmere 49, P. G. Amm 39, K. C. Wessels 31, D. J. Callaghan 39); Western Province* 117 (D. J. Cullinan 65; B. de K. Robey three for 17).

Second leg: At Centurion Park, Verwoerdburg, November 18. Northern Transvaal won by five wickets. Natal* 168 (S. T. Clarke three for 19); Northern Transvaal 171 for five (M. Yachad 33, V. F. du Preez 64, M. D. Haysman 39).

Final

First leg: At St George's Park, Port Elizabeth, November 25. Eastern Province won by 2 runs. Eastern Province* 196 for six (M. W. Rushmere 96, D. J. Richardson 35); Northern Transvaal 194 for nine (M. D. Haysman 56, A. M. Ferreira 41 not out; R. J. McCurdy three for 34).

Second leg: At Centurion Park, Verwoerdburg, December 2. Eastern Province won by seven wickets. Northern Transvaal 130 (M. Yachad 30; J. N. Maguire three for 24, D. J. Callaghan four for 38); Eastern Province* 131 for three (M. W. Rushmere 34, B. W. Lones 36, M. Michau 36 not out; T. Bosch three for 21).

BENSON AND HEDGES TROPHY, 1989-90

(Day/night matches of 45 overs per side)

At Centurion Park, Verwoerdburg, November 1. Natal won by 39 runs. Natal* 218 (H. R. Fotheringham 44, T. R. Madsen 55, K. J. Hughes 35, D. Norman 39; S. T. Clarke five for [illegible]); Northern Transvaal 179 for seven (M. D. Haysman 69, G. Grobler 32 not out).

At Springbok Park, Bloemfontein, November 2. No result, rain having stopped play. Eastern Province* 139 for seven (G. J. Parsons three for 37); Orange Free State 29 for no wkt.

At St George's Park, Port Elizabeth, November 8. Eastern Province won by seven wickets. Border* 192 for eight (G. L. Long 40; J. N. Maguire three for 29); Eastern Province 196 for three (P. G. Amm 69, K. C. Wessels 63).

At Wanderers, Johannesburg, November 9. Northern Transvaal won by six wickets, having been set a revised target of 176 off 43 overs. Transvaal* 183 for eight (S. J. Cook 45, S. B. Smith 45, R. V. Jennings 31; S. Elworthy four for 30); Northern Transvaal 176 for four (M. Yachad 71).

At Wanderers, Johannesburg, November 15. Transvaal won by eight wickets. Impalas 208 for eight (W. S. Truter 65, K. J. Bridgens 53); Transvaal* 209 for two (S. B. Smith 52, S. J. Cook 91 not out, K. J. Rule 30 not out).

At Kingsmead, Durban, November 15. Natal won by six wickets after rain had reduced their target to 178 off 35 overs. Eastern Province 228 for four (K. C. Wessels 88, P. G. Amm 78, M. W. Rushmere 32 not out); Natal* 182 for four (J. N. Rhodes 74 not out, K. J. Hughes 38, K. M. Curran 38; R. J. McCurdy three for 59).

At Harmony Ground, Virginia, November 16. Orange Free State won by five wickets. Border* 177 for five (B. M. Osborne 74 not out; C. J. van Heerden four for 47); Orange Free State 178 for five (W. J. Cronje 50, P. J. R. Steyn 44).

At Newlands, Cape Town, November 22. Natal won by 26 runs. Natal* 203 for nine (H. R. Fotheringham 70, T. R. Madsen 50; E. O. Simons three for 42); Western Province 177 fo eight (P. W. Martin 60, P. N. Kirsten 49; K. M. Curran three for 27).

At Centurion Park, Verwoerdburg, November 23. Orange Free State won by 62 runs Orange Free State* 207 for seven (W. J. Cronje 51, C. J. van Heerden 38; G. Grobler thre for 42); Northern Transvaal 145 (R. C. Ontong 42).

At Newlands, Cape Town, November 29. Eastern Province won by 67 runs. Easter Province* 195 for five (P. G. Amm 136, D. J. Richardson 34 not out); Western Province 12 (P. N. Kirsten 39).

At Wanderers, Johannesburg, November 30. Transvaal won by five wickets. Orange Fre State 140 (P. J. R. Steyn 38, G. C. Victor 35; H. A. Page three for 46); Transvaal* 142 fo five.

At Centurion Park, Verwoerdburg, December 13. Western Province won on faster scorin rate. Western Province* 159 for eight (R. J. Ryall 41 not out); Northern Transvaal 118 for si (M. W. Pringle three for 26).

At St George's Park, Port Elizabeth, December 14. Eastern Province won by seven wicket Northern Transvaal* 184 for nine (M. D. Haysman 61, R. C. Ontong 32, L. J. Barnard 30 Eastern Province 186 for three (K. C. Wessels 84, P. G. Amm 65).

At Kingsmead, Durban, December 15. Natal won by 12 runs. Natal 182 (A. C. Hudson 6 T. R. Madsen 41); Transvaal* 170 (S. J. Cook 66, S. B. Smith 37; R. J. Varner four for 3

At St George's Park, Port Elizabeth, December 19. Transvaal won by three wicke Eastern Province* 144 for seven (M. Michau 42 not out, D. J. Richardson 32; R. P. Sn three for 34); Transvaal 148 for seven (S. B. Smith 41; M. Michau three for 18).

At Kingsmead, Durban, December 20. Natal won by 21 runs. Natal 188 for six (A. Hudson 63, H. R. Fotheringham 36; A. A. Donald three for 35); Orange Free State* 167 (J. Cronje 42, C. J. van Heerden 41, C. J. P. G. van Zyl 48; P. W. E. Rawson three for 8, T. Packer three for 37).

At Newlands, Cape Town, December 21. Western Province won by five wickets after ra had reduced their target to 116 off 32 overs. Transvaal* 162 for seven (S. J. Cook 41, S. Jacc 47); Western Province 116 for five (T. N. Lazard 43, L. Seeff 42).

At Buffalo Park, East London, December 22. Western Province won on scoring-rate after ›rder failed to meet a revised target of 134 off 31 overs. Western Province* 194 for five . N. Kirsten 104, J. J. E. Hardy 46); Border 128 (D. H. Howell 32, I. L. Howell 32; M. W. ringle six for 30).

At Buffalo Park, East London, February 2. Northern Transvaal won by five wickets after eir target had been reduced to 174 off 44 overs following a blackout. Border* 177 for nine i. L. Long 45, B. M. Osborne 50; S. T. Clarke three for 31); Northern Transvaal 176 for five 1. J. R. Rindel 73, L. J. Barnard 32).

At Kingsmead, Durban, February 7. Natal won by 97 runs. Natal* 243 (K. D. Robinson 60, . J. Hughes 59, D. Norman 35); Impalas 146 (G. M. Charlesworth 44 not out; R. J. Varner ye for 25).

At Danie Craven Stadium, Stellenbosch, February 14. Orange Free State won by four ickets. Impalas* 172 (W. S. Truter 38, J. D. du Toit 30; G. J. Parsons three for 46); Orange ree State 177 for six (W. J. Cronje 52 not out).

At Danie Craven Stadium, Stellenbosch, February 28. Border won by two wickets. npalas* 213 for eight (G. F. J. Liebenberg 63, J. M. Arthur 44, R. Marais 32; W. K. Watson ree for 34); Border 214 for eight (G. C. Holmes 51, G. L. Long 30, B. M. Osborne 30).

At Springbok Park, Bloemfontein, March 2. Western Province won by 19 runs. Western ovince* 165 for eight (P. N. Kirsten 32); Orange Free State 146 (J. J. Strydom 32; M. W. ringle three for 19, C. R. Matthews three for 22).

At Newlands, Cape Town, March 6. Western Province won by seven wickets. Impalas* 154 .. J. Bridgens 38, G. M. Charlesworth 30; M. W. Pringle three for 34, P. N. Kirsten three r 32); Western Province 160 for three (P. N. Kirsten 69, D. J. Cullinan 35 not out).

At Centurion Park, Verwoerdburg, March 9. Northern Transvaal won by seven wickets. ıpalas 174 for five (W. S. Truter 74, G. F. J. Liebenberg 65; P. S. de Villiers three for 36); orthern Transvaal* 176 for three (L. J. Barnard 74 not out, M. J. R. Rindel 56 not out).

At Buffalo Park, East London, March 14. No result, rain having stopped play. Natal* 186 r eight (H. R. Fotheringham 36, A. C. Hudson 36, J. N. Rhodes 54 not out; S. J. Base three r 38); Border 2 for one.

At St George's Park, Port Elizabeth, March 16. Eastern Province won by 38 runs. Eastern ovince* 217 for two (K. C. Wessels 100 not out, M. W. Rushmere 57); Impalas 179 (K. J. idgens 61; B. N. Schultz three for 29).

At Wanderers, Johannesburg, March 16. Transvaal won by seven wickets. Border 190 for x (B. M. Osborne 50, E. N. Trotman 53, C. S. Stirk 43); Transvaal* 194 for three (S. J. Cook , R. F. Pienaar 75, K. J. Rule 33 not out).

emi-finals

rst leg: At Wanderers, Johannesburg, March 20. No result, rain having stopped play. ansvaal 216 for eight (S. B. Smith 112, L. P. Vorster 34); Natal* 42 for no wkt.

First leg: At St George's Park, Port Elizabeth, March 21. Eastern Province won by nine ickets. Western Province* 182 for six (A. P. Kuiper 42, B. M. McMillan 54 not out, E. O. mons 32; R. J. McCurdy three for 43); Eastern Province 183 for one (P. G. Amm 89 not out, . C. Wessels 54).

Second leg: At Newlands, Cape Town, March 23. Eastern Province won by virtue of having st fewer wickets with the scores level. Western Province* 160 for eight (B. M. McMillan 63, . B. Rundle 34 not out; J. N. Maguire three for 37, R. J. McCurdy three for 49); Eastern ovince 160 for six (K. S. McEwan 36).

Second leg: At Kingsmead, Durban, March 23. Natal won by 35 runs. Natal 200 (K. J. ughes 46; H. A. Page three for 36); Transvaal* 165 (R. V. Jennings 53, H. A. Page 40; W. E. Rawson three for 15, T. J. Packer three for 30).

Final

At Kingsmead, Durban, March 30. Eastern Province won by one wicket. Natal* 202 (A. Hudson 35, K. J. Hughes 43, K. M. Curran 30; R. J. McCurdy five for 30); Eastern Provin 205 for nine (K. C. Wessels 41, D. J. Callaghan 65, K. G. Bauermeister 48).

ENGLISH XI IN SOUTH AFRICA, 1989-90

The following players were under contract to tour South Africa in 1989-90 and 1990-9 M. W. Gatting (*captain*), D. A. Graveney (*manager*), C. W. J. Athey, K. J. Barnett, B. Broad, C. S. Cowdrey, G. R. Dilley, R. M. Ellison, J. E. Emburey, N. A. Foster, B. French, P. W. Jarvis, M. P. Maynard, R. T. Robinson, J. G. Thomas and A. P. Wells.

COMBINED BOWL XI v ENGLISH XI

At De Beers Country Club, Kimberley, January 26, 27, 28. English XI won by 254 rur Toss: English XI.

English XI

B. C. Broad c Osborne b McLaren	26	– b Lindenberg
C. W. J. Athey c Liebenberg b Watson	43	– b Fourie
R. T. Robinson c Arthur b Lindenberg	26	– c Fourie b Lindenberg
*M. W. Gatting c Bridgens b du Toit	75	
A. P. Wells c McLaren b Watson	0	– (4) not out
J. E. Emburey c Arthur b du Toit	10	– (5) c Truter b Lindenberg
R. M. Ellison c Liebenberg b Fourie	8	– (6) not out
†B. N. French c Lindenberg b Howell	55	
J. G. Thomas c and b McLaren	2	
P. W. Jarvis c and b Howell	35	
D. A. Graveney not out	2	
B 4, l-b 14, w 1, n-b 4	23	B 4, l-b 6, w 1, n-b 3
1/52 2/95 3/109 4/110 5/151 6/174 7/229 8/242 9/300	305	1/69 2/113 3/125 4/153 (4 wkts dec.) 2

Bowling: *First Innings*—Watson 17–4–33–2; Fourie 20–2–58–1; du Toit 24–8–55- McLaren 19–4–64–2; Howell 12.3–4–27–2; Lindenberg 16–3–50–1. *Second Innings*—Wats 11–2–31–0; Fourie 15–2–38–1; Lindenberg 18–3–57–3; Howell 13–7–23–0; McLa 10–0–36–0; du Toit 3–0–11–0.

Combined Bowl XI

J. M. Arthur st French b Graveney	30	– c Robinson b Graveney
G. F. J. Liebenberg b Jarvis	21	– c French b Thomas
W. S. Truter c Gatting b Emburey	31	– st French b Graveney
B. M. Osborne c Athey b Graveney	0	– c Emburey b Graveney
†K. J. Bridgens c Broad b Graveney	17	– c and b Emburey
J. D. du Toit c Emburey b Graveney	4	– b Emburey
*I. L. Howell c Gatting b Emburey	10	– c Gatting b Emburey
P. McLaren c Wells b Emburey	0	– c Broad b Graveney
B. C. Fourie not out	7	– (10) not out
H. C. Lindenberg c Athey b Graveney	4	– (11) b Emburey
W. K. Watson c Thomas b Graveney	26	– (9) c Gatting b Emburey
B 1, w 1	2	L-b 3
1/49 2/57 3/57 4/89 5/99 6/107 7/110 8/115 9/122	152	1/6 2/50 3/62 4/79 5/83 6/85 7/99 8/103 9/105 1

Bowling: *First Innings*—Jarvis 9–3–21–1; Thomas 5–0–20–0; Ellison 6–1–18–0; Graver 23.2–9–45–6; Emburey 21–6–47–3. *Second Innings*—Jarvis 7–0–27–0; Thomas 8–2–19 Emburey 19.2–7–36–5; Graveney 18–6–20–4.

Umpires: K. E. Liebenberg and J. W. Peacock.

SOUTH AFRICAN UNIVERSITIES v ENGLISH XI

At Springbok Park, Bloemfontein, January 30, 31, February 1. Drawn. Toss: South African Universities.

South African Universities

	First innings		Second innings	
P. J. R. Steyn	lbw b Jarvis	20	c Cowdrey b Foster	0
T. N. Lazard	lbw b Jarvis	87	lbw b Jarvis	0
A. C. Hudson	c Maynard b Foster	13	c and b Foster	12
*W. J. Cronje	c Barnett b Cowdrey	104	c French b Cowdrey	12
L. J. Wilkinson	b Jarvis	18	c Wells b Foster	40
J. Payn	not out	24	lbw b Jarvis	2
†A. P. Plantema	b Foster	10	lbw b Foster	12
S. Jacobs	not out	25	c and b Barnett	26
D. R. Laing	(did not bat)		b Foster	6
C. E. Eksteen	(did not bat)		not out	34
T. Bosch	(did not bat)		not out	6
	B 9, l-b 9, w 7, n-b 2	27	B 5, l-b 4, n-b 1	10
	1/51 2/75 3/235 4/253 5/267 6/294	(6 wkts dec.) 328	1/0 2/0 3/19 4/53 5/57 6/79 7/85 8/105 9/127	(9 wkts dec.) 160

Bowling: *First Innings*—Dilley 10–2–30–0; Foster 18–4–54–2; Jarvis 19–5–58–3; Emburey 29–6–70–0; Cowdrey 11–0–44–1; Barnett 19–3–54–0. *Second Innings*—Foster 22–7–37–5; Jarvis 17–6–42–2; Cowdrey 10–1–38–1; Wells 2–0–7–0; Emburey 10–4–11–0; Barnett 6–0–16–1.

English XI

	First innings		Second innings	
B. C. Broad	c Wilkinson b Laing	37	c Laing b Eksteen	32
K. J. Barnett	c Eksteen b Jacobs	19	hit wkt b Bosch	0
R. T. Robinson	c Laing b Jacobs	7	c Jacobs b Bosch	5
M. P. Maynard	b Jacobs	0	st Steyn b Eksteen	8
A. P. Wells	run out	5	not out	11
C. S. Cowdrey	b Eksteen	10	not out	9
*J. E. Emburey	b Wilkinson	57		
†B. N. French	c Hudson b Jacobs	5		
N. A. Foster	c Cronje b Eksteen	46		
P. W. Jarvis	c Bosch b Jacobs	1		
G. R. Dilley	not out	0		
	B 1, l-b 11, w 2, n-b 11	25	B 2, l-b 1, n-b 7	10
	1/35 2/60 3/68 4/75 5/75 6/97 7/117 8/193 9/205	212	1/2 2/26 3/46 4/55	(4 wkts) 75

Bowling: *First Innings*—Bosch 17–1–68–0; Jacobs 24–13–29–5; Eksteen 20–3–58–2; Laing 14–2–32–1; Wilkinson 6.4–1–13–1. *Second Innings*—Bosch 7–0–24–2; Jacobs 4–0–22–0; Eksteen 11.2–4–11–2; Laing 8–4–14–0; Cronje 1–0–1–0.

Umpires: R. E. Koertzen and R. L. Symcox.

SOUTH AFRICAN INVITATION XI v ENGLISH XI

At Jan Smuts Stadium, Pietermaritzburg, February 3, 4, 5. Drawn. Toss: South African Invitation XI.

South African Invitation XI

M. W. Rushmere not out . . . . 150 – (2) not out 151
P. G. Amm lbw b Foster . . . . 7 – (1) c Gatting b Thomas 65
*R. F. Pienaar c Barnett b Thomas . . . . 63 – c Robinson b Ellison 81
D. J. Cullinan not out . . . . 77 – not out 9
L-b 1, w 6, n-b 1 . . . . 8 B 3, l-b 4, w 2 9

1/8 2/131 (2 wkts dec.) 305 1/126 2/276 (2 wkts dec.) 315

J. N. Rhodes, D. J. Callaghan, †T. R. Madsen, O. Henry, M. W. Pringle, P. S. de Villiers and C. R. Matthews did not bat.

Bowling: *First Innings*—Foster 21–5–40–1; Thomas 19–5–40–1; Ellison 20–2–73–0; Gatting 16–3–53–0; Barnett 10–1–40–0; Wells 4–0–23–0; Graveney 8–0–35–0. *Second Innings*—Foster 14–2–46–0; Thomas 13–3–56–1; Graveney 18–2–98–0; Ellison 9–1–42–1; Barnett 7–0–31–0; Gatting 4–0–33–0; Athey 2–0–2–0.

English XI

B. C. Broad c Pringle b Henry . . . . 85 – c Matthews b Henry 36
C. W. J. Athey c de Villiers b Henry . . . . 29 – c Madsen b Matthews 24
*M. W. Gatting c and b Matthews . . . . 71 – (7) not out 20
K. J. Barnett c sub b Henry . . . . 34 – c Matthews b Henry 7
R. T. Robinson not out . . . . 29 – c Pringle b Pienaar 41
A. P. Wells c Cullinan b Callaghan . . . . 12 – c Cullinan b Henry 48
R. M. Ellison not out 13
†B. N. French (did not bat) . . . . – (6) not out 19
B 2, l-b 10, n-b 7 . . . . 19 B 2, n-b 1 3

1/87 2/171 3/208 4/236 5/263 (5 wkts dec.) 292 1/56 2/68 3/87 4/121 5/169 (5 wkts) 198

N. A. Foster, J. G. Thomas and D. A. Graveney did not bat.

Bowling: *First Innings*—de Villiers 17–3–62–0; Pringle 14–2–36–0; Henry 36–10–115–3; Matthews 11–4–32–1; Rhodes 4–1–11–0; Callaghan 9–1–24–1. *Second Innings*—de Villiers 11–3–12–0; Pringle 6–0–18–0; Henry 30.1–7–76–3; Matthews 9–2–18–1; Pienaar 13–1–72–1.

Umpires: S. B. Lambson and C. J. Mitchley.

SOUTH AFRICA v ENGLISH XI

At Wanderers, Johannesburg, February 8, 9, 10. South Africa won by seven wickets. Toss: South Africa.

English XI

B. C. Broad c Jennings b McMillan . . . . 48 – c Jennings b Donald 0
C. W. J. Athey b Donald . . . . 3 – lbw b McMillan 16
R. T. Robinson c Snell b McMillan . . . . 31 – c Jennings b McMillan 17
*M. W. Gatting c McMillan b Snell . . . . 22 – b Kuiper 0
A. P. Wells b Snell . . . . 4 – c Wessels b Donald 11
K. J. Barnett c Fotheringham b Donald . . . . 0 – c Donald b Snell 24
†B. N. French c Jennings b Donald . . . . 1 – c Jennings b Donald 0
J. E. Emburey c Jennings b Snell . . . . 1 – c Jennings b Snell 2
R. M. Ellison b Donald . . . . 6 – c Cook b Rundle 12
N. A. Foster b Snell . . . . 11 – c Jennings b Donald 2
P. W. Jarvis not out . . . . 1 – not out 0
B 4, l-b 17, n-b 7 . . . . 28 B 4, l-b 11, w 2, n-b 2 . . . 19

1/15 2/96 3/106 4/118 5/119 6/123 7/132 8/138 9/152 156 1/2 2/33 3/34 4/42 5/69 6/73 7/78 8/85 9/122 12

Bowling: *First Innings*—Donald 21–10–30–4; Snell 22.5–11–38–4; McMillan 15–2–41–2; Kuiper 6–1–21–0; Rundle 1–0–5–0. *Second Innings*—Donald 18–5–29–4; Snell 15–5–28–2; Kuiper 14–4–23–1; McMillan 11–6–18–2; Rundle 5–2–9–1.

South Africa

*S. J. Cook c Robinson b Ellison	20	– c and b Gatting	15
H. R. Fotheringham lbw b Jarvis	8	– lbw b Ellison	38
K. C. Wessels st French b Emburey	1	– lbw b Gatting	2
P. N. Kirsten c French b Jarvis	4	– not out	17
R. F. Pienaar c French b Ellison	13	– not out	1
A. P. Kuiper b Foster	84		
B. M. McMillan b Ellison	0		
†R. V. Jennings c Emburey b Ellison	23		
D. B. Rundle c French b Foster	23		
R. P. Snell c French b Jarvis	7		
A. A. Donald not out	7		
L-b 7, w 5, n-b 1	13	W 3	3
1/23 2/28 3/40 4/40 5/77 6/77 7/148 8/180 9/189	203	1/56 2/56 3/71	(3 wkts) 76

Bowling: *First Innings*—Jarvis 22.5–7–71–3; Foster 21–6–54–2; Ellison 15–6–41–4; Emburey 14–5–30–1. *Second Innings*—Jarvis 6–2–25–0; Foster 4–0–20–0; Ellison 7–1–13–1; Gatting 6–1–17–2; Athey 1.1–1–1–0.

Umpires: K. E. Liebenberg and J. W. Peacock.

†At Centurion Park, Verwoerdburg, February 16. South Africa won by five wickets. English XI* 217 (54.5 overs) (M. W. Gatting 55, B. N. French 43; R. P. Snell three for 39, A. P. Kuiper three for 22); South Africa 218 for five (52 overs) (S. J. Cook 73, A. P. Kuiper 37, C. E. B. Rice 36 not out). *Man of the Match:* A. P. Kuiper.

†At Kingsmead, Durban, February 18. South Africa won by 14 runs. South Africa* 219 for ive (55 overs) (H. R. Fotheringham 51, C. E. B. Rice 43 not out, T. R. Madsen 42 not out; K. J. Barnett three for 33); English XI 205 for seven (55 overs) (K. J. Barnett 76, C. W. J. Athey 44). *Man of the Match:* K. J. Barnett.

†At Springbok Park, Bloemfontein, February 20. South Africa won by 207 runs. South Africa* 301 for seven (55 overs) (S. J. Cook 73, P. N. Kirsten 40, A. P. Kuiper 117; M. W. Gatting three for 54); English XI 94 (45.1 overs) (C. W. J. Athey 50; A. A. Donald three for 1). *Man of the Match:* A. P. Kuiper.

†At Wanderers, Johannesburg, February 23. English XI won by 134 runs. English XI* 296 or eight (55 overs) (K. J. Barnett 136, C. W. J. Athey 49); South Africa 162 (37.2 overs) H. R. Fotheringham 58, R. F. Pienaar 52; M. W. Gatting six for 26). *Man of the Match:* K. J. arnett. *Man of the Series:* A. P. Kuiper.

CRICKET IN THE WEST INDIES, 1989-90

By TONY COZIER

In winning the 1990 Red Stripe Cup, Leeward Islands not only claimed their first regional first-class title but also created a record by winning all five of their matches. Only Barbados, in the 1979-80 Shell Shield, had previously completed a 100 per cent sequence, but that was when the Leeward and Windward Islands played as a combined team and there were only four matches each.

With six Test players – captain Vivian Richards, Richie Richardson, Curtly Ambrose, Winston Benjamin, Keith Arthurton and Eldine Baptiste – the Leewards had the all-round depth and experience to be considered clear favourites. Nevertheless they had possessed similar strength in past seasons without fulfilling expectations. This time, though, after winning an important opening match against a powerful Barbados team, they confirmed their status in spite of some crucial setbacks. Richards broke a finger dropping a slip catch on the first day of the season and returned only for the final match against Jamaica. By this time the Cup had already been won. Fast bowler Winston Benjamin had only the Barbados match before he succumbed to knee and ankle injuries, which ruled him out for the rest of the season.

In Richards's absence, Richardson assumed the captaincy for the first time, and his 421 runs at 70.16, with two centuries, indicated that he thrived on the additional responsibility. His calm and assured leadership stood him out as a strong candidate for the West Indies captaincy in the coming years. He was the competition's leading run-getter and second in the averages only to Gordon Greenidge of Barbados, who had to shorten his club contract in Australia in order to abide by the West Indies Board's regulation that full participation in the Cup series was mandatory for Test selection. The second of Greenidge's two centuries was made against Windward Islands, batting in the unfamiliar position of No. 6 because of illness.

Jamaica were unfortunate that their defence of the championship, which they had won in 1987-88 and 1988-89, was spoiled by the weather. Rain prevented a ball being bowled in their two away matches, against the Windwards and Guyana, and they had to settle for third place when the Leewards beat them by three wickets in the season's final match. That result could have carried more significance had it not been for Jamaica's earlier washouts; as it was, the Leewards proved their point and their determination with a hard-won victory which gave them their perfect record.

Second place went to Barbados, led by their fifth captain in eight seasons Desmond Haynes. They recovered from losing their opening home match t the Leewards to win their last three matches, against Guyana, Trinidad & Tobago and the Windwards. Guyana, like Jamaica, also suffered from ba weather, with their two home matches at Bourda being abandoned without ball bowled, just as the Second Test against England was later. Howeve successive defeats to the Leewards and Barbados prior to the abandone games had already put them out of contention for the championship. Th Windwards ended three barren years with their first win since 1985-8 beating Trinidad & Tobago who, under the youngest captain in the tourna ment's history, the twenty-year-old left-handed batsman, Brian Lar replaced them in last position. The Trinidadians lost four successive matches, and any hopes that their fifth, against Guyana, might offer some chance for late redemption were dashed by the equatorial Georgetown climate.

The Board's insistence on full participation by all the leading players prevented what could have been an exodus to Australia on profitable contracts. But injuries limited the appearances of several of the stars, and along with the rain, the Leewards' early ascendancy and the imminent arrival of the England team, their absence diminished interest considerably. Malcolm Marshall, like Richards, played just two matches because of back and arm trouble. Tony Gray, the tall Trinidadian fast bowler, whose form for the West Indies B team in Zimbabwe in October had made him a strong contender to regain his Test place, bowled just fifteen overs in one match before being laid up with a back injury, while Winston Benjamin, as mentioned, was also confined to one match. Greenidge missed Barbados's key clash with Jamaica because of a leg strain.

None the less, familiar names again made the biggest impact. Richardson and Greenidge collected two centuries each, while Carlisle Best, Desmond Haynes and Thelston Payne (Barbados), Keith Arthurton (Leewards) and Carl Hooper (Guyana) were other Test players with hundreds. Three batsmen with B team qualifications, the left-handed James Adams (Jamaica), Dawnley Joseph (Windwards) and Andy Jackman (Guyana), as well as one from the 1988 West Indies youth team, Roland Holder of Barbados, also played three-figure innings. Adams took seven hours to reach his hundred against Trinidad & Tobago, his first at first-class level and the slowest on record in regional cricket. Stuart Williams, a stylish twenty-year-old opener from Nevis and playing in his first full season, was the only other century-maker, one of three in the Leewards' 526 for eight declared against the Windwards. This was the highest total of the season.

The top bowlers were also those with established reputations, all medium pace and above. In his ninth season Eldine Baptiste, with accuracy and control, proved that medium-pace swing bowling can be as effective as outright pace and hostility, even in the Caribbean, an example which was followed later by the England team. His 26 wickets (at 17.50) for the Leewards made him the leading wicket-taker in the Red Stripe Cup and earned him a recall to the West Indies team, after six years, for the Antigua Test against England. Others who figured prominently later in the series against England collected twenty or more wickets. Ian Bishop, of Trinidad & Tobago, took 23 at 14.34 each, Ambrose 22 at 17.04 for the Leewards, and Ezra Moseley's 22 wickets at 24.63 were enough to bring him his first Test call at the age of 32, seven years after he disqualified himself from West Indies cricket by touring South Africa with the "rebel" teams. He and fellow-Barbadian all-rounder Franklyn Stephenson were the only two to return to the fold following the International Cricket Council ruling which opened the way for the pardoning of those who had played in South Africa. Jamaica's Patrick Patterson, from a new, shortened run, took seventeen wickets in three matches on the Sabina Park pitch, bowling or having lbw thirteen of his victims. It was an impressive enough return to win him back his Test place, if only briefly.

Not only were the Leewards the strongest, best-led and best-balanced side in the Cup, but they provided the most exciting prospect in Hamesh Anthony. A strongly built nineteen-year-old from Antigua, he had seventeen wickets in four matches with his fast-medium bowling, and his batting potential was obvious. Anthony had played a large part in the Leewards triumph in the junior regional tournament the previous August, and by th end of the season he had signed to play county cricket in England fo Glamorgan. With talent such as his emerging, the Leewards look set t dominate West Indies cricket as Barbados did in the 1960s.

Most of the side has come from Antigua, which advanced a strong case fo entering a team of its own, rather than remaining part of the Leeward Island side. Mainly on financial grounds, the West Indies Board rejected th application – as it did another to accord first-class status to the annua Leeward Islands tournament between Antigua, St Kitts, Nevis, Montserrat Anguilla and the Virgin Islands. Far from extending the first-clas programme, the Board announced that the annual inter-county final i Guyana would not be recognised as first-class from 1990 onwards, havin similarly withdrawn recognition of the annual North versus South match i Trinidad & Tobago in 1985.

The one-day competition for the Geddes Grant Shield provided Trinida & Tobago with some compensation for their shocking season in the Re Stripe Cup. They played steady, well-organised cricket to beat easily a muc stronger, but over-confident, Barbados team by five wickets in the final.

RED STRIPE CUP AVERAGES, 1989-90

BATTING

(Qualification: 200 runs)

	M	*I*	*NO*	*R*	*HI*	*100s*	*Avg*
C. G. Greenidge (*Barbados*)	4	6	1	356	128	2	71.2
R. B. Richardson (*Leeward I.*)	5	9	3	421	125	2	70.1
P. J. L. Dujon (*Jamaica*)	3	5	1	252	92	0	63.0
L. L. Harris (*Leeward I.*)	5	8	3	250	81	0	50.0
D. S. Morgan (*Jamaica*)	3	5	0	226	94	0	45.2
C. B. Lambert (*Guyana*)	3	6	1	212	63	0	42.4
C. L. Hooper (*Guyana*)	3	5	0	201	102	1	40.2
C. A. Best (*Barbados*)	5	8	0	310	175	1	38.7
T. R. O. Payne (*Barbados*)	5	8	1	270	101	1	38.5
D. L. Haynes (*Barbados*)	5	9	1	285	108	1	35.6
K. L. T. Arthurton (*Leeward I.*)	5	9	2	230	101*	1	32.8
D. A. Joseph (*Windward I.*)	4	8	0	260	134	1	32.5
L. D. John (*Windward I.*)	4	8	0	229	75	0	28.6
A. L. Kelly (*Leeward I.*)	5	9	0	241	46	0	26.7

* *Signifies not out.*

BOWLING

(Qualification: 10 wickets)

	O	*M*	*R*	*W*	*BB*	*Avg*
I. R. Bishop (*T & T*)	130	23	330	23	6-81	14.3
B. P. Patterson (*Jamaica*)	88.3	13	277	17	7-53	16.2
H. A. G. Anthony (*Leeward I.*)	105.5	18	285	17	5-40	16.7
C. E. L. Ambrose (*Leeward I.*)	174.2	61	375	22	6-29	17.0
E. A. E. Baptiste (*Leeward I.*)	191.1	60	455	26	5-99	17.5
N. F. Williams (*Windward I.*)	62.5	7	217	11	5-36	19.7
R. Sieuchan (*T & T*)	78.1	16	230	10	4-45	23.0
H. W. D. Springer (*Barbados*)	136	36	290	12	4-40	24.1
E. A. Moseley (*Barbados*)	175.1	28	542	22	5-89	24.6
K. C. G. Benjamin (*Leeward I.*)	141.4	35	346	14	3-22	24.7

	O	*M*	*R*	*W*	*BB*	*Avge*
R. C. Haynes (*Jamaica*)	117	20	356	14	5-28	25.42
C. G. Butts (*Guyana*)	131	34	307	12	5-73	25.58
W. W. Davis (*Windward I.*)	107.3	13	355	13	7-57	27.30
G. E. Charles (*Guyana*)	107.2	24	274	10	5-40	27.40
F. D. Stephenson (*Barbados*)	124.4	25	336	12	3-63	28.00
I. B. A. Allen (*Windward I.*)	83	10	354	11	4-39	32.18

RED STRIPE CUP, 1989-90

	Played	*Won*	*Lost*	*Drawn*	*Abandoned*	*1st-inns Points*	*Points*
Leeward Islands	5	5	0	0	0	0	80
Barbados	5	3	1	1	0	4	52
Jamaica	3	1	1	1	2	13	37
Windward Islands	4	1	2	1	1	4	24
Guyana	3	0	2	1	2	8	16
Trinidad & Tobago	4	0	4	0	1	5	9

Win = 16 pts; 1st-innings lead in drawn match = 8 pts; 1st-innings deficit in drawn match = 4 pts; 1st-innings lead in lost match = 5 pts; Abandoned match = 4 pts each.

*In the following scores, * by the name of a team indicates that they won the toss.*

At Kingston, Jamaica, January 5, 6, 7, 8. Jamaica won by 58 runs. Jamaica 203 (D. S. Morgan 52, R. C. Haynes 38; I. R. Bishop five for 33) and 281 (J. C. Adams 108, R. C. Haynes 55; I. R. Bishop six for 81, R. J. Bishop three for 29); Trinidad & Tobago* 205 (R. J. Bishop 42, B. C. Lara 33, A. L. Logie 41; B. P. Patterson seven for 53) and 221 (P. V. Simmons 65, A. L. Logie 75; M. A. Tucker four for 51, R. C. Haynes three for 68). *Jamaica 16 pts, Trinidad & Tobago 5 pts.*

At Kingstown, St Vincent, January 5, 6, 7, 8. Drawn. Windward Islands 162 (J. D. Charles 60; G. E. Charles five for 40, C. G. Butts three for 32) and 336 (L. D. John 38, D. A. Joseph 134, J. J. Pierre 41, N. F. Williams 43, W. W. Davis 35; G. E. Charles three for 61, C. G. Butts five for 73); Guyana* 289 (A. F. D. Jackman 114, C. L. Hooper 58, R. Seeram 50; N. F. Williams five for 70) and 23 for no wkt. *Windward Islands 4 pts, Guyana 8 pts.*

At Bridgetown, Barbados, January 5, 6, 7, 8. Leeward Islands won by seven wickets. Barbados 185 (T. R. O. Payne 32, F. D. Stephenson 77, E. A. Moseley 37; C. E. L. Ambrose three for 51, W. K. M. Benjamin three for 42) and 262 (C. G. Greenidge 78, D. L. Haynes 39, F. D. Stephenson 46, H. W. D. Springer 32 not out; C. E. L. Ambrose four for 55, K. C. G. Benjamin three for 52); Leeward Islands* 336 (A. L. Kelly 38, E. A. E. Baptiste 46, C. E. L. Ambrose 49, W. K. M. Benjamin 47; E. A. Moseley five for 89) and 112 for three (R. B. Richardson 46 not out). *Leeward Islands 16 pts.*

At Kingston, Jamaica, January 12, 13, 14, 15. Drawn. Barbados* 423 (C. A. Best 175, S. N. Proverbs 58, T. R. O. Payne 59, E. A. Moseley 48; B. P. Patterson five for 59, N. O. Perry three for 68) and 168 for nine (D. L. Haynes 39, S. N. Proverbs 34; N. O. Perry three for 55, R. C. Haynes five for 28); Jamaica 485 for seven dec. (D. S. Morgan 94, J. C. Adams 41, P. J. L. Dujon 76, C. A. Davidson 91, R. C. Haynes 72; F. D. Stephenson three for 63). *Jamaica 8 pts, Barbados 4 pts.*

At Basseterre, St Kitts, January 12, 13, 14, 15. Leeward Islands won by 187 runs. Leeward Islands* 245 (R. B. Richardson 125; R. A. Harper four for 55) and 212 for nine dec. (S. C. Williams 32, R. B. Richardson 36, R. M. Otto 32; L. A. Joseph four for 67); Guyana 129 (K. C. G. Benjamin three for 33, H. A. G. Anthony three for 19) and 141 (C. B. Lambert 63, C. L. Hooper 33; C. E. L. Ambrose six for 29). *Leeward Islands 16 pts.*

At Point-à-Pierre, Trinidad, January 12, 13, 14, 15. Windward Islands won by four wickets. Trinidad & Tobago* 108 (A. L. Logie 30; I. B. A. Allen four for 39, N. F. Williams five for 36) and 211 (R. J. Bishop 50, K. A. Williams 35, R. Nanan 31; W. W. Davis seven for 57); Windward Islands 237 (D. A. Joseph 32, J. J. Pierre 30, N. F. Williams 31, W. W. Davis 30; R. Sieuchan four for 74) and 84 for six (I. R. Bishop five for 28). *Windward Islands 16 pts.*

At Bridgetown, Barbados, January 19, 20, 21, 22. Barbados won by seven wickets. Barbados 452 for eight dec. (C. G. Greenidge 128, D. L. Haynes 59, C. A. Best 43, T. R. O. Payne 101, M. D. Marshall 59; C. L. Hooper three for 80) and 43 for three; Guyana* 231 (C. B. Lambert 51, C. L. Hooper 102) and 260 (S. Dhaniram 31, R. Seeram 71 not out, A. F. Sattaur 35, L. A. Joseph 44; E. A. Moseley four for 66). *Barbados 16 pts.*

At Port-of-Spain, Trinidad, January 19, 20, 21, 22. Leeward Islands won by eight wickets. Trinidad & Tobago 88 (K. C. G. Benjamin three for 22, E. A. E. Baptiste three for 35) and 188 (D. Williams 37, R. Nanan 36 not out, R. Sieuchan 31; E. A. E. Baptiste three for 32, N. C. Guishard five for 24); Leeward Islands* 145 (L. L. Harris 77 not out; I. R. Bishop four for 40, R. Sieuchan four for 45) and 134 for two (A. L. Kelly 36, R. B. Richardson 46 not out). *Leeward Islands 16 pts.*

At Castries, St Lucia, January 19, 20, 21, 22. Abandoned without a ball bowled. *Windward Islands 4 pts, Jamaica 4 pts.*

At Georgetown, Guyana, January 26, 27, 28, 29. Abandoned without a ball bowled. *Guyana 4 pts, Jamaica 4 pts.*

At St John's, Antigua, January 26, 27, 28, 29. Leeward Islands won by an innings and 15 runs. Windward Islands* 257 (D. A. Joseph 31, J. J. Pierre 38, J. Eugene 37, N. F. Williams 39; K. C. G. Benjamin three for 55, H. A. G. Anthony four for 46) and 254 (L. D. John 45, J. R. Murray 38, N. F. Williams 66 retired hurt, W. W. Davis 31; C. E. L. Ambrose three for 68, E. A. E. Baptiste three for 56); Leeward Islands 526 for eight dec. (A. L. Kelly 46, S. C. Williams 123, R. B. Richardson 123, K. L. T. Arthurton 101 not out, L. L. Harris 56; T. Z. Kentish three for 109). *Leeward Islands 16 pts.*

At Point-à-Pierre, Trinidad, January 26, 27, 28, 29. Barbados won by an innings and 87 runs. Trinidad & Tobago 182 (B. C. Lara 45, N. Bidhesi 57; E. A. Moseley three for 38) and 172 (B. C. Lara 33, D. Williams 38; E. A. Moseley three for 66, V. D. Walcott three for 39); Barbados* 441 for eight dec. (D. L. Haynes 108, C. A. Best 44, T. R. O. Payne 33, R. I. C. Holder 124, R. L. Hoyte 46; R. Dhanraj three for 148). *Barbados 16 pts.*

At Georgetown, Guyana, February 1, 2, 3, 4. Abandoned without a ball bowled. *Guyana 4 pts, Trinidad & Tobago 4 pts.*

At Roseau, Dominica, February 1, 2, 3, 4. Barbados won by nine wickets. Windward Islands 185 (L. D. John 37; G. L. Linton four for 79, H. W. D. Springer four for 40) and 213 (L. D. John 75, J. R. Murray 33 not out; E. A. Moseley three for 39); Barbados* 340 (R. I. C. Holder 53, C. G. Greenidge 118, G. L. Linton 42; W. W. Davis three for 62) and 61 for one (D. L. Haynes 33 not out). *Barbados 16 pts.*

At Kingston, Jamaica, February 8, 9, 10, 11. Leeward Islands won by three wickets. Jamaica* 337 (D. S. Morgan 47, P. J. L. Dujon 92, C. A. Davidson 65, C. A. Walsh 34 not out; E. A. E. Baptiste five for 99) and 130 (P. J. L. Dujon 44 not out; E. A. E. Baptiste four for 47, H. A. G. Anthony five for 40); Leeward Islands 281 (K. L. T. Arthurton 53, L. L. Harris 81, N. C. Guishard 48 not out; C. A. Walsh three for 74) and 190 for seven (A. L. Kelly 38, E. A. E. Baptiste 44, N. C. Guishard 40 not out; M. A. Tucker four for 43). *Leeward Islands 16 pts, Jamaica 5 pts.*

SHELL SHIELD AND RED STRIPE CUP WINNERS

The Shell Shield was replaced by the Red Stripe Cup after the 1986-87 season.

1965-66	Barbados	1978-79	Barbados
1966-67	Barbados	1979-80	Barbados
1968-69	Jamaica	1980-81	Combined Islands
1969-70	Trinidad	1981-82	Barbados
1970-71	Trinidad	1982-83	Guyana
1971-72	Barbados	1983-84	Barbados
1972-73	Guyana	1984-85	Trinidad & Tobago
1973-74	Barbados	1985-86	Barbados
1974-75	Guyana	1986-87	Guyana
1975-76	Trinidad / Barbados	1987-88	Jamaica
1976-77	Barbados	1988-89	Jamaica
1977-78	Barbados	1989-90	Leeward Islands

SOOKRAM MEMORIAL TROPHY, 1989-90

Formerly the Guystac Trophy

At Blairmont, Berbice, October 31, November 1, 2, 3. Demerara won by eight wickets. Berbice 212 (A. F. Sattaur 94; D. Butts three for 39, R. A. Harper three for 43) and 248 (A. F. Sattaur 50, D. Persaud 41, N. Baksh 62 not out, D. Fingal 42; R. A. Harper five for 72); Demerara* 410 (N. Barry 35, N. McKenzie 87, R. Seeram 114, M. A. Harper 42, S. Mohammed 36; L. A. Fraser three for 87) and 53 for two.

†GEDDES GRANT SHIELD, 1989-90

Zone A

At Kingston, Jamaica, January 10. Barbados won by three wickets. Jamaica 207 for six (50 overs) (D. S. Morgan 75, C. A. Davidson 40; H. W. D. Springer three for 28); Barbados* 211 for seven (48.2 overs) (D. L. Haynes 74, P. A. Wallace 52; B. P. Patterson three for 34).

At Bridgetown, Barbados, January 17. Barbados won by seven wickets. Guyana 116 for nine (33 overs) (C. B. Lambert 41; F. D. Stephenson five for 26); Barbados* 117 for three (32.1 overs) (C. G. Greenidge 32).

At Georgetown, Guyana, January 24. Guyana v Jamaica. Abandoned without a ball bowled.

Zone B

At Point-à-Pierre, Trinidad, January 10. Trinidad & Tobago won by 64 runs. Trinidad & Tobago 240 for five (49 overs) (P. V. Simmons 125; N. F. Williams three for 34); Windward Islands* 176 for nine (49 overs) (N. F. Williams 38).

At Port-of-Spain, Trinidad, January 17. Trinidad & Tobago won by five wickets. Leeward Islands 101 (36.2 overs) (H. A. G. Anthony 32; I. R. Bishop three for 10, R. Sieuchan three for 36, R. Nanan three for 26); Trinidad and Tobago* 104 for five (37.1 overs) (A. L. Logie 37; K. C. G. Benjamin three for 25).

At St John's, Antigua, January 24. Leeward Islands won by 100 runs. Leeward Islands* 267 for four (50 overs) (R. E. Bassue 64, R. B. Richardson 32, K. L. T. Arthurton 67 not out, R. M. Otto 51); Windward Islands 167 for six (50 overs) (J. D. Charles 54; H. A. G. Anthony three for 30).

Final

At Port-of-Spain, Trinidad, February 10. Trinidad & Tobago won by five wickets. Barbados 178 for nine (47 overs) (A. H. Gray three for 22, R. Sieuchan three for 34); Trinidad & Tobago* 180 for five (44.2 overs) (D. I. Mohammed 57, B. C. Lara 41, A. L. Logie 33). *Player of the Match:* D. I. Mohammed.

CRICKET IN NEW ZEALAND, 1989-90

By C. R. BUTTERY

The 1989-90 Shell Trophy went to Wellington, who won four of their te matches and were the only team to finish the season undefeated. This wa quite a remarkable achievement. At the halfway stage they were in last place and were given little chance of overtaking Auckland, the competition leader and clear favourites for the title. However, victories in their next three game took Wellington to the top of the points table, and despite intensive efforts b Auckland and Canterbury to dislodge them, they were able to maintain thei lead. Batsmen Andrew Jones and Bruce Edgar were a tower of strength, an Jonathan Millmow, a tall fast bowler, took 33 wickets, which earned him place in the New Zealand side to tour England later in the year.

Unfortunately for Wellington, the season will be remembered for thei farcical tactics at the end of the third day of their return match agains Canterbury. In order to narrow the 94-run gap between the two sides, in th hope of then buying the last two wickets to win the game, Wellingto captain Erwin McSweeney incurred the wrath of cricket purists b instructing his bowlers to toss up a series of deliberate no-balls. In th penultimate over, comprising 22 balls, Robert Vance conceded a record 7 runs (1444664614116666600401), 69 coming from the bat of the Canterbur wicket-keeper, Lee Germon. In the circumstances the question of whethe Germon's feat should go in the record books is debatable. As it turned out McSweeney's tactics almost cost him the game, which ended in a draw wit the scores level after the final over, bowled by Evan Gray, had produced further 17 runs. The scoreboard attendants could not keep up with the rapi run-rate from the last two overs, and neither side realised how clos Canterbury were to victory until the match was over.

Canterbury could feel justifiably pleased at finishing runners-up t Wellington, although they were undoubtedly a little frustrated to be only run short of winning their final-round match. Victory then would have mad the Shell Trophy theirs. Even so, it was an excellent result for a team whic had languished in the lower half of the competition for the previous fou seasons. The Canterbury captain, Rod Latham, led by example with 59 runs, and young Chris Harris, son of the former New Zealand Test cricketer P. G. Z. Harris, scored 468 runs at an average of 42.54 in his first season. St Roberts was the most successful bowler, with 39 wickets, while all-rounde Mark Priest continued to make a valuable contribution to the side. Pries took 31 wickets with his left-arm spinners, scored 429 runs, and gaine selection for the tour of England.

The defending Shell Trophy champions, Auckland, were expected to d well, and for the first half of the season they alternated between first an second in the table. However, at crucial times they lost up to six players fo Test duties, including their opening batsmen, John Wright and Trevo Franklin, wicket-keeper Ian Smith, and the fast bowlers, Danny Morriso and Martin Snedden. Their other fast bowler, Willie Watson, was injure midway through the series and took no further part in the competition. A a result, Auckland failed to win any of their last four games and finishe third behind Wellington and Canterbury. Wright had a marvellous season, captaining New Zealand to victory against India and Australia and also heading the national batting averages with 818 runs at 81.80. Dipak Patel and Jeff Crowe batted solidly in support of Wright, while Morrison and Snedden were the leading bowlers with 41 and 39 wickets respectively.

Central Districts were probably the unluckiest team in the competition. They lost to Northern Districts by only 1 run, and two matches later a combination of rain and bad light prevented them from beating Otago. A victory in either of these matches would have won them the Shell Trophy. Nevertheless, their fourth placing was considerably better than the previous year, when they finished last. The batting was very much dependent on Martin Crowe and Mark Greatbatch, both of whom missed games because of international commitments. Greatbatch did not score as freely as in 1988-89, but Crowe was in good form, his 720 runs including a magnificent 242 against Otago. Fast bowler Dave Leonard impressed, taking 29 wickets in his first season, while off-spinner Stu Duff collected 28 wickets.

Fifth-placed Otago defeated Auckland twice but gained no further wins. Ken Rutherford batted extremely well throughout the season to score 940 runs at an average of 55.29. Playing for Otago against the Indian touring side, he hit 226 not out, which was the highest score recorded by a provincial player against an overseas team. Bruce Blair was also in form with 759 runs, average 47.43, and he made a useful score in nearly every match. Stephen Boock was again Otago's chief wicket-taker, his 34 wickets including match figures of fifteen for 104 against Auckland.

Without Graeme Hick to strengthen their batting, Northern Districts struggled for much of the season. They were defeated four times, and although they managed to win two games, they still finished last. Grant Bradburn led both the batting and bowling with 842 runs and 30 wickets, while Shane Thomson also demonstrated his all-round ability. The 21-year-old scored 532 runs, collected 24 wickets bowling fast-medium, and made an impressive Test début against India. Other outstanding performances were by the medium-pace bowler, Derek Beard, whose six for 18 against Central Districts included a hat-trick, and wicket-keeper Bryan Young, who surprised everyone with his batting average of 53.27 for the season.

The format for the one-day Shell Cup tournament changed slightly from that of previous years, when the winner was decided at the end of the fifth round. Instead, five rounds were played as before, but the four leading teams then met in two semi-finals, followed by a final to decide the winner of the Shell Cup. Otago and Canterbury were eliminated after the preliminary rounds, while Northern Districts and Wellington lost their semi-final matches to Auckland and Central Districts, who met in the final. Thanks to a hard-hitting 90 by Patel, Auckland put on 198 for eight, and then restricted Central Districts to 176 for nine in their 50 overs. The Central Districts pair, Martin Crowe and Greatbatch, were the tournament's leading run-scorers. Crowe totalled 307 runs, average 51.16, while Greatbatch's consistency produced scores of 80 not out, 43 not out, 52, 70 not out and 1, earning him an average of 123.00. Snedden was the most successful bowler with eighteen wickets, average 13.27, closely followed by Wellington's Ewen Chatfield, who took twelve wickets in his last season of representative cricket.

FIRST-CLASS AVERAGES, 1989-90

BATTING

(Qualification: 5 completed innings, average 30)

	M	*I*	*NO*	*R*	*HI*	*100s*	*Avge*
J. G. Wright (*Auckland*)	9	12	2	818	185	3	81.80
M. D. Crowe (*C. Districts*)	9	13	2	720	242	3	65.45
A. H. Jones (*Wellington*)	10	16	4	697	170*	1	58.08
K. R. Rutherford (*Otago*)	13	19	2	940	226*	3	55.29
B. A. Young (*N. Districts*)	11	17	6	586	100*	1	53.27
B. R. Blair (*Otago*)	11	16	0	759	131	1	47.43
C. Z. Harris (*Canterbury*)	10	17	6	468	86	0	42.54
R. T. Hart (*C. Districts*)	4	8	0	289	133	1	41.28
S. A. Thomson (*N. Districts*)	9	18	5	532	74	0	40.92
J. J. Crowe (*Auckland*)	11	16	1	609	110	1	40.60
D. N. Patel (*Auckland*)	10	15	1	567	125*	2	40.50
B. A. Edgar (*Wellington*)	10	18	0	720	162	2	40.00
G. E. Bradburn (*N. Districts*)	12	23	1	842	96	0	38.27
C. J. Smith (*C. Districts*)	10	19	3	610	160*	2	38.12
R. T. Latham (*Canterbury*)	10	18	2	593	79	0	37.06
C. M. Kuggeleijn (*N. Districts*)	11	19	3	588	102*	1	36.75
G. R. Larsen (*Wellington*)	10	16	4	440	69	0	36.66
T. J. Franklin (*Auckland*)	11	17	1	569	110	1	35.56
R. H. Vance (*Wellington*)	10	17	1	545	123	1	34.06
K. A. Wealleans (*N. Districts*)	12	23	1	730	112*	2	33.18
M. W. Priest (*Canterbury*)	9	15	2	429	68	0	33.00
L. K. Germon (*Canterbury*)	10	15	6	289	160*	1	32.11
R. L. Glover (*C. Districts*)	4	8	2	191	113	1	31.83
B. Z. Harris (*Otago*)	9	16	1	476	86	0	31.73
R. G. Twose (*N. Districts*)	8	15	2	397	61	0	30.53
B. R. Hartland (*Canterbury*)	9	17	1	482	126*	1	30.12

* *Signifies not out.*

BOWLING

(Qualification: 20 wickets)

	O	*M*	*R*	*W*	*BB*	*Avge*
J. P. Millmow (*Wellington*)	249.5	67	699	33	6-13	21.18
D. J. Leonard (*C. Districts*)	221.4	54	641	29	5-52	22.10
M. C. Snedden (*Auckland*)	392.3	107	877	39	6-20	22.48
P. W. O'Rourke (*Wellington*)	257.4	61	690	29	5-71	23.79
N. A. Mallender (*Otago*)	280.2	75	706	29	4-20	24.34
D. K. Morrison (*Auckland*)	318.4	68	999	41	5-75	24.36
S. J. Roberts (*Canterbury*)	323.4	60	951	39	4-61	24.38
C. Pringle (*Auckland*)	180.5	33	565	23	4-56	24.56
D. N. Patel (*Auckland*)	225.4	55	568	23	5-54	24.69
I. D. Fisher (*C. Districts*)	290.2	95	652	26	5-43	25.07
S. L. Boock (*Otago*)	414.5	153	865	34	8-57	25.44
M. W. Priest (*Canterbury*)	393.4	134	882	31	9-95	28.45
S. W. Duff (*C. Districts*)	305.2	73	810	28	6-46	28.92
E. J. Gray (*Wellington*)	335.4	132	696	24	8-78	29.00
S. A. Thomson (*N. Districts*)	228.1	40	736	24	4-108	30.66
G. E. Bradburn (*N. Districts*)	334.2	78	928	30	6-56	30.93
R. G. Petrie (*Canterbury*)	333.3	68	988	29	5-59	34.06
B. P. Bracewell (*N. Districts*)	324.5	58	912	23	3-47	39.65

SHELL TROPHY, 1989-90

	Played	*Won*	*Lost*	*Drawn*	*1st Inns Pts*	*Total Pts*
Wellington	10	4	0	6	14*	57
Canterbury	10	3	1	6	16	52
Auckland	10	2	3	5	28	50
Central Districts	10	2	5	3	24	48
Otago	10	2	2	6	22*	42
Northern Districts ...	10	2	4	4	16	40

Win = 12 pts; lead on first innings = 4 pts.

* *First-innings points share in one match.*

Wellington were penalised 5 points, Otago 4 points, and Auckland 2 points for failing to achieve an average of seventeen overs per hour during the competition.

*In the following scores, * by the name of a team indicates that they won the toss.*

At Eden Park, Auckland, December 8, 9, 10. Auckland won by an innings and 104 runs. Central Districts* 111 (M. J. Greatbatch 42; D. K. Morrison three for 26, M. C. Snedden five for 30) and 145 (M. D. Crowe 39; W. Watson seven for 60); Auckland 360 (R. B. Reid 88, J. G. Wright 71, J. J. Crowe 31, S. W. Brown 60 not out, Extras 30; G. K. Robertson three for 90, I. D. Fisher five for 82). *Auckland 16 pts.*

At Basin Reserve, Wellington, December 8, 9, 10. Drawn. Northern Districts* 340 for seven dec. (D. J. White 52, K. A. Wealleans 48, G. E. Bradburn 93, S. A. Thomson 71 not out, Extras 35) and 223 for three dec. (K. A. Wealleans 112 not out, R. G. Twose 49, G. E. Bradburn 40); Wellington 261 for nine dec. (B. A. Edgar 40, R. H. Vance 46, A. H. Jones 36; S. A. Thomson three for 39) and 256 for eight (R. H. Vance 63, A. H. Jones 52, G. R. Larsen 53 not out; P. S. Neutze three for 62). *Northern Districts 4 pts.*

At Lancaster Park, Christchurch, December 8, 9, 10. Drawn. Canterbury* 185 (R. G. Petrie 42 not out; N. A. Mallender three for 35) and 297 for three (B. R. Hartland 126 not out, P. G. Kennedy 60, P. E. McEwan 64); Otago 289 for nine dec. (K. R. Rutherford 96, B. R. Blair 39, R. N. Hoskin 63; R. G. Petrie three for 48). *Otago 4 pts.*

At Harry Barker Reserve, Gisborne, December 15, 16, 17. Drawn. Auckland* 350 for six dec. (T. J. Franklin 69, J. G. Wright 90, D. N. Patel 125 not out); Northern Districts 186 (C. M. Kuggeleijn 34, B. A. Young 52 not out; D. K. Morrison four for 57, J. G. Bracewell four for 49) and 238 for six (K. A. Wealleans 44, S. A. Thomson 38, B. A. Young 44 not out, G. W. McKenzie 41 not out; M. C. Snedden three for 29). *Auckland 4 pts.*

At Queen's Park, Invercargill, December 15, 16, 17. Drawn. Wellington* 268 for nine dec. (B. A. Edgar 162, E. B. McSweeney 34; D. J. Hunter four for 74); Otago 131 for two (K. B. K. Ibadulla 34, K. J. Burns 46 not out, K. R. Rutherford 42 not out). *Otago 2 pts, Wellington 2 pts.*

At Nelson Park, Napier, December 15, 16, 17. Drawn. Central Districts 333 for six dec. (P. S. Briasco 60, C. J. Smith 104, M. J. Greatbatch 38, I. D. Fisher 36 not out, S. W. Duff 30 not out; C. Z. Harris three for 53) and 146 for eight dec. (T. E. Blain 30, S. W. Duff 36); Canterbury* 188 for five dec. (P. G. Kennedy 49, R. T. Latham 58; I. D. Fisher three for 29) and 61 for two. *Central Districts 4 pts.*

At Carisbrook, Dunedin, January 6, 7, 8. Otago won by an innings and 61 runs. Otago* 398 (P. W. Dobbs 38, K. J. Burns 61, K. R. Rutherford 119, B. R. Blair 83); Auckland 164 (T. J. Franklin 39, J. J. Crowe 33, D. N. Patel 31; S. L. Boock seven for 47) and 173 (J. J. Crowe 34, M. R. Pringle 42, J. G. Bracewell 30; S. L. Boock eight for 57). *Otago 16 pts.*

At Smallbone Park, Rotorua, January 6, 7, 8. Northern Districts won by 1 run. Northern Districts* 258 (K. A. Wealleans 51, R. G. Twose 56, G. W. McKenzie 35, B. A. Young 31, C. M. Kuggeleijn 32; D. J. Leonard five for 81) and 157 (G. E. Bradburn 35; D. J. Leonard five for 52, S. W. Duff three for 23); Central Districts 260 for six dec. (M. D. Crowe 138 not out, M. W. Douglas 70; S. B. Doull three for 61) and 154 (C. J. Smith 90 not out, carrying his bat; S. B. Doull three for 17, S. A. Thomson three for 40). *Northern Districts 12 pts, Central Districts 4 pts.*

At Basin Reserve, Wellington, January 6, 7, 8. Drawn. Wellington 199 (E. B. McSweeney 92; M. W. Priest three for 56) and 267 for three (B. A. Edgar 81, R. H. Vance 90, A. H. Jones 48 not out, E. B. McSweeney 37 not out); Canterbury* 379 for nine dec. (D. J. Boyle 33, B. R. Hartland 35, P. G. Kennedy 39, M. W. Priest 68, C. Z. Harris 86; P. W. O'Rourke four for 72). *Canterbury 4 pts.*

At Lancaster Park, Christchurch, January 10, 11, 12. Drawn. Auckland 240 for nine dec. (R. B. Reid 48, T. J. Franklin 38, J. J. Crowe 51, S. W. Brown 41; S. J. Roberts three for 54, R. M. Ford four for 49) and 253 for eight dec. (T. J. Franklin 45, J. G. Wright 45, D. N. Patel 98; R. G. Petrie five for 59); Canterbury* 241 for five dec. (D. J. Boyle 31, P. G. Kennedy 50, P. E. McEwan 60, R. T. Latham 58 not out) and 192 for five (B. R. Hartland 32, P. E. McEwan 51, R. T. Latham 48). *Canterbury 4 pts.*

At Fitzherbert Park, Palmerston North, January 10, 11, 12. Wellington won by four wickets. Central Districts* 313 for six dec. (M. D. Crowe 31, M. W. Douglas 114, T. E. Blain 82 not out) and 203 (M. J. Greatbatch 70, M. D. Crowe 55, M. W. Douglas 55; E. J. Gray three for 96); Wellington 255 for seven dec. (B. A. Edgar 55, A. H. Jones 72, T. D. Ritchie 59) and 264 for six (A. H. Jones 67, T. D. Ritchie 86, G. R. Larsen 51 not out). *Wellington 12 pts, Central Districts 4 pts.*

At Molyneux Park, Alexandra, January 10, 11, 12. Drawn. Northern Districts* 416 for six dec. (K. A. Wealleans 41, R. G. Twose 61, G. E. Bradburn 46, S. A. Thomson 74, C. M. Kuggeleijn 51, B. A. Young 100 not out) and 133 for four dec. (S. A. Thomson 50 not out; P. W. Hills three for 25); Otago 270 for seven dec. (B. Z. Harris 86, K. R. Rutherford 31, B. R. Blair 56, N. A. Mallender 43; B. P. Bracewell three for 47) and 168 for eight (K. J. Burns 36, B. Z. Harris 53, N. A. Mallender 46 not out; G. E. Bradburn four for 56). *Northern Districts 4 pts.*

At Lancaster Park, Christchurch, January 14, 15, 16. Canterbury won by two wickets. Northern Districts 326 (K. A. Wealleans 88, G. E. Bradburn 59, S. A. Thomson 57; R. G. Petrie three for 96, S. J. Roberts four for 67, M. W. Priest three for 61) and 243 for nine dec. (K. A. Wealleans 32, B. A. Young 53, C. M. Kuggeleijn 38 not out, G. W. McKenzie 39; S. J. Roberts three for 59, R. G. Petrie three for 57); Canterbury* 329 for six dec. (D. J. Boyle 50, P. G. Kennedy 87, C. Z. Harris 62 not out, M. W. Priest 67; P. S. Neutze three for 61) and 241 for eight (B. R. Hartland 35, P. E. McEwan 75, R. T. Latham 43; C. M. Kuggeleijn three fo 58). *Canterbury 16 pts.*

At Eden Park, Auckland, January 14, 15, 16. Drawn. Auckland 279 (T. J. Franklin 110 S. W. Brown 80; J. P. Millmow three for 65, D. A. Stirling three for 53) and 40 for one Wellington* 276 (B. A. Edgar 61, R. H. Vance 48, A. H. Jones 58, T. D. Ritchie 41; D. K Morrison three for 60, C. Pringle three for 90). *Auckland 2 pts (2 penalty pts deducted).*

At Pukekura Park, New Plymouth, January 14, 15, 16. Drawn. Central Districts 424 (M. J Greatbatch 86, M. D. Crowe 242, T. E. Blain 34; V. F. Johnson three for 114, S. L. Booc three for 97); Otago* 232 (P. W. Dobbs 41, B. Z. Harris 32, K. J. Burns 47; S. W. Duff six fo 46) and 264 for eight (B. Z. Harris 78, B. R. Blair 40; S. W. Duff five for 106). *Central Distric 4 pts.*

At Eden Park, Auckland, January 18, 19. Auckland won by an innings and 112 runs Auckland 368 (T. J. Franklin 39, J. G. Wright 61, D. N. Patel 114, M. R. Pringle 41, J. C Bracewell 42; B. P. Bracewell three for 93, S. B. Doull three for 73); Northern Districts* 7 (C. Pringle three for 31, M. C. Snedden six for 20) and 177 (R. G. Twose 53 not out, B. Bracewell 46; C. Pringle three for 71, M. C. Snedden four for 37). *Auckland 16 pts.*

At Basin Reserve, Wellington, January 18, 19, 20. Wellington won by eight wickets. Otag 57 (J. P. Millmow six for 13) and 290 (K. R. Rutherford 146, B. R. Blair 52; J. P. Millmo four for 70, E. J. Gray three for 85); Wellington* 294 (R. H. Vance 32, A. H. Jones 37, G. Burnett 56, T. D. Ritchie 68; N. A. Mallender three for 54, K. R. Rutherford five for 72) ar 56 for two. *Wellington 16 pts.*

At Lancaster Park, Christchurch, January 18, 19, 20. Central Districts won by eight wickets. Canterbury* 148 (M. W. Priest 31; D. J. Leonard four for 19) and 142 (M. W. Priest 50, R. G. Petrie 49; D. J. Leonard three for 52, I. D. Fisher five for 43); Central Districts 165 (S. W. Duff 40; R. G. Petrie three for 37, C. Z. Harris three for 64) and 126 for two (C. J. Smith 41). *Central Districts 16 pts.*

At Bledisloe Park, Pukekohe, January 27, 28, 29. Wellington won by six wickets. Northern Districts* 293 (D. J. White 43, G. E. Bradburn 94, C. M. Kuggeleijn 42; P. W. O'Rourke four for 60) and 152 (D. J. White 38, R. G. Twose 30, S. A. Thomson 49 not out; P. W. O'Rourke three for 41, G. R. Larsen five for 27); Wellington 297 for five dec. (R. H. Vance 123, T. D. Ritchie 61, M. P. Speight 65 not out) and 149 for four (G. P. Burnett 49 not out; S. A. Thomson three for 18). *Wellington 15 pts (1 penalty pt deducted).*

At Basin Reserve, Wellington, February 2, 3, 4. Wellington won by 49 runs. Wellington 397 for seven dec. (B. A. Edgar 125, G. R. Larsen 69, B. R. Williams 103 not out, G. N. Cederwall 44; G. R. Logan three for 74) and 154 for five dec. (G. N. Cederwall 45); Central Districts* 290 for seven dec. (R. T. Hart 133, I. D. Fisher 71, Extras 30; P. W. O'Rourke five for 71) and 212 (P. S. Briasco 30, R. L. Glover 113, S. W. Duff 31; R. A. Pick five for 57, B. R. Williams three for 32). *Wellington 16 pts.*

At Carisbrook, Dunedin, February 4, 5, 6. Drawn. Otago* 350 (P. W. Dobbs 31, K. J. Burns 50, P. A. Campbell 37, B. R. Blair 131, R. E. W. Mawhinney 47; S. J. Roberts four for 77, M. W. Priest three for 67, G. K. MacDonald three for 77) and 202 (B. Z. Harris 71; M. W. Priest nine for 95); Canterbury 324 (P. G. Kennedy 52, R. T. Latham 79, M. W. Priest 50, G. K. MacDonald 57; N. A. Mallender four for 75) and 114 for five (R. T. Latham 42; N. A. Mallender four for 20). *Otago 4 pts.*

At Queen Elizabeth Park, Masterton, February 6, 7, 8. Drawn. Auckland* 412 for nine dec. (R. B. Reid 107, J. J. Crowe 110, D. N. Patel 61, C. Pringle 33 not out; D. J. Leonard three for 64) and 134 for two dec. (R. B. Reid 63, S. J. Peterson 34, C. Pringle 31 not out); Central Districts 283 for five dec. (R. T. Hart 99, T. E. Blain 96; S. W. Brown three for 55) and 145 for seven (T. E. Blain 54; C. Pringle three for 25, S. W. Brown four for 19). *Auckland 4 pts.*

At Basin Reserve, Wellington, February 10, 11, 12. Drawn. Auckland 217 (J. T. C. Vaughan 106 not out, A. C. Parore 45; J. P. Millmow five for 36, G. N. Cederwall three for 52) and 177 (J. J. Crowe 68 not out; E. J. Gray eight for 78); Wellington* 214 (M. P. Speight 62, E. B. McSweeney 48, E. J. Gray 38, G. N. Cederwall 40; C. Pringle three for 58, R. P. de Groen five for 47) and 165 for nine (B. A. Edgar 44, E. J. Gray 31; C. Pringle three for 42, D. N. Patel five for 54). *Auckland 4 pts.*

At Cobham Oval, Whangarei, February 10, 11, 12. Canterbury won by two wickets. Northern Districts* 295 (D. J. White 52, G. W. McKenzie 39, B. A. Young 41, P. S. Neutze 40; R. G. Petrie three for 92) and 216 for five dec. (C. M. Kuggeleijn 68, B. A. Young 76 not out; M. W. Priest three for 100); Canterbury 233 (R. T. Latham 53, P. E. McEwan 50; D. A. Beard three for 55, G. E. Bradburn six for 56) and 281 for eight (D. J. Boyle 86, B. R. Hartland 46, C. Z. Harris 34, P. E. McEwan 51; C. M. Kuggeleijn four for 92). *Canterbury 12 pts, Northern Districts 4 pts.*

At Carisbrook, Dunedin, February 10, 11, 12. Central Districts won by 85 runs. Central Districts* 233 (R. T. Hart 32, P. S. Briasco 31, M. W. Douglas 56, I. D. Fisher 44 not out; S. L. Boock five for 88) and 114 for two dec. (C. J. Smith 51 not out, M. W. Douglas 53); Otago 84 for two dec. (K. J. Burns 40 not out) and 178 (P. W. Dobbs 35, B. R. Blair 48; M. C. Goodson five for 51, S. W. Duff three for 65). *Central Districts 16 pts.*

At Eden Park, Auckland, February 14, 15, 16. Canterbury won by two wickets. Auckland 411 for nine dec. (T. J. Franklin 40, S. J. Peterson 30, J. J. Crowe 91, D. N. Patel 71, J. G. Bracewell 85, Extras 30; S. J. Roberts three for 91, R. M. Ford four for 76) and 162 for nine dec. (J. J. Crowe 32, J. T. C. Vaughan 36 not out; S. J. Roberts four for 61); Canterbury* 324 (D. J. Boyle 69, B. R. Hartland 36, C. Z. Harris 69, M. W. Priest 50; R. P. de Groen four for 51, M. C. Snedden four for 61) and 253 for eight (B. R. Hartland 40, R. T. Latham 33, C. Z. Harris 39, P. E. McEwan 67; M. C. Snedden four for 66). *Canterbury 12 pts, Auckland 4 pts.*

At Eden Park, Auckland, February 18, 19, 20. Otago won by four wickets. Auckland 225 (S. J. Peterson 57, J. J. Crowe 81, A. J. Hunt 55; J. K. Lindsay four for 22) and 190 (J. G. Bracewell 49, J. T. C. Vaughan 75; D. J. Hunter four for 35, V. F. Johnson three for 38); Otago* 265 (K. B. K. Ibadulla 89, B. R. Blair 72, N. A. Mallender 50; C. Pringle four for 56) and 151 for six (K. B. K. Ibadulla 43; D. N. Patel four for 41). *Otago 12 pts (4 penalty pts deducted).*

At Lancaster Park, Christchurch, February 18, 19, 20. Drawn. Wellington 202 (J. M. Aiken 39, R. H. Vance 51; S. J. Roberts three for 34, C. Z. Harris three for 42) and 309 for six dec. (J. M. Aiken 156 not out, B. A. Edgar 32, G. P. Burnett 48, E. B. McSweeney 30; R. G. Petrie three for 80); Canterbury* 221 for seven dec. (D. J. Boyle 63, P. G. Kennedy 33, R. T. Latham 43; R. A. Pick four for 61) and 290 for eight (P. G. Kennedy 33, L. K. Germon 160 not out; J. P. Millmow three for 59). *Canterbury 4 pts (Wellington 4 penalty pts deducted).*

At Harry Barker Reserve, Gisborne, February 22, 23, 24. Drawn. Northern Districts* 376 (D. J. White 53, G. E. Bradburn 96, G. W. McKenzie 37, M. D. Bailey 34, B. P. Bracewell 57 not out, P. S. Neutze 40; D. J. Hunter four for 53); Otago 397 for seven (K. B. K. Ibadulla 104, K. J. Burns 66, B. R. Blair 94, N. A. Mallender 52 not out, Extras 32). *Otago 4 pts.*

At Trafalgar Park, Nelson, February 26, 27, 28. Northern Districts won by seven wickets. Central Districts* 308 for nine dec. (C. J. Smith 160 not out, carrying his bat, P. S. Briasco 38, S. W. Duff 36; C. W. Ross four for 88, B. P. Bracewell three for 65) and 82 (M. W. Douglas 34; C. W. Ross three for 25, D. A. Beard six for 18 including a hat-trick); Northern Districts 318 for four dec. (D. J. White 110, C. M. Kuggeleijn 102 not out) and 73 for three. *Northern Districts 16 pts.*

PLUNKET SHIELD AND SHELL TROPHY WINNERS

The Plunket Shield was replaced by the Shell Trophy after the 1974-75 season.

1921-22 Auckland
1922-23 Canterbury
1923-24 Wellington
1924-25 Otago
1925-26 Wellington
1926-27 Auckland
1927-28 Wellington
1928-29 Auckland
1929-30 Wellington
1930-31 Canterbury
1931-32 Wellington
1932-33 Otago
1933-34 Auckland
1934-35 Canterbury
1935-36 Wellington
1936-37 Auckland
1937-38 Auckland
1938-39 Auckland
1939-40 Auckland
1940-45 No competition
1945-46 Canterbury
1946-47 Auckland
1947-48 Otago
1948-49 Canterbury
1949-50 Wellington
1950-51 Otago
1951-52 Canterbury
1952-53 Otago
1953-54 Central Districts
1954-55 Wellington
1955-56 Canterbury
1956-57 Wellington
1957-58 Otago
1958-59 Auckland
1959-60 Canterbury
1960-61 Wellington
1961-62 Wellington
1962-63 Northern Districts
1963-64 Auckland
1964-65 Canterbury
1965-66 Wellington
1966-67 Central Districts
1967-68 Central Districts
1968-69 Auckland
1969-70 Otago
1970-71 Central Districts
1971-72 Otago
1972-73 Wellington
1973-74 Wellington
1974-75 Otago
1975-76 Canterbury
1976-77 Otago
1977-78 Auckland
1978-79 Otago
1979-80 Northern Districts
1980-81 Auckland
1981-82 Wellington
1982-83 Wellington
1983-84 Canterbury
1984-85 Wellington
1985-86 Otago
1986-87 Central Districts
1987-88 Otago
1988-89 Auckland
1989-90 Wellington

†SHELL CUP, 1989-90

At Eden Park, Auckland, December 27. Auckland won by seven wickets. Northern Districts* 162 (48 overs) (K. A. Wealleans 30, G. E. Bradburn 39 not out; D. N. Patel four for 18); Auckland 163 for three (36 overs) (R. B. Reid 55, J. G. Wright 50, T. J. Franklin 35 not out).

At Basin Reserve, Wellington, December 27. Wellington won by five wickets. Central Districts* 198 (49.2 overs) (M. W. Douglas 40, I. D. Fisher 34, G. K. Robertson 34 not out; E. J. Chatfield three for 36, P. W. O'Rourke three for 26); Wellington 202 for five (47.5 overs) (B. A. Edgar 54, A. H. Jones 60, G. R. Larsen 30 not out).

At Centennial Park, Oamaru, December 27. Canterbury won by 91 runs. Canterbury 194 for nine (50 overs) (P. G. Kennedy 41, R. T. Latham 44; K. R. Rutherford three for 26); Otago* 103 (40.5 overs).

At Molyneux Park, Alexandra, December 29. Auckland won by three wickets. Otago* 130 (46.5 overs) (A. W. Bligh 33; D. K. Morrison three for 29, M. C. Snedden four for 23); Auckland 133 for seven (48.3 overs) (J. G. Bracewell 43; N. A. Mallender four for 16).

At Basin Reserve, Wellington, December 29. Canterbury won by 57 runs. Canterbury* 186 (49.1 overs) (P. G. Kennedy 77; E. J. Chatfield three for 22, J. P. Millmow three for 24); Wellington 129 for nine (50 overs) (G. P. Burnett 36; M. W. Priest three for 14).

At Tauranga Domain, Tauranga, December 29. Central Districts won by 2 runs. Central Districts* 208 (49.2 overs) (P. S. Briasco 50, T. E. Blain 70; R. G. Twose three for 35); Northern Districts 206 for nine (50 overs) (D. J. White 101; S. W. Duff three for 42).

At Lancaster Park, Christchurch, December 31. Auckland won by 40 runs. Auckland* 209 for nine (50 overs) (J. G. Wright 96, I. D. S. Smith 31; R. G. Petrie five for 24); Canterbury 169 (49.3 overs) (P. G. Kennedy 45).

At Tauranga Domain, Tauranga, December 31. Northern Districts won by 49 runs. Northern Districts* 144 (44.5 overs) (B. A. Young 52; E. J. Chatfield three for 24); Wellington 95 (41.1 overs).

At Cook's Gardens, Wanganui, January 1. Central Districts won by 69 runs. Central Districts 229 for five (50 overs) (M. D. Crowe 86, M. J. Greatbatch 80 not out); Otago* 160 (45 overs) (B. R. Blair 50; D. J. Leonard four for 45).

At Basin Reserve, Wellington, January 2. Wellington won by seven wickets. Otago* 141 for eight (50 overs) (J. P. Millmow three for 25); Wellington 142 for three (44.4 overs) (B. A. Edgar 57, G. P. Burnett 40 not out).

At Aorangi Park, Timaru, January 2. Northern Districts won by 54 runs. Northern Districts* 196 for seven (50 overs) (R. G. Twose 81, B. A. Young 36); Canterbury 142 (45.5 overs) (R. T. Latham 42 not out; S. A. Thomson three for 21).

At Eden Park, Auckland, January 3. Central Districts won by nine wickets. Auckland 192 for nine (50 overs) (J. J. Crowe 32, M. R. Pringle 40; G. R. Logan three for 35); Central Districts* 193 for one (43.1 overs) (M. D. Crowe 104 not out, M. J. Greatbatch 43 not out).

At Molyneux Park, Alexandra, January 4. Northern Districts won by four wickets after being set a revised target of 121 from 30 overs. Otago* 132 for two (33 overs) (P. W. Dobbs 32, B. R. Blair 34, K. J. Burns 39 not out); Northern Districts 122 for six (29.3 overs) (K. A. Wealleans 32, G. E. Bradburn 34; N. A. Mallender three for 14).

At Levin Domain, Levin, January 4. Central Districts won by five wickets. Canterbury* 170 for nine (50 overs) (D. J. Boyle 42, C. Z. Harris 42; D. J. Leonard five for 48); Central Districts 171 for five (42.2 overs) (M. J. Greatbatch 52, R. L. Glover 58 not out).

At Eden Park, Auckland, January 4. Wellington won by 50 runs. Wellington 174 (49.4 overs) (G. P. Burnett 36, G. R. Larsen 45, D. A. Stirling 39; M. C. Snedden three for 24); Auckland* 124 (41 overs) (J. J. Crowe 30; J. P. Millmow three for 31, D. A. Stirling three for 18).

Central Districts 8 pts, Auckland 6 pts, Northern Districts 6 pts, Wellington 6 pts, Canterbury 4 pts, Otago 0 pts.

Semi-finals

At Pukekura Park, New Plymouth, March 21. Central Districts won by eight wickets. Wellington* 153 for five (50 overs) (R. H. Vance 56 not out); Central Districts 154 for two (41.4 overs) (M. D. Crowe 48, M. J. Greatbatch 70 not out).

At Seddon Park, Hamilton, March 22. Auckland won by one wicket. Northern Districts 208 for seven (50 overs) (K. A. Wealleans 74, B. A. Young 50); Auckland* 209 for nine (48.2 overs) (J. J. Crowe 51, D. K. Morrison 30 not out; G. E. Bradburn three for 28).

Final

At McLean Park, Napier, March 24. Auckland won by 22 runs. Auckland* 198 for eight (50 overs) (J. G. Wright 41, D. N. Patel 90; P. S. Briasco four for 48); Central Districts 176 for nine (50 overs) (P. S. Briasco 57, M. W. Douglas 51; M. C. Snedden four for 27).

PAKISTAN v NEW ZEALAND, 1990-91

Pakistan won all three matches. By scoring a hundred in each Test, Shoaib Mohammad took to five his number of centuries in consecutive Tests against New Zealand, while his total of 507 runs at 169.00 was a record for Pakistan in a series between the two countries. When Javed Miandad reached 14 in his second innings at Faisalabad, he became the fifth player to score 8,000 runs in Tests, and he finished the series with 8,041, behind S. M. Gavaskar (10,122), A. R. Border (8,701) and G. Boycott (8,114), having overtaken I. V. A. Richards and G. S. Sobers during his innings. Pakistan's first-innings total of 102 at Faisalabad was their lowest against New Zealand.

First Test: At Karachi, October 10, 11, 12, 14, 15. Pakistan won by an innings and 43 runs. New Zealand 196 (M. J. Greatbatch 43, K. R. Rutherford 79; Wasim Akram four for 44, Waqar Younis four for 40) and 194 (M. D. Crowe 68 not out; Wasim Akram four for 60, Waqar Younis three for 39); Pakistan 433 for six dec. (Ramiz Raja 78, Shoaib Mohammad 203 not out, Salim Malik 43).

Second Test: At Lahore, October 18, 19, 20, 22, 23. Pakistan won by nine wickets. New Zealand 160 (I. D. S. Smith 33, Extras 38; Waqar Younis three for 20) and 287 (M. D. Crowe 108 not out, K. R. Rutherford 60, Extras 44; Waqar Younis seven for 86); Pakistan 373 for nine dec. (Ramiz Raja 48, Shoaib Mohammad 105, Javed Miandad 43, Ijaz Ahmed 86, Salim Yousuf 33; W. Watson six for 78) and 77 for one (Shoaib Mohammad 42 not out).

Third Test: At Faisalabad, October 26, 28, 29, 30, 31. Pakistan won by 65 runs. Pakistan 102 (C. Pringle seven for 52, W. Watson three for 29) and 357 (Shoaib Mohammad 142, Salim Malik 71, Javed Miandad 55; D. K. Morrison four for 105, C. Pringle four for 100); New Zealand 217 (M. D. Crowe 31, I. D. S. Smith 61; Waqar Younis seven for 76) and 177 (D. N. Patel 45, G. E. Bradburn 30 not out; Waqar Younis five for 54, Aaqib Javed three for 57).

Full details of the New Zealanders' tour of Pakistan will appear in the 1992 edition of Wisden

CRICKET IN INDIA, 1989-90

By R. MOHAN and SUDHIR VAIDYA

The Indian season began not on the cricket field but in the court-room. Before the highest court in the land, at a dramatic hearing on a public-interest litigation brought against its sweeping disciplinary and penal action on leading cricketers, the Board of Control for Cricket in India was made to retrace its steps. Forced by the Supreme Court's ruling to annul all decisions made on "arbitrary, ill-advised, incompetent and unjustifiable" grounds, the Board's Working Committee rescinded the fines imposed on several Indian cricketers who had played in the United States and Canada on their way home from the tour of the Caribbean in May 1989. Similarly, the one-year ban from all cricket on six senior players, who were said to be the leaders of the "rebel" tour, was revoked.

The basis of the Board's action had been the players' breach of the contracts they had entered into when selected to represent India. However, the wording of these contracts was shown to be unreasonable, one-sided and coercive: in short, the contract was a document which went well beyond reasonable governance. In the wake of this *cause célèbre*, the entire perspective of player-establishment relations changed, although not all the change was for the good. It did mean that the players got off scot-free. A further outcome of the settlement between the Board and the players was the exoneration of Mohinder Amarnath, whose suit against the Board, pending in the lower courts while he remained banned for a season for the disparaging comments he had made about the selectors, was decided upon as a connected matter.

"Get on with the game", was the sincere advice of the then Chief Justice, Mr E. S. Venkatramaiah. But few were willing to listen. That light-hearted exhibition cricket should lead to such divisions was the saddest aspect of the controversy. And the repercussions of it were to be felt throughout the crowded season that followed, not least in the eccentric selection policies for which India has always been famous. In this respect, it has become standard practice to reduce "domestic" cricket to a trial for picking the national team. Every tournament, barring the Ranji Trophy championship, which runs for close to seven months, gets to be played just before a limited-overs international tournament or a Test series. With the selectors descending on them, the matches are played in such a tense atmosphere that the scores and performances tend to mislead as often as not, and do not mirror the true worth of the players.

When the long season ended, Bengal were the national champions, having won the Ranji Trophy again after a gap of 51 years. Back in 1938-39, when Bengal won the trophy for the first time, their team contained a liberal sprinkling of Englishmen. The 1989-90 side had a few recruits from other states, and two of them, Arun Lal and Raja Venkat [Raja Venkatraman], took a leading part in Bengal's wresting the trophy from the defending champions, Delhi, in the final. But while victory over Delhi in the final proved momentous for Bengal, it was the quotient rule that made the news. Awarding trophies on the basis of a first-innings lead is bad enough; the runs-scored/wickets-lost "tie-break" which decides the winner in the event of interference from the weather before either side has gained a first-innings lead is most unsatisfactory and has complicated the issue further. Bengal won the Ranji Trophy final by virtue of their higher quotient, their cause being helped considerably by time-wasting tactics which not only denied the opposing bowlers a possible vital wicket but also resulted in penalty runs being gained as a result of slow over-rates.

Cricket in India is already a batsman's game. Such an ill-conceived "tie-break" rule renders it even more of one. To Bengal's credit, their players were among those severely critical of the quotient rule, even if they did have the advantage of batting second and knowing exactly what they had to do to get ahead of Delhi's rather poor quotient of 27.80. Bengal were poorly placed at 97 for four, from which point Arun Lal and Raja Venkat took them to 176 without further loss across two days marked by many stoppages owing to rain. No play was possible on the final day, and a total readjusted to 216 by 40 penalty runs gave Bengal their winning quotient of 54. Earlier, in their quarter-final match, Bengal had been the beneficiaries of the quotient rule, even though their 312 for two was a long way from Bombay's 590 for five declared. As Bengal had not beaten Bombay in twelve previous meetings, the significance of the quotient was apparent. Such a match, moreover, illustrates what a "batathon" cricket in India has become. Bombay declared their innings on the third morning of the four-day match, probably believing that a quotient of 118 gave them a clear chance of winning. That such an approach represents a short cut, and should not be allowed precedence over bowling the opposition out, is obvious to all except those who perpetrate this batting-oriented system of quotients.

Four different teams have won the Ranji Trophy in four seasons – Hyderabad, Tamil Nadu, Delhi and Bengal. A far cry from the days of Bombay's domination, when with two exceptions they won every season from 1955-56 to 1976-77), this is a healthy development, indicating that team strengths have evened out. However, it is a different matter that only a few bowlers managed to take 25 wickets in a first-class season which ran from early October to the end of March. And of the nine bowlers who managed 25 wickets or more in the Ranji Trophy, only three were youngsters. Atul Wassan of Delhi, who was selected for the tours of New Zealand and England, was clearly an outstanding prospect with 39 Ranji Trophy wickets at 14.07. Subroto Banerjee of Bihar, a trainee at the school for potential fast bowlers, was not far behind, with a tally of 29 wickets at 14.58 in the championship. Such are the ways of the Indian selection committee, though that it frequently seems there is something in the Indian cricket system which militates against the nurturing and consistent encouragement of bowlers. A case in point was Vivek Razdan. Another to attend the MRF-sponsored Pace Foundation in Madras, where Dennis Lillee is a kind of Professor Emeritus Razdan took five wickets for 79 in an innings against Pakistan at Sialkot in December in only his second Test. Yet before the season was over, he had been overlooked.

The decline in bowling standards was nowhere more apparent than in the Duleep Trophy, which in the main featured India's second-string bowlers One glance at the scores reveals the type of cricket that was played. Central Zone declared at 641 for seven against East and 604 (plus 24 penalty runs) for six against North; South Zone went even better in making 665 against West while in the five-day final they made 527 for six declared in their second innings and won outright through their spinners, Venkatapathy Raju and Margasahayam Venkataramana. There were sixteen centuries by eleven batsmen in four matches, and a few 90s besides. Pravin Amre of Central Zone was most prolific with three three-figure innings of 106, 240 not out and 113, matching Raman Lamba's feat in 1987-88 of three centuries in a Duleep Trophy series. His colleague, at Railways and for Central Zone, U. R. Radhakrishnan, a left-handed opener, made two hundreds in the Duleep, as did V. B. Chandrasekhar and Robin Singh of Tamil Nadu and South Zone. Rakesh Parikh made his double-hundred (218 in 680 minutes) on his first outing in the Duleep Trophy.

The Duleep Trophy matches were played in the south, a region once well known for pitches tending to help spinners. The wickets in 1989-90, however, were kill-joys. No bowler, of spin or pace, could be expected to be enthusiastic about doing his job when the conditions were so thoroughly loaded in favour of batsmen. And though the series was said to be a trial for picking the team to New Zealand, a list of 48 probables had already been announced, which meant that even those who scored most heavily were never seriously in contention.

The selection of the team to New Zealand proved quite contentious, with Mohammad Azharuddin succeeding Krish Srikkanth as captain. Srikkanth had led India in the drawn series in Pakistan, where the honours were fairly even, and that performance was to be the best by India in a season notable for acrimony, controversy, and little memorable cricket as far as India were concerned. Srikkanth, who had to return home from the West Indies after his hand was broken by Ian Bishop before the Test series, was the senior player untainted by the American-tour controversy. However, he did lead the players' revolt with regard to the new contracts offered for the tour of Pakistan, and in addition he was in poor personal form there. This gave the selectors sufficient reasons when the time came to play the toppling game.

With two major Test tours during the season, as well as the six-nation Nehru Cup tournament in India and two visits to Sharjah, with the summer series in England to come, there was plenty of international cricket for the Indian players. Not much of it was of a high quality, unfortunately.

Sachin Tendulkar, the prodigy who burst upon the scene in the previous season, made his first hundred outside the Ranji Trophy, hitting an unbeaten 103 in the second innings of the Irani Cup match at the Wankhede Stadium in Bombay, which remained the one pitch in India with a bit of juice in it. He made all the tours during the season and in New Zealand went close to becoming the youngest century-maker in Tests. He holed out to wide mid-off when 12 runs short in the Test at Napier. Other young batsmen who made their runs with consistency were Rakesh Parikh, the Baroda opener, M. V. Sridhar of Hyderabad, also an opener, who was the quickest to make 1,000 Ranji career runs (in terms of time rather than innings, as he had fourteen to Rusi Modi's seven) and Vivek Jaisimha, son of the Test cricketer, M. L. Jaisimha. They were three of only seven batsmen to score 500 runs in the Ranji Trophy. The fact that, of those seven, four were opening batsmen was, perhaps, a true reflection of bowling standards. Playing the new ball is not as hazardous a task in India as it can be in other parts of the cricket world. – R.M.

FIRST-CLASS AVERAGES, 1989-90

BATTING

(Qualification: 500 runs)

	M	*I*	*NO*	*R*	*HI*	*100s*	*Avge*
Arun Lal (*Bengal*)	8	9	2	828	189*	3	118.28
R. B. Parikh (*Baroda*)	7	11	2	934	218	4	103.77
P. K. Amre (*Railways*)	7	8	1	667	240*	3	95.28
V. B. Chandrasekhar (*Tamil Nadu*)	5	6	0	516	146	3	86.00
R. Venkatraman (*Bengal*)	7	7	1	500	170	2	83.33
Robin Singh (*Tamil Nadu*)	7	9	2	563	141	2	80.42
U. R. Radhakrishnan (*Railways*)	7	11	2	723	214	3	80.33
S. S. Karim (*Bihar*)	8	10	2	631	148	3	78.87
K. Azad (*Delhi*)	7	9	1	580	120	3	72.50
Yusuf Ali Khan (*Railways*)	7	8	0	553	233	2	69.12
M. V. Sridhar (*Hyderabad*)	9	13	0	885	169	3	68.07
V. Vats (*Uttar Pradesh*)	8	11	2	569	130*	1	63.22
S. S. Khandkar (*Uttar Pradesh*)	8	14	2	740	102*	1	61.66
L. S. Rajput (*Bombay*)	8	11	2	506	168	2	56.22
V. Jaisimha (*Hyderabad*)	9	13	1	662	138*	2	55.16
I. B. Roy (*Bengal*)	8	10	0	537	152	2	53.70
Bantoo Singh (*Delhi*)	10	12	1	547	136	2	49.72
R. Sapru (*Uttar Pradesh*)	8	13	2	528	184	1	48.00

** Signifies not out.*

BOWLING

(Qualification: 20 wickets)

	O	*M*	*R*	*W*	*BB*	*Avge*
Deepak Sharma (*Haryana*)	167.2	48	377	22	6-37	17.13
S. Subramaniam (*Tamil Nadu*)	154	38	418	24	5-10	17.41
Bharati Vij (*Punjab*)	228.2	73	455	26	7-27	17.50
S. Banerjee (*Bihar*)	191.2	41	565	30	7-18	18.83
A. S. Wassan (*Delhi*)	259.5	40	903	47	7-36	19.21
A. Kumble (*Karnataka*)	196.4	52	471	24	5-134	19.62
A. Qayoom (*Jammu and Kashmir*)	171.3	18	608	29	7-57	20.96
D. Wasu (*Tamil Nadu*)	152.3	29	462	22	5-40	21.00
S. L. V. Raju (*Hyderabad*)	337.4	115	681	32	6-127	21.28
Sanjeev Sharma (*Delhi*)	263	55	711	31	8-76	22.93
M. V. Rao (*Services*)	150.3	13	593	25	4-33	23.72
A. R. Bhat (*Karnataka*)	248.5	65	600	25	4-36	24.00
Gopal Sharma (*Uttar Pradesh*)	366.5	70	952	37	9-59	25.72
T. Chakradhar Rao (*Andhra*)	156.1	9	572	22	6-92	26.00
S. Mohapatra (*Orissa*)	214.2	36	719	27	7-74	26.62
R. R. Kulkarni (*Bombay*)	216	29	857	32	7-73	26.78
J. Srinath (*Karnataka*)	193.5	28	747	27	5-85	27.66
N. S. Yadav (*Hyderabad*)	285	59	727	25	5-63	29.08
N. D. Hirwani (*Madhya Pradesh*)	329.1	47	1,081	37	7-44	29.21
P. S. Vaidya (*Vidarbha*)	187	23	766	25	4-76	30.64
M. Venkataramana (*Tamil Nadu*)	207.4	29	735	23	6-98	31.95
R. Sett (*Bengal*)	224	37	724	21	5-107	34.47
Arshad Ayub (*Hyderabad*)	291.2	55	825	21	7-45	39.28

*In the following scores, (M) indicates that the match was played on coir matting, and * by the name of a team indicates that they won the toss. It should also be noted that innings' totals may include penalty points added when the fielding side failed to meet the required over-rate.*

RANJI TROPHY, 1989-90

Central Zone

At Karnail Singh Stadium, Delhi, October 15, 16, 17. Drawn. Railways* 478 for eight dec. (Yusuf Ali Khan 90, U. R. Radhakrishnan 214, K. B. Kala 58, P. K. Amre 32, S. M. H. Kirmani 30; M. A. Ansari three for 94); Uttar Pradesh 195 (Indrapal Singh 63; R. Venkatesh five for 64, Ratan Singh four for 43) and 165 for two (S. S. Khandkar 102 not out). *Railways 14 pts, Uttar Pradesh 4 pts.*

At Railway Ground, Jaipur (M), October 15, 16, 17. Rajasthan won by six wickets. Vidarbha 250 (S. Phadkar 96, P. S. Vaidya 72; P. Sunderam seven for 72, Yunus Ali three for 28) and 272 (M. Agasti 39, P. Hingnikar 35, H. R. Wasu 49 not out, P. S. Vaidya 65; P. Sunderam three for 65, Yunus Ali three for 63); Rajasthan* 163 for nine dec. (S. Vyas 30, Padam Shastri 62; S. M. Jugade five for 43, P. S. Vaidya three for 49) and 360 for four (A. Mudkavi 31, D. Jain 167 not out, A. Asawa 79, P. Krishna Kumar 49). *Rajasthan 17 pts, Vidarbha 8 pts.*

At VCA Ground, Nagpur, October 18, 19, 20. Drawn. Vidarbha* 539 (A. Kane 42, U. Phate 31, S. Gujar 126, H. R. Wasu 190, R. Gawande 78 not out; Ratan Singh three for 107, R. Venkatesh four for 108) and 21 for no wkt; Railways 493 (Yusuf Ali Khan 233, U. R. Radhakrishnan 70, K. B. Kala 66, P. K. Amre 38; P. Gandhe five for 165, H. R. Wasu three for 125). *Vidarbha 9 pts, Railways 9 pts.*

At Kamla Club, Kanpur, October 21, 22, 23. Uttar Pradesh won by an innings and 220 runs. Uttar Pradesh* 491 for nine dec. (S. S. Khandkar 49, S. Chaturvedi 85, R. Sapru 184, V. Vats 60, G. Pandey 43; H. R. Wasu five for 152); Vidarbha 144 (P. Hingnikar 37; Gopal Sharma three for 40, M. A. Ansari five for 13) and 127 (Gopal Sharma six for 48). *Uttar Pradesh 24 pts, Vidarbha 1 pt.*

At Maharaja College Ground, Jaipur (M), November 5, 6, 7. Madhya Pradesh won by an innings and 82 runs. Rajasthan 183 (S. Mudkavi 56; T. A. Sekhar six for 46) and 135 (A. Mudkavi 40; N. D. Hirwani seven for 44); Madhya Pradesh* 400 for eight dec. (P. Dwivedi 115, S. Ansari 64, R. Talwar 95). *Madhya Pradesh 20 pts, Rajasthan 2 pts.*

At ITI Ground, Indore, November 18, 19, 20. Drawn. Uttar Pradesh 242 (V. Vats 89, R. P. Singh 49; S. Lahore four for 61) and 269 for five dec. (S. S. Khandkar 46, V. Vats 130 not out; N. D. Hirwani three for 66); Madhya Pradesh* 316 (A. Vijayvargiya 37, K. Patel 43, P. Dwivedi 31, R. Talwar 42, D. Nilosey 49; R. P. Singh four for 69, A. Q. Zaidi three for 103) and 61 for two (A. Vijayvargiya 31). *Madhya Pradesh 13 pts, Uttar Pradesh 11 pts.*

At Roop Singh Stadium, Gwalior, November 26, 27, 28. Drawn. Railways* 509 for six dec. (K. B. Kala 214, P. K. Amre 79, S. M. H. Kirmani 93, A. S. Negi 99) and 1 for no wkt dec.; Madhya Pradesh 408 (S. Ansari 87, K. Patel 54, R. Talwar 64, D. Nilosey 99 not out, R. Chauhan 43; S. Srinivasan three for 90, Ratan Singh four for 81) and 24 for no wkt. *Madhya Pradesh 7 pts, Railways 11 pts.*

At Kamla Club, Kanpur, November 26, 27, 28. Uttar Pradesh won by an innings and 49 runs. Uttar Pradesh* 340 (S. S. Khandkar 83, V. Vats 59, R. Sapru 53, S. Chaturvedi 33; Y. Mathur three for 73, S. Mudkavi five for 95); Rajasthan 125 (Gopal Sharma nine for 59) and 166 (A. Mudkavi 36, Padam Shastri 58; Gopal Sharma four for 47, S. Kesarwani four for 63). *Uttar Pradesh 22 pts, Rajasthan 3 pts.*

At Karnail Singh Stadium, Delhi, December 1, 2, 3. Drawn. Rajasthan* 294 (J. Mathur 125, A. Asawa 58, Extras 33; R. Venkatesh seven for 82) and 186 for eight (Padam Shastri 46, A. Asawa 45; Ratan Singh three for 33); Railways 313 (U. R. Radhakrishnan 93, K. B. Kala 46, P. K. Amre 53, S. M. H. Kirmani 33; S. Mudkavi five for 41). *Railways 13 pts, Rajasthan 10 pts.*

At Postal Ground, Yeotmal (M), December 1, 2, 3. Drawn. Vidarbha 248 (A. Kane 41, P. Hingnikar 36, S. Phadkar 48, H. R. Wasu 30; N. D. Hirwani six for 76) and 262 for seven dec. (M. Gogte 56, S. Phadkar 37, R. Gawande 70 not out; N. D. Hirwani five for 97); Madhya Pradesh* 258 (A. Vijayvargiya 53, P. Dwivedi 49, M. Sahni 41; P. S. Vaidya three for 61, H. R. Wasu three for 39) and 104 for two (S. Ansari 54). *Vidarbha 10 pts, Madhya Pradesh 13 pts.*

Uttar Pradesh 61 pts, Madhya Pradesh 53 pts, Railways 47 pts, Rajasthan 32 pts, Vidarbha 28 pts. Uttar Pradesh and Madhya Pradesh qualified for the knockout stage.

East Zone

At Maligaon Railway Stadium, Gauhati, November 13, 14, 15. Drawn. Assam* 402 (Zahir Alam 99, Deepak Das 154, Rajinder Singh 43, Amal Das 37; S. Banerjee six for 45); Tripura 125 (R. Chowdhary 48 not out, carrying his bat; N. Konwar three for 24, S. Srivastava six for 29) and 233 for six (A. Baig 35, S. Paul 74, Y. K. Chowdhary 43). *Assam 14 pts, Tripura 4 pts.*

At Mecon, Ranchi, November 20, 21, 22. Bihar won by an innings and 5 runs. Bihar* 403 (P. Khanna 85, H. Gidwani 32, S. S. Karim 148, A. Hussain 34; Rajinder Singh four for 125); Assam 120 (S. Banerjee three for 44, Dhananjay Singh four for 43) and 278 (R. Bora 94, B. Majumdar 37; Abinash Kumar three for 42). *Bihar 22 pts, Assam 2 pts.*

At Eden Gardens, Calcutta, November 20, 21, 22. Drawn. Tripura 192 (Vivek Mehra 42, S. Paul 50; Arup Bhattacharya five for 33) and 254 for one (R. Chowdhary 136 not out, A. Baig 106 not out); Bengal* 506 for three dec. (I. B. Roy 90, Arun Lal 166, R. Venkatraman 53, S. Ganguly 66 not out, Arup Bhattacharya 64 not out). *Bengal 13 pts, Tripura 5 pts.*

At Barabatti Stadium, Cuttack, November 25, 26, 27. Orissa won by an innings and 103 runs. Orissa* 401 (S. Das 113, A. Jayaprakash 107, S. Bhuyan 32, Extras 49; Y. K. Chowdhary four for 86); Tripura 127 (Vivek Mehra 50 not out, carrying his bat; H. Praharaj five for 51) and 171 (R. Chowdhary 44, S. Paul 33, Y. K. Chowdhary 35; Sushil Kumar five for 37). *Orissa 22 pts, Tripura 3 pts.*

At Eden Gardens, Calcutta, November 25, 26, 27. Bengal won by an innings and 120 runs. Assam* 246 (Deepak Das 65, Amal Das 72 not out, Extras 31; R. Sett three for 62, Arup Bhattacharya four for 53) and 87 (B. Majumdar 42; S. Sensharma six for 33, R. Sett three for 26); Bengal 453 for five dec. (I. B. Roy 120, R. Venkatraman 170, A. Malhotra 64 not out, G. Shome 34 not out; S. Srivastava three for 161). *Bengal 24 pts, Assam 4 pts.*

At MH Stadium, Patna, November 30, December 1, 2. Drawn. Bihar* 341 (B. S. Gossain 51, S. S. Karim 119, Sunil Singh 36, Abinash Kumar 33 not out; R. Sett five for 107) and 53 for one; Bengal 432 for five dec. (I. B. Roy 152, Arun Lal 58, R. Venkatraman 125, S. Ganguly 52 not out, S. J. Kalyani 34). *Bengal 12 pts, Bihar 6 pts.*

At Barabatti Stadium, Cuttack, December 5, 6, 7. Drawn. Bihar 313 (P. Khanna 83, H. Gidwani 86, S. S. Karim 55 not out; S. Mohapatra five for 104, Sushil Kumar four for 89) and 70 for one dec.; Orissa* 249 (B. Mohanty 47, A. Jayaprakash 74, A. Khatua 51; S. Banerjee three for 73, Dhananjay Singh three for 49) and 54 for no wkt. *Bihar 10 pts, Orissa 8 pts.*

At Baripada Stadium, Baripada, December 12, 13, 14. Drawn. Orissa* 378 (S. Das 54, A. Roy 47, A. Jayaprakash 121, A. Khatua 32, H. Praharaj 46; S. Sensharma three for 44, U. Chatterjee four for 90) and 21 for two; Bengal 211 (Arun Lal 34, R. Venkatraman 46, S. Ganguly 31; S. Mohapatra seven for 74) and 303 for five dec. (I. B. Roy 74, R. Venkatraman 45, U. Chatterjee 39, Rajinder Singh 38 not out, S. J. Kalyani 42 not out). *Orissa 14 pts, Bengal 12 pts.*

At Barabatti Stadium, Cuttack, December 17, 18, 19. Drawn. Assam 380 (S. Neogi 46, Zahi Alam 140, R. Bora 37, B. Majumdar 43, H. Barua 43; H. Praharaj five for 97, S. Mohapatra four for 116) and 171 for six (Zahi Alam 58 not out; S. Mohapatra four for 59); Orissa* 404 for eight dec. (B. Mohanty 55, D. Mahanty 51, R. Biswal 70, A. Jayaprakash 78, A. Khatua 45, Extras 34). *Orissa 15 pts, Assam 8 pts.*

At PTI Ground, Agartala, January 13, 14, 15. Bihar won by an innings and 92 runs. Bihar 265 (H. Gidwani 42, S. S. Karim 35; S. Banerjee five for 59); Tripura 51* (S. Banerjee seven for 18, Dhananjay Singh three for 25) and 122 (Vivek Mehra 50; S. Banerjee five for 58, V. Venkatram four for 26). *Bihar 22 pts, Tripura 4 pts.*

Bengal 61 pts, Bihar 60 pts, Orissa 59 pts, Assam 28 pts, Tripura 16 pts. Bengal and Bihar qualified for the knockout stage.

North Zone

At Sher-I-Kashmir Stadium, Srinagar, October 7, 8, 9. Jammu and Kashmir won by an innings and 61 runs. Jammu and Kashmir 383 (A. Aijaz 36, V. Bhaskar 31, A. Gupta 98, S. Chowdhary 127 not out; Shakti Singh four for 105); Himachal Pradesh* 178 (Jaswant Rai 42, Shakti Singh 61; A. Qayoom five for 57, R. K. Gupta three for 42) and 144 (A. Vij 30 not out; A. Qayoom three for 46, A. Peerzada four for 43). *Jammu and Kashmir 24 pts, Himachal Pradesh 5 pts.*

At Air Force Ground, Palam, Delhi, November 11, 12, 13. Delhi won by 179 runs. Delhi 303 (R. Vinayak 46, Sanjay Sharma 45, Sanjeev Sharma 58, Extras 37; M. V. Rao four for 109, A. Bajpayee five for 93) and 237 for five dec. (R. Vinayak 101 not out, K. Bhaskar Pillai 34, Extras 37; M. V. Rao four for 86); Services* 186 (A. S. Wassan five for 59, S. S. Saini three for 38) and 175 (H. Dutta 39, A. Ghosh 35, Extras 31; A. S. Wassan five for 66, P. Jain three for 23). *Delhi 19 pts, Services 7 pts.*

At Punjab CA Stadium, Patiala, November 17, 18, 19. Drawn. Punjab 426 (D. Pandove 78, R. Kalsi 74, Bhupinder Singh, jun. 35, Krishna Mohan 78, Jaspal Singh 49; A. Qayoom four for 125, S. Parvez three for 50) and 211 (A. Kapoor 57, V. Rathore 33, Jaspal Singh 34; A. Qayoom seven for 73, R. K. Gupta three for 48); Jammu and Kashmir* 331 (Nirmal Singh 44, A. Gupta 104, V. Bhaskar 54, S. Parvez 49; Jaspal Singh six for 97, Bharati Vij four for 68) and 35 for no wkt. *Punjab 13 pts, Jammu and Kashmir 12 pts.*

At Indira Gandhi Stadium, Una, November 19, 20, 21. Drawn. Himachal Pradesh* 189 (R. Nayyar 35, R. Dutt 40; C. Murlidharan five for 45) and 261 (R. Nayyar 141 not out, Brijinder Sharma 32; Subramaniam four for 75); Services 244 (H. Dutta 31, S. Bhatnagar 77, S. C. Sadangi 33; A. Sen three for 52) and 174 for eight (A. Ghosh 50, Chinmoy Sharma 34, Swapan Dutta 34 not out). *Services 14 pts, Himachal Pradesh 11 pts.*

At Vishwakarma High School, Rohtak, November 21, 22, 23. Haryana won by an innings and 31 runs. Jammu and Kashmir 91 (Chetan Sharma four for 30, K. Virdi six for 35) and 223 (A. Aijaz 46, Z. Bhatt 51; Deepak Sharma four for 49); Haryana* 345 (A. Kaypee 151, V. Yadav 63, Extras 30; R. K. Gupta three for 91, A. Gupta four for 66). *Haryana 21 pts, Jammu and Kashmir 3 pts.*

At Vishwakarma High School, Rohtak, November 25, 26, 27. Drawn. Punjab 321 (V. Rathore 46, Krishna Mohan 30, Jaspal Singh 78, Arun Sharma 107; Chetan Sharma four for 85) and 196 for four dec. (D. Pandove 59, V. Rathore 48, A. Kapoor 51 not out); Haryana* 284 (A. Kumar 72, A. Kaypee 111, Yashpal Sharma 31; S. Mehra seven for 68) and 79 for three (Deepak Sharma 41 not out). *Punjab 12 pts, Haryana 10 pts.*

At Punjab Agricultural University Ground, Ludhiana, November 29, 30, December 1. Punjab won by an innings and 163 runs. Punjab* 420 (V. Rathore 98, A. Kapoor 68, Jaspal Singh 41, Bhupinder Singh, jun. 70, S. Mehra 47, M. Inder Singh 64; M. V. Rao three for 146, A. Bajpayee four for 115); Services 149 (Swapan Dutta 50, B. R. Singh 31; S. Mehra three for 46, Bharati Vij five for 30) and 108 (Bharati Vij seven for 27). *Punjab 23 pts, Services 3 pts.*

At Paddal Stadium, Mandi, November 23, 24, 25. Drawn. Himachal Pradesh* 139 (Jaswant Rai 44; Harpreet Singh five for 27); Delhi 186 (R. Vinayak 53, Sanjay Sharma 59, K. Bhaskar Pillai 37 not out). *Delhi 10 pts, Himachal Pradesh 4 pts.*

At Air Force Ground, Palam, Delhi, November 25, 26, 27. Drawn. Jammu and Kashmir 230 (S. Parvez 53, R. K. Gupta 38; V. Kadam five for 80, M. V. Rao three for 61) and 170 (A. Gupta 57; S. C. Sadangi four for 28); Services* 281 (H. Dutta 62, Chinmoy Sharma 109, B. R. Singh 61; A. Qayoom seven for 57). *Services 16 pts, Jammu and Kashmir 9 pts.*

At Feroz Shah Kotla, Delhi, November 29, 30, December 1. Delhi won by an innings and 133 runs. Jammu and Kashmir 105 (A. S. Wassan seven for 36) and 199 (V. Bhaskar 62, Extras 33; A. S. Wassan three for 52, Sanjeev Sharma four for 43); Delhi* 437 for four dec. (M. Nayyar 99, R. Vinayak 99, Sanjay Sharma 76, Bantoo Singh 93, K. Bhaskar Pillai 32 not out, Extras 38). *Delhi 24 pts, Jammu and Kashmir 2 pts.*

At TIT Ground, Bhiwani, November 29, 30, December 1. Haryana won by an innings and 50 runs. Himachal Pradesh 107 and 120 (Jaswant Rai 38; A. Singla three for 27, V. Dutt four for 43); Haryana* 277 (A. Kaypee 110, V. Yadav 42, Chetan Sharma 47 not out; Shakti Singh four for 79). *Haryana 20 pts, Himachal Pradesh 3 pts.*

At Gandhi Ground, Amritsar, December 4, 5, 6. Punjab won by ten wickets. Himachal Pradesh* 143 (Shambu Sharma 50; M. Inder Singh three for 3) and 146 (M. Inder Singh six for 60); Punjab 284 (A. Mehra 108, S. Chopra 60, M. Inder Singh 42; Jaswant Rai six for 80) and 7 for no wkt. *Punjab 17 pts, Himachal Pradesh 4 pts.*

At Feroz Shah Kotla, Delhi, December 4, 5, 6. Drawn. Haryana 234 (Deepak Sharma 43, A. Kaypee 49, Chetan Sharma 54, Extras 31; A. S. Wassan five for 71) and 220 for eight (Yashpal Sharma 52, V. Yadav 36; A. S. Wassan four for 89, Sanjeev Sharma three for 44); Delhi* 375 for five dec. (M. Nayyar 86, Sanjay Sharma 51, Bantoo Singh 77 not out, K. Bhaskar Pillai 45, Sanjeev Sharma 54 not out; Chetan Sharma three for 98). *Delhi 15 pts, Haryana 7 pts.*

At Gandhi Ground, Amritsar, December 9, 10, 11. Drawn. Punjab* 174 (Jaspal Singh 48, Arun Sharma 32; A. S. Wassan six for 56) and 332 for six dec. (A. Kapoor 131 not out, Krishna Mohan 46, S. Chopra 47 not out); Delhi 315 (Bantoo Singh 104, K. Bhaskar Pillai 62, K. Azad 81; Bhupinder Singh, sen. five for 69) and 52 for no wkt. *Delhi 15 pts, Punjab 8 pts.*

At Nehru Stadium, Gurgaon, December 9, 10, 11. Haryana won by six wickets. Services 86 (Deepak Sharma four for 26, A. Singla four for 8 including a hat-trick) and 95 (S. Dutta 41, Deepak Sharma six for 37); Haryana* 98 (R. Puri 50 not out; S. C. Sadangi five for 19, M. V. Rao four for 33) and 92 for four. *Haryana 14 pts, Services 6 pts.*

Delhi 83 pts, Punjab 73 pts, Haryana 72 pts, Jammu and Kashmir 50 pts, Services 46 pts, Himachal Pradesh 27 pts. Delhi and Punjab qualified for the knockout stage.

South Zone

At Gymkhana Ground, Secunderabad, November 18, 19, 20. Drawn. Hyderabad* 261 (V. Jaisimha 138 not out; J. Srinath five for 85 including a hat-trick on dêbut) and 308 (Abdul Azeem 46, V. Jaisimha 46, M. V. Ramanamurthy 39, N. S. Yadav 46, N. R. Yadav 64 not out; A. R. Bhat three for 54); Karnataka 338 (C. Saldanha 55, R. M. H. Binny 32, K. A. Jeshwant 94, J. Srinath 39; N. R. Yadav three for 85) and 48 for seven (N. R. Yadav three for 24). *Hyderabad 13 pts, Karnataka 15 pts.*

At Arlem Ground, Margao, November 25, 26, 27. Hyderabad won by an innings and 180 runs. Hyderabad* 473 for seven dec. (Abdul Azeem 35, C. Jaikumar 63, M. V. Sridhar 136, V. Jaisimha 107, Ehtesham Ali 74 not out); Goa 118 (S. L. V. Raju four for 12) and 175 (S. Shinde 114; S. L. V. Raju four for 44, N. S. Yadav five for 69). *Hyderabad 21 pts, Goa 1 pt.*

At Indira Priyadarshini Stadium, Visakapatnam, December 2, 3, 4. Drawn. Goa 453 (P. Amonkar 70, D. Bangera 47, S. Kangralkar 31, S. Mahadevan 90, R. Raikar 52, H. Angle 70, N. Vernekar 46, Extras 33; M. N. Ravikumar three for 69, T. Chakradhar Rao six for 120) and 41 for no wkt; Andhra* 456 for seven dec. (O. Vinodkumar 65, V. Chamundeswarnath 154, M. S. Kumar 128, M. N. Ravikumar 39 not out; U. Naik three for 120). *Andhra 11 pts, Goa 8 pts.*

At Chidambaram Stadium, Madras, December 2, 3, 4. Drawn. Kerala 74 (S. Subramaniam five for 10, M. Venkataramana three for 12) and 75 for four (Narayan Kutty 31); Tamil Nadu* 202 for five dec. (V. B. Chandrasekhar 73, Robin Singh 35 not out; S. Ramesh three for 43). *Tamil Nadu 13 pts, Kerala 5 pts.*

At Chinnaswamy Stadium, Bangalore, December 9, 10, 11. Drawn. Karnataka* 265 (K. A. Jeshwant 32, A. Kumble 58, J. Srinath 34, Extras 32; B. Arun three for 34) and 224 for five (C. Saldanha 42, P. V. Shashikant 63, V. A. Raja 33, G. Reddy 44; M. Venkataramana three for 73); Tamil Nadu 421 for nine dec. (V. B. Chandrasekhar 53, D. Wasu 46, Arjan Kripal Singh 103, R. Madhavan 50, M. Senthilnathan 55, S. Subramaniam 31 not out; A. Kumble five for 134). *Tamil Nadu 13 pts, Karnataka 7 pts.*

At Prakasham Stadium, Kothagudem (M), December 9, 10, 11. Drawn. Hyderabad* 556 for five dec. (Abdul Azeem 145, C. Jaikumar 140, M. V. Sridhar 87, V. Jaisimha 33, Zakir Hussain 100 not out) and 263 for six dec. (C. Jaikumar 44, M. V. Sridhar 101, V. Jaisimha 43, T. Chakradhar Rao four for 64); Andhra 189 (M. F. Rehman 53, K. V. S. D. Kamaraju 44, N. S. Yadav five for 63) and 190 for six (V. Prasanna Kumar 67, K. V. S. D. Kamaraju 57). *Hyderabad 18 pts, Andhra 8 pts.*

At District Youth Services Stadium, Hassan (M), December 16, 17, 18. Karnataka won by an innings and 118 runs. Kerala* 193 (Narayan Kutty 34, P. G. Sunder 34, Nanda Kumar 40; A. Kumble four for 50, A. R. Bhat three for 39) and 119 (S. Srinath three for 46, A. Kumble three for 11, A. R. Bhat four for 46); Karnataka 430 for nine dec. (C. Saldanha 94, P. V. Shashikant 102, V. A. Raja 68, G. Reddy 36, Extras 37; A. Padmanabhan five for 120). *Karnataka 24 pts, Kerala 3 pts.*

At Arlem Ground, Margao, December 23, 24, 25. Kerala won by seven wickets. Goa* 262 (D. Bangera 30, S. Shinde 105; V. Hariharan three for 58, A. Padmanabhan four for 77) and 182 (S. Shinde 31, H. Angle 33 not out, J. Shetty 30; P. T. Subramaniam five for 67, V. Hariharan three for 47); Kerala 271 (Habib Rehman 70, Nanda Kumar 49, P. G. Sunder 55; U. Naik five for 89, H. Angle five for 57) and 175 for three (Narayan Kutty 44, P. T. Subramaniam 45 not out, Nanda Kumar 41 not out). *Kerala 19 pts, Goa 8 pts.*

At Indira Gandhi Stadium, Vijayawada, December 24, 25, 26. Karnataka won by an innings and 43 runs. Andhra* 137 (A. R. Bhat three for 32) and 87 (J. Srinath three for 22, A. R. Bhat four for 36, A. Kumble three for 12); Karnataka 267 (R. M. H. Binny 71, S. Jeshwant 49; T. Chakradhar Rao six for 92, B. S. Mangesh four for 62). *Karnataka 23 pts, Andhra 4 pts.*

At District Level Stadium, Sirsi (M), January 13, 14, 15. Karnataka won by ten wickets. Goa* 283 (P. Amonkar 34, S. Mahadevan 115, D. Bangera 47; J. Srinath three for 59, A. R. Bhat three for 87, R. Ananth three for 68) and 151 (S. Dhuri 52 not out; J. Srinath four for 51, R. Ananth three for 41); Karnataka 396 for eight dec. (C. Saldanha 79, G. Reddy 93, K. A. Jeshwant 33, R. M. H. Binny 77) and 39 for no wkt. *Karnataka 18 pts, Goa 6 pts.*

At Public Stadium, Thiruvala (M), January 13, 14, 15. Drawn. Kerala 334 (Narayan Kutty 59, P. Ranganathan 92, P. G. Sunder 72, Feroz Rashid 31) and 254 for six (P. Ranganathan 41, P. G. Sunder 33, P. T. Subramaniam 43, Feroz Rashid 54 not out); Hyderabad* 486 (M. V. Sridhar 87, V. Jaisimha 38, Zakir Hussain 45, Ehtesham Ali 154, Arshad Ayub 77; A. Padmanabhan five for 140). *Kerala 9 pts, Hyberabad 15 pts.*

At Kodi Rama Murthy Stadium, Srikakulam (M), January 13, 14, 15. Tamil Nadu won by an innings and 78 runs. Tamil Nadu 358 (M. Senthilnathan 63, R. Madhavan 31, B. Arun 141, A. P. Sureshkumar 36, S. Subramaniam 43; B. S. Mangesh five for 76); Andhra* 121 (B. Arun four for 40, A. P. Sureshkumar four for 20) and 159 (O. Vinodkumar 86; D. Wasu five for 40, R. Madhavan four for 13). *Tamil Nadu 22 pts, Andhra 4 pts.*

At Nehru Stadium, Tiruchi, January 20, 21, 22. Drawn. Tamil Nadu* 331 (K. Srikkanth 86, Robin Singh 39, B. Arun 33, D. Wasu 61 not out; Kanwaljit Singh five for 83) and 207 for seven dec. (K. Srikkanth 56, D. Wasu 37, Robin Singh 50 not out; Arshad Ayub three for 72, Kanwaljit Singh four for 68); Hyderabad 342 (Abdul Azeem 41, M. V. Sridhar 82, P. Rameshkumar 89, Arshad Ayub 45; D. Wasu four for 79) and 45 for one. *Hyderabad 14 pts, Tamil Nadu 10 pts.*

At MSP Ground, Mallapuram (M) January 20, 21, 22. Drawn. Andhra* 244 (B. Sudhakar Reddy 32, M. Surendrakumar 33, V. Vijayasarathy 41, K. V. S. D. Kamaraju 50, B. S. Mangesh 30; P. T. Subramaniam three for 45) and 384 for six dec. (M. Surendrakumar 57, V. Vijayasarathy 39, K. V. S. D. Kamaraju 106, K. B. Ramamurthy 104 not out; V. Hariharan three for 109); Kerala 318 (P. G. Sunder 39, P. T. Subramaniam 149, Feroz Rashid 44; S. Krishnamohan five for 90, T. Chakradhar Rao four for 79) and 76 for two (Narayan Kutty 31). *Kerala 14 pts, Andhra 10 pts.*

At Chidambaram Stadium, Madras, January 27, 28, 29. Tamil Nadu won by an innings and 73 runs. Goa 200 (P. Amonkar 40, S. Dhuri 56 not out; S. Subramaniam five for 37) and 174 (H. Angle 44, S. Dhuri 50; D. Wasu four for 59, S. Subramaniam five for 56); Tamil Nadu* 447 for six dec. (K. Srikkanth 111, Mujib-ur-Rehman 137 on début, Arjan Kripal Singh 36, Robin Singh 69, D. Wasu 39 not out; U. Naik four for 152). *Tamil Nadu 21 pts, Goa 4 pts.*

Karnataka 87 pts, Hyderabad 81 pts, Tamil Nadu 79 pts, Kerala 50 pts, Andhra 37 pts, Goa 27 pts. Karnataka and Hyderabad qualified for the knockout stage.

West Zone

At MTB College Ground, Surat, November 18, 19, 20. Drawn. Gujarat* 361 (M. Parmar 50, P. H. Bhatt 92, B. K. Patel 30, N. A. Patel 61, J. P. Saigal 47 not out; R. R. Kulkarni seven for 114) and 159 for four (S. S. Talati 44, M. Parmar 33); Bombay 495 for five dec. (L. S. Rajput 168, S. S. Hattangadi 64, C. S. Pandit 55, D. B. Vengsarkar 101 not out, V. Kambli 72). *Bombay 14 pts, Gujarat 7 pts.*

At Municipal Ground, Rajkot, November 18, 19, 20. Drawn. Saurashtra* 244 (B. S. Pujara 50, A. Pandya 73; M. Narula three for 36) and 198 for eight dec. (S. S. Tanna 66, A. Pandya 55); Baroda 308 for eight dec. (R. B. Parikh 56, K. S. Chavan 110, T. B. Arothe 60; B. Radia three for 107) and 28 for no wkt. *Baroda 13 pts, Saurashtra 8 pts.*

At Nehru Stadium, Pune, November 25, 26, 27. Drawn. Maharashtra 491 for six dec. (S. S. Bhave 203 not out, A. P. Deshpande 55, M. D. Gunjal 131; B. Radia three for 159) and 6 for no wkt dec.; Saurashtra* 384 (B. S. Pujara 61, S. S. Tanna 110, B. Jadeja 30, A. Pandya 30, C. C. Mankad 63 not out; R. T. Yerwadekar three for 89, S. V. Jedhe three for 86) and 31 for no wkt. *Maharashtra 10 pts, Saurashtra 6 pts.*

At Motibaug Palace Ground, Baroda, November 25, 26, 27. Drawn. Baroda* 467 for eight dec. (R. B. Parikh 198, K. S. Chavan 42, A. D. Gaekwad 65, N. R. Mongia 41; D. T. Patel four for 141) and 258 for three dec. (R. B. Parikh 115 not out, K. S. Chavan 80, T. B. Arothe 51); Gujarat 318 (S. S. Talati 37, B. Mistry 75, P. H. Bhatt 51, N. Laliwala 41; T. B. Arothe five for 53) and 53 for two. *Baroda 16 pts, Gujarat 9 pts.*

At Wankhede Stadium, Bombay, December 1, 2, 3. Drawn. Saurashtra 347 (S. S. Tanna 67, S. Pillai 78, C. C. Mankad 36, R. Mehta 30; R. R. Kulkarni six for 125) and 90 for two dec. (S. Pillai 61 not out); Bombay* 358 for nine dec. (S. S. Hattangadi 44, D. B. Vengsarkar 58, A. Sippy 127 not out, S. Limaye 45; B. Radia four for 123) and 16 for no wkt. *Bombay 12 pts, Saurashtra 9 pts.*

At Nehru Stadium, Pune, December 1, 2, 3. Drawn. Maharashtra* 420 (A. P. Deshpande 89, S. V. Jedhe 111, M. D. Gunjal 97, S. J. Jadhav 68; S. S. Hazare three for 105, S. Dukanwala four for 138) and 30 for no wkt; Baroda 579 for nine dec. (R. B. Parikh 45, K. S. Chavan 44, S. Sawant 51, T. B. Arothe 112, M. Narula 176, N. R. Mongia 80, S. S. Hazare 32; S. J. Jadhav three for 91). *Baroda 11 pts, Maharashtra 9 pts.*

At Motibaug Palace Ground, Baroda, December 9, 10, 11. Drawn. Bombay* 399 (S. S. Hattangadi 32, D. B. Vengsarkar 59, A. Sippy 138, S. K. Talpade 47, S. M. Jadhav 37; R. Patel three for 101, M. Narula five for 75); Baroda 173 (K. S. Chavan 59; R. R. Kulkarni seven for 73) and 219 for three (R. B. Parikh 103 not out, T. B. Arothe 33, S. Sawant 39 not out). *Bombay 12 pts, Baroda 6 pts.*

At Sardar Patel Stadium, Bulsar, December 9, 10, 11. Drawn. Maharashtra* 366 (A. P. Deshpande 123, S. S. Sugwekar 44, S. J. Jadhav 47, S. M. Kondhalkar 43, V. V. Oka 50 not out; D. T. Patel six for 102) and 239 for six (S. S. Bhave 59, S. V. Jedhe 64, S. S. Sugwekar 31); Gujarat 469 (S. D. Pathak 57, M. Parmar 155, B. Mistry 37, P. H. Bhatt 86, N. Laliwala 69; D. Kelavkar six for 104). *Gujarat 16 pts, Maharashtra 11 pts.*

At Brabourne Stadium, Bombay, December 15, 16, 17. Drawn. Bombay* 578 for nine dec. (A. Sippy 84, D. B. Vengsarkar 139, C. S. Pandit 100, S. K. Talpade 131 not out, R. R. Kulkarni 50; R. T. Yerwadekar three for 92) and 55 for two (A. Sippy 30 not out); Maharashtra 439 (S. S. Bhave 98, A. P. Deshpande 83, S. S. Sugwekar 99, V. V. Oka 57; S. S. Patil four for 117). *Bombay 11 pts, Maharashtra 10 pts.*

At Municipal Ground, Rajkot, December 15, 16, 17. Drawn. Gujarat 316 (M. Parmar 63, P. H. Bhatt 56, N. A. Patel 41, B. K. Patel 56; C. C. Mankad four for 97); Saurashtra* 384 for eight (S. S. Tanna 82, B. Jadeja 147, R. Mehta 34, B. Radia 54 not out; J. J. Zinto four for 97). *Saurashtra 10 pts, Gujarat 8 pts.*

Bombay 49 pts, Baroda 46 pts, Maharashtra 40 pts, Gujarat 40 pts, Saurashtra 33 pts. Bombay and Baroda qualified for the knockout stage.

Pre-quarter-finals

At Keenan Stadium, Jamshedpur, February 8, 9, 10, 11. Drawn. Bihar were declared winners by virtue of their first-innings lead. Karnataka* 274 (P. Ramesh Rao 32, K. A. Jeshwant 55, S. Viswanath 70; S. Banerjee five for 57) and 170 for four (P. Ramesh Rao 58 not out, A. Kumble 39 not out); Bihar 567 (Sunil Kumar 32, P. Khanna 64, H. Gidwani 229, B. S. Gossain 47, S. S. Karim 103, S. Banerjee 44; A. Kumble three for 140).

At Wankhede Stadium, Bombay, February 8, 9, 10, 11. Bombay won by an innings and 43 runs. Madhya Pradesh 394 (S. M. Patil 185, M. Sahni 73; R. R. Kulkarni three for 103, R. V. Kulkarni three for 59) and 199 (P. Dwivedi 30, M. Sahni 79, S. Lahore 31 not out; Iqbal Khan three for 13); Bombay* 636 (L. S. Rajput 127, S. K. Talpade 97, R. J. Shastri 79, C. S. Pandit 70, K. D. Mokashi 75 not out, R. R. Kulkarni 52, A. W. Sabnis 33, Extras 51; D. Nilosey three for 186, D. Kapadia three for 78).

uarter-finals

Motibaug Palace Ground, Baroda, February 16, 17, 18, 19. Baroda won by three wickets. tar Pradesh* 405 (V. Vats 59, S. S. Khandkar 72, S. Chaturvedi 44, R. Sapru 45, Indrapal gh 46, R. P. Singh 47; R. Patel three for 77) and 189 (S. S. Khandkar 52, R. P. Singh 32; S. kanwala four for 39); Baroda 320 (K. S. Chavan 52, A. D. Gaekwad 122; Gopal Sharma e for 93) and 275 for seven (R. B. Parikh 94, M. Narula 58 not out, S. S. Hazare 37 not out).

At Eden Gardens, Calcutta, February 16, 17, 18, 19. Drawn. Bengal were declared winners virtue of their quotient of 156 compared with Bombay's quotient of 118. Bombay* 590 for e dec. (L. S. Rajput 67, S. S. Hattangadi 135, A. Sippy 60, R. J. Shastri 169 not out, C. S. ndit 64, Iqbal Khan 35 not out); Bengal 312 for two (P. Roy 107, Arun Lal 189 not out).

At Feroz Shah Kotla, Delhi, February 16, 17, 18, 19. Drawn. Delhi were declared winners virtue of their first-innings lead. Bihar* 249 (B. S. Gossain 76, S. S. Karim 62, Sunil Singh ; Sanjeev Sharma eight for 76); Delhi 264 for eight (K. Bhaskar Pillai 35, K. Azad 113 not t, Extras 30; S. Banerjee three for 64, K. V. P. Rao three for 35).

At Gymkhana Ground, Secunderabad, February 16, 17, 18, 19. Drawn. Hyderabad were clared winners by virtue of their first-innings lead. Hyderabad* 416 (Abdul Azeem 103, V. Sridhar 169, V. Jaisimha 40, Ehtesham Ali 58; Bhupinder Singh, sen. five for 123) and 4 (C. Jaikumar 59; Bharati Vij five for 61, Krishna Mohan four for 75); Punjab 203 (D. ndove 67, Arun Sharma 39; Arshad Ayub seven for 45) and 177 for three (V. Rathore 102 : out, Bhupinder Singh, jun. 37).

emi-finals

Motibaug Palace Ground, Baroda, March 2, 3, 4, 5. Drawn. Delhi were declared winners virtue of their first-innings lead. Delhi* 560 (M. Nayyar 58, R. Lamba 146, Bantoo Singh K. Bhaskar Pillai 33, K. Azad 120, R. Vinayak 46, Sanjeev Sharma 44); Baroda 234 (R. B. rikh 61, A. D. Gaekwad 38, N. R. Mongia 41; Maninder Singh five for 56) and 225 for four Sawant 30, N. R. Mongia 101 not out, S. S. Hazare 32 not out).

At Gymkhana Ground, Secunderabad, March 2, 3, 4, 5. Drawn. Bengal were declared nners by virtue of their first-innings lead. Bengal* 539 for eight dec. (I. B. Roy 40, Arun Lal A. Malhotra 258 not out, Extras 39; Arshad Ayub three for 171) and 81 for one (I. B. Roy ; Hyderabad 417 (Abdul Azeem 31, C. Jaikumar 92, V. Jaisimha 50, Zakir Hussain 81, S. Yadav 97 not out; U. Chatterjee four for 110, S. Mukherjee five for 132 including a -trick on début).

nal

Eden Gardens, Calcutta, March 23, 24, 25, 27, 28. Drawn. Bengal were declared winners virtue of their quotient of 54.00 compared with Delhi's quotient of 27.80. Delhi* 278 Azad 93, Bantoo Singh 36; D. Mukherjee three for 74, R. Sett three for 73); Bengal 216 four (Arun Lal 52 not out, R. Venkatraman 39 not out).

RANJI TROPHY WINNERS

34-35	Bombay	1953-54	Bombay	1972-73	Bombay
35-36	Bombay	1954-55	Madras	1973-74	Karnataka
36-37	Nawanagar	1955-56	Bombay	1974-75	Bombay
37-38	Hyderabad	1956-57	Bombay	1975-76	Bombay
38-39	Bengal	1957-58	Baroda	1976-77	Bombay
39-40	Maharashtra	1958-59	Bombay	1977-78	Karnataka
40-41	Maharashtra	1959-60	Bombay	1978-79	Delhi
41-42	Bombay	1960-61	Bombay	1979-80	Delhi
42-43	Baroda	1961-62	Bombay	1980-81	Bombay
43-44	Western India	1962-63	Bombay	1981-82	Delhi
44-45	Bombay	1963-64	Bombay	1982-83	Karnataka
45-46	Holkar	1964-65	Bombay	1983-84	Bombay
46-47	Baroda	1965-66	Bombay	1984-85	Bombay
47-48	Holkar	1966-67	Bombay	1985-86	Delhi
48-49	Bombay	1967-68	Bombay	1986-87	Hyderabad
49-50	Baroda	1968-69	Bombay	1987-88	Tamil Nadu
50-51	Holkar	1969-70	Bombay	1988-89	Delhi
51-52	Bombay	1970-71	Bombay	1989-90	Bengal
52-53	Holkar	1971-72	Bombay		

IRANI CUP, 1989-90

Ranji Trophy Champions (Delhi) v Rest of India

At Wankhede Stadium, Bombay, November 3, 4, 5, 6, 7. Delhi won by 309 runs. Delhi* 4 (Sanjay Sharma 42, K. Bhaskar Pillai 47, Bantoo Singh 136, K. Azad 111, Sanjeev Sharma 4 V. Razdan three for 113, S. L. V. Raju four for 80) and 383 for eight dec. (M. Nayyar 91, Vinayak 67, Sanjay Sharma 72, Sanjeev Sharma 70; S. L. V. Raju three for 93); Rest of In 290 (L. S. Rajput 39, Gursharan Singh 31, S. S. Karim 51, S. R. Tendulkar 39, W. V. Ram 33; A. S. Wassan three for 76, Sanjeev Sharma three for 66, Maninder Singh four for 51) a 245 (W. V. Raman 41, S. R. Tendulkar 103 not out; Sanjeev Sharma four for 45, Maninc Singh three for 51).

DULEEP TROPHY, 1989-90

At Chidambaram Stadium, Madras, December 25, 26, 27, 28. Drawn. Central Zone w declared winners by virtue of their first-innings lead. Central Zone* 641 for seven dec. (Yu Ali Khan 131, U. R. Radhakrishnan 125, S. S. Khandkar 71, P. K. Amre 106, R. Sapru 36, Gujar 38, V. Vats 64 not out, Gopal Sharma 40, Extras 30) and 129 for two (U. Radhakrishnan 32, S. S. Khandkar 60); East Zone 400 (Arun Lal 183, A. Jayaprakash 41, Ganguly 31, R. Biswal 53; P. S. Vaidya four for 76, N. D. Hirwani five for 146).

Semi-finals

At Indira Priyadarshini Municipal Stadium, Visakapatnam, December 30, 31, January 1, Drawn. Central Zone were declared winners by virtue of their first-innings lead. Cent Zone* 628 for six dec. (U. R. Radhakrishnan 52, S. S. Khandkar 73, P. K. Amre 240 not o R. Sapru 93, R. P. Singh 52 not out, Extras 56; A. S. Wassan three for 181) and 12 for o North Zone 434 (M. Nayyar 61, Gursharan Singh 95, Ajay Sharma 117, K. Bhaskar Pil 113; P. S. Vaidya four for 88, N. D. Hirwani three for 183).

At Chinnaswamy Stadium, Bangalore, December 30, 31, January 1, 2. Drawn. South Zc were declared winners by virtue of their first-innings lead. South Zone* 665 (V. Chandrasekhar 146, M. V. Sridhar 81, M. Azharuddin 69, M. Venkataramana 41, Rot Singh 141, S. L. V. Raju 33, Extras 33; R. R. Kulkarni three for 149, S. A. Ankola four 178); West Zone 465 (R. B. Parikh 218, D. B. Vengsarkar 123, S. S. Sugwekar 33, B. Radia not out; S. L. V. Raju three for 113).

Final

At Gymkhana Ground, Secunderabad, January 5, 6, 7, 9, 10. South Zone won by 322 ru South Zone* 448 (V. B. Chandrasekhar 120, M. V. Sridhar 32, W. V. Raman 96, V. Jaisim 32, Robin Singh 44; N. D. Hirwani four for 125) and 527 for six dec. (M. V. Sridhar 43, W. Raman 30, M. Azharuddin 184, V. Jaisimha 73, Robin Singh 128, Arshad Ayub 51 not o P. S. Vaidya four for 144); Central Zone 345 (Yusuf Ali Khan 34, U. R. Radhakrishnan 1 S. S. Khandkar 86; S. L. V. Raju six for 127, M. Venkataramana three for 78) and 308 (Vats 43, P. K. Amre 113, Yusuf Ali Khan 41, R. P. Singh 40; M. Venkataramana six for 9

M. G. KAILIS-CHEMPLAST TROPHY, 1989-90

At Chidambaram Stadium, Madras, September 16, 17, 18, 19. Drawn. Tamil Nadu* 5 (V. B. Chandrasekhar 119, P. C. Prakash 90, Robin Singh 33, B. Arun 104, D. Wasu M. Venkataramana 44); Western Australia 271 for eight (J. A. Brayshaw 30, M. R. J. Vele 41, W. S. Andrews 89, T. G. Hogan 42; K. Srikkanth three for 61).

CRICKET IN PAKISTAN, 1989-90

By ABID ALI KAZI

akistan's domestic season was heralded in late August by the National Jnder-19 Championship, given added importance because Pakistan's team or the Asia Youth Cup in Bangladesh was selected on the basis of perforiances in it. Karachi beat Lahore City in the final to regain the Grade One itle, while Grade Two was won by Gujranwala, who beat Sukkur to earn a lace in Grade One the following season.

Similarly, the season's Wills Cup one-day matches served as a warm-up for he Sharjah Champions Trophy and the Nehru Cup competitions, both of vhich were won by Pakistan, and they brought to notice several young layers who later toured with the national side. The tournament had its share f problems, however. PIA, who lost to Habib Bank in the final, were fined ₹s25,000 for including Azeem Hafeez, who had left PNSC without obtaining "No Objection" certificate from them. And the final itself was delayed by 0 minutes when Javed Miandad, captain of Habib Bank, took exception to he pitch provided at the National Stadium in Karachi and asked for the rass to be mown. When his request was accepted, the PIA team in turn rotested. Their point of view was that once the stumps had been put in place nd the creases marked, the ground came under the umpires' control, and any ecision on mowing the grass from then became their responsibility. Finally he two teams bowed to the crowd's pressure and agreed to start at 10.30 a.m., lthough the incident was not without a final twist: Miandad did not play in he match, which was won easily by Habib Bank by eight wickets.

The season also saw the start of a series to be played each year between the vinners of the previous season's Wills Cup in Pakistan and Wills Trophy in ndia. The inaugural match was played in Lahore in early October between Jnited Bank and Delhi, with the Indian champions winning by five wickets o become the first holders of the Super Wills Cup. It was in this match that mran Khan noticed the potential of Waqar Younis, which led to his being iven a chance in the national side.

The final of the first-class division of the Patron's Trophy was an all-Karachi affair, in which Karachi Whites beat Karachi Blues by one wicket. The competition was played on a league basis among eight teams, with Karachi Blues finishing on top of the league table with six outright wins. Their success owed much to the all-round talents of Asif Mujtaba, who scored 71 runs, including three centuries, and captured 30 wickets with his slow eft-arm bowling. Lahore City, not helped by internal politics and the somewhat strange policy of not selecting players who were already employed by departments and organisations, finished last and, in accord with the ournament rules, were relegated to Grade Two, leaving Pakistan's major ricketing centre without first-class status for the time being. Their place in the Grade One section was taken by Peshawar, who beat Hyderabad in the Grade Two final. In 1989-90, the non first-class part of the Patron's Trophy was contested by thirteen regional teams divided into two groups. Group A consisted of Islamabad, Peshawar, Gujranwala, Lahore City B, Hazara, Dera Ghazi Khan and Dera Ismail Khan; Group B of Hyderabad, Quetta, Lahore Division, Sukkur, Larkana and Sibi.

The format of the Quaid-e-Azam Trophy changed again, being organise on a "double league" basis to provide the players with more first-clas cricket. With eight departmental teams involved, 56 league matches wer scheduled, although because of the weather six of these were abandone without a ball being bowled and sixteen others were seriously affected. Onl fourteen games produced outright results. Habib Bank headed the league b securing 121 points, closely followed by PIA with 120. The semi-finals wer played between the top four teams from the league, with United Ban beating Habib Bank by six wickets and PIA winning on first innings fror PNSC to go through to the final. The final at Gaddafi Stadium, Lahore, wa badly hit by rain and had to be extended to seven days to allow the teams t complete their first innings. PIA were declared national champions whe United Bank, needing to score 288, were bowled out for 236. Rizwan-u Zaman of PIA and Basit Ali of PACO both topped 1,000 runs in the Troph while Sajjad Akbar and Amin Lakhani, both of PNSC, bagged more than 5 wickets. PACO, who finished last, were relegated, their place being taken b Combined Universities, who beat Pakistan Customs in the Grade Two fina

As in the 1988-89 season, a one-day competition was run concurrently wit the Patron's Trophy and the Quaid-e-Azam Trophy, each first-class matc being followed by a one-day game. The winners of the one-day Patron Trophy were Karachi Whites, who beat Karachi Blues by four wickets, an the one-day Quaid-e-Azam Trophy was won by ADBP, who beat Habi Bank by seven wickets. The most encouraging aspect of the season unde review was that all the major matches were televised by the Pakista Television Corporation. This was an important step towards increasing th popularity of domestic cricket, which had recently lost its appeal for th crowds.

The season's batting averages were headed by Shoaib Mohammad of PIA who averaged 83.20 from five matches and 416 runs, thanks to his unbeate 203 in the Third Test against India. Inzamam-ul-Haq (Multan/United Bank had the highest aggregate of the season: with 1,645 runs at an average c 60.92 from 21 matches, including six hundreds, he just failed to overtake th Pakistan record for most runs in a season held by Saadat Ali, who score 1,649 runs in 1983-84. Ten other batsmen passed 1,000 runs, among the Asif Mujtaba, who also took 57 wickets and held 21 catches, the best al round performance of the season. The highest individual innings was 26 posted by Munir-ul-Haq for HBFC against PACO at Sahiwal in a Quaid-e Azam league match.

Aziz-ur-Rehman of Sargodha headed the bowling averages with 42 wicke at 17.76 apiece. The only bowler to take 100 wickets was the Sargodha an PNSC off-spinner, Sajjad Akbar, who finished with 104 at an average c 22.38 and narrowly missed the Pakistan record of 107 wickets, taken by Ija Faqih in 1985-86. Had PNSC won their Quaid-e-Azam semi-final, he migh well have broken the record in the final. Haaris Khan, for Karachi Blue against Lahore City in the Patron's Trophy, Masood Anwar, the Unite Bank slow left-arm spinner, against National Bank, and the PACO of spinner, Ayaz Jilani, against United Bank, performed the season's hat-trick

The bowling highlight of the season, however, was provided by nineteer year-old Imran Adil. Captaining Bahawalpur in the Patron's Trophy, th former Pakistan Under-19 fast bowler captured all ten wickets i Faisalabad's first innings to become only the second Pakistani to take all ter He collected a further five wickets in the second innings, giving him matc figures of fifteen for 158 – a rare return in Pakistan cricket – and yet he finished on the losing side. In the same match the Bahawalpur wicket-keeper, Imran Zia, took ten catches, seven of them in the second innings, and Bilal Ahmed, Faisalabad's wicket-keeper, held eight catches. In eighteen first-class games, keeping wicket for ADBP as well as Faisalabad, Bilal Ahmed effected 50 dismissals, the season's highest tally, and also scored 950 runs with an average of 33.92.

FIRST-CLASS AVERAGES, 1989-90

BATTING

(Qualification: 500 runs, average 35)

	M	*I*	*NO*	*R*	*HI*	*100s*	*Avge*
Mansoor Rana (*Bahawalpur/ADBP*)	13	18	5	1,036	207*	2	79.69
Saeed Anwar (*Karachi Whites/United Bank*)	11	17	1	1,082	221	5	67.62
Inzamam-ul-Haq (*Multan/United Bank*)	21	36	9	1,645	139*	6	60.92
Asif Mujtaba (*Karachi Blues/PIA*)	22	35	5	1,587	170	6	52.90
Shahid Saeed (*HBFC*)	12	17	2	730	111*	3	48.66
Tariq Mahboob (*Multan*)	7	14	2	579	120	2	48.25
Shafiq Ahmed (*United Bank*)	15	21	4	813	130*	3	47.82
Basit Ali (*Karachi Blues/PACO*)	19	34	3	1,479	157	4	47.70
Zahid Ahmed (*PIA*)	16	23	2	984	128	4	46.85
Rizwan-uz-Zaman (*Karachi Whites/PIA*)	18	29	3	1,197	217*	5	46.03
Raees Ahmed (*United Bank*)	13	20	1	868	138*	3	45.68
Tariq Ismail (*Bahawalpur*)	7	14	1	593	149*	1	45.61
Pervez Shah (*Lahore City/United Bank*)	18	29	7	1,001	116*	2	45.50
Sajid Ali (*Karachi Whites/National Bank*)	17	27	0	1,200	108	3	44.44
Shahid Anwar (*Bahawalpur/PACO*)	17	30	2	1,239	165	3	44.25
Atif Rauf (*ADBP*)	10	13	1	517	113*	1	43.08
Manzoor Elahi (*Multan/ADBP*)	16	25	2	964	119	3	41.91
Shahid Javed (*Rawalpindi/Habib Bank*)	15	26	6	826	207*	3	41.30
Munir-ul-Haq (*Karachi Blues/HBFC*)	18	30	0	1,207	266	3	40.23
Aamer Sohail (*Habib Bank*)	13	19	2	680	104*	1	40.00
Shaukat Mirza (*Karachi Blues/Habib Bank*)	19	31	6	997	111*	3	39.88
Zahoor Elahi (*Multan/ADBP*)	18	30	2	1,111	133	2	39.67
Feroze Mehdi (*PIA*)	12	18	0	670	104	1	37.22
Nasir Wasti (*PNSC*)	15	25	3	799	116*	1	36.31
Saifullah (*United Bank*)	15	25	1	866	92	0	36.08
Tahir Shah (*National Bank*)	12	18	2	577	80	0	36.06

* *Signifies not out.*

BOWLING

(Qualification: 30 wickets)

	O	*M*	*R*	*W*	*BB*	*Avge*
ziz-ur-Rehman (*Sargodha*)	270.5	52	746	42	7-47	17.76
ohammad Zahid (*Bahawalpur*)	263.5	51	711	37	6-68	19.21
qbal Qasim (*Karachi Whites/National Bank*)	517.2	148	1,116	58	8-34	19.24
ohammad Riaz (*Rawalpindi*)	349.4	85	881	44	7-90	20.02
auseef Ahmed (*Karachi Whites/United Bank*)	263.4	64	705	35	6-79	20.14
hakil Khan (*Habib Bank*)	294	60	920	45	7-46	20.44
sif Mujtaba (*Karachi Blues/PIA*)	517.1	150	1,191	57	6-19	20.89

	O	*M*	*R*	*W*	*BB*	*Avge*
Haaris Khan (*Karachi Blues*)	376.1	90	1,003	45	7-90	22.28
Sajjad Akbar (*Sargodha/PNSC*)	913.1	198	2,328	104	8-47	22.38
Zakir Khan (*ADBP*)	291.5	53	910	40	7-73	22.75
Iqbal Sikandar (*Karachi Blues/PIA*)	510.4	118	1,349	58	6-52	23.25
Masood Anwar (*United Bank*)	441.4	111	1,159	48	6-52	24.14
Ali Ahmed (*HBFC*)	275.4	44	970	35	5-83	27.71
Nadeem Khan (*Karachi Whites/PACO*)	408.2	82	1,186	41	5-34	28.92
Shahid Mahboob (*Karachi Whites/PACO*)	592.2	96	1,860	60	7-60	31.00
Amin Lakhani (*PNSC*)	667.2	142	1,844	59	5-116	31.25
Raja Afaq (*Rawalpindi/ADBP*)	567.2	118	1,585	50	6-41	31.70
Akram Raza (*Habib Bank*)	489	82	1,322	41	5-69	32.24
Javed Hayat (*PACO*)	418.3	94	1,210	37	6-69	32.70

*In the following scores, * by the name of a team indicates that they won the toss.*

BCCP PATRON'S TROPHY, 1989-90

Note: First innings closed at 85 overs in the group matches.

Grade I

At Bahawal Stadium, Bahawalpur, October 16, 17. Karachi Whites won by an innings and 34 runs. Karachi Whites 347 (Moin-ul-Atiq 83, Saeed Anwar 39, Babar Basharat 50, Ayaz Jilani 82 not out, Moin Khan 40; Mohammad Zahid four for 107); Bahawalpur* 104 (Shahid Mahboob five for 56, Nadeem Khan five for 34) and 209 (Tariq Ismail 81, Naeem Taj 45; Shahid Mahboob four for 69, Nadeem Khan four for 73). *Karachi Whites 14 pts, Bahawalpur 4 pts.*

At LCCA Ground, Lahore, October 16, 17, 18, 19. Karachi Blues won by three wickets. Lahore City* 353 for nine (Sher Ali 64, Pervez Shah 72, Kashif Khan 35, Wasim Ali 72) and 308 (Kamran Khan 39, Sher Ali 120, Wasim Ali 91; Haaris Khan six for 110 including a hat-trick, Sohail Mehdi three for 77); Karachi Blues 325 for five (Munir-ul-Haq 126, Shaukat Mirza 111 not out, Haseeb-ul-Hasan 32 not out) and 337 for seven (Sajid Riaz 119, Basit Ali 74, Munir-ul-Haq 48, Rashid Latif 37 not out). *Karachi Blues 14 pts, Lahore City 6 pts.*

At Pindi Club Ground, Rawalpindi, October 16, 17, 18, 19. Drawn. Rawalpindi* 252 for nine (Raffat Ijaz 32, Shahid Javed 90, Raja Afaq 34 not out; Amanullah three for 41, Aziz-ur-Rehman three for 78, Raja Nasir three for 74) and 266 (Raffat Ijaz 33, Jamal Siddiqi 39, Masood Anwar 30, Nadeem Abbasi 47; Raja Nasir three for 84, Mohammad Nawaz three for 44); Sargodha 226 for seven (Mohammad Nawaz 70, Asad Malik 46; Mohammad Riaz three for 92, Shakeel Ahmed three for 56) and 209 for seven (Maqsood Ahmed 61; Raja Afaq four for 61). *Rawalpindi 8 pts, Sargodha 7 pts.*

At Montgomery Biscuit Factory Ground, Sahiwal, October 17, 18, 19, 20. Multan won by six wickets. Faisalabad 262 (Mohammad Ramzan 43, Aamer Nazir 35, Sami-ul-Haq 41, Saadat Gul 34, Wasim Hyder 34; Inzamam-ul-Haq five for 93) and 236 (Mohammad Ramzan 40, Mohammad Ashraf 93, Sami-ul-Haq 47; Nadeem Iqbal five for 50); Multan* 286 for eight (Zahoor Elahi 54, Inzamam-ul-Haq 139 not out, Manzoor Elahi 40; Naved Nazir three for 101) and 213 for four (Masroor Hussain 84, Tariq Mahboob 72 not out). *Multan 14 pts Faisalabad 8 pts.*

At Bakhtiari Youth Centre Ground, Karachi, October 23, 24, 25. Karachi Whites won by five wickets. Faisalabad* 175 (Naseer Shaukat 38; Ijaz Faqih three for 37, Nadeem Khan three for 57, Babar Basharat three for 5) and 207 (Bilal Ahmed 35, Aamer Nazir 88; Shahid Mahboob four for 51, Nadeem Khan four for 50); Karachi Whites 254 (Moin-ul-Atiq 37 Sajid Ali 30, Saeed Anwar 55, Moin Khan 41; Fazal Hussain three for 107, Tanvir Afzal five for 53) and 129 for five (Moin Khan 42, Aamer Hanif 31; Fazal Hussain four for 45). *Karachi Whites 14 pts, Faisalabad 5 pts.*

At Sargodha Stadium, Sargodha, October 23, 24, 25. Karachi Blues won by six wickets. rgodha* 258 for nine (Mohammad Nawaz 49, Arshad Pervez 131; Haaris Khan five for 67, hail Mehdi three for 58) and 150 (Azhar Sultan 69; Asif Mujtaba three for 39, Haaris Khan e for 54); Karachi Blues 263 for three (Munir-ul-Haq 110, Shaukat Mirza 105 not out) and 6 for four (Sajid Riaz 60 not out, Asif Mujtaba 45; Amanullah three for 48). *Karachi Blues pts, Sargodha 6 pts.*

At Army Sports Stadium, Rawalpindi, October 23, 24, 25. Rawalpindi won by six wickets. hore City* 235 (Fayyaz Shah 59, Pervez Shah 39, Rizwan Qazi 62; Mohammad Riaz five r 83, Raja Afaq three for 66) and 108 (Mohammad Riaz three for 28, Shakeel Ahmed six for); Rawalpindi 250 for seven (Raffat Ijaz 35, Shahid Javed 107, Mujahid Hameed 61 not t; Shahid Ali five for 98) and 94 for four (Jamal Siddiqi 31). *Rawalpindi 14 pts, Lahore City ts.*

At Montgomery Biscuit Factory Ground, Sahiwal, October 24, 25, 26, 27. Drawn. Multan 2 for six (Inzamam-ul-Haq 78, Tariq Mahboob 116 not out, Manzoor Elahi 38, Shahbaz slam 35, Mohammad Shafiq 31 not out) and 375 for six dec. (Masroor Hussain 37, zamam-ul-Haq 81, Tariq Mahboob 66, Manzoor Elahi 104 not out, Shahbaz Aslam 35); hawalpur* 315 (Shahid Anwar 54, Tariq Ismail 63, Naeem Taj 69, Sohail Iqbal 39; zamam-ul-Haq five for 80) and 243 for four (Shahid Anwar 151 not out, Imran Zia 46). *ultan 9 pts, Bahawalpur 4 pts.*

At National Stadium, Karachi, October 30, 31, November 1. Karachi Whites won by ten ckets. Multan 149 (Zahoor Elahi 55; Shahid Mahboob seven for 60, Iqbal Qasim three for) and 376 (Shahid Hameed 37, Manzoor Elahi 119, Inzamam-ul-Haq 89 not out; kharuddin Baloch four for 94); Karachi Whites* 389 (Saeed Anwar 221, Ijaz Faqih 32, oin Khan 53; Shahbaz Aslam five for 33) and 137 for no wkt (Moin-ul-Atiq 85 not out, zwan-uz-Zaman 52 not out). *Karachi Whites 14 pts, Multan 4 pts.*

At Iqbal Stadium, Faisalabad, October 30, 31, November 1, 2. Faisalabad won by 31 runs. isalabad 226 (Nadeem Arshad 35, Bilal Ahmed 47, Tanvir Afzal 57, Wasim Hyder 62 not t; Imran Adil ten for 92) and 139 (Naseer Shaukat 34; Imran Adil five for 66, Tariq Ismail ree for 52); Bahawalpur* 155 (Saleem Taj 52 not out, Mohammad Zahid 35; Wasim Hyder ree for 39, Saadat Gul three for 30) and 179 (Shahid Anwar 53, Mohammad Zahid 33; ashid Wali four for 50). *Faisalabad 13 pts, Bahawalpur 4 pts.*

At Sargodha Stadium, Sargodha, October 30, 31, November 1, 2. Drawn. Lahore City 155 ervez Shah 60 not out, Fayyaz Shah 31; Naeem Khan four for 36, Aziz-ur-Rehman four for) and 352 for seven dec. (Sher Ali 39, Pervez Shah 101 not out, Haider Jehangir 44, Rizwan azi 67, Naeem Ashraf 50 not out; Raja Nasir four for 112); Sargodha* 211 (Anis-ur-Rehman , Asad Malik 37, Aziz-ur-Rehman 43; Pervez Shah four for 43) and 146 for four (Anis-ur-ehman 52, Mohammad Hasnain 31; Wasim Ali three for 34). *Sargodha 7 pts, Lahore City ts.*

At Army Sports Stadium, Rawalpindi, October 30, 31, November 1. Rawalpindi won by 66 ns. Rawalpindi* 206 (Nadeem Abbasi 66; Haaris Khan seven for 90) and 193 (Raffat Ijaz , Nadeem Abbasi 34; Asif Mujtaba six for 66, Haaris Khan four for 99); Karachi Blues 234 haukat Mirza 58, Asif Mujtaba 45, Haseeb-ul-Hasan 45; Shakeel Ahmed five for 52) and 99 lohammad Riaz five for 47). *Rawalpindi 12 pts, Karachi Blues 7 pts.*

At Bakhtiari Youth Centre Ground, Karachi, November 6, 7, 8. Karachi Whites won by ree wickets. Karachi Whites* 330 for seven (Moin-ul-Atiq 37, Mansoor Akhtar 124, Saeed nwar 117 not out; Ayaz Mahmood three for 87) and 74 for seven (Naeem Ashraf four for); Lahore City 171 (Wasim Ali 35; Iqbal Qasim four for 36) and 227 (Babar Zaman 66, ashif Khan 42 not out, Naeem Ashraf 31; Irfan Habib three for 29, Nadeem Khan three for). *Karachi Whites 14 pts, Lahore City 3 pts.*

At Bahawal Stadium, Bahawalpur, November 6, 7, 8. Bahawalpur won by 49 runs. ahawalpur 227 for nine (Abdul Rahim 32, Naeem Taj 32, Mohammad Altaf 32 not out; ziz-ur-Rehman six for 76) and 138 (Shahid Anwar 55; Sajjad Akbar eight for 47); Sargodha* 5 (Mohammad Hasnain 65; Mohammad Zahid five for 44) and 151 (Anis-ur-Rehman 32, zhar Sultan 34, Aziz-ur-Rehman 35; Mohammad Zahid four for 54, Abdul Rahim five for). *Bahawalpur 13 pts, Sargodha 4 pts.*

At Montgomery Biscuit Factory Ground, Sahiwal, November 6, 7, 8, 9. Multan won by 1 runs. Multan 287 (Zakir Hussain 33, Manzoor Elahi 114; Mohammad Riaz three for 57) a 227 (Zahoor Elahi 30, Zakir Hussain 58, Manzoor Elahi 33, Mohammad Shafiq 43; Sab Azhar six for 55); Rawalpindi* 170 (Nadeem Abbasi 46, Mujahid Hameed 35; Manzoor Ela four for 18, Nadeem Nazar three for 73) and 147 (Raffat Ijaz 36, Jamal Siddiqi 33; Nadee Nazar six for 27). *Multan 14 pts, Rawalpindi 4 pts.*

At Bagh-e-Jinnah Ground, Faisalabad, November 6, 7, 8. Karachi Blues won by eig wickets. Faisalabad* 152 (Naseer Shaukat 41 not out; Iqbal Sikandar three for 2) and 2 (Mohammad Akram 37, Mohammad Ashraf 73 not out; Asif Mujtaba four for 39, Iqb Sikandar three for 43); Karachi Blues 288 for eight (Azam Khan 38, Iqbal Sikandar 41, A Dalpat 92 not out, Shakil Sajjad 36; Naved Nazir five for 126, Tanvir Afzal three for 126) a 72 for two. *Karachi Blues 14 pts, Faisalabad 4 pts.*

At Bakhtiari Youth Centre Ground, Karachi, November 13, 14, 15. Sargodha won by 2 runs. Sargodha* 258 for eight (Anis-ur-Rehman 41, Mohammad Hasnain 35, Azhar Sult 64; Tauseef Ahmed three for 72) and 250 (Mohammad Hasnain 100, Maqsood Ahmed : Sajjad Akbar 31; Tauseef Ahmed six for 79); Karachi Whites 148 (Sajid Ali 33, Manso Akhtar 52; Aziz-ur-Rehman seven for 47) and 92 (Aziz-ur-Rehman six for 31). *Sargod 14 pts, Karachi Whites 4 pts.*

At Bahawal Stadium, Bahawalpur, November 13, 14, 15, 16. Drawn. Rawalpindi* 212 f nine (Raffat Ijaz 50, Shahid Javed 45; Mohammad Altaf four for 74, Mohammad Zahid fo for 86) and 396 for seven dec. (Shahid Javed 207 not out, Mohammad Riaz 62, Mujah Hameed 50 not out); Bahawalpur 312 for nine (Shahid Anwar 101, Shahzad Arshad 7 Naeem Taj 32, Sohail Iqbal 31; Sabih Azhar three for 71) and 166 for four (Shahid Anwar 4 Tariq Ismail 88; Mohammad Riaz three for 57). *Bahawalpur 9 pts, Rawalpindi 6 pts.*

At Montgomery Biscuit Factory Ground, Sahiwal, November 13, 14, 15, 16. Karachi Blu won by 160 runs. Karachi Blues 312 for nine (Basit Ali 106, Asif Mujtaba 107 not ou Inzamam-ul-Haq three for 83) and 351 for eight dec. (Basit Ali 127, Azam Khan 34, A Mujtaba 56, Saeed Azad 42, Haseeb-ul-Hasan 33; Shahbaz Aslam four for 79); Multan* 1 (Masroor Hussain 40, Inzamam-ul-Haq 44; Iqbal Sikandar six for 52) and 337 (Inzamam- Haq 107, Zahoor Elahi 70, Tariq Mahboob 54, Shahbaz Aslam 31; Iqbal Sikandar four for 7 Haaris Khan three for 83). *Karachi Blues 14 pts, Multan 4 pts.*

At LCCA Ground, Lahore, November 13, 14, 15, 16. Lahore City won by seven wicke Faisalabad 203 for nine (Mohammad Ashraf 30, Naseer Shaukat 45, Rashid Wali 31 not ou Pervez Shah six for 74) and 167 (Bilal Ahmed 92; Naeem Ashraf three for 38, Pervez Sh three for 77); Lahore City* 140 (Kashif Khan 55 not out; Naseer Shaukat seven for 42, Tanv Afzal three for 31) and 231 for three (Babar Zaman 57, Sher Ali 71, Pervez Shah 51 not ou *Lahore City 10 pts, Faisalabad 6 pts.*

At LCCA Ground, Lahore, November 20, 21, 22, 23. Drawn. Lahore City 337 for sev (Tariq Baig 112, Babar Zaman 135; Nadeem Nazar three for 106) and 321 for eight dec. (Sh Ali 35, Babar Zaman 78, Pervez Shah 49, Kashif Khan 80 not out; Manzoor Elahi three f 37, Shahbaz Aslam three for 62); Multan* 243 (Zahoor Elahi 96, Manzoor Elahi 43; Qais Waheed seven for 74) and 236 for four (Zahoor Elahi 35, Inzamam-ul-Haq 100 not out, Tar Mahboob 42, Manzoor Elahi 39). *Lahore City 9 pts, Multan 6 pts.*

At Sargodha Stadium, Sargodha, November 20, 21, 22, 23. Drawn. Sargodha* 230 (Anis-u Rehman 30, Arshad Pervez 58, Naeem Khan 45; Saadat Gul three for 65, Tanvir Afzal thr for 63) and 7 for two; Faisalabad 217 for nine (Mohammad Ramzan 53, Bilal Ahmed 4 Saadat Gul 32 not out; Aziz-ur-Rehman three for 53). *Sargodha 8 pts, Faisalabad 6 pts.*

At National Stadium, Karachi, November 21, 22, 23. Karachi Whites won by an innin and 7 runs. Rawalpindi* 183 (Arif Butt 54, Sabih Azhar 42; Fakharuddin Baloch four for 1 and 140 (Shahid Mahboob four for 50, Fakharuddin Baloch five for 54); Karachi Whites 3 (Aamer Hanif 31, Sajid Ali 64, Saeed Anwar 133, Tahir Mahmood 31; Mohammad Riaz fi for 82): *Karachi Whites 14 pts, Rawalpindi 5 pts.*

At KDA Ground, Karachi, November 21, 22, 23. Karachi Blues won by three wicke Bahawalpur* 251 (Tariq Ismail 43, Naeem Taj 46, Nasir Jam 49, Extras 35; Haaris Kha three for 64, Iqbal Sikandar five for 90) and 97 (Tariq Ismail 38; Asif Mujtaba six for 1 Haaris Khan three for 25); Karachi Blues 250 (Shaukat Mirza 62, Asif Mujtaba 10 Mohammad Zahid six for 68) and 102 for seven (Mohammad Zahid five for 29). *Karachi Blu 14 pts, Bahawalpur 8 pts.*

At National Stadium, Karachi, November 27, 28, 29, 30. Karachi Blues won by six wickets. Karachi Whites* 231 (Azeem Ahmed 51, Mansoor Ali 31, Sajid Ali 70; Raza Khan three for 53) and 271 (Sajid Ali 108, Azeem Ahmed 52, Saeed Anwar 62; Raza Khan three for 82, Asif Mujtaba five for 19); Karachi Blues 319 for eight (Rashid Hasan 31, Asif Mujtaba 170, Munir-ul-Haq 44; Irfan Rana three for 114, Tahir Mahmood four for 28) and 184 for four (Basit Ali 32, Ijaz Farooqi 40, Asif Mujtaba 72 not out). *Karachi Blues 14 pts, Karachi Whites 7 pts.*

At Sargodha Stadium, Sargodha, November 27, 28, 29, 30. Drawn. Sargodha* 310 (Mohammad Hasnain 54, Azhar Sultan 116, Arshad Pervez 43, Sajjad Akbar 43; Nadeem Iqbal five for 106, Zahoor Elahi three for 72) and 392 for seven dec. (Mohammad Hasnain 130, Mohammad Atiq 45, Azhar Sultan 30, Arshad Pervez 62, Ahmed Hayat 50, Aziz-ur-Rehman 50 not out); Multan 365 for eight (Zahoor Elahi 33, Tariq Mahboob 120, Inzamam-ul-Haq 107; Sajjad Akbar three for 129, Aziz-ur-Rehman five for 102) and 177 for six (Zahoor Elahi 35, Manzoor Elahi 64 not out, Tariq Mahboob 45). *Multan 9 pts, Sargodha 8 pts.*

At Army Sports Stadium, Rawalpindi, November 27, 28, 29, 30. Faisalabad won by 156 runs. Faisalabad 255 for five (Mohammad Ashraf 102 not out, Bilal Ahmed 58, Shams-ul-Haq 37; Mohammad Riaz four for 100) and 195 (Ijaz Ahmed 43, Bilal Ahmed 47, Shams-ul-Haq 31; Mohammad Riaz seven for 90, Shakeel Ahmed three for 40); Rawalpindi* 135 (Azmat Jalil 30; Naved Nazir nine for 50) and 159 (Raffat Ijaz 34, Mohammad Riaz 34; Naved Nazir four for 55, Tanvir Afzal five for 54). *Faisalabad 14 pts, Rawalpindi 2 pts.*

At LCCA Ground, Lahore, November 30, December 1, 2, 3. Bahawalpur won by five wickets. Lahore City 278 for five (Kamran Khan 33, Tariq Baig 103, Babar Zaman 47, Pervez Shah 36; Mohammad Zahid three for 69) and 249 (Kamran Khan 81, Tariq Baig 103; Mohammad Altaf six for 77, Mohammad Zahid three for 59); Bahawalpur* 314 for two (Tariq Ismail 149 not out, Shahid Anwar 82, Saleem Taj 39) and 219 for five (Tariq Ismail 37, Mansoor Rana 30, Imran Zia 50 not out, Naeem Taj 57 not out). *Bahawalpur 12 pts, Lahore City 5 pts.*

Karachi Blues 91 pts, Karachi Whites 81 pts, Multan 60 pts, Faisalabad 56 pts, Bahawalpur 54 pts, Sargodha 54 pts, Rawalpindi 51 pts, Lahore City 43 pts. Karachi Blues and Karachi Whites qualified for the final.

Final

At National Stadium, Karachi, March 10, 11, 12, 13, 14. Karachi Whites won by one wicket. Karachi Blues 250 (Mohammad Javed 42, Haseeb-ul-Hasan 58; Fakharuddin Baloch five for 88) and 341 (Rashid Mahmood 108, Ijaz Farooqi 85, Rehan Farooqi 30, Riaz Sheikh 38 not out; Irfan Habib five for 78, Ghulam Ali three for 50); Karachi Whites* 340 (Zafar Jamal 68, Moin Khan 129, Nauman Mushtaq 33; Rehan Farooqi three for 65) and 252 for nine (Sajjad Abbas 68, Zafar Ahmed 76; Haseeb-ul-Hasan five for 66).

QUAID-E-AZAM TROPHY, 1989-90

Note: First innings closed at 85 overs in the group matches and semi-finals.

Grade I

At National Stadium, Karachi, December 24, 25, 26, 27. Drawn. Habib Bank 271 (Aamer Sohail 53, Anwar Miandad 74, Akram Raza 75 not out; Sajjad Akbar three for 101, Amin Lakhani three for 82) and 311 for eight dec. (Arshad Pervez 92, Shahid Javed 53 not out, Sohail Fazal 46, Tahir Rasheed 36 not out; Sajjad Akbar five for 98); PNSC* 225 for seven (Sohail Jaffer 39, Nasir Wasti 79, Sohail Miandad 48) and 228 for three (Sohail Jaffer 36, Farrukh Bari 52, Mahmood Hamid 78 not out). *Habib Bank 8 pts, PNSC 7 pts.*

At Bakhtiari Youth Centre Ground, Karachi, December 24, 25, 26, 27. PIA won by 152 runs. PIA* 264 (Feroze Mehdi 79, Asif Mujtaba 33, Zahid Ahmed 73; Shahid Mahboob three for 62, Javed Hayat three for 111) and 281 for eight dec. (Feroze Mehdi 63, Sagheer Abbas 31, Zahid Ahmed 51, Iqbal Sikandar 54; Mian Fayyaz three for 97); PACO 235 for nine (Basit Ali 47, Sanaullah 58 not out, Extras 33; Iqbal Sikandar four for 72, Tanvir Ali three for 27) and 158 (Shahid Anwar 50; Asif Mujtaba five for 43, Iqbal Sikandar four for 43). *PIA 14 pts, PACO 7 pts.*

At KDA Sports Ground, Karachi, December 24, 25, 26, 27. National Bank won by 50 runs. National Bank 181 (Tahir Shah 30, Saleem Anwar 71; Inzamam-ul-Haq four for 30) and 206 (Ameer Akbar 40, Saeed Azad 45, Tahir Shah 39; Masood Anwar six for 52 including a hat-trick); United Bank* 132 (Saifullah 39, Sher Ali 49; Iqbal Qasim five for 44) and 205 (Sher Ali 80, Shafiq Ahmed 33; Iqbal Qasim three for 58, Hafeez-ur-Rehman three for 88). *National Bank 11 pts, United Bank 4 pts.*

At Pindi Club Ground, Rawalpindi, December 24, 25, 26, 27. Abandoned without a ball bowled, owing to rain. *ADBP 3 pts, HBFC 3 pts.*

At National Stadium, Karachi, December 30, 31, January 1. Habib Bank won by six wickets. Habib Bank 310 for four (Agha Zahid 44, Arshad Pervez 68, Aamer Sohail 104 not out, Anwar Miandad 71) and 34 for four (Umar Rasheed four for 10); PACO* 134 (Shahid Nawaz 41; Naved Anjum three for 72, Shakil Khan seven for 46) and 209 (Sanaullah 33 not out; Shakil Khan five for 84). *Habib Bank 14 pts, PACO 2 pts.*

At Bakhtiari Youth Centre Ground, Karachi, December 30, 31, January 1, 2. PIA won by 112 runs. PIA* 238 (Rizwan-uz-Zaman 42, Asif Mohammad 58 not out, Anil Dalpat 35 not out; Amin Lakhani three for 90, Sajjad Akbar three for 67) and 171 (Rizwan-uz-Zaman 42, Asif Mujtaba 41; Sajjad Akbar four for 63, Sohail Farooqi five for 56); PNSC 165 (Farrukh Bari 34, Mahmood Hamid 30; Asif Mujtaba three for 29, Iqbal Sikandar three for 43, Tanvir Ali three for 44) and 132 (Mahmood Hamid 30; Zahid Ahmed seven for 14). *PIA 13 pts, PNSC 4 pts.*

At Gaddafi Stadium, Lahore, December 30, 31, January 1, 2. Drawn. HBFC 243 (Faisal Qureshi 42, Rafat Alam 111 not out, Ali Ahmed 37; Barkatullah eight for 86); National Bank* 224 (Sajid Ali 51, Saeed Azad 79; Ali Ahmed five for 83, Shahid Saeed four for 84). *HBFC 8 pts, National Bank 7 pts.*

At Pindi Club Ground, Rawalpindi, December 30, 31, January 1, 2. United Bank won by 3 runs. United Bank* 270 for seven (Inzamam-ul-Haq 39, Shafiq Ahmed 130 not out, Ashraf Ali 40; Khatib Rizwan three for 74) and 185 (Saifullah 58; Mohammad Asif six for 69); ADBP 252 for eight (Zahoor Elahi 72, Atif Rauf 47, Mansoor Rana 57, Manzoor Elahi 34; Masood Anwar four for 94) and 200 (Mansoor Rana 50, Ghaffar Kazmi 32; Masood Anwar four for 60, Shahid Butt three for 71). *United Bank 14 pts, ADBP 7 pts.*

At National Stadium, Karachi, January 6, 7, 8, 9. Habib Bank won by 213 runs. Habib Bank 197 (Aamer Sohail 43, Naved Anjum 36, Sohail Fazal 36, Tahir Rasheed 34; Rashid Khan three for 51) and 416 for six dec. (Aamer Sohail 89, Arshad Pervez 117, Shaukat Mirza 59, Shahid Javed 50 not out, Naved Anjum 39; Rashid Khan three for 107); PIA* 211 (Asif Mujtaba 89, Anil Dalpat 39, Azeem Hafeez 34; Naved Anjum eight for 87) and 189 (Rizwan-uz-Zaman 80, Sagheer Abbas 41; Shakil Khan seven for 63). *Habib Bank 11 pts, PIA 6 pts.*

At Bakhtiari Youth Centre Ground, Karachi, January 6, 7, 8, 9. Drawn. PNSC* 252 for nine (Sohail Miandad 57, Nasir Wasti 80; Shahid Mahboob three for 46) and 221 (Sohail Jaffer 62, Sohail Miandad 41, Farrukh Bari 34; Shahid Mahboob three for 72, Javed Hayat six for 69); PACO 236 (Shahid Anwar 70, Basit Ali 86; Sajjad Akbar five for 71, Amin Lakhani four for 119) and 123 for nine (Sajjad Akbar six for 35). *PNSC 9 pts, PACO 7 pts.*

At Municipal Stadium, Gujranwala, January 6, 7, 8, 9. Abandoned without a ball bowled, owing to rain. *National Bank 3 pts, ADBP 3 pts.*

At Jinnah Stadium, Sialkot, January 6, 7, 8, 9. Abandoned without a ball bowled, owing tc rain. *United Bank 3 pts, HBFC 3 pts.*

At Gaddafi Stadium, Lahore, January 13, 14, 15, 16. Drawn. PIA* 280 for nine (Asi Mujtaba 34, Wasim Hyder 79 not out, Iqbal Sikandar 68; Sikander Bakht three for 76) anc 511 for five dec. (Rizwan-uz-Zaman 120, Asif Mohammad 110, Zahid Ahmed 109 not out Wasim Hyder 107 not out); United Bank 349 for two (Saifullah 53, Moin-ul-Atiq 32, Raee Ahmed 138 not out, Shafiq Ahmed 116 not out) and 89 for one (Saifullah 35, Moin-ul-Atiq 4 not out). *United Bank 9 pts, PIA 5 pts.*

At LCCA Ground, Lahore, January 13, 14, 15, 16. Drawn. PACO* 280 for five (Uma Rasheed 45, Shahid Nawaz 55, Basit Ali 54, Shahid Anwar 34) and 338 (Shahid Nawaz 44 Basit Ali 74, Yahya Toor 50, Javed Hayat 36, Sanaullah 42; Iqbal Qasim five for 105, Hafeez ur-Rehman three for 137); National Bank 286 for eight (Sajid Ali 43, Saeed Azad 79, Saleer Pervez 41, Shahid Tanvir 74 not out; Javed Hayat three for 90) and 186 for seven (Tahir Sha 63, Sajid Ali 81; Shahid Mahboob five for 52). *PACO 8 pts, National Bank 7 pts.*

At Pindi Club Ground, Rawalpindi, January 13, 14, 15, 16. ADBP won by 259 runs. ADBP* 307 for five (Zahoor Elahi 122, Bilal Ahmed 89, Mansoor Rana 35; Sajjad Akbar five for 113) and 293 for two dec. (Zahoor Elahi 133, Atif Rauf 113 not out); PNSC 170 (Sohail Jaffer 55, Mahmood Hamid 42; Mohammad Asif four for 55, Raja Afaq five for 38) and 171 (Sohail Miandad 46, Sajjad Akbar 51 not out; Khatib Rizwan three for 51, Raja Afaq six for 41). *ADBP 14 pts, PNSC 2 pts.*

At Jinnah Stadium, Sialkot, January 13, 14, 15. Habib Bank won by two wickets. HBFC 171 (Munir-ul-Haq 63, Wasim Ali 34; Naved Anjum five for 64) and 215 (Aamer Kurshid 73; Waheed Niazi four for 65, Akram Raza three for 62); Habib Bank* 268 (Agha Zahid 33, Shaukat Mirza 89, Akram Raza 59, Tahir Rasheed 33; Ali Ahmed three for 57, Shahid Saeed three for 40) and 119 for eight (Arshad Pervez 31; Shahid Saeed four for 46). *Habib Bank 14 pts, HBFC 4 pts.*

At Gaddafi Stadium, Lahore, January 20, 21, 22, 23. Drawn. PIA 252 (Zahid Ahmed 104, Iqbal Sikandar 41; Barkatullah four for 88, Afzaal Butt three for 56) and 260 for eight (Feroze Mehdi 104, Asif Mujtaba 32, Haider Nisar 58); National Bank* 290 for three (Sajid Ali 96, Wasim Arif 105 not out, Saeed Azad 66 not out). *National Bank 9 pts, PIA 6 pts.*

At LCCA Ground, Lahore, January 20, 21, 22, 23. Drawn. PACO* 306 for nine (Aamer Hanif 58, Shahid Nawaz 68, Javed Hayat 55 not out; Masood Anwar three for 110, Raees Ahmed four for 123) and 93 for four; United Bank 329 for eight (Raees Ahmed 131, Shafiq Ahmed 52, Saifullah 50, Inzamam-ul-Haq 32 not out). *United Bank 9 pts, PACO 8 pts.*

At Jinnah Stadium, Sialkot, January 20, 21, 22, 23. Drawn. PNSC 221 (Mahmood Hamid 37, Nasir Wasti 57, Mohsin Kamal 31; Ali Ahmed three for 52, Zulfiqar Butt three for 34); HBFC* 253 for eight (Monis Qadri 71, Munir-ul-Haq 70, Wasim Ali 30; Sajjad Akbar three for 42). *HBFC 9 pts, PNSC 6 pts.*

At Montgomery Biscuit Factory Ground, Sahiwal, January 20, 21, 22, 23. Drawn. ADBP 368 for six (Bilal Ahmed 106, Mansoor Rana 67; Akram Raza three for 83) and 511 for six (Zahoor Elahi 62, Bilal Ahmed 57, Atif Rauf 33, Mansoor Rana 207 not out, Mujahid Hameed 94; Akram Raza four for 178); Habib Bank* 212 (Azhar Khan 100; Zakir Khan three for 46). *ADBP 9 pts, Habib Bank 5 pts.*

At Gaddafi Stadium, Lahore, January 27, 28, 29, 30. Habib Bank won by five wickets. United Bank 300 for six (Saifullah 78, Sher Ali 49, Shafiq Ahmed 74, Inzamam-ul-Haq 50 not out; Shakil Khan four for 107) and 184 (Sher Ali 30, Inzamam-ul-Haq 38, Pervez Shah 34; Waheed Niazi four for 66, Shakil Khan five for 71); Habib Bank* 367 for five (Agha Zahid 0, Anwar Miandad 70, Shaukat Mirza 102 not out, Azhar Khan 79) and 118 for five (Aamer Sohail 31, Azhar Khan 39 not out; Sajid Bashir three for 48). *Habib Bank 13 pts, United Bank pts.*

At LCCA Ground, Lahore, January 27, 28, 29, 30. PNSC won by 3 runs. PNSC* 276 for five (Abdullah Khan 84, Sohail Jaffer 39, Nasir Wasti 80 not out; Tahir Shah three for 77) and 167 (Iqbal Qasim three for 55, Hafeez-ur-Rehman five for 44); National Bank 246 (Sajid Ali 43, Tahir Shah 66, Shahid Tanvir 57; Sajjad Akbar five for 86, Amin Lakhani four for 69) and 194 (Sajid Ali 52; Sajjad Akbar six for 81, Amin Lakhani three for 70). *PNSC 14 pts, National Bank 5 pts.*

At Pindi Club Ground, Rawalpindi, January 27, 28, 29, 30. Drawn. ADBP 323 (Zahoor Elahi 51, Bilal Ahmed 58, Atif Rauf 55, Mansoor Rana 60; Tanvir Ali five for 122); PIA* 309 for six (Rizwan-uz-Zaman 67, Feroze Mehdi 70, Asif Mohammad 31, Asif Mujtaba 55, Zahid Ahmed 51; Mansoor Rana three for 87). *ADBP 8 pts, PIA 8 pts.*

At Jinnah Stadium, Sialkot, January 27, 28, 29, 30. Abandoned without a ball bowled, owing to rain. *PACO 3 pts, HBFC 3 pts.*

At Montgomery Biscuit Factory Ground, Sahiwal, February 3, 4, 5, 6. Drawn. United Bank* 313 for three (Raees Ahmed 91, Shafiq Ahmed 120 not out, Inzamam-ul-Haq 63 not out) and 303 for five (Sher Ali 42, Saifullah 30, Ali Zia 60, Pervez Shah 116 not out, Ashraf Ali 46); PNSC 266 for four (Abdullah Khan 63, Sohail Jaffer 85, Farrukh Bari 49). *United Bank 7 pts, PNSC 6 pts.*

At Gaddafi Stadium, Lahore, February 3, 4, 5, 6. Drawn. National Bank 278 (Sajid Ali 106, Saeed Azad 36, Wasim Arif 32; Akram Raza four for 71, Shakil Khan five for 70) and 154 for four (Tahir Shah 30, Shahid Tanvir 40); Habib Bank* 240 (Aamer Sohail 57, Arshad Pervez 37; Barkatullah three for 63, Iqbal Qasim three for 34). *National Bank 9 pts, Habib Bank 7 pts.*

At LCCA Ground, Lahore, February 3, 4, 5, 6. Drawn. PACO* 341 for five (Aamer Hani 78, Basit Ali 128, Umar Rasheed 51; Raja Afaq three for 108) and 314 for seven (Shahi Nawaz 34, Basit Ali 157; Raja Afaq three for 112); ADBP 257 for nine (Atif Rauf 3 Mansoor Rana 59, Ghaffar Kazmi 57 not out; Javed Hayat four for 77). *PACO 9 pts, ADB 6 pts.*

At Pindi Club Ground, Rawalpindi, February 3, 4, 5, 6. Drawn. HBFC* 213 (Aame Khurshid 96, Shahid Saeed 38; Asif Mujtaba four for 60, Zahid Ahmed six for 59); PIA 25 (Asif Mohammad 109, Sajid Khan 30; Kazim Mehdi three for 85, Sohail Khan five for 78 *PIA 9 pts, HBFC 6 pts.*

At National Stadium, Karachi, February 8, 9, 10, 11. Drawn. ADBP 290 for eight (At Rauf 81, Mansoor Rana 93, Manzoor Elahi 64; Rashid Khan four for 102, Azeem Hafee three for 86); PIA* 283 (Feroze Mehdi 90, Sajid Khan 44, Zahid Ahmed 59, Rashid Khan 34 Zakir Khan seven for 73, Raja Afaq three for 62). *ADBP 9 pts, PIA 8 pts.*

At Pindi Club Ground, Rawalpindi, February 8, 9, 10, 11. Drawn. Habib Bank 360 fc eight (Aamer Sohail 46, Arshad Pervez 34, Shaukat Mirza 48, Shahid Javed 101 not ou Akram Raza 46; Masood Anwar four for 162, Shahid Butt three for 99); United Bank* 253 fc seven (Saifullah 32, Shafiq Ahmed 48, Ali Zia 45, Pervez Shah 49 not out). *Habib Bank 8 pt United Bank 8 pts.*

At Montgomery Biscuit Factory Ground, Sahiwal, February 8, 9, 10, 11. Drawn. HBFC 27 (Monis Qadri 72, Wasim Ali 80, Rafat Alam 42; Javed Hayat three for 87, Ayaz Jilani five fc 58) and 601 for nine (Munir-ul-Haq 266, Wasim Ali 78, Sarfraz Azeem 52, Zulqarnain 3 Zulfiqar Butt 54 not out, Extras 40; Shahid Mahboob four for 188, Umar Rasheed four f 105); PACO* 429 (Shahid Anwar 165, Aamer Hanif 89, Basit Ali 31, Zahid Fazal 57, Um Rasheed 41; Wasim Ali six for 51). *PACO 9 pts, HBFC 8pts.*

At LCCA Ground, Lahore, February 8, 9, 10, 11. National Bank won by seven wicket PNSC 176 for nine (Sajjad Akbar 58 not out; Iqbal Qasim four for 65, Hafeez-ur-Rehma three for 71) and 152 (Sohail Miandad 55, Mohsin Kamal 44; Iqbal Qasim eight for 34 National Bank* 240 (Tahir Shah 34, Sajid Ali 108; Amin Lakhani five for 116, Sajjad Akb five for 85) and 91 for three (Tahir Shah 35 not out, Sajid Ali 35). *National Bank 13 pts, PNS 5 pts.*

At Aga Khan Gymkhana Ground, Karachi, February 12, 13, 14, 15. Drawn. Habib Bank 261 for seven (Aamer Sohail 34, Arshad Pervez 36, Anwar Miandad 36, Agha Zahid 4 Shahid Javed 51 not out; Iqbal Sikandar five for 83); PIA 255 (Feroze Mehdi 68, As Mohammad 75 not out; Akram Raza three for 93, Aamer Sohail three for 71). *Habib Ban 9 pts, PIA 8 pts.*

At National Stadium, Karachi, February 13, 14, 15, 16. Drawn. ADBP 169 (Masood Anw 55; Sikander Bakht four for 69) and 36 for no wkt; United Bank* 164 (Saifullah 32; Zak Khan six for 61). *ADBP 5 pts, United Bank 4 pts.*

At Gaddafi Stadium, Lahore, February 13, 14, 15, 16. Drawn. PNSC* 267 (Qaiser Rashee 73, Nasir Wasti 61, Mohsin Kamal 33; Zulfiqar Butt three for 61); HBFC 279 for eig (Aamer Khurshid 52, Shahid Saeed 74, Munir-ul-Haq 59, Ali Ahmed 31; Amin Lakhani thr for 115, Sajjad Akbar three for 80). *HBFC 9 pts, PNSC 4 pts.*

At LCCA Ground, Lahore, February 13, 14, 15, 16. Drawn. PACO 248 (Aamer Hanif 3 Basit Ali 48, Zahid Fazal 30, Umar Rasheed 36, Yahya Toor 32; Iqbal Qasim five for 61 National Bank* 277 (Wasim Arif 35, Sajid Ali 92, Shakil Sajjad 41; Javed Hayat five for 9 Ayaz Jilani four for 73). *National Bank 9 pts, PACO 7 pts.*

At National Stadium, Karachi, February 18, 19, 20, 21. Drawn. United Bank 286 (Sher A 65, Shafiq Ahmed 65, Saifullah 43; Asif Mohammad five for 54) and 348 for eight dec. (Rae Ahmed 106, Inzamam-ul-Haq 135; Rashid Khan four for 99); PIA* 265 (Sajid Khan 103 n out, Zahid Ahmed 64; Sikander Bakht three for 51, Sajid Bashir three for 61) and 230 for fi (Rizwan-uz-Zaman 51, Zahid Ahmed 115 not out; Sikander Bakht three for 74). *United Ba 9 pts, PIA 8 pts.*

At Bahawal Stadium, Bahawalpur, February 18, 19, 20, 21. Abandoned without a b bowled, owing to rain. *ADBP 3 pts, Habib Bank 3 pts.*

At Gaddafi Stadium, Lahore, February 18, 19, 20, 21. Drawn. HBFC* 303 (Monis Qadri 62, Shahid Saeed 61, Munir-ul-Haq 47, Rafat Alam 37, Sarfraz Azeem 42; Tahir Shah five for 74, Shakil Sajjad three for 77) and 244 for seven dec. (Sarfraz Azeem 60, Shahid Saeed 111 not out; Ameer Akbar four for 48); National Bank 272 for nine dec. (Tahir Shah 67, Ameer Akbar 77; Ali Ahmed three for 90, Shahid Saeed three for 66) and 166 for three (Ameer Akbar 51, Saeed Azad 76 not out). *HBFC 9 pts, National Bank 8 pts.*

At Jinnah Stadium, Sialkot, February 18, 19, 20, 21. PNSC won by four wickets. PACO 124 (Basit Ali 47; Sajjad Akbar four for 33, Amin Lakhani four for 30) and 309 (Shahid Anwar 57, Aamer Hanif 52, Basit Ali 63; Sajjad Akbar five for 123, Amin Lakhani three for 108); PNSC* 251 for five (Qaiser Rasheed 42, Nasir Wasti 116 not out, Aamer Ishaq 39 not out; Umar Rasheed four for 75) and 185 for six (Abdullah Khan 37, Sohail Miandad 50). *PNSC 14 pts, PACO 2 pts.*

At LCCA Ground, Lahore, February 23, 24, 25, 26. Drawn. National Bank* 213 for four (Tahir Shah 47, Saeed Azad 101, Shahid Tanvir 51 not out; Zakir Khan three for 59) v ADBP. *ADBP 2 pts, National Bank 2 pts.*

At Iqbal Stadium, Faisalabad, February 23, 24, 25, 26. Drawn. PIA* 283 for seven (Feroze Mehdi 91, Sajid Khan 60, Zahid Ahmed 39; Sajjad Akbar four for 85); PNSC 253 (Abdullah Khan 34, Sohail Miandad 44, Mahmood Hamid 52, Nasir Wasti 50; Asif Mohammad three for 96, Asif Mujtaba three for 97, Zahid Ahmed three for 30). *PIA 9 pts, PNSC 7 pts.*

At Jinnah Stadium, Sialkot, February 23, 24, 25, 26. Drawn. United Bank 96 (Shafiq Ahmed 30 not out; Ayaz Jilani six for 17 including a hat-trick, Nadeem Khan three for 30); PACO* 122 for two (Shahid Anwar 71, Basit Ali 38 not out). *PACO 5 pts, United Bank 1 pt.*

At Gaddafi Stadium, Lahore, February 23, 24, 25, 26. Drawn. HBFC 258 for seven (Monis Qadri 53, Munir-ul-Haq 83, Tariq Alam 54 not out; Akram Raza three for 69) v Habib Bank*. *HBFC 4 pts, Habib Bank 3 pts.*

At Gaddafi Stadium, Lahore, February 28, March 1, 2, 3. Drawn. HBFC 269 (Aamer Kurshid 30, Tariq Alam 55, Sarfraz Azeem 63 not out, Zulfiqar Butt 41; Sajid Bashir three for 60, Masood Anwar three for 77) and 216 (Aamer Kurshid 56, Shahid Saeed 81; Masood Anwar four for 46, Raees Ahmed four for 65); United Bank* 335 for eight (Raees Ahmed 56, Inzamam-ul-Haq 91, Pervez Shah 97, Ashraf Ali 37; Ali Ahmed three for 65) and 123 for six (Inzamam-ul-Haq 34). *United Bank 9 pts, HBFC 8 pts.*

At Iqbal Stadium, Faisalabad, February 28, March 1, 2, 3. Drawn. PIA* 292 for eight (Asif Mohammad 44, Asif Mujtaba 103, Nasir Khan 69 not out; Barkatullah five for 66, Iqbal Qasim three for 66) and 154 for three (Zahid Ahmed 56, Iqbal Sikandar 46 not out); National Bank 268 (Tahir Shah 80, Ameer Akbar 58, Saeed Azad 30, Shahid Tanvir 31; Zulfiqar Ali four for 117). *PIA 9 pts, National Bank 8 pts.*

At Jinnah Stadium, Sialkot, February 28, March 1, 2, 3. Drawn. PNSC* 293 (Qaiser Rasheed 53, Sohail Miandad 64, Farrukh Bari 46, Aamer Ishaq 53, Mahmood Hamid 41; Zakir Khan four for 32, Khatib Rizwan four for 85); ADBP 258 (Zahoor Elahi 53, Mujahid Hameed 73, Maqsood Kundi 53; Amin Lakhani four for 65). *PNSC 9 pts, ADBP 8 pts.*

At LCCA Ground, Lahore, February 28, March 1, 2, 3. Drawn. Habib Bank* 267 for nine (Agha Zahid 73, Anwar Miandad 52, Azhar Khan 52 not out; Nadeem Khan three for 75); PACO 254 for nine (Shahid Nawaz 60, Shahid Mahboob 33, Yahya Toor 30, Sanaullah 30 not out; Abdul Qadir three for 105). *Habib Bank 9 pts, PACO 8 pts.*

At Gaddafi Stadium, Lahore, March 5, 6, 7, 8. Drawn. PIA 321 (Nasir Khan 41, Iqbal Sikandar 86 not out, Rashid Khan 73, Extras 32; Ali Ahmed four for 82) and 362 for nine dec. (Rizwan-uz-Zaman 133, Nasir Khan 59, Asif Mujtaba 72; Ali Ahmed five for 126, Shehzad Ilyas four for 106); HBFC* 285 (Tariq Alam 76, Rafat Alam 56, Zulfiqar Butt 34 not out; Azeem Hafeez three for 89, Wasim Hyder three for 86) and 252 for six (Shahid Saeed 111 not out, Tariq Alam 35, Sarfraz Azeem 33). *PIA 9 pts, HBFC 8 pts.*

At Jinnah Stadium, Sialkot, March 5, 6, 7, 8. Drawn. ADBP* 250 for six (Bilal Ahmed 40, Mansoor Rana 105 not out, Mujahid Hameed 50; Ayaz Jilani three for 50) and 219 (Manzoor Elahi 68, Mujahid Hameed 42; Nadeem Khan three for 60); PACO 268 (Umar Rasheed 65, Shahid Nawaz 67, Basit Ali 70; Khatib Rizwan three for 94, Raja Afaq five for 89) and 158 for eight (Basit Ali 45, Zahid Fazal 40; Zakir Khan three for 44, Khatib Rizwan three for 42). *ADBP 8 pts, PACO 8 pts.*

At Bagh-e-Jinnah Ground, Lahore, March 5, 6, 7. Habib Bank won by eight wickets. PNSC 220 (Ramiz Raja 64, Sohail Miandad 46, Sajjad Akbar 36; Akram Raza five for 69) and 127 (Nasir Wasti 37; Abdul Qadir three for 41); Habib Bank* 264 for eight (Aamer Sohail 52, Arshad Pervez 40, Shaukat Mirza 73; Sajjad Akbar five for 107, Amin Lakhani three for 113) and 84 for two (Aamer Sohail 48). *Habib Bank 14 pts, PNSC 6 pts.*

At Pindi Club Ground, Rawalpindi, March 5, 6, 7, 8. United Bank won by 264 runs. United Bank* 267 for nine (Saifullah 61, Raees Ahmed 32, Inzamam-ul-Haq 104 not out, Pervez Shah 51; Shahid Tanvir four for 64) and 301 for five dec. (Saifullah 92, Saeed Anwar 115, Raees Ahmed 42); National Bank 134 (Sajid Ali 36; Tauseef Ahmed five for 68) and 170 (Saeed Azad 47, Shahid Tanvir 47; Tauseef Ahmed four for 32, Masood Anwar three for 60). *United Bank 14 pts, National Bank 4 pts.*

At Gaddafi Stadium, Lahore, March 10, 11, 12, 13. Drawn. HBFC 277 (Saleem Taj 70, Tariq Alam 67, Rafat Alam 62; Khatib Rizwan three for 23) and 458 for five dec. (Aamer Kurshid 35, Shahid Saeed 107, Munir-ul-Haq 92, Wasim Ali 104 not out, Tariq Alam 50; Qasim Shera three for 52); ADBP* 292 (Atif Rauf 82, Mansoor Rana 87, Manzoor Elahi 43; Sohail Khan five for 104) and 196 for two (Sabih Azhar 100 not out, Bilal Ahmed 70). *ADBP 9 pts, HBFC 8 pts.*

At LCCA Ground, Lahore, March 10, 11, 12, 13. Drawn. PIA* 287 for one (Rizwan-uz-Zaman 139, Nasir Khan 112 not out, Asif Mohammad 32 not out) and 412 for two dec. (Rizwan-uz-Zaman 217 not out, Nasir Khan 45, Asif Mujtaba 112 not out); PACO 326 for nine (Aamer Hanif 62, Zahid Fazal 51, Ayaz Jilani 50, Javed Hayat 31, Nadeem Khan 37 not out, Aaqib Javed 32 not out; Zahid Ahmed four for 94) and 141 for three (Basit Ali 54, Zahid Fazal 52 not out). *PIA 8 pts, PACO 5 pts.*

At Pindi Club Ground, Rawalpindi, March 10, 11, 12, 13. Abandoned without a ball bowled, owing to rain. *Habib Bank 3 pts, National Bank 3 pts.*

At Arbab Niaz (formerly Shahi Bagh) Stadium, Peshawar, March 10, 11, 12, 13. Drawn. PNSC* 264 (Ramiz Raja 60, Sohail Miandad 71, Sajjad Akbar 48; Masood Anwar six for 88, Tauseef Ahmed three for 71) and 350 (Ramiz Raja 63, Nasir Wasti 57, Mahmood Hamid 92, Extras 31; Tauseef Ahmed six for 110); United Bank 283 (Saeed Anwar 35, Raees Ahmed 50, Inzamam-ul-Haq 34, Tauseef Ahmed 77; Sajjad Akbar four for 85) and 150 for three (Saifullah 37, Saeed Anwar 54). *United Bank 9 pts, PNSC 8 pts.*

Habib Bank 121 pts, PIA 120 pts, United Bank 106 pts, PNSC 101 pts, National Bank 98 pts, ADBP 94 pts, HBFC 90 pts, PACO 88 pts. Habib Bank, PIA, United Bank and PNSC qualified for the semi-finals.

Semi-finals

At Gaddafi Stadium, Lahore, March 15, 16, 17, 18. United Bank won by six wickets. Habib Bank 298 (Aamer Sohail 30, Agha Zahid 50, Shaukat Mirza 49, Tahir Rasheed 70 not out; Waqar Younis four for 130, Masood Anwar three for 55) and 169 (Salim Malik 43, Extras 32; Waqar Younis six for 86, Tauseef Ahmed three for 37); United Bank* 229 (Saeed Anwar 35, Inzamam-ul-Haq 38, Pervez Shah 47, Ashraf Ali 35; Shakil Khan three for 48, Agha Zahid three for 44) and 239 for four (Saifullah 85 not out, Saeed Anwar 30, Shafiq Ahmed 64, Inzamam-ul-Haq 32).

At National Stadium, Karachi, March 15, 16, 17, 18. PIA were declared winners by virtue of their first-innings lead. PNSC 269 for nine (Farrukh Bari 48, Nasir Wasti 33, Mahmood Hamid 116 not out; Iqbal Sikandar three for 72) and 292 (Abdullah Khan 53, Ramiz Raja 36, Sohail Jaffer 81; Rashid Khan four for 65); PIA* 321 for seven (Rizwan-uz-Zaman 117, Asif Mujtaba 110, Asif Mohammad 35; Amin Lakhani four for 120) and 145 for four (Asif Mujtaba 60 not out; Sajjad Akbar three for 37).

Final

At Gaddafi Stadium, Lahore, March 20, 21, 22, 23, 24, 25, 26. PIA were declared winners by virtue of their first-innings lead. PIA 287 (Nasir Khan 53, Asif Mujtaba 38, Zahid Ahmed 128; Waqar Younis five for 84); United Bank* 236 (Saifullah 34, Raees Ahmed 85, Waqar Younis 51; Azeem Hafeez four for 76, Wasim Hyder three for 44).

QUAID-E-AZAM TROPHY WINNERS

1953-54	Bahawalpur	1974-75	Punjab A
1954-55	Karachi	1975-76	National Bank
1956-57	Punjab	1976-77	United Bank
1957-58	Bahawalpur	1977-78	Habib Bank
1958-59	Karachi	1978-79	National Bank
1959-60	Karachi	1979-80	PIA
1961-62	Karachi Blues	1980-81	United Bank
1962-63	Karachi A	1981-82	National Bank
1963-64	Karachi Blues	1982-83	United Bank
1964-65	Karachi Blues	1983-84	National Bank
1966-67	Karachi	1984-85	United Bank
1968-69	Lahore	1985-86	Karachi
1969-70	PIA	1986-87	National Bank
1970-71	Karachi Blues	1987-88	PIA
1972-73	Railways	1988-89	ADBP
1973-74	Railways	1989-90	PIA

LIMITED-OVERS FINALS

†Wills Cup, 1989-90

At National Stadium, Karachi, September 29. Habib Bank won by eight wickets. PIA 177 (46.3 overs) (Rizwan-uz-Zaman 30, Shoaib Mohammad 51; Agha Zahid three for 20, Akram Raza three for 34); Habib Bank* 178 for two (42.3 overs) (Agha Zahid 60, Aamer Sohail 73).

†Super Wills Cup, 1989-90

At Gaddafi Stadium, Lahore, October 6. Delhi won by five wickets. United Bank 243 for five (50 overs) (Mansoor Akhtar 89, Saeed Anwar 74); Delhi* 244 for five (48 overs) (M. Nayyar 63, R. Lamba 40, K. Bhaskar Pillai 74 not out, K. Azad 35).

†One-day Patron's Trophy, 1989-90

At National Stadium, Karachi, March 9. Karachi Whites won by four wickets. Karachi Blues* 191 for six (40 overs) (Sajid Riaz 88, Ijaz Farooqi 45 retired hurt; Fakharuddin Baloch three for 45); Karachi Whites 192 for six (38.4 overs) (Zafar Jamal 62, Azeem Ahmed 56).

†One-day Quaid-e-Azam Trophy, 1989-90

At National Stadium, Karachi, March 25. ADBP won by seven wickets. Habib Bank 247 for six (39 overs) (Agha Zahid 98, Anwar Miandad 66, Salim Malik 31); ADBP* 248 for three (36 overs) (Bilal Ahmed 87, Mansoor Rana 52 not out, Manzoor Elahi 41 not out).

CRICKET IN SRI LANKA, 1989-90

By GERRY VAIDYASEKERA

The 1989-90 Division I tournament for the Lakspray Trophy, Sri Lanka's premier competition, got under way in a somewhat low key on a rain-restricted day in early October. But with the advent of 1990, and a return of peace into the country, cricket took a turn for the better, with keen competition developing among the leading players for places in the Sri Lankan team to be selected for the Austral-Asia Cup in Sharjah in April.

In the final round of the Lakspray, contested by the top nine clubs from the preliminary series, a close contest ensued between Sinhalese SC (SSC), Panadura SC and Moratuwa SC. The final-round matches, accorded first-class status by the Board of Control, were of three days' duration, and when the last of them finished early in March, SSC headed Panadura by just 1.135 points to win the championship. Only a three-point margin separated the top three clubs.

A feature of the season was the inability of Nondescripts and Colombo Cricket Club, two strong teams of the past, to qualify for the final round. SSC, however, were undisputed champions. They maintained an unbeaten record throughout the Lakspray Trophy tournament, and their six wins in eight matches in the first-class round included victory over second-placed Panadura by an innings and 231 runs, with a day to spare, the highest margin in Sri Lankan first-class cricket. They were ably led by Mahinda Halangoda, their left-arm medium-pace bowler and all-rounder, whose figures of eight for 64 and seven for 27 in the match against Sinha SC at Maitland Place included a hat-trick. This was easily the best bowling performance of a season in which bowlers generally reaped a rich harvest. In addition to winning the Lakspray Trophy, SSC made their season a memorable one by winning the Brown's Trophy and the Kandos Trophy, thus landing the three most coveted prizes in Sri Lankan cricket.

The Lakspray Award for the Best Bowler was won by the Galle captain, Jayananda Warnaweera. A right-arm medium-pace and off-break bowler, he was the first to take 100 wickets in the season, doing so on February 11, and he set a new record for the Lakspray with 124 wickets, bettering his return of 121 wickets in 1985-86. Having taken 53 wickets in the preliminary round of the competition, he took 71 more in the first-class matches at an average of 13.47. Warnaweera was also named the Outstanding Cricketer of the Series. But while he had performed well in the Lakspray tournament for a number of years, doubts over his mode of delivery had limited his Test appearances to just one against Pakistan in 1985-86.

A new face, Ajith Wasantha of Moratuwa, headed the batting averages with a first-class aggregate of 519 runs at 57.66 to win the Best Batsman's prize, while another newcomer, Sinha's Rohita Ranjith, was the leading all-rounder, scoring 462 runs and capturing 23 wickets in the final rounds. Rupenath Wickremaratne of Colts hit the fastest hundred of the season, off 69 balls, in scoring 134 against Sinha, and Nishan Dhanasinghe, with 215 for Sinha against Galle at Katunayake, recorded the only double-hundred in a bowler's season.

In June 1990, the much desired inter-provincial competition, officially entitled the Singer Inter-Provincial Cricket Tournament for the President's Trophy, was launched. It comprised six matches of first-class status between teams representing Central, North-Western, Southern and Western provinces and was won by Western Province. Led by Arjuna Ranatunga, the captain of Sri Lanka, Western were the only province to win a match, defeating Southern by three wickets at Galle.

In winning the under-23 limited-overs Brown's Trophy, the first inter-club tournament of the 1989-90 season, SSC routed their arch-rivals, Nondescripts, in the final. All Division I clubs took part, with the exception of Saracens and the four teams which reached the final round of the Division II (Section A) tournament, and the 26 participants were divided into four groups, with the first two from each group qualifying for the quarter-finals. In the final of the Kandos Trophy under-23 limited-overs tournament, SSC beat Colombo CC by virtue of a faster run-rate in an interrupted match.

An invitation tournament for the six clubs which had been eliminated from the Division I Lakspray tournament after the preliminary matches was held for the first time. Sponsored by Delmege Forsyth, it was known as the Delmege Trophy (Division I, Section B) Tournament and was won by Tamil Union. In their match against Bloomfield at Sara Stadium, Tamil Union ran up a total of 690 for four, the highest of the season. In the same competition, Nomads were debarred by the Tournament Committee of the Board of Control for refusing to continue a match after their batsmen walked off the field when the umpire would not revoke his earlier decision to give one of them out.

Sri Lanka's Chaminda Handunnettige, a stylish right-hand batsman from Nalanda College, won the Player of the Series trophy at the inaugural Asia Youth Cup, played in Bangladesh in December. He had the best batting average in the seven-nation tournament, with a top score of 99 (run out) against Malaysia. At home, meanwhile, it was pleasing to note that, after a lapse of some years, schools cricket was revived in Jaffna in the Northern province, with fifteen schools taking part.

LAKSPRAY TROPHY FIRST-CLASS AVERAGES, 1989-90

BATTING

(Qualification: 300 runs)

	M	*I*	*NO*	*R*	*HI*	*100s*	*Avge*
V. A. Wasantha (*Moratuwa*)	8	10	1	519	134	2	57.66
. A. W. Gunawardene (*SSC*)	7	11	1	469	96	0	46.90
. M. R. Ranjith (*Sinha*)	8	13	1	462	124	1	38.50
. S. G. Bulankulame (*Colts*)	7	12	1	420	103	1	38.18
. R. N. S. Fernando (*Air Force*)	6	9	0	335	110	1	37.22
. N. Ranasinghe (*BRC*)	7	9	0	329	65	0	36.55
. M. N. C. Dhanasinghe (*Sinha*)	6	11	0	394	215	2	35.81
. G. Abeynaike (*SSC*)	7	10	1	319	66	0	35.44
. Mendis (*Colts*)	7	13	1	401	95*	0	33.41
Thenuwara (*Panadura*)	8	14	2	398	86*	0	33.16
de Zoysa (*BRC*)	7	14	0	460	127	1	32.85
. Ranatunga (*Moratuwa*)	8	12	1	346	82	0	31.45

	M	I	NO	R	HI	100s	Avge
S. L. Anthonisz (*SSC*)	7	11	0	335	91	0	30.45
A. Bulankulame (*Colts*)	8	13	2	333	83*	0	30.27
C. M. Wickremasinghe (*Moratuwa*)	8	11	0	323	115	1	29.36
S. Sooriyarachchi (*Panadura*)	8	14	1	340	88	0	26.15
S. S. K. Gallage (*Air Force*)	8	13	1	302	62	0	25.16
W. M. Janaka Kumudu (*Sinha*)	8	13	0	310	72	0	23.84

* *Signifies not out.*

BOWLING

(Qualification: 20 wickets)

	O	M	R	W	BB	Avge
M. B. Halangoda (*SSC*)	152	35	424	43	8-64	9.86
K. P. J. Warnaweera (*Galle*)	338.5	72	957	71	7-16	13.47
F. S. Ahangama (*SSC*)	192	49	480	33	7-30	14.54
S. Jayawardene (*Panadura*)	203	23	525	36	6-30	14.58
C. M. Wickremasinghe (*Moratuwa*)	184	38	399	24	4-34	16.62
N. Ranatunga (*Moratuwa*)	199	61	452	27	6-33	16.74
R. G. C. E. Wijesuriya (*Moratuwa*)	266	69	489	28	6-51	17.46
K. A. P. S. Angulugaha (*Air Force*)	122	26	397	22	5-100	18.04
T. Ahamath (*BRC*)	186	44	560	29	6-42	19.31
K. Perera (*Old Cambrians*)	255	47	823	40	7-60	20.57
G. J. Woutersz (*BRC*)	224	60	487	23	4-59	21.17
K. G. Priyantha (*Air Force*)	149	11	578	26	6-56	22.23
S. D. Anurasiri (*Panadura*)	253.3	89	890	40	5-50	22.25
P. Milton (*Sinha*)	244	23	967	40	7-89	24.17
A. Ratnasiri (*Colts*)	172	23	657	27	6-26	24.33
H. M. R. Ranjith (*Sinha*)	217	33	788	23	5-61	34.26

LAKSPRAY TROPHY, 1989-90

	P	W	L	1st Inns Win	1st Inns Loss	No Result	Points
Sinhalese SC (SSC)	8	6	0	1	0	1	88.615
Panadura	8	5	1	2	0	0	87.480
Moratuwa	8	3	1	3	0	1	85.485
Galle	8	3	3	0	1	1	60.545
Air Force	8	1	5	1	0	1	40.110
Colts	8	1	1	2	3	1	39.390
Sinha	8	0	4	2	1	1	36.690
Burgher Recreation Club	8	1	3	0	3	1	31.590
Old Cambrians	8	0	2	1	4	1	28.29

Notes: Clubs were penalised points for slow over-rates and incomplete or delayed score-sheet as follows: Sinhalese SC – 2.250 pts; Panadura – 0.050 pts; Moratuwa – 0.050 pts; Galle – 0.350 pts; Air Force – 1.500 pts; Colts – 5.400 pts; Sinha – 0.200 pts; Burgher Recreation Club – 4.350 pts; Old Cambrians – 2.200 pts.

The preliminary round matches were not considered first-class.

At Sinhalese Sports Club Ground, Colombo, January 5, 6, 7. Drawn. Moratuwa 163 for si (A. Wickrematillake 39, W. A. Wasantha 61) v Sinhalese Sports Club.

At Burgher Recreation Club Ground, Colombo, January 5, 6, 7. Drawn. Burghe Recreation Club 71 for four (A. N. Ranasinghe 32; H. M. R. Ranjith four for 31) v Sinh Sports Club.

At Air Force Ground, Katunayake, January 5, 6, 7. Drawn. Air Force 120 for five (A. D. N. R. de Alwis 37, S. S. K. Gallage 37; N. Peiris four for 13) v Old Cambrians.

At The Esplanade, Galle, January 5, 6, 7. Drawn. Colts 112 (U. Hettiarachchi 47; K. P. J. Warnaweera three for 31); Galle 95 for eight (S. Wijesiri 35; G. Goonasena three for 35, Rupanath Wickremaratne three for 28).

At Panadura Ground, Panadura, January 12, 13, 14. Drawn. Panadura 279 (S. Sooriyarachchi 88, P. M. V. Deshapriya 45, S. D. Anurasiri 74; P. Milton seven for 123) and 281 for three dec. (K. Sanjeewa 60, K. P. J. A. de Silva 47, S. Thenuwara 86 not out, S. Sooriyarachchi 63); Sinha Sports Club 189 (H. M. R. Ranjith 37; S. Jayawardene six for 80) and 167 for six (W. M. Janaka Kumudu 30, K. S. Asoka 46).

At Air Force Ground, Katunayake, January 12, 13, 14. Sinhalese Sports Club won by eight wickets. Air Force 192 (R. A. N. R. Ratnayake 30, E. R. N. S. Fernando 59, N. P. Jayatillake 35; F. S. Ahangama four for 44, M. B. Halangoda three for 60) and 167 (S. S. K. Gallage 56, W. L. R. P. Rodrigo 43; R. Jayawardene seven for 39); Sinhalese Sports Club 336 for eight dec. (S. L. Anthonisz 91, A. A. W. Gunawardene 85, R. G. Abeynaike 32, U. N. K. Fernando 31; P. G. S. R. Ariyathilake four for 52, P. T. S. Fernando three for 118) and 26 for two.

At Colts Ground, Colombo, January 12, 13, 14. Drawn. Colts 86 (H. H. Devapriya 42; N. Ranatunga six for 33) and 403 for four (D. S. G. Bulankulame 87, H. H. Devapriya 93, W. Fernando 111, A. Bulankulame 83 not out); Moratuwa 275 (A. Wickrematillake 60, R. Weerawardene 39, N. Ranatunga 68, L. R. Fernando 43; G. Goonasena four for 72, A. Ratnasiri three for 70).

At Burgher Recreation Club Ground, Colombo, January 12, 13, 14. Galle won by seven wickets. Burgher Recreation Club 131 (K. P. J. Warnaweera seven for 43, H. Munasinghe three for 29) and 216 (A. N. Ranasinghe 61; K. P. J. Warnaweera six for 104, H. Munasinghe three for 46); Galle 254 (S. Fonseka 67, G. Liyanage 31, G. de Silva 36, K. Weerasinghe 33; N. M. Soysa five for 52, G. J. Woutersz four for 89) and 97 for three (G. de Silva 31 not out).

At Colts Ground, Colombo, January 19, 20, 21. Colts won by an innings and 37 runs. Sinha Sports Club 70 (A. Ratnasiri six for 26) and 289 (K. S. Asoka 67, H. M. N. C. Dhanasinghe 109, H. M. R. Ranjith 44; S. Munaweera four for 66); Colts 396 (P. Dissanayake 55, A. Hettiarachchi 51, H. H. Devapriya 47, Rupanath Wickremaratne 134, S. Munaweera 65; P. Milton six for 108).

At Burgher Recreation Ground, Colombo, January 19, 20, 21. Burgher Recreation Club won by 68 runs. Burgher Recreation Club 209 (P. de Zoysa 57, T. Ahamath 48; P. T. S. Fernando four for 45) and 146 (N. Pathirage 31, K. L. S. Sirisena 52 not out; R. N. Weerakkody five for 46, K. A. P. S. Angulugaha four for 42); Air Force 81 (T. Ahamath six for 42, K. L. S. Sirisena three for 18) and 206 (W. L. R. P. Rodrigo 66, E. R. N. S. Fernando 41; T. Ahamath five for 55).

At Tyronne Fernando Stadium, Moratuwa, January 19, 20, 21. Drawn. Panadura 208 (S. Thenuwara 75, S. Sooriyarachchi 34; K. Perera five for 64) and 157 (M. de Mel 35, S. D. Anurasiri 44; K. Perera seven for 60); Old Cambrians 127 (S. D. Anurasiri four for 35) and 111 for seven (S. D. Anurasiri three for 15).

At The Esplanade, Galle, January 19, 20, 21. Sinhalese Sports Club won by 172 runs. Sinhalese Sports Club 172 (A. A. W. Gunawardene 38, S. Ranatunga 33, B. E. A. Rajadurai 30; H. Munasinghe seven for 55, K. P. J. Warnaweera three for 64) and 170 for nine dec. (S. L. Anthonisz 56, S. Ranatunga 53 not out; K. P. J. Warnaweera seven for 54); Galle 58 (M. B. Halangoda five for 7, R. Jayawardene four for 22) and 112 (O. A. P. Udayaratne three for 15).

At Tyronne Fernando Stadium, Moratuwa, January 26, 27, 28. Panadura won by two wickets. Moratuwa 87 (S. Jayawardene six for 40) and 151 (W. A. Wasantha 53 not out, R. G. C. E. Wijesuriya 39; S. Jayawardene four for 70, M. Fernando three for 18, S. D. Anurasiri three for 24); Panadura 135 (K. P. J. A. de Silva 43; N. Ranatunga five for 44) and 104 for eight (M. P. A. Cooray three for 49).

At Burgher Recreation Club Ground, Colombo, January 26, 27, 28. Drawn. Burgher Recreation Club 241 (S. Dissanayake 56, G. J. Woutersz 46; K. Perera five for 69) and 304 for four dec. (P. de Zoysa 56, J. Perera 100 not out, A. N. Ranasinghe 65); Old Cambrians 298 (N. Peiris 50, A. Fernando 78, P. L. J. Fernando 53; T. Ahamath five for 95, N. M. Soysa three for 74) and 116 for three (A. Fernando 36 not out, S. de Silva 30 not out).

At The Esplanade, Galle, January 26, 27, 28. Galle won by ten wickets. Air Force 138 (K. P. J. Warnaweera five for 27) and 56 (K. P. J. Warnaweera seven for 16); Galle 182 (H. Munasinghe 38, L. W. Loos 46; K. G. Priyantha six for 52) and 15 for no wkt.

At Sinhalese Sports Club Ground, Colombo, January 26, 27, 28. Drawn. Colts 194 (A. Bulankulame 35, G. Goonasena 41; F. S. Ahangama three for 65) and 100 for one (C. Mendis 44, D. S. G. Bulankulame 50 not out); Sinhalese Sports Club 442 (S. L. Anthonisz 46, A. A. W. Gunawardene 39, S. Ranatunga 38, R. G. Abeynaike 66, C. N. Fernando 63, B. E. A. Rajadurai 65, M. B. Halangoda 73 not out; A. Ratnasiri three for 115, Rupanath Wickremaratne three for 57, A. Liyanage three for 80).

At Sinhalese Sports Club Ground, Colombo, February 2, 3, 4. Sinhalese Sports Club won by an innings and 110 runs. Sinha Sports Club 121 (H. M. R. Ranjith 65; M. B. Halangoda eight for 64) and 61 (M. B. Halangoda seven for 27 including a hat-trick, F. S. Ahangama three for 28); Sinhalese Sports Club 292 (W. N. Silva 63, R. Jayawardene 80, U. N. K. Fernando 38, C. N. Fernando 45; P. Milton seven for 99).

At Tyronne Fernando Stadium, Moratuwa, February 2, 3, 4. Drawn. Old Cambrians 151 (A. Fernando 31, D. de Silva 57; R. G. C. E. Wijesuriya three for 35) and 217 for seven (L. Dharmasiri 50, D. Rajapakse 98); Moratuwa 378 (A. Wickrematillake 46, W. A. Wasantha 134, M. P. A. Cooray 50; H. Mendis four for 76, K. Perera three for 139).

At Burgher Recreation Club Ground, Colombo, February 2, 3, 4. Panadura won by eight wickets. Burgher Recreation Club 121 (G. J. Woutersz 35; Ravin Wickremaratne three for 26, S. D. Anurasiri three for 15) and 107 (D. S. B. P. Kuruppu 38; S. D. Anurasiri four for 29, M. de Mel four for 25); Panadura 128 (T. Ahamath four for 32) and 102 for two (K. P. J. A. de Silva 44, S. Thenuwara 44 not out).

At Colts Ground, Colombo, February 2, 3, 4. Drawn. Colts 290 (A. Hettiarachchi 50, P. Dissanayake 66, Rupanath Wickremaratne 56, P. T. S. Fernando three for 68) and 220 (C. Mendis 95 not out, A. Bulankulame 35; K. G. Priyantha four for 81, P. T. S. Fernando three for 38); Air Force 302 (S. S. K. Gallage 49, H. M. R. Herath 30, E. R. N. S. Fernando 110; A. Ratnasiri three for 82, E. Jayatillake three for 78, G. Goonasena three for 63) and 30 for no wkt.

At Tyronne Fernando Stadium, Moratuwa, February 9, 10, 11. Drawn. Burgher Recreation Club 133 (A. N. Ranasinghe 54; C. M. Wickremasinghe four for 51) and 232 (P. de Zoysa 64, A. N. Ranasinghe 46, N. Pathirage 42 not out; R. G. C. E. Wijesuriya three for 50, C. M. Wickremasinghe three for 73); Moratuwa 298 (R. Weerawardene 36, N. Ranatunga 42, W. A. Wasantha 100, R. Kumarsiri 34; N. Amerasinghe four for 53, T. Ahamath three for 96) and 64 for three.

At Air Force Ground, Katunayake, February 9, 10, 11. Air Force won by an innings and 173 runs. Sinha Sports Club 96 (K. S. Asoka 37; K. G. Priyantha five for 41, J. S. I. Wijemanne three for 12) and 113 (K. G. Priyantha five for 64, K. A. P. S. Angulugaha four for 32); Air Force 382 (A. D. N. R. de Alwis 85, W. L. R. P. Rodrigo 38, E. R. N. S. Fernando 72, R. N. Weerakkody 32, J. S. I. Wijemanne 50; H. M. R. Ranjith five for 110, P. Milton four for 153).

At The Esplanade, Galle, February 9, 10, 11. Galle won by 95 runs. Galle 180 (S. M. Faumi 42 not out; K. Perera five for 80) and 183 (S. Wijeratne 37; C. Perera four for 26); Old Cambrians 68 (K. P. J. Warnaweera seven for 42, G. Pitigala three for 9) and 200 (S. Fernando 37, B. de Silva 65; K. P. J. Warnaweera five for 93).

At Sinhalese Sports Club Ground, Colombo, February 9, 10. Sinhalese Sports Club won by an innings and 231 runs. Panadura 82 (M. B. Halangoda five for 29, F. S. Ahangama four for 48) and 60 (F. S. Ahangama seven for 30, M. B. Halangoda three for 29); Sinhalese Sports Club 373 (A. A. W. Gunawardene 63, R. G. Abeynaike 59, R. Jayawardene 39, M. B. Halangoda 38, C. N. Fernando 42, B. E. A. Rajadurai 33, F. S. Ahangama 34 not out; P. M. V. Deshapriya three for 72).

At Colts Ground, Colombo, February 16, 17, 18. Drawn. Burgher Recreation Club 216 (A. de Silva 66, G. J. Woutersz 75; A. Ratnasiri five for 85, A. Bulankulame five for 45) and 263 for five dec. (P. de Zoysa 127, N. Pathirage 62; U. Hettiarachchi three for 67); Colts 232 (C. Mendis 63, A. Hettiarachchi 44; K. L. S. Sirisena three for 64, G. J. Woutersz three for 40) and 213 for five (C. Mendis 86, D. S. G. Bulankulame 103).

At The Esplanade, Galle, February 16, 17, 18. Moratuwa won by 140 runs. Moratuwa 259 (R. Weerawardene 121; K. P. J. Warnaweera four for 106) and 166 (W. A. Wasantha 33, C. M. Wickremasinghe 58; K. P. J. Warnaweera five for 80, P. de Silva three for 31); Galle 178 (P. de Silva 43; R. G. C. E. Wijesuriya six for 51) and 107 (R. G. C. E. Wijesuriya four for 30, K. G. Perera three for 27).

At Tyronne Fernando Stadium, Moratuwa, February 16, 17, 18. Drawn. Sinha Sports Club 276 (W. M. Janaka Kumudu 72, K. S. Asoka 31, H. M. R. Ranjith 124; K. Perera five for 85) and 220 (W. M. Janaka Kumudu 55, G. A. Kumara 81 not out; P. L. J. Fernando four for 84); Old Cambrians 159 (A. Fernando 37, C. Perera 32 not out; P. Milton five for 63, R. Priyantha three for 46) and 242 for eight (S. Fernando 53, S. de Silva 48, P. L. J. Fernando 35, C. Perera 39; W. K. Jayalath three for 21).

At Panadura Ground, Panadura, February 16, 17, 18. Panadura won by an innings and 94 runs. Air Force 93 (S. D. Anurasiri four for 20, P. M. V. Deshapriya four for 28) and 169 (N. P. Jayatillake 84; M. Jayasena five for 27, S. Jayawardene three for 33); Panadura 356 (M. de Mel 107, M. Jayasena 99, M. Fernando 42 not out; K. A. P. S. Angulugaha five for 100, K. G. Priyantha four for 99).

At Panadura Ground, Panadura, February 23, 24, 25. Panadura won by five wickets. Galle 149 (H. Munasinghe 43 not out; S. D. Anurasiri four for 38) and 153 (G. Liyanage 73; S. D. Anurasiri four for 36, S. Jayawardene three for 32); Panadura 225 (S. Thenuwara 51, S. Sooriyarachchi 35; K. P. J. Warnaweera six for 81) and 82 for five (P. de Silva three for 35).

At Colts Ground, Colombo, February 23, 24, 25. Drawn. Old Cambrians 162 (L. Dharmasiri 33; G. Goonasena four for 49, A. Liyanage four for 29) and 233 (N. Waduge 60, B. de Silva 37, P. L. J. Fernando 31; A. Liyanage four for 55, A. Ratnasiri three for 60); Colts 192 (P. Dissanayake 59; C. Perera six for 55, K. Perera three for 54) and 171 for seven (A. Bulankulame 36, U. Hettiarachchi 59; P. L. J. Fernando three for 77).

At Tyronne Fernando Stadium, Moratuwa, February 23, 24, 25. Moratuwa won by an innings and 102 runs. Sinha Sports Club 147 (W. M. Janaka Kumudu 63; C. M. Wickremasinghe four for 34) and 160 (H. M. R. Ranjith 53, G. A. Kumara 40; C. M. Wickremasinghe three for 8, K. G. Perera three for 31); Moratuwa 409 (R. Kumarsiri 31, W. A. Wasantha 86, C. M. Wickremasinghe 115, R. G. C. E. Wijesuriya 77 not out; W. K. Jayalath four for 111, P. Milton three for 99).

At Burgher Recreation Club Ground, Colombo, February 24, 25, 26. Sinhalese Sports Club won by four wickets. Burgher Recreation Club 183 (D. S. B. P. Kuruppu 62, P. de Zoysa 36; B. E. A. Rajadurai four for 52, R. Jayawardene four for 31) and 195 (D. S. B. P. Kuruppu 40, T. Ahamath 34; B. E. A. Rajadurai five for 65, O. A. P. Udayaratne three for 34); Sinhalese Sports Club 240 (S. L. Anthonisz 70, A. A. W. Gunawardene 40, M. B. Halangoda 43; N. Amerasinghe four for 69, G. J. Woutersz four for 81) and 142 for six (A. A. W. Gunawardene 30, R. G. Abeynaike 34 not out; G. J. Woutersz three for 56).

At Tyronne Fernando Stadium, Moratuwa, March 2, 3, 4. Moratuwa won by seven wickets. Air Force 156 (W. L. R. P. Rodrigo 52; K. G. Perera five for 42) and 210 (A. D. N. R. de Alwis 61, S. S. K. Gallage 62, H. M. R. Herath 36; C. M. Wickremasinghe four for 69, R. G. C. E. Wijesuriya three for 34); Moratuwa 263 (N. Ranatunga 82, C. M. Wickremasinghe 40, B. Fernando 64; J. S. I. Wijemanne five for 88) and 104 for three (R. Kumarsiri 36 not out, N. Ranatunga 52).

At Air Force Ground, Katunayake, March 2, 3, 4. Drawn. Galle 119 (S. M. Faumi 34; H. M. R. Ranjith five for 61, P. Milton four for 45) and 425 for seven (R. K. Liyanage 71, G. Liyanage 77, S. Fonseka 37, A. Srimanne 31, S. M. Faumi 95, R. Ariyawansa 49 not out); Sinha Sports Club 430 (H. M. N. C. Dhanasinghe 215, H. M. R. Ranjith 80; S. M. Faumi four for 85, K. P. J. Warnaweera four for 183).

At Sinhalese Sports Club Ground, Colombo, March 2, 3, 4. Sinhalese Sports Club won by 260 runs. Sinhalese Sports Club 342 for five dec. (D. Ranatunga 170, A. A. W. Gunawardene 96, R. G. Abeynaike 63; S. de Silva three for 49) and 182 for five dec. (R. G. Abeynaike 34, U. N. K. Fernando 90; K. Perera three for 42); Old Cambrians 60 (M. B. Halangoda seven for 42, F. S. Ahangama three for 14) and 204 (S. Fernando 82, B. de Silva 50; B. E. A. Rajadurai four for 36, M. B. Halangoda three for 45).

At Panadura Ground, Panadura, March 2, 3, 4. Panadura won by an innings and 30 runs. Colts 206 (D. S. G. Bulankulame 48, C. Mendis 30, A. Hettiarachchi 43, A. Bulankulame 50; S. D. Anurasiri five for 50) and 138 (D. S. G. Bulankulame 40; S. Jayawardene three for 36, P. M. V. Deshapriya three for 20); Panadura 374 (K. P. J. A. de Silva 44, S. Thenuwara 49, S. Sooriyarachchi 51, M. Jayasena 57, M. de Mel 103; G. Goonasena four for 109).

SINGER INTER-PROVINCIAL TOURNAMENT, 1989-90

At Sinhalese Sports Club Ground, Colombo, June 15, 16, 17. Drawn. Western Province 193 (C. Mendis 33, E. A. R. de Silva 39; N. Ranatunga five for 63, P. K. Wijetunge three for 45) and 213 for seven dec. (A. Ranatunga 60, S. H. U. Karnain 33 not out, R. J. Ratnayake 33 not out); Central Province 138 (G. F. Labrooy three for 22) and 250 for seven (R. S. Mahanama 45, D. S. B. P. Kuruppu 92, J. R. Ratnayeke 36, S. Ranatunga 41; R. J. Ratnayake three for 51).

At The Esplanade, Galle, June 15, 16, 17. Drawn. Southern Province 265 (D. C. Wickremasinghe 36, S. T. Jayasuriya 54, M. S. Atapattu 36, U. P. Sumathipala 45, A. J. Samarasekera 31 not out; J. S. I. Wijemanne five for 51) and 169 for seven (D. C. Wickremasinghe 37, M. S. Atapattu 48 not out; U. C. Hathurusinghe three for 48). North-Western Province 217 (T. M. Wijesinghe 43; P. Milton three for 54).

At Welagedera Stadium, Kurunegala, June 22, 23, 24. Drawn. North-Western Province 235 (S. Dharmasena 72, A. W. R. Madurasinghe 32; N. Ranatunga three for 42, R. S. Kalpage three for 75) and 200 for seven (G. W. D. S. A. K. Guneratne 31, T. M. Wijesinghe 40, R. J. Jaymon 65 not out; P. K. Wijetunge seven for 51); Central Province 251 for eight dec. (N. Ranatunga 30, J. R. Ratnayeke 76, D. N. Nadarajah 80; R. K. B. Amunugama four for 88, M. P. Jayaratne three for 42).

At The Esplanade, Galle, June 22, 23, 24. Western Province won by three wickets. Southern Province 176 (D. C. Wickremasinghe 30, M. S. Atapattu 41; S. D. Anurasiri five for 44, R. J. Ratnayake three for 26, taking a hat-trick) and 168 (D. C. Wickremasinghe 35, M. S. Atapattu 36; S. D. Anurasiri six for 25); Western Province 177 for nine dec. (A. P. Gurusinha 75; C. P. H. Ramanayake four for 60) and 170 for seven (C. Mendis 38, A. P. Gurusinha 34, B. R. Jurangpathy 36).

At Asgiriya Stadium, Kandy, June 29, 30, July 1. Drawn. Central Province 275 (S. Ranatunga 58, J. R. Ratnayeke 48, D. N. Nadarajah 44; K. P. J. Warnaweera five for 66); Southern Province 9 for no wkt.

At Welagedera Stadium, Kurunegala, June 29, 30, July 1. Drawn. North-Western Province 174 (S. S. Guruge 58) and 9 for no wkt; Western Province 187 (H. P. Tillekeratne 45, G. F. Labrooy 35 not out; R. K. B. Amunugama three for 45).

CRICKET IN ZIMBABWE, 1989-90

By ALWYN PICHANICK

The highlight of the season for Zimbabwe was their third successive triumph in the ICC Associate Members' Trophy, which qualified them to take part in the World Cup to be played in Australia and New Zealand in February 1992. Notwithstanding the general improvement in their competitors, the Zimbabweans were held to be too professional for the other teams – which was understandable bearing in mind their greater experience against opposition from Full Member countries. Before their trip to The Netherlands for the ICC Trophy, Zimbabwe faced two strong touring teams from the West Indies and England, playing three unofficial "Tests" against England A. These were arranged under the agreement with ICC that Zimbabwe should play five-day matches against representative teams from Full Member countries while serving five years' probation before their bid for Full Member status was reconsidered in 1994.

In the first tour, in October and November, Zimbabwe's guests were Young West Indies. Like three previous teams which had visited Zimbabwe, they included players who had already represented West Indies, as well as those on the fringe. Under the captaincy of Brian Lara they were welded into a formidable combination by the end of the tour, and having drawn their first four-day game against Zimbabwe they won both the others by an innings within three days. The tourists also won the one-day series 3-1, with one game abandoned because of the weather, and played two three-day games against Zimbabwe B, winning one and drawing one. Clayton Lambert scored a magnificent double-hundred in the second first-class match, followed a few days later by a one-day century in Bulawayo. There were also hundreds for Lara and the consistent Dawnley Joseph, while Tony Gray's bowling brought him eighteen wickets at 9.00 and Carl Hooper produced some good all-round performances.

For Zimbabwe, David Houghton played four fine innings, including 165 in the first four-day match in Harare, and averaged 101.66. Unfortunately for his team he was not available for the later fixtures, as he was invited to play for the Rest of the World against West Indies in Canada, where he scored 86 to win a Man of the Match award. No other Zimbabwean averaged more than 27.00, but Andy Flower continued to develop, batting well under pressure. Eddo Brandes put in the best bowling performance, taking ten wickets in the first-class matches and showing great hostility throughout.

Zimbabwe's captain during the Young West Indies tour was Andy Waller, but a back injury subsequently put him out not only for the rest of the season but also for the ICC tournament. Houghton took charge of the team for the second tour, in February and March, when England A played three five-day "Tests" against Zimbabwe, two in Harare and one in Bulawayo, and three one-day internationals. The tourists won all three of the latter, but the five-day matches were evenly contested. England A won the series, thanks to Zimbabwe's second-innings batting collapse in the first game, which enabled the visitors to secure a ten-wicket victory. The remaining two "Tests" were drawn, both being intriguingly well balanced.

Houghton continued where he had left off against Young West Indies in establishing his credentials as a world-class batsman. He scored a hundred in the first five-day game and a double-century in the next, which kept his average over 80 in first-class matches throughout the season. Andy Flower emphasised that he had become a batsman of stature, and also kept wicket competently, with six catches and a stumping; meanwhile his younger brother, Grant, a right-hand opener and a left-arm spin bowler, made an impressive début, scoring a half-century in his second game. The marathon spells and economical figures of John Traicos – he conceded 266 runs in 196 overs – fostered the opinion among experienced journalists accompanying the touring team that he was still among the best spin bowlers in the world. Brandes, Kevin Duers and Malcolm Jarvis all bowled well at various times, and there were solid all-round contributions from Ali Shah. In one of the non first-class games between England A and Zimbabwe B, the performances of century-maker Gavin Briant and Wayne James earned them both places on the trip to Europe.

A month after England A's visit, the Zimbabweans embarked on a two-week tour of England, an invaluable preparation for the ICC Trophy tournament in The Netherlands. They lost their two opening fixtures, one-day matches against Sussex and Essex, but played well in their three-day games against Yorkshire, Gloucestershire and Lancashire, all of which were drawn. At Bristol, Shah batted for almost the whole of the second day to score a magnificent 185, while against Lancashire, Colin Robertson recorded his maiden first-class century. Brandes bowled with sustained accuracy and hostility.

Moving on to The Netherlands, Zimbabwe won all the friendly matches played before the ICC tournament, and all their games in the preliminary rounds of the competition, eventually beating Bangladesh in the semi-final and then The Netherlands to secure the Trophy. Zimbabwe remain unbeaten in this competition, which they had previously won in 1982 and 1986; they have won 23 of their 25 matches, with two washed out in England in 1982. Nevertheless, the importance of victory, which qualified them to take part in the World Cup for the third time, and their role as favourites put the team under immense pressure. In this competition, too, they had to adapt to smaller grounds and matting wickets, which few of them had played on before.

The outstanding batting came from the Flower brothers, Andy and Grant, who averaged 70 and 63 with the bat respectively, while in the final the experienced Andy Pycroft played an important innings at a crucial time. Brandes was the pick of the bowlers, well supported by Duers, Traicos, Jarvis and Shah. Zimbabwe's fielding was of the highest order, as could be expected from their previous displays in World Cups, and as captain Houghton revealed qualities of true leadership to supplement his tactical acumen.

FIRST-CLASS MATCHES, 1989-90

Young West Indies in Zimbabwe

At Harare Sports Club, Harare, October 10, 11, 12, 13. Drawn. Toss: Zimbabwe. Zimbabwe 344 for nine dec. (A. Flower 39, D. G. Goodwin 58, D. L. Houghton 165; A. H. Gray five for 70, L. A. Joseph four for 128) and 156 for three (R. D. Brown 34, A. Flower 44 not out, D. L. Houghton 56 not out); Young West Indies 396 (D. S. Morgan 31, B. C. Lara 145, D. A. Joseph 87; E. A. Brandes five for 117).

At Harare Sports Club, Harare, October 24, 25, 26. Young West Indies won by an innings and 230 runs. Toss: Zimbabwe. Zimbabwe 106 (D. L. Houghton 36; A. H. Gray seven for 30) and 102 (D. L. Houghton 48; A. H. Gray three for 24, C. L. Hooper three for 10, R. Dhanraj three for 29); Young West Indies 438 (C. B. Lambert 219, B. C. Lara 35, C. L. Hooper 86, J. C. Adams 31; E. A. Brandes three for 105).

At Harare Sports Club, Harare, October 31, November 1, 2. Young West Indies won by an innings and 56 runs. Toss: Zimbabwe. Zimbabwe 106 (L. A. Joseph three for 37, C. L. Hooper three for 19) and 182 (R. D. Brown 32, A. Flower 43; R. Dhanraj six for 79, N. O. Perry three for 61); Young West Indies 344 (D. A. Joseph 149, J. C. Adams 35, L. A. Joseph 67; D. F. Dolphin three for 59).

Zimbabwe's matches v England A may be found in England A in Kenya and Zimbabwe, 1989-90.

CRICKET IN DENMARK, 1990

By PETER S. HARGREAVES

After the high note on which Danish cricket finished in 1989, a sense of anticlimax was inevitable when, for the first time, the country narrowly failed to reach the ICC Trophy semi-finals. Hopes were dashed when stomach infections afflicted the Danish captain and all-rounder, Søren Henriksen, and his fellow fast bowler, Jens Bredo, at a crucial stage of the competition; a month earlier in Denmark these two had routed Bangladesh, the team which beat them to a place among the last four in the Trophy. The Danes preserved their dignity through their continued ascendancy over Canada, the only side to defeat the host country, The Netherlands, before they lost in the final to the all-conquering Zimbabwe.

On the domestic scene 1989's champions, Svanholm, at one time looked as if they would make a clean sweep of prizes, but in the last few weeks of the season Esbjerg emerged slightly ahead of them, with AB third. At the foot of the first division the two Jutland clubs, Aarhus and Nykøbing Mors, promoted the previous season, went straight down again, the latter losing a challenge match to the second division side, Nørrebro, most of whose players were Pakistani. Further recruits of Pakistani background will strengthen Nørrebro in 1991 as they and Slagelse join the first division. Another of Copenhagen's three Pakistani clubs, Ishøj, were relegated from the second division, along with the Funen team, Kerteminde, to be replaced by Frem, also of Copenhagen, and the Husum club from South Schleswig, which proved far too strong for the third division.

Inconsistency plagued many of Denmark's top batsmen. Tim Jensen of KB, the former Esbjerg player, had the highest aggregate, 905 runs, but at a relatively low average, just under 35. Svanholm's young opener, Jesper Christiansen, boosted his claims to the position in the national team, with 683 runs at an average of just under 57, while the most successful of the middle-order men was Ole Stoustrup of AB, with 889 runs at about 42. Aftab Ahmed, the previous season's find, was somewhat out of form for the first two-thirds of the season, including the ICC Trophy, but recovered well.

The bowlers received a fillip from the newly settled Australian, Ross McLellan, whose 40 wickets at under 11 runs apiece gave him easily the most economical figures and helped his club, Chang, to finish fourth. In Jan A. Nielsen, also of Chang, and Tahir Siddique, of Svanholm, two promising young off-spinners emerged. In England, meanwhile, Ole Mortensen had one of his best seasons at Derbyshire, especially in the limited-overs competitions.

In the youth divisions, the usual clubs held sway. Svanholm beat Esbjerg to win the Under-18 Junior competition, and Ishøj appeared in the finals of both the Under-15 Boys' and the Under-13 Lilleput divisions, losing to Esbjerg in the former but beating Herning with their younger players. Denmark's ladies were less convincing in the second European Cup tournament, played on grass pitches in Leicester and Nottingham, than they had been the previous year. A reasonable total against Ireland proved their best performance. At home AB, women's champions for seven of the past eight seasons, lost their semi-final by 2 runs to Nykøbing Mors, who went on to beat the favourites, Svanholm, by a single run from the last ball of the final. It was not a weekend for those with weak nerves.

CRICKET IN THE NETHERLANDS, 1990

By DAVID HARDY

Although the 1990 season in The Netherlands revolved around the ICC Trophy for Associate Members, which dominated the month of June, this did not prevent the completion of a full programme of league matches. The national Premier League was suspended for the 21 days of the tournament, so that matches were not affected by national call-ups, and reached its conclusion, albeit almost by default, on a damp first weekend in September. By then both Kampong of Utrecht, league champions for the past two seasons, and Koninklijke Utile Dulci, of Deventer, had earned 24 points from seventeen matches. Kampong lost their last game by 13 runs, and KUD, prevented from playing by rain, won the championship by virtue of a higher average of points per match played. The oldest Dutch club, founded in 1875, thus became national champions for the first time, a triumph for captain Steven Lubbers, and a well-deserved consolation for his disappointment in the ICC Trophy final, where he led The Netherlands in their unsuccessful challenge to Zimbabwe.

Lubbers also won the Olivetti Top Performance Trophy, awarded by the umpires, for being the outstanding individual player of the season. He was the leading Dutch run-scorer in the league, with 722 runs at 55.54, but five player-coaches exceeded that total: Zimbabweans Andy Flower (730) at Voorburg and David Houghton (919) at Quick, of The Hague, Trinidadian Rupert Gomes (868) at VRA, Amsterdam, and, most impressively, Nolan Clarke (1,122) at Quick and Peter Cantrell (1,165) at Kampong. Queensland all-rounder Cantrell just failed to beat his all-time Dutch record of 1,214, set in 1988, but the 42-year-old Barbadian, Clarke, hit 265 not out (with fifteen sixes) on May 27 against Bloemendaal to beat the previous highest individual score in Dutch Premier League cricket, 240 by Jan Offerman in 1935. In the return match against Bloemendaal, Clarke scored 193 (seventeen sixes), for a total of 458 runs and 32 sixes against one club. It was undoubtedly a season for batsmen. No Premier League bowler reached 50 wickets, the highest tally going to KUD's professional, the New Zealander, Stuart Roberts, with 46.

The unfortunate Bloemendaal were relegated to the national Second League, to be replaced by the Schiedam club, Hermes DVS, back in the top flight after one year's absence; ACC of Amstelveen just missed promotion for the third year running. Kampong continued their recent run of success by winning the 40-overs Telegraaf Cup, beating second division side Rood en Wit of Haarlem by 5 runs in the final.

Elsewhere in Dutch cricket, the national ladies team finished third in the European Cup in England. Three junior teams toured south-west England, where the Under-16s won all five matches against county opposition, and the Dutch Still Going Strong team once again proved too strong for their Danish and English veteran counterparts. In September the beach cricket open championship was a great success on the Wadden Sea island of Schiermonnikoog.

WOMEN'S CRICKET, 1990

By CAROL SALMON

The staging of the European Cup tournament in the East Midlands in July, and the comfortable retention of the trophy by England, could be classed as the highlight and lowlight of the women's season. From the positive point of view, the tournament was well administered by Ann Woods and a small band of determined East Midlands workers, while on the field of play England were simply too good for the inexperienced opposition provided by Ireland, Denmark and The Netherlands. More critical observers, however, remarked on the almost complete lack of interest shown in the event by the rest of the women's cricket fraternity; on the large bill with which the Women's Cricket Association was left, following a similar lack of interest from major sponsors, despite some admirable local support; and on the fact that much of the 55-overs cricket was too predictable.

The reason the cricket did little to stimulate those who did attend was that the visitors, not unexpectedly, still have much to learn, even when compared with an England team nowhere near the force of old. It was a similar story at the 1988-89 World Cup in Australia, and at the inaugural European Cup in Denmark in 1989. However, with South Africa no longer a viable option, with West Indies failing to build on several tours to England, and with India the essence of administrative unpredictability, new opposition must be encouraged, particularly in the Northern hemisphere. England's role, therefore, is critical. The WCA must be seen as a positive influence by the emerging cricketing nations, while at the same time England's cricketers must retain their own competitive edge, which was not always the case in the East Midlands tournament. Perhaps the full England side should play a European XI, selected from the 1991 European Cup tournament in The Netherlands. If England were to send their B team to the tournament, this should lead to keener competition, and to additional and more meaningful matches for a wider spread of England players.

Thought also needs to be given to the next World Cup, in 1993 in England. Few people will want to watch one-sided limited-overs matches; and in time fewer players will turn up simply to come second. A qualification tournament, such as that run for the men's World Cup, is one possibility. Another is that a stronger, more competitive team would come from a combination of the best from Ireland, Denmark and The Netherlands; but these countries might think otherwise, especially as they have made such great strides in a relatively short time.

The trend of the second European Cup was set on the opening day when England beat the Dutch by eight wickets, and they went on to beat Denmark by 206 runs and Ireland by nine wickets. Denmark were particularly disappointed to lose to The Netherlands, while Ireland qualified for the final by beating both sides. Media coverage of the tournament was good, with the final at Great Oakley CC in Northampton well chronicled. England won the toss there, and after a slow start they blossomed to average 4 an over and reach 109 in the 31st over without losing a wicket. Wendy Watson, who was omitted from the opening match against Holland, went on to demonstrate her increasing value to England by making 107 not out of the side's eventual 22 for three. With vice-captain Karen Smithies, Watson put on 80 in sixteen overs. Ireland, struggling against the bowling of Jo Chamberlain and the controlled Clare Taylor, had only 63 on the board at the halfway mark, although just one wicket was down. The only subsequent alteration to the pattern came with the loss of more wickets, and they were 159 for eight after their 55 overs. It was an indication of Ireland's difficulties that their most experienced player, Mary-Pat Moore, the Irish captain at the 1988 World Cup, and the Yorkshire vice-captain, could manage only 44 from 125 deliveries.

Ireland continued the improvement they had shown signs of in Australia. If anything, the side's leadership qualities had not matched their individual improvement. The Dutch, on the other hand, appeared considerably better organised, and their win over Denmark reversed the position of twelve months previously at the first European Cup. More was expected of Denmark, particularly as they possessed fine individual talents, such as their captain, Jani Jonsson. It was obvious, however, that England were not stretched, and the selectors seemed to endorse this by omitting, for one reason or another, five players, including captain Jane Powell, from the twelve-strong team which toured Ireland shortly afterwards. Visits to Ireland have been commendably regular, but it was questionable whether a team needed to go again so soon after the European Cup, and with the dates clashing with the traditional cricket week in Malvern – not to mention the seemingly never-ending demands on players' time and money.

England's European Cup squad was: Jane Powell (*captain*), Karen Smithies (*vice-captain*), Janet Aspinall, Caroline Barrs, Jo Chamberlain, Cathy Cooke, Alison Elder, Carole Hodges, Debra Maybury, Sue Metcalfe, Lisa Nye, Gill Smith, Clare Taylor and Wendy Watson. The manager was Norma Izard, while Ruth Prideaux was coach. The successful East Midlands captain, Smithies, took over for the two-match tour to Ireland, with all-rounder Suzie Kitson of East Anglia returning after injury had kept her out of the European Cup. Newcomers were Sarah-Jane Cook, a seam bowler from Sussex, and the Yorkshire opener, Linda Burnley. The full tour party to Ireland was: Karen Smithies (*captain*), Gill Smith (*vice-captain*), Linda Burnley, Jo Chamberlain, Sarah-Jane Cook, Cathy Cooke, Alison Elder, Carole Hodges, Suzie Kitson, Debra Maybury, Sue Metcalfe and Clare Taylor. The manager was Norma Izard and the coach Ruth Prideaux.

After this tour, two members of the England selection panel, Gail Donnison (East Midlands) and Jeny Humphries (Kent), announced that they would not be seeking re-election. They were replaced by the former international spinner, Gill McConway (East Anglia), and England coach Ruth Prideaux, who thus joined convenor Sheila Keen and Anne Gordon, both of Surrey. With no more nominations, it appeared that the WCA was content with four selectors instead of the previously preferred five. Both McConway and Gordon started their cricketing careers in their home countries of New Zealand and Australia respectively.

In the domestic game, 22-year-old Smithies led East Midlands to the county championship, scoring 50 and taking three for 35 in 10.4 overs as they beat Yorkshire in an exciting final by 4 runs. The North took the territorial tournament by winning all three games against the South, the East, and the Mid-West, while on the club scene Wakefield completed the league and cup double for the second successive year. They beat Gunnersbury by 80 runs in the cup final, and another London club, Riverside, in the league final by seven wickets.

EUROPEAN CUP, 1990

At Electric Sports Ground, Leicester, July 18. England won by eight wickets. Toss: Th Netherlands. The Netherlands 57 (33 overs) (C. Barrs three for 1); England 58 for tw (19.5 overs).

At Ivanhoe CC, Leicester, July 18. Ireland won by 49 runs. Toss: Denmark. Ireland 234 fc four (M.-P. Moore 99, A. Murray 61; L. Hansen three for 47); Denmark 185 for eight (5 overs) (J. Jonsson 49, B. Langerhuus 42; S. Bray five for 27).

At John Player AC, Nottingham, July 19. Ireland won by 26 runs. Toss: The Netherlands Ireland 198 for four (55 overs) (S. Owens 84 not out); The Netherlands 172 for nine (55 overs (N. Payne 47, I. Schoof 38; S. Bray three for 32).

At John Player Sports Ground, Nottingham, July 19. England won by 206 runs. Toss Denmark. England 270 (54 overs) (J. Powell 98 not out, D. Maybury 56); Denmark 64 (24. overs) (G. A. Smith five for 15).

At Ivanhoe CC, Leicester, July 20. England won by nine wickets. Toss: England. Irelan 169 for nine (52 overs) (E. Owens 40, A. Linehan 39; J. C. Aspinall four for 35); England 17 for one (44.4 overs) (W. A. Watson 93 not out, J. Powell 35 not out).

At Electric Sports Ground, Leicester, July 20. The Netherlands won by 34 runs. Toss Denmark. The Netherlands 123 for seven (S. Nelson three for 27); Denmark 89 (M. Frost 35 I. Oulfer four for 14, E. Velthan four for 26).

Final

At Great Oakley CC, Northampton, July 22. England won by 65 runs. Toss: Englanc England 224 for three (55 overs) (W. A. Watson 107 not out, K. Smithies 41); Ireland 159 fc eight (55 overs) (M.-P. Moore 44).

ENGLAND IN IRELAND, 1990

At Clontarf CC, Dublin, August 16. England won by 62 runs. Toss: Ireland. England 156 fo nine (55 overs) (L. Burnley 30; S. Bray four for 24); Ireland 94 (45.4 overs) (G. A. Smith thre for 12, S. J. Kitson three for 13).

At Leinster CC, Dublin, August 17. England won by ten wickets. Toss: England. Ireland 7 (42.1 overs); England 84 for no wkt (21.2 overs) (D. Maybury 37 not out, A. Elder 37 not out)

BIRTHS AND DEATHS OF CRICKETERS

The qualifications are as follows:

1. All players who have appeared in a Test match or a one-day international for a Test-match playing country.

2. English county players who have appeared in 50 or more first-class matches during their careers and, if dead, were still living ten years ago.

3. Players who appeared in fifteen or more first-class matches in the 1990 English season.

4. English county captains, county caps and captains of Oxford and Cambridge Universities who, if dead, were still living ten years ago.

5. All players chosen as *Wisden* Cricketers of the Year, including the Public Schoolboys chosen for the 1918 and 1919 Almanacks. Cricketers of the Year are identified by the italic notation *CY* and year of appearance. A list of the Cricketers of the Year from 1889 to 1988 appeared in *Wisden* 1989.

6. Players or personalities not otherwise qualified who are thought to be of sufficient interest to merit inclusion.

Key to abbreviations and symbols

CUCC – Cambridge University, OUCC – Oxford University.

Australian states: NSW – New South Wales, Qld – Queensland, S. Aust. – South Australia, Tas. – Tasmania, Vic. – Victoria, W. Aust. – Western Australia.

Indian teams: Guj. – Gujarat, H'bad – Hyderabad, Ind. Rlwys – Indian Railways, Ind. Serv. – Indian Services, J/K – Jammu and Kashmir, Karn. – Karnataka (Mysore to 1972-73), M. Pradesh – Madhya Pradesh (Central India [C. Ind.] to 1939-40, Holkar to 1954-55, Madhya Bharat to 1956-57), M'tra – Maharashtra, Naw. – Nawanagar, Raja. – Rajasthan, S'tra – Saurashtra (West India [W. Ind.] to 1945-46, Kathiawar to 1949-50), S. Punjab – Southern Punjab (Patiala to 1958-59, Punjab since 1968-69), TC – Travanacore-Cochin (Kerala since 1956-57), TN – Tamil Nadu (Madras to 1959-60), U. Pradesh – Uttar Pradesh (United Provinces [U. Prov.] to 1948-49), Vidarbha (CP & Berar to 1949-50, Madhya Pradesh to 1956-57).

New Zealand provinces: Auck. – Auckland, Cant. – Canterbury, C. Dist. – Central Districts, N. Dist. – Northern Districts, Wgtn – Wellington.

Pakistani teams: ADBP – Agricultural Development Bank of Pakistan, B'pur – Bahawalpur, HBFC – House Building Finance Corporation, HBL – Habib Bank Ltd, IDBP – Industrial Development Bank of Pakistan, Kar. – Karachi, MCB – Muslim Commercial Bank, NBP – National Bank of Pakistan, NWFP – North-West Frontier Province, PACO – Pakistan Automobile Corporation, Pak. Rlwys – Pakistan Railways, Pak. Us – Pakistan Universities, PIA – Pakistan International Airlines, PNSC – Pakistan National Shipping Corporation, PWD – Public Works Department, R'pindi – Rawalpindi, UBL – United Bank Ltd, WAPDA – Water and Power Development Authority.

South African provinces: E. Prov. – Eastern Province, Griq. W. – Griqualand West, N. Tvl – Northern Transvaal, NE Tvl – North-Eastern Transvaal, OFS – Orange Free State, Rhod. – Rhodesia, Tvl – Transvaal, W. Prov. – Western Province.

Sri Lankan teams: BRC – Burgher Recreation Club, CCC – Colombo Cricket Club, Mor. – Moratuwa Sports Club, NCC – Nondescripts Cricket Club, Pan. – Panadura Sports Club, SLAF – Air Force, SSC – Sinhalese Sports Club, TU – Tamil Union Cricket and Athletic Club.

West Indies islands: B'dos – Barbados, BG – British Guiana (Guyana since 1966), Comb. Is. – Combined Islands, Jam. – Jamaica, T/T – Trinidad & Tobago.

* *Denotes Test player.* ** *Denotes appeared for two countries. There is a list of Test players country by country from page 85.*

† *Denotes also played for team under its previous name.*

Aamer Hameed (Pak. Us, Lahore, Punjab & OUCC) b Oct. 18, 1954
*Aamer Malik (ADBP) b Jan. 3, 1963
*Aaqib Javed (PACO) b Aug. 5, 1972
Abberley, R. N. (Warwicks.) b April 22, 1944
*a'Beckett, E. L. (Vic.) b Aug. 11, 1907, d June 2, 1989
*Abdul Kadir (Kar. & NBP) b May 10, 1944
*Abdul Qadir (HBL, Lahore & Punjab) b Sept. 15, 1955
*Abel, R. (Surrey; *CY 1890*) b Nov. 30, 1857, d Dec. 10, 1936
Abell, Sir G. E. B. (OUCC, Worcs. & N. Ind.) b June 22, 1904, d Jan. 11, 1989
Aberdare, 3rd Lord (*see* Bruce, Hon. C. N.)
*Abid Ali, S. (H'bad) b Sept. 9, 1941
Abrahams, J. (Lancs.) b July 21, 1952
*Absolom, C. A. (CUCC & Kent) b June 7, 1846, d July 30, 1889
Acfield D. L. (CUCC & Essex) b July 24, 1947
*Achong, E. (T/T) b Feb. 16, 1904, d Aug. 29, 1986
Ackerman, H. M. (Border, NE Tvl, Northants, Natal & W. Prov.) b April 28, 1947
A'Court, D. G. (Glos.) b July 27, 1937
Adam, Sir Ronald, 2nd Bt (Pres. MCC 1946-47) b Oct. 30, 1885, d Dec. 26, 1982
Adams, C. J. (Derbys.) b May 6, 1970
Adams, P. W. (Cheltenham & Sussex; *CY 1919*) b 1900, d Feb. 28, 1962
*Adcock, N. A. T. (Tvl & Natal; *CY 1961*) b March 8, 1931
*Adhikari, H. R. (Guj., Baroda & Ind. Serv.) b July 31, 1919
*Afaq Hussain (Kar., Pak. Us, PIA & PWD) b Dec. 31, 1939
Afford, J. A. (Notts.) b May 12, 1964
*Aftab Baloch (PWD, Kar., Sind, NBP & PIA) b April 1, 1953
*Aftab Gul (Punjab U., Pak. Us & Lahore) b March 31, 1946
*Agha Saadat Ali (Pak. Us, Punjab, B'pur & Lahore) b June 21, 1929
*Agha Zahid (Pak. Us, Punjab, Lahore & HBL) b Jan. 7, 1953
*Agnew, J. P. (Leics; *CY 1988*) b April 4, 1960
*Ahangama, F. S. (SSC) b Sept. 14, 1959
Aird, R. (CUCC & Hants; Sec. MCC 1953-62, Pres. MCC 1968-69) b May 4, 1902, d Aug. 16, 1986
Aitchison, Rev. J. K. (Scotland) b May 26, 1920
*Akram Raza (Sargodha & HBL) b Nov. 22, 1964
Alabaster, G. D. (Cant., N. Dist. & Otago) b Dec. 10, 1933
*Alabaster, J. C. (Otago) b July 11, 1930
Alcock, C. W. (Sec. Surrey CCC 1872-1907 Editor *Cricket* 1882-1907) b Dec. 2, 1842 d Feb. 26, 1907
Alderman, A. E. (Derbys.) b Oct. 30, 1907 d June 4, 1990
*Alderman, T. M. (W. Aust., Kent & Glos. *CY 1982*) b June 12, 1956
Aldridge, K. J. (Worcs & Tas.) b March 13 1935
Alexander of Tunis, 1st Lord (Pres. MCC 1955-56) b Dec. 10, 1891, d June 16, 1969
*Alexander, F. C. M. (CUCC & Jam.) b Nov. 2, 1928
*Alexander, G. (Vic.) b April 22, 1851, d Nov. 6, 1930
*Alexander, H. H. (Vic.) b June 9, 1905
Alikhan, R. I. (Sussex, PIA & Surrey) b Dec. 28, 1962
*Alim-ud-Din (Rajputana, Guj., Sind, B'pur, Kar. & PWD) b Dec. 15, 1930
*Allan, D. W. (B'dos) b Nov. 5, 1937
*Allan, F. E. (Vic.) b Dec. 2, 1849, d Feb. 9, 1917
Allan, J. M. (OUCC, Kent, Warwicks. & Scotland) b April 2, 1932
*Allan, P. J. (Qld) b Dec. 31, 1935
*Allcott, C. F. W. (Auck.) b Oct. 7, 1896, d Nov. 19, 1973
Allen, A. W. (CUCC & Northants) b Dec 22, 1912
Allen, B. O. (CUCC & Glos.) b Oct. 13, 1911, d May 1, 1981
*Allen, D. A. (Glos.) b Oct. 29, 1935
*Allen, Sir G. O. B. (CUCC & Middx; Pres. MCC 1963-64; *special portrait 1987*) b July 31, 1902, d Nov. 29, 1989
Allen, M. H. J. (Northants & Derbys.) b Jan. 7, 1933
*Allen, R. C. (NSW) b July 2, 1858, d May 2, 1952
Alletson, E. B. (Notts.) b March 6, 1884, d July 5, 1963
Alley, W. E. (NSW & Som.; *CY 1962*) b Feb. 3, 1919
Alleyne, H. L. (B'dos, Worcs., Natal & Kent) b Feb. 28, 1957
Alleyne, M. W. (Glos.) b May 23, 1968
*Allom, M. J. C. (CUCC & Surrey; Pres. MCC 1969-70) b March 23, 1906
*Allott, P. J. W. (Lancs. & Wgtn) b Sept. 14, 1956
Altham, H. S. (OUCC, Surrey & Hants; Pres. MCC 1959-60) b Nov. 30, 1888, d March 11, 1965
*Amalean, K. N. (SL) b April 7, 1965
*Amarnath, Lala (N. Ind., S. Punjab, Guj., Patiala, U. Pradesh & Ind. Rlwys) b Sept. 11, 1911
*Amarnath, M. (Punjab & Delhi; *CY 1984*) b Sept. 24, 1950
*Amarnath, S. (Punjab & Delhi) b Dec. 30, 1948

*Amar Singh, L. (Patiala, W. Ind. & Naw.) b Dec. 4, 1910, d May 20, 1940
*Ambrose, C. E. L. (Leewards & Northants) b Sept. 21, 1963
*Amerasinghe, A. M. J. G. (Nomads) b Feb. 2, 1954
*Ames, L. E. G. (Kent; *CY 1929*) b Dec. 3, 1905, d Feb. 26, 1990
**Amir Elahi (Baroda, N. Ind., S. Punjab & B'pur) b Sept. 1, 1908, d Dec. 28, 1980
*Amiss, D. L. (Warwicks.; *CY 1975*) b April 7, 1943
Anderson, I. S. (Derbys. & Boland) b April 24, 1960
*Anderson, J. H. (W. Prov.) b April 26, 1874, d March 11, 1926
*Anderson, R. W. (Cant., N. Dist., Otago & C. Dist.) b Oct. 2, 1948
*Anderson, W. McD. (Otago, C. Dist. & Cant.) b Oct. 8, 1919, d Dec. 21, 1979
Andrew, C. R. (CUCC) b Feb. 18, 1963
*Andrew, K. V. (Northants) b Dec. 15, 1929
Andrew, S. J. W. (Hants & Essex) b Jan. 27, 1966
*Andrews, B. (Cant., C. Dist. & Otago) b April 4, 1945
*Andrews, T. J. E. (NSW) b Aug. 26, 1890, d Jan. 28, 1970
Andrews, W. H. R. (Som.) b April 14, 1908, d Jan. 9, 1989
Angell, F. L. (Som.) b June 29, 1922
*Anil Dalpat (Kar. & PIA) b Sept. 20, 1963
*Ankola, S. A. (M'tra) b March 1, 1968
*Anurasiri, S. D. (Pan.) b Feb. 25, 1966
*Anwar Hussain (N. Ind., Bombay, Sind & Kar.) b July 16, 1920
*Anwar Khan (Kar., Sind & NBP) b Dec. 24, 1955
Appleyard, R. (Yorks.; *CY 1952*) b June 27, 1924
*Apte, A. L. (Ind. Us, Bombay & Raja.) b Oct. 24, 1934
*Apte, M. L. (Bombay & Bengal) b Oct. 5, 1932
*Archer, A. G. (Worcs.) b Dec. 6, 1871, d July 15, 1935
*Archer, K. A. (Qld) b Jan. 17, 1928
*Archer, R. G. (Qld) b Oct. 25, 1933
*Arif Butt (Lahore & Pak. Rlwys) b May 17, 1944
Arlott, John (Writer & Broadcaster) b Feb. 25, 1914
*Armitage, T. (Yorks.) b April 25, 1848, d Sept. 21, 1922
Armstrong, N. F. (Leics.) b Dec. 22, 1892, d Jan. 19, 1990
Armstrong, T. R. (Derbys.) b Oct. 13, 1909
*Armstrong, W. W. (Vic.; *CY 1903*) b May 22, 1879, d July 13, 1947
*Arnold, A. P. (Cant. & Northants) b Oct. 16, 1926
*Arnold, E. G. (Worcs.) b Nov. 7, 1876, d Oct. 25, 1942
*Arnold, G. G. (Surrey & Sussex; *CY 1972*) b Sept. 3, 1944
*Arnold, J. (Hants) b Nov. 30, 1907, d April 4, 1984
*Arshad Ayub (H'bad) b Aug. 2, 1958
Arshad Pervez (Sargodha, Lahore, Pak. Us, Servis Ind., HBL & Punjab) b Oct. 1, 1952
*Arthurton, K. L. T. (Leewards) b Feb. 21, 1965
*Arun, B. (TN) b Dec. 14, 1962
*Arun Lal, J. (Delhi & Bengal) b Aug. 1, 1955
*Asgarali, N. (T/T) b Dec. 28, 1920
Ashdown, W. H. (Kent) b Dec. 27, 1898, d Sept. 15, 1979
*Ashley, W. H. (W. Prov.) b Feb. 10, 1862, d July 14, 1930
*Ashraf Ali (Lahore, Income Tax, Pak Us, Pak Rlwys & UBL) b April 22, 1958
Ashton, C. T. (CUCC & Essex) b Feb. 19, 1901, d Oct. 31, 1942
Ashton, G. (CUCC & Worcs.) b Sept. 27, 1896, d Feb. 6, 1981
Ashton, Sir H. (CUCC & Essex; *CY 1922*; Pres. MCC 1960-61) b Feb. 13, 1898, d June 17,1979
Asif Din, M. (Warwicks.) b Sept. 21, 1960
*Asif Iqbal (H'bad, Kar., Kent, PIA & NBP; *CY 1968*) b June 6, 1943
*Asif Masood (Lahore, Punjab U. & PIA) b Jan. 23, 1946
*Asif Mujtaba (Kar. & PIA) b Nov. 4, 1967
Aslett, D. G. (Kent) b Feb. 12, 1958
Aspinall, R. (Yorks.) b Nov. 27, 1918
*Astill, W. E. (Leics.; *CY 1933*) b March 1, 1888, d Feb. 10, 1948
*Atherton, M. A. (CUCC & Lancs.; *CY 1991*) b March 23, 1968
*Athey, C. W. J. (Yorks. & Glos.) b Sept. 27, 1957
Atkinson, C. R. M. (Som.) b July 23, 1931
*Atkinson, D. St E. (B'dos & T/T) b Aug. 9, 1926
*Atkinson, E. St E. (B'dos) b Nov. 6, 1927
Atkinson, G. (Som. & Lancs.) b March 29, 1938
Atkinson, J. C. M. (Som. & CUCC) b July 10, 1968
Atkinson, T. (Notts.) b Sept. 27, 1930
Attenborough, G. R. (S. Aust.) b Jan. 17, 1951
*Attewell, W. (Notts.; *CY 1892*) b June 12, 1861, d June 11, 1927
Austin, Sir H. B. G. (B'dos) b July 15, 1877, d July 27, 1943
*Austin, R. A. (Jam.) b Sept. 5, 1954
Avery, A. V. (Essex) b Dec. 19, 1914
Aworth, C. J. (CUCC & Surrey) b Feb. 19, 1953

Aylward, J. (Hants & All-England) b 1741, d Dec. 27, 1827
*Azad, K. (Delhi) b Jan. 2, 1959
*Azeem Hafeez (Kar., Allied Bank & PIA) b July 29, 1963
*Azhar Khan (Lahore, Punjab, Pak. Us., PIA & HBL) b Sept. 7, 1955
*Azharuddin, M. (H'bad; *CY 1991*) b Feb. 8, 1963
*Azmat Rana (B'pur, PIA, Punjab, Lahore & MCB) b Nov. 3, 1951

Babington, A. M. (Sussex) b July 22, 1963
*Bacchus, S. F. A. F. (Guyana, W. Prov. & Border) b Jan. 31, 1954
*Bacher, Dr A. (Tvl) b May 24, 1942
*Badcock, C. L. (Tas. & S. Aust.) b April 10, 1914, d Dec. 13, 1982
*Badcock, F. T. (Wgtn & Otago) b Aug. 9, 1895, d Sept. 19, 1982
*Baichan, L. (Guyana) b May 12, 1946
*Baig, A. A. (H'bad, OUCC & Som.) b March 19, 1939
Bailey, Sir D. T. L. (Glos.) b Aug. 5, 1918
Bailey, J. (Hants) b April 6, 1908, d Feb. 9, 1988
Bailey, J. A. (Essex & OUCC; Sec. MCC 1974-87) b June 22, 1930
*Bailey, R. J. (Northants) b Oct. 28, 1963
*Bailey, T. E. (Essex & CUCC; *CY 1950*) b Dec. 3, 1923
Baillie, A. W. (Sec. MCC 1858-63) b June 22, 1830, d May 10, 1867
Bainbridge, P. (Glos.; *CY 1986*) b April 16, 1958
*Bairstow, D. L. (Yorks. & Griq. W.) b Sept. 1, 1951
Baker, R. P. (Surrey) b April 9, 1954
*Bakewell, A. H. (Northants; *CY 1934*) b Nov. 2, 1908, d Jan. 23, 1983
Bakker, P. J. (Hants) b Aug. 19, 1957
*Balaskas, X. C. (Griq. W., Border, W. Prov., Tvl & NE Tvl) b Oct. 15, 1910
*Balderstone, J. C. (Yorks. & Leics.) b Nov. 16, 1940
Baldry, D. O. (Middx & Hants) b Dec. 26, 1931
*Banerjee, S. A. (Bengal & Bihar) b Nov. 1, 1919
*Banerjee, S. N. (Bengal, Naw., Bihar & M. Pradesh) b Oct. 3, 1911, d Oct. 14, 1980
*Bannerman, A. C. (NSW) b March 21, 1854, d Sept. 19, 1924
*Bannerman, Charles (NSW) b July 23, 1851, d Aug. 20, 1930
Bannister, J. D. (Warwicks.) b Aug. 23, 1930
*Baptiste, E. A. E. (Kent & Leewards) b March 12, 1960
*Baqa Jilani, M. (N. Ind.) b July 20, 1911, d July 2, 1941

Barber, A. T. (OUCC & Yorks.) b June 17, 1905, d March 10, 1985
*Barber, R. T. (Wgtn & C. Dist.) b June 23, 1925
*Barber, R. W. (Lancs., CUCC & Warwicks; *CY 1967*) b Sept. 26, 1935
*Barber, W. (Yorks.) b April 18, 1901, d Sept. 10, 1968
Barclay, J. R. T. (Sussex & OFS) b Jan. 22, 1954
*Bardsley, W. (NSW; *CY 1910*) b Dec. 7, 1882, d Jan. 20, 1954
Baring, A. E. G. (Hants) b Jan. 21, 1910, d Aug. 29, 1986
Barker, G. (Essex) b July 6, 1931
Barling, T. H. (Surrey) b Sept. 1, 1906
Barlow, A. (Lancs.) b Aug. 31, 1915, d May 9, 1983
*Barlow, E. J. (Tvl, E. Prov., W. Prov., Derbys. & Boland) b Aug. 12, 1940
*Barlow, G. D. (Middx) b March 26, 1950
*Barlow, R. G. (Lancs.) b May 28, 1851, d July 31, 1919
Barnard, H. M. (Hants) b July 18, 1933
Barnes, A. R. (Sec. Aust. Cricket Board 1960-81) b Sept. 12, 1916, d March 14, 1989
*Barnes, S. F. (Warwicks. & Lancs.; *CY 1910*) b April 19, 1873, d Dec. 26, 1967
*Barnes, S. G. (NSW) b June 5, 1916, d Dec. 16, 1973
*Barnes, W. (Notts.; *CY 1890*) b May 27, 1852, d March 24, 1899
*Barnett, B. A. (Vic.) b March 23, 1908, d June 29, 1979
*Barnett, C. J. (Glos.; *CY 1937*) b July 3 1910
*Barnett, K. J. (Derbys. & Boland; *CY 1989* b July 17, 1960
Barnwell, C. J. P. (Som.) b June 23, 1914
Baroda, Maharaja of (Manager, Ind. i Eng., 1959) b April 2, 1930, d Sept. 1 1988
*Barratt, F. (Notts.) b April 12, 1894, d Jan 29, 1947
Barratt, R. J. (Leics.) b May 3, 1942
*Barrett, A. G. (Jam.) b April 5, 1942
Barrett, B. J. (Auck., C. Dist., Worcs. & N Dist.) b Nov. 16, 1966
*Barrett, J. E. (Vic.) b Oct. 15, 1866, d Feb 9, 1916
Barrick, D. W. (Northants) b April 28 1926
*Barrington, K. F. (Surrey; *CY 1960*) b Nov 24, 1930, d March 14, 1981
Barron, W. (Lancs. & Northants) b Oct. 2 1917
*Barrow, I. (Jam.) b Jan. 6, 1911, d April 1979
*Bartlett, E. L. (B'dos) b March 18, 1906, Dec. 21, 1976

*Bartlett, G. A. (C. Dist. & Cant.) b Feb. 3, 1941
Bartlett, H. T. (CUCC, Surrey & Sussex; *CY 1939*) b Oct. 7, 1914, d June 26, 1988
Bartley, T. J. (Umpire) b March 19, 1908, d April 2, 1964
Barton, M. R. (OUCC & Surrey) b Oct. 14, 1914
*Barton, P. T. (Wgtn) b Oct. 9, 1935
*Barton, V. A. (Kent & Hants) b Oct. 6, 1867, d March 23, 1906
Barwick, S. R. (Glam.) b Sept. 6, 1960
Base, S. J. (W. Prov., Glam., Derbys. & Boland) b Jan. 2, 1960
Bates, D. L. (Sussex) b May 10, 1933
*Bates, W. (Yorks.) b Nov. 19, 1855, d Jan. 8, 1900
*Baumgartner, H. V. (OFS & Tvl) b Nov. 17, 1883, d April 8, 1938
Baxter, A. D. (Devon, Lancs., Middx & Scotland) b Jan. 20, 1910, d Jan. 28, 1986
*Bean, G. (Notts & Sussex) b March 7, 1864, d March 16, 1923
Bear, M. J. (Essex & Cant.) b Feb. 23, 1934
*Beard, D. D. (C. Dist. & N. Dist.) b Jan. 14, 1920, d July 15, 1982
*Beard, G. R. (NSW) b Aug. 19, 1950
Beauclerk, Lord Frederick (Middx, Surrey & MCC) b May 8, 1773, d April 22, 1850
Beaufort, 10th Duke of (Pres. MCC 1952-53) b April 4, 1900, d Feb. 5, 1984
*Beaumont, R. (Tvl) b Feb. 4, 1884, d May 25, 1958
*Beck, J. E. F. (Wgtn) b Aug. 1, 1934
Becker, G. C. (W. Aust.) b March 13, 1936
*Bedi, B. S. (N. Punjab, Delhi & Northants) b Sept. 25, 1946
*Bedser, A. V. (Surrey; *CY 1947*) b July 4, 1918
Bedser, E. A. (Surrey) b July 4, 1918
Beet, G. (Derbys.; Umpire) b April 24, 1886, d Dec. 13, 1946
*Begbie, D. W. (Tvl) b Dec. 12, 1914
Beldham, W. (Hambledon & Surrey) b Feb. 5, 1766, d Feb. 20, 1862
*Bell, A. J. (W. Prov. & Rhod.) b April 15, 1906, d Aug. 2, 1985
Bell, R. V. (Middx & Sussex) b Jan. 7, 1931, d Oct. 26, 1989
*Bell, W. (Cant.) b Sept. 5, 1931
Bellamy, B. W. (Northants) b April 22, 1891, d Dec. 20, 1985
*Benaud, J. (NSW) b May 11, 1944
*Benaud, R. (NSW; *CY 1962*) b Oct. 6, 1930
*Benjamin, W. K. M. (Leewards & Leics.) b Dec. 31, 1964
Bennett, D. (Middx) b Dec. 18, 1933
Bennett, G. M. (Som.) b Dec. 17, 1909, d July 26, 1982
*Bennett, M. J. (NSW) b Oct. 16, 1956
Bennett, N. H. (Surrey) b Sept. 23, 1912
Bennett, R. (Lancs.) b June 16, 1940
*Benson, M. R. (Kent) b July 6, 1958
Bernard, J. R. (CUCC & Glos.) b Dec. 7, 1938
Berry, L. G. (Leics.) b April 28, 1906, d Feb. 5, 1985
*Berry, R. (Lancs., Worcs. & Derbys.) b Jan. 29, 1926
Bessant, J. G. (Glos.) b Nov. 11, 1892, d Jan. 18, 1982
*Best, C. A. (B'dos) b May 14, 1959
*Betancourt, N. (T/T) b June 4, 1887, d Oct. 12, 1947
Bhalekar, R. B. (M'tra) b Feb. 17, 1952
*Bhandari, P. (Delhi & Bengal) b Nov. 27, 1935
*Bhat, R. (Karn.) b April 16, 1958
Bick, D. A. (Middx) b Feb. 22, 1936
Bicknell, D. J. (Surrey) b June 24, 1967
Bicknell, M. P. (Surrey) b Jan. 14, 1969
Biddulph, K. D. (Som.) b May 29, 1932
Biggs, A. L. (E. Prov.) b April 26, 1946
*Bilby, G. P. (Wgtn) b May 7, 1941
*Binks, J. G. (Yorks.; *CY 1969*) b Oct. 5, 1935
*Binny, R. M. H. (Karn.) b July 19, 1955
*Binns, A. P. (Jam.) b July 24, 1929
Birch, J. D. (Notts.) b June 18, 1955
Bird, H. D. (Yorks. & Leics.; Umpire) b April 19, 1933
*Bird, M. C. (Lancs. & Surrey) b March 25, 1888, d Dec. 9, 1933
Bird, R. E. (Worcs.) b April 4, 1915, d Feb. 20, 1985
*Birkenshaw, J. (Yorks., Leics. & Worcs.) b Nov. 13, 1940
*Birkett, L. S. (B'dos, BG & T/T) b April 14, 1904
Birrell, H. B. (E. Prov., Rhod. & OUCC) b Dec. 1, 1927
Bishop, G. A. (S. Aust.) b Feb. 25, 1960
*Bishop, I. R. (T/T & Derbys.) b Oct. 24, 1967
*Bisset, Sir Murray (W. Prov.) b April 14, 1876, d Oct. 24, 1931
*Bissett, G. F. (Griq. W., W. Prov. & Tvl) b Nov. 5, 1905, d Nov. 14, 1965
Bissex, M. (Glos.) b Sept. 28, 1944
*Blackham, J. McC. (Vic.; *CY 1891*) b May 11, 1854, d Dec. 28, 1932
*Blackie, D. D. (Vic.) b April 5, 1882, d April 18, 1955
Blackledge, J. F. (Lancs.) b April 15, 1928
*Blain, T. E. (C. Dist.) b Feb. 17, 1962
Blair, B. R. (Otago) b Dec. 27, 1957
*Blair, R. W. (Wgtn & C. Dist.) b June 23, 1932
Blake, D. E. (Hants) b April 27, 1925
Blake, Rev. P. D. S. (OUCC & Sussex) b May 23, 1927
Blakey, R. J. (Yorks.) b Jan. 15, 1967
*Blanckenberg, J. M. (W. Prov. & Natal) b Dec. 31, 1893, 'presumed dead'

*Bland, K. C. (Rhod., E. Prov. & OFS; *CY 1966*) b April 5, 1938
Blenkiron, W. (Warwicks.) b July 21, 1942
Bligh, Hon. Ivo (*see* 8th Earl of Darnley)
Blofeld, H. C. (CUCC) b Sept. 23, 1939
Blundell, Sir E. D. (CUCC & NZ) b May 29, 1907, d Sept. 24, 1984
*Blunt, R. C. (Cant. & Otago; *CY 1928*) b Nov. 3, 1900, d June 22, 1966
*Blythe, C. (Kent; *CY 1904*) b May 30, 1879, d Nov. 8, 1917
*Board, J. H. (Glos.) b Feb. 23, 1867, d April 16, 1924
*Bock, E. G. (Griq. W., Tvl & W. Prov.) b Sept. 17, 1908, d Sept. 5, 1961
Bodkin, P. E. (CUCC) b Sept. 15, 1924
*Bolton, B. A. (Cant. & Wgtn) b May 31, 1935
*Bolus, J. B. (Yorks., Notts. & Derbys.) b Jan. 31, 1934
*Bond, G. E. (W. Prov.) b April 5, 1909, d Aug. 27, 1965
Bond, J. D. (Lancs. & Notts.; *CY 1971*) b May 6, 1932
*Bonnor, G. J. (Vic. & NSW) b Feb. 25, 1855, d June 27, 1912
*Boock, S. L. (Otago & Cant.) b Sept. 20, 1951
*Boon, D. C. (Tas.) b Dec. 29, 1960
Boon, T. J. (Leics.) b Nov. 1, 1961
*Booth, B. C. (NSW) b Oct. 19, 1933
Booth, B. J. (Lancs. & Leics.) b Dec. 3, 1935
Booth, F. S. (Lancs.) b Feb. 12, 1907, d Jan. 21, 1980
*Booth, M. W. (Yorks.; *CY 1914*) b Dec. 10, 1886, d July 1, 1916
Booth, P. (Leics.) b Nov. 2, 1952
Booth, R. (Yorks. & Worcs.) b Oct. 1, 1926
*Borde, C. G. (Baroda & M'tra) b July 21, 1934
*Border, A. R. (NSW, Glos, Qld & Essex; *CY 1982*) b July 27, 1955
Bore, M. K. (Yorks. & Notts.) b June 2, 1947
Borrington, A. J. (Derbys.) b Dec. 8, 1948
*Bosanquet, B. J. T. (OUCC & Middx; *CY 1905*) b Oct. 13, 1877, d Oct. 12, 1936
Bose, G. (Bengal) b May 20, 1947
Boshier, B. S. (Leics.) b March 6, 1932
*Botham, I. T. (Som., Worcs. & Qld; *CY 1978*) b Nov. 24, 1955
*Botten, J. T. (NE Tvl & N. Tvl) b June 21, 1938
Boucher, J. C. (Ireland) b Dec. 22, 1910
Bourne, W. A. (B'dos & Warwicks.) b Nov. 15, 1952
*Bowden, M. P. (Surrey & Tvl) b Nov. 1, 1865, d Feb. 19, 1892
*Bowes, W. E. (Yorks.; *CY 1932*) b July 25, 1908, d Sept. 5, 1987
Bowler, P. D. (Leics., Tas. & Derbys.) b July 30, 1963
*Bowley, E. H. (Sussex & Auck.; *CY 1930*) b June 6, 1890, d July 9, 1974
Bowley, F. L. (Worcs.) b Nov. 9, 1873, d May 31, 1943
Bowman, R. (OUCC & Lancs.) b Jan. 26, 1934
Box, T. (Sussex) b Feb. 7, 1808, d July 12, 1876
*Boyce, K. D. (B'dos & Essex; *CY 1974*) b Oct. 11, 1943
*Boycott, G. (Yorks. & N. Tvl; *CY 1965*) b Oct. 21, 1940
Boyd-Moss, R. J. (CUCC & Northants) b Dec. 16, 1959
Boyes, G. S. (Hants) b March 31, 1899, d Feb. 11, 1973
*Boyle, H. F. (Vic.) b Dec. 10, 1847, d Nov. 21, 1907
*Bracewell, B. P. (C. Dist., Otago & N. Dist.) b Sept. 14, 1959
*Bracewell, J. G. (Otago & Auck.) b April 15, 1958
*Bradburn, W. P. (N. Dist.) b Nov. 24, 1938
*Bradley, W. M. (Kent) b Jan. 2, 1875, d June 19, 1944
*Bradman, Sir D. G. (NSW & S. Aust.; *CY 1931*) b Aug. 27, 1908
Bradshaw, J. C. (Leics.) b Jan. 25, 1902, d Nov. 8, 1984
Brain, B. M. (Worcs. & Glos.) b Sept. 13, 1940
Bramall, Field-Marshal The Lord (Pres. MCC 1988-89) b Dec. 18, 1923
*Brann, W. H. (E. Prov.) b April 4, 1899, d Sept. 22, 1953
Brassington, A. J. (Glos.) b Aug. 9, 1954
*Braund, L. C. (Surrey & Som.; *CY 1902*) b Oct. 18, 1875, d Dec. 23, 1955
Bray, C. (Essex) b April 6, 1898
Brayshaw, I. J. (W. Aust.) b Jan. 14, 1942
Brazier, A. F. (Surrey & Kent) b Dec. 7, 1924
Breakwell, D. (Northants & Som.) b July 2, 1948
*Brearley, J. M. (CUCC & Middx; *CY 1977*) b April 28, 1942
*Brearley, W. (Lancs.; *CY 1909*) b March 11, 1876, d Jan. 13, 1937
*Brennan, D. V. (Yorks.) b Feb. 10, 1920, d Jan. 9, 1985
Bridge, W. B. (Warwicks.) b May 29, 1938
Bridger, Rev. J. R. (Hants) b April 8, 1920, d July 14, 1986
Brierley, T. L. (Glam., Lancs. & Canada) b June 15, 1910, d Jan. 7, 1989
Briers, N. E. (Leics.) b Jan. 15, 1955
*Briggs, John (Lancs.; *CY 1889*) b Oct. 3, 1862, d Jan. 11, 1902
*Bright, R. J. (Vic.) b July 13, 1954

*Briscoe, A. W. (Tvl) b Feb. 6, 1911, d April 22, 1941
*Broad, B. C. (Glos. & Notts.) b Sept. 29, 1957
Broadbent, R. G. (Worcs.) b June 21, 1924
Brocklehurst, B. G. (Som.) b Feb. 18, 1922
*Brockwell, W. (Kimberley & Surrey; *CY 1895*) b Jan. 21, 1865, d June 30, 1935
Broderick, V. (Northants) b Aug. 17, 1920
Brodhurst, A. H. (CUCC & Glos.) b July 21, 1916
*Bromfield, H. D. (W. Prov.) b June 26, 1932
*Bromley, E. H. (W. Aust. & Vic.) b Sept. 2, 1912, d Feb. 1, 1967
*Bromley-Davenport, H. R. (CUCC, Bombay Eur. & Middx) b Aug. 18, 1870, d May 23, 1954
*Brookes, D. (Northants; *CY 1957*) b Oct. 29, 1915
Brookes, W. H. (Editor of *Wisden* 1936-39) b Dec. 5, 1894, d May 28, 1955
Brooks, R. A. (OUCC & Som.) b June 14, 1943
*Brown, A. (Kent) b Oct. 17, 1935
Brown, A. S. (Glos.) b June 24, 1936
*Brown, D. J. (Warwicks.) b Jan. 30, 1942
Brown, D. W. J. (Glos.) b Feb. 26, 1942
*Brown, F. R. (CUCC, Surrey & Northants; *CY 1933*; Pres. MCC 1971-72) b Dec. 16, 1910
*Brown, G. (Hants) b Oct. 6, 1887, d Dec. 3, 1964
Brown, J. (Scotland) b Sept. 24, 1931
*Brown, J. T. (Yorks.; *CY 1895*) b Aug. 20, 1869, d Nov. 4, 1904
Brown, K. R. (Middx) b March 18, 1963
*Brown, L. S. (Tvl, NE Tvl & Rhod.) b Nov. 24, 1910, d Sept. 1, 1983
Brown, R. D. (Zimb.) b March 11, 1951
Brown, S. M. (Middx) b Dec. 8, 1917, d Dec. 28, 1987
*Brown, V. R. (Cant. & Auck.) b Nov. 3, 1959
*Brown, W. A. (NSW & Qld; *CY 1939*) b July 31, 1912
Brown, W. C. (Northants) b Nov. 13, 1900, d Jan. 20, 1986
*Browne, C. R. (B'dos & BG) b Oct. 8, 1890, d Jan. 12, 1964
Bruce, Hon. C. N. (3rd Lord Aberdare) (OUCC & Middx) b Aug. 2, 1885, d Oct. 4, 1957
Bruce, S. D. (W. Prov. & OFS) b Jan. 11, 1954
*Bruce, W. (Vic.) b May 22, 1864, d Aug. 3, 1925
Bruyns, A. (W. Prov. & Natal) b Sept. 19, 1946
Bryan, G. J. (Kent) b Dec. 29, 1902
Bryan, J. L. (CUCC & Kent; *CY 1922*) b May 26, 1896, d April 23, 1985
Bryan, R. T. (Kent) b July 30, 1898, d July 27, 1970
*Buckenham, C. P. (Essex) b Jan. 16, 1876, d Feb. 23, 1937
Buckingham, J. (Warwicks.) b Jan. 21, 1903, d Jan. 25, 1987
Budd, E. H. (Middx & All-England) b Feb. 23, 1785, d March 29, 1875
Budd, W. L. (Hants) b Oct. 25, 1913, d Aug. 23, 1986
Bull, F. G. (Essex; *CY 1898*) b April 2, 1875, d Sept. 16, 1910
Buller, J. S. (Yorks. & Worcs.; Umpire) b Aug. 23, 1909, d Aug. 7, 1970
Burden, M. D. (Hants) b Oct. 4, 1930, d Nov. 9, 1987
*Burge, P. J. (Qld; *CY 1965*) b May 17, 1932
*Burger, C. G. de V. (Natal) b July 12, 1935
Burgess, G. I. (Som.) b May 5, 1943
*Burgess, M. G. (Auck.) b July 17, 1944
*Burke, C. (Auck.) b March 22, 1914
*Burke, J. W. (NSW; *CY 1957*) b June 12, 1930, d Feb. 2, 1979
*Burke, S. F. (NE Tvl & OFS) b March 11, 1934
*Burki, Javed (Pak. Us, OUCC, Punjab, Lahore, Kar., R'pindi & NWFP) b May 8, 1938
*Burn, E. J. K. (K. E.) (Tas.) b Sept. 17, 1862, d July 20, 1956
Burnet, J. R. (Yorks.) b Oct. 11, 1918
Burns, N. D. (Essex, W. Prov. & Som.) b Sept. 19, 1965
Burnup, C. J. (CUCC & Kent; *CY 1903*) b Nov. 21, 1875, d April 5, 1960
Burrough, H. D. (Som.) b Feb. 6, 1909
*Burton, F. J. (Vic. & NSW) b 1866, d Aug. 25, 1929
*Burtt, T. B. (Cant.) b Jan. 22, 1915, d May 24, 1988
Buse, H. T. F. (Som.) b Aug. 5, 1910
Bushby, M. H. (CUCC) b July 29, 1931
Buss, A. (Sussex) b Sept. 1, 1939
Buss, M. A. (Sussex & OFS) b Jan. 24, 1944
Buswell, J. E. (Northants) b July 3, 1909
*Butcher, A. R. (Surrey & Glam.; *CY 1991*) b Jan. 7, 1954
*Butcher, B. F. (Guyana; *CY 1970*) b Sept. 3, 1933
Butcher, I. P. (Leics. & Glos.) b July 1, 1962
*Butcher, R. O. (Middx, B'dos & Tas.) b Oct. 14, 1953
*Butler, H. J. (Notts.) b March 12, 1913
*Butler, L. S. (T/T) b Feb. 9, 1929
*Butt, H. R. (Sussex) b Dec. 27, 1865, d Dec. 21, 1928
*Butterfield, L. A. (Cant.) b Aug. 29, 1913
*Butts, C. G. (Guyana) b July 8, 1957
Buxton, I. R. (Derbys.) b April 17, 1938
*Buys, I. D. (W. Prov.) b Feb. 3, 1895, dead
Byas, D. (Yorks.) b Aug. 26, 1963
*Bynoe, M. R. (B'dos) b Feb. 23, 1941

Caccia, Lord (Pres. MCC 1973-74) b Dec. 21, 1905, d Oct. 31, 1990
Caesar, Julius (Surrey & All-England) b March 25, 1830, d March 6, 1878
Caffyn, W. (Surrey & NSW) b Feb. 2, 1828, d Aug. 28, 1919
Caine, C. Stewart (Editor of *Wisden* 1926-33) b Oct. 28, 1861, d April 15, 1933
*Cairns, B. L. (C. Dist., Otago & N. Dist.) b Oct. 10, 1949
*Cairns, C. L. (N. Dist. & Notts.) b July 13, 1970
Calder, H. L. (Cranleigh; *CY 1918*) b 1900
*Callaway, S. T. (NSW & Cant.) b Feb. 6, 1868, d Nov. 25, 1923
*Callen, I. W. (Vic. & Boland) b May 2, 1955
*Calthorpe, Hon. F. S. Gough- (CUCC, Sussex & Warwicks.) b May 27, 1892, d Nov. 19, 1935
*Camacho, G. S. (Guyana) b Oct. 15, 1945
*Cameron, F. J. (Jam.) b June 22, 1923
*Cameron, F. J. (Otago) b June 1, 1932
*Cameron, H. B. (Tvl, E. Prov. & W. Prov.; *CY 1936*) b July 5, 1905, d Nov. 2, 1935
*Cameron, J. H. (CUCC, Jam. & Som.) b April 8, 1914
*Campbell, G. D. (Tas.) b March 10, 1964
*Campbell, T. (Tvl) b Feb. 9, 1882, d Oct. 5, 1924
Cann, M. J. (Glam. & OFS) b July 4, 1965
Cannings, V. H. D. (Warwicks. & Hants) b April 3, 1919
*Capel, D. J. (Northants & E. Prov.) b Feb. 6, 1963
Caple, R. G. (Middx & Hants) b Dec. 8, 1939
Cardus, Sir Neville (Cricket Writer) b April 3, 1888, d Feb. 27, 1975
*Carew, G. McD. (B'dos) b June 4, 1910, d Dec. 9, 1974
*Carew, M. C. (T/T) b Sept. 15, 1937
*Carkeek, W. (Vic.) b Oct. 17, 1878, d Feb. 20, 1937
*Carlson, P. H. (Qld) b Aug. 8, 1951
*Carlstein, P. R. (OFS, Tvl, Natal & Rhod.) b Oct. 28, 1938
Carmody, D. K. (NSW & W. Aust.) b Feb. 16, 1919, d Oct. 21, 1977
Carpenter, D. (Glos.) b Sept. 12, 1935
Carpenter, R. (Cambs. & Utd England XI) b Nov. 18, 1830, d July 13, 1901
*Carr, A. W. (Notts.; *CY 1923*) b May 21, 1893, d Feb. 7, 1963
*Carr, D. B. (OUCC & Derbys.; *CY 1960*; Sec. TCCB 1974-86) b Dec. 28, 1926
*Carr, D. W. (Kent; *CY 1910*) b March 17, 1872, d March 23, 1950
Carr, J. D. (OUCC & Middx) b June 15, 1963
Carrick, P. (Yorks. & E. Prov.) b July 16, 1952
Carrigan, A. H. (Qld) b Aug. 26, 1917
Carrington, E. (Derbys.) b March 25, 1914
Carse, J. A. (Rhod., W. Prov., E. Prov. & Northants) b Dec. 13, 1958
*Carter, C. P. (Natal & Tvl) b April 23, 1881, d Nov. 8, 1952
*Carter, H. (NSW) b Halifax, Yorks. March 15, 1878, d June 8, 1948
Carter, R. G. (Warwicks.) b April 14, 1933
Carter, R. G. M. (Worcs.) b July 11, 1937
Carter, R. M. (Northants & Cant.) b May 25, 1960
Cartwright, H. (Derbys.) b May 12, 1951
*Cartwright, T. W. (Warwicks., Som. & Glam.) b July 22, 1935
Carty, R. A. (Hants) b July 28, 1922, d March 31, 1984
Cass, G. R. (Essex, Worcs. & Tas.) b April 23, 1940
Castell, A. T. (Hants) b Aug. 6, 1943
Castle, F. (Som.) b April 9, 1909
Catt, A. W. (Kent & W. Prov.) b Oct. 2, 1933
*Catterall, R. H. (Tvl, Rhod., Natal & OFS; *CY 1925*) b July 10, 1900, d Jan. 2, 1961
*Cave, H. B. (Wgtn & C. Dist.) b Oct. 10, 1922, d Sept. 15, 1989
Chalk, F. G. H. (OUCC & Kent) b Sept. 7, 1910, d Feb. 17, 1943
*Challenor, G. (B'dos) b June 28, 1888, d July 30, 1947
*Chandrasekhar, B. S. (†Karn.; *CY 1972*) b May 17, 1945
Chandrasekhar, V. B. (TN) b Aug. 21, 1961
*Chang, H. S. (Jam.) b July 22, 1952
*Chapman, A. P. F. (Uppingham, OUCC & Kent; *CY 1919*) b Sept. 3, 1900, d Sept. 16, 1961
*Chapman, H. W. (Natal) b June 30, 1890, d Dec. 1, 1941
*Chappell, G. S. (S. Aust., Som. & Qld; *CY 1973*) b Aug. 7, 1948
*Chappell, I. M. (S. Aust. & Lancs.; *CY 1976*) b Sept. 26, 1943
*Chappell, T. M. (S. Aust., W. Aust. & NSW) b Oct. 21, 1952
*Chapple, M. E. (Cant. & C. Dist.) b July 25, 1930, d July 31, 1985
*Charlton, P. C. (NSW) b April 9, 1867, d Sept. 30, 1954
*Charlwood, H. R. J. (Sussex) b Dec. 19, 1846, d June 6, 1888
*Chatfield, E. J. (Wgtn) b July 3, 1950
*Chatterton, W. (Derbys.) b Dec. 27, 1861, d March 19, 1913
*Chauhan, C. P. S. (M'tra & Delhi) b July 21, 1947
Cheatle, R. G. L. (Sussex & Surrey) b July 31, 1953
*Cheetham, J. E. (W. Prov.) b May 26, 1920, d Aug. 21, 1980

Chester, F. (Worcs.; Umpire) b Jan. 20, 1895, d April 8, 1957
Chesterton, G. H. (OUCC & Worcs.) b July 15, 1922
Chevalier, G. A. (W. Prov.) b March 9, 1937
Childs, J. H. (Glos. & Essex; *CY 1987*) b Aug. 15, 1951
Childs-Clarke, A. W. (Middx & Northants) b May 13, 1905, d Feb. 19, 1980
Chipperfield, A. G. (NSW) b Nov. 17, 1905, d July 29, 1987
Chisholm, R. H. E. (Scotland) b May 22, 1927
Chowdhury, N. R. (Bihar & Bengal) b May 23, 1923, d Dec. 14, 1979
Christiani, C. M. (BG) b Oct. 28, 1913, d April 4, 1938
Christiani, R. J. (BG) b July 19, 1920
Christopherson, S. (Kent; Pres. MCC 1939-45) b Nov. 11, 1861, d April 6, 1949
Christy, J. A. J. (Tvl & Qld) b Dec. 12, 1904, d Feb. 1, 1971
Chubb, G. W. A. (Border & Tvl) b April 12, 1911, d Aug. 28, 1982
Clark, D. G. (Kent; Pres. MCC 1977-78) b Jan. 27, 1919
Clark, E. A. (Middx) b April 15, 1937
Clark, E. W. (Northants) b Aug. 9, 1902, d April 28, 1982
Clark, L. S. (Essex) b March 6, 1914
Clark, T. H. (Surrey) b Oct. 4, 1924, d June 15, 1981
Clark, W. M. (W. Aust.) b Sept. 19, 1953
Clarke, A. R. (Sussex) b Dec. 23, 1961
Clarke, Dr C. B. (B'dos, Northants & Essex) b April 7, 1918
Clarke, R. W. (Northants) b April 22, 1924, d Aug. 3, 1981
Clarke, S. T. (B'dos, Surrey, Tvl, OFS & N. Tvl) b Dec. 11, 1954
Clarke, William (Notts.; founded All-England XI & Trent Bridge ground) b Dec. 24, 1798, d Aug. 25, 1856
Clarkson, A. (Yorks. & Som.) b Sept. 5, 1939
Claughton, J. A. (OUCC & Warwicks.) b Sept. 17, 1956
Clay, J. C. (Glam.) b March 18, 1898, d Aug. 12, 1973
Clay, J. D. (Notts.) b Oct. 15, 1924
Clayton, G. (Lancs. & Som.) b Feb. 3, 1938
Clements, S. M. (OUCC) b April 19, 1956
Cleverley, D. C. (Auck.) b Dec. 23, 1909
Clift, Patrick B. (Rhod., Leics. & Natal) b July 14, 1953
Clift, Philip B. (Glam.) b Sept. 3, 1918
Clinton, G. S. (Kent, Surrey & Zimb.-Rhod.) b May 5, 1953
Close, D. B. (Yorks. & Som.; *CY 1964*) b Feb. 24, 1931

Cobb, R. A. (Leics. & Natal) b May 18, 1961
Cobham, 9th Visct (Worcs.) b Oct. 23, 1881, d July 31, 1949
Cobham, 10th Visct (Hon. C. J. Lyttelton) (Worcs.; Pres. MCC 1954) b Aug. 8, 1909, d March 20, 1977
*Cochrane, J. A. K. (Tvl & Griq. W.) b July 15, 1909, d June 15, 1987
*Coen, S. K. (OFS, W. Prov., Tvl & Border) b Oct. 14, 1902, d Jan. 28, 1967
*Colah, S. M. H. (Bombay, W. Ind. & Naw.) b Sept. 22, 1902, d Sept. 11, 1950
Colchin, Robert ("Long Robin") (Kent & All-England) b Nov. 1713, d April 1750
*Coldwell, L. J. (Worcs.) b Jan. 10, 1933
*Colley, D. J. (NSW) b March 15, 1947
Collin, T. (Warwicks.) b April 7, 1911
*Collinge, R. O. (C. Dist., Wgtn & N. Dist.) b April 2, 1946
*Collins, H. L. (NSW) b Jan. 21, 1889, d May 28, 1959
Collins, R. (Lancs.) b March 10, 1934
*Colquhoun, I. A. (C. Dist.) b June 8, 1924
Coman, P. G. (Cant.) b April 13, 1943
*Commaille, J. M. M. (W. Prov., Natal, OFS & Griq. W.) b Feb. 21, 1883, d July 27, 1956
*Compton, D. C. S. (Middx & Holkar; *CY 1939*) b May 23, 1918
Compton, L. H. (Middx) b Sept. 12, 1912, d Dec. 27, 1984
*Coney, J. V. (Wgtn; *CY 1984*) b June 21, 1952
*Congdon, B. E. (C. Dist., Wgtn, Otago & Cant.; *CY 1974*) b Feb. 11, 1938
*Coningham, A. (NSW & Qld) b July 14, 1863, d June 13, 1939
*Connolly, A. N. (Vic. & Middx) b June 29, 1939
Connor, C. A. (Hants) b March 24, 1961
Constable, B. (Surrey) b Feb. 19, 1921
Constant, D. J. (Kent & Leics.; Umpire) b Nov. 9, 1941
*Constantine, Lord L. N. (T/T & B'dos; *CY 1940*) b Sept. 21, 1902, d July 1, 1971
Constantine, L. S. (T/T) b May 25, 1874, d Jan. 5, 1942
*Contractor, N. J. (Guj. & Ind. Rlwys) b March 7, 1934
*Conyngham, D. P. (Natal, Tvl & W. Prov.) b May 10, 1897, d July 7, 1979
*Cook, C. (Glos.) b Aug. 23, 1921
*Cook, F. J. (E. Prov.) b 1870, dead
*Cook, G. (Northants & E. Prov.) b Oct. 9, 1951
*Cook, N. G. B. (Leics. & Northants) b June 17, 1956
Cook, S. J. (Tvl & Som.; *CY 1990*) b July 31, 1953
Cook, T. E. (Sussex) b Feb. 5, 1901, d Jan. 15, 1950

*Cooper, A. H. C. (Tvl) b Sept 2, 1893, d July 18, 1963
*Cooper, B. B. (Middx, Kent & Vic.) b March 15, 1844, d Aug. 7, 1914
Cooper, F. S. Ashley- (Cricket Historian) b March 17, 1877, d Jan. 31, 1932
Cooper, G. C. (Sussex) b Sept. 2, 1936
Cooper, H. P. (Yorks. & N. Tvl) b April 17, 1949
Cooper, K. E. (Notts.) b Dec. 27, 1957
*Cooper, W. H. (Vic.) b Sept. 11, 1849, d April 5, 1939
*Cope, G. A. (Yorks.) b Feb. 23, 1947
*Copson, W. H. (Derbys.; *CY 1937*) b April 27, 1908, d Sept. 14, 1971
Cordle, A. E. (Glam.) b Sept. 21, 1940
*Corling, G. E. (NSW) b July 13, 1941
Cornford, J. H. (Sussex) b Dec. 9, 1911, d June 17, 1985
*Cornford, W. L. (Sussex) b Dec. 25, 1900, d Feb. 6, 1964
Cornwallis, Capt. Hon. W. S. (2nd Lord Cornwallis) (Kent) b March 14, 1892, d Jan. 4, 1982
Corrall, P. (Leics.) b July 16, 1906
Corran, A. J. (OUCC & Notts.) b Nov. 25, 1936
*Cosier, G. J. (Vic., S. Aust. & Qld) b April 25,1953
*Cottam, J. T. (NSW) b Sept. 5, 1867, d Jan. 30, 1897
*Cottam, R. M. H. (Hants & Northants) b Oct. 16, 1944
*Cotter, A. (NSW) b Dec. 3, 1884, d Oct. 31, 1917
Cottey, P. A. (Glam.) b June 2, 1966
Cotton, J. (Notts. & Leics.) b Nov. 7, 1940
Cottrell, G. A. (CUCC) b March 23, 1945
Coulson, S. S. (Leics.) b Oct. 17, 1898, d Oct. 3, 1981
*Coulthard, G. (Vic.) b Aug. 1, 1856, d Oct. 22, 1883
*Coventry, Hon. C. J. (Worcs.) b Feb. 26, 1867, d June 2, 1929
Coverdale, S. P. (CUCC, Yorks., & Northants) b Nov. 20, 1954
Cowan, M. J. (Yorks.) b June 10, 1933
*Cowans, N. G. (Middx) b April 17, 1961
*Cowdrey, C. S. (Kent) b Oct. 20, 1957
Cowdrey, G. R. (Kent) b June 27, 1964
*Cowdrey, M. C. (OUCC & Kent; *CY 1956*; Pres. MCC 1986-87) b Dec. 24, 1932
*Cowie, J. (Auck.) b March 30, 1912
Cowley, N. G. (Hants & Glam.) b March 1, 1953
*Cowper, R. M. (Vic. & W. Aust.) b Oct. 5, 1940
Cox, A. L. (Northants) b July 22, 1907, d Nov. 1986
Cox, G., jun. (Sussex) b Aug. 23, 1911, d March 30, 1985
Cox, G. R. (Sussex) b Nov. 29, 1873, March 24, 1949
*Cox, J. L. (Natal) b June 28, 1886, d July 1971
*Coxon, A. (Yorks.) b Jan. 18, 1916
Crabtree, H. P. (Essex) b April 30, 1906, May 28, 1982
Craig, E. J. (CUCC & Lancs.) b March 2 1942
*Craig, I. D. (NSW) b June 12, 1935
Cranfield, L. M. (Glos.) b Aug. 29, 1909
Cranmer, P. (Warwicks.) b Sept. 10, 19
*Cranston, J. (Glos.) b Jan. 9, 1859, d De 10, 1904
*Cranston, K. (Lancs.) b Oct. 20, 1917
*Crapp, J. F. (Glos.) b Oct. 14, 1912, d Fe 15, 1981
*Crawford, J. N. (Surrey, S. Aust., Wgtn Otago; *CY 1907*) b Dec. 1, 1886, d M 2, 1963
*Crawford, P. (NSW) b Aug. 3, 1933
Crawley, A. M. (OUCC & Kent; Pr MCC 1972-73) b April 10, 1908
Crawley, L. G. (CUCC, Worcs. & Essex) July 26, 1903, d July 9, 1981
Crawley, M. A. (OUCC & Lancs.) b De 16, 1967
Cray, S. J. (Essex) b May 29, 1921
*Cresswell, G. F. (Wgtn & C. Dist.) March 22, 1915, d Jan. 10, 1966
*Cripps, G. (W. Prov.) b Oct. 19, 1865, July 27, 1943
*Crisp, R. J. (Rhod., W. Prov. & Worcs.) May 28, 1911
*Croft, C. E. H. (Guyana & Lancs.) b Mar 15, 1953
Croft, R. D. B. (Glam.) b May 25, 1970
*Cromb, I. B. (Cant.) b June 25, 1905, March 6, 1984
Crookes, N. S. (Natal) b Nov. 15, 1935
Cross, G. F. (Leics.) b Nov. 15, 1943
*Crowe, J. J. (S. Aust. & Auck.) b Sept. 1958
*Crowe, M. D. (Auck., C. Dist. & Som.; *C 1985*) b Sept. 22, 1962
Crump, B. S. (Northants) b April 25, 19
Crush, E. (Kent) b April 25, 1917
Cumbes, J. (Lancs., Surrey, Worcs. Warwicks.) b May 4, 1944
*Cunis, R. S. (Auck. & N. Dist.) b Jan. 1941
*Curnow, S. H. (Tvl) b Dec. 16, 1907, d Ju 28, 1986
Curran, K. M. (Glos., Zimb. & Natal) Sept. 7, 1959
*Curtis, T. S. (Worcs. & CUCC) b Jan. 1 1960
Cuthbertson, G. B. (Middx, Sussex Northants) b March 28, 1901
Cutmore, J. A. (Essex) b Dec. 28, 1898, Nov. 30, 1985
*Cuttell, W. R. (Lancs.; *CY 1898*) b Sept. 1 1864, d Dec. 9, 1929

*Da Costa, O. C. (Jam.) b Sept. 11, 1907, d Oct. 1, 1936
Dacre, C. C. (Auck. & Glos.) b May 15, 1899, d Nov. 2, 1975
Daft, Richard (Notts. & All-England) b Nov. 2, 1835, d July 18, 1900
Dakin, G. F. (E. Prov.) b Aug. 13, 1935
Dalmeny, Lord (6th Earl of Rosebery) (Middx & Surrey) b Jan. 8, 1882, d May 30, 1974
*Dalton, E. L. (Natal) b Dec. 2, 1906, d June 3, 1981
*Dani, H. T. (M'tra & Ind. Serv.) b May 24, 1933
*Daniel, W. W. (B'dos, Middx & W. Aust.) b Jan. 16, 1956
*D'Arcy, J. W. (Cant., Wgtn & Otago) b April 23, 1936
Dare, R. (Hants) b Nov. 26, 1921
*Darling, J. (S. Aust.; *CY 1900*) b Nov. 21, 1870, d Jan. 2, 1946
*Darling, L. S. (Vic.) b Aug. 14, 1909
*Darling, W. M. (S. Aust.) b May 1, 1957
*Darnley, 8th Earl of (Hon. Ivo Bligh) (CUCC & Kent; Pres. MCC 1900) b March 13, 1859, d April 10, 1927
Davey, J. (Glos.) b Sept. 4, 1944
*Davidson, A. K. (NSW; *CY 1962*) b June 14, 1929
Davies, Dai (Glam.) b Aug. 26, 1896, d July 16, 1976
Davies, Emrys (Glam.) b June 27, 1904, d Nov. 10, 1975
*Davies, E. Q. (E. Prov., Tvl & NE Tvl) b Aug. 26, 1909, d Nov. 11, 1976
Davies, H. D. (Glam.) b July 23, 1932
Davies, H. G. (Glam.) b April 23, 1913
Davies, J. G. W. (CUCC & Kent; Pres. MCC 1985-86) b Sept. 10, 1911
Davies, T. (Glam.) b Oct. 25, 1960
Davis, B. A. (T/T & Glam.) b May 2, 1940
Davis, C. A. (T/T) b Jan. 1, 1944
Davis, E. (Northants) b March 8, 1922
Davis, I. C. (NSW & Qld) b June 25, 1953
Davis, M. R. (Som.) b Feb. 26, 1962
Davis, P. C. (Northants) b May 24, 1915
Davis, R. C. (Glam.) b Jan. 1, 1946
Davis, R. P. (Kent) b March 18, 1966
Davis, S. P. (Vic.) b Nov. 8, 1959
Davis, W. W. (Windwards, Glam., Tas. & Northants) b Sept. 18, 1958
Davison, B. F. (Rhod., Leics, Tas. & Glos.) b Dec. 21, 1946
Davison, I. (Notts.) b Oct. 4, 1937
Dawkes, G. O. (Leics. & Derbys.) b July 19, 1920
Dawson, E. W. (CUCC & Leics.) b Feb. 13, 1904, d June 4, 1979
Dawson, O. C. (Natal & Border) b Sept. 1, 1919
Day, A. P. (Kent; *CY 1910*) b April 10, 1885, d Jan. 22, 1969
*de Alwis, R. G. (SSC) b Feb. 15, 1959
*Dean, H. (Lancs.) b Aug. 13, 1884, d March 12, 1957
*Deane, H. G. (Natal & Tvl) b July 21, 1895, d Oct. 21, 1939
*De Caires, F. I. (BG) b May 12, 1909, d Feb. 2, 1959
*De Courcy, J. H. (NSW) b April 18, 1927
*DeFreitas, P. A. J. (Leics. & Lancs.) b Feb. 18, 1966
Delisle, G. P. S. (OUCC & Middx) b Dec. 25, 1934
*Dell, A. R. (Qld) b Aug. 6, 1947
*de Mel, A. L. F. (SL) b May 9, 1959
*Dempster, C. S. (Wgtn, Leics., Scotland & Warwicks.; *CY 1932*) b Nov. 15, 1903, d Feb. 14, 1974
*Dempster, E. W. (Wgtn) b Jan. 25, 1925
*Denness, M. H. (Scotland, Kent & Essex; *CY 1975*) b Dec. 1, 1940
Dennett, E. G. (Glos.) b April 27, 1880, d Sept. 14, 1937
Denning, P. W. (Som.) b Dec. 16, 1949
Dennis, F. (Yorks.) b June 11, 1907
Dennis, S. J. (Yorks., OFS & Glam.) b Oct. 18, 1960
*Denton, D. (Yorks.; *CY 1906*) b July 4, 1874, d Feb. 16, 1950
Deodhar, D. B. (M'tra; oldest living Ranji Trophy player) b Jan. 14, 1892
*Depeiza, C. C. (B'dos) b Oct. 10, 1927
Derrick, J. (Glam.) b Jan. 15, 1963
*Desai, R. B. (Bombay) b June 20, 1939
De Saram, F. C. (OUCC & Ceylon) b Sept. 5, 1912, d April 11, 1983
de Silva, A. M. (CCC) b Dec. 3, 1963
de Silva, D. L. S. (SL) b Nov. 17, 1956, d April 12, 1980
*de Silva, D. S. (SL) b June 11, 1942
*de Silva, E. A. R. (NCC) b March 28, 1956
de Silva, G. N. (SL) b March 12, 1955
*de Silva, G. R. A. (SL) b Dec. 12, 1952
*de Silva, P. A. (NCC) b Oct. 17, 1965
de Smidt, R. (W. Prov.) b Nov. 24, 1883, d Aug. 3, 1986
Devereux, L. N. (Middx, Worcs. & Glam.) b Oct. 20, 1931
de Villiers, P. S. (N. Tvl & Kent) b Oct. 13, 1964
*Dewdney, C. T. (Jam.) b Oct. 23, 1933
*Dewes, J. G. (CUCC & Middx) b Oct. 11, 1926
Dews, G. (Worcs.) b June 5, 1921
*Dexter, E. R. (CUCC & Sussex; *CY 1961*) b May 15, 1935
*Dias, R. L. (CCC) b Oct. 18, 1952
Dibbs, A. H. A. (Pres. MCC 1983-84) b Dec. 9, 1918, d Nov. 28, 1985
*Dick, A. E. (Otago & Wgtn) b Oct. 10, 1936
*Dickinson, G. R. (Otago) b March 11, 1903, d March 17, 1978

*Dilley, G. R. (Kent, Natal & Worcs.) b May 18, 1959
Diment, R. A. (Glos. & Leics.) b Feb. 9, 1927
*Dipper, A. E. (Glos.) b Nov. 9, 1885, d Nov. 7, 1945
*Divecha, R. V. (Bombay, OUCC, Northants, Vidarbha & S'tra) b Oct. 18, 1927
Diver, A. J. D. (Cambs., Middx, Notts. & All-England) b June 6, 1824, d March 25, 1876
Dixon, A. L. (Kent) b Nov. 27, 1933
*Dixon, C. D. (Tvl) b Feb. 12, 1891, d Sept. 9, 1969
Dodds, T. C. (Essex) b May 29, 1919
*Dodemaide, A. I. C. (Vic. & Sussex) b Oct. 5, 1963
Doggart, A. G. (CUCC, Durham & Middx) b June 2, 1897, d June 7, 1963
*Doggart, G. H. G. (CUCC & Sussex; Pres. MCC 1981-82) b July 18, 1925
*D'Oliveira, B. L. (Worcs.; *CY 1967*) b Oct. 4, 1931
D'Oliveira, D. B. (Worcs.) b Oct. 19, 1960
*Dollery, H. E. (Warwicks. & Wgtn; *CY 1952*) b Oct. 14, 1914, d Jan. 20, 1987
Dollery, K. R. (Qld, Auck., Tas. & Warwicks.) b Dec. 9, 1924
*Dolphin, A. (Yorks.) b Dec. 24, 1885, d Oct. 23, 1942
Donald, A. A. (OFS & Warwicks.) b Oct. 20, 1966
*Donnan, H. (NSW) b Nov. 12, 1864, d Aug. 13, 1956
*Donnelly, M. P. (Wgtn, Cant., Middx, Warwicks. & OUCC; *CY 1948*) b Oct. 17, 1917
*Dooland, B. (S. Aust. & Notts.; *CY 1955*) b Nov. 1, 1923, d Sept. 8, 1980
Dorrinton, W. (Kent & All-England) b April 29, 1809, d Nov. 8, 1848
Dorset, 3rd Duke of (Kent) b March 24, 1745, d July 19, 1799
*Doshi, D. R. (Bengal, Notts., Warwicks. & S'tra) b Dec. 22, 1947
*Douglas, J. W. H. T. (Essex; *CY 1915*) b Sept. 3, 1882, d Dec. 19, 1930
Dowding, A. L. (OUCC) b April 4, 1929
*Dowe, U. G. (Jam.) b March 29, 1949
*Dower, R. R. (E. Prov.) b June 4, 1876, d Sept. 15, 1964
*Dowling, G. T. (Cant.) b March 4, 1937
*Downton, P. R. (Kent & Middx) b April 4, 1957
Draper, E. J. (E. Prov. & Griq. W.) b Sept. 27, 1934
*Draper, R. G. (E. Prov. & Griq. W.) b Dec. 24, 1926
Dredge, C. H. (Som.) b Aug. 4, 1954
*Druce, N. F. (CUCC & Surrey; *CY 1898*) b Jan. 1, 1875, d Oct. 27, 1954
Drybrough, C. D. (OUCC & Middx) b Aug. 31, 1938
*D'Souza, A. (Kar., Peshawar & PIA) b Jan. 17, 1939
*Ducat, A. (Surrey; *CY 1920*) b Feb. 16, 1886, d July 23, 1942
*Duckworth, C. A. R. (Natal & Rhod.) b March 22, 1933
*Duckworth, G. (Lancs.; *CY 1929*) b May 9, 1901, d Jan. 5, 1966
Dudleston, B. (Leics., Glos. & Rhod.) b July 16, 1945
*Duff, R. A. (NSW) b Aug. 17, 1878, d Dec. 13, 1911
*Dujon, P. J. L. (Jam.; *CY 1989*) b May 28, 1956
*Duleepsinhji, K. S. (CUCC & Sussex; *CY 1930*) b June 13, 1905, d Dec. 5, 1959
*Dumbrill, R. (Natal & Tvl) b Nov. 19, 1938
*Duminy, J. P. (OUCC, W. Prov. & Tvl) b Dec. 16, 1897, d Jan. 31, 1980
*Duncan, J. R. F. (Qld & Vic.) b March 25, 1944
*Dunell, O. R. (E. Prov.) b July 15, 1856, d Oct. 21, 1929
*Dunning, J. A. (Otago & OUCC) b Feb. 6, 1903, d June 24, 1971
*Du Preez, J. H. (Rhod. & Zimb.) b Nov 14, 1942
*Durani, S. A. (S'tra, Guj. & Raja.) b Dec 11, 1934
Durose, A. J. (Northants) b Oct. 10, 1944
*Durston, F. J. (Middx) b July 11, 1893, April 8, 1965
*Du Toit, J. F. (SA) b April 5, 1868, d Jul 10, 1909
Dye, J. C. J. (Kent, Northants & E. Prov b July 24, 1942
Dyer, D. D. (Natal & Tvl) b Dec. 3, 194
*Dyer, D. V. (Natal) b May 2, 1914, d Jur 18, 1990
*Dyer, G. C. (NSW) b March 16, 1959
Dyer, R. I. H. B. (Warwicks.) b Dec. 2 1958
*Dymock, G. (Qld) b July 21, 1945
Dyson, A. H. (Glam.) b July 10, 1905, June 7, 1978
Dyson, J. (Lancs.) b July 8, 1934
*Dyson, John (NSW) b June 11, 1954

*Eady, C. J. (Tas.) b Oct. 29, 1870, d De 20, 1945
Eagar, E. D. R. (OUCC, Glos. & Hants) Dec. 8, 1917, d Sept. 13, 1977
Eagar, M. A. (OUCC & Glos.) b March 2 1934
Eaglestone, J. T. (Middx & Glam.) b Ju 24, 1923
Ealham, A. G. E. (Kent) b Aug. 30, 194
East, D. E. (Essex) b July 27, 1959
East, R. E. (Essex) b June 20, 1947
Eastman, G. F. (Essex) b April 7, 1903

Eastman, L. C. (Essex & Otago) b June 3, 1897, d April 17, 1941
*Eastwood, K. H. (Vic.) b Nov. 23, 1935
*Ebeling, H. I. (Vic.) b Jan. 1, 1905, d Jan. 12, 1980
Eckersley, P. T. (Lancs.) b July 2, 1904, d Aug. 13, 1940
*Edgar, B. A. (Wgtn) b Nov. 23, 1956
Edinburgh, HRH Duke of (Pres. MCC 1948-49, 1974-75) b June 10, 1921
Edmeades, B. E. A. (Essex) b Sept. 17, 1941
*Edmonds, P. H. (CUCC, Middx & E. Prov.) b March 8, 1951
Edmonds, R. B. (Warwicks.) b March 2, 1941
Edrich, B. R. (Kent & Glam.) b Aug. 18, 1922
Edrich, E. H. (Lancs.) b March 27, 1914
Edrich, G. A. (Lancs.) b July 13, 1918
*Edrich, J. H. (Surrey; *CY 1966*) b June 21, 1937
*Edrich, W. J. (Middx; *CY 1940*) b March 26, 1916, d April 24, 1986
*Edwards, G. N. (C. Dist.) b May 27, 1955
*Edwards, J. D. (Vic.) b June 12, 1862, d July 31, 1911
Edwards, M. J. (CUCC & Surrey) b March 1, 1940
*Edwards, R. (W. Aust. & NSW) b Dec. 1, 1942
*Edwards, R. M. (B'dos) b June 3, 1940
*Edwards, W. J. (W. Aust.) b Dec. 23, 1949
Eele, P. J. (Som.) b Jan. 27, 1935
Eggar, J. D. (OUCC, Hants & Derbys.) b Dec. 1, 1916, d May 3, 1983
*Ehtesham-ud-Din (Lahore, Punjab, PIA, NBP & UBL) b Sept. 4, 1950
*Elgie, M. K. (Natal) b March 6, 1933
Ellcock, R. M. (Worcs., B'dos & Middx) b June 17, 1965
Elliott, C. S. (Derbys.) b April 24, 1912
*Elliott, H. (Derbys.) b Nov. 2, 1891, d Feb. 2, 1976
Elliott, Harold (Lancs.; Umpire) b June 15, 1904, d April 15, 1969
Ellis, G. P. (Glam.) b May 24, 1950
Ellis, J. L. (Vic.) b May 9, 1890, d July 26, 1974
Ellis, R. G. P. (OUCC & Middx) b Oct. 20 1960
Ellison, R. M. (Kent & Tas.; *CY 1986*) b Sept. 21, 1959
Elms, R. B. (Kent & Hants) b April 5, 1949
Emburey, J. E. (Middx & W. Prov.; *CY 1984*) b Aug. 20, 1952
Emery, R. W. G. (Auck. & Cant.) b March 28, 1915, d Dec. 18, 1982
Emery, S. H. (NSW) b Oct. 16, 1885, d Jan. 7, 1967
Emmett, G. M. (Glos.) b Dec. 2, 1912, d Dec. 18, 1976
*Emmett, T. (Yorks.) b Sept. 3, 1841, d June 30, 1904
*Endean, W. R. (Tvl) b May 31, 1924
*Engineer, F. M. (Bombay & Lancs.) b Feb. 25, 1938
*Evans, A. J. (OUCC, Hants & Kent) b May 1, 1889, d Sept. 18, 1960
Evans, D. G. L. (Glam.; Umpire) b July 27, 1933, d March 25, 1990
*Evans, E. (NSW) b March 6, 1849, d July 2, 1921
Evans, G. (OUCC, Glam. & Leics.) b Aug. 13, 1915
Evans, J. B. (Glam.) b Nov. 9, 1936
Evans, K. P. (Notts.) b Sept. 10, 1963
*Evans, T. G. (Kent; *CY 1951*) b Aug. 18, 1920
Every, T. (Glam.) b Dec. 19, 1909, d Jan. 20, 1990
Eyre, T. J. P. (Derbys.) b Oct. 17, 1939

Faber, M. J. J. (OUCC & Sussex) b Aug. 15, 1950
*Fagg, A. E. (Kent) b June 18, 1915, d Sept. 13, 1977
Fairbairn, A. (Middx) b Jan. 25, 1923
*Fairbrother, N. H. (Lancs.) b Sept. 9, 1963
*Fairfax, A. G. (NSW) b June 16, 1906, d May 17, 1955
Fairservice, C. (Kent & Middx) b Aug. 21, 1909
*Fane, F. L. (OUCC & Essex) b April 27, 1875, d Nov. 27, 1960
Fantham, W. E. (Warwicks.) b May 14, 1918
*Farnes, K. (CUCC & Essex; *CY 1939*) b July 8, 1911, d Oct. 20, 1941
*Farooq Hamid (Lahore & PIA) b March 3, 1945
*Farrer, W. S. (Border) b Dec. 8, 1936
*Farrimond, W. (Lancs.) b May 23, 1903, d Nov. 14, 1979
*Farrukh Zaman (Peshawar, NWFP, Punjab & MCB) b April 2, 1956
*Faulkner, G. A. (Tvl) b Dec. 17, 1881, d Sept. 10, 1930
*Favell, L. E. (S. Aust.) b Oct. 6, 1929, d June 14, 1987
*Fazal Mahmood (N. Ind., Punjab & Lahore; *CY 1955*) b Feb. 18, 1927
Fearnley, C. D. (Worcs.) b April 12, 1940
Featherstone, N. G. (Tvl, N. Tvl, Middx & Glam.) b Aug. 20, 1949
'Felix', N. (Wanostrocht) (Kent, Surrey & All-England) b Oct. 4, 1804, d Sept. 3, 1876
*Fellows-Smith, J. P. (OUCC, Tvl & Northants) b Feb. 3, 1932
Feltham, M. A. (Surrey) b June 26, 1963
Felton, N. A. (Som. & Northants) b Oct. 24, 1960
*Fender, P. G. H. (Sussex & Surrey; *CY 1915*) b Aug. 22, 1892, d June 15, 1985

*Ferguson, W. (T/T) b Dec. 14, 1917, d Feb. 23, 1961
*Fernandes, M. P. (BG) b Aug. 12, 1897, d May 8, 1981
Fernando, E. R. (SL) b Feb. 22, 1944
*Fernando, E. R. N. S. (SLAF) b Dec. 19, 1955
Fernando, T. L. (Colts) b Dec. 27, 1962
Ferreira, A. M. (N. Tvl & Warwicks.) b April 13, 1955
Ferris, G. J. F. (Leics. & Leewards) b Oct. 18, 1964
**Ferris, J. J. (NSW, Glos. & S. Aust.; *CY 1889*) b May 21, 1867, d Nov. 21, 1900
*Fichardt, C. G. (OFS) b March 20, 1870, d May 30, 1923
Fiddling, K. (Yorks. & Northants) b Oct. 13, 1917
*Fielder, A. (Kent; *CY 1907*) b July 19, 1877, d Aug. 30, 1949
*Findlay, T. M. (Comb. Is. & Windwards) b Oct. 19, 1943
Findlay, W. (OUCC & Lancs.; Sec. Surrey CCC, Sec. MCC 1926-36) b June 22, 1880, d June 19, 1953
*Fingleton, J. H. (NSW) b April 28, 1908, d Nov. 22, 1981
*Finlason, C. E. (Tvl & Griq. W.) b Feb. 19, 1860, d July 31, 1917
Finney, R. J. (Derbys.) b Aug. 2, 1960
Firth, J. (Yorks. & Leics.) b June 27, 1918, d Sept. 6, 1981
Firth, Rev. Canon J. D'E. E. (Winchester, OUCC & Notts.; *CY 1918*) b Jan. 21, 1900, d Sept. 21, 1957
*Fisher, F. E. (Wgtn & C. Dist.) b July 28, 1924
Fisher, P. B. (OUCC, Middx & Worcs.) b Dec. 19, 1954
*Fishlock, L. B. (Surrey; *CY 1947*) b Jan. 2, 1907, d June 26, 1986
Fitton, J. D. (Lancs.) b Aug. 24, 1965
Fitzgerald, R. A. (CUCC & Middx; Sec. MCC 1863-76) b Oct. 1, 1834, d Oct. 28, 1881
*Flavell, J. A. (Worcs.; *CY 1965*) b May 15, 1929
*Fleetwood-Smith, L. O'B. (Vic.) b March 30, 1910, d March 16, 1971
Fletcher, D. A. G. (Rhod. & Zimb.) b Sept. 27, 1948
Fletcher, D. G. W. (Surrey) b July 6, 1924
*Fletcher, K. W. R. (Essex; *CY 1974*) b May 20, 1944
Fletcher, S. D. (Yorks.) b June 8, 1964
*Floquet, C. E. (Tvl) b Nov. 3, 1884, d Nov. 22, 1963
*Flowers, W. (Notts.) b Dec. 7, 1856, d Nov. 1, 1926
Foat, J. C. (Glos.) b Nov. 21, 1952
*Foley, H. (Wgtn) b Jan. 28, 1906, d Oct. 16, 1948
Folley, I. (Lancs.) b Jan. 9, 1963
Foord, C. W. (Yorks.) b June 11, 1924
Forbes, C. (Notts.) b Aug. 9, 1936
*Ford, F. G. J. (CUCC & Middx) b Dec. 14, 1866, d Feb. 7, 1940
Ford, N. M. (OUCC, Derbys. & Middx) b Nov. 18, 1906
Ford, R. G. (Glos.) b March 3, 1907, d Oct. 1981
Fordham, A. (Northants) b Nov. 9, 1964
Foreman, D. J. (W. Prov. & Sussex) b Feb. 1, 1933
Fosh, M. K. (CUCC & Essex) b Sept. 26, 1957
Foster, D. G. (Warwicks.) b March 19, 1907, d Oct. 13, 1980
*Foster, F. R. (Warwicks.; *CY 1912*) b Jan. 31, 1889, d May 3, 1958
Foster, G. N. (OUCC, Worcs. & Kent) b Oct. 16, 1884, d Aug. 11, 1971
Foster, H. K. (OUCC & Worcs.; *CY 1911*) b Oct. 30, 1873, d June 23, 1950
Foster, M. K. (Worcs.) b Jan. 1, 1889, d Dec. 3, 1940
*Foster, M. L. C. (Jam.) b May 9, 1943
*Foster, N. A. (Essex; *CY 1988*) b May 6, 1962
Foster, P. G. (Kent) b Oct. 9, 1916
*Foster, R. E. (OUCC & Worcs.; *CY 1901*) b April 16, 1878, d May 13, 1914
*Fothergill, A. J. (Som.) b Aug. 26, 1854, d Aug. 1, 1932
Fotheringham, H. R. (Natal & Tvl) b April 4, 1953
*Fowler, G. (Lancs.) b April 20, 1957
Fowler, W. P. (Derbys., N. Dist. & Auck.) b March 13, 1959
*Francis, B. C. (NSW & Essex) b Feb. 18, 1948
Francis, D. A. (Glam.) b Nov. 29, 1953
*Francis, G. N. (B'dos) b Dec. 7, 1897, d Jan. 12, 1942
*Francis, H. H. (Glos. & W. Prov.) b May 26, 1868, d Jan. 7, 1936
Francke, F. M. (SL & Qld) b March 29, 1941
*Francois, C. M. (Griq. W.) b June 20, 1897, d May 26, 1944
*Frank, C. N. (Tvl) b Jan. 27, 1891, d Dec. 26, 1961
*Frank, W. H. B. (SA) b Nov. 23, 1872, d Feb. 16, 1945
Franklin, H. W. F. (OUCC, Surrey & Essex) b June 30, 1901, d May 25, 1985
*Franklin, T. J. (Auck.) b March 18, 1962
*Fraser, A. R. C. (Middx) b Aug. 8, 1965
*Frederick, M. C. (B'dos, Derbys. & Jam.) b May 6, 1927
*Fredericks, R. C. (†Guyana & Glam.; *CY 1974*) b Nov. 11, 1942
*Freeman, A. P. (Kent; *CY 1923*) b May 17, 1888, d Jan. 28, 1965

*Freeman, D. L. (Wgtn) b Sept. 8, 1914
*Freeman, E. W. (S. Aust.) b July 13, 1944
*Freer, F. W. (Vic.) b Dec. 4, 1915
*French, B. N. (Notts.) b Aug. 13, 1959
Frost, G. (Notts.) b Jan. 15, 1947
Frost, M. (Surrey & Glam.) b Oct. 21, 1962
Fry, C. A. (OUCC, Hants & Northants) b Jan. 14, 1940
*Fry, C. B. (OUCC, Sussex & Hants; *CY 1895*) b April 25, 1872, d Sept. 7, 1956
*Fuller, E. R. H. (W. Prov.) b Aug. 2, 1931
*Fuller, R. L. (Jam.) b Jan. 30, 1913, d May 3, 1987
*Fullerton, G. M. (Tvl) b Dec. 8, 1922
Funston, G. K. (NE Tvl & Griq. W.) b Nov. 21, 1948
*Funston, K. J. (NE Tvl, OFS & Tvl) b Dec. 3, 1925
*Furlonge, H. A. (T/T) b June 19, 1934

Gabriel, R. S. (T/T) b June 5, 1952
*Gadkari, C. V. (M'tra & Ind. Serv.) b Feb. 3, 1928
*Gaekwad, A. D. (Baroda) b Sept. 23, 1952
*Gaekwad, D. K. (Baroda) b Oct. 27, 1928
*Gaekwad, H. G. (†M. Pradesh) b Aug. 29, 1923
Gale, R. A. (Middx) b Dec. 10, 1933
*Gallichan, N. (Wgtn) b June 3, 1906, d March 25, 1969
*Gamsy, D. (Natal) b Feb. 17, 1940
*Gandotra, A. (Delhi & Bengal) b Nov. 24, 1948
*Gannon, J. B. (W. Aust.) b Feb. 8, 1947
*Ganteaume, A. G. (T/T) b Jan. 22, 1921
Gard, T. (Som.) b June 2, 1957
Gardner, L. R. (Leics.) b Feb. 23, 1934
Garland-Wells, H. M. (OUCC & Surrey) b Nov. 14, 1907
Garlick, R. G. (Lancs. & Northants) b April 11, 1917, d May 16, 1988
*Garner, J. (B'dos, Som. & S. Aust.; *CY 1980*) b Dec. 16, 1952
Garnham, M. A. (Glos., Leics. & Essex) b Aug. 20, 1960
*Garrett, T. W. (NSW) b July 26, 1858, d Aug. 6, 1943
*Gaskin, B. B. MacG. (BG) b March 21, 1908, d May 1, 1979
*Gatting, M. W. (Middx; *CY 1984*) b June 6, 1957
*Gaunt, R. A. (W. Aust. & Vic.) b Feb. 26, 1934
*Gavaskar, S. M. (Bombay & Som.; *CY 1980*) b July 10, 1949
*Gay, L. H. (CUCC, Hants & Som.) b March 24, 1871, d Nov. 1, 1949
Geary, A. C. T. (Surrey) b Sept. 11, 1900, d Jan. 23, 1989
*Geary, G. (Leics.; *CY 1927*) b July 9, 1893, d March 6, 1981
Gedye, S. G. (Auck.) b May 2, 1929
*Gehrs, D. R. A. (S. Aust.) b Nov. 29, 1880, d June 25, 1953
Ghai, R. S. (Punjab) b June 12, 1960
*Ghavri, K. D. (S'tra & Bombay) b Feb. 28, 1951
*Ghazali, M. E. Z. (M'tra & Pak. Serv.) b June 15, 1924
*Ghorpade, J. M. (Baroda) b Oct. 2, 1930, d March 29, 1978
*Ghulam Abbas (Kar., NBP & PIA) b May 1, 1947
*Ghulam Ahmed (H'bad) b July 4, 1922
*Gibb, P. A. (OUCC, Scotland, Yorks. & Essex) b July 11, 1913, d Dec. 7, 1977
Gibbons, H. H. (Worcs.) b Oct. 10, 1904, d Feb. 16, 1973
*Gibbs, G. L. (BG) b Dec. 27, 1925, d Feb. 21, 1979
*Gibbs, L. R. (†Guyana, S. Aust. & Warwicks.; *CY 1972*) b Sept. 29, 1934
Gibbs, P. J. K. (OUCC & Derbys.) b Aug. 17, 1944
Gibson, C. H. (Eton, CUCC & Sussex; *CY 1918*) b Aug. 23, 1900, d Dec. 31, 1976
Gibson, D. (Surrey) b May 1, 1936
*Giffen, G. (S. Aust.; *CY 1894*) b March 27, 1859, d Nov. 29, 1927
*Giffen, W. F. (S. Aust.) b Sept. 20, 1861, d June 29, 1949
*Gifford, N. (Worcs. & Warwicks.; *CY 1975*) b March 30, 1940
*Gilbert, D. R. (NSW) b Dec. 29, 1960
*Gilchrist, R. (Jam. & H'bad) b June 28, 1934
Giles, R. J. (Notts.) b Oct. 17, 1919
Gill, A. (Notts.) b Aug. 4, 1940
Gilhouley, K. (Yorks. & Notts.) b Aug. 8, 1934
*Gillespie, S. R. (Auck.) b March 2, 1957
Gilliat, R. M. C. (OUCC & Hants) b May 20, 1944
*Gilligan, A. E. R. (CUCC, Surrey & Sussex; *CY 1924*; Pres. MCC 1967-68) b Dec. 23, 1894, d Sept. 5, 1976
*Gilligan, A. H. H. (Sussex) b June 29, 1896, d May 5, 1978
Gilligan, F. W. (OUCC & Essex) b Sept. 20, 1893, d May 4, 1960
*Gilmour, G. J. (NSW) b June 26, 1951
*Gimblett, H. (Som.; *CY 1953*) b Oct. 19, 1914, d March 30, 1978
Gladstone, G. (*see* Marais, G. G.)
Gladwin, Chris (Essex & Derbys.) b May 10, 1962
*Gladwin, Cliff (Derbys.) b April 3, 1916, d April 10, 1988
*Gleeson, J. W. (NSW & E. Prov.) b March 14, 1938
*Gleeson, R. A. (E. Prov.) b Dec. 6, 1873, d Sept. 27, 1919
*Glover, G. K. (Kimberley & Griq. W.) b May 13, 1870, d Nov. 15, 1938

Glover, T. R. (OUCC) b Nov. 26, 1951
Goddard, G. F. (Scotland) b May 19, 1938
*Goddard, J. D. C. (B'dos) b April 21, 1919, d Aug. 26, 1987
*Goddard, T. L. (Natal & NE Tvl) b Aug. 1, 1931
*Goddard, T. W. (Glos.; *CY 1938*) b Oct. 1, 1900, d May 22, 1966
Goel, R. (Patiala & Haryana) b Sept. 29, 1942
Goldstein, F. S. (OUCC, Northants, Tvl & W. Prov.) b Oct. 14, 1944
*Gomes, H. A. (T/T & Middx; *CY 1985*) b July 13, 1953
Gomes, S. A. (T/T) b Oct. 18, 1950
*Gomez, G. E. (T/T) b Oct. 10, 1919
*Gooch, G. A. (Essex & W. Prov.; *CY 1980*) b July 23, 1953
Goodway, C. C. (Warwicks.) b July 10, 1909
Goodwin, K. (Lancs.) b June 25, 1938
Goodwin, T. J. (Leics.) b Jan. 22, 1929
Goonatillake, F. R. M. de S. (SL) b. Aug. 15, 1951
*Goonatillake, H. M. (SL) b Aug. 16, 1952
Goonesena, G. (Ceylon, Notts., CUCC & NSW) b Feb. 16, 1931
*Gopalan, M. J. (Madras) b June 6, 1909
*Gopinath, C. D. (Madras) b March 1, 1930
*Gordon, N. (Tvl) b Aug. 6, 1911
Gore, A. C. (Eton & Army; *CY 1919*) b May 14, 1900, d June 7, 1990
Gothard, E. J. (Derbys.) b Oct. 1, 1904, d Jan. 17, 1979
Gould, I. J. (Middx, Auck. & Sussex) b Aug. 19, 1957
*Gover, A. R. (Surrey; *CY 1937*) b Feb. 29, 1908
*Gower, D. I. (Leics. & Hants; *CY 1979*) b April 1, 1957
Gower, G. M. (Border) b July 10, 1952
Gowrie, 1st Lord (Pres. MCC 1948-49) b July 6, 1872, d May 2, 1955
Grace, Dr Alfred b May 17, 1840, d May 24, 1916
Grace, Dr Alfred H. (Glos.) b March 10, 1866, d Sept. 16, 1929
Grace, C. B. (Clifton) b March 1882, d June 6, 1938
*Grace, Dr E. M. (Glos.) b Nov. 28, 1841, d May 20, 1911
Grace, Dr Edgar M. (MCC) (son of E. M. Grace) b Oct. 6, 1886, d Nov. 24, 1974
*Grace, G. F. (Glos.) b Dec. 13, 1850, d Sept. 22, 1880
Grace, Dr Henry (Glos.) b Jan. 31, 1833, d Nov. 15, 1895
Grace, Dr H. M. (father of W. G., E. M. and G. F.) b Feb. 21, 1808, d Dec. 23, 1871
Grace, Mrs H. M. (mother of W. G., E. M. and G. F.) b July 18, 1812, d July 25, 1884
*Grace, Dr W. G. (Glos.; *CY 1896*) b July 18, 1848, d Oct. 23, 1915
Grace, W. G., jun. (CUCC & Glos.) b July 6, 1874, d March 2, 1905
Graf, S. F. (Vic., W. Aust. & Hants) b May 19, 1957
*Graham, H. (Vic. & Otago) b Nov. 22, 1870, d Feb. 7, 1911
Graham, J. N. (Kent) b May 8, 1943
*Graham, R. (W. Prov.) b Sept. 16, 1877, d April 21, 1946
*Grant, G. C. (CUCC, T/T & Rhod.) b May 9, 1907, d Oct. 26, 1978
*Grant, R. S. (CUCC & T/T) b Dec. 15, 1909, d Oct. 18, 1977
Graveney, D. A. (Glos.) b Jan. 21, 1953
Graveney, J. K. (Glos.) b Dec. 16, 1924
*Graveney, T. W. (Glos., Worcs. & Qld; *CY 1953*) b June 16, 1927
Graves, P. J. (Sussex & OFS) b May 19, 1946
*Gray, A. H. (T/T & Surrey) b May 23, 1963
*Gray, E. J. (Wgtn) b Nov. 18, 1954
Gray, J. R. (Hants) b May 19, 1926
Gray, L. H. (Middx) b Dec. 16, 1915, d Jan. 3, 1983
Greasley, D. G. (Northants) b Jan. 20, 1926
*Greatbatch, M. J. (C. Dist.) b Dec. 11, 1963
Green, A. M. (Sussex & OFS) b May 28, 1960
Green, D. J. (Derbys. & CUCC) b Dec. 18, 1935
Green, D. M. (OUCC, Lancs. & Glos.; *CY 1969*) b Nov. 10, 1939
Green, Brig. M. A. (Glos. & Essex) b Oct. 3, 1891, d Dec. 28, 1971
*Greenhough, T. (Lancs.) b Nov. 9, 1931
*Greenidge, A. E. (B'dos) b Aug. 20, 1956
*Greenidge, C. G. (Hants & B'dos; *CY 1977*) b May 1, 1951
*Greenidge, G. A. (B'dos & Sussex) b May 26, 1948
Greensmith, W. T. (Essex) b Aug. 16, 1930
*Greenwood, A. (Yorks.) b Aug. 20, 1847, d Feb. 12, 1889
Greenwood, P. (Lancs.) b Sept. 11, 1924
Greetham, C. (Som.) b Aug. 28, 1936
*Gregory, David W. (NSW; first Australian captain) b April 15, 1845, d Aug. 4, 1919
*Gregory, E. J. (NSW) b May 29, 1839, d April 22, 1899
*Gregory, J. M. (NSW; *CY 1922*) b Aug. 14 1895, d Aug. 7, 1973
*Gregory, R. G. (Vic.) b Feb. 26, 1916, d June 10, 1942
*Gregory, S. E. (NSW; *CY 1897*) b April 14 1870, d August 1, 1929
*Greig, A. W. (Border, E. Prov. & Sussex *CY 1975*) b Oct. 6, 1946
*Greig, I. A. (CUCC, Border, Sussex & Surrey) b Dec. 8, 1955

*Grell, M. G. (T/T) b Dec. 18, 1899, d Jan. 11, 1976
*Grieve, B. A. F. (Eng.) b May 28, 1864, d Nov. 19, 1917
Grieves, K. J. (NSW & Lancs.) b Aug. 27, 1925
*Grieveson, R. E. (Tvl) b Aug. 24, 1909
*Griffin, G. M. (Natal & Rhod.) b June 12, 1939
*Griffith, C. C. (B'dos; *CY 1964*) b Dec. 14, 1938
Griffith, G. ("Ben") (Surrey & Utd England XI) b Dec. 20, 1833, d May 3, 1879
*Griffith, H. C. (B'dos) b Dec. 1, 1893, d March 18, 1980
Griffith, K. (Worcs.) b Jan. 17, 1950
Griffith, M. G. (CUCC & Sussex) b Nov. 25, 1943
*Griffith, S. C. (CUCC, Surrey & Sussex; Sec. MCC 1962-74; Pres. MCC 1979-80) b June 16, 1914
Griffiths, B. J. (Northants) b June 13, 1949
Griffiths, Rt Hon. The Lord (W. H.) (CUCC & Glam.; Pres. MCC 1990-91) b Sept. 26, 1923
*Grimmett, C. V. (Wgtn, Vic. & S. Aust.; *CY 1931*) b Dec. 25, 1891, d May 2, 1980
Grimshaw, N. (Northants) b May 5, 1911
*Groube, T. U. (Vic.) b Sept. 2, 1857, d Aug. 5, 1927
*Grout, A. T. W. (Qld) b March 30, 1927, d Nov. 9, 1968
Grove, C. W. (Warwicks. & Worcs.) b Dec. 16, 1912, d Feb. 15, 1982
Grover, J. N. (OUCC) b Oct. 15, 1915
Groves, M. G. M. (OUCC, Som. & W. Prov.) b Jan. 14, 1943
Grundy, J. (Notts. & Utd England XI) b March 5, 1824, d Nov. 24, 1873
*Guard, G. M. (Bombay & Guj.) b Dec. 12, 1925, d March 13, 1978
*Guest, C. E. J. (Vic. & W. Aust.) b Oct. 7, 1937
*Guha, S. (Bengal) b Jan. 31, 1946
**Guillen, S. C. (T/T & Cant.) b Sept. 24, 1924
Guise, J. L. (OUCC & Middx) b Nov. 25, 1903
*Gunasekera, Y. (SL) b Nov. 8, 1957
**Gul Mahomed (N. Ind., Baroda, H'bad, Punjab & Lahore) b Oct. 15, 1921
*Guneratne, R. P. W. (Nomads) b Jan. 26, 1962
*Gunn, G. (Notts.; *CY 1914*) b June 13, 1879, d June 29, 1958
Gunn, G. V. (Notts.) b June 21, 1905, d Oct. 14, 1957
Gunn, J. (Notts.; *CY 1904*) b July 19, 1876, d Aug. 21, 1963
Gunn, T. (Sussex) b Sept. 27, 1935
Gunn, William (Notts.; *CY 1890*) b Dec. 4, 1858, d Jan. 29, 1921
*Gupte, B. P. (Bombay, Bengal & Ind. Rlwys) b Aug. 30, 1934
*Gupte, S. P. (Bombay, Bengal, Raja. & T/T) b Dec. 11, 1929
*Gursharan Singh (Punjab) b March 8, 1963
*Gurusinha, A. P. (SSC) b Sept. 16, 1966
Gurr, D. R. (OUCC & Som.) b March 27, 1956
*Guy, J. W. (C. Dist., Wgtn, Northants, Cant., Otago & N. Dist.) b Aug. 29, 1934

Haafiz Shahid (WAPDA) b May 10, 1963
Hacker, P. J. (Notts., Derbys. & OFS) b July 16, 1952
Hadlee, B. G. (Cant.) b Dec. 14, 1941
*Hadlee, D. R. (Cant.) b Jan. 6, 1948
*Hadlee, Sir R. J. (Cant., Notts. & Tas.; *CY 1982*) b July 3, 1951
*Hadlee, W. A. (Cant. & Otago) b June 4, 1915
Hafeez, A. (*see* Kardar)
Hagan, D. A. (OUCC) b June 25, 1966
*Haig, N. E. (Middx) b Dec. 12, 1887, d Oct. 27, 1966
*Haigh, S. (Yorks.; *CY 1901*) b March 19, 1871, d Feb. 27, 1921
Halfyard, D. J. (Kent & Notts.) b April 3, 1931
*Hall, A. E. (Tvl & Lancs.) b Jan. 23, 1896, d Jan. 1, 1964
*Hall, G. G. (NE Tvl & E. Prov.) b May 24, 1938, d June 26, 1987
Hall, I. W. (Derbys.) b Dec. 27, 1939
Hall, J. W. (Sussex) b March 30, 1968
Hall, Louis (Yorks.; *CY 1890*) b Nov. 1, 1852, d Nov. 19, 1915
Hall, T. A. (Derbys. & Som.) b Aug. 19, 1930, d April 21, 1984
*Hall, W. W. (B'dos, T/T & Qld) b Sept. 12, 1937
Hallam, A. W. (Lancs. & Notts.; *CY 1908*) b Nov. 12, 1869, d July 24, 1940
Hallam, M. R. (Leics.) b Sept. 10, 1931
*Halliwell, E. A. (Tvl & Middx; *CY 1905*) b Sept. 7, 1864, d Oct. 2, 1919
*Hallows, C. (Lancs.; *CY 1928*) b April 4, 1895, d Nov. 10, 1972
Hallows, J. (Lancs.; *CY 1905*) b Nov. 14, 1873, d May 20, 1910
*Halse, C. G. (Natal) b Feb. 28, 1935
*Hamence, R. A. (S. Aust.) b Nov. 25, 1915
Hamer, A. (Yorks. & Derbys.) b Dec. 8, 1916
Hammond, H. E. (Sussex) b Nov. 7, 1907, d June 16, 1985
*Hammond, J. R. (S. Aust.) b April 19, 1950
*Hammond, W. R. (Glos.; *CY 1928*) b June 19, 1903, d July 1, 1965
*Hampshire, J. H. (Yorks., Derbys. & Tas.; Umpire) b Feb. 10, 1941
*Hands, P. A. M. (W. Prov.) b March 18, 1890, d April 27, 1951

*Hands, R. H. M. (W. Prov.) b July 26, 1888, d April 20, 1918
*Hanif Mohammad (B'pur, Kar. & PIA; *CY 1968*) b Dec. 21, 1934
*Hanley, M. A. (Border & W. Prov.) b Nov. 10, 1918
Hanley, R. W. (E. Prov., OFS, Tvl & Northants) b Jan. 29, 1952
*Hanumant Singh (M. Pradesh & Raja.) b March 29, 1939
Harbord, W. E. (Yorks. & OUCC) b Dec. 15, 1908
Harden, R. J. (Som. & C. Dist.) b Aug. 16, 1965
Hardie, B. R. (Scotland & Essex) b Jan. 14, 1950
*Hardikar, M. S. (Bombay) b Feb. 8, 1936
*Hardinge, H. T. W. (Kent; *CY 1915*) b Feb. 25, 1886, d May 8, 1965
*Hardstaff, J. (Notts.) b Nov. 9, 1882, d April 2, 1947
*Hardstaff, J., jun. (Notts. & Auck.; *CY 1938*) b July 3, 1911, d Jan. 1, 1990
Hardy, J. J. E. (Hants, Som. & W. Prov.) b Oct. 10, 1960
Harfield, L. (Hants) b Aug. 16, 1905, d Nov. 19, 1985
*Harford, N. S. (C. Dist. & Auck.) b Aug. 30, 1930, d March 30, 1981
*Harford, R. I. (Auck.) b May 30, 1936
Harman, R. (Surrey) b Dec. 28, 1941
*Haroon Rashid (Kar., Sind, NBP, PIA & UBL) b March 25, 1953
*Harper, R. A. (Guyana & Northants) b March 17, 1963
*Harris, 4th Lord (OUCC & Kent; Pres. MCC 1895) b Feb. 3, 1851, d March 24, 1932
Harris, David (Hants & All-England) b 1755, d May 19, 1803
Harris, M. J. (Middx, Notts., E. Prov. & Wgtn) b May 25, 1944
*Harris, P. G. Z. (Cant.) b July 18, 1927
*Harris, R. M. (Auck.) b July 27, 1933
*Harris, T. A. (Griq. W. & Tvl) b Aug. 27, 1916
Harrison, L. (Hants) b June 8, 1922
*Harry, J. (Vic.) b Aug. 1, 1857, d Oct. 27, 1919
Hart, G. E. (Middx) b Jan. 13, 1902, d April 11, 1987
Hart, R. T. (C. Dist.) b Nov. 7, 1961
*Hartigan, G. P. D. (Border) b Dec. 30, 1884, d Jan. 7, 1955
*Hartigan, R. J. (NSW & Qld) b Dec. 12, 1879, d June 7, 1958
*Hartkopf, A. E. V. (Vic.) b Dec. 28, 1889, d May 20, 1968
Hartley, A. (Lancs.; *CY 1911*) b April 11, 1879, d Oct. 9, 1918
*Hartley, J. C. (OUCC & Sussex) b Nov. 15, 1874, d March 8, 1963
Hartley, P. J. (Warwicks. & Yorks.) b April 18, 1960
Hartley, S. N. (Yorks. & OFS) b March 18, 1956
Harvey, J. F. (Derbys.) b Sept. 27, 1939
*Harvey, M. R. (Vic.) b April 29, 1918
Harvey, P. F. (Notts.) b Jan. 15, 1923
*Harvey, R. L. (Natal) b Sept. 14, 1911
*Harvey, R. N. (Vic. & NSW; *CY 1954*) b Oct. 8, 1928
Harvey-Walker, A. J. (Derbys.) b July 21, 1944
Hasan Jamil (Kalat, Kar., Pak. Us & PIA) b July 25, 1952
*Haseeb Ahsan (Peshawar, Pak. Us, Kar. & PIA) b July 15, 1939
Hassan, B. (Notts.) b March 24, 1944
*Hassett, A. L. (Vic.; *CY 1949*) b Aug. 28, 1913
*Hastings, B. F. (Wgtn, C. Dist. & Cant.) b March 23, 1940
*Hathorn, C. M. H. (Tvl) b April 7, 1878, d May 17, 1920
*Hawke, 7th Lord (CUCC & Yorks.; *CY 1909*; Pres. MCC 1914-18) b Aug. 16, 1860, d Oct. 10, 1938
*Hawke, N. J. N. (W. Aust., S. Aust. & Tas.) b June 27, 1939
Hawker, Sir Cyril (Essex; Pres. MCC 1970-71) b July 21, 1900
Hawkins, D. G. (Glos.) b May 18, 1935
*Hayes, E. G. (Surrey & Leics.; *CY 1907*) b Nov. 6, 1876, d Dec. 2, 1953
*Hayes, F. C. (Lancs.) b Dec. 6, 1946
*Hayes, J. A. (Auck. & Cant.) b Jan. 11, 1927
Hayes, K. A. (OUCC & Lancs.) b Sept. 26, 1962
Haygarth, A. (Sussex; Historian) b Aug. 4, 1825, d May 1, 1903
Hayhurst, A. N. (Lancs. & Som.) b Nov. 23, 1962
*Haynes, D. L. (B'dos & Middx; *CY 1991*) b Feb. 15, 1956
Haynes, R. C. (Jam.) b Nov. 11, 1964
Haysman, M. D. (S. Aust., Leics. & N. Tvl) b April 22, 1961
Hayward, T. (Cambs. & All-England) b March 21, 1835, d July 21, 1876
*Hayward, T. W. (Surrey; *CY 1895*) b March 29, 1871, d July 19, 1939
Haywood, P. R. (Leics.) b March 30, 1947
*Hazare, V. S. (M'tra, C. Ind. & Baroda) b March 11, 1915
Hazell, H. L. (Som.) b Sept. 30, 1909, d March 31, 1990
Hazlerigg, Lord, formerly Hon. A. G (CUCC & Leics.) b Feb. 24, 1910
*Hazlitt, G. R. (Vic. & NSW) b Sept. 4 1888, d Oct. 30, 1915
*Headley, G. A. (Jam.; *CY 1934*) b May 30 1909, d Nov. 30, 1983

*Headley, R. G. A. (Worcs. & Jam.) b June 29, 1939
*Healy, I. A. (Qld) b April 30, 1964
Hearn, P. (Kent) b Nov. 18, 1925
*Hearne, Alec (Kent; *CY 1894*) b July 22, 1863, d May 16, 1952
**Hearne, Frank (Kent & W. Prov.) b Nov. 23, 1858, d July 14, 1949
*Hearne, G. A. L. (W. Prov.) b March 27, 1888, d Nov. 13, 1978
*Hearne, George G. (Kent) b July 7, 1856, d Feb. 13, 1932
*Hearne, J. T. (Middx; *CY 1892*) b May 3, 1867, d April 17, 1944
*Hearne, J. W. (Middx; *CY 1912*) b Feb. 11, 1891, d Sept. 14, 1965
Hearne, Thos. (Middx) b Sept. 4, 1826, d May 13, 1900
Hearne, Thos., jun. (Lord's Ground Superintendent) b Dec. 29, 1849, d Jan. 29, 1910
Heath, G. E. M. (Hants) b Feb. 20, 1913
Heath, M. (Hants) b March 9, 1934
Hedges, B. (Glam.) b Nov. 10, 1927
Hedges, L. P. (Tonbridge, OUCC, Kent & Glos.; *CY 1919*) b July 13, 1900, d Jan. 12, 1933
Hegg, W. K. (Lancs.) b Feb. 23, 1968
*Heine, P. S. (NE Tvl, OFS & Tvl) b June 28, 1928
*Hemmings, E. E. (Warwicks. & Notts.) b Feb. 20, 1949
Hemsley, E. J. O. (Worcs.) b Sept. 1, 1943
*Henderson, M. (Wgtn) b Aug. 2, 1895, d June 17, 1970
Henderson, R. (Surrey; *CY 1890*) b March 30, 1865, d Jan. 29, 1931
Henderson, S. P. (CUCC, Worcs. & Glam.) b Sept. 24, 1958
*Hendren, E. H. (Middx; *CY 1920*) b Feb. 5, 1889, d Oct. 4, 1962
*Hendrick, M. (Derbys. & Notts.; *CY 1978*) b Oct. 22, 1948
*Hendriks, J. L. (Jam.) b Dec. 21, 1933
*Hendry, H. S. T. L. (NSW & Vic.) b May 24, 1895, d Dec. 16, 1988
Henry, O. (W. Prov., Boland, OFS & Scotland) b Jan. 23, 1952
Herman, O. W. (Hants) b Sept. 18, 1907, d June 24, 1987
Herman, R. S. (Middx, Border, Griq. W. & Hants) b Nov. 30, 1946
Heron, J. G. (Zimb.) b Nov. 8, 1948
*Heseltine, C. (Hants) b Nov. 26, 1869, d June 13, 1944
Hever, N. G. (Middx & Glam.) b Dec. 17, 1924, d Sept. 11, 1987
Hewett, H. T. (OUCC & Som.; *CY 1893*) b May 25, 1864, d March 4, 1921
Heyn, P. D. (SL) b June 26, 1945
*Hibbert, P. A. (Vic.) b July 23, 1952
Hick, G. A. (Worcs., Zimb. & N. Dist.; *CY 1987*) b May 23, 1966
*Higgs, J. D. (Vic.) b July 11, 1950
*Higgs, K. (Lancs. & Leics.; *CY 1968*) b Jan. 14, 1937
Hignell, A. J. (CUCC & Glos.) b Sept. 4, 1955
*Hilditch, A. M. J. (NSW & S. Aust.) b May 20, 1956
Hill, Alan (Derbys. & OFS) b June 29, 1950
*Hill, Allen (Yorks.) b Nov. 14, 1843, d Aug. 29, 1910
*Hill, A. J. L. (CUCC & Hants) b July 26, 1871, d Sept. 6, 1950
*Hill, C. (S. Aust.; *CY 1900*) b March 18, 1877, d Sept. 5, 1945
Hill, E. (Som.) b July 9, 1923
Hill, G. (Hants) b April 15, 1913
*Hill, J. C. (Vic.) b June 25, 1923, d Aug. 11, 1974
Hill, L. W. (Glam.) b April 14, 1942
Hill, M. (Notts., Derbys & Som.) b Sept. 14, 1935
Hill, N. W. (Notts.) b Aug. 22, 1935
Hill, W. A. (Warwicks.) b April 27, 1910
Hills, J. J. (Glam.; Umpire) b Oct. 14, 1897, d Sept. 21, 1969
Hills, R. W. (Kent) b Jan. 8, 1951
Hill-Wood, C. K. (OUCC & Derbys.) b June 5, 1907, d Sept. 21, 1988
Hilton, C. (Lancs. & Essex) b Sept. 26, 1937
Hilton, J. (Lancs. & Som.) b Dec. 29, 1930
*Hilton, M. J. (Lancs.; *CY 1957*) b Aug. 2, 1928, d July 8, 1990
*Hime, C. F. W. (Natal) b Oct. 24, 1869, d Dec. 6, 1940
*Hindlekar, D. D. (Bombay) b Jan. 1, 1909, d March 30, 1949
Hinks, S. G. (Kent) b Oct. 12, 1960
*Hirst, G. H. (Yorks.; *CY 1901*) b Sept. 7, 1871, d May 10, 1954
*Hirwani, N. D. (M. Pradesh) b Oct. 18, 1968
*Hitch, J. W. (Surrey; *CY 1914*) b May 7, 1886, d July 7, 1965
Hitchcock, R. E. (Cant. & Warwicks.) b Nov. 28, 1929
*Hoad, E. L. G. (B'dos) b Jan. 29, 1896, d March 5, 1986
*Hoare, D. E. (W. Aust.) b Oct. 19, 1934
*Hobbs, Sir J. B. (Surrey; *CY 1909, special portrait 1926*) b Dec. 16, 1882, d Dec. 21, 1963
*Hobbs, R. N. S. (Essex & Glam.) b May 8, 1942
Hobson, D. L. (E. Prov. & W. Prov.) b Sept. 3, 1951
*Hodges, J. H. (Vic.) b July 31, 1856, d Jan. 17, 1933
Hodgkinson, G. F. (Derbys.) b Feb. 19, 1914, d Jan. 7, 1987
Hodgson, A. (Northants) b Oct. 27, 1951

Hodgson, G. D. (Glos.) b Oct. 22, 1966
Hofmeyr, M. B. (OUCC & NE Tvl) b Dec. 9, 1925
*Hogan, T. G. (W. Aust.) b Sept. 23, 1956
*Hogg, R. M. (S. Aust.) b March 5, 1951
Hogg, W. (Lancs. & Warwicks.) b July 12, 1955
*Hohns, T. V. (Qld) b Jan. 23, 1954
Holder, J. W. (Hants; Umpire) b March 19, 1945
*Holder, V. A. (B'dos, Worcs. & OFS) b Oct. 8, 1945
*Holding, M. A. (Jam., Lancs., Derbys., Tas. & Cant.; *CY 1977*) b Feb. 16, 1954
*Hole, G. B. (NSW & S. Aust.) b Jan. 6, 1931, d Feb. 14, 1990
*Holford, D. A. J. (B'dos & T/T) b April 16, 1940
*Holland, R. G. (NSW & Wgtn) b Oct. 19, 1946
*Hollies, W. E. (Warwicks.; *CY 1955*) b June 5, 1912, d April 16, 1981
Hollingdale, R. A. (Sussex) b March 6, 1906, d Aug. 1989
Holmes, Gp Capt. A. J. (Sussex) b June 30, 1899, d May 21, 1950
*Holmes, E. R. T. (OUCC & Surrey; *CY 1936*) b Aug. 21, 1905, d Aug. 16, 1960
Holmes, G. C. (Glam.) b Sept. 16, 1958
*Holmes, P. (Yorks.; *CY 1920*) b Nov. 25, 1886, d Sept. 3, 1971
Holt, A. G. (Hants) b April 8, 1911
*Holt, J. K., jun. (Jam.) b Aug. 12, 1923
Home of the Hirsel, Lord (Middx; Pres. MCC 1966-67) b July 2, 1903
Hone, Sir B. W. (S. Aust. & OUCC) b July 1, 1907, d May 28, 1978
*Hone, L. (MCC) b Jan. 30, 1853, d Dec. 31, 1896
Hooker, J. E. H. (NSW) b March 6, 1898, d Feb. 12, 1982
Hooker, R. W. (Middx) b Feb. 22, 1935
*Hookes, D. W. (S. Aust.) b May 3, 1955
*Hooper, C. L. (Guyana) b Dec. 15, 1966
*Hopkins, A. J. Y. (NSW) b May 3, 1874, d April 25, 1931
Hopkins, J. A. (Glam. & E. Prov.) b June 16, 1953
Hopkins, V. (Glos.) b Jan. 21, 1911, d Aug. 6, 1984
*Hopwood, J. L. (Lancs.) b Oct. 30, 1903, d June 15, 1985
*Horan, T. P. (Vic.) b March 8, 1854, d April 16, 1916
*Hordern, H. V. (NSW & Philadelphia) b Feb. 10, 1883, d June 17, 1938
*Hornby, A. N. (Lancs.) b Feb. 10, 1847, d Dec. 17, 1925
*Horne, P. A. (Auck.) b Jan. 21, 1960
Horner, N. F. (Yorks. & Warwicks.) b May 10, 1926
*Hornibrook, P. M. (Qld) b July 27, 1899, d Aug. 25, 1976
Horsfall, R. (Essex & Glam.) b June 26, 1920, d Aug. 25, 1981
Horton, H. (Worcs. & Hants) b April 18, 1923
Horton, J. (Worcs.) b Aug. 12, 1916
*Horton, M. J. (Worcs. & N. Dist.) b April 21, 1934
Hossell, J. J. (Warwicks.) b May 25, 1914
*Hough, K. W. (Auck.) b Oct. 24, 1928
*Howard, A. B. (B'dos) b Aug. 27, 1946
Howard, A. H. (Glam.) b Dec. 11, 1910
Howard, B. J. (Lancs.) b May 21, 1926
Howard, K. (Lancs.) b June 29, 1941
*Howard, N. D. (Lancs.) b May 18, 1925, d May 31, 1979
Howard, Major R. (Lancs.; MCC Team Manager) b April 17, 1890, d Sept. 10, 1967
*Howarth, G. P. (Auck., Surrey & N. Dist.) b March 29, 1951
*Howarth, H. J. (Auck.) b Dec. 25, 1943
*Howell, H. (Warwicks.) b Nov. 29, 1890, d July 9, 1932
*Howell, W. P. (NSW) b Dec. 29, 1869, d July 14, 1940
Howland, C. B. (CUCC, Sussex & Kent) b Feb. 6, 1936
*Howorth, R. (Worcs.) b April 26, 1909, d April 2, 1980
Hughes, D. P. (Lancs. & Tas.; *CY 1988*) b May 13, 1947
*Hughes, K. J. (W. Aust.; *CY 1981*) b Jan. 26, 1954
*Hughes, M. G. (Vic. & Essex) b Nov. 23, 1961
Hughes, S. P. (Middx & N. Tvl) b Dec. 20, 1959
Huish, F. H. (Kent) b Nov. 15, 1869, d March 16, 1957
Hulme, J. H. A. (Middx) b Aug. 26, 1904
Human, J. H. (CUCC & Middx) b Jan. 13, 1912
Humpage, G. W. (Warwicks. & OFS; *CY 1985*) b April 24, 1954
Humphries, D. J. (Leics. & Worcs.) b Aug. 6, 1953
*Humphries, J. (Derbys.) b May 19, 1876, d May 7, 1946
Hunt, A. V. (Scotland & Bermuda) b Oct. 1, 1910
*Hunt, W. A. (NSW) b Aug. 26, 1908, d Dec. 31, 1983
*Hunte, C. C. (B'dos; *CY 1964*) b May 9, 1932
*Hunte, E. A. C. (T/T) b Oct. 3, 1905, d June 26, 1967
Hunter, David (Yorks.) b Feb. 23, 1860, d Jan. 11, 1927
*Hunter, Joseph (Yorks.) b Aug. 3, 1855, d Jan. 4, 1891
Hurd, A. (CUCC & Essex) b Sept. 7, 1937

*Hurst, A. G. (Vic.) b July 15, 1950
Hurst, R. J. (Middx) b Dec. 29, 1933
*Hurwood, A. (Qld) b June 17, 1902, d Sept. 26, 1982
*Hussain, M. Dilawar (C. Ind. & U. Prov.) b March 19, 1907, d Aug. 26, 1967
*Hussain, N. (Essex) b March 28, 1968
*Hutchings, K. L. (Kent; *CY 1907*) b Dec. 7, 1882, d Sept. 3, 1916
Hutchinson, J. M. (Derbys.) b Nov. 29, 1896
*Hutchinson, P. (SA) b Jan. 26, 1862, d Sept. 30, 1925
*Hutton, Sir Leonard (Yorks.; *CY 1938*) b June 23, 1916, d Sept. 6, 1990
*Hutton, R. A. (CUCC, Yorks. & Tvl) b Sept. 6, 1942
*Hylton, L. G. (Jam.) b March 29, 1905, d May 17, 1955

*Ibadulla, K. (Punjab, Warwicks., Tas. & Otago) b Dec. 20, 1935
*Ibrahim, K. C. (Bombay) b Jan. 26, 1919
*Iddon, J. (Lancs.) b Jan. 8, 1902, d April 17, 1946
*Igglesden, A. P. (Kent & W. Prov.) b Oct. 8, 1964
*Ijaz Ahmed (Gujranwala, PACO & HBL) b Sept. 20, 1968
*Ijaz Butt (Pak. Us, Punjab, Lahore, R'pindi & Multan) b March 10, 1938
*Ijaz Faqih (Kar., Sind, PWD & MCB) b March 24, 1956
*Ikin, J. T. (Lancs.) b March 7, 1918, d Sept. 15, 1984
*Illingworth, R. (Yorks. & Leics.; *CY 1960*) b June 8, 1932
Illingworth, R. K. (Worcs. & Natal) b Aug. 23, 1963
*Imran Khan (Lahore, Dawood, Worcs., OUCC, PIA, Sussex & NSW; *CY 1983*) b Nov. 25, 1952
*Imtiaz Ahmed (N. Ind., Comb. Us, NWFP, Pak. Serv., Peshawar & PAF) b Jan. 5, 1928
*Imtiaz Ali (T/T) b July 28, 1954
Inchmore, J. D. (Worcs. & N. Tvl) b Feb. 22, 1949
*Indrajitsinhji, K. S. (S'tra & Delhi) b June 15, 1937
Ingle, R. A. (Som.) b Nov. 5, 1903
Ingleby-Mackenzie, A. C. D. (Hants) b Sept. 15, 1933
Inman C. C. (Ceylon & Leics.) b Jan. 29, 1936
Innes, G. A. S. (W. Prov. & Tvl) b Nov. 16, 1931, d July 19, 1982
*Inshan Ali (T/T) b Sept. 25, 1949
*Insole, D. J. (CUCC & Essex; *CY 1956*) b April 18, 1926
*Intikhab Alam (Kar., PIA, Surrey, PWD, Sind & Punjab) b Dec. 28, 1941
*Inverarity, R. J. (W. Aust. & S. Aust.) b Jan. 31, 1944
*Iqbal Qasim (Kar., Sind & NBP) b Aug. 6, 1953
*Irani, J. K. (Sind) b Aug. 18, 1923, d Feb. 25, 1982
*Iredale, F. A. (NSW) b June 19, 1867, d April 15, 1926
Iremonger, J. (Notts.; *CY 1903*) b March 5, 1876, d March 25, 1956
*Ironmonger, H. (Qld & Vic.) b April 7, 1882, d June 1, 1971
*Ironside, D. E. J. (Tvl) b May 2, 1925
*Irvine, B. L. (W. Prov., Natal, Essex & Tvl) b March 9, 1944
*Israr Ali (S. Punjab, B'pur & Multan) b May 1, 1927
*Iverson, J. B. (Vic.) b July 27, 1915, d Oct. 24, 1973

*Jackman, R. D. (Surrey, W. Prov. & Rhod.; *CY 1981*) b Aug. 13, 1945
*Jackson, A. A. (NSW) b Sept. 5, 1909, d Feb. 16, 1933
Jackson, A. B. (Derbys.) b Aug. 21, 1933
Jackson, Sir A. H. M. (Derbys.) b Nov. 9, 1899, d Oct. 11, 1983
*Jackson, Rt Hon. Sir F. S. (CUCC & Yorks.; *CY 1894*; Pres. MCC 1921) b Nov. 21, 1870, d March 9, 1947
Jackson, G. R. (Derbys.) b June 23, 1896, d Feb. 21, 1966
*Jackson, H. L. (Derbys.; *CY 1959*) b April 5, 1921
Jackson, John (Notts. & All-England) b May 21, 1833, d Nov. 4, 1901
Jackson, P. F. (Worcs.) b May 11, 1911
Jacques, T. A. (Yorks.) b Feb. 19, 1905
*Jahangir Khan (N. Ind. & CUCC) b Feb. 1, 1910, d July 23, 1988
*Jai, L. P. (Bombay) b April 1, 1902, d Jan. 29, 1968
*Jaisimha, M. L. (H'bad) b March 3, 1939
Jakeman, F. (Yorks. & Northants) b Jan. 10, 1920, d May 18, 1986
*Jalal-ud-Din (PWD, Kar., IDBP & Allied Bank) b June 12, 1959
James, A. E. (Sussex) b Aug. 7, 1924
*James, K. C. (Wgtn & Northants) b March 12, 1904, d Aug. 21, 1976
James, K. D. (Middx, Hants & Wgtn) b March 18, 1961
James, R. M. (CUCC & Wgtn) b Oct. 2, 1934
James, S. P. (Glam. & CUCC) b Sept. 7, 1967
*Jameson, J. A. (Warwicks.) b June 30, 1941
*Jamshedji, R. J. D. (Bombay) b Nov. 18, 1892, d April 5, 1976
*Jardine, D. R. (OUCC & Surrey; *CY 1928*) b Oct. 23, 1900, d June 18, 1958

Jardine, M. R. (OUCC & Middx) b June 8, 1869, d Jan. 16, 1947
*Jarman, B. N. (S. Aust.) b Feb. 17, 1936
Jarrett, D. W. (OUCC & CUCC) b April 19, 1952
*Jarvis, A. H. (S. Aust.) b Oct. 19, 1860, d Nov. 15, 1933
Jarvis, K. B. S. (Kent & Glos.) b April 23, 1953
*Jarvis, P. W. (Yorks.) b June 29, 1965
*Jarvis, T. W. (Auck. & Cant.) b July 29, 1944
*Javed Akhtar (R'pindi & Pak. Serv.) b Nov. 21, 1940
*Javed Miandad (Kar., Sind, Sussex, HBL & Glam.; *CY 1982*) b June 12, 1957
*Jayantilal, K. (H'bad) b Jan. 13, 1948
*Jayasekera, R. S. A. (SL) b Dec. 7, 1957
Jayasinghe, S. (Ceylon & Leics.) b Jan. 19, 1931
Jayasinghe, S. A. (SL) b July 15, 1955
Jayasuriya, S. T. (CCC) b June 30, 1969
Jefferies, S. T. (W. Prov., Derbys., Lancs. & Hants) b Dec. 8, 1959
Jefferson, R. I. (CUCC & Surrey) b Aug. 15, 1941
*Jeganathan, S. (SL) b July 11, 1951
*Jenkins, R. O. (Worcs.; *CY 1950*) b Nov. 24, 1918
Jenkins, V. G. J. (OUCC & Glam.) b Nov. 2, 1911
*Jenner, T. J. (W. Aust. & S. Aust.) b Sept. 8, 1944
*Jennings, C. B. (S. Aust.) b June 5, 1884, d June 20, 1950
Jennings, K. F. (Som.) b Oct. 5, 1953
Jennings, R. V. (Tvl) b Aug. 9, 1954
Jepson, A. (Notts.) b July 12, 1915
*Jessop, G. L. (CUCC & Glos.; *CY 1898*) b May 19, 1874, d May 11, 1955
Jesty, T. E. (Hants., Border, Griq. W., Cant., Surrey & Lancs.; *CY 1983*) b June 2, 1948
Jewell, Major M. F. S. (Sussex & Worcs.) b Sept. 15, 1885, d May 28, 1978
*John, V. B. (SL) b May 27, 1960
Johnson, C. (Yorks.) b Sept. 5, 1947
*Johnson, C. L. (Tvl) b 1871, d May 31, 1908
Johnson, G. W. (Kent & Tvl) b Nov. 8, 1946
*Johnson, H. H. H. (Jam.) b July 17, 1910, d June 24, 1987
Johnson, H. L. (Derbys.) b Nov. 8, 1927
*Johnson, I. W. (Vic.) b Dec. 8, 1918
Johnson, L. A. (Northants) b Aug. 12, 1936
*Johnson, L. J. (Qld) b March 18, 1919, d April 20, 1977
Johnson, P. (Notts.) b April 24, 1965
Johnson, P. D. (CUCC & Notts.) b Nov. 12, 1949
*Johnson, T. F. (T/T) b Jan. 10, 1917, d April 5, 1985
Johnston, B. A. (Broadcaster) b June 24, 1912
*Johnston, W. A. (Vic.; *CY 1949*) b Feb. 26, 1922
Jones, A. (Glam., W. Aust., N. Tvl & Natal; *CY 1978*) b Nov. 4, 1938
Jones, A. A. (Sussex, Som., Middx, Glam., N. Tvl & OFS) b Dec. 9, 1947
*Jones, A. H. (Wgtn) b May 9, 1959
Jones, A. L. (Glam.) b June 1, 1957
Jones, A. N. (Sussex, Border & Som.) b July 22, 1961
*Jones, A. O. (Notts. & CUCC; *CY 1900*) b Aug. 16, 1872, d Dec. 21, 1914
Jones, B. J. R. (Worcs.) b Nov. 2, 1955
*Jones, C. M. (C. E. L.) (BG) b Nov. 3, 1902, d Dec. 10, 1959
*Jones, D. M. (Vic.; *CY 1990*) b March 24, 1961
*Jones, Ernest (S. Aust. & W. Aust.) b Sept. 30, 1869, d Nov. 23, 1943
Jones, E. C. (Glam.) b Dec. 14, 1912, d April 14, 1989
Jones, E. W. (Glam.) b June 25, 1942
*Jones, I. J. (Glam.) b Dec. 10, 1941
Jones, K. V. (Middx) b March 28, 1942
*Jones, P. E. (T/T) b June 6, 1917
Jones, P. H. (Kent) b June 19, 1935
*Jones, S. P. (NSW, Qld & Auck.) b Aug. 1, 1861, d July 14, 1951
Jones, W. E. (Glam.) b Oct. 31, 1916
Jordan, J. M. (Lancs.) b Feb. 7, 1932
Jorden, A. M. (CUCC & Essex) b Jan. 28, 1947
Jordon, R. C. (Vic.) b Feb. 17, 1937
*Joshi, P. G. (M'tra) b Oct. 27, 1926, d Jan. 8, 1987
Joshi, U. C. (S'tra, Ind. Rlwys, Guj. & Sussex) b Dec. 23, 1944
*Joslin, L. R. (Vic.) b Dec. 13, 1947
Jowett, D. C. P. R. (OUCC) b Jan. 24, 1931
Judd, A. K. (CUCC & Hants) b Jan. 1, 1904, d Feb. 15, 1988
Judge, P. F. (Middx, Glam. & Bengal) b May 23, 1916
Julian, R. (Leics.) b Aug. 23, 1936
*Julien, B. D. (T/T & Kent) b March 13, 1950
*Jumadeen, R. R. (T/T) b April 12, 1948
*Jupp, H. (Surrey) b Nov. 19, 1841, d April 8, 1889
*Jupp, V. W. C. (Sussex & Northants; *CY 1928*) b March 27, 1891, d July 9, 1960
*Jurangpathy, B. R. (CCC) b June 25, 1967

*Kallicharran, A. I. (Guyana, Warwicks. Qld, Tvl & OFS; *CY 1983*) b March 21 1949
*Kaluperuma, L. W. (SL) b May 25, 1949
*Kaluperuma, S. M. S. (SL) b Oct. 22, 1961
*Kanhai, R. B. (†Guyana, T/T, W. Aust Warwicks. & Tas.; *CY 1964*) b Dec. 26 1935
*Kanitkar, H. S. (M'tra) b Dec. 8, 1942

*Kapil Dev (Haryana, Northants & Worcs.; *CY 1983*) b Jan. 6, 1959
**Kardar, A. H. (formerly Abdul Hafeez) (N. Ind., OUCC, Warwicks. & Pak. Serv.) b Jan. 17, 1925
Karnain, S. H. U. (NCC) b Aug. 11, 1962
*Keeton, W. W. (Notts.; *CY 1940*) b April 30, 1905, d Oct. 10, 1980
Keighley, W. G. (OUCC & Yorks.) b Jan. 10, 1925
*Keith, H. J. (Natal) b Oct. 25, 1927
Kelleher, H. R. A. (Surrey & Northants) b March 3, 1929
*Kelleway, C. (NSW) b April 25, 1886, d Nov. 16, 1944
Kelly, J. (Notts.) b Sept. 15, 1930
*Kelly, J. J. (NSW; *CY 1903*) b May 10, 1867, d Aug. 14, 1938
Kelly, T. J. D. (Vic.) b May 3, 1844, d July 20, 1893
*Kempis, G. A. (Natal) b Aug. 4, 1865, d May 19, 1890
*Kendall, T. (Vic. & Tas.) b Aug. 24, 1851, d Aug. 17, 1924
Kennedy, A. (Lancs.) b Nov. 4, 1949
*Kennedy, A. S. (Hants; *CY 1933*) b Jan. 24, 1891, d Nov. 15, 1959
*Kenny, R. B. (Bombay & Bengal) b Sept. 29, 1930, d Nov. 21, 1985
Kent, M. F. (Qld) b Nov. 23, 1953
Kentish, E. S. M. (Jam. & OUCC) b Nov. 21, 1916
Kenyon, D. (Worcs.; *CY 1963*) b May 15, 1924
*Kerr, R. B. (Qld) b June 16, 1961
*Kerr, J. L. (Cant.) b Dec. 28, 1910
Kerr, K. J. (Tvl & Warwicks.) b Sept. 11, 1961
Kerslake, R. C. (CUCC & Som.) b Dec. 26, 1942
Kettle, M. K. (Northants) b March 18, 1944
Khalid Hassan (Punjab & Lahore) b July 14, 1937
*Khalid Wazir (Pak.) b April 27, 1936
*Khan Mohammad (N. Ind., Pak. Us, Som., B'pur, Sind, Kar. & Lahore) b Jan. 1, 1928
Khanna, S. C. (Delhi) b June 3, 1956
Kidd, E. L. (CUCC & Middx) b Oct. 18, 1889, d July 2, 1984
Kilborn, M. J. (OUCC) b Sept. 20, 1962
Killick, Rev. E. T. (CUCC & Middx) b May 9, 1907, d May 18, 1953
Kilner, Norman (Yorks. & Warwicks.) b July 21, 1895, d April 28, 1979
*Kilner, Roy (Yorks.; *CY 1924*) b Oct. 17, 1890, d April 5, 1928
Kimpton, R. C. M. (OUCC & Worcs.) b Sept. 21, 1916
King, C. L. (B'dos, Glam., Worcs. & Natal) b June 11, 1951
King, F. McD. (B'dos) b Dec. 14, 1926
King, I. M. (Warwicks. & Essex) b Nov. 10, 1931
King, J. B. (Philadelphia) b Oct. 19, 1873, d Oct. 17, 1965
*King, J. H. (Leics.) b April 16, 1871, d Nov. 18, 1946
*King, L. A. (Jam. & Bengal) b Feb. 27, 1939
Kingsley, Sir P. G. T. (OUCC) b May 26, 1908
*Kinneir, S. P. (Warwicks.; *CY 1912*) b May 13, 1871, d Oct. 16, 1928
*Kippax, A. F. (NSW) b May 25, 1897, d Sept. 4, 1972
Kirby, D. (CUCC & Leics.) b Jan. 18, 1939
*Kirmani, S. M. H. (†Karn.) b Dec. 29, 1949
Kirsten, P. N. (W. Prov., Sussex & Derbys.) b May 14, 1955
*Kischenchand, G. (W. Ind., Guj. & Baroda) b April 14, 1925
Kitchen, M. J. (Som.; Umpire) b Aug. 1, 1940
*Kline, L. F. (Vic.) b Sept. 29, 1934
*Knight, A. E. (Leics.; *CY 1904*) b Oct. 8, 1872, d April 25, 1946
*Knight, B. R. (Essex & Leics.) b Feb. 18, 1938
*Knight, D. J. (OUCC & Surrey; *CY 1915*) b May 12, 1894, d Jan. 5, 1960
Knight, R. D. V. (CUCC, Surrey, Glos. & Sussex) b Sept. 6, 1946
Knight, W. H. (Editor of *Wisden* 1870-79) b Nov. 29, 1812, d Aug. 16, 1879
*Knott, A. P. E. (Kent & Tas.; *CY 1970*) b April 9, 1946
Knott, C. H. (OUCC & Kent) b March 20, 1901, d June 18, 1988
Knott, C. J. (Hants) b Nov. 26, 1914
Knowles, J. (Notts.) b March 25, 1910
Knox, G. K. (Lancs.) b April 22, 1937
*Knox, N. A. (Surrey; *CY 1907*) b Oct. 10, 1884, d March 3, 1935
Kortright, C. J. (Essex) b Jan. 9, 1871, d Dec. 12, 1952
*Kotze, J. J. (Tvl & W. Prov.) b Aug. 7, 1879, d July 7, 1931
Kourie, A. J. (Tvl) b July 30, 1951
Krikken, K. M. (Derbys.) b April 9, 1969
*Kripal Singh, A. G. (Madras & H'bad) b Aug. 6, 1933, d July 23, 1987
*Krishnamurthy, P. (H'bad) b July 12, 1947
*Kuggeleijn, C. M. (N. Dist.) b May 10, 1956
Kuiper, A. P. (W. Prov. & Derbys.) b Aug. 24, 1959
*Kulkarni, R. R. (Bombay) b Sept. 25, 1962
*Kulkarni, U. N. (Bombay) b March 7, 1942
*Kumar, V. V. (†TN) b June 22, 1935
*Kumble, A. (Karn.) b Oct. 17, 1970
*Kunderan, B. K. (Ind. Rlwys & Mysore) b Oct. 2, 1939
*Kuruppu, D. S. B. P. (BRC) b Jan. 5, 1962

*Kuruppuarachchi, A. K. (SL) b Nov. 1, 1964
*Kuys, F. (W. Prov.) b March 21, 1870, d Sept. 12, 1953
Kynaston, R. (Middx; Sec. MCC 1846-58) b Nov. 5, 1805, d June 21, 1874

*Labrooy, G. F. (CCC) b June 7, 1964
Lacey, Sir F. E. (CUCC & Hants; Sec MCC 1898-1926) b Oct. 19, 1859, d May 26, 1946
*Laird, B. M. (W. Aust.) b Nov. 21, 1950
*Laker, J. C. (Surrey, Auck. & Essex; *CY 1952*) b Feb. 9, 1922, d April 23, 1986
*Lall Singh (S. Punjab) b Dec. 16, 1909, d Nov. 19, 1985
*Lamb, A. J. (W. Prov., Northants & OFS; *CY 1981*) b June 20, 1954
Lamb, T. M. (OUCC, Middx & Northants) b March 24, 1953
*Lamba, R. (Delhi) b Jan. 2, 1958
Lambert, C. B. (Guyana) b Feb. 10, 1962
Lambert, G. E. (Glos. & Som.) b May 11, 1919
Lambert, R. H. (Ireland) b July 18, 1874, d March 24, 1956
Lambert, Wm (Surrey) b 1779, d April 19, 1851
Lampard, A. W. (Vic. & AIF) b July 3, 1885, d Jan. 11, 1984
Lampitt, S. R. (Worcs.) b July 29, 1966
*Lance, H. R. (NE Tvl & Tvl) b June 6, 1940
Langdale, G. R. (Derbys. & Som.) b March 11, 1916
Langford, B. A. (Som.) b Dec. 17, 1935
*Langley, G. R. A. (S. Aust.; *CY 1957*) b Sept. 14, 1919
*Langridge, James (Sussex; *CY 1932*) b July 10, 1906, d Sept. 10, 1966
Langridge, J. G. (John) (Sussex; *CY 1950*) b Feb. 10, 1910
Langridge, R. J. (Sussex) b April 13, 1939
*Langton, A. B. C. (Tvl) b March 2, 1912, d Nov. 27, 1942
*Larkins, W. (Northants & E. Prov.) b Nov. 22, 1953
Larsen, G. R. (Wgtn) b Sept. 27, 1962
*Larter, J. D. F. (Northants) b April 24, 1940
*Larwood, H. (Notts.; *CY 1927*) b Nov. 14, 1904
*Lashley, P. D. (B'dos) b Feb. 11, 1937
Latchman, H. C. [A. H.] (Middx & Notts.) b July 26, 1943
*Laughlin, T. J. (Vic.) b Jan. 30, 1951
*Laver, F. (Vic.) b Dec. 7, 1869, d Sept. 24, 1919
*Lawrence, D. V. (Glos.) b Jan. 28, 1964
*Lawrence, G. B. (Rhod. & Natal) b March 31, 1932
Lawrence, J. (Som.) b March 29, 1914, d Dec. 10, 1988

*Lawry, W. M. (Vic.; *CY 1962*) b Feb. 11, 1937
*Lawson, G. F. (NSW & Lancs.) b Dec. 7, 1957
Leadbeater, B. (Yorks.) b Aug. 14, 1943
*Leadbeater, E. (Yorks. & Warwicks.) b Aug. 15, 1927
Leary, S. E. (Kent) b April 30, 1933, d Aug. 21, 1988
Lee, C. (Yorks. & Derbys.) b March 17, 1924
Lee, F. S. (Middx & Som.) b July 24, 1905, d March 30, 1982
*Lee, H. W. (Middx) b Oct. 26, 1890, d April 21, 1981
Lee, J. W. (Middx & Som.) b Feb. 1, 1904, d June 20, 1944
Lee, P. G. (Northants & Lancs.; *CY 1976*) b Aug. 27, 1945
*Lee, P. K. (S. Aust.) b Sept. 14, 1904, d Aug. 9, 1980
*Lees, W. K. (Otago) b March 19, 1952
*Lees, W. S. (Surrey; *CY 1906*) b Dec. 25 1875, d Sept. 10, 1924
Leese, Sir Oliver, Bt (Pres. MCC 1965-66) b Oct. 27, 1894, d Jan. 20, 1978
*Legall, R. A. (B'dos & T/T) b Dec. 1, 1925
Legard, E. (Warwicks.) b Aug. 23, 1935
*Leggat, I. B. (C. Dist.) b June 7, 1930
*Leggat, J. G. (Cant.) b May 27, 1926, d March 8, 1973
*Legge, G. B. (OUCC & Kent) b Jan. 26 1903, d Nov. 21, 1940
Lenham, L. J. (Sussex) b May 24, 1936
Lenham, N. J. (Sussex) b Dec. 17, 1965
*le Roux, F. L. (Tvl & E. Prov.) b Feb. 5 1882, d Sept. 22, 1963
le Roux, G. S. (W. Prov. & Sussex) b Sept 4, 1955
*Leslie, C. F. H. (OUCC & Middx) b Dec 8, 1861, d Feb. 12, 1921
Lester, E. (Yorks.) b Feb. 18, 1923
Lester, G. (Leics.) b Dec. 27, 1915
Lester, Dr J. A. (Philadelphia) b Aug. 1 1871, d Sept. 3, 1969
Lethbridge, C. (Warwicks.) b June 23, 1961
*Lever, J. K. (Essex & Natal; *CY 1979*) b Feb. 24, 1949
*Lever, P. (Lancs. & Tas.) b Sept. 17, 1940
*Leveson Gower, Sir H. D. G. (OUCC & Surrey) b May 8, 1873, d Feb. 1, 1954
*Levett, W. H. V. (Kent) b Jan. 25, 1908
Lewington, P. J. (Warwicks.) b Jan. 30 1950
*Lewis, A. R. (CUCC & Glam.) b July 6 1938
Lewis, C. (Kent) b July 27, 1908
*Lewis, C. C. (Leics.) b Feb. 14, 1968
Lewis, D. J. (OUCC & Rhod.) b July 27 1927
*Lewis, D. M. (Jam.) b Feb. 21, 1946
Lewis, E. B. (Warwicks.) b Jan. 5, 1918, d Oct. 19, 1983

Lewis, E. J. (Glam. & Sussex) b Jan. 31, 1942
*Lewis, P. T. (W. Prov.) b Oct. 2, 1884, d Jan. 30, 1976
Lewis, R. V. (Hants) b Aug. 6, 1947
*Leyland, M. (Yorks.; *CY 1929*) b July 20, 1900, d Jan. 1, 1967
*Liaqat Ali (Kar., Sind, HBL & PIA) b May 21, 1955
Liddicutt, A. E. (Vic.) b Oct. 17, 1891, d April 8, 1983
Lightfoot, A. (Northants) b Jan. 8, 1936
Lill, J. C. (S. Aust.) b Dec. 7, 1933
*Lillee, D. K. (W. Aust., Tas. & Northants; *CY 1973*) b July 18, 1949
*Lilley, A. A. (Warwicks.; *CY 1897*) b Nov. 28, 1866, d Nov. 17, 1929
Lilley, A. W. (Essex) b May 8, 1959
Lilley, B. (Notts.) b Feb. 11, 1895, d Aug. 4, 1950
Lillywhite, Fred (Sussex; Editor of *Lillywhite's Guide to Cricketers*) b July 23, 1829, d Sept. 15, 1866
Lillywhite, F. W. ("William") (Sussex) b June 13, 1792, d Aug. 21, 1854
*Lillywhite, James, jun. (Sussex) b Feb. 23, 1842, d Oct. 25, 1929
*Lindsay, D. T. (NE Tvl, N. Tvl & Tvl) b Sept 4, 1939
*Lindsay, J. D. (Tvl & NE Tvl) b Sept. 8, 1909, d Aug. 31, 1990
*Lindsay, N. V. (Tvl & OFS) b July 30, 1886, d Feb. 2, 1976
*Lindwall, R. R. (NSW & Qld; *CY 1949*) b Oct. 3, 1921
*Ling, W. V. S. (Griq. W. & E. Prov.) b Oct. 3, 1891, d Sept. 26, 1960
*Lissette, A. F. (Auck. & N. Dist.) b Nov. 6, 1919, d Jan. 24, 1973
Lister, J. (Yorks. & Worcs.) b May 14, 1930
Lister, W. H. L. (Lancs.) b Oct. 7, 1911
Livingston, L. (NSW & Northants) b May 3, 1920
Livingstone, D. A. (Hants) b Sept. 21, 1933, d Sept. 8, 1988
Livsey, W. H. (Hants) b Sept. 23, 1893, d Sept. 12, 1978
*Llewellyn, C. B. (Natal & Hants; *CY 1911*) b Sept. 26, 1876, d June 7, 1964
Llewellyn, M. J. (Glam.) b Nov. 27, 1953
Lloyd, B. J. (Glam.) b Sept. 6, 1953
*Lloyd, C. H. (†Guyana & Lancs.; *CY 1971*) b Aug. 31, 1944
*Lloyd, D. (Lancs.) b March 18, 1947
*Lloyd, T. A. (Warwicks. & OFS) b Nov. 5, 1956
Lloyds, J. W. (Som., OFS & Glos.) b Nov. 17, 1954
*Loader, P. J. (Surrey and W. Aust.; *CY 1958*) b Oct. 25, 1929
Lobb, B. (Warwicks. & Som.) b Jan. 11, 1931
*Lock, G. A. R. (Surrey, Leics. & W. Aust.; *CY 1954*) b July 5, 1929
Lockwood, Ephraim (Yorks.) b April 4, 1845, d Dec. 19, 1921
*Lockwood, W. H. (Notts. & Surrey; *CY 1899*) b March 25, 1868, d April 26, 1932
Lockyer, T. (Surrey & All-England) b Nov. 1, 1826, d Dec. 22, 1869
*Logan, J. D. (SA) b June 24, 1880, d Jan. 3, 1960
*Logie, A. L. (T/T) b Sept. 28, 1960
*Lohmann, G. A. (Surrey, W. Prov. & Tvl; *CY 1889*) b June 2, 1865, d Dec. 1, 1901
Lomax, J. G. (Lancs. & Som.) b May 5, 1925
Long, A. (Surrey & Sussex) b Dec. 18, 1940
Longfield, T. C. (CUCC & Kent) b May 12, 1906, d Dec. 21, 1981
Lord, G. J. (Warwicks. & Worcs.) b April 25, 1961
Lord, Thomas (Middx; founder of Lord's) b Nov. 23, 1755, d Jan. 13, 1832
*Love, H. S. B. (NSW & Vic.) b Aug. 10, 1895, d July 22, 1969
Love, J. D. (Yorks.) b April 22, 1955
Lowndes, W. G. L. F. (OUCC & Hants) b Jan. 24, 1898, d May 23, 1982
*Lowry, T. C. (Wgtn, CUCC & Som.) b Feb. 17, 1898, d July 20, 1976
*Lowson, F. A. (Yorks.) b July 1, 1925, d Sept. 8, 1984
*Loxton, S. J. E. (Vic.) b March 29, 1921
*Lucas, A. P. (CUCC, Surrey, Middx & Essex) b Feb. 20, 1857, d Oct. 12, 1923
Luckes, W. T. (Som.) b Jan. 1, 1901, d Oct. 27, 1982
*Luckhurst, B. W. (Kent; *CY 1971*) b Feb. 5, 1939
Lumb, R. G. (Yorks.) b Feb. 27, 1950
*Lundie, E. B. (E. Prov., W. Prov. & Tvl) b March 15, 1888, d Sept. 12, 1917
Lynch, M. A. (Surrey & Guyana) b May 21, 1958
Lyon, B. H. (OUCC & Glos.; *CY 1931*) b Jan. 19, 1902, d June 22, 1970
Lyon, J. (Lancs.) b May 17, 1951
Lyon, M. D. (CUCC & Som.) b April 22, 1898, d Feb. 17, 1964
*Lyons, J. J. (S. Aust.) b May 21, 1863, d July 21, 1927
Lyons, K. J. (Glam.) b Dec. 18, 1946
*Lyttelton, Rt Hon. Alfred (CUCC & Middx; Pres. MCC 1898) b Feb. 7, 1857, d July 5, 1913
Lyttelton, Rt Rev. Hon. A. T. (MCC) b Jan. 7, 1852, d Feb. 19, 1903
Lyttelton, Rev. Hon. C. F. (CUCC & Worcs.) b Jan. 26, 1887, d Oct. 3, 1931
Lyttelton, Hon. C. G. (CUCC) b Oct. 27, 1842, d June 9, 1922
Lyttelton, Hon. C. J. (*see* 10th Visct Cobham)

Lyttelton, Rev. Hon. E. (CUCC & Middx) b July 23, 1855, d Jan. 26, 1942
Lyttelton, Hon. G. W. S. (CUCC) b June 12, 1847, d Dec. 5, 1913
Lyttelton, Hon. R. H. (MCC) b Jan. 18, 1854, d Nov. 7, 1939

*McAlister, P. A. (Vic.) b July 11, 1869, d May 10, 1938
*Macartney, C. G. (NSW & Otago; *CY 1922*) b June 27, 1886, d Sept. 9, 1958
*Macaulay, G. G. (Yorks.; *CY 1924*) b Dec. 7, 1897, d Dec. 13, 1940
*Macaulay, M. J. (Tvl, W. Prov., OFS, NE Tvl & E. Prov.) b April 19, 1939
*MacBryan, J. C. W. (CUCC & Som.; *CY 1925*) b July 22, 1892, d July 14, 1983
*McCabe, S. J. (NSW; *CY 1935*) b July 16, 1910, d Aug. 25, 1968
McCanlis, M. A. (OUCC, Surrey & Glos.) b June 17, 1906
*McCarthy, C. N. (Natal & CUCC) b March 24, 1929
*McConnon, J. E. (Glam.) b June 21, 1922
*McCool, C. L. (NSW, Qld & Som.) b Dec. 9, 1915, d April 5, 1986
McCorkell, N. T. (Hants) b March 23, 1912
*McCormick, E. L. (Vic.) b May 16, 1906
*McCosker, R. B. (NSW; *CY 1976*) b Dec. 11, 1946
McCurdy, R. J. (Vic., Derbys., S. Aust. & E. Prov.) b Dec. 30, 1959
*McDermott, C. J. (Qld; *CY 1986*) b April 14, 1965
*McDonald, C. C. (Vic.) b Nov. 17, 1928
*McDonald, E. A. (Tas., Vic. & Lancs.; *CY 1922*) b Jan. 6, 1891, d July 22, 1937
*McDonnell, P. S. (Vic., NSW & Qld) b Nov. 13, 1858, d Sept. 24, 1896
McEvoy, M. S. A. (Essex & Worcs.) b Jan. 25, 1956
McEwan, K. S. (E. Prov., W. Prov., Essex & W. Aust; *CY 1978*) b July 16, 1952
*McEwan, P. E. (Cant.) b Dec. 19, 1953
McEwan, S. M. (Worcs.) b May 5, 1962
McFarlane, L. L. (Northants, Lancs. & Glam.) b Aug. 19, 1952
*McGahey, C. P. (Essex; *CY 1902*) b Feb. 12, 1871, d Jan. 10, 1935
*MacGibbon, A. R. (Cant.) b Aug. 28, 1924
*McGirr, H. M. (Wgtn) b Nov. 5, 1891, d April 14, 1964
*McGlew, D. J. (Natal; *CY 1956*) b March 11, 1929
*MacGregor, G. (CUCC & Middx; *CY 1891*) b Aug. 31, 1869, d Aug. 20, 1919
*McGregor, S. N. (Otago) b Dec. 18, 1931
McHugh, F. P. (Yorks. & Glos.) b Nov. 15, 1925
*McIlwraith, J. (Vic.) b Sept. 7, 1857, d July 5, 1938
Macindoe, D. H. (OUCC) b Sept. 1, 1917, d March 3, 1986
*McIntyre, A. J. W. (Surrey; *CY 1958*) b May 14, 1918
McIntyre, J. M. (Auck. & Cant.) b July 4, 1944
*Mackay, K. D. (Qld) b Oct. 24, 1925, d June 13, 1982
McKay-Coghill, D. (Tvl) b Nov. 4, 1941
McKechnie, B. J. (Otago) b Nov. 6, 1953
*McKenzie, G. D. (W. Aust. & Leics.; *CY 1965*) b June 24, 1941
McKenzie, K. A. (NE Tvl & Tvl) b July 16, 1948
*McKibbin, T. R. (NSW) b Dec. 10, 1870, d Dec. 15, 1939
*McKinnon, A. H. (E. Prov. & Tvl) b Aug. 20, 1932, d Dec. 2, 1983
*MacKinnon, F. A. (CUCC & Kent) b April 9, 1848, d Feb. 27, 1947
McLachlan, I. M. (CUCC & S. Aust.) b Oct. 2, 1936
*MacLaren, A. C. (Lancs.; *CY 1895*) b Dec. 1, 1871, d Nov. 17, 1944
*McLaren, J. W. (Qld) b Dec. 24, 1887, d Nov. 17, 1921
*Maclean, J. A. (Qld) b April 27, 1946
Maclean, J. F. (Worcs. & Glos.) b March 1, 1901, d March 9, 1986
*McLean, R. A. (Natal; *CY 1961*) b July 9, 1930
MacLeay, K. H. (W. Aust.) b April 2, 1959
*McLeod, C. E. (Vic.) b Oct. 24, 1869, d Nov. 26, 1918
*McLeod, E. G. (Auck. & Wgtn) b Oct. 14, 1900, d Sept. 14, 1989
*McLeod, R. W. (Vic.) b Jan. 19, 1868, d June 14, 1907
McMahon, J. W. (Surrey & Som.) b Dec. 28, 1919
*McMahon, T. G. (Wgtn) b Nov. 8, 1929
*McMaster, J. E. P. (Eng.) b March 16, 1861, d June 7, 1929
McMillan, B. M. (Tvl, W. Prov. & Warwicks.) b Dec. 22, 1963
*McMillan, Q. (Tvl) b June 23, 1904, d July 3, 1948
*McMorris, E. D. A. (Jam.) b April 4, 1935
*McRae, D. A. N. (Cant.) b Dec. 25, 1912
*McShane, P. G. (Vic.) b 1857, d Dec. 11, 1903
McSweeney, E. B. (C. Dist. & Wgtn) b March 8, 1957
McVicker, N. M. (Warwicks. & Leics.) b Nov. 4, 1940
*McWatt, C. A. (BG) b Feb. 1, 1922
*Madan Lal (Punjab & Delhi) b March 20, 1951
*Maddocks, L. V. (Vic. & Tas.) b May 24, 1926
*Madray, I. S. (BG) b July 2, 1934
*Madugalle, R. S. (NCC) b April 22, 1959

*Madurasinghe, A. W. R. (SL) b Jan. 30, 1961
*Maguire, J. N. (Qld & E. Prov.) b Sept. 15, 1956
*Mahanama, R. S. (CCC) b May 31, 1966
Maher, B. J. M. (Derbys.) b Feb. 11, 1958
*Mahmood Hussain (Pak. Us, Punjab, Kar., E. Pak. & NTB) b April 2, 1932
*Mailey, A. A. (NSW) b Jan. 3, 1886, d Dec. 31, 1967
*Majid Khan (Lahore, Pak. Us, CUCC, Glam., PIA, Qld & Punjab; *CY 1970*) b Sept. 28, 1946
*Maka, E. S. (Bombay) b March 5, 1922
*Makepeace, J. W. H. (Lancs.) b Aug. 22, 1881, d Dec. 19, 1952
*Malcolm, D. E. (Derbys.) b Feb. 22, 1963
*Malhotra, A. (Haryana) b Jan. 26, 1957
Mallender, N. A. (Northants, Otago & Som.) b Aug. 13, 1961
*Mallett, A. A. (S. Aust.) b July 13, 1945
Mallett, A. W. H. (OUCC & Kent) b Aug. 29, 1924
*Malone, M. F. (W. Aust. & Lancs.) b Oct. 9, 1950
Malone, S. J. (Essex, Hants & Glam.) b Oct. 19, 1953
*Maninder Singh (Delhi) b June 13, 1965
*Manjrekar, S. V. (Bombay) b July 12, 1965
*Manjrekar, V. L. (Bombay, Bengal, Andhra, U. Pradesh, Raja. & M'tra) b Sept. 26, 1931, d Oct. 18, 1983
*Mankad, A. V. (Bombay) b Oct. 12, 1946
*Mankad, V. (M. H.) (W. Ind., Naw., M'tra, Guj., Bengal, Bombay & Raja.; *CY 1947*) b April 12, 1917, d Aug. 21, 1978
*Mann, A. L. (W. Aust.) b Nov. 8, 1945
*Mann, F. G. (CUCC & Middx; Pres. MCC 1984-85) b Sept. 6, 1917
*Mann, F. T. (CUCC & Middx) b March 3, 1888, d Oct. 6, 1964
Mann, J. P. (Middx) b June 13, 1919
*Mann, N. B. F. (Natal & E. Prov.) b Dec. 28, 1920, d July 31, 1952
Manning, J. S. (S. Aust. & Northants) b June 11, 1924, d May 5, 1988
*Mansell, P. N. F. (Rhod.) b March 16, 1920
*Mansoor Akhtar (Kar., UBL & Sind) b Dec. 25, 1956
Mansoor Rana (ADBP) b Dec. 27, 1962
*Mantri, M. K. (Bombay & M'tra) b Sept. 1, 1921
*Manzoor Elahi (Multan, Pak. Rlwys & IDBP) b April 15, 1963
*Maqsood Ahmed (S. Punjab, R'pindi & Kar.) b March 26, 1925
Maqsood Rana (Lahore) b Aug. 1, 1972
*Marais, G. G. ("G. Gladstone") (Jam.) b Jan. 14, 1901, d May 19, 1978
Marie, G. V. (OUCC) b Feb. 17, 1945
*Markham, L. A. (Natal) b Sept. 12, 1924
*Marks, V. J. (OUCC, Som. & W. Aust.) b June 25, 1955
Marlar, R. G. (CUCC & Sussex) b Jan. 2, 1931
Marner, P. T. (Lancs. & Leics.) b March 31, 1936
*Marr, A. P. (NSW) b March 28, 1862, d March 15, 1940
*Marriott, C. S. (CUCC, Lancs. & Kent) b Sept. 14, 1895, d Oct. 13, 1966
Marsden, Tom (Eng.) b 1805, d Feb. 27, 1843
Marsh, F. E. (Derbys.) b July 7, 1920
*Marsh, G. R. (W. Aust.) b Dec. 31, 1958
*Marsh, R. W. (W. Aust.; *CY 1982*) b Nov. 11, 1947
Marsh, S. A. (Kent) b Jan. 27, 1961
Marshal, Alan (Qld & Surrey; *CY 1909*) b June 12, 1883, d July 23, 1915
Marshall, J. M. A. (Warwicks.) b Oct. 26, 1916
*Marshall, M. D. (B'dos & Hants; *CY 1983*) b April 18, 1958
*Marshall, N. E. (B'dos & T/T) b Feb. 27, 1924
*Marshall, R. E. (B'dos & Hants; *CY 1959*) b April 25, 1930
Martin, E. J. (Notts.) b Aug. 17, 1925
*Martin, F. (Kent; *CY 1892*) b Oct. 12, 1861, d Dec. 13, 1921
*Martin, F. R. (Jam.) b Oct. 12, 1893, d Nov. 23, 1967
Martin, J. D. (OUCC & Som.) b Dec. 23, 1941
*Martin, J. W. (NSW & S. Aust.) b July 28, 1931
*Martin, J. W. (Kent) b Feb. 16, 1917, d Jan. 4, 1987
Martin, S. H. (Worcs., Natal & Rhod.) b Jan. 11, 1909, d Feb. 1988
Martindale, D. J. R. (Notts.) b Dec 13, 1963
*Martindale, E. A. (B'dos) b Nov. 25, 1909, d March 17, 1972
Maru, R. J. (Middx & Hants) b Oct. 28, 1962
*Marx, W. F. E. (Tvl) b July 4, 1895, d June 2, 1974
*Mason, J. R. (Kent; *CY 1898*) b March 26, 1874, d Oct. 15, 1958
Masood Iqbal (Lahore, Punjab U., Pak. Us & HBL) b April 17, 1952
*Massie, H. H. (NSW) b April 11, 1854, d Oct. 12, 1938
*Massie, R. A. L. (W. Aust.; *CY 1973*) b April 14, 1947
*Matheson, A. M. (Auck.) b Feb. 27, 1906, d Dec. 31, 1985
*Mathias, Wallis (Sind, Kar. & NBP) b Feb. 4, 1935
*Matthews, A. D. G. (Northants & Glam.) b May 3, 1904, d July 29, 1977

*Matthews, C. D. (W. Aust. & Lancs.) b Sept. 22, 1962
Matthews, C. S. (Notts.) b Oct. 17, 1929
*Matthews, G. R. J. (NSW) b Dec. 15, 1959
*Matthews, T. J. (Vic.) b April 3, 1884, d Oct. 14, 1943
*Mattis, E. H. (Jam.) b April 11, 1957
Maudsley, R. H. (OUCC & Warwicks.) b April 8, 1918, d Sept. 29, 1981
*May, P. B. H. (CUCC & Surrey; *CY 1952*; Pres. MCC 1980-81) b Dec. 31, 1929
*May, T. B. A. (S. Aust.) b Jan. 26, 1962
Mayer, J. H. (Warwicks.) b March 2, 1902, d Sept. 6, 1981
Mayes, R. (Kent) b Oct. 7, 1921
Maynard, C. (Warwicks. & Lancs.) b April 8, 1958
*Maynard, M. P. (Glam.) b March 21, 1966
*Mayne, E. R. (S. Aust. & Vic.) b July 2, 1882, d Oct. 26, 1961
*Mayne, L. C. (W. Aust.) b Jan. 23, 1942
*Mead, C. P. (Hants; *CY 1912*) b March 9, 1887, d March 26, 1958
*Mead, W. (Essex; *CY 1904*) b March 25, 1868, d March 18, 1954
Meads, E. A. (Notts.) b Aug. 17, 1916
*Meale, T. (Wgtn) b Nov. 11, 1928
*Meckiff, I. (Vic.) b Jan. 6, 1935
Medlycott, K. T. (Surrey & N. Tvl) b May 12, 1965
*Meher-Homji, K. R. (W. Ind. & Bombay) b Aug. 9, 1911, d Feb. 10, 1982
*Mehra, V. L. (E. Punjab, Ind. Rlwys & Delhi) b March 12, 1938
*Meintjes, D. J. (Tvl) b June 9, 1890, d July 17, 1979
*Melle, M. G. (Tvl & W. Prov.) b June 3, 1930
Melluish, M. E. L. (CUCC & Middx) b June 13, 1932
*Melville, A. (OUCC, Sussex, Natal & Tvl; *CY 1948*) b May 19, 1910, d April 18, 1983
Mence, M. D. (Warwicks. & Glos.) b April 13, 1944
Mendis, G. D. (Sussex & Lancs.) b April 20, 1955
*Mendis, L. R. D. (SSC) b Aug. 25, 1952
*Mendonca, I. L. (BG) b July 13, 1934
Mercer, J. (Sussex, Glam. & Northants; *CY 1927*) b April 22, 1895, d Aug. 31, 1987
*Merchant, V. M. (Bombay; *CY 1937*) b Oct. 12, 1911, d Oct. 27, 1987
Merrick, T. A. (Leewards, Warwicks. & Kent) b June 10, 1963
*Merritt, W. E. (Cant. & Northants) b Aug. 18, 1908, d June 9, 1977
*Merry, C. A. (T/T) b Jan. 20, 1911, d April 19, 1964
Metcalfe, A. A. (Yorks. & OFS) b Dec. 25, 1963
Metson, C. P. (Middx & Glam.) b July 2, 1963
*Meuleman, K. D. (Vic. & W. Aust.) b Sept. 5, 1923
*Meuli, E. M. (C. Dist.) b Feb. 20, 1926
Meyer, B. J. (Glos.; Umpire) b Aug. 21, 1932
Meyer, R. J. O. (CUCC, Som. & W. Ind.) b March 15, 1905
Mian Mohammad Saaed (N. Ind. Patiala & S. Punjab; Pak.'s first captain) b Aug. 31, 1910, d Aug. 23, 1979
*Middleton, J. (W. Prov.) b Sept. 30, 1865, d Dec. 23, 1913
**Midwinter, W. E. (Vic. & Glos.) b June 19, 1851, d Dec. 3, 1890
*Milburn, B. D. (Otago) b Nov. 24, 1943
*Milburn, C. (Northants & W. Aust.; *CY 1967*) b Oct. 23, 1941, d Feb. 28, 1990
*Milkha Singh, A. G. (Madras) b Dec. 31, 1941
Miller, A. J. T. (OUCC & Middx) b May 30, 1963
*Miller, A. M. (Eng.) b Oct. 19, 1869, d June 26, 1959
*Miller, G. (Derbys., Natal & Essex) b Sept. 8, 1952
*Miller, K. R. (Vic., NSW & Notts.; *CY 1954*) b Nov. 28, 1919
*Miller, L. S. M. (C. Dist. & Wgtn) b March 31, 1923
Miller, R. (Warwicks.) b Jan. 6, 1941
*Miller, R. C. (Jam.) b Dec. 24, 1924
*Milligan, F. W. (Yorks.) b March 19, 1870, d March 31, 1900
*Millman, G. (Notts.) b Oct. 2, 1934
Millmow, J. P. (Wgtn) b Sept. 22, 1967
*Mills, C. H. (Surrey, Kimberley & W. Prov.) b Nov. 26, 1867, d July 26, 1948
*Mills, J. E. (Auck.) b Sept. 3, 1905, d Dec. 11, 1972
Mills, J. M. (CUCC & Warwicks.) b July 27, 1921
Mills, J. P. C. (CUCC & Northants) b Dec. 6, 1958
Milner, J. (Essex) b Aug. 22, 1937
*Milton, C. A. (Glos.; *CY 1959*) b March 10, 1928
*Milton, W. H. (W. Prov.) b Dec. 3, 1854, d March 6, 1930
*Minnett, R. B. (NSW) b June 13, 1888, d Oct. 21, 1955
"Minshull", John (scorer of first recorded century) b *circa* 1741, d Oct. 1793
*Miran Bux (Pak. Serv., Punjab & R'pindi) b April 20, 1907
*Misson, F. M. (NSW) b Nov. 19, 1938
*Mitchell, A. (Yorks.) b Sept. 13, 1902, d Dec. 25, 1976
*Mitchell, B. (Tvl; *CY 1936*) b Jan. 8, 1909
Mitchell, C. G. (Som.) b Jan. 27, 1929
**Mitchell, F. (CUCC, Yorks. & Tvl; *CY 1902*) b Aug. 13, 1872, d Oct. 11, 1935
*Mitchell, T. B. (Derbys.) b Sept. 4, 1902

*Mitchell-Innes, N. S. (OUCC & Som.) b Sept. 7, 1914
Mobey, G. S. (Surrey) b March 5, 1904
*Modi, R. S. (Bombay) b Nov. 11, 1924
*Mohammad Aslam (N. Ind. & Pak. Rlwys) b Jan. 5, 1920
*Mohammad Farooq (Kar.) b April 8, 1938
*Mohammad Ilyas (Lahore & PIA) b March 19, 1946
*Mohammad Munaf (Sind, E. Pak., Kar. & PIA) b Nov. 2, 1935
*Mohammad Nazir (Pak. Rlwys) b March 8, 1946
*Mohsin Kamal (Lahore, Allied Bank & PNSC) b June 16, 1963
*Mohsin Khan (Pak. Rlwys, Kar., Sind., Pak. Us & HBL) b March 15, 1955
Moin-ul-Atiq (UBL) b Aug. 5, 1964
*Moir, A. McK. (Otago) b July 17, 1919
Moir, D. G. (Derbys. & Scotland) b April 13, 1957
*Mold, A. W. (Lancs.; *CY 1892*) b May 27, 1863, d April 29, 1921
Moles, A. J. (Warwicks. & Griq. W.) b Feb. 12, 1961
*Moloney, D. A. R. (Wgtn, Otago & Cant.) b Aug. 11, 1910, d July 15, 1942
Monckton of Brenchley, 1st Lord (Pres. MCC 1956-57) b Jan. 17, 1891, d Jan. 9, 1965
Mongia, N. R. (Baroda) b Dec. 19, 1969
Monkhouse, G. (Surrey) b April 26, 1954
*Moodie, G. H. (Jam.) b Nov. 25, 1915
*Moody, T. M. (W. Aust. & Warwicks.) b Oct. 2, 1965
*Moon, L. J. (CUCC & Middx) b Feb. 9, 1878, d Nov. 23, 1916
*Mooney, F. L. H. (Wgtn) b May 26, 1921
Moore, D. N. (OUCC & Glos.) b Sept. 26, 1910
Moore, H. I. (Notts.) b Feb. 28, 1941
Moore, R. H. (Hants) b Nov. 14, 1913
Moores, P. (Worcs., Sussex & OFS) b Dec. 18, 1962
*More, K. S. (Baroda) b Sept. 4, 1962
Morgan, D. C. (Derbys.) b Feb. 26, 1929
Morgan, M. (Notts.) b May 21, 1936
*Morgan, R. W. (Auck.) b Feb. 12, 1941
*Morkel, D. P. B. (W. Prov.) b Jan. 25, 1906, d Oct. 6, 1980
*Morley, F. (Notts.) b Dec. 16, 1850, d Sept. 28, 1884
Morley, J. D. (Sussex) b Oct. 20, 1950
*Moroney, J. (NSW) b July 24, 1917
*Morris, A. R. (NSW; *CY 1949*) b Jan. 19, 1922
Morris, H. (Glam.) b Oct. 5, 1963
Morris, H. M. (CUCC & Essex) b April 16, 1898, d Nov. 18, 1984
*Morris, J. E. (Derbys. & Griq. W.) b April 1, 1964
Morris, R. E. (OUCC) b June 8, 1967
*Morris, S. (Vic.) b June 22, 1855, d Sept. 20, 1931
*Morrison, B. D. (Wgtn) b Dec. 17, 1933
*Morrison, D. K. (Auck.) b Feb. 3, 1966
*Morrison, J. F. M. (C. Dist. & Wgtn) b Aug. 27, 1947
Mortensen, O. H. (Denmark & Derbys.) b Jan. 29, 1958
*Mortimore, J. B. (Glos.) b May 14, 1933
Mortlock, W. (Surrey & Utd Eng. XI) b July 18, 1832, d Jan. 23, 1884
*Moseley, E. A. (B'dos, Glam. & E. Prov.) b Jan. 5, 1958
Moseley, H. R. (B'dos & Som.) b May 28, 1948
*Moses, H. (NSW) b Feb. 13, 1858, d Dec. 7, 1938
*Moss, A. E. (Middx) b Nov. 14, 1930
*Moss, J. K. (Vic.) b June 29, 1947
*Motz, R. C. (Cant.; *CY 1966*) b Jan. 12, 1940
Moulding, R. P. (OUCC & Middx) b Jan. 3, 1958
*Moule, W. H. (Vic.) b Jan. 31, 1858, d Aug. 24, 1939
*Moxon, M. D. (Yorks. & Griq. W.) b May 4, 1960
*Mudassar Nazar (Lahore, Punjab, Pak. Us, HBL, PIA & UBL) b April 6, 1956
*Muddiah, V. M. (Mysore & Ind. Serv.) b June 8, 1929
*Mufasir-ul-Haq (Kar., Dacca, PWD, E. Pak. & NBP) b Aug. 16, 1944, d July 27, 1983
Muncer, B. L. (Middx & Glam.) b Oct. 23, 1913, d Jan. 18, 1982
Munden, V. S. (Leics.) b Jan. 2, 1928
*Munir Malik (Punjab, R'pindi, Pak. Serv. & Kar.) b July 10, 1934
Munton, T. A. (Warwicks.) b July 30, 1965
**Murdoch, W. L. (NSW & Sussex) b Oct. 18, 1854, d Feb. 18, 1911
*Murray, A. R. A. (E. Prov.) b April 30, 1922
*Murray, B. A. G. (Wgtn) b Sept. 18, 1940
*Murray, D. A. (B'dos) b Sept. 29, 1950
*Murray, D. L. (T/T, CUCC, Notts. & Warwicks.) b May 20, 1943
*Murray, J. T. (Middx; *CY 1967*) b April 1, 1935
Murray-Willis, P. E. (Worcs. & Northants) b July 14, 1910
Murrell, H. R. (Kent & Middx) b Nov. 19, 1879, d Aug. 15, 1952
Murrills, T. J. (CUCC) b Dec. 22, 1953
*Musgrove, H. (Vic.) b Nov. 27, 1860, d Nov. 2, 1931
*Mushtaq Ahmed (UBL & Multan) b June 28, 1970
*Mushtaq Ali, S. (C. Ind., Guj., †M. Pradesh & U. Pradesh) b Dec. 17, 1914

*Mushtaq Mohammad (Kar., Northants & PIA; *CY 1963*) b Nov. 22, 1943
Mynn, Alfred (Kent & All-Eng.) b Jan. 19, 1807, d Oct. 31, 1861
*Nadkarni, R. G. (M'tra & Bombay) b April 4, 1932
*Nadeem Abbasi (R'pindi) b April 15, 1964
*Nadeem Ghauri (HBL) b Oct 12, 1962
Naeem Ahmed (Kar., Pak. Us, NBP, UBL & PIA) b Sept. 20, 1952
*Nagel, L. E. (Vic.) b March 6, 1905, d Nov. 23, 1971
*Naik, S. S. (Bombay) b Feb. 21, 1945
*Nanan, R. (T/T) b May 29, 1953
*Naoomal Jaoomal, M. (N. Ind. & Sind) b April 17, 1904, d July 18, 1980
*Narasimha Rao, M. V. (H'bad) b Aug. 11, 1954
Naseer Malik (Khairpair & NBP) b Feb. 1, 1950
Nash, J. E. (S. Aust.) b April 16, 1950
*Nash, L. J. (Tas. & Vic.) b May 2, 1910, d July 24, 1986
Nash, M. A. (Glam.) b May 9, 1945
*Nasim-ul-Ghani (Kar., Pak. Us, Dacca, E. Pak., PWD & NBP) b May 14, 1941
*Naushad Ali (Kar., E. Pak., R'pindi, Peshawar, NWFP, Punjab & Pak. Serv.) b Oct. 1, 1943
*Naved Anjum (Lahore, UBL & HBL) b July 27, 1963
*Navle, J. G. (Rajputna, C. Ind., Holkar & Gwalior) b Dec. 7, 1902, d Sept. 7, 1979
*Nayak, S. V. (Bombay) b Oct. 20, 1954
*Nayudu, Col. C. K. (C. Ind., Andhra, U. Pradesh & Holkar; *CY 1933*) b Oct. 31, 1895, d Nov. 14, 1967
*Nayudu, C. S. (C. Ind., Holkar, Baroda, Bengal, Andhra & U. Pradesh) b April 18, 1914
*Nazar Mohammad (N. Ind. & Punjab) b March 5, 1921
*Nazir Ali, S. (S. Punjab & Sussex) b June 8, 1906, d Feb. 18, 1975
Neale, P. A. (Worcs.; *CY 1989*) b June 5, 1954
*Neblett, J. M. (B'dos & BG) b Nov. 13, 1901, d March 28, 1959
Needham, A. (Surrey & Middx) b March 23, 1957
*Nel, J. D. (W. Prov.) b July 10, 1928
Nevell, W. T. (Middx, Surrey & Northants) b June 13, 1916
*Newberry, C. (Tvl) b 1889, d Aug. 1, 1916
Newell, M. (Notts.) b Feb. 25, 1965
*Newham, W. (Sussex) b Dec 12, 1860, d June 26, 1944
Newland, Richard (Sussex) b *circa* 1718, d May 29, 1791
Newman, G. C. (OUCC & Middx) b April 26, 1904, d Oct. 13, 1982
*Newman, Sir J. (Wgtn & Cant.) b July 3, 1902
Newman, J. A. (Hants & Cant.) b Nov. 12, 1884, d Dec. 21, 1973
Newman, P. G. (Derbys.) b Jan. 10, 1959
*Newport, P. J. (Worcs. & Boland) b Oct. 11, 1962
*Newson, E. S. (Tvl & Rhod.) b Dec. 2, 1910, d April 24, 1988
Newstead, J. T. (Yorks.; *CY 1909*) b Sept. 8, 1877, d March 25, 1952
*Niaz Ahmed (Dacca, PWD, E. Pak. & Pak. Rlwys) b Nov. 11, 1945
Nicholas, M. C. J. (Hants) b Sept. 29, 1957
Nicholls, D. (Kent) b Dec. 8, 1943
Nicholls, R. B. (Glos.) b Dec. 4, 1933
*Nichols, M. S. (Essex; *CY 1934*) b Oct. 6, 1900, d Jan. 26, 1961
Nicholson, A. G. (Yorks.) b June 25, 1938, d Nov. 4, 1985
*Nicholson, F. (OFS) b Sept. 17, 1909, d July 30, 1982
*Nicolson, J. F. W. (Natal & OUCC) b July 19, 1899, d Dec. 13, 1935
*Nissar, Mahomed (Patiala, S. Punjab & U. Pradesh) b Aug. 1, 1910, d March 11, 1963
*Nitschke, H. C. (S. Aust.) b April 14, 1905, d Sept. 29, 1982
*Noble, M. A. (NSW; *CY 1900*) b Jan. 28, 1873, d June 22, 1940
*Noblet, G. (S. Aust.) b Sept. 14, 1916
*Noreiga, J. M. (T/T) b April 15, 1936
Norfolk, 16th Duke of (Pres. MCC 1957-58) b May 30, 1908, d Jan. 31, 1975
Norman, M. E. J. C. (Northants & Leics.) b Jan. 19, 1933
*Norton, N. O. (W. Prov. & Border) b May 11, 1881, d June 27, 1968
*Nothling, O. E. (NSW & Qld) b Aug. 1, 1900, d Sept. 26, 1965
*Nourse, A. D. ("Dudley") (Natal; *CY 1948*) b Nov. 12, 1910, d Aug. 14, 1981
*Nourse, A. W. ("Dave") (Natal, Tvl & W. Prov.) b Jan. 26, 1878, d July 8, 1948
Nugent, 1st Lord (Pres. MCC 1962-63) b Aug. 11, 1895, d April 27, 1973
*Nunes, R. K. (Jam.) b June 7, 1894, d July 22, 1958
*Nupen, E. P. (Tvl) b Jan. 1, 1902, d Jan. 29, 1977
*Nurse, S. M. (B'dos; *CY 1967*) b Nov. 10, 1933
Nutter, A. E. (Lancs. & Northants) b June 28, 1913
*Nyalchand, S. (W. Ind., Kathiawar, Guj. & S'tra) b Sept. 14, 1919
Nye, J. K. (Sussex) b May 23, 1914
Nyren, John (Hants) b Dec. 15, 1764, d June 28, 1837
Nyren, Richard (Hants & Sussex) b 1734, d April 25, 1797

Oakes, C. (Sussex) b Aug. 10, 1912
Oakes, J. (Sussex) b March 3, 1916
*Oakman, A. S. M. (Sussex) b April 20, 1930
Oates, T. W. (Notts.) b Aug. 9, 1875, d June 18, 1949
Oates, W. F. (Yorks. & Derbys.) b June 11, 1929
O'Brien, F. P. (Cant. & Northants) b Feb. 11, 1911
*O'Brien, L. P. (Vic.) b July 2, 1907
*O'Brien, Sir T. C. (OUCC & Middx) b Nov. 5, 1861, d Dec. 9, 1948
*Ochse, A. E. (Tvl) b March 11, 1870, d April 11, 1918
*Ochse, A. L. (E. Prov.) b Oct. 11, 1899, d May 6, 1949
*O'Connor, J. (Essex) b Nov. 6, 1897, d Feb. 22, 1977
*O'Connor, J. D. A. (NSW & S. Aust.) b Sept. 9, 1875, d Aug. 23, 1941
Odendaal, A. (CUCC & Boland) b May 4, 1954
*O'Donnell, S. P. (Vic.) b Jan. 26, 1963
*Ogilvie, A. D. (Qld) b June 3, 1951
*O'Keeffe, K. J. (NSW & Som.) b Nov. 25, 1949
*Old, C. M. (Yorks., Warwicks. & N. Tvl; *CY 1979*) b Dec. 22, 1948
*Oldfield, N. (Lancs. & Northants) b May 5, 1911
*Oldfield, W. A. (NSW; *CY 1927*) b Sept. 9, 1894, d Aug. 10, 1976
Oldham, S. (Yorks. & Derbys.) b July 26, 1948
Oldroyd, E. (Yorks.) b Oct. 1, 1888, d Dec. 27, 1964
*O'Linn, S. (Kent, W. Prov. & Tvl) b May 5, 1927
Oliver, P. R. (Warwicks.) b May 9, 1956
O'Neill, M. D. (NSW) b March 5, 1959
*O'Neill, N. C. (NSW; *CY 1962*) b Feb. 19, 1937
Ontong, R. C. (Border, Tvl, N. Tvl & Glam.) b Sept. 9, 1955
Opatha, A. R. M. (SL) b Aug. 5, 1947
Ord, J. S. (Warwicks.) b July 12, 1912
*O'Reilly, W. J. (NSW; *CY 1935*) b Dec. 20, 1905
O'Riordan, A. J. (Ireland) b July 20, 1940
Ormrod, J. A. (Worcs. & Lancs.) b Dec. 22, 1942
O'Shaughnessy, S. J. (Lancs. & Worcs.) b Sept. 9, 1961
Oslear, D. O. (Umpire) b March 3, 1929
*O'Sullivan, D. R. (C. Dist. & Hants) b Nov. 16, 1944
Outschoorn, L. (Worcs.) b Sept. 26, 1918
*Overton, G. W. F. (Otago) b June 8, 1919
*Owen-Smith, H. G. O. (W. Prov., OUCC & Middx; *CY 1930*) b Feb. 18, 1909, d Feb. 28, 1990
Owen-Thomas, D. R. (CUCC & Surrey) b Sept. 20, 1948
*Oxenham, R. K. (Qld) b July 28, 1891, d Aug. 16, 1939

Packe, M. St J. (Leics.) b Aug. 21, 1916, d Dec. 20, 1978
*Padgett, D. E. V. (Yorks.) b July 20, 1934
*Padmore, A. L. (B'dos) b Dec. 17, 1946
Page, H. A. (Tvl & Essex) b July 3, 1962
Page, J. C. T. (Kent) b May 20, 1930
Page, M. H. (Derbys.) b June 17, 1941
*Page, M. L. (Cant.) b May 8, 1902, d Feb. 13, 1987
*Pai, A. M. (Bombay) b April 28, 1945
*Paine, G. A. E. (Middx & Warwicks.; *CY 1935*) b June 11, 1908, d March 30, 1978
*Pairaudeau, B. H. (BG & N. Dist.) b April 14, 1931
*Palairet, L. C. H. (OUCC & Som.; *CY 1893*) b May 27, 1870, d March 27, 1933
Palairet, R. C. N. (OUCC & Som.; Joint-Manager MCC in Australia 1932-33) b June 25, 1871, d Feb. 11, 1955
Palia, P. E. (Madras, U. Prov., Bombay, Mysore & Bengal) b Sept. 5, 1910, d Sept. 9, 1981
*Palm, A. W. (W. Prov.) b June 8, 1901, d Aug. 17, 1966
*Palmer, C. H. (Worcs. & Leics.; Pres. MCC 1978-79) b May 15, 1919
*Palmer, G. E. (Vic. & Tas.) b Feb. 22, 1860, d Aug. 22, 1910
Palmer, G. V. (Som.) b Nov. 1, 1965
*Palmer, K. E. (Som.; Umpire) b April 22, 1937
Palmer, R. (Som.) b July 12, 1942
*Pandit, C. S. (Bombay) b Sept. 30, 1961
Pardon, Charles Frederick (Editor of *Wisden* 1887-90) b March 28, 1850, d April 18, 1890
Pardon, Sydney H. (Editor of *Wisden* 1891-1925) b Sept. 23, 1855, d Nov. 20, 1925
*Parfitt, P. H. (Middx; *CY 1963*) b Dec. 8, 1936
Paris, C. G. A. (Hants; Pres. MCC 1975-76) b Aug. 20, 1911
Parish, R. J. (Aust. Administrator) b May 7, 1916
*Park, R. L. (Vic.) b July 30, 1892, d Jan. 23, 1947
*Parkar, G. A. (Bombay) b Oct. 24, 1955
*Parkar, R. D. (Bombay) b Oct. 31, 1946
Parkar, Z. (Bombay) b Nov. 22, 1957
*Parker, C. W. L. (Glos.; *CY 1923*) b Oct. 14, 1882, d July 11, 1959
*Parker, G. M. (SA) b May 27, 1899, d May 1, 1969
Parker, G. W. (CUCC & Glos.) b Feb. 11, 1912
Parker, J. F. (Surrey) b April 23, 1913, d Jan. 27, 1983

*Parker, J. M. (N. Dist. & Worcs.) b Feb. 21, 1951
Parker, J. P. (Hants) b Nov. 29, 1902, d Aug. 9, 1984
*Parker, N. M. (Otago & Cant.) b Aug. 28, 1948
*Parker, P. W. G. (CUCC, Sussex & Natal) b Jan. 15, 1956
*Parkhouse, W. G. A. (Glam.) b Oct. 12, 1925
*Parkin, C. H. (Yorks. & Lancs.; *CY 1924*) b Feb. 18, 1886, d June 15, 1943
*Parkin, D. C. (E. Prov., Tvl & Griq. W.) b Feb. 18, 1870, d March 20, 1936
Parks, H. W. (Sussex) b July 18, 1906, d May 7, 1984
*Parks, J. H. (Sussex & Cant.; *CY 1938*) b May 12, 1903, d Nov. 21, 1980
*Parks, J. M. (Sussex & Som.; *CY 1968*) b Oct. 21, 1931
Parks, R. J. (Hants) b June 15, 1959
*Parore, A. C. (Auck.) b Jan. 23, 1971
Parr, F. D. (Lancs.) b June 1, 1928
Parr, George (Notts. & All-England) b May 22, 1826, d June 23, 1891
*Parry, D. R. (Comb. Is. & Leewards) b Dec. 22, 1954
*Parsana, D. D. (S'tra, Ind. Rlwys & Guj.) b Dec. 2, 1947
Parsons, A. B. D. (CUCC & Surrey) b Sept. 20, 1933
Parsons, A. E. W. (Auck. & Sussex) b Jan. 9, 1949
Parsons, G. J. (Leics., Warwicks., Boland, Griq. W. & OFS) b Oct. 17, 1959
Parsons, Canon J. H. (Warwicks.) b May 30, 1890, d Feb. 2, 1981
*Partridge, J. T. (Rhod.) b Dec. 9, 1932, d June 7, 1988
Partridge, N. E. (Malvern, CUCC & Warwicks.; *CY 1919*) b Aug. 10, 1900, d March 10, 1982
Partridge, R. J. (Northants) b Feb. 11, 1912
*Pascoe, L. S. (NSW) b Feb. 13, 1950
Pasqual, S. P. (SL) b Oct. 15, 1961
*Passailaigue, C. C. (Jam.) b Aug. 1902, d Jan. 7, 1972
*Patankar, C. T. (Bombay) b Nov. 24, 1930
**Pataudi, Iftikhar Ali, Nawab of (OUCC, Worcs., Patiala, N. Ind. & S. Punjab; *CY 1932*) b March 16, 1910, d Jan. 5, 1952
*Pataudi, Mansur Ali, Nawab of (Sussex, OUCC, Delhi & H'bad; *CY 1968*) b Jan. 5, 1941
Patel, A. (S'tra) b March 6, 1957
*Patel, B. P. (Karn.) b Nov. 24, 1952
*Patel, D. N. (Worcs. & Auck.) b Oct. 25, 1958
*Patel, J. M. (Guj.) b Nov. 26, 1924
*Patel, R. (Baroda) b June 1, 1964
Pathmanathan, G. (OUCC, CUCC & SL) b Jan. 23, 1954

*Patiala, Maharaja of (N. Ind., Patiala & S Punjab) b Jan. 17, 1913, d June 17, 197
*Patil, S. M. (Bombay) b Aug. 18, 1956
*Patil, S. R. (M'tra) b Oct. 10, 1933
*Patterson, B. P. (Jam., Tas. & Lancs.) Sept. 15, 1961
Pauline, D. B. (Surrey & Glam.) b Dec. 15 1960
Pawson, A. G. (OUCC & Worcs.) b Ma 30, 1888, d Feb. 25, 1986
Pawson, H. A. (OUCC & Kent) b Aug. 22 1921
Payn, L. W. (Natal) b May 6, 1915
*Payne, T. R. O. (B'dos) b Feb. 13, 1957
*Paynter, E. (Lancs.; *CY 1938*) b Nov. 5 1901, d Feb. 5, 1979
Payton, W. R. D. (Notts.) b Feb. 13, 1882 d May 2, 1943
Pearce, G. (Sussex) b Oct. 27, 1908, d Jun 16, 1986
Pearce, T. A. (Kent) b Dec. 18, 1910, Aug. 11, 1982
Pearce, T. N. (Essex) b Nov. 3, 1905
*Pearse, C. O. C. (Natal) b Oct. 10, 1884, May 7, 1953
Pearson, D. B. (Worcs.) b March 29, 193
*Peate, E. (Yorks.) b March 2, 1856, March 11, 1900
Peck, I. G. (CUCC & Northants) b Oct. 18 1957
*Peebles, I. A. R. (OUCC, Middx & Scotland; *CY 1931*) b Jan. 20, 1908, Feb. 28, 1980
*Peel, R. (Yorks.; *CY 1889*) b Feb. 12, 1857 d Aug. 12, 1941
*Pegler, S. J. (Tvl) b July 28, 1888, d Sept 10, 1972
*Pellew, C. E. (S. Aust.) b Sept. 21, 1893, May 9, 1981
Penn, C. (Kent) b June 19, 1963
*Penn, F. (Kent) b March 7, 1851, d Dec 26, 1916
Pepper, C. G. (NSW and Aust. Serv. Umpire) b Sept. 15, 1918
Perera, K. G. (Mor.) b May 22, 1964
Perkins, C. G. (Northants) b June 4, 191
Perkins, H. (CUCC & Cambs.; Sec. MCC 1876-97) b Dec. 10, 1832, d May 6, 191
*Perks, R. T. D. (Worcs.) b Oct. 4, 1911, Nov. 22, 1977
Perrin, P. A. (Essex; *CY 1905*) b May 26 1876, d Nov. 20, 1945
Perryman, S. P. (Warwicks. & Worcs.) Oct. 22, 1955
*Pervez Sajjad (Lahore, PIA & Kar.) b Aug 30, 1942
*Petherick, P. J. (Otago & Wgtn) b Sept. 25 1942
*Petrie, E. C. (Auck. & N. Dist.) b May 22 1927
*Phadkar, D. G. (M'tra, Bombay, Bengal & Ind. Rlwys) b Dec. 10, 1925, d March 17 1985

Phebey, A. H. (Kent) b Oct. 1, 1924
Phelan, P. J. (Essex) b Feb. 9, 1938
Philipson, H. (OUCC & Middx) b June 8, 1866, d Dec. 4, 1935
Phillip, N. (Comb. Is., Windwards & Essex) b June 12, 1948
Phillipps, J. H. (NZ Manager) b Jan. 1, 1898, d June 8, 1977
Phillips, R. B. (NSW & Qld) b May 23, 1954
Phillips, W. B. (S. Aust.) b March 1, 1958
Phillipson, C. P. (Sussex) b Feb. 10, 1952
Phillipson, W. E. (Lancs.) b Dec. 3, 1910
Philpott, P. I. (NSW) b Nov. 21, 1934
Piachaud, J. D. (OUCC, Hants & Ceylon) b March 1, 1937
Pick, R. A. (Notts. & Wgtn) b Nov. 19, 1963
Pickles, C. S. (Yorks.) b Jan. 30, 1966
Pickles, L. (Som.) b Sept. 17, 1932
Pienaar, R. F. (Tvl, W. Prov., N. Tvl & Kent) b July 17, 1961
Pieris, H. S. M. (SL) b Feb. 16, 1946
*Pierre, L. R. (T/T) b June 5, 1921, d April 14, 1989
Pierson, A. R. K. (Warwicks.) b July 21, 1963
*Pigott, A. C. S. (Sussex & Wgtn) b June 4, 1958
Pilch, Fuller (Norfolk & Kent) b March 17, 1804, d May 1, 1870
Pilling, H. (Lancs.) b Feb. 23, 1943
*Pilling, R. (Lancs.; *CY 1891*) b July 5, 1855, d March 28, 1891
Pithey, A. J. (Rhod. & W. Prov.) b July 17, 1933
*Pithey, D. B. (Rhod., OUCC, Northants, W. Prov., Natal & Tvl) b Oct. 4, 1936
Pitman, R. W. C. (Hants) b Feb. 21, 1933
*Place, W. (Lancs.) b Dec 7, 1914
Platt, R. K. (Yorks. & Northants) b Dec. 21, 1932
*Playle, W. R. (Auck. & W. Aust.) b Dec. 1, 1938
Pleass, J. E. (Glam.) b May 21, 1923
*Plimsoll, J. B. (W. Prov. & Natal) b Oct. 27, 1917
Pocock, N. E. J. (Hants) b Dec. 15, 1951
*Pocock, P. I. (Surrey & N. Tvl) b Sept. 24, 1946
Pollard, P. R. (Notts.) b Sept. 24, 1968
*Pollard, R. (Lancs.) b June 19, 1912, d Dec. 16, 1985
*Pollard, V. (C. Dist. & Cant.) b Burnley Sept. 7, 1945
Pollock, A. J. (CUCC) b April 19, 1962
*Pollock, P. M. (E. Prov.; *CY 1966*) b June 30, 1941
*Pollock, R. G. (E. Prov. & Tvl; *CY 1966*) b Feb. 27, 1944
*Ponsford, W. H. (Vic.; *CY 1935*; oldest surviving Test player) b Oct. 19, 1900
Pont, K. R. (Essex) b Jan. 16, 1953
*Poole, C. J. (Notts.) b March 13, 1921
Pooley, E. (Surrey & first England tour) b Feb. 13, 1838, d July 18, 1907
*Poore, M. B. (Cant.) b June 1, 1930
*Poore, Brig-Gen. R. M. (Hants & SA; *CY 1900*) b March 20, 1866, d July 14, 1938
Pope, A. V. (Derbys.) b Aug. 15, 1909
*Pope, G. H. (Derbys.) b Jan. 27, 1911
*Pope, R. J. (NSW) b Feb. 18, 1864, d July 27, 1952
Popplewell, N. F. M. (CUCC & Som.) b Aug. 8, 1957
Portal of Hungerford, 1st Lord (Pres. MCC 1958-59) b May 21, 1893, d April 22, 1971
Porter, A. (Glam.) b March 25, 1914
Porter, G. D. (W. Aust.) b March 18, 1955
Pothecary, A. E. (Hants) b March 1, 1906
*Pothecary, J. E. (W. Prov.) b Dec. 6, 1933
Potter, G. (Sussex) b Oct. 26, 1931
Potter, J. (Vic.) b April 13, 1938
Potter, L. (Kent, Griq. W., Leics. & OFS) b Nov. 7, 1962
*Pougher, A. D. (Leics.) b April 19, 1865, d May 20, 1926
Pountain, F. R. (Sussex) b April 23, 1941
Powell, A. G. (CUCC & Essex) b Aug. 17, 1912, d June 7, 1982
*Powell, A. W. (Griq. W.) b July 18, 1873, d Sept. 11, 1948
*Prabhakar, M. (Delhi) b April 15, 1963
*Prasanna, E. A. S. (†Karn.) b May 22, 1940
Pratt, R. L. (Leics.) b Nov. 15, 1938
Pressdee, J. S. (Glam. & NE Tvl) b June 19, 1933
Preston, Hubert (Editor of *Wisden* 1944-51) b Dec. 16, 1868, d Aug. 6, 1960
Preston, K. C. (Essex) b Aug. 22, 1925
Preston, Norman (Editor of *Wisden* 1951-80) b March 18, 1903, d March 6, 1980
Pretlove, J. F. (CUCC & Kent) b Nov. 23, 1932
Price, D. G. (CUCC) b Feb. 7, 1965
Price, E. J. (Lancs. & Essex) b Oct. 27, 1918
*Price, J. S. E. (Middx) b July 22, 1937
*Price, W. F. F. (Middx) b April 25, 1902, d Jan. 13, 1969
Prichard, P. J. (Essex) b Jan. 7, 1965
*Prideaux, R. M. (CUCC, Kent, Northants, Sussex & OFS) b July 31, 1939
Pridgeon, A. P. (Worcs.) b Feb. 22, 1954
*Priest, M. W. (Cant.) b Aug. 12, 1961
*Prince, C. F. H. (W. Prov., Border & E. Prov.) b Sept. 11, 1874, d March 5, 1948
Pringle, C. (Auck.) b Jan. 26, 1968
*Pringle, D. R. (CUCC & Essex) b Sept. 18, 1958
Pringle, M. W. (OFS, Sussex, E. Prov. & W. Prov.) b June 22, 1966
Pritchard, T. L. (Wgtn, Warwicks. & Kent) b March 10, 1917

*Procter, M. J. (Glos., Natal, W. Prov., Rhod. & OFS; *CY 1970*) b Sept. 15, 1946
Prodger, J. M. (Kent) b Sept. 1, 1935
*Promnitz, H. L. E. (Border, Griq. W. & OFS) b Feb. 23, 1904, d Sept. 7, 1983
Prouton, R. O. (Hants) b March 1, 1926
Puckett, C. W. (W. Aust.) b Feb. 21, 1911
Pugh, C. T. M. (Glos.) b March 13, 1937
Pullan, D. A. (Notts.) b May 1, 1944
*Pullar, G. (Lancs. & Glos.; *CY 1960*) b Aug. 1, 1935
Pullinger, G. R. (Essex) b March 14, 1920, d Aug. 4, 1982
*Puna, N. (N. Dist.) b Oct. 28, 1929
*Punjabi, P. H. (Sind & Guj.) b Sept. 20, 1921
Pycroft, A. J. (Zimb.) b June 6, 1956
Pydanna, M. (Guyana) b Jan. 27, 1950

*Qasim Omar (Kar. & MCB) b Feb. 9, 1957
Quaife, B. W. (Warwicks. & Worcs.) b Nov. 24, 1899, d Nov. 28, 1984
*Quaife, William (W. G.) (Warwicks. & Griq. W.; *CY 1902*) b March 17, 1872, d Oct. 13, 1951
Quick, I. W. (Vic.) b Nov. 5, 1933
*Quinn, N. A. (Griq. W. & Tvl) b Feb. 21, 1908, d Aug. 5, 1934

*Rabone, G. O. (Wgtn & Auck.) b Nov. 6, 1921
*Rackemann, C. G. (Qld) b June 3, 1960
*Radford, N. V. (Lancs., Tvl & Worcs.; *CY 1986*) b June 7, 1957
*Radley, C. T. (Middx; *CY 1979*) b May 13, 1944
*Rae, A. F. (Jam.) b Sept. 30, 1922
Raees Mohammad (Kar.) b Dec. 24, 1932
*Rai Singh, K. (S. Punjab & Ind. Serv.) b Feb. 24, 1922
Rait Kerr, Col. R. S. (Sec. MCC 1936-52) b April 13, 1891, d April 2, 1961
Rajadurai, B. E. A. (SSC) b Aug. 24, 1965
*Rajindernath, V. (N. Ind., U. Prov., S. Punjab, Bihar & E. Punjab) b Jan. 7, 1928, d Nov. 22, 1989
*Rajinder Pal (Delhi, S. Punjab & Punjab) b Nov. 18, 1937
*Rajput, L. S. (Bombay) b Dec. 18, 1961
*Raju, S. L. V. (H'bad) b July 9, 1969
Ralph, L. H. R. (Essex) b May 22, 1920
*Ramadhin, S. (T/T & Lancs.; *CY 1951*) b May 1, 1929
*Raman, W. V. (TN) b May 23, 1965
*Ramanayake, C. P. H. (TU) b Jan. 8, 1965
*Ramaswami, C. (Madras) b June 18, 1896, 'presumed dead'
*Ramchand, G. S. (Sind, Bombay & Raja.) b July 26, 1927
*Ramiz Raja (Lahore, Allied Bank & PNSC) b July 14, 1962
*Ramji, L. (W. Ind.) b 1900, d Dec. 20, 1948

Ramprakash, M. R. (Middx) b Sept. 5, 1969
Ramsamooj, D. (T/T & Northants) b July 5, 1932
*Ranasinghe, A. N. (BRC) b Oct. 13, 1956
*Ranatunga, A. (SSC) b Dec. 1, 1963
*Ranatunga, D. (SSC) b Oct. 12, 1962
*Randall, D. W. (Notts.; *CY 1980*) b Feb. 24, 1951
Randhir Singh (Orissa & Bihar) b Aug. 16, 1957
*Rangachari, C. R. (Madras) b April 14, 1916
*Rangnekar, K. M. (M'tra, Bombay & †M. Pradesh) b June 27, 1917, d Oct. 11, 198
*Ranjane, V. B. (M'tra & Ind. Rlwys) b July 22, 1937
*Ranjitsinhji, K. S., afterwards H. H. the Jam Sahib of Nawanagar (CUCC & Sussex; *CY 1897*) b Sept. 10, 1872, d April 2, 1933
*Ransford, V. S. (Vic.; *CY 1910*) b March 20, 1885, d March 19, 1958
Ransom, V. J. (Hants & Surrey) b March 17, 1918
*Rashid Khan (PWD, Kar. & PIA) b Dec. 15, 1959
Ratcliffe, R. M. (Lancs.) b Nov. 29, 1951
Ratnayake, N. L. K. (SSC) b Nov. 22, 196
*Ratnayake, R. J. (NCC) b Jan. 2, 1964
*Ratnayeke, J. R. (NCC) b May 2, 1960
Rawson, P. W. E. (Zimb. & Natal) b Ma 25, 1957
Rayment, A. W. H. (Hants) b May 29, 192
Raymer, V. N. (Qld) b May 4, 1918
*Razdan, V. (Delhi) b Aug. 25, 1969
*Read, H. D. (Surrey & Essex) b Jan. 28, 1910
*Read, J. M. (Surrey; *CY 1890*) b Feb. 9, 1859, d Feb. 17, 1929
*Read, W. W. (Surrey; *CY 1893*) b Nov. 23, 1855, d Jan. 6, 1907
Reddick, T. B. (Middx, Notts. & W. Prov.) b Feb. 17, 1912, d June 1, 1982
*Reddy, B. (TN) b Nov. 12, 1954
Redman, J. (Som.) b March 1, 1926, d Sept. 19, 1981
*Redmond, R. E. (Wgtn & Auck.) b Dec. 29, 1944
*Redpath, I. R. (Vic.) b May 11, 1941
Reed, B. L. (Hants) b Sept. 17, 1937
*Reedman, J. C. (S. Aust.) b Oct. 9, 1865, d March 25, 1924
Rees, A. (Glam.) b Feb. 17, 1938
Reeve, D. A. (Sussex & Warwicks.) b April 2, 1963
Reeves, W. (Essex; Umpire) b Jan. 22, 1875, d March 22, 1944
*Rege, M. R. (M'tra) b March 18, 1924
*Rehman, S. F. (Punjab, Pak. Us & Lahore) b June 11, 1935
*Reid, B. A. (W. Aust.) b March 14, 1963
*Reid, J. F. (Auck.) b March 3, 1956

*Reid, J. R. (Wgtn & Otago; *CY 1959*) b June 3, 1928
Reid, K. P. (E. Prov. & Northants) b July 24, 1951
*Reid, N. (W. Prov.) b Dec. 26, 1890, d June 6, 1947
Reid, R. B. (Wgtn & Auck.) b Dec. 3, 1958
Reidy, B. W. (Lancs.) b Sept. 18, 1953
*Relf, A. E. (Sussex & Auck.; *CY 1914*) b June 26, 1874, d March 26, 1937
*Renneburg, D. A. (NSW) b Sept. 23, 1942
Revill, A. C. (Derbys. & Leics.) b March 27, 1923
Reynolds, B. L. (Northants) b June 10, 1932
Rhodes, A. E. G. (Derbys.) b Oct. 10, 1916, d Oct. 18, 1983
*Rhodes, H. J. (Derbys.) b July 22, 1936
Rhodes, S. D. (Notts.) b March 24, 1910, d Jan. 7, 1989
Rhodes, S. J. (Yorks. & Worcs.) b June 17, 1964
*Rhodes, W. (Yorks.; *CY 1899*) b Oct. 29, 1877, d July 8, 1973
Rice, C. E. B. (Tvl & Notts.; *CY 1981*) b July 23, 1949
Rice, J. M. (Hants) b Oct. 23, 1949
*Richards, A. R. (W. Prov.) b 1868, d Jan. 9, 1904
*Richards, B. A. (Natal, Glos., Hants & S. Aust.; *CY 1969*) b July 21, 1945
*Richards, C. J. (Surrey & OFS) b Aug. 10, 1958
Richards, G. (Glam.) b Nov. 29, 1951
*Richards, I. V. A. (Comb. Is., Leewards, Som., Qld & Glam.; *CY 1977*) b March 7, 1952
*Richards, W. H. M. (SA) b Aug. 1862, d Jan. 4, 1903
*Richardson, A. J. (S. Aust.) b July 24, 1888, d Dec. 23, 1973
Richardson, A. W. (Derbys.) b March 4, 1907, d July 29, 1983
Richardson, D. J. (E. Prov. & N. Tvl) b Sept. 16, 1959
*Richardson, D. W. (Worcs.) b Nov. 3, 1934
Richardson, G. W. (Derbys.) b April 26, 1938
*Richardson, P. E. (Worcs. & Kent; *CY 1957*) b July 4, 1931
*Richardson, R. B. (Leewards) b Jan. 12, 1962
*Richardson, T. (Surrey & Som.; *CY 1897*) b Aug. 11, 1870, d July 2, 1912
*Richardson, V. Y. (S. Aust.) b Sept. 7, 1894, d Oct. 29, 1969
*Richmond, T. L. (Notts.) b June 23, 1890, d Dec. 29, 1957
*Rickards, K. R. (Jam. & Essex) b Aug. 23, 1923
Riddington, A. (Leics.) b Dec. 22, 1911
*Ridgway, F. (Kent) b Aug. 10, 1923
Ridings, P. L. (S. Aust.) b Oct. 2, 1917
*Rigg, K. E. (Vic.) b May 21, 1906
Riley, H. (Leics.) b Oct. 3, 1902, d Jan. 24, 1989
*Ring, D. T. (Vic.) b Oct. 14, 1918
Ripley, D. (Northants) b Sept. 13, 1966
Rist, F. H. (Essex) b March 30, 1914
*Ritchie, G. M. (Qld) b Jan. 23, 1960
*Rixon, S. J. (NSW) b Feb. 25, 1954
*Rizwan-uz-Zaman (Kar. & PIA) b Sept. 4, 1962
*Roach, C. A. (T/T) b March 13, 1904, d April 16, 1988
*Roberts, A. D. G. (N. Dist.) b May 6, 1947, d Oct. 26, 1989
*Roberts, A. M. E. (Comb. Is., Leewards, Hants, NSW & Leics.; *CY 1975*) b Jan. 29, 1951
*Roberts, A. T. (Windwards) b Sept. 18, 1937
*Roberts, A. W. (Cant. & Otago) b Aug. 20, 1909, d May 13, 1978
Roberts, B. (Tvl & Derbys.) b May 30, 1962
Roberts, The Hon. Sir Denys (Pres. MCC 1989-90) b Jan. 19, 1923
Roberts, Pascal (T/T) b Dec 15, 1937
Roberts, S. J. (Cant.) b March 22, 1965
Roberts, W. B. (Lancs. & Victory Tests) b Sept. 27, 1914, d Aug. 24, 1951
*Robertson, G. K. (C. Dist.) b July 15, 1960
*Robertson, J. B. (W. Prov.) b June 5, 1906, d July 5, 1985
*Robertson, J. D. (Middx; *CY 1948*) b Feb. 22, 1917
*Robertson, W. R. (Vic.) b Oct. 6, 1861, d June 24, 1938
Robertson-Glasgow, R. C. (OUCC & Som.) b July 15, 1901, d March 4, 1965
Robins, D. H. (Warwicks.) b June 26, 1914
Robins, R. V. C. (Middx) b March 13, 1935
*Robins, R. W. V. (CUCC & Middx; *CY 1930*) b June 3, 1906, d Dec. 12, 1968
Robinson, A. L. (Yorks.) b Aug. 17, 1946
Robinson, Emmott (Yorks.) b Nov. 16, 1883, d Nov. 17, 1969
Robinson, Ellis P. (Yorks. & Som.) b Aug. 10, 1911
Robinson, H. B. (OUCC & Canada) b March 3, 1919
Robinson, M. (Glam., Warwicks., H'bad & Madras) b July 16, 1921
Robinson, M. A. (Northants) b Nov. 23, 1966
Robinson, P. E. (Yorks.) b Aug. 3, 1963
Robinson, P. J. (Worcs. & Som.) b Feb. 9, 1943
Robinson, Ray (Writer) b July 8, 1908, d July 6, 1982
*Robinson, R. D. (Vic.) b June 8, 1946
*Robinson, R. H. (NSW, S. Aust. & Otago) b March 26, 1914, d Aug. 10, 1965

*Robinson, R. T. (Notts.; *CY 1986*) b Nov. 21, 1958
Robson, E. (Som.) b May 1, 1870, d May 23, 1924
Rochford, P. (Glos.) b Aug. 27, 1928
*Rodriguez, W. V. (T/T) b June 25, 1934
Roe, B. (Som.) b Jan. 27, 1939
Roebuck, P. M. (CUCC & Som.; *CY 1988*) b March 6, 1956
Rogers, N. H. (Hants) b March 9, 1918
Rogers, R. E. (Qld) b Aug. 24, 1916
Romaines, P. W. (Northants, Glos. & Griq. W.) b Dec. 25, 1955
*Roope, G. R. J. (Surrey & Griq. W.) b July 12, 1946
*Root, C. F. (Derbys. & Worcs.) b April 16, 1890, d Jan. 20, 1954
*Rorke, G. F. (NSW) b June 27, 1938
*Rose, B. C. (Som.; *CY 1980*) b June 4, 1950
Rose, G. D. (Middx & Som.) b April 12, 1964
Roseberry, M. A. (Middx) b Nov. 28, 1966
Rosebery, 6th Earl of (*see* Dalmeny, Lord)
*Rose-Innes, A. (Kimberley & Tvl) b Feb. 16, 1868, d Nov. 22, 1946
Ross, C. J. (Wgtn & OUCC) b June 24, 1954
Rotherham, G. A. (Rugby, CUCC, Warwicks. & Wgtn; *CY 1918*) b May 28, 1899, d Jan. 31, 1985
Rouse, S. J. (Warwicks.) b Jan. 20, 1949
Routledge, R. (Middx) b July 7, 1920
*Routledge, T. W. (W. Prov. & Tvl) b April 18, 1867, d May 9, 1927
*Rowan, A. M. B. (Tvl) b Feb. 7, 1921
*Rowan, E. A. B. (Tvl; *CY 1952*) b July 20, 1909
*Rowe, C. G. (Wgtn & C. Dist.) b June 30, 1915
Rowe, C. J. C. (Kent & Glam.) b May 5, 1953
Rowe, E. J. (Notts.) b July 21, 1920, d Dec. 17, 1989
*Rowe, G. A. (W. Prov.) b June 15, 1874, d Jan. 8, 1950
*Rowe, L. G. (Jam. & Derbys.) b Jan. 8, 1949
*Roy, A. (Bengal) b June 5, 1945
*Roy, Pankaj (Bengal) b May 31, 1928
*Roy, Pranab (Bengal) b Feb. 10, 1957
*Royle, Rev. V. P. F. A. (OUCC & Lancs.) b Jan. 29, 1854, d May 21, 1929
*Rumsey, F. E. (Worcs., Som. & Derbys.) b Dec. 4, 1935
Rushmere, M. W. (E. Prov.) b Jan. 7, 1965
*Russell, A. C. [C. A. G.] (Essex; *CY 1923*) b Oct. 7, 1887, d March 23, 1961
Russell, P. E. (Derbys.) b May 9, 1944
*Russell, R. C. (Glos.; *CY 1990*) b Aug. 15, 1963
Russell, S. E. (Middx & Glos.) b Oct. 4, 1937
*Russell, W. E. (Middx) b July 3, 1936
Russom, N. (CUCC & Som.) b Dec. 3, 1958
Rutherford, I. A. (Worcs. & Otago) b June 30, 1957
*Rutherford, J. W. (W. Aust.) b Sept. 25, 1929
*Rutherford, K. R. (Otago) b Oct. 26, 1965
Ryan, M. (Yorks.) b June 23, 1933
*Ryder, J. (Vic.) b Aug. 8, 1889, d April 3, 1977

Saadat Ali (Lahore, UBL & HBFC) b Feb. 6, 1955
*Sadiq Mohammad (Kar., PIA, Tas., Essex, Glos. & UBP) b May 3, 1945
Sadler, W. C. H. (Surrey) b Sept. 24, 1896, d Feb. 12, 1981
*Saeed Ahmed (Punjab, Pak. Us, Lahore, PIA, Kar., PWD & Sind) b Oct. 1, 1937
Saeed Anwar (UBL) b Sept. 6, 1968
*Saggers, R. A. (NSW) b May 15, 1917, d March 1987
Sainsbury, G. E. (Essex & Glos.) b Jan. 17, 1958
Sainsbury, P. J. (Hants; *CY 1974*) b June 13, 1934
*St Hill, E. L. (T/T) b March 9, 1904, d May 21, 1957
*St Hill, W. H. (T/T) b July 6, 1893, d 1957
Sajid Ali (Kar. & NBP) b July 1, 1963
Sajjad Akbar (PNSC) b March 1, 1961
*Salah-ud-Din (Kar., PIA & Pak. Us) b Feb. 14, 1947
Sale, R., jun. (OUCC, Warwicks. & Derbys.) b Oct. 4, 1919, d Feb. 3, 1987
*Saleem Altaf (Lahore & PIA) b April 19, 1944
*Saleem Jaffer (Kar. & UBL) b Nov. 19, 1962
*Salim Malik (Lahore & HBL; *CY 1988*) b April 16, 1963
*Salim Yousuf (Sind, Kar., IDBP, Allied Bank & Customs) b Dec. 7, 1959
Salisbury, I. D. K. (Sussex) b Jan. 21, 1970
Samaranayake, A. D. A. (SL) b Feb. 25, 1962
*Samarasekera, M. A. R. (CCC) b Aug. 5, 1961
Sampson, H. (Yorks. & All-England) b March 13, 1813, d March 29, 1885
*Samuelson, S. V. (Natal) b Nov. 21, 1883, d Nov. 18, 1958
*Sandham, A. (Surrey; *CY 1923*) b July 6, 1890, d April 20, 1982
*Sandhu, B. S. (Bombay) b Aug. 3, 1956
*Sardesai, D. N. (Bombay) b Aug. 8, 1940
*Sarfraz Nawaz (Lahore, Punjab, Northants, Pak. Rlwys & UBL) b Dec. 1, 1948
*Sarwate, C. T. (CP & B, M'tra, Bombay & †M. Pradesh) b June 22, 1920

*Saunders, J. V. (Vic. & Wgtn) b Feb. 3, 1876, d Dec. 21, 1927
Savage, J. S. (Leics. & Lancs.) b March 3, 1929
Savage, R. Le Q. (OUCC & Warwicks.) b Dec. 10, 1955
Savill, L. A. (Essex) b June 30, 1935
Saville, G. J. (Essex) b Feb. 5, 1944
Saxelby, K. (Notts.) b Feb. 23, 1959
Saxena, R. C. (Delhi & Bihar) b Sept. 20, 1944
Sayer, D. M. (OUCC & Kent) b Sept. 19, 1936
Scarlett, R. O. (Jam.) b Aug. 15, 1934
Schofield, R. M. (C. Dist.) b Nov. 6, 1939
Schultz, S. S. (CUCC & Lancs.) b Aug. 29, 1857, d Dec. 18, 1937
*Schwarz, R. O. (Middx & Natal; *CY 1908*) b May 4, 1875, d Nov. 18, 1918
*Scott, A. P. H. (Jam.) b July 29, 1934
Scott, Christopher J. (Lancs.) b Sept. 16, 1959
Scott, Colin J. (Glos.) b May 1, 1919
Scott, C. W. (Notts.) b Jan. 23, 1964
*Scott, H. J. H. (Vic.) b Dec. 26, 1858, d Sept. 23, 1910
Scott, M. E. (Northants) b May 8, 1936
*Scott, O. C. (Jam.) b Aug. 25, 1893, d June 16, 1961
*Scott, R. H. (Cant.) b March 6, 1917
Scott, S. W. (Middx; *CY 1893*) b March 24, 1854, d Dec. 8, 1933
*Scott, V. J. (Auck.) b July 31, 1916, d Aug. 2, 1980
*Scotton, W. H. (Notts.) b Jan. 15, 1856, d July 9, 1893
*Sealey, B. J. (T/T) b Aug. 12, 1899, d Sept. 12, 1963
*Sealy, J. E. D. (B'dos & T/T) b Sept. 11, 1912, d Jan. 3, 1982
Seamer, J. W. (Som. & OUCC) b June 23, 1913
*Seccull, A. W. (Kimberley, W. Prov. & Tvl) b Sept. 14, 1868, d July 20, 1945
Seeff, L. (W. Prov.) b May 1, 1959
*Sekar, T. A. P. (TN) b March 28, 1955
*Selby, J. (Notts.) b July 1, 1849, d March 11, 1894
Sellers, A. B. (Yorks.; *CY 1940*) b March 5, 1907, d Feb. 20, 1981
*Sellers, R. H. D. (S. Aust.) b Aug. 20, 1940
*Selvey, M. W. W. (CUCC, Surrey, Middx, Glam. & OFS) b April 25, 1948
*Sen, P. (Bengal) b May 31, 1926, d Jan. 27, 1970
*Sen Gupta, A. K. (Ind. Serv.) b Aug. 3, 1939
*Serjeant, C. S. (W. Aust.) b Nov. 1, 1951
Seymour, James (Kent) b Oct. 25, 1879, d Sept. 30, 1930
*Seymour, M. A. (W. Prov.) b June 5, 1936

*Shackleton, D. (Hants.; *CY 1959*) b Aug. 12, 1924
*Shafiq Ahmad (Lahore, Punjab, NBP & UBL) b March 28, 1949
*Shafqat Rana (Lahore & PIA) b Aug. 10, 1943
*Shahid Israr (Kar. & Sind) b March 1, 1950
*Shahid Mahboob (Karachi, Quetta & PACO) b Aug. 25, 1962
*Shahid Mahmoud (Kar., Pak. Us & PWD) b March 17, 1939
Shahid, N. (Essex) b April 23, 1969
*Shahid Saeed (HBFC) b Jan. 6, 1966
Shakil Khan (WAPDA) b May 28, 1968
*Shalders, W. A. (Griq. W. & Tvl) b Feb. 12, 1880, d March 18, 1917
*Sharma, Ajay (Delhi) b April 3, 1964
*Sharma, Chetan (Haryana) b Jan. 3, 1966
*Sharma, Gopal (U. Pradesh) b Aug. 3, 1960
*Sharma, P. (Raja.) b Jan. 5, 1948
Sharma, R. (Derbys.) b June 27, 1962
Sharma, Sanjeev (Delhi) b Aug. 25, 1965
Sharp, G. (Northants) b March 12, 1950
Sharp, H. P. (Middx) b Oct. 6, 1917
*Sharp, J. (Lancs.) b Feb. 15, 1878, d Jan. 28, 1938
Sharp, K. (Yorks. & Griq. W.) b April 6, 1959
*Sharpe, D. (Punjab, Pak. Rlwys, Lahore & S. Aust.) b Aug. 3, 1937
*Sharpe, J. W. (Surrey & Notts.; *CY 1892*) b Dec. 9, 1866, d June 19, 1936
*Sharpe, P. J. (Yorks. & Derbys.; *CY 1963*) b Dec. 27, 1936
*Shastri, R. J. (Bombay & Glam.) b May 27, 1962
*Shaw, Alfred (Notts. & Sussex) b Aug. 29, 1842, d Jan. 16, 1907
Shaw, C. (Yorks.) b Feb. 17, 1964
*Sheahan, A. P. (Vic.) b Sept. 30, 1946
Sheffield, J. R. (Essex & Wgtn) b Nov. 19, 1906
*Shepherd, B. K. (W. Aust.) b April 23, 1937
Shepherd, D. J. (Glam.; *CY 1970*) b Aug. 12, 1927
Shepherd, D. R. (Glos.; Umpire) b Dec. 27, 1940
*Shepherd, J. N. (B'dos, Kent, Rhod. & Glos.; *CY 1979*) b Nov. 9, 1943
Shepherd, T. F. (Surrey) b Dec. 5, 1889, d Feb. 13, 1957
*Sheppard, Rt Rev. D. S. (Bishop of Liverpool) (CUCC & Sussex; *CY 1953*) b March 6, 1929
*Shepstone, G. H. (Tvl) b April 8, 1876, d July 3, 1940
*Sherwell, P. W. (Tvl) b Aug. 17, 1880, d April 17, 1948
*Sherwin, M. (Notts.; *CY 1891*) b Feb. 26, 1851, d July 3, 1910
*Shillingford, G. C. (Comb. Is. & Windwards) b Sept. 25, 1944

*Shillingford, I. T. (Comb. Is. & Windwards) b April 18, 1944
*Shinde, S. G. (Baroda, M'tra & Bombay) b Aug. 18, 1923, d June 22, 1955
Shirreff, A. C. (CUCC, Hants, Kent & Som.) b Feb. 12, 1919
*Shivnarine, S. (Guyana) b May 13, 1952
*Shoaib Mohammad (Kar. & PIA) b Jan. 8, 1962
*Shodhan, R. H. (Guj. & Baroda) b Oct. 18, 1928
Short, A. M. (Natal) b Sept. 27, 1947
*Shrewsbury, Arthur (Notts.; *CY 1890*) b April 11, 1856, d May 19, 1903
*Shrimpton, M. J. F. (C. Dist. & N. Dist.) b June 23, 1940
*Shuja-ud-Din, Col. (N. Ind., Pak. Us, Pak. Serv., B'pur & R'pindi) b April 10, 1930
*Shukla, R. C. (Bihar & Delhi) b Feb. 4, 1948
*Shuter, J. (Kent & Surrey) b Feb. 9, 1855, d July 5, 1920
*Shuttleworth, K. (Lancs. & Leics.) b Nov. 13, 1944
Siddons, J. D. (Vic.) b April 25, 1964
*Sidebottom, A. (Yorks. & OFS) b April 1, 1954
*Sidhu, N. S. (Punjab) b Oct. 20, 1963
*Siedle, I. J. (Natal) b Jan. 11, 1903, d Aug. 24, 1982
*Sievers, M. W. (Vic.) b April 13, 1912, d May 10, 1968
*Sikander Bakht (PWD, PIA, Sind, Kar. & UBL) b Aug. 25, 1957
Silk, D. R. W. (CUCC & Som.) b Oct. 8, 1931
*Silva, S. A. R. (NCC) b Dec. 12, 1960
Sime, W. A. (Notts.) b Feb. 8, 1909, d May 5, 1982
Simmons, J. (Lancs. & Tas.; *CY 1985*) b March 28, 1941
*Simmons, P. V. (T/T) b April 18, 1963
*Simpson, R. B. (NSW & W. Aust.; *CY 1965*) b Feb. 3, 1936
*Simpson, R. T. (Notts. & Sind; *CY 1950*) b Feb. 27, 1920
*Simpson-Hayward, G. H. (Worcs.) b June 7, 1875, d Oct. 2, 1936
Sims, Sir Arthur (Cant.) b July 22, 1877, d April 27, 1969
*Sims, J. M. (Middx) b May 13, 1903, d April 27, 1973
*Sinclair, B. W. (Wgtn) b Oct. 23, 1936
*Sinclair, I. McK. (Cant.) b June 1, 1933
*Sinclair, J. H. (Tvl) b Oct. 16, 1876, d Feb. 23, 1913
*Sincock, D. J. (S. Aust.) b Feb. 1, 1942
*Sinfield, R. A. (Glos.) b Dec. 24, 1900, d March 17, 1988
*Singh, Charan K. (T/T) b 1938
Singh, "Robin" [R. R.] (TN) b Sept. 14, 1963
Singh, R. P. (U. Pradesh) b Jan. 6, 1963
Singh, Swaranjit (CUCC, Warwicks., Punjab & Bengal) b July 18, 1931
Singleton, A. P. (OUCC, Worcs. & Rhod b Aug. 5, 1914
*Sivaramakrishnan, L. (TN) b Dec. 31, 196
Skelding, Alec (Leics.) b Sept. 5, 1886, April 17, 1960
Skinner, A. F. (Derbys. & Northants) April 22, 1913, d Feb. 28, 1982
Skinner, D. A. (Derbys.) b March 22, 192
Skinner, L. E. (Surrey & Guyana) b Sept. 1950
*Slack, W. N. (Middx & Windwards) b De 12, 1954, d Jan. 15, 1989
Slade, D. N. F. (Worcs.) b Aug. 24, 1940
Slade, W. D. (Glam.) b Sept. 27, 1941
*Slater, K. N. (W. Aust.) b March 12, 193
*Sleep, P. R. (S. Aust.) b May 4, 1957
*Slight, J. (Vic.) b Oct. 20, 1855, d Dec. 1930
Slocombe, P. A. (Som.) b Sept. 6, 1954
*Smailes, T. F. (Yorks.) b March 27, 1910, Dec. 1, 1970
Smales, K. (Yorks. & Notts.) b Sept. 1 1927
*Small, G. C. (Warwicks. & S. Aust.) b Oc 18, 1961
Small, John, sen. (Hants & All-England) April 19, 1737, d Dec. 31, 1826
*Small, J. A. (T/T) b Nov. 3, 1892, d Apr 26, 1958
*Small, M. A. (B'dos) b Feb. 12, 1964
Smedley, M. J. (Notts.) b Oct. 28, 1941
*Smith, A. C. (OUCC & Warwicks.; Chie Exec. TCCB 1987-) b Oct. 25, 1936
*Smith, Sir C. Aubrey (CUCC, Sussex Tvl) b July 21, 1863, d Dec. 20, 1948
*Smith, C. I. J. (Middx; *CY 1935*) b Aug. 2 1906, d Feb. 9, 1979
*Smith, C. J. E. (Tvl) b Dec. 25, 1872, March 27, 1947
*Smith, C. L. (Natal, Glam. & Hants; *C 1984*) b Oct. 15, 1958
Smith, C. S. (CUCC & Lancs.) b Oct. 1932
*Smith, C. W. (B'dos) b July 29, 1933
*Smith, Denis (Derbys.; *CY 1936*) b Jan. 2 1907, d Sept. 12, 1979
*Smith, D. B. M. (Vic.) b Sept. 14, 1884, July 29, 1963
Smith, D. H. K. (Derbys. & OFS) b Jun 29, 1940
*Smith, D. M. (Surrey, Worcs. & Sussex) Jan. 9, 1956
*Smith, D. R. (Glos.) b Oct. 5, 1934
*Smith, D. V. (Sussex) b June 14, 1923
Smith, Edwin (Derbys.) b Jan. 2, 1934
*Smith, E. J. (Warwicks.) b Feb. 6, 1886, Aug. 31, 1979
*Smith, F. B. (Cant.) b March 13, 1922

*Smith, F. W. (Tvl) No details of birth or death known
Smith, G. (Kent) b Nov. 30, 1925
Smith, G. J. (Essex) b April 2, 1935
*Smith, Harry (Glos.) b May 21, 1890, d Nov. 12, 1937
*Smith, H. D. (Otago & Cant.) b Jan. 8, 1913, d Jan. 25, 1986
Smith, I. (Glam.) b March 11, 1967
*Smith, I. D. S. (C. Dist.) b Feb. 28, 1957
Smith, K. D. (Warwicks.) b July 9, 1956
Smith, M. J. (Middx) b Jan. 4, 1942
*Smith, M. J. K. (OUCC, Leics. & Warwicks.; *CY 1960*) b June 30, 1933
Smith, N. (Yorks. & Essex) b April 1, 1949
*Smith, O. G. (Jam.; *CY 1958*) b May 5, 1933, d Sept. 9, 1959
Smith, P. A. (Warwicks.) b April 5, 1964
Smith, Ray (Essex) b Aug. 10, 1914
Smith, Roy (Som.) b April 14, 1930
*Smith, R. A. (Natal & Hants; *CY 1990*) b Sept. 13, 1963
Smith, R. C. (Leics.) b Aug. 3, 1935
*Smith, S. B. (NSW & Tvl) b Oct. 18, 1961
Smith, S. G. (T/T, Northants & Auck.; *CY 1915*) b Jan. 15, 1881, d Oct. 25, 1963
*Smith, T. P. B. (Essex; *CY 1947*) b Oct. 30, 1908, d Aug. 4, 1967
*Smith, V. I. (Natal) b Feb. 23, 1925
Smith, W. A. (Surrey) b Sept. 15, 1937
Smith, W. C. (Surrey; *CY 1911*) b Oct. 4, 1877, d July 16, 1946
*Smithson, G. A. (Yorks. & Leics.) b Nov. 1, 1926, d Sept. 6, 1970
*Snedden, C. A. (Auck.) b Jan. 7, 1918
*Snedden, M. C. (Auck.) b Nov. 23, 1958
Snellgrove, K. L. (Lancs.) b Nov. 12, 1941
*Snooke, S. D. (W. Prov. & Tvl) b Nov. 11, 1878, d April 4, 1959
*Snooke, S. J. (Border, W. Prov. & Tvl) b Feb. 1, 1881, d Aug. 14, 1966
*Snow, J. A. (Sussex; *CY 1973*) b Oct. 13, 1941
Snowden, A. W. (Northants) b Aug. 15, 1913, d May 7, 1981
Snowden, W. (CUCC) b Sept. 27, 1952
*Sobers, Sir G. S. (B'dos, S. Aust. & Notts.; *CY 1964*) b July 28, 1936
Sohail Fazal (Lahore) b Nov. 11, 1967
*Sohoni, S. W. (M'tra, Baroda & Bombay) b March 5, 1918
Solanky, J. W. (E. Africa & Glam.) b June 30, 1942
*Solkar, E. D. (Bombay & Sussex) b March 18, 1948
*Solomon, J. S. (BG) b Aug. 26, 1930
*Solomon, W. R. T. (Tvl & E. Prov.) b April 23, 1872, d July 12, 1964
Sood, M. M. (Delhi) b July 6, 1939
Southern, J. W. (Hants) b Sept. 2, 1952
Southerton, James (Surrey, Hants & Sussex) b Nov. 16, 1827, d June 16, 1880
Southerton, S. J. (Editor of *Wisden* 1934-35) b July 7, 1874, d March 12, 1935
*Sparling, J. T. (Auck.) b July 24, 1938
Speight, M. P. (Sussex & Wgtn) b Oct. 24, 1967
Spencer, C. T. (Leics.) b Aug. 18, 1931
Spencer, J. (CUCC & Sussex) b Oct. 6, 1949
Spencer, T. W. (Kent) b March 22, 1914
Sperry, J. (Leics.) b March 19, 1910
*Spofforth, F. R. (NSW & Vic.) b Sept. 9, 1853, d June 4, 1926
*Spooner, R. H. (Lancs.; *CY 1905*) b Oct. 21, 1880, d Oct. 2, 1961
*Spooner, R. T. (Warwicks.) b Dec. 30, 1919
Springall, J. D. (Notts.) b Sept. 19, 1932
*Srikkanth, K. (TN) b Dec. 21, 1959
*Srinivasan, T. E. (TN) b Oct. 26, 1950
*Stackpole, K. R. (Vic.; *CY 1973*) b July 10, 1940
Standen, J. A. (Worcs.) b May 30, 1935
Standing, D. K. (Sussex) b Oct. 21, 1963
*Stanyforth, Lt-Col. R. T. (Yorks.) b May 30, 1892, d Feb. 20, 1964
*Staples, S. J. (Notts.; *CY 1929*) b Sept. 18, 1892, d June 4, 1950
Starkie, S. (Northants) b April 4, 1926
*Statham, J. B. (Lancs.; *CY 1955*) b June 17, 1930
*Stayers, S. C. (†Guyana & Bombay) b June 9, 1937
Stead, B. (Yorks., Essex, Notts. & N. Tvl) b June 21, 1939, d April 15, 1980
*Steel, A. G. (CUCC & Lancs.; Pres. MCC 1902) b Sept. 24, 1858, d June 15, 1914
*Steele, D. S. (Northants & Derbys.; *CY 1976*) b Sept. 29, 1941
Steele, J. F. (Leics., Natal & Glam.) b July 23, 1946
Stephens, E. J. (Glos.) b March 23, 1910
Stephenson, F. D. (B'dos, Glos., Tas. & Notts.; *CY 1989*) b April 8, 1959
Stephenson, G. R. (Derbys. & Hants) b Nov. 19, 1942
Stephenson, H. H. (Surrey & All-England) b May 3, 1832, d Dec. 17, 1896
Stephenson, H. W. (Som.) b July 18, 1920
*Stephenson, J. P. (Essex & Boland) b March 14, 1965
Stephenson, Lt-Col. J. R. (Sec. MCC 1987-) b Feb. 25, 1931
Stephenson, Lt-Col. J. W. A. (Essex & Worcs.) b Aug. 1, 1907, d May 20, 1982
Stevens, Edward ("Lumpy") (Hants) b *circa* 1735, d Sept. 7, 1819
*Stevens, G. B. (S. Aust.) b Feb. 29, 1932
*Stevens, G. T. S. (UCS, OUCC & Middx; *CY 1918*) b Jan. 7, 1901, d Sept. 19, 1970
*Stevenson, G. B. (Yorks. & Northants) b Dec. 16, 1955
Stevenson, K. (Derbys. & Hants) b Oct. 6, 1950

Stevenson, M. H. (CUCC & Derbys.) b June 13, 1927
*Stewart, A. J. (Surrey) b April 8, 1963
*Stewart, M. J. (Surrey; *CY 1958*) b Sept. 16, 1932
*Stewart, R. B. (SA) b Sept. 3, 1856, d Sept. 12, 1913
Stewart, R. W. (Glos. & Middx) b Feb. 28, 1945
Stewart, W. J. (Warwicks. & Northants) b Oct. 31, 1934
*Stirling, D. A. (C. Dist.) b Oct. 5, 1961
Stocks, F. W. (Notts.) b Nov. 6, 1917
*Stoddart, A. E. (Middx; *CY 1893*) b March 11, 1863, d April 4, 1915
*Stollmeyer, J. B. (T/T) b April 11, 1921, d Sept. 10, 1989
*Stollmeyer, V. H. (T/T) b Jan. 24, 1916
*Storer, W. (Derbys.; *CY 1899*) b Jan. 25, 1867, d Feb. 28, 1912
Storey, S. J. (Surrey & Sussex) b Jan. 6, 1941
Stott, L. W. (Auck.) b Dec. 8, 1946
Stott, W. B. (Yorks.) b July 18, 1934
Stovold, A. W. (Glos. & OFS) b March 19, 1953
*Street, G. B. (Sussex) b Dec. 6, 1889, d April 24, 1924
*Stricker, L. A. (Tvl) b May 26, 1884, d Feb. 5, 1960
Stringer, P. M. (Yorks. & Leics.) b Feb. 23, 1943
*Strudwick, H. (Surrey; *CY 1912*) b Jan. 28, 1880, d Feb. 14, 1970
Strydom, W. T. (OFS) b March 21, 1942
*Studd, C. T. (CUCC & Middx) b Dec. 2, 1860, d July 16, 1931
*Studd, G. B. (CUCC & Middx) b Oct. 20, 1859, d Feb. 13, 1945
Studd, Sir Peter M. (CUCC) b Sept. 15, 1916
Sturt, M. O. C. (Middx) b Sept. 12, 1940
*Subba Row, R. (CUCC, Surrey & Northants; *CY 1961*) b Jan. 29, 1932
*Subramanya, V. (Mysore) b July 16, 1936
Such, P. M. (Notts., Leics. & Essex) b June 12, 1964
Sudhakar Rao, R. (Karn.) b Aug. 8, 1952
Sueter, T. (Hants & Surrey) b *circa* 1749, d Feb. 17, 1827
*Sugg, F. H. (Yorks., Derbys. & Lancs.; *CY 1890*) b Jan. 11, 1862, d May 29, 1933
Sullivan, J. (Lancs.) b Feb. 5, 1945
Sully, H. (Som. & Northants) b Nov. 1, 1939
*Sunderram, G. R. (Bombay & Raja.) b March 29, 1930
Sunnucks, P. R. (Kent) b June 22, 1916
*Surendranath, R. (Ind. Serv.) b Jan. 4, 1937
Surridge, W. S. (Surrey; *CY 1953*) b Sept. 3, 1917
*Surti, R. F. (Guj., Raja. & Qld) b May 25, 1936
*Susskind, M. J. (CUCC, Middx & Tvl) b June 8, 1891, d July 9, 1957
*Sutcliffe, B. (Auck., Otago & N. Dist.; *CY 1950*) b Nov. 17, 1923
*Sutcliffe, H. (Yorks.; *CY 1920*) b Nov. 24, 1894, d Jan. 22, 1978
Sutcliffe, S. P. (OUCC & Warwicks.) b May 22, 1960
Sutcliffe, W. H. H. (Yorks.) b Oct. 10, 1926
Suttle, K. G. (Sussex) b Aug. 25, 1928
Swallow, I. G. (Yorks. & Som.) b Dec. 18, 1962
*Swamy, V. N. (Ind. Serv.) b May 23, 1924, d May 1, 1983
Swanton, E. W. (Middx; Writer) b Feb. 11, 1907
Swarbrook, F. W. (Derbys., Griq. W. & OFS) b Dec. 17, 1950
Swart, P. D. (Rhod., W. Prov., Glam. & Boland) b April 27, 1946
*Swetman, R. (Surrey, Notts & Glos.) b Oct. 25, 1933
Sydenham, D. A. D. (Surrey) b April 6, 1934
Symington, S. J. (Leics.) b Sept. 16, 1926

*Taber, H. B. (NSW) b April 29, 1940
*Taberer, H. M. (OUCC & Natal) b Oct. 7, 1870, d June 5, 1932
*Tahir Naqqash (Servis Ind., MCB, Punjab & Lahore) b July 6, 1959
Tait, A. (Northants & Glos.) b Dec. 27, 1953
*Talat Ali (Lahore, PIA & UBL) b May 29, 1950
Talbot, R. O. (Cant. & Otago) b Nov. 26, 1903, d Jan. 5, 1983
*Tallon, D. (Qld; *CY 1949*) b Feb. 17, 1916, d Sept. 7, 1984
*Tamhane, N. S. (Bombay) b Aug. 4, 1931
*Tancred, A. B. (Kimberley, Griq. W. & Tvl) b Aug. 20, 1865, d Nov. 23, 1911
*Tancred, L. J. (Tvl) b Oct. 7, 1876, d July 28, 1934
*Tancred, V. M. (Tvl) b July 7, 1875, d June 3, 1904
Tang Choon, R. P. (T/T) b 1914, d Sept. 5, 1985
*Tapscott, G. L. (Griq. W.) b Nov. 7, 1889, d Dec. 13, 1940
*Tapscott, L. E. (Griq. W.) b March 18, 1894, d July 7, 1934
*Tarapore, K. K. (Bombay) b Dec. 17, 1910, d June 15, 1986
Tarrant, F. A. (Vic., Middx & Patiala; *CY 1908*) b Dec. 11, 1880, d Jan. 29, 1951
Tarrant, George F. (Cambs. & All England) b Dec. 7, 1838, d July 2, 1870
*Taslim Arif (Kar., Sind & NBP) b May 1, 1954

*Tate, F. W. (Sussex) b July 24, 1867, d Feb. 24, 1943
*Tate, M. W. (Sussex; *CY 1924*) b May 30, 1895, d May 18, 1956
*Tattersall, R. (Lancs.) b Aug. 17, 1922
*Tauseef Ahmed (PWD, UBL & Kar.) b May 10, 1958
*Tavaré, C. J. (OUCC, Kent & Som.) b Oct. 27, 1954
Tayfield, A. (Natal, Tvl & NE Tvl) b June 21, 1931
*Tayfield, H. J. (Natal, Rhod. & Tvl; *CY 1956*) b Jan. 30, 1929
*Taylor, A. I. (Tvl) b July 25, 1925
Taylor, B. (Essex; *CY 1972*) b June 19, 1932
*Taylor, B. R. (Cant. & Wgtn) b July 12, 1943
*Taylor, Daniel (Natal) b Jan. 9, 1887, d Jan. 24, 1957
*Taylor, D. D. (Auck. & Warwicks.) b March 2, 1923, d Dec. 5, 1980
Taylor, D. J. S. (Surrey, Som. & Griq. W.) b Nov. 12, 1942
Taylor, G. R. (Hants) b Nov. 25, 1909, d Oct. 31, 1986
*Taylor, H. W. (Natal, Tvl & W. Prov.; *CY 1925*) b May 5, 1889, d Feb. 8, 1973
*Taylor, J. M. (NSW) b Oct. 10, 1895, d May 12, 1971
*Taylor, J. O. (T/T) b Jan. 3, 1932
*Taylor, K. (Yorks. & Auck.) b Aug. 21, 1935
Taylor, K. A. (Warwicks.) b Sept. 29, 1916
*Taylor, L. B. (Leics. & Natal) b Oct. 25, 1953
*Taylor, M. A. (NSW; *CY 1990*) b Oct 27, 1964
Taylor, M. L. (Lancs.) b July 16, 1904, d March 14, 1978
Taylor, M. N. S. (Notts. & Hants) b Nov. 12, 1942
Taylor, N. R. (Kent) b July 21, 1959
*Taylor, P. L. (NSW) b Aug. 22, 1956
Taylor, R. M. (Essex) b Nov. 30, 1909, d Jan. 1984
*Taylor, R. W. (Derbys.; *CY 1977*) b July 17, 1941
Taylor, T. L. (CUCC & Yorks.; *CY 1901*) b May 25, 1878, d March 16, 1960
Taylor, W. (Notts.) b Jan. 24, 1947
Tedstone, G. A. (Warwicks. & Glos.) b Jan. 19, 1961
*Tendulkar, S. R. (Bombay) b April 24, 1973
Tennekoon, A. P. B. (SL) b Oct. 29, 1946
*Tennyson, 3rd Lord (Hon. L. H.) (Hants; *CY 1914*) b Nov. 7, 1889, d June 6, 1951
*Terry, V. P. (Hants) b Jan. 14, 1959
*Theunissen, N. H. (W. Prov.) b May 4, 1867, d Nov. 9, 1929
Thomas, D. J. (Surrey, N. Tvl & Glos.) b June 30, 1959
*Thomas, G. (NSW) b March 21, 1938
*Thomas, J. G. (Glam., Border, E. Prov. & Northants) b Aug. 12, 1960
Thompson, A. W. (Middx) b April 17, 1916
*Thompson, G. J. (Northants; *CY 1906*) b Oct. 27, 1877, d March 3, 1943
Thompson, J. R. (CUCC & Warwicks.) b May 10, 1918
*Thompson, Nathaniel (NSW) b April 21, 1838, d Sept. 2, 1896
Thompson, R. G. (Warwicks.) b Sept. 26, 1932
*Thoms, G. R. (Vic.) b March 22, 1927
*Thomson, A. L. (Vic.) b Dec. 2, 1945
*Thomson, J. R. (NSW, Qld & Middx) b Aug. 16, 1950
*Thomson, K. (Cant.) b Feb. 26, 1941
*Thomson, N. I. (Sussex) b Jan. 23, 1929
*Thomson, S. A. (N. Dist.) b Jan. 27, 1969
Thorne, D. A. (Warwicks & OUCC) b Dec. 12, 1964
Thornton, C. I. (CUCC, Kent & Middx) b March 20, 1850, d Dec. 10, 1929
*Thornton, P. G. (Yorks., Middx & SA) b Dec. 24, 1867, d Jan. 31, 1939
Thorpe, G. P. (Surrey) b Aug. 1, 1969
*Thurlow, H. M. (Qld) b Jan. 10, 1903, d Dec. 3, 1975
*Tillekeratne, H. P. (NCC) b July 14, 1967
Tilly, H. W. (Middx) b May 25, 1932
Timms, B. S. V. (Hants & Warwicks.) b Dec. 17, 1940
Timms, J. E. (Northants) b Nov. 3, 1906, d May 18, 1980
Timms, W. W. (Northants) b Sept. 28, 1902, d Sept. 30, 1986
Tindall, M. (CUCC & Middx) b March 31, 1914
Tindall, R. A. E. (Surrey) b Sept. 23, 1935
*Tindill, E. W. T. (Wgtn) b Dec. 18, 1910
Tissera, M. H. (SL) b March 23, 1939
*Titmus, F. J. (Middx, Surrey & OFS; *CY 1963*) b Nov. 24, 1932
Todd, L. J. (Kent) b June 19, 1907, d Aug. 20, 1967
Todd, P. A. (Notts. & Glam.) b March 12, 1953
Tolchard, J. G. (Leics.) b March 17, 1944
*Tolchard, R. W. (Leics.) b June 15, 1946
Tomlins, K. P. (Middx & Glos.) b Oct. 23, 1957
*Tomlinson, D. S. (Rhod. & Border) b Sept. 4, 1910
Tompkin, M. (Leics.) b Feb. 17, 1919, d Sept. 27, 1956
Toogood, G. J. (OUCC) b Nov. 19, 1961
*Toohey, P. M. (NSW) b April 20, 1954
Tooley, C. D. M. (OUCC) b April 19, 1964
Topley, T. D. (Surrey, Essex & Griq. W.) b Feb. 25, 1964
Tordoff, G. G. (CUCC & Som.) b Dec. 6, 1929

*Toshack, E. R. H. (NSW) b Dec. 15, 1914
Townsend, A. (Warwicks.) b Aug. 26, 1921
Townsend, A. F. (Derbys.) b March 29, 1912
*Townsend, C. L. (Glos.; *CY 1899*) b Nov. 7, 1876, d Oct. 17, 1958
*Townsend, D. C. H. (OUCC) b April 20, 1912
*Townsend, L. F. (Derbys. & Auck.; *CY 1934*) b June 8, 1903
*Traicos, A. J. (Rhod. & Zimb.) b May 17, 1947
*Travers, J. P. F. (S. Aust.) b Jan. 10, 1871, d Sept. 15, 1942
*Tremlett, M. F. (Som. & C. Dist.) b July 5, 1923, d July 30, 1984
Tremlett, T. M. (Hants) b July 26, 1956
*Tribe, G. E. (Vic. & Northants; *CY 1955*) b Oct. 4, 1920
*Trim, J. (BG) b Jan. 24, 1915, d Nov. 12, 1960
Trimble, G. S. (Qld) b Jan. 1, 1963
Trimble, S. C. (Qld) b Aug. 16, 1934
*Trimborn, P. H. J. (Natal) b May 18, 1940
**Trott, A. E. (Vic., Middx & Hawkes Bay; *CY 1899*) b Feb. 6, 1873, d July 30, 1914
*Trott, G. H. S. (Vic.; *CY 1894*) b Aug. 5, 1866, d Nov. 10, 1917
*Troup, G. B. (Auck.) b Oct. 3, 1952
*Trueman, F. S. (Yorks.; *CY 1953*) b Feb. 6, 1931
*Trumble, H. (Vic.; *CY 1897*) b May 12, 1867, d Aug. 14, 1938
*Trumble, J. W. (Vic.) b Sept. 16, 1863, d Aug. 17, 1944
*Trumper, V. T. (NSW; *CY 1903*) b Nov. 2, 1877, d June 28, 1915
*Truscott, P. B. (Wgtn) b Aug. 14, 1941
*Tuckett, L. (OFS) b Feb. 6, 1919
*Tuckett, L. R. (Natal & OFS) b April 19, 1885, d April 8, 1963
*Tufnell, N. C. (CUCC & Surrey) b June 13, 1887, d Aug. 3, 1951
Tufnell, P. C. R. (Middx) b April 29, 1966
Tuke, Sir Anthony (Pres. MCC 1982-83) b Aug. 22, 1920
Tunnicliffe, C. J. (Derbys.) b Aug. 11, 1951
Tunnicliffe, H. T. (Notts.) b March 4, 1950
Tunnicliffe, J. (Yorks.; *CY 1901*) b Aug. 26, 1866, d July 11, 1948
*Turnbull, M. J. (CUCC & Glam.; *CY 1931*) b March 16, 1906, d Aug. 5, 1944
*Turner, A. (NSW) b July 23, 1950
Turner, C. (Yorks.) b Jan. 11, 1902, d Nov. 19, 1968
*Turner, C. T. B. (NSW; *CY 1889*) b Nov. 16, 1862, d Jan. 1, 1944
Turner, D. R. (Hants & W. Prov.) b Feb. 5, 1949
Turner, F. M. (Leics.) b Aug. 8, 1934
*Turner, G. M. (Otago, N. Dist. & Worcs.; *CY 1971*) b May 26, 1947
Turner, S. (Essex & Natal) b July 18, 1943
*Twentyman-Jones, P. S. (W. Prov.) b Sept. 13, 1876, d March 8, 1954
Twining, R. H. (OUCC & Middx; Pres. MCC 1964-65) b Nov. 3, 1889, d Jan. 3, 1979
*Tyldesley, E. (Lancs.; *CY 1920*) b Feb. 5, 1889, d May 5, 1962
*Tyldesley, J. T. (Lancs.; *CY 1902*) b Nov. 22, 1873, d Nov. 27, 1930
*Tyldesley, R. K. (Lancs.; *CY 1925*) b March 11, 1897, d Sept. 17, 1943
*Tylecote, E. F. S. (OUCC & Kent) b June 23, 1849, d March 15, 1938
*Tyler, E. J. (Som.) b Oct. 13, 1864, d Jan. 25, 1917
*Tyson, F. H. (Northants; *CY 1956*) b June 6, 1930

Ufton, D. G. (Kent) b May 31, 1928
*Ulyett, G. (Yorks.) b Oct. 21, 1851, d June 18, 1898
*Umrigar, P. R. (Bombay & Guj.) b March 28, 1926
*Underwood, D. L. (Kent; *CY 1969*) b June 8, 1945
Unwin, F. St G. (Essex) b April 23, 1911, d Oct. 1990

*Valentine, A. L. (Jam.; *CY 1951*) b April 29, 1930
*Valentine, B. H. (CUCC & Kent) b Jan. 17, 1908, d Feb. 2, 1983
*Valentine, V. A. (Jam.) b April 4, 1908, d July 6, 1972
*Vance, R. H. (Wgtn) b March 31, 1955
*van der Bijl, P. G. (W. Prov. & OUCC) b Oct. 21, 1907, d Feb. 16, 1973
van der Bijl, V. A. P. (Natal, Middx & Tvl; *CY 1981*) b March 19, 1948
Van der Gucht, P. I. (Glos. & Bengal) b Nov. 2, 1911
*Van der Merwe, E. A. (Tvl) b Nov. 9, 1904, d Feb. 28, 1971
*Van der Merwe, P. L. (W. Prov. & E. Prov.) b March 14, 1937
van Geloven, J. (Yorks. & Leics.) b Jan. 4, 1934
*Van Ryneveld, C. B. (W. Prov. & OUCC) b March 19, 1928
van Zyl, C. J. P. G. (OFS & Glam.) b Oct. 1, 1961
Varachia, R. (First Pres. SA Cricket Union) b Oct. 12, 1915, d Dec. 11, 1981
Varey, D. W. (CUCC & Lancs.) b Oct. 15, 1961
*Varnals, G. D. (E. Prov., Tvl & Natal) b July 24, 1935
Vaulkhard, P. (Notts. & Derbys.) b Sept. 15, 1911
*Vengsarkar, D. B. (Bombay; *CY 1987*) b April 6, 1956
*Veivers, T. R. (Qld) b April 6, 1937

*Veletta, M. R. J. (W. Aust.) b Oct. 30, 1963
*Venkataraghavan, S. (†TN & Derbys.) b April 21, 1946
*Venkataramana, M. (TN) b April 24, 1966
*Verity, H. (Yorks.; *CY 1932*) b May 18, 1905, d July 31, 1943
*Vernon, G. F. (Middx) b June 20, 1856, d Aug. 10, 1902
Vernon, M. T. (W. Aust.) b Feb. 9, 1937
Vigar, F. H. (Essex) b July 7, 1917
*Viljoen, K. G. (Griq. W., OFS & Tvl) b May 14, 1910, d Jan. 21, 1974
*Vincent, C. L. (Tvl) b Feb. 16, 1902, d Aug. 24, 1968
*Vine, J. (Sussex; *CY 1906*) b May 15, 1875, d April 25, 1946
*Vintcent, C. H. (Tvl & Griq. W.) b Sept. 2, 1866, d Sept. 28, 1943
Virgin, R. T. (Som., Northants & W. Prov.; *CY 1971*) b Aug. 26, 1939
*Viswanath, G. R. (†Karn.) b Feb. 12, 1949
*Viswanath, S. (Karn.) b Nov. 29, 1962
*Vivian, G. E. (Auck.) b Feb. 28, 1946
*Vivian, H. G. (Auck.) b Nov. 4, 1912, d Aug. 12, 1983
*Vizianagram, Maharaj Kumar of, Sir Vijay A. (U. Prov.) b Dec. 28, 1905, d Dec. 2, 1965
*Voce, W. (Notts.; *CY 1933*) b Aug. 8, 1909, d June 6, 1984
*Vogler, A. E. E. (Middx, Natal, Tvl & E. Prov.; *CY 1908*) b Nov. 28, 1876, d Aug. 9, 1946
Vonhagt, D. M. (Moors) b March 31, 1965

*Waddington, A. (Yorks.) b Feb. 4, 1893, d Oct. 28, 1959
Waddington, J. E. (Griq. W.) b Dec. 30, 1918, d Nov. 24, 1985
*Wade, H. F. (Natal) b Sept. 14, 1905, d Nov. 22, 1980
Wade, T. H. (Essex) b Nov. 24, 1910, d July 25, 1987
*Wade, W. W. (Natal) b June 18, 1914
*Wadekar, A. L. (Bombay) b April 1, 1941
*Wadsworth, K. J. (C. Dist. & Cant.) b Nov. 30, 1946, d Aug. 19, 1976
*Wainwright, E. (Yorks.; *CY 1894*) b April 8, 1865, d Oct. 28, 1919
*Waite, J. H. B. (E. Prov. & Tvl) b Jan. 19, 1930
*Waite, M. G. (S. Aust.) b Jan. 7, 1911, d Dec. 16, 1985
*Walcott, C. L. (B'dos & BG; *CY 1958*) b Jan. 17, 1926
*Walcott, L. A. (B'dos) b Jan. 18, 1894, d Feb. 27, 1984
Walden, F. I. (Northants; Umpire) b March 1, 1888, d May 3, 1949
Walford, M. M. (OUCC & Som.) b Nov. 27, 1915
Walker, A. (Northants) b July 7, 1962
Walker, A. K. (NSW & Notts.) b Oct. 4, 1925
Walker, C. (Yorks. & Hants) b June 27, 1920
Walker, C. W. (S. Aust.) b Feb. 19, 1909, d Dec. 21, 1942
Walker, I. D. (Middx) b Jan. 8, 1844, d July 6, 1898
*Walker, M. H. N. (Vic.) b Sept. 12, 1948
*Walker, P. M. (Glam., Tvl & W. Prov.) b Feb. 17, 1936
Walker, W. (Notts.; oldest living County Champ. player) b Nov. 24, 1892
*Wall, T. W. (S. Aust.) b May 13, 1904, d March 25, 1981
*Wallace, W. M. (Auck.) b Dec. 19, 1916
Waller, C. E. (Surrey & Sussex) b Oct. 3, 1948
*Walsh, C. A. (Jam. & Glos.; *CY 1987*) b Oct. 30, 1962
Walsh, J. E. (NSW & Leics.) b Dec. 4, 1912, d May 20, 1980
*Walter, K. A. (Tvl) b Nov. 5, 1939
*Walters, C. F. (Glam. & Worcs.; *CY 1934*) b Aug. 28, 1905
*Walters, F. H. (Vic. & NSW) b Feb. 9, 1860, d June 1, 1922
Walters, J. (Derbys.) b Aug. 7, 1949
*Walters, K. D. (NSW) b Dec. 21, 1945
Walton, A. C. (OUCC & Middx) b Sept. 26, 1933
*Waqar Hassan (Pak. Us, Punjab, Pak. Serv. & Kar.) b Sept. 12, 1932
*Waqar Younis (Multan, UBL & Surrey) b Jan. 16, 1971
*Ward, Alan (Derbys., Leics. & Border) b Aug. 10, 1947
*Ward, Albert (Yorks. & Lancs.; *CY 1890*) b Nov. 21, 1865, d Jan. 6, 1939
Ward, B. (Essex) b Feb. 28, 1944
Ward, D. (Glam.) b Aug. 30, 1934
Ward, D. M. (Surrey) b Feb. 10, 1961
*Ward, F. A. (S. Aust.) b Feb. 23, 1909, d March 25, 1974
*Ward, J. T. (Cant.) b March 11, 1937
*Ward, T. A. (Tvl) b Aug. 2, 1887, d Feb. 16, 1936
Ward, T. R. (Kent) b Jan. 18, 1968
Ward, William (MCC & Hants) b July 24, 1787, d June 30, 1849
*Wardle, J. H. (Yorks.; *CY 1954*) b Jan. 8, 1923, d July 23, 1985
*Warnapura, B. (SL) b March 1, 1953
*Warnaweera, K. P. J. (SL) b Nov. 23, 1960
Warne, F. B. (Worcs., Vic. & Tvl) b Oct. 3, 1906
Warner, A. E. (Worcs. & Derbys.) b May 12, 1959
*Warner, Sir P. F. (OUCC & Middx; *CY 1904, special portrait 1921*; Pres. MCC 1950-51) b Oct. 2, 1873, d Jan. 30, 1963

*Warr, J. J. (CUCC & Middx; Pres. MCC 1987-88) b July 16, 1927
*Warren, A. R. (Derbys.) b April 2, 1875, d Sept. 3, 1951
*Washbrook, C. (Lancs.; *CY 1947*) b Dec. 6, 1914
*Wasim Akram (Lahore, PACO, PNSC & Lancs.) b June 3, 1966
*Wasim Bari (Kar., PIA & Sind) b March 23, 1948
*Wasim Raja (Lahore, Sargodha, Pak. Us, PIA, Punjab & NBP) b July 3, 1952
Wass, T. G. (Notts.; *CY 1908*) b Dec. 26, 1873, d Oct. 27, 1953
*Wassan, A. S. (Delhi) b March 23, 1968
Wassell, A. (Hants) b April 15, 1940
Watkin, S. L. (Glam.) b Sept. 15, 1964
*Watkins, A. J. (Glam.) b April 21, 1922
*Watkins, J. C. (Natal) b April 10, 1923
*Watkins, J. R. (NSW) b April 16, 1943
Watkinson, M. (Lancs.) b Aug. 1, 1961
*Watson, C. (Jam. & Delhi) b July 1, 1938
Watson, F. B. (Lancs.) b Sept. 17, 1898, d Feb. 1, 1976
*Watson, G. D. (Vic., W. Aust. & NSW) b March 8, 1945
Watson, G. G. (NSW, W. Aust. & Worcs.) b Jan. 29, 1955
*Watson, W. (Yorks. & Leics.; *CY 1954*) b March 7, 1920
*Watson, W. (Auck.) b Aug. 31, 1965
*Watson, W. J. (NSW) b Jan. 31, 1931
Watson, W. K. (Border, N. Tvl, E. Prov. & Notts.) b May 21, 1955
*Watt, L. (Otago) b Sept. 17, 1924
Watts, E. A. (Surrey) b Aug. 1, 1911, d May 2, 1982
Watts, H. E. (CUCC & Som.) b March 4, 1922
Watts, P. D. (Northants & Notts.) b March 31, 1938
Watts, P. J. (Northants) b June 16, 1940
Waugh, M. E. (NSW & Essex; *CY 1991*) b June 2, 1965
*Waugh, S. R. (NSW & Som.; *CY 1989*) b June 2, 1965
*Wazir Ali, S. (C. Ind., S. Punjab & Patiala) b Sept. 15, 1903, d June 17, 1950
*Wazir Mohammad (B'pur & Kar.) b Dec. 22, 1929
Weale, S. D. (OUCC) b Sept. 16, 1967
*Webb, M. G. (Otago & Cant.) b June 22, 1947
*Webb, P. N. (Auck.) b July 14, 1957
Webb, R. J. (Otago) b Sept. 15, 1952
Webb, R. T. (Sussex) b July 11, 1922
Webb, S. G. (Manager Australians in England 1961) b Jan. 31, 1900, d Aug. 5, 1976
*Webbe, A. J. (OUCC & Middx) b Jan. 16, 1855, d Feb. 19, 1941
Webster, J. (CUCC & Northants) b Oct. 28, 1917
Webster, Dr R. V. (Warwicks. & Otago) b June 10, 1939
Webster, W. H. (CUCC & Middx; Pres. MCC 1976-77) b Feb. 22, 1910, d June 19, 1986
*Weekes, E. D. (B'dos; *CY 1951*) b Feb. 26, 1925
*Weekes, K. H. (Jam.) b Jan. 24, 1912
Weeks, R. T. (Warwicks.) b April 30, 1930
*Weerasinghe, C. D. U. S. (TU) b March 1, 1968
*Weir, G. L. (Auck.) b June 2, 1908
*Wellard, A. W. (Som.; *CY 1936*) b April 8, 1902, d Dec. 31, 1980
*Wellham, D. M. (NSW) b March 13, 1959
Wellings, E. M. (OUCC & Surrey) b April 6, 1909
Wells, A. P. (Sussex & Border) b Oct. 2, 1961
Wells, B. D. (Glos. & Notts.) b July 27, 1930
Wells, C. M. (Sussex, Border & W. Prov.) b March 3, 1960
Wenman, E. G. (Kent & England) b Aug. 18, 1803, d Dec. 31, 1879
Wensley, A. F. (Sussex) b May 23, 1898, d June 17, 1970
*Wesley, C. (Natal) b Sept. 5, 1937
*Wessels, K. C. (OFS, W. Prov., N. Tvl, Sussex, Qld & E. Prov.) b Sept. 14, 1957
West, G. H. (Editor of *Wisden* 1880-86) b 1851, d Oct. 6, 1896
*Westcott, R. J. (W. Prov.) b Sept. 19, 1927
Weston, M. J. (Worcs.) b April 8, 1959
*Wettimuny, M. D. (SL) b June 11, 1951
*Wettimuny, S. (SL; *CY 1985*) b Aug. 12, 1956
Wettimuny, S. R. de S. (SL) b Feb. 7, 1949
*Wharton, A. (Lancs. & Leics.) b April 30, 1923
*Whatmore, D. F. (Vic.) b March 16, 1954
Wheatley, K. J. (Hants) b Jan. 20, 1946
Wheatley, O. S. (CUCC, Warwicks. & Glam.; *CY 1969*) b May 28, 1935
Whitaker, Haddon (Editor of *Wisden* 1940-43) b Aug. 30, 1908, d Jan. 5, 1982
*Whitaker, J. J. (Leics.; *CY 1987*) b May 5, 1962
Whitcombe, P. A. (OUCC & Middx) b April 23, 1923
White, A. F. T. (CUCC, Warwicks. & Worcs.) b Sept. 5, 1915
*White, D. W. (Hants & Glam.) b Dec. 14, 1935
White, E. C. S. (NSW) b July 14, 1913
*White, G. C. (Tvl) b Feb. 5, 1882, d Oct 17, 1918
*White, J. C. (Som.; *CY 1929*) b Feb. 19, 1891, d May 2, 1961

White, Hon. L. R. (5th Lord Annaly) (Middx & Victory Test) b March 15, 1927, d Sept. 30, 1990
White, R. A. (Middx & Notts.) b Oct. 6, 1936
White, R. C. (CUCC, Glos. & Tvl) b Jan. 29, 1941
*White, W. A. (B'dos) b Nov. 20, 1938
Whitehead, J. P. (Yorks. & Worcs.) b Sept. 3, 1925
Whitehouse, J. (Warwicks.) b April 8, 1949
*Whitelaw, P. E. (Auck.) b Feb. 10, 1910, d Aug. 28, 1988
Whitfield, B. J. (Natal) b March 14, 1959
Whitfield, E. W. (Surrey & Northants) b May 31, 1911
Whiting, N. H. (Worcs.) b Oct. 2, 1920
Whitington, R. S. (S. Aust. & Victory Tests; Writer) b June 30, 1912, d March 13, 1984
*Whitney, M. R. (NSW & Glos.) b Feb. 24, 1959
Whittaker, G. J. (Surrey) b May 29, 1916
Whitticase, P. (Leics.) b March 15, 1965
Whittingham, N. B. (Notts.) b Oct. 22, 1940
*Whitty, W. J. (S. Aust.) b Aug. 15, 1886, d Jan. 30, 1974
*Whysall, W. W. (Notts.; *CY 1925*) b Oct. 31, 1887, d Nov. 11, 1930
*Wickremasinghe, A. G. D. (NCC) b Dec. 27, 1965
*Wiener, J. M. (Vic.) b May 1, 1955
*Wight, C. V. (BG) b July 28, 1902, d Oct. 4, 1969
*Wight, G. L. (BG) b May 28, 1929
Wight, P. B. (BG, Som., & Cant.) b June 25, 1930
Wijegunawardene, K. I. W. (CCC) b Nov. 23, 1964
*Wijesuriya, R. G. C. E. (Mor.) b Feb. 18, 1960
Wild, D. J. (Northants) b Nov. 28, 1962
*Wiles, C. A. (B'dos & T/T) b Aug. 11, 1892, d Nov. 4, 1957
Wilkins, A. H. (Glam., Glos. & N. Tvl) b Aug. 22, 1953
Wilkins, C. P. (Derbys., Border, E. Prov. & Natal) b July 31, 1944
*Wilkinson, L. L. (Lancs.) b Nov. 5, 1916
Wilkinson, P. A. (Notts.) b Aug. 23, 1951
Wilkinson, Col. W. A. C. (OUCC) b Dec. 6, 1892, d Sept. 19, 1983
Willatt, G. L. (CUCC, Notts. & Derbys.) b May 7, 1918
*Willett, E. T. (Comb. Is. & Leewards) b May 1, 1953
Willett, M. D. (Surrey) b April 21, 1933
Willey, P. (Northants, E. Prov. & Leics.) b Dec. 6, 1949
Williams, A. B. (Jam.) b Nov. 21, 1949
Williams, C. B. (B'dos) b March 8, 1926
Williams, C. C. P. (Lord Williams of Elvet) (OUCC & Essex) b Feb. 9, 1933
Williams, D. (T/T) b Nov. 4, 1963
Williams, D. L. (Glam.) b Nov. 20, 1946
*Williams, E. A. V. (B'dos) b April 10, 1914
*Williams, N. F. (Middx, Windwards & Tas.) b July 2, 1962
Williams, R. G. (Northants) b Aug. 10, 1957
*Williams, R. J. (Natal) b April 12, 1912, d May 14, 1984
Williamson, J. G. (Northants) b April 4, 1936
*Willis, R. G. D. (Surrey, Warwicks. & N. Tvl; *CY 1978*) b May 30, 1949
*Willoughby, J. T. (SA) b Nov. 7, 1874, d *circa* 1955
Willsher, E. (Kent & All-England) b Nov. 22, 1828, d Oct. 7, 1885
Wilmot, K. (Warwicks.) b April 3, 1911
Wilson, A. (Lancs.) b April 24, 1921
Wilson, A. E. (Middx & Glos.) b May 18, 1910
*Wilson, Rev. C. E. M. (CUCC & Yorks.) b May 15, 1875, d Feb. 8, 1944
*Wilson, D. (Yorks. & MCC) b Aug. 7, 1937
Wilson, E. F. (Surrey) b June 24, 1907, d March 3, 1981
*Wilson, E. R. (CUCC & Yorks.) b March 25, 1879, d July 21, 1957
Wilson, J. V. (Yorks.; *CY 1961*) b Jan. 17, 1921
*Wilson, J. W. (Vic. & S. Aust.) b Aug. 20, 1921, d Oct. 13, 1985
Wilson, P. H. L. (Surrey, Som. & N. Tvl) b Aug. 17, 1958
Wilson, R. C. (Kent) b Feb. 18, 1928
*Wimble, C. S. (Tvl) b Jan. 9, 1864, d Jan. 28, 1930
Windows, A. R. (Glos. & CUCC) b Sept. 25, 1942
Winfield, H. M. (Notts.) b June 13, 1933
Wingfield Digby, Rev. A. R. (OUCC) b July 25, 1950
Winn, C. E. (OUCC & Sussex) b Nov. 13, 1926
*Winslow, P. L. (Sussex, Tvl & Rhod.) b May 21, 1929
Wisden, John (Sussex; founder John Wisden and Co. and *Wisden's Cricketers' Almanack*) b Sept. 5, 1826, d April 5, 1884
*Wishart, K. L. (BG) b Nov. 28, 1908, d Oct. 18, 1972
Wolton, A. V. G. (Warwicks.) b June 12, 1919, d Sept. 9, 1990
*Wood, A. (Yorks.; *CY 1939*) b Aug. 25, 1898, d April 1, 1973
*Wood, B. (Yorks., Lancs., Derbys. & E. Prov.) b Dec. 26, 1942
Wood, C. J. B. (Leics.) b Nov. 21, 1875, d June 5, 1960

Wood, D. J. (Sussex) b May 19, 1914, d March 12, 1989
*Wood, G. E. C. (CUCC & Kent) b Aug. 22, 1893, d March 18, 1971
*Wood, G. M. (W. Aust.) b Nov. 6, 1956
*Wood, H. (Kent & Surrey; *CY 1891*) b Dec. 14, 1854, d April 30, 1919
*Wood, R. (Lancs. & Vic.) b March 7, 1860, d Jan. 6, 1915
*Woodcock, A. J. (S. Aust.) b Feb. 27, 1948
Woodcock, John C. (Editor of *Wisden* 1980-86) b Aug. 7, 1926
*Woodfull, W. M. (Vic.; *CY 1927*) b Aug. 22, 1897, d Aug. 11, 1965
Woodhead, F. G. (Notts.) b Oct. 30, 1912
Woodhouse, G. E. S. (Som.) b Feb. 15, 1924, d Jan. 19, 1988
**Woods, S. M. J. (CUCC & Som.; *CY 1889*) b April 13, 1867, d April 30, 1931
Wookey, S. M. (CUCC & OUCC) b Sept. 2, 1954
Wooler, C. R. D. (Leics. & Rhod.) b June 30, 1930
Wooller, W. (CUCC & Glam.) b Nov. 20, 1912
Woolley, C. N. (Glos. & Northants) b May 5, 1886, d Nov. 3, 1962
*Woolley, F. E. (Kent; *CY 1911*) b May 27, 1887, d Oct. 18, 1978
*Woolley, R. D. (Tas.) b Sept. 16, 1954
*Woolmer, R. A. (Kent, Natal & W. Prov.; *CY 1976*) b May 14, 1948
*Worrall, J. (Vic.) b May 12, 1863, d Nov. 17, 1937
*Worrell, Sir F. M. M. (B'dos & Jam.; *CY 1951*) b Aug. 1, 1924, d March 13, 1967
Worsley, D. R. (OUCC & Lancs.) b July 18, 1941
Worsley, Sir W. A. 4th Bt (Yorks.; Pres. MCC 1961-62) b April 5, 1890, d Dec. 4, 1973
*Worthington, T. S. (Derbys.; *CY 1937*) b Aug. 21, 1905, d Aug. 31, 1973
Wright, A. (Warwicks.) b Aug. 25, 1941
Wright, A. J. (Glos.) b July 27, 1962
*Wright, C. W. (CUCC & Notts.) b May 27, 1863, d Jan. 10, 1936
*Wright, D. V. P. (Kent; *CY 1940*) b Aug. 21, 1914
*Wright, J. G. (N. Dist., Derbys. & Cant.) b July 5, 1954
*Wright, K. J. (W. Aust. & S. Aust.) b Dec. 27, 1953
Wright, L. G. (Derbys.; *CY 1906*) b June 15, 1862, d Jan. 11, 1953
Wyatt, J. G. (Som.) b June 19, 1963
*Wyatt, R. E. S. (Warwicks. & Worcs.; *CY 1930*) b May 2, 1901
*Wynne, O. E. (Tvl & W. Prov.) b June 1, 1919, d July 13, 1975
*Wynyard, E. G. (Hants) b April 1, 1861, d Oct. 30, 1936

Yachad, M. (N. Tvl & Tvl) b Nov. 17, 1960
*Yadav, N. S. (H'bad) b Jan. 26, 1957
*Yajurvindra Singh (M'tra & S'tra) b Aug. 1, 1952
*Yallop, G. N. (Vic.) b Oct. 7, 1952
*Yardley, B. (W. Aust.) b Sept. 5, 1947
*Yardley, N. W. D. (CUCC & Yorks.; *CY 1948*) b March 19, 1915, d Oct. 4, 1989
Yardley, T. J. (Worcs. & Northants) b Oct. 27, 1946
Yarnold, H. (Worcs.) b July 6, 1917, d Aug. 13, 1974
*Yashpal Sharma (Punjab) b Aug. 11, 1954
Yawar Saeed (Som. & Punjab) b Jan. 22, 1935
*Yograj Singh (Haryana & Punjab) b March 25, 1958
Young, D. M. (Worcs. & Glos.) b April 15, 1924
*Young, H. I. (Essex) b Feb. 5, 1876, d Dec. 12, 1964
*Young, J. A. (Middx) b Oct. 14, 1912
*Young, R. A. (CUCC & Sussex) b Sept. 16, 1885, d July 1, 1968
*Younis Ahmed (Lahore, Kar., Surrey, PIA, S. Aust., Worcs. & Glam.) b Oct. 20, 1947
*Yuile, B. W. (C. Dist.) b Oct. 29, 1941

*Zaheer Abbas (Kar., Glos., PWD, Dawood Indust., Sind & PIA; *CY 1972*) b July 24, 1947
Zahid Ahmed (PIA) b Nov. 15, 1961
*Zakir Khan (Sind, Peshawar & ADBP) b April 3, 1963
Zesers, A. K. (S. Aust.) b March 11, 1967
*Zoehrer, T. J. (W. Aust.) b Sept. 25, 1961
*Zulch, J. W. (Tvl) b Jan. 2, 1886, d May 19, 1924
*Zulfiqar Ahmed (B'pur & PIA) b Nov. 22, 1926
*Zulqarnain (Pak. Rlwys & Lahore) b May 25, 1962

OBITUARIES

ALDERMAN, ALBERT EDWARD, who died on June 4, 1990, aged 82, was a member of the Derbyshire side which won the County Championship in 1936 after several years of steady progress up the table. He developed into a reliable, secure opening batsman and a steadying influence when the innings was in its formative stage. Derbyshire's rise from the very depths – in 1920 they lost seventeen out of the eighteen matches in their programme – was largely due to the influence and devoted service of three men: G. R. Jackson, the captain from 1922 to 1930, A. W. Richardson, captain from 1931 to 1936, and Sam Cadman, the former professional and highly respected head coach with a gift for spotting talent. Jackson and Richardson, by firm discipline and positive leadership, engendered a team spirit and efficiency seldom before attained, while Cadman behind the scenes kept bringing forward young players of promise, many of whom went on to successful careers. Alderman was a product of the fine work being done in the nursery. He made his first-class dèbut in 1928, and by 1931 was established as a regular member of the eleven when he had a match at The Oval to be proud of, hitting 113 not out, his maiden century, followed by an unbeaten 50 in the second innings. In 1933 Alderman for a second time failed by a narrow margin to reach his 1,000 runs, but from 1934 to 1939 he was comfortably over this particular hurdle. Also in 1934 his average exceeded 30 for the first time, and among many splendid performances he batted especially well against Hampshire at Portsmouth in both innings in an effort to stave off defeat. In the follow-on, he resisted for five hours and a half in carrying his bat for a chanceless 124. This sort of situation seemed to bring out the best in him.

In Derbyshire's Championship year in 1936, Alderman's contribution in the outfield received special commendation. At The Oval, when Tom Barling of Surrey swept a ball from Copson to leg and everyone thought the hit was carrying for six, Alderman sprinted fully 30 yards round the fine-leg boundary and brought off a wonderful catch, with his outstretched right hand just above the palings. *Wisden* pronounced that the catch "should live in the memories of all those who were present on the Wednesday". Tendulkar's effort at Lord's in 1990 to dismiss Lamb behind the bowler, if not an exact replica, had many points in common with Alderman's brilliant feat. In 1937 he enjoyed his best summer, with 1,509 runs at 33.53 including three centuries. Against Leicestershire at Chesterfield he made 175, his highest score, and his opening stand of 233 with Denis Smith, in three hours, followed by 149 for the second wicket with Stanley Worthington, was the foundation of a crushing victory by an innings and 199 runs. Smith, the fluent left-hander, and Worthington were aggressive players for whom Alderman was often the perfect foil. He also scored 112 against the touring New Zealanders at Derby. The highlight of his 1938 season was a brilliant catch at Trent Bridge, which he brought off by running at full tilt in front of the startled members in the pavilion, once again taking the ball in his outstretched right hand. The victim was G. F. H. Heane. Alderman may at times have been prosaic and almost anonymous at the crease, but in the deep field he was a star of the first magnitude. He resumed his interrupted career in 1946 without ever really getting into his stride again. He had in the end to be satisfied with 12,376 runs for an average of 25.94. In the course of his career he exceeded 1,000 runs six times, hit twelve hundreds and held 202 catches. In assessing his value to his county, a generous estimate of the number of runs he saved by his brilliant fielding should be put into the equation. Alderman stood as an umpire on the county circuit in the mid-1960s and subsequently was coach at Repton.

ALLEN, GEORGE RAYMOND, who died in Montserrat on September 20, 1990, aged 41, made his début in first-class cricket in the West Indies in 1966 when he was only sixteen. As an off-spinning all-rounder, he played in five matches in the Shell Shield for the Combined Islands, for whom he took eleven wickets with a best performance of three for 9 against Trinidad in 1971-72. In the same year he made his highest score of 53 for Leeward Islands against G. T. Dowling's New Zealand tourists.

AMES, LESLIE ETHELBERT GEORGE, CBE, who died suddenly at his home in Canterbury on February 26, 1990, aged 84, was without a doubt the greatest wicket-keeper-batsman the game has so far produced; and yet, at the time he was playing, it used to be said there were better wicket-keepers than Ames, and that he was in the England team because of his batting. If this was so, would Jardine, for example, have preferred him to Duckworth in Australia in 1932-33? Surely not. When fully fit, Ames was England's first-choice wicket-keeper from 1931 to 1939, when he virtually gave up the job. For Kent, he was an integral part of their Championship side from 1927 to the first match of 1951, when a sharp recurrence of back trouble, which had dogged him for so long, brought his career to an end while he was actually at the crease. By this time he had amassed 37,248 runs, average 43.51, made 102 hundreds, including nine double-hundreds, and passed 1,000 runs in a season seventeen times, going on to 3,000 once and 2,000 on five occasions. He had had a direct interest in 1,121 dismissals, of which more than 1,000 were effected when he was keeping wicket. His total of 418 stumpings is easily a record.

Born at Elham near Canterbury on December 3, 1905, Ames went to Harvey Grammar School in Folkestone and at seventeen was brought to the notice of the Kent authorities. It was the county coach at the time, G. J. V. Weigall, who persuaded him to take up wicket-keeping as a second string to his bow, and a year or two passed before the young man began to appreciate the soundness of this advice. However, in 1927, Ames's first full season, his aggressive approach to batting and form behind the stumps repeatedly caught the eye. And all the time his famous partnership with "Tich" Freeman was being cemented. In 1928, these two astounded the world of cricket: Freeman took a record 304 wickets and Ames, making 122 dismissals and 1,919 runs, achieved the wicket-keeper's double for the first time. A year later he repeated what had been a unique achievement, but with a record 128 dismissals, and in 1932, when he was in superlative all-round form, he scored 2,482 runs, including nine centuries, at 57.72 to finish third in the national averages and made a record 64 stumpings in a total of 104 dismissals. In 1933, a batsman's year, he enjoyed an *annus mirabilis*. Far from feeling stale after a gruelling tour of Australia, he discovered an even greater appetite for runs, scoring 3,058 including three double-hundreds and six other three-figure innings. He also made the highest score of his career, 295 against Gloucestershire at Folkestone, and two separate hundreds in a match for the first time, against Northamptonshire at Dover. To cap it all, there were another 68 dismissals. Ames's innings of 295 was an excellent example of the tempo he regularly maintained once he was going; it took a little over 240 minutes and contained a six and 34 fours. It is probably true to say that he scored at around 50 runs per hour throughout his career, and it is hardly surprising that a player of his calibre should have won the Lawrence Trophy twice, in 1936 and 1939, both centuries being made in under 70 minutes. When Kent made 803 for four declared against Essex at Brentwood in 1934, Ames contributed an unbeaten 202, ensuring that the declaration could be made at lunch on the second day. In the season of 1937 he was as busy as ever, passing 2,000 runs for the third time and effecting 74 dismissals, though no longer with the help of Freeman, who had retired.

Ames represented England in 47 Tests, making 2,434 runs, including eight hundreds, and 97 dismissals (74 catches and 23 stumpings). He toured Australia with MCC in 1928-29 as reserve wicket-keeper to Duckworth, and would have played in the final Test at Melbourne, purely as a batsman, but for breaking a finger keeping to Larwood. Instead, he made his début against South Africa at The Oval in 1929 and toured the Caribbean under F. S. G. Calthorpe in the following winter. In the second of the representative matches (since granted full Test status) he helped Hendren in a match-winning stand of 237 for the fourth wicket in England's second innings, his 105 being the first century by an England wicket-keeper. In the fourth and final match, at Kingston, he hit his highest Test score of 149. Against New Zealand in 1931, Ames (137) and G. O. B. Allen (122) put on 246 together for the eighth wicket at Lord's, which has remained a record in Test matches for that wicket. The runs, which rescued England from a paltry 190 for seven, were made in under three hours, while at Christchurch in 1932-33 he and Hammond "flogged the bowling all over the ground" to the tune of 242 in 144 minutes for the fourth wicket. More restraint was expected of him at Lord's in 1934 against Australia on the first afternoon, when he and Leyland came together and added 129 in what was to prove a crucial partnership. Failure then, and England instead of Australia would have been caught on the sticky wicket so brilliantly exploited by Verity. Ames used to say that he was more proud of this innings of 120 than of all his others; *Wisden* simply described it as "inspiring". In 1935, against South Africa at The Oval, he made 123 before lunch on the final day, a tremendous effort and still the most runs in the morning session of a Test match. In 1938 at Lord's, Hammond (240) and Ames (83) added 186 for England's sixth wicket against Australia, and that winter in South Africa, on his last major tour, Ames again helped his captain in a major partnership. At Cape Town, in the Second Test, the pair put on 197 in 145 minutes for the fourth wicket, both scoring hundreds. Ames finished the series with an average of 67.80 and a career average in Tests of 40.56.

Ames was a correct player with a fluent classical style; a magnificent driver, especially when moving out to the pitch. When set, he employed the lofted drive over the inner ring of fielders with rare judgement and skill, and he could turn good-length balls into half-volleys on lightning feet. Woe betide any bowler who started dropping short: he would be hammered to the cover boundary, or despatched to leg with powerful hooks or pulls. A superb entertainer, he was popular with spectators up and down the land, but praise or flattery would leave him unmoved: he could never understand what all the fuss was about. Behind the stumps he maintained a consistently high standard. Among his more notable efforts when playing for England were eight dismissals against West Indies at The Oval in 1933, and against South Africa in 1938-39 he conceded only one bye for every 275 balls delivered in the series. On the Bodyline tour he took the thunderbolts of Larwood and Voce with quiet efficiency. His style was unobtrusive; there were no flamboyant gestures. He saw the ball so early that he was invariably in the right position without having to throw himself about. His glovework was neat and economical, his stumpings almost apologetic.

During the Second World War, Ames rose to the rank of Squadron-Leader in the RAF and played a little one-day cricket, even taking a hat-trick against Epsom CC with his slow spinners. In the five post-war seasons before his retirement, playing now as a batsman, he enjoyed an Indian summer, adding nearly 10,000 runs to his already formidable aggregate. In 1947, and again in 1948, he made seven hundreds, his total of 2,137 runs in the Championship in 1947 being reminiscent of 1933. In 1950 he reached his 100th hundred in brilliant style to win the match against Middlesex during the Canterbury Week, becoming only the twelfth player to achieve this milestone. His batting had lacked none of its old virility and panache, but that winter, captaining the Commonwealth team in

India, he was often worried by the back trouble which was soon to end his playing days.

Well versed in man management and administrative skills from his war service, he was given charge of three MCC tours – the 1966-67 Under-25 team to Pakistan, and the senior sides to the West Indies in 1967-68 and Ceylon and Pakistan in 1968-69 – and he was a selector from 1950 to 1956 and again in 1958, the first professional to be appointed as such. From 1960 to 1974 he was secretary/manager of Kent, a post he filled with conspicuous success, commanding the respect of the players by his sense of discipline and absolute fairness. From years of failure Kent improved steadily until they won the Championship in 1970. The county's second great partnership, with Colin Cowdrey in charge in the middle and Ames working behind the scenes, had had its reward at last, and by now Kent were becoming one of the dominant forces in the limited-overs competitions. Ames was an honorary life member of MCC and was in time elected to the Club's committee. In retirement he remained fit and active, spending many pleasurable days on the golf course, where his natural sense of timing stood him in good stead. If ever there was a true Man of Kent it was he. The attendance of a thousand people at his memorial service in Canterbury Cathedral was a worthy tribute to him.

ARMSTRONG, NORMAN FOSTER, who died at Bournemouth on January 19, 1990, aged 97, was the second-oldest English first-class cricketer at the time of his death. Armstrong had a most unusual career. Having made one appearance as an amateur for Leicestershire in 1919, he was not seen again until 1926, when he embarked on a highly successful professional career at the ripe age of 33, crossing the divide between good club cricket and the first-class game unusually quickly. Armstrong had made 19,002 runs for his county by the end of the 1939 season at an average of 32.98, reaching his 1,000 runs in thirteen consecutive seasons from 1927 and once exceeding 2,000. It is worth noting that for these years he averaged 1,430 runs per season. He put together 36 hundreds.

Armstrong needed no more than the season of 1926 for the inevitable adjustments to his game, making the most of the excellent coaching and advice provided by Leicestershire at this period. His defence, later to become rock-like, was tightened up, but wisely no attempt was made to interfere with his highly idiosyncratic array of scoring strokes on the leg side, of which the most telling was a species of short-arm hook in front of square. For the rest of his runs, he relied on a variety of pushes, nudges and prods, executed at the last minute just as the frustrated bowler thought he had broken through. The special hallmarks of his batting, courage and concentration when faced with high speed, were demonstrated in an innings of 34 not out, in a total of 92, against Nottinghamshire in July 1927 at Leicester: Larwood and Barrett were in full cry, each taking five for 20, all clean bowled. His first hundred, an undefeated 113 at Northampton, took him all of four and a half hours and was a typically painstaking effort. In 1928, going in at No. 3, the position he was to make his own till the end of his career, he enjoyed the distinction of heading the county averages for the first time, with 1,646 runs at 35.78. This was a remarkable advance, and his increase of skill was underlined by the highest score of his career – an innings of 186 against Yorkshire, during which he was given a thorough examination by Wilfred Rhodes, who bowled 69 overs. Impervious to all his wiles, Armstrong stayed at the crease for 400 minutes. Leicestershire made more than 500 and were able to enforce the follow-on. A year later, he took a hundred off the reigning champions, Lancashire. The better the opposition, the better he played. In 1930 he made 147 against a Surrey attack which included Gover and Maurice Allom, and his five centuries and aggregate of more than 1,500 runs were most impressive in the wet summer of 1932. In 1933, a summer of good wickets and continuous sunshine, Armstrong reached a peak of 2,113 runs for an average of 43.12, becoming the first Leicestershire batsman to score 2,000 runs for the county in a season. In 1934, when he took a hundred off Larwood and Voce at Trent Bridge, and again in 1935 he topped the county averages with impressive figures. No-one enjoyed batting conditions much in 1936, but Armstrong made his 1,000 runs, and in 1937, although he played second fiddle to Leslie Berry, his colleague in many a useful partnership over the years, he none the less had a fine season with more than 1,700 runs, at an average of 42, and five hundreds. He was not far short of his 47th birthday when in 1939 he was his county's leading batsman for the fifth time, showing greater freedom than ever before and producing off-side strokes of rare quality, a revelation to those who knew him best.

Owing to his inflexible determination at the crease, and the frequency with which he rescued a lost cause in a weak batting side, he came to be known as "the Valiant Armstrong". But his contribution did not end there: he held 223 catches, mostly in the slips, and was a useful medium-pace bowler who could break a partnership when needed, his 110 wickets costing 40.53 each.

BAINES, LT-COLONEL MICHAEL FITZROY TALBOT, who was a useful right-handed batsman and fast-medium bowler, died at Salisbury on March 9, 1990 at the age of 91. He was a regular soldier and played in one first-class match for the Army, against the University at Cambridge in 1926. He batted at No. 11 in both innings and failed to score, but was once not out; in his eight overs he conceded 39 runs without taking a wicket. He was one of the oldest surviving first-class cricketers.

BRAIN, DESMOND MORRAH, who died at Tumut, New South Wales, on March 1, 1990, aged 80, played for Tasmania in three first-class matches in 1930-31. Against the touring West Indians at Launceston he made 11 and 16, batting at No. 7, and when the West Indians went in, he had the satisfaction of catching George Headley for 3. Brain also played against Victoria at Melbourne, where he scored 93, and altogether he made 156 runs for an average of 26.00.

BRUCE-LOCKHART, RAB BROUGHAM, who died at Burneside in Cumbria on May 1, 1990, aged 73, had made a great reputation for himself as a leg-spinning all-round cricketer at the Edinburgh Academy before going up to Cambridge. Without quoting chapter and verse, it is enough to say that in his five years in the XI he made comfortably more than 2,500 runs for an average of 40 and took more than 100 wickets with his leg-spin at a little more than 12 apiece. He was at the head of both the batting and bowling averages in his last two years, and captain in 1935. Sadly, the high expectations held for him went largely unfulfilled at the University. Loss of form and confidence, a fault in his batting technique, or perhaps lack of subtlety in his bowling may have accounted in one way or another for this disappointing outcome. In the Freshmen's match of 1937, although failing to score, he took six for 34, and a half-century and four wickets for 6 runs for the Perambulators against the Etceteras paved the way for his début for the University, against Nottinghamshire. The match, however, was ruined by rain, and in his second trial, against Middlesex, he made but a few runs in each innings and bowled out Patsy Hendren. His only other first-class game was against Yorkshire in 1938, but again he did not impress. In his three first-class appearances, he scored 32 runs, average 8.00, and his one wicket cost 146 runs. While failing to emulate his father, John, by winning a Blue at cricket, he did follow in his footsteps by playing rugby for Cambridge and Scotland, and by taking up schoolmastering. He was headmaster of Loretto from 1960 to 1976.

COOPER, SIR HENRY, who died in Auckland on September 4, 1990, aged 81, was the manager of the first New Zealand team to tour India and Pakistan, under the captaincy of H. B. Cave in 1955-56. Born in Derbyshire, whence his parents emigrated when he was four, he played three first-class games for Auckland in the war years, scoring 99 runs (average 24.75) with a highest innings of 52 against Wellington in 1943-44. Greatly revered as a secondary school headmaster, he had an association with Auckland Grammar School which lasted 68 years, first as a pupil, then on the teaching staff from 1935 to 1953, and later as headmaster from 1954 to 1973. His knighthood was given for services to the community.

COOPER, RICHARD CLAUDE, who collapsed from a heart attack and died near Malmesbury on March 14, 1990, aged 44, made something of a name for himself in West Country cricket circles from 1967 to 1989 by his aggressive, hard-hitting batting for Wiltshire and various club sides. When he made a hundred in each innings for Wiltshire against their Second Eleven at Devizes in 1970, Somerset were sufficiently impressed to offer him a contract. The door was open. Here was the chance to knuckle down, learn the business and show what the "West Country Milburn", as he was called, could do at a higher level. For Cooper bore a remarkable resemblance to the former England batsman: he was built on the same generous scale; he had the same natural gifts and a flair for hitting the cover off the ball. The difference between the two men lay in their temperaments. The keen edge of competition brought out the best in Milburn when he went to Northampton, and he soon became a Test player; it seemed to inhibit Cooper, whose period with Somerset from 1972 to 1974 brought him little joy. He preferred the more comfortable environment of his native Wiltshire, for whom he made nearly 5,000 runs at an average of 30, and he continued to make hay for clubs such as Malmesbury and Chippenham. In 1972 his 95 on a rain-affected pitch for Somerset against Minor Counties (South), in the Benson and Hedges Cup at Plymouth, rescued his side from an embarrassing position and earned him the Gold Award. His one first-class match was against Nottinghamshire at Trent Bridge in 1972 where he made 4 runs in his two innings. It was unfortunate that such a rare talent could not have yielded richer dividends.

COOTE, CYRIL ERNEST, BEM, who died at the wheel of his car at Cottenham on January 24, 1990, aged 80, was one of the best-known and most widely respected groundsmen in the country. Under him the wicket at Fenner's became famous. Coote, no mean player himself, not only understood thoroughly all the stages of pitch preparation, but was convinced that no young player however gifted, can be expected to develop into a first-class cricketer unless he i given the chance to play his shots on a surface which has both pace and a reasonable bounce. He took over at Cambridge in 1935 and did not finally give up his duties until 1980. During that long period, a whole cavalcade of aspiring undergraduates had the enormous benefit of occupying the crease on his square May and Dexter, for example, were doubly fortunate in moving on from th pitches at Charterhouse and Radley to the perfection of Fenner's. It was n wonder that they both hit the ball so fluently and with such power. But Cyri Coote was much more than a groundsman; he was also a guide, counsellor and friend to all undergraduates who sought his advice when things were not goin well with their game. As a player he would have more than held his own in first class cricket, if he had been able to follow that path. However, he had to live wit an old soccer injury which left him lame. Minor Counties cricket for Cambridge shire, with a programme of eight two-day matches per season, made much mor sense, and as a left-handed opening bat he made nearly 3,000 runs for the between 1932 and 1939. His best year was 1935, when he made 675 runs for a average of 56.25 and also played in four Minor Counties representative matches, having most success against the University at Cambridge, where he scored 49 and 46. He captained Cambridgeshire in 1938 and 1939 and from 1946 to 1949, finishing with a flourish by making 200 against Berkshire.

CROOM, LESLIE CHARLES BRYAN, who died on December 20, 1989, aged 69, was taken on to the Warwickshire staff as a professional in 1949 but was not re-engaged. A sound right-handed batsman, he was given four games, but with a highest score of 26, against Essex at Brentwood, and 73 runs in all for an average of 9.12, he made no real impression. Croom returned to the Birmingham League, playing for West Bromwich Dartmouth. He was the son of A. J. W. Croom, who made more than 17,000 runs for the Midland county between the wars.

DUNKLEY, MAURICE EDWARD FRANK, who died at Preston in Rutland on December 27, 1989, aged 75, played as a young professional for Northamptonshire in the last three pre-war seasons. In 36 matches he made 904 runs at an average of 15.06, suggesting in a number of useful innings, especially in 1938, that he might have improved enough to make the grade. That season he hit his highest score of 70 at Scarborough against the prospective champions, Yorkshire, helping his captain, R. P. Nelson, add 102 for the eighth wicket; a week earlier he had made 50 against Sussex at Northampton. An all-round sportsman, Dunkley played soccer for Manchester City, making 51 first-team appearances before and after the war, and Northampton Town. Later in life he became an excellent golfer.

DYER, DENNIS VICTOR, the South African opening batsman, who died at Durban on June 18, 1990, aged 76, was establishing himself in Currie Cup cricket when the Second World War seriously interrupted his career. He had announced himself in the best possible way in the 1939-40 season by making 185 on his first-class début, for Natal against Western Province at his native Durban. When first-class cricket was resumed in the southern summer of 1945-46, with eighteen "friendly" matches, Dyer made his second century, hitting 117 for Natal against Griqualand West at Pietermaritzburg in what proved to be a low-scoring game. The form he showed a year later in scoring his third and final hundred, 135 against Transvaal at Durban, helped to secure him a place in the team which toured England under Alan Melville in 1947. Melville had planned to open with Bruce Mitchell and Dyer in the Tests, but Dyer was completely out of sorts and was vulnerable to the lifting ball outside his off stump. At the same time it was clear that he was not in the best of health. Nevertheless, picked for the Third Test at Manchester, he made 62 in three hours against an England attack consisting of Edrich, Gladwin, Cranston and, for a few overs, Charles Barnett. He had no further success, although he played at Leeds and The Oval. However, Dyer had probably been carrying a grumbling appendix for some weeks before an immediate operation became necessary; happily he made a swift recovery and was able to sail home with the team. On the tour, he made 673 runs at 25.88, with a highest score of 74 against Gloucestershire at Cheltenham immediately before the Fifth Test. In 1948-49 MCC had a glimpse of him when they played Natal at Durban, but that was his final season and he retired with 1,725 first-class runs to his credit at 37.50, a figure confirming that he was far from his best in England.

EDUN, WILFRED (SONNY), who collapsed and died on June 10, 1990 after addressing a group of young cricketers in Georgetown, Guyana, was a medium-fast bowler in the improving British Guiana teams of the 1950s. He batted in the lower half of the order. In April 1955, playing for British Guiana against an Australian side still smarting from their failure to regain the Ashes from Hutton's team, he was entrusted with the new ball and took one wicket for 78 runs in 22 overs as the tourists ran up 476 for seven declared. Batting at No. 9, he made 17 not out and 6. Early in 1956, he was included in the young side which the West Indies sent to New Zealand to help prepare future Test players, but he had only two first-class matches, taking six wickets at 12.83 and heading the averages. After he had given up playing, he devoted much of his time to the administration of the game in Guyana.

EVANS, DAVID GWILLIAM LLOYD, who died at Cympengraig Drefach, Llandysul, on March 25, 1990, at the age of 56, was Glamorgan's regular wicket-keeper from 1958 to 1969, when he eventually gave way to Eifion Jones, having played in 270 games for his county. Successor to Haydn Davies, he made himself, by hard work and diligent practice, into one of the best wicket-keepers of his time: O. S. Wheatley, his captain from 1961 to 1966, reckoned that Evans dropped no more than two palpable chances during the whole of those six seasons. Apart from Wheatley himself, Evans had such testing bowlers to take as Jeff Jones, McConnon, Peter Walker, Don Shepherd with his sharp off-cut, and Wilfred Wooller. In 1962, he made six catches against Yorkshire at Cardiff, four in succession in the second innings in a match which Glamorgan won by five wickets. A year later, he had his best season, his 89 dismissals making him the leading wicket-keeper in the country and beating the Glamorgan record; with the bat, his stubborn defence, frequently as night-watchman, brought him more than 400 runs. Altogether he accomplished 503 catches and 55 stumpings, and scored 2,875 runs for an average of just over 10. He was awarded a round-the-world Winston Churchill Scholarship in 1967-68 to study coaching methods and generally to promote the game, with special reference to Australia, and in 1971 he went on the first-class umpires' list, making such a good impression that he stood in nine Tests in the first half of the 1980s. At the time of his death he had just returned to the list after a spell of ill health.

EVE, STANLEY CHARLES, who died on January 27, 1990, aged 64, was educated at Upminster School in Essex, and from the school XI he soon joined the Upminster club, for which he was to become a heavy scorer. Diminutive in stature, he did not allow his lack of inches to curb his natural aggression, and word soon reached the county that in Eve they had a promising recruit. He duly made his début in the Championship in mid-May 1949, playing as an amateur and scoring 717 eventful runs in seventeen matches at an average of 27.57. This was a fine performance, but the bare figures give no clue to the vagaries of fortune he experienced. In his second match he hit 120 at Brentwood against Warwickshire in a stay of just over two hours, completely dominating a fourth-wicket stand of 163 with Frank Vigar, whose score was 36. The Essex chronicler in *Wisden* states that he showed "mastery of the drive, cut, glance and hook and hit nineteen 4's". Soon after this, he excelled with an innings of 86 against Northamptonshire at Westcliff, this time sharing in a stand of 146 for the fourth wicket with Peter Smith, and against Leicestershire at Leicester he hit 60 in the first innings, adding 131 for the third wicket with Vigar; he was undefeated with 27 when Essex won by seven wickets. His unbeaten 69 against Surrey at Southend on a worn pitch, with Laker and Lock in full cry and Alec Bedser in support, was a plucky and resourceful effort in a losing cause. The next highest score off the bat was 12 as Essex went down by an innings. Finally, he made 109 runs in the match against the touring New Zealanders. Now for the "downs". He was bowled by Perks for 16 at Worcester, lbw to Wellard at Bath for 2, and lbw to Wooller at Ebbw Vale for 1. Against Derbyshire at Westcliff he made 9 and 0, being caught behind by Dawkes off Gladwin in the first innings and off Jackson in the second. Later on, at Southend, Alec Bedser bowled him for 0, and against Sussex, on the same ground, he twice fell to James Langridge for low scores. It will be seen that he was the victim of six different Test bowlers, exploiting his keenness to push on from the start of an innings. After the excitements of 1949, being unable to free himself from his business commitments for any length of time, Eve played intermittingly for Essex in 1950, 1951 and 1957, but did little to add to his reputation. For Upminster, however, he continued to help himself to runs almost at will, and in 1976, when he was 50, he scored more than 1,000. His full first-class record was 1,041 runs for an average of 22.14.

EVERY, TREVOR, who died at Newport on January 20, 1990, just after his 80th birthday, had to contend with a tragedy which brought to an abrupt end his career with Glamorgan as a wicket-keeper-batsman. At the pre-season nets in 1934, he found to his dismay that he was unable to pick up properly the flight of the ball. However, he started the opening match, against Kent at Cardiff, keeping wicket as usual: the scorecard shows that he must have asked for relief about halfway through Kent's first innings; and batting at No. 10 he was bowled by Freeman for 0. He was never to step on to a cricket field again. Within a day or two a specialist pronounced his optic nerve to be deteriorating so rapidly that he would soon be totally blind. Glamorgan made a moving appeal on his behalf, and more than £1,000 was raised to help him adjust to a very different way of life.

Every, who was born at Llanelli, was playing for the local club when he was spotted by some Glamorgan professionals, who recommended him for a trial with the county. In 1929 he played in nineteen matches, sharing the wicket-keeping duties with two other young professionals, and in 1930 he "trained on into a first-rate keeper". He completed 47 dismissals, a total he equalled in 1932, and his work behind the stumps, standing up to the contrasting spin of J. C. Clay and Frank Ryan, impressed many good judges. His batting also began to pick up, with a maiden fifty against Leicestershire and more than 400 runs to his credit. His 696 runs, average 21, in 1932 included his first and only century in first-class cricket, an aggressive innings of 116 against Worcestershire at Stourbridge. The highlight of his season in 1933 was the day he and Dai Davies, both local boys, made 75 and 70 respectively at Llanelli in a Championship match. They were cheered to the echo by a large and enthusiastic crowd. Then darkness fell. It is clear that, under the captaincy of M. J. Turnbull, a cricketer of high promise, lively personality, and good humour was developing along a path which might have taken him to the top. In his short career he disposed of 179 batsmen, of whom 70 were stumped, and scored 2,518 runs for an average of 16.35. After his loss of sight, he was trained in Cardiff as a stenographer by the Royal National Institute for the Blind, for whom he worked for many years. Nor did he ever lose touch with the game which had promised him so much.

GEARRY, GEORGE NEVILLE, who died in New Zealand in January 1990, aged 66, played in fourteen matches for Canterbury from 1953-54 to 1956-57. A left-hand batsman, and in club cricket a prodigious hitter, he made 337 runs, average 17.74, in first-class matches, while his right-arm medium-pace bowling brought him 32 wickets at 26 apiece. His best return was six for 32 against Wellington at Christchurch in his first season of Plunket Shield cricket.

GORE, BRIGADIER ADRIAN CLEMENTS, DSO, who died at Horton Priory on June 7, 1990, in his 91st year, was a naturally gifted all-round sportsman with a touch of genius. At Eton his talent for cricket when he was a junior or a colt was allowed to lie dormant in house leagues; or possibly he did not bother to play, preferring instead the racquets court and other delights. At all events, whether or not he was a late discovery, he burst upon the cricketing scene at the beginning of the 1918 season fully armed and ready for combat, his chief weapon being a vicious in-swinger which moved late and was delivered at a brisk fast-medium; once the shine was off, his line and length were such that he proved on many occasions to be the very devil to get away. In 1918 Gore took 51 wickets for Eton at an average of 7.51, making such an impact that E. B. Noel obtained and published in *Wisden* his full record. Consequently we know that his strike-rate was as low as 21.18. The same writer went on to say that "at times he might have bowled out anyone" and "did not need the assistance of a wind". Indeed, had he chosen a career other than the Army, and made himself available for regular first-class cricket, he might well have been a handful at a higher level.

In only the second encounter of Eton's 1918 season, Gore demolished RMC Sandhurst on an Agar's Plough pitch affected by overnight rain, his fourteen wickets in the match, including nine for 29 in the second innings, being most unfriendly treatment from one who was destined for the same academy not long after the end of term. The Ramblers were undermined in the next match, when his figures were five wickets for 35. And if that was not enough to satisfy his appetite, he and B. S. Hill-Wood were soon hustling out Charterhouse for 13 and 83, again at Eton. This time, Gore's match figures were nine for 32. Eton and Harrow played home and away matches against each other this year, neither of which was subsequently counted in the official series. At Harrow, Gore was more or less contained, but in the return he claimed four wickets for 33 and, when Eton, 7 runs behind on the first innings, pressed for a two-innings result, he stole the show with an analysis of 16–4–27–5. No wonder the editor of *Wisden* honoured him with a place among the portraits of Five Public School Cricketers of the Year.

Gore played in sixteen first-class matches between 1921 and 1932. Most of these were for the Army, for whom he proved to be a formidable and penetrative spearhead. On his first appearance at Fenner's against the University in 1921, he had figures of 12–4–17–4 and 14–4–34–2. In 1924 he played for the Combined Services against the South Africans, dismissing A. D. Nourse and H. W. Taylor, their two most experienced batsmen, in the first innings; and a year later, in the traditional Services match at Lord's, he sank the Navy with some devastating bowling. His eight wickets cost him 46 runs in 20.1 overs, it being said of his bowling that he "swerved in pronounced fashion and often very late". Probably on the strength of this performance he was chosen for the Gentlemen in the Folkestone Festival, but he achieved little of note. Further success attended his efforts at irregular intervals up until his last match for the Army at Lord's in 1932, when he again tormented the Navy's batsmen with five wickets for 84 in 41 overs. In all first-class matches he took 52 wickets for an average of 21.90. As a tail-end batsman capable of making a useful contribution, he made 142 runs in first-class cricket at 9.46, his highest score being 32 not out for the Army against Oxford University at Folkestone in 1931.

GRIMSTON, LT-COLONEL GEORGE SYLVESTER, who died at Hove on September 18, 1990, aged 85, was educated at Winchester, where he had an excellent season as an all-rounder in 1923, averaging 19 with the bat and taking 30 wickets at a cost of 17.33 with his fast-medium bowling. A year later he made his first-class début for Sussex against Lancashire at Brighton. Far from being overawed by the occasion he contributed 23 invaluable runs, which went a long way to saving the game. At Leicester he punished the bowling freely when making 47 to increase his side's lead to 118 before their opponents were routed for 45. In 1926-27, as a young officer on duty in India, he appeared twice against A. E. R. Gilligan's MCC side for the Army and Southern Punjab, but by the English summer of 1928 he was back at home, playing for Sussex. His best match was against Gloucestershire at Brighton when he made 61 and 25, and earlier he had made a fifty against the West Indians on the same ground. His bowling had hardly been called upon, but in 1929 he had an inspired spell against Middlesex at righton with an analysis of 14.3–3–40–5, including the wickets of Jack Hearne, Nigel Haig, F. T. Mann and R. W. V. Robins. He also took part in the memorable match against Kent at Hastings wherein 1,451 runs were made, with K. S. Duleepsinhji hitting 115 and 246, only the fifth instance of this feat at the time. After 1930 Grimston played no more for Sussex but became an important figure in Army cricketing circles, appearing regularly in their traditional matches. In 1937 he made 95 and 36 against Cambridge, driving "admirably", hitting fourteen fours and putting on 70 for the last wicket with C. T. Orton in the first innings. These splendid efforts could not prevent the University from winning by ten wickets. In 1939, also at Fenner's, he hit his only first-class hundred, helping . W. C. Packe put on 220 for the fifth wicket towards an Army total of 537. Finishing on this high note he raised his aggregate to 826 for an average of 21.73. He also took nine catches and eleven wickets at 38.09. In 1950 he resumed his association with Sussex by taking up the position of secretary and remained such until 1964, a period which, at the end, saw the county win the first two limited-overs finals at Lord's.

GROVES, LESLIE JOSEPH, who died in Dunedin on September 4, 1990, aged 9, had a first-class career which stretched from 1929-30 until 1949-50, but he made only fifteen appearances for his province, Otago. In his first match, at the age of eighteen, Otago used six bowlers against Wellington, but Groves, a leg-spinner, was not among them, and he batted at No. 9. His second match was seven years later, when he took a career-best four for 68 against Wellington. In all he claimed 22 wickets in first-class matches and always commanded respect. He was a useful tail-end batsman, with 285 runs at 11.40 and a best score of 35 against Canterbury in 1948-49.

HARDSTAFF, JOSEPH, junior, who died in hospital at Worksop on January , 1990, aged 78, was one of the most elegant batsmen of his generation. In point of style and suppleness of movement at the crease he could stand comparison with the greatest exponents of the art of batsmanship. He may have lacked the majesty of Hammond or the feline grace of Sobers, but his batting had a certain sheen and glamour about it, all its own. From an early age he had shown clear signs of cricketing ability, receiving invaluable advice from his father, Joe, a highly respected Nottinghamshire and England batsman and later a Test match umpire. When, at the age of sixteen, he was recommended to the Nottinghamshire authorities by Larwood, he proved to be an extremely apt pupil, and in 1930, aged nineteen, he seized his chance by making 53 not out in only his second Championship match. There followed three seasons of consolidation, his captain, Arthur Carr, preferring to nurse him along in the lower order. Carr's patience and judgement proved correct: in 1934 the young man's batting blossomed to the tune of 1,817 runs, including four hundreds. By now he had settled in at No. 4, becoming an integral part of one of the strongest batting sides in the country, and maintaining his form he played in his first Test, against South Africa, in 1935. Chosen for MCC's tour of Australia and New Zealand under E. R. T. Holmes in 1935-36, he was an outstanding success with 1,044 runs in first-class matches, his innings of 230 not out against an Australian XI at Melbourne making such an impression that his future at the highest level seemed assured. Another productive season followed in 1936, including 94 against India at Old Trafford, but on the Ashes tour of 1936-37 his form largely deserted him on the big occasions. He played in all the Tests, but 83 in a lost cause at Melbourne in the final one was his best effort by some way.

However, the disappointing tour gave way to a summer rich in achievement. Looking much sounder in method, Hardstaff made 1937 a memorable year by scoring 2,540 runs, hitting three double-hundreds and five other three-figure scores, and finishing second to Hammond in the averages with 57.72. In August alone he scored 1,150 runs. During Canterbury Week, he produced a phenomenal innings of 126 as Nottinghamshire achieved 310 in three hours to win with 4 minutes to spare. Scoring largely in front of the wicket, he reached 100 in just 5 minutes, which was to win him the Lawrence Trophy, and hit 117 out of 13 scored in an hour. In Nottinghamshire's first innings he had batted three hours for 97, and he showed similar resolve in making 243 to save the game against Middlesex at Trent Bridge when his side were facing a heavy defeat. Moreover his innings, containing two sixes and 31 fours, had a decisive influence on the outcome of the Championship; until then, Middlesex and Yorkshire had been engaged in a thrilling two-horse race. In the Tests against New Zealand he recovered lost ground by hitting two hundreds and making 350 runs with an average of 70.00, but though he maintained this splendid form in 1938, he could not find a place in England's line-up against Australia at Trent Bridge or Lord's. Failure at Leeds on a difficult pitch was made amends for by 169 not out at The Oval, where he added 215 for the sixth wicket with Hutton (364). There was general surprise when he was not chosen to tour South Africa in that winter. In the last pre-war season he was again in fine form, averaging more than 50 and making five hundreds, and he played in all three Tests against West Indies.

Hardstaff was deprived by the war of what would have been six productive seasons. As it was, he came home in November 1945 after three years on the Burma front and the following June announced his fitness and form with 205 not out against India in front of a full house at Lord's. This promised well for the continuation of his Test career, yet he could not command a regular place. On his third tour of Australia, in 1946-47, he played in only one Test, and in 1947, when he repeated his 1937 feat of hitting three double-hundreds and had the splendid aggregate of 2,396 runs with an average of 64.75, he did not play in one of the five Tests against the South Africans. He had fair success in the West Indies in 1947-48, although never happy under Allen's leadership, but the First Test against the Australians in 1948 – when in front of his home crowd he helped Compton put on 93 for the fourth wicket in an atrocious light as England were battling to save the game – proved to be his last. In 23 Tests he had scored 1,636 runs at an average of 46.74.

At county level he remained a formidable player. In 1949 he headed the national averages with 72.61 from 2,251, including eight hundreds, and by the time he retired at the end of the 1955 season he had scored 31,847 runs at an average of 44.35. His 83 hundreds included ten double-hundreds, with a highest score of 266 at Leicester in 1937. In addition to 1935-36 in Australia and New Zealand, he passed 1,000 runs thirteen times, going on to 2,000 four times, and he took 123 catches.

But the figures tell only half the story. Nurtured on the perfect Trent Bridge pitches of the 1930s, Hardstaff stood erect like a sentinel at the crease, hands high up the handle, and he was beautifully poised for attack or defence. Tall, slim and a natural athlete, he drove superbly through the covers, and could cut and force the ball away with wrists of steel generating the power. His footwork, neat and polished, would bring him effortlessly into line for the stroke he needed. He will be remembered also for his running, gathering and throwing in the deep, all of which were in the highest class; less so for his occasionally useful medium-pace bowling.

HASEEB-UL-HASAN, who was murdered by an unknown gunman at Joharabad, Pakistan on April 18, 1990, aged 25, had played in 32 first-class matches for Karachi and Karachi Blues since 1984-85. Only a month earlier, bowling left-arm medium-pace, he had taken five for 66, career-best figures against Karachi Whites in the final of the Patron's Trophy. In all he took 5 wickets at 31.50 apiece, while his left-hand batting produced 1,365 runs for an average of 31.02. His highest score was 104 against HBFC at Karachi in 1986-87.

HAZELL, HORACE LESLIE, who died at Bristol on March 31, 1990, aged 80, was one of a number of effective slow left-arm bowlers who were playing in county cricket in the 1930s, and on into the 1950s. He made his début in first-class cricket in 1929, playing in three Championship games for Somerset, but had to wait on the sidelines until 1932 for another opportunity. Standing in his way was the formidable and taciturn figure of his captain, J. C. White, who, with the retirement of Rhodes, was for a season or two the best bowler of his type in the country. However, Hazell performed so well in 1932 that he took 63 wickets at a cost of 23 each and was awarded his county cap. In 1933, a batsman's year, he found it much easier to contain batsmen than get them out. At Chilvers Coton against Warwickshire, he bowled 61 overs from the same end unchanged, a remarkable example of the metronomic accuracy he could command. He used to say himself that he could not flight the ball like J. C. White; nor was he able to impart enough spin on good wickets to trouble the best players. Nevertheless, in 1936, playing in his first full season in the Championship, he responded splendidly by taking 77 wickets at 21 apiece. In the three matches at Weston-super-Mare against Glamorgan, Hampshire and Sussex, all of whom were beaten, he captured twenty wickets. He headed the Somerset bowling averages for the first time in 1939 and had a major part in the tied game with Worcestershire at Kidderminster, taking five for 6 in their second innings and being bowled out himself when the scores were level.

The first four post-war seasons, in each of which he headed the county's averages, proved to be the most productive period of his career. In 1948 he took 105 wickets at 19.76, and a year later he had his best season with 106 wickets at 19.48, coming sixth in the national averages in a little cluster of left-handers, the other three being A. H. Kardar, Howorth and Jack Young. Once again he revelled in the conditions at Weston-super-Mare, where he dismissed 25 batsmen, an average of four per innings. Earlier in the season, at Taunton on a rain-affected pitch, he had mesmerised the whole Gloucestershire side, Tom Graveney included, returning the extraordinary analysis of 28.3–21–27–8 in the first innings. He had twelve for 63 in the match and was chiefly responsible for Somerset's first victory over their neighbours since 1938. That he was allowed to weave his web and go unscathed seems strange indeed: in the first innings he bowled 105 balls without conceding a run. At the end of 1952, when he again headed Somerset's averages, much to his surprise and disappointment his contract was not renewed. Though he was now 43, it proved to be a serious error of judgement by the committee. Without him, Somerset remained bottom of the Championship in each of the next three seasons. Hazell for his part found employment with Mitchells and Butlers in the Birmingham League.

Hazell, who also batted left-handed, was an accomplished all-round cricketer. A specialist No. 11, he was a pastmaster of the art of passive defence and could lie doggo while his partner went on accumulating, often in tight situations. He seems to have cut loose just once: at Bath in 1936 he despatched Hedley Verity for 28 in an over, including four sixes. His tubby figure and roly-poly gait ruled him out for fielding away from the bat and he developed into a high-class catcher near the wicket, especially in the slips. In the course of his 350 matches for Somerset he held 249 catches. He took 957 wickets at 23.97 and made 2,280 runs for an average of 8.17, figures which do less than justice to the value of many of his innings. He was a splendid team man; always the one to have around in the dressing-room or on the field if things were going wrong and morale was low.

HENRY, DENIS PHILIP, who died on March 27, 1990 at the age of 82, played in just one first-class match, for the Free Foresters against the University at Oxford in 1948. The match was ruined by rain. A middle-order right-hand batsman and off-spin bowler, he made a single in his only innings and conceded 16 runs in three overs without taking a wicket. He played most of his cricket for the Bank of England against good London club sides.

HIGGINS, HENRY JAMES ROY, who died at Brisbane on February 24, 1990, aged 90, was the last surviving member of the first side to represent Queensland in the Sheffield Shield, at the beginning of the 1926-27 season. Queensland performed very creditably in those early encounters, when there was no indication that they were going to have to wait so long for success in the competition. Typical of their skill and nerve was the match they played against New South Wales at Sydney from December 31, 1927 to January 5, 1928. The home state led off with 639, Kippax making 315 not out, and then bowled out Queensland for 276; Higgins, batting at No. 9, failed to score. When they followed on, however, Queensland reached 590 and made a great effort to force a win on a rain-affected pitch. In their recovery, they had owed nearly everything to Rowe (147) and Higgins, who made 179 in four hours and hit 22 fours before being run out. The last four wickets put on 255. Although making some useful scores lower down the order and occasionally going in first, he never approached this sort of form again. In six seasons he played in fourteen Shield games, making 617 runs for an average of 25.70.

HILTON, MALCOLM JAMESON, who died at Oldham on July 8, 1990, aged 61, was the best slow left-arm bowler that Lancashire produced since the turn of the century. In May 1948 he became for a short time the most-discussed young man in the cricket world when, in only his third first-class match, he twice dismissed Bradman at Old Trafford. In the Australians' first innings the nineteen-year-old Hilton bowled the great man for 14, and in the second he had him stumped after beating him with his three previous deliveries. Thereafter, fearing that all the brouhaha might spoil him, Lancashire gradually withdrew him from the front line, but not before he had claimed 41 wickets at 21.07. A year later they sensibly decided to confine Hilton's activities to Second Eleven cricket, in which, so well did he absorb the advice of the coaching staff, he dominated the Minor Counties Championship by taking 103 wickets. In 1950 he came right to the front, putting his trust more in his ability to impart sharp spin than in subtle variations of pace and flight. So impressed were the England selectors that, without any more ado, they picked him for the final Test against West Indies at The Oval. This was a tough baptism, made tougher still when Brown lost the toss, and in a total of 503 he bowled 41 wicketless overs for 91 runs. Berry, his fellow-Lancastrian, was preferred to him for Australia, but it must have been a close thing. Hilton's record of 135 wickets at less than 17 apiece was the more impressive of the two, but Berry's ability on firm pitches undoubtedly influenced the selectors. However, a similar record in 1951 earned Hilton a Test recall against South Africa at Headingley, where the pitch proved to be lifeless, a handicap to batsmen and bowlers alike. The South Africans, largely through the stolid Eric Rowan, ground out 538, and England followed suit with 505 before rain mercifully intervened. Hilton bore much of the burden, taking three for 176 in 61.3 overs, but he joined a skittish Trevor Bailey in a last-wicket stand of 60, of which his own share was 9. This included a "mighty six" off Athol Rowan. In the winter of 1951-52 he toured India with MCC, but took a long time to settle down and did not come into the Test side until the penultimate match at Kanpur, where conditions proved to be more favourable to spin than in any previous match. England won by eight wickets and "Hilton seized his chance magnificently and was one of the leading figures in the success" with match figures of nine for 93. At Madras he disposed of Hazare and Phadkar but could not prevent India from gaining their first-ever Test victory.

A moderate season in 1952 was followed by a disastrous one in Coronation year, when for the first time he was afflicted by a serious loss of control, a bowler's nightmare. He had to sit out the monsoons of 1954 in the pavilion, but when cricket was possible he took nearly 100 wickets at 20 apiece, although at times he looked vulnerable. He passed the coveted figure for the third time in 1955, yet probably had even more satisfaction from his maiden century, 100 not out at Northampton, which was compiled with his unusual repertoire of robust strokes. By 1956 he was well and truly back to his best, claiming 158 wickets at 13.96 with the excellent strike-rate of 45.56 and finishing third in the national averages. He considered his fourteen for 88 in August at Weston-super-Mare to be the highlight of his season. For Somerset, his younger brother, Jim, took eight wickets with his off-spinners. A week later, there were red faces at The Oval when Surrey were bowled out for 96 by Hilton and Tattersall; and even more embarrassment was caused early in September when, in the Champion County's match against The Rest, Surrey were again dismissed on the same ground by the Lancashire pair, losing twenty wickets for a combined total of 143. Hilton captured six wickets for 10 runs in the first innings, spinning the ball viciously from leg in helpful conditions, and the Oval faithful were reminded that there were other spinners around, apart from Lock and Laker. He was chosen as one of the Five Cricketers of the Year for the 1957 edition of *Wisden*.

By now he was still only 28, and as a slow bowler he could reasonably look forward to the best years of his career. He seemed to have put his troubles behind him, and there was an Australian tour in the offing. Instead, he was once more bedevilled by lack of consistency, suddenly losing control of his bowling without being able to account for it. And although the wet summer of 1958 brought the longed-for return to form with 94 wickets, and he achieved the best figures of his career when taking eight for 19 against the New Zealanders in a total of 144, from 1959 to 1961 he obtained only 25 wickets. Lancashire offered to re-engage him, but he preferred to go into league cricket. In 1960 he was awarded a benefit, jointly with Tattersall, which realised £11,701, a measure of their popularity. In 270 first-class matches Hilton took 1,006 wickets with an average of 19.42 and a strike-rate of 55.04. His lusty batting brought him 3,416 runs, average 12.11, and he made 202 catches in virtually all positions. Indeed his brilliant fielding made him a frequent choice as England's twelfth man.

HOLE, GRAEME BLAKE, who died in Adelaide on February 14, 1990, aged 59, played in eighteen Tests for Australia from 1951 to 1955 and toured England under A. L. Hassett in the summer of 1953. The verdict on his Test career must be that it was deeply disappointing both to the player and the selectors, who kept faith with him for as long as they reasonably could. When he was summoned to the colours against England in February 1951, he seemed to have everything in his favour, not least his personal charm, good looks and grace of movement. He batted stylishly, could bowl off-breaks, and fielded in any position. He seemed to possess all the qualities needed for the captaincy of Australia. Hole was nineteen and playing for the St George club in Sydney grade cricket when, in 1949-50, he was picked to represent New South Wales against Victoria in what was in effect the Sheffield Shield final. He managed only 23 and 6 with the bat, but taking six for 61 in the match he helped his side win by 196 runs. It was a useful début. That winter, he moved to Adelaide and became an automatic choice for South Australia until he retired in 1957-58. In 1950-51 he made 478 runs in the Shield for an average of 39.83, and in the state's two matches against MCC he batted well, without scoring heavily. Chosen for the final Test at Melbourne, when Australia had already somewhat fortuitously built up a 4-0 lead in the rubber, he made 63 in the second innings but could do little more than delay England's first victory since 1938. He also helped to make it slightly less emphatic by bowling Hutton for 79. In

1951-52, however, he suffered a considerable setback, scoring only 190 runs in nine innings against West Indies. He achieved little of note, apart from 45 not out in the second innings at Brisbane, when he remained imperturbable in a crisis, and 62 at Sydney in the final game, and his form in the Sheffield Shield, until he made a fine century against Queensland, was moderate. Next season, when the South Africans tested Australia to the full, drawing the series 2-2, he disappointed once again, the highest of some useful scores being a stylish 59 in the Fourth Test at Adelaide. Outside the Tests he fared better against the South Africans, with a well-made 97 for an Australian XI at Sydney and 102 for South Australia in Adelaide at the end of the tour. In the Sheffield Shield, helped by not outs, he averaged more than 80, and South Australia were winners for the first time since the Bradman era.

By the time Hole toured England in 1953, the balance of power was swinging the home country's way, and they recovered the Ashes at The Oval at the end of a fascinating series in which runs were generally hard to come by. Tried as an opener at Trent Bridge, in those days the traditional venue for the First Test, he twice succumbed to Bedser, for 0 and 5. But at Lord's he made a useful 47 in Australia's second innings, as well as taking four catches in the slips, and at Old Trafford he helped Harvey put on 173 for the fourth wicket in Australia's first innings of 318. In the tense struggle which followed at Headingley, Hole was very much in the action: he had scored 53 when he was brilliantly caught by Lock off Bedser in the first innings, and was 33 when, with Australia going for the runs, he was caught by Graveney from a hit which looked like carrying for six over the square-leg boundary. After that, Australia were forced to give up the chase. At The Oval he played very well for 37 on the first day. Finishing with 273 runs for an average of 27.30, he was fourth in the Test averages behind Hassett, Morris and Harvey, and while he had certainly not lost ground, nor had he gained much. For the whole tour he made 1,118 runs at 33.87, as well as taking 22 catches. His bowling was rarely used.

Back at home in 1953-54 Hole made 670 runs for South Australia in a Sheffield Shield season which for once was not overshadowed by Test matches and a touring team. On Christmas Day 1953, against Queensland at Adelaide, he made 171 and then went on to 226, his only double-century. But the next summer, after an excellent 57 at Brisbane against Hutton's team, he was bowled three times in succession by Tyson at Sydney and Melbourne and was swept away in the wreckage of Australia's batting, never to be called upon again. His generous backlift, coupled with a long, lazy swing of the bat as he shaped his strokes, must have left him vulnerable to extreme speed. However, his failure to establish himself as a Test batsman was more one of temperament than technique. There were occasions when he came tantalisingly close to the breakthrough: one large score might well have done the trick. He had three more seasons for South Australia before being forced to retire when he ruptured his spleen taking an acrobatic catch off Dooland's bowling to dismiss Sam Loxton. In all first-class matches he made 5,647 runs for an average of 36.66, including eleven hundreds, and took 61 wickets at 44.03. His 82 catches were mostly at slip, where he became a specialist. In Test matches he scored 789 runs, average 25.45, and took three wickets at 42.00 apiece and 21 catches. He afterwards served the South Australian Cricket Association in several capacities.

HOLMAN, RAYMOND SIDNEY, who died on September 19, 1989, aged 70, played for South Australia against New South Wales at Adelaide in one of the non-competitive matches arranged for the season of 1940-41. New South Wales fielded a side not far short of Test strength and Holman, batting at No. 7, was dismissed by O'Reilly in the first innings for a single and in the second by McCool for 3. That must have been enough leg-spin for him for the time being.

HUTTON, SIR LEONARD, who died in hospital at Kingston-upon-Thames on September 6, 1990, aged 74, was one of the greatest batsmen the game has produced in all its long history. In the Hall of Fame he sits at the high table with the élite, and if English cricket alone is taken into consideration he was one of the two most accomplished professional batsmen to have played for his country, the other being Sir Jack Hobbs with Walter Hammond and Denis Compton coming next *haud longo intervallo*.

He was born at Fulneck near Pudsey into a family in which there was a healthy respect for the old virtues of discipline and self-denial. It was also a keen cricketing family, and the boy seems to have nursed ambitions deep in his heart to become a great player. He devoured anything he could lay his hands on about the art of batting, and by the time he had come to the notice of George Hirst he was already a complete player. Indeed, Hirst proclaimed that there was nothing to teach him; Sutcliffe, more extravagant in his praise, predicted that he would play for England. By 1934, still only seventeen, he was ready for first-class cricket, and in fourteen matches in the Championship he at once made his mark with five fifties and a maiden first-class century – an innings of 196 against Worcestershire at Worcester. Batting with supreme confidence he was last out in a total of 416. He also showed a high degree of skill in batting for four hours on a difficult pitch at Scarborough before being bowled by Goddard for 67. Ill health a year later held him up, but in 1936 he made his 1,000 runs for the first time, often having to bat on rain-affected pitches in that vile summer. Impatient critics complained that he was too defensive. His answer was swift and to the point, and in 1937 he let loose a torrent of runs to show himself magnificently equipped with strokes. Against Derbyshire at Sheffield he made 271 not out, and when Yorkshire entertained Leicestershire at Hull he celebrated his 21st birthday with a fine 153, sharing in an opening partnership of 315 with Sutcliffe. His season's total of 2,888 (average 56.62) was second only to Hammond's. A broken finger in July 1938 put him out of cricket for around six weeks, but in 1939 he was in superlative form with 2,167 runs in the Championship and 2,883 in all matches, including twelve hundreds.

In 1941 Hutton injured his left arm so badly in a gymnasium during commando training that three bone grafts were needed to repair the damage done by the compound fracture. He was in hospital for eight months before he was finally discharged, his left arm weakened and some two inches shorter than the other. However, he set about restoring the strength to the withered arm, and by 1943 he was making plenty of runs in the Bradford League. His top hand was once more in control, as he always insisted it must be, and when in the summer of 1945 he played in the Victory matches against the Australian Services, and one or two other first-class games, all were agreed that his technique was in good working order and promised well for the future. In the post-war seasons he made runs in full measure, exceeding the 2,000 mark comfortably from 1947 to 1953 and never allowing the strain of Test cricket to interfere with his commitment to Yorkshire. In the summer of 1949 he excelled himself. Two years earlier Compton and Edrich had held the stage, and Hutton had merely had a good season. Now it was to be the turn of the Yorkshireman. His total of 3,429 runs, including twelve hundreds, was the fourth-highest aggregate in the all-time list. Furthermore he passed 1,000 runs in two separate months, breaking the record for a single month with 1,294 in June.

A batsman's worth must always be judged by his performances in Test matches. Hutton was chosen to represent his country for the first time in 1937 against New Zealand. He had a rough start at Lord's, making 0 and 1, but he was quickly into his stride with 100 at Old Trafford. A year later he was destined to make history and capture the public's imagination with his 364 at The Oval. Hammond wanted 1,000 on the board to be certain of victory and Hutton, suiting his game perfectly to the needs of the occasion, obliged by staying at the crease for thirteen hours seventeen minutes until 770 had been scored. The following winter in South Africa, without scoring heavily in the Tests, he delighted spectators wherever he played by the sheer quality of his batting. Back at home he was in irresistible form against the West Indians with 196 at Lord's, the last 96 coming in 95 minutes, and he rang down the curtain on Test cricket for six years with 165 not out at The Oval.

MCC's tour of Australia in 1946-47 was reluctantly undertaken, for the prospect of a humiliation as complete as that of 1920-21 was abhorrent to them. But Hutton, although often not in the best of health, had a splendid tour, scoring 1,267 runs and averaging 70. In the Second Test, at Sydney, he savaged the Australian fast bowlers in an innings too scintillating to last, making 37 out of 49 before he unluckily hit his wicket, and he finished on a high note with an unbeaten 122 in the final Test at Sydney before being laid low with tonsillitis between the close of the first day's play and the resumption three days later. Early in 1948 he flew out to the West Indies to reinforce Allen's beleaguered team, but to expect him to rescue the series was asking too much. That summer, however, he was the centre of controversy in the middle of the Australian visit, when the selectors lost their heads and dropped him after he had looked in some discomfort against Lindwall and Miller at Lord's. Promptly restored for Headingley, he had the last laugh by finishing the series with scores of 81, 57, 30 (out of 52) and 64. His partnership of 359 in 310 minutes with Washbrook at Ellis Park, Johannesburg, was the highlight of MCC's successful tour of South Africa under F. G. Mann in 1948-49 and at the time was the highest for the first wicket in Test cricket. When West Indies comprehensively defeated England in 1950, Hutton alone seemed able to fathom the wiles of Ramadhin and Valentine, and his undefeated 202 at The Oval, when he carried his bat, was a magnificent fighting innings. Now he was nearing the final phase of his career, and he seemed to be playing better than ever. With Compton immobilised, Washbrook past his best and Edrich no longer the player he was, Hutton had to carry England's batting. He responded by averaging 88.83 in the 1950-51 Test series in Australia, 50 more per innings than the next Englishman; he again carried his bat, for 156 at Adelaide, and at Melbourne he had the satisfaction of making the winning hit in England's first post-war victory over Australia. But at The Oval in 1951, against South Africa, he had the misfortune to become the first player given out "obstructing the field" in Test cricket.

In 1952, against India, Hutton became England's first professional captain, although he had never captained his county. He at once showed his mastery of the job and kept his side splendidly on their toes. His handling of the young Trueman was exemplary, keeping him sharp and full of energy by restricting him to short bursts. Three of the four Tests were won, rain depriving England of victory at The Oval. In 1953, when the Ashes were regained in a low-scoring but nevertheless absorbing series, his leadership throughout was firm and confident, and with no-one else averaging 40 he with 55 was much the best batsman on either side. His innings of 145 at Lord's was as near perfect an exhibition of the art of batting as one could ever expect to see. The following winter found him leading MCC abroad for the first time, and the West Indians on their own soil presented a formidable challenge. Nothing went right to start with, the first two Tests being lost through feeble batting, but in the end the series was squared 2-2, largely through the efforts of the captain, who followed his 169 at Georgetown in the Third Test with 205 in the Fifth at Kingston. He was at the crease for about sixteen hours for the two innings, and all the time in sweltering heat. It had been a phenomenal feat of concentration. Now one more task remained for him: the retention of the Ashes in Australia. This was done in style in 1954-55, and after a grievous setback at Brisbane in the First Test. Hutton had two young batsmen at his command in May and Cowdrey and a most potent weapon in Tyson, for whose success he deserved much of the credit by encouraging him to shorten his run up to the wicket. England won three Tests in a row and most likely were deprived of a run of four by rain at Sydney. Hutton had little energy left for long innings, but his 80 at Adelaide was the cornerstone of the vital victory. He had to decline the offer of the captaincy for all five Tests against South Africa in 1955, owing to continued ill health, and early in 1956 he announced his retirement. He had captained England 23 times, winning eleven Tests, drawing eight and losing only four. Recognition of his achievements was swift. The previous year MCC had made him an honorary member while he was still playing, and in June he received a knighthood for his great services to the game.

In 513 first-class matches, Sir Leonard Hutton compiled 40,140 runs for an average of 55.51. He reached 100 centuries in 619 innings, the lowest ratio by an Englishman, and of his eventual total of 129 hundreds, eleven exceeded 200. Twelve times in England and five times on tour overseas he passed 1,000 runs in a season. A useful leg-spinner in his early days, he claimed 173 wickets, average 29.51, and made 400 catches, generally in positions near the wicket. In 79 Test matches he scored 6,971 runs for the impressive average of 56.67, hitting nineteen hundreds and twice carrying his bat; he alone had passed 400 runs in a series eight times. He was a selector in 1975 and 1976 and had accepted the presidency of Yorkshire not many months before he died. In his day he had no peer, and in the words of Geoffrey Chaucer, "He was a verray parfit gentil knight".

Many were the tributes paid to Sir Leonard Hutton at the time of his death.

Peter May: "I always admired him tremendously and learned a great deal through watching his technique. He managed to maintain his form extremely well when captaining England."

Raymond Illingworth: "He was simply a god to me as a kid, when I followed him all round the Bradford League playing for Pudsey St Lawrence. Those who played with and against him knew he was the best player and a class above everyone else."

Brian Close: "He was a marvellous player and everybody who played with him was privileged. He was the complete expert, and batting with him you just couldn't help but learn."

Denis Compton: "We were different characters but very good friends, and he was the greatest opening batsman I have ever seen. I say that because in our day we played on uncovered wickets. His powers of concentration were remarkable, but when he wanted to be he was one of the best strokemakers in the game."

Colin Cowdrey: "I was just so lucky to play my earlier matches in the England side under his captaincy. He took all the trouble in the world to help me on my way."

In 1950, *Bill O'Reilly*, in comparing the post-war Hutton with the Hutton of 1938, said: "His footwork is as light and sure and confident as Bradman's ever was. He is the finished player now . . . one cannot fail to be impressed with the fluency and gracefulness of his strokemaking . . . . His control of the game is masterful."

JESSOP, REVD GILBERT LAIRD OSBORNE, who died in St Thomas's Hospital, London, on January 16, 1990, aged 83, was the son of Gilbert Jessop, known as "The Croucher" and a famous hitter in the early years of the century. The younger Jessop was not in the least inhibited by his father's reputation, and became a competent cricketer in his own right at Minor County and good club level. He was educated at Weymouth College, where he played a prominent part in the XI from 1922 to 1924, taking 97 wickets with his off-spin. His batting promised much in 1923, when he made a century and finished third in the averages, but went into sharp decline during the wet summer of 1924, his robust methods being ill suited to the many sodden pitches he must have encountered. After leaving school in the year before going up to Cambridge, he seems to have worked on his batting; we find him in May 1926 making 157 and performing the hat-trick in a club match. In 1927 he showed excellent form in the Freshmen's match at Cambridge, making 57 and 47 not out. *Wisden* was fulsome in its praise: "No one appeared to better advantage than Jessop who displayed a refreshing vigour in the first innings, and in the second, if lucky in some of his hits, again batted with confidence and power." On the strength of this, he was selected for a further trial but failed in both innings. He made his first-class début for MCC against Wales at Lord's in 1929, scoring a useful 29 in the second innings before falling to Sydney Barnes, who had match figures of seven for 99 in 75 overs at the age of 56. Jessop played in three first-class matches for Hampshire in 1933, two in the Championship and the other against the West Indians at Southampton, in which he made 25 in the second innings facing a hostile Martindale. By now he had completed his theological studies and taken Orders. In 1936 he turned out for Cambridgeshire with considerable success; and in 1939 he did even better in his first season for Dorset, averaging 37 with the bat and taking 21 wickets at 11.19 apiece. He was to enjoy a number of successful seasons after the war. In his four first-class matches, Jessop made 86 runs for an average of 12.28, while his one wicket was that of James Langridge.

KERR, ERIC ALAN DAVID, who died at Melbourne on February 16, 1989, aged 65, was a member of the Victoria team which finished runners-up in the Sheffield Shield in 1949-50, the season in which Jack Iverson mystified everyone with his unorthodox grip in taking 46 wickets. Kerr, a solid right-hand batsman and right-arm opening bowler, played in all six matches, usually batting at No. 6 or No. 7, and finished second in the state's averages with 407 runs at 40.70. However, his thirteen wickets cost him 40.53 each. In November 1949 he led off with 79 against Western Australia at Perth and followed this with 95 against New South Wales at Melbourne over the Christmas holiday. His innings pushed Victoria to within 7 runs of New South Wales's opening 360, whereupon they seized the initiative by bowling out the visitors for 123, Kerr taking two for 30 and being at the crease when Victoria completed the good work with a five-wicket victory over the holders. At Brisbane in February Kerr's 97 was top score in the first innings, but in the second Victoria were bowled out for 88 and eventually beaten by two wickets. In 1950-51, when Victoria won the Shield, he made 104 in the second innings of their opening match against South Australia, at Adelaide, sharing in a stand of 192 for the fifth wicket with Neil Harvey, who hit his first Shield century. But after this promising start, he lost his form and his place in the side. Altogether he played in sixteen first-class matches for Victoria, making 825 runs with an average of 41.25 and a highest score of 112 against Tasmania on his début in 1946-47. He also took 22 wickets at 38.22.

KHOT, JEHANGIR BEHRAMJI, who died at Bombay on March 25, 1990, aged 76, played as an all-rounder for Bombay from 1935-36 to 1944-45. His hat-trick against Baroda at the Brabourne Stadium in 1943-44 was the first ever for Bombay, and only the fourth in the Ranji Trophy championship. A right-arm medium-pace swing bowler or off-spinner, he had an outstanding match in the 1941-42 Ranji Trophy final, taking six for 19 and five for 40 against Mysore. Earlier that season he hit his highest score, an innings of 103 not out for the Parsees against the Europeans, and during his career he was twice awarded Dr Pavri's Silver Jubilee Gold Medal for his performances in the Bombay Quadrangular and Pentangular tournaments.

KING, EDMUND POOLE, died at Brampton on September 11, 1990, aged 83. In 1925 and again in 1926, his determined batting in the Winchester second innings saved his side from defeat by Eton. His 50 in the 1926 match was his highest score in his two years in the XI. These innings, and an unbeaten 35 in Winchester's three-wicket victory over Marlborough in 1925 when the game could have gone either way, showed he was at his best in a crisis, a valuable attribute. However, in his three games for Gloucestershire in July 1927 he could manage no more than 14 runs, with 6 in each innings against Kent at Dover as his best effort.

LINTON, BRIGADIER JAMES EDWARD FRYER, DSO, died at Cozumel, Mexico on December 21, 1989, aged 80. A right-arm fast bowler and middle-order batsman, in 1932 he played in two Championship matches for Glamorgan as an amateur. He had the misfortune to bag a "pair" against Middlesex at Cardiff, being bowled by Durston and Sims, but he took one wicket for 34 runs in fourteen overs in the visitors' first innings. Against Hampshire at Bournemouth he managed 3 runs in his two innings, but he was in good company, as no-one else could cope with Alex Kennedy, who took thirteen wickets in the match for 71 runs. Linton was a regular soldier in the Royal Artillery.

MATTHEWS, THOMAS HAROLD, who died on May 5, 1990, aged 85, played in three first-class matches for Tasmania as a batsman and wicket-keeper in 1930-31. He hit 78 on his début against Victoria and in all made 164 runs, average 32.80, and two catches.

MILBURN, COLIN (OLLIE), who died on February 28, 1990, aged 48, after collapsing at Newton Aycliffe, Co. Durham, enjoyed all too brief a career in first-class cricket. On May 23, 1969, he was involved in a car accident and lost the use altogether of his left and master eye. His other eye was slightly damaged as he was thrown forward into the windscreen. This cruel blow was a tragedy not only for the player himself but for the whole world of cricket. For he was a devastating attacking player, with a wide range of orthodox strokes to supplement his cutting and pulling. He was nearing his peak when his injury removed him from the scene he had illuminated during a period of depressing mediocrity.

Milburn was a heavyweight. One winter, after a rigorous course of dieting, he turned the scales at sixteen stones; he normally hovered around the eighteen-stone mark. He was the largest man to play first-class cricket in England since Warwick Armstrong in 1921, but like many large men he was light on his feet, and he never had any difficulty in positioning himself for the shot he wanted to play. Born at Burnopfield, a mining village near Durham, he inherited his large frame and cricketing ability from his father, who was a big hitter in local cricket. By 1953, eleven-year-old Colin was playing in the Burnopfield second team, and two years later he was batting and bowling for the senior side and representing Durham Schoolboys. By 1959, impatient to measure himself against stronger opposition, he moved to Chester-le-Street, where he was a sensation: a string of spectacular performances earned him selection for Durham county against the touring Indians, and he seized on the occasion to make an impressive hundred. Warwickshire and Northamptonshire were soon competing for his services, but Ken Turner, the secretary at Northampton, with an eye for talent, was the one to snap him up. The season of 1960 was spent qualifying and learning his craft. He was encouraged to develop his natural attacking instincts by the county captain, Keith Andrew, and, going in first, he made 1,153 runs for the Second Eleven for an average of 33.91, playing a big part in their carrying off the championship. At this stage of his career, he was also a promising fast-medium bowler with a refreshingly short approach. In 1961 he was given a run in the Championship side, but needed more time for adjustment, especially against off-spinners. Back in the second team, he again passed 1,000 runs for an improved average of 43.34. A year later, however, he gained a regular place in the senior side, and his maiden hundred came at Northampton against Cambridge University. His 129 contained two sixes and nineteen fours, and with Mike Norman he put on 227 in 170 minutes for the first wicket. Such was his weight of stroke that almost 70 per cent of his runs had come in boundaries, a proportion typical of his larger innings. His other century was made on an awkward pitch at Buxton: coming in with the scoreboard reading 23 for four, he hit eighteen fours in his 102 and with Norman (58) put on 152 for the fifth wicket. The other nine batsmen scraped 13 runs between them. In 1963 he made satisfactory progress with more than 1,500 runs. Against Yorkshire at Northampton he hit 48 and, with seven sixes and fourteen fours, 123 in 113 minutes. His 100 and 88 (one six, fourteen fours) against Worrell's West Indians were both magnificent innings and helped to put the county in a winning position before rain interrupted proceedings. Later that year he went on MCC's tour of East Africa under M. J. K. Smith, enjoying himself hugely with five scores of more than 50.

In 1966 Milburn took the step up into Test cricket and quickly showed that he had both the temperament and technique to succeed at the highest level. Against the formidable West Indies side, he hit 94 in England's second innings at Old Trafford in the First Test, and with a memorable 126 not out at Lord's he saved the game by his brilliant attacking strokes. He had come off on the most famous of stages, but to his acute disappointment he was dropped for the final Test at The Oval on the grounds that he was too much of an encumbrance in the field. His answer to the selectors' caution was to put the Essex bowlers to the sword with a superb double-century at Clacton. His 203, which was the lion's share of a county record opening stand of 293 with Roger Prideaux, was an object lesson in how to set up a victory by attacking cricket. Milburn, already first to 1,000 runs that year finished second in the national averages with an aggregate of 1,861 at 48.97. He was one of *Wisden's* Five Cricketers of the Year in the 1967 edition.

That winter came a new departure: he was engaged to play for Western Australia in the 1966-67 Sheffield Shield competition. The enterprise proved an enormous success both on and off the field. Milburn's jovial manner and love of his fellow human beings made him immensely popular in the dressing-room and beyond the boundary. The Australians acclaimed him. He made 571 runs in the Shield for an average of 40.79, and spectators who saw it have not forgotten his hundred in only 77 minutes at Adelaide. The following winter he went to the West Indies with Cowdrey's side, but in 1968-69, omitted from the team to Ceylon and Pakistan, he was able to play once again in Australia. This time he made a royal progress through the states, and at Brisbane he played the most extraordinary innings seen there in Shield matches. On the first day he made 243, and before he was out in the first over after tea, having scored 181 between lunch and tea, he had hit four sixes and 38 fours. He was fifth in the Australian averages that season with 940 runs at 62.66, and when England were in trouble on their riot-torn tour of Pakistan, Milburn was summoned to help out. The players formed a guard of honour as he descended from the plane. Coming into the side for the Third Test at Karachi, he gave England a marvellous start with 139, his hundred arriving off 163 balls. But it was to be his last Test innings. On the third day the match was abandoned because of the civil disturbance, and the team flew home to England. Two months later, in Northamptonshire's first match of the season, he made his final hundred, 158 against Leicestershire, just a day or two before his injury.

A player who always wanted to attack, as he did, was sure to have downs as well as ups. In 1967-68 he failed to win a place in the Test side against West Indies, a setback which did not prevent him from being the liveliest member of the party. But at Lord's in 1968, against Australia, he hit a wonderful 83, one superb pull off Cowper landing high up in the Grand Stand. There were those who liked to sa that he was a mere slogger. Nothing could have been further from the truth. He was fundamentally an orthodox player with a sound defence. He could drive well, but his shots square on either side of the wicket were his special hallmark. He could cut and pull with brutal power and would literally batter an attack into submission. He was only 28 when he lost his eye and there is no knowing what heights he might have reached. He and Botham, who was, appropriately, a pall-bearer at his funeral, might even have joined forces for England.

The cold statistics show that Milburn made 13,262 runs in first-class cricket for an average of 33.07, a figure which would have been substantially higher if he had not attempted a comeback in 1973-74. They give little idea of the pleasure and excitement he gave to thousands. The records also show that he took 99 wickets at 32.03 and made 224 catches, mostly close up on the leg side; that he passed 1,000 runs in six English seasons; that for Northamptonshire he made a hundred before lunch on four occasions; and that he holds the county's record with 43 catches in 1964. In his nine Tests he made 654 runs for an average of 46.71.

OMAR KHAN, who died at Karachi on August 4, 1990, stood as an umpire in the Test match at Lahore between Pakistan and New Zealand in 1969-70. He played as a batsman for Sind in the Ranji Trophy before Partition in 1947.

OWEN-SMITH, DR HAROLD GEOFFREY (TUPPY), who died at Cape Town on February 28, 1990, aged 81, made a great name for himself in England in the 1930s as an exceptional all-round sportsman. His prowess at cricket was at least equalled on the rugby field, where he captained England, and he was a champion lightweight boxer. Born at Rondebosch, Cape Town, on February 18, 1909, he was twenty when he first set foot on English soil as a member of the South African touring side. He had had a thorough grounding as a boy at the Diocesan College from such English professionals as Harry Lee, Newman, Astill and O'Connor, and had already made his presence felt in Western Province's two matches against MCC in 1927-28. In the first match of the tour, bowling on a rain-damaged pitch, he took four for 43 in fourteen overs with his slow leg-breaks, and the records seem to show that Hammond was his first victim in first-class cricket. At the end of the tour, when MCC played a return match with Western Province, Owen-Smith made 32 in the second innings.

He first attracted attention in the early weeks of the 1929 tour by his magnificent fielding in the deep, and especially at cover point. He was fast and he would chase for all he was worth before unleashing a powerful, flat return to the top of the stumps. His anticipation at cover, and his ability to intercept strokes which would leave others standing, made him the star of a fine fielding side, and it is probably safe to say that only two other fielders, Colin Bland and Clive Lloyd, have caused such a stir since his day. In the Second Test at Lord's, going in at No. 7 when his side were in danger of letting a hard-won advantage slip, he first helped Morkel add 48 for the sixth wicket and later took complete control in a last-wicket partnership of 43 with Bell. His judgement and selection of the right ball to hit made a big impression, as did his manipulation of the strike, and he was 52 not out at the close of the innings, having seen South Africa achieve a lead of 20 runs. In the Third Test at Headingley, however, they conceded a lead of 102 on first innings and were only 14 runs ahead when they lost their seventh second-innings wicket in the last over of the second day. The match seemed as good as over, but next morning Owen-Smith, 27 not out overnight, and Quinn took the score to 167 before Quinn was eighth out, stumped by Duckworth off White. Now Owen-Smith went for the bowling in magnificent style and was in such command that he monopolised the strike before being out for 129, having made 102 before lunch. His stand of 103 with Bell, scored in 65 minutes, has remained a record for South Africa's tenth wicket. So loud and prolonged was the applause while the two returned to the pavilion, they might have won the match for their side. However, England got home, thanks to Woolley, though not without some trouble. In all first-class matches on the tour Owen-Smith made 1,168 runs at 35.39 and took 30 wickets at 25.80 apiece. In addition to his hundred at Leeds he scored 126 against Warwickshire, and the editor of *Wisden* had no hesitation in choosing him as one of the Five Cricketers of the Year.

In 1930 Owen-Smith returned to England with a Rhodes Scholarship to study medicine at Oxford, and as expected he won his Blue in all three years. In 1931, saving his best for the big occasion, he made 78 at Lord's and bowled 71 overs for 200 runs and six wickets. His bowling had already brought him excellent analyses against Gloucestershire, Lancashire and the Club Cricket Conference. A year later he made 67 against Cambridge, a valuable effort which helped to save the follow-on, and bowled 76 overs, again taking six wickets. In his final year, with examinations impending, he played less but found the hard, dry pitches of 1933 very much to his liking. He obtained bounce as well as turn. At Lord's he took five for 93 against Cambridge and finished fourth in the national averages. When Owen-Smith continued his medical training at St Mary's Hospital in 1935, he was able to turn out for Middlesex in August, and to a lesser extent in 1936. In 1937 he played in twelve Championship games and took 57 wickets at 19.84, including eight for 103 against Gloucestershire at Lord's. In the Challenge Match that September between Middlesex and Yorkshire at The Oval, which the Yorkshiremen won easily, Owen-Smith made 77 in Middlesex's first innings, the next highest score being 25. His genius with the bat also shone brightly when, playing for MCC at Lord's, he gave his old university a drubbing to the tune of a career-highest 168 not out, "producing a wide variety of strokes with astonishing ease". And to rub it in, he took five for 33 in Oxford's first innings. In South Africa, he played in the Currie Cup before and after the war, and at Cape Town in 1948-49, after service in the Middle East, he took 65 not out off MCC in the opening match of their tour. In all he made 4,059 runs in first-class cricket for an average of 26.88 while his bowling earned him 319 wickets at 23.22. Quite apart from his 93 catches, he must have saved hundreds of runs by his superb fielding. In Test matches he averaged 42.00 in 1929 with 252 runs to take third place in the averages.

Looking back over the years, it is legitimate to ask why Owen-Smith's cricket aroused so much enthusiasm. Quite apart from the exhilarating nature of his play it was the young man himself who had such a wide appeal. Cricket in England in the 1920s had largely been dominated by the older generation; the flower of the nation's young manhood had been cut down in Flanders, and Owen-Smith's play and his debonair attitude seemed to fill the gap. A famous writer on the game likened him to Denis Compton more than anyone else he could think of. Like Compton, Owen-Smith was just as likely to make runs with a borrowed bat a with his own; like Compton he communicated his enjoyment of cricket t thousands.

PERERA, KANKARATNE MUDALIGE MELVILLE TITUS, who died i Sri Lanka on October 3, 1990, just before his 63rd birthday, had played a full pa in the cricket life of the island. A prominent schoolboy all-rounder at St Thoma College in the mid-1940s, he went on to become a leading captain, administrato and, for more than a decade, a national selector. He was manager of the S Lankan team that played in the 1975 World Cup in England, and chairman c selectors when Sri Lanka played their inaugural Test match, against England a Colombo in February 1982. In April 1957, he took six wickets for 68 in 45 ove for Ceylon Cricket Association against Madras CA in the M. J. Gopalan Troph match, and four years later, for Government Services, five for 20 against the sam opponents in a two-day game. Several weeks later, he opened the bowling f

Ceylon in the one-day match against Richie Benaud's England-bound Australian team and took the wickets of the Australian captain and Graham McKenzie. Perera served the Nondescripts club for well over 45 years, first as a player and captain, bringing them the P. Saravanamuttu Trophy in 1960-61, and later on the committee and as a vice-president. At the time of his death he was president-elect of the club.

PETTIT, DAVID WILLIAM, who died suddenly on May 28, 1990, aged 53, at Greta West, Victoria, had five games for Oxford in 1958 and 1959 as an opening bowler but met with little success. In the XI at St Edmund's, Canterbury, he made 261 runs in 1955 at 26.10, with an unbeaten 58 his highest score, and he bowled with great success, his 34 wickets costing only 10.17. In 1958, with Bailey and Sayer unavailable, Oxford gave him a match in The Parks against Derbyshire: he had first use of the new ball in each innings, but was expensive and did not take a wicket. A year later he underwent a trial of four straight games at Oxford, including the match against the Indian touring team. He would have bowled his heart out, but he could manage only six wickets at 62.00 apiece. However, against Yorkshire, with defeat impending, he added some spice to the last rites by hitting three sixes in an innings of 22. The scorecard shows that he was stumped by the ever-present Binks, trying perhaps to hit a fourth.

QUICK, ARNOLD BERTRAM, who died at Clacton on July 17, 1990, aged 75, played in nineteen first-class matches for Essex before and after the Second World War as an exuberant, hard-hitting batsman, invariably confined to one of the lower positions in the order. He made a name for himself in club cricket at Clacton with the sheer power of his straight driving, which not infrequently endangered the life of the bowler's umpire, and once hit six sixes in an over. Inevitably Essex showed an interest as stories of his feats filtered through. In the summer of 1936, in his second match for the county, he struck 39 off Hammond, Sinfield and Goddard (eight for 64) to earn a narrow first-innings advantage. In 1937 he made 239 runs at 18.38, and with 43 in the second innings against Hampshire at Southend was mainly responsible for Essex getting home by two wickets with only two minutes of extra time remaining. He also played useful innings against Worcestershire and Nottinghamshire, reaching 53 at Trent Bridge. He made one other fifty, hitting up 57 against Yorkshire in 1952 on his home territory at Clacton, as a result of which the visitors had to bat again, albeit briefly, for their victory. From 1956 to 1959 Quick captained the Essex Second Eleven in the Minor Counties Championship and in 1959 took charge of their first matches in the newly inaugurated Second Eleven competition. At this level his rigour and impetuosity were less severely punished, and he collected more than 1,000 runs in the four years. When his first-class cricket ended in 1952, he had made 439 runs for an average of 13.71.

REOCH, EARL CLARK, died at Dundee on December 1, 1989, aged 47. A right-hand bat and slow left-arm bowler, he captained his county, Forfarshire, in 1968, 1971 and 1976. In 1973 he represented Scotland against Ireland, batting at No. 3, but expectations that he would make runs were sadly unfulfilled. He mustered just 7 runs in his two innings. In the same year he played for Scotland against the touring New Zealanders and against Essex, neither match being first-class.

RHOADES, CEDRIC SETTLE, who died in hospital at Macclesfield on March 26, 1990, aged 69, will be remembered in Lancashire especially and elsewhere as the man who, almost single-handed, brought about the revival in the county's fortunes in the late 1960s and early 1970s. He came into prominence with the overthrow of the committee in 1964 and by 1969 he was chairman. By this time the county's fortunes were at the lowest ebb in their history. Pride and traditional excellence had gone by the board; Old Trafford itself seemed in danger of losing its status as a major cricketing centre. In the Championship, Lancashire had not finished higher than eleventh between 1961 and 1967; in the Gillette Cup they had met with no tangible success. Fully alive to the commercial possibilities of the one-day game, Rhoades demanded a concerted effort in the new competitions. Success was immediate and captured the public's imagination. Old Trafford was full to the brim with enthusiastic supporters as Lancashire won the Gillette Cup four times in six years from 1970 and carried off the John Player Sunday League in 1969 and 1970. The famous ground itself was given a complete face-lift and sponsorship was encouraged. All that was missing was success in the Championship. Three high finishes were achieved under Rhoades's aegis, but with little else to deliver to the frustrated members he resigned as chairman in 1986 in the face of rebel opposition. The wheel had turned full circle. He had served on the TCCB committee at Lord's for many years and in Lancashire on a large number of bodies connected with the game.

ROBERTS, WILLIAM MAURICE, who died at Adelaide on January 21, 1990, aged 73, played for South Australia on three occasions between 1937-38 and 1946-47 as an off-spin bowler and low-order batsman. His one Sheffield Shield match was against Queensland at Adelaide in December 1946, when the visitors, batting first, ran up a total of 401. Roberts was given a good bowl, taking two wickets for 86 in 24 eight-ball overs, and in his three matches he took nine wickets at 25.89.

ROBINS, COLONEL WILLIAM VERNON HARRY, who died in Cheshire on June 26, 1990, aged 83, was the younger brother of R. W. V. Robins, the England captain and selector. A left-handed bat and occasional leg-spinner, he was in the XI at University College School, London in 1923 and 1924, coming third in the averages in the latter year with a top score of 56. Becoming a regular soldier, he first appeared for the Army in 1931, and altogether played in eight first-class matches, one of them being for Madras against Tennyson's team in 1937-38. He made 207 runs at 17.25, with a highest score of 60 for the Europeans against the Indians at Madras in 1937-38, and took fifteen wickets at 37.53 apiece.

ROTHSCHILD, THE THIRD LORD, GBE, GM, FRS (NATHANIEL MAYER VICTOR), who died in London on March 20, 1990, aged 79, was one of the most versatile and gifted men of his time, and a cricketer of considerable talent. In 1929, his last year at Harrow, he made his mark in all departments of the game: he was one of three boys to score more than 500 runs in schools matches, he took twenty wickets at 25 apiece, and he was a high-class performer in the slips. At Lord's against Eton, opening with Terence Rattigan, he made a dashing 43 out of 68 to launch Harrow's reply to a total of 347, to which his bizarre mixture of pace and spin had made much too generous a contribution. He made runs for the Lord's Schools against the Rest, and towards the end of August he was given a run by Northamptonshire, making an auspicious start in first-class cricket with scores of 27, 31, 11, 16 not out, 36, 5 and 28. His 36 was made against Larwood, Barratt and Voce after five wickets had gone down for 39. In 1930 he played in the Freshmen's match at Cambridge, and in a further trial he drove finely in making 112 for the Perambulators against the Etceteras. This innings and his highest first-class score of 63 against Kent at Peterborough (st Ames b Freeman) earned him a game for the University against Sussex. However, he found Maurice Tate too much of a handful in both innings. He was looked upon as a possible captain of Northamptonshire on the retirement of V. W. C. Jupp, but the job was given to W. C. Brown and Rothschild went on to conquer wider fields. In his eleven first-class matches he made 282 runs for an average of 15.66 and held eight catches

ROWE, EDMUND JOHN, who died at Ellesmere on December 17, 1989, aged 69, kept wicket for Nottinghamshire between 1949 and 1957. After a few matches as an amateur he turned professional in 1951 and was capped in 1954. The tedium of his duties behind the stumps, owing to the poverty of the county's attack, was relieved by the registration of the Australian, Bruce Dooland, a leg-spin and googly bowler of the highest class. Dooland uplifted a demoralised side, with Rowe a competent and grateful lieutenant. Rowe played in 103 matches for his county, effecting 204 dismissals of which 52 were stumpings. With the bat he was a genuine tailender, scraping together 295 runs in 122 visits to the crease. His highest score was 16. After making way for Geoff Millman, Rowe took up a coaching appointment at Ellesmere College, and in 1971 he had a season on the first-class umpires' list.

RUDGE, LLOYD MAURICE, who died at Worcester on October 15, 1990, aged 56, made one first-class appearance, opening the bowling for Worcestershire against Combined Services at Worcester in 1952. For the eighteen-year-old right-arm fast bowler, one of six players in the Worcestershire side aged twenty or younger, it could have been a chastening experience: the Services made century stands for their first four wickets before declaring at 548 for four. However, although failing to take a wicket, Rudge conceded only 36 runs in his twelve overs. Batting at No. 10, he was run out for 1.

RYAN, ALBERT JAMES, who died on July 10, 1990, aged 86, played for South Australia between 1925-26 and 1936-37. In December 1927 he made a solitary appearance in the Sheffield Shield, against Queensland at Adelaide, being one of four young players the state selectors wanted to see. Ryan, a solid, compact type of batsman with a sound defence and enough shots to keep his score on the move, made 86 on this occasion but was not called up again till 1932-33, when he played against Jardine's MCC team in their last match in Australia. He made 61, top score for the innings, and 25. Given a full Shield season in 1933-34, he scored 363 runs for an average of 40.33 in the six matches. His maiden hundred, an innings of 124 at Adelaide against Queensland, came in just about four hours, and his unbeaten 94 against New South Wales, put together with hardly a false stroke, was the foundation of a ten-wicket victory. Two years later we find him supporting Badcock (325) in a fourth-wicket stand of 198 against Victoria at Adelaide, his own contribution being 77. Up in Brisbane he made his highest score of 144, having to face Gilbert at his fastest and being forced to concentrate on defence for long periods. No-one else passed 50 in South Australia's innings. In 1936-37 he showed a liking once again for English bowling with a well-played 71 against Farnes, Allen and Voce. In a career of 33 games, spread over twelve seasons, he hit 1,493 runs for an average of 30.46, while as a useful bowler of slow-medium off-breaks he took twenty wickets at 43.30, with best figures of four for 13.

SCHOFIELD, ROBIN MATTHEW, who was killed in January 1990, aged 50, when a tree he was cutting fell on him, was the first New Zealander to make seven dismissals behind the wicket in an innings in a first-class match. He performed this feat for Central Districts against Wellington at Wellington in 1964-65, all his victims being caught. At the same time he was also the first New Zealand wicket-keeper to make nine dismissals in a match. He completed 26 dismissals that season, a record 25 of them in the Plunket Shield, and altogether in 53 matches for his province he claimed a total of 122. He also scored more than 1,000 runs for an average of 17.98.

SEN, AMARENDRA NATH (MONTU), who died at Calcutta on April 12, 1990, aged 66, played for Bengal in some Ranji Trophy matches between 1943-44 and 1955-56. In January 1951 he appeared for the Governor of Bihar's XI against the powerful Commonwealth team, captained by Leslie Ames, and going in first made 13 and 17, being bowled by Derek Shackleton and George Tribe. He later took two wickets at the end of the match when a draw had become a certainty. After his playing days were over, Sen became a first-class umpire and a selector.

SMITH, GEORGE WILLIAM OSWALD, who died on November 25, 1989 at Worthing, aged 83, received his grounding in batting and wicket-keeping at Bishop's Stortford College, where he had a good record before going up to Cambridge. He was chosen to play in the Seniors' match in his second year in residence but did not play for the University. Given a fairly extensive trial by Essex in 1929 as a batsman, he made 30 opening the innings against Derbyshire at Derby, and 39 not out against Northamptonshire at Northampton lower down the order. This proved to be his highest score in a first-class match. He turned out once in 1930. In ten matches he made 206 runs for an average of 13.73, and later he appeared for Suffolk in Minor Counties cricket.

SMITH, STANLEY ARTHUR JOHN, who died in 1990, played in fourteen first-class matches for Victoria in the first half of the 1930s. He was a leg-spinner and no mean performer with the bat, whose figures suggest that he was unfortunate not to command a regular place in the state team. He had an excellent first-class début against Queensland at Melbourne in 1931-32, when Queensland squeezed home by 22 runs only after Ben Barnett and Smith, with 47, had put on 99 for the last wicket. He took two for 32 in Queensland's first innings of 200 and had the splendid analysis of 35–5–96–5 in the second. Later in the season he took five for 86 against New South Wales at Melbourne. In 1935-36, when he played in four Shield matches, making 151 runs at 30.20, he scored 80 not out, batting at No. 10, when Victoria compiled 522 for nine declared against Queensland at Melbourne. Remembering that he was bowling eight-ball overs, his 14.1–2–56–1 when Bradman was putting together 357 for South Australia at Melbourne showed great control, and two other performances, four for 73 against New South Wales and three for 57 against Queensland, both at the MCG, should not go unnoticed. At a time when Smith's bowling was inevitably overshadowed by the deeds of Grimmett and O'Reilly, his final tally of 56 wickets at 26.43, with a best performance of eight for 44 against Tasmania at Hobart in 1933-34, shows that he was a leg-spinner of genuine quality.

SMITH, WILLIAM ALFRED, who died in Wiltshire during February 1990 aged 89, was the elder brother of C. I. J. (Big Jim) Smith, the Middlesex an England fast bowler and unorthodox hitter. He was himself a right-arm fast medium bowler and low-order batsman, though without his brother's flair for th unexpected, but when offered terms by Middlesex, he showed no interest in professional first-class career. Instead he was for many years both the spearhea and the mainstay of the Wiltshire attack, from 1929 to 1939 taking 387 wickets a 16.84. It was on the strength of his consistent form with the ball that he was twic chosen to play for the Minor Counties in representative matches, against th South Africans at Skegness in 1935 and against Oxford the following year. A Skegness, in front of a record attendance, he stood up well to the punishmer meted out by Eric Rowan and Viljoen, who put on 219 in two and a half hours. I The Parks, going in last, he made 35 to add the final touches to his side's stead recovery from a poor start, and with five for 95 he made the undergraduates wor hard for their runs. In these, his only first-class matches, Smith made 47 runs ar took nine wickets at 23.11.

SMURTHWAITE, JAMES, who died at Middlesbrough on October 20, 1989, aged 73, played in seven matches for Yorkshire in 1938 and 1939. He was a fast-medium swing bowler who could switch to quickish off-breaks when the conditions were right. At Bramall Lane in June 1939, he and Frank Smailes caused a sensation by routing Derbyshire for 20 on a rain-affected pitch after Yorkshire themselves had been dismissed by the Pope brothers for 83. Smurthwaite was the chief executioner with the remarkable figures of five for 7 in 4.2 eight-ball overs. In Derbyshire's second innings, Smailes took all ten wickets for 47, well supported by Smurthwaite, who kept up the pressure at the other end. After a weekend in the headlines, he then withdrew to the obscurity of the Minor Counties Championship, in which he took 36 wickets at 12.94 for Yorkshire's Second Eleven that season. After the war he played for many years with success as a professional in the North Yorkshire and South Durham League.

SPEED, ANDREW WATSON, who died at Bromsgrove on July 16, 1990, aged 91, was the oldest living Warwickshire cricketer at the time of his death. A right-arm fast-medium bowler, he was skilful enough to step straight into the first-class arena and take wickets with apparently little or no preparation. Certainly his impact was immediate. In 1927, given first use of the new ball against Worcestershire at New Road, he removed the first three batsmen and the No. 6, and his figures of 33–9–75–4 testify to his form and fitness. In his only other match of the summer he denied Hampshire first-innings points at Portsmouth by mopping up the tail, finishing with four wickets for 64 runs. Next season, however, he was able to devote a little more time to cricket and played in six matches. When Warwickshire defeated the West Indians at Birmingham by seven wickets, Speed with five for 39 and four for 60 was the outstanding player in the match. Among his victims were C. A. Roach, George Challenor, E. L. G. Hoad and the youthful Learie Constantine. Against Glamorgan at Cardiff he took six for 81, his best return, in a total of 440, the limitations of the rest of the attack having been cruelly exposed. It is not surprising that the Warwickshire committee and supporters were left to regret what might have been when Speed resumed his business career and disappeared from the scene. In eight matches he took 29 wickets at a cost of 18.55, while in seven visits to the crease he made 29 runs with a highest score of 11 not out.

SPITTEL, H. LLEWELYN (LOU), who died in Sri Lanka on September 30, 1990, aged 70, was a younger brother of Malcolm Spittel, a former Ceylon captain. A leading bowler in the 1950s, he specialised in left-arm orthodox spin but also shared the new ball, bowling medium pace. His club cricket was initially for Saracens, but he later joined his brother at Nondescripts: the two once bowled out Bloomfield for 21, Lou taking five for 8 in 7.4 overs, including four maidens, and Malcolm five for 13 in seven overs, the only instance of brothers performing this feat in Sri Lankan cricket. In October 1950, playing for Ceylon against F. R. Brown's MCC team in a one-day match, he captured the prize wicket of Hutton, who died in the same month as Spittel.

STEELE, REVD JOHN WILLIAM JACKSON, who died in Devon on March 29, 1990, aged 84, played seventeen times for Hampshire in 1938 and 1939 while he was based at Winchester as an army chaplain. A quickish bowler, who could make the new ball move about, and a useful lower middle-order batsman, he enjoyed a highly successful début in first-class cricket, making 73 for once out and having a match analysis of seven for 144 against Gloucestershire at Portsmouth early in May. In Gloucestershire's second innings he accounted for the first three batsmen before Hammond and Crapp, exercising all their skill, just about put matters right. In the end Hampshire won at the last gasp by 30 runs and were greatly indebted to their new recruit; who had, incidentally, been passed off by R. C. Robertson-Glasgow as "A Church of England bowler, straight up and down and no funny business"! Steele continued to cause tongues to wag on the county circuit by such performances as eight for 139 in the match against Worcestershire at Basingstoke, and four for 29 when he achieved the breakthrough to bring victory by 37 runs over Derbyshire at Portsmouth. In all he took 39 wickets in the Championship at 24.87. He started 1939 even better. An analysis of 18.7–2–62–6, bowling eight-ball overs, against Warwickshire at Portsmouth was his best performance in the top grade. And a few days later he sent back Ames, Chalk and Valentine in four balls against Kent at Southampton. He had made only a few appearances, however, when he went lame and could play no more. In assessing his achievements it should be remembered that he was no raw recruit but a well-season,ed cricketer of 33 when he made his début, trained in the hard school of regimental contests. Indeed, he played twice for the Army at Lord's, making 77 against the Royal Navy in 1938, and he played there against the Public Schools in 1939. He made 406 runs for Hampshire for an average of 16.91 and took 57 wickets at 26.64, many of them good ones. His first-class figures from nineteen games in all were 434 runs (average 16.69) and 66 wickets at 25.90.

SUGDEN, MARK, who died at Dartmouth on January 21, 1990, three weeks short of his 88th birthday, was educated at Denstone and Trinity College, Dublin. He was a right-hand batsman and an occasional fast-medium bowler. In 1919 he came second in the Denstone averages with 411 runs at 31.69 and was the only member of the XI to make a hundred. But in 1920 his figures suggest either a complete loss of form and confidence, or the possibility that the wet pitches in the West Midlands did not suit his style of play. In eight first-class matches between 1922 and 1930 for Dublin University and the Gentlemen of Ireland he made 263 runs, with an average of 17.53 and a highest score of 51 against Scotland at Greenock in 1926, and took six wickets at 42.50. Sugden, who taught for many years at the Royal Naval College, Dartmouth, was capped 28 times by Ireland at rugby as a scrum-half, and after retiring as a player he developed an interest in coaching, helping to produce a manual which was published in 1946.

SYKES, ERIC, who died at Barnsley on December 7, 1989, aged 83, played in three matches for Derbyshire as an amateur in 1925 and in two more as a professional in 1932. In 1925 he made his highest first-class score with an innings of 50 on his début, against Gloucestershire at Derby. The home side had lost five wickets for 47 when he went in, but he played fluently in a most promising effort. He later turned professional, but Derbyshire were a useful side at this time, well stocked with promising young cricketers, and he did not receive another opportunity to prove himself until 1932. Against Hampshire at Chesterfield that season he made 27, out of 36 scored while he was at the wicket, in the first innings of a tight, low-scoring match when every run counted. His father, E.C., had played for Hampshire before the turn of the century.

THOMPSON, LESLIE BAINES, who died in Canada on April 23, 1990, aged 81, played in six matches as an amateur for Middlesex in the seasons immediately after the Second World War. A swing bowler with the ability to move the ba[ll] both ways, and often late, he took three of his five first-class wickets (averag[e] 49.60) on début, against Northamptonshire at Lord's, when he also made th[e] match safe for Middlesex by coming in at the fall of the ninth wicket and playing [a] maiden over. Most of his cricket was played for the Ealing club, for whom he too[k] 100 wickets eleven times and 2,571 in all at a cost of 12.97. He played fair[ly] regularly for the Middlesex Second Eleven, whom he occasionally captained.

UNWIN, FREDERICK ST GEORGE, who died on October 4, 1990, aged 79, played in 53 first-class matches between 1932 and 1951, all but one of them for Essex. He had been in the Haileybury XI which lost so heavily to Cheltenham at Lord's in 1929, scoring only 3 and 5 as they went down by 185 runs. For Essex he played many useful innings, which makes it more difficult to account for the even more numerous failures. Being a lower middle-order batsman possessing a good range of attacking strokes, he might have been liable to go for the bowling before he had played himself in; certainly the professional bowlers of the day would have found it easy to exploit any technical fault or limitation. In his first match for Essex, against Northamptonshire at Leyton, he helped his side towards an innings lead with 24 containing "some well-executed strokes". Soon after this, he found himself having to cope with the formidable but moody Amar Singh, who was having one of his "on" days when All India visited Leyton. Unwin (29) and Charles Bray (41) stopped the rot after an early collapse. In 1933 at Derby he hit ten fours in his 47, and at Swansea he registered his first Championship fifty, his 56 in the second innings paving the way to victory over Glamorgan by 103 runs. A year later he repeated this score against them in the first county match to be staged at Neath, and in the second innings he helped Jack O'Connor save the game, being 29 not out at the close. In 1939 Unwin shared the captaincy of Essex with D. R. Wilcox and Captain J. W. A. Stephenson, on the face of it a complex and somewhat perilous arrangement. Yet it turned out to be a great success: Essex finished fourth and had their best season since 1933. Unwin scored 226 runs, averaging 17.38. He turned out a few times after the war, notably in 1946 when he made his highest score of 60, helping to save the game against Kent at Colchester, and he finished with 1,138 runs for an average of 14.58. He also held 33 catches.

WATSON, RICHARD MARTIN, died in hospital at Penrhosgarnedd, North Wales, on October 1, 1987, aged 65. Called up at short notice to play for Derbyshire against Worcestershire at Chesterfield in May 1947, to his great credit he held his nerve in a crisis by making the winning hit, a six, with only two balls to go. He helped out on five other occasions that season, his best score being 25 not out against the touring South Africans in a rain-affected match. In the second innings he was one of six batsmen to fall to the leg-spinner, Smith, for 1 run in 4.5 overs. Altogether his left-handed batting produced 68 runs for an average of 8.50. His leg-spin was not called upon.

WEEKS, FREDERICK JAMES, who died at Bristol on February 20, 1990, aged 86, was in the Clifton side in 1920 and 1921. A useful middle-order left-hand batsman, in his two seasons he made more than 400 runs at an average of 17 with two fifties to his credit, one of them unbeaten. His best effort at Lord's against Tonbridge was an innings of 21 in 1920, going in at No. 8. He left on the young side and might have been a real success in 1922. Gloucestershire summoned him to play against Kent at Maidstone in July 1925, and he found himself in such distinguished company as Dipper, Hammond, Sinfield, Charles Parker and Goddard, Test players all. Still, sent in at No. 8, he does not seem to have been too overawed. He made 18 in the first innings, and 17 in the second as Gloucestershire, who had held the whip-hand all through, and even enforced the follow-on, allowed Kent to sneak home by 24 runs. Weeks's 17 was the second-highest score: he must have been not a little surprised at his colleagues' lack of confidence in going for the runs. His highest score was 35 not out against Yorkshire at Hull in 1926; in his seven first-class matches between 1925 and 1928 he made 122 runs for an average of 11.09.

WHITE, HON. LUKE ROBERT (FIFTH BARON ANNALY), who died in London on September 30, 1990, at the age of 63, emerged as a young player of high promise at Eton during the 1943 season. Showing a maturity in technique well beyond his years, he opened the batting and scored 342 runs at 34.20. In 1944 he was their most assured batsman with 503 runs for an average of 50. His most important innings was probably at Harrow, where he removed all possibility of defeat by making an excellent 76 when most of his colleagues were struggling. For the Lord's Schools against the Rest, he showed very good form, and later in the week he confirmed his class with a hundred for the Public Schools against a Lord's XI, his 102 containing fifteen fours in a stay of two hours. The match did not pass without incident. A V1 flying bomb fell fewer than 200 yards from the ground during the first innings, but although the blast sprayed pieces of soil over the pitch, play was barely interrupted. The boys, staying out on the field, apparently unconcerned, were applauded for their pluck by the spectators, some of whom had thrown themselves flat under seats for protection. White made another appearance at Lord's that summer, playing in a one-day match for Middlesex and Essex against Kent and Surrey. Still only seventeen, and in no way intimidated by the presence of many players of first-class experience, he made 77, which was the backbone of his side's total of 218. Lieutenant D. V. P. Wright took six wickets for 76, figures which indicate how well White played. A year later, along with John Dewes and Donald Carr, White was subjected to the gaze of the whole nation when he was chosen to represent England in the third of the hastily arranged "Victory Tests" at Lord's against the Australian Services. He made 11 and 4, and in England's first innings he helped Hutton put on 55 for the fourth wicket, defending well when Hassett crowded him with close fielders. This was his first-class début. He played in five more matches, three for Middlesex and one each for the RAF and MCC, his highest score being 46 for the RAF against Worcestershire at Worcester in June 1946. He had no ambitions to pursue a first-class career, preferring to enjoy his cricket for such clubs as MCC, the Ramblers and I Zingari.

WHITELEY, PETER, who died at Crompton on October 28, 1989, aged 54, played four matches for Lancashire in the Championship in 1957 and 1958. He was a slow left-arm bowler of considerable promise and a useful middle-order batsman whose highest score of 32, against Hampshire at Old Trafford in 1957, was made at a critical time in the match. Lancashire, bowled out for 89 and 74 behind on the first innings, had stood at 16 for four in their second innings before Pullar (138) and Bond put on 115 for the fifth wicket. The escape was finally effected by the 101 added by Pullar with the support of Whiteley for the sixth, and Lancashire went on to win by 95 runs. Whiteley's best bowling was three for 7 against the West Indians. He was a stalwart of the Second Eleven at this time and for a few more years: in 1956 he had bowled 150 overs more than anyone else taking 54 wickets at 18.42. But even though Lancashire were desperately short of talent, and his work in the Second Eleven received favourable comment in three successive years, Whiteley decided his future lay elsewhere and instead played league cricket as a professional for Crompton, Milnrow and Harrogate. In his five first-class matches he made 86 runs, average 14.33, and took nine wickets at 29.55 apiece.

WOLTON, ARTHUR VICTOR GEORGE, who died on September 9, 1990 at Solihull, aged 71, was an integral part of Warwickshire's Championship-winning side of 1951. It is always appreciated when an old player keeps in touch with and takes an active interest in, his county. Wolton was seen frequently

Edgbaston and, having been a stylish, forceful player himself, he would surely have revelled in the season of 1990. He would also have delighted spectators at every version of the game with fielding that would have been outstanding by the standards of any era. In this connection *Wisden* saw fit to comment on his "beautiful action". Born near Maidenhead, Wolton in his youth gained experience with Berkshire, and after the war he sharpened his game in the Birmingham League, a regular recruiting ground for Warwickshire players. Having made a single appearance for the county in 1947, scoring 2 and 0 against the Scottish Cricket Union, he spent the 1948 season, at the mature age of 29, adjusting to the greater demands of the first-class game, not least in point of stamina. Some useful scores at No. 6 or No. 7 were promising, and given a full trial in 1949 he made 978 runs, including his maiden hundred. This innings of 111 not out in just under four hours did much to set up Warwickshire's victory by an innings and 37 runs over Somerset, and a week later he contributed exactly 100 for once out to the win over Sussex at Coventry. A year later Warwickshire were the only county to lower the colours of the West Indians, and Wolton's 89 in the home side's first innings was the foundation-stone of a notable triumph. Strong on the drive, he punished the bowling and was especially severe on Valentine.

Since winning the Championship in 1911, Warwickshire had come no closer than fourth: under R. E. S. Wyatt in 1934, and now in 1949 and 1950. The bold and, as it turned out, inspired appointment of Dollery to the captaincy in 1949, plus a freedom from injury among the players, brought the great prize within reach in 1951. Not a man faltered, and in the end Warwickshire were safely home with sixteen wins and only two defeats. Wolton banked more than 1,000 runs for the second season in succession and hit the highest score of his career to date, an undefeated 157 which helped towards a crucial win over Gloucestershire at Coventry. Loss of form in 1952 was followed by a heartening recovery a year later which led to the second stage of his career. In 1954 he was promoted to No. 3 to take on greater responsibility and, at the age of 35, he finished the season as the county's leading batsman. With 1,770 runs at 41.16 he was ninth in the national averages. Dizzy heights indeed. According to *Wisden*, "nothing was as remarkable as the advance of Wolton". His five-hour 165 against Worcestershire at Dudley, where he opened the innings, proved to be the highest score of his career. His 1955 summer was even more prolific as he took advantage of the drier wickets to harvest 1,809 runs for an average of 34.13. He passed his 1,000 runs comfortably again in 1956, but in 1957, out of the blue, he suffered a severe setback, which may have been psychological. M. J. K. Smith was now ready to play for the county and bat at No. 3. Wolton possibly saw his place in the side threatened as he dropped down to No. 5. Form eluded him, and he had to be demoted to the Second Eleven. In 1958, however, he put the previous year's disappointments behind him and in a dismal season of a mere 146 centuries he finished thirteenth in the averages with 34.88 from 1,186 runs. May 9 to 12, 1959 were happy days for Wolton. The match with Surrey, which had been set aside for his Benefit, was won memorably by Warwickshire, in spite of two separate hundreds from Barrington. Wolton made a useful 49 and received more than £3,000 from the gate and other subscriptions. Not long after, at Oxford, he attacked the University's bowling so enthusiastically that he hit four sixes and nineteen fours in his 136, and he went on to reach 1,000 runs for the seventh and last time. He appeared in only one match in 1960 as more youthful replacements were by now available. In 297 matches, all but one of them for Warwickshire, he scored 12,930 runs for the thoroughly respectable average of 31.00. In addition to his twelve hundreds he chipped in with 37 wickets at 33.13 as a slow off-spinner. He took 117 catches, mostly away from the bat, and saved countless runs with his superb running and throwing from the deep field.

WOOD, RONALD, who died at Wakefield on May 22, 1990, aged 60, played 22 times for Yorkshire from 1952 to 1956, coming into the Championship side at a time when Wardle was at the height of his powers. Wood, whose younger brother, Barry, played for England in the 1970s, was an orthodox slow left-arm bowler, and so his opportunities were limited in what was, in effect, his apprenticeship. His first season was his most successful: he took 27 wickets at 18.92. He had match figures of four for 57 at Lord's on début, claiming Edrich and Compton as his first wickets, followed by seven for 67 at Worcester and four for 48 against Leicestershire at Sheffield. Then against Scotland at Glasgow he wrought havoc by taking six second-innings wickets for 9 runs in his last five overs on a wearing pitch. His full analysis was 21.5–9–45–8. In 1953 he bowled almost exactly the same number of overs in the Championship but claimed only fifteen wickets at 30.33 apiece. He remained on the staff for another three years, doing sterling work for the Second Eleven, before playing as a professional in the leagues. When Lidget Green were Bradford League champions in 1957, Wood took 67 wickets at 8.67 each. In first-class matches his 51 wickets cost 26.39 each, and he scored 60 runs in eighteen innings.

THE LAWS OF CRICKET

(1980 CODE)

INDEX TO THE LAWS

Law 1. The Players ... 1288
Law 2. Substitutes and Runners: Batsman or Fieldsman Leaving the Field: Batsman Retiring: Batsman Commencing Innings ... 1288
Law 3. The Umpires ... 1289
Law 4. The Scorers ... 1291
Law 5. The Ball ... 1292
Law 6. The Bat ... 1292
Law 7. The Pitch ... 1292
Law 8. The Wickets ... 1293
Law 9. The Bowling, Popping and Return Creases ... 1293
Law 10. Rolling, Sweeping, Mowing, Watering the Pitch and Re-marking of Creases ... 1294
Law 11. Covering the Pitch ... 1295
Law 12. Innings ... 1295
Law 13. The Follow-on ... 1296
Law 14. Declarations ... 1296
Law 15. Start of Play ... 1296
Law 16. Intervals ... 1297
Law 17. Cessation of Play ... 1298
Law 18. Scoring ... 1299
Law 19. Boundaries ... 1300
Law 20. Lost Ball ... 1301
Law 21. The Result ... 1301
Law 22. The Over ... 1302
Law 23. Dead Ball ... 1303
Law 24. No-ball ... 1304
Law 25. Wide-ball ... 1305
Law 26. Bye and Leg-bye ... 1306
Law 27. Appeals ... 1306
Law 28. The Wicket is Down ... 1307
Law 29. Batsman Out of His Ground ... 1307
Law 30. Bowled ... 1307
Law 31. Timed Out ... 1308
Law 32. Caught ... 1308
Law 33. Handled the Ball ... 1309
Law 34. Hit the Ball Twice ... 1309
Law 35. Hit Wicket ... 1309
Law 36. Leg Before Wicket ... 1310
Law 37. Obstructing the Field ... 1310
Law 38. Run Out ... 1311
Law 39. Stumped ... 1311
Law 40. The Wicket-keeper ... 1311
Law 41. The Fieldsman ... 1312
Law 42. Unfair Play ... 1312
42.1. Responsibilities of Captains ... 1312
42.2. Responsibilities of Umpires ... 1312
42.3. Intervention by the Umpire ... 1312
42.4. Lifting the Seam ... 1313
42.5. Changing the Condition of the Ball ... 1313
42.6. Incommoding the Striker ... 1313

42.7. Obstruction of a Batsman in Running 1313
42.8. The Bowling of Fast Short-pitched Balls 1313
42.9. The Bowling of Fast High Full Pitches 1313
42.10. Time Wasting 1314
42.11. Players Damaging the Pitch 1314
42.12. Batsman Unfairly Stealing a Run 1314
42.13. Player's Conduct 1314

LAW 1. THE PLAYERS

1. Number of Players and Captain

A match is played between two sides each of eleven players, one of whom shall be captain. In the event of the captain not being available at any time, a deputy shall act for him.

2. Nomination of Players

Before the toss for innings, the captain shall nominate his players, who may not thereafter be changed without the consent of the opposing captain.

Note

(a) More or Less than Eleven Players a Side
A match may be played by agreement between sides of more or less than eleven players, but not more than eleven players may field.

LAW 2. SUBSTITUTES AND RUNNERS: BATSMAN OR FIELDSMAN LEAVING THE FIELD: BATSMAN RETIRING: BATSMAN COMMENCING INNINGS

1. Substitutes

In normal circumstances, a substitute shall be allowed to field only for a player who satisfies the umpire that he has become injured or become ill during the match. However, in very exceptional circumstances, the umpires may use their discretion to allow a substitute for a player who has to leave the field or does not take the field for other wholly acceptable reasons, subject to consent being given by the opposing captain. If a player wishes to change his shirt, boots, etc., he may leave the field to do so (no changing on the field), but no substitute will be allowed.

2. Objection to Substitutes

The opposing captain shall have no right of objection to any player acting as substitute in the field, nor as to where he shall field, although he may object to the substitute acting as wicket-keeper.

Experimental Law: The opposing captain shall have no right of objection to any player acting as substitute on the field, nor as to where he shall field; however no substitute shall act as wicket-keeper. (*It has been recommended that this Experimental Law should apply in all levels of cricket from April 1, 1989*).

3. Substitute not to Bat or Bowl

A substitute shall not be allowed to bat or bowl.

4. A Player for whom a Substitute has Acted

A player may bat, bowl or field even though a substitute has acted for him.

5. Runner

A runner shall be allowed for a batsman who, during the match, is incapacitated by illness or injury. The person acting as runner shall be a member of the batting side and shall, if possible have already batted in that innings.

6. Runner's Equipment

The player acting as runner for an injured batsman shall wear the same external protective equipment as the injured batsman.

7. Transgression of the Laws by an Injured Batsman or Runner

An injured batsman may be out should his runner break any one of Laws 33 (Handled the Ball), 37 (Obstructing the Field) or 38 (Run Out). As striker he remains himself subject to the Laws. Furthermore, should he be out of his ground for any purpose and the wicket at the wicket-keeper's end be put down he shall be out under Law 38 (Run Out) or Law 39 (Stumped), irrespective of the position of the other batsman or the runner, and no runs shall be scored.

When not the striker, the injured batsman is out of the game and shall stand where he does not interfere with the play. Should he bring himself into the game in any way, then he shall suffer the penalties that any transgression of the Laws demands.

8. Fieldsman Leaving the Field

No fieldsman shall leave the field or return during a session of play without the consent of the umpire at the bowler's end. The umpire's consent is also necessary if a substitute is required for a fieldsman, when his side returns to the field after an interval. If a member of the fielding side leaves the field or fails to return after an interval and is absent from the field for longer than fifteen minutes, he shall not be permitted to bowl after his return until he has been on the field for at least that length of playing time for which he was absent. This restriction shall not apply at the start of a new day's play.

9. Batsman Leaving the Field or Retiring

A batsman may leave the field or retire at any time owing to illness, injury or other unavoidable cause, having previously notified the umpire at the bowler's end. He may resume his innings at the fall of a wicket, which for the purposes of this Law shall include the retirement of another batsman.

If he leaves the field or retires for any other reason he may resume his innings only with the consent of the opposing captain.

When a batsman has left the field or retired and is unable to return owing to illness, injury or other unavoidable cause, his innings is to be recorded as "retired, not out". Otherwise it is to be recorded as "retired, out".

10. Commencement of a Batsman's Innings

A batsman shall be considered to have commenced his innings once he has stepped on to the field of play.

Note

(a) Substitutes and Runners

For the purpose of these Laws, allowable illnesses or injuries are those which occur at any time after the nomination by the captains of their teams.

LAW 3. THE UMPIRES

1. Appointment

Before the toss for innings, two umpires shall be appointed, one for each end, to control the game with absolute impartiality as required by the Laws.

2. Change of Umpires

No umpire shall be changed during a match without the consent of both captains.

3. Special Conditions

Before the toss for innings, the umpires shall agree with both captains on any special conditions affecting the conduct of the match.

4. The Wickets

The umpires shall satisfy themselves before the start of the match that the wickets are properly pitched.

5. Clock or Watch

The umpires shall agree between themselves and inform both captains before the start of the match on the watch or clock to be followed during the match.

6. Conduct and Implements

Before and during a match the umpires shall ensure that the conduct of the game and the implements used are strictly in accordance with the Laws.

7. Fair and Unfair Play

The umpires shall be the sole judges of fair and unfair play.

8. Fitness of Ground, Weather and Light

(a) The umpires shall be the sole judges of the fitness of the ground, weather and light for play.

(i) However, before deciding to suspend play, or not to start play, or not to resume play after an interval or stoppage, the umpires shall establish whether both captains (the batsmen at the wicket may deputise for their captain) wish to commence or to continue in the prevailing conditions; if so, their wishes shall be met.

(ii) In addition, if during play the umpires decide that the light is unfit, only the batting side shall have the option of continuing play. After agreeing to continue to play in unfit light conditions, the captain of the batting side (or a batsman at the wicket) may appeal against the light to the umpires, who shall uphold the appeal only if, in their opinion, the light has deteriorated since the agreement to continue was made.

(b) After any suspension of play, the umpires, unaccompanied by any of the players or officials, shall, on their own initiative, carry out an inspection immediately the conditions improve and shall continue to inspect at intervals. Immediately the umpires decide that play is possible they shall call upon the players to resume the game.

9. Exceptional Circumstances

In exceptional circumstances, other than those of weather, ground or light, the umpires may decide to suspend or abandon play. Before making such a decision the umpires shall establish, if the circumstances allow, whether both captains (the batsmen at the wicket may deputise for their captain) wish to continue in the prevailing conditions; if so, their wishes shall be met.

10. Position of Umpires

The umpires shall stand where they can best see any act upon which their decision may be required.

Subject to this over-riding consideration, the umpire at the bowler's end shall stand where he does not interfere with either the bowler's run-up or the striker's view.

The umpire at the striker's end may elect to stand on the off instead of the leg side of the pitch, provided he informs the captain of the fielding side and the striker of his intention to do so.

11. Umpires Changing Ends

The umpires shall change ends after each side has had one innings.

12. Disputes

All disputes shall be determined by the umpires, and if they disagree the actual state of things shall continue.

13. Signals

The following code of signals shall be used by umpires who will wait until a signal has been answered by a scorer before allowing the game to proceed.

Boundary	– by waving the arm from side to side.
Boundary 6	– by raising both arms above the head.
Bye	– by raising an open hand above the head.
Dead Ball	– by crossing and re-crossing the wrists below the waist.
Leg-bye	– by touching a raised knee with the hand.
No-ball	– by extending one arm horizontally.
Out	– by raising the index finger above the head. If not out, the umpire shall call "not out".
Short run	– by bending the arm upwards and by touching the nearer shoulder with the tips of the fingers.
Wide	– by extending both arms horizontally.

14. Correctness of Scores

The umpires shall be responsible for satisfying themselves on the correctness of the scores throughout and at the conclusion of the match. See Law 21.6 (Correctness of Result).

Notes

(a) Attendance of Umpires
The umpires should be present on the ground and report to the ground executive or the equivalent at least thirty minutes before the start of a day's play.

(b) Consultation between Umpires and Scorers
Consultation between umpires and scorers over doubtful points is essential.

(c) Fitness of Ground
The umpires shall consider the ground as unfit for play when it is so wet or slippery as to deprive the bowlers of a reasonable foothold, the fieldsmen, other than the deep-fielders, of the power of free movement, or the batsmen of the ability to play their strokes or to run between the wickets. Play should not be suspended merely because the grass and the ball are wet and slippery.

(d) Fitness of Weather and Light
The umpires should suspend play only when they consider that the conditions are so bad that it is unreasonable or dangerous to continue.

LAW 4. THE SCORERS

1. Recording Runs

All runs scored shall be recorded by scorers appointed for the purpose. Where there are two scorers they shall frequently check to ensure that the score-sheets agree.

2. Acknowledging Signals

The scorers shall accept and immediately acknowledge all instructions and signals given to them by the umpires.

LAW 5. THE BALL

1. Weight and Size

The ball, when new, shall weigh not less than $5\frac{1}{2}$ ounces/155.9g, nor more than $5\frac{3}{4}$ ounces/163g; and shall measure not less than $8\frac{13}{16}$ inches/22.4cm, nor more than 9 inches/22.9cm in circumference.

2. Approval of Balls

All balls used in matches shall be approved by the umpires and captains before the start of the match.

3. New Ball

Subject to agreement to the contrary, having been made before the toss, either captain may demand a new ball at the start of each innings.

4. New Ball in Match of Three or More Days' Duration

In a match of three or more days' duration, the captain of the fielding side may demand a new ball after the prescribed number of overs has been bowled with the old one. The governing body for cricket in the country concerned shall decide the number of overs applicable in that country, which shall be not less than 75 six-ball overs (55 eight-ball overs).

5. Ball Lost or Becoming Unfit for Play

In the event of a ball during play being lost or, in the opinion of the umpires, becoming unfit for play, the umpires shall allow it to be replaced by one that in their opinion has had a similar amount of wear. If a ball is to be replaced, the umpires shall inform the batsman.

Note

(a) Specifications
The specifications, as described in 1 above, shall apply to top-grade balls only. The following degrees of tolerance will be acceptable for other grades of ball.

(i) *Men's Grades 2–4*
Weight: $5\frac{5}{16}$ ounces/150g to $5\frac{13}{16}$ ounces/165g.
Size: $8\frac{11}{16}$ inches/22.0cm to $9\frac{1}{16}$ inches/23.0cm.

(ii) *Women's*
Weight: $4\frac{15}{16}$ ounces/140g to $5\frac{5}{16}$ ounces/150g.
Size: $8\frac{1}{4}$ inches/21.0cm to $8\frac{7}{8}$ inches/22.5cm.

(iii) *Junior*
Weight: $4\frac{5}{16}$ ounces/133g to $5\frac{1}{16}$ ounces/143g.
Size: $8\frac{1}{16}$ inches/20.5cm to $8\frac{11}{16}$ inches/22.0cm.

LAW 6. THE BAT

1. Width and Length

The bat overall shall not be more than 38 inches/96.5cm in length; the blade of the bat shall be made of wood and shall not exceed $4\frac{1}{4}$ inches/10.8cm at the widest part.

Note

(a) The blade of the bat may be covered with material for protection, strengthening or repair. Such material shall not exceed $\frac{1}{16}$ inch/1.56mm in thickness.

LAW 7. THE PITCH

1. Area of Pitch

The pitch is the area between the bowling creases – see Law 9 (The Bowling and Popping Creases). It shall measure 5 feet/1.52m in width on either side of a line joining the centre of the middle stumps of the wickets – see Law 8 (The Wickets).

2. Selection and Preparation

Before the toss for innings, the executive of the ground shall be responsible for the selection and preparation of the pitch; thereafter the umpires shall control its use and maintenance.

3. Changing Pitch

The pitch shall not be changed during a match unless it becomes unfit for play, and then only with the consent of both captains.

4. Non-Turf Pitches

In the event of a non-turf pitch being used, the following shall apply:

(a) Length: That of the playing surface to a minimum of 58 feet/17.68m.

(b) Width: That of the playing surface to a minimum of 6 feet/1.83m.

See Law 10 (Rolling, Sweeping, Mowing, Watering the Pitch and Re-marking of Creases) Note (a).

LAW 8. THE WICKETS

1. Width and Pitching

Two sets of wickets, each 9 inches/22.86cm wide, and consisting of three wooden stumps with two wooden bails upon the top, shall be pitched opposite and parallel to each other at a distance of 22 yards/20.12m between the centres of the two middle stumps.

2. Size of Stumps

The stumps shall be of equal and sufficient size to prevent the ball from passing between them. Their tops shall be 28 inches/71.1cm above the ground, and shall be dome-shaped except for the bail grooves.

3. Size of Bails

The bails shall be each $4\frac{3}{8}$ inches/11.1cm in length and when in position on the top of the stumps shall not project more than $\frac{1}{2}$ inch/1.3cm above them.

Notes

(a) Dispensing with Bails
In a high wind the umpires may decide to dispense with the use of bails.

(b) Junior Cricket
For junior cricket, as defined by the local governing body, the following measurements for the wickets shall apply:

Width – 8 inches/20.32cm.
Pitched – 21 yards/19.20m.
Height – 27 inches/68.58cm.
Bails – each $3\frac{7}{8}$ inches/9.84cm in length and should not project more than $\frac{1}{2}$ inch/1.3cm above the stumps.

LAW 9. THE BOWLING, POPPING AND RETURN CREASES

1. The Bowling Crease

The bowling crease shall be marked in line with the stumps at each end and shall be 8 feet 8 inches/2.64m in length, with the stumps in the centre.

2. The Popping Crease

The popping crease, which is the back edge of the crease marking, shall be in front of and parallel with the bowling crease. It shall have the back edge of the crease marking 4 feet/1.22m from the centre of the stumps and shall extend to a minimum of 6 feet/1.83m on either side of the line of the wicket.

The popping crease shall be considered to be unlimited in length.

3. The Return Crease

The return crease marking, of which the inside edge is the crease, shall be at each end of the bowling crease and at right angles to it. The return crease shall be marked to a minimum of 4 feet/1.22m behind the wicket and shall be considered to be unlimited in length. A forward extension shall be marked to the popping crease.

LAW 10. ROLLING, SWEEPING, MOWING, WATERING THE PITCH AND RE-MARKING OF CREASES

1. Rolling

During the match the pitch may be rolled at the request of the captain of the batting side, for a period of not more than seven minutes before the start of each innings, other than the first innings of the match, and before the start of each day's play. In addition, if, after the toss and before the first innings of the match, the start is delayed, the captain of the batting side shall have the right to have the pitch rolled for not more than seven minutes.

The pitch shall not otherwise be rolled during the match.

The seven minutes' rolling permitted before the start of a day's play shall take place not earlier than half an hour before the start of play and the captain of the batting side may delay such rolling until ten minutes before the start of play should he so desire.

If a captain declares an innings closed less than fifteen minutes before the resumption of play, and the other captain is thereby prevented from exercising his option of seven minutes' rolling or if he is so prevented for any other reason, the time for rolling shall be taken out of the normal playing time.

2. Sweeping

Such sweeping of the pitch as is necessary during the match shall be done so that the seven minutes allowed for rolling the pitch, provided for in 1 above, is not affected.

3. Mowing

(a) Responsibilities of Ground Authority and of Umpires
All mowings which are carried out before the toss for innings shall be the responsibility of the ground authority; thereafter they shall be carried out under the supervision of the umpires. See Law 7.2 (Selection and Preparation).

(b) Initial Mowing
The pitch shall be mown before play begins on the day the match is scheduled to start, or in the case of a delayed start on the day the match is expected to start. See 3(a) above (Responsibilities of Ground Authority and of Umpires).

(c) Subsequent Mowings in a Match of Two or More Days' Duration
In a match of two or more days' duration, the pitch shall be mown daily before play begins. Should this mowing not take place because of weather conditions, rest days or other reasons, the pitch shall be mown on the first day on which the match is resumed.

(d) Mowing of the Outfield in a Match of Two or More Days' Duration
In order to ensure that conditions are as similar as possible for both sides, the outfield shall normally be mown before the commencement of play on each day of the match, if ground and weather conditions allow. See Note (b) to this Law.

4. Watering

The pitch shall not be watered during a match.

5. Re-marking Creases

Whenever possible the creases shall be re-marked.

6. Maintenance of Foot-holes

In wet weather, the umpires shall ensure that the holes made by the bowlers and batsmen are cleaned out and dried whenever necessary to facilitate play. In matches of two or more days' duration, the umpires shall allow, if necessary, the re-turfing of foot-holes made by the bowler in his delivery stride, or the use of quick-setting fillings for the same purpose, before the start of each day's play.

7. Securing of Footholds and Maintenance of Pitch

During play, the umpires shall allow either batsman to beat the pitch with his bat and players to secure their footholds by the use of sawdust, provided that no damage to the pitch is so caused, and Law 42 (Unfair Play) is not contravened.

Notes

(a) Non-turf Pitches

The above Law 10 applies to turf pitches.

The game is played on non-turf pitches in many countries at various levels. Whilst the conduct of the game on these surfaces should always be in accordance with the Laws of Cricket, it is recognised that it may sometimes be necessary for governing bodies to lay down special playing conditions to suit the type of non-turf pitch used in their country.

In matches played against touring teams, any special playing conditions should be agreed in advance by both parties.

(b) Mowing of the Outfield in a Match of Two or More Days' Duration

If, for reasons other than ground and weather conditions, daily and complete mowing is not possible, the ground authority shall notify the captains and umpires, before the toss for innings, of the procedure to be adopted for such mowing during the match.

(c) Choice of Roller

If there is more than one roller available, the captain of the batting side shall have a choice.

LAW 11. COVERING THE PITCH

1. Before the Start of a Match

Before the start of a match, complete covering of the pitch shall be allowed.

2. During a Match

The pitch shall not be completely covered during a match unless prior arrangement or regulations so provide.

3. Covering Bowlers' Run-up

Whenever possible, the bowlers' run-up shall be covered, but the covers so used shall not extend further than 4 feet/1.22m in front of the popping crease.

Note

(a) Removal of Covers

The covers should be removed as promptly as possible whenever the weather permits.

LAW 12. INNINGS

1. Number of Innings

A match shall be of one or two innings of each side according to agreement reached before the start of play.

2. Alternate Innings

In a two-innings match each side shall take their innings alternately except in the case provided for in Law 13 (The Follow-on).

3. The Toss

The captains shall toss for the choice of innings on the field of play not later than fifteen minutes before the time scheduled for the match to start, or before the time agreed upon for play to start.

4. Choice of Innings

The winner of the toss shall notify his decision to bat or to field to the opposing captain not later than ten minutes before the time scheduled for the match to start, or before the time agreed upon for play to start. The decision shall not thereafter be altered.

5. Continuation after One Innings of Each Side

Despite the terms of 1 above, in a one-innings match, when a result has been reached on the first innings, the captains may agree to the continuation of play if, in their opinion, there is a prospect of carrying the game to a further issue in the time left. See Law 21 (Result).

Notes

(a) Limited Innings – One-innings Match
In a one-innings match, each innings may, by agreement, be limited by a number of overs or by a period of time.

(b) Limited Innings – Two-innings Match
In a two-innings match, the first innings of each side may, by agreement, be limited to a number of overs or by a period of time.

LAW 13. THE FOLLOW-ON

1. Lead on First Innings

In a two-innings match the side which bats first and leads by 200 runs in a match of five days or more, by 150 runs in a three-day or four-day match, by 100 runs in a two-day match, or by 75 runs in a one-day match, shall have the option of requiring the other side to follow their innings.

2. Day's Play Lost

If no play takes place on the first day of a match of two or more days' duration, 1 above shall apply in accordance with the number of days' play remaining from the actual start of the match.

LAW 14. DECLARATIONS

1. Time of Declaration

The captain of the batting side may declare an innings closed at any time during a match, irrespective of its duration.

2. Forfeiture of Second Innings

A captain may forfeit his second innings, provided his decision to do so is notified to the opposing captain and umpires in sufficient time to allow seven minutes' rolling of the pitch. See Law 10 (Rolling, Sweeping, Mowing, Watering the Pitch and Re-marking of Creases). The normal ten-minute interval between innings shall be applied.

LAW 15. START OF PLAY

1. Call of Play

At the start of each innings and of each day's play, and on the resumption of play after any interval or interruption, the umpire at the bowler's end shall call "play".

2. Practice on the Field

At no time on any day of the match shall there be any bowling or batting practice on the pitch.

No practice may take place on the field if, in the opinion of the umpires, it could result in a waste of time.

3. Trial Run-up

No bowler shall have a trial run-up after "play" has been called in any session of play, except at the fall of a wicket when an umpire may allow such a trial run-up if he is satisfied that it will not cause any waste of time.

LAW 16. INTERVALS

1. Length

The umpire shall allow such intervals as have been agreed upon for meals, and ten minutes between each innings.

2. Luncheon Interval – Innings Ending or Stoppage within Ten Minutes of Interval

If an innings ends or there is a stoppage caused by weather or bad light within ten minutes of the agreed time for the luncheon interval, the interval shall be taken immediately.

The time remaining in the session of play shall be added to the agreed length of the interval but no extra allowance shall be made for the ten-minute interval between innings.

3. Tea Interval – Innings Ending or Stoppage within Thirty Minutes of Interval

If an innings ends or there is a stoppage caused by weather or bad light within thirty minutes of the agreed time for the tea interval, the interval shall be taken immediately.

The interval shall be of the agreed length and, if applicable, shall include the ten-minute interval between innings.

4. Tea Interval – Continuation of Play

If, at the agreed time for the tea interval, nine wickets are down, play shall continue for a period not exceeding thirty minutes or until the innings is concluded.

5. Tea Interval – Agreement to Forgo

At any time during the match, the captains may agree to forgo a tea interval.

6. Intervals for Drinks

If both captains agree before the start of a match that intervals for drinks may be taken, the option to take such intervals shall be available to either side. These intervals shall be restricted to one per session, shall be kept as short as possible, shall not be taken in the last hour of the match, and in any case shall not exceed five minutes.

The agreed times for these intervals shall be strictly adhered to, except that if a wicket falls within five minutes of the agreed time then drinks shall be taken out immediately.

If an innings ends or there is a stoppage caused by weather or bad light within thirty minutes of the agreed time for a drinks interval, there will be no interval for drinks in that session.

At any time during the match the captains may agree to forgo any such drinks interval.

Notes

(a) Tea Interval – One-day Match
In a one-day match, a specific time for the tea interval need not necessarily be arranged, and it may be agreed to take this interval between the innings of a one-innings match.

(b) Changing the Agreed Time of Intervals
In the event of the ground, weather or light conditions causing a suspension of play, the umpires, after consultation with the captains, may decide in the interests of time-saving to bring forward the time of the luncheon or tea interval.

LAW 17. CESSATION OF PLAY

1. Call of Time

The umpire at the bowler's end shall call "time" on the cessation of play before any interval or interruption of play, at the end of each day's play, and at the conclusion of the match. See Law 27 (Appeals).

2. Removal of Bails

After the call of "time", the umpires shall remove the bails from both wickets.

3. Starting a Last Over

The last over before an interval or the close of play shall be started provided the umpire, after walking at his normal pace, has arrived at his position behind the stumps at the bowler's end before time has been reached.

4. Completion of the Last Over of a Session

The last over before an interval or the close of play shall be completed unless a batsman is out or retires during that over within two minutes of the interval or the close of play or unless the players have occasion to leave the field.

5. Completion of the Last Over of a Match

An over in progress at the close of play on the final day of a match shall be completed at the request of either captain, even if a wicket falls after time has been reached.

If, during the last over, the players have occasion to leave the field, the umpires shall call "time" and there shall be no resumption of play and the match shall be at an end.

6. Last Hour of Match – Number of Overs

The umpires shall indicate when one hour of playing time of the match remains according to the agreed hours of play. The next over after that moment shall be the first of a minimum of twenty six-ball overs (fifteen eight-ball overs), provided a result is not reached earlier or there is no interval or interruption of play.

7. Last Hour of Match – Intervals between Innings and Interruptions of Play

If, at the commencement of the last hour of the match, an interval or interruption of play is in progress or if, during the last hour, there is an interval between innings or an interruption of play, the minimum number of overs to be bowled on the resumption of play shall be reduced in proportion to the duration, within the last hour of the match, of any such interval or interruption.

The minimum number of overs to be bowled after the resumption of play shall be calculated as follows:

(a) In the case of an interval or interruption of play being in progress at the commencement of the last hour of the match, or in the case of a first interval or interruption, a deduction shall be made from the minimum of twenty six-ball overs (or fifteen eight-ball overs).

(b) If there is a later interval or interruption, a further deduction shall be made from the minimum number of overs which should have been bowled following the last resumption of play.

(c) These deductions shall be based on the following factors:

(i) The number of overs already bowled in the last hour of the match or, in the case of a later interval or interruption, in the last session of play.

(ii) The number of overs lost as a result of the interval or interruption allowing one six-ball over for every full three minutes (or one eight-ball over for every full four minutes) of interval or interruption.

(iii) Any over left uncompleted at the end of an innings to be excluded from these calculations.

(iv) Any over left uncompleted at the start of an interruption of play to be completed when play is resumed and to count as one over bowled.

(v) An interval to start with the end of an innings and to end ten minutes later; an interruption to start on the call of "time" and to end on the call of "play".

(d) In the event of an innings being completed and a new innings commencing during the last hour of the match, the number of overs to be bowled in the new innings shall be calculated on the basis of one six-ball over for every three minutes or part thereof remaining for play (or one eight-ball over for every four minutes or part thereof remaining for play); or alternatively on the basis that sufficient overs be bowled to enable the full minimum quota of overs to be completed under circumstances governed by (a), (b) and (c) above. In all such cases the alternative which allows the greater number of overs shall be employed.

8. Bowler Unable to Complete an Over during Last Hour of the Match

If, for any reason, a bowler is unable to complete an over during the period of play referred to in 6 above, Law 22.7 (Bowler Incapacitated or Suspended during an Over) shall apply.

LAW 18. SCORING

1. A Run

The score shall be reckoned by runs. A run is scored:

(a) So often as the batsmen, after a hit or at any time while the ball is in play, shall have crossed and made good their ground from end to end.

(b) When a boundary is scored. See Law 19 (Boundaries).

(c) When penalty runs are awarded. See 6 below.

2. Short Runs

(a) If either batsman runs a short run, the umpire shall call and signal "one short" as soon as the ball becomes dead and that run shall not be scored. A run is short if a batsman fails to make good his ground on turning for a further run.

(b) Although a short run shortens the succeeding one, the latter, if completed, shall count.

(c) If either or both batsmen deliberately run short the umpire shall, as soon as he sees that the fielding side have no chance of dismissing either batsman, call and signal "dead ball" and disallow any runs attempted or previously scored. The batsmen shall return to their original ends.

(d) If both batsmen run short in one and the same run, only 1 run shall be deducted.

(e) Only if 3 or more runs are attempted can more than one be short and then, subject to (c) and (d) above, all runs so called shall be disallowed. If there has been more than one short run the umpires shall instruct the scorers as to the number of runs disallowed.

3. Striker Caught

If the striker is caught, no run shall be scored.

4. Batsman Run Out

If a batsman is run out, only that run which was being attempted shall not be scored. If, however, an injured striker himself is run out, no runs shall be scored. See Law 2.7 (Transgression of the Laws by an Injured Batsman or Runner).

5. Batsman Obstructing the Field

If a batsman is out Obstructing the Field, any runs completed before the obstruction occurs shall be scored unless such obstruction prevents a catch being made, in which case no runs shall be scored.

6. Runs Scored for Penalties

Runs shall be scored for penalties under Laws 20 (Lost Ball), 24 (No-ball), 25 (Wide-ball), 41.1 (Fielding the Ball) and for boundary allowances under Law 19 (Boundaries).

7. Batsman Returning to Wicket he has Left

If, while the ball is in play, the batsmen have crossed in running, neither shall return to the wicket he has left, even though a short run has been called or no run has been scored as in the case of a catch. Batsmen, however, shall return to the wickets they originally left in the cases of a boundary and of any disallowance of runs and of an injured batsman being, himself, run out. See Law 2.7 (Transgression by an Injured Batsman or Runner).

Note

(a) Short Run
A striker taking stance in front of his popping crease may run from that point without penalty.

LAW 19. BOUNDARIES

1. The Boundary of the Playing Area

Before the toss for innings, the umpires shall agree with both captains on the boundary of the playing area. The boundary shall, if possible, be marked by a white line, a rope laid on the ground, or a fence. If flags or posts only are used to mark a boundary, the imaginary line joining such points shall be regarded as the boundary. An obstacle, or person, within the playing area shall not be regarded as a boundary unless so decided by the umpires before the toss for innings. Sightscreens within, or partially within, the playing area shall be regarded as the boundary and when the ball strikes or passes within or under or directly over any part of the screen, a boundary shall be scored.

2. Runs Scored for Boundaries

Before the toss for innings, the umpires shall agree with both captains the runs to be allowed for boundaries, and in deciding the allowance for them, the umpires and captains shall be guided by the prevailing custom of the ground. The allowance for a boundary shall normally be 4 runs, and 6 runs for all hits pitching over and clear of the boundary line or fence, even though the ball has been previously touched by a fieldsman. 6 runs shall also be scored if a fieldsman, after catching a ball, carries it over the boundary. See Law 32 (Caught) Note (a). 6 runs shall not be scored when a ball struck by the striker hits a sightscreen full pitch if the screen is within, or partially within, the playing area, but if the ball is struck directly over a sightscreen so situated, 6 runs shall be scored.

3. A Boundary

A boundary shall be scored and signalled by the umpire at the bowler's end whenever, in his opinion:

(a) A ball in play touches or crosses the boundary, however marked.

(b) A fieldsman with ball in hand touches or grounds any part of his person on or over a boundary line.

(c) A fieldsman with ball in hand grounds any part of his person over a boundary fence or board. This allows the fieldsman to touch or lean on or over a boundary fence or board in preventing a boundary.

4. Runs Exceeding Boundary Allowance

The runs completed at the instant the ball reaches the boundary shall count if they exceed the boundary allowance.

5. Overthrows or Wilful Act of a Fieldsman

If the boundary results from an overthrow or from the wilful act of a fieldsman, any runs already completed and the allowance shall be added to the score. The run in progress shall count provided that the batsmen have crossed at the instant of the throw or act.

Note

(a) Position of Sightscreens
Sightscreens should, if possible, be positioned wholly outside the playing area, as near as possible to the boundary line.

LAW 20. LOST BALL

1. Runs Scored

If a ball in play cannot be found or recovered, any fieldsman may call "lost ball" when 6 runs shall be added to the score; but if more than 6 have been run before "lost ball" is called, as many runs as have been completed shall be scored. The run in progress shall count provided that the batsmen have crossed at the instant of the call of "lost ball".

2. How Scored

The runs shall be added to the score of the striker if the ball has been struck, but otherwise to the score of byes, leg-byes, no-balls or wides as the case may be.

LAW 21. THE RESULT

1. A Win – Two-innings Matches

The side which has scored a total of runs in excess of that scored by the opposing side in its two completed innings shall be the winner.

2. A Win – One-innings Matches

(a) One-innings matches, unless played out as in 1 above, shall be decided on the first innings, but see Law 12.5 (Continuation after One Innings of Each Side).

(b) If the captains agree to continue play after the completion of one innings of each side in accordance with Law 12.5 (Continuation after One Innings of Each Side) and a result is not achieved on the second innings, the first innings result shall stand.

3. Umpires Awarding a Match

(a) A match shall be lost by a side which, during the match, (i) refuses to play, or (ii) concedes defeat, and the umpires shall award the match to the other side.

(b) Should both batsmen at the wickets or the fielding side leave the field at any time without the agreement of the umpires, this shall constitute a refusal to play and, on appeal, the umpires shall award the match to the other side in accordance with (a) above.

4. A Tie

The result of a match shall be a tie when the scores are equal at the conclusion of play, but only if the side batting last has completed its innings.

If the scores of the completed first innings of a one-day match are equal, it shall be a tie but only if the match has not been played out to a further conclusion.

5. A Draw

A match not determined in any of the ways as in 1, 2, 3 and 4 above shall count as a draw.

6. Correctness of Result

Any decision as to the correctness of the scores shall be the responsibility of the umpires. See Law 3.14 (Correctness of Scores).

If, after the umpires and players have left the field in the belief that the match has been concluded, the umpires decide that a mistake in scoring has occurred, which affects the result, and provided time has not been reached, they shall order play to resume and to continue until the agreed finishing time unless a result is reached earlier.

If the umpires decide that a mistake has occurred and time has been reached, the umpires shall immediately inform both captains of the necessary corrections to the scores and, if applicable, to the result.

7. Acceptance of Result

In accepting the scores as notified by the scorers and agreed by the umpires, the captains of both sides thereby accept the result.

Notes

(a) Statement of Results

The result of a finished match is stated as a win by runs, except in the case of a win by the side batting last when it is by the number of wickets still then to fall.

(b) Winning Hit or Extras

As soon as the side has won, see 1 and 2 above, the umpire shall call "time", the match is finished, and nothing that happens thereafter other than as a result of a mistake in scoring (see 6 above) shall be regarded as part of the match.

However, if a boundary constitutes the winning hit – or extras – and the boundary allowance exceeds the number of runs required to win the match, such runs scored shall be credited to the side's total and, in the case of a hit, to the striker's score.

LAW 22. THE OVER

1. Number of Balls

The ball shall be bowled from each wicket alternately in overs of either six or eight balls according to agreement before the match.

2. Call of "Over"

When the agreed number of balls has been bowled, and as the ball becomes dead or when it becomes clear to the umpire at the bowler's end that both the fielding side and the batsmen at the wicket have ceased to regard the ball as in play, the umpire shall call "over" before leaving the wicket.

3. No-ball or Wide-ball

Neither a no-ball nor a wide-ball shall be reckoned as one of the over.

4. Umpire Miscounting

If an umpire miscounts the number of balls, the over as counted by the umpire shall stand.

5. Bowler Changing Ends

A bowler shall be allowed to change ends as often as desired, provided only that he does not bowl two overs consecutively in an innings.

6. The Bowler Finishing an Over

A bowler shall finish an over in progress unless he be incapacitated or be suspended under Law 42.8 (The Bowling of Fast Short-pitched Balls), 9 (The Bowling of Fast High Full Pitches), 10 (Time Wasting) and 11 (Players Damaging the Pitch). If an over is left incomplete for any reason at the start of an interval or interruption of play, it shall be finished on the resumption of play.

7. Bowler Incapacitated or Suspended during an Over

If, for any reason, a bowler is incapacitated while running up to bowl the first ball of an over, or is incapacitated or suspended during an over, the umpire shall call and signal "dead ball" and another bowler shall be allowed to bowl or complete the over from the same end, provided only that he shall not bowl two overs, or part thereof, consecutively in one innings.

8. Position of Non-striker

The batsman at the bowler's end shall normally stand on the opposite side of the wicket to that from which the ball is being delivered, unless a request to do otherwise is granted by the umpire.

LAW 23. DEAD BALL

1. The Ball Becomes Dead

When:

(a) It is finally settled in the hands of the wicket-keeper or the bowler.

(b) It reaches or pitches over the boundary.

(c) A batsman is out.

(d) Whether played or not, it lodges in the clothing or equipment of a batsman or the clothing of an umpire.

(e) A ball lodges in a protective helmet worn by a member of the fielding side.

(f) A penalty is awarded under Law 20 (Lost Ball) or Law 41.1 (Fielding the Ball).

(g) The umpire calls "over" or "time".

2. Either Umpire Shall Call and Signal "Dead Ball"

When:

(a) He intervenes in a case of unfair play.

(b) A serious injury to a player or umpire occurs.

(c) He is satisfied that, for an adequate reason, the striker is not ready to receive the ball and makes no attempt to play it.

(d) The bowler drops the ball accidentally before delivery, or the ball does not leave his hand for any reason.

(e) One or both bails fall from the striker's wicket before he receives delivery.

(f) He leaves his normal position for consultation.

(g) He is required to do so under Law 26.3 (Disallowance of Leg-byes).

3. The Ball Ceases to be Dead

When:

(a) The bowler starts his run-up or bowling action.

4. The Ball is Not Dead

When:

(a) It strikes an umpire (unless it lodges in his dress).

(b) The wicket is broken or struck down (unless a batsman is out thereby).

(c) An unsuccessful appeal is made.

(d) The wicket is broken accidentally either by the bowler during his delivery or by a batsman in running.

(e) The umpire has called "no-ball" or "wide".

Notes

(a) Ball Finally Settled

Whether the ball is finally settled or not – see 1(a) above – must be a question for the umpires alone to decide.

(b) Action on Call of "Dead Ball"

(i) If "dead ball" is called prior to the striker receiving a delivery, the bowler shall be allowed an additional ball.

(ii) If "dead ball" is called after the striker receives a delivery, the bowler shall not be allowed an additional ball, unless a "no-ball" or "wide" has been called.

LAW 24. NO-BALL

1. Mode of Delivery

The umpire shall indicate to the striker whether the bowler intends to bowl over or round the wicket, overarm or underarm, right- or left-handed. Failure on the part of the bowler to indicate in advance a change in his mode of delivery is unfair and the umpire shall call and signal "no-ball".

2. Fair Delivery – The Arm

For a delivery to be fair the ball must be bowled, not thrown – see Note (a) below. If either umpire is not entirely satisfied with the absolute fairness of a delivery in this respect he shall call and signal "no-ball" instantly upon delivery.

3. Fair Delivery – The Feet

The umpire at the bowler's wicket shall call and signal "no-ball" if he is not satisfied that in the delivery stride:

(a) The bowler's back foot has landed within and not touching the return crease or its forward extension; or

(b) Some part of the front foot whether grounded or raised was behind the popping crease.

4. Bowler Throwing at Striker's Wicket before Delivery

If the bowler, before delivering the ball, throws it at the striker's wicket in an attempt to run him out, the umpire shall call and signal "no-ball". See Law 42.12 (Batsman Unfairly Stealing a Run) and Law 38 (Run Out).

5. Bowler Attempting to Run Out Non-striker before Delivery

If the bowler, before delivering the ball, attempts to run out the non-striker, any runs which result shall be allowed and shall be scored as no-balls. Such an attempt shall not count as a ball in the over. The umpire shall not call "no-ball". See Law 42.12 (Batsman Unfairly Stealing a Run).

6. Infringement of Laws by a Wicket-keeper or a Fieldsman

The umpire shall call and signal "no-ball" in the event of the wicket-keeper infringing Law 40.1 (Position of Wicket-keeper) or a fieldsman infringing Law 41.2 (Limitation of On-side Fieldsmen) or Law 41.3 (Position of Fieldsmen).

7. Revoking a Call

An umpire shall revoke the call "no-ball" if the ball does not leave the bowler's hand for any reason. See Law 23.2 (Either Umpire Shall Call and Signal "Dead Ball").

8. Penalty

A penalty of 1 run for a no-ball shall be scored if no runs are made otherwise.

9. Runs from a No-ball

The striker may hit a no-ball and whatever runs result shall be added to his score. Runs made otherwise from a no-ball shall be scored no-balls.

10. Out from a No-ball

The striker shall be out from a no-ball if he breaks Law 34 (Hit the Ball Twice) and either batsman may be run out or shall be given out if either breaks Law 33 (Handled the Ball) or Law 37 (Obstructing the Field).

11. Batsman Given Out off a No-ball

Should a batsman be given out off a no-ball the penalty for bowling it shall stand unless runs are otherwise scored.

Notes

(a) Definition of a Throw
A ball shall be deemed to have been thrown if, in the opinion of either umpire, the process of straightening the bowling arm, whether it be partial or complete, takes place during that part of the delivery swing which directly precedes the ball leaving the hand. This definition shall not debar a bowler from the use of the wrist in the delivery swing.

(b) No-ball Not Counting in Over
A no-ball shall not be reckoned as one of the over. See Law 22.3 (No-ball or Wide-ball).

LAW 25. WIDE-BALL

1. Judging a Wide

If the bowler bowls the ball so high over or so wide of the wicket that, in the opinion of the umpire, it passes out of the reach of the striker, standing in a normal guard position, the umpire shall call and signal "wide-ball" as soon as it has passed the line of the striker's wicket.

The umpire shall not adjudge a ball as being wide if:

(a) The striker, by moving from his guard position, causes the ball to pass out of his reach.

(b) The striker moves and thus brings the ball within his reach.

2. Penalty

A penalty of 1 run for a wide shall be scored if no runs are made otherwise.

3. Ball Coming to Rest in Front of the Striker

If a ball which the umpire considers to have been delivered comes to rest in front of the line of the striker's wicket, "wide" shall not be called. The striker has a right, without interference from the fielding side, to make one attempt to hit the ball. If the fielding side interfere, the umpire shall replace the ball where it came to rest and shall order the fieldsmen to resume the places they occupied in the field before the ball was delivered.

The umpire shall call and signal "dead ball" as soon as it is clear that the striker does not intend to hit the ball, or after the striker has made an unsuccessful attempt to hit the ball.

4. Revoking a Call

The umpire shall revoke the call if the striker hits a ball which has been called "wide".

5. Ball Not Dead

The ball does not become dead on the call of "wide-ball" – see Law 23.4 (The Ball is Not Dead).

6. Runs Resulting from a Wide

All runs which are run or result from a wide-ball which is not a no-ball shall be scored wide-balls, or if no runs are made 1 shall be scored.

7. Out from a Wide

The striker shall be out from a wide-ball if he breaks Law 35 (Hit Wicket), or Law 39 (Stumped). Either batsman may be run out and shall be out if he breaks Law 33 (Handled the Ball), or Law 37 (Obstructing the Field).

8. Batsman Given Out off a Wide

Should a batsman be given out off a wide, the penalty for bowling it shall stand unless runs are otherwise made.

Note

(a) Wide-ball Not Counting in Over
A wide-ball shall not be reckoned as one of the over – see Law 22.3 (No-ball or Wide-ball).

LAW 26. BYE AND LEG-BYE

1. Byes

If the ball, not having been called "wide" or "no-ball", passes the striker without touching his bat or person, and any runs are obtained, the umpire shall signal "bye" and the run or runs shall be credited as such to the batting side.

2. Leg-byes

If the ball, not having been called "wide" or "no-ball", is unintentionally deflected by the striker's dress or person, except a hand holding the bat, and any runs are obtained the umpire shall signal "leg-bye" and the run or runs so scored shall be credited as such to the batting side.

Such leg-byes shall be scored only if, in the opinion of the umpire, the striker has:

(a) Attempted to play the ball with his bat; or

(b) Tried to avoid being hit by the ball.

3. Disallowance of Leg-byes

In the case of a deflection by the striker's person, other than in 2(a) and (b) above, the umpire shall call and signal "dead ball" as soon as 1 run has been completed or when it is clear that a run is not being attempted, or the ball has reached the boundary.

On the call and signal of "dead ball" the batsmen shall return to their original ends and no runs shall be allowed.

LAW 27. APPEALS

1. Time of Appeals

The umpires shall not give a batsman out unless appealed to by the other side which shall be done prior to the bowler beginning his run-up or bowling action to deliver the next ball. Under Law 23.1 (f) (The Ball Becomes Dead), the ball is dead on "over" being called; this does not, however, invalidate an appeal made prior to the first ball of the following over provided "time" has not been called – see Law 17.1 (Call of Time).

2. An Appeal "How's That?"

An appeal "How's That?" shall cover all ways of being out.

3. Answering Appeals

The umpire at the bowler's wicket shall answer appeals before the other umpire in all cases except those arising out of Law 35 (Hit Wicket) or Law 39 (Stumped) or Law 38 (Run Out) when this occurs at the striker's wicket.

When either umpire has given a batsman not out, the other umpire shall, within his jurisdiction, answer the appeal or a further appeal, provided it is made in time in accordance with 1 above (Time of Appeals).

4. Consultation by Umpires

An umpire may consult with the other umpire on a point of fact which the latter may have been in a better position to see and shall then give his decision. If, after consultation, there is still doubt remaining the decision shall be in favour of the batsman.

5. Batsman Leaving his Wicket under a Misapprehension

The umpires shall intervene if satisfied that a batsman, not having been given out, has left hi wicket under a misapprehension that he has been dismissed.

6. Umpire's Decision

The umpire's decision is final. He may alter his decision, provided that such alteration i made promptly.

7. Withdrawal of an Appeal

In exceptional circumstances the captain of the fielding side may seek permission of th umpire to withdraw an appeal provided the outgoing batsman has not left the playing area. I this is allowed, the umpire shall cancel his decision.

LAW 28. THE WICKET IS DOWN

1. Wicket Down

'he wicket is down if:

(a) Either the ball or the striker's bat or person completely removes either bail from the top of the stumps. A disturbance of a bail, whether temporary or not, shall not constitute a complete removal, but the wicket is down if a bail in falling lodges between two of the stumps.

(b) Any player completely removes with his hand or arm a bail from the top of the stumps, provided that the ball is held in that hand or in the hand of the arm so used.

(c) When both bails are off, a stump is struck out of the ground by the ball, or a player strikes or pulls a stump out of the ground, provided that the ball is held in the hand(s) or in the hand of the arm so used.

2. One Bail Off

f one bail is off, it shall be sufficient for the purpose of putting the wicket down to remove the emaining bail, or to strike or pull any of the three stumps out of the ground in any of the ways tated in 1 above.

3. All the Stumps Out of the Ground

f all the stumps are out of the ground, the fielding side shall be allowed to put back one or nore stumps in order to have an opportunity of putting the wicket down.

4. Dispensing with Bails

f owing to the strength of the wind, it has been agreed to dispense with the bails in ccordance with Law 8, Note (a) (Dispensing with Bails), the decision as to when the wicket is own is one for the umpires to decide on the facts before them. In such circumstances and if he umpires so decide, the wicket shall be held to be down even though a stump has not been truck out of the ground.

Vote

(a) Remaking the Wicket
If the wicket is broken while the ball is in play, it is not the umpire's duty to remake the wicket until the ball has become dead – see Law 23 (Dead Ball). A member of the fielding side, however, may remake the wicket in such circumstances.

LAW 29. BATSMAN OUT OF HIS GROUND

1. When out of his Ground

\ batsman shall be considered to be out of his ground unless some part of his bat in his hand r of his person is grounded behind the line of the popping crease.

LAW 30. BOWLED

1. Out Bowled

The striker shall be out *Bowled* if:

(a) His wicket is bowled down, even if the ball first touches his bat or person.

(b) He breaks his wicket by hitting or kicking the ball on to it before the completion of a stroke, or as a result of attempting to guard his wicket. See Law 34.1 (Out Hit the Ball Twice).

Vote

(a) Out Bowled – Not lbw
The striker is out bowled if the ball is deflected on to his wicket even though a decision against him would be justified under Law 36 (lbw).

LAW 31. TIMED OUT

1. Out Timed Out

An incoming batsman shall be out *Timed Out* if he wilfully takes more than two minutes t come in – the two minutes being timed from the moment a wicket falls until the new batsma steps on to the field of play.

If this is not complied with and if the umpire is satisfied that the delay was wilful and if a appeal is made, the new batsman shall be given out by the umpire at the bowler's end.

2. Time to be Added

The time taken by the umpires to investigate the cause of the delay shall be added at th normal close of play.

Notes

(a) Entry in Scorebook
The correct entry in the scorebook when a batsman is given out under this Law "timed out", and the bowler does not get credit for the wicket.

(b) Batsmen Crossing on the Field of Play
It is an essential duty of the captains to ensure that the in-going batsman passes the out going one before the latter leaves the field of play.

LAW 32. CAUGHT

1. Out Caught

The striker shall be out *Caught* if the ball touches his bat or if it touches below the wrist h hand or glove, holding the bat, and is subsequently held by a fieldsman before it touches th ground.

2. A Fair Catch

A catch shall be considered to have been fairly made if:

(a) The fieldsman is within the field of play throughout the act of making the catch.

(i) The act of making the catch shall start from the time when the fieldsman firs handles the ball and shall end when he both retains complete control over th further disposal of the ball and remains within the field of play.

(ii) In order to be within the field of play, the fieldsman may not touch or groun any part of his person on or over a boundary line. When the boundary is marke by a fence or board the fieldsman may not ground any part of his person ove the boundary fence or board, but may touch or lean over the boundary fence o board in completing the catch.

(b) The ball is hugged to the body of the catcher or accidentally lodges in his dress or, i the case of the wicket-keeper, in his pads. However, a striker may not be caught if a ba lodges in a protective helmet worn by a fieldsman, in which case the umpire shall ca and signal "dead ball". See Law 23 (Dead Ball).

(c) The ball does not touch the ground even though a hand holding it does so i effecting the catch.

(d) A fieldsman catches the ball, after it has been lawfully played a second time by th striker, but only if the ball has not touched the ground since being first struck.

(e) A fieldsman catches the ball after it has touched an umpire, another fieldsman c the other batsman. However, a striker may not be caught if a ball has touched protective helmet worn by a fieldsman.

(f) The ball is caught off an obstruction within the boundary provided it has nc previously been agreed to regard the obstruction as a boundary.

3. Scoring of Runs

If a striker is caught, no run shall be scored.

Notes

(a) Scoring from an Attempted Catch
When a fieldsman carrying the ball touches or grounds any part of his person on or over a boundary marked by a line, 6 runs shall be scored.

(b) Ball Still in Play
If a fieldsman releases the ball before he crosses the boundary, the ball will be considered to be still in play and it may be caught by another fieldsman. However, if the original fieldsman returns to the field of play and handles the ball, a catch may not be made.

LAW 33. HANDLED THE BALL

1. Out Handled the Ball

Either batsman on appeal shall be out *Handled the Ball* if he wilfully touches the ball while in play with the hand not holding the bat unless he does so with the consent of the opposite side.

Note

(a) Entry in Scorebook
The correct entry in the scorebook when a batsman is given out under this Law is "handled the ball', and the bowler does not get credit for the wicket.

LAW 34. HIT THE BALL TWICE

1. Out Hit the Ball Twice

The striker, on appeal, shall be out *Hit the Ball Twice* if, after the ball is struck or is stopped by any part of his person, he wilfully strikes it again with his bat or person except for the sole purpose of guarding his wicket: this he may do with his bat or any part of his person other than his hands, but see Law 37.2 (Obstructing a Ball From Being Caught).

For the purpose of this Law, a hand holding the bat shall be regarded as part of the bat.

2. Returning the Ball to a Fieldsman

The striker, on appeal, shall be out under this Law if, without the consent of the opposite side, he uses his bat or person to return the ball to any of the fielding side.

3. Runs from Ball Lawfully Struck Twice

No runs except those which result from an overthrow or penalty – see Law 41 (The Fieldsman) - shall be scored from a ball lawfully struck twice.

Notes

(a) Entry in Scorebook
The correct entry in the scorebook when the striker is given out under this Law is "hit the ball twice", and the bowler does not get credit for the wicket.

(b) Runs Credited to the Batsman
Any runs awarded under 3 above as a result of an overthrow or penalty shall be credited to the striker, provided the ball in the first instance has touched the bat, or, if otherwise, as extras.

LAW 35. HIT WICKET

1. Out Hit Wicket

The striker shall be out *Hit Wicket* if, while the ball is in play:

(a) His wicket is broken with any part of his person, dress, or equipment as a result of any action taken by him in preparing to receive or in receiving a delivery, or in setting off for his first run, immediately after playing, or playing at, the ball.

(b) He hits down his wicket whilst lawfully making a second stroke for the purpose o guarding his wicket within the provisions of Law 34.1 (Out Hit the Ball Twice).

Notes

(a) Not Out Hit Wicket

A batsman is not out under this Law should his wicket be broken in any of the way referred to in 1(a) above if:

(i) It occurs while he is in the act of running, other than in setting off for his firs run immediately after playing at the ball, or while he is avoiding being run ou or stumped.

(ii) The bowler after starting his run-up or bowling action does not deliver the ball in which case the umpire shall immediately call and signal "dead ball".

(iii) It occurs whilst he is avoiding a throw-in at any time.

LAW 36. LEG BEFORE WICKET

1. Out lbw

The striker shall be out *lbw* in the circumstances set out below:

(a) Striker Attempting to Play the Ball

The striker shall be out lbw if he first intercepts with any part of his person, dress o equipment a fair ball which would have hit the wicket and which has not previousl touched his bat or a hand holding the bat, provided that:

(i) The ball pitched in a straight line between wicket and wicket or on the off sid of the striker's wicket, or in the case of a ball intercepted full pitch would hav pitched in a straight line between wicket and wicket; and

(ii) The point of impact is in a straight line between wicket and wicket, even i above the level of the bails.

(b) Striker Making No Attempt to Play the Ball

The striker shall be out lbw even if the ball is intercepted outside the line of the o stump if, in the opinion of the umpire, he has made no genuine attempt to play the ba with his bat, but has intercepted the ball with some part of his person and if th circumstances set out in (a) above apply.

LAW 37. OBSTRUCTING THE FIELD

1. Wilful Obstruction

Either batsman, on appeal, shall be out *Obstructing the Field* if he wilfully obstructs th opposite side by word or action.

2. Obstructing a Ball From Being Caught

The striker, on appeal, shall be out should wilful obstruction by either batsman prevent catch being made.

This shall apply even though the striker causes the obstruction in lawfully guarding hi wicket under the provisions of Law 34. See Law 34.1 (Out Hit the Ball Twice).

Notes

(a) Accidental Obstruction

The umpires must decide whether the obstruction was wilful or not. The accidenta interception of a throw-in by a batsman while running does not break this Law.

(b) Entry in Scorebook

The correct entry in the scorebook when a batsman is given out under this Law i "obstructing the field", and the bowler does not get credit for the wicket.

LAW 38. RUN OUT

1. Out Run Out

Either batsman shall be out *Run Out* if in running or at any time while the ball is in play – except in the circumstances described in Law 39 (Stumped) – he is out of his ground and his wicket is put down by the opposite side. If, however, a batsman in running makes good his ground he shall not be out run out if he subsequently leaves his ground, in order to avoid injury, and the wicket is put down.

2. "No-ball" Called

If a no-ball has been called, the striker shall not be given run out unless he attempts to run.

3. Which Batsman Is Out

If the batsmen have crossed in running, he who runs for the wicket which is put down shall be out; if they have not crossed, he who has left the wicket which is put down shall be out. If a batsman remains in his ground or returns to his ground and the other batsman joins him there, the latter shall be out if his wicket is put down.

4. Scoring of Runs

If a batsman is run out, only that run which is being attempted shall not be scored. If, however, an injured striker himself is run out, no runs shall be scored. See Law 2.7 (Transgression of the Laws by an Injured Batsman or Runner).

Notes

(a) Ball Played on to Opposite Wicket
If the ball is played on to the opposite wicket, neither batsman is liable to be run out unless the ball has been touched by a fieldsman before the wicket is broken.

(b) Entry in Scorebook
The correct entry in the scorebook when a batsman is given out under this Law is "run out", and the bowler does not get credit for the wicket.

LAW 39. STUMPED

1. Out Stumped

The striker shall be out *Stumped* if, in receiving the ball, not being a no-ball, he is out of his ground otherwise than in attempting a run and the wicket is put down by the wicket-keeper without the intervention of another fieldsman.

2. Action by the Wicket-keeper

The wicket-keeper may take the ball in front of the wicket in an attempt to stump the striker only if the ball has touched the bat or person of the striker.

Note

(a) Ball Rebounding from Wicket-keeper's Person
The striker may be out stumped if, in the circumstances stated in 1 above, the wicket is broken by a ball rebounding from the wicket-keeper's person or equipment or is kicked or thrown by the wicket-keeper on to the wicket.

LAW 40. THE WICKET-KEEPER

1. Position of Wicket-keeper

The wicket-keeper shall remain wholly behind the wicket until a ball delivered by the bowler touches the bat or person of the striker, or passes the wicket, or until the striker attempts a run.

In the event of the wicket-keeper contravening this Law, the umpire at the striker's end shall call and signal "no-ball" at the instant of delivery or as soon as possible thereafter.

2. Restriction on Actions of the Wicket-keeper

If the wicket-keeper interferes with the striker's right to play the ball and to guard his wicket, the striker shall not be out except under Laws 33 (Handled the Ball), 34 (Hit the Ball Twice), 37 (Obstructing the Field), 38 (Run Out).

3. Interference with the Wicket-keeper by the Striker

If in the legitimate defence of his wicket, the striker interferes with the wicket-keeper, he shall not be out, except as provided for in Law 37.2 (Obstructing a Ball From Being Caught).

LAW 41. THE FIELDSMAN

1. Fielding the Ball

The fieldsman may stop the ball with any part of his person, but if he wilfully stops it otherwise, 5 runs shall be added to the run or runs already scored; if no run has been scored 5 penalty runs shall be awarded. The run in progress shall count provided that the batsmen have crossed at the instant of the act. If the ball has been struck, the penalty shall be added to the score of the striker, but otherwise to the scores of byes, leg-byes, no-balls or wides as the case may be.

2. Limitation of On-side Fieldsmen

The number of on-side fieldsmen behind the popping crease at the instant of the bowler's delivery shall not exceed two. In the event of infringement by the fielding side the umpire at the striker's end shall call and signal "no-ball" at the instant of delivery or as soon as possible thereafter.

3. Position of Fieldsmen

Whilst the ball is in play and until the ball has made contact with the bat or the striker's person or has passed his bat, no fieldsman, other than the bowler, may stand on or have any part of his person extended over the pitch (measuring 22 yards/20.12m × 10 feet/3.05m). In the event of a fieldsman contravening this Law, the umpire at the bowler's end shall call and signal "no-ball" at the instant of delivery or as soon as possible thereafter. See Law 40.1 (Position of Wicket-keeper).

4. Fieldsmen's Protective Helmets

Protective helmets, when not in use by members of the fielding side, shall be placed, if above the surface, only on the ground behind the wicket-keeper. In the event of the ball, when in play, striking a helmet whilst in this position, 5 penalty runs shall be awarded as laid down in Law 41.1 and Note (a).

Note

(a) Batsmen Changing Ends
The 5 runs referred to in 1 and 4 above are a penalty and the batsmen do not change ends solely by reason of this penalty.

LAW 42. UNFAIR PLAY

1. Responsibility of Captains

The captains are responsible at all times for ensuring that play is conducted within the spirit of the game as well as within the Laws.

2. Responsibility of Umpires

The umpires are the sole judges of fair and unfair play.

3. Intervention by the Umpire

The umpires shall intervene without appeal by calling and signalling "dead ball" in the case of unfair play, but should not otherwise interfere with the progress of the game except as required to do so by the Laws.

4. Lifting the Seam

A player shall not lift the seam of the ball for any reason. Should this be done, the umpires shall change the ball for one of similar condition to that in use prior to the contravention. See Note (a).

5. Changing the Condition of the Ball

Any member of the fielding side may polish the ball provided that such polishing wastes no time and that no artificial substance is used. No-one shall rub the ball on the ground or use any artificial substance or take any other action to alter the condition of the ball.

In the event of a contravention of this Law, the umpires, after consultation, shall change the ball for one of similar condition to that in use prior to the contravention.

This Law does not prevent a member of the fielding side from drying a wet ball, or removing mud from the ball. See Note (b).

6. Incommoding the Striker

An umpire is justified in intervening under this Law and shall call and signal "dead ball" if, in his opinion, any player of the fielding side incommodes the striker by any noise or action while he is receiving the ball.

7. Obstruction of a Batsman in Running

It shall be considered unfair if any fieldsman wilfully obstructs a batsman in running. In these circumstances the umpire shall call and signal "dead ball" and allow any completed runs and the run in progress, or alternatively any boundary scored.

8. The Bowling of Fast Short-pitched Balls

The bowling of fast short-pitched balls is unfair if, in the opinion of the umpire at the bowler's end, it constitutes an attempt to intimidate the striker. See Note (d).

Umpires shall consider intimidation to be the deliberate bowling of fast short-pitched balls which by their length, height and direction are intended or likely to inflict physical injury on the striker. The relative skill of the striker shall also be taken into consideration.

In the event of such unfair bowling, the umpire at the bowler's end shall adopt the following procedure:

(a) In the first instance the umpire shall call and signal "no-ball", caution the bowler and inform the other umpire, the captain of the fielding side and the batsmen of what has occurred.

(b) If this caution is ineffective, he shall repeat the above procedure and indicate to the bowler that this is a final warning.

(c) Both the above caution and final warning shall continue to apply even though the bowler may later change ends.

(d) Should the above warnings prove ineffective the umpire at the bowler's end shall:

- (i) At the first repetition call and signal "no-ball" and when the ball is dead direct the captain to take the bowler off forthwith and to complete the over with another bowler, provided that the bowler does not bowl two overs or part thereof consecutively. See Law 22.7 (Bowler Incapacitated or Suspended during an Over).
- (ii) Not allow the bowler, thus taken off, to bowl again in the same innings.
- (iii) Report the occurrence to the captain of the batting side as soon as the players leave the field for an interval.
- (iv) Report the occurrence to the executive of the fielding side and to any governing body responsible for the match, who shall take any further action which is considered to be appropriate against the bowler concerned.

9. The Bowling of Fast High Full Pitches

The bowling of fast high full pitches is unfair. See Note (e).

In the event of such unfair bowling the umpire at the bowler's end shall adopt the procedures of caution, final warnings, action against the bowler and reporting as set out in 8 above.

10. Time Wasting

Any form of time wasting is unfair.

(a) In the event of the captain of the fielding side wasting time or allowing any member of his side to waste time, the umpire at the bowler's end shall adopt the following procedure:

(i) In the first instance he shall caution the captain of the fielding side and inform the other umpire of what has occurred.

(ii) If this caution is ineffective he shall repeat the above procedure and indicate to the captain that this is a final warning.

(iii) The umpire shall report the occurrence to the captain of the batting side as soon as the players leave the field for an interval.

(iv) Should the above procedure prove ineffective the umpire shall report the occurrence to the executive of the fielding side and to any governing body responsible for that match, who shall take appropriate action against the captain and the players concerned.

(b) In the event of a bowler taking unnecessarily long to bowl an over the umpire at the bowler's end shall adopt the procedures, other than the calling of "no-ball", of caution, final warning, action against the bowler and reporting.

(c) In the event of a batsman wasting time (See Note (f)) other than in the manner described in Law 31 (Timed Out), the umpire at the bowler's end shall adopt the following procedure:

(i) In the first instance he shall caution the batsman and inform the other umpire at once, and the captain of the batting side, as soon as the players leave the field for an interval, of what has occurred.

(ii) If this proves ineffective, he shall repeat the caution, indicate to the batsman that this is a final warning and inform the other umpire.

(iii) The umpire shall report the occurrence to both captains as soon as the players leave the field for an interval.

(iv) Should the above procedure prove ineffective, the umpire shall report the occurrence to the executive of the batting side and to any governing body responsible for that match, who shall take appropriate action against the player concerned.

11. Players Damaging the Pitch

The umpires shall intervene and prevent players from causing damage to the pitch which may assist the bowlers of either side. See Note (c).

(a) In the event of any member of the fielding side damaging the pitch, the umpire shall follow the procedure of caution, final warning, and reporting as set out in 10(a) above.

(b) In the event of a bowler contravening this Law by running down the pitch after delivering the ball, the umpire at the bowler's end shall first caution the bowler. If this caution is ineffective the umpire shall adopt the procedures, as set out in 8 above other than the calling and signalling of "no-ball".

(c) In the event of a batsman damaging the pitch the umpire at the bowler's end shall follow the procedures of caution, final warning and reporting as set out in 10(c) above.

12. Batsman Unfairly Stealing a Run

Any attempt by the batsman to steal a run during the bowler's run-up is unfair. Unless the bowler attempts to run out either batsman – see Law 24.4 (Bowler Throwing at Striker's Wicket before Delivery) and Law 24.5 (Bowler Attempting to Run Out Non-striker before Delivery) – the umpire shall call and signal "dead ball" as soon as the batsmen cross in any such attempt to run. The batsmen shall then return to their original wickets.

13. Player's Conduct

In the event of a player failing to comply with the instructions of an umpire, criticising his decisions by word or action, or showing dissent, or generally behaving in a manner which might bring the game into disrepute, the umpire concerned shall, in the first place, report the matter to the other umpire and to the player's captain requesting the latter to take action. If this proves ineffective, the umpire shall report the incident as soon as possible to the executive of the player's team and to any governing body responsible for the match, who shall take any further action which is considered appropriate against the player or players concerned.

Notes

(a) The Condition of the Ball
Umpires shall make frequent and irregular inspections of the condition of the ball.

(b) Drying of a Wet Ball
A wet ball may be dried on a towel or with sawdust.

(c) Danger Area
The danger area on the pitch, which must be protected from damage by a bowler, shall be regarded by the umpires as the area contained by an imaginary line 4 feet/1.22m from the popping crease, and parallel to it, and within two imaginary and parallel lines drawn down the pitch from points on that line 1 foot/30.48cm on either side of the middle stump.

(d) Fast Short-pitched Balls
As a guide, a fast short-pitched ball is one which pitches short and passes, or would have passed, above the shoulder height of the striker standing in a normal batting stance at the crease.

(e) The Bowling of Fast Full Pitches
The bowling of one fast, high full pitch shall be considered to be unfair if, in the opinion of the umpire, it is deliberate, bowled at the striker, and if it passes or would have passed above the shoulder height of the striker when standing in a normal batting stance at the crease.

(f) Time Wasting by Batsmen
Other than in exceptional circumstances, the batsman should always be ready to take strike when the bowler is ready to start his run-up.

ADDRESSES OF REPRESENTATIVE BODIES

INTERNATIONAL CRICKET COUNCIL: Lt-Col. J. R. Stephenson, OBE, Lord's Ground, London NW8 8QN.

ENGLAND: Cricket Council, A. C. Smith, Lord's Ground, London NW8 8QN.

AUSTRALIA: Australian Cricket Board, D. L. Richards, 90 Jolimont Street, Jolimont, Victoria 3002.

WEST INDIES: West Indies Cricket Board of Control, G. S. Camacho, Kensington Oval, Fontabelle, St Michael, Barbados.

INDIA: Board of Control for Cricket in India, J. Dalmiya, Cricket Association of Bengal, Eden Gardens, Calcutta 700 021.

NEW ZEALAND: New Zealand Cricket Inc., G. T. Dowling, OBE, PO Box 958, 109 Cambridge Terrace, Christchurch.

PAKISTAN: Board of Control for Cricket in Pakistan, A. A. K. Abbasi, Gaddafi Stadium, Lahore.

SRI LANKA: Board of Control for Cricket in Sri Lanka, S. Skandakumar, 35 Maitland Place, Colombo 7.

SOUTH AFRICA: South African Cricket Union, Dr A. Bacher, PO Box 55009, Northlands 2116, Transvaal.
South African Cricket Board, PO Box 54059, Vrededorp 2141, Transvaal.

ARGENTINA: Argentine Cricket Association, R. H. Gooding, c/o The English Club, 25 de Mayo 586, 1002 Buenos Aires.
BAHAMAS: Bahamas Cricket Association, Mrs J. M. Forbes, PO Box N-10101, Nassau.
BANGLADESH: Bangladesh Cricket Board of Control, T. M. Islam, The Stadium, Dhaka.
BERMUDA: Bermuda Cricket Board of Control, C. W. Butterfield, PO Box 992, Hamilton.
CANADA: Canadian Cricket Association, K. R. Bullock, PO Box 1364, Brockville, Ontario, K6V 5Y6.
DENMARK: Danish Cricket Association, J. Holmen, Idraettens Hus, Brøndby, DK 2605.
EAST AND CENTRAL AFRICA: East and Central African Cricket Conference, S. Patel, PO Box 7377, Ndola, Zambia.
FIJI: Fiji Cricket Association, P. I. Knight, PO Box 300, Suva.
FRANCE: Association Française du Cricket, B. Laforgue, Rue Curial 73, 75019 Paris.
GIBRALTAR: Gibraltar Cricket Association, T. J. Finlayson, 21 Sandpits House, Withams Road.
HONG KONG: Hong Kong Cricket Association, J. A. Cribbin, University of Hong Kong, Extra-Mural Studies, Pokfulam Road.
ISRAEL: Israel Cricket Association, N. Davidson, PO Box 93, Ben-Gurion Airport 70100.
ITALY: Associazione Italiana Cricket, S. Gambino, Via S. Ignazio 9, 00186 Rome.
JAPAN: Japan Cricket Association, R. G. Martineau, Shizuoko City, Chiyoda 736, Yamadai Corp. 305, Japan 420.
KENYA: Kenya Cricket Association, B. Mauladad, PO Box 40462, Nairobi.
MALAYSIA: Malaysian Cricket Association, Lt-Cdr K. Selvaratnam (Retd), c/o Royal Selangor Club, PO Box 10137, 50704 Kuala Lumpur.
NEPAL: Cricket Association of Nepal, Jaikumar H. Shah, PO Box 925, Kathmandu.
NETHERLANDS: Royal Netherlands Cricket Board, Hon. Secretary, Neuiwe Kalfjeslaan 21-B, PO Box 898, 1182 AA Amstelveen.
PAPUA NEW GUINEA: Papua New Guinea Cricket Board of Control, W. Satchell, PO Box 1105, Boroko.
SINGAPORE: Singapore Cricket Association, R. Sivasubramaniam, 5000-D Marine Parade Road 22-16, Laguna Park.
SWITZERLAND: Swiss Cricket Association, P. Nixon, Spitzackerstrasse 32, 4103 Bottmingen.
UNITED ARAB EMIRATES: Emirates Cricket Board, Abdul Rahman Bukhatir, Sharjah Cricket Stadium, PO Box 783, Sharjah.
USA: United States of America Cricket Association, Naseeruddin Khan, 2361 Hickory Road, Plymouth Meeting, Pennsylvania 19462.
WEST AFRICA: West Africa Cricket Conference, O. A. Nwokedi, National Sports Commission, National Stadium, PO Box 145, Surulere, Lagos, Nigeria.
ZIMBABWE: Zimbabwe Cricket Union, D. A. Ellman-Brown, PO Box 702, Harare.
BRITISH UNIVERSITIES SPORTS FEDERATION: 28 Woburn Square, London WC1.
CLUB CRICKET CONFERENCE: A. E. F. Stevens, 353 West Barnes Lane, New Malden, Surrey, KT3 6JF.
ENGLAND SCHOOLS' CRICKET ASSOCIATION: C. J. Cooper, 68 Hatherley Road, Winchester, Hampshire SO22 6RR.
IRISH CRICKET UNION: D. Scott, 45 Foxrock Park, Foxrock, Dublin 18, Ireland.
MINOR COUNTIES CRICKET ASSOCIATION: D. J. M. Armstrong, Thorpe Cottage, Mill Common, Ridlington, North Walsham, NR28 9TY.
NATIONAL CRICKET ASSOCIATION. B. J. Aspital, Lord's Ground, London NW8 8QN.
SCARBOROUGH CRICKET FESTIVAL: Colin T. Adamson, Cricket Ground, North Marine Road, Scarborough, North Yorkshire, YO12 7TJ.
SCOTTISH CRICKET UNION: R. W. Barclay, Admin. Office, 18 Ainslie Place, Edinburgh, EH3 6AU.
COMBINED SERVICES: Lt-Col. K. Hitchcock, c/o Army Sport Control Board, Clayton Barracks, Aldershot, Hampshire GU11 2BG.
THE SPORTS COUNCIL: Director-General, 16 Upper Woburn Place, London WC1 0QP.
ASSOCIATION OF CRICKET UMPIRES: L. J. Cheeseman, 16 Ruden Way, Epsom Downs, Surrey, KT17 3LN.
WOMEN'S CRICKET ASSOCIATION: Administration Secretary, 41 St Michael's Lane, Headingley, Leeds LS6 3BR.

The addresses of MCC, the First-Class Counties, and Minor Counties are given at the head of each separate section.

INTERNATIONAL CRICKET COUNCIL

On June 15, 1909, representatives of cricket in England, Australia and South Africa met at Lord's and founded the Imperial Cricket Conference. Membership was confined to the governing bodies of cricket in countries within the British Commonwealth where Test cricket was played. India, New Zealand and West Indies were elected as members on May 31, 1926, Pakistan on July 28, 1952, and Sri Lanka on July 21, 1981. South Africa ceased to be a member of ICC on leaving the British Commonwealth in May, 1961.

On July 15, 1965, the Conference was renamed the International Cricket Conference and new rules were adopted to permit the election of countries from outside the British Commonwealth. This led to the growth of the Conference, with the admission of Associate Members, who were entitled to one vote, while the Foundation and Full Members were each entitled to two votes, on ICC resolutions. On July 12, 13, 1989, the Conference was renamed the International Cricket Council and revised rules were adopted.

CONSTITUTION

Chairman: The nominee of the President of MCC, with the confirmation of the members at the annual conference. Prior to making his nomination, the President of MCC shall have appropriate consultations, including with all Foundation and Full Members. The term of office is for one year, commencing October 1, but subject to the proviso that no Chairman shall remain continuously in office for more than four years, the Chairman may offer himself for re-nomination for a further year.

Secretary: To be appointed by members at the annual conference. Normally the office will be filled by the Secretary of MCC.

Administrator: Appointed for such periods as determined by members at the annual conference.

Foundation Members: Australia and United Kingdom.

Full Members: India, New Zealand, Pakistan, Sri Lanka and West Indies.

Associate Members*: Argentina (1974), Bangladesh (1977), Bermuda (1966), Canada (1968), Denmark (1966), East and Central Africa (1966), Fiji (1965), Gibraltar (1969), Hong Kong (1969), Israel (1974), Kenya (1981), Malaysia (1967), Netherlands (1966), Papua New Guinea (1973), Singapore (1974), United Arab Emirates (1990), USA (1965), West Africa (1976) and Zimbabwe (1981).

Affiliate Members*: Bahamas (1987), France (1987), Italy (1984), Japan (1989), Nepal (1988) and Switzerland (1985).

* *Year of election shown in parentheses.*

MEMBERSHIP

The following governing bodies for cricket shall be eligible for election.

Foundation Members: The governing bodies for cricket in the United Kingdom and Australia are known as Foundation Members (while also being Full Members of ICC) and have certain additional rights as set out in the Rules of the Council.

Full Members: The governing body for cricket recognised by ICC of a country, or countries associated for cricket purposes, or geographical area, from which representative teams are qualified to play official Test matches.

Associate Members: The governing body for cricket recognised by ICC of a country, or countries associated for cricket purposes, or a geographical area, which does not qualify as a Full Member but where cricket is firmly established and organised.

Affiliate Members: The governing body for cricket recognised by ICC of a country, or countries associated for cricket purposes, or a geographical area (which is not part of one of those already constituted as a Full or Associate Member) where ICC recognises that cricket is played in accordance with the Laws of Cricket. Affiliate Members have no right to vote or to propose or second resolutions at ICC meetings.

TEST MATCHES

1. Duration of Test Matches

Within a maximum of 30 hours' playing time, the duration of Test matches shall be a matter for negotiation and agreement between the two countries in any particular series of Test matches.

When agreeing the Playing Conditions prior to the commencement of a Test series, the participating countries may:

(a) Extend the playing hours of the last Test beyond the limit of 30 hours, in a series in which, at the conclusion of the penultimate match, one side does not hold a lead of more than one match.

(b) Allow an extension of play by one hour on any of the first four days of a Test match, in the event of play being suspended for one hour or more on that day, owing to weather interference.

(c) Play on the rest day, conditions and circumstances permitting, should a full day's play be lost on either the second or third scheduled days of play.

(d) Make up time lost in excess of five minutes in each day's play owing to circumstances outside the game, other than acts of God.

Note. The umpires shall determine when such time shall be made up. This could, if conditions and circumstances permit, include the following day.

2. Qualification Rules

A cricketer can be qualified to play in a Test match and one-day international either by birth or by residence.

(a) Qualification by birth. A cricketer, unless debarred by ICC, is always eligible to play for the country of his birth.

(b) Qualification by residence. A cricketer, unless debarred by ICC, shall be eligible to play for any country in which he is residing and has been residing during the four immediately preceding years, provided that he has not played for the country of his birth during that period.

Notes

(a) Notwithstanding anything hereinbefore contained, any player who has once played in a Test match or one-day international for any country shall not afterwards be eligible to play in a Test match or one-day international against that country, without the consent of its governing body.

(b) ICC in conjunction with the governing body of any country may impose more stringent qualification rules for that country.

3. The Appointment of Umpires

The following rules for the selection and appointment of Test match umpires shall be followed as far as is practicable to do so:

(a) The home authority shall appoint a committee for the purpose of nominating umpires to officiate in all Test matches.

(b) Test match umpires will be nominated by this committee from those umpires officiating in first-class matches during the current season.

(c) Wherever possible, umpires likely to be nominated by this committee shall officiate in matches against the visiting team, thus giving the visiting captain an opportunity to judge the umpires to be nominated. As long as possible before each Test match, the manager of the touring team and the secretary of the home authority will be informed of the names of the umpires nominated for the particular Test match. Any objection against either umpire must be lodged within three days of the notice being received or at least seven days before the match, whichever is the later, and will be dealt with by the committee as set up in (a), or by a special committee appointed by the home authority, whose decision shall be final. The names of the umpires shall not be given to the press until after this time has elapsed.

(d) While a captain is entitled to submit objections to a particular umpire nominated for a Test match, he may not ask for a particular umpire to be given precedence for appointment over any other. If either captain raises what is considered by the committee (or by the special committee appointed by the home authority) to be a definite and reasonable objection to any particular umpire, his wishes shall be met.

(e) The sole authority for handling press enquiries shall be the official representative appointed by the home authority for the purpose and not the captains or any of the players.

FIRST-CLASS MATCHES

1. Definitions

(a) A match of three or more days' duration between two sides of eleven players officially adjudged first-class shall be regarded as a first-class fixture.

(b) In the following Rules the term "governing body" is restricted to Foundation Members, Full Members and Associate Members of ICC.

2. Rules

(a) Foundation and Full Members of ICC shall decide the status of matches of three or more days' duration played in their countries.

(b) In matches of three or more days' duration played in countries which are not Foundation Members or Full Members of ICC:

(i) If the visiting team comes from a country which is a Foundation or Full Member of ICC, that country shall decide the status of matches.

(ii) If the visiting team does not come from a country which is a Foundation or Full Member of ICC, or is a Commonwealth team composed of players from different countries, ICC shall decide the status of matches.

Notes

(a) Governing bodies agree that the interest of first-class cricket will be served by ensuring that first-class status is *not* accorded to any match in which one or other of the teams taking part cannot on a strict interpretation of the definition be adjudged first-class.

(b) In case of any disputes arising from these Rules, the Secretary of ICC shall refer the matter for decision to the Council, failing unanimous agreement by postal communication being reached.

3. First-class Status

The following matches shall be regarded as first-class, subject to the provisions of 1(a) being completely complied with:

(a) In the British Isles and Eire
The following matches of three or more days' duration shall automatically be considered first-class:

(i) County Championship matches.

(ii) Official representative tourist matches from Full Member countries unless specifically excluded.

(iii) MCC v any first-class county.

(iv) Oxford v Cambridge and either University against first-class counties.

(v) Scotland v Ireland.

(b) In Australia

(i) Sheffield Shield matches.

(ii) Matches played by teams representing states of the Commonwealth of Australia between each other or against opponents adjudged first-class.

(c) In India

(i) Ranji Trophy matches.

(ii) Duleep Trophy matches.

(iii) Irani Cup matches.

(iv) Matches played by teams representing state or regional associations affiliated to the Board of Control between each other or against opponents adjudged first-class.

(v) All three-day matches played against representative visiting sides.

(d) In New Zealand

(i) Shell Trophy matches.

(ii) Matches played by teams representing major associations of the North and South Islands, between each other or against opponents adjudged first-class.

(e) In Pakistan

(i) Matches played by teams representing divisional associations affiliated to the Board of Control, between each other or against teams adjudged first-class.

(ii) Matches between the divisional associations and the Universities Past and Present XI.

(iii) Quaid-e-Azam Trophy Grade I matches.

(iv) BCCP Patron's Trophy Grade I matches.

(f) In Sri Lanka

(i) Singer inter-provincial tournament matches played over three days for the President's Trophy.

(ii) Inter-association matches played over three days for the Robert Senanayake Trophy.

(iii) Inter-club Division I tournament matches played over three days for the Lakspray Trophy.

(iv) Matches of three days or more against touring sides adjudged first-class.

(g) In West Indies

(i) Matches played by teams representing Barbados, Guyana, Jamaica, Trinidad & Tobago, the Windward Islands and the Leeward Islands, either for the Red Stripe Cup or against other opponents adjudged first-class.

(h) In all Foundation and Full Member countries represented on ICC

(i) Test matches and matches against teams adjudged first-class played by official touring teams.

(ii) Official Test Trial matches.

(iii) Special matches between teams adjudged first-class by the governing body or bodies concerned.

QUALIFICATION AND REGISTRATION

Regulations Governing the Qualification and Registration of Cricketers in Test and Competitive County Cricket

1. QUALIFICATIONS FOR ENGLAND

Subject to the overriding discretion of the Test and County Cricket Board, acting with the consent of the International Cricket Council, the qualifications for playing for England shall be:

(a) That the cricketer was born in the British Isles; or

(b) That the cricketer's father or mother was born in the British Isles and that he himself is residing and has been resident therein during the preceding four consecutive years; or

(c) That the cricketer is residing and has been resident in the British Isles during the preceding seven consecutive years; or

(d) That the cricketer is residing and has been resident in the British Isles both during the preceding four consecutive years and since the day before his fourteenth birthday; and in addition

(e) That the cricketer must be either a British or an Irish citizen.

All these qualifications apply only if the cricketer has not played for any other country in a Test match or (if the Board so decides) any other international match during the specified period of residence or in the case of (a) during the previous four years.

In the case of (b), if the cricketer has played first-class cricket in his country of origin before commencing his period of residence in the British Isles (but only if such period of residence commenced after December 11, 1984), or if he has played first-class cricket in any other country (but only if such period of residence commenced on or after March 6, 1986), the four-year period shall be increased to such number of years (not exceeding seven) as equals four years plus one year for each season of first-class cricket he played there. In the case of (b), (c) and (d), if, at any time after the commencement of the 1985 season, the cricketer plays first-class cricket in any other country (other than as an overseas cricketer in circumstances approved by the Board), then if previously qualified for England under (b), (c) or (d) he shall cease to be so qualified. If he was in the course of acquiring residential qualification, his period of residence in the British Isles shall be treated as terminated. In both instances, a new period of residence will be required.

In the case of a cricketer seeking to become qualified, he will (until he has become an England qualified cricketer) be treated as having been resident within the British Isles for the relevant consecutive years only if he has spent a minimum of 210 days in each year within the British Isles. A year shall mean a year ending April 14.

It is also required that a player shall make, whenever requested by the Board, a declaration in writing that it is his desire and intention to play for England and that he is not seeking to play in a Test match or any other international match for another country.

2. QUALIFICATIONS FOR REGISTRATION FOR COMPETITIVE COUNTY CRICKET

Subject to the overriding discretion of the Board and subject to Extraordinary Registrations:

(a) A cricketer qualified for England shall be qualified for registration only for:

(i) The county of his birth.

(ii) The county in which he is residing and has been resident for the previous twelve consecutive months.

(iii) The county for which his father regularly played.

(b) In addition, a cricketer qualified for England shall be qualified for registration for a county if:

(i) He has none of the above qualifications for any county and is not or was not registered for one for the current or immediately previous season; or

(ii) Although qualified for and/or registered for one or more counties, the county or counties concerned have confirmed in writing that they do not wish to register him or retain his registration and have not included him on List I (see Extraordinary Registrations).

3. REGISTRATION

Normally new registrations take place during the close season, but in exceptional circumstances a county may apply to register a player in the course of a season.

No cricketer may be registered for more than one county at any one time or, subject to the overriding discretion of the Board, for more than one county during any one season. However, this shall not prevent a player qualified to play for England, and already registered for a minor county, from being registered for a first-class county with the consent of the minor county concerned, who will not lose his registration.

Except with the Board's approval no county may have registered for it more than 35 cricketers at any one time.

4. SPECIAL REGISTRATION

The qualification for county cricket may be wholly or partially waived by the Board and a cricketer qualified to play for England may be "specially registered" should the Board conclude that it would be in the best interest of competitive county cricket as a whole. For this purpose the Board shall have regard to the interests of the cricketer concerned and any other material considerations affecting the county concerned including, if applicable, the cricketer's age and the other Special Registrations of the county in previous years.

5. CRICKETERS NOT QUALIFIED TO PLAY FOR ENGLAND

No county shall be entitled to play more than one unqualified cricketer in any competitive match. From 1991 onwards no county may have at any one time more than one registered unqualified cricketer.

From 1991, a county may change its one registered unqualified cricketer only if, after the start of the season, that cricketer is chosen to play for his country for all or part of an official tour of the British Isles. The cricketer's registration must be cancelled in respect of the balance of the season before his replacement is registered.

If a registered overseas player is invited to play for his country for the whole or part of a tour of the British Isles, his county must release him.

Note: A citizen of a country within the European Community, although he is not qualified to play for England, is not regarded as an unqualified cricketer for the purposes of registration, provided he satisfies the requirements as set out in Regulation 1 (except that (a) for "in the British Isles" read "within the EC"; (b) for "any other country" read "any country outside the EC").

6. EXTRAORDINARY REGISTRATIONS

Each first-class county shall, on or before September 21 each year, send to the Board and every other county in the County and Minor Counties Championship:

(a) A list ("List I") of all cricketers, including unqualified cricketers, who either have a contract in writing to play for that county for the whole or part of the next season, or, having had such a contract for the season then about to end, have been offered in writing a contract for the whole or part of the next season.

(b) A list ("List II") of all other cricketers who have had such a contract for the season about to end.

A first-class county wishing to apply for registration for the next season of a cricketer whose name appears on another county's List I must give notice in writing to the Board and to that other county. The Board will not register the cricketer for the applicant county for at least 21 days after receipt of such notice.

If the Board approves the application and registers the cricketer for the applicant county, the registration is treated as an Extraordinary Registration, unless at its discretion the Board decides it will not be so treated. Before the Board's final decision to treat it as an Extraordinary Registration, any county concerned and the cricketer may make representations to the Board, and any of them or the Board may request an Investigating Tribunal to report on the application.

In deciding whether or not to treat a registration as an Extraordinary Registration, the Board shall consider the best interests of competitive county cricket as a whole and, for that purpose, have regard to:

(a) Where applicable, whether the terms of the offer made by the county on whose List I the cricketer appears were, in all the circumstances, fair and reasonable.

(b) The interests of that county.

(c) The interests of the cricketer, taking into account his age.

(d) The interests of the Board, any report by the Investigating Tribunal, and any other matter considered relevant by the Board.

Except in circumstances which in the opinion of the Board are exceptional, no county shall be permitted to make more than one Extraordinary Registration in any period of twelve months or more than two Extraordinary Registrations in any period of five years.

7. NEGOTIATIONS BETWEEN COUNTIES AND CRICKETERS

No county may approach or be involved in discussions with any unregistered cricketer who is not qualified for that county with a view to offering him a trial or registering him:

(a) During the currency of a season without having given not less than fourteen days' previous notice in writing; or

(b) During the close season without having given notice in writing

to any county for which he is qualified for registration by virtue of birth or residence before making any such approach or engaging in any such discussions.

No county may approach or be involved in discussions with any registered cricketer with a view to offering him a trial or registering him or employing him in any capacity without first obtaining the written consent of the county for which he is registered. This does not apply to discussions between a first-class county and a cricketer whose only registration is with a minor county; a cricketer on List II of the county for which he is registered; any other cricketer who has no contract in writing with the county for which he is registered for all or any part of the following season (including such a cricketer on List I), in which case a county may make an approach or begin discussions after October 31, provided that not less than fourteen days' prior notice has been given to the county for which he is registered.

No county may approach or be involved in discussions with any cricketer under the age of sixteen (or who was under sixteen on the last preceding April 15) unless the cricketer is qualified for registration by that county by birth or residence or is not qualified for registration by any other first-class county. A cricketer born in Wales is regarded as qualified by birth for Glamorgan.

8. RESIDENCE

A player does not interrupt his qualifying period of residence by undertaking government service or occasional winter work for business reasons outside the county in which his residence is situated.

The qualifying period cannot run while the cricketer has a contract with or is registered by another county.

CAREER FIGURES OF PLAYERS RETIRING OR NOT RETAINED

BATTING

	M	*I*	*NO*	*R*	*HI*	*100s*	*Avge*	*1,000r/season*
J. P. Agnew	218	232	49	2,118	90	0	11.57	0
P. Bainbridge	257	424	60	12,353	169	22	33.93	8
D. L. Bairstow	459	647	119	13,961	145	10	26.44	3
A. R. Clarke	26	37	9	406	68	0	14.50	0
G. S. Clinton	270	450	53	13,118	192	20	33.04	7
G. Cook	460	793	65	23,277	203	37	31.97	12
I. Folley	136	158	49	1,465	69	0	13.44	0
T. Gard	112	126	25	1,389	51*	0	13.75	0
I. J. Gould	297	399	63	8,756	128	4	26.05	0
J. W. Govan	8	11	1	80	17	0	8.00	0
D. A. Graveney	383	487	142	6,109	119	2	17.70	0
A. M. Green	164	291	17	7,932	179	9	28.94	3
B. R. Hardie	378	608	79	18,103	162	27	34.22	11
G. W. Humpage	351	574	76	18,098	254	29	36.34	11
K. B. S. Jarvis	260	199	87	403	32	0	3.59	0
A. I. Kallicharran	505	834	86	32,650	243*	87	43.64	12+1
G. Miller	383	548	94	12,027	130	2	26.49	0
G. V. Palmer	54	70	11	903	78	0	15.30	0
L. B. Taylor	218	199	86	1,061	60	0	9.38	0
D. A. Thorne	69	113	15	2,523	124	2	25.74	0
D. R. Turner	426	696	74	19,005	184*	28	30.55	9
D. J. Wild	119	167	21	3,688	144	5	25.26	0

* *Signifies not out.*

BOWLING AND FIELDING

	R	*W*	*BB*	*Avge*	*5W/i*	*10W/m*	*Ct/St*
J. P. Agnew	19,485	666	9-70	29.25	37	6	39
P. Bainbridge	9,985	273	8-53	36.57	7	0	110
D. L. Bairstow	308	9	3-25	34.22	—	—	961/13
A. R. Clarke	1,872	53	5-60	35.32	2	0	7
G. S. Clinton	201	4	2-8	50.25	—	—	96
G. Cook	806	15	3-47	53.73	—	—	419/3
I. Folley	8,890	284	7-15	31.30	10	1	58
T. Gard	8	0	—	—	—	—	178/39
I. J. Gould	365	7	3-10	52.14	—	—	536/67
J. W. Govan	614	25	5-54	24.56	1	—	4
D. A. Graveney	23,953	829	8-85	28.89	36	6	201
A. M. Green	2,192	49	6-82	44.73	1	—	85
B. R. Hardie	254	3	2-39	84.66	—	—	349
G. W. Humpage	553	13	2-13	42.53	—	—	671/72
K. B. S. Jarvis	19,998	674	8-97	29.67	20	3	59
A. I. Kallicharran	4,030	84	5-45	47.97	1	—	323
G. Miller	24,854	888	8-70	27.98	39	7	309
G. V. Palmer	4,107	92	5-38	44.64	1	—	30
L. B. Taylor	14,648	581	7-28	25.21	18	1	53
D. A. Thorne	2,078	41	5-39	50.68	1	—	54
D. R. Turner	357	9	2-7	39.66	—	—	191
D. J. Wild	2,910	66	4-4	44.09	—	—	40

MEETINGS IN 1990

TCCB SPRING MEETING

t its Spring Meeting, held at Lord's on March 6, 7, the Test and County Cricket Board iscussed the structure of domestic cricket from 1991 onwards, and after a debate of some ree hours its members voted 12-6 in favour of an amendment – proposed by Kent and conded by Derbyshire – to retain for a further three years the existing County Champion-ip programme of sixteen three-day matches and six four-day matches. A proposal, put rward by the Cricket, England and Marketing committees, for a sixteen-match four-day hampionship had earlier been rejected 14-4. In both votes Minor Counties abstained. lthough the majority of the Board's members accepted that an increase in the number of ur-day matches might well have the effect, in due time, of improving the standard of players the top level, it was felt that the existing programme, introduced in 1988, had not been in peration long enough to make a well-founded judgement on a further change. All the embers of the Board asked that a number of the ancillary points raised by the Cricket ommittee should be taken into account, in particular the need for extra preparation for the ngland team before a Test match. It was hoped that the England team would have two days gether before home Test matches, instead of meeting on the preceding day, and counties xpressed their willingness to release international players in advance of Test matches.

At the end of the debate, the chairman of the Cricket Committee, O. S. Wheatley, said that it were the wish of the members of the Board for him to resign, given the considerable efeat of what he saw as the major plank of his committee's cricketing policy, he would do so. he Board did not take that up, and Mr Wheatley and all the Board's main committee hairmen were re-elected. The Board, expressing its support for the England Committee, hich was established in 1989, agreed to proceed with the principle of A team tours in the inter, to give financial support to England training sessions, and to continue to use more xtensively expert coaches to help cricketers at all levels.

The Board accepted a recommendation from the Pitches Committee to widen the definition pitches considered unsuitable for first-class cricket to include "those which offer consistent, xaggerated sideways movement allowing the ball to dominate the bat". In 1989 the 25-point enalty had been applied to pitches which were so badly prepared that the ball went through e surface early in a match. It was decided also that over-rate fines in the County Champion-ip would in 1990 be paid wholly by the players. Previously they had been shared equally by e county club and the players. As a concession to the players, requested by the Cricketers' ssociation, the Board agreed that the rate at which fines begin would be lowered from ghteen and a half to eighteen overs per hour.

The rules of the Benson and Hedges Cup were amended so that, in the quarter-final round, e teams winning the four groups could in future be drawn against any of the four group inners-up. Previously two counties from the same group had not been able to meet in the uarter-finals. It was felt that the former provision excluded the possibility of local derbies, hich were attractive ties in terms of local interest and revenue. It was agreed to experiment 1990 with machine-stitched balls in Second Eleven matches in order to judge the effects of ich balls against the effects of hand-stitched ones, and the TCCB banned the use of a convex at being promoted by a bat-maker as giving an advantage to batsmen slogging for runs. It as thought that this was not in keeping with the Board's policy of improving the quality of nglish cricket.

TCCB EMERGENCY MEETING

t an Emergency Meeting of the TCCB, held at Edgbaston on May 21, a proposal to increase om six to eight the number of four-day games played by each county in the Championship, ith a corresponding reduction in three-day games from sixteen to fourteen, was defeated hen it failed to acquire a majority. Voting was 9-9, with the Minor Counties abstaining. hose in favour of the proposal were Glamorgan, Hampshire, Leicestershire, Nottingham-ire, Somerset, Surrey, Warwickshire, Worcestershire and MCC.

INTERNATIONAL CRICKET COUNCIL

At its Annual Meeting at Lord's on June 28, 29, ICC was unanimous in its condemnation the deterioration in standards of discipline in the international game. There was a gene consensus that the formation of an independent panel of umpires would go a long way towar resolving the problem, and there was also strong support among Council members for t presence at every Test match of an ICC referee, who would have an independent a authoritative role. The Council decided also that it was essential to bring in an internatior Code of Conduct which, *inter alia*, would take into account such practices as "sledging" distraction and verbal intimidation on the field – at all levels of the game. It was agreed th the chief executives of the seven Test match countries should meet at Lord's in October examine the relevant details and then present their proposed package to a special F Members' meeting in Australia in January 1991, with a view to its implementation in Ap 1991.

A resolution by England and New Zealand to limit fast, short-pitched bowling to one su delivery per over did not receive the necessary two-thirds majority, the vote in favour bei 4-3, and therefore was not approved. However, the Council acknowledged that umpir generally speaking, may have had difficulty in interpreting Law 42.8 as written and it w decided to ask MCC, in its Law-making capacity, to re-examine and rewrite the Law, whe necessary, to help umpires apply it as intended. Confirming its 1989 decision that 90 overs p day (15 overs per hour) should be the absolute minimum in Test cricket, the Council agre that a system of financial penalties would be written into the Code of Conduct for failure achieve the required over-rate.

TCCB SUMMER MEETING

At its Summer Meeting, held at Lord's on August 17, the Test and County Cricket Board ga umpires the power from 1991 to penalise teams whose players roughen one side of the ball replacing that ball with an older and inferior one. This brought the penalty for "roughing u into line with that already in existence for picking the seam. The Board also agreed that county whose overseas player was selected for the 1991 tour of England by West Indies wou be allowed to register a replacement, who may have played for another county, on a one-ye rather than a two-year contract. The decision would be reviewed in 1991 with regard 1992 contracts.

TCCB WINTER MEETING

At its Winter Meeting, held at Lord's on December 5, 6, the Test and County Cricket Boa offered Durham the opportunity to become in 1992 the eighteenth first-class county, subject their having planning permission and initial funding for a new headquarters ground Chester-le-Street, and to their appointing a chief executive, and employing a he groundsman to take charge of preparing their out-grounds as well as their county ground. T recommendation, following the findings of a working party established in September 1989 investigate Durham's application, was unopposed, although two counties abstained. It w agreed that Durham would attend the TCCB Spring Meeting in 1991 as an observer, becor a full voting member from October 1, 1991 and be qualified to benefit financially from t Board's central fund from January 1, 1992. With the admission of Durham, the Coun Championship would continue its current programme of sixteen three-day and six four-d matches, with the proviso that the one county not played against in the three-day match would be played in a four-day one. The Refuge Assurance League would become a straig seventeen-match league competition; the Benson and Hedges Cup would be enlarged to teams, with one group consisting of six teams and the other three groups having five team and Minor Counties' representation in the NatWest Bank Trophy would be reduced by o county.

A proposal by Derbyshire, Kent, Northamptonshire and Yorkshire that pitches be l uncovered in County Championship matches was defeated by fifteen votes to four, havi initially failed to gain the backing of the England and Cricket committees. The Boa however, agreed on a new definition of what constituted a good pitch. "At the commenceme [of a game] the pitch should be completely dry, firm and true, providing pace and even boun throughout, and should ideally wear sufficiently to give spinners some help later in the game

In 1990, groundsmen had been required to produce pitches that were "white or straw-coloured" and contained "no trace of greenness", and the Board now accepted that a green pitch was not necessarily an unacceptable one by virtue of its colour alone. If pitches at county headquarters were thought by the Pitches Committee to need improvement to bring them up to standard, such counties would be ordered to play their games away from their headquarters. The 25-point penalty for an unacceptable pitch was retained for 1991.

The Board agreed to implement a Code of Conduct in line with that being drafted by ICC for international cricket. This would cover all aspects of behaviour both on and off the field in order to uphold the good name of cricket, and it would apply to all involved in the game, such as committee members and officials, as well as to players. Following concern at incidents of fast, head-high full tosses ("beamers"), umpires were empowered to order the immediate removal of a bowler (i.e., without prior warning) for the rest of the innings if they thought such a delivery was deliberate. It was agreed that the minimum over-rate in the County Championship would revert to the 1989 standard of eighteen and a half overs per hour, and that fines would once again be shared equally between a county and its players.

ERRATA

WISDEN, 1987

Page 450 — In Hampshire's second innings, K. D. James's dismissal should read "c C. S. Cowdrey b Tavaré", not c and b Tavaré as stated.

WISDEN, 1990

Page 64 — L. E. G. Ames's hundred in 1939 was against Surrey at The Oval, not Sussex as stated.

Page 268 — I. J. F. Hutchinson, Middlesex v Derbyshire at Lord's (3rd day), was omitted from the list of Hundreds Before Lunch.

Page 328 — R. C. Russell should have a dagger by his name to denote that he was the England wicket-keeper.

Pages 680 and 697 — In the match between Oxfordshire and Gloucestershire, the record eighth-wicket partnership of 83 was between S. N. V. Waterton and D. A. Hale, not between J. S. Hartley and Hale as stated.

Page 1018 — In the Bangladesh innings, Nasir Ahmed scored 9 not out, not 99 not out as stated.

Page 1020 — In the match between Bangladesh and Sri Lanka, Ather Ali Khan was stumped by Kuruppu, not caught as stated. The Man of the Match was J. R. Ratnayeke, not D. S. B. P. Kuruppu.

Page 1082 — The match between Eastern Province B and Northern Transvaal B on January 27, 28, 29 was played at the Old Grey Ground in Port Elizabeth, not at St George's Park.

Page 1207 — S. H. Martin bowled right-arm medium, not left as stated.

CRICKET BOOKS, 1990

By JOHN ARLOTT

For this year, and to some extent as a follow-up to 1989, 93 titles have been submitted for review. Outstandingly, the most impressive cricket history book of this century has been completed, in the five-volume *The Complete History of Australian Cricket 1803-1989*. The general standard of books received is uniformly high and frequently authoritative; moreover, colour illustration is no longer the rarity it once was among cricket books. Six titles include the name of *Wisden*: this appears to represent a development of publishing business, though several of them embody material from its volumes.

The *Australian History*, by Jack Pollard, consists of five octavo volumes comprising, in all, 1,888 pages. Published by Angus & Robertson, they are:

1. *The Formative Years: Australian Cricket 1803-1893* (336 pages; £14.95).
2. *The Turbulent Years: Australian Cricket 1893-1917* (300 pages; £15.95).
3. *The Bradman Years: Australian Cricket 1918-1948* (412 pages; £16.95).
4. *From Bradman to Border: Australian Cricket 1948-1989* (444 pages; £20).
5. *Highest, Most and Best: Australian Cricket Statistics 1850-1990* (Ross Dundas in association with Jack Pollard; 396 pages; £25).

This *magnum opus*, created with immense care, covers all cricket within Australia, as well as visits of touring sides and Australian tours overseas. Mr Pollard is most sound in his perspective and facts, and unbiased in his attitude; he also finds room for anecdotes, often amusing, so far as can be judged veracious, and invariably illuminating. One presumes that this historic series will be added to from time to time but, for the period it covers, it is satisfying and entirely thorough. It is authoritative and has been written with a touch which is never boring. Its readability is aided by the relegation of most statistics to the fifth volume.

Cricket: An Illustrated History (Phaidon Press; £19.95), by David Rayvern Allen, is most decorative, as might be expected from the title and those publishers. Mr Allen's text, too, is of a high order; he clearly cares immensely about cricket, its facts and history, and he deals with them carefully, sensitively and precisely, yet with sufficient humanity to avoid heaviness. The decorations are quite sumptuous: admirably selected, richly varied, from comic postcards to oil paintings, Rowlandson to Phil May, engravings to historic documents. Barely a page is turned without demands for a positive response from the reader's eye or attention. This 160-page quarto, profoundly thought out, will take its place as a standard textbook on the game.

The Illustrated History of the Test Match (Sidgwick & Jackson; £15.95), by Peter Arnold and Peter Wynne-Thomas, with a foreword by Richie Benaud, is of considerable historic value. It deals with every series of Test cricket from England v Australia 1876-77; there is an appendix of Test records and averages, plus a complete register of Test cricketers from 1877 to 1987, giving the playing years and number of Tests of every player concerned. The photographs are prolific, imaginatively chosen, and constantly illuminate their period and subject.

A History of Indian Cricket (André Deutsch; £19.95), by Mihir Bose, with a foreword by Sunil Gavaskar, is an extremely substantial book – a 571-page octavo – with sound illustrations and prolific records. It is most firmly involved with its subject, which it records with typical Indian thoroughness. The chapter headings themselves provide a potted history, from "The era of the princes" through "Vizzy", "The Merchant era", "The age of Gupte", "The Gavaskar era", "The rise of the North" to "World Champions 1983-85" and the "One-day revolution and after, 1986-89". The statistics are admirably thorough, and this is bound to become the standard textbook on Indian cricket.

The Golden Age of Cricket (Macdonald/Queen Anne Press; £14.95), by George Plumptre, is a study of the game in the Edwardian period. It has been most admirably constructed by one who is obviously an enthusiast for that phase of the game. The chapter headings – "The Edwardian Ethos", "The Dawn of Modern Cricket 1895", "Amateurs and Professionals: Pastime or Job?" – show how he develops his theme, down to the point where "The Lustre Gently Fades 1910-14". Mr Plumptre's sources are laid out generously in his bibliography of some 60 titles, from Sir Home Gordon and C. B. Fry to Jack Hobbs, Ranjitsinhji and Neville Cardus, not forgetting Fred Root, Osbert Sitwell, S. M. J. Woods and W. G. Grace. The whole study is illuminated by sympathetic period photographic reproductions: there is an I Zingari team of the early 1900s, and "their attending ladies"; the Yorkshire team and Plum Warner, with his wife, are caught playing croquet. The author notes that "The period saw the matches between England and Australia elevated to a position of unrivalled importance". On the other hand, he does not shrink from the less pleasant events of the period as, for instance, the occasion when "the luckless [J.N.] Crawford" was informed by "Shrimp" Leveson Gower that he was "withdrawing his invitation for Crawford to play in his side at Scarborough and that the MCC would not be considering him for the forthcoming tour to South Africa. Finally he was informed by Surrey that they no longer required his services." Thus one of the most gifted amateurs in the English game of the time departed to Australia. It is a scholarly, readable period piece, and a handsomely made book.

Sketches at Lord's (Collins/Willow; £19.95), by Michael Down and Derek West, is subtitled "The cricket lithographs of John Corbet Anderson". A most generously illustrated quarto, much of it in colour, it does the artist honest justice and is linked with a sound knowledge of cricket. For instance, on the subject of the draw stroke, it notes that "Old Tom [Hearne] was one of the last first-class cricketers to practise this hazardous stroke". It has, too, some admirable anecdotes, notably that about the umpire, Dickie Diver, who once gave out a last man 2 runs short of a win in a match. When the not out batsman protested, "I bet you half-a-crown you were wrong", Diver replied, "Umpires can't bet, sir, but" – pocketing the bails – "*now* I'll bet you a sovereign". It is a book of atmosphere and most handsomely reproduces what is probably the finest popular art the game has spawned.

The Lord's Test 1884-1989 (Spellmount; £15.95), by Steven Lynch, with an introduction by David Frith, is a pleasing history of that great match over the years. The famous names of the game stride through its pages: the frontispiece is a portrait of the young Don Bradman, whose 254 in 1930 was the highest score in those matches. However, A. G. Steel, who made the first century in it, and Arthur Shrewsbury, who with his second hundred there became the first batsman to total 1,000 Test runs, are also accorded portraits. Not only the winners are remembered; so are such as Willie Watson and Trevor Bailey who, in 1953, saved the game for England. A 288-page octavo, it has a lively and free-flowing narrative, with adequate scores, good statistics and pertinent illustrations: an immensely readable history.

Summers In Winter (Kingswood Press; £14.99), by Anthony Meredith, sets out the story of the development of England cricket tours to Australia by reconstructing four tours which the author has taken as being representative of their respective eras. These are, then, Lillywhite's of 1876-77, which saw the beginning of the great rivalry in Test matches between the mother country and its colony; Plum Warner's of 1903-04, the first under the auspices of MCC; Gubby Allen's of 1936-37, intended to heal the wounds to the relationship inflicted by the Bodyline series; and Mike Brearley's of 1978-79, which was played under the shadow of Kerry Packer's floodlit World Series Cricket. "By the time Mike Brearley's England side toured in 1978-79", Tony Lewis writes in his foreword, "the Australian fears were that their team, drastically depleted by the exodus of World Series players, would not be able to give England hard enough competition. They were right; England won 5-1 and the golden history to which every England cricketer wanted to belong became tarnished."

Great Innings (Anaya Publishers; £16.95), by Peter Roebuck, is a most handsome 176-page quarto, prolifically illustrated, often in colour. The innings with which he deals fall mostly within modern times, though sometimes he goes outside them to deal with, for instance, Jack Hobbs, Gilbert Jessop, Arthur Shrewsbury, Herbert Sutcliffe, Victor Trumper and Douglas Jardine. Each of the innings' accounts carries also biographical notes on its scorer. Mr Roebuck writes in his usual forthright style; he knows his cricket well and is not afraid to be critical. Once again, like so many books in this year, it has been physically most handsomely made.

Cricket's Strangest Matches (Robson Books; £14.95) is a collection by Andrew Ward of 100 matches, plus an "Afterword". The accounts, which run from 1837 to 1989 and include many spectacular oddities, are tidily terse, readable, yet invite expansion in the reader's mind. Many of the stories are indeed extraordinary, but Mr Ward has provided scorecards to prove his point; like his text, these also divert. The illustrations, though relatively few, are often illuminating. This theme has attracted writers before, but none has been so full as Mr Ward.

My Lord's (Collins/Willow; £14.95), edited by Tim Heald, and subtitled "A celebration of the world's greatest cricket ground", consists of some 36 essays by various hands. Some of the contributors are firmly connected with current cricket writing, others have been most thoughtfully recruited and with happy results. The illustration is by line drawings with a definitely humorous bent, and it ends with a not generally known poem by Gavin Ewart which also contributes its meed of humour. Most of the essays, it seems, were commissioned especially for this book, wherefore it is, for a cricket anthology, most refreshingly unhackneyed.

The Book of Cricket Quotations (Stanley Paul; £7.99), by Peter Ball and David Hopps, is a 248-page octavo, soft-covered, revision of their 1986 edition dedicated "To the rheumatic hacks who have suffered years of working in primitive wooden press boxes, situated at square leg without a view of the scoreboard". Full of cheerful surprises, it starts with "The Greats and Others – players and teams" and runs through "The Game that Was", "Philosophers All", "Lords and Masters", "They Also Serve" to "Tribes Without the Law – Pakistanis, Aussies, Yorkies, and Others" and "Ladies in

Waiting". That list of chapter headings indicates the course of some amusing selections and extremely shrewd observations.

The Wisden Book of Cricket Quotations (Macdonald/Queen Anne Press; £14.95), edited by David Lemmon, is a more solid – at 309 pages – octavo, enlarging and revising the 1982 edition. It, too, contains much of the humour inseparable from the game. Again and again, the editor has discovered the really penetrative, understanding and human passage, like this quotation from E. W. Swanton on Gubby Allen. "Perfectionists are not always easy people to live with, and 'Gubby' has always been a perfectionist, whether in the Committee Room at Lord's, or on the golf course, re-writing the *MCC Coaching Book*, tending his car and his roses, ordering his dinner, or even describing in close anatomical detail his latest strain or his last hip operation." There are 1,978 quotations in this collection and they suit all moods and all attitudes to the game. Mr Lemmon is a patient and cheerful compiler.

The Wisden Book of Cricket Memorabilia (Lennard Publishing; £25), by Marcus Williams and Gordon Phillips, is concerned with the collection of cricketana whose scope is indicated by a list of its chapter headings: "Auctions", "Paintings", "Prints", "Other Pictorial Matter", "Books and Periodicals", "Ceramics and Sculpture", "Ornamental Objects", "Printed Ephemera", "Equipment and Clothing", "Postcards, Cigarette Cards and Stamps" and, even then, "Miscellaneous". A 328-page quarto, it is a really exhaustive survey of a vast field of collecting, and it has been handsomely, generously and temptingly illustrated, largely in black-and-white, but partly in colour. It is highly informed – a master work on its subject.

The Concise Wisden: An Illustrated Anthology of 125 Years, by Benny Green, has appeared in two editions. The first, published by St Michael (Marks & Spencer) in 1988 as *The Illustrated Wisden Anthology 1864-1988*, has been submitted again for review in this issue and is, therefore, presumably still available at £12.99. The second is issued by Macdonald/Queen Anne Press at £15.95. The two are identical in pagination, illustrations and text. There is only a slight difference in the dust-wrappers, and the St Michael edition is on heavier paper, making the book itself slightly thicker. It is edited by that *Wisden* enthusiast and authority, Benny Green. Moving with both familiarity and respect through the complete history from the start to almost the present day, and arranging his material chronologically, he has selected the riches in match accounts, articles and obituaries. The illustration is highly intelligent and imaginatively laid out. Much of it is in colour, and the whole creation of the book is indeed handsome. There is a seven-page index to its 400 octavo pages, and to look up a fact, a match or a player is to find oneself button-holed and reading on. It is the ideal cricket gift book.

The Wisden Book of Captains on Tour: Test Cricket 1946-1989 (Stanley Paul; £14.99), by Don Mosey, while referring to every tour from 1946 to the end of 1989, looks especially and penetratingly at the men who have been made captain. The author is at pains to show, where possible, why captains were appointed and, often, why they lost the post. A 288-page octavo, it is readable and positive, carries some statistics and has a useful index.

The Wisden Book of Heroic Performances: Highlights from the Eighties (Stanley Paul; £6.99), by Graham Otway, is a paper-bound 140-page collection of 29 outstanding feats of cricket by a collection of players from David Gower in 1981 to Jack Russell in 1989. Thus every one of these performances falls within the author's working life, and his enthusiasm is not to be doubted. The generous illustration is by black-and-white photographs, with some innings charts.

The Daily Telegraph Century of County Cricket: The Hundred Best Matches (Sidgwick & Jackson; £16.99), edited by Simon Heffer, was, in the first place, a bright idea and in its execution has proved most attractively readable. It begins with Nottinghamshire v Sussex in 1890 and ends with Essex v Yorkshire in 1989. The matches are interesting for assorted reasons. They include MacLaren's 424 for Lancashire against Somerset in 1895, Hick's 405 not out for Worcestershire, also against Somerset, 93 years later, and Alletson's historic hitting against Sussex in 1911. There is an account and discussion of the controversy about the great Holmes-Sutcliffe stand of 1932. Indeed, the great men of the county game stalk through these pages: Grace, Fry, Ranji, Hobbs, Trueman, Cowdrey, Botham. The writers range over E. W. Swanton, Thomas Moult and Colonel Philip Trevor, and Mr Swanton also provides the introduction which sets all in proportion. The illustration is by photographs of the famous players of a century. It is all admirably presented, relishable and readable: a happy collection.

Fine Glances: A Connoisseur's Cricket Anthology (Simon & Schuster; £11.95), edited by Tom Graveney and Mike Seabrook, and illustrated with line drawings by Bill Tidy, is a most attractive collection. It is also almost entirely original, many of the pieces having been written specially. If the outstanding contribution is the essay, "Confessions of a Cricketer", by Mike Brearley, there is much more that is attractive in writings that range as far afield as C. H. Rolph, Miles Kington and the Hon. Michael Manley. This is yet another compelling anthology which helps to lift the year's books under review to an unusually high level.

SACA: The History of the South Australian Cricket Association (Sports Marketing [Australia]; £19.95), by Chris Harte, is a weighty 448-page quarto. It is a most carefully made and pertinently illustrated history of that state's cricket, and is yet another indication of Mr Harte's conscientious marshalling of relevant cricket information. Once again he has written an utterly and absolutely authoritative cricket book, which is accepted as the Association's definitive history. It needs only to be kept up to date: it would be difficult indeed for any other addition to be made to it. Nothing is sadder than the news of Mr Harte's withdrawal from the Australian cricket-writing scene, and it will be intriguing to discover how he passes his time in that respect now that he has returned to England.

The History of Gloucestershire County Cricket Club (Christopher Helm; £15.95), by David Green, is prefaced by a personal view from B. D. "Bomber" Wells. It adds to the growing shelf of this publisher's county histories. Mr Green, of course, is authoritative: technically knowledgeable and an experienced writer with a nice turn of wit. His colleague, "Bomber" Wells, contributes a highly personal and diverting introductory nine pages. The illustrations in black-and-white are plentiful, and the statistics are amply satisfying. Again and again, Mr Green goes to the root of the matter, explaining the shape of, and reason for, a single season's outcome.

Gloucestershire Cricketing Greats (Spellmount; £13.95), by Dean Hayes, consists of 46 biographies of Gloucestershire players. The Graces are there, of course, and so is B. D. Wells, not to mention Harry Huggins, Zaheer Abbas and Bev Lyon. There are ample photographs of the players concerned, and Mr Hayes is rarely at a loss for such a final sentence as "Charlie Barnett enjoyed his cricket immensely, always considering himself a public entertainer – something never doubted by those who had the privilege to see him play". There is a useful statistical appendix, and the author most humanly finds himself unable to resist the temptation to pick the greatest eleven of Gloucestershire players. Great it is, too, with the batting by W. G. Grace, Charlie Barnett, Wally Hammond, Tom Graveney and Zaheer Abbas, and Gilbert Jessop there to provide any further entertainment that may be necessary. The photographs are, in many cases, extremely nostalgic.

A History of Cricket in Hampshire (Hampshire Books; published by Hampshire County Council; £7.95), by Norman Gannaway, is a companionable 88-page octavo, with some pleasing black-and-white illustration, written with plenty of knowledge of history and from a personal viewpoint in more recent years. It reads easily, beginning with local cricket in the late seventeenth century and carrying on in a thorough and scholarly fashion to the chapter "Into the Future".

From the Stretford End (Partridge Press; £16.95), by Brian Bearshaw, with an introduction by Cyril Washbrook, is the history of the Lancashire Cricket Club and carries the imprimatur "Official". A bulky, 392-page octavo, it is generous in its coverage. The biographical notes are valuable – that on the Reverend J. R. Napier is particularly intriguing – and there are many triumphs to celebrate: the statistics are extremely thorough. Illustration is in black-and-white, and the whole impression is one of thoroughness, making it a standard work on the subject.

Memories of Somerset Cricket: People, Matches, Grounds (Somerset CCC; no price given) is a 128-page octavo contributed by enthusiasts for cricket in the county; they include players, committee members, journalists, the club's scorer and the senior groundsman. The editor has thus sought to give a variety of views, and the section on grounds is particularly interesting.

The History of the Warwickshire County Cricket Club (Christopher Helm; £15.95), by Jack Bannister, is quite the soundest and most authoritative history of the county written. Mr Bannister himself played for Warwickshire from 1950 to 1968 as a successful bowler; since then he has been secretary of the Cricketers' Association, cricket correspondent of the *Birmingham Post*, and a cricket commentator for BBC radio and television. There is a personal view by M. J. K. Smith, who captained the side for a decade, and his seven-page contribution is characteristic of his shrewd approach to the game. Mr Bannister writes sagely and knowledgeably, frequently from his personal knowledge of the players concerned, and with acceptable touches of both philosophy and humour. It is difficult to imagine an author more closely in touch with his subject. This is a 328-page octavo which is not only sound but immensely readable, and carries the thorough statistical section associated with this series of county histories.

Basingstoke and North Hants Cricket Club 1865-1990 (Basingstoke CC, Hampshire; no price given), subtitled "Celebration of 125 years at May's Bounty", is a 44-page quarto with plenty of black-and-white illustrations. It is a light, often genuinely amusing, history of this club and its ground over rather more than a century, with contributions from officials, including the lady scorer, Derek Dicker and Freddie Butler of that ilk, once known as "Young Fred" but now president of the club. It has an attractive paper cover and adequate statistics.

The History of Bexley Cricket Club (Bexley CC, Manor Way, Bexley, Kent; £10), by Roger B. Hill, is a friendly and enthusiastic history. The opening chapter is of "Matches played in the years before the Battle of Trafalgar"; the eleventh addresses itself to "League cricket"; then come 40 pages of

statistics and scores. It includes some reproductions of rare early photographs. W. G. Grace played on the club's ground, and Arthur Wellard as a young man turned out regularly for the club. The author, Dr Hill, has been hon. secretary, chairman and president of the club and is a qualified coach and umpire.

Chinchilla and District Cricket Association Souvenir Book (1965-1990) (Chinchilla and District CA; $A15) has been published for the silver anniversary of a club which flourishes on the Darling Downs, 200 miles west of Brisbane in Queensland, Australia. A 212-page soft-bound quarto, with the last 47 pages devoted to "Runs, wickets and records", this provides an enthusiastic and lively record of a club which has achieved some appreciable triumphs in its short history.

Honor Oak Cricket Club 1965-1990 (Honor Oak CC, Dulwich Common, London SE21; £3.50 incl. p. & p.), by M. B. Alexander, is a soft-bound 98-page octavo continuing, from the short history 1886-1982, the story of the club originally known as "Star". Its relatively short coverage makes for an extremely personal season-by-season account, and it deals with both a successful second eleven and women's cricket. The most historic name it lists is that of John Emburey of Middlesex and England. Black-and-white illustrations are lively, the statistical appendices short, and the scores adequate.

The History of Llanelli Cricket Club (Llanelli Borough Library; £12, plus £1 p. & p.), by Bob Harragan, is a most ambitious publication to emerge from club cricket. It is a 296-page quarto in stiff boards, generously illustrated in both colour and black-and-white. Llanelli has been a major club of South Wales, producing such prominent Glamorgan players as Dai Davies ("Llanelli's equivalent to W. G. Grace"), Trevor Every, Emrys Davies, Haydn Davies, Willie Jones, Jim Presdee, Ken Lewis, Peter Walker, Brian Edrich, Euros Lewis, Geoff Jones, Kevin Lyons, Alwyn Harris, Winston Davis and Malcolm Nash. This is a book obviously written with immense pride, its 28-page index a mark not only of thoroughness but of the number of people and clubs who share Llanelli's distinguished history.

The Road to Lord's (Toft CC; no price given) was produced by the Toft club of Cheshire to mark their winning of the National Village Championship in 1989. It is a six-page, paperbound, oblong quarto souvenir containing the scores and celebrating the village's victory over Hambledon in the replayed final at Beckenham.

Les Ames (Christopher Helm; £15.95), by Alan Hill, is, rather surprisingly, the first biography of one of the most popular and respected of English cricketers. It is a 175-page hardback octavo, illustrated in black-and-white. Born in 1905, Les Ames was a considerable all-round sportsman: he was a good enough left wing at soccer to appear professionally for Clapton Orient and Gillingham, and as a wicket-keeper-batsman was outstanding to international standard in both departments. He played for Kent from 1926 to 1951, and for England in 47 Tests, and much of his career was involved with those of the great leg-spinners, particularly "Tich" Freeman, but also "Father" Marriott and Doug Wright. At seventeen he joined the county staff and, maturing quickly, at 22 he set a new wicket-keeping record by dismissing 122 batsmen (52 stumpings, 70 catches). It was, as Mr Hill reminds us, P. G. H. Fender who said, at the beginning of the 1928-29 England tour to Australia: "I found everyone regretting that Ames could not keep like Duckworth, or that Duckworth could not bat like Ames." Ames is, of course, much associated also with Frank Woolley, with whom he played for many years; but as this book shows beyond question, Les Ames was his own man and an outstanding cricketer in his own right.

Dolly, subtitled "The life and career of a cricketer of character" (Worcestershire CCC; no price given), is the 104-page quarto issued in support of Basil D'Oliveira's 25-year testimonial. Surely he must find it wryly amusing that the introduction is by the Duke of Westminster. However, many of those who know him have contributed generously and revealingly to this book, which is well illustrated in colour and black-and-white. It is, for a benefit occasion, quite an appreciable volume.

Martin Donnelly (Association of Cricket Statisticians; £2.50), by Wesley Harte, is No. 8 in the Association's "Famous Cricketers" series. In his introduction, Mr Harte gives the opinion that "in the immediate post-war period Martin Donnelly was regarded as the world's finest left-hand batsman". He was, indeed, a magnificent player, and it is surprising to read that he played in only 131 first-class matches, and 231 innings, for his 9,250 runs at 47.43. However, he finished with first-class cricket in England in 1950 by going into business in Australia, and he waited a decade before turning out for Lord Cobham's XI against MCC in his native New Zealand, his final first-class game. The figures of his career are impressive, and detailed in the normal manner of the Association.

Cricket with Grace (Unwin Hyman; £16.95), by David Rayvern Allen, is "An illustrated anthology on W.G.". A 160-page quarto, it has been compiled in scholarly and thorough manner, and its contributors run from Conan Doyle to Neville Cardus. Some of the poems, stories and songs will be new to many readers, though the necessary stock pieces are also included. Mr Allen has chosen well: there is humour and humanity in his collection, and many of the black-and-white illustrations will prove fresh and informative.

Len Hutton, A Pictorial Biography (Collins & Brown; £12.95), by David Lemmon, is a 107-page hardback quarto. The narrative of the success of one of the great cricketers of our time as a batsman, captain and human being is written with the author's characteristic care and has a perceptive foreword by Trevor Bailey. It is most profusely – if not always completely relevantly – illustrated with black-and-white photographs and ends with an obituary notice obviously written immediately after the subject's funeral.

Cheerful Charlie (published by the author, PO Box 271, Shoeburyness, Essex SS3 9UL; £11.95 hardback, £8.95 softback, incl. p. & p.), by Jan Kemp, is a biography of C. P. McGahey. Neville Cardus was a considerable admirer of McGahey's character and humour, but we have not previously seen a full-dress biography. This is a 152-page octavo which comes basically from McGahey's own territory. Many of its themes are captured in the chapter headings: "An East End Lad", "An Essex Player", "Captaincy and Beyond" and "A Great Encourager".

The Test Match Career of Walter Hammond (Nutshell Publishing; £13.95), by Derek Lodge, has a foreword by Brian Johnston. The author informs us that "it was to have been written by the late David Burnett James", who is the first person mentioned in the acknowledgements. In dealing with the career of one of the few truly great players – the author calls him at one point "the world's best batsman" – it is concerned much with his 85 Tests, and particularly his seven series against Australia. It is a well-made, 216-page octavo, with several pages of black-and-white illustrations.

Rhythm and Swing (Souvenir Press; £15.95), by Richard Hadlee, is described as "an autobiography with Richard Becht". It is a 303-page octavo, most generously illustrated in both black-and-white and colour, and it covers the career of the man who retired in 1990 as the most prolific Test wicket-taker of all time. It is a substantially written, often humorous, story which does honest justice to a very great player: attractive to handle, it is absorbing and satisfying to read.

George Lohmann: The Beau Ideal (published by Pluto Press, Australia; available in England from J. W. McKenzie, 12 Stoneleigh Park Road, Ewell, Epsom, Surrey KT19 0QT; £4.95), by Vic Sissons, is the first – but, at 65 pages and soft-covered, brief – biography of the great Surrey and England medium-pace bowler. By 21 he was established in both the county and the national elevens; he had an amazingly successful period from 1886 to 1892, and died in 1901 at the age of 36.

A Double Life (Ringpress; £14.95) is the autobiography of that remarkable all-rounder, Phil Neale, written in conjunction with Patrick Murphy. A generously illustrated 160-page quarto, it relates the story of a most impressive career. Neale played soccer for Lincoln City from 1975 to 1984, a period in which they were twice promoted to the Third Division; at cricket, he has played as a useful batsman and occasional bowler since 1975, and since 1982 as captain, for Worcestershire, county champions in 1988 and 1989. In addition to his games-playing, he gained an Honours degree in Russian at Leeds University. Much of his charm, as well as his clear thinking, comes through in this unusual book.

Harold Larwood (Association of Cricket Statisticians; £2.50) is the sixth in the Association's series of famous cricketers. It is a 56-page octavo with text by Peter Wynne-Thomas and very full statistics.

Bill O'Reilly: A Cricketing Life (Millennium; $A24.95), by Jack McHarg, is described as "The Authorised Biography". Called by Lindsay Hassett in his foreword "The finest spin bowler in living memory", O'Reilly was a man of considerable strength of character, drive and will. Mr McHarg's story is full of the gusto so characteristic of his subject, and he continues it into chapters on "The journalist", "Work and family" and "Bill's thoughts on cricketers". This is a highly professional and readable 226-page octavo, with relevant black-and-white illustration.

Ranji: A Genius Rich and Strange (Kingswood Press; £14.99), by Simon Wilde, is the biography of one of the most romantic figures of English cricket. A 257-page octavo, by a member of *The Times* sporting staff, it fully justifies its publication, with its revelations of previously unprinted material about its subject. Mr Wilde has drawn on secret government papers and hitherto unknown letters to reveal Ranji as far more than the great cricketer and constant debtor everyone knew him to be. He shows him as a vastly different character, and other material uncovers his relationship with an English girl he probably wished to marry. The story sorts oddly with the background of Victorian cricket, but it reads well, convincingly and revealingly.

The "Demon" Spofforth (New South Wales University Press, PO Box 1 Kensington, NSW, Australia 2033; no price given), by Richard Cashman, is surprisingly enough, the first biography of this great figure of Anglo-Australian cricket. The author, Dr Cashman, teaches history at the University of New South Wales and has published several cricketo-social studies, as well as writing regularly on the game. He has gone, typically of the professional scholar, to original sources, including at times his subject. Spofforth, a man of strong and clear opinions, was the first great publ

cricket idol of Australia, and was called by more than one of his supporters the greatest bowler in the world; a claim his figures of the time corroborate. A 275-page octavo, this book contains many valuable and unusual black-and-white illustrations and line drawings.

Bowled Statham (Breedon Books; £12.95), by Tony Derlien, is labelled "The authorised biography". A 167-page octavo, it tells the story of the man whom Fred Trueman described as the "most accurate quick bowler who has ever played cricket". Nearly half of Statham's 2,260 first-class wickets were bowled, and his average of 16.36 is the lowest achieved by any post-1918 bowler who has taken more than 2,000 wickets. Such figures are, indeed, impressive, but the story of the career of this modest, reliable man is here told with careful facts and without flourishes. Indeed, it is typical and sympathetic, carrying the story on past the time when he retired completely from the game to the point at which Statham, unemployed, developed osteoporosis and Trueman arranged a dinner for his benefit. It is, in many ways, a moving account, and it will bring its subject even more admirers.

Cyril Washbrook (Association of Cricket Statisticians; £2.50), by Malcolm Lorimer and Roy Cavanagh, is the seventh in the Association's series of "Famous Cricketers". As the authors remark in their introduction, it was fitting that it should be published in the year when its subject was president of Lancashire CCC. It carries a biographical essay and then Washbrook's innings-by-innings record, followed by his other career statistics.

A Test of Fire (Robson Books; £14.95), by Graham Gooch, is "A personal account of a dramatic year by England's captain". A 185-page octavo, with black-and-white illustrations, it tells the story which first surprised the British and West Indian cricketing publics through England's astonishing win, by nine wickets, at Sabina Park. The series did not continue quite so happily for Gooch's men, but there were comforts to be gained. The whole story is told with the assistance of Steve Whiting, easily and frankly and much more clearly than many such accounts. Mr Gooch's collaborator does not come between the captain and his text. "I'm used to being hit on the hands, but I have never broken a finger before, and I wasn't fully aware of what had happened. I couldn't hold the bat at all and I thought at first it was a dislocation as the small knuckle on my left hand was depressed. It was obvious I couldn't go on as it was. Laurie Brown, our physio, tried to correct it which was simply agony."

The Ultimate Test (Partridge Press; £12.99), by Richard Evans, carries as its subtitle "The story behind the 1990 cricket tours to South Africa and the West Indies". The first part is concerned with Mike Gatting's "rebel" tour with its pervading background of political change, notably Nelson Mandela's release. The second deals with the England side which, under Graham Gooch, rose above all reasonable hopes of English supporters. This is a 248-page octavo with black-and-white photographs and ample scoresheets.

The Hick 'n' Dilley Circus (Macmillan; £14.95), written with the obvious happy assistance of Patrick Murphy, is a 198-page octavo which reflects on the 1989 English season when Worcestershire, with those two, retained the County Championship. Written in diary form, from alternating voices, it tells the story in a friendly fashion and reveals, in addition to some attacking cricket, the genuine friendship that exists between Graeme Hick and Graham Dilley. Hick, of course, broke upon the game like a refreshing shower, and in recent seasons had established himself as a major batsman

)illey, troubled by a knee injury, had chosen to end his official England areer. For all the differences between them, they teamed up effectively, and learly with much enjoyment, in this season which brought considerable uccess.

Cricket Voices, subtitled "Interviews with Mihir Bose" (Kingswood Press; 14.99), is an extremely solid 284-page octavo. It is composed of interviews y a cricket-hungry enquirer with officials, past and present, players, mpires, coaches, and every kind of body about the game. They have bviously spoken frankly with Mr Bose, who has been a faithful reporter. No etail is too small for him to observe, and he has elicited much information 1at some reporters would ignore – and some would never be able to discover.

After the Interval (Crowood Press; £14.95), by Michael Melford, is that ccomplished observer's review of the game since 1947: from "Back to first-lass cricket" down to a very wise review titled "Then and now". It is a 238-age octavo with some extremely interesting black-and-white photographic lustrations. Mr Melford has always been a writer of natural ease and polish: is experience as a correspondent of the *Daily Telegraph*, which lasted for ore than 30 years, took him to much of the best cricket England xperienced, and he has reported it objectively and with obvious pleasure.

The Essential E. W. Swanton (Collins/Willow; £16.95), edited by George lumptre, is subtitled "The 1980s Observed". This, the second anthology of ie author's writing, is a solid 318-page octavo. Reflecting his considerable ricketing travels, wide reading and acquaintance, it takes an authoritative oint of view in a whole series of essays and extracts, some of them short and l to the point. The style is typically Mr Swanton's. He has thought much bout the game and observes a great deal. His essay, "Woodcock's last Visden", from the *Daily Telegraph*, is perceptive and sympathetic, and milarly there are others, not dealing with headline news but perceiving the rogress of the game.

Great Tests Recalled (Bloomsbury; £16.99), edited by Peter Hayter, is a enerous 221-page quarto, profusely illustrated in black-and-white. It deals ith nineteen Test matches, from England versus Australia, the Ashes match : The Oval in 1882, to the First Test between West Indies and England at .ingston in 1990. Its subtitle, "Original reports of the memorable matches", xplains the nature of its contents, and the writers range widely in choice.

Cricket Indulgence (PB Enterprises, Sports Marketing [Australia]; no price iven), edited by D. M. Harding, is a collection of the cricket writings of 'hris Harte. In the course of 37 essays in a 112-page hard-covered octavo, Mr Iarte is, as usual, lucid and readable. He goes straight to the point on all 1atters, and illuminates his enthusiasm for cricket with flashes of wit.

The 23rd of Nico Craven's seasonal offerings, *Summer Pudding* (from the uthor, The Coach House, Ponsonby, Seascale, Cumbria CA20 1BX; £4.35), as a foreword by John Woodcock, and the text from Emerson, "As I am, so see". In a 64-page octavo, this is a collection of ten pieces, taking the reader n a joyous journey from Harrogate to Bath and back to Cumberland before etting down to the serious business at Cheltenham. The illustration by rank Fisher – "Everybody was TALKING . . . *The Listener* will never be a estseller in Yorkshire" – has unexpectedly taken on a nostalgic and historic spect.

Willow, and other Cricket Poems (from the author, 20 Smallbrook Walk, rewe, Cheshire CW2 6LX; £1 incl. p. & p.) by Imogen Grosberg, is her annual offering of verse in a fourteen-page quarto, with her invariable warm feeling for cricket and careful use of cricketing language.

The Five Seasons (Oak Press, 9 Oak Lane, Bradford BD9 4PU; £2: a limited edition of 500 copies), by Colin Shakespeare – which is a handsome start for anyone proposing to utter a book of poetry – contains 25 poems, six of them named for considerable cricketers, but with several on other subjects. This is a 32-page paperbound octavo, obviously produced by one deeply versed in cricket.

New South Wales versus Victoria: A Statistical Survey (obtainable from Roger Page, 55 Tarcoola Drive, Yallambie, Victoria, Australia; $A12.50 and Sport-in-Print, 3 Radcliffe Road, West Bridgford, Nottingham; £6.25) by John King, is a 76-page quarto and yet another of that writer's exhaustive statistical surveys.

One-Day International Cricket Records (Association of Cricket Statisticians £5.50), by V. H. Isaacs and R. K. Whitham, is a 92-page paperbound soft-covered octavo. It is a thorough and useful record, becoming always more so with the proliferation of one-day cricket at representative level.

ICC Trophy Competitions 1979, 1982, and 1986 (Association of Cricket Statisticians; £4) has a preface by Richard Streeton and a foreword by Philip Snow. The preface points out that, "A long existing gap in cricket history is finally filled with this book, which makes available for the first time the full scorecards from the first three ICC Trophy competitions". It is a 113-page soft-covered octavo which gives the scores of the matches between the Associate countries of ICC, who range across the world.

Cricket Matches 1855-1859 (Association of Cricket Statisticians; no price given) is a 170-page octavo which represents another volume in the steady attempt of the Association to complete the records of the game in England while *First Class Matches 1898* (ACS; £8) follows, in a 211-page octavo, the Association's sequence towards its goal.

The Grand Matches of Cricket Played in England from 1771 to 1791 (J. W. McKenzie, 12 Stoneleigh Park Road, Ewell, Epsom, Surrey KT19 0QT; £16) by William Epps, with an introduction by David Rayvern Allen, is a facsimile reproduction of one of the earliest and rarest cricket books originally published in 1799. This edition consists of 104 octavo pages, and with an "apology", Mr Allen's introduction tells its history.

Rupert's Year (Somerset CCC; no price given) is quite surprisingly ample for a benefit brochure: it is a 112-page soft-bound quarto issued in support of Peter Roebuck's benefit fund in 1990. Its contents are many and varied; quite a number of them, as for instance the clerihews, are original. It is a diverting read and should serve Mr Roebuck well.

Wisden Cricketers' Almanack 1990 (John Wisden & Co. Ltd; £18.50 hardback, £15.50 soft cover), edited by Graeme Wright, is the 127th edition and continues as the bulwark of reference on the game. It is a chubby, 1,296-page, smallish octavo which contains all the usual features and references: notes on the game in South Africa; essays by E. W. Swanton and by David Foot. The Five Cricketers of the Year, pictured in colour, are S. J. Cook, D. M. Jones, M. A. Taylor, R. A. Smith and R. C. Russell. All the first-class matches of the 1989 English season are included, and due attention is paid to the game in the schools, the Second Elevens and Minor Counties, and first-class cricket outside England. One can only say that the standard has been maintained.

Benson and Hedges Cricket Year: September 1989 to September 1990 (Pelham Books; £17.99), edited by David Lemmon, with a knowledgeable foreword by Mark Nicholas, is the ninth edition of this very full – 496 pages – strongly bound annual. It is most generously illustrated, partly in colour, and covers cricket all over the world, with a most satisfying final section on the game in England.

ACS International Cricket Year Book, 1990 (Association of Cricket Statisticians; £5) is a 224-page octavo. Its strength, of course, lies in its statistics, which cover Test matches, one-day internationals, the English counties, and the first-class game in ten other countries.

Benson & Hedges West Indies Cricket Annual 1990 (Caribbean Communications, PO Box 40W, Worthing, Christ Church, Barbados; and 116 Queens Road, Hersham, Surrey KT12 5LL; no price given), edited by Tony Cozier, is an 88-page quarto most generously illustrated in black-and-white and colour. It covers West Indies domestic cricket, England's tour, and West Indies tours to Zimbabwe and North America. It has also the usual and invaluable Who's Who in West Indies Cricket. The obituaries include the much lamented C. L. R. James.

ACS First Class Counties' Second Eleven Annual 1990 (Association of Cricket Statisticians; no price given), edited by Les Hatton, is thorough, valuable and, in much of its content, unique among cricket publications. There are more than 600 biographical entries, and the editor hopes strongly for greater completion of his ground.

The 1990 Guide to Minor Counties Cricket (Berry & Radd, "Idsworth", Fair Close, Frankton, near Rugby, Warwickshire CV23 9PL; £1.50), edited by Mike Berry, Niall Campbell and Pete Norton, is a new publication which runs to 56 octavo pages in a soft binding. There are separate notes on each minor county concerned, biographical notes on major figures and players, and plenty of black-and-white portrait illustrations.

The Victorian Cricket Association Annual Reports 1989-1990 (from Victorian Cricket Association, 86 Jolimont Street, Jolimont, Victoria 3002; $A22; overseas $A25 incl. p. & p.) is a most thorough record of the state's cricket and history of its past achievements. It runs to 147 octavo pages, with black-and-white illustration.

ACSSI Cricket Yearbook 1988-89 (The Marine Sports, 53 Gokhale Roac (North), Dadar, Bombay 400 028; Rs60; UK agent: Martin Wood, 12 S John's Road, Sevenoaks, Kent TN13 3LW), edited by Anandji Dossa, Sudhi Vaidya and Mohandas Menon, gives an ample coverage of cricket in Indi with numerous and excellently laid-out statistics. It is a 400-page octavo i soft covers, with a few black-and-white illustrations. Particularly helpful i the register of players who have represented India, including those who hav played in one-day internationals.

Irish Cricket Union Yearbook 1990 (Able Press, 35 Sandymount Avenue Dublin 4; £1, plus 54p p. & p.), edited by Francis Xavier Carty, covers th game in that country with its usual thoroughness within 88 octavo pages.

The County Yearbooks, notices of which follow, may be assumed t include the counties' match scores of the previous season of first and secon elevens, chairmen's reports, averages and biographical notes on the player Only additions to that generalisation are mentioned.

Essex County Cricket Club 1990 Handbook (Essex CCC; £4), edited b Peter Edwards, celebrates what Tom Pearce in his foreword describes as year when "The county side had the best overall record in the country". It

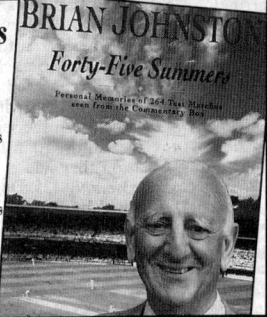

a heavyweight among yearbooks and extremely wide-ranging in its content. There are articles on John Lever's retirement, on Essex and England captaincy by Graham Gooch, by Trevor Bailey on the structure of cricket, David Lemmon on Essex in the 1980s, and Doug Insole on Trevor Bailey, as well as numerous other features and many black-and-white illustrations in its 296 octavo pages.

Glamorgan County Cricket Club 1990 Yearbook (Glamorgan CCC; £4), edited by Steven Watkin, is most pleasingly produced, with black-and-white illustrations in its 160 octavo pages. There are features by the editor, Alan Wilkins, Andrew Hignell, Wilf Jeffreys, Dean Conway, Len Smith, Gordon Lewis and Tom Oldknow.

Hampshire Handbook (Hampshire CCC; £4) is a 200-page octavo. There are features by John Hughes, Andrew Hignell, Patrick Symes, Mike Neasom, Kevan James and Tony Mitchener, plus a poem by Imogen Grosberg. There are a few black-and-white illustrations.

Kent County Cricket Annual 1990 (Kent CCC; £3.50), edited by John Evans, is a 248-page quarto with illustrations in black-and-white and some in colour. It is, understandably and movingly, much concerned with the loss of Leslie Ames. In addition to features by Derek Carlaw, Howard Milton, Alan Ealham and Colin Page, there is an interesting tabulation of cricketers who have played first-class cricket for Kent and also for other counties.

Lancashire Cricket 1990 Yearbook (Lancashire CCC; £4) is edited by Bob Warburton, Malcolm Lorimer, Ken Grime and Robbie Robbins. Although its 368 octavo pages give much attention to Lancashire leagues and statistics, there is ample treatment of the county club and its past achievements. There are features on players, past and present, and articles by Richard Streeton and Malcolm Lorimer.

Somerset County Cricket Club 1990 Yearbook (Somerset CCC; £3.50), edited by Michael Hill, is a 208-page octavo, illustrated in black-and-white and colour. There are player portraits, and features by John Harrison, Vic Marks, Matthew Engel, Jimmy Cook, Peter Roebuck, Peter Robinson and Richard Streeton.

Surrey County Cricket Club Yearbook for 1990 (Surrey CCC; £4.50), introduced by Geoffrey Howard, contains within its 160 octavo pages a most impressive study of the new building of the West Stand and the Ken Barrington Centre by David Seward. There are features by Ian Greig, Geoff Arnold, Chris Waller, Mike Edwards, Penny Davies, Alec Stewart, John Woodcock and Pat Gibson, and the whole is illustrated in black-and-white.

The two English cricket periodicals go steadily ahead. *The Cricketer* (Beech Hanger, Ashurst, Tunbridge Wells, Kent TN3 9ST; £1.60 monthly), edited by Christopher Martin-Jenkins, with spring and winter annuals, was founded in 1920 and as such is much the senior cricket periodical in the world. Main contributors are the editor, Alan Lee, E. W. Swanton and Robert Brooke, while on one occasion they had a contribution from Mr John Major.

Wisden Cricket Monthly (25 Down Road, Guildford, Surrey GU1 2PY; £1.40 monthly), edited by David Frith, has now reached its twelfth annual volume. Contributors include the editor, David Gower, E. M. Wellings, Jonathan Rice and, from Australia, Trevor Grant, while the colour and black-and-white photography of Patrick Eagar adorns its pages each month.

Australian Cricket Journal, edited by Chris Harte, ceased publication with the issue of April 1990 (Vol. 5 No. 3) and Mr Harte's subsequent return to England. It was an enlightened and intelligent periodical.

Notable reprints of books which made their mark on publication are: *Play Resumed with Cardus* (Macdonald/Queen Anne Press; £5.95) by Neville Cardus; *Cardus in the Covers* (Macdonald/Queen Anne Press; £5.95) by Neville Cardus; *In Search of Cricket* (The Pavilion Library; £7.99) by J. M. Kilburn; *Double Century: Cricket in The Times, Volume Two 1935-1990* (The Pavilion Library; £8.99) edited by Marcus Williams; *Masters of Cricket from Trumper to May* (The Pavilion Library; £7.99) by Jack Fingleton; *Cricket Cauldron: With Hutton in the Caribbean* (The Pavilion Library; £7.99) by Alex Bannister; and *The Cricket Captains of England* (The Pavilion Library; £7.99) by Alan Gibson.

Note: Titles published by the Association of Cricket Statisticians may be obtained from the Association, 3 Radcliffe Road, West Bridgford, Nottingham NG2 5FF.

Basingstoke Boy (Collins/Willow; £16.95), by John Arlott, is described on its flyleaf as the first volume of his autobiography, although it frequently brings the reader up to date with its subject's life. The author, referring to himself throughout in the third person, is inclined to see himself as the subject of a story he can scarcely credit is his own. Yet while the progress from boy in the Hampshire country town of Basingstoke and policeman in wartime Southampton, to BBC poetry producer in London and "the voice of cricket", might seem at first glance one of great good fortune, also revealed is John Arlott's enjoyment of and capacity for his work. And although cricket has been essential to his life, it shares its place with other enthusiasms; this story relates a well-lived life. If at times its style makes it seem impersonal, there is no mistaking the author in its observations. "This man, Hobbs, the great one, he played in such ordinary fashion: there was nothing exciting like Mr Crate or Mr Chesterfield hitting their huge sixes on May's Bounty at Basingstoke. Only when one looked at Sutcliffe, painstakingly precise, was it possible to understand that Hobbs was doing it all with the untroubled, easy air of a man pottering in his garden . . . [Hobbs] was all but disappointing in making it all so simple . . . ." Or elsewhere: "No doubt the Birmingham police excelled in some or all of those activities but, in those days, it was simply the hard force. Advancement was by cases, which was taken to mean convictions: it was a force hating, and hated by, its public."

FIXTURES, 1991

** Indicates Sunday play.* † *Not first-class.*

4d = Play over 4 days; where not indicated, first-class matches are of 3 days' duration.

Saturday, April 13

Cambridge* Cambridge U. v Lancs.
Oxford Oxford U. v Hants

Tuesday, April 16

Lord's (4d) MCC v Middx
Cambridge Cambridge U. v Northants

Wednesday, April 17

Oxford Oxford U. v Glam.

Friday, April 19

Cambridge Cambridge U. v Essex

Tuesday, April 23

†**Benson and Hedges Cup** (1 day)

Derby Derbys. v Northants
Bristol Glos. v Combined Universities
Southampton Hants v Notts.
Canterbury Kent v Leics.
Trowbridge Minor Counties v Glam.
Forfar Scotland v Lancs.
Taunton Somerset v Middx
The Oval Surrey v Essex

Thursday, April 25

†**Benson and Hedges Cup** (1 day)

Oxford Combined Universities v Derbys.
Manchester Lancs. v Kent
Lord's Middx v Surrey
Trowbridge Minor Counties v Hants
Nottingham Notts. v Yorks.
Hove Sussex v Leics.
Birmingham Warwicks. v Essex
Worcester Worcs. v Glos.

Saturday, April 27

Derby (4d) Derbys. v Northants
Chelmsford (4d) Essex v Surrey
Southampton* (4d) Hants v Kent
Leicester (4d) Leics. v Glam.
Lord's (4d) Middx v Yorks.
Taunton (4d) Somerset v Sussex
Birmingham (4d) Warwicks. v Lancs.
Worcester* (4d) Worcs. v Glos.
Oxford Oxford U. v Notts.
Hove* (4d) †Sussex 2nd XI v England Under-19

Thursday, May 2

†**Benson and Hedges Cup** (1 day)

Cambridge Combined Universities v Worcs.
Chelmsford Essex v Middx
Bristol Glos. v Northants
Southampton Hants v Glam.
Canterbury Kent v Sussex
Leicester Leics. v Scotland
Birmingham Warwicks. v Somerset
Leeds Yorks. v Minor Counties

Saturday, May 4

†**Benson and Hedges Cup** (1 day)

Cardiff Glam. v Notts.
Leicester Leics. v Lancs.
Lord's Middx v Warwicks.
Northampton Northants v Combined Universities
Taunton‡ Somerset v Surrey
Hove‡ Sussex v Scotland
Worcester Worcs. v Derbys.
Leeds Yorks. v Hants

‡ *Reserve day, Sunday.*

Tuesday, May 7

†**Benson and Hedges Cup** (1 day)

Derby Derbys. v Glos.
Chelmsford Essex v Somerset
Cardiff Glam. v Yorks.
Manchester Lancs. v Sussex
Northampton Northants v Worcs.
Nottingham Notts. v Minor Counties
Glasgow (Hamilton Crescent) Scotland v Kent
The Oval Surrey v Warwicks.

Thursday, May 9

Bristol (4d)	Glos. v Hants
Lord's (4d)	Middx v Sussex
Northampton (4d)	Northants v Essex
Nottingham (4d)	Notts. v Leics.
Taunton (4d)	Somerset v Glam.
The Oval (4d)	Surrey v Kent
Worcester (4d)	Worcs. v Lancs.
Leeds (4d)	Yorks. v Warwicks.
Cambridge	Cambridge U. v Derbys.

Sunday, May 12

Arundel	†Lavinia, Duchess of Norfolk's XI v West Indians (1 day)

Tuesday, May 14

Bristol	†Glos. v West Indians (1 day)

Wednesday, May 15

Worcester	Worcs. v West Indians
Cambridge	Cambridge U. v Middx
Oxford	Oxford U. v Glos.

Thursday, May 16

Swansea (4d)	Glam. v Warwicks.
Folkestone (4d)	Kent v Essex
Manchester (4d)	Lancs. v Derbys.
Northampton (4d)	Northants v Leics.
Hove (4d)	Sussex v Hants
Leeds (4d)	Yorks. v Notts.

Saturday, May 18

Lord's*	Middx v West Indians
Cambridge	Cambridge U. v Surrey

Wednesday, May 22

Derby	Derbys. v Somerset
Chelmsford	Essex v Warwicks.
Cardiff	Glam. v Northants
Nottingham	Notts. v Kent
The Oval	Surrey v Lancs.
Hove	Sussex v Middx
Sheffield	Yorks. v Glos.
Cambridge	Cambridge U. v Leics.

Thursday, May 23

Birmingham	†ENGLAND v WEST INDIES (1st 1-day Texaco Trophy)

Saturday, May 25

Manchester	†ENGLAND v WEST INDIES (2nd 1-day Texaco Trophy)
Cardiff	Glam. v Sussex
Bournemouth	Hants v Surrey
Canterbury	Kent v Derbys.
Leicester	Leics. v Notts.
Taunton	Somerset v Middx
Birmingham	Warwicks. v Glos.
Leeds	Yorks. v Northants
Oxford	Oxford U. v Worcs.

Monday, May 27

Lord's	†ENGLAND v WEST INDIES (3rd 1-day Texaco Trophy)

Wednesday, May 29

†Benson and Hedges Cup – Quarter-Finals (1 day)

Taunton or The Oval	Somerset or Surrey v West Indians

Friday, May 31

Bristol	Glos. v Essex
Manchester	Lancs. v Sussex
Lord's	Middx v Kent
Northampton	Northants v Derbys.
Nottingham	Notts. v Hants
Birmingham	Warwicks. v Yorks.
Worcester	Worcs. v Glam.

Saturday, June 1

Leicester*	Leics. v West Indians

Tuesday, June 4

Ilford	Essex v Leics.
Swansea	Glam. v Somerset
Bristol	Glos. v Middx
Basingstoke	Hants v Lancs.
Tunbridge Wells	Kent v Warwicks.
Northampton	Northants v Worcs.
The Oval	Surrey v Notts.
Oxford	Oxford U. v Yorks.

Thursday, June 6

Leeds*	ENGLAND v WEST INDIES (1st Cornhill Test, 5 days)

Friday, June 7

Chesterfield Derbys. v Glam.
Ilford Essex v Worcs.
Southampton Hants v Glos.
Tunbridge Wells Kent v Sussex
Uxbridge Middx v Leics.
Birmingham Warwicks. v Somerset
Oxford Oxford U. v Lancs.

Saturday, June 8

Lord's †Eton v Harrow (1 day)

Tuesday, June 11

Harrogate †Tilcon Trophy (3 days)

Wednesday, June 12

†Benson and Hedges Cup – Semi-Finals (1 day)

Derby or Southport Derbys. or Lancs. v West Indians

Friday, June 14

Cardiff Glam. v Middx
Gloucester Glos. v Notts.
Leicester Leics. v Surrey
Hove Sussex v Worcs.
Harrogate Yorks. v Kent

Saturday, June 15

Northampton* Northants v West Indians

Tuesday, June 18

Gloucester Glos. v Derbys.
Leicester Leics. v Lancs.
Bath Somerset v Hants
Coventry Warwicks. v Sussex
Worcester Worcs. v Notts.
Cambridge Cambridge U. v Glam.
Oxford Oxford U. v Kent

Thursday, June 20

Lord's* ENGLAND v WEST INDIES (2nd Cornhill Test, 5 days)

Friday, June 21

Derby Derbys. v Surrey
Neath* Glam. v Leics.
Manchester Lancs. v Kent
Northampton* Northants v Hants
Nottingham Notts. v Warwicks.
Bath Somerset v Glos.
Horsham Sussex v Essex
Sheffield Yorks. v Middx

Saturday, June 22

Dublin (Malahide)* Ireland v Scotland

Wednesday, June 26

Oxford †Oxford & Camb. Univs v West Indians (2 days)

†NatWest Bank Trophy – First Round (1 day)

Bedford Beds. v Worcs.
Reading Berks. v Hants
Exmouth Devon v Essex
Bournemouth Dorset v Lancs.
Darlington Durham v Glam.
Bristol Glos. v Norfolk
Bishop's Stortford Herts. v Derbys.
Dublin (Castle Avenue) Ireland v Middx
Canterbury Kent v Cambs.
Leicester Leics. v Salop
Nottingham Notts. v Lincs.
Edinburgh (Myreside) Scotland v Sussex
Bath Somerset v Bucks.
Stone Staffs. v Northants
The Oval Surrey v Oxon.
Birmingham Warwicks. v Yorks.

Friday, June 28

Trowbridge †League Cricket Conference v West Indians (1 day)
Liverpool Lancs. v Glam.
Lord's Middx v Essex
Luton Northants v Glos.
The Oval Surrey v Somerset
Birmingham Warwicks. v Derbys.
Worcester Worcs. v Leics.

Saturday, June 29

Southampton* Hants v West Indians
Hove* Sussex v Cambridge U.

Tuesday, July 2

Chelmsford	Essex v Hants
Cardiff	Glam. v Notts.
Maidstone	Kent v Northants
Hinckley	Leics. v Glos.
Taunton	Somerset v Lancs.
Arundel	Sussex v Surrey
Birmingham	Warwicks. v Middx
Leeds	Yorks. v Worcs.
Lord's	Oxford U. v Cambridge U.

Thursday, July 4

Nottingham	ENGLAND v WEST INDIES (3rd Cornhill Test, 5 days)

Friday, July 5

Derby	Derbys. v Sussex
Southampton	Hants v Yorks.
Maidstone	Kent v Glam.
Leicester	Leics. v Northants
The Oval	Surrey v Essex

Sunday, July 7

Taunton	†Somerset v Glos. (1 day)

Wednesday, July 10

Darlington	†Minor Counties v West Indians (2 days)

Thursday, July 11

†NatWest Bank Trophy – Second Round (1 day)

Luton or Worcester	Beds. or Worcs. v Durham or Glam.
Reading or Southampton	Berks. or Hants v Dorset or Lancs.
Bristol or Lakenham	Glos. or Norfolk v Notts. or Lincs.
Glasgow (Titwood) or Hove	Scotland or Sussex v Devon or Essex
Taunton or Marlow	Somerset or Bucks. v Ireland or Middx
Burton upon Trent (Ind Coope) or Northampton	Staffs. or Northants v Leics. or Salop
The Oval or Oxford (Christ Church)	Surrey or Oxon. v Kent or Cambs.
Birmingham or Leeds	Warwicks. or Yorks. v Herts. or Derbys.

Friday, July 12

Oxford	†MCC Schools Festival (4 days)

Saturday, July 13

Lord's	†BENSON AND HEDGES CUP FINAL (1 day)
Downpatrick	†Ireland v West Indians (1 day)

Monday, July 15

Brecon	†Wales v West Indians (1 day)

Tuesday, July 16

Swansea	Glam. v West Indians
Southend	Essex v Kent
Portsmouth	Hants v Worcs.
Uxbridge	Middx v Northants
Nottingham	Notts. v Lancs.
Guildford	Surrey v Glos.
Hove	Sussex v Somerset
Scarborough	Yorks. v Derbys.
Lord's	†MCC v MCC Schools (1 day)

Wednesday, July 17

Lord's	†MCC Schools v NAYC (1 day)

Thursday, July 18

Lord's	†NCA Young Cricketers v Combined Services (1 day)

Friday, July 19

Southend	Essex v Somerset
Cheltenham	Glos. v Glam.
Portsmouth	Hants v Warwicks.
Uxbridge	Middx v Lancs.
Wellingborough School	Northants v Notts.
Guildford	Surrey v Yorks.
Hove	Sussex v Leics.
Kidderminster	Worcs. v Derbys.

Saturday, July 20

Canterbury*	Kent v West Indians

Tuesday, July 23

Chesterfield — Derbys. v Hants
Cardiff — Glam. v Essex
Cheltenham — Glos. v Sussex
Manchester — Lancs. v Warwicks.
Northampton — Northants v Somerset
Worksop — Notts. v Yorks.
Worcester — Worcs. v Kent

Wednesday, July 24

Wolverhampton — †England Amateur XI v Sri Lankans (1 day)

Thursday, July 25

Birmingham* — ENGLAND v WEST INDIES (4th Cornhill Test, 5 days)

Friday, July 26

Hartlepool — †Durham v Sri Lankans (1 day)
Cheltenham — Glos. v Worcs.
Leicester* — Leics. v Warwicks.
Lord's — Middx v Notts.
Taunton — Somerset v Kent
The Oval — Surrey v Glam.

Saturday, July 27

Leeds* — Yorks. v Sri Lankans

Tuesday, July 30

Swansea or Worcester — Glam. or Worcs. v Sri Lankans

Wednesday, July 31

†NatWest Bank Trophy – Quarter-Finals (1 day)

Nottingham or Bristol — Notts. or Glos. v West Indians
Jesmond — †England XI v Rest of the World XI (1 day)

Thursday, August 1

Jesmond — †England XI v Rest of the World XI (1 day)

Friday, August 2

Derby — Derbys. v Sri Lankans
Canterbury — Kent v Surrey
Manchester — Lancs. v Yorks.
Lord's — Middx v Hants
Weston-super-Mare — Somerset v Leics.
Eastbourne — Sussex v Northants
Worcester — Worcs. v Warwicks.

Saturday, August 3

Chelmsford* — Essex v West Indians

Tuesday, August 6

Bristol — Glos. v Sri Lankans
Derby — Derbys. v Essex
Canterbury — Kent v Hants
Lytham — Lancs. v Northants
Leicester — Leics. v Yorks.
Weston-super-Mare — Somerset v Worcs.
Eastbourne — Sussex v Notts.
Birmingham — Warwicks. v Surrey
Lord's — †England Under-19 v Australia Under-19 (1st 1-day)

Thursday, August 8

The Oval* — ENGLAND v WEST INDIES (5th Cornhill Test, 5 days)
Nottingham — †England Under-19 v Australia Under-19 (2nd 1-day)

Friday, August 9

Swansea — Glam. v Hants
Bristol — Glos. v Lancs.
Leicester — Leics. v Kent
Lord's — Middx v Derbys.
Northampton — Northants v Warwicks.
Nottingham — Notts. v Essex
Middlesbrough — Yorks. v Sussex

Saturday, August 10

Taunton* — Somerset v Sri Lankans

Monday, August 12

†Bain Clarkson Trophy Semi-Finals (1 day)

Tuesday, August 13

†Bain Clarkson Trophy Semi-Finals (1 day) (if not played on August 12)

Wednesday, August 14

†NatWest Bank Trophy – Semi-Finals (1 day)

Manchester‡	†England A v Sri Lankans (1 day)

Thursday, August 15

Manchester‡	†England A v Sri Lankans (1 day)

‡ *At another venue if Lancs. at home in NWB Trophy semi-finals.*

Friday, August 16

Derby	Derbys. v Lancs.
Colchester	Essex v Northants
Bournemouth	Hants v Leics.
Nottingham	Notts. v Somerset
Worcester	Worcs. v Surrey
Leeds	Yorks. v Glam.
Leicester	†England Under-19 v Australia Under-19 (1st "Test") (4 days)

Saturday, August 17

Hove*	Sussex v Sri Lankans

Tuesday, August 20

)erby	Derbys. v Leics.
;olchester	Essex v Yorks.
3ournemouth	Hants v Sussex
;anterbury	Kent v Glos.
3lackpool	Lancs. v Worcs.
'he Oval	Surrey v Middx
3irmingham	Warwicks. v Glam.

Thursday, August 22

,ord's	ENGLAND v SRI LANKA (Cornhill Test, 5 days)

Friday, August 23

lanchester	Lancs. v Essex
lorthampton	Northants v Surrey
lottingham	Notts. v Derbys.
aunton	Somerset v Yorks.
'orcester	Worcs. v Middx

Tuesday, August 27

Chelmsford	†England Under-19 v Australia Under-19 (2nd "Test") (4 days)

Wednesday, August 28

Abergavenny (4d)	Glam. v Glos.
Southampton (4d)	Hants v Somerset
Canterbury (4d)	Kent v Middx
Manchester (4d)	Lancs. v Notts.
Leicester (4d)	Leics. v Derbys.
Northampton (4d)	Northants v Yorks.
The Oval (4d)	Surrey v Sussex
Birmingham (4d)	Warwicks. v Worcs.
Scarborough	Tesco International Match (3 days)

Thursday, August 29

Lord's	†Minor Counties Knockout Final (1 day)

Friday, August 30

Lord's	†National Club Championship Final (1 day)

Saturday, August 31

Scarborough	†Joshua Tetley Festival Trophy (3 days)
Lord's	†National Village Championship Final (1 day)

Sunday, September 1

†Refuge Assurance Cup – Semi-Finals (1 day)

Tuesday, September 3

Chelmsford (4d)	Essex v Derbys.
Bristol (4d)	Glos. v Northants
Nottingham (4d)	Notts. v Middx
The Oval (4d)	Surrey v Hants
Hove (4d)	Sussex v Kent
Worcester (4d)	Worcs. v Somerset
Scarborough (4d)	Yorks. v Lancs.

Saturday, September 7

Lord's	†NATWEST BANK TROPHY FINAL (1 day)
Hove	†Seeboard Trophy (3 days)
Scarborough	†Yorks. v The Yorkshiremen (1 day)

Sunday, September 8

Scarborough †World XI v Yorks. (1 day)
Luton †Minor Counties Championship Final (1 day)

Monday, September 9

Manchester England Under-19 v Australia Under-19 (3rd "Test") (4 days)

†Bain Clarkson Trophy Final (1 day)

Tuesday, September 10

Derby (4d) Derbys. v Notts.
Cardiff (4d) Glam. v Worcs.
Bristol (4d) Glos. v Somerset
Leicester (4d) Leics. v Essex
Lord's (4d) Middx v Surrey
Birmingham (4d) Warwicks. v Northants

Sunday, September 15

Manchester †REFUGE ASSURANCE CUP FINAL (1 day)

Tuesday, September 17

Chesterfield (4d) Derbys. v Yorks.
Chelmsford (4d) Essex v Middx
Southampton (4d) Hants v Glam.
Canterbury (4d) Kent v Leics.
Manchester (4d) Lancs. v Surrey
Nottingham (4d) Notts. v Worcs.
Taunton (4d) Somerset v Warwicks.
Hove (4d) Sussex v Glos.

Sunday, September 22

County champions v 1990-91 Sheffield Shield winners (1 day)

Monday, September 23

County champions v 1990-91 Sheffield Shield winners (4 days)

WEST INDIAN TOUR, 1991

MAY

12 Arundel †v Lavinia, Duchess of Norfolk's XI (1 day)
14 Bristol †v Glos. (1 day)
15 Worcester v Worcs.
18 Lord's* v Middx
23 Birmingham †v ENGLAND (1st 1-day Texaco Trophy)
25 Manchester †v ENGLAND (2nd 1-day Texaco Trophy)
27 Lord's †v ENGLAND (3rd 1-day Texaco Trophy)
29 Taunton or The Oval v Somerset or Surrey

JUNE

1 Leicester* v Leics.
6 Leeds* v ENGLAND (1st Cornhill Test, 5 days)
12 Derby or Southport v Derbys. or Lancs.
15 Northampton* v Northants
20 Lord's* v ENGLAND (2nd Cornhill Test, 5 days)
26 Oxford †v Oxford & Camb. Univs (2 days)
28 Trowbridge †v League Cricket Conference (1 day)
29 Southampton* v Hants

JULY

4 Nottingham v ENGLAND (3rd Cornhill Test, 5 days)
10 Darlington †v Minor Counties (2 days)
13 Downpatrick †v Ireland (1 day)
15 Brecon †v Wales (1 day)
16 Swansea v Glam.
20 Canterbury* v Kent
25 Birmingham* v ENGLAND (4th Cornhill Test, 5 days)
31 Nottingham or Bristol v Notts. or Glos.

AUGUST

3 Chelmsford* v Essex
8 The Oval* v ENGLAND (5th Cornhill Test, 5 days

SRI LANKAN TOUR, 1991

JULY

4	Wolverhampton	†v England Amateur XI (1 day)
[illegible]	Hartlepool	†v Durham (1 day)
7	Leeds*	v Yorks.
[illegible]	Swansea or Worcester	v Glam. or Worcs.

AUGUST

2	Derby	v Derbys.
6	Bristol	v Glos.
10	Taunton*	v Somerset
14	Manchester‡	†v England A (1 day)
15	Manchester‡	†v England A (1 day)

‡ *At another venue if Lancs. at home in NWB Trophy semi-finals.*

17	Hove*	v Sussex
22	Lord's	v ENGLAND (Cornhill Test, 5 days)

†REFUGE ASSURANCE LEAGUE, 1991

APRIL

1–Glam. v Northants (Cardiff); Glos. v Middx (Bristol); Hants v Yorks. (Southampton); Lancs. v Notts. (Manchester); Leics. v Derbys. (Leicester); Surrey v Somerset (The Oval); Warwicks. v Sussex (Birmingham); Worcs. v Kent (Worcester).

8–Essex v Yorks. (Chelmsford); Lancs. v Northants (Manchester); Leics. v Glam. (Leicester); Middx v Surrey (Lord's); Notts. v Warwicks. (Nottingham); Somerset v Sussex (Taunton).

MAY

5–Derbys. v Hants (Derby); Essex v Leics. (Chelmsford); Glam. v Notts. (Cardiff); Glos. v Worcs. (Bristol); Kent v Warwicks. (Canterbury); Middx v Northants (Lord's).

2–Hants v Kent (Southampton); Northants v Leics. (Northampton); Notts. v Essex (Nottingham); Somerset v Glam. (Taunton); Surrey v Glos. (The Oval); Sussex v Middx (Hove); Worcs. v Lancs. (Worcester); Yorks. v Warwicks. (Leeds).

19–Derbys. v Lancs. (Derby); Glam. v Warwicks. (Swansea); Hants v Somerset (Bournemouth); Kent v Essex (Folkestone); Leics. v Yorks. (Leicester); Northants v Worcs. (Northampton); Sussex v Glos. (Hove).

26–Glam. v Sussex (Swansea); Glos. v Hants (Swindon); Kent v Derbys. (Canterbury); Leics. v Notts. (Leicester); Somerset v Middx (Taunton); Surrey v Essex (The Oval); Warwicks. v Worcs. (Birmingham); Yorks. v Northants (Leeds).

JUNE

2–Derbys. v Yorks. (Chesterfield); Glam. v Essex (Pontypridd); Lancs. v Sussex (Manchester); Middx v Kent (Southgate); Northants v Hants (Northampton); Warwicks. v Somerset (Birmingham); Worcs. v Surrey (Worcester).

9–Derbys. v Surrey (Chesterfield); Essex v Worcs. (Ilford); Glos. v Northants (Moreton-in-Marsh); Hants v Sussex (Basingstoke); Lancs. v Glam. (Manchester); Middx v Leics. (Uxbridge); Notts. v Somerset (Nottingham).

16–Derbys. v Somerset (Checkley); Essex v Hants (Chelmsford); Glam. v Middx (Cardiff); Glos. v Notts. (Gloucester); Leics. v Surrey (Leicester); Sussex v Worcs. (Hove); Warwicks. v Lancs. (Birmingham); Yorks. v Kent (Scarborough).

23–Lancs. v Kent (Manchester); Notts. v Middx (Nottingham); Somerset v Glos. (Bath); Sussex v Essex (Horsham); Warwicks. v Surrey (Birmingham); Yorks. v Worcs. (Sheffield).

30–Essex v Derbys. (Chelmsford); Kent v Glos. (Canterbury); Northants v Somerset (Luton); Surrey v Notts. (The Oval); Worcs. v Leics. (Worcester); Yorks. v Glam. (Leeds).

JULY

7–Derbys. v Sussex (Derby); Essex v Warwicks. (Chelmsford); Hants v Worcs. (Southampton); Kent v Glam. (Maidstone); Leics. v Lancs. (Leicester); Middx v Yorks. (Lord's); Northants v Surrey (Tring).

14–Kent v Leics. (Canterbury); Notts. v Hants (Nottingham); Somerset v Lancs. (Taunton); Surrey v Sussex (The Oval); Warwicks. v Middx (Birmingham); Worcs. v Derbys. (Worcester); Yorks. v Glos. (Scarborough). *Note:* Matches involving the Benson and Hedges Cup finalists to be rearranged.

21–Essex v Somerset (Southend); Glos. v Derbys. (Cheltenham); Hants v Warwicks. (Portsmouth); Middx v Lancs. (Lord's); Northants v Notts. (Wellingborough School); Surrey v Yorks. (The Oval); Sussex v Leics. (Hove); Worcs. v Glam. (Worcester).

28–Derbys. v Northants (Derby); Glos. Essex (Cheltenham); Hants v Lan (Southampton); Somerset v Ke (Taunton); Surrey v Glam. (The Ova Sussex v Notts. (Hove).

AUGUST

4–Glam. v Glos. (Swansea); Kent v Surr (Canterbury); Lancs. v Yorks. (Ma chester); Middx v Hants (Lord's); Not v Worcs. (Nottingham); Somerset Leics. (Weston-super-Mare); Sussex Northants (Eastbourne); Warwicks. Derbys. (Birmingham).

11–Glam. v Hants (Ebbw Vale); Glos. Lancs. (Bristol); Leics. v Warwic (Leicester); Middx v Derbys. (Lord's Northants v Essex (Peterborough Notts. v Kent (Nottingham); Yorks. Sussex (Middlesbrough).

18–Derbys. v Glam. (Derby); Essex v Mid (Colchester); Hants v Leics. (Bourn mouth); Kent v Northants (Canterbury Lancs. v Surrey (Manchester); Wa wicks. v Glos. (Birmingham); Worcs. Somerset (Worcester); Yorks. v Not (Scarborough).

25–Lancs. v Essex (Manchester); Leics. Glos. (Leicester); Northants v Warwick (Northampton); Notts. v Derbys. (N tingham); Somerset v Yorks. (Taunton Surrey v Hants (The Oval); Sussex v Ke (Hove); Worcs. v Middx (Worcester).

†SECOND ELEVEN CHAMPIONSHIP, 1991

All matches are of three days' duration.

APRIL

24–Derbys. v Warwicks. (Chesterfield).

30–Middx v Northants (Southgate).

MAY

1–Lancs. v Leics. (Manchester); Surrey v Worcs. (The Oval); Sussex v Glam. (Hastings); Warwicks. v Hants (Mitchells and Butlers).

7–Derbys. v Somerset (Chesterfield).

8–Glam. v Surrey (Swansea); Leic v Northants (Uppingham); Notts. Worcs. (Steetley, Shireoaks); Sussex Lancs. (Hove).

14–Essex v Somerset (Chelmsford); Sussex Northants (Horsham).

15–Derbys. v Lancs. (Chesterfield); Glos. v Worcs. (Bristol); Leics. v Hants (Hinckley); Notts. v Yorks. (Nottingham); Surrey v Kent (The Oval); Warwicks. v Glam. (Griff & Coton, Nuneaton).

21–Glos. v Yorks. (Bristol); Middx v Hants (Harrow); Northants v Essex (Northampton).

22–Derbys. v Glam. (Belper Meadow); Leics. v Kent (Market Harborough); Worcs. v Somerset (Worcester).

28–Essex v Derbys. (Colchester); Northants v Kent (Oundle School); Sussex v Surrey (Eastbourne).

29–Middx v Lancs. (RAF Vine Lane, Uxbridge); Somerset v Glam. (North Perrott); Yorks. v Warwicks. (Bradford).

JUNE

4–Glos. v Essex (Arle Court, Cheltenham); Kent v Warwicks. (Maidstone); Lancs. v Northants (Manchester); Leics. v Glam. (Hinckley); Somerset v Hants (Taunton); Surrey v Derbys. (Banstead); Worcs. v Sussex (Worcester).

11–Hants v Glos. (Bournemouth); Kent v Derbys. (Sittingbourne); Middx v Sussex (Lensbury Club, Teddington); Northants v Surrey (Old Northamptonians); Notts. v Essex (Worthington Simpson); Somerset v Leics. (Glastonbury).

12–Glam. v Worcs. (Abergavenny); Yorks. v Lancs. (Todmorden).

18–Essex v Leics. (Chelmsford); Hants v Yorks. (Southampton); Kent v Middx (Canterbury); Lancs. v Glos. (Northern CC, Crosby); Northants v Worcs. (Oundle School); Sussex v Warwicks. (Hove).

9–Notts. v Somerset (Worksop CC).

5–Essex v Middx (Chelmsford); Glam. v Glos. (BP Llandarcy); Lancs. v Kent (Blackpool); Northants v Notts. (Northampton); Somerset v Sussex (Taunton); Yorks. v Derbys. (Harrogate).

6–Hants v Surrey (Portsmouth); Warwicks. v Leics. (Stratford-upon-Avon).

JULY

2–Glos. v Notts. (Lydney); Hants v Northants (Southampton); Lancs. v Glam. (Manchester); Surrey v Yorks. (The Oval); Worcs. v Essex (Worcester).

3–Warwicks. v Middx (Knowle & Dorridge).

9–Essex v Warwicks. (Chelmsford).

10–Derbys. v Middx (Derby); Glam. v Notts. (Cardiff); Kent v Sussex (Maidstone); Lancs. v Hants (Manchester); Leics. v Glos. (Oakham); Yorks. v Somerset (York).

16–Glam. v Hants (Ebbw Vale); Glos. v Derbys. (Tuffley Park, Gloucester); Kent v Essex (Canterbury); Northants v Yorks. (Northampton); Worcs. v Middx (Flagge Meadow, Worcester).

17–Lancs. v Notts. (Liverpool); Leics. v Surrey (Leicester).

23–Essex v Glam. (Chelmsford); Glos. v Kent (Bristol); Northants v Somerset (Wellingborough School); Notts. v Surrey (Worksop College); Warwicks. v Lancs. (Studley); Yorks. v Worcs. (Marske-by-Sea).

24–Derbys. v Sussex (Heanor); Middx v Leics. (Richmond).

30–Essex v Sussex (Southend); Hants v Notts. (Bournemouth); Kent v Worcs. (Dartford); Leics. v Yorks. (Market Harborough); Somerset v Warwicks. (Clevedon); Surrey v Middx (Oxted).

31–Northants v Derbys. (Oundle School).

AUGUST

6–Essex v Lancs. (Chelmsford); Glam. v Northants (Ammanford); Hants v Kent (Southampton); Middx v Notts. (Watford Town); Somerset v Glos. (Taunton); Surrey v Warwicks. (Guildford); Worcs. v Leics. (Worcester); Yorks. v Sussex (Leeds).

13–Surrey v Essex (Oxted).

14–Glam. v Yorks. (Usk); Notts. v Sussex (Collingham); Somerset v Middx (Devonshire Park Road, Weston); Warwicks. v Glos. (Walmley); Worcs. v Derbys. (Halesowen).

20–Glos. v Northants (Arle Court, Cheltenham); Surrey v Somerset (Guildford); Sussex v Hants (Hove); Worcs. v Lancs. (Barnt Green); Yorks. v Essex (Elland).

21–Glam. v Kent (Cardiff); Warwicks. v Notts. (Leamington Spa).

27–Derbys. v Leics. (Derby); Glos. v Surrey (Bristol).

28–Hants v Essex (Bournemouth); Notts. v Kent (Steetley, Shireoaks); Somerset v Lancs. (Taunton); Worcs. v Warwicks. (Worcester); Yorks. v Middx (Leeds).

SEPTEMBER

3–Derbys. v Hants (Derby); Middx v Glam. (Harrow); Sussex v Glos. (Horsham).

4–Kent v Yorks. (Folkestone); Leics. v Notts. (Leicester); Warwicks. v Northants (Moseley).

11–Hants v Worcs. (Southampton); Kent v Somerset (Canterbury); Lancs. v Surrey (Manchester); Middx v Glos. (Enfield); Notts. v Derbys. (Nottingham); Sussex v Leics. (Hove).

†BAIN CLARKSON TROPHY, 1991

All matches are of one day's duration.

APRIL

30–Lancs. v Leics. (Manchester).

MAY

2–Derbys. v Notts. (Derby); Kent v MCC Young Cricketers (Maidstone).

6–Derbys. v Leics. (Shipley Hall, Ilkeston); Lancs. v Yorks. (Manchester); Warwicks. v Somerset (Birmingham).

7–Glam. v Warwicks. (Swansea); Middx v Essex (Finchley); Sussex v Kent (Eastbourne).

9–Glos. v Warwicks. (Moreton-in-Marsh).

13–Sussex v MCC Young Cricketers (Sidley).

14–Derbys. v Lancs. (Chesterfield); Hants v Worcs. (Southampton); Notts. v Yorks. (Clipstone); Surrey v Kent (The Oval); Warwicks. v Glam. (Birmingham).

20–Essex v Kent (Newbury Park); Leics. v Northants (Leicester); Notts. v Lancs. (Worthington Simpson); Surrey v Middx (The Oval); Warwicks. v Glos. (Coventry & North Warwicks).

21–Leics. v Lancs. (Leicester); Worcs. v Somerset (Worcester).

27–Glos. v Glam. (Bristol); Sussex v Surrey (Eastbourne); Yorks. v Leics. (Bradford).

28–Notts. v Leics. (Worksop College); Somerset v Glam. (Westlands, Yeovil).

30–Worcs. v Glos. (Kidderminster).

31–Essex v Surrey (Colchester).

JUNE

3–Kent v Surrey (Maidstone); Somerset v Hants (Taunton); Yorks. v Northants (Bingley).

4–Middx v MCC Young Cricketers (Richmond); Yorks. v Notts. (Bawtry Road, Sheffield).

7–Notts. v Northants (Nottingham); Somerset v Glos. (Winscombe); Worcs. v Hants (Worcester).

10–Hants v Glos. (Bournemouth); Middx v Sussex (Ealing); Northants v Leics. (Northampton); Surrey v MCC Young Cricketers (The Oval); Worcs. v Warwicks. (Worcester).

11–Glam. v Worcs. (Bridgend); Yorks. v Lancs. (Todmorden).

17–Derbys. v Yorks. (Chesterfield); Essex v MCC Young Cricketers (Ilford); Glam. v Somerset (Llanelli); Surrey v Sussex (The Oval).

21–Hants v Warwicks. (Southampton); Kent v Middx (Canterbury).

24–Essex v Middx (Chelmsford); Glam. v Glos. (Swansea); Hants v Somerset (Southampton); Yorks. v Derbys. (Leeds).

JULY

1–Northants v Notts. (Banbury).

2–Middx v Kent (Birkbeck Coll., Greenford).

3–MCC Young Cricketers v Ken[t] (Norbury).

5–Glos. v Worcs. (Bristol); Northants [v] Derbys. (Northampton).

8–MCC Young Cricketers v Surrey (Nor[bury]); Notts. v Derbys. (Farnsfield); Somerset v Worcs. (Taunton); Sussex [v] Essex (Lewes Priory CC); Warwicks. [v] Hants (Birmingham).

9–Glos. v Hants (Bristol); Kent v Susse[x] (Maidstone); Leics. v Notts. (Leicester); Middx v Surrey (Harrow); Northants [v] Lancs. (Bedford Modern School); Worc[s.] v Glam. (Stourbridge).

15–Glam. v Hants (Panteg); Leics. [v] Derbys. (Leicester); Northants v York[s.] (Northampton); Surrey v Essex (Th[e] Oval).

6–Lancs. v Notts. (Manchester).

9–Glos. v Somerset (Tuffley Park, Gloucester); Kent v Essex (Canterbury); Warwicks. v Worcs. (Old Edwardians CC).

2–Derbys. v Northants (Heanor); Hants v Glam. (Southampton); MCC Young Cricketers v Sussex (Norbury).

3–Sussex v Middx (Hove).

6–Lancs. v Northants (Manchester); MCC Young Cricketers v Essex (Norbury).

29–Essex v Sussex (Southend); Lancs. v Derbys. (Manchester); Leics. v Yorks. (Market Harborough); MCC Young Cricketers v Middx (Norbury); Somerset v Warwicks. (Bristol Imperial).

Semi-finals to be played on August 12 or August 13.

Final to be played on September 9 (reserve day September 10).

†MINOR COUNTIES CHAMPIONSHIP, 1991

All matches are of two days' duration.

MAY

5–Lincs. v Herts. (Sleaford); Northumb. v Beds. (Jesmond); Wales v Oxon. (Llanelli).

7–Dorset v Bucks. (Sherborne School).

8–Cumb. v Beds. (Carlisle); Durham v Herts. (Hartlepool).

9–Suffolk v Cambs. (Bury St Edmunds).

JUNE

9–Beds. v Staffs. (Dunstable); Herts. v Northumb. (Tring); Lincs. v Cumb. (Bourne); Wales v Berks. (Swansea); Wilts. v Oxon. (Swindon).

0–Cheshire v Cornwall (Bowdon).

1–Herts. v Cumb. (Garston, Watford); Suffolk v Northumb. (Ransome, Ipswich).

2–Cambs. v Norfolk (Wisbech); Salop v Cornwall (Shifnal).

9–Salop v Cheshire (Bridgnorth); Staffs. v Cambs. (Ind Coope, Burton upon Trent).

3–Northumb. v Lincs. (Jesmond); Oxon. v Bucks. (Pressed Steel Fisher, Oxford); Wales v Devon (Usk).

0–Bucks. v Berks. (Marlow).

Unless either side is playing in the Knock-out Competition semi-finals.

JULY

1–Beds. v Suffolk (Leighton Buzzard).

3–Cambs. v Lincs. (Cambridge); Staffs. v Durham (Brewood).

7–Cornwall v Wilts. (Falmouth); Cumb. v Staffs. (Netherfield); Dorset v Devon (Weymouth); Herts. v Beds. (Hitchin); Lincs. v Norfolk (Burghley Park); Oxon. v Berks. (Morris Motors, Oxford); Salop v Wales (Shrewsbury).

11–Berks. v Dorset (Kidmore End).

Unless either side is playing in the NatWest Bank Trophy second round.

14–Beds. v Durham (Luton); Cornwall v Bucks. (Truro); Oxon. v Cheshire (Banbury XX); Staffs. v Northumb. (Leek).

15–Norfolk v Cumb. (North Runcton).

16–Cambs. v Durham (Cambridge); Devon v Bucks. (Sidmouth); Wilts. v Cheshire (Trowbridge).

17–Suffolk v Cumb. (Ipswich School).

21–Cumb. v Cambs. (Millom); Devon v Wilts. (Instow); Dorset v Wales (Sherborne School); Oxon. v Salop (Christ Church, Oxford); Staffs. v Lincs. (Stone).

23–Northumb. v Cambs. (Jesmond); Wilts. v Salop (Trowbridge).

24–Norfolk v Beds. (Lakenham).

28–Cheshire v Dorset (Neston); Cornwall v Berks. (St Austell); Cumb. v Durham (Barrow); Norfolk v Herts. (Lakenham); Wales v Bucks. (Colwyn Bay).

30–Devon v Berks. (Bovey Tracey); Salop v Dorset (Wellington); Suffolk v Herts. (Mildenhall).

AUGUST

1–Norfolk v Suffolk (Lakenham).

4–Beds. v Lincs. (Bedford); Bucks. v Cheshire (Slough); Devon v Cornwall (Exmouth); Durham v Northumb. (Gateshead Fell); Herts. v Cambs. (Potters Bar); Wilts. v Wales (Marlborough College).

5–Norfolk v Staffs. (Lakenham).

6–Berks. v Cheshire (Finchampstead); Dorset v Cornwall (Dorchester).

7–Suffolk v Staffs. (Bury St Edmunds).

11–Berks. v Salop (Reading CC); Lincs. v Durham (Lincoln Lindum); Northumb. v Cumb. (Jesmond); Wilts. v Dorset (Devizes).

12–Cornwall v Oxon. (Helston).

13–Bucks. v Salop (Beaconsfield); Cheshire v Wales (Toft).

14–Cambs. v Beds. (March); Devon v Oxo (Torquay).

18–Berks. v Wilts. (Falkland CC).

19–Durham v Norfolk (Durham Univ. Lincs. v Suffolk (Cleethorpes); Wales Cornwall (Ebbw Vale).

20–Dorset v Oxon. (Weymouth); Herts. Staffs. (Hertford).

21–Durham v Suffolk (Stockton on Tees Northumb. v Norfolk (Jesmond).

25–Bucks. v Wilts. (Amersham); Salop Devon (Oswestry).

27–Cheshire v Devon (Warrington).

SEPTEMBER

8–**Final** (Wardown Park, Luton).

†MINOR COUNTIES KNOCKOUT COMPETITION, 1991

All matches are of one day's duration.

Qualifying Round

May 19 Beds. v Bucks. (Henlow); Herts. v Berks. (Stevenage); Lincs. v Cambs. (Sleaford); Norfolk v Suffolk (Postwick).

First Round

June 2 Herts. or Berks. v Beds. or Bucks. (Bishop's Stortford or Reading CC); Lincs. or Cambs. v Norfolk or Suffolk (Sleaford or The Leys School); Cheshire v Cumb. (Stalybridge); Devon v Wilts. (Exmouth); Dorset v Cornwall (Sherbor School); Durham v Northum (Gateshead Fell); Salop v Wal (Perkins, Shrewsbury); Staffs. Oxon. (Walsall).

Quarter-finals to be played on June 16.

Semi-finals to be played on June 30.

Final to be played on August 29 at Lord's

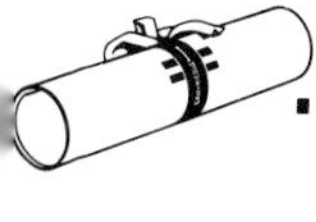